Dictionary of International
Food and Cooking Terms

DICTIONARY OF
International
Food & Cooking
Terms

⟨————❧∞❧————⟩

BY MYRA WALDO

ORIGINALLY PUBLISHED AS VOLUME TWO OF
The International Encyclopedia of Cooking

THE MACMILLAN COMPANY · NEW YORK

COLLIER-MACMILLAN LTD. · LONDON

Illustrated by Sidonie Coryn

Library of Congress Catalog Card Number: 67-27514

FIRST PRINTING

The Macmillan Company, New York
Collier-Macmillan Canada Ltd., Toronto, Ontario

Printed in the United States of America

PREFACE

This book seeks to collect, in one volume, the most important food terms and definitions from all over the world.

It includes the most used classic words, principally derived from France, Germany and Italy, the three countries chiefly responsible for our gastronomic repertoire and vocabulary. In addition, thousands of food terms from the United States are included, among them, local names for various fish, game and berries, and many strictly American dishes and preparations. As a result of the author's years of travel in over eighty foreign countries, there are also included thousands of definitions of food terms from Africa, Asia, the Pacific and South America. A brief description of the food and diet of these countries has also been given. Several hundred words, no longer in general use and now regarded as archaic or obsolete, have been included for those who wish to consult this volume to ascertain the meaning of various literary references, particularly those having a Latin or Old English background. Hundreds of technical food terms with a chemical or technical association are defined for use by students of food chemistry. Local usage and slang expressions have also been included where deemed of sufficient importance.

Obviously, no single book of any size can hope to include every possible food or culinary term from the entire world. For example, so varied are the natural foods of Asia, and so numerous the many local food terms, that a complete volume of equal size could be prepared containing Asiatic food terms alone. However, the more important and representative terms of that vast continent have been included.

A word about spellings: English-speaking people have a tendency to expect the rest of the world to follow in their footsteps and spell every word in the Anglo-Saxon-American fashion. (They tend to overlook the fact that even within their own language British and Americans cannot agree on the spelling of a common word—aluminum, aluminium, for example.) But it is a fact that English is just one language among thousands in the world and is based upon the customary twenty-six letter alphabet of the Romans. In eastern Europe, the Cyrillic alphabet is similar to, but not identical with, our alphabet, thus causing many spelling variations. Much of the remainder of the world uses a different alphabet, many with sounds not duplicated in our own language, leading to what philologists call variant spellings. The Anglo-Indian word *curry*, to use an example, is merely an attempt to imitate the Indian sound of the word. English-speaking people often reproduced that Indian term by such spellings as *kari, khari, curi, currie*, until the present-day spelling of curry became standardized. But then, even in twentieth-century France, is the favorite garlic mayonnaise of Provence more correctly spelled *aïoli, aïolli* or *aïlloli*? If we cannot agree within the scope of our own alphabet, the difficulties of reproducing foreign tongues solely by their imitative sounds to Western ears may be realized. Therefore, in looking up a word it may on occasion be necessary to check possible variations in spelling, such as the use of y for i, s for z, k for c, and c for s.

There is no previous work covering all of the material in this book. The only volume of this type was prepared in France several decades ago, and more recently translated into English. The French, however, are somewhat provincial about the food of countries other than their own, and that work does not encompass much more than the food of France. The rest of the world, and especially the United States, is largely ignored.

I hope this book will fulfill its desired purpose—a needed reference source for food terms from our own country, from Europe, and, in fact, from the entire world.

MYRA WALDO

Dictionary of International Food and Cooking Terms

A

Aal (Norwegian). Eel.

Aal I Gélé (Danish). Jellied eel.

Aalsoep (Dutch). Eel soup.

Aam. A German and Dutch liquid measure for wines varying from 37 to 41 gallons.

Aardappel (Dutch). Potato.

  Aardappel Puree (Dutch). Mashed potatoes.

  Aardappelsoep (Dutch). Potato soup.

Aardbei-Chipolata (Dutch). Mixture of cream, eggs, and crushed fruits.

Aarfugl (Norwegian). Tiny birds.

Aâssida (Algerian). A boiled flour and water mixture, prepared with butter; it is a staple food, low in cost and very filling.

Abacate (Portuguese). Avocado pear.

Abadejo (Spanish). Pollack, a type of fish, having a fairly good taste and texture.

Abaisse (French). Thinly rolled pastry used for lining tarts and making pastry croustades.

Abaisser (French). To roll out dough with a rolling pin. The correct thickness is important. In a pie crust, for instance, the dough will burst if too thin and it will be undercooked if too thick.

Abalone; Sea Ear. Large sea snail or mollusk with a flattened shell. Chinese-Americans in California were the first in the United States to eat the abalone found along the California shores. The central muscle, a broad foot by which the abalone clings to rocks, is the edible portion. When removed from the shell it resembles a large sea scallop, but it has a strong taste similar to that of a clam. Supplies have diminished, and now fresh abalone cannot be sold outside of California. It is available in many specialty-food shops in cans or in dried form in oriental food shops.

As fresh abalone is quite tough, it is best when minced and used in fish soups, chowders, canapes, and sandwiches. It must be sliced and tenderized by being pounded with a mallet before being fried or broiled. It is particularly important not to overcook Abalone.

Abalone is often dried, particularly in Japan. It is very flavorsome, but it must be soaked in water at least 4 days with frequent changes of water.

Abat-Faim (French). The first substantial dish served at a meal of many courses.

Abats (French). Brains, head, heart, kidney, liver, sweetbreads, tongue, tripe, or other internal organs of animals.

Abatte (French). A heavy, double-edged knife, used for many culinary purposes, but especially to flatten meats, particularly veal.

Abattoir. Slaughterhouse.

Abavo. A pumpkin native to India from which a soup is made.

Abbacchio (Italian). Baby lamb.

  Abbacchio alla Cacciatora. Lamb with a spicy sauce of tomatoes and green peppers.

  Abbacchio in Brodetto. Baby lamb in egg sauce.

Abborre (Swedish). Perch.

Abdelavis. An Egyptian melon.

Abendessen (German). Dinner; evening meal.

Aberdeen. A rich, creamy, soft Scotch cheese.

Abernethy Biscuit (Scotch). A crisp biscuit containing caraway seeds; named for the town where it was first made.

Abertam. A hard Czechoslovakian sheep's-milk cheese.

A.B. Goods. An American term used to describe many kinds of gum, jelly, and marshmallow sweets. The origin of the term is obscure.

Abkari. In parts of Asia, the manufacture and sale of liquor.

Able. A fish resembling the salmon but smaller; found on the Swedish coast.

Ablette (French). The bleak, a very small pink fresh-water fish, member of the carp family.

Ablette de Mer. Whitefish.

Abóbora (Portuguese). Pumpkin.

Abomasum. The fourth stomach of the sheep, cow, and other cud-chewing animals; occasionally used for food. It is often used as a source of rennet, much used in making cheese.

Abon (Indonesian). Fried slivers of shredded beef.

Abondance (French). Watered-down wine; wine diluted by water.

Abricock. An alternative name for an apricot.

Abricoté (1) A variety of plum or peach somewhat like the apricot. (2) Candied apricot glazed with apricot marmalade.

Abricoter. In pastry making, to cover with strained apricot paste.

Abricotine; Abricota. An apricot-flavored cordial.

Abrikoos (Dutch). Apricot.

Abrikos (Danish). Apricot.

Absinthe; Absinth. An aromatic licorice-flavored liquor, apéritif, and flavoring made from oils of wormwood, angelica, anise, and marjoram. France outlawed its sale before World War I, and most of the other Western countries followed suit. The dark green oil of the wormwood had been charged with causing sterility, insanity, and sometimes death. Damage to imbibers was probably due to the high alcoholic content. Absinthe generally is bottled at 136° proof; that is, it is 68 percent alcohol, thus very potent.

Absinthe was invented in Switzerland in the late 1700s by an exiled French physician and pharmacist, Dr. Ordinaire, who used a high-proof brandy as a base for the drink. In 1797 he sold the formula to Henri-Louis Pernod, whose name is now linked with absinthe substitutes similarly made but without the wormwood and at a much lower proof.

An ingredient in some mixed drinks, such as a Sazarac, absinthe or its substitutes are more commonly prepared as an *absinthe drip*. For this, a special glass with a drip top is required. A teaspoon of sugar syrup and a jigger of absinthe are placed in the glass. The drip top is filled with finely crushed ice, and water is slowly dribbled into the glass. The liquor turns first milky, then cloudy, then opalescent with glints of green, pink, and gold.

Oysters Rockefeller, a New Orleans specialty, is one of the few dishes in which absinthe substitute is occasionally used. In the United States an absinthe substitute, legally produced, is available.

Absinthin. The bitter element of wormwood.

Absinthium. Wormwood, a bitter aromatic plant.

Abstainer. One who abstains voluntarily from alcoholic drinks.

Abstemious. Extremely moderate in eating and/or drinking; temperate.

Abstinence. Abstaining from food, particularly meat.

Aburage (Japanese). Soybean curd, obtained from cooked soybeans, fried in oil.

Abutilon. A plant native to various parts of the world. Its edible flowers may be used as a vegetable. The leaves are similar to spinach when boiled but have a slightly sour taste.

Abymes. A group of red and white wines from the Savoy region of France.

Acacia. A tree of the mimosa family that yields gum arabic and gum acacia. In France, the flowers are sometimes used for dessert fritters. The flowers are sprinkled with sugar, soaked in brandy or rum, then dipped in batter and fried in deep fat, drained, and sprinkled with sugar.

Acajou. The cashew or cashew nut.

Acanthus. A spiny grass that grows along the shores of the Mediterranean; its leaves, when young and tender, may be used in salads.

Acarajé (Brazilian). Beans covered with a shrimp sauce.

Acarne. The grayling, a fish similar to the sea bream.

Acciúga (Italian). Anchovy.

Accola. Another name for the white tuna.

Accolade. Two (or more) pieces of poultry, meat, or fish arranged back to back on the same dish.

Accomoder (French). To prepare and arrange a dish.

Accote-Pot (French). A three-legged metal utensil designed to support pots, particularly on a kitchen fireplace.

Accoub. A vegetable in the thistle family that tastes like asparagus or artichoke. The entire plant, roots, and shoots are edible when boiled and may be served with melted butter.

Accubation. The ancient custom of reclining rather than sitting at the table.

Accumbent. Reclining at the table while eating.

Accuncciatu (French). A lamb, mutton, and sometimes horsemeat stew made with potatoes; a favorite in Corsica.

Aceite (Spanish). Oil.

Aceituna (Spanish). Olive.

Acephala. One of the two great classes of shellfish.

Acepipes Diversos (Portuguese). Hors d'oeuvre; appetizers.

Acerb; Acerbic. Sour, bitter, harsh, or sharp-tasting.

Acescency. The state of turning sour.

Acescent. To turn sour.

Acetable. An ancient liquid measure equal to a saucerful; sometimes, ½ a gill.

Acetabulum; Acetable. A cup that holds vinegar at the table; equal to ½ gill.

Acetal. A colorless liquid formed during the process of wine making.

Acetarious. Pertaining to plants used in salads.

Acetary. In pears, acid pulp in the form of a mass of particles near the base.

Acetate C-8; Acetate C-10. Colorless liquids used to impart synthetically to candies and other confections the flavors of various fruits.

Acetic. Of or pertaining to vinegar.

Acetic Acid. A colorless, biting, pungent liquid compound. Vinegar contains from 4½−12 percent acetic acid.

Acetify. To change to acid or vinegar.

Aceto (Italian). Vinegar.

Aceto Dolce (Italian). Fruit and vegetables sweetened and preserved in vinegar and mustard; served as a relish.

Acétomel. A vinegar-and-honey mixture sometimes used in the preparation of candied fruit.

Acetose. (1) Having the taste of vinegar. (2) The herb sorrel or sorrel dock.

Acetous. Sour, like vinegar. Acetous fermentation is the chemical reaction that changes sugar or alcohol into vinegar.

Achar; Achard. A condiment, best known in India, consisting of various young fruits and vegetables (palm cabbage, bamboo shoots, etc.) pickled and strongly spiced. Saffron is generally included for color.

Achara (Philippine). Pickle made from green papaya.

Achards, Les (West Indian). Vegetable appetizer made with assorted vegetables.

Ache d'Eau Berle (French). Wild celery.

Achene. A hard dry fruit consisting of a single seed with a thin outer skin or covering that does not break open when the fruit is ripe.

Achiote; Achote. Annatto seeds, often used in Latin cookery to add a reddish coloring to foods; the seeds add little taste.

Achuete (Philippine). Annatto seeds. *See* Achiote.

Acid. (1) Sharp, sour, and biting to the taste. (2) A chemical compound soluble in water, sour to the taste, and identifiable by its ability to turn litmus red.

Acid Curd. In cheese making, the curd produced when lactic acid causes the casein to thicken.

Acid Foods and Basic Foods. In the digestive process some foods leave an acid residue, others an alkaline (or base) residue. Minerals sodium, potassium, magnesium, and calcium are base-forming. Phosphorus, sulfur, and chlorine are acid-forming. Which of these predominates in the food determines whether the food itself leaves an acid or an alkaline residue. An acid residue is left by meat, fish, eggs, cheese, cereals. An alkaline residue is left by milk, vegetables, some fruits. Fats and sugars are neutral, as they contain no minerals.

Acid Ice. A mixture of beaten egg whites, sugar, and lemon juice, similar to a meringue, for use on puddings and pies.

Acidify. To make sour or acid.

Acidimeter. An instrument for measuring the strength of acids.

Acidity. The proportion of acid in a substance.

Acid Number. The number of milligrams of caustic potash required to neutralize the free fatty acids in 1 gram of fat.

Acidophilus (Lactic-Acid) Milk. A fermented milk that tastes like buttermilk, made by mixing the bacteria *lactobacillus acidophilus* with whole milk. It is recommended for easing certain gastrointestinal disorders.

Acidulate. To make somewhat sour or acid by flavoring with an acid food or substance.

Acidulated Water. Water to which a small amount of vinegar or lemon juice is added. The usual ratio is 1 tablespoon to 2 cups of water.

Acidulous. Somewhat sour or acid.

Acini de Pepe (Italian). Very tiny pieces of pasta, used mainly in soup.

Acinus. A berry, such as a raspberry or grape, that grows in a cluster.

Ackee. A vegetable found in the Caribbean, especially Jamaica. A red pod encloses the flesh, which, when boiled, tastes like eggs. Ackee can be baked, roasted, or made into various dishes with meat or fish.

Açores, Fromage des. A round, solid cow's-milk cheese with a peppery taste produced in the Azores; when dry, used for grating.

Acorn. A small brown nut, the fruit of varieties of the oak tree, used primarily as food for pigs. Some types are edible, however. In parts of southern Europe sweet acorns are prepared like chestnuts. In Turkey, acorns provide the base of a popular dish called *racahout*. In times of famine acorns have provided flour for bread and have been roasted, ground, and boiled for use as a coffee substitute.

Acorn Barnacle. A rather small shellfish with a flat, bland taste; found in waters throughout the world.

Acorn Squash. A small hard-shell squash; best when cut in half, the seeds removed, and baked with a little butter and sugar. *See also* Squash.

Acouchy. A small rodent similar to the guinea pig and agouti; the Surinam rabbit. It is occasionally used as food.

Acqua (Italian). Water.

Acqua Cotta (Italian). A mushroom-and-tomato soup with eggs and cheese; prepared in Tuscany.

Acqua di Firenze (Italian). An apéritif wine made with spices and lemon peel.

Acqua di Fiume (Italian). A liqueur with a distinctive aroma and bouquet.

Acqua Minerale (Italian). Mineral water.

Acquavit. *See* Aquavit.

Acqua Vitae. Alcoholic drinks, especially brandy and whisky.

Acquavite (Italian). Brandy.

Acquette. An aromatic afterdinner cordial or liqueur popular in northern Italy and southern France. One type is made with cinnamon, nutmeg, and cloves, and shreds of silver leaf; another type is made with angelica, cloves, cinnamon, lemon peel, and gold leaf.

Acrid. Biting, stinging, or sharp-tasting.

Acronarcotic. Of food, both acrid and narcotic.

Actinie; Actinia. A sea anemone, prepared like crab. Three varieties are edible: the *mule back*, the *actigne*, and the *rastegne*.

Açúcar (Portuguese). Sugar.

Adam-and-Eve Pudding. Cooked apples with a cake mixture spread over the top and baked.

Adam's Fig. *See* Plantain.

Adane. A variety of sturgeon found in the Po River in Italy; often smoked. The caviar is excellent.

Adchempilavi. (Turkish). Pickled meat stewed with rice.

Addict. One compelled to follow a regular habit. Coffee and tea addiction is common, but there are many other food and drink habits.

Additives. Materials added to food to help manufacture and preserve it or to improve its taste and appearance. Examples are emulsifiers, flavors, thickeners, curing agents, humectants, colors, vitamins, minerals, and mold, yeast, and bacterial inhibitors. In the United States the use of most additives is controlled by federal and state laws.

Addle Egg. Rotten or decomposed egg.

Ade. A tall chilled drink of citrus-fruit juice, water, and sugar. Lemonade and orangeade are the most popular, with wine, liquor, or a liqueur sometimes added.

A.D.E.B. Association Pour le Développement de l'Exportation des Vins de Bordeaux—Association for the Development of the Exportation of Bordeaux Wines.

Aderezo (Spanish). Dressing.

Adipic Acid. An acid sometimes used as the acid portion of baking powder in the manufacture of self-raising flour.

Adipose. (1) Fatty. (2) Animal fat or oil.

Adlay. A cereal or grain grown chiefly in Spain and Portugal; used as food.

Admiral. A hot punch consisting of red wine sweetened with sugar, flavored with vanilla and cinnamon, and thickened with egg yolks.

Adobo (Philippine). Stew. *See also* Philippines.

Adoc. A term occasionally applied to curdled milk.

Adoucir (French). To reduce the bitterness, spiciness, or the saltiness of a dish by cooking or by adding water, milk, or a light broth, or by a combination of the two methods.

Adragante. Gum tragacanth, a vegetable gum. Diluted in cold water to form a white jelly or gum paste, it is used by pastry makers to thicken creams and fillings.

Adriatic Fig. *See* Fig.

Adulteration. In food manufacture or processing, the deliberate addition of a cheaper substance or a fraudulent substitution that lowers the quality of a food. To protect the consumer the U.S. Pure Food and Drug laws require that all foods be labeled as to their true contents.

Adure. To scorch or burn (foods) completely.

Absolute. Complete or pure, as absolute alcohol.

Advocaat. (1) A Dutch beverage made with eggs, sugar, and vanilla. (2) A liqueur made with brandy and fresh egg yolks.

Adzuki. A bean grown in several oriental countries, especially Japan; may be cooked as a fresh vegetable or, when dry, ground into a flour.

Aeble (Danish). Apple.

Aebleflaesk. Pork and apples cooked together; a Danish favorite.

    Aeblegrød. Applesauce.

    Aeblekage med Flødeskum. Applecake with whipped cream.

    Aebleskiver. A type of doughnut.

    Aeblesuppe. Apple soup.

Aeg (Danish). Egg.

Aeggekage (Danish). Pork pancake.

Aegilops. A genus of grasses, including the wild oat, or other corn-weed grass.

Aelia. A bug that attacks wheat causing damage to the gluten of flour milled from it.

Aemono (Japanese). Salad.

Aender (Danish). Duck.

Aerate. To charge with carbon dioxide gas or to introduce air by beating or whipping.

Aerated Bread. A bread produced mechanically without leaven or yeast. Carbon dioxide is mixed with water, then mixed with flour in an iron vessel and placed under pressure to form the dough. It is said to be more easily digestible than yeast bread.

Aerated Flour. Another name for self-raising flour.

Aerated Water. Bottled water either deriving from natural springs or artificially produced. In bottling, both kinds of water are charged with a gas, usually carbon dioxide. Some of the well-known mineral waters from natural springs are Perrier (French), Vichy (French), and San Pellegrino (Italian). Artificially aerated waters are sold as soda water, club soda, carbonated water, seltzer water, and effervescent water.

Aerator. A substance capable of introducing air, such as baking powder in dough.

Aerter (Danish). Peas.

Aettekees. A Belgian white cheese, fermented, slightly hardened and rather salty, with a strong flavor and aroma.

Afèlia (Cyprian). Pork (previously marinated in wine for several days) and potatoes.

Affiner (French). To purify; to make finer; in the cheese industry, various treatments are carried out in special cellars maintained at constant temperatures.

Affriander (French). To improve the appearance of dishes with garnishes or decorations.

Affriter (French). To "season" a new skillet by rubbing it with fat or oil, sometimes with salt, before wiping it dry, after which it is heated for 10 minutes and cooled.

Affumicato (Italian). Smoked.

Afikomen (Hebrew). A piece of unleavened bread (matzoth) eaten at the end of Seder, the ritual meal served at Passover.

Africains (French). Small dessert cookies.

African Pigeons. A term used to describe a wide range of small game birds. The three best types are the Speckled, the Olive, and especially the Delalande Green.

Aftercourse. A course usually served after the main course.

Afterdinner Coffee. Very strong black coffee served after a meal, either at the table or in the living room, sometimes with cream and sugar.

Afternoon Tea. A light meal, served in the late afternoon, usually consisting of tea served either with lemon or with milk and sugar, possibly accompanied by plum cake, a light spongecake, thin cucumber sandwiches, and something hot, such as crumpets or muffins with jam. In England, where the custom originated, afternoon country tea was simpler but more substantial, perhaps including homemade bread, butter, watercress, radishes, and hard-cooked eggs. In the United States, afternoon tea, consisting of tea sandwiches, thinly sliced bread with a variety of fillings, and the beverage, is usually served between four and five.

Aftertaste. The taste sensation which remains after eating food or drinking a beverage, or which returns shortly after consumption. The term is generally used with reference to wines.

Agami. A wild game bird, found in various parts of South America, and often used as a food. It tends to be somewhat dry, and should be cooked slowly with plenty of fat.

Agape. A love feast; a meal eaten in remembrance of the Last Supper.

Agar-Agar. A gelatin derived from a red seaweed and used in making gelatin desserts, jellies, and soups. The seaweed originated in Japan and also grows abundantly on the Atlantic and Pacific coasts of the United States. It is marketed in slender sticks, in blocks, and in powder form. In China, swallows use agar-agar in building their nests, which, in turn, are used to make gelatinous bird's-nest soup.

Agaric. A group of fungi including mushrooms with thin, transparent gills. Small quantities are used in making bitter appetite stimulants, such as *Fernet Branca.*

Clouded Agaric. A rather large gray-brown palatable wild mushroom.

Agathon. A Greek poet, renowned for the lavishness of his banquets.

Agave. The American aloe, a plant of the *amaryllis* family, whose fermented sweet sap makes the sour-tasting *pulque* and, when distilled after fermentation, produces *tequila,* Mexico's popular alcoholic drink.

Agavose. A sugar made from the stalks of the century plant by Mexican Indians.

Agemono (Japanese). Deep-fat-fried foods.

Agenaise (French). Eggs cooked and served on a base of sautéed chopped onions, garlic, and parsley.

Agene Process. The treatment of flour during milling with nitrogen trichloride to simulate natural aging.

Agerhøns (Danish). Partridge.

Ägg (Swedish). Egg.

Äggröra. Scrambled eggs.

Agglutinate. Sticky. In oriental countries, agglutinated rice is preferred to the type which produces separate grains, because it is easier to eat with chopsticks; also made into small patties or dumplings.

Agi. *See* Ají.

Aging. The treatment of flour with oxidizing agents. It was originally found that when freshly milled flour was stored for several weeks, it underwent an aging effect and produced a stronger and more resilient dough and a bolder loaf. During storing the flour slowly bleached.

Angel Cake; Angel Food Cake. A light sweet cake made primarily with egg whites and sugar;

usually baked in a special tubular pan with a hole in the center.

Agliata (Italian). Garlic blended with vinegar, used for flavoring, particularly around Genoa.

Aglio (Italian). Garlic.

Agly, Côtes d'. Sweet, odd-tasting, and liqueur-like wines originating in the Agly Valley in the Roussillon region of France.

Agneau de Lait (French). Young lamb; suckling lamb.

Agnello (Italian). Lamb.

Agnello al Forno. Baked lamb.

Agnello Arrosto. Roast lamb.

Agnolotti (Italian). Dough stuffed with various mixtures of minced meat and vegetables.

Agnolotti di Torino. Rather good-sized ravioli filled with ground lamb and served with a sauce.

Agou. A type of grain resembling millet; grown in various parts of Africa.

Agourci; Agoursis. Small cucumbers, resembling gherkins, prepared in the Russian manner with dill.

Agouti. A rodent resembling the guinea pig, native to the West Indies and South America. Its rather strong flesh is usually prepared like suckling pig.

Agraz; Agras (Spanish). A soft cold drink, prepared with almonds, sugar, and the juice of unripened grapes.

Agrestal; Agrestial. Growing wild in cultivated fields or open country.

Agriot. A kind of sour cherry.

Agronomy. Management of rural land; rural economy.

Agrumes (French). Citrus and related fruits.

Aguacates (Spanish). Avocados.

Aguaji. The grouper, a Caribbean food fish.

Aguardiente (Spanish). Literally, "burning water"; strong, raw liquor distilled from molasses or grapes and bottled without aging or rectifying; consumed mainly in Spain, Mexico, Brazil, and other Latin countries.

Aguaxima (Brazilian). A variety of black pepper.

Aguja Palá (Spanish). Another name for the swordfish, other than Pez de Espada.

Agurk (Danish). Cucumber.

Agurkesalat (Danish, Norwegian). Cucumber salad.

Ahzee-uk (Eskimo). Wild arctic blackberries.

Aide de Cuisine (French). Assistant cook.

Ai Ferri (Italian). Grilled.

Aïgo Boulido; Bouïllido (French). A soup of the Cévennes region prepared with olive oil, garlic, and herbs, thickened with an egg yolk, and served with bread crusts.

Aïgo Saou (French). A fish soup strongly flavored with garlic; made with tomatoes, onions, and potatoes.

Aigre (French). Sour; acid.

Aigre au Cédrat; Aigre de Cèdre (French). A beverage made of orangeade, flavored with mulberry juice, lemon juice, and honey.

Aigre-Doux (French). Sweet and sour.

Aigrettes, Cheese. Cheese straws; occasionally, small cheese fritters.

Aiguebelle (French). A yellow or green strong liqueur.

Aiguière. Container made of clay or china, used in medieval times to serve water at the table.

Aiguille à Brider (French). Larding needle used for inserting strips of fat or bacon into meat or poultry.

Aiguillettes (French). (1) Thin strips or slices of meat, poultry, or game cut lengthwise from the body of the carcass or bird. (2) Foods cooked on small skewers.

Ail (French). Garlic.

Ailerons (French). The small wings of birds or fins of certain fish.

Aillade (French). Any preparation which contains a considerable amount of garlic.

Ailler (French). To add garlic.

Aïn-Bessem-Bouira. A type of Algerian red and white wine.

Aïn-El-Hadiar. A type of Algerian red, rosé, and white wine produced in Oran.

Aïoli; Aïolli; Aïlloli (French). A garlic-flavored mayonnaise popular in Provence; usually served with poached hot or cold fish, sea food, vegetables, and eggs; also added to bouillabaisse.

Aïoli garni consists of a variety of foods served with flavored mayonnaise. Garlic cloves must be crushed to a pulp in a mortar or put through a garlic press before being mixed with the mayonnaise. Aïoli is best prepared with homemade mayonnaise.

Aipo (Portuguese). Celery.

Airelle de Marais (French). Cranberry.

Airelle Myrtille (French). Whortleberry or huckleberry.

Airelle Rouge (French). The red bilberry, the cranberry, used for jellies, compotes, and jams.

Aiselle. A species of beetroot used in salads or as a vegetable.

Aisy, Cendré d'. A cow's-milk cheese aged in grapevine ashes; produced in the Armançon Valley of France.

Aitchbone. The cut of beef lying over the rump; the bone of the rump.

Ait-Farle (Scotch). A fourth of a round of oatcake.

Ait-Jannock (Scotch). A thick oatmeal shortbread.

Ajacilo. A medium-hard, rather spicy cheese made in Corsica, France.

Ajam (Indonesian). Chicken.

Ajeel (Iranian). Cocktail snack consisting of pistachios, almonds, watermelon and pumpkin seeds, and puffed peas.

Ají; Agi. A small, red very hot type of pepper grown chiefly in Peru; basis of numerous spicy dishes, such as *ají de pollo*, made with chicken.

Ajiaco (Spanish). Thick soup or stew made in parts of South America with various ingredients, such as potatoes, chili peppers, green peas, eggs, avocados.

Ajinomoto (Japanese). Flavoring powder, mono-sodium glutamate.

Ajo (Spanish). Garlic.

Ajoqueso (Spanish). A Latin-American dish of melted cheese, peppers, etc.

Ajoutées (French). Small garnishes; side dishes.

Akala (Hawaiian). A berry-producing shrub whose purplish or orange fruits are large, juicy, small-seeded, and taste somewhat like the raspberry or strawberry.

Aka Miso (Japanese). A red paste made from fermented soybeans, rice malt, and salt.

Akee. *See* Ackee.

Aku Malu (Hawaiian). Dried salted tuna fish, usually eaten with poi in the Hawaiian and other islands in the Pacific.

Akvavit. *See* Aquavit.

Ål (Danish, Swedish). Eel.

Al, All, Alla (Italian). "In the style or fashion of"; usually followed by the name of the district in Italy where the dish is prepared.

À la Broche (French). Roasted on a spit or skewer, usually in an open fire.

À la Carte. Meals ordered and paid for by separate items.

Alacha (Spanish). A large variety of sardine.

Aladan, Oeufs (French). Eggs served on rice previously cooked with onions, saffron, and tomatoes and garnished with pimientos.

À la Diable (French). Deviled; seasoned with a hot or pungent condiment or spices.

À la Ficelle (French). Tied with string.

Alamang (Philippine). A small shrimp.

À la Mode (French). (1) "In the fashion of"; usually followed by the name of a city or district,

as in *tripe à la mode de Caen*. (2) In the United States a scoop of ice cream on top of pie.

À l'Anglaise (French). Plain boiled.

Albacora (Spanish). A small variety of tunafish. *See* Albacore.

Albacore. A torpedo-shaped tuna weighing 60 pounds or less. It has a delicate flavor and white meat and is used for the white-meat canned tuna.

Albaricoque (Spanish). Apricot.

Albedo. The white pith of the inner peel of citrus fruits. It consists of sugars, cellulose, and pectins, and is a source of pectin for commercial manufacture.

Alberge. A clingstone peach native to France; used chiefly for cooking or for jams.

Albicocca (Italian). Apricot.

Albini. A firm white cheese made from both goat's and cow's milk in northern Italy.

Albino. Lacking pigmentation. Albino sturgeons, for example, produce a pale, gold-colored caviar, which tastes similar to black caviar. During Czarist days in Russia, albino caviar was reserved by royal decree for the czar, who purchased the entire catch for a large price.

Albóndiga (Spanish). Meatball.

Albondigón (Spanish). Meat loaf.

Alboni. A brown sauce made with red-currant jelly and roasted beechnuts; usually served only with venison.

Albran (French). A wild duck known for its inter-esting, gamy taste.

Albufera Sauce. (1) A brown sauce enriched with port wine, served with roast pork, game, etc. (2) A sauce made with meat glaze and pimientos.

Albula. A comparatively little-known Swiss cheese strongly flavored by the herbs eaten by cows.

Albumen. White of egg; it consists primarily of albumin dissolved in water. *See* Albumin.

Albumen Water. A drink for invalids made with egg white beaten with water and a teaspoon of lemon juice.

Albumin. Proteins rich in sulfur and complex in structure. The important albumins are those found in milk, meat, egg white, and in many vegetables. Because the proteins were thought to exist in almost pure form in egg white, they were erroneously called "albumen."

Alburn. A small lake fish, seldom marketed commercially; best when pan-fried.

Al Burro (Italian). With butter.

Alcachofa (Spanish). Artichoke.

Alcachofra (Portuguese). Artichoke.

Alcaparra (Spanish). Caper.

Alcarraza; Alcarazas (Spanish). Any utensil intended for cooling fluids, especially water.

Alcazar (Spanish). A type of pastry made with almonds and apricot jam.

Alchermes. An Italian liqueur prepared with flower essences and spices.

Alcohol. A colorless liquid, with a pleasant mild odor, containing no food nutrients; it is the intoxicating element in wines, spirits, and beers. The Chinese made a rice wine long before the Christian era. The Egyptians and ancient Chaldeans knew how to concentrate alcohol by distillation. The Greeks subsequently learned to make beer from the Egyptians.

To make alcohol, it is necessary to have sugar or a product that can be converted into sugar. The grape sugar in grape juice is the source of alcohol for wine. The sugar is transformed into alcohol by fermentation, a process brought about by the action of yeast. In fermentation the yeast attacks each molecule of sugar, splitting it into two molecules of ethyl alcohol and two molecules of carbon dioxide gas. The gas evaporates and the alcohol remains.

Grains, cereals, potatoes, and other products lack natural sugar, but they are rich in starch, which can be changed to sugar by the action of an enzyme, diastase. Once the sugar is produced, yeast goes to work to cause the fermentation that yields alcohol.

Distilled spirits are produced by concentrating the alcohol. As alcohol is highly volatile, that is, it turns to gas at a lower temperature than water does, it can be heated, the alcoholic vapors caught, then condensed again, resulting in an alcohol of high purity.

An ounce of most alcoholic drinks, like bourbon and Scotch, contains about 100 calories.

Alcohol C-9. A colorless liquid used to supply the synthetic taste of citrus fruits and pineapple to jams, candies, etc.

Alcoholic Beverages. *See* Ale, Beer, Bourbon, Brandy, Cocktail, Gin, Liqueur, Rum, Rye, Scotch, Whisky, Wine, and individual beverages by name.

Alcoholometry. The measurement of the proportion of alcohol in a solution. Such measurements are stated in relation to proof spirit. The instrument used for measuring proof is the *alcoholometer.*

Alcoolat. Alcohol flavored with aromatic herbs or extracts during distillation. The best-known alcoolats are absinthe and mint alcohol.

Alcool Blanc (French). A series of clear white dry liquors, high in alcoholic content, made from fruits and berries.

Aldehyde. (1) A colorless volatile fluid obtained by the oxidation of alcohol. (2) A class of compounds of the same type, each derived from its alcohol by the removal of two atoms of hydrogen.

C-7. A rather oily, colorless liquid used to supply the synthetic flavor of almonds or other nuts to candies, etc.

C-8. A colorless liquid used to supply the synthetic taste of apricot or plum to various foods.

C-14 *Pure.* A slightly yellowish liquid used to supply the synthetic taste of peach and apricot to candies, jams, etc.

C-18. A light yellowish, although sometimes colorless, liquid used to supply a coconut taste to various candies, etc.

Al Dente (Italian). Literally, "to the tooth"; as applied to *pasta*, firm, slightly undercooked; as Italians prefer it.

Alder. A bitter herb sometimes used in making bitters, vermouth, etc.

Alderman's Walk (British). The center cut of a haunch of mutton or venison; the best part of the under-cut or fillet of a sirloin of beef, containing the most delicate slices.

Alderney. A breed of cattle famous for fine milk.

Ale. A brew made by fermenting malt (made from barley) and hops. It is more bitter and heavier than beer, the difference being due to the method of fermentation. Originally it was brewed only from malt, without the hops, in northern Europe, where wine was not produced. *See* Beer.

Aleberry. (1) A fine oatmeal mixed with weak ale and left to soak for a couple of hours, then strained, boiled, and sweetened. (2) A drink made of boiled ale with sugar, spices, and pieces of bread.

Alec. (1) A herring. (2) A relish or pickle made of small herrings.

Aleconner. In medieval times a public official who regulated, supervised, and controlled the price and quality of beer and ale.

Alecost. A vegetable root formerly used as a spice.

Alegar. Sour ale; a malt vinegar.

Alehouse. A place where ale or beer is sold.

Alembic. A piece of equipment used in the distillation process of making alcoholic beverages.

Alénois (French). Cress.

Alentejo. A soft, slightly strong ewe's- or cow's-milk cheese, usually cylindrical; made in the province of Alentejo, Portugal.

Aleurobius. A mite found in old flour stored under adverse conditions, sometimes giving it a slightly purple color.

Aleurometer. An instrument that measures the amount of gluten in flour.

Aleurone Layer. A single layer of large cells under the bran coat and outside the endosperm of cereal grains.

Alewife. A fish of the herring family found along the eastern coast of North America from the Gulf of St. Lawrence to Chesapeake Bay. Closely akin to the herring and the shad in both shape and color, it may be prepared like either. It is called *gasperau* in St. Lawrence Bay, *ellwife* and *sawbelly* in other localities, and *round pompano* in Bermuda.

Alface (Portuguese). Lettuce.

Alfajores (Spanish). A filled-cooky dessert.

Al Forno (Italian). Baked.

Al Fresco. In the open air; refers especially to dining outdoors.

Algae. Flowerless plants, including seaweeds, containing algin, from which edible jellies similar to agar-agar are obtainable. Seaweeds such as Irish moss and dulce, which are algae, have been used as food in various countries for a long time.

Alga Mar. A type of edible seaweed, often used as food in Chile, and other South American countries.

Algarde. A little-known Spanish wine.

Algerian Wine. The vineyards of Algeria, using modern methods and large-scale, assembly-line production introduced by the French, turn out vast quantities of table wine marketed all over the world. Algerian wine is usually strong in alcoholic content and lends itself to blending. It seems to travel well in all climates. Some of the wines can be very good, but since most of them are made from inferior grapes, the better wines suffer from this general reputation.

Algérienne, À l'. A style of preparation; of meat and poultry, garnished with vegetables fried or marinated in oil.

Algin. A gelatin obtained from seaweeds and used as a low-cost additive to food.

Alginates. Salts of alginic acid found free and as calcium salt in many seaweeds. They are used in artificial cherries, as sausage casings, and as thickeners and stabilizers in ice cream, artificial whipped cream, and some kinds of jellies.

Alginic Acid. *See* Alginates.

Alhagi. An oriental vegetable whose skin is covered with a thick, sticky syrup which, under the hot sun, dries up into small black grains which are prepared like tapioca, barley, or other cereals.

Alho (Portuguese). Garlic.

À l'Huile. Cooked or canned in oil; served with oil.

Alicante. A red Spanish dessert wine.

Alicante Bouschet. A mediocre variety of grape used in Algeria and California for making red wine.

Alicot (French). A peasant stew made with leftover duck or goose, bacon, onions, mushrooms, and chestnuts; a specialty of Rouergue.

Alicuit (French). A Basque provincial stew prepared with poultry giblets cooked with carrots, potatoes, and garlic.

Aligoté Wine. A white Burgundy wine, a blend of wine from the comparatively poor Aligoté grape and from the better Pinot Chardonnay. The label on the bottle must indicate the Aligoté pressing.

Aligout (French). Mashed potatoes with cheese and cream; made in the Languedoc region.

Alimango (Philippine). A fine-flavored edible crab.

Aliment. Food, nourishment; anything edible.

Alimentary. Pertaining to food and nutrition.

Alimentation. Nutrition; food.

Alimentary Paste. Dough products, such as macaroni, spaghetti, and other types of *pasta*, made to be cooked in water or stock and served with a sauce; also egg noodles, etc.

Alkalescent. Tending to become alkaline; having an excess of minerals. Certain vegetables, particularly those of the cabbage family, tend to be alkalescent.

Alkanet. A coloring substance, alkannin, sometimes used to color fats, cheese, essences, and inferior port wine.

Alkékenge (French). A kind of ground-cherry; the small tree produces a red berry, often glazed with sugar or used in jams and compotes.

Alkermés. A red Italian liqueur prepared with clove, cinnamon, and vanilla in a mixture of alcohol, sugar syrup, and orange-blossom water.

Alkohol (Swedish). Alcohol.

Alla (Italian). In the style of.

Alla Griglia (Italian). Broiled.

Allasch. Kümmel; a liqueur made with caraway seeds.

Alleluia (French). Pastries of varied shapes and flavors served at Easter.

Allemande, À l'. In the German style; applied to dishes whose ingredients or preparations are typically German; for instance, a dish using sauerkraut and pork, or garnished with dumplings or smoked sausages.

Allemande Sauce; Sauce Parisienne. A white sauce, béchamel or velouté, with heavy cream and egg yolks beaten in. It is the base for many creamed dishes and is served with fish or eggs.

Allerlei; Leipziger Allerlei (German). Dish consisting of stewed early spring vegetables; macédoine of vegetables served mainly in Leipzig.

Allgäuer Bergkäse. A Bavarian cheese similar to Emmentaler.

Allgäuer Rahmkäse. A creamy rich Bavarian cheese that tastes similar to but milder than Limburger; often flavored with caraway.

All-Holland Cake. A cake made to celebrate All-Saints' Day.

Alliaceous. Smelling or tasting like garlic and onions.

Alliance, À la St. Usually indicating braised carrots, artichoke bottoms, and small onions in a particular dish.

Alliaria. A strong-smelling, garlic-flavored plant whose leaves are occasionally used in salads or cooking.

Allice; Allice Shad. A European fish of good quality.

Alligator. Young alligator is edible, although just barely. Its strongly flavored flesh is usually eaten only by primitive natives.

Alligator Pear; Avocado. Soft green or purple pear-shaped tropical fruit. *See also* Avocado.

Alli-Pebre d'Anguiles (Spanish). Eel in garlic sauce.

Allium. A class of plants of the lily family including garlic, onion, leek, chive, and shallot.

Allotrophic. A variation in nutritive properties without change in chemical or physical characteristics.

All-Purpose Flour. Flour made of a blend of hard and soft wheats which has less protein than bread flour and may be used for most baking and cooking. If cake flour is used, cakes will have a more tender texture. In a cake recipe calling for cake flour, 2 tablespoons less per cup of all-purpose flour may be substituted.

Allspice. An aromatic spice, Jamaica pepper or pimenta; the dried berry from the allspice tree of the West Indies. Its taste resembles a combination of nutmeg, cloves, and cinnamon. When ripe and dry the berries are similar to black pepper, but somewhat larger and less pungent.

Allumette. A foodstuff cut in the general shape of a match; thin slivers of meat or fish. By extension, allumettes are small pieces of pastry served as hors d'oeuvre.

Allyl Caproate. A yellowish or sometimes colorless liquid used to furnish a pineapple taste to various foods synthetically.

Almandin. Of confections, containing almonds.

Almavica (Italian). Dessert resembling a semolina pudding.

Almejas (Spanish). Clams.

  Almejas con Arroz. Clams with rice.

Almejones (Spanish). Scallops.

Almendras (Spanish). Almonds.

Almendron. The Brazil-nut tree.

Almoço (Portuguese). Lunch.

Almond. A distinctively flavored nut usually classified in two types: (1) *Sweet almond* (from a pink-flowered tree), which is eaten as a dessert fruit when freshly picked, but is more often used in its dried form, frequently salted as a cocktail accompaniment and with a variety of dishes. (2) *Bitter almond* (from the white-flowered tree), which is used mainly in candy making and for flavoring. Both varieties are grown extensively in California and are imported in quantity from Jordan (the kernel is plump and long) and Valencia, Spain (plump and pointed at one end but broad at the other). Choice nuts are used for making candy, almond paste, or almond butter. The five grades of dried almonds, from the least expensive to the best are: Common, Large, Sultan, Pistache, and Jordan. The nut is easily shelled with the fingers, although there is a "hard-shell" variety which may require a nutcracker.

To blanch almonds: Pour boiling water over almonds and steep 5 minutes or until the skins are wrinkled. Do not soak more than ¼ pound at a time because they become soggy if left too long in the water. Drain water from the nuts and rub the pointed end between the thumb and forefinger until the skin slips from the nut. Almonds may be dried after blanching in a warm oven.

Burnt Almonds. Blanched, toasted sweet almonds cooked with sugar until well coated.

Country Almonds. The Indian almond tree, producing a nut which has a fair taste; the expressed oil of the nut may be used in cooking.

Almond Extract. *See* Extracts.

Almond Icing. An almond paste used to coat cakes before they are iced.

Almond Mill. A machine used for grinding dried blanched almonds; not to be confused with an almond-paste mill in which almond paste and marzipan are milled and cooked.

Almond Oil, Bitter. Oil obtained from the bitter seeds of the almond tree.

Almond Paste. Finely ground blanched almonds used in macaroons and other cookies, in cakes, Danish pastry filling, and as a basis for marzipan candy. It is available in cans in many delicacy shops. The nuts can be ground in an electric blender, put through a meat grinder, or pounded in a mortar.

Almond Syrup. An emulsion of mixed ground kernels of sweet and bitter almonds (apricot or peach kernels may be substituted for the bitter almonds) in barley syrup or in a mixture of orange-flower water and sugar. Ten parts of sweet almonds are generally used to three parts of bitter almonds. It is used by bakers and pastry shops and by soda fountains for fancy iced beverages.

Almôndegas (Portuguese). Meat balls.

Almuerzo (Spanish). Luncheon.

Aloe. A warm-climate plant whose rather narrow thick leaves are used in making bitters.

Aloṣa (Spanish). Shad, a fine food fish.

Alose (French). Shad; fish commonly known as *allice* or *allice shad*.

Alose Avignonnaise. Fried shad baked with sorrel.

Aloxe-Corton. French red and white wines of a limited part of a locality. A district wine rather than an estate wine in or near the town of Aloxe-Corton, close to Beaune in the Burgundy region. *See* France, The Wines of.

Aloyau avec Filet (French). A French cut of beef, resembling the short loin or hip.

Alperche (Portuguese). Apricot.

Alpes. A French cheese imitating Italy's Bel Paese.

Alpestra. A mediocre Austrian smoked cheese.

Alpestro. A slightly salted Italian goat cheese.

Alpha-Laval Centrifuge. A machine that separates liquids of different density or clarifies liquids; widely used for cream separation.

Alphée. A marine crayfish of mediocre flavor; may be prepared like lobster.

Alphenic. White barley sugar; sugar candy.

Al Punto (Italian). Medium well done.

Alque. A small antarctic penguin. The flesh must be well cooked to eliminate the unpleasant oily taste.

Alsace, Muscat d'. A dry Alsatian wine made from the muscat grape.

Alsacienne, À l'. In the Alsatian style; served with smoked meats, sausages, etc. *Choucroute à l'Alsacienne* is sauerkraut with smoked meats and sausages.

Al Sangue (Italian). Rare.

Alsatian Wine. Although Alsatian wines are not in a class with the finest German and French white wines, connoisseurs describe them as fresh, flowery, and delicate. Light and pleasant, they are ideal with almost any kind of food, especially on hot summer days. They should be chilled and drunk when fairly young, preferably 3—5 years old.

The wines of Alsace are named, not for the district from which they come, but for the grape from which they are made. These include Gewerz-Traminer, Riesling, and Sylvaner. Only a small amount of red wine, of inferior quality, is produced in Alsace. *See* France, The Wines of.

Alsatian Yeast. A type of yeast.

Al Sugo (Italian). With sauce.

Altar Wine. Wine plays a part in the ritual of most Western religions. In the Roman Catholic Church, the wine used in the Eucharist must be made of pure grape juice, naturally fermented, with an alcoholic content of not more than 12 percent. Rabbinical law states that the wine used in Jewish rituals must be pure and natural. In both religions the wine may be red or white but it may not be used if soured.

Altavilla. A dry red wine produced in Calabria, Italy.

Altenburger Ziegenkäse. A rather soft goat's-milk cheese made in Germany.

Alternates. *See* Substitutions.

Altesse. A sweet, rich white wine produced in the French Alps; it develops a dry taste as it matures.

Altitude. For the effect on cooking processes of altitudes over 2,500 feet above sea level, *see* High-Altitude Cooking.

Altsohl. *See* Brinza cheese.

Altwater. A German liqueur made from mountain plants.

Alubati. A Philippine green vegetable roughly like spinach.

Aluko Chop (Indian). Fried potato pancake made in Nepal.

Alum. An astringent mineral salt sometimes used to whiten flour and, commercially, to maintain firm texture in pickles and maraschino cherries. Its use is strictly limited by law.

Aluminite. A type of fireproof earthenware, used for cooking utensils.

Aluminum. A silvery, bluish-white metal noted for its lightness, strength, and rapid transmission of heat. It is nontoxic and can be molded into many shapes, which makes it well suited for a wide variety of kitchen uses.

Care and Cleaning. Although aluminum is a naturally shiny metal, it tends to dull if not frequently used and washed. Certain foods, particularly eggs, and water containing iron, sulfur or alkalies, will stain aluminum utensils. Such stains can be removed by scrubbing with a fine steel wool, by rubbing with lemon, or by boiling a weak solution of vinegar and water in the stained pot or pan.

Aluminum Ware. Pots and pans made from aluminum are of two types: *Cast Aluminum* is light in weight but has a heavy appearance and a grainy surface. Walls are comparatively thick so that the utensil heats evenly and holds its heat for a long time; it is best suited for slow-cooking operations and for food containing little water. *Stamped Aluminum* is made from sheet metal and has a shiny, smooth surface. Its thin walls heat rapidly but do not retain the heat; it is best used for quick cooking, boiling, and baking.

Aluminum Foil. Thin aluminum sheeting available in roll form useful for wrapping food to be placed in refrigerator or oven, since it forms an airtight, watertight seal, yet conducts heat. It is also very handy as a pan liner, as a cover for utensils, or to separate different foods being cooked in the same pot.

Alveograph. A machine that measures the stretching quality of dough as an index of protein quality for baking. A standard disk of dough is blown into a bubble and the pressure curve and bursting pressure are measured.

Alvéole (French). Wax cell of the honeycomb.

Amandel (Dutch). Almond.

Amandes, Pâté d' (French). Almond paste; a mixture of powdered almonds, sugar, and egg whites or water, made into a paste used for cake coverings, etc.

Amandes Douces (French). Sweet almonds.

Amandes Pralinées (French). Burnt almonds.

Amandine. As applied to fish, prepared with toasted, slivered almonds in browned-butter sauce.

Amanita Caesarea. A European wild mushroom, orange with a yellow stem; also called *Kaiserling* (Germany).

Amaracus. Dittany, an aromatic herb native to Crete.

Amaranth. A mild-flavored wild herb; may be used as a vegetable if well seasoned.

Amaretti (Italian). Macaroons.

Amaretto. An Italian liqueur made with bitter almonds.

Amargo (Portuguese). Bitter.

Amargosa. An apple tree native to the South Pacific; the leaves are used as a green vegetable.

Amarone. One of Italy's finest wines; a smooth, soft red wine, well rounded and balanced; produced near Verona.

Amassette (French). A small knife used by pastry makers to pack dough.

Amazake (Japanese). Sweet wine.

Amazu (Japanese). A sweet vinegar sauce.

Ambergris. A waxlike substance, produced by sperm whales and found floating in tropical seas; once used in cooking, now used in making perfume.

Amberjack. A very large fish found in the Gulf of Mexico and the Caribbean; prepared like any other large fish that may be cut into steaks.

Ambert. A French cheese similar to cheddar; best during winter months.

Ambigu (French). A kind of buffet at which a variety of dishes are served at the same time.

Ambonnay. A dark red wine produced in small quantities from the Pinot Noir grape in the Champagne district of France.

Ambrette (French). A plant with a musk odor whose seeds are sometimes used to flavor coffee or other beverages.

Ambroisie. A cold milk drink flavored with vanilla or kirschwasser.

Ambrosia. (1) Ambrosia as we know it today is probably very different from the drink and food of the gods in Greek mythology. It is said that the gods partook of ambrosia to preserve their immortality, and that mortals permitted to taste it received additional beauty, strength, and swiftness, becoming in some measure godlike.

In the southern United States, ambrosia is a simple fruit dessert consisting of fresh orange slices or segments sprinkled with freshly grated coconut. At Christmas time it is often served with fruit cake.

Also called ambrosia is an American drink resembling a champagne cocktail in which the bubbling beverage is spiked with Cognac and flavored with Angostura bitters or, in New Orleans, with Cognac and Cointreau.

(2) An herb used to flavor fresh fruit salad, preserves, and jellies; also called *Oke of Cappadocia.*

Ameaux (French). Pastry made of puff paste and eggs.

Ameijoas (Portuguese). Small clams.

Ameixa (Portuguese). Plum.

Ameixa Sêca. Prune.

Amelanchier. A group of trees, related to the medlar, producing small fruits.

Amelcorn (1) An inferior European wheat. (2) French rice.

Améléon. A type of cider produced in Normandy, France.

Amelet. Another name for an Omelet.

Amendoa (Portuguese). Almond.

Amendoim (Portuguese). Peanut.

Amer (French). Bitters. Used extensively in cooking, bitters may be natural (bay leaf, ginger, etc.), or may be added by the cook (caramelized sugar, etc.).

Américaine; Armoricaine, À l' (French). A sauce used chiefly with lobster, other shellfish, and sometimes with meat and eggs; made with butter or olive oil and tomatoes.

American Cheese. The Pilgrims began producing cheese in the colonies, using the English method for making cheddar, about 1620. The product is often distinguished from the European type by being called *American cheddar.* Commercially, American cheddar is marketed in two types, mild and sharp, although there is also a difference as to their respective ages. American cheddar includes the hard-coated Pineapple cheese as well as Monterey Jack and Sage. Other important American cheeses are Brick, Colorado Blackie,

Coon, and, the most original of all, Liederkranz, which is completely American despite its German name. Tillamook (somewhat sharp and creamy) and Wisconsin Longhorn (a cheddar) are also noteworthy. Some commercial cheesemakers market an "American cheese," usually processed, made of very young cheese, customarily sliced.

Americano (Italian). A tall, cooling drink. An ounce of Italian bitters, such as Campari or Carpano, is poured into an 8-ounce glass over cracked ice containing two jiggers of sweet vermouth; then soda water is added to fill the glass. It is stirred gently and garnished with a twist of lemon peel. A smaller drink, the Americano cocktail, is also made. *See* Campari.

American Partridges. The common American varieties of partridge.

American Plan. A system used in hotels, especially in resort hotels, in which the room and all meals are included in the daily rate. It differs from European plan, under which only the room rate is quoted, meals being charged separately.

  Modified American Plan. Like the American plan but with one meal, usually the midday meal, not included in the daily rate. But some hotels allow the guest to have either lunch or dinner as well as breakfast.

Amer Picon. A French apéritif with a slight burntorange flavor; usually served with a little grenadine and ice water.

American Quail. A general term for a number of small game birds, especially the partridge.

Amidon de Blé (French). Cornstarch.

Amincir (French). (1) To cut. (2) To pound (meats or fish) until thinner.

Amiral, À l'. As applied to fish preparations, served with a fish velouté (white sauce) and garnished with crayfish tails, fried mussels and oysters, mushrooms, and truffles.

Ammaperdrix. An excellent-flavored African partridge occasionally found in southern France.

Ammocète; Ammocoete. A young lamprey resembling the eel and usually prepared in the same manner.

Ammonia, Carbonate of. A salt substance, sometimes used in the making of baking powder.

Amomum. An herb, similar to cardamom, highly flavored, and much used in southeast Asia as a cooking ingredient. *See* Cardamom.

Amontillado. A moderately dry, pale, nutty-flavored sherry; best served chilled. *See* Sherry.

Amora (Portuguese). Blackberry.

Amoroso (Spanish). A sweet dark sherry. *See* Sherry.

Amou. A simple cheese made of cow's milk in southwestern France; it resembles the St-Paulin cheese and is best during the cold months.

Amourettes. (1) Marrow cut in strips and crumbed. (2) Lamb's fry.

Ampalaya. A bitter Philippine melon.

Ampelography. The science of raising grapes for wine making.

Amphicarpus. Having fruit of two different kinds or at two different times.

Amphisarca. A hard-rinded succulent berry.

Amphitryon (Greek). A host, one who entertains guests at dinner.

Amphora. A two-handled wine or oil vessel. Verdicchio, an Italian wine, is shipped in an amphora-shaped bottle.

Ampulla. A small two-handled globular flask or bottle, common in ancient Rome.

Amsoi. A plant whose green leaves are used as a vegetable in the Guianas, South America.

Amsterdamse Korstjes (Dutch). Spice cake.

Amulet (Obsolete). Omelet, especially a sweet one made with flour, sugar, egg yolks, and orangeflower water and egg whites beaten separately.

Amygdaline. Relating to almonds.

Amydon. The finest flour.

Amyl. A starch; the finest flour.

Amyl Acetate. A liquid used to produce a pear flavor synthetically.

Amyl Butyrate. A synthetic flavoring agent in essences and liqueurs.

Amyl Phenyl Acetate. A colorless liquid used to give a synthetic honey flavor to candies, etc.

Amyl Propionate. A colorless liquid used to give a fruity flavor to jams, candies, etc.

Amyl Valeriate. A synthetic apple flavoring.

Amylase. An enzyme in saliva that changes starch into sugar.

Amyloid. (1) Any non-nitrogenous starchy food. (2) A starchlike substance that forms the cell walls in the cotyledons of various plants.

Anabiotic. A stimulant or tonic.

Anack. Bread made with oatmeal.

Añada (Spanish). Vintage wine.

Anadama Bread. A cornmeal and white-flour bread made with molasses and yeast leavening.

Anadonta. A large freshwater mollusk; often used as food, although its taste is somewhat inferior.

Anago (Japanese). An edible eel.

Analect. In ancient Roman households the slave who gathered up the dishes and distributed the leftover food.

Analeptique (French). A food of a light consistency but nutritionally rich or stimulating, such as milk, chocolate, and wine.

Ananas (French and German). Pineapple.

Ananasso (Italian). Pineapple.

Ananaz (Portuguese). Pineapple.

Anchiovis (Danish). Anchovies.

Anchoas (Spanish). Anchovies.

Anchoiade (French, Corsican). Mashed anchovies combined with parsley, olive oil, and garlic, and spread on bread soaked with olive oil.

Ancholivette. Olive stuffed with anchovy.

Anchovy. A tiny herringlike fish, never more than 4–5 inches in length, used as a component of many preparations and dishes, such as anchovy butter, sauce, hors d'oeuvre, and garnishes.

Anchovies are native to the Mediterranean and the English Channel, and are caught by the millions during the spring and summer months. Fishermen lure them into nets on dark and moonless nights by means of artificial lights which attract and blind them. Preparation for market is by methods which originated with the ancient Greeks and Romans. The fish are cleaned, graded, and washed, and then packed in layers with salt in small kegs. The fillets may be packed as straight strips or in curls.

The taste of the anchovy tends to sharpen the appetite for both food and drink, and often heightens the flavor of accompaniments. Boned anchovies, pounded or blended into a paste, are the basis for many sauces. Whole fillets are used in hors d'oeuvre, antipasto, smorgasbord, and as a garnish for various cutlets and wiener schnitzel. Anchovy butter is delicious when spread lightly on a steak for broiling or when

used in a sauce or salad dressing. Anchovy as a seasoning rather than as a major ingredient may be used in a wide variety of sauces.

Anchovy Pear. A russet-colored West Indian fruit, frequently pickled. *See also* Mango.

Anchovy Toast. Buttered toast with anchovies; toast spread with anchovy butter.

Anchusa. *See* Bugloss.

Ancien Impérial. A very soft fresh cream cheese made in Normandy, France; packaged in small portions.

Ancienne, À l'. Old-style; with a garnish consisting of kidney beans, hard-cooked eggs, and braised lettuce.

Ancient Eggs (Chinese). Aged eggs, preserved eggs, etc. *See* Preserved Eggs.

And (Danish). Duck.

Andalouse, À l'. With a garnish containing pimientos and tomatoes; much used on poultry and eggs.

Andean Cheese. A Venezuelan cow's-milk cheese shaped into crude cubes and wrapped in aromatic leaves.

Andesteg (Danish). Roast duck.

Andijvie (Dutch). Endive.

And Med Aebler Og Svedsker (Danish). Duck with apples and prunes.

Andorran Cheese. A sheep's-milk cheese of fair quality produced in the valley of Andorra, adjacent to southwestern France.

Andouille (French). A firm fat pork sausage usually served as an hors d'oeuvre, made in the Touraine region; the *andouillet* is much softer. *See also* Andouillet.

Andouille de Vire (French). A lightly smoked black-skinned sausage made of pig's innards in Normandy.

Andouillet (French). Minced veal and bacon or chopped fish made into a paste.

Andrajos (Spanish). Giblets.

Andropogon. A species of edible grass including the sugar cane, used for food or for making flavoring ingredients.

Aneth (French). A plant of the fennel family often used by candy makers because of its distinctive taste. *Sweet aneth* (*anet*) is the herb dill.

Anethene. The most volatile part of the essential oil of dill, fennel, and related herbs.

Anethole; Anethol. White crystals often used to give a synthetic taste of licorice to candies, etc.

Ange de Mer (French). ·The dogfish, a fish of mediocre taste, related to the shark and the ray.

Angelat. A heart-shaped cow's-milk cheese made in Normandy; also called *coeur de Bray.*

Angel Bread (British, Scotch). A purgative cake consisting of spurge, ginger, flour, and oatmeal.

Angelfish. A term applied to many different fish in different parts of the world.

Angelica. (1) A biennial plant cultivated for its roots and stalks. In France, the green stems are candied and used to decorate cakes and pastries. In Lapland, the roots are ground and used for flour to make a bread substitute. Angelica also is used to flavor certain liqueurs, such as Izarra, a yellow Basque beverage of the Chartreuse type. (2) Two beverages from California: (a) a sweet white wine formerly made by the Mission Fathers; (b) a highly fortified white dessert wine.

Angelica, Wild. A species of wild herb, the roots of which are sometimes used in making gin.

Angels on Horseback (British). Savory, served at the conclusion of a meal. Oysters are wrapped individually in bacon slices, skewered, baked 5–6 minutes and served hot on buttered toast. Finely chopped onion and parsley may be sprinkled over the oysters before they are rolled in the bacon. In the United States they are served also as an hors d'oeuvre.

Angels' Pie. A pie in which young pigeons, madeira wine, cayenne pepper, lemon juice, hard-cooked plover's or pigeon's eggs, forcemeat, and gravy are covered with flaky pastry and baked in a slow oven.

Angel Tip. Crème de cacao liqueur with sweet cream floating on top.

Angkak (Philippine). Red-colored rice grains used to lend color to fermented fish preparations.

Anglaise Custard. Molded custard made of sugar, milk or cream, egg yolks, and flavoring.

Anglaise, À l' (French). Boiled, or simply prepared in the English style.

Anglaise Dip. A combination of oil, beaten eggs, and spices into which foods are dipped before being breaded.

Angler. An ugly gray fish without scales and with evil-looking fangs; its flesh must be beaten before being edible.

Angloise. A kind of plum tart.

Angobert. A large cooking pear.

Angostura. A well-known brand of bitters, an aromatic flavoring used a few drops at a time in cocktails, or, when taken neat, medicinally, as a digestive aid. It is made in Trinidad, according to an original and secret recipe of a Dr. Siegert, from the bitter bark of the Cusparia tree and several herbs and spices.

Angoumois. A variety of apricot named for an old province of France.

Angú (Brazilian). Cereal or porridge made of cornmeal, rice, manioc flour, etc.; eaten hot or cooled and sliced.

Angú Paulista (Brazilian). Pork, creamed vegetables, hearts of palm, and cornmeal; prepared in São Paulo.

Anguila (Spanish). Eel.

Anguilla (Italian). Eel; Anguille Eels.

  Anguilla alla Ticinese. Eel cooked with herbs, garlic, and red and white wine; served cold as an appetizer.

  Anguilla alla Veneziana. Young eel cooked in lemon and tuna-fish sauce; a specialty of Venice.

  Anguilla Carpionata. Marinated eel.

  Anguilla in Salsa Rossa. Eel in tomato sauce.

Anguille Berlinoise (French). Eel cooked in beer with pieces of rye bread.

Angula (Spanish). A small variety of eel found in rivers.

Anguria. A gourd; watermelon.

Anice (Italian). Anise.

Anijs (Dutch). Anise.

Animelle di Vitello (Italian). Sweetbreads.

Animelles (French). Lamb's fry.

Anis (Spanish). A sweet anise-flavored liqueur.

Anisado (Philippine). An anise-flavored wine.

Anisated. Mixed or flavored with aniseed.

Anise. An aromatic umbelliferous plant native to the Levant; often confused with dill, which was probably the anise mentioned in the King James Version of the Bible. It is used to flavor sweet puddings, creams, and pastries. *See* Aniseed.

Aniseed. Licorice-flavored seeds of the anise herb used in Italian, Middle East, and oriental dishes. They may be sprinkled on coffee cakes, sweet breads, cookies, shellfish, fresh-fruit salads, sauerkraut, cole slaw, or cooked cabbage. In Germany it is used to flavor a fancy bread called *Anisbrod*. Aniseed oil supplies the licorice flavor in absinthe, anisette, and pernod.

Aniser (French). To stew with aniseed or to mix with aniseed.

Anisette (French). An anise-flavored liqueur.

Anisina (Italian). An anise-flavored liqueur.

Anis Mascado (Philippine). Nutmeg.

Anitra (Italian). Duck.

    Anitra in Casseruola. Casserole of duck.

    Anitra Selvatica. Wild duck.

Anjan (Siamese). A food coloring.

Anjou-Mousseux. The white wines of Anjou made into sparkling wines by the champagne process.

Anjovislåda (Swedish). Anchovy omelet.

Anka (Swedish). Duck.

Anker. A liquid measure used in various parts of the world.

Ankerstoke; Anker Stock. A long oblong loaf of bread originally made of rye but occasionally prepared with wheat.

Annadas. A term applied to young, or the first year's sherry.

Anna Potatoes. Thin round slices of potatoes cooked with plenty of butter, salt and pepper.

Annatto; Anatta (South American, Central American). An orange-red dye derived from the seeds of a Central American plant, used to color cheese and other dishes.

Annette Potatoes. Shoestring potatoes, fried with butter and pressed into a sort of pancake.

Annona; Anona. Various tropical fruits including soursop, cherimoya, and custard apple. The term *anona* refers only to the custard apple in certain parts of the world.

Annotine. Any tree whose fruit does not ripen in one season, such as the fig.

Annotto. *See* Annatto.

Anodon; Anodonta. A genus of shellfish without teeth on the hinge of the shell, such as fresh-water mussels of southern France; the taste is less distinctive than that of regular mussels.

Anon. A fish similar to whiting.

Anona. The custard apple, a tropical fruit native to Central and South America and India.

Anorexy; Anorexia. Lack of appetite.

Anotta. *See* Annatto.

Anschovis-Sosse (German). Anchovy sauce.

Anserine. Pertaining to geese.

Ansjos (Norwegian). Anchovies.

Antepast. Anything eaten or drunk before a meal to sharpen the appetite.

Anteprandial. Before dinner.

Anticuchos (Peruvian). Pieces of beef heart dipped in a spicy sauce and grilled.

Antipasti (Italian). Appetizers.

    Antipasti Almagri. Seafood appetizers.

    Antipasti Assortiti. Assorted appetizers.

    Antipasti Casalinghi. Home-style appetizers.

    Antipasti di Pesce. Fish appetizers.

Antipasto (Italian). Appetizer.

Antispattering Agent. Substances added to frying fats to prevent the formation of water droplets. Examples are lecithin and sucrose esters.

Aoudad. A semiwild North African sheep.

Aoudze; Aoutdze (Ethiopian). A highly flavored sauce prepared with ginger, clove, herbs, and peppers; served with meats.

Apahap (Philippine). A sea bass.

Apeas. A Christmas cooky, made with egg whites, sugar, and chopped hickory nuts.

Apelsin (Swedish). Orange.

Apéritif (French). A short alcoholic drink less potent than a cocktail, drunk before a meal to stimulate the appetite. In Europe it is usually served straight or with a dash of bitters and a twist of lemon peel. The most popular apéritif wines are French dry vermouth, Italian sweet vermouth, the pale dry sherries, Madeira, Dubonnet, Byrrh, and Campari. Some apéritif wines may be mixed with plain or sparkling water, but usually they are served straight. Perhaps influenced by American practice, Europeans now sometimes chill the wines.

Aperitivos (Portuguese). Appetizers.

Apfel (German). Apple.

   Apfelkuchen. An apple pastry dessert made with puréed apples, breadcrumbs, and cinnamon.

   Apfelmus. Applesauce.

   Apfelschnittchen. Apple fritters.

Apfelsinen (German). Oranges.

Apfelstrudel (Austrian, Hungarian, German). Popular dessert, made by stretching dough over a large table covered with a clean cloth until it is almost transparent and as thin as tissue paper; the dough is then filled with apples sprinkled with sugar.

Apfelwein; Apfelmost (German). Cider.

Aphie; Nonnat; Loach. A Mediterranean fish.

Api; Lady Apple; Pomme d'Api. A miniature apple, green and bright red.

Apicius. The name of three famous gourmets of ancient Rome. The second Apicius was the most renowned for his knowledge and culinary skill.

Apio (Spanish). Celery.

Apiol; Apiole. A parsley camphor, obtained by distilling parsley seeds with water.

Aplatir (French). To flatten. Steaks and fillets may be tenderized by being flattened with the side of a cleaver.

Apollinaris Water (German). An alkaline, highly aerated water containing sodium chloride, and calcium and sodium and magnesium carbonates; obtained from a spring in the valley of the Ahr.

Appalam. Round flat wafers made from green chick peas.

Appareil (French). Food mixtures used in preparing various dishes.

Appas; Hoppers (Ceylonese). Thin coconut-flavored pancakes.

Appel (Dutch). Apple.

   Appelbol. Apple dumpling.

   Appelmoes. Applesauce.

   Appeltaart. Apple pie.

   Appelwijn. Cider.

Appelsin (Danish). Orange.

Appelsinsaft (Norwegian). Orange juice.

Appenzeller. A medium-soft cheese made in Switzerland and southern Germany; it resembles Emmentaler and comes in 20-pound wheels. The common type is made with skim milk, the festive type with whole milk.

Appert, François. A French scientist (1750–1841) who experimented with food preservation and developed one of the first practical methods of canning.

Appétissant (French). Appetizing; whetting the appetite; relishing.

Appétissants Suédois (French). Thin slices of rye (or dark) bread covered with anchovy butter and spread with smoked salmon.

Appétit (French). Appetite.

Appetite. According to scientists, an instinctive desire or tendency to satisfy with food the needs of the body. Hunger is the need to eat; appetite is the anticipation of pleasure to be gained from eating or drinking. It can be stimulated by the sight or the smell of food, or may occur independently as a result of regular meal schedules. Also, appetite may disappear suddenly without being gratified or after the consumption of a few mouthfuls. A creative cook prepares foods to stimulate the appetite by appearance, aroma, and taste as well as to satisfy hunger.

Appetitive. Giving an appetite.

Appétits (French). Certain herbs that stimulate the appetite, such as onions, chives, and shallots.

Appetize. To give an appetite to or create hunger.

Appetizer. Any food or drink that stimulates or excites the appetite.

Appetizing. Increasing or exciting the desire for food. Certain Jewish stores that sell smoked fish are referred to as "appetizing stores."

Appetost (Danish). A smooth, mellow cheese, made from sour buttermilk, with caraway seeds added.

Apple. The most extensively grown fruit throughout the temperate zones of the world, the apple was probably one of the first fruits cultivated by man. It is mentioned in many legends from ancient times: golden apples are prevalent in Greek mythology; the apple is the food that supplies wisdom to the gods in Scandinavian folklore; and, traditionally, in the Bible the apple is the fruit of the Tree of Knowledge that tempted Adam and Eve.

Apples are generally classified as eating apples and cooking apples. Eating, or dessert, apples are sweet, fragrant, and are attractive in color, either red, yellow, or, in the case of some early summer varieties, pale green. Cooking apples are large, wholly or partially green, and tart or acid, the latter quality causing the flesh to melt into a soft pulp when cooked.

As the adage about an apple a day keeping the doctor away implies, the fruit is one of our most nutritious foods. It contains vitamins B and C, which are retained even after cooking. A single apple contains from 8–11 percent sugar, the essence of energy. Underripe apples should not be eaten raw because their high starch content is hard to digest. The high amount of starch in underripe apples is converted to sugar in cooking and produces a delicious green-apple pie.

More than 200 species of apples are grown in the United States alone, the leading producer in the world. Cultivation began during colonial times and developed into a commercial large-scale business with the planting of orchards in western New York during the middle 1800s.

Apples keep better than most other fruits; hence they can be purchased in quantity and stored for future use, preferably in a dry, cool place. About 2 pounds of cooking apples should be adequate for a 10-inch pie or for 6 servings of applesauce.

The most popular varieties of American apples are as follows:

Name	Description
Baldwin	deep red flecked with yellow
Ben Davis	red
Crab Apple	red with yellow spots
Delicious	red
Early Harvest	yellow
Golden Delicious	deep yellow
Gravestein	yellow
Greening	red with yellow stripes
Grimes Golden	green
Jonathan	blood red
McIntosh	dark red or green
Northern Spy	red with yellow stripes
Ribston Pippin	yellow
Rome Beauty	yellow with red stripes
Spitzenburg	bright red
Stayman Winesap	red with yellow stripes
Wealthy	yellow with red stripes
Winesap	dark red
Wolf River	yellow with wide red stripes
Worcester Pearman	red
Yellow Newtown	yellow spots and red stripes

Apple Amber. A dish made of apple purée, lemon, eggs, and puff pastry.

Apple Butter. The sweetened, cooked, thickened pulp of apples. In the United States apple butter is associated with Pennsylvania Dutch cookery, though this preserve and spread for bread is now popular throughout the country. German immigrants probably brought the recipe with them, for it had long been made in Germany. There the time for making apple butter was a festive occasion, the whole neighborhood gathering to gather the apples, pare and core them, and drop them into a huge pot to be cooked with cider and spices, usually allspice, cinnamon, and cloves. The apple butter was put up in jars to last through the winter and until the apple crop was ready for harvesting the following autumn.

Apple Cider. *See* Cider.

Apple Corer. A small knife with a deeply curved blade that removes the apple core with one turn.

Apple in Nightgown (British). Apple dumpling. The apples are peeled and cored, then filled with orange conserve or thick marmalade, wrapped in rich crust, and baked.

Applejack; Calvados. Apple brandy prepared by distilling cider.

Apple John (**John-Apple**). An apple said to keep for two years and to be ripe when it is withered.

Apple Juice. In unsweetened form a popular fruit juice. The highest grade of canned apple juice, which is treated at low temperatures to destroy yeast and mold, finely filtered and vacuum-sealed, will retain the delicate flavor and the full vitamin content of fresh juice. Apple juice is a more highly refined product than cider. *See* Cider.

Äpplen (Swedish). Apples.

   Äpplekaka. Apple cake.

   Äpplevin. Cider.

Apple of Love (Obsolete). The tomato.

Apple of the Earth. *See* Camomile.

Applesauce. A preparation made from peeled apples, sugar, and a little water, and cooked until soft; served hot or cold; a classic accompaniment to duck, pork, or goose.

Apples, Dry-Pack. Peeled and cored apples preserved by a sterilization process and canned without added water.

Apple Snow. Apple pulp or purée mixed with meringue and decorated with jelly.

Apple Strudel. *See* Apfelstrudel.

Apple Tansy. Apple rings dipped in a rich batter of eggs, fried in butter, and served with cream.

Apple Treacle. The juice of freshly pressed apples evaporated at low temperature to a thick syrup containing a high percentage of natural sugar.

Appliances, Kitchen. *See* Kitchen Equipment.

Apprète (French). A thin slice of bread.

Apprêté (French). Prepared, cooked, dressed.

Apprêts (French). Dishes; preparations; dressing.

Après-Dîner (French). Afterdinner.

A Prezzo Fisso (Italian). Fixed-price meal.

Apricot. An oval, golden, slick-skinned fruit resembling in flavor both the peach and the plum. It is a native of North China, but is now cultivated in all temperate-zone countries. The large juicy dessert fruit from the Loire Valley in France is acknowledged as the world's best apricot. Smaller varieties are grown on an enormous scale in California, Australia, and South Africa, and are frequently made into jams and preserves or are dried for export. Dried apricots keep their flavor more satisfactorily than any other fruit similarly processed, and are rich in iron; about two-thirds of the world's crop is so treated.

Apricots do not contain as much sugar as apples. They are most healthful and delicious when thoroughly ripe. The mature fruit, plump, firm, and uniform in color, is in season in the United States in June, July, and August.

Fresh apricots are sold by the dozen or by the pound (8 to 16). One pound will make about 2½ cups of cooked apricots. Ripe fruit should be covered and stored in the refrigerator; slightly green fruit can be ripened at room temperature.

Apricots, usually unpeeled, are canned whole or in halves. They are graded according to U.S. standards.

Dried apricots are usually sold halved and unpeeled and are graded according to size. They should be stored in a dark, cool, dry place.

Apricot Brandy. A strong-flavored liqueur made from apricots. There are two types: one in which the brandy is distilled directly from fresh fruit and crushed pit kernels; the other in which brandy or other alcohol is flavored with dried apricots.

Apricot Liqueur. A sweetened apricot brandy of low-to-medium alcoholic content.

Apricot Palm. A palm tree that grows in tropical American countries and produces a small fruit which tastes somewhat like an apricot.

Apricot Pulp. Ripe apricots halved and stoned, then preserved without sugar by sterilization.

Apricot Purée. Sieved apricot pulp with an equal weight of sugar boiled to the consistency of jam.

Aprikosen (German). Apricots.

Apron. (1) An article of clothing worn in front of the body to protect clothes, particularly while cooking. (2) A small fish of the perch family.

Apry. A French afterdinner liqueur with an apricot taste.

Apulid (Philippine). Water chestnut.

Aqua (Latin). Water.

Aqua d'Oro. A liqueur whose predominant flavor is rosemary and rosolio. Invented by the Italians in the thirteenth century, it was introduced into France in 1533 by Catherine de Medici.

Aqua Mirabilis. A water prepared from cloves, galangals, cubebs, mace, cardamom, nutmegs, ginger, and spirits of wine, settled for 24 hours, then distilled.

Aqua Pura (Latin). Pure water.

Aquavit; Akvavit. A potent liquor distilled from grain or potatoes and sometimes flavored with caraway. Each Scandinavian country has its own version. Outsiders, however, agree that the Danish product is the best.

The drink should be chilled but should never be served over ice. In Scandinavia the aquavit bottle is sometimes frozen in a block of ice. The drink is poured into an ounce or an ounce-and-a-half glass and should be swallowed all at once, not sipped. The Swedes follow it with a beer chaser to minimize its effect.

Aqua Vitae (Latin). "Water of life"; brandies and other strong liquors.

Aquavite di Genziana. An Italian liqueur made with gentian.

Aquavite di Ginepro. An Italian liqueur made with juniper.

Arabian Coffee. Coffee made with rose water, cardamom seeds, and sugar or honey.

Arabica. Colombian coffee.

Arachichu. A South American tree producing a fruit of moderate flavor.

Arachide (French). Peanut.

Arachis. The peanut.

Arachis Oil. Peanut oil, obtained from arachis nuts; used as bakery compound fat and in making baker's chocolate. It is a cheap and reasonably effective substitute for olive oil and is used as salad oil.

Aragosta (Italian). Clawless lobster.

Aragosta Fra Diavolo. Lobster cooked in sauce of herbs and tomatoes.

Araignée (French). Spider crab.

Arak; Batavia Arak. A brandylike rum of ancient lineage, having been distilled from sugar cane and rice in the East Indies as far back as 800 B.C. Today in Indonesia arak is produced in factories in and around Djakarta. Molasses is fermented with river water and small cooked cakes of dried red Javanese rice. Wild yeasts also contribute to the distinctive quality of the aged rum, which is dry and pungent. In Indonesia it is usually drunk neat. The Dutch, who took arak to the Netherlands, and the Scandinavians, to whom they introduced it, often serve it mixed with fruit juices.

Aramon. A comparatively unimportant variety of grape used for making red wines in southern France, Algeria, and California.

Arancia (Italian). Orange.

Aranciata (Italian). Orangeade.

Arangini (Italian). Balls of rice, often made with ground meat.

Araqui. A potent Ethiopian liquor. The term probably derives from the word *arak*, used in the Middle East.

Arber. A sour-milk, creamy, semihard cheese made in Germany and Czechoslovakia.

Arbois. Various wines of the Jura Mountain region.

Arbor. Orchard.

Arbouse (French). Berry of the arbutus tree resembling the strawberry but lacking its flavor.

Along the Mediterranean coasts it is used in making wines and liqueurs; the sweet and sour berries are also made into a compote.

Arbre à Pain (French). Fruit of the breadfruit tree.

Arbutus. A shrub or small tree which produces small red berries, often used in making wines or liqueurs. *See* Arbouse.

Arca; Arche. A small mediocre-tasting shellfish found on part of the coast of France.

Arcachon (French). An oyster with a strong flavor.

Archiduc, À l'. As applied to egg dishes, served with a cream sauce, with onions and paprika, and garnished with truffles.

Ardi-Gasna. An air-dried sheep's-milk cheese made in the French Pyrenees.

Areca Nut; Betel Nut. The egg-shaped thick fruit of the Areca palm. The seeds are rolled up in betel leaves and chewed with lime in Southeast Asia.

Arenga Palm. A tropical palm tree whose sap is often used to make a type of palm wine; when evaporated by sunshine or heat, the natural sap may be used as a sweet syrup.

Arenques (Portuguese, Spanish). Herrings.

Aresancocho (Venezuelan). Hearty meat stew.

'Arf and 'Arf (Cockney). A blend of porter and pale ale.

Argali. Asian wild or rock sheep.

Argenteuil (French). Having asparagus as an ingredient.

Argentine. A small fish of the salmon family.

Argol. The crust of crude tartar that forms on the inside of the vats in which wine is fermented. When the argol is purified by boiling and recrystallizing, cream of tartar is formed.

Argus. East Indian pheasants related to the peacock.

Argute. Sharp tasting or spicy.

Aril; Arille. Mace.

Aringhe Marinate (Italian). Marinated herring.

Arista (Italian). Roast loin of pork.

Aristologist. Specialist in aristology, the art or science of dining.

Aristotle's Lantern. A fanciful name for the sea urchin.

Arles. A city in southern France, particularly

noted for its sausage, the famous *saucisson d'Arles*.

Arlésienne, À l' (French). Denotes a garnish of sautéed vegetables, especially tomatoes and eggplant.

Armadillo. A South American mammal which is enclosed in a very hard, shell-like casing. The meat is edible, although far from delicious. In North America, the meat is sometimes combined with bread crumbs and plenty of spices, and made into a type of sausage.

Armagnac. A brandy distilled from wine made in the old province of ·Gascony, France. Sometimes called the *brandy of Lafayette*, Armagnac is considered second only to Cognac in quality. Some prefer it to Cognac because it has a drier taste, but connoisseurs believe Cognac is superior. *See* Brandy, Cognac.

Arménienne, À l' (French). With rice, tomatoes, and lemon.

Arme Ritter (German). A type of sweet fritter.

Armoricaine. An alternative spelling for Américaine.

Armoricaines. Oysters found off the coast of Brittany, France. *Armorica* was the Latin term for "Brittany."

Arnhemse Meisjes (Dutch). Small cookies.

Arnione di Vitello (Italian). Veal kidney.

Aroma. Distinctive odor or fragrance. Applied to all foods but particularly to certain aromatic herbs and spices as well as to wines.

Aromates. Substances, such as herbs, spices, and fruit peels, that exude an aroma most people find pleasing in food. Of all aromates garlic is perhaps the most controversial in that many people find it highly pleasing, while many object to it.

Aromatic. Having a spicy, fragrant, or sweet smell; formerly herbs, spices, and seasonings were called aromatics.

Aromatic Seasoning. *See* Épice Culinaire.

Aromatize. To flavor or season with spice; to supply an aroma or fragrance.

Arquebuse. A liqueur prepared from a group of aromatic herbs.

Arracacha. A South American green plant whose tuberous root is eaten like the potato.

Arrack. Hawaii's contribution to the world's alcoholic beverages, white okolehao, or arrack, is a very pale liquor, distilled from a fermented mash of molasses, rice lees, and coconut juice. The more popular dark okolehao is made from a similar mash, except that baked taro replaces the coconut juice, giving the drink its darker color and smoky aroma.

Both liquors are available from 80 to 90 proof. Neither is widely known outside Hawaii, although both are used as ingredients in some of the exotic drinks served in Polynesian restaurants on the mainland.

Arrack should not be confused with arak. *See* Arak.

Arrigny. A soft cow's-milk cheese produced in the Champagne region of France. It is eaten quite fresh, being aged in cellars only 2—3 weeks.

Arrope. An unfermented grape juice boiled to the thickness of syrup and used to sweeten sherry and other Spanish wines.

Arroser (French). To baste with gravy, sauce, oil, butter, or drippings.

Arrostito (Italian). Roasted.

Arrosto (Italian). Roast.

  Arrosto d'Agnello. Roast young lamb.

Arrowhead; Arrowleaf. *See* Wapatoo.

Arrowroot. A dry, powdery, and very nutritive starch used for thickening soups and sauces. When mixed with boiling water it forms a paste which is easily digested by small children and by convalescents. Arrowroot comes from the pith of the roots of several plants of the *Marcanta* genus of South America, but is now cultivated in many other tropical areas of the world. According to legend, it was used to heal wounds caused by arrows, but in reality its name is an approximation of the American Indian *Araruta*, which means "flour root."

Arroz (Spanish). Rice.

  Arroz à la Parellada. Rice cooked with meats, chicken, and vegetables.

  Arroz con Pollo. Chicken and rice colored and seasoned with saffron, a typical Spanish dish that has traveled to every country settled by Spanish people. *Arroz* (rice) is extensively used in cooking on the eastern coast of Spain because of the proximity of the rice paddies south and west of Barcelona. Saffron is extracted from the crocuses grown near Murcia, a little to the south.

Arroz Doce (Portuguese). Rice pudding.

Arsella (Italian). Mussel.

Arsling Pole. A pole with which bakers move hot embers into different parts of the oven.

Artemisia. A genus of plants with a bitter or aromatic taste.

Ärter med Fläsk (Swedish). Pea soup with pork.

Artichaut des Indes. *See* Patate.

Artichaut d'Hiver (French). Jerusalem artichoke.

Artichauts Maraîchères. Artichokes (Globe) dipped in boiling water, then braised in white wine and oil.

Artichoke. Two completely different vegetables: the *French*, or *Globe*, *artichoke*, a dark green, multileaved plant of the thistle family; and the *Jerusalem artichoke*, a tuber.

French artichoke. The green or sometimes purplish heads vary in size from very small to 4–5 inches in diameter. The smallest heads are usually more tender. Each head is served as a single portion. The vegetable has a delicate nutty flavor, which, oddly enough, does not complement certain beverages, including wines, which tend to lose their taste when taken as an accompaniment.

Artichokes have been cultivated for many centuries and have been improved constantly. They grow well in all temperate regions, but the best variety comes from California. In the United States the season is year-round; in France, from June to September.

To cook artichokes, remove the larger outside leaves, cut off the hooked ends of the remaining leaves and clip off the stem close to its base. Carefully separate the leaves and remove the prickly "choke" in the center. Tie the leaves with a piece of string to hold the shape, and cook in boiling salted water, to which a little vinegar or lemon juice has been added. Boil until the base is tender, 15–20 minutes, depending on size. Remove from water, drain, and discard string.

Artichokes may be served hot with melted butter or Hollandaise sauce, or cold as a salad or appetizer. They are eaten with the fingers. Each leaf is pulled off and dipped into the accompanying sauce, and the tender end is eaten. When the leaves have been stripped, the base, or heart, is cut into pieces and eaten with a fork.

Very small artichokes, preserved in olive oil, may be purchased and used as hors d'oeuvre. These are eaten in their entirety.

Jerusalem artichoke. This vegetable resembles a potato but is more warty and misshapen. It is not often found on the market since it does not keep well, but it is easily grown in most sections of the United States. The tuber has a pleasant flavor and makes an interesting change from potatoes. It should be cooked in its jacket after being well washed and scrubbed. The skin is peeled off easily.

Since the vegetable apparently did not originate in Jerusalem, no logical explanation is known for the name.

Artificial Cream. A mixture made with clouded edible oils that can be whipped like regular cream.

Artillery Punch. *See* Punch.

Artischocken (German). Artichokes.

Artisjok (Dutch). Artichoke.

Artocarpad. A tree in the genus *Artocarpus*, to which the breadfruit belongs.

Arval Cake. Originally a cake served after the funeral of a nobleman in medieval England. The word "arval" comes from "arfwol," "arf" referring to inheritance, and "wol" to ale. Today in certain parts of England, arval cakes are passed to the mourners after a funeral; they are not eaten immediately but are taken home.

Arvejas Partidas (Spanish). Split peas.

Arza. An Arabian mare's-milk brandy.

Asadero; Oaxaca. A Mexican white whole-milk cheese.

Asado (Argentine). (1) Barbecue. (2) Any roast meat.

Asafetida (Indian). A gummy or powdered vegetable substance similar to garlic; used as a flavoring ingredient in curries, meatballs, and pickles. The odor is somewhat repellent to Western peoples.

Asam (Malayan). Tamarind, a tropical tree, the fruit of which is used as a flavoring ingredient.

Asco. A modest Corsican cheese made from sheep's and goat's milk; at its best during the winter months.

Ascorbic Acid. Vitamin C, obtained chiefly from fruits and vegetables.

Ascospores. True yeast cells.

Ascus. A spore wall or case (such as the withered yeast-cell wall) where spores have been reproduced.

Ashaks (Afghan). Dough stuffed with leeks.

Ash Bread. In the southern United States, corn bread wrapped in cabbage leaves and baked in ashes.

Ash; Asch Cake. Cake baked on the hearth.

Ashdrink. A beverage, of low alcoholic content, prepared from leaves of the ash, sugar, and yeast.

Ashet (Scotch). A dish or meat platter.

Asiago (Italian). A sweet-curd, semicooked pungent cheese, originally made from ewe's milk but now made from cow's milk. Although it originated in northern Italy, it is now also made in the United States.

Asiatic Corn. A name erroneously given to Indian corn by herbalists who believed that corn originated in Asia, although it actually originated in America.

Asie (Danish). Pickled cucumber.

Asitia. A loathing of food; lack of appetite.

Asparagi alla Fiorentina (Italian). Asparagus with brown butter and poached egg.

Asparagine. An acid substance found in asparagus, potatoes, beetroots, and licorice juice.

Asparaginous. Similar to or related to asparagus.

Asparagus. A slender white or green vegetable known since the days of ancient Rome and now cultivated in most temperate regions. When cooked, it is edible hot, cold, or tepid. Its tips are used in salads and for a variety of garnishes, fillings, and decorations.

Asparagus contains vitamins A and B. It is also rich in mineral salts and tends to stimulate the bladder. Water makes up 94 percent of its weight.

Both white (blanched) and green asparagus are on the market. The color is controlled by the grower, who forms the white shoots by banking earth deeply over the roots to prevent light from reaching them. They are cut just as the tip shows above the ground. The white asparagus is somewhat milder in flavor than the green and is used mostly for canning.

Asparagus is sold by the pound or by the bunch, which usually weighs about 3½ pounds. Fresh asparagus is one of the first signs of spring in the vegetable market. Its season is short, but canning and freezing methods now make it available throughout the year.

Canned asparagus tips are used for salad or garnishing, and the longer stalks as vegetables. Both white and green are available, and may be served hot or cold. No additional cooking is required. The canning process changes the flavor slightly.

Asparagus soups also may be purchased in cans. These are made from stalks or tips, and can be utilized, in condensed form, as a sauce base.

Frozen asparagus varies little from the fresh in flavor or appearance, but the texture is inferior. The spears may be whole or cut into small pieces. Frozen asparagus should be cooked in boiling salted water until tender. It then may be used like the fresh vegetable.

Asparagus Bean. An edible South American bean.

Asparges (Danish). Asparagus.

Aspargesbönner (Norwegian). String beans.

Aspartic Acid. An amino acid; a colorless crystalline substance found in sugar-beet molasses.

Aspe. A firm sheep's-milk farmer's cheese made in the French Pyrenees.

Asperge (French and Dutch). Asparagus.

Aspergesoep (Dutch). Asparagus soup.

Asperges de Candes. A fine-tasting asparagus grown in the village of Candes, in the Touraine region of France.

Asperge Vauclusienne (French). In spite of the name, which indicates asparagus, a preparation made with artichokes, stuffed with ham, etc.

Aspergillus. (1) Mold commonly found on bread.

(2) A type of yeast used in fermenting liquids and foods.

Asperula. Sweet grass or sweet woodruff, used for flavoring liqueurs.

Aspic. (1) (French) A cold dish coated with or molded in a *gelée*. A *gelée* is a jelly made of beef, veal, chicken, or fish stock which jells when cooled, either because of natural gelatin

or because gelatin has been added. One table-spoon (one envelope) of commercial gelatin is used for each two cups of liquid. (2) (American) The jelly itself.

Aspide (Portuguese). Aspic.

Assado nas Brazas (Portuguese). Broiled.

Assaisonnement (French). Seasoning, condiment, or sauce.

Assaisonner (French). To season or to mix.

Assam. Tea from the province of Assam in north-eastern India. It produces a strong, flavorful brew, and is often blended with less pungent varieties for a milder taste. *See* Tea.

Assamar. The bitter substance produced when gum, sugar, starch, gluten, meat, bread, etc., are roasted in the air until they turn brown.

Asseour; Assewer. In medieval England, an officer who set the banquet table for the king.

Assiette (French). (1) A plate. (2) A plate of hors d'oeuvre.

Assiette Anglaise. A variety of cold meats served on one plate.

Assiette Volante. A small soufflé or other small dish that should be served piping hot.

Assietter (Swedish). A plate of hors d'oeuvre served at the table.

Astacian. Lobsterlike crustacean.

Asti Spumante. A sparkling, sweet wine made from Moscato grapes in Piedmontese vineyards around Asti, Italy. *See* Italy, The Wines of.

Ata. A whole-meal flour produced in India in small crushing mills. It is cooked into flat cakes or loaves called *chapatis* (*chapattis*).

Athenaeus. A Greek writer who wrote several works on dining and the art of good living.

Athénienne, A l' (French). In Athenian style; that is, prepared with tomatoes, braised onions, and sweet pimientos, garnished with fried eggplant, and usually served with Sauce Madère.

Atherine. Varieties of small fish, including the sand smelt, which are distinguishable from the real smelt by the absence of the characteristic cucumber odor.

Athol Brose (Scotch). Drink made with whisky and honey.

Atjar (Indonesian). Pickled vegetables, prepared in the Javanese style. The best atjar is made with radishes.

Atka. A small fish found in parts of the Pacific Ocean.

Attar of Roses. An aromatic liquid produced by the distillation of fresh rose petals with water; used in various candies, cakes, and confections.

Attelet. Small decorative skewer made of silver and used for serving special delicacies, such as truffles.

Atteraux. (1) Skewers. (2) Foods strung on a skewer, dipped in a flavoring sauce, then in breadcrumbs, and fried.

Attiksgurka (Swedish). Vinegar pickles.

Attiser (French). To increase the heat of a wood or charcoal fire when cooking food.

Attorta (Italian). Pastry made with fruit, choc-olate, and nuts.

Atum (Portuguese). Tuna.

Atum de Lata. Canned tuna.

Atum Fresco. Fresh tuna.

Atún (Spanish). Tuna.

Atún en Escabeche. Pickled tuna.

Atún Africano (Spanish). African tuna, a somewhat darker variety.

Au; Aux (French). In menus "with," as *aux pommes de terre*, with potatoes.

Auberge (French). Inn.

Aubergine (French). Eggplant. In England, the French word is preferred.

Auberginen (German). Eggplant.

Aubergiste (French). Innkeeper.

   Aubergiste, À l'. In the inn's or hotel's style of preparing a dish.

Au Beurre Noir (French). With black or brown butter.

Au Blanc (French). Cooked white; with a white sauce. Also, to cook foods gently so that they will not add color, as in making a white sauce or in not permitting onions to brown.

Au Bleu (French). (1) As applied to fish, especially trout, cooked in a court bouillon with vinegar. If the fish is not alive, the tail will not curl, thus it is not truly *au bleu*. (2) Meat cooked blood-rare.

Aubour (French). The chevène, a river fish.

Au Brun (French). Cooked in a brown sauce.

Auflauf (German). A soufflé or puff, such as an omelet or baked soufflé pudding.

Au Four (French). Baked in the oven.

Au Gras (French). Cooked in a rich fatty gravy.

Au Gratin (French). Prepared with breadcrumbs or cheese, browned in the oven or under the broiler, and served in the same dish.

Augurkje (Dutch). Gherkin.

Au Jus (French). Of meat, served with the natural juices.

Au Kari; Cari (French). Curried.

Au Lait (French). With milk or cooked in milk.

Auld Man's Milk (Scotch). An eggnog.

Aulx (French). The plural form of "garlic."

Aum (German). A wine cask holding about 160 liters.

Aumelette. Omelet.

Au naturel (French). (1) Cooked very simply, without garnish. (2) Raw.

Aurantiamarin. A glucoside in the albedo of the bitter orange which is partly responsible for the flavor.

Aurore. (1) A cheese of fair quality, made in Normandy, France. (2) Stuffed, hard-cooked eggs. (3) Any dish cooked in Aurore Sauce.

Aurore Sauce. A sauce prepared with either Béchamel or Mornay Sauce combined with tomato purée and a little butter.

Aurum. An Italian liqueur with a strong orange flavor.

Austern (German). Oysters.

Autoclave. A vessel in which high temperatures can be obtained by using high pressure, as the pressure cooker.

Automatic Bakery. A series of machines connected with one another and with a baking oven, capable of manipulating dough, cake, or sponge batters, shaping, tinning, depositing, proving, and baking them practically untouched by hand.

Autrichienne, À l' (French). In the Austrian style; that is, prepared with cabbage, caraway seeds, and paprika.

Autun, Fromage d'. A medium-soft cow's-milk cheese made in Nivernais, France; aged in cellars.

Ava; Kawa Kava, Yava. An intoxicating drink made from pepper roots in various islands of the South Pacific.

Avant-Goût (French). Foretaste, the gustatory sensation experienced before food is actually placed in the mouth.

Avant-Pêche (French). A variety of peach that ripens very early.

Avelãs (Portuguese). Hazelnuts; filberts.

Aveline (French). Hazelnut.

Avellan. A filbert or hazelnut.

Avellanas (Spanish). Hazelnuts.

Avenalin. The globulin protein in oats.

Avenin. The glutelin protein in oats.

Aver Cake (British). An oatcake.

Aver Corn (British). A rent paid in corn, sometimes in the form of bread, to a rector.

Averin. The cloudberry or knoutberry.

Avern. Wild strawberry found in Scotland during August; often made into a jelly.

Aves. A general zoological class of vertebrates, which includes all birds.

Aves (Portuguese, Spanish). Poultry.

Avezia (Portuguese). Flounder.

Aviner (French). (1) To fill a new barrel with cheap wine in order to remove the odor of its wood. (2) An intoxicated person.

Avocado; Avocado Pear; Alligator Pear. A green pear-shaped fruit native to Africa, and now cultivated extensively in the West Indies, Mexico, Central and South America, and in the United States. The fruit varies in weight from 6 ounces to a pound.

   Those bright and fresh in appearance and just beginning to turn soft are most desirable. If the

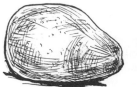

color is right but the fruit is still hard, the fruit may be set aside in a sunny, warm place until soft enough for use. Avocados are easily bruised, and injuries affect the quality of the flesh.

The avocado is rich in unsaturated oil and vitamins, particularly in vitamin B. It has a nutty flavor and a butterlike consistency. Unfortunately, it is quite fattening because of its high oil content.

When cut, the flesh of the avocado tends to turn dark and unappealing in color. To combat this, add a little lemon or lime juice. It has been found that placing the avocado pit in the center of a dish of mashed avocado tends to keep the flesh from darkening.

Avocado Fat. An edible oil prepared from avocado pears.

Avocette; Avocet; Avoset. Long-legged bird of the teal family commonly found along the river banks of western France; prepared like other game birds.

Avoine (French). Oats.

Avola. A Sicilian town that produces excellent sweet almonds.

Avondeten (Dutch). Supper.

Awamori. A very strong Japanese liquor distilled from millet.

Awmous Bannock (Scotch). A bannock or piece of bread given to a beggar.

Awn. A scale or husk; the beard of corn or grass.

Awwamaat (Lebanese). Doughnut.

Axonge; Axunge. Fine white fat obtained from the internal fat of animal kidneys and other organs.

Ayapana. A South American plant whose leaves are dried and used for tea.

Aydes, Fromage des. A home-style cow's-milk cheese produced near Orléans, France, and often aged in wood ashes.

Aygreen. The houseleek, a garden herb or vegetable.

Aylesbury. A variety of English duck of rather good quality.

Ayran (Turkish). A mixture of yoghurt and water.

Ayungin. A Philippine freshwater fish.

Azarole. The reddish fruit of the *Neapolitan medlar*, a Mediterranean plant similar to the hawthorn. Tangy and sweet, it is made into excellent jellies and jams.

Azeitão, Queijo do (Portuguese). A soft, rich, oily sheep's-milk cheese.

Azeitonas (Portuguese). Olives.

Azijn (Dutch). Vinegar.

Azores. A group of islands in the Atlantic Ocean west of Portugal, famous for very sweet, delicious pineapples.

Azúcar (Spanish). Sugar.

Azuki (Japanese). A red bean.

Azukian (Japanese). A paste made from red beans.

Azy. Rennet made of skimmed milk and vinegar.

Azyme (French). A bread made without leavening, such as Norwegian flat breads and Jewish matzos.

Azymous. Unleavened, especially unleavened breads. "Azyme" and "azymous" are often used interchangeably.

B

Baalie (Scotch). A thin underbaked oatmeal cake.

Baba. A light yeast cake, usually baked in a swirl-sided mold and soaked with a rum-and-sugar syrup. The dessert originated in France early in the nineteenth century, and its popularity has spread to many countries. In the United States, babas are available in many bakeries, and canned babas packed in rum syrup are sold also in many grocery stores.

Supposedly, King Stanislas Leszczynski of Poland created and named the cake for one of his favorite literary characters, Ali Baba. It is not known whether the king actually created a new recipe or whether he simply poured rum over *kugelhopf*, a Polish yeast-leavened cake that contains raisins. Many types of baba have been developed since then; some, especially the French version, omit raisins. Others suggest kirsch or Cognac instead of rum in the syrup, and some have a glaze of fruit preserves.

   Baba au Rhum. Either a whole baba or an individual portion soaked in heavy, sweet rum syrup.

Baba Ghannouj (Middle Eastern). Finely chopped or puréed eggplant and sesame seeds.

Babassu Nut Oil. An edible oil made from the babassu palm, greatly resembling coconut oil in taste and aroma.

Babcock Test. A test for fat in milk. A sample is mixed with sulfuric acid in a Babcock bottle, centrifuged, diluted, and recentrifuged. The level of the fat is indicated in the neck of the bottle.

Babeurre (French). Buttermilk.

Babret. Kneading board.

Baby. A quarter bottle of wine or spirits.

Bacalao (Spanish). Codfish.

   Bacalao Madrilena. Dried codfish, boiled with onions, olive oil, and tomatoes.

Bacalhau (Portuguese). Codfish.

   Bacalhau à Gomes de Sa. Dried codfish prepared with onions, garlic, and eggs.

   Bacalhau, Fofos de. Codfish balls.

   Bacalhau Fresco à Portuguesa. Fresh cod with rice and vegetables.

Bacardi. A brand of rum originally distilled in Cuba by the Bacardi family; light in taste and aroma, it is widely used in cocktails and other mixed drinks.

Baccalà (Italian). (1) Codfish. (2) Dried salt codfish prepared as a special Christmas dish.

   Baccalà alla Cappuccina. Dried codfish cooked in oil, garlic, and parsley.

   Baccalà alla Veneziana. Sautéed salt codfish.

Bacchanalia. A festival in honor of the Roman god of wine, Bacchus; drunken revelry; orgy.

Bacchant; Bacchante. A priest, priestess, or worshiper of Bacchus; a drunken reveler.

Bacchus. "The riotous god," the Roman god of wine.

Bacciferous. Producing or bearing berries.

Baci (Italian). Macaroons made with candied lemon peel, cinnamon, and cloves; a specialty of Liguria.

Bacillus Lactis. Bacteria that turn milk sour.

Bacillus Mesentericus Vulgatus. Bacteria or germs

that cause "rope" disease, attacking breads and cakes.

Bacillus Mycoderma Aceti. Bacteria that cause wine to sour.

Backbear (British). The carrying of illegally killed venison on the back (*Forest Laws* of 1667).

Back-Brede. Baking board.

Bäckerei (German). Pastry.

Backhuhn (German). Breaded fried chicken.

Back'n'Bier (German). A strong-flavored beer; a specialty of Bayreuth.

Backspan (Scotch). A baking plate for oatcakes.

Back-Spittle. A wooden shovel or board for baking purposes.

Backsteiner. A German cheese somewhat like Limburger.

Backster. A baker.

Backstone (Scotch). A special stone used for baking bread and oatcakes.

Backward Doughs. Yeast doughs that rise too slowly because they are too cool, contain too much salt, or contain old yeast.

Backwerk (German). Pastry.

Bacoco. Porgy, a kind of fish.

Bacon. Bacon comes from the breast and flank of the pork carcass after the spareribs have been removed. It is either dry- or pickle-cured, then smoked. Bacon is available lean and fat. Qualities vary, the same packers offering luxury bacons as well as inferior grades, the latter being less expensive and perfectly satisfactory as a flavoring ingredient in cooking. Even cheaper cuts are available for flavoring, such as the bacon chunks or squares, and "ends," sold in many supermarkets. For those who prefer thicker bacon slices than those generally available in packages, slab bacon is the answer, as it can be cut to any desired thickness.

Canadian, or Canadian-style, bacon is cut from a different part of the pork carcass. It is a cured, smoked, boneless strip of pork loin, much leaner and more expensive than regular bacon. It comes in a rounded shape rather than in slabs.

Only about a one-week supply of bacon should be bought at one time, because this fat meat is perishable and can be kept only for a week, or two weeks at the most, for the best flavor. It should be stored in the refrigerator in its original wrappings. Bacon cannot be frozen satisfactorily, because the fat turns rancid.

Bacon may be fried, broiled, or baked. Remove the package from the refrigerator a half-hour or so before separating the slices.

To fry bacon: Put bacon in a cold skillet over medium heat. For crisp slices, pour off the fat as it accumulates in the pan. Turn frequently and, when slices are brown and crisp, drain on absorbent paper.

To broil bacon: Arrange the slices on a rack three inches from the source of heat, with control set at 350°. Turn slices frequently until brown.

To bake bacon: The bacon need not be turned as it cooks to provide uniformly well-cooked slices. Place the separated slices on a rack in a baking pan. Bake in a 400° oven 10 minutes or until brown.

The bacon fat may be strained, cooled, and refrigerated to be used for frying potatoes, eggs, or as a seasoning in vegetables, baked beans, or meat loaf.

Baconique (French). A medieval meal consisting chiefly of pork or pork products.

Bacony. Fatty, like bacon.

Bacoreta (Spanish). A dark meat variety of tuna.

Bacum (British). Baked.

Badderlocks. An edible seaweed.

Badet (Javanese). A fermented liquor made from rice, sometimes with spices and fruit juices added; a holiday and party drink.

Badian; Chinese Anise; Star Anise. Fruit of the badian tree, used in flavoring anisette, a sweet liqueur. In India, China, and Japan, badian wood is burned to scent the house. The dried fruit is chewed after meals like an afterdinner mint. Badian seeds have the licorice taste of anise and are used in baking breads and cakes and as a flavoring in sausage.

Badian Anise. An alternative name for Chinese anise and star anise.

Badiane (French). Badian; Chinese anise; star anise.

Badischer (German). Pike.

Badisches Ochsenfleisch (German). Boiled beef with horseradish sauce, a specialty of the Black Forest region.

Badminton Cup. A wine cup made of claret and

herbs. The herbs should be removed as soon as the proper taste balance is achieved.

Bael; Bengal Quince. An East Indian fruit of the orange family. Picked half ripe, it is dried and cut in slices. The ripe fruit is very fragrant and may be enjoyed as it is or be made into preserves.

Baffat (Indian). Curry made with meat and radishes.

Bagasse. Sugarcane pulp after the juice has been extracted under great pressure.

Bagel. A Jewish bread. The dough is shaped like a doughnut, boiled, then baked to a golden brown. Split down the middle, it is buttered, or spread with cream cheese and covered with lox (smoked salmon); popular at Sunday morning breakfast.

Bagna Cauda (North Italian). Dip for raw vegetables prepared by simmering garlic and chopped anchovies in a blend of butter and olive oil and kept hot over a spirit lamp.

Bagnes; Fromage à la Raclette. A very hard Swiss cheese. Half-inch slices are toasted until runny, then spread on bread and eaten hot.

Bagoong (Philippine). Salted, fermented shrimp; also dried shrimp.

Bagozzo; Bresciano. A hard yellow, rather sharp-flavored Parmesan-type cheese.

Bag Pudding. A pudding boiled in cloth. A well-floured cloth is laid in a bowl or colander and filled with the suet crust and meat. The crust is then sealed over and the cloth knotted. The pudding is dropped in boiling water and cooked gently 2–3 hours.

Bagration. (1) A cold sauce of mayonnaise, anchovy purée, and caviar. (2) A salad made with artichoke bottoms, celery root, and macaroni. These are only two of numerous dishes named for the famous Russian general who loved fine food.

Bagre. The common catfish.

Bahamas. The food in the Bahamas was originally British, then it became "international," at least in the luxury hotels, but now it shows strong signs of becoming almost American. However, Nassau does have local specialties, many of which are of interest to the gourmet.

The majority of local strong drinks are based upon rum, but gin and whisky are equally important. There are some good dishes prepared with three local sea specialties—conch, (a large shellfish), turtle (best made into a Bahamian turtle pie), and margot fish, which has a good flavor. Conch (pronounced "conk") is made into chowders, fritters, curries, and *conch souse* (pickled with vinegar and lime juice). The most unusual soups are made of okra, conch, breadfruit, coconut, turtle, and whelk.

Rice dishes, *pilaus*, made of chicken, okra, and the like, are very popular. Roast wild pigeon is a tasty dish. Vegetable dishes are baked papaya, baked kidney beans, a number of breadfruit preparations, and the classic peas and rice, Nassau style. Some good salads are prepared with avocados, breadfruit, and papayas. The desserts are usually based upon fruit—bananas, guava, pineapples, yams, and coconuts.

Bahama Duck; Pintail. An edible herbivorous wild duck native to the West Indies and South America. *See* Duck.

Baicoli (Italian). A sweet pastry.

Baie de Ronce (French). Blackberry.

Baier (Norwegian). Dark beer.

Baik; Bake (Scotch). A cookie or cake.

Baikbred. Kneading trough.

Bain-de-Pieds (French). Literally, a footbath. Colloquially, coffee or tea poured from a cup into a saucer.

Bain-Marie (French). Double boiler. Sauces and custards that must never be allowed to boil can be cooked in the top part over the boiling water in the lower pan; the sauce will stay below the boiling point. The bottom pan should be heavy and flat so that it will not rock when top mixture is being stirred.

Baiser (French). Literally a kiss; in cooking, two very small meringues joined together with whipped cream or jelly.

Baissière (French). Sediment from wine.

Baisure (French). The soft part of the bread where two loaves touch each other.

Bait (Obsolete, British). Food or refreshment. As a noun, a light repast for travelers; a snack between meals. As a verb, to stop for rest or refreshments.

Bajet. A very flat type of oyster found off the coast of Africa; used chiefly for soups.

Bake. (1) To cook food by means of dry heat that does not reach it directly. (2) A social gathering at which food is served, such as a clam bake. (3) To make foods dry or firm by means of heat.

Bake Blind. To bake pie shells unfilled, so that they may be filled later as needed. To keep the pastry flat without bubbling or rising unevenly, lay greaseproof paper on the uncooked pastry, cover with rice, dried peas, or beans, and bake until done.

Baked Alaska. A dessert that must be prepared just before it is to be served. Cake, hard-frozen ice cream, and meringue are baked in a hot oven about 5 minutes or until the meringue is delicately browned but not dry.

Bakemeat. Pie or pastry.

Baken (Obsolete). Baked.

Bake Off. (1) Bakers' term for cooking bread and occasionally cake. (2) A cooking contest.

Baker. (1) One who bakes or makes bread and cakes. (2) A small portable tin oven.

Baker-Crab. A ceramic pie dish.

Baker's Cheese. A skim-milk cheese similar to cottage cheese but softer, more finely grained, and more sour; used commercially for cheesecakes and fillings.

Baker's Dozen. Thirteen.

Bakery. Baker's shop; a place where bread and cakes are made and sold.

Bakewell Pudding. A preserved-fruit pudding named for Bakewell, England, where it originated.

Bakewell Tart (British). A rich tart of pastry, jam, and custard, sometimes almonds, originally made in Derbyshire.

Baking. The process of cooking by dry heat in a confined space, such as a heated oven, at temperatures varying from 250° to 550°. Most recipes indicate the desired oven temperature and time required for baking.

Baking Case (British). Kneading board.

Baking Powder. A mixture used as a leavening agent for cakes, quick breads, and a few puddings. It has been marketed in prepared form since 1850; until then, home-made combinations of sour milk and baking soda (sodium bicarbonate), or baking soda and cream of tartar were used.

All baking powders contain baking soda, dry acid or acid salts, and starch or flour to stabilize the mixture. The soda and acid, when moistened and heated, act together to produce carbon dioxide, the leavening agent. There are three kinds of baking powders, which differ in the acid content:

(1) Double-acting, combination or SAS-phosphate powders containing calcium acid phosphate and sodium aluminum sulfate;

(2) Tartrate powders containing cream of tartaric acid; and

(3) Phosphate powders containing calcium acid phosphate or sodium acid pyrophosphate.

Because of the different acid ingredients used, baking powders vary in reaction speed. These variations in reaction time are due to differences in the quantity of carbon dioxide gas liberated and lost during the mixing of the batters. It is best to follow the proportions suggested in the directions that come with a particular brand of powder.

To check if baking powder is still active: stir 1 teaspoon baking powder into a ¼ cup hot water. If bubbles do not form quickly, the powder is stale and will not be effective.

SAS-Phosphate. A so-called double-acting type of baking powder. A rather small amount of gas is released when the dry ingredient is combined with the liquid, but the larger amount is released when heated.

Tartrate. A type of baking powder that reacts almost immediately when dry ingredients are combined with a liquid.

Phosphate. A type of baking powder in which some gas is released at room temperature when combined with a liquid; however, some gas is retained until heated.

Baking-Powder Residue. The substance remaining after the chemical action in baking powder has taken place.

Baking Sheet. Aluminum sheet on which to cook pastry and cookies.

Baking Soda; Sodium Bicarbonate; Saleratus. One of the chief ingredients in baking powder. It acts as a leavening agent when combined with sour or acidified milk, molasses, and the dry acids and acid salts used in baking powders.

Baking Test. A small amount of bread, cake, or pastry dough baked or cooked to determine the success of the recipe before proceeding with the whole amount.

Bakin-Lotch (British). A bread of very good quality.

Bakken (Dutch). Fry.

Bakli. An aromatic herb used in Middle East cookery.

Bakso (Indonesian). Meatballs.

Baktjang (Indonesian). Rice mixture cooked in banana leaves.

Bakverk (Swedish). Pastry.

Balachan; Balachong (Asian). Condiment used on rice dishes; prepared with dried shrimp or fish, pounded fine with salt or spices, and dried.

Balane; Acorn Shell. A small shellfish whose fine-tasting meat is prepared like crabmeat.

Balaou. A very small West Indian fish resembling the sardine.

Balata. A tropical tree whose sap is used for making chewing gum.

Balatoni Fogas. A delicate fish from Lake Balaton, Hungary.

Balderdash. A jumbled mixture of liquid, such as milk and beer, or beer and wine.

Baldpate. An edible game duck.

Baleares. Some islands of Spain including Majorca, Minorca, and Ibiza. The best food comes from the sea or from the soil; meat is of comparatively poor quality. Fish is served plain, cooked with vegetables, or used in an excellent fish soup, *sopa de pescado. Sopa a la Mallorquina* is a vegetable chowder. *Tumbet* is a mixed-vegetable dish consisting of tomatoes, peppers, and eggplant.

Ballachony (Indian). Appetizer prepared by pounding shrimp or prawns, ginger, chilies, lemon, onion, and salt to a smooth paste.

Ball Cheese. A Pennsylvania Dutch sour-milk cheese.

Balli; Baalic (Scotch, British). A thick cake.

Balling Saccharometer. A machine that measures the density of sugar; used chiefly in candy making.

Ballisten (Scotch). A stone on which oatcakes are baked.

Ballotine (French). Boned, stuffed, and rolled meat, poultry, game, or fish served hot or cold.

Ballotine de Canard. Duck's legs boned and stuffed with ground pork or ham.

Balm. A fragrant herb of the mint family found in most temperate climates. The plant is about two feet tall and has clusters of pale yellow flowers. The strongly aromatic leaves have a decided lemon odor and flavor. The ancient Greeks and Orientals used balm in tea and wine drinks to soothe nerves and reduce fever. Today it is used for perfumes and toilet waters and in such liqueurs as Chartreuse and Benedictine. The fresh or dried leaves give a distinctive taste to fruit drinks and wine cups, salads, soups, sauces, and stuffings.

Balorine A hash made of finely ground or chopped meat with beetroot, spring onions, and caraway seeds.

Balsam Pear. The Chinese bitter melon, so called because its vaguely medicinal bitter taste suggests quinine; used chiefly in soups and braised dishes.

Balthasar. A bottle holding 3.3 gallons of wine, usually champagne.

Balushai (Indian). Cruller or doughnut consisting of a flattened round ball dipped in sugar syrup.

Balut (Philippine). Eggs allowed to form embryos, then boiled and eaten as an accompaniment to beer or other beverages.

Bambèle; Bambella. A diminutive variety of carp found in many of the lakes of central Europe; prepared like the larger, more common varieties.

Bamboche. Eggs fried in oil and served on a bed of diced creamed vegetables topped with sticks of fried fish.

Bamboo Shoots. Young sprouts from a species of bamboo tree cut when just appearing above the ground. They are tender and flavorful and are used extensively as a vegetable in oriental cookery. The taste is roughly comparable to that of the artichoke. Canned varieties are available in the United States. (See illustration p. 34.)

Bamyee (Middle Eastern). Lamb, beef, or chicken combined with okra and onions.

Banan (Swedish). Banana.

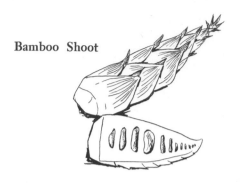

Bamboo Shoot

Banana. The fruit of a large tropical tree cultivated in most countries with hot climates. About 30 species are known, with various tastes. Bananas in the market are usually yellow or red. The red ones are shorter and thicker than the yellow and have a somewhat richer flavor.

The banana is native to India, where it was discovered along the Indus River three centuries before Christ. A legend in the Hindu religion relates that the banana was the fruit forbidden to Adam and Eve in Eden, supposedly located on the island of Ceylon, and that it was with banana leaves that they covered their nakedness. Banana plants were introduced into the New World by Spanish colonials in 1516.

In many tropical regions, natives look upon bananas as their staple food. A diet consisting solely of this fruit will sustain life for a long period because of the relatively high nitrogen content. Grown on a given acreage, bananas will support a larger number of humans than will wheat.

Bananas are harvested and shipped while still green and unripe. Green bananas are composed chiefly of starch and may be indigestible. Properly ripened fruit should have an attractive color, a fresh appearance, and a firm pulp texture. For immediate use, the fully ripe fruit should be purchased. For use over a few days or for cooking purposes, the partly ripe fruit should be bought. This can be matured at room temperature if desired. Ripeness is indicated by the color of the skin, and good flavor is indicated when the solid red or yellow color, depending on the variety, is flecked with brown.

Dried or powdered bananas are available for flavoring.

Banana, Cooking. *See* Plantain.

Banana Essence. A mixture of fats and spice oils dissolved in water and alcohol; used to impart the general taste and aroma of fresh bananas.

Banana Figs. Bananas split lengthwise and sundried without being treated with sulfur dioxide— a dark, sticky product.

Banana Flour. (1) A flour made by drying well-ripened and carefully selected bananas. It is highly nutritious and digestible, and, when mixed with milk or water into a thin gruel, is suitable for invalids and children.

(2) In the West Indies, unripe bananas are dried, then pounded into flour. It contains some moisture, fat, protein, ash, and carbohydrates.

Banane Fritte (Italian). Fried bananas.

Banania. A banana-flavored French liqueur.

Banbury. A rather soft cylindrical cheese made in Banbury, England.

Banbury Cakes (British). A tart of puff pastry filled with mincemeat, famous in Banbury.

Bancha. A coarse Japanese green tea.

B & B. A mixture of Bénédictine (an herb-infused liqueur) and brandy; less sweet than straight Bénédictine.

Bandes (French). Strips of pastry used in lattice-designed tops for tarts or pies.

Bandes des Cervelas (French). Strings of sausages.

B and S. Brandy and soda.

Bangi. (1) A bright green orange-shaped Philippine fruit. (2) A thick barley or oatmeal cake.

Bañgus. Milkfish, a Philippine fish.

Banian. Member of a Hindu caste that does not eat meat.

Banilloes. Vanilla pods or beans; not in liquid or powdered form.

Banitsa (Bulgarian). Very rich, overly sweet pastry often eaten with fruit.

Bank. A bed of oysters, or other shellfish.

Bankebiff (Norwegian). Beefsteak.

Bankekød (Danish). Beef stew.

Bank Fish. A cod caught off the Newfoundland Bank.

Bannock (Scotch). A fairly large round unleavened bread made of barley or wheat flour, oatmeal, or dried peas, and usually cooked on a hot hearth or on a griddle over the fire.

Hogmanay Bannock. An oatcake. *See* Hogmanay.

Bannock-Even. Shrove Tuesday.

Bannock Fluke. Turbot, a fish similar to a small halibut.

Bannock Stick. Rolling pin.

Banon (French). A farmer's goat's-milk cheese wrapped in chestnut leaves, drenched with brandy, and aged two months.

Banquet. Sumptuous meal served to a large number of people at a festive or ceremonial occasion. The term "banquet" comes from the French *banc* and the Italian *banco*, meaning "bench"; thus a meal taken in company derives its name from the seating facilities.

Banquière, Sauce. A sauce prepared with Sauce Suprême, Madeira wine, and chopped truffles; usually served on egg and poultry dishes.

Bantam. A small domestic fowl; named for Bantam, a community in Java.

Banyan. A fig-bearing tree native to India and other warm countries.

Banyuls. A natural sweet wine produced on the west part of France's Mediterranean coast. Its color ranges from light gold to dark red and it is high in alcoholic content.

Baobab. A large downy-skinned fruit native to Africa but also grown in Florida. Its pulp is edible, though faintly acid, and the leaves and bark of the tree are used to treat tropical fever. The fruit is often called *monkey bread* because in some areas it is a staple with monkeys.

Bap (Scotch). A yeast breakfast roll.

Bap-An-Taak. Buns well covered with jam.

Bapper. Baker.

Bara Brith; Speckled Bread (Welsh). A dark yeast bread filled with currants, raisins, and candied fruit peel.

Bar. (1) (Indian) An intoxicating drink made by certain tribes of the Western Ghats. (2) An establishment that sells drinks over a bar, a long counter. (3) Dogfish, white-fleshed salt-water fish. (4) (Swedish) Berry. (5) The bass, a food fish.

Barack (Hungarian). Apricot brandy.

Bara Lawr (Welsh). Bread made with seaweed.

Bara Pikelet (Welsh). A small round leavened cake made with fine flour.

Baraquille (French). A tasty pastry filled with minced partridge, chicken, veal, sweetbreads, truffles, mushrooms, and other ingredients.

Barbacoa Mexicana (Mexican). Barbecue usually made with young goat or lamb.

Barbade. A liqueur made by steeping lemon and orange peels, spices, and sugar in brandy.

Barbados Cream. A heavy sweet spicy liqueur made with mace, cinnamon, citrus fruit peel, and cloves.

Barbados Molasses. A dark cooking molasses treated to resemble cane syrup.

Barbarée. Winter cress; spicy, crisp vegetable used in soups, in salad, or as a vegetable.

Barbaresco. *See* Italy, The Wines of.

Barbarie, À la. As applied to meat, game, or poultry, studded with truffles.

Barbary Almonds. The small Barbary almonds are bitter, and the sweet ones are not of very good quality. They are used chiefly in making low-priced candies and cakes.

Barbe. (1) Wattle of a turkey. (2) The fin of a flatfish.

Barbecue. Originally a pig or steer roasted or broiled whole for a feast, or the feast at which such provender was served. The term comes from the French *barbe à queue*, or "from beard to tail." The English word was in use in colonial

Virginia before 1700 and is probably of southern United States derivation. Formerly, barbecued

meat was cooked in a pit, but today it is broiled on a grate over a live-coal, charcoal, or wood fire. In the southern and western United States, the barbecue is a long-standing tradition.

With outdoor preparation of food becoming increasingly popular in the United States, the principle has been simplified to fit the smallest backyard or terrace. The home barbecue uses a fireplace or outdoor stove in place of a fire pit, and the equipment may vary from a simple portable outdoor grill to an elaborately constructed fireplace with oven and flues.

Barbe de Bouc (French). The garden-variety black salsify and also the wild variety. The green shoots may be eaten in salads, the root may be prepared like similar root vegetables.

Barbe de Capucin (French). A wild chicory, now grown commercially in dark places so that it may acquire a crisp texture and whitish color; particularly good in salads.

Barbe de Chèvre (French). (1) A mediocre wild mushroom. (2) Clematis shoots, which are occasionally pickled.

Barbe de Jupiter (French). A houseleek that grows on roofs and walls. Its succulent leaves may be used as a vegetable.

Barbel. A European freshwater fish of the carp family with a slightly muddy taste.

Barbera. *See* Italy, The Wines of.

Barberey; Fromage de Troyes. A soft, small cheese, similar to Camembert, made of fresh warm cow's milk, in the Champagne district of France.

Barberry. The red fruit of a shrub grown in most temperate regions, especially in New England. Its pleasantly acid flavor is well suited for preserves and jellies as well as for sauces, tarts, and pies. Barberry wine is sweet, but not distinctive.

Barbescue. A floor on which coffee beans are spread to dry.

Barbier. The Mediterranean "sucker" fish; best when lightly sautéed.

Barbillen (French). A young barbel, a small fish of the carp family.

Barbotte. The eelpout, or river burbot.

Bar Bread. Barley bread.

Barbunya (Turkish). Red mullet.

Barcelona Nuts. Small round hazelnuts or filberts native to Spain, Turkey, and Italy.

Bar de Mer (French). Sea bass.

Barding. Wrapping meat or poultry in fat. A thin sheet of bacon or beef fat is sliced and trimmed to fit around or over meat or poultry. It is tied with string and provides moisture and fat during roasting. This process differs from larding, for which the fat is inserted into the poultry or meat in thin, sometimes seasoned, strips.

Bardolino. *See* Italy, The Wines of.

Bareca. A small cask or keg.

Barfi (Indian). A candy resembling fudge.

Bar Goose. The barnacle goose. *See* Barnacle Goose.

Barigoule; Bourigoule; Brigoule. A brownish mushroom found in parts of southern France; good-tasting but somewhat rubbery in texture.

Barigoule, À la (French). Garnished with coarsely chopped mushrooms in a brown sauce and served with artichokes.

Baril Wheat. A soft, weak wheat produced in Argentina and Uruguay.

Bark. The rind, husk, or shell of fruits and grains.

Barkeep; Barkeeper. A person who works behind a bar where alcoholic drinks are prepared and served.

Bar-le-Duc (French). A preserve or jam dating from the early 14th century. Made of whole red or white currants suspended in a clear jelly, it differs somewhat from a jam, a jelly, or a preserve in that the seeds are removed individually from each currant. Although originally made only with currants, strawberries and other berries are now used also. Sometimes called *confiture de groseille*, it is marketed in tiny glass jars, and is comparatively expensive.

Barley. One of the oldest forms of cultivated cereals, probably originating in Western Asia, where it still grows wild. It was planted by the ancient Egyptians, Greeks, and Romans, and traces have been found in Stone Age remains of the lake dwellers of Switzerland. Ears of barley are shown on ancient coins and on statues plaited into the hair of the harvest goddess Ceres.

Barley is adaptable to both warm and cold climates, and has a wider distribution than any other cereal. When the husks have been removed, the grain is used in soups and stews. When steamed, rounded, and polished, the grain is sometimes ground into a fine whole-meal flour for making bread, porridge, or gruel. Barley is also converted into malt for use in brewing and distilling.

Barley Bangers (British). Barley cakes.

Barleycorn, John. *See* John Barleycorn.

Barley Meal. A ground hulled barley; barley flour is ground pearl barley; barley flakes are flattened grains.

Barley Sugar. Sugar heated just to the melting point, then caramelized, resulting in large, coarse grains.

Barley Sugar Candy. A brittle confection of sugar, boiled quickly and drawn into long thin strips; yellow, more or less transparent, and usually flavored with lemon.

Barley Water. A drink for invalids made in proportions of 2 ounces of pearl barley to 5 pints of water boiled until reduced to half the original bulk, then strained and served cold.

Barley Wine. (1) A beverage, probably more like beer than wine, made by the Egyptians, Babylonians, Assyrians, and other ancient peoples. There is a recipe for barley wine on a Babylonian artifact dating back to about 2800 B.C. (2) Beer in medieval England. (3) A liquor brewed from malt, sometimes without hops.

Barm. The frothy, foaming yeast that forms on the surface of malt liquors during fermentation.

Barm Biscuits. Biscuits made with fermented dough that is allowed to rise overnight, mixed the next morning with flour and leavening, then baked.

Barm Brack. A small flat yeast cake made with sugar, fats, fruits, and other ingredients.

Barmaid. In England a girl or woman who prepares and serves drinks behind a bar.

Barmecide. One who offers imaginary food or illusory benefits. The term comes from the name of a family of princes at Bagdad one of whom put a succession of empty dishes before a beggar pretending that they contained food—a fiction which the beggar humorously accepted.

Barming. Forming barm on a fermenting liquor.

Barmy Sponge. Liquid yeast allowed to stand overnight and then used in breadmaking.

Barnacle. An edible mollusk found attached to rocks, wharves, ship bottoms, etc.; when small it may be eaten raw, but older specimens are better cooked in soups or stews.

Barnacle Goose. A type of wild goose found chiefly in the arctic regions, but also in temperate regions during winter. It is edible, but far from delicious, being tough, stringy, and strongly flavored.

Bar Noir (French). Black bass.

Barolo. One of the best red table wines of Italy. *See* Italy, The Wines of.

Baron. An enormous cut of lamb or beef. The term differs in meaning in various countries.

> **Baron of Beef.** A regal joint of beef consisting of both sirloins cooked and carved while joined at the backbone. Too large for most ovens, it is usually roasted over an open fire.

> **Baron of Lamb.** Usually, both hind legs and both loins of a lamb; the hindquarters. Sometimes, the saddle and both legs.

Barquette (French). A boat-shaped piece of pastry.

> **Barquette Écossaise.** Pastry shell filled with smoked salmon.

> **Barquette Ostendaise.** Pastry shell filled with creamed oysters.

Barquillera (Philippine). A wafer iron used in making *barquillos*, a sweet confection.

Barquillos (Philippine). Dessert made with milk, egg yolks, flour, lemon rind, and sugar, and shaped by hot irons.

Barracuda. A pikelike fish that may grow to 6 feet in length, 30 inches in girth, and 100 pounds in weight. It has a long pointed jaw and razor-sharp teeth; some species are maneaters. The barracuda is a popular game fish but is not particularly valuable as food, although it is popular in California. When smoked, it has an interesting taste.

Bar Rayé (French). Striped bass.

Barrel. A liquid measure, usually 36 gallons.

Barrico. A keg.

Barrot (French). An anchovy barrel.

Barsac. A French wine district of the Bordeaux region. *See* France, The Wines of.

Barse. The original name of a fish subsequently corrupted to *base*, and later to *bass*.

Bar, Service. A counter from which drinks are handed to waiters who serve customers at tables.

Bar Spoon. A long-handled spoon with a small cup; used for stirring cocktails in a cocktail mixer.

Bar Syrup. A simple sugar syrup.

Barszcz (Polish). *See* Borscht.

Bartavelles. Red-legged or rock partridge, a game bird native to France.

Barton (British). (1) A pen for poultry. (2) Formerly a large farm.

Barusso Wheat. A reddish, fairly strong South American wheat.

Baryani Pilau (Pakistani). Highly seasoned rice-and-lamb dish made with yoghurt, almonds, and raisins.

Basam. An Asiatic legume much used in India.

Basic Seven Foods Plan. A division of foods into seven groups, with the recommendation that some food from each group be eaten every day to ensure a well-balanced diet.

Group 1—Green and yellow vegetables. *Group 2*—Oranges, tomatoes, grapefruit, and raw salads. *Group 3*—Potatoes and other vegetables and fruits. *Group 4*—Milk and cheese. *Group 5*—Meat, poultry, fish, and eggs. *Group 6*—Bread, flour, and cereals. *Group 7*—Butter and margarine.

Basil; Sweet Basil. A hardy annual herb whose leaves emit a sweet clovelike fragrance. Native to India, the plant is used as a symbol of reverence to the dead, and a pot of it is kept in memory of a departed loved one. It is also one of the symbols of love in Italy. Basil grows 2–2½ feet high, with large heart-shaped leaves and white tubular flowers forming in spikes at the top of its branches. Either the fresh or the dried leaves are used to flavor eggs, fish, meats, poultry, salads, soups, sauces, and vegetables.

Basilic (French). Basil; sweet basil.

Basil Sherry. A flavoring used for enriching soups, especially mock or real turtle soup.

Basmuttee. A fine rice grown in India.

Basquaise, À la. Of meat, garnished with sautéed potatoes, mushrooms sautéed in olive oil, and chopped ham.

Bass. Any one of several kinds of spiny-finned sea and river fishes. Most are excellent for food and may be purchased whole or in fillets or steaks, depending on their size. They may be baked, broiled, or fried.

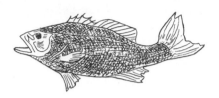

Best-known saltwater varieties

Black sea bass—one of the most abundant and important food fish caught along the east coast of the United States. It has an oblong body, is silvery blue, and is covered with hard, rough scales. The white flesh is particularly delicious.

California white sea bass—a large fish, similar to the weakfish, weighing from 50–100 pounds.

Sea bass—one of the most popular of European food fishes.

Stone bass—a deep-water sea perch of the tropical Atlantic.

Striped bass or rockfish—native to both coasts of the United States. It is green and yellow with black stripes and weighs from 20–100 pounds. It is greatly valued as a game fish and for food.

Best-known freshwater varieties

Black bass—any one of three types of game fish found in rivers and lakes of the eastern United States. It is silvery blue and is best for food when weighing about 5 pounds.

Calico or strawberry bass—found in the rivers and lakes of the Mississippi Valley. It is small and greenish.

Channel bass—found in rivers in the southern United States. It is silvery gray with a reddish tinge; also called *red drum*.

Rock bass—found in the Upper Mississippi and Great Lakes regions. Its flesh is flabby and often has a muddy taste.

White bass—resembles the rock bass and is often found in the same waters. The flesh is decidedly preferable in texture and taste.

Bass, Gray. A food fish of the perch family.

Bassia. A tropical tree from whose seeds a butter-like oil is pressed; named for Bassi, an Italian botanist.

Bassie (Scotch). A wooden basket or other vessel for carrying meal to the board on which dough is kneaded.

Bassin; Bassine (French). (1) A hemispheric-shaped egg bowl usually made of copper. Some cooks claim that egg whites whip up stiffer and better in this type of copper bowl. (2) A cooking utensil for preparing jams and jellies.

Bassinc à Friture (French). A deep frying utensil.

Bassin à Laver les Doigts (French). Finger bowl.

Basswood. A large tree whose flowers may be boiled and made into a kind of tea.

Bastaple Bread (Irish). A flat soda loaf or cake baked in a pot.

Baste. To pour or brush water, melted fat, or a flavoring or seasoning liquid over food to keep it moist while cooking. In basting roast meats the object is to return to the meat the juices and flavors that dry out during cooking. Basting is usually essential for a roast unless a covered pan is used, and it should be repeated several times during a long cooking period. A spoon, ladle, basting syringe, or cup may be used for pouring the liquid.

Bataclan (French). Pastry heavily flavored with almonds and covered with vanilla icing.

Bâtard Montrachet. A fine white Burgundy wine of the Côte d'Or region of France. *See* France, The Wines of.

Batata (Spanish, Portuguese). *See* potato.

Batatas Doces (Portuguese). Sweet potatoes.

Bataw. The hyacinth bean; used as a food in the Philippine Islands.

Bataway. A Philippine fish of the grouper family.

Batch. The quantity produced at one baking.

Batch Flour. Coarse flour.

Batchie. Baker's assistant.

Baten Gen Mihshee (Middle Eastern). Eggplant stuffed with lamb, rice, and spices.

Batfowl. To catch birds at night by blinding them with a light, then knocking them down or netting them.

Bath Chaps (British). Cheeks of pigs, pickled, then smoked; served boiled as a breakfast dish in England. They originated in Bath, and are less popular now than formerly.

Batida (Brazilian). Drink made with white rum and the juice of the marajuca, a local fruit.

Bâton (French). Stick or slice, often of bread.

Bâton de Jacob (French). Small oblong sponge-cake with a flavored cream filling and a chocolate frosting.

Bâtonnets (French). Small cakes, usually shaped in lengths, and made with any desired ingredients, such as nuts and spices.

Bâtons Royaux (French). Minced chicken or game in small patties.

Batow. A string bean native to the South Pacific.

Battelmatt. A large, round, fairly soft cow's-milk cheese made in Switzerland.

Batten. (1) To fatten or gain weight. (2) To eat with great gusto or greedily.

Battenburg. A multicolored butter sponge layer cake, arranged lattice fashion and filled with almond paste.

Batter. A mixture of flour and a liquid (plus salt, eggs, and sometimes sugar) which can be either poured or dropped from a spoon. *Pour batters* usually consist of 1 part liquid to 1 part flour, as in griddlecakes and popovers. *Drop batters* have 1 part liquid to 2 parts flour and are used in muffins and gingerbread.

    Batter Cakes. Griddlecakes and flapjacks.

    Batter Yeast. Dough used as a "starter" for other yeast doughs.

Battered Trotters. Pig's or sheep's trotters or calf's feet stewed with vegetables, covered with thick batter, and deep-fried.

Batterie de Cuisine (French). The complete apparatus or set of utensils used for preparing or serving meals.

Battle; Battel. To feed or nourish; to promote growth.

Battuto (Italian). A flavoring ingredient, used in Rome, consisting of lard, garlic, parsley, and celery.

Batu Geling (Malaysian). A grinding stone used in making curry paste.

Batu Lesong (Malaysian). The pestle and mortar used in preparing the classic spice mixtures.

Bauden Cheese. A sour-milk cheese made in Germany and Austria, usually conical or cylindrical in shape.

Bauernbrot (German). A coarse-grained dark bread.

Bauernomelett (German). Bacon-and-onion omelet.

Bauernsuppe (German). A vegetable soup with macaroni.

Bauletto (Italian). Rolled veal.

Baume. A resin-flavored French liqueur.

Baumkuchen (German). "Tree-cake," Christmas cake shaped cylindrically, like a hollow tree stump.

Baunilha (Portuguese). Vanilla.

Bavarian Cream; Bavarois; Cream Bavarois; Crème Bavarois. A molded dessert prepared with gelatin, whipped·cream, beaten egg whites, and flavorings, combined with a custard mixture. After chilling, it must be unmolded carefully; if properly made, it will have an extremely light, delicate texture. Softer versions may be used as a sauce with desserts, especially those made with fruits.

Bavarois (French). *See* Bavarian Cream.

Bavaroise (French). A hot drink, containing tea as a base, and with any other desired ingredients, usually sugar, milk, rum, kirschwasser, brandy and eggs.

Bavaroise à l'Eau (French). Tea flavored with orange-flower water.

Bavaroise aux Choux (French). Absinth and orgeat, an almond-flavored syrup.

Bavette d'Aloyau (French). The thin skirt or flank of veal or beef.

Baveuse (French). Runny; *Omelette baveuse* is a partially cooked omelet.

Bawang (Malaysian). Onion.

> **Bawang Merah.** Shallots.
>
> **Bawang Puteh.** Garlic.

Bawd (Scottish). Hare.

> **Bawd Bree.** Rabbit soup.

Baxter (British). Baker.

Bay. *See* Bay Leaf.

Bay Leaf. The aromatic leaf of the small evergreen sweet bay or laurel tree, well known in Europe since the days of the ancient Greeks and Romans. Today it is also cultivated extensively in Central America and the southern United States. The dried leaf is used chiefly for seasoning fish, game, meats, pickles, poultry, salads, sauces, soups, stews, stuffings, and vegetables. It forms a part of the classic *bouquet garni.* After use in cooking, the bay leaf should be discarded.

Baya. A Philippine rice wine, having an extremely pleasant, smooth taste; it is a specialty of the Ifugaos tribe, of the northern Philippines.

Bayonnaise, À la (French). Prepared with a garnish made of gherkins, braised onions, and anchovy fillets.

Bayonne. A town in France known chiefly for its *jambon de Bayonne*, a fine type of ham best served as an appetizer.

Bay Salt. (1) Solar salt, obtained in large crystals originally by the slow evaporation of sea water by the sun's heat. (2) A kind of oyster.

Bay Scallops. The best kind of scallop; smaller than sea scallops and superior in flavor. *See* Scallop.

B/B. Of liquor, bottled in bond.

Beach Plum. A small edible fruit, resembling a plum, which grows on bushes along the seashore in the eastern United States. It is made into a tart jelly that is particularly good with roasted meats and poultry.

Beaker. A large, wide-mouthed drinking vessel; a goblet.

Beaming. A scallop with excellent taste and texture.

Bean. The smooth, kidney-shaped edible seed, one of several seeds formed in the long pods of certain legumes. The name "bean" may also be applied to the plant bearing these seeds or to the pod containing them. Many varieties are used in cooking, in either fresh or dried form. In most cases the pod may also be eaten when young and tender.

Fresh varieties

Snap, string, or french beans—different names given to the long, slim, green vegetable usually eaten, pod and all, while the seeds within are very immature. Modern cultivation has made these beans practically stringless. They are the *haricots verts* on French menus.

Lima or butter beans—these are fairly large and flat and are graded according to size. The Ford Hook variety is the larger, and the smaller is marketed as Baby Lima or Butter Bean. They are sold fresh in the pod (which is not generally eaten) or already shelled.

Broad or fava beans—similar to the Lima, but with a rounder pod and seeds. This is the best-known bean in Europe and the only kind cultivated there until the 16th century, when other varieties were introduced from North and South America and the Orient.

Dried varieties

Lima—shelled dried Lima beans useful in many inexpensive dishes.

Navy—the small white beans commonly used for baked beans.

Kidney—large, dark red, kidney-shaped beans used frequently in regional cookery.

Pinto—the dotted pink and white beans of the western United States, known as *frijoles* in Mexican cookery.

Cowpeas or *black-eye peas*—small white beans with a black spot at the eye. A favorite in the southern United States.

Soybeans—formerly used for cattle feed, but now grown extensively for human consumption. They have a distinctive flavor and more food value than any other dried bean.

Bean Curd; Bean Cake. A popular food made with soybeans in China and other oriental countries. White soybeans are cooked until very soft, forced through a sieve, combined with calcium carbonate, and then formed into cakes. Bean curd itself has little taste, but it is high in protein, is very nutritious and inexpensive, and combines well with other foods. It should be cooked a few minutes before being used.

   Dried Bean Curd. Bean curd is often dried into thin, firm sheets; softened by soaking in water, it may be added to any desired dish.

Bean-Curd Cheese. Bean curd prepared with red or white soybeans and fermented in Chinese rice wines, with salt added.

Bean-Curd Leaf. A Siamese soybean pancake.

Bean Filling, Sweet. A sweet soybean filling often used in Chinese cakes, particularly at New Year's time. Black soybeans are cooked until very soft, then forced through a sieve, combined with sugar, and cooked until the moisture evaporates.

Beano (British slang). A gay party at which alcoholic drinks are served.

Bean Oil. Soybean oil.

Bean Sprouts. Tender shoots of germinated beans used frequently in oriental cookery. They are produced by moistening certain varieties of beans, such as mung, or soy, in slightly warmed water, placed under a damp cloth, which keeps out daylight and bleaches the shoots as they appear. Bean sprouts are sold in cans, but they are available fresh only in areas with a large Chinese population.

Bear. (1) Any of a variety of large carnivores native to North America. The flesh is edible, but is unusually strong in flavor, often tough, and should be used for food only after a long marination. (2) (British) Barley.

Bearberry. A shrub, growing wild in Alaska, that produces a shriveled berry; despite its appearance it has an interesting taste.

Béarnaise, Sauce. A French sauce served with steaks, broiled chicken, and boiled or fried fish. It is a variation of Hollandaise, and should be kept and served slightly warm, never hot or cold. If heated too much, the ingredients separate and curdle. Smooth texture may be restored by adding a few drops of cold water or cream. The sauce was named for Béarn, native city of Henry IV.

Bear's Paw. Although the meat of bears is ordinarily coarse and not especially tasty, the paws have an unusual texture and flavor, suggesting that of smoked ham. Bear's paws are popular with Eskimos and Chinese.

Beater. A cooking utensil for whipping, beating, or blending liquids.

Béatilles (French). Delicacies such as cockscombs and pâté de foie gras. *Une assiette de Béatilles* is a plate of dainty, choice food.

Beating. Rapidly turning over part of the contents of a mixing bowl with a beater, whisk, or spoon

in order to introduce a large amount of air into the mixture.

Beaufort. A sharp, distinctive cow's-milk cheese made in the Savoy district of France.

Beaujolais. A French wine and a French wine district. *See* France, The Wines of.

Beaumé Saccharometer. A machine that measures the density of sugar syrup.

Beaumont; Tomme de Beaumont. A delicate semisoft cheese produced in French Savoy from October until June; an imitation of the Trappist Tamie cheese.

Beaune. A town in the Burgundy region of France. The slopes to the north have fine vineyards, including Les Fèves and Les Grèves. Some Beaune winegrowers store their wines in the ancient city walls constructed when the Romans occupied Gaul. The wines are lighter and softer and mature earlier than those of northern Burgundy.

Beaune, Hospice de. A famous group of wines produced near Beaune, France; the Hospice is a charitable organization formed many centuries ago. *See* France, The Wines of.

Beauvilliers, Antoine. French restaurateur who founded the first real restaurant in Paris before the Revolution. Called "La Grande Taverne de Londres," it was situated on the Rue de Richelieu, near the Palais Royal. He was the author of *L'Art du Cuisinier*.

Beauvilliers Cake. A rich spongecake, iced and filled with cream; originally, a foil-wrapped cake intended for travel, named after Beauvilliers by one of his pupils, the pastrycook, Monnier. *See* Beauvilliers, Antoine.

B.E.B. "Best ever bottled"; a boastful claim of liquor bottlers.

Bebidas (Portuguese). Drinks; liquor.

Bécasse (French). The woodcock, a tiny game bird.

Bécasseau (French). A very small game bird, aromatic and delicious, usually eaten bones and all.

Bécasse de Mer (French). The red surmullet, a Mediterranean fish often cooked without being gutted, like the bécasse.

Bécassine (French). Snipe, a game bird.

Beccaccia (Italian). Woodcock.

Béchameil, Louis de (Marquis de Nointel). A seventeenth-century financier who was Lord Steward of the Royal Household of Louis XIV. Béchamel sauce is said to have been invented by him, but is more likely to have been named after him by some court chef. *See* Béchamel.

Béchamel (French). A basic white sauce, usually made with milk, sometimes with stock. It was supposedly created for Louis de Béchameil, Marquis de Nointel, financier and Lord Steward of the Royal Household of Louis XIV, at whose banquets this sauce frequently appeared.

Beckenoffe (Alsatian). Stew made with pork, lamb, and potatoes.

Becker. A Mediterranean fish; found also in warm waters and in African rivers; the freshwater fish is regarded as superior.

Bécune (French). The sea pike.

Bedagosa. A synthetic coffee prepared from cassia seeds; frequently used in Europe for adulterating natural coffee.

Bedfordshire Clanger (British). A two-course meal, both courses of which are contained in the same pastry roll and cooked simultaneously. The main-course end, filled with minced meat and onion, is separated by a pastry strip from the dessert end, spread with jam or molasses.

Bedstraw. A delicate wild herb, yellow and white. The stems and leaves can be used like rennet for curdling milk. The flowers are often used for coloring cheese and butter.

Bee Bread. A honeycomb still containing honey.

Beechnut. Beech trees produce small triangular-shaped nuts that taste much like filberts. Beech trees occasionally grow in groves, or in twos or threes in New England woodlands, but not abundantly enough to warrant commercial gathering of the nuts. New Englanders, however, often go "nutting" in the fall for these delectable kernels.

Beef. The flesh of the ox, cow, heifer, or steer raised for food and usually specially fattened for the market. The best beef is firm to the touch. The lean meat is a brilliant red and the fat nearly white; the lean should be dotted with small flecks of white fat.

Beef is marketed in many cuts, and the quality of an individual joint or piece of meat depends on the part of the carcass from which it comes. The quality of beef in general depends upon breed, age, and methods of feeding, fattening, and slaughter of the animal. "Prime" or "Grade A-1" beef comes from the very choicest steer or heifer. In the case of the "Choice" Grade the animal is usually older when slaughtered and the meat is darker in color, with negligible fat mixed in the lean portions.

Wholesale cuts of beef include: round, rump, flank, loin, plate, rib, brisket, chuck, foreshank, variety meats.

Of these, the most tender and most expensive retail cuts are from the loin and rib: sirloin, porterhouse, shell and T-bone steaks, and rib roasts and rib steaks. Variety meats include: brains, heart, kidneys, liver, lights (or lungs), sweetbreads, tongue and tripe.

Beef is either chilled or frozen for marketing and should be kept under refrigeration until cooked. However, it must not be left too long in the home refrigerator. Chopped or ground beef, in particular, should be used as quickly as possible. Variety meats also keep less well than the regular cuts. Frozen meats should be thawed thoroughly before cooking.

Beef may be prepared for the table by broiling, roasting, pot-roasting or braising, or stewing or boiling. The choice of cooking method is usually determined by the cut.

Boiled Beef. Formerly a favorite preparation in Austria. The meat was cut in a score of different ways, boiled, and served with apple sauce, grated horseradish, pickles, boiled potatoes,

or mustard. Some of the cuts no longer used included *Beinfleisch, Kavalierspitz, Ortschwanzl, Hieferschwanzl,* and *Tafelspitz.*

Dried Beef. Thin slices of beef preserved by air- or heat-drying, or by curing or smoking.

Beefeater. One who eats beef. It is thought that the Yeomen of the Guard, on duty at the Tower of London, were so named because of the enormous amount of beef allotted to and consumed by them.

Beef Olives. Very thin slices of beef filled with a savory stuffing, rolled and tied, browned in a little fat, then simmered in thick gravy until tender.

Beefsteak. A thick cut of beef from the hindquarter suitable for broiling or pan-frying.

Beefsteak Fungus. A large edible mushroom that grows on trees and somewhat resembles a beef tongue.

Beef Tea. A concentrated meat broth, often used in invalid diets, usually made by pouring boiling water over a more or less solid form of beef extract. It can also be made by steaming beef in a very small quantity of water until all the juice is extracted.

Beer. One of the favorite thirst-quenching beverages in the world, particularly in countries where there are no vineyards and where wine or spirits are too expensive for daily use. It is also a popular cooking ingredient. The word "beer," probably derived from the Saxon *bere,* meaning "barley," is a generic term for all fermented malt beverages, including ale, bock beer, lager, and stout.

Beer is made from water and malted barley which are fermented, usually flavored with hops, refined, and filtered. The taste and alcoholic strength depends upon the quantity and quality of the malt and water and also upon the manner and method of brewing and storing. The greater the proportion of water to malt, the less alcohol in the beer.

To make beer, barley is dampened, spread on a floor, and allowed to germinate. The germ, removed and dried in a kiln or oven, becomes malt. The malt is then ground in a mill to become grist. The grist is mixed with hot water in a tub and becomes mash. Hops are then added to the mash (except in the case of ale), which becomes wort. The wort is drawn into a fermenting vat, yeast is added, and fermentation occurs.

The invention of fermented beverages from grain is attributed to the ancient Egyptians, and the Babylonians are known to have made as many as eighteen varieties of beer as early as 2200 B.C. There is no specific mention of beer in the Bible, but many of the references to wine are believed to have been intended to mean beer. According to Assyrian sources, beer was one of the provisions on Noah's Ark. The Greeks learned brewing from the Egyptians, and then taught the Romans. The process spread through the Romans to Britain and to Northern Europe. The Germans were the first to use hops for flavor, and they also discovered a method for aging beer, which became *lager*, after the German word meaning "to store." Beer was stocked on the *Mayflower*, William Penn had a personal brewery, and George Washington his private recipe. It was the discoveries of the French scientist Louis Pasteur that made beer bottling economically feasible and a major industry throughout the world.

Beer and Skittles. The pleasures of life. Skittles, which sounds temptingly edible, is an English game of ninepins.

Beeregar. Vinegar produced from beer.

Beeren Auslese (German). A fine sweet wine produced from grapes individually removed from selected grape clusters. *See also* Germany, The Wines of.

Beery. Like beer; tasting like beer; containing plenty of beer.

Beer Yeast. Brewers' yeast.

Beest; Beestings. The first milk a cow gives after the birth of her calf. The flavor is different from that of later milk.

Beeswing. The second crust that forms on very old port wine.

Beet. Not particularly rich in any nutrient, beets are served mainly because of their flavor and their attractive deep red color. Beet greens, however, are good sources of vitamins A and C, riboflavin, and iron.

The ancient residents of Mediterranean countries knew nothing about vitamins, but they so much enjoyed the refreshing flavor of beet greens that they ignored the roots. It was not until the second century A.D. that Romans began cooking and eating the fleshy red root. Now, of course, beets are a staple vegetable in many countries, being used also in soups and salads.

In the United States, nearly two-thirds of all the beets eaten are canned; they are available whole, sliced, diced, quartered, or cut julienne or shoestring style, and may be plain, pickled, spiced, or in the sweet-sour Harvard sauce. Fresh beets are on the market the year round, but the tiny beets with the greens attached are usually obtainable only in the spring. Beet greens or tops are sold in the summer.

In buying beet greens look for fresh, tender leaves, and cook them within a day or two. Leaves with coarse, heavy veins or ribs are usually too tough to be palatable. Beets should be smooth and firm and free from cracks, ridges or scars around the top. Store them in a cool moist place. The medium-sized ones are likely to be more tender than the larger ones, especially during the winter months.

To retain their color, beet roots should be cooked whole in their skins with the roots and with about an inch of the stem left intact. Beets require at least 20 minutes' cooking in boiling water, depending on the size.

Beetroot. The English preference is for beetroot, the American for plain beet. *See* Beet.

Beeves. Oxen.

Bee Wine. Wine produced by the usual alcoholic fermentation of sugar but with yeast in the form of a clump and lactic bacteria. The clump rises and falls with the bubbles of carbon dioxide produced.

Before-the-Rain Jasmine. A rather aromatic, light, somewhat sweet tea made from early jasmine leaves, those appearing before the rainy season being regarded as the finest.

Beggar's Chicken (Chinese). A whole small young chicken wrapped in many thicknesses of special paper, then covered with clay approximately an inch thick. After being baked, the hard clay is carefully cracked open, the paper unwrapped, and the chicken emerges soft and succulent, though often likely to be lacking in

Benzoyl Peroxide. A substance used chiefly to bleach flour.

Benzyl Acetate. A colorless liquid used to supply the synthetic flavor of apples, plums, or raspberries to candies.

Benzyl Butyrate. A colorless liquid used to supply the synthetic flavor of fruits to candies, jellies, etc.

Benzyl Cinnamate. A white crystalline material used to furnish a pineapple or berry flavor to various foods.

Benzyl Formate. A colorless liquid used to supply the synthetic flavor of pineapple or apricot to various foods.

Benzyl Isobutyrate. A colorless liquid used to supply the synthetic taste and aroma of raspberries or strawberries to various foods.

Benzyl Isovalerate. A colorless liquid used in the manufacture of candy and jelly to supply the taste and odor of various fruits, especially apples.

Benzyl Propionate. A colorless liquid used to supply a synthetic taste of bananas in various foods.

Béquet (French). The lower jaw of a pig's head, which is generally cured and smoked.

Bercy Sauce (French). Sauce made from fish concentrate, white wine, and shallots.

Berenjena (Spanish). Eggplant.

Bergamder (French). A species of duck.

Bergamot. (1) A lemon-flavored herb related to the mint. After the colonial patriots had tossed a shipload of British tea into Boston harbor, they chose as a substitute for their favorite brew, the dried leaves of wild bergamot. Red bergamot, also known as *bee balm* or *Indian's plume*, grows wild in the eastern United States; the Oswego Indians made a beverage from it. (2) A popular English winter pear, cultivated since the Middle Ages, possibly having been introduced into England by the Romans. (3) A pear-shaped orange, the rind of which is used in confections and toilet waters.

Bergamottes de Nancy (French). A famous lemon-flavored sweet confection made in Nancy; prepared with bergamot.

Bergamo. A wine produced in Lombardy, Italy.

Bergère, À la (French). In shepherdess style; that is, with a garnish of mushrooms and parsley.

Bergkäse. A group of Swiss-type cheeses from various Alpine regions. Best known are *Battelmatt*, *Fontina*, *Gruyère*, *Montasio*, *Vacherin*, and *Walliser*.

Bergquara. A Swedish cheese similar to Gouda.

Beringela (Portuguese). Eggplant.

Berigões (Portuguese). A bivalve similar to a cherrystone clam.

Berle, Ache d'Eau (French). Wild celery.

Berliner Art (German). In the Berlin style.

Berliner Pfankuchen (German). A doughnut stuffed with jam and fried, a Berlin specialty.

Berlingot. A kind of caramel made in France.

Berlingozzo (Italian). Cream cake.

Berlinois (French). Ball-shaped light yeast cakes similar to doughnuts.

Bermuda. Bermuda cuisine naturally resembles that of the British homeland. To this may be added the dishes served in the luxury hotels, the vaguely French-type cuisine. However, Bermuda has a few interesting dishes, although no truly distinctive cookery style.

The most unusual local drink is the *Bermuda Swizzle Cup* made with rum, bitters, sugar, and eggs. Bermuda fish chowder is good, as is the *Bermuda codfish breakfast* prepared with potatoes, bananas, and avocados. The most interesting meat dish is the cassava pie, made with pork and chicken and cassava, a locally grown starchy root. Bermuda onions, of course, are known for their delicate flavor, and when baked with grated cheese and eggs are even more delicious. The best desserts contain fruits, particularly coconuts and bananas; there is also an interesting local fruitcake prepared with buttermilk.

Bermuda Onion. A large, very sweet, very mild-flavored onion originally grown in Bermuda but now cultivated also in Texas and California. On the exterior some varieties are pale gold, others are purple-red.

Bermuda Swizzle Cup. A drink made with light rum, bitters, eggs, and sugar.

Bernacle. Barnacle.

Bernaisetunke (German). Béarnaise sauce.

Bernard, Émile. A nineteenth-century chef employed by King Wilhelm I of Prussia; best remembered for his book, *Cuisine Classique*.

Bernarde. A saffron-colored Italian cheese made from a combination of cow's and goat's milk.

Bernard l'Hermite (French). The hermit crab.

Bernkastel. A village in the Moselle region of Germany known for its superb white wines. *See* Germany, The Wines of.

Berried. Of shrub, tree; having berries on its limbs or branches.

Berro (Spanish). Watercress.

Berry. A small pulpy fruit, usually edible, of many varieties. Juices of some berries are used for refreshing drinks or are made into wine or brandy. The whole berry is served raw in fruit cups or salads, or is cooked in pies and tarts,

jellies, jams, and preserves. The most popular varieties are blackberry, blueberry, cranberry, currant, dewberry, gooseberry, huckleberry, loganberry, mulberry, raspberry, and strawberry (*see* under individual names). Botanically the banana, grape, and tomato are classified as berries.

Berry Sugar. A sugar with small, fine crystals that dissolve readily.

Besaigre (French). Of wine; starting to turn sour.

Besi (French). (1) Numerous varieties of pears, usually cold weather types. (2) Salted, dried cow's meat; a term used somewhat derogatorily.

Bésis (French). Stew made with beef simmered with pearl barley, olive oil, and the juices of oranges and lemons.

Besuga de Laredo (Spanish). The red gilthead, a food fish; not so good as the Dorado.

Betaine. Tasteless, colorless crystalline constituent of beet sugar molasses.

Betasuppe (Norwegian). Mutton broth.

Bête (French). Literally, beast; wild game, especially wild boar.

Betel Nut; Areca Nut. Orange nut of the betel palm; mixed with lime, wrapped in leaves, and

chewed as a mild stimulant in Southeast Asia.

Betel Palm. The palm tree, native to Southeast Asia, which produces the betel nut.

Beterrabas (Portuguese). Beets.

Betony. An herb, now rarely cultivated; formerly used for its mint flavor.

Betterave (French). Beetroot.

Betty. (1) A dessert; alternate layers of sliced sweetened fruit and buttered breadcrumbs in a baking dish moistened with a small amount of fruit juice and baked until the top is brown and crisp. Betties can be made of apples, berries, peaches, plums, pineapple, and other fruits. (2) A straw-covered, pear-shaped bottle.

Beurre (French). Butter.

Beurré. A sweet juicy variety of French pear.

Beurre Blanc Sauce (French). A white fish sauce, a specialty of the Loire region. It is prepared from a reduction of shallots, white wine vinegar, and fresh butter; superb with pike.

Beurre d'Escargot (French). Snail butter; usually a combination of softened butter, plenty of garlic, parsley, and chopped shallots.

Beurre de Noisettes (French). Melted butter combined with crushed hazelnuts.

Beurre Fondu (French). Drawn or melted butter.

Beurre Manié (French). Small balls of flour and butter kneaded together to thicken soups, stews, and sauces.

Beurre Noisette. Butter browned to a nut color; usually served with grilled fish.

Beurre Roux, Au (French). With brown butter.

Beurrer (French). To butter (foods).

Bevande (Italian). Drinks; liquor.

Bever (Obsolete). A drink, usually of an alcoholic beverage.

Bever Cake. A cake eaten with ale in the afternoon.

Beverages. All liquids, alcoholic and non-alcoholic, normally consumed by human beings.

Bhahjees (Indian). (1) Fried. (2) The mixture in which the frying is done—a blend of mustard oil, ground turmeric, chilies, and salt.

Bhajia (Indian). Vegetable fritters.

Bhang. Leaves and seeds of Indian hemp, which are chewed and eaten.

Bhartha (Indian). A vegetable roasted over an open fire and then mashed smooth.

Bhatta Rice. An Indian rice, commonly used with curried food.

Bhel Puri (Indian). Crisply fried rounds of dough mixed with onions, chutney, and puffed rice.

Bhujia (Indian). A vegetable dish.

Bianchetti (Italian). Whitebait, a fish.

Bianco Sarti. An Italian apéritif́ drink made from rhubarb.

B.I.B. Of liquor, bottled in bond.

Bibacious. Denoting an alcoholic person.

Bibb Lettuce; Limestone Lettuce. A small head of lettuce with very tender dark green leaves. First grown in the United States around the early 1900s, when it was developed by a Kentucky colonel, John Bibb, who purchased seeds in Europe and brought them to his farm near

Frankfurt, Kentucky. It is becoming increasingly popular in the United States, although it is often difficult to wash the lettuce clear of soil or sand.

Bible Cake. A cake, all of whose ingredients are mentioned in the Bible.

Bibulous. Consuming liquor extensively.

Bica (Portuguese colloquial). Coffee.

Bicarbonate of Soda. An alkali formerly used to brighten the color of green vegetables in cooking; now rarely used.

Bicchiere (Italian). A drinking glass.

Bicker. A beaker, bowl, or dish used for liquor.

Bico (Philippine). A coconut rice pudding.

Bident. A two-year-old sheep.

Biefstuk (Dutch). Beefsteak.

Bien Fatigué (French). Of salad greens, tossed with a hot dressing until limp.

Bien-Me-Sabe (Spanish). "I know it well." Denoting simple, family-style desserts customarily served in Latin countries, such as custard or plain cake with sauce.

Bier (Dutch, German). Beer, ale.

Bierkeller (German). A restaurant whose specialty is beer.

Biersuppe (German). Beer soup.

Bierwurst (German). A large fatty type of sausage, often served with bread and beer.

Bieten met Appelen (Dutch). Beets and apples.

Bife (Portuguese). Beefsteak.

  Bife de Vaca a Marrare. Steak in lemon sauce.

  Bife na Frigideira. Steak served in a mustard sauce on earthenware plates.

Bifer. A plant that bears fruit twice a year.

Biferno. An Italian liqueur flavored with wild herbs.

Biff (Swedish). Beef.

  Biff à la Lindström. A ground-meat dish made with cream, beets, potatoes, and eggs.

  Biffstek. Beefsteak.

Biffin. (1) A cooking apple from Norfolk, England. The name, which comes from "beef," refers to the apple's color. (2) A baked apple flattened into the form of a cake.

Biftec (Spanish). Steak.

Bigarade (French). Orange sauce, usually served with duck; made with a brown sauce or with the juices from the pan in which the bird was roasted, flavored with lemon and orange juices, and sometimes a caramel of vinegar and sugar. Originally the Seville, or bitter, orange, brought to Spain by the Moors, was used, but the more familiar sweet orange is an excellent substitute.

Bigaradier (French). Bitter orange.

Bigarré (French). Describing a method of preparing calf's head.

Bigarreau. A large heart-shaped red and yellow cherry.

Bigarrure (French). A rich stew containing capons, pheasants, or other game.

Bigg. Barley grown in rows of four.

Biggin. A coffeepot with strainer, named for its inventor.

Bignè (Italian). A kind of pastry.

  Bignè al Formaggio. Cheese puffs.

Bignon, Louis. A famous nineteenth-century French restaurateur who owned the Café Riche, at which many dishes of the *haute cuisine* were invented and first served.

Bigos (Polish). Hunters' stew made with sauerkraut, Polish sausage, and a variety of cooked meats, such as beef, veal, pork, and lamb. One of the oldest and best-known national dishes, it is particularly good prepared a day in advance and then reheated.

Bija (Spanish). Achiote, the red coloring ingredient used in cooking in South America.

Bijane (French). Peasant soup made with red wine cooked with breadcrumbs in Anjou.

Bijon (Philippine). A rice noodle.

Bikkurim. The earliest fruits of the harvest at the time of Shavuoth, the Jewish festival.

Biksemad (Danish). Hash with a fried egg on top.

Bilberry. A small shrub producing edible red-purple berries used to make a preserve or jelly particularly good with roast meats or game.

Billard. Coalfish.

Billet. A one-year-old coalfish.

Billingsgate. A fish market near a gate in London.

Bill of Fare. A list of the foods served at a hotel or restaurant. Sometimes the diner is offered a choice, sometimes not.

Billy (Australian slang). A teapot or utensil used for making tea.

Biltong (Afrikaans). Dried strips of lean meat.

Bind. To moisten with milk or egg to keep a mixture together.

Bingen. A wine village in Rheinhessen, Germany. *See* Germany, The Wines of.

Binny. A large barbel found in the Nile River, Egypt.

Bioses. Sugars containing maltose, sucrose, and lactose.

Birch Beer. A soft drink resembling beer but without alcohol, made from the sap of the birch tree.

Birch Sugar. A crude sugar once made in Scotland and Scandinavia from the sap of the sweet birch tree.

Bird's Cherry. A wild fruit tree whose fruit looks like a small cherry and has an interestingly acid taste.

Bird's-Nests. The edible nests of a genus of swift found along the China coast and on certain islands in the Indian Ocean. In oriental cuisine, the nests, partly consisting of mucus secreted by the birds, are prepared as a soup served at the end of a meal. The nests are sold in Chinese stores in the United States.

Bird Spit. A spit on a rotisserie used for grilling poultry.

Biriani; Biryani (Indian). Mainly boiled rice layered with meat or vegetable curry, then baked.

Birk Wine. A wine made in Scotland from the sap of the birch tree with raisins, almonds, and crude tartar.

Birle (Scottish). To pour a drink.

Birlie (British slang). A loaf of bread.

Birlin. A small oatmeal cake.

Birnbrot (Swiss). Fruitcake made with dried pears.

Birnen (German). Pears.

Birra (Italian). Beer.

Birschermuesli (Swiss). Rich, tasty breakfast food, made of cereals, dried fruits, nut fragments, and sugar and usually eaten with milk or cream.

Birt (Obsolete). A turbot, an excellent food fish.

Birwecka (Alsatian). A very rich small cake.

Biryani. *See* Biriani.

Biscotins (French). Small, crisp, slightly sweet cookies served with ice cream, wine, coffee, or chocolate.

Biscottes (French). Brioche paste, sliced thin, baked, buttered, and sugared; usually served with tea.

Biscotti (Italian). Crackers.

Biscotti all' Anice. Anise cookies.

Biscottini (Italian). Small sweet cookies.

Biscottini di Mandorle. Almond macaroons.

Biscotto Tortoni (Italian). *See* Biscuit Tortoni.

Biscuit. A raised bread baked in small shapes and made from dough leavened with baking powder, soda, or yeast. The name is derived from a French term meaning "twice cooked." On the continent and in England "biscuit" refers to the small flat unleavened bread or cakes commonly called crackers in the United States.

Biscuit Glacé. A glazed ice-cream biscuit.

Biscuits de Reims (French). Finger biscuits.

Biscuit Tableware. Dull-finished ware, usually red or tan, prepared from the first firing of earthenware. It may have a scratched or painted pattern and is sometimes finished with a thin coat of transparent glaze.

Biscuit Tortoni (Italian). A frozen ice-cream dessert originated by the famous restaurateur Tortoni, who was the rage of Paris in the mid-nineteenth century. Served in individual paper cups, it is sprinkled with macaroon crumbs soaked in sherry.

Biset (French). A rock pigeon, a delicate game bird.

Bishop. (1) A mixture of citrus fruit, sugar, and wine. (2) To allow a liquid, such as milk, to burn while being cooked.

Bisk. An old dish containing birds' cockscombs and sweetbreads.

Bisky (British slang). Biscuit.

Bismarck. A drink made of champagne and stout.

Bismarck Herring. Fillets of herring pickled in white wine, vinegar, and seasonings; usually served as an hors d'oeuvre or appetizer.

Bisque (French). A smooth rich or thick soup; usually made from shellfish, but sometimes with vegetables.

    Bisque d'Ecrevisse. A thick rich soup made from crayfish.

Bissar (Algerian). A cooked bean dish made with olive oil.

Bistecca (Italian). Steak.

    Bistecca alla Fiorentina. Broiled steak served with lemon and oil.

    Bistecca alla Pizzaiola. Steak with tomatoes, spices, and garlic.

    Bistecca con Salsa di Capperi. Steak with caper sauce.

Bistro. In France a simple bar and restaurant that usually serves good food and wine in comparatively plain surroundings. Gourmets travel miles to dine at famous bistros.

Bitok (Russian). Hamburger made with any ground meat or poultry, onions, and bread.

Bitki Skobilov. Small flat dumplings made of ground veal.

Bitokes à la Russe (French). Fried cutlets of chopped meat and marrow served with a sour-cream sauce and onions.

Bitter. Having a harsh unpleasant taste, like quinine or wormwood; not sweet.

Bitter Ash. Quassia, a strong bitter substance sometimes used in making bitters or apéritifs.

Bitter Melon. A green vegetable similar in shape to a cucumber, with an irregular exterior; commonly used in Chinese cookery. Its rather bitter taste suggests quinine.

Bitter Orange. The Seville orange in Spain, *bigaradier* in France, and *melangolo* in Italy. It is too acid to be eaten raw, and is used in the making of marmalade. The peel oil is used in the liqueur Curaçao. The peel and flower oils (neroli oil) and the oils from the green twigs (petit-grain oils) are used in perfumery.

Bitters. A spirit base flavored with aromatic herbs, barks, roots, and fruits and then distilled; produced by several manufacturers from supposedly secret formulas. Bitters are used either as a digestive aid or as an ingredient of cocktails to lend smoothness or tang. Bitters themselves may serve as an apéritif. Some are diluted with water, flavored with grenadine or other sweeteners, and sipped before meals.

Bitter-Sweet. Tasting both bitter and sweet. The almond is a classic example.

Bitter-Sweeting (Obsolete). A bitter-sweet apple.

Bitto Cheese. A very hard Italian cheese with eyes. When young it is quite smooth and oily; after two years it hardens and becomes suitable for grating.

Bizcochitos (Spanish). Crackers, cookies.

Bizcochuelo (Spanish). Spongecake.

Bizette (French). The female teal, a small duck-like game bird.

Blåbaer (Norwegian). Blueberry.

    Blåbaersuppe. Blueberry soup.

    Blåbaerpannekake. Blueberry pancakes.

Blåbär (Swedish). Blueberry.

Blachan (Malayan). Shrimp paste.

Black-Bean Sauce. Fermented black soybeans puréed until liquid.

Blackberry. The fruit of a variety of thorny bushes which have been cultivated commercially in the United States since the 1850s. Unripe berries are red or green; the mature fruit is shiny black. The tartly sweet berries may be used as a fresh-fruit dessert or in fruit salads, or may be cooked in pies, jams, and preserves.

Blackbird. Any of various birds, the male of which is almost entirely black; rarely eaten, despite the famous nursery rhyme about a blackbird pie. In certain parts of Europe around the Mediterranean, the blackbird is occasionally eaten, especially in the autumn, when its diet gives it a somewhat better taste.

Black Bonito; Black Salmon. The cobia, a salt-water food fish.

Black Bun (Scottish). A type of dark pastry or cake, filled with currants, baked inside a pastry crust during Hogmanay. *See* Hogmanay.

Blackcap. Black raspberry.

Blackcock. The male black grouse.

Black Cumin. A black aromatic herb of the crowfoot family; sometimes used in place of pepper.

Black Currant. A bush fruit popular for pies, puddings, jams, and jellies, and for cordials such as the French *cassis*. It is· cultivated in Europe but grows wild in the United States.

Black Dragon. A Chinese red tea.

Black Drum. The drumfish, a saltwater food fish.

Black-Eyed Pea; Cowpea. A legume botanically classified as a bean, not as a pea. In the United States, California, not the South, is now the principal producer of black-eyed beans, and most of the crop goes to the southern states, where the beans are great favorites. They appear frequently in Hopping John, for which the dried beans are cooked in ham broth with chopped ham and rice.

Blackfish. (1) A food fish found in Atlantic coastal waters. Average weight is 2—3 pounds, but mature specimens may reach 20 pounds in weight and 3 feet in length. (2) The name for numerous dark-skinned fishes. (3) A salmon after spawning.

Black Grouse. The British black game or heath fowl. The hen is gray and the cock black.

Blackhull Wheat. A red winter wheat grown in Kansas.

Black Jack. (1) A mixture of burnt sugar and caramel used in England as a batter coloring for wedding cakes. (2) Licorice flavoring in chewing gum and candy.

Blackjack. In Michigan, the whitefish.

Black Jacks. Leather mugs with silver rims once used for serving drinks, now prized as antiques.

Black Man (British). A rich toffee made with dark molasses.

Black Mission. *See* Fig.

Black Mustard. *See* Wild Mustard.

Black Pepper. A small tropical plant whose dried berries are ground to various degrees of coarseness or fineness and used for seasoning. Freshly ground pepper is far better than commercially ground pepper. *See also* Pepper.

Black Pot (Obsolete). Beer mug.

Black Pudding (British). (1) A mixture of oatmeal, blood from a freshly killed pig, minced liver, chopped suet, and seasoning. It is made up in large sausage-shaped bladders brushed over with blood before being baked, which turns them black and gives them the name. The black puddings are traditionally from the North and Midlands of England. (2) A type of meat loaf prepared with tongue. (3) A kind of large dark frankfurter.

Black Raspberry. A species of raspberry that bears black berries; native to the eastern United States and cultivated in New England.

Black Salmon; Black Bonito. The cobia, a salt-water food fish.

Black Sauce. (1) A mixture of soy sauce and molasses. (2) A dark brown sauce made with beer.

Blackstrap. An inferior grade of molasses with a meager sugar content.

Black Stripe. A drink made with rum and molasses; so called because the dark molasses lies on the rum in a stripe before it is stirred. In summer ice is added to the drink, in the winter boiling water.

Black Sugar. The root extract of licorice.

Black Vinegar (Chinese). *Jit cho*, a vinegar made in Chinkiang; used as a spicy dip for various foods.

Bladder Cherry. *See* Ground Cherry.

Blaeberry (Scotch). The bilberry, a small edible berry.

Blanc (French). A white soup stock, or a *court-bouillon* in which vegetables may be cooked.

Blanc, Au (French). To cook foods gently to prevent their adding color, as in making a white sauce or preventing onions from browning.

Blanc de (French). Indicating a white food, or one served with a white sauce.

Blanc de Blanc (French). White wine made exclusively from white grapes.

Blanc d'Oeuf (French). The white of an egg.

Blanch. (1) To pour boiling water over food and allow it to stand 3—5 minutes to loosen skin, or to set the color. Certain nuts, such as almonds and pistachios, are blanched to soften the skin so that it can be easily removed. (2) To partially cook food for various purposes (for example, in order to harden, cleanse, lighten the color, reduce odor, or remove excess fat). (3) The process of banking earth over a growing vegetable, especially celery and asparagus, to keep out the sun and thus produce white stalks.

Blanchaille (French). The whitebait, a delicate little fish; usually deep-fat fried.

Blanching Machine. A machine that removes the skins from almonds and other nuts.

Blancmange. A dessert made from flour, water, and milk, stiffened with gelatin, and sweetened or flavored and colored as desired, although it should be white to remain true to its name. It is cooked in a mold and served cold.

Blancs (French). Meats served with white sauce.

Bland. Smooth; gentle to the taste; not sharp-flavored.

Blandad Fruktsoppa (Swedish). Soup made with dried fruits.

Blandad Grönsaksfat (Swedish). Assorted vegetables.

Blangah (Malaysian). An earthenware pot having a wooden cover, used to prepare curries. Since the earthenware retains the flavor of the cooked dish, separate pots are used for meat and fish.

Blanquet. A variety of grape and two kinds of pears; all are mediocre in quality.

Blanquette (French). Stew of veal, lamb, chicken, sweetbreads, or any white meat, served in a creamy sauce and garnished with onions and mushrooms.

　　Blanquette d'Agneau. Lamb in a white sauce.
　　Blanquette de Poularde. Chicken stew in a white sauce.
　　Blanquette de Veau. Veal stew.

Blaue Forelle (German). Fresh-killed trout boiled quickly.

Blayais. A wine district of the Bordeaux region of France. *See* France, The Wines of.

Bleaching. The whitening or decolorizing of flour or edible oils.

Bleak. A small European river fish of the carp family, considered a delicacy; best pan-fried.

Blé de Turquie (French). Corn.

Bleeding. Permitting the escape of air and gas from raised dough by cutting it and leaving the cut unsealed.

Blé en Herbe (French). Corn in the husk.

Blemmle (British). To mix flour and water.

Blencorn. Rye and wheat grown together.

Blend. To mix food thoroughly; to mingle or to combine into one product.

Blended Honey. (1) A blend of invert sugar and genuine honey. (2) A blend of different honies to produce a desired mixture.

Blender, Electric. When this electrical appliance was invented in the 1930s its use was limited mainly to the preparation of alcoholic drinks, such as daiquiris. Since then home economists working for the various manufacturers of the appliance have discovered so many other practical uses for the blender that today it is an impor-

tant piece of kitchen equipment. It shortens the time that must be devoted to such chores as puréeing fruits and cooked vegetables, mincing or shredding vegetables, mixing the ingredients for quick breads and for blending dips, spreads, and sandwich fillings. It also simplifies the making of soups, sauces, and gravies; crumbs bread; grates cheese; and also mixes cake frostings, fillings, and toppings.

　　It should be emphasized that the blender is not an all-round appliance. It is not a beater, hence cannot be used for mixing cake batters, nor will it beat egg whites for meringues and frostings. It cannot be used to knead a stiff dough, to grind raw meat, nor to whip cream.

Blenny. A very small freshwater European fish, rarely exceeding 6 inches in length, found in rivers, streams, and lakes. The blenny has white meat with a good flavor, but overly soft texture; best when cooked quickly in butter.

Blé Noir (French). Buckwheat.

Blette (French). Mangold; a vegetable with leaves resembling spinach. *Tarte aux blette* is a specialty of Provence.

Bletting. As applied to fruits, overripening. Certain fruits are not palatable until they are quite soft; many others have by then passed their peak.

Bleu. Blue-veined cheeses made in the Roquefort area of France. They differ from Roquefort cheese in that the latter was formerly made only with ewe's milk, whereas the Bleu cheeses are usually made with cow's milk. *See also* Blue Cheese.

Bleu, Au. A method of quickly cooking fish so as to retain the maximum taste and freshness. Water, vinegar, and sometimes a bay leaf are allowed to boil; the fish (preferably a young trout) is added while still alive. This procedure results in a fish with a curled tail and a bluish color, from which it gets its name of *bleu*. As a rule, fish so prepared should be served only with melted butter; Hollandaise or *beurre blanc* are not nearly so suitable.

Blewits. A comparatively scarce type of wild mushroom which has a good taste.

Blewits, Wood. *See* Wood Blewits.

Blimbing. A rather small greenish fruit with an acid taste; much used in Southeast Asia for cooking, being too acid for eating raw.

Blinde Vinken (Dutch). Stuffed veal.

Blini. (1) A small buckwheat pancake commonly served in Russia and Poland in place of pastry or toast to accompany such hors d'oeuvre as caviar or cheese. (2) A white-flour pancake.

  Blini aux Caviare (French). Small buckwheat pancake, spread with caviar, and served with sour cream.

  Blini aux Saumon Fumé (French). Small buckwheat pancake, spread with slices of smoked salmon, and served with sour cream.

Blintzes. Thin egg pancakes filled with fruit or cheese, and rolled; traditional in Jewish cuisine.

Blite. Wild spinach.

Bloater (British). A specially processed smoked herring. The freshly caught fish is soaked briefly in brine, then dried by stringing through the gills and mouth onto long rods which are hung for several days. The fish then go into the smokehouse for about a week. Yarmouth, England, is world-famous for its bloaters.

  Bloater Paste. A soft paste made from baked bloaters blended with butter; used chiefly as a spread on toast for making hors d'oeuvre.

Blødkogt Aeg (Danish). Soft-boiled egg.

Blodpudding (Norwegian). Blood pudding.

Bloemkool (Dutch). Cauliflower.

Blomkål (Danish, Swedish). Cauliflower.

Blommer (Danish). Plums.

Blond (French). Meat stock made from white meats, such as veal, lamb, or chicken. *Sauce blonde* is a white or cream-colored sauce made of flour and butter.

Blonde de Veau (French). A rich broth made of veal; used to flavor sauces and white soups.

Blood Orange; Malta Orange. A variety of orange with red pulp and juice. It is often used in making Sauce Maltaise, which is like Hollandaise Sauce, but has a red color.

Blood Partridge; Blood Pheasant. A term which describes numerous game birds around the world, particularly those with bright red markings.

Blood Pudding; Blood Sausage. A large sausage made chiefly of pig's blood and suet.

Blood Sugar. The blood sugar in humans is glucose, normally present at 70—100 mg. per 100 ml. It rises after a meal, but rapidly returns to normal except in diabetes mellitus. It is stored in the liver and muscles as glycogen. The energy for muscular activity comes from the oxidation of glucose.

Bloomer Loaf (British). A crusty baton-shaped loaf of bread with many cuts on the top.

Bloom, Fat. The whitish appearance on the surface of chocolate that sometimes occurs in storage. It is due to a change in the form of the fat at the surface or to fat's diffusing outward and being deposited on the surface.

Bløtkake (Norwegian). Spongecake.

Bløtkokt Egg (Norwegian). Boiled egg.

Bludkercake (British). Cake made with hog's blood to be eaten on Easter Sunday.

Blueback. Another name for the trout.

Blue Cap Salmon. A year-old salmon, whose head has a blue spot.

Blue Cod. An ocean fish found off the coast of New Zealand; especially good when smoked or salted.

Blueberries. The edible small blue berries, the fruit of a variety of bushes found in Canada and the United States, used for pies, puddings, jams, jellies, preserves, and sauces. Blueberries were collected by the Indians during colonial times, and were eaten fresh in season and dried for wintertime use. The original wild species (there were dozens of different types) were extremely small and had a distinctive fruity flavor; they grew chiefly in sandy or peaty soil. In the past half-century blueberry cultivation has resulted in rather large, attractive berries which unfortunately lack the fine flavor of the original small berry. In many parts of the country the terms "blueberry" and "huckleberry" are used interchangeably. On the other hand, sometimes the term "blueberry" is used to describe the cultivated berry and the term "huckleberry" to describe the wild species.

Blue Cheese. The Roquefort-type cheese made in the United States, Denmark, and Canada; produced from cow's or goat's milk ripened by Penicillium molds. An imitation of Bleu cheese. *See* Bleu Cheese.

Bluefish; Skipjack. A bluish-green food fish found along the east coast of the United States and ranging in weight from 3–15 pounds.

Blue Gage. A bluish plum.

Bluegill. A freshwater fish resembling the trout; varying from 1–2 feet in length and weighing from 1–3 pounds.

Bluenose. (1) A kind of clam. (2) A Nova Scotia purple potato.

Bluepoint. Properly, an oyster found in a certain section of waters off Long Island, but often any good-sized oyster from the Atlantic Ocean or Gulf of Mexico.

Blue Rose Rice. A variety of rice native to the southern United States.

Blue-Stem Wheat. A white, soft wheat grown in the western United States.

Blue Vinny (British). Blue Dorset cheese, a chalk-white cheese with a bright blue streak running through it. "Vinny" is a corruption of the very old word "vinew," meaning "mold."

Blumenkohl (German). Cauliflower.

Blusher. A pale pink wild mushroom usually found in forests or wooded regions during midsummer.

Blutwurst (German). A sausage in which blood is used as a thickening agent; some types are ready to eat, others require cooking.

Boar. Uncastrated male of the pig family, wild or domesticated, but usually the name refers to the wild animal.

Board (Colloquial). Meals provided in exchange for payment. The American term "room and board" has begun to lose popularity, as few places of accommodation provide meals.

Boarding House. Place where meals or rooms and meals are furnished. Boarding houses are gradually disappearing from the American scene.

Board Wages (British). Formerly, wages paid to servants to buy food when meals were not provided by the employer.

Boar Fish. A mediocre-tasting fish with a turned-up snout; a member of the mackerel family.

Bob. Fava or broad beans.

Bob Veal. Meat from calves under 6 weeks old, considered unfit to eat because of its odd taste and texture.

Bobwhite; American Quail. Small game bird found from Mexico to Canada.

Bocal (French). A low wide glass container used for preserved fruits or vegetables.

Bocca di Dama (Italian). Nut spongecake.

Bocconi (Italian). "A mouthful"; a very small variety of Provolone cheese. *See* Provolone.

Bocconcini (Italian). Small rolled mouthfuls of foods; made with ham, veal, or cheese.

Bocconotti (Italian). Small *pasta* filled with sweetbreads or chicken livers.

Bock (1) A strong dark-colored sweet beer brewed in the winter and drunk in the spring, the only time of the year it is available. (2) A glass tankard holding a half-pint.

Bocksbeutel (German). Squat, stubby bottle used to ship Franconia wines. *See* Germany, The Wines of.

Bockwurst (German). A rather heavy kind of frankfurter.

Bodega (Spanish). (1) A place where wine is stored; a winecellar. (2) A small, cozy nightclub or place where gypsies gather to sell drinks, dance, and collect money from tourists.

Bodenheim. A wine village in Rheinhessen, Germany. *See* Germany, The Wines of.

Bodge (Obsolete). Oat measure of about a half-peck.

Bodwinje. An extra-strong beef soup, often served with sour cream.

Boerenkool met Rookworst (Dutch). Kale (or cabbage) with sausages.

Boerenmeisjes (Dutch). Apricots preserved in brandy.

Boerewors (Afrikaans). Homemade sausage, usually prepared with beef, pork, and spices, then grilled over an open fire.

Boeuf (French). Beef.

Boeuf Bouilli. Boiled beef.

Boeuf Coupe à la Française (French). The term which describes the French style of cutting up beef. *See* separate listings under Aloyau, Tranche, Culotte, Plat, etc.

Boeuf Braisé. Braised beef.

Boeuf Fumé. Smoked beef.

Boeuf Saignant à la Ficelle. Fillet of beef wrapped tightly with string, roasted quickly in a very hot oven, then dipped in boiling consommé for one minute, and served immediately. The combination of quick roasting and dipping produces an excellent juicy meat.

Boeuf Salé. Salted or corned beef.

Bøf (Danish). Beefsteak.

Bøf Raifort. Beef with horseradish.

Bofu (Japanese). An edible leaf from a vegetable resembling the parsnip.

Bogavante (Spanish). Lobster. *Langosta*, the term customarily used, actually describes the sea crayfish.

Bog Butter (Norse, Finnish, Scotch, Irish) (Obsolete). Butter buried in bogs to ripen until it developed a strong flavor.

Bogle. In medieval England a cake eaten at supper on Bogle Day, March 29.

Bohea. A rather poor-quality Chinese black tea named for the mountain where it grows.

Bohnen (German). Beans.

Boiled Dressing. A seasoned-to-taste, home-cooked salad dressing resembling mayonnaise in color and taste.

Boiler. A kitchen utensil, usually large, used for boiling food.

Boiling. A method of cooking foods in liquid, usually water, at the boiling point, which is 212°F. at sea level. The boiling point varies, being lower at high mountain levels. *See* High-Altitude Cookery.

In boiling vegetables it is very important that the vegetables be plunged into boiling water, for the high temperature retards the loss of ascorbic acid in vitamin C. Whenever possible, they should be cooked in minimum time in the smallest amount of water practicable. A tight-fitting cover should be used to prevent the escape of steam and to avoid scorching.

Beef and other meats cooked in liquid should not be prepared at the boiling point but at simmering (185°F.) because the higher water temperature will result in stringy, dry meat difficult to slice.

Boitelle, A la (French). Cooked with mushrooms.

Bokking (Dutch). Bloaters, a kind of herring.

Bokser. St. John's Bread, a long seed pod of the carob tree; it may be chewed and eaten. *See* Carob.

Bok Um Pap (Korean). A fairly spicy dish of fried rice and beef.

Bolachas (Portuguese). Cookies.

Bold Bread. A loaf of bread with an over-all good appearance.

Bolée (French). A brown earthenware container, used for cider in Normandy.

Bolet. *See* Boletus.

Boleti (Italian). Mushrooms.

Boletus. A rather large European mushroom, often measuring 7 inches across the top, with a fine flavor and texture.

Lurid Boletus. A reddish mushroom with a somewhat open, netlike surface; rather uncommon and rarely eaten.

Rough-Stalked Boletus. A mushroom with rough stems and flesh white shading into pink;

commonly found in woods and forests during September and October.

Bolillos (Mexican). Rolls resembling French bread.

Bolitas (Spanish). Fritters.

Bolitas de Queso (Spanish). Cheese balls usually served with drinks.

Bolivia. Because much of this mountainous country is extremely cold, hearty foods, often highly spiced, are the general rule. *Picantes*, small pieces of chicken or meat served in a burning-hot sauce, are popular. A similar dish is *ají de carne*, pork cooked with red peppers. Many restaurants feature *parilladas*, meats broiled over an open fire.

In this invigorating climate hot soups are the rule, not the exception. *Valdiviano con huevos*, a garlicky-beef soup with eggs, is typical. Soups made of chicken, onions, potatoes, and noodles are also very popular. Bolivians enjoy spaghettis and all other *pasta*, possibly because they are heat-producing. Though fish are caught in chilly Lake Titicaca, most people prefer dried codfish, *bacalao*. The Bolivians' true love is for desserts and sweets. Marvelous fruits, particularly pineapples and melons, are produced in the *yungas*, the narrow valleys. Every cook delights in preparing pastries, creams, custards, tortes, cakes, puddings, and the like; *postres*, desserts, are the measure of a cook's talents. Considerable wine is produced in the Cochambamba region, the *muyurina*, but the quality is only fair. The local beer is excellent. Because it is bottled under high pressure and often explodes at sea level, it is usually not exported.

An interesting novelty is *chuño*, the frozen potato, very popular among the Indians. Because of the high altitude, local potatoes are quite small. They are frozen, thawed, and refrozen, sometimes repeatedly. Almost moisture-free, the potato becomes almost pure starch with a unique, vaguely cheeselike flavor.

Boller (Danish). Meatballs or fishballs.

Bollito (Italian). Boiled.

Bollitos. Cornmeal mixed with meats and spices, cut into cubes, and boiled; served on toothpicks, usually with drinks.

Bologna Sausage. A large smoked sausage made

of pork fat, bacon, and veal. Originally produced in Bologna, this Italian specialty is now made all over the world. There is also an all-beef type prepared for kosher use.

Bolos (Portuguese). Cakes.

Bomba di Riso (Italian). Rice, mushrooms, cheese, and chicken livers packed into a mold and baked.

Bombard. To stuff a piece of meat or poultry.

Bombarde (Tyrolean). Dish made of sheep's tongues and minced meat.

Bombay Duck. The small Indian Ocean bummalo fish dried, salted, and lightly roasted; often fried crisp and served with curries.

　　Bombay Duck Salad. Crumbled, toasted, or fried Bombay ducks, combined with thin slivers of fresh ginger, chopped green onions, chopped green chili peppers, and a little vinegar and oil; served with curries in India.

Bombay Wheat. A hard, brittle, dry wheat grown in India.

Bomb Calorimeter. *See* Calorimeter.

Bombe (French). An iced pudding or ice-cream dessert; a rich custard lining with fruit-cream filling.

Böna (Swedish). Bean.

Bonbon (French). Any kind of candy; usually bonbons are fancifully decorated or shaped.

　　Bonbons à la Menthe. Peppermint candies.

Bonbonnières (French). Boxes, usually of china, often elaborately designed, for holding candies (bonbons).

Bon-Chrétien (French). A winter pear.

Bonda (Indian). Balls of mashed potatoes fried in deep fat, eaten as a snack in South India.

Bondepige med Slør (Danish). Dessert made of butter, rye bread, and applesauce, and served with whipped cream.

Bondo Gumbo (Nigerian). Stewed lamb made with okra, pimientos, and tomatoes; served with balls of cooked whole wheat.

Bondon. A French whole-milk cheese made in small cylinders and wrapped in soft white paper. A very small quantity of sugar is added to the milk while the cheese is being made. It comes chiefly from Normandy, and is similar to Gournay cheese but slightly sweeter. The Bondon cheese made near Rouen is different and resembles Neufchâtel.

Bondost. A cylindrical Swedish cow's-milk cheese, often with caraway seeds.

Bonduc. Hazelnut.

Bone. *See* Bones.

Bône. An important wine region of Algeria.

Bone Broth. A broth prepared by prolonged boiling of chopped bones. Consisting of 2—4 percent gelatin and very little calcium, it has little nutritive value.

Bone Marrow. The soft, fatty, edible matter found in certain animal bones; frequently used in cookery, especially in Europe.

Bone Porcelain. A porcelain developed in the latter part of the 19th century by adding bone ash (obtained from animal bones) to the traditional potter's mixtures. It is between hard- and soft-paste porcelain in hardness and whiteness. Also called Bone China.

Bonensla (Dutch). String-bean salad.

Bonensoep (Dutch). Bean soup.

Bones. The skeletal leftovers from meat, fowl, or fish are useful for making soup or stock. Bones are also served as a main course if they are usually large and with some of the original meat left attached, especially roast-beef bones. Broiling is the best method of preparation.

Bon Goût (French). (1) A highly flavored dish. (2) Good taste.

Boniface. Owner of a hotel or restaurant. The term comes from *Boniface*, the jovial innkeeper in Farquhar's *Beaux' Stratagem*.

Bonite (French). Bonito, a fish of the tuna family. *See* Bonito.

Bonito. A small species of saltwater mackerel belonging to the tuna family, found in the Mediterranean and the warmer waters of the Atlantic.

Bonne-Bouche (French). Small tasty dishes, such as hors d'oeuvre.

Bonne Femme (French). (1) Housewife. (2) Of foods, prepared simply, as by a housewife.

Bonnes Mares. A group of Burgundy wines. *See* France, The Wines of.

Bonnet de Turquie (French). Pastry shaped to resemble a Turk's cap.

Bonnet Fleuk (Scotch). A flatfish of the turbot family.

Bonnock (Scotch). *See* Bannock.

Bonnyclabber. Sour clotted milk.

Bonvalet (French). A rich, sweet almond cake.

Boon (Dutch). Bean.

Booze (Slang). Liquor. The term is probably derived from the name of a liquor made from sesame seeds, the national drink of Bulgaria and similarly pronounced.

Boquerones (Spanish). Fish similar to anchovies.

Boquettier (French). A crabapple tree.

Borachio (Obsolete, Spanish). A goatskin bag to hold wine.

Borage. A sturdy annual herb growing in all temperate and warm climates, borage has been a favorite herb since the time of the ancient Greeks. The plant grows 2—2½ feet tall with a course and fuzzy-appearing foliage. Star-shaped blue flowers blossom singly at the tip of the stalk. Fresh young leaves, which smell and taste like cucumber, are used for flavoring iced drinks, salads, and vegetables. Europeans cook them as a vegetable like spinach. Both dried and fresh leaves are used to flavor soups and stews.

Borassus. A sugar- and wine-producing tropical palm.

Bord-de-Plat (French). Round covers for the edge or border of dishes not in use.

Bordeaux. One of the great wine-producing areas of southwestern France, named for the seaport in the Gironde which has shipped overseas more French wines than all the other French ports combined. About three-fourths of the Bordeaux wines, often called claret, are red; they are light, soft, and elegant in taste. The others are white, the best-known being the rather sweet Sauternes and the dry Graves. *See* France, The Wines of.

Bordelaise. A sauce made with beef marrow and red wine; used with steaks, hamburgers, kidneys, and some egg dishes.

Borecale; Borecole; Scotch Kale. A kind of cabbage having coarse, curly green leaves.

Borëk (Turkish). Thin layers of *yufka* dough,

brushed with melted butter and milk, and filled with meat or vegetable mixtures; served hot. When made on a tray and cut into pieces, it is called *tray borek*; boreks may also be individual pastries.

Borelli. A small Italian cheese made from buffalo milk.

Boric Acid. A shiny white crystalline substance used to preserve foods.

Borovička (Czechoslovakian). Gin.

Borrego (Portuguese). Lamb.

Borrel (Dutch). A drink of Dutch gin, *jenever*.

Borscht (Russian, Polish). Soup made of beets or cabbage, and other ingredients; usually served with sour cream.

Borststuk (Dutch). Brisket.

Bosch. An imitation-butter table spread.

Boston Brown Bread. A moist, rather sweet brown bread steamed rather than baked; a favorite Saturday-night food in Boston and elsewhere in New England, particularly when served with baked beans.

Bota (Spanish). Cask used for sherry.

Botarga. A type of caviar.

Botargo. A relish made from fish roe.

Boter (Dutch). Butter.

Boterham (Dutch). Slice of bread; bread and butter.

Boterhamkoek (Dutch). An anise-flavored sweet cake.

Botija. A round earthenware jar with a spout and a handle.

Botling. The chub, a river fish.

Botrys. A fairly good-tasting herb, little used now; sometimes called Oke of Paradise.

Botrytiscinerea (Scientific). The mold that forms on grapes prior to harvest; called *edelfäule* in Germany, and *pourriture noble* in France. *See* France, The Wines of; Germany, The Wines of.

Bottle Sizes. *See* Wine Bottle Sizes.

Bottom Yeast. *See* Low Yeast.

Botuline. A poisonous ptomaine present in decaying foods.

Botulism. Food poisoning due to the toxin produced by *Clostridium botulinus*. The spores can withstand boiling for 3 hours; they require a temperature of 248°F. (120°C.) for total destruction. Hence foods, especially meat and nonacid canned vegetables, though cooked, may still contain these spores. The toxin itself is destroyed at 149°F. (65°C.). Extremely small quantities are fatal. Botulism paralyzes the motor-nerve centers.

Botzaris. Lamb soup with green peas.

Boucan. A kind of frame to hold meats when they are being cured or smoked. The word "buccaneer," meaning pirate, probably comes from boucan, the method used by pirates to preserve meats.

Bouché; Bouchonné (French). As applied to wine, having acquired the unpleasant taste of the cork.

Bouchées (French). Tiny puff pastries, sweet for dessert or savory with a variety of fillings, served either hot or cold as an hors d'oeuvre.

    Bouchées de Femme. Small puff-pastry shapes filled with any desired mixture and served as an hors d'oeuvre.

    Bouchées à la Reine. Very small puff-paste patties filled with a chicken ragoût. The wife of Louis XV, Marie Leczinska, invented this dish.

Boucher (French). Butcher.

Bouchère (French). A strong meat broth with shredded cabbage, marrow, chervil, and parsley.

Bouchots (French, Colloquial). Mussels.

Boudanne. A French cow's-milk cheese.

Boudinade (French). Boned quarter of lamb stuffed with sausage and roasted; served with a rich gravy.

Boudin (French). A type of sausage made of poultry, game, or fish.

    Boudin Blanc (French). White sausage, usually made with pork.

    Boudin de Noël (Belgian). A sausage made from pigs' blood, pork, cabbage, and onions.

    Boudin de Volaille à la Richelieu (French). Chicken, truffles, and mushrooms combined into what is called a sausage but is actually a soft mixture.

    Boudin Noir (French, Belgian). A strong-flavored black sausage, usually made with pig's blood. Though popular in parts of France and Belgium, it is an acquired taste, because of its strong flavor.

Bouff (German). Cake made with eggs, sugar, butter, flour, currants, raisins, and lemon juice.

Bouffis. Smoked or salted herring prepared in northeastern France.

Bough. The animal's shoulder, as bough of beef.

Bough Cake (German). An ancient cake in which dried figs and other dried fruits and almonds are threaded on a piece of twine, then hung and basted with a batter mixture, being turned on a spit so that the batter cooks and sticks to the fruit. When the coatings are sufficiently thick, the bough is taken down and sliced to be eaten with sugar. Today bakers' and confectioners' establishments make a modern version over an electric stove, pouring a much lighter spongecake mixture over a revolving wooden cylinder, thus producing a long, light, smooth cake with a hole through the center for filling. It may be filled with flavored cream, glacé cherries, nuts, and shredded peel.

Bougna. A Melanesian feast, particularly in the area of New Caledonia, closely resembling the *Mangiti* of the Fiji Islands. Foods are wrapped in vegetable leaves and steamed on hot stones in an underground oven.

Bougras (French). A carnival-time soup made in Périgord; prepared from cabbage, onions, and other vegetables, flavored with the water in which blood puddings have been made.

Bouillabaisse (French). Superb fish soup, a specialty of Marseilles. Cities, towns, and hamlets along the Mediterranean coast of France all prepare bouillabaisse, though there may be a slight (or even great) variation in the recipe. But basically bouillabaisse consists of a *variety* of Mediterranean fish—rascasse, chapon, saint-pierre, conger eel, red mullet, whiting, and sometimes lobster, crabs, and other shellfish.

In the United States mackerel, fresh tuna, perch, pike, and trout may be substituted for unobtainable Mediterranean varieties, but the result will be different. The fish is cooked with onions, garlic, tomatoes, fennel, parsley, bay leaf, saffron, olive oil, pepper, and fish stock or water. The cooked fish is placed in a deep dish with chunks of French bread and the soup is strained over them. The dish is served hot, sometimes with a sprinkling of parsley.

Bouillabaisse du Lac. A stew of fish, similar to a bouillabaisse, made of freshwater fish, such as pike, perch, whitefish, etc.

Bouille, La. A popular cheese produced in Normandy, France.

Bouilliture d'Anguilles (French). Very small, young eels cooked in a stew with onions, garlic, white wine, and egg yolks; a specialty of Poitou.

Bouilloire (French). Kettle used almost exclusively for boiling water.

Bouillon (French). Broth; also a clear soup made with various kinds of meat, fowl, or fish.

Bouillon Aveugle. "Blind soup"; a clear soup which lacks "eyes" of fat.

Bouillon de Légumes. Vegetable soup; vegetable stock.

Bouïra. A wine region of Algeria; not so good as Mascara or Bône.

Boulanger (French). Baker.

Boulangerie (French). Bakery.

Boulant (French). A pouter pigeon.

Boule à Riz (French). A perforated-metal bowl or other container in which rice or small patties are suspended to be cooked in the same saucepan with a broth.

Boule de Neige (French). (1) A type of pastry or cake shaped into balls and covered with whipped cream. (2) Balls of ice cream.

Boulettes (French). Little meatballs or breadcrumb balls used chiefly for garnishing.

Bouname; Twelfth-Day Cake (Belgian). A cake baked with honey, butter, cream, and a small piece of rock candy.

Bouquet. The aroma of wine.

Bouquet Garni (French). Herbs, usually thyme, bay leaf, and parsley, tied together and used to flavor soups, stews, or sauces; always to be removed from the food before serving.

Bouquetière, À la (French). A garnish for meat or poultry dishes, consisting of neatly-arranged mounds of vegetables.

Bouquettes (Belgian). Buckwheat pancakes made with raisins.

Boura. A very sweet fig-and-raisin Algerian liqueur.

Bourbon. A whisky distilled in the United States from a fermented mash of grain of which at least 51 percent is corn. It was first distilled in

Kentucky from corn ground at a mill in Bourbon County, hence its name.

Bourbon Barrel. A white-oak barrel, well charred on the inside, used for the storage and maturing of bourbon.

Bourbon Coffee. A commercially important coffee from Santos, Brazil; used chiefly to blend with other coffees.

Bourcette. A corn salad or lamb's lettuce.

Bourdelot des Poires (French). Baked pears.

Bourdelots Normands (French). Apples wrapped in dough and baked; a specialty of Normandy.

Bourgain (French). A fresh unsalted cheese made in Neufchâtel; very perishable.

Bourgeais. A wine district of the Bordeaux region of France. *See* France, The Wines of.

Bourgeoise, À la (French). Prepared home style; that is, simply.

Bourgeois Supérieurs. *See* Crus Bourgeois.

Bourgueil. A wine district of the Loire River region of France. *See* France, The Wines of.

Bourguignonne, À la (French). Usually prepared with Burgundy wine and braised onions.

Bourguignote (French). Truffle ragoût, usually served with game.

Bourrache (French). An aromatic kitchen herb with a cucumber flavor; also called *cucumber herb.*

Bourride (French). Garlic-flavored fish stew or soup made in Provence; usually served with *aioli,* a garlic-flavored mayonnaise.

Bourru (French). (1) New wine; young wine. (2) Spiced or aromatized wine.

Bousa. A crude African beer made from millet.

Bousellouf (Algerian). A cooked sheep's head, prepared with a vinegar and oil dressing.

Boutargue (French). Mullet roe dried and pickled; eaten raw in Provence, parts of Italy, and in the Middle East.

Bouzy (French). A wine district in the Champagne region which produces very good white wines.

Bovril. Trade name for an essence of beef made in England and widely exported; a teaspoonful in a cup of hot water makes a beef-tea drink. It is also used to enhance the flavor of soups and gravies.

Bowback. Whitefish.

Bowfin. Freshwater blackfish.

Bowla. A tart made of sugar, apple, and bread.

Boxberry. *See* Wintergreen.

Boxbeutel (German). A flat, squat bottle of green glass, used for bottling Steinwein.

Box Cheese. A firm, mild German cheese, quite similar to American brick cheese, made from whole cow's milk; usually colored with saffron and flavored with caraway. A soft box cheese is made from skim milk.

Boxings. The coarse offal remaining after bran is separated from flour.

Box Loaf. A loaf of bread covered while baking.

Boxty Bread (Obsolete, Irish). A bread made from grated raw potatoes and flour.

Boxty on the Griddle (Irish). Potato bread.

Boxty on the Pan (Irish). Hot potato pancake.

Boysenberry. A large purple berry, which is shaped like a blackberry, but tastes somewhat like a raspberry.

Braaivleis (Afrikaans). A picnic or barbecue at which traditional native dishes are served.

Bra Cheese. A small, hard white cheese made of partly skimmed milk in Piedmont, Italy. The variety produced around Turin is soft and creamy.

Braciole (Italian). Beef and ham rolls; meat patties; chops.

Bracken; Fiddleheads. A vegetable that has a poor taste when raw but is acceptable when cooked.

Brackish. Salty in quality or taste.

Bräckt Lax (Swedish). Fried salmon.

Brahma. A breed of Indian cattle able to resist high temperatures; raised successfully in very hot areas of the southwestern United States.

Brahma Beer. An excellent Pilsener-type Brazilian beer.

Brains. The "gray matter" contained in the skulls of animals, classed as a variety meat. Gourmets consider calf brains the choicest and pig brains the least desirable.

Brains are much like sweetbreads in tenderness and texture. Since they do not keep well, they should be used soon after purchase, or else precooked to avoid spoilage.

Braise. A method of cooking foods, especially meats, by moist heat. Meats are first browned in a small amount of fat, then cooked covered over low heat in juices from the meat or a small amount of added liquid, either water, milk, cream, meat stock, dilute vinegar, or vegetable juices. Braising is used particularly for meat cuts having considerable connective tissue which the moist heat softens. Pork and veal chops and steaks also may be braised.

Braisière; Daubière (French). Large heavy oval pan; used for braising.

Bramble. (1) Any prickly shrub of the rose family. (2) Berries that grow on prickly shrubs, such as the raspberry and the blackberry, are called *bramble fruits* or *bramble berries*.

    Bramble Jelly. A firm jelly made from bramble fruits and sugar.

Bran. The husk of grain which, when ground, makes a flour for whole-meal bread. When processed, it may be used as a cereal or made into a bread.

Brancino. An Adriatic fish, highly esteemed in Venice, something like pike; may be boiled, fried, or served in aspic.

Brand; Brandkäse (German). A small sour-milk cheese ripened in beer kegs.

Branda. A strong, crude brandy made in Piedmont, Italy.

Brandade de Morue (French). Dried codfish, boiled, then ground very fine and mixed with olive oil, garlic, and cream; often served on toast as an hors d'oeuvre; it is popular in southern France.

Brander (Scotch). A griddle.

    Brander Bannock. A thick oatcake baked on a griddle.

Brandied. Prepared with or preserved in brandy.

Brandy. A spirit distilled from any wine or from the fermented juice of a fruit. The name is a shortened form of the English "Brandywine."

    Brandies may be distilled directly, or they may be a blend of various distillates, fortified with neutral spirits, colored, sweetened, or flavored. They contain 45—60 percent alcohol and are aged in wooden casks at least 3—4 years before bottling. Brandies improve with aging up to a point, then they begin to deteriorate and must be bottled to prevent further evaporation. The color is usually a pale amber.

    A bottled brandy is usually qualified by the name of its country of origin, as in French, Spanish, or Portuguese brandy; by the name of the district where the wine was made from which it was distilled, such as Armagnac or Cognac; or by the name of the fruit from which it is made, such as plum brandy, cherry brandy, blackberry brandy, etc. *See* Cognac.

Brandy Snaps. Brittle taffylike sweet cakes made with syrup, butter, sugar, ginger, and only enough flour to produce a thin batter.

Branja de Brailia (Romanian). A salty sheep's-milk cheese.

Branntwein (German). Brandy.

Brännvin. Aquavit, a clear white strong Scandinavian liquor.

Brant. A small wild goose with a flavor that is good, although slightly gamy.

Branza de Burduf (Romanian). A sheep's-milk cheese shipped in pine- or fir-wood containers, which flavor the cheese.

Branza de Cosulet (Romanian). A sheep's-milk cheese packed in pine bark.

Bräserad Lax med Vittvinsås (Swedish). Fresh salmon in white-wine sauce.

Brasserie (French). A popular type of simple restaurant serving good, plain food.

Braten (German). Roast.

Brathändl; Brathuhn (German). Roast chicken.

Bratwurst (German). A bland-tasting pork sausage.

Braulio. A liqueur made with wild mountain herbs in Lombardy, Italy.

Braune Tunke (German). Brown sauce.

Braunschweig; Braunschweiger (German). Liverwurst sausage; liver paste.

Brawn. Meat and fat diced and set in a thick gelatin with seasonings. It is usually made with pig's or calf's head or leg of veal because these meats, when boiled, make a solid aspic. Brawn is served cold with piquant sauces.

Brawner. A male pig specifically grown to be eaten.

Brazil. Whereas most of South America has been influenced by Spain, in Brazil the Portuguese cooking style is conspicuous. This is evident especially in the use of dried codfish, oil, olives, tomatoes, and onions. There has also been an African influence as well as the effect produced by the local fruits and vegetables. The resulting cuisine is quite interesting and definitely original. In the northern half of the country, dishes are highly spiced, but this is far less true in the south, although the dishes there are full-flavored.

Some of Brazil's outstanding dishes are: *empadinhas de camarões*, miniature shrimp pies; *canja*, a cream of chicken-and-rice soup; *casquinho de caranguejo*, stuffed crab shells; *peito de tartaruga*, breast of turtle cooked with garlic and onions; *pato no tucupi*, duck cooked with *tucupi* (the yellow juice of the manioc root); *golintra marajoara,* a chicken fricassee with coconut milk; and *pato com môlho de laranja*, duck with orange sauce.

The one national dish is *feijoada*, a bean dish cooked with meat, rice, and spices; it is particularly important in the smaller communities. *Palmitos*, hearts of palm, are used to make many different kinds of salads; avocados are also used in salad making, *salada de abacate*. Desserts often follow the Portuguese style—puddings, custards, and creams made of nuts or oranges, or ice creams made of coconuts or other local fruits. The local nuts, *castanha-do-Pará*, which we call Brazil nuts, are used in cooking, and served as salted, toasted nut chips.

Needless to say, coffee is the national drink. It is taken black, preferably in minute cups, heavily sugared, all during the day; an exception is at breakfast, when it is usually served with hot milk. *Maté*, the Paraguayan tea, has its adherents, however. The local beer is delicious; the wines are only fair, sometimes not even that. *Cachaça* is a raw, powerful rum that few visitors like; it, too, has its adherents among the local population. There is a marvelous soft drink, *guaraná*, made from a Brazilian root.

Brazil, The Wines of. *See* South America, The Wines of.

Brazil Nut. The large globular fruit of a South American tree named for its country of origin. A hard woody casing contains 18—24 closely packed, oily, three-angled nuts. They are difficult to crack, but they are very rich in flavor, nutritious, and are widely used in confectionery. Very similar and with an even better taste are *Paradise nuts*, which are seldom exported.

Brazil Nut

Brazo de Gitano (Spanish). A custard-filled spongecake dessert resembling a jelly roll.

Bread. A food made from flour or meal by moistening, kneading, and baking, sometimes with a ferment added. It is the oldest, commonest, and cheapest form of human food, with relics of preparation dating back more than 10,000 years. Flour or meal for bread has been made with one or more kinds of cereal, as well as from various grasses, roots, or seeds. The ancient Chinese, Egyptians, and Hebrews prepared flat cakes made of wheat flour and water without leaven.

The discovery of fermented bread is attributed to the Egyptians, and thus the baking industry was born. Every Egyptian village had its public ovens and all nobles had their private bakers. Still, the use of leavened bread did not supersede the older method. Flat flour and water cakes were the chief sustenance of the Roman legions, and the same forms were used widely throughout the Middle Ages.

The quality of bread, its nutritive value, appearance, and flavor depend on the nature and quality of the grain from which its flour or meal is made; the milling method is also very important. The grains of all cereals consist of four main parts: (1) the outer covering or husk, (2) the bran layers, (3) the germ, and (4) the endosperm, or starch. It is the germ that contains the building material of the plant itself, rich protein and vitamins, which are also essential to the human diet. For centuries flour was obtained laboriously by crushing grain between two stones. This method retained all but the coarsest part of the outer covering of the grain, and the color varied from light brown in the case of wheat, to black when rye was used. In the late 1800s a roller mill invented in Hungary made it possible to crush grain between revolving metal cylinders. This process was much more rapid and economical, and easily separated the bran and germ from the kernel. A snow-white flour was produced which made an attractive bread devoid of almost all nutrients except starch. It is only recently that scientists delving into the whys and wherefores of a healthful diet have provided methods for enriching white bread and replacing the essential vitamins and minerals removed by the milling processes. Whole-grain breads, too, are becoming more popular, since they are now known to be more wholesome and flavor-filled than the staple white loaves.

Bread-and-Butter Plate. A flat plate about 5 inches in diameter used during the meal to hold an individual serving of bread and butter.

Bread and Chumps (British slang). Bread and cheese.

Bread and Dippy (British slang). Bread dipped in thin cream.

Bread Board. Smooth wooden board on which bread or other foods can be cut or sliced. It offers protection both to the knife edge and to the tabletop.

Bread Box. A ventilated container, usually made of sheet metal, used to store breadstuffs, to postpone staleness and prevent mustiness.

Bread Crumbs. There are two kinds of bread crumbs, each serving special purposes. *Dry* bread crumbs, the kind that can be rolled fine, are used for coating foods before frying, for buttered crumbs, and they can also be used for stuffings if a close-textured preparation is desired. Commercial bread crumbs are of this type. *Soft* bread crumbs, used for bread puddings, fondues, timbales, stuffings, and buttered crumbs, are made by crumbling bread 2—4 days old.

Bread Fleke (Obsolete). A rack on which oatcakes were partially dried.

Bread Flour. Flour milled from the firm inner part of spring, or hard, wheat.

Breadfruit. A tropical fruit, resembling a green melon in size and shape and a white potato in taste and texture. A staple food in tropical countries, it is rich in starch. It is usually prepared as a vegetable, boiled and eaten plain or stuffed.

It is also sliced and baked or fried in oil, and used as bread.

Bread-Making Flour. A flour containing fairly strong gluten so as to withstand a period of fermentation. It produces good volume and texture in the bread.

Breadnut. (1) A type of breadfruit tree that produces a fruit with large seeds, resembling chestnuts; the seeds are usually boiled. (2) A tropical starchy root used for stuffings or in soups.

Bread Roast (British). A sandwich loaf of bread with the top removed and the soft center taken out in one piece, leaving a shell of crust about an inch thick. The case is filled with a seasoned mixture of minced meat, vegetables, and sauce. The top crust is put back on as a lid, and the whole is "roasted" in a moderate oven. This very old farmhouse dish was revived during World War II by the British Ministry of Food.

Breadroot. *See* Yam.

Bread Sauce (British). A sauce served with game birds; made of white crustless bread soaked in milk, cooked with onion, spices, and butter.

Breadstuff. (1) All breads. (2) The grains, meal, and flour used in making bread.

Bread Wine. A simple country beverage made with brown bread, sugar, and water, kept in a warm place until it ferments; resembles the Russian *kvass*.

Break Bread. To share a meal.

Breakfast. The first meal of the day, hence the name "to break a fast." Breakfast menus vary widely with country, locality, and occupation.

Breakfast Tea. *See* English Breakfast Tea.

Bream. (1) A European freshwater food fish, member of the carp family. (2) The bluegill.

Brebajes. Beverages.

Brede (Obsolete). Roasted meat.

Brèdes (French). Stew made in certain French colonies, from various vegetable leaves.

Bree (Scottish). (1) Soup stock or broth. (2) (Colloquial) A thick soup.

Breid of Mane (Scotch). An aromatic bread.

Bréjauda (French). Cabbage soup made with bacon in the Auvergne region.

Brème de Mer; Daurade (French). The sea bream, a fish about 18 inches long.

Bremer Kuekenragout (German). A rich mixture of meat and vegetables in a cream sauce.

Brennesnut (Norwegian). Barley-and-frankfurter soup.

Brennevin (Norwegian). Brandy.

Bresí; Brési (French). A substantial piece of beef dried by smoke, a specialty of the Jura region.

Bresolle. (1) An entrée made with several different kinds of meat. (2) A veal ragout.

Bresse. A region of east central France famous for its fine food, especially the excellent chicken, *poulet de Bresse.*

Bret; Brit; Burt (British, Colloquial). A small turbotlike fish.

Breteuil, Baron de (Louis-Auguste Le Tonnelier). French diplomat and Minister under Louis XVI; he was a noted epicure and gourmet.

Bretonne, À la (French). Prepared with beans.

Bretonne, Sauce (French). A thick *velouté* sauce with shredded vegetables added, served with fish or eggs.

Brevas (Spanish). Black figs.

Brevine. A Swiss cheese resembling Emmentaler.

Brew. To make a beverage, especially beer, ale, tea, according to the usual procedures for the drink involved.

Brewery. Place where ale and beer are made.

Brewing. (1) Preparing a particular brew. (2) The quantity brewed at one time.

Brewis. A broth, or bread dipped in broth. *Fish and brewis* is a Newfoundland dish made of codfish and crackers in broth.

Breyes Baylicales (Algerian). Dessert made with small squares of cooked semolina and assorted nuts.

Brezel (German). Pretzel.

Brickbat. A cheese, made in Wiltshire, England, mostly of milk (with added cream) and ripened for a year.

Brick Cheese. A semisoft American cow's-milk cheese with a mild but rather pungent flavor. It is brick-shaped and is distinguished by its numerous holes. Wisconsin is a great producer. *See* American Cheese.

Brick Ice Cream (Italian). Ice cream consisting of three different flavors; usually oblong in shape. Sometimes also called Neapolitan ice cream.

Brick Tea. An old Chinese product still favored in Siberia and other parts of Russia. Tea leaves were pressed into bricks and slabs. The brick was rubbed into a fine powder, then boiled with water to which salt and fat had been added, resulting in a smooth, oily brown liquid resembling cocoa.

Bricotta. A Corsican medium soft sheep's-milk cheese.

Bridage (French). The tying-up with string of the limbs of game or poultry; trussing.

Bride Cup (British). A drinking cup, usually containing wine, passed at a wedding.

Brider (French). To truss poultry.

Brié (French). A kneaded paste used for biscuits and similar products.

Brie. A soft, round, flat cheese from Melun, Coulommiers, and Meaux in France that has been renowned for centuries. Made from whole cow's milk, it is perishable and should be kept under refrigeration. Brie is marketed in three sizes: large—about 16 inches in diameter and weighing about 6 pounds; medium—12 inches, 3½ pounds; and small—8 inches, about 1 pound. The cheese should be removed from refrigeration at least three hours before it is served.

Brie Façon. Imitation Brie cheese.

Brier (French). To flatten paste with a rolling pin.

Brigidini (Italian). Anise-flavored cookies.

Brignoles. Dark red cooking plums grown in the Brignoles district of France.

Brigue. Bass, a food fish.

Brigue, Fromage de la. A round fermented cheese made in France of cow's milk (sometimes sheep's milk).

Brikk (Algerian). Eggs arranged in pastry, then fried.

Brill. A European flatfish of the turbot family with very light, delicate flesh; best served filleted and baked.

Brillat-Savarin. (1) A rather soft cheese made in Normandy, France. (2) Various preparations consisting principally of lamb or mutton cut into small pieces. (3) A light yeast cake.

Brillat-Savarin, Jean Anthelme. A famous French gourmet (1755—1826); the author of numerous aphorisms about the pleasures of the table, and especially famous for his *Physiologie du Goût*, a brilliant exposition on food and eating habits.

Brilliolo. A Corsican chestnut cake served with hot milk.

Brina Dubreala. A fairly soft Romanian sheep's-milk cheese cured in brine.

Brindza. *See* Brinza.

Brine. A saltwater solution used for pickling and preserving fish, butter, and vegetables.

Brine Cheese. Any cheese cured in salted water or brine.

Bringebaer (Norwegian). Raspberries.

Brinjal; Brinjaul. Eggplant.

Brinsen. *See* Brinza.

Brinza; Brinsen. A Hungarian cheese made of sheep's milk (sometimes combined with goat's milk) into a rather creamy, rich, sharp product tasting somewhat like Roquefort. It is also known as Altsohl, Klencz, Landoch, Liptauer, Neusohl, Siebenburgen, and Zips. In the United States the cheese is frequently imitated, particularly in Hungarian communities, where its name is spelled *Brindza*.

Brioche (French). A light-textured yeast bread prepared with butter and eggs, and usually shaped into a bun with a small topknot. Brioches are best served hot with butter and perhaps strawberry jam on the side. At breakfast in France they are always accompanied by a cup of steaming *café au lait* (coffee with hot milk). In recent years brioche has become a breakfast staple in many other countries.

    Brioches au Caviar. Small brioches filled with caviar; may also be sliced.

Brioler; Westphalia Sour-Milk Cheese. A renowned German sour-milk cheese kneaded by hand; it is soft, fatty, and rather strong-tasting.

Briolet (French, Colloquial). Poor quality wine; the name derives from the wine of the Brie district, which is notoriously poor.

Brionne. *See* Custard Marrow.

Briqueton. French name for England's Wiltshire Brickbat cheese.

Brise-Flamme (French). An asbestos pad or wire mat, used to protect cooking utensils from direct heat.

Brisket. Layered lean and fat meat covering the breastbone of an animal. Beef brisket, either plain or corned, is cooked in liquid or braised; best when cut for boiled beef.

Brisler (Danish). Sweetbreads.

Brisling (Norwegian). Smoked sardine.

Brisolette (French). A very small cocktail appetizer or hors d'oeuvre.

Brisotine (French). Any dish containing chopped or minced meat.

Bristol Cream. A special brand of excellent sweet sherry distributed under the trade name "Harvey."

Bristol Milk. A fine-quality sherry, slightly inferior to Bristol Cream, shipped and blended by wine merchants under the trade name "Harvey."

British Guiana. *See* Guianas, The.

Brittle. A hard candy usually containing nuts.

Brix Scale. A scale of densities often used for measuring sugar solutions, fruit juices, etc.

Brizecon. An imitation of authentic Reblochon cheese, made in Savoy, France.

Broad Bean. A tasty bean of pale greenish-gray color enclosed in large plump pods covered with soft white lining. The ancient Greeks thought these beans dulled the wits and caused bad dreams.

Broadbill. The swordfish.

Broccio. A slightly salty sheep's-milk cheese made in Italy and Corsica; it resembles Ricotta.

Broccoli. Two distinct forms of this ancient vegetable, savored in Roman times, are grown in the United States. The most common is the Italian, or *sprouting*, type, which grows 2—2½ feet tall into a somewhat branching head of bud clusters atop a thick green stalk. The *heading* broccoli, the other type, resembles cauliflower.

    The stalks, buds, and the few leaves clinging to the stalk all are edible. The vegetable should be dark green with compact bud clusters and tender, firm stalks. It should be cooked in very little water and only until just tender, for overcooking impairs the color, flavor, and texture. The stalks may be split lengthwise to speed cooking. The tough parts of the stalk should be removed before cooking.

Formerly broccoli was soaked in salted water for 20 minutes before cooking to remove insects. But modern cultivation and spraying methods have eliminated that problem so that a quick rinsing in cold water is sufficient.

Broccoli is fairly strong-flavored, but if it is cooked uncovered for the first few minutes, there is no pronounced flavor. A slice of bread added to the water when cooking broccoli will help to minimize the cooking odor.

Frozen broccoli, available the year round in spears or chopped, is becoming increasingly popular. It is cooked in much the same way as the fresh vegetable.

Broccoli alla Fiorentina (Italian). Broccoli fried in oil.

Brochan (Scottish). Cereal; porridge.

Broche (French). A spit or grill.

Brochet Badoise (French). Baked pike cooked with sour cream.

Brochette (French). A small silver, steel, or wooden skewer put through pieces of meat, cheese, poultry, or fish for broiling or frying.

Brochettes au Fromage. Small pieces of cheese placed on a skewer alternately with bread slices, dipped in milk, flour, and egg, and deep-fat fried.

Brocolos (Portuguese). Broccoli.

Brød (Danish). Bread.

Bröd (Swedish). Bread.

Brodaie (Italian). A rice dish prepared with salami, onions, pig's blood, and cheese in Piedmont.

Brödchen (German). Small dinner rolls.

Brodet (Yugoslavian). Fish soup.

Brodetto (Italian). Mixed-fish stew, sometimes seasoned with saffron.

Brodetto all' Ancona. Fish-and-tomato soup.

Brodetto di Pesce. A fish stew.

Brodo (Italian). Broth.

Brodo di Manzo. Beef broth.

Broil. *See* Broiling.

Broiler. (1) A chicken 8–12 weeks old and weighing 1–2½ pounds, the ideal size for broiling. Broilers are available all year round but are most plentiful from May to September. *See* Chicken. (2) A covered metal pan fitted with a rack on which foods may be broiled. The pan is designed to be used in an oven, but most modern ranges are equipped with a built-in cooking unit, which serves the same purpose.

Broiling. Grilling, a cooking process by which food is prepared under a very hot flame or over hot coals. It produces a coating on the outer surface of the food while the inside warms gradually and cooks more slowly, retaining most of its juices.

Broken Orange Pekoe. A small-leaf tea; it makes a liquid with a good color and is generally used in blending.

Broken Pekoe. A tea leaf slightly larger than broken orange pekoe but having less color when brewed; used in blending rather than marketed straight.

Broken Pekoe Souchong. A tea that has a stronger taste than broken pekoe and is lighter in the cup.

Bromatology. The study, art, and skill of food.

Bromeliaceous. Belonging to the pineapple family.

Bromelin. A proteolytic enzyme found in pineapple juice, used for tenderizing meat and sausage skin casings.

Brominated Oils; Weighting Oils. Olive, peach, apricot kernel, or soya oils combined with bromine; used to help stabilize emulsions of flavoring substances in soft drinks.

Bronx Cocktail. An alcoholic drink made with gin and a little Italian sweet vermouth.

Broo (Scottish). A thick soup, bree; sometimes, juice or liquor.

Brood. Oysters in their second year.

Brood (Dutch). Bread.

Brood en Boter. Bread and butter.

Broodjes (Dutch). Rolls.

Broodkaase. A hard, flat Dutch cheese with a nutty flavor.

Broodpap (Dutch). Bread pudding.

Brooklime; Water Pimpernel. A variety of wild cress, found in various parts of Europe.

Brook Trout. A freshwater game fish common to eastern North America; delicious when broiled or sautéed in butter.

Broon Barnets (British). Bread baked with molasses and flour.

Broschen (German). Sweetbreads.

Brose (Scotch). A seasoned oatmeal dish with boiling water added.

Brot (German). Bread.

Brötchen (German). Rolls.

Broth. A liquid like a soup, but usually thinner and simpler, in which other foods have been boiled, as, for example, chicken broth or beef broth. It may be served as a clear soup or bouillon or with cut-up vegetables or rice added.

Brotola de Roca (Spanish). A fish found in southern European waters; it is similar to burbot.

Brotzeit (German). Between-meal snack of sausages, bread, and beer or coffee.

Brou de Noix. A sweet French afterdinner liqueur made with walnuts steeped in brandy.

Brouet (French). A liquor or broth.

Brouet d'Andouille. The stock obtained from cooking tripe.

Brouilly. A town in the Beaujolais wine district of France. *See* France, The Wines of.

Brousse; Brousso; Braccio. A cheese obtained by boiling whey.

Brousse de la Vézubie. A small sheep's-milk cheese made near Nice, France.

Brousse Tea. A tea made in parts of the United States from the dried and slightly heated leaves of a plant known as *Vaccinium arctosaphylos.*

Broussin (French). A mixture of vinegar, soft cheese, and pepper.

Broutes; Broutons (French). A dish of cabbage, sometimes with leeks added; served with oil and vinegar in the Béarn district.

Browet (Obsolete). The juice from boiled meat made into a broth.

Browis. *See* Brewis.

Brown. To seal the juices within a piece of meat or other food by scorching its surfaces.

Brown Betty. A fruit-and-bread crumb pudding. *See* Betty.

Brown Bread. A sweetish dark bread cooked by steaming; traditionally served with Boston baked beans. *See also* Boston Brown Bread.

Brown Fungus; Cloud Ears. An edible fungus much used in Chinese cookery.

Brown George (British). (1) Coarse brown bread. (2) A hard biscuit. (3) Brown George turnovers are pastry shells filled with apples and baked in tins 12–14 inches by 6 inches.

Brown Gravy. A gravy of meat juice, drippings, flour, and seasonings.

Brownie. A rich chocolate cookie or cake.

Brown Rice. The milled rice grain from which only the husk has been removed; it is more nutritious than white rice, and takes longer to cook.

Brown Sauce. The base for most highly spiced sauces.

Brown Sherry. *See* Spain, The Wines of.

Brown Sugar. A dark sugar not completely refined, containing molasses, produced by a different boiling method from white sugar, and used mostly in the making of confections and cakes. *See also* Sugar.

Brownware (British). Glazed brown earthenware used for stews, potted meats, and similar dishes; manufactured chiefly by Pearsons of Chesterfield.

Browthy Bread (British). Light and spongy bread.

Broye (French). Made with soup, leftover pork meat thickened with corn flour and allowed to cool until firm, then cut and fried in fat.

Broyo (French). Cornmeal cooked in vegetable broth until very thick; eaten hot or cooled and sliced; specialty of Béarn.

Brühe (German). Consommé.

Bruine Boonen (Dutch). Black beans.

Bruise. (1) To crush foods, herbs, or spices in a mortar. (2) Injury to fruits and vegetables.

Brûlant (French). Piping hot or burning.

Brule. An ice-cream dessert made with sweet cream, egg yolks, sugar, and flavorings.

Brûlot (French). A lump of sugar soaked in brandy, ignited, and then added to coffee.

Brûlot, Café. Black coffee prepared with brandy and spices, and served in a tall, narrow cup; specialty of New Orleans.

Bruna Bönor (Swedish). Baked beans.

Brunch. A midmorning meal combining the features of breakfast and lunch.

Brunello. *See* Italy, The Wines of.

Brunkaalssuppe (Danish). Brown cabbage soup.

Brunnenkresse (German). Watercress.

Brunoise (French). (1) A soup, either thick or clear, containing finely cut vegetables. (2) Finely diced vegetables, intended as the basis for a soup, stew, or stuffed food.

Bruns Lapskaus (Norwegian). Brown meat stew.

Brunswick Stew. A meat-and-vegetable stew originated in colonial Virginia and still a favorite in many parts of the southern United States. The traditional version included stewing chicken, lean beef, or veal and rabbit, or squirrel.

Bruss (Italian). A paste made with oil, garlic, pepper, and cheese; used as flavoring.

Brussels Lof (Dutch). Chicory.

Brussels Sprouts. Named for the capital of Belgium, this vegetable has been known to Europeans since the 13th century. An aristocrat of the cabbage family, this tiny "cabbage" has a pronounced, strong flavor. Select specimens are those with bright-green tightly closed leaves. They are not only eye-appealing but also a good source of vitamins A and C. They lend themselves to many different methods of preparation. Most people who do not like Brussels sprouts have never eaten the very young, very small specimens; these have a delightfully delicate flavor quite different from the "cabbagy" taste many people dislike.

Brussoles (French). A dish somewhere between a stuffing and a stew.

Bruststück (German). Brisket.

Brut (French). Of sparkling wines and champagnes, having a dry quality. If *brut*, wines contain ½–1 percent sugar. Peculiarly enough, champagnes marked "dry" are actually sweeter than the *brut* types.

Brutna Skorpor (Swedish). Dry round rusks like toast.

Bruxelles Cheese. A rather soft Belgian skim-milk cheese.

Bruyère, Coq de. Heath cock, a small game bird.

Brylépudding (Swedish). Caramel pudding.

Bryonia; Bryony. A tuberous-rooted perennial vine related to the gourd family. The root is often used for making bitters.

BTU. *See* Unit of Heat, British.

Bual; Boal. A Madeira wine very rich in flavor and delicate in bouquet.

Bub (British). Strong beer.

Bubble and Squeak (British). An everyday dish utilizing leftover meats and vegetables. The meat may be sliced and reheated in fat with the vegetables, or meat and vegetables may be simmered together in a saucepan.

Bubbler. An Ohio River fish, of fair quality.

Bucayo (Philippine). Sugar syrup and freshly grated coconut cooked until translucent.

Buccan (West Indian). A barbecue.

Buccellato (Italian). A cake, usually ring-shaped, filled with any desired cream. Also, a cake with anise and currants.

Bucellas. A wine district of Portugal. *See* Portugal, The Wines of.

Buche de Bacalao. The air-dried lining of a codfish stomach; used as food in many Latin countries.

Buck (1) The male of the roe deer. (2) A basket used by fishermen to catch eels.

Buckbean. A bitter-tasting clover sometimes substituted by dishonest brewers for hops.

Buckeye. A horse-chestnut tree.

Buckie. A mollusk shell.

Bucklings. Very lightly smoked salted herrings.

Buck Rarebit. Welsh rarebit with a poached egg on top.

Buckshee (British Army slang). An allowance of food above the usual amount; extra rations.

Buckwheat. An herb, of Siberian origin, cultivated as a food plant and ground into flour. It is not a true cereal but nevertheless is used to make bread, pancakes, and cakes. Buckwheat groats, known as *kasha*, is very popular in eastern Europe; it is cooked and served like rice.

Budapest Cheese. A very soft fresh-cream Hungarian cheese.

Budare (Venezuelan). A clay pot, sometimes a griddle, used for making bread from corn.

Budbud (South Pacific). Rice dish usually prepared in a banana leaf.

Budderized Milk. Milk preserved illegally by the addition of hydrogen peroxide.

Budding (Danish). Pudding.

Budding of Yeast. The live action of yeast when it is combined with other foods, dissolved in water, and kept at a suitable temperature.

Budín (Spanish). Pudding.

Budino (Italian). Pudding.

　Budino di Pasta. Noodle pudding.

　Budino di Ricotta. Cheese pudding.

　Budino Torinese. Chestnut pudding.

Bue (Italian). Beef.

　Bue alla Spiedo. Beef on skewers.

Buffalo. The American bison. At one time, this large member of the ox family was prevalent across most of the American plains, and used as food. The meat was somewhat tough and stringy, and the flavor variable, occasionally good, usually poor.

Buffalo, À la. Of meat, cooked directly on a griddle or open fire.

Buffalo Berry. A fruit cultivated on the western plains of the United States. Round and tart, it resembles the barberry and is used for jellies and preserves. Its name refers to the custom of serving the cooked berries with buffalo meat.

Buffalo Currant. A currant found in the central United States; at its best when made into jellies, jams, and pies.

Buffalo Fish. A principal food fish of the Mississippi River. Very popular in Jewish cookery.

Buff Caps. Wild mushrooms, found in the autumn, having very bright colors, often yellow or red, and good taste and texture.

Buffet. A popular American way of entertaining, in which foods are arranged on a table or sideboard and guests either help themselves or are served by a waiter or maid. This is a much easier way of serving party foods than a sitdown dinner. Chafing dishes, electric trays, or candle warmers keep the hot dishes hot. The complete party menu, including dessert, may be arranged on one table if it is large enough, or secondary tables may be used.

The term "buffet" comes from the French. Formerly at large receptions the buffet was presented on a tiered table whose arrangement was a work of art. The tiered tables, usually near the entrance in restaurants, on which specialties of the house are displayed are also called buffets.

Buffeter (French). To remove wine, and improperly replace it with an equal amount of water.

Buggle (Scottish). A large bannock, or flat cake, made in Orkney and Shetlands on March 29.

Bugle Horn (Obsolete). A drinking horn.

Bugloss. *Anchusa*; a small plant whose leaves, eaten as a green vegetable, taste much like chard. The flowers may be added to salads, or dried and used as an herb.

Bugnes (French). A kind of doughnut or flat cruller, made of various dough mixtures, fried in deep fat, and dusted with sugar.

　Bugnes Lyonnaises. Sweet dessert fritter, a specialty of Lyons.

Buisson (French). A dish arranged like a pyramid. *Un buisson d'écrevisses* is a pile of crayfish.

Buko (Philippine). Young, immature coconut.

Bulbil. A small bulb which forms on certain plants, such as garlic.

Bulb Kelp. A seaweed found along the Alaskan coast; used in making pickles and jellies.

Bulgaria. In Bulgaria the main meal is served at midday, the evening meal consisting of leftovers or cheese, bread, and fruit. In general, the food is similar to that of the other Balkan countries, Greece, and Turkey. But because Bulgaria is comparatively poor, the national diet is somewhat limited in variety, with strong emphasis on vegetables, fruits, and dairy products.

Vegetables are the chief ingredients in most recipes, especially in the summer months, for meat is too expensive for the low per capita income. Green beans, eggplant, peppers, cucumbers, tomatoes, and radishes are standard fare for every Bulgarian. Lentils, rice, and beans, as well as potatoes, are used to supplement the diet and provide necessary calories. Seasonal fruits and melons include excellent apricots, pears, and grapes.

Simple cheeses, *syréné*, usually the fresh type, and yoghurt are standard daily items. Yoghurt is believed to be the source of continuing health and longevity of the people, an extraordinarily large percentage of whom become octogenarians. The Bulgarians are very fond of sweets and pastries; *banitsa* is a cloying, rich pastry, and *baklawa* is the classic overly rich pastry soaked in honey that originated in Turkey.

Beer is passable, and the local wines are unpretentious, often somewhat crude in taste. *Mastika* is the local potent brandy; and *slivovitza*, also called *slivovice*, is a burning plum brandy. A fermented drink of sesame seed, *booze*, though viscous, gray, and unappetizing, is very popular. The American slang word "booze" might have come from this Bulgarian drink.

Bulgood. Yeast.

Bulimia. Extreme hunger.

Bulimious. Insatiably hungry.

Buljong (Norwegian and Swedish). Consommé.

Bullmeat. The meat of young bulls.

Bullabesa (Spanish). A thick soup made with numerous fish and shellfish.

Bullace. A tree that bears a fruit similar to the damson plum. The fruit is round, not oval like the damson, and does not have the pleasant rough taste characteristic of the damson; it is used in England for pies, puddings, preserves, and jellies.

Bulle. A Gruyère cheese made in Switzerland.

Bullhead. The catfish.

Bullnut. An oblong but somewhat rounded nut native to various parts of the United States; quite similar to the hickory nut.

Bullock. Steer or ox.

Bull's Blood. *Egri Bikaver*, a hearty Hungarian red wine. *See* Hungary, The Wines of.

Bull's-Eyes (British). An old peppermint-flavored sweet made of boiled sugar and formed into round, irregular pieces.

Bull Trout. A large member of the salmon family. Despite its size, it has a surprisingly delicate flavor; prepared like any other type of trout.

Bully Beef (British). Corned beef or pressed beef cured so that it will keep indefinitely in cans.

Bulter (British). Coarse bread with a large percentage of bran.

Bumbo. A rum drink containing nutmeg, water, and sugar.

Bumboat. A small boat that transports food from shore to ships at sea.

Bummalo. Small Indian Ocean fish used to make Bombay duck. *See* Bombay Duck.

Bumper. A glass used for a toast and filled to the brim.

Bun. A small, round sweet roll that may contain raisins or nuts and may be covered with a sugar glaze or cinnamon.

Bun Dough. A sweet rich yeast dough for making most buns.

Buncuit. A decorated cake with a sweet pastry bottom and a yeast-dough top.

Bundenfleisch; Bundnerfleisch (German). Salted beef, a specialty of the Grisons, Switzerland; it is air-dried, sometimes smoked, and sliced paper-thin. As an appetizer, it may be served with figs or melon, and a generous dusting of black pepper. It greatly resembles Italy's prosciutto.

Bundkuchen (German). A sweet, yellow round cake.

Bung. A gingerbread cake.

Bunga Sundal (Malayan). Dried edible flowers used as a flavoring ingredient.

Bun Glaze. A solution brushed over hot buns to create a glossy surface. Gum solutions, mixtures of eggs, sugar, and milk, and sugar solutions are examples.

Bunion. (1) A peanut. (2) A poor Italian almond.

Bun Loaves. Large pieces of bun dough, sometimes containing fruits, baked in bread tins; served sliced and buttered.

Bunting. (1) Gray shrimp. (2) Aquatic wading bird, found in various parts of the world; despite a somewhat gamy taste, often used as food.

Buñuelos (Spanish). Doughnuts.

Burani (Oriental). A kind of consommé of chicken and barley reduced and scented with various herbs.

Buras (Indonesian). Rice served in banana leaves.

Burbot (French). The eelpout, a freshwater fish often mistaken for the true eel.

Burdock. A wild plant or herb, found in temperate regions; its leaves are eaten as a green vegetable.

Burdwan (Indian). Hash or ragout for which small pieces of cooked meat are simmered with stock, seasoned with onion, cayenne pepper, chilies, garlic, and lemon juice.

Burette. Oil-and-vinegar cruet.

Burfi (Indian). A candy or sweet made chiefly from khoa (dried fresh whole milk); it may contain nuts or carrots.

Burgall. The American blue perch.

Burgoo. A kind of soup or highly spiced stew made in the southern United States.

Burgot Beergood. Yeast.

Burgunder Sosse (German). Wine sauce.

Burgundy. (1) A kind of wine. *See* France, The Wines of. (2) A soft white loaf-shaped cheese.

Buri. The star apple, a fruit native to the Philippines and other warm countries.

Buridda; Burrida (Italian). Fish stew.

Burrida di Pesci. A fish soup, specialty of Genoa.

Buriello Calabrese (Italian). Butter wrapped in Caciocavallo cheese.

Burlace. A European grape grown in the 17th century, now supplanted by improved types.

Burma. Unlike Western meals, Burmese food is seldom eaten in courses, nor do the Burmese believe in hors d'oeuvre, appetizers, or cocktails, which, to their way of thinking, spoil the appetite.

Rice, of course, is the basis of most meals. It is eaten with one or more curried dishes made of fish, meat, or poultry. Sometimes, there is a soup; *mon la hingyo*, cabbage soup, is typical. Usually there is a salad or fried vegetables, or both. More elaborate meals might include scores of different dishes, however.

A favorite at all meals is the classic sauce, *nga-pi-gyet*, prepared from shrimp paste, garlic, onions, and hot red chili peppers. Usually Westerners do not like its taste at first, but eventually even foreign residents develop a liking for it. It is quite similar to the *nam prik* sauce so frequently encountered in Thailand. Desserts are rarely served, except on special holidays.

Own thee moant is a coconut cake, which is probably Anglo-Burmese, not indigenous.

The national cuisine bears considerable resemblance to that of neighboring countries, especially the flavoring and spicing ingredients. Garlic, onions, hot peppers, coconut, ginger, saffron, cardamom, cumin, turmeric, and tamarind are typical items in Burmese cookery.

Wine is not served, but the local beer is quite good and very refreshing, for Burma's weather tends toward humidity and extreme high temperatures.

Burmeister. A soft brick-type cheese made in Wisconsin.

Burnet; Pimprenelle; Salad Burnet. An aromatic herb, formerly popular, with a pleasing aroma; particularly suited for salads.

Burning Off. Applying high heat to a new skillet in order to remove the impurities.

Burnt Almond. A praliné flavor created by combining caramel and lightly browned almonds.

Burnt Sugar. Caramel; a solution made by dissolving burnt sugar in boiling water.

Burree (Obsolete). Butter pear, an English pear with a soft pulp.

Burriello. A water-buffalo cheese popular around Naples, Italy.

Burro (Italian). Butter.

Burro e Parmigiano. With butter and Parmesan cheese, a classic way to serve *pasta*.

Burton Ale. An excellent ale produced near the River Trent in England; it is believed that the local water is responsible for the taste.

Busa. *See* Fermented Milk.

Busecca (Italian). Tripe with beans.

Bush Apple. Not an apple, but an Australian plum.

Bushman. A medium-hard yellow Australian cheese.

Bush Tea. A beverage made from the dried leaves of the South African shrub *Cyclopia genistoides*; flavor and aroma are similar to those of the China teas.

Bustard. A rather large game bird with a very good flavor found in Europe, Africa, and Australia.

Buster Crab. A soft-shell crab. However, some gourmets describe it as a crab whose old shell is loosened but not yet discarded. *See also* Crabs.

Butcher. A person who sells meat in a store. With the advent of chain stores in the United States, the butcher selling retail and cutting meats in individual cuts is becoming rare.

Butchery. A slaughterhouse; a butcher shop.

Butifarra (Spanish). A sausage made of pork, spiced with pepper and nutmeg, and shaped into links; popular in Latin countries.

Butler. A man employed in a household to take charge of the pantry, food purchases, wines, and table service. Since domestic help has become rarer, the butler's various household duties may or may not include cooking.

Butlerage. (1) The state of being a butler, especially in a large or royal household. (2) The tax levied on imported wines in England.

Butler's Pantry; Butlery. A rather small space, or small room, located between the dining room and the kitchen, supposedly for the use of a butler or maid; often as not, because of the lack of domestic help, the hostess uses the butler's pantry.

Butt. (1) The thick end of a ham or shoulder. *See also* Ham. (2) A wine cask. (3) Several different types of flatfish. (4) An American cut of beef found between the rear leg and the inside flank, where the leg and body meet.

Butter. The solidified fat of fresh milk or cream separated by churning. It is the most easily digested form of fat and is also best for taste and enriching qualities. Cakes and pastries made with butter have a far better flavor and are richer than those made with other fats, and meats and vegetables served with butter often need no other sauce.

Butter may or may not be salted or colored. The favorite with most Americans, however, is a bright yellow, often tinted with vegetable dyes. Its quality depends on the quality of the milk or cream from which it is made and the manner of production.

Butter has been known to man since earliest times and presumably originated with nomadic tribes who prepared it from the milk of the cows, ewes, goats, mares, asses, buffaloes, and camels raised for their domestic needs. In parts of ancient India butter was considered a sacred food, and the Hebrews used butter not only as a food but also for medicinal purposes. In more recent times butter was made on individual farms and marketed locally, but with modern preservation methods it can now be shipped from local creameries all over the world.

Butter is usually packaged in one-quarter, one-half, one-, two-, or five-pound prints, bars, or loaves. It should always be refrigerated until used. It is most often served in the form of small squares or pats cut from a quarter-pound bar or stick. For special occasions, however, it may be shaped or molded into a variety of attractive forms.

Compound Butter. (1) Melted butters, with flavorings or spices added, used to garnish or dress certain dishes. (2) Softened butters, combined with any desired ingredients.

Savory Butter. Fresh butter beaten until smooth with various seasonings, flavorings, and colorings; used with various dishes and as a spread for sandwiches and garnishes for hors d'oeuvre.

Butterback. A wild duck, of rather gamy flavor, native to various parts of the United States.

Butter Cream; Butter Icing. A mixture of sugar and creamed butter; sometimes made with other ingredients, flavorings, and colors; used in cakes.

Buttered Beer. A mixture of cinnamon, butter, sugar, and beer brewed without hops.

Buttered Syrup. A sweet brown syrup prepared from maple or other sugar syrup and butter; often used on pancakes, French toast, and waffles.

Butterfat. The fat content in milk; by extension, the fat content of ice cream and other dairy products.

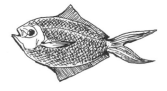

Butterfish. A delicious small, deep-olive-colored fish of the mackerel family found along the Atlantic seaboard.

Butter Flavor. A mixture of almond, nutmeg, and walnut oils used to lend a buttery flavor to cakes and other products. Among the essential oils and synthetic esters used for this purpose are ethyl butyrate, amyl butyrate, and butyric acid.

Butterie (Scotch). A butter biscuit or a butter roll.

Butterine. An imitation butter made from various fats and oils.

Butter Knife. *See* Flatware.

Buttermilk. Originally, the liquid left after butter has been churned from milk. The beverage usually found on the market, however, is often made from skim or whole milk fermented and soured by adding bacteria cultures, then churned to break up the curd. As a source of protein buttermilk is as nutritious as sweet milk, and it is more easily digested, since the casein has been broken up by the souring and churning processes.

Buttermilk Cheese. An American farm-style cheese with a fresh, soft texture much like cottage cheese but finer-grained.

Buttermilk, Cultured. *See* Cultured Buttermilk.

Buttermischungen (German). Butter.

Butternut. A rich, oily nut of the white walnut tree; used in cakes and cookies and also in pickles and catsup, but it tends to become rancid quickly after being shelled.

Butter of Cacao; Cocoa Butter. A thick oily substance produced from cacao seeds; used in making chocolate candies, cosmetics, and pharmaceutical preparations. *See* Cocoa Butter.

Butter Plate; Butter Dish. A large dish used to hold butter for all the diners at a meal or a small plate for individual servings.

Butter Sauce. A simple sauce with butter as its principal ingredient; may be served hot or cold but is usually offered with hot foods.

Butterscotch. (1) A rich flavoring made of brown sugar and butter. (2) A hard candy, made from brown sugar and butter; sold in chunks or coated as candy filling.

Butter-Slag. (British). A slice of bread and butter.

Butter Sponge. A light cake mixture in which clarified butter is added to a stiffly beaten mixture of eggs, sugar, and flour.

Butter Spreader. *See* Flatware.

Button Onions. Small onions picked before maturity; used in stews, eaten raw, or made into pickles.

Butuan. An inferior Philippine banana with seeds.

Butyraceous. Resembling butter.

Butyric. Similar to butter in chemical composition.

Butyric Acid. Acid, induced by low temperatures and exposure to air, which forms in butter, causing it to turn rancid.

Butyrometer. A device used in dairies to measure the butterfat in milk.

Buvette (French). A place to obtain refreshments; a bar; a coffeehouse.

Buzz (Colloquial). To drink the contents of a bottle down to the last drop.

B.W. Bonded warehouse or winery; a liquor term.

Byrrh. Trade name of a slightly bitter French apéritif wine flavored with herbs and fortified with brandy.

Byscute. The finest sort of bran.

C

Caballa (Spanish). Mackerel.

Cabaret. A restaurant featuring entertainment along with food and drink.

Cabassoles (French). The feet and tripe (sometimes also the head) of sheep boiled with vegetables and meat bones; a preparation of the Rouergue region of France.

Cabbage. The cabbage available today is the result of centuries of patient experiments to develop a tender, flavorful, and nutritious vegetable from the wild, nonheading original native to Asia Minor. Modern cabbage comes in many varieties. The heads may be round, pointed, or flat, and green, red, purple, or white. The leaves may be smooth or curly and crinkled. Types of fresh cabbage found in the market include Domestic, Danish, Savoy, Red, and Chinese. The Chinese type, although sold as cabbage, is really a member of the mustard family.

When selecting cabbage, look for solid, firm heads that are heavy for their size. The leaves should have a good color and be free from insect injury or bruises. A small head usually weighs under 2 pounds, a medium head 2–5 pounds and a large head 5 pounds. Cabbage is usually sold by the pound. Four cups of shredded cabbage or two cups of the cooked vegetable can be derived from one pound.

Cabbage provides an inexpensive supplement of ascorbic acid in the diet; 1½ cups or ⅜ pound of raw cabbage provides the average daily allowance of ascorbic acid for a normally active man.

Since cabbage loses moisture rapidly, the leaves tend to wilt or become flabby at room temperature. Remove withered leaves, wash the cabbage, drain, and place in a plastic bag or covered container and store in the refrigerator.

Sauerkraut is shredded or chopped cabbage which has been salted and allowed to ferment naturally. *See* Sauerkraut.

Versatile cabbage may be used either raw or cooked. Raw cabbage is commonly cut or shredded when served in salads. To retain ascorbic acid in shredding cabbage, use a sharp knife rather than a slaw cutter in order to prevent vitamin loss from bruising. The greatest vitamin loss occurs during the first 10–15 minutes after the cabbage is cut; however, cabbage stored in the refrigerator rather than at room temperature loses little additional ascorbic acid.

The strong odors given off by cabbage as it cooks are released during the first 5 minutes of cooking, hence the pan should be uncovered during that period so that the strong aroma may escape from the vegetable. A piece of bread placed in the cooking water helps to minimize the odor.

Cabbage, Dried. When cabbage is dried it develops a strong flavor, quite different from its original taste. Salted dried cabbage is commonly used in oriental cookery.

Cabbage, Preserved. Chinese cabbage may be preserved with salt, unfermented or fermented, sometimes with spices, onions, etc.

Cabbage Lettuce. A type of headed lettuce shaped like a cabbage.

Cabbage Palm. A variety of palm with edible buds cultivated in Florida and grown in many other tropical climates; the buds are used raw in salads and as an hors d'oeuvre or as a cooked vegetable.

Cabecou. A French goat's-milk cheese matured in vine leaves and sometimes soaked in Cognac or vinegar.

Cabernet. A variety of grape used extensively in the production of the wines of Bordeaux, France. The vine also is cultivated in other countries, including Spain and Italy. In California excellent red wines made from that variety are *Cabernet* or *Cabernet Sauvignon.*

Cabidela (Portuguese). Giblets.

Cabillaud; Cabilliau (French). (1) The cod. (2) A dish of mashed cod.

   Cabillaud à l'Anglaise. Boiled cod.

   Cabillaud Navarin. Cod boiled in white wine with mushrooms, mussels, and parsley.

Cabilliau. *See* Cabillaud.

Cabinet Pudding. A custard pudding made of bread or cake crumbs, dried fruit, eggs, and milk; usually served with a sauce.

Cabinet Wines. The term used by some wine-growers or bottlers (especially in Germany and the United States) to denote special quality. The claim may or may not be valid.

Cabis; Chevène (French). The blackfin, a fish.

Cabob (British). A leg of lamb or mutton stuffed with herbs and white herring.

Cabrales (Spanish). A blue cheese.

Cabrières. A full-bodied, fruity French *rosé* wine of fair quality.

Cabrilla. A fish of the perch family similar to the grouper. *See* Grouper.

Cabrito (Portuguese). Kid.

Cabracho (Spanish). A red fish, spotted or otherwise marked, having a fairly good taste.

Caça (Portuguese). Wild game.

Cacahuète (French). Peanut.

Cacao. Long before Columbus discovered America, the natives of Mexico, South America, and the West Indies were using the dried, partly fermented beans of the cacao tree to make a drink that was the forerunner of hot chocolate and cocoa. The cacao tree which bears the beans is native to South and Central America and is extensively cultivated there. *See* Cocoa.

Cacao Mass. A liquid obtained from roasted ground cacao beans.

Cachaça. A very strong, crude Brazilian rum.

Cachar. Small-leaved Indian black tea.

Cachat d'Entrechaux. (1) A medium-hard strong sheep's-milk cheese made with various liquors. It is produced in southern France from May until late autumn. (2) A molded mixture of various cheeses made with vinegar, brandy, and spices in the French Alps; served with red wines.

Cachicato. The blue-striped grunt, a tropical fish.

Cachiment (French). The West Indian tree that produces the custard apple, or *pomme cannelle.* The pulp of the fruit is yellow and of the consistency of custard.

Cachuete (French). Peanut.

Cachuse (French). Fresh pork cooked slowly with onions; a dish made in northeastern France.

Caciocavallo. A spindle-shaped Italian cheese with a pointed bottom and a neck and head at the top; a smooth, firm white cheese made from cow's milk, sometimes from buffalo's milk; also called the "horse" cheese (from the design on the label) and imitated all over the world.

   Caciocavallo Siciliano. Sicilian Caciocavallo; resembles provolone and may be eaten fresh or, when aged, grated.

Cacio Fiore; Caciotta. A very soft, fresh, yellowish, delicate, buttery Italian cheese made from ewe's or goat's milk colored with saffron.

Caciucco (Italian). (1) A spicy seafood soup. (2) Stew made with wine.

Cackerel. A small Mediterranean fish.

Cactus Pear; Prickly Pear. The prickly-skinned fruit of a cactus plant that grows wild in the American Southwest and in southern Italy; often available in late summer and early fall. To prevent pricking the fingers, make an incision lengthwise in the skin and pull it away from the pulp. Do not refrigerate cactus pears.

Caddy. A container with a tight-fitting cover; moisture- and vapor-proof, it is used to store tea. Tin caddies have largely replaced the elaborate boxes of fine wood and delicate china once in vogue. Many experts believe that the caddy should never be washed, for the tea leaves season the box and give a richer aroma and flavor to the fresh tea stored in it.

Cade (Obsolete). A herring barrel.

Cadelinhas (Portuguese). Clams.

Cadger (British). A hard biscuit formerly made in Cumberland.

Cadgery; Kedgeree. A rice-and-fish dish.

Caerphilly Cheese. A semisoft Welsh cow's-milk cheese that ripens in about 3 weeks; also available "green," but it does not keep well.

Caew (Obsolete British). To knead.

Caesar Salad. A California salad of romaine

lettuce, garlic croutons, anchovies, oil, and a raw egg; served as an appetizer.

Café (1) A restaurant or coffeehouse. (2) (French) Coffee.

    Café au Lait. Coffee and hot milk served at breakfast in France. Equal amounts of dark-roasted coffee and hot milk are simultaneously poured into a cup.

Café Brulot. Strong, dark coffee made with liquor and spices, customarily served in a tall, narrow cup; a specialty of New Orleans, Louisiana.

Café Complet. Continental breakfast; that is, coffee with hot milk, rolls (usually *croissants* or *brioches*), jam, and butter.

Café Double. Double-strength black coffee.

Café Frappé. Iced coffee.

Café Noir. Black coffee.

Café Turc. Turkish coffee.

Café Vierge. Coffee made with whole roasted coffee beans.

Café com Leite (Portuguese). Coffee with hot milk.

Cafeteria. A restaurant in which the customer selects his food from an open display.

Cafézinho (Brazilian). A very small cup of extra-strong coffee imbibed steadily throughout the day.

Caffa. The region of ancient Abyssinia from which the word "coffee" is derived.

Caffè (Italian) Coffee.

    Caffè con Panna. Coffee with cream.

    Caffè Freddo. Chilled coffee.

    Caffè in Ghiaccio. Iced coffee.

    Caffè Latte. Coffee with milk.

Caffeic. Pertaining to coffee.

Caffeine. A stimulant alkaloid present in coffee, tea, and cola drinks.

Caffeol. The volatile oil that gives a characteristic flavor and aroma to coffee.

Caffre. Edible pith of a South African tree; used in making Kaffir bread.

Caffre Corn. Indian millet.

Cagmag. (1) An old tough goose. (2) Meat of poor quality.

Cagouille (French). Snails.

Caguama. The sea turtle.

Caillados de Vouillos. A yellowish distinctive cheese made in Combrailles, France.

Caillé (French). Milk curds which have not quite begun to ferment in cheesemaking; cottage cheese, is an example. *Caillé* and *caillebottes* are often used interchangeably, but *caillé* really means the milk curds, whereas *caillebottes* refers to the cheese made with artichoke seeds.

Caillebottes (French). A very fresh, quite soft cheese prepared with artichoke seeds produced chiefly in Poitou and Anjou. *See also* Jonchée.

Caillé de Habas. A fresh sheep's-milk cheese with the texture of newly clotted milk; made in Gascony, France.

Cailletot (French). Young turbot.

Caillot-Rosat. A French pear with an aroma of roses.

Caimito (Spanish). The star apple, a fruit.

Caipirinha (Brazilian). A drink made with limes, sugar, and the crude rum called *cachaca*.

Caisse (French). An oblong serving dish.

Cajassou; Cujassou (French). A strong, pungent goat's-milk cheese made in the Périgord region of France.

Cajeta de Membrillo (Mexican). Quince paste.

Cajú (Portuguese). Cashew nut.

Cajuada (West African). A fermented beverage made from cashew nuts.

Cajuil. The cashew nut.

Cake. The art of baking a perfect cake is perhaps not as important as formerly. The packaged cake mixes on the grocer's shelves take practically all the guesswork out of cake baking. By following the instructions the housewife can use them with a minimum of effort and maximum chances of success. But few convenience products can match the exquisite flavor and delicate texture of a cake prepared from scratch.

    To bake a perfect cake may not require wizardry but it does demand certain standards. The ingredients should be of the best quality. The recipe should be a well-tested one and should be followed accurately. Cake baking is not an area in which to try improvisations. Skill is needed in mixing the ingredients to just the right degree at just the right time. Here, too, the directions in the recipe should be closely followed. Finally, the cake must be baked at the right temperature in a reliable oven. If the temperature gage in the oven is lacking or not accurate, an oven thermometer should be used.

The Flour: Whenever possible, cake flour should be used, for it is milled to the fine, satiny texture essential for a delicate cake. If all-purpose flour is substituted, reduce the quantity; that is, for every cup of cake flour specified in a recipe use only ⅞ cup of all-purpose flour.

The Sugar: Fine-grained sugar is best for cakes. Too coarse a sugar makes a coarse-textured cake. If sugar is lumpy, sift before measuring.

The Fat: Butter, margarine, or hydrogenated fats are best to use in light cakes with a delicate flavor. When the recipe calls for melted fat, vegetable oils may be used satisfactorily.

The Eggs: Use good-quality fresh eggs of medium size.

Cake Pans: For successful results use the size and shape pan specified in the recipe. If the cake contains fat, the pan should be greased by brushing the bottom and sides with liquid fat. If a piece of heavy waxed paper cut to fit the bottom of the pan is inserted, or the greased pan is lightly dusted with flour, the baked cake can be more easily removed. To bake a cake containing no fat the pan should not be greased.

The Baking: The oven should be preheated to the temperature specified in the recipe. The pan or pans should be placed as near the center of the oven as possible. If two or more pans are used, they should not be placed directly over one another nor so close to one another on the shelf that they interfere with the circulation of air. If it is necessary to look at the cake while it is baking, the oven door should be opened gently and closed promptly. Do not open door until 10 minutes before specified baking time.

To Remove Cake from Pan: Let the cake stand for 5 minutes or so in the pan on a cake rack so that steam may form. Run a knife between the edge of the cake and the pan. Invert the pan on a wire rack, lift off the pan, and peel off the waxed paper. If possible, place a second wire rack over the cake and invert so that the cake will be right side up.

In general, all cakes fall into two classes:

(1) cakes with fat, such as butter and pound cakes; and (2) cakes without fat, such as sponge- and angel cakes. Cakes with fat include among the ingredients milk or another liquid and, as a rule, either baking powder or baking soda with an acid. Cakes without fat contain no liquid other than that supplied by eggs, and they rely for leavening mainly on the air incorporated by means of the beaten egg.

But in spite of the best intentions, cake failures do occur. Here are some of the common problems with an explanation of their causes.

Coarse grain or holes in angel or spongecakes: Usually this is caused by underbeating the egg whites or not thoroughly folding them into the batter. The large holes come from folding air into the batter as it is poured into the pan. After the pan has been filled, cutting through the batter with a spatula will break the air bubbles and eliminate the holes. Or the pan can be lifted and hit firmly against a solid surface.

Close-textured or heavy grain: Heaviness usually is the result of overstirring or beating the batter. It is more apt to occur when an electric beater is used. Unless the cake is a very rich one, the batter should be stirred after each addition of dry and liquid ingredients only until well blended and smooth. Using a moderately slow speed in a mixer prevents overbeating. Heaviness also may be caused by too much sugar, shortening, or liquid, or too little leavening.

Humps and cracks in the top of the cake: Too much flour is usually the cause of this problem in a cake. Sift the flour once before measuring, spoon it into a measuring cup, and level it off with a straight-edged knife or spatula. Too hot an oven in the first part of the baking period also may cause humps and cracks, especially in loaf cakes. A crust must not form until the leavening has had time to raise the batter, otherwise it will rise more in the center, where the crust is tender.

Cakebread (British). A roll or small loaf of fine bread.

Cake Cooler. A rectangular or round wire rack or stand, on which a cake is placed to cool after it has been removed from the pan. Racks usually have small legs so that they hold the cake above the table or counter surface and thus allow air to circulate beneath the cake. *See* Cake Rack.

Cake-Creel (Scotch). A rack at the top of a kitchen on which to dry oatcakes.

Cake Decorator. Home cooks can duplicate many of the elaborate frosting designs of professional bakers with the aid of the cake-decorating sets available where kitchenware is sold. The sets consist of a pastry tube or gun, or a cloth or rubber bag for holding the icing or cream. They contain 6–8 tubes which can be used interchangeably with the holders. The pastry is pushed through the holder and through the variously shaped apertures in the tubes which form lines or dots, leaves, flowers, and plain or fancy borders. A little practice is required to gain skill in this art. Icings are now being marketed in cans with decorating tubes attached.

Cake Flour. A fine flour milled from soft wheat. When cake flour is specified in recipes but is not available, ⅞ cup of all-purpose flour may be substituted for every cup of cake flour required.

Cake Liners. Paper liners placed in a pan to hold the batter while baking.

Cake-Night (British). The eve of All Saints' Day.

Cake Pan. A utensil designed for baking cakes. It may be round, square, or oblong with straight or slightly flared sides. Some pans have removable bottoms, as, for instance, the spring form pan; others have a tube in the center, as, for example, the angel-cake pan. Shiny pans are best for cakes.

Cake Rack. A flat wire arrangement, slightly raised, on which cakes may be placed for cooling. *See* Cake Cooler.

Cake Spice. A combination of cinnamon, ginger, cloves, and mace in equal proportions.

Cake-Spittle (Scotch). A thin board with which to turn over oatcakes while in the oven.

Calabacines (Spanish). Squash.

Calabash. A pumpkin or gourd.

Calabaza (Spanish). (1) Edible squash blossoms. (2) Pumpkin.

Calabrese. A variety of sprouting broccoli, sometimes called *asparagus-broccoli* because the side shoots grow quite long and are very good when cut and cooked like asparagus. The flower heads are green, not white like the cauliflower, or purplish green like purple sprouting broccoli.

Caladium. A plant whose root is sometimes used as a substitute for potatoes in oriental countries.

Calamanci; Calamansi. A Philippine sour fruit tasting like lemon or lime; used to prepare a refreshing drink.

Calamaretti (Italian). Baby cuttlefish.

Calamari; Calamary (Italian). Squid, cuttlefish, inkfish; a popular food in many Mediterranean

countries. Squid may be broiled, fried, stewed, or stuffed, and included in fish stews and soups. Not popular in the United States.

    Calamari in Casseruola. Squid in tomato sauce.

Calamint. A small herb whose leaves have an aroma and taste suggesting peppermint, but less suited than peppermint to commercial use.

Calamus; Wild Iris; Sweet Rush; Sweet Flag; Myrtle Sedge. A sweet, aromatic herb usually growing in wet regions; the leaves are used as a salad green and as flavoring for puddings and cooked fruits; the root may be boiled with sugar to make a sort of candy.

Calavo. A trade name for certain avocados grown in California.

Calawaii (South Pacific). Various species of mullet.

Calcagno (Sicilian). A ewe's-milk cheese suitable only for cooking.

Calcavella (Portuguese). A sweet white wine produced near Lisbon.

Calciferol. *See* Vitamin D.

Calcium. A dietary essential associated with phosphorus and vitamin D. It is needed for the formation of bones and teeth, and is an essential constituent of all living cells. Vitamin D aids its absorption, and the lack of the vitamin or calcium can lead to rickets.

The daily requirement is 0.8 gram per day, and the need is increased in growing children, in pregnancy, and particularly in lactation. Rich sources are milk and cheese, and moderate sources are eggs and vegetables. Calcium is now added to bread.

Calcutta Wheat. A hard, brittle Indian wheat.

Caldaro. *See* Italy, The Wines of.

Caldeirada a Pescadora (Portuguese). A thick, rather spicy fish stew.

Caldereta (Spanish). Stew.

    Caldereta Asturiana. A mixed-fish stew.

Caldero. An iron or aluminum pot used in Latin countries; it has a rounded bottom, straight sides, and two rather small handles.

Caldo. (1) (Italian) Hot; warm. (2) (Spanish, Portuguese) Soup.

    Caldo de Carne (Portuguese). Meat bouillon.

    Caldo de Gallina (Spanish). Chicken soup.

    Caldo Gallego (Spanish). A thick stew of meat and vegetables.

    Caldo Verde (Portuguese). Green soup made with potatoes and kale.

Caldron; Cauldron. A large kettle used for boiling in colonial days when cooking was done largely over an open fire.

Calefactor. A small stove.

Calf. (1) A young cow. (2) The back part of flesh on the shank of a leg on any animal.

California Chuck Roast. The bottom chuck of beef with the bone left in; usually prepared by slow braising.

Calf's Brains. *See* Brains.

Calf's-Foot Jelly. *See* Veal.

Calf's Head. *See* Veal.

Calibogus (American). Spruce beer and rum mixed together. *See also* Callebogus, a Nova Scotian and Newfoundland drink.

Cali Butt; Cali Ham. Cured and smoked pork from the shoulder (picnic) of the carcass is sometimes called *cali, calis,* or *calas butt* or *ham.* This cut contains a higher percentage of bone, skin, and connective tissue than regular ham and costs less.

Calid. Warm, sometimes hot.

California Pompano. The whiting.

California Wines. *See* United States, The Wines of.

Calimyrna. Fig.

Calipash; Calipee (British). These words, probably corruptions of the term "carapace," the hard, domed shell covering the backs of turtles, crabs, etc., are used to refer to these creatures. *Calipash* popularly is used to describe the sticky flesh of the turtle under the upper shell. *Calipee* identifies the flesh upon the under shell.

Calisson (French). An almond confection made in Aix-la-Chapelle.

Callalu Soup. A tropical soup made from *eddoe* leaves; that is, taro leaves.

Calle (Italian). A kind of mushroom.

Callebogus. A favorite Nova Scotian and Newfoundland drink made by adding alcohol to spruce beer. *See also* Calibogus, an American drink.

Calling Crab. A land crab with a long claw; occasionally used as food.

Calliste. A heavy, sweet, cloying wine produced in Greece today, as it was in ancient times.

Callos (Spanish). Tripe.

Callou. A mild-flavored Arabian "wine" made from the flowers of the coconut palm. It is unusual in that it matures and is ready for drinking within 24 hours after it is made. A few hours thereafter its vinous quality disappears and it becomes unpleasantly sour.

Calmar. Squid, cuttlefish, inkfish.

Caloric Punsch (Norwegian, Swedish). A rather sweet liqueur prepared with sugar syrup and rum.

Calorie. The foods our bodies burn are measured in units of heat called calories. A calorie is the quantity of heat necessary to raise about one quart of water 8° F. We utilize the calories contained in food as muscular energy, to repair and replace body tissues, and to maintain body temperature and blood circulation.

The problem of gaining or losing weight can be expressed quite simply in terms of calories. If more calories are consumed than the body needs for its work, the excess is deposited as fat and body weight increases. But if the body uses more calories than it takes in, part of the fat reserve is burned and the weight declines.

CALORIE CHARTS

Beverages, Alcoholic

Beer, Bock	8 ounces	180
Beer, Lager	8 ounces	110
Bourbon whisky	1 ounce	100
Brandy	1 ounce	80
Canadian whisky	1 ounce	100
Champagne, dry	4 ounces	110
Champagne, sweet	4 ounces	135
Cognac	1 ounce	80
Gin	1½ ounces	125
Irish whisky	1 ounce	100
Liqueurs	1 ounce	80
Manhattan	2½ ounces	240
Martini, dry	2½ ounces	180
Martini, sweet	2½ ounces	200
Port wine	3½ ounces	100
Rum	1½ ounces	150
Rum and cola	Tall glass	225
Rye whisky	1 ounce	100
Scotch whisky	1 ounce	100
Sherry, dry	3½ ounces	110
Sloe gin	1½ ounces	150
Vermouth, dry	1 ounce	40
Vermouth, sweet	1 ounce	60
Vodka	1½ ounces	125
Whisky sour	3½ ounces	225
Wine, dry	3½ ounces	70
Wine, sweet	3½ ounces	125

Beverages, Non-alcoholic

Apple juice	1 cup	120
Buttermilk	1 quart	340
Buttermilk	1 cup	85
Carbonated drinks	8 ounces	100
Carbonated water (unflavored)		0
Chocolate milk	8 ounces	225
Chocolate syrup	1 tablespoon	40
Club soda		0
Cider	1 cup	125
Cocoa, whole-milk	1 cup	235
Cocoa, dry powder	1 tablespoon	20
Coffee, black		0

Coffee, with milk	1 cup	25
Coffee, cream, sugar	1 cup	100
Cola drinks	1 cup	100
Ginger ale	8 ounces	100
Grape juice	8 ounces	130
Grapefruit juice (canned)	8 ounces	130
Grapefruit juice (fresh)	8 ounces	90
Grapefruit juice (frozen)	1 can (6 oz.)	95
Grapefruit-orange (canned)	8 ounces	130
Ice-cream soda	1 average	325
Lemonade	8 ounces	115
Malted milk	12 ounces	325
Malted milk (with ice cream)	12 ounces	625
Milk, chocolate	8 ounces	225
Milk, whole	1 cup	165
Milk, skim	1 cup	85
Orange juice, fresh	1 cup	108
Orangeade	12 ounces	135
Ovaltine, half milk	1 cup	110
Pineapple juice (canned)	1 cup	125
Postum, black		0
Postum, half milk	1 cup	85
Postum, cream, sugar	1 cup	100
Root beer	8 ounces	105
Seltzer		0
Soda, flavored, carbonated	8 ounces	100
Tea, plain		0
Tea, sugar, milk	1 cup	50
Tomato juice	1 cup	50

Breads

Bagel	1	125
Bread crumbs	½ cup	165
Boston brown bread	¾″ slice	110
Cinnamon bun	1 medium	165
Cinnamon toast	1 slice	125
Cornbread muffin	1 medium	130
Cracked-wheat bread	½″ slice	60
Croutons	½″ cube	5
Date-and-nut bread	½″ slice	155

Frankfurter roll	1	155
French bread	½" slice	50
Gingerbread	2" square	205
Gluten bread	½" slice	45
Graham bread	½" slice	90
Hamburger roll	1	150
Italian bread	½" slice	40
Melba toast	1 slice	20
Muffins	1 average	120
Muffin, blueberry	1 average	135
Muffin, bran	1 large	125
Muffin, English	1	125
Muffin, raisin	1	115
Parkerhouse roll	1 large	125
Protein bread	¼" slice	30
Pumpernickel	½" slice	105
Raisin bread	½" slice	65
Rolls, plain	1 medium	120
Rye bread	½" slice	55
Rye bread, toast	½" slice	55
Rye Krisp	1 piece	15
Soy bread	½" slice	80
Swedish rye wafers	1 wafer	20
White bread	½" slice	65
White bread, toast	½" slice	65
Whole-wheat bread	½" slice	55
Zweiback	1 piece	25

Cakes and Pies
(as purchased commercially)

Almond coffee cake	3"×2"×1"	200
Angel food	3"×2"×2"	300
Apple crumb	3"×2"×1"	200
Apple turnover	1 average	290
Butter cake	3"×2"×1"	200
Cheesecake, cream	2½" wedge	320
Chocolate cake, iced	3"×2"×1"	220
Chocolate cake, plain	3"×2"×1"	150
Coconut cake, iced	3"×2"×1"	300
Coffee cake	3"×3"×1"	150
Cup cake	1 average	120
Cup cake, iced	1 average	170
Fruit cake	3"×3"×1"	225
Ginger cake	2"×2"×1"	175
Gold cake	3"×3"×1"	175
Jelly roll	1" slice	250

Pie, most varieties	1 average cut (4")	300
Pie, custard	1 average cut	265
Pie, mince	1 average cut	385
Pie, pumpkin	1 average cut	265
Pound cake	2"×2"×1"	200
Spice cake	2"×2"×1"	220
Strawberry shortcake	3" wedge	350
White cake, plain	2"×2"×1"	240
White cake, iced	2"×2"×1"	310

Canned Foods
(as purchased commercially)

Fish

Mackerel	½ cup	210
Salmon	½ cup	170
Sardines in oil	5 medium, drained	165
Sardines, tomato sauce	1½ large	225
Shrimp, dry pack	10–12 medium	80
Shrimp, wet pack	10–12 medium	45
Tuna	½ cup, drained	255

Fruits

Apricots	4 medium halves, 2 T. syrup	115
Blackberries	½ cup	95
Blueberries	½ cup	50
Cherries, red	½ cup	60
Grapefruit sections	½ cup	85
Peaches, cling	2 medium halves, 2 T. syrup	95
Peaches, freestone	2 medium halves, 2 T. syrup	100
Pears	2 medium halves, 2 T. syrup	90
Pineapple, sliced	2 small slices or 1 large slice, 2 T. syrup	125
Plums, purple	3 plums, 2 T. syrup	115

Meats and Poultry; Luncheon Dishes

Beef goulash	8 ounces	190
Beef stew	8 ounces	180

Chicken-noodle dinner	8 ounces	170
Chicken stew, dumplings	8 ounces	190
Chili con carne, beans	8 ounces	300
Chop suey with meat	8 ounces	150
Corned-beef hash	8 ounces	320
Lamb stew	8 ounces	180
Macaroni, cheese sauce	8 ounces	210
Macaroni creole	8 ounces	150
Pork and beans	8 ounces	310
Spaghetti, tomato sauce	8 ounces	210
Spanish rice	8 ounces	130

Soups

(Entire contents of can, 1¼ cups, before milk or water is added; compute additional calories for milk, if added.)

Asparagus, cream of	175	Consommé	100
		Green pea	330
Bean with bacon	435	Mock turtle	225
Beef	275	Mushroom, cream of	340
Beef noodle	155		
Black bean	250	Oxtail	230
Bouillon (beef broth)	77	Pepper pot	270
		Scotch Broth	290
Celery, cream of	220	Tomato	205
Chicken, cream of	220	Vegetable	205
Chicken gumbo	155	Vegetable-beef	220
Chicken noodle	160	Vegetarian vegetable	200
Chicken with rice	110		
Clam chowder	190		

Vegetables
(Average)

Asparagus, cuts and tips	20	Cauliflower	20
		Collard greens	30
Asparagus	25	Corn, cut	80
Beans, baby lima	125	Corn on the cob	100
Beans, Fordhook	100	Kale, chopped	30
Beans, French style	30	Mixed vegetables	65
Beans, green cut	30	Mustard greens	20
Beans, wax cut	30	Okra	40
Broccoli, chopped	30	Peas and carrots	55
Broccoli, spears	30	Peas, black-eyed	130
Brussels sprouts	35	Peas, green sweet	75

Potatoes, French-fried	170	Spinach	25
		Squash, crookneck	20
Potatoes, hashed brown	75	Squash, winter	40
		Succotash	95
Potatoes, mashed	75	Turnip greens	25

Cereals and Flours

Barley, raw	1 tablespoon	45
Bran, 100%	½ cup	75
Bran, flakes	½ cup	55
Bran, raisin	½ cup	80
Buckwheat flour	½ cup	175
Cereals, most cooked	1 cup	150
Cheerios	1 cup	100
Cornflakes	1 cup	90
Corn flour	1 cup	405
Cornmeal, cooked	1 cup	125
Cornmeal, dry	1 cup	400
Cream of Wheat	1 cup	120
Farina	1 cup	105
Flour, pastry	1 cup	365
Flour, rye	1 cup	285
Flour, wheat	1 cup	400
Grapenuts	½ cup	160
Griddle cakes, wheat	1 (5")	75
Grits, cooked	1 cup	120
Kix	1 cup	130
Krispies	1 cup	135
Noodles, dry	1 cup	280
Noodles, egg, cooked	1 cup	105
Oat cereal	1 cup	100
Oatmeal, cooked	1 cup	150
Oatmeal, dry	1 cup	310
Pancake mix, dry	1 cup	470
Pancakes, buckwheat	1 (5")	65
Pancakes, wheat	1 (5")	75
Pep	1 cup	125
Pie crust, plain	Double crust (9" pie)	1315
Pie crust, plain	Lower crust (9" pie)	655
Puffed Rice	1 cup	55
Puffed Wheat	1 cup	40
Ralston	1 cup	190
Rice flakes	1 cup	120
Rice, brown raw	1 cup	750

Rice, converted raw	1 cup	680
Rice, white raw	1 cup	690
Rice, converted cooked	1 cup	205
Rice, white cooked	1 cup	200
Rice, precooked dry	1 cup	420
Shredded Wheat	1 large	100
Shredded Wheat	1 medium	80
Soybean flour, low fat	1 cup	230
Soybean flour, medium fat	1 cup	235
Soybean flour, full fat	1 cup	250
Soybean grits	1 cup	365
Spaghetti, dry	1 cup	355
Spaghetti, cooked	1 cup	220
Starches (corn, arrowroot, etc.)	1 cup	465
Starches	1 tablespoon	30
Tapioca, dry	1 cup	545
Tortillas	1 (5")	50
Waffle flour	8 ounces	650
Waffles	1 average	215
Wheat flakes	1 cup	125
Wheat flour	1 cup	400
Wheat germ	1 cup	245
Wheat, rolled	1 cup	175
Whole meal	1 cup	175
Wheat-barley cereal	1 cup	410
Yeast, dry	1 tablespoon	20

Cookies, Sweet Cakes
(as purchased commercially)

	each piece
Animal crackers	9
Chocolate Chip cookies	56
Chocolate grahams	58
Chocolate snaps	17
Devil's-food squares	59
Fig Newtons	53
Frutana biscuits	34
Gaiety Creme Sandwiches	110
Lemon snaps	16
Lorna Doone shortbread	38
Macaroon cookies	21
Mallomars	61
Mello squares	57
Mickey Mouse cookies	7

Nabisco sugar wafers	5
National arrowroot biscuits	22
Oatmeal cookies	18
Oreo Creme Sandwiches	57
Raisin fruit biscuits	34
Social Tea biscuits	20
Trio Creme Sandwiches	55
Vanilla wafers	15
Zuzu ginger snaps	15

Dairy Products

Acidophilus milk	1 cup	95
American cheese	1 ounce	105
Bleu cheese	1 ounce	95
Brie cheese	1 ounce	100
Butter	1 cup	1600
Butter	1 tablespoon	100
Butter	1 pat	50
Buttermilk, skim milk	1 cup	85
Camembert	1 ounce	85
Cheddar, cheese foods	1 ounce	95
Cheddar, processed	1 ounce	105
Cheeses, processed	1 ounce	105
Condensed milk	1 tablespoon, sweetened	60
Cottage cheese	½ cup	105
Cottage cheese	1 ounce	25
Cream cheese	1 ounce	105
Cream cheese	1 tablespoon	55
Cream, light	½ pint	490
Cream, light	1 tablespoon	30
Cream, heavy	½ pint	780
Cream, heavy	1 tablespoon	50
Cream, heavy sour	1 tablespoon	50
Edam cheese	1 ounce	120
Evaporated milk	1 tablespoon, unsweetened	25
Gorgonzola cheese	1 ounce	100
Goat's milk	1 cup	165
Grated cheese	1 tablespoon	35
Gruyère cheese	1 ounce	100
Limburger cheese	1 ounce	100
Malted milk	Tall glass	325
Malted milk (ice cream)	Tall glass	625
Milk, condensed	1 cup	980
Milk, dried skim	1 tablespoon	28

Milk, dried whole	1 tablespoon	39		Mackerel	2″×2″×2″	100
Milk, evaporated	1 cup	345		Mackerel, salt	4 ounces	160
Milk, malted	1 ounce powder	115		Oysters	6 average	90
Milk, skim	1 cup	85		Oysters, fried	6 average	400
Milk, whole	1 cup	165		Oyster stew	1 cup	250
Ovaltine, half milk	1 cup	110		Perch	4 ounces	90
Parmesan cheese	1 ounce	110		Pike	4 ounces	80
Parmesan, grated	1 tablespoon	30		Porgy	4 ounces	100
Pot cheese	1 tablespoon	30		Salmon, broiled	3″×3″×1″	200
Provolone cheese	1 ounce	105		Salmon, canned	1 cup	375
Roquefort cheese	1 ounce	90		Salmon, creamed	½ cup	300
Sour cream	1 tablespoon	50		Salmon, smoked	4 ounces	325
Stilton cheese	1 ounce	110		Sardines, canned	4 ounces	225
Swiss cheese	1 thin slice	100		Scallops	4 ounces	90
Velveeta cheese	1 ounce	100		Shad	3″×3″×1″	150
Welsh rarebit	1 cup	390		Shad Roe	3 ounces	125
Yeast, dry	1 tablespoon	20		Shrimp	9 average	100
Yoghurt, skim milk	1 cup	115		Shrimp, canned	4 ounces	100
Yoghurt, whole milk	1 cup	180		Smelts	3 average	100
				Sole, fillet of	4 ounces	90
				Sturgeon, smoked	4 ounces	175

Fish

				Swordfish	3″×3″×½″	225
Anchovies	1 ounce	10		Trout, brook	8 ounces	125
Anchovy paste	1 tablespoon	30		Trout, lake	8 ounces	160
Bass	2″×2″×1″	100		Tuna, canned with oil	4 ounces	300
Bluefish	2″×2″×1″	100		Tuna, drained	4 ounces	200
Butterfish	4 ounces	125		Tuna, fresh	4 ounces	180
Brook Trout, broiled	8 ounces	125		Whitefish	4 ounces	150
Clam juice	6 ounces	50				
Clams	4 ounces meat	90				
Clams, round	6	100				
Clams, soft shell	12	100				

Frozen Foods
(as purchased commercially)

Fruits

Cod	2″×2″×1″	90			
Crab	4 ounces meat	100			
Crab Meat, canned	4 ounces	110		Apples, sliced	90
Eel	4 ounces	125		Apricots	100
Finnan Haddie	4 ounces	125		Blueberries, sweetened	105
Flounder	2″×2″×1″	75		Blueberries, unsweetened	55
Frogs' Legs	4 ounces	75		Boysenberries, sweetened	95
Haddock	2″×2″×1″	100		Boysenberries, unsweetened	50
Halibut	2″×2″×1″	120		Cherries, red, sweetened	110
Herring, Atlantic	4 ounces	210		Cherries, red, unsweetened	55
Herring, pickled	4 ounces	100		Peaches, sliced	90
Herring, smoked	4 ounces	225		Pineapple, chunks	85
Herring, sour-cream	4 ounces	250		Raspberries, red	100
Lake Trout, sautéed	4 ounces	325		Rhubarb	75
Lobster, 1 pound	4 ounces meat	100		Strawberries, sliced	110
Lobster, canned	½ cup meat	75		Strawberries, whole	90

Fruit Juices

(About 3½ ounces prepared from concentrated, frozen can, according to instructions on label)

Grape juice, sweetened		55
Grapefruit juice		45
Lemonade, sweetened		45
Orange juice		45
Orange-grapefruit juice		45
Pineapple juice		55

Soups

Oyster stew	6 ounces	190
Pea with ham	6 ounces	190
Shrimp, cream of	6 ounces	260

Fruits, Fresh

Apples	1 small	55
Apples	1 medium	75
Apples	1 large	115
Apple butter	1 tablespoon	30
Applesauce	1 cup unsweetened	100
Applesauce	1 cup sweetened	180
Apricots, cooked	½ cup (with sugar)	240
Apricots, dried	½ cup	200
Apricots, fresh	1 medium	20
Avocado	½ average	280
Banana	1 small	80
Banana	1 large	120
Blackberries, raw	1 cup	80
Blueberries, raw	1 cup	85
Cantaloupe	½, 5" melon	40
Cherries, raw	1 cup unpitted	65
Cherries, raw	1 cup pitted	95
Coconut, dried	4 ounce package	630
Coconut, fresh	1 cup shredded	350
Coconut milk	1 cup	60
Crab apple	1 average	20
Cranberries, raw	1 cup	55
Cranberry sauce	1 cup	550
Currants, red, raw	1 cup	60
Dates	½ cup pitted	250
Figs, dried	1 average	50

Figs, fresh	1 average	30
Fruit cocktail, fresh	½ cup	65
Gooseberries, raw	1 cup	60
Grapefruit	½ large, 5"	105
Grapefruit	½ medium, 4"	75
Grapefruit	½ small, 3½"	45
Grapefruit	1 cup sections	80
Grapes, Concord	½ pound	125
Grapes, Delaware	½ pound	125
Grapes, Malaga	½ pound	150
Grapes, Muscat	½ pound	150
Grapes, Niagara	½ pound	125
Grapes, Thompson, seedless	½ pound	150
Guavas	1 average	50
Honeydew melon	1 medium wedge	45
Huckleberries	1 cup	80
Lemon juice	1 tablespoon	4
Lemons	1 medium	20
Limes	1 medium	20
Loganberries	1 cup	90
Mangos	1 average	85
Muskmelons	½, 5" melon	40
Nectarines	1 medium	40
Orange juice	1 cup	108
Oranges	1 large	105
Oranges	1 medium	75
Oranges	1 small	50
Oranges, sections	1 cup	85
Papaya	1 average serving	65
Peaches	1 medium	45
Peaches	1 large	65
Pears	1 average	95
Pears	1 small	70
Persimmon	1 average	90
Pineapple, raw	1 slice, ½" thick	35
Pineapple, raw	1 cup cubes	75
Plums	1 average	30
Pomegranate	1 average	75
Prunes	1 large	25
Raisins	1 cup	430
Raspberries, black	1 cup	100
Raspberries, red	1 cup	70
Rhubarb, raw	1 cup diced	20
Rhubarb, cooked	1 cup (with sugar)	385
Strawberries	1 cup	55
Tangerines	1 medium	35
Tangerine juice	1 cup	95

Watermelon	1 wedge, 4″×8″	120
Watermelon, ¾″ cut	½ slice	50

Meats and Poultry

Bacon	2 medium slices	90
Bacon, Canadian	1 slice	60
Beef, boiled	4 ounces	200
Beef, chuck	3 ounces	265
Beef, corned (lean)	4 ounces	200
Beef, ground	3 ounces	310
Beef liver, fried	4 ounces	240
Beef, pot-roast	4 ounces	275
Beef, rib-roast	1 large slice	300
Beef, round	3 ounces	200
Beef, rump	3 ounces	320
Beef, sirloin	3 ounces	260
Beef, stewing	Average serving	325
Beef tongue	4 thin slices	160
Beef, canned corn-beef hash	3 ounces	120
Bologna	1 average slice	80
Brains	3 ounces	105
Calf's liver	4 ounces	160
Chicken, broilers	½ average	330
Chicken, canned	4 ounces	200
Chicken, fried	4 ounces boneless	275
Chicken, hens	4 ounces boneless	350
Chicken, roasters	4 ounces boneless	225
Chicken fat	1 tablespoon	100
Chicken livers	4 ounces	150
Duck, roasted	4 ounces boneless	350
Duck, roasted	3″×3″×1″	250
Frankfurters	1 small	125
Frankfurters	1 large	200
Goose, roasted	4 ounces boneless	325
Ham, boiled	4 ounces	375
Ham, fresh	4 ounces boneless	450
Ham, smoked	4 ounces	420
Hamburger	3 ounces	310
Heart, beef	3 ounces	110
Kidneys, beef	4 ounces	150
Lamb chop, loin	4 ounces	350
Lamb chop, rib	1 small	225
Lamb, roast leg	3 ounces boneless	230
Lamb, shoulder	3 ounces boneless	290
Lamb stew	1 cup	250
Liverwurst	1 average slice	90

Mutton	2 thin slices	200
Pastrami	4 ounces	350
Pig's feet	4 ounces meat	160
Pork chop, loin	4 ounces	440
Pork chop, rib	4 ounces	375
Pork loin	4 ounces	350
Pork sausage	1 average	225
Pork, spareribs	4 ounces	360
Rabbit	4 ounces	190
Sausage, bologna	1 thick slice	100
Sausage, liverwurst	1 thin slice	75
Sausage, salami	1 thin slice	75
Sausage, summer	1 thin slice	60
Sausage, Vienna	4 ounces	240
Squab	1 average	275
Sweetbreads, broiled	4 ounces	100
Sweetbreads, fried	4 ounces	325
Tongue, beef	4 thin slices	160
Tripe	4 ounces	150
Turkey	4 ounces	300
Veal cutlet, breaded	4 ounces boneless	240
Veal cutlet, broiled	4 ounces boneless	210
Veal, shoulder	4 ounces	270
Veal stew meat	4 ounces	330
Venison	4 ounces	225
Vienna sausage	4 ounces	240

Vegetables, Fresh

Artichokes	1	95
Asparagus	10 spears	25
Asparagus	1 cup spears	35
Bamboo shoots	4 ounces	35
Beans, baked	1 cup	240
Beans, green	1 cup	25
Beans, kidney	1 cup	300
Beans, lima	1 cup	150
Beans, pork, molasses	1 cup	325
Beans, pork, tomatoes	1 cup	295
Beans, white marrow	4 ounces dried	320
Beets	1 cup	70
Beets, pickled	4 ounces	25
Broccoli	1 cup	40
Brussels sprouts	1 cup	40
Cabbage, Chinese	4 ounces	25
Cabbage, cooked	1 cup	40
Cabbage, raw	1 cup	25
Carrots	1 medium	20

Carrots, cooked	1 cup	45		Pumpkin seeds	1 ounce	150
Cauliflower	1 cup	30		Radishes	10	25
Celeriac (celery root)	1 root	10		Rice, boiled	1 cup	200
Celery, cooked	1 cup	25		Rice, brown	½ cup raw	375
Celery, raw	1 large stalk	6		Rice, wild	½ cup raw	300
Chives	1 ounce	10		Rutabagas	1 cup	50
Corn	1 ear	90		Sauerkraut	1 cup	40
Corn, cooked	1 cup kernels	140		Scallions, young	6 small	25
Cucumber	1 average	20		Soybean sprouts	1 cup	45
Eggplant	3 large slices	50		Spinach, boiled	½ cup	50
Endive	4 ounces	20		Squash, Hubbard	1 cup	100
Garlic	1 clove	5		(winter)		
Kohlrabi	1 cup	40		Squash, summer	1 cup	30
Leeks	1 cup	40		Succotash	1 cup	175
Lentils	4 ounces	360		Sweet potatoes	1 average	190
Lettuce	1 large leaf	3		Tomatoes	1 medium	25
Lettuce	1 head	65		Tomatoes, stewed	1 cup	50
Mushrooms	1 cup	30		Turnips	1 cup	40
Mustard greens	1 cup	30		Watercress	4 ounces	20
Okra	1 cup	40		Yams, baked	1 average	200
Olives, green	1	7		Yams, candied	1 average	375
Olives, black	1	10		Zucchini	1 cup	45
Onions, cooked	1 cup	80				
Onions, green	10 large	100				
Onions, raw	1 average	35				
Parsley, chopped	1 tablespoon	1				
Parsnips	1 cup	90				
Peas, cooked	1 cup	110				
Peas, dried	4 ounces	375				
Peas, fresh	4 ounces (in shell)	115				
Peppers	1 average	20				
Pigeon peas, cooked	4 ounces	125				
Pimientos	1 average	10				
Potatoes	1 average	100				
Potatoes au gratin	4 ounces	275				
Potato chips	10 medium	100				
Potatoes, baked	1 Idaho	150				
Potatoes, boiled	1 average	100				
Potatoes, French-fried	8 pieces	160				
Potatoes, fried raw	½ cup	250				
Potatoes, hashed brown	½ cup	240				
Potatoes, mashed	½ cup (with milk)	80				
Potatoes, mashed	½ cup (milk, butter)	120				
Potatoes, sweet	1 average	190				
Pumpkin	1 cup	75				

Calorimeter. An instrument for measuring the amount of oxidizable energy present in a substance. The substance is burned in oxygen and the liberated heat is measured. The heat liberated by burning a food will coincide with the metabolizable energy only if all the material is digestible. It is also known as the *bomb calorimeter* because of its bomblike shape.

Calory. *See* Calorie.

Caltrop. *See* Water Chestnut.

Calumba. An evergreen plant, grown chiefly in southern India, the root of which is used in making bitters, apéritifs, etc.

Caluso. A sweet wine produced in Piedmont, Italy.

Calvados. Apple brandy made in the Department of Calvados in Normandy, France. It is somewhat like American applejack but is aged about 10 years. It has a strong burning taste and only a vague apple flavor, but the aroma is pleasant.
  Calvados du Pays d'Auge. A smooth, soft apple brandy with a remarkable aroma; made in the region of Auge, France.

Calvenzano. A cheese that is an imitation or close relative of Gorgonzola; made in Bergamo, Italy.

Calzone (Italian). Dough stuffed with meat, fish, cheese, or eggs and baked until it puffs up.

Camarão (Portuguese). Shrimp.

Camarguais. A white ewe's-milk cheese flavored with thyme and bay leaf; made in the Camargue region of France.

Camarine (French). A wild crakeberry or crowberry.

Camarón (Spanish). Shrimp.

Camas. The bulb of a plant similar to the lily; formerly eaten by North American Indians.

Cambacérès Jean-Jacques, Régis de. A French nobleman of the early 19th century famous for the food served in his home. Several dishes bear his name.

Cambrel. A hook-shaped piece of wood or metal used by butchers to hang meat.

Cambric Tea. A weak tea, usually diluted with an equal part of warm milk, often served to invalids and young children.

Cambridge Cheese; York Cheese. A soft white, somewhat tangy cow's-milk cheese made in England; eaten fresh.

Cambridge Sauce (British). A thick sauce consisting of mashed yolks of hard-cooked eggs, mashed anchovies, capers, cayenne pepper, oil, and vinegar; served with cold meats.

Cambur. Banana.

Camel. Young camel is edible, and is sometimes eaten by Arabic people.

Camel's Thorn. A pea or bean plant.

Camembert. A cheese, said to have been named by Napoleon, first made in 1791 by a Madame Harel in Camembert, a hamlet in the Department of Orne, France. It is now made also in Normandy. As it comes to market the cheese is a 10-ounce round about 4½ inches in diameter and 1–1½ inches thick, sometimes also a 12-ounce round cheese. The center, yellow and waxy when it is first made, should be quite soft when it is ripe for eating, and is best when made in the summer months. It is encased in a feltlike layer of moldy rind and usually is wrapped in paper or parchment. Pie-shaped wedges, individually wrapped pieces, are also available, but these are inferior in taste. Imitations of Camembert are now made in other countries, including the United States.

Camerain. A French actor in the eighteenth century who invented a soup that cost $30 per serving. Grimod de la Reynière dedicated his gastronomic work *Almanach des Gourmands* to him.

Camerani (French). A garnish consisting of small pastry shells stuffed with goose liver, truffles, macaroni, and a rich cream sauce; usually served with sweetbreads or game.

Camomile. A hardy European perennial, a member of the aster family, whose dried flower heads

are steeped in boiling water to make a tea.

Camomile Beer. A bitter homemade beer made with sugar, water, camomile, cream of tartar, and ginger.

Camomilla Alpina. A liqueur made with wild herbs, especially camomile, in Lombardy, Italy.

Camosun. A medium soft imitation of American Monterey cheese.

Camote (Spanish). Sweet potato.

Campari. An Italian apéritif wine flavored with bitter-orange peel, gentian, quinine, and other ingredients, usually considered as a bitters; often served with ice, a twist of lemon peel, and a dash of soda water. It is also used in making an Americano, containing vermouth, and a Negroni, prepared with gin and vermouth.

Camp Cookery. *See* Outdoor Cookery.

Campden Process. A method of preserving food with sodium bisulfite; also known as *cold preservation*.

Campeachy. The wood or bark of a Mexican tree, sometimes used to add coloring to wine or liqueurs.

Campine (Belgian, French). A variety of fat hen raised near Campine, Belgium.

Caña. A very light Paraguayan rum used with fruit juices in mixed drinks.

Canada. Discussions of Canadian food inevitably lead to disagreement, for Canada stretches from the Atlantic to the Pacific; there are sophisticated city dwellers and farmers who live off the land. In addition to the English influence, Quebec still retains its French style of cooking.

Throughout much of the country, almost any dish served in the United States may be encountered in Canada; this is particularly noticeable with respect to steaks and chops, vegetables and potatoes, and pies and cakes. From their British background, the Canadians show their link to the homeland by their fondness for large breakfasts, roast beef, cheese, and teatime specialties.

Canada, however, has some interesting food items: the salmon is of extraordinary delicacy. On the east coast, the Gaspé and New Brunswick salmon are highly regarded; on the west coast the Coho salmon is the best. In the north, game dishes are common items of the diet. Lobster, shrimp, and crab are all excellent. All meats are liked, but beef may well be the national choice. The Canadians, with a huge supply of milk, produce many fine cheeses; the cheddar and Oka are probably the outstanding types.

However, it is in Quebec, with its French-Canadian cuisine, that the gourmet finds his interest excited. The local pea soup, *soupe aux pois Canadienne*, is satisfying and filling; the cheddar-cheese soup is marvelous in cold weather; *tourtière* is pork-and-veal pie; *ragoût de boulettes* is a stew with ground pork balls; *bouilli* is the Canadian equivalent of a boiled dinner; *tarte au sirop d'érable* is a maple-syrup tart; and *grand-pères* are dumplings in maple syrup. Also worthy of note: lion's-gate pancakes, served with hot applesauce and whipped cream; blueberry crisp pudding, made with brown sugar and oatmeal; the Laurentian family soup, made with beef stock, vegetables, and served with grated cheese; and such homely but delicious fare as baked beans, clam and fish chowders, fruit pies, and home-made breads.

Canada Grouse. A spotted grouse.

Canadian Bacon. *See* Bacon.

Canadian Wines. The wines of Canada are little known, and they are rarely, if ever, exported. Because of the cool summers and early autumns, important grape production is never likely to be realized. However, Canada does produce a fair quantity of red and white wines of at least drinkable quality for local consumption.

Canapé. In the United States canapés are commonly served as cocktail accompaniments. They are small open-faced sandwiches made of toast spread with highly seasoned pastes or well-

flavored butters. Egg salad, caviar, fish or ham paste, or pieces of smoked salmon are among the popular canapé toppings. They may be attractively garnished with pimientos cut like flower petals, with black or green olive slices, etc. Even the simplest are time-consuming to prepare, but they can be made in advance and frozen.

In France the canapé is a rectangular piece of toast or fried bread, plain or spread with a paste, usually served with winged game.

Canard (French). Duck.

Canard à la Presse. Pressed duck, a very rich dish prepared with duck blood; not to everyone's taste. Some restaurants specializing in this dish offer an almost theatrical presentation.

Canard Nantais. Nantes duck.

Canard Rouennais. Rouen duck.

Canard Sauvage. Wild duck.

Canary Grass. A type of grass, originally cultivated in the Canary Islands, which bears an edible seed high in starch content.

Canary Wines. Wines produced in the Canary Islands; many resemble Madeira wine.

Cancalaise, À la (French). Garnished with oysters.

Canch. A large piece of bread.

Cancoillotte; Canquoillotte. A distinctive, very soft strong cheese prepared, in France-Comté and in the Jura region of France, with soured milk and butter and eggs, sometimes with wine added; sold in small containers; not good during the summer months.

Can-Con. A Philippine green vegetable much like spinach.

Cancroid. Belonging to the crab family; related to crabs.

Candied (Crystallized) Fruits. Fruits, fresh or preserved, boiled in sugar until saturated with the syrup, then dried.

Candil. The squirrelfish.

Candling Eggs. Holding eggs to the light to observe transparency and the presence or absence of spots.

Candy. Man first tasted sweets in the juice of the sugar cane and in the honey of the bee. The earliest records of candy, forty centuries old, are found in hieroglyphics on temple walls in ancient Egypt, where the primitive procedures in candy making were depicted. Early Chinese history reveals that a kind of candy was made by boiling barley and water to a hard consistency, spinning it into sticks, then rolling it in sesame seeds. The Venetians brought sugar to Europe in about the 13th century.

Some two thousand (or more) varieties of candy exist today. They are based on one indispensable ingredient, sugar, which is dissolved in a liquid to form a syrup. In structure candies are either crystalline, that is, composed of minute crystals, such as fudges and fondants, or noncrystalline, such as taffies, brittles, and clear hard candies. The temperature or concentration to which the sugar syrup is cooked determines the type of candy—soft, chewy, or hard; the manipulation after cooking determines the texture—grainy or smooth.

Because the temperature is so important in candy cookery it is advisable to use a candy thermometer. Always heat the thermometer gradually with the water or syrup before plunging it into a boiling liquid which may crack the bulb.

Assemble all the needed equipment and ingredients before starting to make candy. The saucepan should be large enough to allow the mixture to boil up—a 2–3-quart capacity pan is best. It should be of heavy metal to avoid the syrup's sticking as it is apt to do in a light-metal container. Wooden spoons are best for stirring and beating.

A few hints on candy making: When sugar and water are being cooked together, they should be stirred when first put over low heat to dissolve the sugar, but then while the mixture boils, it should no longer be stirred. Candies with molasses among the ingredients, however, will need practically continuous stirring to prevent them from boiling over. Creamy candies like fondants and fudges should be cooled quickly without being stirred until they are lukewarm (110° F.), to avoid crystal formation which gives an unpleasant coarseness to the candy.

If a candy thermometer is not available, the cold water test can be used to judge when candy is done. Fill a cup with cold water and test in this way:

Soft Ball: A drop of syrup in the cold water will form a soft ball when shaped with the fingers. It will flatten when removed from the water.

Firm Ball: The syrup can be formed into a ball which does not flatten when removed from water.

Hard Ball: The ball which is formed is distinctly chewy.

Cane, Sugar. The tall reeds which, when pressed, produce sugar cane juice, subsequently made into sugar.

Canel (Obsolete). Cinnamon.

Canela (Spanish). Cinnamon.

Canella. Wild cinnamon.

Canestrato. A strong, firm Sicilian cheese made of a combination of sheep's and goat's milk.

Caneton (French). Duckling.

> **Caneton à la Rouennaise.** Duckling served in a rich sauce of Cognac, red wine, and onions.

> **Caneton de Rouen.** Duckling from Rouen, France. The bird is killed by thrusting a skewer through its brain, thus keeping the blood in the flesh.

Canette (French). A very young duckling.

Cangrejo (Spanish). Crab.

> **Cangrejos de Mar.** Baby crabs.

> **Cangrejos de Rio.** Shrimp.

Canistel. A West Indian sweet yellow-green-orange-colored fruit.

Canister. A can or box for holding coffee, sugar, tea, or flour.

Canistrelli (French). Irregular-shaped anise-and-sugar cookies; a specialty of Corsica.

Canja (Portuguese, Brazilian). A thick soup or stew made with chicken and rice.

Canja com Arroz. Rice-and-chicken soup.

Canja de Galinha. Chicken soup.

Canneberge (French). Cranberry.

Canned Food. In 1795 an obscure French confectioner and chef, Nicolas Appert, after fifteen years' experimentation, developed a method of food preservation that is the fundamental process of canning as practiced today. It was his theory that if food is sufficiently heated, then sealed in a container that excludes air, the food will keep. Appert filled bottles with various foods, sealed them with cork stoppers, and cooked them in boiling water. Samples of his preserved vegetables and fruits carried around the world on sailing vessels retained their wholesomeness.

From Appert's time to the present, the history of canning is a story of the development of better containers, improved equipment, time-saving machinery, and research. This has led to the discovery and understanding of the scientific principles of canning.

Commercial canning today is a multimillion-dollar industry, widely distributed throughout the United States and producing a large variety of fruits, vegetables, juices, soups, meats, fish, milk, and specialty products in both cans and glass containers.

Shoppers will find the label on the can an excellent aid in selecting canned foods. The Federal Food, Drug and Cosmetic Act requires that the label state the name of the manufacturer or distributor of the product, and that the contents of the container be stated in terms of net weight or volume.

Canned-food labels bear additional information to aid the shopper. They give information regarding variety, style of pack, amount of food in the container expressed in terms of cupfuls or number of pieces or servings, consistency, tenderness, and serving advice. *See also* Canning.

Cannelle (French). Cinnamon.

Canneloni (Italian). A *pasta*, served either as an appetizer or as a light main course, for which squares of dough are spread with a finely chopped, well-seasoned chicken, vegetable, or meat mixture, or with seasoned cheese, then rolled, covered with a sauce, and baked. Canneloni are sometimes made with a pancake instead of noodle dough.

Canneloni Florentine. Large pieces of *pasta* colored green with spinach and served with an appropriate sauce or cheese.

Cannelons (French). Small puff-paste forms filled with finely chopped chicken, meat, or fish.

Canner's Alkali. A mixture of sodium hydroxide and sodium carbonate used to remove skin from fruit before canning. Sodium hydroxide alone is more frequently used.

Cannery. A plant where fruit, vegetables, or meats are canned.

Cannikin. A small drinking can.

Canning. Successful home canning is an art that can give pleasure and satisfaction to the home cook. Canning is not difficult, and if directions are carefully followed, the results should be good. The following steps are suggested for successful canning:

I Preparation of Jars and Equipment

Check all equipment carefully and be sure it is in good condition before starting to can. Wash jars and lids and get them fitted together. This saves time and work after the food is on hand.

Canning equipment should include:

A pressure cooker for processing nonacid vegetables; boiling water bath for processing fruits and tomatoes or for the nonacid vegetables if pressure cooker is not available. Any vessel that is deep enough to allow boiling water to come up one to two inches over the top of the jars may be used. This might be a wash boiler, lard can, or bucket. It must be fitted with a lid and rack.

Rack for bottom of cooker—may be made from wood slats or wire meshing.

Jar lifter.

Sieve for making juices.

Pan for sterilizing jars.

Pan for precooking food.

Flat pan for holding hot jar while filling.

Jar funnel.

Measuring cup and spoons.

Tablespoons, long-handled spoon, wooden spoon, knife, and fork.

Jars.

Sharp butcher and paring knives.

Wire basket for scalding tomatoes and fruits for peeling.

Vegetable brush.

Pans for washing and preparing foods.

Types of jars, lids, and rubbers

1. Glass-top jar—has glass disk with rubber ring for sealing gasket. The glass lid is held in place by a metal rim. Top of jar must be smooth.
2. Screw-top or mason jar—with porcelain lining in a zinc screw-top.
3. Lightning-seal jar—glass top with wire bail.
4. Self-seal jar—has metal disk and metal tion (self-seal) by pouring boiling water over them
5. Dip rubber rings in boiling water and place on the jars before filling them.
6. When jars are packed with food, and processed for longer than 20 minutes, they do not need to be sterilized but should be clean and hot when filled. (*Exception:* Jars should be sterilized for such vegetables as corn, beans, and peas, which are generally more difficult to keep.)

Don't spoil good-quality food by using unclean equipment (towels, tabletops, dishcloths, etc.)

ring. Self-sealing as the jar cools after processing. Top of the jar must have a smooth edge. The metal disk can be used only once, but the ring may be used again.

Check jars, lids, and rubbers carefully

Check jars to be sure there are no nicks or cracks.

Use only rubber rings that do not leave a mark when pinched together tightly.

To test mason and lightning-seal jars, fill half full of water, put on rubber ring and cover, seal, and turn upside down to see if it leaks.

Discard mason lids with loose or cracked linings.

Edge of mason lid should be free from dents. If thumbnail can be inserted between lid and glass when closed, lid does not fit and should be discarded.

To test pressure cooker

Open safety valve, scour the steel ball, and make sure that it does not stick. Clean the opening to the gage with a toothpick. The gage indicator should rest at zero when not in use. Steam should not escape from the cooker when completely sealed.

Preparation of jars, rubbers, and lids

1. Wash jars and tops in hot soapy water.
2. Rinse in hot water.
3. Drain by inverting in a clean, flat pan.

II Selection of Food for Canning

Use speed in all steps of canning. Get the food into the processor as soon as possible. Select good, sound food free from bruises or decay.

Vegetables are best at their prime stage of maturity, when they are greenest and tenderest, before beans have started separating from the pod or greens have become thick and fibrous.

Fruits should be ripened on the tree for best flavor and sweetness.

Discard woody stems, fibrous cores, etc.

Remember: The quality of the canned product will be no higher than that of the food that goes into the can.

III Preparation of Food

Wash vegetables and fruits before podding, breaking, peeling, or stemming. This keeps the inside of the food clean and makes it easier to process without spoilage.

Wash greens by lifting up and down in pans of water as many times as needed to remove all sand and dirt.

Scald tomatoes and peaches for peeling by dipping in boiling water until skins loosen; then put into cold water.

Sort and grade food for size and degree of maturity.

IV Sterilizing Jars

Jars must be thoroughly sterilized (all equipment and working surfaces should be as clean as a doctor's office) to destroy all bacteria and to prevent food spoilage.

To sterilize jars:

1. Invert clean jars on a rack or cloth in a pan of warm water. If using zinc or glass lids, place them in the pan also.
2. Boil jars 15–20 minutes.
3. Keep jars in boiling water until ready to be filled.
4. Prepare jar lids that have a seal composi-

V Precooking

Cook all nonacid vegetables and most fruits for a short time before packing into hot jars. This shrinks the product, giving a fuller pack, and saves time in getting the processor up to the correct temperature, which helps to prevent spoilage.

Vegetables. Cover the vegetables with boiling water. Boil until vegetables are heated through 3–5 minutes. Greens should be precooked until wilted, using only the water that clings to the leaves after washing.

Large fruits. Precook peaches, pears, apples, plums in boiling syrup or water until heated through—3–5 minutes.

VI Packing

Have processor on the stove boiling hot and jars hot or sterilized (according to method of canning) and the food boiling. Work quickly so the food remains hot.

When ready to pack, remove one jar at a time from the hot water. Keeping the jars hot helps prevent breakage during packing and processing and prevents cooling of the product.

Place hot jars in flat pan.

If rubber ring is being used, place it in posi-

tion on the jar resting flat on the sealing shoulder of the jar.

Pack the jars quickly so the precooked food remains hot.

For starchy vegetables, pack jar loosely so food moves in liquid freely. Large fruits, such as peaches, should be placed pit side down, shingle fashion.

Fill jars to within one-half inch of top, except for starch vegetables, such as peas, beans, and corn, which should come only to within one inch of the top. This space is called head space.

For vegetables, add one-half teaspoon of salt for each pint.

Cover food with the boiling liquid in which the food has been precooked. If there is insufficient liquid, add boiling water. Allow head space as indicated above.

Work out the air bubbles by inserting a knife blade or spatula down the sides of the jar.

Wipe the rubber ring and sealing edge of the jar with a clean cloth to remove any particles of food.

VII Sealing before Processing

Adjust lid of jar completely or partially according to type of seal used:

Vacuum or self-seal jars should be completely sealed before processing.

Mason and glass-top seals should be screwed on until tight, then turned back one-fourth inch.

Lightning-seal jar—top clamp is snapped into place and side clamp left up.

As the jars are filled, place in hot canner or where they will keep hot until processing begins.

VIII Process at the Temperature and for the Time Indicated in the Time Table

A. Pressure cooker—recommended for nonacid vegetables and meats

1. Put one or two inches of boiling water in canner.
2. Allow space between jars for free circulation of steam.
3. When cooker is loaded, adjust the cover and fasten it securely. If there are several

clamps, fasten moderately tight those opposite each other, a pair at a time; then go back over the whole set and tighten each pair.

4. See that no steam escapes anywhere except at the petcock.
5. Allow the petcock to remain open until the steam escapes in a steady stream 7–10 minutes. This makes sure that all of the air has escaped; otherwise, the pressure gage will indicate air pressure instead of steam pressure.
6. Now close the petcock and allow the pressure to rise until the gage reaches the required pressure.
7. Begin counting time when the proper pressure is reached, and process according to time table.
8. Keep the pressure regulated evenly during the processing by controlling the amount of heat under the cooker. A wavering pressure causes a loss of juice from the jars.
9. After processing time is completed, remove cooker from heat.
10. Allow gage to go back slowly to zero before opening petcock. This requires 30 minutes or more if the processor is full.
11. Open petcock gradually.
12. Remove lid carefully, tilting away from you to prevent steam burns.

B. *Boiling water bath—recommended for fruits and tomatoes. Use for nonacid vegetables only if pressure cooker is not available*

1. Place an open rack in the bottom of the canner to prevent jars from resting on the bottom and to permit free circulation of water.
2. Have water in processor boiling as hot jars are packed and placed in canner.
3. Place hot packed jars on rack as they are filled, allowing sufficient space between jars so water can circulate freely about them.
4. Keep boiling water at least one to two inches above top of jars.
5. Start counting time when the water reaches an active boil, and process for the length of time given in the time table.
6. Keep water boiling steadily throughout the entire processing time.
7. If water boils away, replace with more boiling water.
8. If water should cease to boil for any reason, estimate length of time it has stopped boiling and add to the time given in the time table as follows:
   For fruits and tomatoes, add that much time to the time given in the time table.
   For vegetables, double the time and add to time given in the time table.

IX Sealing the Jars after Processing

Mason and glass-top jars—complete seal by screwing lid tightly.

Lightning-seal—push side clamp down.

Vacuum or self-seal—this type seals as it cools, and should need no further adjustment. If the screw band is loose, after processing, hold the lid in place so it will not turn and tighten the metal ring.

X Cooling

Cool jars quickly. Place on a clean surface 5 inches apart to permit free circulation of air.

Protect hot jars just out of the cooker from drafts to avoid cracking or breaking them.

XI Test the Seal

To make sure the jar of processed food is sealed, test it after the jars have cooled 24 hours.

Mason, glass-top, and lightning-type seal—tilt jar carefully to see if liquid oozes out.

Vacuum seal—tap lid with a spoon. A clear ringing sound indicates a seal.

If a seal has not been made, check lid, rubber ring, and jar. Replace if necessary. The food should then be reprocessed a second time.

XII Storage

Remove metal rings from glass-top jars and vacuum seals after jars have cooled 24 hours. These may be used over again. The seal is made with the glass lid or metal disk—not the screw band.

Wipe jars carefully with a damp cloth. Do not touch rubber or hold jars by top. This may break the seal.

Store in a cool, dry, dark place that is well ventilated.

Caution: All nonacid vegetables which have been canned at home should be boiled 10–15 minutes before tasting.

TIME TABLE FOR PROCESSING VEGETABLES

Vegetables, nonacid	Canning Directions	Boiling Water Bath Glass jars Pts. & Qts.	*Processing Time* Pressure Cooker Time—Min. Glass Jars Pts.	Qts.	Pounds Pressure
Asparagus	Wash. Cut in 1″ lengths or tie in uniform bundles; stand upright with tough portions in boiling water, cover tightly. Boil 2–3 min. Pack hot.	3 hrs.	30	35	10
Beans, lima, fresh	Wash, shell. Boil in water to cover 3 min. Pack loosely while hot.	3 hrs.	50	55	10
Beans, string	Wash, remove tips and cut into desired lengths. Boil in water to cover 5 min. Pack hot.	3 hrs.	30	35	10
Beets, baby	Wash, leave on roots and 1″ of stems to prevent bleeding. Boil about 15 min. or until skins slip off. Skin, trim, cut if desired. Pack hot.	3 hrs.	30	35	10
Corn	Remove husks and silk. For whole kernels—cut from cob without scraping. Cream style, cut shallow and scrape cob. Boil 3–5 min. Pack loosely while hot.	Kernel, 3½ hrs. Cream, 3½ hrs.	60 75	70	10 15
Greens, Spinach, Kale, Dandelion, Etc.	Wash thoroughly, lifting greens from several waters. Remove tough stems. Cook in uncovered vessel without added water until wilted. Pack loosely, while hot. Cut through greens with a sharp knife.	3 hrs.	60	65	15

TIME TABLE FOR PROCESSING VEGETABLES (Cont'd)

Vegetables, nonacid	Canning Directions	Boiling Water Bath Glass jars Pts. & Qts.	Pressure Cooker Time—Min. Glass Jars Pts.	Qts.	Pounds Pressure
Peas, green	Wash, shell, simmer about 5 min. Pack loosely while hot.	3 hrs.	45		10
Pumpkin, Squash	Wash, peel, cut into 1–1½″ cubes. Simmer until heated through. Pack hot.	3 hrs.	60	65	10
Vegetable Soup Mixtures	Wash, trim vegetables, cut into small pieces. Combine two or more vegetables, corn, lima beans, tomatoes, onions, peas, carrots, celery, pimientos. Boil 5 min. Pack loosely while hot.	3 hrs.	60	70	10

The header row spans *Processing Time* over the Boiling Water Bath and Pressure Cooker columns.

Canning Fruits

Small fruits—such as berries and cherries

1. Place graded, washed berries in clean jar.
2. Make juice out of the sound, overripe, or cull berries by crushing and simmering until juice is extracted.
3. Sweeten juice as necessary.
4. Heat juice to simmering, pour over berries in jar, and process in boiling water bath according to time table.

Large fruits

1. Prepare in advance a syrup according to suggestions in following time table.
2. Precook the fruit in the syrup or water until heated through and shrunken.
3. Pack hot fruit into clean hot jars, shingle fashion, to get maximum amount into jars.
4. Fill jars with hot juice.
5. Process in boiling water bath according to the time table.

Tomato juice

1. Wash tomatoes well, remove cores, and cut into small pieces.
2. Handle in small quantities of one to two gallons and avoid delay at any stage of the procedure.
3. Precook to 170°F. or simmer until softened.
4. Put through sieve at once.
5. If for infant or invalid use, omit salt; otherwise, add ½–1 teaspoon to each quart.
6. Reheat to simmering point. Do not boil.
7. Pour into sterilized containers, seal, and process.

TIME TABLE FOR PROCESSING FRUITS

Fruits and Acid Foods	Canning Directions	Processing Time Boiling Water Bath Time—Minutes Pints and Quarts Glass Jars
Apples	Wash, pare, core, cut in quarters. Boil in syrup or water 5 min. Pack hot. Or pack hot in form of apple sauce.	15 5
Cherries	Wash, remove pits or leave unpitted. Cook in syrup 5 min.; pack hot. Or pack raw, cover with boiling syrup.	5 25
Berries other than straw-berries	Wash carefully, remove stems. Precook 3–5 min. in syrup and pack hot. Or pack raw and cover with boiling syrup.	5 20
Peaches, Apricots	Immerse in boiling water until skins will slip off. Dip in cold water. Peel, cut in halves, remove pits, cook in syrup, pack hot. Or pack raw, cover with boiling syrup.	15 25-35
Pears	Wash and peel, cut in halves, core. If hard, cook in syrup 4–8 min. Pack hot. Or pack raw, cover with boiling syrup.	20 20
Pimientos, ripe	Wash, place in hot oven (450°) 6–8 min. Dip in cold water. Remove skins, stems, and core. Fold and pack hot. Add no liquid.	40
Pineapple	Slice, peel, core. Cut in pieces, heat slowly with sugar to taste. Pack hot.	25
Plums	Wash, prick skins, cook in small amount of syrup. Pack hot. Or pack raw, covering with boiling syrup.	5 20
Rhubarb	Trim, wash, cut in half-inch lengths. Boil only until soft, with sugar to taste. Pack hot.	5
Sauerkraut	Allow to be well fermented before canning. Heat to simmering; avoid boiling. Pack hot and closely. Cover with hot juice.	30
Strawberries	Wash, stem. Boil only until soft with sugar to taste. Allow to stand overnight in kettle. In morning, bring quickly to boil. Pack hot.	5

TIME TABLE FOR PROCESSING FRUITS (Cont'd)

Fruits and Acid Foods	Canning Directions	Processing Time Boiling Water Bath Time—Minutes Pints and Quarts Glass Jars
Tomatoes	Wash, put in boiling water (about 1 min.) until skins loosen. Plunge into cold water. Peel, remove core. Simmer until soft, pack hot. Or pack raw, fill jar with hot juice.	5 20
Tomato juice	Wash, skins may be left on. Simmer only until soft. Put through sieve at once. Reheat to simmering. Pour into jars. Process at simmering (180°).	5
Fruit juices	Wash, drain, crush fruit. Heat to simmering. Strain. Add sugar if desired. Reheat. Pour into jar, process at simmering (180°).	20

Syrup for Fruit

	Water	and	Sugar	or	Corn Syrup	or	Honey
Thin syrup	1 c.		¼ c.		½ c.		¼ c.
Medium syrup	1 c.		½ c.		1 c.		½ c.
Heavy syrup	1 c.		1 c.		2 c.		1 c.

Can Opener. The most practical kinds of can opener are those that fasten on the wall or the heavily mounted models that sit securely on a counter surface. If an electrically operated opener can be had, so much the easier for the home cook. But an inexpensive, hand-operated rotary opener readily available in the stores does an excellent job without the hazards of scratched fingers. The safest can openers are those that operate with a revolving motion and press down the fresh cut edge of the can. Some versions have a magnet that lifts the top from the can after it has been cut. The pry-type opener, which is the cheapest, is also the most dangerous because it makes sharp, jagged edges.

Cannoli (Italian). Cream-filled pastry.

Cannonball Fruit. A round fruit with woody flesh from a South American tree; not particularly tasty.

Cannon Bread (British). Bread given to the mayor and aldermen of Exeter as an allowance at Christmas and Easter.

Cannon Roll (Viennese). Bread whose two ends are rolled toward the middle and crossed.

Canonaus. A rather sweet red wine produced in Sardinia, Italy.

Can Swells. Bulges on the ends of food cans caused by the gases produced by the fermentation of the contents.

Cantal Cheese. A hard yellowish cheese with a strong, biting flavor, produced in cylinders weighing from 40 to over 100 pounds in the Department of Cantal, France.

Cantaloupe. The cantaloupe is a member of the muskmelon family, to which the honeydew, honeyball, and Casaba melon also belong. It derives its name from Cantalupo, a 16th-century Papal estate outside Rome, where the first melons in Europe were cultivated from seeds brought from Armenia.

The cantaloupe is easily identified by the coarse, corky netting of its rind with a light green background under the netting. When it is ripe and ready for eating, it has a fragrant, sweet odor and a sweet, fine-textured orangish flesh.

Most popularly, cantaloupe is served halved and in the shell, sometimes with a sprinkling of salt. Freshly ground black pepper on cantaloupe produces an odd but pleasing flavor. The flavor of cantaloupe blends with that of almost all other fruits and berries as well as with sweet liqueurs. Marinating it in port wine produces an exquisite flavor.

Cantarèu. (French). Small snails cooked in a spicy tomato sauce; a specialty around Nice.

Canteen. A store at an army base where soldiers can buy food, sometimes liquor, and other items.

Canterbury Pudding (British). A plain sponge pudding served with a port wine sauce; believed to have originated in cathedral towns.

Cantharelle; Chanterelle (French). An edible mushroom having a good flavor.

Cantle. A slice or piece of bread, cheese, or other food.

Cantonese. A Chinese culinary style, used in the majority of Chinese restaurants in the United States. Most foods are prepared by the "stir-fry" method, in which foods are cut into thin slices or slivers, cooked quickly, and served immediately. One outstanding feature of this style of cuisine is the *dim-sum* (or *dum-sim*) preparation, consisting of small portions of meat or fish-filled pastries, dumplings, etc.

Cantonese Sausage (Chinese). A sausage resembling a long frankfurter, made from pork and wine and flavored with fruit rind; usually boiled.

Canvasback Duck. One of the most prized wild ducks of North America. Because it lives on wild vegetables, especially celery, it develops a fine flavor. The name derives from its light-colored back, suggestive of a rough fabric.

Cap. A wooden drinking bowl.

Cape Brandy. A spirit distilled from grapes and aromatic herbs and spices; popular in Cape Province, Republic of South Africa.

Capelan (French). A fish of the cod family resembling smelt.

Capelli d'Angelo (Italian). Very thin noodles.

Capellini (Italian). Small, thin noodles.

    Capellini e Fegatini in Brodo. Noodles and chicken livers in soup.

Capendu. A French, red apple, of only moderate quality.

Capercailzie. A northern European bird about the size of a small turkey; cooked and served like a grouse.

Capern (German). Capers.

Caperon. A large white strawberry of excellent flavor.

Capers. The small tight round buds of the caper bush native to many Mediterranean countries. They are best when gathered at daybreak before they open. The pickled buds are used in sauces and as a garnish for fish, seafood, and cold meats.

Caper Sauce (British). A popular though mediocre sauce made with mutton stock; milk, and chopped capers and served with boiled mutton or lamb.

Cape Smoke. A crude alcoholic beverage made by the native Bantu population in South Africa.

Capillaire. A sugar syrup, clarified with egg white and flavored with orange-flower water, rose water, or curaçao; usually added to other liqueurs to give them body.

Capillarimeter. An instrument that measures the strength of wine.

Capilotade (French). Stew prepared with leftover meat and a thick, seasoned sauce.

    Capilotade de Volaille. Stewed poultry in a spicy brown sauce.

Capirotada. (1) (Mexican). Sweet bread pudding; usually served with a fruit sauce. (2) (Spanish). Sweet pudding containing bread and cinnamon.

Capitaine. A large fish of excellent taste and texture native to African waters.

Capitone (Italian). Giant eel.

Caplin. (1) A small fish similar to the smelt. (2) A small smelt native to the arctic.

Capocollo (Italian). A highly peppered smoked-pork product.

Capoletti (Italian). Similar to ravioli but triangular.

Capon. An unsexed male chicken, usually less than 10 months old, that has tender meat and soft, pliable, smooth-textured skin. Capons weigh

4–8 pounds and are usually roasted, although many foreign stews use disjointed capons.

Caponata (Sicilian). Appetizer of fried eggplant, tomato sauce, anchovies, capers, black olives, celery, and onion.

Caponatina (Italian). Eggplant relish.

Caponatine (Italian). Spicy salad.

Capone. (1) A rather bony rockfish found near Corsica, France. (2) An eel much used in fish dishes.

Capoun (French). Cabbage stuffed with sausage meat and rice; a specialty around Nice.

Capozzella (Italian). Lamb's head.

Cappa ai Ferri (Italian). Broiled scallops.

Cappellacci alla Zucca (Italian). Small *pasta* similar to ravioli, filled with cheese and squash.

Cappelletti (Italian). Noodle dough stuffed with chicken.

Capperi in Galeri (Italian). Anchovies and capers.

Cappie. (1) A small drinking cup. (2) A beer somewhere betwen ale and ordinary beer.

Cappie-Bake (British, Scotch). A cookie shaped something like a small pie.

Cappone (Italian). Capon.

    Cappone Tartuffato. Roast capon with truffles.

Cappon Magro (Italian). (1) Vegetable salad arranged in a series of different colors and garnished with seafood. (2) Mixed salad of lobster, fish, and anchovies.

Cappuccino (Italian). Coffee prepared with milk in an espresso machine; sometimes served with a sprinkling of cinnamon.

Capretto (Italian). Young goat.

Capri. *See* Italy, The Wines of.

Caprian. A goat's-milk cheese with a very strong taste and odor; made in Capri, Italy.

Capric Acid. A colorless crystalline fatty acid with a goatlike flavor, present in butter and in the oil of the coconut.

Capricot (French). Apricot-flavored liqueur.

Caprino (Argentinian). A biting, spicy goat's-milk cheese.

Caproic Acid. An acid found in butter.

Caps. Candied citrus peels.

Capsicum. Cayenne pepper, paprika, red pepper, chilies and chili powder, pimientoes, and fresh

red and green peppers all belong to the *Capsicum* genus. *Capsicum* is a very large genus of tropical herbs and shrubs yielding a many-seeded berry or fruit which, in some species, for example, *Capsicum grossum* (fresh green pepper), is used in the fresh form, and in other species, such as *Capsicum tetragonum* (paprika) is dried and powdered. Black and white pepper are not related to the capsicums. They are the fruit of a different plant, *Piper nigrum*, native to the East Indies.

Capucin. A mature hare with an unpleasantly strong flavor.

Capucine. Flower of the capucine plant preserved and used like capers; also used fresh in salads.

Caquelon (French). An earthenware cooking utensil, generally used for cheese fondue.

Carabao. Water buffalo. The meat is often used in the Philippines as a holiday food; large cuts are roasted over an open fire.

Caracóis (Portuguese). Snails.

Caracoles (Spanish). Snails.

Carafe. A wide-bottomed tapering plain or engraved glass bottle for beverages, popular in Europe for serving inexpensive wines. Metal carafes with a thermos lining are also available.

Carambola. A yellow ridged, sweet or acid fruit native to Southeast Asia. The sweet types are palatable.

Caramel. Burnt sugar used for flavoring or coloring. *See also* Caramels.

Caramel Color. A caramel solution used to color a wide variety of foods.

Caramel Fruits. Fruits dipped in a sugar glaze.

Caramelize. To melt sugar until browned. Sugar is put in a heavy skillet and placed over very low heat without stirring until a light brown liquid has formed.

    For a caramel syrup, stir water or another liquid into the melted sugar carefully to avoid spattering. Or pour the caramel into a liquid and dissolve. The hardened mass formed will eventually dissolve.

Caramella (Italian). Caramel; hard candy.

Caramelo (Latin American) Dark sugar syrup.

Caramels. Soft, chewy candies prepared with a combination of sugar syrup and corn syrup to which cream and flavoring are added. After cooking, the mixture should be stirred occasionally until cool and then poured into one corner of a lightly buttered pan and allowed to flow at will to form a sheet of uniform thickness. Caramels are usually cut into ¾-inch cubes.

Caramel Slice. Filled layers of cake topped with caramel sauce.

Caramels Mous (French). Taffy.

Caramelvla (Dutch). Caramel custard.

Caramote. A shellfish strongly resembling the shrimp. It often reaches 8 inches in length. When live it is yellow-green; when cooked it turns red. In Italy caramotes are called *scampi*.

Caranguejo (Portuguese). Crab.

Carapace. The upper shell of a crab, turtle, and other crustaceans.

Carapau (Portuguese). A fish similar to a sardine.

Carapulca (Spanish). Cubed pork and sausage slices simmered in broth, then topped with hard-cooked eggs and chopped almonds; served hot in the pan in which they were cooked.

Caratos (South American). A soft drink made with sprouted corn and rice.

Caravansary; Caravanseri. A quadrangular inn in the Middle East where caravans stopped overnight. Meals were served in the enclosed court.

Caraway. The tiny crescent-shaped seeds, fruit of the plant of the umbelliferal family, are most familiarly used as a flavoring for rye bread. But, having a faintly anise aroma, they are also used to flavor cakes; cheese spreads; beef, veal, and lamb stews; baked apples; apple pie; quick and yeast breads; and vegetables, particularly sauerkraut and cabbage. The tender young leaves of the herb may be used in salads and as a flavoring for cheese spreads.

Caraway Loaf. An American imitation of the German cheeses made with caraway seeds; similar to Kümmelkäse. *See* Kümmelkäse.

Caraway Oil. A pale yellow, edible oil obtained from caraway seeds.

Carbohydrates. Sugars and starches found in foods. Bread, cereals and cereal products, syrups, and leguminous vegetables are high in carbohydrates. Refined sugar is the most concentrated carbohydrate. A pound of carbohydrate contains 1,820 calories.

Carbonada (Spanish, South American). Meat stew.

Carbonado. Roasted meat cut, basted, sprinkled with bread crumbs, and grilled.

Carbonated. Containing carbonic acid. Carbonated beverages are bubbly and effervescent.

Carbonated Water. *See* Carbon Dioxide.

Carbonated Wines. Sparkling wines made artificially by adding carbonic acid gas to still wines. The bubbles are larger than those in natural sparkling wines, but do not last as long.

Carbonation. The introduction of carbon dioxide in order to produce bubbles.

Carbon Dioxide. A heavy, colorless, odorless gas. When water is charged with carbon dioxide it becomes soda or carbonated water. Carbon dioxide is released in large quantities during alcoholic fermentation. It is used to make beer and some less expensive sparkling wines. The gas has no liquid state; when cooled it forms a solid mass—the dry ice used for refrigeration. The carbon dioxide formed by the chemical reaction between baking soda and an acid is the leavening agent for many cakes and quick breads.

Carbonnade. Originally this French term referred to meats grilled over charcoal (carbon). Today *carbonnade* usually denotes a meat stew or ragout, the most famous being the Belgian dish *Carbonnades Flamande,* for which slices of beef seasoned with salt and pepper are simmered with sliced onions in beer, preferably Belgian, and brown stock.

Carborundum. Trade name for silicon carbide, an abrasive used for sharpening knives.

Carcake (Scotch). A small cake or pancake made with eggs; eaten on Shrove Tuesday.

Carcassin. The crucian, a very bony fish.

Carciofi (Italian). Artichokes.

  Carciofi alla Giudia. Deep-fried artichokes.

  Carciofi alla Romana. Artichokes stuffed with mint and garlic and cooked in olive oil.

Cardamine; Lady's Smock. A wild plant or herb,

sometimes eaten as a salad green in various parts of the United States; it has a watercress or mustard taste.

Cardamom. A highly aromatic spice available either ground or in whole seeds. Native to India and a member of the ginger family, it is one of the spices in curry. The Scandinavians use the whole or ground seeds in cakes, sweet pastries,

breads, and cookies, but it is most popular in the Near and Far East.

Cardiga (Portuguese). A rather rich, oily sheep's-milk cheese.

Cardinal (Colloquial). A mulled red-wine drink.

Cardinal, À la (French). Of fish, garnished with a preparation of truffles and mushrooms.

Cardinal Fish. Red mullet.

Cardinale. An Italian drink made of gin, bitters, and Italian vermouth.

Cardinaliser (French). Literally "to make red." Usually to place live lobster or other seafood in boiling liquid until it turns red.

Cardinal of the Sea. A fanciful name for the lobster.

Cardinal Sauce. A well-seasoned white or velouté sauce made with fish stock and enriched with lobster or other shellfish butter; served with shellfish or fish.

Cardon (French). Cardoon. *See* Cardoon.

Cardona Salt. A type of salt noted for its purity; found in huge beds near the town of Cardona in northern Spain.

Cardoon. A vegetable related to the globe artichoke. The roots and stems are usually cooked in a seasoned liquid, then chilled and served in a salad, but the delicately flavored vegetable may also be served in a Béchamel sauce or sautéed in butter.

Care Cake. A Shrove Tuesday cake.

Carême, Antonin. A great French chef, creator, and author who lived from 1784 to 1833. He was called the "Cook of kings and the king of cooks." In many respects, Carême was single-handedly the innovator of scores of new dishes and sauces, and more than anyone else, brought French culinary skills to their highest point. He was the author of *L'Art de la Cuisine, Le Pâtissier Pittoresque, Le Maître d'Hotel Français,* and *Le Pâtissier Royal Parisien.*

Carême, Jean de. A noted chef nicknamed "John of Lent" who was cook for Pope Leo X.

Cargolades. Snails; so called in the Roussillon district of France.

Caribbean Food. *See* individual listings under Cuba, Haiti, Jamaica, etc.

Caribou. A reindeer, native to North America, which can be cooked like other venison; that is, broiled, roasted with strips of salt pork over the top, or cooked like pot roast. It is best when marinated in a wine mixture for several days before use. The meat is usually sold frozen in the United States.

Carignane. A very sweet French dessert wine with the distinctive taste of the Carignane grape; also grown for wine making in the French Pyrénées, North Africa, and California.

Caril (Portuguese). Curry.

Carimanolas (Panamanian). Pork fritter made with yuca (yucca), eggs, and vegetables.

Carioca (Portuguese). Coffee served with hot water.

Carioca, A la. In Brazilian style, often with beans, sometimes with hearts of palm.

Carite. (1) The kingfish. (2) The painted mackerel.

Cariucho (South American). Steak dish served with a rich peanut sauce.

Carle (British). Small cakes traditionally baked as gifts for singers at Christmas.

Carlowitz. A red wine, popular in Yugoslavia and Austria, produced along the banks of the Danube River.

Carlsbad. A medium-hard, somewhat salty sheep's-milk cheese made in central Europe, particularly in Czechoslovakia.

Carlsberg. An exceptionally good Danish beer; made in several different styles, including a special export type.

Carmignano. Red Italian wine similar to Chianti.

Carnabyn. A very nutritious malt-and-wine drink with stimulating tonic properties.

Carnation. A variety of cherry.

Carne (Italian). Meat.
  Carne di Bue. Beef.

Carne (Portuguese). Meat.
  Carne Assado. Roast meat.
  Carne de Carneiro. Mutton.
  Carne de Porco. Pork.
  Carne de Porco a Algarvia. Fried pork and clams.
  Carne de Vinha. Pickled pork.
  Carne de Vitella. Veal.
  Carne Picada. Minced or chopped meat.

Carne (Spanish). Meat.
  Carne de Cerdo. Pork.
  Carne de Res. Beef.
  Carne de Ternera. Veal.
  Carne de Vaca. Beef.

Carne de Membrillo (Spanish). Sweet, semisolid fruit paste.

Carneiro (Portuguese). Mutton.

Carob; Bokser. An evergreen tree, native to Mediterranean countries, that bears a sweet, succulent pod that has provided food for man and beast since prehistoric times. It is also called algarroba, locust pod, and St. John's bread, the latter because it may have been the "locust" eaten by John the Baptist in the wilderness (Mark 1:6). The large red-brown pods, rich in sugar, may be dried and ground and used in a syrup to flavor aromatic liqueurs. This is done in Sicily and Egypt. The dried pods are sometimes found in American stores specializing in Near East food. They are chewed for their sweet flavor as a kind of candy.

Carolina Rice. Rice grown in North and South Carolina; noted for its excellent taste; tends to cook with grains separated.

Carolines (French). Small, unsweetened eclairs served as appetizers; sometimes filled with meat or fish mixtures.

Carom Seeds. Vegetable seeds somewhat resembling parsley seeds; used in India for fritters, fish, etc.

Carosella. *See* Italian Fennel.

Carota (Italian). Carrot.

Carotee. An Arabic weight, about 700 pounds, used for dried fruits.

Carotene. An orange pigment present in plants, especially in carrots, covered by chlorophyll in green leaves. It is converted to vitamin A in the body and is important for growth and eyesight.

Carouse. (1) A toast or drink. (2) To drink freely.

Carp. A freshwater fish inhabiting rivers, lakes, and ponds. Its original home was China; it was transported to England about 1614. In 1875, it was brought to the United States. Like the buffalo fish and the catfish, the carp is one of the most important of the commercial fishes caught in the Mississippi River system. Often Midwestern farmers that have a stream or small river on their property fence in a stretch of the water to hatch carp, feeding them until they are plump and ready for market.

Most market carp, weighing 2–6 pounds, is shipped East, where it is in great demand among Chinese and Jewish housewives; it is one of the fishes used in making the classic Jewish dish gefüllte fish.

Carpe (French). Carp.
  Carpe à la Bière. Carp prepared with onions, celery root, ginger, and beer.
  Carpe à l'Alsacienne. Stuffed steamed carp served with sauerkraut.
  Carpe Chambord. Skinless carp cooked in white wine and served with a sauce of truffles, oysters, mushrooms, etc.
  Carpe Hongroise. Carp served in a sauce of sour cream and paprika.

Carpe à Cuir (French). The leather carp, a variety of carp whose body is somewhat wider than that of other varieties.

Carpe à Miroir. The mirror carp, an important fish food in France.

Carpillon; Carpeau (French). Very young carp or mullet.

Carpion (French). A small variety of mountain trout, usually found in the Alps region.

Carquelin. A fruity red wine with a pleasant aroma, made in the Beaujolais region of France. It is good only for a few years, then it deteriorates rapidly.

Carrabin Wheat. An Australian wheat of fairly good quality.

Carrageen. An edible sea moss. *See* Sea Moss.

Carré (French). The rib part of pork, mutton, lamb, and veal.

Carré. A small rich French cream cheese of the Neufchâtel type, marketed in squares measuring about 2 inches; called *Petit Carré*.

Carré de l'Est. A soft, smooth cow's milk cheese with a very light mold; resembles Camembert.

Carrelet (French). The sand dab, also flounder, a flat sea fish with an agreeable flavor but nondescript texture.

Carrot. A root vegetable grown in almost every country; an essential flavoring for soups and stews as well as a delicious vegetable. Carrots are also among the richest and least expensive sources of carotene, which our bodies convert into the essential nutrient vitamin A.

Carrots are equally delicious raw and cooked. Raw carrot curls or sticks are indispensable as a low-calorie appetizer. Shredded or grated raw carrots may be combined with seedless raisins, or with crushed pineapple, or with chopped hard-cooked eggs. Cooked carrots may accompany all kinds of meats, fish, and poultry.

The feathery carrot tops now are usually removed before the vegetable is marketed in one-pound transparent film bags, which yield approximately 1½ cups of diced or shredded carrot and provide 5 half-cup servings.

Buy carrots that are firm and crisp with a smooth, clean skin free from surface blemishes. The brighter the orange in the carrot, the more carotene it contains. But the bright hue does not necessarily indicate tenderness and sweetness. In fact, the larger, more mature carrots, likely to be the most orange in color, are not as tender as smaller specimens. Use the big carrots in stews and pot roasts and the smaller ones for salads or relish trays.

Fresh carrots are available the year round, as are the canned and frozen products.

Carry (Danish). Curry.

Carta (Portuguese). Flounder.

Carta del Giorno (Italian). Menu.

Carte (French). List of items served; bill of fare.

Unlike the menu, it offers individual dishes rather than meals at a fixed price.

Carte del Dia (Portuguese). Daily bill of fare.

Cartilage. Elastic tissue, such as gristle.

Cartilaginous. Similar to or having the texture of cartilage.

Cartouche. A round piece of greased paper used for covering food being cooked.

Carurú (Brazilian). A dish made of okra, shrimp, and dendê oil; occasionally various other ingredients are added.

Carvi. A plant with a root similar to salsify and a seed similar to cumin or anise.

Carvie (Scotch). Caraway seeds.

Carvie Cakes (Scotch). Flat cakes made of oatmeal and caraway seeds.

Carving. Once it was the custom for the man of the house to teach his sons the intricacies of the art of carving. Unfortunately, too few men today are skilled in this art that adds so much charm and graciousness to dining.

Carving is an art that demands practice for perfection and also a knowledge of the various meat cuts so that they can be sliced to best advantage. Important, too, are good tools, for even an expert carver cannot work unless he has the proper utensils. Carving sets are manufactured in a variety of shapes of blades and handles. The blade should be of fine quality steel, carefully forged and tempered so that it will take and hold an edge. The carving set consists of a knife, fork, and steel. The large-size set in which the knife has a 9-inch blade for large roasts and turkeys is perhaps more practical than the smaller set with a knife having an 8-inch blade. The forks should have a guard to protect the hands of the carver. The steel is used to sharpen the edge of the knife. The carving knife should be sharpened as necessary, and the carving set should be kept separate from the rest of the kitchen cutlery in order to keep the edge of the knife in good condition. Electric carving knives, now available, facilitate carving.

The cook also has some responsibility in the carving, for the meat should be done properly. If it is undercooked, it will require too much exertion on the part of the carver, and if it is overdone, it will be impossible to get neat slices.

Poultry, still hot from the oven, is somewhat difficult to slice; it slices better when slightly cool.

Carviol. An Austrian vegetable similar to cauliflower.

Caryopsis. A dry one-seeded fruit that grows like a single grain.

Casaba Melon. A large globular melon with a rough-furrowed rind. The ripe flesh is soft, creamy white with a delicate green tone and is sweet and juicy but has little aroma.

Casabe (Latin American). (1) Round flat dried cakes made of grated yucca (cassava or manioc). (2) Cassava flour.

Casanova. A salad made with celery and truffles.

Casareep; Cassareep. A liquid seasoning or flavoring made from cassava in the Guianas, South America.

Cascalope (Obsolete, French). Escalope; thin round steaks of veal usually dipped in beaten eggs, then bread crumbs, and fried.

Cascaval Penir. A Turkish copy of the cheddar-like cheese similar to Italy's caciocavallo.

Casein. A protein produced when milk is curdled by rennet. The fermentation of casein is the origin of all cheeses.

Case Knife. A large table knife.

Caseous. Cheesy; like cheese.

Caseralla. A medium soft, creamy Greek cheese.

Casere. A unique Greek hard, brittle sheep's-milk cheese with an unusual biting quality.

Cashera. A Greek cow's- or goat's-milk cheese similar to Casere. *See* Casere.

Cashew Nuts. Crescent-shaped golden kernels that are white, plump, fairly firm, sweet, and bland before roasting. They are the most popular nut and represent more than half the annual nut imports of the United States. India and Mozambique produce the principal crop, although the trees grow also in many other tropical regions. Cashews do not grow in shells but hang from an applelike fruit called the *cashew pear*. Cashews are processed mainly in India, as a great deal of hand labor is required.

The nut, roasted or pickled, acquires its delicate flavor only after it has been subjected to a high temperature. The milky juice of the fruit

is fermented to make a wine greatly favored in Brazil.

Cashew nuts are not satisfactory for baking because they become too soft.

Cashew-Nut Paste. A cooked mixture of cashew nuts and sugar.

Casing. The substance in which sausage meats are encased. It may be the cleaned intestines of cattle, pigs, or lamb, or it may be a synthetic material.

Cask. A large wooden vessel used for storing liquor or food; usually smaller than a barrel.

Casquinho de Caranguejo (Portuguese). Baked crab meat.

Cassareep (South American). Seasoning made from cassava root. Sometimes spelled Casareep.

Cassata (Sicilian). Frozen desserts. In some varieties spongecake is layered between ice cream and whipped heavy cream, while in others no cake is used.

Cassava; Manioc. Tropical plant whose root is the source of tapioca. *See* Tapioca. *See also* Farinha.

Casse à Roti (French). A dripping pan.

Casseler Rippsspeer (German). Fried salted pork.

Cassemuse (French). Rather hard pastry made in the Touraine region.

Casse-Noir (French). The hawfinch, a small game bird.

Casserole. A term that refers both to the utensil and to the dish cooked in it. Casserole utensils, which have a venerable history, are made of plain or glazed earthenware, Pyrex, heatproof porcelain, heavy-enameled cast iron, or stainless steel

with cast-aluminum bottom; but they must have a tight-fitting cover. Oval casseroles are more practical than round ones because they can accommodate a whole chicken or a roast.

Casserole dishes are a boon to the busy housewife because most of them contain all the ingredients for a one-dish meal, and they can be prepared in advance and be reheated immediately before serving. Many dishes, in fact, are improved by standing, since it permits the various flavors to develop. There is practically no limit to the ingredients that can be included. Meats, poultry, or fish may be combined with a starchy ingredient, such as macaroni or potatoes, and also with vegetables.

Casserole à l'Ancienne (French). Sauerkraut casserole made with smoked meats and roast partridge.

Casserole à la Russe (French). A casserole with high sides.

Casserole à Sauter (French). A shallow casserole or skillet.

Casserole en Terre (French). An earthenware saucepan or casserole.

Casserole-Sauteuse (French). A shallow type of casserole, designed specifically for sautéeing.

Casseruola (Italian). Casserole.

Cassia. The bark of a tree similar to cinnamon and ground in the same manner, but with a less fragrant flavor. Cassia buds are used whole in pickling or ground in baking.

Cassina. A tea-substitute beverage containing caffeine and tannin, made from the cured leaves of a species of holly found in the southern United States. Indians used its brew for medicinal and festive purposes.

Cassiri. A drink brewed in Guyana from the sweet potato or the root of the sweet cassavas; having a very pleasant flavor. In processing the version in which corn is prepared with sweet potatoes and sugar-cane juice, the natives chew the corn in order to convert the starch to sugar; they then spit it into gourds, where it is blended with the other ingredients for fermentation.

Cassis. (1) Black currants. (2) The apéritif drink that is a mixture of black-currant juice, brandy, and sugar. It is most familiar as an ingredient for the Vermouth Cassis. A teaspoon of cassis is added to a third of a glass of dry vermouth, then filled with ice and soda water. (3) The red, *rosé*, and white wines of Cassis on the Mediterranean coast near Marseilles are an ideal accompaniment to the local seafood dishes.

Cassola (Italian). (1) A peasant dish made with pig's feet and ears, sausages, and vegetables. (2) In Sardinia, a fish soup.

Cassole (French). (1) Small casserole. (2) A small open earthenware pot.

Cassolette (French). (1) Small china container or pot, often coated or glazed. (2) Small casserole.

Cassonade. An unrefined sugar; when flavored with rum it is called *cassonade de canne*.

Cassoulet (French). Dried-bean stew made with pork, lamb, preserved goose or duck, and sausages. It is a specialty of Languedoc, where each of the three cities, Castelnaudary, Carcassonne, and Toulouse, has its own variation.

Cassumunar. A spicy East Indian root similar to ginger. A small amount is sufficient to flavor most dishes.

Castagna (Italian). Chestnut.

Castanaccio; Castagnaci (Italian). A flat cake made of chestnut flour; formerly cooked on hot rocks.

Castagnole (Italian). Macaroons made with chocolate and cinnamon.

Castagnon. A fine-flavored French chestnut.

Castane. Chestnut.

Castanha (Portuguese). Chestnut.

Castanhas do Brazil (Portuguese). Brazil nuts.

Castelane (French). A green plum resembling the greengage.

Castel del Monte. See Italy, The Wines of.

Castelli Romani. See Italy, The Wines of.

Castello. See Crema Danica.

Castelmagno. An Italian cheese similar in taste and texture to Gorgonzola.

Castelo Branco. A medium soft Portuguese goat's- or sheep's-milk cheese.

Castilla la Nueva. The region in Spain including Madrid, Toledo, and environs. Good soups include *sopa de ajo Madrileño* (made with garlic) and *potaje Madrileño* (a vegetable soup). Potatoes and beans are the favorite vegetables. All meats are eaten, although roast suckling pig is particularly popular. The *cocido Madrileño* is a classic meat stew. The best food in Spain is shipped to Madrid, which naturally has the greatest range of cuisine.

Castillon. A very perishable, fresh white cream cheese made in Gascony, France.

Castrato (Italian). Mutton.

Casuy (Philippine). Cashew nut.

Catadromous. Denoting fish going to spawn in the sea after having lived in fresh water.

Catalane, À la. In the style originated in Catalonia, Spain; usually indicating the use of rice, tomatoes, and sautéed eggplant.

Catalonia. *See* Spain, The Wines of.

Catawba. A large grape, native to the Catawba River area in North Carolina, and transplanted to the Finger Lakes area of New York and other eastern vineyards. It produces sweet white wines and champagnes, usually blended with other wines.

Catchup. *See* Catsup.

Catechu. A red-brown sap obtained from certain acacia trees; used as a chewing substance in certain parts of Asia. The sap is high in tannin, and is chewed for its stimulating effect.

Catfish. An oily freshwater fish caught in great quantities in southern rivers, chiefly in the Mississippi and its tributaries. Catfish may weigh as little as one pound or as much as fifty pounds. Common varieties are the channel, blue, spotted, fiddler, yellow cat, or groujon. The fish is easily identified by its horned pout. Catfish should be washed very thoroughly and skinned before cooking, as they have a characteristic muddy taste.

Catigot. Fish preparation made with carp or eel, bacon, onion, garlic, tomatoes, bay leaf, saffron, and seasoning.

Catinat. An Italian liqueur made with wild Alpine grasses and herbs.

Catnip. An herb, member of the mint family; used as a tea base and as an aromatic food seasoning.

Cat's-Head Cheese (Colloquial). Edam cheese.

Cat's Tongue (British). A long thin wafer.

Catsup; Catchup; Ketchup. A thick, well-spiced, slightly sweet tomato sauce used as a condiment. In England walnut and mushroom catsups are also used. The word probably derives from the Malayan *kecap*, meaning "taste," which indicates the Eastern origin of this popular condiment.

Cattail. A wild plant used as a salad green or vegetable; the roots may be ground into a flour.

Caudière (French). Fish soup similar to a *chaudrée. See* Chaudrée.

Caudle. Porridge or gruel containing oatmeal or other cereal, and at least some of the following: spices, wine, liquor, beer, sugar, and eggs. This dish enjoyed great vogue in earlier times as a nourishing dish for convalescents, particularly mothers who had just given birth.

Cauldron. *See* Caldron.

Caul. (1) (Obsolete) Cabbage. (2) A thin membrane enclosing part of certain animals' intestines; eaten in certain parts of the world, and used to wrap or enclose sausage meat.

Caul Fat. A thin membrane, composed mainly of fat, covering the low part of a pig's intestines. Often the French and Chinese wrap food in caul fat to preserve its shape or flavor.

Cauliflower. The aristocrat of the cabbage family, grown for its flowers rather than its leaves, cauliflower ranks sixteenth in United States vegetable production. In winter and early spring, most of the crop comes from California; in summer, from New York, first from the Catskills, later from Long Island. Hence, fresh cauliflower is available almost the year around. The fresh heads should be clean, compact, and white or creamy-white; frozen cauliflower, separated into flowerettes before being subjected to below-zero temperatures, is available all year throughout the United States.

Cauliflower likes a moist, cool place, not only when it is growing but also when it is stored. It should be packed in a moistureproof container and refrigerated.

Raw cauliflowerettes, chilled in ice water, are delectable as a relish or in salads. Cooked cauliflower, buttered or creamed, is a popular accompaniment to main dishes. Scalloped cauliflower makes a satisfying main dish for a light meal. Before cooking, the outer stalks and leaves of cauliflower should be removed. The cauliflower, head down, may be soaked about 15 minutes in cold salted water to remove insects. Whole cauliflower heads require about 25 minutes to cook. Use a pan containing a moderate amount of water and without a cover. Flowerettes should be dropped into a small amount of boiling salted water and cooked covered until just tender, about 10 minutes. For a milder flavor, cook the flowerettes uncovered. A piece of bread added to the water in which cauliflower is cooked helps minimize cooking odors. It is best to serve the vegetable immediately, as standing causes the heads to discolor and taste strong, as does overcooking.

Cauponate (Obsolete). One who sells food and liquor.

Cavalla (South American). A golden, good-tasting saltwater fish of the pompano family; weighs 3 to 35 pounds.

Cavallucci di Siena (Italian). Small fruit-and-nut cakes.

Cavally (Obsolete). Horse mackerel.

Cavatoni Rigati (Italian). Curved, ribbed, tubular pasta about 2 inches long.

Cave (French). Wine cellar.

Caveau (French). Small wine cellar; also a special small enclosure for expensive or rare wines.

Caviale (Italian). Dried fish roe; caviar.

Caviar; Caviare. True black caviar is the roe, or eggs, of several varieties of sturgeon. This expensive delicacy is mostly imported from Russia and Iran. The roe is washed, lightly salted, and either packed in ice and sold fresh, or it is processed and packed in glass or tin containers. The largest caviar egg is the beluga, although some regard the smaller sevruga as the finest.

Pressed caviar is less expensive and is available fresh or pasteurized. Many of the *cognoscenti* prefer the flavor of fresh pressed caviar.

Red caviar is the roe of salmon. Saltier and with larger eggs than its black relative, it is best when served with cream cheese, sour cream, or eggs to minimize the salt flavor.

Before being served, caviar should be thoroughly chilled but never frozen. At fine hotels and restaurants the caviar comes to the table imbedded in a bowl of crushed ice. It may be eaten plain, with a dash of lemon juice, or with a sprinkling of chopped hard-cooked eggs or chopped raw onion. *Blini* and sour cream are excellent served with caviar. Connoisseurs prefer it heaped on buttered or plain toast with no accompaniments.

Chilled vodka or dry champagne are ideal with black caviar.

Caviar of the Sea. The sea urchin.

Cavoletti (Italian). Brussels sprouts.

Cavolfiore alla Romana (Italian). Cauliflower in oil.

Cavolfiore Indorato e Fritto (Italian). Fried breaded cauliflower.

Cavolo (Italian). Cabbage.

Cavy. *See* Guinea Pig.

Cay (Turkish). Tea.

Cayenne Pepper. The ground dried ripe fruit of several members of the *capsicum* family. Very hot and pungent, the spice should be used sparingly. A pinch is enough to add zest to foods. A few grains may be sprinkled over clam chowder or oyster stew, or mixed into cream or cottage cheese for a canapé spread. In barbecue sauces cayenne gives the essential bite.

Cazón (South American). The dogfish.

Cazuela (Spanish). Casserole.

C. E.; Cuvée Extra. Special quality or type of wine; an imprecise term used by wine producers.

Cebada (Spanish). Barley.

Cebola (Portuguese). Onion.

Cebolla (Spanish). Onion.

Ceci (Italian). Chick-peas.

Cecils (British). Tiny meatballs seasoned with chopped anchovies, nutmeg, onions, parsley, salt, and pepper. They are brushed with egg, rolled in bread crumbs and fried in fat, then served with clear beef gravy.

Cecina. Dried or jerked beef.

Cédrat. The fruit of the citron or lemon tree, native to ancient Persia, but now grown in southern France and other hot climates; used chiefly in jams, candies, and pastry. A liqueur made from the fruit is called *Cédratine*.

Cédratine. A heavy, sweet liqueur made from cedrats, the lemons grown in Corsica, France.

Cefali (Italian). Bluefish.

Celeriac. *See* Celery Root.

Celery. Two varieties of celery are found in American markets; the green, or Pascal, variety is relatively new. Its greenish stalks are somewhat coarse but completely stringless; the flavor is slightly sweet and nutlike. Yellow or golden celery has been blanched so that the stalks are quite white; it has a less pronounced flavor than the green variety. Both varieties are best when the fairly solid stalks are of medium length and crisp enough to crackle when snapped, and the leaves are fresh and green.

Americans were not the first to appreciate celery. Homer mentions the vegetable in the *Odyssey,* and the ancient Chinese used it for medicinal purposes. During the Renaissance the Italians developed a fondness for celery, but they liked it cooked, whereas in England and later in America the vegetable was more usually eaten raw. Dutch farmers were the first to grow celery commercially in the United States, beginning its cultivation as early as 1874 in Kalamazoo, Michigan. Raw celery is served in many forms, as celery curls on an appetizer tray, stuffed with cheese or other foods as an hors d'oeuvre, or chopped fine in salads or sandwich fillings.

Like the Italians, the French prefer celery braised or cooked in some other way. It was probably the French who discovered the fine flavor celery contributes to stocks, soups, casseroles, and creamed dishes.

Celery has little nutritive value, but it is low in calories, as it is 90 percent water.

Highly perishable, celery needs a cool, moist temperature to stay crisp. Stalks should be carefully washed, dried slightly, and stored in a covered container or plastic bag in the refrigerator.

Celery Cabbage. *See* Chinese Cabbage.

Celery Root; Knob Celery; Celeriac. Turnip-rooted form of celery with the same flavor as the variety cultivated for the stalks. Select fairly small knobs, because the larger roots tend

to be hollow and woody. The roots can be used raw or cooked. The raw vegetable may be cut in julienne strips and served with a mustard sauce as an hors d'oeuvre, or may be ground and seasoned with salt and vinegar. Cooking the root requires 10–20 minutes in boiling water. It may be served hot with butter, pepper, and salt, or cold in a marinade of French dressing. Matchlike strips of celery knob may be deep-fat fried for an interesting variation.

Celery Salt. A combination of salt and ground celery seed that adds a delightful flavor to oyster stew, fish chowders, cole slaw, tomato juice, soup, or fish salads. When adding it to a recipe, reduce the amount of regular salt by one-half.

Celery Seed. A minute, seedlike fruit of a herbaceous plant related to vegetable celery. The whole seeds may be added to salads, sauces, or pickling mixtures, or sprinkled on cheese, crackers, or rolls. Ground celery seed is a seasoning for soups and other dishes whose flavor is improved by celery. *See also* Celery Salt.

Celestine. Any of a number of French dishes of exceptional quality named in honor of Pope Celestine V (1215–1296).

Cellar. Underground storage place for wine or food.

Cellaret. Compartment for wine bottles.

Cellophane Noodles. Clear, transparent noodles, used in oriental cooking.

Celluflour. A powdered cellulose; used in experimental reducing diets to provide indigestible bulk.

Cellulose. A polysaccharide consisting of a long chain of glucose units that forms the supporting cell structure in plants. It is not digestible in man or other monogastric animals but serves to provide bulk for intestinal functioning.

Cena (Spanish). Supper.

Cenci (Italian). Sweet cakes.

Cendré de la Brie. A soft, creamy white French Brie cheese cured in ashes; not good during hot weather.

Cendrée, La. Flat, firm sheep's-milk cheese made in the Loire Valley in France. Cendrée cheeses are also made in the Burgundy, Aube, and Marne regions.

Cendrillon. Cooked in hot ashes or cinders.

Cenoura (Portuguese). Carrot.

Centerba. Liqueur made in Tocco, Italy, from

aromatic herbs growing in the Apennine Mountains. As these herbs are very numerous, the term *cent-erba,* a hundred herbs, is used.

Centolla; Centollo (Spanish). Large crab.

Central America. (Guatemala, Honduras, El Salvador, Nicaragua, Costa Rica, Panama)

While there is a certain resemblance to the food of Mexico, Central American food is generally milder and less highly spiced. However, the basic pattern of Mexico repeats itself to the south, with the same familiar dishes appearing in almost all the countries.

Guatemalans like mashed avocados and bean appetizers; the *cocida a la Criolla* is similar to a French *pot-au-feu,* a soup made with beef and vegetables; *gallo en chicha* is rooster in *chicha* (much like hard cider); *fiambre* is the traditional dish of assorted meats and vegetables eaten each November 1; vegetables are often squash, beans, and the like. Fruit desserts are best, especially those made with bananas. Of course, *tortillas* and *tamales,* from Mexico, are standard fare. Coffee is the national drink.

Hondurans like coffee and a piece of bread for breakfast; their afternoon and evening meals are many coursed and quite substantial. They enjoy all of the Mexican dishes, although *tamales* are here called *montoucas.* Honduran fruits and melons are particularly good, including many rare, unusual types.

El Salvador prefers to serve its chief meal in the middle of the day. There is a local sweet wine, made from a native fruit called *nance;* a cocktail is made from it and called *nancito.* Another local wine, called *marañón,* is served very cold. Typical first-course dishes might include a corn *tortilla* stuffed with cheese or a corn *tamale* filled with meat; the favorite soups are probably those made of beans or seafood. Blue crabs, gray clams, crawfish, and red snapper are about the best of the local catches of shellfish and fish. *Lomo vincentino* is a loin of beef stuffed with bacon, sausage, green peppers, and tomatoes. Chicken is frequently cooked *en chicha,* as in Guatemala.

Nicaragua has some interesting drinks. *Rompope* is the local version of egg nog; *champola* is a soft drink made from *guanábana,*

a tropical fruit; *tiste* is the favorite soft drink made from ground, roasted corn, with cocoa, sugar, and water. There is also a firewater of considerable potency but quite crude in taste, *aguardiente;* this drink is equally popular throughout Central America. A typical Nicaraguan meal might consist of *vigoron,* an appetizer made of pig cracklings, cassava, and pickled vegetables; *sopa de mondongo,* an excellent tripe soup containing local vegetables like *chayote, yucca,* and *chilotes.* The main course might be *baho,* a steamed dinner of beef, bananas, plantains, and cassava, or possibly a *nacatamal,* made with pork, bacon, potatoes, and rice. A favorite dessert is *curbasa,* a combination of separately cooked jam or compote, made from papaya, mangos, and plums. Desserts prepared from cooked bananas, like *maduro en gloria,* are also very popular.

Costa Ricans like to eat frequently throughout the day; sometimes they have regular meals, but frequently during the day they enjoy snacks and soft drinks. Besides consuming innumerable cups of coffee, Costa Ricans like chocolate, beer, and *chicha,* a favorite local ciderlike beverage. *Elote,* green corn boiled in its husks, is a regular item; soups are substantial and filling. *Tamales ticos* are the local version of *tamales,* made with chick-peas, rice, sweet peppers, pork, raisins, and onions. A roast suckling pig, *asado de tepescuintle,* cooked with herbs, is considered a great treat.

Panama has its own specialties. The single most popular local dish might well be the *sancocho,* the soup-stew classic throughout Latin America. Other dishes of note: *conejo pintado,* a braised wild-rabbit dish; *carne a la ropa vieja,* a sautéed beef hash; and *flan,* the favorite custard dessert of all Spanish-speaking countries.

Centrifuge. A machine that exerts a pull many times stronger than gravity by rapid spinning. It is used to clarify liquids by settling the heavier solid in a few minutes that ordinarily might take several days under gravity. It is also used to separate two liquids of different densities, such as cream from milk.

Cep (French). The vine stock.

Cepaceous; Cepous. Resembling an onion.

Cépage (French). (1) A variety of vine. (2) A plant used for growing wine grapes.

Cèpes. *See* Mushrooms.

Cephalopoda. A group of mollusks including the octopus and the squid.

Cepous (Obsolete). Resembling an onion.

Cerago. (1) Honeycomb with bee's honey. (2) Bee-bread.

Cercelle; Sarcelle (French). Waterfowl similar to the wild duck.

Cerdo (Spanish). Pork.

Cere. To rub with spices.

Cereal. *See* Cereals.

Cereal Coffee. Beverage prepared from roasted cereal grains.

Cerealin. A substance in bran that contains nitrogen.

Cereals. Grasses that produce edible grains, the grains themselves, and the foodstuffs prepared from them. Common cereals include buckwheat, corn, rice, oats, wheat, rye, and semolina. Though flours and meals are actually cereals, the term "cereal" is usually applied only to breakfast foods, both ready to eat and those requiring cooking.

Cerejas (Portuguese). Cherries.

Ceres. Goddess of vegetation in Greek mythology; origin of the term "cereal."

Ceres Wheat. A Canadian wheat used chiefly for breadmaking.

Cerevisial. Pertaining to beer.

Cerezas (Spanish). Cherries.

Cerf (French). (1) Stag, hart, or deer. (2) Venison.

Cerfoil (Obsolete). Chervil.

Ceriman. An Asiatic fruit with a pineapple-banana flavor.

Cerkes Tavagu (Turkish). Dish prepared with chicken, walnuts, and red peppers.

Cerneau (French). Kernel of the green walnut.

Cerneaux (French). (1) Green walnuts, a specialty of the Touraine region. (2) Appetizer made with walnuts, green-grape juice, and chopped chervil; made in Touraine.

Cerneaux Confits. Preserved green walnuts.

Cerons. A moderately sweet white wine with a flowery bouquet, produced in Bordeaux, France.

Certified Milk. Milk produced under very high standards of sanitation so as to have the lowest possible bacteria content.

Certosino (Italian). Honey cake filled with citron and almonds.

Certoso Stracchino. A cow's-milk cheese resembling Tallegio, produced near Milan, Italy. *See* Tallegio.

Cerveja (Portuguese). Beer.

Cervelas (French). Well-seasoned fat pork sausage.

Cervelas aux Pistaches. A mild sausage made with pistachios, a specialty of Lyons.

Cervelas Truffé. A large lightly cured truffled sausage.

Cervelle de Canut. French white cheese flavored with chives, salt, and pepper.

Cervelle de Veau (French). Calf's brains.

Cervello (Italian). Brains.

Cervesa Negra. A Philippine dark or black beer.

Cesanese. An Italian wine. *See* Italy, The Wines of.

Cetrioli (Italian). Cucumbers.

Ceylon. In general, the cuisine of this island resembles that of India. Rice, of course, is the staple food appearing at every meal. The majority of dishes are quite highly spiced with powdered Maldive fish, red chili peppers, ginger, onions, and garlic. As a rule, most meat, poultry, fish, or vegetable preparations are served as a curry, but there are many unusual kinds. Some of the more interesting ones are made from ash-pumpkin (a variety of squash), breadfruit, dried sprats (*halmessan bola ambul*), jackfruit (*kos ambul*), green *cadju, katurumurunga* flowers, *kung-koong* leaves, onion leaves, green papaya, and scores of other rather rare ingredients.

The desserts are usually fresh fruit, of which Ceylon has a superb selection. However, there is an entire school of sweetmeat cookery, *rasa kavili,* which includes many unusual items. The Sinhalese have a sweet tooth, and candies, cookies, and puddings are well liked throughout the country. Some of the better-known ones include *aluvā,* made of rice flour and cadjunuts; *āppa,* which translates as "hoppers," and is made from rice flour and coconut milk; *bittara āppa* is an "egg hopper," and is just like an *āppa,* but with an egg; *idi āppung dodol* is molded rice with coconut milk and cinnamon; *kiribath* is country rice cooked with thick coconut milk, and is usually served with sugar and cinnamon, but there are many more, usually made with rice or rice flour.

Alcoholic drinks are of no importance, and the national taste inclines toward fruit drinks. The national drink is tea, produced locally, which is of excellent quality.

Ceylon Spinach. *Basella,* climbing plant with heavy fleshy leaves resembling spinach; used for cooking or in salads.

Ceylon Tea. Various kinds of black tea from the island of Ceylon having a unique flavor and richness. They are grown from low to very high altitudes and vary widely in quality.

Ch. Château; a Bordeaux term designating a wine grown (and sometimes bottled) on the premises of the vineyard.

Chai. Chinese tea; the term is used in Russia and sometimes also in England, Portugal, and parts of Africa.

Chabichou. Goat's-milk cheese, sometimes cone-shaped, made in Poitou, France.

Chablis. Extremely dry white Burgundy wine having a so-called "flinty" flavor which distinguishes it from all other wines. Excellent with all seafood, Chablis is *the* wine to serve with oysters, experts say. *See* France, The Wines of.

Chaboisseau (French). A scorpion or devil fish, usually cooked with other fish in soups or bouillabaisse.

Chabot. A blackfin fish found in rivers of France.

Chaboute. A freshwater fish similar to trout, found in Iraq.

Cha Ching. The classic scholarly treatise on tea written by Lu Yu, in China, in about 780; also called the *Tea Classic.*

Chack (British). A snack.

Chacoli. (1) A light grape juice, white or red, made from Chilean grapes. (2) Sour green wines produced in the Basque region of Spain.

Chad. (1) The young of the sea bream, a food fish. (2) Shad.

Chafer. A pot for heating water to be used in cooking.

Chaff. (1) To thresh corn or grain to remove husks. (2) The husks.

Chafing Dish. A cooking utensil consisting of a deep metal pan set in a water basin supported on

legs over an alcohol burner. For rapid cooking the basin is removed so that the pan sits directly over the burner. Some French copper chafing dishes have two pans besides the water basin, one a very shallow skillet, the other a deep pan. Crêpes Suzette and fondue are chafing-dish specialties. When the chafing dish is used to keep foods hot, as on a buffet, the basin is filled with hot water and inserted between the pan and the burner.

The chafing dish can be used for cooking on the table.

Chai. A storage place for wines, usually above ground. The man in charge is called the *maître de chai.*

Chaingy, Fromage de. A fairly good cheese made during cool months in Orléans, France.

Chain Oven. Oven that bakes food on trays moving on conveyer belts.

Chainside. The bluegill, a freshwater food fish.

Chaintré. A fruity, full-bodied French wine produced in the Commune of Chaintré, south of the Côte d'Or.

Chair (French). Meat.
> **Chair à Saucisse.** Chopped or ground pork meat, usually highly seasoned, used in sausages or stuffings.
> **Chair Blanche.** White meat.
> **Chair Noire.** Dark meat.

Chakchoucka (Algerian). Mixed vegetables with eggs.

Chalakoa (French, Spanish). A light rosé wine of the Basque country.

Chalk. Calcium oxide. Water which contains too much calcium (hard water) is not suitable for cooking.

Challah; Twist. The classic Jewish Sabbath bread;

made with eggs, colored with saffron to a light gold color, and braided.

Chalon. A wine district of the Burgundy region, France. *See* France, The Wines of.

Châlon, Château. A yellowish-to-amber wine of passable quality produced in the Jura region of France.

Châlonnaise, Côte. Region of east central France noted for its large production of low-priced red and white wines.

Chalots (Spanish). Shallots, a very mild onion.

Chalupas (Spanish). A spicy Mexican dish containing sausage, chili, onions, and seasonings.

Cham. To chew or mash.

Cham. A Swiss cheese strongly resembling Emmentaler.

Chamberat. A cow's-milk cheese, similar to Port du Salut, that requires six months to mature; made in France.

Chambertin. An excellent Burgundy wine. The vineyards of Chambertin on the Côte d'Or comprise about seventy acres divided among about twenty proprietors. Chambertin is said to have been Napoleon's favorite wine. The quality varies considerably according to the different methods of cultivation, bottling, etc., practiced by the individual owners. *See* France, The Wines of.

Chambolle-Musigny. A wine district of the Burgundy region, France. *See* France, The Wines of.

Chambord, À la. A method of dressing carp (or other muddy-water fish) by inserting strips of fat, thus larding the fish to impart flavor.

Chambré (French). Of wine, allowed to come to room temperature. However, room temperature is an imprecise notion. In France during the wintertime room temperature is usually much lower than that in the United States.

Chambrer (French). To bring wines out of a cold cellar in order to allow them to come to room temperature; about two hours is sufficient.

Chamois. Antelope, a favorite with hunters; also known for its excellent milk.

Chamomile. *See* Camomile.

Champ. To chew or munch.

Champ (Irish). A vegetable dish; *See* Ireland.

Champagne. This sparkling white wine probably needs no introduction. Poets have extolled it and toasts have been drunk with it on all kinds of happy occasions from wedding feasts to elegant banquets and bon voyage parties.

Vineyards around Reims and Épernay in northern France, where champagne is produced, have been making wine since Caesar conquered Gaul. But the first wines were still. The bubbles were not put into champagne until sometime in the 17th century. Dom Pérignon, a Benedictine monk, has been credited with inventing champagne as we know it today, but whether he was the true inventor or not, he developed the complex process still used in making the wine. It is a blend of various wines of the area combined to give balance and uniformity to the product. Champagne owes its sparkle to a secondary fermentation that takes place within the tightly corked bottle. The grape varieties used are chiefly Pinot Noir and Chardonnay.

Champagne is produced by the same process in other countries, including the United States. Fine champagne is fermented in the bottle in which it is sold; low-quality champagne is made by the "bulk" process. *See* France, The Wines of.

Champagne-Bottle Sizes. Magnum, 2 bottles; Jeroboam, 4; Rehoboam, 6; Methuselah, 8; Salmanazar, 12; Balthazar, 16; Nebuchadnezzar, 20.

Champagne Brandy. Excellent Cognac from Grande Champagne and Petite Champagne, two of the four Cognac districts of France. The label "Fine Champagne" designates a blend of Grande and Petite Champagne with at least 50 percent Grande Champagne.

Champagne Nature. A nonsparkling dry champagne; a very pleasant white wine, particularly good with shellfish.

Champagniser (French). The process of adding bubbles to a wine, especially champagne; the entire process of making champagne.

Champignon (French). Mushroom.

　Champignon de Paris. A white mushroom much used in the vicinity of Paris.

Champinjon (Swedish). Mushroom.

Champoléon de Queyras. A hard skim-milk cheese made in the region of Hautes-Alpes, France.

Champolo. A soft drink made in El Salvador from the guanábana, a tropical fruit.

Champoreau (French). Black coffee with a liqueur or rum added.

Chancaca (Peruvian). Raw, unprocessed sugar.

Chancelier de Gannat. A cheese formerly made in the Bourbonnaise region of France.

Chandler. A supplier of groceries, particularly to ships.

Chank (Hindu). A large shell for serving wine or other food.

Channel Bass. The drumfish, a saltwater food fish.

Chanoinesse, À la (French). With a garnish consisting of creamed carrots and truffles in a sherry-veal sauce; usually served with sweetbreads, chicken, or poached eggs.

Cha-No-Yu. The classic Japanese ceremony of making tea according to the centuries-old ritual.

Chanquetes (Spanish). Small fried fish.

Chantelle. An American imitation of Port du Salut cheese, but with a milder, more pleasant aroma.

Chanterelle. A small yellowish mushroom with a pleasant odor and excellent taste.

Chanticleer. Rooster.

Chantilly (French). Containing whipped cream. Heavy cream whipped and flavored with sugar and vanilla for desserts is called *crème chantilly*.

   Chantilly Baskets. Fanciful containers for desserts and confections; may be made of marzipan, candied sugar, or of cakes baked, scooped out, dried in the oven, then coated with a sweet glaze. Candied fruits mixed with whipped cream are the traditional filling for a chantilly basket.

   Chantilly Cheese. *See* Hablé Crème Chantilly.

Ch'Ao Fan (Chinese). Fried rice with onions, meat, and shrimp.

Chao Tom (Vietnamese). A snack consisting of sugar cane spread with shrimp paste and cooked.

Chaource. A fresh or slightly fermented cow's-milk cheese made in Champagne, France; good from October to early June.

Chapati; Chapatti; Chappati (Indian). A flat bread made by mixing whole-meal flour with water, rolling small pieces of the dough into thin circles like pancakes, then baking crisp on a griddle. Also called *Indian handbread* or *phulka*.

Chapcha (Korean). Stew of vegetables and meat or poultry.

Chapeler (French). To make bread crumbs by crushing bread.

Chapelle-Chambertin. A dry deep-colored red wine with a fairly high alcoholic content; produced in Burgundy, France.

Chapelure (French). Bread crumbs.

   Chapelure Blanc. Crumbs of trimmed white bread forced through a sieve.

   Chapelure Blonde. Crumbs prepared from toasted bread.

Chapon. A slice of French bread heavily rubbed with garlic and moistened with oil and vinegar; a specialty of Provence, where it is cubed and tossed with green salads to supply the garlic flavor.

Chappit Tatties (Scotch). Mashed potatoes.

Char. A salmonlike fish with only pink flesh caught principally in the deep lakes and rivers of France and Switzerland. This delicately flavored fish is available frozen or canned in the United States. The char strongly resembles the *omble chevalier* found in Swiss and French lakes. The American char is actually a trout.

Charal. A small Mexican lake fish.

Charcoal. In wine making, charcoal is sometimes used to purify or remove unwanted coloring. Charcoal is a favorite fuel for the preparation of meats and poultry because it produces an intense heat, and causes the food to become crusty.

Charcoal Biscuits. Biscuits made of dough containing finely ground charcoal, which was highly regarded as a digestive substance. About the turn of the century charcoal biscuits were eaten after dinner to assist digestion.

Charcuterie (French). Prepared meats, especially pork, sold ready to eat.

Charcutier (French). Caterer of smoked, dressed, and cooked meats.

Chard. A leafy green vegetable prepared like spinach. To retain the fullest flavor it should be steamed with only the water that clings to the leaves after washing. The stalks, also delicious, can be cooked separately like celery. The best chard is crisp and fresh-looking, with full stalks and bright green leaves. It is perishable and doesn't travel well, and should therefore be bought only near where it is grown.

Charentais. An aromatic French melon, usually small, with luscious soft pink-orange meat.

Charger. Large serving platter.

Charleroi, Boulette de. A round Belgian cheese made in the vicinity of Brussels.

Charlock. Field mustard or other field weeds.

Charlotte. A very general term used to describe a wide range of puddings, cakes prepared with creams, fruit desserts, and the like. They may be served either hot or cold. Many charlottes are made with buttered bread, cake slices, sponge fingers, and arranged in a mold; the center is filled with fruit, cream mixtures, meringues, etc. In England, charlottes are frequently made with marmalade and bread crumbs.

> **Charlotte de Pomme** (French). Apple charlotte, made with thin slices of bread steeped in clarified butter, placed in a mold, filled with an apple purée, and baked.

> **Charlotte Russe; Russian Charlotte.** A chilled dessert prepared in a mold lined with ladyfingers and filled with whipped cream or with a Bavarian-cream mixture of any desired flavor.

Charlotte Mold. A round mold with straight sides, usually about eight inches deep; used for making charlottes, a type of dessert.

Charmes-Chambertin. A deep red dry wine with a fine bouquet produced in Burgundy, France.

Charmey Fine. A Swiss cheese roughly like Gruyère.

Charnu (French). A wine with robust, full body.

Charoli. An Indian nut of only moderate taste and quality.

Charolles, Fromage de. A goat's-milk cheese made in the Charolais region of France; at its best in April and May.

Charoseth. The traditional mixture of chopped nuts and apples combined with a little wine and served during the Jewish Seder meal at Passover.

Charost. A goat's-milk cheese made in the Berry region of France.

Charqui (Latin American). Jerked beef; that is, meat cut in long slices or strips and dried in the sun.

Chartreuse. (1) A famous liqueur made by the monks of La Grande Chartreuse near Grenoble, France, from a formula given to them by Henry IV in 1607. The original recipe was deciphered and improved by one of the monks, Brother Gerome Manbec, in 1757. The herb mixture was formerly used as an elixir. As a *medicinal* product, the elixir contained 136 different herbs and was bottled at 110 proof; it is still made and sold today in various parts of the world. It cannot be marketed in the United States because the monks refuse to disclose the formula, and United States law requires that pharmaceutical products be labeled with their ingredients.

The liqueurs are made by merely adding honey, sugar, and brandy to the elixir (which is believed to contain hyssop, angelica, balm, cinnamon bark, saffron, and mace, combined with alcohol). Chartreuse is prepared in both green and yellow varieties. The green is 110 proof and the yellow is 86 proof. In America, green Chartreuse is more popular, possibly because it is less sweet. At one time a white Chartreuse was marketed, but it has been discontinued.

The monks were expelled from France in 1903 and moved to Spain until 1935; pre-expulsion Chartreuse is rare, and, when available, sells for over $100 a bottle. (2) (Obsolete) Partridge preparation, customarily containing vegetables. (3) Any dish prepared in a mold whose ingredients are arranged attractively.

Chaschol. A hard skim-milk cheese produced in Grisons, Switzerland; made in wheels about 20 inches in diameter.

Chasoba (Japanese). Vermicelli made of buckwheat flour and green tea.

Chassagne-Montrachet. A wine district of the Burgundy region of France. *See* France, The Wines of.

Chasse. A small glass of liqueur drunk to remove other tastes.

Chasselas. A white grape grown in the Loire Valley of France; used as a dessert and as a wine ingredient.

Chasse Royale (French). Elaborately arranged game dishes or preparations.

Chasseur, À la (French). Usually, with a sauce of

sautéed mushrooms, shallots, and white wine; served with poultry, meat, or eggs.

Chat. A small potato of poor quality.

Chatak. An Indian measurement, much used in cooking, equal to about 2 ounces.

Château. (1) A thick cut of porterhouse steak. (2) Potatoes cut in rather long strips, cooked in butter or oil, and usually crusted on top.

Château Bottled. The finest-quality Bordeaux wines of France. The label *"mise en bouteilles au château"* indicates that the wines have been bottled, labeled, and packed by the vineyard owner before delivery to the shipper. Château wines delivered to the shipper in casks and bottled in his Bordeaux cellars are generally regarded as second-quality.

Châteaubriand, Viscount François August (1769-1848). A French writer; a double-fillet steak was named for him.

Châteaubriand. A method of cutting and preparing beef fillet originated by Montmireil, chef to Châteaubriand, the French writer. A thick piece, usually large enough to serve two or three, is cut from the beef fillet and broiled. In some versions the fillet is wrapped in chuck steak and broiled under high heat until the chuck is completely charred, leaving the fillet inside hot but very rare. Traditionally it is served with Béarnaise sauce.

Châteaubriand Sauce. Sauce prepared with butter, shallots, white wine, tarragon, pepper, and lemon.

Château Grillet. A wine region of the Rhône district of France. *See* France, The Wines of.

Châteauneuf-du-Pape. A famous full-bodied wine of the Rhône district of France, vaguely resembling a hearty Burgundy. As many as ten different grape varieties may be blended to produce this wine. *See* France, The Wines of.

Châteauroux. A pungent, aromatic goat's-milk cheese made in France.

Château Wines. *See* France, The Wines of; *see also* Château Bottled.

Châtelaine. A garnish consisting of braised quartered artichoke hearts, baked tomatoes, braised celery, and sautéed potatoes; usually served with roast lamb.

Chatouillard. A method of preparing potatoes, by cutting them in long spirals and then deep-frying.

Chatre, Fromage de la. A French goat's-milk cheese.

Chatti (Asian). A saucepan or cooking pot.

Chauchas (Spanish). String beans.

Chaudeau (French). A sweet sauce for puddings and similar dishes.

Chaudemer (Obsolete, French). Freshwater fish broiled, then combined in a wine sauce and cooked gently for an hour or two until stew-like in consistency.

Chaudèu. A very firm cooky made with orange flowers around Nice, France.

Chaud-Froid. (1) Poultry dish, prepared hot but served as a cold preparation. (2) Any dish, including fish dishes, served with a chaud-froid sauce. *See* Chaud-Froid Sauce.

Chaud-Froid Sauce. White or brown sauce served with various cold foods, especially chicken. White chaud-froid sauce is made with béchamel and gelatin; brown chaud-froid sauce is prepared with a demi-glaze and gelatin. Sometimes, food coated with chaud-froid sauce is also covered with an additional glazing of aspic; it is then garnished or decorated.

Chaudrée (French). Fish soup or chowder usually consisting of several varieties of fish, eel, and a sauce made with white wine, onions, garlic, and spices.

Chaudron. A small cauldron or pot.

Chauffer à l'Ébullition (French). To heat to boiling.

Chaumontel. Large variety of pear.

Chausson (French). A flaky pastry in the form of a turnover, filled with pâté, minced chicken, jam, or apples; usually eaten warm.

Chautagne. A group of red and white wines produced in the Savoy region of France. The reds are fairly good, the whites mediocre.

Chavannaz. A dry white wine low in alcohol; produced in the Savoy region of France.

Chavanne. Blackfin fish found in French rivers.

Chavender. The chub, a fairly good food fish found in Britain.

Chavignol. A fair, not completely dry, flowery white wine produced in the Sancerre region of France.

Chaw. (1) To chew. (2) To swallow a large mass without chewing.

Chawal (Indian). Boiled rice.

Chawdron (British). (1) Sauce made of spices and chopped entrails. (2) Entrails used as food. The word *chowder* is believed to have developed from this word.

Chayote. A Central American pear-shaped squash, very popular in the Caribbean; may be sliced, coated with batter, and deep-fat fried, or cooked or baked like other squash. Also known as *christophine* in the French West Indies.

Cheats. An English cake fried in deep fat and served with jam or a sweet sauce.

Chebule (Urdu). A dried prunelike fruit with astringent qualities; also called *myrobolan*.

Checkchuka (Algerian). A dish of tomatoes, squash, onions, peppers, and eggplant fried in olive oil, heavily flavored with garlic. It greatly resembles the *ratatouille* of Provence, France.

Checkerberry; Winterberry. The bright red berry of the wintergreen bush that grows wild in acid soil, usually under evergreen trees, in Canada and the northern United States. The berries may be boiled in water to make a sort of tea. The wintergreen flavoring in candy, chewing gum, and toothpaste is now synthetically produced.

Cheddar. Cheddar is by far the most popular cheese in the United States. Cheddar or cheese of a similar type represents 70 percent of the cheese production, excluding cottage cheese, in the United States. Because of the prevalency of cheddar and cheddar-type cheeses, these cheeses are often called "American cheese."

A hard cheese, made from sweet cow's milk and ranging in color from pale to bright yellow, cheddar was first prepared in the village of that same name in Somersetshire, England, probably in the late 16th century. The first cheddar-cheese factory in the United States was opened in Rome, New York, in 1851. Cheddar is cured for at least 60 days, usually 3–6 months. A good aged cheddar with sharp flavor is cured at least a year. *See also* American Cheese; Cheese.

Cheddaring Process. The consolidation of the curd in the manufacture of cheese. After coagulating the milk, heating of the curd, and draining, the curds are piled along the floor of the vat where, in the case of cheddar cheese, they consolidate into a rubbery sheet of curd.

Cheenesuckur (Hindu). A fine quality rice.

Cheese. About 4,000 years ago an Arab commercial traveler poured his day's supply of milk into a pouch made from the dried stomach of a sheep. After a journey of many hours through the desert, he lifted the pouch to quaff his thirst. The liquid was surprisingly thin and watery; but at the bottom of the bag there were white curds which tasted delicious.

This is the legend, perhaps apocryphal, of how cheese originated. At any rate, the making of cheese dates back thousands of years. Rennet, a curdling agent found in the stomachs of sheep and other young mammals, is still very often used in cheese production.

The art of cheesemaking spread from Asia to Europe, where it gradually found its way to every corner of the continent. As there was no exact formula for making cheese, almost every district developed its own variation. Some varieties have become world-famous; for example, France's Roquefort, which is mentioned as early as 1070, and the Gorgonzola of Italy's Po Valley, which was created about 879.

Cheese is made wherever animals are milked, and cheesemaking is often a way of utilizing surplus milk. Cow's milk is generally used, but goat's milk and ewe's milk are also common. Sometimes the milk of camels, asses, mares, buffaloes, and reindeer is converted into cheese.

Tremendous variation occurs in the formulas for making cheese, but the following process is usually followed: milk is coagulated or curdled, the curd is stirred and heated, the whey is drained off, and the curd is then collected or pressed. The cheeses are cured to obtain the desired flavor and texture.

Cheeses can be classified as follows: Very hard (grating cheeses, like Parmesan and Romano), hard (cheddar and cheeses with "eyes," like Swiss and Gruyère), semisoft (Brick, Port du Salut, and Roquefort). Soft cheeses are divided into two categories: ripened (like Bel Paese, Brie) and fresh (cottage and cream cheeses).

Process cheese, an American innovation, is made from one or more natural cheeses of the same variety or of two or more varieties. The cheeses are cut into small pieces, melted, pasteurized, and blended with an emulsifying agent which helps to produce a smooth texture. The pasteurization halts aging so that the cheese can be held at the desired standard level. Process cheeses slice easily and melt readily, but most connoisseurs deplore their lack of a pronounced flavor and often find the very smooth texture unpleasant. Process cheeses may contain fruits, vegetables, meats, and spices or such flavorings as pimiento, olive, and caraway.

Cheese is one of the most nutritious of foods, rich in protein and calcium, and is one of the most economical protein foods. Cheeses vary slightly in their nutritional makeup, but all are nutritious.

Cheese should be refrigerated in a covered container, wrapped in aluminum foil or Saran Wrap or in its original container. Soft cheeses are perishable, as is fresh milk, and should be used soon after purchase. Hard cheeses keep longer, but they may become dry and moldy unless well wrapped and stored in a cool place. If mold develops, it can be scraped off without harm to the flavor or quality of the cheese.

If cheese is to be sliced, it should be removed from the refrigerator and allowed to reach room temperature before being cut. When cheese is to be served as a dessert, let it stand at room temperature for an hour or two so that full flavor will develop. In cooking, remember that cheese fares best at moderate temperatures. High heat and long cooking make cheese tough, stringy, and leathery and may also cause mixtures of cheese, egg, and milk to curdle. To speed melting and blending cheese with other foods, grate or dice the cheese.

Americans (who eat about 12 pounds of cheese per person each year) include it in all courses, from appetizers to desserts. Cheese dips and spreads are favorite cocktail accompaniments. As a main dish, cheese may appear in soufflés, fondues, omelets, and casseroles. Cheese goes into salads and sandwiches, too, and in sauces for vegetables. For dessert, cheese cake is popular or, borrowing a Continental custom, the cheese may be served with fresh fruits.

In France, cheese is served before the dessert as a separate course, accompanied by a full-bodied red wine. Sometimes it may be presented with the salad after the main course, but inflexible classicists of *haute cuisine* frown on that practice. Crackers or sliced dark and white bread and butter may accompany the cheese in France. With Munster, cumin is offered so that diners can season the cheese to their taste. Cheeses like Gorgonzola or Roquefort are particularly delicious with a pear or an apple.

Cheeses

(See also under individual listings)

Aberdeen	Azy (rennet)
Abertam	Backsteiner
Aettekees	Bagnes
Aisy, Cendré d'	Bagozzo; Bresciano
Ajacilo	Baker's cheese
Albini	Ball cheese
Albula	Banbury
Alentejo	Banon
Allgäuer Bergkäse	Barberey
Allgäuer Rahmkäse	Battelmatt
Alpes	Bauden cheese
Alpestra	Beaufort
Alpestro	Beaumont
Altenburger Ziegenkäse	Bellarno
Altsohl	Bellelay
Ambert	Belo Vrhnje
Amou	Bel Paese
Ancien Impérial	Bergkäse:
Andean cheese	Battelmatt
Andorran cheese	Fontina
Angelat	Gruyère
Appenzeller	Montasio
Appetitost	Vacherin
Appetost	Walliser
Arber	Bergquara
Ardi-Gasna	Bernarde
Arrigny	Bernkastel
Asadero	Bitto cheese
Asco	Bleu cheese
Asiago	Blue cheese
Aspe	Bondon
Aurore	Bondost
Autun, Fromage d'	Borelli
Aydes, Fromage des	Boudanne
Azeitão, Queijo do	Bouille, La

Bourgain
Box cheese
Bra cheese
Brandkäse
Branja de Brailia
Branza de Burduf
Branza de Cosulet
Brazo de Gitano
Bresciano; Bagozzo
Brevine
Brickbat
Brick cheese
Bricotta
Brie
Brie Façon
Brique, Fromage de la
Brillat-Savarin
Brina Dubreala
Brine cheese
Brinsen
Brinza:
    Altsohl
    Klencz
    Landoch
    Liptauer
    Neusohl
    Siebenburgen
    Zips
Brioler
Briqueton
Brizecon
Broccio
Broodkaase
Brousse
Brousse de la Vézubie
Bruxelles
Budapest cheese
Bulle
Burgundy cheese
Buriello Calabrese
    (butter and cheese)
Burmeister
Bushman cheese
Buttermilk cheese
Cabecou
Cabrales
Cachat d'Entrechaux
Caciocavallo Siciliano

Cacio Fiore
Caerphilly
Caillados de Vouillos
Caillebottes
Caille de Habas
Cajassou; Cujassou
Calcagno
Calvenzano
Camarguais
Cambridge cheese
    (York cheese)
Camembert
Camosun
Cancoillotte;
    Canquoillotte
Canestrato
Cantal cheese
Caprian
Caprino
Caraway Loaf
Cardiga
Carlsbad
Carré
Carré de l'Est
Cascaval Penir
Caseralla
Casere
Cashera
Castello (Crema Danica)
Castelmagno
Castelo Branco
Castillon
Cat's-Head cheese
    (Edam cheese)
Cendré de la Brie
Cendrée, La
Certoso Stracchino
Cervelle de Canut
Chabichou
Chaingy, Fromage de
Cham cheese
Chamberat
Champoléon de Queyras
Chancelier de Gannat
Chantelle
Chantilly cheese
Chaource
Charleroi, Boulette de

Charmey, Fine
Charolles, Fromage de
Charost
Chaschol
Châteauroux
Cheddar
Chef-Boutonne,
    Fromage de
Chehanna
Cheshire cheese
Cheshire-Stilton
Chester cheese
Chevre à la Feuille
Chevret; Chevreton
Chevretin
Chevrotin
Chevrotin des Alpes
Chevroton
Chevru de la Brie
Chiavari
Chouzé
Chrisalinna cheese
Cierp
Citeaux, Fromage de
Civray, Fromage de
Clabbered cheese
Claqueret (Ciboulette
    de Lyons)
Club cheese
Coeur à la Creme
Coimbra
Colby cheese
Colombières, Fromage de
Combrailles, Fromage de
Commission cheese
Comte, Fromage de
Conches
Condrieu
Coon cheese
Cornhusker cheese
Cornimont
Corse, Roquefort de
Cotherstone cheese
Cottage cheese
Cottenham
Cottslowe
Couhé-Verac
Coulandon, Fromage de

Coulommiers
Coulommiers frais
Cream cheese
Crèche
Crema Danica
Crème de Gruyère
Crème-Double
Crémets
Crémets d'Angers
Crémets de Saumur
Cremini
Creole cheese
Crescenza
Creusain
Creuse cheese
Croissant cheese
Croissant demi-sel
Croquette Marchoise
Crottin de Chavignol
Crowdy; Crowdie
D'Ambert
Damen
Danablu
Danish Blue
Danish Export
Dansk Schweizerrost
Darling
Dauphin
Daventry
Decize
Délices de Rouvray
Demi-Sel
Derby; Derbyshire
Devonshire Cream
    cheese
Dolce Verde
Domaci Beli Sir
Domiata
Dorset; Dorset Blue
Dotter
Double cheese
Double Cream cheese
Double-Creme
Double Dorset
Dresdener Bierkäse
Dry cheese
Duel
Dunlop

Durak
Dutch cheese
Dutch Cream cheese
Edam
Egg cheese
Elbing; Elbinger
Elbo
Emiliano
Emmental; Emmenthal
Engadine
English Dairy
Époisses, Fromage d'
Erbo
Erce
Eriwani
Ervy
Esrom
Etuve
Evora
Farm cheese;
   Farmer cheese
Farm Vale
Femme, Fromage de
Ferme
Feta
Feuilles de Dreux
Filled cheese
Flamengo
Fleur de Deauville
Flotost
Flower cheese
Foggiano
Fontina; Fontini
Forez cheese
Formagelle
Formaggi di Pasta
   Filata
Formaggini
Formaggini de Lesco
Formaggini di
   Montpellier
Fort, Le
Fort de Béthune
Fourme
Fourme d'Ambert
Frankenwein
Frinot
Fromage à La Pie

Fromage Bavarois
Fromage Blanc
Fromage de Boîte
Fromage de Chèvre
Fromage de Monsieur
Fromage de Vendôme
Fromage Fort
Fromage Gras
Fromageon
Fromage Persillé
Fromage Sec
Frometon
Fromgey
Frühstück
Ftinoporino
Furmai Squaquaron
Gaiskäsli
Gammelöst
Gaperon
Garda
Gascony, Fromage de
Gautrias
Geheimrath
Gérardmer
Géromé
Gervais
Getmesost
Gex
Gex Marbré
Gex-Septmoncel
Gien, Fromage de
Gjetost
Gloucester
Glumse
Glux
Goat cheese
Gorgonzola
Gouda
Gouzon
Goya
Grana Reggiano
Gras
Green Bay
Green cheese
Gruyère
Gueyat
Guéyin
Güssing

Hablé Crème Chantilly
Hand cheese
Harzé
Harzkäse
Hauteluce
Havarti
Hay cheese
Heiltz-le-Maurupt
Herbesthal
Hergårdsost
Herkimer
Herve
Hohenheim
Holstein Health
Holstein Skim-Milk
   cheese
Hop; Hopfen
Horse cheese
Hushållost
Ilha
Imperial Club
Incanestrato
Isigny
Isola, Fromage de
Jack cheese
Jiban Homeed
Joban
Jochberg
Jonchée
Josephine
Journiac
Jumeaux
Jura Bleu
Kaiserkäse
Kajmak
Kajmar
Karab
Karvi
Kash Kwanh
Kasseri
Katschawalj
Kefalotiry
Kefir
Kjargaard
Klatschkäse
Klencz
Kloster
Knost

Kochenkäse
Kolos-Monostor
Kolosvarer
Königskäse
Kopanisti
Koppen
Krauterkäse
Krut
Krutt
Kryddost
Kuminost
Kümmelkäse
Kumminost
Labanee
Laguiole
La Mothe Saint-Herage,
   Fromage de
Lancashire
Landoch
Langlois Bleu
Langres, Fromage de
Lapland
Laqueuille Bleu
Larron
Laumes, Fromage des
Leaf cheese
Lebne
Lecco
Leder
Leicester
Leruns
Lescin
Levroux
Leyden
Liederkranz
Limbourg
Limburger
Lincoln
Linies
Liptau
Livarot
Livernon, Fromage de
Livlander
Locatelli
Loches, Fromage de
Lodigiano
Lombardo
Longhorn

Lormes, Fromage de
Lorraine
Lunch cheese
Lüneberg
Macquelines, Fromage de
Magdeburger-Huhkäse
Maigre
Mainuaer
Mainzer Hand
Maiorchino
Majocchino
Malakoff
Manchego
Manur; Manuri
Mâquée
Maribo
Marienhofer
Märkisch
Maroilles
Marommes
Mascarpone
Melun
Merovingian
Mignot
Migras
Milano, Stracchino di
Mimolette
Minas
Mingaux
Minnesota Blue
Mintzitra
Molbo
Moliterno
Moncenisio
Mondseer
Monkshead
Monsieur, Fromage de
Montagne, Fromage de
Montasio
Montavoner
Mont-Cénis
Mont des Cats
Montdidier
Mont d'Or
Monterey Jack
Monterobbio
Montmarault
Montrachet, Fromage de

Morbier
Mostôffait
Mothéry
Mottais
Motte Valsesiane
Mount Hope
Mouse-Trap cheese
Mozarella
Mozzarelle Affumicata
Münster
Mycella
Mysost; Mytost
Nageles; Nagelkazen
Nagelkassa
Nantais
Nessel
Neufchâtel
Nieheimer
Niolo, Fromage du
Noekkelost; Noekkleost
Nordost
North Wilts
Nostrale
Nuits, Fromage de
Oka
Old English
Old Heidelberg
Oleron, Fromage de
Olivet
Olivet-Bleu
Olivet-Cendré
Olmützer Quargel
Oriental Fromage
Orrys, Fromage d'
Ossau, Fromage d'
Ostiepek
Oswego
Oust, Fromage d'
Óvár
Ovcji Sir
Pabstett
Paglia
Palpuszta
Pamproux
Panir
Pannarone
Papato
Parmesan; Parmegiano

Passaur Rahmkäse
Passin
Patay, Fromage de
Pave de l'Auge
Pelardon; Pelardon de
  Rioms
Pelvoux
Pennsylvania Hand
Penroque
Pentele
Péral
Persillé d'Aravis
Persillé de Savoie
Petafina; Petafine
Petit-Bessay
Petit Carré
Petit Gruyère
Petit Suisse
Pfister
Philadelphia Cream
Picodon
Pie, Fromage à la
Pimp
Pineapple cheese
Piora
Pithiviers au Foin
Platte Kees
Pommel
Ponta
Pontgibaud, Fromage de
Pont l'Évêque
Poona
Port Salut; Port du
  Salut
Potato cheese
Pot cheese
Pourly, Fromage de
Poustagnacq
Prato
Prattigau
Pretost
Primavera
Primula
Promessi
Providence
Provolone
P'teux
Quache

Quagliata
Quatre-Sons
Queso Anejo
Queso de Cincho
Quesong Puti
Queysas
Rabaçal
Radener
Radolfzeller Cream
Ramadoux
Rangiport
Raper
Raviggiolo
Rayon
Reblochon
Récollect
Recuit
Red cheese
Regianita
Reindeer cheese
Remoudou
Rhubarbe
Ribbiole; Robbiolini;
  Robiola
Riceys
Ricotta
Ricotta Romano
Rigotte
Rigotte des Alpes
Rinnen
Riola
Rocamdour
Rocroi
Rokadur
Roll cheese
Rollot
Roma
Romadour
Romalour
Romanello
Romano
Romatour de Kempten
  in Allgau
Roncal
Roquefort
Roquefort de Corse
Rouennais
Rougeret

Royal Sentry
Ruffec
Rumilly
Runesten
Rush Cream
Rygeøst
Saaland Pfarr
Saaner
Sage cheese
Saingorlon
Saint-Affrique
Saint-Amand-Montrond
Sainte-Anne-d'Auray
Saint-Benôit
Saint-Claude
Sainte-Maure
Saint-Émilion
Saint-Fargeol
Saint-Florentin
Saint-Gelay
Saint-Gildas-des-Bois
Saint-Ivel
Saint-Loup
Saint-Marcellin
Saint-Nectaire
Saint-Odile
Saint-Paulin
Saint-Rémy
Salamana
Salame
Salers
Salit
Saloio
Saltee
Samsö; Samsöe
Sancerre, Fromage de
Sansoë
Sapsago
Sardo
Sarraz
Sarsenage
Sassenage
Sault
Sauzé
Savoy
Sbrinz
Scamorze; Scarmorze
Scanno

Schabzieger
Schamser
Scharzberger
Schlesische
   Sauermilchkäse
Schlesischer Weichquarg
Schlosskäse
Schmierkäse
Schoenland
Schwarzenberg
Schweizerst
Sec d'Orléans
Seguin
Selles-Sui-Cher
Septmoncel
Sérac
Serai
Serra, Queijo da
Silesian cheese
Sir Iz Mjesine
Sir Mastny
Sir Posny
Slipcote
Smaltost
Smearcase
Sollies-Toucas
Sospel, Fromage de
Soumaintrain
Soybean cheese
Spalen
Sperrkäse
Spiced Leyden
Spitz
Spitzkäse
Sposi
Spra
Steenworde, Fromage de
Steinkäse
Stirred Curd
Store cheese
Stracchino
Stracchino de Milano
Stringer
Styria
Sveciaost
Sweet-Curd cheese
Swiss Green
Szekely

Tallegio
Tamie
Tanzenburger
Tarare, Fromage de
Taviers
Taworg
Teleme
Terzolo
Tête de Moine
Texel
Thion
Thivers, Fromage de
Thoissey, Fromage de
Tholy
Three Counties
Tignard
Tilsit
Tome; Tomme
Tome de Savoie
Toscano
Touareg
Touloumisio
Toupin
Tournon-Saint-Martin
Trappe, La
Trappiste d'Echourgnac
Trauben
Travnik
Traz
Treccia
Trois Cornes
Troô, Fromage de
Troyen

Truckles
Tulle, Fromage de
Tuscano
Tybo
Tzigenkäse
Urda
Uri
Vacharin Fondu
Vacherin à la Main
Vacherin du Mont d'Or
Valdeblore
Valençay
Valio
Vasterbottensost
Västgotaöst
Veneto
Vézelay, Fromage de
Vieux Lille Puant
Villebarron
Villiers-Vendôme
Viterbo
Void
Volvet Kaas
Weisslacker
Welsh cheese
Wensleydale
West Friesian
Whitethorn
Wiltshire
Xaintray
York
Young American
Ziegel

Cheese Bread. A bread made with any cheese to add flavor; best when lightly toasted.

Cheese Butter. A combination of butter with a soft cheese, such as cream cheese or camembert.

Cheese Cake. A rich, creamy cake made with cream or cottage cheese, milk, eggs, and flavorings.

Cheesie (British). A small biscuit eaten with cheese.

Cheeselip. Rennet used in making cheese.

Cheesemonger (British). A dealer in cheese.

Cheese Paring. Paring the rind off a piece of cheese.

Cheese Press. In cheese manufacture, a machine that presses curds.

Cheese Rennet. Any plant whose leaves, sap, or flowers can curdle milk in the cheesemaking process.

Cheese Straws. Strips of puff paste flavored with cheese.

Cheese Vat. Molds where cheeses are pressed and shaped.

Cheese Wafers. Cheese-flavored biscuits.

Chef. Literally, "chief" or "head"; a person skilled in cooking, particularly when employed in a restaurant. A *sous chef* is second cook.

Chef de Cuisine. Person in charge of a group of chefs; director or executive chef.

Chef-Boutonne, Fromage de. A French cheese matured and drained in clay or wooden molds.

Chehanna. Cow's-milk cheese made in Tibet and Mongolia.

Cheilly-lès-Maranges. A dry wine produced near Beaune, France.

Chěkop Manis. A Malayan shrub with small, somewhat leafy young growths; used as a green vegetable.

Chelas. The pincer-like claws of crabs or lobsters.

Chelo; Chelou (Iranian). Rice cooked with melted butter so that a crisp crust is formed on the bottom.

Chelsea Bun (British). A traditional yeast bun; rolled-out dough is sprinkled with sugar and fruit and baked in squares.

Chemise (French). (1) Skin or jacket of the potato. (2) An edible envelope, such as pastry, in which food is often enclosed in Continental cookery. It is said to be *en chemise*. (3) Lined, such as a mold that has been covered with a paste, jelly, or forcemeat.

Chemiser (French). To line a mold with any desired food, such as paste, jelly, or forcemeat.

Chemitrés (French). A type of waffle made in Lorraine.

Chěmpědak. Small species of jack fruit with a somewhat more intense flavor; both seeds and pulp are edible.

Chenas. A fruity dry red wine produced in the Beaujolais region of France.

Chenu (French). Of wine, denoting excellence.

Chen Ya (Korean). Meat fritters cooked in oil.

Cherimoya. A subtropical green fruit with a soft white, juicy flesh of exquisite flavor. Fancy fruit shops in the northern United States offer cherimoyas grown in California and Florida as well as in Hawaii, Central America, and the Caribbean islands.

Cherries. Sweet or sour, cherries are one of nature's most delectable products. Sweet-cherry trees are believed to have grown first around the Caspian Sea and through the Balkans; but they must have come to Europe very early, for mounds of sweet-cherry pits have been found in prehistoric caves of central Europe. Birds probably carried the seeds from Asia to Europe. Sour cherries, which originated in the same area as the sweet, migrated more slowly, perhaps because the birds did not like their sharp flavor.

In the United States, most sweet cherries grow on the West Coast where the winter is mild and

the summer dry. Sour cherries grow mainly around the Great Lakes, especially in Michigan.

Fresh cherries are marketed during the summer months as they are harvested, with the sweet more plentiful than the sour. The sooner they are eaten after picking, the better cherries are. At full ripeness, they are firm, shiny, plump, and well colored.

Although the season for fresh cherries is limited, the canned and frozen fruit is available the year round. Both sweet and sour are packed in various can sizes, the one-pound tin being most common. Most frozen cherries go to commercial bakers and ice cream and preserve manufacturers; some are sold at retail in ten, sixteen, or twenty-ounce packages. Frozen cherry pies are a recent innovation as are canned cherry pie mixes, jellied cherry sauce, and cherry juice.

White cherries, the Queen Anne variety, are now rarely seen fresh in the markets, since the canners buy up the entire crop.

Cherry Bay; Cherry Laurel. An herb, rarely used now, with an almondlike odor.

Cherry Bounce. A general term for several kinds of alcoholic drink all of which have a cherry taste.

Cherry Brandy. A mixture of steeped cherries and brandy, with a distinctive fruity, semisweet taste.

Cherry Gin. An afterdinner drink made with gin flavored with cherries.

Cherry Heering. A Danish cherry liqueur with a remarkable fruit flavor and aroma.

Cherry Laurel. *See* Cherry Bay.

Cherry Marnier. An afterdinner drink made with cherries; produced in France.

Cherry Olives. Pickled cherries, prepared unsweetened, to serve as an hors d'oeuvre.

Cherry Pepper. An extremely hot-tasting pepper; a type of *capsicum*.

Cherry Rum. A mixture of steeped cherries and rum.

Cherrystone. Hard-shell clam about 3 inches in length when mature, after 2 years; important commercially.

Cherry, West Indian; Malpighia. Fruit which is the richest known source of vitamin C, both in its ripe and its green states.

Cherry Whisky. A cherry-flavored whisky used as an afterdinner liqueur.

Chervil. A European annual whose lacy fernlike leaves have an aromatic flavor similar to that of parsley, but more subtle. The basis of many mixed herb seasonings, chervil is one of the standard ingredients of the French *fines herbes*. Used to flavor salads, sauces, and stuffings for poultry, fish, and shellfish, and in soups, stews, and omelets. In some parts of Europe, chervil root is eaten like carrots.

Chervil, Bulbous. A central European plant with rounded starchy roots, much like small potatoes; the roots may be boiled and eaten like other starchy roots.

Cheshire Cheese; Chester Cheese. A popular English cheese first made in the village of Chester on the River Dee. Cheddar and Cheshire cheeses were well known during the reign of Elizabeth I. Cheshire is firm but more crumbly and less compact than cheddar. The curd may be nearly white but is usually deep yellow.

Cheshire-Stilton. A combination of Cheshire and Stilton cheeses with characteristic blue-green veins.

Chesil. A small, smooth green pear of rather good taste and texture.

Chesky. An English afterdinner drink made with whisky and cherries.

Chessel (British). A vat for making cheese.

Chesteine (Obsolete). Chestnut tree.

Chester Cheese (British). Cheshire cheese.

Chester Pudding. Egg custard with almonds, lemon rind, and butter spread in a pastry shell and topped with a stiffly beaten egg white. The American lemon meringue pie derives from the pudding.

Chestnut. Known in Italy as "the bread of the mountains," the chestnut is a thin-shelled, sweet, edible nut encased in a bristly bur.

Early in this century, the United States was an important producer of chestnuts, but some time before 1935 a virulent fungus disease from the

Orient completely wiped out the crop. Chestnuts sold in the United States are imported, mostly from Italy with a few shipments coming each year from Portugal. Italian chestnuts shipped from northern ports such as Genoa are known as *Piedmont chestnuts*, those from the south as *Naples chestnuts*. Chestnut-growing is also an important industry in France, and some of the best nuts are from the Languedoc region.

Marrons are a special, superior variety of chestnut favored by manufacturers of chestnut preserves because it is large and keeps well. The marron has a far less attractive appearance than some of the lesser specimens, which have an invitingly smooth, glossy skin. The skin of the marron is dull, almost dusty-looking, but the meat is superb.

There are two principal ways of preserving chestnuts—whole and as a paste. The preserved whole chestnuts are generally in a sweetened vanilla syrup, or they may be wrapped in foil. They are expensive but attractive garnishes for desserts. Chestnut paste is an excellent spread and may be served in tarts or with whipped cream or ice cream.

Chestnut, Water. *See* Water Chestnut.

Cheval Blanc, Château. An extraordinarily well-balanced dry red wine produced in Saint-Émilion, Bordeaux, France.

Chevalet (French). A piece of bread or toast, covered with a little fat, on which chicken breasts are placed in the preparation of certain dishes.

Chevalière, À la (French). A style of preparing poached eggs in a pastry crust with mushrooms, with a rich cream sauce, decorated with cockscombs.

Chevalier-Montrachet. An exceptional white wine, not bone-dry, produced in Burgundy, France.

Chevaine; Chevanne; Chevasson; Chevène; Chevenne; Chevesne. The chub, a blackfin fish found in many French rivers; usually served fried or in stews.

Cheveuse d'Ange; Cheveux (French). Candy made with young carrots.

Chevre à la Feuille. A French goat's-milk cheese matured in chestnut leaves.

Chevret; Chevreton. Several pungent goat's-milk cheeses produced in various parts of France.

Chevretin. Small squares of goat's-milk cheese made in Savoy, France.

Chevreuse (French). Small tarts usually made of goose liver and served as an appetizer.

Chevreuse, À la (French). A style of preparation in which hard-cooked eggs are coated with grated Parmesan cheese, fried, and served in a ring of puréed green beans.

Chevrier. A green kidney bean sometimes eaten fresh but usually dried.

Chevrotin. A goat's-milk cheese made in the Bourbonnais region of France. It is kept uncovered, under a tree, then eaten fresh with garlic and salt or with sugar and cream.

Chevrotin des Alpes. A strong, aromatic goat's-milk cheese, made in the Alpes region of France; it is aged in a cave 3–4 months.

Chevroton. A French cheese made of equal parts of cow's- and goat's-milk and matured on a bed of rye.

Chevru de la Brie. A soft, creamy white cheese made near Chevru, France.

Chewet (Obsolete). Mixture of fish or meat, chopped up and seasoned; popular during the Middle Ages.

Chewing Gum. A flavored, chicle substance sweetened as desired and popular in the United States. Not precisely a candy, it keeps the mouth moist.

Chianti. *See* Italy, The Wines of.

Chianti Classico. *See* Italy, The Wines of.

Chiavari. A firm sweet- or sour-milk Italian cheese.

Chich (Italian). Chick-pea or lentil.

Chicha (South American). Fermented corn drink.

Chicharo. Green pea.

Chicharrón (Spanish). Pork skin fried crisp; pork cracklings.

Chichester Pudding (British). A baked pudding made with fine crumbs stirred into a custard mixture with stiffly beaten egg white folded in gently, but not thoroughly blended. The baked pudding has a marble pattern and is served with wine sauce or a vanilla-flavored custard.

Chick. The young offspring of a bird or fowl.

Chicken. A general term for birds ranging from young, tender broilers and fryers to roasting chickens, capons, and stewing chickens or fowl.

According to United States government standards, broilers and fryers are young chickens (usually under 16 weeks old) of either sex; they are tender-meated with soft, pliable, smooth-textured skin and a flexible breastbone cartilage. They weigh 1½–3½ pounds. Roasters are young chickens (usually under 8 months old) of either sex; they, too, are tender-meated with soft, pliable skin and with a breastbone cartilage somewhat less flexible than that of a broiler or fryer. Roasters usually weigh 3–5½ pounds.

A capon is an unsexed male chicken (usually under 10 months old). It is also tender-meated with soft, pliable skin. Capons are excellent for roasting and usually weigh 6–10 pounds.

Hens or stewing chickens or fowl are mature female chickens (usually more than 10 months old) with meat less tender than that of a roaster and with a nonflexible breastbone. They weigh 3–7 pounds. Cocks or old roosters are mature male chickens with a coarse skin, toughened and darkened meat, and a hardened breastbone. Spurs may be present on the legs. They weigh 4–9 pounds and are used for stewing.

Chicken Maryland. Chicken coated in flour or bread crumbs, and fried.

Chicken Steak. A fairly tender, boneless piece of beef from the top of the chuck; may be broiled.

Chickling. A green vegetable of inferior quality; best when very young. Dried seeds may be used like beans or lentils.

Chick-Peas; Ceci. Cultivated since antiquity, chick-peas are a dried legume of minor importance in the United States but they are used extensively in India, the Near East, Italy, France, and in most Spanish-speaking countries. In Spanish and Latin American cooking, where they are known as *garbanzos,* the peas are most popularly prepared in soups and stews. In Mexico, where they are often served in tomato sauce, the peas must be replanted every few years with seeds brought from Spain, for Mexican soil causes the seeds to toughen after a time.

In North Africa, chick-peas are a traditional garnish for the classic *couscous.* A popular hors d'oeuvre in Italy, France, and the Near East consists of cooked chick-peas marinated in oil and vinegar and perhaps further flavored with chopped onion or parsley or bits of pimiento, and served cold. Both dried chick-peas, which must be soaked before cooking, and canned chick-peas, which are ready to use, are available in grocery stores.

Chico. An oriental fruit with a chocolate taste.

Chicon. Romaine lettuce grown in central and southeastern France.

Chicorea (Portuguese). Chicory.

Chicory. A name given to a number of different vegetables. One type, called either chicory or *curly endive,* has narrow, curled, feathery leaves and is sold by the head for salad greens. It is related to the dandelion and closely resembles the parsnip and the sugar beet. This is the plant whose root is roasted and added to coffee. The brew made from a blend of coffee beans and roasted chicory root is particularly favored in New Orleans.

The term *endive* is also used for the tight, blanched heads of a salad vegetable sold in the United States during the winter months. It comes from Belgium, where it was first grown in 1845 on the outskirts of Brussels. This endive, sometimes called chicory in the United States, is called *witloof* in Belgium, and is used in salads or as a braised or a creamed vegetable. It is believed to have originated in Egypt.

Chicoty. Chicken, ham, and tongue rolled around a small gherkin and served as an hors d'oeuvre.

Chifa (Peruvian). The term used in Peru for Chinese restaurant.

Chiffonade (French). Vegetables cut into fine strips or ribbons and generally used to garnish clear or thick soups. In the United States, a chiffonade dressing for salads is one in which French dressing is enhanced with chopped parsley or green pepper, pimiento or pickled beet strips, and hard-cooked egg.

Chiffon Cakes. Light, very fluffy cakes usually made with liquid shortening. Though fine-grained and tender, they do not crumble and tend to remain moist and fresh for quite a while; good unfrosted or frosted. *See* Cake.

Chiffon Pies. Light-textured pies made with gelatin and beaten egg whites.

Chikoo. A dark-brown Indian fruit whose taste suggests both that of a fig and that of an apple.

Chikuwa (Japanese). Broiled fish cake.

Chilbe (Israeli). A type of spicy peanut butter, popular in Israel.

Chile. Chile is undoubtedly the most food-conscious nation in South America and with good reason, for this long, narrow country has better resources than any other Latin American country, especially with respect to seafood. There are ocean fish like swordfish, *congrio,* and *corbina,* all of excellent flavor. But in addition, Chile has some unique shellfish: *locos* (a sort of cross between a scallop and an abalone); *chorros* (giant clams); *jaibas* (crabs); *erizos* (sea urchins); there are also lobster, shrimp, oysters, and mussels, of surpassing excellence of flavor. The classic treatment for shellfish is to prepare it as a *chupe*, which may be described roughly as a spicy seafood chowder. *Caldillo de pescado*, the Chilean fish soup, is also extremely good.

Some favorite dishes: *carbonada*, a beef stew with vegetables; *charquicán*, a type of hash often made with dried meat; *caucau*, tripe cooked with garlic, onions, and potatoes; *valdiviano con huevos*, a soup made of dried beef and eggs; *corderito estofado*, lamb stewed with potatoes and vegetables; *humitas*, a favorite corn dish; *pastel de choclo*, a sort of corn pie made with chicken and hard-boiled eggs; *empanaditas de crema*, small cream pies served for dessert. *Mazamorra morada* is a purple-flavored corn dessert, with a startling color and interesting taste.

An Indian dish of some interest is *curanto en olla*, which means "food in the pot." It is an unusual combination of seafood, poultry, and meat cooked together, often for several hours. Chilean beer is good, but the wines are even better. The local grape cider, raw or boiled, is served before lunch or as a refreshing afternoon beverage. *Chacoli* is a grape cider having a higher degree of fermentation.

Chile, The Wines of. *See* South America, The Wines of.

Chili; Chile; Chilli. The Mexican pepper, varying in color from yellow through brown into deep red. The peppers may be extremely mild, medium, or burning hot. Chilies come in miniature sizes (such as the Tepin or Piquin) up to extremely large types (the Poblano, for example). Chilies may be used in the dried form (Pasilla, Mulato, Piquin, Ancho, and Tepin) or fresh (Pimiento, Poblano, Jalapeño, Chipotle, etc.). Chili peppers should not be confused with chili powder, which is a blend of spices.

Chile con Queso; Chili con Queso (Spanish). A spicy dish made with chilies and cheese.

Chili Sauce. A spicy red sauce made from tomatoes, spices, onions, garlic, sugar, vinegar, and salt. It is similar to catsup (ketchup) but contains more cayenne, onions, and garlic.

Chilled Eggs. Eggs kept just above the freezing point, as a method of cold storage.

Chillie Padi (Malayan). A small very burning chili pepper.

Chimaja. The root of a Mexican wild-cherry tree. Chopped, dried, and ground, it is used as a condiment.

Chimay, À la. Baked stuffed eggs prepared with dried mushrooms and Mornay sauce.

China. Of the four great cuisines—French, German, Italian, and Chinese—the Chinese is sometimes considered the greatest or the second most important culinary style in the world. For pure ingenuity, scope, and variety of dishes, the Chinese cuisine leads all the nations.

Just as there is French provincial food, with dishes varying from one province to another, so there is a wide variation in Chinese cookery styles. China is an enormous country, with the world's largest population, and of course ingredients differ from one region to another. Although the most popular of all Chinese cookery styles in the United States (and in China, for that matter) is Cantonese, it is only one of the styles. Others of importance include those of Honan, Szechuen, Fukien, Shantung, Peking, and Shanghai. *Cantonese* food is usually "scrambled" or "stir-fried" (*chow*) in the pan; it features many noodle dishes and not a few using shellfish and vegetables. *Honan* dishes are somewhat spicy, there are numerous sweet-and-sour preparations, and the food is moderately rich. *Szechuen* is the hottest and spiciest cookery style in China, the dishes tending to be somewhat oily. *Fukien* always features soups, sometimes several at a meal; the food is less heavy than in other provinces. *Shantung* often cooks with wine, and the dishes are quite light. *Peking* food resembles that of Shantung, although it is cooked with more spice; Peking features mutton, Peking-style duck, and steamed bread. *Shanghai*-style dishes are frequently steamed rather than fried, and sweet-and-sour pork is a great specialty.

By Western standards, Chinese cooking uses many exotic and unfamiliar ingredients. Most Americans believe that sharks' fins and ancient eggs are everyday foods; in point of fact, they are not, being too expensive. Much more important for the vast majority of Chinese are such ingredients as fresh ginger root, peanut oil, scallions (green onions), garlic, bean paste, sesame oil, Chinese "vinegar," Chinese "wines," monosodium glutamate, bamboo shoots, bean sprouts, noodles, and soy sauce (this last taking the place of salt, as used in Western cooking).

At present the Chinese government is urging the people to eat all their meals at large catering establishments, and discouraging the traditional custom of family meals. However, the old habits persist, and as Chinese people are fond of tradition, there is considerable resistance by the public. Most families eat three meals a day, at what Westerners would regard as normal hours. Breakfast, early in the morning, consists of boiled noodles or *congee,* rice cereal, and tea. At midday, there is often soup, and about four or five different dishes all served at the same time. The evening meal is similar, but the dishes served at lunch are never repeated. Desserts are unimportant, except that fresh fruit may occasionally be served. Tea is usually the only beverage, and most Chinese drink it after eating, not during the meal. The people like to eat frequently during the day, and are fond of nibbling watermelon seeds, nuts, and the like. Especially popular are *dim sum,* which are small pastries or boiled dough filled with various ingredients. Those who can afford it often enjoy a dish of noodles at bedtime.

Chinese food is eaten with chopsticks, although a spoon is served with soup. Of course, food must be cut into small bite-sized pieces so that it may readily be picked up with chopsticks, for no knives are used. Everyone is served with an individual bowl of boiled rice, and most people call for a second portion.

They do not drink coffee, and there are no strong liquors, although there is a so-called "whisky." However, certain Chinese alcoholic beverages, called "wines," are popular. The best-known include *shiu jo, ching moy, nor mai jo,* and *moy gwai loo.*

China. A thick, fleshy root stalk similar to sarsaparilla; sometimes used as a flavoring ingredient or in soft drinks.

China Orange. (1) A sweet Chinese orange. (2) The *naranja dulce* of Latin America.

Chinchang (Malayan). Water chestnut.

Chincapin. *See* Chinquapin.

Chine. A cut of meat consisting of parts of the backbone and adjoining parts; also known as *saddle.*

Chinese Artichoke; Japanese Artichoke. A type of very white tuber, having an excellent taste, prepared like ordinary white potatoes.

Chinese Cabbage. A green vegetable of the mustard family sold as cabbage. The thick, smooth leaves are light green to white, and the heads average about 4 inches thick and 18–20 inches long. This market garden crop is used in salads or is cooked like spinach.

Chinese Date; Chinese Jujube. A Chinese fruit of various sizes and species. It resembles the date and may be used in preserves and pastries or candied.

Chinese Eggs. Various dishes known as Pidan, Houeidan, and Dsaoudan according to the method of preparation. Fresh duck eggs are covered with a mixture of caustic soda, burnt straw ash, salt, and slaked lime, and are stored for several months. The white and yolk coagulate and become partially discolored.

Chinese Gooseberry. A small round fruit with a brownish hairy exterior. The pale green flesh is delicious and may be eaten plain or with a little sugar. The chief source of supply is New Zealand.

Chinese Ham. Ham cured by a method originally used in China; the taste resembles that of Smithfield ham.

Chinese Mustard; Chinese Cabbage. Another variety of the mustard family cultivated in China for its leaves, which are cooked like spinach. *See* Chinese Cabbage.

In Chinese resaurants in the United States the condiment known as Chinese mustard is dry English mustard or mustard powder to which water is added to release the volatile fiery oils.

Chinese Plum. A very sweet yellow plum.

Chinese Radish. A very large vegetable resembling an overgrown radish but tasting like a turnip.

Chinese Vinegars. White, red, and black vinegars made from rice.

Chinese Watercress. *See* Watercress, Chinese.

Chinese Watermelon. A watermelon with a waxy, hairy skin and white flesh containing cucumberlike seeds; used mainly for making preserves in the oriental cuisine; also used as a soup.

Chinese Wines. In China wines are usually made from rice and are known as *rice wines*. However, wines and beers, either light or dark, are also made from millet, wheat, and beans.

Chingara, À la. With a *sauce espagnole*, made with julienne-cut ham, tongue, truffles, and mushrooms; usually served with veal or poultry. *Chingara* is a corruption of *Zingara* meaning *gypsy*.

Chinguirito. A Mexican alcoholic beverage.

Chinkiang Vinegar (Chinese). A black rice vinegar made in Chinkiang; used as a condiment for dipping foods.

Chinois. (1) A fruit similar to the tangerine. (2) A cone-shaped sieve with fine holes.

Chinon. A wine district of the Loire River region. *See* France, The Wines of.

Chinonaise, À la. With a garnish consisting of stuffed cabbage, apple slices dipped in parsley and baked, with a brown sauce; usually served with roast meats.

Chinquapin; Chincapin. A small sweet chestnut native to Virginia and other southern regions of the United States.

Chin-Ye-Hin (Burmese). Soup flavored with lemons and limes.

Chiodi di Garofoni (Italian). Cloves.

Chipa Paraguay; Chepa Paraguay (Paraguayan). Bread made with cheese and potato flour.

Chipilin (Mexican). Leaf used for flavoring sauces and soups.

Chipolata. (1) A mild, pleasant-tasting onion. (2) A very small pork sausage seasoned with chopped chives.

Chipped Beef; Dried Beef. Beef pickled for 30 days in the same manner as corned beef, then smoked for 2 days, and dried for 2 weeks. The meat is then sliced wafer-thin by machine. Originally dried beef was sold mostly in 2½- and 3½-ounce glass jars. Now much of it is packed in quarter-pound pliofilm envelopes to serve 6, and it can be stored in the freezer.

Chipped beef either in glass jars or pliofilm envelopes is a stand-by for the emergency shelf. It may be used in that old, somewhat tiresome creamed chipped beef on toast, or it may be prepared more elaborately.

Chips. The food most commonly served in the form of chips is the potato. Potato chips are very popular for munching with cocktails and for snacks. Raw potatoes are cut into thin slices, dropped in cold water, dried, and fried in hot fat for a few seconds. They may be served hot or cold. Commercially prepared potato chips are sold in clear paper bags or in large boxes.

Bananas, parsnips, carrots, and turnips may be prepared in the same manner.

Chirimorriñón; Cherimoya (Spanish). The custard apple.

Chirivías (Spanish). Parsnips.

Chisel; Chissel. Bran; coarse flour.

Chiselly Bread. Coarse dry bread.

Chito Melon. A melon of rather poor taste and texture raised almost exclusively for its rind, which makes an excellent pickle or relish.

Chitterlings. Cooked animal intestines, popular in the southern United States.

Chive. A kind of kitchen knife.

Chives. A member of the leek and onion family, chives are cultivated for their thin, tubular green stalks which have many uses in recipes where a mild onion flavor is desired. Also, because of its lilac blooms, the plant is popular for edging herb and kitchen gardens.

Chive plants may be grown from seed or by planting bulblets in fairly rich soil. Plants bought from the grocery store will usually flourish if they are transplanted into larger pots in good soil and placed in the sunlight.

Only the young leaves of the chive plant are used for culinary purposes. The leaves can be clipped with scissors down to the level of the earth. Though they can be quick-frozen satisfactorily, they do not dry well. Since much of their flavor is lost in cooking, it is best to use the chopped green leaves as a last-minute sprinkling atop cream soups and vegetables and in salads, salad dressing, herb butters, and cottage cheese.

Chivey. In Maine, the whitefish.

Chivo (Spanish). Goat.

Chivry, À la. Prepared with a sauce made from a basic cream sauce, white wine, herbs, and spices; usually served with chicken or eggs; a garnish for poached eggs served on sautéed bread, with asparagus.

Chlodnik; Kolodnik (Polish, Russian). Cold sour vegetable soup, prepared with fresh and pickled cucumbers and yoghurt.

Chlorophyll. Green coloring matter found in plants.

Choclo (South American). Corn.

Choco (Portuguese). Cuttlefish.

Chocolade (Danish, Dutch). Chocolate.

Chocolade-Melk (Dutch). Chocolate milk.

Chocolate. (1) A hot beverage made with milk and sugar combined with cocoa. (2) A confection in solid form eaten as candy.

Cacao beans are dried, roasted and polished, then crushed. A thick, brownish liquor results, which contains about fifty percent cocoa fat; when cooled, and some of the fat partially removed, it is made into blocks, or squares called bitter chocolate. With some sugar added, it is known as bittersweet chocolate. *See* Cocoa and Chocolate.

Chocolate Coverture. Chocolate coating.

Chocolate Dipping Table. An area holding several pans of dipping chocolate kept liquid by steam pipes.

Chocolate Enrober. Machine that puts a chocolate coating on cakes and candies.

Chocolate Kettle. Tank where chocolate is mixed.

Chocolat Mélangeur (French). Machine for grinding chocolate into a paste.

Chocozuela (Spanish). Top sirloin of beef.

Choesels (Belgian). Stew made with tripe and sweetbreads, sometimes with oxtails.

Choke Apple. Crab apple.

Choke Cherry. Two kinds of astringent cherries used for jams and preserves.

Choke Pear. A harsh pear; best when cooked as a compote.

Choklad (Swedish). Chocolate.

Chokladglass (Swedish). Chocolate ice cream.

Choko. A bitter Philippine fruit roughly resembling a pear.

Choky. Of fruit, hard to eat.

Cholent. A classic Jewish dish made of beans and meat cooked overnight.

Cholesterol. A fatlike substance found in the human body. Excessive amounts in the blood are believed to be a contributing factor in heart attacks. Cholesterol is measured by milligrams for each 100 cubic centimeters of blood. In the United States, under 225 is considered low; 226–259 is medium, over 260 is regarded as high. The cholesterol content of foods is set forth under Foods, The Composition of (under Fatty Acids).

Cholum. Indian millet grown for food.

Chondrin. A gelatin-type substance sometimes used in the manufacture of food.

Choo-Cha. One of the best Chinese green teas.

Chop. (1) To cut into fine pieces. (2) A cut of meat from the rack or the loin (for example, pork, veal, lamb, or mutton chops). (3) Either the grade of Chinese tea (for example, *first chop*) or a special brand or lot.

Chopa (Spanish). A type of gray bream, found in warm European waters; good taste.

Chop Dish. Small platter for serving chops.

Chope (French). Tankard of beer, usually with a 12-ounce capacity.

Chop House. A restaurant specializing in steaks and chops.

Chopped Beef. *See* Hamburger.

Chopper, Meat. (1) A person, such as a butcher, who cuts up meat. (2) A utensil used for chopping meat.

Chopping Board. Sturdy board, usually made of hard wood, for chopping and mincing foods.

Chopping Bowl and Knife. A sturdy wooden bowl, usually made of hard wood, and a semicircular knife used to dice and chop food.

Chopsticks. Chopsticks, with which all food is eaten in China, Japan, and Southeast Asia, are usually made of a certain species of hard, durable Chinese bamboo, which is stainless and washes easily. Sometimes chopsticks, tapered sticks about 10–12 inches long and 3/16 inch thick, are made of ivory with carving and tracery on their sides.

The proper holding of chopsticks is the first step to using them with ease. Pick up the sticks with the squared ends in the hand, the rounded points being the "business end" of the sticks.

1. Hold them so that the ends are even; even them off by pressing them against the plate.

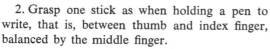

2. Grasp one stick as when holding a pen to write, that is, between thumb and index finger, balanced by the middle finger.

3. Grasp the second chopstick similarly between thumb and index finger, but balanced by the third finger.

4. The basic, or second, chopstick is held motionless, or nearly so, when picking up food; the first, or "pen" chopstick is the one which moves in a pincerlike action to pick up food and hold it between the two sticks.

Chop Suey. The meaning of this term in Cantonese is "odds and ends," but though it has a Chinese name, the dish originated in the United States. Legend has it that during the gold rush in the West some prospectors somewhat inebriated arrived late at a small restaurant and demanded dinner. The Chinese cook protested that there was nothing left, but the men refused to budge until they had been served. Finally the cook tossed together whatever leftovers were available in the kitchen and served them on rice. The men, highly pleased with the dish, asked its name and the cook replied "chop suey."

Whatever the gold-rush cook may have used in his dish, chop suey, which has become one of the most popular dishes in the United States, now usually includes in its melange of ingredients: bean sprouts, water chestnuts, soy sauce, mushrooms, sliced pork or chicken, or assorted chopped vegetables.

Chorizos. Hot Spanish sausages made with lean and fat pork and pork liver seasoned with cayenne pepper, sweet red peppers, salt, and juniper berries; often cooked with chick-peas or *garbanzos*.

Chorley Cakes (British). Round breads with a currant filling.

Chorogi. *See* Chinese Artichoke.

Choron. (1) Béarnaise-tomato sauce served with fish, sea food, or meat. (2) A garnish consisting of the sauce, artichokes, asparagus, and peas, served with beef.

Chotahazri (Anglo-Indian). A light early breakfast.

Chou Paste. A paste made with water, butter, flour, and eggs, which can be made into cream puffs or fried into little puffs and filled with any desired filling. Sometimes Choux. *See* Choux.

Chou (French). Cabbage.

    Chou-au-Lard. German-style cabbage cooked with bacon.

    Chou Blanc. White cabbage.

    Chou de Mer. Sea kale.

Chou de Milan. Savoy cabbage.

Chou de Siam. Kohlrabi, or cabbage turnip. The three varieties are green, purple, and white.

Chou Frisé. Curled Savoy cabbage.

Chou Navet. Turnip-rooted cabbage.

Chou Palmiste. Palm cabbage.

Chou Vert. A variety of cabbage whose leaves grow loosely outward and are very green when ripe.

Chouca. Jackdaw, a bird found in the French Alps and other parts of Europe; prepared like any small game bird.

Chouée (French). Provincial dish consisting of cooked green cabbage soaked liberally in butter, and pressed into any desired shape.

Choucroute Garni; Choucroute à l'Alsacienne. Cooked sauerkraut, served with smoked meats or sausages.

Choupiquel. Freshwater blackfish.

Choux (French). Literally, "cabbages"; a cream-puff pastry (pâte à choux).

Chouzé. A fresh cow's-milk cheese made in the Touraine region of France.

Chow (American, Colloquial). Food, especially in the military service; the term is undoubtedly a variation of pidgin Chinese chow-chow.

Chow-Chow. Relish consisting of sweet pickle mixed with mustard.

Chowder. Soups, usually rich and often containing fish or shellfish, although there are also vegetable chowders. Most fish and sea-food chowders have a seasoned milk base, with the fish and vegetables cooked until tender but not puréed. Manhattan clam chowder is not traditional in that tomatoes are used instead of milk.

Chowder Beer. An alcoholic drink made by boiling black spruce, molasses, and water.

Chowl (Indian). Rice.

Chow Mein. A dish popular in China, containing fried noodles and generally made with chicken, pork, or shrimp.

Chow Yuk (Chinese). Any dish made of pork combined with vegetables.

Chremslach. A kind of pancake, used in the Jewish Passover celebration.

Chrisalinna Cheese. A hard cow's-milk cheese made in the canton of Graubünden, Switzerland.

Christe-Marine. A marine plant used for an inferior gherkin or relish.

Christian IX Cheese. A Danish spiced cheese.

Christmas. This holiday is usually an occasion for an elaborate meal, the menu varying from country to country. In the United States, Christmas dinner may feature such items as clam chowder, shrimp cocktail, roast turkey, ham, or lamb, sweet potatoes, pies (particularly mince), and cakes. In England, the main course may be roast beef or a bird, but the dessert is sure to be a plum pudding. In France, the réveillon is served after Midnight Mass. It is as elaborate as the tastes and means of the family permit, but usually emphasizes rich pâtés, truffled dishes, pastry preparations, and game.

Christmas Melon; Santa Claus Melon. Golden-colored fruit with a mottled green surface. It has a sweet flavor and requires delicate handling. When ripe, it has a pungent, pinelike odor. Ripeness is best determined by the pressure test. Available quite late in the year, often these melons are an expensive December delicacy.

Christopher. Baneberry, a mediocre-tasting berry.

Christophine; Chayote. Pear-shaped vegetable with a taste similar to that of squash.

Chrysanthemum. Edible plant similar in taste to cauliflower; eaten in the Japanese diet.

Chub. Very bony freshwater fish similar to carp; native to southern waters; may be used for cooking.

Chuck. To the wholesale meat dealer, shoulder section of a side of beef, including that portion of the forequarter remaining after the rib, fore shank, brisket, and short plate have been removed.

To the shopper, the boned meat deriving from this cut that is sold either as a roast or as a steak, both of which should be either braised or simmered in liquid.

Chuck Wagon. Originally, a wagon carrying pots, pans, and other cooking equipment as well as food for cowboys and farmhands in the western United States; now, diners, outdoor restaurants, etc.

Chucrut (Spanish). Sauerkraut.

Chu Fan (Chinese). Boiled rice fried with ground

meat, mushrooms, water chestnuts, and a beaten egg.

Chufas; Earth Almonds; Rush Nuts. Small, hard, tuberous roots resembling peanuts; grown in warm climates, where they are eaten either raw or baked, fresh or dried, like peanuts. In Spain *horchata,* a delicious milky drink, is prepared from chufa nuts.

Chuff (British, Colloquial). Bread.

Chukar. An excellent-tasting Indian and Iranian partridge; prepared like all small game birds.

Chuletas (Spanish). Chops.

 Chuletas de Cerdo. Pork cutlets.

 Chuletas de Cordero. Lamb cutlets.

 Chuletas de Ternera. Veal cutlets.

Chu Min (Chinese). Fried noodles combined with pork and vegetables.

Chuño. A Bolivian Indian method of alternately freezing and thawing potatoes to remove most of the moisture. This results in an extremely starchy, very small potato with a distinctive cheeselike flavor. *See* Bolivia.

Chupatty (Indian). Pancakes made of coarse wheat flour and unleavened; shaped by hand and cooked on a griddle.

Chupe (South American). Thick soup or stew made usually with shellfish. An outstanding dish, it is prepared in many different ways, depending upon the ingredients used and the locality.

Church-and-Chapel. A loaf of bread made with enough dough to allow it to rise high in the pan, and deeply slashed down the center so that the rising crust will overlap the sides of the pan like large overhanging eaves.

Churn. (1) Old-fashioned turning appliance, operated by hand, for churning milk into butter. (2) To stir or mix cream to make butter.

Churn Milk. Buttermilk.

Churrasco (South American). Generally, a method of broiling or barbecuing meat, especially beef, over an open fire.

Churros. (1) (Mexican). Crullers. (2) (Spanish). Sweet fritters.

Chu Sun (Chinese). Bamboo shoots.

Chutnee. *See* Chutney.

Chutney; Chutnee. A spicy-sweet relish. There are several brands of chutney on the market, some made in this country, some in England and India. India is the home of chutney, the recipe for which varies considerably, although most popularly it includes tamarinds, mangos, raisins, garlic, shallots, apples, pimientos, mustard, brown sugar, and vinegar. It is usually served with curries. In the United States, home cooks and canners sometimes make tomato, peach, apple, and gooseberry chutneys, all well spiced.

Chyle. A milklike liquid consisting of lymph and partly digested fat, formed out of the chyme in the small intestine of the human being.

Chyme. A spongy substance into which food is changed by the action of the human stomach.

Cibarious. Edible.

Cibation. Eating or taking food into the body.

Ciborium. (1) The vessel used in religious services to hold the consecrated bread of the Eucharist. (2) A drinking cup in ancient Roman times.

Ciboule. A sort of onion-garlic much used in French cooking. Also, the Welsh onion and sometimes the scallion.

Ciboulette; Civette (French). Chives.

Cibrio (Italian). Fricassee or stew of chicken livers, giblets, and cockscombs.

Cicala di Mare (Italian). "Cricket of the sea," a shellfish resembling the shrimp and prepared in similar ways.

Ciceler (French). To score; to make cuts on the surface of meat or fish before cooking.

Cicely, Sweet. An herb in the parsley family, used as a flavoring ingredient since early Roman times. In France, it is used as a food flavoring, and also in the making of liqueurs, notably Chartreuse.

Cicharon (Philippine). Pork cracklings.

Cich Pea (Obsolete). Chick-pea.

Cider. Fermented or unfermented apple juice. Cider should be made from sound apples, especially a blend of two or more varieties; when culls or windfalls are used, the beverage lacks the fine flavor of that made from top-quality fruit.

Cider is made by grinding apples to a pulp, then passing the pulp through a press to extract the juice. The dark liquid thus obtained is apple juice; if it is sterilized at that point, it remains apple juice. Sweet cider may be partially fermented, but fermentation is interrupted while there is still a considerable amount of sugar in the juice. Hard cider is produced when fermentation continues until all the sugar has been converted to alcohol (and carbon dioxide), and tastes sour.

In France, cider has been made since the 13th century. Special apples are used, some sweet, some tart, some acid.

Ciderkin. A weak cider made by adding water to apple juice and pulp, and pressing it again.

Cider Sauce. A sauce made with cider, melted butter, flour, the liquid in which a piece of ham or bacon has been boiled, pepper, and a pinch of sugar; served with hot ham.

Cider Vinegar. *See* Vinegar.

Cieche (Italian). Baby eels cooked in olive oil with garlic and cheese.

Cierp. A French cheese made from cow's milk or with ewe's milk added.

Cigalas (Spanish). Shrimp.

Cigarette Fish (Colloquial). The whiting.

Ciliege (Italian). Cherries.

Cima di Vitello (Italian). Veal in aspic.

Cimier (French). Haunch or saddle of venison.

Cinchona. A rather small tree native to South America and tropical countries. Its bitter bark (also called *Peruvian bark*) is used for making bitters. It was named for Countess Chincón, wife of a Peruvian viceroy.

Cinder Toffee (British). Toffee that has holes and crunches like cinders.

Cinghalaise. A cold sauce made of squash, cucumbers, tomatoes, oil, lemon juice, chopped egg yolks, and curry.

Cinnamon. This most familiar of spices has a long, romantic history. True cinnamon, which

grows only on the island of Ceylon, has a mild, delicate aroma and flavor. *Cassia cinnamon*, the variety used most commonly in cooking, is more pronounced in flavor and aroma and is grown in several parts of the Far East, including the East Indies and China.

When the Mediterranean countries were in the ascendancy, cinnamon was brought to Rome and Venice by way of Arabia. It was very expensive, and traders explained that they had to ask high prices because it was dangerous to collect cinnamon. They claimed that cinnamon grew in the center of a mysterious lake guarded by vicious birds which attacked those trying to get the spices. These birds had to be routed for a brief period at great personal peril while the traders waded into the lake, tore off a few branches of the tree, and hurried to safety. The story was not true.

Cinnamon, or *cassia cinnamon*, is actually the bark of a tree. Peeling begins when it is about 6 years old. The branches to be peeled are cut close to the trunk, then taken to a shelter and scraped, and the bark removed in long sections. As sections dry they curl and form the familiar cinnamon sticks.

Cinnamon sticks are used in pickling, in flavoring puddings, and as stirrers for after-dinner coffee. Ground cinnamon has many uses —in baked goods, as a topping for puddings and hot cereals, rice, and farina. It is especially good with fruits, with baked apples and in apple pie.

Cinnamon Fern. *See* Fiddlehead fern.

Cinnamon Oil. (1) An oil made from cinnamon leaves and used for flavoring foods. (2) A sweet yellowish oil derived from cinnamon bark.

Cinnamyl Isovalerate. A colorless liquid used to supply a nutty taste to packaged and bottled foods.

Cinnamyl Propionate. A colorless liquid commonly used to supply synthetic fruit flavors to food.

Cinque Terre. *See* Italy, The Wines of.

Cinzano Vermouth. Trade name of a fine Italian vermouth made in Turin since 1835. *See* Vermouth.

Cioccolata (Italian). Chocolate.

Ciorba (Romanian). Sour soup. Originally the base used to impart the sour taste was the juice obtained from wheat bran. However, this traditional method required a great deal of work, and in recent years other souring ingredients, such as sorrel leaves, green plums, sour apple juice, green grapes, and sauerkraut juice, have become popular.

Cipolle (Italian). Onions.

Ciriole (Italian). Rather large pasta, usually home-made.

Ciro. A red wine, partly sweet, produced in Calabria, Italy.

Ciruela (Spanish). Plum; prune.

> **Ciruela Pasa.** Prune.

Cisco. A freshwater variety of the herring family caught in the Great Lakes, particularly in Lake Ontario; it has a stronger savor than ordinary herring.

Ciseler. To make an incision carefully in the underskin of a fish.

Cisolo. A wine produced near Piacenza, Italy.

Citeaux, Fromage de. A Port du Salut cheese made by Trappist monks in Citeaux, France; best from April to December.

Citrange. A cross between the sweet orange and an inedible variety; used in making preserves and beverages.

Citric Acid. In the dry state an organic acid having the form of rather large fragile crystals. Citric acid may be extracted from lemon juice, or a synthetic version can be prepared from a special fermentation of glucose. It is found also in gooseberries, raspberries, oranges, and limes. It is used in confectionery, aerated water, and to help set jams and jellies.

Citroen (Dutch). Lemon.

Citron; Cedrat. An aromatic fruit resembling a lemon, much used for crystallization or in jellies and jams. *Citron* is the word for "lemon" in many countries.

Citronat. A French liqueur flavored with bergamot and lemon peel; often home-made.

Citronelle. An herb of the mint family with a strong, penetrating, lemonlike flavor; used in a French cordial of the same name.

Citronellyl Butyrate. A colorless liquid often used to supply a synthetic fruit flavor to jams and jellies.

Citronfromage (Danish). A lemon-flavored dessert.

Citronkräm (Swedish). Lemon dessert.

Citron Melon. A small rather round watermelon with very poor flavor. The rind is used to make relishes and pickles.

Citronnat (French). Candied lemon peel.

Citronné (French). Having a lemon flavor.

Citron Water. A beverage made with citron or lemon peel and brandy.

Citrouillat (French). A pumpkin pie or tart; specialty of the Berry region.

Citrouille (French). A kind of pumpkin or squash.

Citrous. Pertaining to orange, grapefruit, and other citrus fruits.

Citrus. A genus of trees and shrubs whose fruits include oranges, grapefruits, lemons, tangerines, and limes, characterized by a certain tartness and a fairly thick skin.

Citrus Pectin. Pectin obtained from citrus fruits.

Ciupin; Ciuppin. A fish soup or stew similar to bouillabaisse, made in Liguria, Italy.

Civelle. A delicately flavored small eel used in fish soups and stews.

Civet (French). Rabbit or hare stew prepared with red wine, onions, bacon, mushrooms, and the animal's blood. Also, occasionally, stews made with other game, meat, or seafood.

Civette (French). Chives.

> **Civet de Langonste.** Lobster-and-tomato stew with onions, garlic, parsley, and seasonings.

> **Civet de Mouton.** Mutton stew perpared with onions, mushrooms, and red wines, often with pig's blood added.

Civray, Fromage de. A simple, rather pungent, aromatic goat's-milk cheese made in Poitou, France.

Clabber. Thick, curdled sour milk. May be eaten plain or with sugar and other flavorings. It may also be stirred and drunk as a beverage. The term probably derives from the Irish word *clabar*, meaning "curds."

Clabbered Cheese (British). Fresh cottage cheese allowed to mature in a cool place.

Clafoutis (French). Fruit pudding made with black cherries and a rich batter; it resembles a pie, but has no pie dough or crust.

Claires. Oysters grown in the French Marennes region.

Clairet. A spiced or aromatized wine made in France; also an apéritif wine.

Clairette de Bellegarde. An almost dry French white wine; served as an apéritif and as a table wine.

Clairette du Languedoc. A yellow-gold dry white wine produced in Hérault, France; as it ages it turns darker and loses much of its original taste.

Clamart (French). Garnish or dish containing green peas.

Clambake. (1) American outdoor picnic or beach party. Theoretically the principal food is baked clams, but it may also include lobsters, corn, and watermelon. (2) Clams, lobsters, and other foods baked in a bed of hot stones in the ground.

Clam Chowder. A unique American contribution to the world of soups. Although there are hundreds of ways of making clam chowder, there are two principal methods: the New England style is made with milk or cream, while the Manhattan style is prepared with tomatoes. All efforts to reconcile the two opposing schools of thought have been in vain.

Clamming. Digging for clams.

Clams. Of the hundreds of species of clams known, several are widely used for food. In this country, the market varieties on the East Coast are different from those of the West Coast.

On the Atlantic coast, the marketed species are hard clams, soft clams, and surf clams. The hard, or hard-shell, clam is commonly called *quahog* in New England, where "clam" generally refers to the soft-shell variety. In the Middle Atlantic states and southward "clam" is the usual name for the hard clam.

Littlenecks and *cherrystones* are dealers' names for the smaller-sized hard clams generally served raw on the half-shell. The larger sizes of hard clams, called *chowders*, are used mainly for chowders and soups. The larger sizes of soft clams are known as *in-shells,* and the smaller sizes as *steamers*.

On the Pacific coast the most common market species are the butter, littleneck, razor, and Pismo clams. The Pacific littleneck clam is a different species from the Atlantic hard clam.

On each coast there are areas famous for the quality of their clams. Notable among these are Pismo Beach, California, whence comes the delicious Pismo clam, and Long Beach, Washington, famous for the razor clam. Ipswich, Massachusetts, is famous for its soft-shell clams.

Many traditions have grown up around the serving and eating of clams. Annual clam-eating contests are held in various coastal regions of the United States. The connotations of the term "clambake" have extended the use of that word far beyond its original meaning.

Although clams are served most often raw or in chowders, there are several good ways to serve them. It is not only the fine, distinctive flavor that recommends them as a food; they are also an excellent source of proteins, minerals, and vitamins.

Clams may be purchased either in the shell, shucked, or canned. Shell clams, generally sold by the dozen or by the pound, should be alive when bought. With hard clams, gaping shells that do not close when handled mean that the clams are dead and therefore no longer usable. With other varieties, the neck should contract somewhat when touched if the clam is usable. Fresh shell clams may be kept in the refrigerator for several days, as long as they remain alive.

Shucked clams should be plump, with clear liquor, and should be free of shell particles. In recent years shucked clams have been packaged and quick-frozen, a process that makes them available all year. Canned clams are packed in various sizes from 3½ ounces to 4 pounds. Clam juice and clam broth also are available canned or bottled.

Clapshot (Scotch). A potato-and-turnip dish popular in the Orkney Islands.

Claqueret; Ciboulette de Lyon. Soft cow's-milk cheese made in Lyons, France.

Claret. In England, the term used to describe all red Bordeaux wines. *See* France, The Wines of.

Clareteer (British, Colloquial). One who drinks claret.

Clarify. To purify or remove undesired matter. When it is desirable to obtain a clear liquid, such as a soup, food particles and cloudy substances are removed by beating in egg white and egg shell over heat. The soup then is strained. Food particles cling to the egg and are separated from the liquid.

Clarified Butter. The clear yellow liquid poured off after butter has melted and the milky residue sinks to the bottom of the pan. To make clarified butter, which will not burn at high temperatures, cut butter into quite small pieces into a saucepan. Cook over low heat until butter melts (being careful that it does not brown), then carefully skim off the foam. Very cautiously pour the yellow liquid through a strainer, being careful to leave the milky fluid in the saucepan.

Clarified Honey. Warm liquid honey obtained by placing solid honey in water at 140°.

Clary. A potherb resembling sage.

Clary; Clary Wine. Homemade wine containing clary blossoms; may also contain raisins, honey, wine, pepper, ginger, or other flavorings; aged in a cask for 6 months.

Clause, Jean Joseph; Close, Jean Joseph. Legendary names of the originator of *pâté de foie gras.*

Clautie Scone (Scotch). Poorly baked scone or cake.

Clavaire. A firm, rather flavorless wild mushroom native to France and other parts of Europe.

Clavaria. Capless mushrooms found in Europe growing in clumps; somewhat tough and lacking in distinctive flavor.

Clavo de Especie (Spanish). Clove.

Claws. Sharp pincers of crabs, lobsters, and certain other crustaceans.

Clear Distance Tea. A black tea produced in Kwangtung province, China.

Clears. A fair-quality flour made after a quality flour has been produced.

Clear Soup. Clarified stock, a strong clear broth obtained from boiling together meat, bones, and vegetables; consommé, broth, and bouillon possibly containing pieces of meat or vegetables and served without further embellishment.

Cleaver. (1) Large, heavy, sharp instrument used by a butcher to cut up an animal carcass. (2)

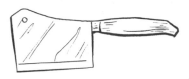

Wide-bladed kitchen tool shaped like a hatchet, used for chopping through bones or for pounding meat thin.

Clementine. A hybrid of the tangerine and orange, a sweet citrus fruit with few seeds.

Clipfish. Smoked cod.

Cloche (French). Cover made of glass or metal, intended to keep foods warm.

Clochettes (French). "Little bells," tasty bell-shaped pastries.

Clod. A part of the shoulder of a beef, or of the neck piece near the shoulder; suitable only for stewing.

Clorty Bread (British). Sticky gingerbread.

Clos. Term describing an enclosure in French vineyards.

Clos de Vougeot. An exceptional type of red wine grown in Burgundy.

Close Bread. Bread made with heavy flour or over-baked bread.

Close, Jean Joseph. *See* Clause, Jean Joseph.

Clos Mariout. A fairly dry white wine produced in the Mariout region of Egypt.

Clotted Cream. Cream (or milk) that has coagulated after being scalded; extremely rich and luscious. *See also* Devonshire Cream.

Cloudberry. A subarctic and arctic red or yellow fruit borne on a vine and resembling a raspberry. It is known for its seeds, and the berries should be swallowed without being chewed. Available in cans in Scandinavian delicacy shops.

Cloud Ear. Tree fungus resembling a mushroom; used in oriental cookery.

Clou de Girofle (French). Clove.

Cloud Mist. An exceptionally fine green tea produced in the Kiansi province of China.

Clouté (French). Studded; as, for example, long

narrow pieces of bacon, tongue, or truffles put into fowl, sweetbreads, or veal. A skewer is used to make the holes.

Clove. A small bulb, such as garlic or onion. *See* Cloves.

Clove Gillyflower. *See* Cloves.

Cloves; Clove Gillyflower. One of the major spices consisting of little brown buds shaped like nails. Cloves were known before the days of the early Egyptians. Clove trees originally were found growing in what is now Indonesia, but the biggest proportion of the world's crop now comes from Madagascar and Zanzibar, islands off the eastern coast of Africa.

An important spice in mincemeat, cloves have many other culinary uses. They are available both ground and whole. Whole cloves stud ham and pork and season pickling fruits. Ground cloves flavor sweet syrups, stews, meat gravies, apple pie, and many other dishes.

Cloven Hoof. The divided hoof of animals like deer. Orthodox Jews eat only the meat of animals having a cloven hoof, thus eliminating the pig.

Clovisse. (French). A type of clam, much like a *palourde*.

Clowsome. Soft, doughy pastry.

Cloy. To satisfy the appetite.

Club Cheese. A group of mashed, spicy cheddar cheeses containing pimientos, olives, onions, and wine usually marketed in small packages or in jars.

Club des Cent. A French organization of 100 experts in food and wine who arrange several elaborate banquets each year.

Club Sandwich; Three-Decker; Decker Sandwich. Sandwich composed of three slices of bread, either plain or toasted, with different fillings in the two layers. The bread or toast, of any type desired, is usually spread with butter or mayonnaise. There may be sautéed Canadian bacon slices in the "lower" layer and thin tomato slices in the "upper." Or one layer may consist of American cheese and ham slices, and the other of thin tomato slices and lettuce. Raw-onion slices, fried-bacon strips, sliced chicken, chopped chicken livers, sliced turkey, or roast beef are other possible fillings.

Club Steak. A cut from the short loin of beef; contains less of the prized loin meat than the porterhouse.

Cludgy (British). Sticky, cloggy, badly baked bread.

Clum (British). Heavy, moist, doughy baked food.

Clupe (French); **Clupeidae** (Latin). Genus of fishes, including the herring, sprat, pilchard, anchovy, and shad.

Clupeidae (Latin). *See* Clupe.

Clupeoid. Belonging to the herring family.

Cluster. Group of similar items, such as a cluster of grapes; growth in a bunch.

Coagulate. To change by chemical reaction from a liquid form into a thickened, curdlike substance. For example, heat causes eggs to solidify; rennet causes milk to curdle.

Coalfish. Pollock, a saltwater fish. In recent years, smoked coalfish has been used as an appetizer.

Coasters. Devices used under glasses to prevent moisture from marring table surfaces. The coaster may be a disk of wood, plastic, metal, or glass. The best kinds have a shallow ridge around the edge to prevent water from dripping off onto the table or other surface. Another type of coaster is the woven jacket that fits over the bottom of the glass and absorbs moisture.

Coat. To cover foods either with plain or seasoned flour, or with an egg-and-bread-crumb mixture. The easiest way to coat with plain or seasoned flour is to put the flour and any other of the dry ingredients into a paper bag, add the food, and, holding the top tightly closed, shake the bag well. Or the flour may be placed in a shallow dish or on heavily waxed paper and the food turned in the flour until it is well coated.

To coat food with egg and crumbs, break the egg into a shallow dish; beat slightly with a fork until the white and yolk are mixed; stir in 2 tablespoonsful of water. In a second shallow dish put finely rolled dry bread crumbs. Dip the food into the egg mixture, turn until all sides are coated, lift with a fork and hold over the dish until the excess egg has dripped off, then turn the egg-coated food in the crumbs until evenly covered.

Cob. (1) The woody spike, or ear of corn on which the kernels grow. *Corn on the cob* is served usually with butter, pepper, and salt. (2) A small round bread weighing 1–2 pounds. (3) The seed of wheat. (4) A male swan, occasionally used for food.

Cobalt. A mineral substance which is probably a dietary essential in small amounts, but a pure cobalt deficiency has never been observed in man. Cobalt is part of the molecule of vitamin B$_{12}$, but nutritionists do not know whether it is essential otherwise.

Cobbler. (1). A drink made with either wine or a spirit, usually combined with a sugar syrup, although a sweet liqueur may be used. An 8- or 10-ounce highball-type glass is filled with crushed ice and the ingredients are poured over it one at a time. The contents are stirred with a bar spoon until frost appears on the outside of the glass. Straws are inserted, and the drink is garnished with fruit and mint leaves. (2) A deep-dish fruit pie with no bottom crust and a top crust made of biscuit dough.

Cobia. A long, slender saltwater fish ranging from brown to black, weighing 15–25 pounds; a fine food fish, but the meat is somewhat dry, lacking natural fat.

Cobloaves (British). Crusty round loaves of bread with a smaller round piece on top.

Cobnut. A nut closely related to the filbert or hazelnut but rounder and bigger.

Coca. A South American plant from whose dried leaves cocaine is obtained. The leaves may be brewed into a tea or may be chewed as a stimulant.

Coca Leaves. Leaves from South American plant *Erythroxylon Cocoa* used as a tea base; because they contain cocaine, also chewed by Peruvian natives as a stimulant.

Cocada (Latin American). Dessert made of coconut preserves, butter, eggs, and flavorings.

Coccagee. A cider apple and its juice.

Cocco. The taro; the tuberous roots are eaten in the West Indies.

Cochevis (French). The crested or copped lark, occasionally eaten.

Cochineal. A dark red liquid obtained from the coccus insect, native to Guatemala and Mexico; used to color icings, creams, and jellies.

Cochinillo Asado (Spanish). Roast suckling pig.

Cochlearia; Scurvy Grass. A kind of wild horse-radish with a spicy, tangy mustard taste.

Cochonailles (French). Pork products.

Cocido (Spanish, South American). Stew prepared with meat, vegetables, and chick-peas (*garbanzos*).

   Cocido Español. Traditional Spanish thick soup made with beef or chicken and vegetables.

Cock. An old rooster; a mature male barnyard or wild fowl with coarse skin, tough dark meat, and a stiff breastbone.

Cockade. Sugar and pastry decorations resembling the ribbon decorations formerly worn on military hats.

Cock-A-Leekie; Cockie-Leekie; Cocky-Leeky. As originally made in Scotland, a capon boiled with white leeks. When the bird is tender, it is removed from the broth, the meat is cut into small pieces and returned to the broth with additional leeks, pepper, salt, and stewed prunes and raisins, then simmered half an hour. In modern versions the capon or fowl is roasted and then simmered with blanched leeks in a beef broth; fruit is not used.

   The English claim the dish originated in England in the 14th century and was "borrowed" by the Scots.

Cockerel. A rooster under one year of age; any young male bird.

Cockie-Leekie. *See* Cock-A-Leekie.

Cock-in-Breeches. Gingerbread shaped like a bird.

Cockle. Small heart-shaped saltwater bivalve with fluted shells; found on the sandy coasts of Great Britain, Ireland, and France; sold shelled and canned in delicacy shops in the United States.

Cockle Cakes. Cakes baked in fluted cockle and scallop shells; formerly popular in fishing towns.

Cockscombs. The jaunty red crests on roosters' heads, once a garnish with the French, who clean and cook them. Cockscombs packed in France are available at delicacy shops and fancy-food stores in the United States.

Cock's Kernels. Hard secretions present in the flesh of the cock. Esteemed as a great delicacy in France, they are rare and expensive.

Cocktail. (1) Alcoholic drink taken before a meal to stimulate the appetite, consisting of a spiritous base, such as whisky, rum, or gin, mixed with a modifying agent to give it a distinctive character and sometimes also with special flavoring or coloring agents. It is served ice cold in special cocktail glasses. (2) Nonalcoholic. In the United States a first course or appetizer, usually consisting of fruit or seafood; sometimes fruit, clam, or vegetable juice.

Cocktail Cheese. Any cheese eaten with alcoholic drinks, usually Camembert, cheddar, Pont l'Evêque, bleu (or blue), Port du Salut, feta, or other sharp or tangy types.

Cocktail Shaker. Utensil for mixing cocktails, available in many shapes, sizes, and materials. A glass shaker with a tight-fitting metal top is particularly convenient because ice does not melt as quickly in it as in an all-metal shaker. The top should be wide enough so that the ice cubes can be inserted easily, and the cover should fit tight and have a small opening through which the drink can be poured. The shaker should be chilled in advance either with ice cubes or in the refrigerator.

Cocktail Strainer. If the cocktail shaker lacks a cover, or if an oversized glass such as bartenders use in pairs to shake cocktails is employed, a strainer is necessary for pouring drinks. There are two types of strainer. One is a very large spoonlike utensil with perforations in the cup and a short handle. The other is a flat disk with a light, coil-spring edge that fits over the top of the shaker or glass.

Cock Turkey. Male turkey.

Cocky-Leeky. *See* Cock-A-Leekie.

Coco. The coconut-producing palm tree.

Coco (Spanish). Coconut.

Côco (Portuguese). Coconut.

Cocoa. (1) The powdered form of cacao beans. (2) The drink made from the powder. *See* Cocoa and Chocolate.

Cocoa and Chocolate. Among the things Columbus discovered in America was the cacao bean. He took samples back to King Ferdinand of Spain. The Spanish explorer Cortez was the first to realize the commercial potentialities of cacao, which, he found, the Aztecs prepared as a drink, "chocolatl." The Indians drank the preparation cold and bitter, but Europeans soon found they preferred it hot and sweetened with sugar. Hot chocolate became a fashionable drink in the Spanish court, later in the court of France, and then in England.

At first the cacao beans were used only for preparing a drink, but in the 19th century Daniel Peter, at Vevey, Switzerland, invented a process for making milk chocolate for eating. In another development *fondant chocolate,* a smooth and velvety variety, replaced the coarse-grained chocolate which had formerly dominated the world market. Today "eating" chocolate is produced far more extensively than "drinking" chocolate.

The cacao beans, which grow on a lush evergreen tree that can be cultivated only in hot, rainy climates within 20 degrees north or south of the equator, yields both eating and drinking chocolate. The first steps of processing are the same for the two products. The beans are cleaned, blended, roasted, then crushed between large grinding stones or heavy steel disks. The process generates enough frictional heat to liquefy the cocoa butter and form what is commercially known as "chocolate liquor." When poured into molds and cooled the liquor forms cakes of the familiar bitter, or unsweetened, chocolate.

It is at this point that the processing of drinking and eating chocolate diverges. For drinking chocolate or cocoa, a proportion of the cocoa butter, a unique vegetable fat, is removed from the chocolate liquor. The rest is cooled, pulverized, and sifted into cocoa powder. In the so-called "Dutch" process the manufacturer introduces an alkali that develops a slightly different flavor and a darker color.

The cocoa butter that was removed goes into the making of eating chocolate, for which additional cocoa butter is needed. The eating chocolate may be light, dark, bittersweet, or milk chocolate. Sweet chocolate is a combination of bitter chocolate with refined sugar, cocoa butter, and sometimes vanilla extract. Milk chocolate is the same with milk added.

The United States is the largest consumer of chocolate and cocoa in the world, with the United Kingdom, West Germany, Holland, and France following.

Instant cocoa, now increasingly popular, especially with young mothers, is a mixture of cocoa, sugar, and an emulsifier. It can be prepared for drinking by merely adding a hot liquid.

Coco de Mer. A nut of the coconut family that grows on the island of Seychelles in the Indian Ocean. The natives believe that Seychelles was the Garden of Eden and that the coco de mer was the forbidden fruit.

Coconut. In tropical areas the coco palm is considered the most useful tree. The coconut shell is fashioned into household utensils, the nut oil is used in cooking, and the shells, or copra residue, provide fuel for cooking. A tropical menu invariably includes coconut milk and grated coconut meat in some form. Mats are woven from the fibrous husk of the nut, and the tropical broom is a coconut-palm branch. These are only a few of the uses to which coconuts are put.

Probably the coconut palm originated in Asia and the Malayan islands and from there was carried by ocean currents to other tropical lands.

Outside the tropics the use of coconuts is more limited, although the whole nuts and prepared coconut products are available the year around.

For making chips for curries and pies, select coconuts that are heavy for their size and in which the milk can be heard or felt to slosh around. Coconuts without liquid and those with wet or moldy "eyes" have spoiled.

New coconut products include: *shredded* sweet coconut, either in long, slender threads for a handsome garnish, or in *shorter* threads for cookies or pies; *flaked* bite-size coconut, used for various dishes; and *toasted-coconut* topping and *fine-grated* coconut for cakes, pies, and puddings.

Coconut Butter. Solidified coconut oil, the result of chilling; used chiefly in commercial bakeries.

Coco Plum. A pleasant, sweet plum native to West Africa.

Cocose. A kind of soft spread or butter made from the meat of coconuts.

Cocotte. (1) A deep iron or copper kitchen utensil, large enough to hold a chicken, with a heavy, close-fitting cover, sometimes of glass. Often cocottes are oval-shaped, but the round ones are also common. They are used for braising meats and chicken, and also for boiling vegetables and for deep-fat frying. (2) Small ramekin in which eggs or other dishes may be cooked and served.

Coco Yam. A tuberous root native to many tropical countries. Dried roots are ground into flour.

Cocozelle. An elongated green squash with white markings. Young specimens, when not overcooked, are palatable.

Coct (Obsolete). To boil or bake.

Coctile. Baked.

Coction. Something cooking or boiling.

Cocuy. A crude Venezuelan cactus brandy.

Cod. A fish important not only as a food but also historically. It has been claimed that it was the cod fisheries that led England to establish colonies in America. They were so important that the cod is represented on the seal of the Colony of Massachusetts, and it is honored with a plaque in the Massachusetts State House.

As a food fish the cod has few peers. It is available almost the year around, appeals to everyone's palate, and leaves little to be desired from the standpoint of nutrition. The merits of cod liver oil are well understood, but they are not so readily recognized in the fish itself.

Because it naturally weighs over 10 pounds, cod is usually marketed in steak or fillet form. Cod prefers cold water and is found along the East Coast of the United States from Cape Hatteras northward. The best source is the Grand Banks of Newfoundland. Cod is caught with otter trawls, trawl lines, hand lines, and gill nets.

Dried cod, *bacalau*, is popular all over the world, particularly in Portugal and Brazil.

Cod Burbot; Coneyfish. A type of freshwater fish which resembles the cod.

Coddle. To boil slowly or parboil, especially eggs.

Coddy. (British). A small cake.

Codfish. A collective term for cod. *See* Cod.

Codiniac (French). A quince marmalade. *See also* Cotignac.

Codlin. An excellent variety of English cooking apple.

Codling. (1) Small cod. (2) Slender, long apple.

Codornices (Spanish). Quail.

Cod's Liver. Liver of the cod, rich in oil and vitamin B. The oil is extracted and used medicinally. The liver was formerly used for making rich forcemeat with bread crumbs, parsley, and seasoning for stuffing other fish.

Cod Sounds. The air bladders of codfish, salted and packed in barrels.

Coelho (Portuguese). Rabbit.

Coeur à la Crème (French). A rich dessert of creamy white cheese characteristically made into a heart shape in a special straw basket which permits the cheese to drain; often eaten with heavy, thick, slightly soured cream.

Coeur de Boeuf Braisé (French). Braised beef heart.

Coeur de Palmier (French). Heart of palm, often used as a salad green.

Coeur de Veau (French). Calf's heart.

Coffea Arabica (Botanical). The coffee plant and its beans.

Coffee. Coffee was discovered about a thousand years ago. The date when the first coffee beans were simmered in water to make a hot, delicious drink is as nebulous as the moment when man first learned to use fire for cooking. According to one popular Syrian legend, the virtues of coffee were first recognized when a monastery goatherd complained to his abbot that the goats, after nibbling the berries of a certain shrub, became so frolicsome that he could not quiet them at night. The abbot tried the berries himself and found them so exhilarating that he took to serving the brew to his monks to keep them from falling asleep during prayers.

It is established that the coffee tree first grew in Africa, probably in Abyssinia and perhaps also in Arabia. The Arabs were the first to discover and promote the use of coffee as a beverage. They were also the first to cultivate the coffee tree. Progress was slow until the 15th and 16th centuries. Then cultivation spread to the East Indies, India, and to Central and South America.

Coffee was praised in its early days for its ability to quicken the wit, restore the weary, comfort the body, and enable the religious to stay awake all night for devotions. But the brew also had Arabic enemies who condemned it as contrary to the teaching of the Koran, as being, if not wine, certainly charcoal and equally objectionable. Coffeehouses were closed in Mecca in 1511, wrecked in Cairo, and forbidden in Constantinople.

But in Europe, coffeehouses became the great centers of political and literary discussions. In Paris, Pascal, an Armenian, opened the first coffeehouse and later at the Café Precope, frequenters included such illustrious personages as Voltaire, Rousseau, Diderot, Marat, and Robespierre. In London, there were 3,000 coffeehouses in 1652, many of them centers of the intellectual life of the times.

The coffee tree is an evergreen with large shiny leaves. The blossoms are white and the fruits resemble and are known as "cherries." These are first green and later turn a dark red. Their flesh is sweet and is frequently eaten. This pulp encloses two seeds, or beans, each inside a thin parchmentlike skin. The beans become hard and flinty on exposure and are the green coffee of commerce. Coffee trees begin to bear three to five years after they are planted as seeds. Modern practice dictates that the coffee berries be washed after picking, when just ripe. After soaking, the beans are dried and packed in bags for shipment.

More than a hundred varieties of coffee are sold in the world's coffee markets, varying widely in price. A number of coffees are named for the port of shipment such as "Rio," "Santos," and "Java."

Coffee is shipped green or unroasted because it keeps well in this state. It is usually roasted in

gas- or oil-heated cylinders at about 450°–
500°. Roasting changes the appearance, consistency, and composition of the bean, bringing
out aroma and flavor.

There are various roasting methods, such as
the medium, most popular in this country; the
French, a longer roast yielding a darker coffee;
and the Italian, the longest roast. After roasting,
the coffees are blended, since each variety has
its own flavor and a blend of several yields a
more pleasing beverage than a straight variety
from one kind of coffee bean.

Coffee beans begin to lose flavor and aroma
after they are roasted; grinding speeds the loss.
To conserve flavor, some large coffee distributors
depend on vacuum canning or other types of
packaging to maintain standards of freshness,
while others rush freshly roasted beans to re-
tailers who do their grinding while the customer
waits. There are several types of grinds to suit
individual tastes in methods of coffee making,
such as coarse, medium, fine, or pulverized
grinds.

The Art of Coffee Making

Brewing coffee is an art. As with all other
arts, a certain amount of knowledge is necessary
before it can be perfected.

1. The first essential is that the coffee grounds
be fresh. No one can make a good beverage with
stale coffee. Since grinding speeds the loss of
flavor and aroma, once the beans have been
ground or once the vacuum seal on the coffee
container has been broken, the coffee should be
used within a week. Refrigeration helps retain
the flavor.

2. Measure coffee and water accurately. For
a richly flavored coffee use 2 level tablespoonfuls
of coffee for each 6-ounce cup of water. These
measurements will produce 40 cups of coffee to
the pound. The amount of water can be varied
slightly if a stronger or weaker brew is desired,
but, for consistent results, once the desired
strength has been obtained, the same measurements should be followed exactly each time
coffee is made.

3. Use fresh cold water. Water that has been
preheated or drawn from the hot-water faucet
may impart an undesirable taste to the brew.

4. Serve the coffee as soon as possible after
brewing.

5. For best results, always brew coffee at full
capacity of the coffee maker.

6. Always use a clean coffee maker. Coffee
oils have a tendency to cling to the inner surfaces of coffee-making utensils, particularly
around rims, ridges, and the spout. They eventually become stale and impart an undesirable taste
to the coffee brew. To avoid this, each time the
container is used, wash thoroughly with soap or
washing powder and rinse carefully with hot
water. When the coffee maker is put in the cupboard between meals, leave the cover off to give
it a chance to air.

Twice a month or oftener the coffee maker
should get a more thorough cleaning. If the coffee
maker is porcelain, enamelware, or glass, put
all parts in a large pot and boil for a few
minutes in a solution of about a tablespoon of
baking soda and a tablespoon of ammonia to
each quart of water. If the coffee maker is a
type that will not stand direct heat, just let it
soak in the hot cleaning solution in a dishpan.
Aluminum coffee makers should be polished with
steel wool and boiled in a solution of vinegar and
water (about one-fourth cup vinegar to one quart
of water). With percolators, fill the percolator
to capacity with whatever solution is used, apply
heat, and let pump operate for several minutes.
This cleans the inside of the percolator tube.
Thoroughly rinse coffee makers in hot water
after any of these processes.

Methods of Coffee Making

The four methods of making coffee are (1)
dripping, (2) percolating, (3) in a vacuum

utensil, and (4) old-fashioned boiling. The drip
method is preferred by many experts because it

brings the water in contact with the coffee for the shortest possible time. This extracts the maximum flavor and aroma and the minimum of bitter taste. However, surveys show that the majority of Americans prefer percolated coffee.

Drip Coffee. There are a number of good drip pots on the market. Some have no filter, only a perforated top; some have cloth and others paper filters, like the Chemex. Scald the pot before making the coffee. Using 2 level tablespoonfuls of coffee to each cup of water, put coffee in top part of pot and pour the freshly boiling water over it, according to the directions that come with the pot. It must be kept hot but never allowed to boil. It should be served hot as soon as possible. Never pour water through more than once.

Percolator Coffee. Electric percolators usually come with an instruction booklet. Some are automatic; that is, perking stops at the correct time and the coffee then is kept hot but not boiling. Others must be disconnected when the coffee has perked to the right degree (after about 6 minutes). If the percolator is not electric, it should be used as follows: put cold water in the coffee maker and heat to boiling. Remove from heat. Insert basket containing ground coffee into percolator. Cover, return to heat, allow to percolate slowly for 6 minutes.

Vacuum Coffee. Put cold water in lower bowl; place on heat; when water boils actively, turn heat low. Insert upper bowl containing coffee grounds. When water has risen to upper level, stir thoroughly. Leave on heat one to three minutes, depending on size of grind.

Boiled Coffee. Boiling is the least satisfactory method for the beginner. With the more general use of percolators, vacuum and drip pots, boiled coffee is more likely to be a feature of the campfire or picnic than of the home breakfast. But for those who wish to know how to do it: measure the required amount of coffee into the pot or saucepan and add a measured amount of cold, hot, or boiling water. Place on heat, stir well, and bring just to a boil. Stir again, remove from heat, and add a dash of cold water to settle the grounds. Do not allow boiling to continue. After coffee has stood a few minutes it is ready to be served. *See also* Decaffeinated Coffee; Espresso Coffee; Instant Coffee.

Coffee Bean. The seed of the coffee tree or shrub.

Coffee Berry. The fruit of the coffee plant.

Coffee Cup. Although any cup can be used for serving coffee, usually the so-called coffee or breakfast cup is either the 6-ounce standard teacup or slightly larger.

Coffee Grounds. The dark brown granular substance remaining after coffee has been prepared. Also, fresh grounds.

Coffeehouse. Small restaurant where coffee is served.

Coffee Maker. *See under* Coffee.

Coffee Mill. *See* Grinder.

Coffee of Sudan (African). A rather stimulating and invigorating beverage made with roasted ground cola nuts.

Coffee Roaster. Apparatus in which green coffee beans are revolved over constant heat until roasted to desired color and flavor.

Coffee Room; Coffee Shop. A room in a hotel or other public place where coffee and simple dishes are served.

Coger Cake (British). In medieval times a common kind of a cake given to farm workers.

Cognac. Brandy produced in a specific geographic district near the town of Cognac, France. Brandy produced outside this region cannot be called *Cognac.*

Cogumelos (Portuguese). Mushrooms.

Cohune Nut. An inferior nut of Central and South America from which an edible oil is extracted.

Coimbra. A somewhat salty Portuguese cheese made from cow's or goat's milk.

Coing. An Alsatian quince-flavored afterdinner liqueur.

Coinguarde. A French quince liqueur.

Coin Silver. A silver alloy used in flat tableware. *See* Silver.

Cointreau. The trade name of a very fine curaçao —a colorless drink with an orange taste. *See* Curaçao.

Cojinúa. The great amber jack, a food fish of South America.

Coke (Colloquial). A dark soft drink, lightly

carbonated, sold under the trade name *Coca-Cola.*

Coker Nut. Another name for coconut.

Cola; Kola. *See* Cola Nut.

Colache (Mexican). Dish consisting of corn, tomatoes, zucchini, and onions.

Colander. A fairly large metal or plastic bowl perforated on the sides and bottom; used for straining hot foods.

Cola Nut. Tropical nut that provides the stimulating quality in cola beverages. About the size of a horse chestnut, it is brown, bitter, and contains two or three times as much caffein as the coffee bean. It first grew in tropical Africa, where the natives prized it as a "pep-up" snack. Later it was transplanted to the Caribbean islands and tropical South America, and is grown commercially for use in beverages and extracts.

Colares. A wine district of Portugal. *See* Portugal, The Wines of.

Colazione (Italian). Lunch.

Colbert Butter; Colbert Sauce. Butter stirred with chopped parsley and tarragon, salt and pepper, a dash of lemon juice, and meat jelly to form a smooth paste; used as an accompaniment to fried fish and broiled fish and meats. Named for Jean Baptiste Colbert, minister under Louis XIV of France.

Colby Cheese. Similar to cheddar, but with a softer body and more open texture, and containing more moisture; more perishable than cheddar.

Colcannon (Irish). Cabbage, boiled potatoes, and sometimes boiled turnips seasoned with butter, pepper, and salt, and baked in a mold.

Cold Dough. Yeast dough below 78°F.

Cold Table. Buffet table, featuring cold cuts, salads, and other cold foods.

Cold-Turkey Pie (British). Bread and cheese.

Cole. (1) Various plants of the mustard family, but usually rape. (2) Kale, a green vegetable. *See* Kale.

Coles (Spanish). Cabbage.

Coles de Bruselas (Spanish). Brussels sprouts.

Cole Slaw; Cold Slaw. A popular salad or relish made of finely sliced or grated cabbage with a dressing. The term derives from the Dutch words *kool sla,* meaning "cabbage salad."

Colewort. (1) Originally cabbage. Now any vegetable green, such as kale, that does not form a head. (2) Young cabbage cooked briefly.

Coliflor (Spanish). Cauliflower.

Colin (French). (1) Pollock, a fish of the cod family. (2) Hake.

Colinabo (Spanish). Kohlrabi.

Collage. The process of clarifying wines.

Collagen. An insoluble protein in the bone, tendons, skin, and connective tissues of animals and fish, converted to soluble gelatin by moist heat.

Collar. To roll and then tie meat with a string.

Collard. A member of the cabbage family whose young, tender leaves are prepared like cabbage; popular in the southern United States.

Collared Beef. A large joint of the thin end of beef flank marinated in spices and salt about 10 days, then boned, rolled, bound tightly, and boiled or baked in a casserole up to 6 hours.

Collation. Light meal; snack.

Colle. (1) A mixture of boiled water and flour used to extend sauces. (2) Gelatin.

Collet. (French). The part of the neck of veal or mutton closest to the head.

Collier (French). A cut of beef, somewhat like the neck and brisket.

Colliers' Foot. Snacks enjoyed by English miners; crusts shaped like the sole of a boot and filled with a mixture of minced meat or bacon, onion, and sometimes also slices of cheese.

Colliflower (Obsolete). Cauliflower.

Collins. Basically a tall alcoholic drink—lemonade and carbonated water spiked with gin or another liquor. The original and still the most popular Collins is prepared with gin, but brandy, rum, vodka, Scotch, or Irish whisky may be substituted. The drink is served in a 14–16-ounce glass with ice cubes or cracked ice, often garnished with an orange slice and a maraschino cherry. It is often sipped through a straw. A commercially prepared Tom Collins Mix is available.

Colloid. Any gelatinous substance composed of insoluble particles that are small enough to remain suspended in a fluid medium without settling to the bottom. Familiar examples are beaten egg white, whipped cream, and emulsions such as milk and salad cream.

Collop. Any small thin slice of meat. The name undoubtedly is derived from the Italian word *scallopini*, which has the same meaning.

Colmar. A pear of fairly good taste and texture.

Colombia. On weekdays the usual Colombian breakfast is coffee with bread, rolls, butter, and jam. On Sundays, however, the traditional breakfast is *tamal* (a cornmeal mixture, wrapped and steamed), together with hot chocolate, bread, and local cheese. If any single food typifies Colombia, it is probably corn, which is used in a wide variety of dishes besides *tamal*. For example, there are: *sopa de maiz* (corn soup), *cocido Bogotano* (beef stew with vegetables and small lengths of corn on the cob), *sopa de mazorca con pollo* (corn and chicken soup), *tortillas de maiz* (corn tortillas), *pastel de maiz*, (corn pie), and *torrejas de maiz tierno* (corn fritters).

Other typical Colombian dishes include: *picante de huevos* (an egg and avocado appetizer), *cuchuco* (a thick soup made from wheat), *piquete* (a pork-and-chicken stew with corn), *ajiaco* (a pork-and-vegetable stew); and *pollo al cazador* (chicken cooked with onions, tomatoes, and chick-peas). Desserts are of little importance, except for the local fruits. The most popular single dessert is *flan*, the Spanish caramel custard found throughout South America.

Coffee and chocolate are favorite beverages. Wines are of small importance, but the local beer is fairly good and makes a good accompaniment to Colombia's many spicy dishes. Many local people like *chicha*, a crude beerlike beverage, or *aguardiente*, the strong brandylike liquor. *Agua de panelo*, which many people enjoy, is made from brown sugar and hot water, and taken with milk or lemon, much like tea.

Colombières, Fromage de. A French semifirm cow's- and goat's-milk cheese similar to Reblochon.

Colombines (French). Mixtures of cooked rice and eggs combined with cheese, shaped as desired, and then cooked.

Coloquinte (French). *Colocynth*, a bitter cucumber.

Coloring, Food. Colorings used to tint cakes, frostings, and other food preparations; usually of either vegetable or mineral origin, although in some countries *cochineal*, an insect, provides carmine.

Colp (Scotch). *See* Collop.

Coltello (Italian). Knife.

Colwick. *See* Slipcote Cheese.

Combrailles, Fromage de. A hard cow's-milk cheese made in the Limousin region of France; used chiefly in fonducs or other melted-cheese dishes.

Comeback Wheat. A good Australian flour used chiefly for bread.

Comestible. Edible; suitable to be eaten.

Comfits. Preserved fruits; sweets, candies, jams.

Comfortable Bread (British). Spiced gingerbread.

Comino (Spanish). Cumin.

Comino Holandés (Spanish). Caraway.

Commendaria. A sweet dessert wine made in Cyprus.

Comminute. To pulverize food, especially spices and herbs. *Comminuted orange drink* is made with the crushed whole orange, including the peel.

Commissariat; Commissary. Department that orders and supplies food for a large number of people, such as a school, institution, army division. The place where the food is prepared is called the *commissary*.

Commission Cheese. A round Dutch cheese closely resembling an Edam but twice as large, weighing up to 8 pounds. Like Edam, it is made in the northern provinces of Holland from slightly skimmed cow's milk.

Common Drum. The saltwater drumfish, a food fish.

Companage (Obsolete). Anything eaten with bread, such as meat, cheese, butter, and jelly.

Compiègne (French). A light cake made with yeast and candied fruit.

Comport. *See* Compote.

Composta di Pesche (Italian). Peach compote.

Compota (Spanish). Stewed fruit.

Compota de Frutas (Portuguese). Fruit compote.

Compote. (1) One or more fresh or dried fruits simmered together with sugar and water and perhaps a flavoring, such as vanilla extract, lemon or orange rind, cinnamon, or cloves. Compotes are usually served cold and may be spiked with a liqueur such as kirsch or brandy. (2) A method of preparing pigeons.

Compotier. Deep dish on a raised base used for serving compotes and other fruit preparations; also used for serving fresh fruit or other cold desserts.

Compounded Butter. A seasoned canapé or sandwich spread prepared with butter, seasoning, and fish paste, minced poultry, or minced watercress. Chilled in balls, it may be used as a garnish.

Compound Fats. Two or more fats combined, such as two animal fats, two vegetable fats, or a vegetable and an animal fat.

Comte, Fromage de. Gruyère cheese made in eastern France.

Coñac (Spanish). Cognac, brandy.

Concassée (French). Peeled tomatoes, with the seeds removed.

Concasser (French). To chop foods forcefully; to grind, pound, or crush foods.

Conch. A large edible shellfish (pronounced konk) uncommon in northern markets but a staple food in the Bahamas and on some Caribbean islands. In Italy, where it is known as *scungilli*, it is also a favorite sea food. Better known in the North than the meat of the conch is the highly decorative shell of the tropical *queen conch*, which opens to show a lustrous interior, deep pink in the center, fading to a pearly white at the rims.

The *channel conch*, or *channel whelk*, found along the cooler northern coast of the United States, is a drab sister to the queen. Its dirty-white shell lacks the flutings and curlicues of the queen's shell. Hold a conch shell to the ear and you will hear the ocean's roar.

The conch has a strong clammy taste, and unless it is prepared just right, the flesh may be tough. People who have learned to eat conch in France or Italy prefer the northern or channel variety.

Both queen and channel conch must be cooked so that the meat does not become tough. This is not easily done. The shellfish may be parboiled and plucked out when the muscle retracts and the conch starts to draw back into the shell. The meat should then be removed quickly and the cooking continued in whatever manner desired.

If conch meat becomes tough during cooking, try to tenderize it by pounding it with the side of a cleaver or plate.

Conch Chowder. Spicy, often peppery chowder made from conchs, the large edible shellfish found in many tropical regions.

Conches. A French cheese closely resembling Switzerland's Emmentaler cheese.

Conchiglie (Italian). Shell-shaped macaroni.

Concoct. To prepare a mixture of foods. The word comes from the Latin *conquere*, "to cook."

Concoction. (1) The act of preparing a dish containing several ingredients. (2) The preparation itself.

Conde (French). Almond-paste cake.

Condé, À la. Dishes named for Prince Louis de Condé (1621–1686): a puréed red bean soup; eggs garnished with puréed red beans; a dessert of rice and apricots; an icing of egg whites, sugar, and almonds.

Condensed Milk. Milk evaporated and sweetened. *See* Milk.

Condiments. Substances added to food either during or after cooking to heighten their flavor and to stimulate the appetite. Salt and pepper are the most common condiments but other spices also fall into this category, as do all members of the onion family, including garlic, shallots, and green onions. Other condiments are capers, pickles, and horseradish, and such prepared products as Tabasco, Worcestershire, and other sauces, prepared mustards, mustard pickles, catsups, and curry powders. Some people regard salt as a seasoning and not as a condiment.

Condimenter (French). To add condiments while cooking.

Condimento (Spanish). Relish, condiment.

Condiment of Condiments. Salt.

Condion (Italian). Salad of pimientos, tomatoes, pickles, and olives with a fish-roe dressing.

Condite. (1) To preserve. (2) A preserve.

Condol (Philippine). Gourd.

Condrieu. (1) An unusual medium-firm, cream goat's-milk cheese prepared during the summer and fall months near Lyons, France. (2) A wine village of the Rhône district. *See* France, The Wines of.

Conejo (Spanish). Rabbit.

Coneyfish. *See* Cod Burbot.

Confarreation. A very solemn marriage ceremony among the ancient Romans at which bread was offered to the witnesses.

Confect. To make a cake, pudding, or candy.

Confection. (1) A mixture of sugar, fruits, and spices. (2) Any cake, pudding, or candy.

Confectionary. Relating to cakes, puddings, and candies.

Confectioner. One who sells or makes candies, ice cream, etc.

Confectioners' Glucose. *See* Starch Syrup.

Confectioners' Sugar. Granulated sugar crushed and screened to a desired fineness, usually containing a little cornstarch to prevent caking. It is used in frostings and icings and for dusting pastries, doughnuts, etc.

Confectionery. (1) Candies, confections, ice cream, sweets. (2) The place where confections are made or sold.

Confectouris. Confectioner.

Confire (French). To preserve foods in syrup, liquor, or vinegar.

Confit (French). Any poultry, game, or meat preserved in its own fat and heavily covered with a layer of fat in a special sealed receptacle.

Confit d'Oie (French). A popular method of preserving goose for several months. The bird is cut into small pieces, sprinkled with salt, and put in a large jar with a weighted board or dish on top. After about 2 weeks the meat is wiped of excess salt and cooked very slowly with the goose fat. When done, the pieces are put into earthenware jars and the hot fat is poured in to cover the meat entirely. The jars are then sealed and kept in a cold place or refrigerator. It is an important ingredient of *cassoulet*, the classic French bean dish.

Congee (Chinese). Rice boiled very soft in a considerable amount of water; eaten as a breakfast food.

Conge Machine. A machine that kneads chocolate blends to a smooth consistency for use as coating.

Conger Eel. *See* Eel.

Conger Eel St. Malo (French). A dish, famous in the restaurants of the seaport of St. Malo, made with sections of a small conger eel dipped in egg and bread crumbs and fried; served with a thick sauce of onions, broth, mustard, anchovy essence, chopped parsley, and white wine.

Congiary. In Roman times, a gift of food divided among soldiers or civilians after an important event, such as a victory.

Congius. A Roman wine measure, a little greater than the modern gallon.

Congou. Black tea produced in various parts of Asia. Congous are usually classified in two principal types: North Chinese and South Chinese.

Congress Tart. A macaroon tart topped with a pastry cross.

Congrio (Spanish). Eel.

Congro (Portuguese). Eel.

Congustable (Obsolete). Pertaining to foods having similar tastes.

Conhas (Mexican). Shell-shaped bread rolls.

Coniglio (Italian). Rabbit.

   Coniglio all' Agrodolce. Rabbit in a sweet-sour sauce.

Conjee; Congee (Chinese). The water from boiled rice and also rice boiled until very soft.

Conocarp. A fruit, such as the raspberry, that contains little cells around a central pith.

Conservation. The preserving of fruit and other foods.

Conserve. Similar to a jam, except that it is usually a blend of two or three fruits. A conserve also contains thin slices of citrus fruit or citrus juice and sometimes raisins or nut meats or both. Small fruits and berries may be conserved whole, but large fruits must be sliced or diced. If desired, one kind of fruit or berry may be used.

Conserven (Dutch). Preserve.

Consolante (French). A drink of wine or beer given to kitchen help during working hours to encourage their efforts.

Consommé (French). Literally, "consumed"; a broth reduced by boiling to about half its original bulk to produce a richer, more intensive flavor. Seasonings must be reduced proportionately: if the original liquid were seasoned to taste with salt, pepper, and other spices, the seasoning would be much too strong for the consommé.

Consommé Américaine. Double-strength beef soup containing green peas and pimientos.

Consommé Croûtes au Pot. Clear beef soup with vegetables, served with large toasted croutons.

Consommé Madrilène. Chicken consommé with tomatoes or tomato paste; served hot or jellied.

Consommé Printanière. Consommé garnished with cut-out pieces of vegetables.

Consumable. Edible.

Consume. To eat or drink.

Consy (Obsolete British). An ancient method of cooking capons in a stew with seasonings and saffron.

Conti, À la. With a garnish consisting of puréed lentils or lentil croquettes.

Contising (French). Cutting slits into fillets of poultry, game, or fish and inserting wedge-shaped slices or truffles or other food.

Contre-Filet; Fauxfilet (French). Loin of beef; fillet of beef; boned sirloin.

Conversation (French). A small puff pastry filled with pastry cream, then iced.

Convive (French). One who eats with others.

Cook. A person who prepares food either in a home or a restaurant.

Cooker. (1) A series of interlocking metal containers for steaming foods. (2) A comparatively airtight container for cooking foods slowly with retained heat.

Cookery. (1) The art or science of preparing food. (2) The place where food is prepared.

Cookie; Cooky. Small, rather flat, sweet cake. The term comes from the Dutch word *koekje,* meaning "little cake." *See also* Cookies.

Cookie Cutter. Dies, usually of metal, sometimes of plastic, for cutting thin cookies into various shapes, such as diamonds, spades, hearts, gingerbread men, Christmas trees, and Easter bunnies. Metal cutters usually make a sharper outline than the plastic variety.

Cookie Jar. Any moistureproof container with a tight-fitting cover for storing cookies. To keep cookies soft, a piece of fresh bread may be stored with them. Crisp cookies should not be stored in the same container as soft ones, for they will absorb the moisture. Crispness can be restored by heating in a moderate oven for a few minutes.

Cookiepress. *See under* Cookies: Pressed Cookies.

Cookies. Cookies require less time in mixing and less skill in baking than cakes. They are especially good for the new cook on which to try her hand, before advancing to more elaborate baking. Cookies keep longer than cakes, too.

The basic ingredients in most cookie recipes include flour, a fat, sugar, eggs, and milk. The flour may be hard wheat, soft wheat, or, in some cases, whole wheat. The fat may be any mild-flavored shortening, and the sugar may be white or brown or a combination of sugar and molasses, syrup, or honey. The liquid may be regular milk, sour milk, buttermilk, water, fruit juice, or even coffee. For flavor it is best to use the freshest eggs available, and in some cases where the unique flavor of butter is important, it should be used in preference to any other shortening.

Cookies may be mixed either by hand or with an electric mixer. In either case, all the ingredients should be assembled and measured before the mixing process is started. The eggs and shortening should be at room temperature.

To speed up the cookie-making process, it is best to have two baking sheets, each about 2 inches smaller than the oven. This makes it possible to arrange cookies on one sheet while the other is baking in the oven. The first time a recipe is used, it is wise to bake a trial cookie to test the consistency of the dough. After baking, the cookies should be removed from the sheet with a spatula and placed in a single layer on a wire cake rack. When cool, they should be transferred to a metal container which can be kept tightly covered.

In general, there are two types of cookies—those made from a soft dough and those from a stiff dough. The soft-dough varieties include drop cookies, which are pushed from a spoon onto a baking sheet and the kind, like brownies, which are spread in a pan like a thin layer of cake. Stiff-dough cookies include rolled cookies, refrigerator or sliced cookies, and cookies shaped by forcing the dough through a cookie press.

Dropped Cookies. The dough should be stiff enough to require pushing from a spoon. To shape, take a little dough on one spoon and push it off the tip with another spoon onto a greased baking sheet, leaving 2–3 inches between drops to allow for spreading. Dropped cookies are likely to be irregular in shape, but they can be kept to fairly uniform size if the quantity of dough put on the spoon is heaped to the same height each time.

Spread Cookies. After baking, these cookies should be cooled, then cut into squares or oblongs.

Rolled Cookies. Thorough chilling of the dough is one of the essentials for success with this variety. If the dough is not well chilled, it will be too soft to roll without adding more flour that will make the cookies tough and dry. Handle only a little of the dough at a time, leaving the rest in the refrigerator. Roll with as few motions as possible to desired thickness. Dip the cooky cutter in flour each time and shake off excess flour so the dough will not stick to the cutter.

Refrigerator or Sliced Cookies. The dough for this type of cookie should be formed into rolls and wrapped tightly in waxed paper or packed into molds and chilled in the refrigerator for at least 5–6 hours, preferably overnight, before cutting. When ready to bake, cut the rolls into slices ⅛- to ¼-inch thick, using a thin sharp knife and a sawing motion, exerting as little pressure as possible.

Pressed Cookies. Pressed cookies are made by forcing a stiff dough through a cookie press, which is a cylindrical instrument usually made of thin metal. The dough is packed into the hollow cylinder and forced by means of a plunger through a small opening to which attachments are fitted to form cookies of various shapes. Some presses have gages to vary the thickness of cookies, one gage for thin crisp ones, another for thicker kinds. Most rolled cookie doughs can be used in a press except those with nuts or fruits which could clog the small openings.

Cookie Sheet. A flat thin metal sheet on which cookies are most easily baked. It may be of any corrosion-resisting or coated metal provided it is thin enough to transmit heat quickly and evenly. The sheet may be flat or it may have a rolled or raised edge, but the edge should not be so high as to interfere with heat circulation.

Cooking Banana. *See* Plantain.

Cooler. (1) Section of a machine where cakes and breads are cooled after being baked. Any commercial appliance for cooling foods. (2) A tall American alcoholic drink served with ice cubes.

Coolie-Hat Pan. A Chinese cooking utensil shaped something like a coolie's hat; used chiefly for deep-fat frying but also for general cooking purposes.

Coon. Oyster native to Florida waters.

Coon Cheese. A very sharp, tangy cheddar cheese, with a dark rind and crumbly texture. It is aged at a higher temperature than most cheddars, from 55°–70°F. *See also* American Cheese.

Coontah. A woody subtropical plant that yields arrowroot.

Cooper. Basket for holding wine bottles.

Cooperatorka Wheat. An excellent-milling Russian red wheat used in making bread.

Coot. A bird similar to the moorhen whose flesh is dark and mild-tasting.

Cooth. *See* Coalfish.

Copa (French). Spiced pork, a specialty of Corsica. Also, sausage made of spiced ground pork.

Copeaux (Obsolete, French). *Petit fours;* small iced cakes.

Copenheering Cocktail (Danish). Drink made of cherry heering and gin shaken with ice; served with a twist of lemon or lime peel.

Coper. A bottle containing an alcoholic beverage formerly given to North Sea fishermen in exchange for fish.

Coppa (Italian). A pork salami.

Coppa Gelata (Italian). Ice-cream dessert.

Coppa Rifredda (Italian). Meat loaf made of tuna fish, veal, and prosciutto.

Coppe (French). A sausage.

Copper-Nosed Bream. The bluegill, a freshwater food fish.

Copra. The dried kernel of the coconut after the oil has been extracted.

Coq. (1) (French). Rooster, cock. (2) (French, Colloquial). The head chef of a ship.

Coq au Coulis d'Ecrevisses (French). Poached chicken served with a creamy shrimp or crayfish sauce.

Coq au Vin Rouge (French). Chicken prepared in red-wine sauce.

Coq de Bois (French). The heath cock, a game bird.

Coq de Bruyère (French). Blackcock, or cock of the heath, a game bird.

Coq d'Inde (French). Turkey cock or cock of India.

Coque (French). A cockle; a shellfish usually eaten cooked but also good raw.

Coque du Lot (French). A rich cake, made in the Lot district, flavored with orange and lemon.

Coquetier (French). An egg vendor.

Coquetière (French). Cooking utensil used for immersing eggs in boiling water.

Coquille. Any small plate shaped like a sea-shell, or a seashell used as a dish.

Coquille St. Jacques (French). A seashell, or similar container, filled with a mixture that includes scallops and mushrooms in a white-wine cream sauce.

Coquilles St. Jacques (French). Scallops.

Coquito. A palm tree native to Chile that yields palm honey.

Coq Vierge (French). An excellent-tasting tender young chicken.

Corach (Indian). Hot sauce for which cayenne pepper, walnuts, mushrooms, pickles, garlic, and cochineal are macerated with vinegar.

Coracine. A soft-textured fish similar to the perch; native to the Nile River.

Coral. Lobster roe, used in French fish cuisine to impart a brilliant color to butter and sauces.

Coral Fish. An insipid fish found on coral reefs.

Coratella (Italian). Stew of lamb, liver, hearts, and tongue.

Corbeille (French). Basket, usually filled with fruit.

Corbières. Group of pleasant nondescript red wines produced in the Pyrénées region of France.

Cordeiro (Portuguese). Lamb.

Cordero (Spanish). Lamb.

Cordes (French). Pastry made in the Touraine region.

Cordial. A sweet afterdinner drink with high alcoholic and sugar content. *See* Liqueurs.

Cordial Glass. *See* Glassware.

Cordial Médoc (French). A mixture of several liqueurs—a blend of crème de cacao, brandy, and orange curaçao.

Cordon. A fruit tree pruned to grow as a single stem.

Core. (1) In fruits the center capsule containing the seeds. (2) To remove this center piece.

Corer. Utensil used for coring fruits.

Corfinio. An Italian cordial, an imitation of Chartreuse.

Coriander, Roman. *See* Fennel Flower.

Coriander. A feathery annual herb, native to Asia and the Mediterranean countries of Europe. Coriander seeds were used by the Romans to flavor many dishes.

Coriander is sold in two forms—whole and ground seeds. Both forms are used in Scandinavian cakes, cookies, and pastries. Whole coriander seed or sometimes the crushed is one of the standard seasonings in sausages and curries.

The fine leaves are used in both Spanish and Chinese cuisine.

Corinthe (French). A vine whose very sweet grapes are used in making white and rosé wines. The grapes may also be dried into raisins, or used in making liqueurs.

Cork. A Portuguese tree, related to the oak, whose bark is used for bottle stoppers.

Corkage. A restaurant charge for opening and serving a bottle of wine.

Corked. Of a wine bottle, having the taste of the cork.

Cork Extractor. A device for retrieving a cork accidentally pushed into a bottle of wine. It has three long wires bent at one end, twisted together, and attached to a handle. When the wires are pushed into the bottle, a sliding ring closes over the cork so that it can be pulled out.

Corkscrews. Instruments for removing corks from bottles have a wide variety of shapes and modes of operation. Some are spiral with a flat or rounded stem. A rounded stem is less likely to cut or break the cork. Another type consists of two rather thin, narrow, parallel steel blades attached at right angles to a heavy handle. The blades are inserted with a gentle rocking motion along opposite sides of the cork; when about halfway down the length of the cork they are pulled with a steady, twisting motion which removes the cork. A new satisfactory type uses a cartridge of compressed gas to force up the cork.

Corky. Of wines, tainted by a bad cork.

Corlieu (French). Curlew, a game bird.

Corme. Shad apple; in France made into a cider.

Corn. A native American cereal believed to have grown wild on the plateaus of Mexico and Central America thousands of years ago. For centuries corn has played a significant part in the religious ceremonies of the Indians, and today tourists travel miles out of their way to see an Indian corn dance.

The white man hails with delight the roasting-ear season. Green corn is at its best when cooked as soon as possible after being picked. It should be immersed in boiling, salted water and cooked until tender, 8–10 minutes.

The yellow varieties of corn are a good source of vitamin A, but the white varieties lack that nutrient. Corn is an excellent source of vitamin B (thiamine) and also contains vitamins C and G (riboflavin) as well as small amounts of minerals, phosphorus, and iron.

Corn is raised in every state of the Union, but most extensively in the area known as the "Corn Belt," which stretches from Ohio to Nebraska and from South Dakota and Minnesota to Missouri.

The only genetic difference between the delicious sweet corn in the produce bins and the field corn that is fed to livestock is a single recessive gene out of the hundreds or thousands of genes in corn. It is this gene that makes the sugary quality of the kernel persist in sweet corn; in other words, it prevents the conversion of some of the sugar into starch. A kernel of field corn lacks the sweetness of the edible variety, even though it may be just as tender.

A good ear of sweet corn has a cob well filled with bright, plump, milky kernels that are just firm enough to offer a slight resistance to pressure and to spurt milk when pricked. The husk should be fresh and green. Dry, yellowed, or straw-colored husks indicate age or damage. Unless properly cooled, corn heats rapidly when packed for shipment. Heating causes the yellowing and drying-out of the husk as well as toughening and discoloration. Immature corn kernels are small and very soft and lack flavor.

About two-thirds of the yearly United States sweet corn crop is marketed fresh, most of the remainder being canned or frozen. Canned corn may be packed either cream style or whole-kernel style; frozen corn usually comes in whole or cut ears or in whole kernels.

Cornas. Crude red wine produced in the Rhône region of France.

Corn Ball. Popcorn ball.

Corn Beef. *See* Corned Beef.

Corn Bread (American). Bread made of corn-meal instead of flour; usually bright yellow. There is also a type of Jewish corn bread, much like rye bread, but heavier.

Corncob; Cob. The rather firm central part of an ear of corn on which the kernels grow.

Corncrakes; Landrails. Migratory birds that spend the spring and summer in the British Isles and the winter in southern France, Spain, Italy, and Greece; popular game bird in England and on the Continent.

Corned. Cured with dry salt or a strong brine solution.

Corned Beef. Cured beef plate or rump. Because of its desirable proportion of tissue fat and lean meat the brisket plate is best suited for corning. The pieces may either be pumped with a pickling solution, or they may be cured by rubbing salt on each piece, packing the pieces in layers, and covering them with a pickle (about 20 percent on a brine salometer), together with sugar, nitrate, and nitrite. The meat is then cured at 36°F. about 4 weeks. Some cures also call for such spices as allspice and cloves to add flavor. Corned beef is not smoked.

Good cuts of corned beef weigh at least 3 pounds and are not too fat. The meat should be washed under running water to remove the brine from the surface, then placed in a large, deep kettle, covered with boiling water, and simmered 3 hours or until a steel fork will easily penetrate to the center.

Cornelian Cherry; Cornel. Olive-sized red fruit, prepared like a pickle in parts of France; occasionally made into a sweet jelly.

Cornet (1) (French). A thin wafer, often cone-shaped; usually made with flour, sugar, cream, eggs, and honey. (2) Cake-decorating devices made of a small sheet of paper rolled and pinned into conical shape. The point of the cornet is cut off to leave an opening as large as may be required. (3) Thin sliced meats are rolled into cone shapes, to be filled and served as an hors d'oeuvre or used as a garnish.

Corn Exchange. Corn market.

Corn Flour. White or yellow corn ground and sifted until the granules are as fine as those of wheat flour; used mainly by commercial bakeries.

Corn Fritter. A fritter batter made with corn.

Corn Husk. The leaves covering ears of corn.

Cornhusker. A moister-than-average cheddar cheese made in the middle western United States.

Cornichon (French). Small, immature gherkin pickled in vinegar; very sharp to the taste. In France it is often served with pâté, cold meats, or the meats from a *pot-au-feu*.

Cornimont. A pungent caraway-flavored French imitation of Münster cheese.

Corning Ware. Trade name of a cold- and heat-resistant material used in various cooking utensils. It can be used for containers of food to be frozen, and can also withstand direct heat.

Cornish Fair Maids. Smoked pilchards.

Cornish Heavy Cake. A light fruit cake which belies its name; baked in a shallow pan and usually served in squares.

Cornish Pastry. Torpedo-shaped pastry containing cubes of meat, potatoes, and other vegetables.

Cornish Sly Cakes. Flat pastry cakes with the dried-fruit filling showing through as a result of being pressed with a rolling pin; similar to eccles cakes.

Corn Meal. White or yellow corn cleaned and ground to a fineness specified by the federal (United States) government. It contains small amounts of fat and not more than 15 percent moisture. Bolted white or yellow corn meal is ground finer than regular corn meal but otherwise is the same. Enriched corn meal contains added vitamins and minerals.

Today corn is ground in steel rollers which break and remove the husk and germ almost entirely. The meal feels dry and granular and keeps very well. Old-fashioned stone-ground or water-ground corn meal was passed through stones to be crushed. Originally water was the source of power for turning the giant grinding stones. Some small mills still produce stone-ground corn meal, which often is sold by mail order. Stone-ground meal is sometimes thought to have a richer flavor than meal ground in steel rollers.

Corn 'n' Oil. A drink made with rum and flavored with falernum in Barbados, British West Indies.

Corn Oil. An edible oil expressed from corn. It is polyunsaturated and therefore desirable for low-cholesterol diets.

Corn Oyster. Corn fritters made with oysters or having an oyster taste.

Corn Parsley. A wild parsley.

Corn Pone. A corn pudding or corn bread made according to different recipes in the southern United States.

Corn Popper. Wire or solid-metal container used for popping corn.

Corn Salad; Field Salad; Lamb's Lettuce. A slightly bitter salad green that grows wild in Europe and Asia and is cultivated commercially in the United States. Served by itself or in combination with another lettuce, it is delectable simply dressed with oil and vinegar appropriately seasoned.

Cornstalk. An ear of corn; sometimes the entire stalk as well as the edible ear.

Cornstarch. A refined starch obtained from corn. It is used as a thickening agent in sauces, puddings, and pie fillings, and yields a more translucent paste than ordinary flour. Cornstarch should be dissolved in a little cold water before being added to a hot liquid, and it must be stirred constantly to prevent lumps. One tablespoonful of cornstarch has a thickening property equal to two tablespoons of regular flour.

Cornstarch Binder. A perfectly smooth mixture of water and cornstarch used to make foods adhere or to thicken sauces and stews.

Corn Syrup. Syrup obtained from cornstarch. Its principal ingredients are dextrose, maltose, and dextrins. Two types are commonly marketed: *Light corn syrup* has undergone a clarification and decolorization. *Dark corn syrup* is a mixture of corn syrup and refiner's syrup (the residual product obtained in the process of refining raw cane or beet sugar). Dark corn syrup is used as a table syrup and in the same ways as light corn syrup when a darker color and distinctive flavor are desired.

Cornucopia. A horn of plenty, usually filled with fruits.

Corny. (British, Colloquial). A strong ale.

Corn Whisky (American). Whisky distilled from a mash containing 80–90 percent corn.

Corona de Cordero (Spanish). Crown of lamb.

Coronata. *See* Italy, The Wines of.

Corroborant. An invigorating or strengthening drink or other substance.

Corsé (French). Wines with substance and body as well as high alcoholic content.

Corser. To reduce or concentrate any liquid or sauce by high heat or boiling.

Corse, Roquefort de. A Corsican imitation of Roquefort.

Corstorphine Cream (Scotch). A preparation of cream named for a village and hill near Edinburgh, where it is commonly made.

Corter. A quarter part of a cake.

Corton. A group of dry red wines produced near Beaune, in the Burgundy region of France. Although mediocre when young, they mature well.

Corton-Charlemagne. An important dry white wine of extraordinary taste and aroma, produced in the Burgundy region of France.

Corymb. A cluster of grapes or berries.

Cos. A type of lettuce native to Cos, Greece; now cultivated in many parts of the world. *See* Romaine.

Coscia di Montone al Marsala (Italian). Leg of lamb with marsala.

Cosido à Portuguesa (Portuguese). Boiled dinner consisting of meat, potatoes, and vegetables.

Cosher (British). One who lives off the food of others.

Coshery (Irish). Feast.

Cossettes. Strips of sugar beet ready to have the sugar removed.

Costalame di Bue (Italian). Ribs of beef.

Costard. Large cooking apple with riblike projections on its sides; formerly favored in England.

Costa Rica. *See* Central America.

Costata (Italian). Rib chop or steak.

Coste (Italian). Short ribs.

Costeletas Porco (Portuguese). Pork chops.

Costellinhas de Carneiro (Portuguese). Mutton chops.

Coster; Costermonger (British). Vendor of vegetables and fruit, who uses a pushcart or stand on the street. The term comes from *costard*, a variety of English apple.

Costillas (Spanish). Chops.

    Costillas de Cerdo. Spareribs.

Costmary. An aromatic herb of the *compositae* family; the dried leaves serve as flavoring for food and, in England, for ale; occasionally used as a tea base.

Costola (Italian). Rib.

Costoletta (Italian). Cutlet or chop.

    Costoletta alla Bolognese. Lightly breaded veal cutlet or chop served with tomato sauce and cheese.

    Costoletta alla Milanese. Fried breaded veal cutlet or chop.

    Costoletta d'Agnello. Lamb chop.

    Costoletta d'Agnello Panato. Breaded lamb chop.

    Costoletta di Maiale. Pork chop.

    Costoletta di Maiale alla Fiorentina. Pork chop cooked with wine and red cabbage.

    Costoletta di Vitello. Veal cutlet or chop.

Costrel. Large drinking bottle with a handle by which it can be hung from the waist.

Côte-à-Côte (French). "Side by side"; dining side by side rather than face to face (*tête-à-tête*).

Côteaux de la Loire. A white-wine region of France, whose products have a good bouquet, are dry or partly sweet, with a delicate fruity or floral quality.

Côte Blonde. A vineyard of the Côte Rôtie vineyards of the Rhône. *See* France, The Wines of.

Côte Brune. A vineyard of the Côte Rôtie vineyards of the Rhône. *See* France, The Wines of.

Côte de Beaune. A wine district of the Burgundy region of France. *See* France, The Wines of.

Côte de Dijon. A wine district of the Burgundy region of France. *See* France, The Wines of.

Côte de Nuits. A wine district of the Burgundy region of France. *See* France, The Wines of.

Côte d'Or. A wine district of the Burgundy region of France. *See* France, The Wines of.

Côte Maconnais. A wine district of the Burgundy region of France. *See* France, The Wines of.

Cotechino; Categhino (Italian). A large spiced pork sausage.

Cotelette (Dutch). Cutlet.

Côtelette (French). (1) Cutlet. (2) Chopped-meat preparation shaped like cutlets.

Côtelette d'Oeufs. Egg croquette, sometimes prepared with ham, tongue, or truffles; usually served with a tomato sauce.

Côte-Rôtie. A rather good, hearty, dry red wine produced in the Rhône Valley of southern France; it has a brilliant purple-red color, strong raspberry taste, and good bouquet. *See also* France, The Wines of.

Côtes Couverts à la Noix (French). A cut of beef, resembling the prime ribs.

Côtes de Boeuf (French). Ribs of beef.

Côtes de Bordeaux Saint-Macaire. A wine district of the Bordeaux region of France. *See* France, The Wines of.

Cotherstone Cheese (British). A blue-veined cow's-milk cheese similar to Stilton; made in Yorkshire, England.

Cotignac (French). A quince preserve, a delicacy prepared in Orléans.

Cotriade (French). Fish soup similar to bouillabaisse but made with butter (instead of olive oil), mackerel, sardines, and without garlic.

Cottabus; Kottabos. An amusement popular at ancient Greek parties; dinner guests took turns flinging the wine left in their cups into a container in a certain way.

Cottage Cheese. A soft uncured cheese usually mixed with some cream. Cheese with 4 percent or more fat is called *creamed cottage cheese*. Flavoring materials, such as peppers, olives, and pimientos may be added. Healthful and relatively inexpensive, it varies in calorie content, depending on whether or not cream is added to moisten the dry curds, Creamed cottage cheese is more fattening than the regular type.

The curds are derived from skim milk or from reconstituted concentrated skim milk or nonfat dry milk solids, and rennet is added. The curd may be cut into rather large pieces; this is usually called *pot cheese* or *popcorn cheese*. When the curds are smaller, the alternate names for cottage cheese are *country-style* or *farm-style* cheese.

Cottage Loaf (British). Two round loaves of bread, one on top of the other, pressed down and allowed to rise, then lightly punched down before baking.

Cottenham. A rich, creamy, medium-hard British cheese with a bluish mold.

Cotto (Italian). Cooked.

Cottonfish. Freshwater blackfish.

Cottonseed Oil. An edible oil prepared from cottonseeds. Refined into a bland-flavored fat, it may be used for almost all cookery purposes that do not require a solid fat. It is used extensively in commercial food preparation. When hardened, the oil is used for margarine.

Cottslowe. A soft, somewhat strong-flavored cream cheese made in the Cotswolds, England.

Coucou (French). A group of fish, particularly the rouget.

Coucoumelle. A rather uncommon wood mushroom found in parts of France.

Couenne; Couenne de Porc (French). The fat-cleaned skin of a pig used to grease pans in France; pork rind.

Cougloff (German, Alsatian). Yeast cake made with fruit.

Couhé-Verac. A plain aromatic goat's-milk cheese made in Poitou, France.

Coulandon, Fromage de. A delicate-flavored goat's-milk cheese similar to Brie, made in the Bourbonnais region of France.

Coulibiac (Russian). Hot fish pie made with salmon, pike, perch, or, as in France, with turbot. The fish is chopped, seasoned with various herbs and spices, and baked in a brioche pastry. Modern versions are also prepared with meat or vegetable fillings.

Coulibiac au Chou. Classic Russian fish dish, consisting of pastry filled with a freshwater-fish mixture; the sauce is served separately.

Coulibiac d'Anguille. Pastry filled with pieces of eel, mushrooms, onions, and hard-cooked eggs.

Coulis; Coullis; Cullis. (1) (Obsolete). Good stock or broth used in making other dishes. An 18th-century recipe calls for bacon, veal, ham, carrots, onions, celery, butter, flour, and parsley cooked until almost dry; then water is added, and it is cooked again until yellowish, then strained. (2) The strained juice of meat, fish, or poultry thickened with bread, flour, or corn-starch. (3) An uncooked purée of tomatoes, or any liquid pulp, used to flavor ragouts and stews.

Coulommiers (French). An excellent-tasting small Brie cheese made near Paris between October and July.

Coulommiers Frais. A fresh cream cheese made around Paris, France.

Coumarin. White crystals used in the food industry to supply a vanilla taste synthetically. *See also* Tonka Bean.

Count Cake (British). Three-cornered cake.

Country Green. A fine-flavored Chinese green tea.

Country-Milled Flour. Flour milled locally, though not always from local wheat.

Country Whites (British). Average white flour.

Coupage (French). The mixture of different wines to obtain a desired result.

Coup d'Avant (French). An alcoholic drink taken before a meal.

Coup d'Après (French). A drink, usually a glass of wine, consumed after a meal.

Coup de Feu (French). A burned joint of meat.

Coupe de Vin (French). The quantity of wine that can be swallowed in one gulp.

Coupe (French). (1) A dessert, usually served in a tall, stemmed glass known as a champagne coupe, consisting of a scoop of ice cream garnished with whipped cream, candied or fresh fruits, and/or chopped nuts. Sometimes syrups or sweeteners are added. (2) A cutting instrument.

Coupe à Légumes (French). Vegetable cutter.

Coupe à Pâte (French). Pastry cutter.

Coupe Jacques (French). Ice-cream dessert decorated with preserved fruit, almonds, cherries, and kirschwasser.

Couperet (French). Very sharp, short knife used for slicing, boning, and cutting meat.

Couque; Couque-Banque (1) (Flemish). Breakfast or tea cake similar to a brioche, usually eaten with apple butter. (2) Pancake made of buckwheat flour and butter. The English borrowed the recipe from the French, who had borrowed it from the Germans. The French term is *couque-banque*, the German *kuchen-gebäcken*.

Couque de Dinant (Belgian). Flat cake made from flour and buckwheat honey and allowed to dry for a few days, then dunked in coffee at the time of eating.

Couronne. (1) Crown-shaped. Pastries, meats, etc, arranged in a ring mold. (2) A round loaf of French bread with fancy twists.

Courseulles. A port in Brittany, France, known particularly for its exceptional-tasting oysters.

Court Bouillon (French). (1) A highly seasoned stock in which fish is simmered to enhance the flavor. (2) Seasoned stock containing vegetables.

Couscous; Couscoussou (North African, particularly Algerian and Moroccan). Preparation made with a prepared cereal called *faufal* (consisting of tiny pellets of semolina) steamed with mutton or chicken together with vegetables and a very hot sauce.

Couscous dates back to the Assyrians and Greeks. The French adopted it from the North Africans. During World War II American soldiers stationed in France became acquainted with couscous and it has since become popular with Americans.

Faufal may be obtained in Near Eastern or oriental food-specialty shops. Otherwise cracked wheat, wheat semolina, or even farina may be used, but the results will be less satisfactory. In North Africa it is proper to eat couscous with the hand. A chick-pea or a raisin, together with a small amount of cooked semolina, is shaped into a small ball and eaten. To avoid spotting clothing a spoon is recommended for beginners.

A sweet couscous is made with raisins and nuts, but the spicy version is far more popular.

Cousinette (French). A rich vegetable soup served with a piece of bread in it; a specialty of the Béarnaise region.

Couteau de Cuisine (French). Standard kitchen knife from 6–9 inches long.

Couteau à Decouper (French). Carving knife, usually about 14–16 inches long.

Couteau à Desosser (French). Boning knife, long and thin.

Couteau Econome (French). Potato-peeling knife.

Couteau à Filets de Sole (French). Knife for filleting fish.

Couteau d'Office (French). Paring knife with a very fine edge.

Couteau Julienne (French). Knife for cutting vegetables into julienne strips.

Couteau Tranche-Lard (French). Fine-edged slicing knife, usually about 16–20 inches long.

Couve (Portuguese). Cabbage.

Couve Flor (Portuguese). Cauliflower.

Couvert. (1) Table setting for a meal, such as bread and butter, silver, and napkins. (2) Cover charge made by restaurants.

Couverture (French). Frosting or topping.

Couveuse. A nondescript wild mushroom.

Cove. An oyster found along the Virginia coast of the United States.

Coventry God Cakes. Ancient English cakes always made at Coventry and given to children by their godparents on New Year's Day. They were made with rough puff pastry and mincemeat, cut into triangles, brushed with egg white, sprinkled with sugar, and baked golden brown and puffy.

Cover Charge. The charge made by a restaurant in addition to the price of what is ordered; intended to cover the cost of a place setting, bread and butter, and the like.

Covey. A brood of partridges, quails, or other game birds.

Cow. A domestic female bovine animal, useful for its milk and flesh; inferior in taste and texture to steer meat.

Coward Sandwich. Half a Hero sandwich. *See* Hero Sandwich.

Cowberry; Red Huckleberry; Red Whortleberry. Different red wild berries growing in the United States; usually the cranberry.

Cow Calf. A female calf; a heifer.

Cow Chervil; Cow Parsley. Wild herb sometimes used for flavoring.

Cow Cress. A wild watercress.

Cowfish. A bony-shelled fish native to the coastal waters of North Carolina; usually cooked in its shell.

Cow Heel. The foot of a cow, with the hoof removed and cleaned; can be stewed with onions or leeks and seasonings until liquid is clear, cut into small pieces and eaten with parsley sauce, or made into rich jellied head cheese.

Cowish. Edible root of a wild plant native to the northwestern United States.

Cow Milker. Mechanical instrument for milking cows.

Cow Parsnip; Hogweed; Meadow Parsnip. A weed found in many temperate countries; used in soups and stews, eaten as a vegetable, and also made into a type of beer.

Cowpea. Black-eyed bean popular in the southern United States; available fresh but generally dried or canned.

Cow Pilot. A mediocre West Indian fish sometimes used for food.

Cowslip. Marsh marigold, an edible wild flower.

Cow Wheat. A plant with seeds similar to wheat grains. When ground, it may be used like ordinary wheat.

Coy. Lobster trap.

Cozida (Portuguese). Boiled.

Cozze (Italian). Mussels.

> **Cozze Acciugate.** Mussels in anchovy sauce.
> **Cozze alla Marinara.** Mussels with herbs, oil, and garlic.
> **Cozze Oreganate.** Baked mussels with oregano.

Crab. A shellfish. The Atlantic and Pacific coasts have their own kinds of this popular shellfish. From the Atlantic and Gulf coasts come *blue crabs*, which compose three-fourths of all the crabs marketed in the United States. *Dungeness* *crabs* are found on the Pacific coast from Alaska to Mexico. *King crabs* are caught in the North Pacific off Alaska. Both New England and California produce *rock crabs*, and of local importance are the *stone crabs* of Florida and the *tanner crabs* of Alaska.

Crabs are available in fish stores in a variety of forms: live, cooked in the shell, cooked and frozen, fresh cooked meat, and canned meat. Live hard-shell crabs are usually sold within a short distance of where they are caught, for they are highly perishable and do not travel long distances. Live soft-shell crabs are shipped hundreds of miles, but they must be packed in ice and seaweed and handled carefully. (Soft-shell crabs are molting blue crabs taken just after they have shed their hard shells and before the new shells are formed.) Fresh hard-shell and soft-shell crabs should be cooked when they are alive. Cooked hard-shell crabs should be refrigerated, iced, or frozen from the time they are cooked until they are used. Crabmeat from blue, Dungeness, king, or rock crab is usually available in cans.

Crab Apple. Fruit of the crab-apple tree, from which tart jellies and preserves are made.

Crab apples are native to both Asia and North America, and are cultivated on a limited commercial scale, New York and Michigan being the leading growers. Crab-apple trees are grown in many yards throughout the United States, for their pinkish white blossoms are decorative.

Crab-Apple Jelly. A bright red jelly made from crab apples.

Crabbed. Bitter.

Crablet. Young crab.

Crab Nut. Nut or seed of a crab tree.

Crab Roe. The roe of crabs; used in the cuisine of many countries. In China crab roe is often prepared with eggs, like a thin pancake, and has a delicate flavor.

Crack. To boil sugar at 280°F.

Cracked Wheat. A coarse flour prepared by cracking or cutting cleaned whole wheat, other than durum, into angular fragments; used for making bread.

Cracker. In the United States, usually a dry, thin wafer, either unsweetened or slightly sweet; in Britain, called a "biscuit."

Crackers come in a wide variety of shapes and forms. The simplest are made of water and flour to which a little salt may be added. They are baked until dry and crisp. Sometimes butter is added for a more crumbly cracker. The hard, unleavened crackers known as *ship biscuits, hardtack,* or *pilot biscuits* are examples of this type. *Soda crackers* are another example, as are the tiny *oyster crackers* served atop oyster stews and bisques. Crackers sometimes are salted, sometimes not.

Crackers should be stored in a moisture- and vapor-proof container to retain crispness. If they become soft, they may be heated in a slow oven until crisp again.

Crackerjack. Candied popcorn sold in a long paper box.

Cracker Meal. Crushed, sifted meal obtained from unsweetened crackers; used to coat croquettes and other foods before deep-fat frying; also used as a topping for casseroles.

Crackling; Cracklings. The appetizing crunchy browned skin on roasted pork. The term *cracklings* is generally used only for crunchy, crisp remains after lard has been cooked out of hog fat. Often "crackling" and "cracklings" are used interchangeably.

Crackling Bread. A bread made with corn meal shortened with salt-pork cracklings; a specialty in the southern United States but popular throughout the country.

Cracknel; Crackle; Crackling; Craqueter; Craquelin. Sweet cake with a hard, shiny, shell-like surface, and a soft fluffy center. *Cracknel,* as used in the King James Version of the Bible, in the list of gifts given by the wife of Jeroboam to the prophet Ahijah (1 Kings 14:3), is probably a corruption which occurred in the translation from the Greek.

Cracknuts. (1) In England, a variety of Spanish nut. (2) A delicious cake that does not, however, contain nuts.

Cradle Spit. A spit with a wire net in the center to hold poultry, small birds, game, or small pieces of meat to avoid piercing before cooking over a barbecue or grill.

Crakeberries. *See* Crowberries.

Cram. To eat hastily; to stuff food into the mouth.

Cramant. A still white wine produced near Épernay, France, from grapes also used in making champagne.

Crambamboli; Crambambuli (German). Traditional punches, now served either hot or iced. A quart of ale is boiled until bubbling, then sugar and ½ pint of rum are added. The hot mixture is removed from the heat and half a dozen beaten eggs are thoroughly stirred into it. It is then poured into a large bowl and served in mugs. Formerly the preparation of these punches was the cause of considerable rivalry and even duels.

Crambe (Obsolete). Cabbage.

Cramique (Belgian). Yeast bread made with raisins.

Cramp (British, Scotch). Heavy cake made with inferior flour.

Crampit. Crumpet.

Cran (1) (French). Wild horseradish. (2) Piece of iron that holds a kettle over a fire.

Cranberry. A tart fruit, native to North America, first cultivated in Massachusetts. The Cape Cod area still produces about 50 percent of the country's annual crop. The Indians used cranberries both as food and as medicine, and taught the Pilgrims the virtues of the fruit. Early New England sailors took barrels of cranberries with them on long ocean voyages to consume as protection against scurvy.

Only in the last century have cranberries been developed into an intensive industry, crops being grown commercially not only in Massachusetts but also in Wisconsin and New Jersey.

At one time the cranberry season was limited. Cranberries came on the market just in time to be prepared in a sauce that was the traditional accompaniment to Thanksgiving turkey, and they were available only until after the Christmas festivities. Formerly whole cranberries, strung on twine, were a popular garland for the Christmas tree.

Even today some people think of cranberries only as an accompaniment to poultry, but the delicious fruit has many other culinary uses. The bright color and pleasantly sharp tang of

the sauce also goes well with meats. And the fresh berries, suitably sweetened, are used in a wide variety of desserts, including sherbets, ices, pies, cakes, and puddings.

Now cranberries are in season almost every month of the year. When the fresh berries are gone, there are frozen whole cranberries, and even more widely distributed are canned cranberry sauces, either whole or strained and jellied. Cranberry juice is a surprisingly refreshing drink.

Fresh cranberries should be put in a boiling sugar syrup and cooked only until they pop. Additional cooking tends to make them bitter. The sauce is at its tangy best if cooked in syrup consisting of two cups of sugar to one cup of water.

Cranson (French). Wild horseradish.

Crany. A crumb.

Crapaudine, À la (French). Cooked game prepared to resemble a frog, as by trussing poultry.

Crapaudine Sauce (French). Brown sauce made with onions, vinegar, and spices.

Crape Fish. Salt cod pressed into a hard, brick-like form, a method formerly used for preserving fish for long voyages.

Crappie. A sunfish native to the Mississippi River and adjacent waters; fairly good-tasting.

Crappin (Scotch). Stuffing for poultry.

Crappit Heads; Crappit Heids (Scotch). Stuffed fish heads.

Craquelin (French). Very crunchy, crisp pastry or cracker.

Craquelot (French). Lightly pickled, salted, or smoked young herring.

Crassane. A deliciously flavored French sweet pear with a gray-green skin; it ripens in the late fall and keeps well.

Cratchern Cakes (British). Cakes made with inferior lard.

Crater. A large bowl for mixing water and wine.

Crattle (British). Crumb.

Cravo (Portuguese). Clove.

Crawfish. *See* Crayfish.

Crawl. (1) A shallow-water enclosure for turtles, fish, etc. (2) A West Indian pigpen.

Crayfish; Crawfish. A freshwater shellfish. The Swedes eat boiled crayfish with gulps of aquavit;

the French prepare it in a bisque, in cold mousses, or au gratin. In the United States crayfish is not common on the East Coast; it is caught in some Midwestern streams and ponds, and is well known on the West Coast. A relative of the lobster, but much smaller, it may be cooked like lobster or shrimp.

Cream. (1) The fat part of milk that rises to the surface when milk is allowed to stand. Commercially it is removed from the milk by centrifugal force in a separator.

Light cream or coffee cream usually contains not less than 18 percent butterfat. *Medium cream* contains 30–36 percent butterfat. *Heavy*, or whipping, cream contains no less than 36 percent butterfat. *Homogenized* cream is light or medium cream treated so as to reduce the size of fat globules; it does not whip well.

(2) A process of rubbing, usually with the back of a spoon, to soften fats and to mix other foods well with fats. Creaming can be done in an electric mixer or with a slotted wooden spoon.

(3) A dessert preparation; either a rich custard, a flavored whipped-cream filling for pies, cakes, tarts, or cream puffs, or a garnish for pastries.

Cream Bun. A cream puff filled with whipped cream, then frosted.

Cream Caramel. Candy made by boiling butter, sugar, cream, and flavorings.

Cream Chantilly. Vanilla-flavored whipped cream.

Cream Cheese. A very rich perishable white cheese, soft, mild-flavored, and uncured, made either wholly with cream or with a mixture of milk and cream. Very popular in the United States, it is used as a sandwich filling, either plain or mixed with chopped olives, pimientos, etc.; as an ingredient in cheesecakes; and as an ingredient in some frostings.

Creamer. (1) A small pitcher or container, part of a tea service, for holding cream. (2) Dairy equipment for separating milk from cream.

Creamery. (1) Place where cheese and butter are made. (2) (British). Shop selling dairy products.

Cream Nut. Brazil nut.

Cream of Tartar. An ingredient of baking powders; a white crystalline substance with a gritty consistency and an acid taste, often obtained from the crystallized scrapings of wine vats in France. It is used for stabilizing egg whites beaten for an angel cake.

Creamometer. Machine that measures the amount of cream in a given quantity of milk.

Cream Pitcher. Usually a fairly small crystal, glass, china, or metal jug in which cream is served; sometimes part of a set with a sugar bowl of similar proportions. The old-fashioned name was *creamer*.

Cream Powders. Acidic powders used in the manufacture of baking powder.

Cream Puffs. Delectable pastries usually prepared in individual portions and consisting of a light, delicate hollow puff of pastry (*pâte à choux*) filled with sweetened whipped cream or with custard. Hot cream puffs, of a smaller size, filled with a seasoned chicken mixture or a sharp cheese, are a popular cocktail accompaniment.

Creams. A rich group of desserts made with cream, sometimes with egg yolks, sugar, and flavorings. Gelatin may be added, but not by perfectionists.

Cream Sauce. A white or velouté sauce enriched with cream.

Cream Separator. Machine that separates cream from milk.

Cream Soup. Thick soup enriched with milk or cream and usually having a cereal, vegetable, fowl, fish, or shellfish base.

Cream, Synthetic. An emulsion of vegetable oil, milk or milk powder, egg yolk, and sugar.

Creamy Batter. A fluffy batter mixture.

Creasy, Highland. *See* Cress, Upland.

Creasy Salad. *See* Cress, Upland.

Crèche. A rather strong, aromatic goat's-milk cheese made in Poitou, France.

Crécy. A French town famous for its excellent carrots. (1) Dishes named "à la Crécy" usually contain carrots or carrot purée. (2) Carrot soup.

Creepie (British). A small speckled fowl.

Creesh (British). Fat or grease.

Crema (Italian). Cream.

Crema di Cioccolata. Chocolate-cream dessert.
Crema di Parmigiano. Parmesan cheese spread.
Crema di Piselli. Cream of pea soup.

Crema di Pollo. Cream of chicken soup.

Crema Rovesciata. Baked custard.

Crema (Spanish). Cream.

Crema Batida. Whipped cream.

Crema Española. A milk-gelatin-and-egg dessert.

Crema Danica. Very popular soft Danish cheese, a cross between Camembert and Brie; particularly good with fresh fruit or red wine. Known as *Castello cheese* in Europe.

Crema di Timo. An Italian liqueur prepared with thyme.

Crémant (French). Pertaining to the light-sparkling quality of wine in contrast to full-sparkling, as in champagne.

Crème (French). (1) Cream. *See under* Cream (3). (2) A group of rich desserts made with cream and flavorings, sometimes with the addition of egg yolks and gelatin.

Crème, À la. Any dish prepared with added cream.

Crème Anglaise. Custard sauce, made with milk, egg yolks, and sugar; cooked gently until the mixture thickens to form a light cream. Sometimes, a small amount of starch may be added. It may be served hot or cold, or used as the basis for Bavarian cream, ice cream, etc.

Crème Bavaroise. Bavarian cream.

Crème Brûlée. Caramel custard made with thin cream, egg yolks, and sugar, with brown sugar sprinkled on top. The custard is placed under a broiler until the sugar melts.

Crème Fouettée. Whipped cream.

Crème Fraîche. Heavy, thickened, slightly soured sweet cream; served with all desserts that require cream. This type of cream is not available in the United States, but it can be duplicated by mixing 1 cup of heavy cream with 1 teaspoon of buttermilk and beating until lukewarm. Pour into a loosely covered container and let stand at room temperature 6–8 hours or until thickened. Stir the cream, cover, and refrigerate until needed. It will thicken even more, and may be kept up to a month. Truly fresh sweet cream is called *fleurette* in France.

Crème d'Arbouse (French). A sweet liqueur. *See* Arbouse.

Crème Chantilly. *See* Hablé Crème Chantilly; *see also* Chantilly.

Crème d'Ananas. A French liqueur made principally from pineapple.

Crème de Bananes. A French liqueur made chiefly from bananas.

Crème de Foie d'Oie (French). A smooth paste containing not less than 50 percent goose liver, the balance consisting of other livers or meats.

Crème de Fromage Frite (French). A mixture of thick Béchamel sauce combined with grated cheese, spread to dry, then cut into any desired shape, rolled in bread crumbs, and fried crisp.

Crème de Gruyère. A bland, softened Gruyère cheese made in France and Switzerland and sold in small tinfoil portions.

Crème de Marrons Glacés (French). Chestnut purée, usually flavored with sugar and vanilla extract.

Crème de Menthe (French). A cordial or liqueur made from several different mints, but usually from peppermint; bottled in two styles— white and green.

Crème de Moka. A French mocha-flavored liqueur.

Crème de Noyaux. A French liqueur flavored from various fruit stones; the taste resembles that of almonds.

Crème de Riz (French). (1) Finely ground rice. (2) A white cream soup containing powdered rice.

Crème de Thé. A French sweet liqueur made with tea.

Crème d'Orge (French). (1) Finely ground barley. (2) A white cream soup containing fine barley.

Crème-Double (French). A white soft cheese made with considerable heavy cream. *See also* Double-Crème.

Crème Renversée (French). Rich custard, usually baked in a round mold, served cold with a caramel syrup.

Crèmes (French). Cordials and liqueurs with a creamlike smoothness.

Crémets; Crémets d'Angers; Crémets de Saumur (French). A fresh-cream cheese dessert, popular around Anjou, prepared from cream whipped with beaten egg whites and served with vanilla, sugar, and added cream in perforated molds; formerly called *mulons*.

Crème Yvette. A purple-colored American cordial with a taste of violets.

Cremini. Small soft, rich cream cheeses made in Cremona, Italy.

Cremor. A thick or viscous juice.

Creole Cheese. Fresh cottage cheese combined with sweet cream; popular in Louisiana.

Creole Sauce. A number of sauces made with tomatoes or tomato sauce, onions, garlic, green pepper, and various other ingredients. Chili powder is sometimes used; in other recipes thyme is the seasoning. The sauce is a Louisiana specialty, usually served on eggs or fish.

Creoved (British). Hardly baked; raw; underdone.

Crêpes (French). Pancakes usually thinner than American pancakes or griddle cakes.

 Crêpes à la Grecque. Thin pancakes served with ground poultry or meat, combined with a rich sauce, and baked in the oven with grated cheese.

 Crêpes Dentelles. Lacy pancakes, specialty of Quimperlé.

 Crêpes Suzette. Very thin French dessert pancakes with curaçao and orange juice flavoring the sauce.

Crepes do Ceu (Portuguese). Pancakes filled with whipped cream and candied fruits.

Crépine de Porc; Crépine (French). The caul of a pig; the membrane surrounding part of the pig's intestine. Pig's cauls are frequently used in French provincial cooking to hold foods in shape.

Crépinette (French). (1) A small flat meat or game sausage, wrapped in a *crépine*, usually served with truffles and a sauce. (2) Fried or roasted chopped meat served with a sauce.

Crépy. A fairly good dry green-gold white wine of Savoy, France.

Crescents. French crescent-shaped breakfast breads (*croissants*) made with leavened dough or sometimes with puff pastry. They originated in Budapest but are very popular in France with *café au lait*.

Crescenz. A German wine term meaning "the growth." *See* Germany, The Wines of.

Crescenza. A soft, rather sweet cow's-milk cheese made in Lombardy, Italy, between September and April.

Cress. Watercress and garden cress, pepper-flavored plants very rich in vitamin A; a nutritious and delicious addition to mixed-green salads or sandwiches. Too often it is regarded only as a garnish and is not eaten.

Cress, Upland. Winter cress, a plant similar to watercress; also called Creasy Salad and Highland Creasy.

Cresson de Fontaine (French). Watercress.

Crêtes (French). Giblets.

Crêtes de Coq. Rooster (cock's) combs; a rather tasteless substance once in great vogue in French *haute cuisine*, but now rarely used.

Creton (French). A cold appetizer made from ground pork and onions, and served in aspic or jelly.

Creusain (French). A round cow's- and goat's-milk cheese with a hard rind.

Creuse Cheese. A distinctive cheese produced in the Department of Creuse, France. Made with skim milk and coagulated with rennet, it is kept in earthenware molds for several days while the whey drips off. Then it is rubbed with salt and may be aged for a year or more. Aged Creuse is dry and firm. Creuse is also sold fresh in tightly closed containers lined with straw. The fresh version is soft, yellow, and quite strong.

Creux (French). Describes a wine that is thin and lacking in substance.

Crevan. A hard dry crust.

Crever (French). To cook a food such as rice or macaroni until it is tender but still firm.

Crever, Faire (French). To boil rice until it bursts.

Crevette (French). Shrimp.

Crevette Liege (French). Plain or fruited brioche.

Crevis (Obsolete). Crayfish.

Crib. Corn-storage bin.

Crimka Wheat. A Russian red winter wheat with good milling qualities.

Crimme (British). To crumble bread.

Crimp. To cut gashes around the edges of food with a sharp knife.

Crimping. (1) Before baking, preventing juices from escaping from fruit pies by tucking the top pastry under the crust at the rim and then pressing the entire circumference against the rim of the pie plate with the tines of a fork or a similar implement.

(2) A method of finely scoring a fish before it is dead so that the muscular fibers are divided before they can become rigid. Crimped fish cooks better and tends to lie flat. Skate is sometimes served in this way when prepared by boiling, but cod and salmon also may be crimped.

Crimping Board. A wooden slab or an iron plate so corrugated that when pastry is rolled over it in different directions a pattern is formed on the surface.

Crin Crin. A green thick-leafed vegetable found in many parts of the world; prepared like spinach.

Criotte-Chambertin. Fine dark, dry red wines produced in Burgundy, France; they age well.

Cripple-Men. Oatcakes toasted before the fire.

Crispeddi (Sicilian). Fritters made with ricotta cheese and anchovies.

Crisps; Cresps (Obsolete). (1) Pancakes. (2) In the United States formerly a favorite thin cracker made with cream, sugar, flour, milk, and eggs, and baked until very dry.

Criss-Cross (or **Lattice**) **Crust.** For the top crust of a two-crust pie the pastry is cut into strips about ½ inch wide. Strips are placed parallel across the top of the filling about ¾ inch apart; a second layer of strips is then placed at right angles to the first layer, forming a criss-cross or lattice pattern.

Croaker. A small American freshwater fish. The name originates from the sound made by the fish when caught.

Crocchette di Riso (Italian). Rice croquettes.

Crocchette di Riso alla Torinese (Italian). Rice fritters.

Crock. Earthenware or other vessel used for storing foods such as butter, pickles, and meats.

Crockery. Earthenware dishes or pots; all of the various types of china.

Crockle (British). A crust of bread.

Crocus. The freshwater drumfish, a food fish.

Croissant Cheese. A small soft, rich cheese, a French specialty.

Croissant Demi-Sel (French). A salty cream cheese.

Croissants. *See* Crescents.

Cromesquis; Kromeskis. Meat, poultry, or fish shaped into croquettes and sometimes rolled in thin slices of bacon, then dipped in batter and fried.

Crookneck. A squash with rough, firm markings and gooselike neck.

Croquant; Croquante (French). (1) A transparent mixture of sugar and fruits. (2) A crunchy confection. (3) A cake usually made with almonds. (4) Crisp pastry used for tarts.

Croque. Crisp, rather hard sugar-coated fruit-paste confection.

Croque au Sel (French). Coarse raw vegetables dipped in salt and eaten plain.

Croquembouche (French). Elaborate pastry in which small individual cream puffs are care-

fully arranged in gradually decreasing concentric circles to form a pyramid, which is then covered with a sugar syrup.

Croque Monsieur (French). Two slices of crustless bread with sliced ham and cheese between, dipped in egg, and sometimes fried, sometimes baked.

Croquet. *See* Croquettes.

Croquetas de Pollo (Spanish). Chicken croquettes.

Croquetjes (Dutch). Croquettes.

Croquette Marchoise. A strong French goat's-milk cheese; not very good during the winter months.

Croquettes. (1) A deep-fat-fried main dish. Finely minced chicken, fish, or meat, appropriately seasoned and usually held together by a thick white sauce, is shaped into cones or rolls, which are dipped in egg and crumbs and fried in deep fat. They are often served with a sauce. (2) A small thin biscuit.

Croquettes de Fromage. Grated cheese and bread crumbs fried in deep fat.

Croquignole. A hard, dry, crisp cake resembling cracknel. *See* Cracknels.

Cros Bout (French). A cut of beef somewhat like the American brisket cut.

Cros du Gîte du Derrière (French). A cut of beef resembling the American leg of beef.

Crosnes (French). Stachys, a vegetable.

Cross Bun, Hot. Small sugar-iced bun marked with a cross; eaten during Lent.

Crossed Buns. Hot cross buns.

Cross Grain. Meat or fowl carved across the grain rather than with the grain.

Crostacei (Italian). Shellfish.

Crostata di Fragole (Italian). Strawberry pie.

Crostini (Italian). A fried cheese sandwich; toast.

Crostino alle Acciughe (Italian). Fried toast with eggs or anchovies.

Crottin de Chavignol. A medium firm, salted goat's-milk cheese made in the Berry district of France.

Crouch Ware. Salt-glazed pottery made in Staffordshire, England.

Crouke (Obsolete). Jug or pitcher.

Croustade Jurassien (French). Flaky cheese-flavored pastry dough served as an appetizer in the Jura region.

Croustades (French). A wide variety of preparations bear this name; though the ingredients may differ, all are encased in a crust, either of bread or of pastry. They are designed in unusual shapes, or they may be contained simply in a hollowed-out loaf of bread. They may be filled with a thick paste of meat, fish, or poultry, or with a thick stew.

Croustadine (French). Pastry shell.

Croustilles (French). Thin slices of potatoes fried in deep fat; potato chips.

Croûte (French). Any of a number of different garnishes or decorations made of bread, and served with soup, stews, and the like.

Croûte-au-Pot (French). A clear soup with crusts of toasted bread floating in it. The English call it *potluck*.

Croûtes à la Moelle (French). Fried pieces of bread with beef marrow and truffles.

Croûtes Délicieuses (French). Fried pieces of bread prepared with mushrooms and cheese.

Croutons. Bread cubes, either buttered or plain, baked in a slow oven or sautéed until crisp and evenly browned; served as a garnish for soups or in Caesar salads. As with toast, day-old bread is better for preparing croutons than a very fresh loaf.

Crow. Crows have at times been used for food. In Germany when food was scarce during World War I crows were in great demand. The young birds are fairly tender, but the meat of older crows is tough and leathery, though it can be converted into a relatively acceptable bouillon.

Crowberries; Crakeberries. Small black, slightly acid, berrylike fruits, which grow on small shrubs in northern climates; popular with youngsters in northern Scotland and northern Russia.

Crowdy; Crowdie. (1) (Scotch). Thick gruel or oatmeal mixed with cold milk, water, or beer. (2) A fresh-cream cheese.

Crow Garlic. Wild garlic sometimes used as a flavoring ingredient.

Crown Roast. A luxury pork or lamb roast. Two racks consisting of unseparated rib chops are formed into a circle, turned meat side inward, and tied tightly. At least 12 chops are usually required.

Crozes-Hermitage. A group of indifferent white and red wines produced in the Dauphiné region of France.

Cru (French). A vineyard; by extension, the wine produced from such a vineyard.

Cru, Vin du (French). Literally, "wine of the country"; local wine.

Crub (British). A crust of bread.

Cruchade (French). A cornmeal cereal, made in parts of France.

Crucian. A fair-tasting fish native to central Europe.

Cruddy Butter. *See* Crowdy.

Crude. Unripe; raw or uncooked.

Crude Gluten. Gluten containing bran and other extraneous matter.

Crudité (French). Raw food, especially radishes, carrots, and celery.

Cruets. Small bottles holding pepper, vinegar, oil, mustard, and other condiments, arranged in a

stand, usually with a handle at the top.

Cruet Sauce. English term for French vinaigrette sauce.

Crule (Scotch). Small oatmeal pancake.

Crullers. Usually twisted lengths of sweet batter fried in deep hot fat, then often sprinkled with granulated or powdered sugar. The term is from the Dutch *krullen*, which means "to curl." *See also* Doughnuts.

Crulls (Obsolete). Potatoes cut in curls and fried in deep fat. "Crull" is a corruption of "curl."

Crumb. (1) A small piece of bread broken from a larger piece. (2) To cover foods with crumbs before frying or baking. (3) To sweep crumbs from a tablecloth.

Crumble. To break doughy foods into small particles; to form into crumbs.

Crumpet (British). A soft unsweetened cake cooked on a griddle; often served at teatime.

Crusades. Fried bread croutons hollowed out, filled with apricot preserves or orange marmalade, and dusted with flavored sugar.

Crus Artisans. A group of good but unimportant wines produced in the Médoc region, Bordeaux, France.

Crus Bourgeois; Bourgeois Supérieurs. A fairly large group of fair wines produced in the Médoc and Graves regions of Bordeaux, France.

Cruse. Earthenware container, pot, bottle, or jug for liquids.

Crush. Fruits and spices ground up or combined into syrups for use as flavorings in creams and fillings.

Crus Paysan. A group of better wines produced in the Médoc and Haut-Médoc regions of Bordeaux, France; inferior to the *crus bourgeois* and the *crus artisans*.

Crust. (1) The firm, sometimes browned surface of baked or cooked foods such as breads, rolls, muffins, and meats, usually of the same composition as the food itself.

A pie crust serves as a container for food as in a one-crust pie, or as an encasing element to hold juices, as in a two-crust fruit pie.

(2) The hardened deposit thrown off by red wines which have been aged long in bottles. *See also* Crusted Port.

Crustaceans. A large group of marine animals with very hard shells, including lobster, crab, shrimp, crayfish, etc., which are edible. The word "crustacean" comes from the Latin *crusta*, meaning "rind."

Crustaceos (Portuguese, Spanish). Crustaceans; shellfish.

Crustas. A short drink for which the inside of the glass is lined with orange or lemon peel; served in either a wineglass or an Old-Fashioned glass.

Crusted Port. Vintage port throws a heavy crust, which is the same as the lees, impurities from wine, found in a cask in which the wine has been stored. All red wines form a certain amount of crust inside the bottle, but that of port is conspicuous. In serving port the bottle must be handled gently so as not to disturb the crust.

Crustose. Having a covering similar to a crust, such as the thick skin of a mushroom.

Crusty Bread. Bread having a hard surface.

Crystallizing. Crystallized flowers, fruits, and confections make attractive decorations for many kinds of desserts. They are not difficult to prepare, although the crystallizing equipment is somewhat complicated. A crystallizing tin is available at stores that offer supplies for professional pastry chefs. It consists of a tin box filled with wire gratings or trays so arranged that they can be let into the box in even stages, one above the other. The trays have four legs arranged so that the legs of the second tray rest on the upper surface of the first tray, and so on for as many trays as are used—the fewer the better. On these trays the articles to be crystallized are carefully spaced so that crystals may form all around each one.

The next step is to fill the box with a sugar syrup made of two parts sugar to one part water. The mixture is boiled until the syrup reaches 220°F. on a candy thermometer. It should be cooled until blood-warm and then poured into the tin well over the top layer. The tin should be kept for several hours in a cool, dry place until a thick, strong, hard crust is formed on the surface. This will indicate that the articles on the trays are crystallized. Then the plug at the bottom of the tin is removed to drain the loose, uncrystallized syrup. The articles should be left on the trays a bit longer to dry and set.

Crystal-White Syrup. A mixture of sugar, vanilla, and corn syrup.

Cuba. The food in Cuba is dominated by a few certain indigenous ingredients, and most of the favorite dishes contain one or more of them. Beans, rice, bananas, plantains, chicken, pork, and seafood are daily fare, and apparently suit the island's taste.

Fish and shellfish are delicious; the favorite single seafood is probably *pargo*, red snapper, which is often prepared with almonds, *con almendras*; it is also very good with avocado sauce. Shrimp and Moro crabs are extraordinarily tasty, often eaten plain, but also used in cooked dishes. Despite all of its available supply of fresh fish, the Cubans contrarily like to eat dried codfish, *bacalao*, usually cooked with onions, garlic, and tomatoes. Pork is decidedly the most popular meat, and the ideal preparation is a roast suckling pig, *lechon asado*. Chicken is often cooked with rice, the classic dish of *arroz con pollo*, or prepared in a stew with potatoes and pimientos, *guisado de pollo*, for example.

Cubans like starchy food and eat all types of potatoes, plantains, green bananas, *yucca*, *taro*, and the like. The fresh vegetables are excellent, but the national preference is for starchy legumes; *frijoles negros*, black beans, and rice and beans are daily foods. Avocados are plentiful and are served as appetizers as well as in salads. Fruit desserts are good, and the Cubans are fond of ice creams, of which the fresh-coconut ice cream is possibly the best. Black coffee is the typical end to a Cuban dinner.

This is a rum country; rum and cola is, of course, a Cuba Libre, and the daiquiri is a classic rum drink. There are no local wines, but the beer is exceptionally good.

Cuba Libre. A rum-and-cola drink served in a tall glass with ice cubes and the juice of half a lime; a favorite drink in many Caribbean countries.

Cubat, Pierre. A famous chef of Alexander II of Russia who was paid for each person served at the Emperor's meals.

Cubeb. The dried berry of a plant native to Southeast Asia used to give a spicy flavor to foods. To Westerners the taste is rather unpleasant, suggesting camphor.

Cube Steak. Inferior meat cut from the flank, top round, or sirloin tip of beef and tenderized by being pressed with a gridlike device to break the fibers.

Cube Sugar. Pure sugar in squares, cubes, or small blocks.

Cucculli (Italian). Small potato dumplings, with nuts and marjoram, breaded and fried crisp; a specialty of Liguria.

Cucharón de Cobre. A dipper shaped like a large spoon.

Cuckold's Cut. The first slice from a loaf.

Cuckoo-Pint (British, Colloquial). Wild arum, a plant whose roots contain a starchy substance.

Cucumber. Cucumbers are not remarkable as far as food value goes. They contain only about 20 calories each and have only fractional quantities of vitamins. But they are so cool and refreshing that they have been a treasured food for hundreds of years.

Cucumbers are believed to be native to India. The Children of Israel, crossing the desert with only manna to eat, remembered with craving the cucumbers they had had in Egypt. Columbus made sure that cucumbers were planted in Haiti in 1494. Seeds were passed on, so that by the middle of the 16th century travelers in colonial America found the American Indians busily hoeing their cucumber patches.

But fresh is only one way in which the cucumber comes to market. It is important, too, as a pickle. The pickles come in numerous styles, brands, container sizes, and prices. *See* Pickles.

Select cucumbers that are firm, well-shaped,

with a bright green color. Store them in the refrigerator until they are to be used. Usually
cucumbers will not keep longer than two weeks.
They should be stored in a humid place at from
45° to 50°; if kept at lower than 45°, dark-
colored watery areas will appear, and the cucumbers will spoil.

Cucumbers range in size from tiny gherkins,
about an inch in length, all the way up to giant
English and Japanese types, 20 inches or even
more. The secret of growing perfectly straight
cucumbers is to place the young vegetable in
a so-called "cucumber glass," a long glass open
at both ends.

Cucumber Tree. Tree whose small, edible fruit
resembles a cucumber.

Cucurbitaceous. Related to fleshy fruits that grow
on climbing or trailing vines, such as melons and
cucumbers.

Cudden. The coalfish, which is of passable quality.

Cuddiruni (Sicilian). Pizza made with sardines.

Cue. A small amount of bread or drink.

Cuiller; Cuillière (French). Spoon.

  Cuiller à Bouche. Tablespoon.

  Cuiller à Café. Teaspoon.

  Cuiller à Entremets. Dessert spoon.

  Cuiller à Pot. Rather small ladle.

  Cuiller à Potage. Soup ladle.

  Cuiller à Soupe. Soup spoon.

Cuillère de Cuisine (French). Wooden spoon;
recommended for stirring sauces instead of metal
spoons, which sometimes cause unpleasant tastes
or dark colors because of certain acids.

Cuillerée (French). A spoonful.

Cuisine (French). A general cooking style; a national or regional manner of preparing food;
sometimes the food served in a hotel, at a
restaurant, or shipboard. In France *bourgeois
cuisine* refers to family-style cooking; *haute
cuisine* means the finest creations of the most
talented chefs.

Cuisinier (French). A chef or cook.

Cuisinière (French). (1) A woman chef or
cook. (2) Range or stove.

Cuissard (French). The leg, haunch, or thigh of
an animal, such as leg of veal.

Cuisse de Volaille (French). Leg of fowl or
chicken.

Cuisse-Madame. A very sweet, delicious French
pear; at its best during July.

Cuisse de Dinde (French). Turkey leg.

Cuisson (French). (1) Meat, fish, or poultry
stock used as a base for sauces. (2) Baking,
cooking.

Cuissot (French). A leg of veal, usually roasted
and braised.

Cuit (French). Boiled and sweetened freshly made
wine.

Cuith (Scotch). Young coalfish.

Cuit Sous la Cendre (French). Cooked under
ashes.

Culantro (Spanish). Coriander.

Culinary. Pertaining to cooking; used in the
preparation of food. The word is derived from
the Latin word *culina* meaning "kitchen."

Cull. Selected, picked over, especially with reference to fruit or fish. *Culls* are rejects.

Cullender. Colander.

Cullen Skink (Scotch). Soup made of finnan
haddie, onions, milk, mashed potatoes, and
parsley.

Culotte (French). Rump of beef.

Culrage. A pepper plant that grows in swamps
or water.

Cultured Buttermilk. A commercial beverage
prepared from skim milk, which is pasteurized,
soured, and then combined with a lactic-acid
culture.

Cumberland Rum Butter. A rich sauce similar to
hard sauce, made with butter, soft brown sugar,
rum, and a little nutmeg. The ingredients are
beaten together, chilled until firm, cut in small
squares, and served on hot puddings or hot
mince pies.

Cumberland Sauce. Sauce for game made of port
wine, currant jelly, orange rind and orange
juice, salt, cayenne pepper, and vinegar; served
hot or cold.

Cumières. An undistinguished red wine produced
in the Champagne region of France.

Cumin Seed; Cummin; Comino Seed. The dried
fruit of an annual plant of the parsley family;
native to Egypt and other Mediterranean countries. Not generally used by home cooks, it is
important in commercial preparations, such as
curry powder, chili powder, chutney, sausages,

cheeses, meats, and pickles. It is excellent for seasoning soups and stews and for flavoring breads and rice.

Cumin, Sweet. *See* Aniseed.

Cumquat. *See* Kumquat.

Cunner. A small saltwater fish native to the Atlantic coast. It is cooked like similar small fish such as sprats. Also called *conner, blue perch, bait-stealer,* and *chogset.*

Cuori di Carciofi (Italian). Hearts of artichokes.

Cup. (1) Round receptacle, with or without handles, in which liquids are served. Cups vary in size, including teacups, coffee cups, demitasse cups. They are made of a variety of materials, from the finest china to metal and glazed earthenware.

A cup serves as a common unit of measure. *See* Weights and Measures.

(2) A drink, such as a wine cup. (3) A dish, such as a fruit cup.

Cupbearer. Head butler who serves wine to the host, especially in a royal household.

Cupboard. A cabinet, closet, or other enclosure for storing food, dishes, and utensils.

Cupcakes. Small confections of cake batter baked in individual portions in special pans or muffin tins. They are baked at the temperature specified for layer cakes but cook about 5 minutes faster.

Cupful. The amount required to fill a cup.

Cup Man. A continuous imbiber of alcoholic beverages.

Cup-Shot (Obsolete). A drunkard.

Curaçao. A liqueur whose flavor is imparted by the rind of a bitter orange that grows on the Dutch Caribbean island of Curaçao. There are orange, green, and white curaçaos. Products based on curaçao include *Grand Marnier, Cointreau,* and *Triple Sec.*

Curaimir (Irish). Venison cutlets previously marinated in wine.

Curassow. A bird similar to the turkey, sometimes used for food.

Curcuma. (1) Certain plants of the ginger family. The dried roots of one species are used to prepare the herb turmeric. Another species is the source of arrowroot. (2) Saffron.

Curcumin. The yellowish coloring substance found in turmeric or in curcuma root.

Curd; Curds. The thicker portion of milk which ordinarily separates from the watery portion (whey) when milk sours. The singular and plural forms are used interchangeably.

Curdle. To thicken or form into curds. *See also* Curdling.

Curdling. Eggs, milk, and sweet cream contain a protein that coagulates when combined with the acids in tomatoes, wines, or lemons. Sour cream itself contains some acid. Heating milk or sweet cream with an acid or with sour cream (with or without additional acid) hastens curdling. To prevent this, add the acid food after cooking, or cook the combination at the lowest possible temperature. For instance, for cream of tomato soup, cook the tomato purée and the white sauce separately. Remove from fire, add purée to sauce a little at a time, stirring steadily; then serve.

If raw eggs are to be used in a hot mixture, beat the eggs, then very gradually add the hot liquid a little at a time, stirring steadily to prevent curdling. The eggs may now be added to all of the hot mixture.

Curds and Butter. A combination of fresh creamery butter and sweet-milk curds pressed together to make a fresh cream cheese. *See also* Crowdy (2).

Curd Tarts. Fillings for pies or cakes made with milk curd.

Cure. To preserve or change the taste of meats by salting and drying processes, or by smoking.

Curer. One who cures fish or other foods.

Curled Oatcake. An oatcake dried by rollers.

Curly Cress; Pepper Grass. A green with curly leaves excellent in a salad or as a garnish.

Curly Murly (Scotch). Yeast cake made with hazelnuts and lemon.

Curn. A Scottish grain or cereal.

Curn of Bread. A bit of bread.

Curnonsky. The outstanding gourmet and food expert of France for several decades before his death in 1956, who wrote many articles and books on food and wine. His real name was Maurice-Edmond Sailland. Sailland never used any first name for his *nom de plume,* Curnonsky.

Curran Dawd (British, Scotch). A lump of currant or raisin bread.

Currant. The dried fruit of a small seedless grape grown in the Mediterranean area.

In the United States fresh currants are on the market for only two or three weeks when the crop is harvested, usually in July. City consumers are probably more familiar with currants in jams and jellies or in the dried form, but many farm gardens include a few currant bushes.

One of the most famous currant jams is *bar-le-duc*, in which the whole berries are suspended in a clear jelly. This delicacy, imported from France, is available in American fine-foods shops. It was first made in France in the 14th century by Perrin Lamothe, cellarer to Duke Robert of France. *See* Bar-le-Duc.

The name "currant" comes from the French *raisins de Corinthe*, since currants were originally imported from Corinth, Greece, and more currants are still raised in the region of the Corinthian Gulf than anywhere else in the world. Currants were first cultivated in Europe in the 16th century.

The three varieties, red, black, and white, may be eaten raw with plenty of sugar; they are less tart when cooked.

Curried. Flavored with curry spices or curry powder.

Curry. This flavorsome powder, originating in India, is not a single spice but a blend of many, sometimes as many as sixteen. Usually it contains coriander, turmeric, cloves, cassia buds, black pepper, red pepper, garlic, cumin seed, and ginger, but the blend may vary considerably from region to region.

Many manufacturers in the United States produce curry powders. In India, curry is not generally purchased as a blend. Indian cooks blend their own spices for curry powder, often varying the ingredients.

Curry powder, which has become increasingly popular in the United States, is used to flavor sauces served with veal, chicken, shrimp, lamb, or rice. Curry powder may be added to the flour with which chicken is coated before frying.

Curry Stuffs. Numerous spices and flavorings used in the making of curries in Asia. In the United States curry powder (actually a blend of spices) can be bought prepared. In Asia most cooks prefer to make their own mixture of "curry stuffs," which may include anise, candlenut, tamarind, nutmeg, cumin, poppy seeds, cinnamon, coriander, turmeric, pepper, dill, nutmeg, cardamom, star anise, saffron, mustard, fenugreek, lemon grass, and ginger.

Cury (Obsolete). All cooked foods.

Cuscinetti (Italian). Fried cheese sandwiches.

Cuscus; Couscous. A North African cereal and meat preparation. *See* Couscous.

Cuscusu (Italian). Fish stew made with onions, garlic, tomatoes, and semolina.

Cuscuz (Brazilian). Corn-flour pudding flavored with any desired fruits or nuts.

Cuscuzeiro (Brazilian). A heavy pot with a tight-fitting cover; resembles the Dutch oven.

Cush. (Obsolete). Prepared according to a recipe the Pilgrims brought from England; usually served in winter. Buttermilk cornbread was fried in bacon or sausage fat with chopped onions. Fresh milk was added, and the dish was seasoned with salt and pepper. It was served hot with a pat of butter.

Cushat. The European ringdove or wood pigeon; sometimes used for food.

Cushion. The part of an animal's leg adjacent to and partly covered by the udder.

Cusk. A large saltwater fish with firm white flesh, related to the cod; native to North Atlantic waters off the coasts of Europe and America.

Cussy, Baron de. A French nobleman who held a high post under Napoleon I and was a great gourmet. Many dishes are named for him.

Cussy (French). Soup composed mainly of Spanish onions simmered in meat stock; supposed to have originated in the village of Cussy.

Custard. A dessert consisting mainly of eggs, milk, sugar, and some flavoring. There are two varieties of custard—the soft or boiled type and the baked type. Soft custards are cooked in the top of a double boiler over boiling water only until the mixture forms a coating on a metal spoon. If the custard is overcooked and the egg separates, it may be beaten with a rotary egg beater to restore the smooth texture. Soft custards may be served as they are, or combined with other foods for such desserts as floating island, trifle, and tipsy pudding.

Baked custards are baked in a moderate oven and may be served warm or chilled.

Custard Apple. Large tropical fruit, often heart-shaped, with a smooth reddish or reddish-brown skin with hexagonal markings somewhat like those of a pineapple, and a sweet, soft pulp. It is grown in Florida and the West Indies. The sweetsop, soursop, and cherimoya belong to the same family.

Custard Bun. Yeast bun topped with hot custard.

Custard Cup. Small earthenware or heatproof glass container in which an individual custard may be baked and served.

Custard Marrow; Custard Squash; Chayote; Brionne. A pear-shaped type of squash with very white flesh.

Custard Powder. A starch mixture that stiffens with the addition of hot milk and sugar to form a sauce.

Custard Tart. Pastry filled with a milk-sugar-and-egg mixture.

Custron (Obsolete). Kitchen servant.

Cut In. The expression "cut in the shortening" means to blend the shortening into the dry ingredients by cutting repeatedly with two knives or by using a pastry blender.

Cutlery. Knives, forks, and spatulas; spoons are often called "cutlery," but this is inaccurate.

Knives in particular should be chosen with care, for they are among the most-used kitchen tools. Most practical for kitchen use are knives of hollow-ground high-carbon or vanadium steel, hammer-forged to develop a fine grain in the steel. Stainless-steel knives of high carbon content also are available, but ordinary stainless-steel knives are not a good investment because they do not last as long as better-quality products.

Before buying, test a knife for spring and balance. Bend the blade; if it is well made, it will remain rigid for about a third of the way down from the handle, the remaining two-thirds being flexible enough to form a slight curve. If the blade is of high-grade steel, it will usually spring back into position.

The way the blade is fastened to the handle is important. In cheap knives the shank of the blade is narrowed to a point which is inserted

into the handle and held by a small nail or merely by a metal collar. In better knives the shaft extends the entire length, or at least half the length, of the handle and is fastened by two or more good-sized rivets. The handle itself, whether made of wood or of plastic, should be easy to grasp and should feel comfortable.

An efficient battery of kitchen knives includes a paring knife with a short blade of 2½–3-inch length; a utility knife with a 4–6-inch blade; a carving knife with a fairly long sturdy blade that is not too pliable; a slicing knife with a long flexible blade, and, if desired, a sturdy butcher knife.

To this list might be added a grapefruit knife with a curved and serrated blade, and the French cook knife with a straight edge and a firm but tapering blade. Useful too is a knife with a scalloped or serrated edge for cutting bread.

Knives should be stored with care in a wooden rack within a drawer or on the wall. A rack with permanently magnetized iron keeps cutlery or other utensils in place.

Forks for the kitchen should include a fork with a long handle for lifting food out of deep pots and a shorter fork for holding meats being carved.

A spatula, either of stainless steel or other metal, does not need to be ruggedly constructed but should be fairly rigid close to the handle and flexible at the end. A broad, rigid spatula can substitute for a pancake turner and can be used to remove cookies from a baking sheet.

Cutlet. Literally, a well-trimmed slice of veal, lamb, or mutton; a corruption of the French word *côtelette*.

Cutlin's Cut (British). Oatmeal.

Cutting Board. Any kind of hardwood board, designed with a scooped-out space and a set of grooves, used to catch meat juices.

Cuttle Bone. In Indian cooking a dried bone in powdered form; baking powder may be used as a substitute.

Cuttlefish. A saltwater mollusk with a very hard shell; used for food in many Mediterranean countries. *See* Squid.

Cuvage (French). Wine fermenting in a vat.

Cuve (French). Any large receptacle used to press grapes in the wine-making process; red wine is allowed to ferment in this receptacle.

Cuveau (French). A small wine-press or vat.

Cuvées (French). (1) The different times or periods at which certain wines were made or fermented in the cask (*cuve*); vintage. (2) Also, the lot of wine from a particular vineyard or wine press.

Cuver (French). To ferment, especially wine.

Cuyos (Brazilian). Drinking cups made of calabash or gourd rind. The fruit is cut into halves, the pulp is removed, and the rind is scraped to the required thinness. When the rinds or shells are sufficiently dry, they are painted both inside and out with various designs.

Cuyte Beer. A high-quality beer made in Brussels, Belgium.

Cyak; Cyauk (British, Scotch). An oatcake spread with cheese or butter.

Cyathus. Wine ladle.

Cydon (Obsolete). Quince.

Cygnets. Young swans, occasionally bagged by hunters in some countries. The flesh is tender and tasty but somewhat odd.

Cymlin; Cymling; Pattypan. A flat white disk-shaped summer squash.

Cynar. An Italian apéritif drink made from artichokes.

Cynareous. Pertaining to plants of the artichoke family.

Cyprine. Belonging to the carp family.

Cyprinidae. The carp family of fish, including carp, barbel, gudgeon, broadsnout, roach, dace, tench, bream, and chub.

Cyprinoid. Of or akin to carp.

Cyprus Wines. The wines of this Mediterranean island include the sweet wines red Commandaria, created by the Knights Templar, Morocannella,

and Xynisteri, all made from grapes dried on the vine, and best when aged 5–10 years. The dry wines tend to be coarse and heady. Formerly Cypriot wines were held in earthenware jars or skins tarred on the inside, thus giving to the wine a taste similar to that of present-day Greek *retsina*. But since pitch no longer is employed, that unpleasant taste no longer is present.

Cyr; Sir (Yugoslavian). Cheese.

Czarny Chleb (Polish). Coarse rye bread.

Czechoslovakia. Many years ago, Czech food had a considerable reputation among gourmets. Today, the average Czech is grateful for enough to eat, without thinking about forgotten delicacies. But many people with long memories look back fondly on the days when Czech food was at its best. Not that Czechoslovakia ever had a truly important cuisine with a wide variety of dishes; even its stanchest admirers admit that it was good home-style cooking, rather than an outstanding cuisine.

The Czechs seldom served appetizer courses. Most meals began with a soup, possibly one made with cabbage, potatoes, or mushrooms. But any soup, *polévka*, worthy of the name, had "something" in it, such as barley, rice, or dumplings. Since the country has no coastline, there was little interest in ocean fish or shellfish. Freshwater fish, like carp, pike, perch, trout, and salmon, on the other hand, were very popular. Carp and pike, with their distinctive, muddy, river-bottom flavor, were prepared in many different styles, of which *ryba na černo*, made with a black sauce, was especially noteworthy.

Boiled beef, *vařené hovězí maso*, may seem like a simple dish, but the Czechs elevated it to a high position, serving it with a variety of sauces flavored with garlic, horseradish, wine, or prunes. Lamb was never a national favorite, but veal was always appreciated. It was for pork, however, that the Czechs reserved their special enthusiasm. The country's national dish was surely roast pork, served with dumplings and sauerkraut. Pork and ham were served in an enormous variety of dishes, almost enough to defy the imagination, and very well prepared, juicy, and succulent.

Dumplings of all sorts, *knedlíky*, were prepared in many different shapes and sizes and combined with many different ingredients; potato dumplings were perhaps the most popular, but the range was limited only by the cook's ingenuity. They were light or heavy, small or giant-sized, tart or sweet, but hardly a day went by without some type of dumpling.

Another unique feature of Czechoslovakia's cookery was the popularity of sausages. Like dumplings, these were prepared with numerous variations—small, plain, smoked, spiced, and so forth—but usually made with pork. Goose, rabbit, and wild game were always enjoyed in this country, and many excellent dishes were prepared from these ingredients. Sauerkraut was often combined with pork or game to make delicious hearty cold-weather dishes.

The Czechs enjoyed cakes and sweet pastries. Poppy seed cake, *makovy dort*, combined their love for sweets with a favorite ingredient, poppy seeds. *Kolache*, yeast pastries, were also very popular. Coffee cakes, rich and filling, were frequently served.

Although some wines are still produced locally, they are of inferior quality. However, the country's Pilsener beer, *Plzeňské pivo*, light, delicate, and crystal clear, is among the finest beers in the world. Cool and refreshing, drawn from a barrel, it can rightly be regarded as a superb beer.

D

Daad. Dough.

Dab; Dabs. A common name for any small flat-fish, but specifically a small flatfish similar to the flounder found off the English coast. It has a thick layer of meat, free from bones, on the upper and lower sides. It is sweet and not oily, with a distinctive flavor and texture.

Dabbies. (1) Cake used at Communion in England. (2) Buttercake, shortbread, and petticoat tails, all British sweet cakes.

Dabbit. Cakes baked on the hearth, covered with hot ashes.

Dabchicks. Small diving water birds. They are difficult to catch, but some hunters like them, especially the young birds, for their flavorful flesh.

Dace. A small silver freshwater fish related to the carp family. In the United States, also fish similar to it, such as the redfin.

Dadhi. *See* Fermented Milk.

Dagh. Dough.

Daging Smoor (Indonesian). Meat cooked into a stew with a dark sauce.

Dag Kebob (Turkish). Preparation similar to shish kebab, consisting of pieces of veal skewered alternately with onions and tomatoes and broiled.

Dagwood (American, Colloquial). A large sandwich with several layers consisting of a variety of ingredients.

Dahi (Indian). Yoghurt.

Dahibara (Indian). A snack consisting of ground lentils and yoghurt shaped into balls and fried crisp.

Dahon Ng Kamote (Philippine). Sweet-potato shoots.

Daikon (Japanese). A long white radish, some of which grow to enormous size. They are usually pickled and eaten as a relish, although they can be eaten raw.

Daing. A dried fish eaten in the Philippine Islands, especially among the Ilocanos.

Dainty. A delicacy or a food of choice quality.

Daiquiri. A drink of Caribbean origin made with 1 part sugar syrup, 2 parts lime juice, and 8 parts white rum; served in a cocktail glass filled with crushed ice. A frozen Daiquiri is prepared with the same proportions but is combined with crushed ice in an electric blender until it forms a snowlike mixture.

Daiquiri, Frozen. A rum drink made with sugar and lime juice, shaken or electrically blended with cracked ice.

Dairy. (1) A building, room, or place where cream and milk are stored for making into cheese and butter. (2) A retail store that sells milk products.

Dairy Butter. Butter prepared fresh and without salt.

Dairy Cream. The original cream separated from the milk with nothing added.

Dairy Farm. A farm that produces milk and cream, for sale as such, or to be converted into butter, cheese, etc.

Dairyman. A person who works, owns, manages, or is otherwise concerned with the production and sale of milk, cream, butter, etc.

Dairy Products. All products based on milk and cream, including buttermilk, yoghurt, butter, cheese, etc.

Dairy Restaurant. A restaurant, usually serving Jewish foods, that does not prepare any meat or poultry dishes.

Daisy. A tall iced alcoholic drink usually with a base of raspberry syrup and citrus juice; may be made with gin, rum, brandy, or whisky. It may be served with straws in a highball glass or strained and presented in a small highball glass. It may also be served in a large goblet and decorated with floating flowers or aromatic leaves.

Dal; Dahl (Indian). Lentils.

Dalag. The Philippine mudfish.

Dalle (French). A thin slice of fish; a *darne* is a thicker slice.

Dallop; Dollop. A moderately large amount of food.

Dama Branca (Portuguese). A white pudding.

Damasco (Portuguese). Apricot.

D'Ambert Cheese. *See* Forez Cheese.

Dambose. A crystallized sugar derived from dambonite, a white crystalline substance.

Dame Blanche. A number of ice-cream preparations, usually made with vanilla ice cream and whipped cream.

Dame Jeanne (French). A wicker-covered glass bottle used for spirits; in English, *demijohn*.

Damen Cheese; Gloire des Montagnes. A soft, mild, uncured cow's-milk cheese made in Austria and Hungary; suitable for ladies, as its name indicates.

Damenkipfel (German). Small crescent-shaped bread rolls.

Damp (British slang). A drink.

Damper (Australian). A crudely-made bread or cake prepared from flour, salt, and water, and baked in hot ashes.

Dampfbraten (German). Beef stew.

Dampfnudeln (German). Dumpling dough enriched with sugar, eggs, and butter, parboiled in milk, steamed in the oven, and served with a custard sauce and stewed fruit.

Damson. A rather small deep-purple plum, eaten fresh, made into compotes, or used for preserves. The name derives from the Latin *Damascenum,* meaning "of Damascus," where the plum may have originated.

Damson Cheese. A preserve made with damson plums boiled to a pulp, rubbed through a sieve, then cooked again with an equal amount of sugar.

Damson Gin. English gin flavored with damson plums and served as a liqueur.

Danablu (Danish). Blue cheese similar to Roquefort.

Dandelion. Wild or cultivated, dandelions are a delectable spring green. The cultivated type is milder in flavor and has more tender leaves than the wild plant. Both kinds should be carefully selected, for the slightest bit of yellow bud will cause an undesirable acrid taste.

Dandelions are sometimes used for making wine, but the tender young leaves are most popularly used in salads, not only in the United States but also in France, England, and Italy. In England the dandelion is known as *blowball, priest's crown, swine's snout, timetable,* or *wiggers.* The French call it *pissenlit,* and the Italians *dente-di-leone,* or lion's tooth.

The greens may be washed, broken into pieces, and served with French dressing, either by themselves or with other greens. Or they may be mixed with thinly sliced scallions, radishes, and cooked beets. Dandelion greens should be cooked like any other green, such as spinach—they should be boiled only in the water that clings to the leaves after washing and cooked only until the leaves wilt.

If, as formerly, they are boiled a long time with several changes of water to remove the bitterness, much of the nutritive value of the greens, a rich source of vitamins A and C, is lost.

D&R. Distiller and rectifier, a liquor-trade term.

Dandy (Colloquial). A bantam fowl, a small domestic bird.

Dango (Japanese). A kind of dumpling.

Danish Blue Cheese. The Danish version of the French *Bleu,* the latter being a cheese made in the Roquefort area but from milk other than that of the ewe.

Danish Butter. An excellent butter with more butterfat than most other butters.

Danish Export. (1) A small, flat, cylindrical cheese resembling Gouda, made in Denmark with the skim milk and buttermilk left over from the production of cream.

(2) A fine Danish beer of fairly high alcoholic content.

Danish Pastry (American). A breakfast pastry (usually filled) made with a yeast dough. The pastry is so popular in some parts of the United States that it is familiarly called a "Danish." The name is undoubtedly a flattering attempt to associate the mediocre copy with an inimitable product, the pastry made in Denmark. For some odd reason, when made in Denmark this pastry is called *Wienerbrød*, or Vienna Bread. In Denmark it is made of a yeast puff paste, resulting in an unbelievably buttery and flaky pastry of matchless delicacy.

Danish Toast. Slices of brown bread spread with horseradish sauce and garnished with strips of smoked salmon and filleted herring.

Dannock. A small loaf of bread; oatcake.

Danskawienerbröd (Swedish). Danish pastry.

Dansk Schweizerrost Cheese. A superb Danish cheese similar to Switzerland's Emmental but with smaller holes.

Danziger Goldwasser. An unusual Polish liqueur containing flecks of gold leaf that present an attractive appearance when the liquid is stirred or shaken. The liqueur itself is flavored with orange peel and various spicy herbs.

Dão. A wine district of Portugal. *See* Portugal, The Wines of.

Daon Bawang (Malayan). Green onions; scallions.

Daon Salam (Malayan). Fresh bay leaf.

Dapifer. Title of the food steward in a nobleman's home in medieval times.

Dara Wheat. Indian wheat of fair-to-average quality.

Dariole Molds. (1) Deep circular pans with a plain side tapering toward the bottom; used in many types of confectionery. (2) In France, the ground meat prepared in the molds.

Darioles (British). Literally, "something produced from a dairy"; individual-size cheesecakes made in special dariole molds.

Darjeeling. The "champagne" of teas. A black tea from the slopes of the Himalayas in India, this leaf colors slowly to a rich red brew with outstanding flavor and aroma. Because of its penetrating, distinctive taste, it is used in many blended teas, especially for the American market.

Darling. A Vermont cheddar cheese with a good flavor.

Darne (French). A thick slice of fish; a thin slice is called a *dalle*.

Dart; Dare; Dace. A fish, *see* Dace.

D'Artois (French). (1) Various dishes named for a French count, but more likely dishes originating in the province of Artois, France. (2) A French pastry of puff paste and jam.

Darum (Indian). A very intoxicating beverage with an offensive odor, made from Mowha flowers; generally diluted considerably before being sold. Because it is so very cheap, it sells better than its aroma would warrant.

Dash. Just a touch, the merest hint of whatever flavoring is being added to food or drink.

Dasheen. A starchy tuber that is a dietary staple in many tropical countries. The Polynesian name is *taro*; in Puerto Rico it is called *yautia*, and in Barbados *eddo*.

A member of the calla lily family, the dasheen is cultivated for its large underground bulb, known as the *corm*, and the smaller tubers sprouting from it, called *cormels*. The corms weigh 1–6 pounds, and the cormels are about the size of a hen's egg. When raw, both have a white flesh encased in a brown fibrous coat. Of about the same food value as the potato, they may be prepared similar to potatoes, except that they do not mash satisfactorily.

Dashi (Japanese). Soup stock or flavoring ingredient prepared from *konbu* (seaweed) and *katsuobushi* (dried flakes of bonito).

Date Palm. Any of a large group of palm trees that bear edible dates. These palms grow around the world wherever the summer seasons are extremely hot and the winters quite mild.

Date Plum. A fruit native to China, where it is called *kaki*. About the size of a small apple, with a reddish hue, it has a juicy, luscious, tawny, semitransparent pulp; often dried with sugar, like figs.

Date. The oblong, single-seeded berry of the date palm. According to legend, dates grew in the Garden of Eden. This is quite possible, for they are mentioned in earliest history. Preserved dates have been found in the tombs of the Egyptian pharaohs, and Assyrian murals depict the cultivation of the date palm. Sacred to all Mohammedans, dates are one of the oldest of staple foods, and they are still used by the Arabs in almost all their dishes. The Arabs also distill vinegar and wine from the fresh fruit and feed cakes of mashed pitted dates to their livestock.

The first date palms in the United States were

grown from seed probably planted by missionaries of the Franciscan and Jesuit orders. Originally they were grown in Florida as well as in southern California. Since the California product proved to thrive better, California became the center of date production. Today the vicinity of Indio produces almost 90 percent of the dates grown in the United States. The Imperial Valley of California and the Salt River Valley of Arizona are other important sources.

When fully ripe, fresh dates are plump and lustrous and have a golden-brown color, a smooth skin, and a sweet pulp. Domestic dates generally are fresh dates. The only processing they require is cleaning, pasteurizing, and either reducing or increasing the moisture as necessary to maintain keeping and eating qualities. The so-called cured date is merely one that has either reached the proper state of dryness on the tree or has been dried after picking. The purpose of curing is to reduce the moisture below the point at which the date would sour or mold.

Dates are one of nature's most complete foods. Beside being 70 percent carbohydrate, in the form of dextrose, they contain vitamins A and B, protein, fat, mineral salts, roughage, and water. Eaten with milk, they are said to constitute a perfect meal.

Date Sugar. The natural sugar in the sap of the wild date tree of India.

Date Wine. The fermented sap of the date palm made into a "wine."

Dátil (Spanish). Date.

Dato. The red tropical fruit of a cactus plant.

Datte de Mer (French). The date shell, an edible mollusk.

Datteri. Roughly date-shaped mussels native to certain Italian waters.

Daube (French). Stews, which may be made of different ingredients and in various styles.

    Daube à l'Avignonnaise. Lamb cubes cooked in red wine with bacon and onions.

    Daube à la Provençale. A beef stew containing mushrooms, olives, tomatoes, and onions.

Daubière (French). (1) A stew pot or other utensil suitable for making stews. (2) Braised meats or poultry.

Daubing. Seasoning certain meats by inserting large pieces of salt pork into the flesh with daubing needles. *See* Larding.

Dauke (Obsolete). A wild carrot.

Dauphin. A superior cow's-milk cheese made in northern France, from April through September; often flavored with herbs or pepper.

Dauphine, À la (French). Garnished with potato balls.

Daurade (French). The gilt-head sea fish; of good flavor, about 18 inches long, and similar to the bream.

Daventry. A small rounded English cheese with bluish-green veins, similar to Stilton.

Daw (British). Underbaked; doughy.

Dayap (Philippine). A lime.

Dazed Bread. Bread insufficiently baked.

Debauchery. The practice of indulging in excessive drinking and eating.

Decaffeinated Coffee. Instant or regular coffee from which almost all the caffein has been removed.

Decanting; Decantation. The process of pouring off red wine from the original bottle into a second container in order to obtain clear wine without sediment. Decanting is not necessary with white wines since they do not collect heavy sediment. To decant wine, a light, preferably a lighted candle, is placed behind the bottle and the wine is poured off slowly only until the sediment begins to move. Decanting should be done about a half-hour before the wine is to be served so that it may have a chance "to breathe." When the wine comes in contact with the air it releases aroma and flavor.

Decanter. A bottle in which wine or liquor is kept. Decanters were popular when it was thought that the label of the wine shipper or liquor manufacturer should not be seen. Today most people unhesitatingly bring a bottle of wine or liquor into the view of their guests.

Decapods; Decapoda. The highest order of shellfish. Crustaceans or mollusks with ten arms or legs, including lobsters, crabs, squid, etc.

Decize. A simple rich, creamy cow's-milk cheese made in the Nivernais region of France.

Deck; Decker. Sandwiches consisting of more than two slices of bread with a filling between the slices. A three-decker sandwich has three slices of bread.

Decoct. To boil away or boil down; to prepare food by boiling.

Decoction. The act of boiling down or reducing a substance to extract soluble parts.

Deep-Dish Pie. Usually a one-crust pie for which sliced, diced, or whole fruit is placed in a shallow baking dish or deep pie pan, covered with a pastry, and baked.

Deep-Fat Frying. A method of cooking in which enough fat is employed to cover the food. For the average frying kettle at least 2 pounds of solid fat or 1 quart of oil is needed for a layer sufficiently deep to cover food. Little of the fat is lost in frying, hence the remainder may be strained after use and reserved for another time. Because of the pronounced odor, deep-fat frying is not desirable in small kitchens.

Any straight-sided saucepan 7–9 inches in diameter and at least 5 inches deep may be used for deep-fat frying. A wire basket that fits inside the kettle is a great convenience. The food is placed in the basket, which is immersed in the hot fat; when done, the food can easily be removed by simply lifting out the basket and holding it over the pan until the excess fat has dripped into the kettle. An electric deep-fat fryer with thermostat control is a good investment for the household in which a lot of this kind of frying is done. So, too, is a deep-fat thermometer that registers the temperature of the fat.

Deep Freeze. The trade name for a home appliance that freezes or stores food; home freezer.

Deer. *See* Venison.

Deerberry. The squaw huckleberry.

Défarde (French). The entrails (sometimes also the feet) of calves.

Defrost. (1) To remove the "snow," or frost, that collects in electric refrigerators or freezers. Many modern appliances have automatic defrosting devices. (2) To thaw frozen foods.

Degchi (Indian). Cooking pan with a saucer-shaped lid.

Degerm. To remove the germ from wheat.

Déglaçage (French). A sauce made by adding liquor (or other liquid) to pan drippings.

Deglaze. To add liquid to a pan in which meat or poultry has been cooked, stirring up the adhering fat particles, to improve sauces, etc.

Deglute. To swallow.

Deglutition. The act of swallowing.

Degorgement. In champagne making, the process of removing sediment from the bottle.

Dégorger (French). To soak in water such foods as calf's head and sweetbreads to remove impurities.

Dégorgeur (French). A skilled technician who quickly removes the cork from champagne bottles, examines the contents, adds small amounts of wine, then recorks.

Dégraisser (French). To skim off grease from the top of soups or sauces.

Déguiser (French). To change foods so completely by the addition of spices or herbs that they are no longer recognized.

Degust. To taste.

Degustation. A French term denoting food or tasting, but not quite translatable. It refers in general to a wide range of possibilities, including a multiple choice of foods and wines.

Dehydrate. To remove moisture from foods. The resulting product may be restored, at least in part, to its original condition by adding water, although sometimes cooking is required.

Dehydrated Foods. Dehydration, that is, the removal of the water from food, was one of man's earliest methods of preserving food, and it is still in use. Much has been done in recent years to improve dehydration methods. The foods to be dried have been developed in such a way that they are particularly adapted to this method of preservation. New processing techniques and more careful application of known methods of preservation by drying and improved equipment, especially dryers, have led to advances in this field. Better equipment for spray drying has resulted in superior dried-egg and dried-milk products. High-vacuum drying has made it possible to produce dehydrated fruit juices, especially citrus juices, of acceptable quality. In France, even wine has been dehydrated, especially for use by soldiers.

Deidesheim. A wine village of the Pfalz region of Germany. *See* Germany, The Wines of.

Deil's Dozen. Thirteen; baker's dozen.

Deipnosophist. A connoisseur in the art of dining. The term is derived from a Greek work of Athenaeus.

Déjeuner (French). The noonday meal, or luncheon.

> **Déjeuner à la Fourchette.** A breakfast or luncheon at which meat is served.

> **Déjeuner de Noce.** A wedding breakfast or lunch.

Delftware. Glazed earthenware, usually blue, made in the Netherlands.

Delibate. To taste a little; to sip.

Delibation. A slight taste; a sip.

Delicacy. A fine food, excellent in taste and texture.

Delicatesse (French). A delicacy.

Delicatessen. (1) Smoked, salted, cured, or otherwise prepared meats, salads, etc., ready to eat. (2) A store that sells such foods. The term comes from the German word *delikatesse*, meaning "delicacy."

Délice (French). Literally, "delight." Any preparation intended to delight the diner, such as an elaborate appetizer or dessert.

Délices de Rouvray. A rich, creamy fresh cheese made in Normandy, France.

Delicia. A stalk of celery stuffed with creamed blue cheese.

Délicieux; Délicieuse (French). Denoting an especially delicious or delightful small food.

Delicious. Highly pleasing to the smell, taste, and palate.

Delicious Apples. An apple discovered in 1872 by Jesse Hiatt of Peru, Iowa, and named the *Hawkeye*. In 1895 it was introduced into commercial

channels by the Stark brothers as the *Delicious*. In 1922 a monument was erected to Jesse Hiatt and his discovery near the original tree. The Delicious is long and has five easily recognized points at the bottom. The flesh is yellowish, firm, a little coarse, tender, and pleasantly subacid in taste. The golden-skinned variety is appropriately called the *Golden Delicious*, and the *Red Delicious* has thick red stripes against a yellow background.

Delikatessassietter (Swedish). A plate of assorted appetizers from the smørgåsbord, containing more selections than an *assietter*.

Delikatesse Kalter Aufschnitt (German). Cold cuts.

Dell Steak. Delmonico steak (shell or club steak), obtained from the short loin of beef.

Demerara. A yellowish-brown cane sugar produced in the Demerara region of Guyana.

Demerara Crystals. Colorless crystals made from refined sugar and blended with a small quantity of molasses or colored sugar syrup.

Demerara Rums. Heavy rums from distilleries in Guyana. Demerara rums of 151 degrees proof, a higher proof than any other liquor, are favored by fishermen off the Grand Banks as a warming drink after battling icy storms.

Demersal Fish. A white fish such as cod, haddock, whiting, hake, ling, halibut, sole, and bream, that lives at the bottom of the sea and contains little fat.

Demi (French, Colloquial). A measure of beer equal to about one-third of a quart.

Demi-Deuil (French). Literally "half-mourning." Veal, fowl, or sweetbreads covered with truffles.

Demidov; Demidoff (French). A dish prepared with Madeira wine, vegetables and truffles.

Demi-Espagnole (French). *See* Demi-Glace.

Demi-Feuilletage (French). Ends or leftovers of pastry dough.

Demi-Glace (French). A brown sauce prepared with an Espagnole sauce base. The Espagnole is reduced, skimmed, and mixed with stock or a clear broth, then flavored with Madeira or sherry.

Demijohn. A large earthenware or glass bottle with a narrow neck and encased in wickerwork with one or two handles. Demijohns range in capacity from 1 to 10 gallons and are used for the storage and shipment of wines.

Demi-Sec (French). In champagne, 7–10 percent sugar.

Demi-Sel Cheese. A salty, soft, light, creamy cheese made in Normandy, France.

Demi-Setier (French). Obsolete measurement for wines, equal to about a half-pint.

Demitasse (French). (1) A short drink of very strong black or dark-roasted coffee. (2) The small cup in which such coffee is served.

Denanthic Ether. A colorless liquid having the synthetic odor of fruit, or sometimes of brandy, often used in making various alcoholic mixed beverages.

Denaturant. A substance added to alcohol to make it unconsumable.

Dendeng (Indonesian). Crisply cooked meat.

Dendé Oil. An oil very popular in the Brazilian cuisine. Its closest equivalent is probably olive oil.

Dénerver (French). To remove membranes or tendons.

Denier, En (French). Potato slices, cut into coin-shaped rounds and deep-fat fried.

Denmark. Danish food is decidedly appetizing and delicious, and immediately palatable to everyone's taste. The ingredients themselves, especially the dairy products, are of unsurpassed quality. The nation's cuisine generally resembles that of its Scandinavian neighbors, but there are a number of local specialties.

Breakfast is a simple meal of bread or rolls, jam and butter, with coffee. Fortunate people, on a visit to Denmark, will manage to have some of the rich breakfast pastry which Americans call "Danish pastry" but which the Danes call "Vienna Bread." At lunchtime the great favorite is *smørrebrød*, literally bread and butter. It consists of slices of dark or whole-grained bread spread with sweet Danish butter, rich and unctuous, and covered with eggs, fish, meat, poultry, or cheese. The sandwiches are never covered, and three sandwiches are considered a fair luncheon, together with dessert and coffee. At about 6 o'clock the Danes serve dinner, consisting of a hot dish and a simple dessert. A great favorite for dinner is *stegt suinekam med aebler*

og svedsker, roast pork with apples and prunes. Another likely selection might be *frikadeller*, miniature meatballs, or *biksemad*, a chopped-meat dish with fried onions and potatoes. Main courses are usually simple but very satisfying and delicious, like superb home-cooked foods. The desserts are often of fruit; the classic dish is *rodgrød med fløde*, a jellied raspberry pudding with cream.

The national strong drink is *snaps*, a clear white liquor almost exactly like Sweden's *aquavit*. *Snaps* (sometimes spelled *snapps*) is usually served with *smørrebrød* and is best when ice cold. Beer is regarded as the ideal chaser for a *snaps*, if that is possible. Denmark produces no wines and is not a real wine-drinking country, although the sophisticated city people drink wine. Beer is the national drink, and the two leading brands are Tuborg and Carlsberg, both excellent. There is a local whisky called Cloc, which is drinkable but scarcely more than that. Many afterdinner cordials are made in the country, but cherry heering, with a pronounced cherry flavor and color, is outstanding.

Dent-de-Lion (French). Dandelion.

Dent-de-Loup (French). (1) A pastry with a pointed end often flavored with anise or cumin. (2) A triangular piece of fried bread upon which other foods are placed.

Dente di Leone (Italian). Dandelion.

Dentex. A gray, round saltwater fish of the perch family with white, firm, savory flesh. Found in the Mediterranean, it is caught off the Italian coast, where it is known as *dentice*.

Dentice (Italian). A fine white-fleshed fish. *See* Dentex.

Denver Sandwich; Western Sandwich. A sandwich made with either scrambled eggs or an omelet combined with chopped sautéed ham, green peppers, and onions.

Dépecer (French). To cut in pieces or carve.

Dépouiller (French). To skim off all possible fat from soups or sauces while cooking.

Derby; Derbyshire Cheese. A hard English cheese made from whole cow's milk; similar to cheddar but flakier and moister.

Derby, À la. Of turkey or capon, stuffed with

rice and served with a sauce of truffles, foie gras and port wine.

Derby Biscuit. A round sweet shortbread biscuit usually containing currants and sometimes flavored with nutmeg.

Derl (British). A broken piece of bread or cake.

Derrière de Paleron (French). A cut of beef, resembling the lower portion of chuck ribs.

Derrin. (1) A thick broad cake or loaf. (2) Mixed oat or barley meal.

Dés (French). Diced food.

Desayuno (Spanish). Breakfast.

Desdemonas. Two rich sponge fingers sandwiched together with cream and then dipped in fondant.

Desessarts. A French gourmet famed in the 18th century; very little of his writings are now available.

Desiccate. To become quite dry. Coconut is often sold in desiccated form.

Désossé (French). Boneless.

Désosser (French). To remove the bones from poultry or game.

Dessécher (French). To stir a pulp, paste, or purée with a wooden spoon while cooking until the mixture is loosened from the pan.

Dessert. A course served at the end of a dinner or supper, usually a sweet dish. In modern American life emphasis is on simplicity. This is reflected in desserts, as in other modes and customs. Because many people try to keep their weight down they often forgo dessert. A survey made a few years ago of New York City families revealed that the most commonly served dessert for everyday meals was fruit, either canned or fresh. Only in week-end menus and on occasions when the family was entertaining at dinner did the more elaborate type of dessert appear.

But this does not necessarily apply in all parts of the United States, especially in rural areas, where pie, cake, or pudding may round out even the heartiest meals.

Desserts range, of course, from the simple fruits already mentioned, served either alone or with cheese, to frosted cake, rich pastries, and elegant puddings. Nor should gelatin desserts be overlooked, for they are particularly favored by weight watchers. The principle in planning a dessert is to have something light like fruit or gelatin if the main course has been substantial. Heartier desserts, such as puddings, custards, and pies, are a more fitting conclusion to a light meal.

Dessert Dumplings. *See* Dumplings.

Desserter (Danish, Norwegian, Swedish). Desserts.

Dessert Fork. The small fork rather than the dinner fork.

Dessert Knife. A small knife, not the dinner knife used for meat, may be used for desserts other than raw fruit. For fruit a special fruit knife with a pointed end is used.

Dessert Plate. A plate about 7 inches in diameter used for serving cakes, pies, and other solid desserts.

Dessert Spoon. A spoon midway in size between the tablespoon and the teaspoon, used not only for desserts but also for fruit and cereal as well as for soup served in a bowl.

Dessert Wines. Chilled sweet wines such as Sauternes, Vouvray, and the Italian Asti Spumante should be served with sweet desserts.

Detergent. A cleansing agent, that is, a soap or synthetic substance used with water for washing dishes, other kitchen utensils, clothes, and for other home-cleaning chores. Soap is usually a combination of several animal or vegetable fats converted into a cleansing agent by means of an alkali. There are both light- and heavy-duty soaps. Synthetic detergents are generally sulfated fatty alcohols and esters, although manufacturers usually keep their formulas secret. The detergents, whether soap or synthetic, are marketed in the form of flakes, beads, powders, and often in liquid form.

Détrempe (French). A pastry dough made with flour and water with butter added.

Deviled; Devilled. (1) Of any food, prepared with a spicy or sharp mixture or sauce. (2) Of poultry, grilled, split, and served brown with bread crumbs.

Deviled Butter. Butter mixed with a large quantity of black and cayenne peppers, ginger, and curry powder.

Deviled Chicken Legs. Legs of chicken (or sometimes other poultry) prepared with a spicy sauce.

Deviled Ham. A mixture of minced ham and various seasonings.

Devil Fish (Colloquial). Octopus, cuttlefish, or other cephalopods.

Devil's Food; Devil Food Cake (American). A very dark chocolate cake.

Devonshire Cream; Clotted Cream (British). Milk heated till quite hot, then set in a cold place for about 24 hours or until it has thickened; used as an accompaniment to desserts.

Devonshire Cream Cheese. An unusual English cream cheese. Whole cow's milk is allowed to set until the cream rises to the top, then it is heated to the boiling point without stirring. Set aside until the layer of cream becomes firm, it is then put into small molds and placed on straw mats to drain. When the cheeses are firm enough to hold their shape, they are sent to market.

Devonshire Junket. The term "junket" probably derives from the Italian *giuncata,* a cream cheese. That word was doubtless derived from *giuncato,* signifying "cover with rushes," that being the way in which cream or "rush" cheeses were prepared in Italy. The French apply *jonc,* a rush, and *joncher,* to prepare with rushes, to cream cheeses in the same way, as *jonchée de crème.*

Devonshire Splits (British). Slightly sweetened soft rolls served with strawberry jam and cream.

Devour. To eat like a beast; to eat greedily.

Dewberry. Brambleberry, a native North American fruit closely related to the blackberry but with a distinctive flavor. It grows on a low, trailing vine.

Dew-Piece (British, Scotch). A piece of bread, oatcake, or scone formerly given to a farm servant before starting work, when the dew was on the ground.

Dextrin. A soluble gummy carbohydrate substance formed when starch is decomposed by heat, acids, or enzymes.

Dextrose. A crystalline sugar present in many fruits, honey, and some vegetables; an important source of energy and a regulator of body temperature.

Dey (British). (1) A woman in charge of a dairy. (2) A baker of bread.

Dhal; Dhall. In India and Southeast Asia, lentils or, occasionally, split peas of various colors. Dhall may consist of split peas, lentils, pigeon peas, and grams (chick-peas) in Malaya.

Dhan Sak (Indian). Rice and curry.

Dhron. A wine village of the Moselle region of Germany. *See* Germany, The Wines of.

Diabetic Bread. A light bread made mainly with gluten and with little starch; intended primarily for diabetics.

Diable (French). (1) A brown porous earthenware pot, usually unglazed; used for preparing chestnuts or potatoes without liquids. (2) A double casserole in which one part fits above the other.

Diablé (French). (1) Deviled. (2) Of various fried or broiled fish, highly seasoned or with hot condiments added.

Diablotins (French). (1) "Little imps." Small meatballs of various kinds. (2) Ball-shaped confections. (3) (Italian) *Gnocchi* dumplings, sprinkled with grated cheese and cayenne, then browned before serving. (4) A small cracker or small toast squares flavored with cheese.

Diablotins de Fromage (French). Cutout rounds of fried bread covered with a cheese sauce and baked.

Diamond-Back Terrapin. *See* Turtle.

Diastase. The specific starch-digesting enzyme present in the kernels of wheat and of other cereal grains. It persists in flours during milling and develops into an active enzyme when flour is moistened and warmed.

Diavolini (Italian). "Little imps." (*See* Diablotins). (1) Sweets, usually consisting of almonds coated with chocolate and perhaps rolled in white or rose-pink nonpareils. (2) Small fried cakes made of deviled rice or farina.

Dibbity. A pancake.

Dibs (Arabic). Wine reduced to a sweet thick syrup.

Dice. To cut food into small cubes.

Dicke Suppen (German). Thick soups.

Dieppoise, À la. Of fish prepared with heavy cream, white wine, shrimp, and mussels.

Diet. (1) A certain prescribed course of food to be eaten daily, usually restricted in quantity or kind. (2) The usual daily intake of food. A balanced diet is essential for a healthy, full life. It includes the variety of foods that supply all the nutrients needed for good health in the proper amounts and in proper proportions.

The observance of a few simple rules will ensure a balanced diet. Six main food groups constitute the balanced diet, and practically every food contains several or all of these groups in varying amounts. The six groups are carbohydrates, fats, proteins, vitamins, minerals, and water. Carbohydrate, fat, and protein supply calories. Carbohydrates (sugars and starches) are the cheapest source of energy. Fats yield twice as many calories as do the same amounts of either carbohydrates or protein. Most of the calories in the diet are furnished by carbohydrates and fat. The primary function of protein is the building, repair, and maintenance of body tissues.

Vitamins and minerals must also be balanced. Each vitamin and mineral has a special function in the body's metabolism or operation. Water furnishes no calories or vitamins, but it may provide various minerals. It helps to maintain body temperature and is needed to facilitate normal intestinal function. The body loses considerable water each day and to replace this loss at least six glasses of water or its equivalent in other liquids should be taken each day.

For a balanced diet there should be a variety of food and a variety at each meal. Balance calories as well as the rest of the diet by maintaining a desirable weight range. Use protective foods (enriched and whole-grain breads and cereals, meats, fish, milk, eggs, legumes, green leafy and yellow vegetables and fruits). Variety is the keynote to the balanced diet.

For balanced and varied meals, the following "basic" foods which supply the essential nutrients should be included each day: milk and milk products; meat, egg, fish, dried beans and other legumes; whole-grain and enriched breads and cereals; green leafy and yellow vegetables; fruits, including citrus fruits and other foods containing vitamin C; fat (including butter or enriched margarine for vitamin A content); potatoes and other vegetables.

Dietary. Pertaining to diet.

Dietary Laws. Orthodox Jewish laws regarding kosher foods.

Diète (French). Diet.

Dietetic. Pertaining to the diet or to the kind of food to be eaten.

Dietetics. The general science of food and its consumption by human beings, including nutritional requirements, caloric counts, and vitamin intake.

Dietician; Dietitian. A person who selects the menu and plans and supervises meals in a hospital, institution, company restaurant, or research institute.

Digby Chicks. Small herrings or pilchards; called *Nova Scotia sprats* by the fishermen at Digby, Nova Scotia.

Digest. To assimilate food in the body so that it may be absorbed into the system.

Digester. A heavy iron cooking pot with a tight-fitting lid that permits the escape of steam only through a valve at the top.

Digestible. Able to be digested.

Digestif (French). Any liqueur or afterdinner drink thought to aid digestion.

Digestion. The process food goes through in the body so that it may be absorbed into the system; the breaking-down of foods into simpler components in the alimentary or digestive tract. Foods may be digested by natural body enzymes in the stomach and intestines, or they may be broken down by chemicals, heat, or microorganisms.

Digestive. (1) Pertaining to digestion. (2) Any substance that aids digestion.

Digestive Biscuits. Crisp whole-meal or wheat-meal biscuits.

Dijon. A city in Burgundy, France, at which a gastronomic fair, the *États Généraux de la Gastronomie*, is held each autumn.

Dika; Dika Butter; Cay-Cay Butter (African). A cake of fat made from the fruit of the mango tree; similar to cacao butter. African natives use it extensively because it does not readily turn rancid; it is also used in the chocolate-making industry.

Dikoya. A rich Ceylonese black tea with a unique flavor.

Dilao (Philippine). Turmeric, a spice.

Dill. A beautiful brilliant green herb with a penetrating odor and an unusual flavor; used to flavor pickles and to give character to many fish dishes. Dill butter is used in sandwiches.

Dill is used extensively in east European and Scandinavian dishes.

Dillkött (Swedish). Veal stew flavored with dill.

Dillkött på Lamm (Swedish). Lamb in dill sauce.

Dill Pickles. French or salted cucumbers pickled and flavored with either fresh dill or dill seeds, and other spices.

Dillsås (Swedish). Dill sauce.

Dilute. To thin or weaken by adding a liquid; to dissolve.

Dimethyl Anthranilate. A colorless or, occasionally, pale yellow liquid used to supply peach and grape taste synthetically to processed foods.

Dinanderie. (1) Brass kitchen utensils made at Dinant, Belgium. (2) Brass items made in India and the Middle East.

Dindon (French). Turkey.

Dindonneau (French). A young turkey.

Dine. Basically, to eat dinner. The term is used more commonly in England than in the United States. In present usage "to dine" implies something more than consuming food. Thus, animals eat, but only man can dine.

Diner. (1) On a railroad train a long car in which meals are served. (2) Roadside restaurant shaped like a railroad car.

Diner (Swedish). Dinner.

Dîner (French). Dinner, the main meal of the day; the dinner hour in France has fluctuated widely.

Dîner d'Andouille (French). A main course consisting of chitterlings (smaller intestines of the pig) made into a sausage.

Dîner de Noce (French). A wedding feast.

Dîner Mi-Carême (French). A dinner served during Lent.

Dinette. A small area, especially in a small modern apartment, set aside for dining.

Dinette Set. A table and chairs, usually small, for use in a dinette.

Dinner. Usually, the principal meal of the day, whether served at midday or at night. Customs vary from country to country.

Dinner Biscuits (British). Unsweetened, rather light biscuits.

Dinner Fork. A large fork used for the meat course.

Dinner Knife. The largest knife in a place setting.

It has a steel blade and is used for the meat course only at dinner or at lunch.

Dinner Party. A dinner more elaborate than usual, to which guests are invited.

Dinner Plate. A flat plate 9–10 inches in diameter, the largest individual plate in the table service.

Dinner Wagon. A tray with shelves below it mounted on four legs equipped with rollers to permit wheeling in and out of the dining room.

Dinuguan (Philippine). Any dish cooked in chicken or pig's blood; similar to *tinumis*.

Diogenes Crab. A hermit crab.

Dionysia. Chief festival of Dionysus, Greek god of wine, held at harvest time.

Diota. A drinking vessel with two handles, used in Greek and Roman times.

Dip. (1) To immerse briefly in a liquid. (2) To place food in a dry mixture, as dipping in flour. (3) A soft mixture, into which crackers, raw vegetables, or potato chips may be dipped; particularly popular at cocktail parties.

Diples (Greek). Cakes made of flour, farina, or Cream of Wheat mixed with eggs, orange juice, and salt, and deep-fat fried. After draining, they are arranged on a platter and heated honey is poured over them; then they are sprinkled with a mixture of powdered sugar, cinnamon, and finely chopped walnuts.

Diplomat; Diplomate. (1) A Béchamel sauce made with brandy, truffles, and shellfish; often served on fish. (2) A fruit pudding made with raisins and liquor.

Dipper. A cup with a long handle used for ladling water, milk, and other liquids; formerly used at wells and other drinking places.

Dipping Chocolate. A special chocolate used for coating cream, nuts, and fruits in candy-making; available from manufacturers and candy-makers.

The chocolate should be grated or cut into fine pieces which will melt and blend more readily over heat than would larger pieces. Not less than one pound and not more than two pounds of dipping chocolate should be used at a time. Less than a pound does not provide sufficient liquid to work with, and more than two pounds is apt to cool and solidify before it can be used up. About 6–7 dozen assorted centers can be dipped with one pound.

Chocolate to be used for dipping should be placed in the top of a double boiler over hot water and stirred continually to produce the proper blend of cocoa butter and to assure a rich, glossy sheen on the finished chocolates.

Important, too, is the proper temperature in the room where the dipping process takes place. It should be a dry day, and the temperature should be 60°–70°F.

Chocolate-coated candies originated sometime before 1870 when a confectioner coated creams with chocolate so they would hold together better. The chocolate-coated creams soon became popular, and other centers, including fruits, nuts, and nougats, were treated in the same manner.

Dipsomania. An uncontrollable desire for alcoholic drinks. A person with this craving is a *dipsomaniac*.

Dishcloth Gourd; Loofah; Snake Squash. A long, narrow squash resembling a cucumber; often used in oriental cookery.

Dishes. (1) An almost infinite variety of utensils suitable for holding foods. (2) Any food preparations.

Dishing Up (British). The art of presenting a roast on a platter in such a manner that it is attractive to the eye as well as convenient for the carver to handle. *Dressage*, the French equivalent of dishing up, includes the garnishing of the dish. The finest art is to have all the dishes to be served at the same course ready and dished up at the same time.

Disjoint. As applied to poultry, to cut into pieces at the joints.

Dispensaire (Obsolete, French). A book of culinary recipes.

Diss Bread (British). A special cake or gingerbread made at Diss, Norfolk.

Dissolve. To make liquid; to combine a food with a liquid and stir until the entire mixture is liquid.

Distillation. A process for separating components in a liquid. Different components in a liquid vaporize, that is, become gas, at differing temperatures. Therefore, if the liquid is heated to the temperature at which some desired component vaporizes, it will separate as a gas, which can then be caught in a condenser, chilled, and returned to what will now be the pure or nearly pure liquid form of that component, called the *distillate*. This is the procedure used for distilling the alcohol from the water in spirits. The place where distillation takes place is called the *distillery*.

Distilled Water. When the distillation process is used to purify water, the liquid is brought to the boiling point so that it vaporizes; the steam is then condensed into pure water, which lacks the air and salts of ordinary water.

Distillers' Yeast. Yeast produced during the fermentation of liquors.

Ditali; Ditalini. Tubes of Italian pasta made in various sizes; often used in making minestrone.

Dittany. Name of a variety of plants. Cretan dittany is an herb that grows abundantly on Mount Dicte in Crete. The European pepperwort, a dittany, is sometimes spelled *dittander*. In England the wood sage, a perennial plant common in open spaces, heaths, and woods, is also known as dittany.

Diuretic Foods. Those foods which stimulate or increase the excretion of urine from the human body. Most vegetables of the cabbage family, radishes, and white wine are known for their diuretic effect.

Divinity. A fudgelike candy made with a heavy sugar syrup added to stiffly beaten egg whites to produce a delicate, light texture. *Nougat*, which contains honey and usually almonds, has more body than divinity, but is otherwise similar. An electric mixer is a great help in making these candies but lacking that, a wire whip works more satisfactorily than a rotary beater.

Dja'Aj (Arabic). Chicken.

Djamur Kuping (Indonesian). Cloud ears, an edible tree fungus.

Djendjelem (North African). A soft white substance made with starch and sugar; used as a cooking ingredient.

Djuvetch (Yugoslavian). Dish of onions, chopped meat or fish, with tomatoes, rice, oil or butter, and stock.

Doagy (British). Sticky, as applied to dough.

Dobbin. A small drinking jug.

Dobosch Torte (Hungarian). A superb multi-layered cake made with chocolate butter-cream filling and a caramel-flavored top.

Dobrada (Portuguese). A stew of tripe, sausages, and white beans.

Dobule (French). The chub. *See* Chub.

Doces (Portuguese). Desserts.

Dock. A large herb family including sorrel and rhubarb. In England other members of this family, such as mountain rhubarb and patience dock, are used as potherbs.

Docker (British). A block of wood with pointed nails to mark or puncture the surface of dough or pastry.

Dodger. A crusty corncake.

Dodine. A white sauce often made with poultry drippings and onions.

Dodine de Canard (French). Boned duck formed into a mold, often with its own jelly. Also, duck stewed with onions.

Doe. Female of the deer, rabbit, and some other animals.

Dog Bramble. A wild currant.

Dogfish. Derogatory term for several species of fish found in different countries. In the Pacific Northwest a coarse variety of salmon is called dog salmon. In France the dogfish is a large oily-fleshed, rather strong-flavored fish caught in the North Atlantic.

Dogmeat. In China and Taiwan, the meat of certain dogs is often used as a food.

Doilies. Chinese-American term for thin wheat pancakes in which foods are rolled and then picked up and eaten with the fingers.

Doily. A circle or oval of lace, linen, paper, or other material placed under dishes, vases, etc. The doily was named for a London dry-goods merchant who is said to have promoted its sale.

Dolce di Castagne (Italian). Chestnut dessert.

Dolcetto delle Langhe. *See* Italy, The Wines of.

Dolce Verde. Literally, "sweet green." A rich, hard Italian cheese, an unsuccessful imitation of Gorgonzola.

Dolci (Italian). Sweets; desserts.

Dolic. Pertaining to several types of pulses, especially the soybean.

Dolichos Bean. A small green vegetable of Southeast Asia, whose pod resembles a string bean.

Dolium (Obsolete). A large earthenware oil or wine jug or vessel used in Roman times.

Dollardee. Bluegill, a freshwater food fish.

Dollarfish. A mediocre small fish, found off the New England coast.

Dollop. A small lump or amount of something, such as a dollop of sour cream.

Dolly. A variety of sweet dishes, fruits, or nuts offered on a tray.

Dolly Varden Trout; Malma. A North American trout noted for its excellent taste and texture.

Dolma; Dolmade (Near Eastern). Grape, cabbage, or (occasionally) lettuce leaves stuffed with a seasoned rice mixture which may include minced lamb, then rolled up and simmered over low heat.

　Dolmas à la Grecque. Stuffed cabbage or vine leaves.

Dolmadakia (Greek). Vine leaves stuffed with rice and meat.

Domaci Beli Sir. A Yugoslavian ewe's-milk cheese cured in a fresh sheep's skin.

Domburi (Japanese). A large bowl.

Dome Molds. Dome-shaped copper or tin pudding molds with or without a shoulder.

Domestic Economy. General housekeeping.

Domiata. A salty, mild, white Egyptian cheese made from buffalo's or cow's milk.

Domiculture. The art of cooking; general housekeeping.

Domineer. To feast luxuriously.

Dominican Republic. The island of Hispaniola, discovered by Columbus, is shared by the Dominican Republic and Haiti, but there is no culinary kinship between the two nations. Haiti has a cuisine influenced by France, whereas that of the Dominican Republic has Spanish overtones.

The local cuisine is based on agricultural produce, and the fruits and vegetables are outstanding. Like the Cubans, the people show a liking for starchy foods, such as beans, rice, plantains, and sweet potatoes. To this basic diet are added the fish and shellfish caught off the coast. Pickled fish, *pescado es escabeche*, is a typical fish preparation, and *sopa hamaca*, a fish soup, is another favorite. *Carne de cerdo*, browned pork strips, is a favorite Dominican food, but all pork dishes are popular here. The classic *sancocho*, a soup-stew of meat and vegetables, is made with seven kinds of meat (at least on special occasions). Sweet desserts, usually made with bananas and coconuts, are much liked. Meals usually end with cups of black Dominican coffee, but tiny cups are frequently served during the day. Other beverages include beer and rum, both made locally.

Dom Pérignon. (1) The renowned monk who lived near Epernay, France, believed to have invented the champagne process. (2) An outstanding brand of champagne, marketed only in exceptional years, in a distinctive bottle shorter than the typical champagne bottle.

Donburi (Japanese). Eel meat served on a bed of rice with a sauce.

Donzelle. A very small fish, native to France, resembling an eel; used in fish soups and stews.

Dooars. Black teas originating in the Dooars, a district of Bengal, India; excellent for blending.

Doodle (Medieval German). The original word for "noodle."

Doogh (Afghan). A buttermilk drink.

Doopiajas; Do Pyaza (Indian). "Two" or "double onions"; a rich highly seasoned rice and meat curry in which two methods of preparing onions are employed.

Dop. A type of brandy usually made by expressing the skins of grapes already used in wine making.

Doppeltes Beefsteak (German). The Chateaubriand cut of steak.

Dorade (French). (1) The gilt head, or the sea bream, excellent food fishes; the dorade is also called the daurade. (2) The term is used, erroneously, to describe any fish with gold or yellow markings.

Dorado (Spanish). A large European saltwater fish having a rather good taste and texture; usually boiled in a court bouillon with white wine or sometimes in salted water.

Dordermeat (Scotch). A bannock or cake formerly given between dinner and supper to servants working on a farm.

Doré (French). Brushed with beaten egg yolks.

Dorking. A breed of poultry raised chiefly in England.

Dormers (Obsolete, British). Croquettes of minced meat and rice, eggs, seasonings, and gravy.

Dorse; Dorsch. A fish caught in the Baltic and believed to be the young of the cod. Some experts, however, believe it is the young of the haddock.

Dorset Cheese; Dorset Blue; Blue Vinny. A hard, blue-veined English cheese with a natural thick rind; made from hand-skimmed milk. It has a round, rich flavor without the pungency of Continental blue cheeses. *Double Dorset* is another version of this cheese, richer and creamier.

Dorure (French). Yolks of beaten eggs brushed over pastry.

Dory; John Dory. A small salt-water fish of golden color.

Dosa (South Indian). Pancake made with a fermented batter of rice and ground lentils or split black beans.

Dosn. Wet unbaked bread.

Dotter Cheese. An unusual cheese, made in Nuremberg, Germany, prepared by mixing egg yolks with skim milk.

Dotterels. Small tame European birds of the plover family, sometimes caught by hand; in season in Europe from October through December.

Double (French). (1) A pair of legs of lamb. (2) The belly or stomach of ruminant animals, thus *gras-double*, tripe.

Double Boiler. Two saucepans, both with handles, one of which fits on top of the other; used with water in the lower pan to prevent the burning of food and to cook foods, such as custards, which must be kept at a temperature below the boiling point. The two parts of the double boiler can be used separately.

Double Cake. A cake made of two layers of pastry sandwiched with currants or jam.

Double Cheese. (1) A cheese made with all cream, as distinguished from a single cheese prepared with some cream removed. (2) A cheese to which some cream has been added when ordinarily it would have been made only from milk.

Double Consommé. Consommé cooked until concentrated and strong; or consommé strengthened by the addition of bouillon cubes.

Double Cream. (1) Very rich, heavy cream that has rested on milk for 24 hours instead of only

12. (2) Any rich, white cheese, high in fat content.

Double Cream Cheese (British). Wensleydale cheese.

Double-Crème; Fromage à la Double-Crème. Several rich fresh cheeses, high in fat, are sold under these names in France.

Double de Mouton. Two legs of mutton in a single piece.

Double Dorset. A rich, creamy blue-mold cheese. *See* Dorset.

Doubler (French). (1) To fold over foods or pastries. (2) To cover with a protective layer of parchment paper, or a baking sheet.

Double Saucepan (British). Double boiler.

Douce-Amère (French). Bittersweet.

Doucet. A French term with many meanings. A variation of *doux*, sweet. (1) A Mediterranean fish of fair quality. (2) A very sweet grape. (3) A cider apple.

Doucette (French). The young edible leaves of the corn salad.

Doucettes. Small fancy cakes and marzipan cookies served with dessert.

Douch (British). A dish of fresh haddock, fried onions, saffron, cider or ale, with bread added to thicken the gravy.

Douf. A small cake.

Dough. A mixture of flour and a liquid, usually with other ingredients, thick enough to knead or roll, as in making yeast bread or rolls. It is too stiff to stir or pour. In various districts of England dough is known as *daafe, daigh, dayegh, deagh, deawh, doaf, doff, doo, dooaf, doof, dow, dye, dowf, duff.*

Dough-Baked. As applied to bread or cake, doughy because incorrectly or incompletely baked.

Dough Cake. A cake made with fat, fruit, and sugar added to a bread dough and allowed to rise, then baked.

Dough Dumplings (British). Leftover risen dough formed into small balls and cooked with boiled beef to make light, fluffy dumplings.

Dough Mixer. A machine used in commercial bakeries for mixing and kneading dough.

Doughnuts. A round of dough, fried in deep fat until brown and crisp. American women of an earlier era, especially in New England and the Midwest, had the art of frying doughnuts down pat. They had a good deal of practice, for the fried cakes were as much a breakfast staple as oatmeal porridge or bacon and eggs. Now when Americans eat less than their predecessors at most meals, and especially breakfast, few home cooks bother making doughnuts. Why should they when every bakery has at least one variety to sell?

But no commercially baked doughnut can measure up to the light, fluffy, flavorful delicacies that grandmother used to make—or so nostalgia may lead some of us to think.

In these days, when thermometers for measuring the temperature of fat are available, some of the trickiness has been eliminated from the art of doughnut making, but it still requires care. If the fat is too low in temperature, the cakes will absorb fat. The temperature should be between 355°–365° during the whole cooking process. It is not a simple matter to keep the temperature at the desired level. The comparatively cold doughnut batter, dropped into the fat, lowers the temperature; hence no more than four to six doughnuts should be fried at one time.

The doughnuts should be slipped into the fat when it has reached the right temperature, then turned quickly with a long-handled fork as soon as they rise to the surface. Turn frequently thereafter until they are well browned on both sides, then remove from pan, allowing grease to drip back in. Place on absorbent paper to cool so that more grease will be drained.

After the doughnuts have been cut but before they are cooked, it is a good idea to let them set a few minutes. In this way the outer surface forms a crust that will prevent excessive grease absorption during frying.

The batter should not contain too much sugar, for that will cause additional fat absorption, and the flour should be kept to the proper proportion or the doughnuts will be tough. Roll the batter out only once, for too much handling also causes toughness.

Dough Room. A room in which temperature and humidity are controlled so that fermentation may take place.

Dough Trough. A container for dough while it is rising.

Douilles Mobiles (French). Pastry tubes used for filling and decorating purposes.

Douillon; Rabotte (French). Any desired fruit wrapped in a short pastry and baked. Pears are the specialty in Normandy, France.

Doum. An Egyptian palm tree that bears an edible fruit about the size of an apple.

Dourada (Portuguese). A kind of fish.

Douro. A district in northern Portugal that produces port wine. *See* Portugal, The Wines of.

Douse. To plunge a food into, or drench it with, water, or another liquid.

Doux. Bottles containing 10–15 percent sugar in champagne. This sweet champagne is seldom sold in the American market, but it is popular in parts of South America and in Russia.

Doux; Douce (French, Colloquial). Any sweet food.

Dove. A bird of the pigeon family, occasionally used for food. Popular opinion opposes the killing of doves, but certain gourmets will not forgo them because they are so delectable.

Dover Splits. Small plain scones eaten hot with butter.

Dowdy. A dessert with biscuit topping, such as an *apple pan dowdy*.

Dowitcher; Brownback; Grayback. The red-breasted or gray snipe.

Dowl. To knead dough rapidly.

Doyenné. A very sweet French pear.

Draff. Refuse; brewer's grains.

Dragée (French). Originally a sugared almond; now, more often, a chocolate drop.

Draggle. To moisten meal, flour, etc., very slightly.

Dragon Fish. A member of the Trachinidae family; used chiefly in France for making bouillabaisse.

Dragon's Beard. A Chinese green tea.

Dragon's Eyes. Lungan, a Chinese fruit, eaten fresh or dried.

Dragon's Well. A green tea produced in Hang-chow, China; often regarded as one of the world's best teas.

Drake. A male duck.

Dram. (1) A very small drink, especially of an alcoholic beverage. (2) Norwegian *snaps*.

Drambuie. A fine Scotch liqueur made of Scotch whisky and heather honey, the formula for which is said to have been brought to Scotland by a French attendant of Prince Charles Edward in 1745. It is served as an afterdinner drink. Translated from the Gaelic, *Drambuie* means "the drink that satisfies."

Draught; Draft. The act of drinking.

Draw. To remove the entrails from, and to clean, poultry or game.

Drawn Butter. Melted butter.

Drawn Poultry. Poultry from which the entrails and usually also the feathers have been removed.

Dredge. To sprinkle or coat foods with flour, sugar, or any other dry substance.

Dreg; Dregs. Matter or sediment from liquors.

Drench. A drink.

Dresdener Bierkäse. A soft skim-milk cheese flavored with caraway seeds; made in Dresden, Germany and considered ideal with beer.

Dress. (1) To mix sauces or flavoring immediately before serving a food. For example, vegetables may be dressed with melted butter, or salad greens with a dressing. (2) To trim, pare, or clean, or to serve well garnished.

Dressage (French). (1) The presentation of food in attractive fashion. (2) The dish or platter, the garnish, arrangement and general appearance of the particular food.

Dressé (French). Garnished or dressed.

Dressed Poultry. The commercial term for birds priced according to their weight after the blood and feathers but not the head, feet, and viscera have been removed. The buyer pays for the waste material. Ready-to-cook poultry is weighed and priced after the bird has been bled, picked, and fully drawn (eviscerated) and after the head, feet, and inedible organs have been removed.

Poultry labeled "ready-to-cook" should be thoroughly cleaned inside and out and should be free of pin feathers. If the ready-to-cook bird is to be sold whole, the giblets (liver, gizzard, and heart) have usually been placed inside the body cavity. The neck may be packed with the giblets.

Dresser en Couronne (French). To arrange foods in a ring shape.

Dressing. *See* Stuffing; Salad Dressings.

Dribble. A small drop of liquid.

Driblet. A very small amount.

Driddlins (British). Knots of dry flour left in bread after baking.

Dried. Lacking moisture.

Dried Beef. *See* Chipped Beef.

Dried Fruits. Drying as a means of preserving food was used successfully in early Egyptian times. It has been applied (even more successfully) in modern times to such fruits as plums, grapes, apricots, figs, dates, and, less frequently, to apples, pears, and peaches. Dried fruit is firm and meaty even though most of its moisture has been removed. Fruit to be dried must be completely ripe before being harvested. Dried fruits contain fruit sugar, several vitamins, and essential minerals.

Dried Limes (Iranian). Limes boiled for a few minutes in lightly salted water and dried in hot sunshine. Small quantities give a piquant flavor to stews, soups, and sauces.

Drikke (Danish). Liquor; drinks.

Drikker (Norwegian). Liquor; drinks.

Drink. To swallow a liquid, alcoholic or non-alcoholic, either to quench the thirst or for nourishment.

Drinkable. Suitable for drinking, such as water or liquor.

Drinker. A person who drinks, especially one who drinks alcoholic beverages excessively.

Drink-Hail (British). Drink to health or good luck; a reply to a toast.

Drinkless. Being dry; without liquor.

Dripolater. *See* Coffee Maker.

Dripping; Drippings. (1) Unbleached and untreated fat from the fatty tissues or bones of cattle. (2) The fats and juices that cook out of meat and poultry; sometimes spread on bread. They are one of the essences that give flavor and character to gravies.

Dripping Pan. A pan used to catch drippings (fat) from meat.

Drop Scone (British, Scotch). A sweet cake or pancake made with a soft batter and dropped on a hot griddle or skillet to fry.

Druid Cake (Scotch). Hogmanay bannock, an oatcake flavored with caraway seeds; made with a hole in the center and marked around the edge with ridged rays symbolic of the sun's rays.

Drumfish; Drum. A saltwater and also a freshwater food fish weighing 25–75 pounds, with sweet, tasty flesh; best when prepared in good-sized steaks. *See also* Sheepshead.

Drumhead. An English variety of cabbage with a flat top.

Drumstick. (1) A long, fibrous Indian bean. (2) In popular usage, the leg of poultry.

Drupe. A fleshy fruit, such as cherry, plum, and olive, at the center of which is a nut or a stone containing a kernel. *See also* Fruit.

Drupel; Drupelet. A small drupe, such as blackberry and raspberry.

Dry. (1) As applied to wines and spirits, not sweet; technically, "lacking in sugar." (2) Having no liquid; solid.

Dry Cheese. Speerkäse or Trockenkäse made in small dairies in the Bavarian Alps and in the Tyrol, Germany. It is produced only in the winter, when the milk cannot be used for other purposes. It is called "dry" because it is placed in a drying room until it becomes very hard through considerable loss of moisture.

Dry Frying. Frying without fat by using an antisticking silicone-finish utensil or a vegetable extract.

Dry Ice. Used commercially for refrigeration, especially of foods being transported. Ice cream is sometimes packed in dry ice to keep it solid.

Dry ice is carbon dioxide in a solid state. The gas is liquefied under pressure, then the pressure is removed and the liquid is allowed to evaporate in a confined space. Some of it returns to a gaseous state and draws heat from the remaining liquid, thereby freezing it to a solid state.

Drycker (Swedish). Drinks; beverages.

Drysalter (British). A person who deals in pickles, oils, and sauces.

Dry Vat. A large container for storing dry foods, such as cereals.

Dubarry (French). With cauliflower; containing cauliflower.

Dubarry Sauce. A sauce prepared with natural meat juices combined with a demi-glace. *See*

Demi-glace.

Dubbelsmörgås (Swedish). Sandwich.

Dubba; Dubber; Duppa (Indian). A skin container used to hold water, ghee (clarified butter), oils, or other liquids; made of gelatin, prepared by boiling skin cuttings and shaping them in earthen molds.

Dublin Bay Prawns. A large excellent-tasting prawn or shrimp found in Dublin Bay, Ireland.

Dublin Pound. A trout.

Dubois, Urbain. The 19th-century chef who wrote *La Cuisine Classique* and invented many notable dishes.

Dubonnet. A French apéritif wine similar to a vermouth; it is based upon a red wine and has a vaguely bitter aftertaste. Dubonnet is drunk either neat or mixed with gin or brandy. *See* Apéritif Wines.

Duchesse; À la Duchesse. A wide variety of French dishes. *Potatoes duchesse* are mashed, mixed with egg yolks, and shaped into various forms. *Duchesse soup* is a purée of chicken garnished with boiled rice.

Duchesse. Small baked cakes made from almond paste.

Duck. The meat of the duck, stronger in flavor than that of chicken or turkey, has long been appreciated by man. Wild ducks have been a favored game ever since Paleolithic man learned to hunt. It is not known when domestication of the birds began. The Peking duck, which is the strain raised domestically now in this country, descends from the Chinese bird that was one of the earliest varieties bred for food.

A major portion of this nation's total production of ducks is provided by Long Island, where some fifty-three duck farmers raise nearly 7,000,-000 birds each year. About 95 percent of the ducks sold are in ready-to-cook frozen form. Long Island ducks are undoubtedly the finest tame ducks in the world.

In buying domestic duck, look for plump, compact birds that are well fleshed and have a clean, unbruised, and unbroken skin. If the duck is frozen, it should not be defrosted until just before it is to be cooked. To defrost, first puncture the moistureproof wrapping in which the bird is encased and place the duck on the shelf of the refrigerator. It will defrost in 30–36 hours and should be cooked immediately after it is completely defrosted. The process of "unfreezing" the duck can be hastened by placing it in the original wrap under running cold water for at least 6 hours.

Duck meat is all dark and furnishes high-quality protein, minerals, and vitamins. It is especially rich in iron and high in thiamin (vitamin B_1) and riboflavin. The large amount of fat in duckling enhances the flavor and makes it a particularly tender and juicy bird for roasting. However, excessive fat should be cut away and dripped away during the roasting process.

The wild duck, such as the *canvasback* and the *mallard*, unlike the domestic duck, possesses little fat. This should be taken into account when cooking. The best way to provide the fat essential to prevent the wild bird from being dry and stringy when it comes to the table is to insert salt pork under the skin with a larding needle. Strips of salt pork or bacon also should be laid across the breast of the duck during roasting.

Duck, Oil-and-Salt Preserved (Chinese preparation). Duck heavily salted, then pressed flat and soaked in peanut oil. Before being cooked, it should be soaked in cold water for an hour and then cut up.

Duck, Salted Dried (Chinese). Duck pressed very flat, then heavily salted and allowed to dry in the sun. It should be soaked in cold water for an hour, then cut up and cooked.

Ducking (British). Shooting or catching wild ducks.

Duckling. A young duck weighing about 3½ pounds.

Duck Potatoes. *See* Wapatoo.

Duck Press. An apparatus consisting of a container to hold duck meat and a press which forces meat down, extracting the juices; similar to a meat or vegetable press, but made particularly for table service and used exclusively for duck dishes, notably *canard à la presse*.

Duck Sauce. *See* Duk Sauce.

Duck's Feet. The cleaned feet of ducks are frequently used in Chinese cookery, where they are highly regarded.

Duck, Wild. *See* Duck.

Due (Danish). Pigeon.

Duel Cheese. A soft cured Austrian cow's-milk cheese prepared in a cube about 2 inches square and 1 inch thick.

Duff (British). A flour-and-egg pudding made with raisins and currants, boiled in a cheese-cloth bag. A *Plum duff* was once a favorite treat aboard British vessels, and tradition dictated that while preparing it the cook keep whistling to show his shipmates that he was not simultaneously eating the dried fruit.

Duglère. A famous French chef who created several dishes.

Duhat. The Java plum, a fruit popular in various Pacific countries, especially in the Philippines; used chiefly for making wines.

Duke Cherry. A hybrid of sweet and sour cherries, popular in France. The American variety is sometimes called *May Duke*.

Duke of Clarence Malmsey. A very dry Madeira wine with a superb flavor and bouquet; often served as an apéritif.

Duk Sauce, Chinese. A rather sweet sauce made of peaches, apricots, vinegar, sugar, and spices, usually served in small dishes, sometimes accompanied by mustard. Foods are dipped into the duk sauce and mustard before eating. Sometimes erroneously spelled "*duck sauce.*"

Duku. A fruit found in the South Pacific, particularly in Indonesia.

Dulce (Spanish). (1) A sweet dish; dessert. (2) Any fruit cooked with sugar until very soft. A coconut sweet is called *dulce de coco*.

Dulceata (Romanian). A group of desserts made of fruits and nuts in a thick syrup.

Dulce de Leche (Spanish). A sweet thick cream made by boiling milk.

Dulcet. Sweet-smelling; sweet-tasting.

Dulcify. To sweeten to the taste.

Dulcite. Madagascar manna purified and used for sweetening.

Dulcitol. A six-carbon sugar-alcohol formed by the reduction of galactose. It occurs in Madagascar manna and is also known as *melampyrin*, *dulcite*, and *galacticol*.

Dulse. A coarse red edible seaweed that grows along sea coasts and is collected in northern countries like Scotland, Iceland, and in the Maritime Provinces of Canada. It is dried and chewed like candy, though it has the salty tang of the sea. It is a rich source of iron. *See* Irish Moss.

Dumalaga (Philippine). A young hen, ideally suited for cooking.

Dumas, Alexandre. A famous French novelist and author of books on cookery, who died in 1870. His *Dictionary of Cuisine*, published in 1872, is still interesting.

Dumb Cake (British). Cake made in silence on the eve of St. Mark's Day. It is made of an egg-shellful each of salt, flour, and wheat meal. The purpose is to enable a young woman to learn something of her future husband; exactly what isn't clear.

Dumbwaiter. (1) In England, shelves or trays that revolve on a pole and hold dishes, etc. (2) A platform or tray that transports dishes, etc., to various parts of a house.

Dumm (Indian). A system of cooking with heat simultaneously above and below the dish.

Dumplings. Americans are familiar with two different kinds of dumplings. One is the light, tender-textured puff made of a farinaceous substance, such as flour, cornmeal, cracker meal, or farina, bound together with egg and usually including butter and salt. These puffs are simmered in a liquid, often the soup or stew with which they are served.

Another kind of dumpling is made with a pastry dough rolled into squares and wrapped around fruits, such as apples, pears, peaches, or cherries, then baked in a moderate oven. It is served as a dessert.

Dumplings for soups and stews should be kept steaming on top of the liquid in which they cook. The liquid should never be brought above the simmering point. The pan should not be crowded, for the dumplings expand as they cook.

Foreign cuisines feature many other varieties of dumplings, such as those made of potatoes, yeast dough, cheese, etc. Czechoslovakia, in particular, emphasizes dumplings in its national cuisine.

Dumpode. Slowly cooked or stewed; probably a corruption of the Persian word *dam-pukht*.

Dun. A method of curing codfish which produces a brown color; it is then called *dunfish*.

Dunan. Two famous French chefs, father and son, who lived in the 18th and 19th centuries. Most of their lives were spent in the service of royalty, particularly the Prince de Condé.

Dunbird. The female pochard. *See* Pochard.

Dun Birds. Birds named for their dun-colored backs; sometimes sought as game in Great Britain; best when roasted.

Dundee Cake (Scotch). A classic cake made with spices, butter, flour, sugar, raisins, candied fruit peel, and almonds.

Dunder. In rum making, the leftover part of the sugar-cane juice; used chiefly in preparing the sweeter, heavier rums.

Dunelin; Dunelm (British). A dish of braised mutton or veal that originated in Durham.

Dunfish. Codfish cured by the dun process. *See* Dun.

Dunk. To dip cake, pastry, or bread into a liquid to soften it. Dunking doughnuts in hot coffee is a popular example.

Dunkles (German). Dark beer.

Dunlop. A medium firm Scotch cheese, with a spicy, sharp taste; somewhat like cheddar.

Dunst. A semolina (starch from the endosperm of the wheat grain) almost as fine as flour; also called *break middlings*.

Dunter. Eider duck.

Durak. A rather smoky, rich Turkish cheese.

Durazno (Spanish). Peach.

Durian. A large Southeast Asian melonlike fruit with a repellent odor. Inside the spiky exterior is a rich, creamy, fine-tasting pulp, which is eaten plain, made into dessert and candy, and recently, in Malaysia, into ice cream. The odor is minimized when the fruit is chilled.

Durra; Doura. Indian millet, a kind of corn; a grain sorghum cultivated in various parts of the world because it is drought-resistant.

Dürre Runde (German). A dried sausage.

Durum Wheat. A very special hard variety of wheat grown chiefly for the making of macaroni, spaghetti, and noodles. In the United States it is raised in Minnesota and the Dakotas. It is also grown in Canada, Spain, North Africa, and Italy.

Dushab (Arabian). Drink consisting of a mixture of date wine and grape juice reduced to a syrup.

Dust Tea. A green Chinese tea that is reduced by rubbing and grinding to a powdery substance.

Dust, Tea. In the tea trade the smallest grade of tea leaf; used mainly in blends. *Fannings* are somewhat larger.

Dutch Cheese. (1) Cottage cheese. (2) Edam or Gouda cheese.

Dutch Cracklings. Small ginger-flavored cookies.

Dutch Cream Cheese. An English cheese made like cream cheese but with eggs added.

Dutch Guiana. *See* Guianas, The.

Dutch Oven. A kitchen utensil that dates back to American colonial days. Originally an iron kettle, it is now made of cast aluminum. It comes in different sizes, but the essential requirement

is a tight-fitting cover that prevents steam from escaping. In it several foods can be cooked at one time. Meat may be seared, placed on a rack, then the vegetables placed around it. A separate, smaller pan holding other foods may be inserted into the oven, a small amount of water added to the bottom and the cover put on top. Usually no additional water is needed.

Dutch Red Balls. Edam cheeses.

Dutch Rusks. Crisp rusks made in Holland from fermented dough.

Dutch Silver. Silverware made in the Netherlands; it contains less pure silver than sterling.

Dutch Treat. A meal or refreshment in which each person pays for the food he consumes.

Duva (Swedish). Pigeon.

Duxelles (French). Mushroom-flavored mixture used for flavoring many kinds of stuffings and sauces; it consists of finely minced mushrooms, onions, shallots, and parsley sautéed in butter or oil, with stock or wine added, then boiled until most of the liquid has evaporated. It can be made in quantity, then refrigerated or frozen. The preparation is named for the Marquis d'Uxelles, a French gourmet of the late 17th century.

Dwarf Cape Gooseberry. *See* Ground Cherry.

Dweller Clam. The giant rock clam.

Dryeryg. (1) (Norwegian). Marinated venison cooked in sour cream. (2) (Danish). Saddle of venison.

Dyrestek (Norwegian). Venison; reindeer or elk meat.

Dyspepsia. Indigestion.

Dzeren. An antelope, often used for food in Mongolia.

E

Earth Apple. A potato or a cucumber; the term is applied to both vegetables in different regions.

Earth Balls. Truffles.

Earth Chestnut. The pignut; sometimes the truffle.

Earthenware. Dishes, pots, casseroles, etc., made of baked clay which cooks and conducts heat well but is breakable.

Earth Nut. (1) *See* Peanut. (2) A tuberous-rooted plant, bearing a nutlike series of bulbs, which, after being boiled, taste like chestnuts.

Easter. An annual Christian church celebration commemorating Christ's resurrection which falls on the first Sunday after the first full moon following March 21. As the end of the Lenten fasting period, Easter, in many countries, is the occasion for rich feasts. The Russian and Greek Orthodox Easter dinners are usually particularly elaborate. Like other religious festivals, this one combines a mixture of pagan and Christian customs. The rabbit and egg symbols came from India and China, where they were features of fertility celebrations occurring about the same time of the year as the Christian Easter. *See* Easter Egg.

Easter Cakes. Large round flat cookies made with flour, eggs, currants, and orange peel.

Easter Eggs. Eggs, perhaps the most traditional food for Easter, have been associated with the spring season since pre-Christian times. They were a feature of the fertility lore of the Indo-European races, and ancient Persians exchanged eggs as gifts at the spring equinox, which for them was the beginning of the new year. Soon after their conversion to Christianity, northern Europeans adopted the egg as an Easter food, to symbolize the tomb from which Christ rose. As eggs were forbidden during Lent, they were particularly welcomed by the devout on Easter Sunday.

The custom of decorating Easter eggs dates back to the earliest Christian times, as does the custom of giving them as presents. Sometimes the eggs were simply colored in gay hues. Some Slavic people used gold and silver painted on in special patterns. The Poles and Ukrainians decorated eggs, either plain or colored, with elaborate designs. Each of these decorated eggs was a masterpiece of art and labor. Melted beeswax was applied to the fresh white eggs with a stylus; the eggs were then dipped in successive baths of dye. After each dipping, wax was painted over the area where the preceding color was to remain. Gradually a complex pattern of lines and colors emerged, the finished egg a jewel-like work of art.

Today in many homes hard-cooked eggs, dyed bright colors, mean tradition to the adults and excitement to the young. They are often arranged in a basket as the centerpiece for the Easter holiday table. They can be as good to eat as they are to look at if they are hard-cooked rather than boiled, for boiling toughens the whites. To hard-cook eggs, cover them with cold water, bring the water slowly to a boil, reduce heat and simmer 12 minutes. Cool eggs in cold water.

Just before Easter, shops offer simple dyes that may be used for decorating eggs. They are easy to apply so that youngsters can participate in the preparation of the eggs. Or gummed papers, such as hearts, signal darts, or even lawyer's seals, may be used.

Not only real eggs but also candy eggs have come to be a part of the holiday fare. These may be sugar-candy eggs, or they may have a cream filling and chocolate coating with appropriate decorations.

Eau de Fleur d'Orange (French). Orange-flower water.

Eau de Framboise. A French raspberry-flavored liqueur.

Eau de la Côte. Several different kinds of alcoholic liqueur made near Vienne, France.

Eau de Mélisse. A French liqueur prepared from the flowers of the balm mint.

Eau de Vie (French). "Water of life"; brandy or other distilled spirits.

    Eau de Vie de Marc. A brandy made from the husks, stems, etc., of the vines after they have been pressed for wine.

    Eau de Vie de Miel. Honey brandy, made by distilling mead, which, in turn, is made by fermenting honey.

Eau Impériale. *Eau de vie*, brandy.

E.B. Of liquor, estate bottled; estate bottling.

Ebarber (French). To remove the outer parts or skin of fish or meat.

Ebbi (Indonesian). Dried shrimp.

Ébouillanter (French). To place foods in boiling water; to scald.

Ebrious. Intoxicated.

Ébullition (French). Boiling point (of a liquid).

Ebulum. A very rich liqueur type of homemade wine with a base of strong ale, a large quantity of elderberries, juniper berries, hops, and numerous spices, left to mature in a cask; served over lumps of sugar.

Ecardine. Species of one-piece shellfish, whose shell has no hinge.

Écarlate, À l' (French). Beef or pork marinated in brine with saltpeter; bright red when cooked.

Eccles Cake (British, Scotch). A round puff pastry filled with brown sugar, currants, and spices.

Échalote (French). Shallot.

Échaudé. A classic, unusual French pastry, actually a kind of bun, mentioned in French texts as far back as 1202. A dough of flour, oil, salt, and water is kneaded and allowed to stand for 2 hours, then divided into small balls and poached in water. The balls are drained, dried, and baked in a hot oven.

Échauder (French). To steep or scald in boiling water.

Echézeaux. An outstanding dry red wine with a remarkable color and excellent bouquet, produced in the Burgundy region of France.

Échine de Porc. Pork skin or backbone.

Echinus. Sea urchin.

Echt (German). Of wine, genuine, authentic. *See* Germany, The Wines of.

Éclair. A small rich French pastry, a finger-shaped cream puff paste (*pâte à choux*), filled with vanilla, chocolate, or coffee cream, or ice cream, and topped with icing or glaze.

Éclanche (French). Shoulder of mutton.

Écossaise, À l' (French). In the Scotch style; usually a soup or stew made of mutton, barley, and vegetables.

Écrevisse (French). Crayfish.

Ecuador. The country has two distinctive food regions—the lowlands and the mountains, each producing its own specialties, for there is wide variation in the produce available and in the daily food requirements of the people. The steamy lowlands feature light foods and cooling drinks to counteract the tropical heat and humidity; the highlands, with their chilly (often cold) weather feature hearty foods and drinks.

The local version of *tamales* (corn mixtures wrapped in husks and steamed) is here called *choclotandas*. A favorite soup is *locro*, made of vegetables, which tastes best with Ecuador's giant corn kernels; *ajiaco* is a sort of soup-stew with varying ingredients. Spicy dishes are well liked, and *ajís*, spicy dishes, are made with a wide variety of ingredients. For example, there are *ají de pollo*, (chicken); *ají de carne* (with meat); *ají de huevos* (with eggs); etc. Other Ecuadorian dishes typical of the country are *chupe de camarones* (shrimp chowder); *camarones con almendras* (shrimp in almond sauce); *mondongo* (cow's feet soup); *fanesca* (a vegetable soup with ground peanuts and codfish); *pescado con coco* (fish cooked with coconut); *patitas de chancho con mani* (pig's feet with peanut sauce); *enrollado de chancho* (pork roll); *fritada* (fried pork); *torta de papa* (potato pudding); *seviche* (pickled fish); *champus* (a dessert made of white hominy); and *buñuelos* (sweet fritters).

Coffee is the national drink. Interesting soft drinks are *rosero* (made from corn and fruit juice) and *fresco de arroz* (made of rice and fruits). *Chicha*, the peasant's drink, has a poor taste but is quite alcoholic. Ecuadorian beer is first rate, however, although efforts at local wines have resulted in poor products.

Écumer (French). To skim.

Écumé. Skimmed.

Écumoire (French). A ladle or perforated spoon used for skimming liquids.

Écuyer (Obsolete, French). Title given to skilled cooks.

Edacious. Eating greedily; devouring food rapidly; voracious.

Edacity. Greediness in eating.

Edam. A famous Dutch cheese named for the village where it originated; made from cow's milk with rennet added, and molded into a ball usually weighing 1–5 pounds. The inside is yellow, the outside a brilliant red. The taste is mild and slightly salty; the body firm and crumbly. Edam is widely imitated in both Denmark and the United States. *See also* Cheese.

Edammer Kaas (Dutch). Edam cheese.

Eddike (Danish). Vinegar.

Eddo; Eddoc. Edible taro leaves used in tropical cooking.

Edel (German). Of wine, noble; generally used in connection with *Spätlese* or *Auslese*. *See* Germany, The Wines of.

Edelbeerenauslese (German). Wine term, more or less the equivalent of *Beeren Auslese*. *See* Germany, The Wines of.

Edelfäule (German). The mold that must be allowed to form on grapes before harvesting. *See* Germany, The Wines of.

Edelweiss. A distinctive, aromatic Italian liqueur.

Edinburgh Rock. A candy made of granulated sugar, water, cream of tartar, and various flavorings.

Edulcorate. To sweeten.

Eel. A voracious snakelike fish with a smooth, slimy skin, found in fresh or sea water. It breeds in the ocean, where millions of eggs are laid by each female, who dies after spawning once. The young instinctively return in armies to the streams or ponds which were the homes of their parents. Maturing after 8 years, they then return to the sea. Eels feed on almost all kinds of animal life from worms and small fish to warm-blooded animals. Those caught in running water tend to have a better flavor than those caught in mud. The color is blackish for the muddy-water specimens, olive-green for the clear-water variety. They should be kept alive until just before eating. The flesh is fat, sweet, and rich in vitamins A and B. It is used in pies and in fish stews, or may be fried, grilled, or jellied. Smoked eel is considered a delicacy in many (especially Scandinavian) countries. Spring, when the eels start their migration back to the ocean, is the eel fisherman's prime season.

Best-known varieties are the *Moray*, which was a favorite food with the ancient Romans, who bred them for food; the *Conger*, or *Sea Eel*, which attains a growth of 7–8 feet; and the *Lamprey*, which is a slightly different species but is similar in appearance and may be cooked in the same manner. Baby eels, the size of matchsticks, are particularly popular in Spain, where they are a favorite snack or appetizer when cooked in olive oil with garlic.

Eelfare. Young eels traveling in a group in a river; they are caught commercially at this time.

Eelpout; Burbot; Lotte. An unusual freshwater fish resembling an eel but larger; found in European and some American rivers. Its hard, coarse flesh is edible but not particularly tasty.

Eend (Dutch). Duck; fowl.

Eette (Obsolete). Eat.

Effervesce. To give off small gas bubbles, as do certain wines.

Effervescence. The formation of bubbles as gas is released in a liquid. *See* Carbonated Water.

Efflate. To puff up, as occurs with a soufflé.

Efó (Brazilian). Dish consisting chiefly of spinach and shrimp.

Egg. The rounded shell-covered product of various birds. The variety most commonly used is the chicken egg. Eggs are a versatile food, being an essential ingredient of most baked products and custards, as well as a food that can be served at any meal. Eggs are graded according to size and freshness. Grades AA and A indicate top quality, with a well-rounded yolk and a firm white; they are especially good for cooking in the shell, poaching, or frying. Grade B eggs have a flatter yolk and thinner white; they may be used in baking and cooking, as they are no different from Grade A in food value. The color of the shell does not affect the quality of the egg. In some areas white eggs are preferred to brown eggs and are therefore higher priced. Eggs come packed according to size, ranging from the jumbo, or extra large, to the very small. If yolks and whites are to be separated, it is easier to do this when the eggs are cold. Eggs should be cooked with low heat to prevent toughening.

Egg Albumen. White of an egg.

Egg-and-Bread-Crumb. To dip food, before frying, into fine dry bread crumbs, then into beaten egg, and again into crumbs to give a crisp crust and to prevent fat from being absorbed by the food. Fish, cutlets, veal, rissoles, and fish cakes are prepared in this way.

Egg Apple. Eggplant.

Egg Beater. An electric or manual rotary mixer or a wire whisk for beating eggs and batters. *See* Kitchen Equipment.

Egg Cheese. Cheese made with eggs added to the curds; a standard cheese-making procedure in Finland.

Egg Cooker. An electrical device for boiling eggs to any desired consistency.

Egg Cup. A small cup without handles designed to hold a boiled egg.

Eggerøre (Norwegian). Scrambled eggs.

Egg Flip. Eggnog.

Egg-Flour Panade. Pancake batter mixed with butter, cooked over hot water in a double boiler, then combined with other foods, often for stuffing.

Egg Fruit (Colloquial). Eggplant.

Egg Glass. A glass that holds a soft-cooked egg conveniently for eating.

Egg Holder. A wire device arranged to hold eggs in the shell; it may be lowered into boiling water to prepare hard-cooked eggs.

Egg Hot. A hot drink containing nutmeg, eggs, sugar, and beer.

Egging and Breading. *See* Egg-and-Bread-Crumb.

Egg Lemonade. A cold drink made of lemon juice, egg yolks, and sugar.

Eggnog. A nourishing beverage resembling a liquid custard, made of milk, beaten eggs, and sugar; often flavored with vanilla, nutmeg, brandy, rum, or whisky. Served hot or cold, it is commonly used as a festive drink, particularly at Christmas time.

Egg Noodles. *See* Macaroni.

Eggplant. An egg- or pear-shaped vegetable, originating in India and cultivated in western Europe since the 17th century; a particular favorite in Asia Minor, Turkey, Greece, Italy, and the Balkan countries. It varies in color from white or yellow to purple. The white variety is popular in Europe, but the purple variety is best liked in America. It ranges in size from several inches to a foot in length. A mature eggplant is heavy, firm, and uniform in color; when overripe, it is soft and shriveled. It may be used as a garnish or as a baked, grilled, fried, or boiled vegetable, and also as an ingredient in stews. The Chinese eggplant is more correctly called *solanum*.

Egg Plum. A light-yellow, oval-shaped plum, a fruit of medium quality.

Egg Poacher. A metal device that holds an egg in a round shape while it is being cooked.

Egg Pop. A kind of eggnog.

Egg Roll; Spring Roll (Chinese). A thin pancake spread with a variety of fillings, rolled up, and fried crisp; eaten with mustard and duk sauce.

Egg Sauce (British). Sauce made of chopped hard-cooked eggs, butter, and lemon juice; occasionally, Hollandaise sauce with chopped hard-cooked eggs.

Eggs, Chinese. *See* Chinese Eggs.

Eggs, Fish. The main ingredient of caviar. The famed black caviar, one of the costliest and greatest of delicacies, is obtained from the sturgeon; red caviar is usually obtained from some species of salmon, sometimes mullet. Herring and shad roe are also highly regarded by gourmets.

Eggshell. The white or light brown exterior of an egg; sometimes used in making coffee to settle the grounds. They may also be used in finishing wine to settle the solid materials.

Egg Slicer. A device used to slice evenly a hard-cooked egg. Usually the egg is fitted into a shallow depression and a grid of fine parallel equally-spaced wires is pressed through it to make uniform slices. One variety of slicer cuts eggs into quarters. The egg slicer can also be used for butter, cheese, and other fairly soft substances.

Eggs, Plover. Small eggs often considered a great delicacy; as a rule, they are hard cooked, then served cold. The taste is delicate, but not necessarily better than that of a hen's egg of comparable size.

Eglantine. Sweetbrier, an herb whose olivelike fruit may be used for a sort of preserve or jelly.

Egrappage (French). The process of removing stems before grapes are pressed to make wine.

Egri Bikaver. An intense, almost purple Hungarian red wine. *See* Hungary, The Wines of.

Egypt. Egyptian food patterns follow those of other Arabic countries. There is strong emphasis on lamb and mutton, on fermented-milk drinks on the order of yoghurt, on various sweet fruit drinks, and honey-laden pastries and candies. Because of the hot climate the main meals are eaten in the early morning or late evening; during the heat of the day, the people satisfy themselves with snacks, nibbling fruits, dates, and nuts, and drinking many refreshing beverages.

In the large cities and along the coast fish is a favorite food. It is usually fried. Only a few soups are served. As in other Mohammedan countries, no pork at all is eaten and comparatively little beef, because of the lack of grazing land; but plenty of lamb and mutton is consumed. As a rule, meat is cooked in stews, often with vegetables, such as eggplant and tomatoes, or with various cereals, like *bourghol*, cracked wheat, for example. Chicken dishes are quite good as a rule. Most people like lentils, beans, and rice, as they are filling and inexpensive. *Couscous*, also found in Algeria, is extremely well liked.

Alcoholic drinks are rarely served. Coffee is drunk all day long from tiny cups holding only a sip or two. Some fairly good wines are made in Egypt but mostly for export, since the vast majority of Egyptians do not drink it. *Clos Mariout,* a dry white wine, is about the best.

Egyptian Onion; Tree Onion. A variety of onion that grows at the top of the plant as well as at the underground root.

Egyptian Lotus. A plant which grows in swampy water in various parts of Asia; the leaves are eaten as a green vegetable, and the seeds, which taste like nuts, are roasted.

Egyptian Wheat. Wheat in which the gluten is not elastic, so that dough made from it breaks when stretched.

Égyptienne, À la. In the Egyptian style, usually featuring leeks, onions, and rice.

Ehrwein (German). Fine wine.

Eier (German). Eggs.

　Hart Gekochte Eier. Hard-boiled eggs.

　Eier in der Schale. Boiled eggs in their shells.

　Eier mit Speck. Bacon and eggs.

　Rühreier. Scrambled eggs.

　Spiegeleier. Fried eggs.

　Verlorene Eier. Poached eggs.

　Weich Gekochte Eier. Soft-boiled eggs.

Eiercrème (German). Custard.

Eieren (Dutch). Eggs.

Eierkückas (Alsatian). Rich pancakes stuffed with a fruit jelly.

Eierpflanzen (German). Eggplant.

Eierspeisen (German). Egg dishes.

Eierteigwaren (German). Pastas, macaroni, spaghetti.

Eigengewachs (German). Of wine, "the growth." *See* Germany, The Wines of.

Eigenes Wachstum (German). Of wine, bottled by the grower of the grapes. *See* Germany, The Wines of.

Eight Precious Pudding (Chinese). Classic rice dessert made with candied fruits, raisins, and nuts.

Einbren (Jewish). Browned flour used for thickening sauces or soups.

Eingemachtes (German). Preserved fruits; preserves.

Eisbein (German). Pork knuckles.

Eisell (Obsolete). Vinegar.

Eiskaffee (German). Iced coffee.

Ejotes (Spanish). String beans.

Elbing; Elbinger. A spicy, rather crumbly German cow's-milk cheese made during cold-weather months.

Elbo. A very mild, butterlike Danish cheese.

El Borjo. A group of Algerian wines 13–15 percent alcohol.

Elbow Macaroni. A narrow, hollow Italian pasta, cut in quarter or half turns.

Elder. Elderberry.

Elderberry. Small black fruit of the elder tree, a shrub found in most temperate regions. The berries are used for making jellies and wine. Oil from the clustered white blossoms is used in perfumes and lotions. *See* Berry.

Elephant Meat. The flesh of this large beast is not regarded as edible by Europeans, but the natives of certain parts of Africa find it satisfactory, although the meat is tough. Elephant's foot, often touted as a great delicacy, is only barely edible.

Elderflower. The fragrant white flower of the elder tree, used for flavoring jams, jellies and wines.

Eldfast Form (Swedish). Casserole.

Elecampe; Elecampane; Scabwort. A rather large herb native to Europe and parts of Asia, sometimes used as a vegetable or made into a candy.

Election Cake, Hartford. A sweet rich yeast cake made with candied fruits.

Electrical Equipment. This modern age offers for the kitchen any number of labor-saving devices powered by electricity. In addition to the conventional range, oven, refrigerator, and freezer, today's cook will find work made much easier by the use of an electric mixer or blender, can opener, clock, coffee grinder, and ice-cream freezer. A toaster, grill, waffle iron, broiler, fryer, casserole, coffee maker, or heating stand can be conveniently used for cooking at the table, and such devices also cut down considerably on kitchen heat during the summer.

Electric Blender. *See* Blender, Electric.

Eledone. An edible octopus; popular in many Mediterranean countries.

Eleme (Turkish). A dried fig.

Elephant's-Foot. A large South African yam.

Elephant Grass. A reed mace, often used as a flavoring ingredient.

Elft (Dutch). Shad.

Elies (Greek). Ripe olives.

Eliquate. To liquefy.

Elixation. The act of boiling; chewing.

Elixate. To steep or boil in water; to chew.

Elixir. (1) Basically, any health-giving drink. (2) A refined liqueur. (3) An alcoholic beverage combined with a sugar syrup.

Elixir di China. An Italian apéritif made from Peruvian bark.

Elk. An extensive variety of deer found in various parts of the world, somewhat resembling the moose. Elk meat is tasty, though somewhat dry. It should be marinated and larded to provide additional fat.

Elmassia (Turkish). A dish made with calf's feet.

Elops. A fish of the herring family.

Elote (Central American). Green corn boiled in its husks.

El Pa y Al (French). A piece of bread heavily rubbed with garlic and olive oil; a favorite in the Roussillon region of France.

Eltville. A wine village of the Rheingau, Germany. *See* Germany, The Wines of.

Elva (Turkish). A pudding made of semolina browned in butter and simmered with sugar, milk, and almonds until a thick paste is formed; it is poured into a mold and chilled before serving.

Elvers. Young eels, born in the depths of the western Atlantic. They are about 2 inches long, transparent pale amber, and very thin; best cooked in deep fat.

Embalm. To prepare foods with oil or spices.

Embden Groats (British). Crushed oats or barley.

Embonpoint. Plumpness, stoutness.

Embrase (Obsolete). To set foods afire.

Embrocher. To impale on a spit or skewer.

Embrown. To make brown.

Embuchado (Spanish). Pork sausage.

Embutidos (Spanish). Pork products.

Ementa (Portuguese). Menu.

Emication. (1) Effervescence, as in sparkling wines. (2) Something that sparkles or bubbles, like champagne.

Émier; Émietter (French). To chop or grind bread into particles.

Emiliano. A very hard cylindrical Italian cheese, similar to Parmesan, whose interior is light yellow and whose exterior is dark and oiled. The flavor varies from mild to rather sharp, and the texture is granular.

Émincé (French). (1) Leftover meat sliced thin and cooked with a special sauce. (2) Finely shredded or sliced. Sometimes the word is erroneously used to describe chopped or ground meats.

Émincer (French). To slice foods thinly.

Emmental; Emmenthal. A hard, rennet Swiss cheese made from cow's milk, an enlarged version of Gruyère but a little softer and with larger and irregular holes. It is made in sizes varying from 100 to 200 pounds. This type is popularly called "Swiss Cheese" in the United States.

Emmer Wheat. A wheat formerly grown in Germany and Switzerland; largely superseded by wheats with better baking qualities.

Émonder (French). To blanch or steep in boiling water to facilitate peeling or skinning.

Empada (Brazilian); **Empanada** (Argentinean, Chilean, Spanish). A small pie or pastry, usually filled with meat or fish.

Empanadillas (Spanish). Small pastries usually stuffed with meat.

Empereur (French). (1) Small rounds of bread with starfish markings spread with any desired mixture and served as an appetizer, often with soups. (2) Swordfish.

Empois (French). A combination of starch and water, such as flour and water.

Emporte-Pièce (French). A metal pastry-making instrument with a small cutting edge by which a piece of rolled pastry may be lifted.

Empotage (French). All of the various ingredients, usually meat and vegetables, contained in a stewpan.

Empoter (French). To assemble and place various stew ingredients in a stewpan.

Em Sangue (Portuguese). Rare.

Emulsifying Agents. Substances, such as gums, soaps, agar, lecithin, glycerol monostearate, alginates, and Irish moss, that aid the uniform dispersion of oil in water; that is, they form emulsions like margarine, ice cream, salad dressing, etc. Stabilizers maintain the emulsions in a stable form.

Emulsifying Salts. Sodium citrate, sodium phosphate, and sodium tartrate, used in the manufacture of milk powder, evaporated milk, sterilized cream, and processed cheese.

Emulsion. A combination of two liquids that will not completely dissolve into each other, such as oil and water, or milk and margarine or butter, beaten together until thoroughly blended to a cream.

Enamelware. Pots, pans, and dishes made of iron or steel sheet with a glasslike material baked on the surface; made in many colors and patterns. It is rust proof, but the exterior coat may chip or flake when exposed to intense heat.

En-Cas (French). Food ready to serve, such as cheese, cold meats, and fruits.

Enchilada (Mexican). A thin corn pancake (*tortilla*) filled with a chicken, meat, bean, or cheese mixture and sometimes covered with a spicy sauce. Popular in Mexico and the southwestern United States.

Encornet (French). A variety of octopus about 20 inches in length when full grown; prepared like squid.

Encratite. An early Christian sect opposed to eating meat and drinking wine.

En-Croûte (French). Wrapped or enclosed in pastry or dough before baking.

Encurtidos (Spanish). Pickles.

Endaubage (French). Ingredients added to a stew, including wine, brandy, herbs, spices, and vegetables.

En Dés (French). Diced.

Endive; Belgian Endive. The white shoots of specially planted chicory roots. These shoots form several thick, fleshy leaves, 4–6 inches long

and 1–2 inches wide, pressed into a long, compact, pointed head. They are good in salads, or boiled, braised, or sautéed. The relatively bitter curly-leaved vegetable known as "chicory" in the United States is called "endive" in England. *See* Chicory.

Endivie (German). Endive.

Endocarp. The third layer of bran around the wheat grain.

End of Steak. The tip or boneless portion of a sirloin steak.

Endorede. To brush pastry with egg yolk, or to dust a cake with sugar to give a bright appearance.

Eneldo (Spanish). Dill.

Enfariner (French). To cover foods with flour prior to frying or some form of cooking.

Engadine. A medium firm, rather mild-tasting Swiss cheese made from whole cow's milk.

Engelsk Bøf (Danish). Sautéed beefsteak.

England. Breakfast in England is generally a very substantial meal, possibly of porridge and heavy, thick cream, or perhaps eggs and crunchy bacon, or a kipper, not to mention toast and marmalade. A more recent development, however, is the trend toward a smaller breakfast followed by "elevenses," a snack in midmorning. Teatime, in the late afternoon, with thin sandwiches, crumpets, scones, buns, or cake, with tea, is perhaps the most interesting meal in England. Breakfast and tea reflect honor upon the culinary standards of England.

But what of lunch and dinner, those two meals which require skill in cooking? As everyone knows, British food is unimaginative, by and large. Many native specialties are unsurpassable, but these are based upon fine ingredients rather than upon good cooking. For example, the local oysters and Scotch smoked salmon are unbeatable, but these items are *naturally* good, before British cooks can cause any damage. In the language of French cooks, *à l'Anglaise*, English style, means plain boiled food, the ultimate insult. Unfortunately, English cooks are largely untrained, and the general level of cookery in the British Isles is poor indeed. There has been some improvement in recent years, but as a rule, although one may now eat better in England, it is only because there are more French and Italian restaurants; British food and cookery remain at a depressingly low level. A gastronomic trip through the countryside will dispel forever any thoughts that English food has improved.

There are, however, numerous British special-

ties worthy of investigation by the gastronomically curious. At random, there are fish preparations such as *kedgeree*, a mixed fish and rice dish, and even *stargazy pie*, also made of fish. Fish and chips are nothing more or less than fried sticks of fish and fried potatoes, a typical snack, but one rarely served in restaurants. The meat stews are tasty when well made, but not exceptional; classic examples are the *Lancashire hotpot* and the *Exeter stew*. Meat pies, usually made from leftover meat, are best avoided, but *Cornish pasties*, miniature pies with assorted fillings, are often worthwhile.

The British serve roast lamb and mutton frequently, and do it fairly well, but seem duty-bound to accompany it with anchovy or mint sauce. The local roast beef is good, but not necessarily better than that in the United States; the British like to slice roast beef very thin, and perhaps they have a valid point. With roast beef there is often *Yorkshire pudding*, a milk, flour, egg, and fat mixture baked in a pan, with a taste reminiscent of popovers. *Bubble and Squeak* is the inelegant name given to a mixture of leftover roast beef and cabbage.

Salads are comparatively poor as a rule. Vegetables are even worse, because British cooks overboil them; potatoes, cabbage, and Brussels sprouts are inevitably overcooked and soggy. The local cheeses, however, are uniformly excellent. *Wensleydale, Stilton*, and *Cheshire* are all delicious. Special mention can be made of *clotted cream*, the superthick, unpourable cream made so well in Devon; clotted cream and strawberries are an unforgettable experience.

The desserts are largely dull, although a few are interesting, such as *Marlborough*, and also *Tipsy puddings*, but local preparations such as bread pudding should be avoided wherever possible. *Fruit fools* are puréed fruits combined with milk and cream, and *trifles* are spongecake with fruit.

England, of course, produces no wines, but wines are very popular with city people, largely disregarded by everyone else. Beer is very good, although usually served at room temperature. The British serve up a great variety of different types—light, dark, ale, bitter, stout, old, pale brown, etc. Combinations are popular; a stout and bitter combination is familiarly called a "mother-in-law."

English Bamboo. The peeled, pickled young shoots of the elder tree.

English Breakfast Tea. A name used in the tea trade for Keemun tea, a black tea originally produced in China but now grown in Formosa.

English Cottage Bread. A crusty loaf of bread consisting of two uneven layers.

English Dairy Cheese. A very hard, dry cheese similar to cheddar; used mostly for cooking.

English Flour. A very soft flour produced in England, suitable for making light baked goods and biscuits.

English Frontignac. A homemade wine made with fresh elder flowers, lemons, sugar, yeast, and chopped raisins. When matured, it vaguely resembles the French white wine after which it is named.

English Monkey. A Welsh rabbit (rarebit), made with melted cheese, eggs, and bread crumbs.

English Muffin. Round flat doughy bread, an American breakfast favorite. Muffins should be torn apart by hand, never sliced.

English Routs. Biscuits made with almond paste, baked in a very hot oven, then glazed.

English Wheat. Though wheat grown in England is weak, the flour has a good flavor. Many of the red and white wheats tend to be runny and soft, and are best used for making biscuits and cakes.

Englut. To gulp foods.

Engorge. To eat more than necessary; to stuff oneself.

Enguia (Portuguese). Eel.

Enhungered (Obsolete). Hungry.

En Jalea (Spanish). Jellied.

Enriched Foods. Everyday foods to which vitamins and minerals have been added.

Ensalada (Spanish). Salad.

    Ensalada de Pepino. Cucumber salad.

    Ensalada Variada. Mixed-green salad.

Enseta. An African plant whose fermented roots and stem are made into a crude bread.

Ensopado (Portuguese). A thick meat-and-bread soup.

En Tasse (French). Served in a cup; usually, of clear soups.

Ente (German). Duck.

Entenbrüstchen (German). Breast of duckling.

Entire-Wheat Flour. Flour milled from whole-wheat grain.

Entonner (French). To open a cask of wine.

Entrecosto de Porco Fresco (Portuguese). Spare-rib.

Entrecôte (French). Sirloin steak cut from the middle part of the loin or sometimes from the rib of beef. It is prepared in a great many different ways: *Anglaise* is with bacon and boiled potatoes; *Béarnaise* is with Béarnaise sauce; *Espagnole* is with sautéed tomatoes and onion rings; *Forestière* is with sautéed mushrooms and potatoes; *Marchand de Vin* is with red wine sauce; *Mirabeau* is with anchovies and olives; *Soubise* is with onion sauce; etc.

Entrecuisse (French). The thigh of poultry, not including the bottom half of the leg, the "drumstick."

Entre-deux-Mers. A wine district of the Bordeaux region of France. *See* France, The Wines of.

Entrée (French); **Entree** (British). Originally, a fish or meat course served before the main course of a many-course dinner. Now, usually the main course; many restaurants lump all their main courses under the heading "entrées." In French practice the entrée is the third or fourth dinner course. The English "entree" refers to side dishes that are handed around to the guests who serve themselves from one large platter or bowl.

Entrelarder (French). To place strips of fat between cuts or slices of meat.

Entremeses Variados (Spanish). Assorted cold appetizers.

Entremets (French). Literally, "go-betweens," or between meals; side dishes of dainties to which guests may help themselves; now almost exclusively dessert sweets of one kind or another. Punch or ices *à la Romaine* may be served as an entremet. The term came into use several centuries ago, when, after a series of meat courses, one sweet dish would appear (between meals, so to speak); thereafter, more meat dishes would be served.

Entremets de Douceur. Sweet dishes; desserts.

Entre Rios Wheat. An Argentine River Plate wheat that produces flour with an average water-absorbing power and average strength.

Enzian. An Italian liqueur made with gentian.

Épaule d'Agneau (French). Shoulder of lamb.

Épaule de Mouton (French). Shoulder of mutton.

Épeautre (French). A kind of wheat, spelt. Sometimes called "German wheat."

Epicarp. The layer of bran beneath the outer coating of the wheat grain.

Épice (French). A spice or seasoning; aromatic plants and their seeds.

Épice Culinaire. A special blend of various herbs and condiments; the ingredients are variable.

Épices Composées (French). A classic spice mixture, often made from basil, sage, bay leaves, thyme, coriander, and mace; when pounded together, about one-fourth of its weight in black pepper is added.

Épices, Quatre (French). Four spices; a mixture of allspice, white pepper, mace, and nutmeg. Sometimes cinnamon, cloves and other spices are added.

Epicure. Connoisseur, gourmet; one who is fastidious about food and drink. See also Epicureanism.

Epicurean. Extremely fond of good food, luxury, and pleasure.

Epicureanism. The philosophy of Epicurus, who believed that happiness is the most important thing in life. Hence the theory that a good life is one filled with good food, wine, pleasure, etc.

Epigram; Épigramme (French). Two cuts of lamb, usually a chop and a slice of breast, braised until dry, then dipped in egg and bread crumbs, and grilled or fried. The name comes from an eighteenth-century marquise, who in a literary conversation mistook the word "epigram" for a new dish and instructed her chef to prepare it. The chef's ingenious creation is still known by the malapropism. "Epigram" is the English menu term for the more correct French word épigramme.

Epileny. A drinking song praising wine.

Épine. A French pear; there are winter and spring varieties.

Épine-Vinette (French). A plant bearing small edible fruit that is sometimes pickled and used as a substitute for capers.

Épinoche. A small mediocre French fish; best when fried.

Epiphany Cake. A round cake made from either pastry or yeast dough, on Epiphany, or Twelfth Night.

Epis de Maïs (French). Miniature corn on the cob, useful as a garnish or served in cocktails.

Eplekake (Norwegian). Applecake.

Eplesno (Norwegian). Apple snow pudding.

Éplucher (French). To peel.

Époisses, Fromage d'. A distinctive cow's milk cheese, 5–6 inches in diameter, prepared with brandy, salt, pepper, cloves, and fennel in the Burgundy region of France; on the market from November till June.

Éponger (French). To place foods on toweling or paper to drain away excess moisture or fat.

Epotation. The act of drinking.

Éprault (French, Colloquial). Celery.

Epulary. Pertaining to a banquet.

Epulation. The act of eating at a banquet.

Equivalents. See Measures.

Érable (French). Sugar cane.

Erbach. A wine village in the Rheingau district of Germany. See Germany, The Wines of.

Erbsensuppe (German). Pea soup.

Erbo. An Italian cheese roughly like Gorgonzola.

Erce. A soft, medium-sharp cheese produced in the wintertime in the Languedoc region of France.

Erdbeeren (German). Strawberries.

Erdbeerkuchen (German). Strawberry tart.

Erf (Obsolete). Cattle.

Ergoos (Turkish, Egyptian). A common drink made from licorice; sold in the streets.

Ergot. A dark-colored fungus that attacks rye and other cereals.

Eriwani. A cheese prepared from ewe's milk and salted in brine in the Caucasus.

Ermitage. The Hermitage wines, produced in the Rhône Valley region of France.

Ersatz (German). Substitute. During World War II ersatz foods were the rule in Germany. Sausages were made with cereals, coffee from chicory and grains, etc.

Erter (Norwegian). Green peas.

Ertesuppe (Norwegian). Pea soup.

Ervanço (Portuguese). Chick-pea.

Ervilhas (Portuguese). Peas.

Ervy. A soft, fatty, round cow's-milk cheese made in the Aube and Champagne regions of France; resembles Camembert.

Erwten (Dutch). Green peas.

Erwtensoep (Dutch). Split-pea soup.

Eryngo; Sea Eryngo; Sea Holly. A weed, with short rigid leaves and stems and a thistlelike blue flower. In England the fleshy cylindrical roots are boiled with sugar and candied. The leaves, when quite young, are sometimes pickled in vinegar and used to garnish salads. In the United States the eryngo is fetid and unedible.

Esau. Indicates a preparation containing lentils.

Escabeche; Escabescia (Spanish). A spicy dish usually made with fish or chicken cooked lightly and then pickled in a marinade; a favorite appetizer in Spain and South America. Escabeche differs from *seviche* in that the food is cooked before pickling; in *seviche* it is eaten raw.

Escalibada (Spanish). Eggplant.

Escalloped. Baked in a special sauce and usually sprinkled with bread crumbs.

Escalope (French). (1) A cut or slice of meat without bones, gristle, or skin. (2) A small, thin round veal steak.

   Escalope de Mouton. Mutton steak.

   Escalope de Porc. Pork cutlet.

Escargots (French). Edible snails.

   Escargots Bourguignonne. Snail shells filled with a mixture of butter, parsley, and garlic, then heated.

Escarole. A variety of endive with wide curly leaves which may be dark green or blanched during cultivation; usually eaten raw in salads, but may be prepared like other leafy vegetables. *See* Chicory.

Escauton (French). Cornmeal cereal cooked with plenty of goose fat; a specialty of Gascony.

Escoffier, Auguste. One of the world's greatest chefs, Escoffier was born in France in 1847 and died in 1935. He created many new dishes, and served European royalty and other dignitaries in famous London hotels. He wrote several books on cookery, notably the *Guide Culinaire,* and is considered a leading authority on cuisine.

Escubac. A sort of ratafia, a liqueur, made with saffron, licorice, cinnamon, and coriander.

Esencia de Menta (Spanish). Peppermint.

Eskimo. A corruption of an American Indian word meaning "eaters of flesh."

Esox. A large fish, such as a salmon.

Espada (Spanish). Swordfish.

Espadin (Spanish). The sprat, a small food fish.

Espagnole Sauce (French). A richly flavored brown sauce, used alone or as the base for other sauces.

Espalier (French). Fruit tree grown against a trellislike arrangement.

Espargos (Portuguese). Asparagus.

Espárragos (Spanish). Asparagus.

Esparregado (Portuguese). Purée; finely ground or mashed.

Especias para Encurtidos (Spanish). Pickling spice.

Espetadas. Pieces of veal, onions and green peppers skewered on a length of wood and broiled; a favorite in the Madeira Islands.

Espinacas (Spanish). Spinach.

Espinafre (Portuguese). Spinach.

Espresso Coffee. The espresso method of brewing coffee originated in Naples. It requires a special mechanism, the espresso coffee maker operated by steam pressure. Water is put into the mechanism and heated until converted into steam. The steam passes through the waiting coffee grounds; then, rich with the flavor and color of coffee, it is reconverted to liquid. Espresso machines are available in many shops in the United States. They range from the two-cup models to large commercial models.

   Many Italian and French restaurants in the United States offer as espresso a brew that is actually made in another Neapolitan coffee maker, the *macchinetta*. This is a drip coffee-pot with a bottom part having a spout, a top part into which the boiling water is poured, and a center basket holding the coffee grounds.

Espresso Joint (American, Colloquial). A small,

usually intimate place where espresso coffee is sold, although other refreshment may also be available.

Esqueixada (Spanish). A fish salad.

Esquinado; Esquinado Toulonais (French). Crabs boiled in water and vinegar, stuffed with a mussel and bread-crumb mixture, and browned in the oven; a specialty of Toulon.

Esquire Trenchant (Obsolete, French). A skilled meat carver at official banquets; also, the presiding officer, a sort of master of ceremonies.

Esrom. A mild, very fat Danish dessert whose taste is cheese similar to that of Port du Salut.

Essai; Essay. The ceremonial tasting of French royalty's food and wine, in order to see if it had been poisoned.

Essence. The taste or food value extracted from any food substance. The natural juice of any substance extracted by distillation so that the maximum flavor is concentrated in the smallest bulk. Meat, fish, poultry, vegetables, and herb essences are marketed as flavoring agents.

Essencia. A type of Tokay wine, rare and expensive. *See* Hungary, The Wines of.

Essig (German). Vinegar.

Essig Fleisch. Pot roast made with vinegar; a favorite in central Europe; also used in the Jewish cuisine.

Estaminet (French). (1) A part of a café reserved for smokers. (2) The front of small restaurants.

Estancia (South American). Cattle ranch.

Estate Bottled. Wine bottled by the owner of the vineyard or, occasionally, by the producer.

Ester. A chemical compound often used for flavoring foods and imparting a synthetic taste; prepared by replacing the acid hydrogen of an acid with the organic radical of an alcohol.

Esterhazy Gulyas (Hungarian). Beef goulash prepared with sour cream.

Est Est Est. A golden Italian wine of mediocre quality made in the Latium region south of Rome. Of two varieties, the sweeter is generally considered to be better. The unusual name, according to legend, is derived from the designations of a servant traveling ahead of his rich master to sample and mark out the best inns along the route. When an inn had good wine, the servant would chalk the Latin word *Est*,

"it is [good]," on the inn's sign. When he encountered this particular wine, then known by another name, he was so enthusiastic that he wrote *Est Est Est* in large letters. Sometimes the name is written as *Est! Est!! Est!!!* with the exclamation marks as shown.

Estocoficado (French). Preparation of codfish cooked with olives, onions, tomatoes, and herbs; the term is used around Nice.

Estofado (Spanish). A stew or casserole.

Estomac (French). Breast of chicken.

Estornino. The Spanish variety of mackerel.

Estouffade (French). Meat cooked very slowly with a little liquid in a covered pan; stew.

> **Estouffade de Boeuf.** Beef stew made with onions, mushrooms, and diced bacon.

Estouffade Chevaline (Belgian). Stewed horse-meat or beef, with vegetables and wine and beer; a favorite around Antwerp.

Estouffée (French). Cooking foods with fat in a tightly-covered cooking container using a minimum of liquid; the term is similar to *à l' étuvée*.

Estragole. A colorless liquid often used in the food industry to supply an anise or licorice flavor to candies, etc.

Estragon (French). Tarragon.

Estufa. (1) (Portuguese). A sort of hothouse or other heated storage room in which Madeira wines are matured. (2) An underground area where the Pueblo Indians of the southwestern United States keep a fire burning constantly for cooking.

Estufada (Portuguese). Stew.

Esturjao (Portuguese). Sturgeon.

Esurient. Hungry.

Esurine. A stimulater of appetite.

Étamine (French). Linen, cotton, or other fabric used for straining sauces and soups.

Ethone. Trade mark of a pale yellow (sometimes white) crystalline material used to supply the synthetic taste of berries or maple to various foods.

Ethyl Alcohol. Ordinary alcohol made by fermenting sugar, cereals, etc.

Ethyl Amyl Ketone. A colorless liquid used in the food industry to supply the synthetic taste of fruit flavors, especially peach, to jellies, candies, etc.

Ethyl Anthranilate. A liquid substance used to supply a synthetic grape flavor to jellies, candies, etc.

Ethyl Cinnamate. A colorless liquid often used to supply a synthetic strawberry taste and odor to various foods.

Ethylene. A colorless gas often used to ripen and color citrus fruits picked when immature and green.

Ethyl Vanillin. Fine, white crystalline material often used to supply a synthetic taste and odor of vanilla.

Etiolate. To blanch or whiten; for example, to make celery whiter.

Etna. A chafing dish used for heating liquids by means of burning alcohol.

Etna. *See* Italy, The Wines of.

Étoile. A group of undistinguished white wines (one of which is sparkling) produced in the Jura region of France.

Étouffé (French). Braised.

Étourneau. The starling, or small black bird, used for food in southwestern France.

Étrille (French). An inferior crab, sometimes called *wooly crab*, used for making soups and stews.

Etuve. A medium-firm, mild Dutch cheese; in half-sizes called *demi-etuve*.

Étuvé (French). Braised or stewed.

Étuvée, À l' (French). Cooked with a considerable amount of fat and without liquids in a covered casserole to retain the flavor of the ingredients.

Eucalyn. A saccharinlike substance produced by the action of yeast on melitose.

Eucharist. The Communion; the Lord's Supper, the bread.

Eugenies. Small cakes or cookies made of almond paste and flavored with curaçao.

Eulachon. *See* Smelt.

Eulogia. The consecrated bread not consumed at Communion.

Euodic. Of herbs, aromatic or pleasant-smelling.

Eupepsia. Good digestion.

Eupeptic. Having a good digestive system.

European Plan. In hotels a system of charging guests for the room (breakfast is sometimes included) only; the meals are charged for as taken. Under the American plan the daily-room rate includes meals.

Evaporated Milk. Milk whose water content has been reduced by half. It is sold unsweetened in cans and can be readily converted into whole milk by the addition of an equal amount of water. Because of its uniform quality it is useful in cooking and for feeding infants.

  Evaporated Milk, Fortified. Evaporated milk fortified by the addition of vitamin D, instead of being irradiated.

Evilhas (Portuguese). Green peas.

Evora. A Portuguese cheese.

Ewa Dodo (Nigerian). Spicy seafood dish made with black-eyed peas, bananas, and red peppers.

Ewe. A female sheep.

Ewer. A wide-mouthed jug holding water to be used by dinner guests for washing the hands before eating. The person who delivered the ewer was called a *ewerer*.

Ewn. An oven in medieval times.

Exalted. Having a strong flavor.

Exenterate. To remove viscera; usually as applied to poultry.

Exesion. Going out to dine.

Exeter Pudding. A pudding made with eggs, fine crumbs, sugar, finely minced suet, lemon, and rum. It is steamed or baked in a buttered mold lined with raisins and tiny almond biscuits, and served with red or black currant wine jelly.

Exossate (Obsolete). To grow fruits without seeds or pits.

Extensometer. An instrument that measures the stretching strength of a dough as an index of its protein quality for baking.

Extract. A concentrated preparation obtained by evaporating animal or vegetable juice, wine, or spirits; used mainly as flavoring agents in food and beverages. The most commonly used is vanilla extract.

Extraction Rate. The yield of flour obtained from wheat in the milling process: 100 percent extraction, or straight-run flour, is whole-meal flour that contains all of the grain; lower extraction rates are the whiter flours from which some of the bran and the germ are excluded, down to a 72 percent extraction, which is the normal white flour of commerce.

Extract of Malt. *See* Malted Barley.

Extract of Meat. *See* Meat Extract.

Extra Dry. *See* Extra Sec.

Extra-Fin. (French). The best quality.

Extrait (French). An extract or concentration, usually of a flavor.

Extra Sec. Very dry; of champagne with 1–2 percent sugar; also sold as *Extra Dry Champagne*.

Eyebrows of Longevity. A Chinese green tea.

F

Faarestek (Norwegian). Leg of mutton.

Fabaceous. Similar to a bean; belonging to the bean plant family.

Fabada Asturiana (Spanish). Pork and beans.

Fabiform. Bean-shaped.

Faca (Portuguese). Knife.

Façon; Façon du Chef. Chef's style of preparation.

Fadge (Irish). (1) Potato bread. (2) A pancake usually made with whole-wheat flour.

Fadøl (Danish). Draught beer.

Faggot; Fagot of Herbs. *Bouquet garni*, a small bundle of herbs, usually parsley, thyme, marjoram, and bay leaf, tied together with cotton for convenient removal after they have served their purpose.

Faggots. A mixture of pork liver, onions, bread crumbs, herbs, and pork fat slowly baked.

Fagiano (Italian). Pheasant.

Fagioli (Italian). Beans.
> Fagioli Assoluti. Kidney beans fried in olive oil with garlic.
> Fagioli di Lima Freschi. Fresh lima beans.

Fagiolini (Italian). Green beans.

Fagottino (Italian). A pastry famous in Venice.

Fahrenheit. A system for measuring temperature in which 32° represents the freezing point and 212° the boiling point. The thermometer was devised by G. D. Fahrenheit, a physicist.

Faience (French). Earthenware or porcelain crockery.

Faire Chabrot (French). In Bordeaux, to add red wine to soup in one's plate, allowing it to warm, then drinking it.

Faire Revenir (French). To brown meat or vegetables lightly without really cooking them.

Faire Ripaille (French). To partake of a marvelous meal or banquet.

Faire Suer (French). To cook meat in a covered pan in its own juices without adding any other liquid.

Faire une Fontaine (French). In making dough, to make a hollow or well in flour into which other ingredients are put.

Fairing (British). Brandy wafers or spiced gingerbread.

Fairy Cake (British). A small rich cake baked in a curved pan.

Fairy Ring. A small white mushroom with a reddish interior that grows in rings; called *mousseron* in France.

Fairy Spuds. A wild plant with a very small edible tuber whose taste resembles that of potato and chestnut.

Faisandage (French). Meat, game, or poultry allowed to age until it becomes "high" or slightly spoiled, *haut-goût*. Because pheasants, in particular, must be aged before using, the term has been derived from *faisan*, the French word for pheasant.

Faisandé (French). Having the flavor of aged game meats or birds; the *haut-goût*.

Faiselle; Faisselle (French). An earthenware pot or reed basket in which soft cheese can be drained.

Fa'i Tao (Samoan). Baked green bananas.

Fait Tout (French). An enamel-lined cooking utensil, suitable for a wide variety of dishes; an all-purpose pot.

Falafel (Israeli). Mashed chick-peas shaped into croquettes and fried in deep fat; a favorite Israeli snack.

Falculella. A Corsican cheesecake made with goat's-milk cheese, eggs, sugar, and milk, and baked on chestnut leaves.

Falernian Wine. An ancient Italian wine, of which little is known today, except that it was highly regarded, especially by the poet Horace.

Falerno. *See* Italy, The Wines of.

Falernum. A Caribbean flavoring syrup containing about 6 percent alcohol, lime juice, almonds, ginger, and simple syrup.

Fallow Deer. A small species of European deer with a golden yellow coat that turns somewhat white, in spots, during the warm weather. The meat is good, but, being somewhat dry, should be marinated before using.

False Banana. *See* Papaw.

Famelic (Obsolete). Appetizing.

Famine. Great lack of food for some length of time in an area; starvation. The word is derived from the Latin *fames*, meaning hunger.

Famish; Famished. To be very hungry; eager for food.

Fan (Chinese). Rice.

Fanchette (French). A pastry filled with a custard or cream mixture and decorated as desired. A small version of the Fanchette is a *fanchonette*.

Fancies. Any small decorated cakes.

Fancy Cakes. Small cream-filled or layered cakes, decorated after baking.

Fanega. A Spanish dry measure equal to 1–1½ bushels; used to measure foodstuffs.

Fanning. A mediocre tea leaf, considerably smaller than broken orange pekoe, that makes tea quickly.

Fantail. An excellent-tasting domestic pigeon that has a fan-shaped tail.

Fantaisie (French). (1) Of food, something imaginative or extraordinary. (2) A food used for other than its ordinary purposes, as, a cereal used as the basis for a dessert.

Fante Kotokyim (Ghanian). A crabmeat or lobster sauce served over rice.

Fante Mbire Flowee (Ghanian). A beef stew made with mushrooms, onions, and tomatoes.

Fantom. A coarse wheat.

Faquir. A coarse wheat.

Far (French Provincial). (1) A stuffing or a dish of boiled meats or poultry. (2) Sometimes, a custard-filled tart.

Far Breton (French). A creamy type of custard tart made in Breton.

Far Poitevin (French). A kind of stuffing made in Poitou from various vegetables and pork, then wrapped in cabbage leaves and cooked. *See also* Farci de Poitou, a quite similar preparation.

Farce (French). A stuffing or forcemeat. The term is derived from the Latin word *farcire*, meaning to stuff or fill.

Farce de Poisson (French). A fish stuffing.

Farci (French). Stuffed, filled.

Farci de Poitou (French). Chopped pork breast, sorrel, lettuce, eggs, and garlic wrapped in lettuce leaves and boiled for several hours; a specialty of Poitou.

Farcidure (French). A buckwheat-flour mixture wrapped in cabbage leaves to form a small ball which is added to cabbage soup; a dish of the Limousin region.

Farcing. The act of stuffing.

Farcir (French). To stuff.

Farcium (Obsolete). Sausage.

Farçon (French). A dish consisting of sweetened potatoes; made in Savoy.

Farçon de l'Aveyron (French). A heavily spiced sausage, prepared in the Rouergue.

Fare. (1) A fish catch; a supply of food. (2) Food served in a hotel or restaurant.

Farfalle (Italian). Egg-noodle bows. A smaller version of Farfalle is called *Farfallette*.

Farfel (Jewish). An egg barley served as a garnish, or as made into dumplings in soups, or used as a substitute for potatoes.

Far i Kal (Norwegian). Lamb stew with cabbage.

Får i Kål (Swedish). A boiled dinner containing lamb and cabbage.

Farina. (1) A creamy white granular cereal made from substantially pure wheat endosperm of the best grade hard wheat; available plain or enriched with thiamine, riboflavin, niacin, and iron. In the preparation the bran, outer coating, and germ of the wheat are removed, leaving only the white inner portion, or endosperm. Farina is available either in the quick-cooking or regular form. (2) A meal or flour made from grains, nuts, beans, and potatoes.

Farináceo (Portuguese). Spaghetti products.

Farinaceous. (1) Pertaining to flour, meal, etc. (2) Of starch, such as pasta and noodles.

Farina Dolce (Italian). Sweet flour made from dried and ground chestnuts; used for cakes and desserts.

Farine (French). Flour.

Fariné. Dredged with flour.

Fariner (French). To cover or dredge with flour.

Farinha (Brazilian). Manioc (cassava) flour. It is sprinkled on foods, especially in rural areas. *See also* Farofa.

Farinha de Avêa (Portuguese). Oatmeal.

Farinose. Mealy; like farina.

Fario. An immature salmon.

Farkleberry. A plant or small tree that produces miniature black berries.

Fårkött (Swedish). Mutton.

Fårkött Kokt Salt (Swedish). Boiled salted lamb.

Farl (Scotch). Three-cornered oatmeal cake, thinner and smaller than a bannock; a favorite at teatime in parts of England.

Farmer Cheese; Farm Cheese. A mild cottage cheese made of whole or skim milk curdled by souring and drained of the whey. Sometimes the curd is enclosed in cloth on which a board and weight are placed to hasten drainage. The curd is kneaded to further expel whey. Then salt and sometimes cream are mixed with the curd and it is molded into various shapes and sizes. It is very low in calories. Mixed with chives, chopped onions, olives, etc., and blended with milk or cream, it may be served as a spread.

The term *Farm Cheese* is sometimes applied to the French product known variously as *fromage à pie, mou, maigre,* and *ferme,* which, being made by individual farmers, varies somewhat from region to region.

Farmhouse Bread (Obsolete). A homemade loaf; now imitated in commercial bakeries using a soft or low-grade flour.

Farm Vale. A small cream cheese marketed in Somerset, England.

Faro. A somewhat sour type of beer made in Belgium.

Farofa (Brazilian). Toasted, lightly browned manioc flour; standard table accessory sprinkled on most dishes to thicken.

Farofa Amarelo (Brazilian). A yellow starchy manioc flour with a dull, floury taste; used in Brazil much as grated cheese is used in Italy.

Farrow. A young pig.

Färserade Tomater (Swedish). Stuffed tomatoes.

Fårstuvning (Swedish). Lamb stew.

Farsumagru Palermitano (Italian). A stew or braised meat served with chopped hard-cooked eggs; a specialty of Palermo.

Farthing Bun (British). Rich fruit bun or cake made from an egg dough.

Fasan (Danish, German). Pheasant.

Faschierter Braten (German). Meat loaf.

Fascine (French). A bundle of foodstuff, such as a bunch of asparagus.

Faséole (French). A type of bean with a very good flavor.

Fasoolia (Middle Eastern). A preparation of cubed lamb, lima beans, onions, and sometimes tomatoes.

Fass (German). A wine cask used in the Rhine Valley. *Fuder* is the equivalent term in the Moselle Valley. *See* Germany, The Wines of.

Fast. (1) To go without food. (2) A period in which no food is eaten.

Fast Day. A day of doing without food, often for a religious purpose. Many religions throughout the world observe a fast day to commemorate an important occasion, to improve one's resolve, or as a penance.

Fasting. Abstaining from food; eating very little.

Fast Yeast. Yeast that rapidly produces carbon dioxide from sugar.

Fats. The fats used for culinary purposes are obtained from animal or vegetable sources. Animal fats derive mainly from milk and meats, yielding such products as butter and lard. Vegetable fats include olive oil and oils from seeds and nuts.

As the terms are commonly used, "fats" refer to substances that are solid at room temperature, and "oils" to those that are liquid at room temperature. *See* Butter; Lard; Margarine; Oils; Hydrogenated Vegetable Shortenings.

Fat is the most concentrated form of body fuel, one tablespoonful yielding approximately 100 calories. It gives "staying" power to the diet in that it leaves the stomach more slowly than protein and carbohydrates, and retards digestion when consumed in combination with either of those nutrients. Hence when fat is included in a meal, one does not feel hungry as soon afterward as when proteins or carbohydrates are eaten without fat. Too much fat, on the other hand, slows up digestion and can cause digestive upsets. As sources of energy and calories the different food fats are practically interchangeable. *See also* Cholesterol.

Fat Hen. *See* Field Salad.

Father-la-Sher. Two types of sea fish bear this name, both of only fair quality, found in European waters.

Fatias Douradas (Portuguese). French toast in sugar syrup.

Fatling. Young barnyard animal fattened with extra food prior to being slaughtered for food.

Fatty. Greasy; containing fat.

Fat Rascals (British). A rich type of scone.

Fattigman (Norwegian). Fried cakes; crullers.

Fatty Cake. A cake made of flour, water, and lard.

Faubonne (French). A bean soup made in several provinces, sometimes with puréed white-shelled beans (*haricots*), sometimes with green peas, sometimes with game and truffles, and occasionally with assorted julienne vegetables.

Faucet. A spigot or tap used to draw liquor from a keg.

Faufal (North African, Arabic). Tiny pellets of semolina used as the basis for making *couscous*, the classic Algerian dish.

Faufel. A palm tree that yields a nut eaten with betel leaves in Southeast Asìa.

Fausen (British). Eel.

Fausse Tortue (French). Mock turtle.

Faux Filet (French). (1) A less expensive cut of beef prepared so as to resemble the more expensive fillet. (2) Loin of beef; also somewhat improperly called *contrefilet*. (3) Tenderloin of beef.

Favas (Portuguese). Beans.

Fava (Italian). A broad bean.

Fave dei Morti (Italian). Pastry; called "beans of the dead" because it is made specially on All Souls' Day.

Faverolles (French). Various types of beans.

Favre, Joseph. A noted Swiss chef, author of several cookery books, including *Académie de Cuisine*.

Fawn. A deer under a year of age, whose meat is rarely eaten. It tastes somewhat like venison but is less gamy.

Faye sur Layon. One of the better white wines of the Coteaux du Layon in the Anjou region of France. *See also* France, The Wines of.

Fayot (French). Dried kidney bean.

Fazenda. In South America, a large farm and the land that goes with it.

F. C. Fine champagne, a Cognac term.

Feaberry. Gooseberry.

Fearnought. A drink to lift one's spirits.

Feast. (1) An elaborate meal or banquet of many courses, usually to celebrate an important occasion. (2) A particularly delicious meal.

Feastful. Festive or gay; in the mood for good food.

Feather Fowlie (Scotch). Chicken soup enriched with cream and egg yolks.

Féchuns (French). Stuffed cabbage; a provincial dish of the Jura.

Fecula (British); **Fécule** (French). Starch extracted in powder form from potatoes, manioc, yams, and other legumes, as distinct from the meals obtained from cereal grains; used as a thickening agent.

Fécule de Marante (French). Arrowroot; flour produced from the root of an American tropical plant. The South American natives extracted a poison for their arrows from the bark of the root; hence the English name.

Fécule de Pommes de Terre (French). Potato flour.

Fécule de Riz (French). Rice flour.

Fedelini (Italian). Pasta shaped into narrow ribbons; used in soup and also prepared in the same way as macaroni.

Federweisser (German). "White feather" young unbottled wine of the Rheinpfalz district. *See* Germany, The Wines of.

Feed. (1) To provide with food. (2) (Colloquial) A meal.

Feeding. The act of eating; generally, eating almost anything merely to satisfy hunger.

Feeii (South Pacific). A banana suitable only for cooking or roasting.

Fegatini (Italian). Chicken livers.

Fegato (Italian). Liver.

> **Fegato alla Veneziana.** Calf's liver with onions.
>
> **Fegato di Pollo.** Chicken-liver spread.
>
> **Fegato di Vitello.** Calf's liver.

Feigen (German). Figs.

Feijão (Portuguese). Bean.

  Feijão Branco. Navy bean.

  Feijão Carrapato. Green bean.

  Feijão Encarnado. Dried red bean.

  Feijão Verde. String bean.

Feijão Vermelho com Molho (Portuguese). Kidney-bean stew.

Feijoada (Portuguese). Beans, meat, and rice.

Feine; Feinste (German). Of wine; "fine" and "excellent." The terms represent only the grower's opinion of his wine. *See also* Germany, The Wines of.

Feints. The "heads and tails," or first and last, as well as the least desirable parts of spirits from a pot still.

Fejões (Portuguese). Kidney beans.

Fel. A red wine produced in the Rouergue region of France.

Felchen (German). Freshwater salmon.

Fell. The parchment-like membrane that covers the exterior fat on lamb. Usually it is removed from the various cuts, except the leg, before it reaches the retail market. Fell helps keep the wholesale lamb cuts fresh and protects the meat if it is being aged. The presence or absence of fell while cooking does not affect the taste of the meat. But if the lamb is to be marinated or otherwise flavored, the flavorings will penetrate the meat more readily if the fell is removed before the marinade or seasoning is added.

Femme, Fromage de. Small rounded cow's-milk or goat's-milk cheese made in northern France.

Femöring (Swedish). Beef fillet.

Fenalår (Norwegian). Smoked leg of mutton.

Fendant. (1) A strong, heady wine made in the Vaud Canton of Switzerland from the Fendant grape. It is a still wine, but often has a bubbly *sémi-petillant* or *spritzing* quality which is quite pleasing. (2) A dry white wine with a fine bouquet produced in certain regions of France.

Fendre (French). To split, as splitting a duck for broiling.

Fennel. A vegetable that resembles celery except that the stalk is bulbular. It is crisp and juicy and has a mild licorice flavor. Chopped small, fresh fennel can be added to a salad; cut into pieces, it makes a marvelous addition to a relish tray. It may be eaten raw or braised like celery.

  Fennel seeds are aromatic and are used to flavor foods as diverse as sweet pickles, cookies, pastries, apple pie, and boiled fish. They are used extensively in Scandinavian as well as Italian baking.

Fennel, Florence. *See* Sweet Fennel.

Fennel Flower. Roman Coriander, a pleasant-tasting, slightly aromatic herb of the buttercup family.

Fennel, Italian. *See* Italian Fennel.

Fennel Pear. A European variety of pear which has a slight taste of fennel.

Fennel, Sicilian. *See* Italian Fennel.

Fennel, Sweet. *See* Sweet Fennel.

Fennel Water; Fenouillette. An after-dinner liqueur or cordial made from fennel.

Fenouillet; Fenouillette (French). A small russet apple or pear with a fennel flavor. (2) A sweet afterdinner liqueur made with fennel. (3) Fennel-flavored water.

Fenugreek. An Asiatic herb whose slightly bitter, aromatic seeds were used by the early Egyptians as doctors today use quinine. Today the seeds are used mainly in the making of curry. Commercially they are also used to flavor candies. Used in very small quantities, they give, surprisingly, a maple-like taste.

Féouse (French). The quiche Lorraine, the famous custard and bacon tart of Lorraine.

Féra. A type of salmon found in certain lakes of Switzerland, Austria, France and surrounding regions. It is found in white, black, and blue stages of development, according to the water, climate, and other conditions. The taste and texture are superb.

Ferchuse (French). A pork stew made in Burgundy.

Ferie (Obsolete, British). A feast day.

Ferme (French). Farm cheese, similar to cottage cheese.

Ferment. Yeast or leavening.

Fermentate. To cause leavening or raising, particularly of a yeast mixture.

Fermentation. The process by which leaven acts on dough mixtures, or upon sugars.

Fermented Goods. Bakery items, such as bread, cakes, buns, and rolls, made with yeast.

Fermented Milks. In several countries, cow's, goat's, and buffalo's milk fermented with a mixture of bacteria and yeasts to convert the lactose to lactic acid, and, in some drinks, to alcohol. Fermented milks include *busa* (Turkestan), *cieddu* (Italy), *dadhi* (India), *kefir* (Balkans), *kumiss* (Caucasus), *leben* (Egypt), *mazun* (Armenia), *kuban*, and *yoghurt*.

Fermière, À la (French). "In the farmer's wife's style," a special method of preparing a dish with carrots, turnips, celery, and onions. A roast is cooked very slowly in butter with the vegetables until tender. Sometimes, various other dishes containing fresh vegetables, or a garnish of carrots, cauliflower, small fried potatoes, and lettuce.

Fernet-Branca. A popular dark brown Italian bitters with a quinine-like taste; used as a flavoring ingredient for cocktails and also, especially by Italians, as a tonic or aid to digestion. The first taste is quite shocking, for the bitters consists of a score of bitter substances in a wine mixture.

Ferns. Ferns are not only ornamental but a few of the wild varieties are also edible in the spring. In the northeastern United States the ostrich fern and the pasture brake may be picked when still in the fiddlehead stages, that is, when the new fronds are still tightly furled. Once they have unfolded so that the green leaflets are open, they are no longer good eating. Thus it is only for a week, or a little longer if the spring is cool, that ferns are edible. Those who cannot identify these edible ferns had best not consider eating them. In recent years canned fiddleheads have appeared in some delicacy shops, indicating that there is an interest in these ferns, which taste like a cross between asparagus and mushrooms.

Ferox. Lake trout.

Ferretti (Italian). A narrow, slightly twisted pasta.

Fersken (Danish). Peach.

Fersk Kjød (Danish). Fresh meat.

Ferskt Kjøtt og Suppe (Norwegian). Vegetable-beef soup.

Ferula. A very large fennel.

Fervence (Obsolete). Glowing heat.

Fervent. Burning hot; boiling.

Festa. An Italian holy day or feast.

Festal. Pertaining to a feast.

Festino (Italian). Feast.

Festival. Relating to a feast; a feast or holiday.

Festival Breads. Loaves of bread made in fancy shapes for special occasions.

Festive. Relating to a feast.

Fet (Obsolete, Swedish). Fat.

Feta. A white goat's- or ewe's-milk cheese made by shepherds in the mountains near Athens, Greece. It is slightly astringent and salty, and is especially good in salads. It is also one of the ingredients in *boerek*, a flaky hors d'oeuvre pastry popular in Greece, Turkey, and the surrounding areas.

Fête. A gala festival or feast in France or Belgium.

Fête-Champêtre (French). An outdoor feast, especially in rural areas.

Féternes. A white wine produced in the Savoy region of France.

Fette (Italian). Slices.

Fette, Le (Italian). A red-cabbage soup with garlic bread, often served in Tuscany.

Fettucine al Burro (Italian). Egg noodles with melted butter.

Fettucine alla Romana (Italian). Egg noodles served with melted butter and grated cheese.

Fettucine Verdi (Italian). Pasta, colored green with spinach.

Feuillage (French). Leaves, usually of pastry.

Feuillantine (French). Tiny puff pastries to accompany tea or ice cream. The flaky butter pastry dough must be rolled out and folded into three layers six different times, then cut into strips and baked with a coating of sugar and egg white, in a moderate oven.

Feuilles de Betterave (French). Beet leaves.

Feuilles de Dreux. A very fatty French cow's-milk cheese.

Feuillet (Obsolete). A wine measurement, equal to one-half of a hogshead.

Feuilletage (French). Puff paste or butter dough.

Feuilleté; Pâte Feuilletée. A baked flaky pastry; it may be round, square, or any other desired shape, and may be plain or filled. The classic feuilleté dessert is the *napoleon*, an oblong pastry.

Feuilleton (French). Slices of pork or veal separated by chopped-meat mixtures, pâté, etc.

Feuillette; Fillette (French, Colloquial). A half-bottle of wine.

Feverfew; Feberfew; Feferfew. A perennial herb of the chrysanthemum family, which comes in white, yellow, and gold. It was once thought to have remarkable powers, especially in reducing fevers, which explains its name. The herb's pleasant flavor made it a favorite flavoring for soups and stews; dried, its leaves and flowers make a soothing tea.

Fèves (French). Beans.

   Fèves de Marais. Broad beans.

Fevettes (French). Very young beans.

Fiambre (Portuguese). Ham.

Fiambres (Spanish). Cold-meat buffet.

Fiasco; Faisque. The typical straw-covered wine bottle in which the more common and less prized Chiantis of Tuscany are marketed. It often has a straw handle, and it requires a straw base, for the bottle is rounded and cannot otherwise stand upright. *See also* Italy, The Wines of.

Fiatole. A gray Mediterranean flat fish; fairly good-tasting.

Ficeler (French). To tie with a string.

Fichi (Italian). Figs.

Fico (Obsolete). Fig.

Fiddlehead Ferns. *See* Ferns.

Fiddler Crab. A small edible crab found chiefly between Tampa and Key West, Florida.

Fidelini (Italian). A type of pasta.

Fideos Gordos (Spanish). Large noodles.

Fiélas. The Mediterranean conger eel, much used in Provence, France for making fish soups and stews.

Field Corn. Corn exposed to air to dry.

Field Basil. Basil, an herb.

Fieldfare. A migratory game bird of the thrush family; known in France as the *grive*.

Field Mushroom. Originally, a wild mushroom which varied considerably in size and color from one region to another. It is now cultivated on a large commercial scale in western European countries and the United States. It has fairly solid texture, but the flavor is inferior to that of other types.

Field Poppy. The white poppy, from which a rather light oil may be obtained by expressing its seeds.

Field Salad. A salad green whose bitter spoon-shaped leaves are also called *corn salad*, *fat hen*, *lamb's lettuce*, and *lamb's quarter*. It is best served with other kinds of lettuce. It grows easily and matures early in the season.

Fiesta. Any holiday or feast. Originally a religious holiday in Spanish-speaking countries. The word derives from the Spanish word meaning "feast."

Fig. A fruit grown in hot climates in many parts of the world. Mentioned frequently in the Bible, figs came from Araby to Syria and thence by caravan to Israel. They were transported by the ancient Semites into their Mediterranean colonies from Phoenicia. The early Greeks eventually introduced figs into their neighboring countries, and the Romans carried the fruit into all the temperate zones of Europe. The French are said to have brought figs to New Orleans.

Because they are available the year around, dried figs are probably more familiar to most Americans than are the fresh. The early missions of California, from San Diego to Monterey, valued the dried figs as a winter fruit. Figs had been brought from Spain as early as 1750. Some of the mission fig trees, over a hundred years old, with trunk girths of more than 18 feet, still stand as testimony to the long life of the tree. The black fig of the mission gardens later was to become an important drying variety. Black Mission figs are famous for their distinctive flavor, both in the fresh and dried state.

Other varieties of figs well adapted to drying include the Adriatic, an Italian variety of white fig; the Kadota, also an Italian importation; and the Calimyrna, originating in Smyrna. The Calimyrna is a large, luscious white fig excellent for eating fresh as well as dried. The dried variety has a deliciously nutlike, sweet flavor.

Fresh figs should be fully ripe when they are eaten. They should be soft and may vary in color from a greenish yellow to a purple or black, depending on the variety.

Figs, which also are canned, are rich in iron and also contain vitamins A, B, C, and G.

Figado (Portuguese). Liver.

Figaro (French). A cold sauce made of mayonnaise flavored with tomato; usually served with fish.

Figatello (Corsican). Sausage made of pork and pork livers, highly spiced and dried; served with heavy bread.

Figo. Fig.

Figos (Portuguese). Figs.

Figue de Barbarie. The red fruit of certain species of cactus found in North Africa and on several islands of the Mediterranean, including Sicily; best when cooked, made into a jam, or prepared as a liqueur.

Figue de Marseille. A small excellent-tasting green fig grown near Marseille and in Provence, France.

Fiji Islands. The fruits and vegetables of the Fiji Islands are not only enormous in size but of excellent flavor. Bananas grow in profusion and in endless variety. In addition, there are such comparatively unusual items as the *soursop, breadfruit, granadilla, mandarin, taro,* and the Fiji equivalent of asparagus, *duruka.*

The local fish are often superb; the *nuqa* is truly excellent. The local shellfish, notably the prawns, are delicious. They are often prepared with coconut milk or with *lolo,* coconut cream. Another favorite cooking ingredient is *dalo,* the Fijian name for taro. *Paulusami,* a great favorite, is made from *dalo* leaves. *Yams* are another favorite, often being roasted or boiled, made into soups or combined with other foods. Also found in the Fijian diet are *cassava* (tapioca root) and *kumala* (sweet potato). The only meat of importance is pork.

Desserts are usually based on fruits, particularly bananas (especially the variety called *vundi ndina*) and coconuts. The national drink is *yaqona,* or *kava,* made from the grated or pounded *yaqona* root, mixed with water (occasionally saliva), and developing a fermented (although nonalcoholic) quality. It is reputed to have curative properties, but this seems doubtful.

Filbert. Cultivated variety of the hazelnut. Until the early 1940s almost the entire filbert crop came to the United States from the Mediterranean countries. But then vastly improved counterparts of wild hazelnuts found in the United States began to be cultivated, mostly in the northwestern states of Oregon and Washington. Filberts had been grown on a commercial basis since the 1900s, but not until about forty years later did the industry expand to major proportions.

In the United States filberts have grown much larger and have an improved flavor over the wild hazelnut. Like the hazelnut, the filbert has a smooth, medium brown shell with a light beige end. The kernel is covered with a clinging brown skin.

Like many other nuts, filberts may be used with or without removing the skins. The tender covering is not objectionable, but many homemakers prefer the lighter appearance of the blanched nut.

The method of blanching filberts is somewhat different from that of other nuts, since a dry blanch is best for the removal of the skin. The nut meats are placed in a shallow pan and toasted in a 250°–275° oven about 20 minutes, or until the skins loosen and can be rubbed off.

Filberts may be ground, sliced, or chopped into large pieces, depending on their use in the many recipes to which they are adaptable.

Filberts are named for St. Philibert, whose day, August 22, is celebrated in France by expeditions into the country to gather nuts. *See also* Hazelnut.

Filbunke (Swedish). Soured milk.

Filé. (1) A powder derived from young leaves of the sassafras tree; a condiment essential to Creole cookery. Gumbo filé and other New Orleans specialties utilize this powder, originally prepared and distributed by the Choctaw Indians. Filé must never be cooked, for it becomes stringy. It should be added to a dish after the pan is removed from the heat, immediately before serving. (2) (French). Spun, such as spun sugar.

Filet. A European wild duck with a good flavor.

Filet (French). Fillet. *See* Fillet.

Filet de Boeuf (French). Fillet of beef. This cut is prepared, in addition to simple cooking, in a variety of different styles: *Béatrix*, with artichokes, carrots, and mushrooms; *Bristol*, with flageolets and potato croquettes; *chipolata*, with fried sausages and vegetables; *flamande*, with cabbage and boiled potatoes; *Godard*, cooked in Madeira wine with truffles;

jardinière, garnished with very small young vegetables; *Niçoise*, with garlic-flavored eggplant, olives, and tomatoes, etc.

Filet de Boeuf Wellington. A fillet of beef spread with *pâté de foie gras*, covered with pastry, and baked; then sliced.

Filet de Chevreuil. Fillet of roebuck or venison.

Filet de Mouton. Fillet of mutton.

Filet de Porc. Fillet of pork; loin of pork.

Filet de Veau. Fillet of veal.

Filet en Chevreuil. Mutton marinated and cooked to taste like venison.

Filetes (Spanish). Fillets.

Filet Mignon. A small thick tenderloin, the tenderest and usually the most expensive cut of beef. For finest flavor the meat should be cooked at high heat only until rare. First, though, it should be trimmed of fat and connective tissue, then the lean meat should be either wrapped in suet or pork fat, or it should be larded with a larding needle. The whole filet mignon weighs 6–8 pounds before trimming.

Filetti di Pesce Oreganato (Italian). Fillets of fish baked with oregano.

Filetto (Italian). Fillet.

  Filetto alla Mignon. Fillet of beef.

  Filetto di Pesce. Fillet of fish.

  Filetto di Sogliole alla Parmigiana. Fillet of sole with Parmesan cheese.

  Filetto di Tacchino alla Crema. Creamed breast of turkey.

Filetto di Tacchino Cardinale. Breast of turkey with cheese and truffles.

Filhó (Portuguese). Fritter; pancake.

Filled Cheese. Cheese made from skim or whole milk mixed with a fat other than natural butterfat. The foreign fat, animal fat or margarine, is either stirred vigorously into the milk with enough rennet to coagulate the milk quickly or is incorporated into the milk by homogenization.

Filled Milk. Milk in which the natural fat has been replaced with fat from another source.

Fillet. Choice meat free from bone. Fillet of beef comes from the tenderloin or underside of the sirloin; fillet of veal and fillet of mutton from the fleshy part of the thigh. Fish fillets are slices free of bone.

Fillette; Feuillette (French). A half-bottle of wine.

Filletti di Tachino alla Bolognese (Italian). Turkey breasts dipped in egg and bread crumbs and sautéed, sometimes with ham; a specialty around Bologna.

Filone (Italian). Bread resembling French bread.

Filoses (Portuguese). Yeast doughnuts.

Filosoof (Dutch). Meat-and-potato pie.

Filter Paper. Porous paper used to filter liquids; available in a variety of styles according to the purpose for which it is to be used.

Filtre (French). Any substance used to clarify liquids. *Café filtre*, not so popular since the advent of the espresso machine, was once the standard style of coffee in France. It took a long time for the coffee to drip from the upper portion of the apparatus through the filter into the cup, during which the coffee became cold.

Filzener. A delicate white wine from the vineyards of Filzen, Germany.

Finage. A wine term denoting all vineyards within a certain rather small area.

Financière (French). (1) A brown sauce flavored with Madeira wine and containing truffles, mushrooms, and pitted olives; served chiefly with sweetbreads and calf's head. (2) Pertaining to various rich dishes.

Findhorn. Smoked haddock.

Fin-Djans (Arabic). Very small egg-shaped cups used to serve coffee.

Findon. Smoked haddock.

Findon Haddock. *See* Finnan Haddie.

Fine. (1) Clear and free from impurities, delicate and superior, as applied to a wide variety of food products, wines, and liquors. (2) To clarify or otherwise purify wines and beer.

Fine (French). Brandy of indifferent quality served in restaurants or other public eating establishments, usually in a carafe and not in the original bottle.

Fine à l'Eau (French). Brandy with water.

Fine Champagne. A cognac or brandy from the Cognac region of France; it contains a blend of liquor from the Grande and Petite Champagne regions, with at least 50 percent Grande Champagne. *See also* Champagne Brandy.

Fin Eggehakk (Norwegian). Scrambled eggs.

Finer. A refiner of food products.

Fines Herbes (French). Parsley, tarragon, chives, chervil, and sometimes thyme all finely minced and used for flavoring sauces, omelets, steaks, and some egg dishes.

Fingan. A small porcelain coffee cup.

Finger Bowl. A small bowl containing water in which to rinse the fingers after the main course and before dessert. The water should be at room temperature. A flower petal may be floated in it. A thin slice of lemon in the water is useful, particularly if the main course consisted of lobster or crab, which soil the fingers.

Fingerling. A very small fish.

Fining. The process whereby liquids, especially wines, are clarified.

Finland. Although adjacent to Russia, Finland's cuisine bears no resemblance to that country's cooking style. If any other country's influence is felt in Finland, it is that of Sweden and possibly that of the other Scandinavian countries. Like the Swedes, Norwegians, and Danes, the Finns are particularly fond of herring, which they prepare in many different ways. Many Finnish families buy herring by the barrelful and serve it at least once daily. In some parts of the country herring is a basic, staple food.

Like their Scandinavian neighbors, the Finns are very partial to the assorted appetizers called *smörgåsbord* in Sweden and *voileipäpöytä* in Finland. Fish dishes are always good, with absolutely fresh, superb seafood available in the market. During August, crayfish come into season, and crayfish-eating parties are common. Fishcakes, fish puddings, and, in fact, fish in all forms are standard fare in this lake-rich country.

All soups are popular, particularly the hearty ones containing solid ingredients, such as fish soups. Local novelties include fruit soups, and an unusually appetizing hot-weather soup called *kurkkukeitto*, a cold cucumber soup. The usual meat dishes are prepared, but the national taste seems to favor stews or casserole dishes. Game of all sorts is highly regarded, and it is not unusual to find bear, venison, elk, hazel hens, grouse, and wild duck on the menu. The favorite vegetables are probably cucumbers and mushrooms.

Worthy of mention is the *piirakka*, a pastry dough stuffed with meat or fish. Occasionally made with a vegetable, such as cabbage, it is called *kaalipiirakka*. The Finns love dairy products and consume them at the highest *per capita* rate in the world. Cream, milk, and especially cheese are staples of the diet for the country folk. Finnish cheeses are extremely wholesome and tasty, though none of them could be considered important or noteworthy. A favorite spread is a mixture of butter and the yolks of hard-cooked eggs, a high-cholesterol combination indeed.

The favorite desserts are fruits or dishes based on fruits. Noteworthy are the delicious strawberries and also cloudberries, which resemble heavily seeded yellow raspberries; the local brambleberries may be said to resemble blackberries. The single outstanding dessert, however, may well be Finnish pancakes, called *suomalainen panukakku*, and generally served with preserved lingonberries. From their fruits and berries the Finns prepare many liqueurs, but *mesimarja* (made from brambleberries) and *lakka* (from cloudberries) are the best. Wines are unimportant, except in the larger cities, but the local beer is quite good. Of course, the potent clear liquor called *snaps* or *aquavit* is the strong drink of the country.

Finnan. Smoked haddock.

Finnan Haddie; Findon Haddock. Smoked haddock, which gets its name from the fishing village of Findon, near Aberdeen, Scotland. The Findons perhaps were the first—certainly they are experts—at preparing it. The haddock is split open, and part of the backbone and the head are removed. It is then lightly salted and smoked, which greatly improves the white meat. Finnan haddie usually is sold in fillets, or split, and is an excellent breakfast fish.

Fino (Italian). Fine.

Fino (Spanish). A dry sherry; *See* Spain, The Wines of.

Finocchi al Burro (Italian). Fennel braised in butter.

Finocchio; Finnocchio; Finochio (Italian). Fennel. *See* Sweet Fennel.

Finocchione (Italian). Salami made with fennel.

Finte. A European fish, thought to be a member of the shad family, although much longer than the usual shad.

Fior d'Agno. An Italian liqueur prepared with wild herbs and which tastes like brandy.

Fior d'Alpe; Flora di Alpi; Flor Alpina. A very sweet yellowish liqueur, usually shipped in a tall, thin bottle inside which is a branch with rock crystals clinging to it.

Fiori di Zucchini Indorati (Italian). Fried squash blossoms.

Fired (Scotch). Baked in an oven.

Fire Fang (British). Cheese or barley with a singed or scorched look or smell.

Fire Pan. A portable pan containing a fire; used for cooking.

Fireproof. Unburnable or slow or hard to burn. Fireproof gloves and handles are important in barbecue cooking.

Firewater (Colloquial). Strong alcoholic drinks; the American Indians called all liquor "firewater."

Firkin. (1) A small wooden cask holding one-fourth barrel. (2) A measure of varying capacity, usually for measuring butter.

Firlot (British). One-fourth of a boll (measurement) of corn.

Firming Agents. Agents such as calcium salts, chloride, or carbonate that form a gel that protects fruit from softening. Fresh fruits contain insoluble pectins as a firm gel around the fibrous tissues and keep the fruit firm. A breakdown of cell structure allows conversion of pectin to pectic acid, with loss of firmness. The addition of calcium salts, chloride, or carbonate forms calcium pectate gel, which protects the fruit against softening. Alum is sometimes used to firm pickles.

First Fruit. The first produce of a season.

Fisch (German). Fish.

Fischgerichte (German). Fish dishes.

Fischschüssel (German). Bacon-and-fish pie.

Fischsupple (German). Fish soup.

Fish. Any aquatic animal that has gills instead of lungs, fins for swimming. Most fish may be used as food. Fish may be found in streams, rivers, lakes and in salt water. Shellfish are sometimes classified as fish, but lack gills and fins. There is a considerable amount of variation in the waste, or inedible parts of fish, generally averaging about 50 percent. Fresh fish has the finest taste of all; iced fish is next, and frozen fish comes in a poor third.

Fish Cake. Ground or chopped fish, seasoned and formed into a patty, then fried.

Fish Day. A certain day of the week, usually Friday, on which fish is eaten.

Fish Eater. One whose diet consists mainly of fish.

Fish Flour. Dried fish, ground finely into a flour, and used in cooking.

Fish Fry. A social gathering at which a large quantity of fish is fried. At one time, in certain parts of the southern United States politicians used the fish fry as an occasion for assembling a group of people who in good mood were ready to listen to their promises.

Fish House Punch. A punch said to have been created at the Fish House Club in Philadelphia two centuries ago; it is made with sugar, peach brandy, rum, cognac, lemon juice and water, served with a large piece of ice in the center of a punchbowl.

Fish Kettle. An oval-shaped pot for cooking fish.

Fish Knife. A wide knife used when eating fish; more popular in Europe than in America.

Fish Liquor. The stock or liquid in which fish is boiled.

Fish Maw. The lining of the stomach of certain fish commonly used in Chinese cookery. The maw is air-dried, cut into strips, and used to flavor various dishes.

Fish Meal. Dried fish ground into a meal.

Fishmonger (British). A dealer in fish.

Fish of the Kings. The whitebait, a food fish.

Fish Pot. (1) (British). Fish soup akin to the Mediterranean bouillabaisse. In some fishing ports it is made from discarded fish. (2) A wicker basket in which fish is caught.

Fish Roe. The roe, or eggs, found in female fish. The most famous and costliest of all is caviar, from the sturgeon.

Fish, Salted (Chinese). Certain salted and dried fish used chiefly for flavoring.

Fish Slicer. A knife used for carving fish.

Fish Stick. Lengths of white fish meat usually frozen, intended to be fried.

Fish, Smoked. *See* Smoked Fish.

Fish Strainer. An earthenware or metal container with holes, used to drain the liquor from cooked fish.

Fishwife. A woman who sells fish.

Fishy. Resembling a fish in odor, appearance, or taste.

Fisk (Danish). Fish.
  Fiskefrikadeller. Fishballs.

Fisk (Norwegian). Fish.
  Fiskeboller. Fishballs.
  Fiskefarse. Chopped or minced fish served as balls or patties.
  Fiskegrateng. Fish soufflé.
  Fiskepudding. Fish pudding.
  Fiskesuppe. Fish soup.

Fisk (Swedish). Fish.
  Fiskbullar. Fishballs.
  Fiskfärs. Fish pudding.
  Fiskfiléer. Fillet of fish.
  Fiskgratin. Fish covered with bread crumbs and baked with a sauce.
  Fisk i Gelé. Jellied fish.
  Fisksås. Fish sauce.

Fisternölleken (German). Corn brandy.

Fistuline. A rather mediocre mushroom found in various parts of France.

Fitou. A passable red wine, about 12 percent alcohol, produced in Languedoc, France.

Fiuggi. An Italian water, frequently sold bottled.

Five-Fragrance Powder (Chinese). A spice mixture containing cloves, cinnamon, aniseed, star anise, and pepper.

Fixes. Sour alcoholic drinks usually served in a tall glass or goblet and sipped through a straw. The traditional base is pineapple syrup, with gin, applejack, whisky, rum, or brandy as the alcoholic ingredient. Lime and lemon juice usually impart the tart or sour taste.

Fixin. A region in Burgundy, France, where many red wines of fairly good quality are produced.

Fizz. A drink that bubbles with a hissing sound. It is made with sugar syrup, lemon juice, and gin. It should be made with freshly charged water and should be drunk quickly while still fizzing. Other fizzes are long iced drinks made with syrups, liquor, and sparkling water.

Fjäderfä (Swedish). Fowl.

Flacket. (1) A flash. (2) A barrel-shaped liquor cask.

Flacon. A small bottle with a cork.

Flaesk (Danish). Pork.
  Flaeskesteg. Roast fresh ham, roast pork.
  Flaeskesteg med Rød Kaal. Roast pork with red cabbage.
  Flaesk i Brunkaal. Pork and brown cabbage.
  Flaesk i Kaal. Pork and cabbage.
  Flaesk med Brunstege Løg. Pork with sautéed onions.
  Flaeskeaeggekage. Bacon-and-egg pancake.

Flaesk (Swedish). Pork.
  Flaeskpannkaka. Pork or bacon pancake.
  Flaeskkorv. Pork sausage.
  Flaeskkotlett. Pork chop.

Flageolet (French). A very small and delicious green kidney bean much used in stews and casseroles.

Flagey-Echézeaux. A wine district of the Burgundy region of France. *See* France, The Wines of.

Flagon. (1) A bottle holding about 2 quarts. (2) Any container intended for liquids, usually with a handle, spout, and lidded cover. (3) (Obsolete). Flask of wine.

Flagon Bun. A bun baked in a can surrounded by hot water to supply moisture.

Flagroot. The pungent root of the sweet flag, a marsh herb; sometimes used as a flavoring ingredient.

Flake. A soft, small loose particle of a given food. Crabmeat, tuna fish, and other foods may be flaked with a fork to separate them into small particles.

Flaked Coconut. Slightly sweetened grated dried coconut.

Flamande, À la (Belgian). In the Flemish or Flanders style; as applied to meat, a sauce of beer, braised carrots, and onions.

Flamber (French). (1) To ignite liquor poured over a dish, such as brandy on pancakes. (2) To singe game or poultry.

Flamengo. A Portuguese cheese similar to Edam.

Flamiche; Flamique (French, Belgian). (1) An open tart, much like a *quiche*, filled with leeks or other ingredients and served as an appetizer. (2) Unsweetened bread dough baked with cheese.

Flamiche Courtraisienne (Belgian). A custard made with leeks and served in a pastry shell; similar to the French *quiche*.

Flampoyntes. Pork pies flavored with cheese and sugar.

Flamri. A cold pudding made with semolina, sugar, eggs, and wine; served with puréed berries, especially currants.

   Flamri Vanille. A vanilla blancmange, usually served with a fruit sauce.

Flamusse (French). A tart filled with eggs and white cream cheese, much like a *quiche* or *flamiche*; made in the Burgundy region.

Flan. An open tart, usually filled with fruits or custard, although in France it may contain a meat *pâté*. It is baked in the flan ring, a ring of metal about an inch high. The pastry is rolled out into a circle, then carefully pressed into the buttered flan ring, which is then placed on a buttered baking sheet. It may be baked before or after the filling is added, depending on the recipe.

   In Latin countries flan is the standard caramel egg custard served at the end of a meal.

Flanc; Flanchet (French). A flank of codfish or beef.

Flan Cremosa (Spanish). Boiled custard.

Flancs (French). Side dishes served at elaborate dinners.

Flan de Manzanas (Spanish). Apple pie.

Flangnarde (French). A type of flan, flavored with vanilla or lemon; made in Auverge and Limousin.

Flank. The meaty part of an animal between the hip and ribs.

Flank Steak. "Steak" is a somewhat misleading name for this beef cut taken from the flank, for it is thin, flat, extremely lean, and, unless from the top quality of beef, tough. Butchers often score it to cut through some of the muscle fibers, thus tenderizing the meat somewhat. This process is necessary because the grain runs lengthwise in this steak, rather than up and down as in the better steaks. Flank steak is often stuffed, rolled, and braised.

   London broil, a popular restaurant beef offering, is made from the flank, but it is worthwhile only with U.S. Prime or U.S. Choice meat. When prepared at home it should be sliced thin, diagonally against the grain.

Flannel. A coarse oatcake.

Flannel Cake. A kind of pancake, so-called because of its somewhat heavy consistency.

Flan Ring. *See* Flan.

Flap (Colloquial). (1) Brandy and soda. (2) A tea crumpet.

Flapjack. Griddle cake. The term probably originated from the cook's habit of turning the cakes over by flapping them into the air with a spatula.

Flare. The fat around pig kidney.

Flash Pasteurization. A process in which the material (usually milk) is held at a higher temperature than in normal pasteurization, but for a shorter period, resulting in less development of the cooked flavor. In ordinary pasteurization milk is heated to 60°C. for 30 seconds; in the flash process it is heated to 74°C. for only a few seconds.

Flask. A small container or bottle to hold liquor, designed to be carried in a pocket.

Fläsk. *See under* Flaesk.

Flat-Dick (British). A coarse sour oatcake.

Flatfish. Fish, including flounder, sole, halibut, and turbot, with a flat body and with both eyes on one side of the body.

Flat Silver. Knives, forks, and spoons.

Flattbröd (Scandinavian). Wafer-thin bread made of various grains.

Flatware. Flat table silver—knives, forks, and spoons.

Flaugnarde (French). A pastry dessert prepared with eggs, flour, sugar, and milk and flavored with vanilla and cinnamon.

Flavedo. The colored outermost layer of citrus fruits, also called the *epicarp*. It contains the oil sacs and numerous yellow plastids (green in the unripe fruit, containing chlorophyll; yellow in the ripe fruit, containing carotene and xanthophyll).

Flavor. (1) The characteristic taste of a food. (2) To furnish foods with added taste, as by flavoring them with spices or sweeteners.

Flavored. Containing an ingredient that imparts flavor.

Flavored Syrup. A low-priced syrup made by combining corn syrup with any desired synthetic flavoring, such as maple or butterscotch.

Flavoring. An ingredient added to food to give it a desired flavor.

Flavorless. Lacking flavor or taste.

Flavorous. Having a good taste or pleasing aroma.

Flead. Lard.

Flead Cakes. (British). Cakes or puff pastries made with lard instead of butter or margarine.

Fleck (German). Tripe.

Fleet. To remove substances floating on the surface of a liquid.

Fleeten. Having the color of skim milk.

Fleisch (German). Meat.
>   Fleischbrühe. Meat soup.
>   Fleischgerichte. Meat dishes.
>   Fleischklösse. Meatballs.
>   Fleischspeisen. Meat preparations.

Fleischig (Yiddish). Meats or meat dishes.

Flensjes (Dutch). Dessert pancakes.
>   Flensjestaart. Pancakes stuffed with stewed fruit.

Flesh. (1) (Colloquial). Meats of animals, fish, and poultry. (2) The soft edible parts of fruits.

Flesher (Scotch). Butcher.

Fleshmonger (Obsolete, British). Butcher.

Fleshpot. Originally a pot exclusively for cooking meats. *Fleshpot* usually denotes good, even luxurious, food and living.

Fleskepannekaker (Norwegian). Breakfast pancakes.

Fleskepølse (Norwegian). Pork sausages.

Flétan (French). Halibut and similar flatfish.

Fleur de Deauville. A French cheese resembling Brie.

Fleur, La. A château that produces one of the better wines of Pomerol, France.

Fleurette (French). Fresh heavy sweet cream. In France *crème fraîche* is slightly matured, which makes it thicker than any cream available in the United States and gives it a very mild sour taste.

Fleurie. A town in the Beaujolais wine district. *See* France, The Wines of.

Fleuriste (French). A tomato shell filled with chopped cooked vegetables.

Fleurons (French). Scraps of puff pastry rolled thin, cut into small crescents or "butterflies" or tied in little knots, fried or baked until golden and crisp; served with soups, entrées, or creamed dishes.

Fleurs de Vin (French). The small flakes which appear prior to fermentation of wine.

Flip. (1) A well-spiced drink made with beer, ale, and cider usually sweetened with sugar; sometimes contains egg. (2) A short drink with either wine or another liquor shaken with sugar and a whole beaten egg. Usually made with 1 teaspoon of sugar syrup, 1 egg, and 2 ounces of liquor for each serving, shaken with finely crushed ice and strained into a sour glass; may be decorated with a dash of grated nutmeg.

Flitch. (1) A side of pig salted and cured. (2) Smoked meat, as a flitch of bacon.

Flitters. Small pancake fritters.

Floating Island. A soft custard with "islands" of meringue floating on top.

Fløde (Danish). Cream.
>   Flødeskum. Whipped cream.
>   Flødsauce. Cream sauce.

Flora Wheat. An Australian wheat, stronger than average.

Florence Fennel. *See* Sweet Fennel.

Florence Oil. A high-quality olive oil.

Florentine, À la. In the style of Florence, Italy; of fish, eggs, or sweetbreads, garnished with spinach purée or leaves.

Florentine. (1) A meat pie. (2) A kind of tart. (3) A lacy crisp flat fruit-and-nut cookie coated with bittersweet chocolate with several recent variations; a specialty of Austria, Germany, and other central European countries.

Florian. A garnish for roasts, usually consisting of braised lettuce, browned tiny white onions, and carrots cut in the shape of olives.

Florida Dusky Duck. A fine wild duck abundant in Florida and other southern states.

Florida Red Snapper. A large red-scaled fish with a very delicate flavor; caught in the waters off the Gulf Coast and weighing as much as 30 pounds. Specimens weighing up to 5 pounds are marketed whole; large specimens are cut into steaks.

Flote (Obsolete). A herd of cattle; a school of fish.

Fløte (Norwegian). Cream.

   Fløtsuppe. Cream soup.

   Fløtevafler. Cream waffles.

Fløtost (Norwegian). Cheese made of boiled whey.

Flotten Milk. Skim milk.

Flounder. A flatfish species of which there are at least 500 varieties. The smallest flounders weigh only a few ounces, the largest are monsters of several hundred pounds. They vary in color from white-cream to brown, but in general their color depends on the bottom surface, for they tend to develop protective coloring. Flounders are not so delicate in taste as sole, but they are occasionally sold as such. In some regions flounders are marketed as fluke, flatfish, etc.

Several varieties are marketed including, in addition to the regular or winter flounder, the fluke or summer flounder, the yellowtail, dab, lemon sole, and gray sole. Caught along the Atlantic Coast from Maine to the Gulf of Mexico, the flounder is a year-round fish suitable when whole for baking and broiling. Fillet of sole often is simply fillet of flounder.

Flour. Finely ground meal made of rye, wheat, buckwheat, or almost any other edible grain. Usually the term applies chiefly to wheat. Flour may also be marketed as "prepared," containing self-leavening ingredients. Flour is usually bleached to give it a better color but, if so, it must be so labeled for the market.

Wheat flours include those milled from durum wheat and used for making semolina, which, in turn, is made into macaroni, spaghetti, and other edible pastes. Hard-wheat flours include the hard winter and hard spring wheats and are used for making bakery flours, bread flours, and all-purpose flours. Soft-wheats are used for pastry, cake, all-purpose, and biscuit flours.

There are, in addition, flours used in combination with wheat flour, including corn, buckwheat, cottonseed, lima-bean, peanut, potato, and soy flours.

When a recipe calls for "flour," it means wheat flour unless some other type is indicated. There may be some qualifying adjective before the word "flour," indicating the specific purpose for which that flour was milled, such as bread, cake, or self-rising flour. But if there is no such qualification, then all-purpose or general-purpose flour is to be used.

Flour, Self-Rising; Self-Raising. Flour to which chemicals have been added that produce carbon dioxide in the presence of water and heat. It thus aerates the dough without prolonged fermentation. Usually "weaker" flours, containing less protein, are used.

Flour Bolt. Flour sieve, sifter.

Flour Cake. A doughnut.

Flouring. Sprinkling lightly with flour, usually before frying.

Flour of Mustard. Powdered mustard seeds.

Floury. Like flour or sprinkled with flour.

Floutes (Alsatian). A type of potato ball or dumpling.

Flower Cheese. A soft-curd rennet cheese prepared from cow's milk with petals of roses, marigolds, or other flowers added in the making.

Fluff. A cooked or uncooked mixture, made with stiffly beaten egg whites, fruit pulp, and sugar.

Fluid Ounce. A liquid measure; 8 fluid ounces equal one standard measuring cup; 16 fluid ounces equal one pint.

Fluke. A large flounder.

Flukies (Scotch). Flounders.

Flummery (British). (1) A simple cold oatmeal dessert. (2) A dessert consisting of raspberries or currants thickened with cornstarch. The early settlers in Virginia brought the flummery recipe from England.

Flunder (German). Flounder.

Fluren. Cakes made with flour.

Flush. The tender young shoots of the tea bush, believed to yield the best leaves.

Flush Cake. A sample of dough placed in the oven to test the heat before baking.

Fluster. To become overheated as a result of drinking.

Flûte (French). (1) A long, narrow roll of crusty bread. (2) A specially designed champagne glass.

Fluting. A method of decorating the edge of a two-crust pie to make it more attractive as well as to prevent the juice of the filling from leaking out. To flute, pinch the top and bottom crusts between the thumb and forefinger all around the rim raising it up slightly to make a standing rim around the edge.

Flying Fish. Two kinds of fish that can jump into the air because they possess winglike fins.

The small, slender fish found in tropical waters, especially in the Caribbean, is popular as food only in Barbados, British West Indies. There it is fried, boiled, baked, and even made into a flying-fish pie topped with a crust of mashed potatoes. Flying fish have a pleasant, somewhat nutty taste. The difficulty of removing their small bones keeps them from being more popular.

Flyndrefilet (Norwegian). Fillet of flounder.

F.O. "Fine old," a liquor term.

Foal (British, Scotch). A small thick bannock or cake of gingerbread sprinkled with sugar-coated caraway seeds.

Foam. (1) Froth or bubbles on a drink; also, a drink filled with froth. (2) A beaten-egg-and-sugar mass, such as a spongecake preparation, before flour is added.

Foamy. Of a mixture or topping; frothy.

F.O.B. "Fine old blend," a liquor term.

Focaccia Castelnovese (Italian). A sweet bun with pine nuts, made during the Christmas and Easter seasons in Liguria.

Focaccia di Vitello (Italian). Veal patties.

F.O.E.S. "Fine old extra special," a liquor term.

Fogash; Fogoch; Fogosch. A delicious unique trout-like fish found in Lake Balaton, Hungary, and in other local waters.

Foggiano. A cheese similar to Pecorino made in southern Italy.

Foglie di Alloro (Italian). Bay leaves.

Foie Gras. One of the greatest and most costly of delicacies, the fattened liver of the goose; produced by force-feeding geese while keeping them in small enclosures, so that the livers grow to enormous size from the rich diet and lack of exercise. Similar *foie gras* is prepared with duck liver, but as this tends to disintegrate in cooking, it is not as widely used.

Hungary ships a large amount of the livers to France, which is the most famous source of *foie gras*, particularly the cities of Strasbourg and Toulouse. For export to the United States, the preparation is most often tinned or packed in earthenware terrines. Livers are graded as *Extra* (the best), *Sur-Choix*, and *Choix*. In tins, *foie gras au naturel* is the finest grade, for it consists solely of a whole liver. *Pâté de foie gras*, the smooth paste made from the liver, consists of at least 75 percent whole *foie gras*, the remainder being minced. *Crème de foie gras* is a lesser grade, consisting of at least 75 percent minced *foie gras* plus such other ingredients as pork livers. *Crème de foie d'oie* consists of 55 percent *foie gras*, and *crème au foie* has 30 percent *foie gras*.

Foie gras, which has a rich yet delicate savor, may be served as a first course, as an accompaniment to cocktails, or as a separate course to follow the roast, accompanied by red wine. Some experts insist that *foie gras* should never be served with a salad, but others recommend that it come with the salad course. *Pâté de foie gras* can be served in its pottery terrine, or, if it is canned, turned out onto a serving dish and accompanied by crusty French bread and a pepper mill.

Foison (Obsolete). An abundant crop.

Foist (Obsolete). A wine cask.

Folatières. A group of dry white wines produced near Puligny, in the Burgundy region of France.

Folle Blanche. A white Chablis table wine made in California from grapes of the same name.

Foncé (French). A dish with a baked pastry bottom.

Foncée, La. A fresh cream cheese made near Pau, France.

Foncer (French). (1) To grease or line a casserole or other dish with fats, ham, or bacon. (2) To line a mold with pastry dough.

Fond (French). (1) Meat stock or concentrated gravy. (2) The bottom of something, as in *fond d'artichaut.*

Fond Blanc. A white stock made by boiling calf's bones with water, onion, bouquet garni, and wine, then strained.

Fond de Gibier. A game stock made by boiling game bones, carcass, wine, and water.

Fond de Volaille. A chicken stock prepared by cooking poultry bones and carcass with soup stock, or by cooking the bones with water, wine, and bouquet garni.

Fondaco (Italian, Arabic). Inn.

Fondant. (1) A smooth, creamy mixture of sugar, water, and sometimes corn syrup, cream of tartar, or lemon juice used as a base of many sweets and as a coating for nuts, fruits, and other confections. (2) A small pear-shaped croquette made of several puréed ingredients dipped in bread crumbs and fried.

Fondas de Alcachofas (Spanish). Artichoke bottoms.

Fondre, Faire (French). To cook fruits or vegetables very slowly in butter in a tightly covered pot without stirring.

Fonds de Braise (French). Ingredients, usually bacon or other fat and vegetables, used to line a mold.

Fonds de Cuisine (French). Liquid or semiliquid sauces or ready mixtures such as meat extracts, basic sauces, *glace de viande*, and *fumets*, etc.

Fondue (Swiss). A bubbling concoction of melted Gruyère cheese (sometimes with other cheeses), Swiss white wine, a sprinkling of pepper, and a bit of kirsch. There are variations on the basic recipe. It is served over a flame in a chafing dish

or casserole. Each diner dips a chunk of bread into the cheese and pops it into his mouth.

Fondue Bourguignonne. A do-it-yourself dish in which the diner places pieces of meat in a container of heated oil, and when the meat is cooked, dips it in an appropriate sauce.

Fondue Oriental. Similar to a Fondue Bourguignonne, except that boiling soup is used instead of oil.

Fondue Parmesan. A cheese appetizer, made with milk, flour, cornstarch, eggs, and Parmesan cheese; the mixture is cooked, allowed to chill, and fried in hot fat.

Fonduta (Italian). Melted Fontina cheese dish made with truffles and eggs.

Fontainebleau (French). A dessert made of soft, rich, white Fontainebleau cream cheese beaten until light; usually served with heavy French sweet-sour cream and sugar.

Fontaine, Faire la (French). "To make a fountain," a dough-making procedure. A circle of flour is made on a board; ingredients placed in the center are combined with the flour to make a dough.

Fontina; Fontini. A very rich, oily, medium-soft, goat's-milk cheese resembling Swiss but spicier, made in northern Italy.

Fontina Valaisan. A fondue made with Goumois cheese, flour, milk, and caraway seeds. *See* Fondue.

Foochow Oolong. A long black-leafed Chinese tea with a rather mild, not very distinctive flavor.

Food; Foodstuff. Edible substances (except alcoholic drinks) that contain nutrients essential for the growth and maintenance of the body.

Food and Wines. *See* Wines and Food.

Food Poisoning. Poisoning due to staphylococci and salmonellae and very rarely to *Clostridium botulinum.*

Staphylococcal poisoning causes rapid symptoms (in 2–4 hours) of nausea, vomiting, diarrhea, and abdominal cramp, with rapid recovery.

Salmonella outbreaks often are connected with meat, milk, fish, and eggs. An endotoxin is produced and when the living organisms are ingested acute gastroenteritis results after 12–24 hours, not often fatal. Nausea, vomiting, diarrhea, abdominal pain, and fever may persist for several weeks.

Botulism is due to the exotoxin produced by *Clostridium botulinum* and is often fatal.

Foods, The Composition of

Food, description, and approximate measure	Food energy Cal.	Protein Gm.	Fat Gm.	Total carbohydrate Gm.	Calcium Mg.	Phosphorus Mg.	Iron Mg.	Vitamin A value I.U.	Thiamine Mg.	Riboflavin Mg.	Niacin Mg.	Ascorbic acid Mg.
Almonds, dried, unblanched:												
Shelled, 1 cup (142 gm.)	848	26.4	76.8	27.8	361	674	6.2	0	.35	.95	6.5	Trace
In shell, 1 cup (78 gm.)	238	7.4	21.6	7.8	102	190	1.8	0	.10	.27	1.8	Trace
Apples:												
Raw, A.P.; refuse, 12 percent:												
1 large (3 in. diam., 230 gm.)	117	.6	.8	30.1	12	20	.6	180	.08	.06	.4	9
1 medium (2½ in. diam., 150 gm.)	76	.4	.5	19.7	8	13	.4	120	.05	.04	.2	6
1 small (2¼ in. diam., 114 gm.)	58	.3	.4	14.9	6	10	.3	90	.04	.03	.2	5
Raw, E.P.:												
1 cup cubed or sliced (142 gm.)	83	.4	.6	21.2	9	14	.4	130	.06	.04	.3	7
Canned. See Applesauce.												
Dried:												
Dehydrated (small pieces), 1 pound	1,606	8.2	10.9	413.1	109	277	8.2	(0)	.33	.47	5.4	53
Uncooked, 1 cup (114 gm.)	315	1.6	1.1	83.4	22	55	1.6	(0)	.11	.11	1.1	14
*Cooked, unsweetened:												
1 pound	358	1.8	1.4	94.4	23	64	1.8	(0)	.09	.14	1.4	9
1 cup (255 gm.)	201	1.0	.8	53.0	13	36	1.0	(0)	.05	.08	.8	5
*Cooked, sweetened:												
1 pound	477	1.8	1.4	124.8	23	54	1.8	(0)	.09	.09	.9	9
1 cup (280 gm.)	294	1.1	.8	77.0	14	34	1.1	(0)	.06	.06	.6	6
Apples and apricots, canned, strained (infant food), 1 ounce.	18	.1	.1	4.7	3	5	.3	300	.01	.01	.1	1
*Apple betty:												
1 pound	680	7.7	13.2	138.9	68	114	.5	730	.26	.18	2.2	5
1 cup (230 gm.)	344	3.9	6.7	70.4	34	58	.2	370	.13	.09	1.1	3
Apple butter:												
1 cup (282 gm.)	518	1.1	2.3	128.0	39	59	1.7	(0)	.03	.06	.4	5
1 tablespoon (18 gm.)	33	.1	.1	8.2	3	4	.1	(0)	Trace	Trace	Trace	Trace
Apple juice, fresh or canned, 1 cup (249 gm.).	124	.2	(0)	34.4	15	25	1.2	90	.05	.07	Trace	2
Applesauce, canned:												
Unsweetened, 1 cup (239 gm.)	100	.5	.5	26.1	10	19	1.0	70	.05	.02	.1	3

Note: Asterisk indicates that values are calculated from a recipe; parentheses indicate imputed value.

Food												
Sweetened, 1 cup (254 gm.)	184	.5	.3	50.0	10	20	1.0	80	.05	.03	.1	3
Strained (infant food), 1 ounce	17	.1	.1	4.5	1	2	.1	20	Trace	Trace	Trace	1
Apricots:												
Raw, 3 apricots (114 gm.); refuse, pits, 6 percent.	54	1.1	.1	13.8	17	25	.5	2,990	.03	.05	.9	7
Canned:												
Water pack, 1 cup halves and liquid (244 gm.).	77	1.2	.2	19.8	24	37	.7	3,300	.04	.05	.8	10
Syrup pack:												
1 cup halves and syrup (256 gm.)	205	1.5	.5	54.8	26	38	.8	3,460	.04	.06	.8	10
4 medium halves and 2 tablespoons syrup (122 gm.).	97	.7	.1	26.1	12	18	.4	1,650	.02	.03	.4	5
Strained (infant food), 1 ounce	17	.3	.1	4.3	6	9	(.3)	(480)	(.01)	(.01)	(.1)	(1)
Dried, sulfured:												
Uncooked:												
Large, 1 cup (28 halves, 162 gm.)	423	8.4	.6	108.4	139	193	7.9	12,040	.02	.25	5.3	20
Small, 1 cup (40 halves, 150 gm.)	393	7.8	.6	100.4	129	178	7.4	11,140	.02	.24	4.9	19
*Cooked, unsweetened, fruit and liquid:												
1 pound	386	7.7	.5	99.0	127	177	7.3	10,990	.02	.23	4.5	14
1 cup (approx. 25 halves, 285 gm.)	242	4.8	.4	62.1	80	111	4.6	6,900	.01	.14	2.8	9
*Cooked, sweetened, fruit and syrup:												
1 pound	559	6.8	.5	143.5	109	154	6.4	9,580	.01	.18	4.1	14
1 cup (approx. 25 halves, 325 gm.)	400	4.9	.4	102.7	78	110	4.6	6,860	.01	.13	2.9	10
Frozen, 3 ounces	70	.6	.1	17.9	9	14	.3	1,410	.02	.03	.4	3
Asparagus:												
Cooked:												
1 pound	92	10.9	.5	16.3	86	241	4.5	4,720	.59	.77	5.4	104
1 cup cut spears (175 gm.)	36	4.2	.4	6.3	33	93	1.8	1,820	.23	.30	2.1	40
Canned, green:												
Solids and liquid:												
1 cup cut spears with liquid (239 gm.).	42	4.5	.5	6.9	43	103	4.1	1,450	.16	.23	2.1	35
6 spears, medium size with 2 tablespoons liquid (126 gm.).	22	2.4	.4	3.7	23	54	2.1	760	.09	.12	1.1	19
Drained solids:												
1 pound	97	10.9	1.8	15.4	86	241	8.6	3,630	.30	.37	4.4	80
1 cup cut spears (175 gm.)	38	4.2	.7	6.0	33	93	3.3	1,400	.11	.14	1.7	31
6 spears, medium size (96 gm.)	21	2.3	.4	3.3	18	51	1.8	770	.06	.08	.9	17
Canned, bleached:												
Solids and liquid:												
1 cup cut spears with liquid (239 gm.).	43	3.8	.7	7.9	36	79	2.2	110	.13	.16	1.8	35
6 spears, medium size with 2 tablespoons liquid (126 gm.).	23	2.0	.4	4.2	19	42	1.1	60	.07	.08	.9	19

[227]

Foods, The Composition of (Continued)

Food, description, and approximate measure	Food energy	Protein	Fat	Total carbohydrate	Calcium	Phosphorus	Iron	Vitamin A value	Thiamine	Riboflavin	Niacin	Ascorbic acid
	Cal.	Gm.	Gm.	Gm.	Mg.	Mg.	Mg.	I.U.	Mg.	Mg.	Mg.	Mg.
Asparagus: (Continued)												
Drained solids:												
1 cup cut spears (175 gm.)	39	3.7	.9	6.3	28	72	1.8	140	.09	.13	(1.5)	31
6 spears, medium size (96 gm.)	22	2.0	.5	3.5	15	39	1.0	70	.05	.07	(.8)	17
Avocados, raw:[1]												
1 cup (½ in. cubes, 152 gm.)	372	2.6	40.1	7.8	15	58	.9	430	.10	.20	1.7	24
½ peeled avocado (3½ by 3¼ in. diam., 114 gm.).	279	1.9	30.1	5.8	11	43	.7	330	.07	.15	1.3	18
Bacon, medium fat, broiled or fried, drained:												
1 pound	2,761	114	250.0	5.0	114	1,158	15.0	(0)	2.16	1.41	21.8	0
2 slices (16 gm.)	97	4	8.8	.2	4	41	.5	(0)	.08	.05	.8	0
Bacon, Canadian, raw, 4 ounces	262	25.1	17.0	(.3)	15	238	3.7	(0)	1.04	.28	5.9	0
Bananas, raw; refuse, skins, 33 percent:												
1 large (8 by 1½ in., 200 gm.)	119	1.6	.3	31.	11	38	.8	570	.06	.06	1.0	13
1 medium (6 by 1½ in., 150 gm.)	88	1.2	.2	23.	8	28	.6	430	.04	.05	.7	10
1 cup slices, E.P. (154 gm.)	136	1.8	.3	35.	12	43	.9	660	.07	.07	1.1	15
Barley, pearled, light, dry, 1 cup (203 gm.).	708	16.6	2.0	160.0	32	384	(4.1)	(0)	.25	.17	6.3	(0)
Beans, common or kidney, mature dry seeds:												
Red kidney:												
Canned (or cooked), solids and liquid, 1 cup (256 gm.).	230	14.6	1.0	42.0	102	317	4.9	(0)	.12	.12	2.0	(0)
Other (including navy, pea bean, white marrow, etc.:												
Raw, 1 cup (190 gm.)	642	40.7	3.0	117.0	310	830	13.1	0	1.28	.44	4.1	3
Canned, baked:												
Pork and molasses, 1 cup (261 gm.)	325	15.1	7.8	50.1	146	295	5.5	90	.13	.09	1.2	7
Pork and tomato sauce, 1 cup (261 gm.).	295	15.1	5.5	48.0	107	295	4.7	220	.13	.09	1.2	7

[1] Data on proximate constituents apply to Fuerte variety.

Beans, lima:												
Immature seeds:												
Cooked:												
1 pound	432	22.7	83.1	1.3	132	350	7.7	1,320	.64	.41	5.0	68
1 cup (160 gm.)	152	8.0	29.3	.5	46	123	2.7	460	.22	.14	1.8	24
Canned:												
Solids and liquid, 1 cup (249 gm.)	176	9.5	33.6	.7	67	182	4.2	330	.09	.11	1.3	20
Drained solids:												
1 pound	432	22.7	83.1	1.3	132	350	7.7	830	.13	.25	2.3	27
1 cup (160 gm.)	152	8.0	29.3	.5	46	123	2.7	290	.04	.09	.8	9
Mature dry seeds, 1 cup (183 gm.)	610	37.9	112.7	2.4	124	697	13.7	0	.88	.32	3.6	3
Beans, snap:												
Green:												
Cooked (small amount of water, short time):												
1 pound	99	6.4	21.3	.9	163	104	3.2	3,000	.32	.45	2.3	64
1 cup (125 gm.)	27	1.8	5.9	.2	45	29	.9	830	.09	.12	.6	18
Cooked (large amount of water, long time):												
1 pound	99	6.4	21.3	.9	163	104	3.2	3,000	.23	.41	1.8	45
1 cup (125 gm.)	27	1.8	5.9	.2	45	29	.9	830	.06	.11	.5	12
Canned:												
Solids and liquid, 1 cup (239 gm.)	43	2.4	10.0	.2	65	45	3.3	990	.08	.10	.7	9
Drained solids:												
1 pound	99	6.4	21.3	.9	163	104	7.7	2,270	.16	.25	1.8	25
1 cup (125 gm.)	27	1.8	5.9	.2	45	29	2.1	620	.04	.07	.5	7
Strained (infant food), 1 ounce	6	.5	1.3	.0	9	7	.2	140	.01	.02	.1	1
Wax or yellow:												
Canned:												
Solids and liquid, 1 cup (239 gm.)	43	2.4	10.0	.2	65	45	3.3	230	.08	.10	.7	9
Drained solids:												
1 pound	99	6.4	21.3	.9	163	104	7.7	540	.16	.25	1.8	25
1 cup (125 gm.)	27	1.8	5.9	.2	45	29	2.1	150	.04	.07	.5	7
Beans, soya. See Soybeans.												
Bean soup. See Soups.												
Bean sprouts, raw. See Mung bean and Soybean sprouts.												
Beef cuts, cooked:[1]												
Chuck:[1]												
1 pound with bone	1,140	96.	0.	81.	40	431	11.4	(0)	.18	.75	15.2	0

[1] Data assume cut to be prepared by braising or pot roasting. Use of proportionate quantity of drippings would add approximately 50 percent more thiamine and niacin and 25 percent more riboflavin.

Foods, The Composition of (Continued)

Food, description, and approximate measure	Food energy	Protein	Fat	Total carbo-hydrate	Cal-cium	Phos-phorus	Iron	Vitamin A value	Thia-mine	Ribo-flavin	Nia-cin	Ascor-bic acid
	Cal.	Gm.	Gm.	Gm.	Mg.	Mg.	Mg.	I.U.	Mg.	Mg.	Mg.	Mg.
Beef cuts, cooked: (Continued)												
1 pound without bone	1,406	118.	100.	0.	50	531	14.1	(0)	.22	.93	18.7	0
3 ounces without bone	265	22.	19.	0.	9	100	2.6	(0)	.04	.17	3.5	0
Flank:[1]												
1 pound with bone	1,381	110.	101.	0.	48	515	13.2	(0)	.22	.89	18.0	0
1 pound without bone	1,425	114.	104.	0.	50	531	13.6	(0)	.22	.92	18.6	0
3 ounces without bone	270	21.	20.	0.	9	100	2.6	(0)	.04	.17	3.5	0
Hamburger:												
1 pound	1,654	100.	136.	0.	41	717	12.7	(0)	.35	.85	21.8	0
3 ounces	316	19.	26.	0.	8	134	2.4	(0)	.07	.16	4.1	0
Lean. See Round.												
Porterhouse:												
1 pound with bone	1,269	86.	100.	0.	41	632	11.2	(0)	.24	.68	17.3	0
1 pound without bone	1,554	104.	123.	0.	50	772	13.6	(0)	.29	.83	21.1	0
3 ounces without bone	293	20.	23.	0.	9	145	2.6	(0)	.05	.15	4.0	0
Rib roast:												
1 pound with bone	1,050	79.	79.	0.	33	612	9.9	(0)	.21	.60	14.2	0
1 pound without bone	1,449	109.	109.	0.	45	840	13.6	(0)	.28	.82	19.5	0
3 ounces without bone	266	20.	20.	0.	9	157	2.6	(0)	.05	.15	3.6	0
Round:												
1 pound with bone	917	107.	51.	0.	43	885	13.4	(0)	.30	.86	21.8	0
1 pound without bone	1,057	123.	59.	0.	50	1,017	15.4	(0)	.35	.99	25.1	0
3 ounces without bone	197	23.	11.	0.	9	191	2.9	(0)	.06	.19	4.7	0
Rump:[1]												
1 pound with bone	1,171	65.	99.	0.	25	263	7.7	(0)	.13	.48	9.6	0
1 pound without bone	1,714	95.	145.	0.	36	386	11.4	(0)	.19	.70	14.1	0
3 ounces without bone	320	18.	27.	0.	7	72	2.1	(0)	.04	.13	2.6	0
Sirloin:												
1 pound with bone	1,173	91.	87.	0.	40	691	11.5	(0)	.26	.74	18.8	0
1 pound without bone	1,346	104.	100.	0.	45	794	13.2	(0)	.30	.85	21.7	0
3 ounces without bone	257	20.	19.	0.	9	149	2.5	(0)	.06	.16	4.1	0
Beef, canned:												
Corned beef hash, 3 ounces	120	11.7	5.2	6.1	22	124	1.1	Trace	.02	.11	2.4	0
Roast beef, 3 ounces	189	21.0	11.0	0.	14	99	2.0	(0)	.02	.19	3.6	0
Strained (infant food), 1 ounce	30	4.9	1.0	0.	3	43	1.2	(0)	Trace	.06	.9	0

[1] Data assume cut to be prepared by braising or pot roasting. Use of proportionate quantity of drippings would add approximately 50 percent more thiamine and 25 percent more riboflavin.

Food	gm.											
Beef, corned, canned:												
Lean, 3 ounces	159	22.5	7.	0.	18	94	3.8	(0)	.01	.21	3.0	0
Medium fat, 3 ounces	182	21.5	10.	0.	17	90	3.7	(0)	.01	.20	2.9	0
Fat, 3 ounces	221	20.0	15.	0.	16	83	3.4	(0)	.01	.19	2.7	0
Beef, dried, or chipped:												
1 cup (165 gm.)	336	56.6	10.4	0.	33	667	8.4	(0)	(.12)	(.53)	(6.3)	0
2 ounces	115	19.4	3.6	0.	11	229	2.9	(0)	(.04)	(.18)	(2.2)	0
*Beef and vegetable stew:												
1 pound	487	25.0	37.2	32.2	59	340	5.0	4,870	.24	.29	6.6	28
1 cup (235 gm.)	252	12.9	19.3	16.7	31	176	2.6	2,520	.12	.15	3.4	15
Beer (average 4 pct. alcohol), 1 cup (240 gm.)	[1]	1.4	.0	10.6	10	62	.0	(0)	Trace	.06	.4	(0)
Beets, common red:												
Raw, peeled root, 1 cup diced (134 gm.)	56	2.1	.1	12.9	36	58	1.3	30	.03	.06	.6	13
Cooked:												
1 pound	187	4.5	.5	44.5	95	141	3.2	90	.09	.18	1.4	30
1 cup diced (165 gm.)	68	1.6	.2	16.2	35	51	1.2	30	.03	.07	.5	11
Canned, solids and liquid, 1 cup (246 gm.)	82	2.2	.2	19.4	37	71	1.5	40	.02	.06	.3	12
Drained solids:												
1 pound	187	4.5	.5	44.5	95	141	3.2	80	.05	.13	.5	21
1 cup diced (165 gm.)	68	1.6	.2	16.2	35	51	1.2	30	.02	.05	.2	8
Strained (infant food), 1 ounce	10	.4	.0	2.2	5	7	.2	Trace	Trace	.01	Trace	2
Beet greens, common, cooked:												
1 pound	125	9.1	1.4	25.4	536[2]	204	14.5	33,780	.23	.73	1.8	68
1 cup (145 gm.)	39	2.9	.4	8.1	171[2]	65	4.6	10,790	.07	.23	.6	22
Beverages, carbonated:												
Ginger ale, 8 fluid ounces (1 cup, 230 gm.)	80	—	—	21.	—	—	—	—	—	—	—	—
Other, including cola type, 8 fluid ounces (1 cup, 230 gm.)	107	—	—	28.	—	—	—	—	—	—	—	—
*Biscuits, baking powder, 1 biscuit (2½ in. diam., 38 gm.) made with:												
Unenriched flour	129	3.1	4.0	19.8	83	73	.2	0	.02	.03	.2	(0)
Enriched flour	129	3.1	4.0	19.8	83	73	.7	0	.09	.08	.7	(0)
Enriched self-rising flour	127	3.0	4.1	19.0	84	95	.7	0	.09	.09	.8	(0)

[1] The value excluding energy derived from alcohol is 48 calories. If the energy from alcohol is considered available, the value is 114 calories.
[2] Calcium may not be available because of presence of oxalic acid.

[231]

Foods, The Composition of (Continued)

Food, description, and approximate measure	Food energy	Protein	Fat	Total carbo-hydrate	Cal-cium	Phos-phorus	Iron	Vitamin A value	Thia-mine	Ribo-flavin	Nia-cin	Ascor-bic acid
	Cal.	Gm.	Gm.	Gm.	Mg.	Mg.	Mg.	I.U.	Mg.	Mg.	Mg.	Mg.
Blackberries:												
Raw, 1 cup (berries about ½ by 1 in., 144 gm.)	82	1.7	1.4	18.0	46	46	1.3	280	.05	.06	.5	30
Canned, solids and liquid:												
Water pack, 1 cup (244 gm.)	104	2.2	1.7	22.9	44	46	(1.7)	450	.03	.05	.5	15
Syrup pack, 1 cup (251 gm.)	216	1.8	.5	57.2	45	48	(1.8)	460	.03	.05	.5	16
Black-eyed peas. See Cowpeas.												
*Blancmange (vanilla cornstarch pudding):												
1 pound	504	15.9	17.7	71.3	531	418	.5	720	.15	.73	.4	3
1 cup (248 gm.)	275	8.7	9.7	38.9	290	228	.2	390	.08	.40	.2	2
Bluberries:												
Raw, 1 cup (140 gm.)	85	.8	.8	21.1	22	18	1.1	400	(.04)	(.03)	(.4)	23
Canned, solids and liquid:												
Water pack, 1 cup (242 gm.)	90	1.0	1.0	21.8	27	15	(1.2)	100	.03	.03	.5	32
Syrup pack, 1 cup (249 gm.)	245	1.0	1.0	64.7	27	15	(1.2)	100	.03	.03	.5	33
Frozen, without sugar, 3 ounces	52	.5	.5	12.8	14	11	.7	200	(.01)	(.01)	(.2)	12
Bluefish:												
Cooked, baked:												
1 pound	704	124.4	19.1	0.	104	1,330	3.2	—	.56	.51	10.0	—
1 piece (3½ by 3 by ½ in., 125 gm.)	193	34.2	5.2	0.	29	366	.9	—	.15	.14	2.8	—
Cooked, fried:												
1 pound	929	103.1	44.5	21.3	86	1,103	2.7	—	.49	.48	9.4	—
1 piece (3½ by 3 by ½ in., 150 gm.)	307	34.0	14.7	7.0	28	364	.9	—	.16	.16	3.1	—
Bologna. See Sausage.												
Boston brown bread. See Breads.												
Bouillon cubes, 1 cube (⅝ in., 4 gm.)	2	(.2)	.1	(0.)	—	—	—	—	—	.07	1.0	0
Brains, all kinds, raw, 3 ounces	106	8.8	7.3	.7	14	281	3.1	0	.20	.22	3.8	15

Food												
Bran (breakfast cereal, almost wholly bran), 1 cup (60 gm.).	145	7.2	2.0	44.5	56	787	6.2	(0)	.22	.23	11.5	(0)
Bran flakes (40 pct. bran), 1 cup (40 gm.)	117	4.3	.8	31.5	24	249	2.0	(0)	.19	.09	3.5	(0)
Bran, raisin, 1 cup (50 gm.)	149	4.5	.9	39.3	30	270	2.4	(0)	.19	.09	3.5	(0)
Brazil nuts:												
Shelled, 1 cup (32 kernels, 140 gm.)	905	20.2	92.3	15.4	260	970	4.8	Trace	1.21	—	—	—
In shell, 1 cup (14 nuts, 122 gm.)	394	8.8	40.2	6.7	113	423	2.1	Trace	.53	—	—	—
***Breads:**												
Boston brown bread made with de-germed cornmeal, 1 slice (3 by ¾ in., 48 gm.):												
Unenriched	105	2.3	1.0	22.1	89	76	1.2	70	.04	.06	.7	(0)
Enriched	105	2.3	1.0	22.1	89	76	1.4	70	.06	.08	.9	(0)
Cracked-wheat bread, 1 slice (½ in. thick, 23 gm.), made with:												
Unenriched flour	60	2.0	.5	11.8	19	29	.2	0	.03	.02	.3	(0)
Toasted, 1 slice	60	2.0	.5	11.8	19	29	.2	0	.02	.02	.3	(0)
Enriched flour	60	2.0	.5	11.8	19	29	.5	0	.06	.04	.6	(0)
Toasted, 1 slice	60	2.0	.5	11.8	19	29	.5	0	.05	.04	.6	(0)
French or Vienna breads, 1 pound:												
Unenriched	1,225	36.8	12.3	236.1	109	322	3.2	0	.21	.28	4.2	(0)
Enriched[1]	1,225	36.8	12.3	236.1	109	322	8.0	0	1.1	.7	10.0	(0)
Italian bread, 1 pound:												
Unenriched	1,195	39.5	3.6	243.8	59	350	3.2	0	.23	.30	4.5	(0)
Enriched[1]	1,195	39.5	3.6	243.8	59	350	8.0	0	1.1	.7	10.0	(0)
Raisin bread, 1 slice (½ in. thick, 23 gm.):												
Unenriched	65	1.6	.7	13.3	18	24	.3	Trace	.02	.02	.2	(0)
Toasted, 1 slice	65	1.6	.7	13.3	18	24	.3	Trace	.01	.02	.2	(0)
Enriched[1]	65	1.6	.7	13.3	18	24	.4	Trace	.06	.04	.5	(0)
Toasted, 1 slice	65	1.6	.7	13.3	18	24	.4	Trace	.04	.04	.5	(0)
Rye bread, American (⅓ rye, ⅔ clear flour), 1 slice (½ in. thick, 23 gm.).	57	2.1	.3	12.1	17	34	.4	0	.04	.02	.4	(0)
White bread, unenriched, 1 slice (½ in. thick, 23 gm.):												
2 percent nonfat milk solids	64	1.9	.8	12.0	15	19	.1	0	.01	.02	.2	(0)
4 percent nonfat milk solids[2]	63	2.0	.7	11.9	18	21	.1	0	.01	.02	.2	(0)
Toasted, 1 slice	63	2.0	.7	11.9	18	21	.1	0	.01	.02	.2	(0)
6 percent nonfat milk solids	63	2.0	.7	12.0	21	23	.1	0	.01	.03	.2	(0)

[1] Iron, thiamine, riboflavin, and niacin are based on the minimum level of enrichment specified in the standards of identity of breads proposed by the Federal Security Agency and published in the Federal Register, August 3, 1943.

[2] When the amount of nonfat milk solids in commercial bread is unknown, use bread with 4 percent nonfat milk solids, for unenriched bread and for enriched.

Foods, The Composition of (Continued)

Food, description, and approximate measure	Food energy	Protein	Fat	Total carbohydrate	Calcium	Phosphorus	Iron	Vitamin A value	Thiamine	Riboflavin	Niacin	Ascorbic acid
	Cal.	Gm.	Gm.	Gm.	Mg.	Mg.	Mg.	I.U.	Mg.	Mg.	Mg.	Mg.
Breads: (Continued)												
White bread, enriched, 1 slice (½ in. thick, 23 gm.):												
2 percent nonfat milk solids	64	1.9	.8	12.0	15	19	.4[1]	0	.06[1]	.04[1]	.5[1]	(0)
4 percent nonfat milk solids[2]	63	2.0	.7	11.9	18	21	.4[1]	0	.06[1]	.04[1]	.5[1]	(0)
Toasted, 1 slice	63	2.0	.7	11.9	18	21	.4	0	.04	.04	.5	(0)
6 percent nonfat milk solids	63	2.0	.7	12.0	21	23	.4[1]	0	.06[1]	.04[1]	.5[1]	(0)
Whole-wheat bread, 1 slice (½ in. thick, 23 gm.)	55	2.1	.6	11.3	22	60	.5	0	.07	.03	.7	(0)
Toasted, 1 slice	55	2.1	.6	11.3	22	60	.5	0	.05	.03	.7	(0)
See also Biscuits, Corn bread, Muffins, Rolls.												
Bread crumbs, dry, grated, 1 cup (88 gm.).	339	10.5	4.0	63.8	98	114	2.3	0	.24	.19	2.7	(0)
Breakfast foods, mixed cereals:												
Corn and soy grits, ready-to-eat (added thiamine and niacin) 1 cup (50 gm.).	177	9.0	.2	37.6	33	91	3.2	(0)	.34	.06	1.0	(0)
Wheat and malted barley, ready-to-eat (added thiamine and niacin), 1 cup (105 gm.).	408	11.6	.6	86.9	49	346	3.7	(0)	.56	.18	4.9	(0)
Breakfast foods. See individual grain, as Corn, Oatmeal, etc.												
Broccoli:												
Cooked, flower stalks:												
1 pound	133	15.0	.9	25.0	590	345	5.9	15,440	.32	.68	3.6	336
1 cup (150 gm.)	44	5.0	.3	8.2	195	114	2.0	5,100	.10	.22	1.2	111
Brown betty. See Apple betty.												
Brussels sprouts, cooked:												
1 pound	212	20.0	2.3	40.4	154	354	5.9	1,820	.18	.54	2.3	213
1 cup (130 gm.)	60	5.7	.6	11.6	44	101	1.7	520	.05	.16	.6	61

[1] Iron, thiamine, riboflavin, and niacin are based on the minimum level of enrichment specified in the standards of identity of breads proposed by the Federal Security Agency and published in the Federal Register, August 3, 1943.

[2] When the amount of nonfat milk solids in commercial bread is unknown, use bread with 4 percent nonfat milk solids, for unenriched bread and for enriched.

Buckwheat flour:												
Dark, 1 cup sifted (98 gm.)	340	11.5	2.4	70.6	32	340	2.7	(0)	.56	.15	2.8	(0)
Light, 1 cup sifted (98 gm.)	342	6.3	1.2	77.9	11	86	1.0	(0)	.08	(.04)	(.4)	(0)
Buckwheat pancake mix. See Pancake mix.												
Butter:												
1 cup (224 gm.)	1,604	1.3	181.4	.9	45	36	.0	7,390[1]	Trace	.02	.2	(0)
1 tablespoon (14 gm.)	100	.1	11.3	.1	3	2	.0	460[1]	Trace	Trace	Trace	(0)
1 pat or square (64 per lb., 7 gm. each)	50	.0	5.7	.0	1	1	.0	230[1]	Trace	Trace	Trace	(0)
Buttermilk, cultured (made from skim milk):												
1 quart (976 gm.)	348	34.2	1.0	49.8	(1,152)	908	.7	40	.35	1.74	1.1	13
1 cup (244 gm.)	86	8.5	.2	12.4	(288)	227	.2	10	.09	.43	.3	3
Cabbage:												
Raw, E.P.:												
1 pound, trimmed	109	6.4	.9	24.1	209	141	2.3	370	.27	.24	1.4	226
1 wedge (3½ by 4½ in., 100 gm.).	24	1.4	.2	5.3	46	31	.5	80	.06	.05	.3	50
1 cup, shredded finely (100 gm.)	24	1.4	.2	5.3	46	31	.5	80	.06	.05	.3	50
Cooked (small amount of water, short time):												
1 pound	109	6.4	.9	24.1	209	141	2.3	410	.23	.23	1.4	141
1 cup (170 gm.)	40	2.4	.3	9.0	78	53	.8	150	.08	.08	.5	53
Cooked (large amount of water, long time):												
1 pound	109	6.4	.9	24.1	209	141	2.3	410	.14	.14	.9	86
1 cup (170 gm.)	40	2.4	.3	9.0	78	53	.8	150	.05	.05	.3	32
Cabbage salad. See Coleslaw.												
Cabbage, celery or Chinese:												
Raw; 1 cup, leaves and stem (1-in. pieces, 100 gm.).	14	1.2	.3	2.4	43	41	.9	260	.03	.04	.4	31
Cooked:												
1 pound	64	5.4	1.4	10.9	195	186	4.1	1,180	.09	.14	1.4	100
1 cup (190 gm.)	27	2.3	.6	4.6	82	78	1.7	490	.04	.06	.6	42
*Cakes:												
Angel food: 2-inch sector (1/12 of 8 in. diam., 40 gm.)	108	3.4	.1	23.5	2	10	.1	0	Trace	.05	.1	(0)
Foundation: 1 square (3 by 2 by 1¾ in., 65 gm.)	228	3.8	7.6	36.3	82	78	.3	100[2]	.02	.05	.2	(0)

[1] Year-round average.

[2] If the fat used in the recipe is butter or fortified margarine, the vitamin A value would be 350 I.U. per square; 390 I.U. per 3-inch sector, iced; and 520 I.U. per 2-inch sector, iced.

Foods, The Composition of (Continued)

Food, description, and approximate measure	Food energy	Protein	Fat	Total carbohydrate	Calcium	Phosphorus	Iron	Vitamin A value	Thiamine	Riboflavin	Niacin	Ascorbic acid
	Cal.	Gm.	Gm.	Gm.	Mg.	Mg.	Mg.	I.U.	Mg.	Mg.	Mg.	Mg.
Cakes: (Continued)												
Foundation, plain icing:												
3-inch sector of layer cake (1/6 of 6 in. diam., 90 gm.).	308	4.5	8.4	54.4	91	86	.4	110[1]	.02	.06	.2	(0)
2-inch sector of layer cake (1/16 of 10 in. diam., 120 gm.).	410	6.0	11.2	72.5	121	115	.5	150[1]	.03	.08	.2	(0)
Foundation, fudge icing:												
3-inch sector of layer cake (1/6 of 6 in. diam., 90 gm.).	314	4.0	10.4	52.6	88	91	.4	110[1]	.02	.07	.2	(0)
2-inch sector of layer cake (1/16 of 10 in. diam., 120 gm.).	419	5.3	13.8	70.2	118	121	.5	140[1]	.03	.10	.3	(0)
Fruit, dark:												
1 piece (2 by 2 by 1/2 in., 30 gm.) ..	106	1.6	4.1	16.8	29	38	.8	50[2]	.04	.04	.3	(0)
Plain cake and cupcakes:												
1 square (3 by 2 by 1 1/2 in., 55 gm.).	180	3.5	4.5	31.4	85	75	.2	70[3]	.02	.05	.2	(0)
1 cupcake (2 3/4 in. diam., 40 gm.) ..	131	2.6	3.3	22.8	62	55	.2	50[3]	.01	.03	.1	(0)
1 cupcake (1 3/4 in. diam.) or 1 square (2 by 2 by 1 in., 25 gm.).	81	1.6	2.0	14.2	39	34	.1	30[3]	.01	.02	.1	(0)
Plain cake and cupcakes, iced:												
3-inch sector of layer cake (1/6 of 6 in. diam., 75 gm.).	241	3.9	4.6	46.6	88	78	.3	70[3]	.02	.05	.2	(0)
2-inch sector of layer cake (1/16 of 10 in. diam., 100 gm.).	322	5.2	6.2	62.1	117	104	.4	90[3]	.02	.07	.2	(0)
1 cupcake (2 3/4 in. diam., 50 gm.) ..	161	2.6	3.1	31.0	58	52	.2	50[3]	.01	.04	.1	(0)
1 cupcake (1 3/4 in. diam.) or 1 square (2 by 2 by 1 in., 40 gm.).	129	2.1	2.5	24.8	47	42	.2	40[3]	.01	.03	.1	(0)
Pound:												
1 slice (2 3/4 by 3 by 5/8 in., 30 gm.).	130	2.1	7.0	14.8	16	31	.5	100[4]	.04	.05	.3	(0)
Rich:												
1 square (3 by 2 by 2 in., 75 gm.) ..	294	3.8	13.3	40.6	79	85	.4	160[5]	.02	.06	.2	(0)

[1] If the fat used in the recipe is butter or fortified margarine, the vitamin A value would be 350 I.U. per square; 390 I.U. per 3-inch sector, iced; and 520 I.U. per 2-inch sector, iced.

[2] If the fat used in the recipe is butter or fortified margarine, the vitamin A value would be 120 I.U.

[3] If the fat used in the recipe is butter or fortified margarine, the vitamin A value would be 200 I.U. per large square; 150 I.U. per cupcake; 90 I.U. per small cupcake or square; 210 I.U. per 3-inch sector, iced; 280 I.U. per 2-inch sector, iced; 140 I.U. per cupcake, iced; and 110 I.U. per small cupcake or square, iced.

[4] If the fat used in the recipe is butter or fortified margarine, the vitamin A value would be 300 I.U.

[5] If the fat used in the recipe is butter or fortified margarine, the vitamin A value would be 620 I.U. square.

Rich, plain icing:

Food												
3-inch sector of layer cake (1/6 of 6 in. diam., 100 gm.).	378	4.4	14.7	58.2	88	94	.5	170[1]	.02	.07	.2	(0)
2-inch sector of layer cake (1/16 of 10 in. diam., 130 gm.).	491	5.7	19.1	75.7	114	122	.6	220[1]	.03	.10	.2	(0)
Sponge: 2-inch sector (1/12 of 8 in. diam., 40 gm.).	117	3.2	2.0	21.8	11	44	.6	210	.02	.06	.1	(0)
Candy:												
Candied or glace peel:												
Citron, 1 ounce	89	.1	.1	22.7	24	7	.2	—	—	—	—	—
Ginger root, crystallized, 1 ounce	97	.1	.1	24.7	—	—	—	—	—	—	—	—
Lemon, orange, or grapefruit peel, 1 ounce.	90	.1	.1	22.9	—	—	—	—	—	—	—	—
*Butterscotch, 1 ounce	116	0.	2.5	24.3	6	2	.5	(0)	(0)	Trace	Trace	(0)
*Caramels, 1 ounce	118	.8	3.3	22.0	36	26	.7	50	.01	.04	Trace	Trace
Chocolate, sweetened, milk, 1 ounce	143	(2.)	9.5	15.8	61	80	.6	40	.03	.11	.2	(0)
Chocolate, sweetened, milk, with almonds, 1 ounce.	151	(2.3)	10.9	14.2	58	71	.8	40	.04	.14	(.3)	(0)
Chocolate creams, 1 ounce	110	1.1	4.0	20.0	—	—	—	—	—	—	—	0
Fondant, 1 ounce	101	0.	0.	26.0	(0)	(0)	(0)	(0)	(0)	(0)	(0)	(0)
*Fudge, plain, 1 ounce	116	.5	3.2	23.0	14[2]	19	.1	60	Trace	.02	Trace	Trace
Hard, 1 ounce	108	0.	0.	28.0	(0)	(0)	(0)	(0)	(0)	(0)	(0)	(0)
Marshmallows, 1 ounce	92	.9	0.	23.0	(0)	(0)	(0)	(0)	(0)	(0)	(0)	(0)
*Peanut brittle, 1 ounce	125	2.4	4.4	20.6	11	35	.6	10	.03	.01	1.4	(0)
Cantaloupes, raw:												
1/2 melon (5 in. diam., 385 gm.); refuse, rind and cavity contents, 53 percent.	37	1.1	.4	8.3	31	29	.7	6,190[3]	.09	.07	.9	59
1 cup diced (145 gm.)	30	.9	.3	6.7	25	23	.6	4,960[3]	.07	.05	.7	47
Carrots:												
Raw:												
1 carrot (5½ by 1 in., or 25 thin strips, 50 gm.).	21	.6	.2	4.6	20	18	.4	6,000	.03	.03	.3	3
1 cup grated (110 gm.).	45	1.3	.3	10.2	43	41	.9	13,200	.06	.06	.7	7
Cooked, 1 cup diced (145 gm.).	44	.9	.7	9.3	38	38	.9	18,130	.07	.07	.7	6
Canned:												
Solids and liquid, 1 cup diced (246 gm.).	69	1.2	1.0	15.0	54	59	1.5	29,520	.06	.05	.8	6

[1] If the fat used in the recipe is butter or fortified margarine, the vitamin A value would be 690 I.U. per 3-inch sector; and 900 I.U. per 2-inch sector, iced.

[2] If the calcium contributed by chocolate is considered unavailable, the value would be 11 mg. per ounce.

[3] Vitamin A based on deeply colored varieties.

[237]

Foods, The Composition of (Continued)

Food, description, and approximate measure	Food energy Cal.	Protein Gm.	Fat Gm.	Total carbohydrate Gm.	Calcium Mg.	Phosphorus Mg.	Iron Mg.	Vitamin A value I.U.	Thiamine Mg.	Riboflavin Mg.	Niacin Mg.	Ascorbic acid Mg.
Carrots: (Continued)												
Drained solids:												
1 pound	138	2.7	2.3	29.1	118	118	2.7	79,750	.10	.10	1.4	12
1 cup diced (145 gm.)	44	.9	.7	9.3	38	38	.9	25,470	.03	.03	.4	4
Strained (infant food), 1 ounce	7	.3	.0	1.7	7	7	.2	2,530	.01	.01	.1	1
Cashew nuts, roasted or cooked, 1 ounce	164	5.2	13.7	7.7	13	121	1.4	—	.18	.05	.6	—
Catsup, tomato. See Tomato catsup.												
Cauliflower:												
Raw, 1 cup flower buds (100 gm.)	25	2.4	.2	4.9	22	72	1.1	90	.11	.10	.6	69
Cooked:												
1 pound	113	10.9	.9	22.2	100	327	5.0	410	.27	.36	2.3	127
1 cup (120 gm.)	30	2.9	.2	5.9	26	86	1.3	108	.07	.10	.6	34
Celery, bleached:												
Raw:												
3 small inner stalks (5 in. long, ¾ in. wide, 50 gm.).	9	.6	.1	1.8	25	20	.2	0	.03	.02	.2	4
1 large outer stalk (8 in. long, 1 in. wide, 1½ in. at root end, 40 gm.).	7	.5	.1	1.5	20	16	.2	0	.02	.02	.2	3
1 cup diced (100 gm.)	18	1.3	.2	3.7	50	40	.5	0	.05	.04	.4	7
Cooked:												
1 pound	82	5.9	.9	16.8	227	182	2.3	0	.18	.14	1.4	23
1 cup diced (130 gm.)	24	1.7	.3	4.8	65	52	.6	0	.05	.04	.4	6
Cereal foods (infant food); dry, precooked, 1 ounce.	103	4.0	.7	20.8	185	194	9.6	(0)	.34	.13	1.4[1]	(0)
See also Oatmeal (infant food).												
Chard:												
Leaves and stalks, cooked:												
1 pound	94	6.4	.9	20.0	477[2]	163	11.4	14,120	.18	.27	1.8	77
1 cup (145 gm.)	30	2.0	.3	6.4	152[2]	52	3.6	4,510	.06	.09	.6	25

[1] Based on products ranging from 0.7 to 1.9 mg. per ounce. The niacin value of some products is as high as 6.5 mg.

[2] Calcium may not be available because of presence of oxalic acid.

Food	gm.											
Leaves, cooked:												
1 pound	122	11.8	1.8	21.8	477[1]	163	11.4	43,990	.18	.73	1.4	77
1 cup (175 gm.)	47	4.6	.7	8.4	184[1]	63	4.4	16,960	.07	.28	.5	30
Cheese:												
Blue mold, domestic type, 1 ounce	104	6.1	8.6	.6	89	96	(.1)	(350)	.01	.17	.1	(0)
Camembert, 1 ounce	85	5.0	7.0	.5	30	52	.1	(290)	.01	.21	.3	(0)
Cheddar:												
1 cup, grated (112 gm.)	446	28.0	36.1	2.4	812	554	1.1	1,570	.03	.47	Trace	(0)
1 ounce (1 in. cube)	113	7.1	9.1	.6	206	140	.3	400	.01	.12	Trace	(0)
Cheddar, processed, 1 ounce	105	6.6	8.5	.6	191	223[2]	.3	(370)	Trace	.12	(Trace)	(0)
Cheese foods, cheddar, 1 ounce	92	5.8	6.8	2.0	162	226	.2	(303)	(.01)	.16	Trace	(0)
Cottage, from skim milk:												
1 cup (225 gm.)	215	43.9	1.1	4.5	216	425	.7	(50)	.04	.69	(.2)	(0)
1 ounce	27	5.5	.1	.6	27	54	.1	(10)	.01	.09	(Trace)	(0)
Cream cheese:												
1 ounce	106	2.6	10.5	.6	19	27	.1	(410)	(Trace)	.06	Trace	(0)
1 tablespoon (15 gm.)	56	1.4	5.6	.3	10	15	.0	(220)	(Trace)	.03	Trace	(0)
Limburger, 1 ounce	97	6.0	7.9	.6	167	111	.2	360	.02	.14	Trace	(0)
Parmesan, 1 ounce	112	10.2	7.4	.8	329	233	.1	(300)	.01	.21	.1	(0)
Swiss, 1 ounce	105	7.8	7.9	.5	262	160	.3	410	Trace	(.11)	(Trace)	(0)
Swiss, processed, 1 ounce	101	7.5	7.6	.5	251	246[3]	.3	390	Trace	.11	Trace	(0)
Cherries, sour, sweet, and hybrid, raw:												
1 cup; refuse, pits, 6 percent (114 gm.)	65	1.2	.5	15.8	19	21	.4	710	.05	.06	.4	9
1 cup, pitted (154 gm.)	94	1.7	.8	22.8	28	31	.6	960	.08	.09	.6	13
Cherries, red, sour, pitted, canned, 1 cup (254 gm.)	122	2.0	.8	30.2	28	30	(.8)	1,840	.07	.04	.4	14
Chicken:[4]												
Raw:												
Broilers, ½ bird (8 oz., bone out)	332	44.4	15.8	0.	31	440	3.3	(0)	.18	.36	22.4	(0)
Roasters (4 oz., bone out)	227	22.9	14.3	0.	16	227	1.7	(0)	.09	.18	9.1	(0)
Hens, stewing chickens (4 oz., bone out)	342	20.4	28.3	0.	16	227	1.7	(0)	.09	.18	9.1	(0)
Fryers:												
Cut-up pieces (commercial cut):												
1 breast (8 oz., bone out)	210	47.0	1.0	0.	28	428	2.2	(0)	.13	.18	21.1	(0)
1 leg (5 oz., bone out)	159	29.1	3.8	0.	21	266	2.6	(0)	.14	.34	8.0	(0)
Canned, boned, 3 ounces	169	25.3	6.8	0.	12	126	1.5	(0)	.03	.14	5.4	(0)

[1] Calcium may not be available because of presence of oxalic acid.
[2] 130 mg. if the added emulsifying agent does not contain phosphorus.
[3] 153 mg. if the added emulsifying agent does not contain phosphorus.
[4] Vitamin values based on muscle meat only.

Foods, The Composition of (Continued)

Food, description, and approximate measure	Food energy Cal.	Protein Gm.	Fat Gm.	Total carbohydrate Gm.	Calcium Mg.	Phosphorus Mg.	Iron Mg.	Vitamin A value I.U.	Thiamine Mg.	Riboflavin Mg.	Niacin Mg.	Ascorbic acid Mg.
Chicken broth. See Soups, canned, bouillon, broth, and consommé.												
Chicken soup. See Soups, canned, chicken.												
Chick-peas or garbanzos, dry, whole seed: Raw, 1 cup (210 gm.)	755	43.7	9.9	127.9	193	788	14.9	Trace	1.16	.37	3.2	(4)
Chili con carne (without beans), canned,[2] 1/3 cup (85 gm.).	170	8.8	12.6	4.9	32	129	1.2	130	.01	.10	1.9	—
Chili sauce:												
1 cup (273 gm.)	268	7.6	1.1	64.7	(33)	(49)	(2.2)	(5,130)	(.25)	(.19)	(6.1)	(31)
1 tablespoon (17 gm.)	17	.5	.1	4.0	(2)	(3)	(.1)	(320)	(.02)	(.01)	(.4)	(2)
Chocolate: Bitter or unsweetened:												
1 ounce	142	(1.6)	15.0	8.3[3]	28[1]	126	1.2	20	.01	.06	.3	(0)
1 cup grated (132 gm.)	661	(7.3)	69.8	38.5[3]	129[1]	589	5.8	80	.06	.32	1.3	(0)
Sweetened: Plain, 1 ounce	133	(.6)	8.4	17.8	(18)[1]	(81)	.8	(10)	(.01)	(.04)	(.2)	(0)
Milk. See Candy.												
Milk, with almonds. See Candy.												
*Chocolate beverage, made with milk, 1 cup (250 gm.).	239	8.2	12.5	26.2	260	230	.5	350	.08	.40	.3	2
Chocolate syrup, 1 tablespoon (20 gm.)	42	(.2)	.2	11.3	(3)[1]	(17)	(.3)	—	—	—	.3	—
Cider. See Apple juice.												
Citron. See Candy.												

[1] Calcium may not be available because of presence of oxalic acid.

[2] Not less than 60 percent meat, not more than 8 percent cereals, seasonings.

[3] Approximately one-third of this total amount of carbohydrate calculated by difference is starch and sugar. The remaining portion is made up of materials thought to be utilized only poorly if at all by the body.

Food											
Clams, long and round:											
Raw, meat only, 4 ounces	92	14.5	1.6	3.9	(109)	(158)	(7.9)	120	.11	.20	(1.8)	—
Canned, solids and liquid, 3 ounces	44	6.7	.9	1.8	74	106	5.4	(70)	(.04)	.08	.9	—
Cocoa, breakfast, plain, dry powder:											
1 cup, stirred before measuring (112 gm.)	329	(9.0)	26.7	54.8[1]	140[2]	797	13.0	(30)	.14	.43	2.6	(0)
1 ounce	83	(2.3)	6.7	13.9[1]	35[2]	202	3.3	(10).	.03	.11	.7	(0)
1 tablespoon (7 gm.)	21	(.6)	1.7	3.4[1]	9[2]	50	.8	(Trace)	.01	.03	.2	(0)
*Cocoa beverage, made with all milk, 1 cup (250 gm.)	236	9.5	11.5	27.2	298	285	1.0	400	.10	.46	.5	3
Coconut:											
Fresh, meat:											
1 cup shredded (97 gm.)	349	3.3	33.7	13.6	20	95	1.9	0	.09	.01	.2	2
1 piece (2 by 2 by ½ in., 45 gm.)	161	1.5	15.6	6.3	9	44	.9	0	.04	Trace	.1	1
Dried, shredded (sweetened):											
1 cup (62 gm.)	344	2.2	24.2	33.0	27	118	2.2	0	Trace	Trace	Trace	(0)
4-ounce package	629	4.1	44.2	60.1	49	216	4.1	0	Trace	Trace	Trace	(0)
Milk only, 1 cup (240 gm.)	60	.7	1.0	12.0	58	70	.2	0	Trace	Trace	.2	4
Cod:											
Raw, 4 ounces E.P.	84	18.7	.5	0.	11	220	.5	0	.07	.10	2.5	2
Dried, 1 ounce	106	23.2	.8	0.	(14)	253	1.0	0	.02	.13	3.1	(0)
*Coleslaw, 1 cup (120 gm.)	102	1.6	7.3	9.2	47	32	.5	80	.06	.05	.3	50
Collards, cooked:											
Boiled in small or moderate amount of water until tender:											
1 pound	182	17.7	2.7	32.7	1,130	263	7.3	34,640	.36	1.09	7.7	200
1 cup (190 gm.)	76	7.4	1.1	13.7	473	110	3.0	14,500	.15	.46	3.2	84
Boiled in large amount of water a long time:											
1 pound	182	17.7	2.7	32.7	1,130	263	7.3	34,640	.32	.95	6.4	150
1 cup (190 gm.)	76	7.4	1.1	13.7	473	110	3.0	14,500	.13	.40	2.7	63
Condensed milk. See Milk, cow.											
Cookies, plain and assorted:											
1 cooky (3 in. diam., ½ in. thick, 25 gm.)	109	1.5	3.2	18.8	6	16	.2	(0)	.01	.01	.1	(0)
2 wafers (2⅛ in. diam., 10 gm.)	44	.6	1.3	7.5	2	6	.1	(0)	Trace	Trace	Trace	(0)

[1] Approximately one-third of this total amount of carbohydrate calculated by difference is starch and sugar. The remaining portion is made up of materials thought to be utilized only poorly if at all by the body.

[2] Calcium may not be available because of presence of oxalic acid.

Foods, The Composition of (Continued)

Food, description, and approximate measure	Food energy	Protein	Fat	Total carbohydrate	Calcium	Phosphorus	Iron	Vitamin A value	Thiamine	Riboflavin	Niacin	Ascorbic acid
	Cal.	Gm.	Gm.	Gm.	Mg.	Mg.	Mg.	I.U.	Mg.	Mg.	Mg.	Mg.
Cooking oil. See Oils, salad or cooking.												
Corn, sweet, white or yellow:												
Cooked:												
1 pound kernels	384	12.3	3.2	91.7	23	236	2.7	1,770[1]	.50	.45	6.4	36
1 cup kernels (165 gm.)	140	4.5	1.2	33.3	8	86	1.0	640[1]	.18	.16	2.3	13
1 ear (5 in. long, 1¾ in. diam., 140 gm.)	84	2.7	.7	20.0	5	51	.6	390[1]	.11	.10	1.4	8
Canned:												
Solids and liquid, 1 cup (256 gm.)	170	5.1	1.3	41.2	10	131	1.3	520[1]	.07	.13	2.4	14
Drained solids:												
1 pound	384	12.3	3.2	91.7	23	236	2.7	1,060[1]	.15	.29	4.1	24
1 cup (165 gm.)	140	4.5	1.2	33.3	8	86	1.0	380[1]	.06	.10	1.5	9
*Corn bread or muffins made with:												
Whole ground cornmeal, 1 muffin (2¾ in. diam., 48 gm.)	103	3.5	2.7	16.7	68	104	.8	60[2]	.07	.09	.4	(0)
Enriched, degermed cornmeal, 1 muffin (2¾ in. diam., 48 gm.)	106	3.2	2.3	17.6	67	74	.9	60[3]	.08	.11	.6	(0)
Corn flakes, 1 cup (25 gm.)	96	2.0	.1	21.2	3	14	.3	(0)	.01	.02	.4	(0)
Corn flakes (added thiamine, niacin, and iron), 1 cup (25 gm.)	96	2.0	.1	21.2	3	14	0.6	(0)	.10	.02	.6	(0)
Corn flour, 1 cup sifted (110 gm.)	406	8.6	2.9	84.5	7	(196)	2.0	370[4]	.22	.06	(1.6)	(0)
Corn grits, degermed:												
Unenriched:												
Dry, 1 cup (160 gm.)	579	13.9	1.3	125.0	6	117	1.6	480[5]	.21	.06	1.8	(0)
*Cooked:												

[1] Vitamin A based on yellow corn; white corn contains only a trace.
[2] Based on recipe using white cornmeal; if yellow cornmeal is used, vitamin A value is 160 I.U.
[3] Based on recipe using white cornmeal; if yellow cornmeal is used, vitamin A value is 120 I.U.
[4] Vitamin A based on yellow corn flour; white corn flour contains only a trace.
[5] Vitamin A based on yellow corn grits; white corn grits contain only a trace.

1 pound	230	5.4	.5	49.9	5	45	.5	190[1]	.07	.03	.8	(0)
1 cup (242 gm.)	122	2.9	.2	26.6	2	24	.2	100[1]	.04	.01	.4	(0)
Enriched:												
Dry, 1 cup (160 gm.)	579	13.9	1.3	125.0	6	117	4.6[2]	480[1]	.71[2]	.42[2]	5.6[2]	(0)
*Cooked:												
1 pound	230	5.4	.5	49.9	5	45	1.4	190[1]	.20	.15	1.9	(0)
1 cup (242 gm.)	122	2.9	.2	26.6	2	24	.7	100[1]	.11	.08	1.0	(0)
Cornmeal, white or yellow:												
Whole ground, dry:												
Unbolted, 1 cup (118 gm.) ...	419	10.9	4.6	87.0	12	302	2.8	600[3]	.45	.13	2.4	(0)
Bolted, 1 cup (127 gm.) ...	459	11.4	4.3	94.6	8	(226)	2.3	570[3]	.38	.10	2.4	(0)
Degermed, unenriched:												
Dry, 1 cup (145 gm.)	527	11.5	1.7	113.7	9	144	1.6	430[3]	.20	.07	1.5	(0)
*Cooked:												
1 pound	227	5.0	.9	48.6	5	64	.9	190[3]	.08	.03	.6	(0)
1 cup (238 gm.)	119	2.6	.5	25.5	2	33	.5	100[3]	.04	.02	.3	(0)
Degermed, enriched:												
Dry, 1 cup (145 gm.)	527	11.5	1.7	113.7	9	144	4.2[3]	430[3]	.64[2]	.38[2]	5.1[2]	(0)
*Cooked:												
1 pound	227	5.0	.9	48.6	5	64	1.8	190[3]	.26	.16	2.2	(0)
1 cup (238 gm.)	119	2.6	.5	25.5	2	33	1.0	100[3]	.14	.09	1.1	(0)
Self-rising, unenriched, dry, 1 cup (118 gm.).	401	10.3	4.4	83.5	309	748	2.7	570[3]	.42	.12	2.2	(0)
Self-rising, enriched, dry, 1 cup (118 gm.).	401	10.3	4.4	83.5	309	748	3.4[3]	570[3]	.52[2]	.31[2]	4.2[2]	(0)

Corn oil. See Oils, salad or cooking.

Corn syrup. See Syrup, table blends.

Corn and soy grits. See Breakfast foods, mixed cereals.

Cornstarch. See Starch.

Cornstarch pudding. See Blancmange.

Cottonseed oil. See Oils, salad or cooking.

[1] Vitamin A based on yellow corn grits; white corn grits contain only a trace.
[2] Iron, thiamine, riboflavin, and niacin are based on the minimum level of enrichment specified in standards of identity promulgated under the Food, Drug, and Cosmetic Act.
[3] Vitamin A based on yellow cornmeal; white cornmeal contains only a trace.

Foods, The Composition of (Continued)

Food, description, and approximate measure	Food energy	Protein	Fat	Total carbo-hydrate	Cal-cium	Phos-phorus	Iron	Vitamin A value	Thia-mine	Ribo-flavin	Nia-cin	Ascor-bic acid
	Cal.	Gm.	Gm.	Gm.	Mg.	Mg.	Mg.	I.U.	Mg.	Mg.	Mg.	Mg.
Cowpeas:												
Immature seed, cooked:												
1 pound	428	32.2	2.7	72.2	168	826	11.4	1,770	1.32	.36	3.6	91
1 cup (160 gm.)	151	11.4	1.0	25.4	59	291	4.0	620	.46	.13	1.3	32
Mature seeds, dry, 1 cup (200 gm.)	684	45.8	2.8	123.2	154	902	13.0	60	1.84	.32	4.5	3
Crabs, Atlantic and Pacific, hard-shell:												
Canned or cooked, meat only, 3 ounces	89	14.4	2.5	1.1	38	155	.8	—	(.04)	(.05)	(2.1)	—
Crackers:												
Graham, 4 small or 2 medium (14 gm.)	55	1.1	1.4	10.4	3	28	.3	(0)	.04	.02	.2	(0)
Saltines, 2 crackers (2 in. square, 8 gm.).	34	.7	.9	5.7	2	7	.1	(0)	Trace	Trace	.1	(0)
Soda, plain:												
2 crackers (2½ in. square, 11 gm.).	47	1.1	1.1	8.0	2	11	.1	(0)	.01	.01	.1	(0)
1 cup oyster crackers, 1 ounce	119	2.7	2.7	20.6	6	27	.3	(0)	.02	.01	.3	(0)
10 oyster crackers or 1 tablespoon cracker meal (10 gm.).	43	1.0	1.0	7.3	2	10	.1	(0)	.01	Trace	.1	(0)
Cracker meal. See Crackers, soda.												
Cranberries, raw, 1 cup (113 gm.)	54	.5	.8	12.8	16	12	.7	50	(.03)	(.02)	.1	13
Cranberry sauce, sweetened, canned, or cooked, 1 cup (277 gm.)	549	.3	.8	142.4	(22)	(19)	(.8)	(80)	(.06)	(.06)	(.3)	5
Cream:												
Light, table, or coffee:												
½ pint (240 gm.)	489	7.0	48.0	9.6	233	185	.1	1,980	.07	.34	.2	3
1 tablespoon (15 gm.)	30	.4	3.0	.6	15	12	.0	120	Trace	.02	Trace	Trace
Heavy or whipping:												
½ pint (approx. 1 pt. whipped, 236 gm.).	779	5.4	82.6	7.6	184	144	.1	3,390	.06	.26	.1	1
1 tablespoon (15 gm.)	49	.3	5.2	.5	12	9	.0	220	Trace	.02	Trace	Trace
Cress, garden:												
Raw, 1 pound E.P.	186	19.1	6.4	24.1	958	(173)	(13.2)	13,470	.49	.75	4.5	396

Cooked:

Boiled in small or moderate amount of water until tender:												
1 pound	186	19.1	6.4	24.1	958	(173)	(13.2)	14,980	.32	.68	3.6	177
1 cup (180 gm.)	73	7.6	2.5	9.5	380	(68)	(5.2)	5,940	.13	.27	1.4	70
Boiled in large amount of water a long time:												
1 pound	186	19.1	6.4	24.1	958	(173)	(13.2)	14,980	.27	.59	3.2	132
1 cup (180 gm.)	73	7.6	2.5	9.5	380	(68)	(5.2)	5,940	.11	.23	1.3	52
Cress, water, leaves and stems, raw, 1 pound	84	7.7	1.4	15.0	885	209	9.1	21,450	.37	.71	3.6	350
Croaker, raw, 4 ounces E.P.	109	20.2	2.5	0.	—	—	—	—	.18	.07	2.0	—
Cucumbers, raw:												
1 cucumber (7½ by about 2 in., 290 gm.)	25	1.4	.2	5.5	20	43	.6	0	.07	.09	.4	17
6 slices, peeled (⅛ in. thick, center section, 50 gm.)	6	.4	.0	1.4	5	10	.2[1]	0[1]	.02	.02	.1	4
Cucumber pickles. See Pickles.												
Currants, red, raw, 1 cup (110 gm.)	60	1.3	2	15.0	40	36	1.0	130	.04	—	—	40
*Custard, baked:												
1 pound	518	24.1	24.5	50.8	518	540	2.3	1,540	.21	.89	.4	2
1 cup (248 gm.)	283	13.1	13.4	27.8	283	295	1.2	840	.11	.49	.2	1
Custard pie. See Pies.												
Custard pudding, canned, strained (infant food), 1 ounce	31	.9	.8	5.2	26	23	.1	60	Trace	.04	Trace	Trace
Dandelion greens:												
Raw, 1 pound E.P.	200	12.3	3.2	40.0	849	318	14.1	61,970	.85	.65	(3.8)	163
Cooked:												
1 pound	200	12.3	3.2	40.0	849	318	14.1	68,870	.59	.54	(3.2)	73
1 cup (180 gm.)	79	4.9	1.3	15.8	337	126	5.6	27,310	.23	.22	(1.3)	29
Dates, "fresh" and dried, 1 cup, pitted, cut (178 gm.)	505	3.9	1.1	134.2	128	107	3.7	100	.16	.17	3.9	(0)
Doughnuts, cake type:												
1 dozen (13½ oz., 383 gm.)	1,626	25.3	80.4	201.8	280	1,095	(2.7)	530	.61	.50	4.8	(0)
1 doughnut (32 gm.)	136	2.1	6.7	16.9	23	92	(.2)	40	.05	.04	.4	(0)

[1] Based on pared cucumber; unpared contains about 0.6 mg. of iron and 130 I.U. vitamin A.

[245]

Foods, The Composition of (Continued)

Food, description, and approximate measure	Food energy	Protein	Fat	Total carbohydrate	Calcium	Phosphorus	Iron	Vitamin A value	Thiamine	Riboflavin	Niacin	Ascorbic acid
	Cal.	Gm.	Gm.	Gm.	Mg.	Mg.	Mg.	I.U.	Mg.	Mg.	Mg.	Mg.
Eels, raw, 4 ounces E.P.	183	21.1	10.3	0.	20	229	.8	2,040	.31	.42	1.6	—
Eggs, hen, fresh, stored, or frozen:												
Raw:												
Whole:												
1 medium (54 gm.); refuse, shell	77	6.1	5.5	.3	26	101	1.3	550	.05	.14	Trace	0
1 cup (5 med., 243 gm.)	394	31.1	27.9	1.7	131	510	6.6	2,760	.23	.70	.2	0
White:												
1 egg white (med., 31 gm.)	15	3.3	0.	.2	2	5	.1	(0)	0.	.08	Trace	0
1 cup (8 med. whites, 243 gm.) ..	121	26.2	0.	1.9	15	41	.5	(0)	0.	.63	(.2)	0
Yolk:												
1 egg yolk (med., 17 gm.)	61	2.8	5.4	.1	25	100	1.2	550	.05	.06	Trace	0
1 cup (14 med. yolks, 243 gm.) ...	878	39.6	77.5	1.7	357	1,424	17.5	7,810	.67	.84	Trace	0
Cooked:												
Hard-cooked:												
1 pound; refuse, shell, 11 percent.	655	51.7	46.5	2.8	218	848	10.9	4,590	0.34	1.11	0.3	0
1 egg in shell; refuse, shell, 11 percent (54 gm.).	77	6.1	5.5	.3	26	101	1.3	550	.04	.13	Trace	0
*Omelet:												
1 pound	775	49.9	58.1	10.0	368	881	9.5	4,720	.35	1.22	.2	0
1-egg omelet (62 gm.)	106	6.8	7.9	1.4	50	120	1.3	640	.05	.17	Trace	0
Poached:												
1 pound	729	57.7	51.8	2.7	245	953	12.3	5,150	.36	1.09	.3	0
1 egg (48 gm.)	77	6.1	5.5	.3	26	101	1.3	540	.04	.12	Trace	0
*Scrambled:												
1 pound	775	49.9	58.1	10.0	368	881	9.5	4,720	.35	1.22	.2	0
1 egg (62 gm.)	106	6.8	7.9	1.4	50	120	1.3	640	.05	.17	Trace	0
1 cup (220 gm.)	376	24.2	28.2	4.8	178	427	4.6	2,290	.17	.59	.1	0
Dried:												
Whole, 1 cup (108 gm.)	640	50.5	45.4	2.7	205	828	9.5	4,040	.36	1.14	.3	0
White, 1 cup (56 gm.)	223	48.1	0.	3.5	27	76	.9	0	0.	1.15	.4	0
Yolk, 1 cup (96 gm.)	666	30.0	58.8	1.2	271	1,078	13.2	5,320	.48	.64	.1	0
Endive, raw, 1 pound E.P.	90	7.3	.9	18.2	359	254	7.7	13,600	.30	.53	1.8	49

Escarole, raw. See Endive.

Evaporated milk. See Milk, cow.

	Calories	Protein	Fat	Carbohydrate	Calcium	Phosphorus	Iron	Vit. A	Thiamine	Riboflavin	Niacin	Asc. acid
Farina:												
Unenriched:												
Raw, 1 cup (169 gm.)	625	18.4	1.4	130.8	47	189	1.7	(0)	.09	.10	1.4	(0)
*Cooked:												
1 pound	198	5.9	.5	41.3	14	59	.5	0	.03	.03	.5	(0)
1 cup (238 gm.)	104	3.1	.2	21.7	7	31	.2	0	.01	.02	.2	(0)
Enriched:												
Raw, 1 cup (169 gm.)	625	18.4	1.4	130.8	47	189	2.2[1]	(0)	.62[1]	.45[1]	2.2[1]	(0)
*Cooked:												
1 pound	198	5.9	.5	41.3	14	59	.9	0	.18	.14	.7	(0)
1 cup (238 gm.)	104	3.1	.2	21.7	7	31	.5	0	.10	.07	.4	(0)
Fats, cooking (vegetable fat):												
1 cup (200 gm.)	1,768	0.	200.	0.	0	0	0	0	0	0	0	0
1 tablespoon (12.5 gm.)	110	0.	12.5	0.	0	0	0	0	0	0	0	0
See also Lard, Oils.												
Figs:												
Raw, 3 small (1½ in. diam., 114 gm.)	90	1.6	.5	22.3	62	36	.7	90	.06	.06	.6	2
Canned, syrup pack, solids and liquid:												
1 cup (265 gm.)	300	2.1	.8	79.5	93	56	1.1	140	.08	.08	.9	1
3 figs and 2 tablespoons syrup (114 gm.).	129	.9	.3	34.2	40	24	.5	60	.03	.04	.4	1
Dried:												
1 large (2 by 1 in., 21 gm.)	57	.8	.3	14.4	39	23	.6	20	.03	.02	.4	(0)
1 cup cut (168 gm.)	453	6.7	2.0	114.9	312	186	5.0	140	.26	.20	2.9	(0)
Fig bars:												
1 small (16 gm.)	56	.7	.8	12.1	11	11	.2	0	Trace	.01	.1	(0)
1 large (25 gm.)	87	1.0	1.2	19.0	17	17	.3	0	.01	.01	.2	(0)
Fish. See individual kind, as Bluefish, Cod, Halibut, etc.												
Flounder, summer and winter, raw, 4 ounces E.P.	78	16.9	.6	0.	69	221	.9	—	.07	.06	1.9	—
Flour. See Corn, Rye, Wheat flours, etc.												
Frankfurters. See Sausage.												
Frog legs, raw, 4 ounces E.P.	82	18.6	.3	0.	20	167	1.2	0	.16	.29	1.3	—
Fruit cocktail, canned, solids and liquid, 1 cup (256 gm.).	179	1.0	.5	47.6	23	31	1.0	410	.03	.03	.9	5

[1] Iron, thiamine, riboflavin, and niacin are based on the minimum levels of enrichment specified in the standards of identity promulgated under the Food, Drug, and Cosmetic Act.

Foods, The Composition of (Continued)

Food, description, and approximate measure	Food energy Cal.	Protein Gm.	Fat Gm.	Total carbo- hydrate Gm.	Cal- cium Mg.	Phos- phorus Mg.	Iron Mg.	Vitamin A value I.U.	Thia- mine Mg.	Ribo- flavin Mg.	Nia- cin Mg.	Ascor- bic acid Mg.
Garbanzos. See Chick-peas.												
Gelatin, dry:												
Plain, 1 tablespoon (10 gm.)	34	8.6	.0	0.	(0)	(0)	(0)	(0)	(0)	(0)	(0)	(0)
Dessert powder, 3 ounce-package, ½ cup	324	8.0	.0	75.6	(0)	(0)	(0)	(0)	(0)	(0)	(0)	(0)
*Gelatin dessert, ready-to-serve:												
Plain:												
1 pound	296	7.3	.0	69.0	(0)	(0)	(0)	(0)	(0)	(0)	(0)	(0)
1 cup (239 gm.)	155	3.8	.0	36.3	(0)	(0)	(0)	(0)	(0)	(0)	(0)	(0)
With fruit added:												
1 pound	324	6.4	.5	79.4	27	50	1.4	510	.13	.09	1.0	13
1 cup (241 gm.)	172	3.4	.2	42.2	14	27	.7	270	.07	.05	.5	7
Ginger ale. See Beverages, carbonated.												
*Gingerbread, 1 piece (2 by 2 by 2 in., 55 gm.)	180	2.1	6.6	28.4	63	39	1.4	50	.02	.05	.6	(0)
Goat milk. See Milk, goat.												
Gooseberries, raw, 1 cup (150 gm.)	59	1.2	.3	14.6	33	42	.8	440	—	—	—	49
Grapefruit:												
Raw; refuse, rind and seeds, 34 percent:												
½ large (5 in. diam., No. 46's, 395 gm.).	104	1.3	.5	26.4	57	47	.5	20	.10	.05	.5	105
½ medium (4¼ in. diam., No. 64's, 285 gm.).	75	.9	.4	19.0	41	34	.4	20	.07	.04	.4	76
½ small (3⅜ in. diam., No. 96's, 190 gm.).	49	.6	.2	12.6	28	22	.2	10	.05	.02	.3	50
1 cup sections (194 gm.)	77	1.0	.4	19.6	43	35	.4	20	.07	.04	.4	78
Canned in syrup, solids and liquid, 1 cup (249 gm.).	181	1.5	.5	47.6	32	35	.7	20	.07	.05	.5	74
Grapefruit juice:												
Fresh, 1 cup (246 gm.)	87	1.2	.2	22.6	20	32	.7	20	.09	.05	.5	99

Food												
Canned:												
Unsweetened, 1 cup (246 gm.)	92	1.2	.2	24.1	20	32	.7	20	.07	.04	.4	85
	131	1.3	.3	34.4	20	33	.8	20	.08	.04	.5	87
Sweetened, 1 cup (251 gm.)												
Grapefruit juice concentrate, frozen, 1 can (6 fluid oz., 202 gm.).	297	3.8	.8	77.0	63	103	2.4	60	.24	.13	1.4	272
Grapefruit-orange juice blend:												
Canned:												
Unsweetened, 1 cup (246 gm.)	99	1.5	.2	25.6	22	37	.7	110	.11	.04	.5	92
Sweetened, 1 cup (251 gm.)	132	1.3	.3	34.9	23	38	.8	110	.12	.04	.5	94
Frozen concentrate, 1 can (6 fluid oz., 202 gm.).	297	4.4	.8	76.6	67	111	2.2	330	.34	.13	1.5	277
Grapes, raw:												
American type (slip skin) as Concord, Delaware, Niagara, and Scuppernong:												
1 bunch (3½ by 3 in., 100 gm.)	55	1.1	1.1	11.6	13	16	.5	60	.05	.03	.2	3
1 cup with skins and seeds (153 gm.)	84	1.7	1.7	17.7	20	25	.7	90	.07	.05	.3	5
European type (adherent skin) as Malaga, Muscat, Sultanina (Thompson Seedless), and Flame Tokay:												
1 cup (40 grapes, ¾ in. diam., 160 gm.).	102	1.2	.6	25.9	26	33	.9	120	.09	.06	.4	6
Grape juice, bottled, commercial, 1 cup (254 gm.).	170	1.0	.0	46.2	25	25	.8	—	.09	.12	(.6)	Trace
Griddlecakes. See Pancakes.												
Guavas, common, raw; refuse, skins, 1 guava (80 gm.).	49	.7	.4	12.0	21	20	.5	180	.05	.03	.8	212
Haddock:												
Cooked, fried:												
1 pound	676	84.9	25.0	31.8	82	826	2.7	—	.20	.43	11.7	—
1 fillet (4 by 3 by ½ in., 100 gm.).	158	18.7	5.5	7.0	18	182	.6	—	.04	.09	2.6	—
Halibut:												
Cooked, broiled:												
1 pound	827	118.9	35.4	0.	64	1,217	3.6	—	.28	.33	47.5	—
1 steak (4 by 3 by ½ in., 125 gm.).	228	32.8	9.8	0.	18	335	1.0	—	.08	.09	13.1	—
Ham. See Pork.												

[249]

Foods, The Composition of (Continued)

Food, description, and approximate measure	Food energy Cal.	Protein Gm.	Fat Gm.	Total carbohydrate Gm.	Calcium Mg.	Phosphorus Mg.	Iron Mg.	Vitamin A value I.U.	Thiamine Mg.	Riboflavin Mg.	Niacin Mg.	Ascorbic acid Mg.
Hamburger. See Beef.												
Heart:												
Beef, lean, raw, 3 ounces	92	14.4	3.1	.6	8	173	3.9	30	.50	.75	6.6	5
Calf, canned, strained (infant food), 1 ounce.	23	3.8	.7	.1	3	43	1.0	—	.02	.23	1.3	—
Chicken, raw, 3 ounces	134	17.4	6.0	1.4	20	121	1.4	30	0.10	0.77	4.4	5
Pork, raw, 3 ounces	100	14.4	4.1	.3	30	112	2.3	30	.36	1.05	5.1	5
Herring, Atlantic, raw, 4 ounces E.P.	217	20.8	14.2	0.	—	290	1.2	130	.02	.17	3.9	—
Herring, lake, raw, 4 ounces E.P.	159	21.0	7.7	0.	14	172	.6	110	.10	.10	3.5	—
Herring, Pacific, raw, 4 ounces E.P.	106	18.8	2.9	0.	—	—	—	110	.03	.25	(2.5)	—
Herring, smoked, kippered, 3 ounces E.P.	180	18.9	11.0	0.	56	216	(1.2)	0	Trace	.24	(2.5)	—
Hominy, dry. See Corn grits.												
Honey, strained or extracted:												
1 cup (338 gm.)	992	1.0	0.	268.7	17	54	3.0	(0)	.02	.13	.7	12
1 tablespoon (21 gm.)	62	.1	0.	16.7	1	3	.2	(0)	Trace	.01	Trace	1
Honeydew melon, raw:												
1 wedge (2 by 7 in., 150 gm., from melon, 6½ by 7 in.), without seeds and rind.	49	.8	0.	12.8	(26)	(24)	(.6)	60	.07	.04	.3	34
*Ice cream, plain:[1]												
1 slice or individual brick (⅛ of quart brick, 81 gm.).	167	3.2	10.1	16.7	100	80	.1	420	.03	.15	.1	1
1 container 3½ fluid ounces (62 gm.)	129	2.5	7.8	12.8	76	61	.1	320	.03	.12	.1	1
1 container 8 fluid ounces (142 gm.)	294	5.7	17.8	29.3	175	141	.1	740	.06	.27	.1	1
Jams, marmalades, preserves, 1 tablespoon (20 gm.).	55	.1	.1	14.2	2	2	.1	Trace	Trace	Trace	Trace	1

[1] Based on 5 pounds of ice cream to the gallon, factory packed.

Food												
Jellies, 1 tablespoon (20 gm.)	50	.0	.0	13.0	(2)	(2)	(.1)	(Trace)	(Trace)	(Trace)	(Trace)	1
Kale, cooked:												
1 pound	182	17.7	2.7	32.7	1,022	281	10.0	38,050	.32	1.04	7.7	232
1 cup (110 gm.)	45	4.3	.7	7.9	248	68	2.4	9,220	.08	.25	1.9	56
Kidneys, raw:												
Beef, 3 ounces	120	12.8	6.9	.8	8	188	6.7	980	.32	2.16	5.5	11
Pork, 3 ounces	97	13.9	3.9	.7	9	209	6.8	110	.50	1.47	8.4	11
Sheep, 3 ounces	89	14.1	2.8	.9	11	202	7.8	(980)	.44	2.06	6.3	11
Kohlrabi:												
Raw, 1 cup diced (138 gm.)	41	2.9	.1	9.2	63	69	.8	Trace	.08	.07	.3	84
Cooked:												
1 pound	136	9.5	.5	30.4	209	227	2.7	Trace	.18	.18	.9	168
1 cup (155 gm.)	47	3.3	.2	10.4	71	78	.9	Trace	.06	.06	.3	57
Lamb:												
Retail items, medium fat:												
Rib chop, cooked:												
1 pound with bone	1,254	72.0	105.0	0.	33	600	9.0	(0)	.43	.77	17.0	0
1 pound without bone	1,900	109.0	159.0	0.	50	908	13.6	(0)	.64	1.17	25.7	0
3 ounces without bone	356	20.0	30.0	0.	9	170	2.6	(0)	.12	.22	4.8	0
Shoulder roast (wholesale 3-rib), cooked:												
1 pound with bone	1,160	71.0	95.0	0.	31	639	8.8	(0)	.41	.75	15.5	0
1 pound without bone	1,551	95.0	127.0	0.	41	854	11.8	(0)	.55	1.01	20.7	0
3 ounces without bone	293	18.0	24.0	0.	8	160	2.2	(0)	.10	.19	3.9	0
Leg roast (wholesale leg), cooked:												
1 pound with bone	981	86.0	68.0	0.	36	923	11.1	(0)	.49	.89	18.4	0
1 pound without bone	1,241	109.0	85.0	0.	45	1,167	14.1	(0)	.62	1.13	23.3	0
3 ounces without bone	230	20.0	16.0	0.	9	219	2.6	(0)	.12	.21	4.4	0
Canned, strained (infant food), 1 ounce	30	4.4	1.3	0.	5	48	.7	(0)	.01	.07	1.1	0
Lamb and vegetable soup, canned, strained (infant food). See Soups, canned vegetable and lamb.												
Lard:												
1 cup (220 gm.)	1,984	0.	220.0	0.	0	0	0	0	0	0	0	0
1 tablespoon (14 gm.)	126	0.	14.0	0.	0	0	0	0	0	0	0	0
Lemons; refuse, rind and seeds, 38 percent; 1 medium lemon (2¾ by 2 in., 100 gm.).	20	.6	.4	5.4	25	14	.4	0	.03	Trace	.1	31

Foods, The Composition of (Continued)

Food, description, and approximate measure	Food energy	Protein	Fat	Total carbohydrate	Calcium	Phosphorus	Iron	Vitamin A value	Thiamine	Riboflavin	Niacin	Ascorbic acid
	Cal.	Gm.	Gm.	Gm.	Mg.	Mg.	Mg.	I.U.	Mg.	Mg.	Mg.	Mg.
Lemon juice:												
Fresh:												
1 cup (246 gm.)	59	1.0	.5	18.9	34	27	.2	0	.11	.01	.3	122
1 tablespoon (15 gm.)	4	.1	.0	1.2	2	2	.0	0	.01	Trace	Trace	7
Canned:												
Unsweetened:												
1 cup (246 gm.)	59	1.0	.5	18.9	34	27	.2	0	.11	.01	.3	104
1 tablespoon (15 gm.)	4	.1	.0	1.2	2	2	.0	0	.01	Trace	Trace	6
Lettuce, headed, raw:												
1 head, loose-leaf (4 in. diam., 220 gm.).	32	2.6	.4	6.4	48	55	1.1	1,200	.10	.18	.4	17
1 head, compact (4¾ in. diam., 1 pound).	68	5.4	.9	13.2	100	114	2.3	2,470	.20	.38	.9	35
2 large or 4 small leaves (50 gm.)	7	.6	.1	1.4	11	12	.2	270	.02	.04	.1	4
Limes; refuse, rind and seeds, 24 percent; 1 medium lime (2 in. diam., 68 gm.).	19	.4	.1	6.4	(21)	(11)	(.3)	0	(.02)	(Trace)	(.1)	14
Lime juice, fresh, 1 cup (246 gm.)	58	1.0	.0	20.4	(34)	(27)	(.2)	0	(.11)	(.01)	(.3)	65
Liver:												
Beef, cooked, fried, 2 ounces	118	13.4	4.4	5.5	5	276	4.4	30,330	.15	2.25	8.4	18
Calf, raw, 3 ounces	120	16.2	4.2	3.4	5	292	9.0	19,130	.18	2.65	13.7	30
Chicken, raw, 3 ounces	120	18.8	3.4	2.2	14	204	6.3	27,370	.17	2.10	10.0	17
Pork, raw, 3 ounces	114	16.7	4.1	1.4	8	308	15.3	12,070	.34	2.53	14.2	19
Sheep or lamb, raw, 3 ounces	116	17.8	3.3	2.5	7	309	10.7	42,930	.34	2.79	14.3	28
Liver, canned, strained (infant food), 1 ounce.	30	4.5	1.1	.3	7	79	2.0	5,440	.01	.61	1.8	—
Liver sausage. See Sausage.												
Liverwurst. See Sausage, liver.												
Lobster, canned, 3 ounces	78	15.6	1.1	.3	55	163	.7	—	(.03)	.06	(1.9)	—

Food											
Loganberries, raw, 1 cup (144 gm.)	90	1.4	.9	21.6	50	27	1.7	(280)	(.04)	(.10)	(.4)	34
Macaroni:												
Unenriched:												
Dry:												
1 cup, elbow type (123 gm.)	463	15.7	1.7	94.1	27	203	1.8	(0)	.11	.07	2.5	(0)
1 cup (1 in. pieces, 110 gm.)	415	14.1	1.5	84.2	24	182	1.6	(0)	.10	.07	2.2	(0)
1 cup (2 in. pieces, 86 gm.)	324	11.0	1.2	65.8	19	142	1.3	(0)	.08	.05	1.7	(0)
*Cooked:												
1 pound	678	23.2	2.7	137.1	41	295	2.7	(0)	.08	.08	2.2	(0)
1 cup (1 in. pieces or elbow type, 140 gm.).	209	7.1	.8	42.3	13	91	.8	(0)	.03	.02	.7	(0)
Enriched:												
Dry:												
1 cup, elbow type (123 gm.)	463	15.7	1.7	94.1	27	203	3.6[1]	(0)	1.08[1]	.46[1]	7.3[1]	(0)
1 cup (1 in. pieces, 110 gm.)	415	14.1	1.5	84.2	24	182	3.2[1]	(0)	.97[1]	.41[1]	6.5[1]	(0)
1 cup (2 in. pieces, 86 gm.)	324	11.0	1.2	65.8	19	142	2.5[1]	(0)	.76[1]	.32[1]	5.1[1]	(0)
*Cooked:												
1 pound	678	23.2	2.7	137.1	41	295	5.0	(0)	.79	.47	6.4	(0)
1 cup (1 in. sticks or elbow type, 140 gm.).	209	7.1	.3	42.3	13	91	1.5	(0)	.24	.15	2.0	(0)
*Macaroni and cheese, baked:												
1 pound	957	36.8	49.9	89.4	867	767	2.3[2]	2,050	.15[2]	.71[2]	1.8[2]	Trace
1 cup (220 gm.)	464	17.8	24.2	43.3	420	372	1.1[3]	990	.07[3]	.35[3]	.9[3]	Trace
Mackerel, canned, solids and liquid:[4]												
Atlantic, 3 ounces	155	16.4	9.4	0.	157	233	1.8	370	.05	.18	4.9	—
Pacific, 3 ounces	153	17.9	8.5	0.	221	245	1.9	20	.02	.28	7.4	—
Mangos, raw, 1 medium (200 gm.); refuse, seeds and skin, 34 percent.	87	.9	.3	22.7	12	17	.3	8,380	.08	.07	1.2	55
Margarine:												
1 cup (224 gm.)	1,613	1.3	181.4	.9	45	36	.0	7,400[5]	(0)	(0)	(0)	(0)
1 tablespoon (14 gm.)	101	.1	11.3	.1	3	2	.0	460[5]	(0)	(0)	(0)	(0)
1 pat (64 per pound, 7 gm.)	50	.0	5.7	.0	1	1	.0	230[5]	(0)	(0)	(0)	(0)

[1] Iron, thiamine, riboflavin, and niacin are based on the minimum level of enrichment specified in the standards of identity promulgated under the Food, Drug, and Cosmetic Act.

[2] If enriched macaroni is used in the recipe the values for iron, thiamine, riboflavin, and niacin would be 3.2 mg., 0.45 mg., 0.91 mg. and 4.1 mg., respectively.

[3] If enriched macaroni is used in the recipe the values for iron, thiamine, riboflavin, and niacin would be 1.5 mg., 0.22 mg., 0.44 mg. and 2.0 mg., respectively.

[4] The vitamin values are based on the drained solids.

[5] Based on the average vitamin A content of fortified margarine. Most of the margarines manufactured for use in the United States have 15,000 I.U. of vitamin A added per pound. The minimum Federal specifications for fortified margarine require the addition of 9,000 I.U. of vitamin A per pound.

Foods, The Composition of (Continued)

Food, description, and approximate measure	Food energy Cal.	Protein Gm.	Fat Gm.	Total carbohydrate Gm.	Calcium Mg.	Phosphorus Mg.	Iron Mg.	Vitamin A value I.U.	Thiamine Mg.	Riboflavin Mg.	Niacin Mg.	Ascorbic acid Mg.
Marmalades. See Jams, marmalades, preserves.												
Mayonnaise. See Salad dressings.												
Meat. See Beef, Lamb, Pork, Veal.												
Melons. See Cantaloupes, Honeydew, Watermelons.												
Milk, cow:												
Fluid (pasteurized and raw):												
Whole:												
1 quart (976 gm.)	666	34.2	38.1	47.8	1,152	908	.7	(1,550)	.35	1.68	1.1	13
1 cup (244 gm.)	166	8.5	9.5	12.0	288	227	.2	(390)	.09	.42	.3	3
Nonfat (skim):												
1 quart (984 gm.)	350	34.4	1.0	50.2	1,210	954	.7	(40)	.35	1.75	1.1	13
1 cup (246 gm.)	87	8.6	.2	12.5	303	239	.2	(10)	.09	.44	.3	3
Canned:												
Evaporated (unsweetened), 1 cup (252 gm.).	346	17.6	19.9	24.9	612	491	.4	1,010	.12	.91	.5	3
Condensed (sweetened), 1 cup (306 gm.).	981	24.8	25.7	167.7	835	698	.6	(1,300)	.16	1.19	.6	3
Dried:												
Whole:												
1 cup (128 gm.)	630	33.0	34.2	48.6	1,215	932	.7	1,790	.39	1.87	.8	8
1 tablespoon (8 gm.)	39	2.1	2.1	3.0	76	58	.0	110	.02	.12	.1	1
Nonfat solids (skim):												
1 cup (120 gm.)	434	42.7	1.2	62.4	1,560	1,236	.7	(50)	.42	2.35	1.4	9
1 tablespoon (7.5 gm.)	28	2.7	.1	3.9	98	77	.0	(Trace)	.03	.15	.1	1
Malted:[1]												
Dry powder, 1 ounce	115	4.1	2.4	20.0	81	107	.6	290	.09	.15	—	(0)
*Beverage, 1 cup (270 gm.)	281	12.4	11.9	31.9	364	332	.8	680	.18	.56	—	3
*Chocolate flavored:												
1 quart (1 kg.)	740	32.0	22.0	106.0	1,090	910	.7	910	.32	1.59	1.0	10
1 cup (250 gm.)	185	8.0	5.5	26.5	272	228	.2	230	.08	.40	.2	2

[1] Based on unfortified products.

Food and approximate measure												
Half and half (milk and cream):												
1 quart (968 gm.)	1,322	31.0	115.2	43.6	1,045	823	.6	4,760	.32	1.52	1.0	12
1 cup (242 gm.)	330	7.7	29.0	10.9	261	206	.1	1,190	.08	.38	.2	3
Buttermilk. See Buttermilk.												
Milk, goat, fluid:												
1 quart (976 gm.)	654	32.2	39.0	44.9	1,259	1,035	1.0	(1,550)	.39	1.04	2.8	10
1 cup (244 gm.)	164	8.1	9.8	11.2	315	259	.2	(390)	.10	.26	.7	2
Molasses, cane:												
First extraction or light:												
1 cup (328 gm.)	825	—	—	213.2¹	541	148	14.1	—	.23	.21	.8	—
1 tablespoon (20 gm.)	50	—	—	13.0¹	33	9	.9	—	.01	.01	Trace	—
Second extraction or medium:												
1 cup (328 gm.)	762	—	—	196.8¹	951	226	19.7	—	—	—	—	—
1 tablespoon (20 gm.)	46	—	—	12.0¹	58	14	1.2	—	—	—	—	—
Third extraction or blackstrap:												
1 cup (328 gm.)	698	—	—	130.4¹	1,899	279	37.1	—	.92	.82	6.9	—
1 tablespoon (20 gm.)	43	—	—	11.0¹	116	17	2.3	—	.06	.05	.4	—
Barbados:												
1 cup (328 gm.)	889	—	—	229.6¹	—	164	—	—	.19	.66	—	—
1 tablespoon (20 gm.)	54	—	—	14.0¹	—	10	—	—	.01	.04	—	—
***Muffins, made with:**												
Unenriched flour, 1 muffin (2¾ in. diam., 48 gm.).	134	3.8	4.0	20.2	99	92	.3	50	.02	.06	.2	(0)
Enriched flour, 1 muffin (2¾ in. diam., 48 gm.).	134	3.3	4.0	20.2	99	92	.8	50	.09	.10	.7	(0)
Mung bean sprouts, raw, 1 cup (90 gm.)	21	2.6	.2	3.7	26	53	.7	10	.06	.08	.5	14
Mushrooms, canned, solids and liquid, 1 cup (244 gm.).	28	3.4	.5	9.0	(17)	(220)	(2.0)	0	.04	.60	4.8	—
Muskmelons. See Cantaloupes and Honey-dew melon.												
Mustard greens, cooked:												
1 pound (140 gm.)	102	10.4	1.4	18.2	999	173	13.2	32,600	0.27	0.82	3.2	204
1 cup (140 gm.)	31	3.2	.4	5.6	308	53	4.1	10,050	.08	.25	1.0	63
Noodles (containing egg):												
Unenriched:												
Dry, 1 cup (1½ in. strips, 73 gm.) . .	278	9.2	2.5	53.4	16	145	1.5	140	.15	.08	1.7	(0)
*Cooked:												
1 pound	302	10.0	2.7	58.1	18	159	1.8	160	.15	.09	1.8	(0)
1 cup (160 gm.)	107	3.5	1.0	20.5	6	56	.6	60	.05	.03	.6	(0)

¹ Total sugars.

Foods, The Composition of (Continued)

Food, description, and approximate measure	Food energy	Protein	Fat	Total carbohydrate	Calcium	Phosphorus	Iron	Vitamin A value	Thiamine	Riboflavin	Niacin	Ascorbic acid
	Cal.	Gm.	Gm.	Gm.	Mg.	Mg.	Mg.	I.U.	Mg.	Mg.	Mg.	Mg.
Noodles (containing egg): (Continued)												
Enriched:												
Dry, 1 cup (1½ in. strips, 73 gm.)	278	9.2	2.5	53.4	16	145	2.1[1]	140	.64[1]	.27[1]	4.3[1]	(0)
*Cooked:												
1 pound	302	10.0	2.7	58.1	18	159	2.3	160	.63	.30	4.8	(0)
1 cup (160 gm.)	107	3.5	1.0	20.5	6	56	.8	60	.22	.10	1.7	(0)
Oat cereal, ready-to-eat (added vitamins and minerals), 1 cup (25 gm.)	100	3.6	1.8	17.6	40	88	1.0	(0)	.20	.05	.5	(0)
Oatmeal or rolled oats:												
Dry, 1 cup (80 gm.)	312	11.4	5.9	54.6	42	324	3.6	(0)	.48	.11	.8	(0)
*Cooked:												
1 pound	285	10.4	5.4	49.9	41	304	3.2	(0)	.43	.10	.8	(0)
1 cup (236 gm.)	148	5.4	2.8	26.0	21	158	1.7	(0)	.22	.05	.4	(0)
Precooked (infant food), dry, 1 ounce.	106	4.3	1.4	19.5	225	226	8.9	(0)	.36	.10	.7[2]	(0)
Oils, salad or cooking:												
1 cup (220 gm.)	1,945	0.	220.	0.	0	0	0.	0	0.	0	0	0
1 tablespoon (14 gm.)	124	0.	14.	0.	0	0	0.	0	0.	0	0	0
Okra, cooked:												
1 pound	148	8.2	.9	33.6	372	281	3.2	3,360	.27	.27	3.6	91
8 pods (3 in. long, ⅝ in. diam., 85 gm.).	28	1.5	.2	6.3	70	53	.6	630	.05	.05	.7	17
Oleomargarine. See Margarine.												
Olives, pickled, "mammoth" size (13⁄16 by 1⅙ in.; refuse, 16 pct.):												
Green, 10 olives (65 gm.)	72	.8	7.4	2.2	48	9	.9	160	Trace	—	—	—
Ripe:												
Mission, 10 olives (65 gm.)	106	1.0	11.6	1.4	48	9	.9	40	Trace	Trace	—	—
Other varieties (as ascalano,	70	.7	7.4	1.7	48	9	.9	30	Trace	Trace	—	—

[1] Iron, thiamine, riboflavin, and niacin are based on the minimum level of enrichment specified in the standards of identity promulgated under the Food, Drug, and Cosmetic Act.

[2] Based on products ranging from .4 to 1.2 mg. per ounce of cereal. The niacin value of some products is as high as 6.5 mg. per ounce.

Omelet. See Eggs, omelet.

manzanilla, and sevilano), 10 olives (65 gm.).

Food												
Onions, mature:												
Raw:												
1 onion (2½ in. diam.). E.P. (110 gm.).	49	1.5	.2	11.3	35	48	.6	60	.04	.04	.2	10
1 tablespoon chopped (10 gm.)	4	.1	.0	1.0	3	4	.0	Trace	Trace	Trace	Trace	1
Cooked, whole:												
1 pound	172	4.5	.9	39.5	145	200	2.3	230	.09	.14	.9	27
1 cup (210 gm.)	79	2.1	.4	18.3	67	92	1.0	110	.04	.06	.4	13
Onions, young green; 6 small onions without tops (50 gm.).	23	.5	.1	5.3	68	12	.4	(30)	(.02)	(.02)	(.1)	12
Oranges; refuse, rind and seeds, 28 percent:												
1 large (3⅜ in. diam., No. 126's, 325 gm.).	106	2.1	.5	26.2	77	54	.9	(440)	.18	.06	.6	116
1 medium (3 in. diam., No. 200's, 215 gm.).	70	1.4	.3	17.4	51	36	.6	(290)	.12	.04	.4	77
1 small (2½ in. diam., No. 288's, 150 gm.).	49	1.0	.2	12.1	36	25	.4	(200)	.08	.03	.3	53
1 cup sections (193 gm.)	87	1.7	.4	21.6	64	44	.8	(360)	.15	.05	.5	95
Orange juice:												
Fresh, 1 cup (246 gm.)	108	2.0	.5	27.1	47	39	.5	(460)	.19	.06	.6	122
Canned:												
Unsweetened, 1 cup (246 gm.)	109	2.0	.5	27.3	25	44	.7	(240)	.17	.04	.6	103
Sweetened, 1 cup (251 gm.)	135	1.5	.5	34.9	25	45	.8	(250)	.18	.05	.6	105
Orange juice concentrate:												
Canned, 1 ounce	65	1.2	.2	16.4	17	25	.5	(140)	.10	.02	.3	63
Frozen, 1 can (6 fl. oz., 202 gm.)	300	5.5	1.4	74.9	69	121	2.0	(670)	.48	.11	1.5	285
Oysters, meat only, raw, 1 cup (13-19 medium size oysters, selects, 240 gm.)	200	23.5	5.0	13.4	226	343	13.4	770	.35	.48	2.8	—
*Oyster stew: 1 part oysters to 3 parts milk by volume:												
1 pound	413	24.1	24.5	24.1	531	499	6.8	1,280	.29	.84	1.8	—
1 cup (with 3-4 oysters, 230 gm.)	209	12.2	12.4	12.2	269	253	3.4	650	.14	.42	.9	—

[257]

Foods, The Composition of (Continued)

Food, description, and approximate measure	Food energy Cal.	Protein Gm.	Fat Gm.	Total carbohydrate Gm.	Calcium Mg.	Phosphorus Mg.	Iron Mg.	Vitamin A value I.U.	Thiamine Mg.	Riboflavin Mg.	Niacin Mg.	Ascorbic acid Mg.
Oyster stew: (Continued)												
1 part oysters to 1 part milk by volume:												
1 pound	461	31.3	25.0	26.8	495	554	13.2	1,560	.40	.86	3.0	—
1 cup (with 6–8 oysters, 240 gm.)	244	16.6	13.2	14.2	262	293	7.0	820	.21	.46	1.6	—
*Pancakes (griddlecakes), baked:												
Wheat (home recipe):												
With unenriched flour:												
1 pound	991	30.9	41.8	120.8	717	699	2.7	890	.26	.59	1.5	2
1 cake (4 in. diam., 27 gm.)	59	1.8	2.5	7.2	43	42	.2	50	.02	.03	.1	Trace
With enriched flour:												
1 pound	991	30.9	41.8	120.8	717	699	5.9	890	.84	.95	5.7	2
1 cake (4 in. diam., 27 gm.)	59	1.8	2.5	7.2	43	42	.4	50	.05	.06	.3	Trace
Buckwheat, with buckwheat pancake mix:												
1 pound	798	27.7	38.1	94.9	1,130	1,643	5.4	490	.72	.72	3.9	3
1 cake (4 in. diam., 27 gm.)	47	1.6	2.3	5.6	67	98	.3	30	.04	.04	.2	Trace
Pancake mix, dry, self-rising:												
Wheat (mixed with other flours):												
Unenriched, 1 cup (135 gm.)	471	12.8	1.9	98.7	628	919	2.7	0	.20	.10	1.9	(0)
Enriched, 1 cup (135 gm.)	471	12.8	1.9	98.7	628	919	4.5	0	.53	.42	3.9	(0)
Buckwheat, 1 cup (135 gm.)	432	14.2	2.6	94.9	630	1,116	4.2	0	.49	.15	3.0	(0)
Papayas, raw, 1 cup (½-in. cubes, 182 gm.).	71	1.1	.2	18.2	36	29	.5	3,190	.06	.07	.5	102
Parsley, common, raw, 1 tablespoon chopped (3.5 gm.).	1	.1	.0	.3	7[1]	3	.2	290	Trace	.01	.1	7
Parsnips, cooked:												
1 pound	274	4.5	2.3	63.1	259	363	3.2	0	.27	.45	.9	54
1 cup (155 gm.)	94	1.6	.8	21.5	88	124	1.1	0	.09	.16	.3	19

Pastry shell, plain. See Pie crust.

[1] Calcium may not be available because of presence of oxalic acid.

Food												
Peaches:												
Raw:												
1 medium; refuse, pits and skins, 12 percent (2½ by 2 in. diam., 114 gm.)	46	.5	.1	12.0	8	22	.6	880	.02	.05	.9	8
1 cup, sliced (168 gm.)	77	.8	.2	20.2	13	37	1.0	1,480	.04	.08	1.5	13
Canned, solids and liquid:												
Water pack, 1 cup (244 gm.)	66	1.2	.2	16.6	12	34	1.0	1,110	.02	.05	1.7	10
Syrup pack:												
1 cup (256 gm.)	174	1.0	.3	46.6	13	36	1.0	1,160	.02	.05	1.8	11
2 medium halves and 2 tablespoons syrup (117 gm.)	79	.5	.1	21.3	6	16	.5	530	.01	.02	.8	5
Strained (infant food), 1 ounce	17	.2	.1	4.3	2	5	.3	180	.01	.01	.2	1
Frozen, 4 ounces	89	.5	.1	22.9	7	17	.5	590	.01	.03	.6	5
Dried, sulfured:												
Uncooked, 1 cup (160 gm.)	424	4.8	1.0	111.0	70	202	11.0	5,200	.02	.31	8.6	30
*Cooked, no sugar added, 1 cup (10-12 halves plus 6 tbsp. liquid, 270 gm.).	224	2.4	.5	58.9	38	105	5.9	2,750	.01	.16	4.3	11
*Cooked, sugar added, 1 cup (10-12 halves plus 6 tbsp. liquid, 305 gm.).	366	2.4	.6	95.5	37	107	5.8	2,750	.01	.15	4.3	12
Peanuts, Virginia type, roasted:												
Shelled:												
1 cup medium halves (144 gm.)	805	38.7	63.6	34.0	107	566	2.7	0	.42	.19	23.3	(0)
1 tablespoon, chopped (9 gm.)	50	2.4	4.0	2.1	7	35	.2	0	.03	.01	1.5	(0)
Peanut butter:												
1 cup (258 gm.)	1,486	67.3	123.3	54.2	191	1,014	4.9	0	.31	.34	41.8	(0)
1 tablespoon (16 gm.)	92	4.2	7.6	3.4	12	63	.3	0	.02	.02	2.6	(0)
Pears:												
Raw:												
1 pear; refuse; skin and core, 17 percent (3 by 2½ in. diam., 182 gm.).	95	1.1	.6	23.9	20	24	.5	30	.03	.06	.2	6
1 cup, quartered (192 gm.)	120	1.3	.8	30.3	25	31	.6	40	.04	.08	.3	8
Canned, solids and liquid:												
Water pack, 1 cup (242 gm.)	75	.7	.2	19.8	19	24	.5	10	.02	.04	.3	4
Syrup pack:												
1 cup (256 gm.)	174	.5	.3	47.1	20	26	.5	10	.02	.04	.4	5
2 medium-size halves plus 2 tablespoons syrup (117 gm.).	79	.2	.1	21.5	9	12	.2	Trace	.01	.02	.2	2
Strained (infant food), 1 ounce	15	.2	.1	3.7	3	4	(.1)	10	Trace	.01	.1	Trace
Peas, green, immature:												
Cooked:												
1 pound	316	22.2	1.8	54.9	100	554	8.6	3,270	1.14	.64	10.4	68
1 cup (160 gm.)	111	7.8	.6	19.4	35	195	3.0	1,150	.40	.22	3.7	24

Foods, The Composition of (Continued)

Food, description, and approximate measure	Food energy	Protein	Fat	Total carbohydrate	Calcium	Phosphorus	Iron	Vitamin A value	Thiamine	Riboflavin	Niacin	Ascorbic acid
	Cal.	Gm.	Gm.	Gm.	Mg.	Mg.	Mg.	I.U.	Mg.	Mg.	Mg.	Mg.
Peas, green, immature: (Continued)												
Canned:												
Solids and liquid, 1 cup (249 gm.)	168	8.5	1.0	32.1	62	167	4.5	1,350	.28	.15	2.6	21
Drained solids:												
1 pound	411	20.4	2.7	78.1	145	350	9.5	3,030	.54	.30	4.5	42
1 cup (160 gm.)	145	7.2	1.0	27.5	51	123	3.4	1,070	.19	.10	1.6	15
Strained (infant food), 1 ounce	14	1.2	.1	2.2	5	18	.4	180	.03	.02	.3	2
Peas, mature dry seeds:												
Entire seeds, 1 cup (200 gm.)	679	47.6	2.8	120.4	114	776	9.4	740	1.53	.56	6.3	4
Split, without seed coat, 1 cup (200 gm.).	689	49.0	2.0	123.4	66	536	10.2	740	1.53	.56	6.3	4
Pea soup, dehydrated. See Soups, dehydrated.												
Pecans:												
1 cup, halves (108 gm.)	752	10.2	78.8	14.0	80	350	2.6	50	.77	.12	1.0	2
1 tablespoon, chopped (7.5 gm.)	52	.7	5.5	1.0	6	24	.2	Trace	.05	.01	.1	Trace
Peppers, green:												
Raw, 1 medium; refuse, stem end, seeds and core, 16 percent (76 gm.).	16	.8	.1	3.6	7	16	.3	400	.02	.04	.2	77
Cooked, parboiled then baked:												
1 pound	119	5.9	.9	27.2	50	114	1.8	3,360	.18	.32	1.8	449
1 pepper, medium (65 gm.)	17	.8	.1	3.9	7	16	.3	480	.03	.05	.3	64
Persimmons, Japanese or Kaki, raw:												
1 persimmon (2¼ in. diam., 125 gm.):												
Seedless kind; refuse, skin, 3 percent	95	1.0	.5	24.2	7	31	.4	3,270	.06	.05	Trace	13
Kind with seeds; refuse, skin and seeds, 24 percent.	74	.8	.4	19.0	6	25	.3	2,570	.05	.04	Trace	10
Pickles:												
Dill, cucumber, 1 large (1¾ in. diam., 4 in. long, 135 gm.).	15	.9	.3	2.8	34	27	1.6	420	Trace	.09	.1	8

Food, approximate measure, and weight (gm.)	Food energy (Cal.)	Protein (gm.)	Fat (gm.)	Carbohydrate (gm.)	Calcium (mg.)	Phosphorus (mg.)	Iron (mg.)	Vitamin A (I.U.)	Thiamine (mg.)	Riboflavin (mg.)	Niacin (mg.)	Ascorbic acid (mg.)
Fresh, cucumber (as bread and butter pickles):												
1 cup (22–24 slices, 170 gm.)	118	1.5	.3	28.9	54	46	3.1	310	.04	.07	.1	15
6 slices (¼ in. by 1½ in. diam., 42 gm.).	29	.4	.1	7.1	13	11	.8	80	.01	.02	Trace	4
Sour, cucumber or mixed, 1 large (1¾ in. diam., 4 in. long, 135 gm.).	15	.7	.3	3.0	34	27	1.6	420	Trace	.09	Trace	8
Sweet, cucumber or mixed:												
1 pickle (2¾ in. long, ¾ in. diam. or 2 pickles 2 in. long, ⅝ in. diam., 20 gm.)	22	.2	.1	5.3	3	4	.3	20	(0)	Trace	Trace	1
1 cup, mixed, chopped (210 gm.)	225	1.7	.8	55.4	34	38	2.7	240	(0)	.04	Trace	15
1 tablespoon, mixed, chopped (13 gm.).	14	.1	.1	3.4	2	2	.2	10	(0)	Trace	Trace	1
Pies:												
*Apple:												
1 pie (9 in. diam., 945 gm.)	2,322	19.8	89.8	373.3	66	227	3.8	1,510	.28	.16	2.3	9
4-inch sector (or 1/7 of 9 in. diam., 135 gm.).	331	2.8	12.8	53.3	9	32	.5	220	.04	.02	.3	1
1-inch sector (of 9 in. diam., 34 gm.).	83	.7	3.2	13.3	2	8	.1	50	.01	.01	.1	Trace
*Blueberry:												
1 pie (9 in. diam., 945 gm.)	2,042	19.8	65.2	354.4	94	208	4.7	1,110	.15	0.28	2.3	34
4-inch sector (or 1/7 of 9 in. diam., 135 gm.).	291	2.8	9.3	50.6	14	30	.7	160	.02	.04	.3	5
1-inch sector (of 9 in. diam., 34 gm.).	73	.7	2.3	12.7	3	7	.2	40	.01	.01	.1	1
*Cherry:												
1 pie (9 in. diam., 945 gm.)	2,388	22.7	92.6	381.8	94	255	3.8	3,610	.25	.16	2.4	13
4-inch sector (or 1/7 of 9 in. diam., 135 gm.).	340	3.2	13.2	54.5	14	36	.5	520	.04	.02	.3	2
1-inch sector (of 9 in. diam., 34 gm.).	85	.8	3.3	13.6	3	9	.1	130	.01	.01	.1	Trace
Coconut custard:												
1 pie (9 in. diam., 910 gm.)	1,859	47.3	79.2	239.3	1,138	1,056	10.9	2,060	.46	1.49	2.7	(0)
4-inch sector (or 1/7 of 9 in. diam., 130 gm.).	266	6.8	11.3	34.2	162	151	1.6	290	.07	.21	.4	(0)
1-inch sector of 9 in. diam., 32 gm.).	66	1.7	2.8	8.6	41	38	.4	70	.02	.05	.1	(0)
Custard:												
1 pie (9 in. diam., 910 gm.)	1,859	47.3	79.2	239.3	1,138	1,056	10.9	2,060	.46	1.49	2.7	(0)
4-inch sector (or 1/7 of 9 in. diam., 130 gm.).	266	6.8	11.3	34.2	162	151	1.6	290	.07	.21	.4	(0)
1-inch sector (of 9 in. diam., 32 gm.).	66	1.7	2.8	8.6	41	38	.4	70	.02	.05	.1	(0)
Lemon meringue:												
1 pie (9 in. diam., 840 gm.)	2,114	30.2	84.8	314.2	168	428	4.2	1,460	.27	.70	1.6	8
4-inch sector (or 1/7 of 9 in. diam., 120 gm.).	302	4.3	12.1	44.9	24	61	.6	210	.04	.10	.2	1
1-inch sector (of 9 in. diam., 30 gm.).	76	1.1	3.0	11.2	6	15	.2	50	.01	.02	.1	Trace

Foods, The Composition of (Continued)

Food, description, and approximate measure	Food energy Cal.	Protein Gm.	Fat Gm.	Total carbohydrate Gm.	Calcium Mg.	Phosphorus Mg.	Iron Mg.	Vitamin A value I.U.	Thiamine Mg.	Riboflavin Mg.	Niacin Mg.	Ascorbic acid Mg.
Pies: (Continued)												
Mince:[1]												
1 pie (9 in. diam., 945 gm.)	2,386	23.6	65.2	430.9	151	378	20.8	70	.64	.33	3.3	6
4-inch sector (or 1/7 of 9 in. diam., 135 gm.).	341	3.4	9.3	61.6	22	54	3.0	10	.09	.05	.5	1
1-inch sector (of 9 in. diam., 34 gm.).	85	.8	2.3	15.4	5	14	.7	Trace	.02	.01	.1	Trace
*Pumpkin:												
1 pie (9 in. diam., 910 gm.)	1,842	38.2	87.4	234.8	491	737	7.3	17,350	.30	1.06	2.9	2
4-inch sector (or 1/7 of 9 in. diam., 130 gm.).	263	5.5	12.5	33.5	70	105	1.0	2,480	.04	.15	.4	(0)
1-inch sector (of 9 in. diam., 32 gm.).	66	1.4	3.1	8.4	18	26	.3	620	.01	.04	.1	(0)
Pie crust, plain:												
*Baked with:												
Unenriched flour:												
1 lower crust, 9 inch shell (135 gm.).	657	10.1	36.3	71.7	15	88	.7	0	.05	.03	.7	(0)
1 double crust, for 9 inch pie (270 gm.).	1,314	20.2	72.6	143.4	30	176	1.4	0	.09	.06	1.4	(0)
Enriched flour:												
1 lower crust, 9 inch shell (135 gm.).	657	10.1	36.3	71.7	15	88	2.7	0	.29	.23	3.0	(0)
1 double crust, for 9 inch pie (270 gm.).	1,314	20.2	72.6	143.4	30	176	5.4	0	.58	.47	5.9	(0)
Unbaked (fresh or frozen), 1 pound	1,946	30.0	107.6	212.0	41	259	1.8	0	.20	.09	2.2	(0)
Pimientos, canned, 1 medium (38 gm.)	10	.3	.2	2.2	3	6	.6	870	.01	.02	.1	36
Pineapple:												
Raw:												
1 cup, diced (140 gm.)	74	.6	.3	19.2	22	15	.4	180	.12	.04	.3	33
1 slice (3/4 in. thick, 3½ in. diam., 84 gm.).	44	.3	.2	11.5	13	9	.3	110	.07	.02	.2	20
Canned, syrup pack, solids and liquid:												
1 cup crushed (260 gm.)	204	1.0	.3	54.9	75	18	1.6	210	.20	.04	.4	23

[1] The proximate constituents, calcium, phosphorus, and vitamin A are calculated from a recipe.

Food												
2 small or 1 large slice plus 2 table-spoons juice (122 gm.).	95	.5	.1	25.7	35	9	.7	100	.09	.02	.2	11
Frozen, 4 ounces	97	.5	.2	25.2	16	11	.3	110	.07	.02	.2	22
Pineapple juice, canned, 1 cup (249 gm.).	121	.7	.2	32.4	37	20	1.2	200	.13	.04	.4	22
Plums (all, excluding prunes) raw:												
1 plum (2 in. diam., 60 gm.); refuse, pits, 5 percent.	29	.4	.1	7.4	10	11	.3	200	.04	.02	.3	3
1 cup halves (2 in. diam., 185 gm.)	94	1.3	.4	23.9	31	37	.9	650	.12	.08	.9	9
Plums (Italian prunes), canned: Syrup pack:												
1 cup, fruit and juice (256 gm.); refuse, pits, 4 percent.	186	1.0	.2	50.2	20	30	2.7	560	.07	.06	.9	3
3 prunes (without pits) plus 2 table-spoons juice (122 gm.).	92	.5	.1	24.9	10	15	1.3	280	.03	.03	.5	1
Popcorn: Popped, 1 cup (14 gm.)	54	1.8	.7	10.7	(2)	(39)	(.4)	(0)	(.05)	(.02)	(.3)	(0)
Pork, fresh: Retail items, cooked: Ham:												
1 pound with bone	1,432	86.0	118.0	0.	39	854	11.1	(0)	1.90	.86	16.9	0
1 pound without bone	1,818	109.0	150.0	0.	50	1,081	14.1	(0)	2.40	1.09	21.3	0
3 ounces without bone	338	20.0	28.0	0.	9	202	2.6	(0)	.45	.20	4.0	0
Loin or chops:												
1 pound with bone	1,149	79.0	90.0	0.	38	811	10.4	(0)	2.86	.83	17.4	0
1 pound without bone	1,508	104.0	118.0	0.	50	1,067	13.6	(0)	3.77	1.09	22.8	0
1 chop (115 gm.)	293	20.0	23.0	0.	10	204	2.6	(0)	.72	.21	4.4	0
3 ounces without bone	284	20.0	22.0	0.	9	200	2.6	(0)	.71	.20	4.3	0
Pork, cured: Ham, smoked, cooked:												
1 pound with bone	1,496	87.0	124.0	(1.5)	38	626	10.9	(0)	2.04	.80	15.7	0
1 pound without bone	1,804	104.0	150.0	(1.8)	45	754	13.2	(0)	2.46	.96	18.9	0
3 ounces without bone	339	20.0	28.0	(.3)	9	141	2.5	(0)	.46	.18	3.5	0
Luncheon meat: Boiled ham, 2 ounces	172	12.9	12.9	0.	5	52	1.5	(0)	.57	.15	2.9	0
Canned, spiced, 2 ounces	164	8.4	13.8	.9	5	91	1.2	(0)	.18	.12	1.6	0
Sausage, pork links or bulk, raw. See Sausage, pork.												
Pork, canned, strained (infant food), 1 ounce.	36	4.8	1.7	0.	4	51	.5	(0)	.10	.08	1.3	0

Foods, The Composition of (Continued)

Food, description, and approximate measure	Food energy	Protein	Fat	Total carbohydrate	Calcium	Phosphorus	Iron	Vitamin A value	Thiamine	Riboflavin	Niacin	Ascorbic acid
	Cal.	Gm.	Gm.	Gm.	Mg.	Mg.	Mg.	I.U.	Mg.	Mg.	Mg.	Mg.
Potatoes:												
Cooked:												
Baked:												
1 pound	446	10.9	.5	102.2	59	300	3.6	110	.50	.21	6.4	77
1 medium potato (2½ in. diam.; peeled, 99 gm., or unpeeled, 128 gm.; refuse, 23 pct.).	97	2.4	.1	22.3	13	65	.8	20	.11	.05	1.4	17
Boiled, unpeeled before cooking:												
1 pound; refuse, cooked skins, 5 percent.	359	8.6	.4	82.3	47	241	3.0	80	.43	.17	5.0	66
1 medium potato (2½ in. diam.; peeled, 142 gm., or unpeeled, 150 gm.; refuse, 5 pct.).	118	2.8	.1	27.1	16	80	1.0	30	.14	.06	1.6	22
Boiled, peeled before cooking:												
1 pound	378	9.1	.5	86.7	50	254	3.2	80	.43	.15	4.6	62
1 medium potato (2½ in. diam.) or 1 cup diced (126 gm.).	105	2.5	.1	24.1	14	71	.9	20	.12	.04	1.3	17
***French-fried:**												
1 pound	1,784	24.5	86.7	236.1	136	690	8.6	250	.82	.49	14.8	126
8 pieces (2 by ½ by ½ in., 40 gm.).	157	2.2	7.6	20.8	12	61	.8	20	.07	.04	1.3	11
***Fried raw:**												
1 pound	1,281	17.3	64.5	164.8	95	481	5.9	170	.57	.35	10.4	88
1 cup (170 gm.)	479	6.5	24.1	61.7	36	180	2.2	60	.21	.13	3.9	33
***Hash-browned after holding overnight:**												
1 pound	1,094	15.0	53.1	144.8	82	422	5.4	150	.36	.26	7.7	34
1 cup (195 gm.)	470	6.4	22.8	62.2	35	181	2.3	60	.15	.11	3.3	14
***Mashed, milk added:**												
1 pound	369	10.0	3.2	77.2	123	281	2.7	190	.37	.25	4.0	34
1 cup (195 gm.)	159	4.3	1.4	33.2	53	121	1.2	80	.16	.10	1.7	14
***Mashed, milk and butter added:**												
1 pound	559	9.5	27.2	72.2	123	268	2.7	1,170	.35	.23	3.7	31
1 cup (195 gm.)	240	4.1	11.7	31.0	53	115	1.2	500	.15	.10	1.6	13
Steamed or pressure-cooked:												
1 pound	378	9.1	.5	86.7	50	254	3.2	80	.45	.18	5.3	65
1 medium potato (2½ in. diam.) or 1 cup diced (126 gm.).	105	2.5	.1	24.1	14	71	.9	20	.12	.05	1.5	18

Canned: Solids and liquid, 1 cup (including some liquid, 250 gm.).	144	4.2	.0	32.8	20	98	1.2	30	.14	.07	2.1	22
Drained solids: 1 pound	378	9.1	.5	86.7	50	254	3.2	80	.36	.15	4.2	57
3–4 very small potatoes (142 gm.)	118	2.8	.1	27.1	16	80	1.0	30	.11	.05	1.3	18
Potato chips, 10 medium (2 in. diam.) or 7 large (3 in. diam., 20 gm.).	108	1.3	7.4	9.8	(6)	(30)	(.4)	(10)	(.04)	(.02)	(.6)	2
Pretzels, 5 small sticks (5 gm.)	18	.4	.2	3.7	1	4	.0	(0)	Trace	Trace	Trace	(0)
Prunes, dried, unsulfured: Uncooked: 4 large prunes; refuse, pits, 12 percent (40–50 per lb., 1⅔ by 1 by ⅔ in., 40 gm.).	94	.8	.2	24.8	19	30	1.4	660	.03	.06	.6	1
4 medium prunes; refuse, pits, 15 percent (50–60 per lb., 1½ by 1 by ½ in., 32 gm.).	73	.6	.2	19.2	15	23	1.1	510	.03	.04	.5	1
4 small prunes; refuse, pits, 18 percent (70–80 per lb., 1⅓ by 1 by ½ in., 24 gm.).	54	.5	.1	14.2	11	17	.8	380	.02	.03	.3	1
1 cup medium; refuse, pits, 15 percent (165 gm.).	375	3.2	.8	99.4	76	119	5.5	2,650	.14	.23	2.4	4
*Cooked, no sugar added (med. size); prunes and liquid; refuse, pits, 8 percent: 1 pound	523	4.6	1.3	137.9	104	167	7.5	3,720	.13	.33	3.3	4
1 cup, 16–18 prunes and ⅓ cup liquid (270 gm.).	310	2.7	.7	81.8	62	99	4.5	2,210	.07	.20	2.0	2
*Cooked, sugar added (med. size); prunes and liquid; refuse, pits, 7 percent: 1 pound	695	4.2	.8	182.3	93	143	6.3	3,160	.13	.25	2.5	4
1 cup, 16–18 prunes and ⅓ cup liquid (315 gm.).	483	2.9	.6	126.6	64	100	4.4	2,200	.09	.18	1.8	3
See also Plums (Italian prunes), canned.												
Prunes, canned, strained (infant food), 1 ounce.	28	.3	.1	7.2	7	8	.4	210	.01	.01	.2	1
Prune juice, canned, 1 cup (240 gm.) ...	170	1.0	0.	46.3	(60)	(96)	(4.3)	—	(.07)	(.19)	1.0	(2)
*Prune whip: 1 pound	674	12.7	1.4	168.4	118	191	8.2	3,910	.17	.49	3.3	9
1 cup (135 gm.)	200	3.8	.4	50.1	35	57	2.4	1,160	.05	.15	1.0	3

Foods, The Composition of (Continued)

Food, description, and approximate measure	Food energy	Protein	Fat	Total carbohydrate	Calcium	Phosphorus	Iron	Vitamin A value	Thiamine	Riboflavin	Niacin	Ascorbic acid
	Cal.	Gm.	Gm.	Gm.	Mg.	Mg.	Mg.	I.U.	Mg.	Mg.	Mg.	Mg.
Pudding, vanilla. See Blancmange.												
Pumpkin, canned, 1 cup (228 gm.)	76	2.3	.7	18.0	(46)	(82)	(1.6)	7,750	.04	.14	1.2	—
Radishes, raw, 4 small (40 gm.); refuse, tops and rootlets, 51 percent.	4	.2	.0	.8	7	6	.2	10	.01	Trace	.1	5
Raisins:												
Dried, unsulfured:												
1 cup (160 gm.)	429	3.7	.8	113.9	125	206	5.3	80	.24	.13	.8	Trace
1 tablespoon (10 gm.)	26	.2	.0	7.1	8	13	.3	Trace	.02	.01	Trace	Trace
*Cooked, sugar added, 1 cup (295 gm.)	572	3.2	.6	150.7	112	186	4.7	60	.18	.12	.6	Trace
Raspberries:												
Black, raw, 1 cup (134 gm.)	100	2.0	2.1	21.0	54	50	1.2	0	.03	(.09)	(.4)	(32)
Red:												
Raw, 1 cup (123 gm.)	70	1.5	.5	17.0	49	46	1.1	160	.03	(.08)	(.4)	29
Frozen, 3 ounces	84	.7	.3	21.0	24	22	.5	70	.01	(.03)	(.2)	14
Rhubarb:												
Raw, 1 cup diced (122 gm.)	19	.6	.1	4.6	62[1]	30	.6	40	.01	—	.1	11
*Cooked, sugar added:												
1 pound	639	1.8	.5	163.4	186[1]	91	1.8	110	.03	—	.3	28
1 cup (272 gm.)	383	1.1	.3	97.9	112[1]	54	1.1	70	.02	—	.2	17
Canned in syrup. See Cooked.												
Rice:												
Brown, raw, 1 cup (208 gm.)	748	15.6	3.5	161.6	81	630	4.2	(0)	.66	.10	9.6	(0)
Converted:												
Raw, 1 cup (187 gm.)	677	14.2	.6	148.5	45	254	1.5	(0)	.38	.06	7.2	(0)
*Cooked:												
1 pound	525	10.9	.5	115.3	36	195	1.4	(0)	.25	.04	4.9	(0)
1 cup (176 gm.)	204	4.2	.2	44.7	14	76	.5	(0)	.10	.02	1.9	(0)
White or milled:												
Raw, 1 cup (191 gm.)	692	14.5	.6	151.7	46	260	1.5	(0)	.13	.05	3.1	(0)

[1] Calcium may not be available because of presence of oxalic acid.

	Calories	Protein (gm.)	Fat (gm.)	Carbohydrate (gm.)	Calcium (mg.)	Phosphorus (mg.)	Iron (mg.)	Vitamin A (I.U.)	Thiamine (mg.)	Riboflavin (mg.)	Niacin (mg.)	Ascorbic acid (mg.)
*Cooked:												
1 pound	542	11.4	.5	118.9	36	204	1.4	(0)	.06	.04	1.9	(0)
1 cup (168 gm.)	201	4.2	.2	44.0	13	76	.5	(0)	.02	.01	.7	(0)
Precooked, dry, 1 cup (110 gm.)	420	9.7	.2	91.6	4	73	.9	(0)	.02	.02	.1	(0)
Rice products:												
Flakes, 1 cup (30 gm.)	118	1.8	.2	26.3	6	35	.5	(0)	.02	.03	.3	(0)
Flakes (added thiamine and niacin), 1 cup, (30 gm.)	118	1.8	.2	26.3	6	35	.5	(0)	.14	.03	1.6	(0)
Puffed, 1 cup (14 gm.)	55	.8	.1	12.3	3	16	.3	(0)	.01	.01	.1	(0)
Puffed (added thiamine and niacin), 1 cup, (14 gm.)	55	.8	.1	12.3	3	16	.3	(0)	.06	.01	.8	(0)
Rice, wild. See Wild rice.												
Rolls:												
Plain, unenriched (pan rolls):												
1 roll (16 per lb., 28 gm.)	86	2.5	1.5	15.4	15	27	.2	0	.02	.03	.3	0
1 roll (12 per lb., 38 gm.)	118	3.4	2.1	20.9	21	36	.3	0	.02	.04	.4	0
1 roll (8 per lb., 57 gm.)	176	5.1	3.1	31.4	31	55	.4	0	.03	.06	.6	0
Plain, enriched (pan rolls):												
1 roll (16 per lb., 28 gm.)	86	2.5	1.5	15.4	15	27	.5[1]	0	.07[1]	.04[1]	.6[1]	0
1 roll (12 per lb., 38 gm.)	118	3.4	2.1	20.9	21	36	.7[1]	0	.09[1]	.06[1]	.8[1]	0
1 roll (8 per lb., 57 gm.)	176	5.1	3.1	31.4	31	55	1.0[1]	0	.14[1]	.09[1]	1.3[1]	0
Sweet:												
Unenriched:												
1 package (6 rolls, 330 gm.)	1,065	28.0	25.7	177.5	208	343	2.0	0	.18	.44	3.3	0
1 roll (55 gm.)	178	4.7	4.3	29.6	35	57	.3	0	.03	.07	.6	0
Enriched:												
1 package (6 rolls, 330 gm.)	1,065	28.0	25.7	177.5	208	343	5.9[1]	0	.80[1]	.51[1]	7.3[1]	0
1 roll (55 gm.)	178	4.7	4.3	29.6	35	57	1.0[1]	0	.13[1]	.08[1]	1.2[1]	0
Rutabagas, cooked:												
1 pound	145	3.6	.5	34.0	250	186	1.8	1,590	.23	.32	3.2	95
1 cup cubed or sliced (155 gm.)	50	1.2	.2	11.6	85	64	.6	540	.08	.11	1.1	33
Rye bread. See Breads.												
Rye flour, light, 1 cup, sifted (80 gm.)	285	7.5	.8	62.3	18	148	.9	(0)	.12	.06	.5	(0)
Rye wafers or "Swedish health bread," 2 wafers (1⅞ by 3½ in., 13 gm.)	43	1.6	.2	9.8	6	52	.6	(0)	.04	.03	.2	(0)

[1] Iron, thiamine, riboflavin, and niacin are based on the minimum level of enrichment specified in the standards of identity of breads proposed by the Federal Security Agency and published in the Federal Register, August 3, 1943.

Foods, The Composition of (Continued)

Food, description, and approximate measure	Food energy Cal.	Protein Gm.	Fat Gm.	Total carbohydrate Gm.	Calcium Mg.	Phosphorus Mg.	Iron Mg.	Vitamin A value I.U.	Thiamine Mg.	Riboflavin Mg.	Niacin Mg.	Ascorbic acid Mg.
Salad dressings:												
Commercial, plain (mayonnaise type):[1]												
1 cup (235 gm.)	902	2.6	86.5	32.7	21	70	.9	340	.04	.07	(0)	0
1 tablespoon (15 gm.)	58	.2	5.5	2.1	1	4	.1	20	Trace	Trace	(0)	0
French:												
1 cup (240 gm.)	945	1.4	85.2	48.7	(0)	(0)	(0)	(0)	(0)	(0)	(0)	(0)
1 tablespoon (15 gm.)	59	.1	5.3	3.0	(0)	(0)	(0)	(0)	(0)	(0)	(0)	(0)
*Home-cooked, boiled:												
1 cup (270 gm.)	446	12.2	27.0	40.5	243	275	1.9	1,350	.16	.46	.7	Trace
1 tablespoon (17 gm.)	28	.8	1.7	2.6	15	17	.1	80	.01	.03	Trace	Trace
Mayonnaise:[2]												
1 cup (205 gm.)	1,451	3.1	159.9	6.2	39	123	2.0	430	.07	.07	(0)	0
1 tablespoon (13 gm.)	92	.2	10.1	.4	2	8	.1	30	Trace	Trace	(0)	0
Salad oil. See Oils, salad or cooking.												
Salmon:												
Cooked, Pacific, broiled or baked:												
1 steak (4 by 3 by ½ in., 120 gm.)	204	33.6	6.7	.2	—	500	1.4	—	.12	.33	9.8	—
Canned, solids and liquid (including bones):												
Chinook or King, 3 ounces	173	16.8	11.2	0.	131[2]	246	.8	200	.02	.12	6.2	(0)
Chum, 3 ounces	118	18.3	4.4	0.	212[2]	299	.6	50	.02	.13	6.0	(0)
Coho or silver, 3 ounces	140	17.9	7.1	0.	197[2]	216	.8	70	.02	.15	6.3	(0)
Pink or humpback, 3 ounces	122	17.4	5.3	0.	159[2]	243	.7	60	.03	.16	6.8	(0)
Sockeye or red, 3 ounces	147	17.2	8.2	0.	220[2]	293	1.0	200	.03	.14	6.2	(0)
Sardines:												
Atlantic type, canned in oil:												
Solids and liquid, 3 ounces	288	17.9	23.0	.9	301	369	3.0	—	(.01)	(.12)	(3.3)	(0)
Drained solids, 3 ounces	182	21.9	9.4	1.0	328	498	2.3	190	.01	.15	4.1	(0)
Pilchards, Pacific type, canned, solids and liquid:												
Natural pack, 3 ounces	171	15.1	11.5	.6	(324)	(143)	(3.5)	(20)	(.01)	(.26)	(6.3)	(0)
Tomato sauce, 3 ounces	184	15.1	12.6	1.4	324	143	3.5	20	.01	.23	4.5	(0)

[1] Minerals and vitamins are calculated from a recipe.
[2] If bones are discarded, calcium content would be much lower. Bones equal about 2 percent of total contents of can.

Food and description												
Sauerkraut, canned:												
Solids and liquid, 1 cup (235 gm.)	39	2.6	.5	8.0	85	42	(1.2)	80	.08	.15	.3	38
Drained solids:												
1 pound	99	6.4	1.4	20.0	163	82	(2.3)	190	.15	.29	.5	74
1 cup (150 gm.)	32	2.1	.4	6.6	54	27	(.8)	60	.05	.10	.2	24
Sausage:												
Bologna:												
1 pound (1 by 2¾ in. diam.)	1,005	67.2	72.2	16.3	(41)	(508)	10.0	(0)	.80	.85	12.2	0
1 piece (1 by 1½ in. diam., 211 gm.).	467	31.2	33.5	7.6	(19)	(236)	4.6	(0)	.37	.40	5.7	0
Frankfurter, cooked:												
1 pound	1,131	64.	91.	9.	27	222	5.4	(0)	.72	.83	11.3	0
1 frankfurter (51 gm.)	124	7.	10.	1.	3	25	.6	(0)	.08	.09	1.3	0
Liver, liverwurst, 2 ounces	150	9.5	11.7	.9	5	135	3.1	3,260	.10	.63	2.6	(0)
Pork, links or bulk, raw, 4 ounces	510	12.2	50.8	0.	7	113	1.8	(0)	.49	.19	2.6	0
Pork, bulk, canned, 4 ounces	340	17.5	29.4	0.	10	188	2.6	(0)	.23	.27	3.4	0
Vienna sausage, canned, 4 ounces	244	17.9	18.6	0.	10	193	2.7	(0)	.11	.14	3.5	0
Scallops, raw, edible muscle, 4 ounces	89	16.8	.1	3.9	29	236	2.0	0	.05	.11	1.6	—
Shad or American shad, raw, 4 ounces E.P.	191	21.2	11.1	0.	—	295	.6	—	(.17)	.27	9.6	—
*Sherbet:[1]												
1 pint (386 gm.)	475	5.8	.2	115.8	193	154	.1	0	.07	.29	.2	(0)
½ cup (96 gm.)	118	1.4	.0	28.8	48	38	.0	0	.02	.07	.0	(0)
*Shortbread (2 squares, 1¾ by 1¾ in., 16 gm.).	81	1.1	3.9	10.3	2	9	.1	0	.01	Trace	.1	(0)
Shrimp, canned:												
Dry pack or drained solids of wet pack, 3 ounces.	108	22.8	1.2	—	98	224	2.6	50	.01	.03	1.9	(0)
Wet pack, solids and liquid, 3 ounces	76	15.9	.8	.3	50	129	1.5	50	.01	.03	1.2	(0)
Syrup, table blends (chiefly corn syrup):												
1 cup (328 gm.)	939	(0.)	(0.)	(242.7)	151	52	13.4	0	0	.03	.3	(0)
1 tablespoon (20 gm.)	57	(0.)	(0.)	(14.8)	9	3	.8	0	0	Trace	Trace	(0)
Soups, canned:[2]												
Bean:												
Condensed, 11 ounces	481	21.5	12.8	73.6	234	256	6.9	—	.25	.25	2.2	—
Ready-to-serve, 1 cup (250 gm.)	191	8.5	5.0	29.5	95	102	2.8	—	.10	.10	.8	—

[1] Based on 6.8 pounds to the gallon, factory packed.
[2] All ready-to-serve soups are calculated from equal weights of the condensed soup and water except cream soup which was based on equal weights of the condensed soup and milk.

Foods, The Composition of (Continued)

Food, description, and approximate measure	Food energy Cal.	Protein Gm.	Fat Gm.	Total carbohydrate Gm.	Calcium Mg.	Phosphorus Mg.	Iron Mg.	Vitamin A value I.U.	Thiamine Mg.	Riboflavin Mg.	Niacin Mg.	Ascorbic acid Mg.
Soups, canned: (Continued)												
Beef:												
Condensed, 11 ounces	248	15.0	8.4	27.8	37	156	.9	—	—	—	—	—
Ready-to-serve, 1 cup (250 gm.)	100	6.0	3.5	11.0	15	62	.5	—	—	—	—	—
Bouillon, broth, and consomme:												
Condensed, 11 ounces	26	(6.)	—	(0.)	6	59	2.8	0	0	.12	1.6	0
Ready-to-serve, 1 cup (240 gm.)	9	(2.)	—	(0.)	2	24	1.0	0	0	.05	.6	0
Chicken:												
Condensed, 11 ounces	187	8.4	5.9	24.6	47	47	.9	—	.06	.34	3.7	—
Ready-to-serve, 1 cup (250 gm.)	75	3.5	2.5	9.5	20	20	.5	—	.02	.12	1.5	—
Strained (infant food), 1 ounce	17	.9	.7	1.7	11	13	.1	70	Trace	.03	.1	Trace
Clam chowder:												
Condensed, 11 ounces	210	10.9	5.9	30.2	84	187	8.7	—	—	—	—	—
Ready-to-serve, 1 cup (255 gm.)	86	4.6	2.3	12.5	36	76	3.6	—	—	—	—	—
Cream soup (asparagus, celery, or mushroom):												
Condensed, 11 ounces	279	6.9	16.2	29.6	162	140	.9	500	.12	.53	.3	3
Ready-to-serve, 1 cup (255 gm.)	201	7.1	11.7	18.4	217	176	.5	200	.05	.20	.1	(0)
Liver soup, strained (infant food), 1 ounce	16	1.2	.3	2.0	5	18	.5	1,340	.02	.12	.5	1
Noodle, rice, or barley:												
Condensed, 11 ounces	291	15.3	10.9	32.4	206	215	.6	60	.06	.12	1.7	0
Ready-to-serve, 1 cup (250 gm.)	117	6.0	4.5	13.0	82	85	.2	30	.02	.05	.7	0
Pea:												
Condensed, 11 ounces	357	16.2	5.0	63.6	81	249	3.7	(1,120)	.44	.19	3.1	9
Ready-to-serve, 1 cup (245 gm.)	141	6.4	2.0	25.0	32	98	1.5	(440)	.17	.07	1.2	5
Tomato:												
Condensed, 11 ounces	230	5.6	5.6	45.5	65	97	2.2	(3,120)	.06	.25	1.9	22
Ready-to-serve, 1 cup (245 gm.)	90	2.2	2.2	17.9	24	39	1.0	(1,230)	.02	.10	.7	10
Vegetable:												
Condensed, 11 ounces	203	10.3	4.4	35.9	81	125	1.9	—	.12	.19	2.8	19
Ready-to-serve, 1 cup (250 gm.)	82	4.2	1.8	14.5	32	50	.8	—	.05	.08	1.0	8
Strained (infant food), 1 ounce	12	.7	.1	2.6	7	11	.3	700	.02	.02	.1	Trace
Vegetable and lamb soup, strained (infant food), 1 ounce.	14	.7	.3	2.2	6	10	.2	740	.01	.01	.3	Trace

Food	Food energy (calories)	Protein (gm.)	Fat (gm.)	Carbohydrate (gm.)	Calcium (mg.)	Phosphorus (mg.)	Iron (mg.)	Vitamin A (I.U.)	Thiamine (mg.)	Riboflavin (mg.)	Niacin (mg.)	Ascorbic acid (mg.)
Soups, dehydrated:												
Navy bean, 1 ounce[1]	92	5.0	.3	17.8	38	120	2.6	0	.12	.05	.6	Trace
Pea, 1 ounce[2]	93	5.8	.3	17.3	19	103	1.5	60	.16	.05	.9	Trace
Soybeans, whole, mature, dried, 1 cup (210 gm.).	695	73.3	38.0	73.1[3]	477	1,231	16.8	230	2.25	.65	4.9	Trace
Soybean curd, 1 cake (2¾ by 2½ by 1 in., 120 gm.).	85	8.4	4.9	3.6	120	114	1.8	—	.07	.06	.4	(0)
Soybean flour, flakes, grits:												
Low fat, 1 cup soy flour, stirred, (101 gm.).	230	45.1	1.1	38.1[3]	268	629	13.1	70	1.11	.35	2.9	(0)
Medium fat:												
1 cup soy flour, stirred (88 gm.)	232	37.4	5.7	32.7[3]	215	537	11.4	100	.72	.30	2.3	(0)
1 cup soy grits (138 gm.)	365	58.6	9.0	51.3[3]	337	842	17.9	150	1.12	.46	3.6	(0)
Full fat, 1 cup (soy flour, stirred, 72 gm.).	250	25.8	14.8	21.5[3]	140	398	8.7	100	.56	.20	1.6	(0)
Soybean milk (without added calcium and vitamins), 4 ounces.	38	3.9	1.7	2.4	24	53	.8	—	.10	.05	.3	(0)
Soybean sprouts, raw, 1 cup (107 gm.)	49	6.6	1.5	5.7	51	72	1.1	190	.24	.21	.9	14
Spaghetti:												
Unenriched:												
Dry, 1 cup (2 in. pieces, 94 gm.)	354	12.0	1.3	71.9	21	155	1.4	(0)	.09	.06	1.9	(0)
*Cooked:												
1 pound	678	23.2	2.7	137.1	41	295	2.7	(0)	.08	.08	2.2	(0)
1 cup (146 gm.)	218	7.4	.9	44.1	13	95	.9	(0)	.03	.02	.7	(0)
Enriched:												
Dry, 1 cup (2 in. pieces, 94 gm.)	354	12.0	1.3	71.9	21	155	2.7[4]	(0)	.83[4]	.35[4]	5.6[4]	(0)
*Cooked:												
1 pound	678	23.2	2.7	137.1	41	295	5.0	(0)	.79	.47	6.4	(0)
1 cup (146 gm.)	218	7.4	.9	44.1	13	95	1.6	(0)	.25	.15	2.1	(0)
Spinach:												
Raw, 4 ounces E.P.	22	2.6	.3	3.6	92[5]	62	3.4	10,680	.13	.23	.7	67
Cooked:												
1 pound	115	14.1	2.7	16.3	563[5]	150	9.1	53,480	.36	.91	2.7	136
1 cup (180 gm.)	46	5.6	1.1	6.5	223[5]	59	3.6	21,200	.14	.36	1.1	54

[1] Navy bean meal with farinaceous flour up to 15 percent.

[2] Pea meal with farinaceous flour up to 15 percent.

[3] Approximately 40 percent of this total amount of carbohydrate calculated by difference is sugar, starch, and dextrin. The remaining portion is made up of materials thought to be utilized only poorly if at all by the body.

[4] Iron, thiamine, riboflavin, and niacin are based on the minimum level of enrichment specified in the standards of identity promulgated under the Food, Drug, and Cosmetic Act.

[5] Calcium may not be available because of presence of oxalic acid.

Foods, The Composition of (Continued)

Food, description, and approximate measure	Food energy Cal.	Protein Gm.	Fat Gm.	Total carbo-hydrate Gm.	Cal-cium Mg.	Phos-phorus Mg.	Iron Mg.	Vitamin A value I.U.	Thia-mine Mg.	Ribo-flavin Mg.	Nia-cin Mg.	Ascor-bic acid Mg.
Spinach: (Continued)												
Canned:												
Solids and liquid, 1 cup (232 gm.)	45	5.3	.9	7.0	209[1]	77	3.7	15,750	.04	.23	.8	34
Drained solids:												
1 pound	115	14.1	2.7	16.3	563[1]	150	9.1	34,650	.10	.54	1.8	65
1 cup (180 gm.)	46	5.6	1.1	6.5	223[1]	59	3.6	13,740	.04	.21	.7	26
Strained (infant food), 1 ounce	4	.5	.1	.7	22[1]	11	.4	1,190	.01	.03	.1	2
Squash, summer, cooked, diced:												
1 pound	74	2.7	.5	17.7	68	68	1.8	1,180	.18	.32	2.7	50
1 cup (210 gm.)	34	1.3	.2	8.2	32	32	.8	550	.08	.15	1.3	23
Squash, winter:												
Cooked:												
Baked, mashed:												
1 pound	215	8.6	1.8	50.0	109	159	3.6	28,100	.23	.68	2.7	31
1 cup (205 gm.)	97	3.9	.8	22.6	49	72	1.6	12,690	.10	.31	1.2	14
Boiled, mashed:												
1 pound	171	6.8	1.4	40.0	86	127	2.7	22,470	.18	.45	1.8	23
1 cup (228 gm.)	86	3.4	.7	20.1	43	64	1.4	11,290	.09	.23	.9	11
Canned, strained (infant food), 1 ounce.	8	.3	.1	1.9	9	5	.1	560	.01	.02	(.1)	1
Starch, pure (including arrowroot, corn, etc.):												
1 cup (128 gm.)	464	.6	.3	111.4	(0)	(0)	(0)	(0)	(0)	(0)	(0)	(0)
1 tablespoon (8 gm.)	29	.0	.0	7.0	(0)	(0)	(0)	(0)	(0)	(0)	(0)	(0)
Strawberries:												
Raw, capped, 1 cup (149 gm.)	54	1.2	.7	12.4	42	40	1.2	90	.04	.10	.4	89
Frozen, 3 ounces	90	.5	.3	22.6	19	19	.5	30	.02	.04	.2	35
Sugars:												
Granulated, cane or beet:												
1 cup (200 gm.)	770	(0.)	(0.)	199.0	—	—	—	(0)	(0)	(0)	(0)	(0)
1 tablespoon (12 gm.)	48	(0.)	(0.)	12.4	—	—	—	(0)	(0)	(0)	(0)	(0)
1 teaspoon (4 gm.)	16	(0.)	(0.)	4.2	—	—	—	(0)	(0)	(0)	(0)	(0)

[1] Calcium may not be available because of presence of oxalic acid.

Food												
1 piece, lump sugar (1⅛ by ⅝ by ⅛ in., 7 gm.)	27	(0.)	(0.)	7.0	—	—	—	(0)	(0)	(0)	(0)	(0)
Powdered:												
1 cup sugar, (stirred before measuring, 128 gm.)	493	(0.)	(0.)	127.4	—	—	—	(0)	(0)	(0)	(0)	(0)
1 tablespoon (8 gm.)	31	(0.)	(0.)	8.0	—	—	—	(0)	(0)	(0)	(0)	(0)
Brown:												
1 cup, firm-packed (220 gm.)	813	(0.)	(0.)	210.1	167[1]	81[1]	5.7	(0)	(0)	(0)	(0)	(0)
1 tablespoon (14 gm.)	51	(0.)	(0.)	13.1	10[1]	5[1]	.4	(0)	(0)	(0)	(0)	(0)
Maple, 1 piece (1¾ by 1¼ by ½ in., 30 gm.)	104	—	—	(27.)	—	—	—	—	—	—	—	—
Sweet potatoes: Cooked: Baked:												
1 pound	691	10.0	4.1	156.2	168	272	4.1	43,160[2]	.45	.29	3.5	105
1 sweet potato, peeled (5 by 2 in., 120 gm.)	183	2.6	1.1	41.3	44	72	1.1	11,410[2]	.12	.08	.9	28
Boiled:												
1 pound	560	8.2	3.2	126.7	136	222	3.2	34,960[2]	.39	.24	2.9	90
1 sweet potato, peeled (5 by 2½ in., 205 gm.)	252	3.7	1.4	57.2	62	100	1.4	15,780[2]	.18	.11	1.3	41
Candied:												
1 pound	813	6.8	16.3	164.3	163	204	4.1	28,380[2]	.18	.18	2.3	41
1 small sweet potato (3½ by 2¼ in., 175 gm.)	314	2.6	6.3	63.4	63	79	1.6	10,940[2]	.07	.07	.9	16
Canned, vacuum or solid pack, 1 cup (218 gm.)	233	4.4	.2	54.5	54	89	1.7	19,300	.12	.09	1.1	31
Swordfish: Cooked, broiled:												
1 steak (3 by 3 by ½ in., 125 gm.)	223	34.2	8.5	0.	25	314	1.4	2,880	.06	.07	12.9	(0)
Tangerines (including other Mandarin type oranges), 1 medium tangerine (2½ in. diam., 114 gm.)	35	.6	.2	8.8	(27)	(19)	(.3)	(340)	.06	(.02)	(.2)	25
Tangerine juice, unsweetened:												
Fresh, 1 cup (246 gm.)	95	2.2	.7	22.6	47	39	(.5)	(1,040)	.17	(.06)	.6	75
Canned, 1 cup (246 gm.)	95	2.2	.7	22.6	47	39	.5	(1,040)	(.15)	(.06)	(.6)	(64)
Tapioca, dry, 1 cup, granulated quick-cooking, stirred (152 gm.)	547	.9	.3	131.3	18	18	(1.5)	(0)	(0)	(0)	(0)	(0)

[1] Calcium and phosphorus are based on dark brown sugar; values would be lower for light brown sugar.

[2] If very pale varieties only were used, the vitamin A value would be very much lower.

Foods, The Composition of (Continued)

Food, description, and approximate measure	Food energy	Protein	Fat	Total carbohydrate	Calcium	Phosphorus	Iron	Vitamin A value	Thiamine	Riboflavin	Niacin	Ascorbic acid
	Cal.	Gm.	Gm.	Gm.	Mg.	Mg.	Mg.	I.U.	Mg.	Mg.	Mg.	Mg.
Tomatoes: Raw:												
1 medium E.P. (2 by 2½ in., 150 gm.)	30	1.5	.4	6.0	16	40	.9	1,640	.08	.06	.8	35
1 small E.P. (1¾ by 2¼ in., 110 gm.)	22	1.1	.3	4.4	12	30	.7	1,210	.06	.05	.6	26
Canned or cooked, 1 cup (242 gm.)	46	2.4	.5	9.4	(27)	(65)	(1.5)	2,540	.14	.08	1.7	40
Tomato juice, canned, 1 cup (242 gm.)	50	2.4	.5	10.4	(17)	(36)	(1.0)	2,540	.12	.07	1.8	38
Tomato catsup:												
1 cup (273 gm.)	268	5.5	1.1	66.9	33	49	2.2	(5,130)	.25	.19	6.1	31
1 tablespoon (17 gm.)	17	.3	.1	4.2	2	3	.1	(320)	.02	.01	.4	2
Tomato purée, canned, 1 cup (249 gm.)	90	4.5	1.2	17.9	(27)	(92)	(2.7)	4,680	.22	.17	4.5	69
Tomato soup. See Soups, canned, tomato.												
Tongue, beef, medium fat, raw, 4 ounces	235	18.6	17.0	.5	10	212	3.2	(0)	.14	.33	5.7	(0)
Tortillas, 1 tortilla (5 in. diam., 20 gm.)	50	1.2	(.6)	9.7	22	37	.4	40[1]	.04	.01	.2	—
Tuna fish, canned:												
Solids and liquid, 3 ounces	247	20.2	17.8	0.	6	250	1.0	(180)	(.04)	(.08)	(9.1)	(0)
Drained solids, 3 ounces	169	24.7	7.0	0.	(7)	(299)	1.2	70	.04	.10	10.9	(0)
Turkey, medium fat, raw, 4 ounces E.P.	304	22.8	22.9	0.	26	363	4.3	Trace	.10	.16	9.1	(0)
Turnips:												
Raw, 1 cup diced (134 gm.)	43	1.5	.3	9.5	54	46	.7	Trace	.07	.09	.6	38
Cooked:												
1 pound	122	3.6	.9	27.2	182	154	2.3	Trace	.18	.27	1.8	82
1 cup diced (155 gm.)	142	1.2	.3	9.3	62	53	.8	Trace	.06	.09	.6	28

[1] Vitamin A value of tortillas made from yellow corn; tortillas made from white corn have no vitamin A value.

Turnip greens:												
Cooked:												
Boiled in small or moderate amount of water until tender:												
1 pound	135	13.2	1.8	24.5	1,176	227	10.9	48,120	.27	1.86	3.2	272
1 cup (145 gm.)	43	4.2	.6	7.8	376	72	3.5	15,370	.09	.59	1.0	87
Boiled in large amount of water, long time:												
1 pound	135	13.2	1.8	24.5	1,176	227	10.9	48,120	.23	1.63	2.7	204
1 cup (145 gm.)	43	4.2	.6	7.8	376	72	3.5	15,370	.07	.52	.9	65
Canned, solids and liquid, 1 cup (232 gm.).	41	3.5	.7	7.4	232	70	3.7	10,210	.03	.21	1.3	45
Veal, cooked:												
Cutlet (wholesale round):												
1 pound without bone	993	127.0	50.0	0.	54	1,171	15.9	(0)	.37[1]	1.26[1]	27.5[1]	0
3 ounces without bone	184	24.0	9.0	0.	10	219	3.0	(0)	.07[1]	.24[1]	5.2[1]	0
Shoulder roast (wholesale chuck):												
1 pound with bone	762	94.0	40.0	0.	40	867	12.1	(0)	.44	1.05	26.5	0
1 pound without bone	1,029	127.0	54.0	0.	54	1,171	16.3	(0)	.60	1.42	35.8	0
3 ounces without bone	193	24.0	10.0	0.	10	219	3.1	(0)	.11	.27	6.7	0
Stew meat:												
1 pound without bone	1,344	114.0	95.0	0.	50	563	13.6	(0)	.23[2]	1.09[2]	21.1[2]	0
3 ounces without bone	252	21.0	18.0	0.	9	105	2.6	(0)	.04[2]	.20[2]	3.9[2]	0
Veal, canned, strained (infant food), 1 ounce.	24	4.5	.5	0.	4	48	.5	(0)	.01	.09	1.6	0
Vegetables, mixed, strained, canned (infant food), 1 ounce.	8	.5	.0	2.0	9	10	.3	[3]	.01	.01	.1	1
Vienna sausage. See Sausage.												
Vinegar:												
1 cup (240 gm.)	29	0.	—	(12.0)	17	24	1.2	—	—	—	—	—
1 tablespoon (15 gm.)	2	0.	—	(.8)	1	2	.1	—	—	—	—	—
***Waffles, baked with:**												
Unenriched flour:												
1 pound	1,304	42.2	48.1	171.6	872	926	4.5	1,630	.29	.82	1.6	(0)
1 waffle (4½ by 5⅝ by ½ in., 75 gm.).	216	7.0	8.0	28.4	144	153	.8	270	.05	.14	.3	(0)
Enriched flour:												
1 pound	1,304	42.2	48.1	171.6	872	926	8.2	1,630	.83	1.22	6.0	(0)

[1] Data assume cut to be prepared by braising or pot roasting. Use of proportionate quantity of drippings would add approximately 50 percent more thiamine and niacin and 25 percent more riboflavin.

[2] Use of proportionate quantity of liquid would double amount of thiamine and niacin and add one-third more riboflavin.

[3] Vitamin A value ranges from 270 to 1,510 I.U. per ounce.

Foods, The Composition of (Continued)

Food, description, and approximate measure	Food energy	Protein	Fat	Total carbo-hydrate	Cal-cium	Phos-phorus	Iron	Vitamin A value	Thia-mine	Ribo-flavin	Nia-cin	Ascor-bic acid
	Cal.	Gm.	Gm.	Gm.	Mg.	Mg.	Mg.	I.U.	Mg.	Mg.	Mg.	Mg.
Waffles, baked with: (Continued) 1 waffle (4½ by 5⅝ by ½ in., 75 gm.).	216	7.0	8.0	28.4	144	153	1.4	270	.14	.20	1.0	(0)
Walnuts, Persian or English:												
1 cup halves (100 gm.)	654	15.0	64.4	15.6	83	380	2.1	30	.48	.13	1.2	3
1 tablespoon chopped (8 gm.)	49	1.1	4.8	1.2	6	28	.2	Trace	.04	.01	.1	Trace
Watercress. See Cress, water.												
Watermelons; refuse, rind and seeds, 54 percent:												
Wedge (4 by 8 in., 1/16 melon 16 by 10 in., 925 gm.).	120	2.1	.9	29.4	30	51	.9	2,530	.20	.22	.7	26
½ slice (¾ by 10 in., 345 gm.)	45	.8	.3	11.0	11	19	.3	950	.08	.08	.3	10
Wheat flours:												
Whole (from hard wheats), 1 cup, stirred (120 gm.).	400	16.0	2.4	85.2	49	446	4.0	(0)	.66	.14	5.2	(0)
80-percent extraction (from hard wheats), 1 cup sifted (110 gm.).	401	13.2	1.4	81.5	26	210	1.4	(0)	.28	.08	2.3	(0)
Self-rising:												
Unenriched, 1 cup sifted (110 gm.)	385	10.1	1.1	81.2	299	532	1.1	(0)	.08	.05	1.3	(0)
Enriched, 1 cup sifted (110 gm.)	385	10.1	1.1	81.2	299[1]	532	3.2[1]	(0)	.48[1]	.29[1]	3.8[1]	(0)
Patent:												
All-purpose or family flour:												
Unenriched, 1 cup sifted (110 gm.)	401	11.6	1.1	83.7	18	96	.9	(0)	.07	.05	1.0	(0)
Enriched, 1 cup sifted (110 gm.)	401	11.6	1.1	83.7	18	96	3.2[2]	(0)	.48[2]	.29[2]	3.8[2]	(0)
Bread flour:												
Unenriched, 1 cup sifted (112 gm.)	408	13.2	1.2	83.7	18	106	1.0	(0)	.09	.06	1.1	(0)
Enriched, 1 cup sifted (112 gm.)	408	13.2	1.2	83.7	18	106	3.2[2]	(0)	.49[2]	.29[2]	3.9[2]	(0)

[1] Iron, thiamine, riboflavin, and niacin are based on the minimum level of enrichment specified in the standards of identity promulgated under the Food, Drug, and Cosmetic Act. Calcium is based on the level usually found in self-rising flour, which is in excess of the minimum (500 mg. per pound) required.

[2] Iron, thiamine, riboflavin, and niacin are based on the minimum level of enrichment specified in the standards of identity promulgated under the Food, Drug, and Cosmetic Act.

Food	Calories	Protein (gm.)	Fat (gm.)	Carbohydrate (gm.)	Calcium (mg.)	Phosphorus (mg.)	Iron (mg.)	Vitamin A (I.U.)	Thiamine (mg.)	Riboflavin (mg.)	Niacin (mg.)	Ascorbic acid (mg.)
Cake or pastry flour, 1 cup sifted (100 gm.)	364	7.5	.8	79.4	17	73	.5	(0)	.03	.03	.7	(0)
Wheat products:												
Bran, breakfast cereals. See Bran.												
Flakes, 1 cup (35 gm.)	125	3.8	.6	28.1	16	115	1.0	(0)	.03	.06	1.7	(0)
Flakes (added iron, thiamine, and niacin) 1 cup (35 gm.)	125	3.8	.6	28.1	16	115	1.5	(0)	.20	.06	2.2	(0)
Germ, 1 cup stirred (68 gm.)	246	17.1	6.8	33.7	57	745	5.5	(0)	1.39	.54	3.1	(0)
Puffed, 1 cup (12 gm.)	43	1.3	.2	9.6	6	39	.4	(0)	.01	.02	.6	(0)
Puffed (added iron, thiamine, and niacin) 1 cup (12 gm.)	43	1.3	.2	9.6	6	39	.5	(0)	.07	.02	.8	(0)
*Rolled, cooked:												
1 pound	341	10.0	1.8	76.7	36	345	3.2	(0)	.33	.12	4.1	(0)
1 cup (236 gm.)	177	5.2	.9	39.9	19	179	1.7	(0)	.17	.06	2.1	(0)
Shredded:												
Plain:												
1 large biscuit (4 by 2¼ in., 1 oz.)	102	2.9	.7	22.7	13	102	1.0	(0)	.06	.03	1.3	(0)
1 small biscuit (2½ by 2 in., 22 gm.)	79	2.2	.6	17.6	10	79	.8	(0)	.05	.03	1.0	(0)
1 round biscuit (24 gm.)	86	2.4	.6	19.2	11	86	.8	(0)	.05	.03	1.1	(0)
With added malt and sugar:												
1 cup bite-size biscuits or 1 cup shreds (60 gm.)	213	5.3	.7	49.7	30	202	2.5	(0)	.11[1]	.09	2.7	(0)
*Whole meal, cooked:												
1 pound	327	12.3	1.4	71.7	41	377	3.2	(0)	.47	.15	4.2	(0)
1 cup (243 gm.)	175	6.6	.7	38.4	22	202	1.7	(0)	.25	.08	2.3	(0)
*Whole meal (added wheat germ, iron, and thiamine), cooked:												
1 pound	248	9.5	1.4	53.6	36	295	22.2	(0)	1.00	.12	3.9	(0)
1 cup (243 gm.)	133	5.1	.7	28.7	19	158	11.9	(0)	.53	.06	2.1	(0)
Wheat and malted barley cereal. See Breakfast foods, mixed cereals.												
*White sauce, medium:												
1 pound	736	18.2	56.8	40.0	522	431	.5	2,310	.16	.70	.5	2
1 cup (265 gm.)	429	10.6	33.1	23.3	305	252	.3	1,350	.09	.41	.3	1
Wild rice, parched, raw, 1 cup (163 gm.)	593	23.0	1.1	122.7	31	553	—	(0)	.73	1.03	10.0	(0)
Yeast:												
Compressed, baker's, 1 ounce	24	(3.0)	.1	3.7	7	172	1.4	(0)	.13	.59	8.0	(0)
Dried, brewer's, 1 tablespoon (8 gm.)	22	(3.0)	.1	3.0	8	151	1.5	(0)	.78	.44	2.9	(0)

[1] For brands that are oven-toasted thiamine will be .03 mg.

Food Values. The relative nourishing power ascribed to foods.

Fool (British). A dessert of stewed fruit that contains a custard, milk, or cream. The name is derived from the French word *fouler*, to force foods through a sieve.

Foot Sugar (British). Dark cane or raw sugar.

Forbidden Fruit. A very sweet citrus-flavored liqueur made with grape brandy and shaddock, a Caribbean grapefruit.

Force (Obsolete). Forcemeat.

Forcemeat. Finely chopped or minced foods, usually but not exclusively meats, and usually well spiced; used in the making of *galantines* and *pâtés*, for stuffing, and for garnishing.

Forchetta (Italian). Fork.

Forcing. The growing of fruits or vegetables in greenhouses out of season.

Forcing Bag. A bag made of strong calico, linen, greaseproof paper, or plastic, fitted with variously

shaped tubes filled with cream, icing, or purées which are forced through the nozzles into fancy shapes. It is also called a *pastry tube* and may be used for cooky dough.

Forcut (Obsolete). Food cut into pieces.

Fordrunken (Obsolete). Intoxicated.

Foreign Export. A style of making beer for export; it is usually stronger in flavor and alcoholic content, so that it keeps well for a longer period of time than ordinary beer.

Forel (Dutch). River trout.

Foreleg Ham. That portion of a pig below the shoulder or ham of both fore and hind legs.

Forelle (German). Trout.

Forelle Blau. Boiled trout quickly cooked.

Forellfisk (Swedish). Trout.

Forebright (British). Bread made from wholewheat or coarse-ground flour.

Forestière, À la. With a garnish of wild mushrooms cooked in butter or diced bacon with small, round potatoes; usually served with meat.

Foretaste. An advance or preliminary taste. Also, a tasting of food before it is served.

Forez Cheese; d'Ambert. A French cheese cured by being placed on a cellar floor and covered with dirt over which water is permitted to trickle. When not spoiled by undesirable mold, it resembles Roquefort in flavor.

Fork. A utensil for conveying food to the mouth; it consists of a handle and two or more long, rather sharp-pointed prongs. Originally forks had two, then three or four prongs; three is now the typical number.

Fork Luncheon. A midday meal; also any repast served with buffet foods, requiring only the use of a fork, without a knife.

Forktail. A four-year-old salmon.

Forlorne (Norwegian). Poached.

Formagelle Cheese. A small, soft ewe's- or goat's-milk cheese made only in spring and autumn and eaten fresh; a specialty of the mountainous areas of northern Italy.

Formaggi di Pasta Filata. A group of Italian cheeses, such as *provolone* and *mozzarella*, prepared by curdling milk with rennet, then heating it and stretching it.

Formaggini (Italian). A fresh, mild, sweet dessert cheese made of cow's and goat's milk, sometimes with spices or sugar mixtures added. *Formaggini di Lecco* and *Formaggini di Montpellier* are examples.

Formaggio (Italian). Cheese.

   Formaggio di Crema. Cream cheese.

Formato di Carne (Italian). Meat loaf.

Formosa Oolong. A fine-tasting green-brown tea produced in Formosa.

Forretter (Norwegian). Appetizers; hors d'oeuvres.

Forst. A wine village in the Pfalz region of Germany. *See* Germany, The Wines of.

Fort de Béthune. A strong French skim-milk cheese with a brownish exterior.

Fort, Le. Several French cheeses, particularly a

cow's-milk cheese made with chopped leeks in southwestern France.

Fortune Cookies. Folded wafers containing a strip of paper with a message served in certain Chinese restaurants. The batter is made with flour (usually rice flour), eggs, powdered sugar, and flavoring, poured in small rounds onto a grill and removed quickly. While the batter is still pliable a strip of paper is placed on each round, which is folded up in a characteristic fashion.

Foster. To nourish by means of food.

Fou (French, Colloquial). An intoxicated person.

Fouace (French). (1) A thin cake made with egg yolks, butter, saffron, spices, and flour, but without leavening. (2) A sweet bun made in the Touraine region.

Fouat. A cake made with butter, flour, and currants.

Fouée (French). (1) An unsweetened pastry made with pieces of fried bacon and moistened with the liquid from walnuts; a specialty of Burgundy. (2) A small rounded bread baked with a crust of melted butter and cream; a specialty of the Poitou region.

Fouet (French). Various kitchen utensils used to beat egg whites, cream, etc.

Fouetté (French). Whipped with a whisk.

Fouler (French). To force foods through a sieve.

Foufou. *See* Fufu.

Four (French). Oven.

  Au Four. Baked.

Four Mendicants. Raisins, almonds, figs, and walnuts (or other nuts) served as a dessert.

Fourchette (French). Fork.

Fourchette, À la (French). Of any meal served, requiring only the use of a fork, not a knife; a buffet meal.

Four, Petit. A bite-size cake covered with fondant, often containing rich fillings.

Forme. A rich French cheese made in the province of Auvergne.

Fourme d'Ambert. A rather spicy blue-veined French cow's-milk cheese; at its best from November to May.

Fourneau (French). A stove or range.

Fourré (French). (1) Coated with cream, sugar, etc. (2) Stuffed, as poultry.

Four Spices. A mixture of cloves, ginger, white pepper, and nutmeg.

Fowl. An edible feathered bird, especially the domestic hen and cock. In the United States the term includes the turkey, goose, duck, etc.

  Usually a fowl is a chicken that has been laying eggs for six months or more. It has a less tender flesh and a coarser skin than younger birds, and the tip of its breastbone is less flexible. It should be cooked with moist heat, that is stewed, fricasseed, boiled, braised, or simmered.

Fowler. A hunter of wild birds.

Fowl's Oyster. Small fatty tissue sometimes found near the tail of certain poultry; formerly popular as a cooking ingredient.

Foxy. (1) Beer or wine not properly fermented. (2) Having a fox-grape flavor, usually describes the taste of native American grapes.

Foy. A gift of food to a person starting on a tour.

Fracassata (Italian). Meat stew with sauce.

Fracid (Obsolete). Overripe food.

Fragole (Italian). Strawberries.

  Fragole di Bosco. Wild strawberries.

  Fragole di Montagna. Wild strawberries.

  Fragole in Vino. Strawberries in wine.

Fragoline (Italian). Wild or small strawberries.

Fragrant Petals. An extremely aromatic, fragrant tea produced in Chinkiang province, China.

Frail. A straw-type basket used to pack raisins, figs, etc., with a 30–75 pound capacity.

Fraischeur. The quality of freshness or crispness.

Fraise (French). Strawberry.

Fraise d'Agneau (French). Lamb's pluck; the lights (lungs), liver, and heart of the lamb.

Fraiser (French). To handle or work raw dough, as by trimming, ridging, braiding, or plaiting.

Fraises des Bois (French). Tiny wood strawberries, eaten either plain or with sugar and heavy half-sweet, half-sour cream, or made into pastry, *tarte aux fraises.*

Fraisia. A French sweet strawberry liqueur.

Framboeza (Portuguese). Raspberry.

Framboos (Dutch). Raspberry.

Frambuesa (Spanish). Raspberry.

Française, À la. The French style; applied to a wide variety of dishes cooked in a simple manner.

Francatelli. The eminent chef of Queen Victoria

and the author of *Cook's Guide* and *Modern Cook*.

France, The Wines of. The wines of France are undoubtedly the finest and the most varied in the world. In the section which follows, we can trace the background of the wines produced in Bordeaux, Burgundy, the Rhône Valley, Loire Valley, Champagne, and Alsace.

Bordeaux

In the extreme southwestern corner of France, near the Atlantic Ocean, there lies the district surrounding the ancient city of Bordeaux, where undoubtedly the world's most famous vineyards may be found. The Bordeaux region produces some of the finest wines in the world. Indeed, only superlatives will suffice to describe these vineyards. True, they furnish the world with some rather ordinary wines as well, but on the whole, Bordeaux wines tend to be above the average even when they are in the *vin ordinaire* category. The red wines range from a very light color to the deepest shades and from a light to a heavy body. In general they tend to be better than the white wines—except for certain dessert types.

When Henri of Anjou married Eleanor of Aquitaine in 1152, he received all of the Bordeaux district as part of her dowry. Two years later, he became King of England, and the region became an English domain. It remained so for almost three hundred years—until 1451.

Henri of Anjou had been eager to acquire Bordeaux because of the vineyards. During the centuries that followed, Bordeaux wines became tremendously popular in England. The British originally called Bordeaux "*claret*," because of its clear color. This second name has endured, and when the English speak of a claret they are talking about Bordeaux wine.

Wars, political upheavals, and economic chaos have marked the history of this region. The wine merchants and the vintners experienced dark periods of unhappy restrictions followed by sunny years of financial success and great prestige. They survived, and the vineyards have continued to produce an unusually high number of vintage wines over the years.

The Bordeaux region consists of five principal districts: Graves, Médoc, Pomerol, St. Émilion, and Sauternes. There are also three districts of less importance: Côtes, Entre-Deux-Mers, and Palus. The Gironde River, running from northwest to southeast, cuts straight through the Bordeaux district. On the left, or southern bank, are Médoc, Graves, and Sauternes; on the right, or northern bank, Pomerol and St. Émilion. In general, these vineyards produce red wines; but Sauternes produces exclusively white, and some portion of the Graves district is also devoted to white. It might be thought that an area producing so many superb wines should be physically impressive, with majestic landscapes, vistas of incomparable beauty. Alas, the truth is that the Bordeaux region is flat and quite dull visually.

In 1855 a most unusual event occurred: the wines of the two districts of Médoc and Sauternes were officially classified. To understand the significance of this, one must consider the commotion that would ensue if there were an attempt to classify the restaurants of New York, or canned goods on the market, or, for that matter, the vineyards of California.

The great occasion which led to this official classification was the Bordeaux exhibit planned for the 1855 Paris World Exposition. The Bordeaux Chamber of Commerce, apparently too timid to undertake the precarious task, delegated it to the *Syndicat des Courtiers*—the Society of Wine Brokers. For almost 125 years the brokers had had their own unofficial method of classification and knew well the greatness of the Bordeaux vineyards. Like merchants all over the world, their opinions were influenced by the market prices of the wines, and this, in itself, may have led to some fallacious conclusions. Nonetheless, the classification was a remarkably accurate one and more than a century later still stands the test of time. With only a few variations, the ratings of the Médoc which follow are even now substantially correct.

MÉDOC WINES
Classification 1855

First Growths
Ch. Lafite-Rothschild

Ch. Margaux
Ch. Latour
Ch. Haut-Brion

Second Growths

Ch. Mouton-Rothschild
Ch. Rausan-Segla
Ch. Rauzan-Gassies
Ch. Leoville-Lascases
Ch. Leoville-Poyferre
Ch. Leoville-Barton
Ch. Durfort-Vivens
Ch. Gruaud-Larose-Sarget
Ch. Gruaud-Larose-Faure
Ch. Lascombes
Ch. Brane-Cantenac
Ch. Pichon-Longueville, Baron de Pichon
Ch. Pichon-Longueville, Ctesse de Lalande
Ch. Ducru-Beaucaillou
Ch. Cos-d'Estournel
Ch. Montrose

Third Growths

Ch. Kirwan
Ch. Issan
Ch. Lagrange
Ch. Langoa-Barton
Ch. Giscours
Ch. Malescot-St-Exupery
Ch. Boyd-Cantenac
Ch. Cantenac-Brown
Ch. Palmer
Ch. La Lagune
Ch. Desmirail
Ch. Calon-Ségur
Ch. Ferrière
Ch. Marquis d'Alesme-Becker

Fourth Growths

Ch. Saint-Pierre
Ch. Talbot
Ch. Branaire-Duluc
Ch. Duhart-Milon
Ch. Pouget
Ch. La Tour-Carnet
Ch. Rochet
Ch. Beychevelle
Ch. Prieuré-Lichine
Ch. Marquis de Termes

Fifth Growths

Ch. Pontet-Canet
Ch. Batailley
Ch. Grand-Puy-Lacoste
Ch. Grand-Puy-Ducasse
Ch. Lynch-Bages
Ch. Lynch-Moussas
Ch. Dauzac
Ch. Mouton-d'Armailhacq
Ch. Le Tertre
Ch. Haut-Bages-Libéral
Ch. Pédesclaux
Ch. Belgrave
Ch. Camensac
Ch. Cos-Labory
Ch. Clerc-Milon
Ch. Cantemerle
Ch. Croizet-Bages

Some explanation of this list is necessary, however, for it is incomplete: only one red wine district—the Médoc—and one white wine district —Sauternes—were considered. (The Sauternes classification will be discussed in detail later.) The red wine districts of St. Émilion, Pomerol, and Graves were not included. In short, the reputation of the Bordeaux district rested upon the Médoc.

The wine brokers divided sixty vineyards into five categories of *crus*, or growths. Of these sixty, fifty-nine were in the Médoc, the only exception being Château Haut-Brion in the Graves district. The wine brokers felt that they could not disregard the immense reputation of Haut-Brion, and they awarded this distinguished wine a place of honor with the Médoc wines. It is difficult today to understand why, having made this exception, the classifiers failed to include some of the outstanding wines of Pomerol, Graves, and St. Émilion. Certainly, a number of wines come to mind, including Cheval Blanc and Petrus, which should have been considered. These two equal, and possibly surpass, many of the third *crus* in the classification.

It has been suggested that the *crus* might well have been divided into three, but certainly not more than four groupings. Many wine experts agree that there is little difference between the third and fourth *crus*, which, during most years, seem fairly equal in quality and bring similar prices on the market. Apparently the wine brokers had second thoughts on the subject in the years after the 1855 classification, for they added many more vineyards; hundreds of additional vineyards have been classified into four new groupings to follow the five original *crus*. These are: superior bourgeois, bourgeois, artisan, and peasant. As recently as 1932, the local Chamber of Commerce added a classification of several hundred bourgeois growths; and in 1953 and 1955, the wines of Graves were classified. This classification was immediately criticized as incomplete. In 1954, when the wines of St. Émilion were classified, there was less criticism, for the job had been done more thoroughly.

Many people have the mistaken impression that only wines in the first *cru* are worth drinking. No one can deny the excellence of the first category, but these wines should be reserved for special occasions. Certain wine snobs (and they do exist) believe that only by paying top prices can they be assured of satisfactory wines. They are wrong, for many fine wines are found in the lower classifications, wines well worth discovering.

Another and not unimportant note on the wines of the Médoc: Each wine is bottled at the château whose name it bears. This fact is stated on the label as *mis en bouteille au château*. Exceptions are Châteaux Kirwan, Léoville-Baron, and Pontet-Canet. Thus, while the Château label offers a degree of assurance to the purchaser, its absence does not always indicate inferiority for these three wines are well above average.

Sauternes and Barsac

The white wines of Sauternes were classified in 1855. With the adjacent district of Barsac, these vineyards occupy about six square miles south of the city of Bordeaux. (There are five subdistricts or communes: Sauternes, Preignac, Bommes, Fargues, and Barsac.) On a rather flinty, gravelly soil, the châteaux grow the Semillon grape (with some Sauvignons and occasionally Muscatelles). The Semillon produces a wine which is unique in its richness and

sweetness combined with a flowery bouquet. Critics describe the wine as too sweet, too cloying for regular consumption. The fact is that Sauternes has an unnecessarily high alcoholic content usually ranging from 13 to 17 percent; it contains a great deal of sugar and a very high percentage of glycerine. This makes the wine precisely what it is: rich and sweet and very smooth. It is a remarkable, a superb wine, but tastes have changed—particularly in the United States. Americans have consistently shown a preference for lighter and drier wines. As a result, Sauternes and Barsac have not had the success in this country that they have had in other parts of the world.

Sauternes wines are produced by a special process. In other parts of the Bordeaux region, when the grapes are perfectly formed and ripe, they are harvested immediately. But here as excitement mounts among the local population, and everyone begins to count the days and watch the skies for portents of weather, the grapes are allowed to remain on the vines. Several days are usually required before they become somewhat overripe and slightly shriveled. Then the skins crack and some of the juice escapes, leaving a higher concentration of sugar in the grape. Now the peasants go carefully through the fields, pulling off the vine leaves by hand to expose the grapes to the direct rays of the sun. To the uninitiated, the grapes look spoiled, for they are shriveled like raisins and covered with a powdery, microscopic fungus, the *bortrytis cinerea*. This is what the pickers have been waiting for. Armed with pairs of tiny scissors, they carefully cut off only those individual grapes—never whole bunches—which are in the proper state of decay. It takes several successive trips through the vineyard to complete the selection of individual grapes; sometimes a half dozen trips are required before the vintner is satisfied that the harvest is completed.

The grapes are placed immediately in the press and squeezed very gently to avoid bitterness. The first run usually furnishes the best wine, the *vin de tête*. Later squeezings are slightly stronger, and the wine is not quite as choice as that from the first pressing. The fungus deposit, which had been allowed to form on the grapes before they were picked, now adds a remarkable bouquet to the wine during the fermentation process. In years when the sun is very hot and there has been little rain, the grapes have a high percentage of sugar. The wine, so high in alcohol and sugar content, requires special treatment. Otherwise it is apt to ferment a second time in a period of hot weather during the summer which follows the original harvest, and the wine will be spoiled. Also, if excess air comes in contact with the young wines, their color darkens. (The ideal color for a fine Sauternes is a brilliant gold.) In certain off years, when there has been too much rain, the grapes swell, which reduces the proper sugar content. In such years, the wine is never sold under châteaux names but is marketed under the simple generic label "Sauternes." These wines have a typical dry-to-medium white wine taste which makes them pleasant with fish dishes. But they are not the Sauternes which live up to the world-wide reputation of this wine.

Here is the classification for Sauternes and Barsac.

Sauternes and Barsac

Classification 1855

First Superior Growth

Ch. d'Yquem

First Growths

Ch. La Tour Blanche
Ch. Lafaurie-Peyraguey
Ch. Haut-Peyraguey
Ch. Rayne-Vigneau
Ch. Suduiraut
Ch. Coutet
Ch. Climens
Ch. Guiraud
Ch. Rieussec
Ch. Rabaud-Promis
Ch. Sigalas-Rabaud

Second Growths

Ch. Mirat
Ch. Doisy-Daëne
Ch. Doisy-Dubroca
Ch. Doisy-Védrines

Ch. d'Arche
Ch. Filhot
Ch. Broustet
Ch. Nairac
Ch. Caillou
Ch. Suau
Ch. Malle
Ch. Romer
Ch. Lamothe

As the chart indicates, only one wine received top classification: Châtcau d'Yquem. Even though this category was determined in 1855, more than a century has failed to shake this wine from its position; it remains today unchallenged. But if it is said that d'Yquem is the greatest sweet white wine in the world, what can be said to those who argue that the great German sweet wines are its equal? In any event, no matter how enthusiastic one may be about Sauternes, its sweetness makes it more a liqueur, an afterdinner drink, than a conventional wine. It is not suitable with food, for its richness masks the flavor of any dish. Yet there arc pcoplc who unhesitatingly order Château d'Yquem and drink it through a meal. Gourmets, on the other hand, rarely drink more than a few sips of d'Yquem, certainly never more than a small glass at any one time.

Since the 1855 classification covered only Médoc and Sauternes, here are those Bordeaux districts which were not included.

Graves

This region extends along the west bank of the Garonne River for about thirty-five miles and is from five to seven miles in width. The soil is pebbly, as in the other wine districts, but it also contains a type of clay called *graves*, for which the district is named. Graves produces fairly good red wines in the upper or northern half of the district, and white wines, both sweet and dry, in the southern or lower half. (Of course, there are exceptions, as a few white wines come from the north.) That great red wine, Château Haut-Brion, is produced in the north and this château also makes a creditable white wine.

The 1953 classification of these wines is:

GRAVES

Official Classification 1953

Classified Red Wines of Graves

Ch. Bouscaut
Ch. Carbonnieux
Domaine de Chevalier
Ch. Couhins
Ch. Haut-Bailly
Ch. Haut-Brion
Ch. La Mission-Haut-Brion
Ch. La Tour-Haut-Brion
Ch. La Tour-Martillac
Ch. Malartic-Lagravière
Ch. Olivier
Ch. Pape Clément
Ch. Smith-Haut-Lafitte

Classified White Wines of Graves

Ch. Bouscaut
Ch. Carbonnieux
Domaine de Chevalier
Ch. Laville-Haut-Brion
Ch. La Tour-Martillac
Ch. Olivier

This classification has been criticized for not including the white wine produced by Château Haut-Brion. Special note should also be taken of the outstanding red wine produced at La Mission-Haut-Brion: Haut-Bailly. And Château Carbonnieux also makes an extraordinarily good white wine.

Saint-Émilion and Pomerol

These two districts, both producing important wines, were also omitted from the 1855 classification. Perhaps the brokers hesitated to include the Saint-Émilion wines because of their lack of typical Bordeaux characteristics, for instead of being light and delicate they have the strong flavor of the more masculine wines of Burgundy. But in 1955 the wines of Saint-Émilion were classified into four *crus*. Heading the list, to no one's surprise, were the two leading vineyards of Château Ausone and Château Cheval-Blanc. Ausone has a long history, reputedly having been planted some two thousand years ago by the Roman poet Ausonius. This wine matures quite slowly and should not be drunk before it is ten years old. Cheval-Blanc, the larger vineyard of

the two, has developed a great reputation among connoisseurs over the years. In some years the wine from this vineyard reaches a surprising perfection and is in great demand. In certain years (1943, for example) it was considered the greatest wine of Bordeaux.

In the Pomerol district, a very short distance away, the outstanding wine is undoubtedly Château Petrus, one that deserves all the recognition it has received.

SAINT-ÉMILION

Official Classification 1955

First Classified Great Growths

Ch. Ausone
Ch. Cheval Blanc
Ch. Beauséjour-Lagarosse
Ch. Beauséjour-Fagouet
Ch. Belair
Ch. Canon
Ch. Clos Fourtet
Ch. Figeac
Ch. La Gaffelière Naudes
Ch. Magdelaine
Ch. Pavie
Ch. Trottevieille

Great Classified Growths

Ch. l'Angelus
Ch. Balestard la Tonnelle
Ch. Bellevue
Ch. Bergat
Ch. Cadet Bon
Ch. Cadet Piola
Ch. Canon la Gaffelière
Ch. Cap de Mourlin
Ch. Chapelle Madeleine
Ch. Chauvin
Ch. Corbin
Ch. Corbin Michotte
Ch. Coutet
Ch. Croque Michotte
Ch. Cure Bon
Ch. Fonplegade
Ch. Fonroque
Ch. Franc Mayne
Ch. Grand Barrail Lamarzelle Figeac
Ch. Grand Corbin Despagne

Ch. Grand Corbin Pecresse
Ch. Grand Mayne
Ch. Grand Pontet
Ch. Grandes Murailles
Ch. Guadet Saint Julien
Ch. Jean Faure
Ch. Clos des Jacobins
Ch. La Carte
Ch. La Clotte
Ch. La Couspaude
Ch. La Dominique
Ch. Clos La Madeleine
Ch. Larcis Ducasse
Ch. Lamarzelle
Ch. Larmande
Ch. Laroze
Ch. Lasserre
Ch. La Tour du Pin Figeac
Ch. La Tour Figeac
Ch. Le Chatelet
Ch. Le Couvent
Ch. Le Prieuré
Ch. Mauvezin
Ch. Moulin du Cadet
Ch. Pavie Decesse
Ch. Pavie Macquin
Ch. Pavillon Cadet
Ch. Petit Faurie de Souchard
Ch. Petit Faurie de Soutard
Ch. Ripeau
Ch. Sansonnet
Ch. Saint Georges Cote Pavie
Ch. Clos Saint Martin
Ch. Soutard
Ch. Tertre Daugay
Ch. Trimoulet
Ch. Trois Moulins
Ch. Troplong Mondot
Ch. Villemaurine
Ch. Yon Figeac

The Lesser Wines

The Bordeaux district has many comparatively undistinguished wines which are, however, worth knowing. *Premières Côtes de Bordeaux*, a narrow strip of land about thirty-eight miles long and two to four miles wide, like the Graves district, produces both red and white wines. The rather sweet white wines are superior to the reds, but the latter are perfectly satisfactory for ordinary occasions, and in special years they deserve to be in a superior category.

Côtes de Bordeaux Saint-Macaire has only white wines, according to the official description, but some rather sweet red wine is produced simply under the name "Bordeaux." These wines are seldom shipped to the United States, but they are found on the European continent where they are used as *vin ordinaire*.

Cérons wine is a kind of lesser Graves. It has a similar light, drinkable quality but with perhaps slightly more bouquet. Like the Graves wines, it tends to be dry, rather than sweet like the Sauternes.

Sainte-Croix-du-Mont is across the river from Sauternes and has many of the same characteristics in the wine it produces: a high percentage of alcohol is the outstanding similarity. By law the wine cannot be classified as Sainte-Croix-du-Mont unless it has a content of 13 percent.

Loupiac is a little district with less than two thousand acres of vineyards. There is little to distinguish the sweet white wines of Loupiac from those of Sainte-Croix-du-Mont, for these wines also have over 13 percent alcoholic content and are fairly high in their percentage of sugar.

Entre-deux-Mers is actually located between the two rivers of the Bordeaux district, the Garonne and the Dordogne. Only white wine may be labeled Entre-deux-Mers, and the red wine produced in the area must be sold as "Bordeaux." The district, a very large one as wine districts go, hasn't one outstanding vineyard, but, on the other hand, the average quality is fair. Entre-deux-Mers is still suffering from the effects of World War II and the postwar years, when much inferior wine bearing this label reached the market. The standard product is a moderately dry white wine, containing by law not less than 11.5 percent of alcohol.

Sainte-Foy-Bordeaux produces a large quantity of unimportant white wine ranging from a medium sweet to sweet type. The red wine tends to be drier.

Graves-de-Vayre's reputation falls between that

of Entre-deux-Mers and the much more distinguished Graves.

Bourgeais and Blayais: In these districts the white wines tend to be dry or at best only slightly sweet. The principal production is red wine, however. Twice as much is produced as of the white wines. The reds are passable, with strong masculine characteristics, robust and full bodied.

Burgundy

The Burgundy region, France's most controversial wine district, lies southeast of Paris between Dijon and Lyons. It produces some of the world's greatest red wines and one superb white wine.

Sometimes the generic term "Burgundy" is extended to include neighboring regions. Strictly speaking, however, only the Côte d'Or is considered true Burgundy wine territory. The Burgundy region is very narrow, on the average only a fraction of a mile wide. Its length is thirty-six miles, beginning at Dijon and extending southwest to Chagny. The vineyards face southeast, the ideal situation for sunshine. The countryside consists of a series of gentle ridges which give the region its name, Côte d'Or or "Slopes of Gold." The vineyards grow on these gentle slopes, usually at altitudes of eight hundred feet; only Corton faces the summer sun at about 975 feet. Peculiarly enough, the wines grown on the lower plains or in the higher altitudes are greatly inferior.

Wine has been produced in the Burgundy region for well over two thousand years. When the Romans came through this country, they found the peasants making excellent wines. The Romans, wine drinkers to a man, consumed enormous quantities, and the conquered Gauls sold them thousands of barrels. The last Caesar tried unsuccessfully in 89 A.D. to prohibit wine growing in Burgundy. Like all good politicians, he gave a plausible reason: the vineyards used land needed for basic food crops. Actually he wanted to protect the Italian wine market. In any event, the prohibition was not conspicuously successful.

During the Middle Ages, the Church gained control of many Burgundy vineyards. France was not a unified country, and the Dukes of Burgundy were among the most powerful and the most belligerent lords of France. During the Hundred Years' War they joined forces with England against the French monarch. Later, when they were defeated by Louis XI, the region was joined to the Crown. But whether cultivated by monk or humble citizen, in war or peace, the vines of Burgundy flourished.

In the Bordeaux region, wines are grown on very large estates—the châteaux owned by syndicates whose corporate existence continues after the death of individual members. The vineyard that grows the grapes also bottles and sells the wines. A great château label offers a reasonable assurance that the wine in the bottle was produced by the vineyard stated on the label, that no other wine has been added, and furthermore that the wine will be similar from year to year because the same châteaux process it.

In Burgundy quite a different situation exists. Instead of the vineyards being owned by a large château, with control in the hands of one family or company, a single vineyard in Burgundy is owned by many people. Under the French law of inheritance, by the principle of *division des biens* (the equal division of property), all children are entitled to inherit equal shares in a particular piece of property. Thus, when the owner of a certain vineyard dies, each of his four children inherits a one-fourth interest. However, when these four children die, leaving a total of perhaps eighteen descendants, the property is split into eighteen shares. The Montrachet vineyard, an extremely important one in Burgundy, is usually cited as an example of the unfortunate result of the French inheritance laws: about nineteen acres of vines are jointly controlled by twelve owners. In some vineyards, the inheritance has been divided to such a point that each owner possesses only several rows of vines.

As Frenchmen are the most individualistic people on earth, it is apparent that when a dozen men own part of the same vineyard, each will tend the vines differently: some will pick earlier than others, each may bottle differently. The net result will be that twelve owners of a certain vineyard will develop twelve different products, although the labels state that it is the same wine of the same year. However, one fact remains: Burgundy has always been in great demand. The supply is inadequate, and it is not surprising that there has been chicanery in the past. In off years when the vintage has been meager, inferior wines were often mixed with superior. This practice became the great scandal of Burgundy. With so many different owners, stabilization and control seemed impossible. But during the 1930s the vintners finally realized that their reputations would be completely ruined unless there were reforms. They devised a complex system of classification by districts, types of grapes, and standards for each. There are checks made on alcoholic content, on tannin, acid, and even the bouquet of both new and aged wines. The results have been more than satisfactory. Fraud has been cut to a minimum, and when a wine merchant or a vintner is caught violating the law regarding adulteration, penalties are severe. Recently a wine grower was fined the equivalent of several hundred thousand dollars.

The Côte d'Or

The true Burgundy region, from Dijon to Chagny, is at present divided by unwritten agreement into two parts. The northern half, called the Côte de Nuits, is world famous for its production of red wines. The southern half, the Côte de Beaune, is famous for its white wines. The interesting fact about the Burgundy route, as one heads southward, is that the wines tend to become lighter in body and color until finally the reds are completely supplanted by the whites. Originally there were three subdivisions—the Côte de Dijon, which included the short stretch of vineyards running for several miles to the south of Dijon, was included with the other two. But this region has declined in productivity until only one important vineyard remains.

Leaving Dijon and heading southward, the road travels through the city suburbs, which now cover many former vineyards. Some fair white wine is produced in the suburban community of Dijon-Larrey, but it is not until the village of Fixin that an important vineyard is encountered. A red wine of quite good quality is produced in the twelve-acre vineyard of Clos de La Perrière. It is a strong wine which improves with age. The Clos du Chapitre is the other vineyard of the town; its product is not up to Clos de La Perrière.

The Côte de Nuits

The district starts with the town of Gevrey-Chambertin and includes Morey-Saint-Denis, Chambolle-Musigny, Gilly-les-Vougeots, Flagey-Echezaux, Vosne-Romanée, Nuits-Saint-Georges, and Premeaux. Several small and unimportant communes have been omitted from this listing.

Many of these villages along the Burgundy wine route have added the name of their most famous vineyard to their own. For example, the insignificant hamlet of Vosne became Vosne-Romanée because within the town lies the great vineyard of Romanée-Conti. Two villages have added Montrachet to their names: Puligny-Montrachet and Chasagne-Montrachet. One gathers that this practice is an attempt to exploit the great vineyards for the benefit of the lesser that lie within the area. A bottle bearing the label of Chambolle-Musigny, for example, does not mean that the wine comes from the Musigny vineyards, but merely that it is produced somewhere within the town limits of Chambolle, now called Chambolle-Musigny. The practice is unquestionably fraudulent.

Gevrey-Chambertin: The great vineyard here is Chambertin, frequently considered only second to Romanée-Conti, the finest in the Burgundy region. In the seventh century these vineyards were given to the Abbey of Béze, a religious order which produced a wine called the Clos de Béze. A peasant named Bertin who owned the adjacent land also planted vineyards; his property became known as *le champ de Bertin* (the field of Bertin), and ultimately Chambertin. This is a remarkable wine with high scores for color and bouquet; it has the masculine characteristics typical of a true Burgundy. The two leading vineyards, each with over thirty acres, are Le Chambertin and Le Clos de Béze. The other vineyards which may legally add Chambertin to their names are Latricières, Mazoyères, Charmes,

Mazys, Clos des Ruchottes, Griotte, and Chapelle. The wines from these vineyards cannot compare with Le Chambertin or Le Clos de Béze, yet they are perfectly satisfactory *vin ordinaire*.

Morey-Saint-Denis: The two leading wines of this district are Clos de Tart and Clos de la Roche. Clos de Tart has had an interesting history, the vineyard having been formerly owned by a nunnery, the ancient order of Notre-Dame-de-Tart. It produces a first-rate wine, slow to mature in most years. Clos des Lambrays is similar in character to Clos de Tart but often surpasses it in quality. Some experts rate it among the ten best wines of Burgundy. The other good wine of this township is Bonnes-Mares, but only a small portion of the vineyard is within the district, and it is usually classified with Chambolle. Clos de la Roche and Clos Saint-Denis are two more vineyards of this commune that produce good red wine.

Chambolle-Musigny: The vineyards here are especially famous for their smoothness, softness, and delicacy. In many respects they resemble the Bordeaux wines. Musigny has a particularly velvet quality. It is produced under the label of the Comte de Vogue. Les Bonnes-Mares is almost, but not quite, as fine.

The other important vineyard here is Les Amoureuses.

Gilley-les-Vougeot: A classic legend of this region is that of Napoleon marching by the Clos Vougeot and ordering his soldiers to salute the great vineyard. The story goes that the French troops still tender their homage to the great wine. Clos Vougeot, with about 125 acres, is a large vineyard by Burgundy standards. Fifty-four people now own the property. A rather small quantity of white wine is also made here and marketed under the name of La Vigne Blanche, but its quality is only fair.

Flagey-Echezaux: Back to back with the renowned Clos Vougeot is the fine vineyard of Les Grands-Echezaux, but it lies within the commune limits of Flagey. When Les Grands-Echezaux has a good year, the wine is likely to be extraordinarily rich and heavy in body.

Four times as large as this vineyard is that of Les Echezaux. Wines from both vineyards are excellent, and no wine lover should fail to know their robust qualities.

Vosne-Romanée: Here in this rather ordinary village are the acknowledged greats of Burgundy. There are those who assert that the best of Vosne-Romanée is far and away the best in the world. These are wines which have every characteristic of superb vintages: delicacy combined with strength (an apparent contradiction, but true in this instance), a fine body, and an attractive ruby color.

The Domaine de la Romanée-Conti, owned by a three-man syndicate, is composed of several great vineyards. The group owns outright the single most important Burgundy, Romanée-Conti. And they also own La Tâche. Incidentally, these two vineyards are among the most valuable pieces of property in the world, although there is neither sign nor impressive building to let the traveler know that the vine-covered field he is passing is anything out of the ordinary. The Domaine also includes part of Richebourg, a wine famous for its rich, full quality. These fortunate people also have portions of Les Grands-Echezaux and Les Echezaux.

Another vineyard worthy of special mention is Les Gaudichots, and a truly superb wine, produced in a tiny, two-vine strip, is La Romanée, owned by Liger-Belair, a well-known shipping firm of the region. If this were any region but Vosne-Romanée, the following wines would have a greater reputation: Romanée-Saint-Vivant, Malconsorts, Beaumonts, and Suchots. They are first-rate.

Nuits-Saint-Georges: This important town of the Côte de Nuits has led a hectic, unsettled existence over the centuries. It was headquarters and bastion for the Dukes of Burgundy and the scene of constant conflict and siege. Peace finally descended on the region in 1870, after the Franco-Prussian War.

The area produces wine of considerable body or "texture." In comparison with other wines, including those from the heart of Burgundy, they seem to be remarkably solid and full. This is the wine for a steak or roast beef. The outstanding vineyard is Saint-Georges. The other vineyard whose wine is familiar to Americans is Les Vaucrains.

Prémeaux: To the south, immediately below Nuits-Saint-Georges, Prémeaux markets the wine from its vineyards not under its own name but under the label of the Nuits-Saint-Georges, and the wines are almost identical in quality. The two vineyards best known to the American market are Les Didiers and Les Corvées.

The remaining hamlets of Prissey, Comblanchien, and Corgoiloin are unimportant; and Ladoix-Serrigny, the last town of the Côte de Nuits, produces a barely adequate white wine.

The Côte de Beaune

The total length of the Côte de Beaune is about sixteen miles. The first 60 percent (roughly) of this ribbonlike strip produces red wines, but commencing at Meursault, the vineyards produce the white. It is the white wines which are the great pride of this district, particularly Montrachet, which is one of the very best of this type. However, the region has some excellent reds, although the quality diminishes as one travels towards Meursault. Fine reds are produced at Aloxe-Corton, Volnay, Beaune, and Pommard.

Aloxe-Corton: Experts consider Le Corton to be the finest red wine of the Côte de Beaune. Although quite close to Nuits-Saint-Georges, which is famous for full-bodied wines, Corton has a very different personality. With its bright color, it is possibly the liveliest of all Burgundies. A Corton under five years of age is not worth drinking, but as it gets older, the roughness wears away, and it develops smoothness and great delicacy. Next in quality to Le Corton is the wine of a much larger vineyard, Les Bressandes.

This is historic country, for it was here in the year 775 that Charlemagne donated his Aloxe vineyard to the Abbey of Saulieu. The great king owned the vineyards that still bear his name: Le Corton Charlemagne, which produce a very fine white wine.

Nearby is the small village of Pernand Vergelesses which has one important vineyard producing a red wine of considerable merit, Les Verglesses. The communes of Chorey and Gamay offer little interest, for the wines are poor.

Beaune: From the tenth century until the present, Beaune has been a center of wine making. Many records indicate that during the Middle Ages the word "Beaune" was a synonym for quality. Even if it were not famous for its vineyards, the Hospice de Beaune would bring the town fame, for the noted wine auction is held here.

The Hospice de Beaune has had a fabulous history. A certain Nicolas Rolin, Chancellor of the Duchy of Burgundy, was the collector of taxes in the reign of Louis XI. Part of the collections stuck to the palm of the honorable collector, and he grew extremely rich, although his pay was modest. Nicolas Rolin anticipated the methods of public relations in the twentieth century: in the year 1443, he and his good wife, Guigone de Salins, founded the Hospice, a home for the ill and aged. Louis XI is said to have remarked that it was just as well that Rolin had made this gift to the poor, as he had impoverished so many. As time went by, other landowners began to make gifts of neighboring vineyards to the Hospice. At present it is the owner of about 180 acres, of which perhaps a dozen are exceptional. As these are scattered throughout the area, their yield is unequal and varies in quality. These wines are somewhat higher in price than competitive wines in the same category.

Beaune vineyards are much larger than those in other districts of Burgundy, with the exception of Les Feves, which consists of only eleven acres that produce an exceptionally smooth wine. Particular note should be made of Le Clos-des-Mouches, a large vineyard whose wine is almost always delicate and distinctive. Ordinary wines of the district labeled simply as "Beaune" are variable and seldom up to expectation.

Pommard: At the beginning of the fifteenth century the Côte d'Or was ravaged by a terrible blight that is supposed to have destroyed the vines of all but a small area on Pommard Mountain. It was from cuttings of these few vines that the devastated vineyards were subsequently replanted all along the Burgundy region from Dijon, south.

Pommard wines are unlike those of their neighbors to the north. Owing to the shift in the position of the slopes, the vineyards face south rather than southeast, and receive the rays of the sun from this different angle. As the road heads southward, the red wines become lighter than those of the Côte de Nuits. The two outstanding vineyards are Les Epenots and Les Rugiens-Bas. Clos de la Commaraine is also worth noting.

Volnay: The brotherhood so active during the Crusades, the Knights of Malta, made Volnay the most publicized and important wine center of the Burgundy region, for it owned several Volnay *climats*, or vineyards. As Volnay is south of Pommard, the wines are just a touch lighter. They are the sort that everyone enjoys, having a berry taste somewhat like the taste of raspberries. Far and away the leading Volnay is Les Caillerets, which in certain years is superb. Champans and Santenots are two other good wines of this region. And of course the Volnay marketed by the Hospice de Beaune is usually worthwhile.

Meursault: This well-known region is the turning point in the transition from red to white wines on the Côte d'Or. From Meursault on, although reds are grown, the emphasis is upon white wines, some of surpassing excellence.

The wine produced at Meursault has a light quality usually described as "fruity." It is generally considered best when young. However, many connoisseurs have a preference for a seven- or even a ten-year-old vintage, for by that time it has developed a "nutty" flavor. But a Meursault older than five years turns dark and loses its gentle, gold cast, becoming *maderisé*— like a Madeira with the latter's characteristic taste and dark color.

It is unfortunately true that good Meursault can seldom be found in a bottle with only "Meursault" and the shipper's name on the label. One usually must pay a little more for a vineyard name, such as Meursault-Charmes, for example. Of course, the best is always costly, and for wines from such fine vineyards as Clos des Perrières and Les Perrières, the price is high.

Puligny-Montrachet: From Meursault, it is just a mile to the village of Puligny, and from Puligny to the next town of Chassagne it is only a little over a mile and a half. Between these two, lies the district producing the white wines known as Montrachet, often called "the divine wine." If Montrachet is not the single greatest white wine in the world (as many experts proclaim), it is without question the greatest white Burgundy. Incidentally, the wine may be pronounced *Montra-chet*, English style, or *Mon-rah-shay*, in the French manner.

If comparisons are made with this wine, the usual one is with Château d'Yquem, the famous sweet white wine of Bordeaux. Defenders of Montrachet point out, with not a little merit to their argument, that d'Yquem is so very sweet that it is more of a liqueur than a wine. But after several glasses of Montrachet, the palate remains clean and dry, refreshed rather than sated.

The oustanding vineyard of the commune of Puligny is Le Montrachet. Its area of about twenty acres extends beyond the boundaries of Puligny into Chassagne to the south. Most experts believe the yield of the two-thirds which lies in Puligny is superior. The other two great vineyards which have a world reputation are Chevalier-Montrachet (which is completely within the limits of Puligny) and Batard-Montrachet (which lies astride the dividing line between Puligny and Chassagne). In certain excellent vintages these two wines are only overshadowed by Le Montrachet.

The production of white wine is more difficult and therefore more expensive than red. More skilled help is required and the process is more intricate. Therefore, when a white wine reaches excellence, it is inevitably expensive. Even the less important Puligny vineyards command fairly high prices for their product: Les Combettes, for instance, is exceptionally good in an average year, and it is not inexpensive.

Chassagne-Montrachet: Everything that has been said about Puligny-Montrachet holds true for this adjacent commune. Only about one-third of the "divine" Montrachet lies within its borders, but it also contains a substantial portion of Batard-Montrachet. The other important white wine is Les Ruchottes, which in good years rivals Batard-Montrachet.

This section also produces red wines of little reputation, comparatively unknown outside France. However, the reds from the Chassaque vineyards represent good value: they are inexpensive and very "drinkable," like Beaujolais, which shall be discussed later.

Santenay: This is the last commune of the Côte de Beaune and also, of course, of the Côte d'Or. The wines grown in the village are red and somewhat thin in quality. They are little known in the United States; light and pleasant, they are quite inexpensive. The leading vineyard is Les Gravières, but because it is not well known, the practice has developed of marketing the wine under the simple name of "Santenay." If the price can be compared to that of Beaujolais, it is a good value.

It is interesting to note that the slopes of the Santenay vineyards turn westward, offering the vines a direct southern exposure, instead of the more desirable southeastern exposure typical of the Côte d'Or. Apparently this factor has much to do with the difference in quality between the Santenay wines and those only a few miles to the north.

Beginning with the town of Chagny, there are three regions of the Burgundy area that are frequently ignored by the connoisseurs. This is unfortunate, for the wines are frequently pleasant and sometimes excellent.

Chalon: Here the vineyards are no longer side by side in a continuous strip as they are in the Côte d'Or. There are open regions of farmlands and pasture. The soil is similar but with some variation which may explain the difference in the wines. The same grapes are grown, however. The leading wine of the district (frequently known as the Côte Chalonnais) is the red wine of Mercurey, which has a certain resemblance to Volnay, that classic wine grown some miles to the north. The main attributes of Mercurey are its pleasant "drinkable" quality and its moderate price.

At the village of Givry, the two leading vineyards are Clos Saint-Paul and Clos Saint-Pierre; both produce wines that are somewhat lighter and thinner than Mercurey.

Maçon: Maçon (the Côte Maçonnais) and Beaujolais are contiguous, separated only by a narrow creek called Le Mauvaise. The cultivation of vines started somewhat later here than in the districts to the north, probably about the eighth century. More than likely the lag was due to the innumerable wars fought in the area.

The Maçon wines were quite unknown in Paris until the latter part of the seventeenth century, when, so the story goes, a peasant named Claude Brosse brought his wines to the capital. Accidentally, they came to the attention of the king, who ordered them for the court. The royal monarch knew wines. The leading wine of Maçon is surely Pouilly-Fuissé, a white of a distinctive, fruity quality, very dry, and ideal with seafood. Its color is distinctive, somewhat golden with a greenish tinge. In France it is often kept until it is ten or more years old, but it is probably at its best when it has aged from two to five years. Most of the Maçonnais wines, other than Pouilly-Fuissé, are sold under the general label of Maçon and a shipper's name. (It should be mentioned that Pouilly-Fuissé has no connection with Pouilly-Fumé, another fine white wine from the Loire Valley.)

Beaujolais: The fascinating region of Beaujolais extends south of Maçon to the outskirts of Lyons, that rendezvous for gourmets. The wines here differ considerably from the other Burgundies, and they are perhaps the most popular reds of France—for they are good, drinkable, and can be sold at a most reasonable price. They make no pretensions to greatness, nor do the producers ask that they be taken seriously like a superb vintage wine of the Côte d'Or. Beaujolais is perfect with a simple dinner, or with cheese and crackers, and it is the most delightful wine for a picnic. The grape from which it comes is the Gamay, known all through France and Europe as a type which produces a great volume of wine of only moderate quality. The vineyards to the north are largely planted to the aristocratic Pinot grape which produces comparatively little wine but of excellent quality. The hot sun of the

Beaujolais region seems to bring out the best qualities of the Gamay grape, however.

In most of France, the wine that comes in a pitcher or carafe is Beaujolais—if it is not an Algerian wine. Beaujolais can be delicious when it is very young, that is, from a few months after harvest to two or three years.

The leading townships producing Beaujolais are Julienas, Moulin-a-Vent, Fleurie, and Brouilly. Of these, the experts are inclined to give first place to the wines of Julienas, but there are others who award honors to the township of Moulin-a-Vent, which produces one of the heaviest of the Beaujolais. The wines of Fleurie are somewhat lighter and fruitier than the others and those of Brouilly have a fine flavor. Morgon and Moulin-a-Vent are exceptional Beaujolais for they keep well for as long as five or six years.

Vineyard names where Beaujolais is concerned are unimportant. However, among Fleurie wines, the label of Clos de la Riolette is worth noting, and from Moulin-a-Vent, Les Carquelins is quite good. Notations on a label that the wine is "Beaujolais Supérieur" are nonsensical—no such wine category exists.

Chablis

Within the Burgundy area one other district remains, located about eighty miles to the northwest of Dijon. Hidden away, off the main route of traffic, in a narrow valley, Chablis seems cut off from the rest of the world in both a physical and a psychological sense. The young people tend to leave the hard work of the vineyards, preferring the more regular hours of factory labor in Paris. During the past century, Chablis vineyards have diminished to the point where only five hundred acres are under cultivation. Of these about a hundred constitute the *grand crus*.

Chablis is extremely dry, almost "flinty." It has a very clear, bright color, quite pale, with a golden-green tinge. Unlike most white wines, it ages well, although there are enthusiasts who claim it is at its best when less than five years old. By tradition, Chablis is the *sine qua non*, the perfect wine, with oysters. But Chablis is also

perfect with other shellfish and with seafood of all types.

Because so little Chablis is available, there have been complaints that unscrupulous shippers are substituting other wines for the authentic Chablis. All Chablis is expensive, even the second growths (the best is the *premier cru supérieur*), the *premier crus*. The small area under cultivation, low production, and great demand create the high prices.

Beginning at the attractive village of Chablis and extending northwest, the *grand crus* vineyards are: Blanchots, Les Clos, Valmur, Grenouilles, Vaudesir, Les Preuses, and Bougros. Unlike other parts of Burgundy, where wines without vineyard labels are somewhat of a risk, Chablis wines marked "Premier Cru," even without a vineyard name, are very apt to be first-rate. Approximately twenty-two vineyards are entitled to sell their products simply as *premier cru*. Some do, but others add their vineyard names. The lesser wines sold as "Petit Chablis" are a gamble, sometimes worthwhile, sometimes not.

Rhône Wines

Although scarcely equal to Bordeaux or Burgundy in importance, the Rhône Valley is a delightful place both for its scenery and for its purple, full-bodied wines. The district begins just a few miles south of Lyons and extends south to Avignon (about 140 miles), with vineyards situated on both banks of the Rhône River. When one remembers that the Beaujolais district lies immediately to the north of Lyons, it is apparent that it is practically a continuation of the Burgundy region. (Indeed, there are some vineyards within the city limits of Lyons, surrounded by factories and housing developments.)

This is a region of both red and white wines, but much more red than white is produced, and as very little white reaches the United States, it is mainly the red wines that Americans know. In addition, there is one excellent pink or *rosé* wine produced at Tavel, one that has become very popular in this country. The red Rhône wines are hearty, the kind that go so well with a juicy, charcoal-broiled steak or with a thick slice of roast beef. They are masculine wines for "masculine" foods, excellent accompaniments to duck or goose or wild game such as venison. They have a fruity quality, a beautiful, rich color and a heavy perfume rather than a bouquet. When young, Rhône wines are drinkable but not at their best. At one time Rhône wines were not considered fit to drink until they were at least six years old, but recently this time has been shortened, not because the nature of the wines has changed, but because the demand for wines has increased, and the public has accepted the taste of the younger wines. It is extremely difficult now to find a Rhône wine over ten years old, and a twenty-year-old bottle is a rarity. Much of the wine is simply labeled as one of three types of the region: Côte-Rôtie, Hermitage, or Chateauneuf-du-Pape. But a simple Chateauneuf-du-Pape is something of a gamble, while a label with the name of a prominent vineyard such as Clos des Papes, for example, should be a guarantee of quality.

Côte-Rôtie: Opposite the old city of Vienne, with its pyramid erected by the Roman conquerors, the first important vineyards of the Rhône Valley begin: Côte-Rôtie—or "the Roasted Slope." This name derives from the fact that the vineyards face the hot southeastern sun; during the summer months temperatures rise in midafternoon to a point where the ground, the vines, and even the grapes themselves seem to be roasting in the shimmering heat. Unlike the Burgundy region farther north, the weather here each summer is more consistently hot and sunny, and failures caused by poor weather are less likely. Also, the Côte-Rôtie vineyards use a different type of grape called the Syrah or Serine. Cultivation is also different here.

Côte-Rôtie vineyards of importance include Les Clos, Le Moulin, and Pavillon Rouge. Leading vineyards are designated as Côte Blonde and Côte Brune. It is said that the *Blonde* wines are best when young and the *Brune* grow better with age. The total production of Côte-Rôtie is never large, and these wines bring somewhat higher prices than those of Chateauneuf-du-Pape.

Condrieu: Just south of Côte-Rôtie is the little community of Condrieu, which produces small quantities of an odd white wine with a distinctive taste. It is interesting but perhaps too unusual for most people. Condrieu wines have never been popular enough to compete with the big three of the Rhône Valley.

Château Grillet: Here a truly outstanding wine is grown, undoubtedly the best in the Rhône Valley. It has been compared to Pouilly-Fuissé, to Pouilly-Fumé, and even to Meursault. In any event, it is an excellent white wine of considerable balance, ideal with any fish or with chicken or veal.

Hermitage: After Château Grillet there comes a lapse of several miles until one reaches the second important region: Hermitage. Both reds and whites are grown here, with the emphasis upon the red. This ruby-colored wine with its purplish cast has the true characteristic shade one thinks of as "wine-color." The bouquet is superb. Hermitage is also famous for its unusual berry taste which leaves a delightful flavor in the mouth after the wine is drunk. When young, it may be somewhat rough and crude, like Chianti, but as Hermitage matures (after at least six years in the bottle), the wine becomes very smooth and velvety. When Hermitage is allowed to age for fifteen or twenty years before being consumed, it has all the qualities of a fine Burgundy. Like the reds, the white Hermitage wines are famous for their keeping qualities, and are really fit to drink only after four years. The leading red wine vineyards include L'Hermite, Croix, and Varogne. The outstanding vineyard for white wine is Chante-Alouette.

Immediately to the north of the Hermitage region are a group of vineyards having the generic name of "Croze-Hermitage"; they produce satisfactory minor wines in most years, seldom as good as those sold under the Hermitage label. Further along the river road are the two small wine districts of Cornas and Saint-Peray. The red wine of Cornas is rarely distinguished, usually being somewhat unbalanced; the white wines of Saint-Peray are also unimportant.

Chateauneuf-du-Pape: After these two little districts there is a region of open spaces; for various reasons the vineyards formerly cultivated on the slopes have been allowed to die out. The soil becomes rocky; the occasional vineyards are strewn with large stones, many the size of boulders. Finally, the river reaches Avignon. Beginning at Chateauneuf-du-Pape, there are miles of vineyards devoted to production of the most plentiful of all Rhône Valley wines. There may be shortages of Hermitage and Côte-Rôtie but rarely of Chateauneuf-du-Pape, which, of course, means that the first two command the higher price.

The beautiful red wines of Chateauneuf-du-Pape are high in alcoholic content: they may not be sold with less than 12 percent, the minimum requirement. The wines are a blend, never made from one single type of grape; at least four different types are used and some wine makers claim they combine as many as ten. Grenache, Syrah, and Picpoul grapes are used more frequently than the others; these are types noted for their bountiful yield rather than their quality. Chateauneuf-du-Pape is a delicious wine with a natural fruit flavor, but it is seldom as good as its neighbors to the north, Hermitage and Côte-Rôtie. The simple label of Chateauneuf-du-Pape is not a sufficient recommendation of quality, but a vineyard name attached to the generic term is usually a guarantee. Good vineyards include Vaudieu, Clos des Papes, La Gardine, and Château de la Nerthe.

Tavel: About eight miles northwest of Avignon is the hamlet of Tavel. In this area the vineyards produce one of the best *rosé* wines of France, if not the best. Like all pink wines, Tavel is not great, yet it is a good wine with almost any food.

Connoisseurs frown upon *rosé* wines, finding them too frivolous for consideration, but they are always pleasant to consider for lunch or a cold supper. They are not recommended, however, with heavy meats.

Loire Wines

France's longest river, the placid Loire, begins its gentle movement in the Cevennes and travels six hundred miles over a landscape shaped like a breakfast *croissant* until it reaches the Atlantic Ocean. Along its course, there are hundreds of miles of vineyards on both banks, many just the simple growths of peasants for their own use, as well as the important commercial vineyards. More than a half million acres of vineyards extend along the shores. It is only between Nevers and Nantes, however, that the important wines are produced. Generally included within the category of Loire River wines are those of the Cher and Arnon rivers where Quincy and Reuilly vintages are made.

Pouilly-sur-Loire and Sancerre: Just past Nevers, there are two wine districts. Pouilly-sur-Loire is the source of one extremely popular white wine, Pouilly-Fumé, a wine with a very dry, distinctive taste. The outstanding vineyard is the Château du Nozet. (Sometimes the label features the family name "de Ladoucette.") This wine should not be confused with Pouilly-Fuissé, although the two are alike in many respects.

Sancerre wine lacks some of the better qualities of Pouilly-Fumé, but it is a pleasant light white wine, with low alcoholic content. It should be consumed within a few years, as it does not keep too long.

On the banks of the Cher and Arnon, which drain into the Loire near Tours, are the Quincy and Reuilly vineyards. Only Quincy wine is exported to the United States. Both vineyards produce similar wines of a light yellow color, quite dry, and fit to drink only when they are young, for their quality, too, fades with age.

Vouvray: Just east of Tours is the Vouvray district, which produces one of the best known of the Loire wines. The vineyards are planted on the slopes which dominate the river that runs through this lovely countryside. The wines are white with an aromatic quality and a fruity taste. In the average year they are quite dry, but certain vintages have a slight, even a pronounced sweetness. Vouvrays are frequently sparkling, or *petillant* as the vintners say. They are perhaps best when they are only a few years old, but there are connoisseurs who claim they are equally good when older—if they are of the sweet type.

Bourgueil: Southwest of Tours and downstream as the Loire flows towards the Atlantic are the districts of Bourgueil and Saint-Nicolas de Bourgueil. Both formerly produced wines regarded as local *vins du pays*, too unimportant to export, but in recent years tourists have discovered them and proclaimed these wines delightful, thereby creating a small market for them. Saint-Nicolas has a very fruity flavor and is good when it is young. These wines are inexpensive, comparable in price to Beaujolais. They taste best when slightly chilled in the refrigerator for half an hour before serving.

Chinon: The Chinon wines are connected with the name of Rabelais, who loved these good wines. They are extremely light in color and body and also in alcoholic content. It is common practice to call them "luncheon wines"—somewhat disparagingly—and let it go at that.

Saumur: Farther down the river lies the ancient town of Saumur, dominated by a castle and surrounded by six different types of vineyards. The sweet white type resembles a mild Sauternes, particularly when the vineyards follow the classic Sauternes method of harvesting and production, and when it is a good year. Saumur is especially known in France for its *mousseaux*, or sparkling wines. For over half a century, the district has made a sparkling Saumur wine by the champagne process: working with individual bottles rather than in bulk with large casks. The finished product is not champagne but a unique Saumur that sparkles. It is seldom shipped to the United States, because as a sparkling wine it would be subject to the high tax levied on wines of this type and could not compete with champagne.

Anjou: The Anjou region, adjacent to Saumur, is a center of wine making. On the south side of the river is the Coteaux du Layon, which is particularly famous for a very sweet white wine, Quart de Chaume. This highly perfumed wine is treated much like Sauternes in the harvesting and fermentation stages. It has a fine reputation, and much of it is exported to the United States. Actually, it is considered the outstanding white wine of the Loire Valley.

Rosé wines, light and pleasant, are produced in a small section called the Coteaux de l'Aubance, as well as farther downstream in the Coteaux de la Loire.

Muscadet: To the east of the city of Nantes are the Muscadet vineyards. Muscadet is the driest of all the wines of the Loire and is satisfactory on several counts, not the least of which is its modest price. At one time ordinary Muscadet was mixed with Chablis to extend the limited quantity of this more famous wine, but the practice is now prohibited.

Champagne

To many people the word "champagne" is synonymous with gaiety and excitement. This connotation has been achieved through a combination of circumstances which include some very intensive publicity.

The champagne district is situated in the French province of Champagne to the east of Paris. For well over two thousand years, a still wine has been produced in the hilly region of the River Marne, as the Roman troops found when they conquered this portion of ancient Gaul. Even then the vineyards were so successful that the Roman Emperor Domitian, in the year 92 A.D., ordered wine production halted and the vines uprooted, for he feared the Gallic product would prove too great competition for Italian wines. However, two centuries later the Emperor Probus rescinded this decree, and the vineyards were again planted in the region.

Champagne was *the* fashionable drink of the seventeenth century. It should be remembered, however, that the sparkling process which makes the champagne we know today was unheard of then. In fact, corks were unknown, and it was customary to cover bottles with a thin film of oil, or with wax or oil-soaked cloth. Toward the end of the seventeenth century, the vintners discovered a way of making the wine sparkle. The individual usually credited with this invention is the monk Dom Perignon, but there is no actual proof of this even though he has been honored with scores of statues, and the best champagne is named after him. It does seem certain, however, that he was the first to think of placing a round cut of cork in the bottle.

The Champagne province has only about six inches of poor soil on top of subterranean beds of chalk; there can be little doubt that it is the chalk which gives champagne its special characteristics. Almost all champagne is made from a blend of black and white grapes, although the finished wine is a bright, pale gold color. (When made from white grapes exclusively, the wine is known as *blanc de blanc*.) *Rosé*, or pink champagne (discounted by the connoisseurs), is prepared by allowing the "must" of red grapes to stand until the wine picks up a small amount of coloring. The climate in the province is poor, frequently erratic, with a cold spring, an early autumn, and considerable rainfall. Some years are excellent for the vineyards, but many others are a total loss.

When harvest time approaches, a committee of the growers meets with a committee of the bottlers to set prices, for when the harvest is ready, there is no time for prolonged negotiations. With such unpredictable weather it is difficult to select the precise harvesting date. But as soon as the grapes are picked, they are brought to the presses and the juice is extracted; the champagne firms store this in casks. The bubbling and fermentation called "boiling" begins, the process lasting anywhere from several days to several weeks depending on the sugar content of the grapes. Winter brings a halt to the fermentation. At each champagne house, old and new wines are blended together to bring out the best qualities of the new wine. Every firm desires to reproduce the qualities which have given it its specific reputation, for unlike Bordeaux and Burgundy, the wines do not come from a particular château or vineyard but represent the skillful blending of different grapes from various parts of the province.

The following February or March the wine is bottled and a mixture of liquid sugar (*liqueur de tirage*) dissolved in old wine is added. This procedure is necessary in order to bring about a second fermentation which occurs a month or two later, in April or May, when the added sugar begins to turn into alcohol, forming carbonic acid, the familar gas which makes the champagne bubble. The bottles are kept on their sides for several years while the wine matures. Then the bottles are placed at angles with the necks pointing downward; gradually they are wiggled, shaken, and maneuvered so that they ultimately stand on their heads, causing the sediment from the fermentation to settle upon the temporary corks.

A skilled technician called the *dégorgeur* care-fully and quickly removes each cork and its sediment, smells the wine, and examines the bottle; the small quantity of wine that is lost by opening the bottle is replaced, together with additional sugar, if it is required. The bottle is recorked, covered with twisted wire, and labeled with the name of the champagne firm. It is then ready for its travels around the world.

Champagnes are prepared for various national tastes and particular purposes. There are champagnes which are almost completely dry, excellent as apéritifs; others, barely past the dry point, are suitable for any purpose with or without food; then there is the dessert type which is definitely sweet. The English market buys the driest of all champagnes, with the absolute minimum of added sugar. (Some small quantity is required in order to produce the second fermentation.) Americans like the dry type, but South America prefers the *douce* or sweet champagne. Here is the classification:

Brut: ½ to 1 percent of sugar.

Extra Dry (or "Extra Sec"): 1 percent to 2 percent

Sec (or dry): 3 percent to 6 percent

Demi-Sec: from 7 percent to 10 percent

Douce; Doux: 10 percent to 15 percent

Which are the best champagnes? This is a matter of individual taste, for the finished product varies from year to year. However, Perrier-Jouet is famous for its very dry wine. (This is a great favorite with the English.) Dom Perignon (produced by Moët & Chandon), a champagne of extraordinary delicacy, is often regarded as the finest.

Market prices of champagne are frequently an indication of the wine buyers' estimate of the various brands. Although comparative prices are not conclusive guides, they do represent an evaluation by both wholesalers and the public. Here, then, are the champagnes, in order of costliness.

Taittinger Blanc de Blancs

Dom Perignon

Louis Roderer Cristal

Mumm's Cordon Rouge

Krug Extra Sec

Bollinger Brut

Pol Roger Brut
Charles Heidsick Rosé
Piper Heidsick Brut
Charles Heidsick Brut
Moët & Chandon Brut
Pommery & Greno Brut
Lanson Brut
Cliquot Yellow Label
Louis Roederer Brut
Perrier-Jouet
St. Marceaux Blanc de Blanc
Mumm's Extra Dry
Besserat de Bellefon
Ayala Gold Label Brut
Marcel Père et Fils Brut

Alsace

The two provinces of Alsace and Lorraine jointly produce wines known as Alsatian, because Alsace has the most important vineyards. Situated in the northeastern corner of France, on the German border, the lovely countryside has had an unhappy history: ceded by France to Germany in 1870, then returned to France in 1918. During the forty-eight years of German control, every effort was made to see that the Alsatian wines were as poor in quality as possible, in order to protect the investments in the German vineyards of the Moselle and Rhine valleys.

Pressure was placed upon the Alsatian vineyards to plant poorer types of vines, which produced high yields but coarse wine. This was then sold as ordinary table wine, unlabeled, from large casks. These wines were also shipped to the Rhine Valley to be blended with German light wines, which are apt to lack sufficient alcoholic strength. With the happy return of Alsace and Lorraine to France, the vineyards began to improve their vines. But for a long time the prewar stigma remained. In order to indicate that the old vines had been replaced with superior ones, the Alsatians hit upon the idea of naming their wines after the type of grape used. Today all Alsatian wines indicate the variety of grape upon the label, sometimes (but not always) as the only identification.

All the wines are white with the exception of a few *rosés*. In general they are light with a slight acid quality which is pleasant and refreshing. The main characteristic is a flowery bouquet reminiscent of a Moselle but not as well balanced or flavorsome. As a rule, most experts recommend that Alsatian wines be drunk when they are a year or two old. Yet they grow smoother with age and are delightful when four or five years old.

Because of their resemblance to German wines, particularly the Moselles, Alsatian wines have suffered in public esteem. People are apt to comment that Alsatians are vaguely similar to German wines—and then draw a critical comparison. The fact is that Alsatian wines do not compare in balance and quality with Moselles, but they should be judged on their own merit as pleasant, light luncheon wines.

Several different types of grapes are grown in Alsace. Riesling is far ahead of its competitors, producing a very dry wine with a pleasant bouquet; Gewurztraminer, next in quality, is known for its remarkable golden cast; the Traminer grape is quite similar to it but has a fruity quality which makes a "spicy" wine. Sylvaner, which is dry with an attractive green color, is not quite as good. The Tokay and Chasselas grapes do not do too well in this region, and wine from these types is little in demand. The excess wine is often blended, several varieties being combined to produce a fair product called Gentil; inferior blends are known as Zwicker or Edelzwicker.

As a rule, labels first mention the type of grape from which the wine is made, but occasionally vineyards of repute will place their names first. The two vineyards most frequently encountered will probably be Clos Sainte-Odile and Clos-Gaensbroennel. With the better wines, the practice is to name the grape and the vineyard, or the grape and the name of the town where the wine was produced. A typical label would be Riesling of Ribeauville, for example. The most important place names include Riquewihr, Ribeauville, Guebwiller, Ammerschwihr, Obernai, Zellenberg, Thann, and Wintzenheim. There has been no official classification of the Alsatian vineyards; it is the only wine district of importance in France not to have some system of classification.

Franchonettes (French). Small custard tarts covered with meringue.

Francillon (French). A hot salad made of potatoes, vinegar, dressing, mussels, etc.; sometimes truffles are added.

Francolin. A tropical bird similar to the pheasant; noted for its delicious white meat.

Franconia. An important wine region of Germany; also called Franken. *See* Germany, The Wines of.

Frangipane. (1) A variety of pear. (2) A sweet cream used in various dessert preparations, made of sugar, flour, eggs, milk, vanilla extract, crushed macaroons or almonds, butter, and salt. (3) A mixture of flour, egg yolk, butter, and milk prepared like a *choux* paste and used in poultry and fish forcemeat.

Frango (Portuguese). Young chicken; broilers.

Franken. An important wine region of Germany; also called Franconia. *See* Germany, The Wines of.

Frankental. A showy, large European grape of fine color but not of exceptional flavor; used chiefly for decorative purposes.

Frankenwein. The Franconia wines of Germany; also called Steinwein. *See* Germany, The Wines of.

Frankfurter; Frankfurt. The most popular type of sausage in America, usually 4–5 inches long, reddish in color, and made from pork or beef. According to the Federal Meat Inspection Division of the United States Department of Agriculture, frankfurters may consist of the ground meat of cattle, swine, sheep, or goat, but no more than 10 percent moisture may be added. The carbohydrate content, which may be cereals, dry milk solids, corn syrup, or vegetable starches, is limited to 2½ percent. Packaged frankfurters in interstate commerce must include on their label a list of all their ingredients in the order of quantity.

In the production of frankfurters, moisture is added in the form of chipped ice, which is needed to blend the ingredients together. Chipped ice is used because it prevents the meat from overheating as it is passed through the grinders. With-

out the ice the meat would get hot and the pork particularly would tend to develop rancidity.

The protein content of a 1.8-ounce frankfurter is 6 grams. Water constitutes 58 percent of the link. Of that total, 48 percent is considered to be the natural liquid content of the meat and the extra 10 percent is the allowable addition.

Although considered typically American, frankfurters are of European origin. There is still dispute among experts as to whether they derive from the Austrian *Wiener* or from the link sausage traditionally made in Frankfurt, Germany.

Franksbrauo (Icelandic). Bread that resembles a French white bread.

Franksbrød (Danish). White bread.

Frappé. Any of several chilled drinks. Fruit frappés are usually puréed fruits mixed in an electric blender or cocktail shaker with chipped ice. For crème de menthe and absinthe frappés the liqueur is poured over crushed ice in a cocktail glass. In some parts of the United States a kind of milk shake blended with ice cream is called a "frappé."

Frapper (French). To freeze or chill liquids, especially creams.

Frascati Melon. A fruit cup with a baked-meringue topping.

Frasvåfflor (Swedish). Small triangular wafflelike cakes usually served with jam.

Frater. The dining area in a monastery.

Freddo (Italian). Cold.

Free Coups (Scotch). Shops that sell stale or sour bread cheaply in the poorer sections of Glasgow.

Free Gallipoli Wheat. An Australian wheat that makes a soft, weak flour.

Free Liver. One who eats at any time and any place.

Free Loader (Colloquial). A person who eats and drinks at the expense of others.

Freestone. A stone or pit that separates readily from the pulp of a fruit, as in the freestone peach or nectarine.

Freeze. To change a substance to a solid or frozen state by reducing the temperature.

Freeze Drying. A food preservation process by which water is removed from frozen foods without substantially changing the shape or color of the product; the cellular structure is also left intact. The substance is frozen and a high vacuum applied; the cooling effect of the evaporation keeps the material frozen while the water distills off as vapor. Foods treated this way can be stored for about 2 years without refrigeration.

Freezer. A specially designed electric appliance that freezes liquids or solids. The home freezer is designed to maintain a temperature well below the freezing point but not so low as that in commercial equipment.

Ice-cream Freezer. An apparatus that turns in a mixture of salt and ice. Inside the machine scrapers mix and aerate the ingredients until frozen into ice cream. Freezers may be operated by hand or by electricity.

Freezing Mixture. A salt-and-ice mixture that freezes other mixtures but is not itself frozen.

Freezing Point. The precise temperature at which water freezes; 32° Fahrenheit or 0° Centigrade.

Freisa. *See* Italy, The Wines of.

Frejon (Nigerian). A preparation, usually served on Good Friday, made from black beans, coconut, and sugar. As a rule, it is eaten with *gurri*, powdered cassava.

Frémir (French). To heat foods to just below the boiling point. *See* Frissoner.

French Dressing. The English name for the dressing with which the French mix salad greens. (There is no French name.) French dressing is a mixture of 3 parts oil (usually olive or walnut oil in France) and 1 part vinegar (red- or white-wine vinegar preferably), seasoned with salt and pepper. Paprika, garlic, dry mustard, or chopped fresh herbs may be added. A mixture including tomato is not a true version of French dressing.

French Dumpling. A dumpling made of eggs, bread crumbs, herbs, etc., then wrapped in cabbage leaves and boiled in soups or stews.

French Fry. (American). Foods, particularly potatoes, cooked in hot deep fat.

French Guiana. *See* Guianas, The.

French Plum. Generally a dried plum prepared in France.

French Rice. Amelcorn, a poor-quality wheat.

French Sticks. Long narrow rolls made from a soft dough.

French Toast. A breakfast dish made of slices of bread dipped in an egg-and-milk batter, then fried in butter; served with jam, powdered sugar, or syrup.

French Wheat. A soft, runny wheat.

French Wines. *See* France, The Wines of.

Frenched. Usually denotes removing meat from the ends of bones leaving them exposed, as with lamb chops.

Fresas (Spanish). Strawberries.

Fresco (Portuguese). Fresh.

Fresco de Arroz (Ecuadorian). A soft drink made of rice and fruit juices.

Fresh. (1) As applied to food, not stale, spoiled, or contaminated; not preserved with salt, etc. (2) As applied to water, free of salt.

Freshwater. Of plants and animals, living or growing in nonsalty water, such as lakes, rivers, ponds, etc., as opposed to seawater.

Fressure (French). Animal lights, or lungs.

Fressure d'Agneau. Lamb's lungs.

Fressure Vendéenne (French). Stew made of pig's liver, heart, lungs, and spleen combined with pig's blood; made in Poitou.

Friable. Readily crumbled, like bread crumbs.

Friand (French). Epicure.

Friandises (French). Small dainty desserts, such as miniature pastries or *petits fours*.

Friand Marseillaise (French). A pastry shell filled with tuna fish.

Friand Champenois (French). A small pastry served hot as an hors d'oeuvre.

Friar's Omelet (British). A sweet baked apple omelet.

Friation (Obsolete). The crumbling of foodstuffs into little pieces.

Fricandeau. A slice of meat, usually veal, stewed and served with a sauce; a sort of fricassee.

Fricandelles (French). Braised small thin game or veal steaks.

Fricandines (French). Small patties filled with minced meat and fried crisp.

Fricassee. A method of preparing poultry, especially older birds, by browning and then simmering the meat in stock well-seasoned and thickened with flour.

Fricassée à la Périgourdine (French). Various vegetables cooked in a beef stock, removed when half cooked, browned in fat, then returned to the stock till completely cooked.

Fricasser (French). To cook foods gently and slowly in a saucepan.

Frichti (German, Colloquial). A breakfast of meat, eggs, etc.

Frico (South American). A casserole containing potato, onion, green pepper, and meat.

Fricot (French, Colloquial). (1) A stew or ragout. (2) A complete but simple dinner.

Friddick. A cake made of oatmeal dough and fried on both sides in fat.

Fridge (British, Colloquial). Refrigerator.

Fried. Cooked in fat.

Fried Cakes. Doughnuts, crullers, etc.

Frigorific. Making cold or freezing.

Frijol; Frijole (Mexican). A small bean that is the basis of numerous bean dishes in Mexico and the southwestern United States.

Frijolada (Spanish). Bean stew with meats and vegetables.

Frijoles Negros (Spanish). Black beans.

Frikadeller (Swedish, Danish). Ground-veal meatballs; fishballs.

Frim. Very juicy, especially vegetables or fruits.

Frinot. A cheese made at Orleans, France; at its best from November to June.

Fripe (French, Colloquial). Something usually eaten on bread, such as jam, butter, cheese, or meat.

Frire (French). To fry in deep fat.

Friske Multer (Norwegian). Cloudberries.

Frissche Kaas (Dutch). Any fresh, mild cheese.

Frissoner (French). To heat foods to just below the boiling point. See Frémir.

Fritada (Brazilian). A heavy deep-dish omelet baked with meat, fish, vegetables, etc., with seasonings.

Friteau (French). A small fritter usually made with savory ingredients, such as sweetbreads, fish, etc.; sometimes sweetened and served as a dessert.

Frito (Spanish). Fried.

Fritot d'Agneau. Deep-fat-fried lamb.

Fritots (French). Small chunks or slices of meat, poultry, fish, etc., dipped in a thick batter and deep fat fried.

Frittata (Italian). A rolled pancake or omelet.

Frittata alla Ciriacese. An omelet made with tuna fish, anchovies, and herbs.

Frittata alla Romana. Vegetable omelet.

Frittata alla Spagnola. Omelet with Spanish sauce.

Frittata con Funghi. Mushroom omelet.

Frittata di Rane. Frogs'-legs omelet.

Frittata di Riso. Rice omelet.

Fritte de Ciliegielle (Italian). Cherry fritters.

Frittella; Frittelle (Italian). Carnival fritters or pancakes, made with pine nuts and raisins.

Frittelle di Polenta. Cornmeal fritters.

Fritter. Batter-dipped foods fried in deep hot fat or sautéed. Fruit, fish, meat, poultry, or vegetables may be used, and may be sliced, like an apple fritter or chopped, like clams, before dipping.

Fritto (Italian). Fried.

Fritto alla Romana. Various fried foods, usually containing artichokes, liver, and sweetbreads.

Fritto di Pollo e Funghi. (Fried chicken with mushrooms.

Fritto Misto. Assorted seafood, meat, or vegetables dipped in batter, fried, and served on the same plate.

Frittons (French). The solid residue left after pork or goose fat is melted; eaten plain or on bread.

Fritturen (German). Fried foods.

Fritura Mixta (Spanish). Assorted meats, chicken, vegetables, or fish dipped in batter and deep-fat fried.

Frituras (Latin American). Fried foods, such as doughnuts, crullers, etc.

Friture (French). (1) Any fried food. (2) The cooking fat. (3) The frying process.

Friture Charentaise (French). Assorted fish, deep-fat fried.

Friture de la Loire (French). Whole small fish breaded and fried; a specialty of the Touraine.

Friturier (French). A cook who specializes in fried food. In large hotels or aboard steamships the *friturier* makes fried potatoes, fish, etc.

Friularo. A common black grape used in making red table wines in the Vento province of Italy.

Frizz. A sizzling noise created by frying.

Frizzle. To cook foods in hot fat until the edges curl or twist.

Frizzled Filbert. A nut resembling the ordinary filbert in taste and texture but having ragged, frizzled husks.

Frogeater. A derogatory term for a Frenchman.

Frogfish. An angler fish.

Frogs' Legs. Most frogs' legs come to the United States from Japan and India, where low labor costs make it possible to process the legs in far greater quantity than is profitable here. Freezing is essential when the product must be shipped great distances. Therefore, although most chefs and fanciers of frogs' legs agree that the fresh legs are superior, they usually have to settle for the frozen ones.

Florida, the principal domestic source of frogs' legs, does ship fresh specimens but in dwindling quantities. Parts of the Everglades, where frogs once abounded, have been converted into state parks, thus cutting off that source of supply. Other subtropical swamps, once the home of the frog, have been drained for housing developments.

But for those who care to catch their own frogs, the cost is minimal. Three edible species can be found in the United States. The American bullfrog, whose croaking song outbooms all others, lives wherever there is permanent deep fresh water. That goggle-eyed amphibian is usually green or greenish brown, and suns on lily pads or logs. The leopard frog, found in open meadows near shallow water, has two bronze or yellow folds of skin running from the eyes to the posterior with brown or olive-green spots between the parallel lines. The familiar green frog, whose skin has a metallic cast, is a ubiquitous fellow, found wherever the bullfrog or leopard frog thrive.

The legs, the only part of the frog that is eaten, should be severed from the body, peeled, and the feet removed. Whether caught fresh or bought, the fresh legs should be soaked about 2 hours in cold water or milk before cooking, to bleach and plump the flesh.

Froise. A big thick pancake, as large as the pan; sometimes made with bacon.

Frokost (Danish). Lunch.

Fromage à la Crème (French). (1) A fresh sheep's-milk cheese with added beaten egg whites. (2) A homemade cottage cheese. (3) Sour milk drained and combined with cream. (4) Sometimes *coeur à la crème*, a cottage-cheese dessert prepared in a heart-shaped wicker basket.

Fromage à la Pie; Fromage Blanc (French). A white cheese, such as cottage or fresh-cream cheese.

Fromage à la Raclette. *See* Bagnes.

Fromage Bavarois (French). A vanilla-flavored dessert cheese.

Fromage Blanc (French). Any white soft cream cheese or cottage cheese.

Fromage de Boîte. A rather soft full-flavored French cheese resembling *Pont l'Évêque*.

Fromage de Chèvre. A hard, astringent French goat's-milk cheese.

Fromage de Monsieur. A rather sharp, pungent cheese made in Normandy, France.

Fromage de Porc (French). An aspic made from a pig's head and trotters.

Fromage de Tête (French). Headcheese prepared with pork scraps shaped to resemble a large cheese.

Fromage de Vendôme. A soft, tangy, cow's-milk cheese matured in ashes; made in the Loire Valley, France.

Fromage d'Italie (French). A headcheese made with pig's heads and livers.

Fromage Fort. Any of several French strong-flavored cheeses.

Fromage Glacé (French). (1) A frozen pudding. (2) Ice-cream dessert in the form of cheese.

Fromage Gras (French). Any fatty cheese, such as the Brie. However, a special *fromage gras* is produced in Savoy.

Fromageon. A white sheep's-milk cheese.

Fromage Persillé. A hard rennet French cheese marbled with bluish mold like a Roquefort.

Fromager (French). To add grated cheese.

Fromage Sec (French). Various white cheeses, prepared by allowing them to drain completely while hung in straw baskets.

Frometon. A cow's-milk cheese made in the Bray region of France.

Fromgey. A simple white cheese made in Lorraine,

France; a slice is customarily placed upon bread and covered with chopped onions.

Frontignac; Frontignan. A group of rich, heavy, sweet muscat wines produced in the Languedoc region of France; usually aged.

Frore (Obsolete). Frozen; frosty foods.

Froschschenkel (German). Frogs' legs.

Frostfish. The whitefish caught in the lakes of New York State.

Frosting. A flavored, sweetened mixture used to cover or decorate certain cakes. With the exception of pound, fruit, and angel cakes, most cakes are enhanced by a frosting spread over the top and sometimes also over the sides. Layer cakes demand a filling between the layers which may be the same as that which covers the cake or may be made by another recipe.

Before frosting, the cakes should be thoroughly cooled. The top and sides should be brushed free of loose crumbs. If the cake rounds very much on the top, the flat bottom should be placed on top and frosted. Layer cakes should be put together with the bottom crusts inside. For frosting, the cakes should be placed on a sheet of heavy waxed paper on a board or cake rack.

The purpose of frosting is to give the final ideal flavor and sweet contrast to the cake. All plain layer and loaf cakes, cup cakes, and French cakes designed for afternoon tea should be frosted. The frosting should fulfill the requisites of color, flavor, and texture.

There are two main types of frosting—a cooked variety, or boiled frosting; and an uncooked or confectioner's-sugar type. The perfect frosting is neither too stiff nor too runny.

Frostfish. A member of the cod family.

Froth. Foam produced when carbonized or fermented liquids are poured.

Frothing. Dredging meat with flour, then browning it quickly with high heat.

Frozen. Made solid under low temperature; turned into ice; sometimes, very cold.

Frozen Custard. A somewhat soft, cold egg-and-milk preparation made in a variety of flavors; it resembles ice cream but is served and eaten in softer form.

Frozen Foods. A general term used to describe the wide range of foods frozen commercially, packaged into convenient portions, and retailed to the general public.

Frucht (German). Fruit.

    Fruchtbrot. Fruit bread.

    Fruchteis. Fruit ices.

    Fruchtpasteten. Fruit pies.

    Fruchtsalat. Fruit salad.

Fructescent. Starting to produce fruit.

Fructiferous. Bearing fruit.

Fructify. To bear fruit; to be fruitful.

Fructose. A fruit sugar found in honey and all sweet fruits.

Frugivorous. Fruit-eating; living chiefly on fruit, rather than meat, fish, or vegetables.

Frugt (Danish). Fruit.

    Frugtcompot. Fruit compote.

    Frugtgrød. Fruit dessert.

Frühlingssuppe (German). Fresh-vegetable soup.

Frühstück (German). Breakfast.

Frühstück Cheese. A round American cheese of the Limburger type, about 2½–3 inches in diameter; also known as *breakfast cheese* or *luncheon cheese.*

Fruit. Any of a wide variety of products of trees, shrubs, vines, cactus, etc., which are edible, and usually, also that portion of a plant which contains the seeds. By this definition, botanists classify the tomato and pea pods, for example, as fruit. It is the fleshy fruits, favored for their pulp, that cooks consider as fruits. These include the *pomes*, which have a seed-bearing core and which include pears and apples; the *drupes*, with a pit or stone in the center usually holding a single seed (cherries and peaches); the so-called *berries* with many seeds in the pulp (blueberries and grapes); the final category, called *aggregate fruits*, includes raspberries and blackberries and is actually made up of a number of drupes held together in one piece.

Before the discovery of the importance of vitamins in the diet, fruits which contained a large proportion of water were generally considered luxuries with little food value. But in addition to furnishing more than their share of such essential minerals as calcium, iron, and vitamins of the B complex, certain fruits make outstanding contributions of vitamins A and C. Apricots, both fresh and dried, and fresh peaches are excellent sources of vitamin A, and vitamin C is furnished in large amounts by citrus fruits.

Fruits are available fresh, canned, dried, and frozen. Improved shipping facilities have extended the season when many fresh fruits are on the market. For example, strawberries in January are now a regular item in northern United States markets.

Fruitage. The bearing of fruit.

Fruitarian. One on a fruit diet.

Fruit Butter. Sieved fruit pulp cooked with sugar, and sometimes spiced, until smooth and thick enough when cooled to spread on bread. Besides apples, fresh or dried apricots, grapes, peaches, plums, or quinces may be made into spreads. Long, slow cooking over very low heat is important to develop the flavor and blend the oils of the spices with the juices and sugars of the fruit. Fruits should be ripe, but they need not be perfect specimens. Small misshapen fruits or the sound portions of windfalls may be used for fruit butter. Commercial fruit butters are available.

Fruit Cake. Two styles of cake made with assorted fruits and nuts evenly distributed in the batter. *Dark fruit cakes* are usually flavored with rum, brandy, or another liquor. *Light fruit cakes* may have fewer fruits than the dark variety. Both should have a moist, tender texture and should slice evenly.

The size of the pieces of fruit and nut in a cake usually depends on the proportion of fruit in a cake. The larger the quantity, the larger the size of the pieces. Currants and seedless raisins are left whole; seeded raisins and cherries are cut in halves. Nuts and dates should be cut in quarters. Candied pineapple and fruit peels should be cut in thin slices.

Fruit cakes are made with fat and are baked longer than other butter cakes and at lower temperatures. They improve with storage. To store fruit cake, cool it completely after baking, wrap in aluminum foil, and store in an airtight tin or stone crock. An apple or orange kept with the cake, and replaced from time to time, helps prevent dryness. Brandy, rum, or whisky may be added during the aging process to retain moisture.

Fruit Cheese. Sieved fruit pulp cooked with sugar and sometimes spice until it is a solid mass; usually served with cream as a dessert.

Fruit Cocktail. A mixture of several fruits all canned, all fresh, or a combination of canned and frozen fruits, usually served in cut-up form. A fruit cocktail is usually served before the main part of a meal, and a fruit cup is regarded as a dessert; frequently the two terms are used interchangeably.

Fruit Cups. Several fruits combined in a cup to bring out a contrast in flavor and texture between the various components. Canned and frozen as well as fresh fruits may be used; they should be served well chilled.

Large fruits may be cut into manageable pieces, but they should never be chopped so fine that they are no longer recognizable. The mixture improves if allowed to steep a while before being served so that the flavors may blend. If acid fruits predominate, it may be necessary to sweeten the cup with sugar or a sweet fruit juice. Small amounts of wine or liqueur may be added if desired. Fruit sherbet added to fruit cup makes a refreshing warm-weather dish.

Fruit Drinks. Drinks made with the juices of fresh fruits, the syrup drained from stewed fruits or from canned or frozen fruits, and canned fruit juices plus fruit-flavored carbonated beverages. The fresh juice by itself is a refreshing beverage as well.

Most fruit-juice combinations are improved by the addition of tart citrus juices, for one of the requirements of a fruit drink is that it not be cloyingly sweet. Sugar should therefore be added with discrimination. Fruit juices should be strained and should be served well chilled.

Fruiter; Fruiterer. One who deals in fruits.

Fruitery. A place where fruit is produced, grown, or stored.

Fruit Kernel. The soft, edible portion found within the hard interior of a stone-centered fruit. It is sometimes made into a liqueur, the best known of which is France's *Noyau*.

Fruit Pectin. A gumlike substance found in some fruits that gives jelly its characteristic texture.

Fruit Salad. (1) Cut-up fruits, much like a fruit cocktail or cup. (2) A luncheon dish consisting of a plate of assorted cut-up fruits, often served with cottage cheese.

Fruits de Mer (French). "Fruits of the sea;" all seafood; in some localities only shellfish.

Fruits Farcis (French). Fruits with pits or stones removed and stuffed with marzipan or other fillings, then dipped in sugar boiled to the hard-crack stage.

Fruit Sieve. A utensil with concentric wires used to remove foreign matter from dried fruits.

Fruits of the Earth. Anything edible grown on the land as distinguished from foods obtained from the sea.

Fruits of the Sea. Seafood—fish, shellfish, edible seaweed, etc.

Fruit Sugar. A sugar consisting of small, fine crystals which dissolve readily. *See* Fructose.

Fruity. (1) Containing fruits; tasting or smelling like fruit. (2) Wine with a grape taste.

Frukost (Swedish). Breakfast.

Frukt (Swedish). Fruit.

Fruktvin (Norwegian). A fruit wine.

Frumenty; Furmenty (Obsolete). Boiled, hulled wheat, drained and sweetened, and served with milk; sometimes fruits such as currants or raisins, were added. It is made by boiling whole wheat for 24 hours until the grains have burst and then set in a thick jelly; it is then boiled with milk.

Frush (Obsolete). To carve meat or poultry.

Fruta (Spanish). Fruit.

Fruta de Bomba (Spanish). Papaya, pawpaw.

Fruta de Pan (Spanish). Breadfruit.

Fruto (Portuguese). Fruit.

Frutta (Italian). Fruit.

    Frutta Composta. Fruit compote.

    Frutta della Stagione. Fruit in season.

    Frutta Secca. Dried fruit.

    Frutti Misti. Mixed fruits.

Frutter. A pancake; a fritter.

Frutti di Mare (Italian). Fruits of the sea; shellfish.

Fry. (1) To cook in fat in a shallow pan. (2) The food so cooked, as, a fish fry.

Fryer. A young, tender chicken, 1½–2½ pounds dressed weight, suitable for frying.

Frying Pan. A shallow metal pan with a long handle used for frying foods.

Ftinoporino Cheese. A Macedonian sheep's-milk cheese similar to Brinsen.

Ftut (Yemenite). Soup stock prepared from meat flavored with garlic and herbs, and combined with squash, potatoes, and green onions.

Fudder (German). A large wine cask.

Fuddled. Confused as a result of over-drinking.

Fuder. A wine cask used in the Moselle Valley of Germany. *Fass* is the equivalent term in the Rhine Valley. *See* Germany, The Wines of.

Fudge. A soft, creamy American candy made of sugar, milk, and butter, and usually flavored with vanilla or chocolate. Unless cooked carefully it becomes gritty. The addition of corn syrup containing a form of sugar which does not readily crystallize, and which also surrounds the particles of crystallizing sugar in the cooling candy, also prevents the formation of the large crystals with an undesirable texture.

Fuel. Food that keeps the body functioning properly.

Fuencaral. A wine made from muscatel grapes grown near Madrid.

Fufu (West African). A staple food; usually a mixture of yams and cassava, although plantain sometimes takes the place of either of the two standard ingredients. When cooked, they are mashed smooth, heavily seasoned with pepper and other spices, and boiled like a thick cereal.

Fuggan. (1) Any bun or cake made of barley meal and lard. (2) A heavy-baked piece of dough, sometimes with a slice of pork pressed on the top.

Fugl (Norwegian). Fowl; poultry.

Fugu (Japanese). A poisonous blowfish. The poison is carefully extracted in licensed restaurants. Fugu is usually served in paper-thin slices with a sour citrus juice and soy-sauce mixture. It is also made into a stew with vegetables and prepared as a soup.

Fukuba. A Japanese agriculturist who developed a method for growing large strawberries. They are planted, surrounded by stone walls (which gives them their other name, *stonewall strawberries*), and given added warmth from the stones which are heated by the sun.

Fukuba Strawberries. *See* Stonewall Strawberries.

Fulbert-Dumonteil. A famous French gastronome of the nineteenth century; his most important work was *La France Gourmande*.

Fulsome. Of food, satisfying or filling.

Fumé (French). Smoked.

Fumer (French). To smoke (meats or fish).

Fumet de Faisan (French). A clear pheasant soup.

Fumet de Poisson (French). Fish bones and head cooked with vegetables, herbs, etc.

Fumets (French). Essences or concentrated liquids or jellies used to flavor stocks and sauces. They are obtained by boiling the desired food in stock or wine. Thus *fish fumet* is obtained by making a stock from the bones and trimmings of fish; the fish stock is then reduced and used with white wine in cooking certain fish.

Funghi (Italian). Mushrooms.

> **Funghi Acciugati al Forno.** Baked mushrooms with anchovies.
>
> **Funghi Ripieni al Forno.** Baked stuffed mushrooms.
>
> **Funghi Rossi.** Red mushrooms.
>
> **Funghi Sott' Olio ed Aceto.** Pickled mushrooms.

Fungi. Cornmeal balls, a favorite in the Virgin Islands.

Fungo (Portuguese). Mushroom.

Fungus. Any plant without green color, leaves, or flowers. The most popular edible fungus is the mushroom. Though the plural is *fungi*, the word *fungus* is often used for both singular and plural.

Funnel. A cone-shaped tube that permits liquid or other mixtures to pass through a small opening.

Funny Cake (Pennsylvania Dutch). A cake batter and sauce baked in a pie shell. When baked the sauce is between the pie shell and cake.

Furfurous. Made from bran; similar to bran.

Furfuryl Acetate. A light, straw-colored substance used to supply a synthetic spicy taste to various foods.

Furmai Squaquaron. A very fresh Italian cream cheese something like ricotta.

Furmenty; Frumenty (British). Barley or hulled wheat boiled in milk, then sweetened with molasses or honey.

Furner. A baker.

Fusel Oil. A mixture of organic acids, higher alcohols (propyl, butyl, and amyl), aldehydes, and esters; alcoholic fermentation produces about 95 percent alcohol and 5 percent fusel oil.

It is present in low concentration in wines and beer, and in higher concentration in pot-still spirit. On maturation of the liquor the fusel oil changes and imparts a special flavor to the spirit.

Fusil. The best type of steel used for sharpening knives.

Fusilli (Italian). Small curls of spiraled spaghetti.

Fust. A wine cask.

Fu Yung (Chinese). Foods prepared with eggs in the form of a thick omelet.

Fuzzle (Obsolete). To make someone drunk.

Fyke. A long fish net.

Fyldt Hvidkaal (Danish). Stuffed cabbage.

Fyldt Svinemørbrad (Danish). Pork with prunes and apples.

Fyllda (Swedish). Stuffed.

Fyrstekake (Norwegian). An almond-flavored cake.

G

Gabi (Philippine). Yams or taro, edible starchy tropical roots.

Gaburatye (French). Mixed fresh green vegetables.

Gädda (Swedish). Pike.

Gade. A family of fish including cod, whiting, haddock, pollack, hake, and ling, with firm white delicately flavored meat.

Gadwall. A wild freshwater duck about the same size as a mallard, found in the United States and Northern Europe. It migrates south in winter and is highly esteemed for the table. Also called *gray widgeon* and *sand widgeon*, it is more strictly a vegetarian than the mallard and other shoal-water ducks and has a less fishy flavor.

Gaffelbitar (Danish). Lightly salted herring.

Gaff Topsail. A sea catfish.

Gage. A quart.

Gai. (1) A European fish noted for its excellent flesh; also called *pucelotte*. (2) A herring after it has spawned. Connoisseurs claim that the taste is better after than prior to spawning.

Gaillac. The most important wine-producing center of the Tarn Department of France for ordinary table wines. Its best-known wine is *Clairette de Gaillac*, a semisparkling rosé.

Gairfish (Obsolete). Garfish.

Gaisburger Marsch (German). (1) Broiled cubes of meat served with onions and noodles. (2) A meat pie.

Gaiskäsli; Ziegenkäse (German, Swiss). A soft goat's-milk cheese.

Gai Tome Ka (Siamese). Chicken stewed in coconut milk.

Gajus (Malayan). The cashew nut.

Galactic. Pertaining to milk; derived from milk. Cheese, for example, is a galactic food.

Galam Butter. A solid fat produced from seeds of a tropical tree and used in cooking.

Galamus. A rather sweet tawny dessert wine with a prematurely old or rancid flavor; made in the vicinity of Roussillon, France.

Galangal. Various Asiatic herbs of the ginger family with aromatic, rather spicy roots; occasionally used for flavoring curries and in making bitters.

Galantina (Italian). A meat aspic.

Galantine (French). An elaborate rolled appetizer covered with aspic, and usually made with chicken, turkey, or duck, but sometimes with meat. When poultry is used, it is boned, and the skin is carefully removed and reserved. The skin is stretched out, covered with part of the boned meat, then with a seasoned forcemeat of the remaining poultry and finely chopped veal or pork. Truffles, pine nuts, or other seasoning may be spread on the meat before it is rolled, after which it is simmered in liquid and chilled before slicing and serving, sometimes with chopped aspic around it.

Galapong (Philippine). A dough made of finely ground rice and water and allowed to ferment overnight.

Galathée. A good-flavored crustacean resembling shrimp but very much larger; may be prepared like shrimp.

Galazyme. Partially fermented milk having a low alcoholic content.

Galeeny. A guinea fowl.

Galeton. A thin buckwheat-flour pancake or crêpe.

Galette (French). (1) A thin round wafer of flaky pastry, sometimes flavored with cheese, or sweetened when served as a dessert. (2) Round light breakfast rolls. (3) A kind of French pastry.

   Galette Piquante. A sweet bread or cake made at Eastertime, consisting of butter, sugar, and eggs combined with regular bread dough, and flavored with orange-flavored water; a specialty of the Poitou region.

Galettes Lausannoise. Small pastry shells filled with onions and cheese.

Galicia. A region of Spain which has excellent food, especially fish, shellfish, and pork products. Fruits and nuts are produced in abundance. Fish soups are featured in the cuisine, notably *caldeirada*, a thick chowder. The *pote gallego* is a heavy, tasty stew of beef, sausages, vegetable, and ham. *Cachelos* is a mixture of vegetables and ham.

Galicien (French). A rich, sweet cake with a butter cream filling and pistachio icing.

Galimafrée; Gallimaufry. (1) Ground shoulder of mutton and chopped bacon cooked in stock and reshaped on the bone, then covered with skin and roasted. (2) A cold meat ragout or stew. (3) (Colloquial). A poorly made stew prepared with scraps of meat.

Galingale. The pleasant-smelling root of an East Indian plant, often used as flavoring.

Galinha (Portuguese). Chicken.

Galinha Cerehada. Lightly fried chicken.

Galinha Corado. Baked chicken.

Gall. The contents of the gall bladder, attached to the liver of poultry. If the gall is broken, the bitter flavor ruins the whole bird. Dark spots should be removed from liver before it is cooked.

Galleta (Spanish). Cracker.

Galley. A ship's kitchen.

Gallina (Spanish). Hen.

Gallina con Garbanzos. Chicken stewed or fried with chick-peas.

Gallina del Mar. A good-sized red fish, having a fairly good taste.

Gallinaceous. Relating to birds that cannot fly well and nest on the ground.

Gallineta (Spanish). Guinea fowl.

Gallinule. Certain birds of the rail family; sometimes, the moor hen.

Gallipot. A very small glazed earthenware jar, pot, or container used for cream. *Pâté de foie gras* was formerly packed only in gallipots.

Gallize. To increase the volume of wine by adding water and sugar.

Gallon. Standard English and American liquid measures. The British imperial gallon weighs 160 ounces, the U.S. gallon 128 ounces. Both are divided into 8 pints; the British pint containing 20 ounces and the American pint 16 ounces. The old English gallon was equal to the present American gallon.

Galuska. Finger-sized dumplings, probably of Hungarian origin; popular in Central Europe.

Gamay. Widely cultivated red wine grapes grown on the slopes of Burgundy in France and in California.

Gamba (Spanish). Prawn, the term used to distinguish it from *camarón*, shrimp.

Gambas (Spanish). Large shrimp.

Gamberetti (Italian). Small shrimp.

Gamberi (Italian). Shrimp.

Gamberi alla Cacciatora. Shrimp in tomato sauce.

Gamberi Fritti. Fried shrimp.

Gambero di Mare (Italian). Clawless lobster.

Game. All wild birds and animals (also some fish) hunted during certain seasons and used for food; also the flesh of these creatures.

Game Bird. An edible wild bird hunted for sport.

Game Knife. A small sharp knife used for carving wild game and fowl; also used as a steak knife.

Gammelöst. A Norwegian semisoft cheese made from sour skim milk, with a grainy texture, a sharp, aromatic flavor.

Gammon (British). (1) A piece of ham or the under part of a side of bacon. Also, cured or smoked ham. (2) To cure bacon by smoking.

Gamy. Having a wild, unusual taste similar to that of game birds or animals. Many people do not, at least at first, enjoy the wild flavor of venison as compared with beef. Nor do they like the taste of wild duck as compared with that of commercially raised ducks. Often the food the particular game has eaten before being killed determines the taste; thus ducks that have eaten fish will develop a somewhat fishy taste. The extremely gamy taste may be minimized by marinating in a wine mixture for at least a day, but this will not always remove the gamy taste.

Gan (Obsolete). Gin.

Ganache Paste. A mixture of boiling fresh dairy cream and granulated sugar.

Gander. The male goose.

Gandul (Latin American). The pigeon pea.

Gang (Danish). Portion.

Ganja. A narcotic and intoxicating Indian hemp mixture.

Ganmodoki (Japanese). Vegetables and fried soybean curd.

Gannet. A web-footed sea bird of mediocre taste sometimes used for food.

Gans (Dutch, German). Goose.

Gänsebrust (German). Breast of goose.

Gänseleber (German). Goose liver.

    Gänseleberpastete. Goose-liver paste.

    Gänseleberwurst. Goose-liver sausage.

Ganses (French). Cookies fried in deep fat and covered with powdered sugar; a specialty of Nice.

Ganso (Portuguese). Goose.

Gantois (French, Belgian). A cylindrical cake made with butter, eggs, cinnamon, pastry dough, and plum jam.

Ganzo (Spanish). Sirloin butt of beef.

Gaper. An edible shellfish resembling a cooky, found in the sand at low-water mark.

Gaperon; Gapron. A cheese made in Limagne, France, from September to July.

Gar; Garfish; Garpike. A fish in the pike family, with a long jaw.

Garam Marsala (Southeast Asian). A flavoring mixture consisting of equal parts of cardamom, black pepper, cloves, cinnamon, and cumin.

Garapiña (Mexican). A soft drink made of pineapple, tamarind, oranges, and sugar.

Garbanzo (Spanish). See Chick-Pea.

Garble (British). Garbage; waste.

Garbure (French). A meatless thick vegetable soup; also a dish made with vegetables.

Garçon (French). A waiter.

    Garçon de Salle. A restaurant waiter.

Garda. A very soft, rich, creamy Italian cheese.

Garda, Chiaretto del. A rosé wine. See Italy, The Wines of.

Garde Manger (French). (1) A meat or larder room. (2) The person in charge of this room.

Garden Balm; Balm Mint; Balm. An herb whose leaves are used in making salads, flavoring foods, and preparing a sort of tea.

Garden Cheese. Medium-quality cream cheese with vegetables.

Garden Cress. A variety of peppergrass, a spring annual.

Gardon (French). The roach fish, a European freshwater fish.

Garetto di Vitello (Italian). Veal knuckle.

Garfish. A long fish with a spearlike nose and an extended jaw.

Garfo (Portuguese). Fork.

Garget. See Poke.

Gargotage (French). Food poorly prepared or served.

Gargote (French, Colloquial). An inferior restaurant.

Gargotier (French). A bad cook; the owner of a low-class restaurant.

Gargoulette (French). A water pitcher.

Garibaldi Biscuit. A currant-filled sandwich cooky.

Garleac (Obsolete, British). Garlic; from gar, spear, and leac, leek.

Garlic. A bulbous annual, a member of the lily family, stronger and more pungent than onions or shallots. The marvelous and unmistakable flavor which garlic imparts to any dish in which it is included has gained increased favor in the United States in the last quarter century. This is an ancient food, referred to by Homer.

Used with discretion, garlic can give a subtle flavoring to a wide variety of foods. When cooked with foods, it may, if desired, be removed before serving. A cut clove of garlic rubbed on a salad bowl before mixed greens and French dressing are tossed in it adds distinctive savor. Slivers of garlic inserted into a leg of lamb before roasting contributes an excellent flavor, and garlic is practically a necessity for hearty stews and pot roasts.

Garlic is usually available fresh or powdered. Fresh garlic comes in cloves, whose color ranges from red to white. It should be stored in a cool dry place. The rather unpleasant breath resulting from eating garlic may be somewhat minimized by chewing several sprigs of fresh parsley shortly after eating the garlic.

    Garlic Butter. Butter flavored with crushed garlic.

    Garlic Oil. Olive oil (or other oil) in which several cut cloves of garlic are steeped.

    Garlic Salt. Salt flavored with garlic. When it is used in recipes, less salt than specified is needed.

Garlic Vinegar. Crushed garlic infused in vinegar.

Garlic, Lesser-Leaved; Rockenbollen. A garlic plant, a smaller, milder variety of *rocambole*; its brown-skinned cloves grow at the top.

Garlicky. Having a garlic odor or taste.

Garmugia (Italian). Beef stew with artichokes.

Garnalen (Dutch, German). Shrimp.

Garner. A grain warehouse.

Garneren (Dutch). Garnish.

Garni (French). (1) Served with such items as pickles, mushrooms, or vegetables. (2) In some countries, small sandwiches.

Garnir (French). To garnish, decorate, or improve.

Garnish. Decoration which enhances the appearance of a prepared dish. A century ago, elaborate garnishes were the rule in French cookery, particularly when practiced in the *haute cuisine*. Hundreds, even thousands, of garnishes were devised, consisting of sauces, fritters, dumplings, pastries, chopped or blended vegetables, fish or meat, and the like. In recent years the garnish has become much simpler, and elaborate preparations are seldom seen except at formal banquets.

A garnish may be nothing more than a sprig of parsley or a twist of lemon. Or it may be more elaborately devised, including expensive black truffles cut to resemble flower buds or leaves, radish roses, or other vegetables cut in attractive shapes. The important thing is that the flavor of the garnish should blend with that of the dish it dresses.

Garniture. The decoration of food; garnish.

Garofolato (Italian). Beef stew with wine, flavored with cloves.

Garpike. The garfish.

Garri (Nigerian). Cracked, roasted cassava, grated and sprinkled over food.

Garum (Latin). A pickled fish sauce, a Roman dish made from the intestines and gills of certain fish.

Gås (Swedish). Goose.

Gascony, Fromage de; Castillon. A French cow's-milk cheese.

Gåsesteg (Danish). Roast goose.

Gåsleverkorv (Swedish). Goose-liver sausage.

Gaspacho. *See* Gazpacho.

Gasperou. The freshwater drum fish, a food fish.

Gas Storage. A method of storing fruit, mainly apples and pears, and vegetables in fresh condition in carbon dioxide gas at 40°F. This doubles the life of the fruit compared with storing at 40°F. without gas.

Gastera. The Greek goddess of gastronomy. The name comes from the Greek *gaster*, stomach.

Gastrique (French). An acidulous base for sweet-and-sour sauces, prepared by boiling sugar and either adding caramel or cooking with sugar.

Gastrology. The study of cooking and eating; the science and art of food preparation.

Gastromania. Excessive or overzealous fondness for foods and wines to the exclusion of other interests in life.

Gastronome; Gastronomer. One who knows and enjoys good food; a gourmet; an expert in fine foods and wines.

Gastronomic. Related to the science and art of food.

Gastronomy. The art of eating, drinking, and dining.

Gastrotechy. The fine art and perhaps also the science of cookery, food, and wine.

Gaststätten. The best type of restaurant in Germany.

Gâteau (French). Cake.

> Gâteau au Fromage. A pastry shell filled with a mixture of eggs, flour, cream, and grated Emmental cheese.
>
> Gâteau de Noce. Wedding cake.
>
> Gâteau des Rois. A special cake frequently prepared in the form of a crown, made with candied fruits and served at Epiphany.
>
> Gâteau Sablé. A sand cake, a rich, light, plain cake.
>
> Gâteau Wallon (Belgian). An apple pie or tart.

Gattinara. An Italian table wine, usually red; made in Piedmont. *See* Italy, The Wines of.

Gaude (French). Cornmeal dumplings or balls boiled and served hot with melted butter, etc.

Gaufer; Gaufre (French). A light cooky, waffle, or wafer baked in a mold similar to a waffle iron.

Gaufrettes (French). Small, fancy thin cookies or wafers.

Gaur. A large ox often used for food in India.

Gautrias. A soft French cheese resembling Port du Salut; marketed weighing about 5 pounds.

Gave, Côtes du. A group of undistinguished red, white, and rosé wines produced in the Pau region of France.

Gavel (British). A certain quantity of corn ready to be bundled.

Gavi. A township of Piedmont, Italy which produces fine-quality white table wines. See Italy, The Wines of.

Gawn (British, Colloquial). A gallon measure of food or liquid capacity.

Gayal. An ox native to Burma; occasionally used for food.

Gayette (French). A small sausage made from pork liver, fat, and spices.

Gay-Lussac. The French scientist who developed the alcoholometer, which measures the alcoholic content of wines.

Gaz (Iranian). A very rich, overly sweet candy.

Gazpacho (Spanish). A chilled soup-salad now popular in America. Most versions are prepared with a purée of fresh tomatoes, garlic, green peppers, onions, olive oil, and vinegar; it is also prepared with broth and garnished with vegetables. It is served ice-cold with small bowls of croutons, chopped cucumbers, green peppers, and tomatoes. When gazpacho is served, a salad course should not be included in the meal.

Gdra (Moroccan). Chicken stew made with chickpeas; served with rice.

Gean (Scotch). Wild cherry.

Geans (Guigne) Cherries. Sweet, firm black, red, or white cherries used in the preparation of a liqueur called guignolet, a specialty of Angers, France.

Gebäck (German). Baked food; pastry.

Gebackene Eier (German). Fried eggs.

Gebak (Dutch). Pastry.

Gebakken (Dutch). Fried.
  Gebakken Bokking. Fried smoked herring.
  Gebakken Panharing. Grilled fresh herring.

Gebonden Soep (Dutch). Cream soup.

Gebraden Kalfsvlees (Dutch). Roast veal.

Gebraden Lamsvlees (Dutch). Roast lamb.

Gebraden Schapenvlees (Dutch). Roast mutton.

Gebratene Lammkeule (German). Roast leg of lamb.

Ged. The pike, an important food fish.

Gedämpfte Kalbsbrust (German). Breast of veal cooked with onions.

Gedämpfte Rinderbrust (German). Potted beef with a natural gravy.

Gedde (Danish). Pike.

Gedroogde Pruimen (Dutch). Prunes.

Geebung. An Australian tree bearing fair-quality fruits.

Geechee Limes. (1) A tart olivelike fruit native only to the banks of the Ogeechee River in Georgia. (2) A condiment made according to a secret recipe by a manufacturer in Savannah, Georgia, and marketed under the name of the fruit.

Geflügel (German). Poultry.
  Geflügelfrikassee. Chicken fricassee.
  Geflügelklein. Chicken giblets.
  Geflügelleber. Chicken liver.

Gefüllter Gänsehals (German). Stuffed goose neck.

Gefüllte Fish; Gefillte Fish; Gefilte Fish (Jewish). Ground boned freshwater fish, usually whitefish, pike, and sometimes carp; prepared with salt, pepper, onions, eggs, and sometimes carrots. The mixture is shaped into balls and simmered in seasoned water and onions or fish stock for about one hour, then chilled. The fish stock forms a jelly, which is served with the fish. Horseradish is the classic accompaniment of this dish.

Gegrillt (German). Grilled.

Gehakt (Dutch). Chopped meatballs or meat loaf.

Geheimrath. A Dutch mass-produced version of better-quality baby Gouda cheese.

Geisenheim. A wine village of the Rheingau, Germany. See Germany, The Wines of.

Gekocht (German). Boiled.

Gekochte Eier (German). Boiled eggs.
  Gekochter Schinken. Boiled ham.
  Gekochtes Fleisch. Boiled beef.
  Gekochtes Ochsenfleisch. Boiled beef.

Gekookte (Dutch). Boiled.

Gel. A coagulated liquid which develops a jellylike consistency.

Gelado (Portuguese). Iced.

Gelant (French). Partly frozen or jelled.

Gelatin. The colorless, odorless substance extracted by boiling hoofs, bones, and animal tissue; as its name suggests, gelatin, dissolved in hot liquid, swells so as to form a viscid, jellylike substance (a gel) when the solution cools.

History tells us that as long ago as the first century the Chinese took advantage of the physical and chemical properties of gelatin.

Gelatin is available in the granulated, unflavored, and unacidulated form, and also in a fruit-flavored mixture of plain gelatin, sugar, fruit acids, flavors, and colorings. The latter is sold in packages standardized to gel one pint of liquid.

Unflavored gelatin is used in making aspics, chiffon pies, Bavarian creams, etc. Either type of gelatin should be mixed with cold liquid, then dissolved over, or in, hot liquid until clear.

Gelatin Dessert Powder. Gelatin, sweetened and flavored, and marketed for the making of simple, easily-prepared desserts.

Gelatina. (1) Jellied meats containing chocolate, a specialty of Salerno, Italy. (2) (Spanish) Gelatin.

Gelatina, En (Spanish). In aspic.

Gelatiniform. In gelatin form.

Gelatinous. Like jelly or gelatin.

Gelation. The process of becoming solid under very low temperatures.

Gelato (Italian). Ice-cream dessert; ice.

　Gelato alla Vaniglia. Vanilla ice cream.

　Gelato Dama Bianca. Almond ice cream.

　Gelato di Caffè. Coffee ice cream.

　Gelato di Crema. Ice cream.

　Gelato di Fragole. Strawberry ice cream.

　Gelato di Frutta. Fruit ice.

　Gelato di Mandorle. Almond ice.

Gelbe Rüben (German). Carrots.

Gelé (Swedish). Jelly.

Gelea (Portuguese). Jelly.

Gelei (Dutch). Jelly.

Gelinotte (French). The hazel hen; ruffled grouse.

Gelo (Portuguese). Ice.

Gelose. Agar-agar, a gelatinous substance found in seaweed and moss.

Gelt. A young female pig.

Gember (Dutch). Ginger.

Gemischter Salat (German). Mixed salad.

Gemüse (German). Vegetables.

　Gemüseplatte. Vegetable plate.

　Gemüsesuppe. Vegetable soup.

Gemsye (Danish). Vegetables.

Gendarme. (1) (French). Pickled herring. (2) A hard, dry Swiss sausage shaped somewhat like a herring.

Génépy des Alpes. An Italian liqueur made with wild mountain herbs.

Geneva. A very dry gin with a smoky quality; distilled in Holland and formerly called *Hollands Geneva* or *Jenever*. It is usually pure white but is sometimes colored with caramel, which results in a straw-colored liquor. It is ready to drink as soon as distilled, and does not improve with aging. The name Geneva is a popularization of the French word *genièvre*, juniper.

Génevoise (French). A fish sauce prepared with sauce Espagnole combined with red wine and mushrooms.

Genièvre (French). The juniper berry, a blue-black berry with a peculiar aromatic flavor used to flavor marinades, liqueurs, syrups, and gins.

Genipap. A rather sour-tasting tropical fruit.

Genoa Cake. A rich fruit cake.

Génoise; Genoese. A rich, light butter sponge-cake, made from sugar, eggs, flour, butter, and vanilla; by extension, any type of cake made from a Génoise mixture. It may be made in lemon and orange variations, with chocolate, nuts, or nougat.

Gentian. A small plant with short leaves, blue flowers, and a bitter-tasting juice, used in making bitters, such as *Fernet-Branca*.

Gentiane. A digestive liqueur flavored with dried ground gentian roots; made in Switzerland and France.

Gentil. A French wine; made with white Pinot grapes in Alsace. *See* France, The Wines of.

Gentleman's Pudding. A simple steamed pudding made with butter, sugar, flour, and eggs, and sweetened with jam; usually served with sherry sauce or cream.

Geoduck. A very large edible Pacific coast clam; best used in chowders and stews.

George Washington Cake. A light fruit cake with white icing.

George Washington Pie. A plain layer cake with

jam as filling and frosting; sometimes with whipped cream.

Georgia Pecans. Nuts from a North American tree related to the hickory. They are available shelled and unshelled.

Gepökelter Schweinekamm (German). Roasted salt pork; a specialty of the Hesse region.

Geräucherter Lachs (German). Smoked salmon.

Geräucherter Schinken (German). Smoked ham.

Gérardmer Cheese. A French cheese, made in Lorraine, from briefly scalded milk curds.

Gerbe. A sheaf of wheat.

Gerber Test. A test for fat used in routine analyses of milk. When sulfuric acid and milk are mixed, heat develops, dissolving the organic matter but not the fat, which separates when amyl alcohol is added. The reaction is carried out in a Gerber bottle with a thin, graduated neck, in which the fat collects and is measured.

Gerbiebenes Gerstl (Austrian). Soup containing noodle dough grated into very small particles like barley.

German Beefsteak. Chopped raw beef.

Germander. A mint-flavored herb.

German Fruit Pudding. A pudding made with butter, sugar, flour, eggs, and milk, topped with several different fruits, then baked; served hot and eaten with heavy sweet cream.

Germna Silver; Nickel Silver. An alloy of zinc, nickel, and copper used for flatware.

German Wines. *See* Germany, The Wines of.

Germany. German food tends toward the substantial and filling rather than toward the light and appetite-provoking as in France. Not that German food can be dismissed as being only heavy, for it is truly one of the world's great cuisines. German cooks prefer to prepare solid, plate-filling dishes that suit the national palate and appetite. The Germans, being healthy, hearty, athletic people have comparatively little interest in dainty appetizers or hors d'oeuvre, and prefer instead a substantial, thick soup.

In the early morning the *Frühstuck*, or breakfast, is the typical Continental breakfast of rolls and coffee. In southern Germany, around Bavaria, a second breakfast is customary; this odd repast, called *Z-nuni* or *Veschperle*, consists of black bread, raw bacon, and a glass of *Kirschwasser*! Lunch is a very substantial meal of several courses, and might typically consist of a bowl of split-pea soup made with ham, possibly followed by pig's knuckles and sauerkraut, accompanied by a large dish of boiled potatoes. Dessert might be a large portion of pudding covered with fruit sauce. With this most Germans would have a glass or two of beer. In the late afternoon everyone heads for a café to have several portions of cake or pastry plus coffee (often with whipped cream). The evening meal, *Abendessen*, usually lighter than the midday repast, may be similar to lunch, or it may consist only of sliced cold delicatessen meats, salad, and the like.

Of the somewhat limited appetizer courses available, surely the most popular are of herring, of which *Rollmöpse* (Rollmop) and *Matjeshering* (Matjes) are quite well known in the United States. Most German soups are very substantial—cabbage, barley, oxtail, and others of similar richness and body. American-style steaks or roast beef are rarely served; beef dishes are likely to be stewed or potted. The classic example is *sauerbraten*, pickled beef, a national favorite. Veal is also quite popular, but lamb is less so. The single favorite meat is pork, and every menu features it in one form or another. From the pig the Germans make sausages in a wide range of sizes and shapes. Popular types include *Weisswurst*, a pale, whitish sausage; *Bratwurst*, a rather large, bland type; *Regensburger*, somewhat spicy; *Cervelat*, a summer sausage. With sausages, sauerkraut is the natural accompaniment. The Germans don't care too much for fresh vegetables, but potatoes are served with every main course. *Knödel*, dumplings, are the only acceptable substitute for potatoes, according to German taste. German cheeses, although not so extensive as French, are noteworthy; the best include *Münster*, *Limburger*, and *Tilsiter*.

German beer is superb, undoubtedly among the best in the world. It comes chiefly in two different styles—light (*helles*) and dark (*dunkles*).

Germany, The Wines of. For the excellence and variety of her wines, France is in a class alone.

However, Germany produces some of the finest and rarest wines in the world. Without exception, the leading German wines are white. (The red wines are quite poor, not suitable for the export market.) Italian wines are mainly red, although there are some satisfactory whites, but no Italian wine, red or white, even in its best year could match a great German wine of a good vintage. France has a wealth of excellent white wines which the French claim not only compete with those of Germany but surpass them—notably the "divine" Montrachet of Burgundy and the sweet dessert wines of Bordeaux. But connoisseurs of German white wines frequently say that their favorites surpass the best French whites, although they admit no country can hope to produce better red wines than France. This discussion, therefore, will be concerned with only the white wines of Germany.

The range of German white wines is limited compared with that of France and Italy, but their reputation is world-wide. All of them fit into a certain general category: their alcoholic content is low, they have a very distinctive flowery bouquet, and they are all of a light gold color with a greenish undertone. They are classified from the very dry to the very sweet.

Wines have been produced in Germany from the time that Caesar's forces invaded the land and taught the people how to plant the vines. Roman ruins and Roman relics may be found throughout the wine districts, and many of the villages bear names adapted from the original Roman place names. The records of Charlemagne contain many references to the excellence of German wines. They reached the apex of popularity with the British during the eighteenth and early nineteenth centuries, when most of the exports were from Hochheimer. The British soon changed the appellation to "Hock," and it is by this name that German wines are still ordered in England.

The wine district of Germany is situated in the western part of the country a short distance from the French provinces of Alsace and Lorraine. The great wines come from two important river valleys, the Rhine and the Moselle. The Rhine cuts across the land from southeast to northwest; on the right, or east, bank of the river is the Rheingau district, producer of many of the finest wines. On the left, or west, bank are Rheinpfalz and Rheinhessen. The other important wine district is situated along the meandering Moselle, which joins the Rhine at Koblenz after traveling in a northeasterly direction. Two other districts frequently considered part of the Moselle region are the Saar and the Ruwer. (Rhine wines can be distinguished immediately from Moselles, for the former come in brown bottles and the latter in green.)

There are comparatively few level vineyards; most of the land devoted to viniculture is steep and precipitous, terraced on the sides of sharp inclines rising from the edge of the river. Each vine must be planted and tended at the cost of great labor and patience. All the work is done by hand, for no horse or machine could possibly cope with the steep slopes to which the vines cling. The soil is quite poor, often extremely rocky. Certain regions contain much slate, while others have none. The weather is a tremendous problem; this is the northern limit at which wine grapes can be raised with any success. Certain vineyards are in the latitude of Newfoundland, and during seasons of late harvest there is always the danger of sudden frost. In the wine towns, sages repeat the old adage that a minimum of 100 days of sunshine is necessary between May and harvest time to produce a satisfactory wine. This happens in about half the years. For a great wine, 120 sunny days are required; this will occur about every fifth year, but two such years may occur close together or may be separated by a decade.

The chief vine is the Riesling, which never produces a large yield. Wines from this grape always have a certain distinctive flowery quality that is unique. The Riesling is small with a greenish-yellow hue. When the weather suits this grape—and with proper soil and cultivation—the wine from it will have rare quality. Riesling grows best in a climate which, though bright and sunny, is not too hot. It also prefers a hilly soil with very good drainage. The best location for it is along the German river banks.

The second most important type is the Sylvaner, a far more productive vine. Next comes the Traminer or a variation of it, the Gewurztraminer, which originated in Alsace. But this type is gradually disappearing from the vineyards and seems likely to be replaced by the Muller-Thurgau, a recent cross between the Sylvaner and the Riesling. The Spatburgunder, actually the Pinot Noir of Burgundy, is used for red wines but never with any conspicuous success.

In all the other wine-making countries of Europe grapes are harvested in late September as a rule and never later than the first week or two in October, for to delay longer would be to risk damage to the vines. In Germany, where the vineyards are so far north, the grapes have seldom obtained enough sunshine to ripen until the middle of October. The harvest never begins before this time and may be delayed even longer. In certain extraordinary years when the sunshine continues, it may extend into November. But in late October and early November the sun lacks warmth, although it may be bright, and only a few of the hardiest types of grape will mature in such cool weather.

German wines are classified by the degree of ripeness of the grape at harvest time; in turn, the degree of ripeness determines the sugar content of the wine. The poorest wines are those which require added sugar to make them palatable. Some vineyards with particularly poor locations, or soil, or improper methods of cultivation, may year after year require the addition of sugar. There are others which may require added sugar in poor years and none in better vintages. At the head of the list are the finest wines needing no sugar at all. These are known as "natural" wines, *Naturwein* the Germans call them. (Sometimes they are known as *Naturrein* or *ungezuckerter Wein*, wine without sugar.) Without sufficient sugar the grapes cannot manufacture alcohol and so cannot be shipped, for wines low in alcohol will not "travel" well. In determining whether a wine is natural, the buyer should look for the designation *Naturwein* on the label; this offers a reasonable degree of assurance. Some of the more important producers may not say the wine is *Naturwein* but instead mark their product *Gewachs* or *Wachstum*, meaning "growth," and

this indicates that the wine is an unblended and therefore a natural wine.

In every vineyard a great deal of thought, effort, and knowledge (combined with a certain amount of luck) goes into the selection of the date for harvesting. This is particularly true in these northern vineyards where a few days' delay can result in great damage from frost. The problem is further complicated by the need to wait for the mold to form on the grapes. In France this mold is called *pourriture noble* (noble mold) and in Germany *Edelfäule*. The weather must be warm during the summer, with enough rain, and then the *Edelfäule* will usually come late, just before harvest time. In some dry years the mold will not appear at all, and then the wines are poor. The *Edelfäule* appears first after several days of bright, warm sunshine followed by cool nights and considerable dew or fog in the morning. At first the grapes seem to be gently dusted with a thin film of powder. This mold is known to scientists as the *Botrytiscinerea*; it is unusual in its action, for it forms an outside coating on the grape that is most unpleasant-looking; the filaments pierce the grape skin, causing a loss of the natural liquid. This loss of moisture makes the remaining sugar more concentrated, but the mold, oddly enough, does not spoil the taste of the grape. Under ordinary circumstances the grapes ready for harvesting contain about 20 percent sugar; after the formation of the *Edelfäule* they have as much as 60 percent.

Not all the vine is touched by the mold; many clusters are protected by their leaves or by other clusters. When the harvesting begins, some vintners delay the picking to wait for the "noble rot" to form. Sometimes they may compromise and pick some of the untouched grapes at the regular harvesting, and then have the pickers delay a week or two before beginning a late harvest when the *Edelfäule* appears. A vineyard may produce its average wine from grapes without the mold, and have a special class known as *spätlese* (late picking) from grapes that have received the *Edelfäule*. *Spätlese* wines are smoother and of better quality, for they have had the benefit of at least a week, sometimes several weeks, of additional sunshine. The result is always a better "finish."

Even finer in quality are the *auslese* (selected picking). Whereas *spätlese* grapes must be at least slightly touched by the mold, *auslese* grapes are those which have been selected by the pickers because they are covered with it and are obviously ripe. Needless to say, *auslese* wines are more expensive because of the time consumed in picking and processing the grapes, which yield less than the ordinary harvest. Sometimes these are classed from *feine auslese* (fine) to *hochfeine auslese* (finest). All these wines will be fairly dry.

Beeren Auslese (selected berries) indicates a wine made from selected, single grapes, each cut by hand from certain selected clusters. Wines of this type are renowned for their bouquet and subtle sweetness. Some vintners, instead of marking the label *Beeren Auslese*, use something more elaborate like *Goldenbeerenauslese* or *Edelbeerenauslese*, but the meaning is the same.

The finest category of German wine is *Trockenbeeren Auslese* (dried berries selection). The berries, of course, are individual grapes. These wines are made from grapes which have hung until almost completely dry and free of any natural liquid, until they are like raisins on the vine. These air-dried raisins are cut from the clusters, one by one, and specially fermented. Making wines of this caliber may be a matter of pride for the vineyard; the risk involved in the delayed harvest and the amount of labor expended may not reimburse the owner even though each bottle sells for twenty or thirty dollars. (In certain fabulous years these wines have been sold for sixty-five dollars a bottle.)

The German vineyards have not been classified, and to know a good wine from a poor one it is necessary to learn to read the label. Most people are appalled by the confusion of long, tongue-twisting German place names, yet, with a little practice, they are not too difficult to understand. German vineyards may be compared roughly to those of the Burgundy district of France, where estate bottling is the rule. The Germans have enacted a series of laws concerning the sale of wines, but the situation leaves

much to be desired. However, a German label tells a great deal more about the wine in the bottle than does one from France or Italy.

In vineyards of reputation great care is taken to identify the product; each daily harvest of grapes is crushed separately and the cask marked. (*Fuder* is the cask mark used in the Moselle Valley, and *Fass* #—— on the Rhine.) This is necessary because every cask will be different from every other cask even though they are all from the same vineyard. At the conclusion of several days' pressing, the wines are not blended together (as they would be in other countries) but are stored separately in their carefully marked casks. An important vineyard may bring to the market in a vintage year great wines of a particular type, but even within that type the casks may vary in quality. For example, a protected corner of a vineyard can produce a wine quite different from a wine that is made from vines in another section more exposed to sun, wind, and rain. A vintner may offer eight casks, each bearing the same name and classification (*Auslese*, for example), yet each cask will be different from the others.

A few minutes spent in reading the label will make its meaning clear. Usually the upper center contains an elaborate coat of arms, a crest, an eagle, or an illustration of some German scene. This is attractive but of no significance. The color of the foil wrapping is usually without meaning also. What is significant is the name of the district or village. (Each district contains its own vineyards, some with famous names, others that are little known. While the majority of vineyards are owned by one proprietor or family, some are jointly owned by a score or more.) A label with only the district name is a risk, for this indicates that while 51 percent of the wine comes from the district, the remaining 49 percent is not specified.

A good vineyard indicates the district, town, and vineyard name, and the name of the grape variety. The exception is when a vineyard has such a tremendous reputation that it is better known than the town; then the town name is dispensed with. Schloss Johannisberger is a famous example. Sometimes the vineyard named is joined to that of the town, like the renowned Piesporter Goldtröpfchen. The omission of the vineyard name, when no grape type is indicated, should signify that the wine comes from an inferior variety.

The label on the better wines will also indicate the degree of ripeness of the grape at the time of harvest: *Auslese* or *Trockenbeeren Auslese*, etc. Of course, the vintage date will also appear.

Determining whether a wine has been artificially sweetened or not requires some knowledge of the terminology: *verbesserte* (improved) is one description; another is *gezuckerte* (sugared). These wines can be good but seldom as good as the natural wines. A wine bottled by the estate indicated on the label has not been sugared, even though this fact is not stated on the label. By law, wines without added sugar specify one (or more) of the following designations on the labels:

Natur, Naturrein, Naturwein, Ungezuckerter: Natural wine, unsugared

Echt, Rein: Genuine

Crescenz, Gewachs, Eigengewächs, Wachstum: The growth; when followed by the grower's name, the wine is unsugared

Original-Abfüllung, Abfüllung, Kellerabfüllung: An original bottling; a bottling (sometimes appears as Orig.-ABFG.)

Kellerabzug, Schlossabzug: Bottled by the estate

Eigenes Wachstum: Bottled by the grower

Kabinett, Kabinettwein: Special, reserved wine

Fass, Bestes Fass, Fuder: Cask #——— indicating an unsugared wine

Edel: Noble; usually in connection with one of the terms denoting ripeness that follows

Spätlese, Auslese, Beeren Auslese, Trockenbeeren Auslese: The degrees of ripeness of the grapes

Other notations interesting to know but not offering any assurance of the quality of the wines include words such as *Feine, Feinste,* or *Hoch-Feinste* which indicate the grower's opinion of his product—or pure salesmanship. Notations concerning aristocratic or royal affiliations *Graf*

(Count), *Freiherr* (Baron), and *Fürst* (Prince) are amusing in themselves, but they are only too frequently meant to confuse and to impress buyers abroad. Other commonly encountered notations are *Winzergenossenschaft* and *Winzerverein*, which indicate the wine is produced and marketed by a vintners' cooperative association.

The Rheingau

On the right bank of the Rhine lies the district producing the finest wines of Germany. Moselle is the only other district that can compete with the Rheingau, and a judgment as to which type is better is a matter of individual taste. The stately Rhine begins in Switzerland, then flows north until it reaches Mainz, where it turns sharply to the southwest. It is here in this bend, for a distance of only twenty miles, that the river flows through the celebrated wine towns from Wiesbaden to Rüdesheim. Located on the north bank of the river, on the moderately steep slopes of the Taunus Hills, are farms which constitute almost one continuous vineyard. Because of their location on the north banks the vineyards face south and sometimes a bit to the southeast, receiving the maximum benefits from the sunshine. The total area under production is quite small, about five thousand acres, only a fraction of that under cultivation in other wine districts of Germany.

Three-quarters of the vineyards are planted to the Riesling, the balance consists of Sylvaner and the Muller-Thurgau cross. Of the fourteen picturesque villages along the river's edge, two-thirds are world-famous for the excellence of their wines.

Hochheim: This little village, generally included in the Rheingau grouping because of its proximity (ten miles to the east) and the similarity of its wines, faces the Main River rather than the Rhine. Unlike the continuous vineyards of the Taunus Hills in the true Rheingau district, those of Hochheim are isolated and surrounded by ordinary farmlands, and instead of being planted on slopes to get the maximum sunshine, the vineyards are on flat ground. In good years Hochheim wines are soft and delicate with a fine fruit flavor; when everything goes well they are superb.

The leading vineyards include the following (all usually preceded with the village name Hochheimer): Domdechaney, Kirchenstück, Stein, Hölle, Daubhaus, Rauchloch.

Eltville: The wine here is produced in substantial quantity. The quality falls below the best Rheingau wines, but it is no less palatable for ordinary occasions. The wines of this township tend to be quite dry with a remarkable bouquet. The outstanding vineyards are Sonnenberg, Taubenberg, Klumbchen, Langenstück.

Rauenthal: Here is a paradox: This village, set back in the hills, rather than on the river bank, has received little publicity, particularly in the United States, where Rauenthaler wines are comparatively unknown even to connoisseurs. Yet it is one of the first wine villages of the Rheingau: prices in Germany are consistently high for wine from these vineyards. It is delicate with an odd, almost spicy, sharp quality. It is interesting to note that the Baiken vineyard, the best in Rauenthal, is classified as the most valuable wine property in Germany. But it is nearly equaled by Gehrn. Worth attention also are Wieshell, Wülfen, Rothenberg, and Herberg.

Erbach: Once again on the shore of the river, we find this superb wine village, famous throughout Germany and wherever connoisseurs gather. The Marcobrunn *Lage*, or vineyard, produces great wines in limited quantities, for the vineyard is small. Marcobrunnen means "fountain marker"; the name derives from the fountain marking the boundary between Erbach and Hattenheim to the west. Sometimes the wine is labeled with the usual combination of place and vineyard—*Erbacher Marcobrunn*—and sometimes (in recognition of its fame) simply as *Marcobrunner*. It is a balanced and rounded wine with a bouquet incomparable in great years. Not in the same class but good are Hohenrain, Siegelsberg, Brühl, and Steinmorgen.

Kiedrich: This village, like its neighbor to the east, Rauenthal, is also far back in the hills, although closer to the river. It has a superb view of the Rhine. The vineyards here are good, although none of them equals those of Erbach or Rauenthal. The wines lack the amazing bouquet that distinguishes their great neighbors. The leading vineyard is Gräfenburg; Turmberg, Sandgrub, and Wasserrose are also good.

Hattenheim: Beautifully situated on the Rhine, this charming town is one that tourists exclaim over and photograph. When all goes well in the vineyards, it produces wines of incomparable excellence. The *spätlese* and *auslese* wines are rich and smooth as silk. Its great vineyard is Steinberg. The wines of this superb vineyard are always sold as Steinberger, or Steinberger and a qualifying designation such as *spätlese*, but the town name never appears on the label. The Steinberg vineyard is a beautiful, completely enclosed property about a mile outside the village proper. Originally it was cultivated by the order of Cistercian monks. Incidentally, the wines with the simple label "Steinberger" (without any further description) are not nearly as expensive or as much in demand as the more highly cultivated types. The other vineyards of this village offer no competition to this foremost *Lage*. But there are over twenty good vineyards, and among them the leaders are generally agreed to be Hassel, Nussbrunnen, Engelmannsberg, Mannberg, and Wisselbrunnen.

Oestrich: Just a short distance to the west of Hattenheim and also on the Rhine, this village has a larger acreage devoted to wine than any other in the Rheingau. The wines are fairly good but not noteworthy. They never develop a truly distinguished bouquet; at best there is always a trace of hardness in them. The two leading vineyards are Lenchen and Doosberg.

Hallgarten: High up in the Taunus Hills behind Hattenheim, this village exhibits the greatest degree of variation between good and bad years. When Hallgartener wines are good they are very, very good, and when they are bad they are almost undrinkable. But in a vintage year, perhaps twice in a decade, Hallgarteners are delicate, low in alcoholic content, and quite dry— all that a superb Rheingau should be. Perhaps this is due to the fact that some of the leading vineyards are just a few hundred yards from that remarkable property which produces the great Steinberger. Although Hallgarten has no truly outstanding *Lagen*, the four which should be noted are Schönhell, Mehrhölzchen, Deutelsberg, and Hendelberg.

Winkel: About two miles down the river to the west of Oestrich is this bustling town with approximately 350 acres devoted to vineyards. Just under a fourth of the total comprises the famous vineyard of Schloss Vollards situated in the hills back of the village. Unlike most of the German vineyards, Schloss Vollards follows a different system with its ordinary wines (those other than *auslese*, *Beeren Auslese*, and *Trockenbeeren Auslese*, which are always clearly labeled). The ordinary wines are shipped in three categories: the most common is sold as "Schloss Vollards" with no further description; next comes Schlossabzug, which is bottled at the castle; and finally there is the best of these wines marked "Kabinett."

Inferior to Schloss Vollards, but excellent, are Hasensprung (the best of the second grade), Dachsberg, and Jesuitengarten.

Johannisberg: The average wine drinker, if asked to name the most famous wine town of the Rhine, would undoubtedly choose Johannisberg, for it has received the most publicity. Although there are about twenty vineyards, all important, they are overshadowed by the reputation of Schloss Johannisberg. It is quite a large vineyard of sixty-six acres, set magnificently on an even slope facing the Rhine. At the top of the hill is the castle itself, which lends its name to the vineyard. (The present building is a reconstruction of the old castle bombed during the war.) From the river the vineyard presents an imposing sight with its terraced acres of grapevines. This wine is marketed in two varieties: the first has a routine label with the name Schloss Johannisberg and the Metternich coat of arms. (The vineyards are still owned by the Metternich family.) The second label has a colored picture of the Schloss. The first type comes in several qualities, and the second has a complex evaluation based upon the color of the seals, an unusual procedure with German wines. Schloss Johannisberg wines have a distinction which is hard to define, but perhaps "balance" is the best word. The wine is fruity with a wonderful bouquet, full-bodied and flavor-some, but no one quality seems predominant. The result is a nearly perfect wine.

Besides this vineyard, about two hundred acres in the village produce very satisfactory wines in the average year and exceptional wines in the vintage years. Johannisberger Klaus is the runner-up, if such a thing is possible, to the great Schloss. Also very good are Hölle, Sterzelpfad, Kahlenberg, and Erntebringer.

Geisenheim: Up in the Taunus Hills is the hamlet which extends from Johannisberg to Rüdesheim, the heart of the Rheingau. Geisenheim wines are excellent but overshadowed by the two magnificent neighbors. Nevertheless, in its best years Geisenheim may surpass Rüdesheim, although it never equals Schloss Johannisberg except in a freak year.

Geisenheim is the site of an important wine school, possibly the best in Germany, called by the tongue-twisting name of Lehr-und-Forschungsanstalt für Wein. This label on a bottle denotes a superior wine from the school's own vineyard. The two leading vineyards of Geisenheim are Rothenberg and Mäuerchen; their nearest competition comes from Lickerstein and Katzenloch.

Rüdesheim: This is the last wine town in the Rheingau, situated picturesquely on the inner corner of the Rhine as it takes a sharp turn toward the northwest, narrows, and begins a swifter, more rapid descent to Koblenz and the sea. Behind the town is a steep hill known as the Berg, on which there are many terraced vineyards banked one upon the other. When the word "Berg" appears with the name of a vineyard it indicates a wine produced on one of these terraces; otherwise it comes from the flat land to the south and east. In great vintage years, when Schloss Johannisberg comes up with a superior wine, Rüdesheim wines are only fair. But, like a contrary woman, Rüdesheim will frequently excel in an off year when the other Rheingau villages are bemoaning a poor vintage. The vineyards of reputation—and there are quite a few—include Bronnen, Rottland, Roseneck, Schlossberg, Lay, Zollhaus, Klosterkiesel, and Hinterhaus.

Assmannshausen: Just north of the Berg of Rüdesheim and not actually in the Rheingau is the village which produces one of the best red wines of Germany. There are those who ridicule the idea that Germany produces any red wine worth mentioning, and it is true that the German red wine is not really important, but it is comparable to the *vin ordinaire* of France. However, after drinking the great flowery white wines day after day, a red wine comes as a delightful change of pace, no matter how insignificant it may be. The grape used is that classic one from Burgundy, the Pinot Noir, but it does not fare so well away from its Gallic homeland. The leading vineyards here are Hinterkirch and Höllenberg.

The Rheinhessen

Across the Rhine River and to the south of the picturesque Rheingau villages is the Hessian wine district, generally known as Rheinhessen. It is an area of rolling country consisting of some five hundred square miles, roughly bounded in the shape of a triangle by the towns of Bingen, Mainz, and Worms, all of which are on the Rhine itself. The system of names and types follow those of the Rheingau. The vineyards, however, do not face south or southeast, and the grape types are not as excellent as those of the Rheingau, but the better wines are very pleasing nonetheless. They have a rounded softness that makes them appealing, and they have always been quite popular in the United States.

Most of the vineyards are planted to the prolific Sylvaner, which accounts for the mediocre quality of a good deal of Rheinhessen wine. The vintners here are more concerned with quantity than quality.

The situation is confused by the peculiar character of a particular wine which in most years is actually poor. This is Liebfraumilch (milk of the Blessed Virgin). Of the 150 villages, all but a handful produce Liebfraumilch. Any wine produced within the Rheinhessen triangle may be called by this name, and much of it is. A fine wine of this district would never have this designation but would be called by its village

name in conjunction with a vineyard—Nackenheimer Engelsberg, for example. Liebfraumilch has so little reputation in Germany that it rarely appears on a wine list; most of it is exported to countries where its uneven qualities are not so well known. As most of the villages produce nothing but this wine and as much of it as possible, we shall consider only the few that produce good wine.

Bingen: This village is across the Rhine from Rüdesheim to the east of the point where the Nahe flows into the larger river. Behind Bingen is the Scharlachberg Hill, which gives its name to the leading vineyard. As Bingen represents the merger of three towns—Bingen, Kempten, and Budesheim—many wines within the old village boundaries have long involved names. Far and away the best vineyard is Binger-Budesheimer Scharlachberg. How much simpler to pronounce and remember the village only second in quality: Binger Ohligberg.

Ingelheim: Northeast toward Mainz, the next important wine town, there is little of interest except the inland village of Ingelheim, often cited as the birthplace of Charlemagne. The white wines are quite ordinary Liebfraumilch. But it is not on white wines that little Ingelheim depends; its inland location and its soil permit it to produce passable light red wines.

Mainz: There are a few vineyards within the city limits, but they produce no wine of importance, and wines from the small suburban areas behind Mainz are mediocre.

Bodenheim: Here the wines produced from vineyards along the banks are unimportant; it is those high on the hillsides that have the reputation. Bodenheimer wines are soft and fragrant and can be outstanding two or three times in a decade. The leading vineyards are Hoch and Kahlenberg.

Nackenheim: With the German experts these wines are favorites; they are a kind of winemaker's wine. The majority of knowledgeable people, however, prefer Nierstein wines. But the Nackenheims deserve comparison with the very best of the Rheinhessen. Their bouquet is famous, and they are extremely smooth. The greatest vineyard is Rothenberg, so called because of the reddish soil on the slopes. Also important are Nackenheimer Stiel and Nackenheimer Engelsberg.

Nierstein: This is the largest wine-producing town of the Rheinhessen and the most famous, leading all the others in the excellence of its wines where its distinguished vineyards are concerned. (But here too a great deal of mediocre wine is sold as Liebfraumilch.) The best vineyards have a happy location facing south and southeast, which certainly has much to do with the unusual finish and roundness of these wines.

The region produces over one and a half million quarts annually, although, as mentioned earlier, only a small proportion is sold under a town and vineyard label. The leading vineyards, all first-rate, include Rehbach, Hipping, Auflangen, Glöck, Kehr, Flächenhahl, and Orbel.

Oppenheim: South of Nackenheim lies this tiny village and its vineyards. Here in somewhat less than five hundred acres some extremely fine wines are produced, highly appreciated in their homeland but less well known in the United States. A great deal of effort has been expended in publicizing the wines of poor quality, but the carefully produced wines of this region have had so little recognition in the export trade that they have to be sold frequently as Liebfraumilch. The four leading vineyards are Kreuz, Sachträger, Goldberg, and Kröttenbrunnen.

Dienheim: Goldberg and Kröttenbrunnen are partially within this town, which is only a mile below Oppenheim, and the only other vineyard here worth consideration is Guldenmorgen.

Worms: This town which produces some wine within its limits has achieved a kind of dubious notoriety as the probable originator of Liebfraumilch. The Liebfrauenkirche (Church of Our Lady) is surrounded by a vineyard. However, the vineyard now wisely markets its wine as Liebfrauenstift. It is fair in quality but without distinction. Other than this wine, which is sometimes sold as Wormser Liebfrauenstift or Liebfrauenstiftswein, there is none here of any importance.

The Pfalz

South of the Rheinhessen is a good wine district variously called the Pfalz, the Rheinpfalz, and—most familiar to us—the Palatinate. The Pfalz region has been famous for wine since the Roman days, and during the Middle Ages it was the chief source of wine for the Holy Roman Empire. Its western border touches France, and the region is usually compared with Alsace-Lorraine: both are agricultural districts with rolling countryside; both have suffered excessively from Franco-German wars over the centuries.

The topography of the Pfalz consists of green plains with some steep hillsides irregularly scattered through the district. From the plains come the most common wines consumed locally, the kind the Germans call *Tischwein* (table wine). But from the slopes of certain special vineyards come the great wines of the region, representing about 15 percent of the total production. Much of the Pfalz is planted to the Sylvaner grape, which produces in abundance the routine wines sold from the barrel because they are not worth bottling. When the wine is freshly fermented, it is low in alcoholic content and cloudy. This wine is called *Federweisser* (white feather). The local folk drink it like water, which it most definitely is not. Later in the year, when the cloudiness is disappearing and the percentage of alcohol is slightly higher, it is served in pitchers and called *Schoppenwein*. None of this is what we recognize as Pfalz wine, for it has a characteristic muddy taste (the vineyards from which it comes lie in the flat regions close to the Rhine), distinctly unpleasant to anyone not accustomed to it. The wines we know are those produced on the hillsides planted to the Riesling. (However, if the Sylvaner is properly planted and cultivated on the hillsides, it can produce an above-average wine, although it can rarely compete with the average Riesling product.)

The vineyards of a large area of the Pfalz are protected by the Haardt Mountains, so that the grapes receive a great deal of sunshine. In an average year the summer weather is warmer in the Pfalz than in the other German wine districts. As a result, the best wines have a well-rounded taste with a suggestion of sweetness— as if they were permeated with the hot sunshine. The wines have a "ripeness" and are quite full-bodied. If these wines have a fault, it is the lack of a fine bouquet; and the latter is the chief characteristic of the greatest Rhine wines.

Unlike most of the German vineyards in the control of families for generations, those of the Pfalz are owned and operated by the Burgundy system; that is, a renowned vineyard may have two or three or even a score of owners, all producing in their own distinctive fashion a different wine yet entitled to the same name. On the other hand, much of the wine is blended with other wines of the same vineyard, and the bottled product may be from one landholder or it may represent the combined product of half a dozen. It would seem safer not to buy wines with only a shipper's name but to look for a vineyard that bottles its own wine.

The district consists of three sections, of which only the center area is of any importance. The first district, called the Unter-Haardt, or Lower Haardt, extends from the border of the Rhein-hessen to the village of Herxheim. Here only routine wines are produced. It is the second section, the Mittel-Haardt, which makes the fine wines. The district extends from Leistaft to Neustadt. The third section, the Ober-Haardt, is the main producer of *Schoppenwein*, the type of carafe wine served in the local inns and taverns.

The center of the Mittel-Haardt has the vineyards which have given the Pfalz its reputation. The strip is about one and a half miles wide and twenty miles in length, but the great vineyards are concentrated from Wachenheim and Ruppertsberg, and between an area of just five miles.

Kellstadt: This is the real beginning of the Mittel-Haardt with a dozen vineyards of importance. But the two vineyards which easily surpass their competitors are Kebnert and Kreuz.

Ungstein: In this village one acre out of five is planted with Riesling and the balance with either Sylvaner or Muller-Thurgau. In addition, a substantial quantity of mediocre red wine is made here. The leading vineyard in the opinion of the local people is Ungsteiner Spielberg.

Bad Durkheim: This region in the middle of a small resort area produces about three times as much wine as Ungstein, but an even smaller percentage of the vineyard is devoted to Riesling. The best wines of the village are sound, pleasant, and drinkable. The local red wine, like that of Ungstein, is barely passable, although the Germans consider it a fairly good wine. The best vineyards here are Michelsberg, Feuerberg, and Spielberg.

Wachenheim: These vineyards need no introduction to wine connoisseurs, whether in Tallahassee or Tokyo. In exceptional years the wines are considered the best in Germany. (This will happen once or twice in a decade.) In good vintage years Wachenheimers have an exceptional bouquet and are full-bodied. About twenty have a reputation, but the best are Gerümpel, Goldbächel, Luginsland, Bächel, and Böhlig.

Forst: This charming village produces the most consistently fine wines of the Pfalz. Over two-thirds of the vineyards are planted to the Riesling grape, and the results are apparent in the delicacy and body of the wine. The excellence of the wine is ascribed to the black basalt in the soil, which has a large quantity of iron. Whatever the reason, these wines are superb. Of the more than fifty vineyards, at least half a dozen are noteworthy: Kirchenstück, Jesuitengarten, Ziegler, Unheheuer, Kranich, and Langenmorgen.

Deidesheim: Whether Forst or Deidesheim is the best of the Pfalz wine villages is one of those delightful questions that may never be resolved. Both have superb wines, produced with the most exacting skill. In an average year only the most knowledgeable of experts could tell one from the other. However, Deidesheim has twice as many acres under cultivation. Of its many vineyards, those with the greatest reputation are Hohenmorgen, Grainhübel, Kränzler, Kieselberg, Reiss, and Leinholc.

Ruppertsberg: Just a hop, skip, and a jump southeast of Deidesheim, this village has less acreage under cultivation and only a third as many vineyards devoted to the Riesling. At least twenty vineyards are entitled to a superior rating here, and of these, there are the leaders: Gaisbohl, Spiess, and Kreuz.

Königsbach: Slightly to the west of Ruppertsberg in beautiful woodland country lies Königsbach, which, while producing good wine, does not rank with the four great villages of the district: Wachenheim, Forst, Deidesheim, and Ruppertsberg. Nevertheless in good years, Königsbacher wines have a marvelous body and a full, fruit flavor; in off years they can be mediocre. The two vineyards to note, out of a dozen that are well known, are Königsbacher Idig and Königsbacher Satz.

The Nahe

The Nahe River, only seventy miles in length, has its beginning at the town of Birkenfeld, then flows northeast to merge with the Rhine at Bingen. Along the shores of the Nahe extend a series of vineyards that have only a moderate reputation. This is unfortunate, for the region produces a number of wines that deserve better recognition. Perhaps they do not get the recognition they deserve because as a group these wines are overshadowed by those of the Rheingau, even as the Nahe itself is merely a tributary of the magnificent Rhine.

Many connoisseurs claim that the Nahe Valley has two different wines, and this claim may add to the confusion and uncertainty regarding the wines. One type is produced in the Langonlonsheim-Odernheim region, close to the junction of the Nahe and the Rhine at Bingen, and is said to resemble that of Rheinhessen. The other type is produced in the Kreuznach district and somewhat resembles a Moselle. But Nahe wines actually have a personality of their own. It is to be hoped that they may soon regain the popularity they had well over a half a century ago. Within Germany itself these wines are increasingly discussed among the experts of the trade. There is an important wine school at Kreuznach, and through the efforts of the faculty the vineyards have been encouraged over the past ten or fifteen years to uproot their poorer vines and replace them with the Riesling. Because of their location and soil (loam in one portion, slate and gravel in another), and because of the short length of time the new vines have been in the

ground, the wines from the Nahe are unusual and interesting.

The wines are offered for sale in brown bottles, much like those of Rheinhessen. There are comparatively few great vineyards, but these deserve complete acceptance and one of them is truly superb. This is the Schloss Böckelheimer-Kupfergrube. At the turn of the century the Schloss did not exist, and the region was covered with brush and small trees. Then a division of the German government created the vineyard, clearing the land and planting the vines. As the vineyard was developed, a truly magnificent wine was produced, recognized everywhere for its delicacy and smoothness.

Bretzenheim: This village produces a wine moderate in quality year after year with few poor vintages. Vogelsang is the leading vineyard.

Kreuznach: The center of the wine district of the Nahe Valley, this town has vineyards within its limits. It is here that the wine producers have their business offices. (The exception is the state-controlled vineyard of Schloss Böckelheim.) There are a dozen excellent vineyards. The best include Hinkelstein, Kröttenpfuhl, Kahlenberg, and Forst.

Münster: This town is sometimes known as Bad Münster-am-Stein. The wines here are frequently quite good but inferior to those of Kreuznach and Niederhäus.

Niederhäus: One of the best wine villages of the Nahe, with a wealth of good wines made year after year in the vineyards. The products of the Niederhäuser Hermannshöhle are far above any others in the area, but also worth attention are Pfingstweide and Hermannsberg.

Norheim: This is another first among the wine villages of the Nahe. Special note should be taken of Norheimer-Kafels, Hinterfels, Kirschheck, and Dellchen, in that order.

Roxheim: Not quite up to Norheim or Niederhäus, but still important for fine wines produced in such vineyards as Hollenpfad, Huttenberg, and Muhlenberg.

Schloss Böckhelheimer: The wines of the State Domain are the best in the Nahe and of these Kupfergrube ranks first and then come Köningsberg and Königsfels.

Franken (Franconia)

Of all German wines, those of Franken have the most labels (many of them erroneously applied), including *Steinwein, Steinwein-in-Bocksbeutel, Steinwein-in-Boxbeutel, Frankenwein*, and so on. The vineyards are in the Main River Valley well to the east of Frankfurt and outside the regular Rhine wine district.

Why should this region have so many unusual labels for wines? The variations of *Bocksbeutel* have to do with the shape of the green bottle that is characteristic: a short, stubby green bottle shaped like a thick army canteen or a flagon. Its correct name is *Bocksbeutel* (*Bock* means goat in German): it is so named because the bottle is supposed to resemble the genitals of the male goat. Some shippers, prudish about this earthy word, have changed the name to *Boxbeutel*. Chileans use the same-shaped bottle for their white wines.

As for the label *Steinwein*, there is a certain outstanding vineyard, the Stein *Lagen*, which is situated in the famous beer city of Würzburg, and the wine from this vineyard became a generic term: people first referred to *Steinwein* meaning the wine from this vineyard, but later the term spread to mean wines from the entire area of Franconia. And, of course, *Frankenwein* simply means a wine from this district.

There have been vineyards in Franconia since the eighth century. The ground is peculiar, consisting of lime, chalk, and shell, which give the wines their earthy taste. The weather is extreme, with very cold winters and early frosts, and the vintners must harvest the grapes early, so that they are not damaged by cold snaps in the autumn. The variety of grape is important here; although the Riesling is grown, it takes longer to mature and frequently fails to ripen. The much quicker ripening qualities of the Sylvaner offer a degree of protection to the grower. The Sylvaner, ripening earlier in this climate, usually produces wine equal to the more hesitant Riesling. However, when the autumn is mild, with cool bright sunshine, the Riesling will bring forth a wine far beyond the powers of the Sylvaner.

Franconia wines have their admirers and critics. The taste is different from the classic German wines, such as Moselle and Rheingau, and this disturbs the connoisseurs. The taste is modified here by the soil and climate; the Franconian wines seem to have more firmness, a fuller body. Some experts find a resemblance between the wines of Alsace and Franconia; others claim that a fine wine of Würzburg is like a good white wine of Burgundy. The bouquet of a Franconian seems less distinctive than that of other German wines; they are not nearly so smooth, but they do keep well, improving as they age—which is not typical of German wines. Again, the average German wine does not go too well with food, but the Franconians do. Incidentally, they represent the best value of all German wines, for they are sold at moderate prices.

Because of the cold weather, late pickings are rare. Bottles of *spätlese* or *auslese* are seldom encountered. The vintage years here rarely correspond to those of the Rhine or Moselle, because of the erratic weather.

The best wines are grown in Würzburg, a charming university city, once filled with magnificent medieval architecture. During the war, the city was heavily bombed and many of the oldest buildings were destroyed. Nevertheless, the city still preserves much of its charm. Würzburg has slightly over five hundred acres under cultivation, and proudly boasts that it produces the best Franken wine. Its claim is based upon the Stein *Lagen* which has maintained its reputation for two centuries. It is handsomely situated on a sharply inclined limestone slope directly opposite the center of Würzburg. Like all the vineyards of Franconia, it faces toward the south-southeast to get all the possible heat and light from the sun. Other important vineyards here include Innere Leiste, Aussere Leiste, Neuberg, Harfe, Schalksberg.

Good wine, although inferior to that of Würzburg, is produced at several other villages and towns in this district. At Randersacker the best vineyards are Hohbug, Teufelskeller, Pfulben. At Escherndorf, which has some two hundred acres under cultivation, the best vineyard is called Lup; also good is Hengstberg. Iphofen is a village which is proud of the wines from Julius-Echter-Berg and the Kammer vineyards. Roedelsee, with only about a hundred acres of vineyards, has Kuchenmeister, Schlossberg, and Schwanleite as the *Lagen* with really distinguished wines. There is also some production at various other villages, including Schloss Saaleck, Veitshoechheim, Castell, and Nordheim.

The Moselle

At Koblenz the Rhine River is joined by a tributary, the Moselle. In turn, the Moselle has two tributary rivers of its own, the Saar and Ruwer. The district through which the rivers run is the homeland of Moselle wines, among the best in Germany.

The vineyards of Moselle are divided into three areas: the Lower Moselle which begins at Koblenz and runs to the border of Enkirch; the Middle Moselle (*Mittel-Mosel*) which runs through Enkirch to Trier; the Upper Moselle which includes every district upstream from Trier. The wines of the Lower and Upper Moselle are what the liquor trade calls "small wines," those which are consumed locally but which are not considered important for export.

It is seldom that tourists find their way into the lovely Moselle Valley, yet actually it is more interesting than the Rhine country. For one thing, it is off the beaten track, the usual tourist route. In fact it is an exceptional American tourist who takes his way through this fascinating valley so rich in history, so extraordinarily picturesque and colorful. The first fifty miles of the Upper Moselle Valley are attractive and the Lower Moselle is interesting, but it is the central section which is surpassingly lovely. The Moselle has worn its way over countless centuries through the rocky soil, until today the river bed is banked on both sides by steep walls. The river twists and turns irregularly, presenting fresh views of incomparable and unexpected beauty.

At the river's edge lie the famous wine towns with names that read like the wine list of a fine restaurant: Zeltingen, Bernkastel, Brauneberg,

Piesport. The river follows a devious, roundabout route, presenting more exciting views at each bend and turn, as it flows northeast to meet the Rhine at Koblenz. On the northwest bank, facing south and southeast, there are miles of terraced vineyards planted on precipitously steep hillsides. As the river twists and turns, the vineyards shift from one bank to the other in order to face south for the maximum benefit of the sun. With slopes averaging five to six hundred feet in height—and occasionally rising to a thousand feet—it is easy to see why viniculture along the Moselle is back-breaking work, possible only for those dedicated to the production of great wines. For anyone else the toil would be unbearable; for the peasants of the Moselle Valley it is an honest labor of love. The ground is difficult to work, and the heavy rains wash down precious soil which must be replaced, returned on the backs of the peasants. Pieces of slate are placed to reflect the sun's rays, and even the larger grape leaves are cut away to keep the shade from the young grapes. The vine shoots, unlike those of the other German wine districts, are trained to grow straight upward on individual stakes, making an imposing sight at harvest time.

The wines are easily distinguished from Rhine wines, which come in brown bottles; Moselles go to market in a distinctive green. They have their own special taste quite unlike the Rheingaus, their only competitor in quality. When very young, they tend to be slightly sparkling, (*petillant*, as the French would say), but this quality disappears gradually with age. They have a tendency to mature quite early and fade rather quickly (with the exception of special sweet wines like *Beeren Auslese*). A Moselle even a year old is worth drinking; it is at its best when two, three, or four years old, and five is about the limit for these wines. In average years the wines have an alcoholic content of 8.5 percent, sometimes 9 percent, but very rarely more than 10 percent. They have one notable quality, a slight bitterness which is pleasant. The Germans call it *angenehine Säure* (a pleasing bitterness). Every third or fourth year the Moselles are unsurpassed. They are light, they are delicate, with a superb bouquet. Which is better, Rheingau or Moselle? It is entirely a matter of individual taste.

Postponing for the moment consideration of the interesting wines grown along the banks of the Ruwer and Saar Rivers, here are the wine villages of the charming Moselle Valley:

Uerzig: This is the first important wine village after Enkirch, Traben, Trarbach, and Kröv, which produce undistinguished products. Here are found several superior vineyards, and one in particular worth remembering. These wines have a light, sparkling quality; they are piquant with a spiciness that is usually ascribed to the soil which is high in iron. In any event, Uerziger wines are distinctive, exceptional when marked *auslese.* The best vineyard is Würzgarten. Schwarzlay, Lay, and Kranklay are also excellent.

Erden: Because of the turns and twists of the river, this little village is on the right bank with vineyards ascending steeply at sharp angles. Many Erdener wines are extraordinarily good. The leading vineyard is Treppchen (meaning "little steps"), in humorous recognition of the steep climb required to reach the vines. Also important are Prälat and Busslay.

Zeltingen: Of all the wine towns of the Moselle, Zeltingen produces the greatest quantity, much of it of first quality, but unfortunately there is also a fair amount of mediocre wine produced. The best way to be certain of a Zeltingen is to purchase one with a vineyard label. These wines are remarkable on several counts: delicacy, softness combined with a full body, and, of course, a bouquet outstanding even for a Moselle. But again, one must beware of wines bearing only the notation "Zeltingen." Out of seventy-odd vineyards, four defy competition: Schlossberg, Sonnenuhr (sometimes spelled Sonnuhr), Rotlay, and Himmelreich.

Wehlen: This unassuming village is fast becoming one of the best wine villages of the Moselle. Unlike its neighbors, which have been making fine wines for a century or more, Wehlen was for a long time not worth considering; its wines were sold in ordinary restaurants and taverns, and only wine dealers knew of its existence. With the turn of the century its fortunes began to improve, and today Wehlener wines usually bring the highest prices of all the Moselles. Local wine dealers pay top prices only for the best, and they don't bid higher and higher without sound judgment and knowledge of what they are buying. When Wehlen vines have the right combination of sunshine and rain, the wines are superb. In those fortunate vintages the wines will be very flowery, well balanced, and delicate. The five leading vineyards are Sonnenuhr, Nonnenberg, Rosenberg, Lay, and Klosterlay.

Graach: Like Wehlen, this village has just over two hundred acres of vineyards set at a sharp incline above the few houses that comprise the small community. Graacher wines are among the best Moselles, noted for their "breed," as the wine experts say. The best vineyard is Josephshof; because of the superior reputation of this vineyard, the label on the wine does not have the village name but is marketed simply as Josephshofer. The other two vineyards of distinction are Himmelreich and Domprobst.

Bernkastel: This is the best known village of the Moselle; even those who have only a modest acquaintance with wines seem to know it. The wine is superb, but the fame of its great vineyard, the Doktor, dates back to a visit from Edward VII of England, who tasted the wine at a nearby spa. The King ordered cases of this wine to be shipped to England, and after that the vineyard's reputation was assured. Bernkasteler Doktor has always commanded high prices. The wines are famous for their full body and remarkable bouquet. There are those who claim to detect a special "smoky" taste in Bernkasteler Doktor—which may or may not be imaginary. On the other hand, gourmets (*Feinschmeckers*, as they are called in Germany) are inclined to question the high prices of these wines. The limited supply (about 1500 cases a year) and the great demand are undoubtedly responsible. But it shouldn't be assumed that no other Moselle can compare with it, for many Moselles are its equal and frequently its superior. This great vineyard is owned by three producers; the best wine is brought to the market under the name "Dr. Thanisch," but those sold under the label of Deinhard and Lauerburg are almost its equal in quality. The other outstanding vineyards include Lay, Bad-stube, Schlossberg, Pfalzgraben, and Schwanen.

Lieser: The wines of this village are pleasant but not in a class with the famous wines we have discussed. Lieser lacks the proper southern expo-sure to mature the grapes properly. The only vineyard worth mentioning is Niederberg.

Brauneberg: Many decades ago, the wines of this village were ranked with the best, but at present its hundred-odd acres produce wine which is good but not truly distinctive. Their full body distinguishes these wines, but their bouquet seems slightly deficient when compared with Piesporter or Bernkasteler. The best vineyard is Juffer, by a long margin. If one thinks of other vineyards here, one should include Falkenberg and Kammer.

Kesten: This hamlet, poorly situated in compari-son with other wine villages of this lovely valley, produces wines that are thin and sourish. Only one is worth considering: this is from the Paulinshofberg vineyards. It is sold exclusively under the vineyard label, for the place name has no reputation.

Wintrich: This village, with its steeply inclined vineyards, is extraordinarily attractive: each ter-race supports a mere handful of vines in a few sparse rows; then there is a sharp, short climb to the next tier with its meager, level surface supporting a few more vines, and so on to the top. From the tourist's point of view these terraces offer a charming sight. The peasant who laboriously carries heavy loads to each succeed-ing level probably has a more jaundiced view. Wintricher wines are fairly good, particularly in exceptional vintage years, when they have con-siderable character. They are best to drink when young, for they don't mature too well. If you encounter a Wintricher wine of a good year at a low price, you will be delighted. None of the vineyards of this village reaches a superior status, but equally good are those of Ohligsberg, Neu-berg, Geyerslay, Sonnseite.

Piesport: This miniature village is squeezed between the Moselle and the hillside covered with vineyards and looks something like a green amphitheater. As far as the eye can see, every inch of soil is devoted to raising the grapes that produce the superb Piesporter. A true Piesporter, one from a distinguished vineyard like Gold-tröpfchen, is always superb. The gold-colored wine is delicate, light in flavor, well balanced, with an incomparable bouquet. It is the favorite of many connoisseurs of German wine and even of experts who find the French counterparts gen-erally superior. Goldtröpfchen is such an out-standing vineyard that it is a byword for excellence all over the world. Other vineyards of considerable reputation are Lay, Güntherslay, and Taubengarten.

Dhron: This village has an unsatisfactory loca-tion. In poor years the wines are thin without a bouquet, and even in good years they are never more than passable. One good vineyard, Dhroner Hofberg, sometimes sells its wines as Dhronhofberger. Two other vineyards in this area are Roterde and Sängerei.

Neumagen: This small village with slightly less than two hundred acres under cultivation is about on a par with Dhron. Its wines are definitely of a minor quality even under the most favorable circumstances. The best thing about Neumagener wines is their comparatively low price. They are best consumed when young, for it is then their bouquet is at its peak. Rosengärtchen is the leading vineyard, and Leienberg and Engelgrube are close competitors.

Trittenheim: At a point where the Moselle River makes a decided U-turn, there is this tiny village in a most attractive location. The wines produced here are light and pleasing but of secondary importance; when they are young and fresh, no wine could be more delightful. None of the vineyards has a reputation. The best are Lauren-tiusberg, Altärchen, and Apotheke.

After Trittenheim there are no vineyards worth mentioning.

The Saar

If one tried to visualize an unlikely wine dis-trict, it would be the Saar surely, with the shores lined by blast furnaces and steel mills, and the air polluted with heavy industrial smoke. The river, a tributary of the Moselle, flows uncon-cernedly through this man-made confusion, along the border of France and Germany near Luxembourg. It is an extraordinary river, for at times it has all the swiftness and power of a mountain stream; then as it winds through quiet communities of a few hundred people and through open fields, it becomes as placid as the landscape through which it flows. Every particle of land facing south is planted to grapevines. This is quite cold country where early frosts in September frequently spoil the harvest, producing a sourish, cranky wine. About once in five years, the moisture and the sunshine balance, and then the Saar shows us a wine worth waiting for! In Germany they say that when a Saar wine is at its best, it is better than any Moselle, and perhaps they are right. Saar wines are light, very light. For some reason, these wines do not seem to accompany food too well. They are best drunk by themselves, purely for pleasure and refreshment. Many years are so cool that the wines require added sugar and are of no importance. In other years the wine is unbalanced. Even in good years Saar wines have a noticeable acid quality. However, it is precisely this sharp quality that gives them the lively taste that Moselles often lack. No one should fail to try a Saar wine of a good year, from a good village, with the name of an outstanding vineyard on the label. Such a wine will stand comparison with a fine Montrachet. Starting at the far end of the Saar River as it flows northward to join the Moselle, here are the wine villages:

Serrig: The wines here are seldom more than passable, and only in a rare year are they accepted by the connoisseurs, for the weather at this end of the valley is quite unpredictable. About every seven or eight years Serrig will come through with a very fine wine, only to return to mediocre, thin, sourish products for many more years. If any vineyards of this village are worth noting, they include Heiligenborn, Würzberg, and Kupp.

Ockfen: This exceptional wine district has had some good years in the past decade or two. Its two-hundred-odd acres are situated to collect the maximum benefits of the sun, and the village escapes many of the heavy rainstorms which seem to plague the region. The leading vineyards are truly noteworthy: Bockstein, Geisberg, and Herrenberg.

Ayl: This is a tiny village with only one area devoted to viniculture. These hundred acres produce some fine wines in good years; routine, however, in lesser vintages. The three best vineyards are Kupp, Neuberg, and Herrenberg.

Niedermennig: Even smaller than Ayl, this toy village also has good wines, although many have a somewhat acid taste which stops just short of being unpleasant. Sonnenberg and Herrenberg are the two vineyards with important names.

Oberemmel: Here we are approaching the best vineyards of the Saar district—the Wiltingen vineyards. Oberemmel lies just a short distance to the east and occasionally competes with them. This is only in rare vintage years, and good as Oberemmeler can be, Wiltingen wines are almost invariably superior. There are many vineyards here, but the two which are outstanding are Rosenberg and Hütte.

Wiltingen: Without question this is the leading village of the Saar, the one area where weather and growing conditions seem consistently better than elsewhere in the valley. Year after year Wiltingen wines are of superior quality. When the weather is exactly right (every ten years or so) Wiltingen produces the finest wine of the entire Moselle district. The village of Wiltingen has the most land under cultivation in the Saar, with about 350 acres of important vineyards. Two *Lagen* have developed such a reputation over the years that their wines are sought after eagerly in good years by gourmets and connoisseurs the world over. For this reason the wines from these vineyards are simply labeled with their names without designating the village: Scharzhofberg and Scharzberg. Roughly in order of merit, the sequence here is Scharzhofberg, Braune Kupp, Gottesfüss, Kupp, Klosterberg, and Scharzberg.

Kanzem: Kanzem wines are usually satisfactory, even delightful in the better years. There are a number of good vineyards such as Berg, Sonnenberg, Altenberg, and Wolfsberg.

Wawern: This village brings to an end the Saar Valley district, for after the next town of Filzen, the Saar makes its juncture with the Moselle.

Wawern has occasional good years when the people of the valley talk about these wines, but in the average year they are not well balanced; they have a kind of bite or sharpness. Herrenberg is the best vineyard.

The Ruwer

This river, the size of a small trout stream, flows for about twenty-five miles to the northwest until it joins the Moselle below the city of Trier. Trier, incidentally, has the most important Roman ruins in northern Europe. It was here that the Romans came as they fanned out through this part of the Continent, conquering everywhere they went. The soldiers found some viniculture along the banks of the Ruwer even two thousand years ago. (Trier was called *Augusta Trevirorum* under the Romans.) For some years during his reign Napoleon had the region under his control. The most recent conquerors of Trier were the American troops who captured the colorful city on March 1, 1945.

The wines of the Ruwer (pronounced rue-ver) are extraordinarily light; their alcoholic content is no more than 10 percent as a rule, possibly because of the weak rays of the sun that reach the grapes during September. The vineyards are planted on steep inclines with staggered rows of terraced vines; the amount of work required to tend them is enormous, and a great deal of careful, methodical labor in the Germanic fashion is necessary to bring the grapes through to a successful harvest. The soil is coarse and intermixed with pieces of slate, but there are no problems involving drainage; after a heavy rain the ground is dry within a matter of hours.

Trier: The vineyards are to the south of the city, approximately midway between the Saar and Ruwer Rivers. At Avelsbach, there are about 150 acres under cultivation, and some quite good wines are turned out. They are rather sharp or hard on the palate, and a taste for this wine must be acquired. However, in good years these wines are superb. The two leading vineyards are Herrenberg and Hammerstein.

Maximin Grünhäus: This is one of the best wine villages of the Ruwer. The wines, like those of Trier and Avelsbach, are light in alcoholic content, gold in color, and with a lovely bouquet in good years. In off years they are not worth drinking. Much of the wine reaches the market under the name of Maximin Grünhäuser.

Eitelsbach: Wines from this village go to market with a very small label around the neck, a somewhat unusual practice for Moselles. The finest wine is produced in the former monastery of the Carthusian order; the label is about as difficult a tongue-twister as any German name can be for an American: Eitelsbacher Karthäuserhofberger.

Casel: Although not equal to the wines of its immediate neighbors, Casel produces good, workmanlike wines at a moderate price. No one goes into raptures about Caseler, but considering the price, the wines are a good value. The three best vineyards are Niesgen, Kohlenberg, and Taubenberg.

Germon (French). White tuna; so named because its flesh is white rather than the more usual pink.

Gerolimo. An Italian cordial made with wild herbs and grasses.

Géromé. A semihard whole-milk cheese made on the western slopes of the Vosges and in eastern France. Its flavor is similar to that of Munster. The cylinders with a brick-red rind weigh up to 11 pounds.

Gerookt (Dutch). Smoked.

Geroosterd Brood (Dutch). Toast.

Geroosterde Kip (Dutch). Roast chicken.

Geropiga (Portuguese). A diluting agent used to adulterate port wine, made of grape juice, brandy, red coloring, and sugar; occasionally used to sweeten wine.

Gerostete Kartoffeln (German). Fried potatoes.

Gerst (Dutch). Barley.

Gerstensuppe (German). Barley soup.

Gerty. Oatmeal.

Gervais. A very rich, delicate, perishable French cream cheese.

Geschmort (German). Braised, stewed.

Gestoofde Makreel (Dutch). Stewed mackerel.

Getmesost. A soft, slightly sweet, Swedish whey cheese made from goat's-milk.

Getränke (German). Drinks; liquor.

Gevogelte (Dutch). Poultry.

Gevrey-Chambertin. A wine district of the Burgundy region in France. *See* France, The Wines of.

Gevulde Broodjes (Dutch). Rolls stuffed with meat, fish, etc.

Gevulde Kool (Dutch). Meat-stuffed cabbage.

Gewachs (German). "Growth," pertaining to wine. *See* Germany, The Wines of.

Gex. A French semihard skim-milk cheese with blue veins.

Gex Marbré. An unusual French cheese with blue-green markings, made with a mixture of cow's, goat's, and sheep's milk.

Gex-Septmoncel. A spicy, salty whole-milk cheese made in the Jura region of France. It is like a blue cheese but without the usual blue veining.

Gezouten Haring (Dutch). Salt herring.

Gezuckerte; Verbesserte (German). Of wine, sugared. *See* Germany, The Wines of.

Ghentsche Peperkoek (Belgian). Honey cake; prepared in Flanders.

Ghentsche Waterzooïe (Belgian). Fish soup or chowder; prepared in Flanders.

Gherkin. A very small variety of cucumber with many prickly protuberances; much used for making pickles. The term probably derives from the old Dutch word *agurkje*.

Ghiacciato (Italian). Iced.

Ghiozzi (Italian). Whitebait, a fish.

Ghirka. A strong spring wheat.

Giant Callista. A brightly colored clam found along the American coast from North Carolina to Texas; best used in cooking.

Giant Rock; Oregon; Vancouver; Dweller. A rather large clam found in the Pacific Northwest region of the United States.

Gibassier; Pompe (French). A cake with a lumpy surface; served on Christmas Eve.

Gibbery; Ginge-Brace. Gingerbread.

Gibel. A central European fish of the carp family.

Gibelotte (French). Rabbit stew.

Gibier (French). Game, wild birds.

Giblets. Poultry liver, heart, and gizzard, often used to stuff poultry and to flavor gravy.

Gien, Fromage de. A French whole-milk cheese of passable quality made from cow's or goat's milk or a combination of the two; then matured in ashes.

Gigondas. Several red and *rosé* wines of fair quality produced in the Rhône Valley.

Gigorit (French). (1) Pig's head cooked slowly in pig's blood and wine; a dish made in Poitou. (2) Lamb's pluck.

Gigot (French). (1) Leg of lamb or mutton. In Brittany it is usually served with white beans, *à la Bretonne*. (2) A simple metal contrivance attached to the bone of cooked meat to prevent the meat from slipping while being carved.

  Gigot à l'Ail. Lamb prepared with a sauce containing a great deal of blanched garlic.

  Gigot d'Agneau. Leg of lamb.

  Gigot de Mouton. Leg of mutton.

Gild. (French). To brush pastry with egg before baking to give it a glossy surface.

Gilka. Gilka Kümmel, a liqueur made with caraway seeds and cumin.

Gill. (1) One-fourth of a pint. (2) To clean a fish or mushroom.

Gilling (British). A young salmon that has returned for the second time to fresh water from the ocean.

Gillyflower (Obsolete). Clove.

Gilly-les-Vougeots. A wine district in the Burgundy region of France. *See* France, The Wines of.

Gilravage. A gay party at which there is a great deal of drinking.

Gilse. A salmon less than one year old weighing about 7 pounds.

Gilt. A female pig.

Gilt Poll. A Mediterranean fish 1–2 feet long.

Gimblette. A large ring-shaped French pastry.

Gimlet. A cocktail made with sugar, lime juice, gin, and carbonated water and served in a sour glass. A *Hong-Kong gimlet* is considered the finest example of this beverage.

Gin. A colorless liquor flavored with juniper berries. A mash of corn, malt, and other grains is fermented and the resulting wort or beer is distilled and rectified to obtain a relatively pure spirit. This in turn is reduced in proof by the addition of distilled water. The diluted spirit is then redistilled with the flavoring agent, predominantly juniper berries. The new spirit is then reduced again with the addition of more distilled water. This is the English method of making gin, a liquor which is never aged. The Dutch use a different method for making Holland gins, fermenting barley malt and juniper berries. *See* Geneva.

The first gin was probably made in northern Europe. The French term for juniper berries, *genièvre*, sooner or later became corrupted and Anglicized, then shortened into the English word "gin."

Three chief types of gin are made: London Dry (unsweetened), Old Tom (similar but sweetened), and the Dutch or Holland type. American gins are usually imitations of the London Dry type, but they seem to lack some of the distinctive quality of the British product, a difference generally attributed to the difference in the waters used. Gins with fruit flavors contain a fruit syrup.

Sloe gin is more properly regarded as a liqueur or cordial than as an ordinary liquor. It is flavored with the sloe berry, sometimes called the *blackthorn.*

Ginal. A solution containing sodium alginate, used to purify beet and cane sugar.

Gingelly Oil. Oil obtained from sesame seeds.

Ginger. A spice derived from the root of a colorful tropical plant which originally grew only in Malabar and Bengal but is now cultivated in tropical areas in many parts of the globe, including the Caribbean, especially Jamaica and Puerto Rico.

Most familiar is powdered ginger, the spice that lends its sweet and pungent flavor to a wide variety of foods, from cakes and cookies to meats and preserves. Whole ginger root, available mostly in oriental food shops, may be cut and added to marinades and many Chinese dishes. The peeled root keeps well when covered with sherry and refrigerated. Preserved ginger, an old Chinese specialty much favored by the English, may be eaten as a candy or used in sauces for desserts. Powdered ginger bears little resemblance in flavor to root ginger, but it may be used as a substitute if the root is not available. Preserved stem ginger, however, when rinsed of the sugar or syrup, closely resembles the root in taste.

Ginger Ale. A carbonated nonalcoholic beverage served plain or as a mixer with liquors. It con-

tains a few drops of essence of ginger mixed with a little caramel coloring, sugar, and soda water.

Ginger Beer. An English creamy white effervescent beverage with a more gingery and less sweet taste than ginger ale. It is made by fermenting ginger, cream of tartar, yeast, sugar, and water, and is bottled before fermentation is completed. It is available in bottles, stone crocks, and tins.

Ginger Brandy. A brandy with a strong ginger taste.

Gingerbread. (1) A dark ginger-flavored spice cake, usually served warm with whipped cream or applesauce. (2) A cooky batter which at Christmas time is baked in such fanciful shapes as gingerbread men, Christmas trees, and Santa Clauses, and decorated with frosting.

Ginger Cordial. A sweet liqueur that contains ginger, raisins, lemon rind, and sometimes whisky or brandy.

Ginger Crush. Stem ginger, sugar-preserved and finely minced.

Ginger Nut. A small hard cooky flavored with ginger.

Ginger Pop. Another name for ginger beer.

Ginger Root. *See* Ginger.

Gingersnap. A thin, slightly aromatic cooky flavored with ginger.

Ginger Spice. Another name for ginger.

Gingery. Containing ginger.

Ginger Wine. (1) A wine containing ginger, sugar, and water. (2) A ginger-flavored cordial made with brandy, ginger, sugar, yeast, and lemon.

Ginkgo; Gingko; Ginko. A rather large oriental tree whose soft edible nuts have a pleasant crunchy quality, much like that of a water chestnut. They are often combined with shellfish and poultry. Ginkgo trees are now grown in the United States.

Ginja (Portuguese). Sour red cherry.

Ginnan (Japanese). The ginkgo nut.

Ginseng. A small shrub or plant with a somewhat solid, thick root; occasionally used in making bitters.

Ginseng Tea (Korean). A tea made from powdered ginseng root; stimulating and refreshing, although probably lacking the miraculous powers frequently attributed to it.

Gin Shop. A liquor store where gin is sold.

Gin Sling. A sweet cold gin drink.

Gioddu (Italian). A fermented milk similar to yoghurt; a specialty of Sardinia.

Gippo (British, Colloquial). Stew, soup, or gravy.

Gipsy Bread. A black-molasses fruit bread; so called because of its dark, gipsylike color.

Giraumon; Giraumont. A West Indian pumpkin of fine taste and texture.

Girdle (British). Griddle.

Girelle; Girella. A rather small brightly colored Mediterranean fish of fair quality.

Girkin. Another spelling of gherkin.

Girnel (Scotch). A place or container for keeping cereals.

Girod. A whole-milk cheese resembling Port du Salut; made in the Savoy region of France.

Giro del Tempio. A sweet white cloying dessert wine produced in Sardinia, Italy.

Giro di Sardegna. A red dessert wine, quite sweet and fairly high in alcoholic content; a popular table wine produced in Sardinia, Italy.

Girofle (French). Clove.

Girrock. A sea fish, found near Great Britain.

Gisbra. An herb whose seeds are often used in fish and meat preparations in the Middle East.

Gitana (Spanish). Cooked "gipsy fashion," that is, with a lot of onions.

Gite à la Noix (French). (1) Veal with a large proportion of bone to meat; used chiefly in making stews, etc. (2) A rather veiny portion of the leg of beef, used for stews and soups.

Gizzard. The second stomach of birds in which food passed from the first stomach is ground fine. In grain-eating birds it is very muscular and thick. In many parts of the world gizzards are considered a delicacy. They may be braised or roasted, included in stews, or used in gravy or in stuffing. They must be cleaned carefully to remove deposits of bird food.

Gjetost. A Norwegian amber-colored goat's-milk cheese firm-textured and somewhat sweet in taste.

Glaçage (French). (1) Glazing; giving a shiny appearance (a) to cakes, by icing or glazing them with sugar icing; (b) to fresh fruit, by dipping it in syrup; or (c) to a sauce or gravy, by concentrating it. (2) Sprinkling foods with sugar. (3) Chilling or freezing foods.

Glace de Sucre; Glace Royale (French). Confectioners' sugar.

Glace de Viande (French). Meat glaze. Marrow bones together with the liquid in which they have been cooked are slowly boiled down (sometimes with vegetables) until very thick, like a firm, very dark jelly. A little will improve the flavor of sauces and stews.

Glacer (French). To glaze foods.

Glacial. Icy, frequently pertains to mint liqueurs.

Glacière (French). Refrigerator.

Glacière à Sucre; Glaçoire (French). A utensil for sprinkling sugar.

Glaçure (French). Icing.

Glair. (1) Egg whites or any similar clear viscous substance. (2) To brush with egg whites.

Glans. Nuts with a hard shell, such as acorns.

Glasgow Tripe. Tripe cooked with a knuckle of veal, salt, and pepper; eaten cold or hot with an onion sauce.

Glass (Swedish). Ice cream; sherbet.

Glassine. A thick translucent greaseproof paper.

Glassware. Objects made of glass, such as drinking glasses. When the Romans conquered England they brought with them the glassmaker's art; when they departed, the English had to return to drinking from wooden or leather receptacles.

Glasswort. A plant with an interesting bitter and salty taste, used to make pickles. A member of the goosefoot family, it grows in salt marshes and has cylindrical, bright green jointed branches.

Glaucous. As applied to fruits such as grapes, lightly covered with a pale, white powder.

Glaze. (1) To spoon or pour a thin coating of chocolate, orange, or lemon flavoring over food. Fish and vegetables covered with a sauce, with grated cheese, or with both may be glazed under the broiler flame to give them a glossy finish. Onions and carrots may be steamed in butter and glazed with a little sugar added at the last minute. (2) To cover cold meat, poultry, or fish with aspic.

Glebe. Land on which food is grown.

Gliadin. A protein of wheat soluble in 70 percent alcohol; a prolamin.

Glister Pudding (Scotch). Pudding made with flour, butter, sugar, eggs, and marmalade.

Globe Artichoke. An edible thistle-type plant

served raw or cooked in various ways. For cooking, small, compact, tightly closed artichokes should be selected, their stems cut off, and about an inch straight across the top also cut away before they are washed and prepared.

Globo de Oro. A round melon with a light yellow rind and pink flesh, native to the southern and southwestern United States.

Glögg. A Swedish red-wine punch flavored with spices, made at Christmastime.

Gloria. A liqueur or cordial made with sugar, rum, and coffee.

Gloucester Cheese. A hard English cheese with a well-developed blue mold on the sides, named for the county where it is produced. There are two types: the *single*, which ordinarily ripens in 2 months, is smaller than the *double*, which requires 6 months to mature and is far better-tasting.

Gloucester Sauce. A mayonnaise dressing flavored with cayenne pepper, chopped chives, lemon juice, and Worcestershire sauce; usually mixed with sour cream, it is served as a dressing for meat salads.

Glucometer. Any of a wide range of devices for measuring the sugar content of fluids, syrups, and wines.

Glucosa (Spanish). Corn syrup.

Glucose. A natural sugar found in many fruits, particularly in grapes. It is used in jams, syrups, and candies.

Glumse. A German cottage cheese.

Glut. To swallow food or drink in one gulp; to stuff oneself with food; to overeat.

Gluten. The rather sticky, firm, edible protein substance remaining after starch has been removed from flour; used in making breads.

Gluten Bread. A bread made with gluten flour and containing less starch than white bread. Though often recommended for reducing and diabetic diets, it contains only slightly fewer calories.

Gluten Fibrin. A casein of vegetable found in gluten.

Glutinous. Sticky; like gluten.

Glutinous Rice. A variety of Asiatic rice that is very sticky when cooked. In the United States rice that cooks as separate grains is preferred.

Glutton. One who overeats or seems never to be satisfied with a normal amount of food.

Gluttonish; Gluttonous. Given to overeating.

Gluttony. Habitual overeating.

Glux. A cheese made the year around in Nivernais, France.

Glycerin. A colorless sweet, syrupy liquid made from vegetable and animal fats; used commercially in the preparation of certain foods.

Gnap the Ween. Very thin cakes; a very light bread.

Gnaw. To chew or bite constantly.

Gnocchi (Italian). Light, tender-textured dumplings made of semolina, other flours, or potatoes. They are cooked in boiling salted water, drained, and served with a cheese sauce; particularly popular in northern Italy.

Gnocchi à la Parisienne. Boiled dumplings combined with Béchamel sauce, covered with melted butter and grated cheese, and baked.

Gnocchi alla Granerese. Noodles with walnuts.

Gnocchi alla Piemontese; Gnocchi Piedmontaise. Dumplings made from potatoes covered with tomato sauce, bread crumbs, grated cheese, and melted butter.

Gnocchi alla Romana. Semolina dumplings.

Gnocchi con le Noci. Potato dumplings filled with nuts.

Gnocchi Leggeri. Noodles with grated Parmesan cheese.

G.N.S. Grain neutral spirits; a liquor term.

Goat. An edible ruminant animal with hollow horns. Goat meat is highly esteemed in southern Europe, especially in France, Spain, and Italy, although it is not popular in the United States. Though usually tougher than mutton, it has a pleasing flavor when it has been roasted, particularly if the animal is young. Male goats are edible only when very young, from 6 weeks to 4 months old; if older, their meat is tough and has a disagreeable aroma.

Goat Antelope. A cross between a goat and an antelope, sometimes used as food.

Goat Cheese. Cheese made chiefly from goat's milk; distinctive and strongly flavored.

Goatling. A goat between one and two years of age.

Goatsbeard; Goat's Bread. (1) A European plant

of the salsify family whose tender new shoots are eaten like asparagus in France. (2) Certain varieties of mushrooms.

Goat's Milk. Pure white and somewhat odd in flavor, goat's milk is similar in composition to cow's milk, but it is richer in protein. In some European countries it is an important part of the diet, and is also used in the production of several cheeses, including the Neufchâtel type.

Goat's Wheat. A wheat similar to buckwheat.

Gobbet. (1) A large piece of food; a large mouthful. (2) To swallow such a piece.

Gobie. A small, rather undistinguished Mediterranean fish, best prepared by frying.

Goblet. A drinking glass, especially one with a stem and base.

Gobo. The great burdock, a vegetable used in oriental countries. The root may be boiled or baked.

Goby. A rather small fish found in oceans and rivers; best when fried.

Godard, À la. Prepared with a rich sauce or garnish consisting of sweetbreads, truffles, mushrooms, and kidneys.

God-Cake (British). A country cake sent on New Year's to children by their godparents.

Godet. A drinking cup.

Godiveau (French). A forcemeat of veal used in the preparation of certain garnishes. *Godiveau lyonnaise* is a forcemeat of pike similar to *quenelles de brochet*.

Godown. (1) A drinking contest in Scotland. (2) A drink or gulp.

God's-Good. Yeast.

Goed Gaar (Dutch). Well done.

Gofer. A kind of wafer.

Gofio. (1) Cornmeal pastry eaten as a snack or as a cereal. (2) A round, roasted mixture of corn, barley, and wheat.

Goggle-Eye Bass. Freshwater bass.

Gogue (French). (1) A moist, heavily spiced meat pudding made in Anjou. (2) A sausage prepared with pork, onions, lettuce, and spinach.

Goguette (French). Gogue without the green herbs. *See* Gogue (1).

Goiaba. Guava.

Gold Caviar. In the days of imperial Russia a rare yellowish "gold" caviar of certain sturgeon.

By law it was reserved for the czar, and the fortunate fisherman was rewarded with a large number of rubles. It was rushed to the czar still fresh and was served as a special treat. Actually "gold" caviar tasted no better than ordinary black or gray caviar. The yellow-gold color is believed to have occurred because the sturgeon was an albino type, lacking regular pigmentation.

Goldenbeeren Auslese (German). A wine term more or less equivalent to *Beeren Auslese*. *See* Germany, The Wines of.

Golden Berry. The Cape gooseberry, a sharp-tasting berry of the *physalis* family. Found in South Africa, it is best used in making jams and jellies.

Goldene Yoich. A yellow chicken soup with globules of fat floating in it, a favorite Jewish Friday-night dish.

Golden Needles. Dried gold-colored lily flowers cooked with meat or poultry in the Orient.

Golden Sauce (British). A very sweet dessert sauce flavored with Cognac.

Golden Syrup. A mixture consisting of cane sugar, invert sugar, and water; thinner and sweeter than molasses. Sometimes, incorrectly, molasses or light syrup.

Golden-Wedding Cake. A tiered frosted cake usually decorated with gold leaves, and served at the celebration of a fiftieth wedding anniversary.

Gold Leaf. Gold pounded into extremely thin sheets that are sometimes used to decorate cakes and chocolates. Though edible, they are tasteless.

Goldline. Saupe, a fish of the sea bream family.

Gold Mullet. A gold-brown Mediterranean food fish about a foot long.

Gold-n-Rich. An American cheese similar to Italy's Bel Paese but blander and sweeter.

Gold Perch. The bluegill, a freshwater food fish.

Gold Riesling. A hybrid wine resembling Riesling, produced in Alsace, France.

Goldwasser. *See* Danziger Goldwasser.

Golosinas (Spanish). Tidbits; snacks.

Goma (Japanese). Sesame seeds.

Gombaut; Gombo. *See* Gumbo; Okra.

Goober. Peanut. Although the term is a popular American one, the word "goober" is Bantu.

Good Friday Buns (British). Hot cross buns,

yeast buns marked with a white cross made of sugar icing; popular during Lent and at Eastertime.

Good Humor. Trade mark of several ice-cream preparations, usually mounted on a stick and sometimes with nuts, fruits, or chocolate coating.

Good King Henry; Wild Spinach. A wild grass native to England which may be cooked like other green vegetables; sometimes used for flavoring.

Goody. Anything particularly delicious, such as candy, pie, cake, or other dessert items.

Goody-Goody. A candy or sweet.

Goose. A bird with rich dark meat and considerable fat. It is on the market usually from Christmastime until April. Geese weigh 8–12 pounds. About 1½ pounds should be allowed for each serving because there is comparatively little meat.

For roasting, the pin feathers should be removed, the goose singed, the cavity washed with cold water, and as much fat as possible removed.

The most common domestic goose is the Toulouse, or gray variety; however, the African, Chinese, and Embden geese are also raised. The Chinese geese are of excellent quality and have been domesticated.

Goose, Wild. A game bird whose distinctive gamy flavor varies according to breed and diet. Wild geese that feed on fish inevitably have a fishy taste. The most popular variety is the Canada goose, but the *snow goose, blue goose, black goose* (the *brant*), as well as the white-fronted American type, all have their adherents.

Gooseberries. Introduced to England from the Continent in the 16th century, gooseberries are one of the fruits of lesser importance in the United States. The season for fresh gooseberries is brief, lasting only for 2–3 weeks in July. The variety most cultivated in America is the European gooseberry, *Ribes grossularia*. It has heavy curved spines at the nodes and scattered weak bristles on the stems; its large round berries may be red or green.

Gooseberries are usually sold in the ½-pint size, although they sometimes come to market in quart containers. Buy bright berries with a clean fresh appearance, each berry plump and juicy. Wash the fruit before using it in a compote, in a preserve, or in tarts or other desserts.

Gooseberry Fool (British). A dish of stewed gooseberries and cream.

Goose Fat. The fat of a goose, one of the most delicately flavored cooking fats. It is usually rendered with a little onion, and when completely melted, strained and refrigerated in a tightly closed jar.

Goosefoot. *See* Pigweed.

Goosenargh Cake (British). A cake containing caraway seeds, flour, butter, and sugar.

Goose Teal. A very small goose.

Gorcock. The male red grouse, an excellent game bird.

Gordyforme Wheat. A very hard durum wheat grown in Russia.

Gorenflot. A large *baba* made with sweet liqueurs, especially kirsch.

Goret. A young suckling pig.

Gorgonzola. A round, creamy, semihard blue-veined cheese produced in northern Italy; particularly good with fresh fruit and buttered crusty bread. A white Gorgonzola also marketed in Italy is not as popular as the ordinary type.

Gormand. *See* Gourmand.

Gormandize. To eat greedily or with extraordinary relish. The word comes from *gourmandise*, the French term for "gluttony."

Gösfilet (Swedish). Pike-perch fillet.

Gosling. A young goose.

Goto (Philippine). Tripe.

Gouda. A yellow Dutch cheese with a red rind, similar to Edam but flatter and larger; usually served for breakfast with black bread and coffee; ideal also with cocoa. A kosher Gouda is prepared for orthodox Jews.

Goudale (French). Vegetable soup to which wine is added after the solid portion has been eaten.

Goudse Kaas (Dutch). Gouda cheese.

Gouffé (French). A creamed chicken soup made with tapioca.

Gouffé, Jules. A 19th-century French chef, author of several books, among them *Le Livre de Pâtisserie*, a culinary classic.

Gougelhopf; Kugelhupf; Kougelhupf; Guglhupf (Alsatian). Sweet yeast cake usually made in a

round mold with spiral markings; particularly good with coffee.

Gougère (French). An unsweetened cheesecake served hot or cold as an appetizer in Burgundy.

Gougère de l'Aube. A pastry made of cheese and eggs, eaten cold or hot.

Gougnette (French). A type of doughnut or fritter especially popular in Quercy.

Goujon (French). Gudgeon, a small freshwater fish.

Goulash (Hungarian). A spicy beef or veal stew. In Magyar, the Hungarian term *gulyás* means "herdsman's meat," a dish that came down from the days of the iron caldron and open fire. Goulash jumped the borders of Hungary long ago to become a staple dish in Vienna and Prague. Through the years each area has developed its own version, so that now there are many variations of goulash.

Basically, goulash is a large amount of onion browned in plenty of butter and combined with cubed meat salted to taste, but no water, stock, or other liquid. The chopped onions supply the moisture as they cook, and they form the characteristic rich gravy. The meat should be so thoroughly cooked that it can be cut with a fork.

Most goulashes call for paprika, an important spice in the Hungarian cuisine.

Goulu Pois. A French green pea, eaten pod and all.

Goumi. A Chinese fruit with orange-colored flesh and a pleasant, slightly acid taste.

Gounerre (French). A smooth paste made from potatoes; a provincial specialty of Burgundy.

Gourd. Any of several plants, such as pumpkins, melons, and cucumbers, that grow on a vine along the ground.

Gourdon (French). Roast guinea hen stuffed with plenty of truffles and served with a rich brandy sauce; a specialty of Quercy.

Gourilos (French). The roots or stump of endive; usually boiled, and eaten as a green vegetable.

Gourmand; Gormand (French). (1) One who is fond of fine food. (2) Sometimes, one who overeats and behaves like a glutton, in contrast to a gourmet, who, though enjoying fine foods, does not overeat.

Gourmandism. Love of good food.

Gourmet. An expert in selecting and judging fine foods and wines; an epicure. The word *gourmet* derives from the French *groumet*, a wine taster.

Gourmette (Rare). A woman gourmet.

Gournay; Malakoff. An extremely rich cheese with a pleasant, creamy white texture, made in Normandy, France.

Gousse d'Ail (French). Clove of garlic.

Goût (French). Taste.

Goût Americain. In the French champagne industry, a sweet champagne; "*Americain*" refers to South America.

Goût de Noisette (French). Of wines and cheeses, having a nutlike taste.

Goûter (French). (1) Afternoon tea. (2) To taste or relish.

Goût Piquant (French). Relish.

Gouzon. A French cow's-milk cheese much like Camembert.

Gowpen (Scotch). An old measure for foodstuffs, especially grain, equal to two handfuls, the quantity held by two hands placed together cupwise.

Goya. An unusually good, dry, hard Argentinean cheese similar to Parmesan.

Gozzard. One who handles or raises geese.

Graach. A wine village in the Moselle region of Germany. *See* Germany, The Wines of.

Gräddvåffler (Swedish). Sour-cream waffles.

Graeskar (Danish). Squash.

Gragnano. *See* Italy, The Wines of.

Graham Bread. Bread made wholly or partly with graham flour.

Graham Flour. Flour containing the outer bran coating of the wheat kernel; named for Sylvester Graham, an early American health-food faddist.

Grainage. Grain crop.

Grain Alcohol. Alcohol made only from grain.

Grained. Containing seeds or particles; having a granular surface.

Graines de Sureau (French). Elderberries.

Grains of Paradise. (1) Cardamom seeds; pungent, aromatic seeds found in Ceylon, East India, Guinea, and West Africa. (2) Often, pepper, much used as a flavoring ingredient in Asia.

Graisse (French). Animal fat.

Graisse Normande (French). A frying fat made by combining suet and pork fat, with added herbs, seasoning, and vegetables; used in Normandy.

Gram (Malaysian). Chick-pea.

Green Gram. Chick-pea; also called *mug*.

Gram Degree. The amount of heat needed to raise one gram of water 1° centigrade.

Gramolata (Italian). (1) Lemonade. (2) A frozen or semifrozen dish made like sherbet; also called *granité*.

Grana (Italian). A popular name in Italy for Parmesan cheese.

Granada (Spanish). Pomegranate.

Granadilla (Latin American). Fruit of the passionflower vine whose pulp is juicy and contains seeds. Sweetened or sprinkled with sherry, it is usually eaten with a spoon as a dessert. Granadilla ice cream is a specialty in some tropical countries.

Granage (Obsolete). Formerly, a tax levied on imported salt in London.

Grana Reggiano. A kind of Parmesan cheese made in Reggio, Italy.

Granary. A warehouse for the storage of threshed grain.

Granate. Pomegranate.

Granatina (Italian). Hamburger patty.

Granchio (Italian). Crab.

Grande Cuilerée (French). A tablespoonful.

Grand Cuisine. The finest art of French cuisine; the ultimate in culinary skill; the entire repertoire of the *haute cuisine* of France.

Grand Ear (Colloquial). Abalone.

Grand Jus (French). A clear or brown liquid obtained by cooking veal bones and vegetables until concentrated.

Grand Marnier. An orange-flavored liqueur with a Cognac base, produced in Cognac, France.

Grand Saint Bernard. A pale green Swiss liqueur flavored with honey, herbs, and mountain flowers.

Grand Veneur. A heavy brown sauce; served with game dishes.

Grange. A place where grain is kept.

Graniferous. Bearing grain or similar seeds.

Graniform. Shaped like grains of corn.

Granita (Italian). A frozen drink; sherbet.

Granita di Caffè. Frozen coffee sherbet or ice.

Granita di Limone. Lemon ice.

Granité (Italian). A half-frozen coffee or fruit water ice served in a glass.

Granivorous. Grain-eating, as applied to animals.

Grantham Gingerbread (British). A highly spiced hard gingerbread.

Granulate. To reduce to small grains or granules.

Granulated. Consisting of small, grainlike particles.

Grape. *See* Grapes.

Grapefrugt (Danish). Grapefruit.

Grapefruit. A large citrus fruit that grows in bunches like grapes. It is, in fact, from the way it grows that it gets its name.

Grapefruit was a slow starter in the fruit field. Its native home is unknown, but it was first described in 1750 as a "forbidden fruit," and was later cultivated in Barbados. About 1840 Don Philippe, a Spanish noble, planted the first grapefruit trees in Florida, presumably from West Indian seed.

Between 1880 and 1885 a group of Florida citrus growers sent the first shipment to New York markets. At the turn of the century production amounted to only a few thousand boxes annually, and the fruit was found only in specialty shops.

Soon grapefruit gained popularity, and by 1910 production reached 1,000,000 boxes a year. Today 50 times as much grapefruit is produced in this country, principally in Florida, California, Arizona, and Texas.

Grapefruit is classed as seeded or seedless. The skin color ranges from pale yellow to reddish yellow or reddish brown. The discoloration, called russeting, does not affect the quality of the pulp. The pink and the seedless varieties are considered by some to be less sweet than the seeded, white-fleshed varieties.

Select firm specimens that are well shaped, smooth-skinned, and springy to the touch. They should be quite heavy for their size for maximum juice.

Fresh juice in quart containers similar to those used for milk are now available. Canned and frozen concentrated grapefruit juice also are popular, as are canned segments.

Grapefruit Peel. Slices of grapefruit rind boiled in a heavy sugar syrup, then dried.

Grapes. Berries that grow in clusters, and the vine on which they grow. They are eaten as a table fruit, and certain varieties are used to make wine. Grapes of one variety or another are in season almost all year, the United States crop being supplemented by imported grapes.

Eating Grapes. This fruit of the vine long has been enjoyed by man, not only in the fresh and dried forms, but also as wine. Moses exempted from military service the husbandman who planted a vineyard, aware of the pleasure and profit vineyards bestow on a community.

An immense number of different varieties of the vine, *Vitis vinifera*, are grown around the world. In the United States western grapes have been developed from Old World varieties. They usually have a higher sugar and solid content, and in many cases are larger than eastern grapes; the skins adhere tightly to the flesh, and the seeds separate easily from the flesh. Western grapes have a sweet, mild flavor, and because they travel well they predominate on fresh-fruit counters throughout the United States. Most eastern grapes have been developed from native species or from hybrids of native species and European varieties. They are generally small and have seeds that cling to the pulp, which separates easily from the skin.

The leading grape varieties in the United States are the *Thompson Seedless*, a greenish white, almost seedless variety of medium size and elongated shape; and the *Emperor*, a light red grape with seeds and an elongated shape. *Muscat* grapes are widely grown in the South.

Raisins are dried grapes, a special product having uses different from fresh grapes. Increasingly popular are grape juices and frozen grape-juice concentrates.

Grapes Used in Wine Making. The first nation to undertake commercial wine making was Rome, which fostered viniculture within its own borders and later in its conquered lands. The Romans were great travelers and businessmen, as well as soldiers, and during the height of their empire-building days they sent specimens of their vine roots to most of Europe and Africa. At the same time they collected all local specimens of roots in the countries through which they traveled.

The type of vine the Romans used in their wine making was the *Vitis vinifera*, which subsequently became the basis for almost all wine making in the world. It is thought that the Romans found it in the Near East, or possibly in a region to the north near the Caucasus. *Vitis vinifera*, the best type of grape for wine, had grown wild in Europe and parts of Asia for thousands of years. After two thousand years of experimenting, only these vines are used, with the exception of native grape stocks grown in vineyards in the United States. When the dread phylloxera struck the European rootstocks, the more resistant American roots were planted in Europe, and native roots were grafted onto the American stock. The grapes produced by the grafted vines were the same as those from the original European roots.

Grapes suitable for eating are rarely good for wine, but several varieties of wine grapes are edible. The *Vitis vinifera* vines have now been classified into about six thousand varieties, and to these must be added the hybrids which are new improved roots. Crosses have been made mainly between European roots, but also between *vinifera* and American *labrusca* roots. The main difference between the American grape and the European is that the skin of the former separates from the pulp quite easily and is therefore known as a "slipskin." European grape skins adhere firmly to the flesh.

The following grapes are most commonly grown for wine:

Albana: A grape grown near Emilia, Italy, producing a medium sweet, occasionally dry white wine.

Albanello: A Sicilian grape which makes a somewhat coarse, unbalanced white wine.

Aleatico: A grape grown chiefly in northern Italy; has a high sugar content and makes a rather sweet red wine.

Alicante-Bouschet: A Spanish grape which yields a high quantity of low-grade red wine with a good deal of sugar; very poor quality.

Aligote: A very ordinary grape used in parts of Burgundy, France, for routine wine; grows in very large clusters.

Aramon: A low-grade red wine grape, used largely for blending with other wines in parts of southern France.

Baco: A series of new grapes hybridized by the French scientist Baco; some have been introduced into the United States.

Barbera: A very dark red-black Italian grape producing a red wine with heavy body and strong deep color.

Black Hamburg: A German black grape of little reputation, having a poor color and taste.

Boal Madeira: A greenish grape grown on the island of Madeira for the production of Madeira wine.

Burger: A Hungarian grape which produces a somewhat thin white wine, used largely for blending.

Cabernet-Sauvignon: A small, thin-skinned black grape of superb quality used for producing the fine red wines of Bordeaux, France; remarkable color and taste.

Carignane: A black grape grown chiefly in southern France, Africa, and California; produces a poor quality red wine, used for blending.

Catarratto: A tough yellow grape, furnishing a wine without much distinction, used for blending.

Catawba: An American red grape which produces a white wine; has a characteristic "foxy" taste; used mainly for white wines and champagne.

Charbono: A black grape grown in Italy and France; has mediocre taste.

Chardonnay: A variety of that famous grape, the Pinot; it is responsible for the reputation of the leading Burgundy white wines.

Chasselas: A French grape with both red and white varieties; produces a wine of low alcoholic content and low acid content.

Concord: An American variety of, a purple-blue color, produces a wine which is low in sugar content; can endure cold weather better than almost all other varieties.

Corinth: An almost seedless grape, thick-skinned, producing an inferior wine; grown as a rule only in Italy.

Cornichon: A mediocre grape with poor color and aroma; grown in parts of France and California.

Dégoutant: A medium-sized black grape grown in parts of France; produces a routine red wine.

Delaware: Small red sweet grape often regarded as one of the best, if not the very best, of the native American varieties; fairly prolific.

Diana: Similar to Catawba, this American grape produces more wine but of a lighter color.

Dutchess: An American variety created by a cross of Concord and Delaware; the wine has a rather good taste, little aroma.

Elvira: A white wine grape producing a wine deficient in sugar content; grown mainly in California and New York.

Feher Szagos: Originally a Hungarian grape, now chiefly used for the making of California sherry.

Flame Tokay: A grape with both red and white varieties; used principally in California for making sweet wines.

Folle Blanche: The grape used for making Cognac in France; also used for California white wines of ordinary quality.

Fresia: An Italian black grape used for making considerable quantities of red wine in the Piedmont of northern Italy.

Furmint: The classic Hungarian grape used in making Tokay; also grown in parts of Germany and California; high in alcohol and sugar.

Gamay: A very large, blackish grape producing large quantities of wine; the standard grape for making Beaujolais in France.

Gewürtztraminer: A black grape raised in Alsace and Germany; similar to the Traminer but spicier and with more bouquet.

Green Hungarian: Originally a Hungarian grape; now used mainly in California for making sweet, dessert-type wines.

Grenache: A black, sweet grape grown in Spain and parts of France; in the United States it is used for making port wine.

Grignolino: An Italian grape, producing a somewhat thin wine generally used for ordinary red table wine, sometimes for *rosé* wines.

Iona: A quite sweet red-purple grape of American stock, principally used in New York state for making champagne.

Ives: An American grape which produces a coarse red wine of little distinction with a wild "foxy" taste.

Malbec: A rather ordinary black grape of France, but an abundant producer, largely used for blending.

Malvasia: A very sweet type of grape grown in Spain, Greece, Madeira, southern France, and northern Italy, used in making dessert wines.

Mataro: A Spanish grape, black and spherical, used for commercial inexpensive wines.

Merlot: A blue-black grape used around Bordeaux, France, as a blending wine for making clarets.

Mission: A European grape grown in California for the production of very sweet wines.

Mourestel: A grape grown in California for low quality red wines.

Müller-Thurgau: A grape much used in Germany; it is a cross between the aristocratic Riesling and the lesser Sylvaner.

Muscadels: A white grape variety, of which there are numerous subtypes, with a strong, fruit flavor, largely used for blending.

Nebbiolo: An outstanding red wine grape grown in Italy on a large scale; Barolo and Barbaresco wines are made from it.

Palomino: A classic grape for the production of sherry wine; also used in California.

Pedro Ximenez: A moderate-size white grape

much used in Spain for adding to sherry wine; extremely sweet.

Petite Sirah: See Sirrah.

Pinot Blanc: An excellent white grape used in making many of the outstanding white Burgundy wines.

Pinot Noir: An excellent black grape, but of very low productivity, used in the making of the finest red Burgundies.

Refosco: A red wine grape, now much less used in Italy, but grown in California for the production of mediocre wine.

Riesling: A small, yellow, round grape which later turns a shade of red-brown; rather moderate yields of superb white wine.

Ruby Cabernet: Not so good as the Cabernet Sauvignon, this grape produces a fairly good, light red wine.

Scuppernong: A hardy American grape which has white and brown types; produces a pale, light wine.

Semillon: The classic white grape of Bordeaux, used in making Graves and Sauternes; also grown extensively in California.

Sirrah: A black grape grown chiefly in the Rhône Valley of France; also in the hot climates of California and South Africa. There are various varieties including the Petite Sirrah, or Petite Sirah.

Sylvaner: A white grape grown mostly in Alsace, Germany, and California; produces a fairly good white wine, not up to Riesling in quality, however.

Thompson Seedless: A small white-green seedless grape used in California for making sherry wine.

Tinta Madeira: A black grape grown in Madeira and Portugal, chiefly used for sweet dessert wines.

Traminer: A sweet, reddish grape producing an oddly flavored white wine, mainly grown in Alsace.

Ugni Blanc: Also known as the Trebbiano grape, used in California for making Chianti.

Valdepenas: A grape grown extensively in parts of Spain for ordinary red table wines of moderately good quality.

Verdot: A small black grape grown in small

quantities in southwestern France, used for ordinary red table wines.

Zinfandel: A European grape, now chiefly used in California for the production of a fruity red table wine.

Grape Stone. The seed found in a grape.

Grape Sugar. Dextrose, the natural sugar present in all green plants but to the greatest extent in grapes. Wine is therefore best made from grapes, although almost all other fruits are used to some extent.

Grape Varietal. A California wine term designating wines chiefly or wholly produced from one particular wine grape.

Grap Fruit (Portuguese). Grapefruit.

Grapiaux (French). Large pancakes cooked in pork fat; a specialty of the Nivernais region.

Grappa. A strong, Italian, somewhat crude brandy-like liquor distilled from skins, seeds, and stalks after the grapes have been pressed for wine.

Grapy. Like grapes; containing grapes.

Gras; Volvet Kaas. (1) A Dutch whole-milk cheese with a very high butterfat content; made the whole year around. (2) (French, Colloquial). Brie cheese.

Gras-Double (French). Tripe.

Grass Lamb (British). A lamb born late in June.

Grass Mushroom. A quite tall, narrow wild mushroom used in Chinese cookery.

Grate. To scrape into small pieces or particles by rubbing against a rough surface.

Grater. A small kitchen utensil with rough surfaces for grating foods.

Gratin; Au Gratin. Foods cooked with a toasted topping of bread crumbs, cheese, or a mixture of both.

Gratinate. To prepare a food with cheese or bread crumbs, then brown in the oven; to prepare food in the gratin style.

Gratiniert (German). Served with cheese or bread crumbs.

Gratin Stuffing. Veal, liver, bacon, chopped shallots, and truffles combined with Madeira wine and brandy, and with beaten egg yolks and butter added.

Grattons; Gratterons (French). The solid residue left when goose or pork fat is melted; eaten plain or on bread.

Graupen (German). Barley.

Graupensuppe (German). Barley soup.

Gravad Lax (Swedish). Pickled raw salmon.

Gravelet; Chevene; Chevesne. A moderate-sized river fish.

Graveling. A young salmon.

Gravenche. A river fish of the salmon family found in parts of France and Switzerland.

Graves. A wine district in the Bordeaux region of France. *See* France, The Wines of.

Graves-de-Vayre. A wine district in the Bordeaux region of France. *See* France, The Wines of.

Graves Official Classification of 1953. *See* France, The Wines of.

Gravlax (Swedish). Marinated or pickled salmon.

Gravy. The natural juice that runs out of meat while it is cooking, as contrasted with a sauce made separately and served with the meat.

Gravy Salt. A dark fluid, chiefly burnt sugar, used to color gravies and soups.

Gray Bass. A food fish of the perch family.

Gray Breid (Scotch). Formerly, bread made of rye or any grain other than wheat.

Grayfish. A small shark; the dogfish, a food fish marketed fresh, smoked, canned, and dried, and prepared like tuna fish. The average market weight is less than 7 pounds although large specimens weigh 20 pounds or more.

Graylag Goose. The European wild goose.

Grayling. A freshwater fish much like trout, with excellent flavor and delicate texture.

Gray Mullet. A fish 1–2 feet long found in the Atlantic and the Mediterranean.

Gray Sole. A variety of flounder. The most renowned type of sole is England's Dover sole; native American gray or lemon soles are so named because of their great similarity to the English species.

Grease Trap. A place where grease collects on a kitchen appliance.

Great Burdock; Wild Gobo. A common weed whose roots, young leaves, and shoots may be eaten like a vegetable.

Greaves (French). Cracklings; rendered fat.

Greece. Although the Greeks are very nationalistic in their conviction that their cuisine is pure and unsullied by outside influences, Greek cookery is similar to that of Turkey, Armenia, and the

Balkan countries. At one time or another the borders of these countries have changed, and it is extremely difficult to determine the origin of a particular dish.

The favorite before-dinner drink is *ouzo*, an anise-flavored white liquor which becomes cloudy when it is mixed with water. Also available is *mesticha*, a kind of brandy, and *tsipouro*. With these drinks it is customary to serve *mezes*, appetizers. Appetizers are quite interesting, especially *taramosalata*, which is made of fish roe and is very much like caviar. Almost all fish preparations are very good, because the Greeks are very fond of seafood, and the local catches ensure freshness. Mullet, *barbuni*, is a great favorite. Greek soups are somewhat limited in scope, but the lemon-and-egg soup, *soupa avgolemono*, is definitely worthwhile.

Lamb is undoubtedly the favorite meat, although beef is becoming increasingly popular. Nevertheless, if meat is available, the chances are that it will be lamb. A standard method of preparing it is to roast it on a spit, much like *shishkebab* in Turkey. Also standard fare are such preparations as *entrather*, lamb and artichokes; *moussaka*, ground lamb and eggplant; and *yuvarlakia*, meatballs in a tomato sauce.

Some specialties should not be overlooked: *spanakopeta*, a cheese-and-spinach mixture in a pastry crust; *dolmadakia*, vine leaves stuffed with meat and rice; *elies*, the marvelous ripe olives; the many types of *pilav*, steamed rice with fish, poultry, or meat. The classic way of preparing vegetables, called *à la Grecque*, is in olive oil. The outstanding Greek cheese is *feta*, a somewhat astringent white cheese which may be eaten plain or crumbled into a green salad. *Kasseri* is a yellowish dry cheese, and fairly good.

Desserts are often of the Near East type—overly sweet honey-soaked pastries and similar cloying confections. *Melachrino* is a cinnamon-laden cake; *karidopita* is a walnut cake, and *kourambiedes* is a better-than-average pastry. The Greeks are excessively fond of pistachio nuts and use them to decorate many cakes and candies. Greek coffee resembles Turkish coffee in that it is served black, usually with the grounds and usually quite sweet.

Although Greek wines are good, none of them matches the French and Italian products. It is a national custom to flavor the wines with resin; this is a holdover from early times when resin was used to seal containers and prevent the wines from leaking. Resinated wines, *retsina*, are unpleasant at first because of their turpentine taste; eventually the palate learns to accept the odd taste, and foreign residents after living in Greece for a number of years often find the unresinated wines insipid by comparison. Good white wines include *Tour-la-Reine* and *Minos*; *Naoussa* and *Chevalier de Rhodes* are probably the best among the reds. *Metaxas*, a sweet brandy, is a popular afterdinner drink. *Mavrodaphne* is a very sweet dessert wine.

Greece, The Wines of. Although wine making was well known three thousand years ago (the Bible is filled with references to wine), it was the Greeks who first developed it into a high skill. Greek wines were famous all over the Southern European and North African world, and the Greeks were so interested in wines of all sorts that traders and merchants brought back foreign wines as valuable cargo. Later, of course, France, Italy, and Germany surpassed the Greeks in their technical innovations. However, in modern times the Greeks have learned from their former pupils, and now follow the methods of the winemakers to the north.

During the heyday of Greece local wines were stored in large pottery containers called *amphoras*. The ancient Greeks found that the wine was extremely perishable, for the jars were unsealed and the action of the air caused deterioration. They experimented and found that if the jars were lined with a sticky substance like tar, the outside air could not make as much contact and the wine kept longer. The tar gave the wine a decidedly resinous taste, but the Greeks soon learned to enjoy the distinctive flavor, preferring it to their ordinary wines. These resinous wines were further flavored with various spices, such as cloves. The Greeks never lost their liking for the resinous flavor, and a great many modern Greeks enjoy *retsina*, resinated wines. The uninitiated person trying Greek wines for the first time is inclined to dismiss them as impossible because of this taste. Today much Greek wine is flavored with sandarac, a resin obtained on several of the magnificent Aegean islands. (Sandarac is used mainly for making varnish!) Fortunately the tourist in Greece finds that most wines come in two types, *retsina* or *aretsinata* (without resin).

A grape that probably originated in Greece is the *Sultana*; it is still cultivated extensively. The · other leading grape type is the *Malvasia*. In addition, there are quite a number of vineyards planted to the sweet *Muscat*. Greeks are inordinately fond of rich, sweet wines. The outstanding example, one which is quite extensively exported, is the Greek dessert wine Mavrodaphne, or "black laurel." It is very rich with almost 20 percent alcoholic content, and it is, roughly, a cross of port, Madeira, and Malaga. A similar wine, but less sweet and less high in alcohol, is Santonin. Samos, Kampa, and Château Decelie are innocuous sweet wines much lighter in character.

Rhodes produces a sweet wine called Santa Helena which is tiresomely rich and cloying to the palate. The Greeks also make imitations of port and muscatel wines, not very high in quality, intended for domestic consumption.

Greek table wines are only fair. Among the whites, the best include Demestica, King Minos, Votrys, Mantineia, Hymettus, Demesticha, and Rodos. All are moderately dry. Zitsa is a medium sweet wine, for those who do not like a very dry white. Among the reds, Beso Roditys, and Naoussa have fairly good body and color. Castel Danielis and the red King Minos are quite good, and they are popular.

Grecque, À la. (1) Preparations made with olive oil or rice, and served cold. (2) Any dish originally of Greek origin.

Greedy. (1) Having a marked tendency to eat or drink hastily and with poor table manners. (2) (British) One who never leaves a scrap of food on his plate.

Greek Wine. (1) Wine produced in Greece. *See* Greece, The Wines of. (2) During the Middle Ages, any sweet, strong dessert wine.

Green. (1) Vegetables, plants, and herbs whose natural color is green. (2) Unripe, as applied to fruits and vegetables.

Greenback. A variety of trout.

Green Bass. The black bass.

Green Bay Cheese. A slightly sharp white cheddar cheese made in Green Bay, Wisconsin.

Green Bone. The gar fish.

Green Butter. *See* Vegetable Butter.

Green Cheese. (1) Sage cheese, a cheddar-type cheese flavored with crushed sage leaves or colored green and with sage extract added for flavoring. (2) A poor-quality cheese made from whey or skim milk.

Green Cod. Salted, undried cod.

Green Corn. Immature corn; most delicious when placed in boiling salted water within an hour or two after picking and cooked only 3–4 minutes, then served with plenty of sweet butter and coarse salt.

Green Crab. A mediocre shore crab.

Green Dough. (1) Unfermented dough. (2) Dough that has not risen.

Green Fat. The greenish gelatinous fatty substance found in the turtle.

Green Ginger Wine. An alcoholic (13%) beverage popular in England, with a piquant, gingery taste; consumed plain or made into cocktails.

Greengage. The sweetest of plums, round and yellow-green with a light red tint where exposed to the sun.

Green Goose. A goose less than 6 months old; a gosling.

Greengrocer. A retail grocer who deals chiefly in fruits and vegetables, especially in England.

Greenhouse. A building made chiefly of glass, where fruits and vegetables may be grown out of season by controlling the light, temperature, and humidity.

Greenland Halibut. A species of white-meat halibut whose taste is often considered finer than that of ordinary halibut.

Green Laver. An edible seaweed.

Green Onions. Young onion shoots; frequently called *scallions*. A green onion is any variety of onion, picked green. Green onions are particularly good when quite small, eaten raw with coarse salt. The greens may be used in salads or may be boiled whole like asparagus and served with any appropriate sauce, including Hollandaise or melted butter. The onions are often chopped and eaten with cottage cheese and sour cream. Green onions are available everywhere in the United States, but California and and Texas are the largest suppliers.

Green Oyster. An oyster whose green color is due to its natural diet.

Green Pepper. A green, rounded, podlike vegetable. Green peppers probably originated in the New World, most likely in warm or tropical climates. They were not liked by the first settlers and became more popular in Europe, where they had been introduced. Later they became a common vegetable in the Americas.

A few peppers are green when mature, but the majority are green when immature; they are brought to market while immature and before the red coloring develops. Green peppers range from tiny to quite large, from globular to long narrow specimens. Peppers may be eaten raw, cut into strips and served in salads, French-fried with or without batter, or stuffed with any desired filling. Roasted peppers, served with oil and vinegar, are a delicious appetizer.

Greens. Leafy green vegetables, such as spinach, chard, broccoli, collards, turnip greens, and beet greens, all very rich sources of vitamin A. The vitamin A content varies with the greenness of the leaves, the paler leaves containing less than the darker-hued ones. Also, the thinner the leaf the richer it is likely to be in vitamin A. Escarole, kale, and parsley have the highest vitamin A content of all vegetables.

Green Sauce. A mayonnaise colored green with the juice of pounded parsley, chervil, and tarragon leaves or spinach.

Green Stuff. Green herbs and green vegetables.

Green Teas. Unfermented teas grown mostly in China and Japan. The Japanese green teas are distinguished and are sometimes referred to as the "white wines of tea."

Grelhados (Portuguese). Grilled.

Gremolada (Italian). An herb and fruit flavoring, consisting of lemon rind, chopped parsley and chopped garlic; customarily added to *osso buco*, a classic dish made with veal knuckles.

Grenache. (1) A variety of grape used for making wine. (2) A group of wines produced from grapes grown chiefly in southern France;

Grenache wines are rich, sweet, and high in alcohol.

Grenade (French). Pomegranate.

Grenade (Obsolete). A dish composed of two layers of bacon with pigeons and thin slices of veal between.

Grenadier. A fish resembling the cod.

Grenadine. A sweet reddish syrup made from pomegranate juice and occasionally from currants; used to color and flavor ice creams, puddings, desserts, etc., and also used in alcohol drinks.

Grenadin; Grenadines; Grenadins (French). A fricassée or stew of meat; larded slices, usually of veal or venison, generally fried lightly in butter.

Grenadins de Brochet (French). Fillets of pike cooked in white wine and served with truffles.

Greyano Vino (Bulgarian). A highly spiced hot wine punch.

Grianneau (French). A young grouse.

Gribenes (Jewish). Cracklings made from the skin of goose, duck, or chicken and flavored with onions.

Gribiche (French). A sauce made with oil and vinegar, egg yolks, mustard, and spices; often served with meats and fish.

Griblette (French). A thin grilled slice of meat or poultry.

Grice. A suckling pig.

Grid. A grill used for cooking.

Griddle. A flat iron pan, rimless or with a very shallow rim, used for cooking pancakes and drop scones.

Griddle Cakes. Pancakes. Flat round cakes baked on a griddle or skillet over direct heat, prepared either from packaged mixes or according to a recipe. They may be made with all-purpose flour, buckwheat flour, or cornmeal, and should be eaten, soon after cooking, with butter and syrup, sausages, bacon, etc.

An ordinary skillet can be used, but a special heavy griddle that does not require greasing is easier to use. The pan should be hot before pouring the batter. A pancake turner aids in turning the cakes to brown both sides.

Gridiron. A cooking utensil consisting of a series of parallel iron bars or bars attached to a handle.

Sometimes any solid sheet of metal used for cooking.

Griessklösschen (German). Semolina dumplings.

Grig. A small freshwater eel.

Grigger (British). A thin pancake baked on a gridiron.

Grignolino. *See* Italy, The Wines of.

Grignon (French). (1) A slice of dry bread baked in a slow oven until very hard, then nibbled like rusk. (2) The heel of a loaf of French bread.

Grill. (1) All broiled foods. (2) To prepare food on a grill or griddle; broil.

Grillade de Poulet. Grilled chicken served with any desired sauce.

Grillardin. A chef, usually in a large hotel, restaurant, or aboard ship, who specializes in grilling foods.

Grilleret Lammehoved (Danish). Grilled lamb's head.

Grillet, Château. A rather good dry white wine produced in the Rhône Valley region of France.

Grill Room. A room in a hotel or restaurant smaller than the main dining room, theoretically specializing in the preparation of grilled foods. Often the second dining room as distinguished from the main one.

Grilse. A young salmon after its first return from the sea and in its second or third year.

Grimod de la Reynière. The French culinary expert and famous gastronome who wrote *Almanach des Gourmands* in 1803.

Grind. To crush into fine particles.

Grinder Sandwich; Hero Sandwich; Submarine Sandwich. A long thin loaf of bread split in two and filled with assorted meats and condiments.

Grindle. The freshwater blackfish.

Grinzing. A suburb of Vienna, Austria renowned for its *heuriger*, places where young wine is sold, perhaps to the accompaniment of zither music. Grinzing produces a fair white wine.

Griotte (French). A dark red cherry also called *Armenian cherry*; not eaten raw but used for jams and compotes.

Grisette. A variety of mushroom found in various parts of Europe; of only mediocre quality.

Grisfötter Kokta (Swedish). Boiled pig's feet.

Griskin. (1) Chine of pork, the cut of pork that is the top of the sparerib and contains the bone

of the spine. In a small pig the sparerib and griskin are not separated. Also called *chine of pork*. (2) The lean loin of pork used for bacon.

Gris-Meunier. A wine of passable quality produced in the Orléans region of France.

Grissini (Italian). Narrow bread sticks about 6 inches long, which are standard items on the tables of most Italian restaurants in the United States. They are made of a dough consisting of wheat flour, vegetable oil, and yeast. Some varieties contain salt, but many are salt-free. Some *grissini* are coated with sesame seeds; others are flavored with cheese or garlic. *Grissini* imported from Italy are usually longer and thinner than those made in the United States.

Antonio Brunero of Turin, is said to have "invented" the bread sticks in 1679, and Turin is famous for its bread sticks.

Grist. Corn ready to be ground.

Gristle. Cartilage.

Gristly. Full of cartilage or gristle.

Grits; Hominy Grits; Corn Grits. Coarsely ground meal. After the bran and the germ have been removed, white or yellow corn is ground coarser than cornmeal and sifted. In the southern United States, grits are popular served either as a breakfast cereal or as a substitute for potatoes.

Grive (French). The fieldfare, a bird of the thrush family.

Grivelette. A small edible thrush; often used as a game food.

Groaning Bread. Christening cake.

Groatcake (British). A cake made with fine oatmeal.

Groats. Oats from which the husk has been entirely removed.

Groats Sugar. A coarse sugar.

Grocer. A retailer who sells food. Originally a grocer was a dealer who bought and sold in gross amounts.

Grocery. A retail store where food products are sold.

Grød (Danish). Porridge.

Groente (Dutch). Vegetables.

Groentesoep (Dutch). Vegetable soup.

Grog. (1) Usually plain rum. The term is derived from *grogram*, a coat once worn by an English admiral, Vernon, who was fond of a rum-and-water combination, but somehow the word "grog" rather than "vernon" has become popular. (2) In the United States, a hot sweetened rum drink containing lemon juice.

Groggery (British). A place where grog is sold.

Grog Shop. A place where one can buy a drink.

Grønaertesuppe (Danish). Green-pea soup.

Grondin (French). Any of a variety of small fish, including the rouget (roach), and gournal (gurnard).

Grønkaal (Danish). Cabbage soup with pork.

Grønlangkaal (Danish). Creamed cabbage.

Grönsaker (Swedish). Vegetables.

Grönsallad (Swedish). Green salad.

Grøntsager (Danish). Vegetables.

Gröntsaker (Norwegian). Vegetables.

Gros-Bec (French). Hawfinch, a small European game bird; best when roasted.

Gros Damas de Tours. An excellent large prune grown near Tours, France.

Grosellas (Spanish). Currants.

Grosert Fool (Scotch). Gooseberry fool, a favorite dessert in England, made of strained sweetened gooseberries mixed with cream.

Gros Michel. "Big Mike," a popular Central American banana.

Gros-Sel (French). Coarse salt.

Grosse-Pièce (French). A large cut of poultry or meat.

Grosset; Grosert (Scotch). Gooseberry.

Gross Feeder. A person who willingly eats unpleasant food that lacks quality or taste.

Gros Soupa (French). The meal served before Midnight Mass on Christmas Eve.

Grote (Obsolete). Groats.

Groumet (French). One who tests, inspects, tastes, or checks wines.

Groundberry. The checkerberry.

Groundbird. A swan, not particularly good for eating.

Ground-Cherry; Bladder Cherry; Dwarf Cape Gooseberry; Husk Tomato; Strawberry Tomato. A wild plant whose small fruit resembles the tomato and tastes like a cross between strawberry and tomato; eaten fresh or made into jams and jellies. The poha, found in Hawaii, is a groundcherry.

Groundfish. Fish that live on the ocean bottom, such as the various flatfish, flounders, and fluke.

Ground Game (British). Rabbits and hares.

Ground Holly. The checkerberry.

Groundling. A small fish that lives at the bottom of the sea.

Groundnut. *See* Peanut.

Groundnut Stew; Moamba (African). A stew consisting of chicken, peanuts, and potatoes.

Ground Pigeon. A pigeon that lives mostly on the ground. It is excellent eating, having a fine flavor and texture.

Ground Rice; Rice Flour. Rice ground to a fine powder.

Grouper. A member of the sea bass family, native to the North Atlantic, the Gulf of Mexico, and the waters near the West Indies; the most abundant species is the *red grouper*. An excellent food fish, but not retailed on a large scale in most of the United States. It is marketed the year round. Although some specimens may weigh as much as 50 pounds, those sent to market usually weigh 5–15 pounds. The smaller fish are sold whole; the larger ones are cut into steaks or fillets. The steak is best broiled.

Grouse. A plump game bird with feathered legs whose feathers match the foliage. It has a delicate, pleasing taste, but must be carefully prepared, for overcooking renders it dry, tough, and flavorless. Basting as frequently as possible is essential, and fresh herbs are indicated. Shallots rather than onions should be used.

Grouse Pigeon. Sand grouse.

Grout. (1) Coarsely ground meal. (2) Malt mixed with water before and during its fermentation.

Groux; Grous (French). A thick cereal made with buckwheat flour and water, particularly in Brittany.

Grovbrød (Norwegian). Rye bread.

Groviera (Italian). Swiss cheese.

Gruau (French). (1) The firm part of wheat containing the gluten portion. (2) Oatmeal or other fine flour.

Gruau d'Avoine (French). Oatmeal.

Grub (Colloquial). Food.

Grudgeons (Obsolete). Gurgeons.

Grudgings. Fine bran.

Gruel. A food for invalids consisting of a cereal, such as oatmeal, boiled with water to the proper consistency, then strained and usually sweetened. Milk or butter is sometimes added just before serving.

Grüne Bohnen (German). Green beans.

Grüne Erbsen (German). Green peas.

Grüne Gurke (German). Cucumber.

Grüne Salat (German). Lettuce.

Grunt. A popular pudding, probably originated in New England, made with fruit or berries, sugar, milk, and butter. Blueberry grunt is a favorite.

Grunt; Pigfish. A fish that makes a sound similar to a grunt. A member of the snapper family, it is caught in the South Atlantic and is one of the staple food fishes of the Key West area. Grunts may be sautéed or pan-broiled. They weigh ½–2 pounds.

Gruntling. A very young pig.

Gruyère. A cheese made from cow's whole milk in much the same manner as Swiss cheese, but it is smaller, has smaller eyes, and a sharper flavor. For more than 200 years Gruyère has been made in the village of Gruyère, Switzerland; it is now also made in France. Gruyère has been imitated all over the world. The American-process Gruyère does not resemble the original in size, color, taste, or texture.

Grynsaadd (Norwegian). Barley soup.

Grystek (Swedish). Pot roast.

Grzyby w Smietanie (Polish). Mushrooms prepared with sour cream.

Guarana. A paste made from seeds of a Brazilian plant; used as food or medicine and in bottled soft drinks.

Guacamole. A cocktail dip of Mexican origin. Very ripe avocados are mashed in a bowl rubbed with garlic, and seasoned with lemon juice, minced onion, salt, and a little chili powder. Corn chips, potato chips, or Mexican tortillas should be served with the guacamole. Raw-vegetable spears may also be dipped in the avocado mixture, which may also contain diced ripe tomatoes, bits of green chilis, or sliced ripe olives.

Guachanche; Guaguanche (Spanish). Barracuda.

Guadeloupe. *See* Martinique.

Guanábana (Spanish). The soursop, a rather large tropical fruit with aromatic white flesh; eaten plain or used in making soft drinks.

Guanimes. A boiled pie or pudding made of coconut milk, sugar, cornmeal, and flavorings.

Guarapo. In Latin countries, water boiled with *papelón*, brown unrefined sugar; in other countries, the juice of raw sugar cane.

Guardanapo (Portuguese). Napkin.

Guardfish. Garfish.

Guards Pudding (British). A steamed light pudding made with bread crumbs.

Guatemala. *See* Central America.

Guava. A tropical fruit, especially plentiful in Mexico and on the Caribbean Islands, varying from round to pearshaped and from yellow to red. Its thin skin encloses the aromatic pulp, which may be sweet or sometimes slightly acid.

Guava paste, a commercial product, is made by boiling the fruit until it is a solid mass that can be sliced. It should be eaten as fresh as possible, for it tends to crystallize with age. It is delicious with fresh white cream cheese.

Guayaba. Guava; may be eaten raw but is used chiefly in making preserves and jams. *See* Guava.

Gudebread. In Scotland, all breads and cakes made between Christmas and New Year. In England gudebread was formerly made for weddings, baptisms, and funerals.

Gudgeon. A small European freshwater fish.

Guébar. A group of Algerian wines, mostly red; full-bodied and alcoholic; quite burning to the taste.

Guédoufle (French). Small bottles, usually joined together, containing oil and vinegar.

Gueulard (French). One extremely fond of food but not a glutton.

Gueuze-Lambic. *See* Lambic.

Gueyat. A cow's-milk cheese prepared in Alsace and Lorraine, France.

Guéyin, Le. A small rather dry cheese seasoned with both salt and pepper, which give it an unusual flavor; made in Lorraine, France.

Gugelhupf; Gugelhopf (German). A yeast coffee cake. *See* Kugelhupf.

Guianas, The. The three regions that make up the Guianas each have their own cuisine. *British Guiana*, now called Guyana, produces rice, coffee, coconuts, molasses, and sugar, which frequently appear in the daily diet. There are no wines, and the favorite local drink is a rum swizzle. The local Demerara rum is 151 proof, making it more than 75 percent alcohol, one of the strongest liquors in the world. Some interesting soups are *breadnut* soup (made from a starchy root), and *callalu* soup (from edible taro leaves, shrimp, and salt beef). A favorite dish is "*coveeched*" fish, often made from a local fish, *queriman*; this pickled fish dish is based on the *escabeche* of the west coast of South America. Also worthy of note are *pepperpot*, a stew made of pork and salt beef and flavored with *cassareep*, a seasoning derived from the cassava; *mettagee*, a dried codfish and coconut dish with local vegetables; and the popular chicken *pilau*, made with rice and raisins. Guavas and soursops are local fruits, often made into ice cream.

Dutch Guiana, now called Surinam, emphasizes its national inheritance, and many Netherlands dishes appear on local menus. Among the interesting food items are *kwie kwie*, a swamp fish; *taja*, a potatolike tuber much used as a starchy vegetable, *puksoi* and *umsoi*, leafy green vegetables often served with pickled meats. Dutch beers and liquors are preferred, although rum is produced in considerable quantities. A popular soft drink is *orgeade*, made of sweet and bitter almonds.

In *French Guiana*, the local cuisine is completely French, and the residents cook as if they lived in a French provincial city. French wines are frequently served, but the high humidity and temperature do not improve their taste.

Guignard (French). A small plover, a game bird.

Guigne. An excellent-tasting French cherry eaten fresh or made into a sweet liqueur called *Guignolet.*

Guignette. (1) The sandpiper, a bird often used as food. (2) The littorine, an edible mollusk found along Mediterranean shores.

Guignolet. *See* Guigne.

Guijones (Spanish). Dill.

Guimauve (French). Marshmallow.

Guinataan (Philippine). A sweet potato-tapioca-yam pudding made with coconut milk.

Guinea Bird. Guinea fowl or hen.

Guinea Deer. The chevrotain, an edible musk deer.

Guinea Fowl; Guinea Hen. A relative of the pheasant, native to Africa and first domesticated by the Greeks, Romans, and Phoenicians. Because the flesh is rather dry, it is best cooked on a spit with frequent basting, or it may be stewed. Guinea fowl eggs are excellent when boiled. In Italy, especially in Messina, roast guinea fowl accompanied by fresh soft figs and perfumed oranges is a festive dish.

Guinea Goose. Swan goose or Chinese goose, an edible goose of fair quality.

Guinea Grains. *See* Amomum.

Guinea Pepper. (1) Cayenne pepper. (2) A pepper plant, *capsicum annum*; source of a certain hot pepper.

Guinea Pig. A rodent. The taste is mediocre, but many primitive people consume it as a regular part of their diet.

Guinea Plum. A West African fruit resembling a plum but not a true plum.

Guinea Wheat (Obsolete). Indian corn.

Guinette (Obsolete, French). Guinea fowl.

Guinness Stout. A rich, strong dark beer made by Guinness, a brewing company in Dublin, Ireland.

Guisado (Spanish). Stew.

   Guisado Español. Spanish national stew; usually made with beef, olive oil, and onions.

Guisantes (Spanish). Green peas.

Gula Malacca. Sugar made from the coconut palm.

Gulaman. An edible Philippine seaweed.

Gular (Obsolete, British). Dedicated to good eating.

Gulbrøtter (Norwegian). Carrots.

Gulch. One who eats or drinks too much and too quickly.

Gule Aerter (Danish). Yellow split-pea soup.

Gulerødder (Danish). Carrots.

Gull. Any young edible bird, especially a goose.

Gulo (Obsolete, British). Glutton.

Gulosity. Gluttony, greediness.

Gulp. To swallow large pieces of food or mouthfuls of liquids.

Gulyás (Hungarian). A stew made of meat or poultry and paprika. Similar to gulyás are *tokány* and *paprikás*. In the tokány the meat is cut somewhat smaller than in the gulyás, and vegetables may be added. Paprikás dishes have a similar taste, but usually sour cream is added. *See* Goulash.

Gum. Various sticky, thick substances obtained from plants and trees, and used for their adhesive or thickening qualities in the preparation of food.

    Gum Arabic. A type of gum obtained from certain species of the acacia tree; used in making confections, especially marshmallows and jellied candies.

Gum Acacia. *See* Gum Arabic.

Gumbo. (1) Okra. (2) A thick New Orleans soup made with okra.

Gumbo Filé. A bland, delicate Creole seasoning made of pulverized dried sassafras leaves. Filé should be added after the gumbo has been removed from the heat; otherwise it will turn the dish into an unpalatable, sticky, gluelike mess.

Gumdrop. A firm, bright-colored, jellylike candy prepared from gelatin, gum arabic, and flavorings.

Gum Paste. A thick sugar icing kneaded with tragacanth or other gum into a paste.

Gum Tragacanth. A gum obtained from plants of the *Astragalus* genus; used chiefly in food preparation for thickening.

Gum Water. A mixture of water and gum arabic, used in making candies, pastes, and jellies.

Gunge. A Middle Eastern food market.

Gunner. The sea bream, a food fish found in various parts of the world.

Gur (Indian). Unrefined cane sugar.

Gurgeons. Coarsely ground cereal or meal.

Gurka (Swedish). Cucumber.

Gurken (German). Cucumbers.

Gurkensalat (German). Cucumber salad.

Gurnard. A rather odd-looking fish found in the Mediterranean and other waters; the three principal varieties are the red, the gray, and the sea swallow. Used in soups and bouillabaisse.

Gurnet (French). Certain fish which exist in many varieties, such as the piper and the streaked, the gray, the red, and the little gurnard.

Güssing. An Austrian skim-milk cheese greatly resembling American brick cheese.

Gust. (1) The flavor or taste of food. (2) A pleasing taste.

Gustable. Able to be tasted.

Gustard (Obsolete). Bustard, a game bird.

Gustation. The act of tasting.

Gustatory. Pertaining or relating to the sense of taste.

Gustful. Tasty; flavorful.

Gustless (Obsolete). Tasteless.

Gusto. (1) Taste, liking. (2) Zest or keen enjoyment of food.

Gut. To remove the inner parts of animals.

Guttle. To eat greedily. A *guttler* is a glutton.

Guyave. *See* Guava.

Guzzle. To swallow an alcoholic beverage in one gulp.

Gwyniad (Welsh). A fish of the trout or salmon family.

Gyle (British). A brew, particularly a beer mixture.

    Gyle-Fat; Gyle-Vat. A vat that contains aging or fermenting wort.

Gymnètre. A silvery Mediterranean fish; usually over a foot long, it tastes like cod.

Gyn. Gin.

Gyu (Japanese). Thin slices of beef used in making sautéed meat dishes, such as sukiyaki.

H

Haas (Dutch). Rabbit.

Habas. Lima bean.

Habas (Spanish). Broad beans.

Habek (Syrian). Basil.

Haberdine. A large cod, used in Britain chiefly for salting.

Habichuelas (Spanish). Kidney beans.

Habiller (French). To prepare foods for eating.

Habitants des Rochers (French). "Inhabitants of rocks," a fanciful name for lobsters, used on pretentious menus.

Hablé Crème Chantilly. An extraordinarily rich, very delicate, soft dessert cheese, generally shipped from Sweden in wedge-shaped wooden containers weighing about 5 ounces. It is best when fresh; when mature, it browns considerably at the edges and loses its delicate taste.

Haché (French). (1) Chopped or minced meat. (2) Diced meat casserole.

Hacher (French). (1) To chop meat. (2) To slice into thin cuts.

    Hacher-Menu. Finely chopping or mincing meat.

Hacinette (French). A small round bowl in which foods are chopped; a crescent-shaped knife is used.

Hachis (1) (Danish). Hash. (2) (French). Hashed meat.

Hachoir (French). A food chopper, usually consisting of a rounded knife, with handles at each end.

Hack. To cut or chop into irregular pieces.

Hackad Biff med Lök (Swedish). Minced steak and onions.

Hackad Kalvfilet (Swedish). Chopped veal.

Hackle. The long narrow feathers on the neck of domestic fowl.

Hackberry. An American tree resembling the elm. Its small, sweet fruit resembles the wild cherry in taste; generally used for making jams, jellies, and preserves.

Haddie (Scotch). Haddock, a food fish.

Haddock. A sea fish of the cod family, smaller than the cod, with a longer dorsal fin, smaller mouth, and a black line running the length of the body on either side. Haddock is in season the year round. Its flesh is firm and keeps well and may be obtained fresh, salted, or smoked. Smoked haddock is known as *finnan haddie*.

Haddyanegg (Scotch). Steamed haddock cooked in milk with butter; poached eggs are placed on the fish, and the stock, slightly thickened with flour, is poured on top.

Hagberry. *See* Hackberry.

Haggis. The national dish of Scotland, the only country where this unique dish is appreciated. The stomach of a sheep is filled with a seasoned stuffing of minced heart, liver, lung, oatmeal, and chopped beef suet, and boiled like a pudding. It is often served with much ceremony, accompanied by bagpipers and a reading of Robert Burns's poem "To a Haggis." More easily appreciated by non-Scots is *pot haggis*, a simpler version prepared in a pot.

Hair Seaweed. An edible Chinese seaweed.

Hairy Brinjal; Hairy Melons. A Chinese green squash often used for flavoring.

Haiti. Haitian food is strongly influenced by that of France, and typical French dishes are served throughout the island. The local Haitian cuisine is very individualistic and original.

    Before meals everyone drinks the *rhum* punch. Typical appetizers include *huitres marinées* (pickled oysters), and an avocado salad with a spicy sauce. Favorite soups are chicken, bean, and *bouillon crabes*, made with crabs, okra, and mushrooms. Chicken dishes are very popular, sometimes being cooked with rice and spices, or made into *poulet à la creole*, with hot pimientos.

Pork is also very popular; *cochon grillo* is fried pork with *ti-malice* sauce. This sauce is frequently served in Haiti; extremely sharp and burning, it is made from lime and sour orange juices, garlic, and hot peppers. *Gruau* is a spicy pork dish made with sour oranges (of an unbelievable acidity). Other Haitian dishes worthy of note are: *diri et djon-djon,* rice and black mushrooms; *mirliton* (much like squash); *conch* (a local shellfish); rice and kidney beans; *mais moulu* (cornmeal with red beans); *tasso* (air-dried meat or poultry cut into thin strips and marinated in lime juice); and *marinade* (fritters made with various ingredients). Typical desserts are baked bananas with molasses and *rhum*-preserved peaches.

Rhum is the local strong drink, served plain, as a punch, and in a cocktail. Strong black demitasse Haitian coffee, heavily sugared, is the invariable conclusion to a local meal.

Hake. (1) Merluche, a sea fish resembling the cod, found along the northern New England coast. Its meat is tender, white, flaky, and rather bland; may be prepared like cod. (2) The whiting, a food fish. (3) A beam or board from which cheeses are hung.

Hakkebøf (Danish). Chopped beefsteak.

Hakket (Danish). Minced, chopped.

Hakket Løg (Danish). Chopped onions.

Hakusai (Japanese). Chinese cabbage.

Halaszlé (Hungarian). Fish soup or stew made with sour cream.

Halb-Fuder. A wine cask containing 480 liters; used in the Moselle Valley, Germany.

Halbran (French). A small variety of duck.

Halb-Stück. A wine cask containing 640 liters; used in the Rhine and the Palatinate districts of Germany.

Halbrot (Swiss). Table wines made from a combination of white and black grapes. In German, *Schillerwein.*

Half-and-Half. (1) In the United States, a mixture of milk and sweet cream. (2) In England, a combination of two types of beer or ale.

Half-Glaze. Semiglaze; demiglaze.

Half om Half (Dutch). A sweet liqueur.

Half-Puff Paste. Paste in which only half the regular quantity of butter or fat is used.

Half-Quartern Loaf (British). A loaf of bread weighing 2 pounds.

Half-Sponge Process. A bread-making process in which most of the water is mixed with the yeast and half of the flour to form a batter. It is left for several hours to ferment, then the rest of the flour is added.

Halia (Malayan). Root ginger.

Halibut. A large flatfish frequenting the cold waters of the North Atlantic and Pacific. Its firm white flesh is much valued as food and may be prepared like cod.

The halibut may grow as long as 10 feet and weigh 300–500 pounds. Its skin can change color in chameleon fashion for camouflage. Both eyes are situated on the right side of the head, and the mouth is large, for gobbling up its prey, usually cod.

Halicot (French). A stewed dish, now called *haricot.*

Halieutic. Pertaining to fishing.

Halite. A natural rock salt.

Hallacas. The national dish of Venezuela consisting of a meat mixture covered with a cornmeal paste, wrapped in banana leaves or corn husks, and cooked until tender. Hallacas are served with a garnish of hard-cooked eggs, raisins, almonds, and olives. *See* Venezuela.

Hallan Cakes (British). Cakes made for All Saints' Day.

Hallaquitas. Small *hallacas,* the classic Venezuelan cornmeal dish, generally prepared in wrapped corn husks. *See* Hallacas; Venezuela.

Hallaur. One of the best-known Swiss red wines.

Hallgartener. A highly esteemed white wine produced in Hallgarten in the Rheingau region of Germany. *See* Germany, The Wines of.

Hallowis. A soft, sweet date found in the Middle East; known for its soft consistency and sweet taste.

Halo Halo (Philippine). An ice cream confection, similar to a soda; made by stirring several scoops of ice cream with syrup or candied fruits.

Halstrad (Swedish). Grilled, broiled.

Halstrad Hummer (Swedish). Broiled lobster.

Halwa (Indian). Dessert made with semolina, wheat, or lentils, or sometimes with carrots, beets, or pumpkin, cooked with milk, butter, and sugar.

Ham. (1) The thigh of any animal, especially the pig, used as food. (2) A cured and smoked leg of pork. Usually, only the hind legs are called hams; the fore legs, which are less delicate, are known as picnics, calas, or shoulders.

The Gauls of ancient France, who were efficient pig breeders, seem to have been the first to produce ham by the salting and smoking of pork. Their skill was so great that they became suppliers of ham not only to Rome but to the whole peninsula.

Ham is a most economical cut of meat, since even the bone can be used to give extra flavor to soup or vegetables.

Hams are cured by soaking in brine or covering with dry salt for 3 days or more, after which they are washed and smoked by any one of a variety of methods. Most American country hams tend to retain their salt, and should be soaked 6–12 hours, then simmered 3 hours or more to remove this excess. When the skin is removed and the fat trimmed, the ham will be ready for baking.

Tenderized hams are partially or entirely cooked before marketing. Proper cooking instructions are stated on the label.

Smithfield or *Virginia hams* come from pigs fed on peanuts and acorns, and are particularly flavorful when baked. They are dry-cured, then smoked and aged.

Many European hams are intended to be eaten uncooked. In this category are *Jambon de Bayonne*, the best-known ham from France; Italian *Prosciutto*; and the hams from Poland, Czechoslovakia, and Hungary. Both the English *York ham* and the *Asturias ham* from Spain should be boiled before eating.

Hambacher. The white wine from the Hambach vineyards of the Neustadt district of the Palatinate in Germany. *See* Germany, The Wines of.

Hamburg. (1) A black grape. (2) A small domestic fowl.

Hamburger; Hamburg Steak. A patty of ground meat, usually beef. The name probably originated about the turn of the century when German sailors asked the short-order cooks along the New York waterfront to prepare small patties of meat in the Hamburg style. The name caught on. At the St. Louis Fair in 1903 hamburgers were an immediate sensation. The hamburger may be a budget dish or a gourmet item, depending on the grade of meat used and on the elaborateness of preparation and service.

Hamburger Art (German). Cooked in the Hamburg style.

Hamburg Parsley; German Parsley. A hardy variety of parsley grown for its fleshy white root; eaten raw or cooked.

Hämchen (German). Pig's knuckles and sauerkraut.

Hamlet. An excellent food fish of the grouper family found in the Caribbean and Gulf of Mexico.

Hamlin. A very sweet type of orange, ideal for juice because of its high proportion of liquid.

Hammantaschen. A traditional three-cornered cake filled with prunes or poppy seeds and served during the Jewish holiday, Purim.

Hammelfleisch (German). Mutton.
>   **Hammelkeule.** Leg of mutton.
>   **Hammelkoteletten.** Mutton cutlets.
>   **Hammelschulter.** Shoulder of mutton.

Hammer. An oyster found in the Pacific Ocean, particularly between the mainland of Asia and the Philippine Islands.

Hanche (French). The loin or leg of lamb, mutton, or venison; the haunch.

Hand. (1) An indefinite quantity of food in a cluster resembling the shape of a hand, such as a hand of bananas. (2) A shoulder of pork.

Handa (Philippine). (1) A menu. (2) A preparation.

Hand Cheese. A small sour-milk, surface-ripened cheese, so called because it was originally molded by hand; sometimes flavored with caraway seeds. When well aged it has a sharp, pungent taste and odor. Local names for the same cheese include: German *Mainzer Handkäse, Berliner Kuhkäse, Satz,* and *Thuringia Caraway*; Russian *Livlander*; and Austrian *Olmutzer Quargeln* and *Olmutzer Bierkäse*. Small quantities are made by farm families of German descent in Pennsylvania.

Handhoven Bread (British). An oatmeal cake or bread.

Handing-Up. The process of weighing pieces of dough, forming them into balls, allowing them to rise, and then remolding them.

Handmade Bread. Bread mixed and prepared without machinery.

Hand of Pork. The foreleg of the pig; usually salted, then boiled; served either cold or hot.

Hand to Mouth. Originally, eating food as soon as it was bought or served; the immediate consumption of food obtained, with nothing saved for the future. Now, lacking provisions.

Hanging. Tenderizing meat or game by allowing it to hang in a cool, well-ventilated, very dry place.

Hangtown Fry. Fried oysters and scrambled eggs.

Hanpen (Japanese). A fishcake.

Haplosporidian. A microscopic member of the protozoan family, a parasite which attacks and destroys oysters; *see* MSX, the term used to describe the disease itself. This parasite is seldom found in waters which have less than a salinity of 15 parts for each 1,000 parts of water, or 1.5 percent of sea salts.

Haptule. A Ceylon tea, regarded as one of the best in the world.

Hard (Colloquial). Of liquors, having high alcoholic content.

Hard-Bake; Hard-Bake Toffee (British). An almond-filled toffeelike candy; made by boiling glucose and sugar to about 305°F., then pouring the mixture over a large amount of almonds.

Hard-Baked Bread. Bread baked too long in too cool an oven.

Hard Corn (British). Rye, wheat.

Harde Eieren (Dutch). Hard-cooked eggs.

Hard Federation Wheat. A hard white wheat grown along the Pacific coast of the United States. It is much stronger than most of the other Pacific coast wheats.

Hard Fish. Salted and dried ling and cod.

Hard Flour. A strong flour which needs a long fermentation period in order to ripen.

Hårdkogt Aeg (Danish). Hard-boiled egg.

Hard Sauce. An uncooked dessert sauce made with sugar and butter, and with flavoring if desired.

Hard-Shell Clam. An excellent clam found along the eastern coast of the United States from Massachusetts to Florida; measures 3–4 inches when mature.

Hardtack. A large, dry, very hard, salt-free biscuit formerly eaten by sailors because it was the only kind of bread that would not spoil on long voyages. New England pilot crackers are similar.

Hare. A wild rodent, closely related to the rabbit; its dark, highly flavored flesh may be prepared much like rabbit, but the flavor is gamier.

Harengiform. Herring-shaped.

Hareng Mariné (French). Pickled herring.

Hareng Bouffi (French). Lightly smoked and perishable herring.

Harenguets (French). Sprats.

Hare Soup (British). A brown cream soup made with hare or rabbit.

Haresteg (Danish). Roast hare.

Haricot (French). A stew of mutton or lamb with beans, turnips, potatoes, and other vegetables.

Haricots (French). Beans, including string beans, butter or lima (either fresh or dried), kidney, and navy beans. *See* Beans.

   Haricots Nains. Dwarf beans.

   Haricots Panachés. A mixture of string beans and flageolets.

   Haricots Rouges. Red beans; scarlet runners.

Harina de Maíz (Spanish). Corn flour.

Haring (Dutch). Herring.

Haringsla (Dutch). Herring salad.

Harlequin. Having several colors, such as harlequin ice cream.

Harness Cask. A covered cask formerly used for holding salted meats on board ship.

Harrach, Couteaux de. Ordinary red, *rosé*, and white Algerian wines. While none of them is important, they are all pleasant for everyday drinking.

Harsh. As applied to wine, unpleasant-tasting.

Harslet (British). A pig's fry (liver, sweetbreads, heart, etc.) sliced, seasoned, mixed with oatmeal or crumbs, wrapped in the skin surrounding the suet, and baked.

Hart. A male deer, particularly over five years old.

Hartford Election Cake. *See* Election Cake, Hartford.

Hartkäse. *See* Saanen.

Hartshorn. (1) A rarely used leavening agent, which must be dissolved in liquid before being used. (2) Fine shavings from a stag's horn; boiled to make jellies in medieval times.

Hartshorn Jelly (Obsolete). A stiff, gelatinous substance prepared in medieval times from the horn of a hart, the male deer; believed to impart strength and good health.

Harusame (Japanese). A noodle made from mung beans.

Harvest. (1) The time of the year when crops are reaped and gathered. (2) The crop.

Harvest Fish. (1) Dollarfish or butterfish. (2) Whiting, particularly in Virginia.

Harvest Home. The last harvest of a particular crop.

Harvesting. Gathering crops from the fields.

Harzé. A strong, aromatic, semicooked cheese made at the Trappist monastery in Belgium; it resembles Port du Salut.

Harzkäse. A very small German hand cheese made from sour milk, sometimes with caraway seeds added.

Hase im Topf (German). A rabbit pâté made with rabbit, pork, red wine, and brandy.

Haselhühner (German). Hazel hens.

Haselnuss (German). Hazelnut.

Hasenbraten (German). Roast hare.

Hasenpfeffer (German). A thick hare or rabbit stew.

Hash. Chopped or ground meats, poultry, fish, etc. (sometimes fresh, sometimes leftover), fried or baked with any desired ingredients, especially with potatoes and onions.

Hashi (Japanese). Chopsticks.

Haslet (Obsolete). A piece of meat ready for roasting.

Hasty Pudding. (1) In the United States, corn-meal mush. (2) In England, a flour or oatmeal mixture. (3) Alternate layers of cream puff paste and sweetened, partly cooked, sliced apples; after the top is sprinkled with a thick layer of sugar and cinnamon, the preparation is baked about 25 minutes in a moderate oven.

Hâtelet (French). Small silver skewers garnished with truffles, mushrooms, and aspic.

Hâtelette; Hâtelle (French). Small pieces of meat or giblets roasted on a skewer.

Hâtereau (French). (1) Sliced pig's liver wrapped in pig's caul and cooked on skewers. (2) Any hot appetizer made of chopped or ground food, dipped in bread crumbs, and fried crisp.

Hâtille (French). Fresh-roasted pork slices.

Hâtiveau (French). (1) Forced hothouse fruits or vegetables. (2) Very young early fruits or vegetables.

Hatted Kit; Hattit Kit (Scotch). Strained curds of milk covered with thick cream; served with sugar, cinnamon, or fruit, especially berries.

Hattenheimer. The white wine of the Hattenheim vineyards, which are among the finest in the Rheingau region of Germany. *See* Germany, The Wines of.

Hauber-Jannock. An oatcake.

Haulm (British). The stalks of beans, peas, or potatoes.

Haunch. The hind quarter of a domestic animal; with reference to game animals, such as a haunch of venison, usually the leg and loin.

Haunchbone. The large bone found in an animal's haunch.

Haupia (Hawaiian). A cornstarch pudding made with coconut cream.

Hausbrot (German). Bread made in the home from a mixture of wheat and rye flour.

Hausen. A large sturgeon.

Hausgeselchtes (German). Smoked pork.

Hautboy. A large white delicate-flavored strawberry.

Haut-Brion. A famous Bordeaux wine. A product of the renowned vineyards of the Château Haut-Brion in the Bordeaux region of France, it is the only wine made in the Graves district which has a "Grand Cru" classification. The red is best known, but a small quantity of excellent white is also produced. *See* France, The Wines of.

Haut-Dahra. A group of fruity Algerian wines. The red wines have good balance, but the white wines tend to be sour.

Hauteluce. A rather plain cow's-milk cheese made in the Savoy district of France.

Hautes-Côtes-de-Bourgogne. A part of the Burgundy wine region of France which produces some of the country's finest wines. *See* France, The Wines of.

Haut-Goût (French). (1) Literally, a high or fine taste. (2) A term describing the flavor of well-aged game; similar to *faisandé*. (3) Strong seasoning.

Haut-Sauternes. A white wine produced in the Bordeaux region of France. *See* France, The Wines of.

Havarti. A slightly sharp Danish cheese kneaded into leaf shapes or rounds and packed in foil.

Haven. An apéritif drink made from oats.

Havercakes (British). Thin, flat barley-meal or oat cakes dried after being baked on a hot plate.

Havermout (Dutch). Oatmeal.

Havers (British). Oat flour.

Havers Oats (British). Wild, uncultivated oats.

Havir (French). To brown quickly.

Hawaii. The cuisine of Hawaii has been influenced by its remarkably varied populations: the native, Japanese, Chinese, Portuguese, and American. Meals may begin with *tariyaki*, a Japanese appetizer of marinated beef on skewers, followed by a native island dish of pickled salmon, and then proceed to an American steak. In few places in the world are there so many different factors influencing the local cuisine.

The fish is usually quite good, although many varieties have an insipid taste; the shellfish is uniformly excellent, particularly the shrimp. Although now a fair amount of beef and lamb is available, the natives much prefer pork, especially when prepared as *kalua puaa*, barbecued pig. *Laulaus*, pork and fish, steamed in *ti* leaves are typical of the island taste in food. Chicken dishes are also well liked, and chicken, spinach, and taro leaves cooked in coconut milk, *moa luau a me wai niu*, is an interesting dish; plain boiled or broiled chicken is seldom served.

The classic feast of the natives is a *luau*, at which all of the traditional dishes of the islands are served. *Lomi*, made with smoked or salted salmon and scallions, is typical. *Laulau*, mentioned above, is another regular *luau* dish. The main course is almost always barbecued pig. The Hawaiians love *poi*, a starchy paste that takes the place of bread, rice, and potatoes. *Poi* is made from the taro root and has a pasty quality which most people dislike at first but eventually learn to tolerate. It comes in varying consisten-cies, is almost tasteless, and is eaten with the fingers; thus, there are two-finger and three-finger *pois*.

The favorite desserts are fruits and melons, but puddings and other sweets are made, usually of coconuts or bananas. The favorite island strong drink is *okolehao*, a homemade firewater.

Hawebake (British). Plain-tasting food; routine fare.

Hawfinch; Grosbeck. A small game bird which, when roasted, has a rather good flavor.

Hawick Bake (British, Scotch). A hard scone flavored with allspice.

Hawker. One who sells foods in the street.

Hawkey. A feast held at harvest time after the crops are in, especially in rural England.

Haws. The fruit of the hawthorn, a hedge-type shrub; used for dessert or in jam, jelly, or preserves.

Haybox Cooking; Fireless Cooking. A method of preparing food in which the food is cooked for a short time, then placed in an insulated container, the haybox, where it remains hot for many hours and cooking continues without further use of fuel.

Hay Cheese; Fromage au Foin. A French cheese allowed to ripen on new-mown hay.

Hay Diet. An outmoded dietetic system based on the theory that carbohydrates and proteins should not be eaten at the same meal.

Hayons. A soft, creamy cheese resembling a Camembert; produced in Normandy, France.

Hazel Grouse. *See* Hazel Hen.

Hazel Hen. The ruffed grouse, a game bird whose white, tender flesh may be prepared like quail. On occasion, the bird may have an unpleasantly gamy taste.

Hazelnut. The fruit of a shrublike tree common in the United States and Europe. Rich in oil and pleasant tasting, it is commonly used in confectionery. *See* Filbert.

Headcheese. A jellied loaf made with the meat from the head of a calf or pig, highly seasoned and molded in its natural aspic.

Heady. As applied to wines or liquors, tending to cause dizziness or intoxication.

Health Foods. A large group of foods eaten in their natural, unprocessed state, such as all whole-grained food, nuts, honey, and unprocessed sugars.

Heart. The hearts of beef, lamb, pork, and veal, when properly cooked, can make a palatable inexpensive dish. Lamb hearts are the most tender; beef hearts are the largest and toughest.

Hearts are washed thoroughly and all veins, arteries, and fat are removed. Long, slow cooking with moist heat gives the best possible results. In Peru, *anticuchos* are pieces of beef heart dipped in a spicy sauce and grilled.

Hearth Cake (British). A cake or loaf baked on the hearth.

Heart of Palm. The very green tender terminal bud of certain palm trees before it grows out of the stem; called *palmito* in Brazil. Heart of palm may be eaten in salads, as garnish for various dishes, etc.

Hearty. As applied to food or drink, satisfying or plentiful.

Heartily. With a good appetite.

Heat. To raise the temperature of liquid or solid foods.

Heath Cock; Mountain Cock. A large European game bird; often 3 feet in length.

Heavies (British). Heavy cakes similar to rock cakes; made in Sussex.

Heavy Syrup. Concentrated mixture of sugar and water.

Hecht (German). Pike.

Heckle Biscuit (British). A cooky pricked before baking to make small holes.

Hedge Garlic. Garlic-flavored wild mustard.

Hedgehog Fruit. The prickly fruit of an Australian tree.

Hedgehog Mushroom. An edible mushroom with a prickly membrane.

Hedgehog Pudding. A spongecake baked in an oval pan, soaked in wine, covered with custard, and studded closely with blanched and split almonds standing upright to resemble hedgehog or porcupine quills.

Hedge Mustard. A South African wild plant often used as a vegetable.

Heel. The end, top, or bottom crust of a loaf of bread.

Hee Maka (Hawaiian). A raw-octopus dish.

Heifer. A young (female) cow that has not yet had a calf.

Heilbot (Dutch). Halibut.

Heilbutt (German). Halibut.

Heiltz-le-Maurupt. A fresh cream cheese produced in the Champagne region of France; eaten fresh.

Helados (Spanish). (1) Ice cream. (2) Any frozen dish.

Heldere Soep (Dutch). Clear soup.

Held-on-Cake (British). An oatcake.

Helgeflundra (Swedish). Halibut.

Helles (German). Light beer.

Helluo (British, Colloquial). One who eats too much.

Helmet Crab. A member of the king crab family with very tasty white flesh; eaten plain or used in cooking.

Helmet Quail. An excellent-tasting American quail with a curled crest.

Helstekt (Norwegian). Fried.

Helvelles; Monk's Morels. A type of wild fungus found in various parts of Europe; the taste is similar to that of mushrooms, but usually not quite so good.

Helzel (Jewish). Stuffed neck of poultry.

Hen. (1) Any female fowl, particularly a chicken. (2) The female of various other birds, fish, or animals, such as the lobster.

Henware. An edible seaweed.

Hepper. A two-year-old salmon.

Heptyl Isobutyrate. A colorless liquid used to supply the synthetic flavor of pineapple, peach, or coconut to food.

Herb. *See* Herbs.

Herbage. The flexible stems and leaves of edible plants.

Herbal. (1) A book about herbs. (2) Pertaining to herbs.

Herbalist. (1) One who has considerable knowledge of herbs. (2) One who sells herbs.

Herbarium. A systematic arrangement of dried plants.

Herb Bennet. A wild plant whose leaves are sometimes used as a flavoring ingredient; the roots are occasionally used as a vegetable.

Herb Bouquet. An assortment or mixture of herbs,

either tied together or inserted in a small cloth bag, used to flavor soups and stews.

Herbesthal. A German cheese strongly flavored with herbs or made from the milk of cows allowed to graze in grasses rich in herbs.

Herb Ivy. A species of chive used for flavoring sauces and salads.

Herbs. A wide variety of seed plants, both wild and cultivated, whose leaves, stems, seeds or roots are used to give flavor or color to almost any food. Herbs are available in fresh or dried form, and they are frequently employed as a garnish to enhance the appearance of a dish as well as to improve its taste. Many have also been used for medicinal purposes.

To give dried herbs a fresh taste, soak them in water for a few minutes before using. Buy small amounts of dried herbs, and keep them in tightly closed jars in a cool place.

The most common herbs are:

Angelica	Lemon Verbena
Anise	Marjoram or Sweet
Balm	Marjoram
Basil or Sweet Basil	Mint
Borage	Oregano
Brunet	Parsley
Camomile	Peppermint
Caraway	Rosemary
Chervil	Saffron
Chives	Sage
Coriander	Savory
Cress	Sesame
Dill	Sorrel
Fennel	Spearmint
Horehound	Tansy
Horseradish	Tarragon
Hyssop	Thyme

Aromatic Herbs. Such herbs as clove, cardamom, cumin, caraway, anise, nutmeg, and ginger.

Stimulant Herbs. Such herbs as pepper, tumeric, and mustard.

Sweet Herbs. Such herbs as marjoram, fennel, thyme, basil, and sage.

Herb Tea. A hot drink made like tea, by pouring boiling water over flavorful leaves, flowers, or the seeds of some herb. Several of such potions are thought to have medicinal value. Best-known herb teas are those made with balm, camomile, dill, fennel, hyssop, marigold, mint, pennyroyal, rosemary, sage, and tansy.

Hereford. A breed of cattle having a white face and a reddish body with white markings.

Heringsalat (German). Herring salad.

Herkimer. A cheddar-type American cheese.

Hermit. A spice cooky containing fruits and nuts.

Hermitage. A hearty red wine produced along the banks of the Rhône River in France. Though rather crude when young, it matures into a smooth wine. The white wines of the region are quite good, too. *See also* France, The Wines of.

Hermit Crab. A crustacean of the crab family that inhabits abandoned mollusk shells; prepared like shrimp or crab.

Hero Sandwich. A long loaf of bread split in two and filled with assorted meats and condiments. Half a hero sandwich is called a *coward*.

Herrgårdsost. A Swedish cheese, medium firm, with a sweet, nutty flavor and a pleasing aroma. It is made from partly skimmed cow's milk, and when cured, contains eyes similar to those in Gruyère.

Herring. An important food fish, not only nutritious but also delicious, plentiful, and economical. Native to the North Atlantic, the herring breeds prodigiously; the average female lays about 50 million eggs annually, so the fish never appear scarce or in danger of becoming extinct, though they are caught by the millions each day in season.

A herring is silvery white on the sides and stomach, with a greenish-blue streak along its back. There are more than 200 varieties. Herring bones have been found in prehistoric caves along the coasts of Denmark, France, and Portugal. Herring fishing was an established industry in Norway at the beginning of the 11th century, and the art of salting the fish dates back to the 14th century. The practice of smoking herring began less than a hundred years later.

Kippers are slightly smoked herring. *Bloaters* are slightly salted and smoked. Young herring are sometimes canned as *sardines*.

Herring Family. Herring is *Clupea Harengus*.

Young herrings are sild. Sprats are *Clupea Sprattus*; the young are brislings. Pilchard is *Clupea Pilchardus*; the young are sardines. Kippers, bloaters, and red-herrings are salted and smoked herrings; bucklings are hot-smoked herrings. *Gaffelbitar* are preserved herring.

Herring Pond. The North Atlantic Ocean, where herring are plentiful.

Herring, Salt. Herring that has been preserved in barrels among layers of salt for about a week.

Herring, Smoked. Lightly salted, smoked herring prepared in somewhat different fashions in various countries. *See also* Bloaters and Kippers.

Herve (Belgian). (1) A strong cheese made from skimmed cow's milk. (2) A soft fermented Limburger-type cheese molded in 6-inch cubes.

Hervido (Venezuelan). A meat-and-vegetable stew.

Hete Bliksem (Dutch). Pork chops with apples and potatoes, highly peppered.

Het Pint (Scotch). A favorite drink during Hogmanay, consisting of hot ale, eggs, sugar, and whisky. *See* Hogmanay.

Heurige. Light young Austrian wines.

Hewe (Obsolete). A domestic servant or cook.

Hicaco. The tropical coco plum.

Hickory Nut. Fruit of an American tree of the walnut family; it contains much fat and is commonly used in cakes, cookies, and candy.

Hickory-Smoked Cheese. Routine cheeses smoked to make them suitable with cocktails and as snacks.

Hickory-Smoked Salmon. Salmon smoked by the burning of hickory wood.

Hielo (Spanish). Ice.

Hierbabuena (Spanish). Mint.

High. Of game or poultry, having acquired a strong odor as a result of aging.

High-Altitude Cooking. Most recipes are devised for cooking at sea level; while the results will not be appreciably different until attempted at altitudes higher than 3,000 feet, from that point on differences in air pressure will affect most cooking processes.

The higher the altitude, the lower the temperature at which water will boil; on very high mountain tops, water boils when almost lukewarm. However, because of differences in air density, it is necessary to increase the length of time when boiling foods.

Certain adaptations have to be made with baking recipes used at 3,000 feet or higher. Inasmuch as flour becomes drier and more compact at high altitudes, slightly less can be used than a standard recipe calls for. Yeast, too, should be used somewhat sparingly, since yeast action is greater at higher altitudes. Baking temperature should be increased slightly; for example, if the recipe calls for 350°F., the oven temperature should be increased to 360°F. However, high-altitude baking varies from recipe to recipe, and only by experimenting will it be possible to find the correct allowances and necessary adjustments.

Highback. The whitefish.

Highball. A tall drink of whisky, usually Scotch, rye, or bourbon, diluted with water or soda or ginger ale, and served with ice.

Highland Creasy. *See* Cress, Upland.

High Tea (British). A late-afternoon meal that sometimes takes the place of dinner. Accompanied by tea, it usually consists of bread and butter, jam, scones, and cakes together with a hot dish or, in summer, of a cold-meat salad with fruit or a tart.

High Yeast. The yeast that rises to the surface when alcoholic liquors are fermenting.

Higos (Spanish). Figs.

Hildesheimer. A German sausage made of two-thirds fat and one-third pork liver; it spreads readily and is used in sandwiches.

Hilsa. A fish similar to mackerel.

Himbeer. An outstanding German liqueur made from raspberries; it has a fine, dry finish, and an excellent aroma reminiscent of fresh berries.

Himbeer Torte (German). Raspberry tart.

Himmel und Erde (German). Sausages, fried onions, applesauce, and mashed potatoes.

Hin. A Jewish liquid measure, especially for wine, containing a little more than a gallon.

Hind. (1) A three-year-old female deer, once considered the choicest of all game. (2) A fish of the grouper family.

Hindbaer (Danish). Raspberries.

Hindberry. Raspberry.

Hindquarter. The hind leg and loin of a domestic animal, such as beef.

Hind Shank. The upper part of a hind leg of beef, veal, or lamb.

Hinojo (Spanish). Fennel.

Hippocras. A medieval spiced and sweetened wine, so named because it was strained through a woolen bag called "Hippocrates' sleeve." It was supposedly invented as a means of making sour wine drinkable by the addition of honey, herbs, and spices.

Hircine. Similar to or resembling a goat.

Hirne (German). Brains.

Hirschbraten (German). Roast venison.

Hishio. A Japanese flavoring or seasoning once popular, especially in medieval times. It was included as a part of the pay for soldiers and officials.

Histy Bread (British). A bread, heavy and streaked because it is underbaked.

Hjemmelaget Gravlaks (Norwegian). Salted salmon.

Hjerne (Danish). Brains.

Hobnob. To drink together; to be friendly with or associate (with someone). In medieval England a drinking term exclusively, from the tavern phrase "hob or nob," that is, to give or take a drink.

Hocco. A South and Central American game bird with an excellent, although gamy flavor.

Hochepot. See Hotch-Potch.

Hochepot de Queue de Boeuf (French). Braised oxtail cooked with vegetables.

Hochfeinste (German). Of wine, fine, excellent, the very best; however, the term represents merely the grower's opinion. See Germany, The Wines of.

Hochgewachs. A German wine term, designating an outstanding growth; its meaning is imprecise inasmuch as each wine grower uses it differently.

Hochheimer. The white wine from the Hochheim vineyards in the Rheingau region of Germany. See Germany, The Wines of.

Hock. The British term for white Rhine wine, probably deriving from the popularity of the vintages from the Hochheimer vineyards. Hock is usually bottled in long, thin, tapering bottles.

Hocket (British). A large lump of bread.

Hoecake (American). A bread or cake made of cornmeal, salt, and water; so named because it was originally baked on the heated blade of a hoe.

Hog. A fully grown pig intended for slaughter.

Hogfat. All fat found on a hog; specifically, the fat surrounding the kidney, which is used in France.

Hogen-Mogen (Obsolete). A strong drink.

Hogfish. A large fish found off the coast of Florida and the West Indies. It is usually good for food, but particularly large specimens are reputed to be poisonous in some areas.

Hoggaster (Obsolete). (1) A three-year-old pig. (2) Any young pig or sheep.

Hoggerel. A two-year-old sheep.

Hoggery. An area where pigs are kept.

Hogget. (1) A two-year-old male pig. (2) A one-year-old sheep.

Hogmanay. The Scottish New Year's Eve; the exact meaning or origin of the term has been lost in a series of conflicting explanations and folklore. Children come to the door of private homes asking for their "Hogmanay" and receive candies, cake, and oranges. A classic food for this holiday is the Hogmanay bannock, an oatcake with a hole in the center, flavored with caraway seeds, and with rays around the edge imitative of the sun's rays. The favorite drink of this celebration is the Het Pint, a mixture of hot ale, eggs, sugar, and whisky. Also popular is Athole brose. See Athole Brose.

Hognut. Earthnut or pignut.

Hogo (Obsolete). A strong, disagreeable flavor.

Hog Plum. (1) Spondias, a tropical fruit resembling a plum but best used for making jams, preserves, etc. (2) A wild lime native to Florida. (3) Kědondong, a small fruit-bearing plant of the mango family.

Hog's Flesh. Pork.

Hog's Grease. Hog fat; lard.

Hogshead. (1) A very large barrel used to hold various liquids; its capacity varies from country to country, but it usually ranges from 63 to 140 gallons. In most instances, 63 gallons is the usual measure. (2) In Britain, 46 gallons of Bordeaux wine, 54 gallons of beer, or 52½ imperial gallons.

Hog's Head Cheese. A jellied preparation made with meat from a hog's head; pork brawn.

Hogweed. An herb fed to hogs; not considered suitable for humans, although edible. *See* Cow Parsnip.

Hohenheim. A soft round German cheese made from partly skimmed milk.

Hojaldre. A spice cake prepared with wine.

Holibut. Another name for halibut.

Hollandaise Collée. Hollandaise sauce extended with a flour-and-water mixture.

Hollandaise Sauce. A golden, rich sauce for eggs, fish, or vegetables, made primarily of butter, egg yolks, and lemon juice.

Hollandässås (Swedish). Hollandaise sauce.

Holländische Sosse (German). Hollandaise sauce.

Hollands Gin. A general term for all dry gins made in the Netherlands.

Hollandse Haring. Dutch herring.

Hollow-Stem Champagne Glass. A stemmed glass chiefly used for sparkling wines, having a hollow stem so that the bubbles máy be seen rising. This type of glass is less popular than formerly because the hollow stem cannot be properly cleaned.

Hollow Ware. Bowl- or tube-shaped metalware or earthenware.

Holsteiner Schnitzel (German). Veal cutlet served with a fried egg and an anchovy.

Holstein Health. A German cooked cheese made of sour milk curd.

Holstein Skim-Milk Cheese. A German saffron-colored cheese made with skim milk and fresh buttermilk.

Holy Bread. Bread blessed and distributed at a church.

Hom. An ancient Persian sacred plant and its edible juice.

Homard (French). Lobster.

   Homard Cardinal. Lobster steamed in court-bouillon, then sliced and combined with mushrooms and truffles in *sauce cardinal*.

   Homard Française. Lobster cooked in white wine, Cognac, and vegetables.

   Homard Newburg. Lobster meat cooked in a court-bouillon, then sliced and combined with sherry, Cognac, and cream.

Homarine. Resembling or pertaining to lobster.

Home Brew. Any homemade alcoholic drink, particularly beer.

Home Economics. The field of subjects related to the management and general welfare of the household, such as nutrition and cookery.

Home Freezer. An electrical appliance for freezing foods or keeping them frozen. "Deep Freeze" is the trade mark of one such appliance.

Homer. A Jewish liquid measure with a capacity of about 80 gallons.

Hominy. Dried and treated corn kernels used as a substitute for rice or potatoes or as a cereal. The kernels may also be ground into a coarse meal, called *hominy grits*, widely popular in the southern United States. *Pearled hominy* is degermed hulled corn.

Homogenized Milk. Milk in which the cream does not separate because it has been forced through fine openings at great pressure to break up the fat and casein, resulting in a liquid much smoother and more easily digestible than regular milk.

Homse (Algerian). Small balls of dough cooked, dried, and served with a honey syrup or coating.

Honan. A province of China which gives its name to a culinary style in which foods are often very spicy, small hot red peppers being used as a flavoring ingredient. Sweet-and-sour dishes are also imaginatively prepared in Honan.

Honde Portie. A combination of shrimp, eggs, steaks, and curry; a favorite in parts of the Dutch West Indies.

Honduras. *See* Central America.

Honey. A sweet viscous food made by bees from flower nectar and secreted in wax honeycombs (masses of wax cells). Its taste, color, and viscosity vary considerably, depending upon the type of plants on which the bees feed. It is one of the oldest sweets known to man, and the Old Testament described the ideal land as one "flowing with milk and honey." It is a wholesome food and may be substituted for any form of sugar in the diet, for it is assimilated completely and easily, and is an excellent source of quick energy.

Originally, wild honey was the only source of supply, but after the technique of artificial hives was devised, beekeeping became an industry in temperate zones.

The outstanding American honeys are the

white clover, basswood, and buckwheat. Honey is produced all over the world, and that of France, Greece, and Scotland is highly regarded. Honey is marketed both in liquid form and with the comb. It has been estimated that bees must extract the nectar from 2½ million flowers to produce one pound of honey.

Comb Honey. Honey sold in the comb. When cut into very small squares and packaged it is known as *cut comb honey*.

Chunk Honey. Bottled honey containing small chunks of the comb.

Extracted Honey. Liquid honey.

Honey-Ball Melon. A small round slightly netted melon varying in color from light green to gray to yellow. The flesh is thick, green, and delicious. The melon keeps well and can be bought and held for several days until properly ripe.

Unripe melons can be identified by their hardness and the greenish white color of the rind. Overripeness shows in mold and in dark sunken damp areas.

Honey Bean. A honey-colored bean. When young the whole pods can be cooked and eaten like green beans; the older beans are shelled and dried to be used like other dried beans.

Honeyberry. A sweet, highly perishable West Indian berry.

Honeyblob. A sweet yellow gooseberry.

Honey Bread. Another name for carob, a fruit found in the Middle East.

Honeycomb. A set of hexagonal wax cells into which bees secrete honey.

Honeycomb Toffee (British). A crunchy hard candy; *See* Cinder Toffee.

Honeydew Melon. An oval-shaped melon, creamy yellow when fully ripe, with green, very sweet, juicy flesh. In a ripe melon the small round scar at one end yields slightly to the touch, and there is a faint pleasant odor. Unripe fruit is hard and whitish-green. Honeydews are available all year but are most plentiful in June and July.

Honeydrop. One drop of honey; a sweet candy.

Honeyed. Covered or sweetened with honey.

Honeyfall. Another name for the honeydew melon.

Honey Fungus. A mediocre green, brown, or yellow mushroom.

Honeyware. An edible seaweed which may be boiled and served as a green vegetable like spinach.

Hong Geong (Chinese). Dried sugared ginger.

Hongos (Spanish). Mushrooms.

Hongroise, À la. In the Hungarian style; a cream sauce liberally seasoned with paprika.

Honing (Dutch). Honey.

Honky-Tonk (Colloquial). A low-class tavern or saloon serving alcoholic drinks.

Honningkake (Norwegian). Honey cake.

Honorius, St. Patron saint of bakers whose day is celebrated on September 30, when he is shown holding a tray containing three loaves of bread.

Høns (Danish). Chicken.

Hønsekødsuppe (Danish). Chicken-and-vegetable soup.

Hønsesalat (Danish). Chicken salad.

Honung (Swedish). Honey.

Hooch (Colloquial). All alcoholic drinks; often applied only to illegally produced liquor.

Hoochow. A Chinese green tea with a light, pleasing flavor.

Hooker (American, Colloquial). A good-sized drink of any alcoholic beverage, such as a hooker of bourbon.

Hootsla (Pennsylvania Dutch). Omelet in which sautéed bread cubes are added to the egg mixture before frying.

Hop; Hopfen. A very small German cheese packed in hops to mature.

Hop Back. A hops strainer used in beer making.

Hop Beer. A homemade drink made with hops, sugar, water, and yeast, and ready to drink within a few days.

Hopjes. Small hard coffee-flavored Dutch candies.

Hopper. (1) One who picks hops. Also, the keg in which hops are prepared for beer making. (2) (Indian). Coconut-flavored pancake or griddle cake made with a fermented batter; also called *Appas*.

Hopper Cake. A seedcake.

Hops. The flowerlike cones of a perennial climbing plant which are dried and used as a flavoring agent for porter, ale, and beer. The hop plant is cultivated extensively in most of Europe and in many parts of the United States. Blossoms are harvested in the late summer. Young shoots, cut in the spring, are delicious as a salad or when boiled and served like asparagus.

Hop Shoots. The tender young flower of the male hop plant; cooked and eaten as a green vegetable.

Hopvine. The vine on which hops grow.

Horchata (Spanish). A milky almond-flavored soft drink.

Hordein. A protein present in barley.

Horehound. A bitter herb related to the mint family; used in flavoring beverages and candies.

Hörnchen Roll. A horseshoe-shaped bread roll popular in Germany and Austria.

Horned Pout. Another name for the catfish.

Hornfish. Another name for the garfish.

Horno, Al (Spanish). Baked.

Horn of Plenty. A brown or gray trumpet-shaped wild mushroom with a pleasing taste and texture.

Hors d'Âge. When appearing on a bottle of French brandy or Cognac, indicates that the contents may well be older than shown on the bottle.

Hors d'Oeuvre (French). "Outside the meal"; tasty tidbits intended to stimulate the appetite, served in addition to the menu. They may be hot or cold, and may accompany drinks or may precede a dinner as do smorgasbord and antipasto.

Horse Bean. Broad bean.

Horse Cheese. Caciocavallo, an Italian cheese whose traditional trade mark is a horse's head.

Horse Chestnut. A seed fruit with a high starch content. When properly processed, the nuts can be ground into a very nutritious flour.

Horse Flesh. *See* Horsemeat.

Horse Mackerel. A fish more akin to tuna than to mackerel, sometimes used as an inferior substitute.

Horsemeat; Horse Flesh. A wholesome and nutritious meat when properly cooked, though far inferior in tenderness and flavor to beef and mutton. It is consumed to some extent among the very poor in certain European countries. In the United States it is used primarily as an additive to dog food.

Horse Mushroom. A field mushroom whose top measures at least 5 inches across. When bruised or cut, its flesh turns an unpleasant brown, and it has a strong taste.

Horse Parsley. A large-leafed parsley.

Horse Plum. A coarse red plum.

Horseradish. A European herb cultivated for its pungent root, which is ground and used as a condiment. It is used in many sauces, particularly to accompany seafood, and tends to stimulate the appetite. The fresh root, grated or shaved into thin slivers, is excellent with roast beef or steak.

Horseradish Tree. A Southeast Asian tree whose long pods, often called "drumsticks," may, when young, be eaten as a green vegetable. The leaves too, are edible.

Horseshoe Crab; King Crab. A crustacean found extensively along the coast of Maine and southward along the shores of the Atlantic.

Horse's Neck. A tall iced nonalcoholic drink made of ginger ale and a long curling strip of lemon peel.

Horse Thistle (Obsolete). Wild lettuce.

Hortaliças (Portuguese). Vegetables.

Hortyard (Obsolete). A fruit orchard.

Hoska (Pennsylvania Dutch). A long sweet yeast raisin bread or coffeecake baked in several braided layers.

Hospice. An inn where travelers may stop overnight and have something to eat.

Hospice de Beaune. *See* France, The Wines of.

Hospitage. A hospice, or inn, where food and refreshment are available.

Hostelry. Hotel; inn.

Hostess. (1) A woman who receives guests in her own home, serving them food and refreshment and entertaining them. (2) A paid employee who greets and seats patrons in a restaurant.

Hostry (Obsolete). Hostelry; inn.

Hot Bread. A quick bread raised with baking powder.

Hot Buttered Rum. A winter rum drink containing butter, particularly popular at ski resorts or wherever it is cold and people want a hot rum drink.

Hotch-Potch (Scotch). A stew or soup made from the neck of mutton, with peas, barley, vegetables, and diced meat.

Hotch-Potchsoppa (Swedish). Stew-soup.

Hot Cross Bun. A small bun with a cross of white sugar icing on top; usually eaten on Good Friday, or, in the United States, during Lent.

Hot Dog. Frankfurter; also called a *red-hot*, *frank*, and *weenie*. It may be boiled or grilled, or may be a main course when accompanied by cabbage or sauerkraut; a quick lunch when served on a long split roll with mustard and relish; or a picnic delight when roasted over an open fire. Hot dogs acquired social acceptance when they were included on a menu served to King George VI and Queen Elizabeth of England during their visit with President and Mrs. Franklin Roosevelt at Hyde Park.

Hotel. A place that offers lodging and meals to paying guests.

Hot Plate. A small portable stove, using either gas or electricity, with one or two burners or heating units mounted on a low frame.

Hot Pot (British). (1) A hot drink of beer. (2) A casserole of potatoes and onions or of beef and potatoes.

Hotspur. An early green pea.

Hot-Water Crust. A pastry dough made with very hot water and fat.

Hot With. A mixture of liquor, sugar, and water.

Hough; Hough Sinew (Obsolete). A leg of beef or venison.

Houting. A whitefish.

Hovis Flour. The trade mark of a flour and bread made with wheat germ.

Howtowdie (Scotch). A young chicken, especially a pullet.

Huacatay. A Peruvian culinary herb, often used to flavor foods at a *pachamanca*, a picnic, together with a spicy *ají*, pepper sauce.

Huachinango (Spanish). Red snapper.

Huasvulcli (Mexican). A dish made of eggs, tomatoes, and cheese, usually served during Holy Week.

Hubert, St. Patron saint of hunters. Many game dishes are named for him.

Huch. A Danube River fish vaguely resembling salmon. In English, *huck*.

Huck. (1) Haunch, the leg and loin of a game animal. (2) *See* Huch.

Huckle. Haunch, the leg and loin of a game animal.

Huckleberry. A widely distributed American wild berry very similar to the blueberry but with larger, harder seeds. Huckleberries are excellent for use in pies, tarts, and puddings, and for jam, jelly, and preserves. *See also* Blueberry.

Huckle-My-Buff (British). A strong punch prepared with beer, brandy, and eggs.

Huevas de Lisa (Venezuelan). Roe of the *lisa* (striped mullet), dried, salted, and eaten as an appetizer.

Huevos (Spanish). Eggs.

> **Huevos al Plato.** Fried eggs.
> **Huevos Blandos.** Poached eggs.
> **Huevos Duros.** Hard-cooked eggs.
> **Huevos Escalfados.** Shirred eggs.
> **Huevos Flamenco.** Fried eggs and sausages.
> **Huevos Fritos.** Fried eggs.
> **Huevos Pasados por Agua.** Boiled eggs.
> **Huevos Revuiltos.** Scrambled eggs.

Huevos Chimbos (Peruvian). Egg custard, made with arrowroot, decorated with almonds, cloves, and raisins, and served with a white wine syrup.

Huffcap (Obsolete). A strong liquor or ale.

Hugmatee (Obsolete, British). A kind of ale.

Huguenote (French). A very large earthenware pan used for baking large fowl; also, a stewpan or soup casserole.

Huhn (German). Chicken.

Hühner (German). Chickens.

> **Hühnerbrühe mit Nudeln.** Chicken soup with noodles.
> **Hühnerbrüstchen.** Breast of chicken.
> **Hühnerflügel.** Chicken wings.
> **Hühnerfrikassee.** Chicken fricassee.
> **Hühnerklein.** Chicken giblets.
> **Hühnerleber.** Chicken livers.

Huile (French). Oil.

> **Huile d'Arachides.** Peanut oil; groundnut oil.
> **Huile d'Oeillette.** Poppy-seed oil, odorless, colorless, and almost tasteless.
> **Huile d'Olive.** Olive oil.

Hukussi (Japanese). Pickled vegetables.

Hull. To remove the calyx of a fruit or vegetable, the stems of berries, or the shells of nuts.

Huller. Small metal tweezers used to remove the calyx or stem of a strawberry.

Hulls. The horny outer covering of cereal grains, maize, buckwheat, rice, etc. Because of the high fiber content they are of limited use as animal feed.

Hummer (Danish, German, Norwegian, Swedish). Lobster.

Hummersalat (Danish). Lobster salad.

Hummus (Arabic). Chick-peas.

Humpback. Another name for the whitefish.

Humpty-Dumpty (British). A boiled brandy-and-ale mixture.

Hungary. A half-century ago, the Hungarian cuisine had so great a variety and scope that even French chefs commented on its originality. Although Hungary was once joined with its neighbor Austria, the Hungarians have always been comparatively unrestrained in their opposition to Austria's conservatism. While Austrians danced to the waltz, the Hungarians showed their preference for free gipsy music. The same tendencies are noticeable in the Hungarian cuisine, which differs sharply from that of Austria and the other Western European countries. Stimulating tastes and bright colors and great imagination in the use of herbs and spices are evident in the Hungarian cuisine.

The classic dish of the country is, of course, goulash (*gulyás*) which may be roughly described as a paprika dish. It may be made with beef, pork, veal, chicken, or fish, and the ingredients may be in large or small pieces, but paprika is always the flavoring ingredient. Of well over two dozen different dishes, certain basic ones are the most popular. *Gulyás* is made of meat; *tokány* has meat cut in smaller pieces and served with a great deal of pepper; *pörkölt* is usually of onions and veal; and *paprikás* has sour cream added.

Since Hungary has no coastline, the ocean or Mediterranean fish are of little importance; the single outstanding fish of the country is the superb Lake Balaton *fogas*. Otherwise the national taste inclines toward river fish, like carp. Soups are likely to be satisfying and filling. *Bableves csipetkével*, bean soup with dumplings, and *gulyásleves*, goulash soup, are good examples.

There is a great liking for noodles, dumplings, and other dough preparations; *gombóc*, flour dumplings, are one of a hundred possibilities. Cheeses are important, and so popular is paprika

that it is added to a cheese called *liptói*. Also worthy of mention is that poppy seeds are served on everything possible—cakes, noodles, and in strudels. There is also considerable use of caraway and dill, as well as paprika.

Desserts are superb, for Hungarians dearly love pastries and cakes of all kinds. The two outstanding desserts are probably strudel (*rétes*) and *dobos torta*, a chocolate-and-caramel cake. Strudel is made with a wide variety of ingredients, poppy seeds, apples, cherries, cheese, or nuts being typical.

Most Hungarian table wines are of fair quality, that is, drinkable but not important to connoisseurs. The most renowned (or publicized) table wine of the country is *Egri Bikavér*, or "Bull's Blood," so called because it is extremely dark red. Other important red wines are produced in Nemes and Szekszard. The most interesting white wine is probably the *Samlyoi Furmint*.

Tokay is, of course, the truly important wine of Hungary, although its reputation was far greater several centuries ago than today, and it is the only important wine produced in Eastern Europe. Tokay wine, is made exclusively from a variety of grape called Furmint in the district called Tokaj, located in northeastern Hungary. In off years, when weather conditions are poor, the vineyards produce mediocre wine. In good years the grapes are picked quite late, having begun to turn to raisins while still on the vine; wine produced from grapes of this type are marketed as *Tokaji Szamarodni*, with about 14 percent alcohol.

The more important Tokay wine is the *Aszu*, and for this wine, grapes which have turned to raisins are collected individually by hand. The pickers select only grapes touched by *edelfäule*, a mysterious type of white rot that settles on the grapes and produces a natural fermentation after harvesting. The grapes are collected in *puttonyos*, baskets holding approximately 30 pounds. A certain number of *puttonyos* are added to regular Tokay wine, and, of course, this sweetens the wine, for the individually picked dried grapes, having lost most of their natural moisture, are quite sweet. Tokay Aszu wine specifies on the label how many *puttonyos* of dried grapes have been added. In many years, the genuine Tokay Aszu is a very important dessert wine, highly regarded by connoisseurs. Even rarer than Aszu is *Essencia*, which is seldom marketed; it is a freakish wine that may remain in good condition for a century or even longer.

Hungary, The Wines of. No one knows when viniculture first began in Hungary, but it is thought that the Romans planted the vines in this region. At any rate, for over two thousand years wines have been produced successfully. Hungary has many quite good table wines, and one great sweet white wine, Tokay. Hungarian wines are of fair quality and the prices they are sold for are reasonable.

Many varieties of the grape are used in wine making, but most of the credit for their unique products must be laid to an unusual grape, the Furming, or Io Furmint. This odd vine produces grapes with a fair amount of natural sugar, ideal for the sweeter white wines. But the great novelty in this grape is that its skin breaks in the heat of sunshine, permitting the juice to escape, and then it produces a second skin that closes over the break. This creates an abnormally high sugar content. This grape will not spoil on the vine. The German Riesling and the Szilvani (Sylvaner) are also used to make white wine. For red wines the leading grape is the Kadarka.

Experts say the best red wine is Egri Bikavér, literally "Bull's Blood," so called because of its intense red color. It is usual in Hungary to combine place names with wine names, so that Egri denotes the town of Eger. This is a hearty wine, high in alcohol, with a strong bouquet. Egri Kadarka from the same region is a generous, full-bodied, rather rough red.

The majority of the wines, however, are white. The Furmint furnishes the characteristic table wine almost completely unknown in the United States. Smolyoi Furmint has a delightful aroma; Debroi Haslevelu is another white famous for its bouquet. Along the shores of lovely Lake Balaton many white wines are produced, including Badacsonyi, Szurkebarat, Auvergnac, Gris, and Rizling. Badacsonyi Keknyelu is very pleasant on a hot summer day.

Tokay

But it is Tokay that is Hungary's pride, a wine impossible to duplicate. Hungarians call it the greatest white wine in the world, a claim also made in Bordeaux for Château d'Yquem, in Burgundy for Montrachet, and in Germany for certain *trockenbeeren auslese* wines.

Tokay is produced only in certain specified areas of northeast Hungary, in the Hegyalja district at the edge of the towering Carpathian Mountains, near the small town of Tokaj (anglicized into Tokay by generations of Englishmen and Americans who could not cope with foreign place names). The wine comes from the Furmint, grown 1600 feet above sea level; protected by the mountains, it escapes much of the weather hazards ordinarily encountered at that altitude. Summer days are hot, followed by mid-September rains, and then clear, sunny weather which permits a late harvest during the last week in October and the first week of November. Without this late harvest Tokay vintages would be impossible; otherwise the region produces only fair white wines.

Tokay is made in three types, although each type is not made every year: Szamorodni, Aszu, and Essencia, or Imperial Tokay. The ordinary harvest with routine treatment develops an above-average white wine with an alcoholic content of about 14 percent—a very heady drink. In certain years Szamorodni changes its character and becomes a medium-sweet wine, occasionally a truly sweet wine, reminiscent of Barsac or of lesser Sauternes. When experts talk of Tokay, however, they are thinking not of this wine but of the two superior types.

Aszu is the Tokay usually exported to the Western world. German methods introduced into imperial Austria-Hungary two centuries ago improved the local product. The Germans followed the methods used in the Rhine and Moselle districts, allowing the grapes to remain on the vines after they were fully ripe so that they would be very high in sugar content. Hungarians call the overripe grapes *trockenbeeren* as they are called in Germany. Of the total produce of the Tokay vineyards less than 2 percent may be classified as Aszu. During the 19th century,

Tokays were considered among the rarest and most valuable wines in the world. They were the standard gifts which the Hungarian government sent on the occasion of a royal marriage or birth abroad, and they became known as the "Imperial wine," a name which has endured.

The overripe grapes are harvested and carefully placed in measures called *puttonyos*, which hold a little less than 7 gallons. These measures are important, for the overripe grapes are combined with ordinary white grapes of the district in precise ratios. The routine Szamorodni whites are measured by the *gonz* cask, which holds about 35 gallons. It is the relationship of *puttonyos* of dried grapes to these that determines the classification of the finished Aszu. On each label of Tokay Aszu there is a notation that the wine is "1 *puttony*" or even "5 *puttonyos*," and this indicates the relative number of dried grapes that have gone into the finished wine: the higher the number, the sweeter the wine. About 5 *puttonyos* is the highest sent to the United States, but certain fortunate gourmets possess fine old bottles marked "9."

The rarest type of all is Essencia. This wine is really a liqueur, for it is too rich and sweet to drink in any quantity. It can be made only in the best years, possibly twice in a decade, when the grapes are at their peak condition: dried and raisinlike and covered with the whitish yeast mold which the French call *pourriture noble*. Individual grapes, rather than bunches, are carefully collected from the vines and mixed together in casks which hang so that the bung is at the bottom. A goose quill is carefully inserted through the bung, and the juice is allowed to drip into a container. The juice drips through naturally, solely from the weight of the grapes, without any additional pressure. This procedure usually takes several months, after which the juice is allowed to ferment. The wine must then develop for at least 10 years, when it has become a liqueur with a nearly unlimited life, possibly as long as 200 years. It continues to improve in the bottle for about 50 years; after this its quality remains more or less constant. Fascinatingly, Essencias are kept in loosely corked bottles so that air can penetrate. It goes without saying

that Essencia is extremely rare, commanding fabulous prices, particularly if the bottle bears a date preceding World War I. The Hungarian government has a small supply of this precious wine which is used to bring up the quality of the Aszu wines in ordinary years.

Hung Beef. Beef hung until tender, then salted, rolled tightly in a cloth, and hung again until dry—about 3 weeks. Sometimes it is smoked; it will then keep almost indefinitely.

Hunger. An unpleasant, sometimes painful feeling due to lack of food. *See also* Appetite.

Hungry Gap. Kale which survives frosts and is available after other vegetables have been destroyed; found in southern regions of the United States.

Hunker Begendi (Turkish). Roasted lamb and eggplant.

Hunter River. A wine-growing region of New South Wales, Australia. Both red and white wines are prepared, but the whites are sometimes regarded as more noteworthy.

Hûre (French). (1) A pig's or boar's head. (2) Head of a large fish.

Huris Hilib (Somalian). Cubed veal cooked with vegetables.

Hurtleberry. The European bilberry or whortleberry; known in America as "huckleberry."

Husbandry. Economic management of a home.

Hushållsost; Household Cheese. A popular Swedish cheese that comes in three varieties: Farmhouse, Swedish, and Westgotland.

Husk. (1) The part of the wheat that encases the grain, the most nutritious and also the richest in gluten. (2) The protective covering of certain fruits and vegetables.

Husking Bee. An American gathering of local people assembled to help a farmer remove corn husks at harvest time; a semisocial event.

Husk Tomato. *See* Ground-Cherry.

Huso. An excellent variety of sturgeon native to the Caspian and Black Seas.

Hussarde, À la (French). With a garnish of tomatoes stuffed with a purée of onions and grated horseradish.

Hutspot (Dutch). A meat stew made with carrots and potatoes; usually eaten on October 3 to commemorate the lifting of the siege of Leyden in 1574.

Hutspot met Klapstuk. Beef stew with soup meats.

Huzarensla (Dutch). Meat salad.

Huzelbrot (German). Fruit bread.

Hverabrauo (Icelandic). Black bread with a strong, distinctive taste.

Hveteboller (Norwegian). Sweet rolls.

Hvetekake (Norwegian). Raisin bread.

Hvid Gjetost. A Norwegian cheese resembling Gjetost but stronger.

Hvidkål (Danish). Cabbage.

Hvidvine (Danish). White wine.

Hyacinth Bean. A type of bean popular in parts of the United States. Young pods are high in Vitamin C and low in calories; mature seeds are rich in protein.

Hyblaean. Sweet; containing honey. The term comes from Hybla, a place in Sicily noted for its bees.

Hybrid. A cross between two different varieties of plants; an improved variety of fruit, etc.

Hydrogenated Fats. Liquid fats converted into solid fats commercially by chemically combining hydrogen atoms with the carbon present in the oil. The fat is then regarded as "saturated." Many scientists regard highly saturated fats as less desirable for human consumption than unsaturated fats.

Hydromel. A honey-water mixture; after fermentation, called *mead*.

Hydrometer. An instrument or apparatus for measuring the density of liquids, such as sugar, syrup, and alcohol.

Hydroponics. The cultivation of plants, especially vegetables, without soil, using water impregnated with salts.

Hyldebaersuppe (Danish). Elderberry soup.

Hymenium. The spore-bearing part of a fungus (mushroom).

Hypocras. An aromatic white wine roughly like vermouth, but spiced. *See also* Hippocras.

Hyson. A Chinese green tea.

Hyssop. A small sweet-scented herb of the mint family; its flowers, which are blue, white, or pink, produce a particularly delicious honey. Both the flowers and the evergreen leaves are used for flavoring salads, soups, tea, and confections, as well as a number of liqueurs, including absinthe. Hyssop is known as a "holy herb" as it is used in purification ceremonies.

I

I'a Lawalu (Hawaiian). Salted fish wrapped in leaves and baked.

I'a Maka (Hawaiian). Salted fresh fish served with poi.

Ibiharage (African). Fried beans prepared with onions, garlic, and hot red peppers in Burundi.

Ibrik (Arabian). A narrow pot with a long handle, used for making coffee.

Ice. (1) The solid form of water; frozen water. From time immemorial it has been used for preserving or chilling foods. Doubtless some primitive cave dweller hit upon the fact that meat buried in the snow or left in an icy stream would keep longer than the same slice of dinosaur lying about in the open air. He also must have discovered the more refreshing qualities of a chilled drink.

In the days of the Roman Empire snow was transported from distant mountaintops to cool foods and drinks. The emperor Nero built huge cellars in the Alps to store winter snows for summer use.

A Scottish surgeon, Dr. William Cullen, made the first known researches into the manufacture of ice in 1755. An American, Dr. John Gorrie, patented the first American practical method for making ice in 1851, and in 1860 a Frenchman, Ferdinand Carre, obtained a U.S. patent for an ice-making machine using ammonia as its freezing agent. Ice plants were then built in the smallest towns, and home delivery of ice was common until the advent of electric and gas refrigerators.

In the culinary arts ice is used mainly for preserving perishables, but today it is also a home necessity for icing drinks, making frozen desserts, and chilling a variety of dishes.

(2) A sweet frozen dessert, concocted of fruit juice, water, and sugar, stirred or whipped during the freezing process to break up the ice crystals and ensure a smooth texture. An ice differs from a sherbet in that the latter is made with milk or cream.

(3) To cover or spread with a creamy sugar or butter-and-sugar mixture.

Iceberg Lettuce. A salad green with a large firm head and thick, broad, wrinkled leaves; not the best variety of lettuce for salads.

Icebox; Ice Refrigerator. An insulated cabinet for the safe storage of perishable foods. A well-made icebox properly supplied with ice will maintain temperatures of 50°F. or lower, sufficient to keep most foods from spoiling. An icebox also prevents dehydration by maintaining adequate humidity as well as coldness inside the cabinet.

The standard icebox is divided into two or more compartments, one holding the ice, the others the food. The ice is placed either above or in an upper portion of the food compartment. If a standard temperature is to be maintained, air must circulate freely between all compartments; therefore racks rather than solid shelves are used. A draining device also keeps the melting ice water out of the rest of the cabinet. The icebox does not manufacture ice; household needs are filled by chipping from the large block in the ice compartment.

The coolest section, that nearest the ice compartment, should be used for more perishable foods, such as milk. Hot foods should be cooled before being stored. In the United States the icebox has been largely supplanted by the electric refrigerator.

Ice Chest. A refrigerator, using blocks of ice.

Ice Closet. A refrigerator.

Ice Chopper. A tool used to chop or shave ice into fine particles. The most efficient type has a flat-toothed blade.

Ice Cream. A frozen dessert made with cream or milk, sugar, and sometimes eggs and flavorings.

It originated in the form of flavored ices, made by the ancient Chinese, and is said to have been brought to Italy by Marco Polo in the 14th century. Italians adopted the delicacy, and about 1660 the Medicis introduced both ice cream and water ices (sherbets) into France. Exported then to England, ice-cream making was brought to America by the early colonists.

Americans contributed the practice of congealing ice-cream custard in a mechanical freezer instead of placing it on ice. George Washington, in an account book dated 1784, mentions a "cream machine for making ice," and Dolly Madison's White House menus frequently included ice cream of many flavors.

In Europe, at the end of the 18th century, a *bombe glacé* was indispensable as the finale to a banquet, and the Italian confectioners Pratti and Tortoni became world-famous for the delicacy of their concoctions. *Coupes* and *parfaits* also came into great popularity at this time.

French Ice Cream. A very rich solid variety of ice cream made from a sweet custard base with cream added.

Neapolitan Ice Cream. An ice-cream brick made in two or more differently colored layers, sometimes with an extra layer of ices.

Parfait. Ice cream with a high fat content and plenty of egg yolks, which produce a characteristic golden color.

Philadelphia Ice Cream. A soft, smooth, creamy ice cream.

Pudding Ice Cream. A rich, creamy ice cream, prepared with nuts, fruits, etc.

Ice-Cream Cone. A cone-shaped, firm piece of pastry, usually of inferior quality, used to hold a ball of ice cream.

Ice-Cream Freezer; Ice Freezer. A device for making ice cream in small quantities. When ice is melted at a forced rate through the use of salt, enough heat is withdrawn from its surroundings to produce freezing temperatures.

The traditional home ice-cream freezer has two parts: an outer wooden bucket holds chipped ice and rock salt and an inner metal can holds the ice cream. The can, suspended from a lateral frame across the bucket, is revolved by a crank in the ice to assure even freezing. Dashers inside the can churn the ice-cream mixture and keep it smooth. As the mixture freezes, it is also aerated, which increases its volume. Both manual and electric versions are available.

Ice-Cream Powder. A mixture of ingredients to which liquid is added in order to make a kind of ice cream.

Ice-Cream Scoop. A device for serving ice cream in neat individual portions. One type has a half-bowl set on the end of a handle. A small blade inside the bowl, operated with a lever on the handle, scrapes loose the scooped-up ball of ice cream.

Ice-Cream Soda. A beverage made of a scoop of ice cream, carbonated water, and a flavoring agent if desired; it is usually named for the flavoring. It is served with both a spoon and a soda straw. The ice-cream soda was probably invented in the Philadelphia drugstore of Elias Durand in 1825, when artificially carbonated water first made its appearance. Mr. Durand, a former pharmacist in Napoleon's army, is credited with opening the first American soda fountain.

Ice Crusher. One of a wide variety of gadgets that deliver ice crushed by manual crank or by electricity. The simplest method of crushing ice is to place chunks in a cloth or bag and beat it with a hammer or a similar heavy instrument.

Ice Cube. *See* Refrigerator.

Iced. (1) Covered or cooled with ice. (2) Covered with icing, as a cake or other confection.

Iced-Tea Spoon. A long teaspoon used to stir iced tea in a tall glass.

Icefish; Caplin. A small good-tasting fish of the smelt family. *See also* Smelt.

Iceland Moss. (1) A moss that may be boiled and eaten as a vegetable. (2) A lichen native to arctic regions which may be dried and ground to be used as flour or brewed into a medicine.

Ice Milk. A preparation of milk, instead of cream, flavorings and other ingredients used as a substitute for ice cream by those who wish to lower their intake of calories.

Ice Pick. A pointed device for chipping small pieces of ice off a larger block.

Ice Pudding. A sweet, frozen pudding.

Ices. *See* Ice, *also* Sherbets.

Ice Tongs. Pincers for handling individual cubes or lumps of ice.

Ichang. A Chinese black tea that produces a rich brew with a fine bouquet and slightly smoky flavor. With the Keemun and Ningchow varieties it is known as one of the "Burgundies of China Teas."

Ichthyophagy. The practice of eating fish exclusively.

Icing. (1) The act of covering or decorating with a sugar or butter-and-sugar mixture. (2) The mixture itself; frosting.

Icing Sugar. Confectioners' sugar.

Igname. The edible root of a Caribbean climbing plant; a source of arrowroot; may also be prepared like a potato.

Iguana. A giant lizard 3–5 feet long, native to the southwestern United States and Central and South America. Despite its frightening appearance, its flesh is white and comparable in taste to that of chicken.

Ijs (Dutch). Ice cream.

Ijswater (Dutch). Ice water.

Ika Vakalolo (Fijian). Raw fish prepared with lime juice; the citric acid "cooks" the fish.

Île-de-France. A region around Paris with a distinctive cuisine. Its food products include cauliflower, leeks, turnips, artichokes, asparagus, cheese (Brie), snails, and cherries.

Île Flottante (French). "Floating island." Elaborate versions consist of liqueur-soaked sponge-cakes covered with whipped cream and nuts floating on a rich custard. Also, poached meringues floating on custard.

Ilha Cheese. A firm cow's-milk cheese made in the Azores and exported to Portugal.

Illipé Butter. See Vegetable Butter.

Il Pesto. An Italian flavoring, made of olive oil, garlic, basil, cheese, pine nuts, etc.; popular around Genoa.

Il Tocco. An Italian flavoring prepared from meat juices with mushrooms, onions, and tomatoes; popular around Genoa.

Imam Bayeldi (Middle Eastern). Eggplant stuffed with onions, tomatoes, and garlic.

Imaret. A Turkish inn where food and wine are provided.

Imbibe. To drink.

Imbottini Delizia (Italian). Veal rolled with ham, cheese, and truffles.

Imbottite (Italian). Stuffed.

Imbrue. To saturate or soak in a liquid; to marinate.

Immerge; Immerse. To dip or plunge (something) into a liquid.

Immi. A Swiss wine measure, equal to about 1⅓ quarts.

Immiscible. Not capable of being mixed. Normally oil and vinegar are immiscible.

Immix. To mix (a food) with another ingredient.

Impanation. The belief that the body of Christ is present in the bread of the Eucharist.

Impératrice, À l'. As applied to desserts, prepared with whipped cream, fruits, and jelly, usually shaped in a mold.

Imperial. (1) A bottle holding 6 liters (equal to slightly more than 6 quarts); sometimes used for Bordeaux wines. (2) A type of plum.

Imperial Quart. The official British quart—40 fluid ounces. The U.S. quart equals 32 fluid ounces.

Imperial Club. A Canadian cheddar cheese.

Impériale. A French bottle holding 6 liters (slightly more than 6 quarts) of champagne or claret. (2) A garnish consisting of foie gras, truffles, mushrooms, and sweetbread dumplings. (3) A prune or prune wine.

Imperial Tokay. Essencia, a type of Tokay wine. See Hungary, The Wines of.

Imperial Water. A nonalcoholic beverage made of lemon juice and rind, water, cream of tartar, and ginger; named for Napoleon Bonaparte, who is said to have originated the drink.

Impeyan. An East Indian pheasant with a crested head; it has an excellent flavor.

Imphee; African Sugar Cane; Broom Corn. A variety of sugar cane.

Imu (South Seas). An underground oven used for baking pigs, taro, etc.

Inamona (Hawaiian). Kukui nuts ground with salt into a paste.

Incanestrato Cheese. An Italian rennet cheese made from cow's, goat's, or sheep's milk combined with various spices and olive oil.

Incasciata (Italian). Layers of pasta, with meat and hard-cooked eggs.

Inchpin. Sweetbread of deer.

Incising. The making of slight cuts with a very sharp knife in meat or fish being prepared for cooking.

Incrassate. Condensed or thickened, as a soup or stew.

Indehiscent. As applied to fruits, not splitting open when mature.

Indelicate. Coarse or rough in taste or texture.

India. Generalizations about a country with the vast area and varied population of India must inevitably be superficial. Sweeping statements are certain to omit exceptions, and even the most routine pronouncements must be carefully phrased in view of the complex religious and climatic variations.

There are many different kinds of cookery, but the chief styles, based upon religion, are probably Mohammedan, Parsee, and Hindu. Gourmets frequently prefer to divide the cuisine into geographical categories. Thus, the Bengal district, for example, features fish preparations; Kashmir is best known for its meat dishes; and the Punjab region is famed throughout the country for its superb food, probably India's best. It should be remembered, however, that the food specialties of one district are rarely served in any other region, although a few preparations are countrywide.

Indian food habits are greatly complicated by religious restrictions. The Moslems will not eat pork; the Hindu Brahmins observe a large number of fast days; the Hindus are vegetarians; other sects eat lamb but not beef, regarding all cattle as holy. Nevertheless, because of the climate, and inasmuch as India is a very poor country, the basic foods and dishes of the country are vegetables or are based on vegetables.

Vegetarianism, practiced by a large proportion of the nation, has led to an entire cuisine based on vegetables, some of great merit. As a rule, most vegetable dishes appear as a curry, or as a *bhujia*, without gravy or liquid. *Boorthas* are often prepared by first roasting the vegetable, then mashing it smooth; eggplant and squash are generally used.

The basic fat of the Indian cuisine is *ghee*, clarified butter, or butter heated so that much of the liquid is removed; untreated butter tends to make curries stick. Certain other foods and spices are basic in the national cuisine. What Westerners call curry powder is actually a selection and combination of various herbs and spices; cardamom, cinnamon, cumin, pepper, cloves, mace, and nutmeg are typical ingredients used to make *garam masala*, "curry powder," but every cook has his own ideas and recipes. *Dahi* (yoghurt) is a frequently used ingredient in many recipes; also important are *khoa* (dried fresh whole milk), *chenna* and *panir* (types of soft cream cheese), *naryal* (coconut), *lal mirch* (hot red chilies), and *kesar* (saffron).

Plain boiled rice, *chawal*, is probably the basis of Indian cookery. Special rice dishes, *pullao*, come in a wide range, including the plainest, *chawal pullao*, made with onions, curry powder, spices, and *ghee*. However, *pullaos* are made with vegetables, nuts, cheese, meat, etc. Curry, needless to say, is India's great contribution to the world of good food; curries can be made with almost any foods or spices, mild, medium, or hot, and heavy with sauce or almost completely dry. With curries it is customary to serve chutney, a type of pickle. One of the nation's outstanding dishes, however, is little known outside India. It is *tandoori murgha*, chicken Tandoori style, that is, prepared with special spices and reddish coloring, and is absolutely delicious. Some other important points of the Indian cuisine include the following: *koftas* (meatballs), *kabobs* (meat on a skewer), bean and lentil dishes, *chapattis* (wholemeal bread), *samosas* (pastry filled with meat), *puri* (fried bread), *pakoras* (fritters), *kulfi* (a sort of ice cream), and a whole range of sweet dishes.

Indian Bread. Bread made with cornmeal.

Indian Chutney. A spicy, smooth chutney made with apples.

Indian Cock (Obsolete). The turkey.

Indian Corn. Corn; maize.

Indian Cress. The nasturtium, a member of the cress family, whose leaves and brilliant flowers are used in salads and sandwiches; the seeds may be used like capers or may be added to pickling spice.

Indian Dumplings. Cornmeal dumplings.

Indianer Krapfen. A Viennese spongecake filled with whipped cream, rich and delicious.

Indian Leaf. An aromatic leaf often used in cooking.

Indian Meal. Cornmeal.

Indian Pear; Indian Fig; Prickly Pear. Fruit of the cactus.

Indian Pudding. A baked cornmeal dessert pudding made with molasses; often served with ice cream.

Indian Rice. (1) The British name for Patna and other Indian-grown rices. (2) In the United States, wild rice.

Indian Sorrel. A wild tropical herb used for flavoring.

Indian Tree Lettuce. A West Indian lettuce with rough, rather tasteless leaves; often cooked like a green vegetable.

Indian Turnip. An edible but rather tasteless tuberous root.

Indian Wheat. (1) A brittle, dry, hard wheat. Dough made from it tends to tear readily when stretched. (2) (Obsolete) Corn.

Indienne, À l' (French). Indian style; usually applied to dishes made with curry or chutney, or both. Plain boiled rice is sometimes served *à l'Indienne.*

Indienne, Sauce (French). A sauce prepared with onions, butter, parsley, celery, thyme, bay leaves, mace, flour, cream, and lemon juice; used on eggs and poultry.

Indische Kruiden (Dutch). Indonesian spices.

Indochina. *See* Vietnam.

Indonesia. In keeping with other countries of Asia, rice is the basic, staple food of Indonesia. Many of the country's national dishes are based on it, and it forms the daily food for the vast majority of people.

Soups are rarely, if ever, served, and appetizers are not common. However, a number of small snacks might well be regarded as appetizers or hors d'oeuvre. *Krupuk udang baroe,* shrimp flakes, are delicious; *saté* are small pieces of marinated spiced meats. There are a number of fish dishes, of which *iekan bandang panggang,* a baked-fish preparation, is typical. But it is rice that makes the meal. Indonesians first help themselves to rice, and then choose from among the various other meat, vegetable, poultry, or fish dishes on the table. At a simple family dinner four or five dishes is the rule. At parties or special dinners a score or more may be served.

The *rijstaffel,* of course, is the high point of the Indonesian cuisine. Most of the side dishes are quite spicy, and to temper the food it is usual to serve *sambals,* relishes, which are often in themselves quite sharp but occasionally cooling. *Sambals* may be made of beans, fish, vegetables, herbs, or almost any ingredients. With a *rijstaffel* only beer is recommended. One of the most interesting rice table dishes is *nasi goreng,* a rice dish with chicken, shrimp, and peanuts. A similar dish, made chiefly with noodles, is *bahmi goreng.*

Familiar ingredients in Indonesian cookery include *ikan terry,* dried fish; *djahe,* ginger; *sajuran kering,* dried vegetables; *trasi,* shrimp paste; *djahe,* ground ginger; *ketumbar,* coriander; *mie,* much like spaghetti; *udang kering,* dried shrimps; *daoen djeroek purut,* lemon balm; *kunjit,* turmeric; *asam,* tamarind; and *kemiri,* nuts.

Indonesische Nasi Goreng. (Dutch). An Indonesian rice dish containing poultry, seafood, ham, and nuts.

Indra. "He who ripens barley," an ancient god of India associated with many religious festivals involving grains, especially barley.

Inebriate. An intoxicated person; to make someone intoxicated.

Inebriated. Drunk; intoxicated.

Inebriant. Intoxicating; an intoxicant.

Inedible. Not fit to eat.

Ineffervescence. As applied to wines, lack of bubbles or sparkle.

Inesculent. Inedible.

Infructuous. Unfruitful; not fruit-bearing.

Infumate. To dry by smoking; applied especially to fish and meats.

Infuse. (1) To pour into or add a liquid ingredient. (2) To steep herbs or other flavorings in boiling liquid in order to extract soluble substances or to absorb the flavor.

Infuser. To infuse; to steep. Tea, for example, is not boiled but allowed to steep in very hot water so that the flavor may be extracted from the leaves.

Infusion. The process of pouring something into a liquid or adding a liquid to something.

Ingefära (Swedish). Ginger.

Ingelheim. A wine village in Rheinhessen, Germany. *See* Germany, The Wines of.

Ingenio. A West Indian sugar mill.

Ingest. To take into the body; to swallow.

Ingesta. Substances eaten to nourish the body.

Ingestion. The act of taking food for nourishment.

Ingluvies. The first stomach of a bird, sometimes used as food.

Ingluvious (Obsolete). Gluttonous; greedy.

Ingredience (Obsolete). Components of a mixture or recipe.

Ingredient. An element or component of a recipe.

Ingurgitate. To swallow greedily in large quantities.

Ingurgitation. The act of swallowing large quantities of food.

Ingwerbrot (German). Gingerbread.

Injelly. To cover a food with jelly.

Injera (Ethiopian). Bread made from *teff*, a cereal grain.

Inkberry. *See* Poke.

Inkfish. Cuttlefish or squid, native to the Mediterranean and the Adriatic. It is usually cut up and fried in oil with a little garlic, deep-fat fried, or used in fish soups and stews.

Inkokt Strömming (Swedish). Pickled sardines or smelts.

Inlagd Sill (Swedish). Pickled herring.

Inmeat. Variety meats, the edible inner parts of an animal, including liver, sweetbreads, etc.

Inn. A house or hotel offering food and lodging to travelers.

Innkeeper. Owner of an inn or hotel.

Innutrient. An edible substance that is not nutritious, such as water.

Innutrition. Lack of nutrition.

Insalata (Italian). Salad.

    Insalata di Cetriolo. Cucumber salad.

    Insalata di Finocchi. Fennel salad.

    Insalata di Peperoni Arrostiti. Roast-pepper salad.

    Insalata di Scarola. Escarole salad.

    Insalata Mista. Combination salad.

    Insalata Paesana. Potato, egg, and mixed-vegetable salad.

    Insalata Verde. Green salad.

Insalivate. To mix (food) with saliva while chewing.

Insalubrity. Unwholesomeness in food.

Insipid. Tasteless; weak-tasting.

Insitiency. Absence of thirst.

Insoluble. Incapable of being dissolved in a liquid.

Inspissate. To thicken or condense; thickened.

Instant Coffee. Coffee evaporated until it becomes a concentrated liquid, then frozen or dried to a powder that is readily soluble in water. In recent years, most of the coffee prepared in the United States is made from instant coffee, but as a rule, it is not prepared properly. Usually not enough coffee is used; furthermore, instant coffee requires steeping, and this cannot be done in an individual cup. Instant coffee should be dissolved in hot water in a small glass container and allowed to steep for a minute or two before being served.

Insteep. To soak or immerse in a liquid.

Instil; Instill. To add by drops, little by little, as to add oil slowly when making mayonnaise.

Insuccate. To steep or soak.

Insulse. Completely tasteless.

Interlard; Interlarding. The adding of fat strips to meat or poultry which would otherwise be somewhat dry because of a lack of natural fat. The fat is usually inserted with a larding needle.

Intingolo (Italian). Stew; ragout.

Intipuff (Malaysian). A coconut and brown-sugar pastry dessert.

Intoxicant. A substance that dulls the senses; for example, an alcoholic beverage.

Intoxicate. To make (someone) drunk; inebriate.

Invasto (Italian). Potted; stewed.

Invertase; Sucrase; Saccharase. An enzyme that splits sucrose into the invert sugars glucose and fructose. Saccharases, widely distributed in plant tissues and the digestive juice of animals, are of two types: glucosaccharases (in animals and the mold *Aspergillus*) and fructosaccharases (in yeast). They respectively attack the glucose and the fructose end of complex sugars. As sucrose is glucose-fructoside, it is attacked by any of the saccharases.

Involtini (Italian). Rolled stuffed meat, usually served with a sauce and sometimes with cheese.
>   Involtini di Vitello alle Acciughe. Rolled veal stuffed with anchovies.

Involto di Carne (Italian). Rolled stuffed meat, usually larger than involtini.

Iodine. An element essential for the development of thyrosin, which regulates the metabolism. It is found in sea water and in all marine plants, such as algae and Irish moss. Small quantities are also found in pineapple, strawberries, asparagus, cabbage, garlic, and leek.

Iota (Italian). Soup made of sauerkraut, dried beans, and garlic.

Iran. Once the fabled land of Persia, modern Iran is gradually changing its food patterns; however, food habits change slowly, and many of the old dishes are still prepared and served.

Caviar is the great specialty, for Iranian caviar is regarded as the finest in the world, superior to that of Russia, and it is not inexpensive, even in Iran. But caviar is reserved for special occasions, and there are many interesting appetizer dishes, such as stuffed grape leaves. Soups are fairly good, especially *ab-goosht*, made with chick-peas and meat, and *shourabat adas*, with lentils and cracked wheat. This last cereal, *bourghol*, has a delicious wheat flavor and is often used like rice.

The most commonly eaten meat is lamb, sometimes served in cubed pieces in a stew, *tasskebab* or *gormeh sabzee*, or ground finely, often to be stuffed into eggplant, *sheikh el-mihshie*. However, most people consider *chelow kebab*, skewered lamb served on rice, the national meat dish. *Chelow*, boiled rice, forms the basis of most Iranian dishes. The breads are chewy and tasty, usually prepared flat and round, and used in place of tableware. The best desserts are fresh fruits, particularly melons, of which there are at least two dozen varieties. Gourmets hang melons in storerooms to ripen slowly, so they may be eaten at the precise moment of their perfection.

To this day, in traditional Iranian households, forks and spoons are not used, and food is picked up with the fingers. But the present generation is getting away from traditional customs, and while they may eat in the traditional fashion at home, they use tableware when dining at hotels and restaurants.

Irancy. A fruity red wine of fair quality produced near Huxerre, France.

Iranian Caviar. Caviar from Iran; often considered better than Russian caviar. *See also* Caviar.

Ireland. The food in Ireland is basically simple. When it is outstanding it is generally because the basic ingredients are superb. Fresh fish, delicious milk and cream, tasty brown bread, and other plain preparations are the rule. There are few outstanding Irish cooked dishes as opposed to natural foods, and Irish cookery is uncomplicated, wholesome but not involved.

Certain basic foods are outstanding. The Irish rely heavily on the potato because they like it and because it is an easily produced crop. Another everyday food is porridge, that is, a coarse, whole-grained oatmeal that takes some time to prepare. Some peasants have a pot of porridge cooking at all hours of the day.

Tea, rather than coffee, is the standard drink. Upon arising, the Irish generally have a cup of strong tea. Then comes breakfast, possibly fresh eggs and the remarkable Irish bacon plus homemade brown bread and more tea. Lunchtime, or dinner, at midday is a typical meal of soup, meat and fish, potatoes, etc. Afternoon tea is usual, and may vary from a simple cup of tea to a more elaborate service with cakes and sandwiches. The evening meal is simpler than lunch.

The best appetizers are Dublin Bay prawns, the local oysters, or smoked salmon. Potato soup is quite good, as are the various fish soups. Freshwater fish, especially salmon, are marvelous, but the ocean fish are more routine because the local chefs show little interest in preparing them well. Beef and lamb are both quite good, sometimes exceptional; the veal is usually mediocre. Irish meat puddings are prepared with doubtful ingredients. The classic Irish stew is made only with lamb, onions, and potatoes; carrots, celery, etc., are variations unauthorized by the originators. As previously mentioned, potatoes are standard, and are the base for a mashed-potato dish called *champ*. *Colcannon champ* is made with cabbage. There are also pea champs, parsley champs, and so forth. Salads are rare and none too good. Local cheeses, though fresh and wholesome, are passable but not subtle. Desserts are of little importance.

The standard strong drink is whiskey, or Irish whiskey, to be precise. (The name of the liquor is usually spelled "whisky" in England and "whiskey" in Ireland.) *Poteen* is home-brewed whiskey still made in Ireland, to the despair of the taxing authorities. *Irish Mist* is the national afterdinner cordial; it is made from whiskey and honey. *Guinness stout*, a strong beer, dark and heavy, is enormously popular in Ireland; porter is popular with most Irish-Americans.

Iriko. A Japanese dried fish.

Irish Coffee. Hot coffee liberally spiked with Irish whiskey and topped with whipped cream, served in a glass; a beverage invented at Shannon Airport, Ireland.

Irish Mist. An Irish afterdinner liqueur made of whiskey and honey.

Irish Moss. An edible purple seaweed, also known as *carrageen*, found on the coasts of Northern Europe and the United States. It is the prime source of iodine. Processed by drying and bleaching, it is used as a thickening agent in jellies and aspics.

Irish Oatmeal. An excellent long-cooking variety of oatmeal produced in Ireland. Recently, quicker-cooking varieties have been marketed, but the flavor is inferior.

Irish Potato; White Potato. A variety of potato with a pale exterior.

Irish Soda Bread. A leavened white bread containing raisins.

Irish Stew. The classic stew made of mutton or lamb, potatoes, and onions, and occasionally with other vegetables.

Irish Whiskey. The national drink of Ireland, a spirit with a distinctive flavor distilled from malted barley.

Irish Wine (Colloquial). Irish whiskey.

Irlandaise, À l'. In the Irish style; usually, with potatoes.

Iron. A mineral vital (in small quantities) to the functioning of the human body. It aids in tissue respiration and in the formation of red corpuscles, and helps carry oxygen to the blood. A deficiency in the body results in anemia. The richest sources of iron are liver, green and leafy vegetables, egg yolk, dried apricots, potatoes, whole-grain and enriched cereals, flour, and bread.

Iron Kwan Yin. An extraordinarily fine Chinese black tea.

Ironware. Kitchen utensils made of iron, mainly skillets and Dutch ovens. Though cumbersome and heavy, ironware is economical, durable, and improves with use; it heats evenly and retains heat. Ironware covered with enamel is even better for cooking.

Iron pans can be "seasoned" by coating their interiors with lard or cooking oil and heating for several hours in a warm oven, then allowing the fat to cool before cleaning it off.

Since ironware has a tendency to rust, it should be carefully dried before storage.

Irouléguy. Red and white wines of better-than-average quality produced in the Basque region of France.

Irradiated Milk. Milk exposed to ultraviolet rays in order to add vitamin D.

Irradiation; Ionizing. Radiation that destroys various microorganisms; the cold-sterilization process. Complete sterilization requires high dosage that causes changes in the flavor, color, and texture of foods. Ionizing irradiation prolongs storage life by suppressing sprouting in potatoes and root vegetables.

Is (Danish, Norwegian). Ice cream; ice.

Isabelita (Spanish). Angelfish.

Iscas de Figado (Portuguese). Slices of liver poached lightly.

Ische Bone. The edge bone, a part of beef over the rump.

Isigny Cheese. An American imitation of Camembert, but with a firmer body and a flavor and aroma similar to Limburger's. It is about the same size and shape as Camembert.

Crème d'Isigny is a heavy, rich cream that greatly resembles England's Devonshire cream.

Isinglass. A gelatinlike material obtained from the air bladder of various fish. As it drifts slowly to the bottom of a liquid, it takes with it all sorts of foreign matter; it is used in this way to clarify liquors and wines.

Isobutyl Benzoate. A colorless liquid used in the food-processing industry to supply the synthetic taste of caraway.

Isobutyl Salicylate. A colorless liquid used occasionally to furnish the synthetic taste of currant or raspberry to jellies, candies, etc.

Isola, Fromage de. A cow's-milk cheese similar to Gruyère, produced north of Nice, France.

Isosafrole. A colorless liquid used in the food-processing industry to supply the synthetic taste of root beer and sarsaparilla.

Israel. The young country of Israel is subject to various influences in its cuisine. The inhabitants include European immigrants, chiefly from colder countries like Poland, Germany, and Austria, as well as the orthodox people who practice ritual *kosher* cooking, abstaining from pork and shellfish and combinations of meat and milk. The very warm climate makes traditional cold-weather dishes inappropriate. Many of the Arabic dishes, more suited to the climate, have therefore become quite popular.

All the classic Jewish dishes, known the world over, are daily items in Israel. Among the appetizers are *gehochte leber*, (chopped chicken liver), pickled herring, herring in sour cream, and chopped eggs and onions. The standard Friday-night soup is chicken soup with noodles; *borscht* (beet soup) and *schav* (made from sorrel, sour grass) are extremely good. *Gefullte fisch*, finely chopped or ground carp and pike, is a universal favorite. Roast chicken and chicken in the pot are classic preparations. Pork is rarely served, but beef appears frequently as boiled beef, or as pot roast, *gedempte fleisch*. American-style steaks or roast beef are seldom seen. Some specialties are *holishkes*, stuffed cabbage with ground meat; *chulent*, a lima-bean-and-meat casserole; stuffed *derma*, beef casing filled with a flour-and-paprika mixture; carrot *tzimmes*, carrots usually cooked with apples and fat; potato *latkes*, potato pancakes; *kreplach*, stuffed pockets of dough, something like Italian ravioli; and *blintzes*, thin, rolled pancakes with a variety of fillings. An interesting egg bread, *challah*, is a Friday specialty. Fried mashed chick-peas, *falafel*, are a popular snack.

Desserts are somewhat routine. Plain cake, honeycake, and cookies usually round out a meal, sometimes accompanied by fresh fruit or compote.

Issues. Miscellaneous parts of an animal, such as inner organs, feet, etc.

Italian Fennel; Sicilian Fennel; Carosella. A type of fennel; best when eaten fresh.

Italian Frangipane. A filling for small tarts, consisting of a mixture of almost equal portions of eggs, almonds, butter, and sugar.

Italian Ice Cream. A rich custard consisting of sugar, milk, and eggs.

Italian Meringue. Hot or boiled meringue.

Italian Pastes. *Pasta*; macaroni. The over-all name for a number of wheat-flour pastes formerly made only in Italy but now made all over the world. The flour, kneaded to a stiff dough is forced through perforated cylinders of different styles to produce flat ribbons, large tubes, or very thin sticks in over a hundred different shapes.

Italian Sauce. A rich sauce made of tomatoes, mushrooms, and ham; often served with pasta.

Italian Squash (Colloquial). Zucchini.

Italienischer Kohl (German). Broccoli.

Italienne, À l' (French). In the Italian style; containing spaghetti or other pasta, tomatoes, mushrooms, and cheese.

Italiensk Salat (Norwegian). Italian salad; varies in preparation, but usually made with several meats, fruits or vegetables, eggs, and mayonnaise.

Italy. Italian cuisine, probably the second greatest in the world, is surely the most misunderstood. Many Americans think of it in terms of spaghetti, tomato sauce, olive oil, and garlic, and believe that every Italian dish is prepared with some of those ingredients. Comparatively few people are aware of the tremendous scope of Italian cookery and of the great number of provincial Italian dishes.

Why do so many people believe that all Italian food is covered with a spicy garlic-laden tomato sauce? It would appear that the reason, at least in retrospect, is that at the turn of the century conditions in southern Italy from Naples through Sicily were extremely bad, with a grinding poverty and even extreme hunger. The more aggressive southern Italians left their homeland and took "steerage" accommodations for the New World, later sending for their families as they earned a little money.

The immigrants' hopes of finding gold on the streets of New York were doomed to disappointment, and they began to seek suitable employment. In many cases they turned to the restaurant business, opening simple establishments and preparing the uncomplicated dishes of southern Italy which they knew so well. Often it was a family affair, with mother in the kitchen; the culinary style was that which she had always known, and which she had learned from her mother. Soon family-style Italian restaurants were springing up all over the country, and Americans learned new food terms—spaghetti, macaroni, pizza, and the like. Possibly because conditions in northern Italy were not quite so bad, comparatively few immigrants came from the region north of Rome to America. For these reasons, even today, few Americans know the dishes of north Italy. Except in a few large cities, most people think of an Italian dinner in terms of antipasto, minestrone, spaghetti with meatballs, and biscuit tortoni. Such a meal might possibly be obtained in Italy, but the odds are against it.

Spaghetti and macaroni dishes are very popular in southern Italy, but in the north the preference is often for a *polenta* (cornmeal) or *risotto* (rice) dish. Tomatoes, onions, and garlic are used in the north, but much more lightly and sparingly than in the south, and in point of fact, more garlic is used on France's Côte d'Azur than in northern Italy. Furthermore, the distinction between northern and southern Italian food is only a beginning, for the food pattern changes quickly from one district to another, often in a matter of a hundred miles or so; in effect, this means that certain provincial dishes are obtainable only in a very limited, circumscribed area and not elsewhere. It is somewhat difficult to understand, at least at first blush, why Italy has so many different cookery styles within its borders.

There is, however, a valid explanation. It should be remembered, as a beginning point, that Italy first became a nation in 1861. For a thousand years before that time, local rulers had controlled limited portions of the peninsula, but these were only small districts, never large areas. Only a little over a century has passed since Italy became unified, supplanting the local dukes, princes, lords, and warriors who controlled their own small regions, often just a small group of villages. Prior to the unification, communications and travel from one district to another were very limited, and in fact, many of them were intermittently at war with one another. For a thousand or more years, people were born and lived out their lives within a limited area, never traveling even to the next district ruled over by an unfriendly prince. Local culinary styles developed within each provincial district, with little modification from outside influences. Of course, it should be pointed out that the entire peninsula had a general culinary style, chiefly because of the availability of ingredients.

Each Italian province now has its food specialties, although the scope is greater and more varied in the north than in the south, as a rule. The Piedmont district in the north features cookery based on butter rather than on olive oil. Local specialties include *agnolotti* (like *ravioli*, but larger), *fonduta*, a melted cheese dish made with Fontina cheese, and *bagna cauda* sauce, a sort of anchovy mixture in which raw vegetables are dipped. Liguria is the region that borders France along the Mediterranean; its specialties include *il pesto*, the basic flavoring sauce of the region, used for almost everything, which is made with cheese, pine nuts, and basil. *Trenette*, thin noodles, are absolutely superb here, as are the fish soups and stews. On the Austrian border, near the city of Bolzano, the favorite preparations include *gnocchi*, made with various fillings; *ravioli alla Trentina*, small squares of dough stuffed with ground meat, chicken, and onions; and the *frittata Trentina*, a pancake served with a delicious mushroom-cheese sauce.

The province of Lombardy also uses butter rather than oil. From this land of good living comes *minestrone*, a thick vegetable soup; *risotto alla Milanese*, rice prepared with white wine and onions; and *costoletta alla Milanese*, a lightly breaded veal chop known the world over. Italians think that the country's best food comes from the region called Emilia-Romagna, which includes the gastronomic city of Bologna. The *pasta*, spaghetti, macaroni, and the like, are extraordinarily good here; *lasagne verdi*, green noodles, and *pappardelle*, flat noodles, are marvels of lightness and delicacy. Many dishes come with a rich meat sauce, locally called *ragu* but usually designated as *alla Bolognese* elsewhere throughout Italy. The province of Tuscany has Florence and Pisa within its borders. Tuscans are known for their love of bean dishes, and frequently dishes designated as *alla Toscana* (in the style of Tuscany) indicate the presence of beans. *Cacciucco* is a marvelous fish soup, often with the thickness and body of a stew; the *bistecca alla Fiorentina* is a thick cut of broiled steak, for the region around Florence is one of the few in Italy where it is possible to obtain an American-style steak.

Around Venice seafood predominates, and *brodetti di pesce*, fish soups, are truly remarkable. *Fegato alla Veneziana* is sautéed calf's liver in white wine with onions; *manzo alla Veneziana* is a rich, succulent beef stew; *risi e bisi* is a classic favorite of rice and peas; and *polenta pastizada* is cornmeal with a chicken-liver and tomato sauce. South of Venice are the Marches, lying along the Adriatic on Italy's east coast; here, too, the basic emphasis is upon fish soups, fresh fish, and shellfish; also worthy of note is the local *lasagne*, made with a rich mixture of ham, cream, mushrooms, and truffles. Umbria is the region that includes Assisi, Orvieto, Spoleto, and Perugia. This district, being somewhat wild and mountainous, has a fair amount of wild game, which are featured in the local cuisine; the sausages are quite interesting; truffles are a local specialty, too; and every town and village makes a cake, pastry, or sweet bread which may be obtained there and nowhere else.

Latium encompasses Rome, and it is here that the cuisine of the entire nation finds its fullest expression. Roman cooking is a complete provincial style by itself, but it also attracts chefs and has restaurants from every province in the country. A great specialty of Rome is *abbacchio*, baby lamb; *stufatino alla Romana* is an excellent, hearty beef stew. The Romans are fond of spaghetti dishes, and especially noteworthy are *spaghetti all'Amatriciana*, with a sauce of pork, onions, and tomatoes; *fettucine alla Romana* is noodles with a rich mixture of butter, cream, and cheese; *alla Carbonara* is extremely interesting, being prepared with bacon and uncooked egg.

Naples is the focal point of Campania, that colorful province where southern Italy truly begins. Here originated *pizza*, that classic open tart covered with tomatoes and other ingredients. Fish soups of all types, but particularly *zuppa di vongole*, a clam soup, are noteworthy here; spaghetti with tomato sauce or with clams are also everyday items; *maccheroni alla Napoletana*, macaroni with a spicy tomato sauce, are typical *pasta* preparations. *Gelati*, the classic ices, are another local specialty.

Further south are Abruzzi and Molise, which features *le virtù*, a vegetable soup with added ingredients like rice and *pasta*; various sausages are well made, and include a liver type with pine nuts, *salsiccia di fegato*; a soft, sweet cream cheese, *ricotta*, is especially good here, as is *provola*, something like *provolone* cheese.

Puglia is comparatively unimaginative in its cookery style, but the local fashion of preparing eggplant with a filling of bread crumbs and capers, *melanzane alla Pugliese*, is quite good; *minestra verde*, a green vegetable soup, is interesting, and so is *calzone*, a *pasta* made with fish and vegetables.

The province of Calabria features hearty, appetizing peasant-style dishes. Soups are made with snails, with celery, *zuppa di Accia*, and with crabs, *zuppa di granchi*. Eggplant cookery is a staple of the diet, especially *alla Calabrese*, diced eggplant with anchovies and tomatoes.

Off the mainland lies the historic island of Sicily, where fish and vegetables are the basis of the diet. Fish soups, *pasta* with fish sauces, *pasta con acciughe*, with anchovies, or baked-macaroni dishes, like *pasta con le sarde*, with whole sardines, raisins, and nuts, are illustrative. Eggplant and artichokes are important vegetables, prepared in a bewildering variety of fashions, and *carciofi alla Siciliana*, artichokes stuffed with bread crumbs, cheese, and anchovies, are typical of the local style. Desserts are extremely popular, and *cassate*, fancy ice creams, are outstanding favorites; *cannoli* are tubes of firm pastry with rich fillings, but dozens of cakes and tarts are made in all the villages that dot the island.

Italy, The Wines of. In no other part of the world except France is so much acreage devoted to the production of wine. Indeed, the per capita consumption in Italy is believed to be the highest in the world, about fifty times that of the United States.

The Greeks, well over two thousand years ago, called the Italians *oenotrii viri*, the men of wineland. Today, with about one-seventh of its total territory devoted to vines, and with an annual wine production of about one million gallons, almost every man, woman, and child in that sunny land drinks wine daily as a matter of habit. (Water is an element in which to wash.) Italian wines are undistinguished and delicious. The Italians think they are no more worth fussing about than bread. Wine is there on the table to drink: it's good and never mind the French nonsense about vintages, bottlers, and particular wines for particular foods. With the exception of special occasions, everyone drinks the wine available and is content.

France has half a dozen important wine districts, and the German vineyards lie along the banks of the principal rivers, the Rhine and the Moselle; in the United States wines are produced mainly in New York, Ohio, and California. But in Italy there are vineyards in all the provinces from the northern mountains to the southern shores of Sicily, from west to east, from the Mediterranean to the Adriatic. It is a rare piece of land on which the Italian farmer does not grow grapes for his own use—intermixed with beans and artichokes, or whatever crop he may be raising.

The weather in Italy is far milder than in France and Germany. Italian summers are hot and sunny, and particular vintage years are seldom important. Like California, where the summer sun is hot, every year is almost always like the previous one. This means that the crop is good, the year's wine is good, but there is never, by contrast, a superb or unusual vintage as there is in France. On the other hand, there is never a year that is a total failure for the vintners.

Wine making in Italy varies greatly: at times it is haphazard to the point of being comical; then again it is methodical and careful, and sometimes one meets the skill that is characteristic of the great *châteaux* of Bordeaux. The Italian tends to bring to his wine making the same attitude that he has toward life. Why save wine in a cellar so that it can age when it tastes good now? It is difficult to find a bottle of Italian wine that is ten years old, while in France such a bottle is a commonplace.

In 1930 the Fascist government instituted a series of regulations concerning wine production which brought a degree of order to a very confused industry. The geographical districts producing the various wines were set, so that the winemakers in the hills behind Sorrento, for example, could not send their excess products north to Piedmont to fill out a shortage of Barolo. If a wine is shipped from one district to another, its label must state that it is a "type" (actually an imitation) of another wine. The word on the label is *Tipo*.

As Italian wines sell at comparatively modest prices, the least desirable have this label. Better assurances of quality are the small round government seal on the top of the bottle marked "Italia" and the words "Marchio Nazionale" on the label. This is a guarantee that the wine has been produced in the district indicated on the label, so that your bottle of Chianti, for example, will contain wine from the prescribed Chianti district.

The Italians make an interesting distinction among red wines, classifying them as "table" wines or "roast" wines (*vini per arrosto*). Young wines of about two years are table wines served with ravioli, spaghetti, noodles, *gnocchi*, or other *pasta* courses. The heavier, more full-bodied wines that take about five years to reach maturity are the "roast" wines. However, people who like the lighter wines frequently drink them with roast meats, whereas people who like the heavier, order them with spaghetti.

Italian white wines are only fair at best. They are pleasant in Italy, but seldom seem as good elsewhere. Of course everyone remembers an exceptional bottle of Soave or Verdicchio he has tasted, but it is true nonetheless that the white wines are undistinguished. The sweet white wines of Italy are not outstanding either, and, with the exception of a few sparkling types, they are difficult to find in the United States.

There is an amusing story about the white wine called Est! Est!! Est!!! In the year 1111, a German bishop traveling to Rome sent his majordomo ahead each day with instructions to find inns where the wine was good. He was to mark on the walls of the taverns the word "Est" (It is good) or "Non est" (It is not good). His man tasted a yellow wine and enjoyed it so much that he wrote on the wall "Est! Est!! Est!!!" When the good bishop saw this, he hastened into the inn. He agreed completely with his majordomo. In fact the bishop never reached Rome: it is said that he died en route from too much good wine. The winemakers of Italy deny the tale, but the story has persisted. Sad to relate, Est! Est!! Est!!! no longer lives up to the exclamation marks; perhaps the bishop was just very thirsty.

Rosé wines have never been important in Italy, and before World War II they were rarely encountered. However, the increase in their popularity in the United States may have encouraged Italian producers to develop them for export. They are light and drinkable, but like most rosés, they seldom have any real character.

The leading wines of Italy, according to districts, follow.

Piedmont

Barolo: A ruby-red wine with a violet bouquet. A very superior roast wine, often compared to a French Hermitage.

Barbaresco: Very much like Barolo, but somewhat lighter in body; an excellent roast wine.

Barbera: A ruby-red wine of only moderate quality, as a rule. Full-bodied, pleasant bouquet, quite inexpensive.

Freisa: A fruity wine, with a deep shade of garnet-red. Available in dry or medium-sweet types; best when several years old.

Gattinara: A deep garnet-red wine with pale highlights, and a slight raspberry taste. Often considered one of Italy's finest wines; a superb roast wine.

Grignolino: A red wine of a brilliant crimson color; fresh to the palate, but with a slightly bitter aftertaste.

Nebbiolo Piedmontese: A table wine when less than two years old; a roast wine when mature. Varies from dry to fairly sweet.

Dolcetto delle Langhe: A ruby-red wine, moderately acid with a slightly bitter aftertaste.

Moscato d'Asti: A gold-colored white wine, low in alcohol; most types are quite sweet.

Asti Spumante: The classic Italian sparkling wine; light and pleasant but quite sweet because it is made of Muscat grapes.

Liguria

Cinque Terre: A yellowish wine which is quite high in alcohol, and has a good bouquet. Dry to medium sweet, but with a somewhat metallic aftertaste.

Coronata: A straw-colored wine, with light and delicate bouquet; usually quite dry.

Lombardy

Sassella: A bright ruby wine with a good deal of bouquet; develops into a fine roast wine as it ages.

Valgella: A red wine with a mild, dry taste, but not quite as good as Sassella.

Chiaretto del Garda: A light-colored *rosé* wine with a pleasant, vaguely bitter taste; low in alcohol.

Lugana: A fairly good dry red wine with a distinctive tartness. It has a moderate amount of alcohol.

Tridentine Venetia

Santa Maddalena: A light, dry red (occasionally very dark) wine, with a slightly bitter aftertaste.

Caldaro: A red wine with a deep, beautiful color and an interesting bouquet; usually quite dry.

Termeno: A dry, sometimes medium-sweet

white wine with a heavy flowery bouquet reminiscent of an Alsatian wine.

Euganean Venetia

Soave: A very light white wine with a greenish cast; dry, vaguely bitter, and quite smooth, low in alcohol.

Bardolino: A bright red wine, with a dry fruity quality; often has a slightly prickling, tart taste. Very good, highly popular table wine.

Valpolicella: A more delicate red wine than most Italian products; has a dry, smooth, slightly bitter taste. Often the nearest thing to a French wine.

Recioto Veronese: A sweet, red wine with a pleasant bouquet; good only for dessert or after dinner.

Vino Veronese: A general term used to describe the quite ordinary table wines of the district; occasional types are slightly better.

Proseco di Conegliano: A yellowish, dry wine with a somewhat bitter aftertaste; often produced as a sparkling wine.

Verdiso: Just like Proseco (above) but much drier, with an interesting bouquet.

Emilia

Lambrusco: A purple-red wine, usually not quite dry; has a distinctive effervescent quality and makes a fair table wine.

Sangiovese di Romagna: A light red wine, with a pleasing bouquet; it leaves a dry, slightly bitter aftertaste. Improves with age.

Marches

Verdicchio: A light-gold and green wine with a pleasing dry but earthy quality; comes in a distinctive amphora bottle.

Rosso Piceno: A dry, sometimes moderately sweet, red wine of fair quality.

Tuscany

Chianti: A bright ruby-red wine (although some white is also shipped), made in several qualities. The ordinary variety, which comes to the market in straw *fiaschi*, is a passable, pleasant wine, but quite crude. When the better types are aged in barrels and sold in regular bottles, they develop a roundness and full flavor that is often surprisingly good. In addition, there is a *Chianti Classico*, produced only in a few designated townships to the south and west of Florence; this is a very superior wine, among the best that Italy offers. The white Chianti has a dry quality, little bouquet, and is only fair.

Brunello: A bright red wine with a distinctive strong taste; improves with age.

Montecarlo: Comes in both red and white types; both are of fair quality.

Vin Santo: This "Holy Wine" with a yellow-gold color and a delicate bouquet is quite sweet.

Umbria

Orvieto: A white wine of moderate quality, with a delicate bouquet and a slightly bitter taste. There is a dry (*secco*) type, and a much sweeter dessert type (*abboccato*).

Latium

Castelli Romani: A descriptive term for the several types of white wine produced in the region around Rome; varies from dry to semi-sweet; only passable in quality. *Frascati* is the gold-colored everyday white wine of Rome and its suburbs.

Aleatico del Viterbese: An unusual red wine with a distinctive aroma; quite sweet, suitable only with dessert.

Cesanese: A ruby-red, dry wine, quite high in alcohol content; varies from dry to slightly sweet.

Abruzzo

Montepulciano d'Abruzzo: A bright red wine with deep undertones of garnet; makes a fairly good roast wine when aged.

Campania

Falerno: This wine comes in both red and white types. The red has a good color and pleasant bouquet. The white is quite dry and yellow in color.

Lacrima Christi: A pale gold wine, with a pleasing bouquet; not absolutely dry, it has a smooth quality. The red is an average table wine.

Vesuvio: A purple-red, rather dry table wine with a fairly good bouquet.

Capri: A straw-colored white wine with a light body; has a very dry, somewhat astringent taste.

Gragnano: A ruby-purple wine with a fine,

fruity flavor, ideal with Neapolitan-style cooking; much like a French Beaujolais, but not quite so dry.

Ravello: This wine is produced in both red and white types; the red is a fair table wine with a ruby color, the white is a sweet dessert wine.

Apulia and Lucania

Castel del Monte: A red wine with a distinctive bouquet and a fruity taste which makes it a very good table wine.

Moscato: A heavy, sweet wine, almost cloying, suitable only for dessert. It has a decided muscat grape taste.

Malvasia: There are two kinds of Malvasia; one type is dry and delicate with a pale straw color, the other is higher in alcohol content and very sweet.

Calabria

Savuto: A strong red wine, dry and smooth, which is much better when old; it is somewhat coarse when fresh and young.

Sicily

Marsala: A fortified dessert wine with about 17 percent alcohol; the types are dry, medium, sweet, or aromatic (with the addition of flavorings).

Etna: The white wine is straw-colored with greenish undertones; has a distinctive dry, almost spicy quality and is probably the best wine of Sicily. The red is fairly good, but somewhat crude.

Sardinia

Vernaccia: An amber-colored wine, quite high in alcoholic content and not too dry; reasonably good.

Oliena: A deep red wine with an extremely fine bouquet. Its taste is dry with a slightly bitter quality.

Ita Palm. A South American tropical palm tree.

Iudabah (Arabian). Sweetened rice stewed in chicken fat.

Iva-Bitter. An Italian liqueur made from *genepi*, a kind of wormwood.

Ivoire, À l' (French). As applied to chicken, served with a pale white or ivory-colored sauce; with ivory sauce.

Ivory Sauce. A well-seasoned cream sauce with meat glaze added to give an ivory tint; served with poultry, sweetbreads, or veal or with other white stews.

Izard. A goatlike antelope native to the Pyrénées, France; highly regarded as a game animal, though the meat is somewhat dry.

Izarra. A French afterdinner liqueur made with angelica.

Izibo. An African tuber that tastes somewhat like a potato.

J

Jachtschotel (Dutch). A pie containing meat, apple, and onion; hunter's stew.

Jack. (1) A young pike-perch and various other fish, including the pompano. (2) An East Indian tree that produces a breadlike fruit; also called *jackfruit*.

Jack Back. In a vinegar factory a tank that holds cooled malt prepared for beer making.

Jack Cheese; Monterey Jack. An American cheddar-type cheese with granular curd; mild and quite smooth when young, but sharper when old.

Jack Crevalle; Jackfish; Pickerel; Pike. Cavalla, a voracious food fish.

Jackfruit. The very large fruit of a tree native to parts of Asia and the South Pacific islands. Both the seeds and pulp are edible. A smaller species of jackfruit is called *chěmpědak* in Malaya.

Jack Mackerel. A rich, oily fish of the mackerel family, which describes various species in different localities of the United States. It is comparatively high in fat content.

Jackrabbit. A rather large rabbit found chiefly on the prairies in the northwestern United States.

Jack Salmon. Pike-perch.

Jacobins (British). Small rounds or fancy shapes made of custard.

Jaddy (British). A cake made with flour and lard or drippings.

Jadra Ichdeedah (Middle Eastern). A preparation containing lentils, rice, onions, and olive oil.

Jaffa; Jaffa Orange. A variety of orange grown in Israel.

Jaffi Almonds. Small bitter North African almonds.

Jagger; Jagging Iron. A utensil with a brass wheel fastened to a handle, used for cutting pastry into fancy shapes.

Jaggery. (1) A crude brown sugar made from the sap of the jaggery palm native to India and other tropical countries. (2) Solidified refined molasses.

Jalea (Spanish). Jelly.

Jalebi (Indian). A dessert consisting of rings of fried dough served in a thick sweet sugar syrup.

Jalousie (French). A trellised puff pastry filled with almond cream.

Jam. A preserve in which the whole fruit or its pulp is cooked with sugar with no attempt to retain the original shape of the fruit. Less sugar is used in proportion to the fruit than when making preserves. If the rind of any citrus fruit is retained, the jam is usually called *marmalade*. Jams may be made from one or more kinds of fruit or from certain vegetables.

Jamaica. As in most British islands of the Caribbean, the favorite dishes show an English derivation. This is true particularly with reference to the fondness for beef, especially roast beef with Yorkshire pudding, and also for curries. In Jamaica the favorite curry is made with small shrimp and fresh coconut milk.

The most popular soups are okra, lobster, Jamaica pepperpot, and red pea (actually kidney beans). Fish dishes include salt salmon cooked with grated coconut, codfish, and *ackees* (a local fruit), and turtle steak. *Solomon Gundy* is an appetizer spread made with kippered herring. *Stamp and Go* are fritters of codfish and onions, usually served with boiled green bananas or plantains. An interesting meat dish is salt beef and red peas cooked with small flour dumplings. Among the vegetables are *chochos* (resembling the squashlike *chayotes*), often baked with onions and meat and served in its own shell. Baked *ackee* with cheese is another favorite, based upon Jamaica's national fruit. Desserts are not complicated; fresh coconut and guava ice cream, and baked bananas with coconut cream are typical.

Jamaica rum, famous the world over, is the most popular island drink. It forms the basis for scores of cocktails and punches, but one of the best is the short rum punch made with lime juice, simple syrup, and dark Jamaica rum and served with nutmeg sprinkled on top.

Jamaica Pepper. Allspice.

Jamaica Rum. Rum distilled in Jamaica from native sugar cane. It usually has a heavy, pungent bouquet and flavor; best when used in mixed drinks.

Jamaica Sorrel; Roselle. A wild green herb, native to Jamaica and other tropical countries; used to flavor foods.

Jambalaya. A Creole dish, native to Louisiana (and several of the Caribbean Islands), made of a variety of fish, shellfish, or meat in a sauce; served with boiled rice.

Jambe de Bois (French). A soup prepared with a beef bone and vegetables.

Jambo; Jambu; Rose Apple. A tropical apple with rose-colored pulp native to Southeast Asia.

Jambon (French). Ham; prepared in many different styles in France. *Bayonnaise* style is with rice, mushrooms, tomatoes, and sausages; *bourguignonne* is with red wine, onions, and mushrooms; *godard* is with red wine, olives, and sweetbreads; *valencienne* is with white wine, tomatoes, Madeira sauces and stuffed tomatoes.

Jambon Blanc; Jambon de Paris (French). Cooked, boned ham.

Jambon d'Ardennes. (1) (Belgian) Ham cured in brine (no sugar) and smoked until dry and quite dark; eaten in paper-thin slices. (2) (French) A pickled, smoked type of ham made in the Béarn region; usually served raw, cut into paper-thin slices.

Jambon de Gibier (French). Leg of a wild pig or other game animal prepared much like ordinary ham; famous in the Touraine region.

Jambon de Montagne (French). Any ham that has been provincially cured.

Jambon de York (French). York ham.

Jambon de Volaille (French). Boned stuffed chicken legs cooked in wine; eaten cold.

Jambon du Pays (French). Any ham that has been locally cured.

Jambonneau (French). The part of a pig between the thigh (or ham portion) and the foot, something like a shin bone. It may be prepared like

ordinary ham, but the flavor is not so good. (2) A small ham.

Jambonneaux de Poulet (French). Stuffed chicken legs.

Jambreads (British). Slices of bread and jam.

Jambu. A comparatively rare Brazilian herb, quite pungent; used to flavor certain local dishes, usually those served with *tucupi* sauce.

Jam Cake. A caramel-frosted cake, originally made in Kentucky, which contains several cups of jams (strawberry, blackberry, etc.).

Jamón (Spanish). Ham.

  Jamón Serrano. Dried ham.

Jantar (Portuguese). Dinner.

Jantong (Southeast Asian). The large edible bud (before the flower) of a fruit-bearing banana shoot; may be prepared like a vegetable or eaten in salads.

Japan. The most conspicuous feature of a Japanese meal is the artistic fashion in which the food is presented. If there is a soup, the soup dish or plate will be carefully selected so as to provide a contrast or to harmonize with the liquid. In the soup there may be tiny perfect bits of star-shaped carrot. Every dish is carefully arranged for maximum eye appeal, and to enhance the diner's appetite. Each meal, in fact each dish, is intended to delight the beholder and increase his pleasure in the food to be eaten.

The Japanese cuisine is not complicated judged by Western standards, but it is frequently interesting. It may be divided into the following groups, for convenience: *suimono* (clear soups); *miso-shiru* (soups made with a fermented malt base); *nimono* (boiled foods), boiled chicken, for example; *yakimono* (broiled foods), such as *kabayaki*, broiled eels; *agemono* (fried food), the best-known being *tempura*, deep-fat fried foods; *mushimono* (steamed food), among which are many egg dishes; and the most famous of all, *nabemono* (open frying-pan foods), particularly *sukiyaki*, sautéed beef with vegetables.

The most tempting to Western palates are *sukiyaki* and *tempura*. Much of the remainder of the Japanese cuisine seems somewhat exotic at first, but after a few meals many Westerners learn to enjoy the local food. An entire cuisine is built around raw fish, but it should be remembered that Japanese fish is far fresher and more tempting than fish anywhere else. *Sashimi* consists of slices of raw fish, usually served as an appetizer. *Sushi* restaurants are highly regarded; at these establishments entire meals of raw fish are served. A simple *sushi* involves a thin slice of raw fish wrapped around a small quantity of boiled rice sprinkled with a little vinegar. *Nigiri sushi* is prepared by adding a little very hot *wasabi* mustard to the rice. More to Western taste are *yakitori*, barbecued chicken; *chawan-mushi*, an egg custard made with fish, chicken, or vegetables; *soba*, buckwheat noodles; *oden*, boiled fish cakes with vegetables; and *oyako domburi*, a chicken-mushroom-and-egg dish. Desserts are unimportant in Japan; two pleasing ones are *awayukikan*, a gelatin dessert, and *kasutera*, a plain cake.

Certain Japanese ingredients give Japanese food its distinctive qualities. Among these are *shoyu* (soy sauce), which is quite salty and almost eliminates the ordinary use of table salt; *miso*, a paste made of fermented soybeans, rice malt and salt; *tofu*, bean curd; *mirin*, a rice wine resembling sherry; and *ajimomoto*, monosodium glutamate, used to bring out the flavors of food. Rice is, of course, the basic food of the country, and fish is more important than meat in the national diet. Chopsticks rather than Western-style tableware are still in use.

There are practically no local wines, although a slight effort has been made; Japanese care little for wine, however. The Japanese are excellent mimics of Western products, and there are many imitations of Scotch whisky, gin, and vodka; their best success, however, is with beer, which is excellent. The national drink is *sake*, often called a rice wine, but it has more of a beerlike quality. It is mild and sweet tasting and is drunk warm from tiny cups. Coffee is becoming increasingly popular in the cities, and Tokyo has many coffeehouses, but tea is still the country's favorite. They drink mainly green tea plain, without milk, sugar, or lemon, and at every meal.

To illustrate the national cuisine, here is a possible holiday menu: *sashimi* (sliced raw fish); *surume* (dried squid); *tai* (broiled fish); *kazu-noko* (fish eggs); and *kinpira gobo*, burdock root.

Foods prepared in advance are stored in tiers of lacquered boxes, one fitting atop the other, called *jubako*.

Japanese Cakes. Brittle cakes made of sugar, egg whites, and almonds.

Japanese Gelatin. Agar-Agar, a gelatin made from seaweed; used in making gelatin desserts, jellies, and soups.

Japanese Horseradish. A pungent Japanese root; grated and served as a condiment with raw fish.

Japanese Medlar. *See* Loquat.

Japanese Persimmon; Kaki. A bright reddish-pink fruit originally cultivated in Japan and China, now grown in the United States. The pulp is extremely juicy and has several long pits.

Japanese Quince. An ornamental Japanese shrub whose berries are too hard to eat but contain an aromatic juice used for making jellies and preserves.

Japanese Radish. The daikon, a very large white radish.

Japanese Teas. The teas of Japan are interesting but are not equal to those prepared in China, Formosa, and India. They are usually classified as natural, pan-fired, and basket-fired.

Jap Mixture. Ground hazelnuts or almonds blended into a semi-meringue, to which melted butter or oil is added.

Japonaise (French). (1) Containing soy sauce or rice. (2) A fruit-and-tomato salad served with a sour-cream sauce. (3) Containing artichokes. (4) Made with mussels and potatoes.

Jar. A deep, wide-mouthed pottery, earthenware, or glass container.

Jardinière, À la (French). "In garden style"; as applied to meat and poultry dishes, served with several fresh-cooked vegetables.

Jarret (French). Knuckle or shin of beef or lamb.
   Jarrets de Mouton. Mutton knuckles.
   Jarrets de Porc. Pickled pig's trotters cooked and served with sauerkraut.
   Jarrets de Veau. Veal knuckles.

Jars (French). A male goose, a gander, having delicious meat.

Jasmine Tea. A fragrant Chinese red tea.

Jasnières. A dry, aromatic white wine of passable quality produced in Maine, France.

Jatropha. A genus of starchy plants, one species of which is the source of tapioca.

Jaune d'Oeuf (French). Yolk of an egg.

Jaune-Mange (French). (1) A yellow dessert made with gelatin, white wine, sugar, eggs, and lemons. (2) A nonstarch custard.

Jaunes. Several European wild mushrooms.

Jause (Austrian; German). Afternoon tea.

Java (Colloquial). Coffee.

Javaanse Sla (Dutch). A Javanese salad made of fruits or vegetables, coconut, and nuts.

Java Tea. Teas native to Java are rich and pungent but are used chiefly for blending.

Jave (British). The top crust of a loaf of bread.

Jay; Jaybird. Certain species of jays, especially those found in Europe, may be eaten like other small game birds; they should be parboiled before being cooked.

Jejune (French). Lacking nutritious qualities. The word derives from the Latin *jejunus*, meaning "hungry."

Jell. To become or cause to become like jelly.

Jellied. Having become like jelly.

Jellied Soup. Soup congealed by being mixed with gelatin; served chilled.

Jelly (1) A gelatinous clear meat or fish stock that becomes solid when chilled. (2) A preserve made by cooking fruit juice and sugar until they are reduced to a required consistency. Proper proportions of acid and pectin, the jellying agent in a fruit juice, are essential for successful jelly making. Natural fruit pectin is available in liquid or powdered form at any grocery.

Jelly Bag. A thin, fine flannel, muslin, or cheesecloth bag into which cooked fruit is poured so that it may retain the pulp but allow the juice to run through clear and unclouded.

Jelly Bean. A small firm, jellylike candy with a glazed exterior; made in many different colors and flavors.

Jelly Crystals (British). A crystalline mixture of powdered gelatin, dry colors, soluble powdered flavors, and sugar.

Jelly Paste. A mixture of fruit pulp and sugar; used chiefly in making certain candies.

Jelly Powder. Packaged sweetened and multiflavored gelatin for use in making desserts and salads, and flavorless or spiced gelatins for many other uses.

Jelly Roll. A popular dessert cake; usually a thin spongecake, prepared flat, spread with jelly or other filling, and rolled up; usually served in slices.

Jelutong. A resinous material used to make chewing gum.

Jengibre (Spanish). Ginger.

Jenever. A very dry, almost musty, gin produced in Holland. *See* Geneva.

Jenny Lind. A round flat two-piece loaf made of lard and sugar, formerly popular in western Scotland.

Jerez (Spanish). Sherry wine.

Jerked Meat. Any meat (usually beef) cut into strips or thin-sliced and dried in the sun. The name is said to be derived from the South American Indian term *charqui*.

Jeroboam. A double magnum of champagne, four times the size of a regular bottle.

Jerusalem Artichoke. *See* Artichoke.

Jerusalem Melon. A melon of passable quality found in various countries around the Mediterranean. It is a natural variety, not a hybrid.

Jesse. A European river mudfish, much like the carp; not very popular because of the great number of bones.

Jésuite (French). A small pastry prepared with almond cream and chocolate and shaped to resemble a Jesuit's habit.

Jésus de Morteau (Alsatian, Swiss). Pork-liver sausage, similar to a fine liverwurst.

Jets d'Houblon (French). Hop sprouts; cooked and eaten like a vegetable.

Jewfish. A large West Indian fish of the grouper family; valued more as a game fish than for food, for its taste is somewhat undistinguished.

Jewish Cooking. A style of preparing food, but with few original dishes, most of them having been copied from Middle European and Russian cuisines. It is usually comparatively simple but well-seasoned, home-style food. *See also* Israel.

Jew's-Ear. A cup-shaped edible fungus of spongy texture.

Jiban Homeed. A Middle Eastern sour cheese made from yoghurt.

Jicara. A rather tall gourd used in Mexico for making chocolate.

Jigger. A metal, glass, or plastic measure for alcoholic drinks; usually holds about 1½ ounces, but varies from region to region.

Jimmies (Colloquial). (1) Hard-shelled crabs. (2) Small flakes of chocolate used to decorate cakes, cookies, etc.

Jingle (British). A mixture of hot ales poured over raisin cake and baked apples.

Jintan Itam (Malayan). Cumin.

Jintan Manis (Malayan). Anise.

Joban. A Syrian cheese simply made from milk and rennet.

Jochberg. A fairly good Tyrolean cheese made of a combination of cow's and goat's milk.

Johannisberg. A wine village of the Rheingau, Germany. See Germany, The Wines of.

Johannisbeersosse (German). Red-currant-jelly sauce.

John (British). Waiter; butler.

John Barleycorn (Colloquial). All intoxicating liquors. The term, which is a personification of "barleycorn," a grain of barley, originally referred only to malt liquors.

John Collins. A tall summer drink made of Holland (Dutch) gin, lemon juice, sugar, and carbonated water over ice and usually garnished with a cherry and a lemon slice. It differs from the Tom Collins only in the type of gin used. See Collins.

John Dory; John Dorée. A small, highly esteemed European food fish.

Johnnycake. (1) A bread made of cornmeal, eggs, and milk. It is a traditional dish in Rhode Island, and family variations of recipes may be jealously guarded. To make the bread authentically, water-ground meal is preferable to the highly refined packaged product ordinarily available. (2) A cornmeal griddle cake. (3) In England it is a sweet roll made of flour, yeast, sugar, butter, eggs, and candied fruit peel. "Johnny" is a popularization of "journey cakes."

Joint. (1) One of the pieces into which the carcass of an animal is cut, such as shoulder, leg, loin, etc. (2) To cut into pieces; to sever poultry at the joints.

Joinville. (1) A butter-and-truffle sauce served with fillet of sole. (2) A layer cake filled with raspberry preserves.

Joinville, À la. Garnished with crayfish or shrimp.

Jojoto (Latin American). Very young corn in the "milk" stage.

Joko (Obsolete, French). An extremely long length of bread; a smaller version was called the joko court.

Jolerie (French). A small freshwater fish similar to perch.

Jollof; Jollov Rice (African). Dish made with chicken, rice, vegetables, meat, and heavily spiced with red peppers.

Jonathan. A variety of apple native to the United States.

Jonchée. (1) A round French cheese prepared from cow's milk (or cream) and drained in green-rush baskets. (2) A French goat's- or sheep's-milk cheese prepared with laurel leaves. (3) A fresh creamy cheese much like Caillebotte, flavored with orange-flower water and sometimes liquor; made in Santonge, France. See Caillebotte.

Jora. Germinated (sprouted) corn. It is often added by Peruvian Indians to chicha, their local beer, in order to make it stronger by fermentation; it is then called chicha de jora.

Jordan. For a discussion of the local food, see Syria; Lebanon.

Jordan Almond. (1) A nut with a long plump kernel native to Jordan. (2) A hard-shell candy-coated almond.

Jordbaer (Danish, Norwegian). Strawberries.

Jorum. (1) A large drinking bowl. (2) Its contents.

Josephine Cheese. A soft Silesian cheese prepared from whole cow's milk and cured in small cylindrical packages.

Joubarbe. A thick, heavy plant somewhat like an artichoke; a vegetable popular in French provincial cooking.

Journiac. A soft, blue-type French cheese resembling Roquefort.

Juan Fernández Langosta. A clawless lobster caught in the waters surrounding the Juan Fernández Islands west of Chile; it has an unusually fine taste and texture.

Judas Tree. A small tree, found in various parts of the world, bearing small flowers which are often pickled in vinegar and used as a flavoring ingredient or relish.

Judías (Spanish). Beans.

Judías Blancas. White beans.

Judic, À la. A style of garnishing a fillet of beef: the fillet is sautéed in butter, arranged on lettuce, then covered with a wine-and-truffle sauce.

Juène (French, Colloquial). The chevesne, a freshwater fish.

Jug. (1) A vessel, usually earthenware and of varying capacity, for storing or carrying liquids; it is narrow-necked, stout, and bulging, and has a handle. (2) A stew, usually made with game and containing the blood of the animal; traditionally cooked in an earthenware pot. (3) To cook very slowly in a casserole or earthenware pot with seasoning, forcemeat balls, and port wine, as in the preparation of jugged hare.

Juglans. The genus of trees that bear walnuts.

Jugo (Spanish). Juice.

Jugo de Naranja. Orange juice.

Jug o' Rum. A type of frog much sought after for its edible legs.

Juice. The natural liquids contained in meats, fruits, and vegetables. The juices of apples, pineapples, and tomatoes are obtained by pulping and straining the fruit; berries must be put through a fine sieve; oranges, lemons, and limes must be squeezed or reamed (*see* Juicer). Juice may be extracted from meat and poultry by means of a press.

Juicer. An implement designed to extract juice from oranges, lemons, and limes. The most common kinds of juicers are the squeezer and the reamer.

The squeezer crushes and presses the fruit. The reamer has a fluted cap that presses into a fruit half with a twisting motion; the juice extracted is full of pulp and seeds and must be strained. More juice is obtained by reaming than by squeezing. Wall and table units are available, both manually and electrically operated. In a smaller, economical type of reamer, usually made of glass, the half of the fruit is placed over the cap and twisted by hand.

Since citrus juice is highly acid, juicers should be carefully cleaned after each use.

Jujube. (1) An oriental fruit resembling a date; used for flavoring foods. Dried jujubes are used in various national cuisines, especially the Chinese. (2) A small flavored candy.

Jujube Plum. A berrylike fruit used for making jellies, pastes, and candies. The tree is native to the Mediterranean, North Africa, and China.

Julekake (Norwegian). Sweet Christmas bread.

Julep. An iced alcoholic drink with a specific sweetening or flavoring. The American mint julep is the best known, but many other kinds of julep "cups" are popular in England. The name is derived from the Persian *gulab*, a highly pungent liquid of distilled rose petals.

Juliénas. A pleasant but unimportant fruity red wine produced in the Beaujolais district of France.

Julienne (French). (1) As applied to meats, fruits, or vegetables, cut into small, matchlike shapes. (2) A vegetable soup served with shredded vegetables. (3) A clear soup or consommé served with thin strips of vegetables.

Julis. A rather small tropical fish with rather good flesh; found in warmer waters.

Jumbles. (1) (Colloquial) Various kinds of mixed cookies and candies. (2) Small lemon-flavored cakes.

Jumbo. Very large. Jumbo olives, however, are smaller than several other sizes.

Jumeaux. A cylindrical goat's-milk (sometimes cow's-milk) cheese made in south-central France.

Jumping Clam. The surf clam. *See also* Clam.

Juneberry. A wild Alaskan edible berry used chiefly for making preserves.

Junges Huhn (German). Spring chicken.

Junges Lamm (German). Spring lamb; baby lamb.

Juniper. An evergreen tree whose aromatic berries are used to flavor gin and also, sparingly, to flavor sauces and stuffings.

Juniper Wine. A beverage resembling wine; flavored with juniper berries, sometimes also with absinthe.

Junket. A dessert consisting of curds and cream or of milk mixed with rennet, then sweetened and flavored. Junket pudding is made of packaged rennet powder mixed with milk.

Junket Tablets. Tablets composed principally of rennin, a substance that coagulates milk; they are made usually from the lining of a calf's stomach.

Jupiter's Beard (Colloquial). Wild artichoke.

Jura Bleu. A spicy, sharp-flavored French blue cheese.

Jura, Côtes du. Wines produced in the Franche-Comté region of France. Both reds and whites are best drunk when fairly young, as they do not mature too well.

Jurançon. The red and white wines produced in Béarn, France. The red wine is passable; in good years the white wine is excellent.

Jus (French). Meat gravy without thickening. A roast or fowl *au jus* is served with only its natural juice.

Jus Lié (French). Natural meat juice thickened with cream or flour.

Jyoshinko (Japanese). Rice flour.

K

Kaalhode (Norwegian). Cabbage.

Kaalrouletter (Norwegian). Stuffed cabbage.

Kaas (Dutch). Cheese.

Kaaslapjes (Dutch). Baked cheese slices.

Kabayaki (Japanese). Broiled eels, sometimes served with rice. *See also* Donburi.

Kab el Ghzal (Moroccan). A crescent-shaped almond pastry.

Kabeljau (German). Cod.

Kabeljauw (Dutch). Cod.

Kabeljo Pudding (Swedish). Dried salted codfish baked with rice, milk, and eggs.

Kabinett; Kabinettwein (German). Special or reserved wine. *See* Germany, The Wines of.

Kabinettpudding (German). Cabinet pudding, served with stewed-fruit sauce.

Kabuni. An Albanian rice pudding.

Kachorn. A Siamese plant, the leaves of which are eaten as a vegetable.

Kadayif (Turkish). A sweet pastry made of shredded wheat strands covered with a thick syrup. Also called Tel Kadayif.

Kadm Budy (Turkish). Ground lamb and onions fried as croquettes.

Kadota. *See* Fig.

Kaernemaelk (Danish). Buttermilk.

Kaernemaelskoldskaal (Danish). Cold buttermilk soup.

Kaffe (Danish). Coffee.

Kaffebröd (Swedish). Coffeecake.

Kaffee (German). Coffee.

Kaffeekuchen (German). Coffeecake.

Kaffir Bread. The edible center of the breadfruit; often eaten as a staple in parts of Africa.

Kaffir Corn. Sorghum grown in Africa and used as a grain, particularly in regions with little rainfall.

Kage (Danish). Cake.

Kager fra Eget Konditori (Danish). Homemade cakes or pastries.

Kahawa (East African). Coffee.

Kail. (1) Kale, a hardy green vegetable of the cabbage family. *See also* Kale. (2) (Scottish) Cabbage broth.

Kail-Yard (British, Scotch). A vegetable garden alongside a small house.

Kaiserfleisch (German). Smoked ribs of pork served with sauerkraut and pease-pudding (dried peas).

Kaiserkäse. A mediocre tangy but mellow German cheese.

Kaiser Rolls. Vienna bread rolls made in various shapes.

Kaiserschmarrn (German). A sweet dessert omelet served cut up into pieces.

Kajmak (Turkish). A fresh cream cheese when young but strongly flavored when mature.

Kajmar Cheese. A Yugoslavian cheese similar to cream cheese that varies considerably in flavor, depending on its age.

Kakao (German, Swedish). Cocoa.

Kaki. *See* Japanese Persimmon.

Kål (Swedish). Cabbage.

Kalakukko (Finnish). A fishcake made with fresh herring, bacon, and pork.

Kalbfleisch (German). Veal.

Kalbfüsse (German). Calf's feet.

Kalbsbeuschl (Austrian). Stew made of calf's lights (lungs).

Kalbsbraten (German). Roast veal.

Kalbsbries (German). Sweetbreads.

Kalbsbrust (German). Breast of veal.

Kalbsfrikassee (German). Veal fricassee.

Kalbshaxe (German). Leg of veal.

Kalbshirn (German). Calf's brains.

Kalbskotelett (German). Veal cutlet.

Kalbsleber (German). Calf's liver.

Kalbsleberwurst (German). Veal sausage.

Kalbslende (German). Fillet of veal.

Kalbsnieren (German). Calf's kidneys.

Kalbsnierenbraten (German). Roast loin of veal.

Kalbsnierenstück (German). Loin of veal.

Kalbsragout (German). Stewed veal.

Kalbsrippchen (German). Veal chop.

Kalbsschlegel (German). Leg of veal.

Kalbsschnitzel (German). Thin cut (fillet) of veal.

Kalbsschulter (German). Shoulder of veal.

Kåldolmar (Swedish). Meat-stuffed cabbage.

Kale. A rather coarse green vegetable of the cabbage family, rich in vitamin A. It does not "head" like cabbage; its leaves have a finely toothed and curly edge. Kale is in heaviest supply during the winter months. Freshly picked kale has dark bluish-green leaves. Yellow or wilted leaves indicate a poor specimen.

Kale is cooked like spinach and other greens. The leaves should be stripped from the tough ribs and cooked, in no water other than that clinging to the leaves after washing, only until tender. Overcooking destroys the flavor and results in a loss of valuable nutrients.

Kaleege. A Himalayan pheasant of exceptionally good taste and texture.

Kalfsborst (Dutch). Breast of veal.

Kalfslapjes (Dutch). Slices of veal.

Kalfslappen (Dutch). Veal steak.

Kalfsvlees (Dutch). Veal.

Kalia (Indian). A highly spiced vegetable dish made with yoghurt; a favorite in Bengal.

Kalkoen (Dutch). Turkey.

Kallstadt. A wine district of the Palatinate, Germany, which produces both red and white wines.

Kålsoppa med Frikadeller (Swedish). Cabbage soup with meat dumplings.

Kalte Ente. Although the words actually mean "cold duck" in German, the term is used to describe a warm weather beverage made of sparkling white wine, soda, slices of lemon, and sometimes dry red wine.

Kaltschale (German). A cold fruit soup or salad prepared with wine.

Kalua Puaa (Hawaiian). A young pig covered with leaves and roasted over stones.

Kalv (Danish). Veal.

Kalvbräss (Swedish). Sweetbreads.

Kalvefilet (Danish). Fillet of veal.

Kalvelever med Løgsauce (Danish). Calf's liver with onion sauce.

Kalvemedaljong (Norwegian). Fillet of veal.

Kalvesteg (Danish). Roast veal.

Kalvestek (Norwegian). Roast veal.

Kalvesuss (Norwegian). Jellied veal.

Kalvfilet (Swedish). Fillet of veal.

Kalvkött (Swedish). Veal.

Kalvkyckling (Swedish). Veal rolls in cream.

Kalvlever (Swedish). Calf's liver.

Kalvrulader (Swedish). Braised veal rolls.

Kalvstek (Swedish). Roast veal.

Kamaboko (Japanese). A steamed fishcake.

Kamano Lomi (Hawaiian). Shredded salt salmon combined with green onions, tomatoes, and ice water.

Kamias (Philippine). A light green fruit sometimes used to impart a slightly sourish taste to certain dishes; it is used like tamarind.

Kamloop. A variety of trout.

Kampfer's Crab. The Dungeness crab, found on the West Coast of North America.

Kan; Kanne (German, Dutch). Wine measure, equal to about 1 quart.

Kandy. City in Ceylon; it is believed that the word "candy" is derived from its name. The Singhalese prepared a sort of candy with sugar and molasses.

Kaneel (Dutch). Cinnamon.

Kanel (Swedish). Cinnamon.

Kangar. An edible cardoon with thistles, a member of the artichoke family; used in Iran in many dishes and in salads.

Kangaroo Apple. An egg-shaped Australian fruit, slightly acid and with a coarse texture.

Kangkong. A Philippine cabbage that grows in wet soil.

Kaninchen (German). Rabbit.

Kannafee Dough (Middle Eastern). Dough made from raw shredded wheat; it is baked with nuts, sugar, and spices and covered with a sugar syrup.

Kansiyé. A meat or chicken stew made with tomatoes, onions, and spices in Guinea.

Kanten. A gelatin made from seaweed in the Orient.

Kanyak. The Turkish imitation of Cognac.

Kaoliang Wine (Chinese). Although called a

Chinese "wine," this is a very strong liquor with about 50 percent alcohol, made from grain.

Kapaun (German). Capon.

Kaper (British). An oat biscuit, usually buttered and served with cheese.

Kaper (German). Caper.

Kapi (Siamese). A spicy, rather strong-smelling paste made of very small shrimp; eaten with boiled rice.

Kapucijners. Pan-fried steak and brown beans in a dark brown sauce, with onions and gherkins; a specialty of Curaçao.

Karab. The Russian sheep's-milk Eriwani cheese.

Karahi (Indian). A deep hemispherical cooking utensil.

Karamel (German). Caramel.

Karamellpudding (Norwegian). Caramel pudding.

Karashi (Japanese). Mustard.

Karbonadekaker (Norwegian). Hamburger made with mixed meats.

Kardemommekaker (Norwegian). Cardamom cookies.

Karelien Steak (Finnish). Mutton and steak cooked together.

Kari (French). Curry.

Karlsbad Fritter (Middle European). A fritter containing pitted red cherries.

Karlsbad Salt Stick (Dutch). A rich yeast or baking-powder dough shaped into a long roll and heavily sprinkled with salt and caraway seeds.

Karnemelk (Dutch). Buttermilk.

Kärnmjölk (Swedish). Buttermilk.

Karonda. A wild gooseberry growing mainly in India.

Karotten (German). Carrots.

Karp (Swedish). Carp.

Karper (Dutch). Carp.

Karpfen (German). Carp.

Kartoffelgerichte (German). Potato dishes.

Kartoffelklösse (German). Potato dumplings.

Kartoffelmos (Danish). Mashed potatoes.

Kartoffeln (German). Potatoes.

    Kartoffeln, Gebackene. Baked potatoes.

Kartoffelpuffer (German). Potato pancakes.

Kartoffelpüree (German). Mashed potatoes.

Kartoffelsalat (Danish, German). Potato salad.

Kartoffelsuppe (German). Potato soup.

Kartoffler (Danish). Potatoes.

Karvi. A soft Norwegian cheese with caraway seeds.

Kasala. A reef fish found in Fijian waters; quite good when fried; when baked, its soft flesh tends to disintegrate.

Käse (German). Cheese.

Käseflädle (German). A pancake or pastry flavored with cheese and sage.

Käseplatte (German). Cheese platter.

Kasha. Russian buckwheat groats, as much a staple in Russia as are rice in China and pasta in Italy. It can be used in place of plain or wild rice or other starches, and may also be used as a stuffing.

Kasher (Jewish). To make foods kosher or ritually proper for eating. *See also* Kosher.

Kash Kwanh. A simple Balkan cheese resembling Parmesan. When young it is a table cheese, when mature a grating cheese.

Kashruth. The ritualistic Hebrew laws for kosher foods and their preparation. *See also* Kosher.

Kassara. A Lebanese wine that tastes fairly good but lacks bouquet.

Kasseri (Greek). A quite firm ewe's-milk cheese.

Kastanien (German). Chestnuts.

Kastanje (Dutch). Chestnut.

Kat. An Arabian tea shrub.

Kataif (Middle Eastern). A sweet pancake stuffed with various fillings.

Katschawalj Cheese. A Yugoslavian sheep's-milk cheese imitating Italy's Cacciocavallo. It comes in a variety of shapes and the cheeses usually weigh about 6 pounds.

Katsuobushi (Japanese). Dried flaked bonito, used particularly for preparing *dashi*.

Kattern Cake (British). A yeast cake made with caraway seeds for St. Catherine's Day.

Katuray (Philippine). The edible flowers of the katuray tree (*Sesbania*).

Katurumurunga (Ceylonese). Flowers; used especially in the preparation of omelets.

Kaviardlåda (Swedish). Baked fish roe.

Kawa Kawa. A bony reef fish with a passably good taste found in Fijian waters.

Kawerma (Turkish). Small balls of ground lamb served as an appetizer.

Käx (Swedish). An unsweetened cracker.

Kayo Manis (Malayan). Cinnamon.

Kebab; Kebob. Small cubes of meat, poultry, or fish threaded on skewers and usually broiled over charcoal but sometimes prepared in an oven

broiler. They are popular in almost every country of the Near East as well as in Russia. The selected food is usually allowed to stand in a well-seasoned marinade, and it may be alternated on the skewers with pieces of vegetables, such as tomatoes, onions, and green peppers. Seasoned ground meat is also prepared on skewers in some countries. Kebabs are usually served with rice.

Kebbuck (Scotch). A type of country cheese.

Kechel (British, Obsolete). A very small cake.

Kecsege. A fish resembling sturgeon; found in the Balkan countries.

Kedgeree (Indian). A fish-and-rice dish. The rice is cooked until dry and firm, then sautéed in butter with onions, spices, and cooked fish; usually garnished with sliced hard-cooked eggs, and served with a curry sauce. It is sometimes a breakfast dish in England.

Kedlock. A wild plant resembling field mustard or kex.

Keech (British). (1) The solid fat of a slaughtered animal formed into a ball. (2) A loaf of bread.

Keeling (Scotch). A codfish.

Kee Mun. A delicious Chinese black tea.

Keep-Ming-Yuk (Eskimo). Edible wild cranberries.

Kefalotir; Kefalotiry. A firm, pungent salty cheese made in the Balkan countries; may be eaten at the table or used for grating.

Kefir; Kephir (Russian). A fermented goat's-milk beverage similar to sour milk; popular in the Caucasus. *See also* Fermented Milk.

Keftedes (Greek, Middle Eastern). Well-seasoned chopped beef combined with mashed potatoes and fried in croquettes or patties.

Keg. A barrel containing 10 gallons or less.

Kĕladi (Southeast Asian). A cylindrical tuber eaten like potatoes. The green leaves of some species may be eaten like a vegetable. When boiled, they are somewhat soapy, but may be satisfactory when fried. If eaten raw, they may cause an irritation in the mouth.

Kelale Narangi (Iranian). *See* Tangerine Shreds.

Kelapa (Indonesian). Coconut.

Kelkel. A slice of salted dried sole.

Kellerabfüllung. Original bottling, a German wine term. *See* Germany, The Wines of.

Kellerabzug. Bottled by the estate, a German wine term. *See* Germany, The Wines of.

Kellermeister (German). Cellarmaster; the man in charge of a wine cellar.

Kemiry. A small nut native to the South Pacific.

Kenchoer (Malayan). A root with a taste similar to that of ginger.

Kengphed (Laotian). A fish chowder made with coconut milk and spices.

Kentish Pudding-Pie (British). A pudding partly boiled and partly baked. An unbaked pie shell is filled with a cooked rice pudding containing currants, then sprinkled with nutmeg and baked.

Kentucky Burgoo. A heavy stew made of meat, poultry, vegetables, and seasonings.

Kentucky Ham. A very salty, heavily cured country ham requiring long soaking in water before cooking. For a milder but still smoky flavor the water should be changed during the cooking. The ham is usually served cold in thin slices.

Kern (Obsolete). Kernel.

Kernel. (1) The soft, edible portion inside the harder shell of a nut or in the pit or stone of a fruit. (2) The seed of wheat, barley, and other grains.

Kern Milk (Scotch). Buttermilk.

Kerrie. Another spelling for curry.

Kers (Dutch). Cherry.

Kesakeitto (Finnish). An elaborate vegetable soup containing numerous vegetables, milk, cream, and shrimp.

Kesari (Indian). A dessert made with vermicelli.

Ket (Obsolete). Raw meat or flesh.

Ketchup; Catsup. A seasoned tomato sauce served with a great variety of foods. It should not be served with a sauced dish, for it would overpower the flavor. Ketchups may be made also from mushrooms, walnuts, anchovies, etc., but such products are rare compared with the bottled tomato sauce.

Ketmie; Gumbo; Lady Fingers. An edible plant; the okra, or a similar vegetable.

Kettle. A household utensil, usually made of metal, for boiling water or other liquids.

Keuftes. Much like Keftedes but made with bread. *See* Keftedes.

Kewane. An excellent Japanese green tea which, when steeped, provides a rich-flavored greenish brew.

Kewra (Indian). A flavoring obtained from the flower of a plant with the same name.

Kex. The dry hollow stalks of wild chervil and cow parsnip; used to flavor foods.

Khā. A Siamese tuber with a distinctive flavor.

Khansamah (Indian). The head of a kitchen.

Kharoff (Kuwaiti). Lamb stuffed with rice, nuts, and raisins.

Khau Mau (Siamese). Unhusked young rice, flattened and then roasted.

Khoa (Indian). Concentrated or boiled-down whole milk cooked and dried to a powder; used in making many sweet preparations.

Khooz Fe Zatore (Middle Eastern). Bread made with zatore, a mixture of herbs.

Khoresh (Iranian). A stew flavored with a sour ingredient, such as lemon or lime juice or verjuice.

Khubiz (Arabian). Bread made either flat in sheets or like a loaf.

Khushkhash (Israeli). Bitter orange.

Kibbee (Middle Eastern). Cracked wheat and meat, lightly or well spiced; served in a wide variety of ways.

　Kibbee Sineea. A baked dish made with ground lamb and cracked wheat.

　Kibbee Sameek. A dish made of cracked wheat, ground shrimp, pine nuts, and onions.

Kibbetz (Israeli). A flat bread.

Kibbled Wheat. Chopped or crushed wheat fragments.

Kichel (German). A small cake.

Kickshaw. Any delicate, unusual, or fancy food item, as, for example, caviar.

Kid. A young goat slaughtered before it has been weaned; a delicacy in several Mediterranean countries.

Kidney Beans. A dark or light red bean that is usually dried; often used in New England in preparing Boston baked beans and in the Southwest for chili.

Kidney Potato. A kidney-shaped potato.

Kidneys. Glandular excretory organs of animals. Veal and lamb kidneys (sold as kidney chops) are rich in nutrients. The outer membrane, fat white veins, and core should be removed before cooking. Veal and lamb kidneys should be cooked only a few minutes to prevent toughness. Beef and pork kidneys should be split in half and soaked in water and vinegar before cooking; they require longer cooking than veal and lamb kidneys.

Kidney Vetch. An herb of the pea family; formerly popular but now seldom used.

Kiedrich. A wine village in the Rheingau, Germany. *See* Germany, The Wines of.

Kiel Sprats. Smoked anchovy.

Kilawin (Philippine). Dish made with onions, garlic, and vinegar.

Kilderkin (British). A barrel with a capacity of 18 English gallons.

Kilkis. Very small Norwegian fish resembling anchovies; preserved like anchovies.

Kill-Devil (West Indian). Any very strong rum.

Kilning. A process in beer making in which malt is heated to stop the germination process.

Kimali Burek (Turkish). A pancake filled with a spiced ground-meat or fish mixture and rolled into a cigar shape.

Kim Chee (Korean). Relish; usually made of cabbage, but may be prepared with any vegetable. *See* Korea.

Kinako (Japanese). Powdered soybean.

Kinchay (Philippine). Chinese celery.

Kinchee (Malayan). Chinese celery or cabbage.

King, À la. In a style consisting of a well-seasoned white or cream sauce mixed with cooked chopped poultry or fish and usually containing mushrooms and pimientos. It may be served on toast or in a croustade or patty shell.

King Coconut. A large, gold-colored coconut, having sweet, soft flesh, and filled with cloudy, sweet water; it grows chiefly in Ceylon.

King Crab; Alaska King Crab. A gigantic horseshoe-shaped shellfish caught off the coast of Alaska. The body contains little that is edible. Neat chunks of meat, often 8–9 inches long and an inch in diameter, are easily extracted from the crab's long, tubular legs. Either frozen or fresh, the white flesh is extremely tender and beautifully flavored.

Kingdom of Fife Pie (Scotch). Rabbit pie.

Kingfish. A large excellent-flavored fish found in both the Atlantic and Pacific Oceans. The many varieties have different names in different regions.

King Minos. A pleasing, moderately dry Greek white wine.

King Mullet. The West Indian goatfish.

King of Bread. A title assumed by Henry IV of France after he stated: "He who rules the nation's bread is a greater ruler than he who rules their souls."

King Pine. Pineapple.

King Salmon. California salmon.

King's Taste. Perfection; the best.

Kip (Dutch). Chicken.

Kipe (British). A basket used to catch fish.

Kipferl (Austrian). A crescent-shaped roll.

Kipkap (Belgian). A headcheese consisting of pig's feet in aspic.

Kippenlever (Dutch). Chicken liver.

Kipper Nut (Colloquial). Peanut.

Kippers. Herring split, salted, dried, and smoked; a popular English breakfast food. Kippers should be wiped with a damp cloth, rubbed with butter, and grilled until crisp. Scotch kippers are the best.

Kir (French). An apéritif drink made of fresh young white Burgundy wine and Crème de Cassis.

Kirn (Scotch). A supper at harvest time.

Kirsch; Kirschwasser. A colorless brandy with a bitter-almond flavor for which cherries are mashed with wooden paddles in a wooden tub, then allowed to ferment, stones and all. The mixture is distilled twice, then stored in earthenware containers to mature. The best kirsch comes from Switzerland and the Black Forest in Germany.

Kirschen (German). Cherries.

Kirschtorte (German). Cherry tart.

Kirschwasser. *See* Kirsch.

Kirsebaer (Danish). Cherry.

Kishek (Middle Eastern). Soup made with eggs, cracked wheat, and yoghurt.

Kissel (Russian). A dessert made from various berries and served in a charlotte mold with heavy cream; eaten either hot or cold.

Kisses. Cookies made with meringue, sometimes with chopped nuts added. Also, a commercial chocolate candy.

Kissing-Crust. The part of the upper crust of a loaf of bread that while baking overhangs the edge of the pan and touches the loaf next to it.

Kitchen. The place where food is prepared.

Kitchen Bouquet. A commercial product for flavoring and coloring soups, stews, and gravies.

Kitchenette. A very small kitchen. In some modern apartments they are like airless, partly equipped closets containing a miniature refrigerator, range, and sink.

Kitchen Equipment. Any item that is used in the preparation of food. A properly equipped kitchen makes cooking easier and better. Equipment should be stored close to where it is used; for example, pots and pans should be kept near the range and oven. Utensils include:

Bottle opener
Brushes, pastry and vegetable
Can opener, electric, hand-operated
Carving board
Chopping board, hardwood
Colander
Cork screw, cartridge, winged metal
Custard cups
Cutters, biscuit, cooky, cheese
Egg beater, rotary, portable electric
Egg slicer
Electric blender
Electric mixer
Food chopper, electric or hand-operated
Forks, long-handled two-prong
Graters
Jar opener
Juice extractor
Kitchen shears
Knives
    Boning knife, for cutting and filleting
    Bread knife, usually with serrated edge
    Butcher knife, for cutting raw poultry and
      meat
    Cake cutter, actually a many pronged utensil
      used for angel and sponge cakes.

Carving knives, for hot and cold meats
Cleaver, for cutting through sinew, flattening, etc.
French knife, for slicing, chopping, etc.
Grapefruit knife, to section citrus fruits
Paring knives
Utility knife, for slicing, icing, etc.
Ladle
Measuring cups, 1 glass cup for liquid, and 1 metal set for dry ingredients
Measuring spoons, in a set ranging in size from ½ teaspoon to 1 tablespoon
Mixing bowls, available nested in several sizes
Mixing spoons, metal and wood
Pancake turner
Pastry blender
Pastry cloth
Pot holders
Pots and pans

Many types of pots and pans are available: aluminum, stainless-steel, stainless-steel with copper bottoms, metal-lined copper, cast-iron, enameled ware, ceramic, glass, pottery. Experiment to find the type you prefer, but tin or aluminum are best for cakes and tortes. Glass is best for pies. You can cook and serve in many of the new Pyroceram pots and casseroles. Most casseroles are flameproof, so they can be used over direct heat or in the oven. Many pans have ovenproof handles so they can be put in the oven. Follow the manufacturer's instructions for seasoning and caring for each type.

Brownie pan, 8 x 8 inches, 2 inches deep
Cake pans
Casseroles, 2-quart, 3-quart
Coffee maker
Cookie sheets
Deep-fat fryer, electric or regular with basket
Double boiler, 1½-quart

Dutch oven, 5-quart
Molds
Muffin pans

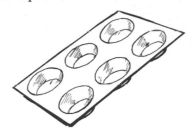

Pie plates, 9-inch, 11-inch
Roasting pan, large, with rack

Saucepans, 1-quart, 1½-quart, 3-quart, 5-quart with covers

Skillets, 5-inch, 7-inch, 10-inch with covers

Soufflé dish, straight-sided, 1½-quart, 2-quart
Tube pan

Racks for cooling cakes

Rolling pin
Rubber scraper
Sifter

Slotted spoon

Spatula

Strainer
Thermometers, meat, deep-fat frying, candy, oven

Timer
Tongs, for lifting hot foods, ice
Wire whisks

Kitchen Garden. A very small garden in which vegetables (and sometimes fruit) are grown only for the use of an individual family.

Kitchenry (British). (1) Kitchen servants. (2) The art of cookery.

Kitchenware. All utensils used in a kitchen.

Kitchines Bread. Thin, soft oatcakes.

Kite (British). A flatfish of the turbot family.

Kiveve (Paraguayan). Squash dish made with cornmeal and cheese.

Kjargaard. A hard rennet Danish cheese made from skimmed cow's milk.

Kjeks (Norwegian). Crackers, cookies.

Kjott (Norwegian). Meat.
　Kjøttboller; Kjøttkaker. Meatballs.
　Kjøttfarse. Hamburger.
　Kjøttpudding. Meat pudding.

Klaben (German). White bread containing currants, almonds, etc.

Klare Suppen (German). Clear soups.

Klatschkäse. A mild, simple German cheese often used to accompany afternoon coffee.

Kleingebäck (German). Fine pastries.

Klejner (Danish). Crullers.

Klencz. *See* Brinza Cheese.

Kletskoppen. A Belgian spiced biscuit.

Klevovaca (Yugoslavian). Plum brandy with juniper berries added, redistilled so as to produce a gin-like beverage.

Klimp (Swedish). Dumplings.

Klipfish. A salted and dried cod boned, kept in salt for a month, then washed and dried slowly. It is known as *bacalao* in Spanish-speaking countries.

Klipfisk (Danish). Dried codfish.

Klippfisk (Norwegian). Fish spread on the cliffs to dry.

Klobásy. A very thick Czechoslovakian frankfurter.

Klopfer. A sausage prepared in Basel, Switzerland.

Klösse (German). Dumplings.

Kloster Cheese. (1) A soft, ripe, finger-shaped cheese made in southern Germany. (2) A soft, ripe rennet cheese made in France from whole cow's milk.

Knaafeh (Arabian). Cheese pastry.

Knab; Knabble (British). To nibble or pick at food.

Knäckebröd (Swedish). A hard-tack rye bread.

Knaidel (Jewish). Dumpling, especially for soups.

Kneading. The process of folding, pushing, and turning yeast dough in order to change its rough, uneven texture to a smooth elastic ball. Kneading helps blend ingredients. It improves flavor and develops the gluten, which in turn develops good grain and texture in bread and rolls. As the dough is kneaded the gluten is rendered more flexible and pliable so that it will stretch when the leavening gas expands and trap the bubbles of gas produced by the yeast.

Knedlíky (Czechoslovakian). Dumplings.

Knife. A cutting instrument with a blade and a handle. *See* Cutlery.

Knipperlé. Alsatian white grapes and the medium-sweet white wine made from them.

Knish (Jewish). An unsweetened pastry filled with a variety of fillings including potato, cheese, or meat; eaten as a snack food, an appetizer, or as an accompaniment to meat dishes.

Knobbards. Small mediocre edible shellfish found along parts of the English coast.

Knoblauch (German). Garlic.

Knobs. (1) Small shellfish-like whelks. (2) Sugar lumps.

Knockit (British). A piece of bread eaten at lunchtime.

Knockwurst (German). A large, thick sausage similar to a frankfurter.

Knödel (German). A type of dumpling; served with butter, cream, cheese, or in soups.

Knoflook (Dutch). Garlic.

Knollensellerie (German). Celery root; celeriac.

Knost; Pulost Cheese. A Norwegian cheese made by treating sour milk with rennet.

Knot Roll (British). A small milk bread roll.

Knotted Marjoram. The sweetest and most fragrant variety of marjoram.

Knoutberry (British). Cloudberry.

Knuckle. Meat which includes a joint.

Knuckle of Veal. Veal from below the knee joint; used mostly for stock and stews.

Knuppel (German). Bread rolls made with a mixture of rye and wheat flours.

Knusper (German). A small cinnamon teacake covered with chopped almonds.

Kob. An African water antelope whose meat, though somewhat dry, has a pleasant taste.

Kobe Beef (Japanese). The excellent-tasting beef from Kobe. Among the many reasons given for its excellence are the daily massaging and the feeding of the cattle with beer, but the type of cattle is equally important.

Koberner. White wine made from grapes grown in Kobern in the Moselle Valley, Germany. *See* Germany, The Wines of.

Kobu. A large variety of Japanese seaweed used in making soup stock.

Kochenkäse. A salt-free white dessert cheese made in Luxembourg.

Kød (Danish). Meat.

Kødboller. Meatballs.

Kødretter. Meat dishes.

Koek (Dutch). Cake.

Koekjes (Dutch). Cakes; cookies.

Koffie (Dutch). Coffee.

Koffie Verkeerd. Coffee with hot milk.

Koffie zonder Melk. Black coffee.

Kofta; Kufta (Middle Eastern). A ground meatball.

Kogt (Danish). Boiled.

Kohada. A small Japanese fish with a rather blue skin; used in preparing *sushi*.

Kohl (German). Cabbage.

Kohlrabi. Cabbage turnip, a variety of cabbage cultivated for the thickened stem that grows just above the ground. The leaves, when young and tender, are eaten as greens. The so-called "root," really the stem, is best diced and cooked like cauliflower. It tastes something like turnip but has a more delicate texture.

Kohlroulade (German). Cabbage stuffed with meat.

Kohlsuppe (German). Cabbage soup.

Kokeboterom. A rather sweet bun containing raisins; made near Dunkirk, France.

Kokonda (Fijian). Fish prepared in coconut milk.

Kokosnoot (Dutch). Coconut.

Kokosnöt (Swedish). Coconut.

Kokt (Swedish). Boiled.

Kokusmakroner (Norwegian). Coconut macaroons.

Kolachi; Kolachy (Middle European). A bun filled or topped with cheese or fruit.

Koldtbord; Koltbord (Norwegian). A cold table containing fish, meats, salads, cheeses, etc.

Kolja (Swedish). Haddock.

Kolodniki (East European). A cold soup made with beet leaves, herbs, and *kvass* (a fermented liquid); usually garnished with sturgeon, cucumber, and sour cream.

Kolodny (Lithuanian). Dumplings, usually filled with marrow and onion, similar to ravioli; sometimes served fried and sprinkled with bread crumbs.

Kolos-Monostor. A Romanian sheep's-milk cheese specially produced by the faculty of an agricultural college.

Kolosvarer. A Romanian cheese imitating Port du Salut.

Kombu (Japanese). A type of saltwater algae which is used as a flavoring in fish soups; dried kombu is used in making tea.

Komkommers (Dutch). Cucumbers.

Kommisbrot (German). Pumpernickel, made with rye flour and meal.

Kompott (German). Fruit compote.

Kona. A region in Hawaii that produces an excellent mild coffee.

Konasansho (Japanese). Powdered or crushed pepper.

Konbu. A Japanese seaweed often used in making *dashi*, a soup stock which forms the base for many dishes.

Konditorei. A German or an Austrian pastry shop.

Königsberger Klopse (German). Meatballs consisting of ground pork and veal, served with capers.

Königskäse. A German cheese imitating Bel Paese.

Konijn (Dutch). Rabbit.

Konjak (Swedish). Brandy; Cognac.

Konjak (Albanian). A type of crude spirit made by peasants.

Koodoo; Kudu. A large brown African antelope often used for food.

Koofteea (Indian). A fried, curried meatball.

Kool (Dutch). Cabbage.

Kop (Dutch). Cup.

Kopanisti. A rather spicy Greek cheese with a blue-green mold.

Kopfsalat (German). Lettuce salad.

Kopje Tart (Dutch). Tart with a raised center and a creamy-mixture filling.

Kopp (Swedish). Cup.

Koppen (German). A rather firm goat's-milk cheese produced in a cup-shaped mold.

Korea. Korean food is somewhat like Chinese food in that it is often cut up small so that it may be eaten with chopsticks; the flavorings used are akin to those of China, especially soy sauce, ginger, rice, mushrooms, and similar ingredients. Unlike the generally bland Chinese food (except in Szechuan), Korean dishes can be hot and spicy, many of them approaching the fiery. Garlic and hot chili peppers are often used freely.

Appetizer courses are seldom served, and meals usually begin with a soup, called *kook*. Typical soups include those made with potatoes, cabbage, bean sprouts, chicken, and they are quite hearty. The most substantial food is white rice, *heen pahb*; it is often combined with beans (*pah pahb*), with bean sprouts (*kong na mool pahb*), and various other ingredients. Koreans like broiled meats and chicken, and also enjoy foods cut up into cubes and broiled on a skewer, *sahn juk*. But a meal would hardly be worth eating, Koreans think, if there were no *kim chee*, the national relish or pickle of the country. *Kim chee* is not readily or easily defined, but it is a kind of fermented, salty vegetable. However, it is also not easily classifiable, for it is made with a very wide range of ingredients, although most usually prepared with Chinese cabbage, *daikon* (Japanese white radish), cucumbers, onions, leeks, but also with fish, fruits, and water chestnuts. There are two principal types of *kim chee*: the summer (or perishable) type, and the more important winter type, which is long-lasting and is used in place of green vegetables during the cold winter months. Incidentally, winter *kim chee* has a peculiarly pungent aroma which often repels Westerners.

During the mild weather Koreans eat as many vegetables as possible, particularly enjoying fried sweet potatoes, *kam ja juhn*, and green peppers, *ko chu juhn*. If dessert is served, it is usually fresh fruit, but occasionally flower cakes, *kwa-juhn*, may be served; *mils sam*, a sort of sesame and cinnamon cooky, is another possibility. Chestnuts and dates often terminate a meal.

The national drink of the country is *cha*, tea,

served plain and quite strong. Ginger-flavored tea is an occasional beverage, and there is a fruit punch, *hwa chiah*.

Korintkaka (Swedish). Fruitcake.

Korma (Indian). Curry, often prepared with dried coconut and ground sesame seeds.

Korv (Swedish). Sausage.

Kørvelsuppe (Danish). Chervil soup.

Kos Ambul (Ceylonese). A curry made with jackfruit.

Kosher. The term "kosher" applies to the selection and preparation of foods for human consumption according to traditional Jewish ritual and dietary laws. Kosher ritual governs which animals and poultry may be used as food; it requires that the livestock or poultry be slaughtered by a *shochet*, an official trained in the laws of *Kashruth*, that is, the state of being kosher. Only the flesh of quadrupeds that chew the cud and have cloven hoofs, such as sheep and cattle, may be consumed, and only the forequarters of such animals may be eaten.

Only fish with scales may be eaten. Orthodox Jews do not eat shellfish. Furthermore, after eating meat, they may not eat dairy foods for a stated period. Meat and dairy foods must be cooked in separate utensils and served on separate dishes. Religious Jews must therefore have two complete sets of dishes, silverware, and pots.

Koteletter (Danish). Chops.

Kotlett (Swedish). Cutlet.

Kött (Swedish). Meat.

Köttbullar. Meatballs.

Köttfärs. Hamburger.

Koud (Dutch). Cold.

Kougelhupf. *See* Kugelhupf.

Koumiss; Kumiss. An ancient fermented milk drink made in the Caucasus Mountains of Russia from either mare's or camel's milk. It is distinguished by a double fermentation—a lactic-acid and an alcoholic stage. To each fresh batch of koumiss a small quantity from the previous making is added. The milk is agitated frequently during fermentation; after about 36 hours the finished beverage is sour, effervescent, and mildly alcoholic.

Kow Paht (Siamese). Fried rice mixed with fish, shellfish, and meat.

Kraasesuppe (Danish). Giblet soup.

Krab (Dutch). Crab.

Krabba (Swedish). Crab.

Krabbe (Danish). Crab.

Krabben (German). Crabs, shrimps.

Kraemmerhuse (Danish). A cone-shaped pastry.

Kräfta (Swedish). Crayfish.

Kraftbrühe (German). Bouillon.

Kraftbrühe mit Hühnerfleisch. Chicken soup.

Kraftsuppe (German). Beef soup.

Kransekage (Danish). Almond cookies.

Kransekake (Norwegian). Pyramid cake.

Kranzkuchen (German). A braided sweet cake.

Krapfen (German). Fritters.

Krauterkäse. A firm grating cheese abounding in herbs; made in Switzerland.

Krebs (German). Crayfish.

Krebsehaler med Dildmayonnaise (Danish). Crayfish with dill mayonnaise.

Kreeft (Dutch). Lobster.

Kremfløte (Norwegian). Cream.

Kremkake (Norwegian). Cream cake.

Krems. A wine district in Austria, not far from Vienna and on the Danube, which produces fairly good white wines, but rather poor red types.

Krenfleisch (Austrian). Boiled pork with horseradish.

Kreuznach. A wine village in the Nahe region of Germany. *See* Germany, The Wines of.

Krevetten (German). Shrimp.

Kriek-Lambic. A Belgian beer flavored with cherries.

Kriekskens (Belgian). Sour cherries pickled in vinegar.

Kringle; Kringli (Norwegian). (1) Coffeecake. (2) A special-shaped loaf of bread.

Kringles. Rich, short, flaky biscuits.

Krokanis (Norwegian). Nougat ice cream.

Kroketten (German). Croquettes.

Kromeskile. A croquette made with rolled slices of bacon filled with seasoned chopped meat or minced chicken, then dipped in batter and fried in deep fat; served as a hot hors d'oeuvre.

Kromeskis (German, Polish). Chopped or ground meat.

Krona Pepper. A mild red pepper.

Kroppkator (Swedish). Potato dumplings.

Kruiden (Dutch). Herbs.

Kruidenomelet (Dutch). Herb omelet.

Kruidnagel (Dutch). Clove.

Kruisbes (Dutch). Gooseberry.

Krupnik. (1) (Russian) A soup made with buckwheat groats. (2) (Polish) A soup prepared with vegetables and roast chicken.

Krupnikopf. A rather sweet liqueur, made with honey and flavored with caraway seeds; popular in Latvia and Lithuania.

Krusbär (Swedish). Gooseberry.

Krusten (German). Pastries.

Krut (Indian). A very dry, hard skim-milk cheese.

Krutt. A primitive cheese made by Mongolians or nomadic Asiatic tribesmen; produced from the sour skim milks of various animals, shaped into balls, and sun-dried.

Krydder (Danish). Rolls cut in half; the upper half is *overkrydder*, the lower half *underkrydder*.

Kryddost (Swedish). A pleasant anise-flavored cheese.

Kryddpeppar (Swedish). Pimiento.

Kryddresild (Norwegian). Spiced herring.

Kuali. A Southeast Asian frying pan or similar utensil.

Kuban. *See* Fermented Milk.

Kubane (Yemenite). A yeast bread cooked overnight.

Kubba Shalgum (Iraqi). A soup prepared with meatballs, vegetables (especially turnips), raisins, and almonds.

Kuchay. A rather mild aromatic garlic native to China and other Asiatic countries.

Kuchen (German). Cake.

Kuchenragout (German). A sweetbread stew containing green peas, mussels, and a cream sauce.

Kuegeli-Pastete (Swiss). A puff pastry filled with mushrooms, sweetbreads, etc.; made in Lucerne.

Kugelhupf. A sweet yeast cake containing flour, yeast, sugar, eggs, candied fruits, and nuts; usually baked in a mold with a swirling pattern. It is of Alsatian origin, and it is believed that Carême popularized it in Paris. It is generally available in Europe and in American bakeries specializing in Continental pastries.

Kuku (Iranian). An egg dish made with meat, fish, and poultry.

Kukui. A Hawaiian nut.

Kulitch; Kulich (Russian). A tall, rich baba baked at Eastertime. The yeast dough, containing white raisins, saffron, chopped almonds, and rum, is raised in a cylinder and best baked in a tin mold.

Kulolo (Hawaiian). Pudding made of taro, brown sugar, and coconut milk.

Kulski (Polish). Cheese dumplings, sometimes prepared with liver or ham.

Kumeras. A New Zealand tuber similar to the sweet potato.

Kumi Kumi. A New Zealand squash similar to the pumpkin.

Kuminost. A medium-firm Norwegian cheese filled with caraway seeds.

Kumiss. *See* Koumiss.

Kumler (Norwegian). Potato dumplings.

Kümmel. (1) Caraway. (2) A liqueur flavored with cumin and caraway. It may have originated in Germany, although the Dutch claim to have been the first to make it. Russia is now a large producer and consumer.

Kümmelkäse. A rather firm German cheese made with caraway seeds; considered ideal with beer.

Kümmelkraut (German). Cabbage with caraway seeds.

Kumminost (Swedish). A cheese containing cumin seeds and sometimes caraway.

Kumquat. A very small, bitter citrus fruit cultivated extensively in Japan and China and in Florida and California. Fresh kumquats are available during the winter. They are delicious sliced thin and included in a fresh-fruit salad. Preserved kumquats are available the year round.

Kundol. A Philippine fruit similar to the jackfruit.

Kunkokee (Korean). Broiled steak in soy sauce.

Kuping Tikus (Southeast Asian). A dry fungus that must be soaked in water before being used.

Kürbis (German). Squash; vegetable marrow.

Kürbissuppe (German). Pumpkin soup.

Kuruma Iraichchi (Ceylonese). A white curry made with lamb.

Kushikatsu (Japanese). Bits of pork placed on a skewer alternately with onion, dipped in batter, and deep-fried; similar to *tonkatsu*.

Kuthra (Syrian). Vegetables.

Kutteln (German). Tripe.

Kuzu (Turkish). Young lamb; baby milk lamb.

Kwali (Malaysian). A deep cooking pan with a large open mouth used for deep-fat frying foods, and preparing noodles.

Kvass; Kwass (Russian). A home-brewed beverage similar to beer, effervescent and mildly alcoholic, made by adding fermented yeast to rye flour mixed with sprouted barley; sometimes flavored with mint leaves or juniper berries. A simpler version is made by fermenting rye bread, sugar, and water.

Kwie-Kwie. A food fish native to the swamp waters of the Guianas, South America.

Kyckling (Swedish). Chicken.

Kyet-u-Hin. A Burmese spicy egg curry.

Kylling (Danish, Norwegian). Chicken.

Kyllingsalat (Norwegian). Chicken salad.

Kyloe. Small Scottish longhorn cattle.

L

Labahita. The surgeon fish, a food fish found in the Pacific.

Laban (Middle Eastern). A cultured-milk drink; yoghurt.

Labanee. A Syrian cheese made from yoghurt and allowed to drain; salt is added later.

Labarde. One of the important wine-growing districts of the Médoc region of France. Its best vintages are sold under the names of their *châteaux. See* France, The Wines of.

Lablab Bean; Egyptian Bean. A black bean native to India and extensively cultivated in Asia and the Middle East. The young bean pods and the matured beans are edible, and the leaves are sometimes cooked as a vegetable.

Labong (Philippine). Bamboo shoots.

Labrus. A brightly colored, rather tasteless Mediterranean fish; best with other seafoods in a bouillabaisse.

Labskaus (German). Herring-and-pork stew.

Lacam. A 19th-century French baker noted for his *petits fours*, cakes, and waffles.

Lac de Marbre. A type of trout found in parts of France.

Lace. To add a dash of liquor, wine, brandy, or cordial to a beverage or soup.

La Chapelle, Vincent. French author of *The Modern Cook* in 1733; many of his recipes are in use today.

Lache. A small, delicate-tasting sea fish; best cooked like smelt.

Lachs (German). Salmon.

Lachsforelle (German). Salmon-trout.

Lachsmedaillons (German). Salmon fillets.

Lacquer, Can. In food cans a layer of gum and gum resin spread on the tinplate and hardened with heat to protect the tin from attack by acid fruit juices.

Lacrima Christi; Lachryma Christi; Lacryme Christi; Lagrima Christi. "Tears of Christ." Popular Italian wines made from grapes grown in the volcanic soil on the lower slopes of Mt. Vesuvius. The white variety is preferred to the red because of its sweeter, more delicate taste. *See* Italy, The Wines of.

Lactalbumin. An albumin present in milk.

Lacteal. Pertaining or relating to milk.

Lactic. Made from milk.

Lactic Acid. The acid produced by the fermentation of milk sugar. It accounts for the flavor of sour milk and promotes the precipitation of the casein curd in cottage cheese. Also used as an acidulant in sugar confectionery, soft drinks, pickles, and sauces.

Lactic Ferment. In breadmaking, in the mixture of milk and flour, lactic-acid bacteria produce from the milk sugar the lactic acid that ripens the gluten in the flour, thus creating a higher loaf of bread. Lactic ferments are also a factor in cheesemaking.

Lactobacillus Bulgaricus. The bacteria that changes milk into yoghurt.

Lactoflavin (Obsolete). Vitamin B_2, so named because it was isolated from milk.

Lactometer. A glass tube used for measuring the density of milk and its cream content.

Lactose. Milk sugar, a natural crystalline sugar present in milk.

Lada (Malayan). Pepper.

Ladies' Delight. A homemade relish consisting of apples, onions, chilies, and white vinegar that can be used after standing only a few days; so named because it can be prepared comparatively quickly.

Ladle. A large cuplike spoon with a long handle, usually used for serving liquids. Varieties may be made of silver for table service, ceramics to match a particular tureen or soup bowl, or metal for kitchen use.

Ladog. A herring found in Lake Ladoga, Russia.

Ladoix-Serrigny. The fair red and white wines produced in Beaune, France. Probably the fruity white wines are better than the red. *See also* France, The Wines of.

Lad's-Love. Southernwood, an herb similar to tarragon; may be cooked like spinach or added to salads.

Ladyfinger. A small, delicate fingerlike piece of spongecake that may be eaten with ice cream or fruit, or may be combined with other ingredients to make a more elaborate dessert.

Lady's-Finger (Colloquial). Okra.

Lady's-Smock. Meadow cress, a weed that grows in moist meadows; the spicy leaves, when young and tender, may be used in salads or to flavor soups. *See* Cardamine.

Lafite-Rothschild, Château. An outstanding red wine produced in the Haut-Médoc (Bordeaux) region of France. The color is brilliant, the taste well balanced, and the bouquet is excellent. *See also* France, The Wines of.

Lagacque. A restaurateur during the French Revolution whose beautiful restaurant in the garden of the Tuileries was famous for elaborate dishes.

Lager; Lager Beer. A light beer that has been aged. Originally produced only in Germany, where the process originated. *See also* Beer.

Lagerøl (Danish). Dark beer.

Lagkage (Danish). A large rich cake.

Lagmi. A North African wine made from the sap of palm trees.

Lagniappe. In Louisiana a little extra, often edible, given to customers making a purchase.

Lagopede; Lagopus. A type of partridge or grouse, native to the Alps and the Pyrénées, having a fine flesh and a light, gamy flavor with a slightly sour aftertaste.

Lagosta (Portuguese). Lobster.

Lagostim (Portuguese). Prawn.

Lagrima. A sweet dessert wine from the vineyards of Malaga, Spain. *See also* Lacrima Christi.

Laguiole. A French hard whole-milk rennet cheese resembling Cantal.

Laguipière. A noted 18th-century French chef with whom Carême studied.

Lahm (Arabic). Meat.

Laie. Female wild boar, often used for food.

Laitance (French). Soft fish roe.

Laitance de Carpe. Soft carp roe.

Lait-de-Poule (Obsolete). A beverage consisting of egg yolks beaten with water, sugar, and spices; formerly a ladies' drink.

Laiteron. A leafy vegetable similar to chicory. Young leaves may be used in salads; mature leaves must be cooked a long time to be edible.

Laitiat (French). Provincial drink made of crushed fruits combined with the whey of milk.

Lake Herring. A herringlike freshwater fish abundant in the Great Lakes. Also called Cisco.

Lake Silverside. Whitebait, a food fish.

Lake Trout. *See* Trout.

Lakka. A Finnish sweet afterdinner liqueur made from the cloudberry.

Laks (Danish, Norwegian). Salmon.

Laksesalat (Danish). Salmon salad.

Lam (Danish, Dutch). Lamb.

Lamb. The young of the sheep before it is a year old. The term applies both to the live animal and to its flesh. After the age of one year, when a lamb has developed its first two incisor teeth, it is called a *yearling*. When the first permanent teeth appear, it becomes a *ewe* or *ram*, depending on its sex, and the flesh is called *mutton*.

Spring lamb is the very young, milk-fed animal, usually born in January and marketed in April of the same year. Its meat is white and delicate, much favored by gourmets and relatively expensive. The yearling is grass-fed, and its meat tends to have more flavor.

Lamb is marketed in cuts, the best of which are the legs, the saddle, and the loins. The neck, breast, and shoulders are also highly edible, and the food value of these less tender cuts is just as good as that of the more tender, expensive portions. Legs of lamb are generally roasted. The loins may be cooked whole, but they are usually cut into chops or cutlets for grilling or frying.

Like most meat marketed in the United States, lamb is graded A-1 for "Choice" or "Prime," A for "Good," B for "Commercial," and C for "Utility." Government stamps indicate the wholesomeness and quality of the meat, and the lower grades are inferior in tenderness and edibility. Wherever government inspectors are available, the lamb is officially stamped before marketing; otherwise the individual butcher must grade his own meat by the rigid governmental standards.

Highest-quality lamb is distinguished by its firm flesh and whiteness of fat. The meat should be eaten as fresh as possible, for it tends to spoil more rapidly than beef.

Lamballe (French). A soup made of meat broth, purée of peas, and tapioca.

Lambert's Filbert. The European cobnut, a very tasty nut; not a true filbert.

Lambertye. A chicken stuffed with goose liver, cooked in white wine, and garnished with Béchamel sauce and truffles.

Lambic (Belgian). A strong sour beer made from barley. *Gueuze-lambic* is generally regarded as the best variety.

Lambrusco. *See* Italy, The Wines of.

Lamb's-Lettuce. *See* Field Salad.

Lamb's-Quarters. *See* Pigweed.

Lamb's-Stove (British). A lamb stew made with the head of a lamb and its lungs, the jaws being stuffed with spinach, onion, and parsley.

Lamb's-Tail Pie (British). A pie made of lambs' tails, mint, salt, and pepper.

Lamb's Wool (British, Obsolete). A 17th-century beverage made with hot ale, the pulp of roasted apples, and spices.

Lamchi-Boonchi. A curry popular in Aruba, Dutch West Indies; it is made with bacon, lamb, tomatoes, green peppers, and pineapple.

Lamellibranchia. Shellfish, including clam, oyster, and scallop.

Lamm (German). Lamb.
    Gebratenes Lamm. Roast lamb.
    Lammfleisch. Lamb.
    Lammkeule. Leg of lamb.
    Lammkoteletten. Lamb cutlets.
    Lammrippstück. Ribs of lamb.
    Lammschulter. Shoulder of lamb.

Lamm (Swedish). Lamb.
    Lammhachi. Chopped lamb.
    Lammkotlett. Mutton chop; lamb chop.
    Lammstek. Roast lamb.

Lammas, Feast of. A harvest festival, held on the first of August in the early English church, at which the first corn was made into bread, consecrated, and served.

Lammas Wheat. Winter wheat.

Lammekotelet (Danish). Lamb chop.

Lammesteg (Danish). Roast lamb.

Lammestek (Norwegian). Leg of lamb.

La Mothe Saint-Heraye, Fromage de. A smooth-textured goat's-milk cheese produced in Poitou, France; best during summer or early autumn.

Lampern. River lamprey.

Lamponi (Italian). Raspberries.

Lamprey. A cylindrical aquatic vertebrate of the eel family with a large snout and no scales. It is greenish yellow with brown markings. The sea lamprey (there are also freshwater varieties) is found most extensively in the Mediterranean and the Atlantic. It has been considered a delicacy since Roman days and is a popular seafood in England today. The flesh is delicate but fatty.

Lampsana. A type of wild endive, although occasionally cultivated; it must be eaten raw, usually in salads, because it toughens and becomes bitter when cooked.

Lamskotelet (Dutch). Mutton chop.

Lamut. A brownish fruit found in Southeast Asia; it has a sweet, smooth taste.

Lancashire. A white, hard, strong English cheese suitable for toasting and for use in Welsh rarebits.

Lancashire Christmas Pudding-Cake (British). Cold leftover Christmas pudding mashed smooth with butter and brandy or rum, spread on pie pastry, brushed with egg, and sprinkled with sugar; served hot with tea, sometimes as small individual pies.

Lancashire Hot Pot (British). A version of Irish stew.

Lanceron. A delicate-flavored fish of the pike family.

Land Crab. Any crab that lives chiefly on land, rather than in the sea.

Land Fish. A freshwater fish.

Land o' Cakes. Scotland, a country famous for its cakes.

Landoch. *See* Brinza Cheese.

Landrail. Corncrake, a fine-flavored game bird.

Landras (Spanish). Sweetbreads.

Ländstycke (Swedish). Sirloin steak.

Land Turtle. Any turtle that stays on land; often used as food.

Landwein (German). A wine term which describes the typical, unpretentious wines served in pitchers or carafes throughout Germany; roughly equivalent to France's *vin du pays*.

Land Winkle. A snail.

Lane Cake. A white cake popular in Alabama and some other southern states. When spiked with moonshine, popularly called "shinny," it is called "shinny cake." The filling is usually made of pecans, raisins, sugar, and egg yolks.

Langenthal Boiled Meat. An assortment of boiled meats and vegetables; the broth is served with toast and grated cheese.

Lang-Loaning Cake (British). A cake made for school children during the holidays.

Langlois Blue. A very creamy, rich blue cheese made in Colorado.

Langosta (Spanish). A clawless variety of lobster.

Langostinos (Spanish). A variety of shellfish similar to shrimp; ocean or deep-sea prawn.

Langouste (French). Crayfish; some clawless varieties of lobster.

Langoustine (French). Prawn.

Langres, Fromage de (French). A yellow smooth-textured fermented cheese from the champagne country. It is cone-shaped, has a yellow crust, and is aged between walnut leaves; eaten fresh from September to April, and dry the rest of the year.

Langshan. A Chinese black fowl; now raised in other parts of the world.

Langue-de-Chat (French). (1) A sponge cooky baked in the shape of a cat's tongue. (2) A variety of mushroom.

Languedoc. A district of southern France famous for fine cooking; *cassoulets* and *pâté de foie gras* are outstanding preparations.

Languedocienne, À la. Of a variety of dishes, prepared with a garlic-flavored sauce and usually garnished with tomatoes, onions, and eggplant.

Languier (French). Smoked pig's tongue.

Languste (German). Clawless, spiny lobster.

Lantau. A South Pacific bean resembling the string bean.

Lap. (1) To take up liquid with the tongue. (2) (Colloquial) Liquor.

Lapereau (French). Very young rabbit.

Lapin (French). A buck rabbit.

Lapje (Dutch). Steak.

Lapland Cheese. A hard reindeer-milk cheese made in Lapland: it resembles Swiss cheese and is dumbbell-shaped.

Lapskaus (Norwegian). Mixed-meat stew.

Lapu-Lapu (Philippine). Grouper, an excellent-tasting food fish.

Lapwing. An edible European bird similar to the plover; its eggs are a delicacy.

Laqueuille Blue Cheese. A rich, hard French cheese.

Laranja (Portuguese). Orange.

Lard. (1) The semisolid oil obtained by melting down pork fat. Properly rendered and strained of impurities, it is as digestible as butter, and is both economical and useful for pastry making, baking of hot breads, and deep-fat frying. (2) To insert strips of fat into lean meats or poultry.

Lard (French). Bacon.

   Lard à Piquer. Larding bacon.

   Lard Fumé. Smoked bacon.

Lardage. The process of placing strips of fat into meats, in order to make them juicier. This is usually done by means of a larding needle, a *lardoire*.

Larder. (1) A place resembling a pantry where foods are stored. (2) Foods that are stored. (3) (French) To interlard.

Larding. The threading of narrow strips of fat through uncooked nonfat meat to make it more

tender and flavorsome. The fat should be white, firm, and dry.

Larding Needle. A long steel implement with a large eye into which strips of fat are threaded to flavor meat, game, and poultry.

Lardo (Italian). Bacon; lard.

Lardoire (French). A greased skewer or larding needle.

Lardons; Lardoons. Strips of bacon or pork fat used for larding meats.

Lardy Cake (British). A cake made of bread

dough rolled out, spread with lard, sugar, and currants, folded and rolled three or four times, then cut into small squares, brushed with milk, sprinkled lightly with sugar, and baked until golden brown.

Lark. Any of numerous singing birds whose sweet, tender flesh is a delicacy in Europe. The lark is not legal game in the United States.

Larron. A French cow's-milk cheese similar to Maroilles but less fatty and oily.

Lasagne; Lasagna (Italian). (1) Wide ribbons of pasta cooked like macaroni. (2) A dish consisting of layers of pasta alternated with a filling of meat, sausage, cheese, tomatoes, or eggs.

> **Lasagne alla Genovese.** Layers of noodles with meat or cheese served with a sauce.
>
> **Lasagne Fatta in Casa.** Homemade lasagne.
>
> **Lasagne Imbottite.** Stuffed lasagne.
>
> **Lasagne Verdi al Forno.** Wide green noodles baked with rich sauce and cheese.

Lasagnes Niçoise (French). Wide noodles covered with tomatoes, garlic, ground beef, etc., and baked with grated cheese.

Lassi; Lhassi (Indian). Beverage made with whipped yoghurt, often with sugar or salt added.

Last (British). A commercial specific weight or measure, depending upon the material involved: for grain and malt, 80 bushels; for herring and cod, 12 barrels; for pilchard and red herring, 12,000–13,200 fish.

La Tâche. A distinctive, extraordinary, dry red wine produced in the Vosne-Romanée region of Burgundy, France. *See also* France, The Wines of.

Latik. The edible precipitate that results when coconut milk is boiled.

Latin America. *See* Central America; *see also* separate listings for the countries of South America.

Latkes (Jewish). Potato pancakes; also, pancakes made of matzos meal.

Latour, Château. An outstanding red wine of Pauillac (Bordeaux), France. *See* France, The Wines of.

Latricières-Chambertin. A fairly important dry red wine with brilliant color and excellent bouquet, produced in Burgundy, France. *See also* France, The Wines of.

Latte (Italian). Milk.

Lattice Crust. *See* Criss-Cross Crust.

Lattich (German). Lettuce.

Lattuga (Italian). Lettuce.

> **Lattuga Romana.** Romaine lettuce.

Lauch (German). Leek.

Laugenbrezel (German). A round twisted roll.

Laugenweck (German). A long roll.

Laulau (Hawaiian). Pork and fish (usually salmon) wrapped in leaves and steamed.

Laumes, Fromage des. A French cheese of passable quality whose crust is washed in brandy and coffee while maturing.

Launce. A sand eel.

Laurel. Bay leaf.

Lavarenne. A famous French chef of the 17th century who wrote books on cooking.

Lavaret (French). A fish of the salmon family found in many European lakes. Its delicate, delicious flesh may be prepared like river trout.

Lavender. A European mintlike herb with spikes of small lilac-purplish flowers; cultivated for its aromatic oil, which is used as a flavoring agent.

Laver. Any of several purple seaweeds, whose fronds are pickled or stewed in Europe.

Laver Bread (Welsh). A bread made with seaweed.

Laver Sauce (British). A sauce with laver, a fine smooth seaweed, and butter; served with mutton.

Lawyer Fish. Another name for the freshwater blackfish.

Lax (Norwegian, Swedish). Smoked salmon.

Lax, Kokt (Swedish). Boiled salmon.

> **Laxforell; Laxöring.** Salmon trout.
>
> **Laxpudding.** Salmon pudding.
>
> **Laxtallrik.** Salmon plate.

Layer Cake. Cake consisting of two or more layers with frostings, whipped cream, or jelly between them.

Layon, Côteau du. The wines of Anjou, France; they are of only fair quality but are pleasant-tasting.

Lazybed (British). A 6-foot-wide section of ground where potatoes are grown. Soil is taken from trenches on each side to cover the potatoes.

Lazy Susan. A revolving tray, usually with several compartments into each of which a different food may be placed. The diner revolves the tray to make his selection.

Leaf. A good year or season for wine; a vintage.

Leaf Cheese; Telpanir; Tschil; Zwirn. Cheese made from sour skimmed ewe's or cow's milk in Eastern Europe.

Leather. *See* Leder.

Leaven. Yeast or any other ferment that causes dough to rise.

Leavening. The agent used to make dough rise.

Lebanon. The cuisines of the Near East countries follow a similar pattern. There is a strong emphasis on lamb (in preference to beef), and no pork is served because it is against Mohammedan religious principles. Lamb dishes predominate, particularly as *kibbe*, lamb with cracked wheat, and a variation of shish kebab here called *lahm mashwi*. Lamb is very often combined with eggplant, a plentiful everyday food, in a dish called *ma'loubeh*. Beef is served occasionally but never as steak or roast beef; usually· it is ground fine and made into meatballs.

Lebanese like to begin a meal with appetizers at a large gathering, the table of *mezza*, or appetizers, laid out for the guests, includes forty or more items such as chick-peas, olives, anchovies, and the like. An eggplant appetizer, *baba gannoj*, is prepared with a sesame sauce. Sesame sauce, *tahini*, is a very frequently used ingredient. It is lemon- and garlic-flavored and is used much as Americans use mayonnaise, as a binder for soft foods and also as flavoring.

The only local liquor is *arak*. With this the Lebanese often serve *sambousiks*, small filled pastries. The people are very fond of *mashie*, stuffed vegetables, particularly tomatoes and peppers; the typical stuffing is ground lamb, rice, and sometimes pine nuts. During the hot weather a favorite salad is *tabouli*, made of cracked wheat, mint, parsley, and onions.

Custards and gelatin desserts are popular, frequently being garnished with pistachio nuts or almonds. Candied fruits, dates, and figs are usually served at the end of a meal. Coffee is always served black, strong, and laden with sediment.

Lebban (Middle Eastern). Coagulated sour milk or yoghurt; used as a drink.

Leber (German). Liver.

    Leberklösse. Liver dumplings.

    Leberknödel. Dumplings made with ground or chopped liver.

    Leberkäse. (1) Goose-liver pâté. (2) A boiled-meat mixture.

    Lebersuppe. Purée of liver soup or soup prepared with white wine and calf's liver.

    Leberwurst. Smoked liverwurst; liver sausage.

Lebkuchen (German). Gingerbread cooky, traditionally served at Christmastime.

Lebne. A sour-milk cottage cheese made in the Middle East.

Lebranche. Brazilian mullet.

Lecco (Italian). A rather soft cow's- or goat's-milk dessert cheese.

Leche (Spanish). Milk.

Lèchefrite (French). A receptacle placed under the skewer of a rotisserie to catch fats and juices.

Lèches (French). Cakes cut into slices.

Lechosa (Spanish). Papaya or pawpaw; a melon with better aroma than taste.

Lechuga (Spanish). Lettuce.

Lecithin. A fatty substance containing phosphorus; present in brains, egg yolk, etc.

Leckerli; Leckerly; Lecrelet (Swiss). A square pastry flavored with lemon or citron and enriched with honey.

Leder. "Leather," a round skim- and buttermilk cheese made in north Germany.

Leek. A hardy biennial plant of the lily family, related to the onion but with a much smaller bulb and broader leaves. It is only occasionally found in a wild state, and the commercial variety is generally believed to be a cultivated form of oriental garlic. It is used for flavoring soups, stews, and stock, and it may be served as a vegetable in any of the ways suitable for asparagus.

Leek was a great favorite with the Egyptians and the Romans. The Emperor Nero is supposed to have drunk leek soup daily, believing that such a diet would deepen his voice. The leek is the floral emblem of Wales, as a result of an ancient battle in which the victorious Welshmen wore the vegetable in their helmets to distinguish themselves from the enemy.

Lees of Wine. The solid matter that settles on the bottom of wine barrels used to ferment wines.

Leftovers. There are two theories regarding leftover foods.

The first views leftovers as a failure and as a state of affairs that ought not to have occurred: failure, that is, in the sense that they are natural results at least of poor planning; the second theory is that leftovers represent potentiality: the cook can demonstrate creative capacity by working within the limitations imposed by the existence of leftovers so as to create novelty within these limitations.

It should be pointed out, however, that there is a third possible analysis, which takes account of reality no less than the other two, namely, that leftovers are the result of intentionality (for the sake of economy, for example), so that they can be viewed simply as the products of voluntary, deliberate human action.

Leghorn. A rather small variety of domestic fowl.

Legumbres (Spanish). Vegetables.

Legumes (French, Portuguese). Fruits and seeds that are formed in pods, such as beans and peas. Their high percentage of protein and carbohydrates makes them almost as important a vegetable food as cereals, but they lack soda and minerals, and tend to be acid-forming if eaten in large quantities without a counterbalancing diet.

Legumi (Italian). Vegetables.

Legumin. A vegetable casein found in such vegetables as beans and peas.

Leguminous. Pertaining to beans, peas, etc.

Leicester (British). A hard reddish-colored cow's-milk cheese with a mildly sharp flavor.

Leipziger Allerlei (German). A mixed-vegetable and bread-crumb dish.

Leiren. Sweet corn root.

Leister (British). A long pronged weapon used to catch salmon.

Leitão Assado (Portuguese). Roast young suckling pig.

Leite (Portuguese). Milk.

Lek (British). A flock of grouse.

Lemon. The yellow, highly scented acid fruit of a citrus tree believed to have been first grown on the foothills of the Himalaya Mountains in India. Arabs introduced the fruit into Europe, and seeds for lemon trees were brought to the New World by Columbus. Lemon cultivation is today a major industry in most Mediterranean countries and in California and Florida.

Lemons are an excellent source of vitamin C, and both the juice and the rind have innumerable uses as flavoring agents for food and beverages. Lemon juice may be substituted for vinegar in any recipe except for pickling. It may be used for cleaning aluminum, for erasing onion or garlic odor from the hands, for removing many stains from linens, and as a shampoo rinse. The rind will clean tarnished copper or brass.

Lemonade. A refreshing drink made of lemon juice, sugar, water, and ice; sparkling water may be used.

Lemon Balm. A lemon-flavored herb of the mint family whose leaves are sometimes used in salads or mint sauce, in fruit, wine, or cider cups, or to make a kind of tea.

Lemon Berry. An acid-flavored wild red berry native to southern California; used for flavoring foods, making soft drinks, etc.

Lemon Cheese. Not a cheese, but a sweet custard that contains lemon, eggs, and butter; used in cakes, tarts, etc.

Lemon Curd. A custard made with lemon juice, eggs, sugar, and butter cooked until the mixture has thickened; it is not a curd.

Lemon Extract. A flavoring agent made of lemon oil and alcohol.

Lemon Fish. Cobia, a saltwater food fish.

Lemon Kali (British). Sodium bicarbonate and tartaric acid combined to form a bubbling drink.

Lemon Oil. A pale yellow liquid pressed from the oil cells of lemon rinds and used to flavor candies, etc.

Lemon Peel. Slices of lemon peel cooked with a heavy sugar syrup, and then dried.

Lemon Pickles. A very hot condiment used with fish, meat, or poultry, and frequently with curry.

Lemon Sole. A small European flatfish resembling the sole but inferior in firmness of flesh and delicacy of flavor; cooked like sole and flounder.

Lemon Squash. A bottled liquid made of soda water, lemon juice, and sugar; used for lemonades, cocktails, and other beverages.

Lemon Squeezer. A manually or electrically operated utensil that removes juice from lemons.

Lemon Verbena. An herb with a slight lemon aroma, used primarily for flavoring salads.

Lendenbraten (German). Roast sirloin of beef.

Lendenschnitten (German). Center cut of beef; fillet.

Lendenstück (German). Sirloin of beef.

Lendestuk (Dutch). Rumpsteak.

Lengua (Spanish). Tongue.

Lenguado (Spanish). (1) The peacock flounder, a tropical food fish. (2) Sole.

Lent. A period of 40 days of penitence before Easter observed by Christians. Most Roman Catholics observe the various fast days during this period, eating no meat on Fridays, Ash Wednesday, and on Holy Saturday morning. The Lenten observance dates back 16 centuries, but the fasting observance began many centuries later. During the Middle Ages abstinence from meat and other prohibitions were far more stringent.

Lentejas (Spanish). Lentils.

Lenten Cakes. Simnel cakes eaten at the middle of the Lenten season.

Lentil. A small branching leguminous plant, originating in Central Asia, and cultivated since ancient times for its round, flat seeds which are among the most nutritious of legumes. Dried lentils can be stored indefinitely. The dried seeds may be green, yellow, orange, or black in color.

Lentilles de Chocolat (French). Chocolate lentil candies.

Lentisk. A bush in the same family as the turpentine tree; it yields an oil or resin used to flavor the Middle Eastern brandy known as *raki*.

Leopard Crab. A crab whose legs are very palatable.

Lepel (Dutch). Spoon.

Lepiote. A large wild mushroom often used in meat stews, casseroles, etc.

Lepisosteus. The gar-pike, a freshwater fish found in Central America; delicately fleshed but covered with hard scales.

Lepre (Italian). Hare.

Lepre in Salmi. Marinated hare.

Lerenes. A tropical plant whose white, rather small tuberous root is boiled and eaten like potato.

Leruns. A simple, salted ewe's-milk cheese made in the Pyrénées, France.

Lescin. A ewe's-milk and rennet cheese made in Caucasian Russia.

Lesser Celandine. A wild plant found in various parts of the world; the leaves are usually cooked and eaten as a green vegetable.

Le To. A stew made in Mali. It has both a ground-beef and a dried-fish sauce. Another version is made with onions and cubed beef. It is usually served with boiled cornmeal.

Letspraengt Oksebryst (Danish). Corned beef.

Lets Vooraf (Dutch). Appetizer or entree.

Lettspraengt Lammebryst (Norwegian). Salted lamb.

Lettuce. A plant, of several varieties, whose crisp, succulent leaves are used primarily for salad. The Romans called it *lactuca*, after the Latin word for milk, since the plant, when cut, exudes a milky substance. Lettuce was cultivated in ancient China and Egypt, and was considered a sacred plant by the Hebrews. It was enjoyed by the Greeks and Romans and was recommended as a health food by their physicians. During the time of the Emperor Augustus, lettuce was served at the end of the meal; under the reign of the Emperor Domitian, however, the fashion changed, and the salad came at the beginning of the repast. The proper place in a meal for enjoying the salad course is still debated among gourmets the world over.

All common varieties of lettuce can be eaten raw, but may also be cooked, like endive.

The four most popular varieties of lettuce on the American market are the following:

Iceberg is characterized by a firm head and crisp, whitish-green leaves.

Boston or *Butter Head* has greener, smoother leaves.

Romaine or *Cos* has a cylindrical, elongated head and coarser leaves.

Leaf has curly leaves.

Lettuce Water. A liquid produced when lettuce is boiled; often used in preparing sauces.

Leucasin. A protein present in wheat.

Levadura (Spanish). Yeast; baking powder.

Levain (French). Levan, a sour-wheat paste used to promote the fermentation of dough; sometimes, yeast.

Levan. Fermented dough without yeast.

Levee. A morning gathering at which coffee or other refreshment is served to guests.

Level. In recipe measurements, in the same plane as the edge of the specified container, as a level teaspoonful or a level cupful.

Lever (Danish). Liver.

Leveret. (1) A young hare. (2) A mature rabbit.

Leverpastej (Swedish). Liver paste; pâté.

Leverpostei (Norwegian). Baked liver loaf.

Leverpostej (Danish). Liver paste; pâté.

Levigate. To rub to a very fine powder.

Levraut (French). Young hare.

Levroux. A rather simple goat's-milk cheese prepared in Berry, France.

Levulose. Fruit sugar, in crystalline form.

Levure. A firm flour-and-water paste used to seal casseroles and ovenproof dishes to prevent the flavor from escaping with the steam.

Lévure (French). A wine term for a yeast culture added to the "must" before fermentation, when the natural yeast mold on the grapes is thought to be insufficient.

Lexias. Raisins made from grapes dipped in a mixture of olive oil and wood ashes which dissolves the waxy coating of the grapes and thus speeds up the drying process.

Leyden. A hard Dutch cheese made from partially skimmed cow's milk and spiced with cumin or caraway seed and cloves.

Liaison. A binding material; flour, cream, or any other foodstuff used to bind or thicken soups and sauces.

Liani (Algerian). Lamb stew with parsley and chick-peas.

Liard (French). Foods cut into thin round slices, as potatoes that are chipped and crisped.

Libament. *See* Libation.

Libant. Sipping.

Libation. (1) Spilling or pouring wine, usually onto the ground, as an offering to a god. (2) (Colloquial) Any alcoholic drink.

Licensed. Having a license permitting the selling of alcoholic beverages; usually, of English pubs.

Lichee; Lichi. *See* Litchi.

Lichia. A tunalike fish.

Licorice. A candy or flavoring agent made from the soaked roots of a European plant of the same name. In solid form it is usually molded into glossy black cylindrical sticks and has a sweetly bitter, sharp taste resembling anise.

Lié (French). Bound or thickened, as applied to soups, creams, and sauces.

Liebre (Spanish). Hare.

Liederkranz. An American soft whole-milk surface-ripened cheese resembling a mild Limburger in body, flavor, and aroma. It was first produced in Ohio.

Lieu. A fish similar to a whiting.

Lièvre à la Royale (French). A rich dish of hare, ground livers, wine, etc.

Light and Mild. In England, a combination of half pale, light ale, and half mild.

Lighten. To soften a mixture by adding eggs or a liquid.

Lightfoot. Deer, hare, and other animals very light on their feet.

Light Horseman. The sweep, an Australian ocean fish.

Lights. A butchers' term for the lungs of beef, lamb, or pork.

Likerish. (1) A cook skilled in creating delicacies. (2) Greedy to eat or taste. (3) Lickerous; delightful or sweet to the palate. (4) Liquorish; very fond of liquor.

Likør (Norwegian). Cordial.

Lillet. A French apéritif wine something like vermouth; best when chilled.

Lima Beans. The seeds of an annual climbing plant native to South America but now cultivated extensively throughout the United States. The beans are short, flat, and kidney-shaped, and are marketed fresh in the pod, frozen, canned, or dried. The fresh beans are also known as *butter beans*.

Limande (French). Lemon sole.

Limandelle; Cardine; Mere de Sole (French). A flat oval fish sometimes 14 inches in length.

Limão (Portuguese). Lemon.

Limas (Spanish). Limes.

Limbourg. A semisoft Belgian cow's-milk cheese with a pungent flavor.

Limburger. A semisoft surface-ripened American

cheese with a very strong flavor and aroma; made from whole fermented cow's milk.

Limburgse Vlaai (Dutch). A pastry tart made with cherries or apricots.

Lime. A small green thin-skinned citrus fruit similar to the lemon. Trees bearing the fruit are cultivated in many subtropical countries, but the world market is supplied mainly by the West Indies and Mexico. The average lime is about half the size of the ordinary lemon and contains about one-third more citric acid. An excellent source of vitamin C, lime juice was once a standard item on long sea voyages for use in preventing scurvy. As a result British sailors are still sometimes referred to as "Limeys." Today lime juice is used chiefly in beverages and for flavoring foods and confectionery.

Lime, Oil of. An essential oil derived from the lime rind and used as a flavoring.

Lime-Blossom Tea. An infusion of dried lime flowers served with a slice of lemon.

Lime Juice. Juice extracted from the lime.

Lime Punch. A beverage containing lime juice.

Limequat. The citrus fruit produced by crossing the lime with the kumquat.

Limewater. Water clarified by the addition of lime.

Limoges. Fine porcelain made in Limoges, France.

Limón (Spanish). Lemon.

Limoncini (Italian). A pasta shaped like a slice of lemon, that is, with "spokes" radiating out from the center.

Limone (Italian). Lemon.

Limonin. A substance present in citrus fruits that causes the juice to become bitter after it has been extracted and has stood awhile.

Limousine, À la (French). A style of cooking in Provence; usually, containing red cabbage and chestnuts.

Limpa (Swedish). Sweet rye bread.

Limpets. Shellfish that cling to rocks on the seashore. Though unattractive in appearance, they have a delicious flavor. They have only one shell and are prepared like cockles and other bivalves.

Limu (Hawaiian). Seaweed; often mixed with peppers and nuts and served as a relish or pickle.

Linalool. A colorless liquid often used in the food-processing industry to supply the synthetic flavor of plum or quince to jellies, etc.

Linalyl Butyrate. A rather light yellow liquid often used to supply the synthetic taste of honey.

Linalyl Isobutyrate. A pale yellow liquid sometimes used to furnish the synthetic taste of black currants to candies, etc.

Lincoln. A soft, perishable English cream cheese.

Lindeman. An Australian winegrower, many of whose products are quite good but lack some of the characteristics of a fine European wine.

Lindemans Riesling. A medium-dry Australian white wine imitative of the European Riesling; often considered one of Australia's best wines.

Line. (1) To line cake pans with fitted pieces of greaseproof paper or aluminum foil. (2) To cover the inside of pie plates and baking dishes with dough. (3) To place a thin coating of gelatin on the inside of a mold before filling it with other ingredients.

Linen Damask. (1) Linen woven with threads in different directions to form a pattern. (2) A kind of tablecloth.

Ling. (1) A long slender Atlantic Ocean fish with a flabby texture and bland taste; any *gadoid* fish. (2) The American burbot. (3) Lingue; any of several species of hake; better when smoked, as the flesh is comparatively poor when fresh.

Linga (Philippine). Sesame seeds.

Lingcod. Another name for ling; sometimes used with reference to larger species of ling found especially in the Gulf of Mexico.

Lingonberry. The mountain cranberry; often used in Scandinavian desserts, sauces, etc.

Lingua (Italian, Portuguese). Tongue.

Lingua di Agnello all' Agrigento (Italian). Lamb tongue with tomato sauce and oranges.

Lingua di Bue (Italian). Beef tongue.

Linguado (Portuguese). Sole.

Linguini (Italian). Narrow noodles.
  Linguini Strascinati. Narrow noodles in egg sauce.

Linies. A simple goat's-milk cheese made in the Champagne region of France.

Linnet. A small edible bird; prepared like most small game birds.

Linoleic Acid. A fatty acid with a low degree of

saturation, found in various edible fats. *See also* Hydrogenated Fats; Saturated Fats; Oleic Acid.

Linoyada (Spanish). A kind of wine lemonade made in the Basque region.

Linsen (German). Lentils.

Linsensuppe (German). Lentil soup.

Linser (Danish). Cream tarts.

Linzertorte (German). Hazelnut cake.

Lipase. A ferment that causes the decomposition of fats and oils.

Lipoproteins. Combinations of protein, fat, and cholesterol created in the body from food.

Lipovitellenin. The lipoprotein part of egg, comprising about one-sixth of the solids of the yolk.

Liptau; Liptauer; Lipto; Liptoi. A salty Hungarian cheese made usually with cow's milk (sometimes with sheep's milk), combined with paprika. *See also* Brinza.

Liquable. Soluble.

Liqueur. An alcoholic drink made from spirits and some aromatic, sweetening, scenting, or coloring agent. It is properly served at the end of a meal, in a relatively small portion, and usually in a special glass. A liqueur may be classed as a stimulant or a digestive. All the liqueurs known as cordials are stimulants. The names are derived from the substance giving the predominant flavor or color, locale, or maker of the drink. The best-known liqueurs are listed under their own names elsewhere in this glossary.

Chief French classifications are: *Crème*, very sweet; *Eau* or *Elixir*, not so sweet.

The alcoholic base for liqueurs may be wine, grain, or molasses, and the resulting drink varies in taste or bouquet depending on the kind and number of additives, which may be fruit, seeds, spices, or flowers. The alcoholic content can vary from 27 percent, as in anisette, to 80 percent in absinthe.

The first liqueurs were developed during the Middle Ages in monasteries throughout Europe, especially in France, for medicinal purposes. From such humble beginnings, thanks to epicures less concerned with matters of health than of the palate, the manufacture has become a major industry.

There are three principal processes for making liqueurs:

Distillation or *Alcoholate* method. The spirit is first mixed with aromatic flavoring substances and is then distilled, often with solid pieces of the additive still remaining. The vintage thus obtained may be sweetened and colored. The best liqueurs are made in this way.

Essence method. The spirit is mixed directly with various flavoring agents, sweetened, and then filtered.

Infusion method. Spirit and sugar are added to fresh fruit juice or a similar substance. Most cordials are made in this manner.

The term "liqueur" is also applied (1) to some outstanding aged liquors fine enough to be enjoyed undiluted and unflavored; and (2) to some very sweet syrups used for flavoring.

Liqueur, Vins de. Red wines made by combining the must and raisins during all or part of the fermentation process. In white or *rosé* wines the must is separated from the pulp.

Liqueur Brandies. Brandies which have been aged and have a thick, almost viscous quality.

Liqueur d'Expédition. Sugar added to champagne at the time the sediment is removed.

Liqueur de Tirage. Liquid sugar added to champagne at the time of bottling.

Liqueur d'Or. A liqueur made from lemon peel and various herbs and having specks of gold leaf floating in it.

Liqueur Jaune. Yellow Chartreuse and various imitations.

Liqueur Vert. Green Chartreuse and various imitations.

Liqueur Whisky. Better-quality whisky, usually aged; best drunk without added water or soda.

Liqueur Wines. Any very sweet, heavy wine.

Liquor. (1) A general term for alcoholic drinks, especially the stronger, distilled ones, such as rye, bourbon, and Scotch. (2) Liquids such as a brine solution.

Liquore della Foresta. An Italian liqueur with a pine taste.

Liquore di Cedro. An Italian liqueur made with citron.

Liquorist. A liqueur maker.

Liquor Thief. A tube used to sample liquors still in their casks.

Lisa. The striped or gray mullet.

Liquors and Liqueurs
  (*see* under individual
  listings).

Abricotine
Absinthe
Acqua di Fiume
Acquavite
Acquette
Advocaat
Aguardiente
Aiguebelle
Alchermes
Alkermès
Allasch
Altwater
Amaretto
Améléon
Amer Picon
Anis
Anisette
Anisina
Apfelwein
Appelwijn
Applejack
Apricot Brandy
Apry
Aquavit
Aquavite di Genziana
Aquavite di Ginepro
Arak
Armagnac
Arquebuse
Arrack
Arza
Athol Brose
Aurum
Ava (kava)
Awamori
Bacardi
Badet
Badminton Cup
Baier
Balderdash
Banania
B & B
B and S
Barack

Barbade
Barbados Cream
Batida
Baume
Bavaroise aux Choux
Benedictine
Biferno
Black Stripe
Bourbon
Bousa
Branda
Brandy
Branntwein
Brännvin
Braulio
Brennevin
Bron de Noix
Bumbo
Byrrh
Caipirinha
Cajuada
Calibogus
Callebogus
Callou
Caloric Punch
Calvados
Calvados du Pays
  d'Auge
Camomilla Alpina
Campari
Caña
Cape Brandy
Cape Smoke
Capillaire
Cappie
Capricot
Cardinale
Carnabyn
Cassiri
Cassis
Catinat
Cédratine
Centerba
Cervesa Negra
Champagne Brandy
Chartreuse
Cherry Bounce
Cherry Brandy

Cherry Gin
Cherry Heering
Cherry Marnier
Cherry Rum
Cherry Whisky
Chesky
Cinzano
Citronat
Cocuy
Cognac
Coing
Coinguarde
Cointreau
Cordial Médoc
Corfinio
Corn 'n' Oil
Corn Whisky
Crambambuli
Crema di Timo
Crème d'Ananas
Crème de Bananes
Crème de Cacao
Crème de Menthe
Crème de Moka
Crème de Noyaux
Crème de Thé
Crème Yvette
Curaçao
Cynar
Damson Gin
Danziger Goldwasser
Darum
Demerara Rum
Dop
Drambuie
Eau de Framboise
Eau de la Côte
Eau de Mélisse
Eau de Vie de Marc
Eau de Vie de Miel
Eau Impériale
Edelweiss
Elixir Di China
Enzian
Escubac
Fennel Water;
  Fenouillette
Fine Champagne

Fior d'Agno
Forbidden Fruit
Fraisia
Génépy des Alpes
Geneva
Gentiane
Gerolimo
Gilka; Gilka Kümmel
Gin
Ginger Brandy
Ginger Cordial
Gloria
Grand Marnier
Grand St. Bernard
Grappa
Guignolet
Half Om Half
Irish Mist
Iva-Bitter
Izarra
Jamaica Rum
Jenever Gin
Kümmel
Kanjak
Kaoliang Wine
Kirsch; Kirschwasser
Lakka
Liqueur d'Or
Liqueur Jaune
Liqueur Vert
Liquore della Foresta
Liquore di Cedro
Maraschino
Marc
Marc de Bourgogne
Marc de Champagne
Marnique
Mastino
Matese
May Cordial
Mazarino
Mekong
Menta Glaciale
Mentuccia di San
  Silvestro
Merisette
Mescal
Mesimarja

Metaxas
Mint Water
Mirabelle
Mistra
Monastine
Monte-Aquilla
Napoleon Brandy
Nocillo
Nocino
Noyau
Noyau Rosé
Ödåkra
Ojen
Okolehao
O. P. Aquavit
Operm
Orange Ratafia
Orasky
Oropa
Ouzo
Överste
Peach Brandy
Pecquet
Peppermint Cordial
Peppermint Get
Persico; Persicot
Pineau des Charentes
Piscarine
Pisco
Poire, Eau de Vie de
Poire William
Pomeranzen
Prunella
Prunelle
Quetsch d'Alsace
Rabinovka
Raki
Rakia
Rakija
Raspail
Raspberry Noyeau
Ratafia

Riabinovka
Rinfresco
Rosolio
Rossol
Rossolis
Rum
Rye
Sambuca
Santa Vittoria
Sassolina
Scotch
Shochu
Shrub
Skåne
Slivovice
Slivovitz
Slivowitz
Sloe Gin
Strega
Szilva
Tafia
Tangerinette
Tari
Tequila
Tokanen
Triple Sec
Tuica
Van der Hum
Vecchia Romagna
Vespetro
Vielle Curé
Villacidro
Vishnevaia
Vlattero
Vodka
Whisky
Wodka; Woudka
Wisniak
Yvette Cream
Zabrouka
Zara

Lisbon. A white wine produced in the province of Estremadura, Portugal. *See* Portugal, The Wines of.

Lisbon Wines. A term occasionally used to describe heavy, sweet wines; sometimes it describes port wine.

Lit (French). Thin slices of meat or vegetables spread in layers to make a bed in cooking.

Litchi; Lichee; Lichi. The nutlike fruit of a Chinese tree widely cultivated also in India, the Philippines, and other countries of the Far East, as well as in southern Florida and California. It is rather like a strawberry in appearance and size; a thin, hard, scaly shell, red when the fruit is completely matured, is easily peeled away from its white, sweet, musty-tasting pulp. For export the fruit is usually allowed to dry in its shell; it then turns black like a raisin and is very sweet, with an acid flavor. Dried, canned, and occasionally fresh varieties are found in most oriental stores.

Lithe (Scotch). To thicken a broth or soup.

Litorne. A variety of thrush with delicious meat; prepared like other game birds.

Little Bustard. (1) A family of game birds, including the great bustard, found in Europe, Asia, and Australia, and related to the cranes and plovers. (2) Local name for the Canada goose and the stone curlew of Europe.

Little Joss Wheat. An English wheat with a red seed. The flour it produces is quite soft and contains about 10.6 percent gluten.

Little-Neck Clams. The smallest hard-shell clams, about 1½ inches in size when over a year old.

Little Salt. A type of cooky, made with sugar, butter, sour cream, flour, salt, and soda.

Littorine. An edible shellfish.

Livarot. A strong-flavored skim-milk cheese made during the summer months in France. It is stored in caves where the temperature is uniformly cold, and takes several months to mature. It is dark red or brown and is at its prime between January and March; marketed in small cylinders.

Live Foods. Fermented foods, such as whole-grain bread, yeast, rennet, sour milk, wine, bean shoots, and sauerkraut.

Lively Ferment. A commercial bakery term for yeast, yeast food, flour, and water mixed at a temperature favorable for the yeast to grow in.

Liver. The largest and most important glandular organ, vital to the digestive processes of both humans and animals, particularly in converting sugars for release into the bloodstream. Medical authorities have discovered that it is rich in vitamins A, B, and C. Therefore the livers of slaughtered animals, poultry, and game are often used as food, stuffing, or garnish. Calf's liver, more highly favored by gourmets, is usually most expensive because of the greater demand for it, but beef, sheep, and pork livers are equally nutritious and equally rich in iron and vitamins.

If liver is overcooked it becomes hard and tough. Slices should be fairly thin and uniform so that they cook evenly until the pink color disappears.

Livernon, Fromage de. A simple goat's-milk cheese made in Quercy, France.

Liver Paste. A general term used to describe any smooth mixture containing liver.

Liver Sausage. Any of a wide range of sausages made with liver.

Liverwurst. A sausage, of German origin, containing a large proportion of liver.

Livestock. Domesticated animals, including cattle, sheep, pigs, and others, many of which are raised for food.

Livetin. A water-soluble protein present in egg yolk.

Livlander; Hand Cheese. A German sour-milk cheese with a pungent taste and odor.

Livornaise Sauce (French). A sauce made with olive oil, egg yolks, and anchovy paste.

Llapingachos (Ecuadorian). Potato pancakes with poached eggs.

Loach. A small European freshwater fish, long, barbed, and eel-like; best when fried in deep fat.

Loaded. (1) As applied to wine, made to appear full-bodied by the use of additives. (2) (American, Colloquial) Intoxicated.

Loaf. (1) A shaped or molded mass, such as bread. (2) A cooked dish of meat or vegetables made into a particular shape.

Loaf Pan. A deep rectangular container used for baking bread or other foods prepared to be served as a loaf.

Loaf Sugar. Sugar pressed into a molded shape.

Loas. Ginger.

Lob. A very thick mixture, a term used especially in beer making.

Lobak. A large white Chinese radish that tastes like a turnip.

Lobescowes (Danish). A thick stew.

Loblolly. A thick cereal made of flour or cornmeal.

Lobscouse. A sailors' stew consisting of salted meat and vegetables left over from a voyage and thickened with ship's biscuit.

Lobster. A large saltwater crustacean found along the Atlantic shoreline from Labrador to North Carolina. It has a smooth, dark, mottled green shell (European varieties are rich purplish-blue with orange joints and red feelers), compound eyes, and five pairs of legs, the front two being large pincers or claws. Supplies are most abundant from June to September, and the most important sources are off the coast of Nova Scotia and Maine. The best-sized lobster for eating purposes weighs about 2 pounds and measures 10–14 inches. It may be cooked in many different ways, and the succulent, highly flavored flesh can be eaten hot or cold with a variety of sauces.

Lobster Creel. Lobster pot.

Lobster Pot. A basket-type net used to catch lobsters.

Lobster, Spiny. A general term for clawless lobsters; the langouste.

Lobster Tail. The tail section of ocean crayfish (crawfish), which resembles the lobster but is smaller and has no claws. It is caught and processed in Australia and South Africa, and the tails are usually available in frozen condition.

Local, The. A British name for a neighborhood saloon, a "local" pub.

Locanda. An inn or lodging house.

Locatelli (Italian). A type of Pecorino cheese with a distinctive granular quality. *See* Pecorino.

Loches, Fromage de. A plain goat's-milk cheese made in Touraine, France.

Locorotondo. A dry white wine made in Puglia, Italy.

Locro. A corn or other vegetable soup-stew popular on the west coast of South America.

Locust Bean. Carob; an edible green bean. *See also* Carob Seed.

Locust Tree; Carob. A subtropical plant found in Europe, Asia, and Africa; its seeds are edible, and the pulp is used for preserves and also for a sweet drink.

Lodigiano. A yellowish cheese made in Lodi, Italy; it is sharp, slightly bitter, and resembles Parmesan in texture; suitable for grating.

Lofschotel (Dutch). Baked endive.

Løg (Danish). Onion.

Loganberry. A hybrid of the blackberry and the raspberry produced by Judge J. H. Logan in 1881. It resembles the blackberry in shape and the raspberry in flavor and in purplish-red color. Highly perishable, loganberries are usually marketed in cans, and may be used as a dessert fruit, a garnish for cereals, in tarts and pies, and as jams and preserves.

Loganiza. *See* Longaniza.

Loifa'i (South Pacific). Green bananas baked and served with coconut milk.

Loin. The front part of the hind quarter of beef, lamb, mutton, pork, or veal with the flank removed.

Loin Chop. A cut of meat taken from the loin of an animal.

Loire Wines. *See* France, The Wines of.

Løk (Norwegian). Onion.

Lök (Swedish). Onion.

Löklåda (Swedish). Onion-and-meat casserole.

Löksås (Swedish). Onion sauce.

Lollipop; Lollypop. A round or oval bright-colored candy usually at the end of a stick.

Loll-Shraub. The Indian name for red Bordeaux wine.

Lolly (British). Bread dipped in beer, tea, or another liquid.

Lolly Banger (British). Thick gingerbread containing raisins.

Lolo (South Pacific). A creamy thick white sauce used for flavoring almost all foods. It is prepared by grating coconut meat and then squeezing the liquid from it.

Lombardo. A Parmesan-type Italian cheese usually used for grating.

Lombo (Portuguese). Loin of meat.

  Lombo de Porco. Loin of pork.

  Lombo de Vitela. Loin of veal.

Lombo di Maiale Tonne (Italian). Pork with a tuna fish sauce.

Lo Mein (Chinese). A dish in which soft noodles are an important ingredient.

Loment (Obsolete). Ground bean meal.

Lomentum. A legume that breaks into single-seed joints when mature.

Lomo (South American). Beef.

London Broil. *See* Flank Steak.

London Buns (British). Plain sweet finger-shaped rolls covered with white icing.

London Dry Gin. A general term for any dry, unsweetened gin, even though made in other countries.

London Eggs (British, Obsolete). Eggs not freshly laid.

London Mixed Grill. A dish consisting of a mutton chop, bacon, a veal cutlet, a piece of beef, grilled tomatoes, and possibly a sausage.

Longan. The edible fruit of an Asiatic evergreen tree.

Longaniza; Loganiza (Spanish). A pork sausage colored with *achote* and spiced with garlic, pepper, and oregano.

Long Bean. Kidney bean.

Longchamp (French). A basic broth consisting of shredded sorrel and vermicelli cooked in consommé and combined with puréed green peas.

Long Clam. Razor clam.

Longe (French). The top part of the loin of an animal, but especially a veal loin.

  Longe de Porc. Loin of pork.

  Longe de Veau. Loin of veal.

Longhorn. (1) A good-quality American cheddar cheese made in Wisconsin. (2) A variety of long-horned cattle.

Long Island Duck. An extraordinarily fine-tasting all-purpose duck; especially suited for roasting.

Long Island Potatoes. Young potatoes.

Long Leek. Common leek.

Long Pepper. Capsicum, especially grown in Africa and India.

Long Pod. A broad bean.

Long Potato. Sweet potato.

Long Rice Noodle; Powdered Silk Vermicelli. A translucent Chinese noodle made from mungo beans.

Lonza di Vitello (Italian). Loin of veal.

Lonzo. Fillet of pork prepared in herbed brine, dried, and cut into thin slices; served as an appetizer in Corsica, France. Also, fillet of smoked pork.

Loofah. A small squash native to Southeast Asia.

Loofah, Angled. A vegetable resembling a large cucumber with steep-angled ridges along its length.

Lookdown. Moonfish; horsehead.

Lop. A variety of rabbit.

Lopper. To congeal or curdle.

Loquat. Japanese medlar; the plumlike fruit of the biwa or medlar tree native to Japan but now cultivated in California and Florida and in southern France; slightly tart and best used for jams and preserves.

Lord Baltimore Cake. A yellow layer cake made with a filling of crushed macaroons, candied cherries, and almonds, and covered with frosting.

Lords and Ladies; Cuckoo-Pint; Wake Robin (British, Colloquial). Wild arum, a plant whose roots contain a starchy substance.

Lord Sugarcane (Colloquial). Rum.

Lorgnettes (French). (1) Fried onion rings. (2) Candied fruit and small dessert cookies.

Lormes, Fromage de. A Camembert cheese produced near Nevers, France.

Lorraine. A small hard sour-milk cheese seasoned with pepper, salt, and pistachio nuts; made in Lorraine, France; usually eaten fresh as a delicacy.

Losange (French). Diamond-shaped food used for garnishing.

Lotah (Anglo-Indian). A round brass or copper water vessel.

Lotophagi. In Greek mythology, eaters of the lotus fruit.

Lotte (French). The eelpout, a freshwater and a saltwater fish. It has excellent flesh and is generally prepared like eel.

Lotus. A water lily; the root and seeds are often used in oriental cookery.

Lotus Seeds. The seeds of the *Nelumbium nelumbo*, used in oriental cookery.

Louche (French). A large long-handled spoon used to serve soup, sauces, etc.

Louise-Bonne (French). A hardy autumn pear with a thick red-and-yellow skin and a pronounced flavor.

Louner (British). A large lump of bread.

Loup; Loup de Mer; Bar (French). A variety of bass found chiefly in the Mediterranean and sometimes in the North Sea; used in the preparation of bouillabaisse.

Loukoumades (Greek). Fritters prepared with a yeast batter heavily flavored with cinnamon; served with a honey syrup.

Loupiac. A wine district of the Bordeaux region of France.

Lovage. A wild form of the herb angelica. Its shoots are used for flavoring liqueurs or are boiled with sugar to make candy. The stems of one variety can be eaten like celery, uncooked in salads, or braised as a vegetable.

Love Apple. The tomato.

Love Feast. A dinner held by early Christians to signify brotherly love.

Love-in-Disguise. Calf's heart filled with savory stuffing, covered with bacon, then wrapped in paper and baked. The paper is removed, and the heart, coated heavily in bread crumbs to disguise it, is then browned in the oven; served with red-currant jelly.

Loving Cup. (1) A large ornamental drinking cup with two handles for convenience in passing from guest to guest for the drinking of toasts. (2) Wines and similar drinks which were once served only in this fashion.

Lovo. An earth oven, much used in parts of the South Pacific, especially the Fiji Islands. A large hole is dug in the ground, and wood is burned to heat the stones. Foods wrapped in vegetable leaves are placed in the *lovo* and allowed to steam for several hours.

Low-Salt Diets. *See* Salt-free Diets.

Low Wines. A liquor industry term, used to describe the first bulk distillate obtained in the whisky-making process.

Low Yeast. The slow-acting yeast used to ferment lager beer. When fermentation is completed, it settles at the bottom of the vat.

Lox (Jewish). Smoked salmon.

Löytens (Swedish). A type of aquavit. *See* Aquavit.

Lozenge. A very small diamond-shaped, flavored candy that dissolves in the mouth.

Lozenge Paste. A mixture of starch, confectioners' sugar, and dissolved gelatin or gum arabic; used to decorate sweets.

Luau. A Hawaiian feast eaten by guests seated on the ground; usually accompanied by music, dancing, drinking, and other activities. *See* Hawaii.

Luau Me Wai Niu (Hawaiian). Fresh taro leaves boiled with coconut milk.

Luberon. Fruity, somewhat sour red wines produced near Maubec, France.

Lucca. A superior-quality Italian olive oil named for a town in northern Italy.

Lucerne Kugeli (Swiss). A pastry ball stuffed with chopped veal and mushrooms.

Luche. An edible seaweed found along the coast of Chile.

Lucines Papillons (French). Soft clams.

Luckshen (Jewish). Noodles.

Lucullus, Lucius Licinius. A Roman epicure and field marshal (114–57 B.C.) noted for his sumptuous banquets. Any dish bearing his name includes such delicacies as truffles, or other costly ingredients.

Lüfer (Turkish). A fish found only in the waters of the Bosporus, with a good taste and delicate white-meat texture; best when grilled plain.

Lugana. *See* Italy, The Wines of.

Luganeghin (Italian). A garlic-flavored sausage.

Luganica. A spicy Italian sausage.

Lukewarm. Neither hot nor cold; rather warm.

Lulas (Portuguese). Squid; cuttlefish; inkfish.

Lumache (Italian). (1) Snails. (2) Snail-shaped pasta.

>**Lumache alla Marchigiana.** Snails in wine sauce.

>**Lumache alla Romana.** Snails in tomato-and-anchovy sauce.

Lumber Pie (Obsolete). Eggs and fish or meat.

Lumpy. As applied to dough, not kneaded thoroughly; as applied to gravy, not smooth.

Lumyai. A Southeast Asian hard-shelled fruit with delicious yellowish flesh.

Lunch; Luncheon. A comparatively light meal usually eaten at midday. Also, any simple repast or refreshment served between meals. Luncheon is usually a formal meal at which guests are present.

Lunchbox. A container in which lunch is carried, usually by schoolchildren and workmen.

Lunch Cheese. A simple, Limburger-type German cheese.

Luncheonette. An eating place that serves mainly lunch but sometimes other meals as well. The menu is usually more limited than that of a restaurant.

Luncheon Meats. A general term for cold cuts and sausages; sometimes, prepared pressed meats.

Luncheon Plate. A plate usually about 7 inches in diameter.

Lüneberg. A saffron-colored cow's-milk cheese made in Austria. It is quite aromatic, and when ripe resembles a cross between Swiss and Limburger.

Lunel Wine. Muscat de Lunel, a sweet dessert wine made from Muscat grapes near Lunel, France.

Lupini (Italian). Flat yellow beans.

Lupus. Pike, a food fish.

Lurcher (Obsolete). One who takes another's share of food.

Lurid. A variety of oyster found on the Pacific coast of the United States.

Lustick (Obsolete). Merrymaking, eating, and drinking.

Lute. (1) To completely encase food with a flour-and-water dough. Hams and old fowl are often cooked in this way to seal in the juices and make the flesh tender. The baked dough is broken off and discarded. (2) To seal casseroles and pâté dishes. (3) The flour-and-water paste used to coat and seal meat.

Lutefisk (Scandinavian). A fish dish made by cutting *torskfisk* (unsalted dry cod) into pieces and soaking it in water for 8 days, on the 9th day placing it in a solution of one pint of potash lye and 12 pints of water and allowing it to soak 3 additional days.

Lutfisk (Swedish). Dried fish, usually cod.

Luxembourg. This small country produces numerous wines, but none is distinctive or of outstanding quality. The white wines tend to be far better than the reds.

Luya (Philippine). Ginger.

Luzinzeth (Arabian). A sweet almond cake; served in a sweet melted-butter sauce.

Lynnhaven. A name given to certain types of flavorsome oysters found in the Chesapeake Bay area of the United States. Although theoretically limited to those oysters brought to market at Lynnhaven, catches from nearby waters are frequently sold under this name.

Lyonnaise, A la (French). In the Lyons style; that is, prepared with sautéed onions.

Lyonnaise Sauce. An onion sauce made with white wine, spices, etc.

Lyst Rugbrød (Danish). Light rye bread.

M

Maalubi (Arabian). A preparation made with rice, veal, and vegetables.

Maan Nezim Nzedo (African). A fish stew made with freshwater fish and okra in Upper Volta.

Maa Tahiti. A Tahitian native feast. *See* Tamaaraa.

Maatjes. Fresh Dutch herrings; usually served on toast, sprinkled with lemon juice, and accompanied by beer.

Mabí. Small pieces of bark of the naked-wood tree in the Caribbean; used to flavor a fermented beverage made in many of the islands.

Maçã (Portuguese). Apple.

Macabeo. A rich, exceedingly sweet wine produced in the Pyrénées region of France; good only with cookies or dessert.

Macabí. Bonefish.

Macadamia Nut. A small round two-kernel nut native to Australia but now grown commercially in Hawaii. Hawaii exports them shelled, roasted, and salted in glass jars; they taste like almonds and have a faint coffee aroma. Available only in delicacy shops, they are served for nibbling with cocktails, but they may be chopped and served atop ice cream and puddings or as an ingredient in certain Hawaiian dishes.

Macarela (Spanish). Mackerel.

Macaroni. Generic name for products including macaroni, spaghetti, and egg noodles in an infinite number of shapes and sizes. Europeans refer to such products as "alimentary pastes."

The most frequently used shapes of macaroni products are: *macaroni*, the tubular shape in short elbows or long lengths; *spaghetti*, the solid rod form available in varying degrees of thickness; and *egg noodles*, the ribbonlike pieces in varying widths. Among the other shapes are corrugated elbows, coiled or bunched rods, alphabets, shells, bows, stars, and seeds.

Best-quality macaroni and spaghetti are made from a mixture of semolina and water. Semolina, the purified middlings of durum wheat, is a granulate amber-colored substance about as fine as sugar. Durum is the hardest variety of wheat known to man. In this country it is grown principally in a small triangular section of twelve North Dakota counties.

Egg noodles may be made from the same mixture of semolina and water used for macaroni and spaghetti but are required by law to contain, in addition, 5.5 percent egg solids. Egg solids may be added in fresh, powdered, or frozen form. Only the yolks are used, since the whites tend to make noodles tough.

The art of making macaroni is so old that its exact origin is lost to history. The Chinese recorded the eating of macaroni products in various forms as early as 5000 B.C.

Among the popular legends is the one about the Chinese maiden who was lured from her breadmaking by her lover, a member of the famous Marco Polo expedition to the Orient. While the maiden neglected her bread dough the wind blew leaves from an overhanging tree into the batter. In an attempt to help her save the dough from waste, the sailor forced the dough through a wicker basket which served as a sieve. The thin strands of dough dried in the sun and, when the sailor departed, the maiden presented him with the dough in this new shape. He cooked the strands of dried dough on his ship and found the dish so delicious that he made it many times thereafter. The food came to be favored by all the members of the crew and finally by the great explorer himself, Marco Polo.

A 13th-century Italian king is credited with naming the food. When he was served the dish, he declared "*Ma Caroni!*", which means "How very dear!"

Some people like macaroni quite tender, others prefer it fairly firm or *al dente*. For the degree of tenderness desired, the cooking time varies from 5 to 20 minutes, according to the shape and brand of macaroni used. As a general rule, cooking directions on the package should be followed. The most important thing is to avoid overcooking—overcooked macaroni is too soft and shapeless.

To cook 8 ounces of macaroni, add a tablespoon of salt to 4 quarts of rapidly boiling water. Gradually add the macaroni so that the water continues to boil. Cook uncovered, stirring occasionally, to prevent sticking, until macaroni is tender.

When tender, drain immediately in a colander or large sieve. If the macaroni is to be served hot, dot it with butter. Macaroni products are best cooked just before serving.

Macaroni and spaghetti approximately double in volume when cooked. Egg noodles do not increase in volume; that is, one cup of uncooked macaroni or spaghetti will give two cups after cooking, one cup of egg noodles will remain one cup.

Package sizes of macaroni products vary throughout the country, the most popular being 8 and 16 ounces.

Macaroni à la Lucerne. A pastry shell filled with macaroni, ham, tongue, sweetbreads, etc.

Macaroni-Cheese. A baked mixture made of cheese and macaroni.

Macaroni Salad. Chilled cooked macaroni may be combined with chilled vegetables, as raw tomato, shredded raw carrot, green pepper or pimiento, and diced celery. Cooked vegetables, like lima beans or peas, may also be used. Leftover vegetables can be utilized in this way. Strips of cold meat make a heartier salad. The entire mixture should be seasoned and moistened, but not drowned, in a mayonnaise or Russian dressing.

An old recipe suggests serving cooked cold macaroni on a platter around a center mound of endive which has been marinated in oil and vinegar, served with a garnish of hard-boiled egg slices, or cold-meat strips, and tomato wedges.

Macaroni Vongole. Spaghetti or other pasta covered with a clam sauce.

Macaroni Wheat. The flour from durum wheat, which is widely used in Italy to make macaroni.

Macaroons. A sweet, porous cooky made with egg whites and sugar and either almonds or shredded coconut. Legend has it that the first macaroons were made by an order of nuns at St. Emilion in the Bordeaux region of France. In the original version, egg whites are stirred into chopped or grated almonds and sugar. To ensure a crisp surface and a soft, chewy interior the mixture should stand half an hour before being put in the oven. The macaroon better known in the United States is made with shredded coconut, egg whites, and sugar. Both varieties should be eaten as fresh as possible and kept in a dry, moderately cool place, protected from the air.

Macarráo (Portuguese). Macaroni.

Macarrones (Spanish). Macaroni.

Maccheroni (Italian). Any type of noodle or spaghetti.

Maccheroni al Forno. Baked macaroni.

Maccheroni alla Chitarra. Macaroni cut on a series of wires; hence the name "guitar." The very sharp edges produce a distinctive taste.

Maccheroni con Piselli. Macaroni with peas.

Maccheroni e Ruta. Macaroni and rue, a bitter herb, served with tomato sauce.

Macchinetta. An Italian coffee-making apparatus. *See* Espresso Coffee.

Mace. A spice used for flavoring cakes, biscuits, preserves, sauces, and fish and meat dishes. It is also used in pickling, and, commercially, in tomato ketchup, mustard sauce, Worcestershire sauce, and frankfurters. Mace is the crimson covering of the nutmeg kernel which, when removed, flattened, and dried, changes to a pale yellowish or reddish brown color. The Banda and Penang varieties are considered the best. The nutmeg kernel, which mace covers, is another spice from the same tree.

Macédoine (French). A mixture of evenly cut fruits or vegetables of different types and colors. A typical macédoine of fresh fruit consists of pears, peaches, apricots, bananas, strawberries, raspberries, and currants sprinkled with sugar syrup, and either kirsch or maraschino, and steeped in the refrigerator for an hour or two before serving.

Macedonia di Frutta (Italian). Fruit cup.

Macerate. To tenderize foods by steeping them in a liquid.

Macéré (French). As applied to food, steeped or soaked in a liquid.

Macérer (French). (1) To soak, pickle, or steep foods. (2) To marinate fruits in sweetened liqueurs.

Machanca (Russian). A dish of pork, sausages, and sour cream prepared in Byelorussia.

Mâche (French). Lamb's-lettuce, a salad green used during cold weather when other salad materials are scarce; corn or field salad.

Macherone (Italian). *See* Mascarpone.

Machiais. Elegant Japanese restaurants with sliding doors, permitting larger or smaller rooms as desired.

Macho. A Mexican banana with extremely firm flesh.

Macis (Spanish). Mace.

Mackerel. A marine fish with high protein and fat content. Each spring tremendous schools of mackerel migrate from deeper waters toward the Atlantic coast from Chesapeake Bay to the St. Lawrence River, and the fish is on the market from April to December. The northern mackerel, also known as *Boston mackerel*, is smaller than the *Florida* and *King mackerel* (both from Florida waters), which are in good supply during January and February.

Mackerel is best either broiled or baked. For baking, it needs no basting. The dressed fish is placed in a shallow pan in a 400° oven: with the head, two minutes for each ounce of dressed weight; without the head, one minute for each ounce. It should be served immediately.

Mackerel Guide. Garfish.

Mâcon. Red wines, somewhat crude in flavor, and less fruity than Beaujolais; these wines are produced near Mâcon, France, and are at their best when 2–4 years old.

Mâconnais. A French wine region with two large subdivisions: Mâcon for red wines and Mâcon-Blanc for white wines.

Mâconnaise. (1) As applied to meats, prepared with red wine. (2) A wine cask.

Macquelines, Fromage de. A soft, mild-flavored cheese similar to Brie, produced in the Valois region of France.

Macque, Pain de la. A French pastry similar to the cream puff.

Macreuse. (1) A migrating wild swamp duck with a very strong, oily flavor. (2) A thin piece of meat found on the spine of beef.

Macrobiotics. A theory of diet which places chief emphasis upon cereals and grains, fish and certain vegetables; it is based upon the vital link between potassium and sodium in the body. Philosophically, macrobiotics is an offshoot of the Yin-Yang theory of forces in the universe.

Madagascar Manna. Dulcite, a sweetening agent.

Madderwort. A wild plant sometimes used to make a kind of beer.

Made Dish. A dish made with leftovers, such as meats, poultry, fish, and vegetables. Made dishes challenge a clever cook to make the second serving of a food, no matter how changed or disguised, as tasty and attractive as the first serving.

Madegrals. Amberfish or amberjack. A small species, called *madregala*, is prepared like cod or halibut.

Madeira. An island about 400 miles off the west coast of Africa whose wines were very popular during American colonial times but are now comparatively rare. Madeiras are fortified wines, usually sweet, although some, such as Sercial, are dry and pale, produced from a grape that came originally from the Rhine Valley of Germany. Madeiras live longer than almost every other wine—a century or more. They may be drunk as an apéritif and may be served with soup and as a dessert wine. They are also used like sherry in soups, sauces, and desserts.

Madeira Cake. Originally an English cake, it is made with flour, butter, sugar, eggs, lemon extract, and lemon rind, decorated with candied citron; a glass of Madeira wine is poured over the cake before serving.

Madeira Nut. A common European walnut.

Madeira Pie. A fruit pie served with Madeira-flavored apricot sauce.

Madeira Sherbet. Fruit sherbet drenched in Madeira wine immediately before serving.

Madeleines (French). Simple small cookies made with butter, flour, eggs, and sugar and flavored usually with either vanilla or almond extract. Baked in special madeleine molds, which are oval and have a ribbed surface, the cookies have ridges on the back.

Madère, Au. Cooked with Madeira wine.

Maderized. As applied to white wine, having darkened and developed a woody taste.

Madras. (1) (Indian) A curry dish. (2) A kind of curry powder.

Madras Tea. A distinctive black tea produced in Madras, India.

Madre Vino. Boiled down, heavily concentrated grape juice, added to various fortified wines as a sweetening agent.

Madrilène, À la. In the Madrid style; denoting a chilled, jellied tomato-flavored broth. Also, containing tomatoes, which are used in many foods in Madrid.

Mad Tomcat. Catfish.

Maelk (Danish). Milk.

Maenad. A drunken female reveler.

Mafai. A yellow grapelike fruit having the taste of apricots; found in Southeast Asia.

Mafalde (Italian). Long twisted noodles.

Magdeburger-Kuhkäse. A rather ordinary cow's-milk cheese made in Magdeburg, Germany.

Maggiorana (Italian). Marjoram.

Magma. The more solid dregs remaining after the liquid part of liquors has been removed.

Magnesium. A mineral found in certain foods which, as magnesium salts, contributes to the firmness and health of bones and teeth, to cells, blood, and tissues.

Magnum. A bottle holding 2 quarts of wine.

Magnum Bonum. (1) A large yellow plum used for cooking. (2) A potato.

Magny. A noted French restaurateur and chef.

Magpie. A bird whose dark flesh is edible, but only barely so; it should be cooked slowly in a casserole over low heat with plenty of fat.

Maguey; Agave. A Mexican plant used to make an intoxicating beverage called *pulque*.

Maguro (Japanese). Tuna.

Mahaya (Indian). A spirit distilled from honey in the Bombay region.

Mahia (Arabian). A spirit distilled from dates.

Mahleb (Middle Eastern). An aromatic herb whose seeds are used in the making of pastries and breads.

Mahogany (British, Obsolete). A drink made of treacle (molasses) and gin.

Mahneek (Middle Eastern). Sausages made from ground lamb flavored with cloves.

Mahseer. An Indian freshwater fish similar to the barbel.

Mahwa. An Indian liquor produced from flowers of the mahwa tree.

Mahzee. A wild potato used by Eskimos.

Maia. (1) A Hawaiian banana. (2) Fermented milk used as a leaven in yoghurt manufacture.

Maiale (Italian). Pork.

 Maiale di Latte. Suckling pork.

 Maiale Tonnato. Pork in tuna sauce.

Maid. Any female who assists with housework, the general care of the family, and the serving and often the preparation of meals.

Maida (Indian). Refined flour.

Maidenhair Fern. A fern whose fine, hairlike composite leaves are dried and used for decorating cakes, especially those on which piped sugar flowers or marzipan is used.

Maids of Honor (British). Curd tarts; a rich cheesecake.

Maifisch (German). Shad.

Maigre (French). As applied to soups and sauces, thin and lean, lacking meat fat.

Maigre Cheese. A simple farm cheese. The French popular name for the rather poor-quality Brie cheese made during the summertime; the springtime cheese is colloquially known as *Migras*, and the finest winter cheese is called *Gras*.

Maïka (North African). A fish stew; made also with shellfish.

Mainauer. A medium-hard, yellowish German cheese.

Maingaux de Rennes (French). A mixture of whipped fresh and slightly soured cream; usually served with berries and sugar.

Maintenon, À la (French). (1) A style of preparing cutlets and sauce; named for the Marquise de Maintenon, consort of Louis XIV. (2) Food wrapped in paper and baked.

Mainzer Hand. An above-average German hand cheese produced in small flat cakes.

Mainzer Rippchen (German). Pork chops.

Maionese (Italian). Mayonnaise.

Maiorchino. An odorous Sicilian sheep's-milk cheese, occasionally made with black pepper.

Mais (French, German). Corn.

Maischlock (Scotch). A coarse bread made from a mixture of grains.

Maison, À la (French). In the style of the house or restaurant.

Maison du Roi. All the departments and personnel of the French royal household. The kitchens, called the *bouche du roi*, had enormous staffs.

Mai Tai (Hawaiian). A mixed rum drink served with an orchid.

Maitrank. May wine, a German wine drunk on May Day; made by adding woodruff, an herb, to young wine.

Maître de Bouche (French). "Master of taste." An honorary title for master chefs or leaders in the culinary field. Also, the person in charge of food and wine for a hotel chain, steamship line, etc.

Maître Butter. *See* Maître d'Hôtel Butter.

Maître d'Hôtel (French). The head of the dining room in a restaurant, private club, or hotel. All other service personnel, including captain, waiters, and busboys, are under his control. A thoroughly trained *maître d'hôtel* understands the kitchen, bar, and wine cellar in addition to the smallest detail of dining-room service. He advises guests in the selection of foods and drinks, and acts as liaison between kitchen and patron. *À la maître d'hôtel* designates elegance of service.

Maître d'Hôtel, À la (French). Pertaining to any specialty suggested by the *maître d'hôtel* of a particular dining room.

Maître d'Hôtel Butter. A creamed butter flavored with lemon juice, parsley, and seasoning; usually served with broiled foods and roast meats.

Maíz (Spanish). Corn.

Maíz Pilado. Pounded corn.

Maíz Cacahuanzincle (Mexican). Hominy; parched corn.

Maize (British). Corn. Also, corn on the cob.

Maíz Retoñado. Sprouted corn, chiefly used in making *carato de acupe*, a Venezuelan fermented drink.

Majarete (Puerto Rican). A dessert prepared from milk and rice flour.

Majocchino. An unusual Sicilian cheese made of a combination of goat's, cow's, and sheep's milk; resembles Incanestrato.

Majonnäs (Swedish). Mayonnaise.

Majorca. A variety of almond native to the island of Majorca, Spain.

Majordomo. The steward or person in charge of a large household, particularly in Europe.

Makapuno (Philippine). The occasional or freak coconut filled with soft meat; often used in making ice cream.

Makaroni (Danish, German). Macaroni.

Makrele (German). Mackerel.

Makrill (Swedish). Mackerel.

Makronen (German). Macaroons.

Makrut. A Siamese citrus plant with edible fruit and leaves.

Malaga. A sweet white wine produced in Andalusia, Spain. *See* Spain, The Wines of.

Malaga Grapes. A good-flavored greenish white grape with numerous seeds; used to make Malaga wine.

Malagkit (Philippine). Glutinous or sticky rice.

Malaguetta Pepper. *See* Amomum.

Malai (Indian). A very thick cream prepared by cooking milk over very low heat for 1½ hours, cooling it, and removing the top surface.

Malakoff Cheese. A very small creamy white French cheese; eaten fresh. *See* Gournay.

Malanga. Taro; an edible starchy tropical root.

Malart (French). The mallard, the common wild duck.

Malassadas (Portuguese). Yeast doughnuts.

Malaxer. To work or knead a mixture to make it more pliable.

Malaysia. Like other Asiatic countries with high temperatures, Malaysia prefers highly spiced dishes. Foods are rarely, if ever, simply broiled or boiled plain; most dishes are cooked with spices and herbs, some of which are familiar to Western palates, and others are quite unusual. In addition to the usual ingredients, ginger, garlic, anise, cumin, cinnamon, coriander, turmeric and other such items, the Malays like mustard seeds (*sawi*), lemon grass (*sĕrai*), tamarind (*asam*), candlenuts (*nuah keras*), fenugreek (*ventayam*), and poppy seeds *kaskas*).

In the lush countryside fruits and vegetables grow profusely. Very popular are such vegetables as Ceylon spinach (*basella*), Indian spinach (*bayam*), yam beans (*bĕngkuang*), breadfruit (*sukun*), Chinese radishes (*lobak*), the Dolichos bean (*kara-kara*), the four-corner bean (*kachang botor*), water chestnuts (*ma thai*), and tapioca (*ubi kayu*). There are more than a dozen varieties of banana (*pisang*), and also the carambola (*blimbing besi*), yellow passion-fruit (*buah susu*), custard apple (*nona srikaya*), the coconut (*kĕlapa*), pomegranate (*delima*), the soursop (*durian blanda*), and the mangosteen (*manggis*).

Malaysian food is based on boiled rice, which is generally served with hot curry dishes made from fish, meat, poultry, or ˙vegetables. *Satai*, small chunks of meat on a skewer, are very popular. Other interesting Malaysian dishes include *kurma*, made with beef or mutton and flavored with cinnamon, cloves, white pepper, garlic, and onions; *opor*, a dish of meat or chicken prepared with coriander, anise, cumin, cinnamon, cloves, and nutmeg; *rendan santan* is a coconut-ginger chicken dish; *dondeng* is spicy bits of steak made with tamarind, garlic, onions, and ginger. There are a few good desserts: *gula malacca*, made with coconut-palm sugar and sago; *sarikauja*, a coconut custard; *kueh blanda*, a coconut cake; and *lapis* cake, made with tapioca.

Malay Apple. A tasty juicy Malaysian fruit that may be eaten raw or cooked.

Malfoof (Middle Eastern). Stuffed cabbage leaves filled with lamb and rice.

Malfoof Mahshie (Yemenite). Cabbage stuffed with ground meat.

Mali. A pure white heavily scented flavoring used in Thailand to flavor tea.

Malic Acid. An acid present in apples and certain other fruits.

Malines. A Belgian asparagus with excellent taste and texture.

Maliputo. A Philippine freshwater fish.

Mallard Duck. A wild duck, a great favorite with hunters. Mallards are considered a great delicacy. Hunters apparently feel duty-bound to approve of the flavor, but many nonhunters find the flesh somewhat gamy.

Mallobet. A cold marshmallow dessert prepared like an ice.

Mallow. A plant whose leaves may be used fresh in making salads; cooked like a green vegetable, it has a sticky, slightly unpleasant texture. There are various species, best known of which are Jews' Mallow and Indian Mallow.

Malma; Dolly Varden. A North American trout.

Malmsey; Malvasia; Malvoisie. A strong, rather sweet wine produced from the Malvasia grape in Madeira, Portugal; usually served with cookies or spongecake.

Maloreddus (Italian). Semolina dumplings; usually served with a sauce.

Malpeque. A flat full-flavored oyster native to the waters around Prince Edward Island, Canada.

Malt. (1) Grain, usually barley, soaked in water and allowed to sprout; used in making beer, distilling liquors, etc. (2) Beer and ale.

Malt Bread. A sweet bread prepared with malt and raisins.

Malted Barley. Barley allowed to sprout in order to produce maltose, from which malt is extracted for brewing purposes.

Malted Milk. A powder made of dried milk plus wheat and malted-barley extracts. Combined with fresh milk it is a delicious nourishing drink.

Maltese Orange. A blood orange with red pulp and red juice.

Malt Extract. A heavy syrup produced when crushed malt is steeped in water.

Malt Extract Barm. A medium for growing yeast, consisting of water and malt extract maintained at a 70°F. temperature.

Malt Flour. Rye, wheat, malted barley, and other cereals ground together.

Malt Liquor. A term used to describe beer, ale, porter, stout, and other similar beverages.

Malt Meals. Mixtures of malt flour, soya flour, white or brown flour, sugar, mineral salts, and aerating chemicals.

Maltose. Malt sugar; a crystalline sugar derived from starch by the action of diastase and/or malt.

Malt Syrup. A bland sweet syrup made with malt and starch.

Malt Whisky. Whisky distilled from a mash containing not less than 51 percent rye or barley.

Malt Wine. Another name for stout beer in England.

Malungay. The Philippine horseradish "tree" or plant.

Malvasia. *See* Malmsey.

Malvoisie. *See* Malmsey.

Mamaliga. Cornmeal, or corn bread, the traditional basic food of Romania. Corn was brought to Europe from America by explorers, and the impoverished peasants of Romania soon adopted cornmeal as their basic food. It is eaten hot or cold, with cheese, vegetables, sauerkraut, and in many other ways.

Mame (Japanese). A type of bean boiled, cooled, and mixed with soy sauce; a favorite with beer.

Mammée; Mamey; Mamey Apple. The tart, round fruit of the mammée tree, a member of the apple group; the fruit has yellow juicy flesh, which may be eaten raw, preserved, or used in cooking.

Mamey Sapote. A reddish-colored tropical fruit having a yellowish pulp with a very large central seed. It has a bland taste, and is best when cooked or made into a jelly with other, more acidulous fruits.

Maná (Peruvian). Almond dessert made with egg yolks and port wine.

Manare (Latin American). A sieve for sifting grated *yucca*.

Manatee. A large whalelike marine animal whose delicate flesh has a flavor reminiscent of pork.

Mancha Manteles (Mexican). "Tablecloth stainer"; chicken and pork served with a sauce consisting of onions, tomatoes, and green peppers.

Manchant (British). A hand-shaped loaf of bread usually not baked in a tin; the term is used in Cornwall.

Manche (French). The bone that projects from a cutlet.

Manchego. A rather bland Spanish cheese, which is pleasant but somewhat undistinguished when young. Aged manchego, *manchego viejo*, on the other hand, is an extraordinarily fine cheese with a nutty taste and crumbly texture.

Manchet (Obsolete). Small 14th-century rolls or loaves made with white flour.

Manchette (French). The small cut-paper decoration used on a bone, especially a lamb chop.

Manchon (French). Small muff-shaped pastries or cookies, usually filled with whipped or butter cream.

Mandalay Beer (Burmese). A good light, refreshing beer prepared in Mandalay.

Mandarina. Tangerine.

Mandarinen (German). Tangerines.

Mandarin Oil. A yellow oil pressed from the rinds of tangerine or mandarin oranges and used to flavor sweets.

Mandarin Orange. A small orange thought to be of Chinese origin.

Mandel (German, Swedish). Almond.

Mandelbrot (German). A partly dry cake made with almonds or flavored with almonds.

Mandelbund (Norwegian). Almond cake.

Mandelsulz (German). A white almond pudding.

Mandeltorte (German). Almond pastry.

Mandler (Norwegian). Almonds.

Mandoletti; Mandorletti (Italian). Sweet almond biscuits.

Mandorle (Italian). Almonds.

Mandrake. Mayapple.

Manducable. Edible.

Manducate. To chew.

Mane (Scotch, Obsolete). In the 14th century, white bread or manchet.

Màneghi (Italian). Dumplings prepared from cracker crumbs, flour, and molasses.

Mange-Tout (French). A young tender pea or bean eaten pod and all.

Mangistan. A fruit native to the South Pacific, particularly to Indonesia.

Mangiti; Mangio (Fijian). A native feast; meats, vegetables, and seafood wrapped in vegetable leaves, lowered into a special earth oven called a *lovo*, and allowed to steam.

Mango. Originally, an Asiatic tree, but now grown in suitable climates around the world. The fruit is long and oval with a green, orange, red, yellow, purple, or occasionally black skin. The flesh is very juicy when ripe, and usually orange-colored, but this may vary according to the variety, of which there are scores. Each fruit contains an extremely large seed or pit, which may be roasted and the kernel eaten. Mangos vary in flavor: the wild types have an extremely acidulous taste, whereas the better cultivated varieties are sweet and luscious. The mango combines the taste of many different fruits, but especially the peach, pineapple, and strawberry. Mangos may be peeled and sliced, or cut in half and eaten with a demitasse spoon; best when chilled, but not ice cold. The fruit is made into jellies, preserves, and relishes, particularly mango chutney. Cooked, sweetened mangos are particularly good with ice cream.

Mango Fish. A bright yellow pleasant-tasting Indian fish.

Mangoit. An orange pear-sized fruit native to the South Pacific; also cultivated in other warm climates.

Mangold. A green vegetable resembling spinach.

Mangold-Wurzel; Mangel-Wurzel. A large field beet sometimes used as food; also used in brewing Mangold-Wurzel beer.

Mango Melon. A melon that must be cooked to be edible; the taste suggests that of squash.

Mango Squash. *See* Chayote.

Mangosteen; Mangostan. A reddish brown East Indian fruit that resembles an orange in size and structure, and tastes like a blend of peach and pineapple.

Mangrove. (1) A tropical fruit, from the tree of the same name whose astringent bark is used in tanning. (2) A tropical fish.

Manhattan Cocktail. A cocktail prepared with rye, Italian vermouth, and bitters in varying proportions; served very cold with a maraschino cherry.

Manicie. White and red wines; also known as the *wines of Bugey* in France.

Manicotti (Italian). Pancake noodles stuffed with cheese and served with sauce.

    Manicotti all' Etrusca. Noodle layers with chicken and mushrooms.

Manié (French). Mixed with the hands; kneaded.

Manier (French). (1) To mix flour with butter or other fat to thicken gravies, stews, etc. The mixture is called *kneaded butter*. (2) To knead butter for making pastry.

Manihot. Manioc flour (cassava flour), made from manioc. *See also* Cassava.

    Manihot Starch. *See* Cassava.

Manioc. *See* Cassava.

Manioc Flour. Flour made from manioc (cassava); much used in tropical countries, especially in Brazil. *See also* Cassava.

Manju (Japanese). Bean-paste buns.

Manna (Biblical). Food miraculously given to the Israelites in the wilderness. Now, food that arrives at an appropriate time or in time of need.

Manna Croup. (1) A Russian coarse hard-wheat cereal used for making puddings. (2) Wheat without bran in a granular preparation, used as food for the sick and for children.

Manna, Madagascar. Dulcite, a sweetening agent.

Mannite. White crystalline scentless juice from the stems of the ash tree, beet roots, and a few other vegetables.

Manouls (French). A provincial dish consisting of tripe combined with ground ham, garlic, eggs, and bread crumbs.

Manqué (French). A butter cake usually flavored with pistachio or lemon.

Mansard (French). Wood pigeon or ring dove.

Mansata. A spirit distilled from bananas.

Manteca (Spanish). Lard, butter, and other fats.

Mantecado (Spanish). (1) A lard cooky. (2) A Puerto Rican custardlike ice cream.

Mantecati (Italian). Ice cream.

Manteiga (Portuguese). Butter.

Mantelikokkare (Finnish). A custard dessert served with huckleberry sauce.

Mantequilla (Spanish). Butter.

Mantu (Korean). Dumplings filled with meat, poultry, or vegetables.

Manur; Manuri. A Yugoslavian slightly salted cow's- or sheep's-milk cheese with buttermilk added.

Manzanas (Spanish). Apples.

Manzanilla. A pale sherry from Spain. *See also* Spain, The Wines of.

Manzano. A South American banana.

Manzo (Italian). Beef.

    Manzo Bollito. Boiled beef.

    Manzo Lesso. Boiled beef.

Manzo Salato. Corned beef.

Manzo Stufato. Beef stew.

Manzo uso Piemontese. Pot roast with wine and ham.

Maple. A medium-sized tree found in North and South America; certain varieties are native only to North America. At certain times of the year, its sweet sap may be tapped and made into maple syrup, sugar, molasses, etc.

Maple Honey. Uncrystallized sap from the sugar-maple tree.

Maple Molasses (British). A syrup made by dissolving maple sugar or evaporating maple sap; maple syrup.

Maple Sugar. A brownish sugar prepared from the sap obtained from certain varieties of maple; the sugar made in northern New England is usually regarded as the best. Maple sugar is sprinkled on fruit or made into candy.

Maple Syrup. A sweet brown syrup made from the sap obtained from certain varieties of maple; the classic accompaniment for griddle cakes and waffles, but also used with French toast, on bread, ice cream, etc.

Mâquée. A Belgian homemade cottage cheese.

Maqui. The berry of a Chilean shrub; used for adulterating wine.

Maraa. The stomach, lungs, liver and other entrails of a ram, eaten raw as a sort of appetizer in the Sudan.

Marabout (French). A large coffeepot.

Maraichère, À la. Of meat, garnished with artichokes and tiny onions; of eggs, garnished with braised sorrel and chervil.

Marajuca. A Brazilian seacoast fruit used in making *batida*, a local drink.

Maraniol. A white crystalline substance often used to furnish the synthetic aroma and taste of walnuts.

Marasca. A small black Yugoslavian cherry.

Maraschino. A very strong alcoholic beverage made from marasca, a black cherry, particularly in Italy and Yugoslavia; usually prepared as a sweet drink, but occasionally made as a dry liquor.

Maraschino Cherry. The marasca cherry. In America maraschino cherries are of the Royal Anne variety, picked and prepared in syrup

before fully ripe, and colored a deep red; used to decorate cakes, puddings, fruit cups, ice-cream desserts, and fancy drinks.

Marble; Marbling (Colloquial). The fat streaks in meat. Marbling indicates the quality; top qualities have more marbling than inferior qualities.

Marble Cake. A cake in which chocolate or cocoa is mixed lightly into the batter to produce a marblelike appearance when baked.

Marbré (French). Marbled, such as cakes.

Marc. A strong French brandy distilled from the skins, stalks, and pips of pressed grapes or from the pulp of apples after the wine or cider has been pressed out. The Italians call this type of brandy *grappa*; although harsh when young, aging helps. *See also* Eau de Vie de Marc.

Marc de Bourgogne. Crude brandies distilled in the Burgundy region, France.

Marc de Champagne. A strong brandy made in the Champagne region of France by distilling the residue of grapes pressed to make champagne.

Marcassin (French). Wild boar slaughtered when less than six months old; marinated before being cooked and usually cooked whole.

March (Obsolete). Uncultivated celery.

Marchpane. *See* Marzipan.

Marcobrunner. An outstanding white wine produced in Rheingau, Germany.

Mardi Gras. In New Orleans, a festive time before the beginning of Lent; the Tuesday before Ash Wednesday.

Maréchale, À la. Garnished with bread crumbs and truffles.

Marée (French). Commercially available seafood.

Marengo. Site of a battle in which Napoleon defeated the Austrians in 1800. Napoleon's chef, Dunand, created a chicken dish which now bears this name, using ingredients available at the time, including olive oil, tomatoes, and garlic. There is some question as to whether or not crayfish and mushrooms were included in the original dish.

Marennes. A small port in the Charente-Maritime district of France where fine white and green oysters are bred. The eating of Marennes oysters amounts to almost a cult in France, and devotees often consume two dozen at a time.

Marennes Vertes. Green oysters from Marennes.

Mare's Tail. A wild plant whose young shoots may be prepared like asparagus.

Margarine. An emulsified blend of vegetable oils or animal fats. In the United States it is usually made from refined corn oil, cottonseed, and soybean oils which are churned, sometimes with milk and salt, and often colored yellow. Vitamin A is generally added. New polyunsaturated margarines, that is, vegetable-oil margarines that are not hydrogenated, have been recommended to people with high cholesterol as a substitute for hydrogenated margarines and butter. Many are available commercially.

Margarita (Mexican). A cocktail made of 3 parts tequila, 1 part cointreau, and the juice of half a lime.

Margaux, Château. One of the most important delicate red wines produced in the Bordeaux region of France. *See also* France, The Wines of.

Margherita. (1) (Italian) A type of twisted pasta. (2) A tequila cocktail. *See* Margarita.

Margot (French). Magpie.

Marguerite. A cookie covered with a combination of nuts or coconut and boiled frosting and baked until brown.

Marguéry. The famous French restaurateur who originated the dish called *filet de sole à la Marguéry.*

Mariage (French). A thick soup made in Provence from beef or lamb and rice.

Maribo. A Danish cheese resembling Gouda.

Marienhofer. A soft, odorous Austrian cheese roughly resembling Limburger.

Marignan Cake (French). A cake made of a Savarin dough, baked and covered with apricot jam and meringue, and soaked in a liqueur-flavored syrup.

Marigold. A yellow garden flower with a pungent aroma, usually cultivated for its decorative value, but the flower petals, either fresh or dried, are sometimes used in foods. The fresh petals may be used sparingly in salads to contribute a pungent taste. Fresh or dried petals may also flavor soups, stews, or broths. The Dutch par-

ticularly use marigold petals in soups and custards; the French flavor and color drinks with the flowers. Butter and cheese sometimes derive their color from the golden powder of marigolds.

The leaves are used for coloring, used raw in salads, and added to meat and fish dishes. Leaves and stems may be boiled and eaten as a vegetable. Baby flower buds may be treated much like capers.

Marigold Pie (British). A very old country pudding made with flaky pastry, egg custard, and marigold petals and baked until the custard is set; served with cheese wedges.

Marigold Wine. Homemade wine, with marigold leaves or petals added.

Marinade. A liquid usually made of vinegar, lemon juice or wine, and spices and herbs, sometimes mixed with oil, in which meats or vegetables are allowed to soak and absorb the flavors.

Marinara (Italian). A spicy, meatless tomato sauce.

Marinate. To allow meats or vegetables to soak in a marinade. *See also* Marinade.

Mariner (French). To pickle or marinate.

Marinerad (Swedish). Pickled; marinated.

Marinerad Strömming (Swedish). Marinated sardines or smelts.

Marineret Sild (Danish). Marinated herring.

Marinière, À la (French). "In marine style." Of seafood or fish, prepared with dry white wine.

Marinierter Hering (German). Marinated herring.

Mariout. A wine region of Egypt that produces passable wines.

Marisco Liso; Marisco Morcillón (Spanish). A type of small scallop, having a smoother shell.

Mariscos (Portuguese, Spanish). Shellfish.

Marissa. A type of beer made locally by tribesmen in the Sudan; it has an oatmeal color, and is quite potent.

Marjolaine (French). *See* Marjoram.

Marjoram. A ubiquitous perennial herb native to the Mediterranean area; also cultivated in more northerly climates, where it is winter-killed and must be replanted annually. Somewhat like sage in flavor but much milder, the leaves, either fresh or dried, are used to flavor soups, fish, eggs, meats, poultry, stews, vegetables, sauces, and salads. Powdered leaves are often used in blends with poultry seasoning and sausage flavoring.

Mark (German). Marrow.

Markhor. A wild goat of northern India; its meat, though stringy, is edible.

Märkisch. A soft, odorous German hand cheese of fair quality.

Marmalade. A jellylike conserve made with oranges or other citrus fruits; formerly also preserves made of apples, cherries, etc., and some tart or acid ingredients, such as lemons. The first marmalades were made from quince. (The word "marmalade" is probably derived from the Spanish word *mermelo* and the Portuguese word *marmelos*, meaning quince.) A good marmalade is a cross between a jam and a jelly; it is somewhat stiff, contains solid ingredients, and is vaguely bittersweet. Most commercial marmalades are prepared from bitter oranges.

Marmalade Plum. The sapote; the fruit of the sapodilla tree.

Marmalade Tree. A quince tree.

Marmelad (Swedish). Jam.

Marmelade (French). Fruit stewed until extremely soft.

Marmite (French). A deep earthenware, enamel, or metal pot with a tight fitting cover used for making meat and chicken soups. Also, the individual china or earthenware bowls in which the soup is served. The soup, called *petite marmite*, usually contains vegetables and pieces of meat or chicken and is served with toasted French bread and grated cheese.

    Marmite à Vapeur. Steam kettle.

    Marmite en Terre. A marmite pot made of earthenware.

Marmorkuchen (German). Marble cake.

Marnique. An orange-flavored Austrian liqueur.

Maroilles; Marrolles. A rich, square whole-milk cheese with a pronounced flavor. During the fermentation process it is beaten and mashed many times, then rolled and dried.

Marommes. A French cow's-milk cheese similar to Neufchâtel.

Maroon. A European sweet chestnut.

Marquer (French). (1) To prepare meats or other foods before stewing, roasting, or braising.

(2) To place foods in a pan lined with strips of pork.

Marquise. (1) A sherbet, usually strawberry or pineapple, flavored with kirschwasser and with whipped cream folded in. (2) A drink of white wine, soda, and a twist of lemon. (3) A sweet, medium-sized pear.

Marrayo or Mampostial. A very sweet Puerto Rican dessert consisting of molasses and grated coconut.

Marroni Canditi (Italian). Candied chestnuts.

Marrons (French). Chestnuts.

Marrons Glacés (French). Chestnuts that have been glazed, candied, or dipped in sugar; used as a confection, decoration, and for *marron glacé* ice cream.

Marrow. The fatty soft tissue in animal bones. Beef marrow is used in many French dishes and sauces. Any dish designated as *à la moelle* indicates the use of marrow in it.

Marrowbone. The large hollow bones of animals that contain marrow, a fatty substance.

Marrowfat. A variety of bean or pea with an oily, rich taste.

Marrow Spoon. A long-handled spoon useful in the removal of bone marrow.

Marry; Marrying. A blending together of two similar items to improve the quality or taste, such as two coffees, or two wines, in order to produce a superior final product.

Marsala. *See* Italy, The Wines of.

Marsala all'Uovo. Marsala wine combined with egg yolks and brandy, and sometimes with added spices.

Marses (Italian). Meringue cut in slices and placed on sheets of baked pastry.

Marsh Hen. The female red grouse; the moor hen.

Marshmallow. A puffy white candy made of gelatin or beaten egg whites, sugar, and a stabilizer.

Marshmallow Cream. A mixture of glucose or corn syrup, sugar syrup, and agar-agar boiled to 250°F., then poured over beaten egg whites and beaten a few minutes.

Martagon. An Alpine lily whose bulbs are used for food in some countries, notably Russia.

Martini. (1) A cocktail varying from 3 parts gin and 1 part dry vermouth to almost pure gin;

usually stirred gently with ice, then poured into a chilled glass. (2) A French apéritif, a type of vermouth.

Martinique and Guadeloupe. Caribbean islands, called the "fortunate islands," Martinique and Guadeloupe are all that remains of the once important French empire in the West Indies. Here is found the best food in the Caribbean, prepared by talented French cooks. In the hotels and restaurants the cuisine follows closely that of France.

The classic drink is the Martinique *rhum* punch, made from sugar cane syrup, water, lime, and *rhum* prepared according to individual preference. French wines are also popular; *rosé* wines seem to suit the climate best.

Appetizers include *acra l'en mori* (codfish fritters) and *chou-chou à la vinaigrette* (coconut-tree heart, sliced, and served with a spicy vinegar sauce). The fish soups are delicious, especially when made with lobster. *Oursins* (sea urchins) are interesting, but not to everyone; *crabes farcis,* stuffed crabs, are a specialty of both islands. The most unusual salad is *salade de chou-coco* (made from the coconut-tree heart or palm heart); a most unusual vegetable is *igname au fromage*, a local yam baked with cheese. As in the other islands of the Caribbean, the inhabitants eat *calalou*, a sort of spicy crab-and-meat stew. The *Colombo Creole* is merely a variation upon curry; the best local curry ingredients are prepared by the Indians of Matouba, who live near the volcano La Soufrière.

Martinoes. A plant that grows in parts of tropical America, with a taste somewhat like that of squash.

Martin-Sec. A European winter pear.

Mary Ann Pan. A special cake pan that forms a depression in the finished cake suitable for fillings.

Märzenbier. March beer, prepared in Munich, Germany.

Marzipan. An icing or candy in which finely ground blanched almonds, sugar, and orange flower or rose water are made into a paste.

Marzipan Fruits. Marzipan molded in the shape of fruits, dried, naturally colored, and glazed.

Masa (Latin American). A corn paste used for general cookery purposes, but especially for the making of cornmeal dishes. White corn is pounded, winnowed, and washed; then cooked and ground into a paste. *Masa* is often made into *arepas*, cornmeal griddle cakes, served with butter and grated cheese.

Masala Paste (Indian). A flavoring mixture of garlic, spices, poppy seeds, ground ginger, and nuts; used to thicken curries, etc.

Mascara. A wine region of Oran, Algiers. The red wines are quite good, the *rosés* are passable, but the whites are quite poor.

Mascarpone. A soft, white, mild Italian cheese much like a Ricotta; it is the basis for a classic cheesecake.

Mascotte (Italian). A Genoese cake filled and iced with mocha butter cream mixed with roasted hazelnuts.

Mascotte, À la. With a garnish consisting of artichoke hearts, sautéed apples, and truffles; usually served with veal, poultry, or beef.

Masgoof (Iranian). A roast-salmon dish made from Tigris River fish.

Mash. Crushed malt or other cereals, soaked in hot water and used in making beer. Corn mash is used for making liquor in some states of the southern United States.

Mashburn. Ground mixed oats, barley, and bran.

Mashelson. A wheat-and-rye mixture.

Mashlock. A coarse bread made from an inferior grain.

Masi (Samoan). Breadfruit allowed to ferment.

Masitas (Spanish). Cupcakes.

Masking. (1) Covering a prepared dish with a sauce or other mixture that completely coats it. (2) A gelatin sauce used for masking.

Maskinonge. *See* Muskellunge.

Maslin; Mashlin. Flour made by grinding a mixture of rye, corn, wheat, barley, and oats. *See* Maslin Bread.

Maslin Bread. A bread made from mixed corn or other grains.

Masquer (French). (1) To coat cooked meat with jelly or a rich gravy; to pour sauce over a dish ready to be served. (2) To cover the inside of a mold with a layer of sauce or gelatin.

Massecuite. Syrups during the process of clarification, concentration, or crystallization, while sugar is being refined.

Massena, À la. With an artichoke garnish; usually applied to beef or birds cooked in truffle sauce; when applied to eggs, indicates the use of artichokes, marrow, and Béarnaise sauce.

Massepains (French). Sweet cookies made with beaten egg whites, almond paste, and sugar.

Massilons; Massillons. Small, almost miniature, almond-paste tarts; served with coffee or tea.

Masthuhn (German). Chicken.

Mastic; Mastiche. The resin of the mastic tree; used in chewing gums and in preparing the spirit Mastic Raki; sometimes used for flavoring cakes and cookies.

Masticate. To chew; mastication. The act of chewing solid food to prepare it for swallowing and digestion.

Mastika. A Greek liquor, somewhat like vodka, flavored heavily with resin.

Mastino. A Sardinian liqueur which tastes somewhat like Chartreuse.

Matai. The water nut; the water chestnut.

Matambre (South American). A rolled slice of beef stuffed with hard-cooked eggs, peppers, and vegetables.

Matcha. The finely powdered green tea used chiefly in the classic Japanese tea ceremony.

Maté; Yerba Maté. A kind of tea, prepared from the dried and chopped leaves of a shrub or small tree called the *Hileia Paraguaiensis*; it is commonly called *Paraguayan tea*, and is the favorite drink of Paraguay, Argentina, Uruguay, and Chile and is also drunk in many other South American countries. The word *maté* refers to the hollowed-out gourd generally used to hold the beverage. A quantity of *yerba* (dried, chopped leaves) is placed in the gourd, and hot water is added. After a few minutes of infusion, the *bombilla* (usually a silver tube about 8 inches long with a fine strainer at the extreme end) is inserted and the *maté* may be drunk. More hot water may be added, for the leaves will flavor several gourdfuls of water. The majority of *maté* drinkers prefer it plain (*maté amargo*), but it may also be drunk with sugar (*maté dulce*). Very often orange peelings are added to the sweetened *maté* for flavor.

It is said to be a very healthful drink, and particularly necessary for the *gauchos* (cowboys) of the South American countries, many of whom live almost exclusively upon beef and *maté*. *Maté* is thought to aid digestion, and supplies certain nutriments required in the diet. Recently *maté* has begun to be served in ordinary cups like tea.

Matefaim (French). "Hunger-tamer"; a large sweet pancake made in Lyons.

Matelote (French). A fish stew prepared with wine, sometimes lighter in texture than a stew. The term cannot properly be used to describe a meat or poultry preparation, although it is sometimes erroneously used in this fashion. For practical purposes, there is no valid distinction between matelote and *Meurette* or *Pochouse*, except that they are somewhat differently prepared according to the province; basically, however, they are all fish stews, made with either white or red wine.

    Matelote de Cervelle. A stew of brains cooked in red wine.

    Matelote Parisienne. A stew of various freshwater fish in red wine with mushrooms and truffles.

Matese. An Italian liqueur made with wild mountain herbs and grasses.

Mateus. A Portuguese *rosé* wine of exceptional quality, produced at Vila Real.

Matie. Herring before the roe or milt is developed.

Matilda (Australian, Colloquial). A billy can, in which hobos make tea.

Matjeshering (German). Pickled herring.

Matjessill (Swedish). Preserved herring; matjes herring.

Matrosengericht (German). Fish stew.

Matsutake (Japanese). Mushroom.

Matsuzaka. A part of Japan famous for its superb beef. The cattle are handled individually, massaged regularly, and often fed on beer.

Mattambala. An edible African tuber resembling the potato.

Mattituck. A fine-flavored oyster.

Maturate. To ripen, especially as applied to fruits.

Mature. Fully ripe; ready to eat.

Matzoon (Middle Eastern). A fermented sourish milk that contains lactic acid.

Matzos. Thin flat pieces of unleavened bread made of flour and water, eaten by religious Jews during Passover; also used for various holiday dishes; may be soaked in milk and crumbled into egg-pancake preparations, etc.

   Matzos Cake. Very finely ground matzos meal.

   Matzos Meal. Ground matzos.

Mauffay (Virgin Islands). A dish consisting of salt pork, fresh pork, beef, fish, and cornmeal, usually served with fungi.

Maultasche (German). Small envelopes of dough stuffed with meat and vegetables.

Maury. A dark red wine of Rousillon, France; best when somewhat mature.

Mauviette (French). A fat lark.

Mavrodaphne. A very sweet Greek dessert wine.

Max (Colloquial). Gin.

Maximin Grunhaus. A wine village in the Ruwer district of Germany. *See* Germany, The Wines of.

Maxixe. A Brazilian cucumberlike vegetable; peeled like a cucumber and served as a salad.

May Apple; Mandrake. An herb of the barberry family, once thought to have magical powers or produce madness; the yellow, rather coarse, well-seeded fruit may be used to prepare a relish or preserve which is good with roast meat or poultry.

May Butter. Unsalted butter placed in storage during the month of May.

May Cordial. A fragrant liqueur, originated in Germany, made by infusing freshly opened hawthorn blossoms in brandy with a little sugar; strained and bottled after 3 months. It is used as a flavoring for other drinks.

May Duke. A very sour wild cherry.

Mayflower. A kind of apple once popular in England.

Mayonesa (Spanish). Mayonnaise.

Mayonnaise. A stable emulsion of eggs, oil, spices, and vinegar or lemon juice used as a dressing or sauce. Commercial mayonnaise should be refrigerated once it has been opened, and all mayonnaise should be kept cold, as it spoils quickly. It should not be frozen, as it separates when thawed.

Mayonnaise Collée. Mayonnaise combined with clear liquid gelatin or jelly; used to coat fish, meat, etc.

Mayonnaise de (French). Either served or mixed with mayonnaise.

Mayonnaise Mousseuse (French). Mayonnaise and whipped cream beaten together.

May Wine; May Bowl. A young German wine drunk in the spring, a few months after the grapes are pressed.

Maza (Syrian). Appetizers.

Mazagran (French). (1) A glass of black coffee with sugar and ice water added; sometimes, a glass of hot coffee. (2) Sliced, buttered potatoes served in a pastry shell.

Mazard; Mazzard. The wild sweet cherry.

Mazarin Cake (Italian). (1) A Genoese cake with a scooped-out well in the center filled with crystallized fruits, apricot purée, and kirsch. The icing is a pink fondant and apricot jam. (2) A small almond cake.

Mazarine. A deep metal plate.

Mazarines. Forcemeat garnishes of fish, poultry, meat, or game. Also, entrées made of fillets of meat and forcemeat.

Mazarino. A tangerine-flavored French liqueur.

Mazer Bowl, Cup, Dish. (Scandinavian). Drinking cups.

Mazis Chambertin. A red wine produced in the Burgundy region of France; it has a fine color, excellent body and aroma, and is well balanced.

Mazum. *See* Fermented Milk.

Mazurrelle (Italian). Pasta shaped like small seashells.

Mazzafegati (Italian). A crude sausage made with pig's liver and other inner organs, pine nuts, and raisins.

Mbisi ye Kalou (Congolese). A fish and green-vegetable dish.

M. d. Ch. (French). *Mis du château*, bottled in the château; a term used in the Bordeaux wine district.

Mead. (1) A fermented mixture of honey and water, flavored with spices. The term is derived from the Teutonic and Indo-European languages; the Celtic term is *medd*. (2) A soft drink containing sarsaparilla and carbonated water.

Mead Bench. A seat at a gala occasion when mead was the drink of the day.

Mead Hall. A large festival hall.

Mead 'n' Ale (British). A Victorian beverage prepared from ale, sugar syrup, oatmeal, and whisky; served at harvest time.

Meadow Chicken. A rail or a coot, edible game birds.

Meadow Garlic. *See* Wild Onion.

Meadow Mussel. A mussel found in salt meadows.

Meadow Parsnip. *See* Cow Parsnip.

Meadowsweet. An herb whose leaves are used to flavor certain liquors, especially vermouth.

Mead Wine. A homemade beverage prepared from mead. *See also* Mead.

Meadwort. A plant whose flowers were used to flavor mead, an alcoholic drink made of fermented honey and water.

Meagre. A large Mediterranean fish with firm white flesh.

Meal. (1) The food served and consumed at one particular time, such as breakfast, lunch, or dinner. (2) Any cereal grain ground to a fine powder, such as cornmeal.

Mealie (South African). An ear of corn.

Mealie-Mealie (South African). Coarsely ground cornmeal, a staple food in many regions of Africa.

Mealing. The act of crushing meal.

Mealman (British, Obsolete). A dealer in flour.

Mealtime. The regular time at which a meal is eaten.

Mealy. Having the consistency of meal; powdery, crumbly, and dry.

Mease. A herring measure equivalent to about 500 herring.

Meat. The flesh of animals, used as food; usually mammals, but often also fish and fowl.

At least 95 percent of animal meat is digested, and it is valuable for its protein content; the more fat, the longer the time required for complete digestion. For this reason, fatty meats provide longer period of satiety, whereas lean meats are not so filling or satisfying. *See* particular meats, such as Beef, Lamb, Pork, etc.

Meat and Drink. All types of food.

Meatballs. Any combination of ground meat shaped into balls. As every nationality has meatballs in its cuisine, there are hundreds of ways in which to prepare them.

Meat Bar. Dehydrated cooked meat and fat; a modern form of pemmican.

Meat Biscuit. A pastry made with meat.

Meat Cleaver. A heavy, sharp metal implement used for cutting through poultry joints and for cutting and flattening meat.

Meat Extract. The water-soluble part of meat is the main source of its flavor. It is produced commercially in the process of preparing corned beef: minced meat is immersed in boiling water when the water-soluble extractives are partially leached out. The liquid is then concentrated by heating.

Meatless. Without meat.

Meat Loaf. Cubed or chopped meat, raw or cooked, combined with vegetables, seasonings, and extenders (such as bread crumbs or rice), shaped into a loaf or pressed into a loaf pan, and baked.

Meat Offering. A food sacrifice offered to gods.

Meat Pie. A combination of meat and vegetables, usually leftovers, topped with either dough or mashed potatoes and baked.

Meat Tea (British). Meat served at an afternoon tea.

Meaty. (1) Containing meat. (2) Having the flavor of, or otherwise resembling, meat.

Méchoui (Arabian). Roasted lamb or mutton, the principal dish of an elaborate dinner.

Medaglioni all' Arlesiana (Italian). Fillet of beef with eggplant and tomatoes.

Medaillons (French). Small cuts or fillets of meat, lobster, or chicken, usually served with a sauce.

Media (Brazilian). A hot drink, half coffee and half milk.

Medicinal Wines. Sweet wines containing various tonic substances, chiefly iron or quinine.

Medisterkaker (Norwegian). Ground-pork patties.

Medisterpolse (Danish). Pork sausage.

Medlar. A brown-skinned fruit edible only when partially decayed. It has a pleasant, acidulous, fruity taste, but the darkened, decayed parts must be cut away before the fruit can be eaten.

Médoc. A French wine district of the Bordeaux region. *See* France, The Wines of.

Médoc Wine Classification of 1855. *See* France, The Wines of.

Mee Fun (Chinese). Very light, delicate rice noodles; a specialty of the Fukien province.

Meel (Dutch). Flour.

Meerrettich (German). Horseradish.

Meeth. Mead.

Megrim. Witch, a flatfish similar in flavor and texture to lemon sole.

Mehlpüt (German). Stewed pears and dumplings.

Mehlsuppe (German). Sweet-and-sour soup, made from flour.

Meinie (British). A family; a household.

Mejillones (Spanish). Mussels.

Mejorana (Spanish). Sweet marjoram.

Mekong. A Siamese whisky made from rice.

Mela (Italian). Apple.

Melada; Melado. A molasses-sugar mixture produced by boiling cane juice.

Melancia (Portuguese). Watermelon.

Mélange (French). (1) A combination or mixture of foods. (2) A preserve made with various fruits.

Melangeur. A mixing vessel consisting of rollers riding on a rotating horizontal bed, used to mix substances of pasty consistency.

Melangolo (Italian). Bitter orange.

Melanzana (Italian). Eggplant.

> Melanzana alla Fiorentina. Baked eggplant with tomato and cheese.

> Melanzana alla Parmigiana. Fried eggplant with tomato and cheese.

> Melanzana Ripiena. Baked eggplant stuffed with capers, olives, and anchovies.

Melanzane (German). Eggplant.

Melão (Portuguese). Melon.

Melba, Nellie. A famous Australian opera star, who was very fond of good living, and who liked to eat elaborate suppers after a performance. Numerous dishes and preparations have been named for her; one of the best known is Peach Melba, ice cream served with peaches.

Melba Sauce. A sweet sauce made with fresh raspberry purée and sugar; served in the dessert called Peach Melba, made with ice cream.

Melba Toast. Very thin slices of white bread baked in a slow oven until very crisp. It was originally made for the opera singer Dame Nellie Melba.

Melboller (Danish). Dumplings.

Mele Fritte (Italian). Apple fritters.

Melet; Melette. (1) Poutine, a small fish; minced, it is used like anchovy paste. (2) Sprat.

Melianopus. A hard durum-type Russian wheat.

Melicrate (British, Obsolete). A honey-and-water beverage.

Melilot. A fragrant French herb used in stews, as a seasoning for freshly killed hare, and for flavoring Sapsago cheese.

Melissa; Melisse. The Mediterranean lemon balm; used as a flavoring for a French liqueur.

Melitose; Melitriose. See Raffinose.

Melk (Dutch, Norwegian). Milk.

Melkevelling (Norwegian). Milk soup.

Melktert (Afrikaans). A milk-custard pie, usually flavored with cinnamon or fruits, and served with tea or coffee.

Mell (Obsolete). Honey.

Mellifluous. Containing honey; very thick and sweet.

Mellow. Of cheese, soft, creamy, or rich; of fruit, fully ripened.

Melocoton (Obsolete). A cross between a quince and a peach.

Melocotones (Spanish). Peaches.

Meloen (Dutch). Melon.

Melon. The fruit of a vine of the cucumber family which probably originated in Asia. One of the most common varieties is the muskmelon or cantaloupe, which has a soft rind and netted surface. The watermelon is a large, juicy, round or ovoid green-skinned fruit with pink flesh and black seeds grown chiefly in Texas and Georgia. Other commercially produced varieties are the honeydew, Casaba, Persian, Spanish, and Cranshaw. Ripe melons are springy to the touch and unblemished. Melons are served in the shell for the first or last course of a meal, sometimes stuffed with other fruits. They are also cut into balls for fruit cup. The rind, particularly of the watermelon, may be pickled and is sold commercially in this form.

Melón (Spanish). Melon.

Melon de Malabar. A Siamese pumpkin; prepared like an American pumpkin.

Melone (Italian). Melon.

Melongene (French). A variety of eggplant.

Melon Seeds. The seeds of any of a variety of

melons; those of watermelon are dried or toasted and eaten as a snack.

Melon Sugar. A sweet liquid obtained from coarse melons; rarely, if ever, prepared today.

Melt. To reduce from a solid to a liquid form, usually by heating.

Melting House. Building where fats from slaughterhouses are melted down.

Melton Mowbray Pie (British). A highly seasoned pork pie; served cold.

Melun. A yellowish, rather firm French cheese with an offensive odor.

Membrillo (Spanish). A firm jellylike dessert made of quinces.

Menazzeleh (Arabian). Chopped meat, onions, and garlic sautéed in a frying pan, with eggs added and cooked only until set; served in wedges, like a pie.

Mendiants (French). Dry fruit, including figs, almonds, raisins, hazelnuts; a traditional dessert for children.

Menestra (Spanish). A stew prepared with a variety of vegetables and small squares of raw ham.

Mengau (Brazilian). A cereal made from green plantains.

Menhaden. A bony fish with rather unpalatable oily flesh.

Menschenfreund (German, Obsolete). Stomach bitters.

Menta (Italian). Mint.

Menta Glaciale. An Italian mint cordial.

Menthe (French). Mint.

Menthyl Acetate. A colorless liquid sometimes used to produce a synthetic mint taste and aroma.

Mentuccia di San Silvestro. An Italian mint cordial.

Menu (French). Bill of fare; sometimes, a meal at a fixed price as opposed to the *carte*, which permits a choice of individual dishes.

Menudillos (Spanish). Giblets.

Menudo. A kind of tripe stew made with green chili peppers; popular in the southwestern United States and northern Mexico.

Menue Viande (French). Fowl and game.

Menu-Gibier (French). Partridges, pheasants, and grouse.

Menu Rôti (French). Small roasted birds.

Menus Droits (French). Pig's ears served as a main course.

Meny (Norwegian). Menu.

Mercurey. A fairly good red wine with pleasing bouquet produced in Burgundy, France.

Mere. Of food, in its pure form.

Mère de Sole; Cardine; Limondelle (French). A flatfish resembling sole.

Mère Goutte (French). Wine made from grape juice extracted without the use of a wine press.

Merenda (Italian). Snack; a small in-between meal.

Merey. Cashew.

Merga (North African). A spicy sauce served with the dish couscous.

Merganser. A wild duck that lives on fish and has a somewhat fishy taste.

Meringue. A preparation consisting of beaten egg whites and sugar. Meringues generally are of two types: the soft type serves as a topping for pies; the hard type may be used as a shell in which to serve ice cream or other desserts. The types vary in the amount of sugar they contain.

Sugar has a great deal to do with the successful making of meringues. The coarseness or fineness of the grain of the sugar is important. If too little sugar is used, the meringue tends to be less fluffy and tender, as well as less sweet than is desirable. If too much sugar is used, the meringue tends to have a gummy crust or be gritty with undissolved sugar crystals.

Meringued. Spread with meringue.

Meringue Petits Fours (French). Beaten egg whites and sugar, shaped as desired, then slowly baked.

Merise (French). Wild cherry.

Merisette. A French wild-cherry cordial.

Merisier (French). A wild-cherry tree whose fruit is used to make kirschwasser.

Merissah (North African). A fermented drink made from dates.

Merlan Colbert (French). Whiting, dipped in eggs and bread crumbs and deep-fat fried.

Merle. Another name for a blackbird.

Merling (Obsolete). Whiting, a food fish.

Merluche (French). Haddock; sometimes hake. *See* Hake (1).

Merluche Fumé. Dried or smoked haddock or hake.

Merluza (Spanish). Codfish.

Merluzzo (Italian). Codfish.

Mermelada (Spanish). Marmalade.

Mero. A variety of sea bass found chiefly in warm waters.

Mérou. A Mediterranean fish of medium size, with a good texture, but an insipid taste.

Merovingian. A French medium-firm, creamy white cheese with a slight bite.

Merrythought (British). Fanciful name for the "wishbone," or part of the breast bone of poultry broken by two persons, the one holding the larger piece getting his unspoken wish.

Mersin. A rather mediocre Turkish liqueur having an orange taste.

Merveille (French). A thin pastry cut into a variety of shapes with a fluted pastry cutter, deep-fried, and sprinkled with vanilla-flavored sugar.

Mes (Dutch). Knife.

Mésange Moustache. (French). Java sparrow, or rice bird, a very delicious small bird.

Mescal; Mezcal. A poor-quality Mexican alcoholic beverage made from the juice obtained from the agave plant, a type of cactus. The cactus tops are often dried and chewed by Mexican Indians for their stimulating effect.

Mesentery. The membrane of a calf's intestines; cooked like calf's head.

Mesimarja. A sweet Finnish afterdinner liqueur made from brambleberries.

Mess. (1) One serving of food at a meal; one portion. (2) A group of people dining together.

Messmate. An eating companion.

Metaxas. A good-quality, rather sweet Greek brandy; best drunk as an afterdinner liqueur. The quality is designated by the number of stars on the label of the bottle.

Metecorn (Obsolete). The giving of a certain amount of corn to medieval servants.

Méteil (French). A mixture of one-third rye flour and two-thirds wheat flour.

Metel. The hairy thorn apple, fruit of the hawthorn.

Metheglin (Celtic). Spiced mead. *See* Mead.

Méthode Champénoise (French). The cham-pagne method; the process of making champagne in individual bottles.

Methyl Anisate. White crystals used to simulate the flavor of melons or other fruit.

Methyl Anthranilate. A colorless or pale yellow liquid used to produce synthetically a grape flavor in making candies, jellies, etc.

Methyl Myristate. A white crystalline substance used to supply a synthetic honey taste in processed foods.

Methyl Nonyl Ketone. A colorless liquid frequently used to supply a synthetic taste and aroma of fruit.

Methyl Salicylate. A colorless liquid with a strong odor similar to wintergreen; used in making chewing gum, soft drinks, etc.

Mets (French). All foods, ready to eat.

Mets de Farine (French). Something mealy.

Mettagee (Guyana). Dried codfish and coconut prepared with tropical vegetables.

Mettre à la Crapaudine (French). To grill in split form, as fowls or pigeons.

Mettwurst (German). A smoked, spiced soft pork-and-liver sausage.

Metwurst (French). A short, medium-thick sausage with a dark covering; made in Strasbourg.

Meunière, À la (French). "In the miller's style." Lightly-floured fish, cooked in plenty of butter, and sprinkled with lemon juice and parsley.

Meurette (French). (1) A wine sauce made with red wine, garlic, shallots, onions, carrots, and butter. (2) A stew prepared with freshwater fish and red wine.

Meursault. A fine-quality white wine produced in Burgundy, France. It has an excellent taste and bouquet, and is best when not too old. *See* France, The Wines of.

Mexilhões (Portuguese). Mussels.

Mezzani (Italian). Curved smooth-textured tubes of pasta about an inch long.

Mezeler (Turkish). Hors d'oeuvre.

Michaelmas (British). The feast of St. Michael, September 29.

Miche de Seigle (French, Obsolete). A round flat loaf of bread, dusted with flour, with criss-cross markings.

Michigan Banana. *See* Papaw.

Michoui. A sheep's stomach stuffed with a mixture of dried fruits and nuts; popular in Mauritania.

Micisca (Corsican). Smoked pork, dried and cooked.

Middag (Danish, Swedish). Dinner.

Middling. (1) The cut of meat on the pig (between the shoulder and the ham) that contains ribs and chops. (2) Average.

Middlings. The rough, coarse particles produced when wheat mixed with bran is ground.

Midi, Vin du. The ordinary red wine produced in the Midi region of France; it is good, but undistinguished.

Midzue-Ame (Japanese). An extract of barley-malt and rice. Combined with milk, it is nutritious for invalids.

Mie de Pain (French). Soft bread or bread crumbs.

Miel (Spanish). Honey; syrup.

   Miel de Abeja. Bee's honey.

   Miel de Caña. Cane syrup.

   Miel de Maíz. Corn syrup.

Mics (Ethiopian). Drink made with honey.

Miette (French). A bread crumb.

Migas (Spanish). Bread crumbs.

Mignardises (French). Small, dainty dishes.

Mignon Fillets; Filet Mignon. Small, rather soft cuts of meat from the tenderloin of beef.

Mignonne (French). (1) A variety of pear. (2) A kind of peach.

Mignonnette. (1) Crushed black pepper. (2) Sauce for oysters made with flavored vinegar and pepper.

Mignot. A famous 17th-century French restaurateur whose popular biscuits Mignot, wrapped in paper, sold on a large scale.

Mignot. A cheese produced in Calvados, France. When young, it is quite mild and fresh. When ripened, it remains soft but resembles Pont l'Evêque.

Migraine. A grape wine produced in the Auxerre region of France.

Migras. Brie cheese made in the springtime. *See also* Maigre Cheese; Gras.

Mijoter (French). To simmer very slowly and gently over low heat.

Miki (Philippine). Wheat noodles prepared with egg.

Milanaise, À la. In the Milan style, usually dipped in eggs, bread crumbs, and grated Parmesan cheese.

Milanese Cake. A cake flavored with anise and iced with apricot jam and anise-flavored fondant.

Milano, Stracchino di. A yellow Italian cheese with a mild taste similar to that of Bel Paese.

Milch (German). Milk.

Milch Cow. A cow that produces milk.

Milchkaffe (German). Coffee with milk.

Milchlamm (German). Young lamb.

Mild. (1) Neither too strong nor too weak; tasting neither biting, sharp, sour, nor bitter. (2) A type of British beer.

Mildew. Many fungi, appearing in whitish spots or other discoloration, that cause foods to decay.

Miliasse; Millat (French). A cornmeal cereal; occasionally cooked with milk instead of water.

Milieu de Poitrine (French). A cut of beef resembling the navel cut, as prepared by American butchers.

Milieu du Gîte à la Noix (French). A cut of beef, resembling the lower portion of bottom round.

Milk. The white fluid obtained from the udders or breasts of certain animals that suckle their young; in common usage, the milk obtained from the cow. In various parts of the world, milk is obtained from goats, camels, sheep, mares, reindeer, etc. This nutritious liquid has been used by man for at least 5,000 years; some experts speculate that this estimate could be doubled. In any event, it has nourished man ever since he learned to keep animals for domestic use.

For thousands of years milk carried potential disease. In 1860 a French scientist, Louis Pasteur, found a simple method of destroying bacteria in milk, the process of *pasteurization*.

Milk is the basis for many other dairy products, such as butter, cream, cheese, and casein. Natural milk is composed of fats, carbohydrates, water, protein, and ash. On the average, milk has about 4 percent fat, but this increases to 18–20 percent when it is made into cream. Most milk sold in the United States is in homogenized form; the milk will not separate from the cream after homogenization. Milk is the raw material of cheeses, the variety being almost endless. It is also marketed as *buttermilk* (the liquid remaining after butter has been made); *condensed milk* (in which the water content is evaporated by means of low heat in a vacuum); *evaporated milk* (similar to condensed milk, but not so sweet or thick); *acidophilus milk* (a fermented milk preparation); *yoghurt* (a semi-solidified fermented milk), etc.

Milk is highly regarded by nutritionists as the perfect food, containing vitamins A, B, C, and G; vitamin D is often added by bottlers. It is high in calories, one measuring cup containing 165 calories. In recent years, however, nutritionists have modified their stand somewhat on the need for milk in the standard diet. While affirming its use as an ideal food for infants and young children, they now no longer urge its consumption by adults. Milk-drinking has been further complicated for adults by the cholesterol problem, for whole milk is fairly high in fat content. A recent outgrowth of this has been the increasing popularity of skim milk, and the improved types of "modified" skim milk, which have a better taste but little fat.

Milk Bread. Bread prepared with milk rather than water.

Milken. Containing milk.

Milk, Frozen. Milk pasteurized, treated with an ultrasonic vibrator, and frozen to 10° F.; it will keep a year.

Milk Punch. Any alcoholic drink containing milk.

Milk Shake. A cold drink in which milk is mixed with a flavoring, such as chocolate, coffee, or vanilla, and beaten or shaken until frothy. Extra richness is achieved by adding ice cream.

Milk Sherbet. A sherbet made with fruit juice, egg whites, and milk; sugar, additional flavoring, and sometimes gelatin are added.

Milk Sop. Bread or bread crusts soaked in milk.

Milk Stout (British). Milk with lactose (milk sugar) added.

Milk Sugar. *See* Lactose.

Milk Tea. Regular-strength tea with an equal amount of hot, but not boiled, milk; served with plenty of sugar; suitable for invalids and convalescents.

Milk Toast. Toast soaked in hot milk and served hot; a nutritious, easily digested food for children and invalids.

Milkweed. A wild plant whose stems have a milky juice. Young shoots may be used in a salad or eaten as a vegetable if cooked with plenty of boiling water to minimize the bitter taste.

Milky. (1) Consisting of milk or of milk and water. (2) Tasting like or resembling milk.

Mill. (1) To beat until fluffy. (2) An apparatus for grinding or crushing an ingredient into a powder.

Millas. A fried pudding made of cooked cornmeal (sometimes flour) flavored with pork fat; sometimes prepared as a dessert pudding, with cooked cherries and kirsch, or as a custard.

Millasses; Millassou; Milles; Milliessou (French). Tarts made with brandied raisins or honey and filled with almond cream; a specialty of Périgord.

Millat. *See* Milliase.

Mill-Bannock (Scottish). A large round oatmeal cake with a hole in the center.

Millecanton. A small fish similar to whitebait.

Mille Feuille (French). "Thousands of layers." A Napoleon, an oblong pastry made of puff-paste layers filled with pastry cream and whipped cream; when baked it separates into paper-thin layers.

Millefoglie (Italian). A flaky pastry.

Miller. A rather small white mushroom with a distinctive odor.

Miller's-Thumb. (1) A very small freshwater fish occasionally used for food. (2) A whiting pout, a bullhead.

Miller Wheat. A soft English wheat with only about 9 percent glutten; the flour is excellent for biscuits and cookies.

Millésimé (French). A wine term, meaning that the wine is dated, or of a particular year's vintage.

Millet. A rather small grain grown for food in Africa and Asia. Also called proso.

Millière (French). A porridge made with corn and rice in Anjou.

Milligram. One one-thousandth of a gram.

Milliliter. One one-thousandth of a liter.

Millstone. One of two round stones used in a mill to grind grain.

Milt. Of fish, the male reproductive glands or their secretion.

Milter. A male fish during the spawning period.

Mimolette. A Dutch cheese similar to Edam but a little harder and more aged.

Mimosa. A garnish of chopped hard-cooked egg yolks. Also, egg salad.

Minas. A fairly good, medium-firm white Brazilian cheese; made in two varieties.

Mince. (1) To cut into small pieces or to grind in a machine. (2) *See* Mincemeat. (3) In British usage, chopped-meat patties.

Minced Meat. Very finely chopped meat.

Mincemeat; Mince. A pie filling consisting of finely chopped meat, suet, raisins, apples, currants, spices, and sugar. Sometimes, a similar mixture made only of fruits.

Mincemeat Pie. A pie with a mincemeat filling.

Mincemeat Spices. A combination of various spices used to flavor mincemeat, usually including cinnamon, cloves, and allspice.

Mincer. Any utensil used to chop foods.

Mineirinhos (Brazilian). Muffins made with green olives and cheese.

Mineraalwater (Dutch). Mineral water.

Mineral Salts. Inorganic salts, including sodium, potassium, calcium, chloride, phosphate, sulfate, etc.

Mineralvatten (Swedish). Mineral water.

Mineralwasser (German). Mineral water.

Mineral Water. Water from a spring or well said to produce a tonic effect because it contains carbon dioxide gas or salts, or both. Many famous spring waters throughout the world are used as beverages with or between meals.

Minestra (Italian). Either pasta or soup.

Minestra alla Cappuccina. Anchovy-and-rice soup.

Minestra alla Romana. A thick dried-pea soup served with macaroni.

Minestrone (Italian). A thick vegetable soup.

Minestry (Austrian). A thick vegetable soup much like Italian minestrone.

Mingaux. A small cream cheese made near Rennes, France.

Minguiche (Mexican). A soup made of onions, green chili peppers, sour cream, and cheese.

Minion Fillets. The small tender underfillets cut from the breasts of birds.

Minnesota Blue. A blue-veined, slightly salty cheese made in Minnesota.

Minnows. Very small freshwater fish, of only passable quality.

Minorca. A domestic fowl that originated in Spain.

Mint. (1) A variety of fragrant herbs including peppermint, spearmint, oregano, marjoram, rosemary, and thyme. When mint is designated in a recipe, however, it refers either to peppermint or spearmint. Mint sauce or jelly is often served with roast lamb, and sprigs of mint are an ideal garnish for fruits and iced tea or fruit drinks. (2) A mint-flavored pastille, candy, or lozenge.

Mint Sauce. A mixture of sugar, vinegar, and chopped mint; usually served with lamb, although not particularly suitable for that purpose.

Mint Tea. A North African green tea flavored with fresh mint; especially popular in Morocco.

Mint Water. A cordial or liqueur made with mint.

Mintzitra; Mitzithra. A soft, oily sheep's-milk cheese made in Greece.

Minute Pudding. Any quickly prepared pudding.

Minute Steak. A boneless steak, about ¼ inch thick, cooked quickly by broiling or pan-frying; theoretically, it cooks in a minute.

Mique Sarladaise (French). A side dish made with wheat- and corn-flour dough mixed with pork fat; served in the Périgord region.

Miques de Mais (French). Cornmeal dough rolled into floured balls and cooked in boiling salted water; eaten in place of bread or, butter-fried and sprinkled with sugar, as dessert.

Mirabeau, À la. Of broiled meats, garnished with black olives and anchovies; of fish, garnished with spicy anchovy butter.

Mirabelle. (1) A small golden yellow plum with exceptional aroma and flavor; grown in France, particularly in Alsace. It is used in Mirabelle jam and in a fruit liqueur, both produced in Alsace. (2) A clear white brandy with a pleasant plum aroma but a strong, burning taste; produced in Alsace and Lorraine.

Mirbane. A synthetic essence of bitter almonds used as a flavoring agent.

Mirepoix (French). A flavoring mixture for stews,

soups, sauces, meat, or fish, which may contain carrots, onions, shallots, bay leaf, thyme, and garlic. It is named for a French duke who lived at the time of Louis XV.

Mirin. A Japanese sweet rice wine, somewhat like sherry.

Mirliton (French). A custard-filled puff-paste tart.

Mirliton de Rouen. A small flaky tart originating in Rouen.

Miroir (French). Any dish, especially eggs, with a bright, shiny finish.

Miroton; Mironton (French). Stew prepared with sautéed onions, tomato, vinegar, spices, and meat heated in the sauce.

Miroton de Boeuf. Slices of beef in a sauce of onions, garlic, and white wine; grated cheese may be added.

Mise-en-Place. A large wooden carving board particularly suitable for carving meats, smoked salmon, etc., at large buffets.

Misericord. A small area within a monastery where the monks were given food and drink.

Misket Karlovo. A Bulgarian gold-colored wine made from the Muscat grape, having an excellent aroma and somewhat sweet taste.

Miso (Japanese). Paste made from fermented soybeans, rice malt, and salt. *Aka miso* is the red type; *shiro miso* the white.

Misoa (Indonesian). Chinese noodles.

Misoshiru (Japanese). Thick, heavy soups.

Missiasoga (Corsican). Narrow lengths of air-dried goat meat.

Missisa (Corsican). Narrow strips of smoked pickled pork cooked over high heat.

Missouri Currant. The fruit of a currant bush growing wild on the banks of streams in Arkansas, Minnesota, Missouri, and farther west. It is round or oval, usually yellow but sometimes black, and is delicious in pies and tarts. The best-known strain is sold as the *Crandall currant.*

Mistelle. A wine term describing the "must" of raisins combined with alcohol in order to stop fermentation.

Misticanza (Italian). Mixed salad.

Mistra. An Italian liqueur made with anise.

Misua (Philippine). Very thin, fine noodles made of wheat.

Misy (Dutch). Truffles or mushrooms.

Mites. Tiny insects that sometimes infest stored products and foods, including cheese, flour, and sugar.

Miti (Samoan). Lime juice, salt water, and coconut cream combined to make a sauce into which foods are dipped.

Miton (French, Obsolete). Middle cut of salmon.

Mitonner (French). To cook soft bread slowly in soup, particularly done in provincial cookery.

Mittagessen (German). Lunch.

Mix. To combine or blend ingredients.

Mixed Grill. A combination of grilled or broiled meats, or, occasionally, seafood; in restaurants, ordinarily lamb chop with bacon, pork sausage and/or kidney, grilled mushrooms and tomatoes, French-fried potatoes, and a garnish of parsley or watercress. It may also include a piece of beef, poultry leg, or sweetbreads.

Mixed Nuts. An assortment of nuts, usually 35 percent walnuts, 25 percent almonds, 20 percent Brazil nuts, 10 percent hazelnuts or filberts, and 10 percent pecans. The mixture may be modified by any packer or distributor; it sometimes includes peanuts.

Mixed Pickles. A variety of vegetables cut small and preserved in clear spiced vinegar; sometimes prepared in a sweetened form.

Mixer. (1) A mechanical shaker-mixer, hand or electrically operated, used to mix, blend, or beat. (2) Any commercially marketed liquid used in the preparation of an alcoholic drink.

Mixing Bowl. A bowl used for mixing foods or liquids.

Mixing Glass. A glass used for measuring as well as mixing liquids.

Mixtelin. A coarse brown bread made of wheat and rye flour.

Mjöl (Swedish). Farina.

Mjölk (Swedish). Milk.

Moambé; Moamba (African). Any dish containing ground peanuts or peanut butter.

Mocha. (1) A very fine coffee that originated in Arabia but is now produced in other parts of the world. It is very smooth and mild, but it lacks sparkle and is therefore best when blended with other types of coffee. (2) A chocolate-coffee flavor; sometimes only a coffee flavor.

Mocha Cream. A coffee-flavored custard or cream mixture.

Mochatine Cakes. Individual mocha-flavored small cakes.

Mochi (Japanese). Rice cake.

Mochi Gome (Japanese). The special *mochi* rice, which is very glutinous.

Mochiko (Japanese). A flour prepared from glutinous rice.

Mock Duck. (1) A skinless piece of pork or veal stuffed with onions and spices and baked. (2) Food molded in the general shape of a duck.

Mock-Turtle Soup. A soup intended to imitate the taste of genuine turtle soup; usually made with veal or calf's head.

Mocoto. A South American calf's-foot stew.

Mode, À la. (1) Of pie, served with ice cream. (2) Of beef, slowly braised and served in a sauce.

Modius. A Roman corn measure, about a peck.

Moella (Portuguese). Gizzard.

Moëlle de Boeuf (French). Beef marrow.

Moe Yee. A black tea produced in Fukien province, China.

Mofongo. Fried ground plantains combined with pork cracklings and shaped into balls.

Mogettes (French). Beans prepared with plenty of heavy cream and butter; a dish of the Poitou region.

Mohn; Mohnsamen (German). Poppy seeds.

Mohnbrötchen (German). Poppy-seed rolls.

Mohrrübensuppe (German). Carrot soup.

Moige. A pancake.

Moilee (Indian). Highly spiced shellfish or fish cooked in coconut milk.

Moist. Any food that is damp or watery.

Moist Sugar. Partly refined sugar with an invert-sugar content, which makes it feel damp.

Moistening. (1) The adding of a small amount of liquid. (2) The liquid added.

Molasses. A thick brownish sweet substance extracted from sugar cane. Before sugar refining was improved, it was the chief sweetening agent. Today it is used for flavoring rather than for sweetening and appears in many Southern and New England recipes. It is also used in the distillation of rum.

Cooking Molasses. A dark molasses with a high iron content.

Table Molasses. A light molasses with less ash and more sugar than cooking molasses.

Molbo. A mild, mellow, rounded Danish cheese coated in red.

Mold. (1) To shape. (2) Any dish or pan in which hot or cold food is prepared so that it

will take the shape of the container. (3) The finished food shaped by the pan. (4) A fuzzy growth, caused by fungi, destructive to many foods. Not all molds are harmful. In the case of cheeses they give distinctive flavors. As part of the fermentation of yeasts they give flavor to wines.

Molé (Mexican). A rich, spicy sauce made of chili peppers, ground nuts, spices, and bitter chocolate; usually served with poultry or meat.

Molé de Guajalote (Mexican). A turkey dish prepared with garlic, tortillas, onion, tomatoes, and chocolate.

Moletas de Vitela (Portuguese). Sweetbreads.

Môlho (Portuguese). Gravy or sauce.

Môlho Ferto de Maçãs (Portuguese). Applesauce.

Molinary. Pertaining to the grinding of corn.

Moliterno. An Italian cheese similar to Cacio-cavallo.

Molle (German). A pint of beer.

Molléra (Spanish). A type of codfish, having somewhat coarse meat.

Molletes (Mexican). Sweet rolls.

Molluschi (Italian). Shellfish.

Mollusk; Mollusc. A group of hard-shelled sea animals that includes oysters, mussels, and snails.

Molosses (Obsolete). Molasses.

Moly. (1) A mythological edible plant supposedly endowed with magic powers. (2) Wild garlic.

Monaco, À la (French). Served with a green-pea-and-caper sauce.

Monastine. A French liqueur made with herbs and plants.

Monbazillac. A sweet white wine produced in

Périgord, France; best when served quite cold. It is often compared with Sauternes but is somewhat different.

Moncenisio. An Italian cheese much like Gorgonzola.

Mondongo (Spanish). A thick soup or stew made with many vegetables.

Mondseer. An Austrian cheese made of skim and whole milk, with a taste resembling Limburger but much milder.

Mongcorn; Mungcorn. Mixed corn.

Monger (British). A dealer in food; for example, costermonger (apple seller) or fishmonger.

Mongo (Philippine). Mung beans.

Mongolian Barbecue (Asian). Various foods, such as meat and poultry, seasoned with many different oils and sauces; eaten with hot sesame cakes.

Monkey Nut. A small nut resembling a peanut. Also, sometimes, the peanut.

Monkfish. Angelfish, spadefish, or porgy.

Monk's Head. A French cheese. *See* Tête de Moine.

Monk's Morels. *See* Helvelles.

Monopole (French). In liquor or wine usage, indicates that the produce is solely owned, a proprietary brand.

Monosodium Glutamate; MSG. A white powder, a vegetable derivative, which has no taste but has the effect of bringing out the flavor of any food to which it is added, with the exception of eggs.

Monselet, Charles. A noted 19th-cenutry French author and writer on cookery.

Monselet, À la. Garnished with artichoke hearts and truffles, often also with fried potatoes.

Monserrato. A sweet Sardinian red wine.

Monsieur, Fromage de. A soft, tasty, somewhat salty, French cheese.

Monstera. A green, cone-shaped, tropical fruit with a tasty whitish pulp and a flavor suggesting banana, mango, and pineapple.

Montagne, Fromage de. A smooth-textured ewe's- or cow's-milk cheese prepared in the Pyrénées region of France.

Montagne, Prosper. A noted French chef and restaurateur, co-author of *Larousse Gastronomique.*

Montasio. A cheese made from cow's and goat's milk near the Austrian-Italian border. When young, it is white, mild, and is eaten fresh; when mature, it becomes yellow and has a spicy taste.

Montavoner. An Austrian cheese made with both sweet and sour milk, and flavored with herbs.

Mont-Blanc. A rich dessert made with chestnuts, whipped cream, and sugar, and shaped into a mound resembling a mountain.

Mont-Cénis. A French goat's- and cow's-milk cheese, partly white shading to yellow, with a salty blue mold much like Roquefort; strongly flavored with parsley.

Mont des Cats. A pasteurized cow's-milk Belgian cheese, made in Flanders; it is the Trappist monks' imitation of Port du Salut, and similar to Saint-Paulin.

Montdidier. A very mild soft French cream cheese.

Mont d'Or. (1) A rather soft, yellow cow's-milk cheese, something like a Brie but with slightly more flavor and aroma; produced near Lyons, France. (2) A large Munster cheese made in the Franche-Comté region of France.

Monte-Aguilla. A Jamaican liqueur spiced with pimientos.

Monte Bianco (Italian). Puréed chestnuts with whipped cream. The Italian version of Mont-Blanc. *See* Mont-Blanc.

Monter (French). To increase the volume of a liquid or soft food by beating or whipping, as by beating egg whites.

Monterey Jack; Jack. (1) A fine California cheddar cheese; mild when young but sharper when aged. (2) A Mexican imitation of California Jack, slightly firmer and with a biting taste.

Monterobbio. A fair-quality wine from the Lombardy region of Italy.

Montecarlo. *See* Italy, The Wines of.

Monte-Cristo; Montpensier Gâteau. A sweet rich cake.

Montepulciano. An Italian red dessert wine. *See* Italy, The Wines of.

Montglas, À la (French). Garnished with liver pâté and truffles poached in Madeira sauce; usually served with seafood or poultry.

Monthélie. A red wine of fair quality produced near Beaune, France.

Monthéry. A soft French cheese made partly of skim milk.

Montmarault; Roujadoux; Saint-Pardoux. A cylindrical blue-veined goat's- or cow's-milk cheese made in the Bourbonnais region of France.

Montmaur. A 17th-century French scholar who had elaborate theories concerning the preparation and cooking of foods.

Montmorency. (1) A variety of cherry native to the Montmorency Valley north of Paris. (2) Various preparations made with cherries.

Montone (Italian). Mutton.

Montpellier Butter. Butter colored green; used as a garnish for fish dishes.

Montpensier. A round cake, rich and sweet, flavored with almonds and vanilla.

Montrachet. One of the world's truly great white wines with excellent aroma and taste; produced in the Burgundy region of France. See France, The Wines of.

Montrachet, Fromage de. A plain goat's-milk cheese made in the Burgundy region of France.

Moole. To knead dough.

Moon Cake (Chinese). A small stuffed cake made with either sweet or savory mixtures; a favorite during the Moon Festival.

Moonfish. Any of a number of short, deep-bodied fish, such as sunfish, harvestfish, spadefish, horsefish; found off the southern Atlantic and Pacific coasts of North America. See also Opah.

Moonshine. A crude intoxicating beverage distilled illegally. The liquor was made secretly at night by light from the moon, hence the term "moonshine."

Moonshiner. A person who makes moonshine.

Moor Cock. The male of the red grouse, an excellent game bird with a rather distinctive taste.

Moor Hen. (1) The female of the red grouse, an excellent game bird. (2) Certain other game birds in various parts of the world.

Moose. A large member of the deer family. The meat, usually only passable, is prepared like venison.

Moque (Belgian). A pastry, the dough for which is shaped into a long sausage, allowed to stand, and then cut into thin rounds for baking.

Morangos (Portuguese). Strawberries.

Morat. A mulberry-flavored drink that contains honey.

Moray. A voracious eel; prepared like any eel, but best in soups, stews, or chowders.

Morbier. A cooked cheese prepared in the Jura region of France; at its best from the late autumn to June.

Mørbrad (Danish). Tenderloin.

Morcheln (German). Morels, a variety of mushroom.

Morcillo. A Puerto Rican pig's-blood sausage.

Morcón (Philippine). Meat roll stuffed with chopped meats, eggs, pickles, and vegetables.

Morel. A variety of mushroom found on the edge of woods in France, the best of which is the small black morel. It has a peculiarly marked exterior, with vertical lines and fairly deep pits.

Morel, Conical. An edible European fungus of excellent taste and fine texture, ranging in color from gray to yellow; it is a springtime mushroom.

Morello Cherry. A very dark red cherry with a slightly bitter flavor; used chiefly for preserving and in jellies and jams.

Morene (Italian). Lamprey or sea eel.

Moretta (Italian). A beverage made of coffee, with anise liqueur, lemon peel, and sometimes other flavorings.

Morey-Saint-Denis. A wine district in the Burgundy region of France. See France, The Wines of.

Morgen Complet (Denmark). Breakfast.

Morg Polo (Iranian). A chicken dish served with chelo, the crunchy rice of Iran.

Mori. A Japanese green tea.

Morille (French). See Morel.

Morillon (French). (1) A black grape. (2) A blue-winged duck.

Moringa. The dessert date, a fruit of the ben-nut or horseradish tree; used as a flavoring agent in cooked foods.

Mornay Sauce (French). A famous sauce used chiefly for vegetables and eggs. It is prepared by reducing 2 parts Béchamel sauce combined with 1 part sweet cream, then adding grated Parmesan or Gruyère cheese, and a little butter. For use on chicken dishes, chicken stock may be substituted for the sweet cream.

Morning Goods (British). All types of confectionery baked and sold fresh daily, including yeast and powder-aerated buns, scones, and pastries.

Morocanella. A sweet, heavy, rich wine prepared in Cyprus.

Moroccan Wheat. The firm flour produced in Morocco; often blended with French flour.

Morocco. Being a Mohammedan country, Morocco has no pork dishes, and alcoholic drinks are not served. Some of the dishes are authentically Moroccan, having originated there, but others come from neighboring Arabic countries. *Couscous*, made of a cereal called *faufal* (tiny bits of wheat), for example, is probably of Algerian origin, although the Moroccans eat it frequently as part of their regular cuisine. *Mashie*, stuffed vegetables, are definitely Syrian and Lebanese in origin, having traveled westward to Morocco with caravans of Arabs many centuries ago.

The morning meal of the country is often soup or *raiff*, small, sweet cakes made from semolina. The other two meals of the day are similar, often beginning with a pastry-filled chicken dish, *bistaela*, for example, followed by a *couscous* with mutton. Salt is never placed on the table, for it is used only in cooking. Garlic is rarely used, but certain other spices and herbs are great favorites—pepper, cinnamon, chervil, saffron, ginger are especially liked. With meals only water is served, although a minted tea may be served in the middle of a repast to refresh the palate.

The usual desserts consist of fruits, semolina puddings, or flaky pastries covered with honey, nuts, and sweet syrups.

Table utensils are rarely used; food is picked up with the fingers of the right hand only, although the left may occasionally be used to tear the bread. Spoons are sometimes provided for eating *couscous*, however.

Moror. A bitter herb such as horseradish served at a Jewish Seder, the ritual Passover meal.

Morot (Swedish). Carrot.

Morro Crab. A large, meaty fine-flavored crab found on the Pacific coast from Mexico to Alaska.

Morsure (Obsolete). Biting (a food) or eating.

Mortadella (Italian). (1) A rather large sausage with an excellent flavor; some versions have pistachio nuts. (2) A soft type of salami.

Mortar and Pestle. The mortar is a bowl, made of metal or some other hard material, in which

substances may be crushed and blended into a powder, using a pestle, a long tool with a rounded end.

Mortifié (French). Of game and meat, well aged.

Morton; Trading Clam. A variety of clam used chiefly for chowders.

Mortress. A soup made with meat, or sometimes only with bread and milk.

Morue Fumée (French). Dried or smoked haddock.

Morue Salée (French). Salt cod.

Moscato. *See* Italy, The Wines of.

Moscovite, À la (French). Garnished with caviar.

Moscovites (French). (1) Canapés or hors d'oeuvres. (2) A group of sweet puddings, creams, or ice cream desserts.

Moscow Mule. A drink made of ginger beer, vodka, and lime.

Moselblümchen (German). A wine term, generally used by shippers to give an elaborate name to an inferior wine, usually prepared with added sugar; literally the term means "Moselle flower."

Moselle. One of Germany's leading wine regions. *See* Germany, The Wines of.

Mossberry. Another name for the cranberry.

Mossel (Dutch). Mussel; clam.

Moss Milk (Icelandic). A drink in which Iceland moss, an edible lichen or *morr*, is added to milk, thus varying the flavor. It may also be used in cooking.

Mostacciole; Mostaccioli; Mostacciolo (Italian). A small sweet chocolate, almond, or fruit cake.

Mostaccioli (Italian). Smooth tubes of pasta, about 2½ inches long, cut with slanted edges.
  Mostaccioli Rigati. Mostaccioli with ridges running down the length of the pasta.

Mostaganem d'Ahra. A group of red and white Algerian wines. In general, the whites are somewhat better than the reds.

Mostarda (Italian, Portuguese). Mustard.

Mostaza (Spanish). Mustard.

Mostelle. A delicate, rather scarce Mediterranean fish somewhat resembling the burbot.

Mostôffait. A rich fresh white cheese flavored with tarragon; made in the Champagne region of France.

Mother Liquid. A stringy liquid left after the fermentation of vinegar.

Mother of Grapes. (1) A brandylike liquor. (2) Marc.

Mother of Thyme. Wild thyme.

Mother of Vinegar. The thick, tough film that forms in wine during the acidulation period.

Mother's Milk (Colloquial). Gin.

Mottais. A soft, creamy, smooth cheese made with a mixture of goat's and cow's milk; somewhat like Camembert; produced in the Touraine region of France.

Motte Valsesiane. A small round Italian cheese containing fennel seeds; made in Piedmont.

Mou de Veau (French). Calf's lights (lungs).

Moufflon. A southern European wild sheep whose meat is fairly good; best when marinated before cooking.

Mouille Bouche (French). A bergamot pear.

Mouiller (French). To add a liquid, such as water or broth, to meats while they are cooking. Also, to add liquid as a means of thinning or flavoring sauces and stews.

Mouillette (French). Toast dipped in a batter or liquid.

Mould (British). Mold, a hollowed-out container.

Moules Frites (French). Mussels fried in deep fat.

Moules Marinières (French). Mussels cooked in white wine with pepper, parsley, and shallots.

Moulin-à-Vent. A town in the Beaujolais wine district of France. See France, The Wines of.

Mouna (Moroccan). A cake made of eggs, butter, yeast, and oranges.

Mountain Cock; Heath Cock. A very large European game bird, often 3 feet long.

Mountain Dew. Scotch whisky.

Mountain Pepper. Capers.

Mountain Wine. A variety of Malaga wine made with mountain grapes.

Mount Hope. A fairly good cheddar-type California cheese.

Mouse Deer. The musk deer native to Java and Ceylon.

Mouselet (French). A garnish of truffles and artichokes.

Mouse-Trap Cheese (Colloquial). Mediocre dry store cheese considered fit only as mouse bait.

Moussache. Flour derived from manioc (cassava) root.

Moussaka (Greek, Turkish). Layers of eggplant slices alternated with chopped lamb or beef; a classic dish.

Mousse (French). A very light, delicate-tasting dish that may be prepared with all kinds of meat or game, fish or shellfish, or as a dessert.

Mousseau (French). A type of wheat flour bread.

Mousseline. A purée strained through a fine sieve and combined with cream; much like a mousse, but prepared in small, individual portions.

Mousseline Sauce. (1) A frothy sauce made with whipped cream and Hollandaise sauce. (2) A sauce made with spinach or a tomato flavoring.

Mousserende Vine (Danish). Sparkling wine; champagne.

Mousseron. Fairy-ring mushroom; a white mushroom, found mainly in southern France, which tends to grow in rings. It averages about 1–2 inches across the top, and has moderately good taste and texture; used mainly in stews and ragouts.

Moustille. A pale red wine of passable quality produced in the Berry region of France.

Moût (French). Grape juice which has not been fermented for wine.

Moutarde (French). Mustard.

Moutarde des Capucins (French). Wild horseradish.

Moutardelle. A variety of horseradish.

Mouton en Daube (French). Stewed mutton, usually prepared with red wine.

Mouton-Rothschild, Château. A truly great dry

red wine produced in the Haut-Médoc region of Bordeaux, France. It keeps well, often for decades. *See also* France, The Wines of.

Mouvettes (French). Round or oval wooden spoons often used in cooking.

Mow. (1) Stacks of peas, corn, beans, or grain. (2) The section of barn in which they are stored.

Mowburn (British). Corn that has a fermented taste because of being stacked while too green.

Moyashi (Japanese). Bean sprout.

Moyeu (French, Obsolete). Egg yolk.

Mozzarella. A white, rubbery, unsalted Italian cheese.

Mozzarella Affumicata; Scamozza (Italian). Mozzarella cheese made up in standard pear shapes weighing about a pound and smoked.

Mozzarella in Carrozza (Italian). A fried-cheese sandwich, often with anchovies.

Mozzarinelli (Italian). A small version of Mozzarella cheese.

MSG. *See* Monosodium Glutamate.

MSX. The popular term used to describe a parasite found in sea or bay waters which is fatal only to oysters. Its scientific name is Multinucleate Sphere-X ("X" meaning unknown); MSX was originally discovered in 1957 in Delaware Bay. *See also* Haplosporidian.

Muckibus (Obsolete). Intoxicated.

Mud Bass. An American freshwater sunfish.

Mud Catfish. Several varieties of American catfish.

Mud Dab. Winter flounder.

Muddle. To mash sugar, fruits, and other nonliquid ingredients before adding the liquid ingredients to alcholic drinks. The implement or rod used is a *muddler* or *stirrer*.

Mudfish. A large variety of fish found all over the world, which likes to burrow into the mud bottom of a river or stream.

Muffin. A quick, light bread made of various kinds of flour, either plain or sweetened, to which may be added berries, nuts, or spices. The batter must be mixed lightly, as overbeating toughens it. It is usually baked in a muffin pan having 6–12 individual cups.

Muffin Bell. The chimes rung in 19th-century England by the muffin man to announce his arrival.

Muffineer (British). A container that holds sugar or salt for sprinkling over muffins.

Mug. (1) The green gram, a Malayan chick-pea. (2) A rather large earthenware, pottery, or metal drinking container with a handle and often with an attached cover.

Muggine. A type of white or gray mullet found in the waters off Liguria, Italy.

Mugle (Jordanian). A heavily spiced rice dish made with nuts.

Mug-Up. In certain parts of the world, especially the far north, the service of hot tea, sometimes accompanied by food.

Mugwort. A slightly bitter tasting and smelling herb that grows in small bushes, wild or cultivated.

Mujaddarah (Arabian). Lentil stew.

Mulberry. Any one of several different varieties of berries grown on the mulberry tree, ranging in color from black through white, red, blue, and purple. The fruit is sweet, but the taste is not distinctive; best used in compotes or jams.

Mull. Wine or beer boiled, sweetened, and flavored with spices; the resulting beverage is said to be *mulled*.

Muller (British). A cooking vessel used for mulling, that is, for boiling with sweet and spicy ingredients.

Mullet. Several different species of fish. Some varieties have a somewhat unpleasant taste, whereas others are quite good. In general, they tend to be oily or fatty.

Mulligan (American). A crude stew made of any sort of meat and any available vegetables, usually outdoors over an open fire; the term is used by hobos.

Mulligatawny; Mulligatunny (Indian). Curry-flavored chicken or lamb soup. The term comes from the Tamil *milagu tannir*, meaning pepper water.

Mulligatawny Paste. A paste of curry and other ingredients used to flavor mulligatawny soup.

Mullons. *See* Crêmets.

Mulse; Hydromel. A drink made of dry red wine, water, and honey brought to the boiling point.

Multum. A licorice-and-quassia additive or adulterant used by brewers.

Multure (Scotch). The fee paid to a miller for grinding wheat into flour or grain into meal.

Mum (British). A strong ale made from malted wheat, oatmeal, ground beans, and herbs.

Mumble. To chew gently, especially as babies do with toothless gums.

Mumbled Hare (British). A dish of cooked hare, eggs, and butter.

Mumme. An ancient beer originally produced in Brunswick, Germany.

Munch. The action of the jaws going up and down in eating.

Mundbissen (German). Patties of meat, fish, or poultry.

Mung Beans; Mung Peas. Small beans or peas which sprout readily in a few days when moistened and kept on a damp cloth; often used in Asiatic cookery.

Mungcorn; Mongcorn. Mixed corn.

Munich Beer. A general term used to describe beers prepared in Munich, Germany; also beers of this type, that is, having a distinctive, malty taste.

Munk (Swedish). Doughnut.

Münster. In the United States, a yellow, quite mild cheese generally available sliced from small oblong loaves. In Germany, a rather strong, flavorsome whole-milk cheese, fairly firm and usually flavored with caraway seeds.

Muqueca. A northeastern Brazilian dish made with fish, various spices, and oil.

Mural (Obsolete). A fruit tree growing next to a wall.

Murat (British). An ancient mulberry preserve.

Mürbeteig (German). Dessert pastry.

Mûre (French). Mulberry.

Mûre de Ronce (French). Blackberry.

Mûre des Haies (French). A bush that yields edible berries.

Murene. A large Mediterranean fish with an excellent flavor; usually prepared with garlic, black olives, tomatoes, and wine.

Muriate. To pickle in brine.

Murin. A Japanese rice wine often used in cooking.

Murphy (Colloquial). Potato.

Murry. The lamprey, or sea eel.

Musa. A plant of the banana or plantain family.

Muscade (French). Nutmeg; mace.

Muscade, Noix de. Nutmeg.

Muscadel. A rich sweet wine made from Muscat grapes and popular several hundred years ago in Europe; not to be confused with Muscatel or Muscadet.

Muscadelle (French). Musk pear.

Muscadet. A medium-dry white wine produced in the Loire region of France; often considered an ideal luncheon wine. *See also* France, The Wines of.

Muscadine. A sweet grape grown in the southern United States.

Muscat. A light-colored, highly aromatic grape, often regarded as having the finest taste of any grape, possibly because of its high sugar content and firm texture.

Muscatel. A very sweet, fairly alcoholic wine made from the muscat grape. Now in poor repute because it is the favorite drink of down-and-out alcoholics, and is the least expensive alcoholic beverage marketed.

Muscatel Sage. Clary, an herb of the mint family; the leaves are occasionally used in Germany to flavor wines.

Muscheln (German). Clams, mussels, shellfish.

Muscoli alla Toscana (Italian). Mussels in tomato sauce.

Muscovado. Unrefined sugar obtained from sugar-cane juice by the evaporation of molasses.

Muscovy Duck; Musk Duck. A game bird; so called because the male has a musky odor.

Museau de Boeuf (French). Ox mouth; usually prepared like tongue.

Muselinas (Spanish). Dumplings.

Musette, En (French, Obsolete). Of shoulder of mutton or beef, braised.

Mush. Cornmeal or Indian meal prepared as a cereal.

Mushimono (Japanese). Steamed foods.

Mushroom. A wide range of edible, gill-bearing fungi ranging in size from that of a button to about a foot in diameter. Mushrooms have been used for thousands of years, Greek writers about 400 B.C. being the first to mention them. It seems clear that earlier civilizations used them as a food and medicine. Certain nations have always shown a liking for mushrooms in their cuisine, notably Poland, Russia, Germany, China, and Japan. The word "mushroom" is believed to be derived from the Old English *muscheron*, having relation to moss. Mushrooms are often found growing wild, and wild varieties often have a better taste than the cultivated varieties, but they should be used only by those who can positively distinguish the poisonous from the nonpoisonous varieties. Truffles, highly regarded flavoring ingredients, are not mushrooms; they grow completely underground, whereas mushrooms grow partly above ground.

Mushrooms have no chlorophyll, which accounts for the lack of green coloring; however, for most culinary purposes they are regarded as vegetables. Mushrooms should be cooked only briefly; overcooking toughens them. Dried mushrooms are expensive, but they make marvelous soups and sauces, providing a concentrated mushroom taste often missing in dishes prepared with fresh specimens. Canned mushrooms do not have a true mushroom flavor, but they are convenient and easy to prepare. While many experts do not believe in washing or peeling mushrooms, claiming that the taste is adversely affected, this seems to be an outmoded belief and modern sanitation demands at least a brief washing.

Oyster Mushroom. A creamy white wild mushroom that grows on trees; the taste is fairly good.

Parasol Mushroom. An extremely large mushroom, often a foot tall with a proportionately large cap, of a brown color shading toward yellow. Only the cap is used, the stem rarely being eaten.

St. George's Mushroom. A wild spring mushroom, white shading toward yellow, about 3 inches across the top.

Mushroom Ketchup. A piquant sauce made with mushrooms and spices.

Musigny. An important dry red wine produced in the Burgundy region of France. It has a beautiful color, fine aroma, but is noted especially for its velvety smoothness. *See* France, The Wines of.

Musk Deer. A small wild deer of the Far East.

Besides providing musk the young are used for food.

Musk Duck. A duck native to Australia and tropical America. *See* Muscovy Duck.

Muskellunge. A rather large pike found chiefly in northern American lakes; a remarkable game fish.

Muskmelon. A sweet, aromatic melon distinguished by its netted or patterned exterior.

Muskrat. Marsh rabbit; its flesh is rather strong-tasting.

Muslinger (Danish). Mussels.

Mu Som (Thai). Barbecued suckling pig, stuffed with oranges and vegetables, a specialty of Chiengmai.

Musoomahn (Siamese). A curry made with beef and peanuts.

Mussakhan. A Middle East chicken dish, well-spiced, and served on soft Arabic bread.

Mussel. An edible mollusk (shellfish) found clinging to rocks along seacoasts. Cold-water mussels are of superior flavor. Cultivated as well as naturally produced mussels are available; the former have a more delicate flavor. Mussels must be scrubbed well and rinsed under running water until the water runs clean. The hairy beards should be cut away, then the mussels steamed until the shells open. Those that do not open must be discarded.

Mussel Brose (Scotch). Mussels cooked with milk, water, and oatmeal.

Mussel Plum. A fair-tasting dark purple plum.

Mussla (Swedish). Mussel.

Must. Young, fresh wine immediately before fermentation begins.

Mustard. (1) A plant, both wild and cultivated; used as a salad green. (2) Table mustard, a preparation made from mustard seeds. The white and black seeds are finely ground, and mixed to a paste with vinegar, oil, and spices; sometimes a fine starch is added to neutralize the natural pungency. English mustard is usually sold in powder form which, when mixed with hot water, is strong and biting; French mustards are prepared in a wide range of styles, the Dijon type (mixed with verjuice) being of medium strength. Bordeaux mustard contains unfermented wine. Bahamian mustard is very mild, and is best used with cheese. Chinese mustard is much like English mustard, although perhaps slightly less pungent and biting. *See* Mustard Seeds.

Mustard Greens. A plant whose tenderest leaves may be used to give a more pungent flavor to salads. Leaves, stems, and flowerheads may be cooked as a vegetable, alone or in combination with blander vegetables.

Mustard Oil. Oil produced from mustard seeds.

Mustard Pot. A small container used to serve mustard.

Mustard Seeds. Small, aromatic seeds, white and dark, from the mustard plant. The whole seed is used in pickling spice and to flavor pickles, relishes, and salads. When the seeds are finely ground to a powder, they are used in making the condiment mustard. Prepared mustard (paste) is chiefly available from France, Germany, Sweden, and the United States, the flavor depending on the seasoning and spices used in the mixture. *See* Mustard.

Mustard Shrub. A West Indian plant with a pungent berry.

Mustard Spinach. A spicy, green vegetable which grows wild in parts of the United States, and which tastes like spinach when cooked; also called Tendergreen.

Mustele; Mostelle. A Mediterranean fish somewhat like the burbot.

Mustewecke (German). Bread or rolls filled with chopped pork.

Mutage. The process of checking fermentation in wine.

Mutchkin. A Scotch measure equal to 1 pint.

Mutton. The flesh of mature sheep, generally over one year of age. The word itself is a modification of the French *mouton*, and was brought into England and the English language by the Norman conquerors. Most Western peoples prefer lamb, the flesh of animals between 6 weeks and 3–4 months of age, for the taste is less pronounced. A century ago the English preferred the taste of mutton, and liked it even when very mature, say, 4 years old. In recent decades European and American palates have shown a decided preference for lamb, with its lighter, less oily flavor. In Oriental and Middle Eastern countries the heavy oily quality of mutton is not looked down upon, however. Mutton flesh varies considerably, depending upon the age, sex, and feeding habits of the particular animal. The U.S. Government grades mutton as prime, choice, good, and medium. Common or Cull mutton is not satisfactory for home culinary use.

Mutton Cabbage. A head of cabbage scooped out and filled with chopped sausage meat and mutton, then covered with cabbage leaves and cooked in meat broth; no longer popular.

Mutton Chop. A cut of mutton containing one rib; may be broiled or fried.

Muttonfish. An eel or other similar sea fish found in the West Indies.

Mutton Ham. A mutton leg cured like ham.

Muttony. Resembling mutton.

Muzenmandelchen (North German). Almond cookies.

Muzzle. To drink alcohol until intoxicated.

Muzzy. Dulled as a result of drinking too much liquor.

Mycella. A Danish imitation of Gorgonzola cheese, but much stronger and heartier.

Myoga. Japanese ginger, used to flavor soups.

Myrtle; Myrtille. The bilberry; used for syrups, fruit compotes, and sweet sauces.

Myrtle Sedge. *See* Calamus.

Mysost; Mytost. A mild, pale brown Swedish cheese with a very buttery taste; also made in the United States.

N

Naal Oil; Sofia Oil. A pale yellow Indian grass containing limonene, which has a mild ginger odor.

Naartje. The South African tangerine, a delicious citrus fruit eaten as dessert or salad, crystallized as a candy, or used in jelly and preserves.

Nabemono (Japanese). Food cooked in a saucepan.

Nabo (Spanish). Turnip.

Nachspeisen (German). Desserts.

Nackenheim. A wine village of the Rheinhessen region of Germany. *See* Germany, The Wines of.

Nacket (Scotch, Obsolete). A small loaf, roll, or cake.

Nage, À la. Of shellfish, served in the broth in which they are cooked, thus retaining the full flavor.

Nageles; Nagelkazen (Dutch). A round, fresh cheese about 16 inches in diameter made of skimmed cow's milk mixed with cloves and cumin seed.

Nägeles. *See* Nagelkassa.

Nagelkassa. A skim-milk cheese made in Austria and Germany.

Nagerechten (Dutch). Desserts.

Nahe. A German river along whose banks are vineyards yielding a distinctive wine. *See* Germany, The Wines of.

Naiboa. (1) Yucca, a starchy tropical root. (2) A confection made from cassava, brown sugar, grated cheese, and aniseed.

Nalesniki (Russian). A pancake filling; a mixture of white cheese and butter rolled into an unsweetened pancake and fried in deep fat.

Name (Latin American). The yam.

Namplā (Siamese). A seasoning sauce made of salted fish or shrimp.

Namprik Phau (Siamese). A pungent condiment of about the consistency of heavy cream, made with garlic, shallots, pepper, and Namplā (salted-shrimp sauce).

Nan (Indian, Pakistani). A flat, soft bread; often served with chicken *tanduri*.

Nana (Syrian). Mint; much used for flavoring.

Nangka (Philippine). Jackfruit.

Nan Roti (Indian) Bread made of slightly leavened dough.

Nantais. (1) A kirsch-flavored almond butter cooky topped with sugar and ground almonds; sometimes iced with an apricot-rum glaze. (2) A duckling from Nantes, France. (3) A salted, curdled cow's-milk cheese made in western France; best from October to June but available all year round.

Nantua, À la (French). Garnished with crayfish tails or covered with crayfish purée.

Nantz. English name for French brandy, most of which, in the 18th century, was smuggled from Nantes.

Naoussa. A rather heavy Greek dry red wine.

Napareuli. A mediocre Russian white wine.

Napa Valley. A wine district north of San Francisco where the vineyards produce some of the best California red and white table wines. *See* United States, The Wines of.

Napery. Household linen, especially table linen.

Napfkuchen (German). A yeast cake usually made with raisins.

Napiform. Resembling a turnip in appearance.

Napkin. A square, or other shape, of cloth or paper used at meals for wiping the fingers and lips and kept on the lap during the meal.

Napoleon (French). A pastry made of puff-paste layers and filled with whipped cream or custard; usually glazed on top.

Napoleon Biscuits. Rich almond cookies sandwiched together with jam.

Napoleon Brandy. If genuine, this liqueur was casked during the time of Napoleon I and is more than a hundred years old; very few bottles are still available. The term is often incorrectly used to describe any aged brandy.

Napolitain. Formerly a very large, fancy cake. Now made in smaller sizes, consisting of layers of an almond-flavored pastry with alternate fillings of jam and jelly between them; coated with apricot jam and piped with icing.

Napolitaine, À la. (1) "In the Neapolitan style." Usually, with garlic and tomatoes. (2) A tri-colored ice cream made in brick form.

Nappe (French). Tablecloth.

Nappé (French). (1) Masked or coated with sauce or jelly. (2) Dipped, as fondants.

Napper (French). To cover with a thick layer of sauce, jam, or jelly; to garnish with slices of truffles, herb leaves, carrot, cucumber, or other decorative edibles.

Napu. The musk deer of Java and Sumatra.

Naranja (Spanish). Orange.

    Naranja Agria. The sour orange, not the bitter orange.

    Naranja Dukc; China. The sweet orange of Latin America.

Naranjilla. An excellent-tasting orange with a bright green interior; native to South America, especially Ecuador.

Narbonne. A town in the Aude district of France that produces passable table wines.

Nardoo. Clover fern, a plant whose seeds are dried and ground into a flour, used chiefly by the Australian aborigines; a flour is also made from the plant.

Naringin. Glucoside found only in the pith of grapefruit, especially when unripe. It often crystallizes in tiny beads in canned grapefruit segments and concentrated juice.

Nasco; Nascol. A sweet white wine made in Sardinia, Italy.

Naseberry. The West Indian tree that produces the sapodilla plum, an edible fruit.

Naseberry Plum. *See* Sapodilla.

Nase, Le. The broadsnout, a member of the carp family.

Nasello (Italian). Whiting.

Nasi (Indonesian). Rice.

Nasi Goreng (Indonesian). A dish consisting of chicken or fish and fried rice.

Nasi Kunung (Indonesian). Yellow rice.

Nasturtium. A decorative and edible plant with bright flowers. The leaves have a distinctive spicy flavor similar to watercress; when young, they can be used in salads, as a garnish, as sandwich fillers, or cooked as a vegetable. They may be sun-dried and kept for later use. The flowers are attractive in salads and fruit cups. The tender buds and seeds may be pickled in vinegar and used as a substitute for capers.

Nata (Portuguese, Spanish). Cream.

Natch-Bonc. The aitch-bone of beef.

Natilla (Mexican). Caramel custard.

Native Orange. A small leathery-skinned orange found in parts of Europe.

Natives. Foods that are indigenous, that is, that grow or are produced naturally in a certain region.

Natur; Naturrein; Naturwein (German). Wine prepared without the addition of sugar.

Nature (French). As applied to wine, not sweetened.

Naturel, Au. Uncooked or boiled in water; plain and simple; prepared simply.

Natur Schnitzel (German). Sautéed veal chops.

Naulet. A yeast pastry baked in the shape of a symbolic figure at Christmas time.

Navarin; Navarin de Mouton (French). Mutton stew made with small onions and potatoes, and sometimes with carrots, peas, and turnips.

Navel Orange. A seedless eating orange distinguished by a navel-like opening at the end opposite the stem; widely grown in California.

Navet (French). Turnip.

Navette (French). Wild turnip.

Navy Bean. The ordinary dried white bean commonly used in cooking. Its name is said to derive from the fact that navies frequently used it as a staple food since it did not spoil on long voyages.

Néac. A passable red wine produced in the Pomerol region of Bordeaux, France. The color is good, but the wine seems to lack finish.

Neapolitan Cream. A dessert made in layers, with different flavors and colors.

Neapolitan Ice Cream. Ice cream prepared in three flavors arranged horizontally in brick form.

Neat (Obsolete). Ox.

Neat's Foot. The foot of a calf or ox.

Neat's Tongue. The tongue of a calf or ox.

Nebbiolo. A black grape cultivated in northern Italy for production of certain varieties of the best Italian wine. (2) Nebbiolo Piedmontese, a moderately sweet red Italian table wine produced in the Piedmont district. *See* Italy, The Wines of.

Nebuchadnezzar. The largest champagne bottle, having a capacity equivalent to 20 ordinary bottles.

Neck. The flesh of the neck of any animal.

Neck Beef (British). Beef from the neck of cattle; suitable only for long stewing or for the preparation of beef tea.

Nectar. (1) Any delicious drink. In Greek mythology, the wine of the gods. (2) The fluid secreted by plants from which bees make honey.

Nectarine. A smooth-skinned variety of peach with firmer flesh and a richer flavor than the ordinary peach; used mostly as a dessert fruit but also for jam and jelly. California and Oregon are the chief areas for cultivation in the United States.

Needle, Larding. A needle pointed at one end with prongs at the other, used for inserting pieces of bacon, ham, or pork fat in meats and poultry before cooking. A *trussing needle*, used for poultry and game, is a pointed steel pin which is pierced at the other end.

Needlefish. A long thin narrow-jawed fish resembling the gar.

Neep (Scotch). Turnip.

Neera (Indian). An unfermented drink made from the coconut palm.

Nefle. *See* Medlar.

Negi (Japanese). Green onion; scallion.

Negroni. An Italian drink made from gin, bitters, and red vermouth; sometimes served with a slice of orange.

Negus. A wine cup, prepared with port or sherry wine, hot water, lemon, and spices; named for its originator, Col. Francis Negus.

Neige (French). "Snow." Shaved ice; beaten egg whites; sweetened chilled fruit juice; or anything served on crushed ice.

Neige de Florence. White flakes of pasta dropped into individual bowls of clear soup at the table.

Nelson Beef. A method of preparing fillet of beef by cooking it in a casserole between sliced onions and sliced potatoes.

Nelumbium; Nelumbo. A kind of water bean occasionally eaten; it belongs to the same family as the lotus of Egypt and Asia.

Nelusko. (1) *Petits fours* made of brandied cherries filled with red-currant jam, dipped in hot icing, then cooled. (2) A frozen chocolate-almond pudding.

Nemes Kadarka. A heavy Hungarian red wine of fair quality.

Nemours. Small flaky tarts baked with jam and a sprinkling of sugar on top.

Nems. A miniature corn native to the South Pacific.

Neoza. A Himalayan pine whose cones contain edible seeds.

Nepal; Nepaul Pepper. A yellowish pepper of the same character as cayenne and Guinea pepper with a sweet, pungent flavor; grown chiefly in India.

Nepenthe. Any drink with sedative properties.

Nerka. The blue-back salmon of Canada, Alaska, and Kamchatka.

Néroli Oil. Oil from orange blossoms; used in candies, confections, and liqueurs. *See also* Orange-Flower Water.

Néroli Pastry. A pastry prepared with néroli oil and candied orange peel, as well as cornstarch, eggs, melted butter, and chopped almonds.

Nerveux (French). A wine with excellent keeping qualities that may be shipped for long distances without losing its taste.

Nesh. (1) Of food, having soft texture or consistency. (2) Tender, succulent, juicy.

Nessel (British). A very thin, round, soft, cured rennet cheese made from whole cow's milk.

Nesselrode, À la. A term indicating several different preparations: a chilled chestnut pudding served with a maraschino or kirsch sauce; a fruit sauce; a game soup garnished with tiny chestnut-stuffed cream puffs; a sturgeon soup; cold pâté-stuffed thrush coated with chaudfroid (jellied mayonnaise sauce); any dessert with candied fruits.

Nests. Edible nests in which various foods are served, particularly dry, fried foods. *Potato nests* are made of matchstick potatoes shaped to a round or oval in a small wire basket and cooked in deep fat. *Pancake nests* are used for stews. *Bird's-nest soup,* a Chinese delicacy now served in many countries, utilizes the natural nests of certain birds after thorough clearing of feathers and other matter, and many washings. *See also* Birds' Nests.

Net Fat; Caul Fat. The thin fatty membrane surrounding the lower portion of a pig's intestine; used to hold foods in a desired shape while boiling or steaming; often used in Chinese cooking.

Netherlands, The. Food is a serious matter in the Netherlands. The people like to eat, and six meals a day are not uncommon. Breakfast is a reasonably substantial meal, usually with hot cereal. About eleven o'clock there is often cake and coffee. Lunch begins about one in the afternoon and is a meal of many courses; it is very similar to dinner, and equally filling. In midafternoon there is teatime, which may include cake, sandwiches, or even some hot food. Before retiring, there is a hasty bedtime snack and possibly a cup of hot cocoa.

The Dutch are very fond of herring and serve it in a variety of ways, but "green" or raw herring is preferred by the local gourmets. The seafood is superb, including oysters, shrimp, mussels, and all of the usual ocean fish. Lobster has become scarce and very expensive. Fishcakes, *vischkoekjes,* are a typical family-style fish preparation. The soups are hearty and rich: *ertwensoep,* the classic split pea soup, and *peensoep,* carrot soup, are examples. There are few steaks as Americans know them, although a Dutch beefsteak with onions is passable, if not outstanding. The Netherlanders much prefer stews with lots of thick gravy, fatty pork dishes, or sausages with mashed potatoes and red cabbage. The type of dishes usually encountered might include *heete bliksem,* heavily peppered pork chops with apples, *gevulde kalfsborst,* stuffed breast of veal, *filosoof,* a meat-and-potato pie, pancakes which come in a wide variety of sizes and shapes, and a standard item, the *uitsmijter,* a meat sandwich with a fried egg, which is available almost everywhere.

Because Holland once owned the islands of Java and Bali, the people are exceedingly fond of Javanese food, and menus frequently feature dishes of that region—*nasi goreng,* fried rice with meat, chicken, etc., *bahmi goreng,* fried noodles with pork and rice, and sometimes even a *rijsttafel,* basically a rice dish with a large assortment of curried foods and relishes. Among the vegetables, baked endive, called *lofschotel,* is worthy of mention, although it is second to potatoes and cabbage in popularity. Desserts are quite unimportant, but the two leading Dutch cheeses, Edam and Gouda, are both world-famous, and deservedly so.

No wines are produced in the Netherlands, but the beers are uniformly excellent. Heineken's is the leading brand. The before-dinner drink is the locally made gin, *jenever,* which has a peculiar musky, or smoky, quality. It is ordered in a restaurant by requesting a *borrel,* the popular term for gin, served ice cold. The afterdinner drinks include a full line of cordials made quite well by Bols; *curaçao,* with its orange-flavored base, is well known, and there is also *advocaat,* made with eggs and liquor.

Netted Carpet. A clam with distinctive crisscross markings, found on parts of the Pacific coast of the United States.

Nettle Tops. In Scotland the young tops of the nettle plant are picked carefully, washed several times and cooked quickly, then served as a vegetable.

Netty Gem. A round melon with a grayish rind and pink or green flesh; cultivated throughout the United States.

Neuchâtel. A canton of Switzerland producing fine white and red wines.

Neufchâtel Cheese. A heart- or square-shaped soft mild rennet cheese made from whole or skim milk in Normandy, France. Best-known varieties, differing only in fat content, size, or shape, are *Bordon, Malakoff, Petit Carré,* and *Petit Suisse.*

Neumagen. A wine village in the Moselle region of Germany. *See* Germany, The Wines of.

Neusohl. Another name for Brinza cheese. *See* Brinza.

Neustadter. A white Rhine wine from the vineyards of Neustadt in the Palatinate district of Germany.

Neutral Fat. Edible bland oils used extensively in the preparation of cakes and candies.

Neutral Spirits. Spirits distilled at a proof of 190 degrees or more; the term is used even though the spirits are subsequently reduced in proof.

Newburg Sauce, A sauce, made of cream, egg yolks, sherry, and butter, created for serving with lobster by a chef of New York's famous Delmonico Restaurant. It is also suitable for shrimp and other seafoods as well as reheated foods.

Newfoundland Fish. The codfish.

New Jersey Tea. A wild plant whose leaves may be dried, then boiled and made into a tea substitute.

New-Laid. Of eggs, newly or freshly laid.

Newport Roast. A rib roast of beef with about three-quarters of the bone removed, or cut short.

Newtown Pippins. A variety of apples of good flavor.

New Zealand. In this scenic paradise the food follows the general pattern of nearby Australia, which in turn follows that of England. The only modifying influence upon the British-Australian cuisine is the native tribes of Maoris, who have shown the New Zealanders some of their local foods and in turn have learned to add European foods to their somewhat limited diet.

Fish, freshly caught in local waters, is superb; there is a unique green clam, the *toheroa*; another rare item is the *pipi*, a shellfish. *Pauas* are a kind of abalone-like shellfish. Wild game dishes are a regular part of the diet, especially wild pig and red deer. There are many interesting vegetables, including *kumi kumi*, which resembles a pumpkin, and *kumeras*, a type of sweet potato. *Rauriki*, a green leaf, is often used for salads.

A particularly interesting specialty is the mutton bird, which makes its nest along the sea and lives on fish. Its natural taste has changed because of its exclusive fish diet, and the mutton bird has been described as tasting "half fish, half bird," being very oily. The bird must be boiled in at least three changes of water to make it palatable, but liking the oily taste, the Maoris seldom bother.

Tea is the national beverage, and afternoon tea a standard meal. New Zealanders are very fond of beer and ale, of which they drink a fair quantity. The local wines are of mediocre quality, including imitations of sherry and port, as well as European table wines.

New Zealand Spinach. A vegetable native to the Southern Hemisphere and now cultivated in the United States. It resembles ordinary spinach in appearance and flavor and may be prepared in the same way. It thrives in hot weather, can be cut repeatedly throughout the summer, and, because its leaves are more open than those of ordinary spinach, is less likely to be sandy.

Nga-Pi-Gyet (Burmese). A garlic-and-shrimp sauce with a strong, spicy taste and aroma.

Ngo Heong (Oriental). An aromatic powdery spice.

Nhoque (Brazilian). Potato fritters or pancakes made with cheese.

Niata. A South American breed of cattle.

Nibbit. Two pieces of oatmeal cake spread with butter and sandwiched together.

Nibble. (1) To take little bites; to bite away little by little. (2) A snack.

Niboshi (Japanese). Small dried sardines.

Nibs. Small pointed pieces of crushed cacao beans. *Almond nibs* are small cube-shaped fragments of whole almonds. *Cocoa nibs* are the fragments of cacao beans after roasting, removal of husk and germ, and slight crushing. *Sugar nibs*, small accumulations of sugar crystals forming little sharp-angled pellets, are used mainly for decoration.

Nicaragua. *See* Central America.

Nickel Silver; German Silver. An alloy of zinc, copper, and nickel used for flat tableware; it contains no silver.

Niçoise. In the style of French Mediterranean cooking in the Nice area; applied mainly to fish and salads: cooked or served with olive oil, tomatoes, garlic, black olives, and often with capers and anchovies.

Nidor. Any strong odor; the odor of cooked food.

Nids. Nests; often made of potatoes, etc.

Nids d'Hirondelles de Chine (French). Chinese birds' nests. *See* Birds' Nests.

Niederhaus. A wine village in the Nahe region of Germany. *See* Germany, The Wines of.

Nieheimer. A slightly salty sour-milk cheese, usually containing caraway seeds, and packed with hops for curing; made in Westphalia, Germany.

Nier (Dutch). Kidney.

Nicren (German). Kidneys.

Niersteiner. A white wine produced at Nierstein, Germany. *See also* Germany, The Wines of.

Niet te Gaar (Dutch). Rare; not too well cooked.

Nigella. A genus·of herbs. The seeds of species are used as a condiment and in making pickles; found in European and Eastern countries.

Niger-Seed Oil. Oil expressed from the seeds of a plant similar to the sunflower. It can be deodorized and used in food.

Nightcap. An alcoholic drink taken late at night, theoretically to induce sleep.

Nightshade; Brèdes. Any of a number of plants; the *deadly nightshade*, a belladonna, was formerly considered poisonous. The green leaves of other nightshades are used like spinach in the West Indies and elsewhere.

Nimono (Japanese). Boiled foods.

Nine-Eyes. The lamprey, a species of eel; besides its two eyes it has seven small holes on its head.

Ninon Sauce. A sauce prepared with vinegar, peanut oil, hard-cooked eggs, shallots, mustard, and spices; served with vegetables, especially artichokes.

Niños Envueltos (Argentinian). Stuffed meat shaped into rolls.

Niolo, Fromage du. A Corsican cow's-milk cheese with a soft texture and piquant flavor; good from October to May.

Niolos (Portuguese). Brains.

Nip. A half pint of any liquor or wine; a small quantity of spirits, usually less than a glass; a very small bottle of champagne containing one drink.

Nipa. A drink obtained from the nipa palm.

Nipper (British). The bluefish.

Nipperkin. A measure for liquors equivalent to a half-pint or less.

Nippitate. Ale or other liquor of prime quality and strength.

Nipplewort. A bitter weed similar to the dandelion

that may be used in salads or may be cooked with other vegetables.

Níspero (Latin American). Sapodilla, a tropical fruit with a brownish skin and beige flesh.

Níspero dc Batata (Latin American). Mashed sweet potato shaped into balls to resemble the *níspero* fruit or sapodilla.

Níspero del Japón (Latin American). Loquat.

Nitrogen. The chemical element in protein which is essential to human life. A gaseous element, it is odorless, colorless, and tasteless. At its boiling point it changes into a liquid, at its melting point into a crystalline white solid.

Nitta. A West African tree whose pods contain edible pulp and seeds.

Niu Jou (Chinese). Beef.

Nivernais. (1) Usually a *sauce allemande*, possibly with fresh vegetables, especially carrots. (2) Fresh vegetables added to any dish. (3) In chicken preparations, served with small dumplings.

Nivernaise, À la. Garnished with glazed onions and carrots cut olive-shape.

Nivette. A variety of peach.

Njure (Swedish). Kidney.

Njursauté (Swedish). Sautéed kidney.

Nocake. Corn parched and pounded into meal; formerly used by North American Indians while on the move.

Noce (French). A wedding; a wedding feast.

Noce Moscata (Italian). Nutmeg.

Nocera. A sparkling water bottled in Italy.

Noci (Italian). Nuts.

Nocillo. An Italian cordial made with nuts.

Nocino. An Italian liqueur prepared with nuts, similar to Nocillo.

No-Cow (West Indian, Colloquial). A drink of coconut water.

Nødder (Danish). Nuts.

Nødder Terte (Norwegian). Nut tart.

Noekkelost; Noekkleost. A hard Norwegian cheese whose taste is similar to that of Edam; made from partly skimmed milk, spiced with cumin seeds, cloves, and sometimes caraway seeds. In loaf form it may weigh 18–32 pounds.

Noël Red-Claret Punch. A wine punch for the Christmas season; its ingredients are flamed in a darkened room just before serving.

Noeuds (Belgian). A heavily spiced biscuit.

Nog. (1) Any mixed drink made of beaten eggs and liquor; nogg. (2) (British) A strong beer brewed in England.

Noggin (British). (1) A small mug or cup. (2) A small quantity of liquor, usually a quarter of a pint.

Noisette (French). (1) A small round piece of lean meat, such as lamb, beef, or veal tenderloins, with the bone and fat removed. (2) Pastry creams or cakes containing or flavored with roasted nuts, particularly hazelnuts or hazelnut praline paste.

> **Noisette d'Agneau.** Small cut of lamb from the loin fillets.

> **Noisette de Boeuf.** Small cut of steak.

> **Noisette de Porc.** Small cut of pork taken from the back and treated like beef.

Noisette Potatoes. Potatoes cut with a ball scoop to the size and shape of a hazelnut and browned in butter.

Noisettine. A cake, or small cakes, made of a short pastry and hazelnut cream; like a noisette cake, but smaller.

Noix (French). Walnut.

Noix de Brésil (French). Brazil nut.

Noix de Coco. Coconut.

Noix de Veau. Cuts of meat taken from the leg of veal; a classic preparation is *à la paysanne,* with onions, carrots, and bacon.

Noizi Nanyama. A side dish, made in Zanzibar, with bananas, onions, tomatoes, and coconut milk; usually served with meat dishes.

Nokhodchi (Iranian). A puffed pea with a nutlike flavor.

Nolet. *See* Naulet.

Noll (British). A dull, drunken person.

Nonat; Nonnat. A very small Mediterranean fish, similar to the whitebait, that must be eaten when fresh and is best when deep-fat fried.

Nonda. An Australian tree of the rose family that yields an edible fruit.

Nonnette (French). Small round glazed spice cakes, usually gingerbread or anise-flavored, the best of which are made in Dijon and Rheims.

Nonpareilles. (1) Bits of colored sugar used for decorating cakes and desserts. (2) Capers grown in Provence. (3) Large slightly acid pears.

Noodles. Long narrow strips of a dried paste usually made from wheat flour and eggs. They may be made at home but can also be bought packaged. Egg noodles are required by United States law to contain a specific quantity of egg yolks.

Noot (Dutch). Nut.

Nopal. (1) An African and Middle Eastern fig. (2) (Spanish) Prickly pear, an edible cactus.

Nopales; Nopalitos (Mexican). Edible leaves of the prickly-pear cactus.

Noques; Nocken (Alsatian). Small dumplings stuffed with a forcemeat and served in soup or eaten sprinkled with bread crumbs, grated cheese, and browned butter.

Noques à la Viennoise. Dessert dumplings served in a cold or hot custard.

Nordost. A white salty, smoky, medium-soft Swedish cheese.

Norfolk Capon. A red herring, found in British waters.

Norfolk Plover. The stone curlew, a small edible bird.

Norfolk Spoon Dumplings (British). Dumplings made from a firm batter consisting of milk, flour, and eggs and cooked in boiling water; served with gravy or eaten as a dessert with butter and sugar or syrup.

Nori. A purple sheet of edible seaweed, used in Japan for making *sushi,* a classic rice-and-fish preparation, and for decorating foods.

Normande, À la. "In Normandy style." Usually with apple flavor; prepared with milk, cream, butter, apples, cider, and apple brandy. Of fish, braised in white wine.

Normandy Pippins. Peeled, pre-cooked, dried apples.

North China Congou. A strong, fragrant, black tea with a rich, full-bodied taste.

North Country Sweet Pie (British). A deep-dish pie made with lamb chops, currants, raisins, salt, pepper, mace, nutmeg, sugar, and lemon juice.

Northern Duluth Wheat. A strong red wheat, generally known as *Northern Spring wheat,* whose small, plump, hard grains produce flour with a high percentage of good-quality gluten.

North Wilts (British). A creamy, excellent-tasting cheddar-type cheese.

Norvégien (French). A pastry flavored with sweet almonds, blanched apricot kernels, and kirsch and baked in round buttered molds.

Norvégienne (French). Any dessert, similar to a Baked Alaska, in which ice cream, enclosed in a hot, nonconductive exterior, such as beaten egg whites, does not melt during the few minutes of baking.

Norway. Breakfast (frokost), served at about 8 o'clock, consists of a table laden with cold fish and meat dishes as well as the more usual breakfast items, hot cereal, eggs, etc. In recent years, more and more Norwegians are developing the Continental breakfast habit, that is, of having a kaffe-complet, rolls, butter, and coffee. The midday meal, called middag, is a hot meal, usually consisting of soup, meat or fish, and dessert. In summer most Norwegians begin their evening meal, aftens, late in the afternoon in order to be free to enjoy the brilliant sunshine. Aftens may be simple or it may be a repetition of the breakfast koldtbord, with additional selections and one hot dish.

The strong drink of the country is aquavit: the best brand is Lindje. Also popular is fruktvin, fruit wine. The local beers are quite good but do not measure up to those of Denmark and Holland, although otherwise of excellent quality. Wines are important only to the well-to-do city people and are seldom seen in rural areas.

The Norwegians enjoy herring, and many people eat it daily because they like it and also because it is available at a low price. It is eaten raw, pickled, fried, baked, smoked, and is even made into a herring soup, sildegryn. Fish is extraordinary and exceptional, particularly salmon and trout. Smoked salmon, though not quite the equal of the Scotch, is very good. Incidentally, the Norwegians often prepare rakørret-raketrout, or salted trout permitted to overripen, which is recommended only to the gastronomically brave. Norwegian soups tend to be rich and creamy, satisfying in cold weather. Steaks or chops are seldom served, but lamb is rather common. Pork is probably the favorite meat. Game of all sorts is routine here, and rensdyrstek, reindeer steak, is first among these. However, elk and bear are reasonably common. Game birds are excellent, the ptarmigan being the best. The Norwegians love cheese, and gammelost, made of cow's milk, and gjetost, an amber-colored goat's-milk cheese, are the most popular. There is a national fondness for crunchy flat breads.

Norwegians love cakes, especially coffee cakes, but these seldom appear at mealtime, being reserved for teatime or late evening. Berries, in season for a very brief time, are superb. Strawberries, of course, are flavorsome, but even better are the cloudberries, yellowish, raspberry-like berries with very hard seeds.

Norwegian Lobster. A lobster, found along the coast of Norway, similar to the ordinary Atlantic lobster but with a peculiar extension of the shell between the eyes.

Nor'wester. A glass of strong liquor.

Nose. The bouquet or aroma of wine.

Nose-Smart (British). Another name for the plant cress.

Nostrale. A rennet cow's-milk cheese made in the mountains of northwestern Italy. A hard variety is produced in the spring when the flocks are grazing in the valleys, and a soft kind is made in summer when the cattle are pastured in the mountains.

Note. A cow's period of lactation.

No-Time Dough (British). Dough made with sufficient yeast to rise as soon as it has been mixed, with no time needed for fermentation.

Notrushki (Russian). Bread flavored with Taworog cheese.

Nottingham Jars (British). Glazed earthenware stew pots.

Nougat. A hard, chewy confection made of honey or sugar syrup and almonds.

Nougatine. A chocolate-almond cube layered with apricots and nuts.

Nouilles (French). Noodles.

Nouilles Fraîches. Fresh homemade noodles.

Nouilles Grand'mère. Boiled noodles with a sauce of mushrooms, pieces of bacon, croutons, and chives.

Nouilles Polonaise. Boiled noodles with bread

crumbs, melted butter, and chopped hard-cooked eggs.

Nouillettes au Gratin. Very fine noodles baked with cheese, bread crumbs, and melted butter.

Nourish. To provide with food and sustenance.

Nourishment. That which nourishes or sustains, such as food or drink.

Nouriture (French). Nourishment; sustenance; food.

Nourrir (French). To enrich by adding butter, cream, oil, etc., to other ingredients.

Nova Scotia Salmon. A very delicate smoked salmon originally prepared in Nova Scotia but now made in the United States.

Nova Scotia Sprats. *See* Digby Chicks.

Nowt (British). Cattle or oxen.

Noxipan. A paste made with hazelnuts; used for cakes and chocolate fillings.

Noyau. A French afterdinner liqueur made by infusing in brandy the pits or stones of cherry, peach, or apricot to produce different flavors.

Noyau Rosé. A pink sweet nut-flavored French liqueur.

Noz (Portuguese). Nut.

N.P.U. *Ne plus ultra*, "nothing better"; the term represents a boast of a wine bottler in reference to his wine.

Nubbin. A small or imperfect ear of corn.

Nuciform. Nut-shaped.

Nuculanium. (1) In the interior of a fleshy fruit, a hard nutlike case enclosing several seeds. (2) A hard-shelled fleshy fruit.

Nudeln (German). Noodles.

Nudelsuppe (German). Noodle soup.

Nueces. (Spanish). Walnuts; nuts.

Nuez Moscada (Spanish). Nutmeg.

Nuits, Fromage de. A French cow's-milk cheese that is eaten fresh or is slightly aged in leaves or vines.

Nuits-Saint-Georges. A red-wine region of Burgundy, France. The wines are good but seldom great; the taste and color are very pleasing. *See also* France, The Wines of.

Numbles. The inner organs (intestines, liver, etc.) of a deer; used for food.

Nuncheon (Obsolete). In medieval times, a light refreshment of liquor or a snack.

Nun's Toast. Pan-fried bread, as French toast.

Nuoc Nam. A very pungent, highly spiced Southeast Asian flavoring ingredient.

Nuss (German). Nut.

Nusskuchen (German). Nutcake.

Nut. One of many varieties of fruit having a separate casing or shell and an edible kernel or meat. Nuts have a high, concentrated nutritive value, containing protein, starch, and fat. Those cultivated in the United States include the peanut (which is actually a bean, or the seed of an herb and matures underground), the English walnut, pecan, almond, and filbert. The United States imports the Brazil nut from South America, the cashew from India, and the chestnut from France and Italy. Coconut comes from most tropical regions.

Nut Bread. Numerous varieties of bread made by mixing nuts and sometimes raisins or other fruits into baking-powder or yeast doughs.

Nut Butter. A thick spread made by grinding and pressing a variety of blanched nuts, peanut butter being the most popular.

Nutcracker. A device for opening nuts by cracking their shells by pressure. The simplest kind

consists of two arms hinged at one end. The nut is placed between the arms and the shell is broken when the arms are squeezed together. A nutcracker is also handy for cracking lobster claws.

Nutgall. A small fruit which grows on bushes in certain subtropical regions; its taste is only passable.

Nut Margarine. A spread made chiefly from the oil of peanut, palm, or coconut.

Nutmeal. Meal produced by grinding the kernels of nuts. Owing to the oiliness of nuts the product is usually in the form of a paste, such as peanut butter, unless most of the oil is extracted before grinding.

Nutmeg. The aromatic seed of an evergreen tree native to the Molucca Islands. The tree also yields mace which comes from a lacy filament between the outer husk and the hard inner shell of the nutmeg proper. Mace is sun-dried. The nutmeg pits are cured over slow-burning fires for several weeks. Most nutmeg is sold in ground form and is used extensively in confections, baked products, puddings, fruit pies, and beverages. *See also* Mace.

Nutmeg Apple. The fruit of the nutmeg tree containing the mace.

Nutmeg Butter. A solid, fatty, reddish brown substance obtained by grinding refuse nutmegs to a fine paste.

Nutmegged. Flavored with nutmeg.

Nutmeg Pigeon. A white pigeon native to Burma and Ceylon; used for food.

Nut Palm. An Australian palm that bears edible nuts.

Nut Pastry. Pastry in which finely ground nut meats are substituted for half the shortening called for in any recipe for a plain pie crust; particularly good with a cream filling.

Nut Pick. A small sharp-pointed instrument for extracting nut meats from broken shells.

Nutrient. A substance that serves as nourishment.

Nutriment. Food; sustenance; nourishment.

Nutrition. (1) All foods. (2) The physical processes by which food is converted into body tissue.

Nutritious. Supplying or serving as nourishment.

Nutritive. Nourishing; nutritious.

Nutshell. The exterior covering or shell of a nut.

Nutting. The gathering of nuts.

Nutty. Abounding in nuts; having a nutlike taste; pleasant and flavorful.

Nuwara. A highly aromatic black tea of Ceylon.

N.V. Nonvintage. Of wine, from a nonvintage year.

Nymphes. Frogs' legs; the term appears on the menus of restaurants serving delicacies and specialties.

Nyre (Danish). Kidney.

Nyresaute (Norwegian). Sautéed kidneys.

Nyrøket Laks (Norwegian). Smoked salmon.

O

Oast. A kiln used to dry hops.

Oast House. A building in which kilns dry malt and hops.

Oaten. Containing oatmeal or grains of oats.

Oatmeal. A cereal consisting of the steamed and flattened grains of husked oats.

Oatmeal Cookies. Small cookies or cakes made of oatmeal.

Oatmeal Saucer. A wide, deep bowl used for an individual serving of oatmeal or other cereals.

Oats. One of the most widely cultivated cereals, serving as fodder for livestock as well as food for humans. It flourishes in colder and wetter climates than other grains, and will grow in climates too hot for wheat or rye. Poor soil is no detriment. Oats for cooking purposes are husked and flattened out into a product known as *rolled oats*. Because oatmeal flour has a low gluten content, and, when mixed with water, does not make a proper dough, it is rarely used for bread.

Oba. An African mango whose stone has a cocoalike flavor.

Oberemmel. A wine village of the Saar region, Germany. *See* Germany, The Wines of.

Ober-Haardt. Part of the Pfalz wine district of Germany. *See* Germany, The Wines of.

Obese. Extra fleshy; very fat.

Obesity. The condition of being very fat.

Oblade. A small Mediterranean fish of fair quality; can be boiled or fried.

Oble. A crisp wafer made of fine wheat flour, often sweetened with honey.

Oblea (Mexican). A thin cracker or wafer used as a base for rich desserts.

Oblete. A thin cake.

Obley. A wafer or altar bread.

O'Brien Potatoes. Small diced potatoes fried with onions and green peppers.

Obst (German). Fruit.

Oca (Italian). Goose.

Oca; Occa; Oka. A South American plant native to Peru that produces walnut-size edible tubers with a flavor similar to that of the sweet potato.

Ocean Perch. The redfish.

Ochsen (German). Oxen.

   Ochsenbraten. Roast beef.

   Ochsenfleisch. Beef.

   Ochsenlende. Fillet of beef.

   Ochsenniere. Beef kidney.

   Ochsenschwanz. Oxtail.

   Ochsenzunge. Ox tongue.

Ochsenmaulsalat (German). A cold-meat salad made with onions and vinegar.

Ockfen. A wine village in the Saar district of Germany. *See* Germany, The Wines of.

Octopus. A marine cephalopod, some species of which are edible. The tough flesh must be tenderized and well cooked, usually by prolonged boiling; it is then sometimes deep-fried.

Ödåkra. A Swedish aquavit with a somewhat spicy taste.

Oenin. A glycoside obtained from the skin of purple grapes.

Oenology. The study or knowledge of wine.

Oenometer. An alcoholometer.

Oenophilist. A lover of wines.

Oenothera. Evening primrose; the roots of one species can be cooked and eaten as a vegetable.

Oester (Dutch). Oyster.

Oestrich. A wine village of the Rheingau region of Germany. *See* Germany, The Wines of.

Oeufs (French). Eggs.

   Oeufs Aigre au Lard. Fried eggs served on bacon with a few drops of vinegar on top.

   Oeufs à la Neige. Floating island; a creamy cold custard dessert made with eggs, milk, sugar, and flavorings and topped with a poached meringue.

   Oeufs à la Turque. Any of several egg dishes;

usually scrambled eggs served with tomatoes and chicken livers; may also be prepared with rice and livers.

Oeufs Alsacienne. Fried eggs served with sausages, fried potatoes, and sauerkraut.

Oeufs Anglaise. Soft-cooked eggs; fried eggs with fried toast and ham; poached eggs with a sort of cheese sauce.

Oeufs aux Écrivisses. Eggs prepared in a variety of fashions but always served with crawfish.

Oeufs Bercy. ·Fried eggs with sausages and tomato sauce.

Oeufs Bouchère. Fried eggs with sausages and green peas; soft-cooked eggs served in a pastry shell with beef marrow.

Oeufs Bretonnes. Eggs stuffed with a mixture of onions, mushrooms, leeks, and spices.

Oeufs d'Alose. Shad roe.

Oeufs Durs. Hard-cooked eggs.

Oeufs Fine Herbes. An egg preparation with chopped chives, parsley, or other appropriate herbs.

Oeufs Fondue. Scrambled eggs with grated Emmental cheese.

Oeufs Joinville. Scrambled eggs with shellfish and mushrooms, usually served in a pastry shell.

Oeufs Meyerbeer. Fried eggs with kidneys, served with tomato sauce.

Oeufs Mollet. Whole medium-cooked eggs with the shells removed. The best way to prepare them is to pour boiling water over the eggs, return the water to a boil, simmer the eggs 5 minutes, remove the eggs and immediately run cold water over them; when they are cool enough to handle, remove the shells by cracking them with the back of a knife. Work slowly to avoid breaking the white. Oeufs Mollet are used for *eggs in aspic*, and can be used wherever poached eggs are specified.

Oeufs Mornay. Scrambled or poached eggs covered with Mornay Sauce.

Oeufs Parisienne. Eggs baked with mushrooms, truffles, and finely ground chicken.

Oeufs Périgourdine. Eggs baked with finely ground goose liver and truffles.

Oeufs Petit-Duc. Soft-cooked eggs or fried eggs served with mushrooms and grated horseradish.

Oeufs de Pluvier. Plovers' eggs.

Oeufs Provençale. Eggs served with sliced sautéed tomatoes.

Oeufs Toupinel. Baked potatoes carefully scooped from their shells, mashed with butter and a little cream, mixed with truffles and strips of ham, then returned to the shells; a poached egg is added to each potato, covered with Mornay Sauce, and browned in the oven.

Oeufs Zingara. Eggs served with ham and tomato sauce.

Offal. (1) The inferior parts of an animal cut off in dressing meat. (2) Inferior or low-priced fish.

Offal, Beef. All variety meats, including liver, heart, kidney, and sweetbreads.

Off-Corn (British). Corn unfit for use.

Offene Torte (German). Open pastry tart.

Officinal Pastilles (French). Jujubes, small pellets of hard-gum consistency, pleasantly flavored as a confection.

Ogliastra. A white Sardinian wine, made in both dry and sweet varieties.

Ognonnade; Oignonade. Any dish containing a large proportion of onions; also, a preparation of sautéed onions.

Ogo. A reef fish, found in Fijian waters, with a fair taste but poor texture.

Oignonade (French). (1) Finely chopped onions sautéed in butter and white wine; used chiefly as a base for stew. (2) A dish with an onion flavor.

Oignonet (French). A delicious summer pear shaped somewhat like an onion.

Oil. Any one of a number of fatty, thick, greasy liquids, high in calories, and used in cooking, and as a food. A substance that leaves a greasy stain on cloth or paper, it is liquid at normal temperatures and soluble in alcohol but not in water. The word "oil" is derived from "olive." Many varieties of oil are used for cooking and in salads. The most common are as follows:

Coconut oil—used principally in tropical countries.

Corn oil—one of the most popular vegetable oils.

Cottonseed oil—when purified and rendered

colorless, used as an ingredient for vegetable cooking fats and margarine.

Olive oil—considered by some gourmets the best oil for culinary use.

Peanut oil—tasteless and odorless; popular in oriental countries.

Palm oil—used for cooking in Africa.

Safflower oil—a favorite among health faddists for its desirable effect upon cholesterol.

Oille (French). A variety of ingredients, such as meat, vegetables, and fruit, cooked in liquid in a kettle; similar to Spanish *cocido*.

Oil-Mill. (1) A machine that crushes fruits and seeds to extract the oil. (2) The factory housing such machines.

Oil Nut. Large nuts and seeds that yield oil; also the plants that produce them.

Oil of Wintergreen. An edible oil extracted from the leaves of a small American evergreen plant and used to flavor candies and chewing gum.

Oil Range. A stove that uses kerosene as fuel.

Oilseed. The wide variety of seeds grown as sources of oils, such as cottonseed, sesame, peanut, sunflower, soya, palm, or any seed yielding an edible oil. After extraction of the oil the residue, the so-called seed cake, is a valuable source of protein.

Oily. Containing oil; greasy or covered with oil.

Oiseaux sans Tête (French). "Birds without heads." Very thin slices of meat spread with a well-seasoned stuffing and rolled up; usually braised.

Oison (French). A young goose or gosling.

Ojen. A rather dry Spanish cordial, made chiefly from star aniseed.

Ojo Gordo (Spanish). Skipjack, a tropical fish.

Oka. (1) *La Trappe*, a medium-soft Canadian cheese made by Trappist monks; similar to Port du Salut. (2) An irregular-shaped, walnut-size tuber known as *occa* or *oxalis*; usually parboiled in salted water, then cooked in butter. In France it is usually made into a purée with cream. (3) (Middle Eastern) A measure of food weight equal to 2¾ pounds.

Oke of Cappadocia. *See* Ambrosia.

Okolehao. A very potent Hawaiian whisky made from a fermented mixture of sugar-cane molasses, Koji rice lees, the juice of baked taro root, and water. The distilled product is dark and has a smoky taste and aroma.

Okra. An ancient vegetable, native to Africa, okra was cooked by Egyptian housewives at the time Antony was courting Cleopatra. It may have been brought to the United States by French settlers in the 18th century, or slave boats may have brought it from Congo regions to the West Indies, thence to the United States.

The okra plant thrives only in southern climates. The part that is eaten is the ridged five-sided pod. If the pod measures more than 3 inches, the vegetable fibers will be tough and the okra is not tender enough for good eating.

Good-quality okra should be fresh and clean-looking. The pods should snap easily when broken. They should be handled carefully, not squeezed tightly.

Okra has a mucilaginous quality. When the vegetable is cut, a stringy kind of liquid sometimes adheres to the knife. When the vegetable is simmered for a short time in water, as is done when okra is stewed with tomatoes and onions to make a favorite southern concoction, the finished product has a gummy consistency, but when okra is fried or simmered a long time, as in Brunswick stew or gumbo, the gumminess disappears.

Okra may be either shallow or deep-fat fried. In the South it is known as "poor man's oysters."

Okse (Danish). Oxen.

    Oksebryst, Kogt. Boiled breast of beef.

    Oksehaleragout. Oxtail stew.

    Oksekoedsuppe. Beef soup.

    Oksesteg. Beef.

    Oksetunge. Beef tongue.

Okse (Norwegian). Oxen.

    Oksefilet. Fillet of beef.

    Oksestek. Roast beef.

Øl (Danish). Beer.

Öl (Norwegian, Swedish). Beer.

Old English Cheese. The brand name of a well-known processed cheese.

Old-Fashioned. One of America's favorite cocktails, made of whisky, bitters, fruit, and sugar; served in a specially shaped glass.

Old Heidelberg. Similar to Liederkranz.

Oldwife. A variety of fishes of the sea bream, alewife, menhaden, and wrasse families.

Oleaginous. Having the properties of oil.

Oleic Acid. An acid found in most fats; it has a partial degree of saturation. *See also* Hydrogenated Fats; Saturated Fats; Linoleic Acid.

Oleomargarine; Margarine. A butter substitute usually made from vegetable oils.

Oleron, Fromage d'. A fresh curd ewe's-milk cheese usually served plain or with cream and sugar or a caramel syrup.

Oliebollen (Dutch). Fried dumplings.

Olijf (Dutch). Olive.

Olio. (1) Various vegetables and meats highly spiced and stewed or boiled together. (2) (Italian) Oil.

Oliva (Italian). Olive.

    Oliva Ripiene. Stuffed olives.

Olive. The fruit of the olive tree, a prized food since ancient times. Its meat has a high calorie content and is very nutritious. The olive is native to the eastern Mediterranean but is now grown in most tropical and subtropical countries. For centuries it has been a staple crop of Greece, Italy, France, and Spain, and the tree was introduced into Mexico and California by Spanish Jesuit missionaries in the 17th century.

    The sweet, nutlike oil pressed from the ripe olive is the chief cooking, frying, and salad oil in many countries, and is a favorite of gourmets. The fruit may be eaten ripe or it may be salted, cured, or pickled in a variety of fashions. Green olives are picked before they are quite ripe. In preparation for the market they are frequently pitted and stuffed with pimiento or anchovy. Black olives are fully ripe when harvested. Ripe olives were first canned in the United States in 1901. Of the many varieties, the best-known in this country are:

Mission—A firm, slightly bitter flesh, but easy to pickle. It makes one of the best olive oils, both in quantity and quality, and as a result more than half of the olives cultivated in California are of this type.

Ascalano—The largest of California olives, a native of Italy. It has a very small pit and slight color even when ripe. The flesh is tender, and

much care is necessary during the pickling process.

Manzanillo I—Of Spanish origin, this olive is deep-colored and bitter when ripe and requires a treatment of lye solution during its curing process.

Manzanillo II—A variety usually processed in Spain. Of excellent quality but usually too small for the American market.

Sevillano—The large Queen olives from Spain are of this type, deeply colored with a big pit, and particularly suited for pickling in both green and black varieties.

Olive, Dried. A variety of olive that is heavily salted and allowed to dry; used in Chinese cookery.

Olive Cream Cheese. A soft cream cheese containing pieces of green olives.

Oliven (German). Olives.

Olive Oil. The pale yellow oil extracted from olives. An excellent oil for cooking or for salads. There are different grades, however. "Pure" or "virgin" oil, extracted cold from the ripe fruit, tends to be greenish and will keep fresh a long time. Second-rate oil, extracted under heat from olive pulp and seeds, is whitish and becomes rancid more quickly. Olive oil is produced in quantity in Italy, Spain, France, and California.

Oliver (British). Bath Oliver biscuit, a semisweet cooky, first made by a Mr. Oliver in the early 19th century.

Olives. Thick slices of veal or beef rolled up with herbs and onions and cooked in a brown sauce.

Olivet. A rather soft sheep's-milk cheese produced in Orléans, France. When fresh, it is mild and creamy. *Olivet-Bleu* is a partly ripened, somewhat salty blue cheese. *Olivet-Cendré* is allowed to mature in ashes.

Olivetti (Italian). Small slices of veal cooked in white wine.

Olla (Spanish). (1) A peasant-style stew. (2) A large earthenware cooking pot.

Olla Podrida (Spanish). The national soup of Spain, actually more like a stew, made of almost any combination of meats and vegetables, but Spanish sausages (*chorizos*) and chick-peas are standard ingredients.

Ollebrød. (1) (Danish) Beer-and-bread soup. (2) (Norwegian) Beer soup.

Olmützer Quargel. An Austrian soft, rather salty skim-milk cheese prepared in very small sizes and often dropped into beer.

Oloroso. A golden, full-bodied, sweet Spanish sherry. *See* Spain, The Wines of.

Oman's Brew. Arabian-style coffee, usually prepared with cardamom seeds.

Omble (French). Three varieties of trout: the *omble commun*, found in rivers; the *omble chevalier*, caught in lakes; the *omble de mer*, found in the sea. *See* Omble Chevalier.

Omble Chevalier. A delicate-tasting fish found in the lakes of Switzerland and the Savoy district of France, believed to be related to the salmon-char family.

Ombre (French). The grayling, a freshwater fish that resembles a trout but is in the salmon family. The flesh has a thyme flavor.

Omelet; Omelette. Eggs beaten to a froth and cooked in a sizzling skillet; served as a main course or as dessert, depending on the filling.

Omelette Agnès Sorel. An omelet filled with mushrooms and ground chicken.

Omelette à la Normande. A sweet omelet stuffed with cooked apples in a sauce of cream and Calvados.

Omelette Américaine. An omelet made with tomatoes, bacon, and mushrooms, sometimes filled with shellfish.

Omelette Bayonnaise. An omelet made with a ham-and-mushroom mixture.

Omelette Demidoff. An omelet filled with artichokes.

Omelette Fourée. A stuffed omelet.

Omelette Jurassienne. An omelet with chopped bacon, cheese, potatoes, and shallots.

Omelette Lorraine. An omelet made with Swiss cheese, cream, tarragon and topped with slices of bacon.

Omelette Mirabeau. An omelet with olives and anchovies.

Omelette Norvégienne. Ice cream covered with meringue and baked in the oven; Baked Alaska; omelette surprise.

Omelette Provençale. An omelet filled with anchovies and spinach, or with garlic, tomatoes, and onions.

Omelette Rossini (Italian). An omelet garnished with truffles and foie gras, often served with a truffle sauce.

Omelette Russe (French). An omelet garnished with caviar.

Omelette Surprise. Ice cream and meringue, browned on top; Baked Alaska.

Omelette Turbigo. An omelet with ham, sausages, and tomatoes.

Omer. A Hebrew food measure equal to slightly more than 5 pints.

Omers. A shellfish found on the rocks of the Channel Islands near England; commonly called the *sea-ear* because the shell resembles the shape of an ear; served locally like scallops.

Omnisbus. A restaurant apprentice whose duties include relaying orders and carrying dishes.

Omnivorous. Disposed to eat all kinds of food.

Omophagia. Appetite for raw food, especially raw flesh.

One-Mix. A cake-mixing method in which all the ingredients are combined and beaten at one time.

Onion. A plant, originating in Asia, with an edible bulb that is pungent both in taste and odor. It has been cultivated since ancient times and at one time was worshiped in Egypt. Leek, chive, garlic, and shallot belong to the onion family, as does the scallion, the young green onion. Scallions are marketed in bunches and may be eaten raw, cut up for salads, or may be boiled and served like asparagus. Mature onions are dried before marketing and should be stored in a cool, dry place to prevent sprouting. The small white or yellow variety is called *pearl* or *button* onion. The types known commonly as *Spanish* or *Bermuda* are very large, somewhat flatter, and have a relatively mild, sweet flavor. They are white, yellow, or red.

Onopordon. A thistlelike plant, one species of which is an edible wild artichoke.

Onos. A Mediterranean fish known as *rockling*; rarely eaten.

Onoto. *Annatto* or *achiote*, the red coloring ingredient used in cooking in Latin countries.

On Tap. Beer or ale in a cask or barrel ready to be sold.

Ontbijt (Dutch). Breakfast.

Ooidal. Egg-shaped.

Oolakan; Oolachan. The candlefish found in the northwestern United States and Canada.

Oolong. (1) A semifermented tea made of a mixture of fully fermented black and unfermented green teas, produced in China and Formosa, those from the latter country usually being of higher quality. (2) (Chinese, Colloquial) Any kind of tea.

Oopak. A black Chinese tea.

Ooze. Sap or juice of a tree, fruit, or plant.

O.P. Aquavit. A Swedish aquavit with a caraway taste.

Opah; Kingfish; Moonfish. A large, comparatively scarce, brilliantly colored fish of the mackerel family; found in the North Atlantic.

Open Tart. A tart shell of short or puff pastry baked without a top. The baked shell is often later filled with fresh or cooked fruit or with custard or another mixture.

Operm. A Continental liqueur with black-currant flavor.

Ophidium. An eel-like Mediterranean fish sometimes used in bouillabaisse.

Oplagt Melk (Norwegian). Clabbered or soured milk.

Opossum. A nocturnal animal native to the southern United States; usually roasted or made into a 'possum stew.

Oppenheim. A wine village of the Rheinhessen region of Germany. *See* Germany, The Wines of.

Opuntia. An Indian fig that grows on a cactus plant.

Oquassa Brook. A variety of trout.

Orach; Orache. Mountain spinach, French spinach, or sea-purslane. The leaves are prepared and eaten as are other green vegetables.

Orange. A green or golden citrus fruit widely cultivated in the countries bordering the Mediterranean and in Florida and California. It grows on a glossy-leaved tree, preceded by waxy-white fragrant blossoms which in the United States are associated with June weddings. The sweet orange was perhaps introduced into Europe from China, possibly by the Portuguese explorer Vasco da Gama. Important varieties include the *California navel*, which is round and deep gold in color and is seedless; it is so named for its navel-like formation at the end opposite the stem. The *Valencia orange* is lighter in color and has seeds. The *blood orange* has red flesh and redder skin. The *bitter orange*, or *bigarade*, is a native of India and was brought from Palestine to Italy by the Crusaders. It was first cultivated in Spain and North Africa by the Arabs.

Orangeade. A refreshing long drink made with orange juice, preferably freshly squeezed, plain or sparkling water, and sugar.

Orangeado (British). Candied orange rind.

Orangeat (French). Candied orange peel.

Orange Bitters. A popular flavoring for mixed drinks made of orange juice and peel.

Orange Blossom Water. A liquid with the aroma of orange blossoms; sometimes used in pastry or cakes.

Orange Butter. Cooked chopped whole orange sweetened and homogenized.

Orange Extract. An orange flavoring agent for confectionery.

Orange-Flower Oil. Oil (néroli) made from orange blossoms; used in confectionery and pastry.

Orange-Flower Water. Néroli oil is made from the flowers of the bitter orange by steam distillation. The condensed water layer from the distillation is orange-flower water. It is used in pastry, confections, and beverages.

Orange Ice. An ice flavored with orange; attractive when served in the skin of a half-orange whose edge has been serrated.

Orange Jelly. A jelly containing orange rind and juice.

Orange Juice. The liquid pressed from oranges.

Orange Peel. Crystallized or candied orange peel, used in pastry making and as a confection.

Orange Pekoe Tea. A black tea with small leaves produced in India and Ceylon.

Orange Pomander. A fresh orange studded with cloves; used to give a pleasing aroma to stored clothing and linens.

Orange Ratafia. A homemade cordial prepared from brandy and orange oils.

Orange Rockfish. A common food fish found off the coast of California.

Orangette. A small orange picked while about 1–1½ inches in diameter and preserved in vinegar to be used as a condiment.

Orangine (French). Orange cake.

Orasky. An English cordial made with whisky and flavored with orange.

Orata, Sergius. A noted Roman gourmet (141 B.C.–82 B.C.) who made oysters a popular food.

Orchard. Generally, a place where fruit trees, nut trees, sugar maples, and herbs grow. Also, a place where fruit trees are cultivated.

Orchard House (British). A greenhouse used to grow fruits out of season or to protect delicate fruits.

Oreanda. A Russian amber-colored dessert wine.

Orecchioni al Burro (Italian). Macaroni with butter and Parmesan cheese.

Oregano. Wild marjoram, an herb with a pungent smell and slightly bitter taste that blends well with veal, lamb, pork, eggs, and cheese.

Oregon Charr. A kind of trout.

Oreille de Porc (French). Pig's ear.

Oreiller de la Belle Aurore (French). An elaborate pâté made of veal, partridge, chicken, duck, pork, ham, rabbit, mushrooms, pistachios, and truffles, baked in pastry.

Oreillette (French). An ear-shaped apple fritter.

Organen (Dutch). Giblets.

Organic. Of food, produced naturally by plant or animal life; recommended by health-food devotees who disapprove of man-made nonorganic foods.

Organt. Wild marjoram, a wild herb.

Orge (French). Barley.

Orgeade. A refreshing soft drink made of sweet and bitter almonds.

Orgeat. A thick syrup made of orange-flower water, almonds, and barley, used for sweetening drinks.

Orientale, A l'. In oriental style or with oriental flavorings; prepared with garlic, tomatoes, peppers, and saffron.

Oriental Fromage. A salted white ewe's-milk cheese made in Middle Eastern countries; similar in taste to the Feta cheese of Greece.

Origan; Origanum. A genus of plants with aromatic leaves, including pot marjoram, sweet marjoram, wild marjoram, and dittany of Crete.

Original-Abfüllung (German). Original bottling. *See* Germany, The Wines of.

Orkney. A rather coarse Scotch cheese; it varies considerably according to the length of time it is allowed to ripen.

Orly. Ground fish formed into croquettes and fried; served with tomato sauce.

Ormeaux. Shellfish found along the coast of Brittany, France; sautéed like scallops.

Ormer. A shellfish somewhat like an abalone, abundant along parts of the English coast.

Oronge. A delicious edible wild mushroom found in European woods in the autumn; particularly good in chicken and meat casseroles.

Oropa. An Italian liqueur made with wild mountain herbs.

Osso Buco (Italian). Veal knuckle, usually prepared with tomatoes and white wine. It is served with *gremolada*—lemon rind, chopped parsley, and chopped garlic—added at the end of the cooking time.

Ost (Danish, Norwegian, Swedish). Cheese.

Osteanretning (Danish). Cheese tray.

Osteria. An Italian inn, hostelry, or low-priced restaurant.

Oster (Danish). Oyster.

Ostesauce (Danish). Cheese sauce.

Orozuz (Spanish). Licorice.

Orred (Danish). Trout.

Orret (Norwegian). Trout.

Orrys, Fromage d'; Castillon; Fromage de Gascony. A summertime cow's-milk cheese similar to Camembert, made in Foix, France.

Ort. Scrap of food left over from a meal.

Ortolan; Bunting. A very small European bird, highly prized for its delicate flavor; usually cooked wrapped in vine leaves and bacon, basted with butter, and served on toast with watercress. The birds are not drawn before cooking.

Orval. (1) A very sweet beer made in Belgium by Trappist monks. (2) An herb, a type of sage.

Orvieto. An excellent white wine, of both sweet and dry types, from the vineyards surrounding Orvieto, Italy. *See* Italy, The Wines of.

Oryx. A large African antelope that has fine-flavored meat.

Orzo (Italian). A kind of pasta about ⅓-inch in length, used chiefly in soups.

Osage Melon. A round melon with a gray rind and pink or green flesh; grown in many parts of the United States.

Os de Moëlle (French). Marrow bone.

Osetra; Osetra Malossol; Osetrova. A dark brown caviar only slightly inferior in taste to Beluga caviar.

Osmazone. The liquid extract of meat which contains the constituents that determine the taste and smell of the meat; the purest essence of meat.

Osoberry. The blue-black fruit of a small tree or shrub in the western United States.

Ossau, Fromage d'. A soft, lightly crusted white ewe's-milk cheese made in Béarn, France.

Osseter. A variety of sturgeon.

Ostiepek. A Czechoslovakian sheep's-milk cheese similar to Italy's Caciocavallo.

Ostion (Spanish). Oyster.

Ostra (Portuguese, Spanish). Oyster.

Ostracean. Pertaining to the oyster.

Ostrica (Italian). Oyster.

Ostrich. The meat of this bird was highly regarded in Roman times, but is now rarely eaten because it is tough and has little taste.

Ostron (Swedish). Oyster.

Ostsufflé (Swedish). Cheese soufflé.

Oswego. A pleasant-tasting cheddar-type cheese made in New York State.

Otaheite Apple. A Tahitian golden yellow fruit. The flavor of the pulp resembles that of the pineapple, but the rind tastes like turpentine.

Othellos. Rich tiny spongecakes hollowed in the center, sandwiched with fresh whipped cream or with liqueur-flavored custard brushed with melted apricot jam, dipped in fondant, and decorated.

Otrea Virginica. The scientific name for the common eastern oyster found chiefly along the middle eastern portion of the United States, especially around Maryland, Virginia, and the Chesapeake Bay area.

Oublie (French). A thin pastry; a dessert cooky.

Ouillat (French). A thin soup made of goose fat, garlic, onions, tomatoes, vinegar, bread, and seasonings; popular in Béarn.

Oukha (Russian). A fish-and-vegetable soup.

Oulade (French). A peasant soup made with potatoes, cabbage, sausage, and salt pork.

Ouliat (French). An onion soup made in the Basque region.

Ounce. A unit of measure. There are 32 ounces to a liquid quart and 16 ounces to the dry pound.

Oursins (French). Sea urchins; round, prickly shellfish with a delicate, reddish-purple, pulplike flesh which is eaten raw. To prepare, trim off the spikes, then cut away the flat side with scissors. Pour off the water and remove the intestine. The edible portion may be scooped out and eaten with a piece of bread, or plain.

Oust, Fromage d'. A soft, white, flavorsome Camembert made in Foix, France.

Outarde (French). Bustard, a large game bird.

Outdoor Cookery. A favorite American way of preparing food, including camp cookery, barbecues, campfire bakes, and the like. The custom originated during the 19th century when it was a favorite device of politicians anxious to draw large crowds. The food was usually simple but appetizing, consisting often of roasted meat, barbecued ribs, corn on the cob, stews of various game meats, watermelon, and other hearty, outdoor-type foods.

Outdrink. To finish a drink completely; to drink more than someone else.

Ouzo. An anise-flavored Greek apéritif resembling absinthe in taste and appearance; served before meals in tall glasses with ice and water.

Ovalbumin. The white of the egg, comprising 55 percent of the total solid content.

Ova Mellita (Roman). Eggs in a honey syrup; popular some 2,000 years ago.

Óvár. A mild, medium-soft Hungarian cow's-milk cheese with a brown-red exterior.

Ovčji Sir. A Yugoslavian firm sheep's-milk cheese.

Oven. A chamber in which food is baked, roasted, or broiled by means of dry heat. It may be of almost any size, shape, or form, built from a variety of materials, and it may utilize almost any efficient heat source. An oven can be warmed internally or externally and it may either be a separate unit or be incorporated in some other device. The so-called Dutch oven is a separate, usually portable unit, with its own heat source.

A constant, even, and exact temperature is

one of the keys to successful oven cookery. Standard oven temperatures, as used in most recipes, are as follows:

Slow .... 250°F.
Moderately slow .... 325°F.
Moderate .... 350°F.
Moderately hot .... 375°F.
Hot .... 400–425°F.
Very hot .... 450–500°F.

Oven Crown (British). The arched roof of the baking oven.

Oven Peel. A flat shovel-like piece of wood with a long handle, used for setting or drawing bread, trays of confectionery, etc., from an oven.

Oven-Ready. Ready to be put into the oven, as applied to poultry that has been plucked, has entrails removed, and needs no further cleaning.

Overripe Dough. Dough that has fermented too long.

Överste. A rather sweet Swedish aquavit.

Ovine. Belonging or pertaining to sheep.

Ovo (Portuguese). Egg.

    Ovos com Fiambre. Ham and eggs.

    Ovos Cozidos. Hard-cooked eggs.

    Ovos Escalfados. Poached eggs.

    Ovos Estrelados. Fried eggs.

    Ovos Mexidos. Scrambled eggs.

    Ovos Quentes. Soft-boiled eggs.

Ovocné Knedlíky (Czechoslovakian). Dumplings prepared with plums, prunes, or other fruit.

Ovoli (Italian). Salad of mushrooms and truffles.

Owunc (British, Obsolete). Oven; a medieval term.

Ox (British). Male cattle, especially beef.

Oxalis; Occa; Oka Plant. A tuberous vegetable with white flesh and a dark exterior, used like the potato. It tastes best when the tubers are allowed to dry for a few days after being harvested; the flavor resembles that of the Jerusalem artichoke.

Ox Antelope. The wild ox.

Ox Cheek. The flesh on the sides of an ox's head.

Oxfilet (Swedish). Fillet of steak.

Oxford Sauce (British). A sauce served with cold meats or venison; prepared from port wine, red-currant jelly, citrus-fruit rind and juice, and ginger, mustard, and shallots.

Ox Horn (Obsolete). The horn of an ox, sometimes used as a drinking container.

Oxkött (Swedish). Beef.

Ox Mushroom. A common large European mushroom.

Ox Palate. The thick white lining on the roof of an ox's mouth.

Oxsteck (Swedish). Rump steak.

Oxtail. The tail of a cow, steer, or ox; it contains very little meat but may be skinned and used to flavor soup; also served braised as a meat dish.

Ox Tongue. Beef tongue.

Oxtunga (Swedish). Beef tongue.

Oxymel. A syrup made of honey and vinegar.

Oyonnade (French). A stew made with goose; a specialty of Burgundy.

Oyster. A marine bivalve mollusk; usually eaten raw, but may be cooked in a number of ways and served hot or cold. The seafood is highly nutritious, containing vitamins, many organic salts, and a high proportion of iodine, all of which are easily assimilated.

Known to man since ancient times, oysters were a great favorite of the Greeks and Romans. After his conquest of Britain, Julius Caesar imported the delicacy in bags packed with snow and ice to embellish his Roman banquets. The American Indians also were hearty oyster eaters.

The United States has vast oyster beds and oyster fishing and farming is an important industry. Oysters from the Atlantic coast are in season from September through April, although the theory that oysters are inedible during breeding time—in months without an "R"—has no basis in scientific fact. Pacific coast oysters are marketed all year round.

The best-known American oysters include the Lynnhaven, Peconic, Mattituck, Robbins Island, Cape Cod, Chincoteague, Gardiner Island, Blue Point, and Bay Salt. In Canada, the Malpeque, from Prince Edward Island, has a considerable reputation with gourmets.

The best-known British varieties are the Colchester and the Whitstable. The best from France are the green Marenne and the Belon.

Oysters keep remarkably well under proper refrigeration and will remain edible in the shell for several months if they are chilled at a temperature below 41°F. Shelled oysters which have been properly chilled and kept at 32°F. will remain good for three weeks or longer. At room temperature they will spoil within two days, and a spoiled oyster can cause serious illness.

Before being opened, oysters should be washed thoroughly in cold water. To open, insert the point of a sharp knife into the hinged or pointed end and push the blade between the two shells until the muscle is cut and the valves begin to separate. Then run the knife around the shell and loosen the oyster.

Oyster Bank. A bed of oysters.

Oyster Bed. The place where oysters are bred or where they breed naturally.

Oyster Brood. Two-year-old oysters.

Oyster Catcher. The sea magpie. The young bird is tender and delicate in flavor.

Oyster Crab. A very small edible crab that lives inside an oyster's shell and feeds as the oyster draws in its own food.

Oysterette. A very small unleavened cracker often served with oysters, clams, or shrimp.

Oyster Farm. A place in certain waters where oysters are reproduced artificially.

Oyster Fork. A small slender-pronged fork used for eating seafood.

Oyster Knife. A knife with a short narrow heavy blade set in a thick wooden handle, used to pry open oysters and clams.

Oyster of Chicken. Two oyster-shaped pieces of meat on the back of a fowl; found in the bone cavities on the lower part of the carcass.

Oyster Plant. A wild plant resembling salsify, with pale blue flowers and gray-green leaves. The leaves, which are very good in salads, have a salty, oysterlike flavor. Salsify is sometimes erroneously called "oyster plant."

Oyster Sauce (Chinese). A sauce or liquid made from oysters. Though the taste is not that of oysters, the sauce adds piquancy and flavor to meats and poultry.

Oyster Stew. Oysters poached in milk or cream, or half and half, served hot with a lump of butter.

Oysters, Dried (Oriental). When oysters are dried, the resulting product is a reddish coarse mass which is added to fish and soups. Because of its extremely strong flavor, it must be soaked in cold water for two days before being used.

P

Pabrica. Another name for paprika.

Pabstett. An American process cheese with little distinctive taste or quality; said to be good with beer.

Pacaret. Wine produced in the Jerez region of Spain.

Pachamanca. A Peruvian picnic, with dancing and music. An oven is made by digging a large pit in the ground, and stones are heated to cook the food. Various seasoned and pickled meats, vegetables, cheese, and poultry are wrapped in banana leaves and cooked in the oven 1½–2 hours. Many like to eat the food with spicy *ají* (pepper) sauce, and the favorite herb called *huacatay*, together with plenty of *chicha de jora*, Indian beer fermented with *jora* (germinated corn), and *pisco*, the local grape brandy.

Pacherenc-du-Vic-Bihl. A crude white wine produced in the Pyrénées, France; best when about two years old. After three years it tends to deteriorate rapidly.

Pachwai. An Indian beer made from rice or other grains.

Packet Cheese (British). Packaged or processed cheese.

Paçoca do Norte (Brazilian). Dish made with dried beef, lard, onions, and manioc flour (*farofa*).

Paddle Fish. A fish of the sturgeon family found in rivers of the Midwestern United States.

Paddy (Indian). Rice in the husk; a place where rice is grown.

Paella (Spanish). The classic rice dish made with chicken, seafood, pimiento, peas, etc. It is made somewhat differently in Barcelona, Valencia, and other parts of Spain.

Paella de Mariscos (Spanish). Rice and seafood.

Paere (Danish). Pear.

Pãesinhos (Portuguese). Biscuits; rolls.

Pagel. A delicate-flavored European sea fish.

Paglia. A Swiss imitation of Italy's Gorgonzola cheese.

Pagnotta (Italian). A large round loaf of bread.

Paila de Cobre. A bowl-shaped copper saucepan.

Pailet Vin. A rather pale, almost straw-colored French red wine, good only when about 2–3 years old.

Paillard di Vitello (Italian). Thin veal cutlet sautéed in butter with lemon juice.

Paillarde (French). A very thin, highly seasoned piece of beef or veal usually sautéed rapidly.

Paillasse (French, Obsolete). A charcoal fire used to grill meat.

Paille, Pommes (French). Julienne strips of apple deep-fat fried; served with broiled meats.

Paille, Vin de. A comparatively scarce French dessert wine high in alcohol, made of raisins.

Pailles (French). Straws; served with soups, etc., to provide a crisp complement.

Pailles au Parmesan (French). Parmesan-cheese straws.

Paillettes (French). (1) Flaky cheese pastry stubs, usually served with syrup. (2) Thin flakes of edible gold or silver, used in such liqueurs as *goldwasser*.

Paillettes au Fromage (French). Cheese straws; like *allumettes au fromage*.

Pain (French). Bread.

Pain Bis. Brown bread.

Pain Buda. A braided type of individual bread.

Pain de Calendre. A loaf of bread baked in Lorraine specially for Christmas.

Pain d'Épice. A kind of gingerbread that originated in the 14th century.

Pain de Ménage. Homemade bread.

Pain de Sarrasin. Buckwheat bread made in the Ardennes region of Belgium.

Pain de Ségovie. Bread with a head in the center; it originated in the Middle Ages.

Pain de Seigle. Rye bread.

Pain de Tortose. A small sweet egg bread strongly flavored with pepper and cinnamon; usually served as a snack.

Pain Fourré. Small rolls used for sandwiches.

Pain Mollet. Light bread.

Pain Noir. Black or dark bread.

Pain Rassis. Stale bread.

Pain Rôti. Toasted bread.

Pain sans Levain. Unleavened bread.

Pain de Cuisine (French). Any loaf-shaped preparation, such as molded chicken or meat.

Pain de Dika. A cocoalike substance obtained by grinding the stone of the *oba*, an African mango.

Pain de Volaille (French). Small shapes or molds of finely minced chicken.

Pains (French). (1) Poached forcemeat dumplings prepared in special loaf molds, served hot or cold. (2) Any loaf-shaped foods, often served in slices.

Paio (Portuguese). Smoked pork tenderloin.

Paj (Swedish). Pie.

Pajuil. Cashew.

Paksiw (Philippine). A dish prepared similarly to an *adobo*, except that the food is not fried.

Pak Bung (Siamese). A wild creeping plant whose tips are used as a vegetable.

Pak Choy. A very dark Chinese cabbage with shiny green leaves.

Pakistan. Pakistan is divided into two parts. The smaller, eastern section borders on Burma; the larger section is west of India.

The Pakistani cuisine is quite spicy, sometimes burningly so, but there are several mild, bland dishes. In general it is similar to that of India. Fish is well liked, but the supply is somewhat limited. *Beckti Kashmiri*, fish prepared in the Kashmiri fashion, is a typical preparation with garlic and hot chili peppers. Rice is the mainstay of the population and is combined with vegetables, fish, meat, and poultry. *Mahi biriani*, fish and rice, and *huzoor pasand pulao*, lamb and rice, are examples.

Pakistanis are inordinately fond of *pulaos*, spiced rice dishes (from the word *pulao* comes our word *pilau*). Since Pakistan is a Mohammedan country, pork is forbidden; beef is not uncommon; lamb is popular. Chicken dishes are very good. *Murgh-i-musallam* is a baked chicken dish found also in the neighboring Middle Eastern countries.

Alcoholic drinks are unimportant here; the national taste is for sweet fruit drinks or tea. Beers and wines are seldom, if ever, served. Milk, buttermilk, and yoghurt are extremely well liked.

Paksoi (South American). A green leaf much used as a vegetable in the Guianas.

Palacsinta (Hungarian). Pancakes.

Pålaeg (Danish). Sandwich spread.

Palais de Boeuf (French). Ox cheek or palate, a cut of meat from the mouth of a steer; boiled or prepared as fritters or croquettes in Europe.

Palamonte (Turkish). A mixture of sugar, spices, and aromatics combined with ground acorns; the basis of a dish called *racahout*.

Palatable. Pleasing to the palate; agreeable to the taste.

Palate. The roof of the mouth; figuratively, the area of taste.

Palatinate. An important German wine region, also known as the Pfalz or Rheinpfalz. *See* Germany, The Wines of.

Palée. A very large type of whitefish.

Palermitana. In Palermo style; Sicilian style.

Paleron. A piece of meat from the shoulder of an animal; best used for stews or ragouts.

Palestine Soup (French). A soup made with Jerusalem artichokes; not an Israeli soup.

Palet (French). A small dry cake flavored with rum, orange, or lemon and sometimes made with almonds or raisins.

Palet de Dames (French). A small frosted cake.

Palette (French). A shoulder cut of pork, sometimes of mutton, salted and prepared in a stew with cabbage. (2) A group of fruity white and red wines produced around Aix-en-Provence.

Palette Knife. A small, broad pastry knife used to spread icings or fillings on cakes and pastries and to work dough mixtures.

Paling op Toast (Dutch). Smoked eel on toast.

Palingsoep (Dutch). Vegetable-and-eel soup.

Palma. A rather dry sherry.

Palmae. The collective name of a group of trees that yield dates, coconuts, palm cabbage, sago, palm wine, and other products.

Palmetto. Cabbage palm; palm tree cabbage.

Palmier (French). A small glazed puff pastry made in the shape of four fingers; when baked it resembles two slightly separated circles.

Palmito (Brazilian). *See* Hearts of Palm.

Palm-Kernel Oil. An oil extracted from the kernels of nuts from the West African oil palm. It is similar to coconut oil and is used in margarine and confectionery.

Palm Nut. The nut from which palm oil is extracted.

Palm Oil. Oil used by West African natives as a soap and a cooking oil.

Palm Wine. An alcoholic beverage usually made from the sap of the date palm or coconut palm.

Paloise, À la (French). With mint-flavored Béarnaise sauce. As applied to broiled meats, garnished with potatoes, hazelnuts, and green beans cooked in cream and covered with a sauce.

Paloma (Spanish). Pigeon.

Palombacce alla Spiedo (Italy). Pigeons roasted on a spit.

Palombette; Palomet (French). A fair-flavored mushroom with a green cap.

Palpuszta. A Hungarian imitation of Limburger cheese, possibly stronger than the original.

Palsternacka (Swedish). Parsnip.

Palta (Latin American). Avocado.

Pamapak (Philippine). Small portion of a dish at which one nibbles. The term is derived from *papak*, "to nibble."

Pambazo (Mexican). A roll hollow in the middle; used for sandwiches.

Pampagana (Philippine). An appetizer.

Pámpano (South American). The round pompano, a tropical fish.

Pamproux. A small round goat's-milk cheese of fair quality produced in Poitou, France.

Pan. (1) A rather flat dish used for various cooking purposes; it may or may not have a cover. (2) (Spanish) Bread. (3) In India, a green betel leaf spread with aniseed, cardamom, chopped betel nut and other spices; chewed after meals for its clean, astringent taste.

Pana. Breadfruit, a large, rather rounded tropical fruit vaguely resembling the sweet potato in taste.

Panaché (French). As applied to any food, mixed; many-colored.

Panada; Panade. (1) A doughlike mixture or paste, sometimes made of flour, bread, or meal with water or milk and butter; used to give consistency to meat or fish forcemeats or stuffings. (2) A peasant soup made of bread in the Jura region of France.

Panage (French). The dipping of foods in bread crumbs before cooking.

Panais (French). Parsnip root.

Panama. *See* Central America.

Panary Fermentation. The action of yeast in dough.

Panatière (French). (1) Variety meats and small game birds baked in scooped-out round loaves of bread. (2) The small latticed sideboard in which bread is kept.

Pan Bagnat (French). A bun or loaf of bread soaked heavily in olive oil and spread with green peppers, olives, tomatoes, onions, anchovies, etc.; a favorite beach or picnic sandwich in Provence.

Pan-Broil. To cook in an uncovered skillet with little or no fat.

Pancakes. A flat, soft cake made of a batter and fried quickly on a griddle or pan. Pancakes are made plain, sweet, or savory or sometimes filled and rolled. They may be very small (measuring just over an inch in diameter, like the famous Silver Dollar pancakes of San Francisco), or they may be the size of a table top, like the enormous German pancakes. Popular all over the world, pancakes are made by almost every civilization where grain products are a staple of the diet. In France, they make *crêpes*, in Sweden, *plättar*; the Dutch prepare *flenjses*; the Russians make *sirniki*; the Italians *cannelloni*; the Austrians enjoy *kaiserschmarren*; in Hungary, it's *palacsinta*; Israel makes *blintzes*; in Alaska, they like sour-dough pancakes.

Pancalier (French). A spring cabbage.

Pancit (Philippines). Any dish containing noodles as a main ingredient.

  Pancit Guisado. A noodle dish made with meat and seafood.

  Pancit Luglug. A noodle dish made with shrimp, green onions, smoked fish, pork cracklings, bean cake, vegetables, and spices.

Pancreas. A gland located near an animal's stomach. When used as food it is called "sweetbread"; it is inferior to the sweetbread obtained from the thymus gland located near the neck. *See also* Sweetbreads.

Pandehorno (Latin American). A crisp ring-shaped cake made with corn-flour dough and sweetened with *papelón*, crude sugar.

Pandekager (Danish). Pancakes.

Pan di Genova (Italian). Almond cake.

Pan di Spagna (Italian). Spongecake.

Pandoras. Fingers of toasted or fried bread spread with a seasoned mixture, dipped in batter, and fried in hot fat.

Pandorato (Italian). French toast.

Pandora (Italian). A yellow cake.

Pandowdy. A deep pie or pudding with only a top crust, usually filled with sliced baked apples, blueberries, or other fruit.

Pane (Italian). Bread.

  Pan' all'Anice. Anise bread.

  Pane Bianco. White bread.

  Pane Bolognese. Sweet cornbread.

  Pane Scura. Dark bread.

  Pane Tostato. Toast.

Pané (French). Crumbed, dipped in egg, and breaded or rolled in bread crumbs.

Paner (French). To coat foods with bread crumbs or with eggs, flour, and/or bread crumbs, usually before frying; sometimes includes the use of grated cheese.

Paner à la Panure (French). To cover with bread crumbs.

Panetière (French). Hollowed-out bread rounds, stuffed, and then baked; croustades.

Panettone; Panetone (Italian). Yeast cake, or yeast bread, usually round, filled with candied fruits, raisins, etc.; a Christmas specialty in Milan.

Panforte (Italian). A cake with candied fruits and nuts made near Siena at Christmas.

Pan-Fry. To cook in an uncovered skillet in shallow fat.

Pang Puay. A Siamese wild watercress.

Panhas (German). Mixture of ground meat, buckwheat, and gravy.

Panicum. A millet used for flour in Italy.

Panier. A basket with a handle. Also, a fancy pastry made to resemble a basket.

Panierte Eier (German). Eggs cooked with bread crumbs.

Panir. A soft cottage cheese made by curdling milk with lemon juice in India.

Panissa (Italian). A rice dish containing bacon, beans, and salami; made in Piedmont.

Panisso (French). Chick-peas and cornmeal boiled together, allowed to cool in small round dishes, then fried in oil, and eaten with sugar; a specialty of Provence.

Panna (Italian). Cream.

  Panna Montata. Whipped cream.

Pannam (Slang). Bread.

Pannarone. A creamy rich Italian cheese similar to Gorgonzola but without blue-green veins.

Pannato (Italian). Breaded.

Panne (French). Melted lard.

Panne de Porc (French). Fat obtained from the kidney of a pig.

Pannekaker (Norwegian). Pancakes.

Pannekoeken (Dutch). Pancakes.

Pannequets (French). Pancakes spread with a sweet or savory mixture, folded in four, and grilled.

Pannino (Italian). Roll, bun.

Pannkaka (Swedish). Pancake.

Panocha; Penuche. (1) (Persian) A candy or dessert made with butter, milk, brown sugar, and nuts. (2) (Mexican, Philippine) Crude, unrefined sugar.

Panon (Italian). An oblong cake containing candied fruits and nuts.

Panoufle (French). The under part of the top of sirloin.

Pantin (French). A small oval or rectangular patty stuffed with a pork forcemeat.

Pantler (European, Obsolete). A royal-household officer in charge of the bread and pastry and usually the cutlery.

Panure (French). A golden brown coating of buttered crumbs or of crumbs combined with beaten egg.

Panyon Tea. An aromatic Chinese black tea.

Panzanella (Italian). A peasant dish consisting of bread served with salad dressing.

Panzarotti (Italian). Squares of pasta stuffed with cheese, meat, etc., and fried.

Pao. An Indian cookery measurement equal to about 8 ounces.

Pão (Portuguese). Bread.

Pap. (1) Soft or semiliquid food suitable for invalids and infants. (2) (Dutch) Porridge.

Papa (South American). Potato.

Papads. *See* Pappadoms.

Papain. Vegetable pepsin, an enzyme with excellent digestive qualities present in the juice of the green fruit of the papaya. A commercial preparation derived from it is used as a meat tenderizer.

Paparetta. A wine produced in the Piedmont region of Italy.

Papaya; Papaw; Pawpaw. A fairly large tropical fruit, much like a melon, with many seeds, pinkish flesh, and a somewhat soapy taste. The terms *papaw* and *papaya* are generally interchangeable, but in a few regions a distinction is drawn between various species.

Papboat (British). A sauceboat or gravy boat used for table service.

Papelón (Latin American). Brown, unrefined sugar made in loaves or cones weighing 1–5 pounds.

Paper Cookery. Cooking in paper; for example, wrapping meat or fish in paper or baking cakes in paper-lined pans. Parchment paper, waxed paper, baking liner paper, and aluminum foil may be used. *See also* Papillote, En.

Paper Towels. A disposable, thick and absorbent paper, usually made into rolls of individual towels joined by perforated lines. Paper towels are used not only for hand drying in the kitchen, but are valuable also for draining fried foods, removing grease from cooking pans, wiping up spilled liquids, and on numerous kitchen occasions requiring a clean cloth that would have to be washed after each use.

Papillote, En (French). (1) Of such foods as fish, poultry, or meat, encased and cooked in parchment paper or foil to retain the juices, and served in the wrapping. (2) Decorated with a paper frill; usually rib ends of chops and crown roasts.

Papin's Digester. An early version of the modern pressure cooker.

Pappa al Pomodoro (Italian). A kind of stew containing tomatoes, olive oil, bread, and garlic; made in Tuscany.

Pappadoms (Indian). Very thin flavored wafers or pancakes fried in oil until very crisp.

Paprika. A mildly pungent red spice prepared by grinding the dried ripe fruits of the bonnet pepper, a member of the *capsicum* family. Valued by cooks both for its flavor and its color, it is used in many dishes. The sweet Hungarian paprika is made from the pods after the stalks and seeds have been removed, and is a standard ingredient of Hungarian cooking, particularly of goulash. The hot Hungarian paprika utilizes the pods, seeds, and stalks. Spanish paprika has a slightly smoky taste and is available sweet and hot. Most imported paprika comes from Hungary and Spain; domestic paprika comes from the valleys of southern California.

Paprikás. Hungarian stews similar to goulash with sour cream added.

Paprikás Csirke. Chicken prepared with paprika in a cream sauce; usually served with boiled noodles.

Paquets Marseillais (French). Pig's feet and tripe cooked with garlic and wine; a favorite dish around Marseille.

Paradise Banana. A small, sweet variety of banana grown in Southeast Asia.

Paradise, Grains of. Pepper; cardamom.

Paradise Nut. (1) Any of various condiments used to adulterate the more expensive black pepper. (2) A nut similar to a Brazil nut but better tasting, although more difficult to harvest and market.

Paraffin. A colorless or white, odorless, tasteless wax used for sealing containers of such foods as jams and jellies, and also for making waxed paper.

Paraguay. One of the staple foods of Paraguay is the orange, eaten plain, served as a garnish, or used in cooking; oranges grow profusely. Another basic food is corn, and although the peasants eat it of necessity, even the more prosperous enjoy it as daily fare. A favorite soup is *locro*, made chiefly of corn. Corn is the principal ingredient of a local cheese bread, *chepa*, prepared with cornmeal.

Paraguayans are very hearty eaters. Although breakfast is skimpy, there are at least three other large, many-coursed meals a day. Besides, in the late afternoon tea, cakes, and other goodies are served. The Paraguayan tea, *maté*, is somewhat like oriental tea but has a distinctive, astringent taste.

Meats and poultry are usually cooked in stews like *zoo-tosopi*, a beef stew with vegetables and plantains; sometimes meats are prepared with rice or starchy roots and vegetables. Beans, manioc, green bananas, and other filling ingredients are popular. Paraguayans are exceedingly fond of noodles and spaghetti dishes, and these are often served.

Desserts are simple, often consisting of fruit pastes or preserves, or of oranges made into puddings, creams, or the like. Local beer is good and the wines are passable. The country's best drink may well be *caña*, a light rum used in making mixed drinks with fruit juices.

Paraguay Tea. *See* Yerba Maté.

Parasol Mushroom. A very large edible mushroom.

Paratha; Parautha. Indian whole-meal pancake or bread fried in ghee (clarified butter).

Parboil. (1) To boil foods for a short time, not until completely cooked. Sweetbreads, for example, are parboiled before being prepared as desired. (2) Sometimes, to overheat.

Parcha. The sweet granadilla, a tropical American fruit.

Pareve (Jewish). In the kosher cuisine, foods that are neither meat nor dairy, such as fruits, vegetables, and eggs, and may therefore be eaten with either meat or dairy foods.

Parfait. (1) An ice-cream dessert served in a tall glass, sometimes with flavorings, sweet syrups, or sauces. (2) A frozen whipped-cream-and-egg mixture often served in a fancy container.

Parfait-Amour. A French liqueur flavored with citron peel.

Parfumer (French). To flavor; to season.

Pargo Criollo; Pargo Rey (Spanish). The red snapper, a tropical fish of unusual quality.

Parillada Inglesa (Spanish). Mixed grill.

Paris-Brest (French). A crown-shaped pastry filled with praline butter cream and sprinkled with almonds.

Pariserfilet (Danish). Smoked fillet of pork.

Parisian Rout Biscuits. Almond biscuits made from sugar, almonds, and egg whites, and piped into small shapes.

Parisian Spice. A varying mixture of spices used, together with salt, to flavor poultry; usually prepared by combining mace, cinnamon, white pepper, red pepper, thyme, bay leaf, rosemary and basil; one part of spice is then mixed with about twenty parts of salt, and used lightly.

Parisien. A spongecake mixture prepared with crystallized fruit, apricot jam, and Italian meringue.

Parisienne, À la. In the Parisian style; elaborately garnished dishes, usually meat.

Parker House Roll. A small yeast roll formed of circles folded in half.

Parkin (British). (1) A ginger cake containing oatmeal and molasses or golden syrup. (2) A spiced cake made in Leeds.

Párky (Czechoslovakian). A long, thin frankfurter.

Parmentier (French). Containing potatoes in one form or another.

Parmentier, Antoine-Auguste. A French agronomist (1737–1817), who championed the idea of eating potatoes, then regarded as unfit for human consumption.

Parmesan; Parmigiana; Parmigiano; Grana. One of Italy's great cheeses; a very firm, sometimes extremely hard cheese, used widely in cooking and also eaten plain. It is used in making appetizers, grated into soups, served on pasta, cooked with meat, poultry, and fish, and so forth. When young, it is nutty and soft; when old, it is perhaps the hardest of cheeses.

Parmesane, À la (French). With Parmesan cheese.

Parmigiana; Parmigiano. *See* Parmesan.

Parmigiana, Alla (Italian). Prepared with cheese.

Päron (Swedish). Pear.

Parperet (Israeli). Corn-flour pudding.

Parr. A very young salmon; saumoneau.

Parrilla (Spanish). Grilled over an open fire.

Parsley. A very versatile green garden herb used as a flavoring or as a garnish. The many varieties include the domestic (curly), Italian (dark green and highly flavored), German, Chinese, single-leaved, etc. Sprigs of parsley are used to flavor soups and stews or to garnish cooked dishes. Chopped parsley may be sprinkled over cooked dishes, or added to foods near the end of cooking.

Parsley, Chinese. A pungent, aromatic variety of parsley used as a garnish by the Chinese.

Parsnip. A carrot-shaped root vegetable used as a flavoring for soups and stews or as a vegetable; best after the first frost.

Parson Brown. A type of orange largely used for fruit juice; its name derives from a parson who first grew the species.

Parson's Nose; Pope's Nose. The tip of the fowl's tail. With the oyster it makes up the *sot-l'y-laisse*, the rump and oyster of the chicken.

Partir, Faire (French). To let dough rise.

Partridge. Several different game birds, found in various parts of the world, belonging to the same family group as the pheasant, grouse, and quail. In the United States, "partridge" is the quail or ruffed grouse. Partridge has a good taste; it is often somewhat dry, but this depends on the species, whether the bird is male or female, the time of the year, and what the bird has been feeding upon. Partridge is best cooked slowly in a casserole with added fat.

Partridgeberry. *See* Wintergreen.

Parures. Trimmings from meat before cooking; used for preparing stock, etc.

Parut (Malaysian). The grater used in preparing tapioca, coconut, and fresh ginger.

Pasas (Spanish). Raisins.

Pascaline d'Agneau (French). Stuffed breast of lamb, served on rice with lamb's liver, brains, and sweetbread added as a garnish.

Pasch Eggs. Easter eggs.

Paska; Pashka (Russian). A molded sour-cream-and-cheese dessert usually made with raisins; an Easter specialty.

Påskebryg (Danish). A highly alcoholic dark beer.

Passa de Uva (Portuguese). Raisin.

Passara (Italian). Flounder.

Passarelles (French). Muscatel grapes dried on the vine, usually used to make very sweet dessert wines. The method of making muscatel raisins from the grapes is called *passerillage*.

Passato di Cipolla (Italian). Cream of onion soup.

Passauer Rahmkäse. A fine German cream cheese.

Passe-Crassane. A very young French winter pear, fair-tasting but not juicy.

Passe-Pomme. A kind of apple of white, red, and Jerusalem varieties.

Passer (French). (1) To pass a soup, vegetable, sauce or meat through a strainer, sieve, or cloth. (2) To quickly get a crust on the surface of meats or vegetables by browning in butter, then cooking by another method.

Passe-Tout-Grain. A combination of Pinot Noir and Gamay wines in Burgundy, France.

Passin. A French imitation of Italy's Parmesan cheese.

Passion Fruit. Granadilla or grenadilla, an aromatic pulpy fruit with small black seeds and a tough purple skin. The flavor is very pleasant, resembling a combination of other fruits. It is so juicy that it is usually eaten with a spoon or made into an ice.

Passoire (French). A strainer or colander.

Passolato. A fairly sweet Sicilian white wine.

Passover Bread. Unleavened bread, matzos; eaten by Jews during Passover.

Passover Cakes. Cakes made in accordance with Jewish dietary laws for Passover foods; they are made either without flour or with matzo or potato flour, and with no leavening.

Passover Wine. A heavy, overly sweet red wine prepared of Concord grapes for use during the Jewish Passover.

Pasta (Italian). Paste; dough; dough products, such as spaghetti and macaroni or pastry.

Pasta Cotta (Italian). The ball of curd (*grana*) used in making Parmesan. The curd drawn into strings is called *pasta filata.*

Pasta di Fegato di Pollo (Italian). Chicken-liver spread, usually served hot.

Pasta e Ceci (Italian). Pasta and chick-peas.

Pasta e Fagioli (Italian). Macaroni and beans.

Pasta Filata. *See* Pasta Cotta.

Pasta Frolla (Italian). A small sweet sugar cooky made of light, very short, delicate, fluffy pastry.

Pastas (Spanish). Pastry.

Pasta Sfogliata (Italian). Puff paste.

Paste. (1) Dough used in pastry making. (2) Any soft, pliable dough. (3) Flour-and-water mixtures such as spaghetti; Italian *pasta.*

Pasteitje (Dutch). Meat-filled pastry.

Pastej (Swedish). Pie.

Pastel (Spanish). Cake; sometimes pie.

Pastél (Portuguese). Pie; tart; pastry.

Pastelão (Portuguese). Pie.

Pastéleis (Portuguese). Pie, pastry.

Pasteler. A pastry maker.

Pasteleriá (Spanish). Pastry; pastry shop.

Pasteles (Spanish). Cakes.

Pastelillos (Spanish). Fried-dough turnovers filled with meat, fish, or cheese.

Pastélinho (Portuguese). Small pie.

Pastelitos. (1) (Spanish) Small cakes. (2) (South American) Small meat pies.

Pastelón. A pie filled with meat, fish, etc.

Pastenague. (1) A parsnip. (2) A fish similar to the skate or ray.

Pastèque (French). Watermelon.

Pastete (German). Pie.

Pasteur, Louis. The French scientist who did important work in connection with wine and also developed the process of treating milk. *See* Pasteurize.

Pasteurize. To heat liquids, especially milk, sufficiently long and to a temperature to kill certain baccili.

Pasteurizer. Equipment used to pasteurize milk, fruit juices, etc., in order to destroy disease-producing bacteria. The liquid to be pasteurized is passed continuously over heated plates or through pipes where it is heated to the required temperature, maintained at that temperature for the required time, then immediately cooled.

Pasticceria (Italian). (1) Bakeries. (2) Baked goods.

Pasticceria con Pan di Spagna (Italian). Small frosted cakes.

Pasticciate (Italian). Baked noodles with cheese, truffles, and cream.

Pasticcio (Italian). Casserole.

Pasticcio di Polenta (Italian). Baked cornmeal pie.

Pasticcio di Tagliatelle (Italian). Noodle pie.

Pasticra (Italian). Pie or tart made with smooth Ricotta cheese; a favorite at Easter.

Pastiera Napoletana (Italian). Puff pastry, often prepared with candied fruits.

Pastillage (Obsolete). A sweet dough or pastry in elaborate shapes used as fancy displays on cakes and confectionery.

Pastilles. Small candy lozenges of many different flavors.

Pastina (Italian). The very small variety of macaroni used mainly in soups.

Pastina al Uovo. Like pastina but made with eggs.

Pasting. In wine and cider making, clarifying or fining.

Pastirma (Turkish). Garlic-flavored, heavily spiced sausage.

Pastis (French). (1) A yellowish licorice-flavored liquor which, when combined with water, becomes a rather sweet, pale green liquid. (2) A light butter cake flavored with Cognac and orange-flower water.

Pastitas (Spanish). Soup dumplings.

Pastrami (Jewish). A cut of beef, usually the shoulder, highly seasoned (especially with garlic) and smoked. Cut into thin slices, it is served either cold or hot.

Pastry. Baked goods, such as tarts, pies, and cakes, made with butter, lard, or vegetable shortening, flour, water, milk, etc. There are several kinds of pastry which differ in the type and amount of shortening and in the way they are blended with flour, such as puff, plain, and flaky pastry. Successful pastry-making requires chilled or cold ingredients and light handling of the dough.

Pastry Bag. A triangular or cone-shaped arrangement of linen or other cloth; nozzles or tubes may be placed at the narrow tip, through which creams, custards, etc. can be piped out into attractive designs.

Pastry Blender. A metal utensil consisting of a series of overlapping loops of wire, used to cut shortening into flour when making pastry.

Pastry Crimper. A small hand instrument used to pinch the edges of pies, tarts, etc.

Pastry Cutter. An instrument to cut sheets of pastry in various shapes with plain or fluted edges.

Pastry Jagger. A small metal wheel used to trim the edges on pastry.

Pastry Shell. An open, unenclosed pastry shape made of any desired dough; usually filled with a selected mixture.

Pastry Tube. A small metal tube which, when attached to a pastry bag, is used to pipe any desired mixture in decorating cakes and other foods. The tubes come in different sizes and shapes which form the basic decorations.

Pastry Wheel. A small instrument, sometimes

used in place of the crimper, to crimp edges on pastry.

Pasty (British). A savory pie, originally prepared with game and venison; now made with any desired ingredient.

Patani (Philippine). Fresh lima beans.

Patatas (Spanish). Potatoes.
    Patatas Asadas. Baked potatoes.
    Patatas Cocidas. Boiled potatoes.
    Patatas Fritas. Fried potatoes.

Patate (Italian). Potatoes.
    Patate Fritte. Fried potatoes.
    Patate Stacciate. Mashed potatoes.

Patay, Fromage de. A plain cow's-milk cheese matured in ashes; produced near Orléans, France.

Pâte (French). Paste, dough, or preparations of paste or dough.
    Pâte à Chou. Puff pastry.
    Pâte à Frire. A light frying batter.
    Pâte à l'Eau. A pastry dough made by adding water to flour very slowly, drop by drop. When the butter is worked in, it is called *détrempe*.
    Pâte à Lever. Fermented dough.
    Pâte Croquante. A crisp almond-and-sugar paste.
    Pâte d'Amandes. Almond paste.
    Pâte d'Anchois. Anchovy paste.
    Pâte de Prunes. A plum cake made in Poitou.
    Pâte des Fruits. A mixture of fruits and sugar cooked until thick, like marmalade, cut into any desired shape, then coated with icing.
    Pâte Feuilletée. Puff paste.
    Pâte Frisée. A rich pastry dough.

Pâté (French). The term *pâté* is derived from *pâte*. Although a *pâté* was originally a dish of ground meat or poultry covered or encased with dough, the term now sometimes refers simply to a ground meat preparation, without a dough covering.
    Pâté à la Flamande. Liver pâté prepared in Belgium from finely ground pork liver, bacon, garlic, pork fat, and spices.
    Pâté de Canard. Duck-liver pâté usually including small pieces of duck meat. *See also* Foie Gras.
    Pâté de Faisan. Pheasant pâté.
    Pâté de Foie d'Oie. A smooth paste theoretically made solely from goose livers, but sometimes from at least 50 percent goose livers and the balance from other livers or meat.
    Pâté de Foie Gras. *See* Foie Gras.
    Pâté de Pâques. "Easter Pie," an unusual dish made with sliced pork, chicken or rabbit, hard-cooked eggs, balls of ground beef, stuffed into a crescent-shaped dough; a specialty of Poitou.
    Pâté de Tête. Ground meat made from pig's head.

Pâté Doré. A home-style pork-liver pâté usually baked in the oven.

Pâté Maison. A paste usually made of finely ground goose or chicken livers, pork or veal, sometimes encased in a dough; prepared at a restaurant or hotel where it is featured.

Pâté Vendéen. A pâté made from wild rabbit and chopped pork in the Poitou region.

Patella; Patelle. Limpet, a delicious-tasting shellfish found clinging to rocks; served raw.

Patent Flour (British). A flour prepared especially for making scones.

Patent Yeast. Compressed yeast.

Patience; Patience Dock. An herblike plant, formerly used as a flavoring in soups or as a vegetable; similar to spinach, with a slightly acid flavor.

Patilla. Watermelon.

Patinho (Portuguese). Young duck; duckling.

Patis (Philippine). A clear liquid sauce obtained from fermented salted shrimp; used for flavoring or seasoning.

Pâtisser (French). To make pastry.

Pâtisserie (French). Pastry, including tarts and tartlets.

Pâtissier (French). A pastry cook.

Patissière (French). A round of veal.

Pâtissière, Crème (French). A thick custard used as a filling for éclairs, Napoleons, tarts, etc.

Patisson. (1) An Asiatic pumpkin with a very dry pulp. (2) A kind of squash.

Pato (Portuguese, Spanish). Duck.

Pato com Môlho de Laranja. Duck in orange sauce.

Pato con Arroz. Duck and rice.

Pato Real. Wild duck.

Pato Silvestre. Wild duck.

Patola. A tasty crunchy Philippine squash with a spongy texture.

Pâtrimonio. An aromatic, rather crude Corsican white wine.

Patronnet (French). Apprentice to a pastry cook.

Patties. Probably a corruption of "pastries." (1) Small pies or pâtés served as hors d'oeuvre or entrée. They may have many different fillings and are most palatable when served piping hot. (2) Any food shaped into small rounds, like hamburgers.

Patty Cases. Puff-paste shells ready to be filled.

Pattypan. *See* Cymling.

Patty Pan. A flat pan used to make tarts.

Paua. A New Zealand abalone, an edible shellfish.

Pauchouse (French). A Burgundian fish stew made with pike, perch, eel, white wine, Cognac, and onions; usually served with garlic croutons.

Paunch. The belly of almost any slaughtered animal.

Paupiettes (French). Thin, flat slices of beef, lamb, or veal stuffed with forcemeat, rolled up, and held together with string; also made from fillets of fish, as paupiettes of sole. Paupiettes may be braised, sautéed, and garnished in various ways.

Pauvre Homme, Sauce au (French). A sauce made with bread crumbs, vinegar, and stock.

Pavé (French). Any dish usually made in a square or rectangular mold. Also, certain square-shaped cakes.

Pave de l'Auge (French). A semisoft cheese similar to Pont l'Évêque but richer and stronger in flavor.

Pavie. A peach whose flesh clings to the stone; less popular since new hybrids have come into the market.

Pavlova. A wide variety of sweet confections, usually containing beaten egg whites or whipped cream, particularly when served with cakes or puddings.

Pavo (Spanish). Turkey.

Pavo Asado. Roast turkey.

Pavot. A black seed, very much like cumin, used in breads and as a flavoring ingredient; poppy seed.

Pawpaw. *See* Papaya.

Pax Bread. A small tablet impressed with a representation of the Crucifixion; kissed by communicants at Mass.

Payasam (Indian). A sweet milk vermicelli pudding.

Payman. A kind of cheese cake.

Payne. Bread.

Paysanne, À la. "In country style"; usually indicating the inclusion of carrots, celery, turnips, onions, potatoes, and bacon in a meat or poultry dish.

Paysan, Vin du (French). Very ordinary wine made by unskilled peasants for their own use.

Pa-Zun Hin (Burmese). A shrimp or prawn curry made with onions, garlic, and spices.

P.D. An abbreviation for Pepper Dust, used as an adulterant for real pepper.

Pea. The rounded seeds of an annual climbing plant native to many parts of the world. Peas have been grown since prehistoric times and are believed to have been eaten daily in the Stone Age. The Egyptians, Greeks, and Romans cultivated peas, storing them against the possibility of war or famine. No one knows, however, when the practice of drying peas began. The peas are shelled when old, dried, and then split, being then called *split peas*. Dried peas are often ground into flour and used for various culinary purposes.

National tastes in peas vary. In England and the United States peas are generally eaten when fairly large; the French prefer the tiniest specimens, the *petit pois*.

Peas are especially delicious fresh when very young; certain types, often called sugar peas, may be eaten whole, pod and all. As a rule canned and frozen peas reach the consumer in rather good condition. Dried (split) peas are marketed in green and yellow styles. Occasionally dried peas reach the market whole, without being split; these are used for making soups. Formerly dried peas had to be soaked overnight before cooking, but the newer types often make this unnecessary.

Pea Bean. The cow pea.

Peach. The delicious fruit of the peach tree. It is thought that the word "peach" derives from *Persica* or *Persicum*, because the fruit probably originated in ancient Persia. When peaches were first brought into Europe, they were popularly called "Persian apples." The flesh is strongly flavored and sometimes aromatic; the stone is rough and has deep furrows. The skin of the peach is often downy or fuzzy, but recent types are quite smooth; it may be pale or marked with red spots.

This juicy fruit comes in two principal varieties: the *freestone*, in which the fruit is readily separated from the stone and is popular for general home use; and the *clingstone*, in which the fruit clings to the stone, used chiefly in canning or commercial products because it holds its shape better. The most important type of freestone peach is the Elberta; other important varieties are the J. B. Hale, Hiley, Mikado, Rochester, Valiant, Golden Jupiter, and Eclipse. Well over 500 varieties are being grown for the market in various parts of the world, although at least 2,500 species are known to botanists.

Georgia and California are particularly known for their production of peaches, but many other states produce a large quantity, notably New Jersey and Maryland.

Peaches are usually eaten raw, sometimes cut into cereals or served with cream and sugar. They may also be baked; used in cakes, tarts, and pies; stewed; brandied; etc. Canned peaches are a staple, somewhat routine dessert for the busy housewife. Baked brandied peaches are very good with poultry.

Peach Bitters. Extract of peach kernels.

Peach Brandy. A sweet liqueur usually made from brandy and peach flavoring.

Peach Nectar. Thickened, sweetened peach juice.

Peach Palm. A South American palm tree with thorny stems and edible fruit.

Peacock. The world's most magnificent bird; in great demand as a food during medieval times but has now almost disappeared from the normal diet. It has a mediocre taste and poor texture.

Peafowl. The peacock and peahen.

Peahen. The female peacock.

Peal (British). A batch of bread.

Peanuts; Earthnuts; Goobers; Groundnuts; Monkey Nuts; Pindars. The edible seeds found in the pods of a low-growing leguminous, vinelike plant native to South America. Although called "peanuts," they are beans. Rich in protein and fat, they are a good source of vitamin B, phosphorus, and iron.

In the United States they are served roasted and salted like nuts, or unsalted in baking and candies. In many other countries, particularly in Africa and the Orient, they are used whole or ground in cooking. Peanut butter is a popular spread, and peanut oil is used in cooking.

Peanut Brittle. A thin brown, brittle candy containing roasted peanuts.

Peanut Butter. A commercial spread made from crushed and ground peanuts; available in chunk style, that is, containing pieces of peanuts, and in a creamy smooth mixture.

Peanut Flour. A flour made from ground dried peanuts.

Peanut Oil. The mild, pleasant-flavored oil extracted from peanuts; used extensively in oriental cooking but may be used like any other vegetable oil.

Peanut Spread. Any mixture containing ground peanuts; usually spread on bread or crackers.

Pea Pods; Snow Peas; Sugar Peas. Edible small whole peas and their pods; used in Chinese cookery.

Pear. The fleshy, smooth-tasting fruit of the pear tree; it has a wide base tapering down to a narrow neck and ending in a thin stem. The pears known today are a tremendous improvement over the wild types, which were hard and had a poor texture. The first good pear reached the market in the 19th century. At present, over 5,000 varieties of pears are being grown all over the world. Commercially, however, the most popular types in the United States are the Kieffer, Bartlett, Bosc, Anjou, Comice, and Seckel. American production is concentrated mainly on the east and west coasts.

The fruit may be eaten fresh, used in fruit cups or salads, cooked in compotes, used in making pies, breads, and cakes, or served with ice cream. The Italians are fond of fresh pears with Gorgonzola cheese.

Pear Nectar. Thickened, sweetened pear juice.

Pearl Barley. Hulled and polished barley.

Pearl Moss. Carrageen, an edible seaweed.

Peas, Dried. Many different types of peas (and beans) are dried for future use; the practice goes back thousands of years. Among the most popular are yellow peas, split peas, chick-peas, and lentils.

Peas and Carrots. A mixture of cooked green peas and carrot cubes, formerly quite popular.

Peas and Rice (Bahamian). Dried pigeon peas cooked with onions, tomatoes, and rice.

Pease. The rarely used plural form of "pea." In Britain the term is still used in parts of the country, as in "pease pudding," or "pease porridge."

Peasecod. Pea pod.

Pease Pudding (British). A pudding made of cooked split peas.

Pea Sprouts. The edible sprouts of the mung pea (or bean).

Peau de Porc (French). Pork skin; crackling; the crisp skin of a roast pork.

Peber (Danish). Pepper.

Peberrod (Danish). Horseradish.

Pec. Salt herring. *Hareng pec* is freshly salted herring barreled without being smoked.

Pecan. An American nut, belonging to the hickory family, found in many parts of North America, particularly the South and Mississippi Valley. The nut has an excellent taste, and comes in two principal types—hard shell, and paper shell, although there are dozens of species cultivated. The tree on which pecans grow is large, and is found in the wild state, although it is an important nut commercially. It is used in cooking, especially for cakes and pies, on ice cream and puddings.

Pecan Pie. A favorite dessert in parts of the southern United States; chopped or whole nuts are combined with molasses or sugar syrup, put into a pastry shell and baked until soft, then served with whipped cream or ice cream.

Peccary. An edible wild pig native to South and Central America; the flesh is good but inclined to be stringy.

Pêcego (Portuguese). Peach.

Pecharmant. A little-known red wine produced in Périgord, France; best when fairly old; often served with cheese.

Pechay (Philippine). A dark Chinese cabbage.

Pecho de Carne (Spanish). Brisket of beef.

Pecho de Ternera (Spanish). Breast of Veal.

Pechugos (Spanish). Breast of chicken.

Peckel (Dutch). Herring in brine.

Pecorino (Italian). Goat's-milk cheese.

Pecquet (Belgian). A coarse, ginlike beverage prepared by peasants from potatoes and juniper berries.

Pecten. The scallop.

Pectin. A colorless carbohydrate substance found in certain plants and trees, but especially in such fruits as the plum, currant, apple, and crabapple. It yields a gel that is used as the basis for fruit jellies. When the fruits are boiled and cooled and the juice extracted, the mass remaining forms into a semisolid (pectin), owing to the action of pectic acid, salts, and enzymes. Pectin is available commercially.

Pediment. A now rare ornamental base or support used to serve elaborate, important dishes, such as desserts.

Peel. The outer coating of a fruit or vegetable.

Peer (Dutch). Pear.

Pegee. A drinking container made from palm leaves by Australian natives.

Pegot. The sticky coating on Roquefort cheese.

Peh Kah (Malaysian). Star anise.

Peigne. A European scallop.

Peixa (Portuguese). Fish.

Peixe Espada (Portuguese). Swordfish.

Pejibave. The fruit of a South American palm, prepared by boiling or by drying and grinding into meal; used in bread and pastries.

Peking Style. A Chinese culinary style based on the cookery of Peking. The outstanding single preparation is Peking-style duck with the skin shiny and crisp.

Pekoe Tea. Fancy Chinese teas, such as orange pekoe, flowery pekoe, etc. They are made fragrant with chulan blossoms, which have an odor similar to jasmine.

Pelagic Fish. Oily fish, including herring, mackerel, and pilchards, found near the surface of the ocean or sea; they contain up to 20 percent fat.

Pelamide. A small mild-flavored Mediterranean tuna.

Pelardon; Pelardon de Rioms. A simple French fermented goat's-milk cheese prepared with white wine.

Péle-Porc (French). Fillet of pork. In parts of the provinces it is customary to present the local priest with this cut of meat just before Christmas.

Pelerine (French). Scallop; also called *scallop of St. James.*

Pelgrim Wheat. A dry, very weak South African grain.

Pelican. A web-footed waterfowl with a large pouch hanging from a long bill and with very

long wings. The flesh is considered edible, although it is tough and oily.

Pelmeni (Russian). Pockets of dough stuffed with various meats, much like Italy's ravioli; eaten plain or in soup.

Pelota (Spanish). Chopped beef.

Pelure d'Oignon. Literally, onionskin; the brownish onionskin color of certain aged wines that have lost their bright color.

Pelures (French). Parings that can be utilized, such as those from mushrooms.

Pelvoux. A rather simple blue cow's-milk cheese made in France.

Pemmican (American, Obsolete). A paste preparation of air-dried finely chopped meat, melted fat, and berries, made sausage-shape in a casing of animal intestine, skin, or canvas. The Indians of North America used venison or bison meat, and later beef. Properly dried and prepared, and sealed against moisture, pemmican kept indefinitely and provided the most nourishment for the least amount of weight. The early North American explorers adopted the Indian method of preparation.

Penates. Ancient Roman household gods.

Pĕnggaga. A Malaysian herblike plant often used as a green vegetable.

Penguin Eggs. Very large eggs of the penguin native to the west coast of South Africa. Their texture and flavor resemble those of plovers' eggs.

Penicillium Glaucum. The tiny mushroomlike spores added to curds that produce the characteristic blue-green veins that give Roquefort cheese its flavor.

Penicillium Roqueforti. The mold or fungus that produces the characteristic blue-green markings in Roquefort cheese.

Penide. A barley sugar twisted like a cord to decorate pastries and confections. Unlike ordinary barley sugar, it becomes opaque in the handling.

Pennòni (Italian). Pasta in the shape of a pen-point.

Pennsylvania Hand Cheese. An imitation of the German hand cheese originally made around Lancaster, Pennsylvania.

Pennyroyal. (1) A pungent herb of the mint

family, often used for flavoring soups, sauces, etc. (2) A tea prepared from it.

Penroque. A Pennsylvania imitation of Roquefort cheese.

Pensacola Snapper. A variety of red snapper. *See* Red Snapper.

Pentele Cheese. A Romanian sheep's-milk cheese whose preparation varies from region to region.

Peoci (Italian). Mussels.

Pepato. An extremely spicy Italian cheese made with whole grains of pepper.

Pepe (Italian). Pepper.

Pepe Forte (Italian). Crushed red-pepper seeds.

Peper (Dutch). Pepper.

Peperkoek (Dutch). Gingerbread.

Peperonata (Italian). Pepper relish.

Peperoni (Italian). Peppers.
  Peperoni Ripieni. Stuffed green peppers.
  Peperoni Saltati. Sautéed peppers.

Pepino. A South American plant with small yellowish fruit of fair quality.

Pepinos (Portuguese, Spanish). Cucumbers.

Pepitoria de Gallina (Spanish). A chicken stew made with olives, tomatoes, and peas.

Pepo. Pumpkins, squash, etc.

Peppar (Swedish). Pepper.

Pepparrotssås (Swedish). Horseradish sauce.

Pepper. A common aromatic and pungent spice prepared from the small fruit of certain plants, chiefly the *piper nigrum*, or black pepper plant, a shrub native to the Travancore and Malabar areas of tropical India.

The true pepper plant is fairly short even when full grown, although there are climbing varieties. When the plants are mature they yield two crops annually for about a decade. Before the tiny berries are completely ripe, they are picked and allowed to dry in the sun. When whole they are called "peppercorns" and are used chiefly in preparing soup stock and sauces. But most pepper is used in ground form. Black pepper is prepared by grinding the entire peppercorn; white pepper is prepared by separating the skin and fleshy exterior from the hard inner portion. White pepper usually has a less burning taste than black pepper and is suitable for preparing dishes with a light or white finish, where flecks

of black pepper would present an unattractive appearance. While American taste favors black pepper, Europeans prize white pepper for its fine flavor, particularly in cooking. The Eastern pepper is not related to cayenne, or red pepper, that comes from a plant of the ginger family.

Pepper is the oldest spice known to man, and one of the oldest staples of world commerce; the demand for it led to the opening of new trade routes through which Europeans gained rich domains in the East. It was on the Malabar coast that Vasco de Gama, the Portuguese navigator, landed after rounding the Cape of Good Hope in 1497. The exorbitant price of pepper in Europe was one of the reasons that Portugal sought a sea route to India. Pepper was later introduced to the East Indies, Malaya, and neighboring areas. It was one of the objectives of Columbus when he sailed westward to discover what he believed was part of the East Indies. Later it was to become a main item of trade for the Dutch and British East India companies.

Pepper purchased in ground form loses its flavor quickly after being opened and should therefore be bought in small quantities. Whole peppercorns, on the other hand, keep their flavor for many years. There is available a wide variety of pepper mills that grind peppercorns into powder.

Pepper, Green and Red. Sweet peppers or bell peppers, the membranous seed pods of certain bushy, wooded plants. The same plant produces both green and red peppers; when young, a pepper is green, the red color appearing with maturity. Sweet peppers are used in relishes, salads, pickles, for stuffing, or as a vegetable. Red peppers are used for canned pimientos.

Pepper Cake (Swedish). A brown spice cake made at Christmas.

Peppercorn. Dried pepper berries, ground into black pepper. *See also* Pepper.

Peppercress. Watercress.

Pepper Dulse. A pungent, biting red seaweed found along the western coast of Scotland; used like a vegetable.

Peppergrass. About 100 members of the American mustard family, some of which are considered weeds, others of which are used as a flavoring ingredient because of their peppery taste. One variety, *garden cress*, is often cultivated.

Pepper Mill. A cylindrical device that holds and grinds peppercorns. Freshly ground pepper is more delicately flavored and more aromatic than the commercially ground. Original pepper mills were simple, but in recent years they have become elaborate, decorative, and often oversized.

Peppermint. An herb much used for flavoring candies and mints; also used in various liqueurs.

Peppermint Cordial. A peppermint-flavored beverage made by blending oil of peppermint and proof spirit with sugar and water.

Peppermint Get. A mint-flavored French cordial.

Peppermint Glacial. A white or green afterdinner drink with a strong mint taste; ideal after a heavy dinner.

Pepperoni (Italian). A dried, firm, spicy sausage.

Pepper Pickle. A sweet pickle made with sweet red and green peppers.

Pepper Pot. (1) A West Indian stew made with meat, poultry, or fish and vegetables, and highly seasoned with red peppers and other spices. (2) Philadelphia pepper pot, a spicy thick soup of tripe, meat, and vegetables.

Pepper Steak. Beef cooked with peppers in a spicy sauce, usually with tomatoes.

Pepper Tabasco. A variety of extremely hot red pepper, used chiefly to make Tabasco pepper sauce.

Pepper Water. An Indian drink made from crushed aromatic peppercorns and water; served as an appetite stimulant.

Pepperwort. *See* Dittany.

Peppery. Sharp and spicy; tasting like pepper.

Pepsi (American, Colloquial). The dark-colored soft drink sold under the trade name "Pepsi-Cola."

Pepsin. An enzyme produced in the human body that aids in the digestion of protein foods such as meat, eggs, and nuts.

Peptic. Pertaining to or aiding digestion.

Pequeno Almoço (Portuguese). Breakfast.

Pera (Italian, Portuguese, Spanish). Pear.

Péral. A round red ewe's-milk cheese with a hazelnut flavor due to its being ripened on a bed of straw; made in the region of Millau, France.

Percebos (Portuguese). A small, odd-shaped shellfish having a very delicate taste.

Perce-Pierre (French). Samphire, an aromatic plant used in making pickles.

Perch. A fine flavored, firmly fleshed freshwater fish found in lakes, streams, and rivers; there are almost innumerable species in various parts of the world.

Perch-Trout. A good-tasting freshwater fish resembling both the perch and the trout.

Perche de Mer (French). Bass.

Perche Goujonnière. The blacktail, a very small fish; best when fried.

Perciatelli (Italian). A pasta similar to spaghetti but somewhat larger.

Percoëll (Hungarian). A stew served with rice and topped with a brown sauce.

Percolator. A type of coffee maker in which boiling water travels through ground coffee; sometimes a filter is used.

Perdiz (Spanish). Partridge.

  Perdiz en Escabeche. Marinated partridge.

Perdizes (Portuguese). Partridge.

Perdrix (French). Mature partridges.

Perejil (Spanish). Parsley.

Pérignon, Dom. (1) The French monk reputed to have originated the sparkling wine now called "champagne." (2) A leading champagne marketed at the present time. *See* France, The Wines of.

Périgord Pie (French). Layers of game, forcemeat, and ham slices combined with bread crumbs, bacon fat, spices, and truffles, baked in a pie dough, and topped with a brown glaze; a specialty of Périgord.

Périgourdine (French). In Périgord style; that is, garnished with truffles, sometimes including *foie gras*.

Perilla. An Asiatic herb resembling mint in taste and aroma.

Periwinkle. A tiny edible sea snail with a round black shell; abundant on the coasts of England and Scotland.

Perkedel (Indonesian). A fried meat patty or fritter.

Perles de Nizam (French). A large pearl barley.

Perles du Japon (French). Small pellets of sago or tapioca.

Perles Suisses (French). A mixture of *chou* (*choux*) paste and grated cheese rubbed through a sieve and cooked in deep fat.

Perlhuhn (German). Guinea hen.

Perlot. A very small oyster found along the coasts of the English Channel.

Perna de Carneiro (Portuguese). Leg of mutton.

Pernand-Vergelesses. A group of fairly good red wines produced in Burgundy, France. *See* France, The Wines of.

Pernice (Italian). Partridge.

Perrier Water (French). A mildly alkaline, well-aerated natural water containing sodium bicarbonate; obtained mainly from Les Bouillens, Vergèze.

Perry. A pear beverage similar to apple cider; contains little alcohol but keeps well in casks.

Persetorsk (Norwegian). Pressed cod.

Persia. *See* Iran.

Persian Berries. Yellow buckthorn berries; used for food coloring.

Persian Melon. A rather large melon with pink-orange flesh; highly aromatic, smooth-tasting, quite juicy, and sweet; best when served cool but not ice-cold.

Persian Wheat. A variety of wheat that produces a stable dough. Red and white Persian wheats are known as *Iranian wheats*.

Persico; Persicot. An aromatic liqueur made from the kernels of peach stones, brandy, sugar, parsley, and other flavorings; used to flavor pastry.

Persil à Grosse Racine (French). A variety of parsley grown for its large root; used chiefly in soup.

Persil Frisé (French). Curled parsley.

Persilja (Swedish). Parsley.

Persillade (French). (1) Any dish containing a large quantity of chopped parsley. (2) Fried leftover meats sprinkled with parsley, such as *persillade de jambon*. (3) A thick white sauce containing considerable parsley.

Persille (Danish). Parsley.

Persillé des Aravis. A goat's-milk cheese produced by mixing old and fresh curds and in-jecting the mixture with molds; made in Savoy, France.

Persillé de Savoie. A cheese heavily laden with parsley; made in Savoy, France.

Persiller (French). To sprinkle with chopped parsley before serving.

Persimmon. A tomato-shaped fruit, either yellow-red or bright orange, whose taste is acid and rather astringent until it is fully ripe and soft. The Japanese variety, *kaki*, tastes somewhat better than the smaller native American type. In Japan, the persimmon is dried.

Peru. Almost all of the traditional South American dishes, such as *sancocho, seviche, escabeche,* and *locro,* are popular in Peru. But there are also many interesting preparations, particularly appetizers, such as *paltas rellenas* (stuffed avocados), *empanaditas* (small pastries filled with meat, cheese, or other ingredients), and *anticuchos* (pieces of beef heart marinated in a spicy sauce and broiled). The outstanding soup is the spicy *chupe*, a chowder made of shrimp (or other shellfish). *Sancochado* is a soup, much like the *sancocho*, a meat stew. Fish dishes are imaginatively cooked; for example, there are *pejerreyes arrebozados*, small mackerel in egg batter, and *arroz con señoritas*, rice with "señoritas," very small scallops. *Paiche* is an Amazon River fish, usually cooked with onions, garlic, and tomatoes.

Important main courses are *picante de gallina*, chicken in a very spicy red-pepper sauce; *chicharrones con camotes*, pork and sweet potatoes; an Indian dish called *olluquitos con charqui*, dried beef prepared with local potatolike tubers; and *tamalitos verdes*, green-corn tamales. Also interesting are *cara pulcra*, a dish of pork, onion, and dried potatoes; *papitas de chancho con mani*, pig's feet in peanut sauce; and *causa*, a fish and yellow potato dish which is very popular. Potatoes are extremely well liked, and *papas a la huancaina* are potatoes served in a classic mayonnaiselike spicy cheese sauce.

The unusual desserts include many cakes, candies, and puddings made of fruits and coconuts. The local doughnuts, *picarones*, are very good. A red-purple corn dessert, *mazamorra morada*, is made with fresh and dried fruits. A rice dish, *arroz zambito*, is classic, and is made with nuts, raisins, and coconut.

A unique local liquor is *pisco*, a very light, pale grape brandy. Although it is taken straight, it also makes an excellent cocktail, the *pisco sour*, prepared with bitters and egg white. The Peruvian Indians make an evil-tasting, evil-smelling beer called *chicha*; it is often "improved" with white *jora* (germinated, sprouted corn), plus some added pisco. *Chicha de jora*, as it is then called, then becomes an extremely strong drink, and is usually imbibed (in enormous quantities) at a *pachamanca*, a Peruvian picnic and fiesta.

Peru, The Wines of. *See* South America, The Wines of.

Perú (Portuguese). Turkey.

Perú Recheado. Stuffed turkey.

Perzik (Dutch). Peach.

Pesca (Italian). Peach.

Pescada (Portuguese). Haddock.

Pescadilla (Spanish). The whiting, a good food fish.

Pescado (Spanish). Fish.

Pescado con Arroz. Fish and rice.

Pescado Guisado. Fish stew.

Pescado a la Veracruz. Fish cooked in the Mexican style, with garlic, olives, etc.

Pesce (Italian). Fish.

Pesce al Cartoccio. Fish baked in a paper wrapper.

Pesce Bollito. Boiled fish.

Pesce in Bianco. Poached fish.

Pesce Marinato. Marinated fish.

Pesce Prete. The star-gazer fish; a tough, somewhat tasteless fish used in stews.

Pêssego (Portuguese). Peach.

Pestle. A tool with a rounded end used to crush any desired substance in a mortar.

Pesto (Italian). A flavoring mixture of garlic, cheese, nuts, and olive oil; popular around Genoa.

Pesto, Il. *See* Il Pesto.

Petafina; Petafine. A French cheese made with cow's and goat's milk, oil, brandy, absinthe, salt, and pepper.

Petcha; Pcha (Jewish). A Middle European and Russian dish of jellied calf's feet; served as an appetizer.

Pétéran (French). A slowly simmered stew of veal, lamb, and potatoes; a specialty in Béarn.

Petersiliensosse (German). Parsley sauce.

Peth. A crumb of bread.

Pétillant (French). Lightly sparkling, a wine term. Although it has bubbles, they are not so pronounced as those in champagne.

Petit-Bessay. A plain French cow's-milk cheese made near Souvigny.

Petit Carré (French). A fresh rich, smooth cream cheese; marketed as *Ancien Impérial* when mature.

Petit Concombre (French). A gherkin.

Petite Cuiller (French). A teaspoon.

Petite Cuillerée. A teaspoonful.

Petite Marmite (French). A clear soup garnished with pieces of meat, cabbage, and other vegetables; usually served with toasted bread and grated cheese in a small earthen casserole or china bowl.

Petites Bouchées (French). Very small shapes made of puff paste with any desired filling; served as an hors d'oeuvre.

Petite Timbale (French). A small mold lined with either forcemeat or pastry and filled with any desired mixture.

Petit Fours (French). (1) Small, fancy, iced cakes. (2) Any small biscuits, cookies, shortbread, or macaroons.

Petit Gruyère. An inferior Danish imitation of Swiss Gruyère cheese marketed in tinfoil wedges.

Petit Lait (French). Whey.

Petit Moule. *See* Coulommiers Cheese.

Petit Pain (French). A small roll made from bread dough.

Petit Pain Fourré. Small rolls scooped out and filled with any desired mixture.

Petit Salé (French). (1) Pig's trotters, usually boiled. (2) Lean salt pork or bacon.

Petits Bourgognes (French). A small soft white sheep's-milk cheese made in the Burgundy region.

Petits Bressans, Les. Rather small goat cheeses individually wrapped in vine leaves; produced in Bresse, France.

Petits Gâteaux Feuilletés (French). Very small pastry shells filled with any desired food.

Petits Gris. French provincial "gray wines," pleasant though not important.

Petits Pâtés (French). Small quantities of force-meat or other mixture wrapped in pastry dough and baked.

Petits-Pieds (French). Small edible game birds, such as larks and ortolans.

Petits Pois; Petits Pois Verts (French). Very small tender garden peas.

Petit Suisse. An outstanding French fresh cream cheese; eaten plain, with sugar, or with half-sweet, half-sour cream.

Petjilis (Indonesian). A slightly sweet fruit-based relish, often made with pineapple.

Peto. The wahoo, a tropical fish.

Pétoncle (French). A round European scallop.

Pétoncles en Ragoût (French). Scallop stew.

Petrus, Château. An exceptionally fine dry red wine of the Pomerol region (Bordeaux), France, with a taste suggesting truffles. See France, The Wines of.

Pe Tsai. Chinese cabbage.

Pets-de-Nonne; Beignets Venteux (French). Tiny fried balls of cream puff paste filled with cream or jam and eaten hot; served with vanilla-flavored sugar in Belgium and France.

Petticoat Tails (Scotch). Small triangular pieces of shortbread.

Petti di Tacchino alla Milanese (Italian). Fried breast of turkey fillets.

Pettitoes. Pig's feet.

Petto di Pollo (Italian). Breast of chicken.

Pewter Ware. An alloy of tin and copper or other metals used for kitchenware and tableware; now also valued as antiques.

Pez de Espada (Spanish). The swordfish.

Pez de Limón (Spanish). The Mediterranean silver fish; generally has a good taste.

Pfalz. An important German wine region, also known as the Rheinpfalz and sometimes as the Palatinate. See Germany, The Wines of.

Pfannkuchen. (1) (German) Pancakes. (2) (Austrian) Round pastry filled with a thick apricot purée.

Pfeffer (German). Pepper.

Pfefferlinge (German). Mushrooms.

Pfefferminz (German). Peppermint, mint.

Pfeffernüss (German). Literally, "peppernuts." The traditional Christmas cooky made with eggs, flour, sugar, butter, and spices including pepper and cardamom; shaped like nuts into small balls.

Pfefferpotthast (German). A spicy meat-and-onion casserole.

Pfirsich (German). Peach.

Pfister. A Swiss skim-milk cheese resembling Emmentaler.

Pflaum (German). Plum.

P.G. Of liquor, proof gallons.

Phaseolin. The globulin protein in the kidney bean.

Pheasant. A long-tailed game bird with bright markings found in various parts of the world. Among the best known species are the common, silver, golden, impeyan, and amherst. Pheasant is highly regarded by gourmets and is recognized as belonging to the world of haute-cuisine; others find its taste disappointingly like that of chicken. Young females are frequently regarded as the best-tasting birds. Pheasant is often aged until somewhat "ripe," or faisandé.

Phenyl Ethyl Benzoate. An almost colorless liquid often used in the food-processing field to imitate synthetically honey or berry flavors.

Phenyl Ethyl Isovalerate. A colorless liquid sometimes used to produce synthetically a peach or apricot flavor in various foods.

Phenyl Ethyl Propionate. A colorless liquid used much like phenyl ethyl isovalerate.

Phenyl Propyl Aldehyde. A colorless liquid often used in the food-processing industry to imitate synthetically the taste of plum, cherry, or bitter almond.

Philadelphia Cream Cheese. A very good American soft white cream cheese.

Philadelphia Ice Cream. A soft, custardy ice cream of smooth, even texture; eaten half melted.

Philadelphia Scrapple. See Scrapple.

Philippines. The food of the Philippines shows native, Chinese, and Spanish influences. Recently there has been a tendency to use American canned and frozen dishes, and to accept typical American foods. But the Philippines still retains its distinctive cooking style.

Breakfast is a surprisingly heavy meal for the

warm climate. It usually consists of fish and rice plus hot chocolate or coffee. In recent years bread and butter have begun to replace the fish and rice. Lunch and dinner are similar meals of several courses, and the midday meal is likely to be the more substantial. A favorite, especially with the island women, is *merienda*, something like teatime. *Merienda* food might consist of banana fritters, *buñuelos* (doughnuts), or *bibingka*, a coconut-milk pudding baked in a banana leaf.

Certain Philippine dishes stand out: *lechon,* a whole barbecued pig, is a national favorite; in the same category is *adobo,* a classic stew made with pork, chicken, shrimp, or mixtures of various ingredients, these being combined with onions and garlic; *morcón* is a stuffed meat roll; *pipi-an,* chicken and pork cooked with peanuts; *escabeche,* pickled, spicy fish; and *lumpia,* various mixtures in a flour-and-water dough wrapper. Soups may or may not be served, because many dishes are prepared with a soup-like liquid. Rice is the staple food and appears at almost every meal; a favorite flavoring ingredient is *patis,* an amber-colored liquid made from fish that tastes something like anchovy paste.

Beer is the national drink and is of excellent quality. *Tuba,* the native strong drink, is made from the sap of palm trees.

Philon (Greek, Obsolete). Carrots. The term derived from *philo,* or loving; because the carrot was thought to have special powers, it was often eaten prior to love-making.

Philopena (Obsolete). A single nut with two kernels, eaten by two persons who make a wager, and in which the loser pays a forfeit.

Pholiota Caperata. A mediocre yellow and white edible fungus found in autumn.

Phong Tom (Vietnamese). Large shrimp chips, similar to potato chips.

Phosphorus. One of the essential minerals in a healthful diet; supplied in varying quantities by eggs, milk, cheese, nuts, many vegetables, fruits, and cereals.

Phulka; Chapatis (Indian). Whole-meal bread.

Physalis. The rather sour Cape gooseberry; best used in making jellies and jams.

Phytolacca. A wild plant whose shoots and young leaves are prepared like spinach.

Pia. Another name for arrowroot.

Piatto (Italian). Plate; dish.

   Piatti del Giorno. The daily special dishes.

Pibronata (Corsican). A heavily flavored sauce.

Picadillo (Spanish). Hash.

Picado (Portuguese). Hash.

Picante (Spanish). Spicy.

Picardan. A European vine that produces the grapes from which muscat wines are made.

Picarel. A small Mediterranean fish; prepared like anchovy.

Piccalilli. A mixture of chopped pickles and sometimes other vegetables preserved in a vinegar-mustard sauce.

Piccata (Italian). (1) Veal scaloppine dipped in beaten egg and fried lightly. (2) Chopped meat.

Piccione (Italian). Pigeon.

   Piccione Arrosto. Roast pigeon.

Piccionetto (Italian). Squab.

Pichelsteiner (German). Meat-and-vegetable casserole.

Picholine. A long black or green olive especially suited for hors d'oeuvre.

Pichones (Spanish). Squabs; pigeons.

Pichon-Longueville, Château. A dry red wine of Bordeaux, France, which matures well and becomes very smooth.

Pickerel. A young or small pike.

Pickle. To preserve fish, vegetables, fruit, or meat in vinegar or brine.

Pickles, Dill. Pickles (usually cucumbers) fermented in a mixture of brine, dill, mixed spices, and sometimes vinegar.

Piclets (British). Muffins.

Picnic. A meal or refreshment eaten outdoors.

Picodon. A soft, lightly salted French goat's-milk cheese ripened in sandstone.

Picpoul de Pinet. A dry white apéritif wine produced in the Languedoc region of France.

Pidan. *See* Chinese Eggs.

Pide (Turkish). Unleavened bread.

Piddock. A mollusk, often eaten in parts of England and France.

Pie. Any food baked in a pastry crust. Pie originated in the fourteenth or fifteenth century in England, where it was usually prepared with fish or chopped meat. It is not known when pies were first made with fruit and vegetables, although the Pilgrims made pumpkin and cranberry pies. In the United States, "pie" usually refers to fruit, custard, or cream pies; however, there are such exceptions as chicken, mince, pumpkin, squash, cranberry, sweet potato, and nut pie. Meat pies are still popular in England, where they are often called "pasties" or "Cornish pasties." In France, pies are made with almost every conceivable filling. One exception to the usual use of the term is "Boston cream pie," which is actually a filled cake.

Pie, Fromage à la. A simple fresh French cheese similar to cottage cheese.

Pie, Mince. A pie filled with a mixture of chopped dried fruits, sometimes with nuts and spices. *Mincemeat pie* also contains chopped meat and fat.

Pie Bird. A small funnel-like utensil inserted in the top crust of a pie to permit steam to escape and thus prevent the pie from becoming soggy. Pie birds were formerly made to resemble a bird with an open mouth, but other versions are now available.

Pièce de Boeuf (French). A piece of beef.

Pièce de Résistance. (French). The most important course or dish of the meal, usually the chef's or cook's best dish.

Pièce Montée. A highly imaginative pastry creation designed for a special occasion or an important event; often inedible.

Pièce Ronde Partie Intérieure (French). A French cut of beef, somewhat like the butt, found between the rear leg and the inside flank.

Pie Cheese. Any rindless cheese suitable to accompany apple or mince pie. Also, any simple cheese that may be cut into wedges, particularly American cheese.

Pied de Cheval (French). A very large European oyster of poor taste.

Pieds (French). Feet.

>**Pieds d'Agneau.** Lamb's feet.
>**Pieds de Boeuf.** Feet of beef or of an ox.
>**Pieds de Mouton.** Mutton feet; usually fried and served in an onion sauce or eaten cold with a vinaigrette sauce.

Pieds de Porc. Pig's feet; pig's trotters.
Pieds De Veau. Calf's feet.

Pieds et Paquets (French). Calf's feet wrapped in tripe and cooked a long time in a spiced white wine and tomato sauce; a specialty of Marseille.

Piémontaise, À la. In an Italian style of cooking, in which beef or game is accompanied by white truffles and *polenta*, a cornmeal mush.

Pieplant (Colloquial). Rhubarb.

Pie Plate. A dish or container suitable for baking pies.

Pierna de Cordero (Spanish). Leg of lamb.

Pierry. A vineyard of the Épernay region of France whose grapes are used for making champagne.

Piesport. A wine village of the Moselle region of Germany. *See* Germany, The Wines of.

Pigeon. A small plump bird with short legs, often used for food.

Pigeonberry. *See* Poke.

Pigeonneau (French). A young pigeon.

Pigeon Pea. A bean native to the West and East Indies; eaten fresh or dried.

Pigeon Pie. A pie consisting of pigeon meat and vegetables covered with a pastry crust.

Piggvarsfilet (Swedish). Fillet of turbot.

Pigments. Artificial coloring used to make foods more attractive.

Pigmeo. A Venezuelan banana.

Pignoli; Pignolia. Pine cone kernels; sometimes roasted but often used in cooking instead of pistachios or almonds; popular in Italian and Middle Eastern cookery.

Pignut. A small oval or pear-shaped bittersweet nut with a heavy shell; it resembles the hickory nut or the almond.

Pig's Fry. The heart, liver, lights, and other internal parts of a pig.

Pigvar (Norwegian). Turbot.

Pigweed; Goosefoot; Lamb's Quarters; Wild Spinach. A wild herb whose leaves may be cooked and eaten like spinach.

Piirakka (Finnish). A pastry dough filled with meat and rice.

Pikante Sosse (German). Piquant sauce; a spicy sauce.

Pike. A large species of game fish found in fresh

waters of North America and Europe; it has long jaws and is a voracious feeder. Pike is a popular fish in Europe, used especially for making *quenelles de brochet*; it is somewhat less popular in the United States, although it is used frequently in Jewish cookery. Young pike is called "pickerel"; a giant species is known as "muskellunge."

Pike-Perch. Any of several fish of the perch family with the general shape of a pike.

Pilaf; Pilaff; Pilau; Pilaw (Near East; Middle East; Eastern Mediterranean). Rice prepared with various other ingredients; may be steamed or sautéed, with meat, poultry, fish, or vegetables.

Pilchard. A small fish resembling the sardine; sometimes the sardine.

Pilet (French). The pintail duck, a European game bird.

Pilgrim. A scallop highly regarded for its flavor.

Pili Nut; Pilipnut. A triangular Philippine wild nut; used in cookery and for making candy.

Pilón (Latin American). The mortar in which foods are chopped or minced with a pestle.

Piloncillo (Mexican). Unrefined brown sugar made into small cones.

Pilot Biscuit; Pilot Bread. A rather large flat cracker; originally carried aboard ship because it kept well.

Pilot Fish. (1) A fair-tasting, oily fish similar to mackerel. (2) The whitefish.

Pils (Dutch). A bottle of beer.

Pilsner Beer; Pilsener Urquell. A famous lager with extraordinarily smooth and delicious flavor; produced in Pilsen, Czechoslovakia.

Pilsnerøl (Danish). Lager beer.

Pilze (German). Mushrooms.

Piment (Dutch). Pimiento.

Piment (French). Various berries from the pepper plant.

Pimenta (Portuguese). Pepper.

Pimenta de Cayenna (Portuguese). Cayenne pepper.

Pimento. (1) The allspice tree, its berry, or the spice made from it, allspice. (2) Pimiento. *See* Pimiento.

Pimentón (Spanish). Paprika.

Pimienta (Spanish). Pepper, the spice.

Pimienta Guayabita (Spanish). Allspice.

Pimiento. The large, very sweet variety of red pepper; eaten raw, used in salads, cooked as a vegetable, pickled and used as a relish, or chopped and added to cream cheese or other soft white cheese.

Pimiento Cheese. Any soft cheese mixed with pimientos, usually cream cheese but sometimes cottage cheese or cheddar.

Pimientos Rellenos (Spanish). Peppers stuffed with rice.

Pimm's Cup (British). Four well-known liquor cups. The original one has gin and bitters as its base; the second whisky, the third brandy, and the fourth rum.

Pimp Cheese. Maine hand cheese, a soft cow's-milk cheese.

Pimpernel. Several herbs, particularly burnt saxifrage and bennet.

Pimprenelle (French). An aromatic leaf; often added to salads to intensify flavor and also used as a condiment in making sauces.

Piña (Spanish). Pineapple.

Pinacbet (Philippine). Several vegetables flavored with *bagoong*, fermented salted shrimp.

Pincer (French). (1) To brown meat and vegetables before adding liquids. (2) To pinch together the edges of pies and pastries.

Pinch. An indefinitely small amount of seasoning, often less than ¼ teaspoonful; the amount that can be held between the thumb and forefinger.

Pinched Shortbread. Shortbread of any size or shape whose ends or edges are pinched together with the thumb and finger for a decoration, as fluting.

Pincisgrasse (Italian). Baked noodles with meat sauce and cheese.

Pindar. The peanut.

Pineapple. A large tropical fruit with an acidulous taste that is often described as a combination of strawberry, apple, mango, and peach, although this varies according to the individual fruit. The pineapple plant has firm, almost stiff foliage with sharp spines running down the edges.

Although its precise origin is in doubt, there is no question that it originated in the New World and was discovered by early explorers. It was first presented to Oliver Cromwell in England and was subsequently mentioned by

Charles II as a great delicacy. Its name originated from its resemblance to a large pine cone.

Many varieties of pineapple are produced and marketed commercially. The *smooth cayenne* is a favorite in the Azores and Hawaii; the *sugar leaf* is grown in Cuba; the *red Spanish*, highly regarded commercially, is grown in Puerto Rico, Florida, and Cuba. Other well-known types are the *Antigua black*, *Antigua white*, and the *bull head*.

The fruit is very juicy and tasty, and is excellent fresh, cooked, made into candy or jelly, used in ice creams and sherbets, glazed with sugar, or squeezed into juice. Unless the fruit is free of bruises, its flavor will be affected; any signs of decay or softness should be cause for rejection. Pineapple contains citric acid, a digestive substance called "bromeline," and a fairly high proportion of sugar.

Pineapple Cheese. A firm, distinctive-tasting cheddar shaped like a miniature pineapple and covered with yellow wax.

Pineapple Cream Cheese. Softened cream cheese combined with flecks of canned pineapple, sometimes with milk or cream added for smoothness.

Pineapple Juice. The yellowish liquid obtained by squeezing fresh pineapple. Although this refreshing beverage has been known a comparatively short time, its popularity has increased steadily and it is now a favorite drink with Americans. The delicacy of fresh pineapple juice is not duplicated by canned or frozen juices, which are satisfactory but lack the true fruit flavor of the original. Pineapple juice may be used, together with brewed tea, as the basis of many liquor punches, and its flavor is excellent when combined with certain liquors, especially rum. Pineapple juice allowed to ferment becomes a sort of wine, somewhat sticky and insipid, but pleasing to those who like rich, unsophisticated fruit wines. Cordials and liqueurs are sometimes made from pineapple juice, but none of them is distinguished for taste or aroma.

Pineapple Orange. A type of tart orange, with a vaguely acid taste reminiscent of pineapple; it is best used for fruit juice.

Pineau. A variety of grape, now generally called *Pinot. See* Pinot.

Pineau des Charentes. A rather sweet liqueur made by combining Cognac with fresh grape juice; served in southwestern France.

Pinée (French). Dried cod.

Pine Nut; Pine Seed; Pignolia; Piñon. The small seeds obtained from the cones of certain varieties of pine tree. They are used in cooking, particularly in the Near East and in Mexican dishes, and are also roasted and served like other nuts.

Pinga. A strong Brazilian liquor much like brandy.

Pinion. The wing tip of poultry; often used in soups and broths.

Pinipig (Philippine). Undeveloped, immature rice roasted, then pounded fine.

Pink Lady. A slightly pink gin cocktail, made with grenadine and egg white.

Pinoccate (Italian). A rich, sweet pastry containing pine nuts.

Pinole. (1) Meal made from parched grains of various edible grass seeds, including parched corn; eaten dry or mixed with water. The Indians of Mexico and the southwestern United States used it on long journeys or in times of war, and it was a staple of the diet of the early American frontiersmen. (2) Roasted wheat-corn, sometimes used as a substitute for coffee or to add flavor to coffee.

Piñon. The pine nut found in the western United States, Mexico, and other parts of the world. The nuts are very small and are used in decorating cakes and cookies and are eaten plain as a snack.

Pinot. A variety of grape of exceptional quality; widely used in wine making in various parts of the world, especially in France, but also in the United States. The grapes are both black and white, quite small, and form in small, very compact clusters.

Pinot Blanc (French). (1) A grape. (2) The wine made from it used by wine producers to add body or strength to better known wines in poor-vintage years.

Pinot Gris (French). (1) A grape; high in sugar but poor in yield. (2) The wine made from it.

Pinson; Gros-Bec. The hawfinch, a small game bird; good when roasted.

Pinson de Neige (French). The snowbird; a game bird; often used as food.

Pint. A unit of measure equal to 2 cups or ½ quart.

Pintade (French). Guinea fowl, a bird of the turkey family, with round white spots sprinkled on bluish gray feathers.

Pintail. A European duck with long greenish black tail feathers.

Pintainho; Pinto (Portuguese). Chicken.

Pinto Bean. A mottled kidney bean, much used in the southwestern United States and Mexico.

Pinwheel. A sandwich or pastry rolled pinwheel fashion.

Piochou (French). A provincial name for green cabbage in Anjou, where it is used extensively.

Piononos. Ripe plantains sliced in circular forms, filled with meat, and fried crisp.

Piora. A Swiss cow's-milk cheese (sometimes with added goat's milk).

Pip. (1) A rhomboid segment on the exterior skin of a pineapple. (2) The seed of a fruit, such as an apple pip.

Pipe. (1) To decorate foods, especially cakes, by forcing any desired mixture through the nozzle of a pastry tube. (2) In England, a standard cask for port wine equivalent to 115 gallons.

Piperade (French). A flat omelet prepared in the Basque region with sautéed onions, green peppers, tomatoes, herbs, and spices.

Piperine. A white crystalline alkaloid obtained from black pepper which has a cooling effect on the body by stimulating perspiration.

Piping Jelly. A flavored, sweetened jelly piped on fancy cakes.

Pipis. An edible New Zealand shellfish.

Pipit. An edible bird so small that it is hardly worth the effort to prepare it.

Pipkin (British). A rather small earthenware pot, sometimes on feet; formerly a standard kitchen utensil.

Pippin. Varieties of apple, including the Ribstone Pippin, Golden Pippin, and the Newtown Pippin.

Pippin Tarts. Pastry shells containing apples cooked with the rind and juice of a bitter orange and a little butter.

Piquancy. Pleasantly sharp; stimulating to the taste buds.

Pique. Trade name of a brown liquid seasoning and coloring agent for soups, stews, etc.; made with spices, water, salt, yeast, and vegetable derivatives.

Piquer (French). (1) To lard foods with fat or salt pork. (2) To prick or gash meats to permit flavoring or to allow fat to draw.

Piquete (Colombian). Chicken, pork, and vegetables stewed together.

Piquette (French). Wine obtained by a second or third pressing of the grapes with unsweetened warm water; consumed locally or used for distilling. (2) A mediocre wine.

Pirao (Brazilian). Cooked cereal or mush consisting of manioc flour combined with the juice or liquid from chicken, fish, or meat; served as a side dish, like potatoes.

Pirau. A New Zealand drink made from fermented corn by the Maoris.

Pirogi; Pirozhki (Russian). Puff paste or brioche dough prepared with a filling of chopped meats, fish, eggs, or rice and vegetables, and baked. Small pies served with soup are called *pirozhki*. Pies cut into portions are called *pirogi*.

Pirurutung (Philippine). A dark purple rice.

Pisang (Javanese). Banana.

Piscarine. A French peach-flavored afterdinner liqueur.

Pisco. A very pale brandy produced from special grapes grown in Ica, a province of southern Peru. It may be drunk straight, added to *chicha* (Peruvian Indian beer) whereupon it is called *chicha de jora*, or made into a pisco sour cocktail.

Piselli (Italian). Peas.

Piselli alla Romana (Italian). Green peas prepared with onions and ham.

Piselli al Prosciutto (Italian). Peas with ham.

Pissala (French). Anchovies mashed into a smooth paste; prepared in Provence.

Pissaladiera; Pissaladière (Italian, French). An

open-faced tart covered with onions, black olives, and anchovies; specialty of the Nice region.

Pissalat. A condiment prepared with fried puréed anchovies and cloves; a specialty of the Provence region of France.

Pistache (French). The pistachio nut.

Pistache, En (French). Leg of mutton prepared with a garlic garnish; also partridges and pigeons similarly prepared.

Pistachio Nut. A small, delicately-flavored nut grown chiefly around the Mediterranean and in California; usually yellow, brown, golden or green; sometimes the outer shells are dyed. Pistachios are eaten plain, used in baking and candy making, and as an ingredient in pork sausages, particularly in Germany and Italy.

Pistachio Substitute. Almonds or other nuts dyed to be substituted for pistachios, which are more expensive.

Pisto alla Genovese (Italian). A mixture of garlic, herbs, and cheese used to flavor soups, etc., in the Genoa area.

Pistole (French). A round, flat sun-dried plum.

Pistolet (Belgian). A hard, smooth, crusty milk bread used as a breakfast roll or for sandwiches.

Pistol Loaf (British). A loaf of bread baked in an enclosed pan so that it will take the shape of the pan.

Pisto Manchego (Spanish). A stew made with onions, eggs, and pork.

Pistou (French). A soup made with tomatoes, green beans, stock, herbs, and pasta; originated on the Riviera.

Pi Tan (Chinese). Duck eggs covered with a mixture of tea leaves, lime, and ashes and allowed to age about 6 months.

Pitanga. The Surinam cherry, a medium tart fruit with a good flavor.

Pitcaithly Bannock (Scotch). Almond short-bread prepared with a paste of flour, butter, sugar, almonds, peel, and caraway seeds.

Pithiviers; Pithiviers Cake (French). A cake made of puff paste and almond paste in the area of Pithiviers, a town famous for its pastries.

Pithiviers au Foin. A soft white cheese produced near Orléans, France.

Pithiviers Cream. A butter cream prepared with butter, sugar, ground almonds, eggs, and liqueur.

Pitraque. An imitation coffee beverage made of ground toasted corn.

Pits. Stones of cherries, plums, peaches, apricots. The oil extracted from them is used in canning sardines and as table oil. The press cake left behind contains the bitter principle amygdalin. It is also made into a French liqueur; *see* Noyau.

Pizza (Italian). Flat baked dough covered with olive oil, tomatoes, anchovies, and cheese; a specialty of Naples.

Pizzadalina (Italian). Onion-anchovy-olive pie.

Pizza di Ricotta (Italian). Cheesecake.

Pizza Figliata (Italian). Pastry with honey and nuts.

Pizzaiola (Italian). Food prepared with a spicy or piquant taste, served with tomato sauce and Mozzarella cheese.

Pizzetta alla Perugina (Italian). Ham and cheese slices cooked between pastry; a specialty of Umbria.

Place Mat. A decorative table covering used as an individual setting under the plate. It may be of linen, plastic, straw, etc., depending on the formality of the occasion.

Plafond (French). Tinned copper baking sheets formerly used for browning small bits of meat.

Plaice. A European flatfish resembling the sole, but inferior in quality; somewhat similar to the American flounder.

Plaisir (French). A small cone-shaped wafer that may be filled as desired.

Plakapon. A very large fine-tasting Siamese fish.

Planked Steak. A large cut of steak served on a special wooden plank or board, usually with several vegetables and an attractive garnish.

Plantain; Adam's Fig; Cooking Banana. A rather large tropical fruit; although superficially resembling the banana, it is usually much larger, less sweet, and is generally inedible without cooking, although a few types may be eaten raw. Plantains, which are high in starch and rich in vitamins, may be boiled, baked, or roasted; thin slices may be fried into crisp chips, much like potato chips.

Planter's Punch (Caribbean) A classic drink made with dark Jamaica rum, sugar, lemon juice, Angostura bitters, and sugar.

Plantillas (Latin American). Halves of ladyfingers

fastened to a piece of paper; a favorite with children.

Plastics. Synthetic dishes and implements much used as kitchenware and for serving as well as for storing foods.

Plastron. A portion of the turtle's shell used to make turtle soup.

Plátano (Latin American). The plantain; a large rather coarse banana, inedible when raw. Ripe plantain is called *plátano amarillo*.

Plat à Sauter (French). A shallow type of casserole or saucepan.

Plat de Côtes (French). A cut of beef resembling the plate cut in American style of butchering beef.

Plat de Joue (French). A cut of beef resembling the beef jowl.

Plat du Général (French). Two center cuts of veal cooked in butter; served with asparagus tips, green peas, sautéed mushrooms, and noodles.

Plate. Any flat or shallow dish, usually china or earthenware, from which food is eaten; may also be made of paper, plastic, or glass.

Plate Beef. The thin portion of meat containing small bones, cut from between the brisket and the flank; a good choice for braising or for soups.

Plate Dinners. A commercial food term for a complete frozen meal, such as fried chicken, vegetables, and potatoes.

Plates Côtes (French). Short ribs of beef.

Platine (French). A small, low baking pan.

Plättar (Swedish). Little pancakes.

Platte Kees. A loose white Belgian cheese, usually eaten with onions or radishes and accompanied by beer.

Plattfisch (German). Plaice, a fish similar to sole.

Platu; Platoo. A small, rather oily Siamese fish.

Pleated Horse (Colloquial). A species of mussels.

Pleurote. An edible fungus, not usually available commercially.

Plie (French). Plaice, a fish similar to sole.

Plomb, Galette de (French). A heavy-textured cake made of butter, egg yolks, cream, and wheat; pressed flat after baking.

Plombières (French). Originally an iced almond-flavored mousse; now also other flavored mousses.

Plommon (Swedish). Plum.

Plover. A good-tasting bird, somewhat scarce; found near marshes or along coastlines. The eggs are highly regarded by gourmets. *See* Plovers' Eggs.

Plovers' Eggs. A delicacy highly regarded by the 19th-century gourmet. The small eggs were hard-cooked, resulting in an orange yolk often considered one of the most delicate-flavored of all foods. Legislation has largely outlawed the sale of plovers' eggs in many countries.

Pluche (French). A soup garnish consisting of shredded leaves of sorrel, lettuce, chervil, parsley, and tarragon.

Pluck. The heart, entrails, and lights of an animal, such as a sheep's pluck.

Plukfisk (Danish). Stewed codfish.

Plukkfisk (Norwegian). Creamed minced fish and potatoes.

Plum. The delicious fruit of a variety of fruit tree botanically known as the *Prunus domestica*. The rather attractive round fruits, technically known as "drupes," contain flat pointed stones surrounded by sweet, colored flesh, and have a light, pleasant aroma. In some parts of the world the term "plum" describes both fresh and dried types, but as a general rule the term "prune" is used to describe the dried version.

Plums have a history going back several thousand years. The plum is grown in many parts of the world, particularly in temperate climates. The three chief regions are North America, Europe, and Japan, and over 100 species are recognized, about 35 of which are American. These have been subdivided into more than 2,000 varieties, ranging from very small to quite large, from bland-flavored to sour, acidulous varieties. They are most frequently yellow, blue, green, and red, but with scores of different color shadings.

The best-known commercial types are the damson, greengage, mirabelle, Santa Rosa, reine-claude, quetsch, black plum, and the "beach plum" found along the Atlantic coast and used for making jellies.

The skin of the fresh plum is firm, tight, and unshriveled; softness or bruise marks indicate overmaturity and poor flavor. Except for the miniature plums, there are 10–15 plums in a pound; when stewed or made into compote a pound usually serves 4 people.

Plum, Naseberry. *See* Sapodilla.

Plump. (1) As applied to food, full, round, and sleek. (2) To soak foods, especially dried fruits, in water, to cause them to swell and to soften the texture.

Plum Sauce. A sweet sauce made from apricots, peaches, and plums (occasionally from other fruits) together with vinegar, sugar, and spices. Because it is frequently served with duck, it is often called *duck* or *duk sauce*.

Plumy. As applied to edible birds, full-feathered.

Plunge. To dip quickly into a liquid.

Pluteus, Common. A wild mushroom with a cap about 6 inches across. The caps are good-tasting, but the stems are quite rubbery.

Pluvier (French). Plover, a small edible water bird; usually wrapped in vine leaves and roasted.

Pluvier Doré (French). The golden plover.

Poach. To cook foods submerged in a liquid kept below the boiling point. Eggs, fish, and chicken may be poached.

Pochage. Poaching; that is, cooking just under the boiling point.

Pochard; Pokard; Poker Bird. The sea duck, a game bird with an extraordinarily fine taste, being much less gamy than most wild ducks. Nevertheless, some specimens occasionally have an unpleasant flavor or dryness, depending upon the sex, the time of year, and what the birds have been eating.

Poché (French, South American). Poached.

Pocher (French). To poach; to cook at a temperature below the boiling point.

Pochero (Philippine). A holiday dish consisting of several meats, potatoes, beans, and onions; undoubtedly related to *puchero*, a South American stew made with vegetables and assorted meats.

Pochlopka (Russian). Onion soup with mushrooms and vegetables.

Pochouse; Pauchouse (French). A fish stew made with several kinds of freshwater fish, particularly eel. *See* Matelote.

Pod. The outer covering of edible seeds such as green peas and lima beans. Some pods are edible.

Podvarek (Yugoslavian). Sauerkraut baked with onions and hot, spicy peppers.

Poêlage (French). The method of cooking in a fair amount of fat, using a tightly-covered cooking utensil.

Poêle. A chef's skillet whose sloping sides and long handle make it easy to toss rather than turn foods; used for frying and browning.

Poêler (French). To brown lightly or braise in a heavy saucepan.

Poêlon (French). (1) A small, low casserole or other cooking container. (2) Any small pan.

Poffertjes (Dutch). Fritters; puffs.

Pogne (French). (1) A very large tart filled with fruit; a specialty of the Dauphiné district. (2) A kind of sweet brioche.

Pogot. A Philippine fish of only passable quality; the liver, considered the best part, is eaten with lime juice and ground chili peppers.

Poha. A Hawaiian name for the ground cherry, a fruit much used in making jelly; the cape gooseberry.

Poi (Hawaiian, South Pacific). A starchy, rather tasteless food made from taro roots. It is prepared in various thicknesses, and is picked up with the fingers, two-finger poi representing a medium thickness.

Poi Fa'I (Samoan). Ripe bananas combined with coconut cream and mashed smooth.

Points d'Asperges (French). Small green asparagus tips.

Poire, Eau de Vie de (French). A clear white pear-flavored liqueur.

Poireau (French). Leek.

Poire Hélène (French). Cooked pears served on ice cream with a chocolate sauce.

Poire William. A large, bright yellow French pear, quite perishable; often used for making a fine brandy, sold under the same name.

Pois Cassés (French). Dried split peas.

Pois Chiches (French). Chick-peas.

Pois Mange-Tout. Sugar peas that are edible pod and all.

Poisson Blanc (Canadian). Whitefish.

Poissonnier (French). The chef in charge of fish cookery, with the exception of fried or grilled fish, which come under the jurisdiction of a *rotisseur* or *grillardin*.

Poissonière (French). A pan or kettle used for cooking fish.

Poi Supper (Hawaiian). A meal consisting of various classic dishes, such as lomi-lomi salmon, chicken in coconut, and poi, the favorite starchy paste.

Poitrine (French). (1) The flank of beef, veal, pork, or lamb. (2) The breast, especially of chicken.

Poitrine d'Agneau. Breast of lamb.

Poitrine de Boeuf. Brisket (breast) of beef.

Poitrine de Mouton. Breast of mutton.

Poitrine de Veau. Breast of veal.

Poivrade Sauce (French). A dark brown sauce containing crushed black pepper, onions, and ham.

Poivré (French). Peppered or spiced.

Poivre de Cayenne (French). Cayenne pepper.

Poivre de Guinée (French). Guinea pepper.

Poivron (French). Red pepper or pimiento.

Poke; Garget; Inkberry; Pigeonberry. A tall wild green plant with edible leaves; they are particularly good in springtime, when they may be cooked like a vegetable. Poke greens, which taste something like spinach, should be boiled in at least two changes of water in order to remove the rank taste.

Pokeweed. The green-red edible shoots of a perennial plant; prepared like asparagus. When picking the shoots one must be careful not to include the poisonous berries and roots.

Poland Water. A mineral water containing carbonic acid; bottled in Maine.

Polco (Portuguese). Octopus.

Polenta (Italian). A cornmeal dish. Polenta is also occasionally made of chestnut flour, as in Corsica.

Polenta Grassa. Layers of cornmeal with plenty of butter and Fontina cheese.

Polentagrøt (Norwegian). Cornmeal pudding.

Polish Wheat. Wheat grown in Poland; usually of poor strength but of good color and flavor.

Pollame (Italian). Poultry.

Pollards. (1) Fine bran containing some flour. (2) Some intermediary products in wheat milling.

Pollastre (Spanish). Baby chicken.

Pollo (Italian). Chicken.

Pollo al Diavolo. Chicken in a spicy sauce.

Pollo al Forno con Uva. Chicken prepared in wine with grapes.

Pollo alla Cacciatora. Chicken cooked in oil, tomatoes, and wine, "hunter's style."

Pollo alla Casalinga. Chicken home style.

Pollo alla Mantovana. Chicken with olives.

Pollo alla Montagnuola. Baked breaded chicken.

Pollo alla Napoletana. Chicken in tomato sauce.

Pollo alla Panna. Chicken in cream.

Pollo alla Romana. Chicken with ham, mushrooms, and rice.

Pollo in Vino Bianco. Chicken in white wine.

Pollo Lesso. Boiled chicken.

Pollo Ripieno. Stuffed chicken.

Pollo (Spanish). Chicken.

Pollo Asado. Roast chicken.

Pollo Frito. Fried chicken.

Pollock; Pollack. An ocean fish much like the cod, noted for its protruding lower jaw; sometimes, the whiting.

Polonaise, À la (French). In the Polish style. (1) Flavored with cream, beets, and red cabbage. (2) Garnished with chopped hard-cooked egg yolks, parsley, and sometimes bread crumbs; often applied to vegetables.

Poloni. A steamed meat dish made of chopped beef and ham with bread crumbs.

Polonies (Colloquial). Bologna sausage.

Polpette (Italian). Meatballs.

Polpette alla Napoletana. Meatballs with rice.

Polpettine (Italian). Small meat or fish patties.

Polpettine di Spinaci (Italian). Spinach dumplings.

Polpettone (Italian). Meat loaf.

Polpi in Purgatorio (Italian). Young octopus prepared with tomatoes; a specialty of Abruzzi and Molise.

Pølse (Norwegian). Sausage.

Pølser (Danish). Sausage.

Pølser og Kartoffelsalat (Danish). Sausages and potato salad.

Polvorones de Canela (Mexican). A cinnamon-flavored teacake.

Polynesian Islands. These South Pacific islands include, besides Hawaii, the Marshall, Gilbert,

Caroline, Tonga, and Samoan islands. Although food resources vary greatly, by and large the population is dependent on catches of fish and shellfish from the local waters and on local agriculture. Few cattle are raised. Pigs are the chief source of meat. Most islanders like chicken and often cook it with fish.

Fishing is usually a reliable source of food; however, it occasionally fails. Warm-water fishing often yields fish with a disappointing and insipid taste and a flabby texture, but the shellfish is usually excellent.

The diet is usually lacking in substance, however, and starchy roots and tubers are used as supplementary foods; sweet potatoes, *uwala momona*, and *taro* are typical. Bananas, mangos, coconuts, and papaya are the usual fruits, and these are always available, even when other foods are in temporarily short supply.

Polynesian islanders all prepare liquors of one sort or another. Sometimes they use palm-tree nuts, sometimes sugar cane. The most renowned drink throughout the islands is *kava*, made by chewing *kava* fibers and spitting them into a bowl filled with water. The mixture becomes intoxicating, but not alcoholic, in a matter of hours.

Polyp. The common octopus, which grows very large. Its flesh is not so good as that of the squid.

Polypodium. Edible ferns.

Poma Rose; Romarrosa (West Indian). The rose apple.

Pombe. African beer prepared from millet seed. The seed is sprouted to break down the starch to fermentable sugar, a process similar to malting in beer manufacture, and then allowed to ferment spontaneously.

Pombo (Portuguese). Pigeon.

Pome. Fruit having a core with seeds surrounded by juicy, rather solid flesh. The apple and pear are pomes.

Pomegranate. A fruit, generally about the size of an apple, ranging from yellow to orange, and from red to deep purple. The pulp is formed around a myriad of seeds, and is somewhat difficult to eat; best when cooled, but not ice cold. The juice is excellent for making refreshing drinks or sherbets; it forms the basis for Grena-

dine, a commercially-available sweet red syrup.

Pomeranzen. Orange-flavored Russian vodka.

Pomeranzensauce; Pomeranzensosse (German). A dark sauce made with sausages.

Pomerol. A wine district of the Bordeaux region of France. *See* France, The Wines of.

Pomfret. A white-meat flatfish found mainly along the Indian coast; particularly good when smoked.

Pomidori (Italian). Tomatoes.

 Pomidori al Forno. Baked tomatoes.

 Pomidori Ripieni al Riso. Tomatoes stuffed with rice.

Pomino. A red Italian wine similar to Chianti.

Pommard. A wine district of the Burgundy region of France. Also, an important dry red wine produced there. *See also* France, The Wines of.

Pomme (French). Apple.

Pomme Cannelle (French). The custard apple, a West Indian fruit.

Pomme d'Amour (French). Tomato.

Pommel. A rich, creamy white French cheese, unsalted and perishable.

Pomme Sauvage (French). The crab apple.

Pommes de Terre (French). Potatoes.

 Pommes de Terre Alumettes. Matchlike strips of potatoes fried in deep fat.

 Pommes de Terre à l'Anglaise. Boiled or steamed potatoes.

 Pommes de Terre Beurre Noir. Potatoes browned in butter with a sauce of capers and a little vinegar.

 Pommes de Terre à la Crème. Sliced boiled potatoes in a Béchamel sauce.

 Pommes de Terre au Fromage. Thin slices of raw potatoes sautéed in butter and baked with cheese.

 Pommes de Terre au Gratin. Mashed or sliced potatoes combined with either butter or cream sauce and cheese.

 Pommes de Terre en Pailles. Potatoes cut in the shape of straws.

 Pommes de Terre Mousseline. Mashed potatoes combined with cream and egg yolks, with melted butter added.

 Pommes de Terre Nature. Potatoes steamed or boiled in salted water.

Pommes de Terre Paille. Potatoes cut into straws and deep-fat fried.

Pommes de Terre Persillées. Boiled potatoes combined with plenty of melted butter and parsley.

Pommes de Terre Soufflées. Potatoes cut into lengths, and fried at two different temperatures so that they puff up.

Pommes en Robe de Chambre. Potatoes boiled in their jackets.

Pommes Purée. Mashed potatoes.

Pomo (Italian). Apple.

Pomology. The science of fruit growing.

Pompadour, À la. Several dishes have been named for the mistress of Louis XV of France, especially sweet preparations, but also dishes containing lamb, asparagus, etc.

Pompano. One of the world's best food fishes, found chiefly in the West Indies and off the coast of Florida. It is noted for its excellent taste and delicate texture. The California pompano is not of similar excellence.

Pompe (French). A light crown-shaped cake served on Christmas Eve.

Pompelmo (Italian). Grapefruit.

Pompettes (French). Orange-flavored sweet pastry.

Pompettes de Marseilles. Fancy shapes of orange-flavored brioche dough.

Pomponnette. A small round fritter made with a puff-pastry dough and filled with finely ground meat or poultry; served as hors d'oeuvre.

Po Nay. A black tea produced in Yunnan province, China.

Pone. A cornmeal bread or pudding.

Ponqué (Puerto Rican). Pound cake.

Ponta. A type of cheese made in the Franche-Comté region of France.

Pontet-Canet, Château. A fine dry red wine produced in Haut-Médoc (Bordeaux), France.

Pontgibaud, Fromage de. A blue-veined cow's-milk cheese made in Auvergne, France.

Pont l'Évêque. A semihard cheese made in France from whole or skim milk; ripened for about 3 months in cellars in a square mold. The cheese has a good taste, medium-firm texture, and an aroma which is not to everyone's pleasure; when ripe, it is yellow-gold.

Pont-Neuf (French). A puff-pastry tartlet filled with frangipane cream and crushed macaroons.

Pony. A small liquor glass, usually of 1–1½ ounce capacity.

Poona. A medium-soft cheese of rather good flavor and texture; produced in New York State.

Poori (Indian). Wheat bread, usually fried.

Poor Knights of Windsor. Fried slices of stale bread spread with marmalade or jam.

Poor-Man's Mustard. Garlic that grows wild on hedges.

Pop. (1) To roast or heat a grain, especially corn, until the kernels burst. (2) (Colloquial) Soda pop; any bottled soft drink.

Popcorn. A special type of dried corn heated until the kernels burst, exposing the inner white part of the grain; usually served with melted butter and salt. Low heat is necessary for proper popping.

Pope. A European fish similar in size and flavor to the perch.

Pope's-Eye. (1) The small circle of fat at the center of a leg of pork or mutton. (2) (Scotch) Rump steak.

Pope's Nose; Parson's Nose. The tip of a fowl's tail.

Popover. A crisp light, hollow muffin made from a thin batter that puffs up over the molds in baking; best eaten hot. Before the molds are filled for baking they must be well greased and very hot, and the batter must be very cold.

Poppadums (Indian). Very light strips or balls, made usually from shrimp and flour, that puff up while frying in hot deep fat.

Popper. A wire or metal container used especially for popping corn.

Poppy-Seed Oil. The oil extracted from poppy seeds; often used in cooking in parts of Europe.

Poppy Seeds. Tiny seeds, with a unique flavor, of a nonnarcotic variety of poppy plant; used extensively in Middle European cooking and baking, but in the United States chiefly on breads.

Porc (French). Pork.

Porc Frais. Fresh pork.

Porc Salé. Salted pork.

Porcelet (French). Suckling pig.

Porchetta (Italian). Roast whole suckling pig.

Porco à Alentejana (Portuguese). Pork cubes cooked with baby clams.

Porcupine. The hedgehog; when young, sometimes used for food.

Porgy; Porgie. A term which describes several ocean food fishes, all of only passable quality, including the sea bream and the scup.

Pork. The meat of the pig commonly used for food around the world. The ideal weight for pigs brought to the market is 200–400 pounds, but this is only a general rule. Good-quality pork meat is rather pink, but the fat should be white. Pork is butchered in scores of different cuts, but the most important ones are hams, spare ribs, loins, butts, shoulders, and feet. The less choice parts, such as brains, tail, ears, tongue, etc., are marketed in low-income districts. Pork is available fresh, frozen, or canned.

Of all animals, the pig has the greatest versatility, and the Midwestern United States packers boast that they use every part of the pig but the squeal. The variety of pork sausages, bacon, and lard products are seemingly endless, being limited only by the ingenuity of the packer or producer.

Because pork has been diagnosed as a carrier of trichinosis, it is always advisable to cook it well, surely until no pink is visible. Lamb or beef may be eaten rare, but pork should be cooked until very well done. About 30 minutes per pound is usual for thick cuts. Pork must never be eaten raw under any circumstances.

Porker. A pig about 6 months old, especially one fattened before being killed.

Pörkölt (Hungarian). Any browned food.

Porotos Negros (Spanish). Black beans.

Porpoise. A fish found in many different waters around the world. It has a rather good taste and firm white flesh, although some species tend to be oily. Although called a fish, it is actually a mammal.

Porridge (British). Cooked oatmeal.

Porringer. A rather small dish intended for the serving of porridge but also used for soups.

Port. A fortified sweet dessert wine prepared in Portugal. It is a blended wine made sweet by arresting the fermentation while the wine still contains sugar. *See* Portugal, The Wines of.

Porter. A strong, very dark English beer, said to have gotten its name from the London porters who liked it so much.

Portet. A French white wine produced in the Béarn region; it may be sweet or dry, but tends to have a slightly unpleasant "bottle stink," which is displeasing.

Porterhouse; Porterhouse Steak. A good cut of beef that contains the tenderloin. The term is said to be derived from a certain New York porterhouse (saloon) that served this cut of steak.

Port Salut; Port du Salut. A creamy, yellowish whole-milk cheese prepared with scalded milk curds by Trappist monks; made in monasteries in various parts of the world.

Portugaise, À la. A style of cooking derived from the Portuguese; with oil, tomatoes, onions, garlic, and pepper.

Portugaises (French). A large type of oyster of fair flavor, theoretically harvested off the coast of Portugal, but often from neighboring regions.

Portugal. Although Portugal shares the Iberian peninsula with Spain, the cuisines of the two countries are quite dissimilar. Portuguese food may be said to have an Italianate quality, with a notable use of tomatoes, olive oil, garlic, and onions. The French culinary expression, *à la Portugaise*, indicates the presence of those ingredients.

Breakfast is of the standard European type: rolls, butter, jam, and coffee. Lunch doesn't begin until one o'clock and is often served at two, somewhat in the Spanish fashion. In the afternoon teatime is a favorite repast, with a wide selection of cakes and pastries, along with several miniature cups of coffee. There are local variations: for example, a *garoto* is coffee with milk, a *carioca* is made with hot water, and is somewhat less strong; and a *bica* is ordinary coffee. Dinner begins at about eight o'clock, but a smart dinner party might not get underway until eleven or so.

Portuguese oysters are mediocre, but the clams, *ameijoas*, are tiny and toothsome. *Percebos*, a shellfish vaguely resembling an elephant's foot, has an excellent taste. *Santola*, crab, is truly worthwhile, and the local *camarãos*, shrimp, are of equal quality. Fresh herring is the national favorite, but its pronounced fishy taste discourages all but the most determined. Actually, the most popular fish in Portugal is *codfish*, fresh sometimes, but inevitably dried and known as *bacalhau*. It is served in a wide variety of fashions: with garlic, onions, and eggs, *à Gomes de Sá*; with a sharp tomato sauce, *à Portuguesa*, and so forth.

The Portuguese like fish soups, which they prepare very well, especially their *caldeirada*. Their national soup is definitely *caldo verde*, a green soup made with potatoes and vegetables. *Canja* is a nourishing chicken soup with rice.

The local meat dishes are of interest to gourmets. The *cosida à Portuguesa*, a peasant-style national dish, consists of boiled meats and vegetables; *iscas*, strips of sautéed calf's liver, is cooked in white wine; *dobrada* is a stew of tripe and beans; *porco à Alentejana* is an interesting mixture of small pieces of pork and tiny clams; *bife na frigideira* is beef in mustard sauce; *carne de vinha*, spicy pickled meat, is also quite popular. Steaks, roast beef, and chops in the American manner are seldom served.

Portuguese cheeses are wholesome and tasty, but not necessarily subtle or distinctive The fresh cream cheese produced in Azeitão, called *queijo fresco*, is nonetheless very tasty and appealing. The most interesting local cheese is probably *queijo da Serra*. Most desserts are on the uninspired side, leaning heavily on eggs and custards. *Pudim d'ovos* is a typical example; *leite-creme con farófias* is just like a floating-island dessert; *pudim Portuguesa* is orange-flavored and slightly above average.

The wines of the country deserve attention. First, there is the everyday drink of the country, *vinho verde*, which translates as "green wine," but the name has reference to the wine's youth and not its color. *Vinho spumoso* is sparkling wine, and the local champagne leaves much to be desired. *Vinho estufado* is wine baked in a hot house, that is, Madeira wine. Of course, there is also *vinho generoso*, wine (usually port) fortified with brandy.

Returning to table wines, the best whites include Bucelas and Colares; among the reds, *vinhos tintos*, Dão and Colares are very good. Portugal produces some good *rosé* wines, and Mateus *rosé* is first-rate. In the north, around Oporto, the famous port wine is produced largely for export because the Portuguese do not show much desire for this drink, which primarily appeals to those in cold climates. Port wine is produced in five general types—ruby, tawny, crusted, vintage, and white. Only the white wine (not actually white, but quite pale) is served before dinner; the others are best with cheese, or after dinner. Ruby port is a blended drink and has a bright reddish color; tawny port remains in the cask longer, and therefore loses some of its color and becomes tawny. Crusted port throws up a considerable amount of sediment in the bottle, and must be poured out with considerable care in order not to disturb the sediment. Vintage port, the finest, is completely unblended; it is the only part that bears a date, and is generally regarded as best at about twenty years of age. On the Portuguese island of Madeira, Madeira wines are produced, but these are now out of public favor. However, Sercial is a dry, interesting appetizer drink, and Malmsey is a dessert wine, rich and sweet. The Portuguese people show little interest in strong liquors, although Scotch is the smart social drink in the fashionable world of Lisbon. The local beers are fairly good, although not distinguished.

Portugal, The Wines of. When Portuguese wines are mentioned, people are apt to think of port, as if no other wine were produced in Portugal. Port is indeed a great wine worthy of its reputation; it is one of the unique wines of the world, and, like Spain's sherry, absolutely inimitable. But port is not the whole story of wine in Portugal. This is a country where people enjoy wine with their meals and between meals. The table wines here are not to be compared with Bordeaux or Burgundies, nor even with the better wines of Italy. They are, however, on a par with the table wines of Spain, being light, pleasant, and ideal for informal meals. They are inexpensive and are excellent values for their prices.

Quite close to Lisbon the vineyards of Colares produce both red and white wines. Of the two, the reds (*Colares tintos*) are superior, with a good dry quality, making them ideal with most meats. This wine is somewhat unusual, and not everyone likes it, but it is a wine that improves with familiarity. Bucellas, also near Lisbon, offers a medium sweet white wine with an odd gold color; it is good, but not superior. Torre Vedras, a neighbor of Bucellas, produces red and white wines of medium quality.

In the center of Portugal, Dão produces wines which are lively and fruity with an excellent bright ruby color, delicious when they are about two or three years old. White Dão is astonishingly like a French *Pouilly-Fuissé*, and, like its Gallic counterpart, it is fine with shellfish.

Around Douro, in the north of Portugal, is the famous wine district. In addition to making the classic port, the region produces its share of table wines. The best, marketed as *Douro Clarete*, vaguely resembles a fair quality of Bordeaux wine. The district also puts up some white and rosé of modest pretensions, which have a subtle undertone of port, as the grapes used are the same.

Further along the Douro Valley, near the Spanish border, is the tiny settlement of Granja de Alligo, where the vintners make a very sweet white wine, *Grandjo*, similar to a *Sauternes*. It is made in the same fashion, the grapes being left on the vines long after the harvest in order to permit the "noble rot" to form. *Grandjo* has never been popular in the United States and is rarely available there.

Most American tourists return from Portugal talking of one wine—*vinho verde*, or green wine. The name derives not from the color but from the youth of the wine, which is made in the extreme north in a district called Entre Douro e Minho. *Vinho verde* is available as either a red or white wine, but it is the consensus that the white is far superior to the red. The whites are low in alcoholic content (they average 9–10 percent) with a slightly sparkling effect and a most pleasing bouquet. They are so delightful to drink that the average person is apt to consume much more than usual. Small quantities of *vinho verde*

are imported into the United States and are exceedingly pleasant to drink during the summer months. (*Lancer* is a light sparkling wine of this general type of fairly good quality.)

Port wine is suited to cold climates, and most of Portugal has mild weather; the national preference, therefore, is for the ordinary table wines. Port's history has always been connected with the Anglo-Saxon countries; in fact, it is called an Englishman's wine. In France, port is looked upon as a specialty wine, while in Germany it is rarely served. But port is the afterdinner drink of England. Until recently, the birth of a boy was the signal for the father to head straight for his favorite wine merchant, where he would order cases of vintage port to be "laid down" for his son and heir. In the next twenty years the port would become a superb aged drink. Now that the stately homes of England are being replaced with three-room apartments, the average English father is more likely to buy a single bottle of port, drink it himself to get over the first shock of parenthood, and let it go at that.

Port is a fortified wine produced in a legally limited area of northern Portugal, the Douro Valley, which is about twenty miles east of the prosperous coast city of Oporto. If the grapes are not grown in this locale, as specified by Portuguese law, a wine is not really port, although there are dozens of imitations, from South Africa to Chile to California. "Port wine types" are pleasant drinks when they are good, but they are far from the quality of genuine port, nor do they taste like it.

The soil of the Douro Valley is believed to have much to do with the character of the wine. The grapes are grown on steeply graded terraces on both sides of the Douro River in a soil which is part granite and part schist, a rock that has been under tremendous pressure from the movement of the earth's crust and vaguely resembles slate. The weather in the valley runs to extremes: very hot in the summer and freezing in the wintertime; rainstorms when they come are fierce. But the vines manage to produce grapes every year, and important vintages occur about three times in a decade.

The grapes used are varieties little known elsewhere: Bastrado, Turigo, Tinta Francisca, and Tinta Carvalha are the most important, but many different types are grown. In fact many vineyards produce more than a dozen varieties, all carefully blended when the wine is made. Around the last week in September the harvest begins. The grapes are brought in and trampled down during a week of high excitement and festival. The fermentation process is quite short, usually not more than three days. The fermentation of the sugar is not allowed to run its course, and when the desired stage is reached, brandy is added in order to stop the action of the yeast. This process brings the alcoholic content to about 20 percent; the remaining unfermented grape sugar acts to sweeten the young wine. This young wine, with the added brandy, is allowed to remain in the vats for several months. The following spring the wines are shipped down the river on picturesque narrow boats to wine lodges located across the river from Oporto at the town of Vila Noval. Here each shipper blends the wine to suit his own taste and that of his customers. Not much wine is actually bottled in Portugal; it is shipped in the cask to England, which for many years has controlled the port industry.

Port may be divided into two general classes: vintage and blended. It may also be broken down into four categories: vintage, crusted, ruby, and tawny. Some people add a fifth category, white port. In years when the vintage has been superior, the port firms may declare a "vintage year," allowing the wine to age for eight to ten years more before it is marketed. Vintage port, scheduled to be sold as an unblended wine, is kept in the cask for only two years, then is shipped to be bottled in England (usually) and allowed to "rest" and improve. After ten years, port wine matures very slowly, if at all. The minimum age at which a vintage port should be drunk is ten years, but many connoisseurs insist on twenty. There is no meeting of minds on this subject.

When port is old, it must be decanted because of the heavy deposit of sediment thrown up on the sides of the bottle. It is poured into another container so that the sediment remains in the original bottle. A very steady hand is required for this delicate operation.

All other port wines are produced by blending. Crusted port also throws up a deposit similar to that of vintage port, so that solid matter forms on the sides of the bottle and constitutes a "crust." Crusted port is a blend of better wines which do not quite meet the requirements of a vintage port. The main difference between the two is one of quality. But, although it may lack some of the extreme flavor and beautiful color of a vintage port, it can be a superb wine nonetheless.

Nonvintage ports are made into ruby or tawny types, and some small quantity is sold as "white" port. For this, only white grapes are used, and the wine is extremely pale and fairly dry. The French like to serve it as an apéritif, but the English consider it a freak wine.

Port is allowed to remain in huge casks called "pipes" for several years. During this period it develops the beautiful color called "ruby" in the port trade. It is the usual color of port. If it is left in the wood casks longer, much of this color disappears and the wine becomes a light brown or "tawny" port. Of course each shipper blends his ruby and tawny wines to produce the finished product in the recognized style of his house. The purchaser can expect to find his favorite type with exactly the same taste from year to year.

It is a pity that port is seldom seen in the United States. It is a superb wine for late afternoon or evening refreshment; but it is at its best at the end of a good dinner. In the fashionable circles of England a century ago, a meal without port was unheard of. The gentlemen at a dinner party always remained at the table for their port with walnuts, which they considered to be the perfect accompaniment. Today's gourmets favor port with cheese. No finer combination can be devised than cheddar cheese, or possibly Roquefort, with a fine glass of port wine.

In France another popular use for port is with melon—a few tablespoons of port are placed in the center of half a chilled melon and allowed to soak into the fruit for ten minutes before serving.

Portuguese Wheat. Wheat of about the same quality as most other European wheats.

Posset. Hot milk curdled with acid or wine.

Possole. A dish prepared with pork shoulder cut into cubes and cooked with fresh hominy, garlic, and chili peppers; popular in parts of the southwestern United States.

Possum Stew. *See* Opossum.

Posta de Carne (Portuguese). Steak.

Posta de Vaca (Portuguese). Beefsteak.

Postres (Spanish). Desserts; sweets.

Pot. (1) (French) Any container for liquids; a wine bottle equal to about three-fourths of a regular wine bottle. (2) A cooking utensil.

Potage (French). A thick (or sometimes clear) soup usually prepared with meat and vegetables. The distinction between a *soupe* and a *potage* is not clear, and the terms are sometimes used interchangeably.

   Potage Agnes Sorel. A creamed chicken soup with mushrooms.

   Potage à l'Ail. A garlic-and-milk soup served with cheese.

   Potage Argenteuil. An asparagus soup made with cream.

   Potage Aurore. A creamy rice soup with tomatoes.

   Potage aux Abatis. A giblet soup, often with rice and vegetables.

   Potage Célestine. A consommé containing strips of pancakes .

   Potage Choisy. A purée of lettuce soup.

   Potage Conti. A lentil soup made with bacon.

   Potage Crécy. A purée of carrot soup.

   Potage Cultivateur. A mixed-vegetable soup, usually made with bacon.

   Potage Dubarry. A cream-of-cauliflower soup; also, a creamy rice soup with cauliflower.

   Potage Écossaise. A mutton-and-barley soup, usually with vegetables.

   Potage Esau. A thick lentil soup.

Potager (French). A soup pot.

Potaje (Spanish). Soup.

Pot Ale. Residue from a grain distillery.

Potassium. A mineral normally plentiful in the diet, important in maintaining the acid-base balance, the osmotic pressure, and the health of nerves and muscles.

Potassium Metabisulfite. A chemical occasionally used as a preservative in citrus soft drinks.

Potatis (Swedish). Potatoes.

Potatismos (Swedish). Mashed potatoes.

Potatispuré (Swedish). Mashed potatoes.

Potatisallad (Swedish). Potato salad.

Potato. An edible tuber of a cultivated plant; first found growing in Peru, and a mainstay of diet during the Irish Famine. Sometimes considered very starchy, but actually contains less starch than certain other foods; besides, it has the advantage of being highly digestible. *White potatoes* are classified into two groups: the long type, a mealy potato, best for baking and mashing (the Idaho potato, excellent for baking, belongs to this group); and the round type, harder and waxier, best for boiling and other uses. New potatoes are those that have not yet reached full maturity and are delicious when boiled and served in their jackets. *Sweet potatoes*, which are the edible roots of a plant of the morning-glory family, also come in two types: one with pale yellow flesh that cooks dry; and the other, with deeper orange flesh, that is sweeter and moister. When buying potatoes, look for specimens that are rot-free, smooth-skinned, and reasonably clean. White potatoes should have shallow eyes and no green coloring on the skin. White potatoes are usually served as a side dish with the main course in baked, boiled, mashed, French- and German-fried, and roast form. They can be made into pancakes or used in casseroles. Sweet potatoes are popular when candied, mashed, or baked. White and sweet potatoes are also sold in frozen form and are made into dehydrated mixes for mashing and pancakes. The potato is the second largest food crop in the world after rice; considering its economical cost and versatility, as well as its nutritional value, this is not surprising. A product made from potatoes that deserves to be better known is *potato flour*, which is excellent as a thickening for sauces, since it cooks quickly and leaves no raw taste; also used in fine baking.

Potato Apple. The seed pod of the potato plant.

Potato Cheese. A German cheese (imitated in the United States) usually made from cow's milk although occasionally from sheep's or goat's milk, together with boiled potatoes.

Potato Crisps; Potato Chips. Potatoes peeled and sliced very thin, washed, soaked 30 minutes in cold water, and drained. They are then dried before deep-fat frying until golden brown and crisp.

Potato Flour. A fine, smooth flour made from potatoes; useful in baking and cooking, and to thicken sauces and stews. Also called Potato Starch.

Potato Masher. A wood or metal utensil of various shapes used to mash cooked potatoes smooth.

Potato Onions. Very early onions harvested, like potatoes, while still underground.

Potato Salad. Boiled, cubed potatoes mixed with mayonnaise or other desired dressing.

Potato Scone (British). A scone containing mashed potatoes; often fried with bacon and served at breakfast.

Potato Starch. A flour made from potatoes; used chiefly to thicken sauces, stews, etc.

Potato Straws (British). Potatoes peeled, cut into matchlike strips, washed, soaked, and drained. They are dried and then fried in deep fat until brown and crisp.

Pot-au-Feu (French). A very popular French soup, prepared with beef, many vegetables, and herbs. The meat is eaten separately, with condiments, usually pickles.

Pot Cake (British). A dumpling made in Norfolk.

Pot Cheese. Cheese similar to cottage cheese but with a much drier curd and with no additional milk or cream.

Pot de Crème (French). A very small individual portion of a rich puddinglike mixture usually made with vanilla or chocolate.

Potée (French). (1) Any dish cooked in an earthenware pot, including soups, stews, and bean dishes. (2) A soup with pork and vegetables.

Potée Limousine (French). A stew made of pork, chestnuts, and red cabbage.

Poteen. Illegally brewed Irish whiskey. *See* Ireland.

Pote Gallego (Spanish). A thick soup made with beans, meat, sausages, and vegetables.

Poteter (Norwegian). Potatoes.

Potetsalat (Norwegian). Potato salad.

Poteteskaker (Norwegian). Potato pancakes.

Potherb. Any plant or herb, such as parsley, used to flavor or season food. Also, any plant whose stems and leaves are boiled and eaten as a vegetable.

Pot Holder. A piece of insulated material used to protect the hands when touching hot cooking utensils.

Pothook. A specially designed hook used to suspend a kettle or other cooking container, particularly over an open fire.

Pothouse (British). Any place that sells beer; a saloon specializing in beer and ale.

Potiron. (1) A brightly colored pumpkin used in France for soups and jams. (2) A variety of mushroom.

Pot Liquor (Southern United States). Liquid left in a cooking container after salt pork has been cooked with green vegetables.

Potluck. A regular meal served to guests without special preparation; food available in the kitchen.

Pot Pie. (1) A stew made with dumplings. (2) A meat, game, or poultry mixture, sometimes with vegetables, covered with biscuit dough and baked.

Pot Posy. A number of herbs tied together and added to a soup or stew for additional flavoring; a *bouquet garni*.

Potpourri. Formerly a mixed meat stew. Sometimes a mixture of spices used to add flavor to soups, stews, etc.

Pot Roast. Meat that is browned, then cooked with very little liquid in a covered pot; variously prepared according to national cuisines.

Potroka. A vegetable bouillon thickened with egg yolks, flour, and cream and sprinkled with dill.

Pots de Crème St. Gervais. A fresh cream cheese often eaten with sugar as a dessert.

Pottage. A very thick, hearty soup.

Pottbrauo (Icelandic). A homemade country bread baked "under a pot" or over an open fire.

Potted Beef (British). Preserved beef.

Potted Meats. Commercially ground or chopped

meat, poultry, or game sold in cans or other containers.

Potting. Preserving in containers, as meats and fish, jams and preserves.

Pottinger (British). A spice merchant of the last century.

Pottle. (1) An old liquid or dry measure which equals two quarts or a half-gallon; a pot or tankard of this capacity. (2) A basket or other small vessel for fruit, particularly strawberries.

Pouding (French). Pudding.

   Pouding au Pain. Bread pudding.

   Pouding au Pain Bis. Brown-bread pudding.

   Pouding de Noël. Plum pudding or Christmas pudding.

Pougues. A salt mineral water bottled in Pougues, France.

Pouillard. A very young partridge.

Pouilly-Fuissé. A dry white wine with a greenish color, produced in the Mâconnais region of France; excellent with shellfish. *See* France, The Wines of.

Pouilly-Fumé. A fruity (sometimes dry) white wine produced in the Nivernais region of France. *See* France, The Wines of.

Pouilly-sur-Loire. A group of pleasant though not important wines produced in the Nivernais region of France. *See* France, The Wines of.

Poularde (French). A medium-sized fat fowl.

Poule (French). A boiling fowl.

Poule-au-Pot (French). A rich soup, made much like a *pot-au-feu*, but with a stuffed chicken added. *See* Pot-au-Feu.

Poule d'Eau (French). A water hen or moor hen; the flesh is very dark and oily, and must be well cooked before being eaten.

Poule de Grain (French). A young or spring chicken.

Poule de Neige (French). The ptarmigan, or white grouse, a game bird.

Poule Dinde (French). A young turkey.

Poule en Compôte (French). Chicken stew; made in the Gascony region.

Poulet à l'Arachide (French). In parts of Africa, a groundnut stew made with chicken, tomatoes, onions, peanuts, and plenty of spices. It is served with rice and an assortment of side dishes, such as onions, green peppers, pawpaws, coconut, fried banana, and pineapple spears.

Poulet de Grain (French). A medium-sized chicken, similar to a poularde.

Poulet Sauté (French). Cut-up pieces of chicken sautéed in butter.

Poulette (French). A hen or female chicken.

Poulette, À la (French). Served with a *velouté* sauce enriched with egg yolks; and sometimes onions and mushrooms; usually served with mussels and oysters.

Poulou (Iranian). Cooked rice combined with poultry, meat, and nuts.

Poulpe (French). Octopus.

Poultry. All domesticated fowl, particularly chickens, ducks, geese, turkeys, pheasants, and guinea hens. Chicken is unquestionably the most popular and important poultry in the United States and in most other countries of the world. Poultry has been raised for food for more than 3,000 years. Wild or game birds are not regarded as poultry.

   Drawn Poultry. Poultry with the viscera, head, and feet removed.

   Dressed Poultry. Poultry which has been bled and picked.

   Oven-Dressed Poultry. Poultry ready to use; not cut up.

   Pan-Dressed Poultry. Disjointed pieces of poultry, ready to use.

   Table-Dressed Poultry. Poultry whole or in parts, ready to use.

Poultry Needle. A long heavy needle with a large eye used to sew up the cavity of fowl, meats, or fish with string.

Poultry Seasoning; Poultry Spices. A commercially prepared combination of spices, usually including thyme, marjoram, and sage, designed for flavoring poultry.

Poumpo (French). A flat cake made with flour and olive oil and decorated on top with crosses made from raised paste; a specialty of Provence.

Pound. (1) To flatten, as meat; to pulverize, as nut meats or other dry ingredients. (2) A unit of weight equal to 16 ounces.

Pounder, Meat. Meat may be pounded with a special meat hammer with sharp-pointed edges, in order to break down the fibers and make the meat more tender. Any mallet, potato masher, or the like may be used.

Poupart; Tourteau. A large crab found on the French coasts; prepared like other types of crab.

Poupelin. A filled pastry made with whipped cream, fruit mousse, or ice cream.

Pourlécheries (French). A sweet pastry; made in the Touraine region.

Pourly, Fromage de (French). A very rich goat's-milk cheese with a somewhat oily quality; made in Burgundy; not good during the winter months.

Pourpier (French). A thick-leaved green used in salads or cooked as a vegetable.

Pousse au Crime (French Army Slang). Red wine.

Pousse-Café. (1) An afterdinner drink made by carefully pouring equal amounts of Cognac, cherry liqueur, orange liqueur, and crème de menthe successively into a glass so that each forms a layer. Any other different-colored liqueurs may also be used. (2) A bottled sweet chocolate-colored cordial.

Poussin (French). A young chicken.

Poussoir (French). A small machine used to make pork sausage.

Poustagnacq (French). A pungent, strong-flavored goat's-milk cheese eaten from April to November.

Poutargue. The salted roe of mullet or tuna, an inferior caviar.

Pouteton; Poulpeton (French). Ground meat rolled inside slices of another kind, often veal; usually braised.

Poutina et Nounat (French). Barely hatched young fish together with its roe boiled and served with lemon juice and olive oil; a specialty of the Nice area.

Poutine. Very small fish, including sardines and anchovies; usually rolled in flour and fried.

Powdered Silk Vermicelli; Long Rice Noodle (Chinese). A translucent noodle, usually made from mungo beans.

Powdered Sugar. Pulverized sugar, very fine in quality, combined with tricalcium phosphate, cornstarch, etc. The more X's after the name the smoother and more delicate the sugar.

Power Cod. A delicately flavored fish of the cod family, roughly resembling a large smelt.

Powsowdie (Scotch). A broth prepared from a sheep's head.

Prager Ham (German). Prague-style ham.

Prague Ham. A delicately flavored, very pink ham originally made in Prague, Czechoslovakia, but now made in other parts of the world. It is best when served cold, cut into paper-thin slices, and accompanied by a glass of Pilsener beer.

Praire (French). A European shellfish much like the clam.

Prairie Hen. An American grouse.

Prairie Oyster. A popular American drink, reputedly a restorative following excessive alcoholic indulgence. It is prepared by placing a whole egg in a glass and adding a little vinegar, salt, and pepper. The whole egg is to be "drunk" before the vinegar. Other versions are made with ketchup, Worcestershire sauce, etc., and some are made with liquor as well.

Praline. In New Orleans, a sweet confection made of pecan nuts and caramel sugar in a characteristic flat shape; in France, a confection made with almonds.

Praliné (French). Flavored with burnt almonds.

Praline Nougat. A confection in which hazelnuts or almonds are added to lemon juice and melted sugar to form a hard nougat, then spread out very thin on an oiled baking sheet to cool.

Praline Paste. Nougat rolled smooth.

Praliner (French). To add praline to such desserts as mousse, custard, or ice cream.

Pranzo (Italian). Dinner.

Pranzo di Legumi all'Uovo (Italian). Vegetable plate with an egg.

Prasline. The original spelling of the name of a confection made of burnt roasted almonds coated with a sugar syrup; as years went by, the letter "s" was dropped.

Pratelle; Pratille des Champs; Psalliote. A good-tasting wild pink mushroom.

Prato. A Brazilian imitation of Edam cheese; yellow and fairly firm.

Pratos de Almoço (Portuguese). Luncheon dishes.

Pratos de Carne (Portuguese). Meat dishes.

Pratos Frios (Portuguese). Cold buffet; cold dishes.

Prattigau. A spicy Swiss cheese resembling Limburger.

Preisselbeeren (German). Red berries similar to cranberries.

Prémeaux. A wine district of the Burgundy region of France. *See* France, The Wines of.

Premières Côtes de Bordeaux. A wine district of the Bordeaux region of France. *See* France, The Wines of.

Premier Garçon (French). Head waiter.

Premier Jus. The best-quality suet prepared from oxen and sheep kidneys. The fat is chilled, chopped, and melted over moderate heat. When pressed, *premier jus*, like rendered tallow, separates into a liquid portion (oleo oil, or liquid oleo) and a solid portion (oleo-stearin, or solid tallow).

Premonata (Corsican). Beef stewed with juniper berries.

Presentoir (French). The surface on which a serving dish rests.

Preserved Eggs; Hundred Year Old Eggs (Chinese). Duck eggs, as a rule, covered with a fairly thick coating of lime, salt, and ashes, then covered with earth and allowed to mature for about 3 months; these are called *pay don*. In another method the eggs are covered only with salt; these are called *harm don*. Because of their unusual taste and consistency, they are considered a delicacy.

Press. (1) Cupboard. (2) A kitchen device for extracting juice from fruits, meats, and vegetables. (3) To force a food through a strainer or fine sieve.

Prés-Salés (French). Young sheep pastured in salt marsh regions of France, where the grass is heavily salted by the ocean winds; they have an unusual delicate taste.

Pressed Caviar. Caviar in which the eggs are gently pressed as a conservation measure. It has a very good taste and is appreciated by connoisseurs. The true natural pressed caviar is sold in glass jars.

Pressgurka (Swedish). Cucumber salad; cucumber relish.

Pressoir (French). A machine that presses apples, grapes, etc.

Pressure Cooker. A cooking vessel with a tightly fitting lid that prevents loss of steam, controlled by a pressure valve. Very little liquid is used, and the steam is generated under high pressure to a temperature much higher than that of boiling water. Foods are therefore cooked in a much shorter time. Manufacturer's instructions indicate how the pressure is to be reduced before removing the lid.

Pressylta (Swedish). Headcheese.

Presunto (Portuguese). Smoked ham.

Pretost. Saaland Pfarr, a Swedish cheese that resembles Holland's Gouda cheese but contains whisky.

Prêtre. A sand smelt found along the Atlantic coast of France. It has a delicate though slightly fishy taste.

Pretzels. Crisp hard twists made from flour, water, shortening, yeast, and salt. The dough is fermented, cut into lengths, and shaped. Pretzels are boiled first, then salted, baked, and dried.

Preziosini al Pomodoro (Italian). Fried dumplings with tomato sauce.

Prezzemolo (Italian). Parsley.

Prickly Pear. A tropical cactus whose pear-shaped fruit is covered with prickles in various colors. The thinnest-skinned ones are quite juicy and flavorsome.

Pricota. An English apricot-flavored afterdinner drink.

Prima Colazione (Italian). Breakfast.

Primavera. A white medium-firm Brazilian cheese.

Primeiro Almoço (Portuguese). Breakfast.

Prime Ribs. The first five ribs of beef, a superior cut for roast beef.

Primeurs (French). (1) The first fruits and vegetables of the season. (2) Hothouse products, obtained before normal season of maturity.

Primitivo. A dry red wine produced in Puglia, Italy.

Primrose. A flowering plant whose leaves are sometimes used in salad.

Primula. A very mild whitish Norwegian cheese, a sort of cross between Gruyère and Brie; marketed in small portions.

Prinsessen Bonen (Dutch). String beans.

Printanier. With fresh vegetables cut in small pieces and usually served with butter. Also, a garnish of vegetables served in soups.

Printanière, À la. Garnished with young tender vegetables, usually including asparagus tips and peas.

Prise (German). Sweetbreads.

Prizzutu (Corsican). Cured ham.

Profiteroles. Small cream puffs filled with any desired sweet mixture, such as custards, creams, or ice cream, and served for dessert. When used as an accompaniment for soups, they are usually not filled and may be fried crisp, or they may be made with savory fillings.

Promessi. A very soft Italian fresh-cream cheese.

Prosanico. An Italian wine made in Umbria.

Prosciutto (Italian). Smoked ham served paper thin.

Prosciutto Crudo (Italian). Raw ham.

Prosciutto di Cinghiale (Italian). A smoked ham much like ordinary prosciutto but made from wild boar; a specialty of Sardinia.

Prosciutto e Melone (Italian). Smoked ham and melon.

Proseco di Conegliano. An Italian table wine. *See* Italy, The Wines of.

Prosen Hot Pot. A lamb or mutton stew made with onions, tomatoes, and carrots.

Protein Milk. Acid milk with curd. It is richer in protein than ordinary milk and is thought to be better tolerated in digestive disorders.

Proteins. Essential constituents of all living cells because they contain nitrogen. Meat, fish, eggs, and cheese are protein foods.

Provençal Aillade (French). Tomatoes, garlic, basil, and olive oil pounded together.

Provençale, À la (French). With olive oil, tomatoes, garlic, spices, and sometimes eggplant.

Provender. Usually, food for animals; occasionally, human food.

Providence. A Port du Salut cheese made in France.

Provolcine; Provole; Provoletti; Provolino; Provoloncini. *See* Provolone.

Provolone. A fairly mild, hard, smoky cheese varying from cream color to pale yellow. The original is made in Italy from water-buffalo milk; American imitations, lacking this kind of milk, are pallid by comparison. The cheese is cured by being allowed to hang in string nets. It comes in all sizes and shapes, from very small to monsters weighing 50 pounds or more; and is called by various names. The young cheeses have a fresh taste, but the older ones are quite biting and sharp.

Pršut. Yugoslavian smoked ham similar in taste to Italian prosciutto.

Prugne (Italian). Prunes.

Pruim (Dutch). Plum.

Prune. *See* Prunes.

Pruneau (French). Dried plum.

Prune de Reine-Claude (French). A small greengage plum.

Prunella. An Italian plum cordial.

Prunelle. A French liqueur made chiefly from plums.

Prunello. A dried plum or small prune.

Prunes. Any kind of dried plum either dried naturally in the sun or in the oven. Although it is not known exactly when the drying of plums first took place, it is surely an ancient practice, probably having had its origins in the Middle East. The American Indians frequently dried plums for future use and as a source of compact food for journeys.

After the plums drop from the tree, they are dipped in a solution (usually lye) to prevent fermentation, and are sun-dried or oven-dried. The pits are almost never removed. The western United States, particularly California and Oregon, is the chief supplier of prunes. The best types are especially treated for eating; the poorer qualities are intended for cooking. In France and Italy excellent-quality prunes are produced. Stewed prunes and prune juice traditionally are recommended for their laxative qualities. Prunes may be used in compotes, in pies, puddings, whips, and cakes; they are frequently stuffed with nuts and eaten like candy.

Prussian Rye Bread. A very dark bread made from coarse rye, particularly good with cheese and beer.

Psalliote; Pratille des Champs. A delicately flavored field or forest mushroom.

P'teux. A French cooked cheese prepared with white wine.

Pucelotte; Pucelette; Gai Fish. An excellent-tasting European fish.

Puchero (Spanish, South American). Soup-stew prepared with meat, chicken, vegetables, and sausage.

Pudding. A wide variety of dishes, savory or sweet, hot or cold, elaborate or simple. Puddings may be divided into two rough categories—those eaten with other foods, and those eaten as a dessert. Yorkshire pudding is a classic example of the first category; plum pudding is a famous sweet dessert pudding. Puddings can be made with a wide variety of ingredients, including rice, fruits, vegetables, tapioca, semolina, noodles, etc. Some culinary experts regard custards as puddings, others classify them separately.

 Pudim (Portuguese). Pudding.

 Pudim de Abobora. Pumpkin pudding.

 Pudim de Nozes. Walnut pudding.

 Pudim de Ovos. Custard.

 Pudim Portuguez. Orange pudding.

Pudín (Spanish). Pudding.

Puerco (Spanish). Pork.

Puerco en Estofado (Spanish). A spicy pork stew.

Puerros (Spanish). Leeks.

Puerto Rico. The local fruits are worthy of note: these include the citron, *cocoplum* (used for preserves), custard apple, *genipap*, *guama*, guava, *guinep*, *hevi*, mango, sour orange, papaya, pineapple, *granada* (pomegranate), roseapple, sapodilla, sea grape, soursop, star apple, tamarind, the yellow mombin, and a wide variety of bananas. Of equal interest are the many unusual vegetables: root vegetables like *apio*, *cassava*, *leren*, *yampee*, *yautía*, and *batata*; there are also fresh vegetables, including breadfruit, chayote, eggplant, plantain, and dozens of kinds of beans.

 The favorite soups are bean or meat soups; very thick soup-stews include the *rancho*, *sancocho*, and *cocido*, which frequently serve as main courses. Fish is often fried with tomatoes, onions, and garlic, or made into *pasteles* (individual portions covered with a paste); perhaps best of all, Puerto Ricans like dried codfish, *bacalao*, surprising as this may seem in view of their bountiful fish supply. Meat and poultry dishes are usually prepared as stews, often with rice. *Asopao* is seafood or chicken and rice, so thin that it might well be called "soupy rice." *Mofongo* is a mixture of plantain, garlic, olive oil, and *chicharrón* (pork skin); *mondongo* is a tripe stew with ham and olives.

 Fruits are favored for desserts, fresh, stewed, or preserved. There are also *ponqué* (undoubtedly derived from pound cake), *sopa borracha* (a cake with liquor or wine), *polvorones* (lard cookies), *besitos de coco* (coconut macaroons), and many puddings made from pumpkin, sweet potato, and the like. Fritters and doughnuts are very popular.

 Fresh-fruit drinks are just about a necessity in the warm climate; almost every fruit is used for making some type of cold drink; *garapiña* is made from pineapple peelings, for example. Of course, the local coffee is the standard hot beverage, but hot chocolate retains a measure of popularity.

Puff. A light pastry, such as cream puff.

Puffball. Wild mushroom.

 Common Puffball. A wild mushroom, measuring about 2 inches across the top; white when immature, then yellow-brown.

 Giant Puffball. A wild mushroom often measuring a foot across the top.

 Mosaic Puffball. A wild mushroom measuring about 6 inches across the top.

Puffed Peas; Nokhodchi (Iranian). Peas treated so that they puff up and have a nutlike flavor.

Puffed Rice. A dry breakfast cereal, usually eaten with sugar and milk or cream.

Puffer. A fritter prepared with flaked oats, water, sugar, salt, and eggs, and dusted with cinnamon.

Puffy. As applied to food, swollen or inflated as a result of beating or of the application of heat.

Puits d'Amour (French). Small crowns of puff pastry filled with custard or jam, usually decorated with whipped cream, jelly, and icing.

Pukeko. A New Zealand bird usually regarded as unsuitable for the table, but when cooked a long time over very low heat, it makes a soup vaguely resembling turtle soup.

Pulao; Pullao (Indian). A rice dish prepared by

sautéing pulao rice in fat, then slowly cooking it with soup stock and other ingredients.

Pulao Rice. A thin, long variety of Indian rice less starchy than the ordinary variety.

Pulassan. A fairly good-tasting Indonesian fruit with a single seed.

Pulauri (Trinidad). A snack specialty consisting of split peas and fried dough dipped in mango chutney.

Puligny-Montrachet. A dry white wine region of Burgundy, France. It produces very good wines known for their bouquet. *See* France, The Wines of.

Pulled Bread. The inside soft part of bread pulled into small pieces while hot and baked until crisp.

Pullet. A rather young hen, especially one less than a year old.

Pulost Cheese. *See* Knost.

Pulp. The fleshy, moist part of a fruit or vegetable.

Pulpe (French). Pulp; the soft part of fruits or melons.

Pulque (Mexican). An intoxicating beverage made from the fermented juice of maguey, a local desert plant.

Pulquerías (Mexican). Saloons and other places where pulque and other beverages are dispensed.

Pulse. The edible seeds of various legumes, such as peas and beans.

Pultost (Norwegian). A sour-milk mixture made with buttermilk.

Pulverized Sugar. A very fine sugar that dissolves instantly; used for delicate cakes, pastry creams, and in iced drinks.

Pumpernickel (German). A dark sourish heavy-textured bread; particularly good with hearty cheese and with sweet butter.

Pumpkin. The fruit, in a wide range of sizes, of a trailing plant. It has not been found growing wild, but was probably first raised in South or Central America. On the other hand, there is some evidence that it may have been grown for food in China over two thousand years ago. The English word is derived from the Greek *pepon*, meaning sun-dried. Pumpkins vary tremendously in size; some are quite small, whereas prize specimens weigh several hundred pounds.

Enormous size does not improve flavor; the fairly small specimens are probably the best-tasting. In most of Europe pumpkin is used chiefly as a vegetable. In the United States it is used for soup, as a vegetable, and classically in pie form. The Pilgrims, at their first Thanksgiving, made pumpkin the popular American favorite that it is. The line that separates pumpkin from squash has never been clearly defined, and the terms are frequently used interchangeably.

Pumpkin-Pie Spices. A mixture of spices, usually including ginger, cinnamon. and cloves. used to flavor pumpkin pie.

Punch à la Romaine. A soft white lemon-flavored ice prepared with lemon juice, water, egg white, sugar, and rum, served between courses to refresh the palate.

Puncheon. A 2-gallon beer cask or a 120-gallon Scotch whisky cask.

Punt e Mes. An Italian apéritif drink similar to vermouth.

Puré de Patatas (Spanish). Mashed potatoes.

Purée. (1) Any food, including fruit, poultry, meat, or vegetable, usually cooked, then made smooth by mashing or smoothing it free of lumps, or by using an electric blender. (2) (French) A puréed soup, such as Purée Saint-Cloud, a green-pea soup.

Purée de Marrons au Naturel. Plain chestnut purée; used for stuffing poultry.

Purée-Presser. A commercial product, of which there are many types, used to press through purées of meats, fish, fruits, and vegetables.

Puri (Indian). Whole-meal bread deep-fat fried in ghee (clarified butter).

Purl (British). An old-fashioned cold-weather drink made of ale and beer heated and added to gin and bitters.

Purry (Scotch). Purée.

Purslane. A very small European wild plant with tender, edible stems; used raw in salads or cooked as a vegetable like spinach. It has a somewhat sticky quality, much like okra.

Pusa Wheat. A strong, glossy Australian wheat.

Puso ng Saging (Philippine). Edible banana blossoms.

Puttonyos. A measure of grapes used in making

Hungarian Tokay wine. *See* Hungary, The Wines of.

Putupap (South African). A type of cornmeal mush, usually served with *Boerwors*, a homemade sausage.

PX. Pedro Ximéniz, a sherry used for blending.

Pyrex. Trade name for a kind of glassware that resists extreme heat and also acids.

Pyrometer. A temperature-indicating instrument; often used to check ovens.

Pytt i Panna (Swedish). Meat hash with onions and potatoes.

Q

Quache. A Greek sheep's-milk cheese.

Quadretti; Quadrucci (Italian). Small squares of pasta served in soup.

Quadrettini (Italian). Elbow macaroni; sometimes flat squares of pasta.

Quadrille. Thin strips of pastry laid across open tarts in a checkered or lattice pattern.

Quaff. To take a long deep drink, or to drink repeatedly in this manner.

Quagliata. A Sicilian goat's-milk cheese.

Quaglie (Italian). Quail.

Quahaug; Quahog. A round hard-shelled clam found chiefly along the New England coast; excellent for chowder.

Quaich (Scotch, Obsolete). A shallow wooden drinking cup.

Quail. A small migratory bird allied to the partridge; found in Europe, Australia, and the United States. The meat is delicate but dry, so it must be basted with fat or liquid.

Quail Dove. A very tasty dove of the West Indies and Florida.

Quail Pigeon. A pigeon in the genus *Geophaps*; eaten as a game bird.

Quail Snipe. A South American plover which has a good taste, although it is sometimes rather tough and stringy.

Quamash. A North American plant of the lily family whose bulbs were formerly used for food by the American Indians.

Quameh (Iranian). A stew made of chopped meat with split peas and a sour-fruit juice.

Quandong. An Australian fruit that resembles a peach; often regarded as the native peach, but it has a different taste and texture. Its edible nut is palatable.

Quarenden (British). A variety of apple common in Devon and Somerset.

Quark (German). Cottage cheese.

Quarkklösse (German). Sweet dumplings made with cottage cheese.

Quart. A measure of liquid capacity, ¼ gallon or 2 pints.

Quart de Chaume. A distinctive yellow-gold-green white wine produced in the Anjou region of France.

Quarter. To cut into four pieces; to divide into four parts.

Quartern Loaf (British). A loaf of bread.

Quarter of Beef. The forepart of beef, including the shoulder and sides.

Quarter of Wheat (British). Eight bushels of grain. To avoid confusion, wheat is now more frequently sold by the cental, or 100 pounds.

Quartier d'Agneau (French). A forequarter of lamb, including the ribs, breast, and shoulder.

Quartier de Derrière (French). A hindquarter of lamb.

Quartier de Devant (French). A forequarter of lamb.

Quartier de Lard (French). The salted and cured side of pork.

Quartier de Porc Salé (French). The ribs or spareribs and shoulder of salted pork.

Quartiolo (Italian). Any Parmesan-type cheese made during September, October, and November.

Quart Pot (British). A pot with a capacity of one quart.

Quasi (French). A cut from the rump of veal.

Quassia. The wood of a tropical tree that provides a medicinal bitters used in apéritifs and sometimes in beer.

Quatourze; Quatorze. White, red, and *rosé* wines produced in the Languedoc region of France. The reds age well; the whites do not.

Quatre-Épices (French). (1) A mixture of spices and herbs (actually more than four) including pepper, allspice, mace, nutmeg, cloves, cinnamon, bay leaves, rosemary, marjoram, and sage, all pounded together. (2) An African tree with a spicy odor.

Quatre-Fruits (French, Obsolete). The four red fruits—red currants, cherries, raspberries, and strawberries.

Quatre-Quarts (French). A cake similar to pound cake, prepared with equal amounts of egg, butter, sugar, and flour.

Quatre Saisons (French). (1) A variety of strawberry. (2) The vegetable and fruit produce of the various seasons.

Quatre-Sous. A comparatively little-known French cheese of good texture but with a strong, sometimes overpowering odor.

Queen Apple. An early apple of moderate quality.

Queen Cake. Many varieties of small plain or fruit cakes baked in fancy molds; often, a currant cake.

Queening. A variety of apple, no longer popular.

Queensland Nut. Another name for the Macadamia nut.

Queen's Taste. Perfect; unsurpassable.

Queen's Ware. Cream-colored Wedgwood ware or a kind of stoneware, usually bordered with a grape-leaf design.

Queijadas de Sintra (Portuguese). Cheesecakes.

Queijo (Portugal). Cheese.

Queimado. A hot, spiced punch formerly prepared by the Portuguese in Bombay from the liquor of the coconut palm.

Quench. To satisfy hunger or thirst completely.

Quenelle (French). A seasoned ball of finely ground or chopped meat or fish, sometimes mixed with a cream puff paste, then poached.

Quenelles de Brochet (French). A classic dish consisting of ground pike mixed with a cream puff paste and gently poached in water; usually served with a shellfish sauce.

Quentao. A Brazilian hot rum drink made with lemon juice, sugar, spices, etc.

Quente (Portuguese). Hot.

Queriman. A rather good-tasting fish found in the Guianas, South America.

Quern. A hand mill for grinding corn; also a small hand mill for grinding pepper, etc.

Quernstone. A millstone.

Quesadilla (Mexican). A *tortilla* stuffed with cheese and peppers or any other desired filling and fried crisp.

Quesadillitas (Mexican). Small *quesadillas*.

Quesillo (Spanish). *Flan*, the favorite caramel custard of Latin countries.

Queso (Spanish). Cheese.

    Queso Blanco. White cheese.

    Queso Fresco. Fresh cream or cottage cheese.

    Queso Gallego. A medium-soft cheese.

Queso Amarillo (Latin American). Yellow cheese, usually cheddar cheese.

Queso Anejo. A Mexican dry white skim-milk cheese.

Queso de Bola (Spanish, Philippine). An Edam cheese or any firm rennet cheese made into a ball shape, usually with a red rind.

Queso de Cincho. A simple Venezuelan cheese marketed in firm orange-colored balls weighing about 4 pounds.

Quesong Puti. A fairly soft white Philippine cheese.

Quetsch d'Alsace. A colorless strong plum liqueur; should be served ice cold; sometimes sipped through a lump of sugar.

Quetsche. An oblong plump plum used for making tarts, jams, and a liqueur.

Queue (French). The tail of an animal.

    Queue d'Agneau. Lamb's tail, usually cooked in soups or stews.

    Queue de Boeuf. Beef tail, used for oxtail soup and stews.

    Queue de Mouton. Sheep's tail.

    Queue de Porc. Pig's tail, usually pickled in brine.

    Queue de Veau. Calf's tail.

Queue de Gîte (French). A cut of beef resembling the shin cut.

Queues d'Écrevisse (French). Crayfish tails.

Queux (Obsolete). A medieval name for cooks.

Queyras. A semisoft white French cheese with a light crust.

Quiche (French). An unsweetened open custard tart to which a variety of ingredients may be added. The classic quiche is made with bacon, but it may also be prepared with cheese, shrimp, etc.

    Quiche Lorraine. An unsweetened custard-and-bacon tart, often served as a first course.

The many variations include *quiche au fromage*, made with cheese; *quiche aux saumon*, made with salmon; and *quiche aux oignons*, made with onions.

Quick Breads. Breads made with baking powder or baking soda instead of yeast; including biscuits, muffins, popovers, waffles, and griddle cakes.

Quicken. The juniper berry.

Quick-Freeze. To place foods in a special apparatus in which they will be frozen rapidly. Slowly frozen foods develop ice crystals, which cause deterioration of both taste and texture.

Quickie. A very small drink of any alcoholic beverage; a drink taken in a hurry.

Quignon (French). A wedge from a large bread.

Quillaja. Soapbark, dried bark that contains sapotoxin, tannin, and quillaja and produces foam in soft drinks.

Quillet (French). A pastry made in round cake tins, filled, then piped with a butter cream and sprinkled with sugar.

Quillettes. Small dessert cookies usually pencil-shaped, sometimes chocolate-coated.

Quill Pig. Porcupine.

Quimbombó. Okra.

Quin. A type of scallop.

Quince. (1) A hard, acid, yellowish pear-shaped fruit; made into a preserve or used to flavor other fruits. (2) Other fruits or trees resembling the quince. Native quince is the Australian *bitterbark*, also called the *emu apple*, or *quinine tree*.

Quinchoncho. The pigeon pea.

Quincy. A dry white French wine with a "flinty" taste, produced in Berry; especially good with shellfish preparations.

Quinnat; Californian Salmon; Chinook Salmon; Columbian Salmon. The king salmon, an excellent food fish found along the North Pacific coast.

Quinoa; Quinua. An annual plant native to the Pacific slopes of the Andes and cultivated in Chile and Peru for its edible cereal-like seeds. The flour obtained from the seeds is similar to, but paler than, buckwheat flour. It is used experimentally in doughs when testing the effects of oxidation, since it apparently has a much higher concentration of oxidizing enzymes than does wheat flour.

Qutaif (Arabian). A dessert similar to pancakes, made of very thin batter, fried in sweet almond oil, and served with a rich syrup and a sprinkling of rose water.

R

Raab. A vegetable native to the southern United States; it resembles broccoli and has a cabbage-like flavor, but no head.

Rabaçal. A fair-quality medium-soft Portuguese cheese made from sheep's or goat's milk.

Rabanadas (Portuguese). A fried sweet bread dessert.

Rabanetes (Portuguese). Radishes.

Rábano (Spanish). Radish.

Rábano Picante (Spanish). Horseradish.

Rabão (Portuguese). Radish.

Rabarbaro. An Italian apéritif drink made from rhubarb.

Rabarber (Danish, Dutch, Swedish). Rhubarb.

Rabinovka. A Balkan sweet liqucur flavored with rowanberry (mountain ash).

Rabiole. A variety of turnip or kohlrabi.

Rabbit. (1) An edible member of the rodent family found in various parts of the world but especially in temperate climates. The distinction between a rabbit and a hare is none too clear, and in many parts of the world the terms are used interchangeably; in other places "rabbit" refers to a young specimen, and "hare" refers to one over a year old.

Young rabbits are far more delicate in taste than the older specimens, which are likely to be tough, dry, and strong. In any event, young or old, rabbit has a better flavor when allowed to age for a few days. Because the flesh is dry, it should be marinated, preferably in wine or vinegar, and cut into pieces for stewing or slow cooking. The best-known rabbit dish is *Hasenpfeffer*, a great favorite in Germany. (2) Rarebit; a mixture made with melted cheese; usually poured over toast; it does not contain rabbit. *See* Rarebit.

Rabbit Cheese (Colloquial). Cheddar cheese.

Rable (French). The back of a hare or rabbit, corresponding to the saddle of lamb.

Rable du Lievre (French). The back of a hare or rabbit prepared in a sort of stew; a French provincial specialty.

Rabo de Buey (Spanish). Oxtail.

Rabotte. Fruit, such as apples or pears, enclosed in a short-crust pastry and baked.

Rabri (Indian). Thick sweet milk.

Racahout; Racachou (Arabian, Turkish). A preparation consisting of acorn flour, potato flour, rice, sugar, cocoa, vanilla, and salep (powdered orchid root). Originally it was a substitute for chocolate, and in France is prepared like chocolate for drinking.

Raccoon. A small wild animal which can be prepared like wild rabbit.

Rachel (French). A garnish for broiled meats; contains poached marrow, artichoke hearts, and Bordélaise sauce.

Rächerkäse (German). All smoked cheeses.

Racines (French). Root vegetables usually served as garnishes.

Racking. Drawing or siphoning off a clear wine from the deposit.

Raclette (Swiss). A dish made by holding Gourmois cheese close to the fire until it melts. It is then scraped onto a plate and eaten with boiled potatoes and pickles.

Radener. A hard, rather dry German cheese greatly resembling Swiss Emmentaler.

Radici (Italian). Radishes.

Radieschen (German). Radishes.

Radijs (Dutch). Radish.

Radish. An annual or biennial plant of the mustard family that has a basal rosette of leaves. Native to China and now grown throughout the world, it is esteemed for its pungent, crisp flesh. It can be red, black, or white; round or elongated; large or small. The Japanese and Chinese grow a turnip-shaped specimen that may weigh up to 50 pounds. Perhaps the most quickly and easily grown vegetable of the home garden, it is eaten raw as a relish, and cut into slices for salads and into elaborate shapes for garnishes, "radish roses" being a familiar accompaniment to cold meats and salads. Radishes are particularly good when dipped in coarse salt and spread with a little sweet butter. Although the roots are useless, the tops can be used in salads if they are very young and finely shredded. Radishes are low in calories, and are recommended for reducing diets because they are bulky and filling and have a diuretic action.

Radolfzeller Cream. A German-Austrian cheese resembling Münster.

Raeker (Norwegian). Shrimp.

Rafano (Italian). Horseradish.

Raffinade. Refined sugar.

Raffinose; Melitose; Melitriose. A sweet substance present in cotton seed, sugar-beet molasses, and Australian manna.

Rafraîchir (French). (1) To refresh or to cool. (2) An ice served between the fish and meat courses.

Rag. The white inner pulp found on oranges and lemons.

Rågbröd (Swedish). Rye bread.

Ragged Parasol. A wild white-gray mushroom, about 5 inches across the top, that tends to grow in clusters. The caps, the best part, are particularly good when young.

Raggmunkar (Swedish). Griddle cakes made with potatoes.

Ragnit. *See* Tilsit.

Ragno (Italian). Bass.

Ragot (French). A wild boar over two years old.

Ragoule; Barigoule (French, Colloquial). The agaric, an edible fungus.

Ragoût (French). (1) A highly seasoned stew made with meat, poultry, or fish, and sometimes with vegetables. (2) A thick sauce, usually made of meat.

> **Ragoût à la Deutsch.** Beef-and-vegetable stew.
> **Ragoût Fin de Sole.** Strips of sole served with mushrooms, asparagus tips, crayfish, and a Hollandaise sauce.

Ragù alla Bolognese (Italian). A rich tomato-and-meat sauce.

Ragueneau. A once-famous Parisian pastry cook who developed many new preparations.

Rahat Lakoum. Turkish delight, a sweet candy.

Rahm. (German). Cream.

Raidir (French). To sear or seal; to brown quickly in butter; to fry in deep fat.

Raie au Beurre Noir (French). Skate cooked in brown butter with a little vinegar.

Raifort (French). Horseradish.

Rail. A wild game bird native to swampy regions; it has a delicate taste and is best in cool weather.

Railway Pudding (British). A plain sponge pudding usually split, filled with jam, topped with a sprinkling of sugar, and served cold.

Rainwater Madeira. A fine type of Madeira wine, originated by a Mr. Habersham. *See* Portugal, The Wines of.

Raiponce. A wild or cultivated bellflower whose edible roots and leaves may be used raw in salads or cooked as a vegetable.

Raised Pies (British). Pies cooked in pastry shells unsupported by pie pans or paper to hold the sides up.

Raisin (French). Grape.

Raisins. Grapes dried naturally in the sun or by artificial means. Most seedless raisins are produced from Sultana or Thompson seedless grapes. The white muscat, a flavorful raisin containing seeds, is sold in clusters for table use. Seedless raisins of pronounced flavor and firm texture are sometimes sold as currants. A good source of sugar, iron, and vitamins A and B, raw raisins make an excellent snack food. Raisins are also used in making cookies, muffins, puddings, and cakes, and in sweet-sour sauces for tongue and ham. Raisins are produced on a large scale in the United States, especially in California, and in Spain, South Africa, and Australia. Sultanas, which are fairly small, light in color, and seedless, are the most important commercially.

Raisin de Corinthe (French). Currant.

Raisiné (French). (1) Food cooked in raisin juice. (2) Jam prepared with raisins, apples, pears, or quince; eaten with bread or used as filling for tarts.

Raising Powder. *See* Baking Powder.

Raisin Sec (French). Raisin.

Raita (Indian). Several dishes, typically consisting

of chopped tomatoes, cheese curd, chili peppers, coriander, and seasoning.

Raite (Greek). A vegetable stew containing tomatoes, walnuts, onions, oil, garlic, wine, and herbs; usually garnished with capers and black olives.

Raiton (French). A small skate.

Raja Fish. The skate.

Raki (Balkan, Middle Eastern). A brandy or strong liquor made of plums, grapes, or mulberries flavored with aniseed and mastic.

Rakia. A sweet, cloying Hungarian liqueur made from grapes with a high sugar content.

Rakija. Another name for slivovitz, a Yugoslavian plum brandy.

Räkor (Swedish). Shrimp.

Rakørret-Raketrout (Norwegian). Salted aged trout; kept until it is moldy and has an odd, spicy taste.

Rakpaprikas (Hungarian). A dish made with a tomato purée, crayfish, and spices, particularly paprika.

Rale. A small, comparatively scarce European game bird of the quail family.

Ramadan. In Moslem countries, the ninth month of the Mohammedan year, a month of stringent fasting. From sunrise to sunset, no Mohammedan may eat or drink.

Ramadoux. A very soft white creamy Belgian cheese made and sold in cubes.

Rambour. An early large red or white tart apple cultivated in the Rambour district of France.

Rambutinn. A Malaysian fruit whose taste resembles that of a very large grape or cherry.

Ramekin; Ramequin. (1) A small baking dish holding only one portion. (2) Pieces of cheese and bread soaked in a mixture of eggs, milk, and melted butter, and baked.

Ramequin Jurassienne (French). Small pastry shells filled with a mixture of cooked leeks, bacon, and cream cheese.

Ramereau (French). A young wood pigeon, often used for food.

Ramier (French). A wild wood pigeon.

Rampion. A European plant, also grown in other parts of the world, whose thick white roots may be eaten raw, used in salads, or cooked as a vegetable.

Ramson. A species of garlic whose leaves are boiled and served as a green vegetable in some parts of Europe.

Rancho (Puerto Rican). A one-dish meal, like a stew, containing meat, noodles, and vegetables.

Rancid. Spoiled, having an unpleasant taste, especially as applied to butter and oils.

Rancio. A mature wine which has passed its peak and whose age may be determined by tasting.

R & R. Rock and rye, a liquor term.

Range. Stove; equipment or apparatus, usually operated by gas or electricity, upon which cooking is done.

Rangiport. A French cheese much like Port du Salut but somewhat lacking its flavor.

Rangpar; Rangpur. A reddish citrus fruit with orange flesh; about the size of a lemon.

Rape. (1) Grape stems and skins from which the must or juice has been expressed; used to make an inferior, thin wine. (2) A plant of the cabbage family, sometimes used in salads. (3) A forage crop whose seeds yield a cooking oil used in India. (4) The frogfish or anglerfish, having an oily taste and soft texture.

Rapé (French). Grated. *Fromage rapé* is grated cheese.

Raper. A French cheese. *See* Rayon.

Râper (French). To grate or shred.

Rapphöna (Swedish). Partridge.

Rare. Undercooked; usually applied to meat cooked just enough to suit the taste of those who like rare meat, such as rare roast beef.

Rarebit. Cheese prepared with seasonings and beer heated together until the cheese melts; served over toast; sometimes also called Rabbit.

Rasam (Indian). A spicy tomato-and-lentil soup.

Rascasio (Spanish). The rockfish; it has a mediocre taste, and is best when cooked slowly in soups and stews.

Rascasse. A Mediterranean fish considered an essential ingredient of bouillabaisse and other French fish soups.

Rasgulla (Indian). A classic dessert made of cream-cheese balls in rose-flavored syrup.

Rasp. A large coarse file with a turned-back handle used by bakers to scrape away burned crusts from bread, rolls, and other baked products.

Raspaduro. *Papelón*, the unrefined brown sugar prepared in several Latin countries.

Raspail. A French sweet liqueur made of herbs and plants.

Raspberry. A fruit produced on certain low perennial shrubs or plants belonging to the genus *Rubus*. Raspberries are usually reddish in color but they may also be white, pink, purple, or yellow. When ripe, the fruit separates quite readily from the plant. Certain varieties have comparatively few seeds, whereas others are filled with them. The fruit has a pleasant, almost delicate taste, but inasmuch as it is quite perishable, fresh fruit should be eaten as soon as possible. It should be eaten when cool, but not ice-cold, to allow the aroma and flavor to be at their peaks. A dark variety of raspberry is properly called the *black raspberry*; it is not a blackberry, according to botanists. Raspberries may be eaten plain, with sugar and cream, made into ice cream or sherbets, used to top cakes or shortbreads, mixed with whipped cream and liqueurs, and used in scores of other different ways. Raspberry preserves are excellent, and a syrup made with raspberries has good aroma, color, and taste.

Raspberry Bun (British). A bun, filled with raspberry jam, that opens while baking.

Raspberry Essence. The concentrated juice of raspberries; used as a flavoring agent.

Raspberry Noyeau. A mixture of raspberry flavoring and an almond-flavored liqueur.

Rasped Rolls. Slightly burned hard rolls.

Rasphead. *See* Rockfish.

Raspings. The scrapings from hard rolls; sometimes sprinkled on boiled ham.

Rasteau. A very sweet, mellow dessert wine made chiefly from Grenache grapes in the Rhône region of France.

Rastegaïs (Russian). Hot hors d'oeuvre.

Rastrello. A sharp-edged spoon used to cut the pulp from halved grapefruit or other citrus fruit.

Rata del Mar (Spanish). A variety of fish found in southern waters of Europe; it is about one foot or slightly more in length. Generally used only in stews or soups.

Ratafia. (1) A sweet wine made from black raisins in the Champagne region of France. (2)

An Italian liqueur made from black cherries. (3) An excellent variety of cherry, known for its good texture. (4) A liqueur made from the pits or stones of cherries, peaches, almonds, etc. (5) A small almond biscuit.

Ratatouille (French). A vegetable dish prepared from various vegetables cooked separately in oil, then combined; served hot or cold; popular in Provence.

Raton. A small cream-cheese tart served as a hot hors d'oeuvre.

Ratonnet (French). Small skewer of meat, usually mutton.

Ratsherrentopf (German). A meat dish consisting of a slice of sautéed beef, a slice of veal, and a slice of calf's liver arranged on top of one another.

Rauchbier (German). Smoked beer; somewhat unusual in taste.

Rauchfleisch (German). Smoked meat.

Rauenthal. A wine village of the Rheingau district of Germany. *See* Germany, The Wines of.

Rauriki. A New Zealand green leaf used for making salads.

Ravanelli (Italian). Radishes.

Ravello. *See* Italy, The Wines of.

Ravier (French). A rather small dish or container suitable for serving appetizers, particularly olives and radishes.

Raviggiolo. A very soft Italian sheep's-milk cheese, somewhat lacking in flavor.

Ravigote (French). A hot or cold well-seasoned sauce prepared with garlic, onions, capers, mustard, and gherkins; usually served with fish.

Ravigote Butter. A mixture of green herbs combined with softened butter and served with broiled meats.

Ravioli (Italian). Pasta dough, cut into small rounds or squares, filled with any desired mixture such as meat, chicken, or cheese, boiled until tender, and served with a sauce.

    Ravioli Dolci. Noodle dough stuffed with sweetened cheese.

    Ravioli Florentine. Ravioli stuffed with spinach and calf's brains.

    Ravioli Niçoise. Ravioli stuffed with garlic-flavored meat and spinach.

Raw Sugar. Brown unrefined sugar 96–98 percent

pure. It is often contaminated with mold spores, bacteria, cane fiber, and dirt, and must be treated.

Ray; Skate. An edible fish with a very large, flat, squarish body; often prepared with black butter.

Rayole (French). A thin layer of dough covered with chopped spinach, pumpkin, and walnuts; a specialty of Provence.

Rayon. A cheese resembling Emmentaler but without holes; when mature, sold as *Raper cheese*.

Ream Bread (British). Bread made from heated corn.

Reamer. A ridged utensil that extracts fruit juice by pressure.

Rebhuhn (German). Partridge.

Reblochon; Roblochon. An outstanding sheep's-milk cheese of unusual flavor made in Savoy, France.

Receipt; Recipe. The ingredients needed and cooking instructions for the preparation of a dish. Local usage determines whether "receipt" or "recipe" is preferred. In colonial America "receipt" was the standard word; today "recipe" seems the more popular.

Réchaud (French). A small portable stove; also a chafing dish or warming vessel designed to keep foods hot on the table.

Réchauffé (French). Reheated.

Recheado (Portuguese). Stuffed.

Recioto Veronese. *See* Italy, The Wines of.

Recipe. A list of ingredients and instructions for the preparation of a specific dish.

Récollet. A cheese similar to Münster made in the Vosges Mountains of France.

Rectify. To purify or refine.

Recuire (French). (1) To cook a second time, as to sauté first, then roast. (2) As applied to certain pastry mixtures, jellies, or syrups, to cook in two separate operations.

Recuit. A soft French cheese similar to Italy's Ricotta, made by heating the whey of cow's milk; eaten plain, with sugar, or used in cooking.

Red Balls. *See* Edam Cheese.

Red-Bean Sauce (Chinese). A sauce with a rather unpleasant odor, made from slightly fermented mashed red soybeans; usually served with meat.

Red Cheese. A Cantonese cheese made from cooked, pressed, and fermented red soybeans combined with salt. When purchased in cans, the solid cubes should be combined with the red liquid until well blended.

Red Currants. Soft, small, tart red berries that grow on bushes in clusters; eaten fresh, cooked in compotes, made into pies, pastries, or jellies.

Red Date. A red date called *hoan joe* by the Chinese; it must be soaked in water for several hours before using.

Reddiker (Norwegian). Radishes.

Red Dog Flour (Colloquial). A poor grade of flour.

Red-Eyed Perch. The freshwater bass.

Red Filbert. A nut similar to the ordinary filbert but with red skin.

Redfish. The blueback salmon; the rosefish or red perch; the red drum or southern red horse; the red phase of a West Indian grouper.

Red Flannel Hash. Corned-beef hash made with beets, chiefly in New England.

Red Grouper. A large delicately flavored, good-textured fish of the bass family.

Red Gurnard. A small fish found along the Atlantic coast from Maine to the Carolinas. It should not be scaled.

Red Herrings. Herrings that have been well salted and allowed to smoke about 10 days. *Bloaters* are salted less and smoked a shorter time. *Kippers* are lightly salted and smoked overnight.

Red Laver. A seaweed sometimes used as food.

Red Mullet. *See* Mullet.

Red Nettle. A plant with edible roots, occasionally used as a vegetable.

Red Pepper. A capsicum known by many different names in various parts of the world (sweet, bell, etc.); used as a vegetable, salad ingredient, or flavoring. Some red-pepper plants are annuals, others are biennials, and generally produce small flowers, followed by edible seed pods. Some varieties are sweet and mild, and may be eaten raw, cooked, or prepared with stuffings. Other types have a strong, biting taste, and still others are scarcely fit for human consumption because of their burning qualities; the last group is usually made into dry or liquid seasonings, a little of which is all that is needed for flavoring. Certain types of red pepper are sweet when mature, others become hot and burning as the color changes from green to red. Very sweet varieties of red pepper are used in preparing pimientos, and are favorites in the Spanish and Italian cuisines.

Red-Pepper Paste. A spicy paste made from hot red peppers, salt, ginger, and chopped onions; it is ground smooth, packed into a glass jar, and covered with a little oil. It will keep well, and a half-teaspoonful may be used to flavor soups and stews.

Red Perch. *See* Perch.

Red Rob Wheat. A Canadian damp-resistant wheat.

Red Snapper. A warm-seas fish of the bass family; the flavor is superior and more delicate than that of bass.

Redstart. A small game bird; prepared like lark.

Red Surmullet. A small good-tasting Mediterranean fish; it should be cooked in sea water to retain the red color.

Reduction; Reducing. To boil down and reduce the liquid content by evaporation, as a sauce or gravy; to thicken; to concentrate a flavor.

Réduire (French). To boil down or reduce the volume of a sauce or mixture to make the flavor more concentrated.

Red Vinegar (Chinese). A red vinegar prepared from rice; used as a dipping sauce for meats, poultry, etc.

Redwing. A small thrush, occasionally eaten as a game bird.

Red Winter Wheat. A soft red wheat grown in the eastern United States.

Reedbird. The bobolink or ricebird; sometimes used for food.

Reeve. *See* Ruff.

Refection. A meal; any refreshment.

Refectory. A place where meals are served, particularly in a school, monastery, etc.

Refiners' Syrup. A sweet liquid obtained after sugar has been refined.

Reflector Oven. An open-front oven that heats on the principle of reflected heat.

Réforme, À la (French). Usually, garnished with strips of cooked carrots, ham, truffles, and hard-cooked egg whites; named for the Reform Club in London.

Refrigerant. A substance that cools; usually a liquid that can be changed into a gas at low temperatures.

Refrigeration. The process of making cold.

Refrigerator. An apparatus, usually shaped like a tall box, in which foods are stored at temperatures usually slightly above the freezing point. Most home refrigerators have a section for making ice cubes, and many have a freezing unit.

Refrigerators must be defrosted and cleaned regularly; some models have self-defrosting features. Most are operated electrically and are thermostatically controlled, which permits the unit to be operated at any desired temperature. Most foods keep best when stored at temperatures between 36° and 46°.

Refrigerator Bag. An airtight bag, usually made of plastic, used to keep foods fresh and to prevent odors from being absorbed by other foods.

Refrigerator Cake. A general term for cakes prepared without baking. Usually biscuits, pieces of previously cooked cakes, ladyfingers, etc., are combined with cream or custard, nuts or fruit, and then chilled in the refrigerator to make the ingredients firm.

Refrigerator Dish. A flat plate with a tight-fitting cover used for storing foods in the refrigerator.

Refroidi (French). Chilled; cooled.

Régal (French). A feast or banquet.

Régalade, À la (French). A Spanish method of drinking wine directly from a flask without allowing the edge of the flask to touch the lips.

Régence, Sauce (French). A sauce containing brandy, pâté, forcemeat balls, truffles, etc.; it originated in the Regency period.

Regianito. An Argentine cheese of the Parmesan type.

Regimen. A special diet or system of food intake.

Reginette. Long narrow wavy curls of pasta.

Régisseur (French). The manager of a vineyard, particularly an important one.

Réglisse (French). Licorice. The aromatic roots of the licorice plant are ground and boiled, and the condensed juice is combined with starch to make black sticks of candy, soft drinks, liqueurs, etc. The root extract is called "black sugar" or "Spanish juice."

Regulo (British). A dial attached to a gas range to regulate the flow of gas.

Mark	½	1	2	3	4	5
Degrees F.	250°	275°	315°	325°	350°	375°
Mark	6	7	8	9	10	11	12
Degrees F.	400°	425°	450°	475°	500°	525°	550°

Reh (German). Venison; deer meat.

Rehoboam. A wine bottle equal to 6 ordinary wine bottles.

Rehrücken (German). Saddle of venison.

Reibkäse. *See* Saanen.

Reignets (African). Fritters or fried foods. The term is a corruption of the French word *beignets*.

Rein (German). Of wine, genuine, authentic. *See* Germany, The Wines of.

Reindeer. An animal of the deer family, with large antlers; found chiefly in cold-weather regions of the world. It supplies milk, and its meat, although somewhat tough and stringy, is similar to venison.

Reindeer Cheese. A salty reindeer-milk cheese made in Lapland and Iceland; resembles Swiss cheese.

Reindeer Milk. Milk obtained from reindeer, particularly in cold-weather countries; used like cow's milk and for making cheese.

Reindeer Tongue. The tongue of a reindeer, usually salted and dried or smoked; eaten in Scandinavian countries.

Reine (French). (1) A medium-size chicken. (2) A chicken purée with mushrooms and truffles. (3) A thick soup made with chicken purée.

Reine, À la (French). An elaborate style of chicken preparation, sometimes including truffles and mushrooms.

Reinette. A soft-textured sweet late-maturing russet apple grown in France.

Reis (German). Rice.

Reiswürstchen (Austrian). Rice sausage.

Réjane (French). A garnish, used chiefly for sweetbreads, consisting of spinach, artichokes, and marrow.

Rejemad (Danish). Shrimp sandwich.

Rejer (Danish). Shrimp.

Réjouissance (French). (1) The bones weighed by the butcher along with the meat purchased. (2) Part of the back of an animal used mainly to supply a gelatinous quality to stews and soups.

Rekecocktail (Norwegian). Shrimp cocktail.

Relâcher (French). To add a liquid in order to thin a sauce.

Relais (French). Roadside restaurant. Formerly a place where horses were changed while the travelers ate or had refreshment.

Relevé (French). The remove, the course which follows either the soup or fish course and precedes the entrée. Sometimes, the main course. A typical *relevé* might be a dish of sweetbreads or tongue.

Relever (French). To season so as to bring out a piquant flavor.

Reliance Wheat. A well-known Canadian wheat, not completely resistant to rust disease.

Reliefs (French). Leftovers.

Religieuses (French). (1) Cream-filled eclairs, iced with fondant, piled up in a pyramid on a pastry base. (2) Puff-paste strips spread with jam and crisscrossed on top with strips of pastry.

Relish. Any item that adds spice, flavor, or zest to the main portion of a meal; a side dish served with a main course; some kind of pickle. In parts of the United States, a relish may consist of applesauce, stewed fruit, or the like. In other areas, a relish is simply any food with a sharp or piquant flavor.

Relish Cream Cheese. Cream cheese to which olives, chives, onions, pimientos, etc., are added for piquancy.

Relleno (Latin American). (1) Stuffed meats or vegetables. (2) Chopped meat.

Remolachas (Spanish). Beets.

Remonter (French). (1) To improve the flavor or texture of foods by the addition of spices, wine, egg yolks, etc. (2) To add alcohol to wine to increase the strength.

Remoudou. A piquant Belgian cow's-milk cheese.

Remouillage (French). A second stock, or a cooking liquid.

Remouiller (French). To recook or boil again completely boiled foods.

Rémoulade. A mayonnaise sauce highly flavored with onion, capers, mustard, gherkins, parsley, spices, and sometimes anchovy paste.

Remove. In elaborate meals, the course that follows either the soup or fish course and precedes the entrée. In France, it is called the *relevé*.

Sometimes, the term is incorrectly applied to the main course of a meal.

Renaissance, À la (French). Garnished with fresh vegetables arranged in small mounds around a roast.

Renne (French). Reindeer.

Rennet. A substance containing rennin, used chiefly in making cheese, junket, and other curdled-milk products.

Rennin. An enzyme in the gastric juices that curdles milk; used in cheese making.

Renovated Butter. Fresh cream, rechurned with rancid melted butter; often used in making inferior commercial cakes.

Renown Wheat. A soft English wheat suitable for cake flour.

Rensdyrstek (Norwegian). Roast reindeer meat.

Renstek (Swedish). Reindeer meat.

Rentschlerizing. Sterilizing by treatment with ultraviolet light. The process is named for Dr. H. C. Rentschler, who developed the lamp.

Renversé (French). As applied to food, dished out. *Crème renversée* is a caramel custard, unmolded from a form or mold.

Repassé (French). Strained several times.

Repast. A meal; food.

Repère (French). A flour-and-egg-white paste used to make a decorative piece adhere to a dish or to other parts of the decoration.

Repollo (Spanish). Cabbage.

Repollo de Bruselas (Spanish). Brussels sprouts.

Requeijão (Portuguese). Recooked cheese.

Requesón (Spanish). A soft white cheese.

Restaurang (Swedish). Restaurant.

Restaurangmatsal (Swedish). Dining room.

Restaurant. A place that serves meals commercially. The name is said to have originated in Paris many centuries ago, when a caterer advertised that his soups had a *restaurant* quality; that is, they would restore energy and well-being.

Restaurateur. A person in the restaurant business.

Restes (French). Leftovers.

Rétes (Hungarian). Strudel, a flaky-leaved pastry dessert; also prepared with sauerkraut or other savory fillings.

Retfo (Ethiopian). A very spicy preparation of ground meat and vegetables.

Reticulum. The second stomach (honeycomb) of ruminants; tripe.

Rettich (German). Radish.

Revalenta Arabica. A mixture of red Arabian or Egyptian lentil and barley flours with a pinch of sugar or salt.

Revbenspjäll (Swedish). Roast spareribs.

Réveillon. In France the traditional sumptuous, elaborate supper served after the Christmas Eve midnight mass; also the supper served at the stroke of midnight on New Year's Eve.

Revenir, Faire (French). To brown foods quickly in butter or other fat until slightly colored.

Reverdir (French). To restore the green color sometimes lost when cooking vegetables by adding synthetic or vegetable coloring.

Revuelto (Spanish). Scrambled eggs.

Rhamnose. A sugar about one-third as sweet as sucrose.

Rheingau. One of the two most important wine districts of Germany, extending from Wiesbaden to Rüdesheim. *See* Germany, The Wines of.

Rheinhessen. An important wine region of Germany. *See* Germany, The Wines of.

Rheinpfalz. An important German wine region, also known as the *Pfalz* and the *Palatinate*. *See* Germany, The Wines of.

Rhenish Wines. Rhine Wine; *see also* Germany, The Wines of.

Rhine River Salmon. *Rheinsalm*, an excellent salmon found in the Rhine River in Germany. When smoked it has a superb flavor and a rather light, delicate taste.

Rhine Wine. *See* Germany, The Wines of.

Rhinskvine (Danish). Rhine wine.

Rhinoceros. A large pachyderm; the flesh of the young animal is sometimes eaten by natives of the countries in which it is found.

Rhône Wines. The product of a French wine district extending from Lyons to Avignon in the general area of the Rhône River. *See* France, The Wines of.

Rhubarb; Pie Plant; Wine Plant. A perennial plant with fairly smooth, rather dark green leaves which grow on firm, thick fleshy stalks. The leaves are used only occasionally as food, but the stalks have a rather unique flavor. Most rhubarb reaches the market in two forms—field-grown and hot-house. The field-grown variety has a more pronounced flavor and darker color than the forced variety.

Old or discolored rhubarb will cook stringy and tough and have a poor flavor. Strawberries combined with rhubarb may be used in compotes, pies, or tarts. Ginger with rhubarb makes an excellent preserve. Rhubarb can be prepared as a simple homemade wine with a rather odd taste. The Italians make a bitter apéritif drink to which they ascribe medicinal powers.

Rhubarbe (French). Rhubarb.

Rhubarbe. A sharp cheese made by kneading Roquefort or blue cheese with Cognac. The mixture is then heavily covered with pepper and left to mature in wine caves. The name has nothing to do with the rhubarb plant.

Rhum (French). Rum.

Rhyton (Obsolete). An ancient drinking horn, sometimes decorated with the head of a goat or of a mythological animal. Since it had no flat base, the contents had to be drunk without putting it down.

Riabinovka. A Russian red vodka flavored with the aromatic oil of ashberries; best as an after-dinner drink.

Ribbed Carpet. A clam with distinctive ribbed markings found along the northwestern coast of the United States.

Ribbon. A well-beaten mixture of egg yolks and sugar that can be folded into ribbonlike strands.

Riblette (French). A small cut of pork; grilled or broiled.

Ribs (Colloquial). Spareribs.

Ricarde. Alternate name for scallops.

Riccio (Italian). Sea urchin, a Mediterranean shellfish.

Rice. The starchy seeds of a widely cultivated grain. The plant is an annual type ranging 2–5 feet in height. Half of the world's rice production comes from the Orient, where it is a staple food. Rice is an important crop in the Carolinas and other parts of the southern United States. The grain is covered with a brown hull, or coating, which is sometimes left on and marketed as brown rice. Since the brown coating is rich in the B-complex vitamins and minerals,

brown rice has greater nutritional value than white rice, which is prepared by removing the hull. Rice is also classified according to kernel shape into short, medium, and long, with the long the most highly esteemed. Boiled rice often accompanies curries and other Far Eastern dishes and is a standby of Creole cookery. In northern Italy rice is often cooked with other ingredients to make *risotti*. The best-known dessert using this grain is rice pudding. Cold rice can be served as a salad in summer. Wild rice is not true rice but a perennial grass seed native to North America.

Rice does not make a satisfactory bread because it lacks certain gluten. It is the basis for many oriental "wines" and liquors, especially *sake*.

  Polished Rice. Rice grain from which the husk and outer bran layers have been removed, then polished with glucose and talc. This is the white rice commonly marketed. It is low in the B vitamins, particularly B_1, which have been largely removed with the bran and germ.

Rice. To press foods through the small holes of a kitchen utensil called a "ricer."

Rice Dust. Rice flour used to prevent dough from sticking.

Rice Flour. A very fine flour made from ground rice; used in Oriental and Middle Eastern baking and produces a fine-textured cake.

Ricer. A utensil used to force a food through its sievelike perforations to give it a light, fluffy consistency.

Rice Starch. Very small starch cells in rice; they jell between 137° and 176°F.

Rice, Synthetic. *See* Synthetic Rice.

Rice Table. The Indonesian *rijsttafel*. *See* Indonesia.

Rice Washing Water (Philippine). The cloudy white water in which raw rice is washed; it gives a slightly starchy taste to food cooked in it.

Rice Wine. *See* Sake.

Riceys. A thin white cheese, slightly aged in ashes of vine branches, which form a gray coating.

Richebourg. One of the finest dry red wines produced in the Burgundy region of France. *See* France, The Wines of.

Richelieu. The name of several preparations. (1)

A garnish for roast meats, composed of stuffed mushrooms, tomatoes, braised lettuce, and baked apples. (2) A dish containing almonds. (3) Breaded sautéed fish fillets garnished with truffles. (4) A layer cake filled with apricot jam and frangipane, and iced with fondant.

Richelieu, Cardinal. A 17th-century French cardinal and general who was also a gourmet, for whom several dishes are named.

Rickey. An American drink made from any desired alcoholic beverage (usually gin), lime juice, and carbonated water.

Ricotta (Italian). Mild, white-curd soft cheese made from sheep's milk.

Ricotta Romana. Fresh cheese, often made with sheep's buttermilk; a great favorite in Rome. It is good alone, with sugar or cinnamon, or with finely ground coffee.

Ricotta Salata. Salted dried Ricotta cheese; used chiefly for grating, but small amounts may be crumbled into a green salad.

Riddle. A sieve with rather large holes.

Riddle of Claret (British, Obsolete). Thirteen bottles of Bordeaux wine, so called because the wine was shipped from France to England in a riddle with 13 openings.

Ridge Cucumber. A variety of cucumber popular in Russia, France, England, and other countries, and now grown in the United States; used for cooking and pickling, and in the same way as ordinary varieties.

Riffle Flumes (British). A food-washing machine consisting of stepped channels along which the food is carried in a flow of water, stones and grit being retained on the steps.

Rigaglie Acciugate (Italian). Giblets in anchovy sauce.

Rigaglie di Pollo (Italian). Chicken livers and hearts with sage flavoring.

Rigatoni. Very large fluted tubes of Italian pasta; often stuffed and covered with sauce.

Rigodon (French). A tart, popular in Burgundy, made of puréed fruit, eggs, milk, small pieces of brioche, and cinnamon.

Rigotte. A small round dry French cheese made from goat's or cow's milk; eaten in summer and autumn.

Rigotte des Alpes. A simple French country cheese, sometimes macerated in white wine.

Rijst (Dutch). Rice.

Rijsttafel; Rijstaffel. The Indonesian rice table. *See* Indonesia.

Rijstpudding (Dutch). Rice pudding.

Rijstrand met Lever (Dutch). A dish consisting of rice, liver, and tomato.

Rijsttaart (Dutch). A rice cake filled with fruits and nuts.

Rikiki. Any alcoholic drink, particularly in 19th-century France.

Rillauds (French). Small pieces of salted pork lightly cooked in lard and served in several different ways, usually as an appetizer similar to a pâté. Rillauds, *rillons*, and *rillots* are similar, but *rillettes* are ground smooth. *See* Rillettes.

Rillettes (French). A spiced ground, pork-meat preparation served as an hors d'oeuvre. Similar to *rillauds*.

Rillettes de Tours. A seasoned pork pâté made in the region of Tours.

Rillon de Blois (French). Fried pork or goose preserved in pork fat. *See* Rillauds.

Rillots. *See* Rillauds.

Rim (Portuguese). Kidney.

Rimmad Oxbringa (Swedish). Salted beef.

Rimote (French). A cornmeal pudding.

Rincette (French). Brandy poured into a coffee cup which is still hot from the coffee in order to warm the brandy and enhance its flavor. *See* Sur-Rincette.

Rind. (1) The outer protective skin or covering of certain fruits and vegetables. (2) The crust on the surface of cheese or bacon. (3) (German) Beef.

Rinderschmorbraten (German). Braised beef.

Rindfleisch (German). Beef.

Rindfleischsuppe (German). Beef consommé.

Rinfresco. An Italian liqueur similar to anisette; made in Modena.

Ring Biscuits. Several small biscuits made in ring form.

Ring Mold. A hollowed-out round container, usually made of metal, with a hole in the center. Foods prepared in ring molds may be attractively served by filling the center with other foods.

Ring-Necked Duck. A wild duck with a distinctive

flavor and good texture due to the water grasses it eats.

Rinnen. A German cheese made from sour milk and caraway seeds.

Riñón (Spanish). The sugar apple.

Riñones (Spanish). Kidneys.

    Riñones al Jerez. Kidneys in sherry-wine sauce.

Rio. The trade term for a certain type of Brazilian coffee.

Rioja. One of the leading wine regions of Spain, which produces wines of considerable quality, as well as many that are routine. *See* Spain, The Wines of.

Riola. A soft cheese made in Normandy, France, usually with sheep's or goat's milk.

Rios Coffee. A Brazilian coffee with a heavy, strong flavor; used to blend with other coffees.

Ripieni di Castagna (Italian). Chestnut stuffing.

Ripieno (Italian). Stuffing.

Ripopée (French). A mixture of leftover wines, sauces, or other liquids.

Rippchen (German). Pork chops.

Rippel (Alsatian). Pork cooked in red wine.

Rippenspeer (German). A fried and boiled pork dish.

Rippenstück (German). Ribs of beef.

Ris (Danish). Rice.

Ris de Veau (French). Sweetbreads.

    Ris de Veau à la Suédoise. Sweetbreads and tongue served with horseradish-flavored sauce.

Risengrød (Danish). Rice porridge or soup.

Risengrynsklatter (Danish). Rice fritters.

Risengrynslapper (Norwegian). Rice pancakes.

Risgrøt (Norwegian). Rice dessert.

Risgryn (Swedish). Rice.

Risgrynsgröt (Swedish). Rice pudding served with cold milk and sugar.

Rishtaya (Syrian). Lamb with noodles and lentils.

Risi e Bisi (Italian). Rice and peas, often with ham.

Riso (Italian). Rice.

    Riso Verde. Green rice.

    Riso alla Calabrese. Baked rice with tomatoes and cheese.

    Riso con Rognoncini Trifolati. Rice-and-kidney casserole.

    Riso e Zucchine in Brodo. Rice and zucchini in soup broth.

Risotto (Italian). Literally, a rice dish; a wide variety of dishes based upon rice. The typical risotto is prepared by cooking rice very slowly with herbs and spices, meat or fish, and perhaps a sauce. The rice absorbs the flavors and develops a distinctive taste and texture.

    Risotto alla Certosina. Rice with crayfish, mushrooms, and peas.

    Risotto alla Finanziera. Rice with chicken livers.

    Risotto alla Milanese. Boiled rice with marrow, mushrooms, saffron, and butter.

    Risotto con Funghi. Rice with mushrooms.

    Risotto con Gamberi. Rice with shrimp.

    Risotto con Salsa di Pesce. Rice with fish sauce.

    Risotto con Vongole. Rice with clams.

    Risotto Florentine. Rice with beef marrow, butter, tomatoes, cheese, and truffles.

    Risotto Paesano. Rice, beans, and vegetables.

    Risotto Piémontese. Steamed rice with fresh white truffles.

    Risotto Torinese. Steamed rice with mushrooms, ham, and peppers, colored with saffron; served with grated cheese and diced tomatoes.

Rissolen (German). Rissoles; ground or chopped mixtures dipped in bread crumbs and fried.

Rissoler (French). To fry foods lightly in butter or fat until browned, especially with bread crumbs.

Rissoles. Small hot meat-, fish-, or mushroom-stuffed crescent-shaped puff pastries. They may

be fried or baked; served as a hot hors d'oeuvre.

Rissolettes. Small rissoles; sometimes pancakes are used instead of puff pastry.

Ristede (Norwegian). Roasted.

Ristet Brød (Danish). Toast.

Ristet Laks (Norwegian). Fried salmon.

Ristet Torskerogn (Danish). Fried roe.

Ritz, César. Founder of the Ritz Hotel chain in Europe and a contributor to elegance and luxury in food service.

Riverfish. Any of various varieties of fish found in freshwater rivers in various parts of the world.

Rivierkreeft. (Dutch). Crayfish.

Riviervis (Dutch). Freshwater fish.

Riz (French). Rice.

> **Riz Caroline.** Long-grained rice.
>
> **Riz, Crème de.** Ground rice.
>
> **Riz Créole.** (1) Rice cooked with tomatoes, okra, and spices. (2) Rice boiled about 10 minutes, drained and spread on a tray, and baked at a low temperature.
>
> **Riz de Camargue.** Rice with assorted shellfish; prepared in the Camargue region.
>
> **Riz de Piedmond.** The round-grained rice of Italy, with a distinctively firm center.
>
> **Riz Sauvage.** Wild rice.

Riz al Maleek (Middle Eastern). A mint-flavored rice dish.

Rizine. A commercial rice preparation used for making puddings.

Riz Sheeyrea Fee Jedgee (Middle Eastern). A preparation consisting of chicken, chick-peas, and vermicelli.

Rizzared Haddie (Scotch). Sun-dried haddock.

Roach. (1) Golden shiner minnow, a European freshwater fish much like the carp. (2) The American sunfish.

Roast. (1) To cook uncovered in an oven or over charcoal, etc. (2) To heat and darken coffee beans, preparatory to grinding. (3) The type and nature of roasted coffee beans, such as a dark roast. (4) Roast meat, especially roast beef.

Roast Beef. A cut of beef which has been roasted and is ready to eat.

Roaster. (1) A young chicken or pig, suitable for roasting. (2) A roasting pan.

Roasting Pan. A rectangular metal or other pan large enough to hold a turkey or ribs of beef. Old-fashioned roasting pans were deep and had covers; modern cookery favors a shallow open pan.

Roastit Bubbly Jock (Scotch). Turkey stuffed with chestnuts, oysters, or sausage.

Rob. Fruit juice cooked over very low heat until it acquires a syruplike heavy consistency.

Robalo (Portuguese). The snook, a tropical fish.

Robbin. A small, poor quality codfish found in European waters.

Robbiole; Robbiolini; Robiola. A rich, mild, creamy yellow cheese made in the Italian Piedmont region; its flavor is similar to that of Brie.

Robert, Sauce. (French). A spicy brown sauce made with mustard, onions, wine, chili, and vinegar; usually served with pork and other meats; available commercially.

Roblochon. *See* Reblochon.

Roblot. A variety of small mackerel.

Rocamadour. (1) A flavorsome goat's-milk cheese made in Quercy, France. (2) A very small sheep's-milk cheese made in southwestern France.

Rocambole. (1) A Spanish shallot, or tree onion; a very mild small onion. (2) A variety of French garlic less pungent than ordinary garlic.

Rochelle Salt. Sodium potassium tartrate, the salt left after sodium bicarbonate and cream of tartar have reacted together.

Rocher. An elaborate pastry of meringue, almonds, coconut, or chocolate, shaped to resemble a rock.

Roches (French). A large Portuguese oyster.

Rock (British). A hard or sticky candy.

Rock and Rye (American). A drink prepared by adding a tablespoon (or less) of rock-candy syrup to rye whisky, then adding a slice of lemon.

Rock Bass. A large number of small American freshwater fish that theoretically live near rocks; sometimes the fish are truly bass, sometimes not.

Rock Cakes (British). Small rock-shaped breads containing fruits.

Rock Candy. Crystallized sugar in its simplest form, usually strung on strings; available white and brown. It is prepared by boiling clarified syrup with a few drops of acetic acid so that the crystals separate readily. It is then allowed to harden for a week or so. Rock candy is good for sore throats, but its culinary use is somewhat limited. Thin lengths of rock candy may be used as muddlers or stirrers in alcoholic drinks.

Rock Cocoa. The hard substance remaining after the oil and cacao butter are removed from the cacao bean.

Rock Cod. Another name for the cod.

Rock Cooky. A drop cooky made with nuts, fruits, and spices.

Rock Eel. The butterfish.

Rockenbollen. *See* Garlic, Lesser-leaved.

Rocket. A salad green. *See* Roquette.

Rockfish. The striped bass. Also, according to locality, the rasphead, bocaccio, and yellowtail.

Rockford Melon. An aromatic melon native to the western United States, especially Colorado; it has pink flesh, a fair texture, and is excellent when in prime condition.

Rock Lobster. The crayfish (crawfish), generally shipped to the American market as frozen *lobster tails*.

Rock Oysters (Australian). The small oysters that grow naturally in rocks but are cultivated on lengths of wood. They have an extraordinarily fine, delicate taste and are eaten plain.

Rock Partridge. The Greek partridge, a small good-tasting game bird found in the mountains of western Europe.

Rock Salmon. The coalfish, a mediocre fish found off the Norwegian and Scottish coasts; best when smoked or dried.

Rock Salt. A common large-crystal salt obtained from mines. It is used in chilling ice cream mixtures, and also for baking oysters and clams because the salt transfers the heat quickly so that the shellfish does not toughen.

Rock Sauce (British). A hard sauce made by beating butter with twice as much sugar, then flavoring it as desired.

Rock Sugar. A porous material made from sugar syrup and royal icing; used to decorate cakes.

Rock Trout. A large, fine-flavored variety of trout found in New Zealand.

Rockweed; Sea Wrack. An edible seaweed found off the coast of Scotland, Ireland, and Iceland.

Rocou. A Brazilian spice with little flavor; used chiefly to color foods.

Rocroi. A skim-milk cheese made in the Ardennes region of Belgium.

Rodaballo (Spanish). Turbot.

Rødbeder (Danish). Beets.

Röd Betor (Swedish). Beets.

Rodekool (Dutch). Red cabbage.

Rodekool met Rolpens (Dutch). Rolled meat, apples, and cabbage.

Rødgrød med Fløde (Danish). A red berry or fruit dessert with cream.

Rødgrøt (Norwegian). Fruit pudding.

Röding (Swedish). The redbelly, a troutlike fish.

Rødkål (Danish). Red cabbage.

Rödkål (Swedish). Red cabbage.

Rod Saus (Norwegian). Fruit sauce.

Rødspaette (Danish). Plaice, a fish similar to sole.

Rödspetta (Swedish). Plaice, a fish similar to sole.

Rødvine (Danish). Red wine.

Roe. The eggs found in the membrane of most fish and the spawn of certain crustaceans. Hard roe is the spawn of the female fish, while soft roe is the milt or sperm of the male fish. The most highly prized of all roes is *caviar*, obtained from the female sturgeon. *Shad roe* is also a great delicacy, but carp, mackerel, and herring all yield good roe. Before serving, roe must be soaked in cold water and the blood vessels carefully removed. *Mullet eggs* are a staple of the Greek cuisine, being prepared into a delicious caviarlike appetizer called *tarama salata*.

Roe; Roebuck. Wild European and Asiatic deer, often eaten as venison.

Rogen (German). Fish roe.

Røget Laks (Danish). Smoked salmon.

Røget Sild (Danish). Smoked herring.

Roggenbrot (German). Rye bread.

Rognon (French). Kidney.

    Rognon de Boeuf. Ox kidney.

    Rognon de Mouton. Sheep's kidney; best when grilled.

    Rognon de Veau. Calf's kidney.

Rognoni (Italian). Kidneys.

    Rognoni al Marsala. Kidneys cooked in Marsala wine.

Rognonnade (French). Loin of veal rolled up with the kidneys attached.

Rognures (French). (1) Trimmings or parings; leftovers. (2) The rolled-out unused leftover portions of puff pastry excellent for pastry shells.

Rohschinken (German). Smoked raw ham.

Roi de Cailles (French). The land rail, a game bird; prepared like quail.

Rokadur. A mediocre Yugoslavian imitation of Roquefort.

Rokam. A small Southeast Asian fruit that resembles the cherry but has less flavor.

Røkelaks (Norwegian). Smoked salmon.

Røket Fisk (Norwegian). Baked smoked fish.

Røketorsk (Norwegian). Smoked codfish.

Rökt Lax (Swedish). Smoked salmon.

Rollata di Pollo (Italian). Boned, rolled, stuffed chicken.

Roll Cheese. A round, very hard English cheese made with cow's whole milk.

Rolling Pin. A cylindrical piece of wood (or other substance) usually with handles at both ends, used to roll out dough.

Rolling Stone. A large, heavy cylindrical stone used to crush cereals and grains.

Rollmops. Pickled herring formed into small rolls with a pickle in the middle.

Rollmöpse (German). Rollmops.

Rollot. A soft cow's-milk cheese with a red rind, made in Picardy, France; resembles Brie.

Roll Out. To spread pastry or other dough thin with a rolling pin.

Rolls. Small amounts of bread dough, made into individual portions, and baked. There are almost innumerable sizes, types, and shapes.

Roly-Poly (British). A flat piece of biscuit dough spread with spices, sugar, sweetened fruits, or jam, then rolled up like a jelly roll and steamed or baked.

Roma. A soft Italian cream cheese.

Romadour. A cheese basically similar to Limburger; made in Austria, Germany, and Switzerland.

Romaine. A variety of lettuce distinctive for its tall, upright pale green leaves. It is often served in halves or quarters with the leaves uncut. It is an essential ingredient of Caesar Salad, for which the leaves are torn (not cut) into inch-long pieces. It is rarely, if ever, cooked in the United States, but in Europe several interesting dishes are prepared with this tasty green. Romaine is called *Cos lettuce* in England and certain other parts of the world.

Romaine, À la. (1) As applied to sherbet, usually champagne-, kirsch-, or rum-flavored. (2) A chilled punch. (3) A style of Italian cooking in which a garnish of spinach and anchovies is served with leg of lamb.

Romalour. A semisoft cow's-milk cheese made in the Lorraine district of France.

Roman Coriander. *See* Fennel Flower.

Romanée, La. An extraordinary dry red wine of excellent taste and remarkable bouquet; produced in Burgundy, France.

Romanée-Conti. The wine considered to be the finest in France and even in the world; it commands a very high price. *See also* France, The Wines of.

Romanello. An American imitation of Italy's Romano cheese; resembles Parmesan.

Romania. Cornmeal, a strictly American food which the first settlers learned about from the Indians, is the staple food of the Romanian people. It was brought from the New to the Old World about two hundred years ago, and immediately took hold. *Mamaliga*, as the Romanians call it, is served plain, hot or cold, as a porridge or cut into slices and fried, with garlic, sausages, meat, sauerkraut, or anything else available. Poor people eat it for every meal, but every Romanian expects it at least once daily.

As in all other Balkan countries, the food follows a certain pattern, with a strong emphasis upon vegetables; *ghivetch*, a vegetable stew, is classic. Beans and potatoes are also standbys in the daily diet. Appetizers find their chief expression in eggplant mixtures, spicy fish dishes, and, best of all, in *ikra*, the local caviar, usually made from carp or pike roe. Soups are a cult, made with a completely original set of recipes. The national soups are *tchorbas*, sour soups, and are based upon a fermenting agent such as wheat bran, vine leaves, lemons, or sauerkraut juice. Meat dishes are not too common; however, *mititei*, spicy chopped meat, and *limba cu masline*, tongue with olives, are interesting.

The best desserts in Romania are fresh fruits in season. Second best are cooked fruits, *pere în compot*, stewed pears, for example. *Alivenca* is a rather good dessert made with cottage cheese and cornmeal.

Local wines are pleasant, and are usually named after the grape type—Riesling, Cabernet, Pinot. The strong drink is plum brandy, *tuica*. Beer is extremely popular. Strong black coffee, *cafea*, is always taken after dinner. The leading cheeses are *urda* and *branza de burduf*, both made from sheep's milk.

Romano. A dry strong Italian cheese much like Parmesan.

Roman Snail. An edible variety of land snail. In October it seals itself in its shell with a layer of calcium; it is then considered ready for use.

Romarin. Rosemary, an aromatic herb; must be used in small quantities because of its strong flavor.

Romatour de Kempten in Allgau. A soft Bavarian cheese with a reddish rind; at its peak between November and April.

Rombo (Italian). Turbot, a fish.

Rombosses (Belgian). Apple slices wrapped in pastry dough; a sort of apple turnover.

Romeritos. A Mexican herb that roughly resembles rosemary.

Romero (Spanish). Rosemary.

Romesco (Spanish). A deliciously flavored lamb stew; particularly popular in the Barcelona area.

Rømmegrøt (Norwegian). Cream porridge.

Rømmesalat (Norwegian). Lettuce salad with sour cream.

Rømmevafler (Norwegian). Sour-cream waffles.

Rompre (French). To knead dough two or three times.

Romsteck (French). Rumpsteak, a cut of meat from the end of the rump and next to the sirloin; less tender than sirloin.

Roncal. A Spanish cow's-milk cheese similar to Parmesan, made in the mountains. After it has aged, the rind is seared with a hot iron.

Rondin (French). A round, large stewpot, made of various materials, with two handles.

Rook. A kind of crow, sometimes used for food.

Rookworst met Stamppot (Dutch). Sausages and crushed vegetables.

Room (Dutch). Cream.

Roomijs (Dutch). Ice cream.

Root. A portion of a plant that grows downward into the ground. Some roots may be eaten raw; others require cooking.

Root Beer. A soft drink prepared from the juices of various roots, including the sassafras and sarsaparilla.

Root Vegetable. A vegetable whose main edible portion is the root, such as the carrot, as opposed to a leafy vegetable like spinach.

Ropa Vieja (Spanish). A beef stew in which pieces of meat are cut into lengths like rope. The meat resembles old rope, which accounts for its name.

Ropiness. Cloudiness in wine.

Ropy. Thick and sticky, like the threads formed when water and sugar are boiled together.

Roquefort. One of the world's truly great cheeses; a distinctive, slightly salty cheese prepared in the village of Roquefort, France. It is white, darkening toward yellow, semisoft, and with a blue-green network of veins. Although it has been copied in various parts of the world, only the authentic French cheese has the true flavor and texture, and may be recognized by the word "France" stamped upon the silver wrapper.

Originally prepared only from ewe's milk, it is now frequently made with added cow's milk. The milk is allowed to curdle, is then drained, and the curds are arranged in layers alternated with specially prepared moldy bread. The mold soon spreads throughout the curds and provides the distinctive salty flavor. It is then aged for two or three months, according to the particular market for which it is intended. Sometimes, in Denmark and the United States, imitation Roquefort is made by injecting a special type of penicillin mold.

Roquefort is extremely versatile. It may be used as an hors d'oeuvre, spread on meats, especially steaks, before broiling, broken or crumbled into green salads, and eaten with fresh fruit. Dry red wine is perfect with Roquefort.

Roquefort de Corse. The Corsican version of Roquefort; it is fairly good but lacks subtlety.

Roquette; Rocket. A green-leafed plant resembling spinach but with a peppery, strong taste; used as a salad green. When purchased, the leaves should be crisp and green, not brown or yellow on the edges.

Roquille (French). (1) Candied orange rind. (2) A wine measure equal to about a half-gallon.

Røraeg (Danish). Scrambled egg.

Rosbif (Italian, Spanish). Roast beef.

Roscas (Spanish). A kind of cooky.

Roschti (Swiss). Fried potatoes, often served with bacon.

Rose Apple. A reddish fruit with a creamy white juicy pulp of inferior flavor.

Rosé aux Fruits. A French sweet wine prepared with fruit extracts and dry white wine.

Rosefish. The ocean perch.

Rose Hips. A portion of the rose plant, occasionally used to flavor jellies and preserves.

Rosell; Rosella. A tart berry native to Asia and Australia; it resembles the cranberry and is used in jellies and preserves.

Roselle. A wild green tropical herb, much like okra, that tastes vaguely like sorrel and is used to flavor soups and stews.

Rosemarin (French). Rosemary.

Rosemary. An herb of the mint family with a strong piney flavor; used in many French and Italian dishes; an ideal flavoring for duck, beef, salmon, and dressings; should be used sparingly because of its strong flavor. If sprigs of rosemary are used in cooking, they must be removed before serving because of their overpowering acrid taste.

Rosenkål (Danish). Brussels sprouts.

Rosenkohl (German). Brussels sprouts.

Rosero (Ecuadorian). A soft drink made from corn and fruit juices; served cold.

Roses. Beautiful flowers whose petals may be used in salads, fruit cups, and special desserts for an exotic effect. A few rose leaves may be used to flavor vinegar and to add aroma and bouquet to jam as it is being made.

Rosetbakkel (German). A waffle fried on rosette-shaped irons; usually served with syrup or honey.

Rosette (French). A very fat pork sausage eaten uncooked as an hors d'oeuvre; prepared in the Lyons district.

Rosinen (German). Raisins.

Rosolio. An Italian liqueur flavored with cinnamon, rose leaves, and orange flowers; known as *rossolis* in France.

Rosquillas (Latin American). Cakes made of corn flour and cheese in spiral or other fancy shapes.

Rossini. A style of preparation using *pâté de foie gras* and truffles.

Rosso Gotta (Indian). Sweet cakes of varying sizes and ingredients.

Rossolis. A French rose-flavored liqueur. *See also* Rosolio.

Rossoll. (1) A liqueur. (2) A confection shaped like coffee berries and flavored with coffee.

Rostat Bröd (Swedish). Toast.

Rostbiff (Swedish). Roast beef.

Rostbratwürste (German). Pork sausages.

Rosticceria (Italian). A small, neighborhood family restaurant.

Rosy Razor. An excellent-tasting California clam with pink-white flesh.

Rota. A passable wine produced in northern Spain; used chiefly in blending with other wines.

Rotary Oven. Trays that rotate on shelves around a large central wheel; they begin and end at the same place.

Rotbarbe (German). Red mullet.

Rotengle. A freshwater European fish, prepared like roach; known in France as *gardon rouge*.

Rote Rüben (German). Beets.

Rôti; Rôt (French). Roast.

Rôtie (French). A baked or toasted slice of bread served buttered at breakfast or tea, or with a spread as a canapé.

Rotis. In Trinidad, curries sold outdoors and eaten picnic-style.

Rotisserie. (1) A revolving spit used for roasting meat; also an electric appliance with a revolving spit. Roasting on a spit over charcoal both indoors and outdoors is very popular. Foods are self-basted and cook evenly. Rotisserie attachments are available for many ovens. (2) A restaurant specializing in roasted foods.

Rôtissoire (French). Roasting pan.

Rôtisson; Chevène. A flavorsome European fish similar to the blackfin, a Great Lakes fish.

Rotkohl (German). Red cabbage.

Rotmos (Swedish). Turnips.

Roucou. Another name for *achiote*, the red-coloring ingredient used in cooking in Latin countries.

Rouelle (French). Food cut in rounds; for example, sliced carrots or round cuts of meat, such as a thick slice of veal cut across the leg.

Rouennais. A cow's-milk cheese made in Rouen, France; best in the spring and autumn.

Rouennaise (French). A highly spiced, very rich

red-wine sauce containing puréed liver and marrow.

Rougail (French). (1) A very spicy thick stew usually made with tomatoes, garlic, eggplant, shrimp, and fish flavored with ginger; served with rice. (2) A spicy condiment made with ginger, peppers, or other hot ingredients.

Rouge de Rivière (French). A tender, excellent-tasting wild duck.

Rougeret. A cow's-milk cheese made in Burgundy, France. Another version is made with goat's milk near Lyons.

Rouget (French). (1) A strong-tasting red-skinned Mediterranean fish; best prepared with a sauce; often used in making bouillabaisse, a fish soup. (2) Red or orange mushrooms.

Rouget Barbet (French). The red mullet, found chiefly in the Mediterranean.

Roughage. Indigestible carbohydrate material in plants, such as cellulose and bran. It passes through the intestine unchanged but absorbs and holds water, adds bulk to the diet, and acts as a laxative.

Rougin; Rougion (French). A very tender excellent-tasting mushroom.

Rouille (French). A garlic sauce (or garlic mayonnaise) popular in Provence.

Roulade. (1) Rolled-up food, such as meat, omelet, etc. (2) A slice of meat, stuffed with a chopped or ground mixture, and served rolled up.

Roulardines (French). Small rolls.

Roulé (French). A biscuit mixture rolled out, covered with a thick jam, made into a roll, and topped with toasted almonds.

Roulette. A small-toothed wooden or metal wheel with a handle; used to cut dough attractively.

Round Dutch Cheese. *See* Edam Cheese.

Roundfish. Whitefish.

Round of Beef. The top and the bottom round of beef. Choice or prime top round is tender and may be pan-broiled, but it should have heavy streaks of fat in the meat. Bottom round is less tender and requires longer cooking, and is best for potting or Swiss steaks.

Round Steak. An oval cut of meat containing a small bone. The cut may be either top round or bottom round. Top round, if of top quality, may be pan-broiled. Bottom round should be braised.

Round Whitefish. An excellent-tasting fish similar to regular whitefish but dark blue on the upper part of its body.

Rouquin (French Army Slang). Red wine.

Rousselet. (1) An excellent-flavored russet pear. (2) A white wine from Béarn, France.

Rousette. (1) (French) A variety of salmon. (2) (New Caledonian) Flying fox; usually prepared in a red wine sauce. (3) (French) *Oreilette*; *merveille*; a corn fritter popular in Périgord.

Roussi (French, Obsolete). Browned flour turned into a *roux*. *See* Roux.

Roussile (French). A rather tough spongy mushroom; barely edible.

Roussillon, Côtes du. The rather sweet natural wines produced in Roussillon, France.

Roussir (French). To color meat or poultry a golden brown by cooking it in smoking hot fat or butter.

Rout Cakes. Small rich almond cookies.

Roux (French). A mixture of fat, usually butter, and flour cooked over low heat to a smooth paste and used to thicken sauces, gravies, and soups. A *white roux* is cooked just long enough to take away the raw taste of the flour; a *brown roux*, until the mixture turns a light brown. Some experts also include a *blond roux*, made exclusively with butter; this type must be used immediately.

Rowan; Serviceberry. The mountain ash, whose small red berrylike fruits are used chiefly for making jelly.

Royale (French). A type of shaped custard, used in clear soups as a garnish.

Royale, À la. (1) With an unsweetened garnish of egg custard; applied to consommé. (2) *Eggs à la royale*, a dish garnished with puff paste and truffles. (3) Served with cream sauces and garnishes; applied to poached egg dishes. (4) Some hot and cold desserts.

Royal Fizz. An effervescent beverage, the basis of which is gin and eggs.

Royal Icing. White sweet icing used to decorate wedding cakes.

Royal Sentry. A mediocre process-type imitation Swiss cheese made in Denmark.

Royan. A large delicate-flavored Mediterranean sardine often used in French provincial cooking.

Rozijn (Dutch). Raisin.

Rozijnen Saus (Dutch). Raisin sauce.

Ruban (French). (1) Egg yolks and sugar beaten together until they combine and fall away, like a ribbon, from a fork lifted from the mixture. (2) A sweet fritter made in many different styles; usually served with powdered sugar.

Rubané (French). Ribbonlike; applied to decorated foods.

Rüben (German). Turnips.

Rubio (Spanish). The red gurnard, a type of red fish of fair quality.

Rudd. A European freshwater fish of the carp family; rather bony and of poor texture.

Ruddy Duck. A good-flavored American wild duck.

Rüdesheim. A wine village of the Rheingau district of Germany. *See* Germany, The Wines of.

Rue. A European plant whose strong-scented, bitter leaves are used for making bitters and flavorings.

Ruff; Reeve. A small European and Asian bird similar to the sandpiper; the female is the *reeve*.

Ruffec. A simple French goat's-milk cheese; sometimes used also as the fermenting agent in the making of other goat's-milk cheeses.

Rugbrød. (1) (Danish) Rye bread. (2) (Norwegian) A rye bread made with yeast, sugar, and milk.

Rühreier (German). Scrambled eggs.

Rull (Norwegian). Spiced beef roll.

Rum. A liquor distilled from various products of tropical sugar cane, such as molasses. Outstanding types are produced in Jamaica, Trinidad, and Martinique.

Rum Cakes. Many different cakes flavored or soaked with rum.

Rum Crustas. An iced rum drink; made in the West Indies.

Rumilly. A soft cow's-milk cheese made in the Savoy district of France.

Rumkin. A medieval drinking vessel.

Rump. A cut of beef from the hip. The piece which is cut from the part closest to the loin,

if of top quality, is tender enough for broiling. The rest of the rump is excellent for pot roasting.

Rumpot. One who drinks a great deal of liquor, especially rum; a drunkard.

Rumpstek (Swedish). Steak.

Rumpy Loaf (Scotch, Obsolete). A crusty, glazed loaf of bread; cut into small squares.

Rum Sauce. A rum-flavored white sauce used on puddings at Christmas.

Rum Shrub. A drink containing rum, lime juice, sugar, water, and spices.

Rumsteack (German). Steak, or sometimes rump steak.

Rundergehakt (Danish, Dutch). A minced-beef dish; hamburger or meat loaf.

Runderlapjes (Dutch). Slices of stewed beef.

Runderlappen (Danish, Dutch). Braised steak.

Runderrolletjes (Dutch). Rolled beef.

Rundlet; Runlet. A wine cask.

Rundstykker (Danish, Norwegian). Rolls.

Rundvlees (Dutch). Beef.

Runesten. A Danish cheese similar to Emmentaler cheese; weighs about 3 pounds.

Ruscus. A plant whose young shoots may be cooked and eaten like a fresh vegetable; the flavor is mediocre.

Rush; Rattan. A scented Indian reed, which is prepared as a spice in some Eastern countries.

Rush Cream Cheese. A European fresh cream cheese allowed to dry on rush mats.

Rusk Paste. A mixture of honey and fat used in making rusk.

Rusks. Slices of sweet or plain bread or cake that have been baked twice, first in a loaf pan, cooled, then sliced and baked again in a slow oven.

Russe, À la. In the Russian style; usually, made with sour cream.

Russel; Russell. Beets and water allowed to ferment until a dark, red juice forms; used to make a kind of Passover borscht.

Russeroles (French). A kind of pastry made in Touraine.

Russet Apple. A good-flavored late-autumn apple with a rough brown skin; used for desserts.

Russet Pear. A reddish summer pear with a pleasant flavor and texture.

Russia. In prerevolutionary days Russian food

was superb. Elaborate banquets consisting of many courses were frequently served, and there was great interest in food. In more recent times, of course, food has become a major production and distribution problem in the Soviet Union, and most people are satisfied with merely getting enough to eat. However, some good cooks still remain, and fine dishes are occasionally prepared, especially for visiting dignitaries.

Appetizers are marvelous. *Zakuska*, as they are called, are among the best in the world. The most famous single one, of course, is *ikra*, caviar. This is eaten plain, with toast, and with lemon juice, sour cream, or grated egg yolk. At the opposite extreme is herring, probably the national favorite, at least on the basis of availability. Salted salmon, much like smoked salmon, is very good, as are the smoked sturgeon and other smoked fish. All the soups tend to be hearty and filling, containing many solid ingredients. The classic soup, needless to say, is *borscht*, made of cabbage or beets; it is sometimes a dairy soup, but often made with meat. There are many *borscht* variations, including some interesting types made with olives, tongue, etc. With *borscht* is often served *pirozhki*, small, filled pastries. The sauerkraut soup, *shchi*, is exceptional, although little known outside Russia.

The best meat in the country is lamb, and *shashlik* (cubes of marinated meat grilled on a skewer) are well known the world over. *Kavkaski shashlik* is similar, but the meat comes in larger pieces. The best-known beef dish is *beef Stroganof*, thin cuts of meat with sour cream. The *koulebiaka* is a sort of yeast dough baked in a loaf with either meat or fish filling; although troublesome to make, it is a truly worthwhile dish. Chicken dishes are good— *cotletki pojarshi* are ground chicken cutlets, and *chicken Kiev* is breast of chicken wrapped around a nugget of butter.

The Russians bother little with cooked vegetables or green salads; as a nation they show a preference for mushrooms, preferably wild, and also for cucumbers. Potatoes are a standby, and *kashoi*, or *kasha*, buckwheat groats, are often eaten as a filling cereal instead of potatoes. The breads are invariably dark and delicious,

and make American pale white bread seem insipid by comparison. There are a few good desserts, especially those made with pastry, like *lomanci z makom*, a Ukrainian poppy-seed-and-honey pastry; *vatroushkis* are cheese pastries. *Mazourka* is a nut-filled walnut cake, and *lakomynkas hrechanyi muky* is a buckwheat cream cake which originated in the Ukraine. Of course there are *blintzes*, delicious pancakes, and also *blinis*, buckwheat pancakes.

The national drink of the country is vodka. It is served ice-cold and straight, never mixed with tomato or orange juice in the American fashion. The Russians like beer, but unfortunately do not make it well. The wines are erratic, sometimes rather good but more often mediocre. The government has strongly pushed the development and consumption of table wines in the hope of cutting down the high national consumption of vodka. White wines lack subtlety as a rule, but the reds are somewhat better. Wines are usually numbered rather than named, being called White No. 3, Red No. 6, and so forth.

As for nonalcoholic beverages, the people like *kvass*, a beerlike drink made from bread, apples, or whatever is available. *Kefir* is a fermented milk drink that tastes like a cross between yoghurt and buttermilk. The Russians are very fond of coffee, but it is quite expensive and is not too well prepared. Tea remains the national drink of the country and is always made with tea leaves rather than with tea bags.

Russia, The Wines of. During the century before the Russian Revolution of 1917, many acres were devoted to viniculture in southern Russia. In Bessarabia, generations of Russian landowners spent large sums growing French vines in an effort to duplicate the French wine they loved so well. But the soil and climate were not the same, and the Bessarabian wines never approached the French in quality, although they were popular in Russia.

Wine production in Czarist Russia was always on a large scale, although less was actually produced than in France, Germany, or Italy. After the Revolution, viniculture continued, but not much wine was made, for the Communists put all their effort into growing foodstuffs. Later more vineyards were planted; the reason is an unexpected one. The Russian economy during 1940–1960 offered little to the consumer in the way of luxuries, so, in an effort to satisfy the growing demand, and also to remove excess currency from circulation, the government determined to bring out a line of luxury wines. These were offered to the public around 1950 and have been increasingly popular, even though the prices, beginning at the equivalent of several dollars a bottle and going up to as much as ten, represent a high price to the Russian public. In recent years the government has been waging a battle against alcoholism, which had increased to the point where it was a matter of serious concern to the authorities. The amount of vodka permitted to be served in restaurants was limited, and simultaneously wine was promoted in an effect to change the drinking habits of the people. Some success has been reported.

Vine growing is mainly in the south, for the northern winters are bitter cold. The leading vineyards are now in the Crimea, particularly in the more protected southern section. There is a large vineyard area again in Bessarabia, but the wines from this region are not so highly regarded as those from Crimea. Other regions include the Volga River country, the Caucasus, and certain parts of old Turkestan.

Russian wines often have no names, only numbers. One selects Red Wine No. 2, White Wine No. 3, and so forth. The whites cover an enormous range; there are scores of imitations of dry French whites, which are unsuccessful, and many sweet French imitations that are reasonably good. The reds seem, in fact, much inferior to the Burgundy or Bordeaux they are imitating. Some local wines are quite interesting, although none challenges the wines of the Western countries. Russia has devoted its greatest efforts in viniculture to the production of quantities of *vin ordinaire* rather than attempting to make small quantities of quality wines.

Champagnes are notoriously bad. The Russian fondness for sweet drinks is evidenced by their sugar content—10–12 percent—so sweet that they set one's teeth on edge.

Russian Cakes. Pieces of Genoese dough mixed with hot apricot jam and rum, and placed between two layers of a spongelike roll.

Russian Dressing. A dressing made with mayonnaise, chili sauce, minced onion, and green pepper. Sour cream may be added. It may be used with any salad other than fruit and with seafood or fish.

Russula; Russule. A tender red-capped wild mushroom native to France; best when picked during the late summer.

Rutabaga. A very large yellow-white turnip.

Ruwer. A small river in Germany along whose banks are vineyards that produce fair wine. *See* Germany, The Wines of.

Rye. A grain grown in many parts of the world, particularly in northern and central Europe. Because it grows in poor soil it is an easier crop to grow than wheat. It is made into flour for breads and is used by distillers for making rye whisky and gin.

Rye Whisky. Whisky distilled from a mash which contains not less than 51 percent rye grain.

Rygeøst. A white Danish cheese.

Rype (Danish, Norwegian). Grouse or ptarmigan.

Rype i Fløtesaus (Norwegian). Ptarmigan served in a thick sauce.

S

Saaland Pfarr. A hard Swedish cheese with a distinctive biting quality; made with whisky.

Saanen; Hartkäse; Reibkäse; Walliskäse. A firm Swiss cow's-milk cheese with small eyes that resembles Emmentaler; its aging period is 3–7 years. Suitable for grating.

Saar. A German wine district along the Saar River, a tributary of the Moselle. *See* Germany, The Wines of.

Saba. A Philippine banana suitable only for cooking or baking.

Sabalo (Spanish). (1) The tarpon, a tropical marine fish. (2) Shad.

Sabayon; Zabaione (French). (1) A dessert of Italian origin, made of egg yolks, sugar, and Marsala or Madeira wine. (2) A sauce for puddings and other desserts.

Sablage. An old form of table decoration made by forming designs in colored sands on a table-cloth.

Sable; Sablefish. Carp, or a similar fish.

Sablé (French). A rich, flat, wedge-shaped cooky, whose crumbly consistency resembles that of shortbread; originated in Normandy.

Sabot au Sang (French, Obsolete). Stew made with blood.

Sabotière (French). An apparatus for making ices.

Saccharin; Saccharine. A crystalline substance several hundred times sweeter than cane sugar. Because it has no calories it is used as a sugar substitute for dietary purposes.

Saccharometer. An instrument that indicates the specific gravity or density of sugar solutions.

Sachertorte (Austrian). A rich chocolate cake.

Sack. (1) Sherry. (2) (British, Obsolete) Most white wines from southern Europe, especially from Spain and the Canary Islands.

Sack Posset. An alcoholic drink made by curdling cream and crumbled biscuits with sherry and other ingredients. Also sometimes made with ale.

Sacrament. The consecrated wine and bread of the Eucharist in the Christian Church.

Sacramental Wine. The heavy, sweet red wine used in various religious ceremonies.

Sacristain (French). A small twisted puff pastry, usually coated with almonds.

Saddle. A cut of meat usually including the upper back portion of an animal from the last rib to the legs on both sides. Saddles of lamb, pork, and beef are usually roasted.

Saddle Cakes (Scotch). Ground-meat patties on fried bread topped with a poached egg.

Safarancho (Mexican). A dish of pork, rice, onions, and green peppers.

Safflower. A European orange flower used as a coloring agent in place of saffron. *See also* Safflower Oil.

Safflower Oil. An edible oil made from the safflower plant. It is a polyunsaturated fat and has been recommended in the diet because of its effect on the cholesterol reading of human beings.

Saffron. A species of crocus whose mildly pungent and aromatic stamens are used to color and flavor foods. It was introduced into Europe by the Arabs and was known in ancient times in Africa, the Near East, and the Far East. It is an essential for bouillabaisse. As a brilliant yellow colorant it is used in confections, vegetables, and beverages. Saffron is also used to season breads, pickles, sauces, fish, meat, and poultry.

Saffron Milk Cap. A mushroom about 4 inches across the top that releases a whitish, milky juice when cut; particularly good when young.

Safrole. A colorless liquid, although occasionally brown, used in the beverage industry to produce synthetically the flavor and aroma of root beer and sarsaparilla.

Saft. (1) (German) Gravy. (2) (Swedish) Fruit juice.

Sage. A strongly aromatic herb whose gray leaves are used fresh and dried to season most types of foods, especially pork and sausage. It was known to the Romans and was brought in the 14th century to England from Swiss and French monasteries. It quickly became one of the most common herbs in English gardens. The United States imports thousands of tons yearly to supply the demand.

Sage Cheese. (1) (British) Cream cheese with sage leaves and green coloring. (2) A green mottled American cheese, usually cheddar, with a distinctive flavor.

Sage Grouse; Sage Hen. The largest of the grouse family, native to the Middle West of the United States. The flesh of the young birds, delicately flavored with the sage on which they feed, is considered excellent eating.

Sago. A red-to-brown flour obtained by grinding the pith in the trunks of the sago and other tropical palms. An easily digested form of starch, it makes tasty and nutritious puddings. Granulated sago is made by mixing the flour with water to form a paste that is then dried and ground.

Sago Palm. The tropical palm tree whose soft pith provides the starchy base from which sago is made.

Sagou (French). Sago.

Saguaro. A giant Mexican cactus whose fruit is used to make an alcoholic beverage.

Sahne (German). Cream.

Sahnenkäse (German). Cream cheese.

Saignant (French). "Bloody." As applied to meats, undergone, that is, red but not raw; equal in the United States to very rare.

Saigneux (French). The neck of veal or mutton.

Saigon Cinnamon. An excellent kind of cinnamon, shipped from Saigon, Vietnam.

Saindoux (French). Rendered pork fat; it keeps well and is used to flavor provincial dishes.

Saingorlon. A French blue-veined cheese similar to Gorgonzola.

Saint-Affrique. A fair-quality goat's-milk cheese made in Guyenne, France.

Saint-Amand-Montrond. An aromatic, strong goat's-milk cheese made near Berry, France.

Saint-Benoît. (1) A soft rennet cheese made in Loiret, France. Charcoal and salt are rubbed on the surface of the cheese and it is aged 12–20 days, depending on the season. (2) A white cow's-milk cheese made in the vicinity of Orléans, France.

Saint-Claude. A small, medium-firm square goat's-milk cheese made in Franche-Comté, France. It is curdled with rennet; may be eaten after 8 hours or aged longer.

Saint-Émilion. A group of red wines produced in the Sainte-Émilion region of Bordeaux, France. In general, they have a good taste and good bouquet. The white wines are usually designated as Bordeaux.

Saint-Fargeol. A firm pungent French cheese.

Saint-Florentin. A fresh white cheese with a high butterfat content made in Burgundy, France; fairly good-tasting but not popular.

Saint-Gelay. A moist goat's-milk cheese about the size and shape of Camembert, produced in Poitou, France,

Saint George's Agaric. A small wild French mushroom of fair flavor but poor texture.

Saint-Germain (French). (1) A thick soup made with fresh green peas. (2) A garnish of fresh peas. (3) Grilled fillets of fish, such as sole, served with Béarnaise sauce.

Saint-Gildas-des-Bois. A very rich cream cheese made from cow's milk in Brittany, France.

Saint-Honoré (French). An elaborate large pastry consisting of a base of pastry garnished with glazed cream puffs arranged in a ring, the center being filled with pastry cream mixed with stiffly beaten egg whites.

Saint-Ivel. An English cream cheese with the general flavor of acidophilus milk or yoghurt.

Saint Jacobskam (Dutch). Scallop.

Saint Jacques, Coquille (French). Scallops.

Saint-John's-Wort. An aromatic plant whose flowering tops are used for infusions and "teas." Formerly the plant was used to make liqueurs.

Saint-Loup. A slightly fermented goat's-milk cheese made in Poitou, France.

Saint Marcellin; Fromage de Chevre. A French cheese, similar to Brie, with a distinctive blue mold on the outside but not on the inside; made of goat's milk to which is added ewe's or cow's milk.

Saint-Michel. A Genoese pastry filled with coffee-flavored butter, covered with vanilla-flavored butter cream, and garnished with chopped almonds.

Saint-Nectaire. A mild cow's-milk cheese with a streaked yellow, red, and white rind; made in the Dore Mountains region of France.

Saint Patrick Soup. A combination of cream-of-spinach soup and cream-of-mushroom soup in equal proportions topped with minced chives or parsley.

Saint-Paulin. A medium-firm French cheese similar to Port du Salut.

Saint-Pierre. A sea fish that yields very delicious white fillets tasting something like sole or turbot.

Saint-Rémy. (1) A smooth, rich cow's-milk cheese made in Lorraine, France. (2) A cheese produced near Combraille, France.

Sainte-Anne-d'Auray. A mild-flavored cow's-milk cheese made in the Brittany region of France.

Sainte-Catharine. A French plum, particularly good when eaten fresh; not suitable for drying into prunes.

Sainte-Croix-du-Mont. A wine district of the Bordeaux region of France. *See* France, The Wines of.

Sainte-Foy-Bordeaux. A wine district of the Bordeaux region of France. *See* France, The Wines of.

Sainte-Maure. A semisoft goat's-milk cheese similar to Camembert, produced in the Touraine region of France.

Sainte-Menehould. A style of cooking calf's and pig's feet. They are cooked, then breaded and baked; served with a piquant sauce.

Sainte-Menehould Sauce. A spicy mustard-and-pickle sauce used chiefly with pig's feet.

Sainte-Odile. An Alsatian white cheese flavored with cumin.

Saisir (French). To brown meat very quickly over high heat to seal in the natural juices.

Saiten. A German sausage, usually served with lentils.

Saithe (Scotch). The coalfish.

Sake; Rice Wine. The national liquor of Japan; a kind of still beer made by a double fermentation of a rice brew. Whole rice grains are fermented in wooden barrels with a yeastlike fungus for about 2 weeks. The alcoholic content is about 14 percent. Saké is served warm in special tiny cups. It is a deceptive drink, having a mild, slightly sweet flavor, but in quantity it can be intoxicating.

Sal (Portuguese, Spanish). Salt.

Sal de Ajo. Garlic salt.

Sal de Apio España. Celery salt.

Sal de Cebolla. Onion salt.

Salad. A cold preparation of vegetables (particularly lettuce, escarole, endive) or herbs (such as watercress) served with a dressing of oil, vinegar, and spices. There are limitless variations, such as hot salads (certain types of German potato salad); salads made of fruit, fish, poultry, meat, or eggs; and the tremendous range of salad dressings made of ingredients other than oil and vinegar.

The classic salad is of the "green" type, made exclusively with a single salad green, or a combination of many different types of salad greens. A section of tomato is sometimes served with a green salad, but purists find this practice objectionable. In the United States the salad is often served with the main course, but in Europe the custom is to serve it as a separate course after the main dish; in California and certain other western states the salad is frequently served as an appetizer course before the main part of the meal. France's *salade Niçoise* is a rare example of a European appetizer salad. The main objection to serving salad with the main course is that the vinegar in the salad dressing destroys the taste of wine, and in Europe wine is always drunk with the main course.

An American novelty is the so-called "luncheon salad," frequently served as a one-dish meal. Unlike the green salad, luncheon salads are usually made of fruit, fish, shellfish, meat, or poultry and classify as salads because they are served with lettuce or other greens. Luncheon salads are often jellied affairs, to the dismay of Europeans, who cannot understand the American taste for sweet and savory ingredients in the same dish.

Although the classic salad dressing is made of oil and vinegar, mayonnaise, "boiled dressing," and other mixtures are now frequently served with luncheon salads; extreme examples are whipped-cream dressings, and combinations of sour cream and mayonnaise, which represent substantial departures from what the French would consider acceptable dressings. In the Middle East, salad dressings made of honey and other sweet liquids are not uncommon. The people of Southeast Asia are particularly fond of salads, because the extreme heat and humidity cause the appetite to yearn for light, crunchy foods. Instead of lettuce they use a tremendous assortment of unusual ingredients—vine leaves, green plants, shrubs, and even the shoots of young fruit trees. The Siamese like to cover their salads with dressings made of soy sauce, or sometimes with a strongly flavored garlicky sauce made of dried fish.

For a good salad, fresh, crisp greens without dark spots or blemishes are used. They are washed thoroughly and then dried, wrapped in towels or Saran Wrap, and chilled. Instead of cutting salad greens, they should be torn into bite-sized pieces by hand. Dressing should be added at the last minute, before serving, except where the instructions direct otherwise.

Salada de Abacate (Portuguese). Avocado salad.

Salada Mixta (Portuguese). Mixed salad.

Salad Basket. A woven wire basket about the size of a colander, used for washing and draining salad greens.

Salad Bowl. A wooden, porcelain, glass, or plastic bowl used for mixing salads. A metal bowl is not advisable because it affects the taste of the salad ingredients.

Salad Burnet. A hardy herb with slightly fuzzy leaves and a mild odor similar to that of cucumbers; used as a salad flavoring ingredient.

Salad Cream. A light-colored mayonnaise.

Salad Dressing. A mixture of ingredients used to give or develop flavor and to bind a salad together; may include oils, vinegar, lemon or other fruit juices, salt, pepper, spices, herbs, cream, eggs (cooked or raw), or many other condiments in varying proportions.

Salad Fork. A fork wider and shorter than a dinner fork with one rather sharp outer edge to facilitate cutting; also used as a dessert fork.

Saladier (French). A salad bowl.

Salad Oil. Any edible oil generally used in pre-paring salad dressings; sometimes only olive oil, the classic salad oil. In France, for example, the term usually refers only to the very finest and most delicate of olive oils, the first or virgin pressing. In other parts of the world the term includes various other oils, such as cottonseed, corn, sesame, walnut, or peanut oil.

Salad Plants. Radishes, chives, scallions, cucumbers, curly endive, watercress, escarole, mustard-and-cress, lettuce and all other tender young greens.

Salad Plate. A plate about 7 inches in diameter used for serving individual salads.

Salaison (French). The salting of foods in order to preserve them.

Salak. A brownish fruit of certain small Asiatic palm trees, with a good but not extraordinary taste.

Salamana. A very soft Italian sheep's-milk cheese with a pronounced flavor, ripened in a sausage-like casing; eaten on bread or mixed with corn-meal and cooked.

Salamander; Salamandre. (1) A heating device, plate, or oven to brown and glaze foods rapidly before serving. (2) (French) To brown bread crumbs in butter before sprinkling over certain foods.

Salambo; Salammbô. A small cake filled with kirsch-flavored French cream. A *chou* pastry is used and the cake is iced.

Salame. A soft cream cheese in sausagelike skins similar to Italian salami.

Salami. A highly spiced long sausage popular in Europe and the United States. It originated in Italy but is prepared differently in various countries, the only similarity being that all versions are sausages. Besides meat they usually contain garlic and spices. Italian salami is generally made with two-thirds pork and one-third beef; Hungarian salamis are smoked and are milder than Italian versions. In the United States salamis fall into two categories: those packed by Midwestern meat concerns are quite mild; the so-called "Jewish," or "kosher," salamis contain no pork and are spicier and far tastier.

Salami may be eaten uncooked as a snack; it may be cut into small cubes and speared with a toothpick, making an ideal hors d'oeuvre; or slices may be fried and made into a sandwich. Salami keeps well, especially if dried.

Salami de Gotha. A German smoked sausage made with beef and pork.

Salami Devil. A chunk of salami dipped in mustard, speared on a toothpick, and served as an hors d'oeuvre.

Salamoia (Italian). Pickle.

Salangane. An Asiatic sea swallow whose nests are used for making soup highly regarded by gourmets. The nests are sold as "swallows'-nests" or "birds'-nests."

Salarium (Latin). Salt money. Roman soldiers were paid an extra amount with which to purchase salt, or sometimes given salt as part of their pay. From this Latin word comes the English word "salary."

Salat (Danish, German). Salad.

Salatagurker (Norwegian). Dill pickles.

Salatplatte (German). Salad platter.

Salbei (German). Sage.

Salber (German). Salt pork.

Salchicha (Portuguese, Spanish). Sausage.

Salchicharia (Portuguese). Smoked-pork products.

Sale (Italian). Salt.

Salé (French). Salted or pickled. *Petit salé* is a small amount of pickled and cooked pork served hot or cold as an hors d'oeuvre. *Agneau de pré salé* is lamb grown on salty marsh lands.

Salées au Fromage (Swiss). Cheesecakes.

Salep. (1) (Near Eastern) A starch made from the tubers of orchids. Mixed with spices, soy sauce, or syrup, it is made into a popular beverage or soup in various parts of Asia. (2) (Arabian) A flavoring agent. *See also* Racahout.

Saler (French). To salt.

Saleratus (Obsolete). Baking soda.

Saler de la Viande (French). To cure, salt, or dry meat.

Salers. A smooth yellow cow's-milk cheese similar to a mild cheddar, made in the Auvergne region of France.

Salgado (Portuguese). Salted.

Salicoque. A small gray variety of shrimp with an inferior flavor; it retains most of its natural color, not turning red when cooked.

Salière (French). Saltcellar.

Saline. Salty; containing salt.

Saline Waters. Natural spring waters, especially those with a high salt content.

Salinometer; Salimeter; Salometer. An instrument that measures the concentration of salt solutions.

Salisbury Steak. Ground beef shaped into a flat oval and broiled; hamburger.

Salit. A cow's-milk cheese produced in Montauban, France; may be used as a table cheese after 8 months' aging. Aged for two years, it is used for grating.

Sallad (Swedish). Salad.

Salladsås (Swedish). Salad dressing.

Sally Lunn. (1) (American) A southern bread made with either baking powder or yeast, baked in a muffin pan or square pan; served with meals. (2) (British) A teacake first made by Sally Lunn at Bath and sold in her teashop in the late 18th century.

Salm (German). Salmon.

Salmagundi; Salmigondis. (1) A mixture of foods, especially chopped meat, onions, anchovies, eggs, and olive oil. (2) A spicy stew or ragout made with several kinds of leftover meats. (3) Sometimes, cold meats prepared in a salad. The word is thought to come from a recipe for *salamis* of an 18th-century French chef named *Salmis de Gonde.*

Salmanasar; Salmanazar. A large wine bottle with the capacity of 12 regular bottles.

Salmão (Portuguese). Salmon.

Salmi; Salmis. An elaborate game preparation, in which the bird is partially roasted, carved, and then cooked in a chafing dish with truffles, mushrooms, and white wine; served on sautéed bread spread with pâté.

Salmigondis (French). *See* Salmagundi.

Salmon. A migratory food fish living in the Atlantic and Pacific oceans but spawning in the rivers of Northern Europe and America. The gray-white-to-pink nutritious flesh is considered excellent eating. The king salmon of the Pacific and the Nova Scotia and Scotch salmon of the Atlantic are considered the finest. Salmon are normally 3–4 feet long and weigh 15–25 pounds, but Pacific salmon can weigh up to 70 pounds.

They are caught while moving from ocean to river, since they do not eat while spawning and the flesh becomes dry.

The salmon move from the ocean to rivers at the beginning of the spawning season. They swim slowly against the current, navigating rapids and leaping waterfalls, sometimes to a height of 25 feet. They spawn in the still water of upper rivers and lakes, the female laying the eggs and the male impregnating them. The exhausted fish are carried back to the ocean by the current. Both male and female Pacific salmon die as they drift back to the sea. The eggs are hatched and the young fish live off the water plants until they are about a foot long (a year or two); then they allow the current to carry them to the ocean.

One of the few fish mentioned by Shakespeare, the salmon was known to ancient Europe, and North American coastal Indians had ritual salmon hunts with torch and spear.

Salmón (Spanish). Salmon.

Salmonberry. A wild raspberry found along the North Pacific coast; eaten as a dessert or used in jams, jellies, or tarts.

Salmone (Italian). Salmon.

Salmonete (Portuguese). Baby salmon.

Salmonete. The red or spotted goatfish, or sometimes red mullet, found in tropical waters.

Salmon Trout. A pink-fleshed trout with unusually delicate taste and texture.

Saloio. A sour Portuguese hand cheese made from cow's milk.

Saloon. A place where liquor is sold; a bar.

Saloop. Sassafras; brought to Europe from North America by Sir Francis Drake. Sassafras tea was widely regarded as a cure-all in 16th-century England.

Salpicon (French). A garnish, filling, or croquette consisting of any variety of finely diced ingredients (meats, vegetables, or fruits) held together with a sauce.

Salpicón de Ave (Spanish). Chicken with mayonnaise.

Salsa (Italian). Sauce.

  Salsa d'Acciughe. Anchovy sauce.

  Salsa d'Aglio. Garlic dressing.

  Salsa di Carne. Meat sauce.

  Salsa di Fegatini. Chicken-liver sauce.

  Salsa di Funghi. Mushroom sauce.

  Salsa di Pomodori. Tomato sauce.

Salsa de Tomatillo (Mexican). A spicy chili sauce made from the *tomatillo*, a vegetable resembling the tomato.

Salsa Español (Spanish). A sauce made of meat, wine, and onions.

Salsa Jalapeña (Mexican). A spicy chili sauce made from the *jalapeña* pepper.

Salsiccia (Italian). Sausage.

  Salsiccia con l'Uva. Sausage with grapes.

Salsify; Salsafy; Oyster Plant. A carrot-shaped root with a mild, sweet flavor suggesting that of parsnip or oyster. It should be soaked in cold water to prevent discoloring, then boiled or deep-fried, or used in salads. Salsify and oyster plant are similar, but not the same, although the terms are often used interchangeably.

Salsify, Black. A variety of salsify with black skin; the young leaves are used in salads.

Salsiz. A miniature Swiss sausage.

Salt. A chemical compound, sodium chloride, found abundantly in the sea, in natural brines, and in a crystalline state known as rock salt. It is the oldest and most important seasoning. In ancient cultures, salt was often an important part of the economy. It was used as a curing agent and preservative and is used today for the same purposes. Part of Roman soldiers' pay was a quantity of salt called a *salarium*, from which our word "salary" comes. European explorers also used salt to barter with primitive tribes in Africa.

No diet can be completely free of salt, since all foods, especially meats, contain it. In the preparation of food, salt must be added, since cooking removes salt. Vegetables, steamed or cooked in their own juices, retain much more of their natural salts than when boiled in water.

One method of preparing commercial salt is by the evaporation of salt water or brine. Several grades of salt crystals are formed, and from these other grades are prepared. Some of the commercial names and uses of these salt crystals are: *cheese salt*, designed for making cheese; *topping flake*, used for crackers; *butter salt*, for making butter; *fine flake*, the general-purpose or table salt used in baking and canning; *fine "pre-*

pared flour" salt, used in self-rising flour and cake mixes; and *kosher salt*, which has the largest crystals. Kosher salt is used by chefs because it melts slower, wilts salads less, and flavors longer. *Maldon salt*, thought by many to be the finest salt produced, is made from the water of the Maldon Sea in Maldon, Essex, England. It is available in fine food shops in most metropolitan areas.

Salt, Below the. An expression for which several interpretations are given; the preferred version relates to the medieval practice of placing salt in the middle of the table. Those seated above the salt were the distinguished guests, those "below the salt" were of lesser importance.

Salt Cellar. A container used to hold salt.

Salted Fish. Many large fish that are often salted when first caught.

Salted Food. Any pickled, preserved, or salted food.

Salted Nuts. Nuts fried in oil and sprinkled with salt.

Saltee. A very firm, rather spicy Irish cheese.

Saltfiskballer (Norwegian). Fish-and-potato dumplings.

Salt-Free Cheese. Various salt-free cheeses intended for those who must limit their intake of salt. Certain pot cheeses, cottage cheese, and French goat cheeses are quite low in salt.

Salt-Free Diets. Retention of fluid in the body depends on the amount of salt present. Therefore, low salt intake reduces the amount of fluid. Low-salt diets are required in cases of hypertension and cardiac insufficiency, which are usually accompanied by edema, nephritis, and nephrosis. Low-salt foods include rice, sugar, flour, fruit, green salads, macaroni, unsalted nuts, and vegetables.

Salt Grinder. A small wooden mill or a mortar, similar to a pepper mill, used to grind rock salt to a powder or fine crystals.

Saltimbocca (Italian). Veal and ham cooked in butter.

> **Saltimbocca alla Romana.** Veal and ham cooked in wine.

Salting Tubs. Tubs of various types and sizes in which meat is pickled in brine.

Saltpeter. Niter, a crystalline mineral salt compound consisting of nitric acid and potassium, used in curing meats. Small quantities add a red color to meat, but an excess toughens it.

Salt Pork. Any portion of a pig that is high in fat and cured in a heavy salt brine; used for flavoring foods and as a fatty base.

Salt-Rising Bread. A bread, usually made with milk, cornmeal, sugar, salt, and baking soda, that undergoes spontaneous fermentation without yeast.

Salt Scone (Scotch). An unsweetened scone containing a little salt.

Salt Stick. A kind of bread or roll, heavily salted with coarse or kosher salt, prepared in a long, comparatively thin shape.

Salts, Indian. The Greek and Roman name for sugar.

Saltsjögädda (Swedish). Archipelago pike.

Salumerie (Italian). Pork products.

Salvador. *See* Central America.

Salvia (Spanish). Sage.

Salvietta (Italian). Napkin.

Salzburger Nockerl (Austrian). A soufflé-like dish that originated in Salzburg; prepared in a skillet with beaten egg yolks and flour into which stiffly beaten egg whites are incorporated.

Salzgurken (German). Small salted cucumbers.

Sam (British). To bake bread in a cool oven. *See also* Sammy.

Samak (Arabic). Fish.

Sambals. (1) (Indian) Relishes and other dishes that cool the palate. (2) A pepper native to South Pacific regions.

Sambar (Indian). A highly seasoned vegetable and lentil dish.

Sambuca. A clear white anise-flavored liqueur made in Italy.

Sammy (British). Soggy or heavy bread.

Samos. A very sweet, somewhat cloying wine made on the Greek island of Samos; popular in Scandinavia and the Low Countries.

Samosa (Indian). A small thin pastry stuffed with a spicy meat or vegetable mixture.

Samovar (Russian). "Self-boiler." A metal urn, usually made of copper or brass, used for heating water for tea over a charcoal grate. The tea itself is not made in a samovar.

Samp. (1) A cereal made from coarsely ground

corn; boiled and eaten with milk. (2) The corn itself.

Samphire; Sea Fennel; Peter's Grass. An aromatic seaweed; cooked and eaten as a vegetable, pickled and eaten like cabbage, or used in preparing pickles.

Samshu; Samsu (Chinese, Malaysian). A rice beer, similar to Japan's *saké*, with a high alcoholic content.

Samsö; Samsöe. A firm white Danish cheese, slightly sweet but sharp; similar to Gruyère or Swiss cheese but with a different texture.

Samztah (Arabian). A dessert prepared with a purée of dates, cream, and cornstarch.

San Bernardo. An Italian bottled sparkling water.

Sancerre. A wine district of the Loire River of France. *See* France, The Wines of.

Sancerre, Fromage de. A French semihard mellow, lightly salted goat's-milk cheese.

Sandalwood Powder. An oriental powder used, especially around Mysore, India, for flavoring ices and sherbets.

Sandboy. The sand eel.

Sand Cake. A crumbly cake made mostly with corn flour and a little wheat flour.

Sand Cherry. A small shrub bearing sweet berries; cultivated in the Midwestern United States.

Sand Clam. A clam found along the Pacific Coast of the United States; especially popular in San Francisco.

Sand Dab. A small ocean fish caught close to shore; a type of flatfish.

Sand Eel; Whitebait. A small fish found along sandy beaches; cooked like smelt.

Sanderlings. Very small edible birds found near the sea in Arctic regions.

Sander; Sandre; Zander. The European giant pike perch, a tasty food fish.

Sanders. Minced beef (or other meat) covered with mashed potatoes and butter and browned in the oven.

Sandía (Spanish). Watermelon.

Sandkage (Danish). Sand cake.

Sandkaker (Norwegian). Sand tarts; a rich pound cake.

Sand Launce. The sand eel.

Sandpiper. A small water sparrow similar to the snipe whose meat is edible but stringy.

Sand Plum. A thick-skinned plum cultivated in the southwestern United States.

Sand Tart. A sweet cake of any desired shape covered with sugar and cinnamon and baked.

Sanduiches (Portuguese). Sandwiches.

Sandwich. Two slices of bread with meat, cheese, etc., between. The name is believed to derive from the Fourth Earl of Sandwich, John Montagu, who liked to eat and gamble at the same time, which made knives and forks cumbersome. He decided to satisfy his hunger with a slice of meat brought to the gaming table, and ate it between two slices of bread.

The sandwich has been known since ancient times, for the Romans ate meat between slices of bread, and the French peasant's midday meal was served in the fields in the same manner.

Sandwiches may be made with fillings of cheese, meat, poultry, fish, peanut butter, jelly, and even salad greens, such as watercress. They can be served open with one slice of bread and can also be broiled. The sandwich has been raised to an art form by the Scandinavians, who serve elaborate compositions based on a single piece of bread. Sandwiches are a staple of lunches, picnic meals, afternoon teas, and midnight suppers.

Sandwich Nut Cheese. A soft mild cheese (such as cream cheese) mixed with chopped nuts and sometimes raisins.

Sandwich Toaster. An electrical device used to grill complete sandwiches, particularly cheese sandwiches.

Sangaree. (1) A tropical sweet cold alcoholic beverage made with brandy, gin or whisky, wine, and sugar. *Barbados sangaree* is made with Madeira wine. (2) An Indian punch prepared with sherry, sugar, lemon juice, and water. (3) *See* Sangri.

Sangiovese di Romagna. *See* Italy, The Wines of.

Sangler (French). To pack ice, or salt and ice, around a mold to freeze ices and ice creams or to keep other desserts frozen.

Sanglier. Wild boar.

Sangri. A beverage made from Madeira wine

mixed with water and sugar with a dash of grated nutmeg; also called *sangaree*.

Sangría. A favorite Spanish warm weather beverage made in a pitcher with ice cubes, red or white wine, slices of fresh fruit and a dash of club soda.

Sangue di Guida. A blood-red, rather bitter Italian table wine from the Broni vineyards of Lombardy.

Sanguette (French). A spiced blood pudding eaten mostly in the provinces.

Sanguinaccio (Italian). Black blood pudding.

Sanguine. A sweet red-fleshed orange with a delicate flavor and fine aroma.

Sanguine; Sanquette (French). A type of pancake made with chicken blood.

San Paolo. An Italian bottled sparkling water.

San Pedro (Spanish). The John Dory, a fine food fish.

San Pellegrino. One of Italy's best sparkling waters.

San Severo. A good white dry table wine produced in the vicinity of Poggia, Italy.

Sansiot (French). A calf's-head dish; made in Burgundy.

Sansoë (French). The Danish cheese Samsö, a firm rich variety of Gruyère.

Sansonnet (French). (1) The starling. (2) Sometimes a small mackerel.

Santa Clara Wines. *See* United States, The Wines of.

Santa Maddalena. *See* Italy, The Wines of.

Santan. Coconut milk.

Santa Vittoria. An Italian liqueur resembling Strega.

Santenay. A wine district of the Burgundy region of France. *See* France, The Wines of.

Santol. A yellowish Philippine sour fruit.

Santola (Portuguese). A large variety of crab.

Sapaceau (French). An egg-and-liquor punch.

Sapid. Savory; pleasant to the taste.

Sapodilla; Naseberry Plum. The large tropical evergreen tree that produces chicle, which is used in making chewing gum. Its large fruit, resembling the pear in both appearance and taste, is eaten raw, used in cooking, or used in desserts and ice creams.

Saporoso (Italian). Relish.

Sapota, Black. A Mexican persimmon with very dark flesh.

Sapporo. A Japanese black (sometimes light) beer with a unique taste.

Sapsago. A small hard green Swiss cheese made from sour skimmed cow's milk and flavored with powdered clover leaves; used mainly for grating. Also produced in the United States.

Sapucaia Nut; Paradise Nut. The fruit of a Brazilian tree; much like the Brazil nut. It tastes better than the Brazil nut but is more difficult to gather.

Saracen Corn. Buckwheat; used mainly for cereal and stuffing, and sometimes as a vegetable. It was brought to Europe by Crusaders who fought in the Holy Land against the Saracens; thus even today the French call buckwheat *blés Sarrasin*.

Saran Wrap. Trade name of a thin clear plastic film used as airtight covering for foods, particularly cheese.

Sarapatel (Brazilian). A somewhat odd sauce made with the blood and inner organs of the pig and sometimes with meat. Duck or chicken may also be used.

Saratoga Chips. Potato chips made of very thin strips of potato soaked in cold water, dried thoroughly, then cooked in very hot fat.

Saratoga Steak. A cut of sirloin steak suitable for broiling.

Sarcelle (French). The teal, a water fowl of the duck family whose meat is a great delicacy and is highly regarded by epicures.

Sarda (Portuguese). Sprat.

Sardella (Italian). Sardines.

Sardelle (German). Anchovy.

Sardellschnitzel (Swedish). Fillet of veal with anchovies.

Sardin (Danish, Swedish). Sardine.

Sardina (Spanish). Sardine.

Sardine. Small migratory fish of the herring family, found abundantly in the Mediterranean Sea, especially near the island of Sardinia; also caught in the Atlantic and Pacific oceans.

Sardines may be eaten fresh, but they are generally canned in oil. French sardines are canned occasionally with truffles and spices. The Scandinavian countries smoke the fish before canning. Portuguese sardines are among the finest canned in oil.

In the United States, sardines are canned on both the Atlantic and Pacific coasts in oil and sometimes with mustard, vegetables, and spices.

Gold Sardine. A fish less than a foot in length found in warm waters around the world; may be prepared in many ways.

Sardinen (German). Sardines.

Sardinha (Portuguese). Sardine.

Sardo. (1) A Pecorino cheese. (2) A somewhat spicy, very firm cheese made in Sardinia, Italy.

Sargasso. A seaweed used in Spain for salad.

Sargo. A very small Mediterranean fish with rather dry flesh; also found in the Caribbean.

Sarladaise. A style of preparing potatoes: they are cut into very small pieces and baked in a casserole with goose fat and truffles.

Sarmalas. Ground or chopped beef combined with chopped onion, ham, parsley, etc., wrapped in vine leaves or other wrappings; and braised in a casserole.

Sarmas (Middle Eastern). Grape leaves stuffed with ground meat and rice; served with a sauce.

Sarrasin; Sarrazin (French). Buckwheat or "Saracen corn." See Saracen Corn.

Sarraz. A Swiss imitation of Roquefort.

Sarriette. Savory, a highly aromatic herb of the mint family.

Sarrubra Wheat. A strong Russian wheat with good milling qualities.

Sarsaparilla. (1) A tropical American climbing plant whose roots are used to make a refreshing beverage. (2) The beverage itself.

Sarsenage. A French blue-mold cheese similar in taste and texture to Roquefort.

Sarsiada. A Philippine fried-fish dish served with a garlic-onion sauce.

Sartadagnano (French). Very small fish, sometimes chopped up, pressed together while cooking in a skillet to form a sort of fish pancake; a specialty of Provence.

Sartizzu (Italian). A pork sausage heavily flavored with cinnamon and pepper; a specialty of Sardinia.

Sås (Swedish). Sauce.

Sashimi (Japanese). Raw fish. Many Japanese preparations are based on raw fish.

Sassafras. An American tree of the laurel family whose bark, twigs, and roots are used for flavoring in cooking and in medicines. Filé powder, an integral part of Creole cookery, is made from the leaves. The roots are also used for making sassafras tea and root beer.

Sassella. A ruby-red table wine of Lombardy, Italy, that has more bouquet than most other Italian wines. See Italy, The Wines of.

Sassenage (French). A salty, hard, bluish rennet cheese made from a combination of sheep's, cow's, and goat's milk.

Sasser (French). To stir in a pan.

Sassolina. An Italian liqueur with a pronounced anise taste.

Satee Ajam (Indonesian). Chicken roasted on a spit.

Satsuma. A mandarin orange.

Satsumage (Japanese). A fried fishcake.

Saturated Fats. All fats have a chemical structure, or "backbone," of carbon atoms ranging from as few as 4 to as many as 20. In the commercial process of converting liquid fats to solid fats (see Hydrogenated Fats) hydrogen is released into the liquid fat, whereupon it combines with the carbon atoms. It is then regarded as "saturated."

Saubohnen (German). Broad beans.

Sauce (French). Sauce. See also separate listings for other sauces in their appropriate alphabetical position, as for example, Béchamel Sauce.

Sauce Américaine. A rich crayfish sauce.

Sauce Anglaise. Apple sauce and horseradish; sometimes mayonnaise flavored with mustard.

Sauce Aurore. A cream-and-tomato sauce.

Sauce Bigarade. A classic sauce for roast duck, consisting of burnt sugar combined with citrus juice, usually with cherries added.

Sauce Bischof. A red-wine sauce made with orange and lemon zest, sugar, and cinnamon; usually served on puddings.

Sauce Bretonne. A sauce made of either cream or white wine, prepared with carrots, leeks, and onions.

Sauce Chantilly. Béchamel sauce combined with cream or with Hollandaise sauce and cream.

Sauce Demidoff. A Madeira sauce with truffles.

Sauce Diable. A spicy sauce made from white wine, shallots, mustard, and peppers; usually served with cold meats.

Sauce Duxelles. A mixture of onions, shallots, mushrooms, and parsley prepared in butter and white wine.

Sauce Financière. Madeira sauce with mushrooms, chicken livers, and truffles.

Sauce Marchand de Vin. Red wine and shallots boiled until concentrated; frequently served with steak.

Sauce Périgord. A Madeira sauce containing truffles.

Sauce Poivrade. A brown sauce highly seasoned with pepper.

Sauce Rémoulade. Mayonnaise with chopped parsley, gherkins, and capers.

Sauce Robert. A mixture of white wine and onion with tomato added.

Sauce Sabayon. A sauce, originally Italian, made by beating wine, sugar, and egg yolks together.

Sauce Soubise. Basically an onion purée but may be enriched with cream and butter.

Sauce Verte. Mayonnaise or any other white sauce colored with green herbs.

Sauce Villeroi. A creamy rich velouté with egg yolks and mushroom purée.

Sauce-Alone; Garlic Mustard (British). A potherb with a strong onion taste combined with the sharpness of mustard; used as a flavoring ingredient.

Sauceboat. An oval, china or silver sauce or gravy

pitcher with a bottom attached to catch drippings.

Saucepan. A container, usually made of metal, used for various cookery purposes.

Saucer. A somewhat shallow dish intended to hold a cup.

Saucer (French). To cover with a sauce.

Sauces. Food flavorings or seasonings in liquid or almost liquid form. Sauces may be divided into several types, but the basic distinction is usually drawn between regular sauces (for fish or meat) and sweet sauces (for desserts, ice cream, and the like). Another basic difference is between hot and cold sauces.

It is believed that sauces first became popular during the height of Greek civilization and subsequently during Roman ascendancy. In any event, the Italians developed the use of sauces, but it was the French, during the 17th and 18th centuries, who created the wide range of present-day sauces. Although still very popular, the last half-century has seen a gradual decline in the popularity of sauces, as skilled kitchen help has become scarcer, and also with the increasing popularity of simple grilled foods served for reducing diets.

Sauces may be made with cream, milk, soup stock, wine, or with almost any ingredient or combination of ingredients. For best results, the liquid in which foods have been cooked should be incorporated into the sauce served with such food. For example, if fish is boiled, the fish stock should be incorporated into the sauce. In the same manner, chicken or meat stock give added flavor to sauces served with chicken or meat. In America, sauces are generally cooked quickly and served at once. In Europe, especially France, the sauce is very frequently prepared with an excess of liquid, then cooked for several hours so that the excess evaporates, leaving a reduced, more concentrated and highly flavored sauce. If this method is followed, salt or salty ingredients must be used with discretion, because the slow-cooking procedure causes a concentration of salt in the finished sauce.

Sauces should have a satisfactory "body," or finish. This holds true regardless of whether the sauce is thin, of medium body, thick, or contains solid ingredients. The French call the body of sauces *du corps*, or sometimes they refer to *la nappe*, with reference to its ability to coat foods. Even the thinnest of sauces should not separate or become watery. Floury, pasty, and lumpy sauces are so bad that food will taste better with no sauce.

Hot sauces are usually made with some form of fat, starch, or flour, and a liquid (wine, stock, milk, cream, etc.). Additional ingredients, spices, and flavorings may be added as desired, according to the dish being prepared. Hot sauces are of two types—white and brown. Brown sauces are prepared by browning flour and sometimes adding vegetables (tomatoes, onions, etc.). Some chefs think that butter sauces (such as Hollandaise) constitute a separate category.

The term "sauce" is also applied to commercially prepared bottled products used to flavor foods, such as Worcestershire, Tabasco, Chili, and similar products.

Sauce Tureen. A covered vessel, smaller than a soup tureen, from which sauces and gravies are dispensed with a ladle at the table.

Saucier (French). One who prepares sauces.

Saucière (French). A deep bowl or dish in which sauce is served.

Saucijsjes (Dutch). Sausages.

Saucijzebroodje (Dutch). Sausage meat in pastry roll.

Saucisse (French). Fresh-pork sausages.

Saucisson (French). Smoked sausages.

> **Saucisson de Lyon.** A pork sausage, usually made with plenty of spices and garlic.

> **Saucisson de Toulouse.** A fairly small, coarsely-textured pork sausage, made in Toulouse; used chiefly in casseroles.

Sauerampfersuppe (German). Sorrel soup.

Sauerbraten (German). Pot roast of beef, marinated in a vinegar-and-spice mixture for several days, then seared on all sides and simmered with carrots and onions; usually served with a well-seasoned thickened sauce or gravy, accompanied by boiled potatoes, red cabbage, or sauerkraut.

Sauerkraut; Sourcrout. Pickled cabbage; prepared with thinly shredded cabbage allowed to pickle in a brine composed of salt and the cabbage juice. It used to be far more popular than it is today; now, however, eating habits have changed and fresh vegetables are more available than formerly during the winter months.

Shredded cabbage is usually prepared in a large wooden cask, alternating in layers with plenty of salt; the mixture is pressed or pounded heavily so as to induce the cabbage juice to flow. It is quite low in calories, and ideal for dieters because it is filling. Sauerkraut is most popular in Germany, where it is frequently served, both hot or cold. In France, it is often made with juniper berries for added flavor. The classic French dish using sauerkraut is *choucroute garni*, in which the sauerkraut is cooked with an assortment of fatty meats. The Russians prepare an excellent sauerkraut soup, *Shchi*, which is hearty and delicious during cold weather.

Sauerkraut Juice. The liquid obtained from crushed cabbage when making sauerkraut. It is a refreshing, acidulous drink and best served cold. Although low in calories, it is stimulating to the appetite and therefore not suited to a reducing diet. Many people find the taste of this juice too strong for their palate, and it is often combined with an equal amount of tomato juice. It has a laxative action.

Sauge (French). Sage.

Saugrené (French). Cooked in little water with butter, herbs, and salt.

Sault. A smooth French cheese made with goat's milk combined with either cow's or sheep's milk and matured in chestnut leaves.

Saumur. A wine region of the Loire River district of France. *See* France, The Wines of.

Saumure (French). A pickling brine; a mixture of water and plenty of salt, sometimes with vinegar, spices, and herbs added.

Saumuré (French). Pickled or marinated.

Saupe. The goldline, a type of sea bream, a salt-water fish.

Saupiquet (French). (1) A red-wine sauce thickened with bread and flavored with onion, vinegar, cinnamon, and ginger; served with game, particularly rabbit. (2) Ham in a heavily seasoned cream sauce; a specialty of Nivernais and Burgundy.

Saur (French). Salted and smoked herring.

Sauré (French). Cured, or dried with smoke.

Saurel. A large fish similar to mackerel.

Saure Sahne (German). Sour cream.

Saurie. A fish found in Japanese waters that resembles a sardine but is somewhat larger and has a sweeter taste.

Saurin. A freshly-cured herring.

Saus (Dutch, Norwegian). Sauce.

Sausage. Meat, usually pork or beef, freshly ground or chopped, salted, pickled, smoked or otherwise cured with added spices, flavorings, flour or filler, and packed into any container or stuffed into an animal gut or a cellulose casing. The variety of sausages is almost limitless, and almost every country produces them. Germany makes the widest variety, but Italy and France follow closely. In the United States a favorite snack is the *frankfurter*, a kind of sausage.

Fish sausages are produced in various parts of the world. Poultry sausages are also popular, particularly in France. Sausages are also prepared with animal's blood, sometimes called blood sausages, made with hog's blood.

One of the most famous sausages is *bologna*, which originated in Bologna, Italy. The frankfurter, or "hot dog," had its beginnings in the town of Frankfurt, Germany. The *salami*, first prepared in Italy, is popular in most of Europe and in the United States.

Some of the popular Spanish sausages include: *longaniza*, prepared with pork, garlic, and herbs; *salchichas*, made with veal and pork and flavored with rum; *butifarra*, a fatty pork sausage prepared with white wine; *salchichon*, one of the best pork sausages of all; *morcilla blanca*, made with chicken, bacon, and hard-cooked eggs; and *morcilta Asturiana*, a type of blood pudding.

"Sausage" also refers to loose sausage meat which is sometimes sold in containers without animal or cellulose wrapping.

Sausage Spices. A combination of spices, usually including coriander, nutmeg, and white pepper, used to season sausages.

Sauté. To brown foods in a small quantity of hot fat, usually in a skillet. Sautéing is also a preliminary step before liquid is added for stews and casseroles. Veal, liver, onions, mushrooms, and other foods are sautéed until cooked. For sautéing, the fat must be hot and the food dry and in a single layer.

Sauté d'Agneau (French). Lamb stew.

Sauté Pan. A skillet with straight sides used for sautéing meats and vegetables; it may vary in size but should have a thick bottom.

Sauter (French). To cook by sautéing, that is, by quick, light frying.

Sauternes. A wine district of the Bordeaux region of France. *See* France, The Wines of.

Sauternes and Barsac Classification of 1855. *See* France, The Wines of.

Sauteuse (French). A shallow heavy pan with a thick bottom, used for sautéing meats and vegetables.

Sautoir (French). A shallow heavy pan, much like a sauteuse and used for the same purposes, but with sides that slope outward.

Sauzé. A strong, aromatic French goat's-milk cheese.

Savarin. A light yeast cake soaked with a rum or kirsch syrup.

Savel. (Portuguese). Shad.

Saveloy. A smoked, red, highly seasoned pork sausage, eaten hot or cold. The first Saveloys were made with pig's brains.

Savoiardi (Italian). Ladyfingers.

Savor. Taste, aroma, or flavor.

Savoring. Enjoying the taste and often the aroma of a food.

Savory. (1) Having a pleasant taste, aroma, or flavor. (2) A dried aromatic herb used to add subtle flavor to meats, salads, soups, and stuffings. (3) *See* Savoury.

Savory, Summer. An herb, bearing light purple flowers; its young leaves may be used as a flavoring ingredient, particularly in making a *bouquet garni*.

Savory, Winter. An herb, bearing white to pink flowers; much like summer savory, except that the flavor is somewhat stronger. It is often used in flavoring egg dishes or in potato preparations.

Savoury (British). A tidbit served after dessert, usually sharp-flavored; often a seafood or something made from cheese.

Savoy. A medium-soft cheese, much like Port du Salut, made in the Savoy region of France.

Savoy Biscuit. Spongecake.

Savoyarde, À la. Describing two different dishes made with potatoes: a pancake omelet filled with sautéed potato slices and thin shavings of Gruyère cheese; and raw potatoes sliced and mixed with grated Gruyère and consommé, and cooked in an earthenware dish.

Savoy Cabbage. A cabbage with loose, wrinkled, curled leaves and with a better flavor than ordinary head cabbage. Its large leaves make it particularly suited for stuffing, or for use where the leaves must be spread or rolled with a filling. It can also be used, finely shredded, for soups, cole slaw, as a green vegetable, and in salads.

Savoy Tubes. Tubes that fit into bags used to pipe batter into pans or creams into pastry.

Savuto. *See* Italy, The Wines of.

SAWFA. South American Wine Farmers Association.

Sawi. (1) Chinese cabbage. (2) Various kinds of Malaysian cabbage.

Sawoh. A South Pacific fruit, particularly popular in Indonesia.

Saxifrage, Burnet; Pimpernel. A dwarf variety of herb, now rarely used.

Saxifrages. Various plants with fleshy leaves that may be used in soups or eaten as vegetables.

Sayadiah (Lebanese). A preparation of fish, rice, onions, and pine nuts.

Sbrinz. A very hard, well-flavored Argentinian cheese that tastes like Parmesan; suitable only for grating.

Scabious. A field plant whose leaves are eaten in salads or cooked like spinach.

Scabwort. *See* Elecampe.

Scad. A coarse-fleshed fish about the size of a herring; more common in Europe than in America.

Scald. (1) To heat any liquid to a temperature just below its boiling point. (2) To plunge a fruit or vegetable into boiling water quickly to make peeling easier.

Scalded Flour. A paste made by adding boiling water to a mixture of cold water and flour, causing the starch cells to burst and thicken.

Scale. To remove the scales of a fish before preparing it for the pan.

Scales, Kitchen. A device used to weigh foods; it is the most accurate method of measuring.

Scallion; Spring Onion. The green, young or spring onion with a mild characteristic onion flavor. Both the white part and the green tops may be eaten raw or cooked.

Scallop. (1) A shellfish popular in various parts of the world. It has an attractive color, strongly marked, regular ridges on the shell, and small "wings" beside the hinge of the shells. Two general types are available: the small *bay scallop* and the much larger *sea scallop*. The bay scallop has the finer taste. Only the adductor muscle, which draws the two parts of the shell together, is edible. Fresh scallops should be firm and without slime on the exterior; otherwise they have a tough, rubbery quality when cooked.

In the United States, scallops are usually prepared quite simply by frying or sautéing. In France, however, there is a wide range of dishes. Along the west coast of South America, notably in Chile and Peru, the chefs prepare imaginative dishes, particularly *chupe*, a thick chowder. Scallops are also marinated in lime juice and onions for several hours and served raw.

(2) To bake in a baking dish, casserole, or ramekin with a slightly thickened liquid, sometimes with bread crumbs on top. Originally, scallop shells were used as containers in this method of preparation.

Scallop, Dried. A Chinese sea scallop that is air-dried; it adds a distinctive, rather fishy taste to foods.

Scaloppine (Italian). Thin slice of meat, usually veal.

Scaloppine al Marsala. Veal cutlet in a Marsala wine sauce.

Scaloppine di Vitello alla Bolognese. A veal slice with ham and cheese.

Scaloppine di Vitello alla Cacciatora. Veal hunter's style, that is, with tomato sauce.

Scaloppine di Vitello alla Pizzaiola. Veal cooked with tomatoes, green peppers, mushrooms, and spices.

Scaloppine di Vitello al Parmigiana. A thin slice of veal with tomato sauce and cheese.

Scaloppine di Vitello Uso di Capri. A fried cut of veal with lemon and peas.

Scamorze; Scarmorze. An Italian buffalo's-milk cheese with a Provolone taste; a favorite around Naples.

Scamozza. *See* Mozzarella Affumicata.

Scampi; Caramote. A delicate, tender shellfish found in the Adriatic Sea. It closely resembles the shrimp but has a finer taste. A favorite Italian method of preparing scampi is grilling them with olive oil and garlic. The American usage of the term "scampi" for all shrimp dishes so prepared is incorrect.

Scanno. A very soft, yellowish sheep's-milk cheese made in southeastern Italy.

Scarlet Runner. A string bean similar to the green bean.

Scarole; Escarole. An endive or chicory plant with wavy broad leaves.

Scarolle (French). Escarole.

Scarus; Parrot Fish. A bright-colored, fine-fleshed Mediterranean fish.

Scaup Duck. The widgeon, a freshwater duck.

Schabzieger. The original sapsago, a cone-shaped Swiss cheese flavored with cloves.

Schafkäse (German). Sheep's-milk cheese.

Schaleth (Jewish). A pastry-covered baked apple-and-noodle dish containing currants, raisins, chopped orange and lemon peel, and eggs.

Schalotten (German). Shallots.

Schaltiere (German). Shellfish.

Schamser. A very large Swiss skim-milk cheese.

Schankbier (German). Light Munich beer.

Schapevlees (Dutch). Mutton.

Scharlachberger. A white Rhine wine. *See* Germany, The Wines of.

Scharzberger. A white wine produced in Scharzhof in the Saar Valley in Germany. *See* Germany, The Wines of.

Schav (Jewish). A cold sorrel soup.

Schellfisch (German). Haddock.

Schenkeli (Swiss). Small rolls fried in butter.

Schiacciato (Italian). Crushed.

Schifela (Alsatian). Shoulder of pork cooked with turnips.

Schikoree (German). Chicory.

Schillerwein. An ordinary table wine, usually pale red, made from both black and white grapes in western parts of Germany.

Schinken (German). Ham.

Schinken, Westfälischer (German). Westphalian ham.

Schinkenomelette (German). Ham omelet.

Schinkenwurst (German). Ham sausage.

Schlachtplatte. Sauerkraut, mashed green peas, boiled pork, liver sausages, and small dumplings; a specialty of Swabia, Germany.

Schlagsahne (German). Whipped cream.

Schlesische Sauermilchkäse. A very firm German or Polish sour-milk cheese; matured one to two months.

Schlesisches Himmelreich (German). (1) Roast pork or goose with dumplings. (2) Purée of peas and sauerkraut; made in Silesia. (3) Mashed fried potatoes covered with bread crumbs and served with smoked bacon and stewed dried fruits.

Schlesischer Weichquarg. A rather soft German or Polish cheese made from sour-curd skim milk.

Schlossabzug (German). Of wine, bottled by the estate. *See* Germany, The Wines of.

Schloss Bockelheimer. A wine produced by a state-owned domain in the Nahe region of Germany. *See* Germany, The Wines of.

Schlosskäse. A cheese produced in Austria and Germany; much like Limburger but with a more delicate flavor.

Schlosskäse, Mondseer. *See* Mondseer.

Schmaltz (Jewish). Chicken or meat fat.

Schmierkäse. A German cottage cheese; many varieties are rather strong and have considerable flavor.

Schmor (German). A pickled-meat dish; sauerbraten.

Schnäpel (German). Trout.

Schnapps (Dutch, German). Strong, hard liquors.

Schnecken (German). Snail-shaped buns or pastry rolled with fruits or nuts.

Schnitzel (Austrian, German). A thin cutlet of veal dipped in egg and bread crumbs or cracker crumbs and cooked in butter, oil, or other fat.

Schnitzel Holstein (German). Veal cutlets served with fried eggs and anchovies.

Schnitz un Gnepp (Pennsylvania Dutch). Ham prepared with dumplings and dried apples.

Schnupfnudel (German). A fairly heavy noodle.

Schoenland. A German imitation of Italy's Bel Paese cheese.

Schokolade (German). Chocolate.

Schooner. An oversized beer stein or goblet.

Schoppenwein. Unbottled young white wine, usually served in pitchers; produced in the Rheinpfalz region of Germany. *See* Germany, The Wines of.

Schüblig. A ground-veal sausage made in St. Gallen, Switzerland.

Sehug (Israeli). A spicy mixture of lemon, garlic, parsley, and red pepper; originally a Yemenite preparation.

Schwarzbrot (German). Dark whole-grained bread.

Schwarzenberg. A German rennet cheese made from partly skimmed cow's milk.

Schwarzwälder Kirschtorte. A cherry tart made in the Black Forest region of Germany.

Schwartzwurst; Schwarzwurst (German). A type of black sausage, prepared with a considerable amount of fat.

Schwedenplatte (German). Tiny assorted sandwiches.

Schwein (German). Hog, pig.

    Schweinebraten. Roast pork.

    Schweinefillets. Fillets of pork.

    Schweinefleisch. Pork.

    Schweinefleischkäse. Pork and other meats in a loaf.

    Schweinehaxe. Leg of pork.

    Schweinekeule. Leg of pork.

    Schweinekotelett. Pork chop.

    Schweinepfeffer. Spiced or peppered pork.

    Schweinerippchen. Spareribs.

    Schweineschenkel. Roast leg of pork.

Schweizerkäse (German). Swiss cheese.

Schweizerøst, Dansk. An undistinguished Danish copy of Swiss cheese.

Scissors, Kitchen. A kitchen instrument for cutting vegetables, disjointing and chopping meat, snipping parsley, trimming salad greens, etc.

Scollop. *See* Scallop.

Scolymus; Spanish Oyster Plant. An edible root similar to salsify.

Scombridae. The mackerel family of fish; it includes the common and Spanish mackerel, the tuna, and the bonito.

Scone (Scotch). A griddle or teacake baked in the oven or on a griddle; cut in quadrants.

Scone Flour. A strong self-rising flour used for scones, which require a great deal of aerating powder.

Scoop. (1) To hollow a fruit, potato, etc., in order to fill it with other food. (2) The instrument for performing this action. (3) A dip for ice cream.

Score. To mark food with small diamonds, cuts, or notches either for decorative purposes or to prevent curling, turning, or crumbling.

Scorpene. The rascasse, a Mediterranean fish used chiefly for making bouillabaisse.

Scorsonère (French). Scorzonera.

Scorzonera. A green plant whose long radishlike root is cooked and eaten as a vegetable.

Scotch Black Bun. A traditional yeast-dough cake stuffed with almonds, fruits, and spices.

Scotch Broth; Scotch Mutton Broth. A soup or stew made with mutton or lamb, mixed vegetables, and barley.

Scotch Eggs. Hard-cooked eggs covered with a layer of sausage or other ground meat, then dipped in beaten eggs and crumbs, and deep fried.

Scotch Farl (Irish, Scotch). A large scone made with whole-meal flour.

Scotch Kale; Kail. (1) A cabbage with coarse, green curly leaves. (2) (Scotch) A broth or thick soup made with kale; the thick soup is served as a main dish.

Scotch Pies. Mutton pies made with a hard, stiff pastry so that the juice does not run out.

Scotch Square Bread. Breads put on boards to rise and pressed together to form squares or rectangles.

Scotch Woodcock. Scrambled eggs served on toast spread with anchovy paste.

Scoter Duck; Scooter Duck. An oily-fleshed duck. The young are passably good if cooked with several changes of water.

Scotland. The best hotels and restaurants in Scotland lean toward French food, or the so-called "international food" so common in de luxe establishments the world over. Authentic Scotch food is obtainable, as a rule, only in private homes.

A comparatively inhospitable, rugged region with cool weather, Scotland has produced only a few specialties for the gourmet, but many of them are noteworthy. Scotch smoked salmon is probably the finest in the world. Dropping down quite a bit, gastronomically speaking, is herring, but Scotch herring, too, is just about the world's best. Another fine specialty is *finnan haddie*, smoked haddock. An unpretentious, simple dish is oatmeal, or porridge. The Scotch oatmeal is slow-cooking, but the whole grains release a nutty flavor that far surpasses all other oatmeals in the world, except possibly the Irish.

Scotch broth is a mutton-and-vegetable soup; *cock-a-leekie*, chicken and leek soup, is quite good. *Bannocks* are flat cakes made with white or barley flour, and *baps* are the typical breakfast rolls. *Haggis*, a classic Scotch preparation, is made with a sheep's pluck (liver, lights, and heart) and cooked in a sheep's stomach; very few non-Scots will take to it. A simpler version is called *pot haggis*, and is a little easier to like. *Skirlie*, or *skirl-in-the-pan*, is a hot oatmeal-and-onion dish; *stovies* are peeled baked potatoes. Desserts are simple British sweets; the Scotch people do their best on teatime cakes and breads, like scones and shortbreads.

The strong drink of the country is whisky. Wine is unimportant, but a considerable amount of beer is consumed.

Scranchum (British). Crisp gingerbread.

Scraper. A rubber or plastic kitchen implement designed to scrape food from dishes and cooking utensils before washing them.

Scrapple. Highly seasoned ground pork cooked with cornmeal, then shaped into loaves or cakes, sliced, and fried. It is served as a breakfast food. Philadelphia scrapple is best known.

Scrod. Young cod split, with the backbone removed, and ready to cook.

Scullery (Obsolete). A butler's pantry or the place where dishes are washed.

Scullion (Obsolete). The servant who performed menial kitchen tasks.

Scum. A skin forming on the top of cold protein liquids; a froth on the surface of a boiling liquid.

Scungilli (Italian). Conch, shellfish.

Scup. Porgy; porgie.

Scuppernong. A fairly large sweet grape, green shading into yellow, native to the southern United States; it is made into a sweet wine.

Sea Anemones. Edible mollusks abundant along the Mediterranean coast of France.

Sea Bass. A good-flavored game fish, found along the Atlantic coast from Florida to Massachusetts, weighing about 1–4 pounds; may be prepared whole or filleted by broiling, pan-frying, sautéing, or baking, with or without a sauce.

Sea Beef (Colloquial). Whale meat.

Sea Bob (Colloquial). Shrimp.

Sea Bream. A delicately flavored fish found in the Mediterranean and along part of the English coast; called *chad* when young.

Sea Chestnut (Colloquial). The sea urchin.

Sea Cow. The manatee, a sea-going mammal; the flesh is sometimes used as food in tropical regions, although it has a somewhat unpleasant, oily taste.

Sea Cucumber. A cucumber-like ocean creature, found in various warm waters of the world. When dried, it is often used in making soups.

Sea Eel. *See* Eel.

Seafood. Edible marine creatures, including, fish, shellfish, and crustaceans. A seafood plate or platter may include various kinds of raw and cooked fish served cold or hot.

Sea Kale. A vegetable that grows wild along the seacoasts of western Europe and is now cultivated in some countries. The thick stalks and leafy crests are cooked like asparagus.

Seal. A marine mammal prized for its skin and the oil extracted from its fat. Eskimos prepare the flesh for food.

Sea Lettuce. An edible green seaweed.

Sea Moss; Carrageen. A seaweed that may be eaten as a vegetable, like spinach.

Sea Needle. A very long eel-shaped fish whose flesh retains its green appearance even when cooked.

Sea Perch. Bass. *See* Bass.

Sea Pheasant. The pintail duck.

Seapure. A type of oyster of fair quality.

Sea Robin. A rather tasteless small fish, found in many localities.

Sea Slug. A small wormlike marine creature; some varieties are considered edible in certain Asiatic countries.

Seasoning Powder. Monosodium glutamate, a vegetable derivative used to improve the taste of food; used originally in oriental cookery.

Seasonings. Ingredients added to foods to enhance the taste; they include salt, pepper, herbs, spices, leaves, and flavorings.

Sea Swallow. The trepang or bêche-de-mer.

Sea Trout. A weakfish found in deep waters off

the Atlantic coast, usually weighing about 5 pounds; prepared in many ways.

Sea Urchin; Sea Hedgehog. A saltwater animal found in various parts of the world. Inside are "sea eggs" that have a distinctive, perhaps fishy, seafood flavor; they are eaten with lemon juice or horseradish much like oysters.

Seawanhaka. A kind of oyster of varying quality.

Sea Wolf. A member of the bass family, the best-known sea wolf being the French *loup* found in the Mediterranean.

Sea Wrack. Edible seaweed, often used as a salad ingredient.

Sebadal. The gray snapper, a tropical food fish.

Sebile (French). A wooden dish used for beating eggs. Also, wooden dishes of various sizes used in the kitchen for chopped ingredients, parsley, and condiments.

Sec. As applied to wine, dry; as applied to champagne, containing 3–6 percent sugar.

Sec d'Orléans. A smooth dry white cow's-milk cheese made in Aydes, France.

Séché (French). Dried.

Sécheur (French). Drying apparatus, used especially for curing meats and fish.

Sedano (Italian). Celery.

Sedelduk (Swedish). Duck.

Seedcake. A cake made with caraway seeds. A caraway powder or flavoring is sometimes substituted for the seeds. Seedcake is sometimes also made with other seeds.

Seekh (Indian). A narrow strip of iron about 2–3 feet long used for grilling foods, especially chicken and kabobs.

Seekrabbe (German). Crab.

Seer. An Indian measurement equal to about 2 pounds.

Seezunge (German). Sole.

Seezungenfilets (German). Fillets of sole.

Segui. A Russian silvery trout.

Seguin. A mild French goat's-milk cheese; at its peak between April and December.

Seibling. A freshwater fish resembling a trout; found in the lakes of Germany. A similar fish, known as *starfish*, is found in the lakes of Scotland.

Seiche; Sèche. Cuttlefish; squid; inkfish.

Seigle (French). Rye flour.

Sekt (German). Sparkling wine.

Selchkarree (German). Smoked pork.

Selderij (Dutch). Celery.

Self-Rising Flour. A commercial flour made from the soft winter wheat with added salt and leavening.

Self-Whiskies. Straight, unblended Scotch whiskies.

Sel Gemme (French). Rock salt.

Selin (French). Mountain parsley.

Selle (French). The saddle of an animal such as veal or lamb; that is, the cut which includes part of the backbone and both loins.

　　Selle de Mouton. Saddle of mutton.

　　Selle de Porc. Saddle of pork.

　　Selle de Veau. Saddle of veal.

Selleri (Danish). Celery.

Sellerie (German). Celery.

Selles-sur-Cher. A French goat's-milk cheese coated with salt and powdered charcoal; produced in Berry.

Selterwasser; Seltzerwasser (German). Seltzer water, a mineral water.

Seltz; Eau de Seltz (French). Seltzer water, a mineral water.

Seltzer Water. (1) An effervescent mineral water from Nieder Selters, Germany. (2) Artificially carbonated effervescent waters used in many beverages.

Seltzer-Water Bottle. A bottle from which seltzer or other carbonated water is siphoned.

Seltzogene Machine. A machine used to make carbonated or soda water.

Selvaggina (Italian). Venison.

Semi di Mellone (Italian). A miniature pasta about ¼ inch long; used mostly in soups.

Semilla de Pana (Latin American). The breadnut tree.

Semillon. A white Bordeaux table wine varying in taste from dry to semisweet. *See* France, The Wines of.

Semini (Italian). Miniature seed-shaped Italian pasta, a fraction of an inch long.

Semisparkling. Of red and white wines, having some effervescence, but not completely sparkling.

Semmel (Austrian). Very small crusty bread rolls, similar to Vienna bread.

Semmelknödel (German). Dumplings consisting

of bread, milk, eggs, onions, and parsley; boiled and served with bread crumbs, butter, and sometimes with chopped ham or bacon.

Semola (Italian). Bran made from wheat flour prepared so as to retain the largest amount of gluten content.

Semolina. The hard portion of wheat remaining after flour has been sifted; used for making macaroni or other pasta. The term derives from the Latin *simila*, meaning "finely ground flour."

Semoule (French). Semolina.

Semuljepudding (Norwegian). Semolina pudding.

Senap (Swedish). Mustard.

Senelle (French). Haw, the fruit of the whitehorn or hawthorn.

Senf (German). Mustard.

Sennep (Danish). Mustard.

Sennepsauce (Danish). Mustard sauce.

Separator. A mechanical device used in dairies to separate cream from milk.

Seppia (Italian). Cuttlefish.

Septmoncel. A semihard blue-veined French cheese made from cow's, sheep's, and goat's milk; resembles Roquefort.

Sept-Oeil (French). The lamprey or its spawn.

Sérac. A strong-flavored cheese made in Savoy, France.

Serai. A hard skim-milk French cheese dried in caves, then crusted and mixed with herbs; usually eaten with butter as a spread.

Serdeau (French, Obsolete). (1) A court official who received the dishes cleared from the king's table. (2) The room to which they were taken.

Serenata. Codfish prepared with vegetables and garnished with hard-cooked eggs and slices of onion and tomato.

Sergeant Fish. The cobia, a saltwater food fish.

Seroendeng (Indonesian). Coconut and peanuts fried together in oil.

Serpolet. A European variety of wild thyme.

Serra, Queijo da. An excellent slightly acid sheep's-milk cheese made in Portugal.

Serran. The sea perch.

Serrer (French). To boil down foods so as to concentrate them.

Serriger. A white wine similar to Moselle from the vineyards of Serrig in the Saar Valley, Germany.

Servet (Dutch). Napkin.

Servett (Swedish). Napkin.

Service. (1) A set of dishes, table utensils, etc., used in serving food. (2) The manner of serving. (3) *Being in service*, an English expression, means "employed in domestic work."

Serviceberry. Small applelike fruit of several species of trees, including the wild service tree, the mountain ash, and the shadbush.

Service Charge. A charge made by certain restaurants, especially those serving food *à la carte*, intended to reimburse the restaurant for table linen, and bread and butter. Also, a 10–15 percent charge made against the total check, and intended to be in lieu of tipping.

Service Plate. A decorative plate on the table used to hold other plates on which food is served and usually removed before the main course is served.

Serviette. Table napkin. Foods served *à la serviette* are served either wrapped in or piled on a napkin.

Sesame. An East Indian aromatic herb known to the ancient Hebrews and Greeks and valued for its oil. Now naturalized to certain parts of the United States, the seeds, pungent and nutlike in flavor, are used in breads, rolls, cookies, and cakes.

Sesbania. A tree, native to the South Pacific and parts of Asia, that bears *katuray* flowers, which are used as food, especially in the Philippines.

Sesos (Spanish). Brains.

Set. The coagulation of liquid foods either by heat, as in the case of custards or other molded dishes, or by cold, as in the case of frozen ice-cream mixtures and jellied preparations.

Setas (Spanish). Mushrooms.

Setier (French, Obsolete). A measure for grain equal to 152 liters; for liquids, equal to 8 pints.

Setubal. A white or amber Portuguese dessert wine made from Muscatel grapes.

Seven-Dish Beef (Vietnamese). Beef prepared in seven different styles, each with its own sauce.

Seviche (Spanish). A raw fish served with onions, garlic, etc., as an appetizer.

Seville Orange. The bitter orange.

Sevruga. Small-grained caviar. Some experts consider the flavor as good as that of the larger-grained type. Beluga roe is the largest-grained caviar on the market.

Sewian (Indian). A thin noodle, like vermicelli, used chiefly for making puddings and desserts.

Sewin (Welsh). A sea trout.

S.F.C. Superior Fine Cognac, a liquor term.

Sfeeha (Syrian). Meat pies.

Sfingi (Italian). Cookies.

Sfogliatine di Crema (Italian). Very flaky pastry with cream.

Sfoglie in Aceto (Italian). Marinated fillet of sole.

Sformato di Tonno (Italian). Tuna pudding.

Sfumatrice (Italian). A machine for obtaining the oil from the peel of citrus fruit.

S.G. (French). *Selon grosseur*, according to size.

Sgombro (Italian). Mackerel.

Shad. Any of the various food fish belonging to the genus *Alosa*. This fish belongs to the herring family, and the shad, having the finest taste, is its most aristocratic member. The flesh is extremely bony, however, and most people find the fish too difficult to eat unless it is first boned, an extremely tedious and painstaking operation. The shad season begins in late January and continues into the first days of summer. It is caught as it ascends streams and rivers to spawn. As a rule, shad picks up the flavors of the waters in which it travels and may often acquire secondary, unpleasant tastes. However, it usually has an extremely light, fine flavor, and is highly prized for its exceptional quality. Once the fish has spawned, the flesh is completely tasteless and insipid.

Shad roe is considered a great delicacy. The roe is fairly large and lends itself well to many different methods of preparation. Before being used, however, it should be parboiled briefly with vinegared water with a little salt added; about a tablespoon of vinegar and a teaspoon of salt for a quart of water is customary. The roe is cooked until it turns white, then baked, broiled, or fried, as desired.

Shadberry. A wide variety of berries which come into season when the shad fish appears in rivers; it includes the juneberry and the serviceberry. The berries are only of fair quality, being somewhat deficient in natural sugar.

Shadbush. Another name for the shadberry; more precisely, the term should be limited to the plant itself. *See* Shadberry.

Shaddock. A large yellow orange. However, the term is usually applied to grapefruit and similar citrus fruit.

Shad of Lake Champlain. The whitefish.

Shad Roe. *See* Shad; *see also* Roe.

Shad Waiter. Whitefish.

Shag (British). A slice of bread.

Shagbark (Colloquial). The hickory nut.

Shaggy Cap. An extremely large mushroom, often 8 inches across the top; good only when young.

Shaggy Ink Cap. An edible wild mushroom with black spores.

Shaker. (1) A household container for various regularly used items, such as salt, pepper, and flour. (2) Any vessel in which drinks can be mixed.

Shallot. A mild, aromatic member of the onion family with bulbs divided like garlic. It adds an excellent flavor, especially to meats and sauces.

Shandygaff. A mixture of beer and ginger beer or ginger ale, both very cold.

Shanghai Cuisine. A sophisticated Chinese culinary style. The fish and shellfish are particularly good, as are the small dumplings, a local specialty. *See* China.

Shank. In beef, veal, or lamb the upper part of the fore leg or the hind leg.

Shank Jelly (British). A lightly seasoned tasty jelly formerly served to invalids.

Sharbat (Indian). A soft drink consisting of a syrup with nuts, flowers, and flavorings.

Sharbati Wheat. Hard, white, amber Indian wheat.

Shark. A carnivorous tough-fleshed fish used as food in certain regions of the world.

Shark's Fins. The dried fins of the shark, used by the Chinese chiefly in soup. When cooked they become gelatinous and are considered a delicacy.

Sharpen. (1) To spice a dish. (2) In pastry making, to render a cream or liquid more acid by adding lemon juice or citric acid.

Shavings (British). Thin biscuits or crackers, twisted into spirals while still hot.

Shchi (Russian). Soup made from pickled shredded cabbage; served with sour cream.

Shea Butter. A solid, greenish-white fat derived from nuts. *See also* Vegetable Butter.

Shearling. A sheep 15–18 months old.

Sheath. The wooden or leather case in which butchers and cooks formerly carried their knives.

Shedder. A soft-shell crab.

Sheep. *See* Lamb.

Sheepberry. A wild berry of the United States; used for jams and jellies.

Sheepshead. (1) A food fish of the porgy family with broad incisor teeth found along the United States coasts of the Atlantic Ocean and the Gulf of Mexico. The flesh is white, flaky, and has a fair flavor. (2) The freshwater drumfish.

Sheep's Milk. Milk of the sheep, which has a higher percentage of sugar and fat than cow's milk and is used for many cheeses, including Roquefort.

Sheep Sorrel. A sour grass with reddish flowers. Also called dock.

Sheep's Trotters. Sheep's feet.

Sheffield Plate. Utensils (plates and flatware) made of copper coated with silver by a method developed in Sheffield, England.

Sheik al Mihshee (Middle Eastern). Baked eggplant with lamb or beef, tomatoes, and onions.

Shell. To remove the hulls from nuts; to detach corn or other cereal grain from the stalk; to separate the meat of shellfish from the shells. Also, the outer covering of nuts, fruits, and some shellfish.

Shellfish. Water animals that have a shell as distinguished from those that have fins and swim about.

Shepherd's Purse; Lamb's Lettuce. A plant somewhat like watercress that grows in shady spots.

Sherbet. (1) An ice usually made from fruit juices, liqueurs, or wines. (2) (Arabian) A cooling fruit drink, usually quite sweet.

Sherris (Obsolete). Sherry wine.

Sherris-Sack. Sherry wine.

Sherry. *See* Spain, The Wines of.

Sherry Cobbler. An iced drink made with sherry, sugar, water, and fruits.

Shewbread. The 12 loaves of bread, referred to in the Bible, that are placed on the altar every Sabbath.

Shiang Soo Ya (Chinese). Duck cooked in deep fat; a Szechuan specialty.

Shifter (British, Obsolete). A cook's apprentice aboard ship.

Shiitake (Japanese). Dried mushrooms.

Shin. The part of an animal's leg behind the knee joint.

Shining Noodles. Clear, transparent noodles made from boiled rice; used in Chinese and Indonesian cooking.

Shinny Cake (American). A white cake with a filling made of raisins, pecans, and liquor, usually moonshine, called "shinny"; made in the South, particularly in Alabama. *See also* Lane Cake.

Shin of Beef. The fore portion of a leg of beef used for soup, stock, etc. Also, the portion behind the knee.

Ship Biscuit. Hardtack, a very dry biscuit that keeps well; formerly a staple aboard ships, where food that did not readily spoil was needed for long voyages.

Shiraz. A wine of passable quality produced in the vicinity of Shiraz, Iran.

Shiro Miso (Japanese). A white paste made from fermented soybeans, rice malt, and salt.

Shirr; Shir. To cook or bake whole eggs that are broken into a baking dish, usually with a little cream.

Shoat. (1) A baking trough. (2) A young pig able to feed itself.

Shochu. A strong Japanese beverage distilled from sweet potatoes.

Shogayaki (Japanese). Slices of beef about a half-inch thick marinated in ginger sauce, then cooked quickly.

Shonkleesh (Middle Eastern). Balls of cottage cheese allowed to ripen about 2 days.

Shoofly Pie (Pennsylvania Dutch). Cake made with brown sugar and molasses in a pie shell.

Shorba (Sudanese). A meat soup made with ground peanuts.

Shortbread. A rich, slightly sweetened cooky or biscuit that crumbles easily because of its high fat content.

Shortcake. A cake filled and covered with fruit (such as strawberries) and sometimes with whipped cream. Originally shortcake consisted of biscuit dough combined with fruit and often with whipped cream; this style is usually called "old-fashioned."

Short Crust. A very rich, slightly sweet pastry dough used for tarts, pies, and pastries.

Short Eating (British). Crisp, like a flaky cracker or shortbread.

Shortening. Any cooking or baking fat such as butter, lard, vegetable fat or oil; available commercially under various trade names.

Short Paste. Paste made with varying amounts of flour, sugar, water, and fats. The shortness depends on the amount of fat used and on proper handling; the less water used, the shorter the end product will be.

Short Ribs. The rib ends of rib roasts, used for braising or in soup.

Short Steak. The smallest of the 3 or 4 sirloin steaks that can be cut from one beef carcass.

Shot Glass. A small whisky glass used to dispense individual servings of liquor.

Shot Pepper. Crushed coarse pepper from white peppercorns.

Shoyu (Japanese). Soy sauce.

Shred. To tear or cut foods into thin slices or strips.

Shredder. An implement used for shredding or slicing vegetables.

Shred Pies (British). Mince pies.

Shrewsbury Biscuit. A crisp cooky-like flat cake.

Shrike. A small bird; prepared like a lark.

Shrimp. A small marine crustacean of which there are numerous varieties. Shrimp have a thin membranelike shell and several pairs of legs attached to the center of the body. They are found in Mexico, England, China, and Japan, and, in the United States, in Florida, Louisiana, Texas, and California. They may be cooked in the shell or may be shelled first; their color, usually grayish, changes to pink when cooked. Shrimp may be prepared in a large variety of ways. The most popular seafood, they are available fresh, frozen, and canned all year round.

Shrimp Butter. A seasoned butter prepared with creamed butter and pulverized cooked shrimp or shells; used as a canapé spread or on cooked seafood dishes.

Shrimp Oil. A flavoring substance used in Taiwan, chiefly with the Mongolian Barbecue.

Shrimp Paste. A salted condiment made from ground shrimp; used extensively in the Orient.

Shrimp Sauce. A fishy black sauce made from shrimp; served with cold foods or as a salad dressing; much used in the Orient.

Shrove Tuesday. The Tuesday before Ash Wednesday; often called Pancake Day.

Shrub. A homemade cordial or liqueur consisting of rum or brandy, lemon juice, and lemon and orange peels mixed together and allowed to stand 60 days; then sweetened to taste, strained, and bottled.

Shuck. To remove the outer coating, as, to shuck oysters or corn.

Shumra. An herb with a distinctive aroma; used in the Middle East, particularly in Israeli and Arabian cookery, for flavoring pickles and relishes and sometimes bread.

Shungiku (Japanese). The edible young leaves of the chrysanthemum.

Shunis. Lovage, a wild plant found in Scotland; eaten fresh or cooked as a vegetable.

Siam. *See* Thailand.

Siberian Crab. A tiny apple, about the size of a large cherry, from a tree native to Siberia.

Siblinger. A white wine made in Switzerland; the best comes from the canton of Schaffhausen.

Sicilian Fennel. *See* Italian Fennel.

Sideboard. A buffet; designed to hold and display table service and sometimes to act as a serving table.

Sidfläsk (Swedish). Bacon.

Sidra (Spanish). Cider.

Sids (British). The inner husks of oat grains.

Siebenburgen. *See* Brinza.

Sierra. The Spanish mackerel, found in tropical waters.

Sieves. Bowl-shaped household utensils of various sizes, with holes or meshes fitted into a frame. They are used to screen various substances, separating the smaller particles that pass through the mesh from larger ones, to drain liquids from solids, and to purée foods. (See illus. p. 557.)

Sieve

Sifter. A sieve with a mechanism for forcing flour or other powders through the mesh.

Sigtebrød (Danish). A smooth rye bread.

Sigtibraud (Icelandic). Bread made of strained rye and wheat.

Sild (Danish). Herring.

Sild (Norwegian). Herring.
  Sildeboller. Herring balls.
  Sildegryn. Herring soup.
  Sildekaviar. Herring caviar.
  Sildesalat. Herring salad.

Sile. (1) A fine strainer or sieve. (2) A very young herring.

Silence Cloth. A large soft cloth or a fitted pad designed to protect the dining table and to reduce the clatter of dishes and silverware.

Silesian Cheese. A German cheese made of skim cow's milk; similar to hand cheese and sometimes flavored with onions or caraway seeds.

Silex. The trade mark for a heat-resistant glass coffee maker. Water rises from the lower bowl into the upper, where it makes contact with the ground coffee, then returns to the lower bowl free of grounds.

Sili (Philippine). The small young tender shoots of the hot red pepper plant.
  Sili Labuyo. A type of very small but extremely hot red pepper.

Silk-Cotton Tree. A tropical African tree whose fruit provides an edible oil.

Silkworms. Silkworm chrysalids were formerly used in Chinese cookery and were considered nutritious and flavorful.

Sill (Swedish). Herring.
  Sillbullar. Herring croquettes.
  Sillgratin. Herring baked with potatoes and bread crumbs.
  Sillsallad. Herring salad.

Sillabub. *See* Syllabub.

Sillery. A vineyard near the Rheims champagne area of France that produces a dry nonsparkling white wine.

Sillock (Scotch). Fried coalfish.

Silure. A rare large fish found in European rivers, similar to an eel.

Silvana (Italian). Chocolate meringue.

Silver. Knives, forks, and spoons intended for table use, though not necessarily made of silver. Originally the finest table utensils were made of silver. Today gold, chrome, stainless steel, and other flatware are still referred to as "silver."

The best flat silver is sterling, which contains a high percentage of pure silver and a small amount of a base metal. Silver plate, less expensive than silver, is made by depositing electrically a thin layer of pure silver upon a baser metal. Coin silver is made on the sterling principle but contains somewhat less pure silver. Nickel silver, despite its name, contains no silver but is made from an alloy.

Silver Birch. A tree whose sap is used to make birch beer.

Silver Cake. A light white cake.

Silver Fizz. An effervescent summer drink made of gin, egg white, and carbonated water.

Silver Hake; Whiting. An American food fish.

Silver Leaf. Pure silver beaten extremely thin and used to decorate foods, especially in the Orient.

Silver Needles. A Chinese green tea.

Silver Plate. Tableware covered with a comparatively thin layer of silver.

Silversides. (1) A small delicate-fleshed fish, found along various seacoasts, about the size of a smelt and cooked similarly. (2) Whitebait. (3) A cut of beef used chiefly in making corned beef.

Silverware. Tableware made from silver.

Simarouba. A South American tree whose bark is made into a bitter tonic.

Simcamas. Yam beans; used for cooking in certain South Pacific and Asiatic countries, especially in the Philippine Islands.

Simgo. A very intoxicating African drink made from the sap of the sagus tree.

Simmer. To cook foods or liquids just below the boiling point; occasionally, to boil gently.

Simmering. A constant but slight movement of a liquid just below the boiling point.

Simnel Cakes. Two kinds of Lenten cake, almond and Bury. The almond cake is rich, contains fruits and marzipan, and is frosted with fondant and icing. The bury is flat, dark, and contains fruits. *See* Lenten Cakes.

Simple Syrup. Sugar dissolved in water and used to sweeten certain cold drinks.

Sinaasappel (Dutch). Orange.

Sinews. The tough tendinous parts of meats, poultry, and game.

Singapore Sling. A cooling drink made of lemon juice, gin, and cherry brandy. It originated in the tropics, possibly in Singapore.

Singe. To expose a plucked fowl to an open flame to facilitate the removal of the pinfeathers.

Singer (French). (1) To add flour to a stew or ragout in order to thicken the sauce. (2) To color a sauce with caramel.

Singha. A good-quality Siamese beer.

Single-Wheat Flour. A flour milled from one kind of wheat rather than from blended wheats.

Sinhalese; Singhalese. The cookery style of Ceylon, which generally resembles that of India but includes many original, novel dishes, such as *kos ambul*, a curry made from jackfruit, and *kuruma iraichchi*, a white curry prepared with lamb. *See* Ceylon.

Sinigang. A Philippine fish or meat stew made with onions, green pepper, and tomatoes.

Sink. A basic piece of kitchen equipment consisting of a large bowl or tub of heavy enamel or metal recessed in a waist-high counter with a drain in the bottom and equipped with hot- and cold-water faucets. It should be conveniently placed with counters on either side and shelves above and below. It is used for general cleaning and especially for washing dishes and foods.

Siphon Bottle. A specially designed bottle in which carbonated or effervescent liquids are held under gas pressure until the desired amount is forced out through a tube or spout.

Sippets. Small triangular pieces of toasted bread used as a garnish or border.

Siri. A South Pacific plant whose leaves are used as a vegetable.

Sir Iz Mjesine. A Yugoslavian sheep's-milk cheese; eaten fresh or salted and allowed to age.

Sirloin. A cut of beef obtained from the part of the loin directly in front of the rump. The precise meaning of this term varies regionally, but it refers to the cut that includes the sirloin and fillet, sometimes also the rumpsteak.

Sirloin Steak. A tender steak cut from the wide end of the loin of beef. It includes a considerable amount of fillet.

Sir Mastny. A Yugoslavian rennet cheese made from ewe's milk and aged in molds.

Sirniki (Russian). A type of pancake made of cheese, eggs, and flour.

Sirop (French). Syrup.

Sirop d'Erable (French). Maple syrup.

Sirop Lié (French). A sugar syrup made with arrowroot and liqueur and colored artificially (often red).

Siroper (French). To cover with or cook in syrup.

Sir Posny; Tord. A hard white Yugoslavian rennet cheese made of skim ewe's milk. After aging it has many holes.

Sirup. *See* Syrup.

Sirupssnipper (Norwegian). Gingersnaps.

Siscowet. A type of lake trout.

Sitaw (Philippine). A rather long thin cowpea.

Sitosterols. Vegetable sterols, derivative compounds resolved from the acids in corn oil and certain other edible oils.

Sitronfromasje (Norwegian). Lemon pudding.

Sitsaron; Cicharon (Philippine). Pork cracklings.

Sizzing (British). Yeast.

Sizzle. The sound of very hot fat or other foods.

Sizzling Platter. A cast-aluminum platter specially made for broiling and serving meat; usually with indentions at the bottom to drain the juices.

Sjömansbiff (Swedish). Beef stew.

Sjøørret (Norwegian). Trout.

Sjøtunge (Norwegian). Sole.

Skåne. Caraway-flavored Swedish aquavit.

Skarpsås (Swedish). Spicy sauce.

Skate; Ray; Rayfish; Raie. A fish with a flattened, disklike body and rather coarse flesh; usually cut up into chunks before cooking.

Skeachan; Ckeechan (Scotch). An ale prepared

from molasses, hops, and yeast at Christmas; an intoxicating malt liquor.

Skeel (British, Obsolete). A wood container used for milk.

Skekt (Swedish). Fried.

Skewer. A short sharp metal pin used to hold meat together while roasting. A long metal

skewer is used for threading meats and vegetables to be grilled barbecue-style. Skewers were originally wooden pins.

Skillet. A frying pan or any other shallow pan suitable for frying.

Skilly (British). A thin, watery gruel or porridge.

Skim. To clear floating matter from the surface of a liquid with a ladle or perforated spoon called a "skimmer."

Skimmed Milk. See Skim Milk.

Skimmer. A rather flat type of large spoon, usually with perforations, used to skim the surface of liquids.

Skim Milk. Milk with the cream content removed.

Skim Milk, Fortified. Skim milk to which milk solids have been added to make it more palatable.

Skim-Milk Powder. A powder made from skim milk; to reconstitute it, water is added and stirred.

Skin. The outside covering of meats, poultry, and game and of fruits and vegetables.

Skink (Scotch). Strong beef soup.

Skinka (Swedish). Ham.

Skinke (Danish). Ham.

Skinkestek (Norwegian). Roast fresh ham.

Skinklåda (Swedish). Ham omelet.

Skipjack; Whitebait. Cavella, a food fish. See also Bluefish.

Skip Mackerel. Bluefish.

Skipperlabskovs (Danish). Sailors' stew; a beef

or veal stew with potatoes, or a pork, veal, and onion stew.

Skirlie (Scotch). Oatmeal, chopped onions, and fat; usually served with meat dishes.

Skirret. An herb introduced into Europe from China and cultivated for its edible root, which is similar to the sweet potato and is hardy enough to be left in the ground during the winter and dug up when needed.

Skirt Steak. A fairly lean, muscled cut of steak taken from under the ribs.

Skoal; Skøl. To drink to the health of a person. The word originated in Scandinavia but is now popular elsewhere.

Skunk Cabbage. A leafy spring vegetable with a skunklike odor when mature. The white leafstalks are delicious but must be boiled with two or three changes of water to remove the offensive odor.

Skyr (Icelandic). A fresh cheese dessert or cream cheese, sometimes very soft, almost liquid; best when eaten with cream and sugar.

Sla (Dutch). Salad; lettuce.

Slab Cakes. Plain and fruited cakes made in large rectangular pans; they weigh about 5 pounds.

Slabonen (Dutch). String beans.

Slack-Baked. A little underbaked.

Slack Dough. Soft dough.

Slagroom (Dutch). Whipped cream.

Slätvarsfilet (Swedish). Brill, a fish.

Slaughter-House. A place where animals are killed and prepared for market.

Slaw. (1) Cole slaw. (2) (Dutch) Cabbage.

Sleepy Cream. Cream that will not churn to butter in a normal period of time.

Slice. A broad flat piece cut from a loaf of bread, a roast, or other foodstuff.

Slicing Knives. Knives designed in a number of sizes and types for particular purposes. Some are preset to cut uniform slices.

Slicing Machine. A machine specially designed to slice a complete loaf of bread at one time.

Sling. Any strong, cooling alcoholic drink; usually made with sugar, liquor, flavorings, and cracked ice. The *Singapore Sling* is the best known.

Slipcoat; Slipcote; Colwick Cheese (British). A small, very soft, rich white rennet cheese made from whole cow's milk. It ripens between cabbage leaves which "slip" off.

Slit. To make an opening, as in piecrust or baked potato, so that steam may escape.

Sliver. (1) A very thin slice of meat, cheese, or any food. (2) The act of cutting meat or vegetables into long thin strips.

Slivovice (Bulgarian). Plum brandy. There are various other spellings, depending upon the locality and local usage.

Slivovitz. A Hungarian brandy-type plum liquor.

Slivowitz. Yugoslavian plum brandy. The stones included with the fruit produce a characteristic bitter flavor.

Sloe; Sloeberry. A small dark astringent fruit resembling a plum; used as a flavoring for gin.

Sloe Gin. A pink alcoholic beverage made of gin and flavored with sloe. *See also* Gin.

Sloe Gin Fizz. An alcoholic drink made with sloe gin.

Sloke. Any of several edible seaweeds, including red laver, sea lettuce, and Irish moss; served as a vegetable in Scotland.

Slop. Weak, watery food not fit to eat.

Slop Bowl. A small round bowl, formerly a regular part of a tea service. Cold dregs were poured into the slop bowl so that fresh, hot tea could be served.

Slottsstek (Swedish). Pot roast with gravy.

Slumgullion (Colloquial). Very bad, almost inedible food.

Smaiskeh (Arabic). Fillet of lamb.

Små Köttbullar (Swedish). Small Swedish-style meatballs.

Smallage. Wild celery.

Small Beer. Weak beer, low in alcoholic strength.

Small Eats (Colloquial). Foods suitable for nibbling, such as olives, cheese, and nuts.

Small Fillet. A small round slice of the fillet of beef cut from the top or bottom end of the tenderloin.

Small Fry. Very small young fish fried in deep hot fat and eaten whole.

Small Salad. Watercress or mustard greens.

Smaltost. A soft or "melting" Swedish cheese.

Smash. A long mixed drink made with crushed mint sprigs and brandy, gin, or whisky.

Småsill (Swedish). Pilchard.

Smearcase; Smierkase (German). Cottage cheese.

Smeiaza (Italian). A tart made with apples, raisins, and nuts; a specialty of Venice.

Smell. To sense or become aware of by means of the olfactory nerves; to perceive the scent or odor of food and wine.

Smelt. A small fish related to the salmon and found in both the Atlantic and Pacific oceans near the shores. Like the salmon, it spawns in fresh water but seldom goes beyond the tide line. It is best sautéed in butter.

Smetana (Russian). Sour cream.

Smitane (French). With, or containing sour cream. The term is a variation on the Russian word for sour cream.

Smitane Sauce. A sauce made with onions, sour cream, and white wine; used with game and fowl.

Smithfield Ham. A type of cured, dried ham prepared in Virginia; it must be sliced very thin. Chinese cooks in the United States often use Smithfield ham, since it closely approximates Chinese-style ham.

Smoked Cheese. Cheese which has been exposed to smoke in order to produce a salty or nutty quality, thus making it suitable for service as an hors d'oeuvre.

Smoked Fish. Fish exposed to smoke in order to preserve it or to change its flavor. (*See* Smoking.) In England kippers and finnan haddie are classic breakfast favorites, and their popularity has spread to Europe and America. In France, smoked salmon is highly regarded, but smoked herring is not overlooked by the gourmet. Smoked sturgeon, perhaps, of all fish, is the most delicate in flavor. Experiments in smoking almost every type of fish have met with varying degrees of success. In recent years, smoked brook trout has been well received and is excellent served with a sauce of sour cream mixed with freshly grated horseradish.

Smoked fish should be kept under refrigeration wrapped in aluminum foil or Saran Wrap, and should be allowed to come to room temperature for about an hour before being served.

Smoked Ham. The cured and smoked hind legs of pork. The fore legs are called *calas*, or picnic hams. Fresh pork is cured either in dry salt or in a brine, then smoked in various ways. *Smithfield* and *Virginia hams* are aged after smoking.

Smoke Dry. To cure fish or meat only by exposure to smoke, during which the food becomes dry.

Smokehouse. A shed or building in which fish or meat is suspended and subjected to many hours of smoke in order to change its taste and/or to preserve it.

Smokejack. An old method of turning a roasting spit by means of a flywheel. Currents of hot air rising in a chimney caused the wheel to revolve.

Smoke Point. In frying oils the temperature at which the decomposition products become visible.

Smoking. The process of changing the taste, or preserving various foods by means of dry smoke. The smoking of foods goes back many centuries when fish and meat were smoked not so much to improve flavor as to provide a compact, convenient food that would not spoil on a journey. In the past century or so, however, smoking has become more popular because of the interesting flavors it produces.

Smoking foods is a fine art, requiring a considerable degree of skill. Although efforts have been made to smoke foods within a small enclosed area, this is rather difficult because, if the food is too close to the source of heat, it will quickly seal and cook rather than absorb the smoked flavor. The food should also be so positioned that the smoke can circulate freely. Small smoking chambers are arranged so as to allow the smoke to escape naturally from a small opening at the top; in commercial smoking, the smoke is forced to travel through chambers by means of fans or compressed air, and is often reused by a continuous circulatory arrangement. Originally only certain hardwoods were used for smoke, but now almost all woods except those with a resinous base are used. Sometimes herbs or aromatic substances are added for additional flavor.

Some meats are pickled before being smoked, such as certain hams and pastrami. As a rule, fish are not pickled before smoking. Smoked salmon and sturgeon are excellent examples of the delicious results to be obtained by smoking. In recent years the popularity of smoking has led to an influx of smoked cheese and of other foods never previously smoked.

Smolt. A salmon about two years old.

Smør (Danish). Butter.

Smör (Swedish). Butter.

Smørbrød (Norwegian). Open-faced sandwiches.

Smørgaas (Norwegian). Appetizers.

Smörgas (Swedish). Slice of bread and butter.

Smörgåsbord (Swedish). A buffet of appetizers, hors d'oeuvre, and hot or cold foods, or both. It may be a few platters or an elaborate collation corresponding to almost a complete dinner, with only dessert and coffee to follow. Smoked fish of various kinds and pickled and jellied foods are favorites for the smörgåsbord. The etiquette of eating smörgåsbord involves three trips to the table: first, for herring; second, for cold cuts; and lastly, for cheese and hot dishes.

Smørrebrød (Danish). Sandwich.

Smother. To cook foods with very little liquid in a tightly covered saucepan.

Smultringer (Norwegian). Doughnuts.

Smyrna. (1) A variety of grape and raisins shipped from Asia Minor. (2) A variety of wheat noted for its large ear.

Snack. Quick between-meal nourishment or refreshment.

Snail. A small shellfish, long considered a delicacy. The land variety is the best. Canned snails, with shells on the side, are exported from France. When fresh snails are used, they should be kept without food for several days, so that they may expel any possible poisonous substances in their system.

Snake Gourd. A gourd with long green and white edible fruits that turn orange when fully ripe.

Snake Juice (Colloquial). Whisky.

Snake Squash; Loofah. A long, cucumberlike vegetable, often used in oriental cookery.

Snap. A small, simple cooky or biscuit, such as a ginger snap.

Snap Bean. String bean.

Snapdragon (Obsolete). A Christmas game in which the participants snatched with their fingers, raisins enveloped in flaming brandy.

Snapper. (1) (Colloquial) A snapping turtle. (2) *See* Bluefish.

Snapper, Red. A firm-fleshed white meat fish with a red skin; found in warm waters. The term is applied to a wide range of different fish in various parts of the world. In the Caribbean, the red snapper is a distinctively flavored fish of excellent quality.

Snapping Turtle. A turtle used for food, especially for soups.

Snaps (Danish, Swedish). Aquavit or other similar liquor.

Snijbonen (Dutch). Young white beans.

Snipe. A delicately flavored small marsh bird; it grows fat in cold weather.

Snitter (Danish). Small sandwiches; canapés.

Snook. Several different warm water fishes, especially the robalo and the sergeant fish.

Snoul. A short thick piece cut from the crusty part of a loaf.

Snow. (1) A white light dessert pudding. (2) A meringue of beaten egg whites with or without sugar. (3) The specially-grated ice on which cold dishes are sometimes served.

Snowball. An ice cream or ice-cream-mixture dessert molded in a ball or globe, sometimes covered with whipped cream, and frequently rolled in grated coconut; often with a chocolate sauce on top.

Snowberry. Many different plants and shrubs that bear edible white berries.

Snowcock. Various partridges and pheasants, particularly those found with white markings.

Snowdrop. (1) A type of wheat. (2) A variety of potato.

Snow Eggs. Meringue poached in milk.

Snow Fungus. A white or brown edible fungus often used in Chinese cookery. The brown type is called *cloud ears.*

Snow Grouse. The ptarmigan, an excellent game bird found chiefly in cold regions.

Snow Partridge. A variety of northern grouse; prepared like grouse or partridge.

Snow Pear. A variety of pear which ripens late in the autumn, often when the first snow has fallen.

Snow Peas; Pea Pods. Whole small edible peas and their pods; often used in Chinese cookery.

S.O. Superior Old, a liquor term.

Soaking. (1) As applied to dried fruits or vegetables, immersing in water for a period of time. (2) The moistening of certain cakes with a syrup.

Soapberry. A mediocre-tasting Alaskan wild berry.

Soave. *See* Italy, The Wines of.

Soba (Japanese). Buckwheat noodles.

Sobremesas (Portuguese). Desserts.

Sobriety. Moderation in the consumption of alcoholic drinks; by extension, moderation in food.

Sobronade (French). A peasant soup-stew made with white beans, ham, fresh pork, onions, and other vegetables, with plenty of seasoning; a specialty of Périgord.

Socca (French). A pastry made from chick-pea flour; often eaten with a glass of white wine around Nice.

Socker (Swedish). Sugar.

Sockerbit (Swedish). Lump of sugar.

Socle (French). A support or decorative pedestal, made of an edible ingredient such as rice or bread, on which is placed the food to be eaten; often the socle is not served or eaten.

Soda. (1) Bicarbonate of soda (baking soda). (2) Ice-cream soda. (3) Sparkling water, such as seltzer and club soda.

Soda Farl (Scotch). A round cake made with baking powder or baking soda and buttermilk and cut in quarters like a scone.

Soda Flour. Bread into which air is incorporated by means of a powder.

Soda Pop (Colloquial). Any nonalcoholic carbonated soft beverage, especially when bottled.

Sodavand (Danish). Soda water; an effervescent drink.

Soda Water. Artificially produced carbonated water used for making effervescent drinks.

Sodium. Salt; a dietary essential usually satisfied by the normal diet. The body contains about 100 grams of sodium and the average diet contains 4–5 grams, equivalent to 10 grams of sodium chloride. Vegetables are relatively poor in sodium; animal foods are rich in sodium.

Sodium Benzoate. (1) A water-soluble food preservative. (2) A crystalline salt.

Sodium Bicarbonate. *See* Baking Soda.

Sodium Metabisulfite. A chemical occasionally used as a preservative in bottled citrus-fruit drinks.

Sødsuppe (Danish). Fruit soup.

Soep (Dutch). Soup.

Soffritto (Italian). Spicy sauce of tomatoes and sautéed pork.

Sofrito (Latin American). A mixture consisting of chopped bacon and ham together with garlic, tomato, onions, and pepper.

Soft-Ball Degree. About 245°F. on a candy thermometer, the temperature at which a drop falling into cold water forms a soft ball.

Soft Dough. Workable dough, not wet.

Soft Drink. A nonalcoholic carbonated beverage such as ginger ale, root beer, and the cola drinks.

Soft Flour. Flour with a weak gluten content, not desirable for making bread.

Softgrass; Spiked Softgrass. An African plant from whose seeds the natives make a crude beer.

Soft Roe. The milt or sperm of fish.

Soft-Shell Crab. A crab that has shed its shell and is covered only by a soft skin. (The shedding is a natural process.) It may be sautéed or broiled and eaten entirely.

Soft Wheat. A wheat that yields a soft flour; usually a winter wheat, which is softer than spring wheat.

Sogliola alla Bella Mugnaia (Italian). Fillet of sole with sauce.

Soissonnais (French). Cooked with white beans.

Soissons. A variety of white bean produced in the area of Soissons, France.

Soja. The fermented juice of the soy bean.

Sol. The threadfish, found in tropical waters.

Solanum. Chinese eggplant.

Sole. A flatfish found only in European waters. Unless imported, the fish available as sole in the United States is likely to be one of a variety of flatfish, such as the flounder or fluke. The true sole has an excellent, delicate flavor which is not duplicated in the American substitutes.

Peculiarly, the taste of sole improves a day or so after it is caught. Its popularity with both chefs and the public is due to its fine flavor, its convenient size, and to the fact that it may

be prepared in many ways because sauces blend successfully with its delicate flesh.

It is marketed chiefly as *true sole* but also as *lemon sole;* the chief difference between them is in the upper skin, that of the true sole being rough and dark.

> **Sole Amélie.** Steamed sole with lobster butter and truffles.
>
> **Sole au Vin Blanc.** Sole cooked with shallots, white wine, and mushrooms, and covered with a white-wine sauce.
>
> **Sole Bénédictine.** Sole stuffed with ground fish and served with mushrooms, truffles, and sliced shellfish.
>
> **Sole Chevreuse.** Stuffed sole cooked in white wine with a sauce of butter and tomato purée.
>
> **Sole Dugléré.** Fillet of sole cooked with tomatoes, parsley, white wine, and shallots, and served with a lemon-juice-and-butter sauce.
>
> **Sole Marcelle.** Steamed sole with mushrooms covered with a white-wine sauce, and garnished with truffles and oysters.
>
> **Sole Normande.** Sole cooked with white wine, covered with sauce Normande and garnished with shellfish.

Sole, Gray. A variety of flounder. *See* Gray Sole.

Solera System. A method of making sherry. *See* Spain, The Wines of.

Solferino. An old name for a confectionery coloring, deep pink with a purplish tinge.

Solha (Portuguese). Plaice, similar to sole.

Solianka (Russian). Vegetable soup with sauerkraut and either meat or fish.

Solilem; Solimeme. A two-layer Alsatian cake.

Solliès-Toucas. A fairly dry goat's-milk cheese made in southern France.

Solmas Loaf (British). A sweet cake made for All Souls' Day.

Solomillo (Spanish). A cut of meat, usually the fillet.

Solomon's Seal. A wild plant whose young shoots can be eaten like asparagus.

Somen (Japanese). Very fine noodles.

Som Sā. A very acid Siamese citrus fruit; may be used for making compotes, etc. The rind and juice are used for flavoring.

Sommelier. The keeper of the wine cellars; the

custodian of all the alcoholic beverages in a restaurant, club, or a royal or great house. He usually wears a large chain with a key around his neck and also serves the wine.

Sommier (French, Obsolete). Kitchen and pantry servants of French kings.

Soncoya. A tropical aromatic mango grown particularly in Central and South America.

Sonoma Wines. *See* United States, The Wines of.

Sop. Anything that has soaked up the liquid into which it has been dipped, as a piece of bread dipped in gravy or milk.

Sopa (Portuguese). Soup.

> **Sopa à Alentejana.** Green-vegetable soup with eggs.
>
> **Sopa à Portuguesa.** Fish soup.
>
> **Sopa de Batata e Agrião.** Potato-and-watercress soup.
>
> **Sopa de Camarão.** Shrimp soup.
>
> **Sopa de Tomate e Ovos.** Tomato-and-egg soup.

Sopa (Spanish). Soup.

> **Sopa de Ajo.** A garlic soup served with eggs.
>
> **Sopa de Legumbres.** Vegetable soup.
>
> **Sopa de Mariscos.** Seafood soup.
>
> **Sopa de Pescado.** Fish soup.
>
> **Sopa de Puchero.** Beef soup containing various other ingredients.
>
> **Sopa de Verduras.** Vegetable soup.
>
> **Sopa Española.** A soup made with rice, tomatoes, peppers, and spices.

Sopa Borracha (Spanish). Literally "drunken soup"; a sort of tipsy cake usually served with a wine sauce.

Sopa de Espuma (Mexican). Foam soup, usually made from chicken stock, flour, eggs, and cheese.

Sopaipillas (Mexican). Fried bread puffed up like miniature pillows; often served with soup.

Sopa Seca (Mexican). A soup containing comparatively little liquid, and having mostly solid ingredients.

Sopavine. An apple that shades to a deep red as though dipped in a rich-colored red wine. The old name is a corruption of "sops of wine."

Sopón (Spanish). A heavy, thick soup.

Soppor (Swedish). Soups.

Sopressata (Italian). Very large pork sausages; a specialty in Molise.

Sorb Apple. The astringent fruit of the sorb, or service, tree, sometimes used for distilling alcohol.

Sorbet (French). Water ice; sherbet.

Sorbetto (Italian). Sherbet.

Sorbitol. A six-carbon sugar alcohol formed by the reduction of fructose; used to sweeten diabetic and other diet foods.

Sore-Heady (British). A small cylindrical cake wrapped in buttered paper.

Sorel, Agnes. Mistress of Charles VII of France, an imaginative French cook whose name is given to many dishes, including omelets and garnishes of truffles, mushrooms, and wine.

Sorghum. A grass resembling broom corn, from which a syrup is extracted.

Sorghum Syrup. A sweet syrup, much like molasses but prepared from the sweet sorghum grass native to tropical Africa and Asia.

Sorrel. A hardy perennial herb, known since 3,000 B.C., with a pungent acid flavor. The young leaves may be used in salads, and the older plants may be cooked like spinach or used as flavoring in soups and sauces. Creamed sorrel soup is particularly good. Sometimes also called dock.

Sorrel Bounce. An acid but pleasant-flavored drink, once popular, made by soaking the leaves and flowers of the hibiscus subdariffa in rum, and sweetening to taste.

Sorvete (Portuguese). Ice cream; ices.

Sospel, Fromage de; Fromage Gras. A French semisoft fermented cow's-milk cheese prepared chiefly in the vicinity of Sospel.

Sotanghon (Philippine). A clear, almost transparent rice noodle.

Sotare (Swedish). Broiled sardines or smelts.

Sot-l'y-Laisse (French). Literally, "a fool leaves it"; the oyster or rump of a chicken; the small bit of flesh above the parson's (or pope's) nose. The small, edible piece found near the tail of a chicken.

Søtsuppe (Norwegian). Sweet fruit soup.

Sottaceti (Italian). Pickled vegetables.

Søtunge (Danish). Sole.

Soubise, À la (French). As applied to food, garnished with onion purée, or having a strong onion flavor. The dishes are named for Prince Charles de Soubise, a noted 18th-century French gastronome who was fond of onions.

Souchet (French). Galingale, the earth almond, an edible tuberous plant.

Souchets; Souchies. Flounder, sole, or other flatfish cut into steaks and poached in salted water and herbs.

Souchong. A smoky-flavored Chinese black tea made from large leaves.

Soucoupe (French). Saucer.

Sou-Fassum (French). Stuffed cabbage cooked in a beef or mutton broth.

Soufflé. A light airy preparation made by combining a thickened sauce, usually of butter, flour, and milk, together with egg whites; when baked, it puffs and expands to develop a delicate texture. Soufflés fall into two chief categories: sweetened and unsweetened. They may be prepared as appetizers, main courses, vegetables, savories, or desserts. Although widely regarded as among the most spectacular of culinary creations, they are not difficult to make, once the rudiments have been learned. Because the light texture of the soufflé is obtained by trapping small pockets of heated air in the cooked mixture, it will fall quickly when cooling begins; therefore, the diners must be ready to eat the soufflé, for it cannot wait and must be served at once.

Soufflé Dish. An ovenproof dish, usually of 1- or 2-quart capacity, made of glass or ceramic, with straight sides. There is no agreement among professional chefs as to whether the dish should be buttered.

Soufflé, Frozen. *See* Soufflé Glacé.

Soufflé Glacé (French). A frozen soufflé; a frozen ice-cream dessert prepared in a soufflé dish with the mixture frozen above the top level to resemble a regular soufflé.

Soufie. A French river fish with a pleasing taste.

Soult (South African). Cooked pig's feet, marinated for several days; eaten cold.

Soumaintrain. A round yellow cheese with an orange exterior made in the Yonne region of France.

Soup. *See* Soups.

Soupçon (French). A vague or slight suggestion of flavor.

Soup Cup. A large double-handled cup used for individual soup servings, sometimes with a removable lid to keep the contents warm.

Soup Dish. A large shallow plate or bowl used for individual soup servings.

Soupe (French). A thick peasant-style soup. A soupe is sometimes distinguished from a potage, in that the former is more of a peasant dish, with many ingredients, whereas the potage is more delicate.

　Soupe à la Chauyotte. An Alsatian soup of milk, water, and butter; used for cooking spaghetti.

　Soupe à la Parisienne. Onion soup with a heavy crust of cheese.

　Soupe d'Épautre. A soup prepared by boiling mutton with vegetables (especially onions) and garlic; made in Provence.

　Soupe Grasse. Fat soup, usually made with salt pork.

　Soupe Vaudoise. An onion soup made with wine; served with a piece of fried bread spread with grated cheese.

Souper (Dutch, French). Supper.

Souper de Bal (French). A elaborate late party supper.

Souper sur l'Herbe (French). A picnic supper to which each guest often brings his own food.

Soupière (French). Soup tureen.

Soupir de Nonne (French). Soufflé fritters; very light delicate fritters.

Soup Ladle. A deep spoon, made in various sizes and of various materials, used to ladle soup into serving dishes.

Soups. Any food specifically prepared to be eaten as a liquid. The differences between soups and various other preparations are difficult to specify. A *stew*, however, usually contains more solid ingredients than are normally found in a soup. A *broth* differs from a soup in being thinner, and is usually a liquid in which some other food has been boiled, as, for example, a chicken broth. Clear soups are often called *bouillons* or *consommés*. A *soupe maigre* is a very thin soup, usually made with vegetables, or sometimes with fish, but never with meat. A *chowder* is most often a rich soup containing solid ingredients; it is frequently made with fish or shellfish, but there are occasional meat or vegetable chowders.

A *cream soup* is thickened with milk or cream. A *puréed soup* is similar to a cream soup, but the thickening comes in part from the pulp used in making the soup. A *bisque* is like a cream or puréed soup but is usually made with shellfish. A *gumbo* is a soup made with fish or shellfish, but with the addition of okra or *filé* powder.

Soups are popular in the cuisines of almost every country, but certain soups have worldwide reputations. For example, America has its clam chowder; Russia is fond of *borscht*; Germany likes oxtail soup; and France has hundreds of good soups, but none so popular as its *pot-au-feu*.

Soup Spoon. A round or oval spoon used for hot or cold soups. The size varies, depending on whether it is used with soup plates or cream-soup cups.

Soup Stick. A long thin roll of bread similar to a bread stick, often served with soup.

Soup Tureen. A large covered soup bowl placed on the table in front of the server who ladles individual servings.

Soupy. Liquidy; like soup.

Sour. Having a characteristic tart taste associated with vinegar or with some citrus fruit, such as lemon.

Sour Braten. *See* Sauerbraten.

Sourcrout. *See* Sauerkraut.

Sourdough (Alaskan). A piece of sour dough saved by prospectors from each day's baking to be available for the following day's baking of homemade bread, to encourage fermentation. Sourdough bread has a distinctive, slightly biting taste.

Sourire (French). To simmer very gently.

Sour Mash. One of two methods of fermentation used to make American-type whiskies. The other method is *sweet mash*. Sour mash whisky must take less than 72 hours in the fermentation process. It is prepared by using about one-third of working yeast used in a previous fermentation.

Sour Milk. Sweet milk may be soured by the addition of a souring agent, such as lemon juice or vinegar, or by a lactic-acid bacteria. Sour milk may be used in preparing Indian dishes, in making cakes and muffins, etc.

Sours. Any alcoholic drinks made with such liquor as whisky, gin, or brandy to which sugar, ice, and fruit juice are added.

Sour Salt. Citric acid, marketed as crystals and used to provide a sour taste to foods, taking the place of vinegar or lemon juice.

Sour Skon (Scotch). A thin cake baked of oatmeal and steeped in water until sour.

Soursop. A West Indian fruit similar to the custard apple.

Sour-Sweet. Having both a sweet and a sour taste.

Souse. (1) To soak in a liquid, such as brine or a marinade. (2) The liquid prepared for pickling foods. (3) (Colloquial) A dish made of the feet, head, and ears of a pig kept in a pickling liquid.

Sous-Noix de Veau (French). The underpart or silverside of a leg of veal.

Souterage (French). The wine blender's term for a mixture of two or more wines.

South Africa, Republic of. There are four major ethnic groups in South Africa—the Dutch, British, Indian, and African. Each group has contributed to a certain extent in the creation of the local culinary style. The Dutch have brought with them from their homeland various Netherlands dishes, the British show their liking for the specialties of their island, and the Indians have their curries and other similar dishes. The African contribution is mostly game and fresh fruits.

Most big-city hotels and restaurants serve what is generally regarded as "international food," that is, food prepared in the pseudo-French cookery style. *Afrikaner* food may be had chiefly in private homes.

The local shellfish is superb; African lobster tails are now shipped frozen around the world, but they are better in their homeland. Two interesting soups are curried potato soup and *melksnysels*, a hot milk soup with noodles. Some of the meat dishes are worthy of note: *sasaties* are skewered meats with a curry flavor; *babottee* is a ground-beef pie; *bean bredee* is a meat stew with beans and lamb; *soutribbetjies* are salted ribs of mutton; and *boerwors* is a kind of farm sausage.

South Africans enjoy homemade breads and

biscuits; *boerbeskuits* are biscuits made with a salt-rising ferment. Pastries include *koeksisters* and *soet koekies.* Unusual desserts are a seaweed jelly and *chippolata*, a gelatin-and-custard dish. The Cape fruits are exceptional, particularly the gooseberries, mangos, apricots, and melons. South African wines are improving constantly; both whites and reds of passable quality are produced in abundance, particularly around Constantia and Drakenstein. The beer is quite good, and there is a local sweet liqueur, *Van der Hum*, which enjoys considerable popularity.

South America, The Wines of. Approximately 10 percent of the world's wine is produced in South America. There is an industry of sorts in every country of the continent. (It should be remembered that large parts of South America were settled by immigrants from Western Europe, particularly from Portugal, Italy, and Germany, who brought with them their love of wine and a knowledge of wine making.) For geographical reasons the wines of the northern portion of the continent are not distinctive and are intended for local consumption.

Brazil: This enormous country on the Atlantic Ocean lacks the climate to produce quality wines. There are only two regions where vineyards are developed on a commercial scale. The first and most important is in Rio Grande do Sul, around Veranopolis and Caxias do Sul. Both family groups and large companies grow the grapes, primarily the Riesling, as white wines are the important type. The reds seem thin and acidulous. The soil is good and the weather satisfactory, although the rainy season brings great downpours which sometimes end in flash floods. But the wines are not distinguished.

The other wine region is in São Paulo Province, north of the city of São Paulo; however, the wines are less worthwhile than those of Rio Grande do Sul. In the whole of Brazil some 30 million gallons are produced, the bulk of it routine wine consumed locally. In fact it is manufactured to discourage the market for imports. The only Brazilian wines one is apt to encounter in the United States are occasional bottles of fair champagne and some passable white wines of the Riesling type.

Peru: On the Pacific side of the continent, the northern portion of the country is arid, and the high mountains along the eastern side prohibit commercial viniculture. The vineyards, then, are south of Lima around Ica, Sicamba, Pativiloa, and Locumba. The chief problem of the vintners is the low rainfall. Then in some years there have been unusual storms which have damaged the vines. A comparatively small amount of wine is produced, and it is only average in quality. Among the reds, Reservado Tacama is fairly good; the whites are sold under the names of Sauterne or Rhin (without the final "e") or other generic descriptions.

Uruguay: Most of the land in this small country is devoted to cattle grazing. But with a large number of Italians in the population, Uruguay produces enough wine to satisfy their demand but seldom exports, for the quality is only fair. As quantity is emphasized rather than quality, the Gamay, known for its high yield, is used more than any other grape. The majority of the wines are white with a rather ordinary finish unsuitable for competition in the world markets.

Argentina: In sheer volume Argentina leads the nations of the Western Hemisphere with nearly 300 million gallons of wine on the market. The main vineyards are around Mendoza in San Juan Province and in the Rio Negro. Of course wines are produced in almost every part of the country, but the three principal areas are those of which Mendoza is the center. Large-scale production emphasizes the mass market. Among Argentina's population of around 20 million, thirteen gallons are consumed annually per person. A low national income keeps prices low.

Mendoza produces the great proportion of table wines. The local industry is controlled by Italian families, descendants of immigrants who started the vineyards. With imported wines, various attempts have been made to imitate French, Italian, and German wines with only moderate success. It is not unusual to see on a wine list a choice of Pinot, Riesling, Tipo Rhin, Sauvignon, Sauterne, Claret, and Chianti.

The wines of San Juan are more apt to be the sweet dessert types, because of the hot sunshine here. A few dry table wines are also produced. Rio Negro makes some of the more expensive, superior white wines, but the production is limited.

In ordinary restaurants or shops the average wines are marketed simply as *tinto* or *blanco*. However, one can find better wines at higher prices. Riva and Company market San Felipe and Gruta Azul, both superior wines in the red and white types. Vieja Abadia has its Seleccion, a better white; Casa de Troya features Gran Reserva which is quite good. The Trapiche Company sells Derby, Fond de Cave, and Puente Viejo at premium prices, because the wines are above average. Canciller markets its Pinot Gris Blanco at comparatively high prices; Urguirena has a Reserve type for both red and white wines. *Chile:* The best wines of South America are produced in this long, narrow land. Although Argentina, its neighbor to the east, produces three times as much wine, the Chilean product is far superior. Argentinian wines are rarely exported, but Chilean wines can be found in the majority of American wine shops and liquor stores, and offer an extraordinarily good value. These wines have that most delightful of all qualities—they are pleasant to drink. Their "drinkable" characteristic, combined with their price, makes them irresistible.

There are three principal areas for the vineyards: in the north around Huasco, in the center near Maipo and Cachapoal, and in the south at Talcahuano and Itata. The grapes are many and varied, including the Semillon, Traminer, and Riesling for white wines, and the Pinot Noir, Cabernet, and similar types for red wines. In addition there are some local grape varieties used, but the European types produce the better wines. The soil is ideal, consisting of volcanic stone, and the climate is ideal for viniculture. It is interesting that *phylloxera*, which nearly destroyed Argentina's vineyards at one time, never attacked the Chilean vines. Although every *hacienda*, small or large, has vineyards for its own use, the industry is controlled by several large concerns which operate and market on a great scale, selling hundreds of thousands of cases.

Chilean wine is sold in a wide variety of bottles: sometimes the Bordeaux-type bottle is used, occasionally the Burgundy, and for the Riesling wines the squat German *bocksbeutel*. This is the type commonly seen in the United States. The labels bear such notations as *Reservado, Especial, Gran Vino,* and *Gran Vino para Banquetes,* in ascending order of merit. Some wines have only a general description on the label, like *Tipo Pommard,* which is pure fantasy on the producer's part. The very good firms prefer to have their vineyards listed and then add a general word indicative of the wine's quality, such as *Santa Rita Reservado* or *Tocornal Gran Vino Tinto.* The leading producers of wines include Cousino, Concha y Toro, Rocornal, Conchali, Carmen, Santa Rita, Undurraga, Tarapaca, Correa Errasuriz, and Ochagavia.

The Burgundy imitations are the poorest, the red Bordeaux are considerably better, but the Chilean white wines are the best. The Chablis type is fair enough, but it cannot match the original. The straight Riesling wines are very good, superior to the Rhine wine types. The sweeter wines which resemble the Barsac and Sauternes are surprisingly pleasant, the best being equal to the average sweet white Bordeaux.

Some *rosés* are made, fair enough but undistinguished. Chilean champagne, however, is a far different matter; the very best types are excellent, to be compared with some of the French second-grade sparkling wines. Because of the high American duty on all sparkling wines, Chilean champagne cannot hope to compete in the American market with the established French product, but this does not alter the fact that Chilean sparkling wines are worth attention. There is some production of a better-than-average sparkling Burgundy which is at least equal to the ordinary wine of this type shipped to the United States from France.

Although there is some variation from year to year in the local climate and the wines vary accordingly, the date on a label of Chilean wine is of secondary importance and may usually be completely ignored.

South China Congou. An excellent light-tasting black tea with slightly red leaves.

Southdown Mutton. An excellent-quality English mutton. A century ago, this mutton was marketed when 3–4 years old. In recent years, however, it is brought to the market sooner, since the new British taste is for younger, less oily meat; besides, the cost of maintaining the animals for 3–4 years was too great in relation to the market price.

South Sea Islands Tea. A tea made from *yapon*, a hollylike plant.

Souvarov. A *petit four* made with fluted-edge pastries sandwiched together two by two after baking, then spread with apricot jam and icing sugar.

Souvarov, À la. As applied to poultry and game birds, prepared in an earthenware casserole sealed with a strip of dough around the cover.

Sow. Female pig.

Sowens; Sowans (Scotch, Obsolete). A dish made of the inner husks of oat grain and sour milk; served with beer.

Sow Thistle. Milkweed; occasionally used as food.

Soybean; Soya Bean. One of the five sacred grains of Old China. The soybean has been known at least 2,500 years as one of the staple foods of the Orient. It is high in vegetable protein, low in starch, and fairly high in fat. It is sometimes called a "vegetarian meat" because some special diets for infants and invalids prescribe it as a substitute for meat.

> **Soybeans, Fermented.** Small, crushed, partly fermented soybeans; often used in Cantonese cookery to produce a slightly spicy taste.

Soybean Cheese. A Chinese "cheese" made from vegetable milk and rennet.

Soybean Curd. A soft, but somewhat firm mixture made from soybeans, with some of the water removed; used in Chinese provincial cookery.

Soybean Jam (Chinese). A condiment made from the residue after soy sauce has been made; often added to various foods.

Soybean Milk. The milklike liquid obtained when soybeans are boiled, crushed to a pulp, and strained.

Soyer, Alexander. A noted French culinary expert who went to Ireland to cook during the famine of 1848 and to the Crimea in 1854. At one time he was chef of the Reform Club in England. He wrote *The Poor Man's Cookery Book* and *A Culinary Campaign*, and also invented a camp stove.

Soy Sauce. The commercially produced extract of the soybean, widely used in oriental cookery to enhance and strengthen the flavor of almost any food. Being salty, it almost eliminates the use of salt in oriental cookery.

Spaghetti (Italian). "Little strings," one of the items in the enormous range of Italian *pasta*. Spaghetti itself is a rather narrow type of long pasta, and is solid rather than hollow. Of all varieties of pasta, spaghetti is purely the most popular in Italy and around the world. Spaghetti should be placed into a large quantity of actively-boiling salted water, and cooked only until barely ready to eat, that is, *al dente*, edible, but chewy, rather than soft. *See also* Macaroni.

> **Spaghetti alla Bolognese.** Spaghetti with a delicate meat-tomato sauce.

> **Spaghetti alla Carbonara.** Spaghetti tossed with a raw egg, cheese, and bits of ham or salt pork.

> **Spaghetti alla Matriciana.** Spaghetti with salt pork and tomatoes.

> **Spaghetti alla Siracusana.** Spaghetti with eggplant, anchovies, and olives.

> **Spaghetti alla Transatlantico.** Spaghetti with mixed seafood.

> **Spaghetti all'Ortica.** Spaghetti with mushrooms.

> **Spaghetti con Aglio ed Olio.** Spaghetti with garlic and oil.

> **Spaghetti con Carne.** Spaghetti with meat sauce.

> **Spaghetti con Salsiccia.** Spaghetti with sausage.

> **Spaghetti con Vongole.** Spaghetti with clams.

Spain. Despite a common misapprehension, most Spanish dishes are on the bland side, and there are comparatively few pungent or spicy preparations. Many dishes, however, do contain onions, garlic, peppers, and other hearty, full-flavored ingredients.

Although parts of Spain experience cold weather during midwinter, generally speaking Spain is a hot-weather country, and meal hours tend to be governed by this pattern. In the morning most people have a simple breakfast of rolls, butter, jam, and coffee. Lunch does not begin, as a rule, before 1:30 P.M., often later. It is a substantial meal consisting of soup, an egg dish, fish and meat, dessert, and sometimes even more. Just before 6 P.M. the cafés serve snacks because dinner never begins before 9:30, often much, much later, because of the intense afternoon and early-evening heat. Dinner is much like lunch, although possibly somewhat lighter.

At odd hours of the day or night Spaniards like tiny appetizers called *tapas*. Meals always begin with an appetizer, often of fish or shellfish. *Angulas*, baby eels, taste quite good. Snails, shrimp, and clams are especially popular. A *zarzuela de mariscos* is a very tasty seafood stew difficult to duplicate outside Spain because of the ingredients required. For some reason, even though fresh seafood is available, the national palate favors dried codfish, *bacalau*, which is prepared in a variety of fashions. A national dish is *paella*, a saffron rice dish with assorted fish and shellfish, plus various other ingredients, such as pimientos, sausage, and sometimes even chicken.

The most interesting soup is *gazpacho*, a cold soup made with vegetables and served with additional chopped raw vegetables and croutons. The precise style varies from district to district, being made sometimes with lamb broth, sometimes with another base, but always ending up as a delicious hot-weather soup. In cold weather piping hot vegetable, chick-pea, and bean soups are favorites. Another national dish is the *cocido*, a soup-stew made in a dozen different styles, for each region prepares it somewhat differently. Basically it is a thick, rich soup having a meat base and containing vegetables and potatoes. The soup is eaten first, then the vegetables, and finally the meat. *Cocido* is sometimes called *pote*, sometimes *olla podrida* and even *caldo*, but it is basically a *cocido*.

There are several interesting main-course meat dishes. *Pollo valenciana* is a delicious, rather complicated dish of chicken, sausage, and occasionally shellfish; *pato y arroz* is duck with rice and ham; *mollejas de ternera al oloroso* is sweetbreads and sherry. Cheeses are good but not unusual or distinguished. There are few salads as Americans understand the term. The classic Spanish dessert is a caramel custard, *flan*. Best of all, however, are the marvelous fruits and melons in season.

The national drink is sherry. The table wines should not be overlooked, however, for although there are no great types, they are quite drinkable. Valdepeñas and Rioja are the two leading types, most experts giving a slight preference for the Rioja wine. Also popular is *Montilla*, a typical dry white wine with little subtlety or finesse. The best-known brands, often the purchaser's surest guide to quality, are *Marqués de Riscal*, *Marqués de Murietta*, and *Paternina*. Little emphasis is placed upon vintage years, and most Spaniards drink wine in the same unpretentious fashion that Italians do. An interesting hot-weather wine drink is the *sangría*, made with wine, sugar, club soda, and pieces of fresh fruit.

Spanish brandy is unique. It is somewhat heavier and slightly sweeter than French Cognac, but in general does not equal the Gallic liquor. Cider, from Asturia, is quite good; the local beer is passable but hardly great. A good soft drink is *horchata*, made from *chufa* nuts (something like peanuts) and quite refreshing. Tea is served only at ladies' smart social afternoon gatherings, when it is regarded as *de rigeur*. Small cups of black coffee and hot chocolate are the usual beverages.

Spain, The Wines of. Hot, sunny Spain has always produced wine. Three thousand years ago the Phoenicians traded wine for other Iberian goods. Later, the Romans enjoyed Spanish wines, and in the ruins of Pompeii guides always show tourists the remains of wine jugs originally made in Spain and brought to Italy by merchant traders. Although the abstinent Moors dominated the mainland for centuries, the production of wine continued.

The average American has never tasted a Spanish wine other than sherry. In the past decade, however, tourists have discovered and enjoyed the local wines, and many have developed a fondness for them. Unfortunately, only a small quantity of Spanish wine reaches the United States, with the exception of sherry.

What makes this situation odd is the fact that Spain exports large quantities of wine to other parts of the world, particularly to regions that cannot afford expensive wines. Only about 40 percent of the export is sherry; the rest are table wines. France, for example, imports the ordinary table wines because of their low price. (And yet at any price the French would not consider the Spanish product if it were not good.)

Spain's total output is approximately 600 million gallons, the bulk of which is table wine consumed within a year or two of production. These wines represent unusual value for the money. It is a rare Spanish wine that can be considered great (with the exception of sherry, of course) but all are light, fresh, and pleasant.

Both red and white wines are produced throughout Spain, and, as in Italy, vintage years are not nearly as important as they are in France. During the Middle Ages, in fact until a century ago, Spanish wines were crudely made. An unexpected event, however, acted indirectly to raise the quality of the wines. A French vineyard owner thought it might be interesting to import a group of American vines and try them out on French soil; he did so and almost completely ruined the French wine industry. The American vines brought with them a small insect called the *Phylloxera vastatrix*, and although the American vines had developed a resistance to the pest, the French ones did not. The insect destroyed vineyard after vineyard. In the year 1868 the damage was incalculable. Vine leaves withered, and grapes, if they appeared at all, were stunted and completely unsuitable for wine making. After several years of effort the vintners faced complete failure, for the pest spread gradually from the Bordeaux region through the Burgundy. In despair many of them moved to Spain, where the phylloxera had not spread. These vintners settled just south of the Pyrénées. They instituted the French methods of planting and tending the vine and followed their ancient ways, introducing the two different systems, so that both Bordeaux and Burgundy wines were made. The Bordeaux type was called *paceta*, and the Burgundy *pomal*; they were shipped to market in the typical bottles of the two French wine districts. Of course, once the phylloxera was defeated in France (by grafting French vines onto the resistant American roots), the French wine makers went home, but the lessons they had taught their Spanish neighbors remained with them.

The two leading table wines of Spain are undoubtedly those from Rioja and Valdepeñas. Rioja is far more important in quality than its nearest competitor, Valdepeñas. The Rioja district centers about the valleys of the River Ebro, southwest of the Bordeaux region of France. The district has several subdivisions. Low Rioja produces a routine wine of passable quality. High Rioja makes a superior wine somewhat resembling a Bordeaux, light and delicate, although slightly rougher. The Alvesa subdistrict produces a wine that is rounded and full, like a good Burgundy. It is here that a good vintage year can be important. Rioja of a good year, aged for 15–20 years, may be as fine as a Richebourg. The Spanish appreciate this, for they have made little effort to ship their aged, superior wines. The leading vineyards (and shippers) are Vina Riscal (Marqués de Riscal), Vina Murrieta (Marqués de Murrieta), Vina Pomal, and Vina Paceta.

Valdepēnas is halfway between Madrid and the Mediterranean. The red and white wines here are hearty, quite dry, and contain considerable alcohol. They have a pleasant taste and are above average in quality, although not as good as the wines of Rioja.

Of the vineyards surrounding the ancient city of Barcelona, Castell del Remy offers fair wines, both red and white. But the best wine is made at Alella, a small village known for its white wine, somewhat on the order of an Alsatian, although it is actually supposed to resemble Rhine wine and is shipped in similar bottles.

Southern Spain produces a special type of fortified wine, Malaga. It is strong (because of the added alcohol) and quite sweet. Once very popular, it is not in vogue in this century which prefers the drier wines.

Sherry is the noted wine of Spain and one of the most imitated in the world. The imitations have never been successful, for the production of authentic sherry is extraordinarily difficult. The *solera* system of making sherry is not only expensive but it involves years for the development of the wine.

Genuine sherry is produced only in southern Spain in a small triangle bounded by the towns of Jerez de la Frontera, Cadiz, and Sanlucar. Jerez is the center of the trade. These wines were originally known as *vino de Jerez*, or wines of Jerez. (The British, the chief consumers of this wine, could not cope with the Spanish name and called it "sherris." This became "sherry" in time.) The small area of production comprises less than 20,000 acres on a soil which is a mixture of clay, chalk, and limestone, subject to tremendous heat during the summer months and very little rain. Temperatures of 110° are not uncommon in Andalusia, but somehow the vines manage to survive. The chief grape used is the sweet Palomina; but Mantuide Pila and Mantui Castellana are also used. For blending purposes a very sweet grape, the Pedro Ximenez, is grown. Incidentally, the grape produces a local wine, familiarly known as PX, which is like a heavy liqueur.

The grapes are harvested about the middle of September and are placed on mats in the sun to evaporate some of the natural moisture. Then they are pressed and allowed to ferment. Several months later the young wines are classified according to type. Sherry is about as unpredictable as a wine can be, and each year's crop is a gamble. Several casks of juice from the same vineyard, picked at the same time and stored in the same warehouse, may produce quite different products: pale and light, or crude and dark—and again of astonishingly fine quality. No one knows why, but undoubtedly the differences are caused by microscopic elements present in the air at the time of the harvest.

In the spring, vintners check their previous year's wine and classify it again, an extremely tedious and painstaking procedure. Some wines will be rejected completely, some will be made into ordinary wine, some into brandy, and the best will be selected for sherry.

During the making of sherry a secondary fermentation called *flor* must take place. At this stage of its life the grape juice is wine but it has not yet become sherry. As the wine is fermenting in casks the bungs are opened to admit air; whereas ordinary wines are destroyed by the air, sherry gains a new distinct flavor from it. The thin, cloudy film that forms on top of the wine is known as the *flor* (a mysterious development not understood even today). This flowering causes complex changes in the wine, adding the characteristic "nutty" flavor that makes sherry what it is. This procedure is followed only in making the drier types of sherry; sweeter sherries are treated with large doses of brandy. The dry sherries are blended afterward in the classic method of the *solera*.

Because of the peculiar qualities of the young wines which are so unpredictable, the *solera* system was developed to assure uniformity from year to year. Sherry is a blended product, for the new young wines are mixed in this process with the old. Visualize a high-vaulted cellar. On the floor is a row of a dozen big casks; above them a tier of identical casks, then a third, fourth, fifth, and even a sixth row at the very top. The casks are all connected, so that the wine from the top casks gradually works its way to the bottom. As orders for sherry are received, quantities are removed from the bottom casks; the wine in the second row gradually works down to the bottom line, and so on from each preceding tier. Young wine is then added at the top; it may take five years for the young wine to reach the bottom and be drawn off for bottling. During these years the new wines take on the characteristics of the older ones (partly because they rest in aged wood casks), thus assuring a uniform product. It is obvious that there can never be a sherry of a particular year, for the wine is made from many different vintages. If a date appears on a bottle, it is not the vintage but represents the date of the oldest wine used in making the blend.

Sherries are marketed in several different styles, according to the country to which they will be shipped. The principal types are as follows:

Manzanilla: Extra dry with a bitter, somewhat salty taste

Fino: Straw-colored with a very dry quality

Amontillado: Dry, but not as dry as Manzanilla or Fino; noted for its "nutty" flavor

Amoroso: Somewhat sweet, with more alcohol, and usually a darker color than other varieties

Oloroso: A very sweet dessert wine, high in alcoholic content. Has a fairly deep color; known also as "cream" sherry

Brown: Even sweeter and richer than Oloroso; distinctively dark brown.

Sherry is necessarily a high-priced wine. The tremendous investment in the *solera* system, the many failures encountered in processing the unpredictable natural wine, and the years of waiting all contribute to the cost of marketing this distinctive wine. Most sherries reach the market under particular trade names like Tio Pepe, Dry Sack, or Harvey's Bristol Cream. After finding a sherry to his liking, the consumer need never be troubled about vintages or variations from year to year, for the bottler will see to it that his product is always uniform. A bottle of sherry bought ten years ago should be identical in taste with one bought today.

Although most wines must be consumed at once after being opened, sherry's peculiar qualities permit it to come into contact with the air. But it will not keep indefinitely; an opened bottle has a life of only a month or so. Then it will begin to deteriorate.

To the novice the very sweet types will seem most attractive. But gradually, as one grows accustomed to the fascinating characteristic taste of the wine, the drier types seem more pleasing. Sweet sherries such as Harvey's Bristol Cream are good only with dessert or after dinner and should never be taken before a meal. The tolerant Spanish rarely drink them and are perfectly willing to export them all; they much prefer the *fino* or *amontillado* sherries, always served slightly chilled.

Spalen; Stringer. A hard rennet-type Emmentaler cheese made in Switzerland of whole cow's milk. It is now produced in many areas of the world, especially in Argentina, and the methods for preparing and aging differ greatly. When fully cured it is used for grating and has a nutty flavor. The name is derived from the wooden containers in which it is shipped.

Spalla di Vitello (Italian). Shoulder of veal.

Spalla di Vitello alla Carabiniera. Veal shoulder with bacon sauce.

Spalla di Vitello al Senape. Veal shoulder with mustard sauce.

Spam. The trade name of a canned luncheon meat made of ground spiced pork; may be served like sausage.

Spanakopeta (Greek). Spinach and cheese served in a pastry crust.

Spanish Bayonet; Spanish Dagger. A wild plant of the yucca family, used for food.

Spanish Cream. A dessert made of gelatin, custard, and egg whites. The stiffly beaten egg whites are folded into the partially-set gelatin custard.

Spanish Juice. *See* Licorice.

Spanish Nuts. Small filbert-type nuts grown in Spain.

Spanish Plant. Spinach.

Spanish Rice. Rice cooked with tomato sauce.

Spanish Shallot. The rocambole, a vegetable similar to garlic, but much less pungent.

Spanish Toast. French toast.

Sparassis. Large, creamy yellow wild mushroom commonly found during the autumn.

Spareribs. All the ribs from the side of pork. Closely trimmed, they are sold fresh, pickled, or smoked. *See* Pork.

Spargel (German). Asparagus.

Sparklet. A small metal vessel containing liquid carbon dioxide for making effervescent drinks.

Sparkling. Effervescent, having bubbles.

Sparkling Wines. A wide range of wines with bubbles or an effervescent quality. Certain wines are naturally sparkling, and must be bottled with special corks and wires. Other wines, including champagne and sparkling burgundy, are given effervescence by the addition of sugar syrup and brandy, generally called the "champagne process."

Sparris (Swedish). Asparagus.

Sparrow. A small bird, similar to the lark, occasionally used as food in some countries.

Sparrowgrass (Colloquial). Asparagus.

Spatchcock. *See* Spitchcock.

Spätlese (German). A late picking of the grapes for wine. *See* Germany, The Wines of.

Spattle. (1) Spatula. (2) To beat well or thoroughly, a baker's term.

Spatula. A kitchen or serving instrument consisting of a thin flat blade set in a handle; used to

spread substances, to scrape, to turn foods over, and to serve them without breaking.

Spatule (French). Spatula.

Spätzle (German). A type of flour dumpling.

Spearfish. A saltwater fish with a long sword-shaped snout; similar to the swordfish and prepared in the same manner.

Spearing. The whitebait, a food fish.

Spearmint; Garden Mint; Lamb Mint. An aromatic herb of the mint family native to Europe but now cultivated in the United States. The oil derived from its leaves is used as a flavoring extract in fillings and frostings, in jelly and in making mint candies.

Specialité de la Maison (French). (1) A dish featured by a restaurant because it is especially well prepared. (2) Any dish prepared in one's home.

Specific Dynamic Action. The increase in metabolism due to the digestion, absorption, and metabolism of foods. It varies with the type of food. For proteins, 30 percent above the basal; for fats and carbohydrates, 4–5 percent.

Proteins are said to be less fattening than the same weight of carbohydrate, as part of the calorie content is dissipated in the specific dynamic action.

Speck (German). Bacon.

Speckled Bread. *See* Bara Brith.

Speculaas (Dutch). Small Christmas cookies.

Speculoos (Belgian). Spice cookies.

Spegepølse (Danish). Salami.

Speilegg (Norwegian). Fried eggs.

Spejlaeg (Danish). Fried egg.

Spek (Dutch). Lard.

Spekelaar (Norwegian). Smoked mutton.

Spekesild (Norwegian). Salt-cured herring.

Spekeskinke (Norwegian). Cured ham.

Spekulatius (German). A sweet almond cooky.

Spelt. A coarse European wheat.

Spent Wash; Spent Beer. Liquor that remains in the whisky still, after the spirit is distilled.

Sperrkäse. A very hard dry cheese made in southern Germany.

Spetzli (Alsatian). Pastry made into pieces the size of a walnut, poached, dried, then tossed lightly in butter in a frying pan.

Spezzatino di Vitello (Italian). Veal stew.

Spiced Beef. Smoked beef prepared with various spices; served sliced very thin.

Spiced Cheese. By United States Government standards any cheese or spread that contains not less than 1½ ounces of spices for each 100 pounds of cheese.

Spiced Leyden. An Edam cheese spiced with caraway seeds.

Spiced Loaf (British). A cake made of highly spiced bread dough and a small amount of sugar.

Spice Islands. The Molucca Islands of the South Pacific, which produce many spices.

Spices; Spice. Any of a very wide range of vegetable substances used to flavor foods. Some spices are pungent, others are fragrant or aromatic; some are low in price, others are quite expensive. Among the most commonly-used spices are ginger, turmeric, mace, nutmeg, clove, allspice, coriander, dill, caraway, cinnamon, and especially pepper, the most widely used of all. Salt is not considered a spice because it is not normally of vegetable origin. The distinction between spices and condiments is not clearly drawn, but the latter generally includes such strong-flavored items as mustard, horseradish, pickle, and the like.

Spices may be used in powdered form, as leaves, bark, flower buds, essential liquids, fruit, seeds, or as whole plants. Spices have been used by mankind since before recorded time, and are frequently mentioned in the Bible, and by Egyptian, Greek, and Roman writers. During the Middle Ages, the search for spices led directly to greater exploration efforts to find new routes and new lands, for the average person's diet was boring and limited; spices were particularly valuable to prevent spoilage because of the lack of refrigeration. In the 16th and 17th centuries, cooks used hundreds of different spices, but most of these have fallen into disuse.

Spicy. Highly flavored with spices or herbs. Spicy foods cause the flow of gastric juices and increase the appetite.

Spider. A cast-iron skillet or frying pan, originally with long legs for use over coals in an open fire.

Spider Crab. (1) Various species of crustaceans allied to crabs. (2) In many coastal regions of France, certain fish of the weever type.

Spiedino (Italian). Fried cheese and bread with anchovy sauce.

Spiegeleier (German). Fried eggs.

Spiermaag (Dutch). Gizzard.

Spigola; Spignola. An Italian fish, a type of striped bass.

  Spigola alla Fiamma. Striped bass in flaming sauce.

  Spigola Bollita con Maionese. Striped bass with mayonnaise.

Spigot. A wooden peg that fits into the vent in a wine cask.

Spijskaart (Dutch). Menu.

Spikenard. (1) A plant often used in making root beer or other soft drinks. (2) (East Indian, Obsolete) An aromatic plant that yielded a fragrant ointment.

Spinach. An annual plant, a member of the goosefoot family, grown for its edible green leaves and stem. It undoubtedly originated in the Middle East.

  Difficult to clean, it should be washed thoroughly under cold running water; sometimes plenty of coarse salt sprinkled on the spinach helps wash away the sand. Spinach marketed in plastic containers is supposedly ready to use, but it should nevertheless be washed. It is available frozen, both in leaf and chopped form. Canned spinach is rather tasteless. Fresh spinach is a delicacy when the young leaves are gently cooked for a short time. No water should be added because the leaves release a considerable amount of fluid naturally. Spinach loses a great deal of volume when cooked. Very fresh spinach leaves, with stems removed, are delicious when mixed into a green salad. A little hot bacon fat poured over the leaves with a little vinegar, salt, and pepper added makes an excellent salad.

Spinach Dock. Sorrel.

Spinaci (Italian). Spinach.

  Spinaci alla Romana. Spinach with raisins and pine nuts.

Spinat (German, Norwegian). Spinach.

Spinazie (Dutch). Spinach.

Spiny Lobster; Cave Lobster; Rock Lobster; Sea Crayfish. A lobster with a very hard spiny shell but no claws; prepared like any other lobster.

Spirits. Distilled liquors, such as whisky, gin, brandy, rum, etc.

Spirituous. Containing spirits or distilled liquors.

Spirlin. The alburn, a European river fish, member of the carp family.

Spirling. The smelt.

Spirtle; Spurtle (Scotch). A round stick used chiefly for stirring oatmeal.

Spit. Any contrivance or arrangement by which foods may be roasted over or before a fire. Sometimes a spit holds the food in a horizontal position, occasionally in a vertical one. Formerly, all spits were operated by hand; now electric power is commonplace.

Spitchcock; Spatchcock (Obsolete). Splitting open and grilling or broiling foods, such as eel or fowl, trussed with small spits or skewers.

Spitz. (1) A small round rennet cheese made in Switzerland. (2) Spitzkäse, a cylindrical German cheese resembling Limburger and flavored with caraway.

Spleen. A glandlike organ found near the stomach of every animal. Ox (beef) spleen is sometimes used in stews.

Split. To cut or open a piece of food into two or more parts, such as fruit, a roll, or poultry.

Split Peas. A variety of pea which splits in half when dried; available in a range of colors, all basically green, but with yellow, red, or gray tones.

Split-Pea Flour. A flour made from finely ground split peas.

Splash. A small quantity of soda water, etc., added to a glass of liquor.

Spoganda (Italian). Spoom, an ice made with

beaten egg whites, cream or partially frozen water, and any flavoring, especially liquor.

Spondias; Hog Apple. A small tropical fruit resembling a plum; used for jam, preserves, and a fermented drink.

Sponge. (1) A very light, porous dough prepared with flour, eggs, and sugar, and usually with leavening, but no fat. (2) A gelatin dessert made with stiffly beaten egg white or whipped cream.

Sponge Biscuit. A type of biscuit with the same texture as a spongecake.

Spongecake. A very light, porous cake prepared with flour, eggs, and sugar, and usually with leavening but no fat. It is comparatively low in calories, because it contains no fat and because its texture is light with many air spaces.

Sponge Finger. A long narrow length of spongecake.

Spoom; Spoum. A frothy sherbet prepared with a light syrup and fruit juices or sweet wines. A meringue, twice the amount of the sherbet, is folded into the mixture; served in chilled sherbet glasses. *See* Spoganda.

Spoon. A utensil with a shallow bowl at the end of a handle in line with the shaft; used at the table for eating or handling liquid or soft foods and in the kitchen for stirring, mixing, ladling, etc. Except for the knife, it is the oldest culinary utensil known. It is made of metal, wood, or plastic, and in various sizes and shapes.

Sposi. A rather small soft Italian cream cheese.

Spot. A name applied to a wide range of small fish found in American waters.

Spotted Callista. An oval-shaped purplish clam; used chiefly in cooking, seldom eaten plain.

Spotted Sand Borer. A greenish silver marine food fish with horizontal bands of greenish brown spots; found off the coasts of China, Japan, Australia, and East Africa at all times of the year.

Spra. A Greek sheep's-milk cheese with a distinctive salty, spicy taste.

Spraengt (Danish). Salted.

Sprat. A small fish of the herring family which may be served fresh grilled with a mustard sauce or may be prepared and preserved like sardines. The young are called *brislings*.

Spread-Eagle Chicken. A plump young chicken split down the back. The breastbone is removed and the meat flattened, seasoned, and buttered. *See also* Spitchcock.

Sprig. A small branch, usually of parsley, thyme, or celery top; used in cooking or as a garnish.

Springerle (German). An anise-flavored cooky in which a design is placed by means of a special rolling pin; a favorite during the Christmas season. The flavor improves with age.

Spring Form Pan. A round straight-sided baking pan with a loose bottom that can be removed or attached by means of a spring.

Spring of Pork. The belly and thin flank or breast of pork.

Spring Onions. Young green onions; scallions.

Spring Roll (Chinese). Egg roll, an appetizer. *See* Egg Roll.

Sprinkle. To scatter in drops or small bits, as lemon juice over fish, paprika over a baked potato, or chopped parsley or any other garnish.

Sprit (Swedish). Liquor.

Sprotten (German). Sprats.

Sprouted Wheat. Wheat berries that sprout and grow while still in the ear during a wet harvesting, causing the wheat to have a high maltose content. Sprouted-wheat flour is a form of malt flour and can make bread small in volume with a gummy texture and a highly colored crust.

Sprouts. Brussels sprouts.

Spruce Beer. (1) Black beer, a fermented beverage made from the twigs and leaves of the spruce tree. (2) A non-alcoholic drink flavored with spruce.

Spuma (Italian). Custard.

　Spuma di Banane. Banana whip.

Spumoni; Spumone (Italian). Ice cream, usually with a combination of several flavors, containing chopped nuts and fruits.

Spun Sugar. Boiled-sugar syrup brought to the long-thread stage, drawn into threads, and usually colored; used to decorate cakes and ice creams.

Spurgee; Spurge. With respect to beer, wine, or other liquor, to throw off impurities naturally during the fermentation process.

Spur Pepper. The pepper plant *capsicum frutescens*, the source of a type of pepper.

Spurs of Bacchus. Various small hors d'oeuvres, salty or highly seasoned to stimulate thirst.

S.Q. (European). Priced according to quantity, a menu term; it refers to the French term *selon quantité*.

Squab. Any young small bird; in some regions, exclusively a young pigeon.

Squab Pie (British). Squabs, or young pigeons, and apples covered with a dough and baked.

Squailing Loaf (British). A badly shaped loaf.

Squarehead Wheat. English red wheat; usually stronger than white wheat.

Squash. The fruit produced on a vine by certain plants belonging to the gourd and pumpkin families. The term "squash" is used to refer to the pumpkin in some regions, and to the gourd in others.

There are three principal kinds of squash: winter, summer, and Canadian. Winter squash, typified by Hubbard squash, have hard exterior shells and keep very well; their texture is firmer and their flavor better than summer varieties. Summer squash have a light, fresh flavor, particularly when eaten young, before the shells harden. Canadian squash, which probably originated in Asia, is typified by crookneck squash. The sizes of squash range from quite small ones to mammoth specimens of enormous weight. Although yellow is the characteristic color, squash come in almost white, many shades of orange, and extend into deep reds, purples, green, and almost black.

The term is undoubtedly of American Indian origin, deriving from the Indian term *askutasquash*. Squash was one of the Indian's principal food crops. In England, squash is called "marrow."

    Squash, Chinese. A long green squash with yellow markings; much used in Chinese cookery.

Squaw Grass. Bear grass, an edible wild grass native to the United States and southwest Canada.

Squeteague. Another name for the weakfish.

Squid. Cuttlefish or calamary. It is closely allied to the octopus, but the American common squid is only about 18 inches long.

    Dried Squid. In many oriental countries squid are air-dried for future use; they must be soaked in cold water for 24 hours before using.

Squill Fish. A small crustacean found along the coast of Europe; it is fairly good, with a taste reminiscent of lobster.

Squirrel. A wild rodent, used as food in parts of the United States and in other countries; often prepared like rabbit. In certain parts of the southern United States, squirrel stews are quite popular.

Stabilizers. Substances that stabilize emulsions of fat and water, such as gums, agar, egg albumin, and cellulose ethers. They are used to produce the texture of meringues and marshmallows.

Stachelbeeren (German). Gooseberries.

Stachys; Chinese Artichoke; Crosnes. A plant whose irregular knotty tubers resemble a string of beads and have a nutty flavor.

Stagbush. A wild shrub bearing a sweet edible berry similar to the black haw.

Stainless-Steel Ware. Kitchenware made of an alloy of steel, chromium, and nickel.

Stake (Colloquial). A small meal.

Stale. (1) Of food, vapid or tasteless because of age; having lost the original freshness but not necessarily inedible. (2) Dry, as stale bread used for making crumbs.

Stalk. (1) The stem of a herbaceous plant, as celery. (2) To remove grapes and berries from a stalk.

Stampot (Dutch). A hash made of smoked sausages served on a bed of cabbage, potatoes, and veal fat.

Stangensellerie (German). Celery.

Stap (Scotch). A dish made in the Shetland Islands of haddock heads and livers; served with fish preparations.

Star Anise; Chinese Anise. An herb with starlike clusters of light, elongated seeds whose flavor is similar to but more pungent than that of licorice; used in oriental cooking.

Starch. A tasteless white substance found in various foods, such as potatoes, beans, corn, etc.; a source of fuel for the body. Starch is prepared for commercial use chiefly from corn and potatoes treated with chemicals and water, ground, and allowed to settle. Various other starches have been prepared from wheat, rice, sago, arrowroot, yams, lentils, peas, chestnuts, bananas, manioc, and nuts. Commercially-prepared starch is generally used for thickening soups and stews, in baking, for preparing batters, and for coating foods.

Starches. Foods with a high starch content.

Starch Jelly. A paste formed when cornstarch is mixed with water. To make it jell, boiling water or fruit juice and sugar are added. Fruit tarts may be glazed with this mixture.

Starch Syrup. A thick liquid, high in starch, usually made from potatoes or corn. It is used extensively as a sweetening agent in candy-making because the syrup prevents crystallization.

Starkbier (German). Heavy Munich beer.

Star of Bethlehem. A plant whose edible roots are prepared like salsify.

Starling. A bird similar to but smaller than the blackbird; prepared like thrush.

Starveling. A hungry or starving person.

Steack (French). Steak.

> **Steack au Poivre.** Steak prepared with crushed black peppercorns.
>
> **Steack de Veau.** Veal steak.
>
> **Steack Haché.** Chopped steak; hamburger steak.

Steak Roll. A cut from a beef round; because it is somewhat tough, meat tenderizer should be used. The steak roll is best when quickly fried.

Steam. To cook in a closed vessel with just enough water to generate steam.

Steam-Bake. When baking, to place in the oven a shallow pan of water with the pan of food to keep the mixture moist; for example, in baking a fruit cake.

Steam Cooker. A covered cooking utensil with one or more insert pans that have special holes.

Steamed Pudding. Any pudding cooked by steaming instead of baking. The pudding mixture is put into a mold, can, or bowl, covered tightly, and placed in boiling water until cooked. Plum pudding is an example.

Steapsin. An enzyme of the digestive system that converts fats into fatty acids and glycerol.

Stearin. Colorless solid portion of animal and vegetable fats.

Stecchini. A variation of a classic Russian soup made of cabbage or sauerkraut.

Stecchini Carlos. Thin slices of veal and ham dipped in egg and flour and fried in butter; usually served with boiled noodles and glazed onions.

Steelhead. A large trout.

Steel Wool. A cleaning device consisting of a mass of fine steel threads; used as an abrasive on metals. It is easy to handle but should be used with care, since it will remove not only stains from surfaces but also part of the surface. Once dampened, it will rust and should be placed in a disposable container, otherwise it will leave rust spots on sinks and drain boards.

Steenworde, Fromages de. Imitation Gouda and Edam cheeses made in Flanders, Belgium.

Steep. To place a dry substance in liquid to extract flavor and color, as steeping tea; to soak a food in an aromatic liquid or brine; to marinate.

Steep Bowl (Obsolete). In medieval times, a bowl in which liquids, especially tea, were steeped.

Steer. Male cattle used for beef; an ox 2–4 years old.

Steg (Danish). Joint of meat.

Stegt Aal (Danish). Fried eel.

Stegte Karbonader (Danish). Fried veal-and-pork balls.

Stegt Fiskefilet (Danish). Fried fish fillets.

Stegt Svinekam (Danish). Roast pork.

Stein (German). A large stone or earthenware container from which beer is drunk.

Steinbutt (German). Turbot.

Stein Käse. A rather smelly United States imitation of a German "beer" cheese.

Steinpilze (German). Mushrooms.

Steinwein; Steinwein-in-Bocksbeutel. Franconia wines of Germany. *See* Germany, The Wines of.

Steirisches Brathuhn (Austrian). Chicken roasted on a spit.

Stekt (Norwegian). Broiled.

Stekt Potatis (Swedish). Fried potatoes.

Stelline (Italian). Miniature star-shaped pasta.

Stemware. Footed drinking glasses, consisting of a bowl set on stems of varying heights. Fine stemware is made of crystal, and it is said that the thinner the glass, the better the beverage tastes, particularly wine. Stemware serves a par-

ticular purpose for champagne and other chilled wine, as the glass can be held by the base or stem, thus keeping the heat of the hand off the bowl containing the wine.

Sterilize. To destroy harmful bacteria by means of high heat.

Sterlet. A small delicately flavored sturgeon native to the Caspian Sea and the rivers that enter into it. Its caviar (roe) is excellent.

Sterling Wheat. A moderately strong South African wheat with average milling qualities.

Sterols. Solid cyclic alcohols found in plants and animal tissues, such as cholesterol. *See* Sisosterols.

Steurkrab (Dutch). Prawn.

Stiacciata (Italian). A flat cake.

Stickleback. A small flavorless river fish.

Stife. A strong-smelling and strong-tasting bread made with beans and peas.

Stillroom (Obsolete). A butler's pantry.

Still Wine. A wine lacking effervescence and sparkle; a table wine.

Stimulant. Any food or liquid that temporarily increases the metabolism or any other activity of the body, such as alcohol, tea, coffee, etc.

Stinger. An intoxicating drink made of brandy and crème de menthe; sometimes served as a cocktail but more properly as a liqueur.

Stint (German). Smelt.

Stirabout (Irish). Porridge.

Stirred Curd Cheeses. A group of cheeses resembling cheddar but with a more granular texture.

Stirrer. A small slender rodlike implement for stirring a drink.

Stirring. The process of moving or mixing a food in a circular motion, usually in a bowl.

Stirrup Cup (British). A last drink; originally the one taken with a guest departing on horseback.

Stoccafisso (Italian). Dried cod usually prepared with anchovies, walnuts, and olives.

Stock. A liquid or jellylike substance containing the juices and soluble parts of meats and vegetables extracted in cooking; used mainly to make sauces, broths, and soups. White stock is white or practically colorless. Brown stock is prepared from partially browned meats or poultry and vegetables. Vegetable stock is the water in which vegetables have been cooked. Fish stock is customarily prepared with the head, bones, and trimming of fish, rarely from the edible portions. Sometimes the meaning of stock is used interchangeably with broth.

Stock Concentrates. Stocks of various sorts reduced by slow, gentle cooking until most of the water content has been eliminated.

Stockfisch (German). Air-dried codfish; must be soaked in water before using.

Stockfish. Dried Norwegian cod.

Stockpot. A large pot in which to cook poultry, soups, or other stocks.

Stokvis (Dutch). Dried haddock.

Stokvis met Rijst (Dutch). Dried fish and rice.

Stollen (German). (1) A rich loaf cake thickly sprinkled with sugar. (2) A yeast bread or coffeecake made with raisins or nuts.

Stomachic Liqueurs (Obsolete). Cordials and liqueurs.

Stone. A sharpening stone or abrasive used to sharpen kitchen cutlery.

Stone-Milled Flour (British). Wheat crushed between heavy stones to make whole meal. Sieved through silk bolting cloths, it yields a fine meal that usually does not keep well.

Stonewall Strawberries; Fukuba Strawberries. Strawberries grown by a process invented by a Japanese agriculturist, Fukuba. The plants are surrounded by stone walls; the sun, heating the stones, provides additional warmth to the young plants, resulting in large, delicious berries.

Stoneware. Fairly coarse glazed pottery.

Stoorum (Scotch). A drink made of oatmeal, water, milk, and salt.

Stopper. The plug, or cork, usually for a bottle or decanter; made of various materials, including glass.

Store Cheese. American cheddar cheese of ordinary quality.

Storeroom. A room or pantry in which foodstuffs are stored; should be kept at an even, cool temperature.

Stor Lammfilet (Swedish). Mutton chops.

Stoup (Obsolete). A medieval drinking vessel; a tankard or flagon.

Stove. Range; the apparatus used to cook foods in the kitchen. The heat may be obtained from wood, coal, gas, electricity, or other sources of energy. The word "stove" has generally been replaced by "range." Various types of stoves have been used since Roman times. It was not until the 15th century, however, that stoves were produced in quantity for use by the general public.

Stoved (Scotch). Stewed.

Stracchino. A soft rich pungent Italian goat's-milk cheese made chiefly in the wintertime.

Stracchino di Milano. A yellow Italian cheese with a flavor similar to that of Bel Paese.

Stracciatella (Italian). Bouillon containing beaten eggs and cheese.

Stradella. A wine made in Lombardy, Italy.

Strain. To pour or force through a strainer.

Strainer. A kitchen utensil used to filter foods or liquids.

Straining Bag. A cloth or felt funnel used to clarify liquids, such as syrups.

Strasbourgeoise, À la. A kind of cooking or garnish involving the use of *pâté de foie gras* or sauerkraut.

Strasbourg Pie. *See* Pâté de Foie Gras. Foie Gras.

Stratford Sauce (British). A horseradish-and-grated-apple sauce mixed with whipped cream, salt, and pepper; good with broiled meats and chicken.

Strawberries Romanoff. Strawberries marinated in a sweet liqueur with whipped cream folded in.

Strawberry. A small reddish fruit produced on a perennial trailing plant. Although most strawberries are red, the color may vary into white, yellow, green, and pink. The sweet, aromatic, juicy pulp is contained in a sort of soft, bag-shaped receptacle marked with small seeded dots. Strawberries range in size from the miniature, or wild, types (including the French *frais des bois*), all the way up to giant specimens produced in Japan, 4–5 inches in length.

The name may have originated in one of three different ways. From its manner of growing along the ground it may be a variation of the word "strewed." Also, the name may have developed because gardeners customarily spread straw around the berries to prevent mildew. The third possibility is that the berries often have a strawlike texture.

Although strawberries grew wild in most of Europe, it was not until the 17th century that commercial production began. Strawberries were also known several centuries ago in parts of Asia, particularly in China, and may have been cultivated there, but the records are not clear. Those who decry the hybridized versions claim that only wild strawberries have full flavor. It is true, despite American thoughts to the contrary, that the smaller berries have the more intense flavor. Very large berries, as a rule, have a somewhat woody texture and a milder taste, but this is not always true.

Strawberries are good with sugar and cream, made into ice cream, cakes, pies, tarts, etc. Strawberry jams and jellies are very popular in the United States.

Strawberry Spinach. *See* Swiss Chard.

Strawberry-Tomato. The Mexican tomato; *see also* Ground Cherry.

Strawberry Tree. The arbutus tree, which produces a red berry from which wines and liqueurs are made. The best known beverage is arbouse. *See* Arbouse.

Straw Potatoes. Potatoes cut lengthwise into very thin strips resembling straws and fried in deep fat.

Straw Wines. Wines made from grapes left to dry on straw mats before pressing.

Strega. An outstanding Italian liqueur with an

orange base; its slightly bittersweet aftertaste suggests yellow Chartreuse.

Streusel (German). A mixture of sugar, crumbs, and sometimes ground nuts used to cover coffeecakes. A streusel cake is one covered with this mixture.

Streuselkuchen (German). Crumb cake.

String Bean; French Bean; Haricot Bean; Snap Bean. Any of various varieties of long beans with meaty pods; used as a vegetable while not completely ripe. *See also* Bean.

Stringer; Spalen: A Swiss skim-milk cheese resembling Emmentaler but much smaller.

Strip. To remove the leaves or petals from the stalk of a plant.

Striped Bass. An Atlantic and Pacific fish ranging in size from 1 pound to over 50 pounds; may be baked, broiled, or cooked with sauces. It is highly regarded, having a fine taste and texture.

Striped Mullet. A fat, strong-flavored mullet; needs a highly seasoned sauce to mask the taste.

Strip Steak. A boneless strip of beef cut from the chuck; best when braised or in a casserole.

Stritzel (Austrian). Yeast cake with raisins; made at Christmas.

Stromateus; Rudderfish. A delicate-fleshed Mediterranean fish; prepared like turbot.

Strömming (Swedish). Cold-water herring; smelts.

Strömmingslåda (Swedish). Baked sardines or smelts.

Strozapreti (Italian). A Parmesan-and-Ricottacheese dumpling made in Tuscany.

Strudel; Strudle; Shtrudel; Shtrudl. A pastry consisting of many thinly rolled layers spread with various fillings, usually fruits and most frequently apples but sometimes with nuts or cheese. First made in Bavaria, strudel is now known to pastry lovers in most parts of the world. No one knows exactly how strudel made the journey to Hungary, but it became very popular there, being called *retes*. Strudel can also be made with cabbage, meat, or spicy mixtures.

Strufoli (Italian). (1) Pastry consisting of balls of sweetened pasta soaked in honey. (2) Fried cookies served with honey.

Stufatino (Italian). Stew.

Stufatino alla Romana (Italian). Roman-style beef stew, that is, prepared with onions, garlic, and red wine.

Stufato di Manzo (Italian). Beef stew.

Stufatu (Corsican). A stew made with macaroni, mushrooms, onions, and sometimes mutton.

Stuffing. Dressing, the filling for the inner cavities of roast poultry to help keep its shape and moistness and to add flavor; also used in rolled meats or other roasted meats. Bread is the usual base for a dry stuffing, but boiled rice, mashed potatoes, corn, or cornmeal are also favored substances. Some stuffings are combined with chestnuts, cashew nuts, livers, and giblets, or with such fruits as apples, cranberries, pineapple, or prunes; also with sausage mixtures or oysters.

Stulle (German). Rye-bread sandwiches with various fillings.

Sturgeon. Various species of a rather large freshwater fish, found in many parts of the world. In many countries, notably England and Russia, it was regarded as a "royal" fish. Sturgeon is best known as the source for caviar, a highlyregarded hors d'oeuvre all over the world. Fresh sturgeon is rich, slightly rubbery in texture, and not particularly distinguished. When smoked, it is oily and has a delicate flavor and somewhat crumbly texture. *See* Caviar.

Sturionian. Pertaining to sturgeon or similar fish.

Stuvad (Swedish). Stewed.

Stuvad Grönsaker (Swedish). Vegetables in cream.

Styria. A cylindrical Austrian whole-milk cheese without distinctive taste.

Sub Gum (Chinese). A dish containing mixed vegetables.

Submarine Sandwich; Grinder; Hero Sandwich. A long loaf of bread split in two and filled

with assorted meats, condiments, etc.; the name and contents vary from region to region.

Subric (French). A sautéed (not fried) fritter

or croquette made with a white sauce, eggs, grated cheese, and ground meat, poultry, vegetables, or rice; usually served as an hors d'oeuvre.

Substitutions. The practice of replacing foods with others which are similar. For example, if sour milk is not available, it may be replaced by fresh milk to which a little lemon juice is added.

Suburek (Turkish). Mutton or beef pie.

Suc. The concentrated liquid obtained by boiling down a juice or by squeezing an animal or vegetable substance.

Sucan. Oat husks steeped until they become sour, particularly in South Wales, Great Britain, where they are an item of food. The liquid is thickened with oatmeal, then eaten with milk like a cereal.

Succo (Italian). Juice.

    Succo d'arancia. Orange juice.

    Succo di Frutta. Fruit juice.

    Succo di Pomodoro. Tomato juice.

Succotash (American). A mixture of cooked sweet corn and lima beans. This preparation probably originated with American Indians, the word itself being of Indian origin.

Succo Tundu; Succu (Italian). A Sardinian soup with dumplings and saffron.

Succulent. (1) Very juicy and tasty. (2) As applied to vegetables, having heavy, fleshy stems and leaves.

Sucées (French). *Petits-fours* containing candied fruits.

Sucet. A small edible eel found in French rivers.

Suckerfish. Several types of fish with either a cup-shaped sucker or a sharp spine on a fin, such as the perch.

Suckling Pig; Sucking Pig. A very young pig still in the nursing stage, varying in size from 12 to 25 pounds; a great favorite, particularly in the South Pacific.

Sucre (French). Sugar.

    Sucre d'Érable. Maple sugar.

    Sucre Candi. Sugar crystals.

    Sucre Crystallisé. Granulated sugar.

    Sucre d'Orge. Barley sugar.

    Sucre en Pain. Lump sugar.

    Sucre en Poudre. Granulated sugar.

    Sucre Glace. Confectioners' sugar.

    Sucre Semoule. Granulated sugar.

Sucre Vanillé. Vanilla sugar; granulated sugar stored in a closed container with a whole vanilla bean.

Sucrin. A melon with a good flavor and a pleasant aroma.

Sucrose. Cane sugar or beet sugar.

Suculento (Spanish). A combination of corn, squash, and other vegetables.

Suédoise (French). Fruits cooked in syrup and placed in layers in an aspic mold, which is then filled with a fruit or a liqueur-flavored jelly.

Suédoise, Sauce (French). A mayonnaise sauce flavored with horseradish and unsweetened apple sauce; usually served with pork or cold goose.

Suer; Faire Suer (French). Literally, "to sweat." This term has come to have two different meanings for professional cooks. (1) To cook foods slowly over gentle heat in a tightly-covered pan until the food "perspires." (2) To sear foods quickly over high heat, in order to seal in the juices.

Suet. In general, almost all kinds of fat; specifically, the firm fat in the region surrounding the kidneys and loins of cattle and sheep.

Sue-wuk (Eskimo). Edible wild blueberries.

Suffle (Italian). Soufflé.

Sufflé (Swedish). Soufflé.

Suffolk Dumplings (British). Small balls of yeast dough cooked in boiling water; served hot with sugar and butter or with a wine sauce.

Sugar. A sweet edible substance obtained from various plants, chiefly from cane, a tall, thick perennial grass, and beets. The term probably derives from the Arabic *sukkar*.

Its precise origin is doubtful, but it is believed to have originated in India because of the common historical references to "Indian salt," as sugar was called over 1,500 years ago. Sugar cane then grew wild; cultivation began much later. Beets were not known to contain sugar until Margraff, a German scientist, discovered its presence about the middle of the 18th century. During several wars it was difficult to import cane sugar, so beet sugar thus became a common substitute.

Sugar is marketed in different forms. The commonest is the ordinary white *granulated* variety. *Powdered* sugar is more finely granulated.

Instant, or *superfine*, sugar dissolves almost immediately. *Confectioners'*, *icing*, or *Four X* sugars are similar; prepared with about 3 percent cornstarch, they are used for candies, icings, etc. *Brown* sugar is made in light and dark types; it is used chiefly in cooking and in making candies, cookies, and cakes. Brown sugar should be stored in a glass container with a tight cover. *Lump*, *tablet*, or *cube* sugar is prepared by moistening granulated sugar with sugar-cane liquor, then pressing it into molds or shapes. Sometimes sugar is colored, often called *confetti sugar*, and used for decoration or other fancy purposes.

Sugar, Brown. A type of sugar, obtained when cane sugar is refined, containing 75–99.7 percent sucrose; it is prepared as light or dark brown sugar. A new type of brown sugar, marketed as Brownulated, keeps dry and pours readily.

Sugar Almond. An almond coated with sugar.

Sugar, Coarse. A refined dry white sugar with rather large crystals that is often colored and used for decoration.

Sugar Apple. *See* Sweetsop.

Sugar Beet. *See* Sugar.

Sugar Cake. A rich cake, made with cream, butter, and sugar.

Sugar Candy. Sweet clear rock crystals formed on strings suspended in a strong solution of sugar that evaporates slowly.

Sugar Cane. *See* Sugar.

Sugar-Cane Flowers. The immature flowers of certain varieties of wild sugar cane eaten as a green vegetable; they resemble a miniature cauliflower.
etc.) served with sauerkraut.

Sugar-Coat. To cover with sugar.

Sugar Cubes. A highly refined white sugar combined with a sucrose syrup and compressed, then dried into cubes.

Sugar Doctor; Candy Doctor. A substance, such as cream of tartar or invert sugar, added in sugar confectionery to prevent the sugar from crystallizing or "graining."

Sugared. Covered with sugar; crystallized with sugar; candied; honeyed.

Sugar Grass. Sorghum.

Sugar Melon. A cantaloupe with sweet, juicy flesh and a gray ribbed skin.

Sugar Off. To boil down maple syrup to make maple sugar.

Sugar Peas. (1) A variety of peas with a high natural sugar content. (2) Peas cooked and served in their pods and eaten whole. *See also* Pea.

Sugarplum. An elaborate piece of candy; a bonbon.

Sugar Plum. A name sometimes used for the persimmon.

Sugarsop. (1) A tropical fruit, the sweetsop found in the West Indies. (2) A fruit dessert made with bread and spices.

Sugar Tablets. A highly refined white sugar combined with a sucrose syrup and compressed into tablets.

Sugar Tongs. A utensil consisting of two lengths of metal with claw ends, joined by a hinge or flexible back; used to pick up lumps of sugar.

Sugar Vinegar. A type of vinegar made with sugar residue from various sugar-making procedures.

Sugar Water. The sap of the sugar maple tree.

Sugary. (1) Containing sugar, or being very sweet. (2) The place where sugar is made or maple syrup is refined.

Sugee. A species of white grain, ground into powder and used as a foodstuff.

Sugo (Italian). Gravy; meat juices.

Suif (French). Mutton fat.

Suilline. Pertaining to pork or pigs.

Suimono (Japanese). A clear soup.

Suisse, Le. Spongecake served with a pudding or custard.

Suisse, À la (French). In the Swiss style; usually containing cheese.

Sukker (Danish). Sugar.

Sukkerbrød (Norwegian). Sweet bread.

Sulfur Waters. Mineral waters from natural springs containing a high proportion of sulfur.

Süllö. Young fogas; a type of river or lake trout found chiefly in Hungary.

Sulperknochen (German). Pig's meat (ears, tail, etc.) served with sauerkraut.

Sultane, À la (French). Finished off with pistachio nuts or pistachio butter.

Sultan Hen. An aquatic web-footed bird; prepared like a coot.

Sülze (German). Cold pork in jelly.

Sumac. A low-growing Middle and Near Eastern herb used in combination with other herbs and spices for picklings, etc.

Sumashijiru (Japanese). Stews.

Sumatra Tea. An Indonesian fermented tea with fairly good flavor. Though not popular in the United States, it is well liked in Asia.

Summer Pudding (British). An uncooked pudding made with bread slices and stewed fruit.

Summer Savory. An aromatic herb whose leaves are used in cooking and flavoring tomato juice.

Summer Snipe. A sandpiper or plover; prepared like woodcock.

Sumo (Portuguese). Juice.

Sundae. Ice cream topped with fruits or fruit sauces or any one of various syrups, as chocolate or butterscotch, often with nuts and whipped cream added.

Sundew. An aromatic plant whose leaves may be eaten either in salads or cooked.

Sunfish. Bluegill, a North American freshwater fish of the perch family.

Sunfish Bass. Rock bass.

Sunflower. A plant, similar in taste to the Jerusalem artichoke, whose long tubers are prepared like salsify and the Chinese artichoke. Certain varieties of sunflower produce seeds that are good when dried and salted.

Suomalainen Pannukakku (Finnish). Pancakes, a national specialty.

Sup. To eat an evening meal.

Supé (Swedish). Supper.

Superfine. Very fine, as superfine sugar.

Supions. A small variety of squid, found in Provence, France.

Suppe (German). Soup.

Suppenfleisch (German). Boiled beef; soup meat.

Suppentopf (German). Strong beef consommé.

Supper. The meal eaten in the evening. If the main meal is eaten during the middle of the day, the evening meal is known as "supper." If the main meal is eaten in the early evening, supper is a meal taken at or near midnight.

Supper (Danish, Norwegian). Soups.

Suppli (Italian). Croquette made with bread, rice, and cheese; sometimes with ham; served very hot.

Suppli al Telefono. Rice croquette stuffed with mozzarella cheese and tomatoes.

Suppli di Riso. Rice croquette stuffed with meat and cheese.

Suprême (French). "Finest," generally with reference to the breast of poultry. *Suprême de volaille* is breast of chicken, served as an entrée.

Suprême, Sauce (French). A rich cream sauce made from chicken stock reduced by boiling, with cream added.

Sur (Swedish). Sour.

Surard (French). Elderberry vinegar.

Surbrauo (Icelandic). Bread with a distinctive sourish taste.

Surbrød (Danish). Sour-rye bread.

Sureau (French). Elderberry.

Surf Clam. A large "jumping" clam found on the Atlantic and Pacific coasts of the United States; there is considerable difference in the size and appearance of surf clams in various localities.

Surfeit. An excess of eating or drinking.

Surfeit Water (Obsolete). A liquid drunk in Victorian times by those who had overindulged in food and liquor. Surfeit water caused people to vomit immediately, thus permitting the sated diner to recover his appetite and begin the process over again.

Surfin (French). Of the best quality, a term used boastfully by food packers or bottlers of alcoholic beverages.

Surinam. *See* Guianas, The.

Surinam Cherry. The Brazilian cherry; eaten fresh or used to make excellent jelly.

Surkal (Norwegian). Sweet-and-sour cabbage.

Surlonge (French). Sirloin.

Surmulet. A strong-tasting Mediterranean fish, similar to the rouget.

Surprise, En (French). Indicating, in the presentation of food, an unusual blend of flavors or temperatures, or a visual surprise; for example, baked Alaska, which has a warm meringue over cold ice cream.

Sur-Rincette. Another drink of Cognac after a rincette. *See* Rincette.

Sursac. An Indonesian fruit having a sweet and

sour taste, vaguely flavored like almonds, and with a soft consistency.

Sur Sild (Norwegian). Pickled herring.

Surstek (Swedish). A beef casserole made with pickled meats and vegetables.

Surstromming (Norwegian). Sour herring.

Surullitos. Cylindrical fritters made of cheese and cornmeal.

Susan. *See* Lazy Susan.

Sushi (Japanese). Vinegared rice; the basis, in small quantities, for a series of raw-fish preparations. *See* Japan.

Süssigkeiten (German). Desserts; sweet dishes.

Süsspeisen (German). Desserts.

Süss-Sauer (German). Sweet-and-sour.

Sûrtout de Table (French). Decorative objects placed on the table at the end of a meal.

Sutler (Obsolete). One who followed an army and sold provisions to soldiers.

Suzanne, Alfred. A French chef who was an authority on eggs and was the author of books on pastry, egg cookery, and other food preparations.

Svamp och Böner (Swedish). Mushrooms and beans.

Svampstuvning (Swedish). Creamed mushrooms.

Sveciaost. A soft, rich Swedish cheese made with whole milk, with all cream, or partly with cream.

Svícková Pečeně (Czechoslovakian). Pickled beef; usually served with a sour-cream sauce.

Svinekoteletter (Danish). Pork chops.

Svinemørbrad (Danish). Spareribs.

Svinestek (Norwegian). Roast pork.

Svinkött (Swedish). Pork.

Swallows. Small birds, which are spit-roasted in some countries.

Swallows' Nests. Nests built by swallows by combining a certain seaweed with their saliva; used by the Chinese in bird's-nest soups.

Swamp Cabbage. A type of wild cabbage with a slightly bitter aftertaste.

Swamp Sugar Pear. A tall wild plant with small good-tasting pear-shaped fruit.

Swan. The flesh of this large aquatic bird was highly regarded during medieval times; it has fallen into disfavor, because of its oily, stringy character.

Swartzain (Dutch). A dish prepared from duck or other fowl.

Sweat Boxes. Warmed containers, used to develop fermentation in vanilla beans to encourage the formation of flavorful oils.

Swede; Swedish Turnip. Rutabaga, a rather coarse yellow root vegetable.

Sweden. The outstanding culinary feature of Sweden is undoubtedly the *smörgåsbord*, the table loaded with appetizers, cold and hot dishes from which the diner helps himself. The proper etiquette involves three trips (at least) to the *smörgåsbord* table, and in a certain prescribed and accepted order. First, one selects herring and other fish. The second plate includes cold meats; and the third, the hot food in the chafing dish as well as some of the cheese. In recent years the *smörgåsbord* has begun to diminish in popularity because the Swedes are beginning to eat less and become more aware of the problems of overweight. As a compromise, restaurants have begun to serve a simple selection of items from the *smörgåsbord* on one plate; this is called the *assietter* and may consist of about a half-dozen items, including herring, sardines, cheese, etc. The more expensive version of *assietter* is called *delikatessassietter*, which might include a few luxury items like smoked salmon, shrimp, and pâté.

Swedish people like to drink at the dinner table rather than have cocktails before the meal. The favorite drink is *snaps*, also called *aquavit*, a clear colorless liquor. This involves the national custom of the *skål* (pronounced "skawl"), and its etiquette is rigidly observed in larger groups. No one drinks snaps without first catching the eye of a person of the opposite sex, saying "*skål*," and then drinking while still holding the other person's eye. Swedish snaps comes in many different types: O.P. and Skåne have a caraway flavor; Angostura is made with bitters; Överste is slightly sweet; Taffel is comparatively unflavored; and Ödåkra is lightly spiced. Swedish beer is very good, varying from 3 to 4.5 percent alcohol. There are no local wines, although wines are popular with city people.

Fish dishes are standard fare; *sillsallad* is an interesting herring salad with apples and beets;

inkokt strömming are pickled fresh sardines; *gravad lax* is marinated salmon; *fiskbullar* are delicious fish balls; *kraftor* are the marvelous crayfish which come into season in August. Soups are rich, thick, and hearty in this cold-weather country. *Vitkålssoppa* is a delicious cabbage soup; *årter med fläsk* is the classic split-pea soup served with pieces of pork. In summertime a cold fruit soup, *blandad fruktsoppa*, is a great favorite.

Meat dishes are represented by *köttbuller*, the famous Swedish meatballs, served with a cream sauce. *Frikadeller* are pork-and-veal meatballs, with a delicate flavor. An interesting method of preparing pot roast is *grytstek*, made with anchovies and molasses. *Sjömansbiff*, a beef stew made with beer, is worthy of notice by those who enjoy succulent stews. There are few vegetable recipes, the people preferring potatoes and dumplings, especially *kroppkakor*, potato dumplings.

Desserts are good. *Plättar* are small plain pancakes, and *pannkakor med sylt* are the favorite Thursday dessert of pancakes with jam. *Äpplekaka med vaniljsås* is Swedish applecake with vanilla sauce. The Swedish people are extremely fond of coffee, which they drink whenever an opportunity arises, and with it they habitually serve coffeecake, *kaffekaka*.

Swedish Punsch. A Scandinavian liqueur consisting of simple sugar syrup combined with Indonesian arak.

Swedish Turnip. The common turnip; rutabaga.

Sweet. (1) (British) A dessert. *Sweets* are candy. (2) Having a taste resembling that of sugar.

Sweet Almond. *See* Almond.

Sweet Basil. An herb cultivated around the world; used to flavor a wide variety of dishes; best with vegetables, particularly cucumbers and tomatoes. *See also* Basil.

Sweet Bay. *See* Bay Leaf.

Sweetbreads. The thymus gland located near the neck of a calf or lamb. Calf's sweetbreads are more highly esteemed than lamb's sweetbreads because of their delicate flavor. Since sweetbreads are very perishable, they should be refrigerated promptly and should be used within 24 hours of purchase. Most recipes call for precooking to improve soft consistency. The pancreas, located near the animal's stomach, is also used as sweetbreads, but the quality and flavor are mediocre.

Sweet Cicely. An aromatic herb sometimes used in cookery.

Sweet Corn; Green Corn. An edible, soft variety of corn usually eaten before it is fully ripe. *See also* Corn.

Sweet Cumin. Anise. *See* Aniseed.

Sweet-Curd Cheese. A hard-type cheddar made by a process in which the milk is set while sweet and the curd cooked firmer.

Sweeten. (1) To make something sweet by adding a sweet substance such as sugar. (2) To lessen the salty or acid taste of a dish by additional cooking, or by adding liquids, especially milk.

Sweetening. Any edible ingredient that sweetens food.

Sweet Fennel; Finochio; Florence Fennel. A sweet licorice-flavored variety of fennel, probably of Italian origin, with a texture similar to that of celery; its appearance is much like that of ordinary fennel, but it is only about half as large. It may be eaten raw or cooked. *See also* Fennel.

Sweet Flag. *See* Calamus.

Sweet Herbs. Herbs such as basil, marjoram, sage, thyme, and mint.

Sweetie-Laif (British). A Christmas cake.

Sweet Lime. A lime native to India and several other Asiatic countries; its flavor is mediocre, but the juice is used in making soft drinks.

Sweet Marjoram. *See* Marjoram.

Sweet Mash. A yeast process used in the United States for making whiskies. Almost all fresh yeast (practically no working yeast from a previous fermentation) is mixed with fresh mash and allowed to ferment about 40–50 hours.

Sweetmeats. Very sweet foods, such as candies, bonbons, candied fruits, etc.

Sweet Oil. Olive Oil.

Sweet Pepper. The very mild, sweet fruit of a particular pepper plant.

Sweet Potato. A trailing-vine plant found in warm climates in various parts of North and South America, grown for its edible roots. The pre-Columbian Indians raised this tasty food, and the Spanish explorers were much impressed by its unusual taste; they took it back to Europe on their return, where it was well received. Sweet potatoes are used much like white potatoes, although they are higher in sugar and caloric content. The flesh may be white, yellow, salmon- or orange-colored. Two types are generally brought to the market: one is light and yellow and has a dry finish; the other is deep orange, heavier-bodied, and has a sweeter, more moist finish. Most experts place the *yam*, a similar type of African tuberous root, in a different classification. As a rule, the public groups the three types in the same category, regarding them all as sweet potatoes.

Sweet potatoes may be boiled, glazed, baked, or fried. Candied sweet potatoes, especially those prepared with orange peel and juice, are classic preparations for Thanksgiving and other holidays. Sweet potatoes may also be prepared like mashed white potatoes. Sweet-potato pie, when prepared like pumpkin, has its adherents.

The sweet potato does not ordinarily keep well in most homes, requiring cool, dry storage at about 55°. Unless such conditions are available, only enough sweet potatoes for use within two or three days should be purchased.

Sweet Rush. *See* Calamus.

Sweets (British). Candy.

Sweetsop. The flavorsome pear-shaped fruit of a tropical plant of the same species as the soursop and custard apple. In the East and West Indies it is used for making pies and preserves and for certain drinks. Sometimes also called the sugar-sop.

Sweet Tooth. A fondness for candies and other sweet foods, such as cakes, ice cream, and other desserts.

Sweet Woodruff. *See* Woodruff, Sweet.

Swift. A swallow sometimes used as food.

Swig. (1) A good-sized drink. (2) To drink a great deal.

Swill. To drink deeply or a great deal.

Swine. Pigs and hogs.

Swiss Chard; Chard; Strawberry Spinach; White Beets. A beet whose leaves are used as a vegetable. The fleshy, firm leaves have a delicate taste when briefly cooked, but become bitter when overcooked. The white stems may be cut into strips or pieces and boiled. Very young chard leaves, with the stems removed, may be used in a mixed-green salad.

Swiss Fondue. A dish of melted cheese, white wine, and potato flour into which small pieces of bread are dunked.

Swiss Green Cheese. Sapsago or Schabziger cheese.

Swiss Roll. A thin spongecake rolled after baking and spread with jam or cream.

Swiss Steak. The less tender cuts of beef, and sometimes of veal or lamb, usually pounded, dipped lightly in flour, braised, and allowed to simmer until tender; served in its own gravy.

Swiss Tart. A Viennese tart; a pastry mixture piped through star-shaped tubes into custard cups and baked; when cool, topped with icing and filled with jam.

Swiss Tea. Any tea prepared with cinnamon.

Switched (Scotch). As applied to foods, whipped.

Switzerland. This tiny mountainous country was formed from segments of France, Germany, and Italy. To this day the languages of these countries are spoken to some extent throughout Switzerland. The national cuisine partakes of the culinary styles of those countries, although modified by the local cooks.

As for a national cookery style, it must be admitted that there is no truly Swiss cuisine. There are many interesting dishes, but no distinctive national style. Swiss food is "international," that is, a combination of the best and worst— dishes in cream sauce, bland food, routine desserts, and, in brief, the sort of food served in deluxe hotels all over the world. True Swiss dishes are served only at home.

Switzerland is usually identified with cheese. What Americans call "Swiss cheese" is known as *Emmentaler*; *Gruyère* is the same as Emmentaler but without holes. Many other cheeses are produced, but none is as famous as the two leading types. A local cheese called *Bagnes* is melted before an open fire and scraped onto a plate, then eaten with boiled potatoes; this is called *raclette*. Tiny individual tarts or pies, ramekins, are also made of cheese. Most famous of all is *fondue*, a mixture of grated cheese, white wine, and potato flour. Everyone dips small crusts of bread into the *fondue* with a fork and drinks white wine. Similar in name but made with meat is *fondue Bourguignonne*, in which individual bits of veal are cooked in oil piece by piece.

Sausages are very good indeed, and the country people eat them almost daily; *klopfer* is a mild sausage, and the *saucisse au foie* is really liverwurst. Sausages also appear in *piccata Luganese*, together with chicken livers and veal. The classic *Bernerplatte* consists of hot sauerkraut with sausages, steamed beef, ham, and potatoes. A few other Swiss specialties are worthy of note: *roesti*, a kind of home-fried-potato dish; *lebèrspiessli*, skewers of bacon and calf's liver; *geschentzeltes*, pieces of veal with a white-wine sauce; *bundnerfleisch*, thin slices of air-dried beef served as an appetizer and tasting something like Italian *prosciutto*.

Swiss beers are mediocre, to say the least. *Moscht* is a kind of apple cider which the Swiss like. The wines are of fair, not great, quality; they are drinkable within the country but do not ship well. *Dôle*, among the red wines, has a somewhat Burgundylike quality and is about the only pleasing red type. The whites are much better, and *Neuchâtel* and *Dezalay* are very good; *Fendant* also has its adherents.

A number of other liquors are produced in the country. *Kirsch*, or *kirschwasser*, is an excellent, clear, colorless, cherry brandy, and an interesting flavoring for cooking and with fruits. *Appensellerbitter* is a liqueur made with alpine roots, herbs, and flowers, and tastes accordingly. *Marc*, a highly alcoholic brandy, is somewhat crude but very potent.

Cakes and cookies are well made in Switzerland, each canton (province or district) featuring its own specialties. Swiss chocolates are smooth and rich and of an unusually creamy consistency. **Switzerland, The Wines of.** When the Romans conquered the territory they called Helvetia, they found the hardy warlike natives knew nothing of the fine skill of making wine. Without delay the tireless conquerors taught the Swiss to plant vines, cultivate them, and produce a respectable product. No wines created by the Swiss could compare with those of Rome, but the Swiss wines were pleasant to drink and helped the soldiers pass their years of duty away from their homeland.

In the twenty centuries that have gone by, the situation is still the same. The Swiss have yet to produce a great wine, or even an important one, but all travelers to this mountainous little country are pleased with a wide choice of satisfactory wines. It is surprising that vineyards can grow in this land of crags and snow-topped mountains, for the terrain would seem unsuitable for raising grapes. But the Swiss are determined and stubborn, and they cultivate their land under circumstances that a less hardy people would regard with despair. They manage to produce about 15 million gallons of wine a year; of this total about 3 million are red and the rest white. This is as it should be, for the reds are only passable (they are apt to be too heavy). But the whites have a pleasant suggestion of the light Rhine wines or those from Alsace.

These wines have never been successfully exported. They are low in alcoholic content, which means that they don't travel well. They arrive in foreign countries with much diminished flavor and sometimes with an unpleasant flat quality.

Some wine is made in each of the twenty-two cantons, but only three are of any importance: Vaud, Valais, and Neuchâtel.

Vaud has two important districts, La Côte and Lavaux. La Côte has vineyards in the villages of Luins, Begnins, and Fechy. Lavaux has excellent white wines, including those from Rivaz and Dezalay. (Two of the Dezalay are bottled under the vineyard names of Clos des Moines and Clos des Abbeyes.)

Valais is a versatile district with some very good (for Switzerland) red wine called Dôle, and a pleasing white wine called Fendant. The vineyard of the Bishop of Sion bottles a Fendant Spätlese that is delightful, far better than most Swiss wines. The Malvoisie, produced here, is a heavy sweet wine often called a "ladies' wine," the implication being that women prefer sweet wines. This region is also the source of several Rhine-wine types, notably the Johannisberg white. A Valais novelty is the Vin du Glacier, a wine prepared and stored at a very high altitude. Its taste is unusual and quite bitter.

Neuchâtel's product is unimportant, even in this land of "little" wines. It is usually pleasant but without much personality. The region also produces a champagne. (The less said . . . !) The local red wine is called Cortaillod and has a fruity and full-bodied flavor not completely dry.

In addition to the three principal wine-producing sections, the Ticino canton, near the Italian border, has a considerable volume of ordinary wines and a few whites, imitations of Italian wines. They are only adequate.

Swiss wines are best when not more than three or four years old. They are marketed under the name of the canton, sometimes under that of a local township, and very rarely under the label of a particular vineyard. The label seldom indicates the merit of the wine. If some bottles have a few bubbles, this does not mean that the wine has gone bad. The Swiss bottle their wines early, and a portion of the natural fermentation is imprisoned in the bottle. The process produces some carbon dioxide, which gives the wine a distinctive effervescent freshness.

Swizzle. An alcoholic drink stirred with a swizzle stick rather than shaken in a cocktail shaker.

Swizzle Stick. A small implement made to whisk the effervescence out of champagne; the use of a swizzle stick is a form of snobbism, for if one doesn't like the bubbles, why drink champagne?

Sword Bean. A broad, long Asiatic bean; when young, it may be eaten as a green vegetable.

Swordfish. A fish found in almost every sea and known to the ancient Greeks and Romans. It grows 7 feet or more in length and weighs several hundred pounds, but the flesh is delicate, white, and flaky. It may be prepared like tuna or mackerel.

Sword Razor; Razor Clam. Any of various kinds of bivalve mollusks with long, thin, curved shells; it can hide in the sand very quickly.

Sybo (Scotch). Green onions; scallions.

Sycamine. The black mulberry.

Sycamore Fig. The fruit of a tree native to Egypt and Syria.

Syes (Scotch). Chives.

Syllabub; Sillabub (Obsolete). An old drink made by mixing wine or cider with milk; also by mixing sweetened cream with wine and beating to a stiff froth. The wine must be used judiciously in order to prevent curdling. The drink may be topped with whipped cream just before serving.

Sylt (Swedish). Jam.

Sylte (Danish). Boiled meatballs.

Syltede Rødbeder (Danish). Pickled beets.

Sylteflesk (Norwegian). Headcheese.

Syltetøj (Danish). Jam.

Synthetic Rice; Tapioca-Macaroni (Indian). A mixture of tapioca flour, groundnut flour, and semolina shaped like rice grains; contains almost twice as much protein as milled rice.

Syra. An acid drink made from whey, prepared in Norway and Iceland.

Syracuse Wine. A rather crude dry white Sicilian wine.

Syria. The foods of Syria, Lebanon, and Jordan are quite similar, although there are a few local variations. Basically, however, these countries follow the general custom and food habits of neighboring Near East Arabic nations.

In Syria there is a great liking for *laban*, or yoghurt. When *laban* is drained of water it becomes *labanee*, a sort of white cheese. *Labanee* is usually eaten with a piece of the delicious local bread, *khobaz*, which is never cut with a knife but torn with the fingers. There are comparatively few *maza*, or appetizer dishes, and only a few soups, *shourabah*, usually made of lentils, chick-peas, or rice.

The classic meat dishes are almost always made of lamb. The favorite dish, probably the national choice, is *kibbe*, made of ground lamb and cracked wheat. When raw it is called *kibbe neeyee*, but it is also fried and baked or made into patties. Beef is occasionally served but pork very rarely. Vegetables are prepared with oil and are usually stuffed with rice or meat in the customary Near East fashion. Squash, eggplant, beans, peppers, cauliflower, and tomatoes are the everyday vegetables.

The Syrians are extremely fond of sweets. *Baklawa*, made of flaky pastry covered with nuts and syrup, is typical. *Knafee* is prepared from shredded wheat and soaked in a rich syrup, and greatly resembles a similar Turkish confection. However, there are dozens of different sweets made with fruits, dates, figs, and nuts.

Syrian Bread. A round flat bread; originally baked on an open hearth.

Syringe. An implement sometimes used by pastry makers to decorate confections.

Syrup; Sirup. A mixture of sugar from such sources as sorghum, corn, and maple, and a liquid, usually water, that is cooked until some of the liquid evaporates, leaving a sticky but pourable substance. Commercial syrups include light and dark corn syrup, pure maple, maple blends and flavors, and fruit flavors. Sugar syrups are used in baking and for icings. To prevent crystallization, the sugar and liquid are combined with a little cream of tartar and cooked over low heat, being stirred constantly until the sugar is dissolved. (Incompletely dissolved sugar results in failure.) The mixture is then cooked over medium heat to the desired consistency. The longer it cooks, the thicker it becomes. A candy thermometer will provide an accurate test as follows:

230°–234°—*Thread stage.* A little slightly cooled syrup will form a thread when rubbed between the fingers.

234°–240°—*Soft-ball stage.* A few drops of syrup dropped into cold water will form a soft ball. This is used for making mousses, etc.

244°–248°—*Firm-ball stage.* A few drops dropped into cold water forms a ball and retains its shape when removed.

250°–266°—*Hard-ball stage.* A few drops dropped into cold water forms a hard ball. This is used for some candies.

270°–290°—*Soft-crack stage.* A few drops dropped into cold water separates into hard but not brittle bits.

300°–310°—*Hard-crack stage.* A few drops dropped into cold water separates into hard, brittle bits.

320°—*Caramelized stage.* Syrup turns brown.

Szamorodni. A Tokay wine. *See* Hungary, The Wines of.

Szechuan. A Chinese province which tends to use spices and hot peppers in some of its dishes; however, many of the dishes are quite mild.

Szekely Cheese. A soft Hungarian ewe's-milk cheese encased in sausage skins.

Szilva. A dry Hungarian plum brandy.

T

Taårta (Swedish). Layer cake.

Taårta med Grädde (Swedish). Cake with whipped cream.

Tabasco, Pepper. *See* Pepper Tabasco.

Tabgle (Scotch). A seaweed eaten as a vegetable.

Table. (1) A raised surface at which people sit to dine. (2) The food or beverages served to a family or guests.

Tablecloth. A cloth, made of any of a wide range of materials; used to cover a table.

Table d'Hôte. In restaurants, a fixed price for all the courses of a meal, as opposed to *à la carte*, according to which each item ordered is paid for separately.

Tablee (Middle Eastern). A cold dish made of barley, chick-peas, and yoghurt.

Tablespoon. The largest spoon normally set at the table, being larger than a dessert spoon. As a standard cooking measurement, the tablespoon is equal to three teaspoons

Tablespoonful. The quantity contained by a tablespoon leveled off.

Tablet. A small flat solid, usually round, confection or sweet; a lozenge.

Tableware. Usually all the eating equipment placed on the table, including the knives, forks, spoons, and plates, and sometimes but not always glassware.

Table Waters. Bottled natural spring or mineral waters.

Table Wines. Light nonsweet red, white, and *rosé* wines, usually consumed with food at the table.

Tabn. A small piece of bread and butter.

Tabooleh (Middle Eastern). A salad of cracked wheat, mint, and parsley.

Taboon (Yemenite). A round primitive oven.

Tacaud; Monie Borgne; Officir. A variety of bony cod.

Tacchino (Italian). Turkey.

Tacchino alla Bolognese. Turkey, cheese, and ham in a thick sauce.

Tacchino Ripieno. Stuffed turkey.

Taccula (Italian). Blackbirds or thrushes baked in myrtle leaves.

Tâche, La. A dry Burgundy red wine of great delicacy and finesse; one of the world's greatest red wines. *See also* France, The Wines of.

Tack (British). Hard biscuits and breads.

Tacon (French). A young salmon.

Tadjin Ahmar (Arabic). Lamb, onions, and prunes heavily flavored with cinnamon and colored with saffron.

Taffaty Tarts (British). Small pastries with layers of apples, sugar, and spice.

Taffy; Toffee. A soft, chewy candy made with either molasses or brown sugar, sometimes with butter added, and various flavorings.

Tafia. (1) (West Indian) Ratafia, a syrupy, sweet liqueur made from cane sugar. (2) A strong brandy-flavored sauce served over puddings and other desserts.

Tagin Orz (Egyptian). Baked rice prepared with chicken livers.

Tagliarini (Italian). Very narrow egg noodles.

Tagliatelle (Italian). Wide, flat egg noodles.

Tagliatelle alla Piemontese. Flat noodles and truffles.

Tagliatelle Verdi. Flat green noodles (colored with spinach).

Taheeni; Taheneh (Arabic). Sesame-seed oil.

Tahiti. A tropical South Pacific island that features mostly French food. However, the native feast, called *tamaaraa* or *maa Tahiti*, consists of tropical foods such as baked bananas and yams, breadfruit, raw fish prepared with citrus juice, and roast young suckling pig.

Tahu (Indonesian). Bean cake.

Taiblet; Tablet (Scotch). A confection made of

sugar, cream, and various flavorings, chiefly cinnamon or clove.

Taillevent; Taillevant. A noted chef of 14th-century France who originated many preparations and wrote the cookbook *Le Viandier*; his real name was Guillaume Tisel.

Tailli-Kataif (Turkish). A sweet molded preparation served with a sweet sauce.

Tailloir; Tranchoir (French). The wooden platter or plate on which meat is cut. Originally, the slices of bread on which food was served and placed on pieces of wood. The same wood was used for every course and the bread discarded, or gathered up and saved for the poor.

Taja. An edible potatolike tuber native to Surinam.

Tajen (Jordanian). A baked dish made with ground beef and assorted vegetables.

Tajima. A Japanese breed of cattle whose meat is especially flavorsome and has an excellent texture. The cattle, slaughtered when young, are not allowed to toughen.

Tajure (Philippine). Fermented soybeans molded into small cakes.

Takenoko (Japanese). Bamboo shoots.

Taki Koji. An oriental malt used to make sake, a Japanese alcoholic beverage.

Talaba (Philippine). Oyster.

Talemeliers (French, Obsolete). In medieval times, the name by which bakers were known.

Talla (Ethiopian). A barley beer of fair quality.

Tallarines (Spanish). Noodles.

Tallegio. A superb soft, flavorsome Italian cheese something like Stracchino, but better.

Talleyrand, Charles Maurice, Marquis de (1754–1838). A French statesman, also the gastronomic expert who originated the eating of cheese with soup. His chef was Carême.

Talmouse. A tart with a cheese-custard filling; served as an appetizer or a dessert.

Talong (Philippine). Eggplant.

Tamaaraa. A native feast in Tahiti, consisting of many tropical foods, such as baked bananas and yams, raw fish prepared with citrus juices, coconuts, fresh fruits, breadfruit, etc. Roast young suckling pig is the main part of the meal. The foods are eaten without forks or knives; they are served on pieces of split bamboo or on banana leaves.

Tamal; Tamales (Mexican). Corn husks spread with *masa* (a ground cornmeal prepared with a lime solution), and wrapped around a spicy mixture, usually of meat. In Oaxaca, banana leaves are used instead of corn husks. Occasionally, sweet tamales are prepared. Tamales are prepared somewhat differently in various parts of Central and South America.

Tamalada. A Mexican party at which tamales are the principal food served.

Tamales Calientes (Mexican, Spanish). Hot tamales.

Tamalitos (Mexican). Miniature tamales, usually served with cocktails.

Tamara. (1) An Italian condiment consisting of crushed cloves, aniseed, cinnamon, coriander seed, and fennel. (2) An Algerian wine.

Tãmaras (Portuguese). Rolls (of food).

Tamarind; Tamarindo. A tropical tree whose fruit is often used for flavoring drinks or eaten raw. The term comes from the Arabic *tamrhindi*, the date of India. The tamarind has a taste similar to that of a plum, but slightly sour.

Tambour (French). (1) A fine-meshed sugar sieve. (2) A small dessert cooky.

Tamie. A kind of Port du Salut cheese made by Trappist monks in Savoy, France.

Tamil Keri (Malaysian). Curry.

Tamis (French). Tammy, a fine cloth used to strain soups and sauces.

Tamisé (French). Rubbed through a sieve or tammy.

Tamiser (French). To press through a fine sieve.

Tammy. A very fine cloth used to strain soups, sauces, etc.

Tan. Of dough, to toughen by kneading.

Tanche. A spring gold-skinned fish of poor quality found in muddy rivers in France.

Tandoori; Tanduri (Indian, Pakistani). (1) A method of barbecuing meat, poultry, or fish. Tanduri chicken with *nan*, a kind of bread, is a great specialty. (2) A simple roasting oven.

Tang. A strong, pungent, or persistent flavor, taste, or aroma associated with food.

Tangelo. A cross between a tangerine and a grapefruit.

Tangerine; Tangerine Orange. A small variety of orange, with a loose soft skin which can be removed easily; the fruit is segmented and quite sweet. Although it may have originated in China, the name derives from the city of Tangiers, Morocco, because the fruit was shipped to Europe from that port.

Tangerine Peel; Tangerine Shreds. Tangerine peel carefully trimmed of the white layer, cut into fine shreds, and dried in hot sunshine. Soaked in cold water, then boiled for a minute, it is used in small amounts for flavoring poultry in the Chinese cuisine.

Tangerinette. A tangerine-flavored French liqueur.

Tangiers. The generic term for oysters brought to market at Tangiers, or nearby points, in the Chesapeake Bay area of the United States.

Tangleberry. A fine-tasting, piquant wild huckleberry native to the eastern United States.

Tango Cocktail. A cocktail prepared with orange juice, gin, orange liqueur, and sweet and dry vermouth.

Tankard. A good-sized beer or ale mug with a handle and a hinged cover that helps prevent the escape of the natural effervescence.

Tannia; Tania. A tropical plant grown for its farinaceous, tuberous root.

Tannin; Tannic Acid. A nonnutritive substance found chiefly in tea, coffee, and red wine, but also in some fruits, nuts, and vegetation. It furnishes an astringent quality to the beverages.

Tansy. A perennial bitter, aromatic herb formerly used as a flavoring for beverages, especially herb teas; now used occasionally to flavor puddings.

Tansy Mustard. A bitter-leafed plant tasting much like cress; used in moderation in salads.

Tantalus. An arrangement in which two or more bottles (of liquor) may be locked so that they are visible but not accessible. In Greek mythology Tantalus was taken to the underworld and made to stand in water up to his chin, but when he tried to drink the water it ebbed away.

Tanzenburger. A sort of Limburger cheese made in Carinthia, Austria.

Tap. A bung or other stopper used to close or seal an opening in a wine or liquor cask.

Tapanda (French). Cured olives, crushed smooth, combined with olive oil and spices; a specialty of Provence.

Tapas (Spanish). Hors d'oeuvre or appetizers served with drinks.

Tapei. A lightly alcoholic drink of Borneo and neighboring islands of the South Pacific.

Tapenade (French). A sauce or spread, originated in Provence, consisting of pounded black olives, anchovies, capers, garlic, lemon juice, and oil; may be served with cold vegetables as a sauce or spread on toast as an hors d'oeuvre.

Tapioca. An important starchy food obtained by heating the manioc, or cassava root. Tapioca, although called by various names, is a widely-used staple food in many different tropical parts of the world. When cooked, it swells in size, becomes transparent, and has a pleasant taste.

  Tapioca, Pearl. Tapioca flour and water cooked a long time until hard-covered pellets are formed.

  Tapioca, Quick-Cooking. Pearl or natural tapioca which has been ground, and cooked tapioca dough that has been crushed, in order to break down the cellular structure and thus permit comparatively quick cooking.

Tapioca-Macaroni. *See* Synthetic Rice.

Tapir. An animal resembling a wild boar or pig; prepared like pork.

Tappit Hen (Scotch). A wine measure holding about 3 English quarts; sometimes made of dark green glass.

Tap Room. A place where beer or ale is sold.

Taproot. The main root of a plant.

Tarare, Fromage de. A small fresh skim-milk cheese, made from cow's milk around Lyons, France.

Taratour (Arabic). A sesame sauce.

Tarbot (Dutch). Turbot.

Tari. A liquor made from the sap of palm trees in certain Pacific islands.

Taro. A starchy tropical root used as a basic food in the South Pacific.

Tarpon. A rather tasteless game fish found in the waters around Florida.

Tarragon. A bright green herb with long narrow leaves; it has a mild licorice flavor and should be used sparingly. Covered with vinegar and sealed, it retains its fresh flavor, and after being rinsed in cold water can be used like the fresh herb. It is essential for Béarnaise sauce and is a fine flavoring for chicken and omelets.

Tarragon Vinegar. An infusion of tarragon leaves in vinegar.

Tart. (1) Having a sour, acid taste. (2) An open-face pastry filled with fruits. (3) (British) Any fruit pie.

Tartare, À la. (1) As applied to breaded fried foods, accompanied by a highly seasoned sauce. (2) Raw chopped lean steak served with a raw egg and condiments. (3) A mayonnaise sauce flavored with herbs, capers, pickles, etc.

Tartaren (German). Raw chopped meat.

Tartarenbrote (German). Raw-meat sandwich.

Tartaric Acid. An acid present in many fruits and prepared commercially from fruits and the lees of wine. Bottlers and packers of many foods and beverages use it to add acidity or effervescence.

Tartar Sauce. Mayonnaise combined with chopped olives, capers, pickles, chives, and lemon juice; usually served with fried or broiled fish and shellfish.

Tarte aux Morilles (French). Puff pastry made with morels in a seasoned cream sauce.

Tarte Bourbonnaise (French). A sweet cheese-cake; a specialty of Burgundy.

Tarteletas (Spanish). Small tarts.

Tartelette (French). A tartlet; a small thin round or oval pastry filled with fruit or a sweet mixture.

Tartine (French). (1) Sandwich with meat or other mixtures. (2) Toast covered with pâté or other spread on which game birds are served.

Tartlets. Small cuplike pastry shells usually filled with fruit or custard.

Tartouffes (French). Potatoes.

Tartufi (Italian). Truffles.

Tartufo di Cioccolato (Italian). A dessert made of chocolate ices or ice cream and containing small pieces of chocolate.

Tasmania. A small island off the south coast of Australia, known best for its fish and game. Especially flavorsome are the local scallops, which are excellent.

Tassau (Haitian). A veal cutlet made with orange and lemon juice.

Tasse (German). Cup.

Taste. The sensation by which a human being evaluates various flavors, such as sweet, sour, bitter, and salt.

Taste Buds. Irregularly arranged cells in the lining of the mouth and on the tongue by which flavors are distinguished.

Taster. One who tastes food or liquor professionally; an expert who can judge the relative qualities of wines, teas, coffees, etc.

Taste-Vin (French). A cup or small flat container used for wine-tasting, usually made of silver or silver plate.

Tasty. Pleasing to the taste.

Tattie (Scotch). Potato.

Tauben (German). Pigeons.

Taufolo Niu (Samoan). Roasted breadfruit mashed smooth and shaped into balls with coconut cream.

Taupo Trout. A delicate-flavored New Zealand trout of the rainbow group.

Tausi (Philippine). Fermented soybeans, much used in local cookery.

Tautog. The blackfish.

Tavá. A lamb, rice, and vegetable stew popular on the island of Cyprus.

Tavel. A wine region in the Rhône area of France that produces a *rosé* wine with a pleasing color and fruity taste. *See also* France, The Wines of.

Tavern. A place where alcoholic beverages are sold and served; a saloon.

Taverna (Greek). A small friendly restaurant where it is customary before ordering to go into the kitchen and examine the dishes being prepared.

Taviers. A quite small aromatic goat cheese made in Périgord, France.

Tavola Fredda (Italian). Cold buffet.

Tawa (Indian). A somewhat concave iron disk about 9 inches in diameter, similar to a griddle; used for making chapati (whole-meal bread).

Tawntatalet (Turkish). A rice-and-chicken dish sweetened with sugar and caramel.

Tawny Grisette. A brownish or grayish fair-tasting mushroom about 3 inches across the top.

Tawny Port. A yellow-brown port. *See* Portugal, The Wines of.

Taworog. A Russian medium-firm sour-milk cheese.

Tazukuri (Japanese). Small dried sardines.

Tazza (Italian). Cup.

T-Bone Steak. A tender steak, cut from the center of the short loin, which has a T-shaped bone and a small tenderloin.

Te (Swedish). Tea.

Té (Spanish). Tea.

Tè (Italian). Tea.

Tea. A hot or cold beverage prepared from the tender leaves, leaf buds, and internodes of various varieties of the tea plant, *Camellia sinensis*, an evergreen native to Asia. It is more widely-used than coffee, and is second only to water as the most important beverage in the world. No one knows who discovered the value and use of tea, but it is generally credited to the Chinese Emperor Shennung about 2,700 B.C. It first reached England during the early 17th century A.D. and soon became popular. The chief tea-production countries are China, Japan, India, Indonesia, Ceylon, and Formosa.

The leaves are picked by hand during active periods of growth—called flushes—and are then dried, rolled, and fired or heated. For black tea, the leaves are fermented about 24 hours before drying. For green tea, which is light-colored and has more tannin than black tea, the leaves are only steamed and dried. Oolong is a sort of compromise between green and black tea, for the leaves are only oxidized or fermented slightly, resulting in a green-brown finish. The best-known black teas are Souchong and Pekoe. Flowering Pekoes are made from the top leaf buds, Orange Pekoe from the first opened leaf, Pekoe from the third leaves, and Souchong from the next leaves. Imperial Hyson and Gunpowder are popular green teas. Various aromatic flowers or herbs are occasionally added; probably jasmine is the most liked additive.

The flavor of tea is produced by volatile oils; the stimulant comes from caffeine; the astringency is furnished by tannin. Tea has no caloric value, but does contain Vitamin B. Tea is best prepared from loose tea, but most Americans use tea bags. A comparatively recent development is the so-called instant tea, in which boiled water is added to powdered tea.

Tea, Brick. In Russia, tea is often pressed into rectangles for convenience.

Tea, Instant. Very finely powdered tea, to which boiling water is added.

Tea Bag. A small paper or cloth container usually holding just enough to make one cupful. When the tea has reached the desired strength, the bag is removed by means of the fine cord attached to it.

Tea Ball. A ball-shaped perforated metal container used to hold tea during steeping.

Teaberry; Checkerberry; Wintergreen. A familiar herb, picked during the autumn when it is red; its dried leaves are mixed with tea leaves or prepared alone as a tea.

Tea Bread (Scotch). Another name for cakes and fancy buns.

Tea Caddy. A jar, canister, or box for storing tea.

Tea Cart. A small wagon or a miniature table on wheels used in serving tea, cakes, etc.

Tea Ceremony. A classic Japanese ceremony, called *cha-no-yu* and based upon Zen principles; an esthetic presentation of the beauties and pleasure of making tea.

Tea Classic. *See* Cha Ching.

Teacup. A rounded container, usually made of china, for drinking tea, coffee, etc.

Teacupful. About 4–4½ ounces, the capacity of the average teacup.

Teakettle. A metal container designed for boiling water quickly.

Teakettle Broth (Obsolete). Various thin broths that require boiling water from the teakettle.

Teal. A delicate-flavored waterfowl of the duck family; usually served roasted, one bird serving two.

Tea Melon. A Chinese cucumber pickle, used like pickles or other condiments.

Teapot. A container, often made of china, with a handle, spout, and cover, used for making and pouring tea.

Tearoom. A place where light meals are served; patronized largely by women. The term has a somewhat derogatory connotation.

Teaseed Oil. Oil prepared from the teaseed nut. Chemically similar to olive oil, but used as an adulterant.

Teaspoon. A spoon commonly served at the table for use with coffee or tea. It is a standard cookery measurement, 3 teaspoons of an ingredient equaling 1 tablespoon.

Tea Strainer. A small round strainer with a spoon-type handle to catch the leaves while tea is being poured through it.

Teawurst. A type of delicately flavored veal sausage, usually lightly smoked.

Tebrød (Norwegian). Teacake.

Te-Complet (Danish). Bread, cake, and tea.

Tedj; Taidge (Ethiopian). A honey drink.

Tee (German). Tea.

Teel Oil. Sesame oil.

Teems (British). A sifting or dredging vessel used for dusting with flour, sugar, or other powder.

Teetotaler. One who abstains from drinking alcoholic beverages.

Teff. (1) An Ethiopian grain whose small seeds are used to make a flour from which *injera,* a coarse bread, is prepared. (2) A type of crude beer.

Teg. A two-year-old sheep.

Teiggemüse (German). Macaroni dishes.

Teiglach (Jewish). Balls of dough cooked in honey and assembled in a mound with nuts.

Tekaka (Swedish). Crumpet.

Teleme. A Balkan sheep's-milk cheese resembling Brinza.

Teller (German). Plate.

Tellerfleisch. An Austrian between-meal snack, served in a large soup plate, containing beef consommé, boiled vegetables, marrow, and some partly cooked boiled beef.

Tellicherry Pepper. An excellent black pepper from the Tellicherry region of India.

Telor Asin (Indonesian). Salted, preserved duck eggs.

Teltower Rübchen (German). Baby turnips cooked in sugar.

Tembleque (Puerto Rican). A pudding made with coconut milk and cornstarch.

Tembo (East African). A rather strong alcoholic beverage prepared with green banana and fermented for several months.

Temple Orange. A thick-skinned sweet orange that segments easily.

Tems Loaf (British). Bread made from finely sifted flour.

Tenareze. A district in Armagnac, France, which produces a fairly good type of brandy.

Tench. A freshwater fish similar to but smaller than the carp.

Tendergreen. A type of wild vegetable green; mustard spinach.

Tenderloin. A cut of beef or pork, especially a tender portion.

Tenderometer. An instrument that measures the stage of maturity of peas to determine whether they are ready for canning.

Tendon. The tough inelastic sinews by which muscles are attached to bones; they are cut away by the butcher or the cook.

Tendret, Lucien. A well-known French jurist and gastronome of the 19th century who published *La Table au Pays de Brillat-Savarin.*

Tendron (French). (1) Gristle or tendon. (2) The piece from the breast of veal or lamb containing the gristle.

Tenmarq Wheat. A high-quality hard winter wheat.

Tent (Obsolete). Very sweet Spanish wines.

Tenthidid. The barber fish or barber sturgeon.

Tepary Bean. A small edible bean of fair quality grown in the southern United States and Mexico because it can withstand extreme heat and drought.

Tepid. Lukewarm.

Tequeños (Venezuelan). Fried cheese strips; served with drinks.

Tequezquite (Mexican). Saltpeter; used chiefly for increasing the "lift," or air, in dough.

Tequila (Mexican). A clear colorless potent liquor made from the fermented juice of a cactus plant called *pulque*; usually served very cold. It is customary to take a sip, then lick a little coarse salt from the top of the hand and suck a wedge of lime.

> **Tequila Sour.** A Mexican drink made of tequila, lemon juice, sugar, and bitters.

Terasi (Indonesian). Shrimp paste.

Terce. *See* Tierce.

Terfez; Terfezia. A large white African truffle without much flavor; generally eaten raw in salad, but may be prepared like the black truffle. It is sometimes dried and used like a mushroom.

Terhonya (Hungarian). A type of spaghetti.

Termeno. *See* Italy, The Wines of.

Ternera (Spanish). Veal.

Terrapin. A small North American freshwater (sometimes tidewater) turtle; used in stews, chowders, and soups.

Terrine. (1) A pâté, prepared in an earthenware baking dish, usually consisting of ground veal, pork, and strips or cubes of game, liver, and truffles highly seasoned and flavored with liquor or wine. (2) The baking dish itself.

Terzolo. An Italian Parmesan-type cheese made during cold-weather months.

Testa Sausage. A rather coarse pork sausage, originally Italian; may be eaten without cooking.

Teste (Nicaraguan). A chocolate-flavored beverage made with roasted corn.

Tête-à-Tête (French). As applied to two people dining together, seated face to face. *Côte-à-côte* means "seated side by side."

Tête à Tête (French). The French term for Dutch Edam cheese.

Tête d'Aloyau (French). Butcher's term for the part of beef forming the end of the rump.

Tête de Cuvée (French). The wine obtained by natural pressure, before the use of a wine-press.

Tête de Moine (French). Monk's-head cheese; a soft, rich cheese shaped into a "head."

Tête de Porc (French). A pig's head; used mostly for its gelatinous qualities or in preparing head-cheese; it is also boiled and served with sauer-kraut.

Tête de Veau (French). Calf's head; usually boiled and served cold with any desired sauce. The classic style is *à la vinaigrette*, with capers, onions, an oil-vinegar dressing, and chopped hard-cooked egg.

Tetine Sautée (French). Boiled cow's udder sliced and fried.

Tetragonia. A New Zealand spinach.

Tetra Pack (British). Square cartons used to pack milk and other beverages.

Tétras (French). A large grouse or prairie chicken with excellent meat.

Texel. A routine sheep's-milk cheese made in Texel, the Netherlands.

Thailand. A century ago the Siamese ate only a midday meal and another meal in the late evening; at the turn of the century a refreshment repast, *krüang wang*, came into popularity, usually being served about three in the afternoon. In postwar years breakfast was introduced, and the three o'clock refreshment has generally been replaced by afternoon tea. Of course, in the countryside, most people adhere to the old customs, eating but two meals a day, with frequent between-meal nibbling of small snacks.

Arak, made from rice or from palm sap, is a favorite drink; there is also a kind of rice whisky called *mekong*. The cuisine of Thailand has been influenced by both China and India. Food is often cut into bite-size pieces in the Chinese fashion; the Indian influence is evidenced by the liking for curries, *kaeng phed*, and spicy foods. Often all the dishes served at a meal are placed on the table at the same time, and thus soup, *kaeng chüd*, may appear with the main course. Salads, *yams*, are extremely popular, and there are many different kinds, some made with fish and meat; the salad "green" may consist of rose petals, *khachorn* flowers, or other equally exotic ingredients. The typical desserts might include the Western equivalent of puddings, made from rice or cassava flour, taro, or tapioca. Desserts are frequently liquid, often of coconut milk or of *saton*, the wood apple.

No discussion of Siamese food could overlook the favorite sauce condiments used regularly on many different foods. *Nam prik* usually does not appeal to Western palates; it is generally made from dried shrimps, garlic, and hot chilies, and has a creamy texture. Just as there are many different types and kinds of *nam prik*, there are many recipes for making *lŏn*, although it is most often made from shellfish, with chili peppers, lemon grass, and garlic; *lŏn* is usually served with fish or vegetables.

Thallus. A plant, such as the mushroom, that does not have the normal arrangement of stem, leaves, and roots. The plural form is *thalli*.

Thann. A type of short dark sausage made in Strasbourg, France.

Thard Cake (British, Scotch). A thin round molasses-and-oatmeal cake.

Thatcher Wheat. A widely grown Canadian

spring wheat that is of good quality and strength and is rust-resistant.

Thee (Dutch). Tea.

Theine. Caffeine, the active principle of tea.

Thermos Bottle. The trade mark for an insulated bottle that keeps foods or liquids hot or cold for several hours.

Thiamine. A very complex compound found in yeast and cereals that aids in maintaining health.

Thickening. Liaison, the process or the substance that gives body to a gravy, a sauce, or to other liquid food; usually brought about by the use of flour, cornstarch, arrowroot, or egg yolks.

Thick Tea. Any tea having flavor, color, and strength.

Thick Yeast. Brewer's yeast with the bulk of the wort removed.

Thimbleberry. A wild red berry native to the western United States; eaten fresh or used in cooking.

Thin Tea. Weak tea that lacks ·body and color.

Thion. A Swiss variety of Emmentaler cheese.

Thiviers, Fromage de. A small rather strong goat's-milk cheese made in Périgord, France.

Thodden (British). Unbaked dough.

Thoissey, Fromage de. A goat's-milk cheese made in Bresse, France; at its best from April to September.

Tholy. A sharp-flavored Camembert produced in the Vosges region of France.

Thon (French). Tuna fish.

Thon à la Provençale. Tuna fish fried in olive oil with anchovies, onions, tomatoes, garlic, and herbs.

Thon Mariné. Pickled tuna fish.

Thonine. A variety of tuna fish.

Thonné (French). A method of preparing veal by marinating it before cooking in herbs, spices, and olive oil.

Thounina (French). In the Languedoc region, a small tuna fish.

Thourins; Tourin (French). Onion soup; differs from traditional onion soups by being thickened with beaten egg yolks and cream.

Thousand Island Dressing. Mayonnaise combined with chopped capers, chili sauce, and parsley.

Three Counties. A routine Irish cheese resembling cheddar.

Thrush. A family of medium-size wild birds, some of which are considered excellent eating.

Thumb Bits. Bite-size tasty mouthfuls of bread or toast with savory spreads; similar to hors d'oeuvre.

Thunder and Lightning (British). Bread with cream and molasses.

Thunder Pumper. Another name for the freshwater drumfish, a food fish.

Thunfisch (German). Tuna fish.

Thunfiski Tomatsauce (Danish). Tuna fish in tomato sauce.

Thuringer Sausage. Summer sausage or dried cervelat.

Thyme. A very pungent aromatic herb of the mint family; to be used sparingly in soups, stews, stuffing, etc. There are over 100 varieties, ranging widely in color; some species are better as a seasoning agent, others are used for making thyme oil.

Thymus. A medium-size gland near the base of the neck in animals; calf thymus is called *sweetbread* and is used for food.

Tia Maria. A Jamaican afterdinner drink with a coffee taste.

Tian (French). (1) A low flat type of casserole used in Provence for preparing vegetable or gratin dishes. (2) The vegetable or gratin preparation itself. (3) A tart filled with young vegetables, pine seeds, and sometimes raisins; a specialty of Nice.

Tidbit; Titbit. Any small pleasing food delicacy.

Tierce (British). A 42-gallon cask in which many foods are packed and sold to the food industry.

Tiered Plinth. A presentation stand for confections, formerly made of wood in several tiers and fancifully decorated. The modern plinth is usually made from sandwich bread.

Tiger Lilies; Golden Needles. Golden flowers that retain their color when dried; often cooked with meat or poultry.

Tiger's Milk. (1) A milklike fortified drink marketed as a health food. (2) An alcoholic beverage.

Tignard. A very firm salty blue-veined sheep's- or goat's-milk cheese made in Savoy, France.

Tilapi (African). Small excellent-tasting freshwater fish.

Ti Leaves (South Pacific). A leaf used in cooking much as banana leaves are used, that is, to hold food in place during the cooking process.

Tilefish. A name given to several different types of American fish, of passable quality.

Tilleul. The lime tree, whose dried flowers are used to make a sort of tea.

Tilsit; Ragnit. A German whole-milk cheese with numerous small holes; a sort of cross between Port du Salut and Brick cheese.

Tilslørte Bondepiker (Norwegian). Bread pudding.

Tilt-Pot. An old way of tilting a pot on the stove by inserting a small piece of iron of the desired thickness under one side.

Timbale. (1) A puff-pastry shell, deeper than a pie shell, filled with meat, poultry, or a sweet mixture. (2) A cooking utensil made of metal or ceramic, made to look like a timbale, a pastry crust.

Timbale à Soufflé. A soufflé dish, generally not very large, used for making soufflés.

Timbale Case. A shaped dough mixture, usually prepared on a special iron, fried in deep fat. The cases are then filled with any desired mixture.

Timbale Iron. A long-handled metal utensil with a small cup at one end, used for making timbale cases by dipping the cup first into batter and then into hot fat.

Timberberry. An Alaskan edible wild berry.

Timer. A device that can be set for a definite period of time and signals the lapse of that time. Modern ranges have built-in timers, but separate spring-driven timers are available. A timer is important in many cooking steps, particularly in baking.

Timo (Italian). Thyme.

Tinamou. A South American bird similar to a partridge; prepared like pheasant.

Tinapa (Philippine). Smoked fish.

Tinola (Philippine). A garlic-flavored chicken soup.

Tinplate. Pressed iron covered with tin, a material formerly used in certain cooking utensils and implements.

Tinta. A dark-colored rough Madeira wine similar to Burgundy.

Tinumis; Dinuguan (Philippine). Any dish cooked in chicken's or pig's blood.

Tinware. Kitchen or household utensils, such as baking pans, made of tin. Tinware has been largely replaced by aluminumware.

Tipparees. The fruit of the Cape gooseberry of South Africa, somewhat like the winter cherry; often used in jams and jellies.

Tipsy Cake. A cake saturated in wine or liquor.

Tipsy Pudding. Any pudding containing wine or liquor.

Tiré (French). Pulled, as pulled sugar.

Tirijala (Puerto Rican). A molasses taffy.

Tisane (French). A medicinal tea or infusion made from herbs, such as camomile, lime blossoms, fennel seeds, etc.; believed to have a sedative effect.

Tisane de Champagne. A champagne lighter than the ordinary type.

Tischweine (German). Ordinary wine of poor quality. The term is used in a derogatory way.

Tisdagssoppa (Swedish). Tuesday soup; made of vegetables and barley.

Tiste. A drink made in El Salvador from pulverized cocoa, dried corn, cold water, sugar, and cracked ice.

Tivela. The three-angled clam, an excellent-tasting clam.

Tjempedak. An Indonesian fruit.

Toad-in-the-Hole (British). Meat baked in batter.

Toalie (British, Scotch). A small round oatmeal pancake.

Toast. (1) A slice of bread partly dried and browned by heat. (2) A person, institution, or sentiment in whose honor people raise their glasses and drink. The term derives from the medieval custom of adding small pieces of browned bread to drinks.

Toaster. An electric appliance used for toasting bread. Toasters are available with vertical or horizontal toasting units and toast both sides of the bread at once. Most models are automatic. Horizontal models are useful for toasting muffins, bagels, and thick slices of bread.

Toasting Fork. A long-handled fork used to hold foods over a fire.

Toasting Rack. A vertical metal frame that supports a vertical grid over a burner; used to toast bread.

Toastmaster. A person, usually at a large dinner, who proposes toasts and also presides at the repast.

Tobago. *See* Trinidad.

Tocane. New champagne from the first pressing of the grapes; fresh grape juice.

Tocco, Il. *See* Il Tocco.

Tocineta (Spanish). Bacon.

Tocino (Spanish). Bacon, pork, salt pork.

Toddy. (1) A drink prepared with whisky and hot water, and sugar. Sometimes brandy or other liquor is used. (2) In tropical countries, a crude liquor prepared from the sap of certain palm trees.

Toddy Palm. *See* Toddy (2).

Toetje (Dutch). Desserts.

Toey. A Siamese leaf used for flavoring food.

Toffee. *See* Taffy.

Toffy (British). *See* Taffy.

Tofu (Japanese). A somewhat firm curd obtained from soybeans; much used in oriental countries. The soybeans are ground and soaked; then made into a paste, boiled, and strained. Various solutions are added to coagulate the curd, and it is molded.

Togue (Philippine). The young sprouts of mongo beans or peas.

Toheroa. A giant New Zealand green clam; best when made into a soup.

Tokanem. A crude rum or strong liquor made in the Malagasy Republic.

Tokány (Hungarian). Meat stew similar to a goulash but with the meat cut in somewhat smaller pieces.

Tokay. A rich sweet Hungarian dessert wine. *See* Hungary, The Wines of.

Tokua (Philippine). The curd prepared from soybeans.

Tom. The male of various animals and birds, such as tom turkey.

Tomalley. The liver of a lobster often incorporated in the sauces served with lobster.

Tom and Jerry. A hot frothy alcoholic drink made with beaten egg yolks, stiffly beaten egg whites, rum, sugar, boiling water, bourbon, and spices; served in mugs with a sprinkling of nutmeg.

Tomat (Danish). Tomato.

Tomate (Portuguese, French, Spanish). Tomato.

Tomates (French). Tomatoes. *Tomates Concassées* are skinned, chopped tomatoes. A *Concentré* is similar to a tomato purée. A *Confiture de Tomates* is somewhat less concentrated than a concentré.

Tomates, Fondue de. Cooked tomatoes with spices and onions.

Tomate Verde (Mexican). Green tomato; a rather small, acid vegetable resembling the tomato; used principally in making sauces.

Tomatillo (Mexican). A small red-yellow-green fruit resembling a miniature tomato. It may be made into a preserve or jam, or prepared like a sauce to serve with meats. It is often sold in small cans.

Tomato. Technically a fruit, it is usually used as a vegetable. An annual plant of the nightshade family, it is native to South America and was brought to Europe by the Spanish explorers. High

in vitamins A and C, tomatoes grow shaped like globes, cherries, plums, or pears. They may be red, yellowish, or green. Beefsteak tomatoes are especially fine and firm-fleshed. Green tomatoes are delicious when fried. They should be purchased only when firm, plump, and unblemished, regardless of type. The small cherry tomatoes may be served as an hors d'oeuvre. Large tomatoes may also be broiled and baked. They are canned in several forms, and made into tomato juice, stewed, puréed, and as paste. Canned Italian plum tomatoes are also packed with tomato paste. Tomatoes are used in almost every style of cooking around the world.

Tomato Juice. The juice of tomatoes, sometimes plain, often with spices added.

Tomato Paste. Tomatoes and their juice, boiled

down to a concentrate, then strained. Used particularly in Italian cooking.

Tomato-Strawberry. A Mexican and Mediterranean fruit that resembles a tomato but tastes like a strawberry; used for preserve or jelly.

Tomatsaft (Norwegian). Tomato juice.

Tomatsås (Swedish). Tomato sauce.

Tomber (French). To cook meat without liquid, allowing the moisture in the meat to "fall down" into the cooking pan and form a "sauce."

Tomber à Glace (French). To reduce a liquid to look like a glaze or thick syrup.

Tomber, Faire (French). To glaze or lightly color a food by cooking in butter.

Tomcod. *See* Cod.

Tom Collins. An alcoholic drink prepared with gin, lemon juice, sugar, and sparkling water; served very cold in a tall glass, usually with a garnish of fruit.

Tome; Tomme; La Tomme. A wide range of cheeses made from cow's, goat's, or sheep's milk in the Alps region of France, particularly near Savoy.

Tome de Savoie. A high-quality soft-textured cow's- or goat's-milk cheese made in Savoy France.

Tomillo (Spanish). Thyme.

Tom Yum Gai (Siamese). A highly spiced soup made with chicken and soy sauce.

Tong (Dutch). Fillet of sole; beef tongue.

Tongs. A kind of pincers, consisting of a small

piece of hinged or pivoted metal, used for lifting sugar, ice cubes, and certain hot foods.

Tongue. The tongue of calf, beef, or lamb, which is good eating. Calf's and lamb's tongues are usually sold fresh; beef tongues are available fresh, smoked, or pickled. As a rule, tongue should be cooked with low or moderate heat, since high heat tends to toughen the connective tissue.

Tongue Cress. Another name for garden cress.

Tonic Water. Carbonated table water containing quinine; used as a mixer, particularly with gin.

Tonijn (Dutch). Tuna.

Tonka Bean. A South American edible aromatic bean, sometimes used as a substitute for the vanilla bean in imitation-vanilla flavorings.

Tonkatsu (Japanese). Batter-dipped slices of pork fried crisp; generally served with shredded cabbage.

Tonno (Italian). Tuna fish.

    Tonno in Crema. Creamed tuna fish.

    Tonno sott' Olio. Tuna fish in olive oil.

Toothpicks. Small thin pointed pieces of wood or plastic, used to spear foods; also used to remove food particles from the teeth.

Topepo. A cross between a red pepper and a tomato.

Toper. One who drinks alcoholic beverages excessively.

Topinambour (French). The Jerusalem artichoke.

Topínky (Czechoslovakian). Slices of dark bread fried with garlic.

Topping. Icing or whipped cream, nuts or fruits for a cake, bread crumbs or cheese for a casserole, or any ingredient that is poured, sprinkled, or spread on top of foods.

Top of Rump. A piece of beef taken from the rump.

Tops-and-Bottoms (British). A rusk-dough biscuit suitable for babies.

Toque. A small hot pastry filled with a *pâté* of game, goose liver, and truffles.

Toque Blanche (French). The tall white hat worn by a chef.

Toranja (Portuguese). Grapefruit.

Tordi allo Spiedo (Italian). Small birds roasted on a spit.

Toro. The cavalla, a food fish.

Torpedo. A fish similar to the skate.

Torrada (Portuguese). Toast.

Torrefy. To roast; to dry out.

Torre Giulia. A dry white aromatic wine from Puglia, Italy.

Torrone (Italian). A nougat made with almonds and honey.

Torsk (Danish, Norwegian, Swedish). Codfish.

Torsk, Kogt (Danish). Boiled cod.

Torskerogn (Danish). Codfish roe.

Torsk Paa Fat (Norwegian). Baked codfish.

Torta (Italian). Cake; pie; tart.

> **Torta di Noci.** Nut tart.
>
> **Torta di Risi.** A rich, creamy rice pudding often made with candied fruit.

Torta Bejarana (Central and South American). A pudding made of spongecake, white cheese, butter, plantains, and brown-sugar syrup.

Torta Pasqualina (Italian). Pocket of dough stuffed usually with cheese, vegetables, and eggs.

Tortas de Carne (Spanish). Meat patties.

Törtchen (German). Little tart; small pastry dessert.

Torte. Very rich cakes, of European origin, usually made with many eggs, nuts or chocolate or fruits, and with little or no flour; also sometimes made of meringue. Tortes are usually iced or covered with whipped cream.

Tortellata alla Crema (Italian). Cream tart.

Tortellini alla Bolognese (Italian). Small dough pockets stuffed usually with chopped chicken and sausage meat.

Tortera (Spanish). A kind of pastry.

Tortilha de Mariscos (Portuguese). Pancake or omelet filled with shellfish.

Tortilla (Mexican). A thin pancake made of mashed corn and baked on a griddle. Used like bread, it is a basic, staple food. Tortillas are available frozen and canned.

Tortilla (Spanish). Omelet.

> **Tortilla à la Española.** (1) Potato omelet. (2) An omelet served with a tomato sauce.
>
> **Tortilla con Jamón.** Ham omelet.
>
> **Tortilla de Huevos.** Plain omelet.

Tortina (Italian). Artichoke omelet.

Tortitas (Spanish). Pancakes.

Tortoise Broth. A broth made from the common tortoise, although tortoise flesh is not considered edible.

Tortue (French). (1) Turtle. (2) A brown sauce made of tomatoes, butter, shallots, pimiento, ham, and Madeira wine.

Tortue Fausse (French). Mock turtle.

Torula. Microscopic fungi cells that reproduce by gemmation, as in yeasts.

Toscano. An Italian sheep's-milk cheese; much like Romano but softer.

Toss. To lift lightly and flip over with a fork and spoon or with two spoons foods such as salad ingredients.

Tostada (Spanish). Toast.

Tostadas (Mexican). Tortillas fried very crisp and sometimes covered with various foods or garnished.

Tostaditas; Totopos (Mexican). Tortillas cut into sections and fried until crisp.

Tostones (Central and South American). Fried plantain flattened down and refried.

Tot (French). A small liquid measure, usually used for alcoholic beverages.

Totani (Italian). Small Mediterranean squid.

Totelots (French). Thin squares of pastry covers with a spicy oil-and-vinegar sauce; served on Good Friday in Briey.

Tôt-Fait (French). (1) (Colloquial) A pancake. (2) A cake similar to a pound cake.

Totopos Tostaditas (Mexican). Small sections of tortilla fried in deep fat; sometimes, round tortillas fried crisp.

Töttchen (German). A spicy meat stew.

Totuava. The ocean bass, a food fish.

Touareg. A primitive dry, crumbly skim-milk cheese made by the Touaregs in France.

Toucinho (Portuguese). Bacon; fat pork.

Touffe (French). Stalks or leaves tied in a bunch.

Toulonnaise Sauce (French). A sauce made with onions, chopped gherkins, white wine, capers, and olives.

Touloumisio. A white crumbly astringent Greek cheese.

Toulouse, À la (French). Usually indicating a rich white stew of veal or chicken, truffles, mushrooms, etc.; used for filling pastry crust, *vol-au-vent* and *bouchées,* or for garnishing.

Toulousaine, À la (French). With or containing butter, oranges, garlic, or duck pâté, cocks' combs, kidneys, sweetbreads, mushrooms, and truffles.

Toupi (French). An earthenware cooking pot with a glazed interior; commonly used in the Béarn region.

Toupin (French). (1) A type of small casserole, distinguished by its high, raised, narrow sides; used chiefly for bean dishes in the Béarn region. (2) A semisoft cow's-milk cheese made in the Savoy region of France.

Touraine. A region of France noted for its fine cooks and excellent dry wines.

Tourd. A Mediterranean fish of the wrasse family.

Tour de Feuilletage (French). The turns and rollings given to pastry to make it flaky.

Tourin (French). A rich onion soup thickened with egg yolks.

    Tourin Bordelais. A peasant-style garlic or onion soup made in the Bordeaux region.

    Tourin Périgourdin. Onion soup made with egg yolks, tomatoes, etc., in the Périgord region.

Tour-La-Reine. A Greek dry white wine.

Tourné (French). Curdled; soured; shaped.

Tourne-Bride (French, Obsolete). A country inn near a great house where the servants of the château guests were housed. Some modern restaurants still like to use the name.

Tournebroche (French). A revolving spit; a turning device for roasting meats.

Tournedos (French). Very small, thin slices of beef fillet weighing about 3 ounces; prepared in dozens of different fashions. For example: *Barigoule* is with slices of foie gras and artichokes; *Bordelaise* is with a red-wine sauce and beef marrow; *Mirabeau* is with anchovy fillets, olives, and shoestring potatoes; *Rossini* is on a slice of fried toast and garnished with foie gras and truffles.

Tourner (French). (1) To peel into rounded shapes, as potatoes, turnips, and other vegetables, either for ragouts and stews or as a garnish. (2) To stir a sauce.

Tournon-Saint-Martin. A white cow's-milk cheese shaped like a pyramid; made in Berry, France.

Touron (French). A ring-shaped cake made with egg whites, sugar, ground almonds, and pistachios.

Tourri. *See* Ouillat.

Tourte (French). A pastry shell filled with meat, fish, or other savory mixture; or one filled with fruit or sweet mixtures. Some experts prefer the term *tourte* for nonsweet mixtures and *tarte* for sweet ones.

Tourte à la Lorraine (French). Pieces of veal and pork, flavored with various seasonings and herbs, placed upon a custard mixture and baked like a pie until the eggs are set.

Tourteau. A large edible crab found along part of the coast of France.

Tourteau Fromagé (French). A cheesecake made in the Poitou region.

Tourte de Mouton (French). Mutton pie.

Tourtelette (French). A small individual serving of filled pastry. *See also* Tartelette.

Tourterelle (French). The turtledove, a game bird.

Tourtière (French). (1) A shallow baking dish, pie dish, or tart mold. (2) A chicken pie made with salsify in Périgord.

Tourtisseau (French). A fritter made with brandy, orange-flower water, and doughs varying from region to region.

Tous-les-Mois (French). A starch prepared from rootstocks of *Canna edulis*; a substitute for arrowroot.

Toute-Bonne (French). A Bartlett pear.

Towkwa. A yellowish Malaysian bean cake.

Trading Clam. The Morton clam, one of only fair quality.

Tragacanth. A gum obtained from several kinds of plants; used to give body to pastries and confections.

Trait (French). A fixed amount of liquor in a cocktail.

Traiteur (French). A caterer; one who supplies food in large quantities.

Tranbär (Swedish). Cranberry.

Tranchant (French). The officer formerly in charge of carving meat at the table in royal households of France.

Tranche Grasse (French). The top part of the leg of beef extending to the rump.

Tranche Grasse Intérieure (French). A cut of beef, somewhat like bottom round.

Trancher (French). To cut up, particularly into slices.

Tranches Petit Os (French). A cut of beef, somewhat like bottom round.

Trancheur (French). The waiter or other person in charge of carving meat in a restaurant.

Tranchoir; Trencher. A wooden platter on which meat is sliced. In the Middle Ages a piece of bread substituted for the dish. Such bread slices were originally called *tailloirs*.

Trandafiri. A type of peasant sausage popular in parts of Romania.

Transparent Icing. A thin clear sugar-and-syrup solution used as a glaze on cakes or on cakes covered with fruit purée.

Transvaal Wheat. A fairly strong South African wheat with good water-absorption properties.

Trappe, La; Oka; Trappist Cheese. An excellent Canadian cheese resembling Port du Salut.

Trappe de Staoueli. A strong, hearty Algerian wine produced in both red and white types.

Trappiste d'Echourgnac. A small cheese similar to Port du Salut, made in Périgord, France.

Traquet (French). The wheatear, a small delicious migratory water bird.

Trauben (German). Grapes.

Trauben. A Swiss Gruyère cheese aged in white wine.

Trautmannsdorff. An Austrian count for whom several desserts were named.

Travailler (French). (1) To beat; also, to work (dough) until well mixed or blended. (2) Of dough, to rise. (3) Of wine, to ferment.

Travancore. A fair-quality Indian black tea used chiefly in a blend of teas.

Travnik. A very soft sheep's-milk cheese made in Yugoslavia and Russia.

Traz os Montes. A rather soft, exceedingly oily sheep's-milk cheese made in Portugal.

Treacle. A very sweet dark brown syrup.

Treacle-Butter Cake (British). Oatcake spread with treacle (molasses).

Treble Palma. A high-grade sherry wine.

Trébuc (French). The meat or poultry added to *garbure*, the vegetable soup made in Béarn.

Treccia. A Neapolitan buffalo's-milk cheese similar to Mozzarella.

Tree Onion. (1) *Egyptian onion*, an onion that grows at the top of the stalk. (2) *Rocambole*, a mild garlic.

Treet Bread (British). A coarse brown loaf made of unbolted flour.

Tree Tomato. An acidulous tomatolike fruit native to New Zealand; best when used in compotes.

Trefoil. A leguminous plant, one species of which is used as a vegetable; another type, the *marsh trefoil*, has bitter leaves sometimes substituted for hops.

Tremper (French). To dip foods, particularly in soups or wines.

Tremper la Soupe (French). To pour soups over bread crusts.

Tremper le Vin (French). To add water to wine.

Trempette (French). A small slice of bread soaked in any liquid.

Trencher. In medieval times a wooden platter or board on which meats and poultry were cut. Also, thick, heavy slices of bread on which dripping hot meats were served. The fatty bread was given to the poor.

Trencherman. One who eats well and enjoys his food.

Trenette col Pesto (Italian). Long noodles with garlic, oil, and herb sauce.

Trepang. The *sea cucumber*, a marine animal; regarded by the Chinese as a great delicacy.

Tress. A plait or braid of dough.

Tressi (South Pacific). Dried fish, especially shrimp.

Trianon, À la (French). In the Trianon style; usually, garnished with three colors.

Trichina Spiralis. A parasitic worm present in underdone meat, especially in pork and pork products, causing a serious disease known as trichinosis.

Tricholoma Terreum. A brownish-gray edible fungus of poor quality.

Triclinium. An ancient Roman dining room.

Trier. A wine town of the Ruwer district of Germany. *See* Germany, The Wines of.

Triggerfish. An armored fish whose spine becomes erect when the fish is threatened with danger. One species is found on the French Mediterranean coast; the so-called pigfish is found on the South Atlantic coast of the United States. The fish is prepared like tuna.

Triglie alla Livornese (Italian). A delicate white-meat fish prepared with tomato-olive sauce.

Trimmings. Parts of meat or fish removed before cooking.

Trinidad and Tobago. Trinidad and Tobago have similar food. In general, it follows a British pattern with an American influence. The native specialties are based on the local produce, as in the other Caribbean islands. The fruits are delicious, especially the mangos, sapodillas, pineapples, papayas (locally known as pawpaws), and bananas. The locally grown vegetables are typical of the West Indies, including tannias, cassavas, eddoes, and various types of sweet potatoes. There is one interesting freshwater fish, the *cascadou* or *cascadura*; also worthwhile are the crabs (often served in their own shell and called *crab backs*), and the small oysters. Another crab dish is *crab matete*, crab meat cooked with farina: The Trinidad *pepperpot* is made with chicken, meats, and spices. The *san coche* (derived from the South American *sancocho*) is a hearty stew of pork, beef, and vegetables; *calaloo* is made with salt beef, pork, and fish or crabs and cooked to the consistency of a thick soup-stew. Also favored are rice dishes, typified by chicken *pelau* (chicken with rice), and pigeon peas with rice, as well as Indian curries.

Rum is the strong drink of these islands. A novelty is the "green swizzle," made with *carypton* (a kind of Angostura bitters).

Trinidad Tea. A kind of tea made in Trinidad from the leaves of the pimiento or allspice tree.

Tripas à Moda do Porto (Portuguese). Tripe cooked with chicken, beans, ham, and sausage.

Tripe. The edible first and second stomachs of certain ruminants, chiefly of beef cattle. However, lamb and pig tripe are also marketed. Tripe is rich in protein but requires long hours of slow cooking. It is regarded highly in much of Europe. France, in particular, prepares an outstanding dish, *tripe à la mode de Caen*. The first stomach of ruminants is quite smooth, the second is honeycombed; ideally, both types should be represented in a tripe dish.

Tripe, À la. Prepared so as to give the appearance of containing tripe, although no tripe is actually contained; that is, with sliced hard-cooked eggs covered with a white sauce containing onions or cucumber cut in thin strips.

Triperie (French). The sale of tripe or the shop in which it is sold.

Tripière (French). A flat round type of casserole used chiefly in the Normandy region for making tripe.

Triple Sec. A clear, colorless, orange-flavored liqueur served as an afterdinner drink and in some cocktails; also used in orange sauces and other cooked dishes.

Tripletail. The grouper, an important tropical food fish.

Trippa (Italian). Tripe.

   Trippa alla Fiorentina. Casserole of tripe served with beans and cheese.

   Trippa in Brodetto. Tripe in a souplike sauce.

   Trippa Ripiena uso Lucania. Tripe stuffed with mixed meat.

Tritato Misto (Italian). Mixed grill.

Triturate. To grind foods to a fine powder.

Trivet. A small, somewhat raised stand on which hot platters, dishes, or pots may be placed without marring the surface of the table. Large trivets are used over open fires.

Trockenbeeren Auslese. A fine, rare, and the most expensive method of preparing certain German wines. *See* Germany, The Wines of.

Trognon (French). The edible heart of certain fruits and vegetables, such as chicory and cabbage.

Trois Cornes. A strong-flavored French goat's-milk cheese.

Trois-Frères (French). A pastry created by the Julien brothers, three famous pastry cooks of the 19th century. The special mold was called *moule à trois frères.*

Tronçon (French). A very thin slice (of meat, etc.). Also, a piece cut from the middle of a large fish; a chunk of any foodstuff longer than it is wide.

Trôo, Fromage de. A French goat's-milk cheese matured in vegetable ashes.

Troto (Italian). Trout.

Trotter Pie (British). A pie made with apples and quinces.

Trotters. The feet portion of such domesticated animals as the calf, lamb, and pig. Calf's and pig's feet are used more often than lamb's. The feet contain a great deal of natural gelatin, and a calf's foot is good added to many stews and for making aspics and jellied soups.

Trou de Milieu (French). A small glass of brandy once drunk in the middle of a banquet, theoretically to refresh the palate.

Troughs. Vessels or containers in which dough is mixed.

Trousse (French). A sheath, suspended from the apron string, designed to hold a butcher's or a cook's tools.

Trout. A delicately flavored fine-textured fish of the salmon family. Trout vary in size from the smallest brook and mountain trout to the river and lake trout, some of which have pink flesh. Because of the fine flavor trout are best when sautéed or broiled. A favorite method of preparing brook trout is to dip the whole fish in seasoned flour, sauté it in butter, and garnish it with sautéed sliced almonds. Many experts think that really fresh trout should just be cooked quickly in water with a few drops of vinegar, then served with melted butter.

Trout, Brook. A general term for numerous species of trout found in swiftly moving streams and brooks.

Trout, Salmon. A name applied to various fish of the trout family, particularly those having a delicate flavor and pink or almost white meat.

Trouxas d'Ovos (Portuguese). A dessert made with eggs and spun sugar.

Troyen. A simple, round cow's-milk cheese made in Champagne, France; best in winter and spring.

Trubu. An East Indian fish similar to a herring; the roe is preserved as a delicacy.

Truchas (Spanish). Trout.

Truches (French, Colloquial). Potatoes.

Truck Garden. Vegetables raised to be sold fresh on the market. The origin of the term is doubtful; it may derive from the practice of bringing the vegetables to the market daily by truck; or it may be a variation on the old French word *troquer,* meaning "to do business."

Truckles. (1) An English skimmed cheese with salty bluish veins. (2) A cheddar cheese made in western England.

Truelle; Trowel. A spatula with a curved handle used for serving fish, pastries, etc.

Trufa (Spanish). Truffle.

Truffe (French). Truffle.

Trüffel (German). Truffle.

Truffiat (French). A sort of potato cake or scone; a specialty of the Berry region.

Trufflage (French). The adding of pieces of truffle to chicken, meat, or game.

Truffle. A highly esteemed edible fungus that grows underground, usually under large oak trees. Truffles are located by the use of trained pigs or dogs which are permitted to develop a taste for them.

Truffles are generally classified as black or white, the black being considered the better. Most connoisseurs think that the best black truffles come from Périgord, in southwestern France, but various parts of France have other types. Both black and white truffles are found in Italy, where the white truffles of Piedmont are very highly regarded; they may be eaten raw or used in making *fonduta* or in pastas, etc. A less flavorsome, less expensive truffle is found in Spain.

Truffle Chocolate. A paste consisting of fresh cream and chocolate, covered with chocolate, and formed into balls.

Truffled. Cooked with truffles.

Trug. (1) A wooden container for milk. (2) An oblong basket used for fruits or vegetables.

Truite (French). Trout.

> **Truite Bleue.** Live trout, cooked quickly in boiling water with a little vinegar.
>
> **Truite Montgolfier.** Boneless trout with a white-wine-and-lobster sauce.

Truite de Mer; Rascasse (French). The sea sow or hogfish.

Truitelle (French). A small trout; a troutlet.

Truite Saumonée (French). Salmon trout.

Truite Vivante (French). Trout kept alive until about to be cooked.

Trumpeter. A South Pacific fish of only passable quality.

Truss. To tie the wings and legs of a bird close to the body with string and skewers so that the bird will hold its shape during cooking.

Truta (Portuguese). Trout.

Truthahn; Truthenne (German). Turkey.

> **Truthahnkeule.** Turkey leg.

Tryblion (Roman, Obsolete). A fairly small plate.

Try Out. To render; to melt fat until it is free from skin and connective tissue so that it can be poured off. The remaining skin and connective tissue are called *cracklings*. Chicken, goose, and pork fat are examples.

Tryps (Roman, Obsolete). A large plate or platter.

Tsamba (Mongolian, Tibetan). A paste made from tea leaves, yak butter, barley flour, salt, and soda; eaten particularly by travelers.

Tuba (Philippine). A rather potent intoxicating beverage made from the sap of palm.

Tube Pan. A round pan with a hole in the center used for baking cakes or as an open-center mold. Some tube pans have legs on the top rim, permitting the pan to be inverted to allow angel, sponge, and chiffon cakes to cool properly in the pan.

Tuber. The edible thickened, sometimes rounded portion of a plant, such as the potato.

Tubettini (Italian). Miniature tubes of pasta; used chiefly in soups.

Tuborg. An outstanding Danish beer; exported to almost all parts of the world.

Tuck (British). Candy or chocolate.

Tuckahoe. A tuberous root dug out of the ground and eaten in North America since Indian times; also used in jellies.

Tucker (Colloquial). A supply of food; a meal.

Tucuma. A Brazilian palm tree that produces an edible fruit of passable quality.

Tucupí Sauce (Brazilian). A sauce made from the manioc root.

Tufoli (Italian). Rather large tubes of pasta; usually stuffed and baked, and served with a sauce.

Tufted Lark. A species of lark whose flesh sometimes has a musky taste.

Tuginar (Turkish). A chopped mutton or veal stew combined with quartered artichokes.

Tuica. A dry Hungarian or Romanian plum brandy.

Tuiles. Small crisp cookies curled while still warm around a rolling pin, then coated with almonds.

Tuinbonen (Dutch). Swamp or wild beans.

Tukemono (Japanese). A type of pickle.

Tulip. A wild tulip, native to southern France, whose edible root is prepared like a Jerusalem artichoke. At various times, tulips have been regarded as a commonplace food; the tuberous root has a starchy quality.

Tulip Glass. A stemmed glass with a narrow bowl shaped roughly like that of a tulip flower; considered ideal for drinking champagne.

Tulle, Fromage de. A salty blue cheese made in Auvergne, France.

Tullibee. A kind of whitefish found in the Great Lakes.

Tumbler. A drinking glass. Before glassmaking was known, drinking containers were made of leather. Since the bases were rounded, they would "tumble" when placed on the table; hence the name "tumbler."

Tun. A very large cask used to hold liquors or wines. The size varies greatly from country to country, but the typical capacity is 252 gallons.

Tuna. The prickly pear, fruit of a cactus plant; may be eaten fresh or made into a dessert. The pulp is boiled and strained, and nuts and spices are added.

Tuna Cardona. A Mexican prickly pear having the general shape of a small pear.

Tuna Cheese. Not a cheese but a chocolate-brown Mexican candy made from tuna cardona, the fruit of a cactus plant.

Tuna Fish; Tunny Fish. A large bullet-shaped fish of the mackerel family found chiefly in the Mediterranean and in the warmer waters of the Atlantic and Pacific oceans. Fresh tuna has a firm, oily texture and should be marinated in a seasoned lemon juice–oil mixture before being sautéed or broiled. By far the largest part of the tuna catch is used for canning.

Tuna Fish, White. *See* Tuna Fish.

Tunge (Norwegian). Tongue.

Tung Gwa (Chinese). A candy made from melons.

Tunken (German). Sauces.

Tunna Pannkakor (Swedish). A pancake dessert.

Tunny; Tunny Fish. *See* Tuna Fish.

Tupelo Honey. An unusual, distinctive honey obtained from bees whose hives are located near tupelo trees, members of the dogwood family.

Turban (French). (1) A dish arranged so as to resemble a turban. *En turban* refers to such an arrangement. (2) Border molds made of various forcemeats.

Turban de Poisson (French). Fish dishes prepared in a ring-shaped mold.

Turban of Veal. A cold dish arranged in the form of a turban, consisting of cold fowl and slices of tongue and cold veal garnished with truffles.

Turbit. A variety of pigeon with a very short beak; often used for food.

Turbot. A European fish resembling the American halibut; sometimes called "king of flatfish" and "pheasant of the sea." The flesh is white and firm but delicate and of excellent flavor.

Turbotière (French). A square-shaped kettle with a removable grid designed to cook turbot and similar flatfish.

Turbotin (French). A small turbot.

Tureen. A fairly deep dish with a cover, used for serving soup. The term is probably a variation upon the French word *terrine*, meaning "earthenware container."

Turkey. A large game and poultry bird related to the pheasant; first discovered in North America. Sixteenth-century explorers found turkeys domesticated in Central America and Mexico. The American colonists ate wild turkey as a staple food. The male bird is known as a *tom turkey*; the female, a *hen*; young ones, as *poults*. A Beltsville small white broad-breasted "baby" turkey weighing 6–9 pounds has been developed by the U.S. Department of Agriculture; it is excellent when broiled. A great deal has been done to improve turkey strains, to make the birds plumper, more tender, and to furnish more white meat. Turkeys are usually roasted, though smaller ones can be broiled. They are sold both fresh and frozen. When purchased, a turkey should be plump, plucked clean, and free from a strong odor. Turkeys are often stuffed. The stuffing should never be put into the bird until shortly before it goes into the oven. About ¾ pound dressed weight makes one serving.

Turkey. The classic drink of Turkey is *raki*, a grape brandy flavored with aniseed, which is usually mixed with water. With *raki* the Turks often have small appetizers, such as chick-peas, stuffed mussels, *midye dolma*, or similar items. *Dolmas*, vine leaves stuffed with various fillings, are extremely popular.

Some of the soups are very interesting, and *düğün chorbasi*, the classic "wedding soup," is made with lamb and egg yolks. Most meals begin with soup, at least in the countryside. Starchy foods, such as lentils, rice, and beans, appear almost daily on the menu. *Pilav* is steamed buttered rice; *iç pilav* is the Turkish style flavored with onions and spices. Lamb is the national meat; it usually appears in stews, combined with vegetables, especially eggplant and tomatoes. *Şiş kebab* is cubes of lamb broiled over charcoal, often with onions and peppers; *döner kebab* a "turning" *kebab*, is a whole piece of lamb held alongside a fire and cut to order. *Şiş köfte* is broiled chopped lamb patties on skewers.

Worthy of note is the very popular *börek*, a flaky pastry filled with cheese or meat. The meat type is called *kiymah börek*. Vegetables are usually cooked with oil and preferably stuffed; for example, *lahana dolmasi* is stuffed cabbage filled with ground lamb and rice. Fresh fruits and melons are marvelous in season. No city except Vienna serves more pastries and sweet confections than does Istanbul. Examples include *tel kadayif*, shredded wheat with chopped walnuts in a thick syrup; *ekmek kadayif*, pastry with a very thick, rich, almost solid cream on top; and *baklava*, flaky layers of fine pastry with a sweet syrup.

Wines are improving steadily; the leading table wines include Kavaklidere, Trakya, Marmara, and Papazkarasi, all of which are of respectable quality and quite drinkable. The champagne-type wines, *köpüklü şarap*, are less successful.

Turkey Corn (British). Green corn.

Turkey Hen. A female turkey.

Turkey Poult. A young turkey.

Turkish Corn (Obsolete). At one time, the name for corn; it had been generally believed that corn originated in Turkey, whereas it actually originated in America.

Turkish Paste. A soft jelly-like candy made in various flavors and coated with sugar; also called Turkish Delight.

Turk's-Head Pan. A round cake pan with a tube in the center and a spiral design on the sides; used for coffeecakes, spongecakes, etc.

Turmeric. An oriental herb of the ginger family whose roots provide the yellowish brown powder used to flavor and color curry powder and mustard.

Turnedo (Italian). Fillet of beef.

Turnedo alla Rossini. Fillet of beef with pâté, truffles, and wine.

Turner. A spatula used to flip over foods such as fried eggs and pancakes cooking in a pan and to remove them without breaking.

Turning. Cutting vegetables into rounded, ornamental shapes either with a small sharp knife or with specially designed instruments.

Turnip. A root vegetable with edible green tops, related to the cabbage and mustard family. The white turnip is fairly small and globelike in shape. The yellow turnip, also called *rutabaga*, is longer and larger. The green leaves of young turnips, cooked briefly, have a mild, slightly spicy flavor.

Turnip Greens; Turnip Tops. The young leaves of the turnip. Cooked as a vegetable, they have a slightly pungent and bitter flavor.

Turnix. A type of quail.

Turnover. A pastry that completely encloses a filling. Turnovers may be large or small, half-round or triangular.

Turnspit. A turning device, of various types, used for revolving meat, poultry, etc., over an open fire.

Turophile. A name proposed by Clifton Fadiman, noted author and lover of cheese, for those who love cheese.

Turrón (Spanish). (1) A confection, something like nougat, made with ground almonds or hazel nuts, sometimes combined with various other ingredients such as candied fruits, pieces of nuts, etc. (2) A small almond-flavored cake.

Turrón de Coco (Mexican, Spanish). A coconut candy or confection.

Turska Kava (Yugoslavian). Thick coffee, heavy with sediment, made in the Turkish style.

Turta, La (Italian). A dish made of rice, spinach, cheese, and egg.

Turtle. An edible reptile native chiefly to warm-water regions, although turtles are found farther north and south. Many experts consider the West Indian turtles the finest. Among land turtles

the best is the *diamondback terrapin* found in the marshes of the Atlantic and Gulf coasts. Turtle soup is usually made with the flesh of water turtle, however. The meat of most turtles is strong-flavored.

Sea Turtle. The green turtle; most highly prized as a food delicacy, being used for the turtle soup and other dishes.

Turtledove. An edible wild bird of the pigeon family.

Turtle Herbs. A ready-mixed group of seasoning herbs including basil, thyme, marjoram, and bay; sold commercially and called *à la torte*.

Tuscano. A medium-firm Italian cheese much like a soft Parmesan.

Tutano (Portuguese). Marrow.

Tutti-Frutti (Italian). (1) All mixed fruits. (2) A preserve made with many different fruits and often spooned over ice cream and puddings. (3) Tutti-frutti ice cream, which was formerly popular in the United States.

Tutú (Brazilian). A dish usually made with puréed leftover beans and manioc flour (sometimes with other ingredients), cooked until quite firm.

Twang. A strong or penetrating taste or smell; has a stronger meaning than "tang."

Twankay. A type of Chinese green tea.

Twist. A cake, pastry, or bread rolled into strips, then braided or twisted before baking. An example is *challah*, the Jewish egg bread.

Tybo. A Danish skim-milk cheese of average quality.

Tykmaelk (Danish). A clabbered-milk (sourmilk) dessert, similar to junket.

Tyrolean Soup. A popular term for split-pea soup.

Tyttebaer (Norwegian). Lingonberries, similar to cranberries and whortleberries.

Tyttebaersyltety (Norwegian). Lingonberry dessert.

Tzigenkäse. A medium-soft salty white Austrian cheese made from sheep's, cow's, or goat's milk.

Tzimmes (Jewish). A classic preparation; basically a sweetened kind of pudding often eaten with meats and poultry. Carrots, and prunes, apples, stewed or baked, are favorite ingredients.

Tzuica. A dry type of Romanian plum brandy.

U

Ubod (Philippine). The edible pith of a coconut tree.

Uccelletti alla Maremmana (Italian). Small birds braised in a spicy sauce of tomatoes, garlic, and anchovies.

Udder. The milk gland of cows, often eaten as food in Central Europe; may be braised or eaten salted or smoked.

Ude. A French chef, author of the *French Cook*, published in 1827. At one time he was cook to Louis XVI and the Earl of Sefton.

Udo. A Japanese plant now cultivated in California for its narrow shoots, which taste like asparagus.

Udon (Japanese). Noodles, macaroni products, etc.

Ugli. An East Indian tree, also grown in the Caribbean area; its fruit, which has a loose, thick, orange skin, tastes like a tangerine.

Ugnsomelett (Swedish). Baked omelet.

Ugnstekt (Swedish). Baked.

Ugnstekt Fläskcarré (Swedish). Roast pork.

Ugnstekt Gädda (Swedish). Oven-fried pike.

Uien (Dutch). Onions.

Uitsmijter (Dutch). An open sandwich, usually made with roast beef or ham, served with a fried egg on top.

Ukha (Russian). Any of a variety of fish soups.

Ullage. (1) The amount by which a wine cask is short of being full. (2) (Colloquial) Liquor left in used wineglasses or casks.

Ulu Tao (Samoan). Green breadfruit baked until very brown and soft.

Ulva. A seaweed used as food in certain countries, notably Japan.

Umber. Grayling, a fish.

Umbles. The edible inner parts of an animal, usually a deer. Inasmuch as the venison was regarded as having a better taste, those who ate this portion were said to be eating "umbles-pie"; the term was later corrupted to "humble-pie."

Umbra; Umbrine. (1) A good-tasting fish, 1–2 feet long, found chiefly in the Mediterranean, but also in the warmer Atlantic waters. (2) The mud-minnow, a small European fish of mediocre quality. (3) A fish similar to perch and sometimes sold for bass.

Umido (Italian). A stew.

Unagi (Japanese). Eel.

Uncooked. Raw; not cooked.

Uncork. To remove the cork from a container. Uncorking a wine bottle involves keeping the contents undisturbed. This is accomplished by using a corkscrew or a special twist drill. Special gas cartridges are now available which remove corks almost effortlessly.

Underdone. Insufficiently cooked; as applied to meats, rare.

Unfermented Wine. Grape or other fruit juices not fermented.

Ungarische Art (German). In the Hungarian style.

Ungarisches Gulasch (German). Hungarian goulash.

Unicorn Plant. A North American herb. *See* Martinoes.

United States. The food to be found in the United States is extremely variable in scope, style, and quality. European visitors, as a rule, find it monotonous and limited, but they frequently praise specific natural foods, particularly the milk and beef. They find the lamb tasteless, the veal tough, and the chicken bland, but some have praise for Long Island ducklings. American fish is superb when fresh, they usually say, but local cooks inevitably fry it to a crisp. Some of this criticism is justified, but the fact remains that much of good American cookery is not visible to the ordinary view, because, like an iceberg, the major portion is hidden. Those who dine only in hotels and restaurants, it is true, will find only standardized, mediocre cookery on the menus. Interesting, truly American specialties are usually found only in private homes.

The food and cookery styles of the United States may be divided into many different categories, but an arbitrary selection would probably include the following: Eastern, Southern, New Orleans-Creole, Western, and Southwestern. Of course, many purists might want to include Maine, Pennsylvania Dutch, the Middle West, or other localities, and with just cause.

The East features a wide range of clam dishes, but especially clam chowder, prepared with cream or milk (New England style) or with tomatoes (Manhattan style). In addition, New England has many pancake preparations, such as blueberry pancakes, plus New England boiled dinner, Maine lobster, various fruit pies, fruit and pastry desserts, cranberry sauce, and many types of relishes.

Moving southward, in the Chesapeake Bay area, crab specialties are popular, notably as stews, bisques, and crab cakes. The Tidelands fish preparations are also worthy of note. Inland and farther south, in Virginia and the Carolinas, the bacon and ham are superb. Other noteworthy southern specialties are the various hot breads, fried chicken, hominy grits, Brunswick stew, corn pone, corn dodgers, rich layer cakes, and old-fashioned shortcakes.

In the south central part of the United States, particularly Louisiana, the food becomes unique and unduplicated, partly American, partly French, and partly African. It is here, and only here, that authentic jambalayas, gumbos, *filés*, and other Creole dishes may be had in the fullest excellence of flavor and made with truly fresh ingredients. New Orleans cookery is unique —not completely French, certainly not American, but an amalgam of several cooking styles.

The southwestern United States specializes in barbecued foods—notably steaks and barbecued spareribs. In addition, because of the proximity to the Mexican border, many Mexican dishes are extremely popular in Texas and other border states. It should be noted for the record that *chili con carne,* often regarded as a Mexican dish, is not; actually, it originated in Texas.

The western part of the country, notably California, has excellent weather. For this reason, outdoor cookery, green salads, and fresh fruits predominate in the local cuisine. The lettuce and other salad greens have a crispness and freshness unsurpassed in almost any other part of the world; an outstanding creation here is the Caesar salad, served as an appetizer.

Of course, this is far from an exhaustive list of American specialities, but merely an attempt to highlight a few local dishes. Often, however, the fine points of American cuisine are natural and inherent in the food—such as the delicate flavor of a freshly caught trout—and not due to the skill of the cook who prepares the fish. This in turn raises the question of whether the simple broiling or roasting of naturally excellent foods constitutes a cuisine, a national style of cooking.

Meal habits in the United States are somewhat different from those of the rest of the Western world. Breakfast, an old-fashioned, American-style breakfast, was formerly a hearty meal of hot cereal, eggs and bacon, pancakes, and other solid fare. However, with weight-watching and lessened physical activity, this has been increasingly replaced by orange juice, toast, and coffee. Lunchtime is generally a simple meal, typified by a sandwich, pie, and coffee, in most parts of the country. There are regions where the big meal of the day is taken at midday, but this custom is disappearing rapidly. The evening meal, sometimes called dinner, sometimes supper, is from 6 to 8:30 P.M., and in general, the earlier time is popular in rural communities, the later in the more populous regions.

Hard liquor is very much in favor in the United States, the consumption per capita running surprisingly high. Rye and bourbon are, of course, the national strong drinks, but Scotch has many adherents, particularly along the two coastlines. American beer is popular, although it somehow lacks the flavor of certain European types. It may well be that coffee is the national drink of the nation.

United States, The Wines of the. The status of American wines is ambiguous. The United States has the greatest technological development of any nation in the world. It has specialists who can solve the most complex problems in both science and industry. Where vineyards are concerned, it has all the authentic vine roots from Europe as well as native varieties, and the soil and the climate in various parts of the country theoretically permit the United States to equal the wines of any nation on earth. And yet most American wine reaching the market is mediocre. If this seems a strong indictment, it should be borne in mind that many European wine experts, after extensive sampling, have completely dismissed American wines. Such a position is too arbitrary; some good, even fine wine is being produced in small quantities, and it is the hope for the future.

Why are not American wines better? Let us begin at the beginning with the earliest records and trace the rather bizarre history of wine making in the United States. When Leif the Lucky with his band of Vikings reached the eastern shore of what is now the United States, about the year 1000, he found so many wild grapes growing that he named the region Vineland.

The Indians of the continent ate the wild grapes, but had no knowledge of how to make wine. It was the European settlers along the eastern seaboard who brought the techniques to this region, as the Spanish settlers brought them to southern California and Mexico. The folklore, completely unsupported by fact, is that Father Junipero Serra planted the first vines at the mission in San Diego about 1769. It is certain, however, that the Franciscan order built many mission houses, twenty-one to be precise, and grew grapes for wine at most of them. The oldest winery is probably the one founded in 1775 at Mission San Gabriel just outside Los Angeles. The early vineyards were in southern California, although there were a few brave beginnings at San Francisco. All the first attempts were made with European roots called *vitis vinifera;* little effort was made to cultivate the native grapes.

About 1830, a Frenchman appropriately named Vignes had considerable success with vine cuttings he had brought from Bordeaux. Later, at the time of the gold rush of 1849, a Hungarian nobleman named Agoston Haraszthy came to California. Always interested in wine making, he planted vines, using European types as Vignes had done. He produced some satisfactory wines, and in 1861 the governor of California asked him to go to Europe to bring back cuttings. He returned with more than a hundred thousand cuttings from some two hundred and fifty different grape varieties. Haraszthy was certain that California would ultimately outproduce Europe in the cultivation of fine wines. In a way, perhaps he is responsible for California's plight today, for he recommended the greatest possible variety of production: white, red, and *rosé,* sweet dessert wines, apéritifs, and sparkling wines. California began then and still continues to imitate the wines of every important area in the world. The vintners defend this position by stating that California is still in the experimental stage, still trying to find the ideal combination of grape, soil, climate, and wine type. In any event, it is just a little more than a century ago that wine making began in a professional way in California. During the 1880's, a dozen important wineries were founded.

The story was somewhat different in the eastern United States. Attempts to grow the European grapes were unsuccessful from the beginning, for the vines would not live in the climate and soil. Success was achieved only with the native vines such as the Delaware, Elvira, and Catawba, and later hybrids. But the vintners had no basis of comparison for these wines. Eventually, however, certain standards were accepted. These wines have an unusual quality which for want of a better word is called "foxy," a rather sharp, wild flavor unlike anything encountered in European wines. As the years have gone by, New York vineyards have concentrated almost exclusively upon white wines, which are far better than any white wines of California; the western vineyards produce some fair red wine, but the white is apt to be routine, while the many imitations of European types are mediocre.

From 1880 to 1920, wine making continued, with serious efforts being made by a number of vintners to produce the best possible product. Then Prohibition began, and the vineyards simply produced raisins, sacramental wines, and table grapes. When they turned again to wine making in 1933, the results were disastrous. The wines shipped were far too young; they were hastily doctored with flavorings, color, syrups. During the late 1930's, the situation improved. But again during World War II, wines were in great demand, and some of the dubious practices returned. Since that time, the majority of wine sold by native vineyards has been mediocre in quality. A few reputable wineries are making efforts to produce fine wines, but the majority seem to be concerned only with making money.

The vineyards claim that the public wants only cheap wines, that their efforts to introduce better products have been unsuccessful. But the fault is not wholly with the public, for in California most of the vineyards are planted with the coarser grape types. No one can say that this choice is not deliberately made. As a generalization, then, it may be said that the wineries are not furnishing a good product, and the public does not seem to demand a better, with the exception of the northeastern part of the United States, where, in any event, European wines have practically monopolized the market. There are, as we have mentioned, a few vintners who are making fine wines, but they account for less than 5 per cent of the total production.

Adding insult to injury, California vintners use pasteurization in order to stop whatever life the wine possesses. Wine is alive, even in the bottle; it continues to breathe, changing slightly for better or worse each day. As this change occurs, many wines throw up a sediment that is a natural, harmless phenomenon. Pasteurization stops the formation of sediment, and the wine becomes flat and lifeless.

There are two categories of American wines —California and the others. About 90 per cent of the wine comes from the former, while the remaining 10 per cent is divided among the Finger Lakes region of upper New York, northern Ohio, and some small areas of New Jersey, Virginia, the Carolinas, Georgia, Michigan, Tennessee, and Missouri. We shall consider the California wines first.

California

Here the soil and climate are so variable that almost any conceivable wine-growing area of the world can be duplicated. There are cool valleys, dry or moist plains, deserts, sloping hills, rolling countryside; every European grape type, every *vitis vinifera* will grow somewhere in California. But there is little or no uniformity in the finished products. A California Burgundy from three different vintners tastes like three different wines, and not one of them has any more than a passing resemblance to the true Burgundy.

California products may be considered from three aspects: the European generic type, the grape varietal (the kind of grape used), and the region in which the vineyard is located.

European generic: This term refers to the European name of the wine which the California vintner attempts to imitate. Of course, in Europe these wines have certain definite characteristics that any wine lover can recognize without difficulty. In the United States, labels are applied according to the judgment of the producer, who decides what wine he thinks his product resembles. A wine maker may bottle and ship any white wine as "Chablis," for example, although his wine resembles Chablis only in its color. The best vintners are getting away from the practice of using European generic names and are substituting the grape varietals, which is more honest. The fact is that well over half the grapes used are not wine grapes at all but ordinary "raisin" or "table" grapes of low quality.

Grape varietal name: At the present time, California laws provide that a wine may be called by its grape varietal name only if 51 per cent of the wine is made from that grape. This is a step forward from the unrestricted practice of selling any red wine as Burgundy or claret— whichever is most in demand. With the grape type on the label, the purchaser knows something of what he is getting. But why should not the law insist on 100 per cent in order for a wine to qualify as a Riesling, a Semillon, or a Sauvignon, for example? However, many of the finer vineyards have disregarded this legal provision, and they do make their wines exclusively from the particular grape name on their labels. Unfortunately, the general public, accustomed to asking for European wine types, have not realized the superior qualities of grape varietal wines, and the sale of European generic types still exceeds the former.

The most successful white wines are made with the Traminer and Sylvaner grapes, which produce a drier wine with a higher alcoholic content than in Germany. The Pinot Blanc and the Chardonnay make a reasonably good American "Chablis." In California, there are two different wines called Sauterne (without the final "s"). The sweet is not a very close approximation of the French, but it is made with the sweet Semillon. The dry Sauterne is offered for sale under the label of the grape type—Sauvignon Blanc and Semillon. These wines with the grape varietals on the label are likely to be much better than the French wines that are sold in the United States at low prices without a vineyard name.

The California *rosés* are becoming popular; the better wine is made from the Grenache Rose, and the routine from the Gamay. For Claret, the vintners use the Cabernet Sauvignon grape and make a reasonably good wine, although it bears only a slight resemblance to the French original. Another important grape varietal is the Pinot Noir, used to make Burgundy. A good bottle of California Pinot Noir is acceptable. Other red wine grapes used on a larger scale are the Gamay, Gamay Beaujolais, Barbera, Zinfandel, and Grignolino. These varietals produce wines that are fruity and pleasant, somewhat like the French Beaujolais or the Italian Chianti.

Many wine makers catering to the unsophisticated demand for a wine that goes with "anything" have come up with several cheap wines without distinction, life, or taste; they are sold as "Vino de Pasta," "Vino de Tavola," "Vino Rosso," or even "Vino de Roma." Wines like these are usually very light, rather sweet, and pasteurized. The vintners defend this practice by saying that it is better to get people to drink wine, any wine, so that ultimately they will learn the difference between the good and the bad. But people who begin by drinking these very bad wines seldom graduate to the better wines. In the same way, inexperienced wine drinkers are frequently sold cheap mixtures of spiked soft drinks, widely advertised by means of television commercials, "wines" like Ripple, Thunderbird, and Golden Spur, which are not truly entitled to be called wines, for they are made from aromatic and sweet flavorings to which alcohol is added. The advertisements say they are like Italian wines. There is a great demand for aromatic wines in Italy, but an Italian knows the difference between a good table wine and an aromatic wine like vermouth or bitters, and he knows the purpose that each serve. No Italian would drink vermouth with dinner, but thousands of Americans buy a bottle of Thunderbird and drink it with steak, find it unpleasant, and end up condemning wine in general. The businessmen who produce such wines are shortsighted, for they cannot see the large market that can be created with honest advertising for genuinely good American wines.

Region: The wines of California can also be distinguished from one another by the region in which they are produced. The University of California scientists have worked out a system based upon weather conditions and disregarding geographical locations. They classify vineyards as in cool, moderately cool, intermediate, moderately hot, and hot zones. A much simpler system, more easily remembered, is based upon location. Almost all the good wines are produced around San Francisco in the counties circling the bay. The physical situation is about the best in the United States for wine making; temperature, sunshine, rainfall, and humidity seem almost ideal. However, wines are also made in the inland valleys and in southern California, but they are comparatively unimportant.

There are four wine-making districts around San Francisco that are important: Sonoma, Napa, Alameda, and Santa Clara-San Benito. Sonoma includes Mendocino County, where red table wines of average quality are produced. Important vineyards of Sonoma are Buena Vista (founded by that remarkable Hungarian, Count Agoston Haraszthy), Sebastiani, Santa Rosa, Korbel and Brothers, Martini and Prati, Italian Swiss Colony, and Parducci Wine Cellars.

Napa includes both the Napa Valley and the Solano region. Here there is a wide selection of excellent wines. Napa and Santa Clara are the two leading counties for fine wines in the United States. From Napa come the wines of Charles Krug, Louis Martini, Beaulieu, Souverain Cellars, Inglenook, the Christian Brothers, and Hanns Kornell Cellars.

Alameda includes Livermore Valley and Contra Costa County. The region produces red wines, sweet white wines, sparkling types, dessert, and aromatic wines—a little of every type—but the white wines are the best. Important firms include Cresta Blanca, Wente, Concannon, and Paul Rhodes Winery.

The Santa Clara district comprises both Santa Cruz and San Benito. However, Santa Clara itself produces the best wines in the United States. The largest vineyard is Almaden, which brings to the market a line of better wines, including sparkling and table wines, as well as many rather ordinary imitations of European specialty wines. Other wineries are Paul Masson, Martin Ray, San Martin, and the Novitiate of Los Gatos.

The inland-valley district extends for about three hundred miles in the middle of the state. The upper portion is reasonably cool, while the southern is extremely hot. From north to south, there are three districts: Lodi-Sacramento, Escalon-Modesto, and Fresno-San Joaquin. In the Lodi-Sacramento region, there are vineyards belonging to the East Side Winery (a farmers' cooperative) and the Guild Wine Company. In the Escalon-Modesto area, there the very large Petri Wineries and E. and J. Gallo, both of which carry out production on an enormous scale. The Fresno-San Joaquin Valley, hot and dry during the summer months, makes many sweet dessert wines, notably in the region around Fresno. The vineyards are Fickling, Cribari & Sons, Roma Wine Company, Cella Vineyards, and Di Giorgio Wine Company.

In southern California (between Los Angeles and the Mexican border), there are scattered vineyards, none of them outstanding. Cucamonga and its surrounding area produces Italian-style red table wines, especially a "Chianti," as well as a variety of dessert wines. The vineyards are Cucamonga Winery, Cucamonga Vineyard Company, Garrett and Company, and the Brookside Vineyard Company.

New York, Ohio, and the Rest of the United States

Most of New York State's wine production is centered about the Finger Lakes region, in the northern part of the state, with additional production in a part of Sullivan County and along certain sections of the Hudson River. Some fifty or so miles from Rochester, and centering about Hammondsport and Penn Yan, the rolling countryside is covered with vineyards. Wines are marketed under European generic names— such as Burgundy, Chablis, sherry, and the like— although the strongest emphasis is upon white wines, which are of better quality than the reds. As a rule, New York State copies of European wine types bear comparatively little resemblance in taste and aroma to the wines they attempt to imitate. However, it should be noted that the white wines are reasonably priced and of good quality. Similarly, New York State sherry wine is a rather good product, but it is not a true sherry in its inherent character.

Possibly the best wine of New York State is "Champagne," usually produced individually in the bottle in the classic French tradition. Some of the better New York "Champagnes" are at least the equal of many lesser French Champagnes, having a fine, clean taste and fairly small bubbles. However, the "Champagnes" made by the bulk process in large vats, usually sold as "Champagne-style," are poor in quality and have little to recommend them. In the vicinity of St. Louis, Missouri, there is also some production of "Champagne"; it is not marketed on a national scale at the present time.

Other important eastern wine regions include the area along Lake Erie from Cleveland to Sandusky, Ohio; a region extending from Virginia through the Carolinas and Georgia; in Michigan, particularly around Benton Harbor; parts of Missouri, notably near the Ozarks; and a small area near Egg Harbor, New Jersey. Of course, almost every state produces a certain amount of local wine, although little of it reaches the national market.

Unit of Heat, British. The British Thermal Unit (BTU) or heat unit is the amount of heat needed to raise the temperature of 1 pound of water 1 degree C. It equals 252 calories.

Universal Sauce. A sauce made of white wine, chicken broth, bay leaves, lemon rind, pepper, and salt; it tastes good on almost everything.

Unleavened Bread. Bread made with dough mixed with water and salt only, with no leavening; matzos.

Unsavory. Unpleasant or unappealing to the taste.

Unsweetened Block Cocoa. Roasted husked cacao beans ground to produce a thick oily liquid which is then allowed to set in molds; widely used as chocolate flavoring for fondant, creams, etc.

Untrussing. Removing the string or other binding from poultry and game.

Uova (Italian). Eggs.

    Uova Acciugate. Anchovy-stuffed eggs.

    Uova Affogate. Poached eggs.

    Uova al Tegame. Scrambled or fried eggs.

    Uova Bollite. Boiled eggs.

    Uova Farcite. Stuffed eggs.

    Uova nel Tegame. Fried eggs.

    Uova Piccante. Deviled eggs.

    Uova Sode. Hard-cooked eggs.

    Uova sott' Aceto. Pickled eggs.

    Uova Strapazzate. Scrambled eggs.

    Uova uso di Sardegna. Eggs cooked in wine with mushrooms.

U.P. Under proof; a liquor term.

Upland Cress. *See* Cress, Upland.

Uppuma (Indian). A preparation of lentils and semolina.

Upriver Wheat. Upriver Plate (Argentine) wheats other than Rosafé. The wheat tends to make slightly runny doughs despite the presence of 11–12 percent gluten.

Upside-Down Cake. A cake in which the sweet ingredients, fruits, nuts, etc., are placed at the bottom of the pan with the batter on top; turned upside down before serving.

Upsy (Dutch). Heavy drinking or carousing.

Uranoscope; Uranoscopus. An edible Mediterranean scorpion, a sea fish.

Urda. A rather aromatic Romanian sheep's-milk cheese.

Uri Cheese. A hard, tangy cow's-milk cheese made in the canton of Uri, Switzerland.

Usé (French). As applied to wine, starting to go bad.

Usquebaugh (Gaelic, Irish). Whiskey. It is from the term *usquebaugh*, which literally means "water of life," that the word "whiskey" originated.

Utensils. Kitchen implements, including pots, pans, bowls, etc.

Uva (British, Italian). Grapes.

Uvaggio. Any Italian wine made from the fermented juices of a mixed variety of grapes.

Uval (French). Pertaining to grapes. *Cure uval*, the grape cure, is a diet of grapes and grape juice.

Uvas (Portuguese, Spanish). Grapes.

Uzenárny (Czechoslovakian). A sausage shop that sells *párky* (frankfurters).

V

Vaca (Portuguese, Spanish). Beef.
  Vaca Cozida. Boiled beef.
  Vaca Estufada. Beef stew.
  Vaca Salada. Corned beef.

Vaccary. A cow pasture; a dairy farm.

Vaccinium. The bilberry.

Vacherin (French). A rich dessert made with meringue or almond-paste circles forming a timbale and filled with Chantilly cream, ice cream, or a *bombe* mixture.

Vacherin Cheese. Any of several varieties of cheese. *Vacherin à la Main*, made in France and Switzerland, is very soft with a hard rind; it spreads well or may be eaten with a spoon. A local name is *Tome de Montagne. Vacherin Fondu* is similar to Swiss cheese. *Vacherin du Mont d'Or*, made in France, is much like Livarot.

Vac-Ice Process (British). Freeze-drying; a method of dehydrating and freezing foods for future use.

Vacreation. A process, developed in New Zealand, of deodorizing cream by steam distillation under reduced pressure.

Vacuum Bottle. A bottle, surrounded by a vacuum and an outercovering, used to keep foods or liquids hot or cold for several hours. *See also* Thermos Bottle.

Vacuum-Packed. Packed in cans or glass jars from which air is extracted, then hermetically sealed.

Vafler (Norwegian). Waffles.

Vainilla (Spanish). Vanilla.

Vairon; Viron. A very small fish found in the rivers of France; best when fried.

Vaisselle (French). All household dishes, including those for the table.

Valdeblore. A goat's-milk cheese made in the mountains around Nice, France.

Valdepeñas (Spanish). Full-bodied, hearty red and white wines produced along the Mediterran-ean shore; the wines are pleasant to drink, but somewhat crude and lack finish. *See* Spain, The Wines of.

Valdostana di Vitello (Italian). Veal with ham and cheese.

Valençay. A very soft goat's-milk cheese in the shape of a pyramid; made in Berry, France. Matured in ashes, it has a distinctive flavor.

Valencia. The generic term for orange in France; the true Valencia is a fairly sweet orange, usually not very large.

Valencia Almonds. Large almonds popular for use in desserts; when blanched they are used whole, slivered, chopped, or ground.

Valencias. Originally raisins produced in Valencia, Spain; now a type also grown in Turkey and California. They are processed in a mixture of potash lye, lavender, and rosemary, then dipped in olive oil.

Valencienne, À la (French). With a tomato sauce containing rice, mushrooms, strips of tongue, and grated cheese.

Valentine Cakes. Gaily decorated heart-shaped cakes presented by sweethearts to each other on St. Valentine's Day.

Valesniki. Hors d'oeuvre made with cream cheese, shaped into croquettes.

Valhalla. In Scandinavian mythology the banquet hall where Odin feasted with those who gave their lives in battle.

Valio. A mediocre Finnish imitation of Swiss cheese.

Valois Sauce. A French sauce used for a variety of dishes, including pastries. Sauces such as Béarnaise, when finished off with meat glaze, are sometimes called "Valois."

Valpolicella (Italian). A light red wine. *See* Italy, The Wines of.

Valtellina. Wines from the Sondrio province,

Italy, including Grumella, Sassella, and red Inferno.

Vanaspati (Indian). Purified, hydrogenated vegetable oil; margarine.

Vand (Danish). Water.

Van Der Hum. A sharp, spicy South African liqueur flavored with herbs and fruits, predominantly tangerine peel; similar to Curaçao.

Vandoise. A French freshwater fish; best used for fish stews or soups.

Vandreuil (French). An excellent fish found in parts of the Mediterranean.

Vangeron. The roach, a small freshwater European fish resembling the dace; usually fried.

Vaniglia (Italian). Vanilla.

Vaniljglass (Swedish). Vanilla ice cream.

Vanilla. The pod of a native Mexican plant now grown in several tropical countries. The dried bean is used as a flavoring extract for many dishes, especially for puddings and ice cream.

The term "vanilla" denotes the entire brownish pod and also the liquid and powder extracts prepared from it. The plant, *Vanilla planifolia*, a member of the orchid family, grows well only in tropical climates or greenhouses. The fruit, 6–10 inches in length, is gathered before it is fully ripe; it is dried and allowed to partly ferment (called "sweat" in the trade) in order to fix the distinctive aroma. Most commercial food packers use synthetically prepared vanilla, but the flavor is not yet completely satisfactory. Synthetic vanillas are not suitable for frozen foods because they tend to develop an "off-taste" in the freezer. The tonka bean is occasionally used as a substitute for vanilla.

Vanilla Bean. The long brown bean from which vanilla flavoring is obtained. It must be kept in a bottle or other container to prevent the flavor from evaporating.

Vanilla Sugar. A sweetener for many desserts and fresh berries; made by sealing a few vanilla beans in a jar with granulated sugar.

Vanille (French). Vanilla.

Vanille, Gousses de (French). Vanilla beans.

Vanillic Acid. An oxidized form of vanillin.

Vanillin. A white, sometimes a yellow-white, substance, much used to produce synthetically the taste and aroma of vanilla; used in many chocolate-flavored products.

Vanilline. A synthetic vanilla.

Vanilline (French). (1) Crystallized extract of vanilla. (2) Sometimes, a synthetic vanilla flavoring.

Vann (Norwegian). Water.

Vannbakkelse (Norwegian). Cream puffs.

Vanneau (French). (1) The lapwing, a small edible game bird whose eggs are considered a delicacy. (2) The fan shell, an edible mollusk.

Vanner (French). To stir a sauce to prevent the formation of a top skin and to keep the mixture smooth.

Vantako Taruwa (Nepalese). A dish of sautéed eggplant flavored with turmeric.

Vapid. Flat; flavorless; lacking quality.

Vaporizing Point. As applied to water, the boiling point.

Vappa. Soured or flat wine.

Varenga. A preparation of boiled, shredded beef with a garlic-onion taste; popular in Madagascar.

Varenikes. Squares or rounds of dough stuffed with meat, fruits, etc. Originally a Ukrainian dish; now also in the Jewish cuisine.

Variety Meats. Sweetbreads, liver, and other parts of beef, mutton, lamb, pork, and veal not usually sold as part of the animal's carcass.

Varkenskotelet (Dutch). Pork chops.

Varkenslapjes (Dutch). Cuts of pork.

Varkensvlees (Dutch). Pork.

Varme (Dutch). Warm; hot.

Varmrätt (Swedish). Hot dishes.

Varmt (Danish). Warm; hot.

Varnishkas (Jewish). Buckwheat groats and noodles.

Vasque. A shallow bowl, usually round, made of varying materials; used for serving cold foods, fruits, or sweets.

Vasterbottensost Cheese; West Bothian Cheese. A pungent Swedish cheese aged 12–18 months.

Västgötaost Cheese; West Gothland Cheese. A semihard, pressed Swedish cheese that ripens in 6 months.

Vat. A vessel or cask that holds beer, wine, or other liquids. Large vats are used for fermenting liquids.

Vatapá (Brazilian). A stew made of chopped

shrimp and fish combined with dendê oil, coconut milk, and flour.

Vatel. A well-known French *maître d'hôtel* in the court of Louis XIV who, according to legend, committed suicide because of an unsuccessful dinner prepared under his direction.

Vatrushki (Russian). Small savory tarts, often made of unsweetened brioche dough with edges crimped, and filled with a cream or onion mixture.

Vaudoise (French). A variety of carp.

Veal. The flesh of a calf at least 6 weeks but less than 3 months old. "Bob" veal, that is, from calves under 6 weeks of age, is hardly fit to be eaten and has a peculiar taste. After 6 weeks of age, the younger the better. As the calf matures the meat becomes baby beef, which is the state in which most veal is sold in the United States. It is definitely not so good as very young veal, as understood by French and Italian chefs. After it is about 10 weeks old, veal becomes stringy and tough, remaining in that undesirable condition until it becomes true beef.

Good veal is pale, the palest meat being best. Although Europeans, especially the French, prepare veal rare, most people prefer it well cooked, but this does not necessarily mean overcooked. Many people complain about veal's dryness; this may easily be remedied by coating it with fat, by inserting fat with a larding needle, or by basting with fat while cooking. Salt pork or bacon strips may be placed across the meat to add juiciness. The chief cuts of veal are leg, loin, shoulder, breast, rib, or roast; the shank is good for stews, etc.

Vecchia Romagna. A fair-quality Italian brandy.

Vedro. A Russian liquid measure equal to about 3 gallons.

Vegan. A person who lives on a strictly vegetarian diet, eating only fruits and vegetables and no eggs or fish.

Vegetabilisk (Swedish). Vegetable.

Vegetable. Any of a wide range of edible plants, roots, herbs, or grass, most of them annuals, commonly eaten either raw or cooked. In certain cases the entire vegetable is edible, as, for example, lettuce and potato. Sometimes the entire vegetable is edible after the skin is removed, as squash. With cauliflower and certain other vegetables, only the flower or other portions can be eaten.

The line separating vegetables from fruits has never been clear in the public mind, although the botanical distinctions are fairly clear. Tomatoes, for example, are usually called a vegetable by the public, but they are classified as a fruit by scientists. Many culinary experts feel that the best distinction between fruits and vegetables may be based on use: fruits are used for dessert, vegetables are served in the main part of a meal. But the pumpkin, for example, is used equally as a dessert (in pies) and as a vegetable.

The Egyptians were the first people who appreciated vegetables. Their favorites were onions and garlic, and they ascribed supernatural powers to those who ate heavily of those odoriferous vegetables. Later, the Greeks and Romans attributed even greater merits to vegetables, and it was believed, at various times, to make heroes out of cowards, intrepid lovers out of timid swains, and the like. Vegetable fads and popularity have come and gone in history. Cabbage, for example, was almost a cult at the beginning of the Dark Ages. Radishes, celery, cucumbers, mushrooms (and, in fact, almost every vegetable) has had its day, for years being regarded as *the* only important food.

The vast majority of the vegetables eaten in the United States today were introduced from Europe, but some came from Africa and South America. Native to the New World are squash, corn, tomatoes, and potatoes.

Vegetables are essential to a balanced diet, and both the green, leafy types as well as the root types should be eaten daily. Most vegetables consist largely of water surrounded by vegetable fiber, mineral salts, starches, protein, and sugars. The vitamin content is always lessened by cooking; since vegetables lose some of the water they contain in cooking, they should always be cooked in the smallest quantity of (salted) water possible. The Chinese method of quickly sautéing cut-up vegetables in hot fat is excellent, but they must be served immediately when ready.

Modern methods of canning and freezing have made almost all vegetables available the entire year, thus broadening the variety of daily menus. However the flavor and texture of garden-fresh vegetables remains superior.

Vegetable Butters. The natural fats present in vegetables. They are solid at ordinary temperatures but melt rather sharply. *Cocoa butter* is derived from the cocoa bean and is used in making chocolate. *Shea butter*, from an African plant, is softer than cocoa butter. *Mowrah* fat is from an Indian plant and is used in making soap and candies.

Vegetable Juices. The juices of certain vegetables, particularly carrots, celery, and tomatoes.

Vegetable Marrow (British). A summer squash with orange flesh and a dark rind.

Vegetable Oyster. The salsify.

Vegetable Pear. Chayote, a flavorsome Mexican squash also grown in Florida. With green skin and green-tinged meat, it is about the size of an acorn squash; may be boiled and mashed, sliced and deep-fat fried, or baked with or without a stuffing. It should be peeled thinly; if very young, it may be cooked unpeeled. The seeds become soft in cooking.

Vegetable Plate. An American term for several vegetables served as a main course, often with a poached egg.

Vegetal. Pertaining or relating to plants.

Vegetarian. A person who eats vegetables and no meat. Some vegetarians eat eggs and fish, others do not.

Vegetarianism. The theory and practice of eating vegetables and no animal flesh.

Velouté. (1) A smooth, rich white sauce for meat, poultry, or fish, made with white veal stock, chicken stock, or fish stock. Thickened with egg yolks it becomes *Allemande sauce*. (2) A cream soup.

Venaco. A Corsican cream cheese.

Vendace. A small lake fish found in parts of Scotland.

Vendôme Cheese. (1) A soft ripened cheese somewhat like Camembert, popular around Paris. (2) A rather hard ewe's-milk cheese ripened in ashes.

Veneto; Vanezza Cheese. A sharp-flavored Italian cheese of the Italian Grana or Parmesan type; used for grating.

Venison. The flesh of deer. Formerly the flesh of any animal hunted and killed for use as food, such as hare, deer, and boar.

Venkel (Dutch). Fennel.

Venta. A Spanish wayside inn that serves meals and wine.

Ventresca Bollita (Italian). Boiled tuna fish.

Venus. A shellfish similar to the cockle; may be eaten raw or cooked like clams.

Verbena; Vervain. A garden plant whose highly scented leaves are dried to make infusions, beverages resembling tea.

Verdel (Spanish). Mackerel.

Verdes (Spanish). As applied to vegetables, greens.

Verdicchio (Italian). A medium-dry white wine, excellent with fish and veal. *See* Italy, The Wines of.

Verdura (Italian). Vegetables.

Verdure Miste (Italian). Mixed vegetables.

Verduresse (French). Various salad herbs and green vegetables.

Verge (French). A whisk, used for beating eggs, usually made of wooden branches or twigs, but sometimes of metal.

Verjuice. The juice of green, unripe grapes, crab apples, etc., with a distinctive sour taste. It was much used during medieval times, being credited with remarkable health-giving qualities; later, in England, it became a standard sour ingredient in cooked dishes, much as vinegar is today. It is still used in oriental cookery, particularly in Iran.

Verjus (French). *See* Verjuice.

Verlorene Eier (German). Poached eggs.

Vendée Fressure (French). An unusual dish prepared with the lungs, liver, spleen, and heart of pigs; made in the Poitou region.

Vermicelli (Italian). Very fine thin strands of pasta; a narrow type of spaghetti.

Vermouth. A type of white wine, produced chiefly in France and Italy, flavored with herbs and bitters; used as an apéritif, in making cocktails, or in cooking. Among the bitter ingredients used in making vermouth are quassia, quinine, anise, absinthe, and orange peel. It is prepared dry, medium, or sweet. Also made in a red, sweet type.

Vernis. The Venus shell, sometimes the clam, both edible varieties of shellfish.

Veron (French). Minnow, a very small freshwater fish.

Vert Bonne (French). A small green plum.

Vert-Pré. (1) A green herb garnish. (2) Certain grilled meats served with a paste of fresh butter, chopped parsley, salt, and pepper, and garnished with straw potatoes and watercress. (3) Fish and poultry coated with green mayonnaise.

Verzata di Riso (Italian). Cabbage-and-rice soup.

Veschperle (German). In Bavaria, the second breakfast, consisting of raw bacon, black bread, and cherry liquor.

Vesiga (Russian). The marrow found in the spine of the sturgeon; dried and used as a food.

Vesou (French). Sugar-cane juice.

Vespetro. A highly spiced homemade Italian and French liqueur containing anise, coriander, angelica, and lemon; rarely made today.

Vessie, En (French). Poached in broth.

Vesture. Anything other than trees that grows on land or covers the soil, such as corn, crops, etc.

Vetch. An edible green seed originally cultivated in the Caucasus, Russia. The starchy root of the tuber-vetch is roasted in hot ash like chestnuts.

Vetebröd (Swedish). Coffee bread.

Vetkoek (South African). A kind of fried bread, prepared with flour, baking powder, sugar, salt, and eggs; usually eaten with preserved fruits.

Ve-Tsin. Monosodium glutamate or Chinese gourmet powder.

Vézelay, Fromage de. A goat's-milk cheese made in Burgundy, France; at its best in the summer.

V.F.C. Very Fine Cognac, a liquor term with little meaning.

Viand. Any article of food; often a choice food.

Viande (French). Meat; viands.

    Viande de Carême. Lenten food.

    Viande Faisandée. Meat with a strong taste due to long aging.

Vichy, À la. Indicating the use of carrots.

Vichyssoise (French). A cream soup prepared with leeks and potatoes; usually served cold.

Vichy Water. Bottled mineral water, chiefly sodium carbonate, obtained from a natural spring at Vichy, France; used mostly to relieve digestive disturbances.

Victoria. (1) A beef garnish consisting of a purée of tomatoes, mushrooms, artichokes, and wine. (2) A sauce of lobster and truffles. (3) An egg dish with lobster. (4) A group of Brazilian coffees. (5) Various fish dishes, salads, and desserts named for Queen Victoria.

Victoria Cake. A cake flavored with cinnamon and cloves, rum, chopped lemon peel and grated rind, and crystallized cherries.

Victorian Wheat. A fairly soft Australian wheat.

Victor Wheat. A white, soft-textured English wheat.

Victual. (1) Food or other items needed and used to support life. (2) Items grown in the soil that are used as food. (3) Items of food or supplies on hand for making meals. (4) To supply with food.

Victualer. One who supplies food and provisions, especially to a ship, army, institution, etc.

Videlle (French). (1) A small confectioner's tool used to pit fruits. (2) Sometimes, a pastry-cutter wheel.

Vider (French). To remove the entrails of meat or poultry; to draw.

Vidonia. A dry, golden, fruity Madeira wine from the Canary Islands.

Vielle Curé. A strong, aromatic afterdinner liqueur made in Bordeaux, France.

Vienna Bread. A highly glazed loaf (or rolls), very crusty from steaming in the oven while baking.

Vienna Coffee. Coffee with whipped cream.

Vienna Flour. A grade of wheat flour of considerable distinction.

Vienna Oven. An oven with a vent for the escape of steam after Vienna bread has attained its glaze.

Vienna Sausage. A type of bland sausage frequently marketed in tinned form.

Viennese Pastry. Pastry made in Vienna, which enjoys one of the greatest reputations in the world. The Viennese are very fond of a great variety of sweet cakes and pastries and are equally devoted to coffee, with which they consume innumerable pastries.

Viennoise, À la. Served with a garnish or sauce

prepared with anchovies, lemon, capers, parsley, and chopped egg. Lightly breaded veal and chicken are prepared *à la viennoise*.

Vierge (French). A frothy whip of butter, lemon juice, salt, and pepper used as a dressing for boiled vegetables.

Vieux Lille Puant. A very strong salty French cheese matured in beer.

Vijg (Dutch). Fig.

Vilain. A fair-tasting small fish found in French rivers.

Vild Hönsfågel (Swedish). Grouse.

Villacidro. A Sardinian brandy with a distinctive aromatic quality.

Villebarron. A white cow's-milk cheese usually aged on the leaves of trees in Blésois, France.

Villeroi, À la. As applied to breaded and fried meat, served with a jellied egg-yolk enriched white sauce.

Villeroux. The famous chef of Count Mirabeau and a friend of the great Carême; he is said to have invented the *omelette au jambon* (ham omelet).

Villiers-Vendôme. A French cow's-milk cheese matured in ashes, then wrapped in vine leaves.

Vin (French). Wine.

Vinaceous. Having the reddish color of wine.

Vinagre (Portuguese, Spanish). Vinegar.

Vinaigre (French). Vinegar.

Vinaigre de Vin (French). Wine vinegar.

Vinaigrer (French). To season with vinegar.

Vinaigrette Sauce (French). A spicy vinegar-and-oil sauce used on cold vegetables, meat, etc.; sometimes prepared with finely chopped parsley.

Vinaigrier (French). A wooden or earthenware barrel-like container used for making vinegar.

Vinal. Started or made in wine.

Vin Blanc (French). White wine.

Vincent. A cold sauce made with herbs and hard-boiled eggs.

Vin de Canne (French). Sugar-cane juice; the liquid obtained by pressing sugar cane.

Vin de Garde (French). A young wine worth buying for future use.

Vin de l'Étoile. Wine produced in Arbois, in the Jura region of France.

Vin de Liqueur (French). Fresh grape juice whose fermentation stops when brandy is added.

Vin de Marché (French). A gift of wine made to someone as part of a business transaction.

Vindemiation. The gathering of grapes or harvesting of other fruit.

Vin de Paille. A rich, sweet French wine made with grapes spread on straw or, occasionally, hung up to dry.

Vin de Sable. Any of the highly alcoholic wines produced in the Basque region of France.

Vin de Sureau (French). Elderberry wine.

Vindrura (Swedish). Grape.

Vine. A plant that grows along the ground or on a trellis or wall, especially a vine that produces grapes used for wine.

Vineal. Related to wine or vines; containing wine; on vines.

Vinedresser. One who cultivates, prunes, and trains vines.

Vinegar. Dilute acetic acid, a sour liquid produced from the fermentation of wines or other alcoholic liquids and various fruits and from the dry distillation of wood (which has an acid taste). It contains, besides acetic and organic acids, sugar, dextrin, extractives, and pigment. It is used as a seasoning and a dressing, and as a digestant, especially with tough or firm-fiber meats and coarse or stringy vegetables. It also has antiseptic properties and is used as a preservative for fish and many vegetables and fruits. Some of the more popular types and flavors of vinegar are wine, cider, garlic, and tarragon.

  Cider Vinegar. Vinegar prepared from apple juice.

  Distilled Vinegar. Vinegar prepared from diluted distilled alcohol.

  Malt Vinegar. Vinegar prepared from malt solutions.

  Sugar Vinegar. Vinegar prepared from sugar solutions.

Vine Leek. A round-headed garlic.

Vinello; Vinetto (Italian). A lesser, unimportant wine.

Vinespinach. A kind of green vegetable resembling spinach, which tends to grow on a vine; basella.

Vineyard; Vinery. An area planted with grape vines.

Vinho (Portuguese). Wine.

Vinho do Porto. Port wine.

Vinho Tinto. Red wine.

Vinho Velho. Old wine.

Vinho Verde. A slightly sparkling young red or white wine.

Vinic. Pertaining to alcohol or wine.

Viniculture. The growing and cultivation of grapes for wine-making purposes.

Vini del Bosco. A group of red and white Sicilian wines.

Vinification. The changing of grape juice by fermentation into an alcoholic beverage.

Vino (Italian). Wine.

Vino Bianco. White wine.

Vino Cotto. Fresh grape juice boiled until it becomes syrupy.

Vino Frizzante. A light, sparkling wine.

Vino Rosso. Red wine.

Vino Secco. Dry wine.

Vino (Spanish). Wine.

Vino de Anada. Fresh young unblended wine produced in Jerez, Spain.

Vino de Jerez. Sherry wine.

Vino de la Casa. The pleasant but undistinguished unbottled wine served in hotels and restaurants in Spain.

Vino de Pasta. Ordinary table wine of the sherry type.

Vino Maestro. A full-bodied, rather sweet wine used to improve lesser wines.

Vino Quemado. Burnt wine; red wine combined with sugar, cinnamon, and orange peel, and drunk in parts of Spain, especially Aragon, on Christmas Eve. It is heated before serving.

Vinolent. Tending to become intoxicated from drinking wine.

Vinous. Like wine; made with wine or smelling or tasting like wine; having the characteristics of wine.

Vin Rosé (French). Pink wine, wine which is neither white nor red.

Vin Rouge (French). Red wine.

Vint. (1) To produce a strong liquor or wine. (2) Vintage.

Vintage. (1) The wine obtained from the vine during a single season. Wine of exceptional quality; usually connotes a particularly good year. (2) The complete grape harvest; the gathering of grapes.

Vintager. One who gathers grapes during the harvest.

Vintage Wine. A fine wine produced during a "vintage" year.

Vintner. A dealer in, or a grower of, wine.

Vintry (Obsolete). A shop where wine is sold and also stored.

Violet Petals. Dried sugar-coated violet petals used as decorations on cakes, puddings, confectionery, and ices.

Violets de Toulouse (French). Sugared or candied violets.

Virgin Brandy. Unblended brandy; natural Cognac.

Virginia Ham. An excellent high-quality kind of ham originally produced in Virginia. The flavor has been ascribed to the kind of pig used, the climate, the method of treatment, and perhaps also to the pig's diet, which includes acorns and other nuts and roots. Usually Virginia hams are baked with a coating of bread crumbs, brown sugar, and cloves.

Virgouleuse (French). A soft sweet winter pear.

Viroplay (French). A garnish consisting of braised spinach, quartered braised artichoke hearts, and sautéed potatoes; usually served with roast lamb.

Virtù (Italian). A provincial soup made of meatballs, pork sausages, and vegetables.

Vis (Dutch). Fish.

Viscid. Thick and syrupy.

Viscogen. A thickening agent consisting of lime, sugar, and water; occasionally used for whipping cream.

Vishnevaia. A Russian cherry brandy made with vodka and crushed wild cherries.

Visigha. Dried marrow from the backbone of the sturgeon; used in making certain Russian dishes.

Viskoekjes (Dutch). Fried fish cakes.

Visniski (Russian). A ball or roll of chopped fish seasoned with fennel, covered with a special dough, and fried in very hot oil.

Viss. A weight equal to about 3½ pounds used to weigh foods in Burma and southern India.

Vitamins. Substances in foods that are essential for normal growth. Originally they were thought to be amines. The word was originated by Casimir Funk, noted lexicographer, by combining *vita* (life) and *amine* (chemical compound).

Vitamins, Loss of. Vegetables lose vitamin C in cooking, mostly by their leaching out into the water. Losses are greatly minimized by steaming or by cooking in a minimum of water.

Pressure cooking: For meat, owing to the higher temperature, there is greater shrinkage and greater expression of extractives into the juice; thus there is also greater destruction of vitamin B_1.

For vegetables, the pressure cooker is used as a steamer, and the greater the speed of cooking and the lessened effect of leaching result in greater preservation of vitamin C than in boiling in an open pan.

Vitamin Losses in Cooking Meat
(percent)

	Vitamin B_1	Vitamin B_2	Nicotinic Acid
Baking	55%	25%	35%
Broiling	30	15	20
Frying	10	10	15
Roasting	35	20	20
Stewing	75	30	50

Vitela (Portuguese). Veal.

Vitellin. A protein found in egg yolk.

Vitelotte (French). The kidney potato, a kind of potato that keeps its firmness when cooked.

Vitello (Italian). Veal.

    Vitello Tonnato. Veal with a cold tuna-fish sauce.

Vitellus. Egg yolk.

Viterbo. An Italian cheese made of sheep's milk curdled with wild artichoke; used chiefly for grating.

Viticulture. The growing and cultivation of grapes for wine.

Viticulturist. A vine grower.

Vitkålsoppa med Frikadeller (Swedish). A cabbage soup served with cut-up pieces of veal.

Vivandier (French). One who follows an army, providing food and supplies to the men.

Vivda (Scotch). Unsalted air-dried or smoked meat.

Vive. A sea perch, found in the waters near France, with white meat of a pleasing taste and texture.

Viveiro de Mariscos (Portuguese). A seafood soup-stew.

Vivers. Things, such as food, used to sustain life.

Viveur en Tasse (French). Very strong bouillon served in cups.

Viveurs. Descriptive of foods, particularly soups, highly seasoned with cayenne or paprika.

Vla (Dutch). Custard.

Vlattero. A sweet Greek liqueur made from currants.

Vlees (Dutch). Meat.

Vleespannekoekjes (Dutch). Meat pancakes.

V.O. Very old; a liquor term.

Vodka. A strong liquor, usually clear and colorless, originally produced in Russia, and now made in other parts of the world. At one time made exclusively from potatoes, it is now produced from grains.

V.O.P. Very old pale; a term used in the port-wine trade.

V.O.T. Very old tawny; a term used in the port-wine trade.

V.O.X. Very old Xerez; a term used in the sherry-wine trade.

Void. A cheese, made in Meuse, France, strongly resembling Pont l'Évêque.

Voider (British). A tray for removing soiled dishes and leftover food from the table during or after a meal.

Volaille Demi-Deuil (French). "Chicken in half-mourning." A dish in which dark truffles are inserted under the skin of a chicken, producing the "half-mourning" effect.

Volatile Oil. An oil that evaporates rapidly on exposure. Examples are oil of onion, garlic, also of lemon and other fruits.

Vol-au-Vent (French). Puff pastry shaped into any desired form, baked, then filled with meat, poultry, or fish.

    Vol-au-Vent Régence. Puff-pastry shell, often oval-shaped, filled with *foie gras*, mushrooms, truffles, and ground poultry quenelles.

    Vol-au-Vent Toulousaine. Puff-pastry shell filled with sweetbreads, mushrooms, and truffles.

Volière, À la (French). As applied to game or poultry, served in its feathers; now rare.

Volnay. A good, often excellent type of red Burgundy wine. *See* France, The Wines of.

Volpalliere (French). Small chicken fillets, larded and braised; served with a truffle sauce.

Volvet Kaas. A Dutch cheese consisting of not less than 45 percent fat when marketed.

Vongole (Italian). Clams.

> Vongole Ripiene al Forno. Baked stuffed clams.

Voorgerechten (Dutch). Appetizers.

Voorjaarssla (Dutch). Spring salad.

Voracious. Gluttonous; devouring food ravenously or greedily. The word comes from the Latin *vorare*, "to devour."

Voracity. Gluttony; greediness in eating.

Vorant. Devouring.

Vork (Dutch). Fork.

Vorspeisen (German). Appetizers.

Vørterkake (Norwegian). Spice bread.

Vougeot, Clos de. One of the most important of all Burgundy wines. *See* France, The Wines of.

Vouvray. A slightly effervescent white wine, usually not completely dry in taste; pleasant, but not very important. *See* France, The Wines of.

Vraie Tortue (French). Real turtle, as contrasted with mock turtle.

Vrilles de Vigne (French). Very young tips of grapevines; often cooked briefly, then soaked in vinegar, and cooked in olive oil.

Vrucht (Dutch). Fruit.

V.S. Very superior; a term used in the liquor trade.

V.S.O. Very superior old; a term used in the liquor trade.

V.S.O.P. Very superior old pale; a term used in the liquor trade.

Vuillemot. A French chef, a friend and culinary adviser of Alexandre Dumas, who owned the Tête Noir restaurant in St. Cloud.

Vuršty (Czechoslovakian). A rather short thick frankfurter.

VVE. *Veuve*, meaning "widow"; a wine term.

V.V.O. Very, very old; a liquor term.

V.V.S. Very, very superior; a liquor term.

W

Wachsbohnen (German). Wax beans; yellow beans.

Wachteln (German). Quail.

Waders. Edible long-legged birds that wade in water in search of food.

Wafer. A very thin layer of baked dough which may be eaten plain or used as the basis of a variety of fancy desserts.

Wafer-Paper. A thin batter of fine flour and water, sweetened and slightly flavored, used as the basis for certain sugary confections, such as macaroons, or for covering certain sugary sweets. White of egg brushed over a hot baking sheet is sometimes substituted.

Wafery (British). The section of the British royal kitchens where pastries are made.

Waffle. A soft, crisp baked batter cooked with a special iron. Waffle batter is similar to but heavier than pancake batter, and before the egg whites are added they are beaten until peaks form. The batter may be varied by the addition of fruits, nuts, cheese, spices, etc. Plain or flavored waffles offer an interesting base for creamed foods, vegetables, ice cream, etc. As a breakfast dish waffles are generally served with butter and syrup and with bacon or ham.

Today waffle irons are electric. As early as the 12th century, long-handled square or round irons were used over open fires. Designs sometimes included a coat of arms or a church symbol as well as the usual indentations of the waffle iron.

Waffle Iron. The modern waffle iron is a hinged metal appliance designed specifically to cook waffles by electricity.

Wagtail. A small European bird with fairly good-tasting flesh; prepared like the lark.

Waiter. (1) A person employed in a restaurant or in a home to serve food at the table. (2) (Obsolete) Salver, a service tray.

Waitress. A woman who serves food at the table in a restaurant, hotel, etc.

Wakame. An edible Japanese seaweed.

Wake. In Ireland, an all-night gathering of friends and relatives to watch over a corpse before burial; usually accompanied by festivities. By extension, the term refers to the food and drink consumed at a wake.

Wake Robin (Colloquial). Wild arum, a plant whose roots contain a starchy substance.

Waldmeister (German). Woodruff, an aromatic herb used to flavor wines and alcoholic drinks.

Waldorf Salad. A salad made with chopped celery, apples, and nuts; often mixed with mayonnaise.

Walewska (French). A garnish for fish, particularly for sole, made of lobster, Mornay sauce, and truffles.

Walla Walla Wheat. A white soft Pacific wheat low in protein; its flour makes very soft dough.

Wall-Eyed. Of various fish, having large, prominent eyes, especially the wall-eyed pike.

Walliskäse. *See* Saanen.

Walnoot (Dutch). Walnut.

Walnut. A two-lobed seed (the edible portion) of the walnut tree encased in a round shell that separates easily into halves. Walnuts originated in the Middle East, have been popular for thousands of years, and were a common article of commerce over a thousand years before the time of Christ. The wrinkled brown nuts have an excellent taste, and they combine well in cakes, cookies, etc. Walnuts with port wine are considered a classic delicacy.

Brought to Southern Europe, walnuts became *the* nut of the Mediterranean area, where the word "nut" actually means walnut. For example, walnuts are *noix* in French, *noci* in Italian, and *nueces* in Spanish. Walnuts became popular in England and were shipped abroad in British vessels; soon a certain variety became known as *English walnut*. Walnuts were introduced into the United States, particularly into California, by the Spanish missionaries.

Walnuts are marketed in several different varieties, chiefly as the white, or butternut, type; English walnut; and black walnut. Green walnuts, immature specimens that have not yet formed shells, are popular in France. Thin-shell walnuts, as the name implies, have thin shells. Pickled walnuts are a popular relish in England.

Walnut Oil. A yellowish green oil made from walnuts; it has a distinctive nutty taste.

Walrus. The large marine animal found chiefly in the Arctic region; its rich, oily flesh is eaten by Eskimos.

Wampi. A very small citrus fruit that tastes like wild grapes.

Wapatoo; Arrowhead; Arrowleaf; Duck-Potato. An aquatic plant with edible tubers, once a great favorite with American Indians; may be used like potatoes.

Wapiti. The elk, or stag, of North America.

Warabi. A Japanese fern sprout used in salads and cooking.

Ward Eight. A whisky-and-grenadine cocktail supposed to have originated in Boston and to have been named for the Eighth Ward.

Wardroom. The space aboard a naval vessel in which meals are served to commissioned officers (except the commanding officer on larger ships).

Ware. (1) Containers, vessels, or dishes made chiefly of baked clay. (2) The spawn of oysters in their third year.

Warek Eenab (Arabic). Stuffed grape leaves.

Wark (Indian). Edible thin silver- or gold-leaf foil used decoratively on sweet preparations.

Warm. (1) To heat food moderately. (2) Neither hot nor cold.

Warming. Heating again foods previously cooked. Also, heating the dishes or plates on which foods are to be served.

Warren's Cooking Pot (British, Obsolete). An old kind of steam cooker.

Warsaw Fish. Any of a number of different fish, but especially the Jewfish.

Warsche (Scotch). Foods lacking salt.

Wasabi. A Japanese herb with a sharp, spicy flavor; horseradish.

Washbrew (British). Oatmeal cooked until it becomes a thick paste.

Washed-Curd Cheese. Cheese in which the curd has been washed to remove acidity.

Washy. As applied to foods, thin or watery.

Wassail. (1) A heated spiced-ale drink that originated during medieval times. (2) In general, a toast to someone's health, or a large, lively drinking party. The term probably derives from the Scandinavian *ves heil*, meaning "to your health."

Wassail Bowl. A large bowl in which the wassail is placed. Often small pieces of toast or small apples are added.

Wastell; Wastel. A yeast oatcake.

Wastle Cake (Scotch). A pancake, similar to a griddle cake.

Wat. (1) (North African) *Zegeni*, a highly spiced meat stew. (2) A rabbit or hare.

Water Bewitched. In relation to liquor, diluted.

Waterbuck. A type of African antelope, often used as food.

Water-Chestnut Flour. Flour made from dried ground water chestnuts; used in Chinese cooking to thicken sauces.

Water Chestnuts. Tubers of an oriental aquatic plant, about the size of chestnuts. They are

peeled before being canned and shipped. Used chiefly in Chinese cookery, they may be used whole or sliced.

Water Convolvulus. An aquatic plant whose immature shoots are often used as a green vegetable.

Watercress. A small perennial aquatic herb. Its pungent peppery green leaves are used raw as a garnish, in salads, and as a sandwich filling, and can also be made into soup. Eaten in considerable quantity, it minimizes the aftereffects of eating onions, garlic, etc.

Watercress, Chinese. A type of watercress with soft, rounded leaves, often used in Chinese cooking.

Water Down, To. To dilute, especially liquors, by adding water or other liquids.

Waterfisch (Dutch). (1) Freshwater fish. (2) A fish sauce consisting of vegetables cooked in fish, bitter orange, pepper, mustard, etc., then strained, and sometimes made into an aspic to coat fish.

Waterfowl. Any of a large range of water birds, many of which are edible.

Watergruel. Cereal cooked with water instead of milk.

Waterhen. The Moorhen, a game bird.

Water Ice. A frozen dessert made of sweetened flavored water and sometimes fruit juice and beaten egg whites; sometimes inaccurately called *sherbet*, which is made with milk and other ingredients.

Water Icing. A syrup and sugar mixture used to ice small cakes. When applied cool, it makes a good glaze; applied hot, it dries with a dull finish.

Watering Place. A resort which features mineral springs.

Water Jacket. A rather shallow pan containing hot water surrounding a smaller container or mold in which a mixture is baked. Because the steam prevents the mixture from drying out, the finished dish is moist. It is quite suitable for moist soufflés.

Watermelon. A thick green-rinded fruit with juicy red pulp. Originally an African fruit, it is now grown abundantly in many parts of the United States and in other countries. Watermelons range in size from the refrigerator size, similar in shape to a honeydew, to the large zeppelin-shaped melons that may be 4–5 feet long. When ripe the melon sounds hollow when thumped; the rind is velvety green and the underside yellow. Watermelon is served cold in wedges or is cut into cubes or balls and served alone or with other fruits. The rind may be pickled and served as a relish.

Water Nymph. A green tea produced in Kwangtung province, China.

Water Oats. Wild rice; Canadian rice.

Water of Life. Strong liquor like brandy; *aqua vitae.*

Water Parsnip. A plant found in marshes which resembles celery; only the leaves are eaten, usually in soups or salads.

Water Pepper; Smartweed. A species called mild water pepper is used in salads in the southern United States.

Water Pimpernel. A type of wild cress found in various parts of Europe. It has a spicy taste, and is good used sparingly in salads.

Water Pitcher. A pitcher primarily used for water.

Water-Soluble. Able to be dissolved in water.

Water Souchet. Chicken or fish stew served in a soup tureen. The term is derived from the Dutch word *waterzoetje.*

Waterzooï (Belgian). A fish stew, sometimes thickened with bread crumbs and cream; may also be made with poultry.

Wax Bean. The yellow relative of the string bean; at its best when the beans within the pod are small and immature. They should be waxy-looking and crisp so that they snap when broken. To prepare them for cooking, the ends should be cut off, the beans washed, and cooked whole, cut crosswise, or in long narrow strips. They may be steamed in a small amount of water, or merely steamed in butter in a tightly closed pan. Wax beans are available frozen and canned.

Waxed Paper; Wax Paper. Thin sheets of paper coated with wax; used to wrap or cover food and to line baking pans.

Wax Gourd. A type of melon with a hard exterior, permitting it to be eaten long after being picked; also called Chinese melon.

Wax Myrtle. Bayberry.

Waxwing. A small game bird with good-tasting though bony flesh.

Wawa (American Indian). The wild goose.

Waybread (British). Plantain.

Weakfish; Squeteague. Any of several saltwater fish with easily torn mouths; found along the Atlantic and Gulf coasts of the United States. Although it is not a trout, the common weakfish is also known as *sea trout* or *deep water trout*. It is prepared like trout and similar fish.

Weckewerk (German). Pork meat and pig skin mixed with bread and fried. Also, a mixture of veal, pork, and pieces of white roll eaten hot or cold.

Wedding Breakfast. The meal served after a morning marriage ceremony and prior to the departure for a honeymoon; by extension, a lunch similarly served.

Wedding Cake. A very large white cake, either plain or filled with fruits or nuts, usually iced; served at wedding receptions. It is customary for the bride, theoretically with the groom's assistance, to make the first cut in the cake, whereupon small pieces are given to all the guests.

Wedge. To cut into triangular pieces, as, for example, a wedge of pie or cake.

Wedgwood. (1) A renowned type of English pottery or ware, available in a wide range of patterns and styles. (2) The pale blue color characteristic of Wedgwood ware.

Weeper. A wine bottle that leaks through the cork.

Weever. An edible European fish of the perch family. The sharp spines in the dorsal fin are poisonous.

Weevil. A small insect, similar to the beetle, that bores into grains and deposits its eggs.

Weihnachtstolle (German). A rich, almond-flavored bread popular in European countries at Christmastime.

Wein Kaltschalen (German). Cold wine soup.

Weinkraut (German). Sauerkraut prepared with white wine.

Weinstuben. In Germany a restaurant specializing in wines.

Weintraube (German). Grape.

Weissbier. A delicate "white" beer with about 2 percent alcohol; made in Berlin, Germany; usually served in a large glass, often with a little raspberry syrup.

Weissbrot (German). White bread.

Weisse Bohnen (German). White string beans.

Weisse Rüben; Weissrüben (German). Turnips, parsnips.

Weisse Sosse (German). White sauce.

Weissfisch (German). Whiting, a fish.

Weissgebäck (German). A kind of pastry.

Weisskohl (German). White cabbage.

Weisslacker. A soft, rather spicy German cheese similar to Allgäuer.

Weissweine (German). White wines.

Weisswurst (German). An uncooked white sausage, prepared with veal and pork.

Well. A hollow or depression. In a mold or cake tin, the center hole; similarly, in pastry or other foods, the space left empty to be filled with a mixture or garnish. Also, in preparing a dough, the depression in a mound of flour into which eggs or liquid are placed.

Well-and-Tree. A large platter, usually made of metal, with a series of connected grooves to catch the juices of meat or poultry and carry them into a trough from which they can be readily removed.

Wellcress. Watercress.

Wels. A large spike-finned freshwater fish. A *dwarf wels*, or freshwater catfish, is delicate-fleshed.

Welsh Barm Cake. A yeast-dough muffin.

Welsh Cakes. Cakes or pancakes prepared with sugar, fat, flour, eggs, raisins, and nutmeg; heavily coated with sugar and cinnamon; cut into triangles.

Welsh Cheese. The classic Welsh cheese, Caerphilly.

Welsh Mutton. A type of mutton obtained from a small breed which grazes on the Welsh mountains; it has a fine taste and texture.

Welsh Rabbit; Welsh Rarebit (British). A dish, now popular in many countries, of melted cheese, mustard, and beer served on slices of toast. The terms are generally used interchangeably.

Wensleydale. A rich, blue-veined English cheese that resembles Stilton. Another variety is whitish, excellent-tasting, and eaten quite fresh.

Western Charr. A variety of trout.

Western Sandwich; Denver Sandwich. A sandwich made with either scrambled eggs or an omelet combined with sautéed ham, peppers, and onions.

West Friesian. A Dutch skim-milk cheese; best when only a week old.

Westphalian Ham. A cured smoked German ham; eaten raw in thin slices, usually as a first course.

Westphalia Sour-Milk Cheese. *See* Brioler.

Wether. A male sheep; a ram.

Wether Gammon. Leg of mutton.

Wet One's Whistle (Colloquial). To have a drink of liquor.

Wey. An English measure used for salt, cheese, corn, and other foods; the measure varies with the particular commodity.

Whale. A large aquatic animal valuable for its oil and bone; its meat is eaten by the Eskimos and the Japanese. Salted whale tongue was formerly considered good eating, as was whale fat. In the Middle Ages the meat was called *Lenten bacon* or sometimes *crapois*.

By modern standards, whale meat is tough and strong-flavored; for this reason it is not a popular food. It is usually sold frozen and should be kept frozen until ready to cook in order to prevent an unpleasant fishy taste. When cooked, its flavor vaguely resembles that of beef.

Whale Oil. Oil obtained from the whale; used, after hardening, for lower-quality margarines, especially in Europe.

Wheat. A very widely grown cereal grain. As one of the first domesticated grains, it has long been the Western world's chief source of bread. In the United States, food products made from wheat contribute one-fourth of the human-energy requirements. There are varieties adapted to growing conditions, as winter wheat (fall-planted) and spring wheat. The grain is transported to mills to be ground into flour. Flour from durum wheat, which is the hardest, is used for macaroni. Hard red winter or spring wheat is used in making bread. Flour from soft red winter wheat is used in making pastry. White wheat is used for pastries and breakfast foods. Leading producers of wheat are the United States, the Soviet Union, China, Canada, Italy, India, and Argentina.

Wheatduck. The American widgeon, a type of wild duck.

Wheatear. (1) Fallowchat, stonechat, or white-tail, small European game birds. (2) Wheat flour.

Wheaten Flour. Flour made of wheat.

Wheatfeed; Millers' Offal; Wheat Offal. Residue from the milling of wheat to produce flour.

Wheat Germ. The part of a wheat kernel containing the fatty substance.

Wheatsheaf Loaf (British). A loaf of bread baked in the shape of a sheaf of wheat; formerly served at harvest festivals.

Whelk. A small edible European mollusk with a spiraled shell.

Whet. (1) To stimulate or sharpen (appetite or thirst). (2) Any food or beverage, but especially liquor, that stimulates the appetite.

Whetstone. An abrasive material or stone on which knives are sharpened; a grinding stone.

Whetstone Cakes (British). Round cakes made with flour, sugar, egg whites, and caraway. The dough is rolled, cut out, and baked in a cool oven on paper.

Whey. The liquid portion of milk after separation from the curd; used in the preparation of cheeses.

Whey Cream. After curd has been removed in cheese making, the cream remaining in the whey.

Whey of Butter. Buttermilk.

Whig. Sour milk, buttermilk, or whey.

Whimberry. Another name for the whortleberry or bilberry.

Whip. (1) Any dessert to which beaten egg white or whipped cream is added. A gelatin whip is made by beating the gelatin before it is firmly set. (2) To beat egg whites, cream, etc. to a froth.

Whipped Butter. Butter into which air has been whipped, causing it to spread readily.

Whipped Cream. Heavy cream beaten with a whisk, rotating beater, or electric mixer until it forms a soft mound; it may be flavored or sweetened; used as a topping for cakes, puddings, ice cream, or any other dessert. A dab of unsweetened whipped cream may be floated in cream soups.

Whisk. (1) A small kitchen tool made of wire loops designed to "whisk" or whip cream, eggs, liquids, and light doughs. A rotary wire whisk, hand-powered or driven by electricity, may also be used. (2) To beat foods, especially egg whites or cream, with a whisk until frothy. (See illus. p. 631.)

Whisk

Whisky; Whiskey. A strong spirit or liquor; in Scotland and Ireland made from malted barley, and in the United States from rye or corn. The word "whisky" derives from two forms of the Gaelic words for "water of life," *usquebaugh* and, later, *whiskybae*. The European liquor trade refers to Scotch "whisky" but adds the "e" for Irish "whiskey"; in America the usual spelling is *whisky*. Although barley, rye, and corn whisky are standard, whiskies are occasionally made with wheat, oats, or potatoes. Whether from Ireland, England, or the United States, all liquors depend on the type of grain used, the distilling process, the type of storage cask used, the manner in which the grain is cured, and, to a surprising extent, upon the character of water.

Scotch whisky is rarely brought to the market in "straight" form; most of it is carefully blended and sold when at least 3 years old, 7–8 years being more typical. Some whiskies are aged for those who like the taste of older liquors. Irish whiskey resembles the Scotch to a considerable extent but is likely to have a lighter, less smoky taste because peat is not used when curing the grain. American whisky is made with two different grains—either corn or rye; it may be bottled as a straight liquor or blended.

According to the best estimates, whisky has been made for at least 600 years.

Any strong liquor, including vodka, may be called whisky. In Burma a local whisky called *Mekong* is prepared.

Whisky and Soda. Whisky combined with club soda, often with ice.

Whisky, Straight. Undiluted whisky, drunk without water.

Whistling Duck. A species of wild duck, the golden-eye, which has a fairly good taste.

White. The whitish viscous fluid surrounding an egg yolk.

Whitebait. A very small, delicate fish prepared like small smelts, or sardines, usually deep-fat fried whole.

White Beet. A name sometimes used for chard. *See* Chard.

White Bread. Bread made with a light-colored flour, as opposed to a dark bread.

White Cap. (1) A type of mushroom with a white, or whitish top. (2) Any of a number of game birds having a white head or markings on the head.

White Cheddar. Cheddar cheese not colored with annatto.

White Cinnamon. The inner bark of wild cinnamon; used as a condiment.

White Crystal Sugar. A very white sugar, 99.7 percent sucrose.

Whitefish. Any of a wide range of freshwater fish known for their white flesh, usually found in lakes, streams, etc. It is prepared like flounder, bass, and pike. Smoked whitefish is a delicately flavored, appetizing fish.

White Friar. Small white flecks floating in wine.

White Fungus; Snow Fungus. An edible fungus much used in the Chinese cuisine.

White Heart. A type of cherry having a light-colored exterior and pink flesh.

White Meal. Oatmeal, as distinguished from bread meal, that is, barley.

White Meat. (1) Any foods that are light in color, such as chicken, veal, or, sometimes, fish. (2) Dairy foods.

White Nougat. A creamy mixture that consists of glucose, boiling sugar, dissolved gelatin, and whipped egg whites, sometimes with fruits, nuts, honey, or cherries added; used as a filling for chocolates.

White Pepper. A powdered white spice. The black outer covering of regular black pepper is removed; the berries are soaked for a week to ten days in water so that the skins loosen. Then they are crushed until loose particles come off, washed, and dried in the sun. The regular milling process is then completed.

Whitepot (British). A preparation of eggs and flour boiled together with milk and cream; a specialty of Devonshire.

White Potato; Irish Potato. A variety of potato with a comparatively light-colored exterior.

White Pudding. A European preparation made like a long sausage coiled round and round in layers.

White Royal Icing. A grayish mixture of icing sugar and beaten egg whites. Small drops of a blue coloring are added commercially to make it a bright white.

White Sauce. A sauce made of flour, butter, and milk (sometimes cream) slowly cooked together until thick; it may be made thin, medium, or thick according to the proportion of flour to liquid. In Europe, any white or light-colored sauce.

Whitetail. Any of several game birds, such as the wheatear.

Whitethorn. A rather firm white Irish cheese.

White Tuna Fish. Germon, a pale-fleshed tuna fish.

White Vinegar. A colorless dilute solution of acetic acid, usually made from malt liquor alcohol.

White Wheat. Any pale or light wheat.

White Wine. As used in the wine trade, any wine, including pink wine, which is not red.

White Wine Vinegar. A vinegar made from white wine.

White Wine Whey. A beverage made from the whey obtained in cheese making combined with white wine.

Whiting. (1) A silvery fish of the codfish family, native to Europe and America. Many local fishes are called whiting because of their similarity to the true whiting. (2) The silver hake.

Whitstables. A fine variety of oyster found off the British coast.

Whittle. To ply with liquor.

Whole-Meal Bread. Bread containing whole-meal flour.

Whole-Wheat. Made with the entire kernel of wheat, such as whole-wheat muffins or bread.

Whortleberry; Blaeberry; Whimberry; Windberry; Wort. A rather small, red flavorsome European berry that tastes much like a huckleberry.

Wickenin' (British). Yeast.

Widerkomm. A medieval ceremonial drinking glass.

Widgeon; Wigeon. A small bird of the wild duck family; usually roasted and basted with butter or bacon drippings because its meat is dry.

Wiener Backhendl (German). Chicken deep-fat fried and baked.

Wienerbrød (Danish, Norwegian). Danish pastry. *See* Danish Pastry.

Wiener Schnitzel (Austrian). A thin slice of lightly-breaded, sautéed veal. When designated *à la Holstein*, it is served with a fried egg and anchovies.

Wies'nbier (German). Meadow beer.

Wig. A rather small cake or bun, just enough for one portion.

Wigeon. *See* Widgeon.

Wigs; Weigs (British). Buns made with currants.

Wijn (Dutch). Wine.

Wild Arum; Lords-and-Ladies. An acrid plant; the starch from its tuberous root is occasionally used in cookery.

Wild Boar. The wild pig or hog native to Asia, Europe, and parts of Africa; its meat is sometimes very good, sometimes extremely gamy.

Wildbrett (German). Game.

Wild Cherry. A blue-black sour fruit used for making jelly and homemade wines.

Wild Chicory. A rather bitter plant; used in salads or pickled.

Wild Cumin. A plant with flower clusters that produce a kind of cumin seed.

Wild Duck. A bird of the mallard family; ancestor of the domestic duck. Its rather coarse, gamy flesh is prepared like that of the domestic duck.

Wilde Appel (Dutch). Crab apple.

Wild Fowl. Game birds, such as partridge, quail, etc.

Wild Goose. A term applied to various wild game birds which are members of the goose family.

Wilding. A crabapple, or wild apple.

Wild Iris. *See* Calamus.

Wild Lettuce. Lettuce that grows wild as large, individual leaves, seldom forming into heads. Some varieties are bland, others spicy.

Wild Mustard. A wild plant, native to the United States, whose edible leaves are best when picked during the early spring, boiled like spinach, and served as a vegetable with plenty of butter. The seeds may be used as a condiment.

Wild Olive. The wild variety of the common olive; it produces a very small fruit.

Wild Onion; Wild Garlic; Wild Shallot; Meadow Garlic. A wild plant whose edible bulbs have a decided onionlike taste and a distinctive odor.

Wild Rice. The grains of a perennial grass native to North America; it is not actually a true rice. Wild rice must be washed very carefully in several changes of water. Although expensive, a small amount is sufficient for several portions.

Wild Spinach. *See* Pigweed.

Wild Thyme. An aromatic plant sometimes used as a flavoring ingredient.

Wild Vine. The fox grape or other clinging or climbing plants.

Wild Yeasts. Yeasts that grow naturally on fruits or plants and readily produce spores; not reliable for commercial use.

Wilhelmina Wheat. A white English wheat, the flour of which makes excellent shortbreads, cookies, and cakes.

William. A sweet juicy pear that matures in September in France and Switzerland. A white liqueur is made from the pears.

Willow Grouse. The ptarmigan. *See* Ptarmigan.

Willow Pattern. A classic dinnerware pattern, executed in blue, featuring willow trees prominently; originated by Thomas Turner.

Willowware. *See* Willow Pattern.

Wiltshire (British). (1) A snappy cheddar cheese made in Wiltshire. (2) An excellent variety of sheep. (3) A kind of flavorsome, smoky bacon.

Windberry. An English bilberry, a small, wild, very juicy blue-black berry; used only for tarts or with apples.

Windegg. An egg with a soft shell; an imperfect egg.

Windfall. Fruit which falls due to the action of the wind.

Windle (British). A corn measure equal to about 3 bushels.

Wine; Wines. In general usage, the fermented juice of certain grapes widely used as a beverage of comparatively low alcoholic content. By extension, the term also includes beverages made from various other fruits, sap of trees, grains, flowers, and the like. Wine can be classified in different ways: either as red or white, European or American, dry or sweet, or according to the method of fermentation. In this last classification, wines are natural, controlled in fermentation with added brandy, and sparkling. By general definition a natural wine is one with an alcoholic content of less than 14 percent. Wines in the second category include all fortified wines like port, sherry, and Madeira which have an alcoholic content of from 14–23 per cent. Because of their high alcoholic content, these wines will not spoil quickly after being opened, whereas the natural wines, low in alcohol, spoil quickly when exposed to the air. These wines improve while they are in the bottle, whereas those with a high alcoholic content rarely show any improvement, with the exception of port.

The making of wine includes the care of the vineyard, the harvesting of the grapes, the fermentation process, and the treatment which follows. Viniculture varies all over the world. In some regions there is not enough sunshine, in others there is far too much. In many places the soil is too dry and must be irrigated, while in others the danger is in excessive rain. Growing ordinary table grapes may not be difficult, but grapes intended for superior wines demand great skill in an extremely complicated process. A lifetime is not sufficient to learn all of the problems and difficulties that a viniculturist must conquer, such as knowing exactly when to harvest. Should the harvest be delayed another day to allow the sugar content of the grapes to increase? But if it rains the grapes will soak up the moisture and the sugar content will be lowered. Even in a good year, some vineyards may harvest too soon or too late and produce wines below the average for the district. On the other hand, even in a bad year, a vineyard may delay the harvest long after the regular period, gambling with the weather and hoping for some sunshine so that in the end it can reap a harvest far better than other vineyards in the district. The vintage year charts are no more than generalizations, for exceptions are always possible. Within a certain district like the Moselle, in Germany, where the river twists and turns and the vineyards receive sun from many angles, a distance of half a mile may mean a completely different wine. In short, vintage charts should be regarded with a certain skepticism.

The proper time for a harvest varies according to the climate of the region. But, in general, when the grapes have developed the greatest possible amount of natural sugar, they are harvested. In the great vineyards, a series of tests quickly reveal the amount of sugar in the grapes; from day to day sugar content may vary as much as 2 percent. The risk involved in selecting the correct date for the harvest can be imagined. Vintners must be certain that the grape skins are covered with the microscopic yeast organisms technically known as *saccharomyces*, which settle on the skins as the grapes ripen. It is a mysterious process, and several centuries of research have failed to disclose its exact nature. What makes this natural yeast more remarkable is the fact that it does not appear until the grapes are ripe, but appear it must, or the fermentation will not occur. When there is a fine, dense layer on the grapes and the time for harvest has almost arrived, the vintners watch the skies with great anxiety—a heavy rain would wash away this yeast. Then it would be necessary to wait until the yeast returned, running the risk of a possible frost with each day of delay. In recent years chemists have worked on the riddle of saccharomyces, so that in years when there is an insufficient amount on the grapes, it is possible now to add prepared laboratory cultures which are synthetic equivalents. Chemical yeasts are used extensively in the United States and, to a limited degree, in Europe. The American wineries claim that the laboratory cultures are satisfactory, while the European vinters find them poor substitutes.

After the grapes are picked, they are rushed to the press. Sometimes the stalks are pressed too. But if the stalks are used, they are gently pressed, for they have a strong tannin content and great care must be taken that they do not add an astringent quality. Some vintners press the stalks separately to obtain the natural sugar. There is considerable difference of opinion on this procedure.

The grapes are crushed by several methods. In California most of the crushing is done by means of hydraulic equipment. In many parts of Europe old hand presses are still in use. What about treading or trampling down the grapes? Surprisingly, some vintners still do this. It is most important that air or oxygen be added to the crushed grapes, and so far no substitute has been found for the regular, rhythmic tramping with the feet. In Spain and Portugal special shoes are used. In much of Italy bare feet are still the rule.

The pressing, whether by mechanical or human means, finally results in a kind of mush of flattened grape skins, pulp, and juice known as *must*. It is now that the natural yeast, the saccharomyces, performs its function. The fermentation process begins, caused by the combination of crushed grapes, oxygen, and the natural yeast. In the absence of any one of these elements, fermentation will not start. Also, if the proportion of any of the three is increased or decreased, the process will proceed differently.

When the must is in this first stage, the mixture is rushed immediately to a vat. The temperature must be carefully controlled or the fermentation will be too slow or too fast, but a reasonable degree of flexibility is allowed, varying from wine district to wine district, and from country to country. The vats are only partially filled; a certain amount of space is left at the top to allow for the violence of the fermentation. Anyone seeing the process for the first time would be amazed at its intensity. In its own small way, within the confines of the vat, it has the fury of a great storm. What is occurring is the conversion of the natural sugar in the grapes into alcohol—more technically, into ethyl alcohol. The bubbling is produced by the action of carbonic gas, formed as sugar is changed into alcohol. The explosive action occurs when each grape sugar molecule is broken into two molecules of carbon dioxide and two of alcohol.

Fermentation time is quite variable; it may last for only a few days, or it may run to several weeks or longer under certain circumstances. The shortest period of fermentation is in Burgundy, where three days is the usual time. In Bordeaux it may take from one and a half to two weeks. Incidentally, this is a sore point with the Bordeaux vintners, for an old Gallic proverb has it that the quicker the period of fermentation, the better the wine. In most of the Rhône Valley, the fermentation varies from two to four weeks; about the same time is taken in the Moselle and Rhine Valleys also. For some of the very sweet wines, there are certain uncharacteristic years in which the fermentation period can extend over a month or more.

When the fermentation comes to a slow conclusion, and the last few bubbles have died away, chemical tests are made to be sure the sugar content is settled—usually to not more than 1 percent, unless the wine is to be a sweet type. The important thing now is to remove the wine from the mass of grape skins, seeds, and stalks, which is known as the *lees*. This process is called *racking*. After being racked, the wine is stored during the winter in wooden casks. During the first month or so in storage, the wine shrinks a little because the wood of the casks absorbs some of it; the wine cools after the heat of fermentation, and some of the wine "breathes" through the pores of the cask. As a rule, between 5 and 10 percent is lost in this manner, and it is necessary to correct the shrinkage—called *ullage*—by adding additional wine.

The following spring, a second period of fermentation begins. Since some carbonic gas is formed, allowance must be made for its escape, and the bung of the wine barrel is loosened slightly. It is during the second fermentation that miscellaneous solid particles gradually drop to the bottom of the cask. With some wines, the process of *fining* is required to clear the wine still more. Fining consists of adding a sticky film of some kind to the top of the wine which will slowly sink to the bottom, carrying with it the foreign matter. This film may be egg whites, gelatine, agar-agar, charcoal, tannin, or any one of a dozen other substances, and the process may take about two weeks. However, even after fining, red wines have a tendency to throw up additional sediment as they age; cream of tartar crystals remain when the wines are stored for the desired length of time in cool temperatures until they are bottled.

At the moment of bottling, the wine is exposed directly to the air for several seconds before the bottle is corked. Something still unexplained happens to the wine, for it develops what has been called "bottle sickness." During the first month or so immediately after it has been bottled, wine is almost undrinkable. But it soon recovers. Wine should never be drunk from a freshly corked bottle, but it is not likely that the average consumer will be faced with this contingency.

Of course this long process has no application to ordinary table wines, the *vin ordinaire*. This is drunk at the spring season immediately after the harvest. Wine of this type receives little special treatment, but good wines warrant all the careful handling described, and some of the very best vineyards go to even more elaborate care and trouble.

Wines. (See also under individual listings.)

Abymes	Bardolino
Açores	Barolo
Acqua di Firenze	Barsac
Agly, Côtes d'	Bâtard Montrachet
Aïn-Bessem-Bouira	Beaujolais
Aïn-el-Hadiar	Beaune, Hospice de
Alicante	Bellet
Aligoté	Bergamo
Aloxe-Corton	Bernkastel
Alsace, Muscat d'	Bingen
Alsatian:	Blanc de Blanc
Gewerz-Traminer	Blayais
Riesling	Bodenheim
Sylvaner	Bonnes Mares
Altavilla	Bordeaux
Altesse	Bouïra
Amarone	Bourgeais
Amazake	Bourgueil
Ambonnay	Bouzy
Amontillado	Briolet
Amoroso	Brouilly
Anisado	Brunello
Anjou-Mousseux	Bual
Arbois	Bucellas
Asti Spumante	Bull's Blood
Banyuls	Burgundy
Barbaresco	Cabernet
Barbera	Cabrières
Barberry wine	Calcavella

Caldaro
Calliste
Callou
Caluso
Canary wines
Canonaus
Capri
Carignane
Carlowitz
Carmignano
Carquelin
Castel del Monte
Castelli Romani
Cerons
Cesanese
Chablis
Chaintré
Chalakoa
Chalon
Châlon, Château
Châlonnaise, Côte
Chambertin
Chambolle-Musigny
Champagne
Champagne nature
Chapelle-Chambertin
Charmes-Chambertin
Chassagne-Montrachet
Château Grillet
Châteauneuf-du-Pape
Chautagne
Chavannaz
Chavignol
Cheilly-lès-Maranges
Chenas
Cheval Blanc, Château
Chevalier-Montrachet
Chianti
Cinque Terre
Ciro
Cisolo
Clairet
Clairette de Bellegarde
Clairette du Languedoc
Claret
Clary
Clos de Vougeot
Clos Mariout

Colares
Condrieu
Corbières
Cornas
Coronata
Corton
Corton-Charlemagne
Côteaux de la Loire
Côte Blonde
Côte Brune
Côte de Beaune
Côte de Dijon
Côte de Nuits
Côte d'Or
Côte Mâconnais
Côte-Rôtie
Côtes de Bordeaux
  Saint-Macaire
Cramant
Crépy
Criotte-Chambertin
Crozes-Hermitage
Cumières
Cyprus wines
Dão
Date wine
Dubonnet
Duke of Clarence
  Malmsey
Ebulum
Echézeaux
Egri Bikaver
El Borjo
English Frontignac
Ermitage
Essencia
Est! Est!! Est!!!
Étoile
Falernian
Federweisser
Fel
Fendant
Féternes
Filzener
Fino
Fitou
Folantières
Folle Blanche

Foncée, La
Frontignac; Frontignan
Fuencaral
Gaillac
Galamus
Garda, Chiaretto del
Gattinara
Gave, Côtes du
Gentil
Gevrey-Chambertin
Gigondas
Gilly-les-Vougeots
Ginger wine
Giro del Tempio
Giro di Sardegna
Gold Riesling
Graves
Graves-de-Vayre
Grenache
Grillet, Château
Grist-Meunier
Guébar
Hallaur
Hallgartner
Hambacher
Harrach, Couteaux de
Hattenheimer
Haut-Brion
Haut-Dahra
Haut-Sauternes
Hermitage
Hochheimer
Hypocras
Imperial Tokay
Irancy
Irouléguy
Jasnières
Julienas
Jura, Côtes de
Jurançon
Kassara
King Minos
Knipperlé
Koberner
Lacrima Christi
Ladoix-Serrigny
Lafite-Rothschild
  Château

Lagmi
Lagrima
Latour, Château
Latricières-Chambertin
Layon, Côteau du
Lillet
Lindemans Riesling
Lisbon
Locorotondo
Luberon
Lunel
Macabeo
Mâcon
Madeira
Maitrank
Malaga
Malmsey
Manicie
Manzanilla
Marcobrunner
Margauxm Château
Marsala
Maury
Mavrodaphne
May wine; May bowl
Mazis Chambertin
Mercurey
Mersault
Migraine
Mirin
Monbazillac
Monserrato
Montepulciano
Monthélie
Montrachet
Morocanella
Mostaganem d'Ahra
Moustille
Mouton-Rothschild
Murin
Muscadel
Muscadet
Muscatel
Musigny
Naoussa
Napareuli
Nasco; Nascol
Néac

Nebbiolo Piedmontise
Nemes Kadara
Neustadter
Niersteiner
Ogliastra
Oreanda
Orkney
Orvieto
Pacaret
Pacherenc-du-Vic-Bihl
Pailet Vin
Paille, Vin de
Palette
Palm wine
Palma
Papparetta
Passolato
Pâtrimonio
Pecharmant
Pernand-Vergelesses
Petrus, Château
Pichon-Longueville,
    Château
Picpoul de Pinet
Pinot Blanc
Pinot Gris
Pomino
Pommard
Pontet-Canet, Château
Port
Pouilly-Fuissé
Pouilly-Fumé
Pouilly-sur-Loire
Primitivo
Prosanico
Quart de Chaume
Quatourze; Quatorze
Quincy
Rainwater Madeira
Rasteau
Ratafia
Richebourg
Romanée, La
Romanée-Conti
Rosé aux Fruits
Rota
Rousselet

Roussilon, Côtes du
Saint-Émilion
Samos
Sangue di Guida
San Severo
Sassella
Sauternes
Scharlachberger
Schillerwein
Schloss Bockelheimer
Semillon
Serriger
Shiraz
Siblinger
Steinwein
Stradella
Syracuse
Szamorodni
Tâche, La
Tamara
Tawny Port
Tinta
Tokay
Torre Giulia
Tour-La-Reine
Trappe de Staoueli
Treble Palma
Trockenbeeren Auslese
Valdepeñas
Valpolicella
Valtellina
Verdicchio
Vermouth
Vidonia
Vin de l'Étoile
Vin de Paille
Vin de Sable
Vinello; Vinetto
Volnay
Vougeot, Clos de
Vouvray
Wormwood wine
Yakja
Yecla
Yvonne
Zilavka

Zinfandel
Zipi Cheese

Zucco
Zwicher

Wine, Chinese. Most "wines" produced in China are made from rice. The closest equivalent is sherry, which may be used as a substitute in making Chinese dishes. Another type of Chinese "wine" is actually a strong liquor; *kaoliang wine*, for example, is high in alcoholic content.

Wineberry. (1) A small, bright orange-red berry that grows on a vine; the taste is mediocre. It is best when crushed and made into a cold drink with water, sugar, and lemon slices. (2) A slightly tart berry related to the raspberry; good fresh or made into jams and jellies.

Winebibber. A person who drinks considerable, perhaps too much, wine.

Wine Biscuit. Fancy-cut shortbread, usually served with wine.

Wine Bottle Sizes. Almost everyone recognizes the standard-sized bottle of wine, usually one of 24 or 25 ounces. Also known to most people are the half bottles or 12–12½ ounces. Some vineyards put up their wines in double bottles, called "magnums," usually about 48 ounces.

The champagne producers frequently bottle their wines in very small sizes, and also in extremely large sizes. However, the U.S. Government does not permit the largest sizes to be imported and these are rarely seen.

Split or nip	6 ounces	
Half-bottle	12½ ounces	
Ordinary wine bottle	24 ounces	
Champagne quart	26 ounces	
Magnum	52 ounces	(2 quarts)
Jeroboam	104 ounces	(4 quarts)
Reheboam	156 ounces	(6 quarts)
Methuselah	208 ounces	(8 quarts)
Salmanazar	312 ounces	(12 quarts)
Balthazar	416 ounces	(16 quarts)
Nebuchadnezzar	520 ounces	(20 quarts)

Wine Cakes. Small cakes or pastries baked in fluted pans; usually made with Madeira wine.

Wine Cellar. A place in a cellar for storing wine; sometimes a closet or other space.

Wine Gallon. By United States tax requirements the official wine gallon contains 231 cubic inches.

Wineglass. A glass intended for use in drinking wine. It may vary considerably in size and shape but should be clear, light, and thin. In general, smaller glasses are used for white wine, larger glasses for red wine.

Winegrower. A person who produces grapes, specifically for use in making wine.

Wine Jelly. A preparation having a jellylike consistency made with red or white wine, gelatin, and flavorings. Sweet versions may be eaten plain or with cream as a dessert; unsweetened versions are often served as an accompaniment to meat or game dishes.

Wine Plant (Colloquial). *See* Rhubarb.

Wine Press. A vat in which grapes are pressed or trodden upon in order to force the juice from the skin.

Winery. A place where wine is produced.

Wines and Liquors, Alcoholic Contents of:

Red Bordeaux	9–11 percent
White Bordeaux	9–12 percent
Moselle and Rhine	9–13 percent
Burgundy	11–14 percent
Champagne	12–13 percent
Tokay Aszu	12–14 percent
Rhône	12–14 percent
Sherry	18–22 percent
Port	19–23 percent
Liqueurs	40 percent or more
Vodka	40–50 percent
Rye, Bourbon, Gin, and Scotch	40–50 percent
Cognac	40–60 percent

Winesap. A reddish apple with a winey flavor; grown chiefly in the United States.

Wineskin. The skin of an animal (sheep, pig, etc.) sewn to form a container for wine.

Wines with Food. The primary function of wine is to make food taste better. Over the years particular affinities have developed. Certain wine connoisseurs would rather not eat oysters than have them without a glass of chilled Chablis; but these people are in the minority, and oysters are very good not only with Chablis but with any dry or medium white wine, such as an Alsatian or a Moselle. Oysters are good, for that matter, without any wine. If you enjoy them with a white Burgundy, that is your privilege, and you may find that chilled Loire Valley white suits your taste better than any other wine. The suggestions that follow, therefore, are only a guide for convenience. They are not meant as rigid rules.

Hors d'Oeuvre: Dry sherry (Fino or Amontillado), dry champagne, Vouvray or other Loire Valley white, dry Moselle, dry California Semillon, any *rosé* wine.

Shellfish: Chablis, Sancerre, Vouvray, Alsatian wines like Riesling or Traminer, dry Moselle, Pinot Blanc, Grey Riesling.

Fish: White Burgundy, Rhine or Moselle, dry white Bordeaux, Dry Semillon or Blanche Folle.

Soups: Usually no wine is advisable, but a medium sherry or Madeira wine is traditional with turtle soup.

Chicken: Ideally, a red wine, like the lighter types of Bordeaux, Burgundy, or Rhône; a Beaujolais is very good, too. Even a *rosé* is suitable, particularly if the chicken is cold. Some people prefer a white wine; if so, an Alsatian or Moselle, or possibly a white Burgundy, are appropriate.

Duck, Goose: A fine heavy red Burgundy, or possibly a Rhône red. A Beaujolais is not too bad, and some of the Italian reds do not make an unsuitable combination. A Cabernet Sauvignon or Gamay are the best American varietal types.

Beef: Any dry red wine including all of the Burgundy, Bordeaux, or Rhône wines; also most of the dry Italian reds. Beaujolais is satisfactory, too. Valdepeñas or Rioja reds are acceptable among the Spanish wines. The Pinot Noir is first choice among the American varietals, and the Gamay second.

Pork and Veal: Either a red, white, or *rosé* wine. The classic wine with pork is a dry German wine, either Rhine or Moselle. With veal, a light red Bordeaux is best. The Cabernet Sauvignon is preferable among American red varietals, the Johannisberger Riesling among the whites.

Spaghetti (*pastas*): If the pasta has a fish

sauce, any Italian dry white wine, or possibly a dry white Bordeaux. All other pastas are best with a dry Italian red; the most popular of these is Chianti, although not necessarily the best. Barbera, Zinfandel, or Grignolino are the most satisfactory of the American red varietals.

Salad: No wine, for the vinegar or lemon juice of the salad spoils the flavor of the wine.

Sausages, tongue, sweetbreads, kidney, liver, etc.: Very light red Bordeaux, or possibly a light Burgundy; sweetbreads may be somewhat better with a white wine if served with a cream sauce; Cabernet Sauvignon among the American types.

Cheese or cheese dishes: Any red wine, particularly Bordeaux or Burgundy; with a separate cheese course at the end of a meal, port wine is superb.

Barbecued foods: Any hearty red wine like Beaujolais, Rhône red, or almost any dry Italian red wine.

Desserts: Sweeter types of champagne, Sauternes, sweet German wines, especially the Beeren Auslese type. Sweet Semillon is the best American variety.

Winetaster. An expert who judges wines for excellence.

Wine Terms. The complex, varied, and extensive production of wines around the world has led to a profusion of terms used in the field of wines. The following are representative:

Abbocato. An Italian term denoting a fairly sweet table wine, but not a completely sweet, dessert-type wine.

Acerbe. A wine with a sour, unpleasant taste.

Acetic. An acid of vinegar produced in wines by the oxidation of ethyl alcohol in combination with a fungus; this causes a distinctive smell. A thin white film forms over such wine.

Aigre. A wine having an acidic quality or taste.

Amontillado. A pale, dry type of sherry.

Amoroso. A medium type of sherry, not so sweet as Oloroso but not so dry as Amontillado.

Añada. A Spanish term for vintage wine.

Apéritif. An appetizer drink, usually one containing bitters, flavorings, or herbs, in combination with a wine base.

Appelation Controlé. A designation on certain French wines indicating that the designation of the wine, and its right to appear on a label, are guaranteed by French liquor laws.

Âpre. A harsh or rough characteristic of certain wines.

Arome. The aroma, or bouquet, of wine.

Arrope. A concentration of grape juice, produced by boiling, used to give color and add sweetness to Spanish sherries.

Auslese. A German wine term denoting a wine made from specially selected grapes. At the time of harvest, some grapes have a white mold deposit called *edelfäule*; these grapes produce a better, smoother wine.

Beerenauslese. A German term indicating wine made from individually selected grapes which are characteristically overripe; the result is an extremely sweet, usually expensive wine.

Beeswing. A very light sediment which often forms in vintage port wine.

Black Rot. A fungus disease of grape vines.

Blanc de Blancs. White wine made exclusively from white grapes.

Blanc de Noirs. White wine made exclusively from black grapes.

Blume. A German term for the aroma or bouquet of wine.

Bocksbeutel. The distinctively shaped green bottle used for Steinwein in Germany; a flagon bottle.

Bottle Sickness. A peculiarity of freshly-bottled wine which causes it to be practically undrinkable for a short period of time.

Bouchonné. A wine that has developed an unpleasant, corky taste.

Bouquet. The pleasing odor or scent given off by a good wine when it is first opened or poured into a glass.

Breed. The quality and personality developed only by wines of the highest caliber.

Brut. A champagne with only very little added sugar; the driest, least sweet champagne.

Butt. A wine cask; for sherry measuring 132 gallons, for Hungarian wines about 13.7 litres.

Cabinettwein. A German wine term used to denote a superior wine, which may or may not be accurate.

Capiteux. A French word for a wine high in alcohol, with a heady quality.

Casse. A disease of wines caused by an excess of iron; when opened, the wine becomes cloudy.

Cep; Cepage. The vine stock.

Chai; Chaix. The wine warehouse, cellar, or storage place.

Chambrer. To bring a bottle of wine gradually to the temperature of the room in which it is to be served by allowing to stand there overnight.

Chaptalisé. The process of adding sugar to wine during the fermentation process in order to increase the alcoholic content.

Charnu. A wine having a great deal of body.

Claret. A general term for wines from the Bordeaux district of France.

Collage. Clearing a wine of any particles or sediment.

Consumo. A term for ordinary Spanish or Portuguese wine intended for regular table use.

Corky. Descriptive of wine with an unpleasant taste caused by a defective or diseased cork.

Corsé. A wine with a heavy or full body.

Coulant. A French expression for a very drinkable, enjoyable wine.

Cru. A French term denoting a vineyard, or the growth of a vineyard.

Crudité. A raw, unfinished wine.

Crust. A deposit cast up on the inside of bottles by certain wines, particularly vintage port wines.

Cuvée. Actually means the vat; in general usage, it refers to the quantity produced by a vineyard. Also means a blend of several different wines.

Decant. The process of transferring wine from one bottle to another bottle or container, usually to eliminate the sediment.

Délicat. A gentle wine, without harshness or crudeness, having a good balance.

Demijohn. A large, round bottle holding at least several gallons, usually covered with wicker.

Demisec. Literally, half dry; actually, a moderately sweet wine, usually champagne.

Deposit. The natural sediment thrown onto the walls of a bottle as the wine matures.

Dosage. The amount of sugar added to champagne before it is finally corked.

Doux. Sweet; a sweet, sugared wine in the champagne trade.

Dry. A term to denote a wine lacking sugar; the opposite of sweet.

Dur. A hard, unpleasant wine.

Echt. A German term for a dry wine, that is, without sugar added to the *must*.

Edelfaule. In Germany, grapes which have become overripe and developed a characteristic white mold.

Egrappage. The process of removing the stems from the grapes before being pressed.

Ehrwein. A German word for fine wine.

Estate Bottled. Wine which is bottled by the owner of the vineyard, or sometimes by the producer; a term used chiefly in Burgundy.

Estufa. A sort of hothouse, where Portuguese Madeiras are heated to improve their quality.

Extra Sec. A seldom-used term to describe a dry champagne.

Faible. A rather weak wine, having a poor body.

Ferme. A firm wine, one with considerable strength and perhaps too much body; often used derogatorily to describe a wine which has failed to mature properly.

Fin; Finesse. A wine with delicacy and pleasantness; one with finesse.

Finings. Substances used to clarify wine, causing foreign particles to settle on the bottom of the container.

Fino. The driest of all Spanish sherries.

Fort. Strong; describes wines of considerable body and strength.

Fortified. Wines whose alcoholic content is increased by the addition of grape spirits (brandy), like port or sherry.

Foxiness. A term used to describe an oxidated wine taste characteristic of many wines of the eastern United States.

Franc de Goût. A wine having a clean cut grape taste, with nothing else apparently added.

Fruité. A characteristic fruitiness apparent in certain wines, the grape aroma and taste.

Fumeux. Having an obvious or strong bouquet; one in which the alcohol rises quickly.

Généreux. A wine having a comparatively high alcoholic content, at least over 12 per cent.

Goût Americain. Used to describe South American taste in champagne, that is, quite sweet.

Goût Anglais. An extremely dry type of champagne; English taste.

Goût de Bois. A wine having a taste of the wood cask in which it was stored.

Goût de Bouchon. Wine with a corky quality.

Goût de Paille. Wine with the taste of straw.

Goût d'Évent. A wine with a dull, flat taste.

Grand Vin. A meaningless term, "Grand Wine," which occasionally appears on poor wine to impress the consumer.

Grossier. An unpleasant or coarse wine which is unfit to drink.

Hock. An English expression for Hochheimer, a German wine; often used as a general term for Rhine wines.

Keller. The German term for cellar.

Kellerabfüllung; Kelle abzug. German terms denoting that the wine was bottled at the cellar of the producer of the wine.

Léger. A French word for a wine with light quality; sometimes it refers to a wine lacking in body or alcoholic strength.

Mâche. A thick wine; one which can almost be "chewed."

Madérisé. A term applied usually to white wines which have darkened, becoming a deep color.

Moelle. A wine which is notable for its mellowness and smoothness.

Mou. A soft, flabby wine without a pronounced character.

Mousseux. A sparkling wine of almost any type, but not including champagne.

Must. The term used to describe unfermented grape juice.

Natur; Naturwein. German terms for undiluted natural wines without added sugar.

Nature. A French term used to denote wine to which nothing has been added; also, still champagne (without bubbles).

Nerf. A strong wine with considerable alcohol.

Nose. The aroma or fragrant bouquet of a wine.

Pasteurization. The process of heating wine to about 145° in order to destroy the active elements in it; this practice is seldom used in Europe, but frequently in California.

Pâteux. A wine with an unpleasant, cloying, thick quality.

Pelure d'Oignon. A wine having a brownish quality, remniscent of the skin of an onion.

Pétillant. Having a slightly sparkling quality, without having bubbles.

Piquant. The somewhat astringent taste found in certain very dry white wines; also denotes a wine which has developed a certain vinegary quality.

Piquette. A very ordinary wine of rather low quality.

Plat. A wine which is flat, dull, or lacking in aroma, body, or strength.

Pot. A wine measure which is about two-thirds of the size of an ordinary "fifth."

Pourriture Noble. A yeast mold or fungus which develops on ripe or overripe grapes; this causes a reduction of the water content of the grape and a higher sugar content.

Race. A French term for the breed, or quality of a wine.

Rancio. The "rancid" taste which develops in certain dessert wines which have been aged too long.

Remuage. The step in the making of champagne in which the bottles are placed on their end and shaken, causing the sediment to collect on the cork.

Rondeur. A French wine term for a "drinkable" wine.

Rosé. Pink wine.

Sec. A descriptive term for a dry champagne.

Sekt. German sparkling wines produced by the champagne process.

Solera. The system by which all Spanish (and some American) sherries are blended, resulting in a uniform product every year.

Soyeaux. A smooth wine, one which is without roughness.

Spatlese. A German term for wine made from

grapes picked late in the harvest, thus resulting in a smooth fuller-bodied wine.

Spritzig. A German term for a lightly sparkling wine.

Spumante. Italian wine expression for a sparkling wine.

Sugaring. The process of adding sugar to grapes low in natural sugar before fermentation.

Tawny. A port wine which has lost some of its natural color because of maturing in wood casks.

Trockenbeeren Auslese. A German wine made from specially selected grapes which have been allowed to overripen on the vine until they have become like raisins.

Ullage. A wine trade term describing wine lost from a bottle or cask because of evaporation.

Varietal. An American wine term describing wines which have a definite and unique character, because of the particular variety of grape from which the wine is made.

Velouté. A wine having velvety-smooth qualities.

Vert. A tart, sharp wine, usually young.

Vignoble. A French vineyard.

Vin Cuit. A highly concentrated wine used to blend with thinner, lighter wines.

Vineux. A wine which has all the worthwhile characteristics a wine should have.

Vino Frizzante. A light, sparkling wine of Italy.

Vinosité. Usually denotes a wine high in alcoholic content.

Vin Rosé. Any pink wine.

Weinberg. A German term for a vineyard.

Xeres. An old name for sherry wine, one still used in France.

Zwicker. An Alsatian blend of several wines.

Wine Vinegar. Any vinegar made from wine; the more usual base is malt.

Winey; Winy. Having the taste and aroma of wine.

Winkle; Periwinkle. A small mollusk eaten raw or sometimes cooked.

Winnow. To allow the air or wind to act naturally upon grain or other substances, so that the lighter particles are blown away and the grain falls to the ground.

Winter Artichoke. The Jerusalem artichoke. *See* Artichoke.

Winter Cress. A wild plant, whose rather spicy, bitter leaves are used as a salad green.

Wintergreen. (1) A small aromatic evergreen plant whose fresh leaves yield a pungent oil used as a flavoring for candies and chewing gum and for various other preparations. (2) A vegetable which keeps well during the winter months.

Wintergreen, Oil of. An oil obtained from the wintergreen, an aromatic plant, and used to flavor candies, mints, etc.

Winter Melon. A large white squash with yellow seeds; often used in Chinese cookery, usually in making winter-melon soup; also pickled or made into the desserts prepared on festivals.

Winter Queening. A type of apple which keeps rather well during the wintertime.

Winter Rocket. Watercress.

Winter Savory. *See* Summer Savory.

Winter Warmer (American, Obsolete). A hot rum drink made with butter, cinnamon, hot water, and spices.

Winter Wheats. Wheats planted in the fall in several countries, their softness depending on the particular climatic conditions.

Winy; Winey. Tasting like or resembling wine.

Wisniak. A Polish cherry liqueur. Often whole cherries are contained in the bottle.

Witch Cake (British). A cake made specially to be used for feats of magic.

Witch Sole. A flatfish similar to plaice or sole but of inferior flavor; cooked like plaice or sole.

Wither. To dry tea leaves, before the roasting process.

Witlof (Dutch). Endive.

Witloof (Belgian). Endive.

Witte Kool (Dutch). Cabbage.

Witte Wyn (Dutch). White wine.

Wodka; Woudka. Polish vodka, regarded by many experts as about the best in the world.

Wolf. (1) A fairly large canine animal, rarely eaten for food except in cases of necessity; the flesh is tough and unpleasant. (2) To swallow foods voraciously with great appetite. (3) Any of a large number of fish found in various parts of the world; probably so called because of their rapacious nature.

Wolffish. The loup, a Mediterranean fish; often used in making bouillabaisse; also good when grilled with fennel leaves.

Wolfsbarsch (German). Bass.

Wolke (British). Rolled or kneaded dough.

Wood Blewits. A rather large blue-purple woodland mushroom found in late autumn.

Woodchuck. Groundhog. The flesh of the young groundhog somewhat resembles that of pig and is prepared like pork.

Woodcock. An excellent game bird with delicious flesh.

Wood Dove. The pigeon.

Wooden Plinth (Obsolete). A base or block on which elaborate cold dishes were presented.

Woodenware. Wooden kitchen utensils, such as rolling pins and salad bowls.

Wood Grouse. A large delicate-flavored game bird; prepared like pheasant.

Wood Hedgehog. A large, somewhat bitter wild mushroom with near-white flesh.

Woodpecker. A bird of undistinguished flavor; occasionally eaten.

Wood Pigeon. The wild pigeon; prepared like domestic pigeon.

Woodruff; Waldmeister. An aromatic herb used for flavoring candies, confections, and wine drinks.

Woodruff, Sweet. A fragrant, sweet herb; used in flavoring wines, wine cups, fresh fruits, and the like.

Wood Sage. A wild herb, also called germander, which smells like sage.

Wood Sorrel. A wild plant whose small heart-shaped sourish leaves are sometimes used for flavorings and soups.

Woozy (Colloquial). Drunk, befuddled.

Worcester. A type of China tableware that originated in Worcester, England.

Worcestershire Sauce (British). A thin spicy sauce of ancient origin; prepared with soya, tamarinds, anchovies, garlic, and condiments and spices from many parts of the world; used for meats, soups, and in many kinds of dressings.

Work. In baking, to mix or knead dough slowly and steadily.

Wormseed. Any of several plants, but especially certain types of fennel, the leaves of which are used to prepare a tea.

Wormwood. (1) Several species of rather bitter astringent plants used in making absinthe and vermouth and in the preparation of herb teas for medicinal purposes. Because wormwood has been found to be habit-forming, many countries regulate its sale. (2) By extension, any food or liquor with a bitter taste.

Wormwood Ale. A highly-flavored type of beer made with an infusion of wormwood.

Wormwood Wine. A sweet cordial or liqueur made with wormwood.

Worst (Dutch). Sausages.

Wort. (1) A cabbagelike plant; an aromatic herb. (2) A malt liquid converted into beer by fermentation. (3) Another name for the whortleberry. *See* Whortleberry.

Worteltjes (Dutch). Carrots.

Wrap. As applied to food, to enfold in fat, pastry, foil, or paper.

Wrasse. A brilliantly colored edible fish, several species of which are found off the Atlantic coast of Europe and in the Mediterranean; best used in soups and stews.

Wreckfish. A name for a variety of fish caught in American waters; the name denotes a different species of fish in various parts of the United States.

Wun Sen (Siamese). A clear noodle made from mung beans.

Wurst (German). Sausage, fresh or smoked.

Wurst in Teig (German). Sausage cooked in dough.

Wurstplatte (German). Platter of assorted sausages.

Wurstspeisen (German). Pork products.

X

Xaintray. A strong-flavored goat's-milk cheese made in Poitou, France.

Xalota (Portuguese). Green onions; scallions.

Xanthia Cocktail. Brandy, gin, and wine with cracked ice, stirred and strained into a cocktail glass.

Xavier. A clear soup garnished with tiny cheese dumplings; named in honor of Count Xavier of Saxony.

Xenium. A present, especially of table delicacies, given to a guest or stranger. In medieval times sometimes a compulsory offering.

Xeres. (1) Jerez, the town in Spain where sherry is produced. (2) (Obsolete) Sherry wine.

Xeres Cocktail. Sherry wine and orange bitters with cracked ice, stirred and strained into a cocktail glass.

Ximenia. A widely distributed plant whose fruit is the tart mountain plum or wild lime.

Y

Yachtwurst. A ready-to-eat coarse-textured sausage made with beef, pork, and pistachio nuts.

Yak. A Tibetan ox whose flesh is edible; its milk resembles goat's milk.

Yak Butter. A butter made from the milk of yaks, long-haired Tibetan cattle. Though flavorsome it is inevitably full of hairs; it is used in tea in Tibet.

Yakhnee (Arabic). Stews.

Yakhni (Indian). Soup; stock.

Yakimono (Japanese). Broiled foods.

Yakju (Korean). A rice wine, not too strong.

Yam. A large sweet tuberous root with a rich moist texture; prepared like the sweet potato, which it resembles. In some parts of the United States the terms "yam" and "sweet potato" are used interchangeably. The yams on the market are ideal for individual servings, but yams often reach a size of 40–50 pounds, occasionally even heavier. Yams are grown commercially in the southern United States, particularly in Florida and Louisiana. The wild varieties are small and have a pleasant taste but a woody texture.

Yam, Round. A yam with a round tuber; the burdekin vine of Australia.

Yamadon. Oil expressed from the yellow nutmeg.

Yamaimo (Japanese). A sweet potato or yam.

Yam-Bean. Two types of tropical plants with starchy pods and tubers that have an odd turnip-like taste.

Yanggona; Yaqona; Yava; Kava (Fijian). A drink prepared from dried pepper roots and water. *See* Yava; *see also* Kava.

Yaourt (French). Yoghurt.

Yapon. A plant similar to holly whose leaves are used to make tea.

Yaqona. *See* Yava.

Yara Yara. White crystalline substances often used to imitate synthetically various flavors, especially those of berries.

Yarmouth Bloater. A slightly salted and smoked herring.

Yarrow. An old-fashioned herb; formerly used to flavor beer, and also made into a sort of tea.

Yasawa (South Pacific). A fried chicken ball.

Yaupon (American Indian). A beverage resembling tea, made from the leaves of a shrub belonging to the holly family.

Yautia (Spanish). Sweet potato.

Yava; Kava (Polynesian). A beverage prepared from dried roots of a certain pepper plant, combined with water or saliva, and allowed to ferment. It is not intoxicating, but produces a pleasant, slightly numbing effect in the mouth.

Yeanling. A young lamb or kid.

Yearling. A four-legged animal a year old or occasionally, in its second year, especially a lamb or calf.

Yearn. To coagulate or curdle milk; to make cheese of curdled milk.

Yearning. Rennet.

Yeast. A minute unicellular fungus that grows in contact with sugar. It is widely used in the preparation of alcoholic beverages, especially beer, and as a leavening agent in baking.

Yeast is 50 percent protein and is rich in vitamins B_1 and B_2, nicotinic acid, and folic acid.

Food yeast is grown as a source of food, for it is able to produce its own protein from simple ammonium salts and waste carbohydrates, such as molasses and sulfite liquors, from wood pulp.

Yeast Cake. (1) Yeast drained and pressed into a cake. (2) A cake using yeast as a leavening agent. As a rule, yeast cakes are flavored much like coffee cakes.

Yeasty. In a ferment; acting like leaven.

Yecla. A pink or *rosé* wine produced in Spain.

Yelk (British, Obsolete). Egg yolk.

Yellowfish. (1) Any of a variety of yellow-colored fishes. (2) A rock trout found off the coast of Alaska.

Yellow Pepper. A podlike vegetable, yellowish when mature; not so strong-tasting as red pepper.

Yellow Perch. A type of bony perch of mediocre quality.

Yellowtail. Any of a variety of fishes found chiefly in North America and in the vicinity of Australia. The flesh is of fair quality.

Yelt. A young sow.

Yeoman Wheat. A variety of English wheat developed specially to produce a stronger flour than that obtainable from most English wheats.

Yerba Buena. A strong aromatic wild mint used in minute quantities mainly for flavoring potatoes and other vegetables.

Yerba Maté. A South American herb tea. *See* Maté.

Yering. A dry Australian red wine.

Yer Shee (Chinese). A coconut candy.

Yex. To belch.

Yield. With reference to cookery and recipes, the number of portions produced, or the quantity of cooked food available.

Yoghurt; Yogurt; Yoghourt; Yagourt; Yoghoort. A curdled milk that originated in the Balkan countries. Methods of preparation differ, but the end product is considered more digestible and nutritious than other milk. Yoghurt is often combined with fresh berries and sugar, or with fruit juice, and eaten as a dessert. Commercially prepared yoghurts have a variety of flavorings.

Yolk. The yellow part of an egg, containing protein and fat. It is surrounded by the white, or albumen, serving as nourishment for the young bird before it is hatched. The yolk is high in both calories and cholesterol.

York Cheese. A perishable English cream cheese.

York Ham. A fine-tasting, distinctive ham produced in England and regarded as that country's best. It has a smoky taste, and may be eaten hot or cold.

Yorkshire Pie. Certain galantines of meat.

Yorkshire Pudding. An English preparation that accompanies roast beef; made with a batter similar to that of popovers and flavored with a few tablespoonfuls of the roast drippings. The finished pudding, somewhat like a thick pancake, is cut in squares and served alongside the roast.

Yorkshire Teacakes. Plain or fruit yeast cakes.

York State Cheese. Cheddars made in New York; a trade term.

Yosenabe (Japanese). Chicken breasts with assorted shellfish; served with a dashi (fish) sauce.

Young American Cheese. Fresh mild cheddar cheese.

Youngberry. A hybrid produced by crossing the blackberry and the dewberry; grown chiefly in the southwestern United States.

Yucca. (1) Spanish bayonet, Spanish dagger, broad-leaved yucca, Adam's needle, bear grass, Eve's darning needle; a wild plant, some varieties of which have an edible fruit. The Indians of the southwestern United States roast the fruit or dry it for future food. Young stalks may be cooked as a vegetable like asparagus. (2) (Central and South American) The cassava, a starchy farinaceous root found in many tropical countries, constituting a cheap source of food.

Yufka (Turkish). Thin leaves of dough, similar to those used for making strudel.

Yule Cakes. Christmas cakes decorated in a wide variety of styles.

Yule Logs. Cake rolls decorated to resemble logs of wood by coating them with chocolate frosting marked to represent the bark.

Yuzu (Japanese). Lemon.

Yvette Cream. A violet-flavored liqueur.

Yvorne. An amber-colored, mildly acid wine produced in the Yvorne district of Switzerland.

Z

Zaatar (Middle Eastern). A mixture of spices and herbs, such as garlic, sumac, and thyme.

Zabaglione; Zabaione (Italian). A foamy egg dessert or runny mousse. It is prepared from egg yolks, wine, sugar, and various flavorings, cooked until thickened, and spooned out into glasses or cups while hot. Sometimes this mixture is used as a sauce atop cakes or puddings. In France, it is called *sauce sabayon*.

Zachte Eieren (Dutch). Boiled eggs.

Zafferano (Italian). Saffron.

Zakouski; Zakuska (Russian). Hors d'oeuvre; appetizers.

Zalm (Dutch). Salmon.

Zambone. Stuffed and salted pig's feet.

Zamia. A species of palmlike trees, some of which have an edible starchy pith.

Zampino; Zampone (Italian). A type of coarse sausage meat forced into a boned pig's foot, then cured and dried.

Zanahoria (Spanish). Carrot.

Zander; Zant (German). Pike-perch; a European freshwater fish somewhat like the whiting.

Zanoibe (Italian). Stuffed pig's feet served hot or cold as an hors d'oeuvre.

Zanzibar Cocktail. A drink made of gin, vermouth, lemon juice, sugar, and orange bitters.

Zapote. The sapodilla, a South American fruit.

Zara. A fine Italian liqueur used to flavor pastries and ices.

Zarda (Indian). A sweet rice dish served at the conclusion of a meal.

Zarf. An ornamental holder for a coffee cup.

Zarzuela (Spanish). A seafood chowder or stew.

Zatore. A Middle Eastern combination of herbs and spices, including sesame seeds, thyme, and savory; used in making bread.

Zaza Cocktail. A cocktail made with dry gin and Dubonnet.

Zea. The botanical genus to which corn belongs.

Two types are commercially important: *flint* and *dent corn.*

Zebu. A cattle native to Asia and Africa whose flesh can be prepared like beef.

Zedoary. An aromatic East Indian tuberous root resembling ginger.

Zeeland Oysters. An excellent oyster found in Zeeland, the Netherlands.

Zeepaling (Dutch). Turbot, a kind of fish.

Zeevis (Dutch). Seafood.

Zegeni (North African). *Wat*, a spicy meat stew.

Zein. A protein similar to gluten found in corn.

Zephires. Small oval-shaped dumplings of force-meat similar to *quenelles*; poached and served with a rich sauce.

Zephyr. A very light, frothy concoction; sometimes, soufflés.

Zeppole (Italian). A fried sweet, doughy cake; a doughnut.

Zest; Zeste. (1) The peel or thin outer skin of a citrus fruit, especially orange or lemon. (2) The skin covering the kernel of a walnut. (3) Anything that stimulates the appetite; a relish.

Zester. An instrument for peeling oranges or lemons.

Zeus. A family of spiny-finned fishes including the John Dory.

Zhug (Yemenite). A mixture of coriander, cardamom, red or green pepper, garlic, and cumin used as a flavoring ingredient.

Zhum (Middle Eastern). A cooked clabbered milk.

Zibet. Asian chives; used for seasoning meats, sauces, and salads.

Zichoriensalat (German). Chicory salad.

Ziegel Cheese. A German cheese made from whole cow's milk.

Ziegenkäse; Gaiskäsli (German). Any cheese made of goat's milk.

Ziger. An inexpensive product resembling cheese, made from whey; may be flavored with such ingredients as vinegar, lemon juice, or cider.

Zilavka. A Yugoslavian dry white wine.

Zimino (Italian). A fish sauce made of white wine, mushrooms, tomatoes, and herbs.

Ziminu (Corsican). A fish chowder.

Zimt (German). Cinnamon.

Zinc (French, Colloquial). A bar where alcoholic drinks are served. The name probably is derived from the fact that bars were originally made of zinc.

Zinfandel. A dry white or red wine produced in California. *See* United States, The Wines of.

Zingara (French). A garnish made of chopped ham, tongue, truffles, and mushrooms in a demi-glacé sauce flavored with tomato and tarragon; usually served with meat and poultry.

Zingel. A slightly muddy-tasting fish of the perch family found in the Danube River.

Zips Cheese. Another name for Brinsen cheese, a soft, sheep's-milk product made originally in Hungary and Romania. *See also* Brinza.

Ziste (French). Zeste, the white substance just underneath the colored skin of citrus fruit.

Ziti (Italian). Quite large smooth tubes of pasta.

Zitoni (Italian). The largest unfluted type of macaroni. *Zitoni rigati* is fluted.

Zitrone (German). Lemon.

Zizanie. Wild rice.

Z'Nuni. In Bavaria, Germany, the second breakfast, consisting of black bread, cherry liquor, and raw bacon.

Zoctwaterkreeft (Dutch). Crayfish.

Zombie. A very strong West Indian and African drink, usually made of several kinds of rum and served cold in a tall glass. The name comes from the Haitian word *zobi*, meaning a dead person brought back to life by magic, which is the reverse of the way the drink usually acts.

Zomotherapy. A treatment using raw meat or raw-meat juice for anemia and neurasthenia in convalescence.

Zoolak. A type of cultured milk with a characteristic acid flavor.

Zout (Dutch). Salt.

Zrazy (Polish). A dish made with very thin rounds of beef garnished with slices of potato fried in butter.

Zubrovka; Zubrowka. A yellowish Russian alcoholic beverage made by steeping zubrowka grass in vodka to flavor and color the liquor.

Zucca (Italian). Squash.

Zucche Ripiene (Italian). Stuffed acorn squash.

Zucchero (Italian). Sugar.

Zucchetti (Italian). A rather small squash; a small zucchini.

Zucchini; Baby Marrows; Courgette. A very tasty Italian squash; green summer Italian marrows. Only the very young specimens have a good flavor. To prepare, it is not necessary to remove the skin.

Zucchini Fritti. Fried summer squash.

Zucco. An Italian dessert wine.

Zucker (German). Sugar.

Zuckererbsen (German). Young green peas.

Zumo de Frutas (Spanish). Fruit drink.

Zunge (German). Tongue.

Zuppa (Italian). Soup.

Zuppa all'Aglio. Garlic soup.

Zuppa d'Erbe. Fresh-greens soup.

Zuppa di Castagne. Chestnut soup.

Zuppa di Ceci. Chick-pea soup.

Zuppa di Cipolle. Onion soup.

Zuppa di Datteri. Mussel soup.

Zuppa di Frutti di Mare. Shellfish soup.

Zuppa di Lenticchie. Lentil soup.

Zuppa di Patate. Potato soup.

Zuppa di Pesce. Fish chowder.

Zuppa di Pesto. Vegetable soup with garlic and herbs.

Zuppa di Scampi. Shrimp soup.

Zuppa di Spinaci. Spinach soup.

Zuppa Genovese. A fish soup made with egg yolks and small *quenelles* of ground fish; popular around Genoa.

Zuppa Pavese. Soup with an egg poached in it; served with cheese and fried bread.

Zuppa Rustica. Peasant soup with beans, potatoes, and sausages.

Zuppa Inglese (Italian). A soft cake soaked in liquor.

Zürchertopf. Chopped beef, macaroni, and tomato sauce baked in a casserole; a specialty of Zurich, Switzerland.

Zuurkool met Worst (Dutch). Sauerkraut and sausages.

Zwack. Trade name of a complete line of Hungarian cordials and liqueurs.

Zwetschgen (German). Plums; prunes.

Zwetschgenknödel (German). Sweet plum dumplings.

Zwicker. An Alsatian blending wine used to combine two other wines in order to obtain a finished product.

Zwieback (German). Crisp dry toast, plain or sweetened; made from a special type of bread sliced when cool, then toasted at low heat. The German term *zweibacken* means "twice baked."

Zwiebelkuchen (German). An onion pastry; a specialty of Hesse.

Zwiebeln (German). Onions.

Zwiebelsuppe (German). Onion soup.

Zwischenrippenstück (German). Ribsteak; entrecôte.

Zymase. Any of a group of enzymes that convert glucose into carbon dioxide and water or into alcohol and carbon dioxide, depending on whether oxygen is present.

Zyme. Yeast. The term *enzyme* means "in yeast," as it was from yeast that the active catalysts were first obtained.

Zymology. The science of fermentation.

Zymoma. Yeast; leaven.

Zymurgy. The chemistry of fermentation in its relation to brewing.

Zythum (Egyptian, Obsolete). An ancient beer prepared from malt and wheat.

S. L. CLEMENS

LIBRARY

OF THE

WORLD'S BEST LITERATURE

Ancient and Modern

CHARLES DUDLEY WARNER

EDITOR

HAMILTON WRIGHT MABIE,   LUCIA GILBERT RUNKLE,
GEORGE H. WARNER

ASSOCIATE EDITORS

THIRTY VOLUMES

VOL. VII

NEW YORK

R. S. PEALE AND J. A. HILL

PUBLISHERS

THE ADVISORY COUNCIL

CRAWFORD H. TOY, A. M., LL. D.,
    Professor of Hebrew, HARVARD UNIVERSITY, Cambridge, Mass.

THOMAS R. LOUNSBURY, LL. D., L. H. D.,
    Professor of English in the Sheffield Scientific School of
        YALE UNIVERSITY, New Haven, Conn.

WILLIAM M. SLOANE, PH. D., L. H. D.,
    Professor of History and Political Science,
        PRINCETON UNIVERSITY, Princeton, N. J.

BRANDER MATTHEWS, A. M., LL. B.,
    Professor of Literature, COLUMBIA UNIVERSITY, New York City.

JAMES B. ANGELL, LL. D.,
    President of the UNIVERSITY OF MICHIGAN, Ann Arbor, Mich.

WILLARD FISKE, A. M., PH. D.,
    Late Professor of the Germanic and Scandinavian Languages
    and Literatures, CORNELL UNIVERSITY, Ithaca, N. Y.

EDWARD S. HOLDEN, A. M., LL. D.,
    Director of the Lick Observatory, and Astronomer,
        UNIVERSITY OF CALIFORNIA, Berkeley, Cal.

ALCÉE FORTIER, LIT. D.,
    Professor of the Romance Languages,
        TULANE UNIVERSITY, New Orleans, La.

WILLIAM P. TRENT, M. A.,
    Dean of the Department of Arts and Sciences, and Professor of
    English and History,
        UNIVERSITY OF THE SOUTH, Sewanee, Tenn.

PAUL SHOREY, PH. D.,
    Professor of Greek and Latin Literature,
        UNIVERSITY OF CHICAGO, Chicago, Ill.

WILLIAM T. HARRIS, LL. D.,
    United States Commissioner of Education,
        BUREAU OF EDUCATION, Washington, D. C.

MAURICE FRANCIS EGAN, A. M., LL. D.,
    Professor of Literature in the ᴵᵃ
        CATHOLIC UNIVERSITY OF AMERICA, Washington, D. C.

9377

TABLE OF CONTENTS

VOL. VII

———

LIVED   PAGE

MARCUS TULLIUS CICERO   106–43 B. C.   3675

BY WILLIAM CRANSTON LAWTON

Of the Offices of Literature and Poetry ('Oration for the Poet Archias')
Honors Proposed for the Dead Statesman Sulpicius (Ninth Philippic)
Old Friends Better than New ('Dialogue on Friendship')
Honored Old Age ('Dialogue on Old Age')
Death is Welcome to the Old (same)
Great Orators and their Training ('Dialogue on Oratory')
Letters: To Tiro; To Atticus
Sulpicius Consoles Cicero after his Daughter Tullia's Death
Cicero's Reply to Sulpicius
A Homesick Exile
Cicero's Vacillation in the Civil War
Cicero's Correspondents: Cæsar to Cicero; Cæsar to Cicero; Pompey to Cicero; Cælius in Rome to Cicero in Cilicia; Matius to Cicero
The Dream of Scipio

THE CID   1045?–1099   3725

BY CHARLES SPRAGUE SMITH

From 'The Poem of My Cid': Leaving Burgos; Farewell to his Wife at San Pedro de Cardeña; Battle Scene; The Challenges; Conclusion

EARL OF CLARENDON (Edward Hyde)   1609–1674   3737
The Character of Lord Falkland

                                                    LIVED   PAGE
MARCUS A. H. CLARKE   1846–1881   3745
  How a Penal System can Work ('His Natural Life')
  The Valley of the Shadow of Death (same)

MATTHIAS CLAUDIUS   1740–1815   3756
  Speculations on New-Year's Day (The Wandsbecker Bote)
  Rhine Wine
  Winter
  Night Song

HENRY CLAY   1777–1852   3761
            BY JOHN R. PROCTER

  Public Spirit in Politics (Speech in 1849)
  On the Greek Struggle for Independence (Speech in 1824)
  South-American Independence as Related to the United
    States (Speech in 1818)
  From the Valedictory to the Senate in 1842
  From the Lexington 'Speech on Retirement to Private
    Life'

CLEANTHES   331–232 B. C.   3784
  Hymn to Zeus

SAMUEL LANGHORNE CLEMENS (Mark Twain)   1835–   3787
  The Child of Calamity ('Life on the Mississippi')
  A Steamboat Landing at a Small Town (same)
  The High River: and a Phantom Pilot (same)
  An Enchanting River Scene (same)
  The Lightning Pilot (same)
  An Expedition against Ogres ('A Connecticut Yankee in
    King Arthur's Court')
  The True Prince and the Feigned One ('The Prince and
    the Pauper')

ARTHUR HUGH CLOUGH   1819–1861   3821
          BY CHARLES ELIOT NORTON

  There is No God
  The Latest Decalogue
  To the Unknown God
  Easter Day — Naples, 1849
  It Fortifies My Soul to Know

                                                                LIVED   PAGE

ARTHUR HUGH CLOUGH — *Continued:*
    Say Not, The Struggle Naught Availeth
    Come Back
    As Ships Becalmed
    The Unknown Course
    The Gondola
    The Poet's Place in Life
    On Keeping within One's Proper Sphere ('The Bothie of
       Tober-na-Vuolich')
    Consider It Again

SAMUEL TAYLOR COLERIDGE   1772–1834   3843

           BY GEORGE E. WOODBERRY

    Kubla Khan
    The Albatross ('The Rime of the Ancient Mariner')
    Time, Real and Imaginary
    Dejection: An Ode
    The Three Treasures
    To a Gentleman
    Ode to Georgiana, Duchess of Devonshire
    The Pains of Sleep
    Song, by Glycine
    Youth and Age
    Phantom or Fact

WILLIAM COLLINS   1721–1759   3871
    How Sleep the Brave
    The Passions
    To Evening
    Ode on the Death of Thomson

WILLIAM WILKIE COLLINS   1824–1889   3879
    The Sleep-Walking ('The Moonstone')
    Count Fosco ('The Woman in White')

GEORGE COLMAN THE ELDER   1733–1794   3901
    The Eavesdropping ('The Jealous Wife')

JOHANN AMOS COMENIUS   1592–1671   3909

           BY BURKE A. HINSDALE

    Author's Preface to the 'Orbis Pictus'
    School of Infancy — Claims of Childhood

	LIVED	PAGE

PHILIPPE DE COMINES   1445–1510   3923

The Virtues and Vices of King Louis XI.
The Virtues of the Duke of Burgundy and the Time of
    his House's Prosperity
The Last Days of Louis XI.
Character of Louis XI.

(All the above from Comines's 'Memoirs')

AUGUSTE COMTE   1798–1857   3935

Evolution of Belief ('Positive Philosophy')
The Study of Law Substituted for That of Causes (same)
Subjection of Self-Love to Social Love ('Positive Polity')
The Cultus of Humanity (same)
The Domination of the Dead (same)
The Worship of Woman (same)

WILLIAM CONGREVE   1670–1729   3945

Mrs. Foresight and Mrs. Frail Come to an Understanding
    ('Love for Love')
Angelica's Proposal (same)
Almeria in the Mausoleum ('The Mourning Bride')

HENRI CONSCIENCE   1812–1883   3957
BY WILLIAM SHARP

The Horse-Shoe ('Rikke-Tikke-Tak')
The Patient Waiter (same)
The Lost Glove
The Iron Tomb
Siska van Roosemael
A Painter's Progress

ROSE TERRY COOKE   1827–1892   3973

The Reverend Thomas Tucker as a Parson ('Some Ac-
    count of Thomas Tucker')

JAMES FENIMORE COOPER   1789–1851   3985
BY JULIAN HAWTHORNE

The Privateer ('The Water-Witch')
The Brigantine's Escape through Hell-Gate (same)
The Doom of Abiram White ('The Prairie')
The Bison Stampede (same)
Running the Gauntlet ('The Last of the Mohicans')
The Prairie Fire ('The Prairie')

	LIVED	PAGE
COPERNICUS	1473–1543	4040

BY EDWARD S. HOLDEN

FRANÇOIS COPPÉE — 1842– — 4045

BY ROBERT SANDERSON

    The Parricide ('For the Crown')
    The Substitute

PIERRE CORNEILLE — 1606–1684 — 4065

BY FREDERICK MORRIS WARREN

    The Lovers ('The Cid')
    Don Rodrigue Describes to King Fernando his Victory
      over the Moors (same)
    The Wrath of Camilla ('Horace')
    Paulina's Appeal to Severus ('Polyeucte')

VICTOR COUSIN — 1792–1867 — 4079

    Pascal's Skepticism ('Les Pensées de Pascal')
    Madame de Longueville ('Life of Madame de Longueville')
    Madame de Chevreuse ('Life of Madame de Chevreuse')
    Comparison between Madame de Hautefort and Madame
      de Chevreuse

ABRAHAM COWLEY — 1618–1667 — 4089

BY THOMAS R. LOUNSBURY

    Of Myself
    On the Death of Crashaw
    On the Death of Mr. William Hervey
    A Supplication
    Epitaph on a Living Author

WILLIAM COWPER — 1731–1800 — 4107

    The Cricket
    The Winter Walk at Noon ('The Task')
    On the Loss of the Royal George
    Imaginary Verses of Alexander Selkirk
    The Immutability of Human Nature (Letter to William
      Unwin)
    From a Letter to Rev. John Newton

GEORGE CRABBE — 1754–1832 — 4117

    Isaac Ashford ('The Parish Register')
    The Parish Workhouse and Apothecary ('The Village')

	LIVED	PAGE

DINAH MARIA MULOCK CRAIK — 1826–1887 — 4123

    The Night Attack ('John Halifax, Gentleman')
    Philip, My King
    Too Late
    Now and Afterwards

MADAME AUGUSTUS CRAVEN (Pauline de la Ferronays)
                                  1820–1891 — 4139

    Albert's Last Days ('A Sister's Story')
    A Generous Enemy ('Fleurange')

FRANCIS MARION CRAWFORD — 1854– — 4151

    The Ghost in the Berth ('The Upper Berth')
    A Thwarted Plan ('Marzio's Crucifix')

PROSPER JOLYOT CRÉBILLON — 1675–1762 — 4167

BY ROBERT SANDERSON

    The Bloody Banquet ('Atreus and Thyestes')
    Mother and Daughter ('Electra')
    The Matricide (same)
    The Reconciliation ('Rhadamistus and Zenobia')

S. R. CROCKETT — 1862– — 4181

    Ensamples to the Flock ('The Stickit Minister')
    Sawny Bean; and the Cave of Death ('The Gray Man')

GEORGE CROLY — 1780–1860 — 4197

    The Firing of Rome ('Salathiel the Immortal')
    A Wife's Influence ('Catiline')
    The Lily of the Valley

GEORGE CUPPLES — 1822–1891 — 4208

    In the Tropics ('The Green Hand')
    Napoleon at St. Helena (same)

GEORGE WILLIAM CURTIS — 1824–1892 — 4221

BY EDWARD CARY

    The Mist at Newport ('Lotus Eating')
    Nazareth ('Howadji in Syria')
    Aurelia as a Grandmother ('Prue and I')
    Prue's Magnolia (same)
    Our Cousin the Curate (same)

LIVED   PAGE

GEORGE WILLIAM CURTIS — *Continued:*

    The Charm of Paris ('Potiphar Papers')
    "Pharisaism of Reform" ('Orations and Addresses')
    The Call of Freedom (same)
    Robert Browning in Florence ('The Easy Chair')

ERNST CURTIUS   1814–1896   4241

    The Causes of Dislike toward Socrates ('History of Greece')
    Socrates as an Influence and as a Man (same)

CUVIER   1769–1832   4251

BY SPENCER TROTTER

    Of Changes in the Structure of the Earth ('The Theory
      of the Earth')
    Of the Fabulous Animals of the Ancient Writers

LIST OF PORTRAITS

IN VOL. VII

Marcus Tullius Cicero	Full page
Earl of Clarendon	Vignette
Matthias Claudius	Vignette
Henry Clay	Full page
Samuel Langhorne Clemens	Full page
Samuel Taylor Coleridge	Full page
William Collins	Vignette
William Wilkie Collins	Vignette
George Colman the Elder	Vignette
Johann Amos Comenius	Vignette
Auguste Comte	Vignette
William Congreve	Vignette
Henri Conscience	Vignette
James Fenimore Cooper	Full page
Copernicus	Vignette
François Coppée	Vignette
Pierre Corneille	Full page
Victor Cousin	Vignette
Abraham Cowley	Vignette
William Cowper	Full page
George Crabbe	Vignette
Dinah Maria Mulock Craik	Vignette
Francis Marion Crawford	Vignette
Prosper Jolyot Crébillon	Vignette
Samuel Rutherford Crockett	Vignette
George William Curtis	Vignette
Ernst Curtius	Vignette
Cuvier	Vignette

CICERO.

MARCUS TULLIUS CICERO

(106–43 B. C.)

BY WILLIAM CRANSTON LAWTON

THE outward life, the political career, of Marcus Tullius Cicero, is to nearly all students of history a tragic and pathetic story. He seems peculiarly unfitted to the people and the time in which his lot was cast. His enlightened love for the traditions of the past, his passionate sentiment of patriotism, his forceful eloquence as a debater in the Senate or as an orator in the Forum,— these qualities of a Burke or a Webster stand out violently dissevered from the lurid history of his time. This humane scholarly life was flung into the midst of the wildest century in all Rome's grim annals; the hundred years of civic turmoil and bloodshed, from the elder Gracchus's murder to the death of Cleopatra.

And yet such was the marvelous activity, the all-sided productiveness, of the Ciceronian intellect, that perhaps no human mind has ever so fully exploited all its powers. Moreover, in each intellectual field which he entered, the chances of time have removed nearly every Roman rival, leaving us no choice save to accept Cicero's guidance. There was many another orator, and history of eloquence. There were other practical treatises on rhetoric. Many a notable correspondence was actually preserved and published, though now lost. Even his free transcriptions from Greek philosophical treatises — hastily conned and perhaps imperfectly understood — have acquired, through the disappearance of the Greek scrolls themselves, an ill-deserved authority as to the tenets of the Epicurean and other schools.

Before and above all else, Cicero was a pleader. Out of that activity grew his ill-starred political activity, while his other literary tastes were essentially but a solace in times of enforced retirement. With the discussion of his oratory, therefore, we may best combine a rapid outline of his life.

By their common birthplace, Arpinum, and by a slight tie of kinship, Cicero was associated with Marius; and he began life, like Disraeli, with radical sympathies. He was the elder son of a wealthy Roman citizen, but no ancestor had ennobled the family by attaining curule office. After a most thorough course of training in Latin and Greek, Cicero began to "practice law." The pleader in ancient Rome was supposed to receive no fee, and even more than with us, found his profession the natural stepping-stone to political honors.

At the age of twenty-six, Cicero (in 80 B. C.) defended his first important client in a criminal case. In the closing days of the Sullan proscriptions, young Roscius, of Ameria in Umbria, was charged with murdering his own father in Rome. A pair of Roscius's kinsmen were probably the real culprits, and had arranged with Chrysogonus, a wealthy freedman and favorite of the Dictator, to insert the dead man's name among the outlawed victims and to divide the confiscated estate. The son was persecuted because he resisted this second outrage. Cicero says he is himself protected by his obscurity, though no other advocate has dared to plead for the unlucky youth. In our present text there are some audacious words aimed at Sulla's own measures: they were probably sharpened in a later revision. The case was won, against general expectation. Cicero may have played the hero that day: certainly the brief remainder of Sulla's life was spent by the young democratic pleader traveling in the East,—"for his health," as Plutarch adds, truly enough. At this time his style was chastened and his manner moderated by the teachers of Athens, and especially by Molo in Rhodes.

Cicero's quæstorship was passed in Sicily, 75–4 B. C. Here he knit close friendships with many Greek provincials, and did a creditable piece of archæological work by rediscovering Archimedes's tomb. His impeachment of Verres for misgovernment in Sicily was in 70 B. C. This time the orator runs a less desperate risk. Since Sulla's death the old constitution has languidly revived. Speech was comparatively free and safe. The "knights" or wealthy middle class,—Cicero's own,—deprived by Sulla of the right to sit as the jurors in impeachment trials like Verres's, partially regain the privilege in this very year. The overwhelming mass of evidence made Verres flee into exile, and Hortensius, till then leader of the Roman bar, threw up the case in despair. Nevertheless Cicero published the stately series of orations he had prepared. They form the most vivid picture, and the deadliest indictments ever drawn, of Roman provincial government,—and of a ruthless art-collector. Cicero instantly became the foremost among lawyers. Moreover, this success made Cicero a leader in the time of reaction after Sulla, and hastened his elevation to posts where only men of sterner nature could be fully and permanently successful.

Pompey, born in the same year, was at this time leading the revolt against Sulla's measures. The attachment now formed, the warmer hearted Cicero never wholly threw off. The young general's later foreign victories are nowhere so generously set forth as in Cicero's too-rhetorical plea "for the Manilian Law," in 66 B. C.

Pompey was then wintering in the East, after sweeping piracy in a single summer from the Mediterranean. This plea gave him the larger command against Mithridates. Despite the most extravagant laudation, however, Pompey remains, here as elsewhere, one of those large but vague and misty figures that stalk across the stage of history without ever once turning upon us a fully human face. Far more distinct than he, there looms above him the splendid triumphal pageant of Roman imperialism itself.

Cicero's unrivaled eloquence won him not only a golden shower of gifts and legacies, but also the prætorship and consulship at the earliest legal age. Perhaps some of the old nobles foresaw and prudently avoided the Catilinarian storm of 63 B. C. The common dangers of that year, and the pride of assured position, may have hastened the full transfer of Cicero's allegiance to the old senatorial faction. Tiberius Gracchus, boldly praised in January, has become for Cicero a notorious demagogue; his slayers instead are the undoubted patriots, in the famous harangues of November. These latter, by the way, were certainly under the file three years afterward, —and it is not likely that we read any Ciceronian speech just as it was delivered. If there be any thread of consistency in Cicero's public career, it must be sought in his long but vain hope to unite the nobility and the *equites*, in order to resist the growing proletariat.

The eager vanity with which Cicero seized the proud title "Father of the fatherland" is truly pathetic. The summary execution of the traitors may have been prompted by that physical timidity so often associated with the scholarly temperament. Whether needless or not, the act returned to plague him.

The happiest effort of the orator in his consular year was the famous plea for Murena. This consul-elect for 62 was a successful soldier. Catiline must be met in the spring "in the jaws of Etruria." Cicero's dearest friend, Servius Sulpicius Rufus, a defeated candidate, accused Murena of bribery. The conditions of Roman politics, the character of Sulpicius, the tone of Cicero himself, bid us adjudge Murena probably guilty. Cicero had supported Sulpicius, but now feels it is no time to "go behind the returns," or to replace a bold soldier by a scholarly lawyer.

To win his case Cicero must heap ridicule upon his own profession in his friend's person, and upon Stoic philosophy, represented by Cato, Sulpicius's chief advocate. This he did so successfully that Cato himself exclaimed with a grim smile, "What a jester our consul is!" Cicero won his case—and kept his friends. This speech is cited *sixteen times* by Quintilian, and is a model of forensic ingenuity, wit, and grace. Its patriotism may be plausibly defended, but hardly its moral standards.

The next year produced the famous and successful defense of
Cluentius,—probably guilty of poisoning,—and also the most delightful of all Cicero's speeches, the oration for the poet Archias.
Whether the old Greek's claim to Roman citizenship was beyond
cavil we neither know nor greatly care. The legal argument is suspiciously brief. The praise of literature and the scholarly life, however, has re-echoed ever since, and still reaches all hearts. Brother
Quintus, sitting in judgment as prætor, is pleasantly greeted.

This is the culmination in Cicero's career of success. Some boastful words uttered in these days make us doubt if he remembered
Solon's and Sophocles's maxim, "Count no life happy before its
close." The fast-growing power of Cæsar presently made the two
successful generals Pompey and Crassus his political tools. Cicero
refused to enter, on similar conditions, the cabal later known as the
"First Triumvirate." Cæsar, about to depart for his long absence in
Gaul, might well regard the patriotic and impulsive orator as the
most serious source of possible opposition in his absence. Marcus
refused, himself, to go along to Gaul a-soldiering, though Brother
Quintus accepted a commission and served creditably. At last,
reluctantly, Cæsar suffered Cicero's personal enemy Clodius to bring
forward a decree outlawing "those who had put Roman citizens to
death without trial" (March, 58 B. C.). Cicero meekly withdrew
from Rome, was condemned by name in absence, and his town
house and villas pillaged.

As to the cowardice of this hasty retreat, none need use severer
words than did the exile himself. It is the decisive event in his
career. His uninterrupted success was ended. His pride could
never recover fully from the hurt. Worst of all, he could never
again pose, even before his own eyes, as the fearless hero-patriot.
In short, Cæsar, the consummate master of action and of men, had
humanely but decisively crippled the erratic yet patriotic rheto-
rician.

In little more than a year the bad conduct of Clodius, the personal good-will of the "triumvirs," and the whirligig of politics,
brought round Cicero's return from Greece. His wings were however effectively clipped. After a brief and slight flutter of independence, he made full, even abject, submission to the dominant
Cæsarian faction. This was in 56 B. C. The next five years, inglo-
rious politically, were however full of activity in legal oratory and
other literary work. In his eloquent defense of Cælius Rufus,
charged with an attempt to poison Clodia, Cicero perforce white-
washes, or at least paints in far milder colors than of old, Catiline,
Cælius's lifelong friend! A still less pleasing feature is the abusive
attack on the famous and beautiful Clodia, probably the "Lesbia" of

Catullus. (The unhappy young poet seems to have preceded Cælius in the fickle matron's favor.)

The events of the year 52 well illustrate the unfitness of Cicero for politics in such an age. Rome was full of street brawls, which Pompey could not check. The orator's old enemy Clodius, at the head of his bravos, was slain by a fellow ruffian Milo in January. At Milo's trial in April Cicero defended him, or attempted to do so. A court-room encircled by a yelling mob and guarded by Pompey's legions caused him to break down altogether. As afterward written out at leisure, the speech is a masterpiece of special pleading. The exiled Milo's criticism on it is well known: "I'm glad you never delivered it: I should not now be enjoying the mullets of Marseilles."

The year 51–50 Cicero spent, most unwillingly, as proconsular governor in far-off Cilicia. Though really humane and relatively honest, he accumulated in these few months a handsome sum in "gifts" from provincials and other perquisites. Even Cicero was a Roman.

Meantime the civil war had all but broken out at home. Cicero hesitated long, and the correspondence with Atticus contains exhaustive analyses of his motives and temptations. His naïve selfishness and vanity at times in these letters seem even like self-caricature. Yet through it all glimmers a vein of real though bewildered patriotism. Still the craving for a triumph — he had fought some savage mountain clans in Asia Minor! — was hardly less dominant.

Repairing late and with many misgivings to Pompey's camp in Epirus, Cicero seems to have been there a "not unfeared, half-welcome" and critical guest. Illness is his excuse for absence from the decisive battle. He himself tells us little of these days. As Plutarch relates the tale, after Pompey's flight to Egypt Cicero refused the supreme command, and was thereupon threatened with death by young Gneius Pompey; but his life was saved by Cato.

One thing at least is undisputed. The last man to decide for Pompey's cause, he was the first to hurry back to Italy and crave Cæsar's grace! For many months he waited in ignoble retirement, fearing the success of his deserted comrades even more than Cæsar's victory. It is this action that gives the *coup de grace* to Cicero's character as a hero. With whatever misgivings, he had chosen his side. Whatever disturbing threats of violent revenge after victory he heard in Pompey's camp, he awaited the decisive battle. Then there remained, for any brave man, only constancy in defeat — or a fall upon his sword.

Throughout Cæsar's brief reign, — or long dictatorship, — from 48 to 44, Cicero is the most stately and the most obsequious of courtiers. For him who would plead for clemency, or return thanks for mercy accorded, at a despot's footstool, there are no more graceful models than the 'Pro Ligario' and the 'Pro Marcello.' Cæsar himself realized, and wittily remarked, how irksome and hateful such a part must be to the older, vainer, more self-conscious man of the twain.

Midway in this period Cicero divorced his wife after thirty years of wedlock, seemingly from some dissatisfaction over her financial management, and soon after married a wealthy young ward. This is the least pleasing chapter of his private life, but perhaps the mortification and suffering it entailed were a sufficient penalty. His only daughter Tullia's death in 45 B. C. nearly broke the father's heart.

Whatever the reason, Cicero was certainly not in the secret of Cæsar's assassination. Twice in letters to members of the conspiracy in later months he begins: "How I wish you had invited me to your glorious banquet on the Ides of March." "There would have been no remnants," he once adds. That is, Antony would not have been left alive.

We have now reached the last two years—perhaps the most creditable time—in Cicero's eventful life. This period runs from March 15th, 44 B. C., to December 7th, 43 B. C. It was one long struggle, first covert, then open, between Antony and the slayers of Cæsar. Cicero's energy and eloquence soon made him the foremost voice in the Senate once more. For the first time since his exile, he is now speaking out courageously his own real sentiments. His public action is in harmony with his own convictions. The cause was not hopeless by any means, so far as the destruction of Antony would have been a final triumph. Indeed, that wild career seemed near its end, when Octavian's duplicity again threw the game into his rival's reckless hands. However, few students of history imagine that any effective restoration of senatorial government was possible. The peculiar pathos of Cicero's end, patriot as he was, is this: it removed one of the last great obstacles to the only stable and peaceful rule Rome could receive—the imperial throne of Augustus.

This last period is however among the most creditable, perhaps the most heroic, in Cicero's career. Its chief memorials are the fourteen extant orations against Antony. The comparative sincerity of these 'Philippics,' and the lack of private letters for much of this time, make them important historical documents. The only one which ranks among his greatest productions—perhaps the classic masterpiece of invective—is the 'Second Philippic.' This was never delivered at all, but published as a pamphlet. This unquestioned fact throws a curious light on passages like—"He is agitated, he perspires, he turns pale!" describing Antony at the (imaginary) delivery of the oration. The details of the behavior of Catiline and others may be hardly more authentic. The 'Ninth Philippic' is a heartfelt funeral eulogy on that same Sulpicius whom he had ridiculed in the 'Pro Murena.'

> « The milestones into headstones turn,
> And under each a friend.»

A fragment from one of Livy's lost books says, "Cicero bore with becoming spirit none of the ills of life save death itself." He indeed perished not only bravely but generously, dissuading his devoted slaves from useless resistance, and extending his neck to Antony's assassins. Verres lived to exult at the news, and then shared his enemy's fate, rather than give up his Greek vases to Antony! Nearly every Roman, save Nero, dies well.

Upon Cicero's political career our judgment is already indicated. He was always a patriot at heart, though often a bewildered one. His vanity, and yet more his physical cowardice, caused some grievous blots upon the record. His last days, and death, may atone for all — save one. The precipitate desertion of the Pompeians is not to be condoned.

The best English life of Cicero is by Forsyth; but quaint, dogged, prejudiced old Middleton should not be forgotten. Plutarch's Cicero "needs no bush."

Cicero's oratory was splendidly effective upon his emotional Italian hearers. It would not be so patiently accepted by any Teutonic folk. His very copiousness, however, makes him as a rule wonderfully clear and easy reading. Quintilian well says: "From Demosthenes's periods not a word can be spared, to Cicero's not one could be added."

Despite the rout of Verres and of Catiline, the merciless dissection of Clodia, and the statelier thunders of the 'Philippics,' Cicero was most successful and happiest when "defending the interests of his friends." Perhaps the greatest success against justice was the 'Pro Cluentio,' which throws so lurid a light on ante-Borgian Italian criminology. This speech is especially recommended by Niebuhr to young philologues as a nut worthy of the strongest teeth. There is a helpful edition by Ramsay, but Hertland's 'Murena' will be a pleasanter variation for students wearying of the beaten track followed by the school editions. Both the failure of the 'Pro Milone' and the world-wide success of the 'Pro Archia' bid us repeat the vain wish, that this humane and essentially modern nature might have fallen on a gentler age. Regarding his whole political life as an uncongenial rôle forced on him by fate, we return devout thanks for *fifty-eight* orations, nearly all in revised and finished literary form! Fragments of seventeen, and titles of still thirty more, yet remain.

From all his rivals, predecessors, pupils, not one authentic speech survives.

The best complete edition of the orations with English notes is by George Long, in the Bibliotheca Classica. The 'Philippics' alone are better edited by J. R. King in the Clarendon Press series. School editions of select speeches are superabundant. They regularly include the four Catilinarians, the Manilian, and the pleas before the dictator, sometimes a selection from the 'Philippics' or Verrine orations.

There is no masterly translation comparable with the fine work done by Kennedy for Demosthenes. The Bohn version is respectable in quality.

Among Cicero's numerous works on rhetoric the chief is the 'De Oratore.' Actually composed in 55 B. C., it is a dialogue, the scene set in 91 B. C., the characters being the chief Roman orators of that day. L. Crassus, who plays the host gracefully at his Tusculan country-seat, is also the chief speaker. These men were all known to Cicero in his boyhood, but most of them perished soon after in the Marian proscriptions. Of real character-drawing there is little, and all alike speak in graceful Ciceronian periods. The exposition of the technical parts of rhetoric goes on in leisurely wise, with copious illustrations and digressions. There is much pleasant repetition of commonplaces. Wilkins's edition of the 'De Oratore' is a good but not an ideal one. The introductions are most helpful. Countless discussions on etymology, etc., in the notes, should be relegated to the dictionaries. Instead, we crave adequate cross-references to passages in this and other works. The notes seem to be written too largely piecemeal, each with the single passage in mind.

In Cicero's 'Brutus,' written in 46 B. C., Cicero, Brutus, and Atticus carry on the conversation, but it is mostly a monologue of Cicero and a historical sketch of Roman oratory. The affected modesty of the autobiographic parts is diverting. Brutus was the chief exponent of a terse, simple, direct oratory,— far nearer, we judge, to English taste than the Ciceronian; and the opposition between them already appears. A convenient American edition is that by Kellogg (Ginn).

The opposition just mentioned comes out more clearly in the 'Orator.' This portrays the ideal public speaker. His chief accomplishments are summed up in versatility,— the power to adapt himself to any case and audience. An interesting passage discusses the rhythms of prose. This book has been elaborately edited by J. E. Sandys. In these three dialogues Cicero says everything of importance, at least once; and the other rhetorical works in the Corpus may be neglected here, the more as the most practical working rhetoric among them all, the 'Auctor ad Herennium,' is certainly not

Cicero's. It is probably by Cornificius, and is especially important as the *first* complete prose work transmitted to us in authentic Latin form. (Cato's 'De Re Rustica' has been "modernized.")

The later history of the Ciceronian correspondence is a dark and much contested field. (The most recent discussion, with bibliography, is by Schanz, in Iwan Müller's Handbuch, Vol. viii., pp. 238–243.) Probably Cicero's devoted freedman Tiro laid the foundations of our collections. The part of Petrarch in recovering the letters during the "Revival of Learning" was much less than has been supposed.

The letters themselves are in wild confusion. There are four collections, entitled 'To Atticus,' 'To Friends,' 'To Brother Marcus,' 'To Brutus': altogether over eight hundred epistles, of which a relatively small number are written *to* Cicero by his correspondents. The order is not chronological, and the dates can in many cases only be conjectured. Yet these letters afford us our chief sources for the history of this great epoch,—and the best insight we can ever hope to have into the private life of Roman gentlemen.

The style of the cynical, witty Cælius, or of the learned lawyer Sulpicius, differs perceptibly in detail from Cicero's own; yet it is remarkable that all seem able to write clearly if not gracefully. Cicero's own style varies very widely. The letters to Atticus are usually colloquial, full of unexplained allusions, sometimes made intentionally obscure and pieced out with a Greek phrase, for fear of the carrier's treachery! Other letters again, notably a long 'Apologia' addressed to Lentulus after Cicero's return from exile, are as plainly addressed in reality to the public or to posterity as are any of the orations.

Prof. R. Y. Tyrrell has long been engaged upon an annotated edition of all the letters in chronological order. This will be of the utmost value. An excellent selection, illustrating the orator's public life chiefly, has been published by Professor Albert Watson. This volume contains also very full tables of dates, bibliography of all Cicero's works, and in general is indispensable for the advanced Latin student. The same letters annotated by Professor Watson have been delightfully translated by G. E. Jeans. To this volume, rather than to Forsyth's biography, the English reader should turn to form his impressions of Cicero at first hand. It is a model of scholarly — and also literary — translation.

The "New Academy," to which Cicero inclined in philosophy, was skeptical in its tendencies, and regarded absolute truth as unattainable. This made it easier for Cicero to cast his transcriptions in the form of dialogues, revealing the beliefs of the various schools through the lips of the several interlocutors. Thus the 'De Finibus Bonorum et Malorum' sets forth in three successive conversations the ideas of Epicureans, of Stoics, and of the Academy, on the Highest Good. It is perhaps the chief of these treatises,—though we would still prefer to have even those later compendiums of the Greek schools through which Cicero probably cited the chief philosophers at second hand! J. S. Reid, an eminent English scholar, has spent many years upon this dialogue, and his work includes a masterly translation.

With a somewhat similar plan, the three books of the 'De Natura Deorum' contain the views of the three schools on the Divine Beings. The speakers are Cicero's Roman contemporaries. This rather sketchy work has been annotated by J. B. Mayor in his usual exhaustive manner. The now fragmentary dialogue entitled 'The Republic,' and its unfinished supplement 'The Laws,' were composed and named in avowed rivalry with Plato's two largest works, but fail to approach the master. The Roman Constitution is defended as the ideal mingling of monarchy, aristocracy, and democracy. The student of pure literature can for the most part neglect these, and others among the hastily written philosophic works, with the explicit approval of so indefatigable a student as Professor B. L. Gildersleeve.

The chief fragment preserved of the 'Republic' is the 'Dream of Scipio.' Its dependence on the vision at the close of Plato's 'Republic' should be carefully observed. It may be fairly described as a free translation and enlargement from Greek originals, of which Plato's passage is the chief. Plagiarism was surely viewed quite otherwise then than now. Still, the Roman additions and modifications are interesting also,—and even as a translator Cicero is no ordinary cicerone! Moreover, in this as in so many other examples, the Latin paraphrase had a wider and more direct influence than the original. It has been accepted with justice ever since, as the final and most hopeful pagan word in favor of the soul's immortality. The lover of Chaucer will recall the genial paraphrase of 'Scipio's Dream' in the 'Parlament of Foules' (stanzas 5-12). We give below, entire, in our quotations from Cicero, the masterly version of the 'Dream,' prepared by Prof. T. R. Lounsbury for his edition of Chaucer's poems. The speaker is the younger Scipio Africanus, and his visit to Africa as a subaltern here described was in 149 B. C., three years previous to his own decisive campaign against Carthage which ended in the destruction of the city.

Cicero shared in full the Roman tendency to give a practical, an ethical turn to all metaphysical discussion. This is prominent in the popular favorite among his larger volumes, the 'Tusculan Disputations.' In each of the five related books a thesis is stated negatively, to be triumphantly reversed later on:—

(1) "Death seems to me an evil."

(2) "I think pain the greatest of all evils."

(3) "Misery seems to me to befall the wise man."

(4) "It does not appear to me that the wise man can be secure from distress of mind."

(5) "Character does not seem to me sufficient for happiness in life."

The original portion of this work is relatively large, and many Roman illustrations occur. Dr. Peabody has included the Tusculans, the two brief essays next mentioned, and the 'De Officiis,' in his excellent series of versions (Little, Brown and Company).

The little dialogue on 'Old Age' is perhaps most read of all Cicero's works. Its best thoughts, it must be confessed, are freely borrowed from the opening pages of Plato's 'Republic.' Still, on this theme of universal human interest, the Roman also offers much pleasant food for thought. The moderation of the Greek is forgotten by Cicero, the professional advocate and special pleader, who almost cries out to us at last:—

> "Grow old along with me:
> The best is yet to be,
> The last of life, for which the first was made!"

It was written in 45–4 B. C. The other little essay 'On Friendship' does not deserve to be bound up in such good company, though it usually is so edited. Bacon's very brief essay has more meat in it. Cicero had many good friends, but fully trusted hardly any one of them — not even Atticus. It was an age which put friendship to fearful trial, and the typical Roman seems to us rather selfish and cold. Certainly this essay is in a frigid tone. Professor Gildersleeve, I believe, has likened it to a treatise of Xenophon on hunting, so systematically is the *pursuit* of friends discussed.

Perhaps the most practical among Roman Manuals of Morals is the treatise on Duties ('De Officiis'), in three books. Here the personal experience of sixty years is drawn upon, avowedly for the edification of young Marcus, the author's unworthy son. This sole Ciceronian survivor of Antony's massacres lived to be famous for his capacity in wine-drinking, and to receive officially, as consul under Augustus, the news of Antony's final defeat and death — a dramatic revenge.

Most of these philosophic treatises were composed near the end of Cicero's life, largely in one marvelously productive year, 45–4 B. C., just previous to the slaying of Cæsar. Not all even of the extant works have been catalogued here. The 'Academica' and 'De Divinatione' should at least be mentioned.

Such were Cicero's distractions, when cut off from political life
and oratory, and above all when bereft by Tullia's death. The especial 'Consolatio,' composed to regain his courage after this blow,
must head the list of lost works. It took a most pessimistic view of
human life, for which it was reproved by Lactantius. Another perished essay, the 'Hortensius,' introducing the whole philosophic
series, upheld Milton's thesis, "How charming is divine philosophy,"
and first turned the thoughts of Augustine to serious study.

Cicero's poems, chiefly translations, are extant in copious fragments. They show metrical facility, a little taste, no creative imagination at all. A final proof of his unresting activity is his attempt
to write history. Few even among professional advocates could have
less of the temper for mere narration and truth. Indeed, reasonable
disregard for the latter trammel is frankly urged upon a friend who
was to write upon the illustrious moments of Cicero's own career!

We said at first that the caprice of fate had exaggerated some
sides of Cicero's activity, by removing all competitors. In any case,
however, his supremacy among Italian orators, and in the ornate dis-
cursive school of eloquence generally, could not have been questioned.

Yet more: as a stylist he lifted a language hitherto poor in
vocabulary, and stiff in phrase, to a level it never afterward surpassed. Many words he successfully coined, chiefly either by translation or free imitation of Greek originals. His clear, copious,
rhythmical phrase was even more fully his own creation. Indeed, at
the present moment, four or five great forms of living speech testify
to Cicero's amazing mastery over both word and phrase. The eloquence of Castelar, Crispi, and Gambetta, of Gladstone and of Everett,
is shot through and through, in all its warp and woof, with golden
Ciceronian threads. The 'Archias' speaks to any appreciative student of Western Europe, as it were, in a mother tongue which dom-
inates his vernacular speech. Human language, then, has become a
statelier memorial of Cicero than even his vanity can ever have
imagined.

(After writing the substance of this paragraph, I was glad to find
myself in close agreement with Mackail's words in his masterly little
'Latin Literature,' page 62.)

RESUMÉ OF GENERAL BIBLIOGRAPHY

The chief encyclopædia of facts and citations for this period is
the cumbrous old 'Geschichte Roms, oder Pompeius Cæsar Cicero
und ihre Zeitgenossen' of W. Drumann (Königsberg: 1834–44). The
plan is ideally bad, being a series of *family chronicles*, while these
three men are more completely isolated from their families and kin

than any other great trio in all Roman history! The book is however an exhaustive, inexhaustible, little acknowledged, but still worked quarry of erudition. The best single book in English is Watson's edition of the (selected) letters (or Jeans's translation), until it shall be superseded by the complete annotated edition of the correspondence, by Tyrrell.

Mommsen's severe judgment on Cicero is well known. The other standard historians are less severe. Forsyth's life is not the final word on the subject by any means, but gives a good general view. The stately Ciceronian Lexicon by Merguet, already complete for the orations, will eventually provide a complete concordance and copious elucidation for all the works. The most accessible complete edition of Cicero's writings in Latin is by Baiter and Kayser, in eleven volumes. The Index Nominum alone fills four hundred closely printed pages of Vol. xi. The great critical edition is that of Orelli (Zurich: 1826–38).

On Cicero as an author, and indeed in the whole field of Latin literature, the 'Geschichte der Römischen Literatur' of Martin Schanz (in I. Müller's 'Handbuch') is most helpful, and even readable.

William Cranston Lawton

OF THE OFFICES OF LITERATURE AND POETRY

From the 'Oration for the Poet Archias'

You ask us, O Gratius, why we are so exceedingly attached to this man. Because he supplies us with food whereby our mind is refreshed after this noise in the Forum, and with rest for our ears after they have been wearied with bad language. Do you think it possible that we could find a supply for our daily speeches, when discussing such a variety of matters, unless we were to cultivate our minds by the study of literature? or that our minds could bear being kept so constantly on the stretch if we did not relax them by that same study? But I confess that I am devoted to those studies; let others be ashamed of them if they have buried themselves in books without being able to produce anything out of them for the common advantage, or anything which may bear the eyes of men and the light. But why need I be ashamed, who for many years have lived in such a manner as never to allow my own love of tranquillity to deny me to the necessity or advantage of another, or my fondness for pleasure to distract, or even sleep to delay, my attention to such claims? Who then can reproach me, or who has any right to be angry with me, if I allow myself as much time for the cultivation of these studies as some take for the performance of their own business; or for celebrating days of festival and games; or for other pleasures; or even for the rest and refreshment of mind and body; or as others devote to early banquets, to playing at dice, or at ball? And this ought to be permitted to me, because by these studies my power of speaking and those faculties are improved, which as far as they do exist in me have never been denied to my friends when they have been in peril. And if that ability appears to any one to be but moderate, at all events I know whence I derive those principles which are of the greatest value. For if I had not persuaded myself from my youth upwards, both by the precepts of many masters and by much reading, that there is nothing in life greatly to be desired except praise and honor, and that while pursuing those things all tortures of the body, all dangers of death and banishment are to be considered but of small importance, I should never have exposed myself in defense of your safety to such numerous and arduous contests, and to these daily attacks of profligate men. But all books are full of such precepts, and all the sayings of philosophers, and all antiquity, are full of precedents teaching the same lesson; but all these things would lie buried in darkness if the light of literature and learning were not applied to them. How many images of the bravest men, carefully elaborated, have both the Greek and Latin writers bequeathed to us, not merely for us to look at and gaze upon, but also for our imitation! And I, always keeping them before my eyes as examples for my own public conduct, have endeavored to model my mind and views by continually thinking of those excellent men.

Some one will ask "What! were those identical great men, whose virtues have been recorded in books, accomplished in all that learning which you are extolling so highly?" It is difficult to assert this of all of them; but still I know what answer I can make to that question: I admit that many men have existed of admirable disposition and virtue, who without learning, by the almost divine instinct of their own mere nature, have been, of their own accord as it were, moderate and wise men. I even add this, that very often nature without learning has had more to do with leading men to credit and to virtue, than learning when not assisted by a good natural disposition. And I also contend that when to an excellent and admirable natural disposition there is added a certain system and training of education, then from that combination arises an extraordinary perfection of character: such as is seen in that godlike man whom our fathers saw in their time—Africanus; and in Caius Lælius and Lucius Furius, most virtuous and moderate men; and in that most excellent man, the most learned man of his time, Marcus Cato the elder: and all these men, if they had been to derive no assistance from literature in the cultivation and practice of virtue, would never have applied themselves to the study of it. Though even if there were no such great advantage to be reaped from it, and if it were only pleasure that is sought from these studies, still I imagine you would consider it a most reasonable and liberal employment of the mind: for other occupations are not suited to every time, nor to every age or place; but these studies are the food of youth, the delight of old age; the ornament of prosperity, the refuge and comfort of adversity; a delight at home, and no hindrance abroad; they are companions by night, and in travel, and in the country.

And if we ourselves were not able to arrive at these advantages, nor even taste them with our senses, still we ought to admire them even when we saw them in others. . . . And indeed, we have constantly heard from men of the greatest eminence and learning that the study of other sciences was made up of learning, and rules, and regular method; but that a poet was such by the unassisted work of nature, and was moved by the vigor of his own mind, and was inspired as it were by some divine wrath. Wherefore rightly does our own great Ennius call poets holy; because they seem to be recommended to us by some especial gift, as it were, and liberality of the gods. Let then, judges, this name of poet, this name which no barbarians even have ever disregarded, be holy in your eyes, men of cultivated minds as you all are. Rocks and deserts reply to the poet's voice; savage beasts are often moved and arrested by song; and shall we who have been trained in the pursuit of the most virtuous acts refuse to be swayed by the voice of poets? The Colophonians say that Homer was their citizen; the Chians claim him as theirs; the Salaminians assert their right to him;

but the men of Smyrna loudly assert him to be a citizen of
Smyrna, and they have even raised a temple to him in their
city.   Many other places also fight with one another for the
honor of being his birthplace.

They then claim a stranger, even after his death, because he
was a poet: shall we reject this man while he is alive, a man
who by his own inclination and by our laws does actually belong
to us? especially when Archias has employed all his genius with
the utmost zeal in celebrating the glory and renown of the
Roman people?   For when a young man, he touched on our
wars against the Cimbri and gained the favor even of Caius
Marius himself, a man who was tolerably proof against this sort
of study.   For there was no one so disinclined to the Muses as
not willingly to endure that the praise of his labors should be
made immortal by means of verse.   They say that the great
Themistocles, the greatest man that Athens produced, said when
some one asked him what sound or whose voice he took the
greatest delight in hearing, " The voice of that by whom his own
exploits were best celebrated."   Therefore, the great Marius was
also exceedingly attached to Lucius Plotius, because he thought
that the achievement which he had performed could be celebrated
by his genius.   And the whole Mithridatic war, great and difficult as it was, and carried on with so much diversity of fortune
by land and sea, has been related at length by him; and the
books in which that is sung of, not only make illustrious Lucius
Lucullus, that most gallant and celebrated man, but they do
honor also to the Roman people.   For while Lucullus was general, the Roman people opened Pontus, though it was defended
both by the resources of the king and by the character of the
country itself.   Under the same general the army of the Roman
people, with no very great numbers, routed the countless hosts
of the Armenians.   It is the glory of the Roman people that by
the wisdom of that same general, the city of the Cyzicenes, most
friendly to us, was delivered and preserved from all the attacks
of the kind, and from the very jaws as it were of the whole war.
Ours is the glory which will be for ever celebrated, which is
derived from the fleet of the enemy which was sunk after its
admirals had been slain, and from the marvelous naval battle off
Tenedos: those trophies belong to us, those monuments are ours,
those triumphs are ours.   Therefore I say that the men by
whose genius these exploits are celebrated make illustrious at

the same time the glory of the Roman people. Our countryman Ennius was dear to the elder Africanus; and even on the tomb of the Scipios his effigy is believed to be visible, carved in the marble. But undoubtedly it is not only the men who are themselves praised who are done honor to by those praises, but the name of the Roman people also is adorned by them. Cato, the ancestor of this Cato, is extolled to the skies. Great honor is paid to the exploits of the Roman people. Lastly, all those great men, the Maximi, the Marcelli, and the Fulvii, are done honor to, not without all of us having also a share in the panegyric. . . .

Certainly, if the mind had no anticipations of posterity, and if it were to confine all its thoughts within the same limits as those by which the space of our lives is bounded, it would neither break itself with such severe labors, nor would it be tormented with such cares and sleepless anxiety, nor would it so often have to fight for its very life. At present there is a certain virtue in every good man, which night and day stirs up the mind with the stimulus of glory, and reminds it that all mention of our name will not cease at the same time with our lives, but that our fame will endure to all posterity.

Do we all who are occupied in the affairs of the State, and who are surrounded by such perils and dangers in life, appear to be so narrow-minded as, though to the last moment of our lives we have never passed one tranquil or easy moment, to think that everything will perish at the same time as ourselves? Ought we not, when many most illustrious men have with great care collected and left behind them statues and images, representations not of their minds but of their bodies, much more to desire to leave behind us a copy of our counsels and of our virtues, wrought and elaborated by the greatest genius? I thought, at the very moment of performing them, that I was scattering and disseminating all the deeds which I was performing, all over the world for the eternal recollection of nations. And whether that delight is to be denied to my soul after death, or whether, as the wisest men have thought, it will affect some portion of my spirit, at all events I am at present delighted with some such idea and hope.

HONORS PROPOSED FOR THE DEAD STATESMAN SULPICIUS

From the ‹Ninth Philippic›

O UR ancestors indeed decreed statues to many men; public sepulchres to few. But statues perish by weather, by violence, by lapse of time; the sanctity of the sepulchres is in the soil itself, which can neither be moved nor destroyed by any violence; and while other things are extinguished, so sepulchres become holier by age.

Let then this man be distinguished by that honor also, a man to whom no honor can be given which is not deserved. Let us be grateful in paying respect in death to him to whom we can now show no other gratitude. And by that same step let the audacity of Marcus Antonius, waging a nefarious war, be branded with infamy. For when these honors have been paid to Servius Sulpicius, the evidence of his embassy having been insulted and rejected by Antonius will remain for everlasting.

On which account I give my vote for a decree in this form: "As Servius Sulpicius Rufus, the son of Quintus, of the Lemonian tribe, at a most critical period of the republic, and being ill with a very serious and dangerous disease, preferred the authority of the Senate and the safety of the republic to his own life; and struggled against the violence and severity of his illness, in order to arrive at the camp of Antonius, to which the Senate had sent him; and as he, when he had almost arrived at the camp, being overwhelmed by the violence of the disease, has lost his life in discharging a most important office of the republic; and as his death has been in strict correspondence to a life passed with the greatest integrity and honor, during which he, Servius Sulpicius, has often been of great service to the republic, both as a private individual and in the discharge of various magistracies: and as he, being such a man, has encountered death on behalf of the republic while employed on an embassy; the Senate decrees that a brazen pedestrian statue of Servius Sulpicius be erected in the rostra in compliance with the resolution of this order, and that his children and posterity shall have a place round this statue of five feet in every direction, from which to behold the games and gladiatorial combats, because he died in the cause of the republic; and that this reason be inscribed on the pedestal of the statue; and that Caius Pansa and

Aulus Hirtius the consuls, one or both of them, if it seem good to them, shall command the quæstors of the city to let out a contract for making that pedestal and that statue, and erecting them in the rostra; and that whatever price they contract for, they shall take care the amount is given and paid to the contractor; and as in old times the Senate has exerted its authority with respect to the obsequies of, and honors paid to, brave men, it now decrees that he shall be carried to the tomb on the day of his funeral with the greatest possible solemnity. And as Servius Sulpicius Rufus, the son of Quintus of the Lemonian tribe, has deserved so well of the republic as to be entitled to be complimented with all those distinctions; the Senate is of opinion, and thinks it for the advantage of the republic, that the curule ædile should suspend the edict which usually prevails with respect to funerals, in the case of the funeral of Servius Sulpicius Rufus, the son of Quintus of the Lemonian tribe; and that Caius Pansa the consul shall assign him a place for a tomb in the Esquiline plain, or in whatever place shall seem good to him, extending thirty feet in every direction, where Servius Sulpicius may be buried; and that that shall be his tomb, and that of his children and posterity, as having been a tomb most deservedly given to them by the public authority.»

OLD FRIENDS BETTER THAN NEW

From the ‹Dialogue on Friendship›

B UT there arises on this subject a somewhat difficult question: Whether ever new friends, if deserving friendship, are to be preferred to old ones, just as we are wont to prefer young colts to old horses?—a perplexity unworthy of a man; for there ought to be no satiety of friendship as of other things: everything which is oldest (as those wines which bear age well) ought to be sweetest; and that is true which is sometimes said, "Many bushels of salt must be eaten together," before the duty of friendship can be fulfilled. But new friendships, if they afford a hope that, as in the case of plants which never disappoint, fruits shall appear, such are not to be rejected; yet the old one must be preserved in its proper place, for the power of age and custom is exceedingly great; besides, in the very case of the horse, which I just mentioned, if there is no impediment, there is no one who does not more pleasurably use that to which he is accustomed than one unbroken and strange to him; and habit asserts its power, and habit prevails, not only in the case of this, which is animate, but also in the cases of those things which are inanimate; since we take delight in the very mountainous or woody scenery among which we have long dwelt.

HONORED OLD AGE

From the 'Dialogue on Old Age'

BUT in my whole discourse remember that I am praising that old age which is established on the foundations of youth: from which this is effected which I once asserted with the great approbation of all present,—that wretched was the old age which had to defend itself by speaking. Neither gray hairs nor wrinkles can suddenly catch respect; but the former part of life honorably spent, reaps the fruits of authority at the close. For these very observances which seem light and common are marks of honor — to be saluted, to be sought after, to receive precedence, to have persons rising up to you, to be attended on the way, to be escorted home, to be consulted; points which, both among us and in other States, in proportion as they are the most excellent in their morals, are the most scrupulously observed. They say that Lysander the Lacedæmonian, whom I mentioned a little above, was accustomed to remark that Lacedæmon was the most honorable abode for old age; for nowhere is so much conceded to that time of life, nowhere is old age more respected. Nay, further: it is recorded that when at Athens during the games a certain elderly person had entered the theatre, a place was nowhere offered him in that large assembly by his own townsmen; but when he had approached the Lacedæmonians, who, as they were ambassadors, had taken their seats together in a particular place, they all rose up and invited the old man to a seat; and when reiterated applause had been bestowed upon them by the whole assembly, one of them remarked that the Athenians knew what was right, but were unwilling to do it. There are many excellent rules in our college, but this of which I am treating especially, that in proportion as each man has the advantage in age, so he takes precedence in giving his opinion; and older augurs are preferred not only to those who are higher in office, but even to such as are in actual command. What pleasures, then, of the body can be compared with the privileges of authority? which they who have nobly employed seem to me to have consummated the drama of life, and not like inexpert performers to have broken down in the last act. Still, old men are peevish, and fretful, and passionate, and unmanageable,— nay, if we seek for such, also covetous: but these are the faults of their characters, not of their old age. And yet that peevishness and those faults which I have mentioned have some excuse, not quite satisfactory indeed, but such as may be admitted. They fancy that they are neglected, despised, made a jest of; besides, in a weak state of body every offense is irritating. All which defects however are extenuated by good dispositions and qualities; and this may be discovered not only in real life, but on the stage, from the two brothers that are represented in 'The Brothers'; how much austerity in the one, and how much gentleness in the other! Such is the fact: for as it is not every wine, so it is not every man's life, that grows sour from old age. I approve of gravity in old age, but this in a moderate degree, like everything else; harshness by no means. What avarice in an old man can propose to itself I cannot conceive: for can anything be more absurd than, in proportion as less of our journey remains, to seek a greater supply of provisions?

DEATH IS WELCOME TO THE OLD

From the 'Dialogue on Old Age'

A N OLD man indeed has nothing to hope for; yet he is in so much the happier state than a young one, since he has already attained what the other is only hoping for. The one is wishing to live long, the other has lived long. And yet, good gods! what is there in man's life that can be called long? For allow the latest period: let us anticipate the age of the kings of the Tartessii. For there dwelt, as I find it recorded, a man named Arganthonius at Gades, who reigned for eighty years, and lived one hundred and twenty. But to my mind nothing whatever seems of long duration, in which there is any end. For when that arrives, then the time which has passed has flowed away; that only remains which you have secured by virtue and right conduct. Hours indeed depart from us, and days and months and years; nor does past time ever return, nor can it be discovered what is to follow. Whatever time is assigned to each to live, with that he ought to be content: for neither need the drama be performed entire by the actor, in order to give satisfaction, provided he be approved in whatever act he may be; nor need the wise man live till the *plaudite*. For the short period of life is long enough for living well and honorably; and if you should advance further, you need no more grieve than farmers do when the loveliness of springtime hath passed, that summer and autumn have come. For spring represents the time of youth and gives promise of the future fruits; the remaining seasons are intended for plucking and gathering in those fruits. Now the harvest of old age, as I have often said, is the recollection and abundance of blessings previously secured. In truth, everything that happens agreeably to nature is to be reckoned among blessings. What, however, is so agreeable to nature as for an old man to die? which even is the lot of the young, though nature opposes and resists. And thus it is that young men seem to me to die just as when the violence of flame is extinguished by a flood of water; whereas old men die as the exhausted fire goes out, spontaneously, without the exertion of any force: and as fruits when they are green are plucked by force from the trees, but when ripe and mellow drop off, so violence takes away their lives from youths, maturity from old men; a state which to me indeed is so delightful, that the nearer I approach to death, I seem as it were to be getting sight of land, and at length after a long voyage to be just coming into harbor.

GREAT ORATORS AND THEIR TRAINING

From the ‹Dialogue on Oratory›

For who can suppose that amid the great multitude of students, the utmost abundance of masters, the most eminent geniuses among men, the infinite variety of causes, the most ample rewards offered to eloquence, there is any other reason to be found for the small number of orators than the incredible magnitude and difficulty of the art? A knowledge of a vast number of things is necessary, without which volubility of words is empty and ridiculous; speech itself is to be formed, not merely by choice, but by careful construction of words; and all the emotions of the mind which nature has given to man, must be intimately known; for all the force and art of speaking must be employed in allaying or exciting the feelings of those who listen. To this must be added a certain portion of grace and wit, learning worthy of a well-bred man, and quickness and brevity in replying as well as attacking, accompanied with a refined decorum and urbanity. Besides, the whole of antiquity and a multitude of examples is to be kept in the memory; nor is the knowledge of laws in general, or of the civil law in particular, to be neglected. And why need I add any remarks on delivery itself, which is to be ordered by action of body, by gesture, by look, and by modulation and variation of the voice, the great power of which, alone and in itself, the comparatively trivial art of actors and the stage proves; on which though all bestow their utmost labor to form their look, voice, and gesture, who knows not how few there are, and have ever been, to whom we can attend with patience? What can I say of that repository for all things, the memory; which, unless it be made the keeper of the matter and words that are the fruits of thought and invention, all the talents of the orator, we see, though they be of the highest degree of excellence, will be of no avail? Let us then cease to wonder what is the cause of the scarcity of good speakers, since eloquence results from all those qualifications, in each of which singly it is a great merit to labor successfully; and let us rather exhort our children, and others whose glory and honor is dear to us, to contemplate in their minds the full magnitude of the object, and not to trust that they can reach the height at which they aim by the aid of the precepts, masters, and exercises that they are all now following, but to understand that they must adopt others of a different character.

In my opinion, indeed, no man can be an orator possessed of every praiseworthy accomplishment unless he has attained the knowledge of everything important, and of all liberal arts; for his language must be ornate and copious from knowledge, since unless there be beneath the surface matter understood and felt by the speaker, oratory becomes an empty and almost puerile flow of words. . . .

"I am then of opinion," said Crassus, "that nature and genius in the first place contribute most aid to speaking; and that to those writers on the art to whom Antonius just now alluded, it was not skill and method in speaking, but natural talent that was wanting; for there ought to be certain lively powers in the mind and understanding, which may be acute to invent, fertile to explain and adorn, and strong and retentive to remember; and if any one imagines that these powers may be acquired by art (which is false, for it is very well if they can be animated and excited by art; but they certainly cannot by art be ingrafted or instilled, since they are all the gifts of nature), what will he say of those qualities which are certainly born with the man himself—volubility of tongue, tone of voice, strength of lungs, and a peculiar conformation and aspect of the whole countenance and body? I do not say that art cannot improve in these particulars (for I am not ignorant that what is good may be made better by education, and what is not very good may be in some degree polished and amended); but there are some persons so hesitating in their speech, so inharmonious in their tone of voice, or so unwieldy and rude in the air and movements of their bodies, that whatever power they possess either from genius or art, they can never be reckoned in the number of accomplished speakers; while there are others so happily qualified in these respects, so eminently adorned with the gifts of nature, that they seem not to have been born like other men, but molded by some divinity. It is indeed a great task and enterprise for a person to undertake and profess that while every one else is silent, he alone must be heard on the most important subjects, and in a large assembly of men; for there is scarcely any one present who is not sharper and quicker to discover defects in the speaker than merits; and thus whatever offends the hearer effaces the recollection of what is worthy of praise. I do not make these observations for the purpose of altogether deterring young men from the study of oratory, even if they be deficient in some natural endowments. For who does not perceive that to C. Cælius, my contemporary, a new man, the mere mediocrity in speaking which he was enabled to attain was a great honor? Who does not know that Q. Varius, your equal in age, a clumsy uncouth man, has obtained his great popularity by the cultivation of such faculties as he has?

"But as our inquiry regards the complete orator, we must imagine in our discussion an orator from whom every kind of fault is abstracted, and who is adorned with every kind of merit. For if the multitude of suits, if the variety of causes, if the rabble and barbarism of the forum, afford room for even the most wretched speakers, we must not for that reason take our eyes from the object of our inquiry. In those arts in which it is not indispensable usefulness that is sought, but liberal amusement for the mind, how nicely, how almost fastidiously, do we judge! For there are no suits or controversies which can force men, though they may tolerate indifferent orators in the forum, to endure also bad actors upon the stage. The orator therefore must take the most studious precaution not merely to satisfy those whom he necessarily must satisfy, but to seem worthy of admiration to those who are at liberty to judge disinterestedly. If you would know what I myself think, I will express to you, my intimate friends, what I have hitherto never mentioned, and thought that I never should mention. To me, those who speak best and speak with the utmost ease and grace, appear, if they do not commence their speeches with some timidity, and show some confusion in the exordium, to have almost lost the sense of shame; though it is impossible that such should not be the case: for the better qualified a man is to speak, the more he fears the difficulties of speaking, the uncertain success of a speech, and the expectation of the audience. But he who can produce and deliver nothing worthy of his subject, nothing worthy of the name of an orator, nothing worthy the attention of his audience, seems to me, though he be ever so confused while he is speaking, to be downright shameless; for we ought to avoid a character for shamelessness, not by testifying shame, but by not doing that which does not become us. But the speaker who has no shame (as I see to be the case with many) I regard as deserving not only of rebuke but of personal castigation. Indeed, what I often observe in you I very frequently experience in myself; that I turn pale in the outset of my speech, and feel a tremor through my whole thoughts, as it were, and limbs. When I was a young man, I was on one occasion so timid in commencing an accusation, that I owed to Q. Maximus the greatest of obligations for immediately dismissing the assembly as soon as he saw me absolutely disheartened and incapacitated through fear." Here they all signified assent, looked significantly at one another, and began to talk together; for there was a wonderful modesty in Crassus, which however was not only no disadvantage to his oratory, but even an assistance to it, by giving it the recommendation of probity.

CICERO TO TIRO

[The following epistles are taken by permission from Jeans's 'Letters of Cicero.' This letter gives a vivid glimpse of Cicero's tenderness to his slaves and freedmen. Tiro was probably the first editor of his former master's letters.]

ÆGYPTA arrived here on the 12th of April. Although he reported that you were now quite rid of your fever and going on very well, he nevertheless caused me some anxiety by his report that you were not able to write to me, the more so because Hermia, who ought to have been here on the same day, has not yet come. I am more anxious than you can believe about your health. Only free me from this anxiety and I will free you from all duties. I would write you more if I thought you could now read more with pleasure. Use all the talents you possess, of which I have no small opinion, to keep yourself safe for my sake as well as your own. Again and again I repeat, take every precaution about your health. Good-by.

P. S.— Hermia is just come. I have your note with its poor weak handwriting— no wonder, too, after so severe an illness. I send out Ægypta to stay with you because he is not a bad companion, and appeared to me to be fond of you; and with him a cook, for you to make use of his services. Good-by.

CICERO TO ATTICUS

[The family affection of Cicero might be illustrated by many such letters as the following:]

IT BEING now eleven days since I left you, I am scrawling this little bit of a note just as I am leaving my country-house before it is light. I think of being at my place at Anagnia to-day, and Tusculum to-morrow; only one day there, so that I shall come up all right to time on the 28th; and oh, if I could but run on at once to embrace my Tullia and give Attica a kiss! Talking of this, by-the-by, do please write and let me know while I am stopping at Tusculum what her prattle is like, or if she is away in the country, what her letters to you are about. Meanwhile either send or give her my love, and Pilia too. And even though we shall meet immediately, yet will you write to me anything you can find to say?

P. S. — I was just fastening up this letter, but your courier has arrived here after a long night journey with your letter. I was very sorry, you may be sure, to find on reading it that Attica is feverish. Everything else that I was waiting for I now know from your note; but when you tell me that to have a little fire in the morning "*sent le vieillard,*" I retort *il le sent plus* for one's poor old memory to begin to totter: because it was the 29th I had promised to Axius; the 30th to you; and the day of my arrival, the 31st, to Quintus. So take that for yourself — you shall have no news. Then what on earth is the good of writing? And what good is it when we are together and chatter whatever comes to our tongues? Surely there is something in *causerie* after all; even if there is nothing under it, there is always at least the delicious feeling that we are talking with one another.

SULPICIUS CONSOLES CICERO AFTER HIS DAUGHTER TULLIA'S DEATH

FOR some time after I had received the information of the death of your daughter Tullia, you may be sure that I bore it sadly and heavily, as much indeed as was right for me. I felt that I shared that terrible loss with you; and that had I but been where you are, you on your part would not have found me neglectful, and I on mine should not have failed to come to you and tell you myself how deeply grieved I am. And though it is true that consolations of this nature are painful and distressing, because those [dear friends and relations] upon whom the task naturally devolves are themselves afflicted with a similar burden, and incapable even of attempting it without many tears, so that one would rather suppose them in need of the consolations of others for themselves than capable of doing this kind office to others, yet nevertheless I have decided to write to you briefly such reflections as have occurred to me on the present occasion; not that I imagine them to be ignored by you, but because it is possible that you may be hindered by your sorrow from seeing them as clearly as usual.

What reason is there why you should allow the private grief which has befallen you to distress you so terribly? Recollect how fortune has hitherto dealt with us: how we have been bereft of all that ought to be no less dear to men than their own children—of country, position, rank, and every honorable office. If one more burden has now been laid upon you, could any addition be made to your pain? Or is there any heart that having been trained in the school of such events, ought not now to be steeled by use against emotion, and think everything after them to be comparatively light?

Or it is for her sake, I suppose, that you are grieving? How many times must you have arrived at the same conclusion as that into which I too have frequently fallen, that in these days theirs is not the hardest lot who are permitted painlessly to exchange their life for the grave! Now what was there at the present time that could attach her very strongly to life? what hope? what fruition? what consolation for the soul? The prospect of a wedded life with a husband chosen from our young men of rank? Truly, one would think it was always in your power to choose a son-in-law of a position suitable to your rank out of our young men, one to whose keeping you would feel you could safely intrust the happiness of a child. Or that of being a joyful mother of children, who would be happy in seeing them succeeding in life; able by their own exertions to maintain in its integrity all that was bequeathed them by their father; intending gradually to rise to all the highest offices of the State; and to use that liberty to which they were born for the good of their country and the service of their friends. Is there any one of these things that has not been taken away before it was given? But surely it is hard to give up one's children? It is hard; but this is harder still—that they should bear and suffer what we are doing.

A circumstance which was such as to afford me no light consolation I cannot but mention to you, in the hope that it may be allowed to contribute equally towards mitigating your grief. As I was returning from Asia, when sailing from Ægina in the direction of Megara, I began to look around me at the various places by which I was surrounded. Behind me was Ægina, in front Megara; on the right the Piræus, on the left Corinth; all of them towns that in former days were most magnificent, but are now lying prostrate and in ruins before one's eyes. "Ah me," I began to reflect to myself, "we poor feeble mortals, who can claim but a short life in comparison, complain as though a wrong was done us if one of our number dies in the course of nature, or has met his death by violence; and here in one spot are lying stretched out before me the corpses of so many cities! Servius, be master of yourself, and remember that it is the lot of man to which you have been born." Believe me, I found myself in no small degree strengthened by these reflections. Let me advise you too, if you think good, to keep this reflection before your eyes. How lately at one and the same time have many of our most illustrious men fallen! how grave an encroachment has been made on the rights of the sovereign people of Rome! every province in the world has been convulsed with the shock: if the frail life of a tender woman has gone too, who being born to the common lot of man must needs have died in a few short years, even if the time had not come for her now, are you thus utterly stricken down?

Do you then also recall your feelings and your thoughts from dwelling on this subject, and as beseems your character bethink yourself rather of this: that she has lived as long as life was of value to her; that she has passed away only together with her country's freedom; that she lived to see her father elected Prætor, Consul, Augur; that she had been the wife of young men of the first rank; that after enjoying well-nigh every blessing that life can offer, she left it only when the Republic itself was falling. The account is closed, and what have you, what has she, to charge of injustice against Fate? In a word, forget not that you are Cicero — that you are he who was always wont to guide others and give them good advice; and be not like those quack physicians who when others are sick boast that they hold the key of the knowledge of medicine, to heal themselves are never able; but rather minister to yourself with your own hand the remedies which you are in the habit of prescribing for others, and put them plainly before your own soul. There is no pain so great but the lapse of time will lessen and assuage it: it is not like yourself to wait until this time comes, instead of stepping forward by your philosophy to anticipate that result. And if even those who are low in the grave have any consciousness at all, such was her love for you and her tenderness for all around her that surely she does not wish to see this in you. Make this a tribute then to her who is dead; to all your friends and relations who are mourning in your grief; and make it to your country also, that if in anything the need should arise she may be able to trust to your energy and guidance. Finally, since such is the condition we have come to, that even this consideration must perforce be obeyed, do not let your conduct induce any one to believe that it is not so much your daughter as the circumstances of the Republic and the victory of others which you are deploring.

I shrink from writing to you at greater length upon this subject, lest I should seem to be doubtful of your own good sense; allow me therefore to put before you one more consideration, and then I will bring my letter to a close. We have seen you not once but many times bearing prosperity most gracefully, and gaining yourself great reputation thereby: let us see at last that you are capable also of bearing adversity equally well, and that it is not in your eyes a heavier burden than it ought to seem; lest we should think that of all the virtues this is the only one in which you are wanting.

As for myself, when I find you are more composed in mind I will send you information about all that is being done in these parts, and the state in which the province finds itself at present. Farewell.

CICERO'S REPLY TO SULPICIUS

Yes, my dear Servius, I could indeed wish you had been with me, as you say, at the time of my terrible trial. How much it was in your power to help me if you had been here, by sympathizing with, and I may almost say, sharing equally in my grief, I readily perceive from the fact that after reading your letter I now feel myself considerably more composed; for not only was all that you wrote just what is best calculated to soothe affliction, but you yourself in comforting me showed that you too had no little pain at heart. Your son Servius however has made it clear, by every kindly attention which such an occasion would permit of, both how great his respect was for myself and also how much pleasure his kind feeling for me was likely to give you; and you may be sure that, while such attentions from him have often been more pleasant to me, they have never made me more grateful.

It is not however only your arguments and your equal share, — I may almost call it, — in this affliction which comforts me, but also your authority; because I hold it shame in me not to be bearing my trouble in a way that you, a man endowed with such wisdom, think it ought to be borne. But at times I do feel broken down, and I scarcely make any struggle against my grief, because those consolations fail me which under similar calamities were never wanting to any of those other people whom I put before myself as models for imitation. Both Fabius Maximus, for example, when he lost a son who had held the consulship, the hero of many a famous exploit; and Lucius Paulus, from whom two were taken in one week; and your own kinsman Gallus; and Marcus Cato, who was deprived of a son of the rarest talents and the rarest virtue,— all these lived in times when their individual affliction was capable of finding a solace in the distinctions they used to carn from their country. For me, however, after being stripped of all those distinctions which you yourself recall to me, and which I had won for myself by unparalleled exertions, only that one solace remained which has been torn away. My thoughts were not diverted by work for my friends, or by the administration of affairs of state; there was no pleasure in pleading in the courts; I could not bear the very sight of the Senate House; I felt, as was indeed too true, that I had lost all the harvest of both my industry and my success. But whenever I wanted to recollect that all this was shared with you and other friends I could name, and whenever I was breaking myself in and forcing my spirit to bear these things with patience, I always had a refuge to go to where I might find peace, and in whose words of comfort and sweet society I could rid me of all my pains and griefs. Whereas now, under this terrible blow, even those old wounds which seemed to have healed up are bleeding afresh; for it is impossible for me now to find such a refuge from my sorrows at home in the business of the State, as in those days I did in that consolation of home, which was always in store whenever I came away sad from thoughts of State to seek for peace in her happiness. And so I stay away both from home and from public life; because home now is no more able to make up for the sorrow I feel when I think of our country, than our country is for my sorrow at home. I am therefore looking forward all the more eagerly to your coming, and long to see you as early as that may possibly be; no greater alleviation can be offered me than a meeting between us for friendly intercourse and conversation. I hope however that your return is to take place, as I hear it is, very shortly. As for myself, while there are abundant reasons for wanting to see you as soon as possible, my principal one is in order that we may discuss together beforehand the best method of conduct for present circumstances, which must entirely be adapted to the wishes of one man only, a man nevertheless who is far-seeing and generous, and also, as I think I have thoroughly ascertained, to me not at all ill-disposed and to you extremely friendly. But admitting this, it is still a matter for much deliberation what is the line,—I do not say of action, but of keeping quiet,—that we ought by his good leave and favor to adopt. Farewell.

A HOMESICK EXILE

I SEND this with love, my dearest Terentia, hoping that you and my little Tullia and my Marcus are all well.

From the letters of several people and the talk of everybody I hear that your courage and endurance are simply wonderful, and that no troubles of body or mind can exhaust your energy. How unhappy I am to think that with all your courage and devotion, your virtues and gentleness, you should have fallen into such misfortunes for me! And my sweet Tullia too,—that she who was once so proud of her father should have to undergo such troubles owing to him! And what shall I say about my boy Marcus, who ever since his faculties of perception awoke has felt the sharpest pangs of sorrow and misery? Now could I but think, as you tell me, that all this comes in the natural course of things, I could bear it a little easier. But it has been brought about entirely by my own fault, for thinking myself loved by those who were jealous of me, and turning from those who wanted to win me. . . . I have thanked the people you wanted me to, and mentioned that my information came from you. As to the block of houses which you tell me you mean to sell—why, good heavens! my dear Terentia, what *is* to be done! Oh, what troubles I have to bear! And if misfortune continues to persecute us, what will become of our poor boy? I cannot continue to write—my tears are too much for me; nor would I wish to betray you into the same emotion. All I can say is that if our friends act up to their bounden duty we shall not want for money; if they do not, you will not be able to succeed only with your own. Let our unhappy fortunes, I entreat you, be a warning to us not to ruin our boy, who is ruined enough already. If he only has something to save him from absolute want, a fair share of talent and a fair share of luck will be all that is necessary to win anything else. Do not neglect your health; and send me messengers with letters to let me know what goes on, and how you yourselves are faring. My suspense in any case cannot now be long. Give my love to my little Tullia and my Marcus.

DYRRACHIUM, Nov. 26.

P. S.—I have moved to Dyrrachium because it is not only a free city, but very much in my interest, and quite near to Italy; but if the bustle of the place proves an annoyance I shall betake myself elsewhere and give you notice.

CICERO'S VACILLATION IN THE CIVIL WAR

BEING in extreme agitation about these great and terrible events, and having no means of discussing matters with you in person, I want at any rate to avail myself of your judgment. Now the question about which I am in doubt is simply this: If Pompeius should fly from Italy (which I suspect he will do), how do you think I ought to act? To make it easier for you to advise me, I will briefly set forth the arguments that occur to me on both sides of the question.

The obligations that Pompeius laid me under in the matter of my restoration, my own intimacy with him, and also my patriotism, incline me to think that I ought to make my decision as his decision, or in other words, my fortunes as his fortunes. There is this reason also: If I stay behind and desert my post among that band of true and illustrious patriots, I must perforce fall completely under the yoke of one man. Now although he frequently takes occasion to show himself friendly to me— indeed, as you well know, anticipating this storm that is now hanging over our heads, I took good care that he should be so long ago—still I have to consider two different questions: first, how far can I trust him; and secondly,—assuming it to be absolutely certain that he is friendly disposed to me,—would it show the brave man or the honest citizen to remain in a city where one has filled the highest offices of peace and war, achieved immortal deeds, and been crowned with the honors of her most dignified priesthood, only to become an empty name and undergo some risk, attended also very likely with considerable disgrace, should Pompeius ever again grasp the helm? So much for this side; see now what may be said on the other.

Pompeius has in our cause done nothing wisely, nothing strongly; nothing, I may add, that has not been contrary to my opinion and advice. I pass over those old complaints, that it was he who himself nourished this enemy of the republic, gave him his honors, put the sword into his hand—that it was he who advised him to force laws through by violence, trampling on the warnings of religion—that it was he who made the addition of Transalpine Gaul, he who is his son-in-law, he who as Augur allowed the adoption of Clodius; who showed more activity in recalling me than in preventing my exile; who took it on him to extend Cæsar's term of government; who supported all his proceedings while he was away; that he too even in his third consulship, after he had begun to pose as a defender of the constitution, actually exerted himself to get the ten tribunes to propose that absence should not invalidate the election; nay more, he expressly sanctioned this by one of his own acts, and opposed the consul Marcus Marcellus, who proposed that the tenure of the Gallic provinces should come to an end on the 1st of March —but anyhow, to pass over all this, what could be more discreditable, what more blundering, than this evacuation of the city, or I had better say, this ignominious flight? What terms ought not to have been accepted sooner than abandon our country? The terms were bad? That I allow; but is anything worse than this? But he will win back the constitution? When? What preparations have been made to warrant such a hope? Have we not lost all Picenum? have we not left open the road to the capital? have we not abandoned the whole of our treasure, public and private, to the foe? In a word, there is no common cause, no strength, no centre, to draw such people together as might yet care to show fight for the Republic. Apulia has been chosen—the most thinly populated part of Italy, and the most remote from the line of movement of this war: it would seem that in despair they were looking for flight, with some easy access to the coast. I took the charge of Capua much against my will—not that I would evade that duty, but in a cause which evoked no sympathy from any class as a whole, nor any openly even from individuals (there was some of course among the good

citizens, but as languid as usual), and where I saw for myself
that the mass of the people, and all the lowest stratum, were
more and more inclined to the other side, many even longing for
a revolution, I told him to his face I would undertake to do
nothing without forces and without money. Consequently I have
had no responsibility at all, because I saw from the very first
that nothing was really intended but flight. Say that I now
follow this; then whither? Not with him; I had already set out
to join him when I found that Cæsar was in those parts, so that
I could not safely reach Luceria. I must sail by the western
sea, in the depth of winter, not knowing where to steer for.
And again, what about being with my brother, or leaving him
and taking my son? How then must I act, since either alternative will involve the greatest difficulty, the greatest mental
anxiety? And then, too, what a raid he will make on me and
my fortunes when I am out of the way — fiercer than on other
people, because he will think perhaps that in outrages on me he
holds a means of popularity. Again, these fetters, remember,—
I mean these laurels on my attendants' staves,— how inconvenient
it is to take them out of Italy! What place indeed will be safe
for me, supposing I now find the sea calm enough, before I
have actually joined him? though where that will be and how
to get there, I have no notion.

On the other hand, say that I stop where I am and find
some place on this side of the water, then my conduct will precisely resemble that of Philippus, or Lucius Flaccus, or Quintus
Mucius under Cinna's reign of terror. And however this decision
ended for the last-named, yet still he at any rate used to say
that he saw what really did happen would occur, but that it was
his deliberate choice in preference to marching sword in hand
against the homes of the very city that gave him birth. With
Thrasybulus it was otherwise, and perhaps better; but still there
is a sound basis for the policy and sentiments of Mucius; as
there is also for this [which Philippus did]: to wait for your
opportunity when you must, just as much as not to lose your
opportunity when it is given. But even in this case, those staves
again of my attendants still involve some awkwardness; for say
that his feelings are friendly to me (I am not sure that this is
so, but let us assume it), then he will offer me a triumph. I
fear that to decline may be perilous—[to accept] an offense with
all good citizens. Ah, you exclaim, what a difficult, what an

insoluble problem! Yet the solution must be found; for what can one do? And lest you should have formed the idea that I am rather inclined towards staying because I have argued more on that side of the question, it is quite possible, as is so frequently the case in debates, that one side has more words, the other more worth. Therefore I should be glad if when you give me your opinion you would look upon me as making up my mind quite dispassionately on a most important question. I have a ship both at Caieta and at Brundisium.

But lo and behold, while I am writing you these very lines by night in my house at Cales, in come the couriers, and here is a letter to say that Cæsar is before Corfinium, and that in Corfinium is Domitius, with an army resolute and even eager for battle. I do not think our chief will go so far as to be guilty of abandoning Domitius, though it is true he had already sent Scipio on before with two cohorts to Brundisium, and written a dispatch to the consuls ordering that the legion enrolled by Faustus should go under the command of one consul to Sicily: but it is a scandal that Domitius should be left to his fate when he is imploring him for help. There is some hope, not in my opinion a very good one, but strong in these parts, that there has been a battle in the Pyrenees between Afranius and Trebonius; that Trebonius has been beaten off; that your friend Fabius also has come over to us with all his troops; and to crown it all, that Afranius is advancing with a strong force. If this be so, we shall perhaps make a stand in Italy. As for me, since Cæsar's route is uncertain — he is expected about equally by way of Capua and of Luceria — I have sent Lepta to Pompeius with a letter, while I myself, for fear of falling in with him anywhere, have started again for Formiæ. I thought it best to let you know this, and am writing with more composure than I have written of late; not inserting any opinion of my own, but trying to elicit yours.

CICERO'S CORRESPONDENTS

IT SEEMS desirable to add a few letters by other hands than Cicero's, to indicate the manifold side-lights thrown on the inner history of this intensely interesting period. Sulpicius's famous attempt at consolation has already been given above. Two brief letters by Cæsar will illustrate the dictator's marvelous ability to comprehend and control other men. Pompey's gruff rudeness forms a contrast which is hardly accidental on the editor's part. Cælius's wit is biting as ever; and lastly, Matius's protest against being persecuted merely because he, who loved Cæsar, openly mourned for his dead friend, has an unconscious tone of simple heroism unequaled in the entire correspondence. W. C. L.

CÆSAR TO CICERO

You know me too well not to keep up your character as an Augur by divining that nothing is more entirely alien from my nature than cruelty: I will add that while my decision is in itself a great source of pleasure to me, to find my conduct approved by you is a triumph of gratification. Nor does the fact at all disturb me that those people whom I have set at liberty are reported to have gone their ways only to renew the attack upon me; because there is nothing I wish more than that I may ever be as true to my own character as they to theirs.

May I hope that you will be near town when I am there, so that I may as usual avail myself in everything of your advice and means of assistance? Let me assure you that I am charmed beyond everything with your relation Dolabella, to whom I shall acknowledge myself indeed indebted for this obligation; for his kindliness is so great, and his feeling and affection for me are such, that he cannot possibly do otherwise.

CÆSAR TO CICERO

Though I had fully made up my mind that you would do nothing rashly, nothing imprudently, still I was so far impressed by the rumors in some quarters as to think it my duty to write to you, and ask it as a favor due to our mutual regard that you will not take any step, now that the scale is so decisively turned, which you would not have thought it necessary to take even though the balance still stood firm. For it will really be both a heavier blow to our friendship, and a step on your part still less judicious for yourself, if you are to be thought not even to have bowed the knee to success — for things seem to have fallen out as entirely favorably for us as disastrously for them; nor yet to have been drawn by attachment to a particular cause — for that has undergone no change since you decided to remain aloof from their counsels; — but to have passed a stern judgment on some act of mine, than which, from you, no more painful thing could befall me; and I claim the right of our friendship to entreat that you will not take this course.

Finally, what more suitable part is there for a good peace-loving man, and a good citizen, than to keep aloof from civil dissensions? There were not a few who admired this course, but could not adopt it by reason of its danger: you, after having duly weighed both the conclusions of friendship and the unmistakable evidence of my whole life, will find that there is no safer nor more honorable course than to keep entirely aloof from the struggle.

POMPEY TO CICERO

To-day, the 10th of February, Fabius Vergilianus has joined me. From him I learn that Domitius with his eleven cohorts, and fourteen cohorts that Vibullius has brought up, is on his way to me. His intention was to start from Corfinium on the 13th, Hirrus to follow soon after with five of the cohorts. I decide that you are to come to us at Luceria; here, I think, you will be most in safety.

CÆLIUS IN ROME TO CICERO IN CILICIA

The capture of his Parthian Majesty and the storming of Seleuceia itself had not been enough to compensate for missing the sight of our doings here. Your eyes would never have ached again if you had only seen the face of Domitius when he was not elected! The election was important, and it was quite clear that party feeling determined the side which people took: only a few could be brought to acknowledge the claims of friendship. Consequently Domitius is so furious with me that he scarcely hates any of his most intimate friends as much as he does me; and all the more because he thinks that it was to do him wrong that his hopes of being in the College of Augurs are snatched away, and that I am responsible for it. He is savage now to see everybody so delighted at his mortification, and myself more active than anybody, with one exception, on behalf of Antonius.

As to political prospects, I have often mentioned to you that I do not see any chance of peace lasting a year; and the nearer that struggle which must infallibly take place, is drawing to us, the more manifest does its danger become. The point at issue about which our lords and masters are going to fight is this: Pompeius has absolutely determined not to allow Cæsar to be elected consul on any terms except a previous resignation of his army and his government, while Cæsar is convinced that he must inevitably fall if he separates himself from his army. He offers however this compromise, that they should both of them resign their armies. So you see their great affection for one another and their much-abused alliance has not even dwindled down into suppressed jealousy, but has broken out into open war. Nor can I discover what is the wisest course to take in my own interests: a question which I make no doubt will give much trouble to you also. For while I have both interest and connections among those who are on one side, on the other too it is the cause and not the men themselves I dislike. You are not, I feel sure, blind to the fact that where parties are divided within a country, we are bound, so long as the struggle is carried on with none but constitutional weapons, to support the more honorable cause, but when we come to blows and to open war, then the safer one; and to count that cause the better which is the less likely to be dangerous. In the present division of feeling I see that Pompeius will have the Senate and all judicially minded people on his side; those who have everything to dread and little to hope for will flock to Cæsar: the army is not to be compared. On the whole, we have plenty of time for balancing the strength of parties and making our decision.

I had all but forgotten my principal reason for writing. Have you heard of the wonderful doings of our censor Appius—how he is rigorously inquiring into our statues and pictures, our amount of land, and our debts? He has persuaded himself that his censorship is a moral soap or toilet powder. He is wrong, I take it; for while he only wants to wash off the dirt, he is really

laying bare his veins and his flesh. Heaven and earth! you
must run, and come to laugh at the things here — Appius questioning about pictures and statues. You must make haste, I
assure you.

Our friend Curio is thought to have acted wisely in giving
way about the pay of Pompeius's troops. If I must sum up my
opinion, as you ask, about what will happen — unless one or
other of them consents to go and fight the Parthians, I see a
great split impending, which will be settled by the sword and
by force; each is well inclined for this and well equipped. If it
could only be without danger to yourself, you would find this a
great and most attractive drama which Fortune is rehearsing.

MATIUS TO CICERO

I RECEIVED great pleasure from your letter, because I found that
your opinion of me was what I had hoped and wished it to
be; not that I was in any doubt about it, but for the very
reason that I valued it so highly, I was most anxious that it
should remain unimpaired. Conscious however that I had done
nothing which could give offense to the feelings of any good
citizen, I was naturally the less inclined to believe that you,
adorned as you are with so many excellences of the most admirable kind, could have allowed yourself to be convinced of anything on mere idle report; particularly seeing that you were a
friend for whom my spontaneous attachment had been and still
was unbroken. And knowing now that it has been as I hoped,
I will answer those attacks which you have often opposed on my
behalf, as was fairly to be expected from your well-known generosity and the friendship existing between us.

For I am well aware of all they have been heaping on me
since Cæsar's death. They make it a reproach against me that I
go heavily for the loss of a friend, and think it cruel that one
whom I loved should have fallen, because, say they, country
must be put before friends — as though they have hitherto been
successful in proving that his death really was the gain of the
commonwealth. But I will not enter any subtle plea; I admit
that I have not attained to your higher grades of philosophy: for
I have neither been a partisan of Cæsar in our civil dissensions,
— though I did not abandon my friend even when his action

was a stumbling-block to me,— nor did I ever give my approval to the civil war, or even to the actual ground of quarrel, of which indeed I earnestly desired that the first sparks should be trampled out. And so in the triumph of a personal friend I was never ensnared by the charms either of place or of money; prizes which have been recklessly abused by the rest, though they had less influence with him than I had. I may even say that my own private property was impaired by that act of Cæsar, thanks to which many of those who are rejoicing at Cæsar's death continued to live in their own country. That our defeated fellow countrymen should be spared was as much an object to me as my own safety. Is it possible then for me, who wanted all to be left uninjured, not to feel indignation that he by whom this was secured is dead? above all when the very same men were the cause at once of his unpopularity and his untimely end. You shall smart then, say they, since you dare to disapprove of our deed. What unheard-of insolence! One man then may boast of a deed, which another is not even allowed to lament without punishment. Why, even slaves have always been free of this — to feel their fears, their joys, their sorrows as their own, and not at anybody else's dictation; and these are the very things which now, at least according to what your "liberators" have always in their mouths, they are trying to wrest from us by terrorism. But they try in vain. There is no danger which has terrors enough ever to make me desert the side of gratitude or humanity; for never have I thought that death in a good cause is to be shunned, often indeed that it deserves to be courted. But why are they inclined to be enraged with me, if my wishes are simply that they may come to regret their deed, desiring as I do that Cæsar's death may be felt to be untimely by us all? It is my duty as a citizen to desire the preservation of the constitution? Well, unless both my life in the past and all my hopes for the future prove without any words of mine that I do earnestly desire this, I make no demand to prove it by my professions.

To you therefore I make a specially earnest appeal to let facts come before assertions, and to take my word for it that, if you feel that honesty is the best policy, it is impossible I should have any association with lawless villains. Or can you believe that the principles I pursued in the days of my youth, when even error could pass with some excuse, I shall renounce now that I am going down the hill, and with my own hands unravel all the web of my life? That I will not do; nor yet will I commit any act that could give offense, beyond the fact that I do lament the sad fall of one who was to me the dearest friend and the most illustrious of men. But were I otherwise disposed, I would never deny what I was doing, lest it should be thought I was at once shameless in doing wrong and false and cowardly in dissembling it.

But then I undertook the management of those games which Cæsar's heir celebrated for Cæsar's victory? Well, this is a matter which belongs to one's private obligations, not to any political arrangement; it was however in the first place a tribute of respect which I was called upon to pay to the memory and the eminent position of a man whom I dearly loved, even though he was dead, and also one that I could not refuse at the request of a young man so thoroughly promising, and so worthy in every way of Cæsar as he is.

Again, I have frequently paid visits of compliment to the consul Antonius. And you will find that the very men who think me but a lukewarm patriot are constantly going to his house in crowds, actually for the purpose of soliciting or carrying away some favor. But what a monstrous claim it is, that while Cæsar never laid any such embargo as this to prevent me from associating freely with anybody I pleased,— even if they were people whom he personally did not like,— these men who have robbed me of my friend should attempt by malicious insinuations to prevent my showing a kindness to whomsoever I will!

I have however no fear that the moderation of my life will hereafter prove an insufficient defense against false insinuations, and that even those who do not love me, because of my loyalty to Cæsar, would not rather have their own friend imitate me than themselves. Such of life as remains to me, at least if I succeed in what I desire, I shall spend in quiet at Rhodes; but if I find that some chance has put a stop to this, I shall simply live at Rome as one who is always desirous that right should be done.

I am deeply grateful to our good friend Trebatius for having thus disclosed to me your sincere and friendly feeling, and given me even an additional reason for honoring and paying respect to one whom it has always been a pleasure to me to regard as a friend. Farewell heartily, and let me have your esteem.

THE DREAM OF SCIPIO

From the Dialogue 'The Republic': Translation of Prof. T. R. Lounsbury

WHEN I went into Africa with the consul Manius Manilius, holding the rank, as you are aware, of military tribune of the fourth legion, nothing lay nearer to my heart than to meet Masinissa, a king who, for good reasons, was on the most friendly terms with our family. When I had come to him, the old man embraced me with tears, and then looking up to heaven, said:—"I give thanks to thee, O supremest Sol, and to you, ye inhabitants of heaven! that before I depart this life I behold in my dominions, and under this roof, Publius Cornelius Scipio, by whose very name I am revived: so never passes away from my mind the memory of that best and most invincible hero." Thereupon I made inquiries of him as to the state of his own kingdom, and he of me as to our republic; and with many words uttered on both sides, we spent the whole of that day.

Moreover, after partaking of a repast prepared with royal magnificence, we prolonged the conversation late into the night. The old man would speak of nothing but Africanus, and remembered not only all his deeds, but likewise his sayings. After we parted to go to bed, a sounder sleep than usual fell upon me, partly on account of weariness occasioned by the journey, and partly because I had stayed up to a late hour. Then Africanus appeared to me, I think in consequence of what we had been talking about; for it often happens that our thoughts and speeches bring about in sleep something of that illusion of which Ennius writes in regard to himself and Homer, of which poet he was very often accustomed to think and speak while awake. Africanus showed himself to me in that form which was better known to me from his ancestral image than from my recollection of his person. As soon as I recognized him I was seized with a fit of terror; but he thereupon said:—

"Be of good courage, O Scipio! Lay aside fear, and commit to memory these things which I am about to say. Do you see that State which, compelled by me to submit to the Roman people, renews its former wars, and cannot endure to remain at peace?" At these words, from a certain lustrous and bright place, very high and full of stars, he pointed out to me Carthage. "To fight against that city thou now comest in a rank but little above that of a private soldier; but in two years from this time thou shalt as consul utterly overthrow it, and in consequence shalt gain by thy own exertions that very surname of Africanus which up to this time thou hast inherited from us. But when thou shalt have destroyed Carthage, shalt have had the honor of a triumph, and shalt have been censor, thou shalt during thy absence be chosen consul for a second time, shalt put an end to to a great war, and lay Numantia in ruins. But when thou shalt be carried in thy triumphal chariot to the capitol, thou wilt find the republic disturbed by the designs of my grandson. Then, O Scipio! it will be necessary that thou exhibit the purity and greatness of thy heart, thy soul, and thy judgment. But I see at that time a double way disclose itself, as if the Fates were undecided; for when thy life shall have completed eight times seven revolutions of the sun, and these two numbers (each one of which is looked upon as perfect; the one for one reason, the other for another) shall have accomplished for thee by their natural revolution the fatal product, to thee alone and to thy name the whole State shall turn; upon thee the Senate, upon thee all good men, upon thee the allies, upon thee the Latins, will fasten their eyes; thou wilt be the one upon whom the safety of the State shall rest; and in short, as dictator, it will be incumbent on thee to establish and regulate the republic, if thou art successful in escaping the impious hands of kinsmen.»

At this point, Lælius uttered an exclamation of sorrow, and the rest groaned more deeply; but Scipio, slightly smiling, said, Keep silence, I beg of you. Do not awake me from my dream, and hear the rest of his words:—

"But, O Africanus! that thou mayest be the more zealous in the defense of the republic, know this: For all who have preserved, who have succored, who have aggrandized their country, there is in heaven a certain fixed place, where they enjoy an eternal life of blessedness. For to that highest God who governs the whole world there is nothing which can be done on earth more dear than those combinations of men and unions, made under the sanction of law, which are called States. The rulers and preservers of them depart from this place, and to it they return.»

I had been filled with terror, not so much at the fear of death as at the prospect of treachery on the part of those akin to me; nevertheless at this point I had the courage to ask whether my father Paulus was living, and others whom we thought to be annihilated. "Certainly," said he: "they alone live who have been set free from the fetters of the body, as if from prison; for that which you call your life is nothing but death. Nay, thou mayest even behold thy father Paulus coming towards thee."

No sooner had I seen him than I burst into a violent fit of tears; but he thereupon, embracing and kissing me, forbade my weeping. I, as soon as I had checked my tears and was able again to speak, said to him, "Tell me, I beseech thee, O best and most sacred father! since this is life, as I hear Africanus say, why do I tarry upon earth? Why shall I not hasten to go to you?"—"Not so," said he; "not until that God, whose temple is all this which thou seest, shall have freed thee from the bonds of the body, can any entrance lie open to thee here. For men are brought into the world with this design, that they may protect and preserve that globe which thou seest in the middle of this temple, and which is called 'Earth.' To them a soul is given from these everlasting fires which you name con- stellations and stars, which, in the form of globes and spheres, run with incredible rapidity the rounds of their orbits under the impulse of divine intelligences. Wherefore by thee, O Publius! and by all pious men, the soul must be kept in the guardianship of the body; nor without the command of Him by whom it is given to you can there be any departure from this mortal life, lest you seem to have shunned the discharge of that duty as men which has been assigned to you by God. But, O Scipio! like as thy grandfather who stands here, like as I who gave thee life, cherish the sense of justice and loyal affection; which latter, in however great measure due to thy parents and kins- men, is most of all due to thy country. Such a life is the way to heaven, and to that congregation of those who have ended their days on earth, and freed from the body, dwell in that place which you see,—that place which, as you have learned from the Greeks, you are in the habit of calling the Milky Way."

This was a circle, shining among the celestial fires with a most brilliant whiteness. As I looked from it, all other things seemed magnificent and wonderful. Moreover, they were such stars as we have never seen from this point of space, and all of such magnitude as we have never even suspected. Among them, that was the least which, the farthest from heaven, and the nearest to earth, shone with a borrowed light. But the starry globes far exceeded the size of the earth: indeed the earth itself appeared to me so small that I had a feeling of mortification at the sight of our empire, which took up what seemed to be but a point of it.

As I kept my eyes more intently fixed upon this spot, Africanus said to me:—"How long, I beg of thee, will thy spirit be chained down to earth? Seest thou not into what a holy place thou hast come? Everything is bound together in nine circles, or rather spheres, of which the farthest is the firmament, which embraces the rest, is indeed the supreme God himself, confining and containing all the others. To that highest heaven are fixed those orbits of the stars which eternally revolve. Below it are seven spheres, which move backward with a motion contrary to that of the firmament. One of these belongs to that star which on earth they call Saturn; then follows that shining orb, the source of happiness and health to the human race, which is called Jupiter; then the red planet, bringing terror to the nations, to which you give the name of Mars; then, almost directly under the middle region, stands the sun,—the leader, the chief, the governor of the other luminaries, the soul of the universe, and its regulating principle, of a size so vast that it penetrates and fills everything with its own light. Upon it, as if they were an escort, follow two spheres,—the one of Venus, the other of Mercury; and in the lowest circle revolves the moon, illuminated by the rays of the sun. Below it there is nothing which is not mortal and transitory, save the souls which are given to mankind by the gift of the gods; above the moon, all things are eternal. For that ninth sphere, which is in the middle, is the earth: it has no motion; it is the lowest in space; and all heavy bodies are borne toward it by their natural downward tendency."

I looked at these, lost in wonder. As soon as I had recovered myself I said, "What is this sound, so great and so sweet, which fills my ears?"—"This," he replied, "is that music which, composed of intervals unequal, but divided proportionately by rule, is caused by the swing and movement of the spheres themselves, and by the proper combination of acute tones with grave, creates with uniformity manifold and diverse harmonies. For movements so mighty cannot be accomplished in silence; and it is a law of nature that the farthest sphere on the one side gives forth a base tone, the farthest on the other a treble; for which reason the revolution of that uppermost arch of the heaven, the starry firmament, whose motion is more rapid, is attended with an acute and high sound; while that of the lowest, or lunar arch, is attended with a very deep and grave sound. For the ninth sphere, the earth, embracing the middle region of the universe, stays immovably in one fixed place. But those eight globes between, two* of which have the same essential action, produce tones, distinguished by intervals, to the number of seven; which number indeed is the knot of almost all things. Men of skill, by imitating the result on the strings of the lyre, or by means of the human voice, have laid open for themselves a way of return to this place, just as other men of lofty souls have done the same by devoting themselves during their earthly life to the study of what is divine. But the ears of men, surfeited by this harmony have become deaf to it; nor is there in you any duller sense: just as, at that cataract which is called Catadupa,— where the Nile rushes down headlong from the lofty mountain-tops,— the people who dwell in that neighborhood have lost the sense of hearing in consequence of the magnitude of the sound. So likewise this harmony, produced by the excessively rapid revolution of the whole universe, is so great that the ears of men are not able to take it in, in the same manner as you are not able to look the sun in the eye, and your sight is overcome by the power of its rays." Though I was filled with wonder, nevertheless I kept turning my eyes from time to time to the earth.

"I perceive," then said Africanus, "that thou still continuest to contemplate the habitation of the home of man. If that seems to thee as small as it really is, keep then thy eyes fixed on these heavenly objects; look with contempt on those of mortal life. For what notoriety that lives in the mouths of men, or what glory that is worthy of being sought after, art thou able to secure? Thou seest that the earth is inhabited in a few small localities, and that between those inhabited places — spots as it were on the surface — vast desert regions lie spread out; and that those who inhabit the earth are not only so isolated that no communication can pass among them from one to another, but that some dwell in an oblique direction as regards you, some in a diagonal, and some stand even exactly opposite you. From these you are certainly not able to hope for any glory.

"Moreover, thou observest that this same earth is surrounded, and as it were, girdled, by certain zones, of which thou seest that two — the farthest apart, and resting at both sides on the very poles of the sky — are stiffened with frost; and that, again,

* Mercury and Venus.

the central and largest one is burnt up with the heat of the sun. Two are habitable: of these the southern one, in which dwell those who make their footprints opposite yours, is a foreign world to your race. But even this other one, which lies to the north, which you occupy,—see with how small a part of it you come into contact! For all the land which is cultivated by you, very narrow at the extremities but wider at the sides, is only a small island surrounded by that water which on earth you call the Atlantic, or the great sea, or the ocean. But though its name is so high-sounding, yet thou beholdest how small it is. From these cultivated and well-known regions can either thy name or the name of any of us surmount and pass this Caucasus which thou seest, or cross yonder flood of the Ganges? Who in the farthest remaining regions of the rising and the setting sun, or on the confines of the north and the south, will hear thy name? When these are taken away, thou assuredly perceivest how immense is the littleness of that space in which your reputation seeks to spread itself abroad. Moreover, even those who speak of us, for how long a time will they speak?

"Nay, even if the generations of men were desirous, one after the other, to hand down to posterity the praises of any one of us heard from their fathers, nevertheless, on account of the chanegs in the earth,—wrought by inundations and conflagration, which are sure to recur at certain fixed epochs,—we are not simply unable to secure for ourselves a glory which lasts forever, but are even unable to gain a glory which lasts for a long time. Moreover, of what value is it that the speech of those who are to be born hereafter shall be about thee, when nothing has been said of thee by all those who were born before, who were neither fewer in number and were unquestionably better men; especially when no one is able to live in the memory of those very persons by whom one's name can be heard, for the space of one year?

"For men commonly measure the year by the return to its place of the sun alone,—that is, of one star; but when all the stars shall have returned to that same point from which they once set out, and after a long period of time have brought back the same relative arrangement of the whole heaven, that, then, can justly be called the complete year. In it I hardly dare say how many ages of human life are contained. For once in the past the sun seemed to disappear from the eyes of men and to be annihilated, at the time when the soul of Romulus made its way into this very temple. When, from the same region of the sky and at the same moment of time, the sun shall have again vanished, then be sure that all constellations and stars have come back to the position they had in the beginning, and that the perfect year is completed. Of that year know that now not even the twentieth part has passed.

"Wherefore, if thou givest up the hope of a return to this place, in which all things exist for lofty and pre-eminent souls, yet of how much value is that human glory which can hardly endure for even the small part of a single year? But if, as I was saying, thou wishest to look on high, and to fix thy gaze upon this abode of the blest and this eternal home, never give thyself up to the applause of the vulgar, nor rest the recompense of thy achievements in the rewards which can be bestowed upon thee by men. It is incumbent on thee that Virtue herself shall draw thee by her own charm to true glory. As for the way in which others talk about thee, let them take care of that themselves; yet without doubt they will talk. But all such renown is limited to the petty provinces of the regions which thou seest: nor in the case of any one is it everlasting; for it both dies with the death of men and is buried in oblivion by the forgetfulness of posterity."

When he had said these things, "O Africanus!" I replied, "if the path that leads to the entrance of heaven lies open to those who have rendered great service to their country, although, in following from my boyhood in thy footsteps and in those of my father, I have not failed in sustaining the honor derived from you, yet henceforth I shall toil with far more zeal, now that so great a reward has been held out before me." — "Do thou indeed," said he, "continue to strive; and bear this in mind, that thou thyself art not mortal, but this body of thine. For thou art not the one which that form of thine proclaims thee to be: but the soul of any one, that alone is he; not that external shape which can be pointed out with the finger. Therefore know thyself to be a god, if that is essentially god which lives, which feels, which remembers, which foresees, which rules and regulates and moves that body over which it is put in authority, as the Supreme Being governs this universe. And as the eternal God moves the world, which in a certain point of view is perishable, so the incorruptible soul moves the corruptible body. For what always moves itself is eternal; but that which communicates to anything a motion which it has itself received from another source, must necessarily have an end of life when it has an end of motion: therefore that alone never ceases to move which moves itself, for the reason that it is never deserted by itself. This indeed is the well-head; this the beginning of motion to all other things that are moved. But to a beginning there is no birth; for all things are born from the beginning. But it itself cannot be born of anything; for that would not be a beginning which sprang from some other source. And just as it is never begotten, so it never dies; for a beginning anni-hilated could neither itself be brought back to life by anything else, nor could it create anything else out of itself, since it is necessary that all things should come from a beginning. So it results that the beginning of motion is in itself, because it is self-moved. And this can neither be born nor die, for if it did, the heavens would fall to ruin, and all nature would stand still; nor could it come into the possession of any power by the original impulse of which it might be put into motion.

"Since therefore it is clear that what is self-moved is eter-nal, who can deny that this essential characteristic has been imparted to the soul? For everything which is moved by a foreign impulse is without a soul; but that which lives is made to go by an inward motion of its own, for this is the special nature and power of the soul. But if it is the one thing among all which is self-moved, then certainly it has had no beginning, and is eternal. Do thou, then, employ it in the noblest duties. But those are the loftiest cares which are concerned with the well-being of our native land. The soul that is inspired by these, and occupied with them, will hasten the quicker into this its real home and habitation. So much the more speedily indeed will it do this, if while it is shut up in the body it shall pass beyond its limits, and by the contemplation of those things which are outside of it shall withdraw itself as far as possible from the body. For the souls of those who have given them-selves up to sensual pleasures, and have made themselves as it were ministers to these, and who under the pressure of desires which are subservient to these pleasures have violated the laws of God and man, when they shall have parted from the body, will fly about the earth itself, nor will return to this place until they shall have suffered torments for many ages." He departed. I awoke from my sleep.

THE CID

(1045? – 1099)

BY CHARLES SPRAGUE SMITH

N THE Cid we have two distinct personages, Rodrigo or Ruy Diaz (Dia son of Diego) who flourished during the last half of the eleventh century; and that legendary hero of Spanish epic poems, ballads, and dramas, whom Philip II. tried to have canonized. We are not left to our own conjectures as to the character and life of the historical Cid. Both Spanish and Arabic records place the main facts beyond all controversy.

He was born at Bivar, a hamlet three miles north of Burgos (circa 1040–1050), of an ancient Castilian family claiming descent from Lain Calvo,—one of the two judges who, tradition declares, was named by the Castilian people as their governor after the Leonese king had treacherously put their counts to death (circa 923).

The period of the Cid coincides with the political disruption of Arabic Spain. The Caliphate of Cordova, which in the preceding century had attained its high point in power and in all the arts of civilization, had fallen. A multitude of petty Moorish States disputed with each other the heritage of the Ommiad caliphs. The Christian States were not slow to profit by their opportunity. Ferdinand I. of Leon-Castile (surnamed the Great, 1037–65) not only extended his territory at the expense of the Moors, but also imposed tribute upon four of their more important States — Saragossa, Toledo, Badajoz, and Seville. Valencia only escaped a similar fate through his death.

The Peninsula was at this time divided among a large number of mutually independent and warring States, Christian and Moslem. The sentiments of loyalty to religion and to country were universally subordinated to those of personal interest; Christians fought under Moorish banners, Moors under Christian. Humanity toward the enemy, loyalty to oaths, were not virtues in the common estimation. Between the Christian States of Leon and Castile great jealousy ruled. Castile had come into being as a border province of the Asturian kingdom, governed by military counts. From the first there seems to have been a spirit of resistance to the overrule of the Asturian kings (later known as kings of Leon). Finally, under its Count Fernan Gonzalez (who died 970), Castile secured its independence. But whether leading a separate political existence, or united with Leon, Castile was ever jealously sensitive of any precedence claimed or exercised by its sister kingdom. Ferdinand I. of Leon-Castile, treating his territorial possessions as personal property,—a policy repeatedly fatal to all advance in Spanish history,—divided them at his death (1005), among his five children. Sancho, the eldest, received Castile, Nahera, and Pampeluna; Alfonso, Leon, and the Asturias; Garcia, Galicia, and that portion of Portugal which had been wrested from the Moors; Urraca received the city of Zamora; and Elvira, Toro.

The expected occurred. Sancho made war on his brothers, compelling both to flee to Moorish territories, and wrested Toro from Elvira. Rodrigo Diaz, the Cid, appears first at this period. He is the *alferez, i. e.*, the standard-bearer, or commander-in-chief under the King, in Sancho's army. The brother Kings, Sancho and Alfonso, had agreed to submit their dispute to a single combat, the victor to receive the territories of both. Alfonso's Leonese army conquered the Castilian, and relying upon the agreement withdrew to its tents. Rodrigo Diaz was already known as the Campeador,—a title won through his having vanquished in single combat the champion of Sancho of Navarre, and signifying probably one skilled in battle, or champion.

Rodrigo gave a wily counsel to the routed Castilians. «The Leonese are not expecting an attack,» he said; «let us return and fall upon them at unawares.» The counsel was followed; the victors, resting in their tents, were surprised at daybreak, and only a few, Alfonso among the number, escaped with their lives. Alfonso was imprisoned at Burgos, but soon released at the entreaty of the Princess Urraca, on condition of his becoming a monk. Availing himself of such liberty, he escaped from the monastery to the Moorish court of Mamoun, King of Toledo. Sancho ruled thus over the entire heritage of his father,—Zamora excepted, the portion of Urraca. While laying siege to that city, he was slain by a cavalier in Urraca's service, Bellido Dolfos, who, sallying from the city, made good his escape, though almost overtaken by the avenging Campeador, 1072.

Alfonso, the fugitive at Toledo, was now rightful heir to the throne; and however reluctant the Castilian nobles were to recognize the authority of a Leonese king, they yielded to necessity. It is asserted—but the historical evidence here is not complete—that before recognizing Alfonso's authority the Castilian nobles required of him an oath that he had no part in his brother's murder, and that it was the Campeador who administered this oath, 1073. Whatever the facts, Alfonso will have thought it wise to conciliate the good-will of the Castilian grandees, and especially that of their leader Rodrigo, until at least his own position became secure. To this we may attribute his giving to Rodrigo in marriage of Jimena, daughter of Diego, Count of Oviedo, and first cousin of the King. The marriage contract, bearing date 1074, is preserved at Burgos.

Some years later Rodrigo was sent to collect the tribute due Alfonso by his vassal Motamid, King of Seville. Finding the King of Granada at war with Motamid, Rodrigo requested him not to attack an ally of Alfonso. But prayers and threats were alike unavailing; it came to battle, and Rodrigo conquered. Among the prisoners were several Christians in the service of Granada, notably Garcia Ordonez, a scion of the royal Leonese house. Not long after, we find Rodrigo charged with having appropriated to his own use a portion of the tribute and gifts sent to Alfonso by Motamid, Garcia Ordonez being his chief accuser. Taking advantage of the pretext — it can have been but a pretext — of Rodrigo's attacking the Moors without first securing the royal consent, Alfonso banished him. Old wrongs still rankling in the King's memory furnished probably the real motive.

And now began that career as soldier of fortune which has furnished themes to Spanish poets of high and low degree, and which, transformed and idealized by tradition, has made of Rodrigo the perfect cavalier of crusading Christian Spain. He offered first, it would seem, his service and that of his followers to the Christian Count of Barcelona, and when refused by him, to the Moorish King of Saragossa. This State was one of the more important of those resulting from the distribution of the Caliphate of Cordova. The offer was accepted, and Rodrigo remained here until 1088, serving successively three generations of the Beni-Hud, father, son, and grandson, warring indifferently against Christians and Moors, and through his successes rising to extraordinary distinction and power.

At this time — 1088 — the attention of both Mostain, the King of Saragossa, and of his powerful captain Rodrigo, was drawn to Valencia. This city after the fall of the Caliphate of Cordova had been ruled for forty-four years by descendants of Almanzor, the great Prime Minister of the last period of the Ommiad dynasty. Mamoun, King of Toledo, who sheltered the fugitive Alfonso, deposed the last of these Valencian kings, his son-in-law, and annexed the State to his own dominion. At Mamoun's death in 1075 Valencia revolted; the governor declared himself independent and placed himself under Alfonso's protection.

Ten years later Mamoun's successor, the weak Cadir, finding his position a desperate one, offered to yield up to Alfonso his own capital Toledo, on condition that the latter should place Valencia in his hands. Alfonso consented. Valencia was too weak to offer resistance, but Cadir proved equally incompetent as king and as general. Depending entirely upon his Castilian soldiery, captained by Alvar

Fañez, a kinsman of Rodrigo, he grievously burdened the people in order to satisfy the demands of this auxiliary troop. But grinding taxes and extortions alike failed; and the soldiery, their wages in arrears, battened upon the country, the dregs of the Moorish population joining them. The territory was delivered at last from their robberies, rapes, and murders, by the appearance of the Almoravides. This new Moslem sect had grown strong in Africa, attaining there the political supremacy; and in their weakness the Moorish kings of Spain implored its assistance in repelling the attacks of the Christian North.

King Alfonso, alarmed at the appearance of these African hordes, recalled Alvar Fañez, was defeated by the Almoravides at Zallaca in 1086, and could think no more of garrisoning Valencia for Cadir. The position of Cadir became thus critical, and he appealed for help both to Alfonso and to Mostain of Saragossa. Mostain sent Rodrigo, ostensibly to his assistance; but a secret agreement had been made, Arabic historians assert, between the king and his general, whereby Cadir was to be despoiled, the city fall to Mostain, the booty to Rodrigo (1088).

The expedition was a successful one: Cadir's enemies were compelled to withdraw, and Rodrigo established himself in Valencian territory. As the recognized protector of the lawful king, in reality the suzerain of Valencia, Rodrigo received a generous tribute; but he had no intention of holding to his agreement with Mostain and assisting the latter to win the city. It is clear on the contrary that he had already resolved to secure, when opportunity offered, the prize for himself. Meanwhile he skillfully held off, now by force, now by ruse, all other competitors, Christian and Moslem alike; including among these King Alfonso, whose territories he wasted with fire and sword when that monarch attempted once, in Rodrigo's absence, to win Valencia for himself.

At another time we find him intriguing simultaneously with four different rivals for the control of the city,—Alfonso and Mostain among the number,—deceiving all with fair words.

As head of an independent army, Rodrigo made now successful forays in all directions; despoiling, levying tribute, garrisoning strongholds, strengthening thus in every way his position. At last the long awaited opportunity came. During his temporary absence, Cadir was dethroned and put to death; and the leader of the insurgents, the Cadi Ibn Djahhof, named president of a republic.

Rodrigo returned, and appealing in turn to ruse and force, at last sat down before the city to reduce it by famine. During the last period of the siege, those who fled from the city to escape the famine were thrown to dogs, or burned at slow fires. The city capitulated on favorable terms, June 15th, 1094. But all the conditions of the capitulation were violated. The Cadi-President was buried in a trench up to his arm-pits, surrounded with burning brands, and slowly tortured to death, several of his kinsmen and friends sharing his fate. Rodrigo was with difficulty restrained from throwing into the flames the Cadi's children and the women of his harem. Yet the lives and property of Ibn Djahhof and his family had been expressly safeguarded in the capitulation. It is probable that Rodrigo's title of "the Cid" or "my Cid" (Arabic, Sid-y = my lord) was given to him at this time by his Moorish subjects.

Master of Valencia, the Cid dreamed of conquering all that region of Spain still held by the Moors. An Arab heard him say, "One Rodrigo (the last king of the Goths) has lost this peninsula; another Rodrigo will recover it." Success crowned his arms for several years. But in 1099 the troops he had sent against the Almoravides were utterly routed, few escaping. The Cid, already enfeebled in health, died, it is said of grief and shame (July, 1099). His widow held the city for two years longer. Besieged at that time by the Almoravides, she sought help of Alfonso. He came and forced the enemy to raise the siege; but judging that it was not possible for him to defend a city so remote from his dominions, counseled its abandonment. As the Christians, escorting the body of the Cid, marched out. Valencia was fired; and only ruins awaited the Almoravides (1102).

The Cid's body was brought to San Pedro de Cardeña, a monastery not far from Burgos; enthroned, it is said, beside the high altar for ten years, and thereafter buried. Jimena survived her husband until 1104.

Ibn Bassam, an Arabic contemporary, writing at Seville only ten years after the death of the Cid, after describing his cruelty and duplicity, adds:—"Nevertheless, that man, the scourge of his time, was one of the miracles of the Lord in his love of glory, the prudent firmness of his character, and his heroic courage. Victory always followed the banner of Rodrigo (may God curse him!); he triumphed over the barbarians, . . . he put to flight their armies, and with his little band of warriors slew their numerous soldiery."

The Cid, a man not of princely birth, through the exercise of virtues which his time esteemed,—courage and shrewdness,—had won for himself from the Moors an independent principality. Legend will have begun to color and transform his exploits already during his lifetime. Some fifty years later he had become the favorite hero of popular songs. It is probable that these songs (*cantares*) were at first brief tales in rude metrical form; and that the epic poems, dating from about 1200, used them as sources. The earliest poetic monument in Castilian literature which treats of the Cid is called 'The

Poem of My Cid.' While based upon history, its material is largely
legendary. The date of its composition is doubtful,—probably about
1200. The poem—the beginning is lost—opens with the departure
of "My Cid" from Bivar, and describes his Moorish campaigns, cul-
minating with the conquest of Valencia. Two Leonese nobles, the
Infantes (Princes) of Carrion, beseech Alfonso to ask for them in
marriage the conqueror's daughters. The Cid assents—to his King
he would refuse nothing—and the marriages are celebrated in Valencia with due pomp. But the princes are arrant cowards. To
escape the gibes of the Cid's companions, after securing rich wedding portions they depart for Carrion. In the oak wood of Carpes
they pretend a desire to be left alone with their wives. Despoiling
them of their outer garments, with saddle-girth and spurred boot
they seek to revenge upon the Cid's daughters the dishonor to which
their own base conduct subjected them while at the Cid's court.
But time brings a requital. The Infantes, called to account, forfeit
property and honor, esteeming themselves fortunate to escape with
their lives from the judicial duels. Princes of Navarre and Aragon
present themselves as suitors, and in second marriages Doña Elvira
and Doña Sola become queens of Spain. The marriages with the
Infantes of Carrion are pure invention, intended perhaps to defame
the Leonese nobility, these nobles being princes of the blood royal.

The second marriages, if we substitute Barcelona for Aragon, are
historical. Of the Cid's two daughters, one married Prince Ramiro
of Navarre and the other Count Raynard Berenger III. of Barcelona.
In 1157 two of the Cid's great-grandchildren, Sancho VI. of Navarre
and his sister Doña Blanca, queen of Sancho III. of Castile, sat on
Spanish thrones. Through intermarriage the blood of the Cid has
passed into the Bourbon and Habsburg lines, and with Eleanor of
Castile into the English royal house.

The 'Poem of My Cid' is probably the earliest monument of
Spanish literature. It is also in our opinion the noblest expression
— so far as the characters are concerned; for the verse halts and
the description sometimes lags — of the entire mediæval folk epic of
Europe. Homeric in its simplicity, its characters are drawn with
clearness, firmness, and concision, presenting a variety true to nature,
far different from the uniformity we find in the 'Song of Roland.'
The spirit which breathes in it is of a noble, well-rounded humanity,
a fearless and gentle courage, a manly and modest self-reliance; an
unswerving loyalty and simple trust toward country, king, kinsmen,
and friends; a child-faith in God, slightly tinged with superstition, for
"My Cid" believes in auguries; and a chaste tender family affection,
where the wife is loved and honored as wife and as mother, and the
children's welfare fills the father's thoughts.

The duplicity of the historical Cid has left indeed its traces. When abandoning Castile he sends to two Jewish money-lenders of Burgos, chests filled, as he pretends, with fine gold, but in reality with sand; borrows upon this security, and so far as we are informed, never repays the loan. The Princes of Carrion, his sons-in-law, are duped into thinking that they will escape from the accounting with the loss of Tizon and Colada, the swords which the Cid gave them. But a certain measure of prudent shrewdness is not out of place in dealing with men of the treacherous character of the Infantes. And as to the Jewish money-lenders, to despoil them would scarce have been regarded as an offense against the moral law in mediæval Spain.

The second poetic monument is variously named. Amadar de los Rios, a historian of Spanish literature, styles it 'The Legend or Chronicle of the Youth of Rodrigo.' Its date also is disputed, some authorities placing its composition earlier, others later than that of the Poem. The weight of evidence seems to us in favor of the later date. It is rude and of inferior merit, though not without vigorous passages. It treats the earliest period of the Cid's life, and is (so far as we know) purely legendary. The realm of Castile-Leon is at peace under the rule of Ferdinand (the First), when the Count Don Gomez of Gormaz makes an unprovoked descent upon the sheep-folds of Diego Lainez. A challenge of battle follows. Rodrigo, only son of Diego, a lad in his thirteenth year, insists upon being one of the hundred combatants on the side of his family, and slays Don Gomez in single combat. Jimena, the daughter of Gomez, implores justice of the King; but when Ferdinand declares that there is danger of an insurrection if Rodrigo be punished, she proposes reconciliation through marriage. Diego and his son are summoned to the court, where Rodrigo's appearance and conduct terrify all. He denies vassalship, and declares to King Ferdinand, "That my father kissed your hand has foully dishonored me."

Married to Jimena against his will (Jimena Diaz, not Jimena Gomez, was his historical wife), he vows never to recognize her as wife until he has won five battles with the Moors in open field. Ferdinand plays a very unkingly rôle in this poem. While his fierce vassal is absent the King is helpless; and Rodrigo draws near only to assert anew his contempt for the royal authority by blunt refusals of Ferdinand's requests. He is always ready, however, to take up the gauntlet and defend the realm against every enemy, Christian or Moor. But this rude courage is coupled with devout piety, and is not insensible to pity. At the ford of the Duero a wretched leper is encountered: all turn from him with loathing save Rodrigo, who gives to him a brother's care. It is Saint Lazarus, who departing blesses him.

At last a formidable coalition is formed against Spain. The Emperor of Germany and the King of France, supported by the Pope and Patriarch, require of Spain, in recognition of her feudal dependence upon the Roman empire, a yearly tribute of fifteen noble virgins, besides silver, horses, falcons, etc. Rodrigo appears when Ferdinand is in despair, and kisses at last the royal hand in sign of vassalship. Though the enemy gather "countless as the herbs of the fields," even Persia and Armenia furnishing contingents, their battle array is vain.

The five Kings of Spain cross the Pyrenees. Arrived before Paris, Rodrigo passes through the midst of the French army, strikes with his hand the gates of the city, and challenges the twelve French peers to combat. The allies in alarm implore a truce. At the council, Rodrigo, seated at the feet of his King and acting as Ferdinand's spokesman, curses the Pope when the latter offers the imperial crown of Spain. "We came for that which was to be won," he declares, "not for that already won." Against Rodrigo's advice the truce is accorded to all. Here the poem is interrupted.

Besides these two epic poems, we have in the earlier Spanish literature two chronicles in prose which describe the life of the Cid, —'The General Chronicle of Alfonso the Learned' and 'The Chronicle of the Cid,' the latter being drawn from the former. Both rest in part upon historical sources, in part upon legend and tradition. Two centuries and more after the Poem, we meet with the Romances or Ballads of the Cid. For the earliest of these do not in their present form date far back of 1500. These ballads derive from all sources, but chiefly from the Cid legend, which is here treated in a lyric, sentimental, popular, and at times even vulgar tone.

Guillem de Castro (1569–1631) chose two themes from the life of the Cid for dramatic treatment, composing a dual drama styled 'Las Mocedades del Cid' (The Youth of the Cid). The first part is the more important. De Castro, drawing from the ballads, told again the story of the insult to Don Diego (according to the ballads, a blow in the face given by Don Gomez in a moment of passion), its revenge, the pursuit of Rodrigo by Jimena, demanding justice of King Ferdinand, and finally the reconciliation through marriage. But De Castro added love, and the conflict in the mind of Rodrigo and in that of Jimena between affection and the claims of honor.

Corneille recast De Castro's first drama in his 'Le Cid,' condensing it and giving to the verse greater dignity and nobility. The French dramatist has worked with entire independence here, and both in what he has omitted and what he has added has usually shown an unerring dramatic instinct. In certain instances, however, through ignorance of the spirit and sources of the Spanish drama he has erred. But the invention is wholly De Castro's, and many of Corneille's most admired passages are either free translations from the Spanish or expressions of some thought or sentiment contained in De Castro's version.

In more recent times Herder has enriched German literature with free renderings of some of the Cid ballads. Victor Hugo has drawn from the Cid theme, in his 'La Legende des Siècles' (The Legend of the Centuries), fresh inspiration for his muse.

Charles Sprague Smith

FROM 'THE POEM OF MY CID'

LEAVING BURGOS

WITH tearful eyes he turned to gaze upon the wreck behind,
    His rifled coffers, bursten gates, all open to the wind:
        Nor mantle left, nor robe of fur; stript bare his castle hall;
Nor hawk nor falcon in the mew, the perches empty all.
Then forth in sorrow went my Cid, and a deep sigh sighed he;
Yet with a measured voice and calm, my Cid spake loftily,—
"I thank thee, God our Father, thou that dwellest upon high,
I suffer cruel wrong to-day, but of mine enemy!"
As they came riding from Bivar the crow was on the right;
By Burgos's gate, upon the left, the crow was there in sight.
My Cid he shrugged his shoulders and he lifted up his head:
"Good tidings, Alvar Fañez! we are banished men!" he said.
With sixty lances in his train my Cid rode up the town,
The burghers and their dames from all the windows looking down;
And there were tears in every eye, and on each lip one word:
"A worthy vassal — would to God he served a worthy Lord!"

FAREWELL TO HIS WIFE AT SAN PEDRO DE CARDEÑA

THE prayer was said, the mass was sung, they mounted to depart;
My Cid a moment stayed to press Jimena to his heart;
Jimena kissed his hand,—as one distraught with grief was she;
He looked upon his daughters: "These to God I leave," said he. . . .
As when the finger-nail from out the flesh is torn away,
Even so sharp to him and them the parting pang that day.
Then to his saddle sprang my Cid, and forth his vassals led;
But ever as he rode, to those behind he turned his head.

Battle Scene

Then cried my Cid—"In charity, as to the rescue—ho!"
With bucklers braced before their breasts, with lances pointing low,
With stooping crests and heads bent down above the saddle-bow,
All firm of hand and high of heart they roll upon the foe.
And he that in a good hour was born, his clarion voice rings out,
And clear above the clang of arms is heard his battle shout:
"Among them, gentlemen! Strike home for the love of charity!
The champion of Bivar is here—Ruy Diaz—I am he!"
Then bearing where Bermuez still maintains unequal fight,
Three hundred lances down they come, their pennons flickering white;
Down go three hundred Moors to earth, a man to every blow;
And when they wheel, three hundred more, as charging back they go.
It was a sight to see the lances rise and fall that day;
The shivered shields and riven mail, to see how thick they lay;
The pennons that went in snow-white came out a gory red;
The horses running riderless, the riders lying dead;
While Moors call on Mohammed, and "St. James!" the Christians cry,
And sixty score of Moors and more in narrow compass lie.

The Challenges

[Scene from the challenges that preceded the judicial duels. Ferrando,
one of the Infantes, has just declared that they did right in spurning the
Cid's daughters. The Cid turns to his nephew.]

"Now is the time, 'Dumb Peter'; speak, O man that sittest mute!
My daughters' and thy cousins' name and fame are in dispute:
To me they speak, to thee they look to answer every word.
If I am left to answer now, thou canst not draw thy sword."
Tongue-tied Bermuez stood; a while he strove for words in vain,
But look you, when he once began he made his meaning plain.
"Cid, first I have a word for you: you always are the same,
In Cortes ever gibing me,—'Dumb Peter' is the name;
It never was a gift of mine, and that long since you knew;
But have you found me fail in aught that fell to me to do?—
You lie, Ferrando, lie in all you say upon that score.
The honor was to you, not him, the Cid Campeador;
For I know something of your worth, and somewhat I can tell.
That day beneath Valencia wall—you recollect it well—
You prayed the Cid to place you in the forefront of the fray;
You spied a Moor, and valiantly you went that Moor to slay;
And then you turned and fled—for his approach you would not stay.
Right soon he would have taught you 'twas a sorry game to play,
Had I not been in battle there to take your place that day.

I slew him at the first onfall; I gave his steed to you;
To no man have I told the tale from that hour hitherto.
Before my Cid and all his men you got yourself a name,
How you in single combat slew a Moor — a deed of fame;
And all believed in your exploit; they wist not of your shame.
You are a craven at the core, — tall, handsome, as you stand:
How dare you talk as now you talk, you tongue without a hand? . . .
Now take thou my defiance as a traitor, trothless knight:
Upon this plea before our King Alfonso will I fight;
The daughters of my lord are wronged, their wrong is mine to right.
That ye those ladies did desert, the baser are ye then;
For what are they? — weak women; and what are ye? — strong men.
On every count I deem their cause to be the holier,
And I will make thee own it when we meet in battle here.
Traitor thou shalt confess thyself, so help me God on high,
And all that I have said to-day my sword shall verify."

Thus far these two. Diego rose, and spoke as ye shall hear:
"Counts by our birth are we, of stain our lineage is clear.
In this alliance with my Cid there was no parity.
If we his daughters cast aside, no cause for shame we see.
And little need we care if they in mourning pass their lives,
Enduring the reproach that clings to scorned rejected wives.
In leaving them we but upheld our honor and our right,
And ready to the death am I, maintaining this, to fight."
Here Martin Antolinez sprang upon his feet: "False hound!
Will you not silent keep that mouth where truth was never found?
For you to boast! the lion scare have you forgotten too?
How through the open door you rushed, across the court-yard flew;
How sprawling in your terror on the wine-press beam you lay?
Ay! never more, I trow, you wore the mantle of that day.
There is no choice; the issue now the sword alone can try:
The daughters of my Cid ye spurned; that must ye justify.
On every count I here declare their cause the cause of right,
And thou shalt own thy treachery the day we join in fight."
He ceased, and striding up the hall Assur Gonzalez passed;
His cheek was flushed with wine, for he had stayed to break his fast;
Ungirt his robe, and trailing low his ermine mantle hung;
Rude was his bearing to the court, and reckless was his tongue.
"What a to-do is here, my lords! was the like ever seen?
What talk is this about my Cid — him of Bivar I mean?
To Riodouirna let him go to take his millers' rent,
And keep his mills a-going there, as once he was content.
He, forsooth, mate his daughters with the Counts of Carrion!"
Upstarted Muño Gustioz: "False, foul-mouthed knave, have done!

Thou glutton, wont to break thy fast without a thought or prayer;
Whose heart is plotting mischief when thy lips are speaking fair;
Whose plighted word to friend or lord hath ever proved a lie;
False always to thy fellow-man, falser to God on high,—
No share in thy good-will I seek; one only boon I pray,
The chance to make thee own thyself the villain that I say.»
Then spoke the king: "Enough of words: ye have my leave to fight,
The challenged and the challengers; and God defend the right."

Conclusion

AND from the field of honor went Don Roderick's champions three.
Thanks be to God, the Lord of all, that gave the victory! . . .
But in the lands of Carrion it was a day of woe,
And on the lords of Carrion it fell a heavy blow.
He who a noble lady wrongs and casts aside — may he
Meet like requital for his deeds, or worse, if worse there be!
But let us leave them where they lie — their meed is all men's scorn.
Turn we to speak of him that in a happy hour was born.
Valencia the Great was glad, rejoiced at heart to see
The honored champions of her lord return in victory:
And Ruy Diaz grasped his beard: "Thanks be to God," said he,
"Of part or lot in Carrion now are my daughters free;
Now may I give them without shame, whoe'er their suitors be."
And favored by the king himself, Alfonso of Leon,
Prosperous was the wooing of Navarre and Aragon.
The bridals of Elvira and of Sol in splendor passed;
Stately the former nuptials were, but statelier far the last.
And he that in a good hour was born, behold how he hath sped!
His daughters now to higher rank and greater honor wed:
Sought by Navarre and Aragon, for queens his daughters twain;
And monarchs of his blood to-day upon the thrones of Spain.
And so his honor in the land grows greater day by day.
Upon the feast of Pentecost from life he passed away.
For him and all of us the grace of Christ let us implore.
And here ye have the story of my Cid Campeador.

Translation of John Ormsby.

EARL OF CLARENDON
(EDWARD HYDE)

(1609 – 1674)

HE statesman first known as Mr. Hyde of the Inner Temple, then as Sir Edward Hyde, and finally as the Earl of Clarendon, belongs to the small but most valuable and eminent band who have both made and written history; a group which includes among others Cæsar, Procopius, Sully, and Baber, and on a smaller scale of active importance, Ammianus and Finlay. Born in Dinton, Wiltshire, 1609, he was graduated at Oxford in 1626, and had attained a high standing in his profession when the civil troubles began, and he determined to devote all his energies to his public duties in Parliament. During the momentous period of the Long Parliament he was strongly on the side of the people until the old abuses had been swept away; but he would not go with them in paralyzing the royal authority from distrust of Charles, and when the civil war broke out he took the royal side, accompanying the King to Oxford, and remaining his ablest adviser and loyal friend.

EARL OF CLARENDON

He was the guardian of Charles II. in exile; and in 1661, after the Restoration, was made Lord Chancellor and chief minister. Lord Macaulay says of him:—"He was well fitted for his great place. No man wrote abler state papers. No man spoke with more weight and dignity in council and Parliament. No man was better acquainted with general maxims of statecraft. No man observed the varieties of character with a more discriminating eye. It must be added that he had a strong sense of moral and religious obligation, a sincere reverence for the laws of his country, and a conscientious regard for the honor and interest of the Crown." But his faults were conspicuous. One of his critics insists that "his temper was arbitrary and vehement. His arrogance was immeasurable. His gravity assumed the character of censoriousness."

He took part in important and dangerous negotiations, and eventually alienated four parties at once: the royalists by his Bill of

Indemnity; the low-churchmen and dissenters by his Uniformity act; the many who suffered the legal fine for private assemblages for religious worship; and the whole nation by selling Dunkirk to France. By the court he was hated because he censured the extravagance and looseness of the life led there; and finally Charles, who had long resented his sermons, deprived him of the great seal, accused him of high treason, and doomed him to perpetual banishment. Thus, after being the confidential friend of two kings (and the future grandfather of two sovereigns, Mary and Anne), he was driven out of England, to die in poverty and neglect at Rouen in 1674. But these last days were perhaps the happiest and most useful of his life. He now indulged his master passion for literature, and revised his 'History of the Rebellion,' which he had begun while a fugitive from the rebels in the Isle of Jersey. In this masterpiece, "one of the greatest ornaments of the historical literature of England," he has described not only the events in which he participated, but noted people of the time whom he had personally known. The book is written in a style of sober and stately dignity, with great acuteness of insight and weightiness of comment; it incorporates part of an autobiography afterwards published separately, and is rather out of proportion. His other works are 'The Essay on an Active and Contemplative Life'; 'The Life of Edward, Earl of Clarendon'; 'Dialogues on Education and the Want of Respect Paid to Age'; 'Miscellaneous Essays,' and 'Contemplation of the Psalms of David.'

THE CHARACTER OF LORD FALKLAND

IF CELEBRATING the memory of eminent and extraordinary persons, and transmitting their great virtues for the imitation of posterity, be one of the principal ends and duties of history, it will not be thought impertinent in this place to remember a loss which no time will suffer to be forgotten, and no success or good fortune could repair. In this unhappy battle was slain the Lord Viscount Falkland; a person of such prodigious parts of learning and knowledge, of that inimitable sweetness and delight in conversation, of so flowing and obliging a humanity and goodness to mankind, and of that primitive simplicity and integrity of life, that if there were no other brand upon this odious and accursed civil war than that single loss, it must be most infamous and execrable to all posterity.

Before this Parliament, his condition of life was so happy that it was hardly capable of improvement. Before he came to twenty years of age he was master of a noble fortune, which descended to him by the gift of a grandfather without passing through his father or mother, who were then both alive, and not well enough contented to find themselves passed by in the descent. His education for some years had been in Ireland, where his father was Lord Deputy; so that when he returned into England to the possession of his fortune, he was unentangled with any acquaintance or friends, which usually grow up by the custom of conversation; and therefore was to make a pure election of his company, which he chose by other rules than were prescribed to the young nobility of that time. And it cannot be denied, though he admitted some few to his friendship for the agreeableness of their natures and their undoubted affection to him, that his familiarity and friendship, for the most part, was with men of the most eminent and sublime parts, and of untouched reputation in the point of integrity; and such men had a title to his bosom.

He was a great cherisher of wit and fancy and good parts in any man; and if he found them clouded with poverty or want, a most liberal and bountiful patron towards them, even above his fortune; of which, in those administrations, he was such a dispenser as if he had been trusted with it to such uses; and if there had been the least of vice in his expense he might have been thought too prodigal. He was constant and pertinacious in whatsoever he resolved to do, and not to be wearied by any pains that were necessary to that end. And therefore having once resolved not to see London, which he loved above all places, till he had perfectly learned the Greek tongue, he went to his own house in the country and pursued it with that indefatigable industry that it will not be believed in how short a time he was master of it, and accurately read all the Greek historians.

In this time, his house being within ten miles of Oxford, he contracted familiarity and friendship with the most polite and accurate men of that university; who found such an immenseness of wit and such a solidity of judgment in him, so infinite a fancy bound in by a most logical ratiocination, such a vast knowledge that he was not ignorant in anything, yet such an excessive humility as if he had known nothing, that they frequently resorted and dwelt with him, as in a college situated in a purer air; so that his house was a university bound in a less volume, whither they came not so much for repose as study, and to examine and refine those grosser propositions which laziness and consent made current in vulgar conversation. . . .

The great opinion he had of the uprightness and integrity of those persons who appeared most active, especially of Mr. Hampden, kept him longer from suspecting any design against the peace of the kingdom; and though he differed commonly from them in conclusions, he believed long their purposes were honest. When he grew better informed what was law, and discerned (in them) a desire to control that law by a vote of one or both Houses, no man more opposed those attempts, and gave the adverse party more trouble by reason and argumentation; insomuch as he was, by degrees, looked upon as an advocate for the court, to which he contributed so little that he declined those addresses and even those invitations which he was obliged almost by civility to entertain. And he was so jealous of the least imagination that he should incline to preferment, that he affected even a morosity to the court and to the courtiers, and left nothing undone which might prevent and divert the King's or Queen's favor towards him, but the deserving it. For when the King sent for him once or twice to speak with him, and to give him thanks for his excellent comportment in those councils which his Majesty graciously termed doing him service, his answers were more negligent and less satisfactory than might have been expected; as if he cared only that his actions should be just, not that they should be acceptable, and that his Majesty should think that they proceeded only from the impulsion of conscience, without any sympathy in his affections; which from a stoical and sullen nature might not have been misinterpreted; yet from a person of so perfect a habit of generous and obsequious compliance with all good men, might very well have been interpreted by the King as more than an ordinary averseness to his service: so that he took more pains and more forced his nature to actions unagreeable and unpleasant to it, that he might not be thought to incline to the court, than any man hath done to procure an office there. . . .

Two reasons prevailed with him to receive the seals, and but for those he had resolutely avoided them. The first, consideration that it [his refusal] might bring some blemish upon the King's affairs, and that men would have believed that he had refused so great an honor and trust because he must have been with it obliged to do somewhat else not justifiable. And this he made matter of conscience, since he knew the King made choice of him before other men especially because he thought him more honest than other men. The other was, lest he might be thought to avoid it out of fear to do an ungracious thing to the House of Commons, who were sorely troubled at the displacing of Harry Vane, whom they looked upon as removed for having done them those offices they stood in need of; and the disdain of so popular an incumbrance wrought upon him next to the other. For as he had a full appetite of fame by just and generous actions, so he had an equal contempt of it by any servile expedients; and he had so much the more consented to and approved the justice upon Sir Harry Vane in his own private judgment, by how much he surpassed most men in the religious observation of a trust, the violation whereof he would not admit of any excuse for.

For these reasons he submitted to the King's command and became his secretary, with as humble and devout an acknowledgment of the greatness of the obligation as could be expressed, and as true a sense of it in his own heart. Yet two things he could never bring himself to whilst he continued in that office, that was to his death; for which he was contented to be reproached, as for omissions in a most necessary part of his office. The one, employing of spies, or giving any countenance or entertainment to them. I do not mean such emissaries as with danger would venture to view the enemy's camp and bring intelligence of their number and quartering, or such generals as such an observation can comprehend; but those who by communication of guilt or dissimulation of manners wound themselves into such trusts and secrets as enabled them to make discoveries for the benefit of the State. The other, the liberty of opening letters upon a suspicion that they might contain matter of dangerous consequence. For the first he would say, such instruments must be void of all ingenuity and common honesty, before they could be of use; and afterwards they could never be fit to be credited: and that no single preservation could be worth so general a wound and corruption of human society as the cherishing such persons would carry with it. The last, he thought such a violation of the law of nature that no qualification by office could justify a single person in the trespass; and though he was convinced by the necessity and iniquity of the time that those advantages of information were not to be declined and were necessarily to be practiced, he found means to shift it from himself; when he confessed he needed excuse and pardon for the omission: so unwilling he was to resign anything in his nature to an obligation in his office.

In all other particulars he filled his place plentifully, being sufficiently versed in languages to understand any that [are] used in business, and to make himself again understood. To speak of his integrity, and his high disdain of any bait that might seem to look towards corruption, *in tanto viro, injuria virtutum fuerit* [in the case of so great a man, would be an insult to his merits]. . . .

He had a courage of the most clear and keen temper, and so far from fear that he was not without appetite of danger; and therefore, upon any occasion of action, he always engaged his person in those troops which he thought by the forwardness of the commanders to be most like to be farthest engaged; and in all such encounters he had about him a strange cheerfulness and companionableness, without at all affecting the execution that was then principally to be attended, in which he took no delight, but took pains to prevent it, where it was not by resistance necessary; insomuch that at Edgehill, when the enemy was routed, he was like to have incurred great peril by interposing to save those who had thrown away their arms, and against whom, it may be, others were more fierce for their having thrown them away: insomuch as a man might think he came into the field only out of curiosity to see the face of danger, and charity to prevent the shedding of blood. Yet in his natural inclination he acknowledged that he was addicted to the profession of a soldier; and shortly after he came to his fortune, and before he came to age, he went into the Low Countries with a resolution of procuring command, and to give himself up to it, from which he was converted by the complete inactivity of that summer: and so he returned into England and shortly after entered upon that vehement course of study we mentioned before, till the first alarm from the North; and then again he made ready for the field, and though he received some repulse in the command of a troop of horse of which he had a promise, he went volunteer with the Earl of Essex.

From the entrance into this unnatural war his natural cheerfulness and vivacity grew clouded, and a kind of sadness and dejection of spirit stole upon him which he had never been used to; yet being one of those who believed that one battle would end all differences, and that there would be so great a victory on the one side that the other would be compelled to submit to any conditions from the victor (which supposition and conclusion generally sunk into the minds of most men, and prevented the looking after many advantages which might then have been laid hold of), he resisted those indispositions, *et in luctu, bellum inter remedia erat* [and in his grief, strife was one of his curatives]. But after the King's return from Brentford, and the furious resolution of the two Houses not to admit any treaty for peace, those indispositions which had before touched him grew into a perfect habit of uncheerfulness; and he who had been so exactly unreserved and affable to all men that his face and countenance was always present and vacant to his company, and held any cloudiness and less pleasantness of the visage a kind of rudeness or incivility, became, on a sudden, less communicable; and thence, very sad, pale, and exceedingly affected with the spleen. In his clothes and habit, which he had intended before always with more neatness and industry and expense than is usual in so great a mind, he was now not only incurious, but too negligent; and in his reception of suitors, and the necessary or casual addresses to his place, so quick and sharp and severe that there wanted not some men (who were strangers to his nature and disposition) who believed him proud and imperious,—from which no mortal man was ever more free.

The truth is, that as he was of a most incomparable gentleness, application, and even a demissness and submission to good and worthy and entire men, so he was naturally (which could not but be more evident in his place, which objected him to another conversation and intermixture than his own election had done) *adversus malos injucundus* [toward evil-doers ungracious] and was so ill a dissembler of his dislike and disinclination to ill men that it was not possible for such not to discern it. There was once in the House of Commons such a declared acceptation of the good service an eminent member had done to them, and as they said, to the whole kingdom, that it was moved, he being present, that the Speaker might in the name of the whole House give him thanks; and then, that every member might as a testimony of his particular acknowledgment stir or move his hat towards him; the which (though not ordered) when very many

did, the Lord Falkland (who believed the service itself not to be
of that moment, and that an honorable and generous person
could not have stooped to it for any recompense), instead of
moving his hat, stretched both his arms out and clasped his
hands together upon the crown of his hat, and held it close
down to his head; that all men might see how odious that flat-
tery was to him, and the very approbation of the person, though
at that time most popular.

When there was any overture or hope of peace, he would be
more erect and vigorous, and exceedingly solicitous to press
anything which he thought might promote it; and sitting amongst
his friends, often, after a deep silence and frequent sighs, would
with a shrill and sad accent ingeminate the word *Peace, Peace;*
and would passionately profess that the very agony of the war
and the view of the calamities and desolation the kingdom
did and must endure, took his sleep from him, and would
shortly break his heart. This made some think or pretend to
think that he was so much enamored on peace, that he would
have been glad the King should have bought it at any price;
which was a most unreasonable calumny. As if a man that
was himself the most punctual and precise in every circumstance
that might reflect upon conscience or honor, could have wished
the King to have committed a trespass against either.   .   .   .

In the morning before the battle, as always upon action, he
was very cheerful, and put himself into the first rank of the
Lord Byron's regiment, who was then advancing upon the
enemy, who had lined the hedges on both sides with musketeers,
from whence he was shot with a musket in the lower part of the
belly, and in the instant falling from his horse, his body was
not found till the next morning; till when, there was some hope
he might have been a prisoner; though his nearest friends, who
knew his temper, received small comfort from that imagination.
Thus fell that incomparable young man, in the four-and-thirtieth
year of his age, having so much dispatched the business of life
that the oldest rarely attain to that immense knowledge, and the
youngest enter not into the world with more innocence: and
whosoever leads such a life needs not care upon how short
warning it be taken from him.

MARCUS A. H. CLARKE

(1846-1881)

ALTHOUGH a native of England, Marcus Clarke is always classed as an Australian novelist. The son of a barrister, he was born in Kensington April 24th, 1846. In 1864 he went to seek his fortune in Australia. His taste for adventure soon led him to "the bush," where he acquired many experiences afterwards used by him for literary material. Drifting into journalism, he joined the staff of the Melbourne Argus. After publishing a series of essays called 'The Peripatetic Philosopher,' he purchased the Australian Magazine, the name of which he changed to the Colonial Monthly, and in 1868 published in it his first novel, entitled 'Long Odds.' Owing to a long illness, this tale of sporting life was completed by other hands. When he resumed his literary work he contributed to the Melbourne Punch, and edited the Humbug, a humorous journal. He dramatized Charles Reade's and Dion Boucicault's novel of 'Foul Play'; adapted Molière's 'Bourgeois Gentilhomme'; wrote a drama entitled 'Plot,' successfully performed at the Princess Theatre in 1873; and another play called 'A Daughter of Eve.' He was connected with the Melbourne press until his death, August 2d, 1881.

Clarke's literary fame rests upon the novel 'His Natural Life,' a strong story, describing the life of an innocent man under a life sentence for felony. The story is repulsive, but gives a faithful picture of the penal conditions of the time, and is built upon official records. It appeared in the Australian Magazine, and before it was issued in book form, Clarke, with the assistance of Sir Charles Gavin Duffy, revised it almost beyond recognition. It was republished in London in 1875 and in New York in 1878. He was also the author of 'Old Tales of a New Country'; 'Holiday Peak,' another collection of short stories; 'Four Stories High'; and an unfinished novel called 'Felix and Felicitas.'

Clarke was a devoted student of Balzac and Poe, and some of his sketches of rough life in Australia have been compared to Bret Harte's pictures of primitive California days. His power in depicting landscape is shown by this glimpse of a midnight ride in the bush, taken from 'Holiday Peak':—

"There is an indescribable ghastliness about the mountain bush at midnight, which has affected most imaginative people. The grotesque and distorted trees, huddled here and there together in the gloom like whispering

conspirators; the little open flats encircled by bowlders, which seem the forgotten altars of some unholy worship; the white, bare, and ghostly gum-trees,
gleaming momentarily amid the deeper shades of the forest; the lonely pools
begirt with shivering reeds and haunted by the melancholy bittern only; the
rifted and draggled creek-bed, which seems violently gouged out of the lacer-
ated earth by some savage convulsion of nature; the silent and solitary places
where a few blasted trees crouch together like withered witches, who, brood-
ing on some deed of blood, have suddenly been stricken horror-stiff. Riding
through this nightmare landscape, a whirr of wings and a harsh cry disturb
you from time to time, hideous and mocking laughter peals above and about
you, and huge gray ghosts with little red eyes hop away in gigantic but
noiseless bounds. You shake your bridle, the mare lengthens her stride, the
tree-trunks run into one another, the leaves make overhead a continuous curtain, the earth reels out beneath you like a strip of gray cloth spun by a
furiously flying loom, the air strikes your face sharply, the bush — always gray
and colorless — parts before you and closes behind you like a fog. You lose
yourself in this prevailing indecision of sound and color. You become drunk
with the wine of the night, and losing your individuality, sweep onward, a
flying phantom in a land of shadows.»

HOW A PENAL SYSTEM CAN WORK

From ‹His Natural Life›

THE next two days were devoted to sight-seeing. Sylvia Frere
was taken through the hospital and the workshops, shown
the semaphores, and shut up by Maurice in a "dark cell."
Her husband and Burgess seemed to treat the prison like a tame
animal, whom they could handle at their leisure, and whose
natural ferocity was kept in check by their superior intelligence.
This bringing of a young and pretty woman into immediate
contact with bolts and bars had about it an incongruity which
pleased them. Maurice Frere penetrated everywhere, questioned
the prisoners, jested with the jailers; even, in the munificence of
his heart, bestowed tobacco on the sick.

With such graceful rattlings of dry bones, they got by-and-by
to Point Puer, where a luncheon had been provided.

An unlucky accident had occurred at Point Puer that morning, however; and the place was in a suppressed ferment. A
refractory little thief named Peter Brown, aged twelve years,
had jumped off the high rock and drowned himself in full view
of the constables. These "jumpings-off" had become rather
frequent lately, and Burgess was enraged at one happening on

this particular day. If he could by any possibility have brought the corpse of poor little Peter Brown to life again, he would have soundly whipped it for its impertinence.

« It is most unfortunate, » he said to Frere, as they stood in the cell where the little body was laid, « that it should have happened to-day. »

« Oh, » says Frere, frowning down upon the young face that seemed to smile up at him, « it can't be helped. I know those young devils. They'd do it out of spite. What sort of a character had he ? »

« Very bad. Johnson, the book. »

Johnson bringing it, the two saw Peter Brown's iniquities set down in the neatest of running-hand, and the record of his punishments ornamented in quite an artistic way with flourishes of red ink.

« 20th November, disorderly conduct, 12 lashes. 24th November, insolence to hospital attendant, diet reduced. 4th December, stealing cap from another prisoner, 12 lashes. 15th December, absenting himself at roll-call, two days' cells. 23d December, insolence and insubordination, two days' cells. 8th January, insolence and insubordination, 12 lashes. 20th January, insolence and insubordination, 12 lashes. 22d February, insolence and insubordination, 12 lashes and one week's solitary. 6th March, insolence and insubordination, 20 lashes. »

« That was the last ? » asked Frere.

« Yes, sir, » says Johnson.

« And then he — hum — did it ? »

« Just so, sir. That was the way of it. »

Just so! The magnificent system starved and tortured a child of twelve until he killed himself. That was the way of it. . . .

After the farce had been played again, and the children had stood up and sat down, and sung a hymn, and told how many twice five were, and repeated their belief in « One God the Father Almighty, maker of Heaven and earth, » the party reviewed the workshops, and saw the church, and went everywhere but into the room where the body of Peter Brown, aged twelve, lay starkly on its wooden bench, staring at the jail roof which was between it and heaven.

Just outside this room Sylvia met with a little adventure. Meekin had stopped behind, and Burgess being suddenly summoned for some official duty, Frere had gone with him, leaving his wife to rest on a bench that, placed at the summit of the cliff, overlooked the sea. While resting thus she became aware of another presence, and turning her head, beheld a small boy with his cap in one hand and a hammer in the other. The appearance of the little creature, clad in a uniform of gray cloth that was too large for him, and holding in his withered little hand a hammer that was too heavy for him, had something pathetic about it.

"What is it, you mite?" asked Sylvia.

"We thought you might have seen him, mum," said the little figure, opening its blue eyes with wonder at the kindness of the tone.

"Him? Whom?"

"Cranky Brown, mum," returned the child; "him as did it this morning. Me and Billy knowed him, mum; he was a mate of ours, and we wanted to know if he looked happy."

"What do you mean, child?" said she, with a strange terror at her heart; and then, filled with pity at the aspect of the little being, she drew him to her, with sudden womanly instinct, and kissed him.

He looked up at her with joyful surprise. "Oh!" he said.

Sylvia kissed him again.

"Does nobody ever kiss you, poor little man?" said she.

"Mother used to," was the reply; "but she's at home. Oh, mem," with a sudden crimsoning of the little face, "may I fetch Billy?"

And taking courage from the bright young face, he gravely marched to an angle of the rock, and brought out another little creature, with another gray uniform, and another hammer.

"This is Billy, mum," he said. "Billy never had no mother. Kiss Billy."

The young wife felt the tears rush to her eyes.

"You two poor babies!" she cried. And then, forgetting that she was a lady, dressed in silk and lace, she fell on her knees in the dust, and folding the friendless pair in her arms, wept over them.

"What is the matter, Sylvia?" said Frere, when he came up. "You've been crying."

"Nothing, Maurice; at least, I will tell you by-and-by."

When they were alone that evening she told him of the two little boys, and he laughed.

"Artful little humbugs," he said, and supported his argument by so many illustrations of the precocious wickedness of juvenile felons that his wife was half convinced against her will.

Unfortunately, when Sylvia went away, Tommy and Billy put into execution a plan which they had carried in their poor little heads for some weeks.

"I can do it now," said Tommy. "I feel strong."

"Will it hurt much, Tommy?" said Billy, who was not so courageous.

"Not so much as a whipping."

"I'm afraid! Oh, Tom, it's so deep! Don't leave me, Tom!"

The bigger boy took his little handkerchief from his neck, and with it bound his own left hand to his companion's right.

"Now I *can't* leave you."

"What was it the lady that kissed us said, Tommy?"

"Lord, have pity of them two fatherless children!" repeated Tommy.

"Let's say it, Tom."

And so the two babies knelt on the brink of the cliff, and raising the bound hands together, looked up at the sky, and ungrammatically said, "Lord, have pity on we two fatherless children." And then they kissed each other, and "did it."

THE VALLEY OF THE SHADOW OF DEATH

From 'His Natural Life'

IT was not until they had scrambled up the beach to safety that the absconders became fully aware of the loss of another of their companions. As they stood on the break of the beach, wringing the water from their clothes, Gabbett's small eye, counting their number, missed the stroke oar.

"Where's Cox?"

"The fool fell overboard," said Jemmy Vetch, shortly. "He never had as much sense in that skull of his as would keep it sound on his shoulders."

Gabbett scowled. "That's three of us gone," he said, in the tones of a man suffering some personal injury.

They summed up their means of defense against attack. Sanders and Greenhill had knives. Gabbett still retained the axe in his belt. Vetch had dropped his musket at the Neck; and Bodenham and Cornelius were unarmed.

"Let's have a look at the tucker," said Vetch.

There was but one bag of provisions. It contained a piece of salt pork, two loaves, and some uncooked potatoes. Signal Hill station was not rich in edibles.

"That ain't much," said the Crow, with rueful face. "Is it, Gabbett?"

"It must do, anyway," returned the giant, carelessly.

The inspection over, the six proceeded up the shore, and encamped under the lee of a rock. Bodenham was for lighting a fire; but Vetch, who by tacit consent had been chosen leader of the expedition, forbade it, saying that the light might betray them. "They'll think we're drowned, and won't pursue us," he said. So all that night the miserable wretches crouched fireless together.

Morning breaks clear and bright, and — free for the first time in ten years — they comprehend that their terrible journey has begun. "Where are we to go? How are we to live?" asks Bodenham, scanning the barren bush that stretches to the barren sea. "Gabbett, you've been out before — how's it done?"

"We'll make the shepherds' huts, and live on their tucker till we get a change o' clothes," said Gabbett, evading the main question. "We can follow the coast-line."

"Steady, lads," said prudent Vetch; "we must sneak round yon sandhills, and so creep into the scrub. If they've a good glass at the Neck, they can see us."

"It does seem close," said Bodenham, "I could pitch a stone on to the guard-house. Good-by, you bloody spot!" he adds, with sudden rage, shaking his fist vindictively at the penitentiary, "I don't want to see you no more till the Day o' Judgment."

Vetch divides the provisions, and they travel all that day until dark night. The scrub is prickly and dense. Their clothes are torn, their hands and feet bleeding. Already they feel outwearied. No one pursuing, they light a fire, and sleep. The second day they come to a sandy spit that runs out into the sea, and find that they have got too far to the eastward, and must follow the shore-line to East Bay Neck. Back through the scrub they drag their heavy feet. That night they eat the last crumb of the loaf. The third day at high noon, after some toilsome walking, they reach a big hill, now called Collins's Mount, and see the upper link of the ear-ring, the isthmus of East Bay

Neck, at their feet. A few rocks are on their right hand, and blue in the lovely distance lies hated Maria Island. "We must keep well to the eastward," said Greenhill, "or we shall fall in with the settlers and get taken." So, passing the isthmus, they strike into the bush along the shore, and tightening their belts over their gnawing bellies, camp under some low-lying hills.

The fourth day is notable for the indisposition of Bodenham, who is a bad walker, and falling behind, delays the party by frequent cooeys. Gabbett threatens him with a worse fate than sore feet if he lingers. Luckily, that evening Greenhill espies a hut; but not trusting to the friendship of the occupant, they wait until he quits it in the morning, and then send Vetch to forage. Vetch, secretly congratulating himself on having by his counsel prevented violence, returns bending under half a bag of flour. "You'd better carry the flour," said he to Gabbett, "and give me the axe." Gabbett eyes him for a while, as if struck by his puny form, but finally gives the axe to his mate Sanders. That day they creep along cautiously between the sea and the hills, camping at a creek. Vetch, after much search, finds a handful of berries, and adds them to the main stock. Half of this handful is eaten at once, the other half reserved for "to-morrow." The next day they come to an arm of the sea, and as they struggle northward Maria Island disappears, and with it all danger from telescopes. That evening they reach the camping-ground by twos and threes; and each wonders — between the paroxysms of hunger — if his face is as haggard and his eyes as blood-shot as those of his neighbor.

On the seventh day Bodenham says his feet are so bad he can't walk, and Greenhill, with a greedy look at the berries, bids him stay behind. Being in a very weak condition, he takes his companion at his word, and drops off about noon the next day. Gabbett, discovering this defection, however, goes back, and in an hour or so appears, driving the wretched creature before him with blows, as a sheep is driven to the shambles. Greenhill remonstrates at another mouth being thus forced upon the party, but the giant silences him with a hideous glance. Jemmy Vetch remembers that Greenhill accompanied Gabbett once before, and feels uncomfortable. He gives hint of his suspicions to Sanders, but Sanders only laughs. It is horribly evident that there is an understanding among the three.

The ninth sun of their freedom, rising upon sandy and barren hillocks, bristling thick with cruel scrub, sees the six famine-
stricken wretches cursing their God, and yet afraid to die.   All
round is the fruitless, shadeless, shelterless bush.   Above, the
pitiless heaven.   In the distance the remorseless sea.   Something
terrible must happen.   That gray wilderness, arched by gray
heaven stooping to gray sea, is a fitting keeper of hideous
secrets.   Vetch suggests that Oyster Bay cannot be far to the
eastward,— the line of ocean is deceitfully close,— and though
such a proceeding will take them out of their course, they
resolve to make for it.   After hobbling five miles they seem no
nearer than before, and nigh dead with fatigue and starvation,
sink despairingly upon the ground.   Vetch thinks Gabbett's eyes
have a wolfish glare in them, and instinctively draws off from
him.   Said Greenhill, in the course of a dismal conversation, "I
am so weak that I could eat a piece of a man."

On the tenth day Bodenham refuses to stir, and the others,
being scarcely able to drag along their limbs, sit on the ground
about him.   Greenhill, eyeing the prostrate man, said slowly, "I
have seen the same done before, boys, and it tasted like pork."

Vetch, hearing his savage comrade give utterance to a
thought all had secretly cherished, speaks out, crying, "It would
be murder to do it; and then perhaps we couldn't eat it."

"Oh," said Gabbett, with a grin, "I'll warrant you that; but
you must all have a hand in it."

Gabbett, Sanders, and Greenhill then go aside, and presently
Sanders, coming to the Crow, said, "He consented to act as
flogger.   He deserves it."

"So did Gabbett, for that matter," shudders Vetch.

"Ay, but Bodenham's feet are sore," said Sanders, "and 'tis
a pity to leave him."

Having no fire, they made a little break-wind; and Vetch,
half dozing behind this, at about three in the morning hears
some one cry out "Christ!" and awakes, sweating ice.

No one but Gabbett and Greenhill would eat that night.
That savage pair, however, make a fire, fling ghastly fragments
on the embers, and eat the broil before it is right warm.   In
the morning the frightful carcass is divided.

That day's march takes place in silence, and at the midday halt Cornelius volunteers to carry the billy, affecting great
restoration from the food.   Vetch gives it him, and in half an

hour afterward Cornelius is missing. Gabbett and Greenhill pursue him in vain, and return with curses. "He'll die like a dog," said Greenhill, "alone in the bush." Jemmy Vetch, with his intellect acute as ever, thinks that Cornelius prefers such a death to the one in store for him, but says nothing.

The twelfth morning dawns wet and misty, but Vetch, seeing the provision running short, strives to be cheerful, telling stories of men who have escaped greater peril. Vetch feels with dismay that he is the weakest of the party, but has some sort of ludicro-horrible consolation in remembering that he is also the leanest. They come to a creek that afternoon, and look until nightfall in vain for a crossing-place. The next day Gabbett and Vetch swim across, and Vetch directs Gabbett to cut a long sapling, which being stretched across the water, is seized by Greenhill and the Moocher, who are dragged over.

"What would you do without me?" said the Crow, with a ghastly grin.

They cannot kindle a fire, for Greenhill, who carries the tinder, has allowed it to get wet. The giant swings his axe in savage anger at enforced cold, and Vetch takes an opportunity to remark privately to him what a *big* man Greenhill is.

On the fourteenth day they can scarcely crawl, and their limbs pain them. Greenhill, who is the weakest, sees Gabbett and the Moocher go aside to consult, and crawling to the Crow, whimpers, "For God's sake, Jemmy, don't let 'em murder me!"

"I can't help you," says Vetch, looking about in terror. "Think of poor Tom Bodenham."

"But he was no murderer. If they kill me, I shall go to hell with Tom's blood on my soul."

He writhes on the ground in sickening terror, and Gabbett, arriving, bids Vetch bring wood for the fire. Vetch going, sees Greenhill clinging to wolfish Gabbett's knees, and Sanders calls after him, "You will hear it presently, Jem."

The nervous Crow puts his hands to his ears, but is conscious, nevertheless, of a dull crash and a groan. When he comes back, Gabbett is putting on the dead man's shoes, which are better than his own.

"We'll stop here a day or so and rest," said he, "now we've got provisions."

Two more days pass, and the three, eying each other suspiciously, resume their march. The third day—the sixteenth of

their awful journey — such portions of the carcass as they have
with them prove unfit to eat.   They look into each other's famine-
sharpened faces, and wonder "Who next?"

"We must all die together," said Sanders, quickly, "before
anything else must happen."

Vetch marks the terror concealed in the words, and when the
dreaded giant is out of ear-shot, says, "For God's sake, let's go
on alone, Alick.   You see what sort of a cove that Gabbett is,—
he'd kill his father before he'd fast one day."

They made for the bush, but the giant turned and strode
toward them.   Vetch skipped nimbly on one side, but Gabbett
struck the Moocher on the forehead with the axe.   "Help! Jem,
help!" cried the victim, cut but not fatally, and in the strength
of his desperation tore the axe from the monster who bore it,
and flung it to Vetch.   "Keep it, Jemmy," he cried; "let's have
no more murder done!"

They fare again through the horrible bush until nightfall,
when Vetch, in a strange voice, called the giant to him.

"He must die."

"Either you or he," laughs Gabbett.   "Give me the axe."

"No, no," said the Crow, his thin malignant face distorted
by a horrible resolution.   "I'll keep the axe.   Stand back!   You
shall hold him, and I'll do the job."

Sanders, seeing them approach, knew his end had come, and
submitted, crying, "Give me half an hour to pray for myself."
They consent, and the bewildered wretch knelt down and
folded his hands like a child.   His big stupid face worked with
emotion.   His great cracked lips moved in desperate agony.
He wagged his head from side to side, in pitiful confusion of
his brutalized senses.   "I can't think o' the words, Jem!"

"Pah," snarled the cripple, swinging the axe, "we can't
starve here all night."

Four days had passed, and the two survivors of this awful
journey sat watching each other.   The gaunt giant, his eyes
gleaming with hate and hunger, sat sentinel over the dwarf.
The dwarf, chuckling at his superior sagacity, clutched the fatal
axe.   For two days they had not spoken to each other.   For two
days each had promised himself that on the next his companion
must *sleep* — and die.   Vetch comprehended the devilish scheme
of the monster who had entrapped five of his fellow-beings to
aid him by their deaths to his own safety, and held aloof.

Gabbett watched to snatch the weapon from his companion, and make the odds even for once and forever. In the daytime they traveled on, seeking each a pretext to creep behind the other. In the night-time when they feigned slumber, each stealthily raising a head caught the wakeful glance of his companion. Vetch felt his strength deserting him, and his brain overpowered by fatigue. Surely the giant, muttering, gesticulating, and slavering at the mouth, was on the road to madness. Would the monster find opportunity to rush at him, and braving the blood-stained axe, kill him by main force? or would he sleep, and be himself a victim? Unhappy Vetch! It is the terrible privilege of insanity to be sleepless.

On the fifth day, Vetch, creeping behind a tree, takes off his belt, and makes a noose. He will hang himself. He gets one end of the belt over a bough, and then his cowardice bids him pause. Gabbett approaches; he tries to evade him, and steal away into the bush. In vain. The insatiable giant, ravenous with famine and sustained by madness, is not to be shaken off. Vetch tries to run, but his legs bend under him. The axe that has tried to drink so much blood feels heavy as lead. He will fling it away. No—he dares not. Night falls again. He must rest, or go mad. His limbs are powerless. His eyelids are glued together. He sleeps as he stands. This horrible thing must be a dream. He is at Port Arthur, or will wake on his pallet in the penny lodging-house he slept at when a boy. Is that the deputy come to wake him to the torment of living? It is not time—surely not time yet. He sleeps—and the giant, grinning with ferocious joy, approaches on clumsy tiptoe and seizes the coveted axe.

On the northeast coast of Van Diemen's Land is a place called St. Helen's Point, and a certain skipper, being in want of fresh water, landing there with a boat's crew, found on the banks of the creek a gaunt and blood-stained man, clad in tattered yellow, who carried on his back an axe and a bundle. When the sailors came within sight of him he made signs to them to approach, and opening his bundle with much ceremony, offered them some of its contents. Filled with horror at what the maniac displayed, they seized and bound him. At Hobart Town he was recognized as the only survivor of the nine desperadoes who had escaped from Colonel Arthur's "natural penitentiary."

MATTHIAS CLAUDIUS

(1740–1815)

ATTHIAS CLAUDIUS, best known as "the Wandsbecker Bote" (the Messenger from Wandsbeck), was born at Reinfeld in Holstein, August 15th, 1740. He was of excellent stock, coming from a long line of clergymen. It was said that scarcely another family in Schleswig-Holstein had given to the church so many sons.

There is but little to record of the quiet boyhood passed in the picturesque stillness of the North German village. At the outset the education of Claudius was conducted by his father, the village pastor. From beginning to end his life was simple, moderate, and well ordered. After finishing his school days at Ploen, he entered the University of Jena (1759), with the intention of studying theology, in order to follow the traditions of the family and enter the ministry. This idea he was soon obliged to relinquish on account of a pulmonary weakness, and he turned instead to the study of jurisprudence. His strongest attraction was towards literature. He became a member of the literary guild in Jena; and later, when he had attained fame as the "Wandsbecker Bote," he was intimately associated with Voss, F. L. Stolberg, Herder, and others of the Göttingen fraternity. His first verses, published in Jena in 1763, under the title 'Tändeleien und Erzählungen' (Trifles and Tales), gave no indication of his talents, and were no more than the usual student efforts of unconscious imitation; they have absolutely no poetic value, and are interesting only as they indicate a stage of development. In editing his works in later years, Claudius preserved of this early poetry only one song, 'An eine Quelle' (To a Spring).

MATTHIAS CLAUDIUS

After leaving the university in 1764, he took a position as private secretary to Count Holstein in Copenhagen; and here, under the powerful influence of Klopstock, whose friendship was at this time the most potent element of his life, and in the brilliant circle which that poet had drawn around him, Claudius entered fully into the life of sentiment and ideas which conduced so largely to his intellectual development. Some years later, after a fallow period spent in the quiet of his father's house at Reinfeld, he settled at Wandsbeck, near Altona (1771), where in connection with Bode he published the Wandsbecker Bote, the popular weekly periodical so indissolubly associated with his name. His contributions under the name of "Asmus" found everywhere the warmest acceptance. In 1775, through Herder's recommendation, Claudius was appointed Chief Land Commissioner at Darmstadt; but circumstances rendering the position uncongenial, he returned to his beloved Wandsbeck, where he supported his family by his pen until 1788, when Crown Prince Frederick of Denmark appointed him revisor of the Holstein Bank at Altona. He died in Hamburg, January 1st, 1815, in the house of his son-in-law, the bookseller Perthes.

A collection of his works, with the title 'Asmus omnia sua secum portans, oder Sämmtliche Werke des Wandsbecker Boten' (The Collected Works of the Wandsbeck Messenger), appeared at Hamburg, 1775–1812. These collected works comprise songs, romances, fables, poems, letters, etc., originally published in various places. The translation of Saint Martin and Fénelon marked the pietistic spirit of his later years, and is in strong contrast to the exuberance which produced the 'Rheinweinlied' (Rhine Wine Song) and 'Urian's Reise um die Welt' (Urian's Journey around the World).

Claudius as a poet won the hearts of his countrymen. His verses express his idyllic love of nature and his sympathy with rustic life. The poet and the man are one. His pure and simple style appealed to the popular taste, and some of his lyrics have become genuine folk-songs.

SPECULATIONS ON NEW YEAR'S DAY

From the Wandsbecker Bote

A HAPPY new year! A happy new year to my dear country, the land of old integrity and truth! A happy new year to friends and enemies, Christians and Turks, Hottentots and Cannibals! To all on whom God permits his sun to rise and his rain to fall! Also to the poor negro slaves who have to work all day in the hot sun. It's wholly a glorious day, the New Year's Day! At other times I can bear that a man should be a little bit patriotic, and not make court to other nations. True, one must not speak evil of any nation. The wiser part are everywhere silent; and who would revile a whole nation for the

sake of the loud ones? As I said, I can bear at other times
that a man should be a little patriotic: but on New Year's Day
my patriotism is dead as a mouse, and it seems to me on that
day as if we were all brothers, and had one Father who is in
heaven; as if all the goods of the world were water which God
has created for all men, as I once heard it said.

And so I am accustomed, every New Year's morning, to sit
down on a stone by the wayside, to scratch with my staff in the
sand before me, and to think of this and of that. Not of my
readers. I hold them in all honor: but on New Year's morning,
on the stone by the wayside, I think not of them; but I sit
there and think that during the past year I saw the sun rise so
often, and the moon,—that I saw so many rainbows and flowers,
and breathed the air so often, and drank from the brook,—and
then I do not like to look up, and I take with both hands my
cap from my head and look into that.

Then I think also of my acquaintances who have died during
the year; and how they can talk now with Socrates and Numa,
and other men of whom I have heard so much good, and with
John Huss. And then it seems as if graves opened round me,
and shadows with bald crowns and long gray beards came out of
them and shook the dust out of their beards. That must be the
work of the "Everlasting Huntsman," who has his doings about
the twelfth. The old pious long-beards would fain sleep. But a
glad new year to your memory and to the ashes in your graves!

RHINE WINE

WITH laurel wreathe the glass's vintage mellow,
    And drink it gayly dry!
  Through farthest Europe, know, my worthy fellow,
    For such in vain ye'll try.

Nor Hungary nor Poland e'er could boast it;
    And as for Gallia's vine,
Saint Veit the Ritter, if he choose, may toast it,—
    We Germans love the Rhine.

Our fatherland we thank for such a blessing,
    And many more beside;
And many more, though little show possessing,
    Well worth our love and pride.

Not everywhere the vine bedecks our border,
      As well the mountains show,
That harbor in their bosoms foul disorder;
      Not worth their room below.

Thuringia's hills, for instance, are aspiring
      To rear a juice like wine;
But that is all; nor mirth nor song inspiring,
      It breathes not of the vine.

And other hills, with buried treasures glowing,
      For wine are far too cold;
Though iron ores and cobalt there are growing,
      And 'chance some paltry gold.

The Rhine,— the Rhine,— there grow the gay plantations!
      Oh, hallowed be the Rhine!
Upon his banks are brewed the rich potations
      Of this consoling wine.

Drink to the Rhine! and every coming morrow
      Be mirth and music thine!
And when we meet a child of care and sorrow,
      We'll send him to the Rhine.

WINTER

A Song to Be Sung Behind the Stove

OLD Winter is the man for me —
      Stout-hearted, sound, and steady;
   Steel nerves and bones of brass hath he:
      Come snow, come blow, he's ready!

If ever man was well, 'tis he;
   He keeps no fire in his chamber,
And yet from cold and cough is free
   In bitterest December.

He dresses him out-doors at morn,
   Nor needs he first to warm him;
Toothache and rheumatis' he'll scorn,
   And colic don't alarm him.

In summer, when the woodland rings,
   He asks " What mean these noises?"

Warm sounds he hates, and all warm things
    Most heartily despises.

But when the fox's bark is loud;
    When the bright hearth is snapping;
When children round the chimney crowd,
    All shivering and clapping;—

When stone and bone with frost do break,
    And pond and lake are cracking,—
Then you may see his old sides shake,
    Such glee his frame is racking.

Near the North Pole, upon the strand,
    He has an icy tower;
Likewise in lovely Switzerland
    He keeps a summer bower.

So up and down—now here—now there—
    His regiments manoeuvre;
When he goes by, we stand and stare,
    And cannot choose but shiver.

NIGHT SONG

THE moon is up in splendor,
    And golden stars attend her;
        The heavens are calm and bright;
Trees cast a deepening shadow;
And slowly off the meadow
    A mist is rising silver-white.

Night's curtains now are closing
Round half a world, reposing
    In calm and holy trust;
All seems one vast, still chamber,
Where weary hearts remember
    No more the sorrows of the dust.

                    Translations of Charles T. Brooks.

HENRY CLAY.

HENRY CLAY

(1777–1852)

BY JOHN R. PROCTER

ENRY CLAY must not be judged as an orator by his reported speeches, which are but skeletons of the masterly originals, but by the lasting effect of these speeches on those who heard them, and by his ability as an originator of important measures and his success in carrying these measures to a conclusion by convincing and powerful oratory. Judged by his achievements and by his wide-spread influence, he must take rank as a statesman and orator of pre-eminent ability. The son of a poor Baptist clergyman, with but scant advantages for acquiring an education; leaving home at an early age and going among strangers to a community where family ties and social connections were a controlling element;—this poor boy, with no family influence, assumed at once, by sheer force of character and ability, a leadership which he held undisputed until his death. And years after he had passed away, it was the "followers of Henry Clay" who kept Kentucky from joining the States of the South in their unsuccessful efforts to withdraw from the Union.

Of his oratory Robert C. Winthrop wrote after a lapse of years: "I can only bear witness to an impressiveness of speech never exceeded, if ever equaled, within an experience of half a century, during which I have listened to many of the greatest orators on both sides of the Atlantic." As a parliamentary leader, Rhodes calls him the greatest in our history. "His leadership," says Mr. Schurz, "was not of that mean order which merely contrives to organize a personal following; it was the leadership of a statesman zealously striving to promote great public interests."

As a presiding officer he was the most commanding Speaker the National House of Representatives has ever had. Winthrop, who served long with him in Congress, said of him:—"No abler or more commanding presiding officer ever sat in the Speaker's chair on either side of the Atlantic. Prompt, dignified, resolute, fearless, he had a combination of intellectual and physical qualities which made him a natural ruler over men." He was six times elected Speaker, sometimes almost by acclamation; and during the many years which he presided over the House not one of his decisions was ever reversed.

VII—236

As a Secretary of State, during his term of four years the treaties with foreign countries negotiated by him exceeded in numbers all that had been negotiated by other secretaries, during the previous thirty-five years of our constitutional history. As a diplomat, he showed himself at Ghent more than a match for the trained diplomatists of the old world.

And with all these he was—at his ideal country home, Ashland, surrounded by wooded lawns and fertile acres of beautiful blue-grass land—a most successful farmer and breeder of thoroughbred stock, from the Scotch collie to the thoroughbred race-horse. I have been told by one who knew him as a farmer that no one could guess nearer to the weight of a Shorthorn bullock than he. He was as much at home with horses and horsemen as with senators and diplomats. I have known many men who were friends and followers of Mr. Clay, and from the love and veneration these men had for his memory, I can well understand why the historian Rhodes says, "No man has been loved as the people of the United States loved Henry Clay."

Clay seemed to have had honors and leadership thrust upon him. Arriving in Kentucky in 1797, he at once advocated the gradual emancipation of slaves, regardless of the strong prejudices to the contrary of the rich slaveholding community in which he had cast his lot; yet, unsolicited on his part, this community elected him to the State Legislature by a large majority in 1803, and before three years of service he was chosen by his fellow members to fill a vacancy in the United States Senate. And until his death in 1852, his constituents in Kentucky vied with each other in their desires to keep him as their representative in either the national Senate or House of Representatives. He entered the latter in 1811, and was selected as Speaker of that body almost by acclamation on the first day of his taking his seat. After a long life spent in his country's service he was elected *unanimously* to the Senate in 1848, despite party strife and the fact that the two parties were almost evenly divided in Kentucky.

No attempt can here be made to even recapitulate the events of importance connected with his long public services. I will call attention only to some of the most important measures which he carried by his magnificent leadership.

WAR OF 1812

Clay assumed the leadership of those who urged resistance to the unjust and overbearing encroachments of Great Britain, and he more than any one else was instrumental in overcoming opposition and forcing a declaration of war. This war — a second war for independence, which changed this country from a disjointed confederacy liable to fall asunder, to a compact, powerful, and self-respecting Union — will ever be regarded as one of the crowning glories of his long and brilliant career. He proved more than a match in debate for Randolph, Quincy, and other able advocates for peace. When asked what we were to gain by war, he answered, "What are we not to lose by peace? Commerce, character, — a nation's best treasure, honor!"

In answer to the arguments that certificates of protection authorized by Congress were fraudulently used, his magnificent answer, "The colors that float from the mast-head should be the credentials of our seamen," electrified the patriots of the country. There is but a meagre report of this great speech, but the effect produced was overwhelming and bore down all opposition. It is said that men of both parties, forgetting all antipathies under the spell of his eloquence, wept together. Mr. Clay's first speech on entering Congress was in favor of the encouragement of domestic manufactures, mainly as a defensive measure in anticipation of a war with Great Britain; arguing that whatever doubts might be entertained as to the general policy of encouraging domestic manufactures by import duties, none could exist regarding the propriety of adopting measures for producing such articles as are requisite in times of war. If his measure for the increase of the standing army had been adopted in time, the humiliating reverses on land during the early part of the war would have been averted. He carried through a bill for the increase of the navy, and the brilliant naval victories of the war of 1812 followed. In the debate on the bill to provide for a standing army, it was argued that twenty-five thousand could not be had in the United States. Clay aroused the people of Kentucky to such enthusiasm that fifteen thousand men volunteered in that State alone, and members of Congress shouldered their muskets and joined the ranks.

TREATY OF GHENT

Henry Clay's faith in the destiny of his country, and his heroic determination that a continuation of the war was preferable to the terms proposed, prevented humiliating concessions. The American Commissioners were Henry Clay, John Quincy Adams, Albert Gallatin, James A. Bayard, and Jonathan Russell, and the British Commissioners Lord Gambier, Henry Goulbourn, and William Adams. The news received by Clay on his arrival in Europe was not calculated to inspire him with hope. From Mr. Bayard he received a letter (dated April 20th, 1814) with news of the triumph of the allies over Napoleon, and stating:—

« There is reason to think that it has materially changed the views of the British Ministry. . . . The great augmentation of their disposable force presents an additional temptation to prosecute the war. »

By the same mail Mr. Gallatin writes from London (April 22d, 1814):—

« You are sufficiently aware of the total change in our affairs produced by the late revolution, and by the restoration of universal peace in the European world, from which we are alone excluded. A well-organized and large army is at once liberated from any European employment, and ready, together with a superabundant naval force, to act independently against us. How ill prepared we are to meet it in a proper manner, no one knows better than yourself; but above all, our own divisions and the hostile attitude of the Eastern States give room to apprehend that a continuation of the war might prove vitally fatal to the United States. »

Mr. Russell writes from Stockholm (July 2d, 1814):—

« My distress at the delay which our joint errand has encountered has almost been intolerable, and the kind of comfort I have received from Mr. Adams has afforded very little relief. His apprehensions are rather of a gloomy cast with regard to the result of our labors. »

Mr. Crawford, our Minister to France, who with Clay favored a vigorous prosecution of the war, writes to him (July 4th, 1814):—

« I am thoroughly convinced that the United States can never be called upon to treat under circumstances less auspicious than those which exist at the present moment, unless our internal bickerings shall continue to weaken the effects of the government. »

With discouraging news from home, the seat of government taken, and the Capitol burned, the Eastern States opposing the war and threatening to withdraw from the Union, and his fellow commissioners in the despondent mood evidenced by the above-quoted letters,—it is amazing that Clay, whom some historians have called a compromiser by nature, opposed any and all concessions and wished that the war should go on.

By the third article of the treaty of 1783 it was agreed that citizens of the United States should not fish in the waters or cure fish on the land of any of the maritime provinces north of the United States after they were settled, without a previous agreement with the inhabitants or possessors of the ground.

By the eighth article of the same treaty, it was agreed that the navigation of the Mississippi River should *ever* remain free and open to the subjects of Great Britain and the United States. It was then supposed that the British Canadian possessions included the head-waters of this river. By the Jay treaty of 1794 this was confirmed, and "that all ports and places on its eastern side, to whichsoever of the parties belonging, might be freely resorted to and used by both parties." At this time Spain possessed the sovereignty of the west side of the river, and both sides from its mouth to 31° north latitude. The United States acquired by the Louisiana purchase of 1803 all the sovereignty of Spain which had previously been acquired by France.

Gallatin proposed to insert a provision for the renewal to the United States of the rights in the fisheries, and as an equivalent to give to Great Britain the right to the navigation of the Mississippi River. This was favored by Gallatin, Adams, and Bayard, and opposed by Clay and Russell. Mr. Clay, seeing that he was in a minority, stated that he would affix his name to no treaty which contained such a provision. After his firm stand Mr. Bayard left the majority. Clay's "obstinacy" in opposing concessions is well shown in Mr. Adams's Journal:—

"To this last article [the right of the British to navigate the Mississippi River] Mr. Clay makes strong objections. He is willing to leave the matter of the fisheries as a nest-egg for another war. . . . He considers it a privilege much too important to be conceded for the mere liberty of drying fish upon a desert, but the Mississippi was destined to form a most important part of the interests of the American Union. . . . Mr. Clay, of all the members, had alone been urgent to present an article stipulating the abolition of impressment. Mr. Clay lost his temper, as he generally does whenever the right of the British to navigate the Mississippi is discussed. . . .

"December 11th. He [Clay] was for war three years longer. He had no doubt but three years more of war would make us a warlike people, and that then we should come out of the war with honor. . . . December 22d. At last he turned to me, and asked me whether I would not join him now and break off negotiations."

After five months of weary negotiations under most adverse conditions so far as the American commissioners were concerned, the treaty was signed on December 24th, 1814. During all these months Clay had resisted any and all concessions, and none were made. The Marquis of Wellesley declared in the House of Lords that the American commissioners had shown a most astonishing superiority over the British during the whole of the correspondence.

During Mr. Clay's absence at Ghent, his admiring constituents returned him to Congress by an almost unanimous vote. A year later in Congress, Clay referred to his part in the bringing on the war as follows:—

« I gave a vote for a declaration of war. I exerted all the little influence and talent I could command to make the war. The war was made. It is terminated. And I declare with perfect sincerity, if it had been permitted to me to lift the veil of futurity and to foresee the precise series of events which had occurred, my vote would have been unchanged. We had been insulted and outraged and spoliated upon by almost all Europe,— by Great Britain, by France, Spain, Denmark, Naples, and to cap the climax, by the little contemptible power of Algiers. We had submitted too long and too much. We had become the scorn of foreign powers and the derision of our own citizens. What have we gained by the war? Let any man look at the degraded condition of this country before the war, the scorn of the universe, the contempt of ourselves; and tell me if we have gained nothing by the war? What is our situation now? Respectability and character abroad, security and confidence at home. »

Clay more than any other man forced the war. It was the successful military hero of this war — the victor of New Orleans — who defeated him in after years for the Presidency.

MISSOURI COMPROMISE

The heated struggle in Congress over the admission of Missouri into the Union first brought prominently forward the agitation of the slavery question. This struggle, which lasted from 1818 to 1821, threatened the very existence of the Union. Jefferson wrote from Monticello:—

« The Missouri question is the most portentous one that has ever threatened the Union. In the gloomiest moments of the Revolutionary War I never had any apprehension equal to that I feel from this source. »

Mr. Schurz, writing of the feeling at the time, says:—

« While thus the thought of dissolving the Union occurred readily to the Southern mind, the thought of maintaining the government and preserving the Union by means of force hardly occurred to anybody. It seemed to be taken for granted on all sides that if the Southern States insisted on cutting loose from the Union, nothing could be done but to let them go. »

The two sections were at this time so evenly balanced that the maintenance of the Union by force could not have been successfully attempted. The compromise which admitted Missouri to the Union as a slave State, and recognized the right of settlers to carry slaves into the territory south of 36° 30', was carried through by the splendid leadership of Clay, who thus earned the title of "the great pacificator." Future historians will accord to him the title of the savior of the Union.

Upon the adoption of the compromise measures Mr. Clay resigned his seat in Congress to give his attention to his private affairs, being financially embarrassed by indorsing for a friend. During his stay at home there was a fierce controversy over the issue of paper money and relief measures to favor debtors who had become involved through the recklessness following such inflation. Against what seemed to be an overwhelming popular feeling, Clay arrayed himself on the side of sound money and sound finance. In 1823 he was again returned to the House of Representatives without opposition, and was chosen Speaker by a vote of 139 to 42.

INTERNAL IMPROVEMENTS

Soon after his entrance into Congress Clay took advanced ground in favor of building roads, improving water-ways, and constructing canals by the general government, in order to connect the seaboard States with the "boundless empire" of the growing West. He became the leader, the foremost champion, of a system which was bitterly opposed by some of the ablest statesmen of the time as unauthorized by the Constitution. Clay triumphed, and during his long public service was the recognized leader of a system which though opposed at first, has been accepted as a national policy by both of the great political parties. That he was actuated by a grand conception of the future destiny of the country, and the needs of such improvements to insure a more perfect union, his able speeches on these questions will show. In one he said:—

« Every man who looks at the Constitution in the spirit to entitle him to the character of statesman, must elevate his views to the height to which this nation is destined to reach in the rank of nations. We are not legislating for this moment only, or for the present generation, or for the present populated limits of the United States; but our acts must embrace a wider scope,— reaching northward to the Pacific and southwardly to the river Del Norte. Imagine this extent of territory with sixty or seventy or a hundred millions of people. The powers which exist now will exist then; and those which will exist then exist now. . . . What was the object of the Convention in framing the Constitution? The leading object was UNION,— Union, then peace. Peace external and internal, and commerce, but more particularly union and peace, the great objects of the framers of the Constitution, should be kept steadily in view in the interpretation of any clause of it; and when it is susceptible of various interpretation, that construction should be preferred which tends to promote the objects of the framers of the Constitution, to the consolidation of the Union. . . . No man deprecates more than I do the idea of consolidation; yet between separation and consolidation, painful as would be the alternative, I should greatly prefer the latter. »

Congress now appropriates yearly for internal improvements a sum far greater than the entire revenue of the government at the time Clay made this speech.

SPANISH-AMERICAN INDEPENDENCE

It was but natural that Clay's ardent nature and his love of liberty would incline him to aid the people of Central and South America in their efforts to free themselves from Spanish oppression and misrule. Effective here as in all things undertaken by him, his name must always be linked with the cause of Southern American independence. Richard Rush, writing from London to Clay in 1825, says: "The South-Americans owe to you, more than to any other man of either hemisphere, their independence." His speeches, translated into Spanish, were read to the revolutionary armies, and "his name was a household name among the patriots." Bolivar, writing to him from Bogotá in 1827, says:—"All America, Colombia, and myself, owe your Excellency our purest gratitude for the incomparable services which you have rendered to us, by sustaining our cause with sublime enthusiasm."

In one of his speeches on this subject Clay foreshadows a great American Zollverein. The failure of the Spanish-American republics to attain the high ideals hoped for by Clay caused him deep regret in after years.

THE AMERICAN SYSTEM

The tariff law of 1824 was another triumph of Clay's successful leadership, since which time he has been called the father of what has been termed the "American System." It must be remembered that Clay was first led to propose protective duties in order to prepare this country for a war which he felt could not be avoided without loss of national honor. When in 1824 he advocated increased tariff duties in order to foster home industries, protection was universal; even our agricultural products were excluded from British markets by the Corn Laws. The man who would now advocate in Congress duties as low as those levied by the tariff law of 1824, would be called by protectionists of the present day a free-trader. When in 1833 nullification of the tariff laws was threatened, Clay, while demanding that the laws should be enforced and that if necessary nullification should be put down by the strong arm of the government, feared that the growing discontent of the South and the obstinacy of a military President threatened the Union, introduced and carried to a conclusion a compromise tariff measure that brought peace to the country.

SECRETARY OF STATE

It was unfortunate that Clay temporarily relinquished his leadership in Congress to accept the premiership in the Cabinet of President Adams. Although the exacting official duties were not congenial, and proved injurious to his health, his administration of this high office was brilliant and able, as is well attested by the number of important treaties concluded, and by his brilliant state papers. His instructions to the United States delegates to the Panama Congress of American Republics will grow in importance in the years to come, because of the broad principles there enunciated,—that private property should be exempt from seizure on the high seas in times of war.

His chivalrous loyalty to President Adams was fully appreciated, and his friendship reciprocated. After the close of his administration Mr. Adams in a speech said:—

«As to my motives for tendering him the Department of State when I did, let the man who questions them come forward. Let him look around among the statesmen and legislators of the nation and of that day. Let him select and name the man whom, by his pre-eminent talents, by his splendid services, by his ardent patriotism, by his all-embracing public spirit, by his fervid eloquence in behalf of the rights and liberties of mankind, by his long experience in the affairs of the Union, foreign and domestic, a President of the United States intent only upon the honor and welfare of his country ought to have preferred to Henry Clay.»

Just before the close of his administration President Adams offered him a position on the bench of the Supreme Court, which he declined.

HIS POSITION ON AFRICAN SLAVERY

Clay was a slaveholder,—a kind master,—but through his entire public life an open advocate of emancipation. He probably received his early predilections against slavery from his association with Chancellor Wythe, before removing from Virginia, as indeed the best part of his education probably came from personal contact with that able man. The intellectual forces of the border slave States were arrayed in favor of emancipation, until, as Clay writes with some feeling in 1849, they were driven to an opposite course "by the violent and indiscreet course of ultra abolitionists in the North"; but Clay remained to his death hopeful that by peaceable means his country might be rid of this great evil. In the letter above quoted, writing of his failure to establish a system of gradual emancipation in Kentucky, he says:—

« It is a consoling reflection that although a system of gradual emancipation cannot be established, slavery is destined inevitably to extinction by the
operation of peaceful and natural causes. And it is also gratifying to believe
that there will not be probably much difference in the period of its existence,
whether it terminates legally or naturally. The chief difference in the two
modes is that according to the first, we should take hold of the institution
intelligently and dispose of it cautiously and safely; while according to the
other it will some day or other take hold of us, and constrain us in some
manner or other to get rid of it. »

As early as 1798, he made his first political speeches in Kentucky
advocating an amendment to the State Constitution, providing for
the gradual emancipation of the slaves. Referring to the failure to
adopt this amendment, he said in a speech delivered in the capital
of Kentucky in 1829: —

« I shall never cease to regret a decision, the effects of which have been
to place us in the rear of our neighbors who are exempt from slavery, in the
state of agriculture, the progress of manufactures, the advance of improvements, and the general progress of society. »

In these days, when public men who should be leaders bend to
what they believe to be the popular wishes, the example of Clay, in
his bold disregard of the prejudices and property interests of his
constituents, is inspiring.

George W. Prentice was sent from New England to Kentucky to
write a life of Clay, and writing in 1830 he says: —

« Whenever a slave brought an action at law for his liberty, Mr. Clay
volunteered as his advocate, and it is said that in the whole course of his
practice he never failed to obtain a verdict in the slave's favor. . . . He
has been the slaves' friend through life. In all stations he has pleaded the
cause of African freedom without fear from high or low. To him more than
to any other individual is to be ascribed the great revolution which has taken
place upon this subject — a revolution whose wheels must continue to move
onward till they reach the goal of universal freedom. »

Three years before this was written, Clay in a speech before the
Colonization Society said: —

« If I could be instrumental in eradicating this deepest stain upon the
character of my country, and removing all cause of reproach on account of it
by foreign nations; if I could only be instrumental in ridding of this foul
blot that revered State which gave me birth, or that not less beloved State
which kindly adopted me as her son, I would not exchange the proud satisfaction which I should enjoy for the honor of all the triumphs ever decreed
to the most successful conqueror. »

He longed to add the imperial domain of Texas to this country, but feared that it would so strengthen the slave power as to

endanger the Union; and when finally he yielded to the inevitable, the Free-Soilers threw their votes to Birney and thus defeated Clay for the Presidency. He deprecated the war with Mexico, yet gave his favorite son as a soldier, who fell at Buena Vista. He stood for the reception of anti-slavery petitions by Congress, against the violent opposition of the leading men of his own section. He continued steadfast to the end, writing in 1849 that if slavery were, as claimed, a blessing, "the principle on which it is maintained would require that one portion of the white race should be reduced to bondage to serve another portion of the same race, when black subjects of slavery could not be obtained." He proposed reasonable schemes for gradual emancipation and deportation, which would, if adopted, have averted the war and settled peaceably the serious problem. He warned the Southerners in 1849 that their demands were unreasonable, and would "lead to the formation of a sectional Northern party, which will sooner or later take permanent and exclusive possession of the Government."

Seeming inconsistencies in Mr. Clay's record on this subject will disappear with a full understanding of the difficulties of his position. Living in a State midway between the North and South, where slavery existed in its mildest and least objectionable form, yet fully alive to its evils, recognizing that the grave problem requiring solution was not alone slavery, but the presence among a free people of a numerous, fecund, servile, alien race; realizing that one section of the country, then relatively too powerful to be ignored, was ready to withdraw from the Union rather than to submit to laws that would endanger slavery; loving the Union with an ardor not excelled by that of any public man in our history; wishing and striving for the emancipation of the slaves, yet too loyal to the Union to follow the more zealous advocates of freedom in their "higher law than the Constitution" crusade,— Mr. Clay in his whole course on this question was consistent and patriotic in the highest degree.

The Compromise of 1850

The crowning triumph of a long life of great achievements was his great compromise measures of 1850. These, with their predecessors of 1821 and 1833, have caused some writers to speak of Clay as a man of compromising nature. The reverse is true. Bold, aggressive, uncompromising, and often dictatorial by nature, he favored compromise when convinced that only by such means could civil war or a disruption of the Union be averted. And he was right. He averted a conflict or separation from the Union when the relative strength of the South was such as to have rendered impossible the preservation of the Union by force. The Constitution was a compromise, without which there would have been no union of States. That the compromise did not long survive him was no fault of Clay's, but chargeable to the agitators of both sections, who cared less for the Union than for their pet theories or selfish interests.

Two years after his death the compromise measures were repealed, and the most destructive civil war of modern times and a long list of resultant evils are the result. Those who knew Henry Clay and had felt his wonderful power as a leader, are firm in the belief that had he been alive and in the possession of his faculties in 1861, the Civil War would have been averted. His name and the memory of his love for the Union restrained his adopted State from joining the South.

The struggle over the passage of the compromise measures, lasting for seven months, was one of the most memorable parliamentary struggles on record. The old hero, Henry Clay, broken in health, with the stamp of death upon him, for six weary months led the fight with much of his old-time fire and ability. Sustained by indomitable will and supreme love of country, "I am here," he said, "expecting soon to go hence, and owing no responsibility but to my own conscience and to God."

In his opening speech, which lasted for two days, he said:—

"I owe it to myself to say that no earthly power could induce me to vote for a specific measure for the introduction of slavery where it had not before existed, either south or north of that line. Sir, while you reproach, and justly too, our British ancestors for the introduction of this institution upon the continent of America, I am for one unwilling that the posterity of the present inhabitants of California and New Mexico shall reproach us for doing just what we reproach Great Britain for doing to us."

He upbraided on the one hand the ultra abolitionists as reckless agitators, and hurled defiance at disunionists of the South, while at the same time appealing to the loftier nature and patriotic impulses of his hearers:—

"I believe from the bottom of my soul that this measure is the reunion of the Union. And now let us discard all resentments, all passions, all petty jealousies, all personal desires, all love of peace, all hungering after gilded crumbs which fall from the table of power. Let us forget popular fears, from whatever quarter they may spring. Let us go to the fountain of unadulterated patriotism, and performing a solemn lustration, return divested of all selfish, sinister, and sordid impurities, and think alone of our God, our country, our conscience, and our glorious Union."

As described by Bancroft, Clay was "in stature over six feet, spare and long-limbed; he stood erect as if full of vigor and vitality, and ever ready to command. His countenance expressed perpetual wakefulness and activity. His voice was music itself, and yet penetrating and far-reaching, enchanting the listeners; his words flowed rapidly without sing-song or mannerism, in a clear and steady stream. Neither in public nor in private did he know how to be dull."

Bold, fearless, commanding, the lordliest leader of his day, he was yet gentle, and as an old friend wrote, "was the most emotional man I ever knew. I have seen his eyes fill instantly on shaking the hand of an old friend, however obscure, who had stood by him in his early struggles." The manliest of men, yet his voice would tremble with emotion on reading aloud from a letter the love messages from a little grandchild.

The following, told me by a gentleman who knew Mr. Clay, illustrates the true gentleman he was:—

"When I was a small boy my father took me with him to visit Mr. Clay at his home Ashland. We found some gentlemen there who had been invited to dinner. Just before they went in to dinner my father told me privately to run out and play on the lawn while they were dining. As the gentlemen came out, Mr. Clay saw me, and calling me to him said, 'My young friend, I owe you an apology.' Turning to the gentlemen he said, 'Go into the library, gentlemen, and light your cigars — I will join you presently.' Taking me by the hand he returned with me to the table, ordered the servants to attend to my wants, and conversed most delightfully with me until I had finished my dinner."

He had the faculty of making friends and holding them through life by ties which no circumstances or conditions could sever.

When Clay passed away there was no one whose Unionism embraced all sections, who could stand between the over-zealous advocates of abolition of slavery on the one side and the fiery defenders of the "divine institution" on the other. Sectionalism ran riot, and civil war was the result. During the many years when the North and South were divided on the question of slavery, and sectional feeling ran high, Henry Clay was the only man in public life whose broad nationalism and intense love for the Union embraced all sections, with no trace of sectional bias. He can well be called "The Great American."

John R Porter

PUBLIC SPIRIT IN POLITICS

From a Speech at Buffalo, July 17th, 1839

ARE we not then called upon by the highest duties to our country, to its free institutions, to posterity, and to the world, to rise above all local prejudices and personal partialities, to discard all collateral questions, to disregard every subordinate point, and in a genuine spirit of compromise and concession, uniting heart and hand to preserve for ourselves the blessings of a free government, wisely, honestly, and faithfully administered, and as we received them from our fathers, to transmit them to our children? Should we not justly subject ourselves to eternal reproach, if we permitted our differences about mere men to bring defeat and disaster upon our cause? Our principles are imperishable, but men have but a fleeting existence, and are themselves liable to change and corruption during its brief continuance.

ON THE GREEK STRUGGLE FOR INDEPENDENCE

From a Speech in 1824

ARE we so mean, so base, so despicable, that we may not attempt to express our horror, utter our indignation, at the most brutal and atrocious war that ever stained earth or shocked high Heaven? at the ferocious deeds of a savage and infuriated soldiery, stimulated and urged on by the clergy of a fanatical and inimical religion, and rioting in all the excesses of blood and butchery, at the mere details of which the heart sickens and recoils?

If the great body of Christendom can look on calmly and coolly while all this is perpetrated on a Christian people, in its own immediate vicinity, in its very presence, let us at least evince that one of its remote extremities is susceptible of sensibility to Christian wrongs, and capable of sympathy for Christian sufferings; that in this remote quarter of the world there are hearts not yet closed against compassion for human woes, that can pour out their indignant feelings at the oppression of a people endeared to us by every ancient recollection and every modern tie. Sir, attempts have been made to alarm the committee by the dangers to our commerce in the Mediterranean; and a wretched invoice of figs and opium has been spread before us to repress our sensibilities and to eradicate our humanity. Ah, sir! "What shall it profit a man if he gain the whole world and lose his own soul?" or what shall it avail a nation to save the whole of a miserable trade and lose its liberties?

SOUTH-AMERICAN INDEPENDENCE AS RELATED TO THE UNITED STATES

From a Speech before the House of Representatives in 1818

IT is the doctrine of thrones that man is too ignorant to govern himself. Their partisans assert his incapacity, in reference to all nations; if they cannot command universal assent to the proposition, it is then demanded as to particular nations; and our pride and our presumption too often make converts of us. I contend that it is to arraign the dispositions of Providence himself, to suppose that he has created beings incapable of governing themselves, and to be trampled on by kings. Self-government is the natural government of man, and for proof I refer to the aborigines of our own land. Were I to speculate in hypotheses unfavorable to human liberty, my speculations should be founded rather upon the vices, refinements, or density of population. Crowded together in compact masses, even if they were philosophers, the contagion of the passions is communicated and caught, and the effect too often, I admit, is the overthrow of liberty. Dispersed over such an immense space as that on which the people of Spanish America are spread, their physical and I believe also their moral condition both favor their liberty.

With regard to their superstition, they worship the same God with us. Their prayers are offered up in their temples to the same Redeemer whose intercession we expect to save us. Nor is there anything in the Catholic religion unfavorable to freedom. All religions united with government are more or less inimical to liberty. All separated from government are compatible with liberty. If the people of Spanish America have not already gone as far in religious toleration as we have, the difference in their condition from ours should not be forgotten.

Everything is progressive; and in time I hope to see them imitating in this respect our example. But grant that the people of Spanish America are ignorant, and incompetent for free government; to whom is that ignorance to be ascribed? Is it not to the execrable system of Spain, which she seeks again to establish and to perpetuate? So far from chilling our hearts, it ought to increase our solicitude for our unfortunate brethren. It ought to animate us to desire the redemption of the minds and bodies of unborn millions from the brutifying effects of a system whose tendency is to stifle the faculties of the soul, and to degrade them to the level of beasts. I would invoke the spirits of our departed fathers. Was it for yourselves only that you nobly fought? No, no! It was the chains that were forging for your posterity that made you fly to arms; and scattering the elements of these chains to the winds, you transmitted to us the rich inheritance of liberty.

FROM THE VALEDICTORY TO THE SENATE, DELIVERED IN 1842

FROM 1806, the period of my entrance upon this noble theatre, with short intervals, to the present time, I have been engaged in the public councils at home or abroad. Of the services rendered during that long and arduous period of my life it does not become me to speak; history, if she deign to notice me, and posterity, if the recollection of my humble actions shall be transmitted to posterity, are the best, the truest, and the most impartial judges. When death has closed the scene, their sentence will be pronounced, and to that I commit myself. My public conduct is a fair subject for the criticism and judgment of my fellow men; but the motives by which I have been prompted are known only to the great Searcher of the human heart and to myself; and I trust I may be pardoned for repeating a declaration made some thirteen years ago, that whatever errors — and doubtless there have been many — may be discovered in a review of my public service, I can with unshaken confidence appeal to that divine Arbiter for the truth of the declaration that I have been influenced by no impure purpose, no personal motive; have sought no personal aggrandizement; but that in all my public acts I have had a single eye directed and a warm and devoted heart dedicated to what, in my best judgment, I believed the true interests, the honor, the union, and the happiness of my country required.

During that long period, however, I have not escaped the fate of other public men, nor failed to incur censure and detraction of the bitterest, most unrelenting, and most malignant character; and though not always insensible to the pain it was meant to inflict, I have borne it in general with composure and without disturbance, waiting as I have done, in perfect and undoubting confidence, for the ultimate triumph of justice and of truth, and in the entire persuasion that time would settle all things as they should be; and that whatever wrong or injustice I might experience at the hands of man, He to whom all hearts are open and fully known, would by the inscrutable dispensations of His providence rectify all error, redress all wrong, and cause ample justice to be done.

But I have not meanwhile been unsustained. Everywhere throughout the extent of this great continent I have had cordial, warm-hearted, faithful, and devoted friends, who have known me, loved me, and appreciated my motives. To them, if language were capable of fully expressing my acknowledgments, I would now offer all the return I have the power to make for their genuine, disinterested, and persevering fidelity and devoted attachment, the feelings and sentiments of a heart overflowing with never-ceasing gratitude. If, however, I fail in suitable language to express my gratitude to them for all the kindness they have shown me, what shall I say, what can I say, at all commensurate with those feelings of gratitude with which I have been inspired by the State whose humble representative and servant I have been in this chamber?

I emigrated from Virginia to the State of Kentucky now nearly forty-five years ago; I went as an orphan boy who had not yet attained the age of majority; who had never recognized a father's smile, nor felt his warm caresses; poor, penniless, without the favor of the great, with an imperfect and neglected education, hardly sufficient for the ordinary business and common pursuits of life; but scarce had I set my foot upon her generous soil when I was embraced with parental fondness, caressed as though I had been a favorite child, and patronized with liberal and unbounded munificence. From that period the highest honors of the State have been freely bestowed upon me; and when in the darkest hour of calumny and detraction

I seemed to be assailed by all the rest of the world, she inter-posed her broad and impenetrable shield, repelled the poisoned shafts that were aimed for my destruction, and vindicated my good name from every malignant and unfounded aspersion. I return with indescribable pleasure to linger a while longer, and mingle with the warm-hearted and whole-souled people of that State; and when the last scene shall forever close upon me, I hope that my earthly remains will be laid under her green sod with those of her gallant and patriotic sons. . . .

That my nature is warm, my temper ardent, my disposition — especially in relation to the public service — enthusiastic, I am ready to own; and those who suppose that I have been assuming the dictatorship, have only mistaken for arrogance or assumption that ardor and devotion which are natural to my constitution, and which I may have displayed with too little regard to cold, calculating, and cautious prudence, in sustaining and zealously supporting important national measures of policy which I have presented and espoused. . . .

I go from this place under the hope that we shall mutually consign to perpetual oblivion whatever personal collisions may at any time unfortunately have occurred between us; and that our recollections shall dwell in future only on those conflicts of mind with mind, those intellectual struggles, those noble exhibitions of the powers of logic, argument, and eloquence, honorable to the Senate and to the nation, in which each has sought and con-tended for what he deemed the best mode of accomplishing one common object, the interest and the most happiness of our beloved country. To these thrilling and delightful scenes it will be my pleasure and my pride to look back in my retirement with unmeasured satisfaction. . . .

May the most precious blessings of Heaven rest upon the whole Senate and each member of it, and may the labors of every one redound to the benefit of the nation and to the advancement of his own fame and renown. And when you shall retire to the bosom of your constituents, may you receive the most cheering and gratifying of all human rewards,— their cor-dial greeting of "Well done, good and faithful servant."

FROM THE LEXINGTON 'SPEECH ON RETIREMENT TO PRIVATE LIFE'

IT WOULD neither be fitting, nor is it my purpose, to pass judgment on all the acts of my public life; but I hope I shall
be excused for one or two observations which the occasion
appears to me to authorize.

I never but once changed my opinion on any great measure
of national policy, or on any great principle of construction of
the national Constitution. In early life, on deliberate consideration, I adopted the principles of interpreting the federal Constitution which have been so ably developed and enforced by Mr.
Madison in his memorable report to the Virginia Legislature;
and to them, as I understood them, I have constantly adhered.
Upon the question coming up in the Senate of the United States
to re-charter the first Bank of the United States, thirty years
ago, I opposed the re-charter upon convictions which I honestly
entertained. The experience of the war which shortly followed,
the condition into which the currency of the country was thrown
without a bank, and I may now add, later and more disastrous
experience, convinced me I was wrong. I publicly stated to
my constituents, in a speech in Lexington (that which I made
in the House of Representatives of the United States not having been reported), my reasons for that change, and they are
preserved in the archives of the country. I appeal to that
record, and I am willing to be judged now and hereafter by
their validity.

I do not advert to the fact of this solitary instance of change
of opinion as implying any personal merit, but because it is a
fact. I will however say that I think it very perilous to the
utility of any public man to make frequent changes of opinion,
or any change, but upon grounds so sufficient and palpable that
the public can clearly see and approve them. If we could look
through a window into the human breast and there discover the
causes which led to changes of opinion, they might be made
without hazard. But as it is impossible to penetrate the human
heart and distinguish between the sinister and honest motives
which prompt it, any public man that changes his opinion, once
deliberately formed and promulgated, under other circumstances
than those which I have stated, draws around him distrust,

impairs the public confidence, and lessens his capacity to serve his country.

I will take this occasion now to say, that I am and have been long satisfied that it would have been wiser and more politic in me to have declined accepting the office of Secretary of State in 1825. Not that my motives were not as pure and as patriotic as ever carried any man into public office. Not that the calumny which was applied to the fact was not as gross and as unfounded as any that was ever propagated. Not that valued friends and highly esteemed opponents did not unite in urging my acceptance of the office. Not that the administration of Mr. Adams will not, I sincerely believe, advantageously compare with any of his predecessors, in economy, purity, prudence, and wisdom. Not that Mr. Adams was himself wanting in any of those high qualifications and upright and patriotic intentions which were suited to the office. . . .

But my error in accepting the office arose out of my underrating the power of detraction and the force of ignorance, and abiding with too sure a confidence in the conscious integrity and uprightness of my own motives. Of that ignorance I had a remarkable and laughable example on an occasion which I will relate. I was traveling in 1828 through — I believe it was Spottsylvania County in Virginia, on my return to Washington, in company with some young friends. We halted at night at a tavern, kept by an aged gentleman who, I quickly perceived from the disorder and confusion which reigned, had not the happiness to have a wife. After a hurried and bad supper the old gentleman sat down by me, and without hearing my name, but understanding that I was from Kentucky, remarked that he had four sons in that State, and that he was very sorry they were divided in politics, two being for Adams and two for Jackson; he wished they were all for Jackson. "Why?" I asked him.—"Because," he said, "that fellow Clay, and Adams, had cheated Jackson out of the Presidency."—"Have you ever seen any evidence, my old friend," said I, "of that?"—"No," he replied, "none," and he wanted to see none. "But," I observed, looking him directly and steadily in the face, "suppose Mr. Clay were to come here and assure you upon his honor that it was all a vile calumny, and not a word of truth in it, would you believe him?"—"No," replied the old gentleman, promptly and emphatically. I said to him in conclusion, "Will you be good enough to show me to bed?" and bade him good-night. The next morning, having in the interval learned my name, he came to me full of apologies; but I at once put him at his ease by assuring him that I did not feel in the slightest degree hurt or offended with him. . . .

If to have served my country during a long series of years with fervent zeal and unshaken fidelity, in seasons of peace and war, at home and abroad, in the legislative halls and in an executive department; if to have labored most sedulously to avert the embarrassment and distress which now overspread this Union, and when they came, to have exerted myself anxiously at the extra session, and at this, to devise healing remedies; if to have desired to introduce economy and reform in the general administration, curtail enormous executive power, and amply provide at the same time for the wants of the government and the wants of the people, by a tariff which would give it revenue and then protection; if to have earnestly sought to establish the bright but too rare example of a party in power faithful to its promises and pledges made when out of power: if these services, exertions, and endeavors justify the accusation of ambition, I must plead guilty to the charge.

I have wished the good opinion of the world; but I defy the most malignant of my enemies to show that I have attempted to gain it by any low or groveling arts, by any mean or unworthy sacrifices, by the violation of any of the obligations of honor, or by a breach of any of the duties which I owed to my country. . . .

How is this right of the people to abolish an existing government, and to set up a new one, to be practically exercised? Our revolutionary ancestors did not tell us by words, but they proclaimed it by gallant and noble deeds. Who are the people that are to tear up the whole fabric of human society, whenever and as often as caprice or passion may prompt them? When all the arrangements and ordinances of existing organized society are prostrated and subverted, as must be supposed in such a lawless and irregular movement as that in Rhode Island, the established privileges and distinctions between the sexes, between the colors, between the ages, between natives and foreigners, between the sane and the insane, and between the innocent and the guilty convict, all the offspring of positive institutions, are cast down and abolished, and society is thrown into one heterogeneous and unregulated mass. And is it contended that the major part of this Babel congregation is invested with the right to build up at its pleasure a new government? that as often, and whenever, society can be drummed up and thrown into such a shapeless mass, the major part of it may establish another and another new government in endless succession? Why, this would overturn all social organization, make revolutions — the extreme and last resort of an oppressed people — the commonest occurrences of human life, and the standing order of the day. How such a principle would operate in a certain section of this Union, with a peculiar population, you will readily conceive. No community could endure such an intolerable state of things anywhere, and all would sooner or later take refuge from such ceaseless agitation in the calm repose of absolute despotism. . . .

Fellow-citizens of all parties! The present situation of our country is one of unexampled distress and difficulty; but there is no occasion for any despondency. A kind and bountiful Providence has never deserted us; punished us he perhaps has, for our neglect of his blessings and our misdeeds. We have a varied and fertile soil, a genial climate, and free institutions. Our whole land is covered in profusion with the means of subsistence and the comforts of life. Our gallant ship, it is unfortunately true, lies helpless, tossed on a tempestuous sea amid the conflicting billows of contending parties, without a rudder and without a faithful pilot. But that ship is our country, embodying all our past glory, all our future hopes. Its crew is our whole people, by whatever political denomination they are known. If she goes down, we all go down together. Let us remember the dying words of the gallant and lamented Lawrence, "Don't give up the ship." The glorious banner of our country, with its unstained stars and stripes, still proudly floats at its mast-head. With stout hearts and strong arms we can surmount all our difficulties. Let us all, all, rally round that banner, and finally resolve to perpetuate our liberties and regain our lost prosperity.

Whigs! Arouse from the ignoble supineness which encompasses you; awake from the lethargy in which you lie bound; cast from you that unworthy apathy which seems to make you indifferent to the fate of your country. Arouse! awake! shake off the dewdrops that glitter on your garments, and once more march to battle and to victory. You have been disappointed, deceived, betrayed; shamefully deceived and betrayed. But will you therefore also prove false and faithless to your country, or obey the impulses of a just and patriotic indignation? As for Captain Tyler, he is a mere snap, a flash in the pan; pick your Whig flints and try your rifles again.

From 'The Speeches of Henry Clay; Edited by Calvin Colton.' Copyright, 1857, by A. S. Barnes and Company.

CLEANTHES

(331–232 B. C.)

CLEANTHES, the immediate successor of Zeno, the founder of Stoicism, was born at Assos, in the Troad, in B. C. 331. Of his early life we know nothing, except that he was for a time a prize-fighter. About the age of thirty he came to Athens with less than a dollar in his pocket, and entered the school of Zeno, where he remained for some nineteen years. At one time the Court of Areopagus, not seeing how he could make an honest livelihood, summoned him to appear before it and give an account of himself. He did so, bringing with him his employers, who proved that he spent much of the night in carrying water for gardens, or in kneading dough. The court, filled with admiration, offered him a pension, which he refused by the advice of his master, who thought the practice of self-dependence and strong endurance an essential part of education. Cleanthes's mind was slow of comprehension but extremely retentive; like a hard tablet, Zeno said, which retains clearest and longest what is written on it. He was not an original thinker, but the strength and loftiness of his character and his strong religious sense gave him an authority which no other member of the school could claim. For many years head of the Stoa, he reached the ripe age of ninety-nine, when, falling sick, he refused to take food, and died of voluntary starvation in B. C. 232. Long afterwards, the Roman Senate caused a statue to be erected to his memory in his native town. Almost the only writing of his that has come down to us is his noble Hymn to the Supreme Being.

HYMN TO ZEUS

Most glorious of all the Undying, many-named, girt round with awe!
    Jove, author of Nature, applying to all things the rudder of law —
Hail! Hail! for it justly rejoices the races whose life is a span
To lift unto thee their voices — the Author and Framer of man.
For we are thy sons; thou didst give us the symbols of speech at our birth,
Alone of the things that live, and mortal move upon earth.

Wherefore thou shalt find me extolling and ever singing thy
 praise;
Since thee the great Universe, rolling on its path round the world,
 obeys:—
Obeys thee, wherever thou guidest, and gladly is bound in thy
 bands,
So great is the power thou confidest, with strong, invincible hands,
To thy mighty ministering servant, the bolt of the thunder, that
 flies,
Two-edged, like a sword, and fervent, that is living and never dies.
All nature, in fear and dismay, doth quake in the path of its stroke,
What time thou preparest the way for the one Word thy lips have
 spoke,
Which blends with lights smaller and greater, which pervadeth and
 thrilleth all things,
So great is thy power and thy nature — in the Universe Highest of
 Kings!
On earth, of all deeds that are done, O God! there is none without
 thee;
In the holy ether not one, nor one on the face of the sea,
Save the deeds that evil men, driven by their own blind folly, have
 planned;
But things that have grown uneven are made even again by thy
 hand;
And things unseemly grow seemly, the unfriendly are friendly to
 thee;
For so good and evil supremely thou hast blended in one by decree.
For all thy decree is one ever — a Word that endureth for aye,
Which mortals, rebellious, endeavor to flee from and shun to obey —
Ill-fated, that, worn with proneness for the lordship of goodly things,
Neither hear nor behold, in its oneness, the law that divinity brings;
Which men with reason obeying, might attain unto glorious life,
No longer aimlessly straying in the paths of ignoble strife.
There are men with a zeal unblest, that are wearied with following
 of fame,
And men with a baser quest, that are turned to lucre and shame.
There are men too that pamper and pleasure the flesh with delicate
 stings:
All these desire beyond measure to be other than all these things.
Great Jove, all-giver, dark-clouded, great Lord of the thunderbolt's
 breath!
Deliver the men that are shrouded in ignorance dismal as death.
O Father! dispel from their souls the darkness, and grant them the
 light

Of reason, thy stay, when the whole wide world thou rulest with
   might,
That we, being honored, may honor thy name with the music of
   hymns,
Extolling the deeds of the Donor, unceasing, as rightly beseems
Mankind; for no worthier trust is awarded to God or to man
Than forever to glory with justice in the law that endures and is
   One.

SAMUEL LANGHORNE CLEMENS (MARK TWAIN)

(1835-)

AMUEL L. CLEMENS has made the name he assumed in his earliest "sketches" for newspapers so completely to usurp his own in public and private, that until recently the world knew him by no other; his world of admirers rarely use any other in referring to the great author, and even to his intimate friends the borrowed name seems the more real. The pseudonym so lightly picked up has nearly universal recognition, and it is safe to say that the name "Mark Twain" is known to more people of all conditions, the world over, than any other in this century, except that of some reigning sovereign or great war captain. The term is one used by the Mississippi River pilots to indicate the depth of water (two fathoms) when throwing the lead. It was first employed by a river correspondent in reporting the state of the river to a New Orleans newspaper. This reporter died just about the time Mr. Clemens began to write, and he "jumped" the name.

Mr. Clemens was born in Hannibal, Missouri, a small town on the west bank of the Mississippi, in 1835. He got the rudiments of an education at a village school, learned boy-life and human nature in a frontier community, entered a printing office and became an expert compositor, traveled and worked as a journeyman printer, and at length reached the summit of a river boy's ambition in a Mississippi steamboat in learning the business of a pilot. It is to this experience that the world is indebted for some of the most amusing, the most real and valuable, and the most imaginative writing of this century, which gives the character and interest and individuality to this great Western river that history has given to the Nile. If he had no other title to fame, he could rest securely on his reputation as the prose poet of the Mississippi. Upon the breaking out of the war the river business was suspended. Mr. Clemens tried the occupation of war for a few weeks, on the Confederate side, in a volunteer squad which does not seem to have come into collision with anything but scant rations and imaginary alarms; and then he went to Nevada with his brother, who had been appointed secretary of that Territory. Here he became connected with the Territorial Enterprise, a Virginia City newspaper, as a reporter and sketch-writer, and immediately opened a battery of good-natured and exaggerated and complimentary description that was vastly amusing to those who were not its targets.

Afterwards he drifted to the Coast, tried mining, and then joined that group of young writers who illustrated the early history of California. A short voyage in the Sandwich Islands gave him new material for his pen, and he made a successful début in San Francisco as a humorous lecturer.

The first writing to attract general attention was 'The Jumping Frog of Calaveras,' which was republished with several other sketches in book form in New York. Shortly after this he joined the excursion of the Quaker City steamship to the Orient, wrote letters about it to American newspapers, and advertised it quite beyond the expectations of its projectors. These letters, collected and revised, became 'The Innocents Abroad,' which instantly gave him a world-wide reputation. This was followed by 'Roughing It,' most amusing episodes of frontier life. His pen became immediately in great demand, and innumerable sketches flowed from it, many of them recklessly exaggerated for the effect he wished to produce; always laughter-provoking, and nearly always having a wholesome element of satire of some sham or pretense or folly. For some time he had charge of a humorous department in the Galaxy Magazine. These sketches and others that followed were from time to time collected into volumes which had a great sale. About this time he married, and permanently settled in Hartford, where he began the collection of a library, set himself to biographical and historical study, made incursions into German and French, and prepared himself for the more serious work that was before him.

A second sojourn in Europe produced 'A Tramp Abroad,' full of stories and adventures, much in the spirit of his original effort. But with more reading, reflection, and search into his own experiences, came 'Old Times on the Mississippi,' 'Tom Sawyer,' and 'Huckleberry Finn,' in which the author wrote out of his own heart. To interest in social problems must be attributed the beautiful idyl of 'The Prince and the Pauper,' and 'The Yankee at the Court of King Arthur,' which latter the English thought lacked reverence for the traditions of chivalry.

During all this period Mr. Clemens was in great demand as a lecturer and an after-dinner speaker. His remarks about New England weather, at a New England dinner in New York, are a favorite example of his humor and his power of poetic description. As a lecturer, a teller of stories, and delineator of character, he had scarcely a rival in his ability to draw and entertain vast audiences. He made a large income from his lectures in America and in England, and from his books, which always had a phenomenally large sale. Very remunerative also was the play of 'Colonel Sellers,' constructed out of a novel called 'The Gilded Age.'

Since 1890 Mr. Clemens and his family have lived most of the time in Europe. For some time before he had written little, but since that his pen has again become active. He has produced many magazine papers, a story called 'Pudd'nhead Wilson,' and the most serious and imaginative work of his life in 'The Personal Recollections of Joan of Arc,' feigned to be translated from a contemporary memoir left by her private secretary. In it the writer strikes the universal chords of sympathy and pathos and heroic elevation. In 1895-6 he made a lecturing tour of the globe, speaking in Australia, New Zealand, South Africa, and India, and everywhere received an ovation due to his commanding reputation. He is understood to be making this journey the subject of another book.

Mr. Clemens is universally recognized as the first of living humorists; but if the fashion of humor changes, as change it may, he will remain for other qualities — certain primordial qualities such as are exhibited in his work on the Mississippi — a force to be reckoned with in the literature of this century. Mr. Clemens's humor has the stamp of universality, which is the one indispensable thing in all enduring literary productions, and his books have been translated and very widely diffused and read in German, French, and other languages. This is a prophecy of his lasting place in the world of letters.

THE CHILD OF CALAMITY

From 'Life on the Mississippi': copyright 1883, by James R. Osgood and Company

B Y WAY of illustrating keelboat talk and manners, and that now departed and hardly remembered raft life, I will throw in, in this place, a chapter from a book which I have been working at by fits and starts during the past five or six years, and may possibly finish in the course of five or six more. The book is a story which details some passages in the life of an ignorant village boy, Huck Finn, son of the town drunkard of my time out West there. He has run away from his persecuting father, and from a persecuting good widow who wishes to make a nice truth-telling respectable boy of him; and with him a slave of the widow's has also escaped. They have found a fragment of a lumber raft (it is high water and dead summertime), and are floating down the river by night and hiding in the willows by day,—bound for Cairo,—whence the negro will seek freedom in the heart of the free States. But in a fog, they

pass Cairo without knowing it. By-and-by they begin to suspect the truth, and Huck Finn is persuaded to end the dismal
suspense by swimming down to a huge raft which they have
seen in the distance ahead of them, creeping aboard under cover
of the darkness, and gathering the needed information by eaves-
dropping:—

But you know a young person can't wait very well when he
is impatient to find a thing out. We talked it over, and by-and-
by Jim said it was such a black night now that it wouldn't be
no risk to swim down to the big raft and crawl aboard and
listen,—they would talk about Cairo, because they would be calculating to go ashore there for a spree, maybe, or anyway they
would send boats ashore to buy whisky or fresh meat or something. Jim had a wonderful level head, for a nigger: he could
'most always start a good plan when you wanted one.

I stood up and shook my rags off and jumped into the river,
and struck out for the raft's light. By-and-by, when I got down
nearly to her, I eased up and went slow and cautious. But
everything was all right—nobody at the sweeps. So I swum
down along the raft till I was 'most abreast the camp fire in the
middle, then I crawled aboard and inched along and got in
amongst some bundles of shingles on the weather side of the
fire. There was thirteen men there—they was the watch on
deck, of course. And a mighty rough-looking lot too. They
had a jug, and tin cups, and they kept the jug moving. One
man was singing—roaring, you may say; and it wasn't a nice
song—for a parlor anyway. He roared through his nose, and
strung out the last word of every line very long. When he was
done they all fetched a kind of Injun war-whoop, and then
another was sung. It begun:—

> " There was a woman in our towdn,
>   In our towdn did dwed'l (dwell),
> She loved her husband dear-i-lee,
>   But another man twyste as wed'l.
>
> " Singing too, riloo, riloo, riloo,
>   Ri-loo, riloo, rilay---e,
> She loved her husband dear-i-lee,
>   But another man twyste as wed'l."

And so on—fourteen verses. It was kind of poor, and when he
was going to start on the next verse one of them said it was

the tune the old cow died on; and another one said, "Oh, give us a rest." And another one told him to take a walk. They made fun of him till he got mad and jumped up and begun to cuss the crowd, and said he could lam any thief in the lot.

They was all about to make a break for him, but the biggest man there jumped up and says:—

"Set whar you are, gentlemen. Leave him to me; he's my meat."

Then he jumped up in the air three times and cracked his heels together every time. He flung off a buckskin coat that was all hung with fringes, and says, "You lay thar tell the chawin-up's done;" and flung his hat down, which was all over ribbons, and says, "You lay thar tell his sufferins is over."

Then he jumped up in the air and cracked his heels together again and shouted out:—

"Whoo-oop! I'm the old original iron-jawed, brass-mounted, copper-bellied corpse-maker from the wilds of Arkansaw!—Look at me! I'm the man they call Sudden Death and General Desolation! Sired by a hurricane, dam'd by an earthquake, half-brother to the cholera, nearly related to the small-pox on the mother's side! Look at me! I take nineteen alligators and a bar'l of whisky for breakfast when I'm in robust health, and a bushel of rattlesnakes and a dead body when I'm ailing! I split the everlasting rocks with my glance, and I squench the thunder when I speak! Whoo-oop! Stand back and give me room according to my strength! Blood's my natural drink, and the wails of the dying is music to my ear! Cast your eye on me, gentlemen!—and lay low and hold your breath, for I'm 'bout to turn myself loose!"

All the time he was getting this off, he was shaking his head and looking fierce and kind of swelling around in a little circle, tucking up his wrist-bands and now and then straightening up and beating his breast with his fist, saying "Look at me, gentlemen!" When he got through he jumped up and cracked his heels together three times, and let off a roaring "Whoo-oop! I'm the bloodiest son of a wildcat that lives!"

Then the man that had started the row tilted his old slouch hat down over his right eye; then he bent stooping forward, with his back sagged and his south end sticking out far, and his fists a-shoving out and drawing in in front of him, and so went around in a little circle about three times, swelling himself up and breathing hard. Then he straightened, and jumped up and cracked his heels together three times before he lit again (that made them cheer), and he begun to shout like this:—

"Whoo-oop! bow your neck and spread, for the kingdom of sorrow's a-coming! Hold me down to the earth, for I feel my powers a-working! whoo-oop! I'm a child of sin; *don't* let me get a start! Smoked glass, here, for all! Don't attempt to look at me with the naked eye, gentlemen! When I'm playful I use the meridians of longitude and parallels of latitude for a seine, and drag the Atlantic Ocean for whales! I scratch my head with the lightning and purr myself to sleep with the thunder! When I'm cold I bile the Gulf of Mexico and bathe in it; when I'm hot I fan myself with an equinoctial storm; when I'm thirsty I reach up and suck a cloud dry like a sponge; when I range the earth hungry, famine follows in my tracks! Whoo-oop! Bow your neck and spread! I put my hand on the sun's face and make it night in the earth; I bite a piece out of the moon and hurry the seasons; I shake myself and crumble the mountains! Contemplate me through leather — *don't* use the naked eye! I'm the man with a petrified heart and biler-iron bowels! The massacre of isolated communities is the pastime of my idle moments, the destruction of nationalities the serious business of my life! The boundless vastness of the great American desert is my inclosed property, and I bury my dead on my own premises!" He jumped up and cracked his heels together three times before he lit (they cheered him again), and as he came down he shouted out: "Whoo-oop! bow your neck and spread, for the pet child of calamity's a-coming!"

Then the other one went to swelling around and blowing again — the first one — the one they called Bob; next, the Child of Calamity chipped in again, bigger than ever; then they both got at it at the same time, swelling round and round each other and punching their fists 'most into each other's faces, and whooping and jawing like Injuns; then Bob called the Child names, and the Child called him names back again: next, Bob called him a heap rougher names, and the Child come back at him with the very worst kind of language; next, Bob knocked the Child's hat off, and the Child picked it up and kicked Bob's ribbony hat about six foot; Bob went and got it and said never mind, this warn't going to be the last of this thing, because he was a man that never forgot and never forgive, and so the Child better look out; for there was a time a-coming, just as sure as he was a living man, that he would have to answer to him with the best blood in his body. The Child said no man was willinger than he was for that time to come, and he would give Bob fair warning, *now*, never to cross his path again, for he could never rest till he had waded in his blood; for such was his nature, though he was sparing him now on account of his family, if he had one.

Both of them was edging away in different directions, growling and shaking their heads and going on about what they was going to do; but a little black-whiskered chap skipped up and says:—

"Come back here, you couple of chicken-livered cowards, and I'll thrash the two of ye!"

And he done it, too. He snatched them, he jerked them this way and that, he booted them around, he knocked them sprawling faster than they could get up. Why, it warn't two minutes till they begged like dogs—and how the other lot did yell and laugh and clap their hands all the way through, and shout "Sail in, Corpse-Maker!" "Hi! at him again, Child of Calamity!" "Bully for you, little Davy!" Well, it was a perfect pow-wow for a while. Bob and the Child had red noses and black eyes when they got through. Little Davy made them own up that they was sneaks and cowards, and not fit to eat with a dog or drink with a nigger; then Bob and the Child shook hands with each other very solemn, and said they had always respected each other and was willing to let bygones be bygones. So then they washed their faces in the river; and just then there was a loud order to stand by for a crossing, and some of them went forward to man the sweeps there, and the rest went aft to handle the after-sweeps.

A STEAMBOAT LANDING AT A SMALL TOWN

From ‹Life on the Mississippi›: copyright 1883, by James R. Osgood and Company

ONCE a day a cheap gaudy packet arrived upward from St. Louis, and another downward from Keokuk. Before these events, the day was glorious with expectancy; after them, the day was a dead and empty thing. Not only the boys but the whole village felt this. After all these years I can picture that old time to myself now, just as it was then: the white town drowsing in the sunshine of a summer's morning; the streets empty, or pretty nearly so; one or two clerks sitting in front of the Water Street stores, with their splint-bottomed chairs tilted back against the wall, chins on breasts, hats slouched over their faces, asleep — with shingle-shavings enough around to show what broke them down; a sow and a litter of pigs loafing along the sidewalk, doing a good business in watermelon rinds and seeds; two or three lonely little freight piles scattered about the "levee"; a pile of "skids" on the slope of the stone-paved wharf, and the fragrant town drunkard asleep in the shadow of them; two or three wood flats at the head of the wharf, but nobody to listen to the peaceful lapping of the wavelets against them; the great Mississippi, the majestic, the magnificent Mississippi, rolling its mile-wide tide along, shining in the sun; the dense forest away on the other side; the "point" above the town and the "point" below, bounding the river-glimpse and turning it into a sort of sea, and withal a very still and brilliant and lonely one. Presently a film of dark smoke appears above one of those remote "points"; instantly a negro drayman, famous for his quick eye and prodigious voice, lifts up the cry, "S-t-e-a-m-boat a-comin'!" and the scene changes! The town drunkard stirs, the clerks wake up, a furious clatter of drays follows, every house and store pours out a human contribution, and all in a twinkling the dead town is alive and moving. Drays, carts, men, boys, all go hurrying from many quarters to a common centre, the wharf. Assembled there, the people fasten their eyes upon the coming boat, as upon a wonder they are seeing for the first time. And the boat *is* rather a handsome sight too. She is long and sharp and trim and pretty; she has two tall fancy-topped chimneys, with a gilded device of some kind

swung between them; a fanciful pilot-house, all glass and "gingerbread," perched on top of the "texas" deck behind them; the
paddle-boxes are gorgeous with a picture or with gilded rays
above the boat's name; the boiler deck, the hurricane deck, and
the texas deck are fenced and ornamented with clean white railings; there is a flag gallantly flying from the jack-staff; the furnace doors are open and the fires glaring bravely; the upper
decks are black with passengers; the captain stands by the big
bell, calm, imposing, the envy of all; great volumes of the black-
est smoke are rolling and tumbling out of the chimneys—a
husbanded grandeur created with a bit of pitch-pine just before
arriving at a town; the crew are grouped on the forecastle; the
broad stage is run far out over the port bow, and an envied
deck hand stands picturesquely on the end of it with a coil of
rope in his hand; the pent steam is screaming through the
gauge-cocks; the captain lifts his hand, a bell rings, the wheels
stop; then they turn back, churning the water to a foam, and
the steamer is at rest.   Then such a scramble as there is to get
aboard, and to get ashore, and to take in freight and to discharge freight, all at one and the same time; and such a yelling
and cursing as the mates facilitate it all with!   Ten minutes
later the steamer is under way again, with no flag on the jack-
staff and no black smoke issuing from the chimneys.   After ten
more minutes the town is dead again, and the town drunkard
asleep by the skids once more.

THE HIGH RIVER: AND A PHANTOM PILOT

From ‹Life on the Mississippi›: copyright 1883, by James R. Osgood and
Company

DURING this big rise these small-fry craft were an intolerable
nuisance.   We were running chute after chute,—a new
world to me,—and if there was a particularly cramped
place in a chute, we would be pretty sure to meet a broad-horn
there; and if he failed to be there, we would find him in a still
worse locality, namely, the head of the chute, on the shoal
water.   And then there would be no end of profane cordialities
exchanged.

Sometimes, in the big river, when we would be feeling our
way cautiously along through a fog, the deep hush would sud-

denly be broken by yells and a clamor of tin pans, and all in an
instant a log raft would appear vaguely through the webby veil,
close upon us; and then we did not wait to swap knives, but
snatched our engine bells out by the roots and piled on all the
steam we had, to scramble out of the way! One doesn't hit a
rock or a solid log raft with a steamboat when he can get excused.

You will hardly believe it, but many steamboat clerks always
carried a large assortment of religious tracts with them in those
old departed steamboating days. Indeed they did. Twenty times
a day we would be cramping up around a bar, while a string of
these small-fry rascals were drifting down into the head of the
bend away above and beyond us a couple of miles. Now a skiff
would dart away from one of them, and come fighting its laborious way across the desert of water. It would "ease all," in the
shadow of our forecastle, and the panting oarsmen would shout,
"Gimme a pa-a-per!" as the skiff drifted swiftly astern. The
clerk would throw over a file of New Orleans journals. If these
were picked up *without comment*, you might notice that now a
dozen other skiffs had been drifting down upon us without saying anything. You understand, they had been waiting to see
how No. 1 was going to fare. No. 1 making no comment, all
the rest would bend to their oars and come on now; and as fast
as they came the clerk would heave over neat bundles of religious tracts, tied to shingles. The amount of hard swearing which
twelve packages of religious literature will command when im-
partially divided up among twelve raftsmen's crews, who have
pulled a heavy skiff two miles on a hot day to get them, is
simply incredible.

As I have said, the big rise brought a new world under my
vision. By the time the river was over its banks we had forsaken our old paths and were hourly climbing over bars that
had stood ten feet out of water before; we were shaving stumpy
shores, like that at the foot of Madrid Bend, which I had always
seen avoided before; we were clattering through chutes like that
of 82, where the opening at the foot was an unbroken wall of
timber till our nose was almost at the very spot. Some of these
chutes were utter solitudes. The dense untouched forest over-
hung both banks of the crooked little crack, and one could
believe that human creatures had never intruded there before.
The swinging grapevines, the grassy nooks and vistas, glimpsed

as we swept by, the flowering creepers waving their red blossoms from the tops of dead trunks, and all the spendthrift richness of the forest foliage, were wasted and thrown away there. The chutes were lovely places to steer in; they were deep, except at the head; the current was gentle; under the "points" the water was absolutely dead, and the invisible banks so bluff that where the tender willow thickets projected you could bury your boat's broadside in them as you tore along, and then you seemed fairly to fly.

Behind other islands we found wretched little farms and wretcheder little log cabins; there were crazy rail fences sticking a foot or two above the water, with one or two jeans-clad, chills-racked, yellow-faced male miserables roosting on the top rail, elbows on knees, jaws in hands, grinding tobacco and discharging the result at floating chips through crevices left by lost teeth; while the rest of the family and the few farm animals were huddled together in an empty wood flat riding at her moorings close at hand. In this flatboat the family would have to cook and eat and sleep for a lesser or greater number of days (or possibly weeks), until the river should fall two or three feet and let them get back to their log cabin and their chills again — chills being a merciful provision of an all-wise Providence to enable them to take exercise without exertion. And this sort of watery camping out was a thing which these people were rather liable to be treated to a couple of times a year: by the December rise out of the Ohio, and the June rise out of the Mississippi. And yet these were kindly dispensations, for they at least enabled the poor things to rise from the dead now and then, and look upon life when a steamboat went by. They appreciated the blessing too, for they spread their mouths and eyes wide open and made the most of these occasions. Now what *could* these banished creatures find to do to keep from dying of the blues during the low-water season!

Once in one of these lovely island chutes we found our course completely bridged by a great fallen tree. This will serve to show how narrow some of the chutes were. The passengers had an hour's recreation in a virgin wilderness while the boat hands chopped the bridge away; for there was no such thing as turning back, you comprehend.

From Cairo to Baton Rouge, when the river is over its banks, you have no particular trouble in the night, for the thousand-mile wall of dense forest that guards the two banks all the way is only gapped with a farm or wood-yard opening at intervals, and so you can't "get out of the river" much easier than you could get out of a fenced lane; but from Baton Rouge to New Orleans it is a different matter. The river is more than a mile wide, and very deep—as much as two hundred feet, in places. Both banks, for a good deal over a hundred miles, are shorn of their timber and bordered by continuous sugar plantations, with only here and there a scattering sapling or row of ornamental China-trees. The timber is shorn off clear to the rear of the plantations, from two to four miles. When the first frost threatens to come, the planters snatch off their crops in a hurry. When they have finished grinding the cane, they form the refuse of the stalks (which they call *bagasse*) into great piles and set fire to them, though in other sugar countries the bagasse is used for fuel in the furnaces of the sugar-mills. Now the piles of damp bagasse burn slowly, and smoke like Satan's own kitchen.

An embankment ten or fifteen feet high guards both banks of the Mississippi all the way down that lower end of the river, and this embankment is set back from the edge of the shore from ten to perhaps a hundred feet, according to circumstances; say thirty or forty feet as a general thing. Fill that whole region with an impenetrable gloom of smoke from a hundred miles of burning bagasse piles, when the river is over the banks, and turn a steamboat loose along there at midnight and see how she will feel. And see how you will feel too! You find yourself away out in the midst of a vague dim sea that is shoreless, that fades out and loses itself in the murky distances; for you cannot discern the thin rib of embankment, and you are always imagining you see a straggling tree when you don't. The plantations themselves are transformed by the smoke and look like a part of the sea. All through your watch you are tortured with the exquisite misery of uncertainty. You hope you are keeping in the river, but you do not know. All that you are sure about is that you are likely to be within six feet of the bank *and* destruction, when you think you are a good half-mile from shore. And you are sure also that if you chance suddenly to fetch up against the embankment and topple your chimneys overboard, you will have the small comfort of knowing that it is about what you were expecting to do. One of the great Vicksburg packets darted out into a sugar plantation one night, at such a time, and had to stay there a week. But there was no novelty about it: it had often been done before.

I thought I had finished this chapter, but I wish to add a curious thing while it is in my mind. It is only relevant in that it is connected with piloting. There used to be an excellent pilot on the river, a Mr. X., who was a somnambulist. It was said that if his mind was troubled about a bad piece of river, he was pretty sure to get up and walk in his sleep and do strange things. He was once fellow pilot for a trip or two with George Ealer, on a great New Orleans passenger packet. During a considerable part of the first trip George was uneasy, but got over it by-and-by, as X. seemed content to stay in his bed when asleep. Late one night the boat was approaching Helena, Arkansas; the water was low, and the crossing above the town in a very blind and tangled condition. X. had seen the crossing since Ealer had, and as the night was particularly drizzly, sullen, and dark, Ealer was considering whether he had not better have X. called to assist in running the place, when the door opened and X. walked in. Now on very dark nights, light is a deadly enemy to piloting; you are aware that if you stand in a lighted room on such a night, you cannot see things in the street to any purpose; but if you put out the lights and stand in the gloom you can make out objects in the street pretty well. So on very dark nights pilots do not smoke; they allow no fire in the pilot-house stove if there is a crack which can allow the least ray to escape; they order the furnaces to be curtained with huge tarpaulins and the skylights to be closely blinded. Then no light whatever issues from the boat. The undefinable shape that now entered the pilot-house had Mr. X.'s voice. This said:—

"Let me take her, George; I've seen this place since you have, and it is so crooked that I reckon I can run it myself easier than I could tell you how to do it."

"It is kind of you, and I swear *I* am willing. I haven't got another drop of perspiration left in me. I have been spinning around and around the wheel like a squirrel. It is so dark I can't tell which way she is swinging till she is coming around like a whirligig."

So Ealer took a seat on the bench, panting and breathless. The black phantom assumed the wheel without saying anything, steadied the waltzing steamer with a turn or two, and then stood at ease, coaxing her a little to this side and then to that, as gently and as sweetly as if the time had been noonday. When Ealer observed this marvel of steering, he wished he had not confessed! He stared and wondered, and finally said: —

"Well, I thought I knew how to steer a steamboat, but that was another mistake of mine."

X. said nothing, but went serenely on with his work. He rang for the leads; he rang to slow down the steam; he worked the boat carefully and neatly into invisible marks, then stood at the centre of the wheel and peered blandly out into the blackness, fore and aft, to verify his position; as the leads shoaled more and more, he stopped the engines entirely, and the dead silence and suspense of "drifting" followed; when the shoalest water was struck, he cracked on the steam, carried her handsomely over, and then began to work her warily into the next system of shoal marks; the same patient, heedful use of leads and engines followed, the boat slipped through without touching bottom, and entered upon the third and last intricacy of the crossing; imperceptibly she moved through the gloom, crept by inches into her marks, drifted tediously till the shoalest water was cried, and then, under a tremendous head of steam, went swinging over the reef and away into deep water and safety!

Ealer let his long-pent breath pour out in a great relieving sigh, and said: —

"That's the sweetest piece of piloting that was ever done on the Mississippi River! I wouldn't believed it could be done, if I hadn't seen it."

There was no reply, and he added: —

"Just hold her five minutes longer, partner, and let me run down and get a cup of coffee."

A minute later Ealer was biting into a pie, down in the "texas," and comforting himself with coffee. Just then the night watchman happened in, and was about to happen out again, when he noticed Ealer and exclaimed: —

"Who is at the wheel, sir?"

"X."

"Dart for the pilot-house, quicker than lightning!"

The next moment both men were flying up the pilot-house companion-way, three steps at a jump! Nobody there! The great steamer was whistling down the middle of the river at her own sweet will! The watchman shot out of the place again; Ealer seized the wheel, set the engine back with power, and held his breath while the boat reluctantly swung away from a "tow-head" which she was about to knock into the middle of the Gulf of Mexico!

By-and-by the watchman came back and said: —

"Didn't that lunatic tell you he was asleep when he first came up here?"

"No."

"Well, he was. I found him walking along on top of the railings, just as unconcerned as another man would walk a pavement; and I put him to bed; now just this minute there he was again, away astern, going through that sort of tight-rope deviltry the same as before."

"Well, I think I'll stay by, next time he has one of those fits. But I hope he'll have them often. You just ought to have seen him take this boat through Helena crossing. *I* never saw anything so gaudy before. And if he can do such gold-leaf, kid-glove, diamond-breastpin piloting when he is sound asleep, what *couldn't* he do if he was dead!"

AN ENCHANTING RIVER SCENE

From 'Life on the Mississippi': copyright 1883, by James R. Osgood and Company

THE face of the water in time became a wonderful book — a book that was a dead language to the uneducated passenger, but which told its mind to me without reserve, delivering its most cherished secrets as clearly as if it uttered them with a voice. And it was not a book to be read once and thrown aside, for it had a new story to tell every day. Throughout the long twelve hundred miles there was never a page that was void of interest, never one that you could leave unread without loss, never one that you would want to skip, thinking you could find higher enjoyment in some other thing. There never was so wonderful a book written by man; never one whose interest was so absorbing, so unflagging, so sparklingly renewed with every re-perusal. The passenger who could not read it was charmed with a peculiar sort of faint dimple on its surface (on the rare occasions when he did not overlook it altogether); but to the pilot that was an *italicized* passage; indeed it was more than that,— it was a legend of the largest capitals, with a string of shouting exclamation-points at the end of it; for it meant that a wreck or a rock was buried there, that could tear the life out of the strongest vessel that ever floated. It is the faintest and simplest expression the water ever makes, and the most hideous to a pilot's eye. In truth, the passenger who could not read this book saw nothing but all manner of pretty pictures in it, painted by the sun and shaded by the clouds; whereas to the trained eye these were not pictures at all, but the grimmest and most dead-earnest of reading matter.

Now when I had mastered the language of this water and had come to know every trifling feature that bordered the great river as familiarly as I knew the letters of the alphabet, I had made a valuable acquisition. But I had lost something too. I had lost something which could never be restored to me while I lived. All the grace, the beauty, the poetry had gone out of the majestic river! I still kept in mind a certain wonderful sunset which I witnessed when steamboating was new to me. A broad expanse of the river was turned to blood; in the middle distance the red hue brightened into gold, through which a solitary log came floating, black and conspicuous; in one place a long slant-ing mark lay sparkling upon the water; in another the surface was broken by boiling tumbling rings that were as many-tinted as an opal; where the ruddy flush was faintest, was a smooth spot that was covered with graceful circles and radiating lines, ever so delicately traced; the shore on our left was densely wooded, and the sombre shadow that fell from this forest was broken in one place by a long ruffled trail that shone like sil-ver; and high above the forest wall a clean-stemmed dead tree waved a single leafy bough, that glowed like a flame in the un-obstructed splendor that was flowing from the sun. There were graceful curves, reflected images, woody heights, soft distances; and over the whole scene, far and near, the dissolving lights drifted steadily, enriching it every passing moment with new marvels of coloring.

I stood like one bewitched. I drank it in, in a speechless rapture. The world was new to me, and I had never seen any-thing like this at home. But as I have said, a day came when I began to cease from noting the glories and the charms which the moon and the sun and the twilight wrought upon the river's

face; another day came when I ceased altogether to note them.
Then, if that sunset scene had been repeated, I should have
looked upon it without rapture and should have commented
upon it inwardly after this fashion: This sun means that we
are going to have wind to-morrow; that floating log means that
the river is rising, small thanks to it; that slanting mark on the
water refers to a bluff reef which is going to kill somebody's
steamboat one of these nights, if it keeps on stretching out like
that; those tumbling "boils" show a dissolving bar and a changing channel there; the lines and circles in the slick water over
yonder are a warning that that troublesome place is shoaling up
dangerously; that silver streak in the shadow of the forest is the
"break" from a new snag, and he has located himself in the
very best place he could have found to fish for steamboats; that
tall dead tree, with a single living branch, is not going to last
long, and then how is a body ever going to get through this
blind place at night without the friendly old landmark?

No, the romance and the beauty were all gone from the
river. All the value any feature of it had for me now was the
amount of usefulness it could furnish toward compassing the
safe piloting of a steamboat. Since those days I have pitied
doctors from my heart. What does the lovely flush in a beauty's
cheek mean to a doctor but a "break" that ripples above some
deadly disease? Are not all her visible charms sown thick with
what are to him the signs and symbols of hidden decay? Does
he ever see her beauty at all, or doesn't he simply view her professionally and comment upon her unwholesome condition all to
himself? And doesn't he sometimes wonder whether he has
gained most or lost most by learning his trade?

THE LIGHTNING PILOT

From 'Life on the Mississippi': copyright 1883, by James R. Osgood and
Company

NEXT morning I felt pretty rusty and low-spirited. We went
booming along, taking a good many chances, for we were
anxious to "get out of the river" (as getting out to Cairo
was called) before night should overtake us. But Mr. Bixby's
partner, the other pilot, presently grounded the boat, and we
lost so much time getting her off that it was plain the darkness

would overtake us a good long way above the mouth. This was a great misfortune; especially to certain of our visiting pilots, whose boats would have to wait for their return, no matter how long that might be. It sobered the pilot-house talk a good deal. Coming up-stream, pilots did not mind low water or any kind of darkness; nothing stopped them but fog. But down-stream work was different; a boat was too nearly helpless, with a stiff current pushing behind her; so it was not customary to run down-stream at night in low water.

There seemed to be one small hope, however: if we could get through the intricate and dangerous Hat Island crossing before night, we could venture the rest, for we would have plainer sailing and better water. But it would be insanity to attempt Hat Island at night. So there was a deal of looking at watches all the rest of the day, and a constant ciphering upon the speed we were making; Hat Island was the eternal subject; sometimes hope was high, and sometimes we were delayed in a bad crossing, and down it went again. For hours all hands lay under the burden of this suppressed excitement; it was even communicated to me, and I got to feeling so solicitous about Hat Island, and under such an awful pressure of responsibility, that I wished I might have five minutes on shore to draw a good full relieving breath, and start over again. We were standing no regular watches. Each of our pilots ran such portions of the river as he had run when coming up-stream, because of his greater familiarity with it; but both remained in the pilot-house constantly.

An hour before sunset, Mr. Bixby took the wheel and Mr. W—— stepped aside. For the next thirty minutes every man held his watch in his hand and was restless, silent, and uneasy. At last somebody said with a doomful sigh:—

"Well, yonder's Hat Island—and we can't make it."

All the watches closed with a snap, everybody sighed and muttered something about its being "too bad, too bad—ah, if we could *only* have got here half an hour sooner!" and the place was thick with the atmosphere of disappointment. Some started to go out, but loitered, hearing no bell-tap to land. The sun dipped behind the horizon, the boat went on. Inquiring looks passed from one guest to another; and one who had his hand on the door-knob and had turned it, waited, then presently took away his hand and let the knob turn back again. We bore steadily down the bend. More looks were exchanged, and nods

of surprised admiration — but no words. Insensibly the men
drew together behind Mr. Bixby, as the sky darkened and one or
two dim stars came out. The dead silence and sense of waiting
became oppressive. Mr. Bixby pulled the cord, and two deep
mellow notes from the big bell floated off on the night. Then a
pause, and one more note was struck. The watchman's voice
followed, from the hurricane deck: —

"Labboard lead, there! Stabboard lead!"

The cries of the leadsmen began to rise out of the distance,
and were gruffly repeated by the word-passers on the hurricane
deck.

"M-a-r-k three! . . . M-a-r-k three! . . . Quarter-less-
three! . . . Half twain! . . . Quarter twain! . . .
M-a-r-k twain! . . . Quarter-less —"

Mr. Bixby pulled two bell-ropes, and was answered by faint
jinglings far below in the engine-room, and our speed slackened.
The steam began to whistle through the gauge-cocks. The cries
of the leadsmen went on — and it is a weird sound always in
the night. Every pilot in the lot was watching now, with fixed
eyes, and talking under his breath. Nobody was calm and easy
but Mr. Bixby. He would put his wheel down and stand on a
spoke, and as the steamer swung into her (to me) utterly invisible marks — for we seemed to be in the midst of a wide and
gloomy sea — he would meet and fasten her there. Out of the
murmur of half-audible talk one caught a coherent sentence now
and then, such as: —

"There; she's over the first reef all right!"

After a pause, another subdued voice: —

"Her stern's coming down just *exactly* right, by *George!*"

"Now she's in the marks; over she goes!"

Somebody else muttered: —

"Oh, it was done beautiful — *beautiful!*"

Now the engines were stopped altogether, and we drifted
with the current. Not that I could see the boat drift, for I
could not, the stars being all gone by this time. This drifting
was the dismalest work; it held one's heart still. Presently I
discovered a blacker gloom than that which surrounded us. It
was the head of the island. We were closing right down upon
it. We entered its deeper shadow, and so imminent seemed the
peril that I was likely to suffocate; and I had the strongest impulse to do *something*, anything, to save the vessel. But still

Mr. Bixby stood by his wheel, silent, intent as a cat, and all the pilots stood shoulder to shoulder at his back.

" She'll not make it! " somebody whispered.

The water grew shoaler and shoaler, by the leadsman's cries, till it was down to —

" Eight-and-a-half! . . . E-i-g-h-t feet! . . . E-i-g-h-t feet! . . . Seven-and — "

Mr. Bixby said warningly through his speaking-tube to the engineer: —

" Stand by, now! "

" Ay-ay, sir! "

" Seven-and-a-half! Seven feet! *Six*-and — "

We touched bottom! Instantly Mr. Bixby set a lot of bells ringing, shouted through the tube, " *Now* let her have it — every ounce you've got! " then to his partner, " Put her hard down! snatch her! snatch her! " The boat rasped and ground her way through the sand, hung upon the apex of disaster a single tremendous instant, and then over she went! And such a shout as went up at Mr. Bixby's back never loosened the roof of a pilot-house before!

There was no more trouble after that. Mr. Bixby was a hero that night; and it was some little time, too, before his exploit ceased to be talked about by river men.

AN EXPEDITION AGAINST OGRES

From 'A Connecticut Yankee in King Arthur's Court': copyright 1889, by Charles L. Webster and Company

M Y EXPEDITION was all the talk that day and that night, and the boys were very good to me, and made much of me, and seemed to have forgotten their vexation and disappointment, and come to be as anxious for me to hive those ogres and set those ripe old virgins loose as if it were themselves that had the contract. Well, they *were* good children — but just children, that is all. And they gave me no end of points about how to scout for giants, and how to scoop them in; and they told me all sorts of charms against enchantments, and gave me salves and other rubbish to put on my wounds. But it never occurred to one of them to reflect that if I was such a wonderful necromancer as I was pretending to be, I ought not to need salves, or instructions, or charms against enchantments, and least of all arms and armor, on a foray of any kind — even against fire-spouting dragons and devils hot from perdition, let alone such poor adversaries as these I was after, these commonplace ogres of the back settlements.

I was to have an early breakfast, and start at dawn, for that was the usual way; but I had the demon's own time with my armor, and this delayed me a little. It is troublesome to get into, and there is so much detail. First you wrap a layer or two of blanket around your body for a sort of cushion, and to keep off the cold iron; then you put on your sleeves and shirt of chain-mail — these are made of small steel links woven together, and they form a fabric so flexible that if you toss your shirt on to the floor it slumps into a pile like a peck of wet fish-net; it is very heavy and is nearly the uncomfortablest material in the world for a night-shirt, yet plenty used it for that — tax collectors and reformers, and one-horse kings with a defective title, and those sorts of people; then you put on your shoes — flatboats roofed over with interleaving bands of steel — and screw your clumsy spurs into the heels. Next you buckle your greaves on your legs and your cuisses on your thighs; then come your backplate and your breastplate, and you begin to feel crowded; then you hitch on to the breastplate the half-petticoat of broad overlapping bands of steel which hangs down in front but is scolloped out behind so you can sit down, and isn't any real improvement on an inverted coal-scuttle, either for looks, or for wear, or to wipe your hands on; next you belt on your sword; then you put your stove-pipe joints on to your arms, your iron gauntlets on to your hands, your iron rat-trap on to your head, with a rag of steel web hitched on to it to hang over the back of your neck — and there you are, snug as a candle in a candle-mold. This is no time to dance. Well, a man that is packed away like that is a nut that isn't worth the cracking, there is so little of the meat, when you get down to it, by comparison with the shell.

The boys helped me, or I never could have got in. Just as we finished, Sir Bedivere happened in, and I saw that as like as not I hadn't chosen the most convenient outfit for a long trip. How stately he looked; and tall and broad and grand. He had on his head a conical steel casque that only came down to his ears, and for visor had only a narrow steel bar that extended down to his upper lip and protected his nose; and all the rest of him, from neck to heel, was flexible chain-mail, trousers and all. But pretty much all of him was hidden under his outside garment, which of course was of chain-mail, as I said, and hung straight from his shoulders to his ankles; and from his middle to the bottom, both before and behind, was divided, so that he could ride and let the skirts hang down on each side. He was going grailing, and it was just the outfit for it, too. I would have given a good deal for that ulster, but it was too late now to be fooling around. The sun was just up; the king and the court were all on hand to see me off and wish me luck; so it wouldn't be etiquette for me to tarry. You don't get on your horse yourself; no, if you tried it you would get disappointed. They carry you out, just as they carry a sun-struck man to the drug-store, and put you on, and help get you to rights, and fix your feet in the stirrups; and all the while you do feel so strange and stuffy and like somebody else — like somebody that has been married on a sudden, or struck by lightning, or something like that, and hasn't quite fetched around yet, and is sort of numb, and can't just get his bearings. Then they stood up the mast they called a spear in its socket by my left foot, and I gripped it with my hand; lastly they hung my shield around my neck, and I was all complete and ready to up anchor and get to sea. Everybody was as good to me as they could be, and a maid of honor gave me the stirrup-cup her own self. There was nothing more to do now but for that damsel to get up behind me on a pillion, which she did, and put an arm or so around me to hold on.

And so we started; and everybody gave us a good-by and waved their handkerchiefs or helmets. And everybody we met, going down the hill and through the village, was respectful to us except some shabby little boys on the outskirts. They said: —

"Oh, what a guy!" and hove clods at us.

In my experience boys are the same in all ages. They don't respect anything, they don't care for anything or anybody. They say "Go up, bald-head!" to the prophet going his unoffending way in the gray of antiquity; they sass me in the holy gloom of the Middle Ages; and I had seen them act the same way in Buchanan's administration; I remember, because I was there and helped. The prophet had his bears and settled with his boys; and I wanted to get down and settle with mine, but it wouldn't answer, because I couldn't have got up again. I hate a country without a derrick.

Straight off, we were in the country. It was most lovely and pleasant in those sylvan solitudes in the early cool morning in the first freshness of autumn. From hilltops we saw fair green valleys lying spread out below, with streams winding through them, and island groves of trees here and there, and huge lonely oaks scattered about and casting black blots of shade; and beyond the valleys we saw the ranges of hills, blue with haze, stretching away in billowy perspective to the horizon, with at wide intervals a dim fleck of white or gray on a wave-summit, which we knew was a castle. We crossed broad natural lawns sparkling with dew, and we moved like spirits, the cushioned turf giving out no sound of footfall; we dreamed along through glades in a mist of green light that got its tint from the sun-drenched roof of leaves overhead, and by our feet the clearest and coldest of runlets went frisking and gossiping over its reefs and making a sort of whispering music comfortable to hear; and at times we left the world behind and entered into the solemn great deeps and rich gloom of the forest, where furtive wild things whisked and scurried by and were gone before you could even get your eye on the place where the noise was; and where only the earliest birds were turning out and getting to business, with a song here and a quarrel yonder and a mysterious far-off hammering and drumming for worms on a tree-trunk away somewhere in the impenetrable remoteness of the woods. And by-and-by out we would swing again into the glare.

About the third or fourth or fifth time that we swung out into the glare—it was along there somewhere, a couple of hours or so after sun-up—it wasn't as pleasant as it had been. It was beginning to get hot. This was quite noticeable. We had a very long pull, after that, without any shade. Now it is curious how progressively little frets grow and multiply after they once get a start. Things which I didn't mind at all at first, I began to mind now—and more and more, too, all the time. The first ten or fifteen times I wanted my handkerchief I didn't seem to care; I got along, and said never mind, it isn't any matter, and dropped it out of my mind. But now it was different: I wanted it all the time; it was nag, nag, nag, right along, and no rest; I couldn't get it out of my mind; and so at last I lost my

temper, and said hang a man that would make a suit of armor
without any pockets in it. You see I had my handkerchief in
my helmet, and some other things; but it was that kind of a
helmet that you can't take off by yourself. That hadn't occurred
to me when I put it there; and in fact I didn't know it.   I
supposed it would be particularly convenient there. And so
now the thought of its being there, so handy and close by, and
yet not get-at-able, made it all the worse and the harder to
bear. Yes, the thing that you can't get is the thing that you
want, mainly; every one has noticed that. Well, it took my mind
off from everything else; took it clear off and centred it in my
helmet; and mile after mile there it stayed, imagining the handkerchief, picturing the handkerchief; and it was bitter and aggra-
vating to have the salt sweat keep trickling down into my eyes,
and I couldn't get at it. It seems like a little thing on paper,
but it was not a little thing at all; it was the most real kind of
misery. I would not say it if it was not so. I made up my
mind that I would carry along a reticule next time, let it look
how it might and people say what they would. Of course these
iron dudes of the Round Table would think it was scandalous,
and maybe raise sheol about it, but as for me, give me comfort
first and style afterwards. So we jogged along, and now and
then we struck a stretch of dust, and it would tumble up in
clouds and get into my nose and make me sneeze and cry; and
of course I said things I oughtn't to have said,— I don't deny
that. I am not better than others. We couldn't seem to meet
anybody in this lonesome Britain, not even an ogre; and in the
mood I was in then, it was well for the ogre; that is, an ogre
with a handkerchief. Most knights would have thought of nothing but getting his armor; but so I got his bandana, he could
keep his hardware for all me.

Meantime it was getting hotter and hotter in there. You
see the sun was beating down and warming up the iron more
and more all the time. Well, when you are hot, that way, every
little thing irritates you. When I trotted I rattled like a crate
of dishes, and that annoyed me; and moreover I couldn't seem
to stand that shield slatting and banging, now about my breast,
now around my back; and if I dropped into a walk my joints
creaked and screeched in that wearisome way that a wheelbar-
row does, and as we didn't create any breeze at that gait, I was
like to get fried in that stove; and besides, the quieter you went

the heavier the iron settled down on you, and the more and more tons you seemed to weigh every minute. And you had to be always changing hands and passing your spear over to the other foot, it got so irksome for one hand to hold it long at a time.

Well, you know when you perspire that way, in rivers, there comes a time when you—when you—well, when you itch. You are inside, your hands are outside: so there you are; nothing but iron between. It is not a light thing, let it sound as it may. First it is one place; then another; then some more; and it goes on spreading and spreading, and at last the territory is all occupied, and nobody can imagine what you feel like, nor how unpleasant it is. And when it had got to the worst, and it seemed to me that I could not stand anything more, a fly got in through the bars and settled on my nose, and the bars were stuck and wouldn't work, and I couldn't get the visor up; and I could only shake my head, which was baking hot by this time, and the fly—well, you know how a fly acts when he has got a certainty: he only minded the shaking enough to change from nose to lip, and lip to ear, and buzz and buzz all around in there, and keep on lighting and biting in a way that a person already so distressed as I was simply could not stand. So I gave in, and got Alisande to unship the helmet and relieve me of it. Then she emptied the conveniences out of it and fetched it full of water, and I drank and then stood up and she poured the rest down inside the armor. One cannot think how refreshing it was. She continued to fetch and pour until I was well soaked and thoroughly comfortable.

It was good to have a rest—and peace. But nothing is quite perfect in this life at any time. I had made a pipe a while back, and also some pretty fair tobacco; not the real thing, but what some of the Indians use: the inside bark of the willow, dried. These comforts had been in the helmet, and now I had them again, but no matches.

Gradually, as the time wore along, one annoying fact was borne in upon my understanding—that we were weather-bound. An armed novice cannot mount his horse without help and plenty of it. Sandy was not enough; not enough for me, anyway. We had to wait until somebody should come along. Waiting in silence would have been agreeable enough, for I was full of matter for reflection, and wanted to give it a chance to work. I wanted to try and think out how it was that rational or even half-rational men could ever have learned to wear armor, considering its inconveniences; and how they had managed to keep up such a fashion for generations when it was plain that what I had suffered to-day they had had to suffer all the days of their lives. I wanted to think that out; and moreover I wanted to think out some way to reform this evil and persuade the people to let the foolish fashion die out: but thinking was out of the question in the circumstances. You couldn't think where Sandy was. She was a quite biddable creature and good-hearted, but she had a flow of talk that was as steady as a mill and made your head sore like the drays and wagons in a city. If she had had a cork she would have been a comfort. But you can't cork that kind; they would die. Her clack was going all day, and you would think something would surely happen to her works by-and-by; but no, they never got out of order; and she never had to slack up for words. She could grind and pump and churn and buzz by the week, and never stop to oil up or blow out. And yet the result was just nothing but wind. She never had any ideas, any more than a fog has. She was a perfect blatherskite; I mean for jaw, jaw, jaw, talk, talk, talk, jabber, jabber, jabber;—but just as good as she could be. I hadn't minded her mill that morning, on account of having that hornet's nest of other troubles; but more than once in the afternoon I had to say:—

"Take a rest, child; the way you are using up all the domestic air, the kingdom will have to go to importing it by to-morrow, and it's a low enough treasury without that."

By permission of S. L. Clemens and his publishers.

THE TRUE PRINCE AND THE FEIGNED ONE

From 'The Prince and the Pauper': copyright 1889, by Charles L. Webster and Company

A T LAST the final act was at hand. The Archbishop of Canterbury lifted up the crown of England from its cushion and held it out over the trembling mock king's head. In the same instant a rainbow radiance flashed along the spacious transept; for with one impulse every individual in the great concourse of nobles lifted a coronet and poised it over his or her head — and paused in that attitude.

A deep hush pervaded the Abbey. At this impressive moment a startling apparition intruded upon the scene — an apparition observed by none in the absorbed multitude, until it suddenly appeared, moving up the great central isle. It was a boy, bare-headed, ill shod, and clothed in coarse plebeian garments that were falling to rags. He raised his hand with a solemnity which ill comported with his soiled and sorry aspect, and delivered this note of warning: —

"I forbid you to set the crown of England upon that forfeited head. *I* am the king!"

In an instant several indignant hands were laid upon the boy, but in the same instant Tom Canty, in his regal vestments, made a swift step forward and cried out in a ringing voice: —

"Loose him and forbear! He *is* the king!"

A sort of panic of astonishment swept the assemblage, and they partly rose in their places and stared in a bewildered way at one another and at the chief figures in this scene, like persons who wondered whether they were awake and in their senses or asleep and dreaming. The Lord Protector was as amazed as the rest, but quickly recovered himself and exclaimed in a voice of authority: —

"Mind not his Majesty, his malady is upon him again — seize the vagabond!"

He would have been obeyed, but the mock king stamped his foot and cried out: —

"On your peril! Touch him not, he is the king!"

The hands were withheld; a paralysis fell upon the house; no one moved, no one spoke; indeed no one knew how to act or what to say, in so strange and surprising an emergency. While all minds were struggling to right themselves, the boy still moved steadily forward, with high port and confident mien; he had never halted from the beginning; and while the tangled minds still floundered helplessly, he stepped upon the platform, and the mock king ran with a glad face to meet him, and fell on his knees before him and said:—

"O my lord the king, let poor Tom Canty be first to swear fealty to thee, and say, 'Put on thy crown and enter into thine own again!'"

The Lord Protector's eye fell sternly upon the new-comer's face; but straightway the sternness vanished away, and gave place to an expression of wondering surprise. This thing happened also to the other great officers. They glanced at each other, and retreated a step by a common and unconscious impulse. The thought in each mind was the same: "What a strange resemblance!"

The Lord Protector reflected a moment or two in perplexity; then he said, with grave respectfulness:—

"By your favor, sir, I desire to ask certain questions which—"

"I will answer them, my lord."

The duke asked him many questions about the court, the late king, the prince, the princesses,—the boy answered them correctly and without hesitating. He described the rooms of state in the palace, the late king's apartments, and those of the Prince of Wales.

It was strange; it was wonderful; yes, it was unaccountable—so all said that heard it. The tide was beginning to turn, and Tom Canty's hopes to run high, when the Lord Protector shook his head and said:—

"It is true it is most wonderful—but it is no more than our lord the king likewise can do." This remark, and this reference to himself as still the king, saddened Tom Canty, and he felt his hopes crumbling under him. "These are not *proofs*," added the Protector.

The tide was turning very fast now, very fast indeed—but in the wrong direction; it was leaving poor Tom Canty stranded on the throne, and sweeping the other out to sea. The Lord Protector communed with himself—shook his head; the thought forced itself upon him, "It is perilous to the State and to us all, to entertain so fateful a riddle as this; it could divide the nation and undermine the throne." He turned and said:—

"Sir Thomas, arrest this — No, hold!" His face lighted, and he confronted the ragged candidate with this question: —

"Where lieth the Great Seal? Answer me this truly, and the riddle is unriddled; for only he that was Prince of Wales *can* so answer! On so trivial a thing hang a throne and a dynasty!"

It was a lucky thought, a happy thought. That it was so considered by the great officials was manifested by the silent applause that shot from eye to eye around their circle in the form of bright approving glances. Yes, none but the true prince could dissolve the stubborn mystery of the vanished Great Seal — this forlorn little impostor had been taught his lesson well, but here his teachings must fail, for his teacher himself could not answer *that* question — ah, very good, very good indeed; now we shall be rid of this troublesome and perilous business in short order! And so they nodded invisibly and smiled inwardly with satisfaction, and looked to see this foolish lad stricken with a palsy of guilty confusion. How surprised they were, then, to see nothing of the sort happen — how they marveled to hear him answer up promptly in a confident and untroubled voice and say: —

"There is naught in this riddle that is difficult." Then, without so much as a by-your-leave to anybody, he turned and gave this command with the easy manner of one accustomed to doing such things: "My lord St. John, go you to my private cabinet in the palace, — for none knoweth the place better than you, — and close down to the floor, in the left corner, remotest from the door that opens from the ante-chamber, you shall find in the wall a brazen nail-head; press upon it and a little jewel-closet will fly open, which not even you do know of — no, nor any soul else in all the world but me and the trusty artisan that did contrive it for me. The first thing that falleth under your eye will be the Great Seal — fetch it hither."

All the company wondered at this speech, and wondered still more to see the little mendicant pick out this peer without hesitancy or apparent fear of mistake, and call him by name with such a placidly convincing air of having known him all his life. The peer was almost surprised into obeying. He even made a movement as if to go, but quickly recovered his tranquil attitude and confessed his blunder with a blush. Tom Canty turned upon him and said sharply: —

"Why dost thou hesitate? Hast not heard the king's command? Go!"

The lord St. John made a deep obeisance — and it was observed that it was a significantly cautious and non-committal one, it not being delivered at either of the kings, but at the neutral ground about half-way between the two — and took his leave.

Now began a movement of the gorgeous particles of that official group which was slow, scarcely perceptible, and yet steady and persistent, — a movement such as is observed in a kaleidoscope that is turned slowly, whereby the components of one splendid cluster fall away and join themselves to another — a movement which little by little, in the present case, dissolved the glittering crowd that stood about Tom Canty and clustered it together again in the neighborhood of the new-comer. Tom Canty stood almost alone. Now ensued a brief season of deep suspense and waiting — during which even the few faint-hearts still remaining near Tom Canty gradually scraped together courage enough to glide, one by one, over to the majority. So at last Tom Canty, in his royal robes and jewels, stood wholly alone and isolated from the world, a conspicuous figure, occupying an elegant vacancy.

Now the lord St. John was seen returning. As he advanced up the mid-aisle, the interest was so intense that the low murmur of conversation in the great assemblage died out and was succeeded by a profound hush, a breathless stillness, through which his footfalls pulsed with a dull and distant sound. Every eye was fastened upon him as he moved along. He reached the platform, paused a moment, then moved toward Tom Canty with a deep obeisance, and said: —

"Sire, the Seal is not there!"

A mob does not melt away from the presence of a plague-patient with more haste than the band of pallid and terrified courtiers melted away from the presence of the shabby little claimant of the crown. In a moment he stood all alone, without friend or supporter, a target upon which was concentrated a bitter fire of scornful and angry looks. The Lord Protector called out fiercely: —

"Cast the beggar into the street, and scourge him through the town — the paltry knave is worth no more consideration!"

Officers of the guard sprang forward to obey, but Tom Canty waved them off and said: —

"Back! Whoso touches him perils his life!"

The Lord Protector was perplexed in the last degree. He said to the lord St. John:—

"Searched you well?—but it boots not to ask that. It doth seem passing strange. Little things, trifles, slip out of one's ken, and one does not think it matter for surprise; but how so bulky a thing as the Seal of England can vanish away and no man be able to get track of it again—a massy golden disk—"

Tom Canty, with beaming eyes, sprang forward and shouted:

"Hold, that is enough! Was it round?—and thick?—and had it letters and devices graved upon it?—Yes? Oh, *now* I know what this Great Seal is, that there's been such worry and pother about! An ye had described it to me, ye could have had it three weeks ago. Right well I know where it lies; but it was not I that put it there—first."

"Who then, my liege?" asked the Lord Protector.

"He that stands there—the rightful king of England. And he shall tell you himself where it lies—then you will believe he knew it of his own knowledge. Bethink thee, my king—spur thy memory—it was the last, the very *last* thing thou didst that day before thou didst rush forth from the palace, clothed in my rags, to punish the soldier that insulted me."

A silence ensued, undisturbed by a movement or a whisper, and all eyes were fixed upon the new-comer, who stood with bent head and corrugated brow, groping in his memory among a thronging multitude of valueless recollections for one single little elusive fact, which, found, would seat him upon a throne—unfound, would leave him as he was for good and all—a pauper and an outcast. Moment after moment passed—the moments built themselves into minutes—still the boy struggled silently on, and gave no sign. But at last he heaved a sigh, shook his head slowly, and said, with a trembling lip and in a despondent voice:—

"I call the scene back—all of it—but the Seal hath no place in it." He paused, then looked up, and said with gentle dignity, "My lords and gentlemen, if ye will rob your rightful sovereign of his own for lack of this evidence which he is not able to furnish, I may not stay ye, being powerless. But—"

"Oh folly, oh madness, my king!" cried Tom Canty in a panic; "wait!—think! Do not give up!—the cause is not lost! nor *shall* be, neither! List to what I say—follow every word—

I am going to bring that morning back again, every hap just as it happened. We talked — I told you of my sisters, Nan and Bet — ah yes, you remember that; and about my old grandam — and the rough games of the lads of Offal Court — yes, you remember these things also; very well, follow me still, you shall recall everything. You gave me food and drink, and did with princely courtesy send away the servants, so that my low breeding might not shame me before them — ah yes, this also you remember."

As Tom checked off his details, and the other boy nodded his head in recognition of them, the great audience and the officials stared in puzzled wonderment; the tale sounded like true history, yet how could this impossible conjunction between a prince and a beggar boy have come about? Never was a company of people so perplexed, so interested, and so stupefied before.

"For a jest, my prince, we did exchange garments. Then we stood before a mirror; and so alike were we that both said it seemed as if there had been no change made — yes, you remember that. Then you noticed that the soldier had hurt my hand — look! here it is, I cannot yet even write with it, the fingers are so stiff. At this your Highness sprang up, vowing vengeance upon that soldier, and ran toward the door — you passed a table — that thing you call the Seal lay on that table — you snatched it up and looked eagerly about, as if for a place to hide it — your eye caught sight of — "

"There, 'tis sufficient! — and the dear God be thanked!" exclaimed the ragged claimant, in a mighty excitement. "Go, my good St. John, — in an arm-piece of the Milanese armor that hangs on the wall, thou'lt find the Seal!"

"Right, my king! right!" cried Tom Canty; "now the sceptre of England is thine own; and it were better for him that would dispute it that he had been born dumb! Go, my lord St. John, give thy feet wings!"

The whole assemblage was on its feet now, and well-nigh out of its mind with uneasiness, apprehension, and consuming excitement. On the floor and on the platform a deafening buzz of frantic conversation burst forth, and for some time nobody knew anything or heard anything or was interested in anything but what his neighbor was shouting into his ear, or he was shouting into his neighbor's ear. Time — nobody knew how much of it — swept by unheeded and unnoted, — At last a sudden hush fell upon the house, and in the same moment St. John appeared upon the platform and held the Great Seal aloft in his hand. Then such a shout went up!

"Long live the true king!"

For five minutes the air quaked with shouts and the crash of musical instruments, and was white with a storm of waving handkerchiefs; and through it all a ragged lad, the most conspicuous figure in England, stood, flushed and happy and proud, in the centre of the spacious platform, with the great vassals of the kingdom kneeling around him.

Then all rose, and Tom Canty cried out:—

"Now, O my king, take these regal garments back, and give poor Tom thy servant his shreds and remnants again."

The Lord Protector spoke up:—

"Let the small varlet be stripped and flung into the Tower."

But the new king, the true king, said:—

"I will not have it so. But for him I had not got my crown again—none shall lay a hand upon him to harm him. And as for thee, my good uncle, my Lord Protector, this conduct of thine is not grateful toward this poor lad, for I hear he hath made thee a duke"—the Protector blushed—"yet he was not a king; wherefore, what is thy fine title worth now? To-morrow you shall sue to me, *through him*, for its confirmation, else no duke, but a simple earl, shalt thou remain."

Under this rebuke his Grace the Duke of Somerset retired a little from the front for the moment. The king turned to Tom, and said kindly:—

"My poor boy, how was it that you could remember where I hid the Seal, when I could not remember it myself?"

"Ah, my king, that was easy, since I used it divers days."

"Used it,—yet could not explain where it was?"

"I did not know it was *that* they wanted. They did not describe it, your Majesty."

"Then how used you it?"

The red blood began to steal up into Tom's cheeks, and he dropped his eyes and was silent.

"Speak up, good lad, and fear nothing," said the king. "How used you the Great Seal of England?"

Tom stammered a moment in a pathetic confusion, then got it out:—

"To crack nuts with!"

Poor child, the avalanche of laughter that greeted this nearly swept him off his feet. But if a doubt remained in any mind that Tom Canty was not the king of England and familiar with the august appurtenances of royalty, this reply disposed of it utterly.

Meantime the sumptuous robe of state had been removed from Tom's shoulders to the king's, whose rags were effectually hidden from sight under it. Then the coronation ceremonies were resumed; the true king was anointed and the crown set upon his head, whilst cannon thundered the news to the city, and all London seemed to rock with applause.

By permission of S. L. Clemens and his publishers.

ARTHUR HUGH CLOUGH

(1819–1861)

BY CHARLES ELIOT NORTON

HE intellectual mood of many of the finest spirits in England and New England during the second quarter of the nineteenth century had something of the nature of a surprise to themselves, no less than to those who came within their influence. It was indeed a natural though unforeseen result of forces, various in kind, that had long been silently at work. The conflicting currents of thought and moral sentiment, which in all ages perplex and divide the hearts of men, took a new direction and seemed to have gathered volume and swiftness. Hardly since the Reformation had there been so deep and general a stirring of the questions, the answers to which, whether they be final or merely provisional, involve conclusions relating to the deepest interests of men. Old convictions were confronted by new doubts; ancient authority was met by a modern spirit of independence. This new intellectual mood was perhaps first distinctly manifest in England in Carlyle's essays, and correspondingly in New England in the essays and poems of Emerson; it was expressed in 'In Memoriam' and 'Maud'; it gave the undertone of Arnold's most characteristic verse, and it found clear and strikingly distinctive utterance in the poems of Clough. His nature was of rare superiority alike of character and intellect. His moral integrity and sincerity imparted clearness to his imagination and strength to his intelligence, so that while the most marked distinction of his poems is that which they possess as a mirror of spiritual conditions shared by many of his contemporaries, they have hardly less interest as the expression and image of his own individuality.

Arthur Hugh Clough was born at Liverpool on New Year's Day, 1819.* His father, who came of an old Welsh family (his mother, Anne Perfect, was from Yorkshire), had established himself in Liverpool as a cotton merchant. Toward the end of 1822 he emigrated with his wife and four children to Charleston, South Carolina, and here for four years was their home. For Arthur they were important years. He was a shy, sensitive boy, "already considered as the genius of the family." He was his mother's darling. She was a woman "rigidly simple in her tastes and habits, of stern integrity"; of cultivated intelligence, fond of poetry, a lover of nature, and

---

* Ruskin and Lowell were his close contemporaries; they were born in February of the same year.

quickly sympathetic with high character, whether in real life or in the pages of romance. While his father taught him his Latin grammar and his arithmetic, his mother read with him from Pope's Iliad and Odyssey, from Scott's novels and other books fitted to quicken the imagination. Her influence was strong in the shaping of his taste and disposition.

In 1828 the family returned for a visit to England, and Arthur was put to school at Chester, whence in the next year he was transferred to Rugby. Dr. Arnold had then very lately become the headmaster at Rugby, and was already giving to the school a tone and quality unknown previously to the public schools of England. He strove to impress upon the boys the sense of personal responsibility, and to rouse their conscience to the doing of duty, not so much as a matter essential to the discipline of the school as to the formation of manly and religious character. The influence of his high, vigorous, and ardent nature was of immense force. But its virtue was impaired by the artificiality of the ecclesiastical system of the Church of England, and the irrationality of the dogmatic creed which, even to a nature as liberal as Dr. Arnold's, seemed to belong to the essentials of religion, and to be indissoluble from the foundation of morality.

Clough became Arnold's devoted disciple, but he had intellectual independence and sincerity enough to save him from yielding his own individuality to any stream of external influence, however powerful. What he called "the busy argufying spirit of the prize schoolboy" stood him in good stead. But the moral stress was great, and it left him early with a sense of strain and of perplexity, as his mind opened to the wider and deeper problems of life, for the solution of which the traditional creed seemed insufficient. His career at school was of the highest distinction; and when he was leaving Rugby for Oxford in 1836, Dr. Arnold broke the rule of silence to which he almost invariably adhered in the delivery of prizes, and congratulated Clough on having gained every honor which Rugby could bestow, and on having done the highest credit to the school at the University,— for he had won the Balliol Scholarship, "then and now the highest honor which a schoolboy could obtain."

Clough went into residence at Oxford in October, 1837. It was a time of stirring of heart and trouble of mind at the University. The great theological controversy which was to produce such far-reaching effects upon the lives of individuals, and upon the Church of England as a whole, was then rising to its height. Newman was at the acme of his popularity and influence. His followers were zealous and active. Ward, his most earnest disciple, was one of Clough's nearest friends. Clough, not yet nineteen years old, but morally and intellectually developed beyond his years and accustomed already to independent speculation in regard to creed and conduct, was inevitably drawn into the deep waters of theological discussion. He heard, too, those other voices which Matthew Arnold in his admirable lecture on Emerson has spoken of as deeply affecting the more sensitive youthful spirits of the Oxford of this time,—the voices of Goethe, of Carlyle, and of Emerson. He studied hard, but his studies seemed, for the moment at least, to be of secondary importance. Although unusually reserved in demeanor and silent in general company, his reputation grew, not merely as a scholar, but as a man distinguished above his fellows for loftiness of spirit, for sweetness of disposition, and for superiority of moral no less than of intellectual qualities. With much interior storm and stress, his convictions were gradually maturing. He resisted the prevailing tendencies of Oxford thought, but did not easily find a secure basis for his own beliefs. In 1841 he tried for and missed his first class in the examinations. It was more a surprise and disappointment to others than to himself. He knew that he had not shown himself in the examinations for what he really was, and his failure did not affect his confidence in his own powers, nor did others lose faith in him, as was shown by his election in the next year to a fellowship at Oriel, and the year later to his appointment as tutor.

His livelihood being thus assured, he led from 1843 to 1848 a "quiet, hard-working, uneventful tutor's life, diversified with reading parties" in the vacations. He was writing poems from time to time, but his vocation as poet was not fully recognized by himself or by others. He had been obliged, in assuming the duties of tutor, to sign the Thirty-nine Articles,—though as he wrote to a friend, "reluctantly enough, and I am not quite sure whether or not in a justifiable sense. However, I have for the present laid by that perplexity, though it may perhaps recur at some time or other; and in general, I do not feel perfectly satisfied about staying in my tutor capacity at Oxford."

The perplexity would not down, but as the years went on, the troubled waters of his soul gradually cleared themselves. He succeeded in attaining independence of mind such as few men attain, and in finding, if not a solution of the moral perplexities of life, at least a position from which they might be frankly confronted without blinking and without self-deception. It became impossible for him to accept, however they might be interpreted, the doctrines of any church. He would not play tricks with words nor palter with the integrity of his soul. This perfect mental honesty of Clough, and his entire sincerity of expression, were a stumbling-block to many of his more conventional contemporaries, and have remained as a rock of offense to many of the readers of his poetry, who find it disturbing to be obliged to recognize in his work a test of their own

sincerity in dealing with themselves. With how few are conviction
and profession perfectly at one! The difficulty of the struggle in
Clough's case, the difficulty of freeing himself from the chains of
association, of tradition, of affection, of interest, which bound him to
conformity with and acceptance of the popular creed in one or the
other of its forms, has led superficial critics of his life and poetry to
find in them evidence that the struggle was too hard for him and
the result unsatisfactory. There could not be a greater error.
Clough's honest acceptance of the insolubility of the vain questions
which men are perpetually asking, and his recognition of the insufficiency of the answers which they are ready to accept or to pretend
to accept, left him as regards his most inward soul one of the seren-
est of men. The questions of practical life, of action, of duty,
indeed presented themselves to his sensitive and contemplative
nature with their full perplexity; but his spiritual life was based on
a foundation that could not be shaken. He had learned the lesson of
skepticism, and accepted without trouble the fact of the limitation
of human faculties and the insolubility of the mystery of life. He
was indeed tired with the hard work of years, and worried by the
uncertainty of his future; when at length, in order to deliver himself from a constrained if not a false position, and to obtain perfect
freedom of expression as well as of thought, he resigned in 1848 both
his fellowship and tutorship.

It was a momentous decision, for it left him without any definite
means of support, it alienated the authorities of the University, it
isolated him from many old friends. Immediately after resigning his
tutorship Clough went to Paris with Emerson, then on a visit to
Europe, as his companion. They were drawn thither by interest in
the strange Revolution which was then in progress, and by desire to
watch its aspects. The social conditions of England had long been
matter of concern to Clough. He had been deeply touched by the
misery of the Irish famine in 1847, and had printed a very striking
pamphlet in the autumn of that year, urging upon the students at
Oxford retrenchment of needless expenditure and restrictions of
waste and luxury. His sympathies were with the poor, and he was
convinced of the need of radical social reform. He therefore
observed the course of revolution on the Continent not merely with
curiosity, but with sympathetic hope.

In the autumn of this year, after his return home, and while at
Liverpool with his mother and sister, he wrote his first long poem,
'The Bothie of Tober-na-Vuolich; a Long-Vacation Pastoral.' It had
no great immediate success, but it made him known to a somewhat
wider public than that of Oxford. It was in its form the fruit of the
reading parties in the Highlands in previous summers. It was in

hexameters, and he asked Emerson to "convey to Mr. Longfellow the fact that it was a reading of his 'Evangeline' aloud to my mother and sister, which, coming after a re-perusal of the Iliad, occasioned this outbreak of hexameters." It is a delightful poem, full of vitality and variety, original in design, simple in incident. It has the freshness and wholesomeness of the open air, the charm of nature and of life, with constant interplay of serious thought and light humor, of gravity and gayety of sentiment.

Its publication was followed speedily by a little volume entitled 'Ambarvalia,' made up of two parts; one, of poems by Clough, and one, of those by an old school and college friend, Mr. Burbidge. Clough's part consisted, as he wrote to Emerson, of "old things, the casualties of at least ten years." But many of these "casualties" are characteristic expressions of personal experience, to which Clough's absolute sincerity gives deep human interest. They are the records of "his search amid the maze of life for a clue whereby to move." They deal with the problems of his own life, and these problems perplex other men as well. "I have seen higher, holier things than these," he writes in 1841:—

> "I have seen higher, holier things than these,
>   And therefore must to these refuse my heart,
>   Yet I am panting for a little ease;
>   I'll take, and so depart."

But he checks himself:—

> "Ah, hold! the heart is prone to fall away,
>   Her high and cherished visions to forget;
>   And if thou takest, how wilt thou repay
>   So vast, so dread a debt?"

The little volume appealed to but a small band of readers. The poems it contained did not allure by fluency of fancy or richness of diction; they were not of a kind to win sudden popularity: but they gave evidence of a poet who, though not complete master of his art, and not arrived at a complete understanding of himself, had yet a rare power of reflection and expression and a still rarer sincerity of imaginative vision. They were poems that gave large promise, and that promise was already in part fulfilled by the 'Bothie.'

Early in 1849 the headship of University Hall in London was offered to Clough and accepted by him. This was an institution professedly non-sectarian, established for the purpose of receiving students in attendance upon the lectures at University College. He was not to enter upon the duties of the place until October, and he spent the greater part of the intervening period in a fruitful visit to

Italy. He reached Rome in April. All Italy was in revolution. The Pope had fled from Rome. The Republic had been declared, and Mazzini was in control of the government. The French army was approaching to besiege the city, and Clough resolved to await the event. No more vivid and picturesque account of aspects of the siege exists than is to be found in his poem of 'Amours de Voyage,' written in great part at Rome, under the pressure and excitement of the moment; then laid aside in the poet's desk, and not published till long afterward. It consists of a series of letters supposed to be written by various persons, in which a narrative of passing events is interwoven with a love story. The hero of the story is a creation of extraordinary subtlety and interest. He has much of the temperament of Hamlet: not wanting in personal courage, nor in resolution when forced to action, but hesitating through sensitiveness of conscience, through dread of mistaking momentary impulse for fixed conviction, through the clearness with which diverging paths of conduct present themselves to his imagination, with the inevitable doubt as to which be the right one to follow. The character, though by no means an exact or complete image of the poet's own, is yet drawn in part from himself, and affords glimpses of his inner nature, of the delicacy of his sensitive poetic spirit, of his tendency to subtle introspective reflection, of his honesty in dealing with facts and with himself. To see things as they are, to keep his eyes clear, to be true to

«The living central inmost I
Within the scales of mere exterior — »

was the principle of his life. The charm of 'Amours de Voyage,' however, consists not merely in animated description, in delicate sentiment, and in the poetic representation of sensitive, impressionable, and high-minded youth, but in its delicate humor in the delineation of character, and in its powerful, imaginative, picturesque reproduction of the atmosphere and influence of Rome, and of the spirit of the moment to which the poem relates. It is as unique and as original in its kind as the 'Bothie.' It is a poem that appeals strongly to the lovers of the poetry of high culture, and is not likely to lack such readers in future generations.

From Rome in July Clough went to Naples, and there wrote another of his most striking poems, 'Easter Day.' In the autumn of 1850 he again went during a short vacation to Italy, but now to Venice; and while there began his third long poem, 'Dipsychus,' of which the scene is in that city. In this poem, which represents the conflict of the soul in its struggles to maintain itself against the temptations of the world and the Devil, Clough again wrote out much of his inner life. It is not so much a piece of strict autobiography of the spirit of an individual, as an imaginative drama of the spiritual experience common in all times to men of fine nature, seeking a solution of the puzzle of their own hearts. In none of his other poems is there such variety of tone, or such an exhibition of mature poetic power. It is indeed loosely constructed; but its separate parts, each contributing to the development of its main theme, with their diversity of imagination, reflection, wit, and sentiment, combine in an impressive unity of effect.

The position at University Hall proved not altogether satisfactory; and no other opening for him offering itself in England, Clough determined after much hesitation and deliberation to try his fortune as a teacher and writer in America. He sailed in October, 1852, on a steamer on which he had Lowell and Thackeray for fellow passengers. He spent the next eight months at Cambridge, employed in tutoring and in literary work, winning the warm regard of the remarkable group of men of letters who then gave distinction to the society of Cambridge and of Boston, and especially keeping up his friendship with Emerson by frequent visits to Concord. There seemed a fair prospect of success for him in his new career. But his friends at home, deeply attached to him, and ill content that he should leave them, obtained for him an appointment as examiner in the Education Department of the Council Office. The salary would give to him a secure though moderate income. He was the more drawn to accept the place, because shortly before leaving England he had become engaged to be married; and accordingly in July, 1853, he returned home and at once entered on the duties of his office. In June 1854 he married. For the next seven years his life was tranquil, laborious, and happy. The account of these years contained in the beautiful sketch of his life by his wife, which is prefixed to the collection of his 'Letters, Poems and Prose Remains,' * gives a picture of Clough's domestic felicity, and of the various interests which engaged him outside of the regular drudgery of official work. His own letters bear witness to the content of his days. He had little leisure for poetry. He was overworked, and in 1860 his health gave way. Leave of absence from the office was given to him. He went to the seashore; he visited the Continent: but though at times he seemed to gain strength, there was no steady recovery. In the autumn of 1861 he went to Italy, accompanied by his wife; he enjoyed the journey, but they had only reached the Lakes when he experienced a touch of fever. They went on to Florence; he became more seriously ill. He began however apparently to recover, but a

---

* It is on this sketch of his life that the present account of him is mainly based.

sudden blow of paralysis struck him down, and on the 13th day of November he died.

Among the most original and beautiful of Matthew Arnold's poems is his 'Thyrsis, a Monody,' to commemorate his friend Arthur Hugh Clough. Thyrsis his mate has gone:—

«No purer or more subtle soul»

than he ever sought the light that

> «leaves its seeker still untired,—
> Still onward faring by his own heart inspired.»

The lament is as true as it is tender. The singer continues:—

> «What though the music of thy rustic flute
> Kept not for long its happy country tone;
> Lost it too soon, and learnt a stormy note
> Of men contention-tost, of men who groan,
> Which tasked thy pipe too sore, and tired thy throat,—
> It failed, and thou wast mute!
> Yet hadst thou always visions of our light.»

Yes, always visions of the light! But Arnold's usual felicity of discrimination is lacking in this last stanza. The stormy note is not the characteristic note of Clough's mature song, nor does his art betray the overtasked pipe. His pipe indeed is not attuned, as was Arnold's own, to the soft melancholy of regret at leaving behind the happy fields of the past in the quest for the light that shines beyond and across the untraveled and dim waste before them; its tone was less pathetic, but not less clear. The music of each is the song of travelers whose road is difficult, whose goal is uncertain. Their only guide is the fugitive light, now faint, now distinct, which allures them with irresistible compulsion. Their pathways at times diverge; but when most divergent, the notes of their accordant pipes are heard in the same direction.

The memory of Clough remains, with those who had the happiness of knowing him in life, distinct and precious. It is that of one of the highest and purest souls. Sensitive, simple, tender, manly, his figure stands as one of the ideal figures of the past, the image of the true poet, the true friend, the true man. He died too young for his full fame, but not too young for the love which is better than fame.

C. E. Norton.

THERE IS NO GOD

« THERE is no God,» the wicked saith,
    « And truly it's a blessing,
For what he might have done with us
    It's better only guessing.»

« There is no God,» a youngster thinks,
    « Or really, if there may be,
He surely didn't mean a man
    Always to be a baby.»

« There is no God, or if there is,»
    The tradesman thinks, « 'twere funny
If he should take it ill in me
    To make a little money.»

« Whether there be,» the rich man says,
    « It matters very little,
For I and mine, thank somebody,
    Are not in want of victual.»

Some others, also, to themselves,
    Who scarce so much as doubt it,
Think there is none, when they are well,
    And do not think about it.

But country folks who live beneath
    The shadow of the steeple;
The parson and the parson's wife,
    And mostly married people;

Youths green and happy in first love,
    So thankful for illusion;
And men caught out in what the world
    Calls guilt, in first confusion;

And almost every one when age,
    Disease, or sorrows strike him,—
Inclines to think there is a God,
    Or something very like him.

THE LATEST DECALOGUE

THOU shalt have one God only: who
    Would be at the expense of two?
No graven images may be
Worshiped, save in the currency.
Swear not at all; since for thy curse
Thine enemy is none the worse.
At church on Sunday to attend
Will serve to keep the world thy friend:
Honor thy parents; that is, all
From whom advancement may befall.
Thou shalt not kill; but need'st not strive
Officiously to keep alive.
Adultery it is not fit
Or safe (for woman) to commit.
Thou shalt not steal: an empty feat,
When 'tis as lucrative to cheat.
Bear not false witness: let the lie
Have time on its own wings to fly.
Thou shalt not covet; but tradition
Approves all forms of competition.

TO THE UNKNOWN GOD

O THOU whose image in the shrine
    Of human spirits dwells divine;
        Which from that precinct once conveyed,
To be to outer day displayed,
Doth vanish, part, and leave behind
Mere blank and void of empty mind,
Which willful fancy seeks in vain
With casual shapes to fill again!

O Thou that in our bosom's shrine
Dost dwell, unknown because divine!
I thought to speak, I thought to say,
"The light is here," — "Behold the way," —
"The voice was thus," — and "Thus the word," —
And "Thus I saw," — and "That I heard," —
But from the lips that half assayed
The imperfect utterance fell unmade.

O Thou, in that mysterious shrine
Enthroned, as I must say, divine!
I will not frame one thought of what
Thou mayest either be or not.
I will not prate of "thus" and "so,"
And be profane with "yes" and "no";
Enough that in our soul and heart
Thou, whatsoe'er Thou may'st be, art.

Unseen, secure in that high shrine
Acknowledged present and divine,
I will not ask some upper air,
Some future day to place Thee there;
Nor say, nor yet deny, such men
And women say Thee thus and then:
Thy name was such, and there or here
To him or her Thou didst appear.

Do only Thou in that dim shrine,
Unknown or known, remain, divine;
There, or if not, at least in eyes
That scan the fact that round them lies,
The hand to sway, the judgment guide,
In sight and sense Thyself divide:
Be Thou but there, in soul and heart,—
I will not ask to feel Thou art.

EASTER DAY

NAPLES, 1849

THROUGH the great sinful streets of Naples as I past,
    With fiercer heat than flamed above my head,
My heart was hot within me; till at last
    My brain was lightened when my tongue had said—
        Christ is not risen!

        Christ is not risen, no—
        He lies and molders low;
        Christ is not risen!

What though the stone were rolled away, and though
        The grave found empty there?—
        If not there, then elsewhere;
If not where Joseph laid him first, why then
        Where other men

Translaid him after, in some humbler clay.
    Long ere to-day
Corruption that sad perfect work hath done,
Which here she scarcely, lightly, had begun:
    The foul engendered worm
Feeds on the flesh of the life-giving form
Of our most Holy and Anointed One.
        He is not risen, no—
        He lies and molders low;
        Christ is not risen!

What if the women, ere the dawn was gray,
Saw one or more great angels, as they say
(Angels, or Him himself)? Yet neither there, nor then,
Nor afterwards, nor elsewhere, nor at all,
    Hath he appeared to Peter or the Ten;
Nor, save in thunderous terror, to blind Saul;
Save in an after-Gospel and late Creed,
        He is not risen, indeed,—
        Christ is not risen!

Or what if e'en, as runs a tale, the Ten
Saw, heard, and touched, again and yet again?
What if at Emmaüs's inn, and by Capernaum's Lake,
    Came One, the bread that brake—
Came One that spake as never mortal spake,
And with them ate, and drank, and stood, and walked about?
        Ah! "some" did well to "doubt"!
Ah! the true Christ, while these things came to pass,
Nor heard, nor spake, nor walked, nor lived, alas!
        He was not risen, no—
        He lay and moldered low;
        Christ was not risen!

As circulates in some great city crowd
A rumor changeful, vague, importunate, and loud,
From no determined centre, or of fact
        Or authorship exact,
        Which no man can deny
            Nor verify;
        So spread the wondrous fame;
            He all the same
        Lay senseless, moldering low;
        He was not risen, no—
            Christ was not risen!

Ashes to ashes, dust to dust;
As of the unjust, also of the just —
    Yea, of that Just One, too!
This is the one sad Gospel that is true —
    Christ is not risen!

Is he not risen, and shall we not rise?
    Oh, we unwise!
What did we dream, what wake we to discover?
Ye hills, fall on us, and ye mountains, cover!
    In darkness and great gloom
Come ere we thought it is *our* day of doom;
From the cursed world, which is one tomb,
    Christ is not risen!

Eat, drink, and play, and think that this is bliss:
    There is no heaven but this;
    There is no hell,
Save earth, which serves the purpose doubly well,
    Seeing it visits still
    With equalest apportionment of ill
Both good and bad alike, and brings to one same dust
    The unjust and the just
    With Christ, who is not risen.

Eat, drink, and die, for we are souls bereaved:
    Of all the creatures under heaven's wide cope
    We are most hopeless, who had once most hope,
And most beliefless, that had most believed.

Ashes to ashes, dust to dust;
As of the unjust, also of the just —
    Yea, of that Just One, too!
It is the one sad Gospel that is true —
    Christ is not risen!

Weep not beside the tomb,
    Ye women, unto whom
He was great solace while ye tended him;
    Ye who with napkin o'er the head
And folds of linen round each wounded limb
    Laid out the Sacred Dead;
And thou that bar'st him in thy wondering womb;
    Yea, Daughters of Jerusalem, depart,
Bind up as best you may your own sad bleeding heart:

Go to your homes, your living children tend,
Your earthly spouses love;
Set your affections *not* on things above,
Which moth and rust corrupt, which quickliest come to end:
Or pray, if pray ye must, and pray, if pray ye can,
For death; since dead is he whom ye deemed more than man,
Who is not risen: no —
But lies and molders low —
Who is not risen!

Ye men of Galilee!
Why stand ye looking up to heaven, where him ye ne'er may see,
Neither ascending hence, nor returning hither again?
Ye ignorant and idle fishermen!
Hence to your huts, and boats, and inland native shore,
And catch not men, but fish;
Whate'er things ye might wish,
Him neither here nor there ye e'er shall meet with more.
Ye poor deluded youths, go home,
Mend the old nets ye left to roam,
Tie the split oar, patch the torn sail:
It was indeed an "idle tale" —
He was not risen!

And oh, good men of ages yet to be,
Who shall believe *because* ye did not see —
Oh, be ye warned, be wise!
No more with pleading eyes,
And sobs of strong desire,
Unto the empty vacant void aspire,
Seeking another and impossible birth
That is not of your own, and only mother earth.
But if there is no other life for you,
Sit down and be content, since this must even do;
He is not risen!

One look and then depart,
Ye humble and ye holy men of heart;
And ye! ye ministers and stewards of a Word
Which ye would preach, because another heard —
Ye worshipers of that ye do not know,
Take these things hence and go: —
He is not risen!

Here, on our Easter Day
We rise, we come, and lo! we find Him not,
Gardener nor other, on the sacred spot:
Where they have laid Him there is none to say;
No sound, nor in, nor out — no word
Of where to seek the dead or meet the living Lord.
There is no glistering of an angel's wings,
There is no voice of heavenly clear behest:
Let us go hence, and think upon these things
In silence, which is best.
Is He not risen? No —
But lies and molders low?
Christ is not risen?

IT FORTIFIES MY SOUL TO KNOW

IT FORTIFIES my soul to know
That though I perish, Truth is so;
That howsoe'er I stray and range,
Whate'er I do, Thou dost not change;
I steadier step when I recall
That if I slip, Thou dost not fall!

SAY NOT, THE STRUGGLE NAUGHT AVAILETH

SAY not, the struggle naught availeth,
The labor and the wounds are vain,
The enemy faints not, nor faileth,
And as things have been, they remain.

If hopes were dupes, fears may be liars;
It may be, in yon smoke concealed,
Your comrades chase e'en now the fliers,
And but for you, possess the field.

For while the tired waves, vainly breaking,
Seem here no painful inch to gain,
Far back, through creeks and inlets making,
Comes silent, flooding in, the main.

And not by eastern windows only,
When daylight comes, comes in the light;
In front, the sun climbs slow, how slowly!
But westward, look, the land is bright.

COME BACK

COME back, come back! behold with straining mast
And swelling sail, behold her steaming fast:
With one new sun to see her voyage o'er,
With morning light to touch her native shore.
          Come back, come back!

Come back, come back! while westward laboring by,
With sailless yards, a bare black hulk we fly.
See how the gale we fight with sweeps her back
To our lost home, on our forsaken track.
          Come back, come back!

Come back, come back! across the flying foam
We hear faint far-off voices call us home:
Come back! ye seem to say; ye seek in vain;
We went, we sought, and homeward turned again.
          Come back, come back!

Come back, come back! and whither back, or why?
To fan quenched hopes, forsaken schemes to try;
Walk the old fields; pace the familiar street;
Dream with the idlers, with the bards compete.
          Come back, come back!

Come back, come back! and whither and for what?
To finger idly some old Gordian knot,
Unskilled to sunder, and too weak to cleave,
And with much toil attain to half-believe.
          Come back, come back!

Come back, come back! yea, back indeed do go
Sighs panting thick, and tears that want to flow;
Fond fluttering hopes upraise their useless wings,
And wishes idly struggle in the strings.
          Come back, come back!

Come back, come back! more eager than the breeze
The flying fancies sweep across the seas,
And lighter far than ocean's flying foam
The heart's fond message hurries to its home.
          Come back, come back!

Come back, come back!
Back flies the foam; the hoisted flag streams back;
The long smoke wavers on the homeward track;
Back fly with winds things which the wind obey:
The strong ship follows its appointed way.

AS SHIPS BECALMED

A s ships becalmed at eve, that lay
    With canvas drooping, side by side,
Two towers of sail, at dawn of day,
    Are scarce long leagues apart descried.

When fell the night, up sprang the breeze,
    And all the darkling hours they plied;
Nor dreamt but each the self-same seas
    By each was clearing, side by side:

E'en so — but why the tale reveal
    Of those whom, year by year unchanged,
Brief absence joined anew, to feel,
    Astounded, soul from soul estranged?

At dead of night their sails were filled,
    And onward each rejoicing steered;
Ah! neither blame, for neither willed
    Or wist what first with dawn appeared.

To veer, how vain! On, onward strain,
    Brave barks!—in light, in darkness too!
Through winds and tides one compass guides
    To that and your own selves be true.

But O blithe breeze! and O great seas!
    Though ne'er that earliest parting past,
On your wide plain they join again,
    Together lead them home at last.

One port, methought, alike they sought,—
    One purpose hold, where'er they fare;
O bounding breeze, O rushing seas,
    At last, at last, unite them there.

THE UNKNOWN COURSE

WHERE lies the land to which the ship would go?
  Far, far ahead, is all her seamen know;
    And where the land she travels from? Away,
Far, far behind, is all that they can say.

On sunny noons upon the deck's smooth face,
Linked arm in arm, how pleasant here to pace!
Or, o'er the stern reclining, watch below
The foaming wake far widening as we go.

On stormy nights, when wild Northwesters rave,
How proud a thing to fight with wind and wave!
The dripping sailor on the reeling mast
Exults to bear, and scorns to wish it past.

Where lies the land to which the ship would go?
Far, far ahead, is all her seamen know.
And where the land she travels from? Away,
Far, far behind, is all that they can say.

THE GONDOLA

AFLOAT; we move—delicious! Ah,
  What else is like the gondola?
    This level flow of liquid glass
Begins beneath us swift to pass.
It goes as though it went alone
By some impulsion of its own.
(How light it moves, how softly! Ah,
Were all things like the gondola!)

How light it moves, how softly! Ah,
Could life, as does our gondola,
Unvexed with quarrels, aims, and cares,
And moral duties and affairs,
Unswaying, noiseless, swift, and strong,
For ever thus—thus glide along!
(How light we move, how softly! Ah,
Were life but as the gondola!)

With no more motion than should bear
A freshness to the languid air;

With no more effort than expressed
The need and naturalness of rest,
Which we beneath a grateful shade
Should take on peaceful pillows laid!
(How light we move, how softly! Ah,
Were life but as the gondola!)

In one unbroken passage borne
To closing night from opening morn,
Uplift at whiles slow eyes to mark
Some palace-front, some passing bark;
Through windows catch the varying shore,
And hear the soft turns of the oar!
(How light we move, how softly! Ah,
Were life but as the gondola!)

THE POET'S PLACE IN LIFE

COME, Poet, come!
       A thousand laborers ply their task
       And what it tends to, scarcely ask,
And trembling thinkers on the brink
Shiver, and know not what to think.
To tell the purport of their pain,
And what our silly joys contain;
In lasting lineaments portray
The substance of the shadowy day;
Our real and inner deeds rehearse,
And make our meaning clear in verse —
Come, Poet, come! for but in vain
We do the work or feel the pain,
And gather up the evening gain,
Unless before the end thou come
To take, ere they are lost, their sum.

Come, Poet, come!
To give an utterance to the dumb,
And make vain babblers silent, come;
A thousand dupes point here and there,
Bewildered by the show and glare;
And wise men half have learnt to doubt
Whether we are not best without.
Come, Poet; both but wait to see
Their error proved to them in thee.

Come, Poet, come!
In vain I seem to call. And yet
Think not the living times forget.
Ages of heroes fought and fell
That Homer in the end might tell;
O'er groveling generations past
Upstood the Doric fane at last;
And countless hearts on countless years
Had wasted thoughts, and hopes, and fears,
Rude laughter and unmeaning tears,—
Ere England Shakespeare saw, or Rome
The pure perfection of her dome.
Others, I doubt not, if not we,
The issue of our toils shall see;
Young children gather as their own
The harvest that the dead had sown —
The dead forgotten and unknown.

ON KEEPING WITHIN ONE'S PROPER SPHERE

From 'The Bothie of Tober-na-Vuolich'

[A party of Oxford men spend their long vacation in Scotland. In due
course they return to their colleges. Adam, one of the party,—
« The grave man nicknamed Adam,
White-tied, clerical, silent, with antique square-cut waistcoat,»
receives a letter at Christmas from Philip (Heuston),
« The Chartist, the poet, the eloquent speaker.»]

WHAT I said at Balloch has truth in it; only distorted.
Plants are some for fruit, and some for flowering only;
Let there be deer in parks as well as kine in paddocks,
Grecian buildings upon the earth, as well as Gothic.
There may be men perhaps whose vocation it is to be idle,
Idle, sumptuous even, luxurious, if it must be:
Only let each man seek to be that for which Nature meant him.
Independent surely of pleasure, if not regardless,
Independent also of station, if not regardless;
Irrespective also of station, as of enjoyment;
Do his duty in that state of life to which God, not man, shall
        call him.

If you were meant to plow, Lord Marquis, out with you and do it;
If you were meant to be idle, O beggar, behold I will feed thee:

Take my purse; you have far better right to it, friend, than the
           Marquis.
If you were born for a groom,—and you seem by your dress to
           believe so,—
Do it like a man, Sir George, for pay, in a livery-stable;
Yes, you may so release that slip of a boy at the corner,
Fingering books at the window, misdoubting the Eighth Command-
           ment.
What, a mere Dean with those wits, that debtor-and-creditor head-
           piece!
Go, my detective D. D., take the place of Burns the gauger.
Ah, fair Lady Maria, God meant you to live and be lovely:
Be so then, and I bless you. But ye, ye spurious ware, who
Might be plain women, and can be by no possibility better!
Ye unhappy statuettes, ye miserable trinkets,
Poor alabaster chimney-piece ornaments under glass cases,
Come, in God's name, come down! the very French clock by you
Puts you to shame with ticking; the fire-irons deride you.
Break your glasses; ye can! come down; ye are not really plaster,
Come, in God's name, come down! do anything, be but some-
           thing!

You, young girl, who have had such advantages, learnt so quickly,
Can you not teach? Oh, yes, and she likes Sunday-school extremely,
Only it's soon in the morning. Away! if to teach be your calling,
It is no play, but a business: off! go teach and be paid for it.
Surely that fussy old dowager yonder was meant for the counter;
Oh, she is notable very, and keeps her servants in order
Past admiration. Indeed, and keeps to employ her talent
How many, pray? to what use? Away! the hotel's her vocation.

Lady Sophie's so good to the sick, so firm and so gentle:
Is there a nobler sphere than of hospital nurse and matron?
Hast thou for cooking a turn, little Lady Clarissa? in with them,
In with your fingers! Their beauty it spoils, but your own it
           enhances;
For it is beautiful only to do the thing we are meant for.

But they will marry, have husbands, and children, and guests, and
           households—
Are there so many trades for a man,—for women one only,
First to look out for a husband and then to preside at his table?

Have you ever, Philip, my boy, looked at it in this way?
When the armies are set in array, and the battle beginning,
Is it well that the soldier whose post is far to the leftward
Say, I will go to the right, it is there I shall do best service?
There is a great Field-Marshal, my friend, who arrays our battalions;
Let us to Providence trust, and abide and work in our stations.

CONSIDER IT AGAIN

"OLD things need not be therefore true."
        O brother men, nor yet the new;
            Ah! still awhile the old thought retain,
And yet consider it again!

The souls of now two thousand years
Have laid up here their toils and fears,
And all the earnings of their pain,—
Ah, yet consider it again!

We! what do you see? each a space
Of some few yards before his face;
Does that the whole wide plan explain?
Ah, yet consider it again!

Alas! the great world goes its way,
And takes its truth from each new day;
They do not quit, nor yet retain,
Far less consider it again.

SAMUEL TAYLOR COLERIDGE.

SAMUEL TAYLOR COLERIDGE

(1772-1834)

BY GEORGE E. WOODBERRY

AMUEL TAYLOR COLERIDGE, the English poet and philosopher, was born at Ottery St. Mary, in Devonshire, October 21st, 1772. He was the ninth and youngest son of the vicar of the parish,—a man characterized by learning and also by some of its foibles,—under whose care he passed his childhood; but on the death of his father he was sent up to London to be educated at Christ's Hospital, and there spent, in companionship with Lamb, his school days from 1782 to 1791. He went in the latter year to Jesus College Cambridge. His career as an undergraduate was marked by an escapade,—his enlistment in the King's Regiment of Light Dragoons in the winter of 1793-94, from which he was released by the influence of his relatives; and in more important ways by his friendship with Southey, whom he found on a visit to Oxford, and his engagement to Sarah Fricker in the summer of 1794. He had already been attached to another young lady, Mary Evans, with whose family he had been intimate. In December 1794 he left Cambridge without taking a degree, and on October 21st, 1795, he was married. His biography from this point is one of confused and intricate detail, which only a long story could set forth plainly and exactly. Its leading external events were a residence in Germany in 1798-99 and a voyage to Malta, with travel in Sicily and Italy in 1804-6; in its inward development, the turning-points of his life were his first intimacy with the Wordsworths in 1797, during which his best poems were composed; his subjection to the opium habit, with increasing domestic unhappiness, in 1801-2; and his retreat under medical control to Highgate in 1816. He was practically separated from his family from the time of his voyage to Malta. Troubles of many kinds filled all these years, but he had always a power to attract friends who were deeply interested in his welfare, and he was never without admirers and helpers. Before he withdrew to Highgate he had resided first at Stowey in the neighborhood of Tom Poole, and later at Greta Hall near the Wordsworths; but he was often away from home, and after he ceased to be an inmate there, from 1806 to 1816, he led a wandering life, either in lodgings frequently changed, or in visits to his friends. His resources were always small, and from the start his friends were his patrons, making up subscriptions, loans, and gifts for him; in 1798 the Wedgwoods gave him a pension of £150 for life, which was soon secured for the support of his family, and in 1812 one-half of this was withdrawn; in 1825 he was granted a royal pension of one hundred guineas, and when this lapsed in 1830 Frere made it up to him. De Quincey had distinguished himself by an act of singular and impulsive generosity to him, upon first acquaintance. He was always cared for, though his indulgence in opium made it difficult for those who knew the fact to assist him directly in a wise way. His pecuniary embarrassment, however, was constant and trying during a great part of his life; his own wretchedness of spirit, under the painful conditions of his bodily state and his moral as well as material position, was very great; but through all these sufferings and trials he maintained sufficient energy to leave behind him a considerable body of literary work. He died July 25th, 1834.

The poetic genius of Coleridge, the highest of his many gifts, found brilliant and fascinating expression. His poems — those in which his fame lives — are as unique as they are memorable; and though their small number, their confined range, and the brief period during which his faculty was exercised with full freedom and power, seem to indicate a narrow vein, yet the remainder of his work in prose and verse leaves an impression of extraordinary and abundant intellectual force. In proportion as his imaginative creations stand apart, the spirit out of which they came must have possessed some singularity: and if the reader is not content with simple æsthetic appreciation of what the gods provide, but has some touch of curiosity leading him to look into the source of such remarkable achievement and its human history, he is at once interested in the personality of the "subtle-souled psychologist," as Shelley with his accurate critical insight first named him; in experiencing the fascination of the poetry one remembers the charm which Coleridge had in life, that quality which arrested attention in all companies and drew men's minds and hearts with a sense of something marvelous in him — "the most wonderful man," said Wordsworth, "that I ever met." The mind and heart of Coleridge, his whole life, have been laid open by himself and his friends and acquaintances without reserve in many volumes of letters and memoirs; it is easy to figure him as he lived and to recover his moods and aspect: but in order to conceive his nature and define its traits, it is necessary to take account especially of his incomplete and less perfect work, of his miscellaneous interests, and those activities which filled and confused his life without having any important share in establishing his fame.

The intellectual precocity which is the leading trait of Coleridge's boyhood, in the familiar portrait of " the inspired charity-boy " drawn by Lamb from schoolboy memories, is not unusual in a youth of genius; but the omnivorousness of knowledge which he then displayed continued into his manhood. He consumed vast quantities of book-learning. It is a more remarkable characteristic that from the earliest period in which he comes into clear view, he was accustomed to give out his ideas with freedom in an inexhaustible stream of talk. The activity of his mind was as phenomenal as its receptivity. In his college days, too, he was fanatical in all his energies. The remark of Southey after Shelley's visit to him, that here was a young man who was just what he himself had been in his college days, is illustrative; for if Southey was then inflamed with radicalism, Coleridge was yet more deeply infected and mastered by that wild fever of the revolutionary dawn. The tumult of Coleridge's mind, its incessant action, the lack of discipline in his thought, of restraint in his expression, of judgment in his affairs, are all important elements in his character at a time which in most men would be called the formative period of manhood, but which in him seems to have been intensely chaotic; what is most noticeable, however, is the volume of his mental energy. He expressed himself, too, in ways natural to such self-abundance. He was always a discourser, if the name may be used, from the London days at the " Salutation and the Cat " of which Lamb tells, saying that the landlord was ready to retain him because of the attraction of his conversation for customers; and as he went on to the more set forms of such monologue, he became a preacher without pay in Unitarian chapels, a journalist with unusual capacity for ready and sonorous writing in the press, a composer of whole periodicals such as his ventures The Watchman and The Friend, and a lecturer using only slight notes as the material of his remarks upon literature, education, philosophy, theology, or whatever the subject might be. In all these methods of expression which he took up one after the other, he merely talked in an ample way upon multifarious topics; in the conversation, sermon, leading article, written discourse, or flowing address, he was master of a swelling and often brilliant volubility, but he had neither the certainty of the orator nor the unfailing distinction of the author; there was an occasional and impromptu quality, a colloquial and episodical manner, the style of the irresponsible speaker. In his earlier days especially, the dominant note in Coleridge's whole nature was excitement. He was always animated, he was often violent, he was always without the principle of control. Indeed, a weakness of moral power seems to have been congenital, in the sense that he was not permanently bound by a practical sense of

duty nor apparently observant of what place duty has in real life.
There was misdirection of his affairs from the time when they came
into his own hands; there was impulsiveness, thoughtlessness, a lack
of judgment which augured ill for him; and in its total effect this
amounted to folly. His intoxication with the scheme known as Pan-
tisocracy, by which he with Southey and a few like-minded projectors were to found a socialistic community on the banks of the
Susquehanna, is the most obvious comment on his practical sense.
But his marriage, with the anecdotes of its preliminaries (one of
which was that in those colloquies with Lamb at the London tavern,
so charmingly described by his boon companion, he had forgotten
his engagement or was indifferent to it), more strikingly exemplifies
the irresponsible course of his life, more particularly as it proved to
be ill-sorted, full of petty difficulties and makeshift expedients, and
in the end a disastrous failure. A radical social scheme and an im-
prudent marriage might have fallen to his share of human folly,
however, without exciting remark, if in other ways or at a later
time he had exhibited the qualities which would allow one to dismiss
these matters as mere instances of immaturity; but wherever Coleridge's reasonable control over himself or his affairs is looked to, it
appears to have been feeble. On the other hand, the constancy of
his excitement is plain. It was not only mental, but physical.. He
was, as a young man, full of energy and capable of a good deal of
hard exercise; he had animal spirits, and Wordsworth describes him
as «noisy» and «gamesome,» as one who

> « His limbs would toss about him with delight,
> Like branches when strong winds the trees annoy;»

and from several passages of his own writing, which are usually disregarded, the evidence of a spirit of rough humor and fun is easily
obtained. The truth is that Coleridge changed a great deal in his
life; he felt himself to be very different in later years from what
he was in the time when to his memory even he was a sort of glorified spirit: and this earlier Coleridge had many traits which are
ignored sometimes, as Carlyle ignored them, and are sometimes
remembered rather as idealizations of his friends in their affectionate
thoughts of him, but in any event are irreconcilable with the figure
of the last period of his life.

It has been suggested that there was something of disease or at
least of ill health in Coleridge always, and that it should be regarded
as influencing his temperament. Whether it were so or not, the plea
itself shows the fact. If excitement was the dominant note, as has
been said, in his whole nature, it could not exist without a physical
basis and accompaniment; and his bodily state appears to have been

often less one of animation than of agitation, and his correspondence frequently discloses moods that seem almost frantic. In the issue, under stress of pain and trouble, he became an opium-eater; but his physical nature may fairly be described as predisposed to such states as lead to the use of opium and also result from its use, with the attendant mental moods. His susceptibility to sensuous impressions, to a voluptuousness of the entire being, together with a certain lassitude and languor, lead to the same conclusion, which thus seems to be supported on all sides,—that Coleridge was, in his youth and early manhood, fevered through all his intellectual and sensuous nature, and deficient on the moral and practical sides in those matters that related to his personal affairs. It is desirable to bring this out in plain terms, because in Coleridge it is best to acknowledge at once that his character was, so far as our part—the world's part—in him is concerned, of less consequence than his temperament; a subtler and more profound thing than character, though without moral meaning. It is not unfair to say, since literature is to be regarded most profitably as the expression of human personality, that with Coleridge the modern literature of temperament, as it has been lately recognized in extreme phases, begins; not that temperament is a new thing in the century now closing, nor that it has been without influence hitherto, but that now it is more often considered, and has in fact more often been, an exclusive ground of artistic expression. The temperament of Coleridge was one of diffused sensuousness physically, and of abnormal mental moods,—moods of weakness, languor, collapse, of visionary imaginative life with a night atmosphere of the spectral, moonlit, swimming, scarcely substantial world; and the poems he wrote, which are the contributions he made to the world's literature, are based on this temperament, like some Fata Morgana upon the sea. The apparent exclusion of reality from the poems in which his genius was most manifest finds its analogue in the detachment of his own mind from the moral, the practical, the usual in life as he led it in his spirit; and his work of the highest creative sort, which is all there is to his enduring fame, stands amid his prose and verse composition of a lower sort like an island in the waste of waters. This may be best shown, perhaps, by a gradual approach through his cruder to his more perfect compositions.

The cardinal fact in Coleridge's genius is that notwithstanding his immense sensuous susceptibilities and mental receptivity, and the continual excitement of his spirit, he never rose into the highest sphere of creative activity except for the brief period called his *annus mirabilis*, when his great poems were written; and with this is the further related fact that in him we witness the spectacle of the imaginative instinct overborne and supplanted by the intellectual faculty exercising its speculative and critical functions; and in addition, one observes in his entire work an extraordinary inequality not only of treatment, but also of subject-matter. In general, he was an egoistic writer. His sensitiveness to nature was twofold: in the first place he noticed in the objects and movements of nature evanescent and minute details, and as his sense of beauty was keen, he saw and recorded truly the less obvious and less common loveliness in the phenomena of the elements and the seasons, and this gave distinction to his mere description and record of fact; in the second place he often felt in himself moods induced by nature, but yet subjective, — states of his own spirit, which sometimes deepened the charm of night, for example, by his enjoyment of its placid aspects, and sometimes imparted to the external world a despair reflected from his personal melancholy. In his direct treatment of nature, however, as Mr. Stopford Brooke points out, he seldom achieves more than a catalogue of his sensations, which though touched with imaginative detail are never lifted and harmonized into lyrical unity; though he can moralize nature in Wordsworth's fashion, when he does so the result remains Wordsworth's and is stamped with that poet's originality; and in his own original work Coleridge never equaled either the genius of Shelley, who can identify nature with himself, or the charm of Tennyson, who can at least parallel nature's phenomena with his own human moods. Coleridge would not be thought of as a poet of nature, except in so far as he describes what he observes in the way of record, or gives a metaphysical interpretation to phenomena. This is the more remarkable because he had to an eminent degree that intellectual power, that overmastering desire of the mind, to rationalize the facts of life. It was this quality that made him a philosopher, an analyst, a critic on the great lines of Aristotle, seeking to impose an order of ethics and metaphysics on all artistic productions. But in those poems in which he describes nature directly and without metaphysical thought, there is no trace of anything more than a sensuous order of his own perceptions. Beautiful and often unique as his nature poems are, they are not creative. They are rather in the main autobiographic; and it is surprising to notice how large a proportion of his verse is thus autobiographic, not in those phases of his own life which may be, or at least are thought of as representative of human life in the mass, but which are personal, such as the lines written after hearing Wordsworth read the 'Prelude,' or those entitled 'Dejection.' When his verse is not confined to autobiographic expression, it is often a product of his interest in his friends or in his family. What is not personal in it, of this sort, is apt to be domestic or social.

If we turn from the poems of nature to those concerned with man, a similar shallowness, either of interest or of power, appears. He was in early years a radical; he was stirred by the Revolution in France, and he was emotionally charged with the ideas of the time, —ideas of equality, fraternity, and liberty. But this interest died out, as is shown by his political verse. He had none but a social and a philosophical interest in any case. Man, the individual, did not at any time attract him. There was nothing dramatic in his genius, in the narrow and exact sense; he did not engage his curiosity or his philosophy in individual fortunes. It results from this limitation that his verse lacks human interest of the dramatic kind. The truth was that he was interested in thought rather than in deeds, in human nature rather than in its concrete pity and terror. Thus he did not seize on life itself as the material of his imagination and reflection. In the case of man as in the case of nature he gives us only an egoistic account, telling us of his own private fortune, his fears, pains, and despairs, but only as a diary gives them; as he did not transfer his nature impressions into the world of creative art, so he did not transfer his personal experiences into that world.

What has been said would perhaps be accepted, were it not for the existence of those poems, 'The Ancient Mariner,' 'Christabel,' 'Kubla Khan,' which are the marvelous creations of his genius. In these it will be said there is both a world of nature new created, and a dramatic method and interest. It is enough for the purpose of the analysis if it be granted that nowhere else in Coleridge's work, except in these and less noticeably in a few other instances, do these high characteristics occur. The very point which is here to be brought out is that Coleridge applied that intellectual power, that overmastering desire of the mind to rationalize the phenomena of life, which has been mentioned as his great mental trait,—that he applied this faculty with different degrees of power at different times, so that his poetry falls naturally into higher and inferior categories; in the autobiographic verse, in the political and dramatic verse which forms so large a part of his work, it appears that he did not have sufficient feeling or exercise sufficient power to raise it out of the lower levels of composition; in his great works of constructive and impersonal art, of moral intensity or romantic beauty and fascination, he did so exercise the creative imagination as to make these of the highest rank, or at least one of them.

'The Ancient Mariner,' apart from its many minor merits, has this distinction in Coleridge's work,—it is a poem of perfect unity. 'Christabel' is a fragment, 'Kubla Khan' is a glimpse; and though the 'Ode to France,' 'Love, Youth, and Age,' and possibly a few other short pieces, have this highest artistic virtue of unity, yet in

them it is of a simpler kind. 'The Ancient Mariner,' on the other
hand, is a marvel of construction in that its unity is less complex
than manifold; it exists, however the form be examined. In the
merely external sense, the telling of the tale to the Wedding
Guest, with the fact that the wedding is going on, gives it unity; in
the merely internal sense, the moral lesson of the salvation of the
slayer of the albatross by the medium of love felt toward living
things, subtly yet lucidly worked out as the notion is, gives it unity:
but in still other ways, as a story of connected and consequential
incidents with a plot, a change of fortune, a climax, and the other
essentials of this species of tale-telling, it has unity; and if its
conception either of the physical or the ethical world be analyzed,
these too—and these are the fundamental things—are found consistent wholes. It nevertheless remains true that this system of
nature as a vitalized but not humanized mode of life, with its bird,
its spirit, its magical powers, is not the nature that we know or
believe to be,—it is a modern presentation of an essentially primitive
and animistic belief; and similarly this system of human life,—if the
word human can be applied to it, with its dead men, its skeleton
ship, its spirit sailors, its whole miracle of spectral being,—is not the
life we know or believe to be; it is an incantation, a simulacrum.
It may still be true therefore that the imaginative faculty of Coleridge was not applied either to nature or human life, in the ordinary
sense. And this it is that constitutes the uniqueness of the poem,
and its wonderful fascination. Coleridge fell heir, by the accidents
of time and the revolutions of taste, to the ballad style, its simplicity, directness, and narrative power; he also was most attracted
to the machinery of the supernatural, the weird, the terrible, almost
to the grotesque and horrid, as these literary motives came into
fashion in the crude beginnings of romanticism in our time; his
subtle mind, his fine senses, his peculiar susceptibility to the mystic
and shadowy in nature,—as shown by his preference of the moon-
light, dreamy, or night aspects of real nature, to its brilliant beauties in the waking world,—gave him ease and finesse in the handling
of such subject-matter; and he lived late enough to know that all
this eerie side of human experience and imaginative capacity,
inherited from primeval ages but by no means yet deprived of
plausibility, could be effectively used only as an allegoric or scenic
setting of what should be truth to the ethical sense; he combined
one of the highest lessons of advanced civilization, one of the last
results of spiritual perception,—the idea of love toward life in any
form,—with the animistic beliefs and supernatural fancies of the
crude ages of the senses. This seems to be the substantial matter;
and in this he was, to repeat Shelley's phrase, the "subtle-souled

psychologist." The material of his imagination, on the sensuous side, was of the slightest: it was the supernaturalism of the romantic movement, somewhat modified by being placed in connection with the animal world; and he put this to use as a means of illustrating spiritual truth. He thus became the first of those who have employed the supernatural in our recent literature without losing credence for it, as an allegory of psychological states, moral facts, or illusions real to the eye that sees them and having some logical relation to the past of the individual; of such writers Hawthorne and Poe are eminent examples, and both of them, it may be remarked, are writers in whom temperament rather than character is the ground of their creative work. The intimate kinship between imagination so directed and the speculative philosophical temper is plain to see. In 'Christabel' on the other hand, the moral substance is not apparent: the place filled by the moral ideas which are the centres of the narrative in 'The Ancient Mariner,' is taken here by emotional situations; but the supernaturalism is practically the same in both poems, and in both is associated with that mystery of the animal world to man, most concentrated and vivid in the fascination ascribed traditionally to the snake, which is the animal motive in 'Christabel' as the goodness of the albatross in the 'The Ancient Mariner.' In these poems the good and the bad omens that ancient augurs minded are made again dominant over men's imagination. Such are the signal and unique elements in these poems, which have besides that wealth of beauty in detail, of fine diction, of liquid melody, of sentiment, thought, and image, which belong only to poetry of the highest order, and which are too obvious to require any comment. 'Kubla Khan' is a poem of the same kind, in which the mystical effect is given almost wholly by landscape; it is to 'The Ancient Mariner' and 'Christabel' what protoplasm is to highly organized cells.

If it be recognized then that the imagery of Coleridge in the characteristic parts of these cardinal poems is as pure allegory, is as remote from nature or man, as is the machinery of fairy-land and chivalry in Spenser, for example, and he obtains credibility by the psychological and ethical truth presented in this imagery, it is not surprising that his work is small in amount; for the method is not only a difficult one, but the poetic machinery itself is limited and meagre. The poverty of the subject-matter is manifest, and the restrictions to its successful use are soon felt. It may well be doubted whether 'Christabel' would have gained by being finished. In 'The Ancient Mariner' the isolation of the man is a great advantage; if there had been any companion for him, the illusion could not have been entire: as it is, what he experiences has the wholeness and truth within itself of a dream, or of a madman's world,—there is no

standard of appeal outside of his own senses and mind, no real
world; but in 'Christabel' the serpentine fable goes on in a world of
fact and action, and as soon as the course of the story involved this
fable in the probabilities and actual occurences of life, it might well
be that the tale would have turned into one of simple enchantment
and magic, as seems likely from what has been told of its continuation; certainly it could not have equaled the earlier poem, or have
been in the same kind with it, unless the unearthly magic, the spell,
were finally completely dissolved into the world of moral truth as is
the case with 'The Ancient Mariner.' Coleridge found it still more
impossible to continue 'Kubla Khan.' It seems a fair inference to
conclude that Coleridge's genius, however it suffered from the misfortunes and ills of his life, was in these works involved in a field,
however congenial, yet of narrow range and infertile in itself. In
poetic style it is to be observed that he kept what he had gained;
the turbid diction of the earlier period never came back to trouble
him, and the cadences he had formed still gave their music to his
verse. The change, the decline, was not in his power of style; it
was in his power of imagination, if at all, but the fault may have
laid in the capacities of the subject-matter. A similar thing certainly
happened in his briefer ballad poetry, in that of which 'Love,' 'The
Three Graces,' 'Alice Du Clos,' and 'The Dark Ladie,' are examples;
the matter there, the machinery of the romantic ballad, was no
longer capable of use; that sort of literature was dead from the
exhaustion of its motives. The great 'Ode to France,' in which he
reached his highest point of eloquent and passionate expression,
seems to mark the extinction in himself of the revolutionary impulse.
On the whole, while the excellence of much of the remainder of his
verse, even in later years, is acknowledged, and its originality in
several instances, may it not be that in his greatest work Coleridge
came to an end because of an impossibility in the kind itself? The
supernatural is an accessory rather than a main element in the interpretation of life which literary genius undertakes; Coleridge so
subordinates it here by making it contributory to a moral truth; but
such a practice would seem to be necessarily incidental to a poet
who was also so intellectual as Coleridge, and not to be adopted as
a permanent method of self-expression.

From whatever cause, the fact was that Coleridge ceased to create
in poetry, and fell back on that fluent, manifold, voluminous faculty
he possessed of absorbing and giving out ideas in vast quantities, as
it were by bulk. He attended especially to the theory of art as he
found it illustrated in the greatest poets, and he popularized among
literary men a certain body of doctrine regarding criticism, its
growth and methods; and in later years he worked out metaphysical

theological views which he inculcated in ways which won for him recognition as a practical influence in contemporary church opinion. In these last years of his lecturing and discoursing in private, the figure he makes is pathetic, though Carlyle describes it with a grim humor, as any one may read in the 'Life of Sterling': over against that figure should be set the descriptions of the young Coleridge by Dorothy Wordsworth and Lamb; and after these perhaps the contrast which Coleridge himself draws between his spirit and his body may enable a reader to fuse the two — youth and age — into one. Whatever were the weaknesses of his nature and the trials of his life, of which one keeps silent, he was deeply loved by friends of many different minds, who if they grew cold, had paid at least once this tribute to the charm, the gentleness, and the delight of his human companionship.

KUBLA KHAN

IN XANADU did Kubla Khan
    A stately pleasure-dome decree,
  Where Alph the sacred river ran
  Through caverns measureless to man
    Down to a sunless sea.
So twice five miles of fertile ground
With wall and towers were girdled round;
And there were gardens bright with sinuous rills,
    Where blossomed many an incense-bearing tree;
And here were forests ancient as the hills,
    Enfolding sunny spots of greenery.

But oh! that deep romantic chasm which slanted
    Down the green hill athwart a cedarn cover:
A savage place! as holy and enchanted
As e'er beneath a waning moon was haunted
    By woman wailing for her demon lover!
And from this chasm, with ceaseless turmoil seething,
As if this earth in fast thick pants were breathing,

A mighty fountain momently was forced;
 Amid whose swift half-intermitted burst
Huge fragments vaulted like rebounding hail,
Or chaffy grain beneath the thresher's flail;
And 'mid these dancing rocks at once and ever
It flung up momently the sacred river.
Five miles meandering with a mazy motion
 Through wood and dale the sacred river ran,
 Then reached the caverns measureless to man,
And sank in tumult to a lifeless ocean:
And 'mid this tumult Kubla heard from far
Ancestral voices prophesying war!

 The shadow of the dome of pleasure
  Floated midway on the waves;
 Where was heard the mingled measure
  From the fountain and the caves.
It was a miracle of rare device,
A sunny pleasure-dome with caves of ice!
  A damsel with a dulcimer
  In a vision once I saw;
  It was an Abyssinian maid,
  And on her dulcimer she played,
  Singing of Mount Abora.
  Could I revive within me
  Her symphony and song,
 To such a deep delight 'twould win me
  That with music loud and long,
  I would build that dome in air —

That sunny dome! those caves of ice!
 And all who heard should see them there,
And all should cry, Beware! beware
 His flashing eyes, his floating hair!
Weave a circle round him thrice,
  And close your eyes with holy dread,
  For he on honey-dew hath fed,
And drunk the milk of Paradise.

THE ALBATROSS

From 'The Rime of the Ancient Mariner'

WITH sloping masts and dripping prow,
  As who, pursued with yell and blow,
  Still treads the shadow of his foe,
  And forward bends his head,
The ship drove fast, loud roared the blast,
  And southward aye we fled.

And now there came both mist and snow,
  And it grew wondrous cold;
And ice, mast-high, came floating by,
  As green as emerald.

And through the drifts the snowy clifts
  Did send a dismal sheen;
Nor shapes of men nor beasts we ken —
  The ice was all between.

The ice was here, the ice was there,
  The ice was all around;
It cracked and growled, and roared and howled,
  Like noises in a swound!

At length did cross an Albatross:
  Thorough the fog it came;
As if it had been a Christian soul,
  We hailed it in God's name.

It ate the food it ne'er had eat,
  And round and round it flew.
The ice did split with a thunder-fit;
  The helmsman steered us through!

And a good south-wind sprung up behind;
  The Albatross did follow,
And every day, for food or play,
  Came to the mariner's hollo!

In mist or cloud, on mast or shroud,
  It perched for vespers nine;
Whilst all the night, through fog-smoke white,
  Glimmered the white moonshine. —

God save thee, ancient Mariner! ·
  From the fiends that plague thee thus!
Why look'st thou so?—With my cross-bow
  I shot the Albatross!

THE Sun now rose upon the right;
  Out of the sea came he,
Still hid in mist, and on the left
  Went down into the sea.

And the good south-wind still blew behind,
  But no sweet bird did follow,
Nor any day for food or play
  Came to the mariner's hollo!

And I had done a hellish thing,
  And it would work 'em woe:
For all averred, I had killed the bird
  That made the breeze to blow.
Ah wretch! said they, the bird to slay,
  That made the breeze to blow!

Nor dim nor red, like God's own head
  The glorious Sun uprist:
Then all averred, I had killed the bird
  That brought the fog and mist.
'Twas right, said they, such birds to slay,
  That bring the fog and mist.

The fair breeze blew, the white foam flew,
  The furrow followed free;
We were the first that ever burst
  Into that silent sea.

Down dropt the breeze, the sails dropt down,
  'Twas sad as sad could be;
And we did speak only to break
  The silence of the sea!

All in a hot and copper sky,
  The bloody Sun, at noon,
Right up above the mast did stand,
  No bigger than the Moon.

Day after day, day after day,
  We stuck, nor breath nor motion;

As idle as a painted ship
    Upon a painted ocean.

Water, water, everywhere,
    And all the boards did shrink:
Water, water, everywhere,
    Nor any drop to drink.

The very deep did rot: O Christ!
    That ever this should be!
Yea, slimy things did crawl with legs
    Upon the slimy sea.

About, about, in reel and rout
    The death-fires danced at night;
The water, like a witch's oils,
    Burnt green, and blue, and white.

And some in dreams assurèd were
    Of the spirit that plagued us so;
Nine fathoms deep he had followed us
    From the land of mist and snow.

And every tongue, through utter drought,
    Was withered at the root;
We could not speak, no more than if
    We had been choked with soot.

Ah! well-a-day! what evil looks
    Had I from old and young!
Instead of the cross, the Albatross
    About my neck was hung.

TIME, REAL AND IMAGINARY

ON THE wide level of a mountain's head
    (I knew not where, but 't was some faery place),
Their pinions, ostrich-like, for sails outspread,
    Two lovely children run an endless race,
      A sister and a brother!
      This far outstript the other;
Yet ever runs she with reverted face,
And looks and listens for the boy behind:
      For he, alas! is blind!
O'er rough and smooth with even step he passed,
And knows not whether he be first or last.

DEJECTION: AN ODE

> Late, late yestreen I saw the new Moon,
>   With the old Moon in her arms;
> And I fear, I fear, my Master dear!
> We shall have a deadly storm.
>
> BALLAD OF SIR PATRICK SPENCE.

WELL! if the bard was weather-wise, who made
    The grand old ballad of Sir Patrick Spence,
    This night, so tranquil now, will not go hence
Unroused by winds that ply a busier trade
Than those which mold yon cloud in lazy flakes,
Or the dull sobbing draft that moans and rakes
    Upon the strings of this Æolian lute,
        Which better far were mute.

For lo! the New Moon, winter-bright
    And overspread with phantom light,
    With swimming phantom light o'erspread,
    But rimmed and circled by a silver thread;
I see the old Moon in her lap, foretelling
    The coming on of rain and squally blast.
And oh! that even now the gust were swelling,
    And the slant night-shower driving hard and fast!
Those sounds, which oft have raised me, whilst they awed,
        And sent my soul abroad,
    Might now perhaps their wonted impulse give —
Might startle this dull pain and make it move and live.

A grief without a pang, void, dark, and drear —
    A stifled, drowsy, unimpassioned grief,
    Which finds no natural outlet, no relief,
        In word, or sigh, or tear —
O Lady! in this wan and heartless mood,
To other thoughts by yonder throstle wooed,
All this long eve, so balmy and serene,
    Have I been gazing on the western sky,
    And its peculiar tint of yellow-green;
And still I gaze — and with how blank an eye!
And those thin clouds above, in flakes and bars,
That give away their motion to the stars, —
Those stars that glide behind them or between,
Now sparkling, now bedimmed, but always seen;

Yon crescent Moon, as fixed as if it grew
In its own cloudless, starless lake of blue:
I see them all so excellently fair —
I see, nor feel, how beautiful they are!

My genial spirits fail;
And what can these avail,
To lift the smothering weight from off my breast?
It were a vain endeavor,
Though I should gaze forever
On that green light that lingers in the west:
I may not hope from outward forms to win
The passion and the life whose fountains are within.

O lady! we receive but what we give,
And in our life alone does Nature live;
Ours is her wedding garment, ours her shroud!
And would we aught behold of higher worth
Than that inanimate cold world allowed
To the poor loveless, ever-anxious crowd —
Ah! from the soul itself must issue forth
A light, a glory, a fair luminous cloud
Enveloping the earth;
And from the soul itself must there be sent
A sweet and potent voice of its own birth,
Of all sweet sounds the life and element!

O pure of heart! thou need'st not ask of me
What this strong music in the soul may be,
What and wherein it doth exist,
This light, this glory, this fair luminous mist,
This beautiful and beauty-making power:
Joy, virtuous lady! Joy that ne'er was given
Save to the pure, and in their purest hour,
Life, and life's effluence, cloud at once and shower —
Joy, lady, is the spirit and the power
Which wedding nature to us, gives in dower
A new Earth and Heaven,
Undreamt-of by the sensual and the proud;
Joy is the sweet voice, Joy the luminous cloud —
We in ourselves rejoice!
And thence flows all that charms or ear or sight,
All melodies the echoes of that voice,
All colors a suffusion from that light.

There was a time when, though my path was rough,
  This joy within me dallied with distress;
And all misfortunes were but as the stuff
  Whence fancy made me dreams of happiness.
For hope grew round me like the twining vine;
And fruits and foliage, not my own, seemed mine.

But now afflictions bow me down to earth,
Nor care I that they rob me of my mirth;
      But oh! each visitation
Suspends what nature gave me at my birth,
  My shaping spirit of imagination.
For not to think of what I needs must feel,
  But to be still and patient, all I can;
And haply by abstruse research to steal
    From my own nature all the natural man —
  This was my sole resource, my only plan:
Till that which suits a part infects the whole,
And now is almost grown the habit of my soul.

Hence, viper thoughts that coil around my mind —
     Reality's dark dream!
I turn from you, and listen to the wind,
  Which long has raved unnoticed. What a scream
Of agony, by torture lengthened out,
That lute sent forth! Thou wind, that ravest without!
  Bare crag, or mountain-tairn, or blasted tree,
Or pine-grove whither woodman never clomb,
Or lonely house, long held the witches' home,
  Methinks were fitter instruments for thee,
Mad lutanist! who in this month of showers,
Of dark-brown gardens, and of peeping flowers,
Makest devils' Yule, with worse than wintry song,
The blossoms, buds, and timorous leaves among!
  Thou actor, perfect in all tragic sounds!
Thou mighty poet, e'en to frenzy bold!
    What tell'st thou now about?
    'Tis of the rushing of a host in rout,
With groans of trampled men, with smarting wounds —
At once they groan with pain, and shudder with the cold.

But hush! there is a pause of deepest silence!
  And all that noise, as of a rushing crowd,
With groans and tremulous shudderings — all is over —
  It tells another tale, with sounds less deep and loud!

A tale of less affright,
And tempered with delight,
As Otway's self had framed the tender lay:
'Tis of a little child
Upon a lonesome wild —
Not far from home, but she hath lost her way;
And now moans low in bitter grief and fear —
And now screams loud, and hopes to make her mother hear.

'Tis midnight, but small thoughts have I of sleep;
Full seldom may my friend such vigils keep!
Visit her, gentle Sleep, with wings of healing!
And may this storm be but a mountain-birth;
May all the stars hang bright above her dwelling,
Silent as though they watched the sleeping earth!
With light heart may she rise, —
Gay fancy, cheerful eyes —
Joy lift her spirit, joy attune her voice;
To her may all things live, from pole to pole —
Their life the eddying of her living soul!
O simple spirit, guided from above!
Dear Lady! friend devoutest of my choice!
Thus mayest thou ever, evermore rejoice.

THE THREE TREASURES

COMPLAINT

How seldom, Friend! a good great man inherits
Honor or wealth, with all his worth and pains!
It sounds like stories from the land of spirits,
If any man obtain that which he merits,
Or any merit that which he obtains.

REPROOF

For shame, dear Friend; renounce this canting strain!
What wouldst thou have a good great man obtain?
Place — titles — salary — a gilded chain —
Or throne of corses which his sword has slain?
Greatness and goodness are not means, but ends!
Hath he not always treasures, always friends,
The good great man? three treasures, — love and light,
And calm thoughts, regular as infant's breath;
And three firm friends, more sure than day and night —
Himself, his Maker, and the angel Death.

TO A GENTLEMAN

COMPOSED ON THE NIGHT AFTER HIS RECITATION OF A POEM ON THE GROWTH OF AN INDIVIDUAL MIND

FRIEND of the Wise! and Teacher of the Good!
 Into my heart have I received that lay
 More than historic, that prophetic lay,
Wherein (high theme by thee first sung aright)
Of the foundations and the building up
Of a Human Spirit thou hast dared to tell
What may be told, to the understanding mind
Revealable; and what within the mind,
By vital breathings secret as the soul
Of vernal growth, oft quickens in the heart
Thoughts all too deep for words!

       Theme hard as high!
Of smiles spontaneous, and mysterious fears,
The first-born they of Reason, and twin-birth;
Of tides obedient to external force,
And currents self-determined, as might seem,
Or by some inner Power; of moments awful,
Now in thy inner life, and now abroad,
When Power stream'd from thee, and thy soul received
The light reflected, as a light bestowed —
Of fancies fair, and milder hours of youth,
Hyblean murmurs of poetic thought,
Industrious in its joy, in Vales and Glens
Native or outland, Lakes and famous Hills!
Or on the lonely High-road, when the Stars
Were rising; or by secret mountain Streams,
The Guides and the Companions of thy way!

Of more than Fancy, of the Social Sense
Distending wide, and Man beloved as Man,
Where France in all her town lay vibrating
Like some becalmèd bark beneath the burst
Of Heaven's immediate thunder, when no cloud
Is visible, or shadow on the Main.
For thou wert there, thine own brows garlanded,
Amid the tremor of a realm aglow,
Amid a mighty nation jubilant,
When from the general heart of humankind

Hope sprang forth like a full-born Deity!
. . . Of that dear Hope afflicted and struck down
So summoned homeward, thenceforth calm and sure,
From the dread watch-tower of man's absolute Self
With light unwaning on her eyes, to look
Far on — herself a glory to behold,
The Angel of the vision! Then (last strain)
Of Duty, chosen laws controlling choice,
Action and Joy! — An Orphic song indeed,
A song divine of high and passionate thoughts,
To their own music chanted!

               O great Bard!
Ere yet that last strain, dying, awed the air,
With stedfast eye I viewed thee in the choir
Of ever-enduring men. The truly Great
Have all one age, and from one visible space
Shed influence! They, both in power and act,
Are permanent, and Time is not with *them*,
Save as it worketh *for* them, they *in* it.
Nor less a sacred roll than those of old,
And to be placed, as they, with gradual fame
Among the archives of mankind, thy work
Makes audible a linkèd lay of Truth,
Of Truth profound a sweet continuous lay,
Not learnt, but native, her own natural notes!
Ah! as I listened with a heart forlorn,
The pulses of my being beat anew:
And even as life returns upon the drowned,
Life's joy rekindling roused a throng of pains —
Keen Pangs of Love, awakening as a babe
Turbulent, with an outcry in the heart;
And Fears self-willed that shunned the eye of Hope,
And Hope that scarce would know itself from Fear,
Sense of past Youth; and Manhood come in vain,
And all which I had culled in wood-walks wild,
And all which patient toil had reared, and all,
Commune with *thee* had opened out — but flowers
Strewed on my corse, and borne upon my bier,
In the same coffin, for the self-same grave!

That way no more! and ill beseems it me
Who came a welcomer in herald's guise
Singing of Glory and Futurity,
To wander back on such unhealthful road,

Plucking the poisons of self-harm! And ill
Such intertwine beseems triumphal wreaths
Strewed before *thy* advancing!

                       Nor do thou,
Sage Bard! impair the memory of that hour
Of my communion with thy nobler mind
By Pity or Grief, already felt too long!
Nor let my words import more blame than needs.
The tumult rose and ceased: for Peace is nigh
Where Wisdom's voice has found a listening heart.
Amid the howl of more than wintry storms,
The Halcyon hears the voice of vernal hours
Already on the wing.

                Eve following eve,
Dear tranquil time, when the sweet sense of Home
Is sweetest! moments for their own sake hailed
And more desired, more precious for thy song,
In silence listening, like a devout child,
My soul lay passive, by the various strain
Driven as in surges now beneath the stars,
With momentary Stars of my own birth,
Fair constellated Foam, still darting off
Into the darkness; now a tranquil sea,
Outspread and bright, yet swelling to the Moon.

And when — O Friend! my comforter and guide!
Strong in thyself, and powerful to give strength! —
Thy long-sustained song finally closed,
And thy deep voice had ceased — yet thou thyself
Wert still before my eyes, and round us both
That happy vision of beloved faces —
Scarce conscious, and yet conscious of its close,
I sate, my being blended in one thought
(Thought was it? or Aspiration? or Resolve?)
Absorbed, yet hanging still upon the sound —
And when I rose, I found myself in prayer.

ODE TO GEORGIANA, DUCHESS OF DEVONSHIRE

On the Twenty-fourth Stanza in Her 'Passage over Mount Gothard'

And hail the Chapel! hail the Platform wild!
   Where Tell directed the avenging Dart,
  With well-strung arm, that first preserved his Child,
Then aim'd the arrow at the Tyrant's heart.

    Splendor's fondly fostered child!
   And did you hail the platform wild
      Where once the Austrian fell
      Beneath the shaft of Tell?
  O Lady, nursed in pomp and pleasure!
  Whence learnt you that heroic measure?

Light as a dream your days their circlets ran;
From all that teaches Brotherhood to Man,
Far, far removed! from want, from hope, from fear.
Enchanting music lulled your infant ear,
Obeisance, praises, soothed your infant heart:
  Emblazonments and old ancestral crests,
With many a bright obtrusive form of art,
  Detained your eye from nature's stately vests
That veiling strove to deck your charms divine;
Rich viands and the pleasurable wine,
Were yours unearned by toil; nor could you see
The unenjoying toiler's misery.
And yet, free Nature's uncorrupted child,
You hailed the Chapel and the Platform wild,
     Where once the Austrian fell
     Beneath the shaft of Tell!
  O Lady, nursed in pomp and pleasure!
  Where learnt you that heroic measure?

  There crowd your finely fibred frame,
    All living faculties of bliss;
  And Genius to your cradle came,
  His forehead wreathed with lambent flame,
    And bending low, with godlike kiss
    Breathed in a more celestial life;
  But boasts not many a fair compeer
  A heart as sensitive to joy and fear?

And some, perchance, might wage an equal strife,
Some few, to nobler being wrought,
Co-rivals in the nobler gift of thought.
Yet *these* delight to celebrate
Laureled War and plumy State;
Or in verse and music dress
Tales of rustic happiness —
Pernicious Tales! insidious Strains!
That steel the rich man's breast,
And mock the lot unblest,
The sordid vices and the abject pains,
Which evermore must be
The doom of Ignorance and Penury!
But you, free Nature's uncorrupted child,
You hailed the Chapel and the Platform wild,
Where once the Austrian fell
Beneath the shaft of Tell!
O Lady, nursed in pomp and pleasure!
Where learnt you that heroic measure?

You were a Mother! That most holy name,
Which Heaven and Nature bless,
I may not vilely prostitute to those
Whose Infants owe them less
Than the poor Caterpillar owes
Its gaudy Parent Fly.
You were a Mother! at your bosom fed
The Babes that loved you. You, with laughing eye,
Each twilight-thought, each nascent feeling read,
Which you yourself created. Oh, delight!
A second time to be a Mother,
Without the Mother's bitter groans:
Another thought, and yet another,
By touch, or taste, by looks or tones,
O'er the growing Sense to roll,
The Mother of your infant's Soul!
The Angel of the Earth, who while he guides
His chariot-planet round the goal of day,
All trembling gazes on the Eye of God,
A moment turned his face away;
And as he viewed you, from his aspect sweet
New influences in your being rose,
Blest Intuitions and Communions fleet
With living Nature, in her joys and woes!

Thenceforth your soul rejoiced to see
The shrine of social Liberty!
O beautiful! O Nature's child!
'Twas thence you hailed the Platform wild,
Where once the Austrian fell
Beneath the shaft of Tell!
O Lady, nursed in pomp and pleasure!
Thence learnt you that heroic measure.

THE PAINS OF SLEEP

ERE on my bed my limbs I lay,
    It hath not been my use to pray
        With moving lips or bended knees;
But silently, by slow degrees,
My spirit I to Love compose,
In humble Trust mine eyelids close,
With reverential resignation;
No wish conceived, no thought expressed!
Only a *sense* of supplication,
A sense o'er all my soul imprest
That I am weak, yet not unblest;
Since in me, round me, everywhere,
Eternal Strength and Wisdom are.

But yesternight I prayed aloud
    In anguish and in agony,
Upstarting from the fiendish crowd
    Of shapes and thoughts that tortured me:
A lurid light, a trampling throng,
Sense of intolerable wrong,
And whom I scorned, those only strong!
Thirst of revenge, the powerless will
Still baffled, and yet burning still!
Desire with loathing strangely mixed
On wild or hateful objects fixed.
Fantastic passions! maddening brawl!
And shame and terror over all!
    Deeds to be hid which were not hid,
Which, all confused, I could not know
    Whether I suffered, or I did:
For all seemed guilt, remorse, or woe,—
My own or others', still the same
Life-stifling fear, soul-stifling shame.

So two nights passed: the night's dismay
Saddened and stunned the coming day.
Sleep, the wide blessing, seemed to me
Distemper's worst calamity.
The third night, when my own loud scream
Had waked me from the fiendish dream,
O'ercome with sufferings strange and wild,
I wept as I had been a child;
And having thus by tears subdued
My anguish to a milder mood,
Such punishments, I said, were due
To natures deepliest stained with sin;
For aye entempesting anew
The unfathomable hell within,
The horror of their deeds to view,
To know and loathe, yet wish to do!

Such griefs with such men well agree,
But wherefore, wherefore fall on me?
To be beloved is all I need,
And whom I love, I love indeed.

SONG, BY GLYCINE

A sunny shaft did I behold,
    From sky to earth it slanted;
        And poised therein a bird so bold —
Sweet bird, thou wert enchanted!

He sunk, he rose, he twinkled, he trolled
    Within that shaft of sunny mist;
His eyes of fire, his beak of gold,
    All else of amethyst!

And thus he sang: "Adieu! adieu!
    Love's dreams prove seldom true.
The blossoms, they make no delay:
The sparkling dewdrops will not stay.
    Sweet month of May,
        We must away;
            Far, far away!
                To-day! to-day!"

YOUTH AND AGE

VERSE, a breeze 'mid blossoms straying,
   Where Hope clung feeding, like a bee —
Both were mine! Life went a-Maying
   With Nature, Hope, and Poesy,
     When I was young!
When I was young?—Ah, woful *when!*
Ah, for the change 'twixt now and then!
This breathing house not built with hands,
   This body that does me grievous wrong,
O'er airy cliffs and glittering sands,
   How lightly *then* it flashed along:—
Like those trim skiffs, unknown of yore,
   On winding lakes and rivers wide,
That ask no aid of sail or oar,
   That fear no spite of wind or tide!
Naught cared this body for wind or weather
When Youth and I lived in't together.

Flowers are lovely; Love is flower-like,
   Friendship is a sheltering tree;
O the joys that came down shower-like,
   Of Friendship, Love, and Liberty!
     Ere I was old!
Ere I was old? Ah, woful *Ere,*
Which tells me Youth's no longer here!
O Youth! for years so many and sweet,
   'Tis known that thou and I were one;
I'll think it but a fond conceit —
   It cannot be that thou art gone!
Thy vesper bell hath not yet tolled:—
And thou wert aye a masker bold!
What strange disguise hast now put on
To *make believe* that thou art gone?
I see these locks in silvery slips,
   This drooping gait, this alter'd size:
But spring-tide blossoms on thy lips,
   And tears take sunshine from thine eyes!
Life is but thought: so think I will
That Youth and I are housemates still.

PHANTOM OR FACT?

AUTHOR

A LOVELY form there sate beside my bed,
    And such a feeding calm its presence shed,
    A tender love, so pure from earthly leaven
That I unnethe the fancy might control,
'Twas my own spirit newly come from heaven,
Wooing its gentle way into my soul!
But ah! the change — it had not stirred, and yet —
Alas! that change how fain would I forget!
That shrinking back like one that had mistook!
That weary, wandering, disavowing Look!
'Twas all another, — feature, look, and frame, —
And still, methought, I knew it was the same!

FRIEND

This riddling tale, to what does it belong?
Is't history? vision? or an idle song?
Or rather say at once, within what space
Of time this wild disastrous change took place?

AUTHOR

Call it a *moment's* work (and such it seems);
This tale's a fragment from the life of dreams;
But say that years matured the silent strife,
And 'tis a record from the dream of Life.

WILLIAM COLLINS

(1721–1759)

THERE is much to inspire regretful sympathy in the short life of William Collins. He was born at Chichester, and received his education at Winchester College and at Magdalen College, Oxford. A delicate, bookish boy, he had every stimulus toward a literary career. With a fine appreciation of beauty in all forms of art, and a natural talent for versification, he wrote poems of much promise when very young. His 'Persian Eclogues' appeared when he was only seventeen. Then Collins showed his impatient spirit and fickleness of purpose by deserting his work at Oxford and going to London with the intention of authorship. His head was full of brilliant schemes,—too full; for with him as with most people, conception was always easier than execution. But finding it far more difficult to win fame than he anticipated, he had not courage to persevere, and fell into dissipated, extravagant ways which soon exhausted his small means.

WILLIAM COLLINS

In 1846 he published the 'Odes, Descriptive and Allegorical,' his most characteristic work. They were never widely read, and it took the public some time to appreciate their lyric fervor, their exquisite imagery, and their musical verse. In spite of occasional obscurities induced by careless treatment, they are among the finest of English odes. His love for nature and sympathy with its calmer aspects is very marked. Speaking of the 'Ode to Evening,' Hazlitt says that "the sounds steal slowly over the ear like the gradual coming on of evening itself." According to Swinburne, the 'Odes' do not contain "a single false note." "Its grace and vigor, its vivid and pliant dexterity of touch," he says of the 'Ode to the Passions,' "are worthy of their long inheritance of praise."

But the inheritance did not come at once, although Collins has always received generous praise from fellow poets. His mortified self-love resented lack of success. With a legacy bequeathed him by an uncle he bought his book back from the publisher Millar, and the unsold impressions he burned in "angry despair."

Meantime he went on planning works quite beyond his power of execution. He advertised 'Proposals for a History of the Revival of Learning,' which he never wrote. He began several tragedies, but his indolent genius would not advance beyond devising the plots. As he was always wasteful and dissipated, he was continually in debt. In spite of his unusual gifts, he had not the energy and self-control necessary for adequate literary expression. Dr. Johnson, who admired and tried to befriend him, found a bailiff prowling around the premises when he went to call. At his instigation a bookseller advanced money to get Collins out of London, for which in return he was to translate Aristotle's 'Poetics' and to write a commentary. Probably he never fulfilled the agreement. Indeed, he had some excuse. "A man doubtful of his dinners, or trembling at a creditor, is not disposed to abstract meditation or remote inquiries," comments Dr. Johnson.

Collins was always weak of body, and when still a young man was seized by mental disease. Weary months of despondency were succeeded by madness, until he was, as Dr. Wharton describes it, with "every spark of imagination extinguished, and with only the faint traces of memory and reason left." Then the unhappy poet was taken to Chichester and cared for by a sister. There he who had loved music so passionately hated the cathedral organ in his madness, and when he heard it, howled in distress.

Among the best examples of his verse, besides the poems already mentioned, are the 'Dirge to Cymbeline,' 'Ode to Fear,' and the 'Ode on the Poetical Character,' which Hazlitt calls "the best of all."

HOW SLEEP THE BRAVE

How sleep the brave, who sink to rest
　　By all their country's wishes blest!
　　When Spring, with dewy fingers cold,
　　Returns to deck their hallowed mold,
She there shall dress a sweeter sod
Than Fancy's feet have ever trod.

By fairy hands their knell is rung,
By forms unseen their dirge is sung;
There Honor comes, a pilgrim gray,
To bless the turf that wraps their clay,
And Freedom shall a while repair,
To dwell a weeping hermit there!

THE PASSIONS

WHEN Music, heavenly maid! was young,
　　While yet in early Greece she sung,
　　The Passions oft, to hear her shell,
　　Thronged around her magic cell.
Exulting, trembling, raging, fainting,
Possest beyond the Muse's painting;
By turns they felt the glowing mind
Disturbed, delighted, raised, refined:
Till once, 'tis said, when all were fired,
Filled with fury, rapt, inspired,
From the supporting myrtles round
They snatched her instruments of sound,
And as they oft had heard apart
Sweet lessons of her forceful art,
Each — for Madness ruled the hour —
Would prove his own expressive power.

First Fear his hand, its skill to try,
　　Amid the chords bewildered laid;
And back recoiled, he knew not why,
　　E'en at the sound himself had made.

Next Anger rushed; his eyes on fire,
　　In lightnings owned his secret stings:
In one rude clash he struck the lyre,
　　And swept with hurried hand the strings.

With woful measures wan Despair —
　　Low solemn sounds — his grief beguiled,
A sullen, strange, and mingled air;
　　'Twas sad by fits, by starts 'twas wild.

But thou, O Hope! with eyes so fair,
　　What was thy delighted measure?
　　Still it whispered promised pleasure,
And bade the lovely scenes at distance hail!
　　Still would her touch the strain prolong,
And from the rocks, the woods, the vale,
　　She called on Echo still through all the song;
　　And where her sweetest theme she chose,
A soft responsive voice was heard at every close,
And Hope enchanted smiled, and waved her golden hair.

And longer had she sung,— but with a frown,
            Revenge impatient rose;
He threw his blood-stained sword in thunder down,
            And with a withering look
            The war-denouncing trumpet took,
            And blew a blast so loud and dread,
        Were ne'er prophetic sounds so full of woe!
            And ever and anon he beat
            The doubling drum with furious heat;
        And though sometimes, each dreary pause between,
            Dejected Pity, at his side,
            Her soul-subduing voice applied,
        Yet still he kept his wild unaltered mien,
While each strained ball of sight seemed bursting from his head.

        Thy numbers, Jealousy, to naught were fixed,
            Sad proof of thy distressful state!
        Of differing themes the veering song was mixed,
And now it courted Love, now raving called on Hate.

            With eyes upraised, as one inspired,
            Pale Melancholy sat retired;
            And from her wild sequestered seat,
            In notes by distance made more sweet,
        Poured through the mellow horn her pensive soul:
            And dashing soft from rocks around,
            Bubbling runnels joined the sound.
        Through glades and glooms the mingled measure stole,
            Or o'er some haunted streams with fond delay,
            Round an holy calm diffusing,
            Love of peace and lonely musing,
            In hollow murmurs died away.

        But oh, how altered was its sprightlier tone
            When Cheerfulness, a nymph of healthiest hue,
            Her bow across her shoulders flung,
            Her buskins gemmed with morning dew,
        Blew an inspiring air that dale and thicket rung!
            The hunter's call, to Faun and Dryad known.
        The oak-crowned Sisters, and their chaste-eyed Queen,
            Satyrs and sylvan boys were seen,
            Peeping from forth their alleys green;
            Brown Exercise rejoiced to hear,
        And Sport leapt up, and seized his beechen spear.

Last came Joy's ecstatic trial;
He with viny crown advancing,
First to the lively pipe his hand addrest;
But soon he saw the brisk awakening viol,
Whose sweet entrancing voice he loved the best.
They would have thought who heard the strain,
They saw in Tempe's vale her native maids,

Amidst the festal sounding shades,
To some unwearied minstrel dancing;
While, as his flying fingers kissed the strings,
Love framed with Mirth a gay fantastic round;
Loose were her tresses seen, her zone unbound;
And he, amidst his frolic play,
As if he would the charming air repay,
Shook thousand odors from his dewy wings.

O Music! sphere-descended maid,
Friend of pleasure, Wisdom's aid!
Why, goddess, why, to us denied,
Lay'st thou thy ancient lyre aside?
As in that loved Athenian bower,
You learned an all-commanding power,
Thy mimic soul, O nymph endeared!
Can well recall what then it heard.
Where is that native simple heart,
Devote to Virtue, Fancy, Art?
Arise, as in that elder time,
Warm, energetic, chaste, sublime!
Thy wonders, in that godlike age,
Fill thy recording Sister's page.
'Tis said — and I believe the tale —
Thy humblest reed could more prevail,
Had more of strength, diviner rage,
Than all which charms this laggard age;
E'en all at once together found
Cecilia's mingled world of sound.
Oh bid our vain endeavors cease,
Revive the just designs of Greece;
Return in all thy simple state!
Confirm the tales her sons relate!

TO EVENING

IF AUGHT of oaten stop, or pastoral song,
 May hope, chaste Eve, to soothe thy modest ear
   Like thy own solemn springs,
   Thy springs and dying gales;

O nymph reserved! while now the bright-haired sun
Sits in yon western tent, whose cloudy skirts,
   With brede ethereal wove,
   O'erhang his wavy bed:—

Now air is hushed, save where the weak-eyed bat
With short shrill shriek flits by on leathern wing;
   Or where the beetle winds
   His small but sullen horn,

As oft he rises 'midst the twilight path,
Against the pilgrim borne in heedless hum:
   Now teach me, maid composed,
   To breathe some softened strain,

Whose numbers, stealing through thy dark'ning vale,
May not unseemly with its stillness suit,
   As, musing slow, I hail
   Thy genial loved return!

For when thy folding-star arising shows
His paly circlet, at his warning lamp
   The fragrant hours, and elves
   Who slept in buds the day,

And many a nymph who wreathes her brows with sedge,
And sheds the freshening dew, and lovelier still,
   The pensive Pleasures sweet,
   Prepare thy shadowy car,—

Then let me rove some wild and heathy scene,
Or find some ruin 'midst its dreary dells,
   Whose walls more awful nod
   By thy religious gleams.

Or if chill blustering winds, or driving rain,
Prevent my willing feet, be mine the hut
   That from the mountain's side
   Views wilds and swelling floods,

And hamlets brown, and dim-discovered spires,
And hears their simple bell, and marks o'er all
   Thy dewy fingers draw
   The gradual dusky veil.

While Spring shall pour his showers, as oft he wont,
And bathe thy breathing tresses, meekest Eve!
   While Summer loves to sport
   Beneath thy lingering light:

While sallow Autumn fills thy lap with leaves;
Or Winter, yelling through the troublous air,
   Affrights thy shrinking train,
   And rudely rends thy robes:

So long, regardful of thy quiet rule,
Shall Fancy, Friendship, Science, smiling Peace,
   Thy gentlest influence own,
   And love thy favorite name!

ODE ON THE DEATH OF THOMSON

IN YONDER grave a Druid lies,
  Where slowly winds the stealing wave!
 The year's best sweets shall duteous rise,
  To deck its poet's sylvan grave!

In yon deep bed of whisp'ring reeds
 His airy harp shall now be laid;
That he whose heart in sorrow bleeds
 May love through life the soothing shade.

Then maids and youths shall linger here,
 And while its sounds at distance swell,
Shall sadly seem in Pity's ear
 To hear the woodland pilgrim's knell.

Remembrance oft shall haunt the shore
 When Thames in summer wreaths is drest;
And oft suspend the dashing oar
 To bid his gentle spirit rest.

And oft as Ease and Health retire
 To breezy lawn, or forest deep,
The friend shall view yon whitening spire,
 And 'mid the varied landscape weep.

But thou, who own'st that earthly bed,
   Ah! what will every dirge avail!
Or tears which Love and Pity shed,
   That mourn beneath the gliding sail!

Yet lives there one, whose heedless eye
   Shall scorn thy pale shrine glimm'ring near —
With him, sweet bard, may Fancy die,
   And Joy desert the blooming year.

But thou, lorn stream, whose sullen tide
   No sedge-crowned sisters now attend,
Now waft me from the green hill's side,
   Whose cold turf hides the buried friend!

And see, the fairy valleys fade,
   Dun Night has veiled the solemn view!
Yet once again, dear parted shade,
   Meek Nature's child, again adieu!

The genial meads, assigned to bless
   Thy life, shall mourn thy early doom!
There hinds and shepherd girls shall dress
   With simple hands thy rural tomb.

Long, long, thy stone and pointed clay
   Shall melt the musing Briton's eyes:
"O vales and wild woods!" shall he say,
   "In yonder grave your Druid lies!"

WILLIAM WILKIE COLLINS

(1824–1889)

WILKIE COLLINS has proved that the charm of a story does not necessarily depend upon the depiction of character or an appeal to the sympathies. As he said:—"I have always held the old-fashioned opinion that the primary object of a work of fiction should be to tell a story." He also aspired to draw living men and women, in which he was less successful. Count Fosco, Miss Gwilt, Armadale, Laura Fairlie, and others, are indeed distinct; but the interest centres not on them but on the circumstances in which they are involved. This is the main reason why the critics, even in admiring his talent, speak of Collins with faint depreciation, as certainly not one of the greatest novelists of the century, although holding a place of his own which forces recognition. For novel-readers have delighted in his many volumes in spite of the critics, and there is a steady demand for the old favorites. Translated into French, Italian, Danish, and Russian, many of them continue to inspire the same interest in foreign lands.

WILKIE COLLINS

Wilkie Collins, born January 8th, 1824, did not show any special precocity in boyhood and youth. He probably learned much more from his self-guided reading than from his schooling at Highbury, especially after his acquisition of French and Italian during two years in Italy in his early teens. The influences about him were strongly artistic. His father, William Collins, was distinguished as a landscape painter. The well-known portrait painter Mrs. Carpenter was his aunt, and the distinguished Scotch artist David Wilkie his godfather. But human action and emotion interested him more than art. He was very young when he expressed a desire to write, and perpetrated blank verse which justified his father in vigorous opposition to his adoption of authorship as a profession. So, his school days ended, he presented the not unusual figure of a bright young Englishman who must earn his bread, yet had no particular aptitude for doing it. He tried business first, and became articled clerk with a City house in the tea trade. But the work was uncongenial; and after a few unsatisfactory years he fell in with his father's views, and was entered at Lincoln's Inn and in due time admitted to the bar, although he never practiced law.

He continued writing for amusement, however, producing sketches and stories valuable as training. On his father's death he prepared a biography of that artist in two volumes (1848), which was considered a just as well as a loving appreciation. His first novel, however, was rejected by every publisher to whom he submitted it. His second, 'Antonina,' a story of the fall of Rome, was mediocre. He was about twenty-six when he met Charles Dickens, then a man of forty, at the height of his fame, and with the kindliest feeling for younger writers still struggling for recognition. Dickens, whose own work was always prompted by sympathetic intuition, and to whom character development came more easily than ingenious plots, cordially admired Collins's skill in devising and explaining the latter. He invited the younger man to become collaborator upon Household Words, and thus initiated a warm friendship which lasted until his own death. Encouraged by him, Collins essayed drama and wrote 'The Light-House,' played at Gadshill by distinguished amateurs, Dickens himself among them. At first thought, his would seem an essentially dramatic talent, and several of his novels have been successfully dramatized. But the very cleverness and intricacy of his situations make them unsuited to the stage. They are too difficult of comprehension to be taken in at a glance by an average audience, in the swift passage of stage action.

It was also the influence of Dickens which inspired Collins to attempt social reform. In 'Man and Wife' he tries to show the injustice of Scotch marriage laws; in 'The New Magdalen,' the possible regeneration of fallen women; in 'Heart and Science,' the abuses of vivisection; and other stories are incumbered with didactic purpose. Mr. Swinburne comments upon this aspect of his career in a jocular couplet —

> «What brought good Wilkie's genius nigh perdition?
> Some demon whispered, 'Wilkie! have a mission!'»

But in all "tendency" novels it is not the discussion of problems that makes them live; and Wilkie Collins, like others, survives by purely literary qualities. Soon after his death the critic of the Spectator gave the following capable summary of his peculiar method:—

"He was a literary chess player of the first force, with power of carrying his plan right through the game and making every move tell. His method was to introduce a certain number of characters, set before them a well-defined object, such as the discovery of a secret, the re-vindication of a fortune, the tracking of a crime, or the establishment of a doubted marriage, and then bring in other characters to resist or counterplot their efforts. Each side makes moves, almost invariably well-considered and promising moves; the counter-moves are equally good; the interest goes on accumulating till the looker-on — the reader is always placed in that attitude — is rapt out of himself by strained attention; and then there is a sudden and totally unexpected mate. It is chess which is being played; and in the best of all his stories, the one which will live for years,— 'The Moonstone,' — the pretense that it is anything else is openly disregarded.»

This analysis however must not be too narrowly construed, as petty critics often do, to mean that the only interest in Mr. Collins's novels is that of disentangling the plot. If this were so, no one would read them more than once; while in fact the best of them are eminently readable again and again. This shallow judgment evidently galled the novelist himself, and 'The New Magdalen' in one aspect was a throwing-down of the gauntlet to the critics; for in it he tells the plot page by page, almost paragraph by paragraph, as he goes along, and even far in advance of the story, yet it is one of the most fascinating of his novels. He proved that he could do admirably what they said he could not do at all — make people read his story with breathless absorption when they knew its end long before they came to it; and it was as interesting backward as forward. 'No Name' is in some sort a combination of the two methods, — a revelation of the end, with perpetual interest in the discovery of means.

'The Moonstone' and 'The Woman in White' are unquestionably his masterpieces. In both he throws light upon a complex plot by means of his favorite expedient of letters and diaries written by different characters, who thus take the reader into their confidence and bewilder him with conflicting considerations, until the author comes forward with an ingenious and lucid solution. 'The Moonstone,' however, is immensely superior in matter even to its fellow; its plot is better (in one place 'The Woman in White' comes to a dead wall which the author calmly ignores and goes on), and some passages are worth reading over and over for pure pathos or description. Mr. Collins was in fact, aside from his special gift, a literary artist of no mean power, even if not the highest: with an eye for salient effects, a skill in touching the more obvious chords of emotion, a knowledge of life and books, that enrich his stories with enough extraneous wealth to prolong their life for many years, and some of them perhaps for generations.

THE SLEEP-WALKING

From 'The Moonstone'

[This episode is related by the physician in charge of Mr. Franklin Blake, whose good name he wishes to clear from a charge of fraud.]

TWO O'CLOCK A. M.—The experiment has been tried. With what result I am now to describe.

At eleven o'clock I rang the bell for Betteredge and told Mr. Blake that he might at last prepare himself for bed. . . . I followed Betteredge out of the room, and told him to remove the medicine chest into Miss Verinder's sitting-room.

The order seemed to take him completely by surprise. He looked as if he suspected me of some occult design on Miss Verinder! "Might I presume to ask," he said, "what my young lady and the medicine chest have got to do with each other?"

"Stay in the sitting-room and you will see."

Betteredge appeared to doubt his own unaided capacity to superintend me effectually, on an occasion when a medicine chest was included in the proceedings.

"Is there any objection, sir," he asked, "to taking Mr. Bruff into this part of the business?"

"Quite the contrary! I am now going to ask Mr. Bruff to accompany me down-stairs."

Betteredge withdrew to fetch the medicine chest without another word. I went back into Mr. Blake's room, and knocked at the door of communication. Mr. Bruff opened it, with his papers in his hand — immersed in Law, impenetrable to Medicine.

"I am sorry to disturb you," I said. "But I am going to prepare the laudanum for Mr. Blake; and I must request you to be present and to see what I do."

"Yes," said Mr. Bruff, with nine-tenths of his attention riveted on his papers, and with one-tenth unwillingly accorded to me. "Anything else?"

"I must trouble you to return here with me, and to see me administer the dose."

"Anything else?"

"One thing more. I must put you to the inconvenience of remaining in Mr. Blake's room to see what happens."

"Oh, very good!" said Mr. Bruff. "My room or Mr. Blake's room,— it doesn't matter which; I can go on with my papers anywhere. Unless you object, Mr. Jennings, to my importing *that* amount of common-sense into the proceedings?"

Before I could answer, Mr. Blake addressed himself to the lawyer, speaking from his bed.

"Do you really mean to say that you don't feel any interest in what you are going to do?" he asked. "Mr. Bruff, you have no more imagination than a cow!"

"A cow is a very useful animal, Mr. Blake," said the lawyer. With that reply he followed me out of the room, still keeping his papers in his hand.

We found Miss Verinder pale and agitated, restlessly pacing her sitting-room from end to end. At a table in a corner stood Betteredge, on guard over the medicine chest. Mr. Bruff sat down on the first chair that he could find, and (emulating the usefulness of the cow) plunged back again into his papers on the spot.

Miss Verinder drew me aside, and reverted instantly to her one all-absorbing interest — the interest in Mr. Blake.

"How is he now?" she asked. "Is he nervous? is he out of temper? Do you think it will succeed? Are you sure it will do no harm?"

"Quite sure. Come and see me measure it out."

"One moment. It is past eleven now. How long will it be before anything happens?"

"It is not easy to say. An hour, perhaps."

"I suppose the room must be dark, as it was last year?"

"Certainly."

"I shall wait in my bedroom — just as I did before. I shall keep the door a little way open. It was a little way open last year. I will watch the sitting-room door; and the moment it moves I will blow out my light. It all happened in that way on my birthday night. And it must all happen again in the same way, mustn't it?"

"Are you sure you can control yourself, Miss Verinder?"

"In *his* interests I can do anything!" she answered fervently.

One look at her face told me I could trust her. I addressed myself again to Mr. Bruff.

"I must trouble you to put your papers aside for a moment," I said.

"Oh, certainly!" He got up with a start—as if I had disturbed him at a particularly interesting place—and followed me to the medicine chest. There, deprived of the breathless excitement incidental to the practice of his profession, he looked at Betteredge and yawned wearily.

Miss Verinder joined me with a glass jug of cold water which she had taken from a side table. "Let me pour out the water," she whispered; "I *must* have a hand in it!"

I measured out the forty minims from the bottle, and poured the laudanum into a glass. "Fill it till it is three parts full," I said, and handed the glass to Miss Verinder. I then directed Betteredge to lock up the medicine chest, informing him that I had done with it now. A look of unutterable relief overspread the old servant's countenance. He had evidently suspected me of a medical design on his young lady!

After adding the water as I had directed, Miss Verinder seized a moment—while Betteredge was locking the chest and while Mr. Bruff was looking back at his papers—and slyly kissed the rim of the medicine glass. "When you give it to him," whispered the charming girl, "give it to him on that side."

I took the piece of crystal which was to represent the Diamond from my pocket and gave it to her.

"You must have a hand in this too," I said. "You must put it where you put the Moonstone last year."

She led the way to the Indian cabinet, and put the mock Diamond into the drawer which the real Diamond had occupied on the birthday night. Mr. Bruff witnessed this proceeding, under protest, as he had witnessed everything else. But the strong dramatic interest which the experiment was now assuming proved (to my great amusement) to be too much for Betteredge's capacity of self-restraint. His hand trembled as he held the candle, and he whispered anxiously, "Are you sure, miss, it's the right drawer?"

I led the way out again, with the laudanum and water in my hand. At the door I stood to address a last word to Miss Verinder.

"Don't be long in putting out the lights," I said.

"I will put them out at once," she answered. "And I will wait in my bedroom with only one candle alight."

She closed the sitting-room door behind us. Followed by Bruff and Betteredge, I went back to Mr. Blake's room.

We found him moving restlessly from side to side of the bed, and wondering irritably whether he was to have the laudanum that night. In the presence of the two witnesses I gave him the dose, and shook up his pillows, and told him to lie down again quietly and wait.

His bed, provided with light chintz curtains, was placed with the head against the wall of the room, so as to leave a good open space on either side of it. On one side I drew the curtains completely, and in the part of the room thus screened from his view I placed Mr. Bruff and Betteredge to wait for the result. At the bottom of the bed I half drew the curtains, and placed my own chair at a little distance, so that I might let him see me or not see me, just as the circumstances might direct. Having already been informed that he always slept with a light in the room, I placed one of the two lighted candles on a little table at the head of the bed, where the glare of the light would not strike on his eyes. The other candle I gave to Mr. Bruff; the light in this instance being subdued by the screen of the chintz curtains. The window was open at the top so as to ventilate the room. The rain fell softly; the house was quiet. It was twenty minutes past eleven by my watch when the preparations were completed, and I took my place on the chair set apart at the bottom of the bed.

Mr. Bruff resumed his papers, with every appearance of being as deeply interested in them as ever. But looking toward him now, I saw certain signs and tokens which told me that the Law was beginning to lose its hold on him at last. The suspended interest of the situation in which we were now placed was slowly asserting its influence even on *his* unimaginative mind. As for Betteredge, consistency of principle and dignity of conduct had become in his case mere empty words. He forgot that I was performing a conjuring trick on Mr. Franklin Blake; he forgot that I had upset the house from top to bottom; he forgot that I had not read ‘Robinson Crusoe’ since I was a child. “For the Lord’s sake, sir,” he whispered to me, “tell us when it will begin to work.”

“Not before midnight,” I whispered back. “Say nothing and sit still.”

Betteredge dropped to the lowest depth of familiarity with me, without a struggle to save himself. He answered by a wink!

Looking next toward Mr. Blake, I found him as restless as ever in his bed; fretfully wondering why the influence of the laudanum had not begun to assert itself yet. To tell him in his present humor that the more he fidgeted and wondered the longer he would delay the result for which we were now waiting, would have been simply useless. The wiser course to take was to dismiss the idea of the opium from his mind by leading him insensibly to think of something else.

With this view I encouraged him to talk to me, contriving so to direct the conversation, on my side, as to lead him back again to the subject which had engaged us earlier in the evening,— the subject of the Diamond. I took care to revert to those portions of the story of the Moonstone which related to the transport of it from London to Yorkshire; to the risk which Mr. Blake had run in removing it from the bank at Frizinghall; and to the expected appearance of the Indians at the house on the evening of the birthday. And I purposely assumed, in referring to these events, to have misunderstood much of what Mr. Blake himself had told me a few hours since. In this way I set him talking on the subject with which it was now vitally important to fill his mind — without allowing him to suspect that I was making him talk for a purpose. Little by little he became so interested in putting me right that he forgot to fidget in the bed. His mind was far away from the question of the opium at the all-important time when his eyes first told me that the opium was beginning to lay its hold upon his brain.

I looked at my watch. It wanted five minutes to twelve when the premonitory symptoms of the working of the laudanum first showed themselves to me.

At this time no unpracticed eye would have detected any change in him. But as the minutes of the new morning wore away, the swiftly subtle progress of the influence began to show itself more plainly. The sublime intoxication of opium gleamed in his eyes; the dew of a steady perspiration began to glisten on his face. In five minutes more the talk which he still kept up with me failed in coherence. He held steadily to the subject of the Diamond; but he ceased to complete his sentences. A little later the sentences dropped to single words. Then there was an interval of silence. Then he sat up in bed. Then, still busy with the subject of the Diamond, he began to talk again—not to me but to himself. That change told me the first stage in the experiment was reached. The stimulant influence of the opium had got him.

The time now was twenty-three minutes past twelve. The next half-hour, at most, would decide the question of whether he would or would not get up from his bed and leave the room.

In the breathless interest of watching him — in the unutterable triumph of seeing the first result of the experiment declare itself in the manner, and nearly at the time, which I had anticipated — I had utterly forgotten the two companions of my night vigil. Looking toward them now, I saw the Law (as represented by Mr. Bruff's papers) lying unheeded on the floor. Mr. Bruff himself was looking eagerly through a crevice left in the imperfectly drawn curtains of the bed. And Betteredge, oblivious of all respect for social distinctions, was peeping over Mr. Bruff's shoulder.

They both started back on finding that I was looking at them, like two boys caught out by their schoolmaster in a fault. I signed to them to take off their boots quietly, as I was taking off mine. If Mr. Blake gave us the chance of following him, it was vitally necessary to follow him without noise.

Ten minutes passed — and nothing happened.

Then he suddenly threw the bedclothes off him. He put one leg out of bed. He waited.

"I wish I had never taken it out of the bank," he said to himself. "It was safe in the bank."

My heart throbbed fast; the pulses at my temples beat furiously. The doubt about the safety of the Diamond was once more the dominant impression in his brain! On that one pivot the whole success of the experiment turned. The prospect thus suddenly opened before me was too much for my shattered nerves. I was obliged to look away from him, or I should have lost my self-control.

There was another interval of silence.

When I could trust myself to look back at him he was out of his bed, standing erect at the side of it. The pupils of his eyes were now contracted; his eyeballs gleamed in the light of the candle as he moved his head slowly to and fro. He was thinking; he was doubting; he spoke again.

"How do I know?" he said. "The Indians may be hidden in the house."

He stopped, and walked slowly to the other end of the room. He turned,— waited,— came back to the bed.

"It's not even locked up," he went on. "It's in the drawer of her cabinet. And the drawer doesn't lock."

He sat down on the side of the bed. "Anybody might take it," he said.

He rose again restlessly, and reiterated his first words. "How do I know? The Indians may be hidden in the house."

He waited again. I drew back behind the half-curtain of the bed. He looked about the room, with the vacant glitter in his eyes. It was a breathless moment. There was a pause of some sort. A pause in the action of the opium? a pause in the action of the brain? Who could tell? Everything depended now on what he did next.

He laid himself down again on the bed!

A horrible doubt crossed my mind. Was it possible that the sedative action of the opium was making itself felt already? It was not in my experience that it should do this. But what is experience where opium is concerned? There are probably no two men in existence on whom the drug acts in exactly the same manner. Was some constitutional peculiarity in him feeling the influence in some new way? Were we to fail, on the very brink of success?

No! He got up again very abruptly. "How the devil am I to sleep," he said, "with *this* on my mind?"

He looked at the light burning on the table at the head of his bed. After a moment he took the candle in his hand.

I blew out the second candle burning behind the closed curtains. I drew back, with Mr. Bruff and Betteredge, into the farthest corner by the bed. I signed to them to be silent, as if their lives depended on it.

We waited — seeing and hearing nothing. We waited, hidden from him by the curtains.

The light which he was holding on the other side of us moved suddenly. The next moment he passed us, swift and noiseless, with the candle in his hand.

He opened the bedroom door and went out.

We followed him along the corridor. We followed him down the stairs. We followed him along the second corridor. He never looked back; he never hesitated.

He opened the sitting-room door and went in, leaving it open behind him.

The door was hung (like all the other doors in the house) on large old-fashioned hinges. When it was opened, a crevice was opened between the door and the post. I signed to my two companions to look through this, so as to keep them from showing themselves. I placed myself — outside the door also — on the opposite side. A recess in the wall was at my left hand, in which I could instantly hide myself if he showed any signs of looking back into the corridor.

He advanced to the middle of the room, with the candle still in his hand; he looked about him, — but he never looked back.

I saw the door of Miss Verinder's bedroom standing ajar. She had put out her light. She controlled herself nobly. The dim white outline of her summer dress was all that I could see. Nobody who had not known it beforehand would have suspected that there was a living creature in the room. She kept back in the dark; not a word, not a movement escaped her.

It was now ten minutes past one. I heard through the silence the soft drip of the rain, and the tremulous passage of the night air through the trees.

After waiting irresolute for a minute or more in the middle of the room, he moved to the corner near the window where the Indian cabinet stood.

He put his candle on the top of the cabinet. He opened and shut one drawer after another, until he came to the drawer in which the mock Diamond was put. He looked into the drawer for a moment. Then he took the mock Diamond out with his right hand. With the other hand he took the candle from the top of the cabinet.

He walked back a few steps toward the middle of the room and stood still again.

Thus far he had exactly repeated what he had done on the birthday night. Would his next proceeding be the same as the proceeding of last year? Would he leave the room? Would he go back now, as I believed he had gone back then, to his bed-chamber? Would he show us what he had done with the Diamond when he had returned to his own room?

His first action, when he moved once more, proved to be an action which he had *not* performed when he was under the influence of the opium for the first time. He put the candle down on a table and wandered on a little toward the farther end of the room. There was a sofa here. He leaned heavily on the back of it with his left hand — then roused himself and returned to the middle of the room. I could now see his eyes.

They were getting dull and heavy; the glitter in them was fast dying out.

The suspense of the moment proved too much for Miss Verinder's self-control. She advanced a few steps,— then stopped again. Mr. Bruff and Betteredge looked across the open doorway at me for the first time. The prevision of a coming disappointment was impressing itself on their minds as well as on mine. Still, so long as he stood where he was, there was hope. We waited in unutterable expectation to see what would happen next.

The next event was decisive. He let the mock Diamond drop out of his hand.

It fell on the floor, before the doorway — plainly visible to him and to every one. He made no effort to pick it up; he looked down at it vacantly, and as he looked, his head sank on his breast. He staggered — roused himself for an instant — walked back unsteadily to the sofa — and sat down on it. He made a last effort; he tried to rise, and sank back. His head fell on the sofa cushions. It was then twenty-five minutes past one o'clock. Before I had put my watch back in my pocket he was asleep.

It was over now. The sedative influence had got him; the experiment was at an end.

I entered the room, telling Mr. Bruff and Betteredge that they might follow me. There was no fear of disturbing him. We were free to move and speak.

" The first thing to settle," I said, " is the question of what we are to do with him. He will probably sleep for the next six or seven hours at least. It is some distance to carry him back to his own room. When I was younger I could have done it alone. But my health and strength are not what they were — I am afraid I will have to ask you to help me."

Before they could answer, Miss Verinder called to me softly. She met me at the door of her room with a light shawl and with the counterpane from her own bed.

" Do you mean to watch him while he sleeps ? " she asked.

" Yes. I am not sure enough of the action of the opium in this case, to be willing to leave him alone."

She handed me the shawl and the counterpane.

" Why should you disturb him ? " she whispered. " Make his bed on the sofa. I can shut my door and keep in my room."

It was infinitely the simplest and the safest way of disposing of him for the night. I mentioned the suggestion to Mr. Bruff and Betteredge, who both approved of my adopting it. In five minutes I had laid him comfortably on the sofa, and had covered him lightly with the counterpane and the shawl. Miss Verinder wished us good-night and closed the door. At my request we three then drew round the table in the middle of the room, on which the candle was still burning, and on which writing materials were placed.

"Before we separate," I began, "I have a word to say about the experiment which has been tried to-night. Two distinct objects were to be gained by it. The first of these objects was to prove that Mr. Blake entered this room and took the Diamond last year, acting unconsciously and irresponsibly, under the influence of opium. After what you have both seen, are you both satisfied so far?"

They answered me in the affirmative, without a moment's hesitation.

"The second object," I went on, "was to discover what he did with the Diamond after he was seen by Miss Verinder to leave her sitting-room with the jewel in his hand on the birthday night. The gaining of this object depended, of course, on his still continuing exactly to repeat his proceedings of last year. He has failed to do that; and the purpose of the experiment is defeated accordingly. I can't assert that I am not disappointed at the result—but I can honestly say that I am not surprised by it. I told Mr. Blake from the first that our complete success in this matter depended on our completely reproducing in him the physical and moral conditions of last year; and I warned him that this was the next thing to a downright impossibility. We have only partially reproduced the conditions, and the experiment has been only partially successful in consequence. It is also possible that I may have administered too large a dose of laudanum. But I myself look upon the first reason that I have given as the true reason why we have to lament a failure, as well as to rejoice over a success."

After saying those words I put the writing materials before Mr. Bruff, and asked him if he had any objection, before we separated for the night, to draw out and sign a plain statement of what he had seen. He at once took the pen, and produced the statement with the fluent readiness of a practiced hand.

"I owe you this," he said, signing the paper, "as some atonement for what passed between us earlier in the evening. I beg your pardon, Mr. Jennings, for having doubted you. You have done Franklin Blake an inestimable service. In our legal phrase, you have proved your case."

Betteredge's apology was characteristic of the man.

"Mr. Jennings," he said, "when you read 'Robinson Crusoe' again (which I strongly recommend you to do), you will find that he never scruples to acknowledge it when he turns out to have been in the wrong. Please to consider me, sir, as doing what Robinson Crusoe did on the present occasion." With those words he signed the paper in his turn.

Mr. Bruff took me aside as we rose from the table.

"One word about the Diamond," he said. "Your theory is that Franklin Blake hid the Moonstone in his room. My theory is that the Moonstone is in the possession of Mr. Luker's bankers in London. We won't dispute which of us is right. We will only ask, which of us is in a position to put his theory to the test first?"

"The test in my case," I answered, "has been tried to-night, and has failed."

"The test in my case," rejoined Mr. Bruff, "is still in process of trial. For the last two days I have had a watch set for Mr. Luker at the bank; and I shall cause that watch to be continued until the last day of the month. I know that he must take the Diamond himself out of his bankers' hands, and I am acting on the chance that the person who has pledged the Diamond may force him to do this by redeeming the pledge. In that case I may be able to lay my hand on the person. And there is a prospect of our clearing up the mystery exactly at the point where the mystery baffles us now! Do you admit that, so far?"

I admitted it readily.

"I am going back to town by the ten o'clock train," pursued the lawyer. "I may hear, when I get back, that a discovery has been made — and it may be of the greatest importance that I should have Franklin Blake at hand to appeal to if necessary. I intend to tell him, as soon as he wakes, that he must return with me to London. After all that has happened, may I trust to your influence to back me?"

"Certainly!" I said.

Mr. Bruff shook hands with me and left the room. Better-edge followed him out.

I went to the sofa to look at Mr. Blake. He had not moved since I had laid him down and made his bed,—he lay locked in a deep and quiet sleep.

While I was still looking at him I heard the bedroom door softly opened. Once more Miss Verinder appeared on the threshold in her pretty summer dress.

"Do me a last favor," she whispered. "Let me watch him with you."

I hesitated—not in the interest of propriety; only in the interest of her night's rest. She came close to me and took my hand.

"I can't sleep; I can't even sit still in my own room," she said. "Oh, Mr. Jennings, if you were me, only think how you would long to sit and look at him! Say yes! Do!"

Is it necessary to mention that I gave way? Surely not!

She drew a chair to the foot of the sofa. She looked at him in a silent ecstasy of happiness till the tears rose in her eyes. She dried her eyes and said she would fetch her work. She fetched her work, and never did a single stitch of it. It lay in her lap—she was not even able to look away from him long enough to thread her needle. I thought of my own youth; I thought of the gentle eyes which had once looked love at *me*. In the heaviness of my heart I turned to my Journal for relief, and wrote in it what is written here.

So we kept our watch together in silence,—one of us absorbed in his writing; the other absorbed in her love.

Hour after hour he lay in deep sleep. The light of the new day grew and grew in the room, and still he never moved.

Toward six o'clock I felt the warning which told me that my pains were coming back. I was obliged to leave her alone with him for a little while. I said I would go up-stairs and fetch another pillow for him out of his room. It was not a long attack this time. In a little while I was able to venture back and let her see me again.

I found her at the head of the sofa when I returned. She was just touching his forehead with her lips. I shook my head as soberly as I could, and pointed to her chair. She looked back at me with a bright smile and a charming color in her face. "You would have done it," she whispered, "in my place!" . . .

It is just eight o'clock. He is beginning to move for the first time.

Miss Verinder is kneeling by the side of the sofa. She has so placed herself that when his eyes first open they must open upon her face.

Shall I leave them together?

Yes!

COUNT FOSCO

From 'The Woman in White'

H E LOOKS like a man who could tame anything. If he married a tigress instead of a woman, he would have tamed the tigress. If he had married *me*, I should have made his cigarettes as his wife does; I should have held my tongue when he looked at me as she holds hers.

I am almost afraid to confess it even to these secret pages. The man has interested me, has attracted me, has forced me to like him. In two short days he has made his way straight into my favorable estimation; and how he has worked the miracle is more than I can tell.

It absolutely startles me, now he is in my mind, to find how plainly I see him! how much more plainly than I see Sir Percival, or Mr. Fairlie, or Walter Hartright, or any other absent person of whom I think, with the one exception of Laura herself. I can hear his voice as if he was speaking at this moment. I know what his conversation was yesterday, as well as if I was hearing it now. How am I to describe him? There are peculiarities in his personal appearance, his habits, and his amusements, which I should blame in the boldest terms or ridicule in the most merciless manner, if I had seen them in another man. What is it that makes me unable to blame them or to ridicule them in *him?*

For example, he is immensely fat. Before this time, I have always especially disliked corpulent humanity. I have always maintained that the popular notion of connecting excessive grossness of size and excessive good-humor as inseparable allies was equivalent to declaring either that no people but amiable people ever get fat, or that the accidental addition of so many pounds of flesh has a directly favorable influence over the disposition of the person on whose body they accumulate. I have invariably combated both these absurd assertions by quoting examples of fat people who were as mean, vicious, and cruel as the leanest and worst of their neighbors. I have asked whether Henry the Eighth was an amiable character? whether Pope Alexander the Sixth was a good man? whether Mr. Murderer and Mrs. Murderess Manning were not both unusually stout people? whether hired nurses, proverbially as cruel a set of women as are to be found in all England, were not, for the most part, also as fat a set of women as are to be found in all England?—and so on through dozens of other examples, modern and ancient, native and foreign, high and low. Holding these strong opinions on the subject with might and main, as I do at this moment, here nevertheless is Count Fosco, as fat as Henry the Eighth himself, established in my favor at one day's notice, without let or hindrance from his own odious corpulence. Marvelous indeed!

Is it his face that has recommended him?

It may be his face. He is a most remarkable likeness, on a large scale, of the great Napoleon. His features have Napoleon's magnificent regularity; his expression recalls the grandly calm immovable power of the Great Soldier's face. This striking resemblance certainly impressed me, to begin with; but there is something in him besides the resemblance, which has impressed me more. I think the influence I am now trying to find is in his eyes. They are the most unfathomable gray eyes I ever saw; and they have at times a cold, clear, beautiful, irresistible glitter in them, which forces me to look at him, and yet causes me sensations, when I do look, which I would rather not feel. Other parts of his face and head have their strange peculiarities. His complexion, for instance, has a singular sallow-fairness, so much at variance with the dark-brown color of his hair that I suspect the hair of being a wig; and his face, closely shaven all over, is smoother and freer from all marks and wrinkles than mine, though (according to Sir Percival's account of him) he is close on sixty years of age. But these are not the prominent personal characteristics which distinguish him, to my mind, from all the other men I have ever seen. The marked peculiarity which singles him out from the rank and file of humanity lies entirely, so far as I can tell at present, in the extraordinary expression and extraordinary power of his eyes.

His manner, and his command of our language, may also have assisted him in some degree to establish himself in my good opinion. He has that quiet deference, that look of pleased attentive interest, in listening to a woman, and that secret gentleness in his voice in speaking to a woman, which say what we may, we can none of us resist. Here too his unusual command of the English language necessarily helps him. I had often heard of the extraordinary aptitude which many Italians show in mastering our strong hard Northern speech, but until I saw Count Fosco I had never supposed it possible that any foreigner could have spoken English as he speaks it. There are times when it is almost impossible to detect by his accent that he is not a countryman of our own; and as for fluency, there are very few born Englishmen who can talk with as few stoppages and repetitions as the Count. He may construct his sentences more or less in the foreign way; but I have never yet heard him use a wrong expression, or hesitate for a moment in his choice of words.

All the smallest characteristics of this strange man have something strikingly original and perplexingly contradictory in them. Fat as he is, and old as he is, his movements are astonishingly light and easy. He is as noiseless in a room as any of us women; and more than that, with all his look of unmistakable mental firmness and power, he is as nervously sensitive as the weakest of us. He starts at chance noises as inveterately as Laura herself. He winced and shuddered yesterday when Sir Percival beat one of the spaniels, so that I felt ashamed of my own want of tenderness and sensibility by comparison with the Count.

The relation of this last incident reminds me of one of his most curious peculiarities, which I have not yet mentioned—his extraordinary fondness for pet animals.

Some of these he has left on the Continent; but he has brought with him to this house a cockatoo, two canary-birds, and a whole family of white mice. He attends to all the necessities of these strange favorites himself, and he has taught the creatures to be surprisingly fond of him and familiar with him. The cockatoo, a most vicious and treacherous bird toward every one else, absolutely seems to love him. When he lets it out of its cage it hops on to his knee, and claws its way up his great big body, and rubs its topknot against his sallow double chin in

the most caressing manner imaginable. He has only to set the
doors of the canaries' cage open, and to call them; and the
pretty little cleverly trained creatures perch fearlessly on his
hand, mount his fat outstretched fingers one by one when he
tells them to "go up-stairs," and sing together as if they would
burst their throats with delight when they get to the top finger.
His white mice live in a little pagoda of gayly painted wire-
work, designed and made by himself. They are almost as tame
as the canaries, and they are perpetually let out, like the canaries. They crawl all over him, popping in and out of his waistcoat, and sitting in couples, white as snow, on his capacious
shoulders. He seems to be even fonder of his mice than of his
other pets; smiles at them, and kisses them, and calls them all
sorts of endearing names. If it be possible to suppose an
Englishman with any taste for such childish interests and amusements as these, that Englishman would certainly feel rather
ashamed of them, and would be anxious to apologize for them
in the company of grown-up people. But the Count apparently
sees nothing ridiculous in the amazing contrast between his
colossal self and his frail little pets. He would blandly kiss his
white mice and twitter to his canary-birds amidst an assembly
of English fox-hunters, and would only pity them as barbarians
when they were all laughing their loudest at him.

It seems hardly credible while I am writing it down, but it
is certainly true that this same man, who has all the fondness
of an old maid for his cockatoo, and all the small dexterities
of an organ-boy in managing his white mice, can talk, when
anything happens to rouse him, with a daring independence of
thought, a knowledge of books in every language, and an
experience of society in half the capitals of Europe, which
would make him the prominent personage of any assembly
in the civilized world. This trainer of canary-birds, this archi-
tect of a pagoda for white mice, is (as Sir Percival himself has
told me) one of the first experimental chemists living, and has
discovered among other wonderful inventions a means of petri-
fying the body after death, so as to preserve it, as hard as
marble, to the end of time. This fat, indolent, elderly man,
whose nerves are so finely strung that he starts at chance
noises, and winces when he sees a house spaniel get a whipping,
went into the stable-yard the morning after his arrival, and put
his hand on the head of a chained bloodhound — a beast so

savage that the very groom who feeds him keeps out of his reach. His wife and I were present, and I shall not forget the scene that followed, short as it was.

"Mind that dog, sir," said the groom; "he flies at everybody!" "He does that, my friend," replied the Count quietly, "because everybody is afraid of him. Let us see if he flies at *me*." And he laid his plump yellow-white fingers, on which the canary-birds had been perching ten minutes before, upon the formidable brute's head, and looked him straight in the eyes. "You big dogs are all cowards," he said, addressing the animal contemptuously, with his face and the dog's within an inch of each other. "You would kill a poor cat, you infernal coward. You would fly at a starving beggar, you infernal coward. Anything that you can surprise unawares — anything that is afraid of your big body, and your wicked white teeth, and your slobbering, bloodthirsty mouth, is the thing you like to fly at. You could throttle me at this moment, you mean miserable bully; and you daren't so much as look me in the face, because I'm not afraid of you. Will you think better of it, and try your teeth in my fat neck? Bah! not you!" He turned away, laughing at the astonishment of the men in the yard; and the dog crept back meekly to his kennel. "Ah! my nice waistcoat!" he said pathetically. "I am sorry I came here. Some of that brute's slobber has got on my pretty clean waistcoat." Those words express another of his incomprehensible oddities. He is as fond of fine clothes as the veriest fool in existence, and has appeared in four magnificent waistcoats already — all of light garish colors and all immensely large, even for him — in the two days of his residence at Blackwater Park.

His tact and cleverness in small things are quite as noticeable as the singular inconsistencies in his character, and the childish triviality of his ordinary tastes and pursuits.

I can see already that he means to live on excellent terms with all of us during the period of his sojourn in this place. He has evidently discovered that Laura secretly dislikes him (she confessed as much to me when I pressed her on the subject), but he has also found out that she is extravagantly fond of flowers. Whenever she wants a nosegay he has got one to give her, gathered and arranged by himself; and greatly to my amusement, he is always cunningly provided with a duplicate, composed of exactly the same flowers, grouped in exactly the same way, to appease his icily jealous wife, before she can so much as think herself aggrieved. His management of the Countess (in public) is a sight to see. He bows to her; he habitually addresses her as "my angel"; he carries his canaries to pay her little visits on his fingers, and to sing to her; he kisses her hand when she gives him his cigarettes; he presents her with sugar-plums in return, which he puts into her mouth playfully, from a box in his pocket. The rod of iron with which he rules her never appears in company—it is a private rod and is always kept up-stairs.

His method of recommending himself to *me* is entirely different. He flatters my vanity by talking to me as seriously and sensibly as if I was a man. Yes! I can find him out when I am away from him; I know he flatters my vanity, when I think of him up here in my own room—and yet when I go downstairs and get into his company again he will blind me again, and I shall be flattered again, just as if I had never found him out at all! He can manage me as he manages his wife and Laura, as he manages the bloodhound in the stable yard, as he manages Sir Percival himself every hour in the day. "My good Percival! how I like your rough English humor!"—"My good Percival! how I enjoy your solid English sense!" He puts the rudest remarks Sir Percival can make on his effeminate tastes and amusements quietly away from him in that manner—always calling the baronet by his Christian name; smiling at him with the calmest superiority; patting him on the shoulder; and bearing with him benignantly, as a good-humored father bears with a wayward son.

The interest which I really cannot help feeling in this strangely original man has led me to question Sir Percival about his past life.

Sir Percival either knows little, or will tell me little about it. He and the Count first met many years ago, at Rome, under the dangerous circumstances to which I have alluded elsewhere. Since that time they have been perpetually together, in London, in Paris, and in Vienna—but never in Italy again; the Count having, oddly enough, not crossed the frontiers of his native country for years past. Perhaps he has been made the victim of some political persecution? At all events, he seems to be patriotically anxious not to lose sight of any of his own countrymen who may happen to be in England. On the evening of his arrival, he asked how far we were from the nearest town, and whether we knew of any Italian gentlemen who might happen to be settled there. He is certainly in correspondence with people on the Continent, for his letters have all sorts of odd stamps on them; and I saw one for him this morning, waiting in his place at the breakfast-table, with a huge official-looking seal on it. Perhaps he is in correspondence with his government? And yet that is hardly to be reconciled, either, with my other idea that he may be a political exile.

How much I seem to have written about Count Fosco! And what does it all amount to?—as poor dear Mr. Gilmore would ask in his impenetrable business-like way. I can only repeat that I do assuredly feel, even on this short acquaintance, a strange, half-willing, half-unwilling liking for the Count. He seems to have established over me the same sort of ascendency which he has evidently gained over Sir Percival. Free and even rude as he may occasionally be in his manner toward his fat friend, Sir Percival is nevertheless afraid, as I can plainly see, of giving any serious offense to the Count. I wonder whether I am afraid too? I certainly never saw a man, in all my experience, whom I should be so sorry to have for an enemy. Is this because I like him, or because I am afraid of him? *Chi sa?*—as Count Fosco might say in his own language. Who knows?

GEORGE COLMAN THE ELDER

(1733-1794)

F THE two George Colmans, father and son, familiar to the student of English drama and humor, the son was for two or three generations much the better known to the public, through the inclusion of some humorous poems — of the coarse practical-joking sort dear to the British public, and not unaptly characterized by Macaulay as "blackguard doggerel" — in popular anthologies. But the improvement in taste has retired these, and the father's work as a dramatist has solider merits.

George Colman was the son of an English diplomatist, and born at Florence, but educated in England; entering Christ Church College, Oxford, in 1751, and becoming M. A. in 1758. He studied law in London; but his tastes and an intimacy with Garrick soon led him to abandon this for poetry and play-writing. His first piece, 'Polly Honeycomb,' was acted at Drury Lane with great success in 1760; and the following year 'The Jealous Wife' — "rich in borrowed excellences" — had an equal

GEORGE COLMAN

welcome. Neither of them has much originality, but they show an excellent sense of stage effect and humorous situation, and are well put together and harmonized. Later it occurred to Garrick and Colman that an entertaining play might be made on the lines of Hogarth's 'Marriage à la Mode,' and the result of their joint labors was 'The Clandestine Marriage' (1766). Garrick made a great hit in this as Lord Ogleby, a faded but witty old man.

Colman also wrote some excellent detached pieces for the Connoisseur, and about 1761 became owner of the St. James's Chronicle and contributed humorous matter to it. In 1764 he published a translation of the comedies of Terence into English blank verse, which was much praised. In 1768 he became an owner of Covent Garden Theatre, and later managed the Haymarket. For many years he wrote and translated pieces for the stage, and was much respected as a manager and liked as a man. In 1783 he published a translation of Horace's 'Art of Poetry.' He died in 1794, after five years of insanity.

THE EAVESDROPPING

From 'The Jealous Wife'

Scene, Mr. Oakly's *House: Enter* Harriot *following a Servant*

HARRIOT — Not at home! are you sure that Mrs. Oakly is not at home, sir?

Servant — She is just gone out, madam.

Harriot — I have something of consequence: if you will give me leave, sir, I will wait till she returns.

Servant — You would not see her if you did, madam.   She has given positive orders not to be interrupted with any company to-day.

Harriot — Sure, sir, if you were to let her know that I had particular business —

Servant — I should not dare to trouble her, indeed, madam.

Harriot — How unfortunate this is! What can I do? Pray, sir, can I see *Mr.* Oakly then?

Servant — Yes, madam: I'll acquaint my master, if you please.

Harriot — Pray do, sir.

Servant — Will you favor me with your name, madam?

Harriot — Be pleased, sir, to let him know that a lady desires to speak with him.

Servant — I shall, madam.   [*Exit Servant.*

Harriot [*alone*] — I wish I could have seen Mrs. Oakly! What an unhappy situation am I reduced to! What will the world say of me? And yet what could I do? To remain at Lady Freelove's was impossible.   Charles, I must own, has this very day revived much of my tenderness for him; and yet I dread the wildness of his disposition.   I must now however solicit Mr. Oakly's protection; a circumstance (all things considered) rather disagreeable to a delicate mind, and which nothing but the absolute necessity of it could excuse. Good Heavens, what a multitude of difficulties and distresses am I thrown into, by my father's obstinate perseverance to force me into a marriage which my soul abhors!

Enter Oakly

Oakly — Where is this lady? [*Seeing her.*] Bless me, Miss Russet, is it you? [*Aside*] — Was ever anything so unlucky? — Is it possible, madam, that I see you here?

Harriot—It is true, sir! and the occasion on which I am now to trouble you is so much in need of an apology, but—the favor, sir, which I would now request of you is that you will suffer me to remain for a few days in your house.

Oakly [*aside*]—If my wife should return before I get her out of the house again!—I know of your leaving your father, by a letter we had from him. Upon my soul, madam, I would do anything to serve you; but your being in my house creates a difficulty that—

Harriot—I hope, sir, you do not doubt the truth of what I have told you?

Oakly—I religiously believe every tittle of it, madam; but I have particular family considerations that—

Harriot—Sure, sir, you cannot suspect me to be base enough to form any connections in your family contrary to your inclinations, while I am living in your house.

Oakly—Such connections, madam, would do me and all my family great honor. I never dreamed of any scruples on that account. What can I do? Let me see—let me see—suppose—
                                                                    [*Pausing.*

Enter Mrs. Oakly *behind, in a capuchin, tippet, etc.*

Mrs. Oakly—I am sure I heard the voice of a woman conversing with my husband. Ha! [*Seeing* Harriot.] It is so, indeed! Let me contain myself! I'll listen.

Harriot—I see, sir, you are not inclined to serve me. Good Heaven, what am I reserved to? Why, why did I leave my father's house, to expose myself to greater distresses?
                                                                    [*Ready to weep.*

Oakly—I would do anything for your sake, indeed I would. So pray be comforted; and I'll think of some proper place to bestow you in.

Mrs. Oakly—So, so!

Harriot—What place can be so proper as your own house?

Oakly—My dear madam, I—I—·

Mrs. Oakly—My dear madam! mighty well!

Oakly—Hush! hark! what noise? No, nothing. But I'll be plain with you, madam; we may be interrupted. The family consideration I hinted at is nothing else than my wife. She is a little unhappy in her temper, madam; and if you were to be admitted into the house, I don't know what might be the consequence.

Mrs. Oakly — Very fine!

Harriot — My behavior, sir —

Oakly — My dear life, it would be impossible for you to behave in such a manner as not to give her suspicion.

Harriot — But if your nephew, sir, took everything upon himself —

Oakly — Still that would not do, madam. Why, this very morning, when the letter came from your father, though I positively denied any knowledge of it, and Charles owned it, yet it was almost impossible to pacify her.

Mrs. Oakly — The letter! How have I been bubbled!

Harriot — What shall I do? what will become of me?

Oakly — Why, look ye, my dear madam, since my wife is so strong an objection, it is absolutely impossible for me to take you into the house. Nay, if I had not known she was gone out just before you came, I should be uneasy at your being here even now. So we must manage as well as we can: I'll take a private lodging for you a little way off, unknown to Charles or my wife or anybody; and if Mrs. Oakly should discover it at last, why the whole matter will light upon Charles, you know.

Mrs. Oakly — Upon Charles!

Harriot — How unhappy is my situation! [*Weeping.*] I am ruined forever.

Oakly — Ruined! not at all. Such a thing as this has happened to many a young lady before you, and all has been well again. Keep up your spirits! I'll contrive, if I possibly can, to visit you every day.

Mrs. Oakly [*advancing*] — Will you so? O Mr. Oakly! I have discovered you at last? I'll visit you, indeed. And you, my *dear* madam, I'll —

Harriot — Madam, I don't understand —

Mrs. Oakly — I understand the whole affair, and have understood it for some time past. You shall have a private lodging, miss! It is the fittest place for you, I believe. How dare you look me in the face?

Oakly — For Heaven's sake, my love, don't be so violent! You are quite wrong in this affair; you don't know who you are talking to. That lady is a person of fashion.

Mrs. Oakly — Fine fashion, indeed! to beguile other women's husbands!

Harriot — Dear madam, how can you imagine —

Oakly — I tell you, my dear, this is the young lady that Charles —

Mrs. Oakly — Mighty well! But that won't do, sir! Did not I hear you lay the whole intrigue together? did not I hear your fine plot of throwing all the blame upon Charles?

Oakly — Nay, be cool a moment! You must know, my dear, that the letter which came this morning related to this lady.

Mrs. Oakly — I know it.

Oakly — And since that, it seems, Charles has been so fortunate as to —

Mrs. Oakly — O, you deceitful man! that trick is too stale to pass again with me. It is plain now what you meant by your proposing to take her into the house this morning. But the gentlewoman could introduce herself, I see.

Oakly — Fie, fie, my dear! she came on purpose to inquire for you.

Mrs. Oakly — For me! Better and better! Did not she watch her opportunity, and come to you just as I went out? But I am obliged to you for your visit, madam. It is sufficiently paid. Pray don't let me detain you.

Oakly — For shame, for shame, Mrs. Oakly! How can you be so absurd? Is this proper behavior to a lady of her character?

Mrs. Oakly — I have heard her character. Go, my fine runaway madam! Now you've eloped from your father, and run away from your aunt, go! You shan't stay here, I promise you.

Oakly — Prithee, be quiet. You don't know what you are doing. She shall stay.

Mrs. Oakly — She shan't stay a minute.

Oakly — She shall stay a minute, an hour, a day, a week, a month, a year! 'Sdeath, madam, she shall stay forever, if I choose it.

Mrs. Oakly — How!

Harriot — For Heaven's sake, sir, let me go. I am frighted to death.

Oakly — Don't be afraid, madam! She shall stay, I insist upon it.

Russet [*within*] — I tell you, sir, I will go up. I am sure that the lady is here, and nothing shall hinder me.

Harriot — Oh, my father, my father!   [*Faints away.*

Oakly—See! she faints. [*Catching her.*] Ring the bell! who's there?

Mrs. Oakly—What, take her in your arms too! I have no patience.

Enter Russet *and servants*

Russet—Where is this—Ha! fainting! [*Running to her.*] Oh, my dear Harriot! my child! my child!

Oakly—Your coming so abruptly shocked her spirits. But she revives. How do you, madam?

Harriot [*to Russet*]—Oh, sir!

Russet—Oh, my dear girl! how could you run away from your father, that loves you with such fondness! But I was sure I should find you here.

Mrs. Oakly—There, there! Sure he should find her here! Did not I tell you so? Are not you a wicked man, to carry on such base underhand doings with a gentleman's daughter?

Russet—Let me tell you, sir, whatever you may think of the matter, I shall not easily put up with this behavior. How durst you encourage my daughter to an elopement, and receive her in your house?

Mrs. Oakly—There, mind that! the thing is as plain as the light.

Oakly—I tell you, you misunderstand—

Russet—Look you, Mr. Oakly, I shall expect satisfaction from your family for so gross an affront. Zounds, sir, I am not to be used ill by any man in England!

Harriot—My dear sir, I can assure you—

Russet—Hold your tongue, girl! you'll put me in a passion.

Oakly—Sir, this is all a mistake.

Russet—A mistake! Did not I find her in your house?

Oakly—Upon my soul, she has not been in the house above—

Mrs. Oakly—Did not I hear you say you would take her to a lodging? a private lodging?

Oakly—Yes; but that—

Russet—Has not this affair been carried on a long time, in spite of my teeth?

Oakly—Sir, I never troubled myself—

Mrs. Oakly—Never troubled yourself! Did not you insist on her staying in the house, whether I would or no?

Oakly — No.

Russet — Did not you send to meet her when she came to town ?

Oakly — No.

Mrs. Oakly — Did not you deceive me about the letter this morning ?

Oakly — No, no, no. I tell you, no!

Mrs. Oakly — Yes, yes, yes. I tell you, yes!

Russet — Shan't I believe my own eyes ?

Mrs. Oakly — Shan't I believe my own ears ?

Oakly — I tell you, you are both deceived.

Russet — Zounds, sir, I'll have satisfaction.

Mrs. Oakly — I'll stop these fine doings, I warrant you.

Oakly — 'Sdeath, you will not let me speak! And you are both alike, I think. I wish you were married to one another, with all my heart.

Mrs. Oakly — Mighty well! mighty well!

Russet — I shall soon find a time to talk with you.

Oakly — Find a time to talk! you have talked enough now for all your lives.

Mrs. Oakly — Very fine! Come along, sir! leave that lady with her father. Now she is in the properest hands.

Oakly — I wish I could leave you in his hands. [*Going, returns.*] I shall follow you, madam! One word with you, sir! The height of your passion, and Mrs. Oakly's strange misapprehension of this whole affair, makes it impossible to explain matters to you at present. I will do it when you please, and how you please.   [*Exit.*

Russet — Yes, yes; I'll have satisfaction.— So, madam! I have found you at last. You have made a fine confusion here.

Harriot — I have indeed been the innocent cause of a great deal of confusion.

Russet — Innocent! what business had you to be running hither after—

Harriot — My dear sir, you misunderstand the whole affair. I have not been in this house half an hour.

Russet — Zounds, girl, don't put me in a passion! You know I love you; but a lie puts me in a passion! But come along; we'll leave this house directly. [*Charles singing without.*] Heyday! what now?

After a noise without, enter Charles, *drunk and singing:* —

> But my wine neither nurses nor babies can bring,
> And a big-bellied bottle's a mighty good thing.

What's here—a woman? a woman? Harriot!—Impossible!— My dearest, sweetest Harriot! I have been looking all over the town for you, and at last, when I was tired and weary and disappointed,— why then the honest Major and I sat down together to drink your health in pint bumpers.

[Running up to her.

Russet—Stand off! How dare you take any liberties with my daughter before me? Zounds, sir, I'll be the death of you!

Charles—Ha, 'Squire Russet, too! You jolly old cock, how do you? But Harriot! my dear girl! [*Taking hold of her.*] My life, my soul, my—

Russet—Let her go, sir! Come away, Harriot! Leave him this instant, or I'll tear you asunder.   [*Pulling her.*

Harriot—There needs no violence to tear me from a man who could disguise himself in such a gross manner, at a time when he knew I was in the utmost distress.

[*Disengages herself, and exit with Russet.*

Charles [*alone*]—Only hear me, sir! Madam! My dear Harriot! Mr. Russet! Gone! She's gone; and egad, in a very ill humor and in very bad company! I'll go after her. But hold! I shall only make it worse, as I did, now I recollect, once before. How the devil came they here? Who would have thought of finding her in my own house? My head turns round with conjectures. I believe I am drunk, very drunk; so egad, I'll e'en go and sleep myself sober, and then inquire the meaning of all this—

> "For I love Sue, and Sue loves me," etc.

[Exit singing.

JOHANN AMOS COMENIUS

(1592–1671)

BY BURKE A. HINSDALE

OHANN AMOS COMENIUS, the Slavic educational reformer, was born March 28th, 1592, at Nivnitz, a village of Moravia. His family belonged to the small but well-known body that takes its name from the country,—"the Moravian Brethren," or simply "the Moravians," whose origin goes back to Huss, the Bohemian reformer. The Brethren are known for their simple evangelical faith, their humble fraternal lives, their interest in education, and particularly their devotion to the cause of missions. Comenius was a Moravian, a minister, and a bishop, and he illustrated the best ideas and inspirations of the Brotherhood in his teachings and life.

COMENIUS

The parents of Comenius died when he was still a child, and he fell into the hands of guardians, who allowed his education to be neglected. He received his elementary education in one of the people's schools that sprang out of the Hussite movement. When sixteen years of age he attended a Latin school, and at twenty he was studying theology at Hebron College, in the duchy of Nassau. Next he spent some time in travel and in study at Heidelberg. and returned to Moravia in 1614, being twenty-two years of age. Too young to be ordained to the ministry, he was made rector of a Moravian school at Prerau, near Olmütz, where his career as a teacher and educator began. His attention had already been turned to the teaching art as practiced in the schools, both by observation and by reading the schemes of educational reform that had been propounded. In 1616 he was ordained to the pastorate, and two years later he was set over the flourishing church of Fulneck, where he also had the supervision of a school. Here he married, and "for two or three years," says Professor Laurie, "spent a happy and active life, enjoying the only period of tranquillity in his native country which it was ever his fortune to experience. For the restoration

of a time so happy he never ceased to pine during all his future
wanderings.»

Soon the Thirty Years' War broke out, and in 1621 Fulneck fell
into the hands of the Spaniards, who dealt with it according to their
usual habit in such cases. Comenius lost all his property, including
his library and manuscripts, and became for the rest of his life an
exile. His wife and child he lost soon after. He had been so unfortunate as to incur the enmity of the Jesuits. We cannot follow
him closely in his wanderings. For some time he lived in secrecy
in Moravia and Bohemia. Then he found a resting-place at Lissa, in
Poland, where in 1621 he published a little work that at once made
him famous. This was the 'Janua Linguarum Reserata,' (the Gate
of Tongues Unlocked), which was translated into the principal languages of Europe and several languages of Asia. The next year he
was elected chief bishop of the Brethren, and henceforth there came
upon him daily, as upon the great Apostle, the care of all the
churches. Still he never ceased reading, thinking, and writing on
educational matters, and was often engaged in the practical work of
teaching. He visited England, called there to confer with the Long
Parliament in reference to the reform of education. He visited
Sweden, where he discussed education and learning with the great
Oxenstierna. Then he lived for a time at Elbing in East Russia.
Next he was called to Transylvania and Hungary on an educational
errand, and then returned to Lissa.

In the course of the war this town was destroyed, and Comenius
again lost all of his possessions. The great Pansophic dictionary
that had engaged him for many years went with the rest,—a loss,
he said, that he should cease to lament only when he should cease
to breathe. His next home was Amsterdam, where he set himself to
collect, revise, and supplement his writings on didactics, and where
they were published in four folio volumes in 1657. At some time, according to Cotton Mather, he was offered the presidency of Harvard
College. After the publication of his works he lived thirteen years,
employed in teaching, in writing, and in pastoral labors. He died
November 15th, 1671, in his eightieth year, having fully merited Von
Raumer's characterization:—"Comenius is a grand and venerable
figure of sorrow. Wandering, persecuted, and homeless during the
terrible and desolating Thirty Years' War, he yet never despaired; but
with enduring truth, and strong in faith, he labored unweariedly to
prepare youth by a better education for a better future." In 1892,
on the three-hundredth anniversary of his birth, the educators of the
world united to honor his memory, and at that time a monument
was erected at Naärden, Holland, the little village where he died
and was buried. At Leipzig there is a pedagogical library founded

in his honor on the two-hundredth anniversary of his birth, which numbers more than 66,000 volumes.

Comenius wrote one hundred and thirty-five books and treatises, most of which were translated during his lifetime into all the languages of Europe and several languages of Asia. Not all of them related to education; he wrote voluminously on religious subjects also. To name and characterize his didactic works would far transcend the limits of this notice; we can do no more than draw an outline of his pedagogical system.

Early in the Renaissance the ancient literatures took complete possession of the minds of scholars and teachers. As these literatures were nowhere the vernacular, the schools were made machines for teaching the Latin and Greek languages. Sometimes the results were better, sometimes worse. We may hope that Comenius spoke of the schools at their worst estate when he said that they were "the terror of boys and the slaughter-houses of minds," — "places where hatred of literature and books was contracted," — "where what ought to be poured in gently was forced in violently," and "where what ought to be put clearly was presented in a confused and intricate manner, as if it were a collection of puzzles." "Ten years," he said, "are given to the study of the Latin tongue, and after all the result is disappointing. Boyhood is distracted for years with precepts of grammar, infinitely prolix, perplexed, and obscure, and for the most part useless. Boys are stuffed with vocabularies without associating the words with things, or indeed with one another." For the time it was impossible, even if desirable, to overturn the established system; and Comenius, while still at Prerau, addressed himself to the problem of simplifying the teaching of Latin. His first book, 'Grammaticæ Facilioris Præcepta,' written for his own pupils, was published at Prague in 1616. The great impression that the 'Janua' produced, shows how ready men were to welcome anything that promised to mitigate the evils of the prevailing methods of teaching.

But deeply interested as he was in teaching languages, Comenius still saw that this was by no means the great educational question of the time. Early in life he had become a disciple of the new inductive philosophy; and of all the titles that have been conferred upon him, that of "the Bacon of education" is the most significant. The impression that he received from Bacon was most profound. Several of his titles, as 'Didactica Magna,' 'Pansophiæ Prodromus,' and 'Silva,' suggest titles before used by his master. Looking at education from the Baconian point of view, Comenius proposed to make it an inductive science. He found in nature the great storehouse of education material. "Do we not dwell in the Garden of Eden," he demanded, "as well as our predecessors? Why should not we use our eyes and ears and noses as well as they? and why need we other teachers than these in learning to know the works of nature? Why should we not, instead of these dead books, open to the children the living book of nature? Why not open their understandings to the things themselves, so that from them, as from living springs, many streamlets may flow?" Holding these views and putting them effectively before the world, he became the founder of the pedagogical school known as the Sense-Realists. But much more than this, he had the rare merit of seeing that modern education must be built on the basis of the modern languages; and so he proposed to call the elementary school the "vernacular school,"—things before words, and vernacular words before foreign words.

Comenius's best known books are the 'Didactica Magna' and the 'Orbis Sensualium Pictus.' The first was written in Czech, the author's vernacular, one of the best of the Slavonic dialects, during his first residence in Lissa; but was not published until a later day, and then in Latin. It is a general treatise on method. "After many workings and tossings of my thoughts," he says, "by setting everything to the immovable laws of nature," he lighted upon this treatise, "which shows the art of readily and solidly teaching all things." The 'Orbis Pictus,' which was only a modification of the 'Janua,' first appeared in 1657. Hoole, the English translator, renders the Latin title thus: 'Visible World; or a Nomenclature and Pictures of all the Chief Things that are in the World, and of Men's Employments Therein.' The 'Orbis Pictus' has been called 'Children's First Picture-Book,' and it obtained much the widest circulation and use of all the reformer's works. It was written to illustrate his ideas of teaching things and words together. Its keynote is struck by the legend, "There is nothing in the intellect that is not first in the sense." The lessons, of which there are one hundred and ninety-four words, are given in Latin and German, and are each illustrated with a copper cut. While the book is wholly unsuited to our use, it is still an interesting pedagogical memorial, archaic and quaint.

But Bacon's influence on Comenius was far greater than has yet appeared. The philosopher had large conceptions of the kingdom of knowledge, and the disciple accepted these conceptions in their most exaggerated form. He became the founder of 'Pansophia': men could attain to universal knowledge if they were rightly taught and guided. When his eye had once caught this vision, it never wandered from it to the day of his death. He projected a Pansophic school, and spent half a lifetime in seeking a patron who would help him to realize his dream. Save some of the first ones, his didactic treatises were written as means to a Pansophic end. The books that have made him immortal he counted but as dust in the balance, compared with the piles of manuscripts that he produced devoted to all knowledge. In fact, he almost despised himself because, partly persuaded by his patrons and advisers and partly compelled by the necessities of livelihood, he gave so much time to things didactic. Thus Comenius was like Bacon, in that his real service to the world was something quite different from what he proposed for its benefit. He was like Bacon also in this, that he put forth the same work — practically so — in more than one form.

The mistakes of Comenius lie upon the surface. He entertained exaggerated views of the results to flow to mankind from the enlargement of knowledge, he greatly overestimated the value of method, and so, very naturally, greatly magnified what the human mind is able to accomplish in the field of learning. He carried much too far his sensational principles, and seriously underestimated the ancient learning and letters. But these mistakes, and even Pansophism itself, may be not only excused but welcomed; since they undoubtedly contributed at the time, and since, to educational progress.

It must not be supposed that Comenius had no precursors. Bacon had disclosed to men his vision of the kingdom of knowledge. Rabelais had published his realistic views of education and his vast scheme of studies. Montaigne had delivered his criticisms on current teaching and submitted his suggestions for reform. Mulcaster had given to the world his far-reaching anticipations of the future. Ratich, the John the Baptist of the new movement, to whom Comenius was probably most indebted next to Bacon, had gone far in revolt from the existing régime. But it was left to Comenius to give the new pedagogy a shaping and an impulse that well entitle him to be called its founder.

Comenius has still other credentials to permanent fame. He advocated popular education, contended for the union of knowledge with morals and piety, proposed the higher education of women, propounded the existing tripartite division of education, and devised a system of graded instruction for schools of a decidedly modern character. His place in the educational pantheon is secure; but not so much by reason of his didactics, which are now largely antiquated, as by reason of his spirit. As Mr. Quick has said: — "He saw that every human creature should be trained up to become a reasonable being, and that the training should be such as to draw out the God-given faculties. Thus he struck the keynote of the science of education."

B. A. Hinsdale

AUTHOR'S PREFACE TO THE 'ORBIS PICTUS'

INSTRUCTION is the means to expel rudeness, with which young wits ought to be well furnished in Schools: but so as that the teaching be — 1, True; 2, Full; 3, Clear; and 4, Solid.

1. It will be true, if nothing be taught but such as is beneficial to one's life; lest there be a cause of complaining afterwards. We know not necessary things, because we have not learned things necessary.

2. It will be full, if the mind be polished for wisdom, the tongue for eloquence, and the hands for a neat way of living. This will be that grace of one's life: to be wise, to act, to speak.

3, 4. It will be clear, and by that, firm and solid, if whatever is taught and learned be not obscure or confused, but apparent, distinct, and articulate as the fingers on the hands.

The ground of this business is, that sensual objects may be rightly presented to the senses, for fear they may not be received. I say, and say it again aloud, that this last is the foundation of all the rest: because we can neither act nor speak wisely, unless we first rightly understand all the things which are to be done, and whereof we are to speak. Now there is nothing in the understanding which was not before in the sense. And therefore to exercise the senses well about the right perceiving the differences of things, will be to lay the grounds for all wisdom, and all wise discourse, and all discreet actions in one's course of life. Which, because it is commonly neglected in our schools, and the things which are to be learned are offered to scholars without being understood or being rightly presented to the senses, it cometh to pass that the work of teaching and learning goeth heavily onward, and affordeth little benefit.

See here then a new help for schools, a Picture and Nomenclature of all the chief things in the world, and of men's actions in their way of living: which that you, good masters, may not be loath to run over with your scholars, I tell you, in short, what good you may expect from it.

It is a little book, as you see, of no great bulk, yet a brief of the whole world, and a whole language; full of Pictures, Nomenclatures, and Descriptions of things.

I. The Pictures are the representations of all visible things (to which also things invisible are reduced after their fashion) of the whole world. And that in that very order of things in which they are described in the 'Janua Latinæ Linguæ'; and with that fullness, that nothing very necessary or of great concernment is omitted.

II. The Nomenclatures are the Inscriptions, or Titles, set every one over their own Pictures, expressing the whole thing by its own general term.

III. The Descriptions are the explications of the parts of the Picture, so expressed by their own proper terms; as the same figure which is added to every piece of the Picture, and the term of it, always showeth what things belongeth one to another.

Which such book, and in such a dress, may (I hope) serve.

I. To entice witty children to it, that they may not conceit it a torment to be in school, but dainty fare. For it is apparent that children (even from their infancy almost) are delighted with pictures, and willingly please their eyes with these lights; and it will be very well worth the pains to have once brought it to pass, that scarecrows may be taken away out of wisdom's gardens.

II. This same little book will serve to stir up the attention, which is to be fastened upon things, and even to be sharpened more and more; which is also a great matter. For the senses (being the main guides of childhood, because therein the mind doth not as yet raise up itself to an abstracted contemplation of things) evermore seek their own objects, and if they may be away, they grow dull, and wry themselves hither and thither out of a weariness of themselves; but when their objects are present, they grow merry, wax lively, and willingly suffer themselves to be fastened upon them, till the thing be sufficiently discerned. This book then will do a good piece of service in taking especially flickering wits, and preparing them for deeper studies.

III. Whence a third good will follow: that children being won thereunto, and drawn over with this way of heeding, may be furnished with the knowledge of the prime things that are in the world, by sport and merry pastime. In a word, this Book will serve for the more pleasing using of the 'Vestibulum' and 'Janua Linguarum,' for which end it was even at the first chiefly intended. Yet if it like any that it be bound up in their native tongues also, it promiseth three good things of itself.

I.   First, it will afford a device for learning to read more
easily than hitherto, especially having a symbolical alphabet set
before it; to wit, the characters of the several letters, with the
image of that creature whose voice that letter goeth about to
imitate, pictured by it.   For the young A B C scholar will easily
remember the force of every character by the very looking upon
the creature, till the imagination, being strengthened by use, can
readily afford all things; and then having looked over a table of
the chief syllables also (which yet was not thought necessary to
be added to this book), he may proceed to the viewing of the
pictures and the inscriptions set over them.   Where again, the
very looking upon the thing pictured suggesting the name of the
thing, will tell him how the title of the picture is to be read.
And thus the whole book being gone over by the bare titles of
the pictures, reading cannot but be learned; and indeed too,
which thing is to be noted, without using any ordinary tedious
spelling, that most troublesome torture of wits, which may wholly
be avoided by this method.   For the often reading over the book,
by those larger descriptions of things, and which are set after the
pictures, will be able perfectly to beget a habit of reading.

II.   The same book being used in English, in English schools,
will serve for the perfect learning of the whole English tongue,
and that from the bottom; because by the aforesaid descriptions
of things, the words and phrases of the whole language are
found set orderly in their proper places.   And a short English
Grammar might be added at the end, clearly resolving the speech
already understood into its parts; showing the declining of the
several words, and reducing those that are joined together under
certain rules.

III.   Thence a new benefit cometh, that that very English
Translation may serve for the more ready and pleasant learning
of the Latin tongue: as one may see in this edition, the whole
book being so translated that everywhere one word answereth to
the word over against it, and the book is in all things the same,
only in two idioms, as a man clad in a double garment.   And
there might be also some observations and advertisements added
at the end, touching those things only wherein the use of the
Latin tongue differeth from the English.   For where there is no
difference, there needeth no advertisements to be given.   But
because the first tasks of the learner ought to be little and
single, we have filled this first book of training one up to see a

thing of himself, with nothing but rudiments; that is, with the chief of things and words, or with the grounds of the whole world, and the whole language, and of all our understanding about things. If a more perfect description of things, and a fuller knowledge of a language, and a clearer light of the understanding, be sought after (as they ought to be), they are to be found somewhere whither there will now be an easy passage by this our little Encyclopædia of things subject to the senses. Something remaineth to be said touching the more cheerful use of this book.

I. Let it be given to children into their hands to delight themselves withal as they please with the sight of the pictures, and making them as familiar to themselves as may be, and that even at home before they are put to school.

II. Then let them be examined ever and anon (especially now in the school) what this thing or that thing is, and is called, so that they may see nothing which they know not how to name, and that they can name nothing which they cannot show.

III. And let the things named them be showed, not only in the picture, but also in themselves; for example, the parts of the body, clothes, books, the house, utensils, etc.

IV. Let them be suffered also to imitate the pictures by hand, if they will; nay, rather let them be encouraged that they may be willing: first, thus to quicken the attention also towards the things, and to observe the proportion of the parts one towards the other; and lastly, to practice the nimbleness of the hand, which is good for many things.

V. If anything here mentioned cannot be presented to the eye, it will be to no purpose at all to offer them by themselves to the scholars; as colors, relishes, etc., which cannot here be pictured out with ink. For which reason it were to be wished that things rare and not easy to be met withal at home might be kept ready in every great school, that they may be showed also, as often as any words are to be made by them, to the scholars.

SCHOOL OF INFANCY

CLAIMS OF CHILDHOOD

THAT children are an inestimable treasure, the Spirit of God
by the lips of David testifies, saying:—"Lo, the children
are the heritages of the Lord; the fruit of the womb his
reward; as arrows in the hand, so are children. Blessed is the
man who has filled his quiver with them; he shall not be confounded." David declares those to be happy on whom God
confers children.

The same is also evident from this: that God, purposing to
testify his love towards us, calls us children, as if there were no
more excellent name by which to commend us.

Moreover, he is very greatly incensed against those who
deliver their children to Moloch. It is also worthy our most
serious consideration that God, in respect of the children of even
idolatrous parents, calls them children born to him; thus indicating that they are born not for ourselves but for God, and
as God's offspring they claim our most profound respect.

Hence in Malachi children are called the seed of God, whence
arises the offspring of God.

For this reason the eternal Son of God, when manifested in
the flesh, not only willed to become the participator of the flesh
of children, but likewise deemed children a pleasure and a
delight. Taking them in his arms, as little brothers and sisters,
he carried them about, and kissed them and blessed them.

Not only this: he likewise uttered a severe threat against any
one who should offend them even in the least degree, commanding them to be respected as himself, and condemning even
with severe penalties any who offend even the smallest of them.

Should any one wish to inquire why he so delighted in little
children, and so strictly enjoined upon us such respectful attention to them, many reasons may be ascertained. And first, if
the little ones seem unimportant to you, regard them not as
they now are, but as in accordance with the intention of God
they may and ought to be. You will see them not only as the
future inhabitants of the world and possessors of the earth, and
God's vicars amongst his creatures when we depart from this
life, but also equally participators with us in the heritage of

Christ, a royal priesthood, a chosen people, associates of angels, judges of devils, the delight of heaven, the terror of hell—heirs of the most excellent dignities throughout all the ages of eternity. What can be imagined more excellent than this?

Philip Melanchthon of pious memory, having upon one occasion entered a common school, looked upon the pupils therein assembled, and began his address to them in these words:— "Hail, reverend pastors, doctors, licentiates, superintendents! Hail! most noble, most prudent, most learned lords, consuls, prætors, judges, prefects, chancellors, secretaries, magistrates, professors, etc." When some of the bystanders received these words with a smile, he replied:—"I am not jesting; my speech is serious; for I look on these little boys, not as they are now, but with a view to the purpose of the Divine mind, on account of which they are delivered to us for instruction. For assuredly some such will come forth from among the number, although there may be an intermixture of chaff among them as there is among wheat." Such was the animated address of this most prudent man. But why should not we with equal confidence declare, in respect of all children of Christian parents, those glorious things which have been mentioned above? since Christ, the promulgator of the eternal secrets of God, has pronounced that "of such is the kingdom of Heaven."

But if we consider only their present state, it will at once be obvious why children are of inestimable value in the sight of God, and ought to be so to their parents.

In the first place, they are valuable to God because, being innocent with the sole exception of original sin, they are not yet the defaced image of God by having polluted themselves with actual guilt, and are "unable to discern between good and evil, between the right hand and the left." That God has respect to this is abundantly manifest from the above words addressed to John, and from other passages of the Sacred Writ.

Secondly, they are the pure and dearly purchased possession of Christ; since Christ, who came to seek the lost, is said to be the Savior of all, except those who by incredulity and impenitence shut themselves out from being participators in his merits. These are the purchased from among men, that they may be the first-fruits unto God and the Lamb; having not yet defiled themselves with the allurements of sin; but they follow the Lamb whithersoever he goeth. And that they may continue so to follow, they ought to be led as it were with the hand by a pious education.

Finally, God so embraces children with abounding love that they are a peculiar instrument of divine glory; as the Scriptures testify, "From the lips of infants and sucklings thou hast perfected praise, because of mine enemies; that thou mayest destroy the enemy and avenger." How it comes to pass that God's glory should receive increase from children, is certainly not at once obvious to our understanding; but God, the discerner of all things, knows and understands, and declares it to be so.

That children ought to be dearer and more precious to parents than gold and silver, than pearls and gems, may be discovered from a comparison between both of these gifts from God: for first, gold, silver, and such other things, are inanimate, being only somewhat harder and purer than the clay which we tread beneath our feet; whereas children are the lively image of the living God.

Secondly, gold and silver are rudimentary objects produced by the command of God; whereas children are creatures in the production of which the all-sacred Trinity instituted special council, and formed them with his own fingers.

Thirdly, gold and silver are fleeting and transitory things; children are an immortal inheritance. For although they yield to death, yet they neither return to nothing, nor become extinct; they only pass out of a mortal tabernacle into immortal regions. Hence, when God restored to Job all his riches and possessions, even to the double of what he had previously taken away, he gave him no more children than he had before; namely, seven sons and three daughters. This, however, was the precise double; inasmuch as the former sons and daughters had not perished, but had gone before to God.

Fourthly, gold and silver come forth from the earth, children come from our own substance; being a part of ourselves, they consequently deserve to be loved by us, certainly not less than we love ourselves: therefore God has implanted in the nature of all living things so strong an affection towards their young that they occasionally prefer the safety of their offspring to their own. If any one transfer such affections to gold or silver, he is, in the judgment of God, condemned as guilty of idolatry.

Fifthly, gold and silver pass away from one to another as though they were the property of none, but common to all:

whereas children are a peculiar possession, divinely assigned to their parents; so that there is not a man in the world who can deprive them of this right or dispossess them of this inheritance, because it is a portion descended from heaven and not a transferable possession.

Sixthly, although gold and silver are gifts of God, yet they are not such gifts as those to which he has promised an angelic guardianship from heaven; nay, Satan mostly intermingles himself with gold and silver so as to use them as nets and snares to entangle the unwary, drawing them as it were with thongs, to avarice, haughtiness, and prodigality: whereas the care of little children is always committed to angelic guardianship, as the Lord himself testifies. Hence he who has children within his house may be certain that he has therein the presence of angels; he who takes little children in his arms may be assured that he takes angels; whosoever, surrounded with midnight darkness, rests beside an infant, may enjoy the certain consolation that with it he is so protected that the spirit of darkness cannot have access. How great the importance of these things!

Seventhly, gold, silver, and other external things do not procure for us the love of God, nor as children do, defend us from his anger; for God so loved children that for their sake he occasionally pardons parents; Nineveh affords an example: inasmuch as there were many children therein, God spared the parents from being swallowed up by the threatened judgment.

Eighthly, human life does not consist in abundance of wealth, as our Lord says, since without God's blessings neither food nourishes, nor plaster heals, nor clothing warms; but his blessing is always present with us for the sake of children, in order that they may be sustained. For if God liberally bestows food on the young ravens calling on him, how much more should he not care for children, his own image? Therefore Luther has wisely said:— "We do not nourish our children, but they nourish us; for because of these innocents God supplies necessaries, and we aged sinners partake of them."

Finally, silver, gold, and gems afford us no further instruction than other created things do, namely, in the wisdom, power, and beneficence of God; whereas children are given to us as a mirror, in which we may behold modesty, courteousness, benignity, harmony, and other Christian virtues, the Lord himself declaring, "Unless ye be converted and become as little children, ye shall

VII—246

not enter into the kingdom of Heaven." Since then God has willed that children should be unto us in the place of preceptors, we judge that we owe to them the most diligent attention.

Thus at last this school would become a school of things obvious to the senses, and an entrance to the school intellectual. But enough. Let us come to the thing itself.

PHILIPPE DE COMINES

(1445–1510)

HE last in date among the great French chroniclers of the Middle Ages was Philippe de Comines (also written Commines or Comynes). He was the scion of an old and wealthy family that attained to nobility by marrying into the house of the barons of Comines, the privilege being a reward for faithful allegiance in the times of trouble and warfare. The approximate date of his birth is the year 1445; his birthplace is not known with certainty, though it may be assumed to have been either on the estate of Comines, near Lille in northern France, or at the Château de Renescure, near Saint-Omer. He lost his mother in 1447, and his father died in 1453, leaving an entangled inheritance that netted a sum of about two thousand five hundred livres, which in those days sufficed to defray the child's current expenses and provide for his education. Under the guardianship of one of his relatives, Jean de Comines, the young orphan was brought up in the true spirit of the feudal times to which he belonged, and was taught the profession of arms. Reading and writing he also acquired, but whatever intellectual training he received beyond this point was owing altogether to his own efforts and exertions.

It was a matter of sincere regret to him that his education never included the study of Latin. He became skilled with the pen, but used it for his own amusement, not with a thought of leaving anything more than notes that might serve others as a basis for fuller historical descriptions. His style is terse, and not devoid of charm; for he was not lacking in imagination, and by quaint simile or other rhetorical effect enlivened many a page of his Chronicles. His vocabulary, without being very rich, is carefully selected, but his syntactical constructions are often abstruse and obscure. On the whole, however, this justice must be done to Philippe de Comines: that what he may lose for want of natural ease of expression is compensated for by his virility of speech and true eloquence. His chief merit lies in his pithy remarks, replete with suggestion. But literary pursuits were not his proper field. In his days such occupations were left almost exclusively to the clergy, in whom alone was supposed to be vested the need and uses of book learning.

He sought, as he grew up, to remedy the shortcomings of his training, and acquired through contact with the numerous foreigners he was in a position to meet, a fair knowledge of Italian, Spanish, and German.

"On coming forth from childhood," he writes, "and being old enough to ride horseback, I was led to Lille before Duke Charles of Burgundy, then Count of Charolais, who took me in his service; and this was in the year 1464." Philippe de Comines was then in his twentieth year, a youth polished in manners, refined in tastes, and above all, a most acute observer,—and these qualities stamped him as a coming diplomat of rare natural ability, in touch with his time, and understanding himself and others sufficiently well to moralize and philosophize about men and things, to reach many a sound conclusion, and to utter many a true and wise saying. He is among the first thinking men of France who committed to paper the results of his labors as a moral philosopher, as a statesman, and as a trusted adviser to royalty.

For eight full years Philippe de Comines remained in the confidential service of the Duke of Burgundy, by whom he was sent, young as he was, on various diplomatic missions of the greatest importance,—first to London, then to Brittany, finally to Orange and Castile. In the course of these expeditions he came in contact with Louis XI., King of France, and knew how to ingratiate himself into his favor. Whatever the reasons for his rupture with the Duke of Burgundy, whatever the special inducements offered by Louis XI., the fact remains that he suddenly left his former master; and possessed of knowledge of the utmost political importance to the King of France, he entered the royal service and remained there until the King's death in August, 1483. His work was generously recognized by Louis XI., and even after his noble patron's death Comines retained his court position for a time. He gradually fell away, however, from his allegiance to the royal cause, and threw himself heart and soul into a movement, set on foot by a number of the feudal lords and directed by the Duke of Orleans himself, against the person of the young King Charles VIII. Arrested on a charge of conspiracy, he spent over two years in various prisons (1486–1489), with ample time to think over the vicissitudes of human happiness. A light sentence was finally passed upon him, and having regained his liberty he was so far restored to favor as to be sent on diplomatic missions, first to Venice and then to Milan.

Though he lived in honor under Louis XII., he retired shortly to private life on his estate of Argenton, where he died in 1510.

It was in the solitude of his prison that Philippe de Comines began to write his reminiscences. The 'Chronique et Hystoire Faicte et Composée par Messire Philippe de Comines' (Paris, 1524) was written between the years 1488 and 1493. It deals with the history of France from 1464 (when Comines went to the court of Charles the Bold) to the death of Louis XI. in 1483. The sequel, 'Chroniques du Roy Charles Huytiesme' (Paris, 1528), written subsequently to 1497, relates the story of the famous expedition to Italy undertaken by Charles VIII. In the pages of 'Quentin Durward,' where Walter Scott has given a graphic portrayal of the great men of that turbulent time, Philippe de Comines stands out beside the crafty and superstitious Louis XI. and the martial Charles of Burgundy as one of the most striking figures of a picturesque age.

THE VIRTUES AND VICES OF KING LOUIS XI.

From the 'Memoirs of Philippe de Comines'

THE chief reason that has induced me to enter upon this subject is because I have seen many deceptions in this world, especially in servants toward their masters; and I have always found that proud and stately princes who will hear but few, are more liable to be imposed upon than those who are open and accessible: but of all the princes that I ever knew, the wisest and most dexterous to extricate himself out of any danger or difficulty in time of adversity was our master King Louis XI. He was the humblest in his conversation and habit, and the most painful and indefatigable to win over any man to his side that he thought capable of doing him either mischief or service: though he was often refused, he would never give over a man that he wished to gain, but still pressed and continued his insinuations, promising him largely, and presenting him with such sums and honors as he knew would gratify his ambition; and for such as he had discarded in time of peace and prosperity, he paid dear (when he had occasion for them) to recover them again; but when he had once reconciled them, he retained no enmity towards them for what had passed, but employed them freely for the future. He was naturally kind and indulgent to persons of mean estate, and hostile to all great men who had no need of him. Never prince was so conversable nor so inquisitive as he, for his desire was to know everybody he could; and indeed he knew all persons of any authority or worth in England, Spain, Portugal, and Italy, in the territories of the Dukes of Burgundy and Bretagne, and among his own subjects: and by those qualities he preserved the crown upon his head, which was in much danger by the enemies he had created to himself upon his accession to the throne.

But above all, his great bounty and liberality did him the greatest service: and yet, as he behaved himself wisely in time of distress, so when he thought himself a little out of danger, though it were but by a truce, he would disoblige the servants and officers of his court by mean and petty ways which were little to his advantage; and as for peace, he could hardly endure the thoughts of it. He spoke slightingly of most people, and rather before their faces than behind their backs; unless he was afraid of them, and of that sort there were a great many, for he was naturally somewhat timorous. When he had done himself any prejudice by his talk, or was apprehensive he should do so, and wished to make amends, he would say to the person whom he had disobliged, "I am sensible my tongue has done me a good deal of mischief; but on the other hand, it has sometimes done me much good: however, it is but reason I should make some reparation for the injury." And he never used this kind of apologies to any person but he granted some favor to the person to whom he made it, and it was always of considerable amount.

It is certainly a great blessing from God upon any prince to have experienced adversity as well as prosperity, good as well as evil, and especially if the good outweighs the evil, as it did in the King our master. I am of opinion that the troubles he was involved in in his youth, when he fled from his father and resided six years together with Philip, Duke of Burgundy, were of great service to him; for there he learned to be complaisant to such as he had occasion to use, which was no slight advantage of adversity. As soon as he found himself a powerful and crowned king, his mind was wholly bent upon revenge; but he quickly found the inconvenience of this, repented by degrees of his indiscretion, and made sufficient reparation for his folly and error by regaining those he had injured. Besides, I am very confident that if his education had not been different from the usual education of such nobles as I have seen in France, he could not so easily have worked himself out of his troubles: for they are brought up to nothing but to make themselves ridiculous, both in their clothes and discourse; they have no knowledge of letters; no wise man is suffered to come near them, to improve their understandings; they have governors who manage their business, but they do nothing themselves: nay, there are some nobles who though they have an income of thirteen livres, will take pride to bid you "Go to my servants and let them answer you," thinking by such speeches to imitate the state and grandeur of a prince; and I have seen their servants take great advantage of them, giving them to understand they were fools; and if afterwards they came to apply their minds to business and attempted to manage their own affairs, they began so late they could make nothing of it. And it is certain that all those who have performed any great or memorable action worthy to be recorded in history, began always in their youth; and this is to be attributed to the method of their education, or some particular blessing of God.

THE VIRTUES OF THE DUKE OF BURGUNDY AND THE TIME OF HIS HOUSE'S PROSPERITY

I SAW a seal-ring of his after his death at Milan, with his arms cut curiously upon a sardonyx, that I have often seen him wear in a riband at his breast; which was sold at Milan for two ducats, and had been stolen from him by a varlet that waited on him in his chamber. I have often seen the duke dressed and undressed in great state and formality, and by very great persons; but at his last hour all this pomp and magnificence ceased, and both he and his family perished on the very spot where he had delivered up the Constable not long before, out of a base and avaricious motive. But may God forgive him! I have known him a powerful and honorable prince, in as great esteem and as much courted by his neighbors (when his affairs were in a prosperous condition) as any prince in Europe, and perhaps more so; and I cannot conceive what should have provoked God Almighty's displeasure so highly against him unless it was his self-love and arrogance, in attributing all the success of his enterprises and all the renown he ever acquired to his own wisdom and conduct, without ascribing anything to God: yet, to speak truth, he was endowed with many good qualities. No prince ever had a greater desire to entertain young noblemen than he, or was more careful of their education. His presents and bounty were never profuse and extravagant, because he gave to many, and wished everybody should taste of his generosity.

No prince was ever more easy of access to his servants and subjects. Whilst I was in his service he was never cruel, but a little before his death he became so, which was an infallible sign of the shortness of his life. He was very splendid and pompous in his dress and in everything else, and indeed a little too much. He paid great honors to all ambassadors and foreigners, and entertained them nobly. His ambitious desire of glory was insatiable, and it was that which more than any other motive induced him to engage eternally in wars. He earnestly desired to imitate the old kings and heroes of antiquity, who are still so much talked of in the world, and his courage was equal to that of any prince of his time. . . .

I am partly of the opinion of those who maintain that God gives princes, as he in his wisdom thinks fit, to punish or chastise their subjects; and he disposes the affections of subjects to their princes as he has determined to exalt or depress them. Just so it has pleased him to deal with the house of Burgundy; for after a long series of riches and prosperity, and sixscore years' peace under three illustrious princes, predecessors to Duke Charles (all of them of great prudence and discretion), it pleased God to send this Duke Charles, who continually involved them in bloody wars, winter as well as summer, to their great affliction and expense, in which most of their richest and stoutest men were either killed or taken prisoners. Their misfortunes began at the siege of Nuz, and continued for three or four battles successively, to the very hour of his death; so much so that at the last the whole strength of the country was destroyed, and all were killed or taken prisoners who had any zeal or affection for the house of Burgundy, or power to defend the state and dignity of that family; so that in a manner their losses equaled if they did not overbalance their former prosperity: for as I have seen these princes puissant, rich, and honorable, so it fared with their subjects; for I think I have seen and known the greatest part of Europe, yet I never knew any province or country, though of a larger extent, so abounding in money, so extravagantly fine in their furniture, so sumptuous in their buildings, so profuse in their expenses, so luxurious in their feasts and entertainments, and so prodigal in all respects, as the subjects of these princes in my time; and if any think I have exaggerated, others who lived in my time will be of opinion that I have rather said too little.

But it pleased God at one blow to subvert this great and sumptuous edifice and ruin this powerful and illustrious family, which had maintained and bred up so many brave men, and had acquired such mighty honor and renown far and near, by so many victories and successful enterprises as none of all its neighboring States could pretend to boast of. A hundred and twenty years it continued in this flourishing condition, by the grace of God; all its neighbors having in the mean time been involved in troubles and commotions, and all of them applying to it for succor or protection,— to wit, France, England, and Spain,— as you have seen by experience of our master the King of France, who in his minority, and during the reign of Charles VII. his father, retired to this court, where he lived six years and was nobly entertained all that time by Duke Philip the Good. Out of England I saw there also two of King Edward's brothers, the Dukes of Clarence and Gloucester (the last of whom was afterwards called King Richard III.); and of the house of Lancaster, the whole family or very near, with all their party. In short, I have seen this family in all respects the most flourishing and celebrated of any in Christendom; and then in a short space of time it was quite ruined and turned upside down, and left the most desolate and miserable of any house in Europe, as regards both princes and subjects. Such changes and revolutions of States and kingdoms, God in his providence has wrought before we were born and will do again when we are dead; for this is a certain maxim, that the prosperity or adversity of princes depends wholly on his divine disposal.

THE LAST DAYS OF LOUIS XI.

THE King towards the latter end of his days caused his castle of Plessis-les-Tours to be encompassed with great bars of iron in the form of thick grating, and at the four corners of the house four sparrow-nests of iron, strong, massy, and thick, were built. The grates were without the wall on the other side of the ditch, and sank to the bottom. Several spikes of iron were fastened into the wall, set as thick by one another as was possible, and each furnished with three or four points. He likewise placed ten bowmen in the ditches, to shoot at any man that durst approach the castle before the opening of the gates; and he ordered they should lie in the ditches, but retire to the sparrow-nests upon occasion. He was sensible enough that this fortification was too weak to keep out an army or any great body of men, but he had no fear of such an attack: his great apprehension was that some of the nobility of his kingdom, having intelligence within, might attempt to make themselves masters of the castle by night, and having possessed themselves of it partly by favor and partly by force, might deprive him of the regal authority and take upon themselves the administration of public affairs; upon pretense that he was incapable of business and no longer fit to govern.

The gate of the Plessis was never opened nor the drawbridge let down before eight o'clock in the morning, at which time the officers were let in; and the captains ordered their guards to their several posts, with pickets of archers in the middle of the court, as in a town upon the frontiers that is closely guarded; nor was any person admitted to enter except by the wicket and with the King's knowledge, unless it were the steward of his household, and such persons as were not admitted into the royal presence.

Is it possible then to keep a prince (with any regard to his quality) in a closer prison than he kept himself? The cages which were made for other people were about eight feet square; and he (though so great a monarch) had but a small court of the castle to walk in, and seldom made use of that, but generally kept himself in the gallery, out of which he went into the chambers on his way to mass, but never passed through the court. Who can deny that he was a sufferer as well as his neighbors? considering how he was locked up and guarded, afraid of his own children and relations, and changing every day those very servants whom he had brought up and advanced; and though they owed all their preferment to him, yet he durst not trust any of them, but shut himself up in those strange chains and inclosures. If the place where he confined himself was larger than a common prison, he also was much greater than common prisoners.

It may be urged that other princes have been more given to suspicion than he, but it was not in our time; and perhaps their wisdom was not so eminent, nor were their subjects so good. They might too, probably, have been tyrants and bloody-minded; but our King never did any person a mischief who had

not offended him first, though I do not say all who offended him
deserved death. I have not recorded these things merely to
represent our master as a suspicious and mistrustful prince, but
to show that by the patience which he expressed in his sufferings (like those which he inflicted on other people) they may be
looked upon, in my judgment, as a punishment which Our Lord
inflicted upon him in this world in order to deal more merci-
fully with him in the next; . . . and likewise, that those
princes who may be his successors may learn by his example
to be more tender and indulgent to their subjects, and less
severe in their punishments than our master had been: although
I will not censure him, or say I ever saw a better prince;
for though he oppressed his subjects himself, he would never
see them injured by anybody else.

After so many fears, sorrows, and suspicions, God by a kind
of miracle restored him both in body and mind, as is his
divine method in such kind of wonders: for he took him out
of this miserable world in perfect health of mind and understanding and memory; after having received the sacraments
himself, discoursing without the least twinge or expression of
pain, and repeating his paternosters to the very last moment of
his life. He gave directions for his own burial, appointed who
should attend his corpse to the grave, and declared that he
desired to die on a Saturday of all days in the week; and
that he hoped Our Lady would procure him that favor, for in
her he had always placed great trust, and served her very
devoutly. And so it happened; for he died on Saturday, the
30th of August, 1433, at about eight in the evening, in the
castle of Plessis, where his illness seized him on the Monday
before. May Our Lord receive his soul, and admit it into his
kingdom of Paradise!

CHARACTER OF LOUIS XI.

SMALL hopes and comfort ought poor and inferior people to
have in this world, considering what so great a king suffered and underwent, and how he was at last forced to
leave all, and could not, with all his care and diligence, protract
his life one single hour. I knew him and was entertained in
his service in the flower of his age and at the height of his
prosperity, yet I never saw him free from labor and care. Of
all diversions he loved hunting and hawking in their seasons;
but his chief delight was in dogs. . . . In hunting, his
eagerness and pain were equal to his pleasure, for his chase was
the stag, which he always ran down. He rose very early in the
morning, rode sometimes a great distance, and would not leave
his sport, let the weather be never so bad; and when he came
home at night he was often very weary, and generally in a violent passion with some of his courtiers or huntsmen; for hunting
is a sport not always to be managed according to the master's
direction; yet in the opinion of most people, he understood it
as well as any prince of his time. He was continually at these
sports, lodging in the country villages to which his recreations
led him, till he was interrupted by business; for during the
most part of the summer there was constantly war between him
and Charles, Duke of Burgundy, and in the winter they made
truces; . . . so that he had but a little time during the
whole year to spend in pleasure, and even then the fatigues he
underwent were excessive. When his body was at rest his mind
was at work, for he had affairs in several places at once, and
would concern himself as much in those of his neighbors as in
his own; putting officers of his own over all the great families,
and endeavoring to divide their authority as much as possible.
When he was at war he labored for a peace or a truce, and
when he had obtained it he was impatient for war again. He
troubled himself with many trifles in his government which he
had better have left alone: but it was his temper, and he could
not help it; besides, he had a prodigious memory, and he forgot
nothing, but knew everybody, as well in other countries as in
his own.

And in truth he seemed better fitted to rule a world than
to govern a single kingdom. I speak not of his minority, for

then I was not with him; but when he was eleven years he was, by the advice of some of the nobility and others of his kingdom, embroiled in a war with his father, Charles VII., which lasted not long, and was called the Praguerie. When he was arrived at man's estate he was married, much against his inclination, to the King of Scotland's daughter; and he regretted her existence during the whole course of her life. Afterwards, by reason of the broils and factions in his father's court, he retired into Dauphiny (which was his own), whither many persons of quality followed him, and indeed more than he could entertain. During his residence in Dauphiny he married the Duke of Savoy's daughter, and not long after he had great disputes with his father-in-law, and a terrible war was begun between them. His father, King Charles VII., seeing his son attended by so many good officers and raising men at his pleasure, resolved to go in person against him with a considerable body of forces, in order to disperse them. While he was upon his march he put out proclamations, requiring them all as his subjects, under great penalties, to repair to him; and many obeyed, to the great displeasure of the Dauphin, who finding his father incensed, though he was strong enough to resist, resolved to retire and leave that country to him; and accordingly he removed with but a slender retinue into Burgundy to Duke Philip's court, who received him honorably, furnished him nobly, and maintained him and his principal servants by way of pensions; and to the rest he gave presents as he saw occasion during the whole time of their residence there. However, the Dauphin entertained so many at his own expense that his money often failed, to his great disgust and mortification; for he was forced to borrow, or his people would have forsaken him; which is certainly a great affliction to a prince who was utterly unaccustomed to those straits. So that during his residence at the court of Burgundy he had his anxieties, for he was constrained to cajole the duke and his ministers, lest they should think he was too burdensome and had laid too long upon their hands; for he had been with them six years, and his father, King Charles, was constantly pressing and soliciting the Duke of Burgundy, by his ambassadors, either to deliver him up to him or to banish him out of his dominions. And this, you may believe, gave the Dauphin some uneasy thoughts and would not suffer him to be idle. In which season of his life, then, was it that he may be said to have enjoyed himself? I believe from his infancy and innocence to his death, his whole life was nothing but one continued scene of troubles and fatigues; and I am of opinion that if all the days of his life were computed in which his joys and pleasures outweighed his pain and trouble, they would be found so few that there would be twenty mournful ones to one pleasant.

AUGUSTE COMTE

(1798–1857)

THE name of Auguste Comte is associated with two such utterly conflicting systems, the «Positive Philosophy» and the «Positive Polity,» that the impression conveyed by his name is apt to be a rather confused one. Littré, Comte's most distinguished disciple, takes no notice of his later speculations, attributing them to a nervous malady complicated by a violent passion for Madame de Vaux; while Carid, on the other hand, considers Comte's return to metaphysical ideas the saving grace in his career. His conception of human knowledge, as defined in the Positive Philosophy, is in a measure the general property of the age. He developed the germs latent in the works of Turgot, Condorcet, and Kant, his immediate predecessors in the world of thought. Universality was the essential characteristic of his intellect, enabling him to penetrate profoundly into the domain of abstract science from mathematics to sociology.

AUGUSTE COMTE

Auguste Comte was born at Montpellier on the 19th of January, 1798, and entered college at the age of nine years. Before attaining his fourteenth year he had already felt the need of fundamental reconstruction in politics and philosophy. This maturity is all the more remarkable that philosophical minds mature slowly. In 1814 he entered the Polytechnic School. When Louis XVIII. suppressed it, Comte, not having graduated, found himself without a career. At the age of twenty he came in contact with Saint-Simon, whose devoted disciple he became. The attraction mutually felt by them was due to their common conviction of the need of a complete social reform, based on a widespread mental renovation.

There was now no place in the national system of education for free-thinkers, and Comte, cut off from all hope of employment in that direction, turned to private instruction for support. At the age of twenty-two, in a pamphlet entitled 'System of Positive Polity,' he announced his discovery of the laws of sociology. The work had no success, and Comte bent his energies during a meditation of twenty-four hours to the conception of a system which would force conviction on his readers. This he so far elaborated that in 1826 he published a plan of the work,—a plan requiring twelve years for its execution.

As his ideas were being appropriated by other people, he now began a dogmatic exposition of Positivism in a course of lectures delivered in his own home. These lectures opened under encouraging auspices, but after the third, Comte's mind gave way. The determining cause of this collapse lay in the excessive strain of his method of work, aided by a bad digestion and mental irritability growing out of the violent attacks made upon him by Saint-Simon's followers. In 1827 he was sufficiently recovered to take up intellectual work again, and the following year he resumed his lectures at the point of their interruption. After the accession of Louis Philippe, Comte was appointed assistant teacher of mathematics at the Polytechnic, and later, examiner of candidates, while he taught in a private school.

Unshakable firmness in philosophical matters and great disinterestedness were characteristic of this social critic, who cared nothing for the money his books might bring. His early sympathies were with the Revolution; he defended the socialist Marrast, though his position in a government school might have been compromised thereby. When in 1830 the Committee of the Polytechnic undertook to give free lectures to the people, he assumed the department of astronomy and lectured on that subject weekly for sixteen years.

The second and great period of Comte's life extends from his recovery in 1828 to the completion of his 'Positive Philosophy' in 1848; though what he calls his "second life" began after that. The intense satisfaction which he felt on the completion of that work became infatuation. He was no longer capable of judging his position sanely, and by his attacks antagonized the scientists.

In 1842 John Stuart Mill gave his adherence to Positivism. When Comte lost his tutorship in the Polytechnic, and shortly after, his position as examiner, Mill raised a small sum for him in England. Afterward Littré organized a subscription, and this formed henceforth Comte's sole resource. He now threw himself more completely than before into the problems of social life, elucidating them in his 'Positive Polity,' whose really scientific elements are almost crowded out of sight by a mass of extravagant theories.

The Positive Calendar, in which the names of great men replace the saints of the Catholic Church, was adopted by Comte in his correspondence. He consecrated an altar to his friend Madame de Vaux, entitled himself High Priest of Humanity, married people, called his letters his briefs, administered the sacraments of his cult in commemoration of birth, the choice of a profession, marriage, etc. He subordinated the intellect to the feelings, wished to suppress independent thought, to center a dictatorship in a triumvirate of bankers, and to concentrate the entire spiritual power of the world in the hands of a single pontiff. He acquired a hatred of scientific and purely literary pursuits, and considered that men reasoned more than was good for them. Comte's absolute faith in himself passes belief. He lauds the moral superiority of fetishism, pronounces the æsthetic civilization of the Greeks inferior to the military civilization of the Romans; is indifferent to proof, provided he attains theoretic coherency; and pushes his spiritual dictatorship to the length of selecting one hundred books to constitute the library of every Positivist, recommending the destruction of all other books, as also that of all plants and animals useless to man. He associates science with sentiment, endows the planets with feeling and will, calls the Earth "le grand fétiche," includes all concrete existence in our adoration along with "le grand fétiche," and names space "le grand milieu," endowing the latter with feeling as the representative of fatality in general. Many of these conceits can be attributed to his ardor for regulating things in accordance with his peculiar conception of unity. He died in Paris at the age of fifty-nine years, on September 5th, 1857.

Throughout life, Comte's method of work was unprecedented. He thought out his subject in its entirety before writing down a word, proceeding from general facts to secondary matters, and thence to details. The general and detailed sketch outlined, he considered the work done. When he began to write, he took up his ideas in their respective order. His memory was wonderful; he did all his reading in his early youth, and the provision then amassed sufficed to elaborate a work for which he had to bear in mind an unusual number of scientific and historical facts. In consequence of his abstention from contemporary literature he became less and less in touch with the age, and missed the corrective force of friction with other minds.

The word "religion," when applied to Comte's later speculations, must not be taken in its ordinary sense. His attitude towards theology was and continued to be purely negative. The obligation of duty was towards the human race as a continuous whole, to whose providence we owe all the benefits conferred by previous generations. If he has not succeeded in suppressing the Absolute, he has co-ordinated all the abstract sciences into one consistent system. Some of them he found ready to hand, and merely revised and rearranged in their philosophical relation, eliminating all non-positive elements. The first three volumes of the 'Positive Philosophy' are devoted to this task. The other three volumes, as well as the last two of the 'Positive Polity,' are dedicated to the solution of the problems of sociology unattempted until then. While they may not have solved these, they have a scientific value independent of any absolute results.

The distinctive characteristic of Positivism is that it subjects all phenomena to invariable laws. It does not pretend to know anything about a future life, but believes that our ideas and intelligence will go to swell the sum total of spirituality, just as our bodies go to fertilize matter.

The complaint has been made that there has been very little serious criticism of the 'Positive Polity,' which Comte regarded as the most original and important of his works. If the form in which he reproduces metaphysics and theology has any value, it is because he has come to see that they are based on perennial wants in man's nature. In the 'Positive Philosophy' he excludes the Absolute; in the 'Positive Polity' he substitutes Humanity in lieu thereof; but his moral intention, however misguided at times, is passionately sincere, and his conviction that his mission was to exalt humanity through all time, sustained him during the course of a long life devoted to a generous ideal, fraught with disappointment, saddened by want of recognition and by persecution and neglect.

THE EVOLUTION OF BELIEF

From the 'Positive Philosophy'

EACH of our leading conceptions passes through three different theoretical conditions: the Theological, or fictitious; the Metaphysical, or abstract; and the Scientific, or positive. Hence arise three philosophies, or general systems of conceptions on the aggregate of phenomena, each of which excludes the others. The first is the necessary point of departure of the human understanding, and the third is its fixed and definite state. The second is merely a state of transition.

In the theological state, the human mind, seeking the essential nature of beings, the first and final causes of all effects,— in short, absolute knowledge,— supposes all phenomena to be produced by the immediate action of supernatural beings.

In the metaphysical state, which is only a modification of the first, the mind supposes, instead of supernatural beings, abstract forces, veritable entities (that is, personified abstractions) inherent in all beings, and capable of producing all phenomena. What is called the explanation of phenomena is, in this stage, a mere reference of each to its proper entity.

In the final, the positive state, the mind has given over the vain search after absolute notions, the origin and destination of the universe, and the causes of phenomena, and applies itself to the study of their laws,— that is, their invariable relations of succession and resemblance. Reasoning and observation, duly combined, are the means of this knowledge. What is now understood when we speak of an explanation of facts, is simply the establishment of a connection between single phenomena and some general facts, the number of which continually diminishes with the progress of science.

The Theological system arrived at the highest perfection of which it is capable, when it substituted the providential action of a single Being for the varied operations of numerous divinities which had been before imagined. In the same way, in the last stage of the Metaphysical system, men substitute one great entity (Nature) as the cause of all phenomena, instead of the multitude of entities at first supposed. In the same way, again, the ultimate perfection of the Positive system would be (if such perfection could be hoped for) to represent all phenomena as particular aspects of a single general fact,— such as gravitation, for instance.

There is no science which, having attained the positive stage, does not bear marks of having passed through the others.

The progress of the individual mind is not only an illustration but an indirect evidence of that of the general mind. The point of departure of the individual and of the race being the same, the phases of the mind of a man correspond to the epochs of the mind of the race. Now each of us is aware, if he looks back upon his own history, that he was a theologian in his childhood, a metaphysician in his youth, and a natural philosopher in his manhood.

THE STUDY OF LAW SUBSTITUTED FOR THAT OF CAUSES

From the ‹Positive Philosophy›

THE first characteristic of the Positive Philosophy is, that it regards all phenomena as subjected to invariable natural Laws. Our business is — seeing how vain is any research into what are called Causes, whether first or final — to pursue an accurate discovery of these Laws with a view to reducing them to the smallest possible number. By speculating upon causes we could solve no difficulty about origin and purpose. Our real business is to analyze accurately the circumstances of phenomena, and to connect them by their natural relations of succession and resemblance. The best illustration of this is in the case of the doctrine of Gravitation. We say that the general phenomena of the universe are explained by it, because it connects under one head the whole immense variety of astronomical facts; exhibiting the constant tendency of atoms towards each other in direct proportion to their masses, and in inverse proportion to the square of their distances; whilst the general fact itself is but a mere extension of one which is familiar to us, and which we therefore say that we know — the weight of bodies on the surface of the earth. As to what weight and attraction are, we have nothing to do with that, for it is not a matter of knowledge at all. Theologians and metaphysicians may imagine and refine about such questions; but Positive Philosophy rejects them. When any attempt has been made to explain them, it has ended only in saying that attraction is universal weight and that weight is terrestrial attraction: that is, that the two orders of phenomena are identical; which is the point from which the question set out.

Before ascertaining the stage which the Positive Philosophy has reached, we must bear in mind that the different kinds of our knowledge have passed through the three stages of progress at different rates, and have not therefore reached their goal at the same time. Any kind of knowledge reaches the positive stage early in proportion to its generality, simplicity, and independence of other departments. Astronomical science, which is above all made up of facts that are general, simple, and independent of other sciences, arrived first; then terrestrial physics; then chemistry; and at length physiology.

It is difficult to assign any precise date to this revolution in science. It may be said, like everything else, to have been always going on, and especially since the labors of Aristotle and the school of Alexandria; and then from the introduction of natural science into the west of Europe by the Arabs. But if we must fix upon some marked period to serve as a rallying-point, it must be that about two centuries ago,—when the human mind was astir under the precepts of Bacon, the conceptions of Descartes, and the discoveries of Galileo. Then it was that the spirit of the Positive Philosophy rose up, in opposition to that of the superstitious and scholastic systems which had hitherto obscured the true character of all science. Since that date, the progress of the Positive Philosophy and the decline of the other two have been so marked that no rational mind now doubts that the revolution is destined to go on to its completion,— every branch of knowledge being, sooner or later, within the operation of Positive Philosophy.

SUBJECTION OF SELF–LOVE TO SOCIAL LOVE

From the 'Positive Polity'

IT is one of the first principles of Biology that organic life always preponderates over animal life. By this principle the sociologist explains the superior strength of the self-regarding instincts, since these are all connected more or less closely with the instinct of self-preservation. But although there is no evading the fact, Sociology shows that it is compatible with the existence of benevolent affections which Catholicism asserted were altogether alien to our nature, and entirely dependent on superhuman grace. The great problem, then, is to raise social feeling by artificial effort to the position which in the natural condition is held by selfish feeling. The solution is to be found in another biological principle; viz., that functions and organs are developed by constant exercise and atrophied by long inaction. Now the effect of the social state is, that while our sympathetic instincts are constantly stimulated, the selfish propensities are restricted; since if free play were given to them, human intercourse would very soon become impossible. Both of the tendencies naturally increase with the progress of humanity, and their increase is the best measure of the degree of perfection that we have attained. Their growth, however spontaneous, may be materially hastened by organized intervention both of individuals and of society; the object being to increase all favorable influences and to diminish unfavorable ones. This is the aim of the science of Morals. Like every other science, it is restricted within certain limits.

The first principle of Positive morality is the preponderance of social sympathy. Full and free expansion of the benevolent emotions is made the first condition of individual and social well-being, since these emotions are at once the sweetest to experience, and the only feelings which can find expression simultaneously in all. This doctrine is as deep and pure as it is simple and true. It is essentially characteristic of a philosophy which by virtue of its attribute of reality subordinates all scientific conceptions to the social point of view, as the sole point from which they can be co-ordinated into a whole.

THE CULTUS OF HUMANITY

From the ‹Positive Polity›

THE cultus of Positivism is not addressed to an absolute, isolated, incomprehensible Being whose existence cannot be demonstrated or compared with reality. No mystery surrounds this Supreme Being. It is composed of the continuous succession of human generations.

Whereas the old God could not receive our homage without degrading himself by a puerile vanity, the new God will only accept praise which is deserved and which will improve him as much as ourselves. This reciprocity of affection and influence can belong only to the final cultus, modifiable and perfectible, addressed to a relative being composed of its own adorers, and better subjected than another to law which permits of foreseeing its wishes and tendencies.

The superiority of demonstrated over revealed religion is shown by the substitution of the love of Humanity for the love of God. To love Humanity constitutes all healthy morality, when we understand the character of such a love and the conditions exacted by its habitual ascendency.

The universal reign of Humanity is to replace the provisory reign of God. Demonstrated religion has its dogmas, its regimen, and its cultus corresponding respectively to three fundamental attributes; viz., thoughts, acts, and sentiments.

The Religion of Humanity transforms the coarse idea of objective immortality into the real objective immortality common to the whole race. The first hypothesis is anti-social; the latter constitutes real sociability.

THE DOMINATION OF THE DEAD

From the 'Positive Polity'

ALWAYS and everywhere, the living are more and more dominated by the dead. This irresistible domination represents the unmodifiable element in all social existence, and regulates the total human movement.

When the "Grand Être" shall occupy the whole planet, each city will live more and more under the weight of preceding generations, not only of its defunct citizens but of the total sum of terrestrial ancestors.

This ascendency was long ignored, and a dominating principle was sought elsewhere, by transporting the human type to external beings, first real, then fictitious. So long as the search for Causes predominated over the study of Law, it was impossible to recognize the true Providence of the race, owing to thus diverting the attention to chimerical influences. At the same time continuous conflicts and discordance made the conception of a collective being impossible. When these fictitious struggles exhausted themselves, Humanity, prepared during their domination, became aroused, and founded on peace and truth the advent of the new religion.

THE WORSHIP OF WOMAN

From the 'Positive Polity'

WOMAN's function in society is determined by the constitution of her nature. As the spontaneous organ of feeling, on which the unity of human nature entirely depends, she constitutes the purest and most natural element of the moderating power; which while avowing its own subordination to the material forces of society, purposes to direct them to higher uses.

First as mother, afterwards as wife, it is her office to conduct the moral education of Humanity.

Woman's mission is a striking illustration of the truth that happiness consists in doing the work for which we are naturally fitted. Their mission is always the same; it is summed up in one word,— Love. It is the only work in which there can never be too many workers; it grows by co-operation; it has nothing to fear from competition. Women are charged with the education of sympathy, the source of real human unity; and their highest happiness is reached when they have the full consciousness of their vocation and are free to follow it. It is the admirable feature of their social mission, that it invites them to cultivate qualities which are natural to them, to call into exercise emotions which all allow to be the most pleasurable. All that is required of them in a better organization of society is a better adaptation of their circumstances to their vocation, and improvements in their internal condition. They must be relieved from outdoor labor, and other means must be taken to secure due weight to their moral influence. Both objects are contemplated in the material, intellectual, and moral ameliorations which Positivism is destined to effect in the life of women. But besides the pleasure inherent in their vocation, Positivism offers a recompense for their services which Catholic Feudalism foreshadowed but could not realize. As men become more and more grateful for the blessing of the moral influence of women, they will give expression to this feeling in a systematic form. In a word, the new doctrine will institute the Worship of Woman, publicly and privately, in a far more perfect way than has ever been possible. It is the first permanent step towards the worship of Humanity; which is the central principle of Positivism viewed either as a philosophy or as a polity.

WILLIAM CONGREVE

(1670–1729)

ONGREVE was the most brilliant of all the English dramatists of the later Stuart period. Born at Bardsley, near Leeds, in 1670, he passed his childhood and youth in Ireland, and was sent to the University of Dublin, where he was highly educated; and on finishing his classical studies he went to London to study law and was entered at the Middle Temple. He had two ambitions, not altogether reconcilable — to shine in literature and to shine in society. His good birth, polished manners, and witty conversation procured him entrance to the best company; but the desire for literary renown had the mastery at the start. His first work was 'Incognita,' a novel of no particular value, published under the name of "Cleophil." In 1693 he wrote 'The Old Bachelor,' a comedy; it was brought out with a phenomenal cast. Under the supervision of Dryden, who generously admired the author, it achieved triumph; and Montagu, then Lord of the Treasury, gave him a desirable place (commissioner for licensing hackney-coaches) and the reversion of another. The plot is not interesting, but the play is celebrated for its witty and eloquent dialogue,

WILLIAM CONGREVE

which even Sheridan did not surpass; it has a lightness which nothing that preceded it had equaled. The characters are not very original, yet it has variety and diverting action.

Returning now to his rival ambition, that of achieving social success, Congreve pretended that he had merely "scribbled a few scenes for his own amusement," and had yielded unwillingly to his friends' desire to try his fortune on the stage. But in 1694 he brought out his second play, 'The Double Dealer.' It was not a favorite, though in it all the powers which made a success of 'The Old Bachelor' were present, mellowed and improved by time. The dialogue is light and natural; but the grim and offensive characters of Maskwell and Lady Touchwood disgusted even an audience of the seventeenth century. Dryden, however, wrote a most ingenious piece of commendatory verse for the play; gradually the public came to his way of thinking; and when, the next year, 'Love for Love' appeared, it was said that "scarcely any comedy within the memory of the oldest man had been equally successful." This play was the triumph of his art; and it won Congreve a share in the theatre in which it was played, —the new theatre which Betterton and others had opened near Lincoln's Inn. Jeremy, the gentleman's gentleman, is delightfully witty, —he has "the seeds of rhetoric and logic in his head,"—and Valentine's mock madness is amusing; but as Sir Sampson remarks of him, "Body o' me, he talks sensibly in his madness! has he no intervals?" Jeremy replies, "Very short, sir."

In about two years Congreve produced 'The Mourning Bride,' a tragedy which was over-lauded, but stands high among the dramas of the century. It ranks with Otway's 'Venice Preserved' and 'The Fair Penitent.' A noble passage describing the temple, in Act ii., Scene 3, was extolled by Johnson. The play was successful, and is more celebrated than some far better plays. But Congreve was unequal to a really great flight of passion; tragedy was out of his range; though he was now hailed, at the age of twenty-seven, as the first tragic as well as the first comic dramatist of his time.

Now, however, a reformer arose who was destined to make his mark on the English drama. The depravation of the national taste which had made the success of Congreve, Wycherley, Farquhar, and others, was the result of a reaction against the Puritan strictness under the Commonwealth. Profligacy was the badge of a Cavalier, and Congreve's heroes exactly reproduced the superficial fine gentleman of a time when to be a man of good breeding it was necessary to make love to one's neighbor's wife, even without preference or passion. In the plays of this period nearly all the husbands are prim, precise, and uncomfortable, while the lovers are without exception delightful fellows. The Puritan writers regarded an affair of gallantry as a criminal offense; the poet of this period made it an elegant distinction.

Jeremy Collier came to change all this. He was a clergyman and a high-churchman, fanatical in the cause of decency. In 1698 he published his 'Short View of the Profaneness and Immorality of the English Stage,' and threw the whole literary world into convulsions. He attacked Congreve, among others, somewhat injudiciously, not only for his sins against decency but for some unreal transgressions; and he had at his command all the weapons of ridicule and indignation. The country sided with the eloquent preacher, but waited for some champion— Dryden presumably—to pick up the gauntlet. Dryden however declined, acknowledging later that Collier was in the right. Congreve stepped in "where angels feared to tread," and succeeded in putting himself entirely in the wrong. His reply was dull,

and he was unwise enough to show anger. Collier's cause remained
in the ascendant, and with the younger race of poets who now came
forward a reform began.

In 1700 Congreve wrote one more play, 'The Way of the World,'
the most brilliant and thoughtful of his works. Lady Wishfort's
character is perhaps too repulsive for comedy, though the reader,
carried on by the ease and wit of the dialogue, will accept her.
Mirabell's brilliant chase and winning of Millamant; the diverting
character of Witwould, an incarnation of feeble repartee; and the
love scene in Act v., Scene 5, in which both lady and gentleman are
anxious and willing to be free and tolerant, are original and amusing
studies. But whether it was the influence of his defeat by Collier
or not, this play, the best comedy written after the civil war, failed
on the stage.

Congreve produced nothing more of consequence, though he lived
for twenty-eight years in the most brilliant society that London
afforded; he suffered from gout and from failing eyesight, and by
way of consolation contracted a curious friendship with the Duchess
of Marlborough, widow of the great Marlborough, with whom he
passed a part of every day. In the summer of 1728 he met with an
accident while driving, and died from the effects of it in January,
1729. The Duchess buried him with pomp; he lay in state in the
Jerusalem Chamber, and was interred in Westminster Abbey.

Congreve was held in the highest esteem by his fellow writers,
and Pope dedicated to him his translation of the Iliad. Yet he
would not hear his literary works praised, and always declared that
they were trifles. When Voltaire during his visit to England
desired to see him, Congreve asked that he would "consider him
merely as a gentleman." "If you were merely a gentleman," said
Voltaire, "I should not care to see you."

Congreve was not a great poet, but he had more wit than any
English writer of the last two centuries except Sheridan; he had at
the same time great skill in character-drawing and in constructing
plots. The profligacy of his plays was the natural consequence of a
period of Puritanical austerity. While not free from the blame of
intentional indecency, he at least lacks the brutality and coarseness
of Wycherley, Vanbrugh, and Farquhar.

MRS. FORESIGHT AND MRS. FRAIL COME TO AN UNDER-STANDING

From 'Love for Love'

Scene:—A Room in the Foresight House. Enter Mrs. Foresight *and* Mrs. Frail

M<small>RS.</small> F<small>RAIL</small>—What have you to do to watch me? 'Slife, I'll do what I please.

Mrs. Foresight—You will?

Mrs. Frail—Yes, marry, will I. A great piece of business, to go to Covent Garden Square in a hackney-coach and take a turn with one's friend!

Mrs. Foresight—Nay, two or three turns, I'll take my oath.

Mrs. Frail—Well, what if I took twenty? I warrant if you had been there, it had been only innocent recreation. Lord, where's the comfort of this life, if we can't have the happiness of conversing where we like?

Mrs. Foresight—But can't you converse at home? I own it, I think there's no happiness like conversing with an agreeable man; I don't quarrel at that, nor I don't think but your conversation was very innocent; but the place is public, and to be seen with a man in a hackney-coach is scandalous; what if anybody else should have seen you alight, as I did? How can anybody be happy, while they're in perpetual fear of being seen and censured? Besides, it would not only reflect upon you, sister, but me.

Mrs. Frail—Pooh, here's a clutter! Why should it reflect upon you? I don't doubt but you have thought yourself happy in a hackney-coach before now. If I had gone to Knightsbridge, or to Chelsea, or to Spring Garden, or Barn Elms, with a man alone, something might have been said.

Mrs. Foresight—Why, was I ever in any of those places? what do you mean, sister?

Mrs. Frail—"Was I?" What do you mean?

Mrs. Foresight—You have been at a worse place.

Mrs. Frail—I at a worse place, and with a man!

Mrs. Foresight—I suppose you would not go alone to the World's-End.

Mrs. Frail—The world's end! what, do you mean to banter me?

Mrs. Foresight — Poor innocent! you don't know that there's a place called the World's-End? I'll swear you can keep your countenance purely; you'd make an admirable player.

Mrs. Frail — I'll swear you have a great deal of confidence, and in my mind too much for the stage.

Mrs. Foresight — Very well; that will appear who has most. You never were at the World's-End?

Mrs. Frail — No.

Mrs. Foresight — You deny it positively to my face?

Mrs. Frail — Your face! what's your face?

Mrs. Foresight — No matter for that; it's as good a face as yours.

Mrs. Frail — Not by a dozen years' wearing. But I do deny it positively to your face, then.

Mrs. Foresight — I'll allow you now to find fault with my face, for I'll swear your impudence has put me out of countenance; but look you here now, — where did you lose this gold bodkin? O sister, sister!

Mrs. Frail — My bodkin?

Mrs. Foresight — Nay, 'tis yours; look at it.

Mrs. Frail — Well, if you go to that, where did you find this bodkin? O sister, sister! sister every way.

Mrs. Foresight [*aside*] — Oh, devil on't, that I could not discover her without betraying myself!

Mrs. Frail — I have heard gentlemen say, sister, that one should take great care, when one makes a thrust in fencing, not to lay open one's self.

Mrs. Foresight — It's very true, sister; well, since all's out, and as you say, since we are both wounded, let us do what is often done in duels, — take care of one another, and grow better friends than before.

Mrs. Frail — With all my heart: ours are but slight flesh wounds, and if we keep 'em from air, not at all dangerous: well, give me your hand in token of sisterly secrecy and affection.

Mrs. Foresight — Here 'tis, with all my heart.

Mrs. Frail — Well, as an earnest of friendship and confidence, I'll acquaint you with a design that I have. To tell truth, and speak openly one to another, I'm afraid the world have observed us more than we have observed one another. You have a rich husband and are provided for; I am at a loss, and have no great stock either of fortune or reputation; and therefore must look sharply about me. Sir Sampson has a son that is expected to-night, and by the account I have heard of his education, can be no conjuror; the estate, you know, is to be made over to him: — now if I could wheedle him, sister, ha? you understand me?

Mrs. Foresight — I do, and will help you to the utmost of my power. And I can tell you one thing that falls out luckily enough; my awkward daughter-in-law, who you know is designed to be his wife, is grown fond of Mr. Tattle; now if we can improve that, and make her have an aversion for the booby, it may go a great way towards his liking you. Here they come together; and let us contrive some way or other to leave 'em together.

ANGELICA'S PROPOSAL

From 'Love for Love'

Scene: — A Room in the Foresight House. Enter Angelica *and* Jenny

Angelica — Where is Sir Sampson? did you not tell me he would be here before me?

Jenny — He's at the great glass in the dining-room, madam, setting his cravat and wig.

Angelica — How! I'm glad on't. If he has a mind I should like him, it's a sign he likes me; and that's more than half my design.

Jenny — I hear him, madam.

Angelica — Leave me; and d'ye hear, if Valentine should come or send, I am not to be spoken with.

Enter Sir Sampson

Sir Sampson — I have not been honored with the commands of a fair lady a great while: — odd, madam, you have revived me! — not since I was five-and-thirty.

Angelica — Why, you have no great reason to complain, Sir Sampson; that is not long ago.

Sir Sampson — Zooks, but it is, madam; a very great while, to a man that admires a fine woman as much as I do.

Angelica — You're an absolute courtier, Sir Sampson.

Sir Sampson — Not at all, madam; odsbud, you wrong me; I am not so old, neither, to be a bare courtier; only a man of words: odd, I have warm blood about me yet, and can serve a lady any way. Come, come, let me tell you, you women think a man old too soon, faith and troth, you do! Come, don't despise fifty; odd, fifty, in a hale constitution, is no such contemptible age.

Angelica—Fifty a contemptible age! not at all; a very fashionable age, I think. I assure you, I know very considerable beaux that set a good face upon fifty. Fifty! I have seen fifty in a side-box, by candle-light, outblossom five-and-twenty.

Sir Sampson—Outsides, outsides; a pize take 'em, mere outsides! hang your side-box beaux! No, I'm none of those, none of your forced trees, that pretend to blossom in the fall, and bud when they should bring forth fruit; I am of a long-lived race; . . . none of my ancestors married till fifty; . . . I am of your patriarchs, I, a branch of one of your antediluvian families, fellows that the flood could not wash away. Well, madam, what are your commands? has any young rogue affronted you, and shall I cut his throat? or—

Angelica—No, Sir Sampson, I have no quarrel upon my hands. I have more occasion for your conduct than your courage at this time. To tell you the truth, I'm weary of living single, and want a husband.

Sir Sampson—Odsbud, and 'tis pity you should!—[*Aside.*] Odd, would she would like me, then I should hamper my young rogues: odd, would she would; faith and troth, she's devilish handsome! [*Aloud.*] Madam, you deserve a good husband, and 'twere pity you should be thrown away upon any of these young idle rogues about the town. Odd, there's ne'er a young fellow worth hanging! that is, a very young fellow. Pize on 'em! they never think beforehand of anything; and if they commit matrimony, 'tis as they commit murder—out of a frolic, and are ready to hang themselves, or to be hanged by the law, the next morning: odso, have a care, madam.

Angelica—Therefore I ask your advice, Sir Sampson. I have fortune enough to make any man easy that I can like, if there were such a thing as a young agreeable man with a reasonable stock of good-nature and sense; . . . for I would neither have an absolute wit nor a fool.

Sir Sampson—Odd, you are hard to please, madam; to find a young fellow that is neither a wit in his own eye nor a fool in the eye of the world, is a very hard task. But faith and troth, you speak very discreetly; for I hate both a wit and a fool.

Angelica — She that marries a fool, Sir Sampson, forfeits the reputation of her honesty or understanding: and she that marries a very witty man is a slave to the severity and insolent conduct of her husband. I should like a man of wit for a lover, because I would have such a one in my power; but I would no more be his wife than his enemy. For his malice is not a more terrible consequence of his aversion than his jealousy is of his love.

Sir Sampson — None of old Foresight's Sibyls ever uttered such a truth. Odsbud, you have won my heart! I hate a wit; I had a son that was spoiled among 'em; a good hopeful lad, till he learned to be a wit; and might have risen in the State. But a pox on't! his wit run him out of his money, and now his poverty has run him out of his wits.

Angelica — Sir Sampson, as your friend, I must tell you, you are very much abused in that matter; he's no more mad than you are.

Sir Samson — How, madam? would I could prove it!

Angelica — I can tell you how that may be done. But it is a thing that would make me appear to be too much concerned in your affairs.

Sir Sampson [*aside*] — Odsbud, I believes she likes me! [*Aloud.*] Ah, madam, all my affairs are scarce worthy to be laid at your feet: and I wish, madam, they were in a better posture, that I might make a more becoming offer to a lady of your incomparable beauty and merit. — If I had Peru in one hand, and Mexico in t'other, and the Eastern Empire under my feet, it would make me only a more glorious victim to be offered at the shrine of your beauty.

Angelica — Bless me, Sir Sampson, what's the matter?

Sir Sampson — Odd, madam, I love you! and if you would take my advice in a husband —

Angelica — Hold, hold, Sir Sampson! I asked your advice for a husband, and you are giving me your consent. I was indeed thinking to propose something like it in jest, to satisfy you about Valentine: for if a match were seemingly carried on between you and me, it would oblige him to throw off his disguise of madness, in apprehension of losing me; for you know he has long pretended a passion for me.

Sir Sampson — Gadzooks, a most ingenious contrivance! if we were to go through with it. But why must the match only be seemingly carried on? Odd, let it be a real contract.

Angelica — Oh fy, Sir Sampson! what would the world say?

Sir Sampson — Say! they would say you were a wise woman and I a happy man. Odd, madam, I'll love you as long as I live, and leave you a good jointure when I die.

Angelica — Ay; but that is not in your power, Sir Sampson; for when Valentine confesses himself in his senses, he must make over his inheritance to his younger brother.

Sir Sampson — Odd, you're cunning, a wary baggage! faith and troth, I like you the better. But I warrant you, I have a proviso in the obligation in favor of myself. Body o' me, I have a trick to turn the settlement! . . .

Angelica — Will you? Well, do you find the estate, and leave the other to me.

Sir Sampson — O rogue! but I'll trust you. And will you consent? is it a match, then?

Angelica — Let me consult my lawyer concerning this obligation; and if I find what you propose practicable, I'll give you my answer.

Sir Sampson — With all my heart: come in with me and I'll lend you the bond. You shall consult your lawyer, and I'll consult a parson. Odzooks, I'm a young man: odzooks, I'm a young man, and I'll make it appear. Odd, you're devilish handsome: faith and troth, you're very handsome; and I am very young, and very lusty! Odsbud, hussy, you know how to choose, and so do I; odd, I think we are very well met. Give me your hand,— odd, let me kiss it; 'tis as warm and as soft — as what? — Odd, as t'other hand; give me t'other hand, and I'll mumble 'em and kiss 'em till they melt in my mouth.

Angelica — Hold, Sir Sampson: you're profuse of your vigor before your time: you'll spend your estate before you come to it.

Sir Sampson — No, no, only give you a rent-roll of my possessions,— ha! baggage! . . . Odd, Sampson's a very good name for an able fellow: your Sampsons were strong dogs from the beginning.

Angelica — Have a care, and don't overact your part. If you remember, Sampson, the strongest of the name, pulled an old house over his head at last!

ALMERIA IN THE MAUSOLEUM

From 'The Mourning Bride'

Enter Almeria *and* Leonora

ALMERIA —   It was a fancied noise, for all is hushed.
   Leonora — It bore the accent of a human voice.
   Almeria — It was thy fear, or else some transient wind
     Whistling through hollows of this vaulted aisle.
     We'll listen.
Leonora — Hark!
Almeria — No, all is hushed and still as death. — 'Tis dreadful!
     How reverend is the face of this tall pile,
     Whose ancient pillars rear their marble heads,
     To bear aloft its arched and ponderous roof,
     By its own weight made steadfast and immovable,
     Looking tranquillity! It strikes an awe
     And terror on my aching sight; the tombs
     And monumental caves of death look cold,
     And shoot a chillness to my trembling heart.
     Give me thy hand, and let me hear thy voice;
     Nay, quickly speak to me, and let me hear
     Thy voice — my own affrights me with its echoes.
Leonora — Let us return; the horror of this place,
     And silence, will increase your melancholy.
Almeria — It may my fears, but cannot add to that.
     No, I will on: show me Anselmo's tomb;
     Lead me o'er bones and skulls and moldering earth
     Of human bodies; for I'll mix with them:
     Or wind me in the shroud of some pale corse
     Yet green in earth, rather than be the bride
     Of Garcia's more detested bed: that thought
     Exerts my spirits; and my present fears
     Are lost in dread of greater ill. Then show me,
     Lead me, for I am bolder grown; lead on
     Where I may kneel, and pay my vows again
     To him, to Heaven, and my Alphonso's soul.
Leonora — I go; but Heaven can tell with what regret.

*The Scene opening discovers a place of tombs; one monument fronting the
view greater than the rest*

Enter Heli

Heli —   I wander through this maze of monuments,
     Yet cannot find him. — Hark! sure 'tis the voice

Of one complaining.— There it sounds: I'll follow it.

[Exit.

Leonora — Behold the sacred vault, within whose womb
The poor remains of good Anselmo rest,
Yet fresh and unconsumed by time or worms!
What do I see? O Heaven! either my eyes
Are false, or still the marble door remains
Unclosed: the iron gates that lead to death
Beneath, are still wide-stretched upon their hinge,
And staring on us with unfolded leaves.

Almeria — Sure, 'tis the friendly yawn of death for me;
And that dumb mouth, significant in show,
Invites me to the bed where I alone
Shall rest; shows me the grave, where nature, weary
And long oppressed with woes and bending cares,
May lay the burden down, and sink in slumbers
Of peace eternal.   Death, grim death, will fold
Me in his leaden arms, and press me close
To his cold clayey breast: my father then
Will cease his tyranny; and Garcia too
Will fly my pale deformity with loathing.
My soul, enlarged from its vile bonds, will mount,
Aud range the starry orbs, and milky ways,
Of that refulgent world, where I shall swim
In liquid light, and float on seas of bliss
To my Alphonso's soul.   O joy too great!
O ecstasy of thought!   Help me, Anselmo:
Help me, Alphonso; take me, reach thy hand;
To thee, to thee I call, to thee, Alphonso:
O Alphonso!

Osmyn *ascends from the tomb*

Osmyn — Who calls that wretched thing that was Alphonso?
Almeria — Angels, and all the host of heaven, support me!
Osmyn — Whence is that voice, whose shrillness, from the grave,
And growing to his father's shroud, roots up Alphonso?
Almeria — Mercy! Providence! O speak!
Speak to it quickly, quickly! speak to me,
Comfort me, help me, hold me, hide me, hide me,
Leonora, in thy bosom, from the light,
And from my eyes!

Osmyn —   Amazement and illusion!
Rivet and nail me where I stand, ye powers;

[Coming forward.

That motionless I may be still deceived.
Let me not stir, nor breathe, lest I dissolve
That tender lovely form of painted air,
So like Almeria.   Ha! it sinks, it falls;
I'll catch it ere it goes, and grasp her shade.
'Tis life! 'tis warm! 'tis she! 'tis she herself!
Nor dead nor shade, but breathing and alive!
It is Almeria, 'tis, it is my wife!

HENRI CONSCIENCE

(1812–1883)

BY WILLIAM SHARP

ENRI CONSCIENCE (not Hendrik Conscience, as commonly written, for though the great romancist was a Fleming by maternal descent and by native sympathy, he was the son of a naturalized Frenchman and was christened Henri), who is popularly known as the Walter Scott of Flanders, is with the exception of Georges Eckhoud the one Belgian author who has succeeded in gaining the ear of Europe. There is not one of the leading languages, and few of the less important, into which one or more of his books have not been translated: indeed, his works are to be found complete or all but complete in French, German, Norwegian, and English. One story for example, 'Rikke-Tikke-Tak,' has not only been rendered into every European tongue, but has been paraphrased to such an extent that variants of it occur, in each instance as an indigenous folk-tale, in every land, from Great Britain in the west to India and even to China in the east.

HENRI CONSCIENCE

To-day to our changed tastes the tales of Conscience may seem somewhat insipid, —that is, in translation; for the style of the original is characterized by singular verve and charm,—but there must be a radical appeal in writings which have reached the home-circle readers of Belgium and Holland, of Germany and of Scandinavia, of France and England and America. Born in Antwerp in 1812, of a French father and a Flemish mother, the childhood of the novelist-to-be was passed during the French domination in the Netherlands. While a youth, he watched with eager intelligence the growing pressure of the Dutch yoke upon Flanders, the restless vicissitudes and memorable events which culminated in the revolution of 1830 and the separation of Belgium from the neighboring country. This uprising of the Flemish people was followed by a re-birth of Flemish literature, of which the informing spirit was Henri Conscience. Thitherto, the young writers of his day modeled themselves upon the then all-potent romantic school of literature in France; moreover, without exception they wrote in French, in accordance with the all-but universal prejudice that Flemish was merely a patois used only by the vulgar people. Although Conscience's first literary efforts—martial songs and poems—were written in French, he exclaimed in 1830, when he was only a youth of eighteen, and with prophetic insight:—"I confess I find in the real Flemish something indescribably romantic, mysterious, profound, energetic, even savage. If ever I gain the power to write, I shall throw myself head over ears into Flemish literature."

The little Henri was a cripple till his seventh year, and the child's mother was wont to amuse him by the narration of wonderful tales of fairies and angels. Later he passed his time in reading forgotten books that were stowed away in the garret, or in exercising his creative faculties in inventing local stories for his admiring companions. At his mother's death his father removed to a lonely spot a mile from the old Antwerp wall, and here was first aroused in the boy the warm love of nature that is so strongly marked in all his writings. After acting as assistant master for two years at Delin College, he in 1830 joined the Belgian patriots as a volunteer. During the six years of his service in the country he gained an insight not only into the beauties of nature, but into the lives and feelings of the Flemish peasantry, into their manners and customs; he grew intimate with the gentle nobility of their character, which underlies the stern melancholy of their outward disposition. Conscience's first important work was written in 1836—after the cessation of the war—to gain him admission to the Olijftak (Olive Branch), a literary club of young enthusiasts. 'Het Wonder Jaar' (1566) was written in Flemish, and was published in Ghent in 1837. This historical romance, full of color and rich in dramatic incident, gave the death-blow to the existing didactic prose and poetry, and was the foundation-stone on which arose the new Flemish school of literature. Pierre Conscience, however, saw his son's partisanship in the Flemish literary movement with such displeasure that eventually the young man had to leave home altogether. His friend Wappers, the eminent painter, procured him a small appointment in the department of political archives, which however he lost, owing to a violent political speech. A funeral oration at the tomb of a director of the Antwerp Academy was the indirect means of his gaining a post in the offices of the Academy, where he remained till 1855. In 1857 he was appointed to the local administration of Courtrai; and in 1868 the Belgian government conferred on him the title of Conservateur des Musées Royaux de Peinture et de Sculpture, a guardianship held by him until his death in 1883.

Conscience's literary career divides itself into two periods, and shows him as historical romancist and as a writer of novels and short tales. The success of 'Het Wonder Jaar' inspired him to a second venture, and in 1858 he published his 'De Leeuw van Vlaenderen' (The Lion of Flanders), an undertaking which despite its subsequent fame brought the author six francs for net profit! He writes of himself that "the enthusiasm of my youth and the labors of my manhood were rooted in my love for my country." To raise Flanders was to him a holy aim. France threatened Flemish freedom: therefore he wrote his two finest historical novels, those which depict the uprising of the Flemings against French despotism, 'The Lion of Flanders' and 'The Peasants' War.'

From the literary point of view the second book is superior to its predecessor; the plot is not so closely linked to history, and though there is less regard to historical accuracy, the story gains more in dramatic unity. As a historical novelist Conscience does not belong to the school of realism and archæology: in a word, he pertains to the school of Walter Scott, not to that of Gustave Flaubert. He writes of himself, "In Holland my works have met with the same favor from Catholics and Lutherans alike;" yet his Catholic predilections have in many instances impaired his historical accuracy, and even deprived his brilliant, vivid 'History of Belgium' of scientific value.

To his second period belong his stories, in which he directs his powers to the task of social regeneration, and of painting the life of his own day as he saw it around him. In such novels as 'De Gierigaerd' (The Miser), 'De Arme Edelman' (The Poor Nobleman), he resolved "to apply the glowing steel to the cankered wounds of which society is dying." He describes the qualities which equipped him for his task when he says, "I am one whom God endowed at least with moral energy and with a vast instinct of affection." It is however in the tales of Flemish peasant life,—'Rikke-Tikke-Tak,' 'How Men Become Painters,' 'What a Mother Can Suffer,' 'The Happiness of Being Rich,' etc.,—that the author's exquisite style shows itself at its finest. There is nothing in the conception of the stories to show great inventive talent; but the execution, the way in which these simple things are recounted, is of the highest artistic excellence. In the matter of style his dual nationality proved an advantage; for to the homely vigor of the Teuton he added the gracefulness, the sobriety, the sense of measure and proportion, which are peculiar to the best French prose. Georges Eckhoud, his celebrated fellow-countryman, says of him:—"In simplicity of form, coupled with the intensity of the idea expressed, lies the eloquence of this Flemish author's tales. Thus is explained the popularity of that delicate casket to the furthest ends of the earth, to the simplest as well as to the most cultivated circles. . . . The work of Conscience is like a sociable country-house, a place where men can regain the simplicity which they had lost through cheating and deception.»

No better summing-up of the writings of Henri Conscience can be given than that penned by himself in his biographical notes:—

«I write my books to be read by the people. I have always made the intellectual development and education of the ignorant my aim. . . . I have sketched the Flemish peasant as he appeared to me. I drew him calm, peaceable, religious, patriotic, attached to his traditions and opposed somewhat vehemently to all innovations; in short, as he appeared to me at that period of my life in 1830, when, hungry and sick, I enjoyed hospitality and the tenderest care amongst them. I have never inspired my heroes with the poetic glamour for which I have been reproached; it is they who inspired me. And then a man may dwell by preference on the defective side and the coarseness of the laborer, may sketch him as the slave of drunkenness and animal passion. I shall not deny the picturesqueness of this work. But between that and the admission of my delusion there is a wide margin. My neighbor's heroes are not necessarily mine, nor do I see them in the same light. People are constantly discussing whether he who paints things in their darkest colors, or he who sees all in a materialistic light, or he who presents everything in its happiest form,—whether he who takes a subjective or an objective point of view,—is right. All I know is,—and it is my settled conviction,—that a conscientious writer is never wrong; and I believe myself to be conscientious.»

This is a frank, manly, and honest pronouncement, and will surely be admitted as such even by those who may not care either for the matter or manner, the method or the literary principles, of Henri Conscience. Perhaps the best commentary is, that after a European success ranking only after that of Scott, Balzac, Dumas, Hugo, and Hans Andersen, Henri Conscience is still (thirteen years after his death at an advanced age) a name of European repute; is still, in his own country, held in highest honor and affection.

William Sharpe

THE HORSE-SHOE

From 'Rikke-Tikke-Tak'

IN THE village of Westmal, some two or three miles from Antwerp, on the road toward Turnhout, stood a little smithy, in which four men — the master and his three journeymen — were busy at various work in the way of their trade; and at the same time were conversing — as much, that is, as the noise of hammers and files would let them — of Napoleon and his mighty deeds of war. One of the journeymen, who had lost two fingers of his left hand, was just beginning a story of the Italian wars, when two horsemen pulled up before the door, and one of them called out, "Hola, my men! my horse wants shoeing."

The journeymen looked curiously at the strangers, who by this time had dismounted. They were evidently both military men. One of them had a great scar right across his face and wore a red riband in his button-hole: the other, though dressed like a gentleman, seemed in some sort his subordinate; he held the horse by the bridle and asked, "Which shoe, colonel?"

"The near forefoot, lieutenant," was the reply.

One of the journeymen took the horse and led it into the shed; and meanwhile the colonel entered the smithy, looked about him, and took up first one, then another, of the tools, as if looking out for an old acquaintance. At last he seemed to have found what he wanted; in one hand he held a heavy pair of tongs, in the other a hammer, both of which he surveyed with so peculiar a smile that the journeymen stood round, gaping and staring in no little amaze.

Meanwhile the iron was in the fire, the bellows panted away, and a garland of sparks spurted from the glowing coals. The journeymen stood by the anvil, hammers in hand, till the master took the iron from the fire; then began the work of forging.

The colonel evidently took a lively interest in what was going on; his features lighted up, as they might have done at the finest music. But when the shoe was taken from the anvil, as ready for putting on, he eyed it a moment not a little disdainfully, took the tongs which held it from the master-smith's hand, and put it back into the fire.

"That will never do," said he; "the shoe's too clumsy by half, master. Now, my lads! look alive! blow away!"

And while one of the journeymen, with an air of great respect, obeyed his directions, he threw off his coat and bared his sinewy arms. Soon the iron was at a white heat: he turned it twice or thrice in the fire with all the air of an experienced hand, laid it on the anvil, and then called to the journeymen in a cheerful tone:—

"Now, my men! look out! I'll give the time, and we'll turn out a shoe fit for the Emperor's nags. So now, attention:—

> 'Rikketikketak,
> Rikketikketoo;
> The iron's warm;
> Up with your arm,
> Now strike,—one, two,
> Rikketikketoo.
>
> 'Rikketikketak,
> Rikketikketoo,
> Strike while it is hot,
> And tarry not.
> Again,—one two,
> Rikketikketoo.'

There, look at the shoe now!"

The journeymen eyed the light neat piece of work agape, and as it were, struck dumb. The master meanwhile seemed to be turning some thought in his head, which he every now and then shook, as though quite unable to come to a satisfactory conclusion. He drew near the stranger, who by this time had resumed his coat; but however closely he scanned him, he seemed unable to recognize him.

The horse was soon shod, and now stood before the smithy ready for its master to mount, who took leave of the party with a friendly shake of the hand to each, laying also a couple of gold pieces on the anvil.

"One for the master, one for the men. Drink my health together and good-by to you."

With these words he threw himself into the saddle and rode off with his companion.

"Well," said the master, "I never in my life knew but one man who could knock off a shoe like that,—so light and neat, and so handily; and I must be greatly mistaken if the colonel isn't just Karl van Milgem himself; he, you know,—but to be sure you don't know,—he that the folks used always to call Rikke-Tikke-Tak."

THE PATIENT WAITER

From 'Rikke-Tikke-Tak'

SHE took her way with the cow toward the brook, which was edged about with a scanty growth of grass. Slowly she went, step by step, leading the creature after her by a cord. At last she reached the line where the heath passed into a range of low-lying boggy pastures, and the alder and juniper bushes formed a closer thicket; there she left the foot-path. A solitary beech stood there — sown probably by a bird, for as far as the eye could see it descried no similar foliage. Magdalen sank down at the foot of the tree. Deeply she bowed her head; motionless she gazed on space; the cord fell from her hand and her accustomed reverie came over her.

Now in the free open air, under the beautiful deep-blue heaven, the sore load of trouble which weighed upon her heart fell from it. Her lips did not move, no sigh escaped from them; but a quiet stream of tears trickled into her lap. Long, very long she sat there without changing her position; but by degrees her tears fell more slowly, till at last she lifted her head, and with a calmer air murmured her old favorite tune:—

> "Rikketikketak,
> Rikketikketoo;
> The iron's warm;
> Up with your arm,
> Now strike,—one, two,
> Rikketikketoo."

What could this strange jingle mean? It would have been useless to ask Magdalen, for she herself knew not how it was that of themselves, almost without will or consciousness of hers, the meaningless words came tripping over her lips. A faint recollection she had of some one having often sung them to her; but that was long, long ago. They spoke but indistinctly, still they had ever more and more fixed themselves in her train of associations, had become ever more and more the accompaniment both of her joys and of her sorrows.

After she had repeated the rhyme a few times, and each time less sadly, she seemed quite to forget her melancholy and the causes of it. She stood up, her face radiant with contentment, briskly led the cow to a place where there was better pasture,

and ran towards a sandy hillock which rose a little above the general surface of the heath. She had often visited this spot. Steadying herself with her hands upon her knees, she fixed her eyes on a bluish point far away upon the extremest verge of the horizon, — a town it was probably, or a large village. . . .
With unwearied eyes she gazed upon the road, doubtless in the unconscious hope that by it he who should release her from her bondage would one day approach that way.

THE LOST GLOVE

"THIS is the celebrated bear-pit of Berne," said the guide. "Pass here when you choose, you will always find people of all ages who are amusing themselves throwing bread and fruit to these ferocious beasts. Here is a good place. See the tricks of these bears, and how they lift up their arms like real beggars."

While Max Rapelings was entirely absorbed in contemplating the amusing antics of the bears, Herman, glancing round, noticed a lady wrapped in a red shawl, who had dropped a yellow glove, and who would probably have lost it, as she continued walking on. He picked up the glove, ran after the lady, and said to her in French, "You have lost something, madam."

The lady turned. Herman seemed transfixed. This lady was no other than the pale maiden of the Aarberggasse, whom he had not recognized at first, owing to her wearing a colored shawl.

She made a step toward him, took her glove with a smile of thanks, and said in a voice whose sweetness was great, "I thank you infinitely, sir."

But at once appeared beside her the old gentleman with the crabbed face, who fixed upon the young man a look both piercing and interrogative.

Just at this moment Max turned toward his friend and cried out: —

"Here, Herman; come quick; there are some bears fighting furiously."

This cry produced upon the young girl and old gentleman an extraordinary effect — it seemed to strike them with terror and affright. They turned away and walked off rapidly, as if in the young doctor they had recognized a dreaded enemy.

Max had observed this inopportune meeting; he left the Swiss, who was still amusing himself by looking into the bear-pit, ran towards his friend, looked at his face attentively, and cried with astonishment: —

"You are pale! What did she say to you? Did her tyrant insult you? You do not answer. Alas! there is an end of all our pleasure for to-day! I would give the poor five francs were you nevermore to meet the pale maiden and her dragon!"

"Hush, hush, Max! I have heard her voice; it is marvelously sweet and fascinating — it still resounds in my ear like a cry of distress."

"A cry of distress! Did she complain to you? What did she say?"

"Only 'I thank you infinitely, sir.'"

"And you call that a cry of distress? You are surely losing your wits!"

"Yes, but her voice was so plaintive, her smile —"

"Oh! she smiled upon you, did she? The Devil! Things begin to look serious."

"Her smile is so sweet, sad, and plaintive."

"There now; you are beginning to talk in verse! This does not seem to me the fitting spot, beside a bear-pit. Come, behave yourself, Herman; here is our host coming. For the love of Heaven, do not mention the pale maiden before him, for he might think you have lost your wits."

THE IRON TOMB

I T WOULD be difficult to describe to you the strange life I led at Bodeghem. I wandered daily along the walks of the uninhabited country-houses, in the woods and shady groves, my mind enveloped as it were in a dream, which like a thick cloud held me aloof from the outer world. It was useless to call to my assistance all my energy and will to dissipate the fog that thus covered my intellect; it was trouble lost. I could only see Rose and her pitiful look; I could only feel the worm of sorrow that gnawed at my heart and only heard the terrible words — "Do you know the news? Rose is going to be married" — that followed me everywhere, without giving me one moment's peace. The violence of passion, the bitterness of despair, had left me entirely. I hated no one, accused no one, not even my cruel fate; not even the future husband, my rival. An intense sorrow, a dreamy resignation, a species of quiet sympathy with my anguish, took the place of all violent emotion in my heart.

Convinced that I was never destined to experience real happiness in this world, I recalled one by one all the recollections of my past life, and with these reminiscences I created for myself an imaginary world, wherein my soul could find a source of peace and consolation.

In walking through the garden I would stop on the bridge and gaze into the water, then returning to less sad thoughts I would contemplate for hours together the lawn that stretched itself before me. I saw in imagination a delicate little girl, pretty as an angel; by her side was a little boy who could not talk, but his eyes at the least word or smile from the little girl would lighten with admiration, gratitude, and pride. I followed these happy children; I trembled with heartfelt emotion when I perceived upon the little girl's face a smile of friendship for the poor boy. I shared in their games as they traced out a bed of flowers in the grass; I ran behind them as they chased the butterflies — I listened to their childish chatterings and each beating of their little hearts, and I recognized with cruel satisfaction that even then a fatal power dominated over these innocent creatures and had already sown in their hearts a seed of a future love. I spoke to the trees, the flowers, the birds, to revive again the memory of my lost happiness, until nightfall and the weary throbbings of my heart warned me that it was time to return home. On other days I would wander in the woods and try to find out those trees to whom I had confided my sorrows and hopes. I recognized the old places where I had once sat, and I thought I could see glittering among the grass the tears I had shed some eight long years ago.

Then I used to weep from pure happiness; the sun of hope inundated my heart with its light. Now I had none; my life was closed by the dark wall of the impossible — it was on that account I had no more tears. Tears are both a prayer and an intercession for help and pity. Why should I complain or implore? — I, to whom no earthly power could give back to my heart what it desired; whose sorrows by their very nature were to be life-lasting.

Again at other times I would sit down on the hedge-side, where the dumb child had worked for weeks carving wooden figures—loved treasures with which he hoped to win a smile. I saw again the spot where the child rolled on the ground, a prey to convulsions of despair, because his tongue refused to utter any intelligible sounds. I saw the white poplar-trees whose bark still bore the mysterious signs with which he tried to make himself understood. The cows that were grazing in the fields, the cracking of the shepherd's whip, the silvery dew arising from the running brook, the splendor of the rising sun, all recalled the memory of my childhood and helped me to forget my mournful sadness, recalling to my mind a picture of happiness that had been, but could never return.

SISKA VAN ROOSEMAEL

Not many years ago, you might have seen in one of the streets behind the green churchyard of Antwerp, a famous old grocer's shop, which through many generations had descended from father to son, and had always been conspicuous for good wares and low prices. The last proprietor of the shop was James van Roosemael, son of Frank, son of Charles, son of Gaspard van Roosemael, and had married Siska Pot, a descendant of the famous Peter Pot, whose name is still to be met in the two Peter-Pot Streets.

This wedded pair, trained from early youth to a life of industry, and now unremittingly busied with their small trade, had never found time to take part in the progress of modern civilization,—or in other words, to *Frenchify* themselves. Their dress, made of stout cloth, was plain, and hardly ever changed its cut; they merely distinguished working dress, Sunday dress, and Easter dress. The latter was never taken from the cupboard but on great holidays, and when the Van Roosemaels took the Holy Communion, or were invited by friends as godparents or marriage guests. It was easily to be seen that the simple people of the old Flemish world, in their quaint though valuable dress, looked rather strangely if compared with many a fine beau, who for a few francs had decked himself out in a fine showy dress, and would, in passing, regard the Van Roosemaels with disdain. But they did not mind it, and thought, "Every man has his own

point to gain — you the shadow, we the substance." They were
sufficiently uneducated not to know that gentlefolks do not dine
at noon, and they therefore were vulgar enough to sit down to
dinner when the clock struck twelve; yea, more, they never
forgot to say grace both before and after dinner. But there
were other imperfections with which they ought to be charged:
for instance, they did not understand a word of French, and
had never felt the want of this accomplishment; they were religious, humble, industrious, and above all peaceable. But the
height of their stupidity was, that they in their Flemish simplicity considered it better every day to lay by an honest stiver,
than by lies and fraud to amass such riches in a few years, that
all the world should exclaim in astonishment, "In what hole
did the rat find it?" In a word, they were Flemish burghers of
the old school.

A PAINTER'S PROGRESS

A T THE funeral of Baron de Erct, a humble vehicle followed
the procession afar off. Arrived at the burial-ground,
three persons alighted from the poor conveyance. They
turned into a by-lane near the cemetery, and did not show themselves during the ceremony. But when all was over, and the
splendid carriages were returning in speed with all the mourners
to the town, three persons were seen entering the churchyard
with slow steps. It was Frank, his aged grandmother leaning
on his arm and supported by his mother on the other side.
Nobody saw them; all was still in the cemetery, and the greatest
silence prevailed around.

Do you mark them all three,— their eyes red with tears, their
breath choked by the agony of grief, approaching a mound of
newly dug-up earth? There rests the man who did good by
stealth. Oh, say not that virtue is not rewarded, not honored!
The tears of these people weigh thousands in the scales of the
heavenly Judge.

Look! the women are kneeling on the mound. They clasp
their hands and bend their heads over the grave; their lips
move. Is theirs a set speech? are their words studied, measured,
written down, in order that they may remember them? Oh no!
They know only one prayer, which the Lord himself has taught

them: they say the Lord's prayer over and over again. Their voices become clearer whilst they pray:—"Forgive us our debts as we forgive our debtors! Holy Mary, Mother of the Lord, pray for us miserable sinners, now and in the hour of death. Amen." Their sobs, their tears, their sighs tell the rest:— "Sleep in peace, kind-hearted friend! we plant no flowers on thy grave; they are not everlasting as the memory of thy countless charities. May thy soul receive in the bosom of thy Maker a reward which the world cannot give!"

And why does not Frank also kneel on the ground? Why? He is absorbed in grief; he feels no life in him, he has forgotten where he is. Look! there he stands like a statue, his head dropping on his breast, his hand pressed to his forehead. How the streaming tears sparkle which burst from his eyes! Unfortunate youth! who could describe the mortal despair which weighs on thy bursting heart!

Awake! seest thou not that the cold ground will injure the health of thy grandmother? Remove her from the grave, else the evening will perhaps still find her kneeling and weeping here. Take courage! return to thy home.

On the following day Frank said in a sorrowful tone to his parents, "We are unfortunate and poor—I am the cause of your sorrow, I know I am. But let me now put a question to you, and answer it candidly! Can we still hold out for three months without earning any money?"

The question remained long unanswered. The mother went up to the invalid husband, and after a long serious conversation with him said, "Three months with the utmost stretch, but no longer." "Well then," said Frank, "I shall make a last attempt. One picture I will paint still—one only, and if I do not sell it soon, then I shall turn sign-painter."

It gave him evident pain to utter this last word; there was a spasm in his throat,—yet he soon composed himself, and asked once more whether they would let him work for three months without trouble or molestation. This his parents readily promised him. Frank then went to Mr. Wappers and received the last twenty-five francs which his generous patron had left for him. With part of this money he purchased colors, and on the following day he shut himself up in the loft where he used to work, and sketched the first outline of the picture which he intended to execute.

It was the churchyard of Hemixem, with a newly thrown-up grave, on which two women were kneeling in prayer; behind them stood a young man weeping and absorbed in the deepest grief; on the side were the walls of the chapel, and in the background a rich landscape. During two months and a half Frank worked without intermission; he went out to the churchyard in order to draw from nature, and made his mother and grandmother sit to him for models.

Never perhaps had an artist worked with more enthusiasm, with more love and industry, at a picture. His soul was full of his subject, and during all the time he was employed in his work his head burnt feverishly. Could this picture turn out ill? No, it must necessarily bear the stamp of inspiration. And so it was.

Frank got on credit an appropriate frame for the exhibition. But this time another thought struck him: he sent his picture to Germany to the exhibition at Cologne. Will he be more successful there? Yet the picture was gone, and stayed away without any news of it whatever.

Poverty, greater than they had ever felt, now broke in upon the longing family. They ate black bread, and were as if crushed by the awaking to the dreadful reality. The good old grandmother showed the greatest courage; she carried quietly her best habiliments and her few trinkets to the pawnbroker's, and consoled the others. But matters could not thus last long. The clothes of Frank and of the mother must at last also be pawned; even the prize medals and other honorable decorations went to the baker as pledges for a little bread. They had already run up an account with the butcher and the grocer — the baker would let them have no more — none would trust the *wretched artist*, as Frank was nicknamed in the neighborhood; the weekly house-rent was unpaid during a whole month, and the landlord had even sent the bailiff to exact payment.

One afternoon in the month of September the destitution of these people reached its height. None of them had tasted a morsel since the preceding evening. The bailiff had just left them with the warning that he would return at six o'clock, and if they did not then pay their rent they would be turned into the street.

Grandmother held Frank's hand in hers, and sought to console him; the mother shed silent tears; the father, who still wore his arm in a sling, sat at the chimney and stared gloomily into the chamber. All at once he burst into a flood of tears and sobbed aloud.

Frank had never seen his father weep: this was the first time in his life; it struck him like a thunderbolt. A shriek of terror burst from him, and he fell on his knees before his father. "Father," he cried, "father, you weep — you! Oh, be at ease; to-morrow I shall turn sign-painter; then I shall at least earn sixpence a day."

The workman raised his son from the floor, and pressed him with his left arm to his heart. "Frank, my boy," he said, "I don't lay blame on you; but we are so wretched. I weep because I am in despair that I cannot work. We are starving, and craving hunger is gnawing at our hearts. Who will give us to eat before the night falls in? Where shall we go when they turn us out to-morrow? Is it not sufficient to turn my brain, or to make me —"

Frank pressed him forcibly to his bosom, and cut short his awful speech by a tender embrace.

Whilst father and son were thus clasped in each other's arms, the door opened, and a man with a leather bag strapped over his shoulder stretched out his hand with a letter in it. With a sudden start Frank disengaged himself from the arm of his father, and attempted to seize the letter; but the postman drew it back and said dryly, "A letter from Germany — two francs!"

Two francs! Where is such a treasure secreted in this poor dwelling? Two francs from people who are starving! Who could describe the tortures and sorrows of this family? The letter contains perhaps what may put an end to their distress; perhaps it would dry up their tears, satisfy their hunger, and protect them from ejectment. And alas! whilst they are staring with beating heart at the letter, and long so ardently to open it, the postman is turning to go off with it and to rob them of all their hopes. It is as if the ground was burning beneath their feet; they stamp the floor from impatience and tear their hair.

Now the mother kneels down before the postman; she raises her hands imploringly! Ha! he weeps — his heart is not of stone. "Here" — he hands the letter to Frank — "take it; I am a poor man too, but I can't stand this any longer." Frank opens the letter slowly with a trembling hand, cautiously undoing each and every fold: but scarcely had he cast his eyes upon the contents, when the muscles of his face began to tremble convulsively; he grows deadly pale, and a strange scream escapes his breast. He supports himself upon the table, and the letter drops from his hands on the floor. The room rings with lamentations, the grandmother raises her hands to heaven, the mother sinks backward from her chair as if paralyzed. Frank was struggling to speak. It was evident he wanted to say something, but he could not make it pass his trembling lips. At last his speech burst forth — "Grandmother, mother, father, I *am* a painter! Five hundred francs for my picture!"

ROSE TERRY COOKE

(1827–1892)

ROSE TERRY was born in Hartford, Connecticut, in 1827, of an old and well-known family, and there nearly all the first half of her life was passed. After that she was little there, spending a number of years with her married sister in Collinsville, and, for fifteen years following her own marriage, in Winsted, Connecticut. The last five years of her life were passed in Pittsfield, Massachusetts, where she died in 1892.

An uneventful life, it might be said; but she had the temperament that makes events. Intensity was the keynote of her nature, the source of her gifts and of her defects. In appearance she was tall and slight, with dark hair, and large dark eyes that dominated her slender oval face, and melted or sparkled with the mood or the occasion. This versatility of temper was deeply founded in her, and is manifest in her work, as in the deep overflowing sentiment of her poems and the almost rollicking humor of her stories, or the tenderness suddenly giving way to bitterness.

Her first literary work was in verse; her earliest venture, before she was twelve years old, being some verses sent privately to the Hartford Courant, and appearing there to the great awe and delight of the little author. As time went on, the creative impulse strengthened and took shape, and she became known as a writer of true poetic feeling and fine rhythmical instinct. In 1860 she gathered her poems into a little volume, which won for her a wider recognition. Quite late in life, in 1888, a complete collection of her poems was made; but she had hardly surpassed that earlier work, which included such gems as 'Then,' 'Trailing Arbutus,' 'The Fishing Song.' Besides these, 'The Two Villages' and 'Nounettes' should be named, as having found their way into many hearts, and as being very perfect specimens of her poetic gift. But it was in her stories that all her rich powers were enlisted. She was one of the first to open by the story-teller's art New England life to the reading public. This field has since been worked to a finer culture, but she brought to the opening of the ground a racy vigor and freshness, a spontaneity, a sparkle, that we could ill spare for the sake of a more delicate finish, and that make her characters stand out with an almost internal force. Among the best of her stories are 'Freedom Wheeler's Controversy

with Providence,' 'The Deacon's Week,' 'Polly Mariner,' 'A Town
Mouse and a Country Mouse,' and 'Odd Miss Todd.' But it is hard
to make an exclusive choice among them. 'The Deacon's Week,'
which she esteemed the best thing she ever did, has had a world-
wide fame and usefulness, having been translated into as many as
four languages, and widely distributed as a tract. Between the years
1881 and 1891 she gathered her stories into book form, under these
titles: 'Somebody's Neighbors,' 'Root-Bound,' 'The Sphinx's Children,' 'Happy Dodd,' 'Huckleberries.' In 1889 appeared her one
novel, 'Steadfast,' an interesting story with much fine character-
drawing. But it is as a writer of short stories of New England life
and of some lovely poems that Rose Terry Cooke will live.

THE REVEREND THOMAS TUCKER AS A PARSON

From 'Some Account of Thomas Tucker'

THE social duties of a settled clergyman might have pressed on
    him onerously; but as if Providence saw that he was best
    fitted for a life of solitude, just as the Green Street Church
had listened to their learned and pious pastor for the first time
after his installation in their pulpit, Keziah, his sister, was seized
with a sudden and dangerous illness. The kind women of the
church rallied around Thomas Tucker in this hour of his need,
and nursed Keziah with unremitting kindness; but all in vain.
She dropped out of life as silently and patiently as she had
endured living, and it remained only to say that the place which
knew her should now know her no more; for she left behind
her no dear friend but her brother, and not an enemy. Even
Thomas missed her rather as a convenience than a companion;
profiting in a certain sense by her death, as it aroused keenly
the sympathy of the church for his loss and loneliness, and
attached them to him by those links of pity that are proverbially almost as strong as love. In any other circumstances the
Green Street Church would no doubt have discovered, early in
their relation, that Mr. Tucker was as unfit for any pastoral
position as he had been for that post in the college chapel; but
much was forgiven him out of his people's abundant kindness,
and their respect for his learning, his simplicity, and his sincere
piety, forbade their objecting at first to his great deficiencies in
those things considered quite as needful to pulpit success as the

power of preaching and the abundance of knowledge. It happened, soon after Keziah's death, that Mr. Tucker was called
to officiate at the funeral of one of his wealthiest parishioners,
a man who had just come back from Europe, and been killed
in a railroad accident on the way to his home in Deerford. He
was personally unknown to Thomas Tucker, but his character
was notorious. He went to church, and bought an expensive
pew there, merely as a business speculation; it gave him weight
in the eyes of his fellows to be outwardly respectable as well
as rich; but he was niggardly to his family, ostentatious, over-
reaching, and cruel as death to the poor and struggling who
crossed his path or came into his employ.

The Reverend Mr. Tucker improved the occasion. He took
for the text of that funeral address, "What shall it profit a man
if he gain the whole world and lose his own soul?" and after a
pungent comparison between the goods of this world and the
tortures of a future state, he laid down his spectacles and wound
up with, "And now, beloved, I have laid before you the two
conditions. Think ye that to-day he whose mortal part lieth
before you would not utter a loud Amen to my statement? Yea,
if there be truth in the Word of God, he who hath left behind
him the gain of life and greed is now crying aloud for a drop of
water to cool his parched tongue, and longing for an hour of
probation wherein to cast off the fetters of ill-gotten gold and
sit with Lazarus gathering crumbs in the company of dogs.
Wherefore, seeing that God hath spoken sharply to you all in
the sudden requirement of this rich man's soul, let his admonition sink into your souls; seek ye first the kingdom of God, and
cast in your lot with the poor of this world, rich in faith, and
be ready to answer joyfully when the Master calls."

Of course the community was outraged; but for a few kindly
souls who stood by the poor parson, and insisted that Keziah's
death had unsettled his mind, and not a few who felt that he
had manfully told the truth without fear or favor, and could
not help feeling a certain respect for him, he would have been
asked, forcibly, to resign that very week. As it was, the indignant widow went over to another denomination without delay.
"I will never set foot in that church again!" she said. "How
can one be safe where a man is allowed to say whatever he
chooses in the pulpit? A ritual never can be personal or
insulting. I shall abide by the Prayer-Book hereafter."

In due time this matter faded out of the popular mind, as all
things do in course of time, and nothing came between pastor
and people except a gradual sense on their part that Solomon
was right when he said, "Much study is a weariness to the flesh;"
not only the student's flesh, but also theirs who have to hear
reiterated all the dry outcome of such study.

But Parson Tucker's career was not to be monotonous. His
next astonishing performance was at a wedding. A very pretty
young girl, an orphan, living in the house of a relative, equally
poor but grasping and ambitious, was about to marry a young
man of great wealth and thoroughly bad character; a man whom
all men knew to be a drunkard, a gambler, and a dissolute fellow, though the only son of a cultivated and very aristocratic
family. Poor Emily Manning had suffered all those deprivations
and mortifications which result from living in a dependent condition, aware that her presence was irksome and unwelcome,
while her delicate organization was overtaxed with work whose
limits were as indefinite as the food and clothing which were its
only reward. She had entered into this engagement in a sort of
desperation, goaded on by the widowed sister-in-law with whom
she lived, and feeling that nothing could be much worse than
her present position. Parson Tucker knew nothing of this, but
he did know the character of Royal Van Wyck; and when he
saw the pallid, delicate, shrinking girl beside this already worn-
out, debased, bestial creature, ready to put herself into his
hands for life, the "daimon" laid hold upon him and spake
again. He opened the service, as was customary in Hartland,
with a short address; but surely never did such a bridal exhort-
ation enter the ears of man and woman before.

"My friends," he began, "matrimony is not to be lightly undertaken, as the matter of a day; it is an awful compact for life
and death that ye enter into here. Young man, if thou hast
not within thyself the full purpose to treat this woman with
pure respect, loyal service, and tender care; to guard her soul's
innocence as well as her bodily welfare; to cleave to her only,
and keep thyself from evil thoughts and base indulgences for
her sake,— if thou art not fit, as well as willing, to be priest
and king of a clean household, standing unto her in character
and act in God's stead so far as man may, draw back even now
from thine intent; for a lesser purpose is sacrilege here, and
will be damnable infamy hereafter."

Royal Van Wyck opened his sallow green eyes with an insolent stare. He would have sworn roundly had not some poor instinct of propriety restrained him; as it was, he did not speak but looked away. He could not bear the keen deep-set eyes fixed upon him, and a certain gaunt majesty in the parson's outstretched arm and severe countenance daunted him for the moment. But Thomas Tucker saw that he had no intention of accepting this good advice, so he turned to Emily.

"Daughter," he said, "if thou art about to enter into this solemn relation, pause and consider. If thou hast not such confidence in this man that thy heart faileth not an iota at the prospect of a lifelong companionship with him; if thou canst not trust him utterly, respect him as thy lord and head, yield him an obedience joyful and secure next to that thou givest to God; if he is not to thee the one desirable friend and lover; if thou hast a thought so free of him that it is possible for thee to imagine another man in his place without a shudder; if thou art not willing to give thyself to him in the bonds of a lifelong, inevitable covenant of love and service; if it is not the best and sweetest thing earth can offer thee to be his wife and the mother of his children,—stop now; stop at the very horns of the altar, lest thou commit the worst sin of woman, sell thy birthright for a mess of pottage, and find no place for repentance, though thou seek it carefully and with tears."

Carried away with his zeal for truth and righteousness, speaking as with the sudden inspiration of a prophet, Parson Tucker did not see the terror and the paleness deepening, as he spoke, on the bride's fair countenance. As he extended his hand toward her she fell in a dead faint at his feet. All was confusion in an instant. The bridegroom swore and Mrs. Manning screamed, while the relations crowded about the insensible girl and tried to revive her. She was taken at once up-stairs to her room, and the wedding put off till the next day, as Mrs. Manning announced.

"And you won't officiate at it, old fellow! I'll swear to that!" roared the baffled bridegroom with a volley of profane epithets, shaking his fist in the parson's calm face.

"Having taken the sword, I am content to perish thereby, even as Scripture saith," answered Thomas Tucker, stalking out of the door.

That night as he sat in his study, the door opened softly, and Emily Manning came in and knelt at the side of the parson's chair. "I have no place to go to, sir," she whispered, with trembling lips. "You saved me to-day; will you help me now? I was going to sin, but I didn't know it till you told me."

"Then it was not sin, my child," said Parson Tucker gently. "Sin is conscious transgression, and from that thou hast instantly departed."

"But what could I do?" she asked, her eyes full of tears. "I have no home. Marcia is tired of me, and I have no other friends. I wanted a home so much. Oh, I was wrong, for I did not love him. And now I have run away from Marcia,—she was so dreadful,—and what shall I do?"

"Poor child!" he said tenderly. "Sit here. I will help. My old woman, in the kitchen below, shall fetch thee to a chamber. Keziah brought her with us; she is kind, and will care for thee, while I go to bring a friend." So saying, the parson rung his bell for old Jane, gave the girl over to her care, and set out himself for President Winthrop's house.

"I have brought you a good work," he said abruptly to Mrs. Winthrop. "Come with me; there is a soul in need at my house."

Mrs. Winthrop was used to this sort of summons from the parson. They had been good friends ever since the eccentric interview brought about by Jack Mason's valentine, and when charity was needed Eleanor Winthrop's heart and hand were always ready for service. She put on hat and shawl, and went with the parson to his house, hearing on the way all the story.

"Mr. Tucker," she said, as he finished the recital, "aren't you going to make much trouble for yourself by your aggressive honesty?"

Thomas looked at her, bewildered.

"But the truth is to be spoken!" he replied, as if that were the end of the controversy. And she was silent, recognizing the fact that here conventions were useless, and self-preservation not the first law of grace, if it is of nature.

All Mrs. Winthrop's kindliness was aroused by the pitiful condition of Emily Manning. She consoled and counseled her like a mother, and soon after took her into her household as governess to the little girls whom Mr. Winthrop's first wife had left him; making for the grateful girl a happy home, which in after years she left to become the wife of a good man, toward whom she felt all that Parson Tucker had required of her on

that painful day which she hated now to remember. And as the
parson performed this ceremony he turned after the benediction
to Eleanor Winthrop, and said with a beam of noble triumph
on his hollow visage, "Blessed be the Lord! I have saved a soul
alive!"

But long before this happy sequel came about, he had other
opportunities to distinguish himself. There came a Sunday when
the service of infant baptism was to be performed; and when
the fair sweet babes, who had behaved with unusual decorum,
were returned to their mothers' arms, and the parson according
to order said, "Let us pray," he certainly offered the most
peculiar petition ever heard in the Green Street Church. After
expressing the usual desire that the baptized children might
grow up in the nurture and admonition of the Lord, he went
on:—"But if it please thee, O Father, to recall these little ones
to thyself in the innocence of their infancy, we will rejoice and
give thanks, and sound thy praises upon the harp and timbrel.
Yea! with the whole heart we will praise thee; for we know the
tribulations and snares, the evil and folly and anguish, of this
life below; and we know that not one child of Adam, coming
to man's estate, is spared that bitter and woful cup that is
pressed out from the fruit of the knowledge of good and evil,
which our progenitors ate of in thy garden of Paradise, and
thereby sinned and fell, and bequeathed to us their evil longings and habitual transgression. They are the blessed who are
taken away in their infancy, and lie forever by green pastures
and still waters in the fields of heaven. We ask of thee no
greater or better gift for these lambs than early to be folded
where none shall hurt or destroy in all thy holy mountain, and
the love that is above all mother's love shall cradle them
throughout eternity. Amen!"

Not a mother in that congregation failed to shiver and tremble at this prayer, and tears fell fast and thick on the babes
who slumbered softly in the tender arms that had gathered them
home, after consecrating them to that God who yet they were
so unwilling should literally accept their offering. Fifty pairs
of eyes were turned on Parson Tucker with the look of a bear
robbed of its cubs; but far more were drowned in tears of memory and regret, poignant still, but strangely soothed by this vivid
presentation of the blessedness wherein their loved and lost were
safely abiding.

Much comment was exchanged in the church porch, after service, on the parson's prayer.

"We ought to hold a special meeting to pray that the Lord will not answer such a petition!" cried one indignant mother, whose little flock were clinging about her skirts, and who had left twin babies, yet unbaptized, at home.

"It *is* rather hard on you, aunty!" said the graceless Jack Mason, the speaker's nephew, now transformed into an unpromising young lawyer in Hartland. "You'd rather have your babies sin and suffer with you than have 'em safe in their little graves, hadn't you? I don't go with the parson myself. I didn't so much mind his funeral gymnastic over old Baker, and his disposition of that party's soul in Hades, because I never before supposed Roosevelt Baker had a soul, and it was quite reassuring to be certain he met with his dues somewhere; but he's worse than Herod about the babies!"

However, the parson did not hear or know what was said of him, and in an ignorance that was indeed bliss continued to preach and minister to his people in strict accordance with his own views of duty. His next essay was a pastoral visit to one of his flock, recently a widow, a woman weak in body and mind both; desirous above all things to be proper and like other people, to weep where she must, smile when she ought, wear clothes like the advance-guard of fashion, and do "the thing" to be done always, whether it was the right and true thing or not.

Her husband had spent all her fortune in speculation, taken to drink as a refuge from folly and reproach at home, and under the influence of the consoling fluid had turned his wife out-of-doors whenever he felt in the mood; kicked her, beaten her, and forced her, in fear of her life, over and over to steal from her own house and take refuge with the neighbors, and ask from them the food she was not allowed at home. At last the end came. Parson Tucker was sent for to see the widow and arrange for funeral services. She had not been present at the Baker funeral, or indeed been in Deerford for some years after that occasion, so she adhered to the conventions; and when Parson Tucker reached the house he was shown into a darkened room, where the disconsolate woman sat posed already in deep mourning, a widow's cap perched upon her small head. A woman would have inferred at once that Mrs. Spring had anticipated the end of Joe's last attack of *mania à potu*, and prepared these funeral garments beforehand; but Thomas Tucker drew no such conclusions. He sat down silently and grimly, after shaking hands with Mrs. Spring, and said nothing. She began the conversation: —

"This is a dreadful affliction, Mr. Tucker. I don't know how I shall live through it."

"It is terrible, indeed," said the parson. "I do not wonder, madam, that you mourn to see your partner cut off in his sins, without time for repentance; but no doubt you feel with gratitude the goodness which hath delivered you from so sore a burden."

"What?" screamed the widow.

"I speak of God's mercy in removing from your house one who made your life a terror, and your days full of fear and suffering; you might have been as others, bereaved and desolate, and mourning to your life's end."

"I don't know what you mean, Parson Tucker," said Mrs. Spring sharply, removing a dry handkerchief from unwet eyes. "Poor dear Joseph is taken away from me, and I'm left a desolate widow, and you talk in this way! I'm sure he had the best of hearts that ever was; it was only, as you may say, accidental to him to be a little overcome at times, and I'm — I'm — o — h!"

Here she gave a little hysterical scream, and did some well-executed sobbing; but the parson did not mind it. He rose up before her, gaunt and gray. "Madam, did not this man beat, and abuse, and insult, and starve you, when he was living? Or have I been misinformed?"

"Well — oh dear, what dreadful questions!"

"Did he?" thundered the parson.

"He didn't mean to; he was excited, Mr. Tucker. He —"

"He was drunk. And is that excuse? Not so, madam. You know, and I know, that his death is a relief and a release to you. I cannot condole with you on that which is not a sorrow;" and he walked rigidly out of the door.

Is it necessary to say that Mr. Spring's funeral did not take place in Deerford? His widow suddenly remembered that he had been born in a small town among the hills of West Massachusetts, and she took his body thither, to be "laid beside his dear payrents," as she expressed it.

Things had now come to a bad pass for Parson Tucker. The church committee had held more than one conference over their duty toward him. It was obvious that they had no real reason for dismissing him but his ghastly honesty, and that hardly offers a decent excuse to depose a minister of the gospel. They hardly knew how to face the matter, and were in this state of perplexity when Mr. Tucker announced, one Sunday, after the sermon, that he would like to see the church committee at his study on Tuesday night; and accordingly they assembled there and found President Winthrop with the parson.

"Brethren," said Thomas Tucker, after the preliminary welcome had passed, "I have sent for you to-night to say, that having now been settled over your church eight years, I have found the salary you paid me so much more than was needed for my bodily support that I have laid by each year as the surplus came to hand, that I might restore to you your goods. The sum is now something over eight thousand dollars, and is placed to the credit of your chairman, in the First Deerford Bank." The committee stared at each other as if each one were trying to arouse himself from sleep. The chairman at last spoke: —

"But Mr. Tucker, this is unheard-of! The salary is yours; we do not desire to take it back; we can't do it."

"That which I have not earned, Brother Street, is not mine. I am a solitary man; my expenses are light. It must be as I said. Moreover, I have to say that I hereby withdraw from your pulpit, of necessity. I have dealt with our best physicians concerning a certain anguish of the breast which seizes me at times unawares, and they all concur that an evil disease lieth upon me. I have not much time to live, and I would fain withdraw from activities and duties that are external, and prepare for the day that is at hand."

The committee were pained as well as shocked. They felt guilty to think how they had plotted this very thing among themselves; and they felt too a certain awe and deep respect for this simple unworldly nature, this supernatural integrity. Mr. Street spoke again; his voice was husky: —

"If this is so, Mr. Tucker, we must of course accept your resignation; but my dear pastor, keep the money! You will need care and comforts, now this trouble has come on you. We can't take it back."

Parson Tucker looked at him with a grave sweet smile. "I thank you, brother, but I have a private store. My sister left her worldly goods to me, and there is enough and to spare for my short sojourn," he answered.

"But it isn't according to the fitness of things that we should take your salary back, Parson Tucker," put in bustling Mr. Taylor. "What upon earth should we do with it?"

"Friend," said the parson, "the eternal fitness of things is but the outcome of their eternal verity. I have not, as I said, earned that wage, and I must restore it: it is for you to decide what end it shall serve in the church."

A few more words passed between them, and then each wrung the parson's hand and left him, not all with unmoved hearts or dry eyes.

"I don't wonder he's going to die!" exclaimed Mr. Street, as the committee separated at a street corner. "He's altogether too honest to live!"

From that day Thomas Tucker sank quietly toward his grave. Friends swarmed about him, and if delicacies of food could have saved him, the dainty stores poured in upon him would have renewed his youth; but all was in vain.

President Winthrop sat by him one summer day, and seeing a sad gleam in his sunken eye, asked gently, "You are ready and willing to go, Brother Tucker?" nothing doubting a glad assent.

But the parson was honest to the last. "No," he said, "I do not want to die; I am afraid. I do not like strange and new things. I do not want to leave my books and my study."

"But, dear brother," broke in the astonished president, "it is a going home to your Father's house!"

"I know not what a home is, friend, in the sense of regret or longing for one. My early home was but as the egg to the bird, a prison wherein I was born, from which I fled; nor was my knowledge of a father one that commends itself as a type of good. I trust, indeed, that the Master will take me by the hand, even as he did Peter upon the water; but the utterance of my secret soul is even that of the apostle with the keys: 'Lord, save, or I perish!'"

"But you have been a power for good, and a close follower of Peter's Lord," said Mr. Winthrop, altogether at a loss for the proper thing to say to this peculiar man.

"One thing alone have I been enabled to do, Brother Winthrop, for which I can with heart and soul thank God, even at this hour. Yea, I thank him that I have been enabled to speak the truth even in the face of lies and deceptions, through his upholding." A smile of unearthly triumph filled every line of the wasted face, and lit his eyes with a flash of divine light as he said this. He grasped close the friendly hand he was holding, turned his cheek to the pillow, and closed his eyes, passing into that life of truth and love that awaited him, even as a child that lies down in the darkness, trembling, fearful, and weary, but awakes, in the dawn of a new day, in the heart of home.

"Still," said President Winthrop to his wife, as they walked home after the funeral, "I believe in the good old proverb, Eleanor, that 'the truth is not to be spoken at all times.'"

"And I never believed in it so little!" she cried, indignantly. "Think what a record he has left; what respect hangs about his memory! Do we know how many weak souls have relied on his example, and held to the truth when it was hard, because he did and could? It is something to be heroic in these days, even if it is unpopular!"

The president shrugged his shoulders.

From 'The Sphinx's Children and Other People's': copyrighted 1886, by Ticknor and Company

JAMES FENIMORE COOPER.

JAMES FENIMORE COOPER

(1789–1851)

BY JULIAN HAWTHORNE

MORE than a century ago, in the town of Burlington, New Jersey, was born a man destined to become one of the best known figures of his time. He was as devout an American as ever lived, for he could arraign the shortcomings of his countrymen as stanchly as he could defend and glorify their ideals. He entered fearlessly and passionately into the life around him, seeing intensely, yet sometimes blind; feeling ardently, yet not always aright; acting with might and conviction, yet not seldom amiss. He loved and revered good, scorned and hated evil, and with the strength and straightforwardness of a bull championed the one and gored the other. He worshiped justice, but lacked judgment; his brain, stubborn and logical, was incongruously mated with a deep and tender heart. A brave and burly backwoods gentleman was he, with a smattering of the humanities from Yale, and a dogged precision of principle and conduct from six years in the navy. He had the iron memory proper to a vigorous organization and a serious, observant mind; he was tirelessly industrious—in nine-and-twenty years he published thirty-two novels, many of them of prodigious length, besides producing much matter never brought to light. His birth fell at a noble period of our history, and his surroundings fostered true and generous manhood. Doubtless many of his contemporaries were as true men as he: but to Cooper in addition was vouchsafed the gift of genius; and that magic quality dominated and transfigured his else rugged and intractable nature, and made his name known and loved over all the earth. No author has been more widely read than he; no American author has won even a tithe of his honorable popularity.

Though Jersey may claim his birthplace, Cooper's childhood from his second to his fourteenth year was passed on the then frontiers of civilization, at Cooperstown on the Susquehanna. There in the primeval forest, hard by the broad Lake Otsego and the wide-flowing river, the old Judge built his house and laid out his town. Trees, mountains, wild animals, and wild men nursed the child, and implanted in him seeds of poetry and wrought into the sturdy fibres of his mind golden threads of creative imagination. Then round about

VII—250

the hearth at night, men of pith and character told tales of the Revolution, of battle, adventure, and endurance, which the child, hearing, fed upon with his soul, and grew strong in patriotism and independence. Nobility was innate in him; he conceived lofty and sweet ideals of human nature and conduct, and was never false to them thereafter. The ideal Man—the ideal Woman—he believed in them to the end. And more than twice or thrice in his fictions we find personages like Harvey Birch, Leatherstocking, Long Tom Coffin, the jailer's daughter in 'The Bravo,' and Mabel Dunham and Dew-of-June in 'The Pathfinder,' which give adequate embodiment to his exalted conception of the possibilities of his fellow creatures. For though portrayal of character in the ultra-refined modern sense of the term was impossible to Cooper, yet he perceived and could impressively present certain broad qualities of human nature, and combine them in consistent and memorable figures. Criticism may smile now and then, and psychology arch her eyebrows, but the figures live, and bid fair to be lusty long after present fashions have been forgotten.

But of the making of books, Cooper, during the first three decades of his life, had no thought at all. He looked forward to a career of action; and after Yale College had given him a glimpse of the range of knowledge, he joined a vessel as midshipman, with the prospect of an admiral's cocked hat and glory in the distance. The glory, however, with which the ocean was to crown him, was destined to be gained through the pen and not the sword, when at the age of five-and-thirty he should have published 'The Pilot.' As a naval officer, he might have helped to whip the English in the War of 1812; but as author of the best sea story in the language he conquered all the world of readers unaided. Meanwhile, when he was twenty-one years old he married a Miss Delancey, whose goodness (according to one of his biographers) was no less eminent than his genius, and who died but a short time before him. The joys of wedded life in a home of his own outweighed with him the chances of warlike distinction, and he resigned his commission and took command of a farm in Westchester County; and a gentleman farmer, either there or at his boyhood's home in Cooperstown, he remained till the end, with the exception of his seven-years' sojourn in Europe.

His was a bodily frame built to endure a hundred years, and the robustness of his intelligence and the vivacity of his feelings would have kept him young throughout; yet he died of a dropsy, at the prime of his powers, in 1851, heartily mourned by innumerable friends, and having already outlived all his enmities. He died, too, the unquestioned chief of American novelists; and however superior to his may have been the genius of his contemporary Walter Scott, the latter can hardly be said to have rivaled him in breadth of dominion over readers of all nationalities. Cooper was a household name from New York to Ispahan, from St. Petersburg to Rio Janeiro; and the copyright on his works in various languages would to-day amount to a large fortune every year. Three generations have passed since with 'The Spy' he won the sympathies of mankind; and he holds them still. It is an enviable record. And although in respect of actual quality of work produced there have been many geniuses greater than he, yet it is fair to remember that Cooper's genius had a great deal of stubborn raw material to subdue before it could proceed to produce anything. It started handicapped. As it was, the man wasted years of time and an immensity of effort in doing, or trying to do, things he had no business with. He would be a political reformer, a critic of society, an interpreter of law, even a master grammarian. He would fight to the finish all who differed from him in opinion; he fought and—incredible as it may seem—he actually conquered the American press. He published reams of stuff which no one now reads and which was never worth reading, to enforce his views and prove that he was right and others wrong. All this power was misdirected; it might have been applied to producing more and better Leatherstockings and Pilots. Perhaps he hardly appreciated at its value that one immortal thing about him,—his genius,—and was too much concerned about his dogmatic and bull-headed Self. Unless the world confessed his infallibility, he could not be quite at peace with it. Such an attitude arouses one's sense of humor; it would never have existed had Cooper possessed a spark of humor himself. But he was uncompromisingly serious on all subjects, or if at times he tried to be playful, we shudder and avert our faces. It is too like Juggernaut dancing a jig. And he gave too much weight to the verdict of the moment, and not enough to that judgment of posterity to which the great Verulam was content to submit his fame. Who cares to-day, or how are we the better or the worse, if Cooper were right or wrong in his various convictions? What concerns us is that he wrote delightful stories of the forest and the sea; it is in those stories, and not in his controversial or didactic homilies, that we choose to discover his faith in good and ire against evil. Cooper, in short, had his limitations; but with all his errors, we may take him and be thankful.

Moreover, his essential largeness appears in the fact that in the midst of his bitterest conflicts, at the very moment when his pamphlets and "satires" were heating the printing-presses and people's tempers, a novel of his would be issued, redolent with pure and serene imagination, telling of the prairies and the woods, of deer and panther, of noble redskins and heroic trappers. It is another world, harmonious and calm; no echo of the petty tumults in which its author seemed to live is audible therein. But it is a world of that author's imagination, and its existence proves that he was greater and wiser than the man of troubles and grievances who so noisily solicits our attention. The surface truculence which fought and wrangled was distinct from the interior energy which created and harmonized, and acted perhaps as the safety-valve to relieve the inward region from disturbance.

The anecdote of how Cooper happened to adopt literature as a calling is somewhat musty, and its only significant feature is the characteristic self-confidence of his exclamation, on laying down a stupid English novel which he had been reading to his wife, « I could write as well as that myself! »   Also in point is the fact that the thing he wrote, 'Precaution,' is a story of English life, whereof at that time he had had no personal experience.   One would like to know the name of the novel which touched him off; if it was stupider and more turgid than 'Precaution' it must have been a curiosity.   Cooper may have thought otherwise, or he may have been stimulated by recognition of his failure, as a good warrior by the discovery that his adversary is a more redoubtable fighter than he had gauged him to be.   At all events, he lost no time in engaging once more, and this time he routed his foe, horse and foot.   One is reminded of the exclamation of his own Paul Jones, when requested to surrender — « I haven't begun to fight! »   'The Spy' is not a perfect work of art, but it is a story of adventure and character such as the world loves and will never tire of.   'Precaution' had showed not even talent; 'The Spy' revealed unquestionable genius.   This is not to say that its merit was actually unquestioned at the time it came out; our native critics hesitated to commit themselves, and awaited English verdicts.   But the nation's criticism was to buy the book and read it, and they and other nations have been so doing ever since.   Nothing in literature lasts longer, or may be oftener re-read with pleasure, than a good tale of adventure.   The incidents are so many and the complications so ingenious that one forgets the detail after a few years, and comes to the perusal with fresh appetite.   Cooper's best books are epics, possessing an almost Homeric vitality.   The hero is what the reader would like to be, and the latter thrills with his perils and triumphs in his success.   Ulysses is Mankind, making sweet uses of adversity, and regenerate at last; and Harvey Birch, Leatherstocking, and the rest are congenial types of Man, acting up to high standards in given circumstances.

But oh! the remorseless tracts of verbiage in these books, the long toiling through endless preliminaries, as of a too unwieldy army marching and marshaling for battle! It is Cooper's way; he must warm to his work gradually, or his strength cannot declare itself. His beginnings abound in seemingly profitless detail, as if he must needs plot his every footstep on the map ere trusting himself to take the next. Balzac's method is similar, but possesses a spiritual charm lacking in the American's. The modern ability of Stevenson and Kipling to plunge into the thick of it in the first paragraph was impossible to this ponderous pioneer. Yet when at length he does begin to move, the impetus and majesty of his advance are tremendous; as in the avalanche, every added particular of passive preparation adds weight and power to the final action. Cooper teaches us, Wellington-like, "what long-enduring hearts can do!" Doubtless, therefore, any attempt to improve him by blue-penciling his tediousness would result in spoiling him altogether. We must accept him as he is. Dullness past furnishes fire to present excitement. It is a mistake to "skip" in reading Cooper; if we have not leisure to read him as he stands, let us wait until we have.

'Precaution' and 'The Spy' both appeared in 1821, when the author was about thirty-two years old. Two years passed before the production of 'The Pioneers,' wherein Cooper draws upon memory no less than upon imagination, and in which Leatherstocking first makes our acquaintance. As a rule (proved by exceptions), the best novels of great novelists have their scene in surroundings with which the writer's boyhood was familiar. 'The Pioneers' and the ensuing series of Leatherstocking tales are placed in the neighborhood of the lake and river which Cooper, as a child, had so lovingly learned by heart. Time had supplied the requisite atmosphere for the pictures that he drew, while the accuracy of his memory and the minuteness of his observation assured ample realism. In the course of the narrative the whole mode of life of a frontier settlement from season to season appears before us, and the typical figures which constitute it. It is history, illuminated by romance and uplifted by poetic imagination. One of our greatest poets, speaking after the second-thought of thirty years, declared Cooper to be a greater poet than Hesiod or Theocritus. But between a poet and a prose-writer capable of poetic feeling there is perhaps both a distinction and a difference.

The birth-year of the 'Pioneers' and of the 'Pilot' are again the same. Now Cooper leaves, for the time, the backwoods, and embarks upon the sea. He is as great upon one element as upon the other: of whom else can that be affirmed? We might adapt the apophthegm on Washington to him: he was "first on land, first on sea, and first in the hearts of his readers." In 'The Pilot' the resources of the writer's invention first appear in full development. His personal experience of the vicissitudes and perils of a seaman's life stood him in good stead here, and may indeed have served him

well in the construction of all his fictions. Fertility in incident and
the element of suspense are valuable parts of a story-teller's outfit,
and Cooper excelled in both; he might have been less adequately
furnished in these respects had he never served on a man-of-war.
Be that as it may, 'The Pilot' is generally accepted as the best sea
story ever written. Herman Melville and his disciple Clark Russell
have both written lovingly and thrillingly of the sea and seamen,
but neither of them has rivaled their common original. Long Tom
Coffin is the peer of Leatherstocking himself, and might have been
made the central figure of as many and as excellent tales. The
three books — 'The Spy,' 'The Pioneers,' and 'The Pilot' — form a
trilogy of itself more than sufficient to support a mighty reputation;
and they were all written before Cooper was thirty-five years old.
Indeed, his subsequent works did not importantly add to his fame;
and many of them of course might better never have been written.
'Lionel Lincoln,' in 1825, fell far short of the level of the previous
romances; but 'The Last of the Mohicans,' in the year following, is
again as good as the best, and the great figure of Leatherstocking
even gains in solidity and charm. As a structure, the story is easily
criticized, but the texture is so sound and the spirit so stirring that
only the cooler after-thought finds fault. Faults which would shipwreck a lesser man leave this leviathan almost unscathed.

At this juncture occurred the unfortunate episode in Cooper's
career. His fame having spread over two continents, he felt a
natural desire to visit the scene of his foreign empire and make
acquaintance with his subjects there; it seemed an act of expedi-
ency too to get local color for romances which should appeal more
directly to these friends across the sea. Upon these pretexts he set
forth, and in due season arrived in Paris. Here however he chanced
to read a newspaper criticism of the United States government;
and true to his conviction that he was the heaven-appointed agent
to correct and castigate the world, he sat down and wrote a sharp
rejoinder. He was well furnished with facts, and he exhibited
plenty of acumen in his statement of them; though his cumbrous and
pompous style, as of a schoolmaster laying down the law, was not
calculated to fascinate the lectured ones. In the controversy which
ensued he found himself arrayed against the aristocratic party,
with only the aged Lafayette to afford him moral support; his arguments were not refuted, but this rendered him only the more
obnoxious to his hosts, who finally informed him that his room was
more desirable than his company. As a Parthian shaft, our redoubtable champion launched a missile in the shape of a romance of
ancient Venice ('The Bravo'), in which he showed how the perversion of institutions devised to insure freedom, inevitably brings to

pass freedom's opposite. It is a capital novel, worthy of Cooper's fame; but it neither convinced nor pleased the effete monarchists whom it arraigned. In the end accordingly he returned home, with the consciousness of having vindicated his countrymen, but of having antagonized all Europe in the process. It may be possible to win the affection of a people while proving to them that they are fools and worse; but if so, Cooper was not the man to accomplish the feat. It should be premised here that during his residence abroad he had written, in addition to 'The Bravo,' three novels which may be placed among his better works; and one, 'The Wept of Wish-ton-Wish,' whose lovely title is its only recommendation. 'The Red Rover' was by some held to be superior even to 'The Pilot'; and 'Heidenhauer' and 'The Headsman of Berne' attempt, not with entire success, to repeat the excellence of 'The Bravo.' He had also published a volume of letters critical of national features, entitled 'Notions of the Americans,' which may have flattered his countrymen's susceptibilities, but did nothing to assuage the wounded feelings of those with whom he contrasted them.

Now, when a warrior returns home after having manfully supported his country's cause against odds, and at the cost of his own popularity, he feels justified in anticipating a cordial reception. What then must be his feelings on finding himself actually given the cold shoulder by those he had defended, on the plea that his defense was impolitic and discourteous? In such circumstances there is one course which no wise man will pursue, and that is to treat his aspersers with anything else than silent disdain. Cooper was far from being thus wise: he lectured his fellow-citizens with quite as much asperity as he had erewhile lectured the tyrants of the Old World; with as much justice too, and with an effect even more embroiling. In 'A Letter to his Countrymen,' 'Monikins,' 'Homeward Bound,' and 'Home as Found,' he admonished and satirized them with characteristic vigor. The last-named of these books brings us to the year 1838, and of Cooper's life the fiftieth. He seemed in a fair way to become a universal Ishmael. Yet once more he had only begun to fight. In 1838 he commenced action against a New York newspaper for slander, and for five years thereafter the courts of his country resounded with the cries and thwackings of the combatants. But Cooper could find no adversary really worthy of his steel, and in 1843 he was able to write to a friend, "I have beaten every man I have sued who has not retracted his libels!" He had beaten them fairly, and one fancies that even he must at last have become weary of his favorite passion of proving himself in the right. Howbeit, peace was declared over the corpse of the last of his opponents, and the victor in so many fields could now apply himself undisturbedly to the vocations from which war had partially distracted him,— only partially, for in 1840, in the heat of the newspaper fray, he astonished the public by producing one of the loveliest of his romances and perhaps the very best of the Leatherstocking series, 'The Pathfinder.' William Cullen Bryant holds this to be "a glorious work," and speaks of its moral beauty, the vividness and force of its delineations, and the unspoiled love of nature and fresh and warm emotions which give life to the narrative and dialogue. Yet Cooper was at that time over fifty years of age.

Nevertheless, so far as his abilities both mental and physical were concerned, the mighty man was still in the prime of his manhood, if not of his youth. During the seven or eight years yet to elapse, after the close of his slander suits in 1843, before his unexpected death in 1851, he wrote not less than twelve new novels, several of them touching the high-water mark of his genius. Of them may be specially mentioned 'Two Admirals' and 'Wing-and-Wing,' 'Wyandotte,' and 'Jack Tier.' Besides all this long list of his works, he published 'Sketches of Switzerland' in 1836; 'Gleanings in Europe,' in a series of eight volumes, beginning 1837; a 'Naval History of the United States' in two octavo volumes; and wrote three or four other books which seem to have remained in manuscript. Altogether it was a gigantic life-work, worthy of the giant who achieved it.

Cooper was hated as well as loved during his lifetime, but at his death the love had quenched the hate, and there are none but lovers of him now. He was manly, sincere, sensitive, independent; rough without but sweet within. He sought the good of others, he devoutly believed in God, and if he was always ready to take his own part in a fight, he never forgot his own self-respect or forfeited other men's. But above all he was a great novelist, original and irresistible. America has produced no other man built on a scale so continental.

Julian Hawthorne

THE PRIVATEER

From 'The Water-Witch'

THE exploits, the mysterious character, and the daring of the Water-Witch and of him who sailed her, were in that day the frequent subjects of anger, admiration, and surprise. Those who found pleasure in the marvelous listened to the wonders that were recounted of her speed and boldness with pleasure; they who had been so often foiled in their attempts to arrest the hardy dealers in contraband reddened at her name; and all wondered at the success and intelligence with which her movements were controlled. It will therefore create no astonishment when we say that Ludlow and the patroon drew near to the light and graceful fabric with an interest that deepened at each stroke of the oars. So much of a profession which, in that age, was particularly marked and apart from the rest of mankind in habits and opinions, had been interwoven into the character of the former, that he could not see the just proportions, the graceful outlines of the hull, or the exquisite symmetry and neatness of the spars and rigging, without experiencing a feeling somewhat allied to that which undeniable superiority excites in the heart of even a rival. There was also a taste in the style of the merely ornamental parts of the delicate machine, which caused as much surprise as her model and rig.

Seamen, in all ages and in every state of their art, have been ambitious of bestowing on their floating habitations a style of decoration which while appropriate to their element, should be thought somewhat analogous to the architectural ornaments of the land. Piety, superstition, and national usages affect these characteristic ornaments, which are still seen, in different quarters of the world, to occasion broad distinctions between the appearances of vessels. In one, the rudder-head is carved with the resemblance of some hideous monster; another shows goggling eyes and lolling tongues from its cat-heads; this has the patron saint, or the ever-kind Marie, embossed upon its moldings or bows; while that is covered with the allegorical emblems of country and duty. Few of these efforts of nautical art are successful, though a better taste appears to be gradually redeeming even this branch of human industry from the rubbish of barbarism, and to be elevating it to a state which shall do no violence to the more fastidious opinions of the age. But the vessel of which we write, though constructed at so remote a period, would have done credit to the improvements of our own time.

It has been said that the hull of this celebrated smuggler was low, dark, molded with exquisite art, and so justly balanced as to ride upon its element like a sea-fowl. For a little distance above the water it showed a blue that vied with the color of the deep ocean, the use of copper being then unknown; while the more superior parts were of a jet black delicately relieved by two lines of a straw color, that were drawn with mathematical accuracy, paralleled to the plane of her upper works, and consequently converging slightly toward the sea beneath her counter. Glossy hammock-cloths concealed the persons of those who were on the deck, while the close bulwarks gave the brigantine the air of a vessel equipped for war. Still the eye of Ludlow ran curiously along the whole extent of the two straw-colored lines, seeking in vain some evidence of the weight and force of her armament. If she had ports at all, they were so ingeniously concealed as to escape the keenest of his glances. The nature of the rig has been already described. Partaking of the double character of brig and schooner, the sails and spars of the forward-mast being of the former, while those of the after-mast were of the latter construction, seamen have given to this class of shipping the familiar name of hermaphrodites. But though there might be fancied, by this term, some want of the proportions that constitute seemliness, it will be remembered that the departure was only from some former rule of art, and that no violence had been done to those universal and permanent laws which constitute the charm of nature. The models of glass which are seen representing the machinery of a ship, are not more exact or just in their lines than were the cordage and spars of this brigantine. Not a rope varied from its true direction; not a sail but it resembled the neat folds of some prudent housewife; not a mast or a yard was there but it rose into the air, or stretched its arms, with the most fastidious attention to symmetry. All was airy, fanciful, and full of grace, seeming to lend to the fabric a character of unreal lightness and speed. As the boat drew near her side, a change of the air caused the buoyant bark to turn like a vane in its current; and as all the long and pointed proportions of her head-gear came into view,

Ludlow saw beneath the bowsprit an image that might be supposed to make, by means of allegory, some obvious allusions to the character of the vessel. A female form, fashioned with the carver's best skill, stood on the projection of the cutwater. The figure rested lightly on the ball of one foot, while the other was suspended in an easy attitude resembling the airy posture of the famous Mercury of the Bolognese. The drapery was fluttering, scanty, and of a light sea-green tint, as if it had imbibed a hue from the element beneath. The face was of that dark bronzed color which human ingenuity has from time immemorial adopted as the best medium to portray a superhuman expression. The locks were disheveled, wild, and rich; the eye full of such a meaning as might be fancied to glitter in the organs of a sorceress; while a smile so strangely meaning and malign played about the mouth, that the young sailor started when it first met his view, as if a living thing had returned his look.

"Witchcraft and necromancy!" grumbled the alderman, as this extraordinary image came suddenly on his vision also. "Here is a brazen-looking hussy! and one who might rob the queen's treasury itself, without remorse! Your eyes are young, patroon: what is that the minx holds so impudently above her head?"

"It seems an open book, with letters of red written on its pages. One need not be a conjurer to divine it is no extract from the Bible."

"Nor from the statute books of Queen Anne. I warrant me 'tis a ledger of profit gained in her many wanderings. Goggling and leers! the bold air of the confident creature is enough to put an honest man out of countenance!"

"Wilt read the motto of the witch?" demanded he of the India shawl, whose eye had been studying the detail of the brigantine's equipment, rather than attending to the object which so much attracted the looks of his companions. "The night air has tautened the cordage of that flying jib-boom, fellows, until it begins to lift its nose like a squeamish cockney when he holds it over salt water! See to it, and bring the spar in line; else we shall have a reproof from the sorceress, who little likes to have any of her limbs deranged. Here, gentlemen, the opinions of the lady may be read as clearly as a woman's mind can ever be fathomed."

While speaking to his crew, Tiller had changed the direction of the boat; and it was soon lying, in obedience to a motion of his hand, directly beneath the wild and significant-looking image just described. The letters in red were now distinctly visible; and when Alderman Van Beverout had adjusted his spectacles, each of the party read the following sentence:—

> "Albeit I never lend nor borrow,
> By taking, nor by giving of excess,
> Yet to supply the ripe wants of my friend,
> I'll break a custom." — 'Merchant of Venice.'

"The brazen!" exclaimed Myndert, when he had gone through this quotation from the immortal bard. "Ripe or green, one could not wish to be the friend of so impudent a thing; and then to impute such sentiments to any respectable commercial man, whether of Venice or Amsterdam! Let us board the brigantine, friend mariner, and end the connection ere foul mouths begin to traduce our motives for the visit."

"The overdriven ship plows the seas too deep for speed; we shall get into port in better season without this haste. Wilt take another look into the lady's pages? A woman's mind is never known at the first answer."

The speaker raised the rattan he still carried, and caused a page of painted metal to turn on hinges that were so artfully concealed as not to be visible. A new surface, with another extract, was seen.

"What is it, what is it, patroon?" demanded the burgher, who appeared greatly to distrust the discretion of the sorceress. "Follies and rhymes! but this is the way of the whole sex; when nature has denied them tongues, they invent other means of speech."

> "Porters of the sea and land
> Thus do go about, about;
> Thrice to thine, and thrice to thine;
> And thrice again to make up nine."

"Rank nonsense!" continued the burgher. "It is well for those who can, to add thrice and thrice to their stores; but look you, patroon — it is a thriving trade that can double the value of the adventure, and that with reasonable risks and months of patient watching."

"We have other pages," resumed Tiller, "but our affairs drag for want of attending to them. One may read much good matter

in the book of the sorceress, when there is leisure and opportunity. I often take occasion, in the calms, to look into her
volume; and it is rare to find the same moral twice told, as these
brave seamen can swear." . . .

If the exterior of the brigantine was so graceful in form and
so singular in arrangement, the interior was still more worthy of
observation. There were two small cabins beneath the main
deck, one on each side of, and immediately adjoining, the limited
space that was destined to receive her light but valuable cargoes.
It was into one of these that Tiller had descended like a man
who freely entered into his own apartment; but partly above and
nearer to the stern was a suite of little rooms that were fitted
and finished in a style altogether different. The equipments were
those of a yacht, rather than those which might be supposed
suited to the pleasures of even the most successful dealer in
contraband.

The principal deck had been sunk several feet, commencing
at the aftermost bulkhead of the cabins of the subordinate officers, in a manner to give the necessary height, without inter-
fering with the line of the brigantine's shear. The arrangement
was consequently not to be seen by an observer who was not
admitted into the vessel itself. A descent of a step or two,
however, brought the visitors to the level of the cabin floor,
and into an ante-room that was evidently fitted for the convenience of the domestic. A small silver hand-bell lay on a table,
and Tiller rang it lightly, like one whose ordinary manner was
restrained by respect. It was answered by the appearance of a
boy, whose years could not exceed ten, and whose attire was so
whimsical as to merit description.

The material of the dress of this young servitor of Neptune
was a light rose-colored silk, cut in a fashion to resemble the
habits formerly worn by pages of the great. His body was
belted by a band of gold, a collar of fine thread lace floated on
his neck and shoulders, and even his feet were clad in a sort
of buskins, that were ornamented with fringes of real lace and
tassels of bullion. The form and features of the child were
delicate, and his air as unlike as possible to the coarse and
brusque manner of a vulgar ship-boy.

"Waste and prodigality!" muttered the alderman, when this
extraordinary little usher presented himself in answer to the
summons of Tiller. "This is the very wantonness of cheap

goods and an unfettered commerce! There is enough of Mech-
lin, patroon, on the shoulders of that urchin, to deck the
stomacher of the Queen. 'Fore George, goods were cheap in the
market when the young scoundrel had his livery!"

The surprise was not confined, however, to the observant and
frugal burgher. Ludlow and Van Staats of Kinderhook manifested equal amazement, though their wonder was exhibited in a
less characteristic manner. The former turned short to demand
the meaning of this masquerade, when he perceived that the hero
of the India shawl had disappeared. They were then alone with
the fantastic page, and it became necessary to trust to his
intelligence for directions how to proceed.

"Who art thou, child?—and who has sent thee hither?"
demanded Ludlow. The boy raised a cap of the same rose-
colored silk, and pointed to an image of a female, with a swarthy
face and a malign smile, painted with exceeding art on its
front.

"I serve the sea-green lady, with the others of the brigantine."

"And who is this lady of the color of shallow water, and
whence come you in particular?"

"This is her likeness: if you would speak with her, she
stands on the cutwater, and rarely refuses an answer."

"'Tis odd that a form of wood should have the gift of
speech!"

"Dost think her, then, of wood?" returned the child, looking
timidly and yet curiously up into the face of Ludlow. "Others
have said the same; but those who know best, deny it. She
does not answer with a tongue, but the book has always something to say."

"Here is a grievous deception practiced on the superstition
of this boy: I have read the book, and can make but little of its
meaning."

"Then read again. 'Tis by many reaches that the leeward
vessel gains upon the wind. My master has bid me bring you
in—"

"Hold—thou hast both master and mistress? You have told
us the latter, but we would know something of the former. Who
is thy master?"

The boy smiled and looked aside, as if he hesitated to
answer.

"Nay, refuse not to reply. I come with the authority of the Queen."

"He tells us that the sea-green lady is our queen, and that we have no other."

"Rashness and rebellion!" muttered Myndert; "but this fool-hardiness will one day bring as pretty a brigantine as ever sailed in the narrow seas to condemnation; and then will there be rumors abroad, and characters cracked, till every lover of gossip in the Americas shall be tired of defamation."

"It is a bold subject that dares say this!" rejoined Ludlow, who heeded not the by-play of the alderman: "your master has a name?"

"We never hear it. When Neptune boards us, under the tropics, he always hails the Skimmer of the Seas, and then they answer. The old god knows us well, for we pass his latitude oftener than other ships, they say."

"You are then a cruiser of some service in the brigantine? no doubt you have trod many distant shores, belonging to so swift a craft?"

"I!—I never was on the land!" returned the boy, thought-fully. "It must be droll to be there: they say one can hardly walk, it is so steady! I put a question to the sea-green lady before we came to the narrow inlet, to know when I was to go ashore."

"And she answered?"

"It was some time first. Two watches were passed before a word was to be seen; at last I got the lines. I believe she mocked me, though I have never dared show it to my master, that he might say."

"Hast the words here?—perhaps we might assist thee, as there are some among us who know most of the sea paths."

The boy looked timidly and suspiciously round; then thrusting a hand hurriedly into a pocket, he drew forth two bits of paper, each of which contained a scrawl, and both of which had evidently been much thumbed and studied.

"Here," he said, in a voice that was suppressed nearly to a whisper. "This was on the first page. I was so frightened lest the lady should be angry, that I did not look again till the next watch; and then," turning the leaf, "I found this."

Ludlow took the bit of paper first offered, and read, written in a child's hand, the following extract:—

> «I pray thee
> Remember, I have done thee worthy service;
> Told thee no lies, made no mistakings, served
> Without or grudge or grumblings.»

"I thought that 'twas in mockery," continued the boy, when he saw by the eye of the young captain that he had read the quotation; "for 'twas very like, though more prettily worded than that which I had said myself!"

"And what was the second answer?"

"This was found in the first morning watch," the child returned, reading the second extract himself:—

> «'Thou think'st
> It much to tread the ooze of the salt deep,
> And run upon the sharp wind of the north!'

"I never dared to ask again. But what matters that? They say the ground is rough and difficult to walk on; that earthquakes shake it, and make holes to swallow cities; that men slay each other on the highways for money, and that the houses I see on the hills must always remain in the same spot. It must be very melancholy to live always in the same spot; but then it must be odd never to feel a motion!"

"Except the occasional rocking of an earthquake. Thou art better afloat, child—but thy master, the Skimmer of the Seas—"

"Hist!" whispered the boy, raising a finger for silence. "He has come up into the great cabin. In a moment we shall have his signal to enter."

A few light touches on the strings of a guitar followed, and then a symphony was rapidly and beautifully executed by one in the adjoining apartment.

"Alida herself is not more nimble-fingered," whispered the alderman; "and I never heard the girl touch the Dutch lute that cost a hundred Holland guilders, with a livelier movement!"

Ludlow signed for silence. A fine manly voice, of great richness and depth, was soon heard, singing to an accompaniment on the same instrument. The air was grave, and altogether unusual for the social character of one who dwelt upon the ocean, being chiefly in recitation. The words, as near as might be distinguished, ran as follows:—

"My brigantine!
Just in thy mold and beauteous in thy form,
 Gentle in roll and buoyant on the surge,
Light as the sea-fowl rocking in the storm,
 In breeze and gale thy onward course we urge —
  My water-queen!

"Lady of mine!
More light and swift than thou none thread the sea,
 With surer keel, or steadier on its path;
We brave each waste of ocean mystery,
 And laugh to hear the howling tempest's wrath! —
  For we are thine!

"My brigantine!
Trust to the mystic power that points thy way,
 Trust to the eye that pierces from afar,
Trust the red meteors that around thee play,
 And fearless trust the sea-green lady's star —
  Thou bark divine!"

"He often sings thus," whispered the boy, when the song was ended: "they say the sea-green lady loves music that tells of the ocean and of her power.—Hark! he has bid me enter."

"He did but touch the strings of the guitar again, boy."

"'Tis his signal when the weather is fair. When we have the whistlings of the wind and the roar of the water, then he has a louder call."

Ludlow would have gladly listened longer; but the boy opened a door, and pointing the way to those he conducted, he silently vanished himself behind a curtain.

The visitors, more particularly the young commander of the Coquette, found new subjects of admiration and wonder on entering the main cabin of the brigantine. The apartment, considering the size of the vessel, was spacious and high. It received light from a couple of windows in the stern, and it was evident that two smaller rooms, one on each of the quarters, shared with it in this advantage. The space between these state-rooms, as they are called in nautical language, necessarily formed a deep alcove, which might be separated from the outer portion of the cabin by a curtain of crimson damask that now hung in festoons from a beam fashioned into a gilded cornice. A luxurious-looking pile of cushions, covered with red morocco, lay along the transom, in the manner of an Eastern divan; and against the bulkhead of each state-room stood an agrippina of mahogany, that was lined with the same material. Neat and tasteful cases for books were suspended here and there, and the guitar which had so lately been used lay on a small table of some precious wood, that occupied the centre of the alcove. There were also other implements, like those which occupy the leisure of a cultivated but perhaps an effeminate rather than a vigorous mind, scattered around; some evidently long neglected, and others appearing to have been more recently in favor.

The outer portion of the cabin was furnished in a similar style, though it contained many more of the articles that ordinarily belong to domestic economy. It had its agrippina, its piles of cushions, its chairs of beautiful wood, its cases for books, and its neglected instruments, intermixed with fixtures of more solid and permanent appearance, which were arranged to meet the violent motion that was often unavoidable in so small a bark. There was a slight hanging of crimson damask around the whole apartment; and here and there a small mirror was let into the bulkheads and ceilings. All the other parts were of a rich mahogany, relieved by panels of rosewood, that gave an appearance of exquisite finish to the cabin. The floor was covered with a mat of the finest texture, and of a fragrance that announced both its freshness and the fact that the grass had been the growth of a warm and luxuriant climate. The place, as was indeed the whole vessel, so far as the keen eye of Ludlow could detect, was entirely destitute of arms; not even a pistol or a sword being suspended in those places where weapons of that description are usually seen, in all vessels employed either in war or in a trade that might oblige those who sail them to deal in violence.

In the centre of the alcove stood the youthful-looking and extraordinary person who, in so unceremonious a manner, had visited La Cour des Fées the preceding night. His dress was much the same, in fashion and material, as when last seen: still it had been changed; for on the breast of the silken frock was painted an image of the sea-green lady, done with exquisite skill, and in a manner to preserve the whole of the wild and unearthly character of the expression. The wearer of this singular ornament leaned lightly against the little table, and as he bowed with entire self-possession to his guests, his face was lighted with a smile that seemed to betray melancholy no less than courtesy. At the same time he raised his cap, and stood in the rich jet-black locks with which nature had so exuberantly shaded his forehead.

The manner of the visitors was less easy. The deep anxiety with which both Ludlow and the patroon had undertaken to board the notorious smuggler had given place to an amazement and a curiosity that caused them nearly to forget their errand; while Alderman Van Beverout appeared shy and suspicious, manifestly thinking less of his niece than of the consequences of so remarkable an interview. They all returned the salutation of their host, though each waited for him to speak.

THE BRIGANTINE'S ESCAPE THROUGH HELL-GATE

From 'The Water-Witch'

AT SUCH moments of intense anxiety, the human mind is wont to seek support in the opinions of others. Notwithstanding the increasing velocity and the critical condition of his own vessel, Ludlow cast a glance in order to ascertain the determination of the "Skimmer of the Seas." Blackwell's was already behind them, and as the two currents were again united, the brigantine had luffed up into the entrance of the dangerous passage, and now followed within two hundred feet of the Coquette, directly in her wake. The bold and manly-looking mariner who controlled her stood between the knight-heads, just above the image of his pretended mistress, where he examined the foaming reefs, the whirling eddies, and the varying currents, with folded arms and a riveted eye. A glance was exchanged between the two officers, and the free-trader raised his sea-cap. Ludlow was too courteous not to return the salutation; then all his senses were engrossed by the care of his ship. A rock lay before them, over which the water broke in a loud and unceasing roar. For an instant it seemed that the vessel could not avoid the danger; then it was already past.

"Brace up!" said Ludlow, in the calm tones that denote a forced tranquillity.

"Luff!" called out the Skimmer, so quickly as to show that he took the movements of the cruiser for his guide. The ship came closer to the wind, but the sudden bend in the stream no longer permitted her to steer in a direct line with its course. Though drifting to windward with vast rapidity, her way through the water, which was greatly increased by the contrary actions of the wind and tide, caused the cruiser to shoot across the current; while a reef, over which the water madly tumbled, lay immediately in her course. The danger seemed too imminent for the observances of nautical etiquette, and Trysail called aloud that the ship must be thrown aback, or she was lost.

"Hard-a-lee!" shouted Ludlow, in the strong voice of authority. "Up with everything — tacks and sheets! — main-top-sail haul!"

The ship seemed as conscious of her danger as any on her decks. The bows whirled away from the foaming reef, and as the sails caught the breeze on their opposite surfaces, they aided in bringing her head in the contrary direction. A minute had scarcely passed ere she was aback, and in the next she was about and full again. The intensity of the brief exertion kept Trysail fully employed; but no sooner had he leisure to look ahead than he again called aloud: —

"Here is another roarer under her bows. Luff, sir, luff, or we are upon it!"

"Hard down your helm!" once again came in deep tones from Ludlow. "Let fly your sheets — throw all aback, forward and aft — away with the yards, with a will, men!"

There was need for all of these precautions. Though the ship had so happily escaped the dangers of the first reef, a turbulent and roaring caldron in the water which as representing the element in ebullition is called "the Pot," lay so directly before her as to render the danger apparently inevitable. But the power of the canvas was not lost on this trying occasion. The forward motion of the ship diminished, and as the current still swept her swiftly to windward, her bows did not enter the rolling waters until the hidden rocks which caused the commotion had been passed. The yielding vessel rose and fell in the agitated water, as if in homage to the whirlpool; but the deep keel was unharmed.

"If the ship shoot ahead twice her length more, her bows will touch the eddy," exclaimed the vigilant master.

Ludlow looked around him for a single moment in indecision. The waters were whirling and roaring on every side, and the sails began to lose their power as the ship drew near the bluff which forms the second angle in this critical pass. He saw by objects on the land that he still approached the shore, and he had recourse to the seaman's last expedient.

"Let go both anchors!" was the final order.

The fall of the massive iron into the water was succeeded by the rumbling of the cable. The first effort to check the progress of the vessel appeared to threaten dissolution to the whole fabric, which trembled under the shock from its mastheads to the keel. But the enormous rope again yielded, and smoke was seen rising round the wood which held it. The ship whirled with the sudden check, and sheered wildly in toward the shore. Met by the helm, and again checked by the efforts of the crew, she threatened to defy restraint. There was an instant when all on board expected to hear the cable snap; but the upper sails filled, and as the wind was now brought over the taffrail, the force of the current was in a great degree met by that of the breeze.

The ship answered her helm and became stationary, while the water foamed against her cutwater as if she were driven ahead with the power of a brisk breeze.

The time from the moment when the Coquette entered the Gate to that when she anchored below "the Pot," though the distance was nearly a mile, seemed but a minute. Certain however that his ship was now checked, the thoughts of Ludlow returned to their other duties with the quickness of lightning.

"Clear away the grapnels," he eagerly cried; "stand by to heave, and haul in!—heave!"

But that the reader may better comprehend the motive of this sudden order, he must consent to return to the entrance of the dangerous passage, and accompany the Water-Witch also in her hazardous experiment to get through without a pilot.

The abortive attempt of the brigantine to stem the tide at the western end of Blackwell's will be remembered. It had no other effect than to place her pursuer more in advance, and to convince her own commander that he had now no other resource than to continue his course; for had he anchored, boats would have insured his capture. When the two vessels appeared off the eastern end of the island, the Coquette was ahead — a fact that the experienced free-trader did not at all regret. He profited by the circumstance to follow her movements, and to make a

favorable entrance into the uncertain currents. To him, Hell-
Gate was known only by its fearful reputation among mariners;
and unless he might avail himself of the presence of the cruiser,
he had no other guide than his own general knowledge of the
power of the element.

When the Coquette had tacked, the calm and observant Skimmer was satisfied with throwing his head-sails flat to the mast.
From that instant the brigantine lay floating in the current,
neither advancing nor receding a foot, and always keeping her
position at a safe distance from the ship, that was so adroitly
made to answer the purposes of a beacon. The sails were
watched with the closest care; and so nicely was the delicate
machine tended, that it would have been at any moment in her
people's power to have lessened her way by turning to the
stream. The Coquette was followed till she anchored, and the
call on board the cruiser to heave the grapnels had been given,
because the brigantine was apparently floating directly down on
her broadside.

When the grapnels were hove from the royal cruiser, the free-
trader stood on the low poop of his little vessel, within fifty feet
of him who had issued the order. There was a smile of indifference on his firm mouth, while he silently waved a hand to his
own crew. The signal was obeyed by bracing round their yards,
and suffering all the canvas to fill. The brigantine shot quickly
ahead, and the useless irons fell heavily into the water.

"Many thanks for your pilotage, Captain Ludlow!" cried the
daring and successful mariner of the shawl, as his vessel, borne
on by wind and current, receded rapidly from the cruiser.
"You will find me off Montauk; for affairs still keep us on the
coast. Our lady has however put on the blue mantle, and ere
many settings of the sun we shall look for deep water. Take
good care of her Majesty's ship, I pray thee, for she has neither
a more beautiful nor a faster."

One thought succeeded another with the tumult of a torrent
in the mind of Ludlow. As the brigantine lay directly under
his broadside, the first impulse was to use his guns; at the next
moment he was conscious that before they could be cleared,
distance would render them useless. His lips had nearly parted
with intent to order the cables cut, but he remembered the
speed of the brigantine, and hesitated. A sudden freshening
of the breeze decided his course. Finding that the ship was

enabled to keep her station, he ordered the crew to thrust the whole of the enormous ropes through the hawse-holes; and freed from the restraint, he abandoned the anchors until an opportunity to reclaim them should offer.

The operation of slipping the cables consumed several minutes; and when the Coquette, with everything set, was again steering in pursuit, the Water-Witch was already beyond the reach of her guns. Both vessels however held on their way, keeping as near as possible to the centre of the stream, and trusting more to fortune than to any knowledge of the channel for safety.

When passing the two small islands that lie at no great distance from the Gate, a boat was seen moving toward the royal cruiser. A man in it pointed to the signal, which was still flying, and offered his services.

"Tell me," demanded Ludlow eagerly, "has yonder brigantine taken a pilot?"

"By her movements, I judge not. She brushed the sunken rock off the mouth of Flushing Bay; and as she passed, I heard the song of the lead. I should have gone on board myself, but the fellow rather flies than sails; and as for signals, he seems to mind none but his own!"

"Bring us up with him, and fifty guineas is thy reward!"

The slow-moving pilot, who in truth had just awakened from a refreshing sleep, opened his eyes, and seemed to gather a new impulse from the promise. When his questions were asked and answered, he began deliberately to count on his fingers all the chances that still existed of a vessel, whose crew was ignorant of the navigation, falling into their hands.

"Admitting that by keeping mid-channel she goes clear of White Stone and Frogs," he said, giving to Throgmorton's its vulgar name, "he must be a wizard to know that the Stepping-Stones lie directly across his course, and that a vessel must steer away northerly or bring up on rocks that will as surely hold him as if he were built there. Then he runs his chance for the Executioners, which are as prettily placed as needs be to make our trade flourish; besides the Middle Ground farther east, though I count but little on that, having often tried to find it myself, without success. Courage, noble captain! if the fellow be the man you say, we shall get a nearer look at him before the sun sets; for certainly he who has run the Gate without a pilot in safety, has had as much good luck as can fall to his share in one day."

The opinion of the East River Branch proved erroneous. Notwithstanding the hidden perils by which she was environed, the Water-Witch continued her course, with a speed that increased as the wind rose with the sun, and with an impunity from harm that amazed all who were in the secret of her situation. Off Throgmorton's there was, in truth, a danger that might even have baffled the sagacity of the followers of the mysterious lady, had they not been aided by accident. This is the point where the straitened arm of the sea expands into the basin of the sound. A broad and inviting passage lies directly before the navigator, while, like the flattering prospects of life, numberless hidden obstacles are in wait to arrest the unheeding and ignorant.

The "Skimmer of the Seas" was deeply practiced in all the intricacies and dangers of shoals and rocks. Most of his life had been passed in threading the one or in avoiding the other. So keen and quick had his eye become in detecting the presence of any of those signs which forewarn the mariner of danger, that a ripple on the surface, or a deeper shade in the color of the water, rarely escaped his vigilance. Seated on the topsail-yard of his brigantine, he had overlooked the passage from the moment they were through the Gate, and issued his mandates to those below with a precision and promptitude that were not surpassed by the trained conductor of the Coquette himself. But when his sight embraced the wide reach of water that lay in front, as his little vessel swept round the headland of Throgmorton, he believed there no longer existed a reason for so much care. Still there was a motive for hesitation. A heavily molded and dull-sailing coaster was going eastward not a league ahead of the brigantine, while one of the light sloops of those waters was coming westward still farther in the distance. Notwithstanding the wind was favorable to each alike, both vessels had deviated from the direct line and were steering toward a common centre, near an island that was placed more than a mile to the northward of the straight course. A mariner like him of the India shawl could not overlook so obvious an intimation of a change in the channel. The Water-Witch was kept away, and her lighter sails were lowered, in order to allow the royal cruiser, whose lofty canvas was plainly visible above the land, to draw

near. When the Coquette was seen also to diverge, there no
longer remained a doubt of the direction necessary to be taken;
and everything was quickly set upon the brigantine, even to her
studding-sails.   Long ere she reached the island the two coasters
had met, and each again changed its course, reversing that on
which the other had just been sailing.   There was in these
movements as plain an explanation as a seaman could desire,
that the pursued were right.   On reaching the island, therefore,
they again luffed into the wake of the schooner; and having
nearly crossed the sheet of water, they passed the coaster, receiving an assurance in words that all was now plain sailing before
them.

Such was the famous passage of the "Skimmer of the Seas"
through the multiplied and hidden dangers of the eastern channel.   To those who have thus accompanied him, step by step,
through its intricacies and alarms, there may seem nothing extraordinary in the event; but coupled as it was with the character previously earned by that bold mariner, and occurring as it
did in the age when men were more disposed than at present to
put faith in the marvelous, the reader will not be surprised to
learn that it greatly increased his reputation for daring, and had
no small influence on an opinion which was by no means uncommon, that the dealers in contraband were singularly favored
by a power which greatly exceeded that of Queen Anne and all
her servants.

THE DOOM OF ABIRAM WHITE

From 'The Prairie'

ABIRAM gave his downcast partner a glance of his eye, and
withdrew towards a distant roll of the land which bounded
the view towards the east.   The meeting of the pair in
this naked spot was like an interview held above the grave of
their murdered son.   Ishmael signed to his wife to take a seat
beside him on a fragment of rock, and then followed a space during which neither seemed disposed to speak.

"We have journeyed together long, through good and bad,"
Ishmael at length commenced: "much have we had to try us,
and some bitter cups have we been made to swallow, my

woman; but nothing like this has ever before lain in my path."

"It is a heavy cross for a poor, misguided, and sinful woman to bear!" returned Esther, bowing her head to her knees, and partly concealing her face in her dress. "A heavy and a burdensome weight is this to be laid upon the shoulders of a sister and a mother!"

"Ay; therein lies the hardship of the case. I had brought my mind to the punishment of that houseless trapper with no great strivings, for the man had done me few favors, and God forgive me if I suspected him wrongfully of much evil! This is, however, bringing shame in at one door of my cabin in order to drive it out at the other. But shall a son of mine be murdered, and he who did it go at large?—the boy would never rest!"

"Oh, Ishmael, we pushed the matter far! Had little been said, who would have been the wiser? Our consciences might then have been quiet."

"Esther," said the husband, turning on her a reproachful but still a dull regard, "the hour has been, my woman, when you thought another hand had done this wickedness."

"I did, I did! the Lord gave me the feeling as a punishment for my sins! but his mercy was not slow in lifting the veil; I looked into the Book, Ishmael, and there I found the words of comfort."

"Have you that book at hand, woman? it may happen to advise in such a dreary business."

Esther fumbled in her pocket, and was not long in producing the fragment of a Bible which had been thumbed and smoke-dried till the print was nearly illegible. It was the only article in the nature of a book that was to be found among the chattels of the squatter, and it had been preserved by his wife as a melancholy relic of more prosperous, and possibly of more innocent days. She had long been in the habit of resorting to it under the pressure of such circumstances as were palpably beyond human redress, though her spirit and resolution rarely needed support under those that admitted of reparation through any of the ordinary means of reprisal. In this manner Esther had made a sort of convenient ally of the Word of God; rarely troubling it for counsel, however, except when her own incompetency to avert an evil was too apparent to be disputed. We shall leave casuists to determine how far she resembled any other believers in this particular, and proceed directly with the matter before us.

"There are many awful passages in these pages, Ishmael," she said, when the volume was opened and the leaves were slowly turning under her finger, "and some there ar' that teach the rules of punishment."

Her husband made a gesture for her to find one of those brief rules of conduct which have been received among all Christian nations as the direct mandates of the Creator, and which have been found so just that even they who deny their high authority admit their wisdom. Ishmael listened with grave attention as his companion read all those verses which her memory suggested, and which were thought applicable to the situation in which they found themselves. He made her show him the words, which he regarded with a sort of strange reverence. A resolution once taken was usually irrevocable in one who was moved with so much difficulty. He put his hand upon the book and closed the pages himself, as much as to apprise his wife that he was satisfied. Esther, who so well knew his character, trembled at the action, and casting a glance at his steady eye, she said:—

"And yet, Ishmael, my blood and the blood of my children is in his veins! Cannot mercy be shown?"

"Woman," he answered, sternly, "when we believed that miserable old trapper had done this deed, nothing was said of mercy!"

Esther made no reply, but folding her arms upon her breast she sat silent and thoughtful for many minutes. Then she once more turned her anxious gaze upon the countenance of her husband, where she found all passion and care apparently buried in the coldest apathy. Satisfied now that the fate of her brother was sealed, and possibly conscious how well he merited the punishment that was meditated, she no longer thought of mediation. No more words passed between them. Their eyes met for an instant, and then both arose and walked in profound silence towards the encampment.

The squatter found his children expecting his return in the usual listless manner with which they awaited all coming events. The cattle were already herded, and the horses in their gears in readiness to proceed, so soon as he should indicate that such was his pleasure. The children were already in their proper vehicle, and in short, nothing delayed the departure but the absence of the parents of the wild brood.

"Abner," said the father, with the deliberation with which all his proceedings were characterized, "take the brother of your mother from the wagon, and let him stand on the 'arth."

Abiram issued from his place of concealment, trembling, it is true, but far from destitute of hopes as to his final success in appeasing the just resentment of his kinsman. After throwing a glance around him with the vain wish of finding a single countenance in which he might detect a solitary gleam of sympathy, he endeavored to smother those apprehensions that were by this time reviving in their original violence, by forcing a sort of friendly communication between himself and the squatter:—

"The beasts are getting jaded, brother," he said; "and as we have made so good a march already, is it not time to camp? To my eye you may go far before a better place than this is found to pass the night in."

"'Tis well you like it. Your tarry here ar' likely to be long. My sons, draw nigh and listen. Abiram White," he added, lifting his cap, and speaking with a solemnity and steadiness that rendered even his dull mien imposing, "you have slain my first-born, and according to the laws of God and man must you die!"

The kidnapper started at this terrible and sudden sentence, with the terror that one would exhibit who unexpectedly found himself in the grasp of a monster from whose power there was no retreat. Although filled with the most serious forebodings of what might be his lot, his courage had not been equal to look his danger in the face, and with the deceitful consolation with which timid tempers are apt to conceal their desperate condition from themselves, he had rather courted a treacherous relief in his cunning, than prepared himself for the worst.

"Die!" he repeated, in a voice that scarcely issued from his chest; "a man is surely safe among his kinsmen?"

"So thought my boy," returned the squatter, motioning for the team that contained his wife and the girls to proceed, as he very coolly examined the priming of his piece. "By the rifle did you destroy my son; it is fit and just that you meet your end by the same weapon."

Abiram stared about him with a gaze that bespoke an unsettled reason. He even laughed, as if he would not only persuade himself but others that what he heard was some pleasantry intended to try his nerves. But nowhere did his frightful merriment meet with an answering echo. All around was solemn and still. The visages of his nephews were excited, but cold towards him, and that of his former confederate frightfully determined. This very steadiness of mien was a thousand times more alarming and hopeless than any violence could have proved. The latter might possibly have touched his spirit and awakened resistance, but the former threw him entirely on the feeble resources of himself.

"Brother," he said, in a hurried unnatural whisper, "did I hear you?"

"My words are plain, Abiram White: thou hast done murder, and for the same must thou die!"

"Esther! sister, sister! will you leave me? O sister! do you hear my call?"

"I hear one speak from the grave!" returned the husky tones of Esther, as the wagon passed the spot where the criminal stood. "It is the voice of my first-born calling aloud for justice! God have mercy, God have mercy on your soul!"

The team slowly pursued its route, and the deserted Abiram now found himself deprived of the smallest vestige of hope. Still he could not summon fortitude to meet his death, and had not his limbs refused to aid him he would yet have attempted to fly. Then by a sudden revolution from hope to utter despair he fell upon his knees and commenced a prayer, in which cries for mercy to God and to his kinsman were wildly and blasphemously mingled. The sons of Ishmael turned away in horror at the disgusting spectacle, and even the stern nature of the squatter began to bend before so abject misery.

"May that which you ask of him be granted," he said; "but a father can never forget a murdered child."

He was answered by the most humble appeals for time. A week, a day, an hour, were each implored with an earnestness commensurate to the value they receive when a whole life is compressed into their short duration. The squatter was troubled, and at length he yielded in part to the petitions of the criminal. His final purpose was not altered, though he changed the means. "Abner," he said, "mount the rock and look on every side that we may be sure none are nigh."

While his nephew was obeying this order, gleams of reviving hope were seen shooting across the quivering features of the kid-

napper. The report was favorable; nothing having life, the retiring teams excepted, was to be seen. A messenger was however
coming from the latter in great apparent haste. Ishmael awaited
its arrival. He received from the hands of one of his wondering
and frighted girls a fragment of that Book which Esther had
preserved with so much care. The squatter beckoned his child
away, and placed the leaves in the hands of the criminal.

"Esther has sent you this," he said, "that in your last moments you may remember God."

"Bless her, bless her! a good and kind sister has she been to
me! But time must be given that I may read; time, my brother,
time!"

"Time shall not be wanting. You shall be your own executioner, and this miserable office shall pass away from my
hands."

Ishmael proceeded to put his new resolution in force. The
immediate apprehensions of the kidnapper were quieted by an
assurance that he might yet live for days, though his punishment
was inevitable. A reprieve to one abject and wretched as
Abiram temporarily produced the same effects as a pardon. He
was even foremost in assisting in the appalling arrangements;
and of all the actors in that solemn tragedy, his voice alone was
facetious and jocular.

A thin shelf of the rock projected beneath one of the ragged
arms of the willow. It was many feet from the ground, and
admirably adapted to the purpose which in fact its appearance
had suggested. On this little platform the criminal was placed,
his arms bound at the elbows behind his back, beyond the possibility of liberation, with a proper cord leading from his neck to
the limb of the tree. The latter was so placed that when suspended the body could find no foot-hold. The fragment of the
Bible was placed in his hands, and he was left to seek his consolation as he might from its pages.

"And now, Abiram White," said the squatter, when his sons
had descended from completing this arrangement, "I give you
a last and solemn asking. Death is before you in two shapes.
With this rifle can your misery be cut short, or by that cord,
sooner or later, must you meet your end."

"Let me yet live! O Ishmael, you know not how sweet life
is when the last moment draws so nigh!"

"'Tis done," said the squatter, motioning for his assistants to
follow the herds and teams. "And now, miserable man, that it

may prove a consolation to your end, I forgive you my wrongs and leave you to your God.»

Ishmael turned and pursued his way across the plain at his ordinary sluggish and ponderous gait. Though his head was bent a little towards the earth, his inactive mind did not prompt him to cast a look behind. Once indeed he thought he heard his name called in tones that were a little smothered, but they failed to make him pause.

At the spot where he and Esther had conferred he reached the boundary of the visible horizon from the rock. Here he stopped, and ventured a glance in the direction of the place he had just quitted. The sun was near dipping into the plains beyond, and its last rays lighted the naked branches of the willow. He saw the ragged outline of the whole drawn against the glowing heavens, and he even traced the still upright form of the being he had left to his misery. Turning the roll of the swell, he proceeded with the feelings of one who had been suddenly and violently separated from a recent confederate forever.

Within a mile the squatter overtook his teams. His sons had found a place suited to the encampment for the night, and merely awaited his approach to confirm their choice. Few words were necessary to express his acquiescence. Everything passed in a silence more general and remarkable than ever. The chidings of Esther were not heard among her young, or if heard, they were more in the tones of softened admonition than in her usual upbraiding key.

No questions nor explanations passed between the husband and his wife. It was only as the latter was about to withdraw among her children for the night, that the former saw her taking a furtive look at the pan of his rifle. Ishmael bade his sons seek their rest, announcing his intention to look to the safety of the camp in person. When all was still, he walked out upon the prairie with a sort of sensation that he found his breathing among the tents too straitened. The night was well adapted to heighten the feelings which had been created by the events of the day.

The wind had risen with the moon, and it was occasionally sweeping over the plain in a manner that made it not difficult for the sentinel to imagine strange and unearthly sounds were mingling in the blasts. Yielding to the extraordinary impulses of which he was the subject, he cast a glance around to see that all were slumbering in security, and then he strayed towards the swell of land already mentioned. Here the squatter found himself at a point that commanded a view to the east and to the west. Light fleecy clouds were driving before the moon, which was cold and watery, though there were moments when its placid rays were shed from clear blue fields, seeming to soften objects to its own mild loveliness.

For the first time, in a life of so much wild adventure, Ishmael felt a keen sense of solitude. The naked prairies began to assume the forms of illimitable and dreary wastes, and the rushing of the wind sounded like the whisperings of the dead. It was not long before he thought a shriek was borne past him on a blast. It did not sound like a call from earth, but it swept frightfully through the upper air, mingled with the hoarse accompaniment of the wind. The teeth of the squatter were compressed and his huge hand grasped the rifle, as if it would crush the metal. Then came a lull, a fresher blast, and a cry of horror that seemed to have been uttered at the very portals of his ears. A sort of echo burst involuntarily from his own lips, as men shout under unnatural excitement, and throwing his rifle across his shoulder, he proceeded towards the rock with the strides of a giant.

It was not often that the blood of Ishmael moved at the rate with which the fluid circulates in the veins of ordinary men; but now he felt it ready to gush from every pore in his body. The animal was aroused, in his most latent energies. Ever as he advanced he heard those shrieks, which sometimes seemed ringing among the clouds, and sometimes passed so nigh as to appear to brush the earth. At length there came a cry in which there could be no delusion, or to which the imagination could lend no horror. It appeared to fill each cranny of the air, as the visible horizon is often charged to fullness by one dazzling flash of the electric fluid. The name of God was distinctly audible, but it was awfully and blasphemously blended with sounds that may not be repeated. The squatter stopped, and for a moment he covered his ears with his hands. When he withdrew the latter, a low and husky voice at his elbow asked in smothered tones:—

"Ishmael, my man, heard ye nothing?"

"Hist!" returned the husband, laying a powerful arm on Esther, without manifesting the smallest surprise at the unlooked-for presence of his wife. "Hist, woman! if you have the fear of Heaven, be still!"

A profound silence succeeded. Though the wind rose and fell as before, its rushing was no longer mingled with those fearful cries. The sounds were imposing and solemn, but it was the solemnity and majesty of nature.

"Let us go on," said Esther; "all is hushed."

"Woman, what has brought you here?" demanded her husband, whose blood had returned into its former channels, and whose thoughts had already lost a portion of their excitement.

"Ishmael, he murdered our first-born: but it is not meet that the son of my mother should lie upon the ground like the carrion of a dog."

"Follow!" returned the squatter, again grasping his rifle and striding towards the rock. The distance was still considerable; and their approach, as they drew nigh the place of execution, was moderated by awe. Many minutes had passed before they reached a spot where they might distinguish the outlines of the dusky objects.

"Where have you put the body?" whispered Esther. "See, here are pick and spade, that a brother of mine may sleep in the bosom of the earth!"

The moon broke from behind a mass of clouds, and the eye of the woman was enabled to follow the finger of Ishmael. It pointed to a human form swinging in the wind, beneath the ragged and shining arm of the willow. Esther bent her head and veiled her eyes from the sight. But Ishmael drew nigher, and long contemplated his work in awe, though not in compunction. The leaves of the sacred book were scattered on the ground, and even a fragment of the shelf had been displaced by the kidnapper in his agony. But all was now in the stillness of death. The grim and convulsed countenance of the victim was at times brought full into the light of the moon, and again, as the wind lulled, the fatal rope drew a dark line across its bright disk. The squatter raised his rifle with extreme care, and fired. The cord was cut, and the body came lumbering to the earth, a heavy and insensible mass.

Until now Esther had not moved nor spoken. But her hand was not slow to assist in the labor of the hour. The grave was soon dug. It was instantly made to receive its miserable tenant. As the lifeless form descended, Esther, who sustained the head, looked up into the face of her husband with an expression of anguish, and said: —

"Ishmael, my man, it is very terrible! I cannot kiss the corpse of my father's child!"

The squatter laid his broad hand on the bosom of the dead, and said: —

"Abiram White, we all have need of mercy; from my soul do I forgive you! May God in heaven have pity on your sins!"

The woman bowed her face, and imprinted her lips long and fervently on the pallid forehead of her brother. After this came the falling clods and all the solemn sounds of filling a grave. Esther lingered on her knees, and Ishmael stood uncovered while the woman muttered a prayer. All was then finished.

On the following morning the teams and herds of the squatter were seen pursuing their course towards the settlements. As they approached the confines of society the train was blended among a thousand others. Though some of the numerous descendants of this peculiar pair were reclaimed from their lawless and semi-barbarous lives, the principals of the family themselves were never heard of more.

THE BISON STAMPEDE

From 'The Prairie'

THE warrior suddenly paused and bent his face aside, like one who listened with all his faculties absorbed in the act.

Then turning the head of his horse, he rode to the nearest angle of the thicket, and looked intently across the bleak prairie in a direction opposite to the side on which the party stood. Returning slowly from this unaccountable, and, to his observers, startling procedure, he riveted his eyes on Inez, and paced back and forth several times with the air of one who maintained a warm struggle on some difficult point in the recesses of his own thoughts. He had drawn the reins of his impatient steed, and was seemingly about to speak when his head again sank on his chest, and he resumed his former attitude of attention. Galloping like a deer to the place of his former observations, he rode for a moment swiftly in short and rapid circles as if still uncertain of his course, and then darted away like a bird that had been fluttering around its nest before it takes a distant flight. After scouring the plain for a minute he was lost to the eye behind a swell of the land.

The hounds, who had also manifested great uneasiness for some time, followed him for a little distance, and then terminated their chase by seating themselves on the ground and raising their usual low, whining, and warning howls.

These movements had passed in so short a space of time that the old man, while he neglected not to note the smallest incident, had no opportunity of expressing his opinion concerning the stranger's motives. After the Pawnee had disappeared, however, he shook his head and muttered, while he walked slowly to the angle of the thicket that the Indian had just quitted:—

"There are both scents and sounds in the air, though my miserable senses are not good enough to hear the one or to catch the taint of the other."

"There is nothing to be seen," cried Middleton, who kept close at his side. "My ears and my eyes are good, and yet I can assure you that I neither hear nor see anything."

"Your eyes are good! and you are not deaf!" returned the other, with a slight air of contempt; "no, lad, no; they may be good to see across a church, or to hear a town bell, but afore you had passed a year in these prairies you would find yourself taking a turkey for a buffalo, or conceiving fifty times that the roar of a buffalo bull was the thunder of the Lord! There is a deception of natur' in these naked plains in which the air throws up the images like water, and then it is hard to tell the prairies from a sea. But yonder is a sign that a hunter never fails to know."

The trapper pointed to a flight of vultures that were sailing over the plain at no great distance, and apparently in the direction in which the Pawnee had riveted his eyes. At first Middleton could not distinguish the small dark objects that were dotting the dusky clouds; but as they came swiftly onward, first their forms and then their heavy waving wings became distinctly visible.

"Listen!" said the trapper, when he had succeeded in making Middleton see the moving column of birds. "Now you hear the buffaloes, or bisons, as your knowing Doctor sees fit to call them; though buffaloes is their name among all the hunters of these regions. And I conclude that a hunter is a better judge of a beast and of its name," he added, winking at the young soldier, "than any man who has turned over the leaves of a book instead of traveling over the face of the 'arth, in order to find out the natur's of its inhabitants."

"Of their habits, I will grant you," cried the naturalist, who rarely missed an opportunity to agitate any disputed point in his favorite studies. "That is, provided always deference is had to the proper use of definitions, and that they are contemplated with scientific eyes."

"Eyes of a mole! as if any man's eyes were not as good for names as the eyes of any other creatur'! Who named the works of His hand? can you tell me that, with your book and college wisdom? Was it not the first man in the Garden, and is it not a plain consequence that his children inherit his gifts?"

"That is certainly the Mosaic account of the event," said the Doctor; "though your reading is by far too literal!"

"My reading! nay, if you suppose that I have wasted my time in schools, you do such a wrong to my knowledge as one mortal should never lay to the door of another without sufficient reason. If I have ever craved the art of reading, it has been that I might better know the sayings of the book you name, for it is a book which speaks in every line according to human feelings, and therein according to reason."

"And do you then believe," said the Doctor, a little provoked by the dogmatism of his stubborn adversary, and perhaps secretly too confident in his own more liberal, though scarcely as profitable attainments, "do you then believe that all these beasts were literally collected in a garden to be enrolled in the nomenclature of the first man?"

"Why not? I understand your meaning; for it is not needful to live in towns to hear all the devilish devices that the conceit of man can invent to upset his own happiness. What does it prove, except indeed it may be said to prove that the garden He made was not after the miserable fashions of our times, thereby directly giving the lie to what the world calls its civilizing? No, no, the garden of the Lord was the forest then, and is the forest now, where the fruits do grow and the birds do sing, according to his own wise ordering. Now, lady, you may see the mystery of the vultures! There come the buffaloes themselves, and a noble herd it is! I warrant me that Pawnee has a troop of his people in some of the hollows nigh by; and as he has gone scampering after them, you are about to see a glorious chase. It will serve to keep the squatter and his brood under cover, and for ourselves there is little reason to fear. A Pawnee is not apt to be a malicious savage.»

Every eye was now drawn to the striking spectacle that succeeded. Even the timid Inez hastened to the side of Middleton to gaze at the sight, and Paul summoned Ellen from her culinary labors to become a witness of the lively scene.

Throughout the whole of those moving events which it has been our duty to record, the prairies had lain in the majesty of perfect solitude. The heavens had been blackened with the passage of the migratory birds, it is true; but the dogs of the party and the ass of the Doctor were the only quadrupeds that had enlivened the broad surface of the waste beneath. There was now a sudden exhibition of animal life which changed the scene, as it were by magic, to the very opposite extreme.

A few enormous bison bulls were first observed scouring along the most distant roll of the prairie, and then succeeded long files of single beasts, which in their turns were followed by a dark mass of bodies, until the dun-colored herbage of the plain was entirely lost in the deeper hue of their shaggy coats. The herd, as the column spread and thickened, was like the endless flocks of the smaller birds whose extended flanks are so often seen to heave up out of the abyss of the heavens, until they appear as countless as the leaves in those forests over which they wing their endless flight. Clouds of dust shot up in little columns from the centre of the mass, as some animal, more furious than the rest, plowed the plain with his horns; and from time to time a deep hollow bellowing was borne along on the wind, as if a thousand throats vented their plaints in a discordant murmuring.

A long and musing silence reigned in the party as they gazed on this spectacle of wild and peculiar grandeur. It was at length broken by the trapper, who, having been long accustomed to similar sights, felt less of its influence, or rather felt it in a less thrilling and absorbing manner, than those to whom the scene was more novel.

«There go ten thousand oxen in one drove, without keeper or master, except Him who made them and gave them these open plains for their pasture! Ay, it is here that man may see the proofs of his wantonness and folly! Can the proudest governor in all the States go into his fields and slaughter a nobler bullock than is here offered to the meanest hand; and when he has gotten his sirloin or his steak, can he eat it with as good a relish as he who has sweetened his food with wholesome toil, and earned it according to the law of natur', by honestly mastering that which the Lord hath put before him?"

"If the prairie platter is smoking with a buffalo's hump, I answer no," interrupted the luxurious bee-hunter.

"Ay, boy, you have tasted, and you feel the genuine reasoning of the thing! But the herd is heading a little this-away, and it behooves us to make ready for their visit. If we hide ourselves altogether, the horned brutes will break through the place and trample us beneath their feet like so many creeping worms; so we will just put the weak ones apart, and take post, as becomes men and hunters, in the van."

As there was but little time to make the necessary arrangements, the whole party set about them in good earnest. Inez and Ellen were placed in the edge of the thicket on the side furthest from the approaching herd. Asinus was posted in the centre, in consideration of his nerves; and then the old man with his three male companions divided themselves in such a manner as they thought would enable them to turn the head of the rushing column, should it chance to approach too nigh their position. By the vacillating movements of some fifty or a hundred bulls that led the advance, it remained questionable for many moments what course they intended to pursue. But a tremendous and painful roar which came from behind the cloud of dust that rose in the centre of the herd, and which was horridly answered by the screams of the carrion-birds that were greedily sailing directly above the flying drove, appeared to give a new impulse to their flight and at once to remove every symptom of indecision. As if glad to seek the smallest signs of the forest, the whole of the affrighted herd became steady in its direction, rushing in a straight line toward the little cover of bushes which has already been so often named.

The appearance of danger was now in reality of a character to try the stoutest nerves. The flanks of the dark moving mass were advanced in such a manner as to make a concave line of the front; and every fierce eye that was glaring from the shaggy wilderness of hair in which the entire heads of the males were enveloped, was riveted with mad anxiety on the thicket. It

seemed as if each beast strove to outstrip his neighbor in gaining this desired cover; and as thousands in the rear pressed
blindly on those in front, there was the appearance of an imminent risk that the leaders of the herd would be precipitated on
the concealed party, in which case the destruction of every one of
them was certain.   Each of our adventurers felt the danger of
his situation in a manner peculiar to his individual character
and circumstances.

Middleton wavered.   At times he felt inclined to rush through
the bushes, and seizing Inez, attempt to fly.   Then recollect-
ing the impossibility of outstripping the furious speed of an
alarmed bison, he felt for his arms, determined to make head
against the countless drove.   The faculties of Dr. Battius were
quickly wrought up to the very summit of mental delusion.   The
dark forms of the herd lost their distinctness, and then the naturalist began to fancy he beheld a wild collection of all the
creatures of the world rushing upon him in a body, as if to
revenge the various injuries which, in the course of a life of
indefatigable labor in behalf of the natural sciences, he had
inflicted on their several genera.   The paralysis it occasioned in
his system was like the effect of the incubus.   Equally unable to
fly or to advance, he stood riveted to the spot, until the infatuation became so complete that the worthy naturalist was beginning, by a desperate effort of scientific resolution, even to class
the different specimens.   On the other hand, Paul shouted, and
called on Ellen to come and assist him in shouting, but his voice
was lost in the bellowings and trampling of the herd.   Furious,
and yet strangely excited by the obstinacy of the brutes and the
wildness of the sight, and nearly maddened by sympathy and a
species of unconscious apprehension in which the claims of nature
were singularly mingled with concern for his mistress, he nearly
split his throat in exhorting his aged friend to interfere.

"Come forth, old trapper," he shouted, "with your prairie
inventions! or we shall be all smothered under a mountain of
buffalo humps!"

The old man, who had stood all this while leaning on his
rifle and regarding the movements of the herd with a steady
eye, now deemed it time to strike his blow.   Leveling his piece
at the foremost bull, with an agility that would have done credit
to his youth, he fired.   The animal received the bullet on the
matted hair between his horns, and fell to his knees; but shaking

his head he instantly arose, the very shock seeming to increase his exertions. There was now no longer time to hesitate. Throwing down his rifle, the trapper stretched forth his arms, and advanced from the cover with naked hands directly towards the rushing column of the beasts.

The figure of a man, when sustained by the firmness and steadiness that intellect can only impart, rarely fails of commanding respect from all the inferior animals of the creation. The leading bulls recoiled, and for a single instant there was a sudden stop to their speed, a dense mass of bodies rolling up in front until hundreds were seen floundering and tumbling on the plain. Then came another of those hollow bellowings from the rear, and set the herd again in motion. The head of the column, however, divided, the immovable form of the trapper cutting it as it were into two gliding streams of life. Middleton and Paul instantly profited by his example, and extended the feeble barrier by a similar exhibition of their own persons.

For a few moments the new impulse given to the animals in front served to protect the thicket. But as the body of the herd pressed more and more upon the open line of its defenders, and the dust thickened so as to obscure their persons, there was at each instant a renewed danger of the beasts breaking through. It became necessary for the trapper and his companions to become still more and more alert; and they were gradually yielding before the headlong multitude, when a furious bull darted by Middleton so near as to brush his person, and at the next instant swept through the thicket with the velocity of the wind.

"Close, and die for the ground," shouted the old man, "or a thousand of the devils will be at his heels!"

All their efforts would have proved fruitless however against the living torrent, had not Asinus, whose domains had just been so rudely entered, lifted his voice in the midst of the uproar. The most sturdy and furious of the bulls trembled at the alarming and unknown cry, and then each individual brute was seen madly pressing from that very thicket which the moment before he had endeavored to reach, with the eagerness with which the murderer seeks the sanctuary.

As the stream divided the place became clear; the two dark columns moving obliquely from the copse, to unite again at the distance of a mile, on its opposite side. The instant the old man saw the sudden effect which the voice of Asinus had produced, he coolly commenced reloading his rifle, indulging at the same time in a heartfelt fit of his silent and peculiar merriment.

"There they go, like dogs with so many half-filled shot-pouches dangling at their tails, and no fear of their breaking their order; for what the brutes in the rear didn't hear with their own ears, they'll conceit they did: besides, if they change their minds, it may be no hard matter to get the jack to sing the rest of his tune!"

"The ass has spoken, but Balaam is silent!" cried the bee-hunter, catching his breath after a repeated burst of noisy mirth, that might possibly have added to the panic of the buffaloes by its vociferation. "The man is as completely dumfounded as if a swarm of young bees had settled on the end of his tongue, and he not willing to speak for fear of their answer."

"How now, friend," continued the trapper, addressing the still motionless and entranced naturalist; "how now, friend; are you, who make your livelihood by booking the names and natur's of the beasts of the fields and the fowls of the air, frightened at a herd of scampering buffaloes? Though perhaps you are ready to dispute my right to call them by a word that is in the mouth of every hunter and trader on the frontier!"

The old man was however mistaken in supposing he could excite the benumbed faculties of the Doctor by provoking a discussion. From that time henceforth he was never known, except on one occasion, to utter a word that indicated either the species or the genus of the animal. He obstinately refused the nutritious food of the whole ox family; and even to the present hour, now that he is established in all the scientific dignity and security of a savant in one of the maritime towns, he turns his back with a shudder on those delicious and unrivaled viands that are so often seen at the suppers of the craft, and which are unequaled by anything that is served under the same name at the boasted chop-houses of London or at the most renowned of the Parisian restaurants.

RUNNING THE GAUNTLET

From 'The Last of the Mohicans'

THERE yet lingered sufficient light in the heavens to exhibit those bright openings among the tree-tops where different paths left the clearing to enter the depths of the wilderness. Beneath one of them, a line of warriors issued from the woods and advanced slowly toward the dwellings. One in front bore a short pole, on which, as it afterward appeared, were suspended several human scalps. The startling sounds that Duncan had heard were what the whites have not inappropriately called the "death-hallo"; and each repetition of the cry was intended to announce to the tribe the fate of an enemy. Thus far the knowledge of Heyward assisted him in the explanation; and as he knew that the interruption was caused by the unlooked-for return of a successful war-party, every disagreeable sensation was quieted in inward congratulations for the opportune relief and insignificance it conferred on himself.

When at the distance of a few hundred feet from the lodges, the newly arrived warriors halted. The plaintive and terrific cry which was intended to represent equally the wailings of the dead and the triumph of the victors, had entirely ceased. One of their number now called aloud, in words that were far from appalling, though not more intelligible to those for whose ears they were intended than their expressive yells. It would be difficult to convey a suitable idea of the savage ecstasy with which the news thus imparted was received. The whole encampment in a moment became a scene of the most violent bustle and commotion. The warriors drew their knives, and flourishing them, they arranged themselves in two lines, forming a lane that extended from the war-party to the lodges. The squaws seized clubs, axes, or whatever weapon of offense first offered itself to their hands, and rushed eagerly to act their part in the cruel game that was at hand. Even the children would not be excluded; but boys, little able to wield the instruments, tore the tomahawks from the belts of their fathers, and stole into the ranks, apt imitators of the savage traits exhibited by their parents.

Large piles of brush lay scattered about the clearing, and a wary and aged squaw was occupied firing as many as might serve to light the coming exhibition. As the flame arose, its power exceeded that of the parting day, and assisted to render objects at the same time more distinct and more hideous. The whole scene formed a striking picture, whose frame was composed of the dark and tall border of pines. The warriors just arrived were the most distant figures. A little in advance stood two men, who were apparently selected from the rest as the principal actors in what was to follow. The light was not strong enough to render their features distinct, though it was quite evident that they were governed by very different emotions. While one stood erect and firm, prepared to meet his fate like a hero, the other bowed his head, as if palsied by terror or stricken with shame. The high-spirited Duncan felt a powerful impulse of admiration and pity toward the former, though no opportunity could offer to exhibit his generous emotions. He watched his slightest movement, however, with eager eyes; and as he traced the fine outline of his admirably proportioned and active frame, he endeavored to persuade himself that if the powers of man, seconded by such noble resolution, could bear one harmless through so severe a trial, the youthful captive before him might hope for success in the hazardous race he was about to run. Insensibly the young man drew nigher to the swarthy lines of the Hurons, and scarcely breathed, so intense became his interest in the spectacle. Just then the signal yell was given, and the momentary quiet which had preceded it was broken by a burst of cries that far exceeded any before heard. The most abject of the two victims continued motionless; but the other bounded from the place at the cry, with the activity and swiftness of a deer. Instead of rushing through the hostile lines as had been expected, he just entered the dangerous defile, and before time was given for a single blow, turned short, and leaping the heads of a row of children, he gained at once the exterior and safer side of the formidable array. The artifice was answered by a hundred voices raised in imprecations, and the whole of the excited multitude broke from their order and spread themselves about the place in wild confusion.

A dozen blazing piles now shed their lurid brightness on the place, which resembled some unhallowed and supernatural arena in which malicious demons had assembled to act their bloody and lawless rites. The forms in the background looked like unearthly beings gliding before the eye and cleaving the air with frantic and unmeaning gestures; while the savage passions of such as passed the flames were rendered fearfully distinct by the gleams that shot athwart their inflamed visages.

It will easily be understood that amid such a concourse of vindictive enemies, no breathing-time was allowed the fugitive. There was a single moment when it seemed as if he would have reached the forest; but the whole body of his captors threw themselves before him, and drove him back into the centre of his relentless persecutors. Turning like a headed deer, he shot with the swiftness of an arrow through a pillar of forked flame, and passing the whole multitude harmless he appeared on the opposite side of the clearing. Here too he was met and turned by a few of the older and more subtle of the Hurons. Once more he tried the throng, as if seeking safety in its blindness; and then several moments succeeded, during which Duncan believed the active and courageous young stranger was lost.

Nothing could be distinguished but a dark mass of human forms tossed and involved in inexplicable confusion. Arms, gleaming knives, and formidable clubs appeared above them, but the blows were evidently given at random. The awful effect was heightened by the piercing shrieks of the women and the fierce yells of the warriors. Now and then Duncan caught a glimpse of a light form cleaving the air in some desperate bound, and he rather hoped than believed that the captive yet retained the command of his astonishing powers of activity. Suddenly the multitude rolled backward, and approached the spot where he himself stood. The heavy body in the rear pressed upon the women and children in front, and bore them to the earth. The stranger reappeared in the confusion. Human power could not, however, much longer endure so severe a trial. Of this the captive seemed conscious. Profiting by the momentary opening, he darted from among the warriors, and made a desperate, and what seemed to Duncan a final, effort to gain the wood. As if aware that no danger was to be apprehended from the young soldier, the fugitive nearly brushed his person in his flight. A tall and powerful Huron, who had husbanded his forces, pressed close upon his heels, and with an uplifted arm menaced a fatal blow. Duncan thrust forth a foot, and the shock precipitated the eager savage headlong, many feet in advance of his intended victim. Thought itself is not quicker than was the motion with which the latter profited by the advantage;

he turned, gleamed like a meteor again before the eyes of Duncan, and at the next moment, when the latter recovered his recollection and gazed around in quest of the captive, he saw him quietly leaning against a small painted post which stood before the door of the principal lodge.

Apprehensive that the part he had taken in the escape might prove fatal to himself, Duncan left the place without delay. He followed the crowd which drew nigh the lodges, gloomy and sullen, like any other multitude that had been disappointed in an execution. Curiosity, or perhaps a better feeling, induced him to approach the stranger. He found him standing with one arm cast about the protecting post, and breathing thick and hard after his exertions, but disdaining to permit a single sign of suffering to escape. His person was now protected by immemorial and sacred usage, until the tribe in council had deliberated and determined on his fate. It was not difficult, however, to foretell the result, if any presage could be drawn from the feelings of those who crowded the place.

There was no term of abuse known to the Huron vocabulary that the disappointed women did not lavishly expend on the successful stranger. They flouted at his efforts, and told him with bitter scoffs that his feet were better than his hands, and that he merited wings, while he knew not the use of an arrow or a knife. To all this the captive made no reply, but was content to preserve an attitude in which dignity was singularly blended with disdain. Exasperated as much by his composure as by his good fortune, their words became unintelligible, and were succeeded by shrill piercing yells. Just then the crafty squaw who had taken the necessary precautions to fire the piles made her way through the throng, and cleared a place for herself in front of the captive. The squalid and withered person of this hag might well have obtained for her the character of possessing more than human cunning. Throwing back her light vestment, she stretched forth her long skinny arm in derision, and using the language of the Lenape, as more intelligible to the subject of her gibes, she commenced aloud:—

"Look you, Delaware," she said, snapping her fingers in his face, "your nation is a race of women, and the hoe is better fitted to your hands than the gun. Your squaws are the mothers of deer; but if a bear or a wild cat or a serpent were born among you, ye would flee. The Huron girls shall make you petticoats, and we will find you a husband."

A burst of savage laughter succeeded this attack, during which the soft and musical merriment of the younger females strangely chimed with the cracked voice of their older and more malignant companion. But the stranger was superior to all their efforts. His head was immovable, nor did he betray the slightest consciousness that any were present, except when his haughty eye rolled toward the dusky forms of the warriors who stalked in the background, silent and sullen observers of the scene.

Infuriated at the self-command of the captive, the woman placed her arms akimbo, and throwing herself into a posture of defiance she broke out anew, in a torrent of words that no art of ours could commit successfully to paper. Her breath was however expended in vain; for although distinguished in her nation as a proficient in the art of abuse, she was permitted to work herself into such a fury as actually to foam at the mouth, without causing a muscle to vibrate in the motionless figure of the stranger. The effect of his indifference began to extend itself to the other spectators, and a youngster who was just quitting the condition of a boy to enter the state of manhood, attempted to assist the termagant by flourishing his tomahawk before their victim and adding his empty boasts to the taunts of the woman. Then indeed the captive turned his face toward the light, and looked down on the stripling with an expression that was superior to contempt. At the next moment he resumed his quiet and reclining attitude against the post. But the change of posture had permitted Duncan to exchange glances with the firm and piercing eyes of Uncas.

Breathless with amazement, and heavily oppressed with the critical situation of his friend, Heyward recoiled before the look, trembling lest its meaning might in some unknown manner hasten the prisoner's fate. There was not, however, any instant cause for such an apprehension. Just then a warrior forced his way into the exasperated crowd. Motioning the women and children aside with a stern gesture, he took Uncas by the arm and led him toward the door of the council lodge. Thither all the chiefs and most of the distinguished warriors followed, among whom the anxious Heyward found means to enter without attracting any dangerous attention to himself.

A few minutes were consumed in disposing of those present in a manner suitable to their rank and influence in the tribe. An order very similar to that adopted in the preceding interview was observed, the aged and superior chiefs occupying the area of the spacious apartment, within the powerful light of a glaring torch, while their juniors and inferiors were arranged in the background, presenting a dark outline of swarthy and marked visages. In the very centre of the lodge, immediately under an opening that admitted the twinkling light of one or two stars, stood Uncas, calm, elevated, and collected. His high and haughty carriage was not lost on his captors, who often bent their looks on his person with eyes which, while they lost none of their inflexibility of purpose, plainly betrayed their admiration of the stranger's daring.

The case was different with the individual whom Duncan had observed to stand forth with his friend previously to the desperate trial of speed; and who, instead of joining in the chase, had remained throughout its turbulent uproar like a cringing statue, expressive of shame and disgrace. Though not a hand had been extended to greet him nor yet an eye had condescended to watch his movements, he had also entered the lodge, as though impelled by a fate to whose decrees he submitted, seemingly, without a struggle. Heyward profited by the first opportunity to gaze in his face, secretly apprehensive he might find the features of another acquaintance; but they proved to be those of a stranger, and what was still more inexplicable, of one who bore all the distinctive marks of a Huron warrior. Instead of mingling with his tribe, however, he sat apart, a solitary being in a multitude, his form shrinking into a crouching and abject attitude, as if anxious to fill as little space as possible. When each individual had taken his proper station, and silence reigned in the place, the gray-haired chief already introduced to the reader spoke aloud, in the language of the Lenni Lenape.

"Delaware," he said, "though one of a nation of women, you have proved yourself a man. I would give you food; but he who eats with a Huron should become his friend. Rest in peace till the morning sun, when our last words shall be spoken."

"Seven nights and as many summer days have I fasted on the trail of the Hurons," Uncas coldly replied; "the children of the Lenape know how to travel the path of the just without lingering to eat."

"Two of my young men are in pursuit of your companion," resumed the other, without appearing to regard the boast of his captive; "when they get back, then will our wise men say to you, 'Live or die.'"

"Has a Huron no ears?" scornfully exclaimed Uncas: "twice since he has been your prisoner has the Delaware heard a gun that he knows. Your young men will never come back."

A short and sullen pause succeeded this bold assertion. Duncan, who understood the Mohican to allude to the fatal rifle of the scout, bent forward in earnest observation of the effect it might produce on the conquerors; but the chief was content with simply retorting:—

"If the Lenape are so skillful, why is one of their bravest warriors here?"

"He followed in the steps of a flying coward, and fell into a snare. The cunning beaver may be caught."

As Uncas thus replied, he pointed with his finger toward the solitary Huron, but without deigning to bestow any other notice on so unworthy an object. The words of the answer and the air of the speaker produced a strong sensation among his auditors. Every eye rolled sullenly toward the individual indicated by the simple gesture, and a low threatening murmur passed through the crowd. The ominous sounds reached the outer door, and the women and children pressing into the throng, no gap had been left between shoulder and shoulder that was not now filled with the dark lineaments of some eager and curious human countenance.

In the mean time the more aged chiefs in the centre communed with each other in short and broken sentences. Not a word was uttered that did not convey the meaning of the speaker, in the simplest and most energetic form. Again a long and deeply solemn pause took place. It was known by all present to be the grave precursor of a weighty and important judgment. They who composed the outer circle of faces were on tiptoe to gaze; and even the culprit for an instant forgot his shame in a deeper emotion, and exposed his abject features in order to cast an anxious and troubled glance at the dark assemblage of chiefs. The silence was finally broken by the aged warrior so often named. He arose from the earth, and moving past the immovable form of Uncas, placed himself in a dignified attitude before the offender. At that moment the withered squaw already mentioned moved into the circle in a slow sidling sort of a dance, holding the torch, and muttering the indistinct words of what might have been a species of incantation. Though her presence was altogether an intrusion, it was unheeded.

Approaching Uncas, she held the blazing brand in such a manner as to cast its red glare on his person and to expose the slightest emotion of his countenance. The Mohican maintained his firm and haughty attitude; and his eye, so far from deigning to meet her inquisitive look, dwelt steadily on the distance as though it penetrated the obstacles which impeded the view, and looked into futurity. Satisfied with her examination, she left him, with a slight expression of pleasure, and proceeded to practice the same trying experiment on her delinquent countryman.

The young Huron was in his war-paint, and very little of a finely molded form was concealed by his attire. The light rendered every limb and joint discernible, and Duncan turned away in horror when he saw they were writhing in inexpressible agony. The woman was commencing a low and plaintive howl at the sad and shameful spectacle, when the chief put forth his hand and gently pushed her aside.

"Reed-that-bends," he said, addressing the young culprit by name, and in his proper language, "though the Great Spirit has made you pleasant to the eyes, it would have been better that you had not been born. Your tongue is loud in the village, but in battle it is still. None of my young men strike the tomahawk deeper into the war-post — none of them so lightly on the Yengeese. The enemy know the shape of your back, but they have never seen the color of your eyes. Three times have they called on you to come, and as often did you forget to answer. Your name will never be mentioned again in your tribe — it is already forgotten."

As the chief slowly uttered these words, pausing impressively between each sentence, the culprit raised his face, in deference to the other's rank and years. Shame, horror, and pride struggled in its lineaments. His eye, which was contracted with inward anguish, gleamed on the persons of those whose breath was his fame; and the latter emotion for an instant predominated. He arose to his feet, and baring his bosom, looked steadily on the keen glittering knife that was already upheld by his inexorable judge. As the weapon passed slowly into his heart he even smiled, as if in joy at having found death less dreadful than he anticipated, and fell heavily on his face at the feet of the rigid and unyielding form of Uncas.

The squaw gave a loud and plaintive yell, dashed the torch to the earth, and buried everything in darkness. The whole shuddering group of spectators glided from the lodge like troubled spirits; and Duncan thought that he and the yet throbbing body of the victim of an Indian judgment had now become its only tenants.

THE PRAIRIE FIRE

From ‹The Prairie›

"SEE, Middleton," exclaimed Inez in a sudden burst of youthful pleasure, that caused her for a moment to forget her situation, "how lovely is that sky; surely it contains a promise of happier times!"

"It is glorious!" returned her husband. "Glorious and heavenly is that streak of vivid red, and here is a still brighter crimson; rarely have I seen a richer rising of the sun."

"Rising of the sun!" slowly repeated the old man, lifting his tall person from its seat with a deliberate and abstracted air, while he kept his eye riveted on the changing and certainly beautiful tints that were garnishing the vault of heaven. "Rising of the sun! I like not such risings of the sun. Ah's me! the imps have circumvented us with a vengeance. The prairie is on fire!"

"God in heaven protect us!" cried Middleton, catching Inez to his bosom, under the instant impression of the imminence of their danger. "There is no time to lose, old man; each instant is a day; let us fly!"

"Whither?" demanded the trapper, motioning him, with calmness and dignity, to arrest his steps. "In this wilderness of grass and reeds you are like a vessel in the broad lakes without a compass. A single step on the wrong course might prove the destruction of us all. It is seldom danger is so pressing that there is not time enough for reason to do its work, young officer; therefore let us await its biddings."

"For my own part," said Paul Hover, looking about him with no equivocal expression of concern, "I acknowledge that should this dry bed of weeds get fairly in a flame, a bee would have to make a flight higher than common to prevent his wings from scorching. Therefore, old trapper, I agree with the captain, and say, mount and run."

"Ye are wrong — ye are wrong; man is not a beast to follow
the gift of instinct, and to snuff up his knowledge by a taint
in the air or a rumbling in the sound; but he must see and
reason, and then conclude. So follow me a little to the left,
where there is a rise in the ground, whence we may make our
reconnoitrings."

The old man waved his hand with authority, and led the way
without further parlance to the spot he had indicated, followed
by the whole of his alarmed companions. An eye less practiced
than that of the trapper might have failed in discovering the
gentle elevation to which he alluded, and which looked on the
surface of the meadow like a growth a little taller than common.
When they reached the place, however, the stunted grass itself
announced the absence of that moisture which had fed the rank
weeds of most of the plain, and furnished a clue to the evidence
by which he had judged of the formation of the ground hidden
beneath. Here a few minutes were lost in breaking down the
tops of the surrounding herbage, which, notwithstanding the advantage of their position, rose even above the heads of Middleton and Paul, and in obtaining a lookout that might command
a view of the surrounding sea of fire.

The frightful prospect added nothing to the hopes of those
who had so fearful a stake in the result. Although the day
was beginning to dawn, the vivid colors of the sky continued to deepen, as if the fierce element were bent on an impious
rivalry of the light of the sun. Bright flashes of flame shot up
here and there along the margin of the waste, like the nimble
coruscations of the North, but far more angry and threatening
in their color and changes. The anxiety on the rigid features
of the trapper sensibly deepened, as he leisurely traced these
evidences of a conflagration, which spread in a broad belt
about their place of refuge, until he had encircled the whole
horizon.

Shaking his head, as he again turned his face to the point
where the danger seemed nighest and most rapidly approaching,
the old man said: —

"Now have we been cheating ourselves with the belief that
we had thrown these Tetons from our trail, while here is proof
enough that they not only know where we lie, but that they
intend to smoke us out, like so many skulking beasts of prey.
See: they have lighted the fire around the whole bottom at the

same moment, and we are as completely hemmed in by the devils as an island by its waters."

"Let us mount and ride!" cried Middleton; "is life not worth a struggle?"

"Whither would ye go? Is a Teton horse a salamander that can walk amid fiery flames unhurt, or do you think the Lord will show his might in your behalf, as in the days of old, and carry you harmless through such a furnace as you may see glowing beneath yonder red sky? There are Sioux too hemming the fire with their arrows and knives on every side of us, or I am no judge of their murderous deviltries."

"We will ride into the centre of the whole tribe," returned the youth fiercely, "and put their manhood to the test."

"Ay, it's well in words, but what would it prove in deeds? Here is a dealer in bees, who can teach you wisdom in a matter like this."

"Now for that matter, old trapper," said Paul, stretching his athletic form like a mastiff conscious of his strength, "I am on the side of the captain, and am clearly for a race against the fire, though it line me into a Teton wigwam. Here is Ellen, who will—"

"Of what use, of what use are your stout hearts, when the element of the Lord is to be conquered as well as human men? Look about you, friends; the wreath of smoke that is rising from the bottoms plainly says that there is no outlet from the spot, without crossing a belt of fire. Look for yourselves, my men; look for yourselves: if you can find a single opening, I will engage to follow."

The examination which his companions so instantly and so intently made, rather served to assure them of their desperate situation than to appease their fears. Huge columns of smoke were rolling up from the plain and thickening in gloomy masses around the horizon; the red glow which gleamed upon their enormous folds, now lighting their volumes with the glare of the conflagration and now flashing to another point as the flame beneath glided ahead, leaving all behind enveloped in awful darkness, and proclaiming louder than words the character of the imminent and approaching danger.

"This is terrible!" exclaimed Middleton, folding the trembling Inez to his heart. "At such a time as this, and in such a manner!"

"The gates of heaven are open to all who truly believe," murmured the pious devotee in his bosom.

"This resignation is maddening! But we are men, and will make a struggle for our lives! How now, my brave and spirited friend, shall we yet mount and push across the flames, or shall we stand here, and see those we most love perish in this frightful manner, without an effort?"

"I am for a swarming time and a flight before the hive is too hot to hold us," said the bee-hunter, to whom it will be at once seen that Middleton addressed himself. "Come, old trapper, you must acknowledge this is but a slow way of getting out of danger. If we tarry here much longer, it will be in the fashion that the bees lie around the straw after the hive has been smoked for its honey. You may hear the fire begin to roar already, and I know by experience that when the flames once get fairly into the prairie grass, it is no sloth that can outrun it."

"Think you," returned the old man, pointing scornfully at the mazes of the dry and matted grass which environed them, "that mortal feet can outstrip the speed of fire on such a path? If I only knew now on which side these miscreants lay!"

"What say you, friend Doctor," cried the bewildered Paul, turning to the naturalist with that sort of helplessness with which the strong are often apt to seek aid of the weak, when human power is baffled by the hand of a mightier Being; "what say you: have you no advice to give away in a case of life and death?"

The naturalist stood, tablets in hand, looking at the awful spectacle with as much composure as if the conflagration had been lighted in order to solve the difficulties of some scientific problem. Aroused by the question of his companion, he turned to his equally calm though differently occupied associate, the trapper, demanding with the most provoking insensibility to the urgent nature of their situation:—

"Venerable hunter, you have often witnessed similar prismatic experiments—"

He was rudely interrupted by Paul, who struck the tablets from his hands with a violence that betrayed the utter intellectual confusion which had overset the equanimity of his mind. Before time was allowed for remonstrance, the old man, who had continued during the whole scene like one much at loss how to proceed, though also like one who was rather perplexed than alarmed, suddenly assumed a decided air, as if he no longer doubted on the course it was most advisable to pursue.

"It is time to be doing," he said, interrupting the controversy that was about to ensue between the naturalist and the bee-hunter; "it is time to leave off books and moanings, and to be doing."

"You have come to your recollections too late, miserable old man," cried Middleton; "the flames are within a quarter of a mile of us, and the wind is bringing them down in this quarter with dreadful rapidity."

"Anan! the flames! I care but little for the flames. If I only knew how to circumvent the cunning of the Tetons as I know how to cheat the fire of its prey, there would be nothing needed but thanks to the Lord for our deliverance. Do you call this a fire? If you had seen what I have witnessed in the eastern hills, when mighty mountains were like the furnace of a smith, you would have known what it was to fear the flames and to be thankful that you were spared! Come, lads, come: 'tis time to be doing now, and to cease talking; for yonder curling flame is truly coming on like a trotting moose. Put hands upon this short and withered grass where we stand, and lay bare the 'arth."

"Would you think to deprive the fire of its victims in this childish manner?" exclaimed Middleton.

A faint but solemn smile passed over the features of the old man as he answered:—

"Your gran'ther would have said that when the enemy was nigh, a soldier could do no better than to obey."

The captain felt the reproof, and instantly began to imitate the industry of Paul, who was tearing the decayed herbage from the ground in a sort of desperate compliance with the trapper's direction. Even Ellen lent her hands to the labor, nor was it long before Inez was seen similarly employed, though none amongst them knew why or wherefore. When life is thought to be the reward of labor, men are wont to be industrious. A very few moments sufficed to lay bare a spot of some twenty feet in diameter. Into one edge of this little area the trapper brought the females, directing Middleton and Paul to cover their light and inflammable dresses with the blankets of the party. So soon as this precaution was observed, the old man approached the opposite margin of the grass which still environed them in a tall and dangerous circle, and selecting a handful of the driest of the herbage, he placed it over the pan of his rifle. The light combustible kindled at the flash. Then he placed the little flame in a bed of the standing fog, and withdrawing from the spot to the centre of the ring, he patiently awaited the result.

The subtle element seized with avidity upon its new fuel, and in a moment forked flames were gliding among the grass, as the tongues of ruminating animals are seen rolling among their food, apparently in quest of its sweetest portions.

"Now," said the old man, holding up a finger, and laughing in his peculiarly silent manner, "you shall see fire fight fire! Ah's me! many is the time I have burnt a smooty path, from wanton laziness to pick my way across a tangled bottom."

"But is this not fatal?" cried the amazed Middleton; "are you not bringing the enemy nigher to us instead of avoiding it?"

"Do you scorch so easily? your gran'ther had a tougher skin. But we shall live to see — we shall all live to see."

The experience of the trapper was in the right. As the fire gained strength and heat, it began to spread on three sides, dying of itself on the fourth for want of aliment. As it increased, and the sullen roaring announced its power, it cleared everything before it, leaving the black and smoking soil far more naked than if the scythe had swept the place. The situation of the fugitives would have still been hazardous, had not the area enlarged as the flame encircled them. But by advancing to the spot where the trapper had kindled the grass, they avoided the heat, and in a very few moments the flames began to recede in every quarter, leaving them enveloped in a cloud of smoke, but perfectly safe from the torrent of fire that was still furiously rolling onwards.

The spectators regarded the simple expedient of the trapper with that species of wonder with which the courtiers of Ferdinand are said to have viewed the manner in which Columbus made his egg stand on its end, though with feelings that were filled with gratitude instead of envy.

COPERNICUS

(1473–1543)

BY EDWARD S. HOLDEN

T HAS been the fortune of other men than Copernicus to render immense services to science: but it has never before been given to any philosopher to alter, for every thinking man, his entire view of the world; to face the whole human race in a new direction; to lay the foundations for all subsequent intellectual progress. To comprehend the new universe which he opened to mankind, it is necessary to understand something of the age in which he lived, and its critical relations to the past and future.

The life of Copernicus covered the years 1473 to 1543. The astronomy of the Greeks came to its flower with Ptolemy (circa A. D. 150), who was followed by a host of able commentators. Their works were mostly lost in some one of the several destructions of the Alexandrian library. Many important treatises survived, of course, though Grecian science was then dead. Bagdad became the seat of astronomy under the Abbasside Caliphs. It is said that Al Mamun (circa A. D. 827) stipulated in a treaty with the Emperor for copies of the manuscripts of Greek philosophers in the Constantinople libraries, and that these were translated for the benefit of Arabian scholars. The Arabs carried this learning, improved in many details, to the lands they conquered. Bagdad, Cordova, Seville, Tangier, have been successively the homes of exact science. Under the Moguls the seat of astronomy was transferred to Samarkand (1405). It was not firmly rooted in Europe until Tycho Brahe built Uranienborg in Denmark in 1576.

The Arabs touched Europe in Spain (711–1492) and through the Crusaders (1099). The ancient Ptolemaic system of the world, which counted the earth as the centre of the universe, was successively amended by new devices,

«With centric and eccentric scribbled o'er,
Cycle and epicycle, orb in orb—»

until it had reached a complexity past belief. King Alfonso X. of Castile expended an enormous sum for the construction of the Alfonsine Tables (1252), which were designed to give, by a comparatively simple calculation, the positions of the sun and planets for past and future epochs,—employing the theories of Ptolemy as a basis. Alfonso's critical remark upon these theories is well known: to wit, that if he had been present at the creation, he could have given the Creator much good advice. As the determination of the places of the planets (their latitudes and longitudes) became more exact, it was increasingly difficult to account for their observed movements by the devices introduced by Ptolemy. New contrivances were required, and each successive epicycle made the system more complex and cumbrous. It was on the point of breaking by its own weight.

There is hardly a glimmer of scientific light in the darkness of the two centuries following. From Roger Bacon (1214–94) to the birth of Leonardo da Vinci (1452) there is scarcely a single date to record except that of 1438, when the art of printing was invented — or re-invented — in Europe.

The writings of Purbach (1460) and of Regiomontanus (1471) brought astronomy in Germany to the same level as the Arabian science of five centuries earlier in Spain, and marked the beginning of a new era for Northern lands. In Italy the impulse was earlier 'felt, though it manifested itself chiefly in literature. Mathematics was not neglected, however, at the ancient University of Bologna; and it was to Bologna that Copernicus came as a student in 1496.

The voyages of Columbus in 1492 and of Vasco da Gama in 1498 were other signs of the same impulsion which was manifest through out the Western lands.

Nicolas Copernicus was born in 1473, in the town of Thorn in Poland. His father was originally from Bohemia, and his mother was the sister of the Bishop of Ermeland. The father died when the lad was but ten years old, and left him to the care of his uncle. His studies were prosecuted at the best schools and at the University of Cracow, where he followed the courses in medicine, and became in due time a doctor. Mathematics and astronomy were ardently studied under learned professors, and the young man also became a skillful artist in painting. At the termination of his studies he turned his face towards Italy, entered the universities of Padua and Bologna, and finally received the appointment of Professor of Mathematics at Rome in 1499, at the age of twenty-seven years. Here his duties were to expound the theories of Ptolemy as taught in the 'Almagest,' and he became entirely familiar with their merits and with their deficiencies.

Astronomers everywhere were asking themselves if there might not be simpler methods of accounting for the movements of the planets and of predicting their situations in the sky than the Ptolemaic methods, loaded down as they were with new complexities.

We know that these questions occupied Copernicus during the seven years of his stay in Italy, 1496 to 1502. He made a few astronomical observations then and subsequently, but he was not a born observer like his successor Tycho Brahe. His observations were directed towards determining the positions of the planets, as a test of the tables by which these positions had been predicted; and they were sufficient to show the shortcomings of the accepted Ptolemaic theory. He was a theoretical astronomer, but his theory was controlled by observation.

In 1502 Copernicus returned to his native land and at once entered holy orders. In 1510 he became canon of Frauenburg, a small town not far from Königsberg. Here he divided his time between his religious duties, the practice of medicine, and the study of astronomy —a peaceful life, one would say, and likely to be free from vexations.

It became necessary for the priest to leave his cloister, however, to defend the interests of the Church in a lawsuit against the Knights of the Teutonic Order. The lawsuit was won at last, but Copernicus had raised up powerful enemies. His conclusions with regard to the motion of the earth were not yet published, but it was known that he entertained such opinions. Here was an opportunity for his enemies to bring him to ridicule and to disgrace, which was not neglected. Troupes of strolling players were employed to turn himself and his conclusions into ridicule; and it requires no imagination to conceive that they were perfectly successful before the audiences of the day. But these annoyances fell away in time. The reputation of the good physician and the good priest conquered his townsfolk, while the scholars of Europe were more and more impressed with his learning.

His authority grew apace. He was consulted on practical affairs, such as the financial conduct of the mint. In 1507 he had begun to write a treatise on the motion of the heavenly bodies — 'De Revolutionibus Orbium Cœlestium' — and he appears to have brought it to completion about 1514. It is replete with interest to astronomers, but there are few passages suitable for quotation in a summary like the present. The manuscript was touched and retouched from time to time; and finally in 1541, when he was nearly seventy years of age, he confided it to a disciple in Nuremberg to be printed. In the month of May, 1543, the impression was completed, and the final sheets were sent to the author. They reached him when he was on his death-bed, a few days before he died.

His epitaph is most humble:— "I do not ask the pardon accorded to Paul; I do not hope for the grace given to Peter. I beg only the favor which You have granted to the thief on the cross." His legacy to the world was an upright useful life, and a volume containing an immortal truth:—

The earth is not the centre of the universe; the earth is in motion around the sun.

The conception that the earth might revolve about the sun was no new thing. The ancients had considered this hypothesis among others. Ptolemy made the earth the centre of all the celestial motions. As the motions became more precisely known, Ptolemy's hypothesis required new additions, and it was finally overloaded. It is the merit of Copernicus that he reversed the ancient process of thought and inquired what hypothesis would fit observed facts, and not what additions must be made to an *a priori* assumption to represent observations. He showed clearly and beyond a doubt that the facts were represented far better by the theory that the sun was the centre of motion of the earth, and not only of the earth, but of all the planets. He says:—

«By no other combination have I been able to find so admirable a symmetry in the separate parts of the great whole, so harmonious a union between the motions of the celestial bodies, as by placing the torch of the world—that Sun which governs all the family of the planets in their circular revolutions—on his royal throne, in the midst of Nature's temple.»*

He did not demonstrate this arrangement to be the true one. It was left to Galileo to prove that Venus had phases like our moon, and hence that its light was sunlight, and that its motion was heliocentric. The direct service of Copernicus to pure astronomy lay in his *method*. What theory will best fit the facts? How shall we test the theory by observation? Indirectly he laid the foundations for the reformation of astronomy by Kepler and Galileo; for Newton's working out of the conception of the sun as a centre of force as well as a centre of motion; for the modern ideas of the relations between force and matter.

The Church, which regarded all sciences as derivatives of theology, placed the work of Copernicus on the Index Expurgatorius at Rome, 1616. The Reformation maintained an official silence on the mooted questions. Luther condemned the theory of Copernicus. But the service of Copernicus to mankind was immense, revolutionary,— incalculable. For thousands of years the earth, with its inhabitants, was the centre of a universe created for its benefit. At one step all this was changed, and man took his modest place. He became a creature painfully living on a small planet—one of many—revolving

* Quoted from the French of Flammarion's 'Life of Copernicus,' page 122.

around one of the smaller stars or suns; and that sun was only one of the millions upon millions shining in the stellar vault. Man's position in the universe was destroyed. The loss of kingship would seem to be intolerable, were it not that it was by a man, after all, that Man was dethroned. All our modern thought, feeling, action, is profoundly modified by the consequences of the dictum of Copernicus—« *The earth is not the centre of the universe.*» Mankind was faced in a new direction by that pronouncement. Modern life became possible. Modern views became inevitable. The end is not yet. When in future ages the entire history of the race is written, many names now dear to us will be ignored: they have no vital connection with the progress of the race. But one name is sure of a place of honor: Copernicus will not be forgotten by our remotest descendants.

Edward S. Holden

FRANÇOIS COPPÉE

(1842–)

BY ROBERT SANDERSON

AMONG writers of the present day whose influence on French letters is strongly felt, François Coppée occupies a foremost rank. Indeed, poets of the new generation look up to him as a master and take him for a model. Born in 1842, at the age of twenty-four he first began to draw attention by the publication in 1866 of a number of poems, collected under the name of 'Le Reliquaire' (The Reliquary or Shrine). Since then he has gone on writing poems, plays, and novels; but it is on his work as a poet that his fame will stand. We cannot do better than turn to one of his books, not for his biography alone, but also for the manner of thinking and feeling of this author. 'Toute une Jeunesse' (An Entire Youth) is not strictly an autobiography; but Coppée informs us that the leading character in this work, Amédée Violette, felt life as he felt it when a child and young man.

FRANÇOIS COPPÉE

Here we learn that Coppée's father was a clerk in the War Offices, earning barely enough to keep his family. The boy was of weakly constitution, nervous and sentimental. The mother died; François grew up with his three sisters, two of whom painted for a living, while the third kept house. Then the father died, and his son also obtained employment in the government offices.

François's boyhood and part of his youth were spent in sadness, almost misery; and the shadow cast over his life by this gloomy period of his existence is very perceptible in the poet's writings. It did not however make him a cynic, a pessimist, or a rebel against the existing social conditions. To be sure, his verse is not unfrequently ironical; but it is the irony of fate that the poet makes you keenly feel, although he touches it with a light hand. The recollection of those joyless days filled Coppée with an immense feeling of sadness and sympathy for all who suffer on this earth, especially for those who struggle on, bravely concealing from all eyes their griefs and sorrows. His life, he tells us, was composed of desires and reveries. His only consolation was in his literary work. He felt the inclination and the need of expressing in a way both simple and sincere what passed under his eyes; of extracting what humble ideal there might be in the small folk with whom he had lived, in the melancholy landscapes of the Parisian suburbs where his childhood had been spent,— in short, to paint from nature. He made the attempt, felt that he was successful, and lived then the best and noblest hours of his life; hours in which the artist, already a master of his instrument and having still that abundance and vivacity of sensations of youth, writes the first work that he knows to be good, and writes it with complete disinterestedness, without even thinking that others will see it; working for himself alone, for the sole joy of producing, of pouring out his whole imagination and his whole heart. Hours of pure enthusiasm, Coppée goes on to say, and of perfect happiness, that he will nevermore find when he shall have bitten into the savory fruit of success, when he shall be spurred on by the feverish desire for fame! Delightful and sacred hours, that can be compared only to the rapture of first love!

Rising at six, Coppée would vigorously begin his battle with words, ideas, pictures. At nine he left for his office. There, having blackened with ink a sufficient number of government foolscap sheets, he would find himself with two or three spare hours, which he employed in reading and taking notes. Every night found him up until twelve at his writing-table. The whole of Sunday was given to his favorite occupation of writing verse. Such a continuous effort, he says, kept up in his mind that ardor, spirit, and excitement without which no poetical production is possible.

Such was Coppée's life until, his name becoming known, he earned enough with his pen to give himself up entirely to his art. Then came his success with 'Le Passant' (The Passer-by: 1869), a one-act play; and the following year, the war, the siege of Paris, through which Coppée served in the militia. «Amédée Violette» has now become famous, and his reputation as a poet rests upon the sincerity of his work. He is esteemed for the dignity of his life, wholly taken up with art; and in the world of French letters his place is in the very first rank. He lives out of the world, in the close intimacy of those he loves, and knows nothing of the wretchedness of vanity and ambition. Like many writers and thinkers of the present day, he feels the weariness of life, and finds oblivion in the raptures of poetry and dreams. Such is the man: a wonderfully delicate organization, of a modest shrinking nature, — notice the name of *Violette* he gives himself, — sensitive to a degree of morbidness.

The Academy elected him a member in 1884. Let us now consider the writer. The general character of Coppée's poetry is tender and melancholy, and the greater part of his work may be summed up as the glorification of the lowly, the weak, the ill-favored by nature or fortune; his heroes are chosen by preference among those who fill the humblest stations in life. One naturally associates poetry with a higher order of things than those presented to our eyes by the contemplation of daily events; but Coppée possesses the art of extracting from the humblest creature, from the meanest occupation, the beautiful, the poetic, the ideal. In the treatment in familiar verse of these commonplace subjects, Coppée is an accomplished master; and therein lies his originality, and there also will be found his best work. The poems comprised in the collections called 'Les Humbles,' 'Contes et Poésies,' and certain stanzas of 'Promenades et Intérieurs,' contain the best specimens of this familiar and sympathetic style of poetry.

There is another key that Coppée touches in his poems, with a light and tender hand; a tone difficult to analyze,—the expression of one's inner emotions, especially that of love; a yearning for an ideal affection of woman; the feeling buried in the hearts of all who have lived, loved, and suffered; regret in comparing what is with what might have been: all these varied emotions more easily felt than defined, all that the French sum up by the term *vécu*, have been rendered by Coppée in some of the poems contained in 'Le Reliquaire,' in 'Intimites,' 'Le Cahier Rouge' (The Red Note-Book), 'Olivier,' under whose name the poet has portrayed himself; 'L'Exilée'; 'Les Mois' (The Months), in the collection having for title 'Les Récits et les Élégies'; 'Arrière-Saison' (Martinmas, or what in this country might be called Indian Summer).

The patriotic chord resounds in several of Coppée's compositions,—usually straightforward, manly; here and there however with a slight touch of chauvinism. The 'Lettre d'un Mobile Breton,' a letter written by a Breton soldier to his parents during the siege of Paris; 'Plus de Sang!' (No More Blood!) 'Aux Amputés de la Guerre' (To the Maimed in Battle), will serve to illustrate Coppée's treatment of subjects inspired by the events of the war, the siege, and the Commune.

Among the various well-known poems of this writer, the fame of which was increased by their being recited in Parisian salons by skilled artists, should be mentioned 'Les Aïeules' (The Grandmothers); 'La Grève des Forgerons' (The Blacksmiths' Strike); 'Le Naufragé' (The Shipwrecked Sailor); and 'La Bénédiction,' an episode of the taking of Saragossa by the French in 1809.

François Coppée has written for the stage; but he is too elegiac, too sentimental a poet to be a first-class playwright, although some of his plays have met with great success: 'Le Passant' (The Passer-by: 1869), a one-act comedy whose great charm lies in the expression of suffering love; 'Le Luthier de Crémone' (The Musical Instrument Maker of Cremona: 1876), probably the best of his dramatic compositions, a one-act comedy in which the leading character is again one of the humble,—Filippo the hunchback, whose deformity covers a brave heart and a magnanimous spirit; and 'Pour la Couronne' (For the Crown: 1895), a five-act drama with more action than is usually found in Coppée's plays. The scene is laid in the Balkans. The character of Constantine Brancomir, who is falsely accused of selling his country to the Turks and submits to an ignominious punishment to save his father's memory, is a very noble one. With these exceptions, Coppée's plays lack action. Remaining titles are: 'Deux Douleurs' (Two Sorrows), a one-act drama, the story of two women who love the same man, and from being rivals become reconciled at his death; 'Fais ce que Dois' (Do What You Ought), a dramatic episode in one act, of a patriotic nature,—somewhat commonplace, however; 'L'Abandonnée,' a two-act drama presenting the picture of a young girl abandoned by her lover, who meets again with him at her death-bed in a hospital ward; 'Les Bijoux de la Délivrance' (The Jewels of Ransom, Freedom), simply a scene, in which a lady dressed for the ball suddenly reflects that the foreigner is still occupying the territory of France until the payment of the ransom, and removes her glittering jewels to be used for a nobler purpose. Still other plays are 'Le Rendezvous,' 'La Guerre de Cent Ans' (The Hundred Years' War), 'Le Trésor' (The Treasure), 'Madame de Maintenon,' 'Severo Torelli,' 'Les Jacobites'; and 'Le Pater' (The Father), which was prohibited by the French government in 1889.

In common with other modern French writers, with Daudet, Maupassant, and others, Coppée excels in the writing of tales. His prose is remarkable for the same qualities that appear in his poetical works: sympathy, tenderness, marked predilection for the weak, the humble, and especially a masterly treatment of subjects essentially Parisian and modern. These *contes* or tales have been collected under various titles:—'Contes en Prose'; 'Vingt Contes Nouveaux' (Twenty New Tales); 'Longues et Brèves' (Long and Short Ones); 'Contes Tout Simples' (Simple Stories). The following may be mentioned as among some of the best of this writer's prose tales:—'Le Morceau de Pain' (The Piece of Bread); 'Une Mort Volontaire' (A Voluntary Death); 'Le Pain Bénit' (The Consecrated Bread); 'La Soeur de Lait' (The Foster-Sister); 'Un Accident'; 'Les Vices du Capitaine';

'Les Sabots du Petit Wolff'; 'Mon Ami Meutrier' (My Friend Meutrier).

Coppée's other prose works are 'Une Idylle Pendant le Siége,' 'Henriette,' 'Rivales,' *nouvelles* or novelettes; 'Toute une Jeunesse'; 'Mon Franc-Parler' (Freely Spoken Words), essays on different subjects, books, authors, celebrities, etc.

Robert Sanderson

THE PARRICIDE

From 'For the Crown'

The scene represents a rocky plateau in the Balkans. In the background and centre of the stage, a ruined Roman triumphal arch. A huge signal-pyre is prepared for firing, near the path. Beside it burns a torch, stuck into the rock. On all sides are pine-trees and crags. In the distance are the Balkans, with snowy summits. It is the middle of a fine starlight night. Michael Brancomir, solus:—

I HAVE promised—have sworn. 'Tis the moment, the place—
  Michael, naught is left but to hold to thy oath.
    What calm! Far below there, the torrent scarce drips—
Othorgul soon will come: I shall speedily hear
On the old Roman high-road the tramp of his horse;
I shall see him approach, he, the foe, 'neath the arch
Built by Dacia's conqueror, Trajan the Great.
What matters it? Ripe for all daring am I,
Basilide! Ah, thy amorous arms, whence I come,
Have embraces to stifle and smother remorse.
Yes, thy hand have I kissed, pointing out shame's abyss;
With joy throbs my heart that I love thee to crime!
And since crime must ensue that thy pleasure be done,
I feel in such treason an awful content.
Enmeshed in the night of thy locks, I have sworn
That in place of the Turk, should the Prince of the Pit
Rise up with a sneer and stretch forth to my hand
This crown I desire, all with hell-fires aglow,
To thee, Basilide, my seared hand should it bring!
Starry night! All thy splendors undaunted I meet.

[*Perceiving his son* Constantine *suddenly approaching over the rocks at the right hand, exclaims, loud and harshly:* —]

What's there? Do I dream? Near the crag there's a man!
Ho, prowler! stand off, 'tis forbid to approach!
Further back, and at once! The command is most strict.
Further back there, I say!

Constantine [*drawing nearer*] —   Fear not, father! 'Tis I.
Michael —
Constantine! Thou, my son!
Constantine —   Yes.
Michael —   What brings thee here,— say,—
To this waste at this hour of the night? Tell me, too,
Why so trembling thy lip? why so pallid thy face?
What thy errand?

Constantine —   Say, rather, what doest *thou* here?
Michael —
First, my answer! My patience thou bring'st to an end!
Say, what brings thee thus here?

Constantine —   Duty, father. I *know*.
Michael [*starting back*] —
What "knowest" thou, boy?
Constantine —   That the clamor of arms
In the Balkans will rise — the Turk comes — that yon pyre
Has beside it this moment no warder of faith —
That this night, if all Christendom's world shall be saved,
I shall fire yonder signal, in spite even of — you!

Michael [*aside*] —
Just God! To a demon defiance I cast —
And the spirit of hell takes the shape of my son!
[*Aloud.*] What madness inspires thee? What folly, what dream?
Constantine —
Nay, spare thyself, father, the shame of a lie.
Thy bargain is made — thy throne offered — the Turk
Meets thee here. I know all — I have heard *all*, I say!

Michael —
Damnation!
Constantine —   — Or no! Let it be, 'tis not true!
Let it be I'm abused — that a horror I dream;
That a madness beset me; that truth is with thee;
That when such a compact of shame thou didst make,
Thy aim was deceiving the traitress, whose kiss
Thou hadst wiped from thy lips, rushing forth into night.
I divine it — thy traitorous part is a ruse!
'Tis alone for thy country, the war for the Cross,

That the mask of disloyalty shadows thy face.
To fire with thine own hand yon signal thou'rt here.
Othorgul in an ambush shall fall and be crushed;
On the Balkans, the girdle of fire — our defense —
Shall flare from Iskren to remote Kilandar —
Ah, I wake! I cast from me this nightmare of shame.
Take the torch, light the pyre — let it burst to its blaze!

Michael —

So suspected I stand? So my son is a spy?
A new order, sooth! What, the heir of my name
Dares to ask to my face if a treason I work!
Since when did a father endure to be told
That his son sets his ears to the cracks of the door?
Say, when did I ask *thy* opinions? Since when
Does the chief take his orderly's counsels in war?
I deign no reply to thy insolent charge.
Thou hast not now to learn that my frown means "Obey."
Hearken then: 'tis my wish to abide here alone
This night at the post. To the fortress at once!
Choose the path the most short! Get thee hence, boy, I
      say.
The signal I light when shall seem to me good.
In the weal of our land I am not to be taught.
I have spoken. Return to thy post, sir. Obey!

Constantine —

It is true, then! No hideous dream of disgrace!
The villainy ripe to its finish! I stay.

Michael —

Thou darest?

Constantine —   Ay, father, thy wrath I can brook.
It is love, yes, the last throbs of love for thyself
That have drawn me to seek thee alone on these heights,
To stand between thee and that hideous crime.
Filial duty? Obedience unto my chief?
To the winds with them both! In my heart rules one
      thought —
I would save thee — to God must I render account —
I must rescue my country, must pluck thee from shame.
Give place there, I say! Stand aside from that torch!
Let the mountain heights glow with their fires!

Michael —   No, by God!

Constantine —

O father, bethink thee! O father, beware!
From above God looks down, and the eyes of the stars.

Of myself I have asked, when thy treason I knew,
What by honor was set?—where lay duty from me?
Alas, it was clear! To denounce to the world
Thy plot—and thyself—and that woman most vile;
To unmask too thy spy. But for thee this means death!
(Death held in reserve through the torture's dread scenes)
—It means in an instant thy glory effaced.
I have pictured thy end at the gibbet, through me.
I could not denounce thee! I held back in dread
From the part of a son who to death yields a sire.
I could not endure that thy name so renowned
Should be scorned—that thy glory should take such dark
          flight.
But at present I act as I must. Time is swift.
I shall kindle yon signal, I say. Give me place!
Calm the woes of thy country!—appease Heaven's wrath!
Think, think, that my silence has turned from thyself
A death on a scaffold, and tortures before.
Think, think that my silence had meant for thee chains,
And the doomsman's dread hand laying clutch upon thee. . .
O father, thou wilt not that I should—regret!

Michael—

Too late. Regret now to have saved thus my life.
O son too devoted, best gained were thy wish
Hadst thou told all—hadst seen me a Judas, disgraced,
Cut down by my soldiers before thine own eyes.
The worse now for thee! Thy heart questions, disputes;
That thing whereon mine is resolved, that I do.
Who has nothing foreseen, he can nothing prevent:
I permit that no hand yonder beacon shall fire.

Constantine—

Thou wouldst yield then, defenseless, our ancient frontier?
Thou wilt suffer the Turk to make Europe his prey,
To all Christendom's ruin—

Michael—   'Tis ingrate to me.
Constantine—

And thy Christ, and thy God?

Michael—   Has God made of me king?
Spite of God, king I would be, will be!

Constantine—   Say—*perhaps*.

Oft a crown is too large for a traitorous head.
It can suddenly prove a garrote—for the stake.

Michael—

Thou insultest! The folly is passing all bounds!

Constantine [*in sudden emotion*]—

Ah yes, I am wrong! O my father, forgive!—
What I utter I know not; for aid I must call!
To my help, then, O memories great of days sped,
Ye evenings of rapture that followed fights won.
Come, turmoils of booty, flags snatched as in sheaves,
Shouts of joy and of pride when from fray I returned
And felt on my forehead, blood-scarred, his hot kiss!—
O ye visions like these, of past glory, crowd thick!
The valor of old years, of old time the deeds,
Quick, rank yourselves here, face this wretchedest man,
Bring a blush to his face at his treason so vile!
Speak, speak to him! Say that at morn, in the town,
The standards that hang at the gates of his halls
Will stoop, as he passes, to smite at his face.
Say, oh say, to this hero become renegade,
That the soldiers long dead on his battle-fields past
In this hour know the crime unexampled he plots,—
That they whisper in dread, 'twixt themselves, 'neath the
     earth,
And if passes some wanderer to-night by their graves,
Indignant the murmur is breathed through the grass.
No, no! to such falsity thou wilt not go;
Even now you repent—all unwilling to leave
A name to be cursed in the memories of all!
Seest thou not, O my father, thy victories come
Like suppliants imploring, to close round your knees?
Will you hold them in hate, will you drive them away?—
The triumphs that all this West-world has acclaimed,
Will you treat them as prostitutes, bowed, to be scorned?
No, this crime so debased you will dare not commit!
It cannot be, father—it never must be!
See me cast at your feet, in last hope, in last prayer;
I shall find the lost hero—the father I've lost!
You will catch up the torch, you will fire yon dry pile:
With an effort supreme from your heart you will tear
This project unspeakable,—promise debased;
You will cast them away to the pyre's fiercest glow
As one burns into naught some foul herb, root and fruit:
You will stand purified as by fire, and the wind
Of the night will bear off on its wings this dark dream
In a whirlwind uproaring of sparks and of flame.

Michael—

'Tis enough, I say! Up! By all devils in hell,
Of the hills and the plains of this land I'll be king!

Ay, and crown my fair queen — be revenged on the priest.
As that sky is unstained, so shall all this be done.
Thy heroics thou wastest — thy insolence too.
Go, dispute with the lion the quarry he holds
When thou seest him tear with his talons the prey.
Of no use all thy menaces — vain sobs, vain prayers:
Be sure once for all that thy childishness fails.
While I live, no man kindles this signal to-night!

Constantine —

While thou *livest!* What word do I catch from thy mouth?
While thou *livest?* O bloody and terrible thought!
In my brain is set loose worse than horror, than death!

Michael —

I guess not thy meaning. Wouldst see me a corpse?

Constantine —

I dream in this moment that one thou — *shouldst* be —
By a doom full of shame, by the traitor's own fate!

Michael —

What dost mean?

Constantine —   Ah, I think, while we parley so long,
Othorgul and his Turks in the valleys approach —
Each instant that's spent makes accomplice of — me!
I think of the duty that I must fulfill.

Michael —

What "duty"?

Constantine [*with desperate resolution*] —
                              I say to myself that, unjust,
I have wished from the chastisement — death — thee to save.
Lo, thy life is a menace, escaping the axe,
A menace to all. And I have here my sword!

Michael [*in horror*] —

Thou! Thy sword!

Constantine —   Yes, of old, without blemish, my blade
Has known well how to stand between death and thy brow;
Still witness to that is the wound that I bear —
But since such keen envy, such ignoble love,
Have made of my hero a creature so base,
Since to scorn of all men, toward the Turk thou dost turn,
To beg at his hands for the crown thou usurp'st —
See, my sword, in its honor, leaps out from its sheath
And commands me thy judge and thy doomsman to be.

                                        [*He draws his sword.*]

Michael [*drawing his sword in turn*] —

My sword then behold! It is fearless of thine!

Constantine —
      'Tis my land I defend — Christian Europe I keep,
      And my duty as soldier, the truth of my line;
      But you, 'tis for treason alone that you draw.
      God beholds us. He watches the lists. Let him judge!
      Traitor, die!

[*Constantine leaps at his father. The swords cross for a moment in quick
    combat. Then Michael receives a stroke full in the breast, and falls.*]

Michael —   Ah!
Constantine —   My God! What a deed!
Michael [*on the ground expiring*] —   Parricide!
      Be cursed!   [*He dies.*
Constantine —   First the signal! The fire to the pile!

[*He takes the torch and sets the signal blaze burning, which soon mounts
    high. Then gradually one sees far along the mountain-chain the
    other signals flashing out, and alarm-guns begin to be heard below.*]

Constantine —
      O ye stars, eyes of God! Be the witnesses, ye!
      But before yonder corpse in the face of that flame,
      I dare to look up and to show you my soul.
      My father his country, his faith would betray.
      I have killed him, O stars! Have I sinned? Ye shall say!

Unrhymed version, in the metre of the original, by E. Irenæus Stevenson.

THE SUBSTITUTE

From 'Ten Tales,' by François Coppée: copyright 1890, by Harper and
Brothers

H<small>E WAS</small> scarcely ten years old when he was first arrested as a
vagabond.

    He spoke thus to the judge: —

"I am called Jean François Leturc, and for six months I was
with the man who sings and plays upon a cord of catgut between
the lanterns at the Place de la Bastille. I sang the refrain with
him, and after that I called, 'Here's all the new songs, ten
centimes two sous!' He was always drunk and used to beat
me. That is why the police picked me up the other night.
Before that I was with the man who sells brushes. My mother
was a laundress; her name was Adèle. At one time she lived

with a man on the ground-floor at Montmartre. She was a good workwoman and liked me. She made money, because she had for customers waiters in the cafés, and they use a good deal of linen. On Sundays she used to put me to bed early, so that she could go to the ball. On week-days she sent me to Les Frères, where I learned to read. Well, the sergeant-de-ville whose beat was in our street used always to stop before our windows to talk with her — a good-looking chap, with a medal from the Crimea. They were married, and after that everything went wrong. He didn't take to me, and turned mother against me. Every one had a blow for me, and so to get out of the house I spent whole days in the Place Clichy, where I knew the mountebanks. My father-in-law lost his place, and my mother her work. She used to go out washing to take care of him; this gave her a cough — the steam. . . . She is dead at Lariboisière. She was a good woman. Since that I have lived with the seller of brushes and the catgut scraper. Are you going to send me to prison?"

He said this openly, cynically, like a man. He was a little ragged street-arab, as tall as a boot, his forehead hidden under a queer mop of yellow hair.

Nobody claimed him, and they sent him to the Reform School.

Not very intelligent, idle, clumsy with his hands, the only trade he could learn there was not a good one, — that of reseating straw chairs. However, he was obedient, naturally quiet and silent, and he did not seem to be profoundly corrupted by that school of vice. But when in his seventeenth year he was thrown out again on the streets of Paris, he unhappily found there his prison comrades, all great scamps, exercising their dirty professions: teaching dogs to catch rats in the sewers, and blacking shoes on ball nights in the passage of the Opera; amateur wrestlers, who permitted themselves to be thrown by the Hercules of the booths; or fishing at noontime from rafts: all of these occupations he followed to some extent, and some months after he came out of the House of Correction, he was arrested again for a petty theft — a pair of old shoes prigged from a shop window. Result: a year in the prison of Sainte Pélagie, where he served as valet to the political prisoners.

He lived in much surprise among this group of prisoners, — all very young, negligent in dress, who talked in loud voices, and carried their heads in a very solemn fashion. They used to meet in the cell of one of the oldest of them, a fellow of some thirty years, already a long time in prison and quite a fixture at Sainte Pélagie; a large cell, the walls covered with colored caricatures, and from the window of which one could see all Paris — its roofs, its spires, and its domes — and far away the distant line of hills, blue and indistinct upon the sky. There were upon the walls some shelves filled with volumes and all the old paraphernalia of a fencing-room: broken masks, rusty foils, breast-plates, and gloves that were losing their tow. It was there that the "politicians" used to dine together, adding to the everlasting "soup and beef," fruit, cheese, and pints of wine which Jean François went out and got by the can; a tumultuous repast, interrupted by violent disputes, and where, during the dessert, the 'Carmagnole' and 'Ça Ira' were sung in full chorus. They assumed, however, an air of great dignity on those days when a newcomer was brought in among them, at first entertaining him gravely as a citizen, but on the morrow using him with affectionate familiarity and calling him by his nickname. Great words were used there: "Corporation," "responsibility," and phrases quite unintelligible to Jean François — such as this, for example, which he once heard imperiously put forth by a frightful little hunchback who blotted some writing-paper every night: —

"It is done. This is the composition of the Cabinet: Raymond, the Bureau of Public Instruction; Martial, the Interior; and for Foreign Affairs, myself."

His time done, he wandered again around Paris, watched afar by the police, after the fashion of cockchafers made by cruel children to fly at the end of a string. He became one of those fugitive and timid beings whom the law, with a sort of coquetry, arrests and releases by turn; something like those platonic fishers who, in order that they may not exhaust their fish-pond, throw immediately back in the water the fish which has just come out of the net. Without a suspicion on his part that so much honor had been done to so sorry a subject, he had a special bundle of memoranda in the mysterious portfolios of the Rue de Jérusalem. His name was written in round hand on the gray paper of the cover, and the notes and reports, carefully classified, gave him his successive appellations: "Name, Leturc;" "The prisoner Leturc;" and at last, "The criminal Leturc."

He was two years out of prison, — dining where he could, sleeping in night lodging-houses and sometimes in lime-kilns, and taking part with his fellows in interminable games of pitch-penny on the boulevards near the barriers. He wore a greasy cap on the back of his head, carpet slippers, and a short white blouse. When he had five sous he had his hair curled. He danced at Constant's at Montparnasse; bought for two sous to sell for four at the door of Bobino, the jack of hearts or the ace of clubs serving as a countermark; sometimes opened the door of a carriage; led horses to the horse-market. From the lottery of all sorts of miserable employments he drew a goodly number. Who can say if the atmosphere of honor which one breathes as a soldier, if military discipline might not have saved him? Taken in a cast of the net with some young loafers who robbed drunkards sleeping on the streets, he denied very earnestly having taken part in their expeditions. Perhaps he told the truth, but his antecedents were accepted in lieu of proof, and he was sent for three years to Poissy. There he made coarse playthings for children, was tattooed on the chest, learned thieves' slang and the penal code. A new liberation, and a new plunge into the sink of Paris; but very short this time, for at the end of six months at the most he was again compromised in a night robbery, aggravated by climbing and breaking,—a serious affair, in which he played an obscure rôle, half dupe and half fence. On the whole, his complicity was evident, and he was sent for five years at hard labor. His grief in this adventure was above all in being separated from an old dog which he had found on a dung-heap and cured of the mange. The beast loved him.

Toulon, the ball and chain, the work in the harbor, the blows from a stick, wooden shoes on bare feet, soup of black beans dating from Trafalgar, no tobacco money, and the terrible sleep in a camp swarming with convicts: that was what he experienced for five broiling summers and five winters raw with the Mediterranean wind. He came out from there stunned, was sent under surveillance to Vernon, where he worked some time on the river. Then, an incorrigible vagabond, he broke his exile and came again to Paris. He had his savings,—fifty-six francs, —that is to say, time enough for reflection. During his absence his former wretched companions had dispersed. He was well hidden, and slept in a loft at an old woman's, to whom he represented himself as a sailor, tired of the sea, who had lost his papers in a recent shipwreck, and who wanted to try his hand at something else. His tanned face and his calloused hands, together with some sea phrases which he dropped from time to time, made his tale seem probable enough.

One day when he risked a saunter in the streets, and when chance had led him as far as Montmartre, where he was born, an unexpected memory stopped him before the door of Les Frères, where he had learned to read. As it was very warm, the door was open, and by a single glance the passing outcast was able to recognize the peaceable school-room. Nothing was changed: neither the bright light shining in at the great windows, nor the crucifix over the desk, nor the rows of benches with the tables furnished with inkstands and pencils, nor the table of weights and measures, nor the map where pins stuck in still indicated the operations of some ancient war. Heedlessly and without thinking, Jean François read on the blackboard the words of the Evangelist which had been set there as a copy:—

"Joy shall be in heaven over one sinner that repenteth, more than over ninety-and-nine just persons which need no repentance."

It was undoubtedly the hour for recreation, for the Brother Professor had left his chair, and sitting on the edge of a table, he was telling a story to the boys who surrounded him with eager and attentive eyes. What a bright and innocent face he had, that beardless young man, in his long black gown, and a white necktie, and great ugly shoes, and his badly cut brown hair streaming out behind! All the simple figures of the children of the people who were watching him seemed scarcely less childlike than his; above all when, delighted with some of his own simple and priestly pleasantries, he broke out in an open and frank peal of laughter which showed his white and regular teeth, —a peal so contagious that all the scholars laughed loudly in their turn. It was such a sweet simple group in the bright sunlight, which lighted their dear eyes and their blond curls.

Jean François looked at them for some time in silence, and for the first time in that savage nature, all instinct and appetite, there awoke a mysterious, a tender emotion. His heart, that seared and hardened heart, unmoved when the convict's cudgel or the heavy whip of the watchman fell on his shoulders, beat oppressively. In that sight he saw again his infancy; and closing his eyes sadly, the prey to torturing regret, he walked quickly away.

Then the words written on the blackboard came back to his mind.

"If it wasn't too late, after all!" he murmured; "if I could again, like others, eat honestly my brown bread, and sleep my fill without nightmare! The spy must be sharp who recognizes me. My beard, which I shaved off down there, has grown out thick and strong. One can burrow somewhere in the great ant-hill, and work can be found. Whoever is not worked to death in the hell of the galleys comes out agile and robust, and I learned there to climb ropes with loads upon my back. Building is going on everywhere here, and the masons need helpers. Three francs a day! I never earned so much. Let me be forgotten, and that is all I ask."

He followed his courageous resolution; he was faithful to it, and after three months he was another man. The master for whom he worked called him his best workman. After a long day upon the scaffolding in the hot sun and the dust, constantly bending and raising his back to take the hod from the man at his feet and pass it to the man over his head, he went for his soup to the cook-shop, tired out, his legs aching, his hands burning, his eyelids stuck with plaster, but content with himself and carrying his well-earned money in a knot in his handkerchief. He went out now without fear, since he could not be recognized in his white mask, and since he had noticed that the suspicious glances of the policeman were seldom turned on the tired workman. He was quiet and sober. He slept the sound sleep of fatigue. He was free.

At last — oh supreme recompense! — he had a friend!

He was a fellow-workman like himself, named Savinien, a little peasant with red lips who had come to Paris with his stick over his shoulder and a bundle on the end of it, fleeing from the wine-shops and going to mass every Sunday. Jean François loved him for his piety, for his candor, for his honesty, for all that he himself had lost, and so long ago. It was a passion, profound and unrestrained, which transformed him by fatherly cares and attentions. Savinien, himself of a weak and egotistical nature, let things take their course, satisfied only in finding a companion who shared his horror of the wine-shop. The two friends lived together in a fairly comfortable lodging, but their resources were very limited. They were obliged to take into their room a third companion, an old Auvergnat, gloomy and rapacious, who found it possible out of his meagre salary to save something with which to buy a place in his own country. Jean François and Savinien were always together. On holidays they together took long walks in the environs of Paris, and dined under an arbor in one of those small country inns where there are a great many mushrooms in the sauces and innocent rebuses on the napkins.   There Jean François learned from his friend all that lore of which they who are born in the city are ignorant: learned the names of the trees, the flowers and the plants; the various seasons for harvesting; he heard eagerly the thousand details of a laborious country life,— the autumn sowing, the winter chores, the splendid celebrations of harvest and vintage days, the sound of the mills at the water-side and the flails striking the ground, the tired horses led to water and the hunting in the morning mist, and above all the long evenings, shortened by marvelous stories, around the fire of vine-shoots. He discovered in himself a source of imagination before unknown, and found a singular delight in the recital of events so placid, so calm, so monotonous.

One thing troubled him, however: it was the fear lest Savinien might learn something of his past.   Sometimes there escaped from him some low word of thieves' slang, a vulgar gesture,— vestiges of his former horrible existence,— and he felt the pain one feels when old wounds reopen; the more because he fancied that he sometimes saw in Savinien the awakening of an unhealthy curiosity.   When the young man, already tempted by the pleasures which Paris offers to the poorest, asked him about the mysteries of the great city, Jean François feigned ignorance and turned the subject; but he felt a vague inquietude for the future of his friend.

His uneasiness was not without foundation.   Savinien could not long remain the simple rustic that he was on his arrival in Paris. If the gross and noisy pleasures of the wine-shop always repelled him, he was profoundly troubled by other temptations, full of danger for the inexperience of his twenty years.   When spring came he began to go off alone, and at first he wandered about the brilliant entrance of some dancing-hall, watching the young girls who went in with their arms around each others' waists, talking in low tones.   Then one evening, when lilacs perfumed the air and the call to quadrilles was most captivating, he crossed the threshold, and from that time Jean François observed a change, little by little, in his manners and his visage. He became more frivolous, more extravagant. He often borrowed from his friend his scanty savings, and he forgot to repay. Jean François, feeling that he was abandoned, jealous and forgiving at the same time, suffered and was silent. He felt that he had no right to reproach him, but with the foresight of affection he indulged in cruel and inevitable presentiments.

One evening, as he was mounting the stairs to his room, absorbed in his thoughts, he heard, as he was about to enter, the sound of angry voices, and he recognized that of the old Auvergnat who lodged with Savinien and himself. An old habit of suspicion made him stop at the landing-place and listen to learn the cause of the trouble.

"Yes," said the Auvergnat angrily, "I am sure that some one has opened my trunk and stolen from it the three louis that I had hidden in a little box; and he who has done this thing must be one of the two companions who sleep here, if it were not the servant Maria. It concerns you as much as it does me, since you are the master of the house, and I will drag you to the courts if you do not let me at once break open the valises of the two masons. My poor gold! It was here yesterday in its place, and I will tell you just what it was, so that if we find it again nobody can accuse me of having lied. Ah, I know them, my three beautiful gold pieces, and I can see them as plainly as I see you! One piece was more worn than the others; it was of greenish gold, with a portrait of the great emperor. The other was a great old fellow with a queue and epaulettes; and the third, which had on it a Philippe with whiskers, I had marked with my teeth. They don't trick me. Do you know that I only wanted two more like that to pay for my vineyard? Come, search these fellows' things with me, or I will call the police! Hurry up!"

"All right," said the voice of the landlord; "we will go and search with Maria. So much the worse for you if we find nothing, and the masons get angry. You have forced me to it."

Jean François's soul was full of fright. He remembered the embarrassed circumstances and the small loans of Savinien, and how sober he had seemed for some days. And yet he could not believe that he was a thief. He heard the Auvergnat panting in his eager search, and he pressed his closed fists against his breast as if to still the furious beating of his heart.

"Here they are!" suddenly shouted the victorious miser. "Here they are, my louis, my dear treasure; and in the Sunday vest of that little hypocrite of Limousin! Look, landlord, they are just as I told you. Here is the Napoleon, the man with a queue, and the Philippe that I have bitten. See the dents? Ah, the little beggar with the sanctified air! I should have much sooner suspected the other. Ah, the wretch! Well, he must go to the convict prison."

At this moment Jean François heard the well-known step of Savinien coming slowly up the stairs.

"He is going to his destruction," thought he. "Three stories. I have time!"

And pushing open the door he entered the room, pale as death, where he saw the landlord and the servant stupefied in a corner, while the Auvergnat, on his knees in the disordered heap of clothes, was kissing the pieces of gold.

"Enough of this," he said, in a thick voice; "I took the money and put it in my comrade's trunk. But that is too bad. I am a thief, but not a Judas. Call the police; I will not try to escape, only I must say a word to Savinien in private. Here he is."

In fact, the little Limousin had just arrived; and seeing his crime discovered, believing himself lost, he stood there, his eyes fixed, his arms hanging.

Jean François seized him forcibly by the neck, as if to embrace him; he put his mouth close to Savinien's ear, and said to him in a low supplicating voice:—

"Keep quiet."

Then turning towards the others:—

"Leave me alone with him. I tell you I won't go away. Lock us in if you wish, but leave us alone."

With a commanding gesture he showed them the door. They went out.

Savinien, broken by grief, was sitting on the bed, and lowered his eyes without understanding anything.

"Listen," said Jean François, who came and took him by the hands, "I understand! You have stolen three gold pieces to buy some trifle for a girl. That costs six months in prison. But one only comes out from there to go back again, and you will become a pillar of police courts and tribunals. I understand it. I have been seven years at the Reform School, a year at Sainte Pélagie, three years at Poissy, five years at Toulon. Now, don't be afraid. Everything is arranged. I have taken it on my shoulders."

"It is dreadful," said Savinien; but hope was springing up again in his cowardly heart.

"When the elder brother is under the flag, the younger one does not go," replied Jean François. "I am your substitute, that's all. You care for me a little, do you not? I am paid. Don't be childish — don't refuse. They would have taken me again one of these days, for I am a runaway from exile. And then, do you see, that life will be less hard for me than for you. I know it all, and I shall not complain if I have not done you this service for nothing, and if you swear to me that you will never do it again. Savinien, I have loved you well, and your friendship has made me happy. It is through it that since I have known you I have been honest and pure, as I might always have been, — perhaps if I had had, like you, a father to put a tool in my hands, a mother to teach me my prayers. It was my sole regret that I was useless to you, and that I deceived you concerning myself. To-day I have unmasked in saving you. It is all right. Do not cry, and embrace me, for already I hear heavy boots on the stairs. They are coming with the *posse*, and we must not seem to know each other so well before those chaps."

He pressed Savinien quickly to his breast, then pushed him from him, when the door was thrown wide open.

It was the landlord and the Auvergnat, who brought the police. Jean François sprang forward to the landing-place, held out his hands for the handcuffs, and said, laughing, "Forward, bad lot!"

To-day he is at Cayenne, condemned for life as an incorrigible.

P. CORNEILLE.

PIERRE CORNEILLE

(1606–1684)

BY FREDERICK MORRIS WARREN

ORNEILLE'S life, apart from the performance and publication of his works, is but imperfectly known, owing to the lack of contemporaneous records and allusions. He was born at Rouen, capital of the old province of Normandy, on June 6th, 1606. At his christening on June 9th he received the name of Pierre, after his father and godfather. He was educated in the Jesuit college (academy) at Rouen, and obtained in 1620 a prize for excellence. Choosing his father's profession, he studied law, and was admitted to the bar on June 18th, 1624. The office of attorney-general in the department of waters and forests was purchased by him on December 16th, 1628. The year following, Mondory, who with a company of actors was probably playing at Rouen, persuaded him to give his (Mondory's) troupe a comedy he had already written; and the season of 1629-30 saw the play produced in Paris, at the newly established Marais Theatre.

The success of this comedy, 'Mélite,' confirmed Corneille in his purpose of writing for the stage and led him to study the principles of dramatic art. While he continued to discharge his legal duties at Rouen, he would frequently visit Paris in order to offer some new play to Mondory, or mingle in the literary society of the capital. So 'Mélite,' made up entirely of conversations where nothing happened, was followed by 'Clitandre,' a tragi-comedy of the popular type, full of bloody episodes. Like 'Mélite,' it was in twelve-syllable verse (Alexandrine) and contained five acts. It also showed Corneille's first attempt to observe unity of time. When it was published in March 1632, a selection of Corneille's poetry, a part of which antedated 'Mélite,' was put with it.

The next two years saw the publication of occasional poems by him in French, and some Latin verse in honor of the King and Richelieu. Before March 1634 he also composed four more comedies: 'The Widow,' a character study, noticeable for the attempt to compromise on unity of time by allowing a day to each act; 'The Gallery of the Palace,' where the action takes place in the fashionable shops of the day, and in which the modern character of the soubrette displaces the traditional nurse of Renaissance comedy, taken by a man in disguise; 'The Lady's Maid,' a study of this successful substitute, where finally Corneille observes both the unities of time and place, and makes his five acts equal, line for line; and 'The Palais Royal,' another topical comedy for Parisians. These four plays are much like their predecessors in lack of action and superfluity of complimentary talk. The same may be said of Corneille's collaboration on Richelieu's 'Comedy of The Tuileries' (1635). His superiority to his colleagues at this time consisted mainly in his poetic talent and common-sense.

In the season of 1634–35 he tried a tragedy, 'Medea,' patterned after Seneca's Latin drama of that name. It shows an advance on his previous efforts, yet did not come up to his high standard; and he sought a diversion for his disappointment by eulogizing the theatrical profession in a play within a play, 'The Dramatic Illusion,' which he gave to the actors of the Hôtel of Burgundy, probably in 1635.

About this time Corneille's attention was drawn to the Spanish drama, then at its highest point. The storied deeds of Spain's national hero especially appealed to his temperament, and he selected Guillen de Castro's 'First Exploits of the Cid' as a model for his imitation. A year or more he may have been busy in adapting its complexity of scene and character to the orderly, simple requirements of the French stage. For it was not till the last days of 1636, after unusual preparations in rehearsals and costuming, that Mondory's company brought out 'The Cid.' Its success was instantaneous. The theatre was crowded for many nights. The stage even was filled in with seats for the nobility, to the great annoyance of the actors and the detriment of the scenery. And sixteen years later, Pellisson, the historian of the Academy, could still write:—"It is difficult to conceive the approbation with which this play was received by the Court and public. People never tired of going to it; you could hear nothing else talked about; everybody knew some part of it by heart; children were made to learn it, and in several places in France it gave rise to the proverb, 'That is as beautiful as The Cid.'"

The history of modern French drama dates from the first performance of 'The Cid.' The theme here selected became the typical one. It shows the struggle between love and honor on the part of the hero, love and duty on the part of the heroine. Jimena's father has insulted Rodrigo's, enfeebled by his advanced years. He calls upon his son to avenge his honor. In spite of his love for Jimena, Rodrigo shows no hesitation. He challenges the Count and kills him. In the lovers' interview which follows, Jimena is more distracted from her duty by her love than Rodrigo was, but yet resolves on vengeance. She demands a champion of the king, who objects that Rodrigo should be pardoned, having just saved the city from the invading Moors. Jimena insists: a champion appears, is overthrown, and is spared by Rodrigo, whereupon the king intervenes and orders the betrothal of the lovers.

Since 'The Cid' ends happily, so far as the hero and heroine are concerned, Corneille first called it a tragi-comedy, but later substituted the title of tragedy. Its general structure is the same as that of his other plays,— five fairly equal acts, subdivided into scenes, with rhymed Alexandrine couplets, excepting in a few lyric strophes. The time of the action is limited to twenty-four hours, but the scene of the action is restricted only by the boundaries of the town (Seville), the different places being marked by a fixed scenery, which presented several localities to the audience at the same time.

His dramatic form and stage properties Corneille had obtained from his French predecessors of the classical school. The mediæval Miracle Plays had practically fallen out of favor nearly a century before 'Mélite,' and had been prohibited in Paris in 1548. But the Fraternity of the Passion still occupied the only theatre in the city, and had a monopoly of all the performances in the city and suburbs. Into its theatre of the Hôtel of Burgundy it had put as much of its old multiplex scenery as it could fit into the new and narrow stage. And while it could no longer act the old Mysteries, still it clung to dramatic stories which knew neither unity of time, place, nor even action.

Outside of these playwrights, however, the Renaissance had created a set of men who looked towards classical antiquity for their literary standards. In 1552 Jodelle and his friends of the Pléiade had appealed to this class by acting in Boncourt College a tragedy modeled on Seneca's Latin dramas. This example was subsequently followed by many writers, who however rarely got their pieces acted, and therefore fell into the way of writing without having the necessities of stage effects in view. Consequently for nearly half a century the best dramatists of France were strangers to the public of the Hôtel of Burgundy, and were drifting more and more from a dramatic conception of the theatre into a lyric one. Long declamatory monologues, acts varying greatly in length and separated by elaborate choruses, were the chief features of this school. Nothing happened on the stage; all was told by messengers.

Yet these dramas, by their very lack of action and scenery, were suited to the limited means of strolling companies of actors; and modifications of them were being played more and more to provincial audiences. Finally in 1599 one of these companies came to Paris, leased the Hôtel of Burgundy from the Fraternity, now tired of its avocation, and laid there the foundations of modern French drama. The purveyor to this troupe was Alexandre Hardy, a man of some education, of considerable theatrical endowments, but lacking in literary taste. True to his classical models so far as the unlettered public of the Hôtel and its scenery would allow, he managed by cutting down the monologues, equalizing the acts, restricting or suppressing the choruses, and leading the dialogue to some climax visible to his audience, to effect a compromise between the partisans of the two schools and educate a new body of theatre-goers. His scenery he could not change, and it still remained a constant temptation to diversity of place and multiplication of episodes. Hardy labored for more than thirty years. It is to his dramatic form, audience, and stage that Corneille succeeded, continuing his work while avoiding his excesses. And aided by the growing taste and intelligence of his public, Corneille could further simplify and refine the style of play in vogue.

Now De Castro's 'Cid' had enjoyed the freedom of the Miracle Plays. It numbered three acts, divided into fifty-three scenes. Its episodes, many of them purely digressive, occupied nearly two years of time and were bounded in place only by the frontiers of Spain. In order to reduce this epic exuberance to the severity of the classical mold, Corneille had to eliminate the digressive episodes, cut down and combine the essential ones, connect the places where the action took place, and lessen the time of its duration. In the French 'Cid,' Rodrigo kills Jimena's father and is betrothed to her in less than twenty-four hours.

This instance alone illustrates the effort Corneille made on himself. It caught also the eye of his rivals and critics. 'The Cid' was fiercely assailed for its "inhumanity" and "improbability," and with the connivance of Richelieu the newly organized Academy was called upon to condemn it. While the opinion of this body was not indeed unfavorable, yet the dispute had so irritated Corneille that he retired to Rouen and for a time renounced his art. When he reappeared, it was as a dramatizer of classical subjects, that dealt with but one episode to a play. But the romantic side still survived in the love affair invariably interwoven with his nobler, sterner theme.

So 'Horace' (1640) treated of the fight of the Horatii and the Curatii, and the immolation of a woman's love to the Roman fatherland. 'Cinna' (1640–41) narrated a conspiracy against Augustus, which was undertaken through love for the heroine, but was pardoned by the Emperor's magnanimity. 'Polyeuctus' (1643) showed how a steadfast Christian husband could preserve his wife's fidelity against the memory of a first love, and how his martyrdom could result in her conversion. 'Pompey' (1643–44) recited the death of that leader and the devotion of Cornelia, his wife, to his memory.

These four plays, tragedies all, represent in their eloquence, their diction, nobility of thought, and lofty aspiration, the highest development of Corneille's dramatic genius.

After this period of serious composition Corneille sought relaxation in comedy, and produced from Spanish models 'The Liar' (1644) and 'The Sequel to the Liar' (1645). Both are superior in dialogue, action, and verse to his earlier plays, and the first remained the best comedy of the new school up to the appearance of Molière. Towards the end of 1645 'Rodogune' was acted, a tragedy to which Corneille was ever partial on account of its highly wrought, exciting solution. 'Théodore' (1646), the fate of another Christian martyr, and 'Heraclius' (1646–47), preceded their author's election to the Academy (January 22d, 1647). The Fronde then intervened, and it was not till 1649 that Corneille's best tragi-comedy, 'Don Sancho,' was performed. A spectacular play or opera, 'Andromeda' (1650), closely followed it. 'Nicomedes' (1651) was a successful tragedy, 'Pertharite' (1652) a failure. Consequently for the next few years Corneille devoted himself to religious poetry and a verse translation of the 'Imitation of Christ.'

But the visit of Molière's company to Rouen in 1658 incited him to write again for the stage. 'Œdipus' (1659), 'Sertorius' (1662), 'Sophonisba' (1663), 'Otho' (1664), 'Agesilas' (1666), and 'Attila' (1667), all tragedies, were the result. Some were successful, but others were not. Molière was now in full career, and Racine was beginning. Corneille's defects were growing. His plays were too much alike, and gallant talk supplied in them the place of deeds. In 1660 a second spectacular drama, 'The Golden Fleece,' had been performed; and the same year he had edited a general edition of his plays, with a critical preface to each play and three essays on the laws and theories of the drama. All this time he had not neglected society and religious verse, and probably in 1662 he had moved from Rouen to Paris.

A retirement of three years followed 'Attila.' Then in 1670 Corneille reappeared with the tragedy 'Titus and Berenice,' neglected by the public for Racine's 'Berenice.' In 1671 he collaborated with Molière and Quinault on a comedy-ballet, 'Psyche.' In 1672 he wrote 'Pulcheria,' a tragi-comedy, and in 1674 gave his last play, the tragedy of 'Surena,' to the stage. Henceforth only supplicatory poems addressed to the King reminded the Parisians of Corneille's existence. In 1682 he published the final revision of his dramas, and in 1684, on the night of September 30th, he passed away. He had married in 1641. Four children survived him.

Corneille's contemporaries complain of his slovenliness, his timidity, quick temper, and wearying conversation. He could never read his own plays successfully, and is even said to have spoken French incorrectly. He was reputed avaricious, but was continually lamenting his poverty, and seems to have died in want. He was quite tall, well set, with large eyes and strongly marked features.

Besides his services to French comedy, Corneille may be said to have established the higher comedy in verse, with its decent manners and self-respecting characters. In this departure he undoubtedly owed much to Plautus and Terence, but probably more to Hardy's tragi-comedies and lighter plays. The chief merit of his style was fine diction, eloquence, and harmony of phrase. His thought was high and noble. As a dramatist he excelled in the invention and variety of his situations. His defects were the reverse of these qualities: rhetoric, subtle sentiment, stiff characters.

The best complete edition of Corneille is Marty-Laveaux's in the Hachette series of 'Les Grands Écrivains de la France' (Great Writers of France), 12 volumes, 1862–68. This edition contains a biographical notice. The most complete bibliography is E. Picot's 'Bibliographie Cornélienne' (Paris, 1865). J. Taschereau's 'Histoire de la Vie et des Œuvres de Corneille' (History of the Life and Works of Corneille) is the best biography (published Paris, 1829: 3d edition, 1869). F. Guizot's 'Corneille and His Times' is the only life that has been translated into English (London, 1857). Of the separate plays, 'The Cid,' 'Horace,' and 'Polyeuctus' have been rendered into English blank verse by W. F. Nokes (Hachette and Company), and these three, together with 'Cinna,' have been literally translated by R. Mongan and D. McRae (London: 1878–86.)

F. M. Warren.

THE LOVERS

From 'The Cid'

The scene is an apartment in the house of Chimène's *father in Seville.* Chimène *and* Elvire *are conversing, after* Chimène *has learned that her father, the* Count de Gormas, *has lost his life in a duel with* Don Rodrigue, *the son of an aged nobleman insulted by* De Gormas.

CHIMÈNE—At stake is my honor; revenge must be mine;
   Whate'er the desire love may flattering stir,
   To the soul nobly born all excuse is disgrace.

Elvire —
    Thou lov'st Don Rodrigue; he can never offend.
Chimène —
    I admit it.
Elvire —   Admitting it, how canst thou act?
Chimène —
    By sustaining my honor, by casting my care —
    Pursue him, destroy him, and after him — die.
Don Rodrigue [*entering as she speaks the last words*] —
    'Tis well! Without taking the pains of pursuit,
    Be secure in the pleasure of ending my days.
Chimène —
    Elvire, oh where are we? What, what do I see?
    Rodrigue in this house! Before me, Rodrigue!
Don Rodrigue —
    Oh, spare not my blood; unresisted, pray taste
    Of my ruin the sweetness, of vengeance the joy.
Chimène —
    Alas!
Don Rodrigue — Hear me, lady!
Chimène —   I die!
Don Rodrigue —   But one word —
Chimène —
    Go, I say; let me die!
Don Rodrigue —   Ah, vouchsafe me a word!
    And once I have spoke, make reply with — this sword.
Chimène —
    What! The sword e'en now red with the blood of my sire!
Don Rodrigue —
    Chimène, my Chimène!
Chimène —   Hide that hideous steel,
    That rebuketh my eyes for thy crime and thy life.
Don Rodrigue —
    Nay, rather behold it, thy hate to excite,
    Thy wrath to increase — and my doom so to speed.
Chimène —
    It is tinged with my blood.
Don Rodrigue —   Plunge it then into mine,
    That so it may lose the dread tint of thy veins.
Chimène —
    Ah, fate all too cruel! that slays in one day
    The father by steel, and the daughter by sight!
    Take away, as I bid, what I cannot endure;
    Thou will'st that I hearken — and kill'st me meantime!

Don Rodrigue —

What thou wishest I do; but with no less desire
That my life, now deplorable, ends by your hand;
For expect not, I beg, from my passion itself
A coward's repentance of deed so deserved.
From thy father's rash hand came a blow — past recall;
It dishonored my sire in his honored old age.
What are blows to a man of due honor thou knowest.
In the shame I had part, and its author must seek;
Him I saw — both my father and honor I 'venged;
I would do it again, if I had it to do.
Yet think not 'gainst duty to father and self
My love for thee, lady, no contest has made;
Of thy power in this moment do thou be the judge.
Too well might I doubt if such vengeance I dared.
Bound to please thee, Chimène, or to suffer affront,
Too rash seemed my arm — I would fain hold it back;
With a deed all too violent blamed I myself:
Thy beauty had weighed down the balance at last,
Had I not, to thy charms, countervailing, opposed
That a man lost to honor could not thee deserve;
That once having loved me when blameless I lived,
She who cared for me stainless must hate me disgraced;
That to hearken to love, to obey its soft voice,
Was to find myself shameful — thy favor to stain.
Again do I tell thee — and while I shall breathe
Unchanged shall I think and unchanging will say —
I have done thee offense, but I could not halt back,
A disgrace to remove and thyself to deserve.
But now, quits with honor, and quits toward my sire,
'Tis thee, thee alone, I would fain satisfy;
'Tis to proffer my blood that thou seest me here.
I have done what I should — what is left I would do.
Well I know that thy father's death arms thee toward mine;
Not thee have I wished of thy victim to cheat.
Boldly immolate, now, the blood he has spilled —
The being who glories that such was his deed.

Chimène —

Ah, Rodrigue! True it is that though hostile I am,
No blame can I speak that disgrace thou hast fled;
Howe'er from my lips this my dolor break forth,
I dare not accuse thee — I weep for my woes.
I know that thy honor, on insult so deep,
Demanded of ardor a valorous proof.

Thou hast done but the duty enjoined on the brave:
Yet more, in its doing 'tis mine thou hast taught.
By thy courage funest, and thy conquest, I'm schooled;
Thy father avenged and thine honor upheld,
Like care, see, is mine; for to load me with grief,
I must father avenge, *I* must honor uphold!
Alas, 'tis thy part here that brings me despair.
Had aught other misfortune bereft me of sire,
My heart in the joy of beholding thyself
The sole solace that heart could receive would have found
Against my affliction a charm would be strong,
My tears would be dried by the dearest of hands.
But lo! I must lose thee, my father a loss;
And the more that my soul may in torment be thrown,
My star has decreed that I compass thy end.
Expect not, in turn, from the passion I own,
That my hand I shall stay from thy punishment meet;
Thy direful offense makes thee worthy of me;
By thy death I shall show myself worthy of thee.

Unrhymed literal version in the metre of the original, by E. Irenæus
Stevenson.

DON RODRIGUE DESCRIBES TO KING FERNANDO HIS VICTORY OVER THE MOORS

From 'The Cid'

UNDER me, then, the troop made advance,
   With soldierly confidence marked on each brow.
   Five hundred we started, but soon reinforced,
Three thousand we were when the port we had reached;
So much did mere sight of our numbers, our mien,
New courage revive in all timorous hearts.
Two-thirds did I ambush, as soon as arrived,
In the vessels in harbor, that ready were found;
But the others, whose numbers each hour did increase,
With impatience on fire, all about me encamped,
Stretched out on the earth passed the beauteous night.
In the harbor, I order the guards to like watch;
Their concealment my stratagem further assists;—
I dared to declare, Sire, as thine the command
That I so followed out, and enjoined upon all.
In the radiance pallid that fell from the stars,
At last, with the flood-tide we spy thirty sails;

Beneath swells the wave, and in movement therewith,
The sea and the Moors into harbor advance.
We permit them a passage — to them all seemed calm,
Our soldiers unseen, and the walls without ward.
Our silence profound well deluded their wit;
No longer they doubt our surprise is achieved;
Without fear they draw nearer — they anchor — they land —
They run to the hands that are waiting to strike.
Then rise we together, and all in a breath
Utter clamorous shoutings that heavenward rise.
From the ships to such signal our troops make response;
They stand forth in arms, and the Moors are dismayed;
By dread they are seized when but half-disembarked;
Ere the battle's begun they have deemed themselves lost.
They have come but to pillage — 'tis fight that they meet.
We assail them on sea, we assail them on land;
On the ground runs the blood we set flowing in streams
Ere a soul can resist — or fly back to his post.
But soon in our spite the chiefs rallied their host,
Their courage awoke, and their fear was o'ercome:
The shame of their dying without having fought,
Their disorder arrests, and their valor restores.
A firm stand they take, and their swords are unsheathed;
The land and the stream, ay, the fleet and the port,
Are a field where, triumphant o'er carnage, is death.
Oh, many the deeds, the exploits worthy fame,
In that horror of darkness are buried for aye,
When each, the sole witness of blows that he struck,
Could not guess whither Fortune the conflict would steer!
I flew to all sides to encourage our force,
Here to push into action, and there to restrain,
To enrank the newcoming, to spur them in turn,
Yet naught could I know till the breaking of day.
But with dawn and the light, our advantage was plain;
The Moors saw their ruin; their courage declined;
And beholding new succor approach to our side,
Changed their ardor for battle to sheer dread of death.
Their vessels they seek, — every cable is cut;
For farewells to our ears are sent up their wild cries;
Their retreat is a tumult — no man ever heeds
If their princes and kings have made good their escape.
Even duty itself yields to fear so extreme.
On the flood-tide they came, the ebb bears them away;
Meantime their two Kings with our host still engaged,

'Mid a handful of followers, slashed by our blows,
In valiance contending, are selling life dear.
In vain to surrender I beg them — entreat,
With the cimeter gripped, not a word will they hear:
But at sight of their troops falling dead at their feet,
The brave who alone make so vain a defense,
Our chief they demand; and to me they submit.
To you, O my Sire, have I sent them, each one —
And the combatants lacking, the combat was done.

THE WRATH OF CAMILLA

From the ‘Horace›

Horatius, *the only survivor of the combat, advances to meet his sister
Camilla with Proculus at his side, bearing the swords of the three
slain Curatii — one of whom was Camilla's betrothed. Camilla surveys him with horror and disdain as he advances.*

HORATIUS — Lo, sister, the arm that hath brothers avenged! —
The arm that our fate so contrary has checked,
The arm that makes Alba our own; and to-day
By one deed the lot of two nations hath fixed.
See these tokens of honor — my glory's attest.
Do thou pay the tribute now due to my fame.

Camilla —
Receive then my tears: for my tears are thy due.

Horatius —
Nay, Rome likes them not, after action so bold.
Our brothers, both slain by the combat's dark fate,
Are avenged by this blood — no more weeping demand.
If a loss be so paid, then the loss is no more.

Camilla —
Since thou deemest my brothers by blood so appeased,
I will cease to show sign of my grief for their death;
But who shall avenge me my lover's death, say?
And make me forget in one moment such loss?

Horatius —
What sayest thou, unhappy?

Camilla —
                  O beloved Curiace!

Horatius —
O boldness disgraceful, from sister disgraced!
The name on thy lips and the love in thy heart
Of the foe of our people, whose conquest is mine!

Thy criminal flame to such vengeance aspires!
Thou darest to utter such thought of thy heart!
Follow passion the less, better rule thy desire:
Make me not so to blush that thy sighs are not hid;
From this moment thou owest to smother thy flame,
Free thy heart from them—dwell on these trophies instead,
And make *them* from this hour thy sole pleasure in life.

Camilla—

Nay, first give me, cruel, a heart hard as thine,
And if thou wilt seek all my spirit to read,
Give me back Curiace, or my passion let glow.
My joy and my grief of his lot are a part;
Him living I loved—him in death I deplore.
No more find me sister—deserted by thee!
Behold in me only a woman outraged,
Who—like to some Fury pursuing thy steps—
Unceasing shall charge thee with trespass so great!
O tiger, blood-gorged, who forbiddest my tears,
Who would see me find joy in this death thou hast wrought,
Who vauntest to Heaven itself such a deed,
Shall I by approval bring death to him—twice?
Misfortunes so dire, may they follow thy life
That thou fallest to envying even my own!
Oh, soon by some cowardice mayest thou blot
This glory thy brutal soul reckons so dear!

Horatius—

O heavens! hath any an equal rage seen?
Dost thou think I could brook, all unmoved, such offense?
That race could endure a dishonor so deep?
Love, love thou the death which means good to thy State,
Prefer to thy passion and thoughts of this man
The sentiment due to a daughter of Rome!

Camilla—

Rome! Object supreme of the wrath that I feel!
This Rome, to whose aid came thy arm—and my loss;
Rome, city that bore thee—by thee so adored!
Rome, hated the more for its honoring thee!
O may each of her neighbors together in league
Sap every foundation, as yet so unsure!
Nay, if Italy be not enough to the fall,
Let the East and the West for her ruin unite;
Let peoples conjoined from the four winds of heaven,
Be met to her downfall; let hills aid, and seas;
O'erthrown on her walls may she prostrate be cast,

Torn out by her own hands, her entrails be strewn!
May the anger of Heaven, here kindled by me,
Rain down on her dwellings a deluge of fire!
O grant that mine own eyes such thunderbolt see!—
See her mansions in ashes, her laurels in dust,
See the latest of Romans yielding his last breath,
I cause of it all — I dying of joy!

[*With the last words* Camilla *rushes from the apartment.* Horace *snatches his sword and pursues her, exclaiming:*—]

Oh too much! Even reason to passion gives place.
Go, weep thou thy lost Curiace in the shades!

[*After an instant is heard behind the scenes the shriek of the wounded* Camilla:—]

Ah, traitor!

Horace [*returning to the stage*]—

Receive thou quick chastisement, due
Whomsoever shall dare Roman foe to lament.

Unrhymed literal version in the metre of the original, by E. Irenæus Stevenson.

PAULINA'S APPEAL TO SEVERUS

From 'Polyeucte'

SEVERUS —   I stand agaze,
Rooted, confounded, in sheer wonderment.
Such blind resolve is so unparalleled,
I scarce may trust the witness of mine ears.
A heart that loves you — and what heart so poor
That knowing, loves you not?— one loved of you,
To leave regretless so much bliss just won!
Nay, more — as though it were a fatal prize —
To his corrival straight to yield it up!
Truly, or wondrous manias Christians have,
Or their self-happiness must be sans bourn,
Since to attain it they will cast away
What others at an empire's cost would win.
For me, had fate, a little sooner kind,
Blessed my true service with your hand's reward,
The glory of your eyes had been my worship;
My twin kings had they reigned — kings? nay, my gods!
To dust, to powder, had I grinded been
E'er I had —

Paulina —   Hold! let me not hear too much;
Let not the smoldering embers of old time

Relume to speech unworthy of us both.
Severus, know Paulina utterly:
His latest hour my Polyeuctus nears;
Nay, scarce a minute has he yet to live.
You all unwittingly have been the cause
Of this his death. I know not if your thoughts,
Their portals opening to your wish's knock,
Have dared to some wild hope give harboring,
Based upon his undoing; but know well,
No death so cruel I would not boldly front,
Hell hath no tortures I would not endure,
Or e'er my stainless honor I would spot,
My hand bestowing upon any man
Who anywise were his death's instrument.
And could you for such madness deem me apt,
Hate would replace my erstwhile tender love.
You're generous — still be so, to the end:
My father fears you; is in mood to grant
All you might ask; ay, I e'en dare aver
That if my husband he do sacrifice,
'Twill be to you. Save then your hapless victim;
Bestir yourself; stretch him your helping hand!
That this is much to claim of you, I know,
But more the effort's great, the more the glory!
To save a rival 'spite of rivalry
Were greatness all particular to you.
And — be that not enough for your renown —
'Twere much to let a woman erst so loved,
And haply who may yet be somewhat dear,
Her greatest treasure owe to your great heart.
In fine, remember that you are Severus!
Adieu! alone determine of your course;
For if you be not all I think you are,
I'd still, not knowing it, believe you such.

English Translation by W. F. Nokes.

VICTOR COUSIN

(1792–1867)

ALL Philosophy, past and present, has been based on the attempt to make abstract ideas clear. The questions Cousin endeavors to answer are:—"Do ideas exist apart from Being and Knowledge; and if so, on what are they founded?" and his answer involves his whole doctrine.

Victor Cousin, the son of a watchmaker of Voltairean principles and of a laundress of strong religious convictions, was born in Paris on November 28th, 1792. But in spite of his humble origin he obtained a brilliant education, and through the force of his genius lived to have precedence at court over his social superiors. The little gamin owed his start in life to Madame Viguier, who placed him at school.

VICTOR COUSIN

On leaving college, from which he was graduated first in his class at the age of eighteen, he could have obtained a position in the Council of State at a yearly salary of five thousand francs; but he preferred to enter the Normal School, then but recently established, with the intention of teaching literature. The impression made upon him by Laromiguière's lectures on philosophy decided him to devote himself to the latter branch of study. Philosophy, to Cousin, was not only a keen delight but a battle as well. Many systems were then arrayed against each other; these in turn fascinated his imagination and excited his enthusiasm,—first the sensual school, then Scottish philosophy as developed by Royer-Collard and Maine de Biran; then Kant, Schelling, Hegel, whose genius he was the first to recognize; and later, Plotinus, Descartes, and Leibnitz. All these doctrines, as he expounded them in his lectures, simmered in his imagination for a while, and unconsciously modifying each other, left a deposit from which arose eclecticism.

There was a dearth of French men of letters when Cousin reached manhood. To become a fashionable lecturer it was only necessary to speak of literature and philosophy in elegant language; and as to these requirements the young orator added a poetic imagination, he became famous at once.

One of Cousin's distinguishing qualities was the impetus he gave to other minds. His lectures created positive fanaticism. But twenty years of age, his delicate face was lighted up with magnificent dark eyes which emitted fire as his own enthusiasm grew. He had a fine voice, was a finished comedian, a poet rather than a deep or original thinker, a preacher rather than a professor, and looked like "a tribune and apostle in one."

It is difficult to understand nowadays the enthusiasm aroused by Cousin's philosophy, or the attacks upon it. He advanced no new truths. No objection could be made to a belief in God, the spirituality and immortality of the soul, and moral liberty. But Cousin went further. He wished to establish philosophy on an independent basis; to found an intermediate school that would not clash with religion, but subsist side by side with, though independent of and in a certain measure controlling it. This aroused the hostility of the Church without satisfying the extremists, who clamored for more radical doctrines. After 1820, when the Normal School was suppressed, Cousin had recourse to private teaching, and devoted his leisure to editing the classics. His edition of Plato occupied him many years. "Every man's life should contain one monument and several episodes," he declared; and his Plato, he believed, was destined to be his "monument."

When Cousin was restored to his chair in 1828, he brought with him a new philosophy which fulfilled the aspirations of the rising generation, whose idol he became. During this course he propounded a few transcendental theories borrowed from Hegel and Schelling, emitted several contestable historical views, and distributed all the doctrines he knew,—and, add his enemies, all those he did not know,—into four divisions. Taken as a whole, Cousin's system has far more in common with Christianity than with pantheism.

During the next three years he made rapid strides in his career. He had taken no part in the July Revolution, but his friends were placed in office by that event, and through their influence he became successively member of the Royal Council of Public Instruction, member of the Academy, and Peer of France.

Cousin was in virtual control of French philosophy when, in 1830, he resigned his chair to become Director of the Sorbonne. To his new task he brought an intelligence matured by time; and the twenty years of his administration were fruitful of good results. He formed a corps of learned professors, perfected the study of French, and placed philosophy on a sound basis. His indefatigable activity, breadth of view, and devotion to teaching made him an admirable director of a school destined to train the professors of a nation. Each one was encouraged to take up an original line of research. He regulated the position of the Sorbonne towards religion, instructing the teachers that belief in God, free-will, and duty was to be inculcated.

Not being of a naturally tender disposition, Cousin may not have loved the students for themselves, but he passionately loved talent, and exerted himself to foster and develop it. Of a disdainful, sarcastic turn of mind, Cousin's mordant wit was well known and greatly feared. His habits were frugal, and though he dressed badly, he was prodigal with regard to books. He nowhere appeared to better advantage than in his library at the Sorbonne, where so many of his books were written. He could talk magnificently on any subject — for an hour; after that, his own eloquence carried him beyond all bounds and he was apt to indulge in paradox. Guizot said of him: "C'est l'esprit qui a le plus besoin de garde-fou." (His is a mind which has the greatest need of restraint.) His voice was wonderfully expressive: witty sayings, comparisons, anecdotes, crowded upon his tongue; as a rule he absorbed the entire conversation and created a sensation, as he loved to do.

Liberal in matters of philosophy rather than in politics, Cousin engaged in a battle with the clergy, to whom however he cheerfully conceded the rights granted by the Charter, and a certain preponderance in the schools. He considered it criminal to attack religion, and required it to be taught in the primary schools, though he excluded it from the University, where it might clash with philosophy. Towards the end of his life he entered into a correspondence with the Pope to prevent ‹ The True, the Beautiful, the Good › from being placed on the Index Expurgatorius, and obtained his point only after lengthy negotiations.

In the earlier years of his life, Cousin's poetic temperament, aided by youth, carried him towards pure philosophy and German ideas. The word pantheism however grew to be a very abomination to him; but storm and protest as he would, it pursued him all his life; his lyric descriptions of God were rigidly interpreted according to pantheistic formulæ, and hurled at his head until he cried "Enough!" "This is the truth," was answered back, though he had long since erased that compromising indorsement of Schelling's system.

Debarred from both politics and teaching at the age of sixty, with intellect and vitality unimpaired, Cousin devoted the fourteen remaining years of his life to literature; and now that the eclectic philosophy is considered merely a brilliant but fleeting system which has lived its day, we still turn with pleasure to his ‹ Biographies. ›

It was by study of the seventeenth century that Cousin's purely literary career began. He relates facts and penetrates the nature of his characters. Taine declares that when at last the lovely face of Madame de Longueville does appear, crash goes a pile of folios to the floor! Nevertheless, strength and energy characterize Cousin's style, and make good his dictum «Style is movement.» To the very end, Cousin retained the spontaneous emotion of youth. The quality of vehemence everywhere so apparent in these 'Biographies' presupposes an intense emotion which is communicated from the writer to the reader.

It was a current joke among the professors of the Sorbonne that her biographer was in love with Madame de Longueville. «Every one knows that Cousin is the *chevalier servant* of Madame de Longueville,» writes Taine. «This noble lady has had the rare privilege of making post-mortem conquests, and the solid walls of the Sorbonne have not protected M. Cousin from the darts of her beautiful eyes. He is so deeply in love with her that he speaks of Condé (her brother) as a brother-in-law, and of La Rochefoucauld (her lover) as a rival.»

Cousin's critics take this retrospective infatuation too seriously. It was merely an «episode» in his life; and when Sainte-Beuve said, «Cousin's bust would one day have engraved beneath it: 'He wished to found a great system of philosophy, and he loved Madame de Longueville,'»—he was more witty than just. It is only fair to add that Sainte-Beuve considered Cousin the most brilliant meteor that had flashed across the sky of the nineteenth century.

In his later years, Cousin recommended 'The True, the Beautiful, the Good' and his 'Philosophy of History' for perusal, in preference to his other books. He was conscious of the drawback attendant upon scattering his doctrines over so many books, and condensed them in the former volume. Composed of brilliant and incomplete fragments, if it does not constitute a systematic whole, the pages relating to God and necessary and universal principles are however full of grandeur, and will always endear it to humanity.

On the 2d of January, 1867, Cousin passed away during his sleep, having been until the last in full possession of the lucidity and vigor which characterized his mind. He left his fine library to the State, with ample funds for its maintenance. He has had the privilege of living in the books of many distinguished men whose minds he trained, whose careers he advanced, and who have recorded in brilliant pages the debt owed him, not by themselves alone, but by all Frenchmen of succeeding generations.

PASCAL'S SKEPTICISM

From 'Les Pensées de Pascal'

Pascal was skeptical of philosophy, not of religion. It is
because he is skeptical in philosophical matters, and recognizes the powerlessness of reason and the destruction of
natural truth among men, that he clings desperately to religion
as the last resource of humanity.

What is philosophical skepticism? It is a philosophical opinion
which consists in rejecting philosophy as unfounded, on the ground
that man of himself is incapable of reaching any truth, and still
less those truths which constitute what philosophy terms natural
morals and religion, such as free-will; the law of duty; the
distinction between good and evil, the saint and the sinner; the
holiness of virtue; the immateriality of the soul; and divine
providence. Skepticism is not the enemy of any special school
of philosophy, but of all.

Pascal's 'Pensées' are imbued with philosophical skepticism;
Pascal is the enemy of all philosophy, which he rejected utterly.
He does not admit the possibility of proving God's existence;
and to demonstrate the impotence of reason, he invented a
desperate argument. We can ignore truth, but we cannot ignore
our own interest, the interest of our eternal happiness. According to him, we must weigh the problem of divine Providence
from this point of view. If God does not exist, it cannot hurt
us to believe in him; but if by chance he should exist, and
we do not believe in him, the consequences to us would be terrible.

"Let us examine this point of view and say: God is, or he is
not," writes Pascal. "To which belief do we incline? Reason is
powerless to solve the question for us. Chaos separates us from
its solution. At the extreme end of this infinite distance, a game
is being played in which heads or tails will turn up. What do
we win in either case? Through the power of mere reason we
can neither prove nor disprove God's existence; through the
power of reason we can defend neither proposition."

On this foundation, not of truth but of interest, Pascal founds
the celebrated calculation to which he applies the law of chance.
Here is the conclusion he reaches:— "In the eyes of Reason, to
believe or not to believe in God (the for and against, or as I
say, the game of '*croix ou pile*') is equally without consequence;

but in the eyes of interest the difference is infinite, because the Infinite is to be gained or lost thereby."

Pascal considers skepticism legitimate, because philosophy or natural reason is incapable of attaining to certitude; he affirms "the sole rôle of reason to be the renouncement of reason; that true philosophy consists in despising philosophy."

The God of Abraham, the God of Jacob, not the God of savants and philosophers, is the God of Pascal. He caught a gleam of light, and believed he had found peace in submission to Christ and his confessor. Doubt yielded to grace; but vanquished doubt carried reason and philosophy in its train.

MADAME DE LONGUEVILLE

From the 'Life of Madame de Longueville'

WHAT a number of accomplished women the seventeenth century produced,—women who inspired adoration, drew all hearts towards them, and spread among all ranks the cultus of beauty, termed by Europe, French gallantry! They accompany this great century upon its too rapid flight, and mark its principal moments. Madame de Longueville has her place in the brilliant galaxy of seventeenth-century women by the right of true beauty and rare charm.

Born in 1619, in the prison of Vincennes, during the captivity of her father, Henri de Bourbon,—whose wife, the beautiful Marguerite de Montmorency, shared his imprisonment,—Mademoiselle de Bourbon grew in grace under the care of her mother, dividing her time between the Carmelite Convent and the Hôtel de Rambouillet, nourishing her soul upon pious and romantic books. Married at the age of twenty-three to a man twenty-three years her senior, she found that M. de Longueville, instead of trying by tenderness to make his young wife forget this disparity, followed the triumphal car of the famous Duchesse de Montbazon, the veriest coquette of the century. Insulted by her rival, neglected by her husband, Madame de Longueville yielded by degrees to the contagion in the midst of which she lived, and after having spent some time at the frivolous court of Münster, was fascinated on her return to Paris by the wit, chivalrous appearance, and distinguished manners of the Prince de Marcillac, afterwards Duc de la Rochefoucauld. This intimacy decided her career, the first part of which it closed in 1648.

The vicissitudes of the Fronde; love, as it was understood at the Hôtel Rambouillet,—that is, love *à la Scudéry*, with its enchantments, its sufferings, intermingled with danger and glory, crossed by adventures, triumphant over the greatest tests, yielding finally to its own weakness and exhausting itself,—such is the second period of Madame de Longueville's life, a period so short, and yet so crowded with events, which began in 1648 and ended towards the middle of 1654. After 1654 Madame de Longueville's life was one long repentance, daily growing in austerity; passed first by the bedside of her husband, and then at the Carmelite Convent and at Port-Royal, where she died in 1679.

First, spotless brilliancy; then sin and prompt expiation. Thus is divided the career of Madame de Longueville. A famous beauty, she possessed height and a fine figure. Her eyes were of the tenderest blue; her light-brown hair, of exceptional fineness, fell in abundant curls around the graceful oval of her face and rippled over her shoulders, which were fully exposed in accordance with the fashion of the time. Add to these attractions a complexion whose fairness, delicacy, and soft brilliancy justified its being compared with a pearl. Her charming skin reflected all the emotions of her soul. She spoke in the softest voice; her gestures harmonized with her face and voice, making perfect music. But her greatest charm was a graceful ease of manner, a languor which had brilliant awakenings when she was moved by passion, but which in every-day life gave her an appearance of aristocratic indifference, of indolence, frequently mistaken for ennui or disdain.

Madame de Longueville loved but one person. For his sake she sacrificed repose, interest, duty, and reputation. For his sake she embarked upon the rashest and most contradictory enterprises. La Rochefoucauld drew her into the Fronde; it was he who made her advance or retreat, who separated her from or reconciled her with her family, who controlled her absolutely. In his hands she became a heroic instrument. Passion and pride had their share in the life of adventure she faced so bravely; but what a soul she must have possessed, to find consolation in struggles such as these! And as so often happens, the man for whom she made these sacrifices was unworthy of them. Witty but selfish, he judged others by himself. Subtle in evil as she was in good, full of selfish cunning in the pursuit of his interests, the least chivalrous of men though he affected the semblance of the highest chivalry, when he believed that Madame de Longueville was yielding to the influence of the Duc de Nemours, he turned against her, blackened her reputation, revealed the weaknesses by which he had profited, and when she was struggling to repair her mistakes by the rigid mortification of the cloister, he published those 'Mémoires' in which he tore her to pieces.

La Rochefoucauld made his peace with the court. He even rode in Mazarin's carriages, saying with inimitable aplomb, "Everything comes to pass in France;" he obtained a pension for himself, a fine position for his son; and was worshiped by lovely women, one of whom, Madame de Lafayette, replaced Madame de Longueville and consecrated her life to him.

How different was Madame de Longueville's conduct! Love led her into the Fronde, love kept her there; when love failed her, everything failed her. The proud heroine who waged war against Mazarin, who sold her jewels, braved the ocean, aroused the North and South, and held the royal authority at bay, withdrew from the scene at the age of thirty-five, in the full maturity of her beauty, when her own interest was alone at stake.

To understand Madame de Longueville's character, to exonerate her from the charge of inconsistency or want of purpose, the unity of her life must be sought in her devotion to the man she loved. It is there in its entirety and unchangeableness; at once triumphant, absurd, and pathetic in the midst of the greatest follies. Her recklessness was inspired by the fickle restless mind of La Rochefoucauld. It was he who drifted from one faction to another, moved by his own interest alone. To Madame de Longueville herself belong her courage in the face of danger; a certain secret delight in the extremity of misfortune; and in defeat a pride not inferior to that of De Retz himself. She does not drop her eyes; she directs her gaze towards worthier objects. Once wounded in that which was most precious to her — her love — she bade adieu to the world, without currying favor with the court, and asking pardon of God alone.

MADAME DE CHEVREUSE

From the 'Life of Madame de Chevreuse'

MADAME DE CHEVREUSE was endowed with almost all the qualities constituting political genius. One alone was wanting,
and this was precisely the master quality without which
all the others lead but to the ruin of their possessor. She was
incapable of keeping in view a steady aim, or rather of choosing
her own aim; some one else always directed her choice. She
had an essentially feminine temperament; therein lay the secret
of her strength and weakness. Her spring of action was love, or
rather gallantry; and the interest of the man she loved became
for the time being her main object in life. This accounts for
the wonderful sagacity, subtlety and energy she expended in the
pursuit of a chimerical aim which constantly eluded her grasp,
and which seemed to charm her by the spell of its difficulty and
danger. La Rochefoucauld accuses her of bringing misfortune
upon all who loved her. It were more just to say that all whom
she loved drew her into foolhardy enterprises.

Richelieu and Mazarin left no stone unturned to attach
Madame de Chevreuse to their interests. Richelieu considered
her an enemy worthy of his steel; he exiled her several times,
and when after his death the doors of France were opened to
the men he had proscribed, the Cardinal's implacable resentment
survived in the soul of the dying Louis XIII., who closed them
to her.

If you turn to Mazarin's confidential letters you will see what
intense anxiety this beautiful conspirator caused him in 1643.
During the Fronde, he had reason to congratulate himself on
having effected a reconciliation with her and followed her wise
advice. In 1660, when the victorious Mazarin signed the treaties
of Westphalia and the Pyrenees, and Don Luis de Haro congratulated him on the peace which was about to succeed to years
of storms, the Cardinal answered that peace was not possible in
a country where even women were to be feared. "You Spaniards can speak lightly of such matters, since your women are
interested in love alone; but things are different in France, where
there are three women quite capable of upsetting the greatest
kingdom in the world; namely, the Duchess of Longueville, the
Princess Palatine, and the Duchess of Chevreuse."

COMPARISON BETWEEN MADAME DE HAUTEFORT AND MADAME DE CHEVREUSE

From the ‹Life of Madame de Chevreuse›

FATE placed them both in the same century, in the same party and in the midst of the same events; but far from resembling each other, they illustrate opposite poles of the character and destiny of women. Both were ravishingly beautiful, brilliantly intelligent, unflinchingly courageous: but one was as pure as she was beautiful, uniting grace with majesty and inspiring respect as well as love. The favorite of a king, not a suspicion touched her; proud to haughtiness with the great and powerful, sweet and compassionate to the oppressed; loving greatness and prizing virtue above the esteem of the world; combining the wit of a précieuse, the daintiness of a fashionable beauty, with the intrepidity of a heroine and the dignity of a great lady,— she left an odor of sanctity behind her.

The other possessed even greater powers of fascination and an irresistible charm. Witty but ignorant; thrown into the midst of party excesses and thinking but little of religion; too great a lady to submit to restraint; bowing only to the dictates of honor; abandoned to gallantry and making light of all else; despising danger and public opinion for the sake of the man she loved; restless rather than ambitious, freely risking her life and that of others; and after spending her youth in intrigues and plots, and strewing her path with victims, traveling through Europe as captive and conqueror and turning the heads of kings; having seen Chalais ascend the scaffold, Châteauneuf dismissed from the ministry, the Duc de Lorraine stripped of his possessions, Buckingham assassinated, the King of Spain launched upon a disastrous war, Queen Anne humiliated, and Richelieu triumphant; defiant to the last, always ready to play a part in that game of politics which had become a passion with her, to descend to the lowest intrigues or to take the most reckless course of action; seeing the weakness of her enemy, and daring enough to undertake his ruin:— Madame de Chevreuse was a devoted friend, an implacable enemy, the most redoubtable adversary of both Richelieu and Mazarin.

ABRAHAM COWLEY

(1618–1667)

BY THOMAS R. LOUNSBURY

ABRAHAM COWLEY, the posthumous son of a citizen and stationer of London, was born in that city in the latter half of 1618. His early education was received at Westminster school. In 1637 he became a scholar of Trinity College, Cambridge, where in 1639 he took the degree of B. A., and in 1642 that of M. A. During the civil commotions that followed, he was ejected from Cambridge University and withdrew to Oxford, which had become for the time being the headquarters of the royalist party. While there he not only continued his studies, but was present and in service in several of King Charles's journeys and expeditions. He finally became secretary to Lord Jermyn, who at the Restoration was created Earl of St. Albans. In this capacity he followed to France the Queen Henrietta Maria, who had left England for that country in 1644, and was there busily engaged in political intrigues to aid the cause of her husband. In her service Cowley was diligently employed, and was dispatched on missions to Jersey, Scotland, Flanders, and Holland. His principal and most absorbing occupation, how-

ABRAHAM COWLEY

ever, was carrying on the cipher correspondence that took place between the King and the Queen. This, and duties allied to this, were so engrossing that according to Sprat, his intimate friend and first biographer, they "for some years together took up all his days and two or three nights every week."

After the execution of Charles, Cowley remained in France until 1656. Then he returned to England, practically to play the part of a spy, if the testimony of the authority already quoted can be trusted. Once there, he was arrested and imprisoned, but subsequently was allowed to go at liberty on bail. After the death of Cromwell he went back to France. He returned at the Restoration, only to meet with the neglect which was incurred by all the followers of the exiled monarch who made the mistake of combining an objectionable sobriety and decency of life with loyalty to the house of Stuart. Furthermore, certain things he had done had made him an object of pretended suspicion. He had been created in 1657 a Doctor of Medicine by the University of Oxford, in obedience to an order of the government. There were passages also in the preface prefixed to the edition of his works published in 1656, which were taken to imply submissive acquiescence on his part in the new order of things. These were satisfactory pretexts for disregarding claims which the self-sacrificing service of years had established. The mastership of the Savoy, which he expected and which he had a right to expect, was given to another. But at last, more fortunate than many of his fellow-sufferers, he received through the influence of the Earl of St. Albans and the Duke of Buckingham a provision sufficient to maintain him in comfort. Withdrawing entirely from public life, he lived successively at Barn Elms and at Chertsey in Sussex. At the latter place he died on July 18th, 1667, and was buried in Westminster Abbey.

Such is a brief outline of the career of the man who during his lifetime was the most popular of English poets. In spite of occasional intervals of good fortune, it is on the whole a melancholy story. Such it seemed to Cowley himself. In the essay entitled 'Of Myself,' quoted below, and in 'The Complaint,' we get not only further details of the author's personal fortunes, but an insight into the feelings of disappointment and dejection which came over him, as he contrasted the difference between what he had hoped and expected and what he had succeeded in achieving or gaining. We learn from the preface to the volume published in 1656, that long before that time he had been eager to withdraw from the harassing occupations in which much of his time had already been wasted, and to spend the remainder of his days in seclusion and study. " My desire," he then wrote, " has been for some years past (though the execution has been accidentally diverted), and does still vehemently continue, to retire myself to some of our American plantations; not to seek for gold or to enrich myself with the traffic of those parts, which is the end of most men that travel thither, . . . but to forsake this world forever, with all the vanities and vexations of it, and to bury myself in some obscure retreat there, but not without the consolations of letters and philosophy."

There seems no reason to doubt the genuineness of the feeling thus expressed, and there is little difficulty in tracing it to its cause. Unquestionably the political situation had a good deal to do with its manifestation at that particular time; but the source of his dejection lay deeper than any temporary overthrow of the side with which he sympathized. Cowley's career, however successful, had not fulfilled the extraordinary promise of his youth. He made his appearance as a man of letters long before he became a man. Of all authors in our own tongue, perhaps in any tongue, he was the most precocious. This is not to say that others have not written as early as he, but that no one who wrote so early has written so well. In 1633, when he was but fifteen years old, he brought out a little volume containing over a thousand lines and entitled 'Poetical Blossomes.' It was made up mainly of two productions, entitled respectively 'Constantia and Philautus' and 'Pyramus and Thisbe.' Of this work a second edition appeared in 1636, with a number of additional poems. In the epistle prefixed to this impression, he states that 'Pyramus and Thisbe' was composed at ten years of age and 'Constantia and Philautus' at thirteen. But much more important than either, appeared in this volume of 1636 a poem entitled 'A Vote.' It consists of eleven stanzas, the last three of which, with a few slight verbal alterations, were cited by Cowley in his essay upon himself. This poetry, which he never surpassed, he there tells us was written when he was thirteen years old. The early date given to its composition may have been due to a slip of memory; at any rate it was not until 1636 that the piece appeared in print. But even were it not written till the very year in which it was published, it must be regarded as a marvelous production for a boy, not alone for the poetic ability displayed in it, but for the philosophic view it takes of life.

A third edition of 'Poetical Blossomes' appeared in 1637. In 1638 came out a pastoral comedy, written while he was king's scholar in Westminster School, and called 'Love's Riddle.' During that same year a Latin comedy entitled 'Naufragium Joculare' had been acted by the students of Trinity College, and a little later was published. All the works mentioned, it will be seen, had been produced by him before he had completed, and most of them in fact before he had reached, his twentieth year. For one further dramatic production he is also responsible at a very early age. In 1641, when the King's son Charles (afterwards Charles II.) passed through Cambridge, Cowley "made extempore," as he says, a comedy which was acted, for the entertainment of the Prince, at Trinity College on March 12th. It was called 'The Guardian,' and in 1650 it was published. At a later period it was rewritten by the author, and in 1661 was brought out at the theatre in Lincoln's Inn Fields with a fair degree of success. It was then entitled 'Cutter of Coleman Street.'

From the time of leaving Cambridge, though he did not cease writing, nothing of his was published for a long while, at least under his own name. In 1647 appeared a volume entitled 'The Mistress'; but even this the publisher professed to bring out wholly on his own responsibility. The work consisted entirely of love poems,

and the very doubtful assertion is steadily repeated in all notices of
Cowley's life that they became the favorite ones of the age.   If so,
the age must have been peculiarly frigid in its feelings.   Whatever
excellences these pieces possess, they are not the excellences that
characterize love poetry.   It is hardly possible to speak of them as
the transcript of any personal experiences.   They are rather aca-
demic exercises, intellectual disquisitions upon the general subject of
love, than the impassioned utterances of a man whose feelings have
ever been profoundly stirred.   The Greek scholar Joshua Barnes,
who flourished a little later, declared that in spite of the sentiments
expressed in these pieces, and in a subsequent poem called 'The
Chronicle,' Cowley was never in love but once in his life.   It could
not be proved on the evidence of the verses contained in 'The Mistress' that he was ever in love at all.   Still, if the poems lack
fervor, they often exhibit ingenuity and grace.

On his return to England during the Protectorate he brought out
a collected edition of his works in folio.   It was published in 1656,
and amongst the matter which then appeared for the first time were
the odes written in professed imitation of Pindar.   The composition
of these set a literary fashion which did not die out till the latter
half of the next century.   To write so-called Pindaric odes became
one of the regular duties of all who were in doubt about their poetic
inspiration, and felt called upon to convince others as well as themselves of their possession of it.   But Cowley introduced the term and
not the thing.   He seems to have fancied that to produce lines with
a different number of feet, and stanzas with a different number of
lines, was the proper method of representing the measure.   But Pindar's verse, if it can be called irregular at all, was regularly irregular.
Cowley's imitation was irregular and nothing else.   Still, so great
was his influence, that a plentiful crop of these spurious reproduc-
tions of an imaginary metrical form sprang up in the literature of the
hundred years following the Restoration.   Among them can occasionally be found genuine imitations of Pindar's measure, such as are the
odes of Congreve and of Gray; but of the countless number of all
kinds produced, those of the last-named author are the only ones
that can be said still to survive.

Another production that made its first appearance in the folio of
1656 was part of an epic poem, which Cowley had begun while he
was at the university.   Its subject was the life and exploits of King
David, and his intention was to complete it in the orthodox number
of twelve books.   It would appear from his preface that the theme
was chosen from a sense of duty as well as from inclination.   Poetry,
he there tells us, should no longer be pressed into the service of
fable.   The Devil had stolen it and alienated it from the service of

the Deity; and it was time to recover it out of the tyrant's power and restore it to the kingdom of God. If this doctrine be true, it must be conceded that Cowley's hands were not the ones to effect the restoration. From what he did towards bringing about the result he deemed desirable, it looks rather as if the craft of the great Adversary of mankind had been put forth to defeat the end in view by instigating this particular poet to undertake this particular task. The 'Davideis' is written in rhymed heroic verse, of which Cowley never gained the full mastery. There is nothing in the matter to make amends for the versification, which is rarely well finished and is not unfrequently rough and inharmonious. In truth, the distinguishing characteristic of the work as a whole is its well-sustained tediousness. Fortunately it was not completed beyond the fourth book; it would not have lessened Cowley's reputation if the first had never been begun.

Cowley continued to write after this volume was published; but a good deal of his later production was in the Latin tongue, and has in consequence been condemned to perpetual obscurity. Interest in that could be least expected to survive the general decay of interest which gradually overtook his writings. His fame stood highest in his own century, and he is perhaps as much underestimated now as he was overestimated then. His collected works passed through edition after edition, and by 1681 had reached the seventh. Such a sale in those days of mighty folios and comparatively few readers indicated great and general popularity. But by the end of the century his influence had begun to decline. Dryden at the outset of his literary career had been one of his most fervent admirers; but in the preface to his last book, which appeared in 1700, he censured his faults severely, and declared that he had so sunk in his reputation that for ten impressions which his works had had in so many successive years, scarcely a hundred copies were purchased during a twelvemonth at the time of his writing. This statement reflected more the feelings of the critic than it represented the actual facts, for between 1699 and 1721 four editions of Cowley's works appeared. Still it is none the less true that Cowley's reputation was then steadily sinking, and was destined to sink still lower. In 1737 Pope directly referred to the fact in the following lines, which have been repeatedly quoted in connection with it:—

«Who now reads Cowley? If he pleases yet,
It is his moral pleases, not his wit;
Forgot his epic, nay, Pindaric art,
But still I love the language of his heart.»

Between 1721 indeed and 1802 not a single separate edition of his works was published; though selections were edited by Bishop Hurd in the interval, and of course his poems were included in the great collections of the booksellers, and of Anderson and Chalmers. In 1881 an edition limited to one hundred copies of his works in verse and prose, for the first time completely collected, was brought out by Grosart as a part of the Chertsey Worthies' Library.

The reasons for the decay of Cowley's reputation are not hard to find. It was due to what Pope called his wit, or what more specifically was criticized by Addison in No. 62 of the Spectator as his false wit. "He could never," says Dryden, "forgive any conceit which came in his way, but swept like a drag-net great and small." There are accordingly but few poems of his that can be read with unmixed pleasure. Even when the piece as a whole is admirable, the reader is always in danger of finding somewhat to jar upon his taste in details. A passage containing lofty thoughts nobly expressed is liable to be followed by another, in which forced and unnatural images or far-fetched conceits utterly destroy the impression wrought by the majestic simplicity of what has preceded. This inequality began early to lower him in general esteem. Even as far back as the seventeenth century, Lord Rochester is reported by Dryden as having said of him very pertinently, if somewhat profanely, that "Not being of God, he could not stand."

From this censure, which is too applicable to most of his work, there are portions that are absolutely free. These are his translations and his prose pieces. In the former — especially in his versions of Anacreon — the necessity of adhering to his original rendered it impracticable for him to go straying after these meretricious beauties of style. But for them in the latter he seems never to have had the least inclination. Here his expression never suffered from the perversion of his taste. He preceded Dryden in introducing into our language that simple structure, that easy natural mode of expression which is peculiarly adapted to the genius of our tongue, and forms the greatest possible contrast to the Latinized diction, the involved constructions, the sometimes stately but frequently cumbrous sentences of the men of the former age, like Hooker and Milton. Cowley was in fact the first regular writer of modern prose. In certain particulars his work in that line has rarely been surpassed. It is simple and straightforward, never sinking into commonplace when treating of the common, never lacking in dignity when occasion demands it to rise. The longest and most important of these prose pieces — nearly all of which are interspersed with poetry — is the one entitled 'A Discourse concerning the Government of Oliver Cromwell.' It was written shortly after the Protector's death, though not published until 1661. In spite of the fact that it is mainly an elaborate attack upon that great ruler, the opening pages prove how profound had been the impression produced upon Cowley by the personality of the man.

Cowley is perhaps the chief of the poets who for some inexplicable reason have been termed metaphysical. The peculiarities of style which led to this school being so designated, were exemplified in passages taken from his works, in the elaborate criticism given of him by Dr. Johnson in the biography he prepared. To most persons that account is now better known than the productions of the man who was its subject. It is not to be expected indeed that Cowley will ever again be a popular author. But he will always be a favorite to a certain extent of a small body of cultivated men, who will overlook his faults for the sake of the lofty morality couched in lofty diction that is scattered through his writings, and even more for that undertone of plaintive tenderness which Pope aptly styled «the language of his heart.» In literary history he will have a place of his own, as having founded in the so-called Pindaric odes a temporary fashion of writing; and a more exalted position for having been the pioneer in the production of our present prose style.

Thomas R. Lounsbury.

OF MYSELF

IT IS a hard and nice subject for a man to write of himself; it grates his own heart to say anything of disparagement, and the reader's ears to hear anything of praise from him. There is no danger from me of offending him in this kind: neither my mind nor my body nor my fortune allow me any materials for that vanity. It is sufficient for my own contentment that they have preserved me from being scandalous or remarkable on the defective side. But besides that, I shall here speak of myself only in relation to the subject of these precedent discourses, and shall be likelier thereby to fall into the contempt than rise up to the estimation of most people.

As far as my memory can return back into my past life, before I knew, or was capable of guessing, what the world or the glories or business of it were, the natural affections of my soul gave me a secret bent of aversion from them, as some plants are said to turn away from others by an antipathy imperceptible to themselves and inscrutable to man's understanding. Even when I was a very young boy at school, instead of running about on holy-days and playing with my fellows, I was wont to steal from them and walk into the fields, either alone with a book, or with some one companion if I could find any of the same temper. I was then too so much an enemy to all constraint, that my masters could never prevail on me, by any persuasions or encouragements, to learn without book the common rules of grammar; in which they dispensed with me alone, because they found I made a shift to do the usual exercise out of my own reading and observation. That I was then of the same mind as I am now (which I confess I wonder at, myself) may appear by the latter end of an ode which I made when I was but thirteen years old, and which was then printed with many other verses. The beginning of it is boyish; but of this part, which I here set down (if a very little were corrected), I should hardly now be much ashamed.

> This only grant me, that my means may lie
> Too low for envy, for contempt too high.
> Some honor I would have,
> Not from great deeds, but good alone;
> The unknown are better, than ill known:
> Rumor can ope the grave.
> Acquaintance I would have, but when't depends
> Not on the number, but the choice of friends.
>
> Books should, not business, entertain the light,
> And sleep, as undisturbed as death, the night.
> My house a cottage more
> Than palace; and should fitting be
> For all my use, no luxury.
> My garden painted o'er
> With nature's hand, not art's; and pleasures yield,
> Horace might envy in his Sabin field.
>
> Thus would I double my life's fading space;
> For he that runs it well, twice runs his race.
> And in this true delight,
> These unbought sports, this happy state,
> I would not fear, nor wish, my fate;
> But boldly say each night,
> «To-morrow let my sun his beams display,
> Or in clouds hide them; I have lived to-day.»

You may see by it, I was even then acquainted with the poets (for the conclusion is taken out of Horace); and perhaps it was the immature and immoderate love of them, which stampt first, or rather engraved, these characters in me: they were like letters cut into the bark of a young tree, which with the tree still grow proportionably. But how this love came to be produced in me so early, is a hard question: I believe I can tell the particular little chance that filled my head first with such chimes of verse as have never since left ringing there: for I remember, when I began to read, and to take some pleasure in it, there was wont to lie in my mother's parlor (I know not by what accident, for she herself never in her life read any book but of devotion),—but there was wont to lie Spenser's works: this I happened to fall upon, and was infinitely delighted with the stories of the knights and giants and monsters and brave houses, which I found everywhere there (though my understanding had little to do with all this); and by degrees with the tinkling of the rhyme and dance of the numbers; so that I think I had read him all over before I was twelve years old, and was thus made a poet as immediately as a child is made an eunuch.

With these affections of mind, and my heart wholly set upon letters, I went to the university; but was soon torn from thence by that violent public storm, which would suffer nothing to stand where it did, but rooted up every plant, even from the princely cedars to me the hyssop. Yet I had as good fortune as could have befallen me in such a tempest; for I was cast by it into the family of one of the best persons, and into the court of one of the best princesses, of the world. Now, though I was here engaged in ways most contrary to the original design of my life,—that is, into much company, and no small business, and into a daily sight of greatness, both militant and triumphant (for that was the state then of the English and French courts), yet all this was so far from altering my opinion, that it only added the confirmation of reason to that which was before but natural inclination. I saw plainly all the paint of that kind of life, the nearer I came to it; and that beauty which I did not fall in love with when for aught I knew it was real, was not like to bewitch or entice me when I saw that it was adulterate. I met with several great persons, whom I liked very well; but could not perceive that any part of their greatness was to be liked or desired, no more than I would be glad or content to be in a storm, though I saw many ships which rid safely and bravely in it: a storm would not agree with my stomach, if it did with my courage. Though I was in a crowd of as good company as could be found anywhere, though I was in business of great and honorable trust, though I ate at the best table, and enjoyed the best conveniences for present subsistence that ought to be desired by a man of my condition in banishment and public distresses; yet I could not abstain from renewing my old school-boy's wish, in a copy of verses to the same effect:—

> "Well then, I now do plainly see
> This busy world and I shall ne'er agree," etc.

And I never then proposed to myself any other advantage from his Majesty's happy Restoration, but the getting into some moderately convenient retreat in the country; which I thought, in that case, I might easily have compassed as well as some others, who with no greater probabilities or pretenses have arrived to extraordinary fortune: but I had before written a shrewd prophecy against myself, and I think Apollo inspired me in the truth though not in the elegance of it:—

> "THOU neither great at court, nor in the war,
> Nor at th' exchange shalt be, nor at the wrangling bar.
>   Content thyself with the small barren praise
>   Which neglected verse does raise."
>   She spake; and all my years to come
>   Took their unlucky doom.
>   Their several ways of life let others chuse,
>   Their several pleasures let them use;
>   But I was born for Love and for a Muse.
>
>   With Fate what boots it to contend?
> Such I began, such am, and so must end.
>   The star that did my being frame
>   Was but a lambent flame,
>   And some small light it did dispense,
>   But neither heat nor influence.
> No matter, Cowley; let proud Fortune see
> That thou canst her despise no less than she does thee.
>
>   Let all her gifts the portion be
>   Of folly, lust, and flattery,
>   Fraud, extortion, calumny,

> Murder, infidelity,
> Rebellion and hypocrisy.
> Do thou nor grieve nor blush to be,
> As all th' inspired tuneful men,
> And all thy great forefathers were, from Homer down to Ben.

However, by the failing of the forces which I had expected, I did not quit the design which I had resolved on; I cast myself into it *à corps perdu*, without making capitulations, or taking counsel of fortune. But God laughs at a man who says to his soul, "Take thy case." I met presently not only with many little incumbrances and impediments, but with so much sickness (a new misfortune to me) as would have spoiled the happiness of an emperor as well as mine; yet I do neither repent nor alter my course. "Non ego perfidum dixi sacramentum;" nothing shall separate me from a mistress which I have loved so long and have now at last married; though she neither has brought me a rich portion, nor lived yet so quietly with me as I hoped from her:—

> "Nec vos, dulcissima mundi
> Nomina, vos Musæ, Libertas, Otia, Libri,
> Hortique Sylvæque, anima remanente, relinquam,"

> (Nor by me e'er shall you,
> You, of all names the sweetest and the best,
> You, Muses, books, and liberty, and rest;
> You, gardens, fields, and woods, forsaken be,
> As long as life itself forsakes not me.)

But this is a very pretty ejaculation; because I have concluded all the other chapters with a copy of verses, I will maintain the humor to the last.

ON THE DEATH OF CRASHAW

> POET and Saint! to thee alone are given
> The two most sacred names of earth and heaven;
> The hard and rarest union which can be,
> Next that of Godhead with humanity.
> Long did the Muses banished slaves abide,
> And build vain pyramids to mortal pride;
> Like Moses, thou (though spells and charms withstand)
> Hast brought them nobly home back to their holy land.

Ah, wretched we, poets of earth! but thou
Wert, living, the same poet which thou'rt now;
Whilst angels sing to thee their airs divine,
And joy in an applause so great as thine.
Equal society with them to hold,
Thou need'st not make new songs, but say the old;
And they, kind spirits! shall all rejoice, to see
How little less than they exalted man may be.

Still the old heathen gods in numbers dwell;
The heavenliest thing on earth still keeps up hell;
Nor have we yet quite purged the Christian land;
Still idols here, like calves at Bethel, stand.
And though Pan's death long since all oracles broke,
Yet still in rhyme the fiend Apollo spoke:
Nay, with the worst of heathen dotage, we
Vain men! the monster woman deify;
Find stars, and tie our fates there in a face,
And paradise in them, by whom we lost it, place.

What different faults corrupt our Muses thus?
Wanton as girls, as old wives fabulous!
Thy spotless Muse, like Mary, did contain
The boundless Godhead; she did well disdain
That her eternal verse employed should be
On a less subject than eternity;
And for a sacred mistress scorned to take
But her, whom God himself scorned not his spouse to make.

It (in a kind) her miracle did do;
A fruitful mother was, and virgin too.
How well, blest swan, did Fate contrive thy death,
And make thee render up thy tuneful breath
In thy great mistress's arms, thou most divine
And richest offering of Loretto's shrine!
Where, like some holy sacrifice t' expire,
A fever burns thee, and Love lights the fire.
Angels, they say, brought the famed Chapel there,
And bore the sacred load in triumph through the air:
'Tis surer much they brought thee there; and they,
And thou their charge, went singing all the way.

Pardon, my Mother-Church, if I consent
That angels led him when from thee he went;
For ev'n in error seen no danger is,
When joined with so much piety as his.

Ah, mighty God! with shame I speak't, and grief;
Ah, that our greatest faults were in belief!
And our weak reason were ev'n weaker yet,
Rather than thus our wills too strong for it.
His faith, perhaps, in some nice tenets might
Be wrong; his life, I'm sure, was in the right;
And I myself a Catholic will be,
So far at least, great Saint, to pray to thee.

Hail, bard triumphant, and some care bestow
On us, the poets militant below!
Oppressed by our old enemy, adverse chance,
Attacked by envy and by ignorance;
Enchained by beauty, tortured by desires,
Exposed by tyrant Love to savage beasts and fires.
Thou from low earth in nobler flames didst rise,
And like Elijah, mount alive the skies.
Elisha-like, but with a wish much less,
More fit thy greatness and my littleness,
Lo! here I beg — I, whom thou once didst prove
So humble to esteem, so good to love —
Not that thy spirit might on me doubled be,
I ask but half thy mighty spirit for me:
And when my muse soars with so strong a wing,
'Twill learn of things divine, and first of thee, to sing.

ON THE DEATH OF MR. WILLIAM HERVEY

IT WAS a dismal and a fearful night;
  Scarce could the moon disk on th' unwilling light,
    When sleep, death's image, left my troubled breast,
        By something liker death possest.
My eyes with tears did uncommanded flow,
        And on my soul hung the dull weight
        Of some intolerable fate.
What bell was that? ah me! too much I know.

My sweet companion and my gentle peer,
Why hast thou left me thus unkindly here,
Thy end forever, and my life to moan?
        Oh, thou hast left me all alone!
Thy soul and body, where death's agony
        Besieged around thy noble heart,
        Did not with more reluctance part,
Than I, my dearest friend, do part from thee.

My dearest friend, would I had died for thee!
Life and this world henceforth will tedious be;
Nor shall I know hereafter what to do,
  If once my griefs prove tedious too.
Silent and sad I walk about all day,
  As sullen ghosts stalk speechless by,
  Where their hid treasures lie;
Alas! my treasure's gone! why do I stay?

He was my friend, the truest friend on earth;
A strong and mighty influence joined our birth:
Nor did we envy the most sounding name
  By friendship given of old to fame.
None but his brethren he and sisters knew,
  Whom the kind youth preferred to me;
  And ev'n in that we did agree,
For much above myself I loved them too.

Say — for you saw us, ye immortal lights —
How oft unwearied have we spent the nights,
Till the Ledæan stars, so famed for love,
  Wondered at us from above!
We spent them not in toys, in lusts, or wine;
  But search of deep philosophy,
  Wit, eloquence and poetry;
Arts which I loved, for they, my friend, were thine.

Ye fields of Cambridge, our dear Cambridge, say
Have ye not seen us walking every day?
Was there a tree about which did not know
  The love betwixt us two?
Henceforth, ye gentle trees, forever fade;
  Or your sad branches thicker join,
  And into darksome shades combine,
Dark as the grave wherein my friend is laid!
Henceforth, no learnèd youths beneath you sing,
Till all the tuneful birds to your boughs they bring;
No tuneful birds play with their wonted cheer,
  And call the learned youths to hear;
No whistling winds through the glad branches fly:
  But all, with sad solemnity,
  Mute and unmovèd be,
Mute as the grave wherein my friend does lie.

To him my muse made haste with every strain,
Whilst it was new and warm yet from the brain:

He loved my worthless rhymes, and like a friend,
        Would find out something to commend.
Hence now, my Muse! thou canst not me delight:
        Be this my latest verse,
        With which I now adorn his hearse;
And this my grief, without thy help, shall write.

Had I a wreath of bays about my brow,
I should contemn that flourishing honor now,
Condemn it to the fire, and joy to hear
        It rage and crackle there.
Instead of bays, crown with sad cypress me;
        Cypress, which tombs does beautify;
        Not Phœbus grieved so much as I,
For him who first was near that mournful tree.

Large was his soul, as large a soul as e'er
Submitted to inform a body here;
High as the place 'twas shortly in heaven to have,
        But low and humble as his grave:
So high, that all the Virtues there did come,
        As to their chiefest seat,
        Conspicuous and great;
So low, that for me too it made a room.

He scorned this busy world below, and all
That we, mistaken mortals! pleasure call;
Was filled with innocent gallantry and truth,
        Triumphant o'er the sins of youth.
He like the stars, to which he now is gone,
        That shine with beams like flame,
        Yet burn not with the same,
Had all the light of youth, of the fire none.

Knowledge he only sought, and so soon caught,
As if for him knowledge had rather sought:
Nor did more learning ever crowded lie
        In such a short mortality.
Whene'er the skillful youth discoursed or writ,
        Still did the nations throng
        About his eloquent tongue;
Nor could his ink flow faster than his wit.

So strong a wit did nature to him frame,
As all things but his judgment overcame;

His judgment like the heavenly moon did show,
Tempering that mighty sea below;
Oh! had he lived in learning's world, what bound
Would have been able to control
His overpowering soul!
We've lost in him arts that not yet are found.

His mirth was the pure spirits of various wit,
Yet never did his God or friends forget;
And when deep talk and wisdom came in view,
Retired, and gave to them their due:
For the rich help of books he always took,
Though his own searching mind before
Was so with notions written o'er,
As if wise nature had made that her book.

So many virtues joined in him, as we
Can scarce pick here and there in history;
More than old writers' practice e'er could reach;
As much as they could ever teach.
These did Religion, queen of virtues, sway;
And all their sacred motions steer,
Just like the first and highest sphere,
Which wheels about, and turns all heaven one way.

With as much zeal, devotion, piety,
He always lived, as other saints do die.
Still with his soul severe account he kept,
Wiping all debts out ere he slept:
Then down in peace and innocence he lay,
Like the sun's laborious light,
Which still in water sets at night,
Unsullied with his journey of the day.

Wondrous young man! why wert thou made so good,
To be snatched hence ere better understood?
Snatched before half of thee enough was seen!
Thou ripe, and yet thy life but green!
Nor could thy friends take their last sad farewell;
But danger and infectious death
Maliciously seized on that breath
Where life, spirit, pleasure, always used to dwell.

But happy thou, ta'en from this frantic age,
Where ignorance and hypocrisy does rage!

A fitter time for heaven no soul e'er chose,
    The place now only free from those.
There 'mong the blest thou dost forever shine,
    And wheresoe'er thou cast thy view
    Upon that white and radiant crew,
Seest not a soul clothed with more light than thine.

And if the glorious saints cease not to know
Their wretched friends who fight with life below,
Thy flame to me does still the same abide,
    Only more pure and rarefied.
There, whilst immortal hymns thou dost rehearse,
    Thou dost with holy pity see
    Our dull and earthly poesy,
Where grief and misery can be joined with verse.

A SUPPLICATION

AWAKE, awake, my Lyre!
    And tell thy silent master's humble tale
    In sounds that may prevail;
Sounds that gentle thoughts inspire
    Though so exalted she,
    And I so lowly be,
Tell her, such different notes make all thy harmony.

    Hark! how the strings awake;
And though the moving hand approach not near,
    Themselves with awful fear
A kind of numerous trembling make.
    Now all thy forces try,
    Now all thy charms apply;
Revenge upon her ear the conquests of her eye.

    Weak Lyre! thy virtue sure
Is useless here, since thou art only found
    To cure, but not to wound,
And she to wound, but not to cure.
    Too weak, too, wilt thou prove
    My passion to remove;
Physic to other ills, thou'rt nourishment to love.

    Sleep, sleep again, my Lyre!
For thou canst never tell my humble tale
    In sounds that will prevail,

Nor gentle thoughts in her inspire;
    All thy vain mirth lay by;
    Bid thy strings silent lie;
Sleep, sleep again, my Lyre, and let thy master die.

EPITAPH ON A LIVING AUTHOR

HERE, passenger, beneath this shed,
    Lies Cowley, though entombed, not dead;
    Yet freed from human toil and strife,
And all th' impertinence of life.

Who in his poverty is neat,
And even in retirement great,
With Gold, the people's idol, he
Holds endless war and enmity.

Can you not say, he has resigned
His breath, to this small cell confined?
With this small mansion let him have
The rest and silence of the grave:

Strew roses here as on his hearse,
And reckon this his funeral verse;
With wreaths of fragrant herbs adorn
The yet surviving poet's urn.

WILLIAM COWPER.

WILLIAM COWPER

(1731–1800)

THE poet Cowper, who stands in the gap that separates Pope from Wordsworth, belongs to the group that includes Thomson, Young, Goldsmith, and Crabbe. If he is unimportant to-day in comparison with his importance to his own time, yet his service to English poetry is great, for he dispersed the artificial atmosphere which Pope had thrown around it. His moods and his keys were alike limited, and he was soon overshadowed by Wordsworth. Cowper saw Nature; Wordsworth saw into Nature, and touched chords undreamed of by the gentle poet of rural scenes and fireside pleasures. Cowper's simplicity of diction was in his day almost daring; and he broke away from all the sentimental Arcadian figures with which Thomson's landscapes were peopled. Therefore his value lies in the note of sincerity that he sounded. Singularly enough, he has been admired by French critics. He has been compared to Rousseau, and Sainte-Beuve calls him "the bard of domestic life." His fame as a serious poet rests chiefly on 'The Task,' which Hazlitt calls "a poem which, with its pictures of domestic comfort and social refinement, can hardly be forgotten but with the language itself."

His life is briefly told. He was born at Berkhampstead, England, November 26th, 1731. Through his mother he was descended from the family of the poet John Donne. She died when he was but six years of age, and he was sent to school in Hertfordshire and to Westminster. For three years he studied law at the Temple, but although called to the bar in 1754, he never practiced. As a young man he had an attack of madness, attempted suicide, and was confined at St. Albans for two years. When released he retired to Huntington, where he formed a friendship with the Unwins. On the death of Rev. William Unwin, he and Mrs. Unwin removed to Olney, where most of Cowper's poems were written, and afterward to Weston, where Mrs. Unwin died in 1796. Cowper survived her four years, dying on April 25th, 1800.

At Olney, Cowper lived in seclusion, amusing himself with his garden and greenhouse, raising pineapples, mending windows, writing, reading, and playing with his pets. The chief of them were his three hares, Puss, Tiny, and Bess, which formed the topic of an essay in the Gentleman's Magazine for June, 1784. It is this simple parlor at Olney which Cowper describes in 'The Task,' where he says:—

> « Now stir the fire, and close the shutters fast,
> Let fall the curtains, wheel the sofa round,
> And while the bubbling and loud-hissing urn
> Throws up a steamy column, and the cups
> That cheer, but not inebriate, wait on each,
> So let us welcome peaceful evening in. »

In this retreat from the haunts of the worldly, whom he deemed so trivial and sinful, the poet found happiness in watching the flickering fire and listening to the wild blasts of winter that swept the panes with swirling snow. Here he sat in his easy-chair, while the dog dozed at his feet, the hares gamboled, and the linnets twittered until silenced by a quaint bit of music on the harpsichord. Cowper would twine "silken thread round ivory reels," wind crewels, or read aloud to his two devoted companions as they knitted, or

> « — the well-depicted flower
> Wrought patiently into the snowy lawn. »

The one, Mrs. Unwin, was somewhat prim and puritanical; the other, Lady Austen, a handsome woman of the world, was gay and vivacious, and banished Cowper's dark moods by her grace and charm. To dispel his morbid fancies she told him the old story of the London citizen riding to Edmonton, which, says Hazlitt, "has perhaps given as much pleasure to as many people as anything of the same length that ever was written."

"Lady Austen," says his biographer Wright, "seeing his face brighten, and delighted with her success, wound up the story with all the skill at her command. Cowper could no longer control himself, but burst out into a loud and hearty peal of laughter. The ladies joined in his mirth, and the merriment had scarcely subsided by supper-time. The story made such an impression on his mind that at night he could not sleep; and his thoughts having taken the form of rhyme, he sprang from his bed and committed them to paper, and in the morning brought down to Mrs. Unwin the crude outline of 'John Gilpin.' All that day and for several days he secluded himself in the greenhouse, and went on with the task of polishing and improving what he had written. As he filled his slips of paper, he sent them across the market-place to Mr. Wilson, to the great delight and merriment of that jocular barber, who on several other occasions had been favored with the first sight of some of Cowper's smaller poems."

The portrait of John Gilpin was taken from John Beyer, a linen-draper who lived at No. 3 Cheapside. 'John Gilpin' was published anonymously in the Public Advertiser, and was received with enthusiasm. Printed as a ballad, copies of it, with pictures of John Gilpin flying past the "Bell" at Edmonton, were sold by hundreds; but Cowper did not acknowledge the poem until 1785, when he brought out 'The Task.'

This was also suggested by Lady Austen, who asked him to write something in blank verse. Cowper replied that he lacked a subject. "Subject—nonsense!" she said: "you can write on anything. Take this sofa for a subject." Following her command, the poet named the first book of 'The Task' 'The Sofa.' She suggested also the verses on 'The Loss of the Royal George.'

At Weston Cowper appears to have enjoyed the society of the county-side. His companions here were Puss, the last surviving hare, and the Spaniel Beau, "a spotted liver-color and white, or rather a chestnut" dog, the subject of several poems.

Cowper never married. His attachment to Theodora—the "Delia" of his verses—the daughter of his uncle, Ashley Cowper, lasted through his life, and her sister, Lady Hesketh, was one of his kindest and best friends. It was she who made for him those peculiar muslin caps which he wears in his portraits. Many short poems addressed to her attest his affection and gratitude for her friendship and ministrations, and to Mrs. Unwin belong the verses and the sonnet inscribed 'To Mary.'

Lives of Cowper are numerous. His old friend, John Newton, attempted one immediately after his death, but this was not completed; and the first to appear was a life by Hayley (1803-6), extended in the 'Life and Letters of Cowper,' by T. S. Grimshawe (1835). There are also Cowper's own 'Memoirs' (a description of his mental derangement and religious experiences), published in 1816; 'Life and Letters of Cowper' by Southey in 1835; and two books by T. Wright, 'The Town of Cowper' (1886); and 'Life of Cowper' (1892). An interesting biography has also been written by Goldwin Smith, in the series of 'English Men of Letters,' in which he says:—

"In all his social judgments Cowper is at a wrong point of view. He is always deluded by the idol of his cave. He writes perpetually on the two-fold assumption that a life of retirement is more favorable to virtue than a life of action, and that 'God made the country and man made the town.' . . . His flight from the world was rendered necessary by his malady and respectable by his literary work; but it was a flight and not a victory. His misconception was fostered and partly produced by a religion which was essentially ascetic, and which, while it gave birth to characters of the highest and most energetic beneficence, represented salvation too little as the reward of effort, too much as the reward of passion, belief, and of spiritual emotion."

Yet despite this gloom, Cowper possessed the humor which finds admirable expression in many small poems, in 'John Gilpin' and in his 'Letters.' These are the real mirror of his life. Southey considers his letters the most delightful in the language. They contain nothing but the details of his daily life, and such happenings as the flowering of pinks, the singing of birds in the apple-blossoms, the falling of the dew on the grass under his window, the pranks of his pets, the tricks of the Spaniel Beau, the frolics of the tortoise-shell kitten, the flight of his favorite hare, and the excitements of a morning walk when the once nodding grass is "fledged with icy feathers." Their English is so easy and graceful, and their humor so spontaneous, that the reader feels a sense of friendship with the modest poet of 'The Task,' who, despite his platitudes, wins a certain respectful admiration.

THE CRICKET

LITTLE inmate, full of mirth,
    Chirping on my kitchen hearth,
    Wheresoe'er be thine abode,
Always harbinger of good,
Pay me for thy warm retreat
With a song more soft and sweet;
In return thou shalt receive
Such a strain as I can give.

Thus thy praise shall be expressed,
Inoffensive, welcome guest!
While the rat is on the scout,
And the mouse with curious snout,
With what vermin else infest
Every dish, and spoil the best;
Frisking thus before the fire,
Thou hast all thine heart's desire.

Though in voice and shape they be
Formed as if akin to thee,
Thou surpassest, happier far,
Happiest grasshoppers that are;
Theirs is but a summer song—
Thine endures the winter long,
Unimpaired and shrill and clear,
Melody throughout the year.

THE WINTER WALK AT NOON

From 'The Task'

THE night was winter in his roughest mood;
    The morning sharp and clear. But now at noon
    Upon the southern side of the slant hills,
And where the woods fence off the northern blast,
The season smiles, resigning all its rage,
And has the warmth of May. The vault is blue
Without a cloud, and white without a speck
The dazzling splendor of the scene below.
Again the harmony comes o'er the vale;
And through the trees I view the embattled tower
Whence all the music. I again perceive
The soothing influence of the wafted strains,
And settle in soft musings as I tread
The walk, still verdant, under oaks and elms,
Whose outspread branches overarch the glade.
The roof, though movable through all its length,
As the wind sways it, has yet well sufficed;
And intercepting in their silent fall
The frequent flakes, has kept a path for me.
No noise is here, or none that hinders thought.
The redbreast warbles still, but is content
With slender notes, and more than half suppressed:
Pleased with his solitude, and flitting light
From spray to spray, where'er he rests he shakes
From many a twig the pendent drops of ice
That tinkle in the withered leaves below.
Stillness, accompanied with sounds so soft,
Charms more than silence. Meditation here
May think down hours to moments. Here the heart
May give a useful lesson to the head,
And Learning wiser grow without his books.
Knowledge and Wisdom, far from being one,
Have ofttimes no connection. Knowledge dwells
In heads replete with thoughts of other men;
Wisdom in minds attentive to their own.
Knowledge, a rude unprofitable mass,
The mere materials with which Wisdom builds,
Till smoothed and squared, and fitted to its place,
Does but encumber whom it seems to enrich.
Knowledge is proud that he has learned so much;

Wisdom is humble that he knows no more.
Books are not seldom talismans and spells,
By which the magic art of shrewder wits
Holds an unthinking multitude enthralled.
Some to the fascination of a name
Surrender judgment, hoodwinked. Some the style
Infatuates, and through labyrinths and wilds
Of error leads them, by a tune entranced;
While sloth seduces them, too weak to bear
The insupportable fatigue of thought,
And swallowing therefore without pause or choice
The total grist unsifted, husks and all.
But trees and rivulets, whose rapid course
Defies the check of winter, haunts of deer,
And sheep-walks populous with bleating lambs,
And lanes, in which the primrose ere her time
Peeps through the moss that clothes the hawthorn root,
Deceive no student. Wisdom there, and truth,—
Not shy, as in the world, and to be won
By slow solicitation,—seize at once
The roving thought, and fix it on themselves.

ON THE LOSS OF THE ROYAL GEORGE

WRITTEN WHEN THE NEWS ARRIVED

TOLL for the brave—
    The brave that are no more!
  All sunk beneath the wave,
    Fast by their native shore!

Eight hundred of the brave,
    Whose courage well was tried,
  Had made the vessel heel,
    And laid her on her side.

A land breeze shook the shrouds,
    And she was overset—
  Down went the Royal George,
    With all her crew complete.

Toll for the brave!
    Brave Kempenfelt is gone;
  His last sea fight is fought,
    His work of glory done.

It was not in the battle;
  No tempest gave the shock;
She sprang no fatal leak;
  She ran upon a rock.

His sword was in its sheath;
  His fingers held the pen,
When Kempenfelt went down
  With twice four hundred men.

Weigh the vessel up,
  Once dreaded by our foes!
And mingle with our cup
  The tear that England owes.

Her timbers yet are sound,
  And she may float again,
Full charged with England's thunder,
  And plow the distant main.

But Kempenfelt is gone —
  His victories are o'er;
And he and his eight hundred
  Shall plow the waves no more.

IMAGINARY VERSES OF ALEXANDER SELKIRK

DURING HIS SOLITARY ABODE ON JUAN FERNANDEZ

I AM monarch of all I survey —
  My right there is none to dispute;
From the centre all round to the sea,
  I am lord of the fowl and the brute.
O Solitude! where are the charms
  That sages have seen in thy face?
Better dwell in the midst of alarms
  Than reign in this horrible place.

I am out of humanity's reach;
  I must finish my journey alone,
Never hear the sweet music of speech —
  I start at the sound of my own.
The beasts that roam over the plain
  My form with indifference see;
They are so unacquainted with man,
  Their tameness is shocking to me.

Society, friendship, and love,
　　Divinely bestowed upon man!
O, had I the wings of a dove,
　　How soon would I taste you again!
My sorrows I then might assuage
　　In the ways of religion and truth—
Might learn from the wisdom of age,
　　And be cheered by the sallies of youth.

Religion! What treasure untold
　　Resides in that heavenly word!—
More precious than silver and gold,
　　Or all that this earth can afford;
But the sound of the church-going bell
　　These valleys and rocks never heard,
Never sighed at the sound of a knell,
　　Or smiled when the Sabbath appeared.

Ye winds that have made me your sport,
　　Convey to this desolate shore
Some cordial endearing report
　　Of a land I shall visit no more!
My friends—do they now and then send
　　A wish or a thought after me?
Oh tell me I yet have a friend,
　　Though a friend I am never to see.

How fleet is the glance of the mind!
　　Compared with the speed of its flight,
The tempest itself lags behind,
　　And the swift-wingèd arrows of light.
When I think of my own native land,
　　In a moment I seem to be there;
But alas! recollection at hand
　　Soon hurries me back to despair.

But the sea-fowl has gone to her nest,
　　The beast is laid down in his lair;
Even here is a season of rest,
　　And I to my cabin repair.
There's mercy in every place,
　　And mercy—encouraging thought!
Gives even affliction a grace,
　　And reconciles man to his lot.

THE IMMUTABILITY OF HUMAN NATURE

From a Letter to William Unwin (1780)

WHEN we look back upon our forefathers, we seem to look back upon the people of another nation; almost upon creatures of another species. Their vast rambling mansions, spacious halls, and painted casements, the Gothic porch smothered with honeysuckles, their little gardens and high walls, their box-edgings, balls of holly, and yew-tree statues, are become so entirely unfashionable now, that we can hardly believe it possible that a people who resemble us so little in their taste should resemble us in anything else. But in everything else, I suppose, they were our counterparts exactly; and time, that has sewed up a slashed sleeve and reduced the large trunk-hose to a neat pair of silk stockings, has left human nature just where it found it.

The inside of the man at least has undergone no change. His passions, appetites, and aims are just what they ever were. They wear perhaps a handsomer disguise than they did in the days of yore, for philosophy and literature will have their effect upon the exterior; but in every other respect a modern is only an ancient in a different dress.

FROM A LETTER TO REV. JOHN NEWTON

OLNEY, NOVEMBER 30TH, 1783.

My dear Friend: —

I HAVE neither long visits to pay nor to receive, nor ladies to spend hours in telling me that which might be told in five minutes; yet often find myself obliged to be an economist of time, and to make the most of a short opportunity. Let our station be as retired as it may, there is no want of playthings and avocations, nor much need to seek them, in this world of ours. Business, or what presents itself to us under that imposing character, will find us out even in the stillest retreat, and plead its importance, however trivial in reality, as a just demand upon our attention. It is wonderful how by means of such real or seeming necessities my time is stolen away. I have just time to observe that time is short, and by the time I have made the observation, time is gone.

I have wondered in former days at the patience of the antediluvian world, that they could endure a life almost millenary,
and with so little variety as seems to have fallen to their share.
It is probable that they had much fewer employments than we.
Their affairs lay in a narrower compass; their libraries were indifferently furnished; philosophical researches were carried on
with much less industry and acuteness of penetration, and fid-
dles perhaps were not even invented. How then could seven
or eight hundred years of life be supported? I have asked this
question formerly, and been at a loss to resolve it; but I think
I can 'answer it now. I will suppose myself born a thousand
years before Noah was born or thought of. I rise with the sun;
I worship; I prepare my breakfast; I swallow a bucket of goat's
milk and a dozen good sizable cakes. I fasten a new string to
my bow, and my youngest boy, a lad of about thirty years of
age, having played with my arrows till he has stripped off all
the feathers, I find myself obliged to repair them. The morning
is thus spent in preparing for the chase, and it is become necessary that I should dine. I dig up my roots; I wash them; boil
them; I find them not done enough, I boil them again; my wife
is angry; we dispute; we settle the point; but in the mean time
the fire goes out, and must be kindled again. All this is very
amusing.

I hunt; I bring home the prey; with the skin of it I mend
an old coat, or I make a new one. By this time the day is far
spent; I feel myself fatigued, and retire to rest. Thus, what
with tilling the ground and eating the fruit of it, hunting, and
walking, and running, and mending old clothes, and sleeping
and rising again, I can suppose an inhabitant of the primeval
world so much occupied as to sigh over the shortness of life,
and to find, at the end of many centuries, that they had all
slipped through his fingers and were passing away like a
shadow. What wonder then that I, who live in a day of so
much greater refinement, when there is so much more to be
wanted and wished, and to be enjoyed, should feel myself now
and then pinched in point of opportunity, and at some loss for
leisure to fill four sides of a sheet like this?

GEORGE CRABBE

(1754–1832)

GEORGE CRABBE was born at Aldborough in Suffolk, the son of a customs officer. He received a fair education for a village lad, and at the age of fourteen was apprenticed to a country surgeon. He early showed an inclination toward letters, versifying much while a schoolboy. In 1778 he abandoned his profession of medicine, in which he was not successful, and came up to London with a few pounds and some manuscript in his pocket, determined to make his way in literature. He met with the usual reverses of a beginner without reputation or patronage, and soon was desperately in need of money. He wrote many letters to well-known people, without response. In his extremity he applied to Burke, who, although a stranger, received him most kindly into his own house, gave him advice and criticism, recommended him to Dodsley the publisher, and introduced him to many notable men of the day, among them Reynolds, Johnson, and Fox.

GEORGE CRABBE

During this time Crabbe wrote 'The Library' and the 'The Village'; and also at the suggestion of his patron qualified himself for the ministry. He took holy orders in 1782, and became shortly after chaplain to the Duke of Rutland. Subsequently he held a number of small livings, procured for him by his friends. The last of these, the rectory of Trowbridge, given him in 1813, he held until his death in 1832.

'The Village,' published in 1783, made the poet's reputation. His next work, 'The Newspaper,' published two years later, was much inferior. For twenty years thereafter he wrote and destroyed vast quantities of manuscript. Not until 1809 did he publish again. 'The Parish Register,' coming out in that year, was even more successful than his first work. In 1810 appeared 'The Borough,' containing his best work; 'Tales in Verse' following in 1812. With 'Tales of the Hall,' appearing in 1819, he took leave of the public.

Crabbe is an important link in the transition period between the poetry of the eighteenth and the nineteenth centuries. Men were

growing tired of the artificiality and the conventional frigidity
of the current verse in the hands of the imitators of Pope. A feeling for change was in the air, manifested in the incipient romantic
movement and in what is called "the return to nature." Goldsmith was one of the first to lead the way back to simplicity, but
he enveloped in a tender, somewhat sentimental idealism whatever
he touched. Then came Thomson with his generalizations of nature,
Cowper, a more faithful painter of rural scenes, and Burns, who
sang of the thought and feeling of the common man. The work
of these poets was a reaction against the poetry of town life, too apt
to become artificial with its subject. Yet, being poets and singers,
they expressed not so much the reality as what lies behind — its
beauty and its tenderness. To give the right perspective to this
return to nature, there was needed a man who should paint life as it
is, in its naked realism, unveiled by the glamour of poetic vision.

Crabbe was this man. The most uncompromising realist, he led
poetry back to human life on its stern dark side. Born and bred
among the poor, he described, as no one else in the whole range of
English verse has done, the sordid existences among which he had
grown up. He dispelled all illusions about rural life, and dealt the
death-blow to the Corydons and Phillises of pastoral poetry. He
showed that the poor man can be more immoral and even more
unprincipled than the rich, because his higher spiritual nature is
hopelessly dwarfed in the desperate struggle to keep the wolf from
the door. He supplied harrowing texts to the social economist. He
is a gloomy poet, especially in the first part of his work, for he
paints principally the shadows that hang over the lives of the lowly;
he does not deal with that life imaginatively as Wordsworth and
Burns do, but realistically, narrating with photographic accuracy
what he saw. He excels in graphic delineations of external facts,
but is also a powerful painter of the passions, especially the more
violent ones, such as remorse and despair. 'Sir Eustace Grey' is a
masterful portrayal of madness.

Crabbe has at times been denied the name of poet. There is little
music in his verse, little of that singing quality that goes with all
true poetry. His versification is often slipshod and careless. His
lack of taste and artistic feeling shows itself not only in the manner
but also in the matter of his work. He dwells by preference on the
unlovely; he does not choose his details as an artist would. He is
too minute, too like those Dutch painters who bestow as much care
on the refuse as on the burnished platters of their interiors. And
again he is trivial or too literal. But the steady admiration his
poetry has excited in men of the most different tastes for several
generations shows that it has deeper qualities. The truth is, that his

mean and squalid details are not mere heaps of unrelated things, nor irrelevant to his story; they are not even mere "scenery." They are part of the history, in general the tragedy, of human hearts and souls; and owe their validity as poetic material, and their power of interesting us, to their being part of the influences that bear on the history.

Scott had Crabbe's poems read aloud in his last illness. Horace Smith called him "Pope in worsted stockings." Jane Austen said she "could fancy being Mrs. Crabbe." Cardinal Newman read the 'Tales of the Hall' with extreme delight on their first appearance, and fifty years later still thought well of them. These different opinions testify that whatever the shortcomings of Crabbe as craftsman, the earnestness and the genuineness of his work give him a secure place among English poets.

ISAAC ASHFORD

From 'The Parish Register'

NEXT to these ladies, but in naught allied,
    A noble peasant, Isaac Ashford, died.
      Noble he was, contemning all things mean,
His truth unquestioned and his soul serene:
Of no man's presence Isaac felt afraid;
At no man's question Isaac looked dismayed;
Shame knew he not; he dreaded no disgrace;
Truth, simple truth, was written in his face:
Yet while the serious thought his soul approved,
Cheerful he seemed, and gentleness he loved;
To bliss domestic he his heart resigned,
And with the firmest had the fondest mind.

Were others joyful, he looked smiling on,
And gave allowance where he needed none;
Good he refused with future ill to buy,
Nor knew a joy that caused reflection's sigh;
A friend to virtue, his unclouded breast
No envy stung, no jealousy distressed;
(Bane of the poor! it wounds their weaker mind
To miss one favor which their neighbors find.)
Yet far was he from stoic pride removed;
He felt humanely, and he warmly loved.
I marked his action when his infant died,
And his old neighbor for offense was tried:

The still tears, stealing down that furrowed cheek,
Spoke pity plainer than the tongue can speak.
If pride were his, 'twas not their vulgar pride
Who in their base contempt the great deride;
Nor pride in learning: though my Clerk agreed,
If fate should call him, Ashford might succeed;
Nor pride in rustic skill, although we knew
None his superior, and his equals few:
But if that spirit in his soul had place,
It was the jealous pride that shuns disgrace;
A pride in honest fame, by virtue gained,
In sturdy boys to virtuous labors trained:

Pride in the power that guards his country's coast,
And all that Englishmen enjoy and boast;
Pride in a life that slander's tongue defied —
In fact a noble passion, misnamed Pride.
He had no party's rage, no sectary's whim;
Christian and countryman was all with him:
True to his church he came; no Sunday shower
Kept him at home in that important hour;
Nor his firm feet could one persuading sect
By the strong glare of their new light direct;
"On hope in mine own sober light I gaze,
But should be blind and lose it, in your blaze."

In times severe, when many a sturdy swain
Felt it his pride, his comfort, to complain,
Isaac their wants would soothe, his own would hide,
And feel in *that* his comfort and his pride.   .   .   .
I feel his absence in the hours of prayer,
And view his seat, and sigh for Isaac there:
I see no more those white locks thinly spread
Round the bald polish of that honored head;
No more that awful glance on playful wight,
Compelled to kneel and tremble at the sight,
To fold his fingers, all in dread the while,
Till Mr. Ashford softened to a smile:
No more that meek and suppliant look in prayer,
Nor the pure faith (to give it force), are there; —
But he is blest, and I lament no more
A wise, good man, contented to be poor.

THE PARISH WORKHOUSE AND APOTHECARY

From 'The Village'

THEIRS is yon house that holds the parish poor,
    Whose walls of mud scarce bear the broken door;
    There, where the putrid vapors flagging play,
And the dull wheel hums doleful through the day;
There children dwell who know no parents' care;
Parents who know no children's love dwell there;
Heart-broken matrons on their joyless bed,
Forsaken wives, and mothers never wed;
Dejected widows with unheeded tears,
And crippled age with more than childhood-fears;
The lame, the blind, and — far the happiest they! —
The moping idiot and the madman gay.

Here too the sick their final doom receive,
Here brought amid the scenes of grief to grieve,
Where the loud groans from some sad chamber flow,
Mixed with the clamors of the crowd below;
Here, sorrowing, they each kindred sorrow scan,
And the cold charities of man to man:
Whose laws indeed for ruined age provide,
And strong compulsion plucks the scrap from pride;
But still that scrap is bought with many a sigh,
And pride embitters what it can't deny.

Say ye, oppressed by some fantastic woes,
Some jarring nerve that baffles your repose;
Who press the downy couch, while slaves advance
With timid eye, to read the distant glance;
Who with sad prayers the weary doctor tease,
To name the nameless ever-new disease;
Who with mock patience dire complaints endure,
Which real pain and that alone can cure:
How would ye bear in real pain to lie,
Despised, neglected, left alone to die?
How would ye bear to draw your latest breath
Where all that's wretched paves the way for death?

Such is that room which one rude beam divides,
And naked rafters form the sloping sides;
Where the vile bands that bind the thatch are seen,
And lath and mud are all that lie between;

Save one dull pane, that, coarsely patched, gives way
To the rude tempest, yet excludes the day:
Here on a matted flock, with dust o'erspread,
The drooping wretch reclines his languid head;
For him no hand the cordial cup applies,
Or wipes the tear that stagnates in his eyes;
No friends with soft discourse his pain beguile,
Or promise hope till sickness wears a smile.

But soon a loud and hasty summons calls,
Shakes the thin roof, and echoes round the walls.
Anon a figure enters, quaintly neat,
All pride and business, bustle and conceit,
With looks unaltered by these scenes of woe,
With speed that, entering, speaks his haste to go;
He bids the gazing throng around him fly,
And carries fate and physic in his eye:
A potent quack, long versed in human ills,
Who first insults the victim whom he kills;
Whose murderous hand a drowsy bench protect,
And whose most tender mercy is neglect.

Paid by the parish for attendance here,
He wears contempt upon his sapient sneer;
In haste he seeks the bed where misery lies,
Impatience marked in his averted eyes;
And some habitual queries hurried o'er,
Without reply he rushes to the door:
His drooping patient, long inured to pain,
And long unheeded, knows remonstrance vain;
He ceases now the feeble help to crave
Of man; and silent sinks into the grave.

DINAH MARIA MULOCK CRAIK

(1826–1887)

LTHOUGH the daughter of a clergyman of the Established Church, Dinah Mulock was not herself a Churchwoman, and in her earlier works she frequently declares her belief in freedom of religious thought and action. She was led to take this attitude by her conviction that her mother was unkindly treated by her father, who in her opinion did not live up to the principles he professed. In a blaze of youthful indignation she carried her delicate mother and younger brothers away from their home at Stoke-on-Trent, Staffordshire, and undertook to support them all by her pen. 'The Ogilvies,' her first novel, was published in 1849, and her first struggle was successful. But she was soon deprived of the cause which she had gone forth to champion. Her mother and one of her brothers died, and she was left alone with her youngest brother to continue her work. Her loving description of her mother in 'My Mother and I' will be remembered as the picture of a pure, tender, and gentle woman.

DINAH M. M. CRAIK

'Olive' and 'The Head of the Family' soon followed 'The Ogilvies,' and in the second of these stories she showed highly imaginative and dramatic qualities, though the plot is simplicity itself. After 'Agatha's Husband' was issued in 1852, no other work of consequence appeared from her pen until the publication in 1857 of 'John Halifax, Gentleman,' her most popular novel. It was the portraiture of a gentleman by instinct, though not by social position. He is a middle-class business man, an inventor who has solved certain problems of capital and labor, and upholds "a true aristocracy," which he defines as "the best men of the country." "These," he says, "ought to govern and will govern one day, whether their patent of nobility be birth and titles or only honesty and brains."

She always maintained that 'A Life for a Life' was her best book, a judgment shared by many of her friends and critics. 'John Halifax,' however, continues to hold the heart and imagination of the many most strongly; perhaps on account of its democratic principles. Mrs. Craik was an earnest advocate of legalizing marriage with a deceased wife's sister, and 'Hannah,' a strong but painful story, deals with this subject. She published between forty and fifty works,— novels, tales for the young, volumes of travel, and poems. She is a writer of the best sort of English domestic novels, full of strong moral purpose. She avoids over-romantic or over-emotional themes, but the tender and poetical ideals of ordinary womanhood find in her a satisfactory exponent. As a poet her position, though not a high one, is lasting. Her versification is good, and her sentiment is always tender, truthful, and noble. Perhaps her best verses are those given below. In 1865 she made a happy marriage, and as her life grew larger and fuller her home became the centre of a group of affectionate friends,— artists, literary men, musicians, and many others full of intellectual interests and aspirations. She died suddenly but peacefully at her home at Shortlands, Kent, near London, on October 12th, 1887.

THE NIGHT ATTACK

From 'John Halifax, Gentleman'

I COULD not sleep—all my faculties were preternaturally alive; my weak body and timid soul became strong and active, able to compass anything. For that one night at least I felt myself a man.

My father was a very sound sleeper. I knew nothing would disturb him till daylight; therefore my divided duty was at an end. I left him and crept down-stairs into Sally Watkins's kitchen. It was silent; only the faithful warder Jem dozed over the dull fire. I touched him on the shoulder, at which he collared me, and nearly knocked me down.

"Beg pardon, Mr. Phineas—hope I didn't hurt 'ee, sir!" cried he, all but whimpering; for Jem, a big lad of fifteen, was the most tender-hearted fellow imaginable. "I thought it were some of them folk that Mr. Halifax ha' gone among."

"Where is Mr. Halifax?"

"Doan't know, sir; wish I did! wouldn't be long a-finding out, though—on'y he says: 'Jem, you stop here wi' they,'" (pointing his thumb up the staircase). "So, Master Phineas, I stop."

And Jem settled himself, with a doggedly obedient but most dissatisfied air, down by the fireplace. It was evident nothing would move him thence; and he was as safe a guard over my poor old father's slumber as the mastiff in the tan-yard, who was

as brave as a lion and as docile as a child. My last lingering
hesitation ended.

"Jem, lend me your coat and hat; I'm going out into the
town."

Jem was so astonished that he stood with open mouth while
I took the said garments from him and unbolted the door. At
last it seemed to occur to him that he ought to intercept me.

"But sir, Mr. Halifax said —"

"I am going to look for Mr. Halifax."

And I escaped outside. Anything beyond his literal duty did
not strike the faithful Jem. He stood on the doorsill and gazed
after me with a hopeless expression.

"I s'pose you mun have your way, sir; but Mr. Halifax said,
'Jem, you stop y'ere,' and y'ere I stop."

He went in, and I heard him bolting the door with a sullen
determination, as if he would have kept guard behind it — waiting for John — until doomsday.

I stole along the dark alley into the street. It was very
silent — I need not have borrowed Jem's exterior in order to
creep through a throng of maddened rioters. There was no
sign of any such, except that under one of the three oil-lamps
that lit the night-darkness of Norton Bury lay a few smoldering hanks of hemp, well rosined. They then had thought of
that dreadful engine of destruction — fire. Had my terrors been
true? Our house — and perhaps John within it!

On I ran, speeded by a dull murmur which I fancied I
heard; but still there was no one in the street — no one except
the abbey watchman, lounging in his box. I roused him and
asked if all was safe — where were the rioters?

"What rioters?"

"At Abel Fletcher's mill; they may be at his house now —"

"Ay. I think they be."

"And will not one man in the town help him — no constables,
no law?"

"Oh, he's a Quaker; the law don't help Quakers."

That was the truth, in those days. Liberty, justice, were idle
names to Nonconformists of every kind; and all they knew of
the glorious constitution of English law was when its iron hand
was turned against them.

I had forgotten this; bitterly I remembered it now. So,
wasting no more words, I flew along the churchyard until I

saw, shining against the boles of the chestnut-trees, a red light. It was one of the hempen torches. Now at last I had got in the midst of that small body of men — "the rioters."

A mere handful they were, not above twoscore; apparently the relic of the band which had attacked the mill, joined with a few plow-lads from the country round. But they were desperate; they had come up the Coltham road so quietly that, except this faint murmur, neither I nor any one in the town could have told they were near. Wherever they had been ransacking, as yet they had not attacked my father's house; it stood upon the other side of the road, — barred, black, silent.

I heard a muttering, "Th' old man bean't there" — "Nobody knows where he be." No, thank God!

"Be us all y'ere?" said the man with the torch, holding it up so as to see round him. It was well then that I appeared as Jem Watkins. But no one noticed me, except one man who skulked behind a tree, and of whom I was rather afraid, as he was apparently intent on watching.

"Ready, lads? Now for the rosin! Blaze 'un out!"

But in the eager scuffle the torch, the only one light, was knocked down and trodden out. A volley of oaths arose, though whose fault it was no man seemed to know: but I missed my man from behind the tree — nor found him till after the angry throng had rushed on to the nearest lamp. One of them was left behind, standing close to our own railings. He looked round to see if none were by, and then sprung over the gate. Dark as it was, I thought I recognized him.

"John?"

"Phineas?" He was beside me in a bound. "How could you do—"

"I could do anything to-night. But you are safe — no one has harmed you. Oh, thank God, you are not hurt!"

And I clung to his arm — my friend whom I had missed so long, so sorely.

He held me tight — his heart felt as mine, only more silently; and silent hearts are strong.

"Now, Phineas, we have not a minute's time. I must have you safe — we must get into the house."

"Who is there?"

"Jael; she is as good as a staff of constables; she has braved them once to-night, but they're back again, or will be directly."

"And the mill?"

"Safe, as yet; I have had three of the tan-yard men there since yesterday morning, though your father did not know. I have been going to and fro all night between there and here, waiting till the rioters should come back from the Severn mills. Hist! there they are — I say, Jael."

He tapped at the window. In a few seconds Jael had unbarred the door, let us in, and closed it again securely; mounting guard behind it with something that looked very like my father's pistols, though I would not discredit her among our peaceful society by positively stating the fact.

"Bravo!" said John, when we stood all together in the barricaded house and heard the threatening murmur of voices and feet outside. "Bravo, Jael! The wife of Heber the Kenite was no braver woman than you."

She looked gratified, and followed John obediently from room to room.

"I have done all as thee bade me — thee art a sensible lad, John Halifax. We are secure, I think."

Secure? Bolts and bars secure against fire? For that was threatening us now.

"They can't mean it — surely they can't mean it," repeated John, as the cry of "Burn 'un out!" rose louder and louder.

But they did mean it. From the attic window we watched them light torch after torch, sometimes throwing one at the house — but it fell harmless against the staunch oaken door, and blazed itself out on our stone steps. All it did was to show, more plainly than even daylight had shown, the gaunt ragged forms and pinched faces, furious with famine.

John, as well as I, recoiled at that miserable sight.

"I'll speak to them," he said. "Unbar the window, Jael;" and before I could hinder he was leaning right out. "Halloo, there!"

At his loud and commanding voice a wave of upturned faces surged forward, expectant.

"My men, do you know what you are about? To burn down a gentleman's house is — hanging."

There was a hush, and then a shout of derision.

"Not a Quaker's! Nobody'll get hanged for burning out a Quaker!"

"That be true enough," muttered Jael between her teeth. "We must e'en fight, as Mordecai's people fought, hand to hand, until they slew their enemies."

"Fight!" repeated John half to himself, as he stood at the now closed window, against which more than one blazing torch began to rattle.

"Fight with these?—What are you doing, Jael?" For she had taken down a large book—the last book in the house she would have taken under less critical circumstances, and with it was trying to stop up a broken pane.

"No, my good Jael, not this;" and he carefully put back the volume in its place—that volume, in which he might have read, as day after day, year after year, we Christians generally do read such plain words as these: "Love your enemies;" "Bless them that curse you;" "Pray for them that despitefully use you and persecute you."

A minute or two John stood by the book-shelves, thinking. Then he touched me on the shoulder.

"Phineas, I am going to try a new plan—at least one so old that it is almost new. Whether it succeeds or no, you'll bear me witness to your father that I did it for the best, and did it because I thought it right. Now for it."

To my horror, he threw up the window wide, and leaned out.

"My men, I want to speak to you."

He might as well have spoken to the roaring sea. The only answer was a shower of missiles, which missed their aim. The rioters were too far off—our spiked iron railing, eight feet high or more, being a barrier which none had yet ventured to climb. But at length one random shot hit John on the chest.

I pulled him in; but he declared he was not hurt. Terrified, I implored him not to risk his life.

"Life is not always the first thing to be thought of," said he, gently. "Don't be afraid; I shall come to no harm. But I *must* do what I think right, if it is to be done."

While he spoke, I could hardly hear him for the bellowings outside. More savage still grew the cry:—

"Burn 'em out! burn 'em out! They be only Quakers!"

"There's not a minute to lose. Stop, let me think—Jael, is that a pistol?"

"Loaded," she said, handing it over to him with a kind of stern delight. Certainly Jael was not born to be a Friend.

John ran down-stairs, and before I guessed his purpose had unbolted the hall door, and stood on the top of the flight of steps in full view of the mob.

There was no bringing him back, so of course I followed. A pillar sheltered me; I do not think he saw me, though I stood close behind him.

So sudden had been his act that even the rioters did not seem to have noticed, or clearly understood it till the next lighted torch showed them the young man standing there, with his back to the door — *outside* the door.

The sight fairly confounded them. Even I felt for the moment he was safe. They were awed — nay, paralyzed, by his daring.

But the storm raged too fiercely to be lulled, except for one brief minute. A confusion of voices burst out afresh.

"Who be thee?" "It's one o' the Quakers." "No, he bean't." "Burn 'un anyhow." "Touch 'un, if ye dare!"

There was evidently a division rising. One big man, who had made himself very prominent all along, seemed trying to calm the tumult.

John stood his ground. Once a torch was flung at him — he stooped and picked it up. I thought he was going to hurl it back again, but he did not; he only threw it down and stamped it out safely with his foot. This simple action had a wonderful effect on the crowd.

The big fellow advanced to the gate, and called John by his name.

"Is that you, Jacob Baines? I am sorry to see you here."

"Be ye, sir?"

"What do you want?"

"Naught wi' thee. We want Abel Fletcher. Where is 'un?"

"I shall certainly not tell you."

As John said this, again the noise arose, and again Jacob Baines seemed to have power to quiet the rest.

John Halifax never stirred. Evidently he was pretty well known. I caught many a stray sentence, such as "Don't hurt the lad;" "He were kind to my lad, he were;" "He be a real gentleman;" "No, he comed here as poor as us," and the like. At length one voice, sharp and shrill, was heard above the rest.

VII—259

"I say, young man, didst ever know what it was to be pretty nigh vamished?"

"Ay, many a time."

The answer, so brief, so unexpected, struck a great hush into the throng. Then the same voice cried:—

"Speak up, man! we won't hurt 'ee! You be one o' we!"

"No, I am not one of you. I'd be ashamed to come in the night and burn my master's house down."

I expected an outbreak, but none came. They listened, as it were by compulsion, to the clear manly voice, that had not in it one shade of fear.

"What do you do it for?" John continued. "All because he would not sell you, or give you, his wheat. Even so; it was *his* wheat, not yours. May not a man do what he likes with his own?"

That argument seemed to strike home. There is always a lurking sense of rude justice in a mob—at least a British mob.

"Don't you see how foolish you were? You tried threats too. Now, you all know Mr. Fletcher; you are his men—some of you. He is not a man to be threatened."

This seemed to be taken rather angrily; but John went on speaking, as if he did not observe the fact.

"Nor am I one to be threatened, neither. Look here—the first one of you who attempted to break into Mr. Fletcher's house, I should most certainly have shot. But I'd rather not shoot you, poor starving fellows! I know what it is to be hungry. I'm sorry for you—sorry from the bottom of my heart."

There was no mistaking that compassionate accent, nor the murmur which followed it.

"But what must us do, Mr. Halifax?" cried Jacob Baines. "Us be starved a'most. What's the good o' talking to we?"

John's countenance relaxed. I saw him lift his head and shake his hair back, with that pleased gesture I remembered so well of old. He went down to the locked gate.

"Suppose I gave you something to eat, would you listen to me afterward?"

There rose up a frenzied shout of assent. Poor wretches! they were fighting for no principle, true or false, only for bare life. They would have bartered their very souls for a mouthful of bread.

"You must promise to be peaceable," said John again, very resolutely, as soon as he could obtain a hearing. "You are Norton Bury folk. I know you. I could get every one of you hanged, even though Abel Fletcher is a Quaker. Mind, you'll be peaceable?"

"Ay, ay! Some'at to eat; give us some'at to eat."

John Halifax called out to Jael, bade her bring all the food of every kind that there was in the house, and give it to him out of the parlor window. She obeyed — I marvel now to think of it, but she implicitly obeyed. Only I heard her fix the bar to the closed front door, and go back, with a strange sharp sob, to her station at the hall window.

"Now, my lads, come in!" and he unlocked the gate.

They came thronging up the steps, not more than twoscore, I imagined, in spite of the noise they had made. But twoscore of such famished, desperate men, God grant I may never again see!

John divided the food as well as he could among them; they fell to it like wild beasts. Meat, cooked or raw, loaves, vegetables, meal — all came alike, and were clutched, gnawed, and scrambled for in the fierce selfishness of hunger. Afterward there was a call for drink.

"Water, Jael; bring them water."

"Beer!" shouted some.

"Water," repeated John. "Nothing but water. I'll have no drunkards rioting at my master's door."

And either by chance or design, he let them hear the click of his pistol. But it was hardly needed. They were all cowed by a mightier weapon still — the best weapon a man can use — his own firm indomitable will.

At length all the food we had in the house was consumed. John told them so; and they believed him. Little enough, indeed, was sufficient for some of them: wasted with long famine, they turned sick and faint, and dropped down even with bread in their mouths, unable to swallow it. Others gorged themselves to the full, and then lay along the steps, supine as satisfied brutes. Only a few sat and ate like rational human beings; and there was but one, the little shrill-voiced man, who asked me if he might "tak a bit o' bread to the old wench at home!"

John, hearing, turned, and for the first time noticed me.

"Phineas, it was very wrong of you; but there is no danger now."

No, there was none — not even for Abel Fletcher's son. I stood safe by John's side, very happy, very proud.

"Well, my men," he said, looking around with a smile, "have you had enough to eat?"

"Oh, ay!" they all cried.

And one man added, "Thank the Lord!"

"That's right, Jacob Baines. And another time *trust* the Lord. You wouldn't then have been abroad this summer morning" — and he pointed to the dawn just reddening in the sky — "this quiet, blessed summer morning, burning and rioting, bringing yourself to the gallows and your children to starvation."

"They be nigh that a'ready," said Jacob, sullenly. "Us men ha' gotten a meal, thankee for i'; bu' what'll become o' the 'ittle uns a' home? I say, Mr. Halifax," and he seemed waxing desperate again, "we must get food somehow."

John turned away, his countenance very sad. Another of the men plucked at him from behind.

"Sir, when thee was a poor lad, I lent thee a rug to sleep on; I doan't grudge 'ee getting on; you was born for a gentleman, surely. But Master Fletcher be a hard man."

"And a just one," persisted John. "You that work for him, did he ever stint you of a halfpenny? If you had come to him and said, 'Master, times are hard; we can't live upon our wages;' he might — I don't say he would — but he *might* even have given you the food you tried to steal."

"D'ye think he'd give it us now?" And Jacob Baines, the big gaunt savage fellow who had been the ringleader — the same too who had spoken of his "little uns" — came and looked steadily in John's face.

"I knew thee as a lad; thee'rt a young man now, as will be a father some o' these days. Oh! Mr. Halifax, may 'ee ne'er want a meal o' good meat for the missus and the babies at home, if 'ee'll get a bit of bread for our'n this day."

"My man, I'll try."

He called me aside, explained to me, and asked my advice and consent, as Abel Fletcher's son, to a plan that had come into his mind. It was to write orders, which each man presenting at our mill should receive a certain amount of flour.

" Do you think your father would agree ? "

" I think he would."

" Yes," John added, pondering, "I am sure he would. And besides, if he does not give some he may lose all. But he would not do it for fear of that. No, he is a just man. I am not afraid. Give me some paper, Jael."

He sat down as composedly as if he had been alone in the counting-house, and wrote. I looked over his shoulder, admiring his clear firm handwriting; the precision, concentrativeness, and quickness with which he first seemed to arrange and then execute his ideas. He possessed to the full that "business" faculty so frequently despised, but which out of very ordinary material often makes a clever man, and without which the cleverest man alive can never be altogether a great man.

When about to sign the orders, John suddenly stopped.

" No; I had better not."

" Why so ? "

" I have no right; your father might think it presumption."

" Presumption, after to-night! "

" Oh, that's nothing! Take the pen. It is your part to sign them, Phineas."

I obeyed.

" Isn't this better than hanging ? " said John to the men, when he had distributed the little bits of paper, precious as pound-notes, and made them all fully understand the same. " Why, there isn't another gentleman in Norton Bury who, if you had come to burn *his* house down, would not have had the constables or the soldiers shoot down one-half of you like mad dogs, and sent the other half to the county jail. Now, for all your mis-doings, we let you go quietly home, well fed, and with food for your children too. *Why*, think you ? "

" I doan't know," said Jacob Baines, humbly.

" I'll tell you. Because Abel Fletcher is a Quaker and a Christian."

" Hurrah for Abel Fletcher! hurrah for the Quakers! " shouted they, waking up the echoes down Norton Bury streets: which of a surety had never echoed to *that* shout before. And so the riot was over.

John Halifax closed the hall door and came in — unsteadily — all but staggering. Jael placed a chair for him — worthy soul! she was wiping her old eyes. He sat down shivering, speechless.

I put my hand on his shoulder; he took it and pressed it hard.

"O Phineas, lad, I'm glad; glad it's safe over."

"Yes, thank God!"

"Ay indeed, thank God!"

He covered his eyes for a minute or two, and then rose up, pale, but quite himself again.

"Now let us go and fetch your father home."

We found him on John's bed, still asleep. But as we entered he woke. The daylight shone on his face — it looked ten years older since yesterday. He stared, bewildered and angry, at John Halifax.

"Eh, young man — oh! I remember. Where is my son — where's my Phineas?"

I fell on his neck as if I had been a child. And almost as if it had been a child's feeble head, mechanically he soothed and patted mine.

"Thee art not hurt? Nor any one?"

"No," John answered; "nor is either the house or tan-yard injured."

He looked amazed. "How has that been?"

"Phineas will tell you. Or stay — better wait till you are at home."

But my father insisted on hearing. I told him the whole without any comments on John's behavior; he would not have liked it, and besides, the facts spoke for themselves. I told the simple plain story — nothing more.

Abel Fletcher listened at first in silence. As I proceeded, he felt about for his hat, put it on, and drew its broad brim down over his eyes. Not even when I told him of the flour we had promised in his name, the giving of which would, as we had calculated, cost him considerable loss, did he utter a word or move a muscle.

John at length asked him if he was satisfied.

"Quite satisfied."

But having said this, he sat so long, his hands locked together on his knees, and his hat drawn down, hiding all the face except the rigid mouth and chin — sat so long, so motionless, that we became uneasy.

John spoke to him gently, almost as a son would have spoken.

"Are you very lame still? Could I help you to walk home?"

My father looked up, and slowly held out his hand.

"Thee hast been a good lad, and a kind lad to us. I thank thee."

There was no answer; none. But all the words in the world could not match that happy silence.

By degrees we got my father home. It was just such another summer morning as the one two years back, when we two had stood, exhausted and trembling, before that sternly bolted door. We both thought of that day; I knew not if my father did also.

He entered, leaning heavily on John. He sat down in the very seat, in the very room where he had so harshly judged us — judged him.

Something perhaps of that bitterness rankled in the young man's spirit now, for he stopped on the threshold.

"Come in," said my father, looking up.

"If I am welcome; not otherwise."

"Thee are welcome."

He came in — I drew him in — and sat down with us. But his manner was irresolute, his fingers closed and unclosed nervously. My father too sat leaning his head on his two hands, not unmoved. I stole up to him, and thanked him softly for the welcome he had given.

"There is nothing to thank me for," said he, with something of his old hardness. "What I once did was only justice, or I then believed so. What I have done, and am about to do, is still mere justice. John, how old art thee now?"

"Twenty."

"Then for one year from this time I will take thee as my 'prentice, though thee knowest already nearly as much of the business as I do. At twenty-one thee wilt be able to set up for thyself, or I may take thee into partnership — we'll see. But " — and he looked at me, then sternly, nay fiercely, into John's steadfast eyes — "remember, thee hast in some measure taken that lad's place. May God deal with thee as thou dealest with my son Phineas — my only son!"

"Amen!" was the solemn answer.

And God, who sees us both now — ay, *now!* and perhaps not so far apart as some may deem — he knows whether or no John Halifax kept that vow.

PHILIP, MY KING

Look at me with thy large brown eyes,
    Philip, my King!
   For round thee the purple shadow lies
Of babyhood's regal dignities.
Lay on my neck thy tiny hand,
   With love's invisible sceptre laden;
I am thine Esther to command,
    Till thou shalt find thy queen-handmaiden,
      Philip, my King!

Oh the day when thou goest a-wooing,
    Philip, my King!
When those beautiful lips are suing,
And some gentle heart's bars undoing,
Thou dost enter, love-crowned, and there
   Sittest all glorified! — Rule kindly,
Tenderly, over thy kingdom fair,
For we that love, ah, we love so blindly,
    Philip, my King!

I gaze from thy sweet mouth up to thy brow,
    Philip, my King:
Ay, there lies the spirit, all sleeping now,
That may rise like a giant, and make men bow
As to one God — throned amidst his peers.
   My Saul, than thy brethren higher and fairer,
Let me behold thee in coming years!
    Yet thy head needeth a circlet rarer,
    Philip, my King!

A wreath, not of gold, but palm. One day,
    Philip, my King,
Thou too must tread, as we tread, a way
Thorny, and bitter, and cold, and gray:
Rebels within thee and foes without
   Will snatch at thy crown. But go on, glorious,
Martyr, yet monarch! till angels shout,
    As thou sittest at the feet of God victorious,—
      "Philip, the King!"

TOO LATE

COULD ye come back to me, Douglas, Douglas,
    In the old likeness that I knew, ·
  I would be so faithful, so loving, Douglas,
    Douglas, Douglas, tender and true.

Never a scornful word should grieve ye,
    I'd smile on ye sweet as the angels do:
Sweet as your smile on me shone ever,
    Douglas, Douglas, tender and true.

Oh to call back the days that are not!
    My eyes were blinded, your words were few:
Do you know the truth now, up in heaven,
    Douglas, Douglas, tender and true?

I never was worthy of you, Douglas;
    Not half worthy the like of you;
Now all men beside seem to me like shadows —
    I love *you*, Douglas, tender and true.

Stretch out your hand to me, Douglas, Douglas,
    Drop forgiveness from heaven like dew,
As I lay my heart on your dead heart, Douglas,
    Douglas, Douglas, tender and true.

NOW AND AFTERWARDS

«Two hands upon the breast, and labor is past.»
                                    RUSSIAN PROVERB.

  «Two hands upon the breast,
        And labor's done;
      Two pale feet crossed in rest,—
        The race is won;
    Two eyes with coin-weights shut,
        And all tears cease;
    Two lips where grief is mute,
        Anger at peace:»
So pray we oftentimes, mourning our lot;
God in his kindness answereth not.

« Two hands to work addressed
        Aye for his praise;
Two feet that never rest
        Walking his ways;
Two eyes that look above
        Through all their tears;
Two lips still breathing love,
        Not wrath, nor fears: »
So pray we afterwards, low on our knees.
Pardon those erring prayers; Father, hear these!

MADAME AUGUSTUS CRAVEN

(PAULINE DE LA FERRONAYS)

(1820–1891)

ADAME CRAVEN has told the story of her home life in 'Récit d'une Sœur: Souvenirs de Famille' (The Story of a Sister). She has given a charming idyllic picture of a Catholic French family — cultivated, simple-minded, and loving, and all animated by religious fervor. She has depicted with the strength of a personal experience the hopes and fears of those who see their dearest friends dying of consumption. She loves to show the gradual renunciation of life, the ennobling influence of sorrow, the triumph of faith over death and bereavement. Her affectionate nature, full of admiring enthusiasm for those she loved, led her to idealize real people as the characters of her books.

She was born at Paris, but had early advantages of travel unusual for a French girl. Her father was Ambassador to Berlin; the family were in Italy for a time; and after her marriage with Augustus Craven she lived a great deal in his native England. So the titles of her books reflect a certain cosmopolitan spirit. She was interested in English politics, and wrote a number of sketches on the subject. The lives of devout Catholic friends appealed to her strongly, and she wrote that of Sister Nathalie Narishkine of the Charity Saint Vincent de Paul, which was cordially indorsed by Cardinal Newman; and that of Lady Georgiana Fullerton.

Her 'Reminiscences,' recollections of England and Italy, show the same keenly sympathetic power of observation. She also translated from the Italian. But her most popular work has been stories. 'The Story of a Sister' (1866), a collection of memoirs, was enthusiastically admired by Catholic readers, and translated into English, was widely read in England and America. It was followed by several novels, of which the most popular have been 'Anne Séverin,' 'Le Mot de l'Énigme' (The Veil Withdrawn), and 'Fleurange.' These have all been translated into English, and the last especially has continued in favor for twenty years. Here, as in her other books, the author's strongest desire is to bear witness to the helpful discipline of trouble and the satisfactions of religion. She treats simple problems of love and duty, depicts primitive emotion, and deals very little in the complex psychology of later fiction. In a strong, fluent, fervid style she demonstrates that religious ecstasy is the most perfect of all joy, and that in Catholicism alone all difficulties may find solution.

ALBERT'S LAST DAYS

From 'A Sister's Story'

ONE of these latter days, Albert suddenly threw his arm round me and exclaimed: "*I am going to die, and we might have been so happy!*" O my God! I felt then as if my heart would really break.

JUNE 26TH. — Before mass, which was again said at twelve o'clock at night in his room, Albert looked at me a long time, and then said with deep feeling, "God bless you!" Then he made the sign of the cross on my forehead, and added, "And God bless your mother, too." After a while he said, "Good-by." I seemed surprised, and perhaps frightened, and then he said, "Good-night," as if to change the sad meaning of the word he had used. And all the while I wished so much to speak openly to him of his death. It was I perhaps who prevented it, by my fear of exciting him. During that last mass, every time that I looked at him he made me a sign to look at the altar. The window was open, but the night was quite dark. At the moment of communion the Abbé Martin de Noirlieu and Albert's father, who was serving mass, came up to him. The Abbé gave one-half of the sacred Host to him, and the other to me. Even in this solemn moment there was something very sweet to me in this. Albert could not open his lips without much suffering — it was for this reason that the Abbé Martin had divided the Host; but even so, he had some difficulty in swallowing, and they were obliged to give him some water. This disturbed him, but the Abbé Gerbet — who was present — assured him it did not signify. Then Albert exclaimed: "My God! Thy will be done!" O my God! this thanksgiving of his must, I think, have been pleasing to thee!

Before mass he had said to the Abbé Martin, who was speaking to him of his sufferings, "The only thing I ask of God now is strength to fulfill my sacrifice." "You are nailed to the cross with our Lord Jesus Christ," the Abbé said, and Albert answered in a very sweet and humble way, "Ah! but I am such a miserble sinner!" The altar had a blue-silk frontal, and was dressed with flowers. It was Eugénie who had arranged it. The blue silk was one of my trousseau dresses that had never been made up, and now was applied to this use.

JUNE 27TH.— Albert was light-headed; was continually talking of going into the country, and pointing to me, cried, "She is coming with me! She is coming with me!" (I was in the habit of writing down every word he said on these latter days of his life; and these words, "She is coming with me," were the last I wrote.)   After dinner that same day we were sitting by his side, without speaking.   Eugénie bent over him and gently suggested his receiving extreme unction.   His countenance did not change in the least.   He said gently and quite quietly, "Will it not be taking advantage of the graces the Church bestows to receive it yet?"   He was anointed however that same evening, and during the whole time I was standing near him, with my hand on his right shoulder.   Eugénie was on the other side of me.

An explanation of this sacrament, which we had read together in our happy days, made me understand all that was going on.   The thought flashed through me with a wild feeling of grief: "What, must his soul be purified even of its ardent love for me?   Must that too be destroyed?"   But I did not shed a single tear.   His own wonderful calm was so holy.   When it was over, Albert made a little sign of the cross on the Abbé Dupanloup's forehead, who received it with respect, and affectionately embraced him.   Then I approached, feeling that it was my turn to receive that dear sign of the cross, which was a sweet habit of happier days.   He kissed me, his parents, Eugénie, Fernand, Montal, and then Julian (his servant), who was weeping bitterly.   When it came to that, Albert burst into tears, and that was more than I could bear; but he quickly recovered fortitude when I kissed him again, and beckoned to the Sister, whom he would not leave out in this tender and general leave-taking, but with his delicate sense of what was befitting, and in token of gratitude he kissed the hand which had ministered to him, in spite of her resistance.   M. l'Abbé Dupanloup, who gave him extreme unction, had prepared him for his first communion, and never forgot the edification it had given him at that time to find Albert on his knees praying in the same place where he had left him three hours before in the Church of St. Sulpice — that church in which his beloved remains were so soon to be deposited.   I sat down by his side.   He was asleep, and I held his hand in mine while Eugénie was writing the following lines to Pauline: —

"O Pauline, what a night has this been! and yet not terrible,—no, a most blessed night. Albert has just received extreme unction. What wonderful graces God bestows: but why were you not here to receive that dear angel's blessing, who, fitter for Heaven than ourselves, is going before us there. . . . ?" After relating all that has been mentioned, she adds: "Pauline, I could not have conceived anything more touching, more holy, more soothing, or a more heavenly peace. I bless God that nothing in all this time has troubled my notions of happiness in death."

ALEXANDRINE TO THE ABBÉ GERBET

THE SAME DAY.

I should feel it a great mercy if you could come, but I am however perfectly composed. I entreat you, continue your prayers for me, for I can no longer pray for myself. I can only think of God, and remind him that I asked for faith in exchange for happiness.   ALEXANDRINE.

ALEXANDRINE'S JOURNAL

JUNE 28TH.— To-night I called Albert's attention to the rising moon. I thought it had the lurid aspect which once before I saw at Rome, when I thought he was dying at Civita Vecchia. The window was open. We looked on the fine trees of the Luxembourg, and the perfume of the honeysuckles and many flowers was sometimes almost too powerful on the night air. Montal came in later and brought me Albert's letters to him, which I had asked for. It was as if a dagger had been driven into my heart. Still I immediately began to read those pages, which though heart-rending were very sweet. The Abbé Martin gave Albert absolution and the plenary indulgence for the night. I was kneeling by his side, and said to him afterwards, "Do kiss me." He raised his feeble head, put up his lips, and kissed me. Then I asked him to let me kiss his eyes. He shut them in token of assent. Later still, feeling unable any longer to forbear pouring my whole heart into his, and longing to take advantage of the few moments yet remaining to us of life, I said to him:— "Albert, Montal has brought me your letters. They comfort me very much. . . ." "Stop!" he cried feebly. "Stop! I cannot bear it—it troubles me!"—"O Albert! I *worship* you!"—The cry burst forth in the anguish of not being able to speak to him, for the fear of troubling his soul forced me to be silent; but those were the last words of my love for him that my lips ever uttered, and he heard them, as he had asked — even as he lay dying. O my God! whom alone I now worship, thou hast forgiven me for that rash word which I never again shall use but to thee, but which I cannot help being glad — and thou wilt pardon my weakness — to have said to my poor dying love. I wanted to sit up, but from grief and want of sleep my head was confused, and wandered so much that I thought I was speaking to Fernand at the window when he was not even there. Then I became afraid of losing my senses, and Eugénie forced me to lie down on the bed. I trusted more to her than any one else to waken me in time. Already, once or twice, I had experienced that terrible feeling when roused from sleep, of thinking that the dreadful moment was come. I was resolved at any cost to be there.

At about three o'clock in the morning, the 29th of June, I saw Eugénie at my bedside, and was terrified; but she calmed me, and said that Albert had asked, "Where is Alex?" "Do you want her?" Eugénie had said. "Of course I want her," he replied, and then began to wander again. I behaved as if I had lost my senses. I passed twice before Albert's bed, and then went into the next room, not the least knowing what I was about. Eugénie came in, holding clasped in her hands the crucifix indulgenced for the hour of death, which the Abbé Dupanloup had lent her. She appeared then as a meek angel of death, for that crucifix was a sign that the end drew near. Albert saw it, seized it himself, kissed it fervently, and exclaimed, "I thank thee, my God!" After that he became quite calm. They changed his position, and turned his head towards the rising sun. He had fallen into a kind of sleep, with his beloved head resting on my left arm. I was standing, and afraid of slipping from my place. The Sister wanted to relieve me, but Eugénie told her not to do so, and that I was glad to be there. When Albert awoke he spoke in his usual voice, and in quite a natural way, to Fernand. . . .

At six o'clock he was then lying in an arm-chair near the window. I saw and knew that the moment was come. . . . Then I felt so great a strength pass into me that nothing could have driven me from my place as I knelt by his side. My sister Eugénie was close to me. His father was kneeling on the other side. His poor mother stood leaning over him, the Abbé Martin by her side. O my God! No one spoke except his father, and each one of his words were words of blessing, the worthiest that could accompany the dying agony of a son. "My child, who hast never caused us pain,— the very best of sons,— we bless you. Do you hear me still, my child? You are looking at your Alexandrine,"— his dying eyes had turned towards me,—"and you bless her also." The Sister began to say the Litany for the Agonizing. And I—his wife—felt what I could never have conceived; I felt that death was blessed, and I said in my heart: "Now, O Lord Jesus, he is in Paradise!" The Abbé Martin began to give the last absolution, and Albert's soul took flight before it was over.

A GENEROUS ENEMY

From 'Fleurange': by permission of American Publishers' Corporation

A S THE silence lengthened, and she looked at Vera with ever-increasing surprise, a sudden apprehension seized her, and a fugitive and remote glimpse of the truth crossed her mind.

Nothing in the world was more vague than her recollection of the name murmured a single time in her presence; but that once was in a conversation of which Count George was the subject, and she remembered that she had then believed that they were talking of a marriage desired by the Princess for her son.

Was it regretfully now that Vera brought to another this permission to accompany him?

Such was the question that Fleurange asked herself. Then approaching Vera, she said to her gently:—

"If you have been intrusted with a message for me, Mademoiselle, how can I thank you sufficiently for having taken the trouble to bring it to me yourself?"

But Vera hastily withdrew her hand, retreating a few steps as she did so. Then as if she were a prey to some emotion which she could not conquer, she fell back in an arm-chair placed near the table; and for some minutes remained pale, panting for breath, her expression gloomy and wild, from time to time brushing away fiercely the tears that in spite of all her efforts escaped from her eyelids.

Fleurange, motionless with surprise, looked at her with mingled terror and interest; but soon the frank decision of her character conquered her timidity. She went straight to the point.

"Countess Vera," she said, "if I have not conjectured rightly the motive which brings you here, tell me the truth. There is going on between us at this moment something which I do not understand. Be sincere; I will be so too. Let us not remain like this toward one another. Above all, do not look at me as if I were not only a stranger, but an enemy."

At this word Vera raised her head.

"Enemies!" she repeated: "Well, it is true; at this moment we are so!"

What did she mean to say? Fleurange folded her arms, and looked at her attentively, seeking to find an explanation to this enigma of her words; to the still more obscure enigma of her face, which expressed by turns the most conflicting sentiments; to the enigma of her eyes, which now regarded her with hate, now with the gentleness and almost the humility of a suppliant.

At last Vera seemed to decide to go on:—

"Yes, you are right," she said: "I must put an end to your suspense, and explain to you my strange conduct; but I need courage to do it, and to come here as I have done, to address myself to you as I am about to do, there must have been—without my knowing why—"

"Well," Fleurange said with a smile, "what else?"

"There must have been in my heart a secret instinct which assured me that you were good and generous!"

This conclusion, after this beginning, did not clear up the situation,—on the contrary, rendered it more involved than ever.

"This is enough by way of introduction," Fleurange said, with a certain tone of firmness. "Speak clearly, Countess Vera; tell me all without reserve; you may believe me when I beseech you to have no fear. Though your words were to do me a harm which at this moment I can neither foresee nor comprehend, speak; I require it of you; hesitate no longer."

"Well then,—here!" said Vera, throwing suddenly upon the table a paper which till then she had held concealed.

Fleurange took it, looked at it, and at first blushed; then she grew pale.

"My petition!" she said; "you bring it back to me? It has been refused then."

« No, it has not been sent. »

« You mean to say that the Empress, after having shown so much kindness towards me, has changed her mind and refused to undertake it ? »

« No. She has given orders to me, on the contrary, to send your petition, and to add to it her own recommendation. »

« Well ? »

« I have disobeyed her orders. »

« I await the explanation which you are no doubt intending to give me. Go on without interrupting yourself; I shall listen. »

« Well then, first of all, answer me. Did you know that George von Walden was the husband who was promised to me, — for whom my father destined me from childhood ? »

« Who was promised you ? — from childhood ? No, I did not know it. But no matter; go on. »

« It is true, it is no matter: this is not the question, although I was obliged to refer to it. It is no longer a question of his misfortune, of his fearful sentence, of that frightful Siberia to which you propose to accompany him — to share a fate which you can neither alleviate, nor, possibly, endure yourself. The question is now, to save him from this destiny; to give back to him life, honor, liberty, all that he has lost. His estates, his fortune, his rank, all may yet be restored to him! This is what I have come to tell you, and to ask you to aid in its accomplishment. »

« All this can be restored to him ! » said Fleurange, in an altered voice. « By what means ? By whose power ? »

« That of the Emperor, invoked, and of his clemency obtained through my entreaties; but upon two conditions, one of which is imposed upon George, the other of which depends upon me. To these two conditions is joined a third, and that one rests with you, with you only ! »

The great eyes of Fleurange were fixed upon Vera, with an expression of profound astonishment, mingled with anguish.

« Finish, I implore you ! » she said. « Finish, if you are not dreaming in saying such words to me, or I in hearing them; — if we are not both mad, you and I ! »

Vera clasped her hands together and cried passionately: —

« Oh, I beseech you, have mercy upon him ! »

She stopped, suffocated by her emotion.

Fleurange continued to look at her with the same expression, and without speaking made a sign to her to go on.

She seemed to concentrate her attention to understand the words that were said to her.

"I am listening," she said at last; "I am listening quietly and attentively; speak to me with the same composure."

Vera resumed in a calmer tone: —

"This morning, at the moment when I had just read your petition, and learned for the first time who the exile was whom you desired to follow, — at this very moment the Emperor arrived at the palace, and sent for me."

"The Emperor?" said Fleurange, with surprise.

"Yes. And do you know what he wished to say to me? You do not guess what it was, and I can understand readily why you should not, for you do not know with what ardor I have solicited pardon for George, how eagerly I have brought together, to this end, all the facts in the case which might disarm his Sovereign's anger against him. What the Emperor wished to say was this, that he deigned to grant me this favor — to grant it to *me*, Fleurange! do you understand? — but on two conditions."

"His pardon?" cried Fleurange. "Go on, I am listening."

"The first, that he should pass four years on his estates in Livonia, without stirring thence — "

Vera ceased suddenly. Fleurange looked up. "And the second?" she said.

"Then," said Vera, slowly and speaking with difficulty, "that the wish of my father and of his should be fulfilled before his departure."

Fleurange shuddered. An icy chill crept towards her heart, and her head grew dizzy. She remained perfectly motionless, however.

"His pardon is upon that condition?" she said.

"Yes. The Emperor has taken an interest in me from my childhood. He loved my father, and it has pleased him to attach this act of clemency to this fulfillment of my father's wish."

There was a long silence. Vera trembled herself as she saw the pale lips and colorless cheeks of Fleurange, and her eyes gazing fixedly into space.

"And he?" she said at last. "He will accept his pardon with this condition without hesitating, will he not?"

"Without hesitation?" repeated Vera, coloring with a new emotion; "that is what I cannot say; this very doubt humiliates and alarms me; for the Emperor would regard the least hesitation as a new ingratitude, and perhaps might retract this pardon."

"But why should he hesitate?" said Fleurange in a voice scarcely audible.

"Fleurange!" said Vera in the same passionate tone she had used more than once during this interview. "Let us break each other's heart, if we must, but let us go to the very end of this. It has been permitted you to see George since you have been here?"

"No."

"But he is expecting you; he knows that you have come, and what devotion has brought you to him?"

"No; he knows nothing of it as yet, and is not to know until to-morrow."

A flash of joy shone in the black eyes of Vera.

"Then it rests with you that he does not hesitate, that he is saved! Yes, Fleurange, let him never know that you are here, let him never see you — never again," she added, looking at her with a jealous terror that she could not conceal, "and life will once more become for him beautiful, brilliant, happy, — what it was, — what it ought always to be, — and the memory of these few months will fade away like a dream!"

"Like a dream!" — Fleurange repeated mechanically these two words, passing her hand across her forehead as she spoke.

"I have not told you all," Vera said; "I have done you an injury that I understand better than any other person can. But," she continued, in a tone which went to the very depths of her listener's heart, "I wished to save George! I desired him to be restored to me! and I have believed — I know not why, for it seems most unreasonable, and I am ordinarily distrustful — yes, I have believed that you would be willing to aid me, against yourself!"

Fleurange, her hands clasped and resting upon her knees, her eyes gazing steadfastly before her, had seemed for a few moments past not to have heard what was said. She was listening, — but it was to that clear distinct voice that rang so true in her own soul, that voice she had always so well known how to recognize, and to which she had never denied obedience.

If George were free, if he recovered his name, his rank, his former position, would she not at once find herself in the same position toward him which she had formerly occupied?—would it not be treason to avail herself in this case of his mother's permission, and that too to the detriment of her who sat there, the wife chosen for him from his childhood? Would it not, still further, be a treason towards him to present herself before him as a danger, as an obstacle, which might, perhaps at the very moment when he recovered his liberty, cause him to lose it anew, with that momentary favor which had restored it to him!

She laid her cold hand upon the hand of Vera, and lifted to hers her gentle and steady gaze.

"It is enough," she said in a calm voice. "You have done right. Yes, I have understood; be tranquil."

Vera, astonished at the look and tone, gazed at her in wonder.

"Act fearlessly," pursued Fleurange. "Act as if I were far away,—as if I had never come."

And taking the petition which lay upon the table, she tore it across, and threw it into the fire! The paper blazed up for a few seconds, then went out. She watched the cinders fly up the chimney.

Vera with an irresistible impulse seized the hand of Fleurange and raised it to her lips; then she remained silent and abashed. She had come resolved to overpower her rival, to convince her, to struggle against her at every point, if she failed in her first attempt; but her victory had taken a character which she had not at all foreseen.

Certainly it had been an easy victory, and yet Vera understood that it had been a cruel one. She felt at this moment more pain than joy, and her attitude no more expressed triumph than did that of Fleurange express defeat. While the one remained with drooping head and downcast eyes, the other had risen to her feet; a fugitive color lingered in her cheeks,—the effort of the sacrifice had lighted up her face and given it unwonted brilliancy.

"I think," she said, "you have nothing more to say to me."

"No—for what I should like to say I cannot and I dare not."

Vera rose and went towards the door, but a recollection brought her back.

"Pardon my forgetfulness," she said. "Here is your bracelet which you dropped this morning, and which I was desired to return to you."

At sight of the talisman Fleurange started; her unnatural color faded, she became deadly pale, and as she looked at it in silence, a few tears, the only ones which she had shed during that interview, slid down her cheeks. But it was only for an instant. Before Vera could think what she was about to do, Fleurange had attached to the arm of her rival the bracelet which the latter had just restored to her.

"This talisman was a present from the Princess Catherine to her son's betrothed; it would bring happiness, she said. It is mine no longer. I give it up to you; it is yours."

Fleurange held out her hand. "We shall never see each other again," she said. "Let us not remember each other with bitterness."

Vera took the hand without looking up. Never had she felt herself so touched and humiliated, and her very gratitude was a wound to her pride. The grave and sweet voice of Fleurange was however irresistible at this moment, and spoke to her heart in spite of herself. She was hesitating between these two feelings, when Fleurange resumed:—

"You are right. It is not my place to wait for you at this moment, for you have nothing now to forgive,—and as for me, I forgive you all."

And while Vera still stood motionless with bowed head, Fleurange bent towards her and kissed her.

FRANCIS MARION CRAWFORD

(1854–)

ANDREW LANG has justly called Crawford the "most versatile and various of modern novelists." Since the appearance of 'Mr. Isaacs' in 1882, he has written nearly thirty novels, distinguished for their variety of subject and treatment. He belongs to the race of cosmopolitan Americans; men who, having no mental boundaries, accept for their literary inheritance the romantic traditions and customs of all nationalities. This natural taste, quickened by European education and extensive travel, has made him swift to comprehend all lands and races, with their types of character developed by social or national conditions. His adaptability of mind is partially explained by him in 'The Three Fates,' supposed to be autobiographic, which describes the career of an author. "The young man's true talent," he says, "lay in his ready power of assimilating unfamiliar knowledge by a process of intuition which escapes methodical learners."

MARION CRAWFORD.

Mr. Crawford was born in Bagni di Lucca, Italy, August 2d, 1854. He is of mingled ancestry. His father, Thomas Crawford the sculptor, was a native of Ireland, and his mother was an American. He spent his early childhood in New York. After studying at Cambridge, Heidelberg, Carlsruhe, and Rome, he went to India in 1879 and edited the Indian Herald at Allahabad. There he became acquainted with a Persian jewel merchant who suggested the mysterious personality of 'Mr. Isaacs.' Returning to America in 1881, he wrote the romance which bears this title. The fantastic creation, with its Oriental flavor, its hints of Anglo-India, the introduction of Ram Lal, the shadowy adept of occultism, and the striking figure of Mr. Isaacs, with his graceful languor, Iranian features, blazing eyes, and luxurious tastes, bestowed immediate celebrity upon its author. This was followed by 'Dr. Claudius,' which, although less romantic, showed increase in constructive skill. This became more marked in 'To Leeward,' the unlovely and tragic story of a wife's infidelity and of society in Rome. The tale of a peasant boy who

became a famous tenor is the theme of 'A Roman Singer,' issued in
1884; and in the same year he published 'An American Politician,'
in which are discussed the party spirit and corruption of American
politics.   In 1885 'Zoroaster' was issued, a story of ancient Persia,
introducing the court of King Darius and the aged prophet Daniel.
After 'A Tale of a Lonely Parish,' a sketch of rural life in England,
one of his most popular books appeared — 'Saracinesca,' which with
'Sant' Ilario' and 'Don Orsino' forms a trilogy describing the
history of an Italian noble family of that day, and indeed forms a
complete study of Rome from 1865 to 1887.   Cardinal Antonelli is
brought upon the scene, and the bewildered and stormy period of
the last struggles of the Papacy for temporal power are painted with
vigorous skill and rapid generalization, until at last, as he says in
'Don Orsino,' —

«Old Rome is dead, never to be old Rome again.   The last breath has
been breathed, the aged eyes are closed forever; corruption has done its
work, and the grand skeleton lies bleaching upon seven hills, half covered
with the piecemeal stucco of a modern architectural body.»

'Marzio's Crucifix' (1887) is the tale of an atheistic artisan who
carves in silver.   This possesses a psychological interest, and that
element deepens in the 'Witch of Prague' (1892), a bold and thrilling
tale of hypnotism.   'Paul Patoff' (1887) relates personal experiences
of a visit to Turkey; 'With the Immortals' (1888) is an attempt to
reanimate dead celebrities.   'Greifenstein' is a tragedy which takes
place in the Black Forest, and tells the fortunes of two noble German families.   It is valued for its accurate descriptions of the Korps
Studenten, with their extraordinary ideals of romance and honor,
tempered with foaming beer and sabre-cuts.   'The Cigarette Maker's
Romance' is a pathetic story of the madness of Count Skariatine;
'Khaled' a fanciful tale of a genie, who is promised a soul if he
can gain a woman's love.   From romance and fancy, Mr. Crawford
turns to New York life in 'The Three Fates,' and in 'Katharine
Lauderdale' with its sequel 'The Ralstons.'   'Marion Darche' is
also an American story.   'Adam Johnston's Son' depends upon a
simple tale of love for its interest; in 'Casa Braccio,' 'The Children
of the King,' and his last book 'Taquisara' (1896), the author returns
again to his familiar *milieu*, Italy.

This is a list of extraordinary variety and voluminousness.   Since
1884 Mr. Crawford has lived near Sorrento.   Here and in his yacht
he writes his novels.   Although he has devoted much time to philology, he never intrudes dialect in his books, which are written
with the idea of pleasing instead of instructing his enormous audience.   His works have been translated into various languages.   He

has received many honors for his literary achievements. He considers 'Pietro Ghisleri' the most realistic of his books. In 1893 Mr. Crawford published a small essay entitled 'The Novel: What it Is.' In this he defines the novel as an "intellectual artistic luxury," a "definition which can be made to include," he says, "a great deal, but which is in reality a closer one than appears at first sight. It covers the three principal essentials of the novel as it should be, of a story, or romance; which in itself and in the manner of telling it shall appeal to the intellect, shall satisfy the requirements of art, and shall be a luxury, in that it can be of no use to a man when he is at work, but may conduce to a peace of mind and delectation during his hours of idleness."

Born Aug. 2, 1854 died April 9, 1909, at Sorrento, Italy. His father, Thomas Crawford was sculptor of "Liberty" on dome of Capitol at Washington. His mother was a sister of Mrs. Julia Ward Howe and a descendant of Gen. Francis Marion. His uncle the celebrated "Sam" Ward induced him to write his first novel "Mr. Isaacs" after hearing him tell a story gathered in his Eastern travels. Written in one month, rejected by two magazines, accepted by the London house of Macmillan.

THE GHOST IN THE BERTH

From 'The Upper Berth,' in the 'Autonym Library': copyrighted by G. P. Putnam's Sons

WE PLAYED whist in the evening, and I went to bed late. I will confess now that I felt a disagreeable sensation when I entered my state-room. I could not help thinking of the tall man I had seen on the previous night, who was now dead,—drowned, tossing about in the long swell, two or three hundred miles astern. His face rose very distinctly before me as I undressed, and I even went so far as to draw back the curtains of the upper berth, as though to persuade myself that he was actually gone. I also bolted the door of the state-room. Suddenly I became aware that the port-hole was open, and fastened back. This was more than I could stand. I hastily threw on my dressing-gown and went in search of Robert, the steward of my passage. I was very angry, I remember, and when I found him I dragged him roughly to the door of one hundred and five, and pushed him towards the open port-hole.

"What the deuce do you mean, you scoundrel, by leaving that port open every night? Don't you know it is against the regulations? Don't you know that if the ship heeled and the water began to come in, ten men could not shut it? I will report you to the captain, you blackguard, for endangering the ship!"

I was exceedingly wroth. The man trembled and turned pale, and then began to shut the round glass plate with the heavy brass fittings.

"Why don't you answer me?" I said roughly.

One of his finest works (historical) Ave Roma Immortalis, 1898.

"If you please, sir," faltered Robert, "there's nobody on board as can keep this 'ere port shut at night. You can try it yourself, sir. I ain't a-going to stop hany longer on board o' this vessel, sir; I ain't indeed. But if I was you, sir, I'd just clear out and go and sleep with the surgeon, or something, I would. Look 'ere, sir, is that fastened what you may call securely, or not, sir? Try it, sir; see if it will move a hinch."

I tried the port, and found it perfectly tight.

"Well, sir," continued Robert, triumphantly, "I wager my reputation as a A1 steward, that in 'arf an hour it will be open again; fastened back too, sir, that's the horful thing — fastened back!"

I examined the great screw and the looped nut that ran on it.

"If I find it open in the night, Robert, I will give you a sovereign. It is not possible. You may go."

"Soverin' did you say, sir? Very good, sir. Thank ye, sir. Good night, sir. Pleasant reepose, sir, and all manner of hin-chantin' dreams, sir."

Robert scuttled away, delighted at being released. Of course I thought he was trying to account for his negligence by a silly story intended to frighten me, and I disbelieved him. The con-sequence was that he got his sovereign, and I spent a very peculiarly unpleasant night.

I went to bed, and five minutes after I had rolled myself up in my blankets the inexorable Robert extinguished the light that burned steadily behind the ground-glass pane near the door. I lay quite still in the dark trying to go to sleep, but I soon found that impossible. It had been some satisfaction to be angry with the steward, and the diversion had banished that unpleasant sensation I had at first experienced when I thought of the drowned man who had been my chum; but I was no longer sleepy, and I lay awake for some time, occasionally glancing at the porthole, which I could just see from where I lay, and which in the darkness looked like a faintly luminous soup-plate suspended in blackness. I believe I must have lain there for an hour, and, as I remember, I was just dozing into sleep when I was roused by a draught of cold air and by distinctly feeling the spray of the sea blown upon my face. I started to my feet, and not having allowed in the dark for the motion of the ship, I was instantly thrown violently across the state-room upon the couch which was placed beneath the porthole. I recovered myself

immediately, however, and climbed upon my knees.   The port-
hole was again wide open and fastened back!

Now these things are facts.   I was wide awake when I got
up, and I should certainly have been waked by the fall had I
still been dozing.   Moreover, I bruised my elbows and knees
badly, and the bruises were there on the following morning to
testify to the fact, if I myself had doubted it.   The port-hole was
wide open and fastened back — a thing so unaccountable that I
remember very well feeling astonishment rather than fear when
I discovered it.   I at once closed the plate again and screwed
down the looped nut with all my strength.   It was very dark in
the state-room.   I reflected that the port had certainly been
opened within an hour after Robert had at first shut it in my
presence, and I determined to watch it and see whether it would
open again.   Those brass fittings are very heavy and by no
means easy to move; I could not believe that the clump had
been turned by the shaking of the screw.   I stood peering out
through the thick glass at the alternate white and gray streaks
of the sea that foamed beneath the ship's side.   I must have
remained there a quarter of an hour.

Suddenly, as I stood, I distinctly heard something moving
behind me in one of the berths, and a moment afterwards, just
as I turned instinctively to look — though I could of course see
nothing in the darkness — I heard a very faint groan.   I sprang
across the state-room and tore the curtains of the upper berth
aside, thrusting in my hands to discover if there were any one
there.   There was some one.

I remember that the sensation as I put my hands forward was
as though I were plunging them into the air of a damp cellar,
and from behind the curtain came a gust of wind that smelled
horribly of stagnant sea-water.   I laid hold of something that
had the shape of a man's arm, but was smooth and wet and
icy cold.   But suddenly, as I pulled, the creature sprang violently
forward against me, a clammy, oozy mass, as it seemed to me,
heavy and wet, yet endowed with a sort of supernatural strength.
I reeled across the state-room, and in an instant the door opened
and the thing rushed out.   I had not had time to be frightened,
and quickly recovering myself I sprang through the door and
gave chase at the top of my speed; but I was too late.   Ten
yards before me I could see — I am sure I saw it — a dark
shadow moving in the dimly lighted passage, quickly as the

shadow of a fast horse thrown before a dog-cart by the lamp on a dark night. But in a moment it had disappeared, and I found myself holding on to the polished rail that ran along the bulk-head where the passage turned towards the companion. My hair stood on end, and the cold perspiration rolled down my face. I am not ashamed of it in the least: I was very badly frightened.

Still I doubted my senses, and pulled myself together. It was absurd, I thought. The Welsh rare-bit I had eaten had disagreed with me. I had been in a nightmare. I made my way back to my state-room, and entered it with an effort. The whole place smelled of stagnant sea-water, as it had when I had waked on the previous evening. It required my utmost strength to go in and grope among my things for a box of wax lights. As I lighted a railway reading lantern which I always carry in case I want to read after the lamps are out, I perceived that the port-hole was again open, and a sort of creeping horror began to take possession of me which I never felt before, nor wish to feel again. But I got a light and proceeded to examine the upper berth, expecting to find it drenched with sea-water.

But I was disappointed. The bed had been slept in, and the smell of the sea was strong; but the bedding was as dry as a bone. I fancied that Robert had not had the courage to make the bed after the accident of the previous night — it had all been a hideous dream. I drew the curtains back as far as I could, and examined the place very carefully. It was perfectly dry. But the port-hole was open again. With a sort of dull bewilder-ment of horror I closed it and screwed it down, and thrusting my heavy stick through the brass loop, wrenched it with all my might till the thick metal began to bend under the pressure. Then I hooked my reading lantern into the red velvet at the head of the couch, and sat down to recover my senses if I could. I sat there all night, unable to think of rest — hardly able to think at all. But the port-hole remained closed, and I did not believe it would now open again without the application of a considerable force.

The morning dawned at last, and I dressed myself slowly, thinking over all that had happened in the night. It was a beau-tiful day, and I went on deck, glad to get out in the early pure sunshine, and to smell the breeze from the blue water, so different from the noisome, stagnant odor from my state-room. Instinct-ively I turned aft, towards the surgeon's cabin. There he stood, with a pipe in his mouth, taking his morning airing precisely as on the preceding day.

"Good-morning," said he, quietly, but looking at me with evident curiosity.

"Doctor, you were quite right," said I. "There is something wrong about that place."

"I thought you would change your mind," he answered, rather triumphantly. "You have had a bad night, eh? Shall I make you a pick-me-up? I have a capital recipe."

"No, thanks," I cried. "But I would like to tell you what happened."

I then tried to explain as clearly as possible precisely what had occurred, not omitting to state that I had been scared as I had never been scared in my whole life before. I dwelt particularly on the phenomenon of the port-hole, which was a fact to which I could testify, even if the rest had been an illusion. I had closed it twice in the night, and the second time I had actually bent the brass in wrenching it with my stick. I believe I insisted a good deal on this point.

"You seem to think I am likely to doubt the story," said the doctor, smiling at the detailed account of the state of the port-hole. "I do not doubt it in the least. I renew my invitation to you. Bring your traps here, and take half my cabin."

"Come and take half of mine for one night," I said. "Help me to get at the bottom of this thing."

"You will get at the bottom of something else if you try," answered the doctor.

"What?" I asked.

"The bottom of the sea. I am going to leave the ship. It is not canny."

"Then you will not help me to find out —"

"Not I," said the doctor, quickly. "It is my business to keep my wits about me — not to go fiddling about with ghosts and things."

"Do you really believe it is a ghost?" I inquired, rather contemptuously. But as I spoke I remembered very well the horrible sensation of the supernatural which had got possession of me during the night. The doctor turned sharply on me.

"Have you any reasonable explanation of these things to offer?" he asked. "No, you have not. Well, you say you will find an explanation. I say that you won't, sir, simply because there is not any."

"But, my dear sir," I retorted, "do you, a man of science, mean to tell me that such things cannot be explained?"

"I do," he answered, stoutly. "And if they could, I would not be concerned in the explanation."

I did not care to spend another night alone in the state-room, and yet I was obstinately determined to get at the root of the disturbances. I do not believe there are many men who would have slept there alone, after passing two such nights. But I made up my mind to try it, if I could not get any one to share a watch with me. The doctor was evidently not inclined for such an experiment. He said he was a surgeon, and that in case any accident occurred on board he must always be in readiness. He could not afford to have his nerves unsettled. Perhaps he was quite right, but I am inclined to think that his precaution was prompted by his inclination. On inquiry, he informed me that there was no one on board who would be likely to join me in my investigations, and after a little more conversation I left him. A little later I met the captain, and told him my story. I said that if no one would spend the night with me I would ask leave to have the light burning all night, and would try it alone.

"Look here," said he, "I will tell you what I will do. I will share your watch myself, and we will see what happens. It is my belief that we can find out between us. There may be some fellow skulking on board, who steals a passage by frightening the passengers. It is just possible that there may be something queer in the carpentering of that berth."

I suggested taking the ship's carpenter below and examining the place; but I was overjoyed at the captain's offer to spend the night with me. He accordingly sent for the workman and ordered him to do anything I required. We went below at once. I had all the bedding cleared out of the upper berth, and we examined the place thoroughly to see if there was a board loose anywhere, or a panel which could be opened or pushed aside. We tried the planks everywhere, tapped the flooring, unscrewed the fittings of the lower berth and took it to pieces: in short, there was not a square inch of the state-room which was not searched and tested. Everything was in perfect order, and we put everything back in its place. As we were finishing our work, Robert came to the door and looked in.

"Well, sir — find anything, sir?" he asked with a ghastly grin.

"You were right about the port-hole, Robert," I said; and I gave him the promised sovereign. The carpenter did his work silently and skillfully, following my directions. When he had done he spoke.

"I'm a plain man, sir," he said. "But it's my belief you had better just turn out your things and let me run half a dozen four-inch screws through the door of this cabin. There's no good never came o' this cabin yet, sir, and that's all about it. There's been four lives lost out o' here to my own remembrance, and that in four trips. Better give it up, sir—better give it up!"

"I will try it for one night more," I said.

"Better give it up, sir—better give it up! It's a precious bad job," repeated the workman, putting his tools in his bag and leaving the cabin.

But my spirits had risen considerably at the prospect of having the captain's company, and I made up my mind not to be prevented from going to the end of the strange business. I abstained from Welsh rare-bits and grog that evening, and did not even join in the customary game of whist. I wanted to be quite sure of my nerves, and my vanity made me anxious to make a good figure in the captain's eyes.

A THWARTED PLAN

From 'Marzio's Crucifix': copyrighted 1887, by F. Marion Crawford, and reproduced by permission of the Macmillan Company, Publishers

MARZIO entered the inner studio when Gianbattista was gone, leaving a boy who was learning to cut little files—the preliminary to the chiseler's profession—in charge of the outer workshop. The artist shut himself in and bolted the door, glad to be alone with the prospect of not being disturbed during the whole afternoon. He seemed not to hesitate about the work he intended to do, for he immediately took in hand the crucifix, laid it upon the table, and began to study it, using a lens from time to time as he scrutinized each detail. His rough hair fell forward over his forehead, and his shoulders rounded themselves till he looked almost deformed.

He had suffered very strong emotions during the last twenty-four hours—enough to have destroyed the steadiness of an ordinary man's hand, but with Marzio manual skill was the first habit of nature, and it would have been hard to find a mental impression which could shake his physical nerves. His mind, however, worked rapidly and almost fiercely, while his eyes searched the minute lines of the work he was examining.

Uppermost in his thoughts was a confused sense of humiliation and of exasperation against his brother. The anger he felt had nearly been expressed in a murderous deed not more than two or three hours earlier, and the wish to strike was still present in his mind. He twisted his lips into an ugly smile as he recalled the scene in every detail; but the determination was different from the reality, and more in accordance with his feelings. He realized again that moment during which he had held the sharp instrument over his brother's head, and the thought which had then passed so rapidly through his brain recurred again with increased clearness. He remembered that beneath the iron-bound box in the corner there was a trap-door which descended to the unused cellar, for his workshop had in former times been a wine-shop, and he had hired the cellar with it. One sharp blow would have done the business. A few quick movements, and Paolo's body would have been thrown down the dark steps beneath, the trap closed again, the safe replaced in its position. It was eleven o'clock then, or thereabouts. He would have sent the workmen to their dinner, and would have returned to the inner studio. They would have supposed afterwards that Don Paolo had left the place with him. He would have gone home and would have said that Paolo had left him — or no — he would have said that Paolo had not been there, for some one might see him leave the workshop alone. In the night he would have returned, his family thinking he had gone to meet his friends, as he often did. When the streets were quiet he would have carried the body away upon the hand-cart that stood in the entry of the outer room. It was not far — scarcely three hundred yards, allowing for the turnings — to the place where the Via Montella ends in a mud bank by the dark river. A deserted neighborhood too — a turn to the left, the low trees of the Piazza de' Branca, the dark, short, straight street to the water. At one o'clock after midnight who was stirring? It would all have been so simple, so terribly effectual.

And then there would have been no more Paolo, no more domestic annoyances, no more of the priest's smooth-faced disapprobation and perpetual opposition in the house. He would have soon brought Maria Luisa and Lucia to reason. What could they do without the support of Paolo? They were only women after all. As for Gianbattista, if once the poisonous influence of Paolo were removed — and how surely removed! Marzio's lips twisted as though he were tasting the sourness of failure, like an acid fruit — if once the priest were gone, Gianbattista would come back to his old ways, to his old scorn of priests in general, of churches, of oppression, of everything that Marzio hated. He might marry Lucia then, and be welcome. After all, he was a finer fellow for the pretty girl than Gasparo Carnesecchi, with his claw fingers and his vinegar salad. That was only a farce, that proposal about the lawyer — the real thing was to get rid of Paolo. There could be no healthy liberty of thought in the house while this fellow was sneaking in and out at all hours. Tumble Paolo into a quiet grave, — into the river with a sackful of old castings at his neck, — there would be peace then, and freedom. Marzio ground his teeth as he thought how nearly he had done the thing, and how miserably he had failed. It had been the inspiration of the moment, and the details had appeared clear at once to his mind. Going over them he found that he had not been mistaken. If Paolo came again, and he had the chance, he would do it. It was perhaps all the better that he had found time to weigh the matter.

But would Paolo come again? Would he ever trust himself alone in the workshop? Had he guessed, when he turned so suddenly and saw the weapon in the air, that the blow was on the very point of descending? Or had he been deceived by the clumsy excuse Marzio had made about the sun shining in his eyes?

He had remained calm, or Marzio tried to think so. But the artist himself had been so much moved during the minutes that followed that he could hardly feel sure of Paolo's behavior. It was a chilling thought, that Paolo might have understood and might have gone away feeling that his life had been saved almost by a miracle. He would not come back, the cunning priest, in that case; he would not risk his precious skin in such company. It was not to be expected — a priest was only human, after all, like any other man. Marzio cursed his ill luck again as he bent over his work. What a moment this would be if Paolo would take it into his head to make another visit! Even the men were gone. He would send the one boy who remained to the church where Gianbattista was working, with a message.

They would be alone then, he and Paolo. The priest might scream and call for help — the thick walls would not let any sound through them. It would be even better than in the morning, when he had lost his opportunity by a moment, by the twinkling of an eye.

" They say hell is paved with good intentions — or lost opportunities," muttered Marzio. " I will send Paolo with the next opportunity to help in the paving."

He laughed softly at his grim joke, and bent lower over the crucifix. By this time he had determined what to do, for his reflections had not interfered with his occupation. Removing two tiny silver screws which fitted with the utmost exactness in the threads, he loosened the figure from the cross, removed the latter to a shelf on the wall, and returning laid the statue on a soft leathern pad, surrounding it with sand-bags till it was propped securely in the position he required. Then he took a very small chisel, adjusted it with the greatest care, and tapped upon it with the round wooden handle of his little hammer. At each touch he examined the surface with his lens to assure himself that he was making the improvement he contemplated. It was very delicate work, and as he did it he felt a certain pride in the reflection that he could not have detected the place where improvement was possible when he had worked upon the piece ten years ago. He found it now, in the infinitesimal touches upon the expression of the face, in the minute increase in the depressions and accentuated lines in the anatomy of the figure. As he went over each portion he became more and more certain that though he could not at present do better in the way of idea and general execution, he had nevertheless gained in subtle knowledge of effects and in skill of handling the chisel upon very delicate points. The certainty gave him the real satisfaction of legitimate pride. He knew that he had reached the zenith of his capacities. His old wish to keep the crucifix for himself began to return.

If he disposed of Paolo he might keep his work. Only Paolo had seen it. The absurd want of logic in the conclusion did not strike him. He had not pledged himself to his brother to give this particular crucifix to the cardinal, and if he had he could easily have found a reason for keeping it back. But he was too much accustomed to think that Paolo was always in the way of his wishes, to look at so simple a matter in such a simple light.

"It is strange," he said to himself. "The smallest things seem to point to it. If he would only come!"

Again his mind returned to the contemplation of the deed, and again he reviewed all the circumstances necessary for its safe execution. What an inspiration, he thought, and what a pity it had not found shape in fact at the very moment it had presented itself! He considered why he had never thought of it before, in all the years, as a means of freeing himself effectually from the despotism he detested. It was a despotism, he reflected, and no other word expressed it. He recalled many scenes in his home, in which Paolo had interfered. He remembered how one Sunday in the afternoon they had all been together before going to walk in the Corso, and how he had undertaken to demonstrate to Maria Luisa and Lucia the folly of wasting time in going to church on Sundays. He had argued gently and reasonably, he thought. But suddenly Paolo had interrupted him, saying that he would not allow Marzio to compare a church to a circus, nor priests to mountebanks and tight-rope dancers. Why not? Then the women had begun to scream and cry, and to talk of his blasphemous language, until he could not hear himself speak. It was Paolo's fault. If Paolo had not been there the women would have listened patiently enough, and would doubtless have reaped some good from his reasonable discourse. On another occasion Marzio had declared that Lucia should never be taught anything about Christianity; that the definition of God was reason; that Garibaldi had baptized one child in the name of Reason and that he, Marzio, could baptize another quite as effectually. Paolo had interfered, and Maria Luisa had screamed. The contest had lasted nearly a month, at the end of which time Marzio had been obliged to abandon the uneven contest, vowing vengeance in some shape for the future.

Many and many such scenes rose to his memory, and in every one Paolo was the opposer, the enemy of his peace, the champion of all that he hated and despised. In great things and small his brother had been his antagonist from his early manhood, through eighteen years of married life to the present day. And yet without Paolo he could hardly have hoped to find himself in his present state of fortune.

This was one of the chief sources of his humiliation in his own eyes. With such a character as his, it is eminently true that it is harder to forgive a benefit than an injury. He might have felt less bitterly against his brother if he had not received at his hands the orders and commissions which had turned into solid money in the bank. It was hard to face Paolo, knowing that he owed two-thirds of his fortune to such a source. If he could get rid of the priest he would be relieved at once from the burden of this annoyance, of this financial subjection, as well of all that embittered his life. He pictured to himself his wife and daughter listening respectfully to his harangues and beginning to practice his principles; Gianbattista an eloquent member of the society in the inner room of the old inn, reformed, purged from his sneaking fondness for Paolo,— since Paolo would not be in the world any longer,— and ultimately married to Lucia; the father of children who should all be baptized in the name of Reason, and the worthy successor of himself, Marzio Pandolfi.

Scrutinizing the statue under his lens, he detected a slight imperfection in the place where one of the sharp thorns touched the silver forehead of the beautiful tortured head. He looked about for a tool fine enough for the work, but none suited his wants. He took up the long fine-pointed punch he had thrown back upon the table after the scene in the morning. It was too long, and over-sharp, but by turning it sideways it would do the work under his dexterous fingers.

"Strange!" he muttered, as he tapped upon the tool. "It is like a consecration!"

When he had made the stroke he dropped the instrument into the pocket of his blouse, as though fearing to lose it. He had no occasion to use it again, though he went on with his work during several hours.

The thoughts which had passed through his brain recurred, and did not diminish in clearness. On the contrary, it was as though the passing impulse of the morning had grown during those short hours into a settled and unchangeable resolution. Once he rose from his stool, and going to the corner dragged away the iron-bound safe from its place. A rusty ring lay flat in a little hollow in the surface of the trap-door. Marzio bent over it with a pale face and gleaming eyes. It seemed to him as though if he looked round he should see Paolo's body lying on the floor, ready to be dropped into the space below. He raised the wood and set the trap back against the wall, peering down into the black depths. A damp smell came up to his nostrils from the moist staircase. He struck a match and held it into the opening, to see in what direction the stairs led down.

Something moved behind him and made a little noise. With a short cry of horror Marzio sprang back from the opening and looked round. It was as though the body of the murdered man had stirred upon the floor. His overstrained imagination terrified him, and his eyes started from his head. He examined the bench and saw the cause of the sound in a moment. The silver Christ, unsteadily propped in the position in which he had just placed it, had fallen upon one side of the pad by its own weight.

Marzio's heart still beat desperately as he went back to the hole and carefully re-closed the trap-door, dragging the heavy safe to its position over the ring. Trembling violently, he sat down upon his stool and wiped the cold perspiration from his forehead. Then, as he laid the figure upon the cushion, he glanced uneasily behind him and at the corner.

With an anxious heart he left the house and crossed the street to the workshop, where the men were already waiting for the carts which were to convey the heavy grating to its destination. The pieces were standing against the walls, wrapped in tow and brown paper, and immense parcels lay tied up upon the benches. It was a great piece of work of the decorative kind, but of the sort for which Marzio cared little. Great brass castings were chiseled and finished according to his designs without his touching them with his hands. Huge twining arabesques of solid metal were prepared in pieces and fitted together with screws that ran easily in the thread, and then were taken apart again. . . . It was slow and troublesome work, and Marzio cared little for it, though his artistic instinct restrained him from allowing it to leave the workshop until it had been perfected to the highest degree.

At present the artist stood in the outer room among the wrapped pieces, his pipe in his mouth and his hands in his pockets. A moment after Gianbattista had entered, two carts rolled up to the door and the loading began.

"Take the drills and some screws to spare," said Marzio, looking into the bag of tools the foreman had prepared. "One can never tell in these monstrous things."

"It will be the first time, if we have to drill a new hole after you have fitted a piece of work, Maestro Marzio," answered the foreman, who had an unlimited admiration for his master's genius and foresight.

"Never mind; do as I tell you. We may all make mistakes in this world," returned the artist, giving utterance to a moral sentiment which did not influence him beyond the precincts of the workshop. The workman obeyed, and added the requisite instruments to the furnishing of his leather bag.

"And be careful, Tista," added Marzio, turning to the apprentice. "Look to the sockets in the marble when you place the large pieces. Measure them with your compass, you know; if they are too loose you have the thin plates of brass to pack them; if they are tight, file away, but finish and smooth it well. Don't leave anything rough."

Gianbattista nodded as he lent a helping hand to the workmen who were carrying the heavy pieces to the carts.

"Will you come to the church before night?" he asked.

"Perhaps. I cannot tell. I am very busy."

In ten minutes the pieces were all piled upon the two vehicles, and Gianbattista strode away on foot with the workmen. He had not thought of changing his dress, and had merely thrown an old overcoat over his gray woolen blouse. For the time, he was an artisan at work. When working hours were over, and on Sundays, he loved to put on the stiff high collar and the checked clothes which suggested the garments of the English tourist. He was then a different person, and in accordance with the change he would smoke a cigarette and pull his cuffs over his hands, like a real gentleman, adjusting the angle of his hat from time to time, and glancing at his reflection in the shop windows as he passed along. But work was work; it was a pity to spoil good clothes with handling tools and castings, and jostling against the men, and moreover the change affected his nature. He could not handle a hammer or a chisel when he felt like a real gentleman, and when he felt like an artisan he must enjoy the liberty of being able to tuck up his sleeves and work with a will. At the present moment, too, he was proud of being in sole charge of the work, and he could not help thinking what a fine thing it would be to be married to Lucia and to be the master of the workshop. With the sanguine enthusiasm of a very young man who loves his occupation, he put his whole soul into what he was to do, assured that every skillful stroke of the hammer, every difficulty overcome, brought him nearer to the woman he loved.

PROSPER JOLYOT CRÉBILLON

(1674–1762)

BY ROBERT SANDERSON

PROSPER JOLYOT, tragic poet, called De Crébillon from the name of the estate his father purchased near Dijon, France, was born in that city January 13th, 1674. The elder Jolyot held an office in the magistracy of the province of Burgundy, and he intended that his son should follow in his footsteps. This the young man did for a time. He was admitted to the bar as advocate to the Parliament of Paris, and at the same time entered the office of a *procureur* (prosecuting magistrate), there to study the forms of procedure and practice of law. This *procureur*, whose name was Prieur, appears to have worked a decisive influence over Jolyot's career, as he was the first to discover in the young man strong aptitudes for tragedy. Being a man of letters, he was struck by the correctness of his clerk's criticisms of some of the French tragic poets, and urged him to try his hand at writing a tragedy himself. This Crébillon did at once, and composed his maiden play, 'La Mort des Enfants de Brute' (The Death of Brutus's Children), a subject more than once treated before. The king's troupe of players refused it, and it was not even printed. Cré-

CRÉBILLON

billon was greatly disappointed, but encouraged by the good Prieur, he very soon conceived and wrote another tragedy, 'Idoménée' (1705), which this time was received and played with some success.

'Idoménée' was followed by 'Atrée et Thyeste' (1707), a play that put Crébillon in the very first rank of tragic poets. Called back to his native place by his father's death, and detained there a long time by a family lawsuit, he brought back from the country his third tragedy, 'Électre' (1708), which was as much admired as the preceding one. 'Rhadamiste et Zénobie,' Crébillon's masterpiece, appeared in 1711. It formed part of the repertoire of the Comédie Française up to the year 1829. 'Xerxès,' played in 1714, met with flat failure; 'Sémiramis' (1717) fared somewhat better. Disgusted with the poor success of his last two tragedies, it was nine years before Crébillon wrote again for the stage. 'Pyrrhus' appeared in 1726, and remained for a long time on the play-bills. Of his last two tragedies 'Catilina' (1748) was for its author a renewal of success, whilst 'Le Triumvirat,' written by Crébillon in his eightieth year, contains here and there fine passages.

Crébillon was elected to the French Academy in 1731. He held several offices during life. He was first receiver of fines, then royal censor, and lastly king's librarian; but neither from these various employments nor from his plays did he derive much profit. The most prosperous epoch of his existence seems to have been about the year 1715, during the brilliant but corrupt time of the *Régence;* part of his life was spent in actual penury, and we find him fifteen years later living in a poor quarter of the capital, having for sole companions of his misery a lot of dogs and cats that he picked up in the streets. However, Louis XV. gave him in his old age a proof of his royal favor. After the representation of 'Catilina,' the King ordered that the poet's complete works be printed at his expense. The edition appeared in 1750, and yielded enough to save Crébillon at least from actual want during his remaining lifetime. It may be easily imagined that in his position of royal censor he incurred the enmity of his colleagues whose plays he refused; and in addition to his pecuniary embarrassments his life was embittered by the attacks of his enemies, among whom Voltaire was not the least conspicuous. Crébillon, who was a man of fine presence and strong constitution, died on June 14th, 1762, in his eighty-ninth year.

Taking the writer's tragedies as they appeared, 'Idoménée,' the first one, is borrowed from Homer's Iliad. It is the story of Idomeneus, King of Crete, who returning from the siege of Troy and being assailed by a frightful tempest, took a vow of sacrificing to Neptune the first human creature he should meet on landing. His own son, Idamantus, was the first person he encountered, and his father at once sacrificed him. Such is the Greek legend; but it being too atrocious in its nature to suit modern taste, in Crébillon's tragedy Idamantus kills himself. We can in a measure understand the terrible struggle going on in the father's breast, obliged by his vow to kill his own child; but only in a measure, for our modern ideas will not admit that under such circumstances a parent should be held to his vow. Nor does it help matters that Idamantus should kill himself to save his father from committing the atrocious deed: the subject is repulsive. The speech of Idomeneus in the first act, recounting the storm scene, is not unfrequently mentioned as a piece of rhetoric.

'Atrée et Thyeste' is far superior to 'Idoménée' both in conception and construction. If the object of tragedy be to excite terror, that condition is certainly fulfilled in 'Atrée et Thyeste.' The subject, taken from Seneca, is well known. Atreus, King of Argos, to avenge the wrong done him by his own brother Thyestes, who had carried off his wife, had the latter's son killed and served to him at a feast. Crébillon carries this fierce cruelty even farther, for in his play he makes Atreus offer his brother a cup filled with the blood of Plisthène, son of Thyestes. On being criticized for this refinement of cruelty the poet bluntly answered, "I never should have believed that in a land where there are so many unfortunate husbands, Atreus would have found so few partisans." The strongest scenes are the closing ones. Although the general opinion at the time was that Crébillon had chosen too horrible a subject, he revealed his power as a tragic poet; and his reputation as such really dates from the production of 'Atrée et Thyeste.'

Crébillon's 'Électre' is in the main the same as that of Sophocles, Euripides, and others. Electra, whose father Agamemnon has been murdered by Ægisthus, induces her brother Orestes to slay the murderer. The change introduced into the plot by the French poet is this one: he makes Electra love the son of her father's slayer, whilst Orestes, who is ignorant of his own birth, loves the daughter. The admirers of the classic models were up in arms at these changes, and 'Électre' was attacked on all sides; but if it had its defects, it had also its merits, and these were finally recognized as being of high order. The scene between Clytemnestra and Electra in the first act, the meeting between Electra and Orestes, and the latter's ravings when he discovers that he has killed his mother, are among the best.

'Rhadamiste et Zénobie' is generally considered Crébillon's masterpiece: it is the only one of his tragedies that contains the romantic element. As narrated in Tacitus, the legend upon which this play is founded runs thus: Rhadamistus, son of Pharasmanes, King of Iberia, had married his cousin Zenobia, daughter of his uncle Mithridates, King of Armenia. The latter was put to death by order of Rhadamistus, who took possession of his uncle's provinces. An insurrection broke out, and Rhadamistus had to flee for his life. He carried off Zenobia with him, but she, owing to her condition, unable to bear the fatigues of the flight, begged her husband to put her to death. After piercing her with his sword and throwing her into the Araxes, he hurriedly made off for his father's kingdom. Zenobia, however, was not dead. She was found on the bank of the river by some shepherds, who carried her to the court of the King Tiridates, who received her kindly and treated her as a queen.

In his tragedy Crébillon makes the husband and wife meet again at the court of Pharasmanes; and Zenobia, believing herself to be a widow, shows her love for Prince Arsames, own brother to Rhadamistus. This invention is certainly no more improbable than the whole story itself. The interview between Pharasmanes and his son in the second act, and the meeting between Rhadamistus and Zenobia in the third, are both remarkable, the first for its grandeur, the second for its pathos and passion.

'Xerxès' is an inferior tragedy. The strongest character in the play is that of the prime minister Artaban, who sows discord between the two sons of Xerxès, intending to seize the throne of Persia for himself. Inferior also is 'Sémiramis.' The famous queen is in love with Agénor, who proves to be her own son Ninias; but even after this discovery, Sémiramis perseveres in her passion. Such a subject can be tolerated on the stage only on condition that the spectator be made to feel the victim's struggle and remorse, as in Racine's 'Phèdre.'

'Pyrrhus' differs from Crébillon's previous tragedies in this one point: no blood is spilled upon the stage; the poet does not rely upon his usual method of striking terror to gain success. For the first time his characters are heroic and express noble sentiments. Pyrrhus, King of Epirus, has been brought up by his guardian Glaucias under the name of Helenus, and believes himself to be his son. It is only when the usurper Neoptolemes demands of Glaucias the surrender of Pyrrhus, that the latter discovers the truth. The courage and magnanimity of Glaucias in refusing to give up his trust; of his son Illyrus in taking the place of Pyrrhus; of Pyrrhus in revealing his true name and offering himself to the usurper, and lastly of Neoptolemes in showing clemency, are worthy of admiration.

Twenty-two years intervene between 'Pyrrhus' and 'Catilina' (1748). As might be expected in a tragedy having for its principal characters Cicero and Cato, political speeches are plentiful. The scene between Catiline, Cato, and Cicero, in the fourth act, is perhaps the strongest. Another interval of six years, and Crébillon wrote his last tragedy 'Le Triumvirat' or 'Le Mort de Cicéron,' which may be termed a rehabilitation of Cicero, who, the critics said, should not have been made a subordinate character to that of Catiline in Crébillon's previous tragedy. Although written in his eightieth year, it cannot be said that this composition shows any sign of mental decay.

With two such masters as Corneille and Racine towering with their mighty height over all other French dramatic poets, it is often difficult to be just towards the latter. They must always suffer by comparison; yet all they wrote did not deserve almost entire oblivion. In the case of Crébillon, the only tragedy by which he is now remembered is that of 'Rhadamiste et Zénobie,' and that principally because it is the only one that has in it an element of romance. But his others contain also qualities of their own: grandeur of conception, great force and energy, together with a severe and sober language. As to his defects, they consist in too great a predilection for the horrible, and in a style which at times is inflated. Voltaire, who could brook no superiority or even equality in any line of literature, did not spare Crébillon his sarcasms. The best outcome of this rivalry between the two poets was the emulation it stimulated in Voltaire, causing him to write over five of Crébillon's tragedies— 'Sémiramis,' 'Électre,' 'Catilina,' 'Le Triumvirat,' 'Atrée et Thyeste,'—under the respective names of 'Sémiramis,' 'Oreste,' 'Rome Sauvée,' 'Le Triumvirat,' 'Les Pélopides.'

Robert Sanderson

THE BLOODY BANQUET

From 'Atreus and Thyestes'

ATREUS—Now in this cup, the pledge of brotherhood,
  Behold the sacred earnest of our peace!
How timely has it come, to still the fears
That bid thee doubt a brother's bounteous love!
If dark distrust of Atreus linger still
Within thy heart—give me the sacred cup.
That shame may fill Thyestes, to withhold
His share in this fraternal festival:
That brothers' hearts, whom love hath set at twain,
Love's holy bonds may reunite again:
Give me the cup! that I, in drinking first,
May drown thy doubts.—Eurysthenes, the cup!

[*He takes the cup from the hand of Eurysthenes, his confidant.*]

Thyestes—

Have I not said, my lord, thou takest ill
My groundless doubts and coward quavering fears?
What henceforth could thy hate deprive me of,
Since son, and provinces, have been restored?
Whate'er the cause and meaning of this wrath,

Have I deserved that thou shouldst crown my days,
My wretched days, with kindness such as this?
Nay; first, Eurysthenes, give me the cup.
Let me be first to pledge all gratitude,
And drown my heart's misgivings, that have lain
Like bitter lees within the cup I drain.

[*He takes the cup from the hand of Atreus, saying:* —]
Yet why delays my son?

Atreus [*addressing his guards*]—   Give answer, guards!
Has he not yet returned?
[*Addressing Thyestes*]—   Be not uneasy.
You soon shall see him, soon to him be joined;
More near and close your union than you dream;
Most sacred pledge, he, of our solemn bond.

Thyestes —
Be thou the voucher, then, of Atreus's faith,
And of Thyestes's safety from his hate,—
Cup of our ancestors! And you, ye gods,
Whom I to witness call! may you strike dead
With swift avenging thunderbolt of wrath
Him who first breaks this pact of peace.— And thou,
Brother as dear as daughter or as son,
Receive this proof of firmest faith.

[*He drains the cup, and recoils.*
Ah, wretch!
What do I see? Great gods, 'tis blood, blood, blood!
Ah, horror! Blood!— mine own runs cold within
My frozen heart, my heart with horror chilled.
The sun grows dim around me; and the cup,
Dyed with such dreadful crimson, seems to shrink
From touch of this my trembling hand.— I die!
'Tis death I feel upon me. O my son!
What has become of thee?

[*Turning to Atreus*]—   My son is dead!
My son is dead, thou cruel one! who offerest
False promises of peace to me bereavèd
In the same instant which has snatched him from me.
And lest this frightful blow should leave me living,
Monster! 'tis wine of blood thy hand is giving!
O Earth! canst thou support us at this moment?
My dream, my ghastly dream returned upon me!
Was it thy blood, my son! they gave thy father?

Atreus —
And canst thou recognize this blood?

Thyestes —   My brother
  I recognize.
Atreus —   Thou shouldst have recognized him
  And known his nature, in the past, nor wronged him,
  And forced him, ingrate! thus to hurl his vengeance!
Thyestes —
  O mighty gods! what crimes are ye avenging?
  Thou fiend spewed forth by hell to blight the earth,
  More fully spend the rage that fills thy breast;
  Send an unhappy father to his son!
  Give this new victim to his bloody manes,
  Nor stop half-way in thy vile path of crime.
  How canst thou spare me, barbarous wretch! to mourn
  Within a world whence thou hast driven away
  The gods, and even the wholesome light of day?
Atreus —
  Nay; I should wish thee back again to life,
  Which I can stuff so bravely with disasters.
  I know thy grief, I hear it in thy moans,
  I see thy sorrows wound thee as I wished;
  And in thy tears I find fulfilled the hope
  That fast was fading in my heart,—revenge!
  Thou callest on death, and I have left thee life,
  'Tis my revenge.
Thyestes —   Ah, vain and flattering hope!
  Thyestes's hand can rob thee of that joy!
             [*He kills himself.*

Theodamia, daughter of Thyestes —
  Ah, heaven!
Thyestes —   Be thou comforted, my daughter;
  Hence, and leave justice to the most high gods,
  Whose hearts your tears will move. Hence! and await
  His punishment, whose perjuries turned pale
  The very gods themselves: they promise it;
  'Tis pledged me in this bloody cup, and now—
  Just gods!—I die!
Atreus —   And I accept the omen;
  For thy self-slaying hand hath crowned my wishes,
  And I enjoy at last my crimes' fell fruitage!

MOTHER AND DAUGHTER

From ‘ Electra ›

CLYTEMNESTRA — So! far from answering a mother's kindness.
　　　Thou heap'st defiance on that sacred name!
　　　And when my pity seeks her happiness,
　　　Electra scorns me still. Ay, ay, defy me,
　　　Proud princess, unrelenting! but accuse
　　　None save thyself, that Fate so frowns on thee!
　　　From a great monarch, jealous of his power,
　　　I won a hero-husband for my daughter;
　　　And hasty Hope had shown to me the sceptre
　　　Within our house once more, bought by that union;
　　　Yet she, ungrateful, only seeks our ruin!
　　　But one word more: thou hold'st the heart of Itys,
　　　And this same day shall see your lots united.
　　　Refuse him at thy peril! for Ægisthus
　　　Is weary of the slave within his palace,
　　　Whose tears move men and gods to pity.

Electra —　　　　　　　　　　　　　　　　Pity!
　　　Against so proud a tyrant, O ye heavens,
　　　What weapon? Can he fear my harmless tears,
　　　Who thus defies remorse? Ah, madam,— mother!
　　　Is it for thee to add to my misfortunes?
　　　I, I Ægisthus's slave — alack, how comes it?
　　　Ah, hapless daughter! who such slave has made me?
　　　And say, of whom was this Electra born?
　　　And is it fitting thou shouldst so reproach me?
　　　Mother!— if still that holy name can move thee,—
　　　And if indeed my shame be known to all
　　　Within this palace,— show compassion on me,
　　　And on the griefs thy hand hath heaped upon me;
　　　Speed, speed my death! but think not to unite me
　　　To him, the son of that foul murderer!
　　　That wretch whose fury robbed me of a father,
　　　And still pursues him in his son and daughter,
　　　Usurping even the disposal of my hand!
　　　Canst speak of such a marriage, and not shudder?
　　　Mother! that lovedst me once,— how have I lost it,
　　　Thy tender love? Alas! I cannot hate thee;
　　　Despite the sorrows that have hedged me round,
　　　The bitter tears I shed within this place,
　　　'Tis only for the tyrant I invoke
　　　The high gods' wrath. Ah, if I must forget

That I have lost a father — help me, madam,
To still remember that I have a mother!

Clytemnestra —

What can I do? how act? Naught save thy marriage
Will satisfy the King. I pray thee, yield.
Repine no longer at thy destined lot,
And cease bewailing o'er a dead barbarian
Who — had he found another Ilion —
Thyself full quickly would have made an offering
Upon the altar of his own ambition.
Thus did he dare — oh dark and cruel heart! —
Before mine eyes to sacrifice my daughter!

Electra —

Cruel — ay, madam; yet was he thy husband.
If thus he purchased for him punishment,
What gods or men appointed *thee* avenger?
If Heaven in extremity of harshness
Compelled him, hapless hero! to outpour
His own blood — answer! was it not for Heaven
He spilled it? But thou, most unnatural mother
Of sorrow-scourged Electra and Orestes,
Thou too wouldst spill the last drops of that blood;
Not for high Heaven, jealous of its altars,
But for the vilest mortal. Ah, behold him!
He comes, inhuman wretch! and at the sight
Fierce passions stir within my seething soul.

THE MATRICIDE

From 'Electra'

ORESTES —   Strike, ye gods!
Ye gods all-powerful, summoned by my fury;
Avenging gods! if there be such, then strike!
Since still I live. My crime, my hideous crime,
Is yours alone to reckon, yours to judge.
Has Heaven only gentle torments for me?
Alas! I see what stays your righteous vengeance:
You know not how to punish crime so foul,
Ye horror-stricken gods!

Electra —   Ah, brother, brother!
Calm this blind frenzy; cure thee of this madness;
Have I not weight enough of grief to bear?
Wouldst thou, Orestes, slay me as I stand?

Orestes —

Hush! utter it no more, that name abhorred.
And thou who shudderest at my odious presence —
Nature! so oft, so deeply outraged here —
I have avenged thee of my murdered father;
But who my murdered mother shall avenge?
Speak, Justice! if thine arm have lost its power, —
Filled with the fury of a just despair,
Behold, myself will aid it to strike home!
If man's remorse can move divinity,
Gods! turn ye to the tears, the blood I spill —
Ha! seest thou, mother?

[*He tries to kill himself, but is disarmed by his guardian
Palamedes.*]

Palamedes —   O my lord!

Orestes —   Leave, leave me!

From thee I will have nothing, wretch inhuman!
Nor from Electra. Was it not your hearts,
Thirsting for blood and victims, that compelled me
To stain my hands with guilt unspeakable?
But how now? whence this mist that darkens round me?
Thanks be to heaven, the way to hell is opened.
Let us to hell! there's nothing that affrights me, —
And in the horror of eternal night,
Hide and enwrap ourselves! — But what pale light
Shines on me now? who to this dark abode
Dares to bring daylight back? What do I see?
The dead of hell look shuddering upon me!
Oh hear the moans, the painful cries — "Orestes!"
Who calls me in this horrible retreat?
It is Ægisthus! oh, too much, too much!
And in my wrath — but soft: what sight is here?
What holds he in his hands? My mother's head!
Ah, what a gaze! Where shall Orestes flee!
Atrocious monster! what a spectacle
Thou venturest to show me! Stay thy fury!
Behold my sufferings; and that awful head —
Hide, hide it from these terror-smitten eyes!
Ah, mother, spare me; spare thy unhappy son!
Ye shades of Agamemnon, hear my cries;
Shades of mine honored father, give thine aid;
Come, shield thy son from the pursuing anger
Of Clytemnestra! ah, show pity on me!
What! even into thy protecting arms

She, furious, still pursues me. All is over!
I yield me to the life-consuming torture.
My guiltless heart, that bore nor part nor share
In the black crime committed by my hand,
Is torn with torments. O ye gods! what culprit
Of deepest guilt could bear worse punishment?

THE RECONCILIATION

From 'Rhadamistus and Zenobia'

ZENOBIA —   My lord, a hapless woman
Whom Fate has fastened to a tyrant's yoke,—
Dare she appeal, disgraced in chains of bondage,
To Romans, masters of the universe?
Ah! yet indeed what better part to play,
For these same masters of the universe,
Than to relieve my great misfortunes? Heaven,
That to their august laws subjected all —

Rhadamistus —
What do I see? Ah, wretched man! Those features —
That voice — Just gods! what sight do ye present
Before mine eyes?

Zenobia —   How comes it that your soul,
My gracious lord, so stirs at sight of me?

Rhadamistus —
Had not my hand deprived of life —

Zenobia —   What is it
I see and hear in turn? Sad recollection!
I tremble, shudder! where and what am I?
My strength fast leaves me. Ah, my lord, dispel
My terror and confusion. All my blood
Runs cold to my heart's core.

Rhadamistus —   Ah me! the passion
That fills my being, leaves no further doubt.
Hast thou, my hand, achieved but half thy crime?
Victim of man's conspiring cruelty,
Sad object of a jealous desperate love
Swept on by rage to fiercest violence,—
After such storm of madness, frenzy, fury —
Zenobia, is it thou?

Zenobia —   Zenobia!
Ah, gods! O Rhadamistus, thou my husband,
Cruel but yet beloved — after trials
So many and so bitter, is it thou?

Rhadamistus —
        Can it be possible thine eyes refuse
        To recognize him? Yes, I am that monster,
        That heart inhuman; yes! I am that traitor,
        That murderous husband! Would to highest Heaven
        That when to-day he stood unknown before thee,
        Forgetting him, thou hadst forgot his crimes!
        O gods! who to my mortal grief restore her,
        Why could ye not return to her a husband
        Worthy herself? What happy fate befalls me,
        That Heaven, touched to pity by my torments
        Of sharp regret, hath granted me to gaze
        Once more upon such charms? But yet — alas!
        Can it be, too, that at my father's court
        I find a wife so dear weighed down with chains?
        Gods! have I not bewailed my crimes enow,
        That ye afflict my vision with this sight?
        O all too gentle victim of despair
        Like mine! How all I see but fills afresh
        The measure of thy husband's guilt! — How now:
        Thou weepest!

Zenobia —
                    Wherefore, thou unhappy being,
        Should I not weep, in such a fateful hour?
        Ah, cruel one! would Heaven, thy hand of hatred
        Had only sought to snatch Zenobia's life!
        Then would my heart, unstirred to depths of anger
        At sight of thee, beat quickly on beholding
        My husband; then would love, to honor lifted
        By rage of jealousy, replace thy wife
        Within thine arms, fresh filled with happiness.
        Yet think not that I feel for thee no pity,
        Or turn from thee with loathing.

Rhadamistus —
                            Ye great gods!
        Far from reproaches such as should o'erwhelm me,
        It is Zenobia who fears to hate me,
        And justifies herself! Ah, punish me,
        Rather than this; for in such fatal kindness,
        Such free forgiveness, I am made to taste
        Of mine own cruelty! Spare not my blood,
        Dear object of my love! be just; deprive me
        Of such a bliss as seeing thee again!
                          [*He falls at her feet.*
        Must I, to urge thee, clasp thy very knees?
        Remember what the price, and whose the blood,

That sealed me as thy spouse! All, even my love,
Demands that I should perish.   To leave crime
Unpunished, is to share the culprit's guilt.
Strike! but remember — in my wildest fury
Never wast thou cast down from thy high place
Within my heart; remember, if repentance
Could stand for innocence, I need no longer
Rouse thee to hatred, move thee to revenge.
Ay! and remember too, despite the rage
Which well I know must swell within thy soul,
My greatest passion was my love for thee.

Zenobia —

Arise! it is too much.   Since I forgive thee,
What profit in regrets? The gods, believe me,
Deny to us the power of wreaking vengeance
On enemies so dear.   But name the land
Where thou wouldst dwell, and I will follow thee
Whithersoe'er thou wilt.   Speak! I am ready
To follow, from this moment forth, forever,
Assured that such remorse as fills thy heart
Springs from thy virtues, more than thy misfortunes;
And happy, if Zenobia's love for thee
Could some day serve as pattern to Armenia,
Make her like me thy willing, loyal subject,
And teach her, if no more, to know her duty!

Rhadamistus —

Great Heaven! can it be that lawful bonds
Unite such virtues to so many crimes?
That Hymen to a madman's lot should link
The fairest, the most perfect of all creatures
To whom the gods gave life? Canst look upon me,
After a father's death? My outrages,
My brother's love — that prince so great and generous —
Can they not make thee hate a hapless husband?
And I may tell myself, since thou disdainest
The proffered vows of virtuous Arsames,
Thou to his passion turn'st a heart of ice?
What words are these? too happy might I live
To-day, if duty in that noble heart
Might take for me the place of love!

Zenobia —   Ah, quiet
Within thy soul the groundless doubts that fill it;
Or hide at least thy unworthy jealousy!
Remember that a heart that can forgive thee

Is not a heart to doubt, — no, Rhadamistus,
Not without crime!

Rhadamistus —   O thou dear wife, forgive me
My fatal love; forgive me those suspicions
Which my whole heart abhors. The more unworthy
Thy inhuman spouse, the less should thy displeasure
Visit his unjust fears. O dear Zenobia!
Give me thy heart and hand again, and deign
To follow me this day to fair Armenia.
Cæsar hath o'er that province made me monarch;
Come! and behold me henceforth blot my crimes
From thy remembrance with a list of virtues.
Come, here is Hiero, a faithful subject,
Whose zeal we trust to cover o'er our flight.
Soon as the night has veiled the staring sky,
Assured that thou shalt see my face again,
Come and await me in this place. Farewell!
Let us not linger till a barbarous foe,
When Heaven has reunited us, shall part us
Again forever. O ye gods, who gave her
Back to my arms in answer to my longings,
Deign, deign to give to me a heart deserving
Your goodness!

S. R. CROCKETT

(1862–)

S. R. CROCKETT

HAT Samuel Rutherford Crockett was born in Little Duchrae, Galloway, Scotland, in 1862, of a long line of tenant farmers; that, a small white-haired boy, beginning at three and a half years of age, he did his daily work on the farm and walked three miles to the parish school, where, under a master who was "a dungeon of learning," he wrestled with Latin as far as "Omnis Gallia" and through the Greek alphabet till he was fifteen; that he then entered Edinburgh University, where he added to his sparse resources by tutoring and journalistic work; and that after severe theological training he was in 1884 ordained to the ministry of the Free Church of Scotland,—reads like a familiar story which with a few changes, such as dates and identities, might have been told of a host of his distinguished countrymen.

Between the covers of his books one may learn all that is essential and characteristic of Mr. Crockett, the most important fact in his literary life being an honorable loyalty to his own home and people and faith. It is his good fortune that that home is in a region of romance and legend and daring adventure; that his people are of an austere race, whose shrewd humor underlies a solemn gravity, whose keenest joy is intellectual controversy, and whose highest ambition is that at least one representative of the whitewashed farm-house shall "wag his head in a pulpit." And fundamentally, for his art's sake, it is his good fortune that his faith is their faith, a stern conviction of a stern creed whose tenderest traditions are fostered by the sight of the Martyrs' Monument on Auchenreoch Muir, and the kirk-yards of Balweary and Nether Dullarg, where under the trees the heroes of Scotland lie as thick as gowans on the lea.

Nor should the influence of the scenery of Galloway be ignored on Mr. Crockett's work. Its trackless moors and lairy coverts, the green woodlands of Earlston and the gray Duchrae craigs, the sleeping pools guarded by dark firs standing bravely like men-at-arms on every rocky knoll, the river Ken flowing silver clear, and the great Kells range, ridge behind ridge of hills "whose very names make a storm of music,"—this is the background of wild deeds and wilder passions, in whose recounting in 'The Raiders' and 'The Men of the Moss-Hags' we have as yet the highest exhibition of his genius.

Construction is not perhaps his strong point, but in these stirring scenes and dramatic situations, chronicled by the hero who creates an atmosphere of fond credulity in his adventures and personality, the author is kept to his work by the stress of hard times. The action is swift, for in 'The Raiders' the hill outlaws come down like the blast of a terrible trumpet; and in 'The Men of the Moss-Hags' Lauderdale and Claverhouse are hunting the Covenanters into the caves of the earth, so that in the rush of events both he who tells the tale and he who listens are hurried along. The feature of these fine romances, especially 'The Raiders,' is their Homeric spirit of generous simplicity and bellicose cheerfulness. Mr. Crockett is a fighter for his loves, his fireside, and his Shorter Catechism. And though there are pathetic passages, the robustness of the men and the heroism of the women remove them from our pity to our proud enthusiasm. Were one to seek the source of Mr. Crockett's inspiration, he would probably find it in the Old Testament.

In this class of novels are included the short, sombre story 'Mad Sir Uchtred' and 'The Gray Man.' Nor are these works lacking in the characteristics of his other manner yet to be spoken of. The long hours in which we ride with John Faa, Lord of Little Egypt, and with Willie Gordon of Earlston, are enlivened with shrewd comment and brilliant narration. Humanity in its least complex aspect, and robust faith in God, transport us to the other and sturdier age in which they dwelt.

The other field in which Mr. Crockett has made a reputation, his earlier field, is his presentment of contemporary Scotch peasant life. Robert Fraser and Janet Balchrystie, in 'The Stickit Minister,' are the descendants of John Faa and May Mischief and of Willie Gordon and Maisie Lenox. They dwell in the same sweet holms and by the levels of the same lochs, bonny and broad, and their faith is nurtured on the rugged Caledonian doctrine for which these, their literary forbears, fought and died. As the shepherd knows his sheep that to us who are not shepherds show so little unlikeness, so Mr. Crockett knows the lines and lineaments of his characters. The pathos of their brave lives is kept in shadow with the fine reserve of one who will not suffer a stranger to intermeddle, but it is felt as we feel that there are dark depths to the sea whose surface waves sparkle in the sun.

In this earlier manner 'A Galloway Herd,' 'The Play-Actress,' and the delicate fantasy 'The Lilac Sunbonnet,' are written. If in 'Cleg Kelly,' the story of an Edinburgh waif, there is a touch of the melodramatic, much may be forgiven an author who with the mastery of subtle peculiarities of individual types combines the power to make a novel vibrate with dramatic action.

ENSAMPLES TO THE FLOCK

From 'The Stickit Minister': the Macmillan Company, Publishers

THE family of the late Tyke M'Lurg consisted of three loons and a lassie. Tyke had never done anything for his children except share with a short-lived and shadowy mother the responsibility of bringing them into the world. The time that he could spare from his profession of poacher he had systematically devoted to neglecting them. Tyke had solved successfully for many years the problem of how to live by the least possible expenditure of labor. Kind ladies had taken him in hand time and again. They had provided clothes for his children, which Tyke had primarily converted into coin of the realm, and indirectly into liquid refreshment, at Lucky Morgan's rag store in Cairn Edward. Work had been found for Tyke, and he had done many half-days of labor in various gardens. Unfortunately, however, before the hour of noon it was Tyke's hard case to be taken with a " grooin' in his inside " of such a nature that he became rapidly incapacitated for further work.

" No, mem, I canna tak' it. It's mony a year since I saw the evil o't. Ye'll hae to excuse me, but I really couldna. Oh, thae pains! O sirce, my inside! Weel, gin ye insist, I'll juist hae to try a toothfu' to obleege ye, like."

But Tyke's toothfu's were over for this world, and his shortcomings were lying under four feet of red mold. Half a dozen kindly folk who pitied his " three loons and a lassie " gathered a few pounds and gave him a decent burial,—not for his own sake, but in order that the four little scarecrows might have a decent start in life. It is the most fatal and indestructible of reproaches in the south of Scotland to have a father buried by the parish.

The lassie was the eldest of the children. She was thirteen, and she hardly remembered what it was to have a mother or a new frock. But ever since she was eleven she had never had a dirty one. The smith's wife had shown her how to wash, and she had learned from the teacher how to mend. "Leeb" had appeared on the books of the school as Elizabeth M'Lurg, and she had attended as often as she could — that is, as often as her father could not prevent her; for Tyke, being an independent man, was down on the compulsory clause of the Education Act, and had more than once got thirty days for assaulting the School Board officer.

When he found out that Leeb was attending school at the village he lay in wait for her on her return, with a stick, and after administering chastisement on general principles he went on to specify his daughter's iniquities:—

"Ye upsettin' blastie, wad ye be for gangin' to their schule, learnin' to look doon on yer ain faither that has been at sic pains to rear ye?"— (a pause for further correction, to which poor Leeb vocalized an accompaniment). "Let me see gin ye can read! Hae, read that!" he said, flinging a tattered lesson-book, which the teacher had given her, to his daughter. Leeb opened the book, and punctuating the lesson with her sobs, she read in the high and level shriek of a locomotive engine, "And so brave Bobby, hav-ing sa-ved the tr-r-r-em-bling child, re-turn-ed with the res-cu-ed one in his mouth to the shore."

"Davert! but ye *can* read!" said her father, snatching the book and tearing it up before her eyes. "Noo, listen; I'll hae nane o' my bairns teached to despise their faither by no Schule Boards. Look you here, Leeb M'Lurg, gin ever I catch you within a mile o' the schule, I'll skin ye!"

But for all this tremendous threat, or maybe all the more because of it, and also because she so much desired to be able to do a white seam, Leeb so arranged it that there were few days when she did not manage to come along the mile and half of lochside road which separated her from the little one-roomed, whitewashed schoolhouse on the face of the brae. She even brought one of the "loons" with her pretty often; but as Jock, Rab, and Benny (otherwise known as Rag, Tag, and Bobtail) got a little older, they more easily accommodated themselves to the wishes of their parent; and in spite of Leeb's blandishments they went into "hidie holes" till the School Board officer had passed by.

M'Lurg's Mill where the children lived was a tumble-down erection, beautiful for situation, set on the side of the long loch of Kenick. The house had once been a little farm-house, its windows brilliant with geraniums and verbenas; but in the latter days of the forlorn M'Lurgs it had become betrampled as to its doorsteps by lean swine, and bespattered as to its broken floor by intrusive hens. It was to M'Lurg's Mill that the children returned after the funeral. Leeb had been arrayed in the hat and dress of a neighbor's daughter for the occasion, but the three loons had played "tig" in the intervals of watching their father's funeral from the broomy knoll behind the mill. Jock, the eldest, was nearly eleven, and had been taken in hand by the kind neighbor wife at the same time as Leeb. At one time he looked as though he would even better repay attention, for he feigned a sleek-faced submission and a ready compliance which put Mistress Auld of the Arkland off her guard. Then as soon as his sister, of whom Jock stood much in awe, was gone out, he snatched up his ragged clothes and fled to the hill. Here he was immediately joined by the other two loons. They caught the Arkland donkey grazing in the field beside the mill-dam, and having made a parcel of the good black trousers and jacket, they tied them to the donkey and drove him homeward with blows and shoutings. A funeral was only a dull procession to them, and the fact that it was their father's made no difference.

Next morning Leeb sat down on the "stoop" or wooden bench by the door, and proceeded to cast up her position. Her assets were not difficult to reckon. A house of two rooms, one devoted to hens and lumber; a mill which had once sawn good timber, but whose great circular saw had stood still for many months; a mill-lade broken down in several places, three or four chairs and a stool, a table, and a wash-tub. When she got so far she paused. It was evident that there could be no more school for her, and the thought struck her that now she must take the responsibility for the boys, and bring them up to be useful and diligent. She did not and could not so express her resolve to herself, but a still and strong determination was in her sore little heart not to let the boys grow up like their father.

Leeb had gone to Sabbath school every week, when she could escape from the tyranny of home, and was therefore well known to the minister, who had often exercised himself in vain on the thick defensive armor of ignorance and stupidity which encompassed the elder M'Lurg. His office-bearers and he had often bemoaned the sad example of this ne'er-do-weel family which had intrenched itself in the midst of so many well-doing people. M'Lurg's Mill was a reproach and an eyesore to the whole parish, and the M'Lurg "weans" a gratuitous insult to every self-respecting mother within miles. For three miles round the children were forbidden to play with, or even to speak to, the four outcasts at the mill. Consequently their society was much sought after.

When Leeb came to set forth her resources, she could not think of any except the four-pound loaf, the dozen hens and a cock, the routing wild Indian of a pig, and the two lean and knobby cows on the hill at the back. It would have been possible to sell all these things, perhaps, but Leeb looked upon herself as the trustee for the rest of the family. She resolved therefore to make what use of them she could, and having most of the property under her eye at the time, there was the less need to indite an inventory of it.

But first she must bring her brothers to a sense of their position. She was a very Napoleon of thirteen, and she knew that now that there was no counter authority to her own, she could bring Jock, Rab, and Benny to their senses very quickly. She therefore selected with some care and attention a hazel stick, using a broken table-knife to cut it with a great deal of deftness. Having trimmed it, she went out to the hill to look for her brothers.

It was not long before she came upon them engaged in the fascinating amusement of rooting for pignuts in a green bankside. The natural Leeb would instantly have thrown down her wand of office and joined them in the search, but the Leeb of to-day was a very different person. Her second thought was to rush among them and deal lusty blows with the stick, but she fortunately remembered that in that case they would scatter, and that by force she could only take home one, or at most two. She therefore called to her assistance the natural guile of her sex.

"Boys, are ye hungry?" she said. "There's sic a graun' big loaf come frae the Arkland!" By this time all her audience were on their feet. "An' I'll milk the kye, an' we'll hae a feast."

"Come on, Jock," said Rab, the second loon, and the leader in mischief, "I'll race ye for the loaf."

"Ye needna do that," said Leeb calmly; "the door's lockit."

So as Leeb went along, she talked to her brothers as soberly as though they were models of good behavior and all the virtues, telling them what she was going to do and how she would expect them to help her. By the time she got them into the mill-yard she had succeeded in stirring their enthusiasm, especially that of Jock, to whom with a natural tact she gave the wand of the office of "sairgint," a rank which on the authority of Sergeant M'Millan, the village pensioner, was understood to be very much higher than that of general. "Sairgint" Jock foresaw much future interest in the disciplining of his brothers, and entered with eagerness into the new ploy. The out-of-doors live stock was also committed to his care. He was to drive the cows along the roadside and allow them to pasture on the sweetest and most succulent grasses, while Rab scouted in the direction of the village for supposititious "poalismen" who were understood to take up and sell for the Queen's benefit all cows found eating grass on the public highway. Immediately after Jock and Rab had received a hunch of the Arkland loaf and their covenanted drink of milk, they went off to drive the cows to the loch road, so that they might at once begin to fill up their lean sides. Benny, the youngest, who was eight past, she reserved for her own assistant. He was a somewhat tearful but willing little fellow, whose voice haunted the precincts of M'Lurg's mill like a wistful ghost. His brothers were constantly running away from him, and he pattering after them as fast as his fat little legs could carry him, roaring with open mouth at their cruelty, the tears making clean watercourses down his grimy cheeks. But Benny soon became a new boy under his sister's exclusive care.

"Noo, Benny," she said, "you an' me's gaun to clean the hoose. Jock an' Rab will no' be kennin' it when they come back!" So, having filled the tub with water from the mill-lade, and carried every movable article of furniture outside, Leeb began to wash out the house and rid it of the accumulated dirt of years. Benny carried small bucketfuls of water to swill over the floor. Gradually the true color of the stones began to shine up, and the black incrustation to retreat towards the outlying corners.

"I'm gaun doon to the village," she said abruptly. "Benny, you keep scrubbin' alang the wa's."

Leeb took her way down rapidly to where Joe Turner, the village mason, was standing by a newly begun pig-stye or swine-ree, stirring a heap of lime and sand.

"G'ye way oot o' that!" he said instantly, with the threatening gesture which every villager except the minister and the mistress of Arkland instinctively made on seeing a M'Lurg. This it is to have a bad name.

But Leeb stood her ground, strong in the consciousness of her good intentions.

"Maister Turner," she said, "could ye let me hae a bucketfu' or twa o' whitewash for the mill kitchen? an' I'll pey ye in hen's eggs. Oor hens are layin' fine, an' your mistress is fond o' an egg in the mornin'."

Joe stopped and scratched his head. This was something new, even in a village where a good deal of business is done according to the rules of truck or barter.

"What are ye gaun to do wi' the whitewash?" he inquired, to get time to think. "There was little whitewash in use about M'Lurg's Mill in yer faither's time!"

"But I'm gaun to bring up the boys as they should," said Leeb, with some natural importance, sketching triangles on the ground with her bare toe.

"An' what's whitewash got to do wi' that?" asked Joe, with some asperity.

Leeb could not just put the matter into words, but she instinctively felt that it had a good deal to do with it. Whitewash was her badge of respectability both inside the house and out, in which Leeb was at one with modern science.

"I'll gie three dizzen o' eggs for three bucketfu's," she said.

"An' hoo div I ken that I'll ever see ane o' the eggs?" asked Joe.

"I've brocht a dizzen wi' me noo!" said Leeb, promptly, producing them from under her apron.

Leeb got the whitewash that very night, and the loan of a brush to put it on with. Next morning the farmer of the Crae received a shock. There was something large and white down on the loch-side, where ever since he came to the Crae he had seen naething but the trees which hid M'Lurg's mill.

"I misdoot it's gaun to be terrible weather. I never saw that hoose o' Tyke M'Lurg's aff our hill afore!" he said.

The minister came by that day, and stood perfectly aghast at the new splendors of the M'Lurg mansion. Hitherto when he had strangers staying with him he took them another way, in order that his parish might not be disgraced. Not only were the walls of the house shining with whitewash, but the windows were cleaned, a piece of white muslin curtain was pinned across each, and a jug with a bunch of heather and wild flowers looked out smiling on the passers-by. The minister bent his steps to the open door. He could see the two M'Lurg cows pasturing placidly with much contented head-tossing on the roadside, while a small boy sat above, laboring at the first rounds of a stocking. From the house came the shrill voice of singing. Out of the firwood over the knoll came a still smaller boy, bent double with a load of sticks.

In the window, written with large sprawling capitals on a leaf of a copy-book under the heading "Encourage Earnest Endeavor," appeared the striking legend:—

SOWING & MENDING DUN
GOOD COWS MILK
    STICKS FOR FIREWOOD CHEEP
NEW LAID EGGS
       BY ELIZABETH McLURG

The minister stood regarding, amazement on every line of his face. Leeb came out singing, a neatly tied bundle of chips made out of the dry débris of the saw-mill in her hand.

"Elizabeth," said he, "what is the meaning of this?"

"Will ye be pleased to step ben?" said Leeb. The minister did so, and was astonished to find himself sitting down in a spotless kitchen, the walls positively painfully white, the wooden chairs scoured with sand till the very fibre of the wood was blanched, and on a floor so clean that one might have dined off it, the mystic whorls and crosses of whiting which connect all good Galloway housekeepers with Runic times.

Before the minister went out of M'Lurg's Mill he had learned the intentions of Leeb to make men of her brothers. He said, "You are a woman already, before your time, Elizabeth!" which was the speech of all others best fitted to please Leeb M'Lurg. He had also ordered milk and eggs for the manse to be delivered by Benny, and promised that his wife would call upon the little head of the house.

As he went down the road by the loch-side he meditated, and this was the substance of his thought: — "If that girl brings up her brothers like herself, Tyke M'Lurg's children may yet be ensamples to the flock."

But as to this we shall see.

SAWNY BEAN; AND THE CAVE OF DEATH

From 'The Gray Man': copyright 1896, by Harper and Brothers

FOR a moment in the darkness I stood dazed, and my head swam. For I bethought me of the earl's words, and I knew that my fate stood upon tiptoe. For here in the finding of this box lay all my life, and it might be my love also. But again another thought crossed the first, damming back and freezing the current of hot blood which surged to my heart. The caird's words in the Grieve's kitchen came to me:— "You will find the treasure of Kelwood in the cave of Sawny Bean, in the head of Benanback over against Benerard."

If this were to be, there was little doubt that we stood in instant and imminent danger of our lives. Yet I could not bring myself to leave the treasure. Doubtless I ought to have done so, and hastened our escape for the sake of the girls. But I thought it might be possible to convey the chest out, and so bring both our quests to an end at once — that for the treasure by the recovery of the box which had been lost and found and lost upon the Red Moss, and that of vengeance by the certain condemnation of the Auchendraynes upon Marjorie's evidence.

The next moment great fear took hold on me. All that I had heard since my childhood about the Unknown who dwelt upon the shore-side, and lived no man knew how, ran through my mind,— his monstrous form; his cloven feet that made steads on the ground like those of a beast; his huge hairy arms, clawed at the finger-ends like the claws of a bear. I minded me of the fireside tales of the travelers who had lost their way in that fastness, and who, falling into the power of his savage tribe, returned no more to kindlier places. I minded also how none might speak to the prowler by night or get answer from him; how every expedition against him had come to naught, because that he was protected by a power stronger, warned and advised by an intelligence higher than his own. Besides, none had been able to find the abode or enter into the secret defenses where lurked the Man-beast of Benerard.

And it was in this abode of death that I, Launce Kennedy, being as I supposed in my sane mind, had taken refuge with two women, one the dearest to me on earth. The blood ran pingling and pricking in my veins. My heart-cords tightened as though it had been shut in a box and the key turned.

Hastily I slipped down, and upon a pretext took the dominic aside to tell him what it was that I had found.

"Ye have found our dead-warrant, then. I wish we had never seen your treasures and banded boxes!" said he roughly, as if I had done it with intent.

And in truth I began to think he was right. But it was none of my fault, and we had been just as badly off in that place if I had not found it.

After that I went ranging hither and thither among all the passages and twinings of the cave, yet never daring to go very far from the place where we were, lest I should not be able to find my way back. For it was an ill place, where every step that I took something strange swept across my face or slithered clammily along my cheek, making one grue to his bone marrows. I am as fond of a nimble fetch of adventures as any man, as every believing reader of this chronicle kens well by this time. But I want no more such experiences. Specially now that I am become a peaceable man, and no longer so regardlessly forward as I was in thrusting myself into all stirs and quarrels up to the elbows.

Then in a little I went soft-footed to where Marjorie and Nell had bestowed themselves. When I told them how we had run into danger with a folly and senselessness which nothing could have excused, save the great necessity into which by the hellish fury of our enemies we had been driven, it was cheerful to hear their words of trust, and their declaration that they could abide the issue with fortitude.

So we made such preparations as we could — as preparing our pistols and loosening our swords. Yet all had to be done by touch in that abode of darkness and black unchristian deeds.

It was silent and eery in the cave. We heard the water lapping further and further from us as it retreated down the long passage. Now and then we seemed to catch a gliff of the noise of human voices. But again, when we listened, it was naught but the wind blowing every way through the passages and halls of the cave; or the echo of the wing-beatings of uncanny things that battened in the roofs and crevices of the murtherous cavern where we abode, unfathomed, unsounded, and obscure.

But we had not long to wait ere our courage and resolution were tested to the uttermost. For presently there came to us clearly, though faintly at first, the crying and baying of voices, fearful and threatening: yet more like the insensate howling of dogs or shut-up hounds in a kennel than human creatures. Then there was empty silence, through which again the noise came in gusts like the sudden deadly anger of a mob; again more sharp and edged with fear, like the wailing of women led to their unpitied doom. And the sound of this inhuman carnival, approaching, filled the cave.

The direful crying came nearer and nearer, till we all cowered pale-faced together, save Marjorie alone — who, having been as it were in hell itself, feared not the most merciless fiends that had broken loose therefrom. She stood a little apart from us, so far that I had not known her presence but for the draught of air that blew inward, which carried her light robe towards me so that its texture touched my face, and I was aware of the old subtle fragrance which in happy days had turned my head in the gardens of Culzean.

But Nell Kennedy stood close to me — so close that I could hear her heart beating and the little sound of the clasping and unclasping of her hands. Which made me somewhat braver, especially when she put both her hands about my arm and gripped convulsively to me, as the noises of the crying and howling waxed louder and nearer.

"I am vexed that I flouted you, Launce!" she whispered in my ear. "I do not care what you said to Kate Allison. After all, she is not such a truth-telling girl, nor yet very by-ordinary bonny."

I whispered to her that I cared not either, and that I was content to die for her.

.   .   .   .

Thus we sat waiting. Suddenly there was a pause in the noise which filled the cavern below. I thought they had discovered us. But Marjorie moved her hand a little to bid me keep down. So very carefully I raised my head over the rock, so that through the niche I could, as before, look down upon them.

The water-door of the cave was now entirely filled by a black bulk, in shape like a monstrous ape. Even in the flickering light I knew that I had seen the monster before. A thrill ran through me when I remembered the Man-beast with which I had grappled in the barn of Culzean the night I outfaced the Gray Man. And now by the silence, and the crouching of the horde beneath me, I learned also that their master had come home. The thing stood a moment in the doorway as though angered at something. Then he spoke, in a voice like a beast's growl, things which I could not at all understand. Though it was clear that his progeny did, for there ensued a rushing from side to side. Then Sawny Bean strode into the midst of his den. He stumbled, and set his foot upon a lad of nine or ten, judging by the size of him, who sprawled in the doorway. The imp squirmed round like a serpent and bit Sawny Bean in the leg. Whereat he stooped, and catching the lad by the feet, he dashed his head with a dull crash against the wall, and threw him like a dead rabbit in the corner.

The rest stood for a moment aghast. But in a trice, and without a single one so much as going to see if the boy were dead or only stunned, the whole hornets' byke hummed again, and the place was filled with a stifling smell of burning fat and roasting victual, upon which I dared not let my mind for a moment dwell.

When Sawny Bean came in, he had that which looked like a rich cloth of gold over his arm — the plunder of some poor butchered wretch, belike. He stood with his trophy, examining it, before the fire. Presently he threw it over his shoulders with the arms hanging idly down, and strode about 'most like a play-actor or a mad person, but manifestly to his own great content and to the admiration of his followers, who stood still and gaped after him.

When he had satisfied himself with this, I saw him look towards our place of refuge. A great spasm gulped my heart when I saw him take the first step towards us, for I knew that it was his forbidden treasure-house in which we lurked.

So I thought it had come to the bitter push. But something yet more terrible than the matter of the boy diverted for the moment the monster's attention. The lad whom he had cast to the side had been left alone, none daring to meddle. But now, as he passed him, Sawny Bean gave the body a toss with his foot. At this, quick as a darting falcon on the stoop, a woman sprang at him from a crevice where she had been crouching — at least by her shape she was a woman, with long elf-locks twisting like snakes about her brow. She held an open knife in her hand, and she struck at the chieftain's hairy breast. I heard the knife strike the flesh, and the cry of anger and pain which followed. But the monster caught the woman by the wrist, pulled her over his knee, and bent back her head. It was a horrid thing to see, and there is small wonder that I can see it yet in many a dream of the night. And no doubt also I shall see it till I die — hear it as well.

Then for a long season I could look no more. But when I had recovered me a little, and could again command my heart to look, I saw a great part of the crew swarm like flies, fetching, carrying, and working like bees upon spilled honey, from the corner where had been the bodies of the lad and the woman. But it was not in the ordinary way that they were being prepared for burial. In the centre of the cave was Sawny, with some of the younger sort of the women pawing over him and bandaging his wounded shoulder. He was growling and spitting inarticulately all the time like a wildcat. And every time his shoulder hurt him, as the women worked with it, he would take his other hand and strike one of them down, as though it was to her that he owed the twinge of pain.

Presently the monster arose and took the gold brocade again in his hand. I thought that of a certainty now the time was come. And I looked at Nell Kennedy.

God knows what was in my eyes. My heart was like to break. For the like of this pass was never man in. That I should have to smite my love to the death within an hour of the first kiss and the first owning of her affection!

But she that loved me read my thought in mine eyes.

She bared her neck for me, so that I could see its tender whiteness in the flicker of the fire.

"Strike there," she said, "and let me die in your arms, who are my heart's love, Launcelot Kennedy."

I heard the Beast-man's step on the stair. I looked from Nell's dear neck to her eyes and back again to her bosom. I lifted my hand with the steel in it, and nerved myself for the striking, for

I must make no mistaking. And even in that moment I saw a dagger also in Marjorie's hand.

Suddenly a tremendous rush of sound filled the cave. The dagger fell from my hand, and Nell and I clasped one another. The clamor seemed to be about us and all round us. Roaring echoes came back to us. The bowels of the earth quaked. Yet methought there was something familiar in the sound of it. I turned me about, and there, standing erect with all his little height, was the dominie. His cheeks were distended, and he was blowing upon his great war-pipes such a thunderous pibroch as never had been heard in any land since the pipes skirled on the Red Harlaw.

What possession had come upon his mind I know not. But the effect I can tell. The pack of fiends that caroused and slew beneath stood stricken a moment, in amaze at the dreadful incomprehensible sounds. Then they fled helter-skelter, yelly-hooing with fear, down the narrow sea-way, from which the tide had now fully ebbed. And when I looked over, there was not a soul to be seen. Only over the edge of a caldron the body of the murdered woman, or at least a part of it, lay — a bloody incentive to haste out of this direful Cave of Death.

The dominie stepped down as though he had been leading a march, strutting and passaging like the king's piper marching about the banqueting-table at Holyrood. I declare, the creature seemed fey. He was certainly possessed with a devil. But the fearlessness of the man won into our veins also. For with steel or pistol in each of our hands we marched after him, ready to encounter aught that might come in our way. Aye, and even thus passed out of the cave, hasting down the long passage without a quiver of the heart or a blenching of the cheek, so suddenly and so starkly, by way of sudden hope, had the glorious music brought the hot blood back to our hearts, even as it had stricken our cruel foes with instant terror.

Thus dry-shod we marched out of the cave of Sawny Bean, and not so much as a dog barked at us. But when in the gray of a stormy morning we reached the cliff's edge, we heard inland the wild voices of the gang yelling down the wind, as though the furies of fear were pursuing them and tearing at their vitals. What they expected I know not. But I guess that they must have taken us for whatever particular devil they happened to believe in, come to take them quick to their own place. Which, after all, could not be much worse than the den in which we had seen them at their disport, nor could all the torturing fiends of lowest hell have been their marrows in devilish cruelty.

.　　.　　.　　.　　.　　.　　.　　.　　.

So once more the world was before us, and strangely quiet it seemed, as if we had died in stress and riot and been born again into an uncanny quiet. There remained now for us only the bringing to pass of righteous judgments upon the wicked ones who had compassed and plotted all this terrible tale of evils. These murders without end, the hellish cruelties and death-breeding deceits, must not fall alone on the crazed outlaw and his brood, for the chief criminals were those that were greater than Sawny Bean and his merciless crew.

GEORGE CROLY

(1780–1860)

THE versatile Irishman George Croly turned to literature as his means of livelihood when about thirty years old. He had been educated in his native town of Dublin, where he had graduated from Trinity College when only fifteen. Even thus early he had distinguished himself as a classical student and for grace in extempore speaking. He next studied for the ministry, and in 1804 was ordained, and obtained a small curacy in the North of Ireland.

But George Croly had a great fund of ambition, which kept him dissatisfied in this humble position. Hopes of preferment were several times held out to him, but they all failed; and tired of disappointment, he gave up his curacy in 1810 and moved to London with his mother and sisters. There he soon found an opening in journalism, and became dramatic critic on the New Times, and a regular contributor to the Literary Gazette and Britannia. He also wrote for Blackwood's Magazine, and as fellow contributor met the young lady whom he afterwards married.

In spite of his scholarship and great facility in expression, Croly's cannot be called an original mind. His verse is mostly a reflection of the literary influences he experienced. A certain exaggeration of emotion, the romance of Byron and Moore then in highest favor, appealed to him, and he emulated it in his most ambitious poems. 'Paris' (1815), although much weaker, strongly suggests 'Childe Harold.' Like Moore, his imagination delighted in Oriental color and richness, and he often chose Eastern subjects, as in 'The Angel of the World.'

The 'Traditions of the Rabbins' has been called an imitation of De Quincey, and indeed a portion of it is wrongly included in the collection of De Quincey's works. His 'Life and Times of George IV.' is more valuable as entertaining reading than for historical significance. To religious literature he contributed a 'Commentary on the Apocalypse,' and a book upon 'Divine Providence, or the Three Cycles of Revelation.' But although he loved literature and had read extensively, Croly's appreciation of it seems to have been entirely emotional. He could not analyze his impressions, and his critical work is vague enthusiasm rather than suggestive discrimination.

He essayed drama successfully. 'Catiline,' in spite of bombastic reminiscences of Marlowe, has tragic strength and richly rhythmic verse. 'Pride Shall Have a Fall,' a clever exposure of social weaknesses, was successfully given at the Covent Garden Theatre.

Although happy in authorship, Croly was anxious to resume his clerical profession, and in 1835 gladly accepted the rectorship of St. Stephen's Church, Walbrook, where a fashionable congregation accorded him a great reputation for eloquence. He was less successful in 1847, when appointed afternoon lecturer at the Foundling Hospital. The orphans and servant-maids failed to appreciate his flowery periods and emotional fervors. He was evidently quite beyond them, and soon resigned in disgust at their ingratitude.

Croly's poems and several other works, highly praised when they appeared, have been nearly forgotten. His fame rests now upon his fiction: 'Tales of the Saint Bernard,' 'Marston,' and 'Salathiel the Immortal.' The last especially, with the enduring fascination of the Wandering Jew legend, is always interesting. It has been often said that no one else has told the story so well. All the romance-loving side of Croly's nature comes out in the glowing descriptions of Eastern scenery, and in the appeal to heroic sentiment. The fantastic figure of Nero, ancient passions and vices, a spirit of former barbarity interwoven with ideality, the tragedy of unending human life, are curiously impressed on the picturesque pages.

THE FIRING OF ROME

From 'Salathiel the Immortal'

INTELLIGENCE in a few days arrived from Brundusium of the Emperor's landing, and of his intention to remain at Antium on the road to Rome, until his triumphal entry should be prepared. My fate now hung in the scale. I was ordered to attend the imperial presence. At the vestibule of the Antian palace my careful centurion deposited me in the hands of a senator. As I followed him through the halls, a young female richly attired, and of the most beautiful face and form, crossed us, light and graceful as a dancing nymph. The senator bowed profoundly. She beckoned to him, and they exchanged a few words. I was probably the subject; for her countenance, sparkling with the animation of youth and loveliness, grew pale at once; she clasped both her hands upon her eyes, and rushed into an inner chamber. She knew Nero well; and dearly she was yet to pay for her knowledge. The senator, to my inquiring glance, answered in a whisper, "The Empress Poppæa."

A few steps onward, and I stood in the presence of the most formidable being on earth. Yet whatever might have been the natural agitation of the time, I could scarcely restrain a smile at the first sight of Nero. I saw a pale, undersized, light-haired young man sitting before a table with a lyre on it, a few copies of verses and drawings, and a parrot's cage, to whose inmate he was teaching Greek with great assiduity. But for the regal furniture of the cabinet, I should have supposed myself led by mistake into an interview with some struggling poet. He shot round one quick glance on the opening of the door, and then procceded to give lessons to his bird. I had leisure to gaze on the tyrant and parricide.

Physiognomy is a true science. The man of profound thought, the man of active ability, and above all the man of genius, has his character stamped on his countenance by nature; the man of violent passions and the voluptuary have it stamped by habit. But the science has its limits: it has no stamp for mere cruelty. The features of the human monster before me were mild and almost handsome; a heavy eye and a figure tending to fullness gave the impression of a quiet mind; and but for an occasional restlessness of brow, and a brief glance from under it, in which the leaden eye darted suspicion, I should have pronounced Nero one of the most indolently tranquil of mankind.

He remanded the parrot to his perch, took up his lyre, and throwing a not unskillful hand over the strings, in the intervals of the performance languidly addressed a broken sentence to me. « You have come, I understand, from Judea; — they tell me that you have been, or are to be, a general of the insurrection; — you must be put to death; — your countrymen give us a great deal of trouble, and I always regret to be troubled with them. — But to send you back would only be encouragement to them, and to keep you here among strangers would only be cruelty to you. — I am charged with cruelty: you see the charge is not true. — I am lampooned every day; I know the scribblers, but they must lampoon or starve. I leave them to do both. Have you brought any news from Judea? — They have not had a true prince there since the first Herod; and he was quite a Greek, a cut-throat, and a man of taste. He understood the arts. — I sent for you to see what sort of animal a Jewish rebel was. Your dress is handsome, but too light for our winters. — You cannot die before sunset, as till then I am engaged with my music master. — We all must die when our time comes.—Farewell—till sunset may Jupiter protect you!"

I retired to execution! and before the door closed, heard this accomplished disposer of life and death preluding upon his lyre with increased energy. I was conducted to a turret until the period in which the Emperor's engagement with his music-master should leave him at leisure to see me die. Yet there was kindness even under the roof of Nero, and a liberal hand had covered the table in my cell. The hours passed heavily along, but they passed; and I was watching the last rays of my last sun, when I perceived a cloud rise in the direction of Rome. It grew broader, deeper, darker, as I gazed; its centre was suddenly tinged with red; the tinge spread; the whole mass of cloud became crimson: the sun went down, and another sun seemed to have risen in his stead. I heard the clattering of horses' feet in the courtyards below; trumpets sounded; there was confusion in the palace; the troops hurried under arms; and I saw a squadron of cavalry set off at full speed.

As I was gazing on the spectacle before me, which perpetually became more menacing, the door of my cell slowly opened, and a masked figure stood upon the threshold. I had made up my mind; and demanding if he was the executioner, I told him "that I was ready." The figure paused, listened to the sounds below, and after looking for a while on the troops in the court-yard, signified by signs that I had a chance of saving my life. The love of existence rushed back upon me. I eagerly inquired what was to be done. He drew from under his cloak the dress of a Roman slave, which I put on, and noiselessly followed his steps through a long succession of small and strangely intricate passages. We found no difficulty from guards or domestics. The whole palace was in a state of extraordinary confusion. Every human being was packing up something or other: rich vases, myrrhine cups, table services, were lying in heaps on the floors; books, costly dresses, instruments of music, all the appendages of luxury, were flung loose in every direction, from the sudden breaking up of the court. I might have plundered the value of a province with impunity. Still we wound our hurried way. In passing along one of the corridors, the voice of complaining struck the ear; the mysterious guide hesitated; I glanced through the slab of crystal that showed the chamber within. It was the one in which I had seen the Emperor, but his place was now filled by the form of youth and beauty that had crossed me on my arrival. She was weeping bitterly, and reading with strong and sorrowful indignation a long list of names, probably one of those rolls in which Nero registered his intended victims, and which in the confusion of departure he had left open. A second glance saw her tear the paper into a thousand fragments, and scatter them in the fountain that gushed upon the floor.

I left this lovely and unhappy creature, this dove in the vulture's talons, with almost a pang. A few steps more brought us into the open air, but among bowers that covered our path with darkness. At the extremity of the gardens my guide struck with his dagger upon a door; it was opened: we found horses outside; he sprang on one; I sprang on its fellow; and palace, guards, and death, were left far behind.

He galloped so furiously that I found it impossible to speak; and it was not till we had reached an eminence a few miles from Rome, where we breathed our horses, that I could ask to whom I had been indebted for my escape. But I could not extract a word from him. He made signs of silence, and pointed with wild anxiety to the scene that spread below. It was of a grandeur and terror indescribable. Rome was an ocean of flame.

Height and depth were covered with red surges, that rolled before the blast like an endless tide. The billows burst up the sides of the hills, which they turned into instant volcanoes, exploding volumes of smoke and fire; then plunged into the depths in a hundred glowing cataracts, then climbed and consumed again. The distant sound of the city in her convulsion went to the soul. The air was filled with the steady roar of the advancing flame, the crash of falling houses, and the hideous outcry of the myriads flying through the streets, or surrounded and perishing in the conflagration.

Hostile to Rome as I was, I could not restrain the exclamation:— "There goes the fruit of conquest, the glory of ages, the purchase of the blood of millions! Was vanity made for man?" My guide continued looking forward with intense earnestness, as if he were perplexed by what avenue to enter the burning city. I demanded who he was, and whither he would lead me. He returned no answer. A long spire of flame that shot up from a hitherto untouched quarter engrossed all his senses. He struck in the spur, and making a wild gesture to me to follow, darted down the hill. I pursued; we found the Appian choked with wagons, baggage of every kind, and terrified crowds hurrying into the open country. To force a way through them was impossible. All was clamor, violent struggle, and helpless death. Men and women of the highest rank were on foot, trampled by the rabble, that had then lost all respect of conditions. One dense mass of miserable life, irresistible from its weight, crushed by the narrow streets, and scorched by the flames over their heads, rolled through the gates like an endless stream of black lava.

We turned back, and attempted an entrance through the gardens of the same villas that skirted the city wall near the Palatine. All were deserted, and after some dangerous leaps over the burning ruins we found ourselves in the streets. The fire had originally broken out upon the Palatine, and hot smoke that wrapped and half blinded us hung thick as night upon the wrecks of pavilions and palaces: but the dexterity and knowledge of my inexplicable guide carried us on. It was in vain that I insisted upon knowing the purpose of this terrible traverse. He pressed his hand on his heart in reassurance of his fidelity, and still spurred on.

We now passed under the shade of an immense range of lofty buildings, whose gloomy and solid strength seemed to bid defiance to chance and time. A sudden yell appalled me. A ring of fire swept round its summit; burning cordage, sheets of canvas, and a shower of all things combustible, flew into the air above our heads. An uproar followed, unlike all that I had ever heard,— a hideous mixture of howls, shrieks, and groans. The flames rolled down the narrow street before us, and made the passage next to impossible. While we hesitated, a huge fragment of the building heaved as if in an earthquake, and fortunately for us fell inwards. The whole scene of terror was then open. The great amphitheatre of Statilius Taurus had caught fire; the stage with its inflammable furniture was intensely blazing below. The flames were wheeling up, circle above circle, through the seventy thousand seats that rose from the ground to the roof. I stood in unspeakable awe and wonder on the side of this colossal cavern, this mighty temple of the city of fire. At length a descending blast cleared away the smoke that covered the arena. The cause of those horrid cries was now visible. The wild beasts kept for the games had broken from their dens. Maddened by affright and pain, lions, tigers, panthers, wolves, whole herds of the monsters of India and Africa, were inclosed in an impassable barrier of fire. They bounded, they fought, they screamed, they tore; they ran howling round and round the circle; they made desperate leaps upwards through the blaze; they were flung back, and fell only to fasten their fangs in each other, and with their parching jaws bathed in blood, died raging.

I looked anxiously to see whether any human being was involved in this fearful catastrophe. To my great relief I could see none. The keepers and attendants had obviously escaped. As I expressed my gladness I was startled by a loud cry from my guide, the first sound that I had heard him utter. He pointed to the opposite side of the amphitheatre. There indeed sat an object of melancholy interest; a man who had either been unable to escape, or had determined to die. Escape was now impossible. He sat in desperate calmness on his funeral pile. He was a gigantic Ethiopian slave, entirely naked. He had chosen his place, as if in mockery, on the imperial throne; the fire was above him and around him; and under this tremendous canopy he gazed, without the movement of a muscle, on the combat of the wild beasts below: a solitary sovereign with the whole tremendous game played for himself, and inaccessible to the power of man.

I was forced away from this absorbing spectacle, and we once more threaded the long and intricate streets of Rome. As we approached the end of one of these bewildering passages, scarcely wide enough for us to ride abreast, I was startled by the sudden illumination of the sky immediately above; and rendered cautious by the experience of our hazards, called to my companion to return. He pointed behind me, and showed the fire bursting out in the houses by which we had just galloped. I followed on. A crowd that poured from the adjoining streets cut off our retreat. Hundreds rapidly mounted on the houses in front, in the hope by throwing them down to check the conflagration. The obstacle once removed, we saw the source of the light — spectacle of horror! The great prison of Rome was on fire. Never can I forget the sights and sounds — the dismay — the hopeless agony — the fury and frenzy that then overwhelmed the heart. The jailers had been forced to fly before they could loose the fetters or open the cells of the prisoners. We saw those gaunt and woe-begone wretches crowding to their casements, and imploring impossible help; clinging to the heated bars; toiling with their impotent grasp to tear out the massive stones; some wringing their hands; some calling on the terrified spectators by every name of humanity to save them; some venting their despair in execrations and blasphemies that made the blood run cold; others, after many a wild effort to break loose, dashing their heads against the walls, or stabbing themselves. The people gave them outcry for outcry; but the flame forbade approach. Before I could extricate myself from the multitude a whirl of fiery ashes shot upwards from the falling roof; the walls rent into a thousand fragments; and the huge prison with all its miserable inmates was a heap of red embers.

Exhausted as I was by this restless fatigue, and yet more by the melancholy sights that surrounded every step, no fatigue seemed to be felt by the singular being that governed my movements. He sprang through the burning ruins,— he plunged into the sulphurous smoke,— he never lost the direction that he had first taken; and though baffled and forced to turn back a hundred times, he again rushed on his track with the directness of an arrow. For me to make my way back to the gates would be even more difficult than to push forward. My ultimate safety might be in following, and I followed. To stand still and to move were equally perilous. The streets, even with the improvements of Augustus, were still scarcely wider than the breadth of the little Italian carts that crowded them. They were crooked, long, and obstructed by every impediment of a city built in haste, after the burning by the Gauls, and with no other plan than the caprice of its hurried tenantry. The houses were of immense height, chiefly wood, many roofed with thatch, and all covered or cemented with pitch. The true surprise is that it had not been burned once a year from the time of its building.

The memory of Nero, that hereditary concentration of vice, of whose ancestor's yellow beard the Roman orator said, "No wonder that his beard was brass, when his mouth was iron and his heart lead,"— the parricide and the poisoner — may yet be fairly exonerated of an act which might have been the deed of a drunken mendicant in any of the fifty thousand hovels of this gigantic aggregate of everything that could turn to flame.

We passed along through all the horrid varieties of misery, guilt, and riot that could find their place in a great public calamity: groups gazing in woe on the wreck of their fortunes, rushing off to the winds in vapor and fire; groups plundering in the midst of the flame; groups of rioters, escaped felons, and murderers, exulting in the public ruin, and dancing and drinking with Bacchanalian uproar; gangs of robbers trampling down and stabbing the fugitives to strip them of their last means; revenge, avarice, despair, profligacy, let loose naked; undisguised demons, to swell the wretchedness of this tremendous infliction upon a guilty and blood-covered empire.

Still we spurred on, but our jaded horses at length sank under us; and leaving them to find their way into the fields, we struggled forward on foot.

A WIFE'S INFLUENCE

From 'Catiline'

AURELIA — One hope there is, worth all the rest — Revenge!
    The time is harassed, poor, and discontent;
    Your spirit practiced, keen, and desperate, —
    The Senate full of feuds, — the city vext
    With petty tyranny — the legions wronged —

Catiline [*scornfully*] —
    Yet who has stirred? Woman, you paint the air
    With Passion's pencil.

Aurelia —   Were my will a sword!

Catiline — Hear me, bold heart! The whole gross blood of Rome
    Could not atone my wrongs! I'm soul-shrunk, sick,
    Weary of man! And now my mind is fixed
    For Sylla: there to make companionship
    Rather of bear and tiger — of the snake —
    The lion in his hunger — than of man!

Aurelia — I had a father once, who would have plunged
    Rome in the Tiber for an angry look!
    You saw our entrance from the Gaulish war,
    When Sylla fled?

Catiline —   My legion was in Spain.

Aurelia — We crept through Italy, a flood of fire,
    A living lava, rolling straight on Rome.
    For days, before we reached it, the whole road
    Was thronged with suppliants — tribunes, consulars;
    The mightiest names o' the State. Could gold have bribed,
    We might have pitched our tents, and slept on gold;

But we had work to do! Our swords were thirsty.
We entered Rome as conquerors, in arms;
I by my father's side, cuirassed and helmed,
Bellona beside Mars.

Catiline [*with coldness*] —   The world was yours!

Aurelia — Rome was all eyes; the ancient tottered forth;
The cripple propped his limbs beside the wall;
The dying left his bed to look, and die.
The way before us was a sea of heads;
The way behind a torrent of brown spears:
So, on we rode, in fierce and funeral pomp,
Through the long living streets, that sunk in gloom,
As we, like Pluto and Proserpina,
Enthroned, rode on — like twofold destiny!

Catiline [*sternly, interrupting her*] —
Those triumphs are but gewgaws. All the earth, —
What is it? Dust and smoke. I've done with life!

Aurelia [*coming closer and looking steadily upon him*] —
Before that eve, one hundred senators
And fifteen hundred knights had paid in blood
The price of taunts, and treachery, and rebellion!
Were my tongue thunder, I would cry — Revenge!

Catiline [*in sudden wildness*] —
No more of this! In to your chamber, wife!
There is a whirling lightness in my brain,
That will not now bear questioning. — Away!

         [*Aurelia moves slowly towards the door.*

Where are our veterans now? Look on these walls;
I cannot turn their tissues into life.
Where are our revenues — our chosen friends?
Are we not beggars? Where have beggars friends?
I see no swords and bucklers on these floors!
I shake the State! *I* — what have I on earth
But these two hands? Must I not dig or starve? —
Come back! I had forgot. My memory dies,
I think, by the hour. Who sups with us to-night?
Let all be of the rarest, — spare no cost.
If 'tis our last, — it may be, — let us sink
In sumptuous ruin, with wonderers round us, wife!
One funeral pile shall send up amber smoke!
We'll burn in myrrh, or — blood!

         [*She goes.*

I feel a nameless pressure on my brow,
As if the heavens were thick with sudden gloom;

A shapeless consciousness, as if some blow
Were hanging o'er my head. They say such thoughts
Partake of prophecy.

                    [He stands at the casement.

The air is living sweetness. Golden sun,
Shall I be like thee yet? The clouds have passed —
And, like some mighty victor, he returns
To his red city in the west, that now
Spreads all her gates, and lights her torches up
In triumph for her glowing conqueror.

THE LILY OF THE VALLEY

WHITE bud, that in meek beauty so dost lean
    Thy cloistered cheek as pale as moonlight snow,
Thou seem'st beneath thy huge high leaf of green,
    An eremite beneath his mountain's brow.

White bud! thou 'rt emblem of a lovelier thing,
    The broken spirit that its anguish bears
To silent shades, and there sits offering
    To Heaven the holy fragrance of its tears.

GEORGE CUPPLES

(1822–1891)

LTHOUGH the Scotch Lowlands were settled by men of pure Anglican blood, the neighboring Highlands and the original Celtic inhabitants of the locality have contributed a strain from another of the primitive Aryan stocks, to the great enrichment in fervor and emotional expressiveness of the people. The Scotchman retains the energy, perseverance, and executive masterfulness of his brothers in Yorkshire and Northumberland, but has in addition a vein of romantic imagination and a touch of Celtic excitability. He may be "dour and canny," and yet not destitute of an instinct for music and color. His name may contain the Celtic "Mac" or "Col," or the English "ton" or "son," but even when his name comes from one source his genius may derive from the other. Stevenson's name is English; but his literary work has the Celtic vividness, brilliancy, pathos, and sense of congruous form. Carlyle's name is Celtic; but in him lies the grim hardness of the Norse seafarers, and the deification of duty, and the impulse to subordinate form to substance, characteristic of the Saxon.

The Scotchman is born to a rich inheritance of tradition,—English wars, border forays, centuries of turbulent life embalmed in legend and ballad. He lives on the scene of action of historical personages, who become as real to him as Holyrood or Arthur's Seat. Scotch national consciousness lies deep in the soul of Scotchmen, though the kingdom be merged into Great Britain, and gives them an individuality and pride of lineage which colors their literature. They are loyal to the Bruce even when they sing 'God Save the Queen.' Blackwood's of the middle of the century, though reckoning the Englishmen Bulwer-Lytton and De Quincey among its honored contributors, was an intensely Scottish magazine; and its Scottish staff was marked by a distinctive literary tone,—a compound of boyish high spirits and old-fashioned conservatism such as we sometimes notice in the cadets of a noble house, to whom their family traditions are sacred, but the necessity of a decorous bearing before the world not at all apparent. The wit of the 'Noctes' is not very subtle, but it is hearty and clean, though it needs high spirits to make it seem amusing. The scholarship is not very profound, but it reaches back to traditions of gentlemanly culture and thoroughly distrusts modern preciosity. Nothing is literature in the estimation of these writers unless it is classic or Scotch. All of them are marked by a hearty love for outdoor sports, and a patriotism enthusiastic indeed, but rather circumscribed, though perhaps on that very account all the more intense. Professor Wilson is the most typical individual of these writers, and George Cupples of the next generation one of the most interesting, and on the whole the one whose literary gift was the most decided and original.

George Cupples was born at Legerwood, August 2d, 1822, and died October 7th, 1891. His father was a minister of the Free Kirk, and his paternal ancestors had been Calvinistic ministers for at least three generations. It was natural that the young man should be intended for the same profession, but he did not feel drawn to it, and when about seventeen went to sea for two years. Although of a firm physical constitution, the life of the seaman wearied him, and he resumed his education at the University of Edinburgh. He fell naturally into a literary career, and though much of his work was journalistic, he was reckoned in his day a critic of true insight. His novels are his best title to reputation, and show a vein of genuine creative power. Cupples combined some of the sterling and attractive traits of the cultured Scotchman of the period into a genuine, manly, and winning personality. Though slightly whimsical, his peculiarities were of the kind that endear a man to his friends; and Cupples numbered among his, Dr. John Brown, Dr. Stirling, Blackwood, and many others of the cultivated Scotchmen of the period.

'The Green Hand,' which came out in Blackwood from 1848 to 1851, is one of the best sea stories ever written. If we put Stevenson's 'Treasure Island' first for balance of description and narration, and sureness in the character touches, 'The Green Hand' and 'Tom Cringle's Log' are close seconds. Cupples's book is perhaps slightly overloaded with description, and deficient in technical construction as a narrative; but it is nevertheless a story which we read without skipping, for the descriptive pages are highly charged with the poetic element, and bear the unmistakable marks of being based on actual observation. Life in a sailing vessel has closer contact with the elemental moods of nature than in a steamer, where the motive power is a mechanical contrivance with the tiresome quality of regularity. To be in alliance or warfare with the wind, and dependent on its fitful moods, brought an element of variety and interest into the seaman's life which steam navigation, with its steadily revolving screw and patent valves, must always lack. Of this Cupples avails himself to the fullest extent; and it would be difficult to find a better presentation of the mysterious life and vastness of the ocean, and of the subtle impression it makes on those brought in daily contact with it, not excepting Victor Hugo's 'Toilers of the Sea.' This is due to

the fact that he spent two years before the mast when a young man.
Especially noticeable too is his admirable use of adjectives denoting
color, which are descriptive because they image truly the observations
of a man of genius, and are not, as in so much modern writing,
purple patches sewed on without any real feeling for the rich and
subtle scheme of nature. In calling up to the imagination the sounds
of the sea,— the creaking of the blocks, the wind in the rigging, the
wash of the water on the sides, the ripple on the bow, and the
infinite variety of the voice of the waves,— Cupples shows true poetic
power. It is not too much to say that 'The Green Hand' does not
suffer from the fact that one of the parts stands in the magazine in
juxtaposition to De Quincey's 'Vision of Sudden Death.'

'Kyloe Jock and the Weird of Wanton-Walls' is a transcript from
the boy life of the author. It appeared in Macmillan's Magazine, in
the autumn numbers of 1860. It is but a short sketch of a group of
simple people in a secluded border parish, but the quality of the
writer is shown as well in small things as in great ones. In it the
wintry scenes especially are given with broad and sure touches, for
the author is a genuine lover of nature; but the characters of Kirstie
the nurse, and of Kyloe Jock, the half-savage herd-boy who knows
so well the wild creatures of the woods and fields that he has even
given names to the foxes, show the feeling for human nature and the
ability to embody it which marks the artist. Kyloe Jock's Scotch is
said to be an absolutely perfect reproduction of the vernacular; and
it might be said that this book, like some of our modern Scotch
stories, would be better if the dialect were not quite so good.

The peculiar qualities of the author are not seen to such good
advantage in another book of his, 'Scotch Deerhounds and Their
Masters.' He was a breeder and unquestioned authority on the
"Grand Dog," and accumulated a store of curious information on its
origin and history; but his enthusiasm for this noble breed, or
"race" as he loves to call it,— and it certainly is the finest and most
striking of all the varieties of the "friend of man,"— led him into
some strange vagaries. One would almost suspect him of holding
the theory that dogs domesticated man, so high does he rank them
as agents of early civilization. His etymology and his ethnology are
alike erratic. He holds that every ancient people in whose name can
be found the combinations "gal," "alb," or "iber," or any other
syllable of a Celtic word, was of the Celtic family, and that the
Scotch deerhound and the Irish greyhound are descendants of the
primeval Celtic dog. In this way he proves that the Carthaginians
and the shepherd kings of Egypt were undoubtedly Celts, for their
sculpture shows that they hunted with large swift dogs that sprang
at the throat of their prey. On the other hand, every tribe that

owned large clumsy dogs that barked is probably non-Celtic. Mr. Cupples's contempt for such dogs is too intense for definite statement, and he evidently thinks that the tribe that owns them cannot hope to rise very high in the scale of civilization. This is certainly Philo-Celticism run mad, and is the more remarkable because Mr. Cupples could discover no Celtic strain in his own ancestry. He gave his dogs, however, Celtic names, as Luath, Shulach, Maida, Morna, Malvina, Oscar, etc. It would have been quite impossible for him to disgrace one of his "tall, swift, venatic hounds" with so Saxon a name as Rover or Barkis. But his enthusiasm is so genuine, and there is such a wealth of curious information in his pages, that his book has a charm and a substantial value of its own.

The other work of Mr. Cupples was, like that of most of the journalistic men of letters of the period, largely anonymous. His essay on Emerson, contributed to the Douglas Jerrold's Magazine, is very highly spoken of. Personally, Mr. Cupples must have been a man of great simplicity and charm, a happy combination of the genuine and most agreeable traits of that hearty and outspoken variety of man, the literary Scotchman.

IN THE TROPICS

From 'The Green Hand'

I LOOKED up the after-hatchway. It seemed still quite dark; and a patch of the deep dark-blue sky showed high over the square opening, with two or three keen sparks of stars, green ones and blue ones — you'd have thought the ladder, short as it was, went up to somewhere clean above the world. But the moment I got on deck I saw it was really lighter — the heavy fog creeping slowly astern off the ship on both hands; the white mist rolling faster over it before the sea breeze against her bows, which had swung seaward by this time from the tide, that rushed like a mill-stream upon both her tight cables; while the muddy river water, bubbling, eddying, and frothing away past, spread far up in the middle, into the dusk astern. *Such* a jabbering, croaking, hissing, shrieking, and yelling, too, as burst into one's ears out of the dark, as if whole legions of monkeys, bullfrogs, parrots, parrakeets, and what not, were coming together full upon us from both sides, one band nearer than the other; till the heavy boom of the surf round the point, and the roar of the tide coming in over the shallows about the river-mouth, pretty well drowned it. The sudden change was a good

relief,— Babel though it seemed after the closeness below,—
with what had been going on; and I looked ahead toward the
sea, which lay away out off our larboard bow, round the headland, and over the opposite point; a cold watery streak of light
showing it from where the breakers rose plunging and scattering
along the sandy bar, to the steady gray line of horizon, clipped
by one of the two brown chops we had got into. It looked
dreary enough as yet, the mouth of it being wider than I'd
fancied it from seaward at night: though even with full water
over the long spit of sand in the middle, there was no draught
at all for the Indiaman except by the channel betwixt it and the
bold point on our right; and pretty narrow it appeared from our
present berth, heaving as it did with the green swell that set in,
while meantime the mist scudding across the face of the headland let us see but the hard lump of bare black rock underneath.

In less time than I've taken to speak, however, the full space
of sky aloft was turning clear; the sea far away suddenly shone
out blue, with the surges tipped white; you saw a sparkling star
high over it sink slowly in, and the fog spread off the water
near us, till here and there you caught the muffled-up shape of
a big tree or two looming through, not half a mile off our starboard quarter; the mist creeping over the headland till the sharp
peak of it stood out against its shadow on the shoulder of a hill
beyond, and old Bob Martin's single clump of cocoas on the rise,
waving in landward from the brisk sea breeze. One passenger
after another came peeping sleepily out of the companion-hatch,
at the men clearing away the wreck of the spars and swabbing
the quarter-deck down; but scarce had Smith, one of the young
writers, reached the poop, when he gave a shout that covered
both poop ladders in no time, with people scrambling over each
other to get up. Next minute you'd have fancied them a knot
of flamingoes with their wings out, as the bright red daybreak
brought out the edge of the woods far astern, through a hazy
lane in the purple mist, topped so with stray cocoanut-trees and
cabbage-palms, dabbled like brushes in the color, that they
scarce knew them to be woods at all, and not a whole lot of
wild savages fresh from other business of the kind, coming down
with all sorts of queer tools upon us; more especially when one
heard such a chorus of unaccountable cries, whistling, and
screaming, as seemed to struggle with the sound of the sea
ahead of us, and the splash alongside. The huge round sun

struck hot crimson along the far turn of the beach, with all manner of twisted blots upon him, as it were, and the very grass and long reeds seemingly rustling into his face, so one didn't for the moment know *him* either; while the muddy, chocolate-colored eddies, sweeping and closing beyond the ship's rudder, glittered and frothed up like blood; and every here and there, along the streak of light, the head of a log or a long branch came dipping up terribly plain; no wonder the old Seringapatam had apparently turned tail to it all, ready to bolt if she could. Almost as soon as you took your hands off your eyes, though, and could see without a red ball or two before them, *there* was the nearest shore growing out toward our starboard bulwark all along, crowded with wet green woods, up into steaming high ground—all to eastward a dazzle of light, with two or three faint mountain peaks shooting up far off in it, and a woody blue hill or so between; while here and there a broad bright hazy spoke off the sun came cutting down into the forest, that brought a patch full of long big leaves, ten times greener than the rest, and let look off the deck into the heart of it among the stems over the bank. The jabber in the woods had passed off all at once with the dusk, the water deepening over the bar, and the tide running slower, so that every one's confused face turned breathless with delight and it grew stiller and stiller. The whole breadth of the river shone out by this time, full and smooth, to the opposite shore three times as far away, where the wood and bulrushes seemed to grow out of the water; a long thick range of low muddy-looking mangroves, with a cover of dark green, rounding from the farthest point one saw, down to some sandy hummocks near the mouth, and a ridge of the same drifted up by the wind off the beach. Beyond that side there was nothing apparently but a rolling sweep of long coarse grass, with a few straggling cocoanut-trees and baobabs like big swollen logs on end, and taken to sprouting at top; a dun-colored heave of land in the distance, too, that came out as it got hotter, in a long, desert-like, red brick-dust sort of a glare. The sole living things to be seen as yet were some small birds rising up out of the long grass, and the turkey-buzzards sailing high over all across, as if on the look-out.

The air was so cool and clear, however, from the tornado over night,—not a cloud in the sky, and the strange scent of the land reaching us as the dew rose off it,—you could see far and wide, with a delicious feeling of it all, that kept every one standing there on the spot where he first gained the deck, even the men looking over their shoulders with the ropes in their fists, and the fresh morning breeze lifting one's hair.

NAPOLEON AT ST. HELENA

From 'The Green Hand'

I HAD to get fairly off the saddle,—rather sore, I must say, with riding up St. Helena roads after so many weeks at sea, —and flung myself down on the grass, with little enough fear of the hungry little beast getting far adrift. This said crag, by the way, drew my eye to it by the queer colors it showed—white, blue, gray, and bright red—in the hot sunlight; and being too far off to make out clearly, I slung off the ship's glass I had across my back, just to overhaul it better. The hue of it was to be seen running all down the deep rift between, that seemingly wound away into some glen toward the coast; while the lot of plants and trailers half covering the steep front of it would no doubt, I thought, have delighted my old friend the Yankee, if he *was* the botanizing gentleman in question. By this time it was a lovely afternoon far and wide to Diana's Peak, the sky glowing clearer deep blue at that height than you'd have thought sky could do, even in the tropics—the very peaks of bare red rock being softened into a purple tint, far off around you. One saw into the rough bottom of the huge Devil's Punch Bowl, and far through without a shadow down the green patches in the little valleys, and over Deadwood Camp,—there was *nothing*, as it were, between the grass, the ground, the stones, and leaves, and the empty hollow of the air; while the sea spread far round underneath, of a softer blue than the sky over you. You'd have thought all the world was shrunk into St. Helena, with the Atlantic lying three-quarters round it in one's sight, like the horns of the bright new moon round the dim old one; which St. Helena pretty much resembled, if what the star-gazers say of its surface be true, all peaks and dry hollows—if indeed you weren't lifting up out of the world, so to speak, when one looked through his fingers right into the keen blue overhead!

If I lived a thousand years I couldn't tell half what I felt lying there; but as you may imagine, it had somewhat in it of the late European war by land and sea. Not that I could have said so at the time, but rather a sort of half-doze, such as I've known one have when a schoolboy, lying on the green grass the same way, with one's face turned up into the hot summer heavens; half of it flying glimpses, as it were, of the French Revolution, the battles we used to hear of when we were children — then the fears about the invasion, with the channel full of British fleets, and Dover Cliffs — Trafalgar and Nelson's death, and the battle of Waterloo, just after we heard *he* had got out of Elba. In the terrible flash of the thing all together, one almost fancied them all gone like smoke; and for a moment I thought I was falling away off, *down* into the wide sky, so up I started to sit. From that, suddenly I took to guessing and puzzling closely again how I should go to work myself, if I were the strange Frenchman I saw in the brig at sea, and wanted to manage Napoleon's escape out of St. Helena. And first, there was how to get into the island and put *him* up to the scheme — why, sure enough, I couldn't have laid it down better than they seemed to have done all along: what could one do but just dodge about that latitude under all sorts of false rig, then catch hold of somebody fit to cover one's landing. No Englishman *would* do it, and no foreigner but would set Sir Hudson Lowe on his guard in a moment. Next we should have to get put on the island — and really a neat enough plan it was, to dog one of the very cruisers themselves, knock up a mess of planks and spars in the night-time, set them all ablaze with tar, and pretend we were fresh from a craft on fire; when even Captain Wallis of the Podargus, as it happened, was too much of a British seaman not to carry us straight to St. Helena! Again, I must say it was a touch beyond me — but to hit the governor's notions of a hobby, and go picking up plants around Longwood, was a likely enough way to get speech of the prisoner, or at least let him see one was there!

How should I set about carrying him off to the coast, though? That was the prime matter. Seeing that even if the schooner — which was no doubt hovering out of sight — were to make a bold dash for the land with the trade-wind, in a night eleven hours long, — there were sentries close round Longwood from sunset, the starlight shining mostly always in the want of a moon; and at any rate there was rock and gully enough betwixt here and the coast to try the surest foot aboard the Hebe, let alone an emperor. With plenty of woods for a cover, one might steal up close to Longwood, but the bare rocks showed you off to be made a mark of. Whew! but why were those same blacks on the island, I thought: just strip them stark naked, and let them lie in the Devil's Punch Bowl, or somewhere beyond military hours, when I warrant me they might slip up, gully by gully, to the very sentries' backs! Their color wouldn't show them, and savages as they seemed, couldn't they settle as many sentries as they needed, creep into the very bedchamber where Bonaparte slept, and manhandle him bodily away down through some of the nearest hollows, before any one was the wiser? The point that still bothered me was, why the fourth of the blacks was wanting at present, unless he had his part to play elsewhere. If it was chance, then the *whole* might be a notion of mine, which I knew I was apt to have sometimes. If I could only make out the fourth black, so as to tally with the scheme, on the other hand, then I thought it was all sure; but of course this quite pauled me, and I gave it up, to work out my fancy case by providing signals betwixt us plotters inside and the schooner, out of sight from the telegraphs. There was no use for her to run in and take the risk, without good luck having turned up on the island; yet any sign she could profit by must be both sufficient to reach sixty miles or so, and hidden enough not to alarm the telegraphs or the cruisers. Here was a worse puzzle than all, and I only guessed at it for my own satisfaction — as a fellow can't help doing when he hears a question he can't answer — till my eye lighted on Diana's Peak, near three thousand feet above the sea. There it was, by Jove! 'Twas quite clear at the time; but by nightfall there was always more or less cloud near the top, and if you set a fire on the very peak 'twould only be seen leagues off: a notion that brought to mind a similar thing which I told you saved the Indiaman from a lee-shore one night on the African coast — and again, by George! I saw *that* must have been meant at first by the negroes as a smoke to help the French brig easier in! Putting that and that together, why it struck me at once what the fourth black's errand might be — namely, to watch for the schooner, and kindle his signal as soon as he couldn't see the island for mist. I was sure of it; and as for a dark night coming on at sea, the freshening of the breeze there promised nothing more likely; a bright white haze was softening out the horizon already, and here and there the egg of a cloud could be seen to break off the sky to windward, all of which would be better known afloat than here.

The truth was, I was on the point of tripping my anchor to hurry down and get aboard again; but on standing up, the head of a peak fell below the sail I had noticed in the distance, and seeing she loomed large on the stretch of water, I pretty soon found she must be a ship of the line. The telegraph over the Alarm House was hard at work again, so I e'en took down my glass and cleaned it to have a better sight, during which I caught sight, for a minute, of some soldier officer or other on horseback, with a mounted redcoat behind him, riding hastily up the gully a good bit from my back, till they were round the red piece of crag, turning at times as if to watch the vessel. Though I couldn't have a better spy at him for want of my glass, I had no doubt he was the governor himself, for the sentries in the distance took no note of him. There was nobody else visible at the time, and the said cliff stood fair up like a look-out place, so as to shut them out as they went higher. Once or twice after, I fancied I made out a man's head or two lower down the gully than the cliff was; which, it occurred to me, might possibly be the botanists, as they called themselves, busy finding out how long St. Helena had been an island; however, I soon turned the glass before me upon the ship, by this time right opposite the ragged opening of Prosperous Bay, and heading well up about fourteen miles or so off the coast, as I reckoned to make James Town harbor. The moment I had the sight of the glass right for her,—though you'd have thought she stood still on the smooth soft blue water,—I could see her whole beam rise off the swells before me, from the dark side and white band, checkered with a double row of ports, to the hamper of her lofty spars, and the sails braced slant to the breeze; the foam gleaming under her high bows, and her wake running aft in the heave of the sea. She was evidently a seventy-four; I fancied I could make out her men's faces peering over the yards toward the island, as they thought of "Boneypart"; a white rear-admiral's flag was at the mizenroyal masthead, leaving no doubt she was the Conqueror at last, with Admiral Plampin, and in a day or two at farthest the Hebe would be bound for India.

I had just looked over my shoulder toward Longwood, letting the Conqueror sink back again into a thing no bigger than

a model on a mantelpiece, when all at once I saw some one
standing near the brow of the cliff I mentioned, apparently
watching the vessel, with a long glass at his eye like myself.
'Twas farther than I could see to make out anything, save so
much; and ere I had screwed the glass for such a near sight,
there were seven or eight figures more appearing half over the
slope behind; while my hand shook so much with holding the
glass so long, that at first I brought it to bear full on the cracks
and blocks in the front of the crag, with the large green leaves
and trailers on it flickering idly with the sunlight against my
eyes, till I could have seen the spiders inside, I daresay. Next
I held it too high, where the admiral and Lord Frederick were
standing by their horses, a good way back; the governor, as I
supposed, sitting on his, and two or three others along the rise.
At length, what with kneeling down to rest it on one knee, I
had the glass steadily fixed on the brow of the rocks, where I
plainly saw a tall dark-whiskered man in a rich French uniform,
gazing to seaward. I knew him I sought too well by pictures,
however, not to be sadly galled. Suddenly a figure came slowly
down from before the rest, with his hands behind his back, and
his head a little drooped. The officer at once lowered the telescope and held it to him, stepping upward as if to leave him
alone — what dress he had on I scarce noticed; but there he was
standing, single in the round bright field of the glass I had hold
of like a vise — his head raised, his hands hiding his face, as I
kept the telescope fixed fair in front of me — only I saw the
smooth broad round of his chin. I knew, as if I'd seen him in
the Tuileries at Paris, or known him by sight since I was a boy,
— I *knew* it was Napoleon.

During that minute the rest of them were out of sight, so
far as the glass went — you'd have supposed there was no one
there but himself, as still as a figure in iron; watching the same
thing, no doubt, as I'd done myself five minutes before, where
the noble seventy-four was beating slowly to windward. When
I *did* glance to the knot of officers twenty yards back, 'twas as
if one saw a ring of his generals waiting respectfully while he
eyed some field of battle or other, with his army at the back of
the hill; but next moment the telescope fell in his hands, and
his face, as pale as death, with his lip firm under it, seemed
near enough for me to touch it — his eyes shot stern into me
from below his wide white forehead, and I started, dropping my

glass in turn. That instant the whole wild lump of St. Helena, with its ragged brim, the clear blue sky and the sea, swung round about the dwindled figures above the crag, till they were nothing but so many people together against the slope beyond.

'Twas a strange scene to witness, let me tell you; never can I forget the sightless, thinking sort of gaze from that head of his, after the telescope sank from his eye, when the Conqueror must have shot back with all her stately hamper into the floor of the Atlantic again! Once more I brought my spy-glass to bear on the place where he had been, and was almost on the point of calling out to warn him off the edge of the cliff, forgetting the distance I was away. Napoleon had stepped, with one foot before him, on the very brink, his two hands hanging loose by his side with the glass in one of them, till the shadow of his small black cocked hat covered the hollows of his eyes, and he stood as it were looking down past the face of the precipice. What he thought of, no mortal tongue can say: whether he was master at the time over a wilder battle than any he'd ever fought; but just then, what was the surprise it gave me to see the head of a man, with a red tasseled cap on it, raised through among the ivy from below, while he seemed to have his feet on the cracks and juts of the rock, hoisting himself by one hand round the tangled roots till no doubt he must have looked right aloft into the French Emperor's face; and perhaps he whispered something—though for my part it was all dumb show to me, where I knelt peering into the glass. I saw even *him* start at the suddenness of the thing—he raised his head upright, still glancing down over the front of the crag, with the spread hand lifted, and the side of his face half turned toward the party within earshot behind, where the governor and the rest apparently kept together out of respect, no doubt watching both Napoleon's back and the ship of war far beyond. The keen sunlight on the spot brought out every motion of the two in front—the *one* so full in my view, that I could mark his look settle again on the other below, his firm lips parting and his hand out before him like a man seeing a spirit he knew; while a bunch of leaves on the end of a wand came stealing up from the stranger's post to Napoleon's very fingers. The head of the man on the cliff turned round seaward for one moment, ticklish as his footing must have been; then he looked back, pointing with his loose hand to the horizon,—there was one minute between them without a motion, seemingly — the captive Emperor's chin was sunk on his breast, though you'd have said his eyes glanced up out of the shadow on his forehead; and the stranger's red cap hung like a bit of the bright colored cliff, under his two hands holding among the leaves. Then I saw Napoleon lift his hand calmly, he gave a sign with it — it might have been refusing, it might have been agreeing, or it might be farewell, I never expect to know; but he folded his arms across his breast, with the bunch of leaves in his fingers, and stepped slowly back from the brink toward the officers. I was watching the stranger below it, as he swung there for a second or two, in a way like to let him go dash to the bottom; his face sluing wildly seaward again. Short though the glance I had of him was, — his features set hard in some bitter feeling or other, his dress different too, besides the mustache being off, and his complexion no doubt purposely darkened, — it served to prove what I'd suspected: he was no other than the Frenchman I had seen in the brig; and mad or sensible, the very look I caught was more like that he faced the thunder-squall with, than aught beside. Directly after, he was letting himself carefully down with his back to my glass; the party above were moving off over the brow of the crags, and the governor riding round, apparently to come once more down the hollow between us. In fact, the seventy-four had stood by this time so far in that the peaks in the distance shut her out; but I ran the glass carefully along the whole horizon in my view, for signs of the schooner. The haze was too bright, however, to make sure either way; though, dead to windward, there were some streaks of cloud risen with the breeze, where I once or twice fancied I could catch the gleam of a speck in it. The Podargus was to be seen through a notch in the rocks, too, beating out in a different direction, as if the telegraph had signaled her elsewhere; after which you heard the dull rumble of the forts saluting the Conqueror down at James Town as she came in: and being late in the afternoon, it was high time for me to crowd sail downward, to fall in with my shipmates.

GEORGE WILLIAM CURTIS

(1824–1892)

BY EDWARD CARY

GEORGE WILLIAM CURTIS was born in Providence, R. I., February 24th, 1824, of a New England family, his ancestry on the father's side running back in unbroken line to the Massachusetts settlers of the first half of the seventeenth century. Though his home was in New York from early boyhood, he was through life a type—one of the best—of New England manhood. The firm, elastic, sometimes hard, fibre of a steadfast and intense moral sense was always found, occasion requiring, beneath the social grace and charm and the blithe and vivid fancy of the author. His schooling was brief—a few years only before the age of eleven. The rest of his education, which was varied and in some lines thorough, was gained by reading, with private tutors, with his accomplished and gifted stepmother, and—richest of all—alone. In 1842, while yet a lad of eighteen, he went for a couple of years as a boarder to Brook Farm. There, to quote his own words, "were the ripest scholars, men and women of the most æsthetic culture and accomplishment. young farmers, seamstresses, mechanics,

GEORGE W. CURTIS

preachers, the industrious, the lazy, the conceited, the sentimental. But they associated in such a spirit and under such conditions that, with some extravagance, the best of everybody appeared." "Compared with other efforts upon which time and money and industry are lavished, measured by Colorado and Nevada speculations, by California gold-washings, by oil-boring and the Stock Exchange, Brook Farm was certainly a very reasonable and practical enterprise, worthy of the hope and aid of generous men and women. The friendships that were formed there were enduring. The devotion to noble endeavor, the sympathy with what is most useful to men, the kind patience and constant charity that were fostered there, have been no more lost than the grain dropped upon the field."

These two years, and one spent on a farm at Concord, Massachusetts, near the homes of Emerson, Hawthorne, Thoreau, were followed by four years in Europe,— in Germany, Italy, France, Egypt; and in 1851, at the age of twenty-seven, Curtis took up seriously the work of a writer. Within a year he published two small volumes, 'The Nile Notes of a Howadji,' and 'The Howadji in Syria.' For a couple of years he was a writer on the New York Tribune, where his Brook Farm friends, Ripley and Dana, were engaged; and 'Lotus-Eating' was made up of letters to that paper from the then famous "watering-places." He dropped newspaper work to become an editor and writer with Putnam's Magazine, and the 'Potiphar Papers' and 'Prue and I' were written for that periodical. For a time he formed a connection with the printer of Putnam's in a publishing business; in which, and through the fault of others, he failed; assuming, quite beyond the requirements of the law, debts which it took a score of years to discharge. Finally he found his publishing home with the house of Harper and Brothers. At first a contributor to the Magazine and the Weekly, he became the editor of the Weekly and the writer of the "Easy Chair"; and from those two coignes of vantage, until his death on August 31st, 1892, he did what, apart from his lectures and addresses, was the work of his life. He made no more books, save the one not successful novel of 'Trumps,' written as a serial for the Weekly, and the volumes from the Addresses and the "Easy Chair" published after his death; yet he fulfilled the prophecy of Hawthorne on the appearance of the 'Nile Notes'—"I see that you are forever an author."

It would not be easy, were it worth while, exactly to classify Curtis; and if in general phrase we say that he was an essayist, that only betrays how comprehensive a label is needed to cover his work. Essays, long or short, the greater number of his writings were; each practically embraced a single subject, and of this presented one phase, important perhaps and grave, or light, amusing, tender, and sometimes satiric to the verge of bitterness—though never beyond it.

The Howadji books, which first gave him a name and fairly launched him as a writer, were a singular and original product, wholly different from what could have been expected of his training and associations; a venture in a field which, curiously enough, since the venture was in every sense more than ordinarily successful, he promptly and forever abandoned. "I aimed," he says in one of his private letters, "to represent the essentially sensuous, luxurious, languid, and sense-satisfied spirit of Eastern life." The style was adapted with courage, not to say audacity, to the aim. No American at that time had ever written English so riotously beyond the accepted conventions, so frankly, almost saucily, limited only by what the writer chose to say of what he felt or fancied under the inspiration of the East. Leigh Hunt compared the 'Nile Notes' to 'Eothen' and to 'Hyperion,' but the relation was extravagantly remote. The Howadji books were as individual as the lavish and brilliant bloom of a plant in the hot rays of the southern spring — and as passing. Once the shining and slightly gaudy flowers were shed, the normal growth proceeded to substantial fruitage.

The 'Potiphar Papers' were like the Eastern books in this, that they were at the time a still more successful venture in a field which, if not wholly abandoned by Curtis, was not continuously cultivated, but was only entered occasionally and never quite in the same spirit. They were a series of satires, fanciful enough in conception, but serious and almost savage in spirit, on the most conspicuous society of the day: its vulgarity, vanity, shallowness, and stupidity, the qualities inherent in the prevalent rivalry in money-spending. They were of marked importance at the time, because they were the brilliant and stinging comment of a gentleman and a patriot on a portion of society whose wealth gave dangerous prominence to the false standards set up and followed. Happily the vices Curtis scourged were those of an over-vigorous and unchastened youth of society, and the chief value of the satire now is as a picture of the past.

'Prue and I' was a series of papers written, as Curtis's letters show, in odd moments and with great rapidity, to meet the exigencies of the magazine. But the papers survive as an example of the pure literary work of the author. The opulence and extravagance of the 'Howadji' books disappear; but the rich imagination, the sportive fancy, the warm and life-giving sentiment, the broad philosophy, are expressed in a style of singular beauty, flexibility, and strength.

And it was in this line that the "Easy Chair" essays were continued, forming one of the most remarkable bodies of literary product of the time. They were written for Harper's Magazine, four or five monthly, equivalent each year to an ordinary duodecimo volume, and the series closed with the death of the writer some thirty-five years from their beginning. Their variety was very great. Some of them touched the events and questions of the time, and the time embraced the political contest with slavery, the Civil War, and the marvelously rapid and complex development of the nation after the war. But when the events or questions of the day were touched, it was at at once lightly and broadly, to illuminate and fix some suggestion of philosophy; through all ran the current of wise and gracious and noble thought or sentiment. Many of the essays were woven of reminiscence and comment on persons. In the little volume selected by himself and published shortly before his death, a dozen of the

twenty-seven were of this nature, embracing such varying person-
alities as Edward Everett, Browning, Wendell Phillips, Dickens,
Thoreau, Jenny Lind, Emerson, Joseph Jefferson. Whoever was thus
brought under the clear, soft, penetrating light of Curtis's pen lived
thereafter in the mind of the reader with a character more real and
just. In many of the essays of the "Easy Chair" there was a tone of
gentle satire, but always hopeful and helpful, not bitter or discouraging; as if in "Titbottom's Spectacles," that broke the heart of the
wearer with their revelation of the evil in those who passed before
them, new lenses had been set, revealing the everlasting beauty and
power of the ideal which evil violates, and to whose gracious and
blessing sway the writer, with a kindly smile at the incongruities of
the actual, invited his friend the reader. The very title had a gleam
of this subtle humor, it being well known to the profession, and
established by the experience of successive generations, that in
reality there is no such thing as an "editor's easy-chair." Even if
we allow for the fact that Curtis's seat was in his tranquil library on
Staten Island, remote from the complications and vexations of the
magazine's office, we must still recognize that the ease was not in the
chair, but in that firm high poise of the writer's spirit which enabled
him, with wisdom as unfailing as his gracious cheer, "to Report and
Consider all Matters of What Kind Soever."

Curtis was, perhaps, in his lifetime even more widely known as a
speaker than as a writer. At the very outset of his career he became one of the half-dozen lecturers under the curious and potent
lyceum system, that in the third quarter of the century did so much
to arouse and satisfy a deep interest in things of the mind in the
widely scattered communities of the American republic. At the
very outset, too, he entered with all his soul into the political agitation against slavery, and became one of the most stirring and most
highly regarded popular orators of the Republican party. Later he
was eagerly sought upon occasions of historical interest and for
memorial addresses. Still later he delivered the remarkable series of
addresses on the reform of the civil service, in what was in effect a
second struggle for political emancipation, waged with as broad a
human purpose, with as high courage, as was the struggle against
slavery, and with even a riper knowledge of the conditions of safety
for the republic. The great body of these addresses, many of the
slightest as well as the more elaborate, were essentially literary.
Most of them were written out and committed to memory, and many
were marked by more of the polish and completeness of the scholar's
conscientious and deliberate work than most of the writing intended
only for publication. But they were still the orator's work, addressed
to the ear, though fitted to bear the test of study, and intended

through the ear to touch the conscience and the heart and sway the will. Apart from the unfailing and lofty moral purpose that pervades them, their lasting charm lies in their music. They were the *emmelia*, the «well-tuned speech,» of the Greeks. But the hidden monitor who kept the orator true to the carefully chosen «pitch» was not the freedman of Gracchus, it was the sensitive and faithful artistic sense of the speaker. A writer lives in the world's literature, necessarily, by those of his writings that find a permanent form in books. Of these Curtis left few. But fairly to judge of his influence on the thought, and so on the life as well as the literature, of his country, we must remember that the unusual gifts and the rare spirit revealed in these few books pervaded also his work in the magazine and the journal; that the fruit of his work would fill a hundred volumes, and that it reached readers by the hundred thousand. Had Curtis sought only the fame of the writer, he could hardly have failed to gain it, and in notable measure. In pursuing the object he did, he might rightly believe at the close of his career — it is doubtful if he ever gave it a thought — that he had rendered to American literature a service unrecognized and untraceable, but singularly, perhaps uniquely, great.

Edward Cary.

THE MIST AT NEWPORT

From 'Lotus Eating.' Copyright, 1852, by Harper & Brothers

I RODE one afternoon with Undine along the southern shore of the Island, by the lonely graves of which I have spoken. We could see only a few feet over the water, but the ocean constantly plunged sullenly out of the heavy fog, which was full of hoarse roars and wailings,— the chaotic sound of the sea. We took the homeward path through the solitary fields, just unfamiliar enough to excite us with a vague sense of going astray. At times, gleams of sunlight, bewildered like ourselves, struggled, surprised, through the mist and disappeared. But strange and beautiful were those estrays; and I well understand why Turner studied vapors so long and carefully.

Two grander figures are not in contemporary biography than that of Coleridge, in Carlyle's 'Sterling,' looking out from Highgate over the mingled smoke and vapor which buries London, as

in lava Pompeii is buried; and that of Turner, in some anonymous but accurate sketches of his latter days, at his cottage on
the edge of London, where, apart from his fame and under a
feigned name, he sat by day and night upon the housetop, watching the sun glorify the vapors and the smoke with the same
splendor that he lavishes upon the evening west, and which we
deemed the special privilege of the sky. Those two men, greatest in their kind among their companions, illustrate with happy
force what Wordsworth sang:—

> «In common things that round us lie,
>   Some random truths he can impart,—
> The harvest of a quiet eye
>   That broods and sleeps on his own heart.»

Gazing from his Highgate window with "large gray eye," did
Coleridge see more than the image of his own mind and his own
career, in that limitless city, wide-sparkling, many-turreted, fading and mingling in shining mist,—with strange voices calling
from its clouds,—the solemn peal of cathedral chimes and the
low voice of the vesper bell; and out of that London fog with
its irresistible splendors, and out of the holy vapors which float
serene amid the Alps, has Turner quarried his colossal fame.
There is no grander lesson in any history of any art than the
spectacle of the greatest painter of our time, sitting upon his
house-top, and from the mist which to others was but a clog and
inconvenience, and associated in all men's minds only with link-
boys and lanterns, plucking the heart of its mystery and making
it worshiped and remembered.

NAZARETH

From 'Howadji in Syria.' Copyright, 1856, by Harper & Brothers

THE traditions which cluster around Nazareth are so tender and
domestic that you will willingly believe, or at least you will
listen to, the improbable stories of the friars as a father
to the enthusiastic exaggerations of his child. With Jerusalem
and its vicinity the gravity of the doctrine is too intimately
associated to allow the mind to heed the quarrels and theories
about the localities. It is the grandeur of the thought which
commands you. But in Nazareth it is the personality of the
Teacher which interests you. All the tenderness of the story

centers here. The youth of the Madonna and the unrecorded years of the Child belong to Nazareth. Therefore imagination unbends to the sweet associations of domestic life. The little picture in the Uffizi recurs again, and the delicate sketches of Overbeck, illustrating the life of Christ, in which as a blooming boy in his father's shop he saws a bit of wood into the form of a cross, looking up smilingly to the thoughtful Joseph and the yearning Mary, as when he brings her the passion-flower in the pleasant room.

The tranquil afternoon streams up the valley, and your heart is softened as if by that tender smile of Mary; and yielding to soliciting friars, you go quietly and see where Joseph's house stood, and where the Angel Gabriel saluted Mary, and the chimney of the hearth upon which she warmed food for her young child, and baked cakes for Joseph when he came home from work, and the rock whence the Jews wished to cast Jesus, and another rock upon which he ate with his disciples.

You listen quietly to these stories, and look at the sights. The childish effort to give plausible form to the necessary facts of the history of the place is too natural to offend. When the pretense is too transparent you smile, but do not scold. For whether he lived upon this side of the way or upon that, this is the landscape he saw for thirty years. A quiet workman, doubtless, with his father, strolling among the melancholy hills of Galilee, looking down into the lake-like vastness of Esdraëlon, where the great captains of his nation had fought,— hearing the wild winds blow from the sea, watching the stars, and remembering the three days of his childhood when he sat in the temple at Jerusalem.

Walking in the dying day over the same solitary hills, you will see in the sunset but one figure moving along the horizon,— a grave manly form, outlined upon the west.

Here was the true struggle of his life — the resolve to devote himself to the work. These are the exceeding high mountains upon which he was lifted in temptation; here in the fullness of his youth and hope Satan walked with him, seductive. For every sin smiles in the first address, says Jeremy Taylor, and carries light in the face and honey in the lip. Green and flowery as Esdraëlon lay the valleys of ease and reputation at his feet; but sternly precipitous as the heights of Galilee, the cliffs of duty above him buried their heads in heaven.

Here too was he transfigured; and in the light of thought he floats between Moses and Elias, between faith and duty, and the splendor of his devotion so overflows history with glory that men call him God.

AURELIA AS A GRANDMOTHER

From 'Prue and I.' Copyright, 1856, by Harper & Brothers

THERE will be a time when you will no longer go out to dinner; or only very quietly, in the family. I shall be gone then; but other old bookkeepers in white cravats will inherit my tastes, and saunter on summer afternoons to see what I loved to see.

They will not pause, I fear, in buying apples, to look at the old lady in venerable cap who is rolling by in the carriage. They will worship another Aurelia. You will not wear diamonds or opals any more, only one pearl upon your blue-veined finger,— your engagement ring. Grave clergymen and antiquated beaux will hand you down to dinner, and the group of polished youth who gather around the yet unborn Aurelia of that day will look at you, sitting quietly upon the sofa, and say softly, "She must have been very handsome in her time."

All this must be; for consider how few years since it was your grandmother who was the belle, by whose side the handsome young men longed to sit and pass expressive mottoes. Your grandmother was the Aurelia of a half-century ago, although you cannot fancy her young. She is indissolubly associated in your mind with caps and dark dresses. You can believe Mary Queen of Scots, or Nell Gwyn, or Cleopatra, to have been young and blooming, although they belonged to old and dead centuries; but not your grandmother. Think of those who shall believe the same of you — you, who to-day are the very flower of youth.

Might I plead with you, Aurelia, — I, who would be too happy to receive one of those graciously beaming bows that I see you bestow upon young men, in passing,— I would ask you to bear that thought with you always, not to sadden your sunny smile, but to give it a more subtle grace. Wear in your summer garland this little leaf of rue. It will not be the skull at the feast, it will rather be the tender thoughtfulness in the face of the young Madonna.

For the years pass like summer clouds, Aurelia, and the children of yesterday are the wives and mothers of to-day. Even I do sometimes discover the mild eyes of my Prue fixed pensively upon my face, as if searching for the bloom which she remembers there in the days, long ago, when we were young. She will never see it there again, any more than the flowers she held in her hand, in our old spring rambles. Yet the tear that slowly gathers as she gazes is not grief that the bloom has faded from my cheek, but the sweet consciousness that it can never fade from my heart; and as her eyes fall upon her work again, or the children climb her lap to hear the old fairy-tales they already know by heart, my wife Prue is dearer to me than the sweetheart of those days long ago.

PRUE'S MAGNOLIA

From 'Prue and I.' Copyright, 1892, by Harper & Brothers

IF I meet Charles, who is bound for Alabama, or John, who sails for Savannah, with a trunk full of white jackets, I do not say to them, as their other friends say:—

"Happy travelers, who cut March and April out of the dismal year!"

I do not envy them. They will be seasick on the way. The Southern winds will blow all the water out of the rivers; and, desolately stranded upon mud, they will relieve the tedium of the interval by tying with large ropes a young gentleman raving with delirium tremens. They will hurry along, appalled by forests blazing in the windy night; and housed in a bad inn, they will find themselves anxiously asking, "Are the cars punctual in leaving?"—grimly sure that impatient travelers find all conveyances too slow. The travelers are very warm indeed, even in March and April,—but Prue doubts if it is altogether the effect of the Southern climate.

Why should they go to the South? If they only wait a little, the South will come to them. Savannah arrives in April; Florida in May; Cuba and the Gulf come in with June; and the full splendor of the Tropics burns through July and August.

Sitting upon the earth, do we not glide by all the constellations, all the awful stars? Does not the flash of Orion's scimitar dazzle as we pass? Do we not hear, as we gaze in hushed midnights, the music of the Lyre; are we not throned with Cassiopeia; do we not play with the tangles of Berenice's hair, as we sail, as we sail?

When Christopher told me that he was going to Italy, I went into Bourne's conservatory, saw a magnolia, and so reached Italy before him. Can Christopher bring Italy home? But I brought to Prue a branch of magnolia blossoms, with Mr. Bourne's kindest regards, and she put them upon her table, and our little house smelled of Italy for a week afterward. The incident developed Prue's Italian tastes, which I had not suspected to be so strong. I found her looking very often at the magnolias; even holding them in her hand, and standing before the table with a pensive air. I suppose she was thinking of Beatrice Cenci, or of Tasso and Leonora, or of the wife of Marino Faliero, or of some other of those sad old Italian tales of love and woe. So easily Prue went to Italy.

Thus the spring comes in my heart as well as in the air, and leaps along my veins as well as through the trees. I immediately travel. An orange takes me to Sorrento, and roses, when they blow, to Pæstum. The camellias in Aurelia's hair bring Brazil into the happy rooms she treads, and she takes me to South America as she goes to dinner. The pearls upon her neck make me free of the Persian Gulf. Upon her shawl, like the Arabian prince upon his carpet, I am transported to the vales of Cashmere; and thus, as I daily walk in the bright spring days, I go around the world.

But the season wakes a finer longing, a desire that could only be satisfied if the pavilions of the clouds were real, and I could stroll among the towering splendors of a sultry spring evening. Ah! if I could leap those flaming battlements that glow along the west — if I could tread those cool, dewy, serene isles of sunset, and sink with them in the sea of stars.

I say so to Prue, and my wife smiles.

OUR COUSIN THE CURATE

From 'Prue and I.'   Copyright, 1856, by Harper & Brothers

WHEN Prue and I are most cheerful, and the world looks fair
—we talk of our cousin the curate. When the world
seems a little cloudy, and we remember that though we
have lived and loved together we may not die together—we talk
of our cousin the curate. When we plan little plans for the boys
and dream dreams for the girls—we talk of our cousin the
curate. When I tell Prue of Aurelia, whose character is every
day lovelier—we talk of our cousin the curate. There is no
subject which does not seem to lead naturally to our cousin the
curate. As the soft air steals in and envelops everything in the
world, so that the trees, and the hills, and the rivers, the cities,
the crops, and the sea, are made remote and delicate and beautiful by its pure baptism, so over all the events of our little lives
—comforting, refining, and elevating—falls like a benediction the
remembrance of our cousin the curate.

He was my only early companion. He had no brother, I
had none; and we became brothers to each other. He was
always beautiful. His face was symmetrical and delicate; his
figure was slight and graceful. He looked as the sons of kings
ought to look; as I am sure Philip Sidney looked when he was
a boy. His eyes were blue, and as you looked at them they
seemed to let your gaze out into a June heaven. The blood ran
close to the skin, and his complexion had the rich transparency
of light. There was nothing gross or heavy in his expression or
texture; his soul seemed to have mastered his body. But he
had strong passions, for his delicacy was positive, not negative;
it was not weakness, but intensity.

There was a patch of ground about the house which we tilled
as a garden. I was proud of my morning-glories and sweet-
peas; my cousin cultivated roses. One day—and we could
scarcely have been more than six years old—we were digging
merrily and talking. Suddenly there was some kind of difference; I taunted him, and raising his spade he struck me upon
the leg. The blow was heavy for a boy, and the blood trickled
from the wound. I burst into indignant tears, and limped
toward the house. My cousin turned pale and said nothing; but
just as I opened the door he darted by me, and before I could

interrupt him he had confessed his crime and asked for punishment.

From that day he conquered himself. He devoted a kind of ascetic energy to subduing his own will, and I remember no other outbreak. But the penalty he paid for conquering his will was a loss of the gushing expression of feeling. My cousin became perfectly gentle in his manner; but there was a want of that pungent excess which is the finest flavor of character. His views were moderate and calm. He was swept away by no boyish extravagance; and even while I wished he would sin only a very little, I still adored him as a saint. The truth is, as I tell Prue, I am so very bad because I have to sin for two — for myself and our cousin the curate. Often, when I returned panting and restless from some frolic which had wasted almost all the night, I was rebuked as I entered the room in which he lay peacefully sleeping. There was something holy in the profound repose of his beauty; and as I stood looking at him, how many a time the tears have dropped from my hot eyes upon his face while I vowed to make myself worthy of such a companion,— for I felt my heart owning its allegiance to that strong and imperial nature.

My cousin was loved by the boys, but the girls worshiped him. His mind, large in grasp and subtle in perception, naturally commanded his companions, while the lustre of his character allured those who could not understand him. The asceticism occasionally showed itself in a vein of hardness, or rather of severity, in his treatment of others. He did what he thought it his duty to do; but he forgot that few could see the right so clearly as he, and very few of those few could so calmly obey the least command of conscience. I confess I was a little afraid of him, for I think I never could be severe.

In the long winter evenings I often read to Prue the story of some old father of the church, or some quaint poem of George Herbert's; and every Christmas Eve I read to her Milton's 'Hymn of the Nativity.' Yet when the saint seems to us most saintly, or the poem most pathetic or sublime, we find ourselves talking of our cousin the curate. I have not seen him for many years; but when we parted, his head had the intellectual symmetry of Milton's, without the Puritanic stoop, and with the stately grace of a Cavalier

THE CHARM OF PARIS

From 'The Potiphar Papers.' Copyright, 1858, by Harper & Brothers

"Yes, my dear Madame," answered the Pacha, "this is indeed making the best of one's opportunities. This is well worth coming to Europe for. It is in fact for this that Europe is chiefly valuable to an American, as the experience of an observer shows. Paris is notoriously the great centre of historical and romantic interest. To be sure, Italy, Rome, Switzerland, and Germany—yes, and even England—have some few objects of interest and attention; but the really great things of Europe, the superior interests, are all in Paris. Why, just reflect. Here is the Café de Paris, the Trois Frères, and the Maison Dorée. I don't think you can get such dinners elsewhere. Then there is the Grand Opera, the Comic Opera, and now and then the Italian—I rather think that is good music. Are there any such theatres as the Vaudeville, the Variétés, and the Montansier, where there is the most dexterous balancing on the edge of decency that ever you saw? and when the balance is lost, as it always is at least a dozen times every evening, the applause is tremendous, showing that the audience have such a subtle sense of propriety that they can detect the slightest deviation from the right line. Is there not the Louvre, where, if there is not the best picture of a single great artist, there are good specimens of all? Will you please to show me such a promenade as the Boulevards, such fêtes as those of the Champs Elysées, such shops as those of the Passages and the Palais Royal? Above all, will you indicate to such students of mankind as Mr. Boosey, Mr. Firkin, and I, a city more abounding in piquant little women, with eyes, and coiffures and toilettes, and *je ne sais quoi*, enough to make Diogenes a dandy, to obtain their favor? I think, dear madame, you would be troubled to do it. And while these things are Paris, while we are sure of an illimitable allowance of all this in the gay capital, we do right to remain here. Let who will, sadden in moldy old Rome, or luxuriate in the orange groves of Sorrento and the South, or wander among the ruins of the most marvelous of empires, and the monuments of art of the highest human genius, or float about the canals of Venice, or woo the Venus and the Apollo, and learn from the silent lips of those teachers a lore sweeter than the French novelists impart; let who will, climb the tremendous Alps, and feel the sublimity of Switzerland as he rises from the summer of Italian lakes and vineyards into the winter of the glaciers, or makes the tour of all climates in a day by descending those mountains towards the south; let those who care for it, explore in Germany the sources of modern history, and the remote beginnings of the American spirit; — ours be the boulevards, the demoiselles, the operas, and the unequaled dinners. Decency requires that we should see Rome, and climb an Alp. We will devote a summer week to the one, and a winter month to the other. They will restore us, renewed and refreshed, for the manly, generous, noble, and useful life we lead in Paris."

«PHARISAISM OF REFORM»

From ʿOrations and Addresses.ʾ Copyright, 1893, by Harper & Brothers

No AMERICAN, it seems to me, is so unworthy the name as he who attempts to extenuate or defend any national abuse, who denies or tries to hide it, or who derides as pessimists and Pharisees those who indignantly disown it and raise the cry of reform. If a man proposes the redress of any public wrong, he is asked severely whether he considers himself so much wiser and better than other men, that he must disturb the existing order and pose as a saint. If he denounces an evil, he is exhorted to beware of spiritual pride. If he points out a dangerous public tendency or censures the action of a party, he is advised to cultivate good-humor, to look on the bright side, to remember that the world is a very good world, at least the best going, and very much better than it was a hundred years ago.

Undoubtedly it is; but would it have been better if everybody had then insisted that it was the best of all possible worlds, and that we must not despond if sometimes a cloud gathered in the sky, or a Benedict Arnold appeared in the patriot army, or even a Judas Iscariot among the chosen twelve? Christ, I think, did not doubt the beloved disciple nor the coming of his kingdom, although he knew and said that the betrayer sat with him at the table. I believe we do not read that Washington either thought it wiser that Arnold's treachery should be denied or belittled, or that he or any other patriot despaired although the treason was so grave. Julius Cæsar or Marlborough or Frederick would hardly be called a great general if he had rebuked the soldier who reported that the lines were beginning to break. When the sea is pouring into the ship through an open seam, everybody is aware of it. But then it is too late. It is the watch who reports the first starting of the seam who saves the ship.

It is an ill sign when public men find in exposure and denunciation of public abuses evidence of the pharisaic disposition and a tendency in the critic to think himself holier than other men. Was Martin Luther, cheerfully defending his faith against the princes of Christendom, a Pharisee? Were the English Puritans, iconoclasts in Church and State but saviors of liberty, pessimists? Were Patrick Henry demanding liberty or death, and Wendell Phillips in the night of slavery murmuring the music of the morning, birds of ill omen? Was Abraham Lincoln saying of the American Union, "A house divided with itself cannot stand," assuming to be holier than other Americans? To win a cheap cheer, I have known even intelligent men to sneer at the scholar in politics. But in a republic founded upon the common school, such a sneer seems to me to show a momentary loss of common-sense. It implies that the political opinions of educated men are unimportant and that ignorance is a safer counselor of the republic. If the gentleman who in this very hall last stooped to that sneer, had asked himself what would have been the fortune of this State and this country without its educated leadership, from Samuel Adams to Charles Sumner,— both sons of Massachusetts, both scholars in politics from Harvard College,— he might have spared his country, his party, and himself, the essential recreancy to America and to manhood which lies in a sneer at education. To the cant about the pharisaism of reform there is one short and final answer. The man who tells the truth *is* a holier man than the liar. The man who does not steal *is* a better man than the thief.

THE CALL OF FREEDOM

From 'Orations and Addresses.' Copyright, 1893, by Harper & Brothers

INTO how many homes along this lovely valley came the news of Lexington and Bunker Hill eighty years ago; and young men like us, studious, fond of leisure, young lovers, young husbands, young brothers, and sons, knew that they must forsake the wooded hillside, the river meadows golden with harvest, the twilight walk along the river, the summer Sunday in the old church, parents, wife, child, mistress, and go away to uncertain war. Putnam heard the call at his plow, and turned to go without waiting. Wooster heard it, and obeyed.

Not less lovely in those days was this peaceful valley, not less soft this summer air. Life was as dear and love as beautiful to those young men as to us who stand upon their graves. Bnt because they were so dear and beautiful, those men went out bravely to fight for them and fall. Through these very streets they marched, who never returned. They fell and were buried; but they never can die. Not sweeter are the flowers that make your valley fair, not greener are the pines that give your river its name, than the memory of the brave men who died for freedom. And yet no victim of those days, sleeping under the green sod of Connecticut, is more truly a martyr of Liberty than every murdered man whose bones lie bleaching in this summer sun upon the silent plains of Kansas.

Gentlemen, while we read history we make history. Because our fathers fought in this great cause, we must not hope to escape fighting. Because two thousand years ago Leonidas stood against Xerxes, we must not suppose that Xerxes was slain, nor, thank God! that Leonidas is not immortal. Every great crisis of human history is a pass of Thermopylæ, and there is always a Leonidas and his three hundred to die in it, if they cannot conquer. And so long as Liberty has one martyr, so long as one drop of blood is poured out for her, so long from that single drop of bloody sweat of the agony of humanity shall spring hosts as countless as the forest leaves and mighty as the sea.

Brothers! the call has come to us. I bring it to you in these calm retreats. I summon you to the great fight of Freedom. I call upon you to say with your voices, whenever the occasion offers, and with your votes when the day comes, that upon these fertile fields of Kansas, in the very heart of the continent, the upas-tree of slavery, dripping death-dews upon national prosperity and upon free labor, shall never be planted. I call upon you to plant there the palm of peace, the wine and the olive of a Christian civilization. I call upon you to determine whether this great experiment of human freedom, which has been the scorn of despotism, shall by our failure be also our sin and shame. I call upon you to defend the hope of the world.

The voice of our brothers who are bleeding, no less than our fathers who bled, summons us to this battle. Shall the children of unborn generations, clustering over that vast western empire, rise up and call us blessed or cursed? Here are our Marathon and Lexington; here are our heroic fields. The hearts of all good men beat with us. The fight is fierce — the issue is with God. But God is good.

ROBERT BROWNING IN FLORENCE

From 'The Easy Chair.' Copyright, 1891, by Harper & Brothers

IT is more than forty years since Margaret Fuller first gave distinction to the literary notices and reviews of the New York Tribune. Miss Fuller was a woman of extraordinary scholarly attainments and intellectual independence, the friend of Emerson and of the "Transcendental" leaders; and her critical papers were the best then published, and were fitly succeeded by those of her scholarly friend, George Ripley. It was her review in the Tribune of Browning's early dramas and the 'Bells and Pomegranates' that introduced him to such general knowledge and appreciation among cultivated readers in this country, that it is not less true of Browning than of Carlyle that he was first better known in America than at home.

It was but about four years before the publication of Miss Fuller's paper that the Boston issue of Tennyson's two volumes had delighted the youth of the time with the consciousness of the appearance of a new English poet. The eagerness and enthusiasm with which Browning was welcomed soon after were more limited in extent, but they were even more ardent; and the devoted zeal of Mr. Levi Thaxter as a Browning missionary and pioneer forecast the interest from which the Browning societies of later days have sprung. When Matthew Arnold was told in a small and remote farming village in New England that there had been a lecture upon Browning in the town the week before, he stopped in amazement, and said, "Well, that is the most surprising and significant fact I have heard in America."

It was in those early days of Browning's fame, and in the studio of the sculptor Powers in Florence, that the youthful Easy Chair took up a visiting-card, and reading the name Mr. Robert Browning, asked with eager earnestness whether it was Browning the poet. Powers turned his large, calm, lustrous eyes upon the youth, and answered, with some surprise at the warmth of the question:—

"It is a young Englishman, recently married, who is here with his wife, an invalid. He often comes to the studio."

"Good Heaven!" exclaimed the youth, "it must be Browning and Elizabeth Barrett."

Powers, with the half-bewildered air of one suddenly made conscious that he had been entertaining angels unawares, said reflectively, "I think we must have them to tea."

The youth begged to take the card which bore the poet's address, and hastening to his room near the Piazza Novella, he wrote a note asking permission for a young American to call and pay his respects to Mr. and Mrs. Browning; but wrote it in terms which, however warm, would yet permit it to be put aside if it seemed impertinent, or if for any reason such a call were not desired. The next morning betimes the note was dispatched, and a half-hour had not passed when there was a brisk rap at the Easy Chair's door. He opened it and saw a young man, who briskly inquired:—

"Is Mr. Easy Chair here?"

"That is my name."

"I am Robert Browning."

Browning shook hands heartily with his young American admirer, and thanked him for his note. The poet was then about thirty-five. His figure was not large, but compact, erect, and active; the face smooth, the hair dark; the aspect that of active intelligence, and of a man of the world. He was in no way eccentric, either in manner or appearance. He talked freely, with great vivacity, and delightfully, rising and walking about the room as his talk sparkled on. He heard with evident pleasure, but with entire simplicity and manliness, of the American interest in his works and in those of Mrs. Browning; and the Easy Chair gave him a copy of Miss Fuller's paper in the Tribune.

It was a bright, and to the Easy Chair a wonderfully happy hour. As he went, the poet said that Mrs. Browning would certainly expect to give Mr. Easy Chair a cup of tea in the evening; and with a brisk and gay good-by, Browning was gone.

The Easy Chair blithely hied him to the Café Doné, and ordered of the flower-girl the most perfect of nosegays, with such fervor that she smiled; and when she brought the flowers in the afternoon, said with sympathy and meaning, "Eccola, signore! per la donna bellissima!"

It was not in the Casa Guidi that the Brownings were then living, but in an apartment in the Via della Scala, not far from the place or square most familiar to strangers in Florence — the Piazza Trinità. Through several rooms the Easy Chair passed, Browning leading the way; until at the end they entered a smaller room arranged with an air of English comfort, where at a table, bending over a tea-urn, sat a slight lady, her long curls drooping forward. "Here," said Browning, addressing her with a tender diminutive, "here is Mr. Easy Chair." And, as the bright eyes but wan face of the lady turned towards him, and she put out her hand, Mr. Easy Chair recalled the first words of her verse he had ever known:—

> "'Onora, Onora!' her mother is calling;
> She sits at the lattice, and hears the dew falling,
>   Drop after drop from the sycamore laden
> With dew as with blossom, and calls home the maiden:
>   'Night cometh, Onora!'"

The most kindly welcome and pleasant chat followed, Browning's gayety dashing and flashing in, with a sense of profuse and bubbling vitality, glancing at a hundred topics; and when there was some allusion to his 'Sordello,' he asked, quickly, with an amused smile, "Have you read it?" The Easy Chair pleaded that he had not seen it. "So much the better. Nobody understands it. Don't read it, except in the revised form, which is coming." The revised form has come long ago, and the Easy Chair has read, and probably supposes that he understands. But Thackeray used to say that he did not read Browning, because he could not comprehend him, adding ruefully, "I have no head above my eyes."

A few days later—

"O gift of God! O perfect day!"—

the Easy Chair went with Mr. and Mrs. Browning to Vallombrosa, and the one incident most clearly remembered is that of Browning's seating himself at the organ in the chapel, and playing,—some Gregorian chant, perhaps, or hymn of Pergolesi's. It was enough to the enchanted eyes of his young companion that they saw him who was already a great English poet sitting at the organ where the young Milton had sat, and touching the very keys which Milton's hand had pressed.

ERNST CURTIUS

(1814–1896)

ERNST CURTIUS, a noted German archæologist and historian, was born at Lübeck September 2d, 1814. He studied philology at Bonn, Göttingen, and Berlin. When in 1837 Christian August Brandis was appointed confidential adviser to Prince Otho of Bavaria, the newly elected king of Greece, Curtius accompanied Brandis's family to Athens as a private tutor. He remained with the Brandises until 1840, when he joined Ottfried Müller's archæological expedition to Delphi. No sooner were the excavations well under way, however, than Müller died. Curtius thereupon returned to Germany, stopping at Rome on the way; and in 1841 took his doctor's degree at Halle.

In 1844 he was appointed tutor to the Crown Prince of Prussia (the late Emperor Frederick), being at the same time made a professor extraordinary at the University of Berlin. He held his position as tutor to the Crown Prince until 1850, when the latter matriculated at Bonn. In 1856 he succeeded Hermann as professor of classical philology at Göttingen, but returned some twelve years later to Berlin to occupy the chair of classical archæology and to act as director of the cabinet of antiquities in the Royal Museum

ERNST CURTIUS

Curtius also much advanced the study of classical archæology as presiding officer of the Archæological Society, as editor of the Archæological Journal, as perpetual secretary of the Royal Academy, and as the founder of the German Archæological Institute at Athens. He undertook a number of scientific missions in the service of the Prussian government, and in 1874 concluded with the Greek government a convention which secured to the German Empire for a term of years the exclusive right to make excavations in the Greek kingdom. The following year the first excavation was begun at Olympia in Elis, the site of the ancient Olympic games, under the direction of Curtius, who with others published the results in a voluminous and most interesting report.

Curtius's chief work is his 'History of Greece,' which appeared in 1867. It was originally published in three volumes as one of a series of manuals for classical students issued by a Berlin house, and was consequently intended for popular use; a circumstance that necessitated the omission of the copious notes in which the text of a German scientific work is commonly lost. It showed a remarkable familiarity with the climate, resources, and physical characteristics of Greece; and interpreted ancient life with much eloquence from the classical literature and from the monuments of ancient art. But the monarchical leaning of the author prevented him from entering fully into and appreciating the public life of the democratic communities which he described; and his enthusiastic temperament led him sometimes to exaggerate and to be too eager a partisan, to accept unproven hypotheses too readily and press them too hard.

Besides his 'History of Greece,' Curtius's most notable works are 'Peloponnesos' (1850–51), which describes in detail the ancient remains on the Peloponnesus; 'Die Stadtgeschichte von Athen' (Municipal History of Athens: 1891), and 'Sieben Karten zur Topographie von Athen nebst erläuterndem Text' (Seven Maps of Athens: 1886). His life was a busy and eminently distinguished one, as an archæologist, historian, and instructor, and his death in the summer of 1896 was generally lamented by his associates.

THE CAUSES OF DISLIKE TOWARD SOCRATES

From the 'History of Greece'

THE Athenians disliked men who wished to be different from every one else; particularly when these eccentrics, instead of quietly pursuing their own path and withdrawing from the world like Timon, forced themselves among their neighbors and assumed towards them the attitude of pedagogues, as Socrates did. For what could be more annoying to an Athenian of repute than to find himself, on his way to the council meeting or the law court, unexpectedly involved in a conversation intended to confuse him, to shake his comfortable self-assurance, and to end by making him ridiculous? In any other city such conversation would have been altogether hard to manage; but at Athens the love of talk was so great that many allowed themselves to be caught, and that gradually the number became very large of those who had been the victims of this inconvenient questioner, and who carried about with them the remembrance of a humiliation inflicted on them by him. And most of all was he hated by those who had allowed themselves to be touched and moved to tears of a bitter recognition of their own selves by his words, but who had afterwards sunk back into their former ways and were now ashamed of their hours of weakness. Thus Socrates had daily to experience that the testing of men was the most ungrateful of tasks which could be pursued at Athens; nor could he, without the sacred resolution of an absolutely unselfish devotion to his mission, have without ceasing obeyed the divine voice which every morning anew bade him go forth among men.

But that there were also more general and deep-seated grounds for the sense of annoyance manifested by the Attic public, is most clearly proved by the attacks of the comic stage. "To me too," it is said in a comedy by Eupolis, "this Socrates is offensive: this beggarly talker, who has considered everything with hair-splitting ingenuity; the only matter which he has left unconsidered is the question how he will get a dinner to-day." Far more serious were the attacks of Aristophanes. His standpoint, as well as that of Eupolis and Cratinus, was the ancient Attic view of life: he regarded the teachers of philosophy, round whom the young men gathered, as the ruin of the State; and although he could not possibly mistake the difference between Socrates and the Sophists,—although moreover he by no means belonged to the personal enemies of Socrates, with whom he rather seems to have enjoyed a certain degree of intimacy,—yet he thought it both his right and his duty, as a poet and a patriot, to combat in Socrates the Sophist, nay, the most dangerous of Sophists. The Athenian of the old school hated these conversations extending through whole hours of the broad daylight, during which the young men were kept away from the *palæstræ;* these painful discussions of topics of morality and politics, as to which it behooved every loyal citizen to have made up his mind once for all. If everything was submitted to examination, everything was also exposed to rejection; and what was to become of the city, if only that was to be allowed as valid which found gracious acceptance at the hands of this or that professor of talk? If everything had to be learnt, if everything was to be acquired by reflection, then there was an end of true civic virtue, which ought to be a thing inborn in a citizen and secured by his training as such. In these days all action and capability of action

was being dissolved into an idle knowledge; the one-sided cultivation of the intellect was loosening the sinews of men, and
making them indifferent to their country and religion. From
this standpoint the poet rejects all such culture of youth as is
founded upon the testing of the mind, and leading it to perfect
knowledge, and lauds those young Athenians who do not care
for wasting their time by sitting and talking with Socrates.

The priestly party, again, was adverse to Socrates, although
the highest authority in religious matters which existed in Hel-
las, and had at all events not been superseded by any other,
had declared in his favor,— at the suggestion of Chærephon,
who from his youth up was attached with devoted affection to
his teacher. His was an enthusiastic nature; and he desired
nothing so ardently as that the beneficent influence which he
had experienced in his own soul might be shared by the largest
possible number of his fellow-citizens. For this reason he was
anxious for an outward recognition of the merits of his so frequently misjudged friend; and he is said to have brought home
from Delphi the oracle which declared Socrates to be the wisest
of all men. Now, although this oracle was incapable of giving
a loftier assurance of his mission to the philosopher himself,
although it could not even remove the antipathy of the public,
yet it might be expected that it would disarm the calumny representing Socrates as a teacher of dangerous heresies; and in
this sense he could not but personally welcome the Delphic
declaration. For it must be remembered that he continued to
regard the oracle as the reverend centre of the nation, as the
symbol of a religious communion among the Hellenes; and in
disallowing all presumptuous meditation on the right way of
venerating the gods, he entirely followed the precedent of the
Delphic oracle, which was in the habit of settling questions of
this kind by the answer that it was according to the usage of
their fathers that men should venerate the gods. At Delphi,
on the other hand, there could be no question as to the importance of one who was leading the revolted world back to reverence for things holy, and who, while his contemporaries were
derisively despising the obsolete ways of the past, and running
after the *ignes fatui* of the wisdom of the day, held up before their eyes the primitive sayings of the temples; a serious
consideration of which he declared to be sufficient to reveal
the treasure of immortal truth contained in them. If it was

confessedly impossible to put an end to the prevailing desire
for independent inquiry, then the priests could not but acknowledge that this was the only way by which the old religion could
be saved.

Even the recognition by Delphi, however, was unable to protect Socrates against the suspicion of heresy. The fanaticism of
the priestly party increased in inverse ratio to its prospects of
real success; it regarded any philosophical discussion of religious
truths as a desecration, and placed Socrates on the same level as
Diagoras. Finally, the democrats, who after the restoration of
the constitution were the ruling party, hated philosophy, because
out of its school had issued a large proportion of the oligarchs;
not only Critias and Theramenes, but also Pythodorus the archon
of the days of anarchy, Aristoteles one of the Four Hundred and
of the Thirty, Charmides, and others, were known as men of
philosophical culture. Philosophy and the tendency towards
political reaction accordingly seemed to be necessarily connected
with one another. In a word, Socrates found opposition everywhere: some deemed him too conservative and others too liberal;
he had against him both the Sophists and the enemies of the
Sophists, both rigid orthodoxy and infidelity, both the patriots of
the old school and the representatives of the renovated democracy.

Notwithstanding all this hostile feeling, the personal security
of Socrates was not endangered, because he pursued his path as
a blameless man, and because it was a matter of conscience with
him to avoid every offense against the law. But after the restoration of the constitution a variety of circumstances continued
to imperil his position at Athens.

SOCRATES AS AN INFLUENCE AND AS A MAN

From the ‹History of Greece›

IF WE contemplate Socrates in his whole way of living and
being (and in truth no other personage of Greek antiquity is
so distinctly brought before our eyes), it seems to us in the
first place as if at Athens he were not in his natural place; so
foreign to Athens are his ways, and so dissociated from it is
his whole individuality. He cannot be fitted into any class of

Athenian civil society, and is to be measured by no such standard as we apply to his fellow-citizens.   He is one of the poorest
of all the Athenians, and yet he passes with a proud step
through the streets of the city and confronts the richest and
best born as their equal; his ungainly and neglected exterior
makes him an object of public derision, and yet he exercises an
unexampled influence upon high and low, upon learned and
unlearned alike.   He is a master both of thought and of speech,
yet at the same time an opponent on principle of those who
were the instructors of the Athenians in both; he is a man of
free thought, who allows nothing to remain untested, and yet he
is more diligent in offering sacrifices than any of his neighbors,
he venerates the oracles, and reposes a simple faith in many
things which the age laughs at as nursery tales; he blames
without reticence the dominion of the multitude, and yet is an
adversary of oligarchs.   Entirely his own master, he thinks differently from all other Athenians; he goes his own path without troubling himself about public opinion; and so long as he
remains in harmony with himself, no contradiction, no hostile
attack, no derision vexes his soul.   Such a man as this seemed
in truth to have been transplanted into the midst of Athens as
it were from some other world.

     And yet, unique in his kind as this Socrates was, we are
unable on closer examination to mistake him for aught but a
genuine Athenian.   Such he was in his whole intellectual tendency, in his love of talk and skill in talk,— growths impossible
in any but Athenian air,— in the delicate wit with which he con-
trived to combine the serious and the sportive, and in his
unflagging search after a deep connection between action and
knowledge.   He was a genuine Athenian of the ancient stamp,
when with inflexible courage he stood forth as the champion of
the laws of the State against all arbitrary interference, and in
the field shrank from no danger or hardship.   He knew and
loved the national poets; but above all it is in his indefatigable
impulse towards culture that we recognize the true son of his
native city.   Herein lay a spiritual affinity between him and the
noblest among the Athenians, a Solon and a Pericles.   Socrates,
like Solon, thought that no man is too old to learn; that to learn
and to know is not a schooling for life, but life itself, and that
which alone gives to life its value.   To become by knowledge
better from day to day, and to make others better, appeared to

both to be the real duty of man. Both found the one true happiness in the health of the soul, whose greatest unhappiness they held to lie in wrong and ignorance.

Thus with all his originality Socrates most decidedly stood on the basis of Attic culture; and if it is taken into consideration that the most celebrated representatives of Sophistry and the tendencies akin to it all came from abroad,—*e. g.*, Protagoras from Abdera, Prodicus from Ceos, Diagoras from Melos,—it may fairly be affirmed that as against these foreign teachers the best principles of Attic wisdom found their representative in Socrates. Far, however, from merely recurring to the ancient foundations of patriotic sentiment,—fallen into neglect to the great loss of the State,—and from opposing himself on an inflexible defensive to the movement of the age, he rather stood in the very midst of it; and merely sought to lead it to other and higher ends. What he desired was not a turning back, but a progress in knowledge beyond that which the most sagacious teachers of wisdom offered. For this reason he was able to unite in himself elements which seemed to others irreconcilably contradictory; and upon this conception was based what most distinguished him above all his fellow countrymen, the lofty freedom and independence of his mind. Thus, without becoming disloyal to his home, he was able to rise above the restrictions of customary ideas; which he most notably achieved by making himself perfectly independent of all external things, in the midst of a people which worshiped the beauty of outward appearance, and by attaching value exclusively to the possessions which are within, and to moral life. For this reason too his personal ugliness — the broad face with the snub nose, thick lips and prominent eyes — was a characteristic feature of his individuality; because it testified against the traditional assumption of a necessary union between physical and intellectual excellence; because it proved that even in a form like that of Silenus there might dwell a spirit like that of Apollo, and thus conduced to a loftier conception of the being of man. Thus he belonged to his people and to his age, but stood above both; and such a man the Athenians needed, in order to find the path whereon it was possible to penetrate through the conflict of opinions to a moral assurance, and to reach a happiness containing its own warrant.

Socrates appears before us as an individuality complete and perfect, of which the gradual development continues to remain

a mystery. Its real germ, however, doubtless lies in the desire
for knowledge, which was innate in him with peculiar strength.
This desire would not allow him to remain under pupilage to
his father: it drove him forth out of the narrow workshop into
the streets and the open places of the city, where in those days
every kind of culture, art, and science, was offered in rich
abundance; for at the time when Socrates was in his twentieth
year, Pericles stood at the height of his splendid activity, which
the son of a sculptor might be supposed to have had occasion
fully to appreciate. The youthful Socrates however brought with
him out of his father's house a certain one-sided and so to
speak *bourgeois* tendency, — *i. e.*, a sober homely sense for the
practically useful, which would not allow itself to be dazzled by
splendor and magnificence. Accordingly he passed by with tol-
erable indifference the much admired works of art with which
the city was at that time filled; for the ideal efforts of the
Periclean age he lacked comprehension; nor do the tragedies of
a Sophocles appear to have exercised much attraction upon him.
If there was one-sidedness in this, on the other hand it bore
good fruit in so far as it confirmed the independence of his
judgment, and enabled him to recognize and combat the defects
and diseases from which Athens suffered even in the midst of
her glories.

But although the son of Sophroniscus carried the idea of the
practically useful into the domain of science, he gave to it in
this so deep and grand a significance that for him it again
became an impulse towards searching with unflagging zeal for
all real means of culture offered by Athens; for he felt the
impossibility of satisfactorily responding to the moral tasks which
most immediately await man, without the possession of a connected knowledge. Thus he eagerly associated with men and
women esteemed as highly cultured; he listened to the lectures
of the Sophists; acquainted himself with the writings of the
earlier philosophers, which he found to be still of vital effect
upon his contemporaries; thoroughly studied with friends desirous
of self-improvement the works of Heraclitus and Anaxagoras;
and in this constant intercourse he gradually became himself
another man,— *i. e.*, he grew conscious of the unsatisfactory
standpoint of the wisdom of the teachers of the day, as well as
conscious of his own aims and mission. For in putting questions
of a kind which could meet with no reply, and in searching for

deeper things than could be offered to him by his hearers, he
gradually became himself the person from whom the impulse
proceeded, and from whom in the end was expected an answer
to the questions which had remained unsolved. He, the seeker
after instruction, became the centre of a circle of younger men
who were enthusiastically attached to him. In how high a
degree that which he endeavored to supply corresponded to the
deeply felt needs of the age, is evident from the fact that men
of the most utterly different dispositions and stations in life gave
themselves up to him: youths of the highest class of society, full
of self-consciousness, buoyancy, and reckless high spirits, such
as Alcibiades; and again, men of a melancholy and timid turn of
mind, such as the well-known eccentric Apollodorus of Phalerus,
who, perpetually discontented with himself and others, led a
miserable existence until in Socrates he found the sole individuality appeasing his wants, and in intercourse with him the satisfaction for which he had longed. To him Socrates was all in
all, and every hour during which he was away from Socrates he
accounted as lost. Thus Socrates was able to re-awaken among
the Athenians — among whom personal intercourse between those
of the same age, as well as between men and youths, was disturbed or desecrated either by party interests or by impure
sensuality — the beneficent power of pure friendship and unselfish
devotion. Sober and calm himself, he excited the noblest enthusiasm, and by the simplest means obtained a far-reaching influence such as before him no man had possessed at Athens; even
before the Peace of Nicias, when Aristophanes made him the
principal character in his 'Clouds,' he was one of the best known
and most influential personages at Athens.

As Socrates gradually became a teacher of the people, so his
mode and habits of life, too, formed themselves in indissoluble
connection with his philosophical development. For this was the
most pre-eminent among his qualities: that his life and his teachings were formed in the same mold, and that none of his disciples could say whether he had been more deeply affected by
the words or by the example of his master. And this was connected with the fact that from the first his philosophy directed
itself to that which might make man better and more pleasing
to Heaven, freer and happier at once. To this tendency he could
not devote himself without rising in his own consciousness to a
continuously loftier clearness and purity, and without subjecting

to reason the elements inborn in him, of sensual impulses, of inertia and passion. Thus he became a man in whom the world found much to smile and mock at, but whom even those who could not stomach his wisdom were obliged to acknowledge as a morally blameless and just citizen. He was devoted with absolute loyalty to his native city, and without desiring offices and dignities, he was from an inner impulse indefatigably active for her good.

For the rest, Socrates, with all his dislike of the pursuit of profit and pleasure, was anything but a morose eccentric like Euripides; from this he was kept by his love of humankind. He was merry with the merry, and spoilt no festive banquet to which he had been bidden. In the friendly circle he sat as a man brave at his cups, and herein likewise offered an example to his friends how the truly free can at one time suffer deprivation, and at another enjoy abundance, without at any time losing his full self-control. After a night of festivity his consciousness was as clear and serene as ever; he had after a rare fashion made his body an ever ready servant of his mind; even physically he could do things impossible to others, and as if protected by some magic charm, he passed unhurt through all the pestilences of Athens without ever timidly keeping out of the way of danger. Fully assured of the inner mission which animated him, he allowed nothing to derange or to confound him. Hostile attacks and derision touched him not; nay, he was known to laugh most heartily of all the spectators when that sinner Aristophanes exhibited him as a dreamer, abstracted from the world and hanging in a hammock between heaven and earth; and when the other comic poets made the public merry with his personal appearance. For the same reason, lastly, he was inaccessible to all the offers made to him by foreign princes, who would have given much to attract the most remarkable man of the age to their courts. The Thessalian grandees in particular, Scopas at Crannon and Eurylochus at Larissa, emulated one another in their endeavors to secure him. But he was no more tempted by their gold than by that of Archelaus, the splendor of whose throne, obtained by guile and murder, failed to dazzle Socrates. He replied with the pride of a genuine republican that it ill befitted any man to accept benefits which he had no power of returning.

CUVIER

(1769–1832)

BY SPENCER TROTTER

ODERN zoölogical science is indebted, in a large measure, to the mind and labor of the three French savants — Lamarck, Saint-Hilaire, and Cuvier. Throughout the troubled times of the French Revolution these three friends and co-laborers pursued their studies, arranging and interpreting the facts which they accumulated, and enriching the literature of the science to which they devoted their lives. Of the three, Cuvier stands forth with greatest prominence to-day as the one who by his studies in the structure and classification of animals, and through his reconstruction of the fossil animals of the Paris Basin, has left the most enduring mark upon the literature of the subject.

CUVIER

George Leopold Christian Frederic Dagobert Cuvier was born at Montbéliard in Alsace, on the 23d of August, 1769. His mother devoted herself to the careful training and development of his growing mind, and in very early life he gave evidence of extraordinary intellectual endowment. Naturally industrious, and possessed of a remarkable memory and the power of concentration, young Cuvier by the age of fourteen had mastered the rudiments of several languages, both ancient and modern, had acquired a considerable knowledge of mathematics, had read widely in history, and was proficient in drawing. He very early showed a decided bent toward scientific pursuits, and drew his first inspiration from the works of Buffon, who was then at the zenith of his fame. While at school he formed a society among his fellows for the reading and discussion of various subjects of a scientific and literary nature. Cuvier's talents became known to Prince Charles, the reigning Duke of Würtemberg, who gave him a free education in the University of Stuttgart. After completing his

university course with honor he sought for a public office under the
government of Prince Charles, but his parents' circumstances (his
father being a retired officer of a Swiss regiment in the service of
France) forced him to abandon this idea, and at the age of nineteen
he accepted the position of a tutor in the family of a nobleman who
resided at Caen in Normandy.

This proved to be the determining event in Cuvier's life. He
found in the mollusk fauna of the near-by sea-coast a fascinating
subject for study, and devoted all of his spare time to the investigation of the structure and relations of the various forms that came to
his notice. The Abbé Tessier, a member of the Academy of Sciences,
who had fled to Normandy from Paris during the Reign of Terror,
made the acquaintance of the young naturalist, and introduced him
by correspondence to a number of the most eminent scientific men of
Paris. One of these men was Geoffroy Saint-Hilaire; and through his
influence Cuvier was invited to assist Mertrud, the professor of comparative anatomy in the Museum of Natural History at the Jardin des
Plantes. From this time on he threw all the energies of his remarkable mind into the study of animals and the building up of the
Museum. The collections which he originated rank among the finest
in the world. In 1802 Cuvier was appointed one of six inspector-
generals to organize lyceums in a number of the French towns,
and ever after gave a great part of his time and thought to the
subject of education. The influence of his work in this direction is
felt to-day in every institution of public instruction throughout France.
On the annexation of Italy he made three different visits to that
country in order to reorganize the old academies, and although a
Protestant he was intrusted with the organization of the University
at Rome. In a similar manner he remodeled the educational systems
throughout Holland and Belgium; and his reports on these questions
are teeming with interest. Cuvier felt that the strength of a nation
lay in the sound education of all classes, the lower as well as the
upper; and to his enlightened views may be traced much of the
excellent system of primary education that prevails in these countries
to-day. Under the bigoted Bourbon government, the despotic rule of
Napoleon, and the liberal reign of Louis Philippe, Cuvier maintained
his post; and throughout the events of the Hundred Days of 1815 he
still held a high position in the Imperial University, of which he had
been made a life member of the council at its foundation in 1808.
He held a distinguished place as a member of the Council of State,
as Minister of the Interior, as Chancellor of the University, and
member of the Protestant faculty of theology. Louis Philippe conferred on him the title of Baron. He lived at the Jardin des Plantes,
surrounded by his family and friends, and his home was the centre

of men of science from all parts of the world. On the 8th of May, 1832, after delivering an unusually eloquent introductory lecture at the College of France, he was stricken with paralysis; and though he rallied sufficiently to preside the next day at the Council of State, he died on the following Sunday.

The chief value of Cuvier's work in general literature lies in the philosophical deductions which he drew from his studies. Lamarck had advanced the theory of the origin of species as a result of the action of the natural conditions of existence impressing and molding the plastic organism. Saint-Hilaire had advanced the doctrine of "homology,"—*i. e.*, the same structure appearing in a different form in different animals as a result of a difference of function. Cuvier opposed both of these theories, holding that each animal was a separate and distinct result of a special creative act, and that each part of its organization was expressly created to meet certain wants. Though the point of view of these three friends differed, yet each held the germ of truth. The action of the environment and the doctrine of homology are vital questions to-day; and Cuvier's deductions are equally pregnant with the truth, only their author viewed the facts as special creative acts of the Divine intelligence. Probably the most wide-reaching effects of Cuvier's work came from his study and restoration of the fossil animals of the Paris Basin, and the consequent recognition of the Tertiary as a distinct geological age. From his investigations in comparative anatomy he proved "that the parts of an animal agree so exactly that from seeing one fragment the whole can be known." This recognition of the *correlation of parts* was one of the grandest achievements of his master mind.

Cuvier's scientific publications were numerous. His best known works are 'Le Règne Animal' (The Animal Kingdom), published in four octavo volumes in 1817, and 'Recherches sur les Ossements Fossiles' (Inquiry Concerning Fossil Bones). This latter work is probably the most enduring monument to his fame, as it laid the basis of the present science of palæontology. The first volume of this work is a masterpiece of scientific literature, and has been widely translated. The English translation by Professor Jameson of Edinburgh, entitled 'Essay on the Theory of the Earth,' has passed through several editions.

OF CHANGES IN THE STRUCTURE OF THE EARTH
From 'The Theory of the Earth'

THE lowest and most level parts of the earth, when penetrated to a very great depth, exhibit nothing but horizontal strata composed of various substances, and containing almost all of them innumerable marine productions. Similar strata, with the same kind of productions, compose the hills even to a great height. Sometimes the shells are so numerous as to constitute the entire body of the stratum. They are almost everywhere in such a perfect state of preservation that even the smallest of them retain their most delicate parts, their sharpest ridges, and their finest and tenderest processes. They are found in elevations far above the level of every part of the ocean, and in places to which the sea could not be conveyed by any existing cause. They are not only inclosed in loose sand, but are often incrusted and penetrated on all sides by the hardest stones. Every part of the earth, every hemisphere, every continent, every island of any size, exhibits the same phenomenon. We are therefore forcibly led to believe not only that the sea has at one period or another covered all our plains, but that it must have remained there for a long time, and in a state of tranquillity; which circumstance was necessary for the formation of deposits so extensive, so thick, in part so solid, and containing exuviæ so perfectly preserved.

The time is past for ignorance to assert that these remains of organized bodies are mere *lusus naturæ*,—productions generated in the womb of the earth by its own creative powers. A nice and scrupulous comparison of their forms, of their contexture, and frequently even of their composition, cannot detect the slightest difference between these shells and the shells which still inhabit the sea. They have therefore once lived in the sea, and been deposited by it; the sea consequently must have rested in the places where the deposition has taken place. Hence it is evident the basin or reservoir containing the sea has undergone some change at least, either in extent, or in situation, or in both. Such is the result of the very first search, and of the most superficial examination.

The traces of revolutions become still more apparent and decisive when we ascend a little higher, and approach nearer to the foot of the great chains of mountains. There are still found many beds of shells; some of these are even larger and more solid; the shells are quite as numerous and as entirely preserved: but they are not of the same species with those which were found in the less elevated regions. The strata which contain them are not so generally horizontal; they have various degrees of inclination, and are sometimes situated vertically. While in the plains and low hills it was necessary to dig deep in order to detect the succession of the strata, here we perceive them by means of the valleys which time or violence has produced, and which disclose their edges to the eye of the observer. At the bottom of these declivities huge masses of their débris are collected, and form round hills, the height of which is augmented by the operation of every thaw and of every storm.

These inclined or vertical strata, which form the ridges of the secondary mountains, do not rest on the horizontal strata of the hills which are situated at their base and serve as their first steps; but on the contrary are situated underneath them. The latter are placed upon the declivities of the former. When we dig through the horizontal strata in the neighborhood of the inclined strata, the inclined strata are invariably found below. Nay sometimes, when the inclined strata are not too much elevated, their summit is surmounted by horizontal strata. The inclined strata are therefore more ancient than the horizontal strata. And as they must necessarily have been formed in a horizontal position, they have been subsequently shifted into their inclined or vertical position, and that too before the horizontal strata were placed above them.

Thus the sea, previous to the formation of the horizontal strata, had formed others which by some means have been broken, lifted up, and overturned in a thousand ways. There had therefore been also at least one change in the basin of that sea which preceded ours; it had also experienced at least one revolution: and as several of these inclined strata which it had formed first are elevated above the level of the horizontal strata which have succeeded and which surround them, this revolution, while it gave them their present inclination, had also caused them to project above the level of the sea so as to form islands, or at least rocks and inequalities; and this must have happened whether one of their edges was lifted up above the water, or the depression of the opposite edge caused the water to subside.

This is the second result, not less obvious nor less clearly demonstrated than the first, to every one who will take the trouble of studying carefully the remains by which it is illustrated and proved.

If we institute a more detailed comparison between the various strata and those remains of animals which they contain, we shall soon discover still more numerous differences among them, indicating a proportional number of changes in their condition. The sea has not always deposited stony substances of the same kind. It has observed a regular succession as to the nature of its deposits: the more ancient the strata are, so much the more uniform and extensive are they; and the more recent they are, the more limited are they, and the more variation is observed in them at small distances. Thus the great catastrophes which have produced revolutions in the basin of the sea were preceded, accompanied, and followed by changes in the nature of the fluid and of the substances which it held in solution; and when the surface of the seas came to be divided by islands and projecting ridges, different changes took place in every separate basin.

Amidst these changes of the general fluid, it must have been almost impossible for the same kind of animals to continue to live; nor did they do so in fact. Their species, and even their genera, change with the strata: and though the same species occasionally recur at small distances, it is generally the case that the shells of the ancient strata have forms peculiar to themselves; that they gradually disappear, till they are not to be seen at all in the recent strata, still less in the existing seas, in which indeed we never discover their corresponding species, and where several, even of their genera, are not to be found; that on the contrary the shells of the recent strata resemble, as respects the genus, those which still exist in the sea; and that in the last formed and loosest of these strata there are some species which the eye of the most expert naturalists cannot distinguish from those which at present inhabit the ocean.

In animal nature, therefore, there has been a succession of changes corresponding to those which have taken place in the chemical nature of the fluid; and when the sea last receded from our continent, its inhabitants were not very different from those which it still continues to support.

Finally, if we examine with greater care these remains of organized bodies, we shall discover, in the midst even of the most ancient secondary strata, other strata that are crowded with animal or vegetable productions, which belong to the land and to fresh water; and amongst the most recent strata — that is, the strata which are nearest the surface — there are some of them in which land animals are buried under heaps of marine productions. Thus the various catastrophes of our planet have not only caused the different parts of our continent to rise by degrees from the basin of the sea, but it has also frequently happened that lands which had been laid dry have been again covered by the water, in consequence either of these lands sinking down below the level of the sea, or of the sea being raised above the level of the lands. The particular portions of the earth also, which the sea has abandoned by its last retreat, had been laid dry once before, and had at that time produced quadrupeds, birds, plants, and all kinds of terrestrial productions; it had then been inundated by the sea, which has since retired from it and left it to be occupied by its own proper inhabitants.

The changes which have taken place in the productions of the shelly strata, therefore, have not been entirely owing to a gradual and general retreat of the waters, but to successive irruptions and retreats, the final result of which, however, has been an universal depression of the level of the sea.

These repeated irruptions and retreats of the sea have been neither slow nor gradual; most of the catastrophes which have occasioned them have been sudden: and this is easily proved, especially with regard to the last of them, the traces of which are most conspicuous. In the northern regions it has left the carcasses of some large quadrupeds which the ice had arrested, and which are preserved even to the present day with their skin, their hair, and their flesh. If they had not been frozen as soon as killed, they must quickly have been decomposed by putrefaction. But this eternal frost could not have taken possession of the regions which these animals inhabited except by the same cause which destroyed them; this cause therefore must have been as sudden as its effect. The breaking to pieces and overturnings of the strata, which happened in former catastrophes, show plainly enough that they were sudden and violent like the last; and the heaps of débris and rounded pebbles which are found in various places among the solid strata demonstrate the vast force of the motions excited in the mass of waters by these overturnings. Life, therefore, has been often disturbed on this

VII—267

earth by terrible events: calamities which, at their commencement, have perhaps moved and overturned to a great depth the
entire outer crust of the globe, but which, since these first commotions, have uniformly acted at a less depth and less generally.
Numberless living beings have been the victims of these catastrophes; some have been destroyed by sudden inundations, others
have been laid dry in consequence of the bottom of the seas
being instantaneously elevated.   Their races even have become
extinct, and have left no memorial of them except some small
fragment which the naturalist can scarcely recognize.

Such are the conclusions which necessarily result from the
objects that we meet with at every step of our inquiry, and which
we can always verify by examples drawn from almost every
country.   Every part of the globe bears the impress of these
great and terrible events so distinctly, that they must be visible
to all who are qualified to read their history in the remains
which they have left behind.

But what is still more astonishing and not less certain, there
have not been always living creatures on the earth, and it is
easy for the observer to discover the period at which animal
productions began to be deposited.

As we ascend to higher points of elevation, and advance
towards the lofty summits of the mountains, the remains of
marine animals — that multitude of shells we have spoken of —
begin very soon to grow rare, and at length disappear altogether.
We arrive at strata of a different nature, which contain no vestige at all of living creatures.   Nevertheless their crystallization,
and even the nature of their strata, show that they also have
been formed in a fluid; their inclined position and their slopes
show that they also have been moved and overturned; the oblique
manner in which they sink under the shelly strata shows that
they have been formed before these; and the height to which
their bare and rugged tops are elevated above all the shelly
strata, shows that their summits have never again been covered
by the sea since they were raised up out of its bosom.

Such are those primitive or primordial mountains which traverse our continents in various directions, rising above the clouds,
separating the basins of the rivers from one another, serving by
means of their eternal snows as reservoirs for feeding the springs,
and forming in some measure the skeleton, or as it were the
rough framework of the earth.   The sharp peaks and rugged

indentations which mark their summits, and strike the eye at a great distance, are so many proofs of the violent manner in which they have been elevated. Their appearance in this respect is very different from that of the rounded mountains and the hills with flat surfaces, whose recently formed masses have always remained in the situation in which they were quietly deposited by the sea which last covered them.

These proofs become more obvious as we approach. The valleys have no longer those gently sloping sides, or those alternately salient and re-entrant angles opposite to one another, which seem to indicate the beds of ancient streams. They widen and contract without any general rule; their waters sometimes expand into lakes, and sometimes descend in torrents; and here and there the rocks, suddenly approaching from each side, form transverse dikes over which the waters fall in cataracts. The shattered strata of these valleys expose their edges on one side, and present on the other side large portions of their surface lying obliquely; they do not correspond in height, but those which on one side form the summit of the declivity often dip so deep on the other as to be altogether concealed.

Yet amidst all this confusion some naturalists have thought that they perceived a certain degree of order prevailing, and that among these immense beds of rocks, broken and overturned though they be, a regular succession is observed, which is nearly the same in all the different chains of mountains. According to them, the granite, which surmounts every other rock, also dips under every other rock; and is the most ancient of any that has yet been discovered in the place assigned it by nature. The central ridges of most of the mountain chains are composed of it; slaty rocks, such as clay slate, granular quartz (_grès_), and mica slate, rest upon its sides and form lateral chains; granular, foliated limestone or marble, and other calcareous rocks that do not contain shells, rest upon the slate, forming the exterior ranges, and are the last formations by which this ancient uninhabited sea seems to have prepared itself for the production of its beds of shells.

On all occasions, even in districts that lie at a distance from the great mountain chains, where the more recent strata have been digged through and the external covering of the earth penetrated to a considerable depth, nearly the same order of stratification has been found as that already described. The crystallized marbles never cover the shelly strata; the granite in mass never rests upon the crystallized marble, except in a few places where it seems to have been formed of granites of newer epochs. In one word, the foregoing arrangement appears to be general, and must therefore depend upon general causes, which have on all occasions exerted the same influence from one extremity of the earth to the other.

Hence it is impossible to deny that the waters of the sea have formerly, and for a long time, covered those masses of matter which now constitute our highest mountains; and farther, that these waters during a long time did not support any living bodies. Thus it has not been only since the commencement of animal life that these numerous changes and revolutions have taken place in the constitution of the external covering of our globe: for the masses formed previous to that event have suffered changes, as well as those which have been formed since; they have also suffered violent changes in their positions, and a part of these assuredly took place while they existed alone, and before they were covered over by the shelly masses. The proof of this lies in the overturnings, the disruptions, and the fissures which are observable in their strata, as well as in those of more recent formation, which are there even in greater number and better defined.

But these primitive masses have also suffered other revolutions, posterior to the formation of the secondary strata, and have perhaps given rise to, or at least have partaken of, some portion of the revolutions and changes which these latter strata have experienced. There are actually considerable portions of the primitive strata uncovered, although placed in lower situations than many of the secondary strata; and we cannot conceive how it should have so happened, unless the primitive strata in these places had forced themselves into view after the formation of those which are secondary. In some countries we find numerous and prodigiously large blocks of primitive substances scattered over the surface of the secondary strata, and separated by deep valleys from the peaks or ridges whence these blocks must have been derived. It is necessary, therefore, either that these blocks must have been thrown into those situations by means of eruptions, or that the valleys, which otherwise must have stopped their course, did not exist at the time of their being transported to their present sites.

Thus we have a collection of facts, a series of epochs anterior to the present time, and of which the successive steps may be ascertained with perfect certainty, although the periods which intervened cannot be determined with any degree of precision. These epochs form so many fixed points, answering as rules for directing our inquiries respecting this ancient chronology of the earth.

OF THE FABULOUS ANIMALS OF THE ANCIENT WRITERS

PERHAPS some persons may be disposed to employ an opposite train of argument, and to allege that the ancients were not only acquainted with as many large quadrupeds as we are, as has been already shown, but that they actually described several others which we do not now know; that we are rash in considering the accounts of all such animals as fabulous; that we ought to search for them with the utmost care, before concluding that we have acquired a complete knowledge of the existing animal creation; and in fine, that among those animals which we presume to be fabulous we may perhaps discover, when better acquainted with them, the actual originals of the bones of those species which are now unknown. Perhaps some may even conceive that the various monsters, essential ornaments of the history of the heroic ages of almost every nation, are precisely those very species which it was necessary to destroy in order to allow the establishment of civilized societies. Thus Theseus and Bellerophon must have been more fortunate than all the nations of more modern days, who have only been able to drive back the noxious animals into the deserts and ill-peopled regions, but have never yet succeeded in exterminating a single species.

It is easy to reply to the foregoing objections, by examining the descriptions that are left us by the ancients of those unknown animals, and by inquiring into their origins. Now the greater number of those animals have an origin purely mythological, and of this origin the descriptions given of them bear the most unequivocal marks; as in almost all of them we see merely the different parts of known animals united by an unbridled imagination, and in contradiction to every established law of nature. Those which have been invented by the poetical fancy of the

Greeks have at least some grace and elegance in their composition, resembling the fantastic decorations which are still observable on the ruins of some ancient buildings, and which have been
multiplied by the fertile genius of Raphael in his paintings.
Like these, they unite forms which please the eye by agreeable
contours and fanciful combinations, but which are utterly repug-
nant to nature and reason; being merely the productions of
inventive and playful genius, or perhaps meant as emblematical
representations of metaphysical or moral propositions, veiled under mystical hieroglyphics after the Oriental manner.   Learned
men may be permitted to employ their time and ingenuity in
attempts to decipher the mystic knowledge concealed under the
forms of the Sphinx of Thebes, the Pegasus of Thessaly, the
Minotaur of Crete, or the Chimera of Epirus; but it would be
folly to expect seriously to find such monsters in nature.   We
might as well endeavor to find the animals of Daniel, or the
beasts of the Apocalypse, in some hitherto unexplored recesses
of the globe.   Neither can we look for the mythological animals
of the Persians,—creatures of a still bolder imagination,—such
as the *martichore*, or destroyer of men, having a human head on
the body of a lion, and the tail of a scorpion; the *griffin*, or
guardian of hidden treasures, half eagle and half lion; or the
cartazonon, or wild ass, armed with a long horn on its forehead.

Ctesias, who reports these as actual living animals, has been
looked upon by some authors as an inventor of fables; whereas
he only attributes real existence to hieroglyphical representations.
These strange compositions of fancy have been seen in modern
times on the ruins of Persepolis.   It is probable that their
hidden meanings may never be ascertained; but at all events we
are quite certain that they were never intended to be representations of real animals.

Agatharcides, another fabricator of animals, drew his information in all probability from a similar source.   The ancient
monuments of Egypt still furnish us with numerous fantastic
representations, in which the parts of different kinds of creatures
are strangely combined,—men with the heads of animals, and
animals with the heads of men,—which have given rise to cynocephali, satyrs, and sphinxes.   The custom of exhibiting in the
same sculpture, in bas-relief, men of very different heights, —
of making kings and conquerors gigantic while their subjects
and vassals are represented as only a fourth or fifth part of their

size,—must have given rise to the fable of the pigmies. In some corner of these monuments Agatharcides must have discovered his carnivorous bull, whose mouth, extending from ear to ear, devoured every other animal that came in his way. But scarcely any naturalist will acknowledge the existence of any such animal, since nature has never joined cloven hoofs and horns with teeth adapted for cutting and devouring animal food.

There may have been other figures equally strange with these, either among those monuments of Egypt which have not been able to resist the ravages of time, or in the ancient temples of Ethiopia and Arabia which have been destroyed by the religious zeal of the Abyssinians and Mahometans. The monuments of India teem with such figures; but the combinations in these are so ridiculously extravagant that they have never imposed even upon the most credulous. Monsters with a hundred arms and twenty heads of different kinds are far too absurd to be believed.

Nay, the inhabitants of China and Japan have their imaginary animals, which they represent as real, and that too in their religious books. The Mexicans had them. In short, they are to be found among every people whose idolatry has not yet acquired some degree of refinement. But is there any one who could possibly pretend to discover, amidst the realities of animal nature, what are thus so plainly the productions of ignorance and superstition? And yet some travelers, influenced by a desire to make themselves famous, have gone so far as to pretend that they saw these fancied beings; or, deceived by a slight resemblance into which they were too careless to inquire, they have identified these with creatures that actually exist. In their eyes, large baboons or monkeys have become *cynocephali*, and sphinxes real men with long tails. It is thus that St. Augustine imagined he had seen a satyr.

Real animals, observed and described with equal inaccuracy, may have given rise to some of these ideal monsters. Thus we can have no doubt of the existence of the hyena, though the back of this animal is not supported by a single bone, and though it does not change its sex yearly, as alleged by Pliny. Perhaps the carnivorous bull may only have been the two-horned rhinoceros falsely described. M. de Weltheim considers the auriferous ants of Herodotus as the *corsacs* of modern naturalists.

The most famous among these fabulous animals of the ancients was the *unicorn*. Its real existence has been obstinately asserted even in the present day, or at least proofs of its existence have been eagerly sought for. Three several animals are frequently mentioned by the ancients as having only one horn placed on the middle of the forehead. The *oryx* of Africa, having cloven hoofs, the hair placed reversely to that of other animals, its height equal to that of the bull, or even of the rhinoceros, and said to resemble deer and goats in its form; the *Indian ass*, having solid hoofs; and the *monoceros*, properly so called, whose feet are sometimes compared to those of the lion and sometimes to those of the elephant, and is therefore considered as having divided feet. The horse unicorn and the bull unicorn are doubtless both referable to the Indian ass, for even the latter is described as having solid hoofs. We may therefore be fully assured that these animals have never really existed, as no solitary horns have ever found their way into our collections, excepting those of the rhinoceros and narwhal.

After careful consideration, it is impossible that we should give any credit to rude sketches made by savages upon rocks. Entirely ignorant of perspective, and wishing to represent the outlines of a straight-horned antelope in profile, they could only give the figure one horn, and thus they produced an oryx. The oryxes that are seen on the Egyptian monuments, likewise, are probably nothing more than productions of the stiff style imposed on the sculptors of the country by religious prejudices. Several of their profiles of quadrupeds show only one fore and one hinder leg; and it is probable that the same rule led them also to represent only one horn. Perhaps their figures may have been copied after individuals that had lost one of their horns by accident, a circumstance that often happens to the chamois and the saiga, species of the antelope genus; and this would be quite sufficient to establish the error. All the ancients, however, have not represented the oryx as having only one horn. Oppian expressly attributes two to this animal, and Ælian mentions one that had four. Finally, if this animal was ruminant and cloven-footed, we are quite certain that its frontal bone must have been divided longitudinally into two, and that it could not possibly, as it is very justly remarked by Camper, have had a horn placed upon the suture.

It may be asked, however: What two-horned animals could have given an idea of the *oryx* in the forms in which it has been transmitted down to us, even independent of the notion of a single horn? To this I answer, as already done by Pallas, that it was the straight-horned *antelope oryx* of Gmelin, improperly named *pasan* by Buffon. This animal inhabits the deserts of Africa, and must frequently approach the confines of Egypt, and appears to be that which is represented in the hieroglyphics. It equals the ox in height, while the shape of its body approaches to that of a stag, and its straight horns present exceedingly formidable weapons, hard almost as iron, and sharp-pointed like javelins. Its hair is whitish; it has black spots and streaks on its face, and the hair on its back points forward. Such is the description given by naturalists; and the fables of the Egyptian priests, which have occasioned the insertion of its figure among their hieroglyphics, do not require to have been founded in nature. Supposing that an individual of this species may have been seen which had lost one of its horns by some accident, it may have been taken as a representative of the entire race, and erroneously adopted by Aristotle to be copied by all his successors. All this is quite possible and even natural, and gives not the smallest evidence for the existence of a single-horned species of antelope.

In regard to the Indian ass, of the alexipharmic virtues of whose horn the ancients speak, we find the Eastern nations of the present day attributing exactly the same property of counteracting poison to the horn of the rhinoceros. When this horn was first imported into Greece, nothing probably was known respecting the animal to which it belonged; and accordingly it was not known to Aristotle. Agatharcides is the first author by whom it is mentioned. In the same manner, ivory was known to the ancients long before the animal from which it is procured; and perhaps some of their travelers may have given to the rhinoceros the name of *Indian ass*, with as much propriety as the Romans denominated the elephant the *bull of Lucania*. Everything which they relate of the strength, size, and ferocity of their wild ass of India corresponds sufficiently with the rhinoceros. In succeeding times, when the rhinoceros came to be better known to naturalists, finding that former authors mentioned a single-horned animal under the name of Indian ass, they concluded without any examination that it must be quite a distinct creature, having solid hoofs. We have remaining a detailed description of the Indian ass, written by Ctesias; but as we have already seen that this must have been taken from the ruins of Persepolis, it should go for nothing in the real history of the animal.

When there afterwards appeared more exact descriptions of an animal having several toes or hoofs on each foot, the ancients conceived it to be a third species of one-horned animals, to which they gave the name of *monoceros*. These double and even triple references are most frequent among ancient writers, because most of their works which have come down to us were mere compilations; because even Aristotle himself has often mixed borrowed facts with those which had come under his own observation; and because the habit of critically investigating the authorities of previous writers was as little known among ancient naturalists as among their historians.

From all these reasonings and digressions, it may be fairly concluded that the large animals of the ancient continent with which we are now acquainted were known to the ancients; and that all the animals of which the ancients have left descriptions, and which are now unknown, were merely fabulous. It also follows that the large animals of the three anciently known quarters of the world were very soon known to the people who frequented their coasts.

It may also be concluded that no large species remains to be discovered in America, as there is no good reason that can be assigned why any such should exist in that country with which we are unacquainted; and in fact none has been discovered there during the last hundred and fifty years. . . .

From all these considerations it may be safely concluded, as shall be more minutely explained in the sequel,— that none of the large species of quadrupeds, whose remains are now found imbedded in regular rocky strata, are at all similar to any of the known living species; that this circumstance is by no means the mere effect of chance, or because the species to which these fossil bones have belonged are still concealed in the desert and uninhabited parts of the world, and have hitherto escaped the observation of travelers, but — that this astonishing phenomenon has proceeded from general causes, and that the careful investigation of it affords one of the best means for discovering and explaining the nature of these causes.